The Original

W9-BYB-666

THOROUGHBRED TIMES
RACING
ALMANAC™
2004

THOROUGHBRED TIMES BOOKS

The Original

THOROUGHBRED TIMES

RACING ALMANAC™

2004
A Thoroughbred Times Book™

Editor in Chief: Mark Simon
Almanac Editor: Don Clippinger
Director of Research: John P. Sparkman
Editors: Tom Law, Michele MacDonald, Amy Owens
Information Technology: Alan Johnson, Jonathan McKinney
Editorial Research: Frank Angst, Steve Bailey, Liane Crossley, Ed DeRosa, Bill Heller, Myra Lewyn, Jeff Lowe, Tom Musgrave, Steve Schuelein, Alicia Wincze
Statistical Research: Gail Allensworth, Andrew Cary, Melissa Humphrey, Billy Huntington Jr., Katie Lossen, Aylett Melton, Vicky Van Camp
Editorial Assistants: Sarah Hatfield, Deanna Lyons, Denise Steffanus, Laura Tucker
Production Director: Jeanette Vance
Production Staff: Nicole Elliott, Betty Gee, Tami Helmreich-Zigo, Laura Lacy, Erica Mitchell
Cover Design: Tami Helmreich-Zigo
Cover Photo: Enzina Mastrippolito

Thoroughbred Times Company Inc.
Publisher: Norman Ridker
Vice President Editorial: Mark Simon
Editorial Office: 2008 Mercer Rd., Lexington, KY 40511

THOROUGHBRED TIMES RACING ALMANAC welcomes comments and suggestions from readers.
Every communication is read by the editors and receives consideration and attention.
THOROUGHBRED TIMES RACING ALMANAC does not decide wagers.

THOROUGHBRED TIMES RACING ALMANAC OF 2004™
Copyright © 2003 Thoroughbred Times Company Inc.
All rights reserved. No part of this book may be reproduced in any form or by any electronic or mechanical means, including information storage and retrieval systems, without permission in writing from the publisher.

Statistics provided herein are compiled by Thoroughbred Times Company Inc. from data supplied by Jockey Club Information Systems Inc., Daily Racing Form Inc., and Equibase Co. Data provided or compiled by Jockey Club Information Systems Inc. generally are accurate but occasionally errors and omissions occur as a result of incorrect data received from others, mistakes in processing, and other causes. The Jockey Club Information Systems Inc. disclaims responsibility for the consequences, if any, of such errors, but would appreciate it being called to their attention. Information as to races, race results, earnings, and other statistical data for races run subsequent to December 31, 1990, was obtained from Equibase Co. and is utilized only with permission of the copyright owner. Such information for periods prior to January 1, 1991, was obtained from Daily Racing Form Inc. Information pertaining to pedigree and production records contained herein copyright the Jockey Club Information Systems Inc.

THOROUGHBRED TIMES RACING ALMANAC™ and THOROUGHBRED TIMES ®
are registered trademarks of Thoroughbred Times Company Inc.
International Standard Serial Number (ISSN) 1540-5486
ISBN Number 1-931993-41-6

THOROUGHBRED TIMES RACING ALMANAC ™
Thoroughbred Times Books™
An imprint of BowTie Press™
www.thoroughbredtimes.com
e-mail: letters@thoroughbredtimes.com

Foreword

Wow, what a year this has been.

In the months since the Premiere Edition of the *Thoroughbred Times Racing Almanac* was published, Thoroughbred racing has hit the depths and the heights. The sport was rocked by an attempted fix of the Breeders' Cup Ultra Pick Six wager, and the scam was discovered largely because the perpetrators held the only winning tickets. The fixed-bet scandal produced front-page headlines, most of them unflattering to the sport. But six months later, the game was on the front pages again, when a gelding owned by a group of high-school friends went for the Triple Crown. Funny Cide did not pull off the feat, but he drew plenty of favorable attention to the sport.

The Premiere Edition of the *Thoroughbred Times Racing Almanac* attracted plenty of favorable attention, too. From everyday and occasional fans to media members to industry leaders, the reviews were unfailingly positive. Clearly, the *Racing Almanac* fulfilled a need for comprehensive, easily accessible, and affordable information on all aspects of Thoroughbred racing and breeding. We at Thoroughbred Times Co. are gratified by the encouraging feedback from users of the *Racing Almanac*. But the Premiere Edition was only the beginning. To quote a well-worn phrase, you ain't seen nothin' yet.

This, the 2004 edition of the *Racing Almanac*, is bigger (by approximately 120 pages) and in all ways better. From beginning to end, new data and statistics explore the many facets of the Thoroughbred sport. Starting on the first pages, we have added tables and charts that delve into the economics of the Thoroughbred industry, including data on claiming activity by state and on aggregate stud fees, also by state. The Triple Crown section has been expanded, with new information on the Kentucky Derby (G1), Preakness Stakes (G1), and Belmont Stakes (G1). The Racetracks chapter is more comprehensive, and major world tracks now are profiled in the International section. The expanded Organizations chapter now includes profiles of the major industry organizations, as well as the major publicly traded companies in Thoroughbred racing. Included with the graded stakes histories is how each race derives its name.

Many sets of hands are involved in producing a volume of this size and scope, and the contributions of several individuals are noteworthy. Norman Ridker, publisher of Thoroughbred Times Co., perceived the need for the *Racing Almanac* and has been its most ardent supporter. Mark Simon, editor in chief, again brought his unerring judgment to the project and guided the many additions to the 2004 *Racing Almanac*. John P. Sparkman, director of research, contributed his voluminous knowledge of both racing and breeding, and he wrote insightful new sections on the development of the commercial breeding industry and the history of Thoroughbred auctions.

Also deserving special mention are the *Racing Almanac*'s chief problem solvers. Alan Johnson, director of information technology, found new ways to squeeze meaningful information out of mountains of data. Production Director Jeanette Vance worked tirelessly to package all the information and to make it easily accessible for our readers. We have some new hands at work for the 2004 *Racing Almanac*, including researchers Andrew Cary and Katie Lossen.

We also are without a set of hands. John Harrell, a former THOROUGHBRED TIMES staff writer, died on April 1, 2003, of a cerebral hemorrhage. He was only 37 and had carried his vast skills and knowledge to a new job as Thoroughbred-industry writer for the Louisville *Courier-Journal*. John Harrell had many passions, starting with his wife, Laura, and their young daughter, Hannah, the light of John's life. He loved Australian rules football, and he loved to study history. Outside his family, though, his greatest passion was for the Kentucky Derby. He consumed every bit of information he could find on the Derby, and he was one of the sport's great historians on the subject. John's significant contributions are a part of the *Thoroughbred Times Racing Almanac*, and they will always be. He lives on in this volume, and in our hearts.

Don Clippinger
Lexington, Kentucky
June 13, 2003

Table of Contents

Table of Contents

General Index

Abbreviations and symbols

The following abbreviations and symbols are used throughout the *Racing Almanac*. Besides the abbreviations below, also used are standard postal abbreviations for states and Canadian provinces.

* See asterisk (*).

4yo Four-year-olds.

4yo & up Four-year-olds and up.

3yo Three-year-olds.

3yo & up Three-year-olds and up.

2yo Two-year-olds.

abt About.

Arg Country code for Argentina.

asterisk (*) In racing and breeding in North America, from 1906 through '74, an asterisk before a name indicates that the horse had been imported to North America in those years. For example: *Nasrullah, *Mahmoud, *Princequillo. Beginning in 1975, the asterisk was replaced by a country code, which designates the country in which the imported horse had been bred (see country code).

Aus Country code for Australia.

Avg. Average.

b. Bay coat color.

blk. Black coat color.

boldface type Typography that indicates a stakes winner, in boldface capital letters, or a stakes-placed horse, indicated by boldface capital and lowercase letters.

br. Brown coat color.

Brz Country code for Brazil.

c. Colt, an ungelded male horse from birth to age five.

c. & g. Colts and geldings.

ca. About, approximately.

Can Country code for Canada.

ch. Chestnut coat color.

Chi Country code for Chile.

Cond. Condition of track.

Corp. Corporation.

country code Beginning in 1975, the asterisk (*) (see above) was replaced by a country code, which designated the country in which the imported horse had been bred. For example: Black Tie Affair (Ire), Waya (Fr), Siphon (Brz). A horse whose name is followed by a country code has been imported to the United States.

CTHS California Thoroughbred Horse Society.

Dist. Distance of race.

Div. A stakes race split and run in divisions.

DRF *Daily Racing Form*.

dk. b. or br. Dark bay or brown coat color.

Eng England; an indication of where a race was run but not a country code for where a horse was bred. (see GB)

f Furlong.

f. A female horse from birth to age five.

f. & m. Fillies and mares.

Fr Country code for France.

g. A gelding of any age.

G1 Grade 1 or Group 1. Grade is used for North America; group is used everywhere else in the world.

G2 Grade 2 or Group 2. Grade is used for North America; group is used everywhere else in the world.

G3 Grade 3 or Group 3. Grade is used for North America; group is used everywhere else in the world.

GB Country code for Great Britain.

Ger Country code for Germany.

gr. Gray coat color.

gr. or ro. Gray or roan coat color.

GSWs Graded stakes winners (for sire references) or graded stakes wins (for runner references).

H. Handicap.

h. An ungelded male horse five years old or older.

HBPA Horsemen's Benevolent and Protective Association.

HK Country code for Hong Kong.

Imp. Imported. Used to designate horses imported to North America for racing or breeding prior to 1906.

Ind Country code for India.

Inc. Incorporated.

Ire Country code for Ireland.

Ity Country code for Italy.

Jpn Country code for Japan.

KSA Country code for Kingdom of Saudi Arabia.

L Listed race, a stakes race that is eligible for grading in the United States but is not graded.

Ltd. Limited.

m Mile.

m. A female horse five years old or older.

MLRS Mare reproductive loss syndrome (see veterinary terms section).

NTRA National Thoroughbred Racing Association.

NZ Country code for New Zealand.

OBSC Ocala Breeders' Sales Co.

OTB Off-track betting.

Pan Country code for Panama.

Per Country code for Peru.

Ph.D. Doctor of Philosophy.

Pol Country code for Poland.

PR Country code for Puerto Rico.

R A restricted race, such as for state-breds or horses sold at a specific sale.

rig. Ridgling, a lay term used to describe either a monorchid or a cryptorchid.

ro. Roan coat color.

Rus Country code for Russia.

S. Stakes.

SAf Country code for South Africa.

Sca Country code for Norway and Sweden.

Sin Country code for Singapore and Malaysia.

spl Stakes placed.

Strs Starters.

St.Wns Stakes wins.

SWs Stakes winners or stakes wins

T A stakes race run on turf.

TCP Triple Crown Productions.

TOBA Thoroughbred Owners and Breeders Association.

TRA Thoroughbred Racing Associations.

TVG Television Games Network.

UAE Country code for United Arab Emirates.

U.S. or USA Country code for United States.

Ven Country code for Venezuela.

Wnrs Winners.

Wnrs/Strs Percentage of winners from starters.

yds Yards.

yo Years old.

YOB Year of birth.

STATE OF THE INDUSTRY
Thoroughbred Economy in 2002

North America's Thoroughbred economy had marked parallels to the United States economy in 2002, and both generally treaded water after sustaining painful economic blows in 2001. Just as with the U.S. economy, important measures of prosperity in racing were down for the year.

Perhaps no statistic is more important than purses, and the accompanying table shows that purses were up again in 2002, with the average purse per race approaching $20,000. That is a good sign, although in inflation-adjusted dollars (see chart) the gain was very modest. But a gain is a gain, although All About Purses (page 10) makes it clear that a larger supply of runners in 2002 translated into lower average earnings per starter. More horses on the racetrack also translated into more claiming horses, more claims, and a lower average claim price from 2001.

The national economy in 2002 was still re-

North American Purses

Year	Total Purses	Average Purse
2002	$1,170,169,267	$19,597
2001	1,146,337,367	18,936
2000	1,093,661,241	18,053
1999	1,008,162,608	16,770
1998	968,366,929	15,838
1997	888,667,752	13,997

covering from the effects of a stock-market bubble in the late 1990s—the roof started to collapse in March 2000—and from the September 11, 2001, terrorist attacks on the World Trade Center in Manhattan and the Pentagon building in suburban Washington, D.C. Those events certainly affected the Thoroughbred industry, most clearly in the bloodstock markets.

While the Standard and Poor's 500 index of large-capitalization stocks was declining 23% for the year, average auction prices for yearlings fell 17%. The total auction market was more than 20% off its 2000 peak. The leading auctions of Keeneland and Fasig-Tipton also were hurt by mare reproductive loss syndrome, which reduced the supply of yearlings in both 2002 and 2003. For the first time in its history, the Keeneland July sale of selected yearlings was canceled in 2003 due to the relative paucity of top-level yearlings.

The economic measures of 2002 reveal another

U.S. Pari-Mutuel Handle
(millions of dollars)

Year	On-Track	Off-Track	Total	Change
2002	$2,029	$13,033	$15,062	+3.2%
2001	2,112	12,487	14,599	+1.9%
2000	2,270	12,051	14,321	+4.4%
1999	2,359	11,365	13,724	+4.7%
1998	2,498	10,617	13,115	+4.6%
1997	2,703	9,839	12,542	+7.9%

North American Purses in Nominal and Real Dollars, 1976-2002

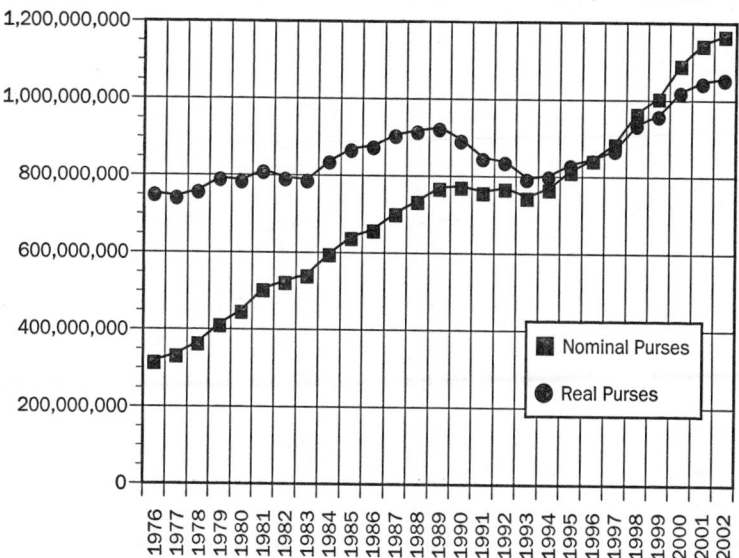

trend, toward more mares and fewer stallions. The reduction in the number of commercial stallions is particularly noteworthy in Kentucky. While auction prices were declining, aggregate stud fees continued to climb. In general, stud fees tend to lag behind other economic indicators, and a change very likely will occur—either higher auction prices or lower stud fees—to permit breeders to achieve a return on their investments.

The figures reveal one important fact: the Thoroughbred industry is a multibillion-dollar enterprise. Wagering in 2002 exceeded $15-billion, purses were again above $1-billion, and auction sales exceeded $750-million. As the national economy continued its slow recovery in the first half of 2003, the major question for the Thoroughbred industry was when it would again return to a path of solid growth.—*Don Clippinger*

Racing Dates, Races, Runners, Starts, Purses by State and Province in 2002

	Racing dates	Races	Runners	Starts	Purses
NORTH AMERICA	**7,054**	**59,758**	**72,765**	**494,230**	**$1,174,242,702**
Alabama	0	0	0	0	0
Arizona	268	2,153	3,271	17,465	14,777,193
Arkansas	52	527	1,691	4,706	11,409,700
California	756	5,111	8,062	39,161	159,354,492
Colorado	41	332	817	2,918	2,957,300
Delaware	141	1,264	3,530	9,872	41,059,780
Florida	365	3,752	7,415	31,356	80,265,582
Georgia	2	10	61	65	347,525
Idaho	48	271	477	1,745	957,952
Illinois	329	3,141	5,007	25,566	78,261,749
Indiana	69	741	2,550	6,719	11,746,915
Iowa	98	780	1,663	6,614	16,284,827
Kansas	50	259	866	1,998	1,596,249
Kentucky	271	2,621	6,889	23,117	82,056,127
Louisiana	330	3,255	6,782	28,353	49,764,894
Maine	0	0	0	0	0
Maryland	230	2,019	4,656	16,047	44,079,310
Massachusetts	155	1,363	2,114	11,249	14,854,014
Michigan	146	1,093	1,451	7,878	10,189,634
Minnesota	61	515	1,104	4,251	6,465,418
Missouri	0	0	0	0	0
Montana	19	94	219	655	198,655
Nebraska	100	886	1,370	7,764	4,898,364
Nevada	6	28	85	157	61,715
New Hampshire	75	711	1,389	5,670	6,826,854
New Jersey	144	1,329	3,274	10,123	38,462,159
New Mexico	234	1,343	2,287	11,567	16,965,943
New York	421	3,797	6,600	29,963	132,167,137
North Carolina	4	16	80	92	240,150
North Dakota	8	40	122	250	107,725
Ohio	447	3,509	5,959	30,619	28,284,730
Oklahoma	186	968	2,275	8,755	7,919,464
Oregon	72	569	1,265	4,559	1,870,471
Pennsylvania	415	3,844	6,215	30,598	44,625,372
Rhode Island	0	0	0	0	0
South Carolina	5	24	128	159	556,250
South Dakota	0	0	0	0	0
Tennessee	1	6	40	40	270,150
Texas	213	1,977	4,609	18,238	31,725,285
Unknown	1	8	62	62	117,100
Utah	0	0	0	0	0
Vermont	0	0	0	0	0
Virginia	35	304	1,728	2,729	5,971,704
Washington	101	884	1,626	6,700	8,651,366
West Virginia	484	4,589	9,468	42,373	71,611,381
Wyoming	16	35	116	243	74,996
UNITED STATES	**6,399**	**54,168**	**66,951**	**450,396**	**1,028,035,632**
Alberta	163	1,169	1,495	8,843	12,366,237
British Columbia	92	846	1,151	6,264	12,108,584
Manitoba	74	589	882	4,529	5,336,660
New Brunswick	0	0	0	0	0
Ontario	282	2,722	3,786	22,580	115,687,788
Saskatchewan	42	260	350	1,592	702,501
Unknown	2	4	24	26	5,300
CANADA	**655**	**5,590**	**7,230**	**43,834**	**$146,207,070**

Claiming Activity by State and Claiming Category in 2002

NORTH AMERICA	No. claims	Value	Average
Maiden claiming	1,610	$32,058,200	$19,912
$0-$4,999	3,184	11,229,850	3,527
$5,000-$9,999	4,923	30,475,375	6,190
$10,000-$19,999	4,336	55,736,000	12,854
$20,000 and up	3,466	110,329,000	31,832
Total	**15,909**	**207,770,225**	**13,060**
UNITED STATES			
Maiden claiming	1,302	25,669,700	19,716
$0-$4,999	2,976	10,479,000	3,521
$5,000-$9,999	4,414	27,163,000	6,154
$10,000-$19,999	3,866	49,583,000	12,825
$20,000 and up	2,902	93,012,500	32,051
Total	**14,158**	**180,237,500**	**12,730**
Arizona			
Maiden claiming	41	260,500	6,354
$0-$4,999	280	937,650	3,349
$5,000-$9,999	193	1,164,500	6,034
$10,000-$19,999	67	802,000	11,970
$20,000 and up	6	135,000	22,500
Total	**546**	**3,039,150**	**5,566**
Arkansas			
Maiden claiming	21	530,000	25,238
$0-$4,999	0	0	0
$5,000-$9,999	59	347,000	5,881
$10,000-$19,999	61	717,500	11,762
$20,000 and up	71	1,966,000	27,690
Total	**191**	**3,030,500**	**15,866**
California			
Maiden claiming	330	9,099,000	27,573
$0-$4,999	271	896,000	3,306
$5,000-$9,999	415	2,654,250	6,396
$10,000-$19,999	722	9,305,500	12,889
$20,000 and up	858	29,466,500	34,343
Total	**2,266**	**42,322,250**	**18,677**
Colorado			
Maiden claiming	1	10,000	10,000
$0-$4,999	23	76,800	3,339
$5,000-$9,999	20	111,000	5,550
$10,000-$19,999	5	55,000	11,000
$20,000 and up	0	0	0
Total	**48**	**242,800**	**5,058**
Delaware			
Maiden claiming	64	1,395,500	21,805
$0-$4,999	0	0	0
$5,000-$9,999	267	1,655,750	6,201
$10,000-$19,999	324	4,320,000	13,333
$20,000 and up	229	6,905,000	30,153
Total	**820**	**12,880,750**	**15,708**
Florida			
Maiden claiming	135	3,021,500	22,381
$0-$4,999	35	143,000	4,086
$5,000-$9,999	159	1,075,500	6,764
$10,000-$19,999	357	4,689,000	13,134
$20,000 and up	266	8,655,500	32,539
Total	**817**	**14,563,000**	**17,825**
Idaho			
Maiden claiming	4	15,000	3,750
$0-$4,999	15	35,700	2,380
$5,000-$9,999	4	22,500	5,625
$10,000-$19,999	0	0	0
$20,000 and up	0	0	0
Total	**19**	**58,200**	**3,063**
Illinois			
Maiden claiming	91	1,423,200	15,640
$0-$4,999	125	465,600	3,725
$5,000-$9,999	288	1,806,250	6,272
$10,000-$19,999	398	5,152,000	12,945
$20,000 and up	200	5,815,000	29,075
Total	**1,011**	**13,238,850**	**13,095**

Indiana	No. claims	Value	Average
Maiden claiming	12	$70,000	$5,833
$0-$4,999	56	206,000	3,679
$5,000-$9,999	88	477,500	5,426
$10,000-$19,999	5	62,500	12,500
$20,000 and up	1	20,000	20,000
Total	**150**	**766,000**	**5,107**
Iowa			
Maiden claiming	11	165,000	15,000
$0-$4,999	11	44,000	4,0000
$5,000-$9,999	38	228,750	6,020
$10,000-$19,999	34	417,500	12,279
$20,000 and up	13	335,000	25,769
Total	**96**	**1,025,250**	**10,680**
Kansas			
Maiden claiming	0	0	0
$0-$4,999	1	3,500	3,500
$5,000-$9,999	2	10,000	5,000
$10,000-$19,999	0	0	0
$20,000 and up	0	0	0
Total	**3**	**13,500**	**4,500**
Kentucky			
Maiden claiming	106	2,200,000	20,755
$0-$4,999	17	68,000	4,000
$5,000-$9,999	229	1,498,500	6,544
$10,000-$19,999	246	3,367,000	13,687
$20,000 and up	212	6,653,000	31,382
Total	**704**	**11,586,500**	**16,458**
Louisiana			
Maiden claiming	61	1,255,000	20,574
$0-$4,999	128	427,500	3,340
$5,000-$9,999	303	1,809,750	5,973
$10,000-$19,999	205	2,565,000	12,512
$20,000 and up	137	3,892,500	28,412
Total	**773**	**8,694,750**	**11,248**
Maryland			
Maiden claiming	90	1,457,500	16,194
$0-$4,999	3	13,000	4,333
$5,000-$9,999	231	1,543,000	6,680
$10,000-$19,999	286	3,898,500	13,631
$20,000 and up	213	5,607,500	26,326
Total	**733**	**11,062,000**	**15,091**
Massachusetts			
Maiden claiming	5	32,000	6,400
$0-$4,999	77	309,500	4,019
$5,000-$9,999	109	667,750	6,126
$10,000-$19,999	63	775,000	12,302
$20,000 and up	2	45,000	22,500
Total	**251**	**1,797,250**	**7,160**
Michigan			
Maiden claiming	2	15,000	7,500
$0-$4,999	13	50,000	3,846
$5,000-$9,999	10	60,000	6,000
$10,000-$19,999	3	35,000	11,667
$20,000 and up	0	0	0
Total	**26**	**145,000**	**5,577**
Minnesota			
Maiden claiming	3	33,000	11,000
$0-$4,999	23	80,500	3,500
$5,000-$9,999	34	221,500	6,515
$10,000-$19,999	18	208,000	11,556
$20,000 and up	1	20,000	20,000
Total	**76**	**530,000**	**6,974**
Montana			
Maiden claiming	0	0	0
$0-$4,999	2	4,100	2,050
$5,000-$9,999	0	0	0
$10,000-$19,999	0	0	0
$20,000 and up	0	0	0
Total	**2**	**4,100**	**2,050**

	No. claims	Value	Average		No. claims	Value	Average
Nebraska				**Texas**			
Maiden claiming	0	$0	$0	Maiden claiming	34	$431,000	$12,676
$0-$4,999	40	115,500	2,888	$0-$4,999	22	88,000	4,000
$5,000-$9,999	12	63,750	5,313	$5,000-$9,999	178	1,126,250	6,327
$10,000-$19,999	2	20,000	10,000	$10,000-$19,999	176	2,037,500	11,577
$20,000 and up	1	20,000	20,000	$20,000 and up	72	1,900,000	26,389
Total	**55**	**219,250**	**3,986**	**Total**	**448**	**5,151,750**	**11,499**
Nevada				**Virginia**			
Maiden claiming	0	0	0	Maiden claiming	3	26,500	8,833
$0-$4,999	1	2,500	2,500	$0-$4,999	1	4,500	4,500
$5,000-$9,999	0	0	0	$5,000-$9,999	8	56,500	7,063
$10,000-$19,999	0	0	0	$10,000-$19,999	2	23,000	11,500
$20,000 and up	0	0	0	$20,000 and up	6	152,500	25,417
Total	**1**	**2,500**	**2,500**	**Total**	**17**	**236,500**	**13,912**
New Hampshire				**Washington**			
Maiden claiming	4	30,000	7,500	Maiden claiming	50	503,000	10,060
$0-$4,999	28	113,000	4,036	$0-$4,999	42	144,800	3,448
$5,000-$9,999	48	294,250	6,130	$5,000-$9,999	102	678,500	6,652
$10,000-$19,999	28	332,000	11,857	$10,000-$19,999	58	786,500	13,560
$20,000 and up	1	50,000	50,000	$20,000 and up	12	307,000	25,583
Total	**105**	**789,250**	**7,51**	**Total**	**214**	**1,916,800**	**8,957**
New Jersey				**West Virginia**			
Maiden claiming	18	344,500	19,139	Maiden claiming	70	411,000	5,871
$0-$4,999	8	32,000	4,000	$0-$4,999	1,191	4,158,250	3,491
$5,000-$9,999	69	433,750	6,286	$5,000-$9,999	880	5,001,500	5,684
$10,000-$19,999	85	1,021,500	12,018	$10,000-$19,999	278	3,327,500	11,969
$20,000 and up	74	2,029,500	27,426	$20,000 and up	9	200,000	22,222
Total	**236**	**3,516,750**	**14,901**	**Total**	**2,358**	**12,687,250**	**5,381**
New Mexico							
Maiden claiming	14	102,000	7,286	**CANADA**	**Canada**		
$0-$4,999	60	220,900	3,682	Maiden claiming	308	6,388,500	20,742
$5,000-$9,999	120	738,000	6,150	$0-$4,999	208	750,850	3,610
$10,000-$19,999	17	187,500	11,029	$5,000-$9,999	509	3,312,375	6,508
$20,000 and up	0	0	0	$10,000-$19,999	470	6,153,000	13,091
Total	**197**	**1,146,400**	**5,819**	$20,000 and up	564	17,316,500	30,703
New York				**Total**	**1,751**	**27,532,725**	**15,724**
Maiden claiming	51	2,101,500	41,206	**Alberta**			
$0-$4,999	50	200,000	4,000	Maiden claiming	23	238,000	10,348
$5,000-$9,999	31	209,750	6,766	$0-$4,999	54	210,750	3,903
$10,000-$19,999	191	2,644,000	13,843	$5,000-$9,999	143	926,500	6,479
$20,000 and up	476	17,850,000	37,500	$10,000-$19,999	91	1,145,000	12,582
Total	**748**	**20,903,750**	**27,946**	$20,000 and up	45	979,000	21,756
Ohio				**Total**	**333**	**3,261,250**	**9,794**
Maiden claiming	27	144,000	5,333	**British Columbia**			
$0-$4,999	213	781,500	3,669	Maiden claiming	34	384,000	11,294
$5,000-$9,999	134	774,500	5,780	$0-$4,999	34	136,000	4,000
$10,000-$19,999	17	189,500	11,147	$5,000-$9,999	67	444,500	6,634
$20,000 and up	0	0	0	$10,000-$19,999	72	946,000	13,139
Total	**364**	**1,745,500**	**4,795**	$20,000 and up	44	1,129,000	25,659
Oklahoma				**Total**	**217**	**2,655,500**	**12,237**
Maiden claiming	2	17,500	8,750	**Manitoba**			
$0-$4,999	29	105,000	3,621	Maiden claiming	3	17,500	5,833
$5,000-$9,999	28	177,500	6,339	$0-$4,999	75	219,625	2,928
$10,000-$19,999	4	50,000	12,500	$5,000-$9,999	38	232,375	6,115
$20,000 and up	0	0	0	$10,000-$19,999	10	112,000	11,200
Total	**61**	**332,500**	**5,451**	$20,000 and up	1	20,000	20,000
Oregon				**Total**	**124**	**584,000**	**4,710**
Maiden claiming	2	14,000	7,000	**Ontario**			
$0-$4,999	53	157,200	2,966	Maiden claiming	248	5,749,000	23,181
$5,000-$9,999	9	54,750	6,083	$0-$4,999	35	158,000	4,514
$10,000-$19,999	1	10,000	10,000	$5,000-$9,999	260	1,704,000	6,554
$20,000 and up	0	0	0	$10,000-$19,999	297	3,950,000	13,300
Total	**63**	**221,950**	**3,523**	$20,000 and up	474	15,188,500	32,043
Pennsylvania				**Total**	**1,066**	**21,000,500**	**19,700**
Maiden claiming	49	548,500	11,194	**Saskatchewan**			
$0-$4,999	158	595,000	3,766	Maiden claiming	0	0	0
$5,000-$9,999	346	2,200,500	6,360	$0-$4,999	10	26,475	2,648
$10,000-$19,999	212	2,570,500	12,125	$5,000-$9,999	1	5,000	5,000
$20,000 and up	42	987,500	23,512	$10,000-$19,999	0	0	0
Total	**758**	**6,353,500**	**8,382**	$20,000 and up	0	0	0
				Total	**11**	**31,475**	**2,861**

Total Auction Sales by State and Province in 2002

	Yearling	Two-Year-Old	Weanling	Broodmare	Racing Stock	Total
NORTH AMERICA	$390,820,438	$129,926,434	$49,062,617	$192,012,919	$3,196,141	$765,018,549
Arizona	869,800	0	2,200	7,400	1,700	881,100
Arkansas	469,050	153,850	38,200	150,400	5,200	816,700
California	8,527,000	18,253,800	470,600	4,109,300	1,507,600	32,868,300
Florida	13,725,200	78,241,500	2,534,900	5,584,700	48,900	100,135,200
Idaho	81,350	12,500	6,550	20,500	0	120,900
Illinois	0	297,600	0	1,700	0	299,300
Indiana	23,950	1,000	5,000	14,750	8,000	52,700
Iowa	296,350	800	13,200	13,200	0	323,550
Kentucky	301,658,700	17,832,200	44,245,500	178,904,300	900,900	543,541,600
Louisiana	1,141,650	372,300	34,200	232,800	25,750	1,806,700
Maryland	9,220,000	10,557,400	1,386,600	1,490,100	488,800	23,142,900
Michigan	143,700	0	0	0	0	143,700
Minnesota	115,200	4,700	0	9,900	3,200	133,000
New Mexico	1,038,450	11,750	1,700	205,200	0	1,257,100
New York	40,587,500	0	0	0	0	40,587,500
Ohio	151,000	14,200	21,900	29,800	0	216,900
Oklahoma	166,275	51,575	0	389,850	115,725	723,425
Oregon	94,125	0	26,400	70,925	700	192,150
Texas	2,863,150	3,733,800	152,400	378,400	75,900	7,203,650
Washington	2,939,100	0	38,400	80,800	7,000	3,065,300
UNITED STATES	384,111,550	129,538,975	48,977,750	191,694,025	3,189,375	757,511,675
Alberta	698,836	4,461	1,068	44,793	1,759	750,917
British Columbia	533,608	1,256	4,522	14,575	0	553,961
Manitoba	106,859	0	0	0	0	106,859
Ontario	5,328,595	381,742	79,277	259,526	5,007	6,054,147
Saskatchewan	40,990	0	0	0	0	40,990
CANADA	6,708,888	387,459	84,867	318,894	6,766	7,506,874

Auction Prices in Current and Deflated Dollars, 1990-2002

		All Horses			Yearlings	
Year	No. Sold	Nominal Dollars	Deflated Dollars	No. Sold	Nominal Dollars	Deflated Dollars
2002	18,398	$767,118,402	$693,277,424	9,000	$390,820,438	$353,201,000
2001	19,168	846,346,171	773,512,257	9,075	473,475,656	432,729,816
2000	21,209	1,091,345,649	1,021,008,382	9,556	519,553,332	486,068,101
1999	19,970	986,842,275	942,641,801	8,757	440,149,579	420,435,365
1998	19,653	828,664,233	802,938,096	8,263	354,200,540	343,204,275
1997	18,698	700,362,250	686,979,882	8,067	307,711,712	301,832,024
1996	15,508	577,839,670	577,839,670	6,512	257,384,021	257,384,021
1995	15,349	457,152,394	466,001,768	6,903	215,649,263	219,823,715
1994	15,664	414,746,588	431,996,196	6,982	188,869,093	196,724,294
1993	10,376	298,068,222	316,928,646	5,218	167,252,430	177,835,416
1992	11,602	283,515,748	308,692,727	5,620	158,459,617	172,531,267
1991	11,901	332,552,530	370,895,731	4,926	179,907,991	200,651,325
1990	10,763	355,044,288	410,394,147	5,181	209,987,357	242,723,472

Includes stallion seasons and shares sold at public auction.

Average Auction Sales by State and Province in 2002

	Yearling	Two-Year-Old	Weanling	Broodmare	Racing Stock	Total
NORTH AMERICA	$43,424	$48,318	$31,131	$40,732	$10,244	$41,824
Arizona	7,248	0	1,100	1,057	1,700	6,777
Arkansas	5,270	6,993	2,728	3,269	2,600	4,720
California	13,753	45,294	6,446	8,651	15,228	19,681
Florida	12,580	54,409	9,458	8,224	4,075	28,708
Idaho	2,085	2,500	1,310	1,205	0	1,831
Illinois	0	12,400	0	1,700	0	11,972
Indiana	2,395	1,000	2,500	1,638	1,600	1,951
Iowa	5,810	800	3,300	1,015	0	4,689
Kentucky	69,314	148,601	47,220	72,401	28,153	68,698
Louisiana	4,622	6,894	2,280	1,862	2,145	3,988
Maryland	15,760	29,164	9,629	5,458	8,575	16,286
Michigan	4,105	0	0	0	0	4,105

	Yearling	Two-Year-Old	Weanling	Broodmare	Racing Stock	Total
Minnesota	8,228	1,175	0	1,414	3,200	5,115
New Mexico	8,800	2,937	1,700	3,206	0	6,722
New York	163,659	0	0	0	0	163,659
Ohio	3,212	1,577	1,684	961	0	2,169
Oklahoma	2,052	1,778	0	2,334	1,961	2,153
Oregon	3,036	0	2,640	1,541	700	2,183
Texas	9,060	20,182	3,242	2,910	3,162	10,261
Washington	11,436	0	2,400	2,126	7,000	9,824
UNITED STATES	**45,995**	**48,680**	**31,578**	**41,681**	**10,422**	**43,365**
Alberta	4,451	1,487	534	1,317	586	3,773
British Columbia	5,558	628	904	2,082	0	5,036
Manitoba	3,053	0	0	0	0	3,053
Ontario	15,626	16,597	4,404	3,507	1,669	13,189
Saskatchewan	2,049	0	0	0	0	2,049
CANADA	**10,337**	**13,837**	**3,394**	**2,772**	**1,127**	**9,121**

Median Auction Sales by State and Province in 2002

	Yearling	Two-Year-Old	Weanling	Broodmare	Racing Stock	Total
NORTH AMERICA	**$10,500**	**$19,000**	**$11,000**	**$6,500**	**$4,000**	**$10,000**
Arizona	4,500	0	1,100	800	0	4,000
Arkansas	2,200	2,450	1,350	2,100	2,600	2,200
California	5,500	15,000	3,200	3,700	8,500	6,000
Florida	6,000	23,500	4,700	4,000	3,700	9,500
Idaho	1,200	2,100	800	750	0	975
Illinois	0	7,850	0	0	0	7,500
Indiana	2,000	0	2,500	1,200	1,100	1,400
Iowa	2,700	0	3,550	800	0	2,000
Kentucky	25,000	100,000	25,000	20,000	8,250	24,500
Louisiana	2,300	4,900	1,900	1,300	1,450	2,100
Maryland	8,500	20,000	4,500	3,000	4,000	7,500
Michigan	3,700	0	0	0	0	3,700
Minnesota	7,000	1,150	0	1,500	0	1,725
New Mexico	3,500	2,600	0	1,600	0	2,500
New York	105,000	0	0	0	0	105,000
Ohio	1,400	1,300	1,200	700	0	1,100
Oklahoma	1,500	1,000	0	1,300	1,500	1,400
Oregon	2,300	0	1,850	1,300	0	1,700
Texas	4,050	12,000	1,700	2,000	2,200	4,000
Washington	6,000	0	1,250	1,200	0	4,500
UNITED STATES	**11,500**	**19,000**	**12,000**	**7,000**	**4,000**	**11,000**
Alberta	2,966	1,822	534	1,005	565	1,978
British Columbia	4,083	628	942	1,885	0	3,298
Manitoba	1,947	0	0	0	0	1,947
Ontario	9,423	16,048	3,434	1,926	1,027	6,910
Saskatchewan	1,790	0	0	0	0	1,790
CANADA	**5,274**	**12,838**	**2,182**	**1,605**	**825**	**4,083**

Average, Median Yearling Prices in Current and Deflated Dollars, 1990-2002

Year	Average	Change	Deflated Average	Median	Change	Deflated Median	S&P 500	Change
2002	$43,424	−17%	$39,244	$10,500	+17%	$9,489	880	−23%
2001	52,173	−4%	47,683	9,000	−22%	8,225	1,148	−13%
2000	54,369	+8%	50,865	11,500	−4%	10,759	1,320	−10%
1999	50,262	+17%	48,011	12,000	+3%	11,463	1,469	+20%
1998	42,865	+12%	41,534	11,626	+6%	11,265	1,229	+27%
1997	38,144	+9%	37,415	11,000	+10%	10,790	971	+31%
1996	34,857	+14%	34,857	10,000	−5%	10,000	741	+20%
1995	30,636	+15%	31,229	10,500	+11%	10,703	616	+34%
1994	26,662	−17%	27,771	9,500	−10%	9,895	459	−2%
1993	32,052	+14%	34,080	10,500	+17%	11,164	466	+7%
1992	28,195	−21%	30,699	9,000	−5%	9,799	436	+4%
1991	35,740	−12%	39,861	9,500	−24%	10,595	417	+24%
1990	40,530	−20%	46,848	12,500	−4%	14,449	336	−5%

North American Mares Bred, 1997-2002

Year	Mares Bred	Change
2002	61,978	+0.1%
2001	61,889	+4.0%
2000	59,487	+3.2%
1999	57,629	+2.0%
1998	56,472	−0.6%
1997	56,791	

North American Mares Bred, 1998-2002

	2002	2001	2000	1999	1998
NORTH AMERICA	61,978	61,889	59,487	57,629	56,472
Alabama	93	90	98	107	146
Alaska	0	0	0	1	1
Arizona	503	402	448	472	507
Arkansas	634	550	572	599	614
California	5,716	5,720	5,376	4,967	4,501
Colorado	416	407	325	328	300
Connecticut	0	5	0	3	4
Delaware	5	0	32	4	5
District of Columbia	21	0	0	0	0
Florida	7,136	6,813	7,047	6,893	6,381
Georgia	114	92	90	102	80
Idaho	254	272	249	299	314
Illinois	1,172	1,211	1,180	952	1,093
Indiana	825	752	682	474	285
Iowa	632	708	626	811	672
Kansas	155	177	182	157	161
Kentucky	19,984	20,962	20,807	19,783	18,849
Louisiana	2,157	2,064	1,975	1,688	1,711
Maine	3	3	2	5	3
Maryland	1,835	1,851	1,750	1,910	1,959
Massachusetts	106	104	85	94	103
Michigan	429	526	357	319	400
Minnesota	299	240	167	159	127
Mississippi	72	68	28	20	26
Missouri	140	139	113	102	121
Montana	231	219	248	236	250
Nebraska	298	326	286	313	272
Nevada	10	15	9	5	8
New Hampshire	0	5	7	12	0
New Jersey	435	238	252	298	327
New Mexico	1,402	1,149	1,036	746	716
New York	2,554	2,206	2,027	1,879	1,853
North Carolina	55	55	58	88	66
North Dakota	71	80	76	60	83
Ohio	823	789	712	693	758
Oklahoma	1,613	1,858	1,557	1,769	1,695
Oregon	356	420	291	357	395
Pennsylvania	996	952	930	858	861
Puerto Rico	679	704	631	839	929
South Carolina	165	229	175	200	175
South Dakota	138	166	72	121	86
Tennessee	93	83	66	65	77
Texas	3,323	3,297	2,882	2,919	3,411
Utah	107	197	247	294	135
Vermont	11	39	0	0	0
Virginia	484	505	580	798	853
Washington	1,090	1,263	1,481	1,308	1,531
West Virginia	878	587	457	348	306
Wisconsin	35	24	26	25	40
Wyoming	29	47	32	49	34
UNITED STATES	58,577	58,609	56,329	54,529	53,224
Alberta	864	825	748	752	845
British Columbia	700	790	821	901	1,030
Manitoba	196	221	152	210	174
New Brunswick	1	7	1	1	3
Northwest Territories	5	0	0	0	0
Nova Scotia	5	5	5	2	4
Ontario	1,445	1,276	1,256	1,053	1,047
Prince Edward Island	14	0	0	0	0
Quebec	16	7	11	4	10
Saskatchewan	155	149	164	177	135
CANADA	3,401	3,280	3,158	3,100	3,248

North American Stallions in Production, 1997-2002

Year	Stallions Standing	Change
2002	3,828	−4.5%
2001	4,007	+11.1%
2000	3,608	−3.9%
1999	3,754	−3.5%
1998	3,889	−6.9%
1997	4,178	

North American Stallions in Production, 1998-2002

	2002	2001	2000	1999	1998
NORTH AMERICA	3,828	4,007	3,608	3,754	3,889
Alabama	20	16	17	20	25
Alaska	0	0	0	1	1
Arizona	60	58	66	69	75
Arkansas	71	61	58	73	69
California	355	385	356	353	347
Colorado	70	66	46	48	52
Connecticut	0	1	0	1	2
Delaware	1	0	1	1	1
District of Columbia	1	0	0	0	0
Florida	260	268	251	270	272
Georgia	24	19	18	18	15
Idaho	45	52	34	50	53
Illinois	110	122	130	110	133
Indiana	99	87	80	63	48
Iowa	56	63	57	60	57
Kansas	23	27	28	24	31
Kentucky	368	429	399	423	411
Louisiana	176	172	143	157	153
Maine	2	3	1	1	1
Maryland	92	95	90	88	101
Massachusetts	24	21	17	18	18
Michigan	53	64	44	53	56
Minnesota	35	27	18	25	26
Mississippi	14	12	9	7	6
Missouri	28	25	21	21	28
Montana	38	38	40	46	49
Nebraska	28	32	28	32	37
Nevada	4	4	4	3	2
New Hampshire	0	1	1	2	0
New Jersey	37	43	39	35	45
New Mexico	135	133	113	100	102
New York	141	121	106	121	118
North Carolina	16	16	14	19	15
North Dakota	9	12	13	11	11
Ohio	92	95	85	101	107
Oklahoma	196	217	190	208	208
Oregon	32	44	35	48	58
Pennsylvania	100	106	98	94	91
Puerto Rico	62	62	69	82	92
South Carolina	26	24	22	22	23
South Dakota	13	18	8	15	11
Tennessee	24	23	18	23	20
Texas	346	363	317	311	332
Utah	18	42	35	36	30
Vermont	5	3	0	0	0
Virginia	56	69	64	80	86

	2002	2001	2000	1999	1998
Washington	89	105	105	96	124
West Virginia	60	47	41	32	24
Wisconsin	13	12	9	7	12
Wyoming	10	14	10	16	13
UNITED STATES	**3,537**	**3,717**	**3,348**	**3,494**	**3,591**
Alberta	81	74	64	72	92
British Columbia	61	74	66	66	79
Manitoba	22	22	19	21	19
New Brunswick	1	2	1	1	1
Northwest Territories	1	0	0	0	0
Nova Scotia	2	2	2	1	1
Ontario	92	91	82	74	83
Prince Edward Island	1	0	0	0	0
Quebec	7	4	3	1	5
Saskatchewan	23	21	23	24	18
CANADA	**291**	**290**	**260**	**260**	**298**

	2002	2001	2000	1999	1998
Kansas	91	107	104	70	104
Kentucky	12,276	14,615	13,903	13,084	12,165
Louisiana	1,305	1,309	1,007	997	1,018
Maine	2	3	1	1	0
Maryland	1,189	1,213	1,229	1,193	1,265
Massachusetts	48	58	52	53	71
Michigan	317	236	176	241	280
Minnesota	138	90	90	52	77
Mississippi	37	26	10	14	24
Missouri	69	92	85	97	100
Montana	93	149	119	133	174
Nebraska	159	173	174	107	123
Nevada	18	5	5	14	15
New Hampshire	1	6	7	0	2
New Jersey	179	184	182	205	215
New Mexico	650	580	397	372	360
New York	1,423	1,411	1,176	1,142	1,036
North Carolina	35	54	50	50	64
North Dakota	56	46	37	39	43
Ohio	453	477	407	390	452
Oklahoma	1,016	1,069	893	863	940
Oregon	267	213	247	219	204
Pennsylvania	546	601	493	461	446
Puerto Rico	530	629	562	679	663
South Carolina	117	89	106	83	75
South Dakota	63	64	45	32	25
Tennessee	31	38	31	34	31
Texas	1,979	2,009	1,623	1,656	1,774
Utah	121	124	132	124	152
Vermont	3	0	7	0	2
Virginia	323	373	461	462	333
Washington	823	987	874	850	907
West Virginia	350	295	189	151	134
Wisconsin	15	27	25	14	15
Wyoming	25	20	20	15	17
UNITED STATES	**35,788**	**38,258**	**34,751**	**32,790**	**32,232**
Alberta	446	485	418	445	370
British Columbia	473	511	547	579	550
Manitoba	95	106	104	76	112
New Brunswick	1	1	1	1	0
Nova Scotia	3	3	1	1	5
Ontario	896	832	659	622	662
Quebec	4	5	1	2	13
Saskatchewan	90	108	85	78	86
CANADA	**2,008**	**2,051**	**1,816**	**1,804**	**1,798**

North American Live Foals, 1997-2002

Year	Live Foals	Change
2002	37,796	−6.2%
2001	40,309	+10.2%
2000	36,567	+5.7%
1999	34,594	+1.7%
1998	34,030	+1.8%
1997	33,443	

North American Live Foals, 1998-2002

	2002	2001	2000	1999	1998
NORTH AMERICA	**37,796**	**40,309**	**36,567**	**34,594**	**34,030**
Alabama	55	61	74	64	56
Alaska	0	0	1	0	2
Arizona	267	316	263	256	333
Arkansas	317	323	305	264	316
California	4,022	3,796	3,301	2,857	3,075
Colorado	217	205	203	159	149
Connecticut	4	5	3	7	4
Delaware	0	24	4	4	16
Florida	4,517	4,527	4,381	3,979	3,622
Georgia	58	51	71	41	94
Hawaii	1	0	0	0	2
Idaho	142	201	163	171	196
Illinois	658	630	444	559	622
Indiana	379	363	271	175	115
Iowa	403	384	348	357	324

Aggregate North American Stud Fees, 1998-2002

	2002	2001	2000	1999	1998
NORTH AMERICA	**$470,079,200**	**$445,807,075**	**$381,291,150**	**$318,405,625**	**$279,863,225**
Alabama	20,250	18,800	25,750	29,600	13,250
Arizona	68,800	110,300	194,800	176,400	277,750
Arkansas	262,750	327,000	204,150	146,950	177,550
California	19,627,650	17,902,850	8,686,150	7,976,400	6,837,850
Colorado	85,600	73,000	80,000	54,300	49,900
Connecticut	2,250	3,750	2,250	5,000	1,650
Delaware	0	2,500	4,000	0	0
Florida	18,906,050	17,980,100	18,976,500	16,003,100	13,150,450
Georgia	31,050	7,950	17,900	8,500	16,850
Idaho	129,150	126,800	109,800	76,950	131,400
Illinois	722,200	673,150	387,250	333,300	265,600
Indiana	295,450	324,700	236,150	169,600	42,850
Iowa	354,750	328,750	260,400	270,550	220,875
Kansas	50,800	62,250	52,500	42,400	29,250
Kentucky	399,538,250	379,143,300	327,608,300	270,748,000	238,505,400
Louisiana	1,348,050	1,223,250	985,500	877,850	787,850
Maryland	7,626,850	7,117,200	7,235,500	6,475,050	5,573,350
Massachusetts	26,500	35,950	17,000	29,250	11,500
Michigan	287,050	135,450	74,650	136,250	225,000

	2002	2001	2000	1999	1998
Minnesota	80,600	45,150	34,850	14,350	15,000
Mississippi	6,000	6,500	0	2,500	3,500
Missouri	34,100	23,500	30,200	24,300	21,550
Montana	48,450	45,300	40,750	34,300	49,300
Nebraska	88,450	174,750	103,350	38,500	40,450
Nevada	2,500	0	5,000	2,500	2,500
New Hampshire	12,000	15,250	3,000	0	200
New Jersey	167,750	194,000	134,500	152,900	234,400
New Mexico	433,650	402,100	308,350	268,300	148,150
New York	6,450,300	7,577,650	4,376,650	4,277,200	3,565,500
North Carolina	30,100	14,550	27,500	9,350	41,400
North Dakota	30,500	10,400	17,400	11,600	4,500
Ohio	413,200	419,200	265,950	256,300	184,000
Oklahoma	774,950	834,275	747,250	691,725	711,600
Oregon	378,350	335,900	154,900	132,500	111,000
Pennsylvania	793,550	942,050	780,050	606,550	585,800
Puerto Rico	204,000	208,500	272,500	15,500	237,750
South Carolina	113,000	116,000	120,250	63,500	1,750
South Dakota	20,200	5,700	5,300	6,900	9,000
Tennessee	2,800	2,000	5,200	12,500	11,400
Texas	3,136,000	2,443,150	2,279,600	2,412,400	1,925,400
Utah	74,500	129,000	127,350	89,300	93,450
Virginia	421,500	520,100	716,350	628,750	298,050
Washington	1,362,700	1,252,700	1,168,900	1,123,950	1,345,050
West Virginia	385,050	224,550	142,750	106,500	55,900
Wisconsin	1,200	4,000	2,950	2,100	3,500
Wyoming	1,000	400	1,500	500	1,600
UNITED STATES	**$464,849,850**	**$441,543,725**	**$377,030,900**	**$314,544,225**	**$276,020,025**
Alberta	595,700	596,750	565,750	516,600	408,400
British Columbia	1,026,100	612,550	1,271,800	1,463,450	1,145,550
Manitoba	62,350	66,250	69,600	53,850	56,750
Ontario	3,483,600	2,913,050	2,307,750	1,778,750	2,196,250
Quebec	400	0	600	0	18,000
Saskatchewan	61,200	74,750	44,750	48,750	18,250
CANADA	**$5,229,350**	**$4,263,350**	**$4,260,250**	**$3,861,400**	**$3,843,200**

Average North American Stud Fees, 1998-2002

	2002	2001	2000	1999	1998		2002	2001	2000	1999	1998
NORTH AMERICA	$15,025	$13,552	$12,319	$11,230	$10,561	New Mexico	1,668	1,535	1,421	1,427	903
Alabama	920	940	954	871	663	New York	4,981	5,990	4,133	4,483	4,296
Arizona	983	985	1,325	1,389	1,335	North Carolina	1,075	1,039	1,058	850	881
Arkansas	1,257	1,428	972	875	925	North Dakota	847	693	1,243	1,055	900
California	5,764	5,766	3,258	3,377	2,904	Ohio	1,440	1,310	1,141	1,176	1,195
Colorado	1,259	890	920	920	846	Oklahoma	1,298	1,328	1,148	1,143	1,259
Connecticut	750	750	750	714	550	Oregon	1,674	1,836	1,040	953	847
Delaware		500	1,000			Pennsylvania	1,816	1,892	1,871	1,805	1,786
Florida	4,634	4,367	4,656	4,521	4,080	Puerto Rico	2,400	2,044	2,620	1,192	1,524
Georgia	1,194	795	778	944	991	South Carolina	1,527	1,657	1,542	1,176	583
Idaho	1,389	1,075	955	884	1,035	South Dakota	721	633	530	767	750
Illinois	1,550	1,562	1,222	1,111	1,121	Tennessee	700	667	867	962	1,267
Indiana	1,349	1,510	1,389	1,731	874	Texas	2,306	2,017	2,140	2,289	1,991
Iowa	1,186	1,162	1,050	1,078	944	Utah	1,433	1,654	1,384	1,374	1,639
Kansas	1,058	1,270	795	785	750	Virginia	1,960	1,838	1,957	1,668	1,656
Kentucky	32,982	26,328	23,927	21,032	19,897	Washington	2,016	1,939	1,835	1,810	2,060
Louisiana	1,398	1,429	1,309	1,302	1,338	West Virginia	1,226	854	881	934	726
Maryland	6,816	6,366	6,168	5,725	5,057	Wisconsin	600	500	590	700	875
Massachusetts	2,038	1,892	1,545	1,045	767	Wyoming	500	400	1,500	500	400
Michigan	1,586	1,411	1,204	1,434	1,490	**UNITED STATES**	**$15,659**	**$14,004**	**$12,793**	**$11,680**	**$10,933**
Minnesota	1,089	1,328	830	718	789						
Mississippi	667	650		500	500	Alberta	1,773	2,072	1,892	1,806	1,882
Missouri	1,795	904	774	868	673	British Columbia	2,890	2,211	2,611	2,842	2,683
Montana	1,242	1,105	926	746	1,174	Manitoba	1,057	989	1,088	1,197	1,158
Nebraska	1,638	1,165	1,123	837	749	Ontario	4,333	4,216	3,802	3,217	4,144
Nevada	2,500		2,500	2,500	2,500	Quebec	400		600		2,000
New Hampshire	1,500	1,271	750		200	Saskatchewan	1,330	1,699	1,946	2,031	830
New Jersey	1,598	1,528	1,269	1,514	1,711	**CANADA**	**$3,266**	**$3,119**	**$2,877**	**$2,714**	**$3,065**

All About Purses 2002

by Mark Simon

Purses for racehorse owners in 2002 were never better. They also took a turn for the worse. Those contradictory trends summarized racetrack purse distribution in 2002. Changes in the racing industry over the past decade, principally full-card simulcasting, have helped to push purses to the most favorable levels for racehorse owners in years. That trend is relatively intact, but the number of runners increased again in 2002, which drove down earnings opportunities for owners. North American purses increased to a record $1.17-billion in 2002, and, coupled with another dip in the total number of races carded in North America, average purses reached a record $19,597. But a 2.2% increase in the number of runners—following a 2.5% increase the previous year—meant that average earnings per runner declined in 2002, to $16,139. While the decrease was just 0.1%, it marked the first time since 1986 that average earnings per runner have declined. Highlights of the data included in this comprehensive annual review of purses and runners in North America are:

- A record $1,170,169,267 in purses was distributed in 59,712 North American races.
- The total number of races continued its long descent after peaking at 82,726 in 1989 and reached its lowest level since 1972.
- Average purse increased to $19,597, a rise of 40% since 1997.
- The total number of runners increased for the fourth straight year, the first time it has increased in four consecutive years since the 1980s.

- Average earnings per runner declined 0.1% to $16,139.
- Nominal median earnings per runner also declined 0.1%, the first such decline since 1986.
- Real average earnings per runner—adjusted for inflation—declined 1.3%.
- 7,555 runners—10.4% of all starters—failed to earn any part of a purse.
- More than half of all starters—52.2%—failed to win a race in 2002.
- Horses that won a race earned an average of $30,099; horses that failed to win a race earned an average of $3,351.
- Horses that won a stakes race earned an average of $147,864.
- Winners collectively earned 89.2% of all purse money.
- 17.6% of all runners earned $25,000 or more and collectively won 68.7% of all purse money.
- 61.6% of all runners earned less than $10,000.
- Races at 1¼ miles accounted for just 0.3% of total races but distributed 2.8% of all purse money, an average of $156,657.
- Stakes races constituted 4.2% of all races and offered 22.8% of all purses.
- 41.8% of all races offered a purse of less than $10,000.
- Claiming races—straight claiming and maiden claiming—accounted for 65.9% of all races but distributed just 38% of all purses.
- Almost half of all races were carded at six furlongs or less.
- The average number of starts per horse continued its long decline, falling to 6.8 in 2002, the fewest ever.

Table 1
Selected Racing Statistics, North American Thoroughbred Racing, 1993-2002

Year	No. of Runners	No. of Races	Total Purses	Average Purse	Earnings Per Runner Average	Earnings Per Runner Median
1993	78,763	72,224	$ 748,415,925	$10,362	$ 9,502	$2,850
1994	74,939	70,617	770,426,193	10,910	10,280	3,314
1995	72,316	68,197	815,987,125	11,965	11,283	3,702
1996	70,371	64,263	845,916,706	13,163	12,021	3,937
1997	69,067	63,491	888,667,752	13,997	12,867	4,425
1998	68,419	61,141	968,366,929	15,838	14,153	4,939
1999	68,435	60,118	1,008,162,608	16,770	14,732	5,310
2000	69,230	60,579	1,093,661,241	18,053	15,798	5,796
2001	70,942	60,538	1,146,337,367	18,936	16,159	6,010
2002	72,504	59,712	1,170,169,267	19,597	16,139	6,003
Change:						
1993-2002	−7.9%	−17.3%	56.4%	89.1%	69.8%	110.6%
2001-2002	2.2%	−1.4%	2.1%	3.5%	−0.1%	−0.1%
Average Change:						
1993-2002	−0.8%	−1.7%	5.6%	8.9%	7.0%	11.1%

Table 2
Distribution of Earnings of Runners for 2002

Earnings Range	No. of Runners	Percent of Runners	Earnings	Percent of Earnings	Average Earnings
$300,000 or more	177	0.2%	$102,163,720	8.7%	$577,196
$200,000 - 299,999	172	0.2%	41,943,444	3.6%	243,857
$100,000 - 199,999	1,084	1.5%	144,054,522	12.3%	132,892
$75,000 - 99,999	1,064	1.5%	91,548,163	7.8%	86,042
$50,000 - 74,999	2,537	3.5%	153,820,482	13.1%	60,631
$25,000 - 49,999	7,759	10.7%	269,978,693	23.1%	34,796
$20,000 - 24,999	3,314	4.6%	74,069,359	6.3%	22,350
$15,000 - 19,999	4,686	6.5%	81,232,387	6.9%	17,335
$10,000 - 14,999	7,067	9.7%	87,155,881	7.4%	12,333
$9,000 - 9,999	1,868	2.6%	17,729,488	1.5%	9,491
$8,000 - 8,999	2,007	2.8%	17,031,335	1.5%	8,486
$7,000 - 7,999	2,174	3.0%	16,291,015	1.4%	7,494
$6,000 - 6,999	2,379	3.3%	15,444,496	1.3%	6,492
$5,000 - 5,999	2,535	3.5%	13,901,326	1.2%	5,484
$4,000 - 4,999	2,733	3.8%	12,265,557	1.0%	4,488
$3,000 - 3,999	2,973	4.1%	10,357,943	0.9%	3,484
$2,000 - 2,999	3,693	5.1%	9,174,521	0.8%	2,484
$1,000 - 1,999	5,004	6.9%	7,297,696	0.6%	1,458
$1 - 999	11,723	16.2%	4,709,239	0.4%	402
None	7,555	10.4%	0	0.0%	0
Totals	**72,504**	**100.0%**	**$1,170,169,267**	**100.0%**	**$16,139**

• Average field size moved up marginally to 8.3 starters per race, the second consecutive increase.

These statistics reflect all Thoroughbred purses distributed to racehorses in North America in 2002, excluding Mexico and Puerto Rico, and were based on data obtained from Jockey Club Information Systems Inc. Steeplechase races are excluded.

Purses Up, Races Down

For the ninth consecutive year, total purses distributed in North America rose from the previous year. The record $1,170,169,267 distributed in 2002 represents a 2.1% increase over 2001. The last time total purses did not increase over the previous year was in 1993, shortly before the full-card simulcasting boom. The big-picture details of total purses are found in Table 1. Purses have increased 56.4% over the last ten years, fueled by full-card simulcasting, which allows fans to bet on races at virtually any track in the country. While on-track attendance is down at almost every track nationally, pari-mutuel handle—the engine that drives purses—increased again in 2002, by 3.2%, to a record $15,048,033,312, according to Equibase. The total number of races run in North America has declined steadily since peaking at 82,726 races in 1989. In 2002, with races again declining 1.4% to 59,712, average purse in North America reached a record $19,597. The number of races run in 2002 was the fewest since 1972, when 59,417 were held. Since 1993, average purse has climbed 89.1%. That is the good news. The bad news is that the number of runners increased again, for the fourth straight year, causing a slight decrease in average earnings per runner. The annual registered foal crop in North America peaked at 51,296 in 1986 and dropped to 34,977 by 1995, a 32% decline. Since then, the number of registered foals in North America has climbed, to an estimated 36,800 for the 2001 crop, though the 2002 foal crop (estimated at 35,600) will be smaller due to the effects of mare reproductive loss syndrome.

Median earnings—half of all runners earned more than the median figure, and half earned less—were just $6,003 in 2002, roughly $10,000 per runner less than the average. Over a ten-year period, median earnings have increased 110.6%, far more than the increase in average earnings but still nowhere close to covering an owner's training costs, let alone the cost of the horse. Adjusted for inflation, the picture was even worse. In current dollars, average earnings per runner declined 0.1%, but in real terms the decline was 1.3%; it was the first decline in real average earnings per runner in 11 years. Over the past ten years, real average earnings per runner increased 44.5%, more than doubling the 17.5% rate of inflation during that time period as measured by the federal government's implicit price deflator. One encouraging measure is deflated average purse, which increased 2.3% in 2002. Over the past ten years, deflated average purses have increased 60.9%. Among the inflation-adjusted statistics, median earnings per runner have experienced the biggest increase in the last decade, jumping 79.2%, to $5,425. Table 2, which breaks down all runners in 2002 by earnings categories, illustrates how hard it is to get a top earner. A mere 2% of all runners earned $100,000 or more in 2002. Those 1,433 horses earned a total of $288,161,686, or 24.6% of all purse money available in North America. The 177 runners that earned $300,000 or more had an average of $577,196, taking 8.7% of all purses. At the other end of the spectrum, 7,555 runners, 10.4% of the total, earned nothing. In 2001, 9.4% of all runners had failed to earn any part of a purse. In 2002, 11,723 runners earned less than $1,000 each, meaning that 26.6% of all runners earned less than $1,000. In 2002, 1,753 horses won stakes races (there were a total of 2,515 stakes races), meaning 2.4% of the 72,504 runners won a stakes. Stakes winners earned an average of $147,864, or 9.2 times the average, and they earned a total of $259,205,384, which is 22.2% of all purses. Stakes distributed 22.8% of all purses in 2002, down from 23% in 2001.

Starts and Wins

Table 3 breaks down earnings as a function of starts in 2002. Horses that started fewer than six times earned less on average than the overall average for all runners, $16,139. Average earnings per runner increase with each start until leveling off in the mid-$20,000 range at eight or more starts.

Horses that started more than ten times— 22% of the total—earned $412.2-million, 35.2% of all purse money. Average earnings per start in 2002 were $2,369, and horses with three or fewer starts did not attain that average. The av-

erage per race peaks at $3,169 for eight starts and gradually diminishes with greater numbers of starts. Fragility of today's horses is evident from starts data over the years. In 2002, 22% of all horses started more than ten times; in 1992, the percentage was 30.7%; in 1982, 37%; in 1972, 42.4%; and in 1967, 47.5%. Horses that failed to win—52.2% of all runners—earned an average of just $3,351. Horses that won just one race earned more than five times as much, $18,140. Since more than half of all runners could not win a race and those runners earned an aggregate of $126.8-million, the 34,665 winners divvied up the remaining $1.04-billion. With so much money available to winners, earnings rose dramatically with every victory. Horses that won two races earned an average of $33,633; three races, $51,129; four races, $67,962; and on up the ladder. Winners collectively earned 89.2% of all purse money.

Table 4, which examines how purses are distributed by age and sex, reveals significant disparities in both categories. Three-year-olds have the best opportunity to earn money. The average purse for races exclusively for three-year-olds is $29,293, 49.5% higher than the overall average purse of $19,597. While just 11.1% of all races are for three-year-olds, those 6,633 races distributed 16.6% of all purses in 2002. Among the major categories, two-year-olds had the fewest races, accounting for 8% of all races in 2002 and 11.2% of all purse money. They also had the second-highest average purse, $27,441. The category with the most races was three-year-olds and up, offering 65.4% of all races and 58.7% of all purses. The category's average purse of $17,593 was less than the $19,597 overall average. Races open to either sex—which

Table 3
Earnings as a Function of Number of Wins for 2002

Races Won	No. of Runners	Percent of Runners	Total Earnings	Percent of Earnings	Average Earnings
More than 13	0	0.0%	$ 0	0.0%	$ 0
13	0	0.0%	0	0.0%	0
12	0	0.0%	0	0.0%	0
11	1	0.0%	67,855	0.0%	67,855
10	1	0.0%	95,680	0.0%	95,680
9	7	0.0%	925,607	0.1%	132,230
8	27	0.0%	5,269,824	0.5%	195,179
7	58	0.1%	6,485,519	0.6%	111,819
6	171	0.2%	20,382,546	1.7%	119,196
5	551	0.8%	50,242,503	4.3%	91,184
4	1,494	2.1%	101,534,738	8.7%	67,962
3	3,980	5.5%	203,494,401	17.4%	51,129
2	9,047	12.5%	304,278,254	26.0%	33,633
1	19,328	26.7%	350,607,908	30.0%	18,140
0	37,839	52.2%	126,784,432	10.8%	3,351
Totals	**72,504**	**100.0%**	**$1,170,169,267**	**100.0%**	**$16,139**

for all practical purposes are for males—were far more abundant than races exclusively for females, with 58.9% of all races open to either sex and 40.7% restricted to females. Just 0.4%, 259 races, were restricted to males. Races restricted to females featured purses higher on average than those open to all sexes. Average purse for races restricted to females was $20,076, while the average for either sex was $19,118.Table 5 examines the differences in earnings by age and sex. While females have the opportunity to run in more races than males, fillies and mares earned an average of $15,520, 6.6% less than the male average of $16,622. In every age bracket, males earned more than females. In the three-year-old category, males earned an average of $19,938, compared with

$17,934 for fillies. The largest difference was in the five-year-old category, with males earning an average of 16.7% per runner more than females. Three-year-olds were the largest age group, with 28.9% of all runners, followed by four-year-olds with 22.7%. Three-year-olds also earned the largest share of purses, taking 33.9% of all money available.

Claiming Statistics

The prevalence of claiming races on the American scene is illustrated by Table 6, which shows the distribution of races in 2002 by class of race. Almost two out of every three North American races, 65.9%, in 2002 featured claimers, including maiden claimers, which were 16.4% of all races. Claiming races fea-

Table 4
Distribution of Races and Purses by Age and Sex for 2002

Sex	No. of Races	Percent of Races	Purses	Percent of Purses	Avg. Purse Per Race
			Two-Year-Olds		
Females	2,179	3.6%	$ 60,831,323	5.2%	$27,917
Males	93	0.2%	5,377,269	0.5%	57,820
Either sex	2,519	4.2%	65,262,935	5.6%	25,908
Overall	4,791	8.0%	131,471,527	11.2%	27,441
			Three-Year-Olds		
Females	3,126	5.2%	84,685,493	7.2%	27,091
Males	99	0.2%	3,059,111	0.3%	30,900
Either sex	3,408	5.7%	106,556,365	9.1%	31,267
Overall	6,633	11.1%	194,300,969	16.6%	29,293
			Three-Year-Olds and Up		
Females	15,526	26.0%	281,678,527	24.1%	18,142
Males	61	0.1%	1,542,244	0.1%	25,283
Either sex	23,464	39.3%	403,801,700	34.5%	17,209
Overall	39,051	65.4%	687,022,471	58.7%	17,593
			Four-Year-Olds		
Females	89	0.1%	2,127,236	0.2%	23,902
Males	3	0.0%	48,400	0.0%	16,133
Either sex	103	0.2%	2,876,213	0.2%	27,924
Overall	195	0.3%	5,051,849	0.4%	25,907
			Four-Year-Olds and Up		
Females	3,358	5.6%	58,074,962	5.0%	17,295
Males	3	0.0%	263,248	0.0%	87,749
Either sex	5,674	9.5%	93,964,806	8.0%	16,561
Overall	9,035	15.1%	152,303,016	13.0%	16,857
			Five-Year-Olds and Up		
Females	0	0.0%	0	0.0%	0
Males	0	0.0%	0	0.0%	0
Either sex	7	0.0%	19,435	0.0%	2,776
Overall	7	0.0%	19,435	0.0%	2,776
			Totals		
Females	24,278	40.7%	487,397,541	41.7%	20,076
Males	259	0.4%	10,290,272	0.9%	39,731
Either sex	35,175	58.9%	672,481,454	57.5%	19,118
Overall	59,712	100.0%	1,170,169,267	100.0%	19,597

Table 5
Distribution of Runners and Earnings by Age and Sex for 2002

Sex	No. of Runners	Percent of Runners	Earnings	Percent of Earnings	Average Earnings
			Two-Year-Olds		
Females	5,891	8.1%	$ 62,855,496	5.4%	$10,670
Males	6,072	8.4%	68,607,631	5.9%	11,299
Overall	11,963	16.5%	131,463,127	11.2%	10,989
			Three-Year-Olds		
Females	10,432	14.4%	187,084,194	16.0%	17,934
Males	10,487	14.5%	209,090,951	17.9%	19,938
Overall	20,919	28.9%	396,175,145	33.9%	18,939
			Four-Year-Olds		
Females	7,640	10.5%	140,580,330	12.0%	18,401
Males	8,847	12.2%	168,504,248	14.4%	19,046
Overall	16,487	22.7%	309,084,578	26.4%	18,747
			Five-Year-Olds and Up		
Females	4,229	5.8%	62,825,245	5.4%	14,856
Males	6,164	8.5%	110,005,300	9.4%	17,846
Overall	10,394	14.3%	172,858,175	14.8%	16,631
			Six-Year-Olds and Up		
Females	3,562	4.9%	39,470,088	3.4%	11,081
Males	9,178	12.7%	121,117,114	10.4%	13,196
Overall	12,741	17.6%	160,588,242	13.7%	12,604
			Totals		
Females	**31,754**	**43.8%**	**492,815,353**	**42.1%**	**15,520**
Males	**40,748**	**56.2%**	**677,325,244**	**57.9%**	**16,622**
Overall	**72,504**	**100.0%**	**1,170,169,267**	**100.0%**	**16,139**

tured below-average purses, distributing just 38% of all purses. The average claiming purse of $11,306 was 42.3% lower than the overall average of $19,597.

The number of claiming races has declined 23.4% in the past decade, though in recent years the trend has reversed. In the early 1970s, claiming races consistently composed approximately 73% of all races. After whole-card simulcasting took off, the percentage of claiming races began to decline, dropping to an all-time low of 64.5% in 2000. That trend has reversed modestly in the past two years, however, as the number of starters has increased. Allowance races are the second-most common races and in 2002 featured an average purse of $27,469, distributing 18.2% of all purses. The third-most common race type was straight maiden races, making up 10.6% of all races and

distributing 12.9% of all purses. Despite the rich purses in stakes events, average field size in stakes in 2002 was 7.8, lower than the overall average for the year. Both straight maiden and maiden claiming races featured average fields of 8.9 starters.

Number of starts per runner has been in a long, steady decline since reaching a peak in the 1950s. In 2002, average number of starts per horse breeched the downside of the seven-start mark for the first time, falling to 6.8. The average number of starts per horse in 1960 was slightly more than 11 per year. In 2002, average field size inched up to 8.3, from 8.2 in 2001, as the number of races declined. Sprint races, the most common race on a typical race card, carry the lowest purses on average, while races at more than one mile carry the highest average purses. The de-

Figure 2
Distribution of purses by best finish position

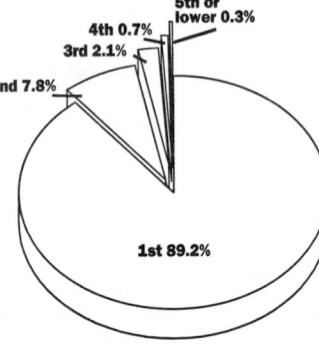

5th or lower 0.3%
4th 0.7%
3rd 2.1%
2nd 7.8%
1st 89.2%

Table 6
Distribution of Races by Class for 2002

	No. of Races	Percent of Races	Average Starters	Purses	Percent of Purses	Avg. Purse Per Race
Maiden Claiming	9,785	16.4%	8.9	$106,379,969	9.1%	$10,872
Claiming	29,566	49.5%	8.2	338,521,749	28.9%	11,450
$0 to 999	0	0.0%	0.0	0	0.0%	0
$1,000 to 1,999	147	0.2%	6.6	286,435	0.0%	1,949
$2,000 to 2,999	1,637	2.7%	8.2	7,174,394	0.6%	4,383
$3,000 to 3,999	3,449	5.8%	8.6	19,606,673	1.7%	5,685
$4,000 to 4,999	4,396	7.4%	8.6	30,571,778	2.6%	6,954
$5,000 to 5,999	4,695	7.9%	8.5	37,973,629	3.2%	8,088
$6,000 to 6,999	1,161	1.9%	7.9	10,250,467	0.9%	8,829
$7,000 to 7,999	2,215	3.7%	8.4	20,808,157	1.8%	9,394
$8,000 to 8,999	929	1.6%	7.7	9,488,717	0.8%	10,214
$9,000 to 9,999	80	0.1%	8.9	601,494	0.1%	7,519
$10,000 to 14,999	4,642	7.8%	8.0	58,332,938	5.0%	12,566
$15,000 to 19,999	2,089	3.5%	7.9	32,400,955	2.8%	15,510
$20,000 and up	4,126	6.9%	7.7	111,026,112	9.5%	26,909
Total Claiming	39,351	65.9%	8.4	$444,901,718	38.0%	$11,306
Optional Claiming	50	0.1%	7.5	516,625	0.0%	10,333
Starter Allowance	1,258	2.1%	7.5	19,517,694	1.7%	15,515
Starter Handicap	63	0.1%	7.9	1,110,114	0.1%	17,621
Maiden	6,339	10.6%	8.9	150,869,884	12.9%	23,800
Allowance	7,732	12.9%	7.8	212,388,141	18.2%	27,469
Handicap	35	0.1%	7.1	860,244	0.1%	24,578
Stakes	2,515	4.2%	7.8	266,561,679	22.8%	105,989
Total Nonclaiming	17,992	30.1%	8.2	$651,824,381	55.7%	$36,229
Total All Races	59,712	100.0%	8.3	$1,170,169,267	100.0%	$19,597

marcation line is at one mile. While the overall average purse in 2002 was $18,913 (excluding juvenile races), the average purse at less than one mile was $14,988 and at more than one mile was twice as much, $30,479. Average purse for races at one mile was $19,565. Slightly more than half of all purse money, 51.2%, was distributed in races at less than one mile, but almost three times as many races were carded at less than one mile than at more than one mile.

The most common distance of races was six furlongs, with 17,167 races, almost one in every three races held in North America for horses older than age two. Though six-furlong races were the most common, they offered below-average purses of $15,570. Highest average purse was offered at the American classic distance of 1¼ miles, which featured an average purse of $156,657. That category, which encompasses the Breeders' Cup Classic (G1) and Kentucky Derby (G1), had only 184 races in 2002. Table 7 presents the actual distribution of races by purse in North America in 2002. Only 78 races, or 0.1% of the total, carried a purse of $500,000 or more. Another 830 races, or 1.4% of the total, offered purses of $100,000 or more. Those 908 races distributed $192.4-million, or 16.4% of purse money.

Mark Simon is editor of Thoroughbred Times.

Table 7
Distribution of All North American Races by Purse for 2002

Range of Purses	No. of Races	Total Purses
$499 or less	14	$ 0
$500-999	12	11,320
$1,000-1,999	443	716,272
$2,000-2,999	1,146	2,736,328
$3,000-3,999	1,333	4,663,459
$4,000-4,999	3,401	15,425,342
$5,000-5,999	4,534	24,658,647
$6,000-6,999	3,685	23,622,865
$7,000-7,999	4,098	30,329,719
$8,000-8,999	3,199	26,603,957
$9,000-9,999	3,109	28,981,894
$10,000-12,499	6,864	76,224,481
$12,500-14,999	4,659	63,381,657
$15,000-19,999	5,824	98,652,826
$20,000-24,999	4,061	89,702,282
$25,000-29,999	3,275	87,918,773
$30,000-39,999	3,808	128,086,588
$40,000-49,999	2,974	131,138,686
$50,000-74,999	2,011	116,252,692
$75,000-99,999	354	28,622,306
$100,000-199,999	615	76,005,556
$200,000-299,999	157	35,550,187
$300,000-399,999	35	11,175,050
$400,000-499,999	23	9,492,900
$500,000-749,999	44	22,911,550
$750,000-999,999	17	13,699,490
$1,000,000 and up	17	23,604,440
Totals	**59,712**	**$1,170,169,267**

Racetrack Purses by Region in 2002

In January 2003, American Gaming Association President Frank J. Fahrenkopf predicted that the future of gambling expansion over the next decade would be fueled not by casinos such as those in Las Vegas, but by racinos, the hybrid of a racetrack and a casino.

The racino movement is reviled by racing purists, but it increasingly is being viewed as a tool for boosting state revenues in a period of budget deficits and a need for new sources of funds. By the first half of 2003, many states were considering whether to place slot machines or video lottery terminals at racetracks.

In some states, racinos are a method for increasing purses to a level where a horse owner has a fighting chance to break even on his or her racing operations. Slot machines made Delaware Park the Mid-Atlantic region's leading track, as measured by purse payments, and because of slots the West Virginia tracks no longer are the poor relatives of the industry's elite. New Mexico is blossoming, and Delta Downs in Louisiana has emerged from the bush to pay per-race purses that are approaching the national average, which was $19,597 in 2002.

In a year when North American purses struggled to keep pace with inflation, the states and Canadian provinces that performed the best in 2002 were those with alternative forms of gaming and provisions for those games to benefit purses. With benefits of full-card simulcasting having generally run their course, most racetracks stood still or slipped back slightly without the revenue stream from alternative gaming, which generally meant slot machines. In the following sections, purses are reviewed by racetrack by region.

Northeast

Northeast tracks have been waiting for slot machines, but by 2003 no track had yet installed them. New York has had authorization to install video lottery terminals since late 2001. New Jersey legislators have put forward bills to authorize slot machines at three state tracks, but the bills often run headlong into the big-money opposition of Atlantic City casinos.

In November 2002, Pennsylvania elected a pro-slots governor, Edward G. Rendell, but a flurry of proposals to build the Keystone State's last authorized Thoroughbred racetrack may slow the process of authorizing slot machines there.

New Hampshire's Rockingham Park gave up on Thoroughbred racing for 2003 and instead raced a 100-date Standardbred meet. But track owners have made it clear the historic Salem property might be offered for sale if the state Legislature does not authorize slot machines. Suffolk Downs in Massachusetts picked up some of the slack from Rockingham's breed change.

While it does not have slot machines, the New York Racing Association has one of the most potent racing programs in North America, and it has ridden the full-card boom to a strong purse structure.

Monmouth Park, the gem of the Jersey Shore, offers very good purses for its spring-summer meet, and Meadowlands's fall meet beats the national average purse. But, without a legislative purse supplement in 2002, the two New Jersey Sports and Exposition Authority tracks paid significantly lower purses than in '01, and another decline was expected for '03.

Every other track in the Northeast pays purses below that of the national average. One particularly bright spot on the 2002 calendar was Suffolk, where a 2001 law put pari-mutuel tax money into purses and resulted in a 16% increase in average daily purse distribution.

Mid-Atlantic

When Robert Ehrlich Jr. scored an upset victory in November 2002 to become Maryland's governor, it appeared the Free State's racetracks were speeding toward getting slot machines, which the tracks say they need to compete with Delaware Park.

Maryland's track operators repeatedly have harbored the hollow hope that they were on the brink of getting slots ever since the machines began to transform Delaware Park from a beautiful track with relatively small purses into the Mid-Atlantic region's heavy hitter among horse owners and trainers.

As legislators kicked around slots proposals, Laurel Park and Pimlico Race Course continued to lose ground. Laurel's daily purse distribution dropped 6% across its three race meets in 2002. At Pimlico, which held spring and fall meets, the decline was 2%. Magna Entertainment Corp. bought a majority interest in the tracks in 2002 and pledged improvements, but uncertainties related to slots slowed backstretch renovations.

While turmoil roiled Maryland, Delaware continued to have the region's best purses in 2002 and will remain its purse leader in '03. Slots were installed at Delaware Park in late 1995, and they have resulted in a substantial increase in purse payments, both for stakes races and overnight races. In 2002, Delaware's average purse increased 10% to more than $32,000. The Wilmington-area track also became one of the best places to run claiming horses, with an average claiming purse well above the North American average for all purses.

West Virginia also has slots, and its two Thoroughbred tracks have used the money to upgrade both their facilities and purses, although not on the same scale as Delaware. Mountaineer Race Track continued to pour money into its racing program, and its purses approached the North American average in 2002. Charles Town Races had a decline in its average purse per race in 2002, but its pots still are well above the subsistence-level purses paid before Penn National Gaming bought the track and installed slots.

Colonial Downs, Virginia's only pari-mutuel track, continues to be hampered by a state government that is ambivalent about any type of gambling and by enmity between Colonial owner Jeffrey Jacobs and the chairperson of the Virginia Racing Commission, Robin Traywick Williams. Still, Virginia pays purses above the national average and was on course to maintain that distinction in 2003.

Southeast

Caught by a horse shortage caused in part by Hialeah Park's closing, Gulfstream Park's average daily purses fell 18% in 2002. But the managers of the Magna track recognized the effects of smaller fields and undertook construction of Palm Meadows Training Center in Boynton Beach, Florida, approximately 45 miles north of the Hallandale track. Horses based at the training center helped the handle in 2003, and Gulfstream's purses moved above $34,000 per race.

Calder Race Course expanded its season in 2002 to make up for Hialeah's closing, and the main Calder meet had a 5.8% increase in purses to more than $22,000 per race. Purses at the end-of-year Tropical Park at Calder meet rose 4.6% from year-earlier levels.

After Tampa Bay Downs resolved a dispute with its horsemen at the beginning of its 2001-'02 season, daily purse distribution rose 3% from the previous year. The improvement in purse payments accelerated in 2002-'03, with purses up more than 10%.

Midwest

In the late 1990s, the Midwest was one of the brightest spots on the map of North American racing. But, as the full-card simulcasting revolution matured, pressures grew on several states and on individual tracks within some states, especially Kentucky.

Some bright spots remain. Keeneland Race Course and Churchill Downs in Kentucky pay some of the highest purses in the nation. During the late 1990s, Turfway Park and Ellis Park also rode the full-card simulcasting boom to much-improved racing programs, but those gains have been chipped away by full-card competition in neighboring states and the arrival of riverboat casinos on their doorsteps.

Although its purses declined in 2002, Keeneland continued to pay the best purses in North America, with an average purse per race of more than $65,000 for its two three-week meets, one in the spring and another in the fall. Churchill had an increase in purses for its spring meet, which features the Kentucky Derby (G1) and other races, but the average purse per race declined in the fall meet.

Churchill Downs Inc., which owns Ellis, said it was offering the Western Kentucky track for sale after a decline in business in 2002. Ellis's purses increased, however. Turfway continued its slide, with purses declining in each of its three meets from 2001 levels. The Northern Kentucky track is owned by Keeneland Association and subsidiaries of GTECH and Harrah's Entertainment.

Arlington Park in suburban Chicago is arguably one of the most beautiful racetracks in the world. But attractive surroundings do not necessarily pay the electric bill or purses, and Illinois tracks in 2003 were confronted with new challenges after outgoing Governor George Ryan pulled the plug on a $15-million supplement to purses. Still, purses at Churchill-owned Arlington rank behind only those of Keeneland and Churchill in the Midwest. Also in 2003, Illinois was without Sportsman's Park, which fell victim to a financially disastrous remodeling of the Cicero track into a dual-use auto and horse facility. Sportsman's merged with its neighbor, Hawthorne Race Course, which offered long spring and fall meets in 2003.

Iowa's Prairie Meadows Racetrack, which depends upon revenue from slot machines, was scheduled to have a sizable cut in purses in 2003 under a new contract with its landlord, Polk County, although an underpayment of purses in 2002 limited the reduction. As a result of the new contract, Prairie Meadows went from paying purses per race above the North American average to below that figure in 2003.

Since it opened in 1994 under the management of Churchill Downs, Hoosier Park in Anderson, Indiana, has operated without a competitor, but that situation changed in late 2002 with the opening of Indiana Downs in Shelbyville. Hoosier paid an average purse in 2002 that was modestly above '01 levels.

Minnesota's Canterbury Park had virtually no change in its 2002 purses, but the suburban Minneapolis track also did not have the Claiming Crown, which pumped $550,000 into the track's purses in 2001. Card club revenues have boosted

Canterbury's purses, and the track is seeking slots.

Great Lakes Downs in Muskegon saved live Thoroughbred racing in Michigan after Ladbroke Racing shut down Detroit Race Course, but owner Magna Entertainment has put the track on a watch list as an unprofitable operation. Magna paid $1.7-million for the former Standardbred track but said in February 2003 that it might write down the value on its corporate books. Magna was seeking approvals to build a new Detroit-area track in Romulus.

Southwest

While slot machines benefited Delta Downs, Fair Grounds in New Orleans experienced its second consecutive decline in purses and average purse per race in the 2002-'03 season. Still, Fair Grounds paid the best purses in the Southwest region. Using the fruits of full-card simulcasting in the late 1990s, Fair Grounds built a strong racing program that emphasized stakes and allowance races. The program remained strong in the 2002-'03 meet, but a substantial purse overpayment in the prior season and declining business resulted in a 3% reduction in purses, with another decline likely for the 2003-'04 season because of another purse overpayment.

Purses at Delta Downs in Vinton exploded in the 2002-'03 meet as a result of slot machines, and Louisiana Downs near Shreveport was on track to install slot machines in 2003, with a substantial increase in purses likely. Evangeline Downs is moving from near Lafayette to Opelousas in St. Landry Parish, which has authorized slot machines. Evangeline has obtained approval for its slots facility, and the new track is scheduled to open by the end of 2004.

The region's second largest purses are paid by Lone Star Park in the Dallas-Fort Worth metroplex, and its first five years were sufficiently impressive that Magna Entertainment paid nearly $100-million, including assumption of debt, for the track in 2002. After riding the crest of full-card simulcasting, Lone Star had minor declines in its average daily purses in both 2001 and '02. The state's two other one-mile tracks, Sam Houston Race Park and Retama Park, had disappointing openings in the mid-1990s, but both had increases in average purse per race, Sam Houston for its 2002-'03 meet and Retama for its 2002 season.

Just as Delta has used slots revenue to improve its racing program, Sunland Park in New Mexico has boosted purses to the point where they were above the national average for the 2002-'03 meet.

West Coast

For many decades, America's West Coast has been considered the trendsetter for the rest of the country. In the world of Thoroughbred racing, however, California has been reluctant to adopt some of the developments that have transformed the sport in the past decade.

Full-card simulcasting is an example. While full-card benefited horsemen elsewhere, California limited incoming simulcasting signals to 10,000 out-of-state races a year, or about 21 a day. Similarly, California got around to authorizing phone-account wagering in 2002, but it has made no difference in purses while making up about 8% of total handle.

Of course, California racing has been sufficiently healthy, so it did not need the survival tools that have turned around the fortunes of racetracks elsewhere. All the Southern California meets ranked in the top ten by average daily handle in 2002, with Del Mar third behind Saratoga Race Course's and Belmont Park's fall meet.

California's horse owners have made it clear they believe changes need to be made to improve the state's purse structure. Thoroughbred Owners of California officials said that slot machines at the track were one of the organization's 2003 legislative goals.

Del Mar was the state's leader by average purse payment, the third highest in North America after Keeneland Race Course and Saratoga in 2002. Among Southern California tracks, the second-highest purses were paid by the Oak Tree meet at Santa Anita Park. Horsemen at Santa Anita's main winter-spring meet lost ground to inflation over the last decade, and they had an actual, current-dollar decline in the 2001-'02 season. Owned by Magna Entertainment, Santa Anita had a 5.6% increase in purses for its 2002-'03 meet after a 2.8% drop in average purse for its previous season. Hollywood Park, owned by Churchill Downs Inc., had the lowest purses of the Southern California tracks, but they were more than double the North American average per race. Purses at the two Northern California tracks, Bay Meadows Race Course and Golden Gate Fields, managed modest increases in 2002.

Emerald Downs in Washington recorded a 4% increase in purses for its 2002 meet.

Canada

A quiet revolution in purse payments has occurred in Canada, especially in Ontario. Even with a Canadian dollar that is worth 68% of its United States counterpart, purses at Woodbine near Toronto have become some of the best in North America. Average daily distribution at Woodbine rose 13% in 2002, to more than $380,000 in U.S. dollars. Woodbine's 2002 purses were comparable to those at Aqueduct, Gulfstream Park, and Monmouth Park.

—Don Clippinger

Purse Distribution by Track for 2002

Northeast

Track, state	No. racing days	Average daily purse distribution (% change from previous year)		Average purse	Average stakes purses (% total purse)	
Aqueduct, NY	134	$367,404	(0%)	$41,233	$126,723	(18%)
Atlantic City Race Course, NJ	1	$110,000	(−5%)	$15,714	$0	(0%)
Belmont Park, NY	88	$546,520	(4%)	$59,156	$233,820	(39%)
Finger Lakes, NY	161	$78,223	(0%)	$8,722	$55,969	(7%)
Meadowlands, NJ	64	$210,678	(−50%)	$23,822	$88,068	(20%)
Monmouth Park, NJ	78	$312,670	(−13%)	$32,518	$96,569	(23%)
Northampton Fair, MA	9	$27,670	(1%)	$3,307	$15,750	(6%)
Penn National Race Course, PA	196	$67,577	(−4%)	$7,599	$39,603	(2%)
Philadelphia Park, PA	216	$144,153	(−3%)	$14,920	$95,656	(10%)
Saratoga Race Course, NY	37	$600,386	(2%)	$64,576	$259,395	(41%)
Suffolk Downs, MA	146	$100,064	(20%)	$11,334	$44,690	(12%)
Rockingham Park, NH	75	$91,025	(0%)	$9,602	$46,379	(10%)

Mid–Atlantic

Track, state	No. racing days	Average daily purse distribution (% change from previous year)		Average purse	Average stakes purses (% total purse)	
Charles Town, WV	254	$131,273	(−8%)	$13,359	$54,979	(6%)
Colonial Downs, VA	27	$197,331	(5%)	$20,105	$80,779	(21%)
Delaware Park, DE	141	$291,204	(14%)	$32,484	$99,334	(15%)
Laurel Park, MD	144	$178,035	(−6%)	$20,575	$74,577	(15%)
Mountaineer Park, WV	230	$166,383	(14%)	$18,284	$100,093	(7%)
Pimlico, MD	74	$232,033	(−2%)	$25,066	$110,654	(27%)
Timonium, MD	8	$124,271	(−11%)	$13,256	$40,000	(8%)

Southeast

Track, state	No. racing days	Average daily purse distribution (% change from previous year)		Average purse	Average stakes purses (% total purse)	
Calder Race Course, FL	181	$231,807	(5%)	$22,141	$86,002	(25%)
Gulfstream Park, FL	90	$314,291	(−15%)	$31,605	$138,818	(28%)
Ocala Training Center, FL	1	$370,000	(−3%)	$61,667	$61,667	(100%)
Tampa Bay Downs, FL	92	$103,711	(−1%)	$10,033	$69,611	(13%)

Midwest

Track, state	No. racing days	Average daily purse distribution (% change from previous year)		Average purse	Average stakes purses (% total purse)	
Anthony Downs, KS	6	$11,663	(30%)	$2,916	$4,997	(50%)
Arlington Park, IL	107	$301,119	(−3%)	$32,414	$136,613	(22%)
Atokad Park, NE	1	$126,500	(1%)	$15,812	$0	(0%)
Beulah Park, OH	138	$53,428	(−10%)	$6,770	$39,692	(7%)
Canterbury Park, MN	61	$105,990	(−4%)	$12,554	$43,502	(19%)
Chippewa Downs, ND	8	$13,466	(8%)	$2,693	$7,312	(41%)
Churchill Downs, KY	82	$428,248	(3%)	$42,929	$252,590	(29%)
Columbus, NE	25	$34,731	(2%)	$4,235	$11,657	(13%)
Ellis Park, KY	41	$195,257	(2%)	$19,431	$91,086	(13%)
Eureka Downs, KS	20	$8,839	(3%)	$2,806	$9,812	(22%)
Fairmount Park, IL	110	$72,221	(38%)	$7,235	$29,648	(6%)
Fonner Park, NE	37	$54,684	(5%)	$5,498	$27,615	(23%)
Great Lakes Downs, MI	118	$84,943	(1%)	$9,537	$62,331	(19%)
Hawthorne Race Course, IL	66	$216,522	(5%)	$23,049	$108,494	(16%)
Hoosier Park, IN	69	$170,245	(3%)	$15,853	$80,522	(16%)
Horsemen's Park, NE	3	$131,083	(1%)	$32,771	$43,300	(55%)
Keeneland, KY	33	$608,385	(−5%)	$67,598	$225,929	(43%)
Kentucky Downs, KY	7	$270,000	(3%)	$42,955	$110,000	(47%)
Lincoln State Fair, NE	34	$43,737	(−3%)	$5,075	$13,359	(11%)
Mt. Pleasant Meadows, MI	28	$5,941	(11%)	$3,961	$0	(0%)
Prairie Meadows, IA	98	$166,172	(4%)	$20,878	$87,994	(21%)
River Downs, OH	122	$63,924	(4%)	$7,822	$65,333	(13%)
Sportsman's Park, IL	46	$239,164	(−2%)	$26,132	$145,114	(18%)
Thistledown, OH	187	$70,123	(−5%)	$9,215	$64,167	(12%)
Turfway Park, KY	106	$159,001	(−6%)	$16,190	$100,455	(17%)
Woodlands, KS	24	$56,229	(12%)	$7,846	$21,359	

Southwest

Track, state	No. racing days	Average daily purse distribution (% change from previous year)		Average purse	Average stakes purses (% total purse)	
Blue Ribbon Downs, OK	84	$9,865	(5%)	$2,857	$8,707	(7%)

Southwest, continued

Track, state	No. racing days	Average daily purse distribution (% change from previous year)	Average purse	Average stakes purses (% total purse)
Delta Downs, LA	88	$106,421 (115%)	$12,115	$89,904 (17%)
Downs at Albuquerque, NM	64	$59,890 (13%)	$11,545	$37,756 (31%)
Evangeline Downs, LA	82	$79,104 (4%)	$7,872	$47,500 (6%)
Fair Grounds, LA	80	$265,740 (−2%)	$26,674	$125,486 (31%)
Fair Meadows at Tulsa, OK	31	$43,892 (−7%)	$13,472	$39,582 (17%)
Gillespie County Downs, TX	8	$5,912 (22%)	$3,638	$11,500 (49%)
Lone Star Park, TX	70	$228,065 (−1%)	$23,512	$127,943 (26%)
Louisiana Downs, LA	80	$158,176 (27%)	$14,697	$57,688 (21%)
Oaklawn Park, AR	52	$219,417 (4%)	$21,650	$129,423 (29%)
Remington Park, OK	71	$80,706 (−9%)	$9,931	$55,161 (23%)
Retama Park, TX	51	$98,061 (8%)	$10,290	$53,182 (22%)
Ruidoso Downs, NM	57	$43,458 (4%)	$8,571	$35,801 (30%)
Sam Houston Race Park, TX	84	$127,528 (25%)	$13,407	$79,353 (32%)
Sunland Park, NM	78	$102,135 (31%)	$15,997	$77,909 (24%)
SunRay Park, NM	35	$76,840 (65%)	$12,006	$51,235 (23%)

West Coast

Track, state	No. racing days	Average daily purse distribution (% change from previous year)	Average purse	Average stakes purses (% total purse)
Apache County Fair, AZ	4	$8,583 (0%)	$1,635	$3,112 (9%)
Arapahoe Park, CO	41	$72,129 (0%)	$8,908	$37,824 (24%)
Bay Meadows, CA	105	$173,639 (3%)	$20,417	$85,378 (18%)
Bay Meadows Fair, CA	12	$139,099 (−1%)	$16,527	$48,160 (9%)
Cochise County Fair, AZ	4	$7,007 (2%)	$1,752	$0 (0%)
Del Mar, CA	43	$470,444 (0%)	$54,673	$164,576 (37%)
Eastern Oregon Livestock Show, OR	3	$10,776 (188%)	$2,020	$0 (0%)
Elko County Fair, NV	6	$10,286 (−5%)	$2,204	$10,545 (34%)
Emerald Downs, WA	91	$94,094 (4%)	$10,341	$54,329 (24%)
Fairplex Park, CA	17	$246,120 (2%)	$24,758	$62,792 (27%)
Ferndale, CA	10	$17,684 (−1%)	$4,534	$9,251 (26%)
Flagstaff, AZ	4	$22,306 (−6%)	$4,461	$0 (0%)
Fresno, CA	10	$71,942 (27%)	$11,241	$75,715 (21%)
Gila County Fair, AZ	4	$6,713 (−8%)	$1,678	$2,428 (18%)
Golden Gate Fields, CA	104	$165,274 (2%)	$19,488	$81,689 (14%)
Graham County Fair, AZ	4	$7,195 (12%)	$1,599	$2,257 (8%)
Grants Pass, OR	19	$17,541 (75%)	$2,564	$4,070 (12%)
Greenelee County Fair, AZ	4	$8,940 (14%)	$1,703	$4,842 (14%)
Hollywood Park, CA	100	$402,511 (0%)	$47,077	$181,407 (36%)
Kalispell, MT	1	$1,800	$1,800	$0 (0%)
Les Bois Park, ID	47	$20,371 (7%)	$3,546	$13,813 (39%)
Los Alamitos, CA	188	$10,442 (−1%)	$5,483	$0 (0%)
Minidoka County Fair, ID	1	$500	$500	$0 (0%)
Mohave County Fair, AZ	4	$8,300 (1%)	$1,747	$3,095 (9%)
Pleasanton, CA	11	$144,018 (−1%)	$17,409	$49,992 (19%)
Portland Meadows, OR	47	$31,127 (4%)	$3,630	$10,501 (13%)
Rillito Park, AZ	10	$9,354 (−15%)	$1,701	$3,827 (4%)
Sacramento, CA	12	$99,626 (10%)	$13,585	$59,775 (10%)
Santa Anita Park, CA	111	$438,928 (1%)	$50,963	$166,883 (36%)
Santa Cruz County Fair, AZ	4	$7,073 (−14%)	$1,886	$3,832 (14%)
Santa Rosa, CA	12	$122,965 (0%)	$15,698	$56,107 (23%)
Solano County Fair, CA	11	$103,211 (−6%)	$13,357	$50,260 (13%)
Stockton, CA	10	$62,960 (−15%)	$9,539	$0 (0%)
Sun Downs, WA	10	$8,885 (−1%)	$1,587	$3,125 (7%)
Tillamook County Fair, OR	3	$13,972 (37%)	$2,096	$3,686 (9%)
Turf Paradise, AZ	170	$74,219 (−9%)	$8,006	$37,538 (18%)
Western Montana Fair, MT	1	$1,900	$1,900	$0 (0%)
Wyoming Downs, WY	16	$4,687 (0%)	$2,143	$5,443 (58%)
Yavapai Downs, AZ	56	$31,463 (0%)	$4,686	$15,029 (12%)
Yellowstone Downs, MT	17	$11,468 (−23%)	$2,119	$6,526 (13%)

Canada

Track, state	No. racing days	Average daily purse distribution (% change from previous year)	Average purse	Average stakes purses (% total purse)
Assiniboia Downs, MB	74	$72,117 (19%)	$9,061	$33,037 (21%)
Fort Erie, ON	116	$197,936 (16%)	$19,879	$99,583 (9%)
Grand Prairie, AB	15	$7,106 (37%)	$2,600	$3,273 (25%)
Hastings Park Racecourse, BC	77	$155,359 (31%)	$15,297	$59,211 (23%)
Kamloops, BC	11	$10,316 (−2%)	$2,316	$5,694 (20%)
Kin Park, BC	4	$8,118 (−19%)	$2,165	$2,800 (9%)
Lethbridge, AB	38	$19,051 (11%)	$3,620	$8,887 (27%)
Marquis Downs, SK	32	$19,514 (20%)	$2,946	$9,550 (26%)
Millarville, AB	1	$15,000 (−9%)	$3,000	$4,100 (27%)
Northlands Park, AB	67	$108,996 (3%)	$12,767	$50,694 (22%)
Queensbury Downs, SK	10	$7,805	$1,626	$3,012 (15%)
Stampede Park, AB	42	$100,428 (14%)	$12,017	$45,833 (13%)
Woodbine, ON	166	$558,598 (13%)	$59,175	$193,283 (26%)

North American Racetrack Stocks in 2002
Revenues and Profit or Loss in Millions of Dollars

Company (Symbol)	Revenues	Profit (Loss)	Year-end stock price
Boyd Gaming Corp. (BYD)	1,228.9	40.0	14.05
Canterbury Park Holding Corp. (ECP)	41.7	2.3	13.27
Churchill Downs Inc. (CHDN)	439.2	21.0	38.18
Gemstar-TV Guide International Inc. (GMST)	1,001.4	-6,423.1	3.25
GTECH Holdings Corp. (GTK)	1,009.7	83.6	27.86
Harrah's Entertainment Inc. (HET)	4,136.4	235.0	39.60
International Game Technology (IGT)	1,847.6	271.1	75.92
Magna Entertainment Corp. (MECA)	549.4	-14.4	6.20
MAXXAM Inc. (MXM)	446.6	-84.0	9.30
MTR Gaming Group Inc. (MTRG)	266.3	17.9	7.96
Penn National Gaming Inc. (PENN)	657.5	30.8	15.86
Scientific Games Corp. (SGMS)	455.3	52.1	7.26
Youbet.com Inc. (UBET)	6.3	-14.8	0.77

Racetrack Stock Closing Prices by Year

Company (Symbol)	2002	2001	2000	1999	1998	1997
Boyd Gaming Corp. (BYD)	14.05	6.50	3.4375	5.1825	3.1325	6.625
Canterbury Park Holding Corp. (ECP)	13.27	7.20	7.50	5.6875	4.125	2.875
Churchill Downs Inc. (CHDN)	38.18	36.97	29.8125	22.5625	32.875	43.875
Gemstar-TV Guide International Inc. (GMST)	3.25	27.70	46.125	71.25	57.25	24.375
GTECH Holdings Corp. (GTK)	27.86	45.29	20.5625	22.00	25.625	31.9375
Harrah's Entertainment Inc. (HET)	39.60	37.01	26.375	26.4375	15.6875	18.875
International Game Technology (IGT)	75.92	68.30	48.00	20.3125	24.3125	25.25
Magna Entertainment Corp. (MECA)	6.20	7.00	4.75			
MAXXAM Inc. (MXM)	9.30	17.50	15.1875	42.875	57.375	43.625
MTR Gaming Group Inc. (MTRG)	7.96	16.00	4.75	3.0675	2.4375	2.00
Penn National Gaming Inc. (PENN)	15.86	30.34	10.1875	9.00	7.00	9.75
Scientific Games Corp. (SGMS)	7.26	8.75	2.95	3.25	1.875	2.4375
Youbet.com Inc. (UBET)	0.77	0.51	0.9687	4.3125	6.375	4.50

2002 in Review: An Ultra-Sized Scam
Scheme to Fix Breeders' Cup Wager Is Year's Top Story

On October 28, when it was announced that he was the sole winner of the Breeders' Cup Ultra Pick Six wager, Baltimore resident Derrick Davis said he believed his luck was changing for the better, now that he was getting a presumed payout exceeding $3-million. "I got divorced at the beginning of the year," Davis told THOROUGHBRED TIMES correspondent Bill Heller that day. "It's been a crappy year up to now."

For Davis and two former fraternity brothers at Philadelphia's Drexel University, the year took a decided turn for the worse. By early December, all three—Davis, reputed mastermind Chris Harn, and Glen DaSilva—had pleaded guilty to charges related to what may have been the biggest swindle in the history of Thoroughbred racing. The scheme, though aborted with no money from the Ultra Pick Six wager reaching Davis or his co-conspirators, sent shockwaves through the Thoroughbred racing industry and the totalizator companies that handle billions of dollars of wagers each year. The fix made clear that security measures of the tote companies and racetracks were penetrated by thieves who used technology

to take advantage of the system's vulnerable points.

The fix unraveled because Volponi won the Breeders' Cup Classic (G1) at odds of 43.50-to-1. If one of the betting favorites had won the Classic and produced dozens of Ultra Pick Six ticket winners, the scheme might never have been discovered. Thus, the good luck of Davis and his Delta Kappa Epsilon fraternity brothers in having the sole winning ticket turned out to be their ticket to federal prison.

The scheme was put in motion on October 18, 2002, when Davis, then 29, opened a phone-betting account at Catskill Off-Track Betting Corp. The location of the account was selected by Harn, a Delaware-based programmer for totalizator company Autotote Corp. Harn, also 29, was aware of a crucial shortcoming in the Catskill OTB's phone-betting system: Calls made into it were not recorded. Most phone-bet systems, whether using operators or telephone touch tones to record wagers, record all transactions.

Harn also was aware of a shortcoming in the way wagers were transmitted to the host race-track's computers and thus into the track's wagering pools. In pick six and other multirace wagers, Autotote did not transmit bets into the host computer as they were being made. The Ultra Pick Six bets were not transmitted from Autotote's computers to those of Arlington Park until immediately after the first five of the pick six races had been run. The lack of an industrywide system for transferring bets to the host track as they are made and Autotote's outdated computer software helped the former Drexel students—none of whom graduated—in their scam.

At 2:14 p.m. EDT on October 26, approximately 23 minutes before the first of the Ultra Pick Six races, the Breeders' Cup Mile (G1), Davis entered his wager from Baltimore into the Catskill OTB system. Apparently unwilling to have just one winning ticket, Davis placed a $12 wager—the equivalent of six tickets—on the Ultra Pick Six. He selected one horse in each of the first four races and every horse in the last two races, the bet totaling $1,152. Court documents revealed that Harn, operating out of Autotote offices in Wilmington, Delaware, accessed the Catskill OTB computers and changed Davis's bet to the winning numbers for the first four races. Before the bet left Autotote's computer, it was a sure winner.

The pattern of the wager set off alarms with veteran bettors and with persons aware of the delay in the transmission of Ultra Pick Six bets to Arlington's computers. Alerted by New York Racing Association officials who thought the bet seemed fishy, Breeders' Cup Ltd. and the National Thoroughbred Racing Association immediately asked the New York State Racing and Wagering Board to investigate the matter. On October 31, Autotote's parent company, Scientific Games Corp., fired Harn, referring to him as a "rogue software engineer" without identifying him by name, and turned over information from its own investigation to federal and state authorities.

Events moved quickly as evidence of a kingsized fix accumulated. The United States Attorney General's office received evidence on November 7, and on November 8, arrest warrants were issued for Harn, Davis, and DaSilva. On November 12, they surrendered to face federal mail fraud and conspiracy charges. Harn pleaded guilty on November 20, and DaSilva and Davis followed on successive days, December 11 and 12.

Their guilty pleas did not close the book on the Ultra Pick Six scandal. As evidence of the fix mounted, racetracks, racing organizations, totalizator companies, and racing commissions moved to shore up confidence in the pari-mutuel system.

Scientific Games in mid-November indicated that it would supply its horse-racing clients with the same computer-security systems it uses for state lotteries. The system alerts company security personnel of any attempt to alter the data. The NTRA moved quickly to restore the betting public's confidence in the pari-mutuel system. Among other steps, it hired Giuliani Partners, operated by former New York Mayor Rudolph Giuliani, to work with Ernst & Young to evaluate the current security system and to propose a more secure alternative.—*Don Clippinger*

Each year, THOROUGHBRED TIMES editors and staff writers collectively determine the year's top stories. The Breeders' Cup Ultra Pick Six scam was 2002's leading story, and following are the other major news items.

2. War Emblem's rags-to-riches saga. War Emblem's year began in New Orleans with trainer Frank "Bobby" Springer and ended on the Japanese island of Hokkaido at the Yoshida family's Shadai Stallion Station. Shortly after his victory in the Illinois Derby (G2) for owner Russell Reineman, War Emblem was purchased by Ahmed bin Salman's The Thoroughbred Corp. for $900,000, plus commissions, and was transferred to trainer Bob Baffert. Less than four weeks after the sale, War Emblem won the Kentucky Derby (G1) at 20.50-to-1 odds. Controversy erupted, however, when Reineman, who retained 10% interest in the colt, attempted to lay claim to the entire $1-million bonus from Sportsman's Park that War Emblem earned for winning the Illinois Derby and Kentucky Derby. War Emblem then won the Preakness Stakes (G1) and a chance to become the 12th Triple Crown winner. But he stumbled badly at the start of the Belmont Stakes (G1) and finished a well-beaten eighth behind longshot winner Sarava. On July 22, Salman, 43, died after suffering a heart attack at his home in Riyadh, Saudi Arabia. Less than two weeks later, War Emblem registered a powerful 3½-length victory in the Haskell Invitational Handicap (G1). Despite a sixth-place finish in the Pacific Classic Stakes (G1), War Emblem was purchased by the Yoshida family from Salman's estate for $17-million. He again disappointed in the Breeders' Cup Classic (G1), finishing eighth in his last career start.

3. Death of Seattle Slew. Exactly 25 years after his triumph in the 103rd Kentucky Derby, Triple Crown winner Seattle Slew died peacefully at Hill 'n' Dale Farm near Lexington on May 7. A month earlier, the 28-year-old son of Bold Reasoning had been moved from his longtime residence, Three Chimneys Farm near Midway, Kentucky, to Hill 'n' Dale by owners Mickey and Karen Taylor after undergoing a second surgery to ease pressure on his vertebrae earlier in the year. Slew was one of the most influential sires of the late 20th century. He was leading general sire of 1984, leading juvenile sire of '88, and leading broodmare sire of '95 and '96 (due mainly to Cigar, the two-time Horse of the Year). He sired more than 100 stakes winners, including champions A.P. Indy, Slew o' Gold, Swale, Landaluce,

Surfside, and Capote, and his progeny earned more than $78-million. He was the broodmare sire of champions Lemon Drop Kid, Escena, and Golden Attraction.

4. Magna continues its acquisitions. By its own fast-paced standards, 2002 started rather quietly for Magna Entertainment Corp. The company began the year working to start up its XpressBet account-wagering service in California and launching construction of the Palm Meadows training facility in South Florida. The pace picked up significantly in mid-March when Magna bought Lone Star Park in Texas for $80-million in cash and the assumption of some liabilities. The addition of Lone Star gave Magna 11 racetrack holdings, nine of which conduct Thoroughbred racing. Magna later in the year agreed to buy a majority interest in the Maryland Jockey Club's Pimlico Race Course and Laurel Park in a deal worth $117.5-million.

5. Downturn in major bloodstock markets. Two years after the stock market and the bloodstock markets reached new heights, the nation's premier yearling auctions took significant hits in 2002. Buyers continued to bid aggressively for only the very best offerings and, although the middle to lower portions of the market suffered serious declines, the top tiers also were affected. Nowhere was the dip more evident than at the Keeneland July selected yearling sale, where total sales dipped to the lowest level since 1978 and average dropped to $487,134, the lowest since '98. Fasig-Tipton, which once again enjoyed profitable returns for its Calder selected two-year-olds in training and its Kentucky July selected yearling sales, had significant declines at its Saratoga selected yearling sale, where average plummeted 43.5% compared with its excellent 2001 sale.

6. Japan loses Sunday Silence and other stallions. The Japanese breeding industry suffered a significant blow on August 19 when Sunday Silence died at age 16 at the Yoshida family's Shadai Stallion Station on Hokkaido. The world's all-time leading sire by progeny earnings (more than $339-million), Sunday Silence died after a 14-week battle with bacterial peritendinitis in his right foreleg and laminitis in his left front foot. Voted 1989 Horse of the Year after defeating his nemesis Easy Goer in the Kentucky Derby, Preakness, and Breeders' Cup Classic, Sunday Silence was sold after his championship season. He easily was Japan's best stallion ever, siring no fewer than 79 stakes winners and ten champions through 2002. Japan's breeding industry also lost two young stallions: End Sweep, North America's record-setting freshman sire of 1998, and multiple Group 1 winner El Condor Pasa.

7. Chris McCarron retires on top. Chris McCarron had reached almost every goal he had in racing by the time he got a leg up for the Affirmed Handicap (G3) on June 23 at Hollywood Park. Then 47, McCarron had been inducted into the Racing Hall of Fame, had won the Kentucky Derby, Preakness Stakes, and Belmont Stakes each twice, and had ridden five Breeders' Cup Classic winners. The only thing left for McCarron was to go out a winner in Hollywood style, which is exactly what he did, guiding Came Home to victory in the final race of his legendary 28-year career. An Eclipse Award winner as outstanding jockey in 1980 and as outstanding apprentice jockey in '74, when he won a then-record 546 races, McCarron retired with 7,139 career victories, placing him sixth on the all-time list. His mounts earned $264,380,651, which placed him atop the all-time earnings list until Pat Day surpassed him on August 10, 2002.

8. Workers' compensation crisis in California. More than 300 California-based trainers were left scrambling for affordable options when Pennsylvania-based Legion Insurance Co., one of California's largest providers of workers' compensation insurance, notified the horsemen that coverage would be discontinued on March 1. Only the government-backed State Fund, obligated by law to provide coverage to all California businesses, offered to carry the trainers, but its rates were significantly higher than Legion's. When the balance of the trainers' old policies expired on July 1, the full force of higher rates hit home.

9. Continuing research on causes of MRLS. As 2002 began, Central Kentucky's Thoroughbred industry hoped that the previous year's catastrophic late-term fetal deaths and early-term abortions—collectively known as mare reproductive loss syndrome (MRLS)—would not occur again. While some cases were reported, in general the breeding and foaling seasons were uneventful. Researchers continued to explore the cause of the 2001 outbreak, which cost the Thoroughbred industry approximately $300-million through 2003. Studies increasingly pointed toward the Eastern tent caterpillar, but not in the way theorized in 2001, when it was suspected that the caterpillars carried cyanide toxin from wild cherry trees to pastures.

10. Illinois tracks merge. Chicago racing changed dramatically on July 31 when Sportsman's Park officials announced they planned to terminate Thoroughbred and auto racing at their Cicero, Illinois, facility and move the National Jockey Club meeting to adjacent Hawthorne Race Course. The 74-acre Sportsman's facility, converted into a dual-purpose auto and horse racing facility in 1999, is to be sold. Terms of the deal between the two family-owned entities, which agreed to a 99-year lease, called for the National Jockey Club to share profits from its Thoroughbred meeting with Hawthorne's owners.—*Tom Law*

Chronology 2002

January 1—Ramon Dominguez is crowned as the winningest rider of 2001 with 431 wins, edging out Racing Hall of Fame jockey Russell Baze by eight. Scott Lake is the leading trainer by wins with 406 victories, second only to Jack Van Berg's 496 in 1976. Patrick Valenzuela, who was granted a jockey's license in late December after a long absence related to substance abuse, wins his first race back at Santa Anita Park.

January 5—Keeneland Association, Kentucky Thoroughbred Association, and Kentucky Horsemen's Benevolent and Protective Association endorse alternative forms of gaming at the state's tracks. Florida sire Valid Appeal dies.

January 8—Jungle Pocket, winner of the 2001 Japan Cup (Jpn-G1), named Japanese Horse of the Year; Kent Desormeaux honored as Japan's outstanding jockey by winning percentage. New Jersey Governor Donald T. DiFrancesco vetoes $18-million purse subsidy and reduces it to $6-million. Ben Huffman named racing secretary at Keeneland Race Course, succeeding Howard Battle.

January 9—ESPN Classic wins Eclipse Award for national television in the features category for its one-hour program on Bill Shoemaker.

January 12—The National Thoroughbred Racing Association formally relinquishes control of an Oregon wagering hub to Television Games Network. The changeover effectively took place on July 1.

January 15—Belinda Stronach, daughter of Frank Stronach, takes over as Magna International Inc. president. Louisiana Gaming Control Board approves Boyd Gaming Corp.'s request for slots at Delta Downs.

January 16—Russell Baze is awarded National Turf Writers Association's Isaac Murphy Award for highest winning percentage in 2001. Baze, the award's only recipient, won for the seventh consecutive year.

January 17—Florida breeder Harry T. Mangurian Jr. and longtime California steward Pete Pedersen are selected as co-recipients of the Eclipse Award of Merit.

January 18—Sheikh Mohammed bin Rashid al Maktoum to receive Special Eclipse Award. Magna Entertainment Corp. introduces XpressBet, a new on-line wagering platform.

January 24—California Horse Racing Board grants licenses to Magna Entertainment Corp. and TVG for advance deposit wagering by telephone.

January 25—Robert S. Strauss elected chairman of Del Mar Thoroughbred Club, succeeding John Mabee, who retired.

January 28—John Henry undergoes successful colic surgery.

January 30—Louisiana Downs and Hastings Park leaving National Thoroughbred Racing Association. Johannesburg and Tempera, winners of their respective Breeders' Cup races, selected as top weights for the 2001 Experimental Free Handicap. NTRA purchases EquiSource, a group-purchasing company, and forms new subsidiary, NTRA Purchasing.

February 7—Barn fire at Evangeline kills eight horses.

February 8—Robert and Janice McNair purchase minority interest in Houston Texans professional football team held by disgraced Enron Chairman Kenneth Lay.

February 12—Chris McCarron resigns from Youbet.com Inc. board of directors.

February 13—Delta Downs slot machine casino opens.

February 14—Saratoga County Board of Supervisors approves video lottery terminals at the Saratoga Equine Sports Center, a Standardbred track. Arkansas Horsemen's Benevolent and Protective Association drops out of National Thoroughbred Racing Association.

February 15—Russell Baze announced as winner of 2002 George Woolf Memorial Jockey Award.

February 18—Point Given named 2001 Horse of the Year at annual Eclipse Awards dinner. Laura Hillenbrand, author of *Seabiscuit: An American Legend*, receives Turf Publicists of America's Big Sport of Turfdom award.

February 20—Kris, a leading English sire, is pensioned. New Hampshire Senate rejects video-lottery terminals and purse subsidy measures.

February 21—Youbet.com Inc. receives license to operate account wagering in California. Doug Bredar named Churchill Downs racing secretary, succeeding the late Jerry Botts.

February 23—Fire in Ocala Stud barn kills 22 horses.

February 25—Seattle Slew to have neurological examination and is removed from stud duty. Lonesome Glory, five-time steeplechase champion, is euthanized after a paddock accident in Cochranville, Pennsylvania.

March 2—Seattle Slew undergoes surgery to fuse two vertebrae in his neck.

March 3—Eddie Delahoussaye elected to Louisiana Sports Hall of Fame.

March 5—Atlantic Ocean brings record price for juvenile filly sold at auction, $1.9-million at Barretts March two-year-olds in training sale.

March 6—Magna Entertainment Corp. agrees to purchase Lone Star Park for $80-million in cash and assumption of $20-million in debt.

March 14—NTRA board approves operating budget of $59.3-million.

March 18—Bill to legalize video lottery terminals at Kentucky racetracks approved by House of Representatives Licensing and Occupations Committee.

March 20—Missouri House of Representatives passes measure to encourage construction of a racetrack in St. Louis area and to allow simulcasting.

March 25—Kris S. is pensioned.

March 27—Maryland Racing Commission approves William Rickman Jr.'s permit to open an off-track betting facility in Cambridge on the Eastern Shore.

March 28—Longchamp opening day canceled after employees strike over pay.

April 1—Seattle Slew moves to Hill 'n' Dale Farm.

April 2—Andy Stronach resigns as Magna executive vice president and director.

April 9—American Horse Council releases updated figures showing a United States horse population of almost seven-million and an equine industry national economic impact of more than $112.1-billion.

April 12—Minimum weight for flat race riders raised to 110 pounds in Great Britain.

April 15—Transfer of Les Bois Park to Arnell Jones is approved by the Idaho Racing Commission.

April 17—John Ertmann named president and chief operating officer of Equibase Co.

April 22—Industry leader, owner-breeder Ogden Phipps, 93, dies. Youbet.com Inc. agrees to one-year co-marketing deal with Churchill Downs Inc.

April 24—Eclipse Award breeder, former Del Mar Chairman John Mabee, 80, dies. Turko's Turn, dam of Point Given, named Broodmare of the Year.

April 25—Mare reproductive loss syndrome study reveals no lasting effects on foals of 2001. Three New York Racing Association pari-mutuel clerks plead guilty to money laundering. Mid-Atlantic Thoroughbred Championships series canceled for 2002.

April 26—California jockeys authorized to wear logos on riding breeches at Hollywood and Bay Meadows.

April 28—Champion Tempera dies after bout of colitis.

April 30—Racing Hall of Fame inductees—Cigar, Serena's Song, *Noor, Grover G. "Buddy" Delp, Jack Westrope—are announced.

May 3—Spain becomes all-time leading distaff earner with her victory in the Louisville BC Handicap (G2).

May 4—War Emblem wins Kentucky Derby (G1). Kentucky Derby horses wear color-coded saddle towels for the first time.

May 6—Television Games Network allows America TAB Ltd. to begin to accept wagers on races.

May 7—Triple Crown winner and leading sire Seattle Slew dies at Hill 'n' Dale Farm. Sire Kris S. dies.

May 10—*Seabiscuit: An American Legend* named nonfiction book of the year by BookSense. Massachusetts House of Representatives rejects slot machines at state's racetracks.

May 13—Blythe Miller wins 200th American steeplechase race, seventh in history to reach milestone.

May 17—Richard Dos Ramos named recipient of the Avelino Gomez Memorial Award.

May 18—War Emblem becomes fourth horse in six years to take first two legs of Triple Crown, winning Preakness Stakes (G1) over Magic Weisner.

May 22—Leading British trainer Major Dick Hern 81, dies.

May 23—Eric Nelson, a Las Vegas real-estate broker, signs ten-year lease with an option to buy Playfair Race Course in Spokane, Washington.

May 29—California Horse Racing Board ordered to reimburse Bob Baffert $102,780 for legal costs incurred while fighting positive drug finding that was thrown out by courts.

May 30—Hong Kong bars wagering with overseas bookmakers.

June 3—Nebraska Supreme Court rules wagering on horse races by telephone violates the state constitution and halts phone betting after seven months. Terry Houghton scores his 3,000 career win. British trainer John Dunlop sends out his 3,000th winner.

June 4—Yearling Thoroughbred colt tests positive for West Nile virus. Former Kentucky Governor Brereton C. Jones and wife Libby buy historic Woodburn Stud.

June 5—Magna Entertainment Corp. to purchase Flamboro Downs, a half-mile harness track in Hamilton, Ontario, for $46-million.

June 8—Sarava ends War Emblem's bid for Triple Crown with 70.25-to-1 upset win in Belmont Stakes (G1).

June 9—John Hettinger donates use of 30 acres in Pawling, New York, to Thoroughbred Retirement Foundation.

June 11—Study confirms that frozen Eastern tent caterpillars ingested by mares can cause mare reproductive loss syndrome.

June 12—Flying Dash (Ger) disqualified from May 11 Hawthorne Derby (G3) win for positive drug test.

June 13—Television Games Network purchases 16.6% interest of Youbet.com. Inc. Explosive device found in grandstand at Sha Tin racecourse in Hong Kong.

June 16—Racing Hall of Fame trainer Horace A. "Jimmy" Jones, who died in September 2001, leaves $6-million to St. Francis Hospital Foundation in Maryville, Missouri.

June 17—Ron Anderson, Angel Cordero Jr., Drew Mollica file lawsuit against New York Racing Association contesting rule limiting agents to one journeyman jockey.

June 18—Language exempting horse racing from Internet gambling prohibition bill deleted.

June 21—Pat Eddery moves into second place on Great Britain's all-time leading jockeys list with 4,494 wins, passing Lester Piggott. The record, 4,870 wins, is held by the late Sir Gordon Richards.

June 23—Chris McCarron retires a winner, guiding Came Home to victory in the Affirmed Handicap (G3) at Hollywood Park in his last career ride. Sadler's Wells records his 200th stakes winner, Morozov, winner of the Prix du Lys (Fr-G3) at Longchamp.

June 26—California Horse Racing Board rejects transfer of Los Angeles County Fair Association's racing dates to Santa Anita from Fairplex Park in Pomona.

June 28—Society of International Thoroughbred Auctioneers raises minimum purse for black type to $35,000, effective January 1, 2003. Lone Star Park signs contract to operate Hipodromo de Maronas, a racetrack in South America.

June 29—Jerry Bailey honored by National Academy of Sports Editors with the 2002 Victor Sports Award for outstanding jockey.

July 1—Charles Town Races installs an additional 587 slot machines, for a total to 2,587.

July 8—Cash Asmussen named Lone Star Park's international spokesman. Jim Greene and Shirley Edwards of The Eighth Pole at New England tracks named winners of 2002 Dogwood Dominion Award.

July 10—Alex Harthill, D.V.M., resigns as president of the Kentucky Horsemen's Benevolent and Protective Association after objecting to board decision to terminate a conflict-of-interest investigation involving Executive Director Marty Maline and others.

July 11—Sire End Sweep dies in Japan.

July 12—Breeders' Cup Ltd. elects 13 new board members as part of reorganization sought by Magna Entertainment Corp. Chairman Frank Stronach. Breeders' Cup approves rules setting minimum qualifications to start in a World Thoroughbred Championships race. Lone Star Park to host Breeders' Cup races in 2004 in place of Churchill Downs, which is undergoing extensive renovation. Churchill tentatively slated to host Breeders' Cup World Thoroughbred Championships in 2005. Suffolk Downs begins account wagering. Wimborne Farm near Paris, Kentucky, is sold at auction for $1.7-million. Fairplex Equine Sales agrees to purchase interest in Barretts Equine Ltd. Susan Bunning, a Lexington bank executive, is elected president of the Kentucky HBPA.

July 14—Racing official Howard Battle, 71, dies.

July 15—Magna Entertainment Corp. agrees to purchase 51% interest in the Maryland Jockey Club, which owns Pimlico Race Course and Laurel Park, for about $50.6-million, with an option to buy out Joseph and Karin De Francis's interests. Race Track Chaplaincy of America creates White Horse Fellowship, White Horse Award.

July 16—Colt by Storm Cat tops Keeneland July yearling sale at $3.1-million. Pat Eddery presented with lifetime achievement award by Goodwood Racecourse.

July 18—Sunday Silence has third surgery on right foreleg.

July 19—Seattle Slew memorialized at public ceremony, unveiling of statue at Hill 'n' Dale Farm.

July 21—Patrick Valenzuela clinches riding title at Hollywood Park, his first in 11 years.

July 22—Owner-breeder Ahmed bin Salman, 43, dies in Saudi Arabia.

July 27—Van Nistelrooy, a $6.4-million Keeneland September yearling, wins the Tyros Stakes at the Curragh and becomes Storm Cat's 100th stakes winner.

July 29—Television Games Network forms partnership with FOXSports.com. Sunline wins third Australian Horse of the Year title.

July 30— Financially strapped Sportsman's Park to merge with Hawthorne Race Course; new entity, Hawthorne National LLC, will assume none of Sportsman's $80-million debt from failed attempt to create a dual-use facility for auto and horse racing.

August 1—NTRA approves extension of television contract with ESPN through 2008.

August 2—Cynthia Medina, aboard Treatwithkidgloves at Fairmount Park, wins her 1,000th career race.

August 3—Yankees Entertainment and Sports network presents inaugural horse racing broadcast in conjunction with National Thoroughbred Racing Association. Bomb threat forces evacuation at Newmarket.

August 4—Early-morning fire at Woodbine kills 32 Thoroughbreds, destroys two barns.

August 5—Del Mar President Joe Harper resigns from Magna board of directors, citing a need to devote all of his time to Del Mar.

August 9—Owner-breeder Bayard Sharp, 89, dies.

August 10—Garrett Gomez wins his 2,000th career race aboard Adalgisa at Del Mar.

August 14—Shane Sellers retires from race riding.

August 16—Sunline wins her fourth New Zealand Horse of the Year title.

August 17—G. Watts Humphrey Jr. elected to Jockey Club's board of stewards. Farda Amiga wins Alabama Stakes (G1) off 105-day layoff.

August 19—Horse of the Year and leading Japanese sire Sunday Silence dies after long battle with laminitis. Laffit Pincay Jr. wins his 1,000th race at Del Mar.

August 20—Irish Turf Club establishes new minimum weight for jockeys in flat racing, 110 pounds.

August 22—Damien Oliver receives his fourth Scobie Breasley Medal for riding excellence in Australia.

August 23—Sire Slew o' Gold pensioned.

August 29—Harrah's Entertainment signs letter of intent to purchase 95% of Louisiana Downs. Magna Entertainment Corp. applies to build a racetrack in Romulus, Michigan, about 17 miles west of Detroit.

August 30—Philadelphia Park's owners apply to build a five-furlong Thoroughbred track in Chester, Pennsylvania, located south of Philadelphia. Through his EQTAH Group, Andy Stronach applies to build a mixed-breed racetrack with a simulcast facility near Detroit.

August 31—J. Terrence Lanni resigns from Magna Entertainment Corp's board of directors.

September 5—Peninsula Gaming Partners completes purchase of Evangeline Downs and land in St. Landry Parish, Louisiana, where a new Evangeline Downs with slot machines will be built. Jorge Valdivieso, aboard Mac Royal at Hipodromo La Plata, wins his 4,000th race. Mark Johnston, aboard Komba at Pimlico Race Course, wins his 3,000th race.

September 6—Keeneland scraps Internet auction of horses failing to meet their minimum bids. Justin Shepherd, 16, wins his first race, aboard Stormie Britches at Remington Park.

September 7—Mario Pino, riding Outdone at Delaware Park, wins his 5,000th career race.

September 8—New England trainer Ron Dandy records his 2,000th career win with Heat of the Night at Rockingham Park. Rock of Gibraltar (Ire) wins Prix du Moulin de Longchamp (Fr-G1) for record seventh consecutive Group 1 victory.

September 9—Patti Cooksey becomes first woman to be inducted into the Kentucky Athletic Hall of Fame.

September 10—Preakness Stakes (G1) runner-up Magic Weisner diagnosed with West Nile virus.

September 11—Racing participants at Doncaster observe moment of silence in memory of terrorist attack victims a year earlier in America. Racetracks in United States observe one-year anniversary of terrorist attacks. Kentucky Derby and Preakness Stakes winner War Emblem sold for $17-million, to enter stud in 2003 at the Yoshida family's Shadai Stallion Station in Japan.

September 14—Doncaster racecourse names St. Leger Stakes (Eng-G1) trophy after late trainer Major Dick Hern.

September 17—Lord Avie, 24, pensioned.

September 19—Jockey Club reports 34,605 live foals of 2002. Don Pettinger, aboard Notable Okie at Remington Park, wins his 3,000th career race.

September 25—American Insurance Group agrees to provide workers' compensation coverage to California trainers.

September 26—Pennsylvania Horse Racing Commission approves racing license for proposed Presque Isle Downs, to be built by MTR Gaming Group.

September 28—Robert Messina, aboard Twisting Coast at Finger Lakes, wins his 2,000th career race.

September 30—Delaware Racing Commission bans use of erythropoietin, known widely as EPO.

October 1—Rick Bozich, Jennie Rees, Lewis Freedman, and Mike Kane receive Red Smith awards for Kentucky Derby stories. John and Donna Ward receive Kentucky Thoroughbred Media's Ambassadors of Racing award for 2002. Robert Mikols, a Long Island crane operator, pleads guilty in hit-and-run death of former jockey Marjorie Clayton Cordero in Greenvale, New York, on January 22, 2001.

October 7—Left Bank euthanized after complications from colic surgery.

October 8—Frank Stronach buys more than 1.8-million shares of Magna Entertainment Corp. stock, raising his ownership to above 10-million.

October 9—Leading sire Raja Baba dies.

October 13—John Gaines, Preston Madden, and Dinwiddie Lampton Jr. inducted into Culver Academies Horsemanship Hall of Fame.

October 16—Charismatic, 1999 Horse of the Year, sold to stand in Japan. Texas Racing Commission approves sale of Lone Star Park to Magna. Churchill Downs seeks bids for 59 luxury box suites, the first 20 of which are to be completed for the 2003 Kentucky Derby.

October 19—Breeders' Cup World Thoroughbred Champions sold out for the first time in history; all tickets at Arlington Park are reserved.

October 20—Sire Saint Ballado dies.

October 21—Winston Thompson, aboard Princess Terlingua at Suffolk Downs, wins his 2,000th race.

October 23—Richard Duchossois and Eugene Melnyk receive the National Turf Writers Association's Joe Palmer Award. Chris McCarron is recipient of the Mr. Fitz Award, and Billy Reed is honored with Walter Haight Award. Alan Marzelli to become president of Jockey Club, succeeding Hans Stahl, who retires on December 31.

October 26—Volponi registers 43.50-to-1 upset win in Breeders' Cup Classic (G1). Azeri wins Breeders' Cup Distaff (G1) to help her secure eventual Horse of the Year honors. Russell Baze, 44, wins aboard Ourwhistlebritches at Bay Meadows Race Course to record his 8,000th victory, becoming the fourth jockey to reach that milestone.

October 28—National Thoroughbred Racing Association announces sole winner of Breeders' Cup Ultra Pick Six, worth more than $3-million. Derrick Davis, a Baltimore computer programmer, holds six winning $2 bets, singling the first four race winners and selecting all horses in the fifth and sixth races of the wager.

October 30—Magna Entertainment Corp. completes purchase of Lone Star Park.

October 31—Scientific Games, owner of Autotote, fires software engineer Chris Harn for alleged wrongdoing involving the Breeders' Cup Ultra Pick Six.

November—Sire Fly So Free, 14, pensioned.

November 1—Playfair Race Course to open as Eric Nelson receives a license to operate the track.

November 2—Patti Cooksey receives Lombardi Symbol of Courage.

November 3—Street Cry (Ire) named United Arab Emirates Horse of the Year.

November 5—Derrick Davis, Chris Harn, and third person under investigation for Ultra Pick Six wager scam. Champion Xtra Heat sells privately to David Plummer's ClassicStar after being bought back at Fasig-Tipton Kentucky November select mixed sale.

November 6—Ernst & Young hired to assess and test tote security systems in light of Ultra Pick Six scam.

November 7—Racing Hall of Fame jockey Julie Krone, who retired in 1999, scores first victory of her comeback at Santa Anita Park.

November 8—U.S. Attorney General's office takes over investigation on Breeders' Cup Ultra Pick Six wager.

November 9—Federal Bureau of Investigation joins probe of Breeders' Cup Ultra Pick Six wager.

November 11—Cliff Berry, aboard Ed's Best Man at Remington Park, wins his 2,000th career victory.

November 12—Former Drexel University fraternity brothers Derrick Davis, Chris Harn, and Glen DaSilva arrested by federal officials and charged with conspiracy to commit wire fraud by fixing Breeders' Cup Ultra Pick Six ticket and at least two other wagers.

November 13—Maryland Racing Commission approves sale of Laurel and Pimlico to Magna.

November 18—National Thoroughbred Racing Association Wagering Technology Working Group to have thousands of multirace wagers audited.

November 20—Virginia Racing Commission approves sale of Laurel and Pimlico to Magna. Chris Harn pleads guilty to wire fraud and money laundering conspiracy. Proposed legislation authorizing 14,000 racetrack slot machines unveiled in Ohio.

November 22—Dermot Browne, former jockey and trainer, receives 20-year ban from English Jockey Club for doping horses. Aqueduct jockey Victor Carrero receives a 15-day suspension and $2,000 fine for throwing his whip and a clod of dirt at his mount, Saltaat, who broke down fatally the previous day. California's workers' compensation insurance plan deal finalized.

November 24—Kentucky Derby winner and sire Spend a Buck dies in Brazil.

November 25—British Horseracing Board restricts field sizes to 20 beginning in 2003.

November 26—Owner-breeder Verne Winchell, 87, dies.

November 28—Russell Baze records his 400th win in a season for the tenth time.

November 29—Palm Meadows Training Center, built by Magna, opens in Boynton Beach, Florida. Dean Kutz receives the 2002 Mike Venezia Memorial Award. Charlotte Weber's Live Oak Stud pays world-record price of $2.95-million for Giant's Causeway weanling filly at Tattersalls December sale.

December 1—Jerry Bailey breaks his own single-season earnings record, with $22.6-million in purses.

December 2—Dick Boushka, developer of the Woodlands racetrack, pleads guilty to defrauding bank.

December 3—Dianna Timm receives 14-year sentence for embezzling money from the Idaho Thoroughbred Association.

December 4—Autotote Systems Inc. sued in class action suit for negligence in maintaining security in light of Ultra Pick Six scam.

December 7—Wake At Noon named Canadian Horse of the Year. Damien Oliver, aboard Legend of Ace at Australia's Sandown racecourse, wins his 1,500th career race. NTRA holds inaugural Great State Challenge at Sam Houston.

December 9—Settlement reached in dispute over horses owned by Allen Paulson Living Trust. As part of settlement between co-trustees Michael Paulson and Nicholas Diaco, champion older female Azeri is to be sold at Barretts March sale. (However, a subsequent agreement reached in 2003 canceled her sale.)

December 10—Steve Sexton named Churchill Downs president. Cliff Goodrich named Arlington president.

December 11—Glen DaSilva pleads guilty to computer fraud conspiracy and money laundering. Michele Blanco, Calder Race Course's publicity director, is elected president of the Turf Publicists of America.

December 12—Derrick Davis, the last of the three Breeders' Cup Ultra Pick Six defendants, pleads guilty to wire fraud conspiracy and money laundering. Todd Pletcher receives the John K. Goodman Alumni Award at the University of Arizona's Symposium on Racing. Betty Mabee, and her late husband John, are recipients of the Clay Puett Award.

December 14—Magna Entertainment Corp. purchases site in suburban Detroit for future racetrack. Falbrav named Italian Horse of the Year.

December 17—Classic winner and sire Conquistador Cielo dies.

December 22—Owner-breeder Virginia McKnight Binger, 86, dies.

December 26—Julie Krone wins Malibu Stakes (G1) aboard Debonair Joe, making her the first female jockey to win a Grade 1 race in California.

December 31—Classic winner and sire Pleasant Colony dies in Virginia. Robert Decker, Churchill Downs Inc. executive vice president and chief financial officer, resigns.

2002 Obituaries

Charles Raymond Allen, 76, veterinarian who worked primarily at New York Racing Association tracks and cared for many high-profile runners for such operations as Rokeby Stable; on December 10 in Palm Desert, California.

Walter H. Annenberg, 94, former owner and publisher of *Daily Racing Form;* his Triangle Publications also owned *TV Guide* and *Seventeen* magazine before its sale for $3-billion in 1988; a close friend of President Ronald Reagan, he served as President Richard Nixon's ambassador to Great Britain from 1969 to '74; patron of the arts and philanthropist who created schools of journalism at the University of Pennsylvania, University of Southern California, and Temple University; on October 1 in Wynnewood, Pennsylvania, of complications from pneumonia.

Edwin Anspach, 92, New England-based trainer who conditioned four-time stakes winner Historian, on July 29 in Ocala.

Roone Arledge, 71, television-sports pioneer who shaped ABC's coverage of the Triple Crown; the creator of Monday Night Football consolidated all three Triple Crown broadcasts as an ABC product in the mid-1980s and installed such top-level talent as Howard Cosell and Jim McKay as the racing shows' anchors; on December 5 in New York City after a lengthy bout with cancer.

Luis Barrera, 80, New York-based trainer who won 1981 Belmont Stakes (G1) with Summing; former assistant to brother Lazaro Barrera, Racing Hall of Fame member; on May 1 of a heart attack at his Belmont Park barn.

Howard Battle, 71, Keeneland racing secretary for nearly 30 years; was instrumental in establishing a ranking system for horses worldwide that was used by the American Graded Stakes Committee; on July 14 in Lexington of stomach cancer.

Virginia McKnight Binger, 86, daughter of Tartan Farms founder William L. McKnight; in Tartan name, breeder of classic winners Unbridled and Codex; on December 22 at her Wayzata, Minnesota, home.

Sir Cecil "Monkey" Blacker, 86, former deputy senior steward of the English Jockey Club, on October 18.

Phil Borgemenke, 64, former jockey on Ohio circuit, on January 29 in Cincinnati.

Jerry Botts, 54, longtime Churchill Downs racing secretary, on January 1 of lung and liver cancer in Louisville.

Stewart Bowie, 76, owner-breeder and Del Mar Thoroughbred Club director, on January 1, in Rancho Santa Fe, California.

Clarence Breedlove, 87, retired trainer best known as the conditioner of multiple stakes winner Zuppardo's Prince, on May 26 in Louisville.

David Brown, 67, neurosurgeon and breeder of multiple graded stakes winner College Town, on February 7 in Claremont, California, of cancer.

Michael Byrne, 77, Irish Turf Club handicapper from 1970 to '90 and subsequently chairman of International Classifications Committee for six years, on April 23 in Dublin after suffering a stroke.

Robert "Uncle Bob" Carey, 67, brother of and assistant to Hawthorne Race Course President Thomas Carey; on June 29 in Riverside, Illinois, from complications of a head injury suffered in a fall seven months earlier.

Jefferson Carr, 77, who helped found Retama Park, on January 15 in Papalote, Texas.

Karri Casner, 23, daughter of WinStar Farm co-owners Bill and Susan Casner, on October 12 in a terrorist attack in Bali, Indonesia.

Albert Clay, 85, owner and breeder who helped found the American Horse Council and was instrumental in establishing the University of Kentucky's Maxwell H. Gluck Equine Research Center; bred or co-bred at least 20 stakes winners, including Grade 1 winners Albert the Great, Seaside Attraction, Gorgeous, Pompeii, and George Navanod; father of Three Chimneys Farm owner Robert Clay; on August 20 at his Mount Sterling, Kentucky, home.

Robert Connors, 66, East Coast-based trainer whose stakes winners included Escaping and Felter On the Quay, on November 15 at his Parkesburg, Pennsylvania, home.

Claude Cowen, 77, owner and breeder since the 1950s, based primarily in the South and Southwest, on April 14 of a stroke.

Matty Cowing, 65, former agent for leading European jockey Frankie Dettori; on May 30 in Cambridge, England.

Milton "Laddie" Dance Jr., 76, co-owned 2000 champion older male and '99 Belmont Stakes (G1) winner Lemon Drop Kid with wife Jeanne Vance; auctioneer for Fasig-Tipton for 40 years; of a heart attack on November 28 in Manalapan, Florida.

William "Billy" Daniels, 41, former jockey, on March 18 of cancer in Providence, Rhode Island.

Guilford Dudley Jr., 95, owner and jockey in flat and steeplechase racing, on June 11 in Palm Beach, Florida.

Guido Federico, 84, retired New England-based trainer who conditioned Grade 2 winner Waquoit; on May 25 in Hallandale Beach, Florida.

Robert Fisher, 74, former jockey who owned and trained Canadian stakes winner Swamp Line, on October 23 after a lengthy illness.

John Foggiano, Midwest-based trainer won training titles at Hazel Park and Detroit Race Course, on August 24 in Muskegon, Michigan.

Natalie Friendly, 74, successful California owner with husband Ed; best horses included Grade 1 winner Vivid Angel and Grade 3 winners Gray Slewpy and Purely Cozzene; author of children's science books; on May 9 in Rancho Santa Fe, California, after a long battle with cancer.

Albert Funk, 73, operated Caliente Racetrack in Tijuana, Mexico, in 1947 as first combined greyhound and horse racing facility in North America, on December 10 at Scripps Clinic in La Jolla, California.

Ron Gallon Sr., 59, trainer in Southern California, Ohio, West Virginia, and Kentucky, on January 8 in Dayton, Ohio, after a brief illness.

John M. "Jack" Gaver Jr., 61, who trained champions Bowl Game and Late Bloomer during his stint for Greentree Stable, on January 5 in Hollywood, Florida.

James "Father Gill" Gill, an owner who also worked as a trainer, jockey's agent, and pony boy, on January 22 in Pennsylvania.

Phil Greally, 20, English-based apprentice jockey, on December 21 after being kicked in the head while tending horses.

Mack Thomas Hall, 68, Phoenix-based owner and trainer, on February 1.

A. R. "Ham" Hamilton, 72, retired trainer and former manager of Payson Park training center near Indiantown, Florida, and Hermitage Farm near Goshen, Kentucky; on January 10 in Lexington.

Bill Hedge, 85, owner of ranch where Oklahoma's first pari-mutuel track, Blue Ribbon Downs, was developed, on July 6 in Sallisaw, Oklahoma.

Major Dick Hern, 81, four-time leading British trainer; won 17 classics, including once-beaten Brigadier Gerard, the 1971 Two Thousand Guineas winner; won the Epsom Derby three times, with Troy (1979), Henbit ('80), and Nashwan ('89); trained for Queen Elizabeth II, including 1977 Epsom Oaks (Eng-G1) winner Dunfermline (GB); confined to a wheelchair after 1984 hunting accident; retired in 1997; on May 22.

William O. Hicks, 92, retired New York-based trainer who conditioned graded stakes winners Clout and Turn of the Coin, on April 16 at the Aiken (South Carolina) Regional Medical Center.

Robert Hindman, 64, owner and breeder from Grand Island, Nebraska, and father of Television Games Network Vice President John Hindman, on November 12 in Omaha, Nebraska.

Barbara Holbrook, 52, Kentucky- and Ohio-based trainer, found dead from a gunshot wound on November 5 at her Yorkville, Indiana, home.

Leonard Imperio, 70, New York-based trainer who conditioned Grade 2 winner Star Gallant, on June 12 in Syosset, New York, of cancer.

Johnie Jamison, 64, New Mexico-based trainer who saddled 44 stakes winners in the previous four years, on September 9.

Walter Johns, 91, former Thistledown publicity director, on August 24 in Parma, Ohio.

Jack Jones, 83, bred 1980 Epsom Derby (Eng-G1) winner Henbit and operated Mineola Farm near Lexington, on July 12 in Lexington.

Audrey Skirball-Kenis, 87, founded Southern California-based 3 Plus U Stable with husband, Charles Kenis; campaigned Grade 1 winners Super Quercus (Fr) and See You Soon (Fr); major contributor to Jewish organizations, including museums in Jerusalem, Cincinnati, and Los Angeles; on June 19 in Los Angeles.

Bob Lee, 71, former member of the New York State Racing and Wagering Board and owner of popular Wishing Well restaurant near Saratoga Springs, New York, on September 1.

Gerald Leigh, 71, England-based owner and breeder of Grade 1- and Group 1-winning full siblings Barathea (Ire) and Gossamer (GB); for 20 years based his breeding operation at 600-acre Eydon Hall Farm, Eydon, Northamptonshire; on June 23 after a long battle with cancer.

Leif Linkfield, 56, former trainer who worked as a clocker's assistant at Keeneland Race Course, on May 26 in Lexington of cancer.

Lucille Caudill Little, 93, widow of owner-breeder W. Paul Little and major donor to Kentucky Horse Park, on October 8 in Lexington.

John C. Mabee, 80, guided Del Mar to national prominence as its president or chairman of the board for 25 years; contributed to revival of California breeding industry with his and wife Betty's Golden Eagle Farm operation near Ramona; three-time Eclipse Award-winning breeder (1991, '97, and '98); Grade 1 winners included Best Pal, General Challenge, Excellent Meeting, River Special, and Jeanne Jones; on April 24, ten days after suffering a stroke, at Casa

Palmera Care Center near Del Mar.

George Maker, 61, Michigan trainer and father of long-time D. Wayne Lukas assistant Mike Maker, on January 18 of cancer in Westland, Michigan.

Eugene "Gene" Sylvester Mandella, 79, former blacksmith and father of Racing Hall of Fame trainer Richard Mandella, on November 12 in Ashton, Idaho.

Armando Martinez, 88, rode more than 5,000 winners in five nations and father of 2001 Penn National Race Course leading trainer Jose Martinez, on January 2 in Harrisburg, Pennsylvania.

Ronald McDonald, 57, owner of Hidden Springs Farm near Versailles, Kentucky; campaigned homebred multiple graded stakes winner Degenerate Gal; on August 29 of brain cancer.

Eddie McMullen, 74, former jockey best remembered as press box manager at Pimlico Race Course and Laurel Park from the 1970s into the '90s, on April 1 in Laurel, Maryland.

Katharine Merryman, 79, Maryland-based owner, breeder, and trainer who bred Grade 1 winner Twixt, on November 15 at her family's farm, The Orebanks, near Sparks, Maryland.

Alice duPont Mills, 88, breeder and owner of Hickory Tree Farm in Middleburg, Virginia; known for philanthropic endeavors; leading runners campaigned by Hickory Tree included 1983 champion two-year-old male Devil's Bag and Grade 1 winners Gone West and Believe It; on March 13.

Don Mularkey, 42, Canterbury Park-based trainer, assistant trainer, and exercise rider, on June 1 in Minneapolis of a head injury suffered in an off-track accident.

Chuck Murphy, 83, exercised Citation and later owned and operated Rancho Delta Paraiso near Stockton, California, on May 18 in Stockton.

Sir Peter Nugent, 83, retired auctioneer and director of Tattersalls Ltd. and Tattersalls Ireland, on December 12.

Rodney O'Domski, 48, farrier who shod a number of high-caliber runners, on March 10 in Camden, South Carolina.

Jason Oliver, 33, jockey and brother of champion rider Damien Oliver, on October 29 at Belmont racecourse in Perth, Australia, of head injuries suffered in a spill the previous day.

Wayne Opperman, 73, Chicago- and Florida-based trainer; founding member of the Florida Horsemen's Benevolent and Protective Association; on October 25 in Keller, Texas.

William Passmore, 92, former flat and steeplechase rider who trained for such clients as John Sanford, Deborah Rood, and Bayard Sharp before retiring in 1963; father of former jockey and Maryland steward Bill Passmore; on November 7 in Seaford, Delaware.

Billy Pearson, 82, retired jockey, quiz-show winner, and actor, on November 28 in Kingston, New York, after a long battle with emphysema.

Christo Philipson, 73, owner-breeder who worked for the British Bloodstock Agency for 37 years, on August 19 in Scotland of cancer.

Ogden Phipps, 93, industry leader who campaigned more than 100 homebred stakes winners, including champions Buckpasser, Easy Goer, Personal Ensign, Impressive, Queen of the Stage, Numbered Account, Heavenly Prize, and Relaxing; won Eclipse Award in 1988 and '89 as outstanding owner and in '88 as outstanding breeder; former Jockey Club chairman was instrumental in forming the New York Racing Association; received posthumous Eclipse Award of Merit in 2003; father of Jockey Club Chairman Ogden Mills "Dinny" Phipps and well-known horse owner Cynthia Phipps; on April 22 in West Palm Beach, Florida.

Harry Quadracci, 66, owner of 2001 graded stakes winner Silver Tornado, on July 29 near his Chenequa, Wisconsin, home of accidental drowning.

Bud C. Rapp, 87, Midwest-based trainer who conditioned multiple stakes winner Little by Little, on July 13 in Hot Springs, Arkansas, of kidney failure and pneumonia.

Georgia Ridder, 87, widow of Southern California owner B. J. Ridder, campaigned Grade 1 winners Alphabet Soup and Cat's Cradle; on June 14 in Pasadena, California.

Paul Rizzo, 49, trainer of a small string for John and Deborah Oxley; trained Grade 3 winner Scottish Halo and stakes winners Superduper Miss, Anclote, and Unlimited Go Go; on March 21 in Wellington, Florida, of cancer.

Conrad Roundtree, 64, Arlington Park outrider, on October 12 after suffering a heart attack in the stable area the previous day.

Ahmed bin Salman, 43, owner of The Thoroughbred Corp., which campaigned 2002 Kentucky Derby (G1) and Preakness Stakes (G1) winner War Emblem and homebreds 2001 Horse of the Year Point Given and leading distaff earner Spain; one of four owners to win Kentucky Derby and Epsom Derby (Eng-G1); on July 22 of a heart attack in Riyadh, Saudi Arabia.

Donna Salmen, 64, wife of Kentucky-based trainer Pete Salmen Jr.; mother of Kentucky Horsemen's Benevolent and Protective Association President Susan Bunning and breeder Peter Salmen III; co-owner of Grade 3 winner Bourbon Belle; on October 12 in Lexington after an illness.

Enrique Sarasola, 65, owner of 1996 Prix de l'Arc de Triomphe (Fr-G1) winner Helissio, on November 3 in Madrid, Spain, after a long illness.

John Schapiro, 87, former owner of Laurel Race Course who inaugurated the Washington, D. C., International Stakes in 1952, on January 5 of heart failure in Baltimore.

Bayard Sharp, 89, Delaware-based owner and breeder; father-in-law of William S. Farish; best horses bred included Grade 1 winners Mississippi Mud (dam of Dixieland Band, bred in his wife's name) and Papal Power; on August 9 at his Centreville, Delaware, home.

Jan Siegel, 69, co-owner with husband, Mace, and daughter, Jan, of Grade 1 winners, including Urbane, I Ain't Bluffing, and Stormy But Valid; on April 4 in Los Angeles after a long battle with cancer.

James P. Simpson, 82, former trainer who conditioned multiple graded stakes winner Cormorant, on September 16 in Winchester, Virginia.

William W. R. Smith, 75, former president of Florida HBPA and former operator of Copper Place Farms, on May 27 in Ocala.

Joseph Solomon, 84, pioneer veterinarian and a founder of the American Association of Equine Practitioners, on January 12 in Hollywood, Florida.

Santiago Soto, 50, international jockey won 1986 Pan American Handicap (G1) on Powder Break and 772 other races in the United States in the 1980s, on September 2 in Milan, Italy, of cancer.

Dusty Stimpson, 29, jockey, of injuries suffered in a one-vehicle accident near Los Angeles on January 1.

Don Sturgill, 74, owner, breeder, and Lexington-based lawyer specializing in the Thoroughbred industry, on October 2 of a heart attack.

Cora Mae Trotsek, 81, who campaigned Lady Golconda, dam of three-time Horse of the Year Forego and widow of Racing Hall of Fame trainer Harry Trotsek, on February 9 in Coral Gables, Florida.

C. L. "Jack" Utley, 85, Northern California-based trainer, on May 14 of cancer in Hayward, California.

Marvin Warner, 83, bred, raced, or owned more than 100 stakes winners solely or in partnership, including Grade 1 or Group 1 winners Stalwart, Desert Wine, Groom Dancer, and 1973 English juvenile champion filly *Bitty Girl. Owned Warnerton Farm in Lexington, Ocala, and Clermont County, Ohio, and an interest in Walmac-Warnerton Farm; imprisoned for the 1985 collapse of Home State Savings Bank; on April 8 in Cape Canaveral, Florida, of a heart attack.

Robert G. Wehle, 82, bred multiple Grade 1 winner Win and owned a 300-acre farm near Scottsville, New York, on July 26 in Syracuse.

Lord Arnold Weinstock, 77, one of Great Britain's leading industrialists who revived England's biggest electric company, GEC, and managed it until his retirement in 1996; raced 1979 Epsom Derby (Eng-G1) winner Troy; owned and bred 1996 Breeders' Cup Turf (G1) winner Pilsudski (Ire); on July 23 at his home in Wiltshire.

Steve Williams, 44, an assistant to Churchill Downs-based trainer Paul McGee, killed with his wife, Grace, when their vehicle was hit by a tractor-trailer just south of Louisville on February 15.

Verne Winchell, 87, owner-breeder campaigned more than 40 stakes winners, including champions Mira Femme and Tight Spot; one of his first horses was Donut King, an early favorite for the 1962 Kentucky Derby named after Winchell and his chain of doughnut shops; on November 26 of a heart attack at his Las Vegas home.

Warren Wolf, 79, longtime racing secretary at River Downs and Tampa Bay Downs, on April 4 in Ocala.

Lucy Maddox Young, 82, wife of Overbrook Farm owner William T. Young, on January 13.

2002 Horse Deaths

ALEXANDRINA, 1987 b. m., Conquistador Cielo—La Lorgnette, by Val de l'Orne (Fr). 26-3-3-3, $214,322. Won 1989 Yearling Sales S. (first division). Dam of 1999 Canadian Horse of the Year Thornfield. Died on February 16.

ALYWOW, 1991 b. m., Alysheba—Triple Wow, by Coastal. 19-7-6-3, $648,431. 1994 Canadian Horse of the Year. Dam of 2002 Goffs International S. (Ire-G2) winner Century City. Euthanized on March 2 after a long battle with a bone infection at Kilcarn Stud in Ireland.

ANDOVER WAY, 1978 dk. b. or br. m., His Majesty—On the Trail, by Olympia. 18-9-6-2, $372,471. Won 1982 Top Flight H. (G1), etc. Dam of at least two stakes winners, including Grade 2 winner Dynaformer. Died on May 9 at Claiborne Farm near Paris, Kentucky, of foaling complications.

ANTESPEND, 1993 b. m., Spend a Buck—Auspiciante (Arg), by *Practicante. 24-10-4-2, $1,011,954. Won 1996 Del Mar Invitational Oaks (G1), etc. Euthanized on April 16 at Chestertown Farm near Chestertown,

New York, after foaling complications.

ARCHERS BAY, 1995 b. h., Silver Deputy—Adorned, by Val de l'Orne (Fr). 13-4-3-2, $666,200. 1998 Canadian champion three-year-old colt. Won Queen's Plate Stakes, etc. Euthanized on October 3 at Windfields Farm near Oshawa, Ontario, due to complications of colic surgery.

AT THE THRESHOLD, 1981 ch. h., Norcliffe—Winver, by Vertex. 18-9-2-5, $695,930. Won 1984 Arlington Classic (G1), etc. Sire of at least eight stakes winners, including 1992 Kentucky Derby (G1) winner Lil E. Tee. Euthanized on March 23 after suffering an apparent stroke at the Purdue University School of Veterinary Medicine in West Lafayette, Louisiana.

BANKER'S LADY, 1985 ch. m., Nijinsky II—Impetuous Gal, by Briartic. 10-8-1-0, $594,297. Won 1988 Ladies H. (G1), etc. Dam of 1998 Tom Fool H. (G1) winner Banker's Gold. Euthanized on March 4 because of foaling complications at Stonerside Farm near Paris, Kentucky.

BANNOCKBURN, 1978 ch. m., Count Brook—Fatal Conflict, by *River War. 19-5-4-3, $91,034. Won 1981 Drop Me a Note S. Dam of ten winners, including graded stakes winners Bella Chiarra and David Copperfield. Died on October 22.

BELIEVE THE QUEEN, 1980 b. h., Believe It—Raise a Queen, by Raise a Native. 20-8-4-3, $452,335. Won 1984 Monmouth H. (G1), etc. Sire of at least five stakes winners, including Grade 2 winner Wait for the Lady. Died on August 1.

BELIEVE IT, 1975 ch. h., In Reality—Breakfast Bell, by Buckpasser. 17-6-6-2, $350,483. Won 1978 Wood Memorial Stakes (G1), etc. Third behind Affirmed and Alydar in '78 Kentucky Derby (G1) and Preakness Stakes (G1). Sire of at least 30 stakes winners, including 1989 Panamanian champion Creemelo and Grade 1 winners Al Mamoon and Garthorn. Died on June 5 at Clear Creek Stud near Folsom, Louisiana, of natural causes.

BIEN BIEN, 1989 ch. h., Manila—Stark Winter, by Graustark. 26-9-8-1, $2,331,875. Won 1992-'93 Hollywood Turf Cup S. (G1), etc. Sire of at least three stakes winners, including 2000 Hollywood Turf Cup S. (G1) winner Bienamado. Died on March 11 after suffering a heart attack at Kirtlington Stud in England.

BIREME, 1977 ch. m., Grundy—Ripeck, by *Ribot. 4-3-0-1, $199,016. Won 1980 Epsom Oaks (Eng-G1). Dam of at least eight winners, including Group 3 winner Yawl. Died on January 14.

BLACK KNIGHT, 1979 b. g., Silver Knight—Brenta, by Coeur Volant. Won 1984 Melbourne Cup (Aus-G1). Ten-year member of Victoria Mounted Police. Euthanized on July 4 after suffering kidney infection.

CAREFOLIE (Ire), 1985 b. h., Caerleon—Balilla, by Balidar. 18-5-3-4, $138,834. Won 1987 Ardenode Stud Leopardstown S. (Ire-G3), etc. Sire of at least six stakes winners, including Group 1 winner Campesino. Died during an unspecified surgical procedure at Haras El Tala in Argentina.

CASHIER'S DREAM, 1999 ch. f., Service Stripe—Jerry's Sister, by Monetary Gift. 7-5-2-0, $423,042. Won 2001 Spinaway S. (G1), etc. Euthanized on July 1 at Hagyard-Davidson-McGee equine clinic near Lexington due to complications of colic.

CASSOWARY, 1981 b. m., Cormorant—Aunt Marion, by What Luck. 17-2-2-2, $72,562. Second in 1984 Post-Deb S. (G3), etc. Dam of at least eight winners, including Grade 2 winner Meadow Flight and Grade 3

winner People's Princess. Died on May 8.

CEE DREAMS, 1996 gr. or ro. m., Cee's Tizzy—Dreamsbury, by Doonesbury. 40-11-5-9, $439,336. Won 2001 California Cup Matron H. Euthanized on March 12 because of complications of having right front leg amputated due to injuries suffered in a January 18 workout.

CONQUISTADOR CIELO, 1979 b. h., Mr. Prospector—KD Princess, by Bold Commander. 13-9-0-2, $474,328. 1982 Horse of the Year, won '82 Belmont S. (G1), Metropolitan H. (G1), etc. Sire of at least 65 stakes winners, including multiple Slovakian and Hungarian champion Montaciel, Grade 1 winners Marquetry and Wagon Limit. Euthanized on December 17 at Claiborne Farm near Paris, Kentucky, because of laminitis.

COUNTRY LIGHT, 1983 b. h., Majestic Light—Harbor Flag, by Hoist the Flag. 6-4-2-0, $196,349. Won 1986 Louisiana Derby (G3), etc. Sire of at least eight stakes winners, including 1991 Canadian champion three-year-old Bolulight. Euthanized on March 11 after fracturing a leg at Double G Ranch near Pinon Hills, California.

COUNTRY QUEEN, 1975 b. m., Explodent—Carrie's Rough, by Rough'n Tumble. Won 1979 Yellow Ribbon Invitational S. (G1), etc. Dam of at least six winners, including stakes winner River Char. Grandam of English and Italian highweight Slickly (Fr). Died on November 3.

DISTINCTLY NORTH, 1988 dk. b. or br. h., Minshaanshu Amad—Distinctiveness, by Distinctive. 10-3-4-0, $250,107. Won 1990 Flying Childers S. (Eng-G2). Sire of at least 16 stakes winners, including Grade 2 winner Innit (Ire). Leading first-crop sire in Europe in 1995. Died in late April after suffering an apparent heart attack at Allevamento di Besnate in Italy.

DIXIE BRASS, 1989 dk. b. or br. h., Dixieland Band—Petite Diable, by Sham. 15-6-2-2, $631,563. Won 1992 Metropolitan Mile H. (G1), etc. Sire of at least 30 stakes winners, including 2000 champion imported filly in Puerto Rico Collect the Brass, 1998-'99 Jamaican Horse of the Year Blumenthal, '99 San Fernando Breeders' Cup S. (G2) winner Dixie Dot Com, etc. Died on January 28 at The Stallion Station near Millbrook, New York.

DOUBLE LOCK (GB), 1975 b. m., Home Guard—St Padina, St. Paddy. 5-1-0-0, $12,922. Won 1978 Sandleford Priory S. Dam of at least four stakes winners, including Group 2 winner Sure Blade and Group 3 winner Sure Sharp. Died on May 1.

DOYOUN, 1985 b. h., Mill Reef—Dumka, by Kashmir II. 7-3-0-3, $356,189. Won 1988 Two Thousand Guineas (Eng-G1). Sire of at least 31 stakes winners, including 1999 North American champion grass male and European Horse of the Year Daylami (Ire); and 2000 champion grass male Kalanisi (Ire). Died on December 5 at Veliefendi equine hospital in Istanbul, Turkey, after suffering from an undisclosed health problem.

DR. PATCHES, 1974 ch. g., Dr. Fager—Expectancy, by Intentionally. 47-17-14-3, $737,612. 1978 co-champion sprinter. Best remembered for defeating Seattle Slew in the 1978 Patterson H. at the Meadowlands. Euthanized on July 30 at Tartan Farms near Ocala due to infirmities of old age.

EGYPTBAND, 1997 b. m., Dixieland Band—Egyptown (Fr), by Top Ville. 9-4-2-2, $669,651. Won 2000 Prix de Diane (French Oaks [Fr-G1]), etc. Died on February 23 from complications of colic at Hagyard Farm near Lexington.

EL CONDOR PASA, 1995 dk. b. or br. h., Kingmambo—Saddlers Gal (Ire), by Sadler's Wells. 11-8-3-0, $3,502,404. 1999 Japanese Horse of the Year, highweighted on European Free Handicap, 1998 Japanese champion three-year-old colt. Died on July 16 after suffering from colic at Shadai Stallion Station in Japan.

ENCINO, 1977 ch. h., Nijinsky II—Crimson Saint, by Crimson Satan. 5-1-1-2, $34,900. Second in 1979 Haggin S., etc. Sire of at least 19 stakes winners, including graded stakes winners The Name's Jimmy and Down Again. Died on June 27 at Beckett Ranch near Colton, California, of natural causes.

END SWEEP, 1991 b. h., Forty Niner—Broom Dance, by Dance Spell. 18-6-6-3, $372,563. Won 1994 Jersey Shore Breeders' Cup S. (G3), etc. Set North American record of 33 two-year-old winners from his first crop in 1998. Sire of at least 23 stakes winners, including Grade 1 winners Swept Overboard, Trippi, and Nany's Sweep. Euthanized on July 11 at Shadai Stallion Station due to complications from an injury to his withers.

EPERVIER BLEU, 1987 b. h., Saint Cyrien—Equadif (Fr), by Abdos. 9-6-3-0, $1,046,873. Highweighted older horse on 1991 European Free Handicap. Sire of at least nine stakes winners, including 2000 Swiss Horse of the Year Minet Bleu. Died on May 20 at Haras du Pin in France of a heart attack.

FIVE STAR FLIGHT, 1978 b. h., Top Command—Sweeping Beauty, by Eddie Schmidt. 12-7-1-0, $351,129. Won 1981 Haskell Invitational H. (G1), etc. Sire of at least six stakes winners, including Grade 3 winner Faster Than Sound. Died on September 1.

FLAWLESSLY—1988 b. m., Affirmed—La Confidence, by Nijinsky II. 28-16-4-3, $2,572,536. 1992-'93 champion grass female. Won '93 Beverly D. S. (G1), etc. Died on September 26 at Elmwood Farm near Versailles, Kentucky, of kidney problems.

FORTUNATE MOMENT, 1984 ch. h., For The Moment—Restless Cat, by Restless Wind. 34-10-3-2, $385,012. Won 1987 American Derby (G1), etc. Sire of at least one stakes winner. Euthanized on June 7 at Oklahoma State University's College of Veterinary Medicine Ranch near Stillwater due to complications of laminitis.

FOURSTARDAVE, 1985 ch. g., Compliance—Broadway Joan, by Bold Arian. 100-21-18-16, $1,636,737. Won 1988 St. Paul Derby (G2), '90 and '91 Daryl's Joy S. (G3) (later renamed for him), etc. Renowned for winning at Saratoga Race Course every year from 1987 to '94. Died of a heart attack at Belmont Park on October 15, four days before a scheduled public appearance at the track.

FREEDOM'S DAUGHTER, 2000 b. f., Saint Ballado—Carezza, by Caro (Ire). 2-2-0-0, $109,200. Won 2002 Schuylerville S. (G2). Died on August 12 at a clinic near Saratoga Springs, New York, from colitis X.

FRENCH ASSAULT, 1999 ch. h., French Deputy—Carly's Crown, by Wild Again. 9-2-3-0, $141,090. Won 2001 El Jovan S. Euthanized on July 10 after failing to respond to treatment for chronic inflammation of the intestines.

GORGEOUS, 1986 dk. b. or br. m., Slew o' Gold—Kamar, by Key to the Mint. 14-8-4-1, $1,171,370. Won 1989 Ashland S. (G1), '90 Vanity Invitational H. (G1), etc. Dam of at least five winners, including stakes winner Stunning. Died on October 4 after suffering an

internal hemorrhage at Three Chimneys Farm near Midway, Kentucky.

HALORY, 1984 ch. m., Halo—Cold Reply, by Northern Dancer. 14-0-2-2, $9,042. Dam of at least five graded stakes winners, including 1998 Blue Grass S. (G2) winner Halory Hunter and '02 Galileo E. B. F. Futurity S. (Ire-G2) winner Van Nistelrooy. Died on March 13 after suffering a ruptured uterine artery.

HAL'S HOPE, 1997 dk. b. or br. h., Jolie's Halo—Mia's Hope, by Rexson's Hope. 33-9-5-3, $1,098,422. Won 2000 Florida Derby (G1), etc. Died on July 12 at Palm Beach Equine Hospital in Florida due to complications of intestinal surgery.

HIGHLAND LEGACY, 1998 b. g., Highland Ruckus—Nonfiction, by Lord Avie. 15-4-2-1, $403,064. 2000 Canadian champion two-year-old male. One of 32 horses killed in a barn fire on August 4 at Woodbine.

HONOR GRADES, 1988 b. h., Danzig—Weekend Surprise, by Secretariat. 24-5-3-5, $173,953. Second in 1991 Derby Trial S. (G2). Sire of at least 23 stakes winners, including 1997 Secretariat S. (G1) winner Honor Glide, '01 Pan American H. (G2) winner Whata Brainstorm. Found dead in paddock on March 31 at Darby Dan Farm near Lexington.

IMADEED, 1997 b. m., Alydeed—Imah, by Gate Dancer. 17-6-3-0, $213,380. Second in the 2001 NBC S. at Belmont Park. Euthanized on June 20 at Rood and Riddle Equine Clinic near Lexington due to complications of suspensory ligament injury suffered in spill in the '02 NBC on June 8.

INGOLDSBY, 1985 b. m., Screen King—Dorothy Kay, by Irish Castle. 2-1-1-0, $12,960. Dam of at least two stakes winners, including Grade 1 winner Formal Gold. Died on June 17 at The Meadows near Georgetown, Kentucky, after a bout with colic.

INGOT WAY, 1981 gr. m., Diplomat Way—Ingot, by Iron Ruler. 37-5-1-6, $66,149. Won 1985 Skipat H. Dam of 1998 Horse of the Year Skip Away. Died on March 27 at Summer Wind Farm near Georgetown, Kentucky, from colic.

IT'S A GIGGLE, 1994 b. g., Northern Baby—Martie's Delighted, by Mo Bay. 19-9-3-1, $356,910. Won 2002 Royal Chase for the Sport of Kings Hurdle S., etc. Finalist for 2002 champion steeplechaser. Euthanized on December 13 at an equine clinic in Tyron, North Carolina, after a bout with colic.

JARRINHO, 1995 b. h., Jarraar—Fortuna Rich, by Faranloy. 33-11-2-2, $141,879. 2001 champion miler in Brazil. Died after suffering broken neck and internal injuries in a paddock accident at Haras Rocavaro in Brazil.

JEBLAR, 1982 b. h., Alydar—City Girl, by Lucky Debonair. 40-14-4-6, $320,618. Won 1987 Broward H., etc. Sire of at least 27 stakes winners, including 1995 Hawthorne Derby (G3) winner Cuzzin Jeb. Struck by lightning in mid-September at Farnsworth Farm near Ocala.

KERALI, 1984 ch. m., High Line—Sookera, by Roberto. 4-1-0-0, $5,212. Dam of at least three stakes winners, including Hasili, the dam of European and North American champion Banks Hill (GB). Died on July 10.

KINGDOM BAY, 1981 ch. h., Otehi Bay—Golden Praise, by Golden Plume. 18-10-5-3, $8,067. Won New Zealand Two Thousand Guineas (NZ-G1), etc. Leading sire in New Zealand 1994 and '96. Sire of at least 24 stakes winners, including 1994 New Zealand champion three-year-old Snap. Euthanized on October 8 at Trelawney Stud near Cambridge, New Zealand, after failing to respond to treatment for a hind leg infection.

KINGRANDI, 1979 b. h., Leigo—Cajopita, by Major's Dilemma. Won 1982 Grande Premio Derby Paulista (Brazilian Derby) (Brz-G1). Sire of at least six stakes winners, including Group 1 winners Ardito, Jack Grandi. Died in November in Brazil.

KRIS S., 1977 dk. b. or br. h., Roberto—Sharp Queen, by *Princequillo. 5-3-1-0, $53,350. Won 1980 Bradbury Stakes. Sire of at least 67 stakes winners, including 1993 champion three-year-old filly Hollywood Wildcat, '99 champion grass female Soaring Softly, '89 Breeders' Cup Turf (G1) winner Prized. Euthanized on May 7 at WinStar Farm near Versailles, Kentucky, due to complications of a neck injury and laminitis.

LANDSEER (GB), 1999 b. c., Danehill—Sabria, by Miswaki. 13-4-4-1, $993,928. Won 2002 Poule d'Essai des Poulains (French Two Thousand Guineas [Fr-G1]), Shadwell Keeneland Turf Mile S. (G2), etc. Euthanized on October 26 after breaking down in the Breeders' Cup Mile (G1) at Arlington Park.

LARIDA, 1979 ch. m., Northern Dancer—Kittiwake, by *Sea-Bird. 25-10-7-1, $328,319. Won 1983 Orchid H. (G2) (second division), etc. Dam of at least four winners, including Group 1 winner Magic of Life, who sold for a record $2.5-million as a weanling at the 1985 Newstead Farm Trust dispersal at Fasig-Tipton Kentucky. Larida's price of $4-million at the sale was believed to have set a record for a barren mare. Died on February 16.

LARLA, 1977 ch. m., Singh—Sweeping Beauty, by Eddie Schmidt. 32-11-7-2, $167,561. Won 1980 Milky Way S., etc. Half sister to Five Star Flight. Dam of at least 12 winners, including Grade 3 winner Western Larla. Died on April 20.

LEFT BANK, 1997 ch. h., French Deputy—Marshesseaux, by Dr. Blum. 24-14-2-0, $1,402,806. 2002 champion older male. Won 2002 Whitney H. (G1) (equaled track record), '01 Cigar Mile H. (G1), etc. Died on October 7 at Ashford Stud near Versailles, Kentucky, of complications of colic surgery.

LIFE AT THE TOP, 1983 b. m., Seattle Slew—See You At the Top, by Riva Ridge. 27-9-6-5, $989,504. Won 1986 Mother Goose S. (G1), etc. Dam of at least four winners, including Group 3 winner Elizabeth Bay. Died on January 4.

LINES OF POWER, 1977 b. h., Raise a Native—Exotic Garden, by Bold Ruler. 28-13-6-2, $239,487. Won 1981 Gravesend H., etc. Sire of at least 22 stakes winners, including graded winners Loach, Clever Power, All Thee Power, etc. Euthanized on June 12 at Iron Horse Farm near Little Rock, Arkansas, due to infirmities of old age.

LEO CASTELLI, 1984 b. h., Sovereign Dancer—Suspicious Native, by Raise a Native. 11-3-3-1, $274,497. Won 1987 Peter Pan S. (G2). Sire of at least 24 stakes winners, including Grade 2 winner Da Devil. Euthanized in February at the College of Veterinary Medicine at Texas A&M University after suffering an intestinal infection.

LISTEN HERE, 1999 ch. c., Gulch—Listen Now, by Storm Bird. 10-4-3-1, $287,480. Won 2002 Amsterdam S. (G2), etc. Euthanized on August 19 at Saratoga Race Course after breaking sesamoid bones in his left foreleg while training.

LONESOME GLORY, 1988 ch. g., Transworld—Stronghold Farm (Fr), by Green Dancer. 44-24-5-6, $1,325,868. Champion steeplechaser 1992, '93, '95, '97, and '99; won Colonial Cup Steeplechase H. three times, etc.; first steeplechase horse to earn more than $1-million. Euthanized on February 25 after breaking a hind leg in a paddock accident at Fox Ferret Farm near Cochranville, Pennsylvania.

LUSHKIN STAR, 1974 ch. h., Kaoru Star—Promising, by Idomeneo. 20-17-3-0, $440,585. 1976 champion two-year-old in Australia. Won 1977 Golden Slipper S. (Aus-G1), etc. Sire of at least 32 stakes winners. Euthanized on July 1 at Newhaven Park Stud near Boorowa, New South Wales, due to severe arthritis.

MARASCA—1999 dk. b. or br. c., Take Me Out—Rajas Secret, by Storm Bird. 7-2-3-1, $196,460. Won 2002 Aventura S. Euthanized on May 10 after breaking two bones in his right foreleg on May 4 while training at Fair Hill Training Center in Maryland.

MARAUDING, 1984 b. h., *Sir Tristram—Biscalowe, by Biscay. 5-3-1-1, earnings not available. Won 1987 Golden Slipper S. (Aus-G1), etc. Sire of at least 28 stakes winners, including 1992 Australian champion two-year-old Burst. Euthanized on November 20 at Newhaven Park Stud near Boorowa, New South Wales after dislocating a pastern joint.

MEADOW STAR, 1988 ch. m., Meadowlake—Inreality Star, by In Reality. 20-11-1-2, $1,445,740. 1990 champion two-year-old filly. Won 1990 Breeders' Cup Juvenile Fillies (G1), '91 Mother Goose S. (G1), etc. Died on April 11 from foaling complications at Hagyard-Davidson-McGee Associates equine hospital in Lexington.

MELLOW ROLL, 1995 b. h., Distinctive Pro—Tim's Lady, by Oh Say. 24-7-4-4, $555,772. Won 1998 Empire Classic H., etc. Euthanized in April due to complications of a shattered pastern suffered in a paddock accident two months earlier.

MI QUIMERA (Arg), 1977 b. m., Good Manners—La Gran Muneca, by Aristophanes. 1980 champion two-year-old filly in Argentina. Dam of Argentine Group 3 winner My Swinger. Died on April 10 of foaling complications at Buena Vista Farm near Ocala.

MOZART (Ire), 1998 b. c., Danehill—Victoria Cross, by Spectacular Bid. 10-5-1-2, $819,900. 2001 champion European sprinter. Died on May 12 at Coolmore Stud in Ireland of acute colitis.

MR PURPLE, 1992 dk. b. or br. h., Deputy Minister—Turk O Witz, by Stop the Music. 21-6-3-5, $1,133,538. Won 1996 Santa Anita Handicap (G1), etc. Sire of at least two stakes winners. Euthanized on May 30 at Victory Rose Thoroughbreds in California due to complications from heart-valve failure.

NASHWAN, 1986 ch. h., Blushing Groom (Fr)—Height of Fashion (Fr), by Bustino. 7-6-0-1, $1,447,003. Highweighted on 1989 European Free Handicap, won '89 Epsom Derby (Eng-G1), Two Thousand Guineas (Eng-G1), etc. Sire of at least 28 stakes winners, including 1998 European champion older horse Swain (Ire), 1996 champion grass mare Wandesta (GB). Euthanized on July 19 at Nunnery Stud in England after complications arose following minor surgery on his right hind leg.

NATSKI, 1984 b. h., Ela-Mana-Mou—Sweet Rhapsody, by *Sea-Bird. 20-7-3-0-. Won Metropolitan (Aus-G1), etc. Sire of at least 39 winners. Died in June at Corrumbene Stud in Australia of an apparent heart attack.

NIMBLE FOLLY, 1977 ch. m., Cyane—Instant Sin, by Restless Native. Unraced. Dam of 11 winners, including Grade 1 winner Contredance, Grade 2 winner Skimble (dam of Grade 1 winner Skimming), and Grade 3 winner Shotiche. Died on October 1.

OH SAY, 1978 b. h., Hoist the Flag—Light Hearted, by Cyane. 9-7-1-1, $78,543. Won 1982 Hannibal H. Sire of at least 25 stakes winners, including Chilean champion Oh Reason and Grade 1 winner Sham Say. Euthanized in late July due to aging problems, including a tumor in his sinus area.

OVERALL, 1985 ch. m., Mr. Prospector—Full Tigress, by El Tigre Grande. 14-6-1-0, $411,828. Won 1987 Spinaway S. (G1), etc. Dam of at least three winners, including stakes winner Hustler. Died on March 23.

PARTYGOER, 1984 b. m., Secretariat—Quiet Charm, by Nearctic. 10-1-3-0, $17,160. Dam of at least eight winners, including Grade 1 winner Dare and Go. Died on March 3.

PENNYHILL PARK, 1990 ch. m., Ascot Knight—Middlemarch, by Buckpasser. 36-10-7-6, $694,569. 1994 Canadian champion older female. Won 1994 Turfway Breeders' Cup S. (G2), etc. Dam of at least two winners, including stakes-placed Penny Perfect. Euthanized in late June after developing a neurological disorder at Springland Farm near Paris, Kentucky.

PENTELICUS, 1984 b. h., Fappiano—Charedi, by In Reality. 37-11-3-5, $267,742. Won 1986 Mayflower S., etc. Sire of at least 17 stakes winners, including graded stakes winners Penny Blues, Hair Spray, How About Now, Dontletthebigonego. Euthanized on August 29 at Ocala Stud Farms due to complications of laminitis.

PHARLY, 1974 ch. h., Lyphard—Comely (Fr), by Boran. 13-5-5-1, $321,976. Won 1977 Prix Lupin (Fr-G1), etc. Fifth leading sire in France in 1983 and '84. Sire of at least 45 stakes winners, including Further Flight, 1995 European champion older horse and winner of the Jockey Club Cup S. (Eng-G3) 1991-'95. Euthanized on November 9 at Woodland Stud near Newmarket, England, after fracturing pelvis in a paddock accident.

PLEASANT COLONY, 1978 dk. b. or br. h., His Majesty—Sun Colony, by Sunrise Flight. 14-6-3-1, $965,383. 1981 champion three-year-old male, won Kentucky Derby (G1), Preakness Stakes (G1), etc. Sire of at least 73 stakes winners, including 1992 European Horse of the Year St. Jovite, 1992 champion older male Pleasant Tap, 1991 champion two-year-old filly Pleasant Stage. Died on December 31 at Blue Ridge Farm near Upperville, Virginia, of natural causes.

POLISH NUMBERS, 1987 b. h., Danzig—Numbered Account, by Buckpasser. 11-4-2-1, $80,493. Second in 1989 J. O. Tobin S. Sire of at least 35 stakes winners, including 1997 Peruvian champion miler Eithan, Grade 1 winner Tenski, Grade 3 winner Biogio's Rose. Euthanized on November 29 after shattering his tibia in a paddock accident at Northview Stallion Station near Chesapeake City, Maryland.

POMPEYO (Chi), 1994 dk. b. or br. g., Nureyev Dancer—Pouliche, by Domineau. 33-11-6-5, $528,325. 2001 champion steeplechaser. Euthanized on January 19 after suffering complications from an injury suffered when kicked in the left front elbow four months earlier.

PRINCE SPELLBOUND, 1979 b. h., Dimaggio—Arctic Spell, by *Arctic Prince. 22-8-8-3, $935,343. Won 1983 Eddie Read H. (G2), etc. Sire of at least 26 winners, including stakes winner Correra. Died on November 18.

PROUD TOWER, 1998 dk. b. h., Proud Irish—Dora's Tower, by Irish Tower. 6-4-1-1, $280,660. Won 2000 Hollywood Prevue S. (G3). Euthanized on February 7 after suffering two fractured sesamoids in a workout at Santa Anita Park.

QUESTELAVIE, 1991 ch. m., Conquistador Cielo—Captivating Grace, by Damascus. 16-3-3-0, $107,816.

Won 1993 Ontario Debutante S. Dam of 1999 Selene S. (Can-G1) winner Roaring Twenties. Died in August.

RAJA BABA, 1968 b. h., Bold Ruler—Missy Baba, by *My Babu. 41-7-12-9, $123,287. Won 1971 Francis Scott Key S., etc. Leading sire in 1980. Sire of 62 stakes winners, including 1987 champion three-year-old filly Sacahuista, 1985 Canadian champion sprinter Summer Mood, 1978-'79 Mexican Horse of the Year Gran Zar (Mex). Euthanized on October 9 at Hermitage Farm near Goshen, Kentucky, following a sudden decline in health.

ROSEDON, 1983 gr. m., Vice Regent—Dobbinee, by Ruritania. 6-2-0-3, $16,750. Dam of at least four winners, including 1992 Canadian Horse of the Year Benburb. Died on January 1.

ROSE OF KINGSTON (Aus), 1978 ch. m., Claude—Kingston Rose (Aus), by Better Boy. 17-8-4-5, earnings not available. 1981 Australian Horse of the Year, '82 Australian champion older mare. Dam of 1990 Melbourne Cup (Aus-G1) winner Kingston Rule.

RUBIANO, 1987 gr. or ro. h., Fappiano—Ruby Slippers, by Nijinsky II. 28-13-6-1, $1,252,817. 1992 champion sprinter. Won '91 NYRA Mile H. (G1), etc. Sire of at least 21 stakes winners, including Grade 1 winner Burning Roma. Euthanized on November 19 at Lane's End near Versailles, Kentucky, due to complications from laminitis.

RUBY SLIPPERS, 1982 ro. m., Nijinsky II—Moon Glitter, by In Reality. 14-5-0-2, $83,760. Dam of at least eight winners, including 1992 champion sprinter Rubiano. Died on July 25.

SAFE PLAY, 1978 b. m., Sham—Bori, by Quadrangle. 27-11-7-3, $393,085. Won 1982 La Canada S. (G1), etc. Dam of at least five winners, including Grade 1 winner Defensive Play. Euthanized in early October at Juddmonte Farms near Lexington because of severe arthritis.

SAINT BALLADO, 1989 dk. b. or br. h., Halo—Ballade, by *Herbager. 9-4-2-0, $302,820. Won 1992 Arlington Classic (G2), etc. Sire of at least 40 stakes winners. Euthanized on October 20 at Taylor Made Farm near Nicholasville, Kentucky, due to complications from surgery for progressive cervical myelopathy.

SEATTLE SLEW, 1974 dk. b. or br. g., Bold Reasoning—My Charmer, by Poker. 17-14-2-0, $1,208,726. Won 1977 Triple Crown while undefeated. 1977 Horse of the Year, '76 champion two-year-old male, '77 champion three-year-old male, '78 champion older male. Leading sire of '84, leading broodmare sire '95, '96. Sire of at least 107 stakes winners, including '92 Horse of the Year A.P. Indy, '83 champion three-year-old male and '84 champion older male Slew o' Gold, '84 champion three-year-old male Swale. Died on May 7 from infirmities of old age at Hill 'n' Dale Farms near Lexington, where he had been moved a month earlier after standing at Three Chimneys Farm near Lexington since 1985.

SECRET HELLO, 1987 dk. b. or br. h., Private Account—Ciao, by Silent Screen. 22-6-3-6, $784,259. Won 1989 Arlington-Washington Futurity (G1), etc. Sire of at least 15 stakes winners, including Grade 2 winner Secret Firm. Euthanized on December 19 due to complications from chronic neurological disease.

SHADAYID, 1988 ro. m., Shadeed—Desirable (Ire), by Lord Gayle. 11-5-2-3, $671,520. 1990 English champion two-year-old filly. Won One Thousand Guineas (Eng-G1), etc. Dam of at least two stakes winners, including English Group 3 winner Bint Shadayid. Died on April 27 from a ruptured uterine artery.

SHANEKITE, 1978 b. h., Hoist Bar—Win Shane, by Anyoldtime. 50-12-13-3, $455,375. Won 1981 National Sprint Championship S. (first division), etc. Sire of at least 16 stakes winners. Euthanized on August 14 at Blooming Hills Farm near Clements, California, due to infirmities of old age.

SHARP PERFORMANCE, 1998 b. h. Kris S.—Theatre Flight, by Theatrical (Ire). 7-4-0-2, $279,780. Won 2001 Lexington S. (G3), etc. Euthanized on June 9 at Belmont Park after developing an infection in his left foreleg following a ligament injury.

SHE WON'T TELL, 1979 ch. m., Exclusive Native—Won't Tell You, by Crafty Admiral. 9-3-1-0, $42,450. Full sister to 1978 Triple Crown winner Affirmed. Dam of Grade 1 winner Senor Pete. Died on March 17 at Manchester Farm near Lexington from foaling complications.

SHIBBOLETH, 1997 b. h., Danzig—Razyana, by His Majesty. 12-5-1-0, $187,624. Won 2002 Jaipur H. (G3), etc. Full brother to leading international sire Danehill. Euthanized in the fall after contracting laminitis.

SIPHONIC, 1999 b. c., Siphon (Brz)—Cherokee Crossing, by Cherokee Colony. 7-3-2-2, $774,778. Won 2001 Hollywood Futurity (G1), etc. Died on October 2 of cardiac arrest about 20 minutes after finishing second in a Santa Anita Park allowance race.

SIX CROWNS, 1976 ch. m., Secretariat—Chris Evert, by Swoon's Son. 15-5-3-5, $136,274. Won 1979 Meadow Queen S. Dam of 1984 champion two-year-old colt Chief's Crown and '87 Frizette S. (G1) winner Classic Crown. Euthanized on February 15 because of infirmities of old age at Three Chimneys Farm near Midway, Kentucky.

SNIPPETS, 1984 b. h., Lunchtime—Easy Date, by Grand Chaudiere. 9-7-2-0, earnings not available. Won 1987 Australia Jockey Club Sires Produce Stakes (Aus-G1), etc. Sire of at least 40 stakes winners, including Mr. Vitality, two-time champion sprinter in Hong Kong. Euthanized on January 20 after suffering an internal hemorrhage.

SPEND A BUCK, 1982 b. h., Buckaroo—Belle de Jour, by Speak John. 15-10-3-2, $4,220,689. 1985 Horse of the Year, won '85 Kentucky Derby (G1), etc. Sire of at least 31 stakes winners, including Grade 1 winner Antespend. Died on November 24 at Haras Bage do Sul in Brazil of anaphylactic shock.

SUNDAY SILENCE, 14-9-5-0, $4,968,554. 1989 Horse of the Year, champion three-year-old male. Won '89 Breeders' Cup Classic (G1), Kentucky Derby (G1), Preakness S. (G1), etc. Preakness duel with Easy Goer is considered one of the greatest races of all time. Leading sire in Japan 1995-2002. World's all-time leading sire by progeny earnings. Sire of at least 79 stakes winners, including ten Japanese champions. Died on August 19 after a long battle with peritendinitis in his right foreleg and laminitis in his left front foot at the Shadai Stallion Station in Japan.

SUPREME LEADER, 1982 b. h., Bustino—Princess Zena, by Habitat. 16-3-0-4, $129,343. Won 1986 Earl of Sefton Stakes (Eng-G3), etc. One of Europe's most active sires with an average book of 244 mares per year. Sire of at least nine stakes winners, including 2001 Gold Cup Steeplechase winner What's Up Boys, runner-up in the '02 Grand National Steeplechase. Died on May 17 at Grange Stud in County Tipperary, Ireland, of a heart attack.

SUSPICIOUS NATIVE, 1972 ch. m., Raise a Native—Be Suspicious, by Porterhouse. Unraced. Dam of nine winners, including graded stakes winners Meadowlake and Leo Castelli. Died on May 23 at Crestfield Farm near Lexington.

TACTICAL ADVANTAGE, 1990 ch. h., Forty Niner—Twitchet, by Roberto. 17-3-2-3, $174,630. Won 1992 Saratoga Special S. (G2). Sire of at least ten stakes winners, including Grade 2 winners Forty One Carats, Prime Directive. Euthanized on December 26 at the University of Florida Large Animal Clinic in Gainesville due to an incurable neurological disorder.

TEMPERA, 1999 dk. b. or br. f., A.P. Indy—Colour Chart, by Mr. Prospector. 7-3-2-2, $770,240. 2001 champion two-year-old filly. Won Breeders' Cup Juvenile Fillies (G1), etc. Euthanized on April 28 after developing laminitis in connection with colitis at Hagyard-Davidson-McGee equine clinic in Lexington.

TEMPLADO (Ven), 1993 b. h., Mazag—Lady Avie, by Lord Avie. 33-13-3-3, $213,044. 1995 Horse of the Year in Venezuela, won '97 Deputy Minister H. Died on February 15 of a heart attack at Haras Gran Derby in Venezuela.

THINGS CHANGE, 1996 gr. or ro. m., Stalwart—Romanticat, by Gato Del Sol. 8-3-2-1, $330,188. Won 1998 Spinaway S. (G1), etc. Died on October 25.

VALID APPEAL, 1972 b. h., In Reality—Desert Trial, by Moslem Chief. 36-8-7-3, $201,733. Won 1975 Dwyer H. (G2), etc. Sire of at least 86 stakes winners, including Sportsmaster (champion in the Dominican Republic), 1998 Meadowlands Cup Handicap (G1) winner K. J.'s Appeal, '90 Santa Monica Handicap (G1) winner Stormy But Valid; died on January 5 at Mockingbird Farm near Ocala.

WARNERS, 1999 ch. c., Dehere—Sweet Gold, by Gilded Time. 6-2-3-0, $101,000. Second in 2002 Bay Shore S. (G3), etc. Sold for $1,050,000 as two-year-old in training at Ocala Breeders' Sales Co. March sale. Euthanized on August 20 at Saratoga Equine Veterinary Services Clinic in Saratoga Springs, New York, due to laminitis resulting from complications of colitis X.

WEEKEND MADNESS (Ire), 1990 b. m., Dance of Life—Spring Break, by Cure the Blues. 27-10-5-1, $660,623. Won 1994 Keeneland Breeders' Cup S. (G3), etc. Died on June 8 due to foaling complications.

WIN, 1980 b. g., Barachois—Par Ci Par La, by Buckpasser. 44-14-10-3, $1,408,980. Won 1985 Man o' War S. (G1), etc. First New York-bred to earn more than $1-million. Euthanized in late May at Tanrankin Farm near Bedford Hills, New York, after sustaining an ankle injury.

WOLF POWER (SAf), 1978 gr. h., Flirting Around—Pandora, by Casabianca. 31-18-7-0, $758,071. 1984 South African Horse of the Year, etc. Sire of at least 38 stakes winners, including Grade 1 winner Freedom Cry. Died on November 15 of a ruptured aorta at Gainesway Farm near Lexington.

ZAFONIC, 1990 b. h., Gone West—Zaizafon, by The Minstrel. 7-5-1-, $669,681. Highweighted on 1992 and '93 European Free Handicap, '93 champion two-year-old colt; won '93 Two Thousand Guineas (Eng-G1), etc. Sire of at least 28 stakes winners, including '97 European champion two-year-old colt Xaar and graded or group winners Ibn Al Haitham (GB), Count Dubois, Zipping, etc. Died on September 7 at Arrowfield Stud in New South Wales, Australia, from injuries suffered in a paddock accident.

HISTORY OF RACING

by Mary Simon

Horse racing officially appeared in the annals of history in approximately 1000 B.C. when Greeks started racing horses with chariots drawn behind them, a dangerous game that subsequently was adopted by the Romans and Egyptians. For the 33rd Olympiad in 644 B.C., formal competition began with riders astride the horses. The Romans, who conquered England in 43 A.D. under Emperor Claudius and ruled it until 410 A.D., carried their horses and their sport to the island nation, where a millennium later it would blossom into the sport known as Thoroughbred racing.

By the late 1500s, racing had become a favorite pastime of English noblemen. King Henry VIII and his daughter Queen Elizabeth I both maintained racing stables, and Elizabeth's cousin King James I established Newmarket racecourse early in the 17th century. His son Charles I also was a racing enthusiast, but he was overthrown and beheaded in 1649, and Lord Protector Oliver Cromwell banned horse racing. After the restoration of the monarchy in 1660, racing flourished under its ardent devotee King Charles II.

Because of Charles II's love for the sport, racing became known as the sport of kings, and during his rule the first of three imported Arabian stallions began the genetic progression toward the Thoroughbred of today. In 1688, Capt. Robert Byerly returned from Hungary with a captured stallion who became known as the Byerly Turk. Sixteen years later, British consul Thomas Darley smuggled an Arabian stallion out of Syria and transplanted him to Yorkshire; he became known as the Darley Arabian. In approximately 1730, an Arabian stallion of unknown lineage appeared in the stable of the Earl of Godolphin and became known as the Godolphin Arabian. These three stallions would become the foundation sires of the Thoroughbred. The Darley Arabian sired Flying Childers, generally regarded as the first great Thoroughbred, in 1714. (For more on the development of the Thoroughbred, see Evolution of the Breed.)

In the late 18th century, racing began to assume a formal structure. Racecourses were established, and the first of the English classics, the St. Leger Stakes, was run in 1776. The Epsom Derby followed four years later, and the Two Thousand Guineas had its first running in 1809. As racing developed in England, it found its way to the American colonies. In 1665, New York Governor Richard Nicholls gave the name Newmarket to America's first racetrack. Although the first track was located in New York, horse racing tended to be frowned upon by religious leaders and communities in the North, but the sport flourished in the South. The first known Thoroughbred sire imported to North America from England was *Bulle Rock, an aged son of the Darley Arabian. Although *Bulle Rock had no lasting influence, pre-Revolution imports such as *Fearnought, pint-sized *Janus, and the *Cub mare influenced the breed's development.

19th Century

Early American presidents, particularly those from the South, were racing fans. Thomas Jefferson approved the Senate's practice of adjourning early to attend local meets. Senators of the day might have marveled at the fabled 28-foot stride of the great colt Florizel or witnessed the unbeatable brilliance of First Consul during his 21-race winning streak.

It was an era of often unrecorded and disputed genealogies, and races were crudely timed, if at all. The 1823 victory of American Eclipse over Henry in the North-South match at Long Island's Union Course proved a milestone in post-Colonial racing. The $20,000-a-side event drew a significant portion of the New York populace and helped American Eclipse stake his claim as the first American earnings champion, with $56,700. At the same time, *Leviathan was standing for America's highest known fee—$75—but he was not the most notable stallion of the period. That honor went to *Diomed, a British castoff after the Revolutionary War. The inaugural Epsom Derby winner in 1780, he arrived on American shores in Virginia in 1798, acquired for a meager $220. *Diomed proceeded over 11 seasons to reshape the American Thoroughbred in his own remarkable image, getting runners that were uniformly taller, heavier of bone, stouter, stronger, and faster than their contemporaries.

Unlike England, where the Epsom Derby and St. Leger heralded a trend toward shorter races, America maintained its long heat races for the first half of the century. While the style of racing evolved over time, change of another kind arrived on March 17, 1850, when *Diomed's great-great grandson Lexington was born on a Central Kentucky farm. Brilliant on the racecourse and even more accomplished at stud, Lexington would reign 16 times—including 14 in succession—as the country's leading sire.

As the century progressed, races became shorter, purses rose, and racing began to become organized. Saratoga Race Course, Pimlico Race Course, Churchill Downs, and Fair Grounds opened for business. The Travers Stakes had its first running in 1864, and the Belmont Stakes was run for the first time in 1867. The Preakness Stakes followed in 1873, and the Kentucky Derby was staged for the first time in 1875. Late in the century, the Jockey Club was established to oversee the growing sport, and it soon assumed control of the *American Stud Book.* In 1889, Miss Woodford became the first American Thoroughbred to top $100,000 in career earnings. Two-year-old racing gained popularity with the inaugural 1888 Futurity, worth $40,000 to the winner; five years later, a juvenile named Domino set a single-season earnings record of $170,790 that would stand for decades. Kingston—last of the great iron horses of a dying era—retired in 1894 with 89 victories, a record to this day. By the end of the 19th century, Kentucky had become the heart of America's Thoroughbred business, with more professional horsemen than any other region. America and its Thoroughbred industry were thus poised to enter a modern era of even greater change.

1901-'10

The American century's first decade was one of promise and turmoil for the Thoroughbred racing industry. Trouble brewed even as financier James R. Keene's great Commando blistered the track at the dawn of the century and as Commando's unbeatable son Colin carried the Keene colors to victory after brilliant victory a few years later. Even as Keene's stable racked up unprecedented earnings, as record purses were dispensed, and as Belmont Park opened its glorious gates, a dark cloud was settling ominously on racing's horizon.

Racing may have been the sport of kings, but it was also part of a larger gambling industry. Increasingly, the taint of corruption eroded public confidence in the sport as high-profile incidents were exposed. Keene's Sysonby, one of the sport's all-time greats, suffered his only loss in the 1904 Futurity after being drugged by a groom. Delhi, the 1904 Belmont Stakes winner, later ran sluggishly and was found to have sponges inserted far up into his nostrils. Electric prods, dopings, ringers, crooked jockeys, and diverse gambling scams involving track bookmakers were daily journalistic fodder.

By 1907, anti-racetrack wagering laws had been simmering for some time on legislative back burners across America. In June 1908, New York passed the Agnew-Hart bill with the ardent blessing of Governor Charles Evans Hughes, who used the legislation as a weapon against the Tammany Hall political machine, a major beneficiary of racing in the New York metropolitan area. Without revenues from legalized gambling, racing soon found it impossible to support itself. In 1910, historic Saratoga was among the racetracks that ceased operation, and E. J. "Lucky" Baldwin's original Santa Anita Park was forced to close.

A domino effect occurred as other states rushed to pass similar legislation. The national purse structure collapsed, declining from a 1907 average of $949 per race to $643 in '09. Top stables, including Keene's, shipped overseas in a European invasion so successful that it would pave the way for the next great blow to the American Thoroughbred industry—England's 1913 passage of the "Jersey Act." In 1908, Churchill Downs's energetic general manager, Col. Matt Winn, pulled some old pari-mutuel machines out of storage, dusted them off, and put them back into use. When racing resumed in the next decade, the pari-mutuel wagering system quickly would become dominant.

Despite all, several great competitors appeared on racing's stage to illuminate the era. Colin was one of nine future Racing Hall of Fame members who campaigned during the decade. Man o' War's fiery sire, Fair Play, was another, along with Commando, Sysonby, Artful, Beldame, Roseben, Broomstick, and Peter Pan.

1911-'20

As indignation among the American populace swelled over the puritan campaigners' assault on gambling and alcohol consumption, a group of wealthy horsemen began to stockpile a fund with which to hold future race meets. The future came quickly. Although the Agnew-Hart legislation moldered on the books until 1934, the penalties associated with it were stripped away by May 30, 1913, when Belmont Park opened for the first time since 1910. Between 1908 and '13, however, American breeders had sent overseas more than 1,500 horses, among them at least 24 champions. Some eventually came back, but many did not. Leading sires *Rock Sand and *Meddler, also part of the exodus, were lost forever to American breeding.

The British responded with the Jersey Act in 1913, which effectively barred many old American lines from England's *General Stud Book,* but the first shots of World War I one year later quickly changed the United States from an exporter of bloodstock into an aggressive importer. Between 1916-'20, numerous English-breds and French-breds became American champions, including *Short Grass, *Sun Briar, *Hourless, *Omar Khayyam, *Johren, *Sunbonnet, *Enfilade, and *Constancy.

Even in the shadow of war, the decade was memorable for its outstanding runners, including future Racing Hall of Fame geldings Roamer, Old Rosebud, and Exterminator. Together, they won 129 races and set or equaled 29 records from five furlongs to 2¼ miles at 14 different racetracks. Iron Mask set a North American record for 5½ furlongs that would stand for 30 years, and the mare Pan Zareta took a back seat to no male in the realm of blazing speed. H. P. Whitney's Regret routinely whipped the boys and in 1915 became the first filly to win the Kentucky Derby. The Triple Crown was won for the first time in 1919 by Sir Barton, although the sweep did not take on its popular name until the 1930s.

Sir Barton won the Belmont on June 11, five days after the decade's finest specimen made his first career start at Belmont Park. Man o' War, considered the greatest American horse of all time, was ineligible for admission to the *General Stud Book*, but in 16 months of competition redefined greatness. He lost one race at two that he should have won, failing to overcome a bad start in the Sanford Stakes at Saratoga Race Course and losing to Upset, but he never lost again. In 1920, "Big Red" established five American and two track records in 11 starts and won his races by a combined 164 lengths. Man o' War capped his extraordinary career on October 12, 1920, by galloping away from Sir Barton in a winner-take-all race at Kenilworth Park in Canada. The $80,000 purse sent him to stud as the richest American Thoroughbred in history with $249,465.

1921-'30

On the surface at least, the Roaring Twenties were a time of outrageous fun—flappers and the fox trot are indelible images of the era—and horse racing rode the crest of this postwar celebration. Elaborate new racetracks were the overt symbol of this prosperity—at least 15 of note were constructed in the United States during the 1920s, including Arlington and Washington Parks in Chicago and Hialeah Park in Florida. Purses went through the roof. In 1923, Zev became the first American racehorse to bank $200,000 in a season and, by 1930, Gallant Fox—the second Triple Crown winner and the first to be recognized for sweeping the three American classics—had raised that bar to $300,000. Jockey Earle Sande, trainer James Fitzsimmons, breeder Harry Payne Whitney, and owner Harry Sinclair each established earnings records that would stand for years. Bloodstock prices also went into orbit, with a yearling commanding a record $75,000 in 1928.

Because the Jersey Act remained in force, horses mostly migrated to the west. Future leading sires *St. Germans, *Sickle, and *Challenger

II were among the importees, as was the great matron *La Troienne. In late 1925, *Sir Gallahad III arrived at Claiborne Farm, where he would reign four times as America's premier sire and 12 times as its leading broodmare sire. *Sir Gallahad III's American-bred counterpart was Man o' War, a private stallion who had seven of his eight champions in his first four crops and in 1926—with only three crops racing—set a progeny earnings record of $409,927.

No single racehorse towered above all others in the 1920s as Man o' War and Colin had before, but the decade nonetheless yielded 15 Racing Hall of Fame members. Foremost among them was Exterminator, the wonderful gelding who scored a 20th-century record 34 stakes victories and retired as America's richest Thoroughbred. Grey Lag flirted with greatness, as did champions Sarazen, Blue Larkspur, Reigh Count, and Gallant Fox. Zev, Crusader, and Sun Beau were big money winners. Princess Doreen won 34 races and broke Miss Woodford's 40-year female earnings record with $174,745. Other notable fillies included 1924 Preakness winner Nellie Morse; multiple champions Black Maria and Bateau; and Rose of Sharon, considered best of either sex at three in 1929. For a time, it appeared the good times would go on forever, but the stock market crashed in October 1929, which led to events that caused the Great Depression.

1931-'40

As the depression shrunk race purses 40%, the average yearling price slumped to $570 in 1932. But, as the Depression eased, the Thoroughbred industry entered one of its healthiest eras. Purses rose by decade's end to record heights, and yearling sales gained strength. Racing also had some wealthy, influential leaders. Joseph E. Widener, vice chairman of the New York Jockey Club, crusaded tirelessly to return the sport in the Empire State to its former glory. Jockey Club Chairman William Woodward campaigned 1935 Triple Crown winner Omaha, but more importantly that year he fired some of the angriest, most articulate words at England's discriminatory Jersey Act. During the decade, increasingly sophisticated stall starting gates were developed, photo-finish cameras were installed, and saliva testing for drugs gained widespread use. Keeneland Race Course, Del Mar Thoroughbred Club, Santa Anita Park, and Hollywood Park opened for business.

Although the 1930s featured many standout racehorses, including 17 future Racing Hall of Fame members and two Triple Crown winners, three in particular captured the hearts of America—C. V. Whitney's Equipoise, Australasian wonder *Phar Lap, and claimer-turned-champion Seabiscuit. Although bred in the purple and owned by one of America's wealthiest bluebloods, there was nothing pretentious about Equipoise, a son of Pennant who was a champion at two in 1930, a three-time handicap champion, and a world-record miler. Seabiscuit, an undersized Wheatley Stable reject, developed into a megastar, reigning as 1938 Horse of the Year and twice as America's handicap champion. In one of the decade's greatest moments, Seabiscuit defeated 1937 Triple Crown winner War Admiral in the two-horse 1938 Pimlico Special Stakes. *Phar Lap illuminated the Depression's darkest hour by winning the 1932 Agua Caliente Handicap in record time, but the huge New Zealander died just 17 days later under suspicious circumstances.

The 1930s launched a feminine revolution of sorts. Top Flight defeated males in the 1931 Futurity to become the first $200,000 juvenile earner and richest American female. Mrs. Payne Whitney's Twenty Grand won that year's Kentucky Derby, and Isabel Dodge Sloane became America's leading owner in 1934. As war in Europe approached, America imported several top stallions. In 1936, Hancock organized a syndicate to purchase *Blenheim II, for $250,000; four years later, Whitney acquired the stallion's classic-winning son, *Mahmoud.

1941-'50

Despite a world at war for half the decade, the 1940s very well may have been racing's finest hour, with four Triple Crown winners crowning the decade. The war years were grim for the sport, however. California's tracks were shut down—Santa Anita was an internment camp for Japanese-Americans, Hollywood was an army storage unit, and Del Mar was used for assembling aircraft wings. Travel restrictions crippled the Saratoga yearling sale and led to the creation of the Breeders' Sales Co., precursor of the Keeneland July sale. In late 1944, the government banned racing, and only victory in Europe saved the 1945 Triple Crown.

Leavening the somber news from overseas were the exploits of Whirlaway, Calumet's "Mr. Longtail," winner of the 1941 Triple Crown. Then there was Alsab, a $700 yearling of peasant lineage who outgamed Whirlaway by a nose in a famous 1942 match race at Narragansett Park. Mrs. John D. Hertz's 1943 Triple Crown winner, Count Fleet, habitually crushed his opposition and romped to a 25-length Belmont Stakes victory, despite a career-ending injury. High-headed, flame-coated Stymie was not the best, but he was nevertheless beloved by fans who made him the

people's horse. Claimed for $1,500 from King Ranch by trainer Hirsch Jacobs, Stymie became the first Thoroughbred to surpass $900,000 in career earnings. King Ranch had Assault, who overcame a deformed right fore foot to win the 1946 Triple Crown. The 1940s also produced several top fillies, including Racing Hall of Fame members Twilight Tear, Busher, Gallorette, Bewitch, Two Lea, and Bed o' Roses. Argentine-bred *Miss Grillo set a 2½-mile world record in the 1948 Pimlico Cup Handicap.

The decade virtually belonged to Warren Wright's magnificent Calumet Stable, whose champions were trained by Ben and Jimmy Jones and in many cases ridden by Eddie Arcaro—all Racing Hall of Fame members. Calumet reigned as America's top owner seven times during the decade, edged only by a trio of prominent women—Mrs. Payne Whitney (1942), Elizabeth Graham ('45), and Isabel Dodge Sloane ('50). Runners who carried the feared devil's red and blue silks during the 1940s included Racing Hall of Fame members Whirlaway, Twilight Tear, Armed, Citation, Bewitch, Coaltown, and Two Lea, and father-son Kentucky Derby winners Pensive and Ponder. Citation was not only Calumet's best but also one of the century's most talented runners. Champion at two and three, American Triple Crown hero, and winner of 16 consecutive races, Citation would become the sport's first millionaire in 1951.

Late in the decade, Claiborne acquired *Nasrullah, a rogue stallion who would transform the American bloodstock industry. Also in 1949, England's Jockey Club backed down after 36 years and rescinded the despised Jersey Act, by now long outdated and hindering rather than helping the British breeding industry. America thus regained its former stature as a respected source of international bloodstock.

1951-'60

As it entered the second half of the 20th century, the U.S. confronted a rapidly changing world. It was at war in Korea, the threat of Nazism had been replaced by the peril of nuclear cataclysm, television was helping to create a truly national society, and polio had been conquered. America's appetite for racing seemed utterly insatiable; attendance and handle records were established almost annually. Perhaps it was too successful. In this decade, racing failed to build a lasting partnership with television—an arrogant decision that the industry would regret into the 21st century.

The 1950s were a time of rising incomes and rising expectations. In 1956, Nashua became the first million-dollar stallion syndication. Also that year, jockey Bill Hartack became the first to ride winners of $2-million in a single season; he topped $3-million the following year. The 1950s witnessed a growing interest in early competition—particularly after the spectacular 1953 debut of the world's richest race, the $270,000 Garden State Stakes for two-year-olds at Garden State Park in New Jersey. Soundness became an issue in the 1950s, with the high-profile breakdowns of such stars as Hail to Reason and Swaps. In 1960, phenylbutazone—an anti-inflammatory drug popularly known as Bute—came into wide use to ease the aches and pains of racing.

Racing in the 1950s had several stars but no Triple Crown winner. (Jockey Eddie Arcaro blamed himself for Nashua's loss to Swaps in the 1955 Derby. Nashua subsequently won the Preakness and Belmont.) The first equine superhero of the TV age was Native Dancer—the "Gray Ghost of Sagamore," whose only loss in 22 starts was by a head in the 1953 Kentucky Derby. Also racing at that time was Tom Fool, who carried heavy imposts to ten straight victories. As Native Dancer and Tom Fool exited the stage, the prodigiously talented pair of Nashua and Swaps took their place. They met twice, with Swaps winning the 1955 Derby and Nashua the '55 $100,000 Washington Park match race. The foal crop of 1954 contained Bold Ruler, Round Table, and *Gallant Man, all Racing Hall of Fame members. Round Table lasted the longest, 66 races, and was America's first great grass horse. Talent was so widespread that no one noticed an ordinary-looking bay gelding who won only a maiden race in 1959. But Kelso went on to become one of the major heroes of the 1960s.

1961-'70

The 1960s were a watershed for America and American racing. Inaugurated in January 1961 was John F. Kennedy, the first President born in the 20th century. Racial segregation was overthrown in the South, but lives were lost in the battle. Kennedy's assassination in 1963 shook America to its core, and soon the collective conformism of the 1950s crumbled. As men walked on the moon, young soldiers were dying in an unpopular Vietnam war.

Racing increasingly became a game of haves and have-nots. In 1967, Damascus banked a single-season record $817,941. That same year, North America's earnings per runner averaged $3,359, or about half of training costs for a year. Medication also became an issue, especially when Dancer's Image was disqualified from his 1968 Kentucky Derby victory over a Bute positive.

State legislators looked to racing to plug budget gaps; at the end of the decade, proposed federal tax changes led to the creation of the American Horse Council to help lobby on behalf of horse racing and breeding interests. Simultaneously, racing was losing some of its audience as other professional sports and entertainment forms gained popularity. National attendance declined in 1967 for the first time since World War II, despite nearly 100 added racing days. During the 1960s, total racing days increased 35%, while average daily attendance declined 3%. At decade's end, off-track betting was approved in New York, which would lead to even larger attendance declines.

Against this chaotic and disquieting backdrop, Kelso—and others like him—redeemed this troubled era and made it one of the most remarkable in 200 years. Allaire duPont's Kelso tore through the handicap ranks, ruling as Horse of the Year from 1960 through '64. Carry Back emerged from Florida to win the 1961 Kentucky Derby and Preakness Stakes. Other outstanding performers of the era were Arts and Letters, Majestic Prince, Nodouble, Northern Dancer, and Fort Marcy, but the second half of the decade belonged to Buckpasser, Damascus, and Dr. Fager. Together, they started 85 times and compiled a 64-13-5 record.

Fillies of the 1960s deserve special mention. Cicada, Old Hat, Affectionately, Straight Deal, Tosmah, Politely, Gamely, and Shuvee averaged 56 career starts. Cicada set an earnings record; Moccasin became the first juvenile filly to take Horse of the Year honors in the 1965 Thoroughbred Racing Associations poll; Dark Mirage was first to sweep New York's filly triple crown in 1968; Dr. Fager's younger half sister, Ta Wee, toted an average of 136 pounds in 1970. Women gained the right to ride in races in 1969, and trailblazer Diane Crump rode in the 1970 Derby. Bloodstock prices were heating up, and Nijinsky II was syndicated for a record $5.44-million in 1970.

1971-'80

In some respects, the decade between 1971 and '80 was one of the century's most satisfying periods for American Thoroughbred racing. Great runners and big money energized the era, but they also disguised some troubling problems, such as race fixing, increasingly lenient medication rules, and a declining audience. The 1970s were racing's best years since the '40s, with three Triple Crown winners within five years. The bloodstock markets were supercharged as well, with the beginning of the Northern Dancer era and the speculative buying that eventually damaged the markets in the 1980s.

Secretariat, Seattle Slew, and Affirmed, the

three Triple Crown winners, attracted most of the attention, and they shared the limelight with Forego, Ruffian, and Spectacular Bid, among others. It has been said that Secretariat appeared at the precise moment when America and racing needed him most. A transcendent, larger-than-life figure bursting with almost supernatural vitality, he streaked across racing's stage in 1972 and '73, leaving behind an impression of pure greatness unrivaled since Man o' War. After he won the 1973 Kentucky Derby (G1) in record time (1:59⅖, a mark that still stands) and the Preakness Stakes (G1) with consummate ease (also probably a record even though the timing was botched), Secretariat quieted every skeptic with his 31-length triumph in the Belmont Stakes (G1) in 2:24, 2⅕ seconds—11 lengths—faster than the existing world record. Seattle Slew blazed through the Triple Crown, becoming the first to complete the sweep with an unbeaten record, and one year later Affirmed won the Triple Crown over his nemesis Alydar, who was second in all three races.

The Triple Crown winners did not stand alone in the spotlight. Twenty-two future Racing Hall of Fame members campaigned during this decade, including six from a remarkable 1970 foal crop. Among them were the first distaff millionaire, Dahlia, 12-for-12 juvenile La Prevoyante, and Forego, who was Horse of the Year three times. Ruffian cruised unbeaten through ten starts until the ill-fated 1975 match race with Kentucky Derby winner Foolish Pleasure that took her life. The era closed with yet another performer for the ages. The Triple Crown eluded Spectacular Bid, but not much else did between 1978 and '80. The compact gray colt set nine track, American, and world standards. In 1980, Genuine Risk became only the second filly in 106 years to wear the blanket of roses.

The 1970s signaled the dramatic rise of top Hispanic jockeys, with none more prominent than Laffit Pincay Jr. Among trainers, the torch passed to Charlie Whittingham and Laz Barrera, whose West Coast-based stables also hailed the arrival of California as a centerpiece of American racing. The industry was changing in other ways, due in part to the 1971 introduction of off-track betting in New York. By 1977, OTB wagers finally exceeded money wagered on track in New York, and the gap would widen thereafter.

1981-'90

The breeding industry follows the fortunes of the racetrack, but for a few years in the 1980s that relationship became temporarily detached, or so it seemed, as rich foreign buyers pursued yearlings by Northern Dancer and his sons. In 1985, a Nijinsky II colt sold for a record $13.1-million at the Keeneland July sale of selected yearlings, but by then the bloodstock markets had entered a slide that would last into the 1990s. Stud fees climbed to unsupportable levels on the fantasy, and everything came crashing down. On the track, attendance was falling while wagering and purses stagnated.

In 1982, at the peak of the bloodstock boom, horseman John Gaines worried over the industry's fundamentals and came up with an idea to market it. One year earlier, the Arlington Million had been inaugurated at Arlington Park as the world's first $1-million Thoroughbred race. Enthusiastically received, it had drawn a field of international grass stars and was won by John Henry. Gaines envisioned a single championship day of racing, offering millions of dollars in purse money, paid for by stallion and foal nomination fees. In November 1984 at Hollywood Park, his dream became reality at the first Breeders' Cup championship day, arguably the sport's greatest innovation since the Triple Crown.

Although he missed the first Breeders' Cup and never raced again, Dotsam Stable's John Henry proved once again that the American Dream was alive and well. He was a gelded son of an obscure sire, and he earned more than $6.5-million. In the 1980s, fillies shined brightest. Eight of the decade's 13 Racing Hall of Fame performers thus far have been members of the distaff set, including Horses of the Year All Along (Fr) and Lady's Secret, 1988 Kentucky Derby winner Winning Colors, undefeated champions Personal Ensign (13-for-13) and Landaluce (5-for-5 before her death), and two-time champion Go for Wand, who died on the track in the 1990 Breeders' Cup Distaff (G1). Also notable were two-time champions Bayakoa (Arg) and Miesque.

Although males of the 1980s lacked the brilliance of their female counterparts, they did provide memorable moments. Ferdinand gave Whittingham his first Kentucky Derby victory at age 73 in 1986, and in '87 he fought to the bitter end under Racing Hall of Fame member Bill Shoemaker to edge Derby winner Alysheba in the Breeders' Cup Classic (G1). The fierce 1989 rivalry between Sunday Silence and Easy Goer ranks among the sport's best, and also memorable was Conquistador Cielo's 14-length triumph in the 1982 Belmont Stakes, the first of trainer Woody Stephens's historic five straight wins in that classic. One of the decade's most poignant moments was trainer Carl Nafzger's spontaneous televised description of Unbridled's 1990 Kentucky Derby stretch run for 92-year-old owner Frances Genter. Trainer D. Wayne Lukas rewrote the record books repeatedly during these years, setting and breaking his own earnings standards.

1991-2000

The century's final decade was a breakthrough for America's racetracks, which built a solid foundation first on intrastate intertrack wagering and then on the true bonanza, interstate full-card wagering. The full-card explosion forever altered the sport. By mid-decade, off-site wagering accounted for 74% of racing's handle, a figure that jumped to 82% by 1999. Some tracks added slot machines to boost both purses and profits without putting any new patrons in the stands. The bloodstock markets recovered from a prolonged recession and rose to new heights as the decade ended.

Lexington ad executive Fred Pope, with counsel from John Gaines, in 1996 proposed an industry alliance to revitalize the sport and create a "major league of racing." Their National Thoroughbred Association, an owner-driven organization, soon was swallowed up by the National Thoroughbred Racing Association (NTRA), which was launched in April 1998 and reached into every corner of the sport. Racing series added hours of television coverage, and in 1999 Television Games Network (TVG) debuted on satellite and a few cable stations.

In the bloodstock market, stallion owners began breeding their stars to large books of mares and sent them to the Southern Hemisphere for double duty. A record for a stallion syndication was set in 2000 when Fusaichi Pegasus commanded a record $60-million to $70-million price tag.

A trio of sensational grays—Holy Bull, Silver Charm, and Skip Away—and Allen Paulson's marvelous bay Cigar captured the imagination of the racing public in the 1990s. Together they won classics, championships, and $30-million, but they were sired by stallions with average stud fees of just $7,800. Among females, Serena's Song and Dance Smartly were the decade's standouts.

It was an exciting classics decade, with the Triple Crown on the line each year between 1997 and '99, with Silver Charm, Real Quiet, and Charismatic winning the Derby and Preakness before coming up short in the Belmont. Silver Charm and Real Quiet were trained by Bob Baffert, but the classics of the 1990s virtually belonged to Lukas, who won six consecutive classic races with five different horses and also trained Charismatic for Robert and Beverly Lewis, Californians who owned Silver Charm and Serena's Song. Cigar, a two-time Horse of the Year, won 16 consecutive races but proved sterile.

Class I racing returned to Texas, but the first two tracks to open, Sam Houston Race Park and Retama Park, struggled initially. Lone Star Park in the populous Dallas-Fort Worth area was a success from its opening in April 1997. An important trend that began toward the end of the decade was the consolidation of racetrack ownership under Magna Entertainment Corp. and Churchill Downs Inc. That consolidation would continue into the 21st century.

2001-'03

The beginning of the new century was indelibly scarred by an act of unspeakable horror, a terrorist attack with commercial jetliners that killed approximately 3,000 innocent people in New York's World Trade Center towers, at the Pentagon, and in a rural Pennsylvania field, where brave passengers sacrificed their lives to protect American institutions from Islamic terrorists bent on destruction. September 11, 2001, forever will be seared on the American psyche, along with December 7, 1941, and November 22, 1963. On each of those dates, America lost some of its innocence and confronted a changing and frightening world.

The terrorist attacks on the United States came at a time of recession, both for the American economy and the Thoroughbred industry, which had boomed with the stock market through the late 1990s and into 2000. Bloodstock-market revenues declined approximately 20% in 2001, and the drops were particularly sharp after the September 11 attacks, which fell on the second scheduled day of the Keeneland September yearling sale. The declines continued through 2002.

Also contributing to the bloodstock-market declines was a mysterious disorder known as mare reproductive loss syndrome (MRLS), which caused the loss of more than 500 late-term fetuses and almost 3,000 early-term fetuses in Central Kentucky. Reliably attributed to Eastern tent caterpillars, MRLS cost the Kentucky Thoroughbred industry an estimated $300-million and led to the cancellation of the 2003 Keeneland July sale of selected yearlings. On the racetrack in 2001, The Thoroughbred Corp.'s Point Given won the Preakness Stakes and Belmont Stakes on his way to being voted Horse of the Year. Tiznow, the California-bred overachiever, won the Breeders' Cup Classic (G1) for the second consecutive year with a gutsy late surge. On the international front, trainer Aidan O'Brien won a record 23 Group/Group 1 races in 2001.

The 2002 racing season, which produced a rags-to-riches story in Kentucky Derby and Preakness winner War Emblem, ended with a scandal that, both in its haul and audacity, rivaled the 1950 Brink's heist in Boston. The heist of 2002 was electronic, and it involved three former fraternity brothers from Philadelphia's Drexel University who conspired to electronically alter a wager after it was placed to win the lucrative Breeders' Cup Ultra Pick Six wager. They were caught because they fixed it too well; when 43.50-to-1 longshot Volponi won the Breeders' Cup Classic, one of the men held the only winning tickets, worth more than $3-million. The strange configuration of the wager set off alarm bells throughout the industry and an investigation was launched before any payout was made. The fixers never collected and within seven weeks all three men pleaded guilty to federal wire-fraud charges. All three were sentenced to prison in early 2003. But the Ultra Pick Six scam exposed massive security breaches in the pari-mutuel wagering system, and industry leaders sought to plug the holes in succeeding months.

After a lull in 2001, Magna Entertainment Corp. resumed its racetrack acquisitions, buying Lone Star Park in Texas and controlling interest in the major Maryland tracks, Pimlico Race Course and Laurel Park. During 2002, the industry lost owner-breeder Ogden Phipps and Seattle Slew, the last surviving Triple Crown winner. Ahmed bin Salman, whose The Thoroughbred Corp. owned War Emblem and Point Given, died of a heart attack in Saudi Arabia. Azeri, winner of the Breeders' Cup Distaff (G1), was voted Horse of the Year after dominating the older female division in the colors of the Allen E. Paulson Living Trust. Internationally, Rock of Gibraltar (Ire) won a record seven consecutive Group 1 races in 2002, but he finished second in his only North American start, in the Breeders' Cup Mile (G1).

Condensed from "Racing Through the Century," for which Mary Simon was awarded the 2000 Eclipse Award for outstanding features-enterprise writing and which was later published as a book with additional material.

History of Racing Silks

Worn by each jockey to represent a horse's owner, racing silks have been associated with horse racing for nearly two millennia. *Kennets Roman Antiquities* (1696) cites colors worn at chariot races: "At these races, the Romans rode in different colours, particularly the companies of Charioteers, to distinguish themselves." Nero was so fond of his green colors that he often wore a green toga when he attended the races during the first century.

The records of England's King Henry VIII mention jockeys' attire in the first half of the 16th century. His 1530 purse accounts show payments for "doublets (shirts) of Bruges Satin for the boys that runne the gueldings" and for "ryding cappes of Black Satin lyned with black vellute (velvet)." Silk, though expensive, was used for jockeys' jackets and caps because of its light weight and soft, smooth texture. Velvet also was used through the first half of the 19th century.

On October 4, 1762, 19 members of the English Jockey Club registered their colors at Newmarket "for the greater convenience of distinguishing the horses in running." Across the Atlantic Ocean just four years later, Philadelphia horsemen registered their silks with the Philadelphia Jockey Club. Registering yellow silks was Lewis Morris Jr., a signer of the Declaration of Independence.

One of the longest-used silks in America belonged to Howell E. Jackson, a relative of President Andrew Jackson who chose all-maroon colors first used in the early 1820s. The all-scarlet silks of Francis Morris (no relation to Lewis) were first worn in 1862 at the Union Course on Long Island. The Morris family used those colors for four generations through John A. Morris.

Rules published for the October 17-19, 1826, race meeting in Lexington required jockeys to wear a silk jacket and cap. The American Jockey Club, founded in 1894, registered silks for $1 annually or $25 lifetime. The most famous silks in American racing have been those of prominent, private stables—the devil's red and blue of Calumet Farm, the plain black jacket with cherry cap of the late Ogden Phipps, and the all-orange silks of Claiborne Farm.

Sporadically, racetracks have experimented with color-coded silks and jockeys' caps. In 1947, Portland Meadows assigned silks colors by post positions, an idea that was copied at Sportsman's Park and Prescott Downs. Narragansett Park matched the colors of jockeys' caps with post positions. Neither experiment caught on nationally.

In the evolution of Thoroughbred racing in the United States, silk has mostly yielded to nylon or Lycra as the preferred fabric of jockeys' colors. Aerodynamic silks have become commonplace in American racing. First unveiled in 1988 when trainer D. Wayne Lukas used them on all 12 of his horses in the Breeders' Cup, aerodynamic silks, though more costly, are widely available today.

Approximately 28,000 sets of silks are registered with the Jockey Club. Owners pay an annual fee of $15 or $60 every five years. The Jockey Club ceased registering lifetime silks in 1964 while perpetually reserving 3,500 designs.

The Jockey Club has registered silks with various punctuation marks, geometric figures, riding equipment, racetracks, vegetables, musical notes, instruments, birds, dogs, horses, foxes, and even an elephant. Though silks can vary from state to state, roughly 95% of all silks designs are registered with the Jockey Club.—*Bill Heller*

Key Dates in American Racing History

1665 New York Governor Richard Nicolls establishes America's first formal racecourse on Long Island, names it "New Market."

1730 The Darley Arabian's son *Bulle Rock becomes the first recognized Thoroughbred imported to America, into the Virginia colony.

1752 The great racemare *Selima wins an intercolonial race in Virginia worth $10,000 **(December)**.

1764 Undefeated racehorse and foundation sire Eclipse is born in England during a solar eclipse. Future influential sire *Fearnought is imported to America.

1780 The inaugural Epsom Derby is won by Sir Charles Bunbury's *Diomed **(May 4)**.

1798 *Diomed is imported to Virginia at age 21 for the equivalent of $250; he becomes America's most important early sire. *Spread Eagle, 1795 Epsom Derby winner, is imported into Virginia.

1801 *Spread Eagle reportedly covers 234 mares. Leviathan, American racing's first great gelding, concludes a 23-race win streak, which remains an American record for more than two centuries.

1802 Leviathan wins a five-mile race carrying 180 pounds.

1804 *Sir Harry, 1798 Epsom Derby winner, is imported into Virginia.

1805 American foundation sire Sir Archy is foaled.

1806 Northern champion First Consul runs his undefeated streak to 21.

1808 *Diomed dies in Virginia at age 31 **(March 10)**.

1810 Maria runs five four-mile heats to win a $500 purse at Fairfield, Virginia **(October 3)**.

1820 American Eclipse covers 87 mares for a $12.50 fee.

1821 Union Course opens on Long Island, becomes America's first famous racetrack **(October 15)**.

1823 American Eclipse defeats Henry in North-South match over the Union Course; he becomes America's leading earner, with $56,700 **(May 27)**.

1833 Leading sires Sir Archy and his best son, Sir Charles, die on same day **(June 7)**.

1836 *Glencoe, winner of the 1834 Two Thousand Guineas, is imported into Alabama.

1842 Fashion defeats Boston in a Union Course match race before a crowd of more than 50,000 **(May 10)**.

1845 Peytona defeats Fashion in a $20,000 match race over two four-mile heats at the Union Course and surpasses American Eclipse as the leading American money winner, with $62,400 **(May 13)**. Fashion defeats Peytona in two four-mile heats at Camden, New Jersey **(May 28)**.

1850 Lexington is born **(March 17)**.

1852 Black Swan defeats Governor Pio Pico's non-Thoroughbred stallion Sarco in a nine-mile match race at Los Angeles for a $2,000 purse and 1,000 head of cattle **(March)**.

1855 Lexington sets a four-mile world record of 7:19¾ **(April 2)**. Lexington defeats Lecomte in a match race at New Orleans **(April 14)**.

1856 Lexington sells for an American record $15,000 to Robert A. Alexander.

1857 American-bred Prioress wins England's Cesarewitch Handicap at Newmarket **(October 13)**. Lexington retires to Woodburn Stud in Kentucky.

1860 Don Juan wins the first running of Canada's Queen's Plate **(June 27)**. Revenue becomes America's first leading sire based on progeny earnings instead of winners.

1861 Lexington leads the American sire list for the first of a record 16 times. Planet surpasses Peytona as America's leading money winner, with $69,700.

1864 Lexington's unbeaten son Norfolk wins America's first Derby—the $1,000 Jersey Derby at Paterson **(June 7)**. Saratoga Race Course opens; the inaugural Travers Stakes is won by Lexington's son Kentucky **(August 2)**. Asteroid, another undefeated son of Lexington, is stolen from Woodburn Stud by Confederate guerillas **(October 22)**, recovered a week later. Norfolk is sold for an American record $15,001.

1866 Jerome Park opens in New York **(September 25)**.

1867 The inaugural Belmont Stakes is won by the filly Ruthless at Jerome Park **(June 19)**. Robert A. Alexander dies at Woodburn at age 48 **(December)**.

1868 The Ladies Handicap is inaugurated at Jerome Park, becoming the first major American race to be carded annually for fillies and mares **(June 16)**.

1870 Monmouth Park opens in New Jersey **(July 30)**. Pimlico Race Course opens in Maryland **(October 25)**.

1872 Fair Grounds racetrack opens in New Orleans **(April 13)**.

1873 The inaugural Preakness Stakes at Pimlico is won by Survivor **(May 27)**. Volume I of the *American Stud Book* is published.

1874 Pari-mutuel wagering is introduced at Jerome Park.

1875 *Kentucky Livestock Record* begins publication **(February 5)**, with a subscription cost of $3 per year. Churchill Downs opens; the inaugural Kentucky Derby is won by Aristides **(May 17)**. Lexington dies **(July 1)**.

1877 Congress adjourns to watch Parole defeat Tom Ochiltree and Ten Broeck at Pimlico **(October 24)**.

1878 Ten Broeck defeats Mollie McCarthy in East-West match at Louisville **(July 4)**.

1880 America's first recorded post parade is held before the Belmont Stakes **(June 14)**. Sheepshead Bay racecourse opens in New York **(June 19)**. Blue Gown, the 1868 Epsom Derby winner, dies en route to America.

1881 Pierre Lorillard's Iroquois becomes the first American-owned and -bred Epsom Derby winner **(June 1)**. Hindoo wins his 18th consecutive race **(September 1)**. Parole retires as the leading American money winner, with $82,816.

1882 Fair Grounds racetrack installs electric lights in its grandstand.

1883	The Louisville Jockey Club racetrack is renamed Churchill Downs.
1884	Buchanan becomes the first maiden Kentucky Derby winner **(May 16)**.
1886	Miss Woodford becomes the first American Thoroughbred to top $100,000 in earnings **(June 2)**. Two-year-old Tremont wins each of his 13 career starts in a ten-week span that ends on **August 7**.
1887	Hanover wins 17 consecutive races.
1888	Trainer Robert Walden saddles a record seventh Preakness Stakes winner, Refund **(May 11)**. King Thomas brings an American yearling auction record of $40,000 **(June 26)**. The inaugural Futurity Stakes at Sheepshead Bay is worth $40,900 to winner Proctor Knott **(September 3)**.
1889	Hanover ends Miss Woodford's reign as the leading American money winner **(August 29)**, retiring with earnings of $118,887. U.S. purse distribution is $2.4-million; 4,820 races are run.
1890	The Preakness Stakes is run at Morris Park in New York **(June 10)**. Salvator runs a world-record 1:35½ mile down the straightaway at Monmouth Park **(August 28)**.
1891	Hawthorne Race Course opens near Chicago **(May 20)**. *St. Blaise sells for a world auction record $100,000 at the August Belmont I estate dispersal **(October 16)**.
1892	Kingston surpasses Hanover as America's top money winner, with $138,917.
1893	Boundless wins the American Derby at Washington Park, after an hour and 40-minute delay at the starting post **(June 24)**. *Ormonde, regarded as Europe's best horse of the 19th century, arrives for stud duty in California **(September 8)**. Two-year-old Domino sets a single-season earnings record of $170,890 and becomes America's leading money winner **(September 29)**. Himyar sets a single-season progeny earnings record of $249,502.
1894	The Jockey Club is incorporated **(February 9)**. Kingston scores a record 89th career victory **(August 21)**. Aqueduct racetrack opens in New York **(September 27)**. *Daily Racing Form* begins publication **(November 17)**. *Sir Modred becomes the only California-based stallion to lead the American year-end sire list.
1895	*Livestock Record* changes its name to *The Thoroughbred Record* **(February 2)**. August Belmont II heads the new Westchester Racing Association, the controlling body of New York racing **(August 14)**. Domino retires with record American earnings of $193,550 **(September 17)**.
1896	Domino arrives in Lexington and makes his last public appearance before entering stud **(February 3)**.
1897	Jockey Club buys the *American Stud Book* from H. Sanders Bruce for $35,000 **(May 17)**. Lucretia Borgia races against time at Oakland, California, setting a world four-mile record of 7:11 that remains on the books today. Domino dies of meningitis at age six **(July 29)**.
1898	Fasig-Tipton auction company is incorporated. American-born jockey Tod Sloan introduces his high-stirrup, crouched ("monkey-on-a-stick") riding style to England.
1899	Fasig-Tipton Co. conducts its first Thoroughbred auction, under electric lights at Madison Square Garden, New York **(June 19)**. Champion and four-time leading sire Hanover dies **(March 23)**.
1900	Pari-mutuel wagering is introduced at Fair Grounds. The Jockey Club registers 3,476 foals. Johnny Reiff becomes the first American to top the English jockey standings, with 143 victories.
1901	William Collins Whitney becomes the second American owner to win the Epsom Derby, with Volodyovski **(June 5)**. James R. Keene's American-bred Cap and Bells, by Domino, wins the Epsom Oaks **(June 7)**. Racing Hall of Fame racehorse and leading sire Hindoo dies at age 23 **(July 4)**. Champion Hamburg sells for $60,000 at the Marcus Daly estate dispersal **(October 1)**. Future five-time leading sire *Star Shoot is imported.
1902	Savable earns the decade's largest winner's purse, $44,500, in the Futurity Stakes **(August 30)**.
1903	Flocarline is the first filly to win the Preakness Stakes **(May 30)**. Africander is the first three-year-old Suburban Handicap winner **(June 18)**.
1904	Oaklawn Park opens in Arkansas **(February 24)**. Leading owner W. C. Whitney dies **(March 7)**. Elwood becomes the first Kentucky Derby winner owned and bred by women **(May 2)**. Hamburg sells for $70,000 at the W. C. Whitney estate dispersal **(October 10)**.
1905	Champion Commando dies of tetanus at age seven **(March 13)**. Belmont Park opens **(May 4)**. Tanya becomes the second filly to win the Belmont Stakes **(May 24)**. Artful hands Sysonby his only defeat, in the Futurity Stakes **(August 27)**. Roseben sets an American six-furlong record of 1:11⅗ under 147 pounds in the Manhattan Handicap **(October 6)**.
1906	An earthquake destroys San Francisco's Ingleside racetrack **(April 18)**. Sysonby dies of septic poisoning at age four **(June 17)**. Roseben wins the Manhattan Handicap for a second time under 147 pounds **(October 12)**. Kentucky appoints the first state racing commission.
1907	Colin launches his perfect 15-for-15 career with a maiden victory at Belmont Park **(May 29)**. The original Santa Anita Park opens in California **(December 7)**. Commando posthumously breaks his grandsire Himyar's single-season progeny earnings record, with $270,345.
1908	California-bred Rubio wins England's Grand National Steeplechase **(March 26)**. Bookmakers are barred from Churchill Downs and 15 pari-mutuel machines are installed **(March)**. Agnew-Hart legislation outlaws public betting in New York, though racing continues without wagering **(June 13)**. Colin ends his career in the Tidal Stakes, a betless exhibition at Sheepshead Bay **(June 20)**. The Locke Law ends racing in New Orleans.
1909	The Walker-Otis Anti-Racetrack Gambling Bill is passed in California, effectively blacking out racing there for a quarter-century **(February 19)**. The Preakness winner's silks are painted on the Pimlico Clubhouse's weathervane for the first time **(May 12)**.
1910	New York passes the Director's Criminal Liability Act, making racetrack operators and executives subject to imprisonment if gambling is found to occur on track premises. All New York tracks cease

	operation. A mass exodus of American breeding stock and racehorses to Europe begins.

1911   Laurel Race Course opens in Maryland **(October 2)**. 390 yearlings average $230 at U.S. auctions. The average U.S. purse reaches a 20th-century low $371.

1912   Wishing Ring wins at Latonia, paying a record $1,885.50 for a $2 wager **(June 17)**. James R. Keene sells Castleton Stud in Kentucky for $225 an acre. Star Charter is the season's leading money winner, with $14,655. Influential sire *Rock Sand and champion Tanya are included in the mass exportation of bloodstock to Europe.

1913   The English Jockey Club passes the Jersey Act, excluding most American pedigrees from admission to the *General Stud Book* **(April)**. Donerail wins the Kentucky Derby at record odds of 91-to-1 **(May 10)**. Belmont Park reopens without legal wagering **(May 30)**. Whisk Broom II becomes the first to sweep New York's handicap triple crown—the Metropolitan, Brooklyn, and Suburban Handicaps **(June 28)**. James R. Keene's estate dispersal is conducted at Madison Square Garden, and future Racing Hall of Fame member Peter Pan tops the sale at $38,000 **(September 2)**.

1914   Iron Mask carries 150 pounds to victory at Juarez, setting a 5½-furlong world record of 1:03⅗ that stands for 30 years **(March 8)**. Old Rosebud sets a Kentucky Derby record of 2:03⅖ that stands for 17 years **(May 9)**.

1915   Pan Zareta gives ten pounds to Joe Blair and beats him in a match race at Juarez, setting a five-furlong world record of :57⅕ that stands for 36 years **(February 10)**. Pan Zareta carries 146 pounds to victory at Juarez, giving rivals from 31 to 54 pounds **(March 26)**. Regret becomes the first filly to win the Kentucky Derby **(May 8)**. The Preakness Stakes is run in two divisions for the only time **(May 15)**.

1916   *Star Shoot sires a record 27 juvenile winners.

1917   The New York State Racing Commission recommends to the Legislature that pari-mutuel wagering be legalized **(January)**. Man o' War is born **(March 29)**. *Omar Khayyam becomes the first foreign-bred Kentucky Derby winner **(May 12)**. Borrow wins the Brooklyn Handicap over Kentucky Derby winners Regret, Old Rosebud, and *Omar Khayyam **(June 25)**.

1918   Exterminator wins the Kentucky Derby at 30-to-1 odds **(May 11)**. Man o' War is sold to Samuel D. Riddle for $5,000 at the Saratoga yearling sale **(August 17)**. Roamer is the first to crack a 1:35 mile, running in 1:34⅘ at Saratoga **(August 21)**.

1919   Sir Barton, a maiden, wins the Kentucky Derby **(May 10)**; he becomes the first American Triple Crown winner in winning the Belmont Stakes **(June 18)**. Man o' War wins his first start, at Belmont Park **(June 6)**; he suffers his only career defeat, to Upset, in Saratoga's Sanford Memorial **(August 13)**. Purchase walks over in the inaugural Jockey Club Gold Cup **(September 13)**. The American Jockey Club registers a century-low 1,665 foals.

1920   Man o' War smashes the world record for 1⅜ miles in winning the Belmont Stakes by 20 lengths **(June 12)**; wins the Lawrence Realization Stakes by approximately 100 lengths **(September 4)**; carries 138 pounds to win the Potomac Handicap at Havre de Grace while setting a 1¹⁄₁₆-mile track record **(September 18)**; defeats Sir Barton in an $80,000 match race at Kenilworth Park in Canada **(October 12)**; retires as America's leading earner, with $249,465.

1921   Man o' War makes a farewell public gallop around the Kentucky Association racetrack in Lexington **(January 28)**. Counterclockwise racing begins at Belmont Park.

1922   Morvich scores his 11th victory in 11 starts in the Kentucky Derby **(May 13)**, joining Regret as the only undefeated Kentucky Derby winners to that time. Kentucky Derby winner and future Racing Hall of Fame member Old Rosebud breaks down in a race at Jamaica racetrack and dies at age 11 **(May 23)**.

1923   Exterminator scores a record 34th stakes victory **(April 21)**. Kentucky Derby winner Zev defeats Epsom Derby winner *Papyrus in a Belmont Park match **(October 20)**. Zev becomes the first American racehorse to top $200,000 in single-season earnings ($272,008). Earl Sande rides the winners of $569,394, a record that stands for 20 years.

1924   Nellie Morse is the fourth and final filly Preakness winner **(May 12)**. Nine-year-old Exterminator finishes third in his 100th and final career start **(June 21)**. Three "international specials" are staged in the U.S. and are won by American-breds Wise Counsellor at Belmont Park **(September 1)**, Ladkin at Aqueduct **(September 27)**, and Sarazen at Latonia **(October 11)**. French star *Epinard finishes second in all three. Man o' War is represented by his first stakes winner when By Hisself wins the Autumn Days Handicap at Empire City **(October 20)**.

1925   Hialeah Park opens in Florida, ushering in an era of big-time winter racing **(January 15)**. Network radio's first broadcast of a Kentucky Derby is aired from Louisville's WHAS **(May 16)**. River Downs opens near Cincinnati **(July 6)**. War Feathers, a Man o' War—*Tuscan Red filly, sells at Saratoga for $50,500, an American yearling auction record **(August 10)**. *Sir Gallahad III arrives at Claiborne Farm from France, becoming the first major American stallion syndication **(December 15)**.

1926   Boot to Boot wins Washington Park's American Derby, the first U.S. race to offer a $100,000-added purse **(July 31)**. Man o' War sets a single-season progeny earnings record of $408,137 with just two crops racing. North American yearling sales average is $2,640.

1927   John Longden scores the first of his 6,032 career victories aboard Hugo K. Asher at Salt Lake City **(October 4)**. Arlington Park racetrack opens near Chicago **(October 13)**.

1928   New Broom, a yearling son of Whisk Broom II, sells for $75,000, an auction record that stands for 26 years **(August 7)**. Wirt G. Bowman becomes America's first flying Thoroughbred, traveling by airplane from San Diego to San Francisco **(October)**.

1929   The $100,000 Coffroth Handicap at Tijuana, Mexico, is won by Golden Prince **(March 17)**. Clyde Van Dusen becomes the eighth gelding to win the Kentucky Derby **(May 18)**. Whichone wins the Futurity Stakes, earning America's first six-figure winner's purse, $105,730 **(September 14)**.

1930 The Preakness Stakes is the first American classic to be started from a gate **(May 9)**. Gallant Fox sweeps the Triple Crown **(June 7)**. Jim Dandy defeats Gallant Fox at 100-to-1 odds in the Travers Stakes **(August 16)**. Gallant Fox becomes the first racehorse to surpass $300,000 in single-season earnings **(September 17)**.

1931 Agua Caliente in Mexico becomes the first North American racetrack to install an electronic timer **(January)**. Hawthorne Park is the first track in the U.S. to use an electronic timer **(August 3)**. Top Flight becomes the leading distaff money winner and the first juvenile to top $200,000 in earnings **(November 7)**. Tropical Park racetrack opens in Florida **(December 26)**. Influential broodmare *La Troienne is imported.

1932 Eddie Arcaro rides his first winner, at Agua Caliente **(January 14)**. Australian wonder horse *Phar Lap wins the $50,000 Agua Caliente Handicap **(March 20)**; dies in California under mysterious circumstances **(April 5)**. Sportsman's Park opens near Chicago **(May 2)**. The North American yearling sales average declines to $570.

1933 The Woolwine-Maloney Bill legalizes pari-mutuel wagering in California **(February 19)**. Broker's Tip, a maiden, wins the Kentucky Derby in a "fighting finish" involving jockeys Don Meade and Herb Fisher, aboard Head Play **(May 6)**. Longacres racetrack opens in Washington state **(August 3)**. Saliva drug testing instituted at Hialeah Park. Legal bookmaking returns to New York. Walter Vosburgh compiles weights for the first Experimental Free Handicap. Mary Hirsch is denied a trainer's license by the Jockey Club.

1934 Bay Meadows Race Course opens in Northern California and is the first in America to use a photo-finish camera **(November 3)**. Santa Anita Park opens in Southern California **(December 25)**. The Kentucky Derby purse is reduced from $50,000 to $30,000. Hialeah Park builds the first modern American grass course.

1935 The inaugural $100,000 Santa Anita Handicap is won by *Azucar, with Twenty Grand and Equipoise in the beaten field **(February 23)**. Mary Hirsch is the first woman awarded a trainer's license from the Jockey Club **(April)**. Omaha becomes the third Triple Crown winner **(June 8)**. Suffolk Downs opens in Massachusetts **(July 10)**.

1936 Jockey Ralph Neves pronounced "dead" after a racing accident at Bay Meadows; he returns to the track that day **(May 12)**. Keeneland Race Course opens in Kentucky **(October 15)**. *Daily Racing Form* begins formal recognition of annual divisional champions, names Granville the first Horse of the Year. Black Toney stands for an American-high $2,000 fee.

1937 Stagehand receives 30 pounds from Seabiscuit and beats him by a nose in the Santa Anita Handicap **(March 5)**. War Admiral becomes the fourth Triple Crown winner **(June 5)**. Delaware Park opens **(June 26)**. Bing Crosby and Pat O'Brien open Del Mar racetrack in California **(July 3)**. Sir Barton, America's first Triple Crown winner, dies in Wyoming **(October 30)**.

1938 Hollywood Park opens in California **(June 10)**. Equipoise dies at age ten **(August 10)**. Seabiscuit defeats *Ligaroti in a Del Mar match race **(August 12)**; Seabiscuit defeats War Admiral in a two-horse Pimlico Special **(November 1)**.

1939 Gulfstream Park opens in Florida **(February 1)**. Ben A. Jones becomes Calumet Farm's trainer **(July)**. The Grayson Foundation is established to finance equine research **(August 12)**. Bay Meadows Race Course installs America's first electric, enclosed starting gate, developed by Clay Puett.

1940 In his third try, Seabiscuit wins the Santa Anita Handicap and retires as the world's leading money winner, with $437,730 **(March 2)**. Pari-mutuel wagering is legalized in New York **(April 1)**; Jamaica racetrack opens in New York with pari-mutuel wagering **(April 15)**.

1941 Golden Gate Fields opens in California **(February 1)**. Merrick dies at age 38, as the oldest known Thoroughbred **(March 13)**. Whirlaway becomes the fifth American Triple Crown winner **(June 7)**.

1942 Thoroughbred Racing Associations is formed **(March 19)**. Garden State Park opens in New Jersey **(July 18)**. Future leading American sire and broodmare sire *Princequillo is claimed for $2,500 **(August 20)**. Alsab defeats Whirlaway in a $25,000 match at Narragansett Park **(September 19)**. Jockey Eddie Arcaro is suspended by Jockey Club stewards for one year for dangerous riding in the Cowdin Stakes **(September 26)**. Whirlaway becomes the first $500,000 earner **(October 3)**. Santa Anita is used as an internment center for Japanese-Americans. Del Mar racetrack becomes a training ground for Marines. Hollywood Park is utilized as a storage facility by the North American Aviation Co. North American yearlings average $638, about half the 1941 average.

1943 Man o' War is pensioned from stud duty at age 26 **(March)**. Stymie is claimed by trainer Hirsch Jacobs for $1,500 **(June 2)**. Tanforan racetrack in California is utilized as a naval training base **(June 3)**. Count Fleet wins the Belmont Stakes by 25 lengths to become the sixth Triple Crown winner **(June 5)**. The Breeders' Sales Co. is organized in Kentucky **(September)**. A wartime ban on "pleasure driving" causes the cancellation or relocation of several race meetings.

1944 The only triple dead-heat in a North American stakes race occurs in Aqueduct's Carter Handicap, between Bossuet, Wait a Bit, and Brownie **(June 10)**. The Breeders' Sales Co. conducts its first yearling auction, at Keeneland **(July 31-August 3)**.

1945 Horse racing in the United States is called off by order of the War Mobilization Board **(January 3)**. American racing resumes four days after Nazi Germany surrenders **(May 12)**. Owner Fred Hooper wins the Kentucky Derby with his first horse, Hoop, Jr. **(June 9)**. North American yearling average soars to $5,146.

1946 Jockey George "The Iceman" Woolf dies following a spill at Santa Anita **(January 4)**. The first transcontinental flight with a Thoroughbred passenger is recorded when Historian flies from Chicago to Los Angeles **(May 29)**. Assault becomes the seventh Triple Crown winner **(June 1)**. Atlantic City Race Course opens **(July 22)**. *Fair Truckle is first to break 1:09 for six furlongs, running 1:08$\frac{4}{5}$ at Golden Gate Fields **(October 4)**. Assault becomes the first $400,000 single-season earner **(November 9)**. The first transatlantic flight with racehorses on board takes place, from Ireland to New Jersey **(November 26-27)**. Lip tattoos are adopted as a method of identifying racehorses.

1947 Stepfather brings a world auction record of $200,000 at the Louis B. Mayer dispersal **(February 27)**. Seabiscuit dies at age 14 **(May 17)**. Armed defeats Assault at Belmont Park in the first $100,000 winner-take-all match race **(September 27)**. Man o' War dies at age 30 **(November 1)**. Stymie retires with record earnings of $918,485. Calumet is the first stable to top $1-million in a season. Automatic hotwalking machines are introduced.

1948 *Alibhai is syndicated for a record $500,000. Citation becomes the eighth Triple Crown winner **(June 12)**. Gallorette is the first racemare to top $400,000 in career earnings **(July 17)**. Citation ends his campaign with a new single-season earnings record of $709,470 **(December 11)**. *Shannon II becomes the first to crack 2:00 for 1$\frac{1}{4}$ miles, running the distance in 1:59$\frac{4}{5}$ at Golden Gate Fields **(October 23)**.

1949 Apprentice Bill Shoemaker rides his first winner, at Golden Gate Fields **(April 20)**. Hollywood Park's grandstand and clubhouse are destroyed by fire **(May 6)**. England's Jockey Club rescinds the Jersey Act after 36 years **(June)**. *Nasrullah is purchased by an American syndicate for $340,000. Keeneland installs America's first aluminum rail.

1950 Detroit Race Course opens **(May 25)**. Future five-time leading American sire *Nasrullah arrives at Claiborne Farm in Kentucky **(July)**. The National Museum of Racing is chartered at Saratoga Springs, New York **(October)**. Gordon Glisson wins the first George Woolf Memorial Jockey Award.

1951 The Santa Anita Maturity offers a record $205,700 purse, with a record winner's share of $144,325 going to Great Circle **(February 3)**. Citation becomes racing's first equine millionaire, winning the Hollywood Gold Cup in his final start **(July 14)**. Bewitch passes Gallorette as leading distaff earner with $462,605. **(July 14)**. The Pimlico Special, won by Bryan G., becomes the first nationally televised race **(November 16)**. Lloyd's of London pays off a $250,000 insurance claim on gravely injured Your Host, who survives to sire Kelso.

1952 The Kentucky Derby is broadcast for the first time on national television, by CBS, and is won by Hill Gail, Ben Jones's record sixth winner **(May 3)**. English representative *Wilwyn wins the inaugural Washington, D.C., International at Laurel Park **(October 18)**. Apprentice jockey Tony DeSpirito scores a single-season record 390 victories **(December 31)**.

1953 Dark Star, 24.90-to-1, hands Native Dancer his only defeat, in the Kentucky Derby **(May 2)**. Charlie Whittingham saddles his first career stakes winner, Porterhouse **(June 10)**. Tom Fool is the second New York handicap triple crown winner, taking the Brooklyn Handicap under 136 pounds **(July 11)**. The Garden State Stakes is inaugurated as the world's richest race, worth $239,000 **(October 31)**. R. H. "Red" McDaniel becomes the first trainer to saddle 200 winners in a season **(December 1)**. Santa Anita opens its Camino Real grass course **(December 26)**. Bill Shoemaker smashes the single-season win record, with 485 victories **(December)**. *Royal Charger is advertised at an American record $10,000 stud fee.

1954 The San Juan Capistrano Handicap is America's first $100,000 grass race **(March 6)**. Bold Ruler and Round Table are foaled at Claiborne Farm in Kentucky **(April 6)**. Determine becomes the first gray Kentucky Derby winner **(May 1)**. Never Say Die is the second American-bred Epsom Derby winner, 73 years after Iroquois **(June 2)**.

1955 The National Museum of Racing opens at Saratoga Springs; the Racing Hall of Fame is instituted **(August 6)**. Camarero's undefeated streak concludes after a world-record 56 consecutive victories, in Puerto Rico **(August)**. Nashua defeats Swaps in a $100,000 match race at Washington Park **(August 31)**. Nashua becomes the first $1-million stallion syndication, for $1,251,000. **(December 15)**. New York Racing Association Inc. is established. *Sir Gallahad III leads the American broodmare sire list for a record 12th time.

1956 Turf Paradise opens in Arizona **(January 7)**. Nashua becomes racing's second equine millionaire **(February 18)**. Woodbine opens in Canada **(June 12)**. John Longden becomes the world's winningest jockey, with 4,871 victories **(September 3)**. Bill Shoemaker and Bill Hartack become the first to ride winners of $2-million in a season. Swaps carries 130 pounds to a 1:39 clocking for 1$\frac{1}{16}$ miles, a mark that stands as a dirt record for 27 years **(June 23)**. The original Aqueduct racetrack is torn down.

1957 Florida Breeders' Sales Co. conducts the first two-year-olds in training sale, at Hialeah **(January 28)**. Bold Ruler defeats Round Table and *Gallant Man in the three-horse Trenton Handicap, described as the race of the year **(November 9)**. Bill Hartack is the first jockey to top $3-million in single-season earnings. The American foal crop tops 10,000 for the first time.

1958 Round Table becomes racing's third equine millionaire **(May 11)**. Future Hall of Fame jockey Jack Westrope is killed in a spill during the Hollywood Oaks **(June 19)**. Round Table supplants Nashua as the world's all-time leading money winner **(October 11)**.

1959 *Tomy Lee is the second foreign-bred winner of the Kentucky Derby **(May 2)**. Jamaica racetrack in New York is torn down to make way for a housing development **(August)**. Modern $32-million Aqueduct racetrack opens in New York **(September 14)**.

1960 Undefeated *Ribot arrives in the U.S. for stud duty **(June 23)**. Kelso wins the first of five Horse of the Year titles. The Animal Insurance Co. of America pays off a $1-million policy on Bally Ache, who died on October 28 **(December)**.

1961 Northern Dancer is born **(May 27)**. Ben A. Jones, Racing Hall of Fame trainer, dies **(June 13)**. A son of Swaps, Swapson, becomes the first six-figure American auction yearling, selling for $130,000 at Keeneland July **(July 24)**. National Association of State Racing Commissioners recommends a general ban on all drugs, narcotics, anesthetics, and analgesics. Kelso becomes the third winner of New York's handicap triple crown **(July 22)**. Racing Hall of Fame jockey Eddie Arcaro retires **(November 18)**.

1962 Champion Crimson Satan is the first high-profile positive finding for phenylbutazone after winning the Leonard Richards Handicap at Delaware Park **(July 23)**. Angel Cordero Jr. rides his first North American winner **(July 26)**. Crazy Kid is first to break 1:08 for six furlongs, clocking 1:07⅘ at Del Mar **(August 18)**. Never Say Die becomes the first American-bred to lead the English sire list.

1963 Bold Ruler leads the American sire list for the first of eight times.

1964 Northern Dancer wins the Kentucky Derby in track-record time of 2:00 **(May 2)**. Laffit Pincay Jr. scores his first career victory, in Panama **(May 19)**. Seven-year-old Kelso wins a fifth Jockey Club Gold Cup **(October 31)** and earns a record fifth Horse of the Year title. Wagering in the United States tops $3-billion.

1965 Admirably runs the fastest six furlongs ever recorded by a filly or mare, tying the world record of 1:07⅘, at Golden Gate Fields **(April 7)**. Affectionately wins the Vagrancy Handicap under 137 pounds, the most weight successfully carried by a filly in 49 years **(July 26)**. Buckpasser breaks the juvenile earnings record, with $568,096 **(October 16)**. Northern Dancer stands his first season for a $10,000 stud fee. Moccasin becomes the first juvenile filly to be named Horse of the Year, in the Thoroughbred Racing Associations poll.

1966 Graustark is syndicated for a record $2.4-million **(June)**. Kelso retires as the world's leading money winner, with $1,977,165 **(March 2)**. John Longden wins the San Juan Capistrano aboard George Royal in his final career ride and retires with a world record 6,032 victories **(March 12)**. Three-year-old Buckpasser becomes the youngest equine millionaire **(August 20)**. American foal registrations top 20,000 for the first time.

1967 Buckpasser concludes a 15-race win-streak in the Metropolitan Handicap at Aqueduct **(May 30)**. Damascus defeats Buckpasser and Dr. Fager by ten lengths in the Woodward Stakes **(September 30)**; banks record single-season earnings of $817,941. Future double classic winner Majestic Prince brings a yearling auction record of $250,000 at Keeneland July **(July 24)**. National racetrack attendance declines for the first time since World War II. Buckpasser is syndicated for a record $4.8-million. Bold Ruler becomes the first to sire juvenile winners of more than $1-million in a season.

1968 Dancer's Image becomes the only disqualified Kentucky Derby winner, after the then-illegal phenylbutazone shows up in his post-race test **(May 4)**. American-bred Sir Ivor wins the Epsom Derby **(May 29)**. Dark Mirage is the first New York filly triple crown winner **(June 22)**. A *Sea-Bird filly sets a world auction record of $405,000 at Keeneland July **(July 23)**. Native Diver becomes the first California-bred millionaire **(July 15)**. Dr. Fager wins the Washington Park Handicap with 134 pounds, in a world-record 1:32⅕ mile **(August 24)**. Dr. Fager carries 139 pounds to victory in the Vosburgh Handicap, his final career start **(November 2)**. *Vaguely Noble is syndicated for $5-million.

1969 Male riders boycott a race at Tropical Park in which Barbara Jo Rubin was scheduled to ride **(January 15)**. Diane Crump becomes the first female to compete in an American Thoroughbred pari-mutuel race, finishing tenth at Hialeah **(February 7)**. Rubin becomes the first of her sex to a win a pari-mutuel Thoroughbred race in America, at Charles Town Races **(February 22)**; Tuesdee Testa is the first female jockey to win at a major American racetrack, aboard Buz On at Santa Anita **(March 1)**. Diane Crump is the first female rider to win a stakes, on Easy Lime in Fair Grounds's Spring Fiesta Cup **(March 29)**. Richard Nixon is the first sitting 20th century President to attend the Kentucky Derby **(May 3)**. Not-for-profit Oak Tree Racing Association launches its first meeting, at Santa Anita **(October 7)**.

1970 Secretariat is foaled in Virginia **(March 30)**. The New York Legislature votes to legalize city-operated off-track betting parlors **(April 8)**. New York Governor Nelson Rockefeller signs a bill legalizing OTB in the Empire State **(April 22)**. Diane Crump finishes 15th as the first female to ride in the Kentucky Derby **(May 2)**. Exacta wagering is introduced in New York and New Jersey **(June)**. Crowned Prince sets a $510,000 world yearling record at Keeneland July **(July 20)**. Citation dies at age 25 **(August 8)**. Bill Shoemaker passes John Longden as the all-time winning jockey, with victory number 6,033 **(September 7)**. Canadian-bred Nijinsky II sweeps undefeated through the English Triple Crown **(September 12)**. Nijinsky II is syndicated for a record $5.44-million. Santa Anita institutes exacta wagering **(October 6)**.

1971 Eclipse Awards are instituted by Thoroughbred Racing Associations, *Daily Racing Form*, and National Turf Writers Association. Off-track betting begins in New York **(April 8)**. Canonero II, a $1,200 auction yearling, wins the Kentucky Derby **(May 1)** and Preakness Stakes **(May 15)**. Eight-time leading sire Bold Ruler dies at age 17 **(July 12)**. Former Illinois Governor Otto Kerner is indicted on federal charges that included bribery to influence racing matters **(December)**. National purse distribution tops $200-million.

1972 European racing authorities institute pattern system to rate best races. Jockey Bill Shoemaker sets an all-time stakes record with win number 555 **(March 2)**. What a Treat brings a $450,000 auction record for a female Thoroughbred **(March 6)**. *Morning Telegraph* daily racing newspaper suspends publication after 139 years **(April 10)**. Kentucky's Court of Appeals awards Forward Pass the winner's purse from the 1968 Kentucky Derby, making him Calumet Farm's eighth Derby winner **(April 28)**. American-owned and -bred Roberto wins the Epsom Derby (Eng-G1) **(June 7)**. Convenience defeats Typecast in a $250,000 Hollywood match race **(June 17)**. Secretariat finishes fourth in his debut **(July 4)** but goes on to win seven of nine starts and is voted Horse of the Year at the conclusion of his two-year-old season. Roberto ends Brigadier Gerard's 15-race win streak, in the Benson and Hedges Gold Cup (Eng-G1) **(August 15)**. Four-time leading breeder Arthur B. "Bull" Hancock Jr. dies **(September 14)**.

1973 At urging of European racing authorities, North American Graded Stakes Committee is formed and begins grading of North American races. Champion mare Typecast brings a world auction record of $725,000 **(January 28)**. Secretariat's record $6.08-million syndication is announced **(February 26)**. Sunday racing begins in California at Hollywood Park **(April 15)**. Secretariat sets a Kentucky Derby (G1) record of 1:59⅖ **(May 5)**. *Cougar II becomes the first foreign-bred millionaire **(May 5)**. Secretariat wins the Belmont Stakes (G1) by 31 lengths in a world record 2:24 for 1½ miles, becoming the ninth Triple Crown winner **(June 9)**. Secretariat is featured simultaneously on the covers of *Time*, *Newsweek*, and *Sports Illustrated* **(June 11)**. Wajima, from the last crop of Bold Ruler, brings a world record yearling price of $600,000 at Keeneland July **(July)**. Secretariat defeats stablemate Riva Ridge in the inaugural Marlboro Cup, setting a world record of 1:45⅖ for 1⅛ miles **(September 15)**. Secretariat ends his career triumphantly in the Canadian International Championship (G2) **(October 28)**. Count Fleet dies at age 33 **(December 3)**. Sandy Hawley is the first jockey to ride 500 winners in a season **(December 15)**.

1974 The centennial Kentucky Derby (G1) is won by Cannonade before a crowd of 163,628 **(May 4)**. Chris Evert defeats Miss Musket by approximately 50 lengths in a $350,000 match race at Hollywood **(July 20)**. Dahlia is the first distaff millionaire **(August 20)**. D. Wayne Lukas saddles his first Thoroughbred stakes winner, Harbor Hauler, in a division of the Foothill Stakes at Pomona **(September 13)**. Dahlia becomes a stakes winner in five countries **(October 27)**. Louisiana Downs opens **(October 30)**. Apprentice jockey Chris McCarron sets a single-season win record of 546. Dan Lasater nearly doubles the previous single-season earnings record for an owner, with $3,020,521.

1975 Ruffian breaks down in Belmont Park's "battle of the sexes" match race against Foolish Pleasure **(July 6)**; dies following surgery and is buried in the Belmont infield **(July 7)**. Seattle Slew sells as a yearling for $17,500 at the Fasig-Tipton Kentucky July sale **(July 19)**. Two yearling colts are stolen from their stalls at the Keeneland fall sale **(September 7)** and are never recovered. On-track betting in the United States tops $5-billion for the first time. On-track attendance tops 50-million for the first time. Champion Wajima is syndicated for a world-record $7.2-million.

1976 Secretariat's son Canadian Bound is the world's first seven-figure auction yearling, bringing $1.5-million at Keeneland July **(July 20)**. Connecticut opens its Teletrack satellite wagering site. Forego wins his third straight Horse of the Year title. What a Pleasure is syndicated for a world-record $8-million.

1977 Washington Park is destroyed by fire **(February 5)**. Garden State Park's grandstand and clubhouse are destroyed by fire **(April 14)**. Seattle Slew becomes the first undefeated American Triple Crown winner **(June 11)**. Champion Fanfreluche is stolen from a pasture at Claiborne Farm **(June 24)**; recovered unharmed six months later. Seattle Slew suffers his first career loss in the Swaps Stakes at Hollywood Park **(July 3)**. Maryland Governor Marvin Mandel is convicted on racing-related racketeering and mail fraud charges **(August 23)**. The Meadowlands in New Jersey opens its first Thoroughbred meet **(September 6)**. American foal registrations top 30,000 for the first time. Lebon-*Cinzano ringer scandal breaks in New York **(September 23)**. Steve Cauthen becomes the first to ride winners of $6-million in a single season **(December 10)** and is later named *Sports Illustrated*'s Sportsman of the Year and Professional Athlete of the Year by the Associated Press. The Minstrel is syndicated for a world record $9-million.

1978 John Henry wins a $25,000 claiming race **(May 21)**; switches to turf and wins for $35,000 claiming tag at Belmont Park **(June 1)**. Affirmed becomes the 11th Triple Crown winner **(June 10)**. Triple Crown winners meet for the first time, with Seattle Slew defeating Affirmed in the Marlboro Cup Handicap (G1) **(September 16)**. Affirmed is syndicated for a world-record $14.4-million.

1979 Affirmed becomes the first career $2-million earner **(June 24)**. Affirmed defeats Kentucky Derby (G1) and Preakness Stakes (G1) victor Spectacular Bid in the Jockey Club Gold Cup (G1); becomes the first to earn $1-million in a single season **(October 6)**. Hollywood Park introduces pick-six wagering **(April 23)**. Turf female division added to annual North American championships, won by Trillion.

1980 Genuine Risk becomes the second filly Kentucky Derby winner **(May 3)**. Ex-jockey Con Errico is convicted of race fixing in New York **(May 19)**, is later sentenced to ten years in prison. Spectacular Bid is unchallenged for Woodward Stakes (G1) and walks over **(September 20)**. Prerace drug testing of horses begins at Aqueduct **(October 14)**. Spectacular Bid is syndicated for a record $22-million.

1981 Julie Krone rides her first winner, at Tampa Bay Downs **(February 12)**. The Arlington Million is inaugurated at Arlington Park as the world's first $1-million Thoroughbred race, with John Henry defeating The Bart by a nose. **(August 30)**. Storm Bird is syndicated for a record $30-million.

1982 Mary Russ becomes the first female jockey to win a North American Grade 1 race, with Lord Darnley in the Widener Handicap **(February 27)**. Trainer Woody Stephens saddles the first of five consecutive Belmont Stakes (G1) winners, Conquistador Cielo **(June 5)**. A son of Nijinsky II—Spearfish brings a record $4.25-million at Keeneland July. Simulcasting begins at Woodbine and Fort Erie in Canada. John Gaines conceives the idea for the Breeders' Cup. Conquistador Cielo is syndicated for a record $36.4-million.

1983 European champion Shergar is stolen from Ballymany Stud in Ireland **(February 8)**; he was never recovered. Genuine Risk produces a stillborn colt by Secretariat, the first offspring of two Kentucky Derby (G1) winners **(April 4)**. Shareef Dancer is syndicated for a record $40-million. Jockey Angel Cordero Jr. rides to a record $10-million season. All Along (Fr) becomes America's first foreign-bred Horse of the Year. Simulcasting begins from the Meadowlands to Atlantic City Race Course **(September 28)**. John Henry becomes the first $4-million earner **(December 11)**. Fourteen Northern Dancer sales yearlings average $3,320,357. The Hollywood Futurity (G1) is carded as racing's first $1-million event for two-year-olds **(December 18)**. Devil's Bag is syndicated for $1-million a share ($36-million). Horse racing loses its status as the nation's number one spectator sport, to baseball.

1984 A share in Seattle Slew sells for $3-million **(May)**. Swale collapses and dies eight days after winning the Belmont Stakes (G1) **(June 17)**. Equine viral arteritis (EVA) halts Kentucky breeding season two weeks early **(June)**. Fit to Fight becomes the fourth horse to sweep New York's handicap triple crown **(July 21)**. The inaugural Breeders' Cup is run at Hollywood Park before 64,625 on-track fans and 50-million television viewers; Wild Again wins the $3-million Breeders' Cup Classic (G1) **(November 10)**. Nine-year-old John Henry retires with record earnings of $6,597,947; he later earns a second Horse of the Year title.

1985 Bill Shoemaker is the first jockey to reach $100-million in purse winnings **(March 3)**. Garden State Park, rebuilt at a cost of approximately $200-million, reopens **(April 1)**. Spend a Buck earns $2.6-million in purse and bonus money following his Jersey Derby (G3) victory **(May 27)**. Steve Cauthen becomes the first American jockey to win both a Kentucky Derby (G1) and Epsom Derby (Eng-G1) **(June 5)**. Creme Fraiche becomes the first gelding to win the Belmont Stakes (G1) **(June 8)**. Seattle Dancer sells for a world auction record of $13.1-million at Keeneland July **(July 23)**. Arlington Park's grandstand is destroyed by fire **(July 31)**. Teleprompter (GB) wins the Arlington Million (G1) in front of a razed grandstand and an on-track crowd of 35,651 **(August 25)**. THOROUGHBRED TIMES weekly news magazine publishes its inaugural edition **(September 20)**. Miss Oceana brings a world-record broodmare price of $7-million at the Newstead Farm dispersal **(November 10)**. American foal registrations top 50,000 for the first time.

1986 A season to 25-year-old Northern Dancer sells at auction for $710,000 **(January)**. The Santa Anita Handicap (G1) becomes the first $1-million-guaranteed handicap, won by Greinton (GB) **(March 2)**. Jan Ciochetti is the first woman to call a race at a major track (Hialeah) **(March 21)**. Woody Stephens saddles his fifth straight Belmont Stakes (G1) winner, Danzig Connection **(June 7)**. Laurel Park inaugurates the Maryland Million **(October 18)**. Lawmaker breaks *Star Shoot's 70-year-old record by siring his 28th juvenile winner **(December 12)**; ends the year with 30 two-year-old winners. Jockey Club foal registrations reach an all-time annual high of 51,293. The Jockey Club launches a mandatory blood-typing program. Joint nomination to Triple Crown races begins.

1987 Jockey Chris Antley wins a record nine races in a single day, at Aqueduct and Meadowlands **(October 31)**. Tejano becomes the first juvenile millionaire **(December 12)**. Northern Dancer retires from breeding. Chrysler Corp. announced as the first sponsor of the $5-million Triple Crown Challenge.

1988 Winning Colors is the third filly Kentucky Derby (G1) winner **(May 7)**. Personal Ensign ends her 13-for-13 career with a thrilling victory over Winning Colors in the Breeders' Cup Distaff (G1) **(November 5)**. Alysheba wins the Breeders' Cup Classic (G1) and retires as the leading American money earner, with $6,679,242 **(November 5)**.

1989 E. P. Taylor, breeder of Northern Dancer and Nijinsky II, dies at age 88 **(May 14)**. Belmont Park is the first American racetrack to time races in hundredths of a second. Arlington International Racecourse opens **(June 28)**. Northern Park, the last Northern Dancer yearling sold at auction, brings $2.8-million at Keeneland **(July 18)**. Secretariat dies at age 19 **(October 4)**. Pari-mutuel wagering on horse racing returns to Texas for the first time since 1937 **(October 6)**. Jockey Kent Desormeaux establishes a single-season win record of 547 **(November 30)**; ends the year with 598 winners.

1990 Bill Shoemaker retires as the world's winningest jockey, with 8,833 victories **(February 3)**. D. Wayne Lukas becomes the first trainer to saddle career winners of $100-million **(May 12)**. Champion Go for Wand breaks down fatally in the Breeders' Cup Distaff (G1) **(October 27)**. Santa Anita hosts the inaugural California Cup Day **(November 3)**. Northern Dancer dies at age 29 **(November 16)**. Alydar dies at Calumet Farm under suspicious circumstances **(November 17)**.

1991 The American Championship Racing Series is launched as a designed-for-television event. Bill Shoemaker is paralyzed in a California car accident **(April 8)**. Equibase, a joint venture of the Jockey Club and Thoroughbred Racing Associations, is formed and begins gathering past-performance data in competition with *Daily Racing Form.*

1992 Video lottery terminals (VLTs) are installed at West Virginia and Louisiana racetracks. Henryk de Kwiatkowski buys Calumet Farm for $17-million at a bankruptcy auction **(March 26)**. Gilded Time runs the fastest six furlongs ever recorded by a two-year-old, 1:07.84, in the Sapling Stakes at Monmouth Park **(August 8)**.

1993 At age 16, Kentucky Derby (G1) winner Genuine Risk produces her first live foal, a colt by Rahy (**May 15**). Julie Krone becomes the first female jockey to win an American classic, with Colonial Affair in the Belmont Stakes (G1) (**June 5**). Champion Prairie Bayou breaks down fatally in the Belmont (**June 5**). Claude R. "Shug" McGaughey III saddles five graded stakes winners at Belmont Park in single day (**October 16**). Arcangues wins the Breeders' Cup Classic (G1) at record 133.60-to-1 odds (**November 6**). Fair Grounds's historic grandstand is destroyed by fire (**December 17**).

1994 Thoroughbred Racing Associations appoints Brian McGrath as its first and only commissioner (**January 17**). The American Championship Racing Series is canceled. Class 1 racing begins in Texas at Sam Houston Race Park (**April 29**). Hollywood Park's casino and card club opens (**July 1**). Cigar begins his 16-race win-streak (**October 28**). Thoroughbred Owners of California is launched.

1995 New York becomes the last North American racing jurisdiction to legalize race-day use of the antibleeder medication furosemide (**September 1**). Hoosier Park opens (**September 1**). Visa International begins sponsorship of the American Triple Crown races. Jockey Jerry Bailey wins a single-season record $16-million in purse money. Delaware Park and Prairie Meadows install slot machines.

1996 Cigar scores his 16th consecutive victory, tying Citation's modern record (**July 13**). Cigar retires as the world's leading money winner, with $9,999,815 (**October 26**). Serena's Song becomes the top North American distaff earner, with $3,283,388. The Breeders' Cup is held outside of the United States for the first time, at Woodbine in Canada (**October 26**).

1997 Atticus is the first to crack a 1:32 mile, running the distance on grass in 1:31.89 (**March 3**). A $25-million infertility insurance claim is paid off on Cigar (**March 24**). Racing Hall of Fame member Exceller is killed in a Swedish slaughterhouse at age 24 (**April 7**). Keeneland utilizes a public address system for the first time, at its spring meeting. Colonial Downs opens as Virginia's first pari-mutuel racetrack (**September 1**). Arlington International announces that it will suspend racing because of financial losses, political climate in Illinois (**September 8**). Chelsea Zupan sets an American record for a female jockey by winning seven consecutive races at Emerald Downs (**September 18-19**). Racing Hall of Fame jockey Eddie Arcaro dies at age 81 (**November 14**). Japanese-based Hokuto Vega retires as the world's richest Thoroughbred mare ($8,300,301).

1998 The National Thoroughbred Racing Association (NTRA) is launched (**April 1**). Tim Smith is named NTRA commissioner (**April 21**). Real Quiet fails by a nose in his quest for the Triple Crown (**June 6**). Elusive Quality clocks a world-record 1:31.63 mile on Belmont Park's grass (**July 4**). NTRA debuts the Lori Petty "Go, Baby, Go" ads. Company controlled by Frank Stronach buys Santa Anita Park. Equibase becomes the sport's sole provider of past-performance data and acquires *Daily Racing Form* database. End Sweep sires a record 33 juvenile winners in his first crop.

1999 Julie Krone retires as the all-time winningest female jockey, with 3,546 victories (**April 18**). ESPN honors Secretariat as one of the top 50 athletes of the 20th century (**May 19**). Mr. Prospector dies at age 29 (**June 1**). Television Games Network (TVG) debuts (**July 14**). Dale Baird becomes the first trainer to saddle 8,000 winners (**July 22**). Churchill Downs Inc. purchases Hollywood Park for $140-million (**September 10**). Laffit Pincay Jr. passes Bill Shoemaker as the world's winningest jockey (**December 10**), with 8,834 victories. Off-site wagering is responsible for 82% of racing's total handle. Frank Stronach-controlled Magna Entertainment Corp. buys Gulfstream Park, Golden Gate Fields, Thistledown, and Remington Park. Churchill Downs Inc. acquires Calder Race Course.

2000 Julie Krone becomes the first female elected to the Racing Hall of Fame (**May 2**). Arlington Park reopens after a two-year hiatus (**May 14**). NTRA and Breeders' Cup Ltd. consolidate (**May 18**). Fusaichi Pegasus becomes the first favorite to win the Kentucky Derby in 21 years (**May 6**); syndicated for a reported record $60-million to $70-million (**June 25**). Hallowed Dreams ties Cigar's and Citation's 20th century consecutive win record, with 16 (**July 15**). Leading breeder Allen Paulson dies at 78 (**July 19**). Breeder Fred Hooper dies at 102 (**August 3**). Churchill Downs Inc. buys Arlington Park (**September**). Laffit Pincay Jr. becomes the first jockey to ride 9,000 career winners (**October 28**). North American purses exceed $1-billion for the first time. Japanese-based Sunday Silence gets single-season progeny earnings of $54-million.

2001 Triple Crown winner Affirmed dies at 26 (**January 12**). The Breeders' Cup becomes formally known as the Breeders' Cup World Thoroughbred Championships (**June 26**). Jerry Bailey becomes the first jockey to ride winners of $20-million in a season (**October 7**). Tiznow becomes the first two-time winner of the Breeders' Cup Classic (**October 27**). Storm Cat stands for a $400,000 fee. The horse racing industry raises more than $5-million to benefit victims of the September 11 terrorist attacks. Laura Hillenbrand's *Seabiscuit: An American Legend* tops the New York *Times* bestseller list for nonfiction.

2002 Japan-based T.M. Opera O, the world's richest Thoroughbred, retires with earnings of $16,200,337 (**January 25**). Seattle Slew, the last living American Triple Crown winner, dies at age 28 (**May 7**). Racing Hall of Fame jockey Chris McCarron retires after career victory number 7,139 (**June 23**). Volponi scores the second-biggest upset in Breeders' Cup Classic (G1) history, with an $89 payoff (**October 26**). Ultra Pick Six wager on Breeders' Cup races is found to have been fixed, and three former Drexel University fraternity brothers plead guilty to $3-million scam. Julie Krone wins at Santa Anita in comeback after 3½ years in retirement (**November 7**). Sadler's Wells is represented by his 209th stakes winner, a world record. Magna International buys Lone Star Park (**October 30**), and the Maryland Racing Commission approves sale of controlling interest in Maryland tracks to Magna (**November 13**).

2003 Laffit Pincay Jr. retires as all-time leading jockey by wins, with 9,530 (**April 29**). Funny Cide becomes first gelding to win Kentucky Derby since Clyde Van Dusen in 1929 (**May 3**).

Great Horses in Racing

Racing Hall of Fame members are listed in italics

The name of each horse is followed by year of birth and year of death, if known. Color and sex (colt, filly, or gelding) are followed by sire, dam, and broodmare sire. The horse's race record is detailed by number of starts, wins, seconds, thirds, and earnings, followed by championship honors and most important wins. Records from the 18th and 19th centuries may be incomplete, and earnings may be impossible to determine. If the horse sired or produced significant stakes winners, that information follows the race record. A sire's or dam's place in important male or female lines is also noted.

ACK ACK, 1966-1990. B. c., Battle Joined—Fast Turn, by *Turn-to. 27-19-6-0, $636,641, Horse of the Year in 1971, champion sprinter, champion older male, Santa Anita H., Hollywood Gold Cup H., etc. Sire of 54 stakes winners, including Youth, Broad Brush, Ack's Secret, Rascal Lass, Caline. Broodmare sire of Sharp Cat, Royal Anthem, Benny the Dip, North Sider, Lost Code.

AFFECTIONATELY, 1960-1979. Dk. b. or br. f., Swaps—Searching, by War Admiral. 52-28-8-6, $546,659, champion two-year-old filly, champion sprinter, champion older mare, Top Flight H., Spinaway S., etc. Dam of Personality.

AFFIRMED, 1975-2001. Ch. c., Exclusive Native—Won't Tell You, by Crafty Admiral. 29-22-5-1, $2,393,818, Horse of the Year in 1978-'79, champion two- and three-year-old male, Triple Crown, Jockey Club Gold Cup (G1), etc. Sire of more than 80 stakes winners, including Flawlessly, Quiet Resolve, Affirmed Success, Peteski, Zoman, Charlie Barley, Bint Pasha. Broodmare sire of Chelsey Flower, Harlan's Holiday, Stinger, Balanchine.

AFRICANDER, 1900-unknown. B. c. *Star Ruby—Afric Queen, by *Darebin. 60-19-15-8, $102,325, champion three-year-old, Belmont S., Suburban H., etc.

ALARM, 1869-1895. B. c., *Eclipse—*Maud, by Stockwell. 9-6-2-1, $12,500, match race with Inverary. Sire of Himyar, Panique, Danger, Ann Fief, Fidele.

ALCIBIADES, 1927-1957. Ch. f., Supremus—*Regal Roman, by Roi Herode. 23-7-2-4, $47,860, champion two-year-old filly, Kentucky Oaks, etc. Dam of Menow, Lithe, Salaminia. Foundation mare of family that includes Sir Ivor, Firm Policy, Rash Statement, Twice the Vice, Shine Again, Halo America.

ALL ALONG (FR), 1979- . B. f., Targowice—Agujita (Fr), by Vieux Manoir. 21-9-4-2, $2,125,809, Horse of the Year in 1983, champion older female, champion older horse in France, Prix de l'Arc de Triomphe (Fr-G1), Turf Classic S. (G1), etc. Dam of Along All, Arnaqueur.

ALLEGED, 1974-2000. B. c., Hoist the Flag—Princess Pout, by Prince John. 10-9-1-0, $623,187, champion three-year-old in England and France, champion older horse in Europe, Prix de l'Arc de Triomphe (Fr-G1) twice, etc. One of only five horses to win consecutive runnings of the Prix de l'Arc de Triomphe. Sire of more than 100 stakes winners, including Miss Alleged, Law Society, Midway Lady, Shantou, Muhtarram, Romanette. Broodmare sire of Suave Dancer, Dr Devious (Ire), Dream Well (Fr), Go and Go (Ire), Sulamani.

ALLEZ FRANCE, 1970-1989, B. f., *Sea-Bird—Priceless Gem, by Hail to Reason. 21-13-3-1, $1,262,801, Horse of the Year in France in 1974, champion two- and three-year-old filly, champion older mare twice, Prix de l'Arc de Triomphe (Fr-G1), etc. Dam of Action Francaise. Considered greatest filly ever trained in France.

ALMAHMOUD, 1947-1971. Ch. f., *Mahmoud—Arbitrator, by Peace Chance. 11-4-0-1, $32,760, Vineland H., etc. Dam of Cosmah, Natalma. Foundation mare of family that includes Northern Dancer, Halo, Danehill, Tosmah, Flawlessly, Arctic Tern, Machiavellian, Coup de Genie, L'Emigrant, Cannonade, La Prevoyante.

ALSAB, 1939-1963. B. c., Good Goods—Winds Chant, by Wildair. 51-25-11-5, $350,015, champion two- and three-year-old colt, Preakness S., American Derby, etc. Sire of 17 stakes winners, including Myrtle Charm, Armageddon, Sabette. Defeated Triple Crown winner Whirlaway in match race. Tail-male ancestor of line that leads to Broad Brush.

ALYDAR, 1975-1990. Ch. c., Raise a Native—Sweet Tooth, by On-and-On. 26-14-9-1, $957,195, Travers S. (G1), Florida Derby (G1), etc. Leading sire in 1990. Sire of 77 stakes winners, including Alysheba, Easy Goer, Criminal Type, Turkoman, Althea, Alydaress, Strike the Gold, Miss Oceana, Endear, Peinture Bleue, Winglet. Broodmare sire of Ajina, Amilynx, Anees, Cat Thief, General Meeting, Lakeway, Lure, Peintre Celebre.

ALYSHEBA, 1984- . B. c., Alydar—Bel Sheba, by Lt. Stevens. 26-11-8-2, $6,679,242, Horse of the Year in 1988, champion three-year-old male, champion older male, Kentucky Derby (G1), Preakness S. (G1), Breeders' Cup Classic (G1), etc. Sire of more than 15 stakes winners, including Alywow, Bright Moon, Moonlight Dance.

AMERICAN ECLIPSE, 1814-1847. Ch. c., Duroc—Millers Damsel, by *Messenger. 8-8-0-0, $56,700, North-South Match Race with (Sir) Henry. Sire of Black Maria, Ariel, Medoc, Fanny, Lance. First great American champion.

AMERICAN FLAG, 1922-1942. Ch. c., Man o' War—*Lady Comfey, by Roi Herode. 17-8-1-1, $82,725, champion three-year-old colt, Belmont S., Withers S., etc. Sire of stakes winners Nellie Flag, Gusto. Broodmare sire of Raise You, Mar-Kell.

ANCIENT TITLE, 1970-1981. Dk. b. or br. g., Gummo—Hi Little Gal, by Bar Le Duc. 57-24-11-9, $1,252,791, Hollywood Gold Cup Invitational H. (G1), Charles H. Strub S. (G1), etc. Won 20 stakes; leading California-bred money earner at the time of his death.

ANITA PEABODY, 1925-1934. B. or br. f., Luke McLuke—*La Dauphine, by The Tetrarch. 8-7-0-1, $113,105, champion two-year-old filly, Futurity S., Debutante S., etc. Dam of Our Count.

A.P. INDY, 1989- . Dk. b. or br. c., Seattle Slew—Weekend Surprise, by Secretariat. 11-8-0-1, $2,979,815, Horse of the Year in 1992, champion three-year-old male, Belmont S. (G1), Breeders' Cup Classic (G1), etc. Sire of at least 50 stakes winners, including Tempera, Golden Missile, Aptitude, Lu Ravi, Secret Status, A P Valentine, Old Trieste.

ARAZI, 1989- . Ch. c., Blushing Groom (Fr)—Danseur Fabuleux, by Northern Dancer. 14-9-1-1, $1,212,351, champion two-year-old male, Horse of the Year in Europe, Breeders' Cup Juvenile (G1), Grand Criterium (Fr-G1), etc. Sire of at least 15 stakes winners, including Congaree, First Magnitude (Ire), America (Ire).

ARIEL, 1822-1843. Gr. f., American Eclipse—Young Empress, by Financier. 57-42-14-1, about $25,000. Ran four-mile heats 28 times, winning 18. Dam of three foals, no winners.

ARISTIDES, 1872-1893. Ch. c., *Leamington—Sarong, by Lexington. 21-9-5-1, $18,325, Kentucky Derby, Withers S., Jerome S., etc. First winner of Kentucky Derby in 1875.

ARMED, 1941-1964. Br. g., Bull Lea—Armful, by Chance Shot. 81-41-20-10, $817,475, Horse of the Year in 1947, champion handicap horse twice, Suburban H., Widener H. twice, Gulfstream Park H., etc.

ARTFUL, 1902-1927. B. f., Hamburg—Martha II, by Dandie Dinmont. 8-6-2-0, $81,125, Futurity S., Brighton H., etc. Tail-female ancestor of family that includes Education, Runaway Groom.

ARTS AND LETTERS, 1966-1998. Ch. c., *Ribot—All Beautiful, by Battlefield. 23-11-6-1, $632,404, Horse of the Year in 1969, champion three-year-old colt, champion handicap horse, Belmont S., Jockey Club Gold Cup, etc. Sire of 30 stakes winners, including Codex, Winter's Tale, Illiterate.

ASSAULT, 1943-1971. Ch. c., Bold Venture—Igual, by Equipoise. 42-18-6-7, $675,470, Horse of the Year in 1946, champion three-year-old colt, Triple Crown, Suburban H., Brooklyn H. twice, etc. Sterile at stud.

ASTEROID, 1861-1886. B. c., Lexington—Nebula, by *Glencoe. 12-12-0-0, $12,800, Woodlawn Vase, etc. One of three sons of Lexington, along with Kentucky and Norfolk, to be considered the best racehorses of the 1860s, called the "great triumvirate." Sire of Creedmoor, Ballankeel.

*AUSTRALIAN, 1858-1879. Ch. c. West Australian—*Emilia, by Young Emilius. 10-3-3-3, $12,150, Doswell S., Galt House S. Sire of Spendthrift, Wildidle, Baden Baden, Fellowcraft, Joe Daniels, Springbok. American founder of male line that includes Man o' War, War Admiral, In Reality, Tiznow.

AZERI, 1998- . Ch. f., Jade Hunter—Zodiac Miss (Aus) by Ahonoora. 12-11-1-0, $2,527,740, Horse of the Year in 2002, champion older female, Breeders' Cup Distaff (G1), Apple Blossom H. (G1) twice, etc.

BALD EAGLE, 1955-1977. B. c., *Nasrullah—Siama, by Tiger. 29-12-5-4, $692,946, champion older horse, Metropolitan H., Suburban H., etc. Sire of 12 stakes winners, including Too Bald, San San. Broodmare sire of 33 stakes winners, including Exceller, Capote.

BALLOT, 1904-1937. Ch. c., *Voter—*Cerito, by Lowland Chief. 38-20-6-6, $154,545, Suburban H., etc. Sire of Midway, Chilhowee, Star Voter. Broodmare sire of Bull Lea.

BATTLEFIELD, 1948-1964. Ch. c., War Relic—Dark Display, by Display. 44-22-14-2, $474,727, champion two-year-old colt, Futurity S., Hopeful S., Travers S., etc. Sire of Yorktown. Broodmare sire of Arts and Letters, Steeple Jill.

BATTLESHIP, 1927-1958. Ch. c., Man o' War—*Quarantaine, by Sea Sick. 55-24-6-4, $71,641, Grand National Steeplechase in England and U.S., etc. Sire of Shipboard, War Battle.

BAYAKOA (Arg), 1984-1997. B. f., Consultant's Bid—Arlucea (Arg), by Good Manners. 39-21-9-0, $2,861,701, champion older female twice, Breeders' Cup Distaff (G1) twice, Spinster S. (G1) twice, etc.

BED O' ROSES, 1947-1953. B. f., Rosemont—Good Thing, by Discovery. 46-18-8-6, $383,925, champion two-year-old filly, champion handicap mare, Santa Margarita H., Matron S., etc.

BELDAME, 1901-1923. Ch. f., Octagon—*Bella Donna, by Hermit. 31-17-6-4, $102,135, Suburban H., Alabama S., Ladies H., etc. Dam of Belvale. Tail-female ancestor of family that includes Revoked, Insouciant.

BEN ALI, 1883-unknown. Br. c., Virgil—Ulrica, by Lexington. 40-12-3-5, $25,090, Kentucky Derby, Hopeful S., etc.

BEN BRUSH, 1893-1918. B. c., Bramble—Roseville, by Reform. 40-25-5-5, $65,208, Kentucky Derby, Suburban H., etc. Leading sire in 1909. Sire of Broomstick, Sweep, Delhi, Meridian, Pebbles, Theo Cook, Von Tromp.

BEND OR, 1877-1903. Ch. c., Doncaster—Rouge Rose, by Thormanby. 14-10-2-0, $90,304, Epsom Derby, Champion S., etc. Sire of *Ormonde, Bona Vista, Kendal, Orvieto. Tail-male ancestor of Phalaris, *Teddy lines.

BEST PAL, 1988-1998. B. g., *Habitony—Ubetshedid, by King Pellinore. 47-18-11-4, $5,668,245, Santa Anita H. (G1), Hollywood Gold Cup H. (G1), etc. Leading California-bred money earner at retirement.

BEWITCH, 1945-1959. Br. f., Bull Lea—Potheen, by Wildair. 55-20-10-11, $462,605, champion two-year-old filly, champion handicap mare, Arlington Lassie S., Vanity H., etc. Defeated stablemate Citation in 1947 Washington Park Futurity.

BIMELECH, 1937-1966. B. c., Black Toney—*La Troienne, by *Teddy. 15-11-2-1, $248,745, champion two- and three-year-old colt, Preakness S., Belmont S., etc. Sire of 30 stakes winners, including Better Self, Be Faithful, Guillotine, Hilarious, Brookfield. Full brother to Black Helen.

BIRDCATCHER, 1833-1860. Ch. c., Sir Hercules—Guiccioli, by Bob Booty. 18-6-4-4, $6,666 in Ireland, Madrid Plate, Peel Cup, etc. Sire of *Alfred, Bird on the Wing, Chanticleer, Daniel O'Rourke, Kingfisher. Tail-male ancestor of Phalaris, *Teddy, Blandford male lines. Famous for passing on dark spots in his chestnut coat, known as "Birdcatcher spots."

BLACK GOLD, 1921-1928. Bl. c., Black Toney—Useeit, by Bonnie Joe. 35-18-5-4, $110,553, champion three-year-old colt, Kentucky Derby, Ohio Derby, etc. Broke down fatally at seven and buried in the infield at Fair Grounds.

BLACK HELEN, 1932-1957. B. f., Black Toney—*La Troienne, by *Teddy. 22-15-0-2, $61,800, champion three-year-old filly, Coaching Club American Oaks, Florida Derby, etc. Tail-female ancestor of family that includes Pleasant Tap, Go for Gin, But Why Not, Princess Rooney. Full sister to Bimelech.

BLACK MARIA, 1826-unknown. Bl. f., American Eclipse—Lady Lightfoot, by Sir Archy. 26-13-(placings unknown), $14,900, Jockey Club Purse, etc. Ran 17 times in four-mile heats. Won a five-heat, four-mile heat race that caused death of one opponent from exhaustion.

BLACK MARIA, 1923-1932. Bl. f., Black Toney—*Bird Loose, by Sardanapale. 52-18-14-6, $110,350, champion three-year-old filly, champion older mare twice, Kentucky Oaks, Metropolitan H., Ladies H. twice, etc. Tail-female ancestor of family that includes Polynesian, Air Forbes Won.

BLACK TIE AFFAIR (Ire), 1986- . Gr. or ro. c., Miswaki—Hat Tab Girl, by Al Hattab. 45-18-9-6, $3,370,694, Horse of the Year in 1991, champion older male, Breeders' Cup Classic (G1), Philip H. Iselin H. (G1), etc. Sire of more than 30 stakes winners, including Formal Gold, Evening Attire. Exported from the United States to Japan in 1997.

BLACK TONEY, 1911-1938. Br. c., Peter Pan—Belgravia, by Ben Brush. 37-12-10-7, $12,815, Independence H., Valuation S., etc. Sire of 34 stakes winners, including Balladier, Big Hurry, Bimelech, Black Gold, Black Helen, Black Maria, Black Servant, Brokers Tip, Miss Jemima. Broodmare sire of more than 25 stakes winners, including Bridal Flower, Elkridge, Relic, Searching. Foundation sire of Col. E. R. Bradley's Idle Hour Farm.

BLANDFORD, 1919-1935. Br. c., Swynford—Blanche, by White Eagle. 4-3-1-0, $16,041, Princess of Wales's S., etc. Leading sire three times in England. Sire of *Blenheim II, *Bahram, Brantome, Windsor Lad, Campanula, Trigo, Dalmary, Mistress Ford, Pasch, Udaipur, Umidwar. Tail-male ancestor of line leading to The Axe II, Quadrangle, Crepello, Mtoto.

***BLENHEIM II**, 1927-1958. Br. c., Blandford—Malva, by Charles O'Malley. 10-5-3-0, $73,060, Epsom Derby, etc. Leading sire in 1941. Sire of 47 stakes winners, including Whirlaway, *Mahmoud, Donatello II, Mar-Kell, Fervent, A Gleam, Jet Pilot. Broodmare sire of A Glitter, Coaltown, Hill Gail, Kauai King, Le Paillon, *Nasrullah, Wistful. Tail-male ancestor of line leading to The Axe II, Quadrangle, Crepello, Mtoto.

BLUE LARKSPUR, 1926-1947. B. c., Black Servant—Blossom Time, by *North Star III. 16-10-3-1, $272,070, Horse of the Year in 1929, champion three-year-old colt, champion handicap horse, Belmont S., Classic S., etc. Sire of 44 stakes winners, including But Why Not, Myrtlewood, Painted Veil, Blue Swords, Alablue, Revoked, Blue Delight, Bee Ann Mac. Broodmare sire of Alanesian, Be Faithful, Busanda, By Jimminy, Cohoes, Durazna, Real Delight, Twilight Tear.

BLUSHING GROOM (Fr), 1974-1992. Ch. c., Red God—Runaway Bride (GB), by Wild Risk. 10-7-1-2, $407,153, champion two-year-old in France, champion miler in France, Grand Criterium (Fr-G1), Poule d'Essai des Poulains (French Two Thousand Guineas) (Fr-G1), etc. Leading sire in England in 1989. Sire of 92 stakes winners, including Nashwan, Rainbow Quest, Arazi, Sky Beauty, Rahy, Blushing John, Runaway Groom, Al Bahathri, Blush With Pride, Mt. Livermore. Broodmare sire of Awesome Again, Flute, Kahyasi, Lammtarra, Macho Uno, Stravinsky, T.M. Opera O.

BOLD FORBES, 1973-2000. Dk. b. or br. c., Irish Castle—Comely Nell, by Commodore M. 18-13-1-4, $546,536, champion three-year-old male, champion two-year-old in Puerto Rico, Kentucky Derby (G1), Belmont S. (G1), etc. Sire of 29 stakes winners, including Tiffany Lass, Air Forbes Won.

BOLD LAD, 1962-1986. Ch. c., Bold Ruler—Misty Morn, by *Princequillo. 19-14-2-1, $516,465, champion two-year-old, Metropolitan H., Futurity S., Hopeful S., etc. Sire of 28 stakes winners, including Sirlad (Ire), Bold Fascinator, Gentle Thoughts, Rube the Great.

BOLD 'N DETERMINED, 1977-1997. B. f., Bold and Brave—Pidi, by Determine. 20-16-2-0, $949,599. Winner of six Grade 1 races at three in 1980, including the Coaching Club American Oaks and the Kentucky Oaks, she had the misfortune of being in the same crop as Kentucky Derby (G1) winner and champion three-year-old filly Genuine Risk. Owned by Corbin Robertson's Saron Stable and trained by Neil Drysdale, she defeated Genuine Risk in the 1980 Maskette Stakes (G2).

BOLD RULER, 1954-1971. Dk. b. or br. c., *Nasrullah—Miss Disco, by Discovery. 33-23-4-2, $764,204,

Horse of the Year in 1957, champion three-year-old colt, champion sprinter, Preakness S., Futurity S., Suburban H., etc. Leading sire eight times, seven in succession (1963-'69). Sire of 82 stakes winners, including Secretariat, Gamely, Lamb Chop, Bold Lad (out of Misty Morn), Bold Lad (out of *Barn Pride), Bold Bidder, Wajima, Queen Empress, Queen of the Stage, Boldnesian, Chieftain, Dewan, Reviewer. Broodmare sire of Autobiography, Christmas Past, Private Terms, Sensational. Tail-male ancestor of Seattle Slew line.

BOLD VENTURE, 1933-1958. Ch. c., *St. Germans—Possible, by Ultimus. 11-6-2-0, $68,300, champion three-year-old colt, Kentucky Derby, Preakness S. Sire of 12 stakes winners, including Assault, Middleground. Broodmare sire of Miss Cavandish, Prove Out.

BONNOUVEL, 1960-unknown. B. g., Duc de Fer—Good News, by *Happy Argo. 51-16-11-7, $176,148, champion steeplechaser three times, Temple Gwathmey Stp. H., Brook Stp. H. twice, etc.

BORROW, 1908-unknown. Ch. g., Hamburg—Forget, by Exile. 91-24-20-12. $87,275, Middle Park Plate (in England), Brooklyn H., etc. Defeated three Kentucky Derby winners in 1917 Brooklyn H.

BOSTON, 1833-1850. Ch. c., Timoleon—Sister to Tuckahoe, by Ball's Florizel. 45-40-2-1, $51,700, champion of his era. Leading sire three times. Sire of Lexington, Lecomte, Commodore, Madeline, Nina, Ringgold, Red Eye. Won 70 of 81 heats, 47 at 4 miles. Lost famous match race with Fashion.

BOURTAI, 1942-1970. B. f., Stimulus—Escutcheon, by *Sir Gallahad III. 12-2-1-2, $3,850, 3rd Pimlico Nursery S. Dam of Bayou, Levee, Delta, Banta, Ambassador. Tail-female ancestor of Aptitude, Big Spruce, Coastal, Dike, Sacahuista, Shuvee, Sleepytime, Slew o' Gold, Talking Picture.

BOWL OF FLOWERS, 1958-unknown. Ch. f., Sailor—Flower Bowl, by *Alibhai. 16-10-3-3, $398,504, champion two- and three-year-old filly, Coaching Club American Oaks, Spinster S., etc. Dam of sires Whiskey Road, Big Burn.

BROAD BRUSH, 1983- . B. c., Ack Ack—Hay Patcher, by Hoist the Flag. 27-14-5-5, $2,656,793, Santa Anita H. (G1), Suburban H. (G1), etc. Leading sire in 1994. Sire of more than 80 stakes winners, including Farma Amiga, Concern, Include, Broad Appeal, Pompeii.

BROOMSTICK, 1901-1931. B. c., Ben Brush—*Elf, by Galliard. 39-14-11-5, $74,730, Travers S., Brighton H., etc. Leading sire 1913-'15; leading broodmare sire 1932-'33. Sire of 69 stakes winners, including Regret, Whisk Broom II, Bostonian, Broomspun, Cudgel, Halcyon, Sweeper, Traffic, Transmute, Wildair, Escoba, Flying Witch, Remembrance, Rowes Bud. Broodmare sire of Equipoise, Mother Goose, Whichone.

BROWN BESS, 1982- . Dk. b. or br. f., *Petrone—Chickadee, by Windy Sands. 36-16-8-6, $1,300,920, champion grass female, Santa Barbara H. (G1), Ramona H. (G1), Yellow Ribbon Inv. S. (G1), etc.

BUCKPASSER, 1963-1978. B. c., Tom Fool—Busanda, by War Admiral. 31-25-4-1, $1,462,014, Horse of the Year in 1966, champion two- and three-year-old colt, champion handicap horse twice, Jockey Club Gold Cup, Metropolitan H., etc. Leading broodmare sire 1983-'84, '88-'89. Sire of 35 stakes winners, including Numbered Account, Relaxing, La Prevoyante, L'Enjoleur, Norcliffe, State Dinner, Silver Buck, Buckaroo, Quick as Lightning, Lassie Dear, Passing Mood. Broodmare sire of Slew o' Gold, Seeking the Gold, Coastal, Woodman, Private Account, Easy Goer, El Gran Senor, Miswaki, Touch Gold.

*BULL DOG, 1927-1954. Dk. b. or br. c., *Teddy—Plucky Liege, by Spearmint. 8-2-1-0, $7,802 Prix Daphnis, etc. Leading sire in 1943; leading broodmare sire in 1953, '54, '56. Sire of 52 stakes winners, including Bull Lea, Occupy, Our Boots, Occupation, Johns Joy, The Doge, Canina, Miss Dogwood, Miss Mommy, Tiger. Broodmare sire of Tom Fool, Decathlon, Dark Star, Rough'n Tumble. Full brother to *Sir Gallahad III; half brother to Bois Roussel, Admiral Drake.

*BULLE ROCK, 1709-unknown. B. c., Darley Arabian—Byerley Turk mare, by Byerley Turk. Earliest Thoroughbred recorded as imported (in 1730) in the United States in the *American Stud Book*. No horse matching his description and pedigree appears in the *General Stud Book*, but he is generally accepted as America's first Thoroughbred.

BULL LEA, 1935-1964. Br. c., *Bull Dog—Rose Leaves, by Ballot. 27-10-7-3, $94,825, Widener H., Blue Grass S., etc. Leading sire in 1947, '48, '49, '52, '53; leading broodmare sire 1958-'61. Sire of 58 stakes winners, ten champions, including Citation, Coaltown, Hill Gail, Two Lea, Twilight Tear, Bewitch, Real Delight, Iron Liege, Armed, Durazna, Next Move. Broodmare sire of Barbizon, Bramalea, Gate Dancer, Idun, Leallah, Pucker Up, Quadrangle, Tim Tam.

BUSHER, 1942-1955. Ch. f., War Admiral—Baby League, by Bubbling Over. 21-15-3-1, $334,035, Horse of the Year in 1945, champion two- and three-year-old filly, champion handicap mare, Hollywood Derby, Santa Margarita H., etc. Dam of Jet Action. Tail-female ancestor of family that includes Beau's Eagle, Play On.

BUSHRANGER, 1930-1937. Ch. g., *Stefan the Great—War Path, by Man o' War. 21-11-3-1, $20,635, champion steeplechaser, Grand National Stp. H., Broad Hollow Stp. H. twice, etc.

BYERLEY TURK, ca. 1680. Bl. c. of unknown parentage. Sire of Jigg, Basto, Black Hearty. One of three Thoroughbred male-line foundation sires. Tail-male ancestor of the Herod line leading to *Ambiorix, The Tetrarch, Dr Devious (Ire), Indian Ridge.

CAFE PRINCE, 1970-unknown. B. g., Creme dela Creme—Princess Blair, by Blue Prince. 52-18-5-4, $228,238, champion steeplechaser twice, Colonial Cup International Stp. twice, etc.

CANONERO II, 1968-1981. B. c., *Pretendre—Dixieland II, by Nantallah. 23-9-3-4, $360,933, champion three-year-old male, Kentucky Derby, Preakness S.-ntr, etc. Sire of five stakes winners, including Cannon Boy. First foreign-trained horse to win Kentucky Derby.

CAPOT, 1946-1974. Br. c., Menow—Piquet, by *St. Germans. 28-12-4-7, $347,260, Horse of the Year in 1949, champion three-year-old colt, Preakness S., Belmont S., etc. Sired 13 foals, no stakes winners.

CARBINE, 1885-1913. B. c., Musket—Mersey, by Knowsley. 43-33-6-3, $143,982, Melbourne Cup twice, Sydney Cup twice, etc. Sire of Amberite, *Bomba, Fowling-Piece, Greatorex, Miss Gunning, Ramrod, Spearmint, Wallace. Won 1890 Melbourne Cup under 145 pounds. Still widely considered best New Zealand-bred of all time.

CARRY BACK, 1958-1983. Br. c., Saggy—Joppy, by Star Blen. 62-21-11-11, $1,241,165, champion three-year-old colt, Kentucky Derby, Preakness S., etc. Sire of ten stakes winners, including Taken Aback, Sharp Gary, Back in Paris.

CAVALCADE, 1931-1940. Br. c., *Lancegaye—*Hastily, by Hurry On. 22-8-5-3, $127,165, Horse of the Year in 1934, champion two- and three-year-old colt, Kentucky Derby, American Derby, etc. Sire of three stakes winners.

CHALLEDON, 1936-1958. B. c., *Challenger II—Laura Gal, by *Sir Gallahad III. 44-20-7-6, $334,660, Horse of the Year in 1939 and '40, champion three-year-old colt, champion handicap horse, Preakness S., Whitney S., etc. Sire of 13 stakes winners, including Ancestor, Tenacious, Donor.

CHARISMATIC, 1996- . Ch. c., Summer Squall—Bali Babe, by Drone. 17-5-2-4, $2,038,064, Horse of the Year in 1999, champion three-year-old male, Kentucky Derby (G1), Preakness S. (G2), etc. Exported to Japan in 2002.

CHIEF'S CROWN, 1982-1997. B. c., Danzig—Six Crowns, by Secretariat. 21-12-3-3, $2,191,168, champion two-year-old male, Breeders' Cup Juvenile (G1), Travers S. (G1), etc. Sire of more than 50 stakes winners, including Erhaab, Grand Lodge, Chief Bearhart, Concerto, Chief Honcho.

CHRIS EVERT, 1971-2001. Ch. f., Swoon's Son—Miss Carmie, by T. V. Lark. 15-10-2-2, $679,475, champion three-year-old filly, filly triple crown, Coaching Club American Oaks (G1), Hollywood Special S. (match race with Miss Musket), etc. Dam of Six Crowns, Wimbledon Star. Second dam of Chief's Crown.

CICADA, 1959-1981. B. f., Bryan G.—Satsuma, by Bossuet. 42-23-8-6, $783,674, champion two- and three-year-old filly, champion older mare, Kentucky Oaks, Beldame S., etc. Dam of Cicada's Pride. Retired as world's leading money-winning female.

CIGAR, 1990- . B. c., Palace Music—Solar Slew, by Seattle Slew. 33-19-4-5, $9,999,815, Horse of the Year in 1995 and '96, champion older male twice, Breeders' Cup Classic (G1), Dubai World Cup, etc. Leading earner of all-time in North America. Sterile at stud. Resides at Kentucky Horse Park.

CITATION, 1945-1970. B. c., Bull Lea—*Hydroplane II, by Hyperion. 45-32-10-2, $1,085,760, Horse of the Year in 1948, champion two- and three-year-old colt, champion handicap horse, Triple Crown, Jockey Club Gold Cup, Hollywood Gold Cup, etc. First $1-million earner. Sire of 12 stakes winners, including Silver Spoon, Fabius.

CLEOPATRA, 1917-unknown. Ch. f., Corcyra—*Gallice, by Gallinule. 26-8-10-4, $55,937, champion three-year-old filly, Coaching Club American Oaks, Alabama S., etc. Dam of Pompey, Laughing Queen; third dam of Tom Fool. Tail-female ancestor of family that includes Ambiopoise, Dust Commander.

CLIFFORD, 1890-1917. B. c., Bramble—Duchess, by Kingfisher. 63-42-14-5, $59,757 Second Special S., Flight S. twice, Phoenix S., etc. Defeated three Racing Hall of Fame members. Regarded as one of the worst gate horses ever, a trait that cost him several races he should have won.

COALTOWN, 1945-1965. B. c., Bull Lea—Easy Lass, by *Blenheim II. 39-23-6-3, $415,675, Horse of the Year in 1949, champion sprinter, champion handicap horse, Jerome H., Blue Grass S., etc. Never sired a stakes winner. Exported to France in 1955.

COLIN, 1905-1932. Br. c., Commando—*Pastorella, by Springfield. 15-15-0-0, $178,110, champion two- and three-year-old colt, Belmont S., Futurity S., etc. Sire of Jock, Neddie, On Watch. Shy breeder. Tail-male ancestor of line that leads to Broad Brush.

COMMANDO, 1898-1905. B. c., Domino—Emma C., by *Darebin. 9-7-2-0, $58,196, champion two- and three-year-old colt, Belmont S., Junior Champion S., etc. Leading sire in 1907. Sire of ten stakes winners from 27 foals, including Colin, Peter Pan, Celt, Hippodrome, Superman, Transvaal, and of Ultimus.

CONQUISTADOR CIELO, 1979-2002. B. c., Mr. Prospector—K D Princess, by Bold Commander. 13-9-0-2, $474,328, Horse of the Year in 1982, champion three-year-old male, Belmont S. (G1), Metropolitan H. (G1), etc. Sire of more than 85 stakes winners, including Marquetry, Forty Niner Days, Wagon Limit. Broodmare sire of more than 70 stakes winners, including Apelia, Dixie Dot Com, Thornfield.

CORRECTION, 1888-unknown. B. f., Himyar—Mannie Gray, by Enquirer. 122-38-35-22, $45,600, Toboggan Slide H., etc. Dam of Yankee, Miss Malaprop, Nature. Tail-female ancestor of family that includes Affirmed, Royal Native, Haste. Full sister to Domino.

COSMAH, 1953-1979. B. f., Cosmic Bomb—Almahmoud, by *Mahmoud. 30-9-5-2, $86,525, Astarita S., etc. Broodmare of the Year in 1974. Dam of Tosmah, Halo, Fathers Image, Maribeau. Foundation mare of family that includes Flawlessly, L'Emigrant, Cannonade, Stephan's Odyssey.

*COUGAR II, 1966-1989. Dk b. or br. c., Tale of Two Cities—*Cindy Lou II, by Madara. 50-20-7-17, $1,172,625, champion grass horse, Santa Anita H. (G1), Sunset H. (G1), etc. Sire of 24 stakes winners, including Gato Del Sol, Exploded.

COUNTERPOINT, 1948-1970. Ch. c., Count Fleet—Jabot, by *Sickle. 21-10-3-1, $284,575, Horse of the Year in 1951, champion three-year-old colt, Belmont S., Jockey Club Gold Cup, etc. Sire of 11 stakes winners, including Dotted Swiss, Harmonizing, Honey Dear, Snow White.

COUNT FLEET, 1940-1973. Br. c., Reigh Count—Quickly, by Haste. 21-16-4-1, $250,300, Horse of the Year in 1943, champion two- and three-year-old colt, Triple Crown, Champagne S., Withers S., etc. Leading sire in 1951; leading broodmare sire in 1963. Sire of 39 stakes winners, including Counterpoint, One Count, Kiss Me Kate, Count Turf, Straight Face, Count of Honor, Countess Fleet, County Delight, Juliets Nurse. Broodmare sire of Kelso, Prince John, Quill, Fleet Nasrullah, Gallant Romeo, Lamb Chop.

CREME FRAICHE, 1982- . B. g., Rich Cream—Likely Exchange, by Terrible Tiger. 64-17-12-13, $4,024,727, Belmont S. (G1), Jockey Club Gold Cup (G1) twice, Super Derby (G1), etc.

CRIMINAL TYPE, 1985- . Ch. c., Alydar—Klepto, by No Robbery. 24-10-5-3, $2,351,274, Horse of the Year in 1990, champion older male, Hollywood Gold Cup (G1), Pimlico Special H. (G1), Metropolitan H. (G1), etc. Sire of seven stakes winners, including Hoolie. Exported to Japan in 1992.

CRIMSON SATAN, 1959-1982. Ch. c., Spy Song—*Papila, by Requiebro. 58-18-9-9, $796,077, champion two-year-old colt, Garden State S., Charles H. Strub S., etc. Sire of 33 stakes winners, including Crimson Saint, Krislin, Whitesburg.

CRUSADER, 1923-1940. Ch. c., Man o' War—Star Fancy, by *Star Shoot. 42-18-8-4, $203,261, Horse of the Year in 1926, champion three-year-old colt, Belmont S., Jockey Club Gold Cup, Suburban H. twice, etc. Sire of six stakes winners, including *Crossbow II.

DAHLIA, 1970-2001. Ch. f., *Vaguely Noble—Charming Alibi, by Honeys Alibi. 48-15-3-7, $1,489,105, Horse

of the Year in England in 1974 and '75, champion three-year-old in Ireland, champion three-year-old in England, champion grass horse in U.S., champion older mare twice in England, King George VI and Queen Elizabeth S. (Eng-G1) twice, Washington, D. C., International (G1), etc. Dam of Dahar, Rivlia, Delegant, Dahlia's Dreamer, Wajd, Llandaff. First distaff millionaire.

DAMASCUS, 1964-1995. B. c., Sword Dancer—Kerala, by *My Babu. 32-21-7-3, $1,176,781, Horse of the Year in 1967, champion three-year-old colt, champion handicap horse, Preakness S., Belmont S., Jockey Club Gold Cup S., etc. Sire of 71 stakes winners, including Private Account, Desert Wine, Highland Blade, Ogygian, Honorable Miss, Time for a Change, Judger, Bailjumper, Timeless Moment, Cutlass. Broodmare sire of 153 stakes winners, including Boundary, Chilukki, Coronado's Quest, Shadeed.

DANCE SMARTLY, 1988- . Dk. b. or br. f., Danzig—Classy 'n Smart, by Smarten. 17-12-2-3, $3,263,835, champion three-year-old filly in U.S., Canadian Horse of the Year, champion two- and three-year-old filly in Canada, Canadian Triple Crown, Breeders' Cup Distaff (G1), Queen's Plate S., etc. Dam of Queen's Plate winners Scatter the Gold, Dancethruthedawn.

DANEHILL, 1986-2003. B. c., Danzig—Razyana, by His Majesty. 9-4-1-2, $321,064, Ladbroke Sprint S. (Eng-G1), etc. Brother to Eagle Eyed, Harpia, Shibboleth, half brother to Euphonic. Leading sire in Australia six times, leading sire in France twice, leading sire in U.S. Sire of more than 215 stakes winners, including Rock of Gibraltar (Ire), Flying Spur, Danewin, Fairy King Prawn, Dane Ripper, Banks Hill (GB).

DANZIG, 1977- . B. c., Northern Dancer—Pas de Nom, by Admiral's Voyage. 3-3-0-0, $32,400. Leading sire 1991-'93. Sire of at least 179 stakes winners, including Chief's Crown, Polish Precedent, Dayjur, Danehill, Dance Smartly, Langfuhr, Anabaa, Green Desert, Pine Bluff. Broodmare sire of Caller One, Dancethruthedawn, Fusaichi Pegasus.

DARK MIRAGE, 1965-1969. Dk. b. or br. f., *Persian Road II—Home by Dark, by Hill Prince. 27-12-3-2, $362,788, champion three-year-old filly, first winner of the filly triple crown in New York, Kentucky Oaks, Delaware Oaks, etc. Won nine consecutive stakes and broke down trying for tenth. Died at four.

DARK STAR, 1950-1972. Br. c., *Royal Gem II—Isolde, by *Bull Dog. 13-6-2-2, $131,337, Kentucky Derby, Derby Trial, etc. Only horse to defeat Native Dancer. Sire of 26 stakes winners, including *Gazala II, My Dad George, Hidden Treasure.

DARLEY ARABIAN, 1700. B. c. of unknown parentage. Sire of Flying Childers, Aleppo, Almanzor, Bartlett's Childers. One of three male-line foundation sires of the Thoroughbred breed. Tail-male ancestor of the Eclipse male line leading to Phalaris, Blandford, Hyperion, *Teddy lines.

DAVONA DALE, 1976- . B. f., Best Turn—Royal Entrance, by Tim Tam. 18-11-2-1, $641,612, champion three-year-old filly, filly triple crown, Kentucky Oaks (G1), etc.

DECATHLON, 1953-1972. B. c., Olympia—Dog Blessed, by *Bull Dog. 42-25-8-1, $269,530, champion sprinter twice, Oceanport H. twice, Hutcheson S., etc. Sire of 12 stakes winners, including Juanita.

*DELANCEY'S CUB MARE, 1762. F., Cub—Second mare (dam of Amaranthus), by Second. One of the first great imported American foundation mares. Dam of (Maria) Slamerkin. Tail-female ancestor of family that includes Nearco, Neckar, Golden Trail, Parole,

Imp, Black Gold, Mad Hatter, Sun Beau, Flirtilla, Sumpter, Artful, Delhi, Falsetto, Halma.

DEPUTY MINISTER, 1979- . Dk. b. or br. c., Vice Regent—Mint Copy, by Bunty's Flight. 22-12-2-2, $696,964, champion two-year-old male in U.S., Horse of the Year in Canada in 1981, champion two-year-old male in Canada, Laurel Futurity (G1), Donn H. (G2), etc. Leading sire in 1997 and '98. Sire of more than 70 stakes winners, including Go for Wand, Open Mind, Awesome Again, Dehere, Touch Gold, Deputy Commander, Keeper Hill, Victory Speech, Clear Mandate, Salt Lake, French Deputy.

DESERT VIXEN, 1970-1982. Dk. b. or br. f., In Reality—Desert Trial, by Moslem Chief. 28-13-6-3, $421,538, champion three-year-old filly, champion older female, Alabama S. (G1), Beldame S. (G1) twice, etc. Dam of Real Shadai; full sister to Valid Appeal.

DETERMINE, 1951-1972. Gr. c., *Alibhai—Koubis, by *Mahmoud. 44-18-7-9, $573,360, Kentucky Derby, Santa Anita Derby, etc. First gray winner of the Kentucky Derby. Sire of 21 stakes winners, including Decidedly, Warfare, Donut King. Broodmare sire of Bold 'n Determined, Gummo, Princess Pout.

DEVIL DIVER, 1939-1961. B. c., *St. Germans—Dabchick, by *Royal Minstrel. 47-22-12-3, $261,064, champion handicap horse twice, Metropolitan H. twice, Suburban H., Whitney S., etc. Sire of 17 stakes winners, including Beau Diable, Call Over, Ruddy.

***DIOMED**, 1777-1808. Ch. c., Florizel—Spectator mare (sister to Juno), by Spectator. 20-11-5-3, $38,200, champion three-year-old in England. First winner of the Epsom Derby. Sire of Sir Archy, Haynie's Maria, Ball's Florizel, Duroc, Fanny, Young Giantess, Potomac, Virginius. Imported to U.S. in 1798. Tail-male ancestor of Boston, Lexington.

DISCOVERY, 1931-1958. Ch. c., Display—Ariadne, by *Light Brigade. 63-27-10-10, $195,287, Horse of the Year in 1935, champion handicap horse twice, Whitney S. three times, Brooklyn H. three times, etc. Sire of 25 stakes winners, including Conniver, Miss Disco, Find, Loser Weeper, Traffic Court. Broodmare sire of Bold Ruler, Native Dancer, Intentionally, Hasty Road, Traffic Judge, Bed o' Roses. Famed as a weight carrier.

DISGUISE, 1897-1927. B. c., Domino—*Bonnie Gal, by Galopin. 8-3-0-4, $40,275, Jockey Club S., 3rd Epsom Derby, etc. Sire of Maskette, Court Dress, Harmonicon, Helmet, Miss Puzzle, Wonder, Comely.

DISPLAY, 1923-1944. B. c., Fair Play—*Cicuta, by *Nassovian. 103-23-25-27, $256,326, Preakness S., Hawthorne Gold Cup, etc. Sire of 11 stakes winners, including Discovery, Parade Girl.

DOMINO, 1891-1897. Br. c., Himyar—Mannie Gray, by Enquirer. 25-19-2-1, $193,550, Champion two-year-old, Futurity S., Withers S., etc. Sire of Commando, Cap and Bells, Disguise, Noonday, Running Stream, Pink Domino. Sired only 20 foals in two crops, eight stakes winners, two classic winners.

DR. FAGER, 1964-1976. B. c., Rough'n Tumble—Aspidistra, by Better Self. 22-18-2-1, $1,002,642, Horse of the Year in 1968, champion older horse, champion sprinter twice, champion grass horse, Whitney S., Vosburgh H. twice, etc. Leading sire in 1977. Sire of 35 stakes winners, including Dr. Patches, Dearly Precious, L'Alezane, Dr. Blum, Tree of Knowledge, Lie Low, Lady Love. Broodmare sire of Cure the Blues, Equalize, Fappiano, Quiet American, Sewickley. Won every championship for which he was eligible in 1968.

DUKE OF MAGENTA, 1875-1899. B. c., Lexing-

ton—Magenta, by *Yorkshire. 19-15-3-1, $45,913, Belmont S., Preakness S., Travers S., etc. Sire of Duke, Eric, Ballyhoo. Sent to England with Parole after three-year-old season, but became a roarer and never raced again.

EASY GOER, 1986-1994. Ch. c., Alydar—Relaxing, by Buckpasser. 20-14-5-1, $4,873,770, champion two-year-old male, Belmont S. (G1), Jockey Club Gold Cup (G1), etc. Sire of nine stakes winners, including Will's Way, My Flag, Furlough.

ECLIPSE, 1764-1789. Ch. c., Marske—Spiletta, by Regulus. 18-18-0-0, undefeated champion in England, won 11 King's Plates. Never leading sire but runner-up 11 times. Sire of Pot8O's, King Fergus, Serjeant, Dungannon, Alexander, Joe Andrews, Mercury, Meteor, Saltram, Volunteer. Tail-male line ancestor of more than 95% of modern Thoroughbreds, including Phalaris, Hyperion, Blandford lines.

***ECLIPSE**, 1855-1878. B. c., Orlando—Gaze, by Bay Middleton. 9-4-0-1, $9,015, Newmarket S., Clearwell S. Sire of Alarm, Ruthless, Scathelock. Tail-male line ancestor of Domino, Plaudit, Dr. Fager, Holy Bull, Broad Brush.

EIGHT THIRTY, 1936-1965. Ch. c., Pilate—Dinner Time, by High Time. 27-16-3-5, $155,475, Travers S., Whitney S., Metropolitan H., etc. Sire of 45 stakes winners, including Sailor, Bolero, Royal Coinage, Rare Perfume, Sunday Evening, Make Tracks, Anyoldtime. Broodmare sire of Cornish Prince, Evening Out, Hold Your Peace, Jaipur, Rare Treat.

ELKRIDGE, 1938-1961. B. g., Mate—Best by Test, by Black Toney. 123-31-18-15, $230,680, champion steeplechaser twice, North American Stp. H. four times, Indian River Stp. H. four times, etc.

EMPEROR OF NORFOLK, 1885-1907. B. c., Norfolk—Marian, by Malcolm. 29-21-2-4, $72,400, American Derby, Brooklyn Derby, etc. Sire of Americus (Rey del Carreras), Cruzados. Buried at Santa Anita Park.

ENDURANCE BY RIGHT, 1899-1908. B. f., Inspector B.—*Early Morn, by Silvester. 18-16-0-2, $27,645, champion two-year-old filly, Champagne S., Clipsetta S., etc. Dam of Stamina. Tail-female ancestor of family that includes Plucky Play, Windjammer, Racing Room, Porter's Cap.

ENQUIRER, 1867-1895. B. c., *Leamington—Lida, by Lexington. 11-7-0-0, $17,550, champion three-year-old, Kenner S., Phoenix S., etc. Sire of Falsetto, Inspector B., Blue Eyes, Mannie Gray.

***EPINARD**, 1920-unknown. Ch. c., Badajoz—Epine Blanche, by *Rock Sand. 20-12-6-0, $46,688, champion two-year-old in France, Grand Criterium, Prix d'Ispahan, etc. Great French champion who ran second in each of three international races in U.S. in 1925. Sire of Rodosto, Marica, Epithet.

EQUIPOISE, 1928-1938. Ch. c., Pennant—Swinging, by Broomstick. 51-29-10-4, $338,610, Horse of the Year in 1932 and '33, champion handicap horse three times, champion two-year-old colt, Metropolitan H. twice, Whitney S., etc. Leading sire in 1942. Sire of nine stakes winners, including Shut Out, Level Best, Bolingbroke, Attention, Swing and Sway. Broodmare sire of Assault, Myrtle Charm.

EXCELLER, 1973-1997. B. c., *Vaguely Noble—Too Bald, by Bald Eagle. 33-15-5-6, $1,674,587, Jockey Club Gold Cup (G1), Grand Prix de Paris (Fr-G1), etc. Sire of 19 stakes winners, including Slew's Exceller, Squan Song.

EXTERMINATOR, 1915-1945. Ch. g., *McGee—Fair Empress, by Jim Gore. 100-50-17-17, $252,996, Kentucky Derby, Saratoga Cup twice, etc. Won record 34 stakes races. Won 19 times carrying 130 pounds or more.

FAIRMOUNT, 1921-unknown. Ch. g., Fair Play—Sunflower, by *Rock Sand. 22-12-5-0, $74,075, Temple Gwathmey Memorial Stp. H. three times, Manley Memorial Stp. H., etc.

FAIR PLAY, 1905-1929. Ch. c., Hastings—*Fairy Gold, by Bend Or. 32-10-11-3, $86,950, Flash S., Coney Island Jockey Club S., etc. Leading sire in 1920, '24, '27; leading broodmare sire in 1931, '34, '38. Sire of Man o' War, Chance Play, Mad Hatter, Display, Chance Shot, Mad Play, Ladkin, Chatterton, Olambala, Stagecraft, Masda, Native Wit, Oval. Broodmare sire of High Quest, Jamestown, Stagehand, Sun Beau. Tail-male ancestor of line of In Reality, Valid Appeal, Tiznow.

FAIRWAY, 1925-1948. B. c., Phalaris—Scapa Flow, by Chaucer. 15-12-1-0, $194,685, champion three-year-old in England, St. Leger S., Champion S. twice, etc. Leading sire in England four times; leading broodmare sire in England in 1946 and '47. Sire of Blue Peter, Fair Copy, Fair Trial, Full Sail, Garden Path, Honeyway, Ribbon, Tide-Way, *Watling Street. Founder of sire line that includes Shergar, Troy, Ela-Mana-Mou, Brigadier Gerard, Lord At War (Arg).

FALLASPEN, 1976-1998. Ch. f., Pretense—Change Water, by Swaps. 20-8-3-0, $198,037, Matron S. (G1), Prioress S., etc. Broodmare of the Year in 1994. Dam of nine stakes winners, including Timber Country, Northern Aspen, Hamas (Ire), Elle Seule, Colorado Dancer (Ire), Fort Wood. Tail-female ancestor of family that includes Dubai Millennium, Charnwood Forest (Ire), Elnadim, Mehthaaf, Occupandiste.

FASHION, 1837-1860. Ch. f., *Trustee—Bonnets o' Blue, by Sir Charles. 36-32-0-0, $41,500, won Match race with Boston, etc. Dam of A la Mode. Greatest of four-mile heat fillies.

FAVORITE TRICK, 1995-. Dk. b. or br. c., Phone Trick—Evil Elaine, by Medieval Man. 16-12-0-1, $1,726,793, Horse of the Year in 1997, champion two-year-old male, Breeders' Cup Juvenile (G1), Hopeful S. (G1), etc. First two-year-old since Secretariat in 1972 to be voted Horse of the Year.

*FEARNOUGHT, 1755-1776. B. c., Regulus—Silvertail, by Heneage's Whitenose. Five wins in England, won three King's Plates. Early American foundation sire. Sire of Symme's Wildair, Fitzhugh's Regulus, Spotswood's Apollo, Eden's Whynot, Gallant, Othello, Harris's Eclipse, Goldfinder.

FERDINAND, 1983-. Ch. c., Nijinsky II—Banja Luka, by Double Jay. 29-8-9-6, $3,777,978, Horse of the Year in 1987, champion older male, Kentucky Derby (G1), Breeders' Cup Classic (G1), etc. Sire of eight stakes winners, including Bull Inthe Heather. Exported to Japan in 1995.

FIRENZE (FIRENZI), 1884-1902. B. f., Glenelg—Florida, by Virgil. 82-47-21-9, $112,471, Gazelle S., Monmouth H., Jerome S. (beating Hanover), etc. Tail-female ancestor of family that includes Carry Back, Paul Jones, Petrify.

FIRST FLIGHT, 1944-1975. B. f., *Mahmoud—Fly Swatter, by *Dis Donc. 24-11-3-3, $197,965, champion two-year-old filly, Matron S., Monmouth Oaks, etc. Defeated Jet Pilot in Futurity S.

FIRST LANDING, 1956-1987. B. c., *Turn-to—Hildene, by Bubbling Over. 37-19-9-2, $779,577, champion two-year-old colt, Champagne S., Hopeful S., etc. Sire of 27 stakes winners, including Riva Ridge, First Family, Gladwin.

FLATTERER, 1979-. Dk. b. or br. g., Mo Bay—Horizontal, by Nade. 51-24-7-5, $534,854, four-time champion steeplechaser 1983-'86, Marion duPont Scott Colonial Cup International Stp. three times, Temple Gwathmey Stp. H. twice, etc.

FLAWLESSLY, 1988-. B. f., Affirmed—La Confidence, by Nijinsky II. 28-16-4-3, $2,572,536, champion grass female twice, Beverly D. S. (G1), Matriarch S. (G1) 3 times, etc.

FLOWER BOWL, 1952-1968. B. f., *Alibhai—Flower Bed, by *Beau Pere. 32-7-4-3, $174,625, Ladies H., Delaware H., etc. Dam of Bowl of Flowers, Graustark, His Majesty.

FOOLISH PLEASURE, 1972-1994. B. c., What a Pleasure—Fool-Me-Not, by Tom Fool. 26-16-4-3, $1,216,705, champion two-year-old male, Kentucky Derby (G1), Suburban H. (G1), Great Match S. (with Ruffian), etc. Sire of 43 stakes winners, including Baiser Vole, Marfa, Kiri's Clown, Maudlin, Prayers'n Promises.

FOREGO, 1970-1997. B. g., *Forli—Lady Golconda, by Hasty Road. 57-34-9-7, $1,938,957, three-time Horse of the Year 1974-'76, champion older male 1974-'77, champion sprinter, Marlboro Cup H. (G1), Metropolitan H. (G1) twice, Woodward H. (G1) 3 times, etc. Last of the great weight carriers. Retired to Kentucky Horse Park.

*FORLI, 1963-1988. Ch. c., Aristophanes—Trevisa, by Advocate. 10-9-1-0, $156,648, Horse of the Year in Argentina, Quadruple Crown, Gran Premio Carlos Pellegrini, Gran Premio Nacional (Argentine Derby), Coronado S.-ncr, etc. Brother to *Tirreno, Tibur. Sire of 60 stakes winners, including Forego, Thatch, Intrepid Hero, Sadeem, Formidable.

FORT MARCY, 1964-1991. B. g., *Amerigo—Key Bridge, by *Princequillo. 75-21-18-14, $1,109,791, Horse of the Year in 1970, champion grass horse twice, champion handicap horse, Washington, D. C., International S. twice, Man o' War S., etc.

FORWARD GAL, 1968-1984. Ch. f., Native Charger—Forward Thrust, by Jet Action. 26-12-4-6, $438,933, champion two-year-old filly, Frizette S., Monmouth Oaks, etc. Third dam of Freedom Cry (GB).

FOURSTARDAVE, 1985-2002. Ch. g., Compliance—Broadway Joan, by Bold Arian. 100-21-18-16, $1,636,737, St. Paul Derby (G2), Daryl's Joy S. (G3) twice, etc. Won a race at Saratoga Race Course for eight consecutive years. Full brother to Irish classic winner Fourstars Allstar.

FREE FOR ALL, 1942-1964. Br. c., Questionnaire—Panay, by *Chicle. 7-6-0-0, $111,225, Arlington Futurity, Washington Park Futurity, etc. Sire of Rough'n Tumble. Tail-male ancestor of Dr. Fager, Holy Bull.

FRIAR ROCK, 1913-1928. Ch. c., *Rock Sand—*Fairy Gold, by Bend Or. 21-9-1-3, $20,365, champion three-year-old, Belmont S., Suburban H., Brooklyn H., etc. Sire of Pilate, Friar's Carse, Apprehension, Inchcape, Black Curl, Emotion, Heloise, Tenez.

FRIZETTE, 1905-unknown. B. f., Hamburg—*Ondulee, by St. Simon. 36-12-8-7, $16,135, Rosedale S., Laureate S., etc. Dam of Banshee, Durzetta, *Lespedeza II. Foundation mare of family that includes Myrtlewood, Seattle Slew, Mr. Prospector, Tourbillon, Sinndar, Cordova, Darshaan, Corejada, *Apollonia, Akiyda, Acamas, Akarad, *Priam II, *Djeddah, Sing Sing, Jet Pilot, Shecky Greene, Typecast, Bahri, Forestry, Chief Bearhart, Escena, Dahlia, Vitriolic, Vagrancy, Anees, Truly Bound, Baldric, Honorable Miss.

FUSAICHI PEGASUS, 1997-. B. c., Mr. Prospector—Angel Fever, by Danzig. 9-6-2-0, $1,994,400, Kentucky Derby (G1), Wood Memorial S. (G2), etc. Syndicated for a world-record $60-million to $70-million in 2000.

GALLANT BLOOM, 1966-1991. B. f., *Gallant Man—Multiflora, by Beau Max. 22-16-1-1, $535,739, champion two- and three-year-old filly, champion handicap mare, Santa Margarita Invitational H., Spinster S., Monmouth Oaks, etc.

GALLANT FOX, 1927-1954. B. c., *Sir Gallahad III—Marguerite, by Celt. 17-11-3-2, $328,165, Horse of the Year in 1930, champion three-year-old colt, Triple Crown, Jockey Club Gold Cup, etc. Sire of 18 stakes winners, including Omaha, Granville, Flares.

**GALLANT MAN*, 1954-1988. B. c., *Migoli—*Majideh, by *Mahmoud. 26-14-4-1, $510,355, Belmont S., Jockey Club Gold Cup, etc. Sire of 51 stakes winners, including Gallant Bloom, Gallant Romeo, War Censor, Spicy Living, Ring Twice. Broodmare sire of Genuine Risk, *Habitony, Lord Avie.

GALLORETTE, 1942-1959. Ch. f., *Challenger II—Gallette, by *Sir Gallahad III. 72-21-20-13, $445,535, champion handicap mare, Metropolitan H., Whitney S., Beldame H., etc. World's leading money-earning female at retirement. Dam of Mlle. Lorette, Courbette. Foundation mare of family that includes Minstrella, Misty Gallore, Silver Ghost, White Gloves, Greenwood Lake, Dancing Moss.

GAMELY, 1964-1975. B. f., Bold Ruler—Gambetta, by *My Babu. 41-16-9-6, $574,961, champion three-year-old filly, champion older mare twice, Alabama S., Beldame S. twice, etc. Dam of Cellini.

GENUINE RISK, 1977-. Ch. f., Exclusive Native—Virtuous, by *Gallant Man. 15-10-3-2, $646,587, champion three-year-old filly, Kentucky Derby (G1), Ruffian H. (G1), etc. Second filly to win Kentucky Derby.

**GLENCOE*, 1831-1858. Ch. c., Sultan—Trampoline, by Tramp. 10-8-1-1, $33,459, Two Thousand Guineas, Ascot Gold Cup, etc. Sire of Pocahontas, Peytona, Reel, Pryor, Star Davis, Vandal. Male-line ancestor of Hanover, Hamburg.

GODOLPHIN ARABIAN, 1724-1753. Br. c. of unknown parentage. Leading sire in England three times. Sire of Cade, Lath, Dismal, Regulus, Babraham, Blank. One of three male-line foundation sires of the Thoroughbred breed. Tail-male ancestor of Matchem line leading to Man o' War, In Reality, Tiznow.

GO FOR WAND, 1987-1990. B. f., Deputy Minister—Obeah, by Cyane. 13-10-2-0, $1,373,338, champion two- and three-year-old filly, Alabama S. (G1), Breeders' Cup Juvenile Fillies (G1), etc. Died at three in Breeders' Cup Distaff (G1). Buried in infield at Saratoga Race Course.

GOOD AND PLENTY, 1900-1907. B. g., Rossington—Famine, by Jils Johnson. 21-14-4-1, $45,815, Grand National Stp. H., Westbury Stp. H., etc.

GRANVILLE, 1933-1951. B. c., Gallant Fox—Gravita, by *Sarmatian. 18-8-4-3, $111,820, Horse of the Year in 1936, champion three-year-old colt, Belmont S., Travers S., etc. Sired only two stakes winners.

GREY LAG, 1918-1942. Ch. c., *Star Shoot—Miss Minnie, by *Meddler. 47-25-9-3, $136,715, Horse of the Year in 1921, champion three-year-old colt, champion handicap horse twice, Belmont S., Metropolitan H., Suburban H., etc. Shy breeder, sired only one stakes winner from 17 foals.

GUN BOW, 1960-unknown. B. c., Gun Shot—Ribbons and Bows, by War Admiral. 42-17-8-4, $798,722,

Metropolitan H., Whitney S., etc. Sire of six stakes winners, including Pistol Packer. Exported to Japan in 1973.

HAIL TO REASON, 1958-1976. Br. c., *Turn-to—Nothirdchance, by Blue Swords. 18-9-2-2, $328,434, champion two-year-old colt, Hopeful S., Sanford S., etc. Broke down and retired at end of two-year-old season. Leading sire in 1970. Sire of 43 stakes winners, including Roberto, Halo, Stop the Music, Mr. Leader, Bold Reason, Trillion, Priceless Gem, Straight Deal, Hail to All, Regal Gleam, Personality, Proud Clarion, Admiring. Broodmare sire of Allez France, Escaline (Fr), Royal Glint, Silver Buck, Triptych. Tail-male ancestor of line that includes Saint Ballado, Sunday Silence, Red Ransom, Brian's Time.

HALO, 1969-2000. Dk. b. or br. c., Hail to Reason—Cosmah, by Cosmic Bomb. 31-9-8-5, $259,553, United Nations H. (G1), Tidal H. (G2), etc. Leading sire in 1983 and '89. Sire of 63 stakes winners, including Sunday Silence, Sunny's Halo, Glorious Song, Devil's Bag, Saint Ballado, Rainbow Connection, Goodbye Halo, Lively One, Jolie's Halo, Coup de Folie. Broodmare sire of Halo America, Machiavellian, Pine Bluff, Rahy, Singspiel (Ire).

HAMBURG, 1895-1915. B. c., Hanover—Lady Reel, by Fellowcraft. 21-16-3-2, $60,380, champion three-year-old colt, Lawrence Realization, Brighton Cup, etc. Leading sire in 1905. Sire of Artful, Borrow, Burgomaster, Frizette, Prince Eugene, Lady Hamburg II, Biturica, Jersey Lightning, Rosie O'Grady.

HANOVER, 1884-1899. Ch. c., Hindoo—Bourbon Belle, by *Bonnie Scotland. 50-32-14-2, $118,887, champion three-year-old colt, Belmont S., Lawrence Realization, etc. Won 17 consecutive races. Leading sire 1895-'98. Sire of Hamburg, Abe Frank, Blackstock, David Garrick, Halma, Handspun, Rhoda B., Tea's Over, The Commoner, Urania, Yankee.

HARRY BASSETT, 1868-1878. Ch. c., Lexington—Canary Bird, by *Albion. 36-23-6-3 $59,450, champion three-year-old colt, Belmont S., Travers S., etc.

HASTINGS, 1893-1917. Br. c., Spendthrift—*Cinderella, by Tomahawk or Blue Ruin. 21-10-8-0, $16,340, Belmont S., Toboggan H., etc. Leading sire 1902, '08. Sire of Fair Play, Gunfire, Don Enrique, Flittergold, Masterman. Notorious for his savage temperament.

HAYNIE'S MARIA, 1808-unknown. Ch. f., *Diomed—Bellair mare, by Bellair. 9-8-1-0. Won at distances from four furlongs to four-mile heats. Famed as the nemesis of the stable of Andrew Jackson who said, "I could not beat her."

**HELIOPOLIS*, 1936-1959. B. c., Hyperion—Drift, by Swynford. 15-5-2-1, $71,216, Prince of Wales's S., Imperial Produce S., etc. Leading sire in 1950, '54. Sire of 53 stakes winners, including High Gun, Olympia, Helioscope, Grecian Queen, Parlo, Berlo, Aunt Jinny, Summer Tan, Princess Turia, Camargo. Broodmare sire of Riva Ridge, Summer Guest.

HENRY (SIR HENRY), 1819-1837. Ch. c., Sir Archy—Diomed mare, by *Diomed. Southern representative in first great North-South four-mile heat match race against American Eclipse at the Union Course, New York, in 1823. Won first heat, but beaten in second and third. Won four-mile and three-mile heat races, including 1823 Jockey Club Purse at Petersburg, Virginia. Sire of Post Boy, Decatur, Alice Grey.

HENRY OF NAVARRE, 1891-1917. Ch. c., Knight of Ellerslie—Moss Rose, by *The Ill-Used. 42-29-8-3, $68,985, champion three-year-old colt, Belmont S., Travers S., etc. Sire of Grave and Gay, Orienta.

HEROD, 1758-1780. B. c., Tartar—Cypron, by Blaze.

10-6-3-0, Match against Antinous, etc. Leading sire in England eight times. Sire of Highflyer, Florizel, Woodpecker, Bridget, Bagot, Maid Of The Oaks, Phenomenom. Tail-male line ancestor of The Tetrarch, Tourbillon, *Ambiorix, Ahonoora, Dr Devious (Ire), Indian Ridge.

HIGHFLYER, 1774-1793. B. c., Herod—Rachel, by Blank. 12-12-0-0, Grosvenor S., Great Subscription Race, etc. Leading sire in England a record 13 times, record 12 in succession. Sire of Sir Peter Teazle, Delpini, Huncamunca, Noble, Rockingham, Skyscraper, Maid Of All Work, Prunella.

HIGH GUN, 1951-1962. Br. c., *Heliopolis—Rocket Gun, by Brazado. 24-11-5-4, $486,025, champion three-year-old colt, champion handicap horse, Belmont S., Jockey Club Gold Cup, etc. Virtually sterile; sired only four foals.

HILL PRINCE, 1947-1970. B. c., *Princequillo—Hildene, by Bubbling Over. 30-17-5-4, $422,140, Horse of the Year in 1950, champion two- and three-year-old colt, champion handicap horse, Preakness S., Jockey Club Gold Cup, etc. Sire of 23 stakes winners, including Bayou, Levee, Royal Living, Middle Brother. Broodmare sire of Dark Mirage, Shuvee.

HILLSDALE, 1955-1972. B. c., Take Away—Johann, by Johnstown. 41-23-6-4, $646,935, Hollywood Gold Cup H., Californian S., etc. Sire of nine stakes winners, including Bravery II and Hi Q., and of stakes-placed Acroterion.

HINDOO, 1878-1901. B. c., Virgil—Florence, by Lexington. 35-30-3-2, $71,875, champion two- and three-year-old colt, Kentucky Derby, Travers S., etc. Won 18 consecutive races at two and three. Sire of Hanover, Buddhist, Hindoo Rose, Jim Gore, Sallie McClelland.

HOLY BULL, 1991- . Gr. c., Great Above—Sharon Brown, by Al Hattab. 16-13-0-0, $2,481,760, Horse of the Year in 1994, champion three-year-old male, Travers S. (G1), Metropolitan H. (G1), etc. Sire of at least 17 stakes winners, including Macho Uno.

HONEYMOON, 1943-unknown. B. f., *Beau Pere—Panoramic, by Chance Shot. 78-20-14-9, $387,760, Top Flight H., Hollywood Oaks, etc. Dam of Honeys Gem, Honeys Alibi from only three foals.

HYPERION, 1930-1960. Ch. c., Gainsborough—Selene, by Chaucer. 13-9-1-2, $124,386, champion three-year-old in England, Epsom Derby, St. Leger S., etc. Leading sire in England six times; leading broodmare sire in England four times. Sire of *Alibhai, Aristophanes, Aureole, Godiva, Gulf Stream, *Heliopolis, High Hat, *Khaled, Owen Tudor, Pensive, Sun Chariot. Broodmare sire of Alycidon, *Aunt Edith II, *Carrozza, Citation, Nearctic, Pretense. Foundation sire of line that leads to *Forli, Star Kingdom, *Vaguely Noble, Marscay, Nodouble, Efisio.

IDLEWILD, 1859-1883. B. f., Lexington—Florine, by *Glencoe. 25-18-1-1, $9,700, Post S., etc. Dam of Wildidle. Full sister to Aerolite, dam of Spendthrift.

IMP, 1894-1909. Br. f., Wagner—Fondling, by Fonso. 171-62-35-29, $70,069, champion older mare twice, Suburban H., etc. Immortalized in verse as "My Coal Black Lady."

IRISH LAD, 1900-unknown. Dk. b or br. c., *Candlemas—Arrowgrass, by Enquirer. 23-12-5-2, $98,210, champion older horse, Metropolitan H., Brooklyn H., etc. Sire in France of Banshee, Blarney.

IROQUOIS, 1878-1899. B. c., *Leamington—Maggie B.B., by *Australian. 26-12-4-3, $99,707, champion three-year-old in England, Epsom Derby, St. Leger S.,

etc. First American-bred winner of the Epsom Derby in 1881. Leading sire in 1892. Sire of Tammany, Huron.

JAIPUR, 1959-1987. Dk. b. or br. c., *Nasrullah—Rare Perfume, by Eight Thirty. 19-10-6-0, $618,926, champion three-year-old colt, Belmont S., Travers S., etc. Sire of Amber Rama, Mansingh, Pontifex.

JANUS (LITTLE JANUS), 1746-1780. Ch. c., Janus—Fox mare, by Fox. Won twice in England and once in the U.S. at four-mile heats. Sire of Meade's Celer, Clodius, Goode's Old Twigg. Early Colonial Thoroughbred foundation sire and foundation sire of the original Virginia Quarter Horse.

JAY TRUMP, 1957-1988. Dk. b. or br. g., Tonga Prince—Be Trump, by *Bernborough. 29-13-5-2, Grand National Stp. H. in England, etc. Also won three Maryland Hunt Cups.

JIM DANDY, 1927-unknown. Ch. g., Jim Gaffney—Thunderbird, by *Star Shoot. 141-7-6-8, $49,570, Travers S., Grand Union Hotel S., etc. Upset Gallant Fox and Whichone in 1930 Travers S. at 100-to-1.

JOHN HENRY, 1975- . B. g., Ole Bob Bowers—Once Double, by Double Jay. 83-39-15-9, $6,591,860, Horse of the Year 1981, '84, champion grass male four times, Santa Anita H. (G1) twice, Jockey Club Gold Cup (G1), Oak Tree Invitational (G1) three times, Hollywood Invitational H. (G1) three times, etc.

JOHN P. GRIER, 1917-1943. Ch. c., Whisk Broom II—Wonder, by Disguise. 17-10-4-2, $37,006, Queens County H., Aqueduct H., etc. Sire of 27 stakes winners, including Boojum, El Chico, Jack High, Miyako, White Lies. Pressed Man o' War to narrowest victory in 1920 Dwyer H.

JOHNSTOWN, 1936-1950. B. c., Jamestown—La France, by *Sir Gallahad III. 21-14-0-3, $169,315, Kentucky Derby, Belmont S., etc. Sire of Flood Town, Acoma. Broodmare sire of Nashua.

JOLLY ROGER, 1922-1948. Ch. g., Pennant—Lethe, by *All Gold. 49-18-9-9, $143,240, Grand National Stp. H. twice, Brook Stp. H., etc.

KAYAK II, 1935-1946. Dk. br. c., Congreve—Mosquita, by Your Majesty. 26-14-8-1, $213,205, champion handicap horse, Santa Anita H., Hollywood Gold Cup, etc. Shy breeder.

KELSO, 1957-1983. Dk. b. or br. g., Your Host—Maid of Flight, by Count Fleet. 63-39-12-2, $1,977,896, Horse of the Year 1960-'64, champion three-year-old male, champion older horse four times, handicap triple crown, Jockey Club Gold Cup five times, Woodward S. three times, etc. Only five-time Horse of the Year.

KENTUCKY, 1861-1875. B. c., Lexington—Magnolia, by *Glencoe. 23-21-0-0, $33,700, Travers S., Saratoga Cup twice, etc. Won 20 consecutive races; first winner of the Travers S. Sire of Nina, Woodbine. Along with Norfolk and Asteroid, one of three dominant sons of Lexington, called the "great triumvirate."

KHALED, 1943-1968. Br. c., Hyperion—Eclair, by Ethnarch. 12-6-1-1, $38,860, Middle Park S., Coventry S., etc. Sire of 61 stakes winners, including Swaps, Terrang, Going Abroad, New Policy, Correspondent, A Glitter, Bushel-n-Peck. Broodmare sire of Candy Spots, Outing Class, Prove It.

KINCSEM, 1874-unknown. B. f., Cambuscan—Waternymph, by Cotswold. 54-54-0-0. Goodwood Cup, etc. All-time leader in number of wins among unbeaten horses. Greatest horse ever bred in Hungary. Raced all over continental Europe and in England.

KING'S BISHOP, 1969-1981. B. c., Round Table—Spearfish, by Fleet Nasrullah. 28-11-4-3, $308,079,

Carter H. (G2), Fall Highweight H. (G3), etc. Sire of 30 stakes winners, including King's Swan, Possible Mate, Queen to Conquer, Queen Lib, Bishop's Ring.

KINGSTON, 1884-1912. Br. c., Spendthrift—*Kapanga, by Victorious. 138-89-33-12, $140,195, First Special S., etc. Leading sire in 1900, '10. Sire of Novelty, Wild Mint, Lida B. Holds American record for most races won at 89.

KOTASHAAN (Fr), 1988- . Dk. b. or br. c., Darshaan—Haute Autorite, by Elocutionist. 22-10-5-2, Horse of the Year in 1993, champion grass male, Breeders' Cup Turf (G1), Eddie Read H. (G1), etc. Exported to Japan in 1994.

LADY LIGHTFOOT, 1812-1834. Br. f., Sir Archy—Black Maria, by *Shark. Won at least 23 races, 15 at four-mile heats. Dam of Black Maria, Terror.

LADY'S SECRET, 1982-2003. Gr. f., Secretariat—Great Lady M., by Icecapade. 45-25-9-3, $3,021,325, Horse of the Year in 1986, champion older female, Breeders' Cup Distaff (G1), Whitney H. (G1), etc. All-time distaff leading earner at time of retirement.

LANDALUCE, 1980-1982. Dk. b. or br. f., Seattle Slew—Strip Poker, by Bold Bidder. 5-5-0-0, $372,365, champion two-year-old filly, Oak Leaf S. (G1), Del Mar Debutante S. (G2), etc. Died at two.

LA PREVOYANTE, 1970-1974. B. f., Buckpasser—Arctic Dancer, by Nearctic. 39-25-5-3, $572,417, champion two-year-old filly in U.S., Horse of the Year in Canada in 1972, champion two-year-old filly in Canada, champion older female in Canada, Frizette S., Spinaway S., etc. Won all 12 of her starts at two. Died at four.

LA TROIENNE, 1926-1954. B. f., *Teddy—Helene de Troie, by Helicon. 7-0-1-1, $146. Greatest American foundation mare of the 20th century. Dam of Bimelech, Black Helen. Foundation mare of family that includes Buckpasser, Easy Goer, Allez France, Affectionately, Busher, Glamour, Numbered Account, Private Account, Woodman, Bee Ann Mac, Autobiography, Cohoes, The Axe II, Big Hurry, Searching, Relaxing, Bridal Flower, Caerleon, Straight Deal, Glowing Tribute, Sea Hero, Lite Light, Go for Gin, Pleasant Tap, Princess Rooney, Prairie Bayou.

LECOMTE, 1850-1856. Ch. c., Boston—Reel, by *Glencoe. 16-11-5-0, $12,630, Jockey Club Purse, etc. Only horse to defeat Lexington. Sire of Umpire, Sherrod.

L'ESCARGOT, 1963-1984. Ch. g., Escart III—What a Daisy, by Grand Inquisitor. 63-14-15-8, $237,572, champion steeplechaser, Cheltenham Gold Cup Stp. H. twice, Meadow Brook Stp. H., etc.

LEXINGTON, 1850-1875. B. c., Boston—Alice Carneal, by *Sarpedon. 7-6-1-0, $56,600, Great State Post S., etc. Leading sire 1861-'74, '76, '78. Sire of Asteroid, Norfolk, Kentucky, Tom Ochiltree, Duke of Magenta, Tom Bowling, Harry Bassett, Sultana, Maiden, Florence, General Duke, Hira, Idlewild, Lida, Preakness, Salina, Ulrica, War Dance. Leading sire record 16 times, 14 in succession.

LONESOME GLORY, 1988-2002. Ch. g., Transworld—Stronghold (Fr), by Green Dancer. 44-24-5-6, $1,325,868, champion steeplechaser five times, Carolina Cup Hurdle S. twice, Colonial Cup Stp. S. twice, etc. First steeplechase millionaire.

LONGFELLOW, 1867-1893. Br. c., *Leamington—Nantura, by Brawner's Eclipse. 16-13-2-0, $11,200, Monmouth Cup twice, Saratoga Cup, etc. Leading sire in 1891. Sire of Freeland, The Bard, Thora, Longstreet, Leonatus, Riley.

LUKE BLACKBURN, 1877-1904. B. c., *Bonnie Scotland—Nevada, by Lexington. 39-25-6-2, $49,460, Champion S., Kenner S., etc. Won 22 of 24 races at three. Sire of Proctor Knott.

LYPHARD, 1969- . B. c., Northern Dancer—Goofed, by *Court Martial. 12-6-1-0, $195,427, Prix Jacques le Marois, Prix de la Foret, etc. Leading sire in U.S. in 1986, leading sire in France 1978 and '79; leading broodmare sire in France in 1985 and '86. Sire of 115 stakes winners, including Dancing Brave, Manila, Three Troikas (Fr), Reine de Saba (Fr), Jolypha, Dancing Maid (Fr), Pharly, Bellypha (Ire), Sangue (Ire), Sabin, Al Nasr (Fr), Elliodor, Featherhill (Fr), Lypheor (GB), Skimble. Broodmare sire of Bering (GB), Groom Dancer, Hatoof, Skimming.

MAD HATTER, 1916-1935. Dk. b. or br. c., Fair Play—Madcap, by *Rock Sand. 98-32-22-15, $194,525, champion handicap horse, Jockey Club Gold Cup twice, Toboggan H., etc. Sire of 22 stakes winners, including Snowflake, The Nut.

MAGGIE B.B., 1867-1889. B. f., *Australian—Madeline, by Boston. 7-3-4-0, $2,950, Sequel S. Greatest American broodmare of 19th century. Dam of Iroquois, Harold, Jaconet, Pera, Panique, Red and Blue. Tail-female ancestor of family that includes Alanesian, Boldnesian, Lawrin, Idun, Top Flight, Whisk Broom II, Life's Magic, Bald Eagle, Dubai Millennium.

MAHMOUD, 1933-1962. Gr. c., *Blenheim II—Mah Mahal, by Gainsborough. 11-4-2-3, $85,413, champion three-year-old in England, Epsom Derby, Champagne S., etc. Leading sire in 1946; leading broodmare sire in 1957. Sire of 66 stakes winners, including The Axe II, Oil Capitol, Cohoes, First Flight, Vulcan's Forge, Mount Marcy, Adile, Snow Goose, Almahmoud, Happy Mood, Mahmoudess. Broodmare sire of Cosmah, Determine, *Gallant Man, *Grey Dawn II, Misty Morn, Silver Spoon, Your Host. Made the gray coat color popular in America.

MAIDEN, 1862-1880. B. f., Lexington—Kitty Clark, by *Glencoe. 15-5-8-3, $5,500, Travers S., Produce S., etc. Second Travers S. winner. Dam of Parole, sixth dam of Nearco.

MAJESTIC PRINCE, 1966-1981. Ch. c., Raise a Native—Gay Hostess, by *Royal Charger. 10-9-1-0, $414,200, Kentucky Derby, Preakness S., etc. Sire of 33 stakes winners, including Majestic Light, Coastal, Sensitive Prince, Eternal Prince.

MAN O' WAR, 1917-1947. Ch. c., Fair Play—Mahubah, by *Rock Sand. 21-20-1-0, $249,465, champion two- and three-year-old colt, Belmont S., Travers S., etc. Leading sire in 1926. Sire of 62 stakes winners, including War Admiral, Crusader, American Flag, War Relic, Bateau, Scapa Flow, Edith Cavell, Maid at Arms, Florence Nightingale, Battleship, Clyde Van Dusen, Hard Tack. Broodmare sire of Blue Swords, Helioscope, Mata Hari, Pavot, Vagrancy. Tail-male ancestor of line that leads to In Reality, Tiznow. Still considered by many to be the greatest racehorse of all time.

MASKETTE, 1906-c.1930. B. f., Disguise—Biturica, by Hamburg. 17-12-3-0, $77,090, champion two- and three-year-old filly, Futurity S., Alabama S., Matron S., Spinaway S., etc.

MATA HARI, 1931-1957. Br. f., Peter Hastings—War Woman, by Man o' War. 16-7-0-2, $66,699, champion two- and three-year-old filly, Breeders' Futurity, Kentucky Jockey Club S., Illinois Derby, etc. Dam of Spy Song, Mr. Music.

MATCHEM, 1748-1781. B. c., Cade—Partner mare, by Partner. 8 wins, The Whip, etc. Leading sire three times in England. Sire of Conductor, Pantaloon, Alfred, Hollandaise, Tetotum. Male-line ancestor of Man o' War, In Reality, Tiznow, Hurry On, Sassafras (Fr).

MATE, 1928-1953. Ch. c., Prince Pal—Killashandra, by *Ambassador IV. 75-20-14-19, $301,810, Preakness S., American Derby, etc. Great rival of Equipoise, Twenty Grand. Sire of five stakes winners, including two-time champion steeplechaser Elkridge.

***MEDLEY**, 1776-1792. Gr. c., Gimcrack—Arminda, by Snap. 13 wins. Sire of Bellair, Calypso, Grey Diomed, Grey Medley, Lamplighter. Early American foundation sire.

***MESSENGER**, 1780-1808. Gr. c., Mambrino—Turf mare, by Turf. 10 wins, $7,365. Sire of Miller's Damsel, Tippoo Saib, Potomac, Bright Phoebus, Mambrino. Early American foundation sire; also foundation sire of the American Standardbred breed.

MIDDLEGROUND, 1947-1972. Ch. c., Bold Venture—Verguenza, by Chicaro. 15-6-6-2, $237,725, Kentucky Derby, Belmont S., Hopeful S., etc. Sire of seven stakes winners, including Resaca. Shy breeder.

MIESQUE, 1984- . B. f., Nureyev—Pasadoble, by Prove Out. 16-12-3-1, $2,070,163, champion grass female in U.S., champion two-year-old in France, champion miler in England, champion older female in France, Breeders' Cup Mile (G1) twice, One Thousand Guineas (Eng-G1), etc. Dam of Kingmambo, East of the Moon, Miesque's Son, Moon Is Up.

MISS WOODFORD, 1880-1899. Br. f., *Billet—Fancy Jane, by Neil Robinson. 48-37-7-2, $118,270, Alabama S., Spinaway S., Pimlico S., etc. First American horse to earn $100,000.

MOCCASIN, 1963-1986. Ch. f., Nantallah—*Rough Shod II, by Gold Bridge. 21-11-2-4, $388,075, Horse of the Year in 1965 Thoroughbred Racing Associations poll, champion two-year-old filly, Gardenia S., Test S., etc. Dam of Apalachee, Scuff, Flippers.

MODESTY, 1881-unknown. Ch. f., War Dance—Ballet, by Planet. 82-35-8-11, $49,135, Kentucky Oaks, American Derby, etc. First filly winner of the American Derby. Tail-female ancestor of family that includes Regret, Thunderer, First Fiddle.

MOLLIE MCCARTHY, 1873-unknown. B. f., Monday—Hennie Farrow, by Shamrock. 17-15-0-0, $18,750, Winter S., Garden City Cup, etc. One of the last great four-mile heat fillies.

MONSIEUR TONSON, 1822-unknown. B. c., Pacolet—Madame Tonson, by Top Gallant. 12-11-0-0. Leading sire in 1834. Sire of Argyle. First horse bred west of the Appalachians to win in the East.

MORVICH, 1919-unknown. Bl. c., Runnymede—Hymir, by Dr. Leggo. 16-12-2-1, $172,909, Kentucky Derby, Hopeful S., etc. First California-bred winner of the Kentucky Derby in 1922, won first 12 starts. Sire of 12 stakes winners.

MOTHER GOOSE, 1922-unknown. Br. f., *Chicle—Flying Witch, by Broomstick. 10-3-1-3, $72,755, champion two-year-old filly, Futurity S. (defeated 28 others in a record field), Fashion S., etc. Dam of Arbitrator. Full sister to Whichone. Tail-female ancestor of family that includes Northern Dancer, Halo, Arctic Tern, Machiavellian, La Prevoyante, Tosmah, Danehill.

MR. PROSPECTOR, 1970-1999. B. c., Raise a Native—Gold Digger, by Nashua. 14-7-4-2, $112,171, Gravesend H., Whirlaway S., etc. Leading sire in 1987-'88; leading broodmare sire in 1997-2001. Sire of at least 179 stakes winners, including Forty Niner, Fusaichi

Pegasus, Seeking the Gold, It's in the Air, Fappiano, Woodman, Gulch, Carson City, Conquistador Cielo, Gone West, Gold Beauty, Kingmambo, Machiavellian, Miswaki. Broodmare sire of Dayjur, Fasliyev, Hollywood Wildcat, Pulpit.

MUMTAZ MAHAL, 1921-1945. Gr. f., The Tetrarch—Lady Josephine, by Sundridge. 10-7-2-0, $67,421, champion two-year-old, champion sprinter, Champagne S., Nunthorpe S., etc. Dam of Mirza II, Badruddin. Tail-female ancestor of *Nasrullah, *Royal Charger, Abernant, Petite Etoile, Shergar, Octagonal, Oh So Sharp (GB), *Migoli, Nishapour, Aliya, Risen Star, *Diableretta, Left Bank, Kalamoun. Known as "the Flying Filly." Still considered by many the fastest filly ever to race in England.

MY CHARMER, 1969-1993. B. f., Poker—Fair Charmer, by Jet Action. 32-6-4-2, $34,133, Fair Grounds Oaks. Dam of Seattle Slew, Lomond, Seattle Dancer (record $13.1-million yearling).

MYRTLEWOOD, 1932-1950. B. f., Blue Larkspur—*Frizeur, by *Sweeper. 22-15-4-2, $40,620, champion sprinter, champion handicap female, Ashland S., Hawthorne Sprint H., etc. Set five track records and equaled three. Dam of Durazna, Miss Dogwood. Foundation mare of family that includes Seattle Slew, Mr. Prospector, Myrtle Charm, Lomond, Typecast, Siberian Express, Highest Trump, Bahri, Ajina, Escena, Sewickley, Forestry, Chief Bearhart.

NASHUA, 1952-1982. B. c., *Nasrullah—Segula, by Johnstown. 30-22-4-1, $1,288,565, Horse of the Year in 1955, champion two- and three-year-old colt, Preakness S., Belmont S., Jockey Club Gold Cup twice, etc. Sire of 77 stakes winners, including Shuvee, Noble Nashua, Diplomat Way, Producer, Marshua, Bramalea, Bombay Duck, Good Manners, Nalee. Broodmare sire of Mr. Prospector, Roberto. First $1-million syndicated stallion.

***NASRULLAH**, 1940-1959. B. c., Nearco—Mumtaz Begum, by *Blenheim II. 10-5-1-2, $15,259, champion two-year-old colt in England, Champion S., Coventry S., etc. Leading sire in 1955-'56, '59-'60, '62 in U.S.; leading sire in England. Sire of 93 stakes winners, including Bold Ruler, Nashua, Never Bend, Nearula, *Musidora, Never Say Die, Jaipur, Bald Eagle, Red God, Delta, Grey Sovereign. Broodmare sire of Drumtop, Natashka, *Sovereign II, Talking Picture, Turkish Trousers. Tail-male ancestor of Bold Ruler, Never Bend, Blushing Groom (Fr), Caro (Ire) lines.

NATIVE DANCER, 1950-1967. Gr. c., Polynesian—Geisha, by Discovery. 22-21-1-0, $785,240, Horse of the Year in 1952, '54, champion two- and three-year-old colt, champion handicap horse, Belmont S., Preakness S., Travers S., Futurity S., etc. Sire of 44 stakes winners, including Raise a Native, Hula Dancer, Dan Cupid, Secret Step, Kauai King, Dancer's Image, Native Charger, Native Street, Exclusive Dancer. Broodmare sire of Northern Dancer, General Assembly, Icecapade, Ruffian. Founder of male line that includes Mr. Prospector, Alydar, *Sea-Bird, Forty Niner, Seeking the Gold, Woodman, Thunder Gulch.

NATIVE DIVER, 1959-1967. Br. g., Imbros—Fleet Diver, by Devil Diver. 81-37-7-12, $1,026,500, Hollywood Gold Cup three times, San Carlos H. twice, etc. Won 33 stakes. Became the first California-bred millionaire.

NEARCO, 1935-1957. B. c., Pharos—Nogara, by Havresac II. 14-14-0-0, $85,974, champion two- and three-year-old in Italy, Grand Prix de Paris, Derby Italiano, etc. Leading sire three times in England; leading broodmare sire three times in England. Sire of *Nasrullah, Dante, *Masaka, *Amerigo, Mossborough, Narrator, Nimbus, *Royal Charger, Sayajirao, Felucca, Infatuation, *Malindi, Neasham Belle, Netherton Maid, Noorani, Neocracy, Noble Lassie, *Rivaz. Broodmare sire of *Arctic Prince, Charlottesville, Saint Crespin III, Sheshoon, *Tulyar, *Vaguely Noble. Tail-male ancestor of Northern Dancer, Bold Ruler, Blushing Groom (Fr), Never Bend, Caro (Ire) male lines.

NEARCTIC, 1954-1973. Br. c., Nearco—*Lady Angela, by Hyperion. 47-21-5-3, $152,384, Horse of the Year in Canada in 1958, Michigan Mile, Saratoga Special S., Canadian Maturity, etc. Sire of 49 stakes winners, including Northern Dancer, Icecapade, Nonoalco, Briartic, Cool Reception, Cold Comfort, Cool Moon, Arctic Dancer, Christmas Wind. Broodmare sire of Kennedy Road, La Prevoyante.

NEEDLES, 1953-1984. B. c., Ponder—Noodle Soup, by Jack High. 21-11-3-3, $600,355, champion two- and three-year-old colt, Kentucky Derby, Belmont S., etc. Sire of 21 stakes winners, including Irish Rebellion. First Florida-bred winner of the Kentucky Derby.

NEJI, 1950-1982. Ch. g., *Hunters Moon IV—Accra, by Annapolis. 46-17-11-8, $270,694, champion steeplechaser three times, Temple Gwathmey Stp. H. twice, Grand National Stp. H. twice, etc.

NELLIE FLAG, 1932-1953. Ch. f., American Flag—Nellie Morse, by Luke McLuke. 22-6-5-1, $59,665, champion two-year-old filly, Kentucky Jockey Club S., Matron S., etc. Dam of Mar-Kell, Sunshine Nell, Nellie L. Foundation mare of family that includes Forego, Bold Forbes, Bet Twice, Lakeway, Mark-Ye-Well, Dewan, Saratoga Six.

NELLIE MORSE, 1921-1941. B. f., Luke McLuke—La Venganza, by Abercorn. 34-7-9-3, $73,565, champion three-year-old filly, Preakness S., Fashion S. etc. Dam of Nellie Flag, Count Morse.

NEVER SAY DIE, 1951-1975. Ch. c., *Nasrullah—Singing Grass, by War Admiral. 12-3-1-3, $89,200, champion three-year-old in England, Epsom Derby, St. Leger S., etc. Leading sire in England in 1962. Sire of 41 stakes winners, including Never Too Late, Saidam, Die Hard. Broodmare sire of 95 stakes winners. Second American-bred to win the Epsom Derby. First American-bred to lead English sire list.

NEXT MOVE, 1947-1968. Br. f., Bull Lea—Now What, by Chance Play. 46-17-11-3, $398,550, champion three-year-old filly, champion older mare, Coaching Club American Oaks, Beldame H. twice, etc. Dam of Good Move, Restless Native. Fourth dam of Peteski.

NIJINSKY II, 1967-1992. B. c., Northern Dancer—Flaming Page, by Bull Page. 13-11-2-0, $667,220, Horse of the Year in Europe in 1970, champion two- and three-year-old in England and Ireland, English Triple Crown, King George VI and Queen Elizabeth S., etc. Last winner of the English Triple Crown. Leading sire in England in 1986; leading broodmare sire in U.S. in 1993-'94. Sire of 155 stakes winners, including Caerleon, Lammtarra, Ferdinand, Ile de Bourbon, Sky Classic, Golden Fleece, Royal Academy, Green Dancer, Number, Javamine, Maplejinsky. Broodmare sire of more than 230 stakes winners, including Fantastic Light, Flawlessly, Forest Flower, Heavenly Prize, Java Gold, Rubiano, Sky Beauty.

NODOUBLE, 1965-1990. Ch. c., *Noholme II—AblaJay, by Double Jay. 42-13-11-5, $846,749, champion handicap horse twice, Santa Anita H., Metropolitan H., etc. Leading sire in 1981. Sire of 91 stakes winners, including Overskate, Mairzy Doates, Coolawin, Chain

Store. Broodmare sire of 89 stakes winners, including Sky Classic, Regal Classic.

***NOOR**, 1945-1974. Br. c., *Nasrullah—Queen of Baghdad, by *Bahram. 31-12-5-3, $356,940, champion handicap horse, Santa Anita H., Hollywood Gold Cup H., etc. Sire of Yours, Flutterby, Noureddin. Broodmare sire of Dancer's Image, Delta Judge. Defeated Citation four times at five.

NORFOLK, 1861-1890. B. c., Lexington—Novice, by *Glencoe. 5-5-0-0, $10,550, Jersey Derby, etc. Sire of Emperor of Norfolk, El Rio Rey, Flood, Ralston. Member of sire Lexington's "great triumvirate" with Asteroid and Kentucky.

***NORTHERN DANCER**, 1961-1990. B. c. Nearctic—Natalma, by Native Dancer. 18-14-2-2, $580,647, champion three-year-old colt, Horse of the Year in 1964 in Canada, champion two-year-old colt in Canada, Kentucky Derby, Preakness S., etc. Leading sire in U.S. in 1971, leading broodmare sire in U.S. in 1991; leading sire in England four times. Sire of 146 stakes winners, including Nijinsky II, Sadler's Wells, Nureyev, The Minstrel, El Gran Senor, Storm Bird, Lyphard, Northern Taste, Northfields, Unfuwain, Northernette, Fanfreluche, Shareef Dancer, Try My Best, Be My Guest, Cool Mood, Dixieland Band. Broodmare sire of more than 235 stakes winners, including Arazi, Eillo, L'Alezane, L'Enjoleur, Narita Brian, Noverre, Rhythm, Ryafan, Southern Halo.

NUREYEV, 1977-2001. B. c., Northern Dancer—Special, by *Forli. 3-2-0-0, $42,522, champion miler in France, Prix Thomas Bryon (Fr-G3), Prix Djebel. Disqualified from victory in 1980 Two Thousand Guineas (Eng-G1). Leading sire twice in France. Sire of more than 135 stakes winners, including Miesque, Peintre Celebre, Theatrical (Ire), Soviet Star, Sonic Lady, Fasliyev, Polar Falcon, Reams of Verse, Stravinsky, Zilzal, Skimming. Broodmare sire of more than 110 stakes winners, including Desert King, East of the Moon, Kingmambo, Peteski, Zabeel.

***OEDIPUS**, 1946-1978. Br. g., Blue Larkspur—Be Like Mom, by *Sickle. 58-14-12-9, $132,405, champion steeplechaser three times, Grand National Stp. H., Brook Stp. H. twice, etc.

***OLD ROSEBUD**, 1911-1922. B. g., Uncle—Ivory Bells, by Himyar. 80-40-13-8, $74,729, Kentucky Derby, Carter H., Flash S., etc. Set Kentucky Derby record that stood for 17 years.

***OMAHA**, 1932-1959. Ch. c., Gallant Fox—Flambino, by *Wrack. 22-9-7-2, $154,705, champion three-year-old colt, Triple Crown, Dwyer S., Classic S., etc. Sire of seven stakes winners, including Prevaricator. Broodmare sire of Summer Tan.

ONE COUNT, 1949-1966. Dk. br. c., Count Fleet—Ace Card, by Case Ace. 23-9-3-3, $245,625, Horse of the Year in 1952, champion three-year-old colt, Belmont S., Travers S., etc. Sire of 12 stakes winners, including Airmans Guide. Broodamre sire of Fit to Fight, Obeah.

***ORMONDE**, 1883-1904. B. c., Bend Or—Lily Agnes, by Macaroni. 16-16-0-0, $138,340, Champion at two, three, and four in England, English Triple Crown. Sire of Orme, Ormondale, *Gold Finch, Ossary. Progressively sterile. Tail-male ancestor of *Teddy line. Widely considered the greatest English racehorse of 19th century; he was a roarer.

***PAN ZARETA**, 1910-1918. Ch. f., Abe Frank—Caddie Griffith, by Rancocas. 151-76-31-21, $39,082, Juarez H., Rio Grande H., etc. Won carrying 140 pounds or more five times. Died at eight and is buried in infield at Fair Grounds.

*PAPYRUS, 1920-1941. Br. c., Tracery—Miss Matty, by Marcovil. 18-9-5-1, $110,068, Epsom Derby, Chester Vase, etc. First Epsom Derby winner to race in the U.S. in international match race against Zev in 1923. Sire of Barbara Burrini, *Cosquilla, *Osiris II, Honey Buzzard.

PARLO, 1951-1978. Ch. f., *Heliopolis—Fairy Palace, by Pilate. 34-8-6-3, $309,240, champion three-year-old filly, champion handicap mare twice, Alabama S., Beldame H., etc. Tail-female ancestor of Arts and Letters, Silverbulletday, Saudi Poetry, Zaccio, Waquoit.

PAROLE, 1873-1903. Br. g., *Leamington—Maiden, by Lexington. 127-59-22-16, $82,111, Saratoga Cup, Epsom Gold Cup (in England), etc. Leading American money winner 1881-1885.

PASEANA (Arg), 1987- . B. f., Ahmad—Pasiflin (Arg), by Flintham. 36-19-10-2, $3,317,427, champion older female twice, Breeders' Cup Distaff (G1), Milady H. (G1) twice, Apple Blossom H. (G1) twice, etc.

PAVOT, 1942-1975. Br. c., Case Ace—Coquelicot, by Man o' War. 32-14-6-2, $373,365, undefeated champion two-year-old colt, Belmont S., Futurity S., etc. Sire of 14 stakes winners, including Andre, Cigar Maid.

PERSONAL ENSIGN, 1984- . B. f., Private Account—Grecian Banner, by Hoist the Flag. 13-13-0-0, $1,679,880, champion older female, Breeders' Cup Distaff (G1), Beldame S. (G1) twice, etc. Broodmare of the Year in 1996. Dam of My Flag, Miner's Mark, Traditionally, Our Emblem; grandam of Storm Flag Flying.

PETER PAN, 1904-1933. B. c., Commando—*Cinderella, by Hermit. 17-10-3-1, $115,450, Belmont S., Hopeful S., etc. Sire of Black Toney, Pennant, Peter Hastings, Tryster, Prudery, Vexatious, Panoply, Wendy.

PEYTONA, 1839-1858. Ch. f., *Glencoe—Giantess, by *Leviathan. 8-6-1-0, $62,400, Peyton S., North-South Match, etc. One-time leading American money earner; defeated Fashion in last great North-South match race.

PHALARIS, 1913-1931. B. c., Polymelus—Bromus, by Sainfoin. 24-16-2-1, $26,376, Challenge S. twice, Stud Produce S., etc. Leading sire twice in England. Sire of 65 stakes winners, including Pharos, Fairway, Colorado, Manna, Fair Isle, *Sickle, *Pharamond II, Chatelaine. Broodmare sire of *Easton, Godiva, Mid-day Sun, Picture Play. Tail-male ancestor of *Nasrullah, Northern Dancer, Native Dancer, Buckpasser sire lines.

PHARIS, 1936-1957. Br. c., Pharos—Carissima, by Clarissimus. 3-3-0 0, $47,531, champion three-year-old in France, Prix du Jockey-Club (French Derby), Grand Prix de Paris, etc. Leading sire in France four times. Sire of *Ardan, Auriban, Philius, Dynamiter, *Priam II, Asterblute. Greatest horse bred in France in first half of 20th century. Racing career cut short by World War II; confiscated by the Nazis during the war and spent five years in Germany.

*PHAR LAP, 1926-1932. Ch. g., Night Raid—Entreaty, by Winkie. 51-37-3-2, $305,921, AJC Derby, Victoria Derby, W. S. Cox Plate (twice); won Agua Caliente H. in only start in North America; died shortly after under mysterious circumstances. Considered Australia's greatest racehorse.

PLANET, 1855-1875. Ch. c., Revenue—Nina, by Boston. 31-27-4-0, $69,700, Great Post S. twice, etc. Sire of Katy Pease, Hubbard, Ballet. Replaced Peytona as America's leading money earner.

PLAUDIT, 1895-1919 B. c., Himyar—*Cinderella, by Tomahawk or Blue Ruin. 20-8-5-0, $32,715, Kentucky Derby, Champagne S., etc. Sire of King James, Casuarina, Rosa Mundi, Spoonful. Tail-male ancestor of Dr. Fager, Holy Bull.

POCAHONTAS, 1837-1870. B. f., *Glencoe—Marpessa, by Muley. 9-0-3-0, $0. Greatest English broodmare of 19th century, dam of Stockwell, King Tom, Rataplan. Ancestress of modern families that include foundation mares Rosy Legend, Kizil-Kourgan, Traverse, Traffic Court, Segula as well as racehorses and sires Dante, Sayajirao, *Ksar, *Kantar, Traffic Judge, Hasty Road, Nashua, Louis Quatorze.

POINT GIVEN, 1998- . Ch. c., Thunder Gulch—Turko's Turn, by Turkoman. 13-9-3-0, $3,968,500, Horse of the Year in 2001, champion three-year-old male, Belmont S. (G1), Preakness S. (G1), etc.

POT8O'S, 1773-unknown. Ch. c., Eclipse—Sportsmistress, by Sportsman. 30 wins in England, Craven S., Jockey Club Plate three times, etc. Sire of Champion, Coriander, Mandane, Waxy. Tail-male line ancestor of Phalaris, Hyperion, Blandford, Domino lines.

PREAKNESS, 1867-1881. B. c., Lexington—Bayleaf, by *Yorkshire. 39-18-11-5, $43,679, Dinner Party S., Saratoga Cup, etc. Sire in England of Fiddler, Piccadilly.

PRECISIONIST, 1981- . Ch. c., Crozier—Excellently, by *Forli. 46-20-10-4, $3,485,398, champion sprinter, Breeders' Cup Sprint (G1), Woodward S. (G1), etc. Virtually sterile. Sired only four foals.

PRETTY POLLY, 1901-1931. Ch. f., Gallinule—Admiration, by Saraband. 24-22-2-0, $187,780, champion two- and three-year-old in England, Epsom Oaks, St. Leger S., Coronation Cup twice, etc. Dam of Molly Desmond, Polly Flinders. Tail-female ancestor of Abadan, Arabella, Brigadier Gerard, Carroll House, *Daumier, Donatello II, Flute Enchantee, Flying Water, Luthier, Marwell, Nearctic, Northern Taste, Premonition, Psidium, St. Paddy, Supreme Court, Swain (Ire). Widely regarded as the greatest English racemare of all time; known as "the peerless Pretty Polly."

PRIMONETTA, 1958-1993. Ch. f., Swaps—Banquet Bell, by Polynesian. 25-17-2-2, $306,690, champion older mare, Alabama S., Spinster S. twice, etc. Broodmare of the Year in 1978; dam of Prince Thou Art, Maud Muller, Cum Laude Laurie, Grenfall. Sister to Chateaugay.

*PRINCEQUILLO, 1940-1964. B. c., Prince Rose—*Cosquilla, by *Papyrus. 33-12-5-7, $96,550, Jockey Club Gold Cup, Saratoga Cup, etc. Leading sire 1957-'58; leading broodmare sire 1966-'70, '72, '73, '76. Sire of 65 stakes winners, including Round Table, Dedicate, Prince John, How, Quill, Hill Prince, Misty Morn, Princessnesian, Cherokee Rose, Discipline. Broodmare sire of Bold Lad, *Comtesse de Loir, Fort Marcy, Key to the Mint, Kris S., Mill Reef, Secretariat, Sham, Sir Gaylord.

PRINCESS DOREEN, 1921-1952. B. f., *Spanish Prince II—Lady Doreen, by Ogden. 94-34-15-17, $174,754, Coaching Club American Oaks, Saratoga H., etc. Dam of Miss Doreen. Tail-female ancestor of Brown Bess, Caller I. D.

PRINCESS ROONEY, 1980- . Gr. f., Verbatim—Parrish Princess, by Drone. 21-17-2-1, $1,343,339, champion older female, Breeders' Cup Distaff (G1), Spinster S. (G1), etc.

PRIORESS, 1853-1868. B. f., *Sovereign—Reel, by *Glencoe. 24-10-1-3, $22,637, Cesarewitch H., two Queen's Plates, etc. First American-bred to win in England, victorious in a runoff after a dead heat in the 1857 Cesarewitch H.

PROCTOR KNOTT, 1886-unknown. Ch. g., Luke Blackburn—Tallapoosa, by *Great Tom. 26-11-6-4,

$80,040, Futurity S., Junior Champion S., 2nd Kentucky Derby, etc. First winner of the Futurity Stakes (now at Belmont Park) in 1888, the race that swung the pendulum of American racing toward two-year-old speed because of its large purse.

PRUDERY, 1918-1930. B. f., Peter Pan—Polly Flinders, by Burgomaster. 22-7-6-5, $47,625, champion two-year-old filly, Alabama S., Spinaway S., etc. Dam of Whiskery, Victorian, Halcyon. Tail-female ancestor of Taylor's Special.

QUESTIONNAIRE, 1927-1950. B. c., Sting—Miss Puzzle, by Disguise. 45-19-8-4, $89,611, Metropolitan H., Brooklyn H., etc. Sire of 24 stakes winners, including Requested, Free For All, Carolyn A., Hash, Stefanita, Third Degree. Tail-male line ancestor of Dr. Fager, Holy Bull.

RAISE A NATIVE, 1961-1988. Ch. c., Native Dancer—Raise You, by Case Ace. 4-4-0-0, $45,955, champion two-year-old colt, Juvenile S., Great American S. Sire of 78 stakes winners, including Alydar, Mr. Prospector, Exclusive Native, Majestic Prince, Laomedonte, Crowned Prince, Native Royalty, Marshua's Dancer, Native Partner, Where You Lead. Broodmare sire of Ajdal, Meadowlake, Slightly Dangerous.

REAL DELIGHT, 1949-1969. B. f., Bull Lea—Blue Delight, by Blue Larkspur. 15-12-1-0, $261,822, champion three-year-old filly, champion handicap mare, Coaching Club American Oaks, Kentucky Oaks, etc. Dam of Plum Cake, No Fooling, Spring Sunshine. Foundation mare of family that includes Alydar, Our Mims, Codex, Rich Cream, Christmas Bonus, Grand Slam, Sugar and Spice, Christmas Past.

REEL, 1838-unknown. Gr. f., *Glencoe—*Gallopade, by Catton. 8-7-1-0. Dam of Lecomte, Prioress, Starke, War Dance. Tail-female ancestor of modern family that includes Two Lea, Tim Tam, Miz Clementine, Best Turn, Chris Evert, Chief's Crown, Winning Colors.

REGRET, 1912-1934. Ch. f., Broomstick—Jersey Lightning, by Hamburg. 11-9-1-0, $35,093, Kentucky Derby, Hopeful S., etc. First filly to win the Kentucky Derby. Tail-female ancestor of family that includes First Fiddle, Divine Comedy.

REIGH COUNT, 1925-1948. Ch. c., *Sunreigh—*Contessina, by Count Schomberg. 27-12-4-0, $178,170, champion two- and three-year-old colt, Kentucky Derby, Jockey Club Gold Cup S., Coronation Cup (in England), etc. Sire of 22 stakes winners, including Count Fleet, Triplicate, Count Arthur. Broodmare sire of Gallahadion.

REVENUE, 1843-unknown. B. c., *Trustee—Rosalie Somers, by Sir Charles. 21-16-5-0. Jockey Club Purse, Proprietor's Purse, etc. Leading sire in 1860. Sire of Planet, Fanny Washington, Revolver.

*RIBOT, 1952-1972. B. c., Tenerani—Romanella, by El Greco. 16-16-0-0, $288,648, champion at two, three, and four in Italy, champion at four in England and France, Prix de l'Arc de Triomphe twice, King George VI and Queen Elizabeth S., etc. Leading sire three times in England. Sire of 65 stakes winners, including Arts and Letters, Tom Rolfe, Graustark, His Majesty, Ragusa, Molvedo, Romulus, Boucher, Long Look, *Prince Royal II, Regal Exception, Arkadina. Broodmare sire of more than 100 stakes winners, including Bireme, Cannonade, Cascapedia, Majestic Light, Treizieme.

RIVA RIDGE, 1969-1985. B. c., First Landing—Iberia, by *Heliopolis. 30-17-3-1, $1,111,497, champion two-year-old male, champion handicap male, Kentucky Derby, Belmont S., etc. Sire of 29 stakes winners, including Tap Shoes, Rivalero, Blitey. Broodmare sire of nearly 50 stakes

winners, including Dancing Spree, Life At the Top.

RIVERMAN, 1969-1999. B. c., Never Bend—River Lady, by Prince John. 8-5-2-1, $223,960, Poule d'Essai des Poulains (French Two Thousand Guineas), etc. Leading sire in France in 1980-'81. Sire of 128 stakes winners, including Irish River (Fr), Triptych, Bahri, Gold River (Fr), Detroit (Fr), Imperfect Circle, Korveya. Broodmare sire of Bosra Sham, Carnegie (Ire), Erhaab, Hector Protector, Highest Honor (Fr), Saint Cyrien, Spinning World.

ROAMER, 1911-1919. B. g., *Knight Errant—*Rose Tree II, by Bona Vista. 98-39-26-9, $98,828, Travers S., Carter H., Saratoga H. three times, etc.

ROBERTO, 1969-1988. B. c., Hail to Reason—Bramalea, by Nashua. 14-7-4-0, $332,272, champion three-year-old in England in 1972, champion two-year-old in Ireland in 1971, Epsom Derby, etc. Sire of 85 stakes winners, including Sunshine Forever, Brian's Time, Plenty of Grace, Dynaformer, and of Red Ransom. Broodmare sire of 135 stakes winners, including Blushing K.D., Commander in Chief, Warning (GB).

ROSEBEN, 1901-1918. B. g., *Ben Strome—Rose Leaf, by Duke of Montrose. 111-52-25-12, $75,110, Carter H., Manhattan H. twice, etc. Great sprinter who won 14 races under 140 pounds or more, known as "the big train."

ROUGH'N TUMBLE, 1948-1968. B. c., Free For All—Roused, by *Bull Dog. 16-4-5-4, $126,980, Santa Anita Derby, Primer S., etc. Sire of 24 stakes winners, including Dr. Fager, My Dear Girl, Flag Raiser, Ruffled Feathers, Minnesota Mac, Treasure Chest. Florida foundation sire.

*ROUGH SHOD II, 1944-1965. B. f., Gold Bridge—Dalmary, by Blandford. 7-1-1-1, $1,306. Dam of Moccasin, Ridan, Lt. Stevens, Gambetta, Thong. Foundation mare of family that includes Sadler's Wells, Nureyev, Thatch, Gamely, Drumtop, Fairy King, King Pellinore, El Condor Pasa, Number, Bienamado.

ROUND TABLE, 1954-1987. B. c., *Princequillo—*Knight's Daughter, by Sir Cosmo. 66-43-8-5, $1,749,869, Horse of the Year in 1958, champion grass horse three times, champion handicap horse twice, Santa Anita H., Hollywood Gold Cup H., etc. Leading sire in 1972. Sire of 83 stakes winners, including Baldric, Apalachee, Flirting Around, Targowice, Royal Glint, King Pellinore, Drumtop, Knightly Manner, Advocator, King's Bishop, Artaius, Dancealot, Foreseer, Poker, Tell. Broodmare sire of 125 stakes winners, including Bowl Game, Caerleon, Hidden Lake, Outstandingly, Topsider.

*ROYAL CHARGER, 1942-1961. Ch. c., Nearco—Sun Princess by Solario. 20-6-7-2, $20,291, Queen Anne S., Ayr Gold Cup, etc. Sire of 54 stakes winners, including *Turn-to, Mongo, *Royal Serenade, Royal Native, Idun, Royal Orbit, Gilles de Retz, Happy Laughter, Royal Palm, *Banri an Oir. Broodmare sire of Majestic Prince, Tudor Queen. Tail-male ancestor of Roberto, Halo lines.

ROYAL HEROINE (Ire), 1980- . Dk. b. or br. f., Lypheor (GB)—My Sierra Leone, by Relko. 21-10-4-2, $1,229,449, champion grass female, Breeders' Cup Mile (G1), Matriarch S. (G1), etc. Second dam of Carmine Lake (Ire).

RUFFIAN, 1972-1975. Dk. b. or br. f., Reviewer—Shenanigans, by Native Dancer. 11-10-0-0, $313,428, champion two- and three-year-old filly, filly triple crown, Spinaway S. (G1), etc. Broke down in match race with Foolish Pleasure and euthanized when she reinjured leg after surgery. Buried in infield at Belmont Park.

RUTHLESS, 1864-1876. B. f., *Eclipse—Barbarity, by *Simoom. 11-7-4-0, $11,000, Belmont S., Travers S., etc. Won first Belmont S. Best of five high-class sisters out of Barbarity nicknamed "the barbarous battalion."

SABIN, 1980- . Ch. f., Lyphard—Beaconaire, by *Vaguely Noble. 25-18-0-2, $1,098,341, Yellow Ribbon Invitational S. (G1), etc. Dam of Sabina, Al Sabin.

SADLER'S WELLS, 1981-. B. c., Northern Dancer—Fairy Bridge, by Bold Reason. 11-6-3-0, $713,690, Irish Two Thousand Guineas (Ire-G1), Eclipse S. (Eng-G1), etc. Leading sire in England 12 times. Sire of at least 215 stakes winners, including Galileo (Ire), High Chaparral (Ire), In the Wings (GB), Salsabil (Ire), Old Vic, Northern Spur (Ire), El Prado (Ire), Montjeu (Ire), Carnegie (Ire), Barathea (Ire), Imagine, King of Kings (Ire), Fort Wood.

SAFELY KEPT, 1986-. B. f., Horatius—Safely Home, by Winning Hit. 31-24-2-3, $2,194,206, champion sprinter, Breeders' Cup Sprint (G1), Test S. (G1), etc.

SALVATOR, 1886-1909. Ch. c., *Prince Charlie—Salina, by Lexington. 19-16-1-1, $113,240, champion three-year-old, Suburban H., Lawrence Realization, etc. Sire of Salvation. Subject of the Ella Wheeler Wilcox poem "How Salvator Won."

SARAZEN, 1921-1940. Ch. g., High Time—Rush Box, by Box. 55-27-2-6, $225,000, Champagne S., Carter H., Dixie H. twice, etc. Defeated *Epinard in third race of the International Series of 1924.

SCEPTRE, 1899-1927. Br. f., Persimmon—Ornament, by Bend Or. 25-13-4-4, $192,544, champion three-year-old, champion older horse, Epsom Oaks, Two Thousand Guineas, One Thousand Guineas, St. Leger S., etc. Dam of Curia, Grosvenor. Tail-female ancestor of Buchan, Commanche Run, Craig an Eran, Relko, Reliance, *Match II, *Noor, *St. Germans, Sunny Jane, Torbido. One of two fillies to win four of the five English classics.

SEA-BIRD, 1962-1973. Ch. c., Dan Cupid—Sicalade, by Sicambre. 8-7-1-0, $645,283, Horse of the Year in France and England, Epsom Derby, Prix de l'Arc de Triomphe, etc. Sire of 33 stakes winners, including Allez France, Little Current, Gyr, Arctic Tern, Kittiwake. Broodmare sire of Alydar's Best, Assert (Ire), Bikala, Miss Oceana.

SEABISCUIT, 1933-1947. B. c., Hard Tack—Swing On, by Whisk Broom II. 89-33-15-13, $437,730, Horse of the Year in 1938, champion handicap male twice, Pimlico Special, Santa Anita H., etc. Sire of four stakes winners, including Sea Swallow.

SEARCHING, 1952-1973. B. f., War Admiral—Big Hurry, by Black Toney. 89-25-14-16, $327,381, Maskette H., Diana H. twice, etc. Dam of Affectionately, Priceless Gem, Admiring. Foundation mare of family that includes Allez France, Sea Hero, Lite Light, Personality, Al Mamoon.

SEATTLE SLEW, 1974-2002. Dk. b. or br. c., Bold Reasoning—My Charmer, by Poker. 17-14-2-0, $1,208,726, Horse of the Year in 1977, champion two- and three-year-old male, champion older male, Triple Crown, Woodward S. (G1), etc. Leading sire in 1984; leading broodmare sire 1995-'96. Sire of at least 107 stakes winners, including A.P. Indy, Swale, Slew o' Gold, Surfside, Capote, Landaluce, Vindication, Slew City Slew, Taiki Blizzard, Lakeway, Honest Lady, General Meeting, Avenue of Flags, Slewvescent, Slewacide. Broodmare sire of more than 110 stakes winners, including Cigar, Agnes World, Escena, Lemon Drop Kid, Golden Attraction, Seeking the Pearl. Only horse to win Triple Crown while undefeated.

SECRETARIAT, 1970-1989. Ch. c., Bold Ruler—Somethingroyal, by *Princequillo. 21-16-3-1, $1,316,808, Horse of the Year in 1972-'73, champion two- and three-year-old male, champion grass male, Triple Crown, Marlboro Cup H., etc. Leading broodmare sire in 1992. Sire of 56 stakes winners, including Lady's Secret, Risen Star, Medaille d'Or, Terlingua, General Assembly, Tinners Way, Weekend Surprise, Secrettame, Six Crowns. Broodmare sire of nearly 100 stakes winners, including A.P. Indy, Chief's Crown, Dehere, Gone West, Secreto, Storm Cat, Summer Squall.

SELIMA, 1745-1766. B. f., Godolphin Arabian—Shireborn mare, by Hobgoblin. 2-2-0-0, $10,200, Great Intercolonial Match Race with Tryal. Dam of Ariel, Selim, Ebony, Bellair, Lightfoot's Partner. Tail-female ancestor of family that includes Hanover, Inspector B., Peytona, Foxhall, The Vid, Pirate's Revenge, Cherokee Run.

SENSATION, 1877-1899. Br. c., *Leamington—Susan Beane, by Lexington. 8-8-0-0, $20,250, champion two-year-old colt, Flash S., Nursery S., etc. Sire of Democrat.

SERENA'S SONG, 1992- . B. f., Rahy—Imagining, by Northfields. 38-18-11-3, $3,283,388, champion three-year-old filly, Mother Goose S. (G1), Beldame S. (G1), etc. Leading North American money-earning female at time of retirement. Dam of Serena's Tune, Sophisticat.

SHIRLEY JONES, 1956-1978. B. f., Double Jay—L'Omelette, by *Alibhai. 49-18-9-5, $282,313, Test S., Maskette H., etc.

SHUVEE, 1966-1986. Ch. f., Nashua—Levee, by Hill Prince. 44-16-10-6, $890,445, champion handicap mare, champion older female, filly triple crown, Jockey Club Gold Cup twice, etc. Dam of Tom Swift, Shukey, Benefice.

SICKLE, 1924-1943. Br. c., Phalaris—Selene, by Chaucer. 10-3-4-2, $23,629, Prince of Wales's S., etc. Leading sire in 1936, '38. Sire of 41 stakes winners, including Stagehand, Brevity, Unbreakable, Star Pilot, Cravat, Reaping Reward, Misty Isle, Jabot. Broodmare sire of Bornastar, Counterpoint, Dan Cupid, How, Social Outcast. Tail-male ancestor of Native Dancer sire line.

SILVERBULLETDAY, 1996-. B. f., Silver Deputy—Rokeby Rose, by Tom Rolfe. 23-15-3-1, $3,093,207, champion two- and three-year-old filly, Breeders' Cup Juvenile Fillies (G1), Kentucky Oaks (G1), etc.

SILVER CHARM, 1994-. Gr. or ro. c., Silver Buck—Bonnie's Poker, by Poker. 24-12-7-2, $6,944,369, champion three-year-old male, Kentucky Derby (G1), Preakness S. (G1), Dubai World Cup (UAE-G1), etc.

SILVER SPOON, 1956-1978. Ch. f., Citation—Silver Fog, by *Mahmoud. 27-13-3-4, $313,930, champion three-year-old filly, Santa Anita Derby, Milady H., etc. Dam of Inca Queen. Tail-female ancestor of family that includes Catinca, Metfield.

SIR ARCHY, 1805-1833. Ch. c., *Diomed—*Castianira, by Rockingham. 7-4-1-0, Post S. Leading Colonial sire. Sire of Sir Charles, Timoleon, Flirtilla, Bertrand, Henry, Kosciusko, Lady Lightfoot, Sumpter, Reality. Oldest member of the Racing Hall of Fame.

SIR BARTON, 1916-1937. Ch. c., *Star Shoot—Lady Sterling, by Hanover. 31-13-6-5, $116,857, champion three-year-old colt, Triple Crown, Saratoga H., etc. First winner of the American Triple Crown. Sire of seven stakes winners, including Easter Stockings.

SIR GALLAHAD III, 1920-1949. B. c., *Teddy—Plucky Liege, by Spearmint. 24-11-3-3, $17,009, Poule d'Essai des Poulains (French Two Thousand Guineas), Prix Jacques le Marois, Match race with *Epinard, etc. Leading sire 1930, '33-'34, '40; leading broodmare sire '39, '43-'52, '55. Sire of 56 stakes winners, including Gallant Fox, Gallahadion, High Quest, Vagrancy, Foxbrough, Fighting Fox, Hoop, Jr., Roman. Broodmare sire of 180 stakes winners, including Beaugay, Challedon, *Galatea II, Gallorette, Johnstown, Royal Native. Greatest American broodmare sire of the 20th century. First major stallion syndication.

SKIP AWAY, 1993- . Gr. or ro. c., Skip Trial—Ingot Way, by Diplomat Way. 38-18-10-6, $9,616,360, Horse of the Year in 1998, champion three-year-old male, champion older male twice, Breeders' Cup Classic (G1), Jockey Club Gold Cup (G1) twice, etc.

SKY BEAUTY, 1990- . B. f., Blushing Groom (Fr)—Maplejinsky, by Nijinsky II. 21-15-2-2, $1,336,000, champion older female, filly triple crown, Alabama S. (G1), Ruffian H. (G1), etc.

SLEW O' GOLD, 1980- . B. c., Seattle Slew—Alluvial, by Buckpasser. 21-12-5-1, $3,533,534, champion three-year-old male, champion older male, Jockey Club Gold Cup (G1) twice, Woodward S. (G1) twice, etc. Sire of 30 stakes winners, including Golden Opinion, Gorgeous, Dramatic Gold, Thirty Six Red, Awe Inspiring. Broodmare sire of Kona Gold.

SOMETHINGROYAL, 1952-1983. B. f., *Princequillo—Imperatrice, by Caruso. 1-0-0-0, $0. Broodmare of the Year in 1973. Dam of Secretariat, Sir Gaylord, First Family, Syrian Sea, Somethingfabulous. Foundation mare of family that includes Saratoga Dew, Alada, John Cherry, Personal Business.

SPECTACULAR BID, 1976-2003. Gr. or ro. c., Bold Bidder—Spectacular, by Promised Land. 30-26-2-1, $2,781,608, Horse of the Year in 1980, champion two- and three-year-old male, champion older male, Kentucky Derby (G1), Preakness S. (G1), etc. Sire of more than 40 stakes winners, including Lotus Pool, Double Feint, Spectacular Love. Broodmare sire of nearly 70 stakes winners.

SPEND A BUCK, 1982-2002. B. c., Buckaroo—Belle de Jour, by Speak John. 15-10-3-2, $4,220,689, Horse of the Year in 1985, champion three-year-old male, Kentucky Derby (G1), Monmouth H. (G1), etc. Sire of more than 30 stakes winners, including Antespend, Investor's Dream. Exported to Brazil in 1997.

SPENDTHRIFT, 1876-1900. Ch. c., *Australian—Aerolite, by Lexington. 13-10-5-0, $27,250, Belmont S., Jersey Derby, etc. Sire of Kingston, Hastings, Lamplighter, Bankrupt. Tail-male ancestor of line that leads to Fair Play, Man o' War, War Admiral, In Reality, Tiznow.

SPINAWAY, 1878-unknown. Ch. f., *Leamington—Megara, by *Eclipse. 9-7-2-0, $16,225, champion two-year-old filly, Hopeful S., Juvenile S., etc. Dam of Lazzarone. Tail-female ancestor of family that includes Giant's Causeway, Tanya, Floradora, Star Pilot, By Land By Sea, Gummo, Spearfish, Gaily, King's Bishop.

SPY SONG, 1943-1973. Br. c., Balladier—Mata Hari, by Peter Hastings. 36-15-9-4, $206,325, Arlington Futurity, Clang H., etc. Sire of 28 stakes winners, including Crimson Satan, Sly Pola, Sari's Song. Broodmare sire of 91 stakes winners, including Blue Tom, Faraway Son, Liloy (Fr), Singh.

STAR SHOOT, 1898-1919. B. c., Isinglass—Astrology, by Hermit. 10-3-1-1, $34,747 in England, National Breeders' Produce S., etc. Leading sire 1911-'12, '16-'17, '19; leading broodmare sire 1924-'26, '28-'29. Sire of Sir Barton, Grey Lag, Uncle, Wistful, Daylight

Saving, Mindful, Priscilla. Broodmare sire of Blazes, Crusader, Gusto, Jack High. Sired a record 27 juvenile winners in 1916 that stood for 70 years.

STOCKWELL, 1849-1870. Ch. c., The Baron—Pocahontas, by *Glencoe. 16-11-3-0, $48,457, champion three-year-old in England, Two Thousand Guineas, St. Leger S., etc. Leading sire in England seven times. Sire of Doncaster, Achievement, Caller Ou, Cantiniere, Chevisaunce, Lord Lyon, Regalia, St. Albans, The Marquis. Known as the "Emperor of Stallions." Tail-male ancestor of Phalaris male line.

STRAIGHT DEAL, 1962-1982. B. f., Hail to Reason—No Fiddling, by King Cole. 99-21-21-9, $733,020, champion handicap mare, Delaware H., Santa Margarita H., etc. Dam of Desiree, Reminiscing.

ST. SIMON, 1881-1908. Br. c., Galopin—St. Angela, by King Tom. 9-9-0-0, $23,121, Ascot Gold Cup, Epsom Gold Cup, Goodwood Cup, etc. Leading sire in England nine times. Sire of Persimmon, Diamond Jubilee, St. Frusquin, Rabelais, Chaucer, Memoir, La Fleche. Tail-male ancestor of *Ribot, *Princequillo male lines.

STYMIE, 1941-1962. Ch. c., Equestrian—Stop Watch, by On Watch. 131-35-33-28, $918,485, champion handicap horse, Metropolitan H. twice, Whitney S., etc. Sire of 12 stakes winners, including Rare Treat, Joe Jones, Paper Tiger. Broodmare sire of Regal Gleam, What a Treat. Retired as world's leading money earner in 1950.

SUN BEAU, 1925-1944. B. c., *Sun Briar—Beautiful Lady, by Fair Play. 74-33-12-10, $376,744, champion handicap horse three times, Hawthorne Gold Cup three times, Aqueduct H., etc. Sire of six stakes winners, including Sun Lover. Leading money earner at his retirement in 1931.

SUN BRIAR, 1915-1943. B. c., Sundridge—*Sweet Briar II, by St. Frusquin. 22-8-4-5, $74,355, champion two-year-old colt, Travers S., Hopeful S., etc. Sire of more than 30 stakes winners, including Sun Beau, Pompey, Firethorn.

SUNDAY SILENCE, 1986-2002. Dk. b. or br. c., Halo—Wishing Well, by Understanding. 14-9-5-0, $4,968,554, Horse of the Year in 1989, champion three-year-old male, Kentucky Derby (G1), Preakness S. (G1), Breeders' Cup Classic (G1), etc. Leading sire in Japan 1995-2002. Sire of more than 88 stakes winners, including Air Shakur, Dance Partner, Marvelous Sunday, Dance in the Dark, Bubble Gum Fellow, Fuji Kiseki, Special Week, Stay Gold, Genuine, Tayasu Tsuyoshi. All-time leading sire by earnings, exceeding $372-million.

SUSAN'S GIRL, 1969-1988. B. f., Quadrangle—Quaze, by *Quibu. 63-29-14-11, $1,251,668, champion three-year-old filly, champion older female twice, Spinster S. (G1) twice, Delaware H. (G1) twice, etc. Dam of Copelan, Paramount Jet.

SWALE, 1981-1984. Dk. b. or br. c., Seattle Slew—Tuerta, by *Forli. 14-9-2-2, $1,583,660, champion three-year-old male, Kentucky Derby (G1), Belmont S. (G1), etc. Died eight days after winning Belmont Stakes.

SWAPS, 1952-1972. Ch. c., *Khaled—Iron Reward, by *Beau Pere. 25-19-2-2, $848,900, Horse of the Year in 1956, champion handicap horse, Kentucky Derby, Hollywood Gold Cup H., etc. Sire of 35 stakes winners, including Affectionately, Chateaugay, Primonetta, No Robbery. Broodmare sire of Best Turn, Fall Aspen, Numbered Account, Personality.

SWOON'S SON, 1953-1977. B. c., The Doge—Swoon, by Sweep Like. 51-30-10-3, $970,605, American Derby, Arlington Classic, etc. Sire of 22 stakes winners, including Chris Evert, Loom, Mr. Washington. Won 22 stakes.

SWORD DANCER, 1956-1984. Ch. c., Sunglow—Highland Fling, by By Jimminy. 39-15-7-4, $829,610, Horse of the Year in 1959, champion three-year-old colt, champion handicap horse, Belmont S., Jockey Club Gold Cup, etc. Sire of 15 stakes winners, including Damascus, Lady Pitt.

SYSONBY, 1902-1906. B. c., *Melton—*Optime, by Orme. 15-14-0-1, $184,438, champion two- and three-year-old colt, Metropolitan H., Saratoga Special, etc. Died at four.

TANYA, 1902-1929. Ch. f., *Meddler—Handspun, by Hanover. 10-6-1-1, $73,127, Belmont S., Hopeful S., Spinaway S., etc. Second filly to win the Belmont S.

TA WEE, 1966-1980. Dk. b. or br. f., Intentionally—Aspidistra, by Better Self. 21-15-2-1, $284,941, champion sprinter twice, Vosburgh H., Fall Highweight H. twice, etc. Dam of Great Above, Tax Holiday, Entropy, Tweak.

TEDDY, 1913-1936. B. c., Ajax—Rondeau, by Bay Ronald. 8-5-1-2, Grand Premio de San Sebastian, Prix des Trois Ans, etc. Leading sire in France twice. Sire of *Sir Gallahad III, *Bull Dog, *La Troienne, *Ortello, Aethelstan, Asterus, Rose of England, Brumeux, Case Ace, Sun Teddy, Anne de Bretagne, Anna Bolena, Assignation, Boxeuse, Coeur a Coeur, La Moqueuse. Tail-male ancestor of line leading to Damascus, Private Account, Captain Steve.

TEMPTED, 1955-unknown. Ch. f., *Half Crown—Enchanted Eve, by Lovely Night. 45-18-4-9, $330,760, champion handicap mare, Alabama S., Ladies H., etc. Dam of Lead Me On.

TEN BROECK, 1872-1887. B. c., *Phaeton—Fanny Holton, by Lexington. 30-23-3-1, $27,550, Phoenix Hotel S., Louisville Cup, etc. Sire of Jim Gray. Once held every major American record from one to four miles.

TENNY, 1886-1909. B. c., *Rayon d'Or—Belle of Maywood, by Hunter's Lexington. 65-25-15-12, $88,442, Brooklyn H., First Special S., etc. Defeated Racing Hall of Fame members Firenze, Hanover, and Kingston, but consistently beaten by Racing Hall of Famer Salvator.

THAD STEVENS, 1865-unknown. Ch. g., Langford—Mary Chilton, by *Glencoe. Great California four-miler.

THE TETRARCH, 1911-1935. Gr. c., Roi Herode—Vahren, by Bona Vista. 7-7-0-0, $55,206, Champagne S., Coventry S., etc. Leading sire in England in 1924. Sire of Mumtaz Mahal, Tetratema, Salmon Trout, *Stefan the Great, Caligula, Polemarch, Paola, Snow Maiden, *The Satrap. Called "the Spotted Wonder," revived the Herod male line in England and popularized the gray coat color.

THE VERY ONE, 1975-1992. B. f., One for All—*Veruschka, by Venture. 71-22-12-9, $1,104,623, Santa Barbara H. (G1), Black Helen H. (G2), etc.

THUNDER GULCH, 1992- . Ch. c., Gulch—Line of Thunder, by Storm Bird. 16-9-2-2, $2,915,086, champion three-year-old male, Kentucky Derby (G1), Belmont S. (G1), etc. Sire of nearly 30 stakes winners, including Point Given, Spain.

TIMOLEON, 1813-1836. Ch. c., Sir Archy—Saltram mare, by *Saltram. 16-14-0-0. Sire of Boston, Hotspur, Sally Walker, Saluda, Omega, Washington.

TIM TAM, 1955-1982. Dk. b. or br. c., Tom Fool—Two Lea, by Bull Lea. 14-10-1-2, $467,475, champion three-year-old colt, Kentucky Derby, Preakness S., etc. Sire of 14 stakes winners, including Tosmah, Timmy

Lad, Nancy Jr. Broodmare sire of Before Dawn, Davona Dale, Known Fact, Mac Diarmida, Tentam.

TIPPITY WITCHET, 1915-unknown. B. g., Broomstick—*Lady Frivoles, by St. Simon. 266-78-52-42, $88,241. Raced to age 14, beginning his career in stakes but descending to the claiming ranks.

TIZNOW, 1997- . B. c., Cee's Tizzy—Cee's Song, by Seattle Song. 15-8-4-2, $6,427,830, Horse of the Year in 2000, champion three-year-old male, champion older male, Breeders' Cup Classic (G1) twice, Santa Anita H. (G1), etc. Only dual winner of the Breeders' Cup Classic.

T.M.OPERA O, 1996-. Ch. c., Opera House (GB)—Once Wed, by Blushing Groom (Fr). 26-14-6-3, $16,200,337, Horse of the Year in Japan, champion three-year-old in Japan, Japan Cup (Jpn-G1), etc. World's leading money-winning Thoroughbred.

TOM BOWLING, 1870-unknown. B. c., Lexington—Lucy Fowler, by *Albion. 17-14-3-0, $35,000, champion three-year-old colt, Travers S., Jersey Derby, Jerome S., Monmouth Cup, etc. Sire of General Monroe.

TOM FOOL, 1949-1976. B. c., Menow—Gaga, by *Bull Dog. 30-21-7-1, $570,165, Horse of the Year in 1953, champion two-year-old colt, champion handicap horse, champion sprinter, handicap triple crown, Futurity S., etc. Leading broodmare sire in England in 1965. Sire of 36 stakes winners, including Buckpasser, Tim Tam, Silly Season, Tompion, Dunce, Jester, Funloving, Sweet Folly, Dinner Partner, Dunce Cap II. Broodmare sire of 90 stakes winners, including Foolish Pleasure, Hatchet Man, Late Bloomer, *Meadow Court, Stop the Music, Majesty's Prince.

TOM ROLFE, 1962-1989. B. c., *Ribot—Pocahontas, by Roman. 32-16-5-5, $671,297, champion three-year-old colt, Preakness S., American Derby-ntr, etc. Sire of 49 stakes winners, including Hoist the Flag, Run the Gantlet, Droll Role, Bowl Game. Broodmare sire of more than 105 stakes winners, including Diminuendo, Environment Friend, Forty Niner, Life's Magic, Niniski, Notebook, Silverbulletday.

TOP FLIGHT, 1929-1949. Dk. br. or br. f., *Dis Donc—Flyatit, by Peter Pan. 16-12-0-0, $275,900, champion two- and three-year-old filly, Coaching Club American Oaks, Futurity S., etc. Dam of Flight Command. Tail-female ancestor of family that includes Watch Fob, Sikeston. World's leading money-winning female at time of retirement.

TOSMAH, 1961-1992. B. f., Tim Tam—Cosmah, by Cosmic Bomb. 39-23-6-2, $612,588, champion two- and three-year-old filly, champion handicap mare, Frizette S., Beldame S., etc. Dam of La Guidecca.

TREMONT, 1884-1901. Bl. c., Virgil—Ann Fief, by Alarm. 13-13-0-0, $39,135, champion two-year-old colt, Great American S., etc.

TURNBACK THE ALARM, 1989- . Gr. or ro. f., Darn That Alarm—Boomie's Girl E., by *Figonero. 22-8-6-4, $960,504, Coaching Club American Oaks (G1), Mother Goose S. (G1), etc.

TURN-TO, 1951-1973. B. c., *Royal Charger—*Source Sucree, by Admiral Drake. 8-6-1-1, $280,032, Garden State S., Flamingo S., etc. Sire of 25 stakes winners, including First Landing, Hail to Reason, Sir Gaylord, Best Turn, Cyane, Turn to Talent. Broodmare sire of 63 stakes winners, including Ack Ack, Bessarabian, Chinook Pass.

T. V. LARK, 1957-1975. B. c., *Indian Hemp—Miss Larksfly, by Heelfly. 72-19-13-6, $902,194, champion grass horse, Washington, D. C., International S., United

Nations H., etc. Leading sire in 1974. Sire of 53 stakes winners, including Quack, T. V. Commercial, Pink Pigeon, Buffalo Lark, Golden Don, T. V. Vixen, Romeo. Broodmare sire of 85 stakes winners, including Bates Motel, Chris Evert.

TWENTY GRAND, 1928-1948. B. c., *St. Germans—Bonus, by *All Gold. 23-14-4-3, $261,790, Horse of the Year in 1931, champion three-year-old colt, Kentucky Derby, Belmont S., etc. Sterile at stud.

TWILIGHT TEAR, 1941-1954. B. f., Bull Lea—Lady Lark, by Blue Larkspur. 24-18-2-2, $202,165, Horse of the Year in 1944, champion two- and three-year-old filly, champion handicap mare, Coaching Club American Oaks, Pimlico Special, etc. Dam of A Gleam, Bardstown, Coiner. Tail-female ancestor of family that includes Before Dawn, Gleaming, A Glitter.

TWO LEA, 1946-1973. B. f., Bull Lea—Two Bob, by The Porter. 26-15-6-3, $309,250, champion three-year-old filly, champion handicap mare, Hollywood Gold Cup H., Santa Margarita H., etc. Dam of Tim Tam, On-and-On, Pied d'Or.

ULTIMUS, 1906-1921. Ch c., Commando—Running Stream, by Domino. Unraced. Sire of Luke McLuke, High Time, High Cloud, Infinite, Stimulus, Supremus. Broodmare sire of Bold Venture, Case Ace, Flying Heels. One of the very few unraced successful sires; inbred 2x2 to Domino.

UNBRIDLED, 1987-2001. B. c., Fappiano—Gana Facil, by *Le Fabuleux. 24-8-6-6, $4,489,475, champion three-year-old male, Kentucky Derby (G1), Breeders' Cup Classic (G1), etc. Sire of Banshee Breeze, Anees, Unbridled's Song, Manistique.

UPSET, 1917-1941. Ch. c., Whisk Broom II—Pankhurst, by *Voter. 17-5-7-1, $37,504, Sanford S., etc. Only horse to defeat Man o' War. Sire of 11 stakes winners, including Misstep.

VAGRANCY, 1939-1964. Dk. b. or br. f., *Sir Gallahad III—Valkyr, by Man o' War. 42-15-8-8, $102,480, champion three-year-old filly, champion handicap mare, Coaching Club American Oaks, Alabama S., etc. Dam of Black Tarquin, Vulcania. Tail-female ancestor of family that includes Ferdinand, Fiddle Isle, Natashka, Tallahto, Hidden Light, Truly Bound, Anees.

VANDAL, 1850-unknown. B. c., *Glencoe—Tranby Mare, by *Tranby. 6-4-1-1. Sire of Vandalite, Survivor, Virgil, Capitola, Vicksburg, Mollie Jackson, Ella D.

VERTEX, 1954-1981. Ch. c., The Rhymer—Kanace, by Case Ace. 25-17-3-1, $453,424, Pimlico Special, Gulfstream Park H., etc. Sire of 25 stakes winners, including Lucky Debonair, Top Knight, Vertee. Broodmare sire of 50 stakes winners.

VICTORIA PARK, 1957-1985. B. c., Chop Chop—Victoriana, by Windfields. 19-10-4-2, $250,076, Horse of the Year in Canada, Queen's Plate, Remsen S., etc. Sire of 25 stakes winners, including Kennedy Road, Solometeor, Victorian Era, Floral Victory. Broodmare sire of Northern Taste, The Minstrel.

VOLANTE, 1882-unknown. B. c., Grinstead—Sister Anne, by Glenelg. 84-35-28-12, $72,099, American Derby, Saratoga Cup, etc.

VOTER, 1894-unknown. Ch. c., Friar's Balsam—*Mavourneen, by Barcaldine. 49-26-6-7, $34,217, Metropolitan H., Toboggan H., etc. Sire of Ballot, Runnymede, Curiosity, Inaugural, Pankhurst.

WAGNER, 1834-1862. Ch. c., Sir Charles—Maria West, by Marion. 18-12-6-0, $34,150, Jockey Club Purse, etc. Sire of Imp, Starke, Lavender, Rhynodyne, Neil Robinson, Endorser.

WANDA, 1882-1905. Ch. f., *Mortemer—Minnie Minor, by Lexington. 24-12-8-0, $58,160, Monmouth Oaks, Champion Stallion S., etc. Tail-female ancestor of family that includes Swaps, Iron Liege, Flying Ebony, Creme dela Creme, Cascapedia, Althea, Green Desert, *Durbar II, Kauai King.

WAR ADMIRAL, 1934-1959. Br. c., Man o' War—Brushup, by Sweep. 26-21-3-1, $273,240, Horse of the Year in 1937, champion three-year-old colt, Triple Crown, Jockey Club Gold Cup, Belmont S., etc. Leading sire in 1945; leading broodmare sire '62, '64. Sire of 40 stakes winners, including Busher, Blue Peter, Searching, Admiral Vee, Busanda, War Date, Blue Banner, Mr. Busher, Bee Mac, Striking. Broodmare sire of 112 stakes winners, including Affectionately, Better Self, Buckpasser, Crafty Admiral, Gun Bow, Hoist the Flag, Iron Liege, Never Say Die, Priceless Gem.

WAR RELIC, 1938-1963. Ch. c., Man o' War—Friar's Carse, by Friar Rock. 20-9-4-2, $89,495, Massachusetts H., Kenner S., etc. Sire of Battlefield, Intent, Relic, Missile. Broodmare sire of Hail to All, My Dear Girl. Tail-male ancestor of male line that includes Tiznow, In Reality, Relaunch.

WEEKEND SURPRISE, 1980-2001. B. f., Secretariat—Lassie Dear, by Buckpasser. 31-7-5-10, $402,892, Golden Rod S. (G3), Schuylerville S. (G3), etc. Broodmare of the Year in 1992. Dam of A.P. Indy, Summer Squall, Welcome Surprise, Horror Grades.

WHICHONE, 1927-1944. Br. c., *Chicle—Flying Witch, by Broomstick. 14-10-2-1, $192,705, champion two-year-old colt, Futurity S., Champagne S., etc. Sire of ten stakes winners, including Handcuff, Today. Rival of Gallant Fox; first winner of $100,000 first-prize purse. Full brother to Mother Goose.

WHIRLAWAY, 1938-1953. Ch. c., *Blenheim II—Dustwhirl, by Sweep. 60-32-15-9, $561,161, Horse of the Year in 1941-'42, champion two- and three-year-old colt, champion handicap horse, Triple Crown, Jockey Club Gold Cup, Travers S., etc. Sire of 18 stakes winners, including Scattered, Kurun, Whirl Some. Exported to France in 1950.

WHISK BROOM II, 1907-1928. Ch. c., Broomstick—Audience, by Sir Dixon. 26-10-8-0, $38,776, first winner of America's handicap triple crown, Victoria Cup (in England), etc. Sire of Whiskery, Diavolo, Victorian, Whiskaway, John P. Grier, Broomshot, Swing On, Upset, Weno.

WINNING COLORS, 1985- . Ro. f., Caro (Ire)—All Rainbows, by Bold Hour. 19-8-3-1, $1,526,837, champion three-year-old filly, Kentucky Derby (G1), Santa Anita Derby (G1), etc. Third filly to win Kentucky Derby.

YO TAMBIEN, 1889-1896. Ch. f., Joe Hooker—Marian, by Malcolm. 73-44-11-9, $89,480, Garfield Park Derby, etc. Half sister to Emperor of Norfolk, El Rio Rey.

YOUR HOST, 1947-1961. Ch. c., *Alibhai—*Boudoir II, by *Mahmoud. 23-13-5-2, $384,795, Santa Anita Derby, Del Mar Futurity, etc. Sire of 16 stakes winners, including Kelso, Social Climber, Windy Sands.

ZACCIO, 1976- . Ch. g., *Lorenzaccio—Delray Dancer, by Chateaugay. 42-22-7-3, $288,124, champion steeplechaser three times, Colonial Cup International Stp. twice, Temple Gwathmey Stp. H., etc.

ZEV, 1920-1943. Br. c., The Finn—Miss Kearney, by *Planudes. 43-23-8-5, $313,639, champion two- and three-year-old colt, Kentucky Derby, Belmont S., International Race S., etc. Sire of two stakes winners. Defeated *Papyrus in first international race in U.S. Retired as world's leading money earner.

ECLIPSE AWARDS
History of the Eclipse Awards

Thoroughbred racing's first official champions were recognized for the 1936 racing season by *Daily Racing Form*, which named Granville as Horse of the Year and selected champions in six divisions.

Beginning in the 1950 racing season, Thoroughbred Racing Associations, formed eight years earlier, announced its own set of champions. Usually the *Form*'s and TRA's separate lists of champions coincided, but sometimes they did not. For example, Horse of the Year titles went separately to One Count and Native Dancer in 1952, Bold Ruler and Dedicate in '57, Roman Brother and Moccasin in '65, and Fort Marcy and Personality in '70.

In 1971, J. B. Faulconer, then president of the Turf Publicists of America, an organization of marketing and public-relations representatives from racetrack and industry organizations, was asked by Monmouth Park executive Philip H. Iselin to head a special committee to consolidate the year-end championship honors. Faulconer helped to bring together the *Form*, TRA, and the National Turf Writers Association, to select one set of champions.

Faulconer is credited with naming the Eclipse Award, which honors the great 18th-century English racehorse and sire from whom many modern-day Thoroughbreds descend. He selected Lexington artist Adalin Wichman to design the award statuette of a lone Thoroughbred tacked in preparation for a race, and he served as master of ceremonies at the inaugural awards dinner on January 26, 1972, at New York's Waldorf Astoria. Faulconer was the host through 1976. Today, the National Thoroughbred Racing Association has replaced the TRA in the three voting groups. Members of the three eligible organizations vote on winners of the ten divisional categories and then select the Horse of the Year. In addition, the groups vote on the outstanding breeder, owner, trainer, jockey, and apprentice jockey. In the equine categories, each voting group's first choice counts ten points, with five points for second and one point for third, for a maximum of 30 points. In balloting for Horse of the Year and outstanding owner, breeder, trainer, jockey, and apprentice jockey, each voting group receives one vote counting one point for a maximum of three points. Additionally, an Award of Merit and a Special Award are given on occasion for noteworthy contributions to Thoroughbred racing.

Eclipse Awards generally are presented shortly after the conclusion of the previous year's racing season. Since the awards were founded, a few notable events have occurred. In 1978, a tie in the voting for outstanding two-year-old filly resulted in It's in the Air and Candy Eclair being named co-champions, while Dr. Patches and J. O. Tobin were voted co-champion sprinters. Voting procedures were changed to eliminate ties. In 1979, the champion turf horse division was divided into male and female categories. In Eclipse history, two-year-olds have been voted Horse of the Year just twice: Secretariat (1972) and Favorite Trick ('97).

While horses and horsemen are honored with Eclipse Awards, so too are members of the media. Selected committees vote on the outstanding submissions in several media categories.

Eclipse Award-Winning Horses

Horse of the Year
2002	Azeri (female)
2001	Point Given
2000	Tiznow
1999	Charismatic
1998	Skip Away
1997	Favorite Trick
1996	Cigar
1995	Cigar
1994	Holy Bull
1993	Kotashaan (Fr)
1992	A.P. Indy
1991	Black Tie Affair (Ire)
1990	Criminal Type
1989	Sunday Silence
1988	Alysheba
1987	Ferdinand
1986	Lady's Secret (female)
1985	Spend a Buck
1984	John Henry
1983	All Along (Fr) (female)
1982	Conquistador Cielo
1981	John Henry
1980	Spectacular Bid
1979	Affirmed
1978	Affirmed
1977	Seattle Slew
1976	Forego
1975	Forego
1974	Forego
1973	Secretariat
1972	Secretariat
1971	Ack Ack

Two-Year-Old Male
2002	Vindication
2001	Johannesburg
2000	Macho Uno
1999	Anees
1998	Answer Lively
1997	Favorite Trick
1996	Boston Harbor
1995	Maria's Mon
1994	Timber Country
1993	Dehere
1992	Gilded Time
1991	Arazi
1990	Fly So Free
1989	Rhythm
1988	Easy Goer
1987	Forty Niner
1986	Capote

1985	Tasso
1984	Chief's Crown
1983	Devil's Bag
1982	Roving Boy
1981	Deputy Minister
1980	Lord Avie
1979	Rockhill Native
1978	Spectacular Bid
1977	Affirmed
1976	Seattle Slew
1975	Honest Pleasure
1974	Foolish Pleasure
1973	Protagonist
1972	Secretariat
1971	Riva Ridge

Two-Year-Old Filly
2002	Storm Flag Flying
2001	Tempera
2000	Caressing
1999	Chilukki
1998	Silverbulletday
1997	Countess Diana
1996	Storm Song
1995	Golden Attraction
1994	Flanders

1993	Phone Chatter
1992	Eliza
1991	Pleasant Stage
1990	Meadow Star
1989	Go for Wand
1988	Open Mind
1987	Epitome
1986	Brave Raj
1985	Family Style
1984	Outstandingly
1983	Althea
1982	Landaluce
1981	Before Dawn
1980	Heavenly Cause
1979	Smart Angle
1978	†It's in the Air
	†Candy Eclair
1977	Lakeville Miss
1976	Sensational
1975	Dearly Precious
1974	Ruffian
1973	Talking Picture
1972	La Prevoyante
1971	Numbered Account
†Tied in voting, named co-champions	

Three-Year-Old Male

2002	War Emblem
2001	Point Given
2000	Tiznow
1999	Charismatic
1998	Real Quiet
1997	Silver Charm
1996	Skip Away
1995	Thunder Gulch
1994	Holy Bull
1993	Prairie Bayou
1992	A.P. Indy
1991	Hansel
1990	Unbridled
1989	Sunday Silence
1988	Risen Star
1987	Alysheba
1986	Snow Chief
1985	Spend a Buck
1984	Swale
1983	Slew o' Gold
1982	Conquistador Cielo
1981	Pleasant Colony
1980	Temperence Hill
1979	Spectacular Bid
1978	Affirmed
1977	Seattle Slew
1976	Bold Forbes
1975	Wajima
1974	Little Current
1973	Secretariat
1972	Key to the Mint
1971	Canonero II

Three-Year-Old Filly

2002	Farda Amiga
2001	Xtra Heat
2000	Surfside
1999	Silverbulletday
1998	Banshee Breeze
1997	Ajina
1996	Yanks Music
1995	Serena's Song
1994	Heavenly Prize
1993	Hollywood Wildcat
1992	Saratoga Dew
1991	Dance Smartly
1990	Go for Wand
1989	Open Mind
1988	Winning Colors
1987	Sacahuista
1986	Tiffany Lass
1985	Mom's Command
1984	Life's Magic
1983	Heartlight No. One
1982	Christmas Past
1981	Wayward Lass
1980	Genuine Risk
1979	Davona Dale
1978	Tempest Queen
1977	Our Mims
1976	Revidere
1975	Ruffian
1974	Chris Evert
1973	Desert Vixen
1972	Susan's Girl
1971	Turkish Trousers

Older Male

2002	Left Bank
2001	Tiznow
2000	Lemon Drop Kid
1999	Victory Gallop
1998	Skip Away
1997	Skip Away
1996	Cigar
1995	Cigar
1994	The Wicked North
1993	Bertrando
1992	Pleasant Tap
1991	Black Tie Affair (Ire)
1990	Criminal Type
1989	Blushing John
1988	Alysheba
1987	Ferdinand
1986	Turkoman
1985	Vanlandingham
1984	Slew o' Gold
1983	Bates Motel
1982	Lemhi Gold
1981	John Henry
1980	Spectacular Bid
1979	Affirmed
1978	Seattle Slew
1977	Forego
1976	Forego
1975	Forego
1974	Forego
1973	Riva Ridge
1972	Autobiography
1971	Ack Ack

Older Female

2002	Azeri
2001	Gourmet Girl
2000	Riboletta (Brz)
1999	Beautiful Pleasure
1998	Escena
1997	Hidden Lake
1996	Jewel Princess
1995	Inside Information
1994	Sky Beauty
1993	Paseana (Arg)
1992	Paseana (Arg)
1991	Queena
1990	Bayakoa (Arg)
1989	Bayakoa (Arg)
1988	Personal Ensign
1987	North Sider
1986	Lady's Secret
1985	Life's Magic
1984	Princess Rooney
1983	Ambassador of Luck
1982	Track Robbery
1981	Relaxing
1980	Glorious Song
1979	Waya (Fr)
1978	Late Bloomer
1977	Cascapedia
1976	Proud Delta
1975	Susan's Girl
1974	Desert Vixen
1973	Susan's Girl
1972	Typecast
1971	Shuvee

Turf Male[1]

2002	High Chaparral (Ire)
2001	Fantastic Light
2000	Kalanisi (Ire)
1999	Daylami (Ire)
1998	Buck's Boy
1997	Chief Bearhart
1996	Singspiel (Ire)
1995	Northern Spur (Ire)
1994	Paradise Creek
1993	Kotashaan (Fr)
1992	Sky Classic
1991	Tight Spot
1990	Itsallgreektome
1989	Steinlen (GB)
1988	Sunshine Forever
1987	Theatrical (Ire)
1986	Manila
1985	Cozzene
1984	John Henry
1983	John Henry
1982	Perrault (GB)
1981	John Henry
1980	John Henry
1979	Bowl Game

Turf female[1]

2002	Golden Apples (Ire)
2001	Banks Hill (GB)
2000	Perfect Sting
1999	Soaring Softly
1998	Fiji (GB)
1997	Ryafan
1996	Wandesta (GB)
1995	Possibly Perfect
1994	Hatoof
1993	Flawlessly
1992	Flawlessly
1991	Miss Alleged
1990	Laugh and Be Merry
1989	Brown Bess
1988	Miesque
1987	Miesque
1986	Estrapade
1985	Pebbles (GB)
1984	Royal Heroine (Ire)
1983	All Along (Fr)
1982	April Run (Ire)
1981	De La Rose
1980	Just a Game (Ire)
1979	Trillion

Turf Horse[1]

1978	Mac Diarmida
1977	Johnny D.
1976	Youth
1975	*Snow Knight
1974	Dahlia (female)
1973	Secretariat
1972	*Cougar II
1971	Run the Gantlet

[1] One turf category prior to 1979

Sprinter

2002	Orientate
2001	Squirtle Squirt
2000	Kona Gold
1999	Artax
1998	Reraise
1997	Smoke Glacken
1996	Lit de Justice
1995	Not Surprising
1994	Cherokee Run
1993	Cardmania
1992	Rubiano
1991	Housebuster
1990	Housebuster
1989	Safely Kept (female)
1988	Gulch
1987	Groovy
1986	Smile
1985	Precisionist
1984	Eillo
1983	Chinook Pass
1982	Gold Beauty (female)
1981	Guilty Conscience
1980	Plugged Nickle
1979	Star de Naskra
1978	†Dr. Patches
	†J. O. Tobin
1977	What a Summer (female)
1976	My Juliet (female)
1975	Gallant Bob
1974	Forego
1973	Shecky Greene
1972	Chou Croute (female)
1971	Ack Ack

†Tied in voting, named co-champions

Steeplechaser

2002	Flat Top
2001	Pompeyo (Chi)
2000	All Gong (GB)
1999	Lonesome Glory
1998	Flat Top
1997	Lonesome Glory
1996	Correggio (Ire)
1995	Lonesome Glory
1994	Warm Spell
1993	Lonesome Glory
1992	Lonesome Glory
1991	Morley Street (Ire)
1990	Morley Street (Ire)
1989	Highland Bud
1988	Jimmy Lorenzo (GB)
1987	Inlander (GB)
1986	Flatterer
1985	Flatterer
1984	Flatterer
1983	Flatterer
1982	Zaccio
1981	Zaccio
1980	Zaccio
1979	Martie's Anger
1978	Cafe Prince
1977	Cafe Prince
1976	Straight and True
1975	Life's Illusion
1974	*Gran Kan
1973	Athenian Idol
1972	Soothsayer
1971	Shadow Brook

Eclipse Award-Winning Individuals

Owner

2002	Richard Englander
2001	Richard Englander
2000	Frank Stronach
1999	Frank Stronach
1998	Frank Stronach
1997	Carolyn Hine
1996	Allen E. Paulson
1995	Allen E. Paulson
1994	John Franks
1993	John Franks
1992	Juddmonte Farms
1991	Sam-Son Farm
1990	Mrs. Frances Genter
1989	Ogden Phipps
1988	Ogden Phipps
1987	Mr. and Mrs. Eugene Klein
1986	Mr. and Mrs. Eugene Klein
1985	Mr. and Mrs. Eugene Klein
1984	John Franks
1983	John Franks
1982	Viola Sommer
1981	Dotsam Stable
1980	Mr. and Mrs. Bertram Firestone
1979	Harbor View Farm
1978	Harbor View Farm
1977	Maxwell Gluck
1976	Dan Lasater
1975	Dan Lasater
1974	Dan Lasater
1973	Not awarded
1972	Not awarded
1971	Mr. and Mrs. E. E. Fogelson

Breeder

2002	Juddmonte Farms
2001	Juddmonte Farms
2000	Frank Stronach
1999	William S. Farish & Partners
1998	John and Betty Mabee
1997	John and Betty Mabee
1996	Farnsworth Farms
1995	Juddmonte Farms
1994	William T. Young
1993	Allen E. Paulson
1992	William S. Farish
1991	John and Betty Mabee
1990	Calumet Farm
1989	North Ridge Farm
1988	Ogden Phipps
1987	Nelson Bunker Hunt
1986	Paul Mellon
1985	Nelson Bunker Hunt
1984	Claiborne Farm
1983	E. P. Taylor
1982	Fred W. Hooper
1981	Golden Chance Farm
1980	Adele Paxson
1979	Claiborne Farm
1978	Harbor View Farm
1977	E. P. Taylor
1976	Nelson Bunker Hunt
1975	Fred W. Hooper
1974	John W. Galbreath
1973	Not awarded
1972	Not awarded

1971	Not awarded

Owner-Breeder

1973	Meadow Stable-Meadow Stud (C. T. Chenery)
1972	Meadow Stable-Meadow Stud (C. T. Chenery)
1971	Paul Mellon

Trainer

2002	Bobby Frankel
2001	Bobby Frankel
2000	Bobby Frankel
1999	Bob Baffert
1998	Bob Baffert
1997	Bob Baffert
1996	Bill Mott
1995	Bill Mott
1994	D. Wayne Lukas
1993	Bobby Frankel
1992	Ron McAnally
1991	Ron McAnally
1990	Carl A. Nafzger
1989	Charles Whittingham
1988	C. R. McGaughey
1987	D. Wayne Lukas
1986	D. Wayne Lukas
1985	D. Wayne Lukas
1984	Jack Van Berg
1983	Woody Stephens
1982	Charles Whittingham
1981	Ron McAnally
1980	Grover G. "Buddy" Delp
1979	Lazaro Barrera
1978	Lazaro Barrera
1977	Lazaro Barrera
1976	Lazaro Barrera
1975	Steve DiMauro
1974	Sherrill Ward
1973	H. Allen Jerkens
1972	Lucien Laurin
1971	Charles Whittingham

Jockey

2002	Jerry Bailey
2001	Jerry Bailey
2000	Jerry Bailey
1999	Jorge Chavez
1998	Gary Stevens
1997	Jerry Bailey
1996	Jerry Bailey
1995	Jerry Bailey
1994	Mike Smith
1993	Mike Smith
1992	Kent Desormeaux
1991	Pat Day
1990	Craig Perret
1989	Kent Desormeaux
1988	Jose Santos
1987	Pat Day
1986	Pat Day
1985	Laffit Pincay Jr.
1984	Pat Day
1983	Angel Cordero Jr.
1982	Angel Cordero Jr.
1981	William Shoemaker

1980	Chris McCarron
1979	Laffit Pincay Jr.
1978	Darrel McHargue
1977	Steve Cauthen
1976	Sandy Hawley
1975	Braulio Baeza
1974	Laffit Pincay Jr.
1973	Laffit Pincay Jr.
1972	Braulio Baeza
1971	Laffit Pincay Jr.

Apprentice jockey

2002	Ryan Fogelsonger
2001	Jeremy Rose
2000	Tyler Baze
1999	Ariel Smith
1998	Shaun Bridgmohan
1997	Roberto Rosado, Philip Teator (tie)
1996	Neil Poznansky
1995	Ramon Perez
1994	Dale Beckner
1993	Juan L. Umana
1992	†Rosemary Homeister Jr.
1991	Mickey Walls
1990	Mark Johnston
1989	Michael Luzzi
1988	Steve Capanas
1987	Kent Desormeaux
1986	Allen Stacy
1985	Art Madrid Jr.
1984	Wesley Ward
1983	Declan Murphy
1982	Alberto Delgado
1981	Richard Migliore
1980	Frank Lovato Jr.
1979	Cash Asmussen
1978	Ron Franklin
1977	Steve Cauthen
1976	George Martens
1975	Jimmy Edwards
1974	Chris McCarron
1973	Steve Valdez
1972	Thomas Wallis
1971	Gene St. Leon

†Jesus Bracho was originally awarded the title but relinquished it in 1994.

Eclipse Award of Merit

2002	Ogden Phipps
	Howard Battle
2001	Harry T. Mangurian Jr.
	Pete Pedersen
2000	Jim McKay
1999	Not awarded
1998	D. G. Van Clief Jr.
1997	Bob and Beverly Lewis
1996	Allen E. Paulson
1995	James E. "Ted" Bassett III
1994	Alfred G. Vanderbilt
1993	Paul Mellon
1992	Robert P. Strub, Joe Hirsch
1991	Fred W. Hooper
1990	Warner L. Jones
1989	Michael Sandler

1988	John Forsythe	1998	Oak Tree Racing Association	1978	Not awarded
1987	J. B. Faulconer	1997	Not awarded	1977	Not awarded
1986	Herman Cohen	1996	Not awarded	1976	William Shoemaker
1985	Keene Daingerfield	1995	Russell Baze	1975	Not awarded
1984	John Gaines	1994	Eddie Arcaro, John Longden	1974	Charles Hatton
1983	Not awarded	1993	Not awarded	1973	Not awarded
1982	Not awarded	1992	Not awarded	1972	Not awarded
1981	William Shoemaker	1991	Not awarded	1971	Robert J. Kleberg
1980	John D. Schapiro	1990	Not awarded		
1979	Frank E. "Jimmy" Kilroe	1989	Richard L. Duchossois		**Man of the Year**
1978	Ogden Mills "Dinny" Phipps	1988	Edward J. DeBartolo Sr.	1975	John A. Morris
1977	Steve Cauthen	1987	Anheuser-Busch	1974	William L. McKnight
1976	Jack J. Dreyfus Jr.	1986	Not awarded	1973	Edward P. Taylor
		1985	Arlington Park	1972	John W. Galbreath
	Special Award	1984	C. V. Whitney		
2002	Keeneland Library	1983	Not awarded		**Outstanding Achievement**
2001	Sheikh Mohammed bin Rashid	1982	Not awarded	1972	Arthur B. Hancock
	al Maktoum	1981	Not awarded		(posthumously)
2000	John Hettinger	1980	John T. Landry, Pierre E. Bellocq	1971	Charles Engelhard
1999	Laffit Pincay Jr.	1979	Not awarded		(posthumously)

Eclipse Award Media Winners

Outstanding Newspaper Writing
1999 Maryjean Wall, Lexington *Herald-Leader*
1998 Tom Keyser, Baltimore *Sun*
1997 Maryjean Wall, Lexington *Herald-Leader*
1996 Tom Keyser, Baltimore *Sun*
1995 Stephanie Diaz, Riverside *Press-Enterprise*
1994 Mike Downey, Los Angeles *Times*
1993 Jennie Rees, Louisville *Courier-Journal*
1992 James Wallace, Seattle *Post Intelligencer*
1990 Paul Moran, *Newsday*
1989 Ronnie Virgets, *Gambit*
1988 Billy Reed, Lexington *Herald-Leader*
1987 Tim Layden, Capital Newspapers
1986 Edwin Pope, Miami *Herald*
1985 Paul Moran, *Newsday*
1984 Bill Christine, Los Angeles *Times*
     Eddie Donnally, Dallas *Morning News*
1983 Dave Koemer, Louisville *Times*
1982 Edwin Pope, Miami *Herald*
1981 Dave Kindred, Washington *Post*
1980 Maryjean Wall, Lexington *Herald*
1979 Billy Reed, Louisville *Courier-Journal*
1978 Joe Hirsch, *Daily Racing Form*
1977 Skip Bayless, Los Angeles *Times*
1976 Edwin Pope, Miami *Herald*
1975 Bob Harding, Newark *Star-Ledger*
1974 William H. Rudy, New York *Post*
1973 Red Smith, New York *Times*
1972 Phil Ranallo, Buffalo *Courier Express*
1971 Scott Young, Toronto *Telegram*

Outstanding Magazine Writing
1999 Tom Keyser, Baltimore *Sun*
1998 Laura Hillenbrand, *American Heritage*
1997 Bill Heller, *The Backstretch*
1996 Don Clippinger, *Mid-Atlantic Thoroughbred*
1995 Not awarded
1994 Jay Hovdey, *The Blood-Horse*
1993 Stephanie Diaz, *The Backstretch*
1992 Joseph P. Pons Jr., *The Blood-Horse*
1990 Bill Nack, *Sports Illustrated*
1989 Bill Nack, *Sports Illustrated*
1988 Jennie Rees, Lexington *Courier-Journal* (Sunday Magazine)

1987 Jack Mann, *Spur*
1986 Bill Nack, *Sports Illustrated*
1985 Bill Mooney, *The Thoroughbred Record*
1984 Frank Deford, *Sports Illustrated*
1983 Arnold Kirkpatrick, *Keeneland*
1982 Jay Hovdey, *Horsemen's Journal*
1981 Joseph P. Pons Jr., *The Blood-Horse*
1980 Clive Gammon, *Sports Illustrated*
1979 William Leggett, *Sports Illustrated*
1978 Bill Nack, *Sports Illustrated*
1977 Whitney Tower, *Classic*
1976 Whitney Tower, *Classic*
1975 Frank Deford, *Sports Illustrated*
1974 Chet Hagan, *Spur*
1973 Pete Axthelm, *Newsweek*
1972 Edward L. Bowen, *The Blood-Horse*
1971 Bill Surface, *Reader's Digest*

Outstanding Feature and Enterprise Writing
2002 John Jeremiah Sullivan, *Harper's*
2001 Laura Hillenbrand, *EQUUS*
2000 Mary Simon, Thoroughbred Times

Outstanding Feature Writing
1991 Bill Nack, *Sports Illustrated*

Outstanding News Writing
1991 Bill Nack, *Sports Illustrated*

Outstanding News and Commentary Writing
2002 Joe Drape, New York *Times*
2001 Janet Patton, Lexington *Herald-Leader*
2000 Jay Hovdey, *Daily Racing Form*

Local Television Achievement
2002 Fox Sports Net Southwest
2001 WTVI, Charlotte, NC
2000 WMAR-TV, Baltimore
1999 Amy Zimmerman and Michael Ewing, Fox-TV Sports West
1998 Jeff Lifson, WHAS-TV, Louisville
1997 Brian Blessing, Ontario Jockey Club
1996 Kenny Rice, WTVQ-TV, Lexington
1995 JCM Productions, New York
1994 Ronnie Virgets, WNXO, New Orleans

1993   Stephen Sadis, KBTC, Tacoma
1992   Rick Cushing, WKPC-TV, Louisville
1991   WABC-TV, New York
1990   Philip Von Borries, WKPC-TV, Louisville
1989   Chris Thomas, WFLA-TV, Tampa
1988   Joseph Kwong, KCET-TV, Los Angeles
1987   Arlington Park
1986   Louisiana Downs
1985   Oak Tree Racing Association
1984   NYRA/Cinema Mistral
1983   Cawood Ledford Productions
1982   ON-TV, Los Angeles
1981   WHAS, Louisville
1980   WCAU, Philadelphia
1979   Dave Johnson, ON-TV
1978   Cawood Ledford, WHAS, Louisville
1977   Jane Chastain, KABC, Los Angeles
1976   NYRA-OTB Race of the Week
1975   Cawood Ledford, WHAS, Louisville

National Television Achievement

1999   Mark Shapiro and William Rapaport, ESPN-TV
1998   E. S. Lamoreaux III, *CBS News Sunday Morning*
1997   E. S. Lamoreaux III, *CBS News Sunday Morning*
1996   NBC Sports
1995   ABC's Wide World of Sports
1994   ABC's Wide World of Sports
1993   E. S. Lamoreaux III, CBS News, *Sunday Morning with Charles Kuralt*
1992   ABC Sports
1991   CBS News, *Sunday Morning with Charles Kuralt*
1990   ABC Sports
1989   ABC Sports
1988   Thoroughbred Sports, *Racing Across America*
1987   ABC
1986   ABC
1985   CBS
1984   NBC
1983   CBS
1982   ESPN
1981   Canadian Broadcasting Corp.
1980   ABC
1979   Don Ohlmeyer, NBC
1978   Roger Murphy, Public Broadcasting System
1977   Jack Whitaker, CBS
1976   CBS
1975   CBS
1974   Pen Densham, John Watson, Insight Productions
1973   Chuck Milton, Tony Verna, CBS
1972   Chuck Milton, Tony Verna, CBS
1971   Burt Bacharach, CBS

National Television— Live Racing Programming

2002   NBC Sports
2001   NBC
2000   ABC Sports
1999   Curt Gowdy Jr., Craig Janoff, Howard Katz, and John Filippelli, ABC Sports

National Television Features

2002   NBC Sports
2001   ESPN Classic

Radio Achievement

2002   Shelby Whitfield, Premiere Radio

2001   WBAL, Baltimore
2000   Shelby Whitfield, Premiere Radio
1999   Tom Leach, WVLK-AM, Lexington
1998   Not awarded
1997   John Patti, WBAL, Baltimore
1996   Robin Dawson, CJCL, Toronto
1995   Vic Stauffer, KKAR, Omaha
1994   John Asher, WHAS, Louisville
1993   Tom Leach, WVLK, Lexington
1992   John Asher, WHAS, Louisville
1991   Julia McEvoy, National Public Radio
1990   John Asher, WHAS, Louisville
1989   John Asher, WAVG, Louisville
1988   John Asher, WAVG, Louisville
1987   Bob Lauder, WHAS, Louisville
1986   ABC Radio Network
1985   Bob Lauder, WHAS, Louisville
1984   WBAL, Baltimore
1983   Tom Davis, WCBM, Baltimore
1982   ABC Radio Network
1981   WBAL, Baltimore
1980   Not awarded
1979   Dick Woolley, WITH, Baltimore
1978   Ted Patterson, WBAL, Baltimore
1977   Not awarded
1976   Win Elliot, CBS
1975   Not awarded
1974   Not awarded
1973   Not awarded
1972   Not awarded
1971   Win Elliot, CBS

Film Achievement

1972   Joseph Burnham

Photography Achievement

2002   Michael Clevenger, Louisville *Courier-Journal*
2001   Barbara Livingston, *The Thoroughbred Chronicle*
2000   Dave Landry, *Canadian Thoroughbred*
1999   Michael Marten, *Daily Racing Form*
1998   Ryan Haynes, Northlands Park
1997   Jean Raftery, Calder Race Course
1996   Skip Dickstein, *The Blood-Horse*
1995   Michael J. Marten, *Daily Racing Form*
1994   Tony Leonard, Thoroughbred Times
1993   Michael Burns, Ontario Jockey Club
1992   Barbara Livingston, *The Blood-Horse*
1991   Rayetta Burr, Benoit and Associates
1990   Michael Cartee, *Thoroughbred of California*
1989   Ron Cortes, Philadelphia *Inquirer*
1988   Ben Van Hook, Louisville *Courier-Journal*
1987   Dan Farrell, New York *Daily News*
1986   Janice Wilkman, Los Angeles *Times*
1985   Kim Pratt, Garden State Park
1984   Bill Straus, *The Thoroughbred Record*
1983   Rayetta Burr, *Paddock*
1982   Kay Coyte, *Horsemen's Journal*
1981   Tom Baker, River Downs
1980   Bob Coglianese, New York Racing Association
1979   Skip Ball, *Maryland Horse*
1978   Douglas Lees, Fauquier *Democrat*
1977   John Walther, Miami *Herald*
1976   John J. Vasile, Covina (California) *Sentinel*
1975   John Pineda, Miami *Herald*
1974   Michael Burns, Ontario Jockey Club
1973   Harry Leder, United Press International
1972   Bob Coglianese, New York Racing Association
1971   Art Rogers, Los Angeles *Times*

Owners of Eclipse Award Winners

Aga Khan—Kalanisi (Ire).

Aykroyd, David, Helen Alexander, and Helen Groves—Althea.

Alexander, Helen, David Aykroyd, and Helen Groves—Althea.

Allbritton, Joseph—Hansel.

Anderson, Frank, Verne H. Winchell, and Rick Carradini—Tight Spot.

Arnemann, Jurgen and Calumet Farm—Criminal Type.

Augustin Stables—Cafe Prince (1977-'78), Pompeyo (Chi).

Bacharach, Burt C.—Heartlight No. One.

Bailey, Richard E.—Dearly Precious.

Beal, Barry and L. R. French—Landaluce, Sacahuista.

Beal, Barry, L. R. French, and Eugene Klein—Capote.

Bell III, John A.—Epitome.

Blue Vista—Possibly Perfect.

Brant, Peter M.—Gulch, Just a Game (Ire), Waya (Fr).

Bray Jr., Dana S.—Johnny D.

Buckland Farm—Pleasant Colony, Pleasant Stage, Pleasant Tap.

Caibett, Edgar—Canonero II.

Calbourne Farm—Brown Bess.

Calumet Farm—Before Dawn, Davona Dale, Our Mims.

Calumet Farm and Jurgen Arnemann—Criminal Type.

Carradini, Rick, Verne H. Winchell, and Frank Anderson—Tight Spot.

Cee's Stable—Tiznow (2001).

Cella, Charles—Northern Spur (Ire).

Centennial Farms—Rubiano.

Christiana Stables—Go for Wand (1989-'90).

Claiborne Farm—Swale, Forty Niner.

Clark Jr., Mrs. F. Ambrose—*Gran Kan.

Clark Jr., Stephen C.—Shadow Brook.

Class Racing Stable, Barry Fey, Moon Han, Larry Opas, Frank Sinatra, and Craig Dollase—Reraise.

Clay, Robert and Tracy Farmer—Hidden Lake.

Cooper, Audrey H. and Michael Fennessy—Yanks Music.

Cooper, Michael and Cecilia Straub-Rubens—Tiznow (2000).

Couvercelle, Jean—Cardmania.

Cowan, Irving and Marjorie—Hollywood Wildcat.

Craig, Sidney and Jenny—Paseana (Arg) (1992-'93).

Croll Jr., Warren A.—Holy Bull.

Crown Stable—Eillo.

Darby Dan Farm—Little Current, Sunshine Forever, Tempest Queen.

Davison, Mrs. Richard—Guilty Conscience.

De Camargo, Jose, Winner Silk Inc., and Old Friends Inc.—Farda Amiga.

De Kwiatkowski, Henryk—Conquistador Cielo, De La Rose.

Dogwood Stable—Inlander (GB), Storm Song.

Dollase, Craig, Barry Fey, Moon Han, Class Racing Stable, Larry Opas, and Frank Sinatra—Reraise.

Dotsam Stable—John Henry (1980-'81, 1983-'84).

Due Process Stables—Dehere.

East-West Stable—Wajima.

Elmendorf Farm—Protagonist, Talking Picture.

Engel, Charles F.—Saratoga Dew.

Envoy Stable—Ambassador of Luck.

Equusequity Stable—Slew o' Gold (1983-'84).

Evergreen Farm—Lit de Justice.

Fares, Issam M.—Miss Alleged.

Farish, Will, William Kilroy, Harold Goodman, and Tomonori Tsurumaki—A.P. Indy.

Farmer, Tracy and Robert Clay—Hidden Lake.

Fennessy, Michael and Audrey H. Cooper—Yanks Music.

Fey, Barry, Moon Han, Class Racing Stable, Larry Opas, Frank Sinatra, and Craig Dollase—Reraise.

Firestone, Mr. and Mrs. Bertram R.—April Run (Ire), Genuine Risk, Honest Pleasure, Jimmy Lorenzo (GB), What a Summer.

Firestone, Bertram R., and Allen E. Paulson—Theatrical (Ire).

505 Farms and Ed Nahem—Bertrando.

Flying Zee Stables—Wayward Lass.

Folsom Farm and J. Merrick Jones Jr.—Chou Croute.

Forked Lightning Ranch—Ack Ack.

Fradkoff, Serge and Baron Thierry Van Zuylen de Nyevelt—Perrault (GB).

Franks, John—Answer Lively.

French, L. R. and Barry Beal—Landaluce, Sacahuista.

French, L. R., Barry Beal, and Eugene Klein—Capote.

Fuller, Peter—Mom's Command.

Gaillard, Dr. Ernest, Arthur Hancock III, and Charlie Whittingham—Sunday Silence.

Gainesway Farm, Robert and Beverly Lewis, and Overbrook Farm—Timber Country.

Genter, Frances A. Stable—Smile, Unbridled.

Gerry, Nancy—Flat Top (1998, 2002).

Godolphin Racing—Daylami (Ire), Fantastic Light, Tempera.

Goodman, Harold, William Kilroy, Will Farish, and Tomonori Tsurumaki—A.P. Indy.

Green, Dolly—Brave Raj.

Grinstead, Carl and Ben Rochelle—Snow Chief.

Greentree Stable—Bowl Game, Late Bloomer.

Greer, John L.—Foolish Pleasure.

Griggs, John K.—Warm Spell.

Groves, Helen, Helen Alexander, and David Aykroyd—Althea.

Guest, Virginia—Life's Illusion.

Hamilton, Emory Alexander—Queena.

Han, Moon, Barry Fey, Class Racing Stable, Larry Opas, Frank Sinatra, and Craig Dollase—Reraise.

Hancock III, Arthur, Charlie Whittingham, and Dr. Ernest Gaillard—Sunday Silence.

Harbor View Farm—Affirmed (1977-'79), Flawlessly (1992-'93), It's in the Air, Outstandingly.

Harris, George, William L. Pape, and Jonathan Sheppard—Flatterer (1983-'86).

Hatley, Melvin E. and Eugene V. Klein—Life's Magic.

Hawksworth Farm—Spectacular Bid (1978-'80).

Headley, Bruce, Irwin and Andrew Molasky, and High Tech Stable (Michael Singh)—Kona Gold.

Henley Jr., Mrs. Jesse M.—Highland Bud.

Hersh, Trust of Philip and Sophie—The Wicked North.

Hibbert, Robert E.—Roving Boy.

Hickory Tree Stable—Devil's Bag.

High Tech Stable (Michael Singh), Bruce Headley, and Irwin and Andrew Molasky—Kona Gold.

Hine, Carolyn H.—Skip Away (1996-'98).

Hi Yu Stable—Chinook Pass.

Hofmann, Mrs. Philip B.—Gold Beauty, Sky Beauty.

Hooper Sr., Fred W.—Precisionist, Susan's Girl (1972-'73, 1975).

Horton, Robert P.—Gallant Bob.

Houghland, Calvin—All Gong (GB).

Hunt, Nelson Bunker—Dahlia, Youth.

Hunt, Nelson Bunker and Frank Stronach—Glorious Song.

Hunt, Nelson Bunker and Edward L. • Stephenson—Trillion.

Hunter Farm—Spend a Buck.

Icahn, Carl—Meadow Star.

Jackson, Michael—Morley Street (Ire) (1990-'91).

Jayeff B Stables and Barry Weisbord—Safely Kept.

Jayeff B Stables, James Tafel, and Richard Santulli—Banshee Breeze.

Jeffords Jr., Mrs. Walter M.—Lonesome Glory (1992-'93, '95, '97, '99).

Jhayare Stables—Itsallgreektome.

Jones, Aaron U.—Lemhi Gold, Tiffany Lass.

Jones, Aaron and Marie—Riboletta (Brz).

Jones Jr., J. Merrick and Folsom Farm—Chou Croute.

Jones, Mrs. Mary F.—*Cougar II.

Juddmonte Farms—Banks Hill (GB), Ryafan, Wandesta (GB).

Karkenny, Alex, Robert Levy, and William Roberts—Smoke Glacken.

Kaster, Mr. and Mrs. Richard and Mr. and Mrs. Donald Propson—Countess Diana.

Keck, Mrs. Howard B.—Ferdinand, Turkish Trousers.

Kellman, Joseph—Shecky Greene.

Kilroy, William, Will Farish, Harold Goodman, and Tomonori Tsurumaki—A.P. Indy.

Klein, Eugene V.—Family Style, Open Mind (1988-'89), Winning Colors.

Klein, Mr. and Mrs. Eugene V.—Lady's Secret.

Klein, Eugene, L. R. French, and Barry Beal—Capote.

Klein, Eugene V. and Melvin E. Hatley—Life's Magic.

LaCombe, Joseph—Favorite Trick.

Lamarque Racing Stable and Louis J. Roussel III—Risen Star.

Lancaster Jr., Carlyle, et al.—Star de Naskra.

Lanzman, David—Squirtle Squirt.

La Presle Farm—Kotashaan (Fr).

Lazy F Ranch—Forego (1974-'77).

Levesque, Jean-Louis—La Prevoyante.

Levy, Morton and Marjoh, and Donald and David Willmot—Deputy Minister.

Levy, Robert P.—Housebuster (1990-'91).

Levy, Robert, William Roberts, and Alex Karkenny—Smoke Glacken.

Lewis, Robert and Beverly—Charismatic, Orientate, Serena's Song, Silver Charm.

Lewis, Robert and Beverly, Gainesway Farm, and Overbrook Farm—Timber Country.

Lickle, William C.—Correggio (Ire).

Loblolly Stable—Prairie Bayou, Temperence Hill, Vanlandingham.

Locust Hill Farm—Ruffian (1974-'75).

Lukas, D. Wayne and Paul Paternostro—North Sider.

Magnier, Susan and Michael Tabor—High Chaparral (Ire), Johannesburg.

Maktoum, Sheikh Maktoum bin Rashid al—Hatoof.

Maktoum, Sheikh Mohammed bin Rashid al—Pebbles (GB), Singspiel (Ire).

Maktoum, Sheikh Mohammed bin Rashid al and Allen E. Paulson—Arazi.

Mangurian Jr., Harry T.—Desert Vixen.

Meadow Stable—Riva Ridge, Secretariat (1972-'73).

Milch, David, and Marc Silverman, and Jack Silverman—Gilded Time.

Mill House—Sensational.

Molasky, Irwin and Andrew, Bruce Headley, and High Tech Stable (Michael Singh)—Kona Gold.

Montpelier—Proud Delta, Soothsayer.

Murdock, Mrs. Lewis C.—Zaccio (1980-'82).

Nerud, John A.—Cozzene.

Niarchos, Stavros—Miesque (1987-'88).

Nishiyama, Masayuki—Paradise Creek.

Oak, Harry A.—Rockhill Native.

Old Friends Inc., Winner Silk Inc., and Jose de Camargo—Farda Amiga.

Opas, Frank, Barry Fey, Moon Han, Class Racing Stable, Frank Sinatra, and Craig Dollase—Reraise.

Overbrook Farm—Boston Harbor, Flanders, Golden Attraction, Surfside.

Overbrook Farm, Gainesway Farm, and Robert and Beverly Lewis—Timber Country.

Oxley, John C.—Beautiful Pleasure.

Padua Stables—Vindication.

Pape, William L.—Athenian Idol, Martie's Anger.

Pape, William L., George Harris, and Jonathan Sheppard—Flatterer (1983-'86).

Paraneck Stable—Artax.

Paternostro, Paul and D. Wayne Lukas—North Sider.

Paulson, Allen E.—Ajina, Blushing John, Cigar (1995-'96), Eliza, Escena, Estrapade.

Paulson, Allen E. Living Trust—Azeri.

Paulson, Allen E. and Bertram R. Firestone—Theatrical (Ire).

Paulson, Allen E. and Sheikh Mohammed bin Rashid al Maktoum—Arazi.

Paxson, Adele—Candy Eclair.

Pegram, Mike—Real Quiet, Silverbulletday (1998-'99).

Perry, William H.—Revidere.

Phillips, Neil and Windfields Farm—*Snow Knight.

Phillips Racing Partnership—Soaring Softly.

Phipps, Cynthia—Christmas Past.

Phipps, Mrs. Ogden—Straight and True.

Phipps, Ogden—Easy Goer, Heavenly Prize, Numbered Account, Personal Ensign, Relaxing.

Phipps, Ogden Mills—Inside Information, Rhythm, Storm Flag Flying.

Pin Oak Stable—Laugh and Be Merry.

Pollard, Carl F.—Caressing.

Pope Jr., George A.—J. O. Tobin.

Prestonwood Farm—Groovy, Victory Gallop.

Propson, Mr. and Mrs. Donald and Mr. and Mrs. Richard Kaster—Countess Diana.

Quarter B. Farm—Buck's Boy.

Russell Reineman and The Thoroughbred Corp.—War Emblem.

Ridder, Bernard R.—Cascapedia.

Riordan, Michael D.—Bates Motel.

Roberts, William, Alex Karkenny, and Robert Levy—Smoke Glacken.

Robins, Gerald W. and Timothy Sams—Tasso.

Robinson, Jill E.—Cherokee Run.

Rochelle, Ben and Carl Grinstead—Snow Chief.

Rokeby Stable—Key to the Mint, Run the Gantlet.

Rosen, Carl—Chris Evert.

Rosenthal, Mrs. Morton—Maria's Mon.

Roussel III, Louis J. and Lamarque Racing Stable—Risen Star.

Ryehill Farm—Heavenly Cause, Smart Angle.

Salman, Prince Fahd bin—Fiji (GB).

Sams, Timothy and Gerald W. Robins—Tasso.

Sam-Son Farm—Chief Bearhart, Dance Smartly, Sky Classic.

Sangster, Robert E.—Royal Heroine (Ire).

Santulli, Richard, James Tafel, and Jayeff B Stables—Banshee Breeze.

Sarkowsky, Herman—Phone Chatter.

Saron Stable—Turkoman.

Scharbauer, Dorothy and Pamela—Alysheba (1987-'88).

Schiff, John M.—Plugged Nickle.

Shannon, Bradley M.—Manila.

Sheppard, Jonathan E., George Harris, and William L. Pape—Flatterer (1983-'86).

Silverman, Marc and Jack, and David Milch—Gilded Time.

Sinatra, Frank, Barry Fey, Moon Han, Class Racing Stable, Larry Opas, and Craig Dollase—Reraise.

SKS Stable—Lord Avie.

Sommer, Sigmund—Autobiography.

Star Crown Stable—Chief's Crown.

Stephen, Martha and Richard and The Thoroughbred Corp.—Jewel Princess.

Stephenson, Edward L. and Nelson Bunker Hunt—Trillion.

Stone, Mrs. Whitney—Shuvee.

Stonerside Stable—Chilukki.

Straub-Rubens, Cecilia, and Michael Cooper—Tiznow (2000).

Stronach, Frank and Nelson Bunker Hunt—Glorious Song.

Stronach Stable—Macho Uno, Perfect Sting.

Sullivan, Jeffrey—Black Tie Affair (Ire).

Summa Stable—Track Robbery.

Tabor, Michael—Left Bank, Thunder Gulch.

Tabor, Michael and Susan Magnier—High Chaparral (Ire), Johannesburg.

Tafel, James, Richard Santulli, and Jayeff B Stables—Banshee Breeze.

Tanaka, Gary—Golden Apples (Ire), Gourmet Girl.

Tartan Stable—Dr. Patches.

Tayhill Stable—Seattle Slew (1978).

Taylor, Mrs. Karen L.—Seattle Slew (1976-'77).

The Thoroughbred Corp.—Anees, Point Given.

The Thoroughbred Corp. and Russell Reineman—War Emblem.

The Thoroughbred Corp. and Martha and Richard Stephen—Jewel Princess.

Tizol, E. Rodriguez—Bold Forbes.

Torsney, Dr. Jerome M.—MacDiarmida.

Tsurumaki, Tomonori, Will Farish, William Kilroy, and Harold Goodman—A.P. Indy.

Tucker, Paula—Princess Rooney.

Valando, Thomas—Fly So Free.

Vance, Jeanne—Lemon Drop Kid.

Van Worp, Robert—Not Surprising.

Van Zuylen de Nyevelt, Baron Thierry, and Serge Fradkoff—Perrault (GB).

Weasel Jr., George—My Juliet.

Weinsier, Randolph—Lakeville Miss.

Weisbord, Barry and Jayeff B Stables—Safely Kept.

Westerly Stud—Typecast.

Whitham, Mr. and Mrs. Frank E.—Bayakoa (Arg) (1989-'90).

Whittingham, Charlie, Arthur Hancock III, and Dr. Ernest Gaillard—Sunday Silence.

Wildenstein, Daniel—All Along (Fr).

Wildenstein Stable—Steinlen (GB).

Willmot, Donald and David, and Morton and Marjoh Levy—Deputy Minister.

Winchell, Verne H., Frank Anderson, and Rick Carradini—Tight Spot.

Windfields Farm and Neil Phillips—*Snow Knight.

Winner Silk Inc., Old Friends Inc., and Jose de Camargo—Farda Amiga

Breeders of Eclipse Award Winners

Adams, Mrs. Vanderbilt—Desert Vixen.

Adena Springs—Macho Uno, Perfect Sting.

Aga Khan—Daylami (Ire), Kalanisi (Ire).

Alexander, Emory—Queena.

Alexander, Helen, David Aykroyd, and Helen Groves—Althea.

Allez France Stables—Steinlen (GB).

Augustus, Peggy—Johnny D.

Aykroyd, David, Helen Alexander, and Helen Groves—Althea.

Baker, Dr. Howard—Serena's Song.

Ballydoyle Stud—Correggio (Ire).

Barnhart, Anna Marie—Skip Away (1996-'98).

Bell, H. Bennett, and Jessica Bell Nicholson—Epitome.

Benjamin, Edward Bernard—Canonero II.

Benjamin, E. V. III, and William G. Clark—Chou Croute.

Bettersworth, J. R.—My Juliet.

Blue Diamond Ranch—Snow Chief.

Blue Seas Music Inc.—Heartlight No. One.

Brant, Peter M.—Gulch, Thunder Gulch.

Calbourne Farm—Brown Bess.

Calumet Farm—Before Dawn, Criminal Type, Davona Dale, Our Mims.

Cannata, Carl and Olivia—Gourmet Girl.

Carolaine Farm and Dr. E. W. Thomas—Rockhill Native.

Carondelet Farm and Vinery—Artax.

Carrion, Jaime S.—Meadow Star.

Castleman, Ben S.—Seattle Slew (1976-'78).

Centurion Farms—Deputy Minister.

Chenery, Helen B.—Saratoga Dew.

Christiana Stables—Go for Wand (1989-'90).

Cisley Stable and Robert P. Levy—North Sider.

Claiborne Farm—Wajima, Revidere, Slew o' Gold (1983-'84), Swale, Forty Niner.

Clark, William G., and E. V. Benjamin III—Chou Croute.

Cleaboy Farms Co.—Inlander (GB).

Clear Creek and Highclere Inc.—Silverbulletday (1998-'99).

Cohen, Ollie A.—Eillo.

Cojuangco, Edwardo M. Jr.—Manila.

Coughlan, Sean—High Chaparral (Ire).

Cowan, Irving and Marjorie—Hollywood Wildcat.

Danada Farm—Proud Delta.

Darley Stud Management—Tempera.

Davison, Mrs. Richard—Guilty Conscience.

Dayton Ltd.—All Along (Fr), Waya (Fr).

Delta Thoroughbreds Inc.—Cardmania.

De Mestre, J. W.—Jimmy Lorenzo (GB).

Due Process Stables—Dehere, Open Mind (1988-'89).

Eaton Farms Inc. and Red Bull Stable—Bold Forbes.

Echo Valley Horse Farm Inc.—Chris Evert, Winning Colors.

Egan, James and David Hanley—Golden Apples (Ire).

Elmendorf Farm—Protagonist, Shadow Brook, Talking Picture.

Evans, Thomas Mellon—Pleasant Colony, Pleasant Tap.

Evans, Mrs. Thomas Mellon—Pleasant Stage.

Farfellow Farms Ltd.—Anees.

Farish, William S., and G. Watts Humphrey Jr.—Sacahuista.

Farish, William S., and W. S. Kilroy—A.P. Indy, Lemon Drop Kid.

Farish, William S., and Ogden Mills Phipps—Storm Song.

Leading breeders
By number of titles won

7—Harbor View Farm

6—Claiborne Farm

6—Allen E. Paulson

5—William S. Farish and Partners

5—William L. Pape

5—Ogden Phipps

5—Jonathan Sheppard

5—Walter M. Jeffords Jr.

4—Calumet Farm

4—Golden Chance Farm

4—Nelson Bunker Hunt

4—Lazy F Ranch

4—Overbrook Farm

3—Anna Marie Barnhart

3—Blue Bear Stud

3—Ben Castleman

3—Due Process Stables

3—Elmendorf Farm

3—Mr. & Mrs. Thomas Mellon Evans

3—Mr. and Mrs. John W. Galbreath

3—Mrs. William Gilmore

3—Fred W. Hooper Jr.

3—Mrs. William M. Jason

3—Juddmonte Farms

3—Meadow Stud

3—Ogden Mills Phipps

3—Verne H. Winchell

Farish, William S., and Parrish Hill Farm—Charismatic.

Farnsworth Farms—Beautiful Pleasure, Jewel Princess.

Feeney, F.—April Run (Ire).

Financiera, Mimika, and Warren Hill Stud—Pebbles (GB).

Firestone, Mr. and Mrs. Bertram R.—Paradise Creek, Theatrical (Ire).

Flaxman Holdings Ltd.—Miesque

(1987-'88).

Floyd, William—Highland Bud.

Franks, John—Answer Lively.

Freeman, Carl M.—Miss Alleged.

Fuller, C. T.—Ambassador of Luck.

Fuller, Peter—Mom's Command.

Gainesway Thoroughbreds Ltd.—Orientate.

Gainsborough Farm—Fantastic Light, Hatoof.

Galbreath, John W.—Little Current, Sunshine Forever.

Galbreath, Mrs. John W.—Tempest Queen.

Galbreath/Phillips Racing Partnership—Soaring Softly.

Garrison, Wayne and Bruce Hundley—Fly So Free.

Genter Stable Inc., Frances A.—Smile.

Gilmore, Mrs. William, and Mrs. William M. Jason—Spectacular Bid (1978-'80).

Golden Chance Farm Inc.—John Henry (1980-'81, 1983-'84).

Gray, Fletcher and John Youngblood—Left Bank.

Greentree Stud Inc.—Bowl Game, Late Bloomer.

Groves, Helen, Helen Alexander, and David Aykroyd—Althea.

Guest, Raymond R.—Cascapedia.

Guest, Virginia D.—Life's Illusion.

Guggenheim, Harry F.—Ack Ack.

Hancock, Arthur B. III, and Leone J. Peters—Risen Star.

Hanley, David and James Egan—Golden Apples (Ire).

Happy Valley Farm—It's in the Air.

Haras El Huerton—*Gran Kan.

Haras General Cruz—*Cougar II.

Haras Principal—Bayakoa (Arg) (1989-'90).

Haras Santa Ana do Rio Grande—Riboletta (Brz).

Haras Santa Amelia—Pompeyo (Chi).

Haras Vacacion—Paseana (Arg) (1992-'93).

Harbor View Farm—Affirmed (1977-'79), Athenian Idol, Outstandingly, Flawlessly (1992-'93).

Harper, Rowe W., and Irish Hill Farm—Spend a Buck.

Hartigan, John H.—Mac Diarmida.

Hayden, Mr. and Mrs. David—Safely Kept.

Hibbert, Robert E.—Roving Boy.

Hickey, P. Noel—Buck's Boy.

Highclere Inc. and Clear Creek—Silverbulletday (1998-'99).

Hi Yu Stables—Chinook Pass.

Hofmann, Mr. and Mrs. Philip B.—Gold Beauty.

Homan, J. L.—Gallant Bob.

Hooper Jr., Fred W.—Susan's Girl (1972-'73, 1975).

Hooper Sr., Fred W.—Precisionist.

Humphrey, G. Watts Jr., and William S. Farish III—Sacahuista.

Humphrey, Mrs. G. Watts Jr.—Genuine Risk.

Hundley, Bruce, and Wayne Garrison—Fly So Free.

Hunt, Nelson Bunker—Dahlia, Estrapade, Trillion, Youth.

Iandoli, Lewis E.—Conquistador Cielo.

Irish American Bloodstock Agency Ltd.—Yanks Music.

Irish Hill Farm and Rowe W. Harper—Spend a Buck.

Janney, Mr. and Mrs. Stuart S. Jr.—Ruffian (1974-'75).

Jason, Mrs. William M., and Mrs. William Gilmore—Spectacular Bid (1978-'80).

Jayeff B Stables and W. G. Lyster III—Johannesburg.

Jeffords, Walter M. Jr.—Lonesome Glory (1992-'93, '95, '97, '99).

Jones, Aaron U.—Lemhi Gold, Tiffany Lass.

Jones, Brereton C.—Caressing.

Juddmonte Farms—Banks Hill (GB), Ryafan, Wandesta (GB).

Karutz, Dr. Wallace—Brave Raj.

Kaster, Richard S.—Countess Diana.

Keck, Howard B.—Ferdinand, Turkish Trousers.

Kellman, Joseph—Shecky Greene.

Kernan, Francis, and Spendthrift Farm—Landaluce.

Kilroy, W. S., and William S. Farish—A.P. Indy, Lemon Drop Kid.

Kirtlington Stud Ltd. and the Kris syndicate—All Gong (GB).

Kitchen, Edgar—Track Robbery.

Kluener, Robert G.—Warm Spell.

Knight, Landon—Flat Top (1998, 2002).

Kris syndicate, the, and Kirtlington Stud Ltd.—All Gong (GB).

Lancaster, Carlyle J.—Star de Naskra.

Lazy F Ranch—Forego (1974-'77).

Levesque, Jean-Louis—La Prevoyante.

Levy, Blanche P., and Murphy Stable—Housebuster (1990-'91).

Levy, Robert P., and Cisley Stable—North Sider.

Lilley, J. A. C.—*Snow Knight.

Little Hill Farm—Real Quiet.

Little, Marvin A. Jr.—Hansel.

Loblolly Stable—Prairie Bayou, Vanlandingham.

Lowquest Ltd.—Timber Country.

Luro, Horatio A.—Wayward Lass.

Lyster III, W. G. and Jayeff B Stables—Johannesburg.

Madden, Preston—Alysheba (1987-'88).

Maktoum, Sheikh Mohammed bin Rashid al—Singspiel (Ire).

Mangurian, Mr. and Mrs. Harry T. Jr.—Gilded Time.

Maynard, Richard D.—Chief Bearhart.

Meadow Stud—Riva Ridge, Secretariat (1972-'73).

Mellon, Paul—Key to the Mint, Run the Gantlet.

Mill House—Sensational.

Miller, MacKenzie, and Dr. and Mrs. R. Smiser West—De La Rose.

Miller, Mr. and Mrs. MacKenzie, and

Dr. and Mrs. R. Smiser West—Chilukki.

Murphy Stable and Blanche P. Levy—Housebuster (1990-'91).

Nahem, Ed—Bertrando.

Narducci, M.D., Audrey—Squirtle Squirt.

Nerud, John A.—Cozzene.

Newgate Stud Company—Fiji (GB).

Nicholson, Jessica Bell, and H. Bennett Bell—Epitome.

North Ridge Farm—Blushing John, Capote.

Nuckols Brothers—Typecast.

Nuckols, Charles Jr. and Sons—Hidden Lake, War Emblem.

Oak Cliff Thoroughbreds Ltd.—Sunday Silence.

Onett, George C.—Cherokee Run.

Overbrook Farm—Boston Harbor, Flanders, Golden Attraction, Surfside.

Pancoast, Mrs. Jean R.—Dearly Precious.

Pape, William L., and Jonathan Sheppard—Flatterer (1983-'86), Martie's Anger.

Parkhill, Marshall—Morley Street (Ire) (1990-'91).

Parrish, Dr. David C. III, Estate of Emma Haggin Parrish, and Douglas Parrish—Life's Magic.

Parrish, Douglas, Estate of Emma Haggin Parrish, and Dr. David C. Parrish III—Life's Magic.

Parrish, Estate of Emma Haggin, Douglas Parrish, and Dr. David C. Parrish III—Life's Magic.

Parrish Hill Farm and William S. Farish—Charismatic.

Paulson, Allen E.—Ajina, Azeri, Cigar (1995-'96), Eliza, Escena.

Payson Stud—Farda Amiga, Vindication.

Paxson, Adele—Candy Eclair.

Pelican Stable—Holy Bull.

Perez, Carlos—Kona Gold.

Peskoff, Stephen D.—Black Tie Affair (Ire).

Peters, Leone J., and Arthur B. Hancock III—Risen Star.

Phillips, Mrs. Jacqueline Getty—Bates Motel.

Phillips Racing Partnership/Galbreath—Soaring Softly.

Phipps, Cynthia—Christmas Past.

Phipps, Mrs. Ogden—Straight and True.

Phipps, Ogden—Easy Goer, Heavenly Prize, Numbered Account, Personal Ensign, Relaxing.

Phipps, Ogden Mills—Inside Information, Rhythm.

Phipps, Ogden Mills, and William S. Farish—Storm Song.

Phipps Stable—Storm Flag Flying.

Pin Oak Farm—Laugh and Be Merry.

Polinger, Milton—What a Summer.

Polk, Dr. Albert F. Jr.—Temperence Hill.

Pope, George A. Jr.—J. O. Tobin.

Ravenbrook Farm Inc.—Not Surprising.

Rathvale Stud—Just a Game (Ire).

Red Bull Stable and Eaton Farms Inc.—Bold Forbes.

Roach, Dr. Ben, and Tom Roach—Princess Rooney.

Robertson, Corbin—Turkoman.

Robins, Gerald W. and Timothy H. Sams—Tasso.

Robinson, Marshall T.—Groovy.

Rosebrock, Perry M.—Smoke Glacken.

Rosen, Carl—Chief's Crown.

Rosenthal, Morton—Maria's Mon.

Ryan, B. L.—Royal Heroine (Ire).

Ryehill Farm—Heavenly Cause, Smart Angle.

Sam-Son Farm—Dance Smartly, Sky Classic.

Sams, Timothy H. and Gerald W. Robins—Tasso.

Sarkowsky, Herman—Phone Chatter.

Sasse, F. H. and A. D. Shead—Perrault (GB).

Schiff, John M.—Plugged Nickle.

Scott, Mrs. Marion duPont—Soothsayer.

Selective Seasons—Family Style.

Sergent, Willard—Reraise.

Shead, A. D. and F. H. Sasse—Perrault (GB).

Sheppard, Jonathan, and William L. Pape—Flatterer (1983-'86), Martie's Anger.

Spendthrift Farm and Francis Kernan—Landaluce.

Spreen, Robert H.—Lady's Secret.

Stone, Whitney—Shuvee.

Straub-Rubens, Cecilia—Tiznow (2000-'01).

Sugar Maple Farm—Itsallgreektome, Sky Beauty.

Swettenham Stud—Lit de Justice.

Swettenham Stud and Partners—Northern Spur (Ire).

Tafel, James B.—Banshee Breeze.

Tall Oaks Farm—Victory Gallop.

Tartan Farms Corp.—Dr. Patches, Unbridled.

Taylor, E. P.—Devil's Bag, Glorious Song.

The Thoroughbred Corp.—Point Given.

Third Kirsmith Racing Associates—Rubiano.

Thomas, Dr. E. W., and Carolaine

Farm—Rockhill Native.

Viking Farms Ltd.—Lord Avie.

Vinery and Carondelet Farm—Artax.

Waldemar Farms Inc.—Foolish Pleasure, Honest Pleasure.

Warren Hill Stud and Mimika Financiera—Pebbles (GB).

Weinsier, Randolph—Lakeville Miss.

Wertheimer and Brother—Kotashaan (Fr).

West, Dr. and Mrs. R. Smiser, and MacKenzie Miller—De La Rose.

West, Dr. and Mrs. R. Smiser and Mr. and Mrs. MacKenzie Miller—Chilukki.

Wheatley Stable—Autobiography.

Wilson, Ralph C. Jr.—Arazi.

Winchell, Verne H.—Cafe Prince (1977-'78), Tight Spot.

Witt, Mr. and Mrs. Robert—Possibly Perfect.

Wood, Mr. and Mrs. M. L.—Favorite Trick.

Wootton, Mary Lou—Silver Charm.

Youngblood, John and Fletcher Gray—Left Bank.

Zurek, Edward N.—The Wicked North.

Trainers of Eclipse Award Winners

Albertrani, Louis—Artax.

Alexander, Frank—Cherokee Run.

Allard, Edward T.—Mom's Command.

Anderson, Laurie—Chinook Pass.

Arias, Juan—Canonero II.

Badgett Jr., William—Go for Wand (1989-'90).

Baffert, Robert—Chilukki, Point Given, Real Quiet, Silverbulletday (1998-'99), Silver Charm, Vindication, War Emblem.

Balding, Gerald B. "Toby"—Morley Street (Ire) (1990-'91).

Barnett, Robert—Answer Lively.

Barrera, Lazaro S.—Affirmed (1977-'79), Bold Forbes, It's in the Air, J. O. Tobin, Lemhi Gold, Tiffany Lass.

Bary, Pascal—Miss Alleged (with Charles Whittingham).

Belanger Jr., Gerald W.—Glorious Song.

Bernstein, David—The Wicked North.

Biancone, Patrick L.—All Along (Fr).

Bin Suroor, Saeed—Daylami (Ire), Fantastic Light.

Bohannan, Thomas—Prairie Bayou.

Boutin, Francois—April Run (Ire), Arazi, Miesque (1987-'88).

Brittain, Clive E.—Pebbles (GB).

Brothers, Frank—Hansel.

Burch, J. Elliot—Key to the Mint, Run the Gantlet.

Byrne, Patrick—Countess Diana, Favorite Trick.

Campbell, Gordon C.—Cascapedia.

Campo, John P.—Pleasant Colony, Protagonist, Talking Picture.

Cantey, Joseph B.—Temperence Hill.

Carroll, Henry—Smoke Glacken.

Cecil, Ben—Golden Apples (Ire).

Cocks, W. Burling—Zaccio (1980-'82).

Croll Jr., Warren A.—Holy Bull, Housebuster (1990-'91).

Curtis Jr., William—Gold Beauty.

Day, Jim—Dance Smartly, Sky Classic.

Delp, Grover G.—Spectacular Bid (1978-'80).

De Seroux, Laura—Azeri.

DiMauro, Steve—Dearly Precious, Wajima.

Dollase, Craig—Reraise.

Dollase, Wallace—Itsallgreektome, Jewel Princess.

Doyle, A. T.—Typecast.

Drysdale, Neil—A.P. Indy, Fiji (GB), Hollywood Wildcat, Princess Rooney, Tasso.

Dunham, Robert G.—Chou Croute.

Elliot, Janet E.—Correggio (Ire), Flat Top (1998, 2002).

Euster, Eugene—My Juliet.

Fabre, Andre—Banks Hill (GB).

Fenstermaker, L. Ross—Precisionist, Susan's Girl (1975).

Fenwick, Charles—Inlander (GB).

Ferris, Richard D.—Star de Naskra.

Fout, Paul R.—Life's Illusion.

Frankel, Robert—Bertrando, Possibly Perfect, Ryafan, Squirtle Squirt, Wandesta (GB).

Freeman, W. C.—Shuvee.

Furr, C.—*Gran Kan.

Frostad, Mark—Chief Bearhart.

Gambolati, Cam—Spend a Buck.

Gaver, John M.—Late Bloomer.

Gaver Jr., John M.—Bowl Game.

Goldberg, Alan E.—Safely Kept.

Goldfine, Lou M.—Shecky Greene.

Gosden, John H. M.—Bates Motel, Royal Heroine (Ire).

Griggs, John K.—Warm Spell.

Harty, Eoin—Tempera.

Hassinger Jr., Alex—Anees, Eliza.

Hauswald, Phil—Epitome.

Head, Christiane—Hatoof.

Headley, Bruce—Kona Gold.

Hertler, John O.—Slew o' Gold (1983-'84).

Hickey, P. Noel—Buck's Boy.

Hine, Hubert—Guilty Conscience, Skip Away (1996-'98).

Howe, Peter M.—Proud Delta, Soothsayer.

Inda, Eduardo—Riboletta (Brz).

Jenda, Charles J.—Brown Bess.

Jerkens, H. Allen—Sky Beauty.

Jolley, LeRoy—Foolish Pleasure, Genuine Risk, Honest Pleasure, Manila, Meadow Star, What a Summer.

Jones, Gary—Turkoman.

Kay, Michael—Johnny D.

Kelly, Thomas J.—Plugged Nickle.

Kimmel, John—Hidden Lake.

King Jr., S. Allen—Candy Eclair.

Laurin, Lucien—Riva Ridge, Secretariat (1972-'73).

Laurin, Roger—Chief's Crown, Numbered Account.

Lepman, Budd—Eillo.

Lobo, Paulo—Farda Amiga.

Lukas, D. Wayne—Althea, Boston Harbor, Capote, Charismatic, Criminal Type, Family Style, Flanders, Golden Attraction, Gulch, Lady's Secret, Landaluce, Life's Magic (1984-'85), North Sider, Open Mind (1988-'89), Orientate, Sacahuista, Serena's Song, Steinlen (GB), Surfside, Thunder Gulch, Timber Country, Winning Colors.

Lundy, Richard J.—Blushing John.

Mandella, Richard—Kotashaan (Fr),

Phone Chatter.

Manzi, Joseph—Roving Boy.

Marquette, Joseph D.—Gallant Bob.

Marti, Pedro—Heartlight No. One.

Martin, Frank—Autobiography, Outstandingly.

Martin, Jose—Groovy, Lakeville Miss, Wayward Lass.

McAnally, Ronald—Bayakoa (Arg) (1989-'90), John Henry (1980, 1983-'84), Northern Spur (Ire), Paseana (Arg) (1992-'93), Tight Spot.

McAnally, Ronald and Victor J. Nickerson—John Henry (1981).

McGaughey III, Claude R.—Easy Goer, Heavenly Prize, Inside Information, Personal Ensign, Queena, Rhythm, Storm Flag Flying, Vanlandingham.

Meredith, Derek—Cardmania.

Miller, F. Bruce—All Gong (GB), Lonesome Glory (1992-'93, '95, '97, '99).

Miller, MacKenzie—*Snow Knight.

Mott, Bill—Ajina, Cigar (1995-'96), Escena, Paradise Creek, Theatrical (Ire).

Neilson, Sanna—Pompeyo (Chi).

Nafzger, Carl A.—Banshee Breeze, Unbridled.

Nerud, Jan H.—Cozzene.

Nerud, John A.—Dr. Patches.

Nickerson, Victor J. and Ronald McAnally—John Henry (1981).

Nobles, Reynaldo—Dehere.

O'Brien, Aidan—High Chaparral (Ire), Johannesburg.

O'Brien, Leo—Yanks Music.

Orseno, Joseph F.—Macho Uno, Perfect Sting.

Penna, Angel—Relaxing.

Penna Jr., Angel—Christmas Past, Laugh and Be Merry.

Perlsweig, Daniel—Lord Avie.

Perdomo, Pico—Gourmet Girl.

Peterson, Douglas—Seattle Slew (1978).

Pletcher, Todd—Left Bank.

Poulos, Ernie—Black Tie Affair (Ire).

Preger, Mitchell C.—Ambassador of Luck.

Robbins, Jay—Tiznow (2000-'01).

Rondinello, Thomas L.—Little Current, Tempest Queen.

Root Sr., T. F.—Desert Vixen.

Roussel III, Louis J.—Risen Star.

Russell, John W.—Susan's Girl (1972-'73).

Sahadi, Jenine—Lit de Justice.

Schosberg, Richard—Maria's Mon.

Schulhofer, Flint S.—Fly So Free, Lemon Drop Kid, Mac Diarmida, Rubiano, Smile.

Sciacca, Gary—Saratoga Dew.

Sheppard, Jonathan E.—Athenian Idol, Cafe Prince (1977-'78), Flatterer (1983-'86), Highland Bud, Jimmy Lorenzo (GB), Martie's Anger.

Smithwick, D. Michael—Straight and True.

Speckert, Chris—Pleasant Stage, Pleasant Tap.

Starr, John—La Prevoyante.

Stephens, Woodford C.—Conquistador Cielo, De La Rose, Devil's Bag, Forty Niner, Heavenly Cause, Sensational, Smart Angle, Swale.

Stevens, Herbert—Rockhill Native.

Stoute, Sir Michael—Kalanisi (Ire), Singspiel (Ire).

Stute, Mel—Brave Raj, Snow Chief.

Tammaro, John—Deputy Minister.

Toner, James J.—Soaring Softly.

Trovato, Joseph A.—Chris Evert.

Turner Jr., William H.—Seattle Slew (1976-'77).

Van Berg, Jack—Alysheba (1987-'88).

Vance, David R.—Caressing.

Van Worp, Judson—Not Surprising.

Veitch, John M.—Before Dawn, Davona Dale, Our Mims, Sunshine Forever.

Vienna, Darrell—Gilded Time.

Walden, W. Elliott—Victory Gallop.

Ward, John T.—Beautiful Pleasure.

Ward, Sherrill W.—Forego (1974-'75).

Watters Jr., Sidney—Shadow Brook,

Leading trainers
By number of titles won

24—D. Wayne Lukas
10—Ron McAnally
10—Jonathan Sheppard
10—Charlie Whittingham
8—Bob Baffert
8—Lazaro Barrera
8—Claude McGaughey III
8—Woody Stephens
6—LeRoy Jolley
6—F. Bruce Miller
6—Bill Mott
5—Neil Drysdale
5—Robert Frankel
5—Flint S. Schulhofer
4—Francois Boutin
4—Hubert Hine
4—John Veitch
4—Frank Y. Whiteley Jr.
3—John Campo
3—W. Burling Cocks
3—Warren A. Croll Jr.
3—Grover G. Delp
3—Janet Elliot
3—Lucien Laurin
3—Jose Martin
3—Sidney Watters Jr.
3—David Whiteley
3—Maurice Zilber

Slew o' Gold (1983-'84).

Wheeler, Robert L. and John W. Russell—Track Robbery.

Whiteley, David A.—Just a Game (Ire), Revidere, Waya (Fr).

Whiteley Jr., Frank Y.—Forego (1976-'77), Ruffian (1974-'75).

Whittingham, Charles—Ack Ack, *Cougar II, Estrapade, Ferdinand, Flawlessly (1992-'93), Miss Alleged (with Pascal Bary), Perrault (GB), Sunday Silence, Turkish Trousers.

Zilber, Maurice—Youth, Dahlia, Trillion.

Zito, Nicholas P.—Storm Song.

Sires of Eclipse Award Winners

Ack Ack—Youth.

Affirmed—Flawlessly (1992-'93).

Ahmad—Paseana (Arg) (1992-'93).

Air Forbes Won—Yanks Music.

***Alcibiades II**—Athenian Idol.

Alleged—Flat Top (1998, 2002), Miss Alleged.

Alydar—Althea, Alysheba (1987-'88), Criminal Type, Easy Goer, Turkoman.

A.P. Indy—Tempera.

Bagdad—Turkish Trousers.

Battle Joined—Ack Ack.

Best Turn—Davona Dale.

Blushing Groom (Fr)—Arazi, Blushing John, Sky Beauty.

Bold Bidder—Spectacular Bid (1978-'80).

Bold Forbes—Tiffany Lass.

Bold Reasoning—Seattle Slew (1976-'78).

Bold Ruler—Secretariat (1972-'73), Wajima.

Broad Brush—Farda Amiga.

Buckaroo—Spend a Buck.

Buckpasser—La Prevoyante, Numbered Account, Relaxing.

Bucksplasher—Buck's Boy.

Capote—Boston Harbor.

Caro (Ire)—Cozzene, Winning Colors.

Cee's Tizzy—Gourmet Girl, Tiznow (2000-'01).

Cherokee Run—Chilukki.

Chief's Crown—Chief Bearhart.

Chieftain—Cascapedia.

Cohoes—Shadow Brook.

Consultant's Bid—Bayakoa (Arg) (1989-'90).

Cormorant—Saratoga Dew.

Court Ruling—Guilty Conscience.

Cox's Ridge—Cardmania, Life's Magic

1984-'85), Vanlandingham.

Creme dela Creme—Cafe Prince (1977-'78).

Crozier—Precisionist.

Cryptoclearance—Victory Gallop.

Danehill—Banks Hill (GB).

Danzatore—Reraise.

Danzig—Chief's Crown, Dance Smartly.

Darshaan—Kotashaan (Fr).

Deep Run—Morley Street (Ire) (1990-'91).

Deerhound—Countess Diana.

Delta Judge—Proud Delta.

Deputy Minister—Dehere, Go for Wand (1989-'90), Open Mind (1988-'89).

Djakao—Perrault (GB).

Doyoun—Daylami (Ire), Kalanisi (Ire).

Dr. Fager—Dearly Precious, Dr. Patches.

El Gran Senor—Lit de Justice.

Erins Isle (Ire)—Laugh and Be Merry.
Exclusive Native—Affirmed (1977-'79), Genuine Risk, Outstandingly.
Fappiano—Tasso, Unbridled, Rubiano.
Faraway Son—Waya (Fr).
Far North—The Wicked North.
Firestreak—*Snow Knight.
First Landing—Riva Ridge.
***Forli**—Forego (1974-'77).
French Deputy—Left Bank.
Gallant Romeo—Gallant Bob, My Juliet.
Graustark—Key to the Mint, Tempest Queen.
Great Above—Holy Bull.
***Grey Dawn II**—Christmas Past, Heavenly Cause.
Gulch—Thunder Gulch.
Habitat—Steinlen (GB).
Hail the Pirates—Wayward Lass.
Hail to Reason—Trillion.
Halo—Devil's Bag, Glorious Song, Sunday Silence.
Hennessy—Johannesburg.
***Herbager**—Our Mims.
His Majesty—Pleasant Colony, Tight Spot.
Hoist the Flag—Sensational.
Holy Bull—Macho Uno.
Honour and Glory—Caressing.
Horatius—Safely Kept.
Ile de Bourbon—Inlander (GB).
In Reality—Desert Vixen, Smile.
In the Wings (GB)—Singspiel (Ire).
Irish Castle—Bold Forbes.
Irish River (Fr)—Hatoof, Paradise Creek.
Jade Hunter—Azeri.
Java Gold—Kona Gold.
Key to the Mint—Jewel Princess, Plugged Nickle.
Kingmambo—Lemon Drop Kid.
Kris—All Gong (GB).
Kris S.—Hollywood Wildcat, Soaring Softly.
Lear Fan—Ryafan.
Licencioso—*Gran Kan.
Little Missouri—Prairie Bayou.
Lively One—Answer Lively.
Lord Gaylord—Lord Avie.
***Lorenzaccio**—Zaccio (1980-'82).
Lt. Stevens—Chou Croute.
Lyphard—Manila.
Lypheor (GB)—Royal Heroine (Ire).
Marquetry—Artax, Squirtle Squirt.
Maudlin—Beautiful Pleasure.
Meadowlake—Meadow Star.
Medieval Man—Not Surprising.
Minnesota Mac—Mac Diarmida.
Miswaki—Black Tie Affair (Ire).
Mo Bay—Flatterer (1983-'86).
Mr. Prospector—Conquistador Cielo, Eillo, Forty Niner, Gold Beauty, Golden Attraction, Gulch, It's in the Air, Queena, Rhythm.
Mt. Livermore—Housebuster (1990-'91), Eliza, Orientate.
Mystic II—Life's Illusion, Soothsayer.
Nashua—Shuvee.
Nashwan—Wandesta (GB).
Naskra—Star de Naskra.

Native Born—Chinook Pass.
Never Bend—J. O. Tobin, Straight and True.
Nijinsky II—De La Rose, Ferdinand, Sky Classic.
***Noholme II**—Shecky Greene.
Norcliffe—Groovy.
No Robbery—Track Robbery.
Northern Baby—Highland Bud, Possibly Perfect, Warm Spell.
Northern Jove—Candy Eclair.
Nureyev—Miesque (1987-'88), Theatrical (Ire).
Nureyev Dancer—Pompeyo (Chi).
Olden Times—Roving Boy.
Ole Bob Bowers—John Henry (1980-'81, 1983-'84).
Our Emblem—War Emblem.
Our Jimmy—Jimmy Lorenzo (GB).
Our Native—Rockhill Native.
Palace Music—Cigar (1995-'96).
***Petrone**—Brown Bess.
Phone Trick—Favorite Trick, Phone Chatter.
Pivotal—Golden Apples (Ire).
Pleasant Colony—Pleasant Stage, Pleasant Tap.
***Pretendre**—Canonero II.
Prince John—Protagonist, Typecast.
Private Account—Inside Information, Personal Ensign.
Quadrangle—Smart Angle, Susan's Girl (1972-'73, 1975).
Quiet American—Hidden Lake, Real Quiet.
Rahy—Fantastic Light, Serena's Song.
Rainbow Quest—Fiji (GB).
Rainy Lake—Lakeville Miss.
Raise a Cup—Before Dawn.
Rajab—Brave Raj.
Raja Baba—Sacahuista.
Red Ransom—Perfect Sting.
Reflected Glory—Snow Chief.
Reviewer—Revidere, Ruffian (1974-'75).
Roberto—Sunshine Forever.
Rock Talk—Heartlight No. One.
Roi Normand—Riboletta (Brz).
Runaway Groom—Cherokee Run.
Run the Gantlet—April Run (Ire).
Sadler's Wells—Correggio (Ire), High Chaparral (Ire), Northern Spur (Ire).
***Sea-Bird**—Little Current.
Seattle Slew—A.P. Indy, Capote, Landaluce, Slew o' Gold (1983-'84), Surfside, Swale, Vindication.
Secretariat—Lady's Secret, Risen Star.
Seeking the Gold—Flanders, Heavenly Prize.
Sharpen Up (GB)—Pebbles (GB).
Silver Buck—Silver Charm.
Silver Deputy—Silverbulletday (1998-'99).
Sir Ivor—Bates Motel.
Skip Trial—Skip Away (1996-'98).
***Sky High II**—Autobiography.
Skywalker—Bertrando.
Sovereign Dancer—Itsallgreektome.
Speak John—Talking Picture.
Spring Double—Martie's Anger.

Leading sires
By number of titles won

9	Mr. Prospector
8	Seattle Slew
6	Alydar
5	Deputy Minister
5	Exclusive Native
5	Transworld
4	Cox's Ridge
4	*Forli
4	Mo Bay
4	Mt. Livermore
4	Ole Bob Bowers
4	Quadrangle
3	Alleged
3	Blushing Groom (Fr)
3	Bold Bidder
3	Bold Reasoning
3	Bold Ruler
3	Buckpasser
3	Cee's Tizzy
3	Fappiano
3	Halo
3	*Lorenzaccio
3	Nijinsky II
3	Northern Baby
3	Nureyev
3	Reviewer
3	Sadler's Wells
3	Skip Trial
3	*Vaguely Noble

Stage Door Johnny—Johnny D., Late Bloomer.
State Dinner—Family Style.
Stop the Music—Temperence Hill.
Storm Cat—Storm Flag Flying.
Strawberry Road (Aus)—Ajina, Escena.
Summer Squall—Charismatic, Storm Song.
Summing—Epitome.
Swoon's Son—Chris Evert.
Tale of Two Cities—*Cougar II.
Tarboosh—Just a Game (Ire).
Targowice—All Along (Fr).
Thunder Gulch—Point Given.
Time for a Change—Fly So Free.
Timeless Moment—Gilded Time.
Tom Rolfe—Bowl Game, Run the Gantlet.
Top Command—Mom's Command.
Topsider—North Sider.
Transworld—Lonesome Glory (1992-'93, '95, '97, '99).
Two Punch—Smoke Glacken.
Unbridled—Anees, Banshee Breeze.
***Vaguely Noble**—Dahlia, Estrapade, Lemhi Gold.
Verbatim—Princess Rooney.
Vice Regent—Deputy Minister.
Wavering Monarch—Maria's Mon.
What a Pleasure—Foolish Pleasure, Honest Pleasure.
What Luck—What a Summer, Ambassador of Luck.
Woodman—Hansel, Timber Country.

2002 Eclipse Award Winners

AZERI
Horse of the Year
Older female
1998 ch. f., Jade Hunter—Zodiac Miss (Aus),
by Ahonoora
Breeder: Allen E. Paulson (Ky.)
Owner: Allen E. Paulson Living Trust
Trainer: Laura de Seroux
2002 record: 9-8-1-0, $2,181,540
Career record: 11-10-1, $2,227,740
2002 stakes victories: Breeders' Cup Distaff (G1),
Apple Blossom H. (G1), Santa Margarita H. (G1),
Milady Breeders' Cup H. (G1), Vanity H. (G1), Clement
Hirsch H. (G2), Lady's Secret Breeders' Cup H. (G2).

A virtual unknown at the beginning of 2002, Azeri dominated
the older female division and was an overwhelming choice as
Horse of the Year in North America, becoming the first female
winner since Lady's Secret in 1986. She was a unanimous winner
of an Eclipse Award in the older female division. Bred by the late
Allen Paulson, the chestnut filly with the fluid motion grew stronger
as the year progressed. She won her last seven starts—five in
Grade 1 stakes—over five different racetracks. Trained by Laura
de Seroux at San Luis Rey Downs and ridden by Mike Smith,
Azeri came from a few lengths off the pace to win the Santa
Margarita (G1) and Apple Blossom (G1) Handicaps but used
her natural speed to capture the last five on the lead. As her
victories accumulated, so did her weight assignments, rising to
127 pounds for the Lady's Secret Breeders' Cup Handicap (G2),
and she often spotted her rivals double-digit concessions. In the
weight-for-age Breeders' Cup Distaff (G1), Azeri put an exclamation
point on her season with a dominating five-length victory.

VINDICATION
Two-year-old male
2002 dk. b. or br. c., Seattle Slew—Strawberry
Reason, by Strawberry Road (Aus)
Breeder: Payson Stud (Ky.)
Owner: Padua Stables
Trainer: Bob Baffert
2002 and career record: 4-4-0-0, $680,950
2002 stakes victories: Breeders' Cup Juvenile (G1),
Kentucky Cup Juvenile (G3)

Trainer Bob Baffert often takes the road less traveled with his
two-year-olds. When he shipped Captain Steve into Turfway Park
for the 2000 Kentucky Cup Classic (G2), he brought along a
lightly raced two-year-old colt for the Kentucky Cup Juvenile
(G3). Captain Steve won, and so too did the two-year-old, Point
Given. The following year, Point Given dominated his division
and was voted Horse of the Year. Baffert considers the Turfway
juvenile race to be an educational exercise, because just about
anything can go wrong—and often does. In 2002, Baffert turned
back the entreaties of Padua Stables co-owner Satish Sanan
and ran Vindication in the Kentucky Cup Juvenile rather than
the Champagne Stakes (G1). The Seattle Slew colt had some
trouble at the Northern Kentucky track, overcame it, and won
easily. In the Breeders' Cup Juvenile (G1), his next start, Vindication
vindicated his $2.15-million purchase price by running on the
early pace, opening daylight in the stretch, and winning by 2¾
lengths over stablemate Kafwain to lock up his Eclipse Award.

STORM FLAG FLYING
Two-year-old filly
2002 dk. b. or br. f., Storm Cat—My Flag,
by Easy Goer
Breeder: Phipps Stable (Ky.)
Owner: Ogden Mills Phipps
Trainer: Claude R. McGaughey III
2002 and career record: 4-4-0-0, $967,000
2002 stakes victories: Breeders' Cup Juvenile Fillies
(G1), Matron S. (G1), Frizette S. (G1)

Storm Flag Flying's bottom line is a tribute to the late Ogden

Phipps's breeding operation. Her dam, Breeders' Cup Juvenile
Fillies (G1) winner My Flag, was the product of two Phipps
champions and Racing Hall of Fame members, Easy Goer and
undefeated Personal Ensign. Storm Flag Flying had champion
written all over her when she arrived at trainer Claude R. "Shug"
McGaughey III's barn, and the big question was how often her
difficult temperament would becloud her talents and cause her
defeat. Storm Flag Flying's oft-stormy personality did not stop
her from winning all four of her 2002 starts, although she ran
greenly each time. After a maiden win, she waltzed through
victories in the Matron (G1) and Frizette (G1) Stakes. The trainer
waited until the last possible moment to send her to Arlington
Park for the Breeders' Cup Juvenile Fillies (G1). His efforts
appeared for naught when Composure blew past her in the stretch,
but Storm Flag Flying rallied impressively to win by a half-length.

WAR EMBLEM
Three-year-old male
1999 dk. b. or br. c., Our Emblem—Sweetest Lady,
by Lord At War (Arg)
Breeder: Charles Nuckols Jr. & Sons (Ky.)
Owner: The Thoroughbred Corp.
Trainer: Bob Baffert
2002 record: 10-5-0-0, $3,455,000
Career record: 13-7-0-0, $3,491,000
2002 stakes victories: Kentucky Derby (G1),
Preakness S. (G1), Haskell Invitational H. (G1),
Illinois Derby (G2).

After winning the Illinois Derby (G2) on April 6 at Sportsman's
Park, War Emblem was purchased by The Thoroughbred Corp.
from Russell Reineman, who retained a 10% interest, and was
transferred to trainer Bob Baffert. The nearly black colt turned in
a front-running, 20.50-to-1 victory in the Kentucky Derby (G1)
under Victor Espinoza and then delivered a three-quarter-length
victory in the Preakness Stakes (G1), giving Baffert his fourth
straight Triple Crown race victory. (Point Given, 2001's Horse of
the Year, won the Preakness and Belmont Stakes [G1]). But War
Emblem stumbled out of the gate in the Belmont and, despite
making a run to take the lead, faded to eighth behind upset winner
Sarava. War Emblem delivered another front-running victory in
Monmouth Park's Haskell Invitational Handicap (G1) on August
4 before closing out the year with a sixth-place finish in the Pacific
Classic Stakes (G1) at Del Mar and an eighth-place finish in the
Breeders' Cup Classic (G1) at Arlington Park, performances that
cost War Emblem any chance of winning Horse of the Year honors.

FARDA AMIGA
Three-year-old filly
1999 b. f., Broad Brush—Fly North,
by Pleasant Colony
Breeder: Payson Stud
Owners: Old Friends Inc., Winner Silk Inc., and Jose de
Camargo
Trainer: Paulo Lobo
2002 record: 6-3-1-0 $1,248,902
Career record: 8-4-1-0, $1,282,302
2002 stakes wins: Kentucky Oaks (G1), Alabama S. (G1).

Farda Amiga made only six starts in 2002, but two of her three
triumphs, coupled with her second-place finish in the Breeders' Cup
Distaff (G1), were significant enough to earn her an Eclipse Award.
After winning an $80,000 allowance/optional claiming race at Santa
Anita Park, she finished fourth in the Santa Anita Oaks (G1). Shipped
to Churchill Downs, she won the Kentucky Oaks (G1) with a late
run at 20-to-1 odds, evoking a lively celebration from her Brazilian
connections, led by owners Julio Camargo, Marcos Simon, and
Jose de Camargo. Trainer Paulo Lobo charted a conservative course
for her next start, waiting until August for Saratoga Race Course's
Alabama Stakes (G1), which she won by three-quarters of a length.
Her next and final stop was the Breeders' Cup Distaff, in which she
finished five lengths behind Horse of the Year Azeri. She came out
of the race with bone chips in her ankle, and her owners opted to
retire her and breed her to Gone West in 2003.

LEFT BANK
Older male
1997 ch. h., French Deputy—Marshesseaux,
by Dr. Blum

Breeders: John Youngblood and Fletcher Gray (Ky.)
Owner: Michael Tabor
Trainer: Todd Pletcher
2002 record: 4-3-0-0, $626,146
Career record: 24-14-2-0, $1,402,806
2002 stakes victories: Whitney H. (G1), Tom Fool H. (G2), Bold Ruler H. (G3).

Left Bank was posthumously named champion older male on the strength of two outstanding performances within 31 days during the summer of 2002. In those two races, he flashed both speed and versatility by breaking Belmont Park's seven-furlong track record and equaling the 1⅛-mile mark at Saratoga Race Course. Left Bank certainly had credentials up to a mile; he closed out his 2001 season with a victory in Aqueduct's Cigar Mile Handicap (G1). After winning the six-furlong Bold Ruler Handicap (G3), Left Bank was parked wide in the one-mile Metropolitan Handicap (G1) and finished fifth. He came back with a 1:20.17 track-record victory in Belmont's seven-furlong Tom Fool Handicap (G2), which he won by 6¼ lengths. He then defeated one of the best fields of older horses in Saratoga's Whitney Handicap (G1), winning by 1¼ lengths over Dubai World Cup (UAE-G1) victor Street Cry (Ire) in a record-equaling 1:47.04 on August 3. Left Bank underwent emergency colic surgery one week after the Whitney and died on October 7 of complications from the surgery.

HIGH CHAPARRAL (Ire)
Turf Male
1999 b. c., Sadler's Wells—Kasora, by Darshaan
Breeder: Sean Coughlan
Owner: Michael Tabor and Susan Magnier
Trainer: Aidan P. O'Brien
2002 Record: 6-5-0-1, $3,436,410
Career Record: 9-7-1-1, $3,614,107
2002 stakes wins: Epsom Derby (Eng-G1), Irish Derby (Ire-G1), Breeders' Cup Turf (G1), Derrinstown Stud Derby Trial (Ire-G3), Ballysax S.

For the fourth consecutive year and seventh time in history, America's champion turf male was trained abroad, and also for the third straight year, made only one start in the United States during his championship season, the Breeders' Cup Turf (G1). A solid, professional victory in the Turf capped a stellar year for High Chaparral (Ire), who might well have gone unbeaten except for a midsummer virus. Trained at Ballydoyle in Ireland by Aidan O'Brien, High Chaparral began the year regarded as his stable's second best middle-distance three-year-old and prepared for the Epsom Derby (Eng-G1) by winning the Ballysax and Derrinstown Derby Trial Stakes (Ire-G3). He proved his superiority to highly touted stablemate Hawk Wing at Epsom, outstaying the stable favorite by two lengths. High Chaparral then added a comfortable Irish Derby (Ire-G1) win over stablemate Sholokov before falling seriously ill with a respiratory virus. The Prix de l'Arc de Triomphe (Fr-G1) came just too soon for him, and he finished third before returning to his best at Arlington Park, where he defeated With Anticipation handily.

GOLDEN APPLES (Ire)
Turf female
1998 b. f., Pivotal—Loon, by Kaldoun
Breeders: James Egan and David Hanley (Ire.)
Owner: Gary A. Tanaka
Trainer: Ben Cecil
2002 Record: 7-3-3-0, $1,111,680
Career Record: 15-6-5-2, $1,621,917
2002 stakes victories: Beverly D. S. (G1), Yellow Ribbon S. (G1), Santa Ana H. (G2).

Golden Apples (Ire) was her division's most consistent performer, racing from March until December and only in Grade 1 or Grade 2 events. She beat Starine (Fr) in the Santa Ana Handicap (G2) and was second in the Santa Barbara Handicap (G2), after which she was found to have a cyst nearly the size of a golf ball in her throat. She underwent surgery and returned three months later to run second in Del Mar's John C. Mabee Ramona Handicap (G1). Trainer Ben Cecil sent her to Arlington Park for the Beverly D. Stakes over the same course that would play host to the Breeders' Cup Filly and Mare Turf (G1). Golden Apples won that race, returned home to win the Yellow Ribbon Stakes (G1) at Santa Anita Park over a field that included reigning champion Banks Hill (GB), and was the 2.80-to-1 favorite for the Filly and Mare Turf. She encountered early trouble in the race and had to race wide but still managed to finish fourth behind Starine. Golden Apples closed her campaign in the Matriarch Stakes (G1) in which she was upset by a head by Dress To Thrill (Ire). She is the first champion for Cecil.

ORIENTATE
Sprinter
1998 dk. b. or br. c., Mt. Livermore—Dream Team, by Cox's Ridge
Breeder: Gainesway Thoroughbreds, Ltd. (Ky.)
Owners: Robert and Beverly Lewis
Trainer: D. Wayne Lukas
2002 record: 10-6-1-0, $1,412,970
Career record: 19-10-3-0, $1,716,950
2002 stakes victories: Breeders' Cup Sprint (G1), Forego H. (G1), Commonwealth Breeders' Cup S. (G2), A. G. Vanderbilt H. (G2), Aristides H. (G3), Smile Sprint H.

Once Hall of Fame trainer D. Wayne Lukas pinpointed Orientate's strength—sprinting on dirt—Bob and Beverly Lewis's four-year-old Mt. Livermore colt was unbeatable. A $250,000 purchase at the 1999 Keeneland September yearling sale, he won all six dirt sprints he contested in 2002. Twelfth in the 2001 Breeders' Cup Classic (G1), he began his four-year-old season by finishing second in the San Fernando Breeders' Cup Stakes (G2) and sixth in the Strub Stakes (G2). Switched to sprinting, Orientate won the seven-furlong Commonwealth Breeders' Cup Stakes (G2) at Keeneland Race Course on April 14. Following ninth- and fourth-place finishes in graded turf stakes, Lukas returned Orientate to dirt sprints. The colt ripped off victories in the Aristides Handicap (G3) at Churchill Downs by 4¼ lengths, the Smile Sprint Handicap by six lengths at Calder Race Course, the A.G. Vanderbilt (G2) and Forego (G1) Handicaps at Saratoga Race Course by two and 2¼ lengths, respectively, and then the Breeders' Cup Sprint (G1) at Arlington Park, by a half-length, to sew up his Eclipse Award.

FLAT TOP
Steeplechaser
1993 dk. b. or br. g., Alleged—Lady of the Light, by The Minstrel
Breeder: Landon Knight (Ky.)
Owner: Nancy Gerry
Trainer: Janet Elliot
2002 record: 5-2-0-3, $237,831
Career record: 20-9-3-2, $592,306
2002 stakes victories: Breeders' Cup Steeplechase, Colonial Cup Hurdle S.

Flat Top won his second Eclipse Award as champion steeplechase horse in 2002, but he did not make it easy for trainer Janet Elliot. He was a stall walker when she mercifully ended his flat career in 1996, and he grew worse after his championship season in 1998. Sidelined by a suspensory-ligament injury in 1999 and a bowed tendon in late 2000, Flat Top returned in the Royal Chase for the Sport of Kings at Keeneland Race Course in April. Elliot shipped him to a Kentucky farm, but Flat Top fretted the whole time and ran a poor third. From then on, Elliot shipped him directly from her Pennsylvania farm to his race sites, with better results. A competitive third in the Iroquois Steeplechase and New York Turf Writers Cup Steeplechase Handicap, Flat Top found his best form in the fall and reeled off victories in the Breeders' Cup Steeplechase and Colonial Cup Hurdle Stakes, both races he had won on his way to the 1998 title.

Champions Before Eclipse Awards

Daily Racing Form (DRF) began naming champions in 1936. Beginning in 1950, the Thoroughbred Racing Associations (TRA) began naming its own champions. The following tables reflect the horses named champions by those two organizations. Where neither the letter (D) or (T) follow the name of the horse, both the DRF and the TRA named that horse champion.

When there were different champions named in any category, the DRF champion is noted with the letter (D) and the TRA with the letter (T). *Daily Racing Form*, the TRA, and the National Turf Writers Association joined forces in 1971 to create the Eclipse Awards, which now recognize the champions of racing in North America.

†-filly, *-imported horse; (D) *Daily Racing Form*; (T) Thoroughbred Racing Associations

Horse of the Year

1970	Fort Marcy (D)
	Personality (T)
1969	Arts and Letters
1968	Dr. Fager
1967	Damascus
1966	Buckpasser
1965	Roman Brother (D)
	†Moccasin (T)
1964	Kelso
1963	Kelso
1962	Kelso
1961	Kelso
1960	Kelso
1959	Sword Dancer
1958	Round Table
1957	Bold Ruler (D)
	Dedicate (T)
1956	Swaps
1955	Nashua
1954	Native Dancer
1953	Tom Fool
1952	One Count (D)
	Native Dancer (T)
1951	Counterpoint
1950	Hill Prince
1949	Capot
1948	Citation
1947	Armed
1946	Assault
1945	†Busher
1944	†Twilight Tear
1943	Count Fleet
1942	Whirlaway
1941	Whirlaway
1940	Challedon
1939	Challedon
1938	Seabiscuit
1937	War Admiral
1936	Granville

Two-Year-Old Male

1970	Hoist the Flag
1969	Silent Screen
1968	Top Knight
1967	Vitriolic
1966	Successor
1965	Buckpasser
1964	Bold Lad
1963	Hurry to Market
1962	Never Bend
1961	Crimson Satan
1960	Hail to Reason
1959	Warfare
1958	First Landing
1957	Nadir (D)
	Jewel's Reward (T)

1956	Barbizon
1955	Needles
1954	Nashua
1953	Porterhouse
1952	Native Dancer
1951	Tom Fool
1950	Battlefield
1949	Hill Prince
1948	Blue Peter
1947	Citation
1946	Double Jay
1945	Star Pilot
1944	Pavot
1943	Platter
1942	Count Fleet
1941	Alsab
1940	Our Boots
1939	Bimelech
1938	El Chico
1937	Menow
1936	Pompoon

Two-Year-Old Filly

1970	Forward Gal
1969	Fast Attack (D)
	Tudor Queen (T)
1968	Gallant Bloom (D)
	Process Shot (T)
1967	Queen of the Stage
1966	Regal Gleam
1965	Moccasin
1964	Queen Empress
1963	Tosmah (D)
	Castle Forbes (T)
1962	Smart Deb
1961	Cicada
1960	Bowl of Flowers
1959	My Dear Girl
1958	Quill
1957	Idun
1956	Leallah (D)
	Romanita (T)
1955	Doubledogdare (D)
	Nasrina (T)
1954	High Voltage
1953	Evening Out
1952	Sweet Patootie
1951	Rose Jet
1950	Aunt Jinny
1949	Bed o' Roses
1948	Myrtle Charm
1947	Bewitch
1946	First Flight
1945	Beaugay
1944	Busher
1943	Durazna
1942	Askmenow

1941	Petrify
1940	Level Best
1939	Now What
1938	Incoselda
1937	Jacola
1936	Apogee

Three-Year-Old Male

1970	Personality
1969	Arts and Letters
1968	Stage Door Johnny
1967	Damascus
1966	Buckpasser
1965	Tom Rolfe
1964	Northern Dancer
1963	Chateaugay
1962	Jaipur
1961	Carry Back
1960	Kelso
1959	Sword Dancer
1958	Tim Tam
1957	Bold Ruler
1956	Needles
1955	Nashua
1954	High Gun
1953	Native Dancer
1952	One Count
1951	Counterpoint
1950	Hill Prince
1949	Capot
1948	Citation
1947	Phalanx
1946	Assault
1945	Fighting Step
1944	By Jimminy
1943	Count Fleet
1942	Alsab
1941	Whirlaway
1940	Bimelech
1939	Challedon
1938	Stagehand
1937	War Admiral
1936	Granville

Three-Year-Old Filly

1970	Office Queen (D)
	Fanfreluche (T)
1969	Gallant Bloom
1968	Dark Mirage
1967	Furl Sail (D)
	Gamely (T)
1966	Lady Pitt
1965	What a Treat
1964	Tosmah
1963	Lamb Chop
1962	Cicada
1961	Bowl of Flowers

1960	Berlo
1959	Royal Native (D)
	Silver Spoon (T)
1958	Idun
1957	Bayou
1956	Doubledogdare
1955	Misty Morn
1954	Parlo
1953	Grecian Queen
1952	Real Delight
1951	Kiss Me Kate
1950	Next Move
1949	‡Two Lea
	‡Wistful
1948	Miss Request
1947	But Why Not
1946	Bridal Flower
1945	Busher
1944	Twilight Tear
1943	Stefanita
1942	Vagrancy
1941	Painted Veil
1940	Not awarded
1939	Unerring
1938	Not awarded
1937	Not awarded
1936	Not awarded

‡ (D) co-champions

Handicap Male

1970	Fort Marcy (D)
	Nodouble (T)
1969	Arts and Letters (D)
	Nodouble (T)
1968	Dr. Fager
1967	Damascus (D)
	Buckpasser (T)
1966	Buckpasser (D)
	Bold Bidder (T)
1965	Roman Brother
1964	Kelso
1963	Kelso
1962	Kelso
1961	Kelso
1960	Bald Eagle
1959	Sword Dancer (D)
	Round Table (T)
1958	Round Table
1957	Dedicate
1956	Swaps
1955	High Gun
1954	Native Dancer
1953	Tom Fool
1952	Crafty Admiral
1951	Hill Prince
1950	*Noor
1949	Coaltown
1948	Citation
1947	Armed
1946	Armed
1945	Stymie
1944	Devil Diver
1943	Market Wise
	Devil Diver
1942	Whirlaway
1941	Mioland
1940	Challedon

1939	*Kayak II
1938	Seabiscuit
1937	Seabiscuit
1936	Discovery

Handicap Female

1970	Shuvee
1969	Gallant Bloom (D)
	Gamely (T)
1968	Gamely
1967	Straight Deal
1966	Open Fire (D)
	Summer Scandal (T)
1965	Old Hat
1964	Tosmah (D)
	Old Hat (T)
1963	Cicada
1962	Primonetta
1961	Airmans Guide
1960	Royal Native
1959	Tempted
1958	Bornastar
1957	Pucker Up
1956	Blue Sparkler
1955	Misty Morn (D)
	Parlo (T)
1954	Parlo (D)
	Lavender Hill (T)
1953	Sickle's Image
1952	Real Delight (D)
	Next Move (T)
1951	Bed o' Roses
1950	Two Lea
1949	Bewitch
1948	Conniver
1947	But Why Not
1946	Gallorette
1945	Busher
1944	Twilight Tear
1943	Mar-Kell
1942	Vagrancy
1941	Fairy Chant
1940	War Plumage
1939	Lady Maryland
1938	Marica
1937	Not awarded
1936	Myrtlewood

Sprinter

1970	†Ta Wee
1969	†Ta Wee
1968	Dr. Fager
1967	Dr. Fager
1966	Impressive
1965	†Affectionately
1964	Ahoy
1963	Not awarded
1962	Not awarded
1961	Not awarded
1960	Not awarded
1959	Intentionally
1958	Bold Ruler
1957	Decathlon
1956	Decathlon
1955	Berseem
1954	White Skies
1953	Tom Fool
1952	Tea-Maker

1951	Sheilas Reward
1950	Sheilas Reward
1949	Delegate
	Royal Governor
1948	Coaltown
1947	Polynesian

1947: first year category included

Turf Horse

1970	Fort Marcy
1969	*Hawaii
1968	Dr. Fager (D)
	Fort Marcy (T)
1967	Fort Marcy
1966	Assagai
1965	Parka
1964	*Turbo Jet II
1963	Mongo
1962	Not awarded
1961	T. V. Lark
1960	Not awarded
1959	Round Table
1958	Round Table
1957	Round Table
1956	Career Boy
1955	*St. Vincent
1954	*Stan
1953	*Iceberg II

1953: first year category included

Steeplechase

1970	Top Bid
1969	*L'Escargot
1968	Bon Nouvel
1967	Quick Pitch
1966	Mako (D)
	Tuscalee (T)
1965	Bon Nouvel
1964	Bon Nouvel
1963	Amber Diver
1962	Barnabys Bluff
1961	Peal
1960	Benguala
1959	Ancestor
1958	Neji
1957	Neji
1956	Shipboard
1955	Neji
1954	King Commander
1953	The Mast
1952	Jam (D)
	Oedipus (T)
1951	Oedipus
1950	Oedipus
1949	Trough Hill
1948	American Way
1947	War Battle
1946	Elkridge
1945	Mercator
1944	Rouge Dragon
1943	Brother Jones
1942	Elkridge
1941	Speculate
1940	Not awarded
1939	Not awarded
1938	Not awarded
1937	Jungle King
1936	Bushranger

RACING HALL OF FAME

The Racing Hall of Fame was founded in 1955 to honor the all-time greats of the sport, though it is limited to horses, jockeys, and trainers. Housed in the National Museum of Racing in Saratoga Springs, New York, the Racing Hall of Fame contains plaques that summarize the accomplishments of each inductee.

In addition to the horses, jockeys, and trainers, the Hall of Fame has a special category, Exemplar of Racing, reserved for a handful of people who have made a lasting impact on the sport as owners, breeders, or racing executives. Otherwise, the Hall of Fame does not individually recognize the accomplishments of owners, breeders, Turf writers, racing secretaries, racetrack owners, or other industry participants.

Each spring, a panel votes on the horses and people nominated for induction into the Hall of Fame. The results are usually announced in the week preceding the Kentucky Derby (G1). The induction ceremonies usually take place the second Monday of August in Saratoga Springs.

Categories under consideration each year are Contemporary Male, Contemporary Female, Horse of Yesteryear, Jockey, and Trainer.

Nominees for induction into the Hall of Fame are first obtained from the 125 members of the Hall of Fame voting panel. The suggestions then go before a nomination committee, which narrows the names down to three for each category for that year's ballots. Names of the three finalists in each division then go before the entire voting panel. The top vote-getter in each category is selected as that year's inductee.

From time to time, additional selections to the Hall of Fame are made by the Historical Review Committee and the Steeplechase Committee. Candidates in these categories must meet the General Eligibility Criteria for consideration. The Historical Review Committee meets to consider if a jockey, trainer, or horse merits consideration for induction into the Hall of Fame but otherwise would remain unrecognized. The Steeplechase Committee meets to consider if a steeplechase jockey, trainer, or horse merits consideration for induction into the Hall of Fame.

Hall of Fame Eligibility Criteria:
To earn a place on the annual ballot, nominees must meet the following criteria:

1. Thoroughbreds become eligible when five calendar years have elapsed between their final racing year and their year of nomination.

2. Eligible Thoroughbreds are classified as Contemporary Male or Female if they have been retired between five and 25 years ago. Horses that have been retired for more than 25 years are classified as Horses of Yesteryear.

3. Active jockeys become eligible after riding Thoroughbreds for 15 years (any interruptions in their careers for injury are not counted against them).

4. Active trainers become eligible after 25 years as licensed Thoroughbred trainers.

5. The 15- and 25-year requirements may be waived for retired jockeys and trainers, but a five-year waiting period is then observed before they become eligible. In cases of fragile health, the Hall of Fame Committee may request that the five-year waiting period be waived at the discretion of the Executive Committee.

Members of the National Museum of Racing Hall of Fame

Exemplars of Racing (Year inducted)

John W. Hanes (1982)	Walter M. Jeffords (1973)	Paul Mellon (1989)	George D. Widener (1971)
C. V. Whitney (1991)			

Jockeys (Year inducted)

Frank D. "Dooley" Adams (1970)	Robert H. "Specs" Crawford (1973)	John P. Loftus (1959)	John L. Rotz (1983)
John Adams (1965)	Pat Day (1991)	John Longden (1958)	Earl Sande (1955)
Joe Aitcheson Jr. (1978)	Eddie Delahoussaye (1993)	Daniel A. Maher (1955)	Carroll H. Schilling (1970)
Edward Arcaro (1958)	Lavelle "Buddy" Ensor (1962)	J. Linus McAtee (1956)	William Shoemaker (1958)
Ted Atkinson (1957)	Laverne Fator (1955)	Chris McCarron (1989)	Willie Simms (1977)
Braulio Baeza (1976)	Earlie Fires (2001)	Conn McCreary (1975)	James "Tod" Sloan (1955)
Jerry Bailey (1995)	Jerry Fishback (1992)	Rigan McKinney (1968)	Mike Smith (2003)
George Barbee (1996)	Andrew "Mack" Garner (1969)	James McLaughlin (1955)	Alfred P. "Paddy" Smithwick (1973)
Carroll K. Bassett (1972)		Walter Miller (1955)	
Russell Baze (1999)	Edward "Snapper" Garrison (1955)	Isaac B. Murphy (1955)	Gary Stevens (1997)
Walter Blum (1987)		Ralph Neves (1960)	James Stout (1968)
George "Pete" Bostwick (1968)	Avelino Gomez (1982)	Joe Notter (1963)	Fred Taral (1955)
Sam Boulmetis Sr. (1973)	Henry F. Griffin (1956)	George M. Odom (1955)	Bayard Tuckerman Jr. (1973)
Steve Brooks (1963)	Eric Guerin (1972)	Winfield "Winnie" O'Connor (1956)	Ron Turcotte (1979)
Don Brumfield (1996)	William J. Hartack (1959)		Nash Turner (1955)
Thomas H. Burns (1983)	Sandy Hawley (1992)	Frank O'Neill (1956)	Robert N. Ussery (1980)
James H. Butwell (1984)	Albert Johnson (1971)	Ivan H. Parke (1978)	Jacinto Vasquez (1998)
J. Dallett "Dolly" Byers (1967)	William J. Knapp (1969)	Gilbert W. Patrick (1970)	Jorge Velasquez (1990)
Steve Cauthen (1994)	Julie Krone (2000)	Laffit Pincay Jr. (1975)	Jack Westrope (2002)
Frank Coltiletti (1970)	Clarence Kummer (1972)	Samuel Purdy (1970)	George M. Woolf (1955)
Angel Cordero Jr. (1988)	Charles Kurtsinger (1967)	John Reiff (1956)	Raymond Workman (1956)
		Alfred Robertson (1971)	Manuel Ycaza (1977)

Trainers (Year inducted)

Lazaro S. Barrera (1979)
H. Guy Bedwell (1971)
Edward D. Brown (1984)
J. Elliott Burch (1980)
Preston M. Burch (1963)
William P. Burch (1955)
Fred Burlew (1973)
Frank E. Childs (1968)
Henry S. Clark (1982)
W. Burling Cocks (1985)
James P. Conway (1996)
Warren A. "Jimmy" Croll Jr. (1994)
Grover G. "Buddy" Delp (2002)
Neil Drysdale (2000)
William Duke (1956)
Louis Feustel (1964)
James Fitzsimmons (1958)
Robert Frankel (1995)
John M. Gaver Sr. (1966)
Thomas J. Healey (1955)

Sam C. Hildreth (1955)
Hubert "Sonny" Hine (2003)
Max Hirsch (1959)
William J. "Buddy" Hirsch (1982)
Thomas Hitchcock Sr. (1973)
Hollie Hughes (1973)
John J. Hyland (1956)
Hirsch Jacobs (1958)
H. Allen Jerkens (1975)
Philip G. Johnson (1997)
William R. Johnson (1986)
LeRoy Jolley (1987)
Ben A. Jones (1958)
Horace A. "Jimmy" Jones (1959)
Andrew Jackson Joyner (1955)
Thomas J. Kelly (1993)
Lucien Laurin (1977)
J. Howard Lewis (1969)
D. Wayne Lukas (1999)

Horatio Luro (1980)
John E. Madden (1983)
James W. Maloney (1989)
Richard Mandella (2001)
Frank "Pancho" Martin (1981)
Ron McAnally (1990)
Henry McDaniel (1956)
MacKenzie "Mack" Miller (1987)
William Molter Jr. (1960)
William I. Mott (1998)
Winbert Mulholland (1967)
Edward A. Neloy (1983)
John A. Nerud (1972)
Burley Parke (1986)
Angel Penna Sr. (1988)
Jacob Pincus (1988)
John W. Rogers (1955)
James G. Rowe Sr. (1955)
Flint S. "Scotty" Schulhofer (1992)
Jonathan Sheppard (1990)

Robert A. Smith (1976)
Tom Smith (2001)
D. M. "Mike" Smithwick (1971)
Woodford C. "Woody" Stephens (1976)
Meshach "Mesh" Tenney (1991)
Henry J. Thompson (1969)
Harry Trotsek (1984)
Jack C. Van Berg (1985)
Marion H. Van Berg (1970)
Sylvester Veitch (1977)
Robert W. Walden (1970)
Michael Walsh (1997)
Sherrill Ward (1978)
Frank Whiteley Jr. (1978)
Charles Whittingham (1974)
Ansel Williamson (1998)
G. Carey Winfrey (1975)
William C. Winfrey (1971)

Horses (Year inducted, year foaled)

Ack Ack (1986, 1966)
Affectionately (1989, 1960)
Affirmed (1980, 1975)
All Along (Fr) (1990, 1979)
Alsab (1976, 1939)
Alydar (1989, 1975)
Alysheba (1993, 1984)
American Eclipse (1970, 1814)
A.P. Indy (2000, 1989)
Armed (1963, 1941)
Artful (1956, 1902)
Arts and Letters (1994, 1966)
Assault (1964, 1943)
Battleship (1969, 1927)
Bayakoa (Arg) (1998, 1984)
Bed o' Roses (1976, 1947)
Beldame (1956, 1901)
Ben Brush (1955, 1893)
Bewitch (1977, 1945)
Bimelech (1990, 1937)
Black Gold (1989, 1921)
Black Helen (1991, 1932)
Blue Larkspur (1957, 1926)
Bold 'n Determined (1997, 1977)
Bold Ruler (1973, 1954)
Bon Nouvel (1976, 1960)
Boston (1955, 1833)
Broomstick (1956, 1901)
Buckpasser (1970, 1963)
Busher (1964, 1942)
Bushranger (1967, 1930)
Cafe Prince (1985, 1970)
Carry Back (1975, 1958)
Cavalcade (1993, 1931)
Challedon (1977, 1936)
Chris Evert (1988, 1971)
Cicada (1967, 1959)
Cigar (2002, 1990)
Citation (1959, 1945)
Coaltown (1983, 1945)
Colin (1956, 1905)
Commando (1956, 1898)
Count Fleet (1961, 1940)

Crusader (1995, 1923)
Dahlia (1981, 1970)
Damascus (1974, 1964)
Dance Smartly (2003, 1988)
Dark Mirage (1974, 1965)
Davona Dale (1985, 1976)
Desert Vixen (1979, 1970)
Devil Diver (1980, 1939)
Discovery (1969, 1931)
Domino (1955, 1891)
Dr. Fager (1971, 1964)
Easy Goer (1997, 1986)
Eight Thirty (1994, 1936)
Elkridge (1966, 1938)
Emperor of Norfolk (1988, 1885)
Equipoise (1957, 1928)
Exceller (1999, 1973)
Exterminator (1957, 1915)
Fairmount (1985, 1921)
Fair Play (1956, 1905)
Fashion (1980, 1837)
Firenze (1981, 1884)
Flatterer (1994, 1979)
Foolish Pleasure (1995, 1972)
Forego (1979, 1970)
Fort Marcy (1998, 1964)
Gallant Bloom (1977, 1966)
Gallant Fox (1957, 1927)
*Gallant Man (1987, 1954)
Gallorette (1962, 1942)
Gamely (1980, 1964)
Genuine Risk (1986, 1977)
Go for Wand (1996, 1987)
Good and Plenty (1956, 1900)
Granville (1997, 1933)
Grey Lag (1957, 1918)
Gun Bow (1999, 1960)
Hamburg (1986, 1895)
Hanover (1955, 1884)
Henry of Navarre (1985, 1891)
Hill Prince (1991, 1947)

Hindoo (1955, 1878)
Holy Bull (2001, 1991)
Imp (1965, 1894)
Jay Trump (1971, 1957)
John Henry (1990, 1975)
Johnstown (1992, 1936)
Jolly Roger (1965, 1922)
Kelso (1967, 1957)
Kentucky (1983, 1861)
Kingston (1955, 1884)
Lady's Secret (1992, 1982)
La Prevoyante (1995, 1970)
*L'Escargot (1977, 1963)
Lexington (1955, 1850)
Longfellow (1971, 1867)
Luke Blackburn (1955, 1877)
Majestic Prince (1988, 1966)
Man o' War (1957, 1917)
Maskette (2001, 1906)
Miesque (1999, 1984)
Miss Woodford (1967, 1880)
Myrtlewood (1979, 1932)
Nashua (1965, 1952)
Native Dancer (1963, 1950)
Native Diver (1978, 1959)
Needles (2000, 1953)
Neji (1966, 1950)
*Noor (2002, 1945)
Northern Dancer (1976, 1961)
Oedipus (1978, 1946)
Old Rosebud (1968, 1911)
Omaha (1965, 1932)
Pan Zareta (1972, 1910)
Parole (1984, 1873)
Paseana (Arg) (2001, 1987)
Personal Ensign (1993, 1984)
Peter Pan (1956, 1904)
Precisionist (2003, 1981)
Princess Doreen (1982, 1921)
Princess Rooney (1991, 1980)
Real Delight (1987, 1949)

Regret (1957, 1912)
Reigh Count (1978, 1925)
Riva Ridge (1998, 1969)
Roamer (1981, 1911)
Roseben (1956, 1901)
Round Table (1972, 1954)
Ruffian (1976, 1972)
Ruthless (1975, 1864)
Salvator (1955, 1886)
Sarazen (1957, 1921)
Seabiscuit (1958, 1933)
Searching (1978, 1952)
Seattle Slew (1981, 1974)
Secretariat (1974, 1970)
Serena's Song (2002, 1992)
Shuvee (1975, 1966)
Silver Spoon (1978, 1956)
Sir Archy (1955, 1805)
Sir Barton (1957, 1916)
Slew o' Gold (1992, 1980)
Spectacular Bid (1982, 1976)
Stymie (1975, 1941)
Sun Beau (1996, 1925)
Sunday Silence (1996, 1986)
Susan's Girl (1976, 1969)
Swaps (1966, 1952)
Sword Dancer (1977, 1956)
Sysonby (1956, 1902)
Ta Wee (1994, 1966)
Ten Broeck (1982, 1872)
Tim Tam (1985, 1955)
Tom Fool (1960, 1949)
Top Flight (1966, 1929)
Tosmah (1984, 1961)
Twenty Grand (1957, 1928)
Twilight Tear (1963, 1941)
Two Lea (1982, 1946)
War Admiral (1958, 1934)
Whirlaway (1959, 1938)
Whisk Broom II (1979, 1907)
Winning Colors (2000, 1985)
Zaccio (1990, 1976)
Zev (1983, 1920)

Owners of Racing Hall of Fame Members

H. C. Applegate—Old Rosebud
Augustin Stables—Cafe Prince
E. J. "Lucky" Baldwin—Emperor of Norfolk
Edith W. Bancroft—Damascus
Belair Stud—Gallant Fox, Granville, Johnstown, Nashua, Omaha
August Belmont II—Beldame, Fair Play, Henry of Navarre
Col. E. R. Bradley—Bimelech, Black Helen, Blue Larkspur, Busher
William Brann—Challedon, Gallorette
Briardale Farm—Tosmah
Brookmeade Stable—Cavalcade, Sword Dancer
Ed Brown and Eugene Leigh—Ben Brush
S. S. Brown—Broomstick
Calumet Farm—Alydar, Armed, Bewitch, Citation, Coaltown, Davona Dale, Real Delight, Tim Tam, Twilight Tear, Two Lea, Whirlaway
Christopher T. Chenery—Hill Prince
Christiana Stable—Go for Wand
Claiborne Farm—Round Table
Gen. Nathaniel Coles—American Eclipse
E. T. Colton—Pan Zareta
Brownell Combs—Myrtlewood
Sidney H. Craig—Paseana (Arg)
Warren A. "Jimmy" Croll Jr.—Holy Bull
J. F. Cushman and E. V. Snedeker—Kingston
D & H Stable—Needles
Marcus Daly—Hamburg
Dotsam Stable—John Henry
Allaire duPont—Kelso
Mike Dwyer—Ben Brush
Phil and Mike Dwyer—Hanover, Hindoo, Kingston, Luke Blackburn, Miss Woodford
Rex Ellsworth—Swaps
Equusequity Stable—Slew o' Gold
Tomonori Tsurumaki and Farish-Goodman-Kilroy—A.P. Indy
Diana Firestone—Genuine Risk
Mr. and Mrs. E. E. Fogelson—Ack Ack
Dr. Ernest Gaillard, Arthur B. Hancock III, and Charles Whittingham—Sunday Silence
Gedney Farm—Gun Bow
Martha F. Gerry—Forego
William Gibbons—Fashion
Greentree Stable—Devil Diver, Tom Fool, Twenty Grand
John L. Greer—Foolish Pleasure
Harry Guggenheim—Ack Ack
James Ben Ali Haggin—Firenze, Salvator
Arthur B. Hancock III, Dr. Ernest Gaillard, and Charles Whittingham—Sunday Silence
Harbor View Farm—Affirmed

Dan Harness—Imp
Frank Harper—Ten Broeck
John Harper—Longfellow
George Harris, William Pape, and Jonathan Sheppard—Flatterer
Hawksworth Farm—Spectacular Bid
Mrs. John D. Hertz—Count Fleet, Reigh Count
Max Hirsch—Grey Lag
Thomas Hitchcock—Elkridge, Good and Plenty
Fred Hooper—Precisionist, Susan's Girl
Rosa M. Hoots—Black Gold
Charles S. Howard—*Noor, Seabiscuit
Nelson Bunker Hunt—Dahlia, Exceller
John Hunter, William Travers, and George Osgood—Kentucky
Ethel Jacobs—Affectionately, Searching, Stymie
Col. William R. Johnson—Sir Archy
Davy C. Johnson—Roseben
B. B. and Monfort Jones—Princess Doreen
James R. Keene—Colin, Commando, Maskette, Peter Pan, Sysonby
James R. and Foxhall Keene—Domino
Kerr Stable—Round Table
Willis Sharpe Kilmer—Exterminator, Sun Beau
King Ranch—Assault, Gallant Bloom
Eugene Klein—Winning Colors
Mr. and Mrs. Eugene Klein—Lady's Secret
Eugene Leigh and Ed Brown—Ben Brush
Jean-Louis Levesque—La Prevoyante
Robert and Beverly Lewis—Serena's Song
Locust Hill Farm—Ruffian
Pierre Lorillard—Parole
Ralph Lowe—*Gallant Man
John Madden—Hamburg
Harry Mangurian Jr.—Desert Vixen
Louis B. Mayer—Busher
Bryon McClelland—Henry of Navarre
Rigan McKinney—Neji
Frank McMahon—Majestic Prince
Meadow Stable—Cicada, Riva Ridge, Secretariat
Paul Mellon—Arts and Letters
J. Cal Milam—Exterminator
Andrew Miller—Roamer
Kent Miller—Elkridge
Lloyd Miller—Dark Mirage
Francis Morris—Ruthless
Mrs. Lewis C. Murdock—Zaccio
J. F. Newman—Pan Zareta
Stavros Niarchos—Miesque
George Osgood, William Travers, and John Hunter—Kentucky
William Pape, George Harris, and Jonathan Sheppard—Flatterer

Allen E. Paulson—Cigar
William Haggin Perry—Gamely
Lillian Bostwick Phipps—Neji, Oedipus
Ogden Phipps—Buckpasser, Easy Goer, Personal Ensign
Powhatan—*L'Escargot
Jack Price—Carry Back
Rancocas Stable—Zev
Mrs. Theodore Randolph—Bon Nouvel
Samuel D. Riddle—Crusader, Man o' War, War Admiral
Nathaniel Rives—Boston
Rokeby Stable—Fort Marcy
Carl Rosen—Chris Evert
Commander J. K. L. Ross—Sir Barton
Albert Sabath—Alsab
Walter J. Salmon Jr.—Battleship
Sam-Son Farm—Dance Smartly
Saron Stable—Bold 'n Determined
Dorothy and Pamela Scharbauer—Alysheba
Marion duPont Scott—Battleship
Mr. and Mrs. L. K. Shapiro—Native Diver
Jonathan Sheppard, William Pape, and George Harris—Flatterer
Harry Sinclair—Grey Lag
E. V. Snedeker and J. F. Cushman—Kingston
Mrs. Mary Stephenson—Jay Trump
Mrs. Whitney Stone—Shuvee
Tartan Farms—Dr. Fager, Ta Wee
Tayhill Stable—Seattle Slew
E. P. Taylor—Northern Dancer
Richard Ten Broeck—Lexington
William Travers, John Hunter, and George Osgood—Kentucky
Tomonori Tsurumaki and Farish-Goodman-Kilroy—A.P. Indy
Paula Tucker—Princess Rooney
Cornelius W. Van Ranst—American Eclipse
Alfred G. Vanderbilt—Bed o' Roses, Discovery, Native Dancer
Mrs. W. K. Vanderbilt III—Sarazen
Wheatley Stable—Bold Ruler
Frank and Janis Whitham—Bayakoa (Arg)
C. V. Whitney—Equipoise, Silver Spoon, Top Flight
Harry Payne Whitney—Artful, Regret, Whisk Broom II
Mrs. Payne Whitney—Jolly Roger
Charles Whittingham, Dr. Ernest Gaillard, and Arthur B. Hancock III—Sunday Silence
George D. Widener—Eight Thirty
Joseph E. Widener—Bushranger, Fairmount
Daniel Wildenstein—All Along (Fr)
Capt. Jim Williams—Luke Blackburn

Breeders of Racing Hall of Fame Members

Muriel Vanderbilt Adams—Desert Vixen
H. H. Aga Khan—*Noor
H. H. Aga Khan and Prince Aly Khan—*Gallant Man
Lucien O. Appleby—Henry of Navarre

F. Wallis Armstrong—Cavalcade
Dr. Howard Baker—Serena's Song
Mrs. Thomas Bancroft—Damascus
Belair Stud—Gallant Fox, Granville, Nashua, Omaha

August Belmont II—Beldame, Fair Play, Man o' War
Bieber-Jacobs Stables—Affectionately
Blue Bear Stud—Zaccio
Col. E. R. Bradley—Bimelech, Black Helen,

Blue Larkspur, Busher, Oedipus
William L. Brann—Challedon
Brookmeade Stable—Sword Dancer
S. S. Brown—Whisk Broom II
Preston Burch—Gallorette
Calumet Farm—Alydar, Armed, Bewitch, Citation, Coaltown, Davona Dale, Real Delight, Tim Tam, Twilight Tear, Two Lea, Whirlaway
Mrs. Thomas J. Carson—Roseben
Ben Castleman—Seattle Slew
Christopher T. Chenery—Hill Prince
Christiana Stables—Go for Wand
Claiborne Farm—Gamely, Round Table, Slew o' Gold
John Clay—Kentucky
Clay Brothers—Roamer
Gen. Nathaniel Coles—American Eclipse
Brownell Combs—Myrtlewood
Leslie Combs II—Majestic Prince
Dayton Ltd.—All Along (Fr)
Allaire duPont—Kelso
Echo Valley Farm—Chris Evert, Winning Colors
Rex Ellsworth—Swaps
Mrs. Charles W. Engelhard—Exceller
Con Enright—Hamburg
William S. Farish and W. S. Kilroy—A.P. Indy
Joseph F. Flanagan—Elkridge
Flaxman Holdings Ltd.—Miesque
Capt. James and A. C. Franklin—Luke Blackburn
Martha F. Gerry—Forego
William Gibbons—Fashion
Mrs. William Gilmore and Mrs. William Jason—Spectacular Bid
Golden Chance Farm—John Henry
Greentree Stable—Devil Diver, Jolly Roger, Twenty Grand
Harry Guggenheim—Ack Ack
Arthur B. Hancock Sr.—Johnstown

Haras Principal—Bayakoa (Arg)
Haras Vacacion—Paseana (Arg)
Harbor View Farm—Affirmed
Dan Harness—Imp
Frank B. Harper—Good and Plenty
John Harper—Ten Broeck, Longfellow
Duval Headley—Dark Mirage, Tom Fool
Mrs. John D. Hertz—Count Fleet
Max Hirsch and King Ranch—Stymie
Fred Hooper—Precisionist, Susan's Girl
Rosa M. Hoots—Black Gold
Sally Humphrey—Genuine Risk
Nelson Bunker Hunt—Dahlia
Mr. and Mrs. Stuart S. Janney Jr.—Ruffian
Mrs. William Jason and Mrs. William Gilmore—Spectacular Bid
Marius E. Johnston—Sarazen
James R. Keene—Colin, Commando, Maskette, Peter Pan, Kingston, Sysonby
Willis Sharpe Kilmer—Reigh Count, Sun Beau
King Ranch—Assault ,Gallant Bloom
King Ranch and Max Hirsch—Stymie
Dixie Knight—Exterminator
Gordon E. Layton—Bold 'n Determined
W. E. Leach—Needles
Jean-Louis Levesque—La Prevoyante
John Madden—Grey Lag, Old Rosebud, Princess Doreen, Sir Barton, Zev
Preston Madden—Alysheba
Maine Chance Farm—Gun Bow
Meadow Stud—Cicada, Riva Ridge, Secretariat
Paul Mellon—Fort Marcy
Eugene Mori—Tosmah
Francis Morris—Ruthless
J. F. Newman—Pan Zareta
Oak Cliff Thoroughbreds—Sunday Silence
Mrs. B. O'Neill—L'Escargot
William Pape and Jonathan Sheppard—Flatterer
Allen E. Paulson—Cigar
Pelican Stable—Holy Bull

Ogden Phipps—Buckpasser, Easy Goer, Personal Ensign, Searching
Thomas Piatt—Alsab
Jack Price—Carry Back
A. C. Randolph—Bon Nouvel
Capt. Archibald Randolph and Col. John Tayloe III—Sir Archy
Samuel D. Riddle—Crusader, War Admiral
Ben Roach and Tom Roach—Princess Rooney
Rokeby Stable—Arts and Letters
Runnymeade Farm—Ben Brush, Hanover
Walter J. Salmon—Discovery, Battleship
Sam-Son Farm—Dance Smartly
Marion duPont Scott—Neji
Jan Sensenich—Jay Trump
Mr. and Mrs. L. K. Shapiro—Native Diver
Robert H. Spreen—Lady's Secret
Whitney Stone—Shuvee
Daniel Swigert—Firenze, Hindoo, Salvator
Tartan Farms—Dr. Fager, Ta Wee
Col. John Tayloe III and Capt. Archibald Randolph—Sir Archy
E. P. Taylor—Northern Dancer
Maj. Barak Thomas—Domino
Alfred G. Vanderbilt—Bed o' Roses, Native Dancer
Waldemar Farms—Foolish Pleasure
Elisha Warfield—Lexington
Aristides Welch—Parole
Wheatley Stable—Bold Ruler, Seabiscuit
C. V. Whitney—Silver Spoon
Harry Payne Whitney—Equipoise, Regret, Top Flight
William C. Whitney—Artful
John Wickham—Boston
George D. Widener—Eight Thirty
Joseph E. Widener—Bushranger, Fairmount
Verne H. Winchell—Cafe Prince
Theodore Winters—Emperor of Norfolk
Woodford and Clay—Miss Woodford
Col. Milton Young—Broomstick

Trainers of Racing Hall of Fame Members

Note: In instances when more than one trainer had a Hall of Fame horse during the horse's career, all are credited.

William Badgett—Go for Wand
Lazaro Barrera—Affirmed
Guy Bedwell—Sir Barton
John Belcher—Boston
Fred Burlew—Beldame
Patrick Biancone—All Along (Fr)
George H. "Pete" Bostwick—Oedipus
Francois Boutin—Miesque
William Brennan—Twenty Grand
Charles Brossman—Imp
Ed Brown—Ben Brush
Henry Brown—Lexington
William Brown—Parole
J. Elliott Burch—Arts and Letters, Sword Dancer, Fort Marcy
Matt Byrnes—Firenze, Salvator
Don Cameron—Count Fleet
Hardy Campbell—Kingston
Edward A. Christmas—Gallorette
W. Burling Cocks—Zaccio

Harry Colston—Ten Broeck
E. T. Colton—Pan Zareta
George Conway—Crusader, War Admiral
Warren A. "Jimmy" Croll—Holy Bull
James E. Day—Dance Smartly
Grover G. "Bud" Delp—Spectacular Bid
Neil Drysdale—A.P. Indy, Bold 'n Determined, Princess Rooney
Ross Fenstermaker—Precisionist, Susan's Girl
Louis Feustel—Man o' War
James "Sunny Jim" Fitzsimmons—Bold Ruler, Gallant Fox, Granville, Johnstown, Nashua, Omaha
Hugh Fontaine—Needles
E. Foucon—Pan Zareta
Willard C. Freeman—Shuvee
John M. Gaver Sr.—Devil Diver, Tom Fool
Jack Goldsborough—Roamer
Carl Hanford—Kelso
John Harper—Longfellow
J.H. "Casey" Hayes—Cicada, Hill Prince
Thomas J. Healey—Equipoise, Top Flight
S. M. Henderson—Princess Doreen

John Hertler—Slew o' Gold
Sam Hildreth—Grey Lag, Zev
Max Hirsch—Assault, Gallant Bloom, Sarazen
William Hirsch—Gallant Bloom
Reg Hobbs—Battleship
Freddy Hopkins—Equipoise
Will Hurley—Bimelech, Black Helen
John Hyland—Beldame, Henry of Navarre
Hirsch Jacobs—Affectionately, Searching, Stymie
LeRoy Jolley—Foolish Pleasure, Genuine Risk
Ben A. Jones—Armed, Bewitch, Citation, Coaltown, Real Delight, Twilight Tear, Two Lea, Whirlaway
Horace A. "Jimmy" Jones—Citation, Coaltown, Tim Tam, Two Lea
Andrew J. Joyner—Fair Play, Whisk Broom II
Charles Kiernan—Good and Plenty
Ray Kindred—Myrtlewood
Everett King—Dark Mirage
Billy Lakeland—Domino, Hamburg

Thomas Larkin—Sir Archy
Lucien Laurin—Riva Ridge, Secretariat
John Lee—Kelso
J. Howard Lewis—Bushranger, Fairmount
John Longden—Majestic Prince
D. Wayne Lukas—Lady's Secret, Serena's Song, Winning Colors
Horatio Luro—Northern Dancer
John Madden—Hamburg
James W. Maloney—Gamely
Ron McAnally—Bayakoa (Arg), John Henry, Paseana (Arg)
Frank McCabe—Hanover
Byron McClelland—Henry of Navarre
John McClelland—Emperor of Norfolk
Henry McDaniel—Exterminator, Reigh Count
Claude R. "Shug" McGaughey III—Easy Goer, Personal Ensign
Joe Mergler—Tosmah
Francois Mathet—Exceller
B. S. Michell—Reigh Count
Kent Miller—Elkridge
Buster Millerick—Native Diver
A. J. Minor—Ruthless
William Molter—Round Table
D. L. Moore—Neji, *L'Escargot
William I. Mott—Cigar
W. F. "Bert" Mulhoiland—Eight Thirty
Tom Murphy—Twenty Grand
Edward Neloy—Buckpasser, Gun Bow

John Nerud—Dr. Fager, *Gallant Man, Ta Wee
H. S. Newman—Pan Zareta
J. L. Newman—Susan's Girl
Victor J. "Lefty" Nickerson—John Henry
George Odom—Busher
Burley Parke—*Noor
Chuck Parke—Susan's Girl
Douglas R. Peterson—Seattle Slew
Vincent Powers—Jolly Roger
Jack Price—Carry Back
John B. Pryor—Lexington
John W. Rogers—Artful
Tommy Root Sr.—Desert Vixen
James Rowe Sr.—Colin, Commando, Hindoo, Luke Blackburn, Maskette, Miss Woodford, Peter Pan, Regret, Sysonby, Whisk Broom II
James Rowe Jr.—Twenty Grand
John Russell—Precisionist, Susan's Girl
Louis J. Schaefer—Challedon
Flint S. "Scotty" Schulhofer—Ta Wee
Jonathan Sheppard—Cafe Prince, Flatterer
A. Shuttinger—Sun Beau
Robert A. Smith—Cavalcade
Thomas Smith—Seabiscuit
Crompton "Tommy" Smith Jr.—Jay Trump
D. Michael Smithwick—Bon Nouvel, Neji
E. V. Snedeker—Kingston

John Starr—La Prevoyante
J. H. Stotler—Discovery
Sarge Swenke—Alsab
Arthur Taylor—Boston, Sir Archy
M. A. "Mesh" Tenney—Swaps
Bob Thomas—Emperor of Norfolk
H. J. Thompson—Blue Larkspur
G. R. Tompkins—Crusader
Joseph Trovato—Chris Evert
Bob Tucker—Broomstick
William H. Turner Jr.—Seattle Slew
Jack Van Berg—Alysheba
John Veitch—Alydar, Davona Dale
Sherrill Ward—Forego
Sidney Watters Jr.—Slew o' Gold
Hanley Webb—Black Gold
Frank D. Weir—Old Rosebud, Roseben
R. L. Wheeler—Silver Spoon
Frank Whiteley Jr.—Damascus, Forego, Ruffian
Charles Whittingham—Ack Ack, Dahlia, Exceller, Sunday Silence
J. Whyte—Sun Beau
Capt. Jim Williams—Luke Blackburn
Peter Wimmer—Broomstick, Imp
William C. Winfrey—Bed o' Roses, Buckpasser, Native Dancer
Maurice Zilber—Dahlia, Exceller
Unknown—American Eclipse, Fashion, Kentucky

Sires of Racing Hall of Fame Members

Abe Frank—Pan Zareta
Ahmad—Paseana (Arg)
Alydar—Alysheba, Easy Goer
*Amerigo—Fort Marcy
Battle Joined—Ack Ack
Ben Brush—Broomstick
*Ben Strome—Roseben
Best Turn—Davona Dale
*Billet—Miss Woodford
Black Servant—Blue Larkspur
Black Toney—Bimelech, Black Gold, Black Helen
*Blenheim II—Whirlaway
Blue Larkspur—Myrtlewood, Oedipus
Bold and Brave—Bold 'n Determined
Bold Bidder—Spectacular Bid
Bold Reasoning—Seattle Slew
Bold Ruler—Gamely, Secretariat
Bold Venture—Assault
*Bonnie Scotland—Luke Blackburn
Boston—Lexington
Bramble—Ben Brush
Broomstick—Regret, Whisk Broom II
Bryan G.—Cicada
Buckpasser—La Prevoyante
Bull Lea—Armed, Bewitch, Citation, Coaltown, Real Delight, Twilight Tear, Two Lea
Caro (Ire)—Winning Colors
*Challenger II—Challedon, Gallorette
Citation—Silver Spoon
Commando—Colin, Peter Pan
Consultant's Bid—Bayakoa (Arg)
Creme dela Creme—Cafe Prince

Crozier—Precisionist
Danzig—Dance Smartly
Deputy Minister—Go for Wand
*Diomed—Sir Archy
Disguise—Maskette
*Dis Donc—Top Flight
Display—Discovery
Domino—Commando
Duc de Fer—Bon Nouvel
Duroc—American Eclipse
*Eclipse—Ruthless
Equestrian—Stymie
Escart III—*L'Escargot
Exclusive Native—Affirmed, Genuine Risk
Fair Play—Fairmount, Man o' War
First Landing—Riva Ridge
*Forli—Forego
Gallant Fox—Granville, Omaha
*Gallant Man—Gallant Bloom
Glenelg—Firenze
Good Goods—Alsab
Great Above—Holy Bull
Gun Shot—Gun Bow
Halo—Sunday Silence
Hamburg—Artful
Hanover—Hamburg
Hard Tack—Seabiscuit
Hastings—Fair Play
High Time—Sarazen
Himyar—Domino
Hindoo—Hanover
*Hunters Moon IV—Neji
Imbros—Native Diver
In Reality—Desert Vixen

Intentionally—Ta Wee
Jamestown—Johnstown
*Khaled—Swaps
*Knight Errant—Roamer
Knight of Ellerslie—Henry of Navarre
*Lancegaye—Cavalcade
*Leamington—Longfellow, Parole
Lexington—Kentucky
*Lorenzaccio—Zaccio
Man o' War—Battleship, Crusader, War Admiral
Mate—Elkridge
*McGee—Exterminator
*Melton—Sysonby
Menow—Tom Fool
*Migoli—*Gallant Man
Mo Bay—Flatterer
*Nasrullah—Bold Ruler, Nashua, *Noor
Nearctic—Northern Dancer
Norfolk—Emperor of Norfolk
Nureyev—Miesque
Octagon—Beldame
Ole Bob Bowers—John Henry
Palace Music—Cigar
Pennant—Equipoise, Jolly Roger
*Persian Road II—Dark Mirage
*Phaeton—Ten Broeck
Pilate—Eight Thirty
Polynesian—Native Dancer
Ponder—Needles
*Prince Charlie—Salvator
*Princequillo—Hill Prince, Round Table
Private Account—Personal Ensign
Quadrangle—Susan's Girl

Rahy—Serena's Song
Raise a Native—Alydar, Majestic Prince
Reigh Count—Count Fleet
Reviewer—Ruffian
*Ribot—Arts and Letters
Rosemont—Bed o' Roses
Rossington—Good and Plenty
Rough'n Tumble—Dr. Fager
Saggy—Carry Back
Seattle Slew—A.P. Indy, Slew o' Gold
Secretariat—Lady's Secret
*Sir Gallahad III—Gallant Fox
*Spanish Prince II—Princess Doreen

Spendthrift—Kingston
*St. Germans—Devil Diver, Twenty Grand
*Star Shoot—Grey Lag, Sir Barton
*Stefan the Great—Bushranger
*Sun Briar—Sun Beau
Sunglow—Sword Dancer
*Sunreigh—Reigh Count
Swaps—Affectionately
Swoon's Son—Chris Evert
Sword Dancer—Damascus
Targowice—All Along (Fr)
The Finn—Zev
Tim Tam—Tosmah

Timoleon—Boston
Tom Fool—Buckpasser, Tim Tam
Tonga Prince—Jay Trump
*Trustee—Fashion
Uncle—Old Rosebud
*Vaguely Noble—Dahlia, Exceller
Verbatim—Princess Rooney
Virgil—Hindoo
Wagner—Imp
War Admiral—Busher, Searching
What a Pleasure—Foolish Pleasure
Your Host—Kelso

Regional Halls of Fame

A plaque in Saratoga Springs, New York, is the ultimate honor for a horse, jockey, or trainer, and racing organizations around the continent have followed the Racing Hall of Fame's lead and established halls of fame honoring racing participants who have made a difference in their regions. The Fair Grounds Hall of Fame, founded in 1971 and thus one of the oldest regional institutions, honors horses and horsemen who have raced in New Orleans. Several regional halls of fame have gone beyond the Racing Hall of Fame categories to include owners-breeders, racing officials, and other industry participants. The Canadian Horse Racing Hall of Fame appears in the International section.

Arlington Park

The Arlington Park Hall of Fame was destroyed with the grandstand on July 31, 1985, and is no longer active. No new members have been inducted since 1989.

Horses
Armed
Buckpasser
Candy Spots
Citation
Coaltown
Dr. Fager
Equipoise
Nashua
Native Dancer
Round Table
Secretariat
Tom Rolfe
T. V. Lark
Twilight Tear

Jockeys
Eddie Arcaro

Braulio Baeza
Steve Brooks
Doug Dodson
Bill Hartack
Johnny Sellers
Bill Shoemaker

Trainers
William Hal Bishop
Ben Jones
H. A. "Jimmy" Jones
Harry Trotsek
Arnold Winick

Stables
Calumet Farm
Hasty House Farm
William Hal Bishop Stable

Calder Race Course

Calder Race Course created its Hall of Fame in 1995 and annually inducts at least one new member in each of four categories. Honorees are selected by a panel of the Calder's administrative, racing, marketing, and publicity departments and members of the local racing media. The Hall of Fame is on the second floor of the grandstand.

Horses (Year inducted)
Brave Raj (1995)
Chaposa Springs (2003)

Cherokee Run (1998)
Flying Pidgeon (2000)
Hollywood Wildcat (2002)

Judy's Red Shoes (1996)
Mecke (1999)
Princess Rooney (1995)
Smile (1995)
Spend a Buck (1995)
Spirit of Fighter (1997)
The Vid (2001)

Jockeys
Mike Gonzalez (2001)
Walter Guerra (1998)
Michael Lee (1996)
Gene St. Leon (1995)
Miguel Rivera (2000)
Mary Russ (2003)
Alex Solis (2002)
Jacinto Vasquez (1999)
Jose Velez Jr. (1997)

Owners-Breeders
Arthur Appleton (1999)

Cobble View Stable (2001)
Farnsworth Farms (1997)
John Franks (2003)
Frances Genter Stable (1998)
Fred Hooper (1995)
James Lewis Jr. (2000)
Harry T. Mangurian Jr. (1995)
Ocala Stud Farm (2002)
Tartan Farms (1996)

Trainers
James Bracken (2000)
Frank Gomez (1995)
Stanley Hough (1996)
Luis Olivares (2002)
Harold Rose (1997)
John Tammaro (1999)
Emanuel Tortora (1998)
Martin D. Wolfson (2003)
Ralph Ziade (2001)

Canterbury Park

Created to honor those who contributed both to the track and Minnesota racing, the Canterbury Park Hall of Fame inducts from one to three new members each year.

Horses
Blair's Cove
Come Summer
Hoist Her Flag
Honor the Hero
John Bullit (NZ)
K Z Bay
Northbound Pride
Princess Elaine
Timeless Prince
Who Doctor Who

Jockeys
Sandy Hawley
Dean Kutz
Luis Quinonez
Mike Smith
Scott Stevens

Trainers
Carl Nafzger

Doug Oliver
Bernell Rhone

Owners
Chuck Bellingham
Frances Genter
Bobbi Knapper
Paul Knapper
Dan Mjolsness

Breeders
Almar Farms
Robert Morehouse

Others
Brooks Fields
Tom Ryther Sr.
Dark Star
Jim Wells

Fair Grounds

Fair Grounds established its Hall of Fame in 1971 to honor those who made lasting contributions to racing on both the local and national levels. Inductees are determined by an 11-member committee composed of the track's administrative staff and members of the New Orleans media. Induction ceremonies are traditionally held on the eve of the Louisiana Derby in March.

Horses

A Letter to Harry
Black Gold
Blushing K. D.
Cabildo
Chou Croute
Colonel Power
Davona Dale
Diplomat Way
Dixie Poker Ace
Furl Sail
Grindstone
Lecomte
Lexington
Marriage
Master Derby
Mike's Red
Monarchist
Monique Rene
No Le Hace
Pan Zareta
Quatrain
Reel
Risen Star
Scott's Scoundrel
Silverbulletday
Spanish Play
Taylor's Special
Tenacious
Tiffany Lass
Tippety Witchet
Whirlaway
Yorktown

Jockeys

Eddie Arcaro
Ron Ardoin
Robert L. Baird
Raymond Broussard
Pat Day
Eddie Delahoussaye
Andrew "Uncle Mack" Garner
Edward "Snapper" Garrison
Eric Guerin
Abe Hawkins
Johnny Heckmann
John Longden
J. D. Mooney
Jimmy Nichols
Winnie O'Conner
Craig Perret
Randy Romero
Earle Sande
Bill Shoemaker
James Forman "Tod" Sloan
Larry Snyder
David Whited

Owners-Breeders

Col. Edward R. Bradley

Dorothy Brown
Jack DeFee
Joseph P. Dorignac Jr.
John Franks
T. A. Grissom
William G. Helis Sr.
Samuel Clay Hildreth
Duncan Farrar Kenner
Harvey Peltier
J. R. Strauss Sr.
Thomas Jefferson Wells
Roger W. Wilson
Anthony Zuppardo

Trainers

Tom Amoss
Bobby Barnett
Angel Barrera
W. Hal Bishop
Frank Brothers
Grover "Bud" Delp
Joey Dorignac III
Henry Forrest
Ben Jones
Jack Lohman
J. O. Meaux
Bill Mott
Homer Pardue
Anthony Pelleteri
Louie Roussel III
Clifford Scott
Dewey Smith
Harry Trotsek
Jack Van Berg
Marion H. Van Berg
C. W. "Cracker" Walker
Vester R. "Tennessee" Wright

Others

Frank "Buddy" Abadie
Eric Wolfson Blind
Richard Ten Broeck
John Blanks Campbell
John F. Clark Jr.
Capt. William Cottrill
Francis Dunne
Marie Krantz
Sylvester W. Labrot Jr.
Allen "Black Cat" LaCombe
John S. Letellier
John G. Masoni
Claude Mauberret Jr.
Gardere "Gar" Moore
Mervin H. Muniz Jr.
Joseph A. Murphy
John Kenneth "Jack" O'Hara
Thomas P. Scott
Albert Stall Sr.

Gulfstream Park

Gulfstream Park's Garden of Champions, located behind the grandstand, features commemorative bronze plaques and a life-size statue of Cigar, Horse of the Year in 1995 and '96. Inductees must be retired, have competed at Gulfstream at least once, and have been named divisional champions or have competed against the highest caliber of competition.

Horses

A.P. Indy
Ajina
Armed
Artax
Arts and Letters
Bald Eagle
Banshee Breeze
Battlefield
Bayakoa (Arg)
Black Tie Affair (Ire)
Beautiful Pleasure
Blushing John
Bold Ruler
Bowl Game
Candy Eclair
Carry Back
Cigar
Cherokee Run
Chief's Crown
Christmas Past
Cicada
Coaltown
Counterpoint
Crafty Admiral
Cryptoclearance
Dark Star
Davona Dale
Daylami (Ire)
Decathlon
Dehere
De La Rose
Deputy Minister
Easy Goer
Eillo
Eliza
Escena
Favorite Trick
Fly So Free
Foolish Pleasure
Forego
Fort Marcy
Forty Niner
Forward Gal
Fraise
Genuine Risk
Gilded Time
Go for Wand
Groovy
Hansel
Heavenly Prize
Hollywood Wildcat
Holy Bull
Housebuster
Inside Information

Izvestia
Kelso
Lady's Secret
La Prevoyante
Late Bloomer
Lemon Drop Kid
Lord Avie
Little Current
Mac Diarmida
Nashua
Needles
Nodouble
Northern Dancer
Office Queen
Old Hat
Open Mind
Paradise Creek
Parka
Paseana (Arg)
Perfect Sting
Pleasant Colony
Pleasant Tap
Plugged Nickle
Princess Rooney
Roman Brother
Round Table
Rubiano
Sabin
Safely Kept
Sailor
Shecky Greene
Silverbulletday
Silver Charm
Skip Away
Sky Beauty
Sky Classic
Smile
Snow Chief
Soaring Softly
Spectacular Bid
Steinlen (GB)
Sunday Silence
Sunshine Forever
Swale
Swaps
Swoon's Son
Sword Dancer
Thunder Gulch
Tim Tam
Unbridled
Vanlandingham
Victory Gallop
Winning Colors
White Skies
With Approval

Hawthorne Race Course

Hawthorne Race Course launched its Hall of Fame on November 10, 1996, with a tribute to 21 jockey inductees during a luncheon ceremony hosted by Eddie Arcaro and Chicago-area track announcer Phil

Georgeff. Trainers were honored for the first time in 1998. Portraits and plaques honoring the Hall of Fame members are on display in the clubhouse.

Jockeys (Year inducted)
Johnny Adams (1996)
Eddie Arcaro (1996)
Ted Atkinson (1996)
Braulio Baeza (1996)
Jerry Bailey (1996)
Robert L. Baird (1997)
Steve Brooks (1996)
Steve Cauthen (1996)
Angel Cordero Jr. (1996)
Pat Day (1996)
Eddie Delahoussaye (1996)
Juvenal Diaz (1998)
Earlie Fires (1997)
Gerland Gallitano (1997)
Chris McCarron (1996)
Randall Meier (1997)

Isaac Murphy (1996)
Laffit Pincay Jr. (1996)
Earle Sande (1996)
Shane Sellers (1997)
Bill Shoemaker (1996)
Ray Sibille (1998)
Carlos Silva (1998)
Ron Turcotte (1996)
Jorge Velasquez (1996)
George Woolf (1996)

Trainers
Ernie Poulos (1998)
Jere Smith Sr. (1998)

Other
Phil Georgeff (1996)

Monmouth Park

The Hall of Champions is located on the first floor of the grandstand and is where honorees are commemorated with banners containing their names, silks, and years they raced at Monmouth Park. The hall was established in 1986 to honor Monmouth-raced horses that achieved success on the national level.

Affectionately
Alydar
Alysheba
Bet Twice
Black Tie Affair (Ire)
Blue Sparkler
Bold Ruler
Buckpasser
Carry Back
Damascus
Dan Horn
Dearly Precious
Decathlon
Dehere
Desert Vixen
First Flight
Forego
Formal Gold
Forty Niner
Friendly Lover
Frisk Me Now
Hansel
Helioscope
Holy Bull
Inside Information
John Henry
Kelso

Lady's Secret
Lord Avie
Lost Code
Majestic Light
Misty Morn
Mongo
Nashua
Needles
Open Mind
Personal Ensign
Point Given
Politely
Polynesian
Riva Ridge
Ruffian
Safely Kept
Serena's Song
Silverbulletday
Skip Away
Smoke Glacken
Spectacular Bid
Spend a Buck
Stymie
Sword Dancer
Ta Wee
Teddy Drone
Touch Gold

Nebraska Racing Hall of Fame

The Nebraska Racing Hall of Fame was established in 1966 to recognize outstanding contributions to Thoroughbred racing in the state. The hall was originally located at Ak-Sar-Ben in Omaha but was relocated to Fonner Park in Grand Island after Ak-Sar-Ben closed in 1995. No inductions have been made since 1993.

Horses (Year Inducted)
Gate Dancer (1991)
Omaha (1969)

Rose's Gem (1971)
Who Doctor Who (1993)

Jockeys
Irving Anderson (1976)
Steve Brooks (1971)
Earl Dew (1978)
Fred Ecoffey (1981)
Dave Erb (1972)
Ira Hanford (1968)
John Lively (1979)
Charley Thorpe (1978)

Trainers
Earl Beezley (1972)
Carl Hanford (1968)
Hoss Inman (1992)
C. B. Irwin (1979)
Robert Irwin (1973)
John Nerud (1970)
Lyman Rollins (1992)
Jack Van Berg (1976)
Marion H. Van Berg (1966)
Don Von Hemel (1991)
Robert L. Wheeler (1972)

Owners-Breeders
Mr. and Mrs. Al Cascio (1993)

Omer "Pete" Hall (1970)
Jack Fickler (1985)
Barton Ford (1978)
Mike Ford (1967)
William Fudge (1973)
Orville Kemling (1981)
Paul Kemling (1981)
Ken Opstein (1985)

Others
Warren Albert (1978)
Dale Becker (1985)
James E. "Tom" Bock (1973)
Ralph Boomer (1971)
Don Fair (1979)
Harry Farnham (1971)
J. J. "Jake" Isaacson (1969)
Don Lee (1992)
Earl Moyer (1967)
Murdock Platner (1979)
Grover Porter (1969)
Al Swihart (1992)
Howard Wolff (1969)

Prairie Meadows

Iowa's first horse-racing facility conducted its inaugural program on March 1, 1989, and established its Hall of Fame nine years later.

Horses (Year inducted)
Dontforgethisname (1999)
Railroad Red (1998)
Prince Ariba (1999)
Vaguely Who (2001)

Owners-Breeders
Jim Bader (1998)

Bob and Marlene Bryant (2002)
Jim and Sandra Rasmussen (2000)

Others
Keith Hopkins (2001)
Ed Skinner (1999)
Jim Woodward (1999)

Remington Park

The Remington Hall of Fame was established in 1999. No others have been inducted since the original group.

Jockey
Pat Steinberg

Trainer
Donnie K. Von Hemel

Owner-Breeder
Ran Ricks Jr.

Horse
Clever Trevor

Texas Horse Racing Hall of Fame

The Texas Horse Racing Hall of Fame was created in 1999 at Retama Park to pay tribute to the people and horses who have influenced the state's racing industry. Honorees are selected by track management, media, horsemen's organizations, and *Daily Racing Form*.

Horses (Year inducted)
Assault (1999)
Groovy (2001)
Middleground (2000)
Pan Zareta (1999)
Staunch Avenger (2002)
Stymie (2000)

Jockeys
Jerry Bailey (2000)
Bill Shoemaker (1999)

Trainer
Max Hirsch (2000)

Owners-Breeders
Robert Kleberg Jr. (1999)
Walter Merrick (2000)
Clarence Scharbauer Jr. (2001)
Joe R. Straus Sr. (2001)
Emerson Woodward (2001)

Others
Charles "Doc" Graham (2002)
B. F. Phillips (1999)
W. T. Waggoner (2001)

TRIPLE CROWN
History of the Triple Crown

As with other great sporting events such as the Olympics and the World Series, the Triple Crown has a rich tradition and history. While modern memory places the Triple Crown in a fixed format—the Kentucky Derby (G1) on the first Saturday in May, the Preakness Stakes (G1) two weeks later, and the Belmont Stakes (G1) three weeks after the Preakness—the series has undergone changes ranging from subtle to seismic in its history.

Origins

The Triple Crown did not start with the inauguration of the three races—the Belmont in 1867, the Preakness six years later, and the Derby in 1875. Of the three races, only the Derby has been run continuously, with gaps in the history of the Preakness (1891-'93) and the Belmont (1911 and '12, when antigambling legislation shut down New York racing). In some years, the Derby and Preakness were run within days of each other, and in two years (1917 and '22) they were run on the same day. In some years, the Preakness was run before the Derby.

Far from being one of the three most-prestigious races for American three-year-olds, the Derby in the early 20th century was a struggling regional race. The marketing and showmanship genius of Churchill track executive Col. Matt J. Winn elevated the race to national and international prominence during the first quarter of the century.

When Sir Barton became the first Triple Crown winner in 1919, he was not recognized as a Triple Crown winner, just as a fast-developing three-year-old who went from maiden to multiple major stakes winner within two months.

In fact, the origin of the term "Triple Crown" (which had been in use in England for decades) has been disputed for many years. For decades, credit for coining the expression generally was accorded to legendary *Daily Racing Form* columnist Charlie Hatton. While Hatton's stature and repeated use of the term closely associated him with the Triple Crown, the phrase arguably was first put in print by New York *Times* writer Bryan Field, who used the expression in 1930 after Gallant Fox won the Belmont.

The Triple Crown has been characterized by clusters of winners, especially in the 1930s, '40s, and '70s, and long droughts in between. After Gallant Fox won the 1930 Triple Crown for owner-breeder Belair Stud, only five years passed before Gallant Fox's son Omaha won for Belair. Two years later in 1937, Man o' War's son War Admiral took the Triple Crown for Samuel D. Riddle's Glen Riddle Farm.

The Triple Crown sweep was achieved four

Triple Crown television ratings and share

Year	Kentucky Derby Rating	Kentucky Derby Share	Preakness Stakes Rating	Preakness Stakes Share	Belmont Stakes Rating	Belmont Stakes Share
2003	6.4	17	5.6	13	9.5	23
2002	7.1	18	5.7	14	7.6	21
2001	8.1	21	5.6	16	4.5	13
2000	5.8	17	3.6	10	2.8	9
1999	6.3	19	3.4	10	6.0	17
1998	6.1	18	3.6	11	5.9	18
1997	7.1	19	4.8	14	5.3	16
1996	7.4	21	3.7	11	2.9	9
1995	6.0	17	3.2	10	3.5	11
1994	7.5	21	4.4	14	3.9	12
1993	7.3	22	4.7	15	4.2	11

Each rating point represents 1,067,000 viewers in 2003; share is the percentage of televisions tuned to that program.

times in the 1940s. First, Calumet Farm and jockey Eddie Arcaro won in 1941 with Whirlaway, and Mrs. John D. Hertz's Count Fleet rolled to victory two years later with Johnny Longden in the saddle. In 1946, King Ranch's homebred Assault scored the triple, and two years later Arcaro and Calumet collected their second Triple Crown sweep with Citation.

In 1950, the Thoroughbred Racing Associations formally recognized the three-race series as the Triple Crown and commissioned Cartier to craft a three-sided trophy, one side for each race. The trophy was in storage many years before Secretariat breezed to a Triple Crown victory in 1973, the first sweep in a quarter-century. Four years later, the brilliant Seattle Slew became the first to win the series without a defeat on his record. In 1978, the first back-to-back Triple Crown sweep occurred when Affirmed defeated Alydar in three classic battles. Harbor View Farm's Affirmed would be the last Triple Crown winner of the 20th century as another long drought took hold.

Modern Triple Crown

The perception that the Triple Crown's prestige made it an irresistible goal for the connections of leading three-year-olds was shaken twice in the 1980s. Gato Del Sol won the 1982 Derby, but trainer Edwin Gregson, speaking for owners-breeders Arthur Hancock III and Leone J. Peters, declined to run the colt in the Preakness. Well aware that Gato Del Sol was unsuited to a speed-favoring Pimlico Race Course track for the Preakness, Gregson and his owners awaited the Belmont, in which Gato Del Sol finished a distant second to Conquistador Cielo.

Dennis Diaz's speedy Spend a Buck crushed his competition in the 1985 Derby, but Diaz turned his back on the Preakness and Belmont, opting for the $1-million Jersey Derby (G3) at the newly rebuilt Garden State Park. Spend a Buck had won two Derby prep races at the New Jersey track, making him eligible for a $2-million bonus if he swept the track's three races for three-year-olds and the Kentucky Derby. Diaz was courted by Garden State officials, and two factors led to Spend a Buck running in the Jersey Derby. First, a serious question arose over Spend a Buck's ability to stay the Belmont's 1½ miles after a rigorous spring campaign. The money also was a factor. Spend a Buck ran for (and collected) $2.6-million in purse and bonus monies in the Jersey Derby. The winner's purses for that year's Triple Crown raced totaled $1,137,740.

The Spend a Buck affair, wrought with acrimony and recrimination, led to a positive event—the creation of Triple Crown Productions late in 1985 to market the three races as a single, unified entity.

Through the remainder of the 20th century, five horses came within one race of winning the Triple Crown, but none collected the $5-million—first offered as a purse and bonus and exclusively as a bonus beginning in 1998. Alysheba won the first two races in 1987 but was a distant fourth to Bet Twice in the Belmont. Sunday Silence won two spirited battles with Easy Goer in 1989 and finished a well-beaten second to his nemesis in the Belmont. The Triple Crown bids of the 1990s occurred in three consecutive years, 1997-'99. In 1997, Derby and Preakness winner Silver Charm could not repel the late charge of Touch Gold in the Belmont. The following year, Real Quiet appeared to have the Belmont won but fell by a nose in the last stride to Victory Gallop. Charismatic, the 1999 Derby and Preakness winner, finished third by less than two lengths despite sustaining a leg fracture in the Belmont's late stages. At the start of the 21st century, War Emblem won the first two legs in 2002, only to finish a well-beaten eighth in the Belmont. In 2003, Funny Cide won the Derby and Preakness before finishing third in the Belmont. With Funny Cide's defeat, racing had its longest gap without a Triple Crown winner.—*John Harrell*

Triple Crown Productions

Charged with marketing the Kentucky Derby (G1), Preakness Stakes (G1), and Belmont Stakes (G1), Triple Crown Productions was created at a time of turmoil within the industry and especially at the three tracks that stage the races. Threatened with a hostile takeover, Churchill Downs Inc. reorganized in 1984 and hired Thomas Meeker, a lawyer, as its president. The following year, Garden State Park reopened and lured the Derby winner, Spend a Buck, off the Triple Crown trail to the Jersey Derby (G3) with a $2-million bonus. Robert E. Brennan, then Garden State's chairman, spoke of the Jersey Derby taking the place of the Preakness at Pimlico Race Course in the Triple Crown. The New York Racing Association also was mired in internal turmoil.

Incorporated in September 1985, Triple Crown Productions opened its office at Churchill Downs in January '86, with Audrey R. Korotkin as its first executive director. In addition to its marketing function, Triple Crown Productions inaugurated a common nomination form and fees for the races, with early nominations of $600 each closing in mid-January and late nominations, originally $3,000 and now $6,000, closing three weeks before the Derby. Previously, each track obtained nominations for its own races. Supplemental entries ($150,000 for the Derby and $100,000 each for the Preakness and Belmont) were permitted beginning in 1990.

In 1987, the company offered the first Triple Crown Challenge—$5-million in purse money and bonuses to a Triple Crown winner and a $1-million bonus to the horse with the best overall performances in all three races. Triple Crown Productions financed the first bonus year (Bet Twice collected $1-million after he finished second to Alysheba in the Derby and Preakness and won the Belmont). In September 1987, the company announced that Chrysler Corp. would become the sponsor of the bonus beginning in '88.

Meeker, chairman of Triple Crown Productions, eliminated the executive director position in August 1989, but media attention the following winter led to hiring Edward Seigenfeld, a former NYRA marketing vice president, as the organization's executive director. Seigenfeld was given the title of executive vice president in 1996. In 1993, the $1-million bonus for the best overall finish was eliminated.

Nominations Since Unified Under Triple Crown Productions

Year	Early	Late	Total	Total Fees	Each Track's Share
2003	446	8	454	$315,600	$105,200
2002	405	12	417	315,000	105,000
2001	440	7	447	306,000	102,000
2000	387	13	400	310,200	103,400
1999	396	11	407	303,600	101,200
1998	384	6	390	266,800	88,933
1997	375	13	388	303,000	101,000
1996	354	7	361	254,800	84,800
1995	317	7	324	232,400	77,400
1994	354	9	363	266,400	88,800
1993	342	25	367	317,700	105,900
1992	389	18	407	314,400	104,800
1991	369	8	377	257,400	85,800
1990	315	33	348	282,000	94,000
1989	381	13	394	267,600	89,200
1988	381	20	401	288,600	96,200
1987	398	24	422	310,800	103,600
1986	422	30	452	343,200	144,400

Early nomination fee has been $600 since 1986; late nomination fee: 1986-'90, $3,000; 1991-'93, $4,500; 1994-present, $6,000.

Chrysler bowed out as the Triple Crown Challenge sponsor after 1995 and was replaced by Visa USA, the credit-card marketing company. Beginning in 1998, a Triple Crown sweep would earn a $5-million bonus in addition to purse earnings from the three races. In 1999, Visa extended its sponsorship through 2005.

Triple Crown Productions board of directors (on June 10, 2003): Representing Churchill Downs, Thomas H. Meeker (TCP president), Arthur B. Modell; representing the Maryland Jockey Club, Joseph A. De Francis (TCP vice president-treasurer), Jim McAlpine; and representing the New York Racing Association, Barry K. Schwartz, Terence J. Meyocks (TCP vice president-secretary).

$5-Million Visa Triple Crown Bonus

Triple Crown Productions will pay a bonus of $5-million to the owner of any horse that is declared the official winner of the Kentucky Derby (G1), the Preakness Stakes (G1), and the Belmont Stakes (G1). The Visa Triple Crown Challenge Bonus for 2003 had the following rules:

1. In the event of a dead heat for first in any race, each horse involved in the dead heat shall be considered to have finished first for purposes of determining whether or not any horse has won all of the races.

2. In the event of a dead heat for first between the same horses in all three races, the bonus money shall be divided equally.

Triple Crown Productions will present the Triple Crown trophy to the owner of a horse winning all of the races.

The Visa Triple Crown Challenge Bonus of $5-million shall be paid by Triple Crown Productions within 30 days after the result of the final race is declared official, but only after any dispute arising with regard to the eligibility, disqualification, or finish of a horse or the official result of any race has been finally adjudicated. Pending final determination of any such dispute, the Triple Crown Challenge Bonus and the Triple Crown trophy shall be held by Triple Crown Productions until such dispute is finally adjudicated and, if the Triple Crown Challenge Bonus and/or the Triple Crown trophy have been awarded to an owner prior to such dispute, the owner agrees that such bonus and/or trophy shall be returned immediately to Triple Crown Productions to be held as provided herein.

No horse has won the Triple Crown since a bonus first was offered in 1987.

From 1987 through '93, a $1-million bonus was offered to the horse that started in all three races and accumulated the most points based on order of finish in each race. Points were: 10 for a win, 5 for second, 3 for third, and 1 for fourth. The following horses received $1-million bonus payments, with the totals below including the bonus and any purse money won in any of the Triple Crown races:

1987—Bet Twice, second in the Kentucky Derby and Preakness Stakes, first in the Belmont Stakes, with earnings of $1,499,160.

1988—Risen Star, third in the Kentucky Derby, first in the Preakness and Belmont, with earnings of $1,767,420.

1989—Sunday Silence, first in the Kentucky Derby and Preakness, second in the Belmont, with earnings of $2,164,053.

1990—Unbridled, first in the Kentucky Derby, second in the Preakness, and fourth in the Belmont, with earnings of $1,759,360.

1991—Hansel, tenth in the Kentucky Derby and first in the Preakness and Belmont, with earnings of $1,850,250.

1992—Pine Bluff, fifth in the Kentucky Derby, first in the Preakness, and third in the Belmont, with earnings of $1,575,896.

1993—Sea Hero, first in the Kentucky Derby, fifth in the Preakness, and seventh in the Belmont, with earnings of $1,735,900.

Triple Crown Race Conditions

(Note: All conditions below are based on 2003 conditions and are subject to change.)

First deadline: January 18, 2004, $600
Second deadline: March 29, 2004, $6,000

Nominations to each and all of the Triple Crown races, the Kentucky Derby, the Preakness Stakes, and the Belmont Stakes (the "races"), may be made by payment of a single nomination fee to Triple Crown Productions LLC as agent for Churchill Downs Inc., the Maryland Jockey Club of Baltimore City Inc., and the New York Racing Association Inc. (the "association" or "associations," as the case may be). The nomination fee for nominations postmarked or hand delivered by January 18, 2004, is $600, and for nominations postmarked or hand delivered from January 19 through March 29, 2004, is $6,000. Horses nominated on or before March 29, 2004, shall be considered original nominees ("original nominees").

At any time prior to the closing for the Kentucky Derby, as defined below, additional nominations to all three races may be made, and the nominee will be eligible for the Visa Triple Crown Challenge Bonus upon payment of a supplementary fee of $150,000 to Churchill Downs Inc. Following the running of the Kentucky Derby, horses may be nominated at any time prior to closing for the Preakness Stakes or the Belmont Stakes (time of closing being defined below) but will not be eligible for the Visa Triple Crown Challenge Bonus. The supplementary fee payable for such nomination shall be $100,000, payable to the Maryland Jockey Club of Baltimore City Inc. for supplemental nomination to the Preakness Stakes and the Belmont Stakes, or $100,000 payable to the New York Racing Association Inc. for supplemental nomination to the Belmont Stakes only.

All supplemental fees will be included in the purse distribution for the race run by the association to which the supplemental nomination is paid, unless otherwise specified in the specific race rules below.

The ability of horses nominated by payment of the foregoing supplementary fees ("supplemental nominees") to enter any race will be determined in accordance with the conditions of that race. All nominees, original, supplemental or otherwise, will be required to pay entry and starting fees for the race or races in which they participate before they may start.

Triple Crown Productions will pay a bonus of $5-million to the owner of any horse that is declared the official winner of all the races in 2004. The bonus will be paid in accordance with the official rules of the Visa Triple Crown Challenge Bonus, which are incorporated herein by reference.

130th running of the Kentucky Derby (G1)
$1-million guaranteed minimum purse
To be run on Saturday, May 1, 2004
One mile and a quarter

For three-year olds, with an entry fee of $15,000 each and a starting fee of $15,000 each. Supplemental nominations may be made upon payment of $150,000 and in accordance with the rules set forth.

All fees, including supplemental nominations, in excess of $500,000 in the aggregate shall be paid to the winner. Churchill Downs Inc. shall guarantee a minimum gross purse of $1,000,000 (the "guaranteed purse").

The winner shall receive $700,000, second place shall receive $170,000, third place shall receive $85,000, and fourth place shall receive $45,000 from the guaranteed purse (the guaranteed purse to each place to be divided equally in the event of a dead heat).

Starters shall be named through the entry box on Wednesday, April 28, 2004, at 10 a.m. EDT (the "closing"). The maximum number of starters shall be limited to 20. Colts and geldings shall each carry a weight of 126 pounds; fillies shall each carry 121 pounds. Supplemental nominees will be allowed to enter but will not have preference over any original nominee and will not be allowed to start the race if the maximum number of starters has otherwise been reached by original nominees prior to the closing.

If the number of nominees exceeds the number of available starting positions at the closing, these conditions shall be applied to determine which nominees will be allowed to start. In the event that more than 20 entries pass through the entry box at the closing, the starters shall be determined at the closing from original nominees first, then supplemental nominees if starting positions are still available, with preference given to those horses that have accumulated the highest earnings in graded stakes races, including all monies actually paid for performance in such graded stakes races. For purposes of this preference, the graded status of each race shall be the graded status assigned to the race by the International Cataloguing Standards Committee in Part I of the International Cataloguing Standards as published by the Jockey Club Information Systems Inc. each year.

Should additional starters be needed to bring the field to 20, the remaining starters shall be determined at the closing with preference given to those horses that have accumulated the highest earnings in nonrestricted sweepstakes. For purposes of this preference, a "nonrestricted sweepstakes" shall mean those sweepstakes whose conditions contain no restrictions other than that of age or sex.

In the case of ties resulting from preferences or otherwise, the additional starter(s) shall be determined by lot.

Any horse excluded from running because of the aforementioned preference(s) shall be refunded the $15,000 entry fee and the $150,000 supplemental fee, if applicable. An "also-eligible" list will not be maintained, and in no event will starters be added or allowed to run in the race that are not determined to be starters at the closing.

Post position shall be determined as follows: A nontransferable lot number shall be drawn for each horse named as a starter at the closing. The lot number drawn for each starter shall determine the numerical order for selection of post position. Selection of post position shall be made by each owner of a horse (or, if more than one, the owners collectively) or the authorized agent of the horse's owner(s).

Horses having common ties through ownership or training shall each be treated separately for purposes of selecting post position. Detailed rules governing the post position draw process are available from the racing secretary's office and will be distributed prior to the closing. These rules shall control. The owner of the winner of the race shall receive a gold trophy.

129th running of the Preakness Stakes (G1)
$1-million guaranteed purse
To be run on Saturday, May 15, 2004
One mile and three-sixteenths

For three-year-olds, $10,000 to pass the entry box, starters to pay $10,000 additional. Supplemental nominations may be made in accordance with the rules, upon payment of $100,000; 65% of the purse to the winner, 20% to second, 10% to third, and 5% to fourth. Weight: 126 pounds for colts and geldings, 121 pounds for fillies.

Starters to be named through the entry box on Wednesday, May 12, 2004, three days before the race by the usual time of closing (the "closing").

The Preakness field will be limited to 14 entries and shall be determined on the Wednesday immediately preceding the day of the race.

In the event that more than 14 horses are properly nominated and pass through the entry box by the usual time of closing, the starters will be determined at the closing with the first seven horses given preference by accumulating the highest earnings in graded stakes (lifetime). For purposes of this preference, the graded status of each race shall be the graded status assigned to the race by the International Cataloguing Standards Committee in Part 1 of the International Cataloguing Standards as published by the Jockey Club Information Systems Inc. each year.

The next four starters will be determined by accumulating the highest earnings (lifetime) in all nonrestricted stakes. "Nonrestricted sweepstakes" shall mean those sweepstakes whose conditions contain no restrictions other than that of age or sex.

The remaining three starters shall be determined by accumulating the highest earnings (lifetime) in all races. Should this preference produce any ties, the additional starter(s) shall be determined by lot.

In application of the above-described rule, each horse will be separately considered without regard to identity of its owner. If the rules described in this paragraph result in the exclusion of any horse, the $10,000 entry fee previously paid will be refunded to the owner of said horse. The above conditions notwithstanding, no horse that earns purse money in the Kentucky Derby shall be denied the opportunity to enter and start in the Preakness Stakes.

Post position shall be determined as follows: A nontransferable lot number shall be drawn for each horse named as a starter at the closing. The lot number drawn for each starter shall determine the numerical order for selection of post position. Selection of post position shall be made by each owner of a horse (or, if more than one, the owners collectively) or the authorized agent of the horse's owner(s).

Horses having common ties through ownership or training shall each be treated separately for purposes of selecting post position. Detailed rules governing the post position draw process are available from the racing secretary's office and will be distributed prior to the closing. These rules shall control. A replica of the Woodlawn Vase will be presented to the winning owner to remain his or her personal property.

136th running of the Belmont Stakes (G1)
$1-million gross purse
To be run on Saturday, June 5, 2004
One mile and a half

For three-year olds, by subscription of $600 each, to accompany the nomination, if made on or before January 18, 2004, or $6,000, if made on or before March 29, 2004, $10,000 to pass the entry box, and $10,000 additional to start. At any time prior to the closing time of entries, horses may be nominated to the Belmont Stakes upon payment of a supplementary fee of $100,000 to the New York Racing Association Inc. All entrants, supplemental or otherwise, will be required to pay entry and starting fees. The purse to be divided 60% to the winner, 20% to second, 11% to third, 6% to fourth, and 3% to fifth. Colts and geldings, 126 pounds; fillies, 121 pounds.

Starters to be named at the closing time of entries. The Belmont field will be limited to 16 starters. In the event more than 16 entries pass through the entry box at the closing, starters will be determined at the closing with the first eight starters given preference by accumulating the highest earning in graded sweepstakes at a mile or over. For purposes of this preference, the graded status of each race shall be the grade assigned by the International Cataloguing Standards Committee in Part 1 of the International Cataloguing Standards as published annually by the Jockey Club Information Systems Inc.

The next five starters will be determined by accumulating the highest earning in all nonrestricted sweepstakes. "Nonrestricted sweepstakes" shall mean those sweepstakes whose conditions contain no restrictions other than age or sex. The remaining three starters shall be determined by accumulating the highest earnings in all races.

Should this preference produce any ties, the additional starter (s) shall be determined by lot. If the rules described result in the exclusion of any horse, the $10,000 entry fee will be refunded to the owner of said horse.

The above conditions notwithstanding, any horse that earns purse money in either the Kentucky Derby or the Preakness Stakes shall be included in the initial eight starters of the Belmont Stakes.

The winning owner will be presented with the August Belmont Memorial Cup, to be retained for one year, as well as a trophy for permanent possession and trophies to the winning trainer and jockey.

Preakness Stakes shall be included in the initial eight starters in the Belmont Stakes. These rules shall control.

The winning owner will be presented with the August Belmont Memorial Cup, to be retained for one year, as well as a trophy for permanent possession and trophies will be presented to the winning trainer and jockey.

Road to the Triple Crown

The following races are traditionally used as preps for the Triple Crown races. The table includes the dates and winners of the races in 2003.

Date	Race	Trk	Dist.	Time	First three finishers
1/1	Tropical Park Derby-G3	Crc	1⅛mT	1:50.45	**NOTHING TO LOSE**, Millennium Storm, **Supah Blitz**
1/3	Spectacular Bid S.-G3	GP	6f	1:10.97	FIRST BLUSH, **Crafty Guy**, Silver Squire
1/4	Count Fleet S.	Aqu	1m70yd	1:42.17	**GREY COMET, Mustang Jock, Penobscot Bay**
1/11	Golden Gate Derby-G3	GG	1 1/16m	1:43.76	STANDARD SETTER, **Ozzie Cat, Pine for Java**
1/12	San Miguel S.-G3	SA	6f	1:08.65	**OMEGA CODE**, Only the Best, Jimmy O
1/18	Holy Bull S.-G3	GP	1 1/16m	1:43	**OFFLEE WILD, Powerful Touch, Bham**
1/18	Santa Catalina S.-G2	SA	1 1/16m	1:42.20	**DOMESTIC DISPUTE, Our Bobby V., Scrimshaw**
1/25	Lecomte S.-G3	FG	1m	1:37.62	**SAINTLY LOOK**, Call Me Lefty, **Winning Fans**
2/1	San Vicente S.-G2	SA	7f	1:21.12	**KAFWAIN, Sum Trick, Southern Image**
2/1	Turf Paradise Derby	TuP	1 1/16m	1:41.74	ROBLEDO, **Siberland, Double Intrigue**
2/8	Whirlaway S.	Aqu	1 1/16m	1:44.74	**BOSTON PARK, Grey Comet**, Go Rockin' Robin
2/9	Golden State Mile S.	GG	1m	1:36.89	**MINISTERS WILD CAT**, Winning Stripes, Clover Situation
2/15	Fountain of Youth S.-G1	GP	1 1/16m	1:43.33	**TRUST N LUCK, Supah Blitz, Midway Cat**
2/15	Hutcheson S.-G2	GP	7f	1:22.60	**LION TAMER, Strength Within, Crafty Guy**
2/16	Risen Star S.-G3	FG	1 1/16m	1:42.99	**BADGE OF SILVER, Lone Star Sky, Defrere's Vixen**
2/21	Palm Beach S.-G3	GP	1⅛mT	1:48.28	**NOTHING TO LOSE**, White Cat, Imitation
2/22	Best Turn S.	Aqu	6f	1:10.68	SECOND IN COMMAND, Super Fuse, **Mustbinthefrontrow**
2/23	Baldwin S.-G3	SA	abt6½fT	1:12.56	**BUDDY GIL**, King Robyn, **Flirt With Fortune**
3/1	San Rafael S.-G2	SA	1m	1:35.89	**ROJO TORO, Spensive**, Crowned Dancer
3/1	Southwest S.	OP	1m	1:38.96	**GREAT NOTION, Alke, Comic Truth**
3/1	John Battaglia Memorial S.	TP	1 1/16m	1:46.23	**CHAMPALI**, Chicken Soup Kid, **Grey Comet**
3/8	El Camino Real Derby-G3	GG	1 1/16m	1:42.26	**OCEAN TERRACE, Ministers Wild Cat, Ten Most Wanted**
3/9	Louisiana Derby-G2	FG	1 1/16m	1:42.67	**PEACE RULES, Funny Cide, Lone Star Sky**
3/15	Florida Derby-G1	GP	1⅛m	1:49.05	**EMPIRE MAKER, Trust N Luck, Indy Dancer**
3/15	Swale S.-G3	GP	7f	1:21.06	**MIDAS EYES**, Posse, **Whywhywhy**
3/16	San Felipe S.-G2	SA	1 1/16m	1:43.64	**BUDDY GIL, Atswhatimtalknbout, Brancusi**
3/16	Gotham S.-G3	Aqu	1m	1:40.60	**ALYSWEEP, Grey Comet**, Spite the Devil
3/16	Tampa Bay Derby-G3	Tam	1 1/16m	1:44.61	**REGION OF MERIT, Aristocat, Hear No Evil**
3/22	Lane's End S.-G2	TP	1⅛m	1:50.68	**NEW YORK HERO, Eugene's Third Son, Champali**
3/22	Rebel S.	OP	1 1/16m	1:44	CROWNED KING, **Great Notion, Comic Truth**
3/22	San Pedro S.	SA	6½f	1:15.21	KING ROBYN, **Truckle Feature, Eye of the Tiger**
3/30	WinStar Derby	Sun	1 1/16m	1:42.84	**EXCESSIVEPLEASURE, Spensive, Apalachian Thunder**
4/5	Santa Anita Derby-G1	SA	1⅛m	1:49.36	**BUDDY GIL, Indian Express, Kafwain**
4/5	Illinois Derby-G2	Spt	1⅛m	1:51.47	**TEN MOST WANTED, Fund of Funds, Foufa's Warrior**
4/6	Lafayette S.-G3	Kee	7f	1:23.14	POSSE, **Roll Hennessy Roll**, Bossanova
4/12	Blue Grass S.-G1	Kee	1⅛m	1:51.73	**PEACE RULES, Brancusi, Offlee Wild**
4/12	Arkansas Derby-G2	OP	1⅛m	1:48.39	**SIR CHEROKEE, Eugene's Third Son, Christine's Outlaw**
4/12	Wood Memorial S.-G1	Aqu	1⅛m	1:48.70	**EMPIRE MAKER, Funny Cide, Kissin Saint**
4/12	Bay Shore S.-G3	Aqu	7f	1:23.19	**HALO HOMEWRECKER**, Don Six, **Stanislavsky**
4/17	Forerunner S.	Kee	1⅛mT	1:52.10	CALIFORNIAN (GB), **Rapid Proof, Color Me Gone**
4/19	Coolmore Lexington S.-G2	Kee	1 1/16m	1:45.47	**SCRIMSHAW, Eye of the Tiger, Domestic Dispute**
4/19	Federico Tesio S.	Pim	1⅛m	1:49.86	**CHEROKEE'S BOY, Penobscot Bay**, High Watermark
4/26	Derby Trial-G3	CD	1m	1:36.22	**MIDAS EYES, Champali**, Desert Warrior
5/3	Kentucky Derby-G1	CD	1¼m	2:01.19	**FUNNY CIDE, Empire Maker, Peace Rules**
5/10	Lone Star Derby-G3	LS	1⅛m	1:50.43	**DYNEVER, Most Feared, Commander's Affair**
5/17	Preakness S.-G1	Pim	1 3/16m	1:55.61	**FUNNY CIDE, Midway Road, Scrimshaw**
5/24	Peter Pan S.-G2	Bel	1⅛m	1:48.47	**GO ROCKIN' ROBIN, Alysweep, Supervisor**
6/7	Belmont S.-G1	Bel	1½m	2:28.26	**EMPIRE MAKER, Ten Most Wanted, Funny Cide**

Horses in bold face were Triple Crown nominees

Triple Crown Winners

America's Triple Crown Winners

Year	Horse	Owner	Trainer	Jockey
1919	Sir Barton	J. K. L. Ross	H. Guy Bedwell	John Loftus
1930	Gallant Fox	Belair Stud	James Fitzsimmons	Earle Sande
1935	Omaha	Belair Stud	James Fitzsimmons	William Saunders
1937	War Admiral	Samuel D. Riddle	George Conway	Charles Kurtsinger
1941	Whirlaway	Calumet Farm	Ben A. Jones	Eddie Arcaro
1943	Count Fleet	Mrs. John D. Hertz	Don Cameron	John Longden
1946	Assault	King Ranch	Max Hirsch	Warren Mehrtens
1948	Citation	Calumet Farm	H. A. "Jimmy" Jones	Eddie Arcaro
1973	Secretariat	Meadow Stable	Lucien Laurin	Ron Turcotte
1977	Seattle Slew	Karen L. Taylor	William Turner Jr.	Jean Cruguet
1978	Affirmed	Harbor View Farm	Lazaro Barrera	Steve Cauthen

Triple Crown Trophy

The Triple Crown trophy was commissioned in 1950 by the Thoroughbred Racing Associations, which copyrighted the term Triple Crown, and has three sides to symbolize the three races in the series. The trophy was presented retroactively to the eight previous winners of the three races.

The first three-year-old with a chance to claim the silver Triple Crown trophy was Tim Tam, who won the 1958 Kentucky Derby and Preakness Stakes but finished second to *Cavan in the Belmont Stakes. Secretariat in 1973 was the first horse to be presented the trophy after sweeping the three races.

Sir Barton

At the start of 1919, Sir Barton was far down the pecking order in trainer H. Guy Bedwell's stable. Commander J. K. L. Ross had purchased the *Star Shoot colt at Saratoga for $10,000 in 1918, but Sir Barton was winless in his six starts as a two-year-old and made his three-year-old debut in the '19 Kentucky Derby. His role in the Derby on May 10, 1919, was to serve as a pacemaker for his highly fancied stablemate, Billy Kelly. They went off at 2.60-to-1, second choice behind the 2.10-to-1 entry of Sailor and Eternal. Ridden by Johnny Loftus, Sir Barton bucked the odds, leading all the way and winning the Derby by five lengths over his stablemate. He immediately shipped to Baltimore and won the Preakness Stakes on May 14 (a Wednesday) by four lengths over Eternal as the 7-to-5 favorite. In the Belmont Stakes on June 11, Sir Barton was 2-to-5 against the entry of Sweep On, third in the Preakness, and Natural Bridge. Sir Barton allowed Natural Bridge to set the pace for three-quarters of a mile before taking the lead and winning by five lengths. Between his Preakness and Belmont victories, Sir Barton won the Withers Stakes.

Sir Barton's achievement was unprecedented, but he was overshadowed by the appearance of Man o' War, who sustained the only defeat of his career in that year's Sanford Memorial Stakes at Saratoga Race Course.

As a four-year-old in 1920, Sir Barton alternated

Ch. c., 1916, by *Star Shoot—Lady Sterling, by Hanover

Owner: Commander J. K. L. Ross
Breeders: Madden and Gooch (Ky.)
Trainer: H. Guy Bedwell
Jockey: Johnny Loftus

		Race record			
Year	Starts	1st	2nd	3rd	Earnings
1918	6	0	1 (1)	0	$ 4,113
1919	13	8 (8)	3 (2)	2 (1)	88,250
1920	12	5 (5)	2 (2)	3 (3)	24,494
	31	13 (13)	6 (5)	5 (4)	$116,857

1919—1st Kentucky Derby, Preakness S., Belmont S., Withers S., Potomac H., Maryland H., Pimlico Fall Series No. 2, Pimlico Fall Series No. 3
1920—1st Saratoga H., Merchants' and Citizens' H., Dominion H., Climax H., Rennert H.

between the brilliant and the ordinary, winning five of 12 starts but finishing off the board twice. Because of his chronically sore feet and difficult temperament, he lost several races that he should have won against overmatched opponents.

After losing a match race to Man o' War, Sir Barton faded from view. Retired to stud at the end of the 1920 season, he enjoyed only moderate success, was sold to the United States Cavalry Remount Station, and lived on a Wyoming ranch until his death in 1937.

Gallant Fox

Bred and owned by Belair Stud of William Woodward, Gallant Fox marked a shift in the standards of American breeding. The introduction of *Sir Gallahad III to the United States from France in the late 1920s represented an important step forward for the American breeding industry. For the next several decades, American breeders went to Europe for proven stallions or prospects, particularly in England. The result was a significant increase in the quality of American racehorses. Woodward was one of the syndicate members involved in the purchase of *Sir Gallahad III, who stood at Claiborne Farm in Kentucky.

Gallant Fox was a good but not outstanding two-year-old, winning the Flash and Junior Champion Stakes and placing in three other stakes in his seven starts in 1929. In the care of trainer James "Sunny Jim" Fitzsimmons, Gallant Fox developed into an imposing physical specimen at three.

A four-length winner in Aqueduct's 1930 Wood Memorial Stakes, Gallant Fox hurtled through the Triple Crown, winning the Preakness on May 9 by three-quarters of a length, the Kentucky Derby eight days later by two lengths, and the Belmont on June 7 by three lengths over Whichone, his leading rival. Three weeks later,

	B. c., 1927, by *Sir Gallahad III— Marguerite, by Celt			
Owner-breeder: Belair Stud (Ky.)				
Trainer: James Fitzsimmons				
Jockey: Earl Sande				
		Race record		
Year	Starts	1st	2nd	3rd	Earnings
1929	7	2 (2)	2 (1)	2 (2)	$ 19,890
1930	10	9 (9)	1 (1)	0	308,275
	17	11 (11)	3 (2)	2 (2)	$328,165

1929—1st Flash S., Junior Champion S.
1930—1st Kentucky Derby, Preakness S., Belmont S., Wood Memorial S., Dwyer S., Classic S., Saratoga Cup, Lawrence Realization S., Jockey Cup Gold Cup

Gallant Fox added the Dwyer Stakes to his list of triumphs.

His only loss of the year occurred in the Travers Stakes at Saratoga, where he ran second to 100-to-1 longshot Jim Dandy.

At the end of the year, Gallant Fox was retired to stud at Claiborne, where he sired 1935 Triple Crown winner Omaha and '36 Belmont Stakes winner Granville. Gallant Fox died on November 13, 1954, and was buried at Claiborne alongside his sire and dam.

Omaha

Five years after his Gallant Fox became the second Triple Crown winner, William Woodward saw his decision to participate in the syndication of French runner *Sir Gallahad III for stud duties in the United States pay off with a second Triple Crown winner. Omaha, a son of Gallant Fox and grandson of *Sir Gallahad III, won nine of 22 starts, but his career did not measure up to that of his sire. At two, he won only once in nine starts, although he finished second in the Sanford and Champagne Stakes.

Once again, trainer James "Sunny Jim" Fitzsimmons's patient hand allowed the chestnut colt to fill out nicely over the winter between his two- and three-year-old years. On May 4, 1935, Omaha stepped onto an off track at Churchill Downs as the 4-to-1 second choice for the Kentucky Derby (favored at 3.80-to-1 was the filly Nellie Flag). Omaha made his move for the lead on the far turn, led by two lengths at the top of the stretch, and won by a relatively easy 1½ lengths over Roman Soldier.

One week later, Omaha was a runaway, six-length winner of the Preakness Stakes over Firethorn, who had skipped the Derby. Despite losing two weeks later in the Withers Stakes, Omaha won the Belmont Stakes by 1½ lengths

	Ch. c., 1932, by Gallant Fox— Flambino, by *Wrack			
Owner-breeder: Belair Stud (Ky.)				
Trainer: James Fitzsimmons				
Jockey: Willie Saunders				
		Race record		
Year	Starts	1st	2nd	3rd	Earnings
1934 (U.S.)	9	1	4 (3)	0	$ 3,850
1935 (U.S.)	9	6 (5)	1 (1)	2 (2)	142,255
1936 (Eng.)	4	2 (2)	2 (2)	0	8,650
	22	9 (7)	7 (6)	2 (2)	$154,705

1935—1st Kentucky Derby, Preakness S., Belmont S., Dwyer S., Classic S.
1936—(In England) 1st Victor Wild S., Queen's Plate

on June 8. Omaha finished third in the Brooklyn Handicap in his next start but won his next two starts, the Dwyer Stakes and the Arlington Classic, before an injury ended his season.

As a four-year-old, Omaha was shipped to England and finished second in the Ascot Gold Cup. Omaha failed at stud, and Claiborne in 1943 sent him to a New York farm. Moved to a farm in Nebraska in 1950, Omaha died in 1959 and was buried at Ak-Sar-Ben racetrack in Omaha.

War Admiral

Glen Riddle Farms owner Samuel Riddle owned War Admiral's famous father, Man o' War, but chose to skip the Kentucky Derby with him in 1920. In Riddle's estimation, Churchill Downs was too far west, and the Derby was too early in the year for his comfort.

War Admiral, a striking brown colt out of the Sweep mare Brushup, had won three of six starts as a two-year-old, and his one stakes victory was in the minor Eastern Shore Handicap at Havre de Grace in Maryland. He returned to Havre de Grace for his first start of 1937 and won the Chesapeake Stakes. Riddle then decided to give War Admiral a shot at the Kentucky Derby.

Sent off as the 8-to-5 favorite in a Derby field of 20, War Admiral led at every point of call and easily held off two-year-old champion Pompoon in the final furlong to win by 1¾ lengths.

One week later, War Admiral was put to a much sterner test in the Preakness Stakes by Pompoon, who battled the Derby winner from the top of Pimlico Race Course's stretch. War Admiral won by a head. In the Belmont Stakes on June 5, War Admiral stumbled at the start, injuring his right foreleg, but the diminutive colt cruised to an easy, three-length victory over Sceneshifter.

Br. c., 1934, by Man o' War—Brushup, by Sweep				
Owner: Glen Riddle Farms				
Breeder: Samuel Riddle (Ky.)				
Trainer: George Conway				
Jockey: Charles Kurtsinger				

		Race record			
Year	Starts	1st	2nd	3rd	Earnings
1936	6	3 (1)	2 (2)	1 (1)	$ 14,800
1937	8	8 (6)	0	0	166,500
1938	11	9 (8)	1 (1)	0	90,840
1939	1	1	0	0	1,100
	26	21 (15)	3 (3)	1 (1)	$273,240

1936—1st Eastern Shore H.
1937—1st Kentucky Derby, Preakness S., Belmont S., Chesapeake S., Pimlico Special, Washington H.
1938—1st Whitney S., Jockey Club Gold Cup, Saratoga Cup, Saratoga H., Wilson S., Queens County H., Rhode Island H., Widener H.

Voted Horse of the Year and champion three-year-old, War Admiral lost a 1938 match race to Seabiscuit in the Pimlico Special.

At stud, War Admiral sired 40 stakes winners and two champions in 320 starters, 12.5% of starters, in his 20-year stud career. He died in 1959.

Whirlaway

Prone to wild trips around the racetrack, Whirlaway could be a danger to himself and those around him, but he was worth the risk to train and run. In his three- and four-year-old seasons, he made 42 starts, won 25 times, finished second 13 times, and was third in four of those four starts. Handled patiently by Racing Hall of Fame trainer Ben Jones, Whirlaway became the first of eight Kentucky Derby winners and two Triple Crown winners for Calumet Farm.

For the Derby on May 3, 1941, Jones fashioned new blinkers for Whirlaway, cutting away the left cup but leaving the right cup intact. He also made a riders change, with Eddie Arcaro replacing Wendall Eads. On Derby day, Whirlaway displayed his customary tendency to run near the back of the pack early. With a quarter-mile left, Whirlaway had moved up to fourth place and was flying. He exploded through a final quarter-mile, running it in :24, and won by eight lengths.

Despite walking out of the gate and trailing by more than nine lengths after a half-mile of the Preakness on May 10, Whirlaway again came on late and won by 5½ lengths. Nearly one month later in the Belmont Stakes, Whirlaway stunned his three rivals by taking off after a half-mile and opening up a seven-length lead after six furlongs. Despite entering the stretch a bit wide, he won

Ch. c., 1938, by *Blenheim II—Dustwhirl, by Sweep				
Owner-breeder: Calumet Farm (Ky.)				
Trainer: Ben A. Jones				
Jockey: Eddie Arcaro				

		Race record			
Year	Starts	1st	2nd	3rd	Earnings
1940	16	7 (4)	2 (2)	4 (3)	$77,275
1941	20	13 (8)	5 (5)	2	272,386
1942	22	12 (10)	8 (6)	2 (2)	211,250
1943	2	0	0	1	250
	60	32 (22)	15 (13)	9 (5)	$561,161

1940—1st Saratoga Special, Hopeful S., Breeders' Futurity, Walden S.
1941—1st Kentucky Derby, Preakness S., Belmont S., Travers S., Lawrence Realization S., Saranac H., Dwyer S., American Derby
1942—1st Brooklyn H., Jockey Club Gold Cup, Massachusetts H., Narragansett Special, Dixie H., Washington H., Louisiana H., Trenton H., Governor Bowie H., Clark H.

by 2½ lengths to become the fifth Triple Crown winner.

The colt maintained his brilliance through 1942, when he was named Horse of the Year a second time.

Sold to French interests, Whirlaway died in southern Normandy on April 6, 1953.

Count Fleet

In 1927, Yellow Cab founder John D. Hertz watched a two-year-old race in which one of the runners reached out and bit another horse dueling with him for the lead. It was a remarkable display of aggression and a single-minded will to win. Hertz was sufficiently impressed to buy the colt, Reigh Count, who won the 1928 Kentucky Derby. Hertz never had much faith in Reigh Count as a stallion and bred him to only a few mares each year, including Quickly, who on March 24, 1940, gave birth to a gangly brown package named Count Fleet. The youngster was so clumsy and awkward that Hertz considered selling him as a yearling and again early in his two-year-old campaign. At two, Count Fleet won ten of 15 starts, was voted champion two-year-old colt, and on the Experimental Free Handicap was accorded highweight of 132 pounds, still the highest weight ever assigned.

As a three-year-old, Count Fleet had no equal. He usually went to the lead early, discouraged his competition by the stretch, and won as he pleased.

In the Kentucky Derby on May 1, Count Fleet went off as the 2-to-5 favorite in the field of ten. He broke sharply under John Longden, went

Br. c., 1940, by Reigh Count—Quickly, by Haste				
Owner-breeder: Mrs. John D. Hertz (Ky.)				
Trainer: Don Cameron				
Jockey: John Longden				
		Race record		
Year	Starts	1st	2nd	3rd	Earnings
1942	15	10 (4)	4 (2)	1 (1)	$ 76,245
1943	6	6 (5)	0	0	174,055
	21	16 (9)	4 (2)	1 (1)	$250,300

1942—1st Champagne S., Pimlico Futurity, Walden S., Wakefield S.
1943—1st Kentucky Derby, Preakness S., Belmont S., Wood Memorial S., Withers S.

immediately to the lead, opened two lengths after six furlongs, and won by an easy three lengths over Blue Swords. One week later, Count Fleet won the Preakness by eight lengths. In the Belmont Stakes on June 5, Count Fleet, at odds of 1-to-20, won by 25 lengths in 2:28⅕.

A seemingly minor injury to Count Fleet's left fore ankle refused to respond to treatment and ended his career. At stud, he sired champions Counterpoint and Kiss Me Kate as well as Count Turf, upset winner of the 1951 Kentucky Derby. Count Fleet died on December 3, 1973.

Assault

As a foal, Assault stepped on a surveyor's stake at King Ranch, which left him with a malformed right fore hoof. As a result, he was called the club-footed comet.

Trainer Max Hirsch initially was unsure that Assault could withstand training because of the injury, but the Bold Venture colt won two of nine starts at two in 1945. He went off at 8.20-to-1 in the Kentucky Derby on May 4, 1946. Assault, with jockey Warren Mehrtens up, blew past Spy Song and Knockdown early in the stretch and won by eight lengths.

One week later in the Preakness Stakes, Assault's Triple Crown dreams nearly ended. Mehrtens decided to go for the knockout punch and sent Assault after the leaders going into the far turn. Assault tired and staggered home, winning by a fast-diminishing neck over Lord Boswell.

When the Belmont Stakes came around on June 1, many racing fans believed the 1½ miles would expose Assault. Lord Boswell was sent off as the 1.35-to-1 favorite, with Assault the second choice at 7-to-5. Mehrtens allowed Assault to reach contention gradually. Trailing Natchez by two lengths in midstretch, Assault exploded past him in the final 200 yards and won by three lengths.

Horse of the Year in 1946, Assault won five of

Ch. c., 1943, by Bold Venture—Igual, by Equipoise				
Owner-breeder: King Ranch (Tx.)				
Trainer: Max Hirsch				
Jockey: Warren Mehrtens				
		Race record		
Year	Starts	1st	2nd	3rd	Earnings
1945	9	2 (1)	2	1 (1)	$ 17,250
1946	15	8 (8)	2 (2)	3 (3)	424,195
1947	7	5 (5)	1	1 (1)	181,925
1948	2	1	0	0	3,250
1949	6	1 (1)	1	1 (1)	45,900
1950	3	1	0	1	2,950
	42	18 (15)	6 (2)	7 (6)	$675,470

1945—1st Flash S.
1946—1st Kentucky Derby, Preakness S., Belmont S., Wood Memorial S., Dwyer S., Westchester H., Pimlico Special, Experimental Free H. No. 1
1947—1st Suburban H., Brooklyn H., Butler H., Grey Lag H., Dixie H.
1949—1st Brooklyn H.

seven starts in '47 and spent much of the year battling fellow handicappers Stymie and Armed for the all-time earnings crown.

Assault was retired in early 1948 but proved to be sterile at stud. Returned to the racetrack, he ran until he was seven. Pensioned at King Ranch, he was euthanized in 1971 after fracturing a leg.

Citation

Citation resulted from a mating of Calumet Farm's premier sire, Bull Lea, with *Hydroplane II, whom Warren Wright purchased from Lord Derby in the spring of 1941. Citation was foaled on April 11, 1945, and joined trainer Jimmy Jones's Maryland division in the spring of '47 to begin his racing career.

At two, his only loss was in the Washington Park Futurity to stablemate Bewitch.

Citation began his three-year-old season with two victories over older horses at Hialeah Park before winning the Everglades and Flamingo Stakes. His jockey, Al Snider, died in a boating accident after the Flamingo, and Jones induced Eddie Arcaro to take the mount.

In the Kentucky Derby against only five opponents on May 1, Citation spotted stablemate Coaltown six lengths in the opening half-mile and ran him down to win by 3½ lengths.

In the Preakness two weeks later, Citation set the pace and won by 5½ lengths as the 1-to-10 favorite. With four weeks between the Preakness and Belmont, Jones sent out Citation for an 11-length victory in the Jersey Stakes. On June 12 in the Belmont Stakes, Citation, at 1-to-5 odds, scored an eight-length triumph over Better Self.

Citation won 19 times in 1948, including a walkover in the Pimlico Special. At the end of his three-year-

| | | | B. c., 1945, by Bull Lea— | | |
| | | | *Hydroplane II, by Hyperion | | |

Owner-breeder: Calumet Farm (Ky.)
Trainers: Ben A. Jones and H. A. "Jimmy" Jones
Jockey: Eddie Arcaro

Year	Starts	Race record 1st	2nd	3rd	Earnings
1947	9	8 (3)	1 (1)	0	$ 155,680
1948	20	19 (16)	1 (1)	0	709,470
1949	—	—	—	—	—
1950	9	2 (1)	7 (5)	0	73,480
1951	7	3 (2)	1 (1)	2	147,130
	45	32 (22)	10 (8)	2	$1,085,760

1947—1st Futurity S., Pimlico Futurity, Elementary S.
1948—1st Kentucky Derby, Preakness S., Belmont S., Jockey Club Gold Cup, Pimlico Special, Belmont Gold Cup, American Derby, Flamingo S., Jersey S., Stars and Stripes H., Tanforan H., Sysonby Mile, Chesapeake S., Seminole H., Derby Trial, Everglades H.
1950—1st Golden Gate Mile H.
1951—1st American H., Hollywood Gold Cup

old season, Citation had 27 victories and two seconds in 29 starts, with earnings of $865,150.

In 1951, Citation won the Hollywood Gold Cup, becoming racing's first $1-million earner. Immediately retired to Calumet, he was an undistinguished sire. He died on August 8, 1970.

Secretariat

Like Man o' War, Secretariat was known as Big Red, and both were big in accomplishments. Secretariat, by leading sire Bold Ruler out of the *Princequillo mare Somethingroyal, made his career debut on July 4, 1972, in a 5½-furlong maiden race at Aqueduct and finished fourth with a late surge. Secretariat subsequently won five stakes impressively and was voted Horse of the Year.

In February 1973, as Secretariat was being prepared for the Triple Crown campaign, he was syndicated by Claiborne Farm for a record $6.08-million. Secretariat easily won his first two starts of the year, the Bay Shore (G3) and the Gotham (G2) Stakes, but the colt ran third in the Wood Memorial Stakes (G1) on April 20, most likely due to a lip abscess. His Kentucky Derby (G1) was one that will forever be remembered. After breaking near the back of the pack, Secretariat began picking up horses on the first turn, collared Sham at the top of the lane, and drew away to a 2½-length victory in a Derby record 1:59⅖ for 1¼ miles.

In the Preakness Stakes (G1), jockey Ron Turcotte sensed a slow early pace and allowed Secretariat to surge to the lead as the six-horse field entered the backstretch. Secretariat dominated the rest of the race and again won by 2½ lengths over Sham. A timer malfunction effectively nullified what should have been a track record.

| | | | Ch. c., 1970, by Bold Ruler— | | |
| | | | Somethingroyal, by *Princequillo | | |

Owner: Meadow Stable
Breeder: Meadow Stud (Va.)
Trainer: Lucien Laurin
Jockey: Ron Turcotte

Year	Starts	Race record 1st	2nd	3rd	Earnings
1972	9	7 (5)	1 (1)	0	$ 456,404
1973	12	9 (9)	2 (2)	1 (1)	860,404
	21	16 (14)	3 (3)	1 (1)	$1,316,808

1972—1st Hopeful S., Futurity S., Garden State S., Laurel Futurity, Sanford S.,
1973—1st Kentucky Derby (G1), Preakness S. (G1), Belmont S. (G1), Man o' War S. (G1), Canadian International Championship S. (G2), Marlboro Cup H., Arlington Invitational S. (G1), Gotham S. (G2), Bay Shore S. (G3)

Only Sham and three others showed up to oppose Secretariat in the Belmont Stakes (G1) on June 9. Secretariat and Sham dueled through the first six furlongs in 1:09⅘ before Sham surrendered. Secretariat steadily pulled away to win by 31 lengths while running 1½ miles in 2:24, an American record.

Retired to Claiborne, Secretariat was a good, but not great, sire. He died of complications from laminitis on October 4, 1989.

Seattle Slew

A son of Bold Reasoning out of My Charmer, by Poker, Seattle Slew was brought along patiently by his young trainer, William H. Turner Jr. He was voted champion two-year-old male after a stunning Champagne Stakes (G1) win in just his third start.

At three, Seattle Slew won Hialeah's Flamingo Stakes (G1) by four lengths on March 26 and took Aqueduct's Wood Memorial Stakes (G1) by 3¼ lengths on April 23.

For the Derby on May 7, Seattle Slew went off as the 1-to-2 favorite. Disaster nearly struck at the start when he swerved out and was sharply taken up by jockey Jean Cruguet. At the top of the stretch, Seattle Slew put away For The Moment and then cruised home by 1¾ lengths over Run Dusty Run.

Two weeks later in the Preakness Stakes (G1), 2-to-5 Seattle Slew took command leaving the backstretch and won by 1½ lengths over Iron Constitution. Seattle Slew then dominated the Belmont Stakes (G1), winning by four lengths over Run Dusty Run. Seattle Slew was the first to complete the series without a defeat. Turner suggested a rest, but owners Karen and Mickey Taylor and Sally and Jim Hill insisted on running in Hollywood Park's Swaps Stakes (G1). Slew finished fourth and did not race again in 1977.

Seattle Slew made seven starts as a four-year-old, and his five victories included an epic win

---

Dk. b. or br. c., 1974, by Bold Reasoning—My Charmer, by Poker

Owners: Mickey and Karen L. Taylor, Dr. Jim and Sally Hill
Breeder: Ben S. Castleman (Ky.)
Trainers: William H. Turner Jr. (1976-'77); Doug Peterson (1978)
Jockey: Jean Cruguet

Year	Starts	Race record			Earnings
		1st	2nd	3rd	
1976	3	3 (1)	0	0	$ 94,350
1977	7	6 (5)	0	0	641,370
1978	7	5 (3)	2 (2)	0	473,006
	17	14 (9)	2 (2)	0	$1,208,726

1976—1st Champagne S. (G1)
1977—1st Kentucky Derby (G1), Preakness S. (G1), Belmont S. (G1), Wood Memorial S. (G1), Flamingo S. (G1)
1978—1st Marlboro Cup Invitational H. (G1), Woodward S. (G1), Stuyvesant S. (G3)

---

over Affirmed in the Marlboro Cup Invitational Handicap (G1), the first ever meeting of Triple Crown winners. Standing first at Spendthrift Farm and then at Three Chimneys Farm, he sired A.P. Indy, 1992 Horse of the Year, and more than 100 stakes winners. He died May 7, 2002, at Hill 'n' Dale Farm, where he was moved shortly before his death.

Affirmed

The 1978 Triple Crown, the first won in back-to-back years, belonged to Affirmed, but his name will forever be linked with Alydar, the first horse to finish second in all three races to a Triple Crown winner.

Both colts dominated their arenas at three, and the Kentucky Derby (G1), in which Alydar went off as the 6-to-5 favorite with Affirmed at 9-to-5, was a clash of titans. Third early under jockey Steve Cauthen, Affirmed surged past Believe It early in the stretch and opened a two-length lead in midstretch. Alydar made a late charge but finished second, beaten 1½ lengths.

Two weeks later on May 20, the two would stage an epic duel in the Preakness Stakes (G1). Affirmed, 1-to-2, once again stalked the early pace and inherited the lead after a quarter-mile. Jorge Velasquez asked Alydar for speed on the backstretch, and the Raise a Native colt reached Affirmed's side leaving the turn. They fought to the wire, with Affirmed winning by a neck.

In the Belmont Stakes (G1) three weeks later, 3-to-5 Affirmed was the only speed in a field of five, and 1.10-to-1 Alydar shadowed him practically from the start. After a half-mile, Affirmed led by one length, and by the top of Belmont's stretch they were a head apart. Alydar appeared to take

---

Ch. c., 1975, by Exclusive Native—Won't Tell You, by Crafty Admiral

Owner-breeder: Harbor View Farm (Fl.)
Trainer: Lazaro Barrera
Jockey: Steve Cauthen

Year	Starts	Race record			Earnings
		1st	2nd	3rd	
1977	9	7 (6)	2 (2)	0	$ 343,477
1978	11	8 (7)	2 (2)	0	901,541
1979	9	7 (6)	1 (1)	1 (1)	1,148,800
	29	22 (19)	5 (5)	1 (1)	$2,393,818

1977—1st Hopeful S. (G1), Futurity S. (G1), Laurel Futurity (G1), Sanford S. (G2), Hollywood Juvenile Championship S. (G2), Youthful S.
1978—1st Kentucky Derby (G1), Preakness S. (G1), Belmont S. (G1), Santa Anita Derby (G1), Hollywood Derby (G1), San Felipe H. (G2), Jim Dandy S. (G3)
1979—1st Jockey Club Gold Cup (G1), Hollywood Gold Cup (G1), Santa Anita H. (G1), Woodward S. (G1), Californian S. (G1), Charles H. Strub S. (G1)

---

a narrow lead inside the furlong pole, but Affirmed fought back and won by a head. He was voted Horse of the Year and repeated in 1979 with six consecutive Grade 1 victories. The sport's first $2-million earner, he sired more than 80 stakes winners. He died on January 12, 2001, at Jonabell Farm.

Near Triple Crown Winners

While the Triple Crown has been swept on 11 occasions, in 47 other years three-year-olds have won two legs of the Triple Crown. Among the 47 near successes are 19 horses who won the Kentucky Derby and Preakness Stakes but not the Belmont Stakes.

Of those 19, injury felled several in the Belmont (including Tim Tam and Charismatic), several have come agonizingly close (Silver Charm, Real Quiet), and two did not run in the Belmont (Burgoo King, Bold Venture) because of injuries before the race.

Following are the 47 horses who won two of the three races. Winner of the race the Triple Crown hopeful lost is in parentheses.

Year	Horse	Kentucky Derby	Preakness	Belmont
2003	Funny Cide	Won	Won	3rd (Empire Maker)
2002	War Emblem	Won	Won	8th (Sarava)
2001	Point Given	5th (Monarchos)	Won	Won
1999	Charismatic	Won	Won	3rd (Lemon Drop Kid)
1998	Real Quiet	Won	Won	2nd (Victory Gallop)
1997	Silver Charm	Won	Won	2nd (Touch Gold)
1995	Thunder Gulch	Won	3rd (Timber Country)	Won
1994	Tabasco Cat	6th (Go for Gin)	Won	Won
1991	Hansel	10th (Strike the Gold)	Won	Won
1989	Sunday Silence	Won	Won	2nd (Easy Goer)
1988	Risen Star	3rd (Winning Colors)	Won	Won
1987	Alysheba	Won	Won	4th (Bet Twice)
1984	Swale	Won	7th (Gate Dancer)	Won
1981	Pleasant Colony	Won	Won	3rd (Summing)
1979	Spectacular Bid	Won	Won	3rd (Coastal)
1976	Bold Forbes	Won	3rd (Elocutionist)	Won
1974	Little Current	5th (Cannonade)	Won	Won
1972	Riva Ridge	Won	4th (Bee Bee Bee)	Won
1971	Canonero II	Won	Won	4th (Pass Catcher)
1969	Majestic Prince	Won	Won	2nd (Arts and Letters)
1968	Forward Pass	Won†	Won	2nd (Stage Door Johnny)
1967	Damascus	3rd (Proud Clarion)	Won	Won
1966	Kauai King	Won	Won	4th (Amberoid)
1964	Northern Dancer	Won	Won	3rd (Quadrangle)
1963	Chateaugay	Won	2nd (Candy Spots)	Won
1961	Carry Back	Won	Won	7th (Sherluck)
1958	Tim Tam	Won	Won	2nd (*Cavan)
1956	Needles	Won	2nd (Fabius)	Won
1955	Nashua	2nd (Swaps)	Won	Won
1953	Native Dancer	2nd (Dark Star)	Won	Won
1950	Middleground	Won	2nd (Hill Prince)	Won
1949	Capot	2nd (Ponder)	Won	Won
1944	Pensive	Won	Won	2nd (Bounding Home)
1942	Shut Out	Won	5th (Alsab)	Won
1940	Bimelech	2nd (Gallahadion)	Won	Won
1939	Johnstown	Won	5th (Challedon)	Won
1936	Bold Venture	Won	Won	Did not start
1932	Burgoo King	Won	Won	Did not start
1931	Twenty Grand	Won	2nd (Mate)	Won
1923	Zev	Won	12th (Vigil)	Won
1922	Pillory	Did not start	Won	Won
1920	Man o' War	Did not start	Won	Won
1895	Belmar	Did not start	Won	Won
1881	Saunterer	Did not start	Won	Won
1880	Grenada	Did not start	Won	Won
1878	Duke of Magenta	Did not start	Won	Won
1877	Cloverbrook	Did not start	Won	Won

†Won on disqualification of Dancer's Image. Winner of race is in parentheses.

Leading Breeders of Triple Crown Race Winners

18 Calumet Farm: Kentucky Derby: Whirlaway (1941), Pensive ('44), Citation ('48), Ponder ('49), Hill Gail ('52), Iron Liege ('57), Tim Tam ('58), Forward Pass ('68), Strike the Gold ('91); Preakness: Whirlaway ('41), Pensive ('44), Faultless ('47), Citation ('48), Fabius ('56), Tim Tam ('58), Forward Pass ('68); Belmont: Whirlaway ('41), Citation ('48)

15 A. J. Alexander: Kentucky Derby: Baden-Baden (1877), Fonso ('80), Joe Cotton ('85), Chant ('94); Preakness: Tom Ochiltree ('75), Shirley ('76), Grenada ('80), Duke of Magenta ('90); Belmont: Harry Bassett ('71), Joe Daniels ('72), Springbok ('73), Duke of Magenta ('78), Spendthrift ('79), Grenada ('80), Burlington ('90)

12 Harry P. Whitney: Kentucky Derby: Regret (1915), Whiskery ('27); Preakness: Royal Tourist ('08), Buskin ('13), Holiday ('14), Broomspun ('21), Bostonian ('27), Victorian ('28); Belmont: Tanya ('05), Burgomaster ('06), Prince Eugene ('13), *Johren ('18)

11 John E. Madden
  8—John E. Madden: Kentucky Derby: Old Rosebud (1914), Paul Jones ('20), Zev ('23), Flying Ebony ('25); Belmont: Joe Madden ('09), The Finn ('15), Grey Lag ('21), Zev ('23)
  3—John E. Madden and Vivian A. Gooch: Kentucky Derby: Sir Barton (1919); Preakness: Sir Barton ('19); Belmont: Sir Barton ('19)

10 Belair Stud: Kentucky Derby: Gallant Fox (1930), Omaha ('35); Preakness: Gallant Fox ('30), Omaha ('35), Nashua ('55); Belmont: Gallant Fox ('30), Faireno ('32), Omaha ('35), Granville ('36), Nashua ('55)

August Belmont II: Preakness: Margrave (1896), Don Enrique (1907), Watervale ('11), Damrosch ('16), Man o' War ('20); Belmont: Masterman ('02), Friar Rock ('16), *Hourless ('17), Man o' War ('20), Chance Shot ('27)

8 E. R. Bradley (Idle Hour Stock Farm): Kentucky Derby: Behave Yourself (1921), Bubbling Over ('26), Burgoo King ('32), Brokers Tip ('33); Preakness: Burgoo King ('32), Bimelech ('40); Belmont: Blue Larkspur ('29), Bimelech ('40)

7 Greentree Stud: Kentucky Derby: Twenty Grand (1931), Shut Out ('42); Preakness: Capot ('49); Belmont: Twenty Grand ('31), Shut Out ('42), Capot ('49), Stage Door Johnny ('68)

6 William S. Farish
  3—William S. Farish and William S. Kilroy: Preakness: Summer Squall (1990); Belmont: A.P. Indy ('90), Lemon Drop Kid ('99)
  2—Parrish Hill Farm and William S. Farish: Kentucky Derby: Charismatic (1999); Preakness: Charismatic ('99)
  1—William S. Farish and E. J. Hudson: Belmont: Bet Twice (1987)

James Ben Ali Haggin: Kentucky Derby: Stone Street (1908); Preakness: Old England ('02), Cairngorm ('05), Rhine Maiden ('15); Belmont: Commanche (1893), Africander (1903)

6 Meadow Stud (C. T. Chenery): Kentucky Derby: Riva Ridge (1972), Secretariat ('73); Preakness: Hill Prince ('50), Secretariat ('73); Belmont: Riva Ridge ('72), Secretariat ('73)

5 Ezekiel F. Clay
  4—Clay and Woodford: Kentucky Derby: Ben Brush (1896); Preakness: Buddhist ('89); Belmont: Hanover ('87), Sir Dixon ('88)
  1—Ezekiel F. Clay: Kentucky Derby: Agile (1905)

John W. Galbreath: Kentucky Derby: Chateaugay (1963), Proud Clarion ('67); Preakness: Little Current ('74); Belmont: Chateaugay ('63), Little Current ('74)

James R. Keene: Belmont: Commando (1901), Delhi ('04), Peter Pan ('07), Colin ('08), Sweep ('10)

King Ranch: Kentucky Derby: Assault (1946), Middleground ('50); Preakness: Assault ('46); Belmont: Assault ('46), Middleground ('50)

Samuel D. Riddle: Kentucky Derby: War Admiral (1937); Preakness: War Admiral ('37); Belmont: American Flag ('25), Crusader ('26), War Admiral ('37)

4 Arthur B. Hancock III
  3—Arthur B. Hancock III and Leone J. Peters: Kentucky Derby: Gato Del Sol (1982); Preakness: Risen Star ('88); Belmont: Risen Star ('88)
  1—Arthur B. Hancock III and Stonerside Ltd.: Kentucky Derby: Fusaichi Pegasus (2000)

Arthur B. Hancock Sr.
  3—Arthur B. Hancock: Kentucky Derby: Johnstown (1939); Preakness: Vigil ('23); Belmont: Johnstown ('39)
  1—Arthur B. Hancock and Mrs. R. A. Van Clief: Kentucky Derby: Jet Pilot (1947)

Aristides Welch: Preakness: Harold (1879), Saunterer ('81); Belmont: Saunterer ('81), Panique ('84)

3 August Belmont I: Preakness: Jacobus (1883); Belmont: Fenian ('69), Forester ('82)

A. J. Cassatt: Preakness: Montague (1890); Belmont: Foxford ('91), Patron ('92)

Ben S. Castleman: Kentucky Derby: Seattle Slew (1977), Preakness: Seattle Slew ('77); Belmont: Seattle Slew ('77)

Claiborne Farm: Kentucky Derby: Swale (1984); Belmont: Coastal ('79), Swale ('84)

Harbor View Farm: Kentucky Derby: Affirmed (1978); Preakness: Affirmed ('78); Belmont: Affirmed ('78)

Mrs. John D. Hertz: Kentucky Derby: Count Fleet (1943); Preakness: Count Fleet ('43); Belmont: Count Fleet ('43)

George J. Long: Kentucky Derby: Azra (1892), Manuel (1899), Sir Huon (1906)

H. Price McGrath (McGrathiana Stud): Kentucky Derby: Aristides (1875); Preakness: Paul Kauvar ('97); Belmont: Calvin ('75)

Paul Mellon: Kentucky Derby: Sea Hero (1993); Belmont: Quadrangle ('64), Arts and Letters ('69)

3   Overbrook Farm
   2—Overbrook Farm and David Reynolds:
      Preakness: Tabasco Cat (1994); Belmont:
      Tabasco Cat ('94)
   1—Overbrook Farm: Kentucky Derby: Grindstone
      (1996)
   Daniel Swigert: Kentucky Derby: Hindoo (1881),
      Apollo ('82), Ben Ali ('86)
2   Mrs. Thomas Bancroft: Preakness: Damascus
      (1967); Belmont: Damascus ('67)
   E. B. Benjamin: Kentucky Derby: Canonero II
      (1971); Preakness: Canonero II ('71)
   Bieber-Jacobs Stable: Preakness: Personality
      (1970); Belmont: High Echelon ('70).
   Peter M. Brant: Kentucky Derby: Thunder Gulch
      (1995); Belmont: Thunder Gulch ('95)
   Brookmeade Stable: Preakness: Bold (1951);
      Belmont: Sword Dancer ('59)
   E. A. Clabaugh: Preakness: Cloverbrook (1877);
      Belmont: Cloverbrook ('77)
   John M. Clay: Kentucky Derby: Day Star (1878);
      Preakness: Survivor ('73)
   Leslie B. Combs II: Kentucky Derby: Majestic
      Prince (1969), Preakness: Majestic Prince ('69)
   Eaton and Red Bull Stable: Kentucky Derby:
      Bold Forbes (1976); Belmont: Bold Forbes ('76)
   Rex C. Ellsworth: Kentucky Derby: Swaps
      (1955); Preakness: Candy Spots ('63)
   Thomas Mellon Evans: Kentucky Derby: Pleasant
      Colony (1981); Preakness: Pleasant Colony ('81)
   R. A. Fairbairn: Kentucky Derby: Gallahadion
      (1940), Hoop, Jr. ('45)
   James Galway (Preakness Stable): Preakness:
      Belmar (1895); Belmont: Belmar ('95)
   Mrs. William Jason and Mrs. William Gilmore:
      Kentucky Derby: Spectacular Bid (1979);
      Preakness: Spectacular Bid ('79)
   W. G. Harding: Belmont: Tyrant (1885), Inspector
      B. ('86)
   Walter M. Jeffords: Belmont: Pavot (1945), One
      Count ('52)
   W. E. Leach: Kentucky Derby: Needles (1956);
      Belmont: Needles ('56)

2   Little Hill Farm: Kentucky Derby: Real Quiet
      (1998); Preakness: Real Quiet ('98)
   Marvin Little Jr.: Preakness: Hansel (1991);
      Belmont: Hansel ('91)
   Loblolly Stable: Preakness: Pine Bluff (1992),
      Prairie Bayou ('93)
   Preston Madden: Kentucky Derby: Alysheba
      (1987); Preakness: Alysheba ('87)
   Dr. J. D. Neet: Kentucky Derby: Plaudit (1898);
      Belmont: Hastings ('96)
   Charles Nuckols & Sons: Kentucky Derby:
      War Emblem; Preakness: War Emblem
   Oak Cliff Thoroughbred Breeders Ltd.:
      Kentucky Derby: Sunday Silence (1989);
      Preakness: Sunday Silence ('89)
   Jack A. Price: Kentucky Derby: Carry Back
      (1961); Preakness: Carry Back ('61)
   Pine Brook Farm: Kentucky Derby: Kauai King
      (1966); Preakness: Kauai King ('66)
   Walter J. Salmon: Preakness: Display (1926),
      Dr. Freeland ('29)
   M. H. Sanford: Kentucky Derby: Vagrant (1876);
      Preakness: Vanguard ('82)
   Morton L. Schwartz: Kentucky Derby: Bold
      Venture (1936); Preakness: Bold Venture ('36)
   Tartan Farms Corp.: Kentucky Derby: Unbridled
      (1990); Preakness: Codex ('80)
   E. P. Taylor: Kentucky Derby: Northern Dancer
      (1964); Preakness: Northern Dancer ('64)
   The Thoroughbred Corp.: Preakness: Point
      Given (2001); Belmont: Point Given ('01)
   Alfred G. Vanderbilt: Preakness: Native Dancer
      (1953); Belmont: Native Dancer ('53)
   C. V. Whitney: Preakness: Dauber (1938);
      Belmont: Counterpoint ('51)
   Joseph E. Widener: Belmont: Hurryoff (1933),
      Peace Chance ('34)
   WinStar Farm: Kentucky Derby: Funny Cide
      (2003); Preakness: Funny Cide (2003)
   Mary Lou Wooton: Kentucky Derby: Silver Charm
      (1997); Preakness: Silver Charm ('97)
   Milton Young: Kentucky Derby: Montrose (1887),
      Donau (1910)

Leading Owners of Triple Crown Race Winners

17 Calumet Farm: Kentucky Derby: Whirlaway
      (1941), Pensive ('44), Citation ('48), Ponder
      ('49), Hill Gail ('52), Iron Liege ('57), Tim Tam
      ('58), Forward Pass ('68); Preakness: Whirlaway
      ('41), Pensive ('44), Faultless ('47), Citation
      ('48), Fabius ('56), Tim Tam ('58), Forward
      Pass ('68); Belmont: Whirlaway ('41), Citation
      ('48)
12 Belair Stud: Kentucky Derby: Gallant Fox (1930),
      Omaha ('35), Johnstown ('39); Preakness:
      Gallant Fox ('30), Omaha ('35), Nashua ('55);
      Belmont: Gallant Fox ('30), Faireno ('32), Omaha
      ('35), Granville ('36), Johnstown ('39), Nashua
      ('55)
10 Harry P. Whitney: Kentucky Derby: Regret
      (1915), Whiskery ('27); Preakness: Royal Tourist
      ('08), Broomspun ('21), Bostonian ('27), Victorian
      ('28); Belmont: Tanya ('05), Burgomaster ('06),
      Prince Eugene ('13), *Johren ('18)
9   E. R. Bradley (Idle Hour Stock Farm): Kentucky

      Derby: Behave Yourself (1921), Bubbling Over
      ('26), Burgoo King ('32), Brokers Tip ('33);
      Preakness: Kalitan ('17), Burgoo King ('32),
      Bimelech ('40); Belmont: Blue Larkspur ('29),
      Bimelech ('40)
8   Dwyer Brothers:
   6—Dwyer Brothers (M. F. and Phil J.): Kentucky
      Derby: Hindoo (1881); Belmont: George
      Kinney ('83), Panique ('84), Inspector B.
      ('86), Hanover ('87), Sir Dixon ('88)
   1—M. F. Dwyer: Kentucky Derby: Ben Brush
      (1896)
   1—Phil J. Dwyer: Preakness: Half Time (1899)
   George L. Lorillard: Preakness: Duke of
      Magenta (1878), Harold ('79), Grenada
      ('80), Saunterer ('81), Vanguard ('82);
      Belmont: Duke of Magenta ('78), Grenada
      ('80), Saunterer ('81)
7   August Belmont II: Preakness: Margrave (1896),
      Don Enrique (1907), Watervale ('11); Belmont:

Hastings (1896), Masterman (1902), Friar Rock ('16), *Hourless ('17)

7 Glen Riddle Farms: Kentucky Derby: War Admiral (1937); Preakness: Man o' War ('20), War Admiral ('37); Belmont: Man o' War ('20), American Flag ('25), Crusader (1926), War Admiral ('37)

Greentree Stable: Kentucky Derby: Twenty Grand (1931), Shut Out ('42); Preakness: Capot ('49); Belmont: Twenty Grand ('31), Shut Out ('42), Capot ('49), Stage Door Johnny ('68)

James R. Keene:
6—James R. Keene: Belmont: Spendthrift (1879), Commando (1901), Delhi ('04), Peter Pan ('07), Colin ('08), Sweep ('10)
1—James R. Keene and Foxhall P. Keene: Preakness: Assignee (1894)

6 Robert and Beverly Lewis:
5—Robert and Beverly Lewis: Kentucky Derby: Silver Charm (1997), Charismatic ('99); Preakness: Silver Charm ('97), Charismatic ('99); Belmont: Commendable (2000)
1—Gainesway Farm, Robert and Beverly Lewis, and Overbrook Farm: Preakness: Timber Country (1995)

Meadow Stable (C. T. and Penny Chenery): Kentucky Derby: Riva Ridge (1972), Secretariat ('73); Preakness: Hill Prince ('50), Secretariat ('73); Belmont: Riva Ridge ('72), Secretariat ('73)

5 Overbrook Farm (W. T. Young):
2—Overbrook Farm: Kentucky Derby: Grindstone (1996); Belmont: Editor's Note ('96)
2—Overbrook Farm and David Reynolds: Preakness: Tabasco Cat (1994); Belmont: Tabasco Cat ('94)
1—Gainesway Farm, Robert and Beverly Lewis, and Overbrook Farm: Preakness: Timber Country (1995)

King Ranch: Kentucky Derby: Assault (1946), Middleground ('50); Preakness: Assault ('46); Belmont: Assault ('46), Middleground ('50), High Gun ('54)

Darby Dan Farm: Kentucky Derby: Chateaugay (1963), Proud Clarion ('67); Preakness: Little Current ('74); Belmont: Chateaugay ('63), Little Current ('74)

4 Brookmeade Stable: Kentucky Derby: Cavalcade (1934); Preakness: High Quest ('34), Bold ('51); Belmont: Sword Dancer ('59)

Mrs. John D. Hertz: Kentucky Derby: Reigh Count (1928), Count Fleet ('43); Preakness: Count Fleet ('43); Belmont: Count Fleet ('43)

J.K.L. Ross: Kentucky Derby: Sir Barton (1919); Preakness: Damrosch ('16), Sir Barton ('19);

Belmont: Sir Barton ('19)

4 The Thoroughbred Corp: Kentucky Derby: War Emblem (2002); Preakness: Point Given ('01), War Emblem ('02); Belmont: Point Given ('01)

3 William Condren:
1—B. Giles Brophy, William Condren, and Joseph Cornacchia: Kentucky Derby: Strike the Gold (1991)
1—William Condren and Joseph Cornacchia: Kentucky Derby: Go for Gin (1994)
1—William Condren, Georgia Hofmann, and Joseph Cornacchia: Preakness: Louis Quatorze (1996)

Joseph Cornacchia:
1—B. Giles Brophy, William Condren, and Joseph Cornacchia: Kentucky Derby: Strike the Gold (1991)
1—William Condren and Joseph Cornacchia: Kentucky Derby: Go for Gin (1994)
1—William Condren, Georgia Hofmann, and Joseph Cornacchia: Preakness: Louis Quatorze (1996)

Arthur B. Hancock III:
1—Arthur B. Hancock III and Leone J. Peters: Kentucky Derby: Gato Del Sol (1982)
2—Arthur B. Hancock III, Ernest Gaillard, and Charlie Whittingham: Kentucky Derby: Sunday Silence (1989); Preakness: Sunday Silence ('89)

Harbor View Farm: Kentucky Derby: Affirmed (1978); Preakness: Affirmed ('78); Belmont: Affirmed ('78)

Loblolly Stable: Preakness: Pine Bluff (1992), Prairie Bayou ('93); Belmont: Temperence Hill ('80)

David McDaniel: Belmont: Harry Bassett (1871), Joe Daniels ('72), Springbok ('73)

Preakness Stable (James Galway): Preakness: Montague (1890), Belmar ('95); Belmont: Belmar ('95)

Rokeby Stable: Kentucky Derby: Sea Hero (1993); Belmont: Quadrangle ('64), Arts and Letters ('69)

Walter J. Salmon: Preakness: Vigil (1923), Display ('26), Dr. Freeland ('29)

H. F. Sinclair: Belmont: Grey Lag (1921), Zev ('23), Mad Play ('24)

Karen and Mickey Taylor and Sally and James Hill: Kentucky Derby: Seattle Slew (1977); Preakness: Seattle Slew ('77); Belmont: Seattle Slew ('77)

Joseph E. Widener: Belmont: Chance Shot (1927), Hurryoff ('33), Peace Chance ('34)

Richard T. Wilson Jr.: Preakness: The Parader (1901), Pillory ('22); Belmont: Pillory ('22)

Leading Trainers of Triple Crown Race Winners

13 James "Sunny Jim" Fitzsimmons: Kentucky Derby: Gallant Fox (1930), Omaha ('35), Johnstown ('39); Preakness: Gallant Fox ('30), Omaha ('35), Nashua ('55), Bold Ruler ('57); Belmont: Gallant Fox ('30), Faireno ('32), Omaha ('35), Granville ('36), Johnstown ('39), Nashua ('55)

D. Wayne Lukas: Kentucky Derby: Winning

Colors (1988), Thunder Gulch ('95), Grindstone ('96), Charismatic ('99); Preakness: Codex ('80), Tank's Prospect ('85), Tabasco Cat ('94), Timber Country ('95), Charismatic ('99); Belmont: Tabasco Cat ('94), Thunder Gulch ('95), Editor's Note ('96), Commendable (2000)

11 James Rowe Sr.: Kentucky Derby: Hindoo (1881), Regret (1915); Preakness: Broomspun

(1921); Belmont: George Kinney (1883), Panique (1884), Commando (1901), Delhi ('04), Peter Pan ('07), Colin ('08), Sweep ('10), Prince Eugene ('13)

11 R. Wyndham Walden: Preakness: Tom Ochiltree (1875), Duke of Magenta ('78), Harold ('79), Grenada ('80), Saunterer ('81), Vanguard ('82), Refund ('88); Belmont: Duke of Magenta ('78), Grenada ('80), Saunterer ('81), *Bowling Brook ('98)

9 Max Hirsch: Kentucky Derby: Bold Venture (1936), Assault ('46), Middleground ('50); Preakness: Bold Venture ('36), Assault ('46); Belmont: Vito ('28), Assault ('46), Middleground ('50), High Gun ('54)

B. A. "Ben" Jones: Kentucky Derby: Lawrin (1938), Whirlaway ('41), Pensive ('44), Citation ('48), Ponder ('49), Hill Gail ('52); Preakness: Whirlaway ('41), Pensive ('44); Belmont: Whirlaway ('41)

8 Bob Baffert: Kentucky Derby: Silver Charm (1997), Real Quiet ('98), War Emblem (2002); Preakness: Silver Charm ('97), Real Quiet ('98), Point Given (2001), War Emblem ('02); Belmont: Point Given ('01)

Woodford C. "Woody" Stephens: Kentucky Derby: Cannonade (1974), Swale ('84); Preakness: Blue Man ('52); Belmont: Conquistador Cielo ('82), Caveat ('83), Swale ('84), Creme Fraiche ('85), Danzig Connection ('86)

7 H. A. "Jimmy" Jones: Kentucky Derby: Iron Liege (1957), Tim Tam ('58); Preakness: Faultless ('47), Citation ('48), Fabius ('56), Tim Tam ('58); Belmont: Citation ('48)

Sam Hildreth: Belmont: Jean Bereaud (1899), Joe Madden (1909), Friar Rock ('16), *Hourless ('17), Grey Lag ('21), Zev ('23), Mad Play ('24)

6 Thomas J. Healy: Preakness: The Parader (1901), Pillory ('22), Vigil ('23), Display ('26), Dr. Freeland ('29); Belmont: Pillory ('22)

Lucien Laurin: Kentucky Derby: Riva Ridge (1972), Secretariat ('73); Preakness: Secretariat ('73); Belmont: Amberoid ('66), Riva Ridge ('72), Secretariat ('73)

5 John M. Gaver: Kentucky Derby: Shut Out (1942); Preakness: Capot ('49); Belmont: Shut Out ('42), Capot ('49), Stage Door Johnny ('68)

Lazaro Barrera: Kentucky Derby: Bold Forbes (1976), Affirmed ('78); Preakness: Affirmed ('78); Belmont: Bold Forbes ('76), Affirmed ('78)

5 H. J. "Dick" Thompson: Kentucky Derby: Behave Yourself (1921), Bubbling Over ('26), Burgoo King ('32), Brokers Tip ('33); Preakness: Burgoo King ('32)

4 Henry Forrest: Kentucky Derby: Kauai King (1966), Forward Pass ('68); Preakness: Kauai King ('66), Forward Pass ('68)

George Conway: Kentucky Derby: War Admiral (1937); Preakness: War Admiral ('37); Belmont: Crusader ('26), War Admiral ('37)

Frank McCabe: Preakness: Half Time (1899); Belmont: Inspector B. ('86), Hanover ('87), Sir Dixon ('88)

3 H. Guy Bedwell: Kentucky Derby: Sir Barton (1919); Preakness: Sir Barton ('19); Belmont: Sir Barton ('19)

J. Elliott Burch: Belmont: Sword Dancer (1959), Quadrangle ('64), Arts and Letters ('69)

G. D. Cameron: Kentucky Derby: Count Fleet (1943); Preakness: Count Fleet ('43); Belmont: Count Fleet ('43)

Peter Coyne: Kentucky Derby: Sir Huon (1906); Belmont: Chance Shot ('27), Peace Chance ('34)

Edward Feakes: Preakness: Montague (1890), Belmar ('95); Belmont: Belmar ('95)

Thomas P. Hayes: Kentucky Derby: Donerail (1913); Preakness: Paul Kauvar (1897), Head Play (1933)

William Hurley: Preakness: Kalitan (1917), Bimelech ('40); Belmont: Bimelech ('40)

Horatio Luro: Kentucky Derby: Decidedly (1962), Northern Dancer ('64); Preakness: Northern Dancer ('64)

David McDaniel: Belmont: Harry Bassett (1871), Joe Daniels ('72), Springbok ('73)

James Rowe Jr.: Kentucky Derby: Twenty Grand (1931); Preakness: Victorian ('28), Belmont: Twenty Grand ('31)

William H. Turner Jr.: Kentucky Derby: Seattle Slew (1977); Preakness: Seattle Slew ('77); Belmont: ('77)

James Whalen: Preakness: Don Enrique (1907), Watervale ('11), Buskin ('13)

Frank Y. Whiteley Jr.: Preakness: Tom Rolfe (1965), Damascus ('67); Belmont: Damascus ('67)

Charles Whittingham: Kentucky Derby: Ferdinand (1986), Sunday Silence ('89); Preakness: Sunday Silence ('89)

Nicholas P. Zito: Kentucky Derby: Strike the Gold (1991), Go for Gin ('94); Preakness: Louis Quatorze ('96)

Leading Jockeys of Triple Crown Race Winners

17 Eddie Arcaro: Kentucky Derby: Lawrin (1938), Whirlaway ('41), Hoop, Jr. ('45), Citation ('48), Hill Gail ('52); Preakness: Whirlaway ('41), Citation ('48), Hill Prince ('50), Bold ('51), Nashua ('55), Bold Ruler ('57); Belmont: Whirlaway ('41), Shut Out ('42), Pavot ('45), Citation ('48), One Count ('52), Nashua ('55)

11 William Shoemaker: Kentucky Derby: Swaps (1955), *Tomy Lee ('59), Lucky Debonair ('65),

Ferdinand ('86); Preakness: Candy Spots ('63), Damascus ('67); Belmont: *Gallant Man ('57), Sword Dancer ('59), Jaipur ('62), Damascus ('67), Avatar ('75)

9 Pat Day: Kentucky Derby: Lil E. Tee (1992); Preakness: Tank's Prospect ('85), Summer Squall ('90), Tabasco Cat ('94), Timber Country ('95), Louis Quatorze ('96); Belmont: Easy Goer ('89), Tabasco Cat ('94), Commendable (2000)

9   **William J. Hartack**: Kentucky Derby: Iron Liege (1957), Venetian Way ('60), Decidedly ('62), Northern Dancer ('64), Majestic Prince ('69); Preakness: Fabius ('56), Northern Dancer ('64), Majestic Prince ('69); Belmont: *Celtic Ash ('60)

Earl Sande: Kentucky Derby: Zev (1923), Flying Ebony ('25), Gallant Fox ('30); Preakness: Gallant Fox ('30); Belmont: Grey Lag ('21), Zev ('23), Mad Play ('24), Chance Shot ('27), Gallant Fox ('30)

8   **James McLaughlin**: Kentucky Derby: Hindoo (1881); Preakness: Tecumseh ('85); Belmont: Forester ('82), George Kinney ('83), Panique ('84), Inspector B. ('86), Hanover ('87), Sir Dixon ('88)

Gary Stevens: Kentucky Derby: Winning Colors (1988), Thunder Gulch ('95), Silver Charm ('97); Preakness: Silver Charm ('97), Point Given (2001); Belmont: Thunder Gulch (1995), Victory Gallop ('98), Point Given (2001)

6   **Jerry Bailey**: Kentucky Derby: Sea Hero (1993), Grindstone ('96); Preakness: Hansel ('91), Red Bullet (2000); Belmont: Hansel (1991), Empire Maker (2003)

Angel Cordero Jr.: Kentucky Derby: Cannonade (1974), Bold Forbes ('76), Spend a Buck ('85); Preakness: Codex ('80), Gate Dancer ('84); Belmont: Bold Forbes ('76)

Charles Kurtsinger: Kentucky Derby: Twenty Grand (1931), War Admiral ('37); Preakness: Head Play ('33), War Admiral ('37); Belmont: Twenty Grand ('31), War Admiral ('37)

Chris McCarron: Kentucky Derby: Alysheba (1987), Go for Gin ('94); Preakness: Alysheba ('87), Pine Bluff ('92), Belmont: Danzig Connection ('86), Touch Gold ('97)

Ron Turcotte: Kentucky Derby: Riva Ridge (1972), Secretariat ('73); Preakness: Tom Rolfe ('65), Secretariat ('73); Belmont: Riva Ridge ('72), Secretariat ('73)

5   **Eddie Delahoussaye**: Kentucky Derby: Gato Del Sol (1982), Sunny's Halo ('83); Preakness: Risen Star ('88); Belmont: Risen Star ('88), A.P. Indy ('92)

Lloyd Hughes: Preakness: Tom Ochiltree (1875), Harold ('79), Grenada ('80); Belmont: Duke of Magenta ('78), Grenada ('80)

John Loftus: Kentucky Derby: George Smith (1916), Sir Barton ('19); Preakness: *War Cloud ('18), Sir Barton ('19); Belmont: Sir Barton ('19)

Willie Simms: Kentucky Derby: Ben Brush (1898), Plaudit ('98); Preakness: Sly Fox ('98); Belmont: Comanche ('93), Henry Of Navarre ('94)

4   **Braulio Baeza**: Kentucky Derby: Chateaugay (1963); Belmont: Sherluck ('61), Chateaugay ('63), Arts and Letters ('69)

George Barbee: Preakness: Survivor (1873), Shirley ('76), Jacobus ('83); Belmont: Saxon ('74)

William "Billy" Donohue: Kentucky Derby: Leonatus (1883); Preakness: Culpepper ('74), Dunboyne ('87); Belmont: Algerine ('76)

Eric Guerin: Kentucky Derby: Jet Pilot (1947); Preakness: Native Dancer ('53); Belmont: Native Dancer ('53), High Gun ('54)

Albert Johnson: Kentucky Derby: Morvich (1922), Bubbling Over ('26); Belmont: American Flag ('25), Crusader ('26)

Clarence Kummer: Preakness: Man o' War

(1920), Coventry ('25); Belmont: Man o' War ('20), Vito ('28)

4   **Conn McCreary**: Kentucky Derby: Pensive (1944), Count Turf ('51); Preakness: Pensive ('44), Blue Man ('52)

Laffit Pincay Jr.: Kentucky Derby: Swale (1984); Belmont: Conquistador Cielo ('82), Caveat ('83), Swale ('84)

James Stout: Kentucky Derby: Johnstown (1939); Belmont: Granville ('36), Pasteurized ('38), Johnstown ('39)

Fred Taral: Kentucky Derby: Manuel (1899); Preakness: Assignee ('94), Belmar ('95); Belmont: Belmar ('95)

Ismael "Milo" Valenzuela: Kentucky Derby: Tim Tam (1958), Forward Pass ('68); Preakness: Tim Tam ('58), Forward Pass ('68)

3   **Chris Antley**: Kentucky Derby: Strike the Gold (1991), Charismatic ('99); Preakness: Charismatic ('99)

William Boland: Kentucky Derby: Middleground (1950); Belmont: Middleground ('50), Amberoid ('66)

James H. "Jimmy" Butwell: Preakness: Buskin (1913); Belmont: Sweep ('10), *Hourless ('17)

Steve Cauthen: Kentucky Derby: Affirmed (1978); Preakness: Affirmed ('78); Belmont: Affirmed ('78)

T. Costello: Preakness: Saunterer (1881), Vanguard ('82); Belmont: Saunterer ('81)

Jean Cruguet: Kentucky Derby: Seattle Slew (1977), Preakness: Seattle Slew ('77); Belmont: Seattle Slew ('77)

Kent Desormeaux: Kentucky Derby: Real Quiet (1998), Fusaichi Pegasus (2000); Preakness: Real Quiet (1998)

Eddie Dugan: Preakness: Royal Tourist (1908), Watervale ('11); Belmont: Joe Madden ('09)

Mack Garner: Kentucky Derby: Cavalcade (1934); Belmont: Blue Larkspur ('29), Hurryoff ('33)

C. Holloway: Preakness: Cloverbrook (1877), Duke of Magenta ('78); Belmont: Cloverbrook ('77)

John Longden: Kentucky Derby: Count Fleet (1943); Preakness: Count Fleet ('43); Belmont: Count Fleet ('43)

J. Linus "Pony" McAtee: Kentucky Derby: Whiskery (1927), Clyde Van Dusen ('29); Preakness: Damrosch ('16)

Warren Mehrtens: Kentucky Derby: Assault (1946); Preakness: Assault ('46), Belmont: Assault ('46)

Isaac Murphy: Kentucky Derby: Buchanan (1884), Riley ('90), Kingman ('91)

Jose Santos: Kentucky Derby: Funny Cide (2003); Preakness: Funny Cide (2003); Belmont: Lemon Drop Kid (1999)

William "Smokey" Saunders: Kentucky Derby: Omaha (1935); Preakness: Omaha ('35); Belmont: Omaha ('35)

John Sellers: Kentucky Derby: Carry Back (1961); Preakness: Carry Back ('61); Belmont: Hail to All ('65)

Bobby Swim: Kentucky Derby: Vagrant (1876); Belmont: General Duke ('68), Calvin ('75)

Wayne D. Wright: Kentucky Derby: Shut Out (1942); Preakness: Polynesian ('45); Belmont: Peace Chance ('34)

Kentucky Derby History

The Kentucky Derby was the dream of Col. Meriwether Lewis Clark Jr., grandson of William Clark of Lewis and Clark Expedition fame. Just 29 when the first Derby was run in 1875, Meriwether Clark had the family's sense of adventure and ambition but devoted his energies to equine pursuits.

Racing in Louisville was essentially dead in the early 1870s following the closure in 1870 of Woodlawn Course, located east of the city. In 1872, Clark traveled to England to observe its racing scene.

He returned with grand ambitions of creating a racing palace in Louisville with races modeled on such leading events in England as the Epsom Derby, Epsom Oaks, and St. Leger Stakes. With $32,000 in investment capital, Clark set about building Louisville's new racetrack in 1874. The facility, built on 80 acres of land leased from Clark's uncles, John and Henry Churchill, was called the Louisville Jockey Club.

The Louisville Jockey Club opened on Monday, May 17, 1875, with four races. It was a sunny day with a crisp breeze, according to an account in the *Live Stock Record* (precursor of *The Thoroughbred Record* and THOROUGHBRED TIMES), and the "course was in splendid order, and all the appurtenances requisite for the comfort and convenience of racing was ready to hand."

All 42 nominees for the inaugural Derby were listed in the program and 15 started, with H. P. McGrath's nobly named Aristides becoming the first Derby winner.

One week after the first meet ended, the *Live Stock Record*'s editor, Benjamin G. Bruce, noted that, while he had attended the inaugural meet at Jerome Park and had visited Saratoga and Long Branch, "never have we seen such a grand success, taking it from its beginning to its close, as the late inaugural meeting of the Louisville Jockey Club."

While the first race meet was an artistic success, at least in Bruce's view, the financial situation of the Louisville Jockey Club was perilous almost from its start. For most of its first 40 years, the Derby would be regarded as a strong regional race at best and an embarrassing farce at worst. There were many reasons for the race's decline. Louisville was still considered western territory to many leading Eastern stables, and the situation grew worse when a track official insulted leading owner James Ben Ali Haggin in 1886. The race's initial 1½-mile distance was considered too taxing for three-year-olds in the spring.

The revival of the track and its signature race began in 1902. Col. Matt Winn, a Louisville tailor with no racetrack management experience but an undying love for the track—he attended every

Kentucky Derby Attendance			
Year	Attendance	Year	Attendance
2003	148,530	1986	123,819
2002	145,033	1985	108,573
2001	154,210	1984	126,453
2000	153,204	1983	134,444
1999	151,051	1982	141,009
1998	143,215	1981	139,195
1997	141,981	1980	131,859
1996	142,668	1979	128,488
1995	144,110	1978	131,004
1994	130,594	1977	124,038
1993	136,817	1976	115,387
1992	132,543	1975	113,324
1991	135,554	1974	163,628
1990	128,257	1973	134,476
1989	122,653	1972	130,564
1988	137,694	1971	123,284
1987	130,532	1970	105,087

Kentucky Derby from 1875 to 1949—recruited a group of Louisvillians to purchase the track for $40,000. Winn spent a decade straightening out the financial mess at the track, which by then was known as Churchill Downs. Then, he set out to revive the Kentucky Derby.

The years 1913-'15 would establish the race's credentials from both a romantic and qualitative standpoint. The 1913 running was won by 91.45-to-1 longshot Donerail, who remains the race's longest-priced winner. The race also picked up an unofficial ambassador in winning rider Roscoe Goose, who lived for a half-century mere blocks from the track, dispensing wisdom and schooling such prospective jockeys as two-time Derby winner Charlie Kurtsinger.

The next year, the gallant gelding Old Rosebud won, enhancing the race's reputation. And, in 1915, New York owner Harry Payne Whitney shipped his marvelous, unbeaten filly Regret to Louisville, where she became the first filly to win the Derby. While some Eastern stables still shied away from shipping west for the Derby—most notably Samuel Riddle's decision not to run Man o' War in 1920—the Derby's reputation was set after 1915.

Winn was a showman who combined a promoter's instincts with a passion for the Derby. The Kentucky Derby benefited from Winn's skill until he died on October 6, 1949. At the time of his death, the Derby had become a national racing institution, traditionally run on the first Saturday in May and part of the Triple Crown, a three-race series for three-year-olds considered as the ultimate test for young horses. The track's Twin Spires, constructed in 1895 when the physical plant was rebuilt on what had been the backstretch side of the original track, were transformed from a unique architectural feature to an iconic symbol.

Before he died, however, Winn witnessed some amazing Derbys. Longshot Exterminator won the 1918 Derby in his three-year-old debut after he was purchased to help train another horse who did not make the race. There were two famous victories by maidens: Sir Barton's 1919 victory launched the first successful Triple Crown campaign, while Brokers Tip won in '33 after his jockey, Don Meade, fought with Head Play's rider, Herb Fisher, down the stretch.

Winn also had to adjust to the circumstances of World War II. Travel restrictions in 1943 gave that Derby a distinctly local flavor, and it became known as the "Street Car Derby." Further war restrictions shut down the sport in early 1945; when the restrictions were lifted after V-E Day, the Derby was scheduled for June 9, the only time the race has been run in June. Three years later, Citation won the Triple Crown—the eighth during Winn's tenure at Churchill.

History flows easily through the Kentucky Derby. Each year seems to bring an amazing, astounding, or simply amusing story. From the sublime (Bill Shoemaker standing up at the sixteenth pole and possibly costing *Gallant Man the 1957 Derby) to the ridiculous (the antics of unraced Nevada gelding One Eyed Tom, who failed to make it to the starting gate in 1972), the Derby has something to offer every racing fan.

Over the last 30 years, the Derby's story has been about the growth of the event as a local and international event. Attendance rose from the 120,000-to-130,000 level in the late 1980s to more than 150,000 starting in 1999. (Security restrictions following the September 11, 2001, terrorist attacks held the 2002 crowd to 145,033 and the 2003 crowd to 148,530.) Unsuccessful Triple Crown bids by Silver Charm, Real Quiet, and Charismatic from 1997-'99 and by War Emblem and Funny Cide in 2002 and '03 created a heightened level of awareness in the Triple Crown races. The efforts of Godolphin Racing (Dubai), The Thoroughbred Corp. (Saudi Arabia and owner of War Emblem), and Michael Tabor and John Magnier (Monaco and Ireland, respectively) to win the race in the late 1990s and early 2000s have given the race an international flavor. —*John Harrell*

Presidents at the Derby

Since World War II, attending the Kentucky Derby has become a pastime of United States Presidents. Getting them to attend while they are actually in office, however, has proved to be a challenge.

Eight U.S. Presidents have been seen under the twin spires on the first Saturday in May, but Richard Nixon is the only one to attend the race while in office. He attended the event in 1968 while he was running for his first term and then fulfilled a promise when he returned the next year, his first in the Oval Office.

Also attending the Derby in 1969 were two future Presidents, Gerald Ford and Ronald Reagan. Ford returned in 1983, along with Jimmy Carter, who defeated him in the 1976 presidential race, and future President George H. W. Bush. Bush returned in 2000, along with his son and future President, George W. Bush.

Other Presidents who have attended the race—though they were not in the Oval Office at the time—are Harry Truman and Lyndon B. Johnson.

Kentucky Derby Trophy

The Kentucky Derby trophy, featuring a simple but classic design with a horse and garland of roses on top, was first presented in 1924, when Black Gold won the 50th running of the Derby.

The trophy had been commissioned for the golden anniversary Derby by Churchill Downs President Col. Matt Winn, who wanted a standard trophy for the connections of each Derby winner. The original design remains to this day, except for one change, when the horseshoe on the trophy was inverted upward starting with the 1999 Derby. The horseshoe had been pointed down for 75 years, according to ancient belief that an upside-down shoe afforded protection. But, since racing superstition maintains that luck runs out of horseshoes that are pointed down, the shoe was inverted.

The only other changes made to the Derby trophy were for the 75th (1949), 100th ('74), and 125th ('99) runnings, when additional jewels were added. Several Derby trophies are on display at the Kentucky Derby Museum; the oldest is Flying Ebony's trophy from the 1925 Derby.

Enduring Twin Spires

The twin spires that top Churchill Downs's grandstand are arguably the best-known architectural feature of any racetrack in the world. They date from the reconstruction of the Louisville track in 1894-'95. Designed by 24-year-old Louisville architect Joseph D. Baldez, the twin spires were intended only as an ornamental feature of the new grandstand, which was constructed at a cost of $100,000. Col. Matt Winn, Churchill's longtime president, once told Baldez, "Joe, when you die there's one monument that will never be taken down, the twin spires."

The spires are checked periodically for structural soundness, and they underwent a renovation in 2002 as part of the $27-million, first phase of Churchill's $127-million renewal project. Workmen inspecting the spires found a copy of the Louisville *Courier-Journal* from 1907 and a flag wrapped around a 1908 copy of the *Courier-Journal*.

Glasses and Mint Julep Cups

The popularity of the mint julep as the official Kentucky Derby drink grew in proportion with the introduction of Derby glasses and sterling silver julep cups as Derby souvenirs in the middle years of the 20th century.

The Derby glass made its introduction in 1938 after Churchill officials noted that patrons took water glasses from their tables on Derby day as souvenirs. In 1939, glass manufacturers were encouraged to add color to the glasses, making them attractive as mint julep glasses. Sales of mint juleps increased threefold, according to track officials, and the glasses have gone on to become the most prominent of Derby souvenirs.

The sterling silver cups were introduced in 1951 as part of the legacy of Col. Matt Winn, who had died two years earlier. Winn wished to make the cups an official Derby souvenir, and they have been part of Derby lore now for more than a half-century. The cups, which hold 12 fluid ounces, were unchanged in design until 1984, when noted owner-breeder Leslie Combs II pointed out that the horseshoe on the glass pointed down, a superstitious sign of bad luck in racing, although an upside-down shoe was regarded in folklore as affording protection. The horseshoe was turned upright and remains so to this day.

Although some relatively minor errors have occurred in the printing on the glasses, two significant mistakes occurred on approximately 100,400 of the half-million Derby glasses manufactured for the 2002 Derby. The erroneous glasses had Burgoo King winning the Triple Crown in 1932 (he won the Derby and Preakness but did not compete in the Belmont Stakes) and War Admiral failing to win the 1937 Triple Crown (he did). These erroneous glasses immediately became collectors' items.

Kentucky Derby Festival

Conducted annually since 1956, the Kentucky Derby Festival has grown into a weeks-long celebration of Louisville's premier attraction. A not-for-profit community organization, the Kentucky Derby Festival recruits 4,000 volunteers for 70 special events that annually attract approximately 1.5-million people to venues in and around Louisville. Financed by corporate contributions and the sale of Pegasus Pins, the festival contributes an estimated $93-million to the local economy.

Three of the best-known events of the Kentucky Derby Festival are the Pegasus Parade, the Great Balloon Race, and the Great Steamboat Race. In 1990, the Kentucky Derby Festival added a new attraction, Thunder Over Louisville. Held about three weeks before the Derby, it is billed as the nation's largest fireworks display and attracts thousands to the banks of the Ohio River each April.

The schedule of events for the 2003 Kentucky Derby Festival included:

They're Off! Luncheon	April 11
Fillies' Derby Ball	April 11
Thunder Over Louisville	April 12
Great Balloon Race	April 26
Basketball Classic	April 26
Great Bed Races	April 28
Knights of Columbus Charity Dinner	April 28
Run for the Rose	April 29
Derby Trainers Dinner	April 29
Great Steamboat Race	April 30
Pegasus Parade	May 1

"My Old Kentucky Home"

As the Kentucky Derby field parades onto the racetrack from the paddock, the University of Louisville Marching Band plays "My Old Kentucky Home," a song whose meaning and involvement with the Derby are shrouded in some mystery. Stephen Collins Foster (1826-'64) wrote the song in 1853, while visiting cousins at Federal Hill in Bardstown, Kentucky, a short distance from Louisville.

According to contemporary accounts, the song was first played at the Derby in 1921, and Damon Runyon reported in '29 that the song was played several times on Derby day. The following year, according to the Philadelphia *Public Ledger*, the song was played as the field came onto the track

Kentucky Derby Handle

Year	On-track	Off-track	Total
2003	$9,079,841	$78,583,822	$87,663,663
2002	8,630,408	70,464,398	79,094,806
2001	8,360,273	59,192,483	67,552,756
2000	8,737,659	53,059,793	61,797,452
1999	8,025,318	46,171,266	54,196,586
1998	7,890,907	44,586,385	52,477,292
1997	7,401,141	41,891,506	49,292,647
1996	7,488,725	37,734,438	45,223,163
1995	7,297,050	37,518,438	44,815,488
1994	7,449,744	37,289,274	44,739,018
1993	6,811,130	33,458,735	40,269,865
1992	6,690,746	28,250,209	34,940,955
1991	6,744,979	27,499,222	34,244,201
1990	6,948,762	27,452,177	34,400,939
1989	6,751,067	23,089,515	29,840,582
1988	7,346,411	25,525,312	32,871,723
1987	6,362,673	20,829,236	27,191,909
1986	6,165,119	19,932,231	26,097,350
1985	5,770,074	14,474,555	20,244,629
1984	5,420,787	13,521,146	18,941,933
1983	5,546,977	—	5,546,977
1982	5,011,575	—	5,011,575
1981	4,566,179	455,163	5,021,342

Kentucky Derby simulcast wagering began in 1981, as three tracks (Longacres, Yakima Meadows, and Centennial) wagered a total of $455,163. Simulcast wagering was shelved for two years and resumed in 1984. Off-track wagering includes interstate and intrastate wagering.

for the Derby.

The sentimental melody and its lyrics may well have foreshadowed the sadness that would fall upon the nation in the Civil War. A Pittsburgh native who lived many years of his brief life there, Foster began writing minstrel songs and had a national hit with "Oh, Susanna" in 1848. His view of slaves and slavery apparently changed in the next few years. According to some accounts, Foster may have been inspired to write "My Old Kentucky Home" after reading Harriet Beecher Stowe's *Uncle Tom's Cabin*, published in 1851. Foster's first draft in his song workbook was entitled "Poor Uncle Tome, Good Night."

"My Old Kentucky Home" came in the midst of Foster's most productive period. He wrote "Old Folks at Home" in 1851 and "Jeannie With the Light Brown Hair" in 1854. Foster died in January 1864 after sustaining a cut, probably alcohol-related, at a New York boarding house. One of his best-known songs, "Beautiful Dreamer," was published posthumously.

"My Old Kentucky Home, Good-Night!" was adopted by Kentucky as its state song in 1928. The official lyrics were subsequently changed to remove references to "darkies" in the original version. The song had three verses, but only the first is now sung. Here are the modern lyrics.

The sun shines bright in the old Kentucky home
'Tis summer, the people are gay;
The corn top's ripe and the meadow's in the bloom,
While the birds make music all the day;
The young folks roll on the little cabin floor,
All merry, all happy, and bright,
By'n by hard times comes a-knocking at the door,
Then my old Kentucky home, good night!
Chorus
Weep no more, my lady,
Oh weep no more today!
We will sing one song for the old Kentucky home,
For the old Kentucky home far away.

Kentucky Derby Future Wager

For years, future-book wagers on the Kentucky Derby has enriched Las Vegas casinos, and Churchill Downs tapped into that bet in 1999 with the Kentucky Derby Future Wager. The bet is offered three times each year, with four days in each wagering period.

Bettors choose the horse they believe will win, with the final pool being offered approximately four weeks before the Derby. From modest beginnings, the wager gained popularity and exceeded $1.5-million in handle in 2002 before falling back to $1,130,169 in 2003.

Here are the amounts wagered by year:

Year	Pool 1	Pool 2	Pool 3	Total
2003	$516,906	$391,002	$222,261	$1,130,169
2002	577,889	401,070	524,847	1,503,806
2001	510,815	372,961	425,871	1,309,647

Year	Pool 1	Pool 2	Pool 3	Total
2000	465,454	306,259	387,206	1,158,919
1999	267,748	178,811	229,674	676,233

Future Pool Payoffs

Year	Winner	Pool 1 Win Price	Pool 2 Win Price	Pool 3 Win Price	Derby Day Win Price
2003	Funny Cide	$188.00	$120.80	$107.40	$27.60
2002	War Emblem	7.60†	16.00†	24.00†	43.00
2001	Monarchos	36.60	13.00	15.80	23.00
2000	Fusaichi Pegasus	27.80	26.40	8.00	6.60
1999	Charismatic	10.20†	30.20†	26.60†	64.60

† Part of mutuel field

Leading Derby Owners by Wins

8 Calumet Farm: Whirlaway, 1941; Pensive, 1944; Citation, 1948; Ponder, 1949; Hill Gail, 1952; Iron Liege, 1957; Tim Tam, 1958; Forward Pass, 1968.

4 Col. E. R. Bradley: Behave Yourself, 1921; Bubbling Over, 1926; Burgoo King, 1932; Brokers Tip, 1933.

3 Belair Stud: Gallant Fox, 1930; Omaha, 1935; Johnstown, 1939.

2 Bashford Manor Stable: Azra, 1892; Sir Huon, 1906.

Harry Payne Whitney: Regret, 1915; Whiskery, 1927.

Mrs. John D. Hertz: Reigh Count, 1928; Count Fleet, 1943.

Greentree Stable: Twenty Grand, 1931; Shut Out, 1942.

King Ranch: Assault, 1946; Middleground, 1950.

Darby Dan Farm: Chateaugay, 1963; Proud Clarion, 1967.

Meadow Stable: Riva Ridge, 1972; Secretariat, 1973.

William Condren and Joseph Cornacchia: Strike the Gold, 1991; Go for Gin, 1994.

Robert and Beverly Lewis: Silver Charm, 1997; Charismatic, 1999.

Leading Breeders of Kentucky Derby Winners

9 Calumet Farm: Whirlaway, 1941; Pensive, 1944; Citation, 1948; Ponder, 1949; Hill Gail, 1952; Iron Liege, 1957; Tim Tam, 1958; Forward Pass, 1968; Strike the Gold, 1991.

5 John Madden: Old Rosebud, 1914; Sir Barton, 1919; Paul Jones, 1920; Zev, 1923; Flying Ebony, 1925.

4 A. J. Alexander: Baden-Baden, 1877; Fonso, 1880; Joe Cotton, 1885; Chant, 1894.

E. R. Bradley (Idle Hour Stock Farm):
1 E. R. Bradley: Behave Yourself, 1921.
2 Idle Hour Stock Farm: Bubbling Over, 1926; Brokers Tip, 1933.
1 H. N. Davis and Idle Hour Stock Farm: Burgoo King, 1932.

3 Bashford Manor Stable (George J. Long): Azra, 1892; Manuel, 1899; Sir Huon, 1906.

Daniel Swigert: Hindoo, 1881; Apollo, 1882; Ben Ali, 1886.

2 Belair Stud: Gallant Fox, 1930; Omaha, 1935.

Claiborne Farm: Johnstown, 1939; Swale, 1984.

R. A. Fairbairn: Gallahadion, 1940; Hoop, Jr., 1945.

2   John W. Galbreath: Chateaugay, 1963; Proud Clarion, 1967.
Greentree Stable: Twenty Grand, 1931; Shut Out, 1942.
Arthur B. Hancock III:
1 A. B. Hancock III and Leone J. Peters: Gato Del Sol, 1982.
1 A. B. Hancock III and Stonerside Ltd.: Fusaichi Pegasus, 2000.
King Ranch: Assault, 1946; Middleground, 1950.
Meadow Stud: Riva Ridge, 1972; Secretariat, 1973.
Harry Payne Whitney: Regret, 1915; Whiskery, 1927.
Milton Young: Montrose, 1887; Donau, 1910.

Leading Derby Trainers by Wins

6   Ben A. Jones: Lawrin, 1938; Whirlaway, 1941; Pensive, 1944; Citation, 1948; Ponder, 1949; Hill Gail, 1952.
4   H. J. "Dick" Thompson: Behave Yourself, 1921; Bubbling Over, 1926; Burgoo King, 1932; Brokers Tip, 1933.
D. Wayne Lukas: Winning Colors, 1988; Thunder Gulch, 1995; Grindstone, 1996; Charismatic, 1999.
3   Bob Baffert: Silver Charm, 1997; Real Quiet, 1998; War Emblem, 2002.
James "Sunny Jim" Fitzsimmons: Gallant Fox, 1930; Omaha, 1935; Johnstown, 1939.
Max Hirsch: Bold Venture, 1936; Assault, 1946; Middleground, 1950.
2   John McGinty: Leonatus, 1883; Montrose, 1887.
James Rowe Sr.: Hindoo, 1881; Regret, 1915.
H. A. "Jimmy" Jones: Iron Liege, 1957; Tim Tam, 1958.
Horatio Luro: Decidedly, 1962; Northern Dancer, 1964.
Henry Forrest: Kauai King, 1966; Forward Pass, 1968.
Lucien Laurin: Riva Ridge, 1972; Secretariat, 1973.
W. C. "Woody" Stephens: Cannonade, 1974; Swale, 1984.
LeRoy Jolley: Foolish Pleasure, 1975; Genuine Risk, 1980.
Lazaro Barrera: Bold Forbes, 1976; Affirmed, 1978.
Charlie Whittingham: Ferdinand, 1986; Sunday Silence, 1989.
Nicholas P. Zito: Strike the Gold, 1991; Go for Gin, 1994.

Trainers With Most Derby Starters

Trainer	Strs.	Wins	2nd	3rd	Unplaced
D. Wayne Lukas	41	4	1	5	31
H. J. Thompson	24	4	2	1	17
James Rowe Sr.*	18	2	1	1	14
Max Hirsch	14	3	0	2	9
W. C. Stephens	14	2	3	3	6
LeRoy Jolley	13	2	2	1	8
Bob Baffert	13	3	1	2	7
Nicholas P. Zito	12	2	0	0	10
James Fitzsimmons	11	3	1	0	7
Ben A. Jones	11	6	2	1	2

*Information on James Rowe Sr. is incomplete

Female Trainers in the Derby

A woman has yet to win the Kentucky Derby (G1) as either a jockey or a trainer, but several female trainers have come close to landing one of

racing's biggest prizes.
Northern California-based trainer Shelley Riley came closest to notching a Kentucky Derby victory when her 29.90-to-1 longshot, Casual Lies, finished second to Lil E. Tee in 1992.
Mary Hirsch, daughter of Racing Hall of Fame trainer Max Hirsch, was the first female trainer to saddle a Derby starter. No Sir, also owned by Mary Hirsch, finished 13th in 1937.
The women who have trained Derby starters:

Trainer	Horse	Year	Finish
Jenine Sahadi	The Deputy (Ire)	2000	14th
Akiko Gothard	K One King	1999	8th
Kathy Walsh	Hanuman Highway	1998	7th
Shelly Riley	Casual Lies	1992	2nd
Patti Johnson	Fast Account	1985	4th
Dianne Carpenter	Kingpost	1988	14th
	Biloxi Indian	1984	12th
Mary Keim	Mr. Pak	1965	6th
Mrs. Albert Roth	Senecas Coin	1949	DNF
Mary Hirsch	No Sir	1937	13th

Leading Derby Jockeys by Wins

5   Eddie Arcaro: Lawrin, 1938; Whirlaway, 1941; Hoop, Jr., 1945; Citation, 1948; Hill Gail, 1952.
Bill Hartack: Iron Liege, 1957; Venetian Way, 1960; Decidedly, 1962; Northern Dancer, 1964; Majestic Prince, 1969.
4   Bill Shoemaker: Swaps, 1955; *Tomy Lee, 1959; Lucky Debonair, 1965; Ferdinand, 1986.
3   Isaac Murphy: Buchanan, 1884; Riley, 1890; Kingman, 1891.
Earl Sande: Zev, 1923; Flying Ebony, 1925; Gallant Fox, 1930.
Angel Cordero Jr.: Cannonade, 1974; Bold Forbes, 1976; Spend a Buck, 1985.
Gary Stevens: Winning Colors, 1988; Thunder Gulch, 1995; Silver Charm, 1997.

Jockeys With Most Derby Mounts

Jockey	Strs.	Wins	2nd	3rd	Unplaced
Bill Shoemaker	26	4	3	4	15
Eddie Arcaro	21	5	3	2	11
Laffit Pincay Jr.	21	1	4	2	14
Pat Day	21	1	4	2	14
Angel Cordero Jr.	17	3	1	0	13
Chris McCarron	18	2	3	0	13
Gary Stevens	17	3	2	1	11
Jerry Bailey	16	2	2	1	11
Jorge Velasquez	14	1	1	2	10
Mack Garner	14	1	0	1	12
Don Brumfield	13	1	0	1	11
Johnny Adams	13	0	2	0	11

African-American Jockeys in the Derby

African-American jockeys dominated the Kentucky Derby during the race's first quarter-century. Between 1875 and 1902, 11 African-American riders won 15 runnings of the Derby. The most famous were Isaac Murphy, the first jockey to win the Derby three times, and Jimmy Winkfield, who won the Derby in 1901 and '02.
Marlon St. Julien became the first African-American rider in the Derby in 79 years when he

finished seventh aboard Curule in the 2000 renewal.

African-American riders who have won the Derby:

Jockey	Year	Mount
Jimmy Winkfield	1902	Alan-a-Dale
	1901	His Eminence
Willie Simms	1898	Plaudit
	1896	Ben Brush
James "Soup" Perkins	1895	Halma
Alonzo "Lonnie" Clayton	1892	Azra
Oliver Lewis	1875	Aristides
Isaac Murphy	1891	Kingman
	1890	Riley
	1884	Buchanan
Isaac Lewis	1887	Montrose
Erskine Henderson	1885	Joe Cotton
Babe Hurd	1882	Apollo
George Garret Lewis	1880	Fonso
William Walker	1877	Baden-Baden

Female Jockeys in the Derby

Jockey	Mount	Year	Finish
Rosemary Homeister	Supah Blitz	2003	13th
Julie Krone	Suave Prospect	1995	11th
	Ecstatic Ride	1992	14th
Andrea Seefeldt	Forty Something	1991	16th
Patricia Cooksey	So Vague	1984	11th
Diane Crump	Fathom	1970	15th

Leading Sires of Derby Winners

3 **Virgil:** Vagrant, 1876; Hindoo, 1881; Ben Ali, 1886.
Falsetto: Chant, 1894; His Eminence, 1901; Sir Huon, 1906.
***Sir Gallahad III:** Gallant Fox, 1930; Gallahadion, 1940; Hoop, Jr., 1945.
Bull Lea: Citation, 1948; Hill Gail, 1952; Iron Liege, 1957.

2 **King Alfonso:** Fonso, 1880; Joe Cotton, 1885.
Longfellow: Leonatus, 1883; Riley, 1890.
Broomstick: Meridian, 1911; Regret, 1915.
***McGee:** Donerail, 1913; Exterminator, 1918.
The Finn: Zev, 1923; Flying Ebony, 1925.
Black Toney: Black Gold, 1924; Brokers Tip, 1933.
Man o' War: Clyde Van Dusen, 1929; War Admiral, 1937.
***St. Germans:** Twenty Grand, 1931; Bold Venture, 1936.
***Blenheim II:** Whirlaway, 1941; Jet Pilot, 1947.
Bold Venture: Assault, 1946; Middleground, 1950.
Bold Bidder: Cannonade, 1974; Spectacular Bid, 1979.
Exclusive Native: Affirmed, 1978; Genuine Risk, 1980.
Halo: Sunny's Halo, 1983; Sunday Silence, 1989.
Alydar: Alysheba, 1987; Strike the Gold, 1991.

Derby Winners Who Sired Winners

2 **Bold Venture (1936):** Assault, 1946; Middleground, 1950.

1 **Halma (1895):** Alan-a-Dale, 1902.
Bubbling Over (1926): Burgoo King (1932)
Reigh Count (1928): Count Fleet, 1943.
Gallant Fox (1930): Omaha, 1935.
Count Fleet (1943): Count Turf (1951)

1 **Pensive (1944):** Ponder, 1949.
Ponder (1949): Needles, 1956.
Determine (1954): Decidedly, 1962.
Swaps (1955): Chateaugay, 1963.
Seattle Slew (1977): Swale, 1984.
Unbridled (1990): Grindstone, 1996.

Fastest Derby Winning Times

1¼ miles

Year	Winner	Time	Cond.
1973	Secretariat	1:59⅖	Fast
2001	Monarchos	1:59.97	Fast
1964	Northern Dancer	2:00	Fast
1985	Spend a Buck	2:00⅕	Fast
1962	Decidedly	2:00⅖	Fast
1967	Proud Clarion	2:00⅗	Fast
1996	Grindstone	2:01.06	Fast
2000	Fusaichi Pegasus	2:01.12	Fast
2002	War Emblem	2:01.13	Fast
1978	Affirmed	2:01⅕	Fast
1965	Lucky Debonair	2:01⅕	Fast
1995	Thunder Gulch	2:01.27	Fast

1½ miles

Year	Winner	Time	Cond.
1889	Spokane	2:34½	Fast
1886	Ben Ali	2:36½	Fast
1879	Lord Murphy	2:37	Fast
1878	Day Star	2:37¼	Dusty
1885	Joe Cotton	2:37¼	Good

Times recorded in hundredths of a second beginning in 1991

Evolution of Derby Stakes Record at 1¼ miles

Year	Winner	Time
1896	Ben Brush	2:07¾
1900	Lieut. Gibson	2:06¼
1911	Meridian	2:05
1913	Donerail	2:04⅘
1914	Old Rosebud	2:03⅖
1931	Twenty Grand	2:01⅘
1941	Whirlaway	2:01⅖
1962	Decidedly	2:00⅖
1964	Northern Dancer	2:00
1973	Secretariat	1:59⅖

Slowest Derby Winning Times

1¼ miles

Year	Winner	Time	Cond.
1908	Stone Street	2:15⅕	Heavy
1907	Pink Star	2:12⅗	Heavy
1897	Typhoon II	2:12½	Heavy
1899	Manuel	2:12	Fast
1918	Exterminator	2:10⅘	Muddy
1929	Clyde Van Dusen	2:10⅘	Muddy
1905	Agile	2:10¾	Heavy
1928	Reigh Count	2:10⅖	Heavy
1919	Sir Barton	2:09⅘	Heavy
1912	Worth	2:09⅖	Muddy

1½ miles

Year	Winner	Time	Cond.
1891	Kingman	2:52¼	Slow
1890	Riley	2:45	Muddy
1883	Leonatus	2:43	Heavy
1892	Azra	2:41½	Heavy
1894	Chant	2:41	Fast

Fastest Derby Fractions

Quarter-mile: :21⅘, Top Avenger (1981)
Half-mile: :44.86, Songandaprayer (2001)
Six furlongs: 1:09.25, Songandaprayer (2001)
One mile: 1:34⅘, Spend a Buck (1985)

Longest Winning Odds

Year	Horse	Odds
1913	Donerail	91.45-to-1
1940	Gallahadion	35.20-to-1
1999	Charismatic	31.30-to-1
1967	Proud Clarion	30.10-to-1
1918	Exterminator	29.60-to-1
1953	Dark Star	24.90-to-1
1995	Thunder Gulch	24.50-to-1
1908	Stone Street	23.72-to-1
1982	Gato Del Sol	21.20-to-1
2002	War Emblem	20.50-to-1
1936	Bold Venture	20.50-to-1
1923	Zev	19.20-to-1
1986	Ferdinand	17.70-to-1

Shortest-Priced Derby Beaten Favorites

Year	Horse	Odds	Finish
1976	Honest Pleasure	.40-to-1	2nd
1940	Bimelech	.40-to-1	2nd
1953	Native Dancer	.70-to-1	2nd
1989	Easy Goer	.80-to-1	2nd
1949	Olympia	.80-to-1	6th
1936	Brevity	.80-to-1	2nd
1992	Arazi	.90-to-1	8th
1911	Governor Gray	1-to-1	2nd
1916	Thunderer	1.05-to-1	5th
1960	Tompion	1.10-to-1	4th
1962	Ridan	1.10-to-1	3rd
1946	Lord Boswell	1.10-to-1	4th
1921	Prudery	1.10-to-1	3rd

Shortest-Priced Winning Favorites

Year	Winner	Odds
1948	Citation	.40-to-1
1943	Count Fleet	.40-to-1
1977	Seattle Slew	.50-to-1
1979	Spectacular Bid	.60-to-1
1939	Johnstown	.60-to-1
1912	Worth	.80-to-1
1914	Old Rosebud	.85-to-1
1931	Twenty Grand	.88-to-1
1952	Hill Gail	1.10-to-1
1906	Sir Huon	1.10-to-1
1930	Gallant Fox	1.19-to-1

Largest Winning Margins

Year	Winner	Lengths
1946	Assault	8
1941	Whirlaway	8
1939	Johnstown	8
1914	Old Rosebud	8
1880	Fonso	7
1945	Hoop, Jr.	6
1894	Chant	6
1985	Spend a Buck	5¾
1970	Dust Commander	5
1932	Burgoo King	5
1926	Bubbling Over	5

Year	Winner	Lengths
1919	Sir Barton	5
1895	Halma	5

Smallest Winning Margins

Year	Winner	Lengths
1996	Grindstone	nose
1959	*Tomy Lee	nose
1957	Iron Liege	nose
1933	Brokers Tip	nose
1902	Alan-a-Dale	nose
1898	Plaudit	nose
1896	Ben Brush	nose
1892	Azra	nose
1889	Spokane	nose
1997	Silver Charm	head
1953	Dark Star	head
1947	Jet Pilot	head
1936	Bold Venture	head
1927	Whiskery	head
1921	Behave Yourself	head
1920	Paul Jones	head

Birthplace of Derby Winners

State	Winners
Kentucky	97
Florida	6
Virginia	4
California	3
Tennessee	3
New Jersey	2
Texas	2
Canada	2
Great Britain	2
Illinois	1
Kansas	1
Maryland	1
Missouri	1
Montana	1
New York	1
Ohio	1
Pennsylvania	1

Fillies in the Derby

In the long history of the Kentucky Derby, only three fillies have won the 1¼-mile classic: Regret in 1915, Genuine Risk in 1980, and Winning Colors in 1988.

Fillies to start in the Derby:

Year	Filly	Finish
1999	Excellent Meeting	5th
	Three Ring	19th
1995	Serena's Song	16th
1988	**Winning Colors**	1st
1984	Life's Magic	8th
	Althea	19th
1982	Cupecoy's Joy	10th
1980	**Genuine Risk**	1st
1959	Silver Spoon	5th
1945	Misweet	12th
1936	Gold Seeker	9th
1935	Nellie Flag	4th
1934	Mata Hari	4th
	Bazaar	9th
1932	Oscillation	13th
1930	Alcibiades	10th
1929	Ben Machree	18th
1922	Startle	8th
1921	Prudery	3rd

Year	Filly	Finish
	Careful	5th
1920	Cleopatra	15th
1919	Regalo	9th
1918	Viva America	3rd
1915	**Regret**	1st
1914	Bronzewing	3rd
	Watermelon	7th
1913	Gowell	3rd
1912	Flamma	3rd
1911	Round the World	6th
1906	Lady Navarre	2nd
1883	Pike's Pride	6th
1879	Ada Glenn	7th
	Wissahickon	9th
1877	Early Light	8th
1876	Lizzie Stone	6th
	Marie Michon	7th
1875	Ascension	10th
	Gold Mine	15th

Maiden Winners of the Derby

Year	Winner
Brokers Tip	1933
Sir Barton	1919
Buchanan	1884

Maiden Starters Since 1950

Only three maidens have won the Kentucky Derby—Buchanan (1884), Sir Barton (1919), and Brokers Tip (1933)—but maidens in the Derby were a common occurrence until the mid-1930s. Since 1950, only seven maidens have run in the Derby, and none have come close to winning. The connections of several runners, most notably Great Redeemer in 1979, were harshly criticized for running.

Year	Horse	Finish
1998	Nationalore	9th
1990	Pendleton Ridge	13
1979	Great Redeemer	10th
1971	Fourulla	19th
1959	The Chosen One	14
1958	Flamingo	13th
1950	On the Mark	8th

Gelding Winners of the Derby

With Funny Cide's victory in the 2003 Derby, the losing streak for geldings ended after 74 years, dating to Clyde Van Dusen in 1929. In the 1990s, three geldings finished second: Best Pal (1991), Prairie Bayou ('93), and Cavonnier ('96). The winning geldings:

Year	Gelding
2003	Funny Cide
1929	Clyde Van Dusen
1920	Paul Jones
1918	Exterminator
1914	Old Rosebud
1888	Macbeth II
1882	Apollo
1876	Vagrant

Geldings in the Derby

In all, 106 geldings have started in the Derby since 1908. Before then, records of starters were incomplete. The geldings that have started in the Kentucky Derby since 1980:

Year	Gelding	Finish
2003	**Funny Cide**	1st
	Buddy Gil	6th
2002	Perfect Drift	3rd
2002	Easy Grades	13th
2001	Balto Star	14th
1999	General Challenge	11th
1998	Hanuman Highway (Ire)	7th
1997	Celtic Warrior	10th
1996	Cavonnier	2nd
	Alyrob	8th
	Zarb's Magic	13th
1993	Prairie Bayou	2nd
	Truth of It All	10th
1991	Best Pal	2nd
1989	Wind Splitter	11th
	Clever Trevor	13th
1988	Kingpost	14th
1986	Bachelor Beau	14th
1984	Raja's Shark	14th
1983	My Mac	14th
1982	Real Dare	19th
1981	Television Studio	5th
	Beau Rit	13th
1980	Rockhill Native	5th
	Execution's Reason	11th

Front-Running Derby Winners

The following Kentucky Derby winners were on the lead at all points of call.

Year	Winner	Winning margin
2002	War Emblem	4
1988	Winning Colors	neck
1985	Spend a Buck	5¼
1976	Bold Forbes	1
1972	Riva Ridge	3¼
1966	Kauai King	½
1955	Swaps	1½
1953	Dark Star	head
1947	Jet Pilot	head
1945	Hoop, Jr.	6
1943	Count Fleet	3
1939	Johnstown	8
1937	War Admiral	1¾
1929	Clyde Van Dusen	2
1926	Bubbling Over	5
1923	Zev	1½
1922	Morvich	1½
1920	Paul Jones	head
1919	Sir Barton	5
1915	Regret	2
1914	Old Rosebud	8
1912	Worth	neck
1911	Meridian	3/4
1910	Donau	1/2
1909	Wintergreen	4
1905	Agile	3
1902	Alan-a-Dale	nose
1901	His Eminence	1½
1900	Lieut. Gibson	3
1897	Typhoon II	neck
1895	Halma	5
1894	Chant	6
1893	Lookout	4
1887	Montrose	2
1883	Leonatus	3

Year	Winner	Winning margin
1881	Hindoo	4
1880	Fonso	1
1878	Day Star	1
1875	Aristides	2

Winning Derby Post Positions
Winning Derby post positions since 1900:

Post	Winners	Post	Winners
1	12	11	3
2	9	12	3
3	8	13	3
4	10	14	2
5	11	15	3
6	6	16	3
7	7	17	0
8	8	18	1
9	4	19	0
10	9	20	1

Undefeated Starters
Seattle Slew, the 1977 Triple Crown winner, was only the fourth undefeated horse to win the Derby. The other three were Regret in 1915, Morvich in '22, and Majestic Prince in '69.

The undefeated Derby starters since Regret in 1915:

Year	Horse	Pre-Derby starts	Derby finish
2000	China Visit	2	6th
	Trippi	4	11th
1998	Indian Charlie	4	3rd
1990	Mister Frisky	16	8th
1988	Private Terms	7	9th
1982	Air Forbes Won	4	7th
1978	Sensitive Prince	6	6th
1977	**Seattle Slew**	6	**1st**
1969	**Majestic Prince**	7	**1st**
1963	Candy Spots	6	3rd
	No Robbery	5	5th
1953	Native Dancer	11	2nd
1948	Coaltown	4	2nd
1940	Bimelech	8	2nd
1922	**Morvich**	11	**1st**
1916	Thunderer	3	5th
1915	**Regret**	3	**1st**

Derby Winners Sold at Public Auction and Privately

Derby	Winner	Year	Sale	Price
2003	Funny Cide	2001	FT Sara	$22,000
		2002	Private	$75,000
2002	War Emblem	2000	Kee Sept	$20,000
		2002	Private	900,000
2001	Monarchos	1999	FT Sara	90,000 (RNA)
		2000	FT Calder	170,000
2000	Fusaichi Pegasus	1998	Kee July	4,000,000
1999	Charismatic	1996	Private	200,000
1998	Real Quiet	1996	Kee Sept	17,000
1997	Silver Charm	1995	OBSC Aug	16,500
		1996	OBSC April	100,000
1995	Thunder Gulch	1993	Kee July	40,000
		1994	Kee April	120,000 (RNA)
1994	Go for Gin	1991	FT Ky	32,000
		1992	FT Sara	150,000
1992	Lil E. Tee	1991	OBSC April	25,000
1990	Unbridled	1987	Tartan Dis	90,000
1989	Sunday Silence	1987	Kee July	17,000 (RNA)
		1988	CTS March	32,000

Derby	Winner	Year	Sale	Price
1988	Winning Colors	1986	Kee July	575,000
1987	Alysheba	1985	Kee July	500,000
1985	Spend a Buck	1983	Private	12,500
1980	Genuine Risk	1978	FT Ky	32,000
1979	Spectacular Bid	1977	Kee Sept.	37,000
1977	Seattle Slew	1975	FT Ky	17,500
1976	Bold Forbes	1974	FT Ky	15,200
1975	Foolish Pleasure	1973	FT Sara	20,000
1971	Canonero II	1969	Kee Sept	1,200
1970	Dust Commander	1968	Kee Sept	6,500
1969	Majestic Prince	1967	Kee July	250,000
1966	Kauai King	1968	FT Sara	42,000
1960	Venetian Way	1958	Kee July	10,500
1959	*Tomy Lee	1956	Tatt Dec	6,762
1954	Determine	1952	Kee July	12,500
1953	Dark Star	1951	Kee July	6,500
1951	Count Turf	1949	FT Sara	3,700
1947	Jet Pilot	1945	Kee July	41,000
1945	Hoop, Jr.	1943	Kee July	10,200
1940	Gallahadion	1938	FT Sara	5,000
1934	Cavalcade	1932	FT Sara	1,200

FT Fasig-Tipton
CTS California Thoroughbred Sale
RNA Reserve Not Attained

Derby Winners Who Did Not Start at Two
A juvenile campaign of some sort is virtually a prerequisite for winning the Kentucky Derby. Only one horse, Apollo, has won the Derby without racing as a two-year-old, and he accomplished that feat in 1882, in the eighth running.

In recent years, only three horses have won the Derby after making only one start as a two-year-old. Tim Tam, trained by H. A. "Jimmy" Jones, won in 1958 after finishing unplaced in his only start at two. Also unplaced in his only juvenile start was Lucky Debonair, who won the 1965 Derby. Fusaichi Pegasus finished second in his only start as a two-year-old and won the Derby as the 2.30-to-1 favorite in 2000.

Derby Weather, Track Condition, and Temperature Since 1940

Year	Winner	Weather	Track condition	Temp
2003	Funny Cide	Partly cloudy	Fast	67
2002	War Emblem	Clear	Fast	71
2001	Monarchos	Clear	Fast	83
2000	Fusaichi Pegasus	Clear	Fast	82
1999	Charismatic	Clear	Fast	72
1998	Real Quiet	Clear	Fast	70
1997	Silver Charm	Overcast	Fast	51
1996	Grindstone	Thunderstorm	Fast	75
1995	Thunder Gulch	Partly cloudy	Fast	72
1994	Go for Gin	Thunderstorm	Sloppy	57
1993	Sea Hero	Overcast	Fast	69
1992	Lil E. Tee	Overcast	Fast	78
1991	Strike the Gold	Overcast	Fast	80
1990	Unbridled	Mostly cloudy	Good	63
1989	Sunday Silence	Overcast	Muddy	51
1988	Winning Colors	Clear	Fast	72
1987	Alysheba	Mostly cloudy	Fast	79
1986	Ferdinand	Partly cloudy	Fast	63
1985	Spend a Buck	Partly cloudy	Fast	72
1984	Swale	Overcast	Fast	71
1983	Sunny's Halo	Thunderstorm	Fast	81
1982	Gato Del Sol	Partly cloudy	Fast	75
1981	Pleasant Colony	Clear	Fast	55

Year	Winner	Weather	Track condition	Temp
1980	Genuine Risk	Clear	Fast	72
1979	Spectacular Bid	Clear	Fast	55
1978	Affirmed	Clear	Fast	67
1977	Seattle Slew	Partly cloudy	Fast	69
1976	Bold Forbes	Overcast	Fast	62
1975	Foolish Pleasure	Overcast	Fast	63
1974	Cannonade	Partly cloudy	Fast	68
1973	Secretariat	Partly cloudy	Fast	69
1972	Riva Ridge	Partly cloudy	Fast	75
1971	Canonero II	Partly cloudy	Fast	73
1970	Dust Commander	Partly cloudy	Good	64
1969	Majestic Prince	Partly cloudy	Fast	87
1968	Forward Pass	Partly cloudy	Fast	71
1967	Proud Clarion	Overcast	Fast	61
1966	Kauai King	Partly cloudy	Fast	67
1965	Lucky Debonair	Clear	Fast	84
1964	Northern Dancer	Overcast	Fast	76
1963	Chateaugay	Partly cloudy	Fast	80
1962	Decidedly	Partly cloudy	Fast	81
1961	Carry Back	Overcast	Good	81
1960	Venetian Way	Partly cloudy	Good	64
1959	*Tomy Lee	Partly cloudy	Fast	94
1958	Tim Tam	Partly cloudy	Muddy	86
1957	Iron Liege	Overcast	Fast	47
1956	Needles	Clear	Fast	82
1955	Swaps	Overcast	Fast	85
1954	Determine	Overcast	Fast	84
1953	Dark Star	Clear	Fast	76
1952	Hill Gail	Clear	Fast	79
1951	Count Turf	Partly cloudy	Fast	67
1950	Middleground	Overcast	Fast	70
1949	Ponder	Partly cloudy	Fast	57
1948	Citation	Overcast	Sloppy	72

Year	Winner	Weather	Track condition	Temp
1947	Jet Pilot	Overcast	Fast	57
1946	Assault	Overcast	Slow	68
1945	Hoop, Jr.	Partly cloudy	Muddy	77
1944	Pensive	Partly cloudy	Good	54
1943	Count Fleet	Clear	Fast	54
1942	Shut Out	Partly cloudy	Fast	87
1941	Whirlaway	Partly cloudy	Fast	76
1940	Gallahadion	Clear	Fast	62

Derby Trivia

Largest field: 23 in 1974.

Smallest field: Three in 1892 and 1905.

Longest-priced runner since 1908: A Dragon Killer, seventh in 1958 at 294.40-to-1.

Most maidens in one race: Six in 1882 (Highflyer, seventh; Pat Malloy colt, ninth; Wallensee, tenth; Newsboy, 11th; Mistral, 12th; Robert Bruce, 14th).

Most lifetime starts going into Derby: 66, Florizar, 1900 (second).

Fewest lifetime starts going into Derby: Zero, 11 times, most recently by Col. Hogan, 1911 (seventh).

Mutuel field horses who won the Derby: Canonero II, 1971; Count Turf, 1951; Flying Ebony, 1925.

Derby winners who never started again: Grindstone, 1996; Bubbling Over, 1926.

Derby winner as both jockey and trainer: Johnny Longden, rider of Count Fleet in 1943 and trainer of Majestic Prince in 1969.

Longest-priced Derby favorite: Harlan's Holiday, 6-to-1, in 2002.

Status of Kentucky Derby Winners Since 1970

Year	Winner	Birthdate	Status	Where Stands/Stood	Location	Death Date
2003	Funny Cide	4/20/00	In training			
2002	War Emblem	2/20/99	Stallion	Shadai Stallion Station	Hokkaido, Japan	
2001	Monarchos	2/9/98	Stallion	Claiborne Farm	Paris, KY	
2000	Fusaichi Pegasus	4/12/97	Stallion	Ashford Stud	Versailles, KY	
1999	Charismatic	3/13/96	Stallion	JBBA Shizunai Stallion Station	Hokkaido, Japan	
1998	Real Quiet	3/7/95	Stallion	Taylor Made Farm	Nicholasville, KY	
1997	Silver Charm	2/22/94	Stallion	Three Chimneys Farm	Midway, KY	
1996	Grindstone	1/23/93	Stallion	Overbrook Farm	Lexington, KY	
1995	Thunder Gulch	5/23/92	Stallion	Ashford Stud	Versailles, KY	
1994	Go for Gin	4/18/91	Stallion	Claiborne Farm	Paris, KY	
1993	Sea Hero	3/4/90	Stallion	Karacabey Pension Stud	Izmit, Turkey	
1992	Lil E. Tee	3/29/89	Stallion	Old Frankfort Stud	Lexington, KY	
1991	Strike the Gold	3/21/88	Stallion	Karacabey Pension Stud	Izmit, Turkey	
1990	Unbridled	3/5/87	Deceased	Claiborne Farm	Paris, KY	10/18/01
1989	Sunday Silence	3/25/86	Deceased	Shadai Stallion Station	Hokkaido, Japan	8/19/02
1988	Winning Colors	3/14/85	Broodmare	Gainesway	Lexington, KY	
1987	Alysheba	3/3/84	Stallion	Janadriyah Stud Farm	Aljanadriya, Saudi Arabia	
1986	Ferdinand	3/12/83	Stallion	Arrow Stud	Hokkaido, Japan	
1985	Spend a Buck	5/15/82	Deceased	Haras Bage do Sul	Sao Paulo, Brazil	11/24/02
1984	Swale	4/21/81	Deceased			6/17/84
1983	Sunny's Halo	2/11/80	Deceased	Double S Thoroughbred Farm	Tyler, TX	6/2/03
1982	Gato Del Sol	2/23/79	Pensioned	Gestut Goerlsdorf	Gorlsdorf, Germany	
1981	Pleasant Colony	5/4/78	Deceased	Lane's End	Versailles, KY	12/31/02
1980	Genuine Risk	2/15/77	Pensioned	Newstead Farm	Upperville, VA	
1979	Spectacular Bid	2/17/76	Deceased	Milfer Farm	Unadilla, NY	6/9/03
1978	Affirmed	2/21/75	Deceased	Jonabell Farm	Lexington, KY	1/12/01
1977	Seattle Slew	2/15/74	Deceased	Three Chimneys Farm	Midway, KY	5/7/02
1976	Bold Forbes	3/31/73	Deceased	Stone Farm	Paris, KY	8/9/00
1975	Foolish Pleasure	3/23/72	Deceased	Horseshoe Ranch	Dayton, Wyoming	11/17/94
1974	Cannonade	5/12/71	Deceased	Gainesway	Lexington, KY	8/3/93
1973	Secretariat	3/30/70	Deceased	Claiborne Farm	Paris, KY	10/4/89
1972	Riva Ridge	4/13/69	Deceased	Claiborne Farm	Paris, KY	4/21/85
1971	Canonero II	4/24/68	Deceased	Gainesway	Lexington, KY	11/11/81
1970	Dust Commander	2/8/67	Deceased	Springland Farm	Paris, KY	10/7/91

Starts of Kentucky Derby Winners at Two and Three

Year	Winner	Starts At 2	Starts Before Derby at 3	Total Pre-Derby Starts	Total Starts At 3	Total Starts at 2-3	Derby Prep	Finish
2003	Funny Cide	3	3	6			Wood Memorial S. (G1)	2
2002	War Emblem	3	4	7	10	13	Illinois Derby (G2)	1
2001	Monarchos	2	2	4	7	9	Wood Memorial S. (G2)	2
2000	Fusaichi Pegasus	1	5	5	8	9	Wood Memorial S. (G2)	1
1999	Charismatic	7	7	14	10	17	Lexington S. (G2)	1
1998	Real Quiet	9	3	12	6	15	Santa Anita Derby (G1)	2
1997	Silver Charm	3	3	6	7	10	Santa Anita Derby (G1)	2
1996	Grindstone	2	3	5	4	6	Arkansas Derby (G2)	2
1995	Thunder Gulch	6	3	9	10	16	Blue Grass S. (G2)	4
1994	Go for Gin	5	4	9	11	16	Wood Memorial S. (G1)	2
1993	Sea Hero	7	3	10	9	16	Blue Grass S. (G2)	4
1992	Lil E. Tee	4	4	8	6	10	Arkansas Derby (G2)	2
1991	Strike the Gold	3	4	7	12	15	Blue Grass S. (G2)	1
1990	Unbridled	6	4	10	11	17	Blue Grass S. (G2)	3
1989	Sunday Silence	3	3	6	9	12	Santa Anita Derby (G1)	1
1988	Winning Colors	2	4	6	10	12	Santa Anita Derby (G1)	1
1987	Alysheba	7	3	10	10	17	Blue Grass S. (G1)	1, pl 3
1986	Ferdinand	5	4	9	8	13	Santa Anita Derby (G1)	3
1985	Spend a Buck	8	3	3	7	15	Garden State S.	1
1984	Swale	7	4	11	7	14	Lexington S.	2
1983	Sunny's Halo	11	2	13	9	20	Arkansas Derby (G1)	1
1982	Gato Del Sol	8	4	12	9	17	Blue Grass S. (G1)	2
1981	Pleasant Colony	5	8	8	9	14	Wood Memorial S. (G1)	1
1980	Genuine Risk	4	3	7	8	12	Wood Memorial S. (G1)	3
1979	Spectacular Bid	9	5	14	12	21	Blue Grass S. (G1)	1
1978	Affirmed	9	4	13	11	20	Hollywood Derby (G1)	1
1977	Seattle Slew	3	3	6	7	10	Wood Memorial S. (G1)	1
1976	Bold Forbes	8	5	13	10	18	Wood Memorial S. (G1)	1
1975	Foolish Pleasure	7	4	11	11	18	Wood Memorial S. (G1)	1
1974	Cannonade	17	4	21	8	25	Churchill allowance	1
1973	Secretariat	9	3	12	12	21	Wood Memorial S. (G1)	3
1972	Riva Ridge	9	3	12	12	21	Blue Grass S.	1
1971	Canonero II	4	8	12	11	15	Series 4A-5A H.	3
1970	Dust Commander	14	8	22	23	37	Blue Grass S.	1
1969	Majestic Prince	2	5	7	8	10	Churchill allowance	1
1968	Forward Pass	10	7	17	13	23	Blue Grass S.	1
1967	Proud Clarion	3	5	8	13	16	Blue Grass S.	2
1966	Kauai King	4	8	12	12	16	Governor's Gold Cup	1
1965	Lucky Debonair	1	8	9	10	11	Blue Grass S.	1
1964	Northern Dancer	9	5	14	9	18	Blue Grass S.	1
1963	Chateaugay	5	3	8	12	17	Blue Grass S.	1
1962	Decidedly	8	4	12	12	20	Blue Grass S.	2
1961	Carry Back	21	7	28	16	37	Wood Memorial S.	1
1960	Venetian Way	9	5	14	11	20	Churchill allowance	2
1959	*Tomy Lee	8	4	12	7	15	Blue Grass S.	1
1958	Tim Tam	1	10	11	13	14	Derby Trial S.	1
1957	Iron Liege	8	9	17	17	25	Derby Trial S.	5
1956	Needles	10	3	13	8	18	Florida Derby	1
1955	Swaps	6	3	9	9	15	Churchill allowance	1
1954	Determine	14	8	22	15	29	Derby Trial S.	1
1953	Dark Star	6	5	11	7	13	Derby Trial S.	2
1952	Hill Gail	7	7	14	8	15	Derby Trial S.	1
1951	Count Turf	10	10	20	14	24	Wood Memorial S.	5
1950	Middleground	5	4	9	10	15	Derby Trial S.	2
1949	Ponder	4	8	12	21	25	Derby Trial S.	2
1948	Citation	9	7	16	20	29	Derby Trial S.	1
1947	Jet Pilot	12	2	14	5	17	Jamaica H.	1
1946	Assault	9	3	12	15	24	Derby Trial S.	1
1945	"Hoop, Jr."	5	2	7	4	9	Cedar Manor Purse	2
1944	Pensive	5	7	12	17	22	Chesapeake S.	2
1943	Count Fleet	15	2	17	6	21	Wood Memorial S.	1
1942	Shut Out	9	2	11	12	21	Blue Grass S.	1
1941	Whirlaway	16	7	23	20	36	Derby Trial S.	2
1940	Gallahadion	5	9	14	17	22	Derby Trial S.	2
1939	Johnstown	12	3	15	9	21	Wood Memorial S.	1
1938	Lawrin	15	8	23	11	26	Derby Trial S.	2
1937	War Admiral	6	2	8	8	14	Chesapeake S.	1
1936	Bold Venture	8	1	9	3	11	South Shore Purse	1

Year	Winner	Starts At 2	Starts Before Derby at 3	Total Pre-Derby Starts	Total Starts At 3	Total Starts at 2-3	Derby Prep	Finish
1935	Omaha	9	2	11	9	18	Wood Memorial S.	3
1934	Cavalcade	11	2	13	7	18	Chesapeake S.	1
1933	Brokers Tip	4	1	5	5	9	Lexington allowance	2
1932	Burgoo King	12	1	13	4	16	Lexington allowance	2
1931	Twenty Grand	8	2	10	10	18	Preakness S.	2
1930	Gallant Fox	7	2	9	10	17	Preakness S.	1

Kentucky Derby

Grade 1, Churchill Downs, three-year-olds, 1¼ miles, dirt. Held on May 3, 2003, with gross value of $1,100,200. First run in 1875. Weights: colts and geldings, 126 pounds; fillies, 121 pounds.

Year	Winner	Jockey	Second	Third	Strs	Time	Track	1st purse
2003	**‡Funny Cide**	J. Santos	Empire Maker	Peace Rules	16	2:01.19	ft	$800,200
2002	**War Emblem**	V. Espinoza	Proud Citizen	Perfect Drift	18	2:01.13	ft	**1,875,000**
2001	**Monarchos**	J. Chavez	Invisible Ink	Congaree	17	1:59.97	ft	812,000
2000	**Fusaichi Pegasus**	K. Desormeaux	Aptitude	Impeachment	19	2:01.12	ft	888,400
1999	**Charismatic**	C. Antley	Menifee	Cat Thief	19	2:03.29	ft	886,200
1998	**Real Quiet**	K. Desormeaux	Victory Gallop	Indian Charlie	15	2:02.38	ft	738,800
1997	**Silver Charm**	G. Stevens	Captain Bodgit	Free House	13	2:02.44	ft	700,000
1996	**Grindstone**	J. Bailey	‡Cavonnier	Prince of Thieves	19	2:01.06	ft	869,800
1995	**Thunder Gulch**	G. Stevens	Tejano Run	Timber Country	19	2:01.27	ft	707,400
1994	**Go for Gin**	C. McCarron	Strodes Creek	Blumin Affair	14	2:03.72	sy	628,800
1993	**Sea Hero**	J. Bailey	‡Prairie Bayou	Wild Gale	19	2:02.42	ft	735,900
1992	**Lil E. Tee**	P. Day	Casual Lies	Dance Floor	18	2:03.04	ft	724,800
1991	**Strike the Gold**	C. Antley	‡Best Pal	Mane Minister	16	2:03.08	ft	655,800
1990	**Unbridled**	C. Perret	Summer Squall	Pleasant Tap	15	2:02	gd	581,000
1989	**Sunday Silence**	P. Valenzuela	Easy Goer	Awe Inspiring	15	2:05	my	574,200
1988	**†Winning Colors**	G. Stevens	Forty Niner	Risen Star	17	2:02⅕	ft	611,200
1987	**Alysheba**	C. McCarron	Bet Twice	Avies Copy	17	2:03⅖	ft	618,600
1986	**Ferdinand**	W. Shoemaker	Bold Arrangement (GB)	Broad Brush	16	2:02⅘	ft	609,400
1985	**Spend a Buck**	A. Cordero Jr.	Stephan's Odyssey	Chief's Crown	13	2:00⅕	ft	406,800
1984	**Swale**	L. Pincay Jr.	Coax Me Chad	At the Threshold	20	2:02⅖	ft	537,400
1983	**Sunny's Halo**	E. Delahoussaye	Desert Wine	Caveat	20	2:02⅕	ft	426,000
1982	**Gato Del Sol**	E. Delahoussaye	Laser Light	Reinvested	19	2:02⅖	ft	428,850
1981	**Pleasant Colony**	J. Velasquez	Woodchopper	Partez	21	2:02	ft	317,200
1980	**†Genuine Risk**	J. Vasquez	Rumbo	Jaklin Klugman	13	2:02	ft	250,550
1979	**Spectacular Bid**	R. Franklin	General Assembly	Golden Act	10	2:02⅖	ft	228,650
1978	**AFFIRMED**	S. Cauthen	Alydar	Believe It	11	2:01⅕	ft	186,900
1977	**SEATTLE SLEW**	J. Cruguet	Run Dusty Run	Sanhedrin	15	2:02⅕	ft	214,700
1976	**Bold Forbes**	A. Cordero Jr.	Honest Pleasure	Elocutionist	9	2:01⅗	ft	165,200
1975	**Foolish Pleasure**	J. Vasquez	Avatar	Diabolo	15	2:02	ft	209,600
1974	**Cannonade**	A. Cordero Jr.	Hudson County	Agitate	**23**	2:04	ft	274,000
1973	**SECRETARIAT**	R. Turcotte	Sham	Our Native	13	**1:59⅖**	ft	155,050
1972	**Riva Ridge**	R. Turcotte	No Le Hace	Hold Your Peace	16	2:01⅘	ft	140,300
1971	**Canonero II**	G. Avila	Jim French	Bold Reason	20	2:03⅕	ft	145,500
1970	**Dust Commander**	M. Manganello	My Dad George	High Echelon	17	2:03⅖	gd	127,800
1969	**Majestic Prince**	W. Hartack	Arts and Letters	Dike	8	2:01⅘	ft	113,200
1968	**Forward Pass**	I. Valenzuela	Francie's Hat	T. V. Commercial	14	2:02⅕	ft	122,600
1967	**Proud Clarion**	R. Ussery	Barbs Delight	Damascus	14	2:00⅗	ft	119,700
1966	**Kauai King**	D. Brumfield	Advocator	Blue Skyer	15	2:02	ft	120,500
1965	**Lucky Debonair**	W. Shoemaker	Dapper Dan	Tom Rolfe	11	2:01⅕	ft	112,000
1964	**Northern Dancer**	W. Hartack	Hill Rise	The Scoundrel	12	2:00	ft	114,300
1963	**Chateaugay**	B. Baeza	Never Bend	Candy Spots	9	2:01⅘	ft	108,900
1962	**Decidedly**	W. Hartack	Roman Line	Ridan	15	2:00⅖	ft	119,650
1961	**Carry Back**	J. Sellers	Crozier	Bass Clef	15	2:04	gd	120,500
1960	**Venetian Way**	W. Hartack	Bally Ache	Victoria Park	13	2:02⅖	gd	114,850
1959	***Tomy Lee**	W. Shoemaker	Sword Dancer	First Landing	17	2:02⅕	ft	119,650
1958	**Tim Tam**	I. Valenzuela	Lincoln Road	Noureddin	14	2:05	my	116,400
1957	**Iron Liege**	W. Hartack	*Gallant Man	Round Table	9	2:02⅕	ft	107,950
1956	**Needles**	D. Erb	Fabius	Come On Red	17	2:03⅖	ft	123,450
1955	**Swaps**	W. Shoemaker	Nashua	Summer Tan	10	2:01⅘	ft	108,400
1954	**Determine**	R. York	Hasty Road	Hasseyampa	17	2:03	ft	102,050
1953	**Dark Star**	H. Moreno	Native Dancer	Invigorator	11	2:02	ft	90,050
1952	**Hill Gail**	E. Arcaro	Sub Fleet	Blue Man	16	2:01⅗	ft	96,300
1951	**Count Turf**	C. McCreary	Royal Mustang	‡Ruhe	20	2:02⅗	ft	98,050
1950	**Middleground**	W. Boland	Hill Prince	Mr. Trouble	14	2:01⅗	ft	92,650
1949	**Ponder**	S. Brooks	Capot	Palestinian	14	2:04⅕	ft	91,600
1948	**CITATION**	E. Arcaro	Coaltown	My Request	6	2:05⅖	sy	83,400
1947	**Jet Pilot**	E. Guerin	Phalanx	Faultless	13	2:06⅘	sl	92,160
1946	**ASSAULT**	W. Mehrtens	Spy Song	Hampden	17	2:06⅗	sl	96,400
1945	**Hoop, Jr.**	E. Arcaro	Pot o'Luck	‡Darby Dieppe	16	2:07	my	64,850

Year	Winner	Jockey	Second	Third	Strs	Time	Track	1st purse
1944	**Pensive**	C. McCreary	Broadcloth	‡Stir Up	16	2:04⅕	gd	64,675
1943	**COUNT FLEET**	J. Longden	Blue Swords	Slide Rule	10	2:04	ft	60,725
1942	**Shut Out**	W. Wright	Alsab	Valdina Orphan	15	2:04⅖	ft	64,225
1941	**WHIRLAWAY**	E. Arcaro	Staretor	Market Wise	11	2:01⅖	ft	61,275
1940	**Gallahadion**	C. Bierman	Bimelech	‡Dit	8	2:05	ft	60,150
1939	**Johnstown**	J. Stout	Challedon	Heather Broom	8	2:03⅖	ft	46,350
1938	**Lawrin**	E. Arcaro	Dauber	Can't Wait	10	2:04⅘	ft	47,050
1937	**WAR ADMIRAL**	C. Kurtsinger	Pompoon	Reaping Reward	20	2:03⅕	ft	52,050
1936	**Bold Venture**	I. Hanford	Brevity	Indian Broom	14	2:03⅗	ft	37,725
1935	**OMAHA**	W. Saunders	Roman Soldier	Whiskolo	18	2:05	gd	39,525
1934	**Cavalcade**	M. Garner	Discovery	Agrarian	13	2:04	ft	28,175
1933	**Brokers Tip**	D. Meade	Head Play	Charley O.	13	2:06⅘	gd	48,925
1932	**Burgoo King**	E. James	Economic	Stepenfetchit	20	2:05⅕	ft	52,350
1931	**Twenty Grand**	C. Kurtsinger	Sweep All	Mate	12	2:01⅘	ft	48,725
1930	**GALLANT FOX**	E. Sande	Gallant Knight	Ned O.	15	2:07⅗	gd	50,725
1929	**‡Clyde Van Dusen**	L. McAtee	Naishapur	Panchio	21	2:10⅘	my	53,950
1928	**Reigh Count**	C. Lang	Misstep	Toro	22	2:10⅖	hy	55,375
1927	**Whiskery**	L. McAtee	‡Osmand	Jock	15	2:06	sl	51,000
1926	**Bubbling Over**	A. Johnson	Bagenbaggage	Rock Man	13	2:03⅘	ft	50,075
1925	**Flying Ebony**	E. Sande	Captain Hal	Son of John	20	2:07⅗	sy	52,950
1924	**Black Gold**	J. Mooney	Chilhowee	Beau Butler	19	2:05⅕	ft	52,775
1923	**Zev**	E. Sande	Martingale	Vigil	21	2:05⅖	ft	53,600
1922	**Morvich**	A. Johnson	Bet Mosie	John Finn	10	2:04⅗	ft	53,775
1921	**Behave Yourself**	C. Thompson	Black Servant	†Prudery	12	2:04⅕	ft	38,450
1920	**‡Paul Jones**	T. Rice	Upset	On Watch	17	2:09	sl	30,375
1919	**SIR BARTON**	J. Loftus	‡Billy Kelly	*Under Fire	12	2:09⅘	hy	20,825
1918	**‡Exterminator**	W. Knapp	Escoba	†Viva America	8	2:10⅘	my	14,700
1917	***Omar Khayyam**	C. Borel	Ticket	Midway	15	2:04⅗	ft	16,600
1916	**George Smith**	J. Loftus	Star Hawk	Franklin	9	2:04	ft	9,750
1915	**†Regret**	J. Notter	Pebbles	‡Sharpshooter	16	2:05⅖	ft	11,450
1914	**‡Old Rosebud**	J. McCabe	‡Hodge	†Bronzewing	7	2:03⅖	ft	9,125
1913	**Donerail**	R. Goose	Ten Point	†Gowell	8	2:04⅘	ft	5,475
1912	**Worth**	C. Schilling	Duval	†Flamma	7	2:09⅖	my	4,850
1911	**Meridian**	G. Archibald	‡Governor Gray	Colston	7	2:05	ft	4,850
1910	**Donau**	F. Herbert	Joe Morris	Fighting Bob	7	2:06⅖	ft	4,850
1909	**Wintergreen**	V. Powers	‡Miami	Dr. Barkley	10	2:08⅕	sl	4,850
1908	**Stone Street**	A. Pickens	‡Sir Cleges	Dunvegan	8	2:15⅕	hy	4,850
1907	**Pink Star**	A. Minder	Zal	Ovelando	6	2:12⅗	hy	4,850
1906	**Sir Huon**	R. Troxler	†Lady Navarre	James Reddick	6	2:08⅘	ft	4,850
1905	**Agile**	J. Martin	Ram's Horn	Layson	3	2:10¾	hy	4,850
1904	**Elwood**	F. Prior	Ed Tierney	Brancas	5	2:08½	ft	4,850
1903	**Judge Himes**	H. Booker	Early	Bourbon	6	2:09	ft	4,850
1902	**Alan-a-Dale**	J. Winkfield	Inventor	The Rival	4	2:08¾	ft	4,850
1901	**His Eminence**	J. Winkfield	Sannazarro	Driscoll	5	2:07¾	ft	4,850
1900	**Lieut. Gibson**	J. Boland	Florizar	Thrive	7	2:06¼	ft	4,850
1899	**Manuel**	F. Taral	‡Corsine	Mazo	5	2:12	ft	4,850
1898	**Plaudit**	W. Simms	Lieber Karl	Isabey	4	2:09	gd	4,850
1897	**Typhoon II**	F. Garner	Ornament	Dr. Catlett	6	2:12½	hy	4,850
1896	**Ben Brush**	W. Simms	Ben Eder	Semper Ego	8	2:07¾	dy	4,850
1895	**Halma**	J. Perkins	Basso	Laureate	4	2:37½	ft	2,970
1894	**Chant**	F. Goodale	Pearl Song	Sigurd	5	2:41	ft	4,020
1893	**Lookout**	E. Kunze	Plutus	Boundless	6	2:39¼	ft	3,840
1892	**Azra**	A. Clayton	Huron	Phil Dwyer	3	2:41½	hy	4,230
1891	**Kingman**	I. Murphy	Balgowan	High Tariff	4	2:52¼	sl	4,550
1890	**Riley**	I. Murphy	Bill Letcher	Robespierre	6	2:45	my	5,460
1889	**Spokane**	T. Kiley	‡Proctor Knott	Once Again	8	2:34½	ft	4,880
1888	**‡Macbeth II**	G. Covington	Gallifet	White	7	2:38¼	ft	4,740
1887	**Montrose**	I. Lewis	Jim Gore	‡Jacobin	7	2:39¼	ft	4,200
1886	**Ben Ali**	P. Duffy	Blue Wing	Free Knight	10	2:36½	ft	4,890
1885	**Joe Cotton**	E. Henderson	Bersan	‡Ten Booker	10	2:37¼	gd	4,630
1884	**Buchanan**	I. Murphy	Loftin	Audrain	9	2:40¼	gd	3,990
1883	**Leonatus**	W. Donohue	‡Drake Carter	Lord Raglan	7	2:43	hy	3,760
1882	**‡Apollo**	B. Hurd	Runnymede	Bengal	14	2:40¼	gd	4,560
1881	**Hindoo**	J. McLaughlin	‡Lelex	Alfambra	6	2:40	ft	4,410
1880	**Fonso**	G. Lewis	Kimball	‡Bancroft	5	2:37½	dy	3,800
1879	**Lord Murphy**	C. Shauer	Falsetto	Strathmore	9	2:37	ft	3,550
1878	**Day Star**	J. Carter	Himyar	Leveller	9	2:37¼	dy	4,050
1877	**Baden-Baden**	W. Walker	Leonard	King William	11	2:38	ft	3,300
1876	**‡Vagrant**	B. Swim	Creedmore	Harry Hill	11	2:38¼	ft	2,950
1875	**Aristides**	O. Lewis	Volcano	Verdigris	15	2:37¾	ft	2,850

†—filly, ‡—gelding, *—imported horse

1875-'95: 1½ miles; 1973-present: Grade 1; 1968: Dancer's Image finished first but was disqualified from purse money; bold indicates records set in number of starters, time, and winning purse; War Emblem's record winning purse includes a $1-million bonus awarded by Sportman's Park for winning the Illinois Derby (G2) and a Triple Crown race. Triple Crown winners are in all capitalized letters.

History of the Preakness Stakes

Born out of a party boast and named for a horse who met an unfortunate end, the Preakness Stakes (G1) is the second jewel of the American Triple Crown and the second-oldest American classic.

Both the Preakness Stakes and Pimlico Race Course, the track where the classic race is staged annually on the third Saturday of May, trace their roots to a party hosted by Milton H. Sanford in Saratoga Springs, New York, in 1868. At the party, Maryland Governor Oden Bowie promised that a new racetrack would open in Baltimore to play host to the Dinner Party Stakes, to which he pledged a hefty purse.

A 70-acre track site, which had been known as Pimlico since the 1850s and had been used for racing since then, was purchased by the Maryland Agricultural Society from Robert Wylie in 1866. The organization held a fair meet at the site in 1869 but failed to raise enough money to complete the track.

Bowie, a horse owner and sportsman, helped another group, the Maryland Jockey Club, to negotiate a lease of the property—$1,000 annual rent for ten years. Gen. John Elliott designed the track, and Pimlico opened on October 25, 1870. Among the amenities was the Pimlico Clubhouse, a Baltimore landmark until it was destroyed by fire in 1966.

Sanford, a New York horseman who made a portion of his fortune by selling blankets to the army in the Civil War, sent his three-year-old colt Preakness to make his only start of that year in the new Dinner Party Stakes. Bred in Kentucky by A. J. Alexander, Sanford bought the Kentucky-bred colt by Lexington out of Bay Leaf, by *Yorkshire, as a yearling for $2,000. He named the colt after his farms in New Jersey and Kentucky, which also bore the name Preakness. The name is derived from the language of the Minisi Indians in northern New Jersey; in their language, "pra-qua-les" meant "quail woods."

Under English jockey Billy Hayward, Preakness won the first Dinner Party Stakes, which today is known as the Dixie Stakes (G2) and is run on grass. Three years later, in 1873, the Maryland Jockey Club staged its first spring meeting and honored the winner of the first Dinner Party Stakes by naming the 1½-mile race for three-year-olds the Preakness Stakes.

Second race on a three-race program on Tuesday, May 23, 1873, the first Preakness Stakes attracted a field of seven to compete for the $2,050 total purse. A crowd estimated at 12,000 made Bowie's Catesby the favorite, but John Chamberlin's Survivor won by ten lengths,

Preakness Attendance					
Year	On-track	Total	Year	On-track	Total
2003	100,268	109,931	1985		81,235
2002	101,138	117,055	1984		80,566
2001	104,454	118,926	1983		71,768
2000	98,304	111,821	1982		80,724
1999	100,311	116,526	1981		84,133
1998	91,122	103,269	1980		83,455
1997	88,594	102,118	1979		72,607
1996	85,122	97,751	1978		81,261
1995	87,707	100,818	1977		77,346
1994	86,343	99,834	1976		62,256
1993	85,495	97,641	1975		75,216
1992	85,294	96,865	1974		54,911
1991	87,245	96,695	1973		61,657
1990	86,531	96,106	1972		48,721
1989	90,145	98,896	1971		47,221
1988	81,282	88,654	1970		42,474
1987		87,945			
1986		87,652			

Attendance figures from 1988 include combined intertrack sites (Laurel, Rosecroft, Delmarva Downs) and exclude Maryland off-track betting sites.

which remains the race's largest winning margin.

Preakness, the horse for whom the race was named, continued to race until age eight, winning the 1875 Baltimore Cup and finishing in a dead heat with Springbok in that year's Saratoga Cup. Sold to England for stud, Preakness became difficult to handle in his later years and was shot to death by his owner, the Duke of Hamilton.

Pimlico staged the first 17 runnings of the Preakness, but the Maryland Jockey Club encountered financial difficulties in 1889 and the race was run the following year at Morris Park in New York. It was not run in 1891, '92, and '93—thus, though two years older than the Kentucky Derby, the Preakness has had one fewer running—and reappeared in 1894 at Gravesend Race Course in Brooklyn, where it would be renewed for 15 years.

Pimlico regained its financial health early in the new century, but the Preakness did not return to Baltimore until May 12, 1909, when Effendi set the pace and won by one length over Fashion Plate while running a mile in 1:39⅖. Unlike the Belmont Stakes, which was not run in 1911 and '12 because of New York antigambling legislation, the Preakness was run with betting through those years.

The race proved so popular that in 1918 the Preakness—then at 1⅛ miles—was run in two divisions, the only American classic race to be split. On May 14 of the following year, J. K. L. Ross's Sir Barton won the Preakness only four days after scoring his maiden victory in the Kentucky Derby. On June 11, 1919, the *Star

Shoot colt defeated two opponents in the Belmont Stakes to become the first Triple Crown winner. The feat was noted after the fact when *Daily Racing Form* columnist Charles Hatton popularized the designation for the three races beginning in 1930.

The Preakness's reputation was sealed in 1920 when the great Man o' War opened his three-year-old season with a 1½-length victory over Upset, the only horse ever to defeat him. The Preakness remained at 1⅛ miles until 1925, when it was changed to its present 1³⁄₁₆ miles.

In 1930, the Preakness was the first race of Gallant Fox's Triple Crown, but after '31 the race took its place as second in the series. In 1945, after victory in Europe led to the lifting of a voluntary ban on racing, the Preakness was run one week after the Derby and one week before the Belmont.

Pimlico was the scene of three memorable Triple Crown efforts in the 1970s: Secretariat's sweeping move to the lead on the clubhouse turn in 1973, Seattle Slew's brilliance in '77, and the stretch-long battle of Affirmed and Alydar in '78.

The race has had its share of controversy as well. In 1962, Greek Money won by a nose over Ridan, whose rider, Manuel Ycaza, claimed foul. A head-on photo, however, disclosed that Ycaza was in fact using his hands and elbows to restrain Greek Money. In 1980, Kentucky Derby winner Genuine Risk was herded wide at the top of the stretch by winner Codex, ridden by Angel Cordero Jr. An objection by Genuine Risk's jockey, Jacinto Vasquez, was disallowed, and Bertram Firestone, the filly's co-owner, forced a long Maryland Racing Commission hearing into the result. The original order of finish was upheld.

The Preakness in the 1980s and '90s was notable for two close finishes: Sunday Silence's 1989 nose victory over Easy Goer and the '97 race, in which Silver Charm won by a head over Free House, with third-place finisher Captain Bodgit another head farther back.

In 2002 and '03, the Derby winners scored victories in the Preakness. War Emblem won the black-eyed Susan garland in 2002, and Funny Cide romped by 9¾ lengths, the second-largest margin ever, in '03. Funny Cide was only the seventh gelding to win the Preakness. The 2003 Preakness was the first run under the management of Magna Entertainment Inc., which bought a 51% interest in the Maryland Jockey Club in 2002.—*Don Clippinger*

Woodlawn Vase

The Woodlawn Vase, said to be the most valuable trophy in sports, is presented annually to the owner of the Preakness Stakes winner. The trophy, 34 inches tall and weighing almost 30 pounds, was created in 1860 by Tiffany and Co. for the Woodlawn Racing Association in Louisville.

After being buried during the Civil War to prevent it from being melted down, the trophy was unearthed and remained in Louisville until 1878, when the Dwyer brothers won it. They presented it to the Coney Island Jockey Club, and it was subsequently presented at two other New York tracks, Jerome Park and Morris Park.

Thomas C. Clyde won the trophy in 1904 and gave it to the Maryland Jockey Club, of which he was a director, in 1917. That year, E. R. Bradley's Kalitan was the first horse to win the Woodlawn Vase at Pimlico.

A Preakness Tradition

A Preakness Stakes tradition observed each year is the painting of the winner's silks on a weather vane atop the Preakness presentation stand. The practice dates to 1909, when lightning destroyed a weather vane atop the Members' Clubhouse, which dated to 1870. The track's directors commissioned a new weather vane depicting a horse and rider, and the weather vane was adorned with the colors of Effendi that year.

The clubhouse structure, an ornate Victorian building that contained dining rooms, sleeping rooms, and a library, burned to the ground in

Added Value of the Preakness

The purse value of the Preakness Stakes (G1) has increased from $1,000 in 1873 to $1-million guaranteed, with the winner currently collecting a check for $650,000. The increase is significant; $1,000 in 1873 would equal only $14,210 today, which is the purse level of a good-quality claiming race.

The Preakness purse has been decreased on occasion, including once during the Great Depression (1933) and in consecutive years, 1949 and 1950. Following is the progression of the Preakness purse:

Year	Added Value	Year	Added Value
1873	$1,000	1933	25,000
1890	1,500	1937	50,000
1894	1,000	1946	100,000
1895	2,000	1949	75,000
1899	1,000	1950	50,000
1902	1,500	1951	75,000
1904	2,000	1953	100,000
1907	2,500	1959	150,000
1909	2,000	1979	200,000
1912	1,500	1983	250,000
1917	5,000	1985	350,000
1918	15,000**	1989	500,000
1919	25,000	1998	1,000,000*
1921	40,000	* guaranteed purse	
1922	50,000	** each division	

Supplemental Nominations to the Preakness

When Triple Crown Productions launched a common nomination in 1986, no supplemental entries were permitted. The rules were changed in 1991 to allow supplemental entries, although no horse owner has yet to put up $100,000 to gain a place in the Preakness Stakes (G1) starting gate.

Supplemental entries to the Preakness were first permitted in 1938, and the first supplemental entrant to win was Citation, who won the 1948 Triple Crown. Calumet Farm owner Warren Wright supplemented both Citation and Coaltown for $3,000 each, but only Citation started. Hill Prince (1950) and Master Derby (1975) were supplemental winners.

Here are the supplemented Preakness starters since 1959:

Year	Horse	Supplement	Finish	Purse winnings
1985	Tajawa	$20,000	6th	$ 0
	Sport Jet	20,000	10th	0
	Hajji's Treasure	20,000	11th	0
1984	Fight Over	15,000	3rd	30,000
1982	Reinvested	10,000	6th	0
1981	Paristo	10,000	3rd	20,000
1980	Lucky Pluck	10,000	8th	0
1975	**Master Derby**	10,000	1st	158,100
	Native Guest	10,000	7th	0
1974	Super Florin	10,000	10th	0
1970	Dust Commander	10,000	9th	0
1968	Nodouble	10,000	3rd*	15,000
1967	Barb's Delight	10,000	6th	0
1959	Manassah Mauler	10,000	8th	0

* moved up from fourth via disqualification

June 1966. Since then, winner's colors have been painted on a weather vane atop an infield replica of the old clubhouse's cupola.

Black-Eyed Susans in the Spring

The black-eyed Susan, Maryland's state flower since 1918, blooms each summer and fall in Maryland and other states, but not in the spring. Thus, the black-eyed Susans that adorn the Preakness Stakes (G1) winner's garland are not black-eyed Susans. Actually, they are Viking daisies in disguise.

The ersatz black-eyed Susans were first draped across Bimelech's withers after the 1940 Preakness. Today, the garland is 18" wide and 90" long, and assembling it requires two days. First, greenery is attached to a spongy rubber base, and then more than 80 bunches of daisies are secured to the base. Heavy felt is then attached to the back to protect the horse. After that, black lacquer is daubed on the center of the daisies to simulate black-eyed Susans.

"Maryland, My Maryland"

While the roots of "My Old Kentucky Home" most likely were opposition to slavery, "Maryland, My Maryland" was originally a nine-stanza poem written in support of the Confederacy.

The author was James Ryder Randall, who wrote it in April 1861 to protest Union troops marching through Baltimore. A Maryland native, Randall was then teaching in Louisiana.

His poem was set to the tune of "Lauriger Horatius" ("O, Tannenbaum"), and the song achieved wide popularity in Maryland and throughout the South before becoming the official state song in 1939.

The two stanzas that are sung:

The despot's heel is on thy shore,
*   Maryland!*
His torch is at thy temple door,
*   Maryland!*
Avenge the patriotic gore
That flecked the streets of Baltimore,
And be the battle queen of yore,
*   Maryland! My Maryland!*

Thou wilt not cower in the dust,
*   Maryland!*
Thy beaming sword shall never rust,
*   Maryland!*
Remember Carroll's sacred trust,
Remember Howard's warlike thrust,
And all thy slumberers with the just,
*   Maryland! My Maryland!*

Origins of the Alibi Breakfast

The Alibi Breakfast, a Preakness-week tradition, is a direct descendant of the informal gatherings on the porch of the historic Old Clubhouse in the 1930s, when trainers, journalists, racing officials, and others would gather during training hours to watch the horses and swap stories.

David Woods, Pimlico Race Course's publicity director in the 1940s, formalized the get-togethers in the Preakness event at which owners and trainers could explain why they believed their horses would win, or take the opportunity to propose an alibi or two in case they did not win.

The track's principal awards—the Old Hilltop

Award, Special Award of Merit, and the David F. Woods Memorial Award—are presented during the breakfast, now held a day before the Preakness.

Preakness Trivia

• Derby winners in recent years were not necessarily favored in the Preakness. Since 1986, the following Derby winners did not go off as the Preakness favorites: Ferdinand, 1986, second; Sunday Silence, 1989, won; Lil E. Tee, 1992, fifth; Sea Hero, 1993, fifth; Silver Charm, 1997, won; Real Quiet, 1998, won; Charismatic, 1999, won.

• Two individuals have won the Preakness both as jockeys and trainers. Louis Schaefer rode Dr. Freeland to victory in 1929 and one decade later trained Challedon to a Preakness win. Johnny Longden rode Count Fleet in 1943 and trained Majestic Prince in '69.

• A starting gate was first used for the Preakness in 1930.

• The Preakness has been run at seven different distances since 1873. The race was as short as one mile in 1909 and '10, as long as 1¾ miles in 1889, and 1³⁄₁₆ miles since 1925.

• Two African-American jockeys have won the Preakness: George B. "Spider" Anderson aboard Buddhist in 1889 and Willie Simms on Sly Fox in '98. The only black jockey to ride in the Preakness in modern times was Wayne Barnett, who finished eighth aboard Sparrowvon in 1985.

• The Preakness preceded the Kentucky Derby on the racing calendar 11 times between 1888 and 1931.

• In 1890, the Preakness and the Belmont Stakes were run on the same card at Morris Park.

• From 1910 through '16, the Preakness was run as a handicap. From 1895 through 1907, the race was under allowance conditions, limiting it to horses that had not won a race worth a certain amount.

• The Preakness was run in divisions in 1918, when *War Cloud and Jack Hare, Jr. won.

Leading Preakness Owners by Wins

7 **Calumet Farm:** Whirlaway, 1941; Pensive, 1944; Faultless, 1947; Citation, 1948; Fabius, 1956; Tim Tam, 1958; Forward Pass, 1968.

5 **George L. Lorillard:** Duke of Magenta, 1878; Harold, 1879; Grenada, 1880; Saunterer, 1881; Vanguard, 1882.

4 **Harry Payne Whitney:** Royal Tourist, 1908; Broomspun, 1921; Bostonian, 1927; Victorian, 1928.

3 **Belair Stud:** Gallant Fox, 1930; Omaha, 1935; Nashua, 1955.

   E. R. Bradley: Kalitan, 1917; Burgoo King, 1932; Bimelech, 1940.

   Robert and Beverly Lewis: Timber Country (co-owners), 1995; Silver Charm, 1997; Charismatic, 1999.

3 **Walter J. Salmon:** Vigil, 1923; Display, 1926; Dr. Freeland, 1929.

2 **August Belmont II:** Don Enrique, 1907; Watervale, 1911.

   Brookmeade Stable: High Quest, 1934; Bold, 1951.

   J. F. Chamberlin: Survivor, 1873; Tom Ochiltree, 1875.

   Glen Riddle Farm: Man o' War, 1920; War Admiral, 1937.

   Loblolly Stable: Pine Bluff, 1992; Prairie Bayou, 1993.

   Overbrook Farm: Tabasco Cat (co-owner), 1994; Timber Country (co-owner), 1995.

   Preakness Stable: Montague, 1890; Belmar, 1895.

   J. K. L. Ross: Damrosch, 1916; Sir Barton, 1919.

   The Thoroughbred Corp.: Point Given, 2001; War Emblem 2002.

Owners with Most Starters

Owner	Starters	Wins
Greentree Stable	20	1
Harry Payne Whitney	15	4
Calumet Farm	14	7
August Belmont II	11	2
George L. Lorillard	11	5
Overbrook Farm	11	2
Brookmeade Stable	9	2
King Ranch	8	1
Pierre Lorillard	8	1
Wheatley Stable	7	1
Rancocas Stable	6	0
Mrs. Ethel D. Jacobs	6	1

Leading Preakness Breeders by Wins

7 **Calumet Farm :** Whirlaway, 1941; Pensive, 1944; Faultless, 1947; Citation, 1948; Fabius, 1956; Tim Tam, 1958; Forward Pass, 1968.

6 **Harry Payne Whitney:** Royal Tourist, 1908; Buskin, 1913; Holiday, 1914; Broomspun, 1921; Bostonian, 1927; Victorian, 1928.

   August Belmont II: Jacobus, 1883; Margrave, 1896; Don Enrique, 1907; Watervale, 1911; Damrosch, 1916; Man o' War, 1920.

4 **A. J. Alexander:** Tom Ochiltree, 1875; Shirley, 1876; Duke of Magenta, 1878; Grenada, 1880.

3 **Belair Stud:** Gallant Fox, 1930; Omaha, 1935; Nashua, 1955.

   James Ben Ali Haggin: Old England, 1902; Cairngorm, 1905; Rhine Maiden, 1915.

2 **William S. Farish:** Summer Squall (co-breeder), 1990; Charismatic (co-breeder), 1999.

   Idle Hour Stock Farm: Burgoo King (co-breeder), 1932; Bimelech, 1940.

   Loblolly Stable: Pine Bluff, 1992; Prairie Bayou, 1993.

   Raceland Stud: Whimsical, 1906; Colonel Holloway, 1912.

   Walter J. Salmon: Display, 1926; Dr. Freeland, 1929.

   R. W. Walden: Vanguard, 1882; Refund, 1882.

   Aristides Welch: Harold, 1879; Saunterer, 1881.

Preakness Wagering, 1980-2003

Year	Preakness Winner	Preakness In-state handle	Preakness Simulcasting	Preakness Total handle
2003	Funny Cide	$3,151,864	$38,008,281	$41,620,145
2002	War Emblem	3,440,321	44,254,871	47,695,192
2001	Point Given	3,342,237	37,352,557	40,694,884
2000	Red Bullet	2,482,262	26,550,064	29,032,326
1999	Charismatic	3,056,891	26,438,761	34,435,703
1998	Real Quiet	2,103,027	17,624,933	23,640,365
1997	Silver Charm	2,667,000	18,087,214	26,602,245
1996	Louis Quatorze	2,352,900	20,545,618	22,898,518
1995	Timber Country	2,519,388	20,869,915	23,389,303
1994	Tabasco Cat	2,548,282	21,461,540	24,009,822
1993	Prairie Bayou	2,269,946	19,293,287	21,563,233
1992	Pine Bluff	2,365,023	19,338,393	21,703,416
1991	Hansel	2,504,693	18,289,622	20,794,315
1990	Summer Squall	2,257,916	16,625,833	18,883,749
1989	Sunday Silence	2,519,893	17,306,821	19,826,714
1988	Risen Star	2,392,384	18,519,289	20,911,673
1987	Alysheba	1,846,768		
1986	Snow Chief	1,680,923		
1985	Tank's Prospect	1,461,997		
1884	Gate Dancer	1,358,444		
1983	Deputed Testamony	1,251,931		
1982	Aloma's Ruler	1,257,244		
1981	Pleasant Colony	1,387,797		
1980	Codex	1,215,664		

Leading Preakness Trainers by Wins

7 Robert W. Walden: Tom Ochiltree, 1875; Duke of Magenta, 1878; Harold, 1879; Grenada, 1880; Saunterer, 1881; Vanguard, 1882; Refund, 1888.

5 Thomas J. Healey: The Parader, 1901; Pillory, 1922; Vigil, 1923; Display, 1926; Dr. Freeland, 1929.

D. Wayne Lukas: Codex, 1980; Tank's Prospect, 1985; Tabasco Cat, 1994; Timber Country, 1995; Charismatic, 1999.

4 Bob Baffert: Silver Charm, 1997; Real Quiet, 1998; Point Given, 2001; War Emblem, 2002.

James E. "Sunny Jim" Fitzsimmons: Gallant Fox, 1930; Omaha, 1935; Nashua, 1955; Bold Ruler, 1957.

H. A. "Jimmy" Jones: Faultless, 1947; Citation, 1948; Fabius, 1956; Tim Tam, 1958.

3 James Whalen: Don Enrique, 1907; Watervale, 1911; Buskin, 1913.

2 Thomas Bohannan: Pine Bluff, 1992; Prairie Bayou, 1993.

Edward Feakes: Montague, 1890; Belmar, 1895.

Henry Forrest: Kauai King, 1966; Forward Pass, 1968.

T. P. Hayes: Paul Kauvar, 1897; Head Play, 1933.
J. S. Healey: Layminster, 1910; Holiday, 1914.
Max Hirsch: Bold Venture, 1936; Assault, 1946.
William Hurley: Kalitan, 1917; Bimelech, 1940.
B. A. "Ben" Jones: Whirlaway, 1941; Pensive, 1944.

Andrew W. Joyner: Cairngorm, 1905; Royal Tourist, 1908.

2 Jack Van Berg: Gate Dancer, 1984; Alysheba, 1987.

Frank Y. Whiteley Jr.: Tom Rolfe, 1965; Damascus, 1967.

Trainers with Most Starters

Trainer	Starters	Wins
D. Wayne Lukas	30	5
Max Hirsch	19	2
James E. Fitzsimmons	18	4
James Rowe Sr.	14	1
Nicholas Zito	12	1
Bob Baffert	9	4
Woody Stephens	9	1
Preston Burch	8	1
John P. Campo	8	1

Female Trainers in the Preakness

Here are the female trainers with Preakness starters:

Year	Horse	Trainer	Finish
2003	New York Hero	Jennifer Pedersen	6th
	Kissin Saint	Lisa Lewis	10th
2002	Magic Weisner	Nancy H. Alberts	2nd
2001	Griffinite	Jennifer Leigh-Peterson	5th
1998	Silver's Prospect	Jean Rolfe	10th
1996	In Contention	Cynthia Reese	6th
1993	Hegar	Penny Lewis	9th
1992	Casual Lies	Shelley Riley	3rd
	Speakerphone	Dean Gaudet	14th
1990	Fighting Notion	Nancy Heil	5th
1980	Samoyed	Judith Zouck	6th
1968	Sir Beau	Judy Johnson	7th

Leading Preakness Jockeys by Wins

Eddie Arcaro, known as "The Master," held sway over the Preakness Stakes in his storied career, winning the race six times in 15 starts. His closest challenger is Pat Day, who has won the race three consecutive times, 1994-'96, and has five victories with 15 Preakness starters.

The leading Preakness jockeys with two or more victories:

6   Eddie Arcaro: Whirlaway, 1941; Citation, 1948; Hill Prince, 1950; Bold, 1951; Nashua, 1955; Bold Ruler, 1957.

5   Pat Day: Tank's Prospect, 1985; Summer Squall, 1990; Tabasco Cat, 1994; Timber Country, 1995; Louis Quatorze, 1996.

3   George Barbee: Survivor, 1873; Shirley, 1876; Jacobus, 1883.
William Hartack: Fabius, 1956; Northern Dancer, 1964; Majestic Prince, 1969.
L. Hughes: Tom Ochiltree, 1875; Harold, 1879; Grenada, 1880.

2   Jerry Bailey: Hansel, 1991; Red Bullet, 2000.
Angel Cordero Jr.: Codex, 1980; Gate Dancer, 1984.
Costello: Saunterer, 1881; Vanguard, 1882.
Fisher: Knight of Ellersie, 1884; The Bard, 1886.
C. Holloway: Cloverbrook, 1877; Duke of Magenta, 1878.
Clarence Kummer: Man o' War, 1920; Coventry, 1925.
Charles Kurtsinger: Head Play, 1933; War Admiral, 1937.
John Loftus: War Cloud, 1918; Sir Barton, 1919.
Chris McCarron: Alysheba, 1987; Pine Bluff, 1992.
Conn McCreary: Pensive, 1944; Blue Man, 1952.
Bill Shoemaker: Candy Spots, 1963; Damascus, 1967.
Gary Stevens: Silver Charm, 1997; Point Given, 2001.
Fred Taral: Assignee, 1894; Belmar, 1895.
Ismael Valenzuela: Tim Tam, 1958; Forward Pass, 1968.

Most Preakness Mounts

Jockey	Starts	Wins
Pat Day	17	5
Eddie Arcaro	15	6
Angel Cordero Jr.	13	2
Chris McCarron	13	2
Gary Stevens	14	2
Bill Shoemaker	12	2
Jerry Bailey	13	2
William Hartack	11	3
Jorge Velasquez	11	1
Braulio Baeza	10	0
Linus McAtee	10	1

Female Jockeys in the Preakness

Only two female jockeys have ridden in the Preakness, and the best finish was by Patricia Cooksey, who was sixth aboard Tajawa in 1985. Andrea Seefeldt, a Maryland-based rider, finished seventh in 1994 aboard Looming.

Jockey	Year	Horse	Finish
Andrea Seefeldt	1994	Looming	7th
Patricia Cooksey	1985	Tajawa	6th

Leading Preakness Sires by Wins

3   Lexington: Tom Ochiltree, 1875; Shirley, 1876; Duck of Magenta, 1878.
Broomstick: Holiday, 1914; Broomspun, 1921; Bostonian, 1927.

2   *Leamington: Harold, 1879; Saunterer, 1881.
***Watercress:** Watervale, 1911; Rhine Maiden, 1915.
Fair Play: Man o' War, 1920; Display, 1926.
***Sir Gallahad III:** Gallant Fox, 1930; High Quest, 1934.
Bull Lea: Faultless, 1947; Citation, 1948.
***Nasrullah:** Nashua, 1955; Bold Ruler, 1957.
Sovereign Dancer: Gate Dancer, 1984; Louis Quatorze, 1996.
Woodman: Hansel, 1991; Timber Country, 1995.

Preakness in the Pedigree

Preakness winners who have sired other Preakness winners:

Man o' War (1920): War Admiral (1937)
Gallant Fox (1930): Omaha (1935)
Bold Venture (1936): Assault (1946).
Polynesian (1945): Native Dancer (1953)
Citation (1948): Fabius (1956)
Native Dancer (1953): Kauai King (1966)
Bold Ruler (1957): Secretariat (1973)
Secretariat (1973): Risen Star (1988)
Summer Squall (1990): Charismatic (1999)

Fastest Preakness Fractions

First quarter-mile: :22⅖ Flag Raiser (1965), Fight Over (1984), Eternal Prince (1985), Vicar (1999).
First half-mile: :45, Bold Forbes (1976).
First six furlongs: 1:09, Bold Forbes (1976).
Fastest first mile: 1:34⅕, Chief's Crown (1985), Sunday Silence (1989).
Fastest final three-sixteenths: :18, Summer Squall, 1990.

Evolution of Preakness Stakes Record

Year	Winner	Time
1925	Coventry	1:59
1934	High Quest	1:58⅕
1942	Alsab	1:57
1949	Capot	1:56
1955	Nashua	1:54⅗
1971	Canonero II	1:54
1984	Gate Dancer	1:53⅗
1985	Tank's Prospect	1:53⅗
1996	Louis Quatorze	1:53⅗ (1:53.43)

Fastest Runnings of the Preakness

Tank's Prospect and Louis Quatorze share the record for the fastest running of the

Preakness Stakes, 1:53⅖. Louis Quatorze, the 1996 winner, was timed in 1:53.43, but Tank's Prospect in 1985 was timed in one-fifths of a second, the standard at that time.

Unofficially, Secretariat ran the Preakness's $1\frac{3}{16}$ miles in the same time. He was caught in 1:53⅖ by *Daily Racing Form* clockers who were hand-timing the race. A malfunctioning official timer recorded a time of 1:55, but that was subsequently adjusted to 1:54⅖.

Year	Winner	Time	Cond.
1996	Louis Quatorze	1:53.43	Fast
1985	Tank's Prospect	1:53⅖	Fast
1984	Gate Dancer	1:53⅗	Fast
1990	Summer Squall	1:53⅘	Fast
1971	Canonero II	1:54	Fast
1979	Spectacular Bid	1:54⅕	Fast
1995	Timber Country	1:54.45	Fast
1980	Codex	1:54⅕	Fast
1973	Secretariat	1:54⅖*	Fast
1977	Seattle Slew	1:54⅖	Fast
1978	Affirmed	1:54⅖	Fast

* Hand-timed in 1:53⅖

Slowest Preakness Times

Citation, a Triple Crown winner and regarded as one of the greatest Thoroughbreds of the 20th century, ran the slowest Preakness Stakes ever, 2:02⅖. But the *Daily Racing Form* chart characterized the track as heavy, which would have been considerably slower than today's speed-tuned racing surfaces.

Following are the slowest Preakness runnings since 1925, when the race's distance became $1\frac{3}{16}$ miles.

Year	Winner	Time	Cond.
1948	Citation	2:02⅖	Heavy
1933	Head Play	2:02	Slow
1927	Bostonian	2:01⅗	Good
1929	Dr. Freeland	2:01⅗	Fast
1946	Assault	2:01⅖	Fast
1930	Gallant Fox	2:00⅗	Fast
1928	Victorian	2:00⅕	Fast
1932	Burgoo King	1:59⅘	Fast
1938	Dauber	1:59⅘	Sloppy
1939	Challedon	1:59⅘	Muddy
1926	Display	1:59⅘	Fast
1950	Hill Prince	1:59⅕	Slow
1944	Pensive	1:59⅕	Fast

Largest Winning Margins

Year	Winner	Lengths
1873	Survivor	10
2003	Funny Cide	9¾
1943	Count Fleet	8
1889	Buddhist	8
1991	Hansel	7
1974	Little Current	7
1951	Bold	7
1938	Dauber	7
1968	Forward Pass	6
1935	Omaha	6
1878	Duke of Magenta	6
1979	Spectacular Bid	5½
1948	Citation	5½
1941	Whirlaway	5½
1950	Hill Prince	5
1912	Colonel Holloway	5

Smallest Winning Margins

Year	Winner	Margin
1989	Sunday Silence	nose
1962	Greek Money	nose
1936	Bold Venture	nose
1934	High Quest	nose
1928	Victorian	nose
1902	Old England	nose
1997	Silver Charm	head
1985	Tank's Prospect	head
1969	Majestic Prince	head
1949	Capot	head
1937	War Admiral	head
1932	Burgoo King	head
1926	Display	head
1922	Pillory	head
1905	Cairngorm	head
1900	Hindus	head

Preakness Odds-On Beaten Favorites

The shortest-priced beaten favorites in the Preakness Stakes were Riva Ridge in 1972 and Fusaichi Pegasus in 2000. Both entered the Preakness off Derby victories and both went off at 3-to-10. Riva Ridge fell to Bee Bee Bee on a sloppy track, and Fusaichi Pegasus finished second to Red Bullet.

Here are the odds-on beaten favorites in the Preakness:

Year	Horse	Odds	Finish
2000	Fusaichi Pegasus	.30-to-1	2nd
1972	Riva Ridge	.30-to-1	4th
1939	Gilded Knight- Johnstown entry	.45-to-1	2nd 5th
1982	Linkage	.50-to-1	2nd
1989	Easy Goer	.60-to-1	2nd
1956	Needles	.60-to-1	2nd
1984	Swale	.80-to-1	7th
1964	Hill Rise	.80-to-1	3rd
1976	Honest Pleasure	.90-to-1	5th
1954	Correlation	.90-to-1	2nd

Winning Preakness Favorites Since 1979

Year	Winner	Odds
2003	Funny Cide	1.90-to-1
2002	War Emblem	2.80-to-1
2001	Point Given	2.30-to-1
1994	Timber Country	1.90-to-1
1993	Prairie Bayou	2.20-to-1
1992	Pine Bluff	7-to-2
1987	Alysheba	2-to-1
1981	Pleasant Colony	3-to-2

Shortest-Priced Preakness Winners

Year	Winner	Odds
1979	Spectacular Bid	.10-to-1
1948	Citation	.10-to-1
1943	Count Fleet	.15-to-1
1953	Native Dancer	.20-to-1
1973	Secretariat	.30-to-1
1955	Nashua	.30-to-1
1937	War Admiral	.35-to-1
1977	Seattle Slew	.40-to-1
1934	High Quest	.45-to-1
1978	Affirmed	.50-to-1

Longest-Priced Preakness Winners

Year	Winner	Odds
1975	Master Derby	23.40-to-1
1925	Coventry	21.80-to-1
1926	Display	19.35-to-1
1972	Bee Bee Bee	18.70-to-1
1983	Deputed Testamony	14.50-to-1
1974	Little Current	13.10-to-1
1924	Nellie Morse	12.10-to-1
1945	Polynesian	12-to-1
1922	Pillory	11.15-to-1
1962	Greek Money	10.90-to-1
1976	Elocutionist	10.10-to-1

Preakness Front-Running Winners

The following Preakness winners were on the lead at all points of call, beginning at a quarter-mile (approaching the clubhouse turn). Regarded as speed horses, neither Seattle Slew nor Affirmed led the opening quarter-mile in the Preakness.

Year	Winner	Winning margin
1996	Louis Quatorze	3¼
1982	Aloma's Ruler	½
1972	Bee Bee Bee	1½
1960	Bally Ache	4
1957	Bold Ruler	2
1954	Hasty Road	neck
1951	Bold	7
1948	Citation	5½
1945	Polynesian	2½
1943	Count Fleet	8
1940	Bimelech	3
1937	War Admiral	head
1934	High Quest	nose
1933	Head Play	4
1920	Man o' War	1½
1919	Sir Barton	4
1918	Jack Hare Jr.	2
1915	Rhine Maiden	1½
1914	Holiday	¾
1911	Watervale	1
1909	Effendi	1
1902	Old England	nose
1899	Half Time	1
1896	Margrave	1
1889	Buddhist	8
1882	Vanguard	neck

Winning Preakness Post Positions

Since 1909, Preakness Stakes winners have come out of the sixth post position 14 times. Only two Preakness winners, Display in 1926 and Point Given in 2001, have come out of the 11th starting position.

Twelve winners have come out of the fourth hole, and 11 each have broken from the second, third, and seventh slots.

Here are the winning post positions since 1909:

Post	Winners	Post	Winners
1	9	7	11
2	11	8	9
3	11	9	3
4	12	10	2
5	10	11	2
6	14	12	2

Preakness Wins by Geldings

Year	Winner
2003	Funny Cide
1993	Prairie Bayou
1914	Holiday
1913	Buskin
1910	Layminster
1907	Don Enrique
1876	Shirley

Geldings were barred from 1920-'34.

Fillies in the Preakness

Since Genuine Risk finished second behind Codex in the controversial 1980 Preakness Stakes (G1), only two other fillies have run in the race. Winning Colors finished a valiant third behind Risen Star after Forty Niner pressed her early, and Excellent Meeting did not finish in the 1999 Preakness.

Four fillies have won the Preakness: Flocarline in 1903, Whimsical in '06, Rhine Maiden in '15, and Nellie Morse in '24.

Here are the 52 fillies to compete in the Preakness:

Year	Horse	Owner	Finish
1875	Australind	Harbeck & Johnson	7th
1880	Emily F.	J. J. Bevins	3rd
1881	Aella	George L. Lorillard	6th
1894	Flirt	Manhattan Stable	13th
1895	Sue Kittie	O. A. Jones	3rd
	Bombazette	C. Littlefield Jr.	7th
1896	Intermission	J. E. McDonald	3rd
	Cassette	A. Clason	4th
1901	Sadie S.	P. H. Sullivan	2nd
1902	Barouche	W. H. McCorkle	6th
	Sun Shower	Jere Dunn	7th
1903	**Flocarline**	M. H. Tichenor & Co.	1st
1904	Possession	C. Oxx	7th
	Flammula	W. H. Kraft	8th
1905	Kiamesha	Oneck Stable	2nd
	Coy Maid	Kenilworth Stable	3rd
	Bohemia	Albemarle Stable	5th

Year	Horse	Owner	Finish
	Iota	H. B. Duryea	9th
1906	Whimsical	T. J. Gaynor	1st
	Content	W. Clay	2nd
	Flip Flap	J. A. Bennet	7th
	Fatinitza	Palestine Stable	8th
1909	Hill Top	R. Angarola	3rd
	Arondack	Mrs. J. McLaughlin	6th
	Sans Souci II	G. J. Kraus	7th
	Grania	A. Garson	8th
1911	Heatherbroom	E. B. Cassatt	6th
1912	Jeannette B.	C. C. Smithson	5th
1913	Cadeau	J. G. Oxnard	5th
1915	Rhine Maiden	E. F. Whitney	1st
1917	Fruit Cake	E. T. Zollicoffer	4th
	Fox Trot	J. E. Griffith	14th
1918	Mary Maud	C. E. Clements	6th
	Quietude	A. H. Morris	9th
1918	Kate Bright	A. Neal	3rd
1919	Milkmaid	J.K.L. Ross	8th
1921	Polly Ann	S. L. Jenkins	2nd
	Careful	W. J. Salmon	12th
	Lough Storm	E. B. McLean	13th
1922	Miss Joy	Montford Jones	10th
1923	Sally's Alley	W. S. Kilmer	11th
1924	Nellie Morse	H. C. Fisher	1st
1925	Maid At Arms	Glen Riddle Farm	11th

Year	Horse	Owner	Finish
1927	Fair Star	Foxcatcher Farm	6th
1928	Bateau	W. M. Jeffords	8th
1930	Snowflake	W J. Salmon	3rd
1935	Nellie Flag	Calumet Farm	7th
1937	Jewell Dorsett	J. W. Brown	8th
1939	Ciencia	King Ranch	6th
1980	Genuine Risk	Diana Firestone	2nd
1988	Winning Colors	Mr. & Mrs. Eugene V. Klein	3rd
1999	Excellent Meeting	Golden Eagle Farm	DNF

Where Preakness Winners Were Foaled

State	Winners
Kentucky	87
Maryland	8
Florida	6
Virginia	6
Pennsylvania	5
California	4
New Jersey	4
New York	3
Tennessee	2
Ohio	1
Texas	1
Canada	1
England	1

Status of Preakness Winners Since 1970

Year	Winner	Birthdate	Status	Where Stands or Stood	Location	Death date
2003	Funny Cide	4/20/2000	In training			
2002	War Emblem	2/20/1999	Stallion	Shadai Stallion Station	Hokkaido, Japan	
2001	Point Given	3/27/1998	Stallion	Three Chimneys Farm	Midway, KY	
2000	Red Bullet	4/13/1997	Stallion	Adena Springs South	Ocala, FL	
1999	Charismatic	3/13/1996	Stallion	JBBA Shizunai Stallion Station	Hokkaido, Japan	
1998	Real Quiet	3/7/1995	Stallion	Taylor Made Farm	Nicholasville, KY	
1997	Silver Charm	2/22/1994	Stallion	Three Chimneys Farm	Midway, KY	
1996	Louis Quatorze	3/13/1993	Stallion	Ashford Stud	Versailles, KY	
1995	Timber Country	4/12/1992	Stallion	Shadai Stallion Station	Hokkaido, Japan	
1994	Tabasco Cat	4/15/1991	Stallion	JBBA Shizunai Stallion Station	Hokkaido, Japan	
1993	Prairie Bayou	3/14/1990	Deceased			6/5/1993
1992	Pine Bluff	5/10/1989	Stallion	Lane's End	Versailles, KY	
1991	Hansel	3/12/1988	Stallion	Hidaka Stallion Station	Hokkaido, Japan	
1990	Summer Squall	3/12/1987	Stallion	Lane's End	Versailles, KY	
1989	Sunday Silence	3/25/1986	Deceased	Shadai Stallion Station	Hokkaido, Japan	8/19/2002
1988	Risen Star	3/25/1985	Deceased	Walmac International	Lexington, KY	3/13/1998
1987	Alysheba	3/3/1984	Stallion	Janadriyah Stud Farm	Aljanadriya, Saudi Arabia	
1986	Snow Chief	3/17/1983	Stallion	Eagle Oak Ranch	Paso Robles, CA	
1985	Tank's Prospect	5/2/1982	Deceased	Venture Farms	Pilot Point, TX	3/2/1995
1884	Gate Dancer	3/31/1981	Deceased	Silverleaf Farm	Orange Lake, FL	3/6/1998
1983	Deputed Testamony	5/7/1980	Stallion	Bonita Farm	Darlington, MD	
1982	Aloma's Ruler	4/21/1979	Stallion	B & B Farm	Monee, IL	
1981	Pleasant Colony	5/4/1978	Deceased	Lane's End	Versailles, KY	12/31/2002
1980	Codex	2/28/1977	Deceased	Tartan Farms	Ocala, FL	8/20/1984
1979	Spectacular Bid	2/17/1976	Deceased	Milfer Farm	Unadilla, NY	6/9/2003
1978	Affirmed	2/21/1975	Deceased	Jonabell Farm	Lexington, KY	1/12/2001
1977	Seattle Slew	2/15/1974	Deceased	Three Chimneys Farm	Midway, KY	5/7/2002
1976	Elocutionist	3/4/1973	Deceased	Airdrie Stud	Midway, KY	3/30/1995
1975	Master Derby	4/24/1972	Deceased	Not Just Another Horse Farm	Chino, CA	1/22/1999
1974	Little Current	4/5/1971	Deceased	Pacific Equine Clinic	Monroe, WA	1/19/2003
1973	Secretariat	3/30/1970	Deceased	Claiborne Farm	Paris, KY	10/4/1989
1972	Bee Bee Bee	4/3/1969	Deceased	JBBA Stallion Station	Hokkaido, Japan	
1971	Canonero II	4/24/1968	Deceased	Gainesway	Lexington, KY	11/11/1981
1970	Personality	5/27/1967	Deceased		Japan	1990

Preakness Stakes

Grade 1, Pimlico Race Course, three-year-olds, $1\frac{3}{16}$ miles, dirt. Held on May 17, 2003, with gross value of $1,000,000. First run in 1873. Weights: colts and geldings, 126 pounds; fillies, 121 pounds.

Year	Winner	Jockey	Second	Third	Strs	Time	Track	1st purse
2003	‡Funny Cide	J. Santos	Midway Road	Scrimshaw	10	1:55.61	gd	$650,000
2002	War Emblem	V. Espinoza	Magic Weisner	Proud Citizen	13	1:56.36	ft	650,000
2001	Point Given	G. Stevens	A P Valentine	Congaree	11	1:55.51	ft	650,000
2000	Red Bullet	J. Bailey	Fusaichi Pegasus	Impeachment	8	1:56.04	gd	650,000
1999	Charismatic	C. Antley	Menifee	Badge	13	1:55.32	ft	650,000
1998	Real Quiet	K. Desormeaux	Victory Gallop	Classic Cat	10	1:54.75	ft	**650,000**
1997	Silver Charm	G. Stevens	Free House	Captain Bodgit	10	1:54.84	ft	488,150
1996	Louis Quatorze	P. Day	Skip Away	Editor's Note	12	**1:53.43**	ft	458,120
1995	Timber Country	P. Day	Oliver's Twist	Thunder Gulch	11	1:54.45	ft	446,810
1994	Tabasco Cat	P. Day	Go for Gin	Concern	10	1:56.47	ft	447,720
1993	‡Prairie Bayou	M. Smith	Cherokee Run	‡El Bakan	12	1:56.61	ft	471,835
1992	Pine Bluff	C. McCarron	Alydeed	Casual Lies	14	1:55.60	gd	484,120
1991	Hansel	J. Bailey	Corporate Report	Mane Minister	8	1:54	ft	432,770
1990	Summer Squall	P. Day	Unbridled	Mister Frisky	9	1:53⅗	ft	445,900
1989	Sunday Silence	P. Valenzuela	Easy Goer	Rock Point	8	1:53⅘	ft	438,230
1988	Risen Star	E. Delahoussaye	Brian's Time	†Winning Colors	9	1:56⅕	gd	413,700
1987	Alysheba	C. McCarron	Bet Twice	Cryptoclearance	9	1:55⅘	ft	421,100
1986	Snow Chief	A. Solis	Ferdinand	Broad Brush	7	1:54⅘	ft	411,900
1985	Tank's Prospect	P. Day	Chief's Crown	Eternal Prince	11	**1:53⅖**	ft	423,200
1984	Gate Dancer	A. Cordero Jr.	Play On	Fight Over	10	1:53⅗	ft	243,600
1983	Deputed Testamony	D. A. Miller Jr.	Desert Wine	High Honors	12	1:55⅖	sy	251,200
1982	Aloma's Ruler	J. Kaenel	Linkage	Cut Away	7	1:55⅖	ft	209,900
1981	Pleasant Colony	J. Velasquez	Bold Ego	Paristo	13	1:54⅗	ft	200,800
1980	Codex	A. Cordero Jr.	†Genuine Risk	Colonel Moran	8	1:54⅕	ft	180,600
1979	Spectacular Bid	R. Franklin	Golden Act	Screen King	5	1:54⅕	gd	165,300
1978	AFFIRMED	S. Cauthen	Alydar	Believe It	7	1:54⅖	ft	136,200
1977	SEATTLE SLEW	J. Cruguet	Iron Constitution	Run Dusty Run	9	1:54⅖	ft	138,600
1976	Elocutionist	J. Lively	Play the Red	Bold Forbes	6	1:55	ft	129,700
1975	Master Derby	D. G. McHargue	Foolish Pleasure	Diabolo	10	1:56⅖	ft	158,100
1974	Little Current	M. A. Rivera	‡Neapolitan Way	Cannonade	13	1:54⅗	gd	156,500
1973	SECRETARIAT	R. Turcotte	Sham	Our Native	6	1:54⅖	ft	129,900
1972	Bee Bee Bee	E. Nelson	No Le Hace	Key to the Mint	7	1:55⅗	sy	135,300
1971	Canonero II	G. Avila	Eastern Fleet	Jim French	11	1:54	ft	137,400
1970	Personality	E. Belmonte	My Dad George	Silent Screen	14	1:56⅕	ft	151,300
1969	Majestic Prince	W. Hartack	Arts and Letters	Jay Ray	8	1:55⅗	ft	129,500
1968	Forward Pass	I. Valenzuela	Out of the Way	Nodouble	10	1:56⅘	ft	142,700
1967	Damascus	W. Shoemaker	In Reality	Proud Clarion	10	1:55⅕	ft	151,500
1966	Kauai King	D. Brumfield	Stupendous	Amberoid	9	1:55⅖	ft	129,000
1965	Tom Rolfe	R. Turcotte	Dapper Dan	Hail to All	9	1:56⅕	ft	128,100
1964	Northern Dancer	W. Hartack	The Scoundrel	Hill Rise	6	1:56⅘	ft	124,200
1963	Candy Spots	W. Shoemaker	Chateaugay	Never Bend	8	1:56⅕	ft	127,500
1962	Greek Money	J. L. Rotz	Ridan	Roman Line	11	1:56⅕	ft	135,800
1961	Carry Back	J. Sellers	Globemaster	Crozier	9	1:57⅗	ft	126,200
1960	Bally Ache	R. Ussery	Victoria Park	*Celtic Ash	6	1:57⅗	ft	121,000
1959	Royal Orbit	W. Harmatz	Sword Dancer	Dunce	11	1:57	ft	136,200
1958	Tim Tam	I. Valenzuela	Lincoln Road	Gone Fishin'	12	1:57⅕	ft	97,900
1957	Bold Ruler	E. Arcaro	Iron Liege	Inside Tract	7	1:56⅕	ft	66,300
1956	Fabius	W. Hartack	Needles	No Regrets	9	1:58⅖	ft	84,250
1955	Nashua	E. Arcaro	Saratoga	Traffic Judge	8	1:54⅗	ft	67,550
1954	Hasty Road	J. Adams	Correlation	Hasseyampa	11	1:57⅖	ft	91,600
1953	Native Dancer	E. Guerin	Jamie K.	Royal Bay Gem	7	1:57⅘	ft	65,200
1952	Blue Man	C. McCreary	‡Jampol	One Count	10	1:57⅖	ft	86,135
1951	Bold	E. Arcaro	Counterpoint	Alerted	8	1:56⅖	ft	83,110
1950	Hill Prince	E. Arcaro	Middleground	Dooly	6	1:59⅕	sl	56,115
1949	Capot	T. Atkinson	Palestinian	Noble Impulse	9	1:56	ft	79,985
1948	CITATION	E. Arcaro	Vulcan's Forge	Bovard	4	2:02⅖	hy	91,870
1947	Faultless	D. Dodson	On Trust	Phalanx	11	1:59	ft	98,005
1946	ASSAULT	W. Mehrtens	Lord Boswell	Hampden	10	2:01⅖	ft	96,620
1945	Polynesian	W. D. Wright	Hoop, Jr.	‡Darby Dieppe	9	1:58⅘	ft	66,170
1944	Pensive	C. McCreary	Platter	‡Stir Up	7	1:59⅕	ft	60,075
1943	COUNT FLEET	J. Longden	Blue Swords	Vincentive	4	1:57⅖	gd	43,190
1942	Alsab	B. James	dh-Requested	dh-Sun Again	10	1:57	ft	58,175
1941	WHIRLAWAY	E. Arcaro	King Cole	Our Boots	8	1:58⅘	gd	49,365
1940	Bimelech	F. A. Smith	Mioland	Gallahadion	9	1:58⅗	ft	53,230
1939	Challedon	G. Seabo	Gilded Knight	Volitant	6	1:59⅘	my	53,710
1938	Dauber	M. Peters	Cravat	Menow	9	1:59⅘	sy	51,875
1937	WAR ADMIRAL	C. Kurtsinger	Pompoon	Flying Scot	8	1:58⅖	gd	45,600

Year	Winner	Jockey	Second	Third	Strs	Time	Track	1st purse
1936	**Bold Venture**	G. Woolf	Granville	Jean Bart	11	1:59	ft	27,325
1935	**OMAHA**	W. Saunders	Firethorn	Psychic Bid	8	1:58⅗	ft	25,325
1934	**High Quest**	R. Jones	Cavalcade	Discovery	7	1:58⅕	ft	25,175
1933	**Head Play**	C. Kurtsinger	Ladysman	Utopian	10	2:02	sl	26,850
1932	**Burgoo King**	E. James	Tick On	Boatswain	9	1:59⅘	ft	50,375
1931	**Mate**	G. Ellis	Twenty Grand	Ladder	7	1:59	ft	48,225
1930	**GALLANT FOX**	E. Sande	Crack Brigade	†Snowflake	11	2:00⅗	ft	51,925
1929	**Dr. Freeland**	L. Schaefer	Minotaur	African	11	2:01⅗	ft	52,325
1928	**Victorian**	R. Workman	Toro	Solace	**18**	2:00⅕	ft	60,000
1927	**Bostonian**	A. Abel	Sir Harry	Whiskery	12	2:01⅗	gd	53,100
1926	**Display**	J. Malben	Blondin	Mars	13	1:59⅘	ft	53,625
1925	**Coventry**	C. Kummer	‡Backbone	Almadel	12	1:59	ft	52,700
1924	**†Nellie Morse**	J. Merimee	Transmute	Mad Play	15	1:57⅕	sy	54,000
1923	**Vigil**	B. Marinelli	Gen. Thatcher	‡Rialto	13	1:53⅗	ft	52,000
1922	**Pillory**	L. Morris	Hea	June Grass	12	1:51⅗	ft	51,000
1921	**Broomspun**	F. Coltiletti	†Polly Ann	Jeg	14	1:54⅕	sl	43,000
1920	**Man o' War**	C. Kummer	Upset	Wildair	9	1:51⅗	ft	23,000
1919	**SIR BARTON**	J. Loftus	Eternal	Sweep On	12	1:53	ft	24,500
1918	***War Cloud**	J. Loftus	Sunny Slope	*Lanius	10	1:53⅗	gd	12,250
	Jack Hare, Jr.	C. Peak	The Porter	†Kate Bright	6	1:53⅖	gd	11,250
1917	**Kalitan**	E. Haynes	Al. M. Dick	‡Kentucky Boy	14	1:54⅖	ft	4,800
1916	**Damrosch**	L. McAtee	Greenwood	Achievement	9	1:54⅘	ft	1,380
1915	**†Rhine Maiden**	D. Hoffman	Half Rock	Runes	6	1:58	my	1,275
1914	**‡Holiday**	A. Schuttinger	Brave Cunarder	Defendum	6	1:53⅘	ft	1,355
1913	**‡Buskin**	J. Butwell	Kleburne	‡Barnegat	8	1:53⅖	ft	1,670
1912	**Col. Holloway**	C. Turner	Bwana Tumbo	Tipsand	7	1:56⅗	sl	1,450
1911	**Watervale**	E. Dugan	Zeus	‡The Nigger	7	1:51	ft	2,700
1910	**‡Layminster**	R. Estep	Dalhousie	Sager	12	1:40⅕	ft	2,800
1909	**Effendi**	W. Doyle	Fashion Plate	†Hill Top	10	1:39⅘	ft	2,725
1908	**Royal Tourist**	E. Dugan	Live Wire	‡Robert Cooper	4	1:46⅖	ft	2,455
1907	**‡Don Enrique**	G. Mountain	Ethon	Zambesi	7	1:45⅖	hy	2,260
1906	**†Whimsical**	W. Miller	†Content	Larabie	10	1:45	ft	2,355
1905	**Cairngorm**	W. Davis	†Kiamesha	†Coy Maid	10	1:45⅘	ft	2,145
1904	**Bryn Mawr**	E. Hildebrand	Wotan	‡Dolly Spanker	10	1:44⅕	ft	2,355
1903	**†Flocarline**	W. Gannon	Mackey Dwyer	Rightful	6	1:44⅘	ft	1,875
1902	**Old England**	L. Jackson	Major Daingerfield	Namtor	7	1:45⅘	hy	2,240
1901	**The Parader**	F. Landry	†Sadie S.	Dr. Barlow	5	1:47⅕	hy	1,605
1900	**Hindus**	H. Spencer	*Sarmatian	Ten Candles	10	1:48⅖	ft	1,900
1899	**Half Time**	R. Clawson	Filigrane	Lackland	3	1:47	ft	1,580
1898	**Sly Fox**	W. Simms	The Huguenot	Nuto	4	1:49¾	gd	1,450
1897	**Paul Kauvar**	C. Thorpe	Elkin	On Deck	7	1:51¼	sy	1,420
1896	**Margrave**	H. Griffin	Hamilton II	*Intermission	4	1:51	ft	1,350
1895	**Belmar**	F. Taral	‡April Fool	†Sue Kittie	7	1:50½	ft	1,350
1894	**Assignee**	F. Taral	Potentate	‡Ed Kearney	14	1:49¼	ft	1,830
1890	**Montague**	J. Martin	Philosophy	Barrister	4	2:36¾	ft	1,215
1889	**Buddhist**	G. Anderson	Japhet	———	2	2:17½	ft	1,130
1888	**Refund**	F. Littlefield	Judge Murray	Glendale	4	2:49	hy	1,185
1887	**Dunboyne**	W. Donohue	Mahony	Raymond	4	2:39½	ft	1,675
1886	**The Bard**	S. Fisher	Eurus	Elkwood	5	2:45	gd	2,050
1885	**Tecumseh**	J. McLaughlin	Wickham	‡John C.	4	2:49	hy	2,160
1884	**Knight of Ellerslie**	S. Fisher	Welcher	———	2	2:39½	ft	1,905
1883	**Jacobus**	G. Barbee	Parnell	———	2	2:42½	gd	1,635
1882	**Vanguard**	T. Costello	Heck	‡Col. Watson	3	2:44½	gd	1,250
1881	**Saunterer**	T. Costello	‡Compensation	Baltic	6	2:40½	gd	1,950
1880	**Grenada**	L. Hughes	Oden	†Emily F.	5	2:40½	ft	2,000
1879	**Harold**	L. Hughes	Jerico	‡Rochester	6	2:40½	ft	2,550
1878	**Duke of Magenta**	C. Holloway	Bayard	‡Albert	3	2:41¾	gd	2,100
1877	**Cloverbrook**	C. Holloway	Bombast	Lucifer	4	2:45½	sl	1,600
1876	**‡Shirley**	G. Barbee	Rappahannock	Compliments	8	2:44¾	gd	1,950
1875	**Tom Ochiltree**	L. Hughes	Viator	†Bay Final	9	2:43½	sl	1,900
1874	**Culpepper**	W. Donohue	*King Amadeus	Scratch	6	2:56½	my	1,900
1873	**Survivor**	G. Barbee	John Boulger	Artist	7	2:43	sl	1,800

†—filly; ‡—gelding; *—imported horse; dh-dead heat; bold indicates records set in starters, time, and 1st purse; Triple Crown winners are in all capitalized letters.

1894, 1½ miles; 1889, 1¼ miles; 1894-1900,1908, 1 1/16 miles; 1901-'07, 1 mile and 70 yards; 1909,1910, 1 mile; 1911-'24, 1⅛ miles. 1891-'93, not run. 1890 held at Morris Park, New York; 1894-1908 Gravesend, New York. Run in two divisions in 1918. 1973-present, Grade 1. Dancer's Image disqualified from third to eighth in 1968. Secretariat's time in 1973 originally reported as 1:55; hand-timed by *Daily Racing Form* clockers in 1:53⅖

Belmont Stakes History

Unforgettable horses, jockeys, and trainers punctuate the glorious history of the Belmont Stakes, a compelling race if only because two three-year-olds carrying equal weights of 126 pounds can battle its testing 1½-mile distance and be separated at the finish line by inches. It has happened more than once in the final race of the Triple Crown.

First run in 1867, the Belmont Stakes is named for August Belmont I, a prominent investment banker and Thoroughbred owner who was president of the American Jockey Club. The Belmont Stakes preceded the Preakness by six years and the Kentucky Derby by eight. Francis Morris's filly Ruthless won the first Belmont Stakes, which was contested at Jerome Park in the Bronx on a Thursday afternoon at 1⅝ miles, "cleverly by a head" over De Coursey. The purse was $2,500.

The first 23 runnings of the Belmont Stakes were held on a ribbon-like course at Jerome Park. In 1890, the Belmont Stakes moved to Morris Park, a 1⅜-mile track a few miles east of what is now Van Cortland Park in the Bronx.

Fifteen years later, in 1905, the Belmont Stakes had a new home, Belmont Park, but the race was not run in 1911 and '12 because antigambling legislation shut down racing in New York in those years. Unlike the Belmont's current counter-clockwise path, the race was run clockwise—like many English and European races—until 1921. By then, two great champions with a unique link had won the race known as the Test of Champions in strikingly different styles.

Colin is one of only two undefeated American champions with more than five starts in the past 95 years (the other is Personal Ensign). Colin nearly lost his unbeaten record because of a mistake by Joe Notter, his jockey in the 1908 Belmont Stakes. In a driving rainstorm so intense that no final time was taken, Notter misjudged the finish line on Colin, and his five-length lead was shaved to a head by a fast-closing Fair Play.

Colin continued to a perfect 15-for-15 record. Fair Play sired Man o' War, the once-beaten champion who won the Belmont by 20 lengths over his only challenger, Donnacona, at odds of 0.04-to-1.

Gallant Fox is one of only two Triple Crown winners who was not the favorite in the Belmont Stakes. The previous year, Whichone had beaten Gallant Fox in the 1929 Futurity and also had won the Champagne and Saratoga Special Stakes. Whichone missed the Kentucky Derby and Preakness Stakes the following spring because of knee problems, but he returned to win the

Belmont Attendance

Year	Attendance	Year	Attendance
2003	101,864	1986	42,555
2002	103,222	1985	43,446
2001	73,857	1984	46,430
2000	67,810	1983	56,677
1999	85,818	1982	46,050
1998	80,162	1981	61,200
1997	70,682	1980	58,883
1996	40,797	1979	59,073
1995	37,171	1978	65,417
1994	42,695	1977	71,026
1993	45,037	1976	58,788
1992	50,204	1975	60,611
1991	51,766	1974	52,153
1990	50,123	1973	67,605
1989	64,959	1972	54,635
1988	56,223	1971	82,694
1987	64,772	1970	54,299

Withers Stakes and went off the 7-to-10 favorite in the 1930 Belmont Stakes.

Gallant Fox had won the Wood Memorial Stakes, Preakness, and Kentucky Derby (in that order), but he went off at odds of 8-to-5 in the field of just four in the Belmont. Gallant Fox uncharacteristically took the lead immediately and scampered to a surprisingly easy three-length victory in a stakes record of 2:31⅗ for 1½ miles.

Gallant Fox's winning Belmont Stakes margin paled next to the 25-length romp of Count Fleet, who completed his 1943 Triple Crown at odds of 1-to-20 "galloping," according to the Belmont chart. Three years later, Assault went off as the 7-to-5 second choice in the Belmont but, like Gallant Fox, he completed his Triple Crown with a three-length victory. Favored Lord Boswell finished fifth in the field of seven at 1.35-to-1.

In 1948, Citation cruised to an eight-length win in the Belmont to become the fourth Triple Crown winner in eight years. There would not be another for a quarter-century.

Plenty of upsets occurred in those 25 years from Citation to Secretariat, and none was more shocking than Sherluck's 1961 victory over 2-to-5 favorite Carry Back at odds of 65.05-to-1, resulting in a then-record Belmont Stakes win payout of $132.10.

Carry Back, who finished seventh, joined Pensive (1944) and Tim Tam ('58) as Kentucky Derby and Preakness winners who lost in the Belmont Stakes. Five more followed Carry Back in the next ten years: Northern Dancer (1964), Kauai King ('66), Forward Pass ('68), Majestic Prince ('69), and Canonero II, who attracted 82,694, then the largest crowd in Belmont Park history, on June 5, 1971, in his four-place finish to Pass Catcher, a 34.50-to-1 longshot.

Just when everybody thought there might not ever be another Triple Crown winner—the tremendous growth in the number of foals was frequently cited as a reason—along came Secretariat. To provide a perspective on his 31-length 1973 Belmont Stakes victory in a world record 2:24, consider that the next-fastest winners, Easy Goer in '89 and A.P. Indy in '92, went in 2:26, the equivalent of ten lengths slower.

Secretariat's 1973 Triple Crown was followed by two more in the ensuing five years: Seattle Slew, who became the only undefeated Triple Crown winner in 1977, and Affirmed one year later.

The Triple Crowns of 1977 and '78 were starkly different. Seattle Slew dominated his generation, while Affirmed was pushed to the limit by his nemesis, Alydar. The final sixteenth of a mile of the 1978 Belmont Stakes, with Affirmed on the inside under Steve Cauthen and Alydar at his throat under Jorge Velasquez, was a dramatic test of will in which Affirmed prevailed by a head. That was not the closest Belmont Stakes finish. Colin had won by the same margin, and Granville in 1936, Jaipur in '62, and Victory Gallop in 1998 prevailed by a nose.

Spectacular Bid had a shot at becoming the third consecutive Triple Crown winner in 1979 but checked in third at 3-to-10 to Coastal in the Belmont after reportedly stepping on a safety pin that morning. Two years later, Derby and Preakness winner Pleasant Colony failed to sweep the series, finishing third to Summing.

Then, Woody Stephens took over. People questioned the Racing Hall of Fame trainer's judgment when he announced that Conquistador Cielo, who had just routed older horses by 7¼ lengths in the one-mile Metropolitan Handicap (G1) five days earlier, would start in the Belmont Stakes. Stephens knew his horse, and the colt won the Belmont by 14 lengths under Laffit Pincay Jr. Stephens-trained Caveat won the 1983 Belmont, and ill-fated Swale won in '84. Then Stephens ran first and second with Creme Fraiche and Stephan's Odyssey in 1985. In 1986, Stephens won his fifth consecutive Belmont Stakes with Danzig Connection, at odds of 8-to-1.

Three consecutive blowouts occurred in the late 1980s, with Bet Twice winning by 14 lengths over Derby and Preakness winner Alysheba (who finished fourth) in '87, Risen Star adding to his Preakness triumph with a 14¾-length Belmont romp, and Easy Goer avenging his

Derby and Preakness losses to Sunday Silence by winning the '89 Belmont Stakes by eight lengths.

The middle years of the 1990s were dominated by Racing Hall of Fame trainer D. Wayne Lukas, who secured consecutive victories with Tabasco Cat (1994), Thunder Gulch ('95), and Editor's Note ('96).

Julie Krone became the first female rider to win a Triple Crown race when she guided Colonial Affair to a 2¼-length win in the 1993 Belmont for trainer Flint S. "Scotty" Schulhofer. The Racing Hall of Fame trainer collected his second Belmont victory in 1999 when Lemon Drop Kid denied Lukas-trained Charismatic a Triple Crown before a record crowd of 85,818.

Charismatic's loss marked the third straight year that a Triple Crown was on the line. In 1997, Silver Charm, trained by Bob Baffert, led 100 yards before the finish but was passed by Touch Gold, who won by three-quarters of a length. One year later, Baffert-trained Real Quiet looked home free in the Belmont before weakening late and losing by a nose in the final stride to Victory Gallop. Two years later, Baffert recorded his first Belmont victory with Point Given's 2001 victory before 73,857, the largest Belmont Stakes crowd without a Triple Crown on the line. In 2002, a record crowd of 103,222 watched Baffert-trained War Emblem stumble at the start and finish eighth in his attempt to sweep the Triple Crown. One year later, Derby and Preakness winner Funny Cide could not overcome a sloppy track and finished third.—*Bill Heller*

Belmont Trophy and Tray

The Belmont Stakes trophy is a solid silver bowl originally crafted by Tiffany's, and it was the trophy that August Belmont I's Fenian won in 1869 after taking the third running of the race. The Belmont family presented it as a perpetual trophy for the Belmont Stakes in 1926, and each winning owner is given the option of keeping the trophy for the year his horse wins. Atop the cover of the trophy is a silver figure of Fenian. The bowl is supported by three horses representing influential sires Eclipse, Herod, and Matchem. The winning owner also receives a permanent large silver tray with the names of previous Belmont Stakes winners engraved on it. Trays also are presented to the winning trainer, jockey, exercise rider, and groom.

Carnation Blanket

The Kentucky Derby (G1) has its roses, the Preakness Stakes (G1) has ersatz black-eyed Susans, and the carnation is the official flower of the Belmont Stakes (G1). Imported from either

California or Colombia, between 300 and 400 carnations are glued onto a green velveteen backing to create the blanket that adorns the Belmont winner.

From "Sidewalks" to "New York, New York"

Until 1997, the song that escorted the Belmont Stakes (G1) field onto the track was "Sidewalks of New York," written in 1894 by Charles Lawlor, a vaudevillian, and James W. Blake, a hat salesman and lyricist. More than one version of the lyrics exist, but the best-known stanza is:

"East Side, West Side, all around the town
"The kids sang 'ring around rosie,' 'London Bridge is falling down'
"Boys and girls together, me and Mamie O'Rourke
"We tripped the light fantastic on the sidewalks of New York."

"New York, New York" is of much more recent vintage, written by John Kander and Fred Ebb in 1977 for the movie of the same name. Composer Kander and and lyricist Ebb are one of Broadway's most successful teams; their credits include *Cabaret, Funny Lady, Woman of the Year,* and *Zorba. New York, New York,* not regarded as one of director Martin Scorsese's better films, starred Liza Minelli, who performed the song in the movie, and Robert de Niro. The song subsequently was recorded by Frank Sinatra and rose to number 32 on the hits chart in 1980.

Its lyrics:
"Start spreading the news
"I'm leaving today
"I want to be a part of it, New York, New York
"These vagabond shoes
"Are longing to stray
"And make a brand new start of it
"New York, New York
"I want to wake up in the city that never sleeps
"To find I'm king of the hill, top of the heap
"These little town blues
"Are melting away
"I'll make a brand new start of it
"In old New York
"If I can make it there
"I'll make it anywhere
"It's up to you, New York, New York."

Belmont Trivia

• The Belmont Stakes has not always been contested at 1½ miles. Prior to 1874, the race was run at 1⅝ miles. The Belmont was held at 1¼ miles from 1890 through '92, and in '95, 1904, and 1905. It was 1⅛ miles in 1893 and '94; at 1⅜ miles 1896 through 1903 and from 1906 through 1925. The Belmont was run at 1½ miles from 1874 through 1889 and from 1926 to the present.

• The Belmont Stakes was run at Aqueduct from 1963 through '67 while Belmont Park was being rebuilt.

• The smallest Belmont Stakes field was two. It happened in 1887, '88, '92, 1910, and '20. The

Belmont Wagering, 1980-2003

Year	Winner	On-track handle	OTB handle	Simulcasting	Total handle
2003	Empire Maker	$3,440,151		$44,642,048	$48,082,199
2002	Sarava	3,753,983		54,503,406	58,257,389
2001	Point Given	2,707,574		34,959,635	37,667,209
2000	Commendable	2,046,835		28,354,418	30,401,253
1999	Lemon Drop Kid	3,143,508		40,839,558	43,983,066
1998	Victory Gallop	2,521,457		25,864,228	28,385,685
1997	Touch Gold	2,229,860		22,546,860	24,776,720
1996	Editor's Note	1,639,134		18,714,712	20,353,846
1995	Thunder Gulch	1,571,891	3,672,079	15,310,597	20,554,567
1994	Tabasco Cat	1,717,684	3,299,616	13,848,321	18,865,621
1993	Colonial Affair	2,793,320	4,567,493	17,472,438	24,833,251
1992	A.P. Indy	2,058,039	4,365,205	12,581,848	19,005,092
1991	Hansel	2,222,049	5,206,757	12,877,258	20,306,064
1990	Go and Go (Ire)	1,588,767	3,832,777	8,985,594	14,407,138
1989	Easy Goer	2,565,156	4,062,020	12,269,211	18,896,387
1988	Risen Star	1,439,045	4,135,493	8,685,408	14,259,946
1987	Bet Twice	2,703,924	6,794,377	8,242,290	17,740,591
1986	Danzig Connection	2,038,445	4,469,831	5,869,281	12,377,557
1985	Creme Fraiche	1,840,198	4,982,800	4,518,679	11,341,677
1884	Swale	2,063,135	5,540,202	4,080,482	11,683,819
1983	Caveat	1,530,010	3,724,455	2,961,256	8,215,721
1982	Conquistador Cielo	1,201,491	2,248,366	2,488,107	5,937,964
1981	Smarten	1,420,517	3,204,415	465,950	5,090,882
1980	Temperence Hill	1,603,057	3,769,868		5,372,925

Beginning in 1996, figures for OTB and simulcasting handle were combined.

largest Belmont Stakes field was 15 in 1983.
- Point Given was the 50th chestnut to win the Belmont. Fifty-two winners have been bay, 28 dark bay or brown, three black, two gray, and one roan.
- Thirty-six of the 135 runnings of the Belmont have been run on off tracks, the most recent in 2003 when Empire Maker won.
- The 2001 Belmont drew a crowd of 73,857, the largest ever for the race without a horse going for the Triple Crown and sixth highest behind 103,222 in 2002, 101,864 in 2003, 85,818 in 1999, 82,694 in 1971, and 80,162 in 1998.
- Sarava was the 17th Belmont winner whose name began with the letter 'S'. Twenty Belmont winners had names beginning with 'C'.

Leading Belmont Owners by Wins

6 **James R. Keene:** Spendthrift, 1879; Commando, 1901; Delhi, 1904; Peter Pan, 1907; Colin 1908; Sweep, 1910.

    Belair Stud: Gallant Fox, 1930; Faireno, 1932; Omaha, 1935; Granville, 1936; Johnstown, 1939; Nashua, 1955.

5 **Mike and Phil Dwyer:** George Kinney, 1883; Panique, 1884; Inspector B., 1886; Hanover, 1887; Sir Dixon, 1888.

4 **Glen Riddle Farms:** Man o' War, 1920; American Flag, 1925; Crusader, 1926; War Admiral, 1937.

    Greentree Stable: Twenty Grand, 1931; Shut Out, 1942; Capot, 1949; Stage Door Johnny, 1968.

3 **August Belmont II:** Masterman, 1902; Friar Rock, 1916; *Hourless, 1917.

    King Ranch: Assault, 1946; Middleground, 1950; High Gun, 1954.

Owners with Most Belmont Starters

Name	Starts	Wins	2nd	3rd	Unplaced
C. V. Whitney	20	2	2	4	12
August Belmont	19	2	4	4	9
Greentree Stable	15	4	1	2	8
Belair Stud	14	6	0	1	7
King Ranch	14	3	2	1	8
James R. Keene	12	6	2	1	3
Calumet Farm	11	2	5	2	2
Brookmeade Stable	11	2	1	1	7
Wheatley Stable	11	0	0	3	8
George D. Widener	10	1	3	2	4
George Lorillard	8	3	3	0	2
Marcus Daly	8	1	1	2	4
Pierre Lorillard	8	1	0	3	4
Ogden Phipps	8	1	0	1	6
Dwyer Brothers	7	5	1	0	1
August Belmont II	7	3	2	0	2
D. McDaniel	7	3	0	0	4
Darby Dan Farm	7	2	0	1	4
Meadow Stable	7	2	0	1	4
Walter M. Jeffords	7	1	1	0	5
Buckland Stable	7	0	0	1	6

Leading Belmont Breeders by Wins

7 **A. J. Alexander:** Harry Bassett, 1871; Joe Daniels, 1872; Springbok, 1873; Duke of Magenta, 1878; Spendthrift, 1879; Grenada, 1880; Burlington, 1890.

5 **Belair Stud:** Gallant Fox, 1930; Faireno, 1932; Omaha, 1935; Granville, 1936; Nashua, 1955.

    J. R. Keene: Commando, 1901; Delhi, 1904; Peter Pan, 1907; Colin, 1908; Sweep, 1910.

    John E. Madden: Joe Madden, 1909; The Finn, 1915; Sir Barton, 1919; Grey Lag, 1921; Zev, 1923.

4 **August Belmont II:** Masterman, 1902; Friar Rock, 1916; *Hourless; Man o' War, 1920.

    Greentree: Twenty Grand, 1931; Shut Out, 1942; Capot, 1949; Stage Door Johnny, 1968.

    H. P. Whitney: Tanya, 1905; Burgomaster, 1906; Prince Eugene, 1913; *Johren, 1918.

3 **W. S. Farish:** Bet Twice, 1987; A.P. Indy, 1991; Lemon Drop Kid, 1999.

    Sam Riddle: American Flag, 1925; Crusader, 1926; War Admiral, 1937.

Leading Belmont Trainers by Wins

8 **James Rowe:** George Kinney, 1883; Panique, 1884; Commando, 1901; Delhi, 1904; Peter Pan, 1907; Colin, 1908; Sweep, 1910; Prince Eugene, 1913.

7 **Sam Hildreth:** Jean Bereaud, 1899; Joe Madden, 1909; Friar Rock, 1916; Hourless, 1917; Grey Lag, 1921; Zev, 1923; Mad Play, 1924.

6 **James "Sunny Jim" Fitzsimmons:** Gallant Fox, 1930; Faireno, 1932; Omaha, 1935; Granville, 1936; Johnstown, 1939; Nashua, 1955.

5 **W. C. "Woody" Stephens:** Conquistador Cielo, 1982; Caveat, 1983; Swale, 1984; Creme Fraiche, 1985; Danzig Connection, 1986.

4 **Max Hirsch:** Vito, 1928; Assault, 1946; Middleground, 1950; High Gun, 1954.

    D. Wayne Lukas: Tabasco Cat, 1994; Thunder Gulch, 1995; Editor's Note, 1996; Commendable, 2000.

    R. W. Walden: Duke of Magenta, 1878; Grenada, 1880; Saunterer, 1881; *Bowling Brook, 1898.

3 **Elliott Burch:** Sword Dancer, 1959; Quadrangle, 1964; Arts and Letters, 1969.

    John M. Gaver: Shut Out, 1942; Capot, 1949; Stage Door Johnny, 1968.

    Lucien Laurin: Amberoid, 1966; Riva Ridge, 1972; Secretariat, 1973.

    Frank McCabe: Inspector B., 1886; Hanover, 1887; Sir Dixon, 1888.

    David McDaniel: Harry Bassett, 1871; Joe Daniels, 1872; Springbok, 1873.

2 **Tom Barry:** *Cavan, 1958; *Celtic Ash, 1960.

    Flint S. "Scotty" Schulhofer: Colonial Affair, 1993; Lemon Drop Kid, 1999.

    Sylvester Veitch: Phalanx, 1947; Counterpoint, 1951.

    Oscar White: Pavot, 1945; One Count, 1952.

Trainers with Most Belmont Starters Since 1972

Name	Starts	Wins	2nd	3rd	Unplaced
D. Wayne Lukas	18	4	0	1	13
Nicholas P. Zito	11	0	5	1	5
LeRoy Jolley	10	0	2	1	7
John P. Campo	10	0	0	1	8

Name	Starts	Wins	2nd	3rd	Unplaced
Woodford C. Stephens	9	5	1	1	2
Flint S. Schulhofer	7	2	1	9	4
Bob Baffert	6	1	2	0	3
Lou Rondinello	6	1	0	2	3
C. R. McGaughey III	5	1	1	1	2
Alfredo Callejas	5	0	0	0	5

Female Trainers in the Belmont

Seven women have trained Belmont Stakes (G1) starters, and the best finish was that by Dianne Carpenter-trained Kingpost, who finished a distant second behind Risen Star in 1988. In 2002, owner-breeder-trainer Nancy Alberts saddled Magic Weisner for a fourth-place finish behind upset winner Sarava.

Women who have trained Belmont starters:

Year	Trainer	Horse	Finish
2003	Linda Rice	Supervisor	5th
2002	Nancy Alberts	Magic Weisner	4th
1996	Cynthia Reese	In Contention	9th
1992	Shelley Riley	Casual Lies	5th
1988	Dianne Carpenter	Kingpost	2nd
1985	Patricia Johnson	Fast Account	4th
1984	Sarah Lundy	Minstrel Star	11th

Leading Belmont Jockeys by Wins

6 **James McLaughlin:** Forester, 1882; George Kinney, 1883; Panique, 1884; Inspector B., 1886; Hanover, 1887; Sir Dixon, 1888.

Eddie Arcaro: Whirlaway, 1941; Shut Out, 1942; Pavot, 1945; Citation, 1948; One Count, 1952; Nashua, 1955.

5 **Earle Sande:** Grey Lag, 1921; Zev, 1923; Mad Play, 1924; Chance Shot, 1927; Gallant Fox, 1930.

Bill Shoemaker: Gallant Man, 1957; Sword Dancer, 1959; Jaipur, 1962; Damascus, 1967; Avatar, 1975.

3 **Braulio Baeza:** Sherluck, 1961; Chateaugay, 1963; Arts and Letters, 1969.

Pat Day: Easy Goer, 1989; Tabasco Cat, 1994; Commendable, 2000.

Laffit Pincay Jr.: Conquistador Cielo, 1982; Caveat, 1983; Swale, 1984.

James Stout: Granville, 1936; Pasteurized, 1938; Johnstown, 1939.

Jockeys with Most
Belmont Starters Since 1938

Name	Starts	Wins	2nd	3rd	Unplaced
Eddie Arcaro	22	6	3	2	11
Angel Cordero Jr.	21	1	2	4	14
Jerry Bailey	18	2	1	1	14
Pat Day	16	3	2	1	10
Braulio Baeza	14	3	2	0	9
Laffit Pincay Jr.	13	3	3	0	7
Jorge Velasquez	13	0	1	5	7
Bill Shoemaker	11	5	1	1	4
Eric Guerin	11	2	2	1	6
Chris McCarron	11	2	1	2	6
Edward Maple	11	2	0	1	8

Name	Starts	Wins	2nd	3rd	Unplaced
Jose Santos	12	1	2	1	8
Jacinto Vasquez	10	0	3	1	6
Mike Smith	8	0	1	1	7
Ron Turcotte	9	2	1	9	6
Jorge Chavez	9	0	0	1	8
Ruben Hernandez	8	1	0	0	7
Bobby Ussery	8	0	1	0	7
Gary Stevens	8	3	1	1	3
John Sellers	7	1	1	1	4

Only One Female Jockey in Belmont

Julie Krone, the only female jockey in the Racing Hall of Fame, is the only female rider to have had a mount in the Belmont. Krone won the 1993 Belmont Stakes (G1) aboard Colonial Affair. She retired in 1999 but resumed her career in 2002.

Krone's Belmont Stakes mounts:

Year	Mount	Finish
1991	Subordinated Debt	9th
1992	Colony Light	6th
1993	**Colonial Affair**	1st
1995	Star Standard	2nd
1996	South Salem	DNF

Leading Sires of Belmont Winners

5 **Lexington:** General Duke, 1868; Kingfisher, 1870; Harry Bassett, 1871; Duke of Magenta, 1878; Saunterer, 1881.

3 ***Australian:** Joe Daniels, 1872; Springbok, 1873; Spendthrift, 1879.

Fair Play: Man o' War, 1920; Mad Play, 1924; Chance Shot, 1927.

Man o' War: American Flag, 1925; Crusader, 1926; War Admiral, 1937.

2 **Commando:** Peter Pan, 1907; Colin, 1908.

Count Fleet: Counterpoint, 1951; One Count, 1952.

Gallant Fox: Omaha, 1935; Granville, 1936.

Hamburg: Burgomaster, 1906; Prince Eugene, 1913.

*Nasrullah: Nashua, 1955; Jaipur, 1962.

*Negofol: *Hourless, 1917; Vito, 1928.

Seattle Slew: Swale, 1984; A.P. Indy, 1992.

*Star Shoot: Sir Barton, 1919; Grey Lag, 1921.

Derby-Preakness Winners
Not Favored in the Belmont

Twenty-nine three-year-olds swept the Kentucky Derby and Preakness to earn a chance at the Triple Crown. Ironically, the only two who were not the betting favorites in the Belmont Stakes became Triple Crown champions.

Gallant Fox in 1930 was the 8-to-5 second choice to 4-to-5 Whichone, who finished second. Assault in 1946 was the 7-to-5 second choice to 1.35-to-1 Lord Boswell, who finished fifth.

Fastest Belmont Times

Year	Winner	Time	Cond.
1973	Secretariat	2:24	Fast
1989	Easy Goer	2:26	Fast
1992	A.P. Indy	2:26	Good
1988	Risen Star	2:26⅖	Fast
2001	Point Given	2:26.56	Fast
1957	Gallant Man	2:26⅗	Fast
1978	Affirmed	2:26⅘	Fast
1994	Tabasco Cat	2:26.82	Fast

Fastest Fractions

Quarter-mile	:23	Another Review, 1991
Half-mile	:46⅕	Secretariat, 1973
Six furlongs	1:09⅘	Secretariat, 1973
One mile	1:34⅕	Secretariat, 1973
1¼ miles	1:59	Secretariat, 1973

Evolution of Belmont Stakes Record at 1½ Miles

Year	Winner	Time	Cond.
1874	Saxon	2:39½	Fast
1926	Crusader	2:32⅕	Sloppy
1930	Gallant Fox	2:31⅗	Good
1931	Twenty Grand	2:29⅗	Fast
1934	Peace Chance	2:29⅕	Fast
1937	War Admiral	2:28⅗	Fast
1943	Count Fleet	2:28⅕	Fast
1957	Gallant Man	2:26⅗	Fast
1973	Secretariat	2:24	Fast

Slowest Winning Times

Year	Winner	Time	Cond.
1970	High Echelon	2:34	Sloppy
1928	Vito	2:33⅕	Fast
1932	Faireno	2:32⅘	Fast
1929	Blue Larkspur	2:32⅘	Sloppy
1933	Hurryoff	2:32⅗	Fast
1927	Chance Shot	2:32⅖	Fast
1944	Bounding Home	2:32⅕	Fast
1926	Crusader	2:32⅕	Fast
1995	Thunder Gulch	2:32.02	Good
1930	Gallant Fox	2:31⅗	Fast
2000	Commendable	2:31.19	Fast
1941	Whirlaway	2:31	Fast

Belmont Winners Who Sired Belmont Winners

3 **Man o' War (1920):** American Flag, 1925; Crusader, 1926; War Admiral, 1937.

2 **Commando (1901):** Peter Pan, 1907; Colin, 1908.

Gallant Fox (1930): Omaha, 1935; Granville, 1936.

Count Fleet (1943): Counterpoint, 1951; One Count, 1952.

Seattle Slew (1977): Swale, 1984; A.P. Indy, 1992.

1 **Duke of Magenta (1878):** Eric, 1889.

Spendthrift (1879): Hastings, 1896.

Hastings (1896): Masterman, 1902.

The Finn (1915): Zev, 1923.

Sword Dancer (1959): Damascus, 1967.

Secretariat (1973): Risen Star, 1988.

Shortest-Priced Winning Favorites

Winner	Year	Odds
Man o' War	1920	.04-to-1
Hanover	1887	.05-to-1
Count Fleet	1943	.05-to-1
George Kinney	1883	.08-to-1
Sweep	1910	.10-to-1
Secretariat	1973	.10-to-1
Johnstown	1939	.12-to-1
Nashua	1955	.15-to-1
Tim Tam	1958	.15-to-1
Forester	1882	.20-to-1
Citation	1948	.20-to-1
*Hourless	1917	.25-to-1
Whirlaway	1941	.25-to-1
Chance Shot	1927	.29-to-1
Sir Dixon	1888	.36-to-1
Burgomaster	1906	.40-to-1
Seattle Slew	1977	.40-to-1
American Flag	1925	.45-to-1
Native Dancer	1953	.45-to-1
Grenada	1880	.50-to-1
Jean Bereaud	1899	.50-to-1
Colin	1908	.50-to-1

Longest Winning Odds

Year	Horse	Odds
2002	Sarava	70.25-to-1
1961	Sherluck	65.05-to-1
1980	Temperence Hill	53.40-to-1
1971	Pass Catcher	34.50-to-1
1999	Lemon Drop Kid	29.75-to-1
2000	Commendable	18.80-to-1
1944	Bounding Home	16.35-to-1

Odds-On Beaten Favorites

Year	Horse	Odds	Finish
1958	Tim Tam	.15-to-1	2nd
1979	Spectacular Bid	.30-to-1	3rd
1922	*Snob II	.33-to-1	2nd
1938	Dauber	.33-to-1	2nd
1942	Alsab	.40-to-1	2nd
1928	Victorian	.45-to-1	5th
1961	Carry Back	.45-to-1	7th
1900	Missionary	.50-to-1	3rd
1944	Pensive	.50-to-1	2nd
1952	Blue Man	.50-to-1	2nd
1963	Candy Spots	.50-to-1	2nd
1915	Pebbles	.60-to-1	3rd
1966	Kauai King	.60-to-1	4th
1913	Rock View	.70-to-1	2nd
1930	Whichone	.70-to-1	2nd
1971	Canonero II	.70-to-1	4th
1947	Faultless	.75-to-1	5th
1889	Diablo	.80-to-1	2nd
1891	Montana	.80-to-1	2nd
1895	Counter Tenor	.80-to-1	2nd
1936	Brevity	.80-to-1	5th
1949	Ponder	.80-to-1	2nd
1964	Northern Dancer	.80-to-1	3rd
1981	Pleasant Colony	.80-to-1	3rd
1987	Alysheba	.80-to-1	4th
1998	Real Quiet	.80-to-1	2nd

Year	Horse	Odds	Finish
1950	Hill Prince	.85-to-1	7th
1960	Tompion	.85-to-1	4th
1957	Bold Ruler	.85-to-1	3rd
1989	Sunday Silence	.90-to-1	2nd

Belmont Front-Runners

Since Capot in 1949, only six horses have won the Belmont while leading at every point of call, and none since Swale in '84. The following Belmont Stakes winners were on the lead at all points of call.

Year	Winner	Winning margin
1898	*Bowling Brook	8
1901	Commando	½
1902	Masterman	2
1904	Delhi	3½
1905	Tanya	½
1906	Burgomaster	4
1907	Peter Pan	1
1908	Colin	Head
1910	Sweep	6
1915	The Finn	4
1916	Friar Rock	3
1917	*Hourless	10
1920	Man o' War	20
1923	Zev	1½
1927	Chance Shot	1½
1930	Gallant Fox	3
1932	Faireno	1½
1937	War Admiral	3
1939	Johnstown	5
1943	Count Fleet	25
1948	Citation	8
1949	Capot	½
1972	Riva Ridge	7
1973	Secretariat	31
1976	Bold Forbes	Neck
1977	Seattle Slew	4
1978	Affirmed	Head
1984	Swale	4

Winning Belmont Post Positions

Post	Winners	Post	Winners
1	23	7	11
2	11	8	5
3	13	9	3
4	8	10	2
5	13	11	2
6	7		

Largest Winning Margins

Year	Horse	Margin in lengths
1973	Secretariat	31
1943	Count Fleet	25
1920	Man o' War	20
1988	Risen Star	14¾
1987	Bet Twice	14
1982	Conquistador Cielo	14
2001	Point Given	12¼
1888	Sir Dixon	12
1931	Twenty Grand	10
1917	*Hourless	10

Smallest Winning Margins

Year	Horse	Margin
1998	Victory Gallop	nose
1962	Jaipur	nose
1936	Granville	nose
1999	Lemon Drop Kid	head
1991	Hansel	head
1978	Affirmed	head
1908	Colin	head
1900	Ildrim	head
1899	Jean Bereaud	head
1895	Belmar	head
1893	Commanche	head
1889	Eric	head
1876	Algerine	head
1867	Ruthless	head
1981	Summing	neck
1976	Bold Forbes	neck
1975	Avatar	neck
1965	Hail to All	neck
1956	Needles	neck
1954	High Gun	neck
1953	Native Dancer	neck
1938	Pasteurized	neck
1936	Granville	neck
1896	Hastings	neck
1891	Foxford	neck
1881	Saunterer	neck
1874	Saxon	neck

Fillies in the Belmont

Ruthless left a tough act to follow when she won the inaugural Belmont Stakes in 1867. Only 20 other fillies have raced in the Belmont Stakes, and just one other, Tanya, in 1905, has won. Kentucky Derby winner and Preakness runner-up Genuine Risk was second to Temperence Hill in 1980, and six other fillies have finished third, most recently My Flag in '96.

Year	Filly	Finish
1867	**Ruthless**	1st
1868	Fanny Ludlow	3rd
1869	Invercauld	3rd
	Viola	7th
1870	Midday	3rd
	Nellie James	4th
	Stamps	6th
1871	Nellie Gray	4th
	Mary Clark	9th
1885	Miss Palmer	9th
1905	**Tanya**	1st
	Funders	7th
1913	Flying Fairy	3rd
1923	Miss Smith	8th
1927	Flambino	3rd
1932	Laughing Queen	10th
1954	Riverina	7th
1980	Genuine Risk	2nd
1988	Winning Colors	6th
1996	My Flag	3rd
1999	Silverbulletday	7th

Geldings in the Belmont

Creme Fraiche, owned by Elizabeth Moran's Brushwood Stable, remains the only gelding ever to have won the Belmont Stakes (G1). In its early years, the Belmont conditions allowed geldings to run in the classic race, but America subsequently bowed to European practice, which barred geldings from major races. Lanius, a gelding, ran in the 1918 Belmont, but it was not until '57 that geldings again were permitted in the race. Creme Fraiche was the first gelding to compete in the Belmont since 1979 champion juvenile male Rockhill Native finished third in '80.

Geldings who have started in the Belmont since 1985:

Year	Gelding	Finish
2003	Funny Cide	3rd
2002	Perfect Drift	10th
2001	Balto Star	8th
2000	Unshaded	3rd
1998	Thomas Jo	3rd
1997	Irish Silence	5th
1996	Rocket Flash	6th
	Jamies First Punch	8th
	Saratoga Dandy	11th

Year	Gelding	Finish
	Cavonnier	DNF
1995	Citadeed	3rd
	Ave's Flag	7th
	Colonial Secretary	9th
1993	Only Alpha	11th
	Prairie Bayou	DNF
1991	Quintana	6th
	Subordinated Debt	9th
1989	Imbibe	7th
1988	Kingpost	2nd
1985	**Creme Fraiche**	1st

Birthplaces of Belmont Winners

Place of Birth	Winners
Kentucky	87
Virginia	11
New Jersey	7
England	6
Florida	5
New York	3
Pennsylvania	3
Tennessee	3
California	2
Ireland	2
Maryland	2
Texas	2
Canada	1
Montana	1

Status of Belmont Stakes Winners, Since 1970

Year	Winner	Birthdate	Status	Where Stands/Stood	Location	Death Date
2003	Empire Maker	4/27/2000	In training			
2002	Sarava	3/2/1999	In training			
2001	Point Given	3/27/1998	Stallion	Three Chimneys Farm	Midway, KY	
2000	Commendable	4/13/1997	Stallion	Mill Ridge Farm	Lexington, KY	
1999	Lemon Drop Kid	5/26/1996	Stallion	Lane's End	Versailles, KY	
1998	Victory Gallop	5/30/1995	Stallion	WinStar Farm	Versailles, KY	
1997	Touch Gold	5/26/1994	Stallion	Adena Springs Kentucky	Versailles, KY	
1996	Editor's Note	4/26/1993	Stallion	Overbrook Farm	Lexington, KY	
1995	Thunder Gulch	5/23/1992	Stallion	Ashford Stud	Versailles, KY	
1994	Tabasco Cat	4/15/1991	Stallion	JBBA Shizunai Stallion Station	Hokkaido, Japan	
1993	Colonial Affair	4/19/1990	Stallion	Arrow Stud	Hokkaido, Japan	
1992	A.P. Indy	3/31/1989	Stallion	Lane's End	Versailles, KY	
1991	Hansel	3/12/1988	Stallion	Hidaka Stallion Station	Hokkaido, Japan	
1990	Go and Go (Ire)	3/21/1987	Deceased	Waldorf Farm	North Chatham, NY	3/2000
1989	Easy Goer	3/21/1986	Deceased	Claiborne Farm	Paris, KY	5/1/1994
1988	Risen Star	3/25/1985	Deceased	Walmac International	Lexington, KY	3/13/1998
1987	Bet Twice	4/20/1984	Deceased	Muirfield East	Chesapeake City, MD	3/5/1999
1986	Danzig Connection	4/6/1983	Stallion	Collin Stud	Newmarket, England	
1985	Creme Fraiche	4/7/1982	Gelding	Brushwood Farm	Malvern, PA	
1984	Swale	4/21/1981	Deceased			6/17/1984
1983	Caveat	3/16/1980	Deceased	Northview Stallion Station	Chesapeake City, MD	2/1/1995
1982	Conquistador Cielo	3/20/1979	Deceased	Claiborne Farm	Paris, KY	12/17/2002
1981	Summing	4/16/1978	Stallion	Getaway Thoroughbred Farms	Romoland, CA	
1980	Temperence Hill	3/6/1977	Stallion	Swang Jei Farm	Nontaburi, Thailand	
1979	Coastal	4/16/1976	Pensioned	Summerhill Stud	Mooi River, South Africa	
1978	Affirmed	2/21/1975	Deceased	Jonabell Farm	Lexington, KY	1/12/2001
1977	Seattle Slew	2/15/1974	Deceased	Three Chimneys Farm	Midway, KY	5/7/2002
1976	Bold Forbes	3/31/1973	Deceased	Stone Farm	Paris, KY	8/9/2000
1975	Avatar	3/10/1972	Deceased	Frisch's Farm	Morrow, OH	12/3/1992
1974	Little Current	4/5/1971	Deceased	Pacific Equine Clinic	Monroe, WA	1/19/2003
1973	Secretariat	3/30/1970	Deceased	Claiborne Farm	Paris, KY	10/4/1989
1972	Riva Ridge	4/13/1969	Deceased	Claiborne Farm	Paris, KY	4/21/1985
1971	Pass Catcher	4/6/1968	Deceased	Ocala Stud Farm	Ocala, FL	1993
1970	High Echelon	3/22/1967	Deceased	Franks Farms	Ocala, FL	5/15/1991

Belmont Stakes

Grade 1, Belmont Park, three-year-olds, 1½ miles, dirt. Held on June 7, 2003, with gross value of $1,000,000. First run in 1867. Weights: colts and geldings, 126 pounds; fillies, 121 pounds.

Year	Winner	Jockey	Second	Third	Strs	Time	Track	1st purse
2003	**Empire Maker**	J. Bailey	Ten Most Wanted	Funny Cide	6	2:28.26	sy	$600,000
2002	**Sarava**	E. Prado	Medaglia d'Oro	Sunday Break (Jpn)	11	2:29.71	ft	600,000
2001	**Point Given**	G. Stevens	A P Valentine	Monarchos	9	2:26.56	ft	600,000
2000	**Commendable**	P. Day	Aptitude	‡Unshaded	11	2:31.19	ft	600,000
1999	**Lemon Drop Kid**	J. Santos	Vision and Verse	Charismatic	12	2:27.88	ft	600,000
1998	**Victory Gallop**	G. Stevens	Real Quiet	‡Thomas Jo	11	2:29.16	ft	**600,000**
1997	**Touch Gold**	C. McCarron	Silver Charm	Free House	7	2:28.82	ft	432,600
1996	**Editor's Note**	R. Douglas	Skip Away	†My Flag	14	2:28.96	ft	437,880
1995	**Thunder Gulch**	G. Stevens	Star Standard	‡Citadeed	11	2:32.02	ft	415,440
1994	**Tabasco Cat**	P. Day	Go for Gin	Strodes Creek	6	2:26.82	ft	392,280
1993	**Colonial Affair**	J. Krone	Kissin Kris	Wild Gale	13	2:29.97	gd	444,540
1992	**A.P. Indy**	E. Delahoussaye	My Memoirs (GB)	Pine Bluff	11	2:26.13	gd	458,880
1991	**Hansel**	J. Bailey	Strike the Gold	Mane Minister	11	2:28.10	ft	417,480
1990	**Go and Go (Ire)**	M. Kinane	Thirty Six Red	Baron de Vaux	9	2:27⅕	gd	411,600
1989	**Easy Goer**	P. Day	Sunday Silence	Le Voyageur	10	2:26	ft	413,520
1988	**Risen Star**	E. Delahoussaye	‡Kingpost	Brian's Time	6	2:26⅖	ft	303,720
1987	**Bet Twice**	C. Perret	Cryptoclearance	Gulch	9	2:28⅕	ft	329,160
1986	**Danzig Connection**	C. McCarron	Johns Treasure	Ferdinand	10	2:29⅘	sy	338,640
1985	**‡Creme Fraiche**	E. Maple	Stephan's Odyssey	Chief's Crown	11	2:27	my	307,740
1984	**Swale**	L. Pincay Jr.	Pine Circle	Morning Bob	11	2:27⅕	ft	310,020
1983	**Caveat**	L. Pincay Jr.	Slew o' Gold	Barberstown	**15**	2:27⅘	ft	215,100
1982	**Conquistador Cielo**	L. Pincay Jr.	Gato Del Sol	Illuminate	11	2:28⅕	sy	159,720
1981	**Summing**	G. Martens	Highland Blade	Pleasant Colony	11	2:29	ft	170,580
1980	**Temperence Hill**	E. Maple	†Genuine Risk	Rockhill Native	10	2:29⅘	my	176,228
1979	**Coastal**	R. Hernandez	Golden Act	Spectacular Bid	8	2:29⅗	ft	161,400
1978	**AFFIRMED**	S. Cauthen	Alydar	Darby Creek Road	5	2:26⅘	ft	110,580
1977	**SEATTLE SLEW**	J. Cruguet	Run Dusty Run	Sanhedrin	8	2:29⅗	my	109,080
1976	**Bold Forbes**	A. Cordero Jr.	McKenzie Bridge	Great Contractor	10	2:29	ft	117,000
1975	**Avatar**	W. Shoemaker	Foolish Pleasure	Master Derby	9	2:28⅕	ft	116,160
1974	**Little Current**	M. Rivera	Jolly Johu	Cannonade	9	2:29⅕	ft	101,970
1973	**SECRETARIAT**	R. Turcotte	Twice a Prince	My Gallant	5	**2:24**	ft	90,120
1972	**Riva Ridge**	R. Turcotte	Ruritania	Cloudy Dawn	10	2:28	ft	83,540
1971	**Pass Catcher**	W. Blum	Jim French	Bold Reason	13	2:30⅗	ft	97,710
1970	**High Echelon**	J. Rotz	Needles n Pens	Naskra	10	2:34	sy	115,000
1969	**Arts and Letters**	B. Baeza	Majestic Prince	Dike	6	2:28⅘	ft	104,050
1968	**Stage Door Johnny**	H. Gustines	Forward Pass	Call Me Prince	9	2:27⅕	ft	117,700
1967	**Damascus**	W. Shoemaker	Cool Reception	Gentleman James	9	2:28⅘	ft	104,950
1966	**Amberoid**	W. Boland	Buffle	Advocator	11	2:29⅗	ft	117,700
1965	**Hail to All**	J. Sellers	Tom Rolfe	First Family	8	2:28⅖	ft	104,150
1964	**Quadrangle**	M. Ycaza	Roman Brother	Northern Dancer	8	2:28⅖	ft	110,850
1963	**Chateaugay**	B. Baeza	Candy Spots	Choker	7	2:30⅕	gd	101,700
1962	**Jaipur**	W. Shoemaker	Admiral's Voyage	Crimson Satan	8	2:28⅘	ft	109,550
1961	**Sherluck**	B. Baeza	Globemaster	Guadalcanal	9	2:29⅕	ft	104,900
1960	***Celtic Ash**	W. Hartack	Venetian Way	Disperse	7	2:29⅗	ft	96,785
1959	**Sword Dancer**	W. Shoemaker	Bagdad	Royal Orbit	9	2:28⅗	sy	93,525
1958	***Cavan**	P. Anderson	Tim Tam	‡Flamingo	8	2:30⅕	ft	73,440
1957	***Gallant Man**	W. Shoemaker	Inside Tract	Bold Ruler	6	2:26⅗	ft	78,350
1956	**Needles**	D. Erb	Career Boy	Fabius	8	2:29⅘	ft	83,600
1955	**Nashua**	E. Arcaro	Blazing Count	Portersville	8	2:29	ft	83,700
1954	**High Gun**	E. Guerin	Fisherman	*Limelight	13	2:30⅘	ft	89,000
1953	**Native Dancer**	E. Guerin	Jamie K.	Royal Bay Gem	6	2:28⅗	ft	82,500
1952	**One Count**	E. Arcaro	Blue Man	Armageddon	6	2:30⅕	ft	82,400
1951	**Counterpoint**	D. Gorman	Battlefield	Battle Morn	9	2:29	ft	82,000
1950	**Middleground**	W. Boland	Lights Up	Mr. Trouble	9	2:28⅗	ft	61,350
1949	**Capot**	T. Atkinson	Ponder	Palestinian	8	2:30⅕	ft	60,900
1948	**CITATION**	E. Arcaro	Better Self	Escadru	8	2:28⅕	ft	77,700
1947	**Phalanx**	R. Donoso	Tide Rips	Tailspin	9	2:29⅗	ft	78,900
1946	**ASSAULT**	W. Mehrtens	Natchez	Cable	7	2:30⅘	ft	75,400
1945	**Pavot**	E. Arcaro	Wildlife	Jeep	8	2:30⅕	ft	52,675
1944	**Bounding Home**	G. L. Smith	Pensive	Bull Dandy	7	2:32⅕	ft	55,000
1943	**COUNT FLEET**	J. Longden	Fairy Manhurst	‡Deseronto	3	2:28⅕	ft	35,340
1942	**Shut Out**	E. Arcaro	Alsab	Lochinvar	7	2:29⅕	ft	44,520
1941	**WHIRLAWAY**	E. Arcaro	Robert Morris	‡Yankee Chance	4	2:31	ft	39,770
1940	**Bimelech**	F. Smith	Your Chance	Andy K.	6	2:29⅗	ft	35,030
1939	**Johnstown**	J. Stout	Belay	Gilded Knight	6	2:29⅗	ft	37,020
1938	**Pasteurized**	J. Stout	Dauber	Cravat	6	2:29⅖	ft	34,530
1937	**WAR ADMIRAL**	C. Kurtsinger	Sceneshifter	Vamoose	7	2:28⅗	ft	38,020
1936	**Granville**	J. Stout	Mr. Bones	Hollyrood	10	2:30	ft	29,800
1935	**OMAHA**	W. Saunders	Firethorn	Rosemont	5	2:30⅗	sy	35,480

Year	Winner	Jockey	Second	Third	Strs	Time	Track	1st purse
1934	**Peace Chance**	W. Wright	High Quest	Good Goods	8	2:29⅕	ft	43,410
1933	**Hurryoff**	M. Garner	Nimbus	Union	9	2:32⅗	ft	49,490
1932	**Faireno**	T. Malley	Osculator	Flag Pole	11	2:32⅘	ft	55,120
1931	**Twenty Grand**	C. Kurtsinger	Sun Meadow	Jamestown	3	2:29⅗	ft	58,770
1930	**GALLANT FOX**	E. Sande	Whichone	Questionnaire	4	2:31⅗	gd	66,040
1929	**Blue Larkspur**	M. Garner	African	Jack High	8	2:32⅘	sy	59,650
1928	**Vito**	C. Kummer	Genie	Diavolo	6	2:33⅕	ft	63,430
1927	**Chance Shot**	E. Sande	Bois de Rose	†Flambino	6	2:32⅖	ft	60,910
1926	**Crusader**	A. Johnson	Espino	Haste	9	2:32⅕	sy	48,550
1925	**American Flag**	A. Johnson	Dangerous	Swope	7	2:16⅘	ft	38,500
1924	**Mad Play**	E. Sande	Mr. Mutt	Modest	11	2:18⅘	gd	42,880
1923	**Zev**	E. Sande	Chickvale	‡Rialto	8	2:19	gd	38,000
1922	**Pillory**	C. H. Miller	*Snob II	Hea	4	2:18⅘	ft	39,200
1921	**Grey Lag**	E. Sande	Sporting Blood	Leonardo II	4	2:16⅘	ft	8,650
1920	**Man o' War**	C. Kummer	*Donnacona	—	2	2:14⅕	ft	7,950
1919	**SIR BARTON**	J. Loftus	Sweep On	Natural Bridge	3	2:17⅖	ft	11,950
1918	***Johren**	F. Robinson	*War Cloud	‡Cum Sah	4	2:20⅖	ft	8,950
1917	***Hourless**	J. Butwell	Skeptic	Wonderful	3	2:17⅘	gd	5,800
1916	**Friar Rock**	E. Haynes	Spur	Churchill	4	2:22	my	4,100
1915	**The Finn**	G. Byrne	Half Rock	Pebbles	3	2:18⅖	ft	1,825
1914	**Luke McLuke**	M. Buxton	‡Gainer	‡Charlestonian	3	2:20	ft	3,275
1913	**Prince Eugene**	R. Troxler	Rock View	†Flying Fairy	4	2:18	ft	3,075
1910	**Sweep**	J. Butwell	Duke of Ormonde	—	2	2:22	ft	9,700
1909	**Joe Madden**	E. Dugan	Wise Mason	‡Donald Macdonald	5	2:21⅗	ft	24,550
1908	**Colin**	J. Notter	Fair Play	King James	4	n/a	sy	22,765
1907	**Peter Pan**	G. Mountain	Superman	Frank Gill	5	n/a	ft	22,765
1906	**Burgomaster**	L. Lyne	The Quail	Accountant	6	2:20	gd	22,700
1905	**†Tanya**	E. Hildebrand	Blandy	Hot Shot	7	2:08	ft	17,240
1904	**Delhi**	G. Odom	Graziallo	Rapid Water	8	2:06⅗	ft	14,685
1903	**Africander**	J. Bullman	Whorler	Red Knight	4	2:21¾	ft	12,285
1902	**Masterman**	J. Bullman	Ranald	King Hanover	6	2:22⅗	ft	12,020
1901	**Commando**	H. Spencer	The Parader	All Green	3	2:21	ft	11,595
1900	**Ildrim**	N. Turner	‡Petruchio	Missionary	7	2:21¼	ft	14,790
1899	**Jean Bereaud**	R. Clawson	Half Time	Glengar	4	2:23	ft	10,680
1898	***Bowling Brook**	F. Littlefield	Previous	Hamburg	4	2:32	hy	7,810
1897	**Scottish Chieftain**	J. Scherrer	On Deck	Octagon	6	2:23¼	ft	3,350
1896	**Hastings**	H. Griffin	Handspring	Hamilton II	4	2:24½	gd	3,025
1895	**Belmar**	F. Taral	Counter Tenor	Nanki Pooh	5	2:11½	hy	2,700
1894	**Henry of Navarre**	W. Simms	Prig	Assignee	3	1:56½	ft	6,680
1893	**Comanche**	W. Simms	Dr. Rice	Rainbow	5	1:53¼	ft	5,310
1892	**Patron**	W. Hayward	Shellbark	—	2	2:12	my	6,610
1891	**Foxford**	E. Garrison	Montana	Laurestan	6	2:08¾	gd	5,070
1890	**Burlington**	S. Barnes	Devotee	Padishah	9	2:07¾	ft	8,560
1889	**Eric**	W. Hayward	Diablo	Zephyrus	3	2:47¼	gd	4,960
1888	**Sir Dixon**	J. McLaughlin	Prince Royal	—	2	2:40¼	ft	3,440
1887	**Hanover**	J. McLaughlin	Oneko	—	2	2:43½	hy	2,900
1886	**Inspector B.**	J. McLaughlin	The Bard	Linden	5	2:41	ft	2,720
1885	**Tyrant**	P. Duffy	‡St. Augustine	Tecumseh	6	2:43	gd	2,710
1884	**Panique**	J. McLaughlin	Knight of Ellerslie	Himalaya	4	2:42	gd	3,150
1883	**George Kinney**	J. McLaughlin	‡Trombone	Renegade	4	2:42½	ft	3,070
1882	**Forester**	J. McLaughlin	Babcock	‡Wyoming	3	2:43	ft	2,600
1881	**Saunterer**	T. Costello	Eole	Baltic	6	2:47	hy	3,000
1880	**Grenada**	W. Hughes	Ferncliffe	Turenne	4	2:47	gd	2,800
1879	**Spendthrift**	G. Evans	‡Monitor	Jericho	6	2:24¾	sy	4,250
1878	**Duke of Magenta**	W. Hughes	Bramble	Sparta	6	2:43½	my	3,850
1877	**Cloverbrook**	C. Holloway	‡Loiterer	Baden-Baden	13	2:46	hy	5,200
1876	**Algerine**	W. Donohue	Fiddlesticks	Barricade	5	2:40½	ft	3,700
1875	**Calvin**	R. Swim	Aristides	Milner	14	2:42¼	ft	4,450
1874	**Saxon**	G. Barbee	Grinstead	Aaron Pennington	9	2:39½	ft	4,200
1873	**Springbok**	J. Rowe	Count d'Orsay	Strachino	10	3:01¾	fr	5,200
1872	**Joe Daniels**	J. Rowe	‡Meteor	Shylock	9	2:58¼	fr	4,500
1871	**Harry Bassett**	W. Miller	Stockwood	By the Sea	11	2:56	ft	5,450
1870	**Kingfisher**	Dick	Foster	†Midday	7	2:59½	ft	3,750
1869	**Fenian**	C. Miller	Glenelg	†Invercauld	8	3:04¼	hy	3,350
1868	**General Duke**	R. Swim	Northumberland	†Fanny Ludlow	6	3:02	ft	2,800
1867	**†Ruthless**	J. Gilpatrick	DeCourcey	Rivoli	4	3:05	hy	1,850

†—filly, ‡—gelding, *—imported horse

1867-'73, 1⅝ miles; 1890-'92, 1895, 1904-'05, 1¼ miles; 1893-'94, 1⅛ miles; 1896-1903, 1906-'25, 1⅜ miles. 1867-'89, held at Jerome Park; 1890-1904, Morris Park; 1963-'67, Aqueduct. Not run 1911 and '12. 1973-present, Grade 1. Hansel (1991), Risen Star (1988), and Bet Twice (1987) earned $1-million bonus from Triple Crown Productions. 1907-'08 no official time recorded; bold-faced type shows records in starters, time, and purse earnings.

2003 Kentucky Derby: Funny Cide of Racing

In the weeks leading up to the Kentucky Derby on May 3, Funny Cide essentially went unnoticed. Trainer Barclay Tagg liked it that way, and kept the New York-bred gelding at Belmont Park until three days before the race, avoiding the frenzied scene that fills the barn area at Churchill Downs in the days leading up to the race.

Funny Cide, a son of leading 2002 North American freshman sire Distorted Humor, had not always been overlooked. On three occasions in late 2000 and early '01, Funny Cide caught Tagg's eye when the trainer visited Tony Everard's New Episode Training Center near Ocala while the gelding, a $22,000 Fasig-Tipton Saratoga preferred yearling sale purchase, was being prepped for entry in a two-year-olds in training sale. Tagg eventually purchased Funny Cide for $75,000, thinking he would be a useful New York-bred for the state's lucrative restricted events.

Funny Cide had plenty of reasons to be lost in the shuffle in the Derby mix after being defeated once each by trainer Bobby Frankel's formidable Derby duo, first by Peace Rules in the Louisiana Derby (G2) in March and then by Empire Maker in the Wood Memorial Stakes (G1) in April.

He also was trying to overcome history by attempting to become the first gelding to win the Derby since Clyde Van Dusen in 1929 and the first New York-bred to capture the storied race. Sackatoga Stable managing partner Jackson Knowlton and Tagg had never started a horse in the Derby, and jockey Jose Santos had never

finished better than fourth in six prior starts.

Strange, unconventional, and funny things often mark the road to the Triple Crown, and, in the case of the Kentucky Derby, Funny Cide happened. In a race that was all but conceded to Frankel and Empire Maker, it was the unassuming gelding at 12.80-to-1 who won the 129th edition of the Derby. Funny Cide finished 1¾ lengths in front of Juddmonte Farms' homebred Empire Maker, who made a languished late run in the stretch and finished a head in front of Peace Rules, with the late-running Atswhatimtalknbout another head farther back in fourth. Funny Cide ran the Derby's 1¼ miles in 2:01.19 on a fast track.

Funny Cide stole the spotlight that had been shining almost solely on Empire Maker throughout the three weeks leading up to the Derby. The son of Unbridled out of 2002 Broodmare of the Year Toussaud had won the Florida Derby (G1) and Wood Memorial, but a minor foot bruise incurred in the Wood flared up during Derby week. Frankel dismissed its significance, but bettors did not, sending him off as the 5-to-2 favorite after being listed at 6-to-5 in the morning line.

Although Empire Maker visually gave the impression he was posting an easy, half-length victory over Funny Cide in the Wood on April 12, Tagg, Santos, and Knowlton thought differently. "Empire Maker was all out," Santos said.

After a half-mile breeze in :48.01 on April 22 at Belmont Park, Funny Cide served notice that he was prepared for the Derby with a sharp five-furlong move in :58.43 on April 29 with Tagg's assistant, Robin Smullen, aboard. Funny Cide shipped to Churchill the next day.

The gelding entered the Derby with no 2003 victories after an undefeated juvenile season against New York-breds. Funny Cide ended his juvenile campaign with back-to-back victories in the restricted Bertram F. Bongard and Sleepy Hollow Stakes at Belmont. Stabled at Palm Meadows training center over the winter, Funny Cide finished fifth in the Holy Bull Stakes (G3) behind winner Offlee Wild and was moved up to second in the Louisiana Derby on the subsequent clenbuterol disqualification of Kafwain. Funny Cide showed a new dimension in the Louisiana Derby when he set the pace, was passed in the stretch, but came back again while racing on the inside.

In the Derby, Funny Cide broke from the fifth post position and bumped with Offlee Wild at the start. But he was quickly in the clear when Peace Rules and Edgar Prado came out slightly and left a large hole for the eventual winner. Blue Grass Stakes (G1) runner-up Brancusi took the field into the first turn, with Peace Rules, Funny Cide, Eye of the Tiger, and

Owner

Sackatoga Stable, a partnership with ten members, derives its name from two New York communities: Sackets Harbor, the town on Lake Ontario where six members of the stable grew up, and Saratoga Springs, where managing partner Jackson Knowlton and partner Lou Titterton now reside. Funny Cide is one of three horses in the stable. The partnership has owned only nine Thoroughbreds since it was formed in 1995. Ownership of Funny Cide is divided into five shares, with Knowlton, David Mahan, and Gus Williams each owning full shares. The remaining two shares are split among Harold Cring, Peter Phillips, Mark Phillips, Jon Constance, Larry Reinhardt, Eric Dattner, and Titterton. All but Reinhardt attended the Derby, and they rented a yellow school bus to take their entourage from their hotel to Churchill Downs.

Trainer

Barclay Tagg, born December 30, 1937, in Lancaster, Pennsylvania, was for many years a Maryland-based trainer before moving his operation to New York in January 2001. He graduated from Pennsylvania State University with a degree in animal husbandry in 1961 and managed a farm in his home state. After a brief career as a steeplechase jockey, he began training in 1971. His first winner was Tooter's Fancy at Liberty Bell Park on January 25, 1972. His first prominent horse was Roo Art, who became a millionaire Grade 1 winner after he was transferred to D. Wayne Lukas. His best horse before Funny Cide was Miss Josh, who won the 1991 Gamely Handicap (G1).

Scrimshaw right behind.

Jerry Bailey kept Empire Maker eighth while racing wide around the first turn as Brancusi clicked off splits of :22.78 and :46.23 for the opening half-mile. As Peace Rules and Brancusi continued to battle on the front end, Funny Cide was traveling smoothly and making steady progress up the backstretch. Peace Rules, the 6.30-to-1 second choice off his win in the Blue Grass, took command after six furlongs in 1:10.48. Midway around the turn, Santos pushed Funny Cide past a tiring Brancusi and took dead aim at Peace Rules.

A quarter-mile from the finish and past the mile in 1:35.75, Peace Rules held a half-length advantage over Funny Cide, with Empire Maker another length behind. Racing between the two Frankel runners, with Peace Rules to the inside and Empire Maker to the outside, Santos called on Funny Cide with three right-handed cracks of the whip outside the furlong marker, and the gelding responded. Santos switched to his left hand with a sixteenth to run, and Funny Cide spurted clear again as Peace Rules started to tire on the inside and Empire Maker failed to sustain his bid.—*Tom Law*

TENTH RACE
Churchill
May 3, 2002

1¼ MILES (1:59⅖). 129th running of the Kentucky Derby. Grade 1. 3-year-olds. Purse $1,000,000.

Value of race $1,100,200; Winner $800,200; second $170,000; third $85,000; fourth $45,000. Mutuel WPS Pool $36,610,341. Exacta Pool $17,429,596. Trifecta Pool $19,040,971. Superfecta Pool $4,908,214.

Horse	M/Eqt.	Wt.	PP	¼	½	¾	1 mi.	Str.	Fin.	Jockey	Odds $1
Funny Cide	L	126	5	$4^{\frac{1}{2}}$	$3^{\frac{1}{2}}$	$3^{1\frac{1}{2}}$	2^{1}	1^{hd}	$1^{1\frac{3}{4}}$	J. Santos	12.80
Empire Maker	Lb	126	11	$8^{\frac{1}{2}}$	$8^{2\frac{1}{2}}$	$8^{1\frac{1}{2}}$	$3^{1\frac{1}{2}}$	$3^{1\frac{1}{2}}$	2^{hd}	J. Bailey	*2.50
Peace Rules	L	126	4	$2^{1\frac{1}{2}}$	$2^{1\frac{1}{2}}$	$2^{1\frac{1}{2}}$	$1^{\frac{1}{2}}$	$2^{\frac{1}{2}}$	3^{hd}	E. Prado	6.30
Atswhatimtalknbout	Lb	126	3	$10^{1\frac{1}{2}}$	12^{2}	11^{2}	$10^{\frac{1}{2}}$	$5^{\frac{1}{2}}$	$4^{2\frac{3}{4}}$	D. Flores	8.90
Eye of the Tiger	L	126	12	3^{hd}	$4^{1\frac{1}{2}}$	$4^{\frac{1}{2}}$	4^{1}	$4^{1\frac{1}{2}}$	5^{1}	E. Coa	41.50
Buddy Gil	L	126	7	13^{hd}	$13^{2\frac{1}{2}}$	13^{4}	11^{1}	$6^{\frac{1}{2}}$	$6^{\frac{3}{4}}$	G. Stevens	7.20
Outta Here	L	126	14	$15^{1\frac{1}{2}}$	14^{hd}	16	15^{3}	$14^{1\frac{1}{2}}$	7^{1}	K. Desormeaux	39.70
Ten Cents a Shine	L	126	13	16	16	$15^{\frac{1}{2}}$	$14^{3\frac{1}{2}}$	11^{1}	8^{nk}	C. Borel	37.20
Ten Most Wanted	L	126	15	$12^{1\frac{1}{2}}$	$10^{\frac{1}{2}}$	$10^{1\frac{1}{2}}$	$9^{\frac{1}{2}}$	$10^{\frac{1}{2}}$	$9^{1\frac{3}{4}}$	P. Day	6.60
Domestic Dispute	L	126	10	$7^{\frac{1}{2}}$	7^{1}	5^{hd}	7^{hd}	$7^{\frac{1}{2}}$	10^{1}	A. Solis	44.00
Scrimshaw	Lb	126	16	$5^{\frac{1}{2}}$	$6^{\frac{1}{2}}$	7^{hd}	8^{hd}	$8^{\frac{1}{2}}$	11^{1}	C. Velasquez	16.50
Offlee Wild	L	126	6	$11^{1\frac{1}{2}}$	$11^{1\frac{1}{2}}$	$9^{1\frac{1}{2}}$	$6^{\frac{1}{2}}$	9^{1}	$12^{5\frac{1}{2}}$	R. Albarado	29.90
Supah Blitz	Lb	126	1	$9^{2\frac{1}{2}}$	$9^{\frac{1}{2}}$	$12^{2\frac{1}{2}}$	13^{hd}	12^{1}	$13^{1\frac{3}{4}}$	R. Homeister	43.10
Indian Express	L	126	8	$6^{\frac{1}{2}}$	5^{hd}	6^{hd}	12^{hd}	$15^{2\frac{1}{2}}$	$14^{1\frac{1}{4}}$	T. Baze	10.80
Lone Star Sky	L	126	9	$14^{1\frac{1}{2}}$	15^{1}	$14^{\frac{1}{2}}$	16	16	15^{1}	S. Sellers	52.10
Brancusi	L	126	2	$1^{\frac{1}{2}}$	$1^{\frac{1}{2}}$	1^{hd}	5^{hd}	$13^{1\frac{1}{2}}$	16	T. Farina	29.30

Scratched—Sir Cherokee.

OFF AT 6:08. Times: :22.78, :46.23, 1:10.48, 1:35.75, 2:01.19.
Start: Good for all. Track: Fast. Weather: Cloudy.

$2 Mutuel Prices:			
6—FUNNY CIDE	**27.60**	**12.40**	**8.20**
12—EMPIRE MAKER		**5.80**	**4.40**
5—PEACE RULES			**6.00**

$2 EXACTA 6-12 PAID $97.00 $2 TRIFECTA 6-12-5 PAID $664.80
$1 PICK THREE 2-9-6 PAID $1,042.50 $1 PICK FOUR 4-2-9-6 PAID $7,017.50
$1 SUPERFECTA 6-12-5-4 PAID $2,795.80

Ch. g., by Distorted Humor out of Belle's Good Cide, by Slewacide. Trainer: Barclay Tagg. Breeder: WinStar Farm (NY)

FUNNY CIDE came out at start, bumped, rated near inside, four to five wide far turn, stiff drive. EMPIRE MAKER six to seven wide early, five wide backstretch, bold bid, drew even, not good enough. PEACE RULES pressed three wide, gained clear lead, held third, good courage. ATSWHATIMTALKNBOUT forced out bit at start, inside to lane, angled seven wide between rivals, closing late. EYE OF THE TIGER four wide early, tracked, leaned in and bumped at five-sixteenths, flattened out in lane. BUDDY GIL bumped at start, unhurried, three to four wide to lane, angled to rail, slight gain. OUTTA HERE eight to nine wide early, checked, angled in, lost position first turn, 12 wide in lane, mild bid. TEN CENTS A SHINE worked way in three to four wide, moved six wide backstretch, ten wide in lane, slight gain. TEN MOST WANTED slow start, bumped, checked, six wide trip, failed to rally. DOMESTIC DISPUTE in contention, five to six wide, empty in last eighth. SCRIMSHAW drifted in and bumped at start, tracked pace, five wide, bid three-eighths, flattened out. OFFLEE WILD bumped repeatedly after start, bid between horses far turn, weakened. SUPAH BLITZ drifted out and brushed at start, inside, no factor. INDIAN EXPRESS rank early, steadied repeatedly early, weakened far turn. LONE STAR SKY steadied, shuffled back first turn, never reached contention. BRANCUSI drifted out and brushed at start, pace inside, dueled, faded.

Copyright © 2003 Equibase Co. LLC

2003 Preakness Stakes: A Laugher for Funny Cide

Finally, after he and Funny Cide had romped to a near-record victory in the Preakness Stakes on May 17, Jose Santos could let it all out. Following a painful week in which he had been accused in a Miami *Herald* article of carrying an illegal electrical device and then cleared of the baseless charges, he and Funny Cide had earned the last laugh.

Standing up in the irons, Santos kissed his fingers and flashed a victory sign to the crowd of 100,268, the fourth largest in racing history at Pimlico Race Course. And, then, grinning, he opened his hand to reveal only his palm.

"The only machine I was carrying with me was the horse, the red horse," Santos proclaimed. "He showed it to you today; he can run like a nice machine. He was rolling at the end."

In fact, Funny Cide's *tour de force* over nine rivals had to convert doubters who pooh-poohed his Derby triumph on May 3 as a fluke. The unlikely chestnut hero—a gelding bred in New York, trained by a veteran who used to climb atop the barn roofs at Pimlico to get a glimpse of the Preakness, and owned by a bunch of New Yorkers who travel in a yellow school bus to watch the runner they call their lottery ticket—had earned a chance to win the Triple Crown.

"He doesn't know he's a gelding, he doesn't know he's a New York-bred, and he runs like hell, so we'll just let him do it," jubilant trainer Barclay Tagg said of Sackatoga Stable's $75,000 private purchase as an unraced juvenile.

Even though the storm caused by the Miami *Herald* allegations—which Kentucky stewards reviewed after receiving a photograph that showed what turned out to be a shadow in Santos's hand—dissipated somewhat after the jockey was cleared

just five days before the Preakness, emotions surged deep for the second jewel of the Triple Crown.

Despite a chilling mist in the air and a record low temperature for the Preakness of 50° following a day of heavy rain that left the surface rated as good for the classic, Santos's vindication on the track sparked an unusual warmth in the crowd.

"That was nice," the rider said almost shyly of the infield cheering, which marked a sharp contrast with the jolting verbal blows he had endured in New York immediately after the allegations surfaced.

Tagg drew some criticism when he opted to keep Funny Cide at Belmont, not shipping to Pimlico until the afternoon before the race. Even then, he chose to stable the son of Distorted Humor far away from the congested stakes barn in stalls allotted to an old friend, trainer Mary Eppler. He also made clear that the barn was off limits to the media.

Funny Cide drew last choice for post position and got the nine hole in the ten-horse field. Only two horses in the previous 127 runnings of the Preakness had won from that post. Funny Cide also had to buck the statistics against geldings; only six had triumphed in the middle jewel of the Triple Crown, with Prairie Bayou in 1993 being the most recent.

Press box pundits hopped aboard Bobby Frankel-trained Peace Rules, who had defeated Funny Cide in the Louisiana Derby (G2) and had finished third in the Derby.

The Preakness also featured a rare classic entry: Scrimshaw and Senor Swinger, trained respectively by rivals D. Wayne Lukas and Bob Baffert, who together had won seven of the last nine runnings of the Preakness. The colts were coupled, since Bob and Beverly Lewis own both of them.

When the gate opened following a slight delay as Ten Cents a Shine refused to be loaded, Coolmore Lexington Stakes (G2) winner Scrimshaw shot to the front, with Peace Rules just to his outside. Santos said Funny Cide broke more sharply than he ever had before and his speed allowed them to clear the rest of the field and save ground going into the clubhouse turn behind a first quarter-mile in :23.37.

"It was a piece of cake," Santos said.

Riding with a loose rein into the backstretch, Santos watched Peace Rules gain the lead and complete a half-mile in :47.14. When Santos asked, Funny Cide easily passed Scrimshaw, and, as they ranged into the far turn, he bounded to Peace Rules's flank and passed him with virtually no challenge. From there, the only questions seemed to be his margin of victory and who would claim second. "At about the

---

Sire

Distorted Humor, 1993 ch. h., Forty Niner—Danzig's Beauty, by Danzig. 23-8-5-3, $769,964. Bred by Charles Nuckols Jr. and Sons, and raced by Russell Reineman and Prestonwood Farm; graded stakes winner at three, four and five. Distorted Humor stood his first season at Prestonwood Farm in 1999, and Funny Cide is from his first crop. Distorted Humor also shuttled to Australia in 1999 and 2000. Prestonwood purchased majority interest in Distorted Humor from Reineman in 1994. When Kenny Troutt and Bill Casner purchased Prestonwood early in 2000, they acquired Prestonwood's interest in Distorted Humor. Stood for a $20,000 stud fee in 2003.

Dam

Belle's Good Cide, 1993 ch. m., Slewacide—Belle of Killarney, by Little Current. 26-2-1-6, $26,696. Dam of two starters, two winners; one graded stakes winner (Funny Cide, Kentucky Derby [G1], Preakness Stakes [G1], etc.). Only a minor winner herself, but half sister to graded winner Belle of Cozzene, stakes winners Quackerbell, Zee Oh Six. Died from colic after foaling a Mojave Moon colt in 2003.

sixteenth pole, it hit me—I'm going to win the Preakness," Santos said of his first win in the race. "I've been riding for 27 years and this is the best horse I've ridden in my life."

Funny Cide crossed the finish line in 1:55.61. His 9¾-length winning margin was unsurpassed but for Survivor's ten-length win in 1873. William S. Farish's homebred Midway Road stole inside Peace Rules and grabbed second, three-quarters of a length in front of a courageous Scrimshaw, who nosed out Peace Rules for third.

Senor Swinger, who raced last most of the way after switching surfaces from turf, rallied late to finish fifth, followed by New York Hero, Foufa's Warrior, Cherokee's Boy, Ten Cents a Shine, and Kissin Saint.

While jockey Gary Stevens said Scrimshaw ran a huge race, Lukas saved praise for Funny Cide. "The winner certainly earned a shot at the Triple Crown," said Lukas, who tried for the triangular trophy in 1999 with the Lewises' Charismatic.

Funny Cide, who increased his career earnings to $1,889,385 with his Preakness victory, was bound for stardom in tourism advertising even before he started in the Belmont Stakes (G1). "There's an 'I Love New York' series they have promoting tourism in New York, and they're going to have one for Funny Cide," Sackatoga managing partner Jackson Knowlton said. "It will generate a lot of interest—it will be statewide on TV—and we're just really excited about showcasing our great horse."

—*Michele MacDonald*

12TH RACE
PIMLICO
May 17, 2003

1³⁄₁₆ MILES. Purse $1,000,000. Open. 3-year-olds. 128th running of the Preakness Stakes. Grade 1.

Value of race $1,000,000; Winner $650,000; second $200,000; third $100,000; fourth $50,000. Mutuel WPS Pool $14,711,833. Exacta Pool $9,205,919. Trifecta Pool $11,041,055. Superfecta Pool $3,198,747.

Horse	M/Eqt.	Wt.	PP	St	¼	½	¾	Str.	Fin.	Jockey	Odds $1
Funny Cide	LA	126	9	6	3^1	2^1	$21½$	1^5	$19¾$	J. Santos	*1.90
Midway Road	L	126	6	7	7^2	$51½$	$3½$	4^3	$2¾$	R. Albarado	20.00
Scrimshaw	Lb	126	2	3	1^{hd}	$31½$	4^1	2^{hd}	3no	G. Stevens	4.90
Peace Rules	L	126	7	2	2^2	1^1	$1½$	3^1	4^2	E. Prado	2.40
Senor Swinger	Lf	126	10	10	10	10	10	6^{hd}	5^{hd}	P. Day	4.90
New York Hero	LAbf	126	8	5	5^{hd}	$61½$	6^1	$53½$	$63¼$	J. Chavez	19.60
Foufa's Warrior	LAbf	126	3	9	$94½$	8^{hd}	7^3	7^{hd}	$71¼$	R. Dominguez	22.40
Cherokee's Boy	LAb	126	1	4	$41½$	$4½$	5^2	8^3	$85¾$	R. Fogelsonger	9.70
Ten Cents a Shine	L	126	5	8	8^{hd}	$94½$	$82½$	$93½$	9^1	J. Bailey	8.50
Kissin Saint	LA	126	4	1	$61½$	$72½$	9^{hd}	10	10	R. Migliore	10.20

L=Lasix   LA=Lasix and adjunct bleeder medication   b=blinkers   f=front bandages

OFF AT: 6:14. Weather: Cloudy. Track: Good. Start: Good.
Times of :23.37, :47.14, 1:11.62, 1:36.42, 1:55.61.
Winner: Bumped at break, rated three wide, clear.

$2 Mutuel Prices:

9—FUNNY CIDE	5.80	4.60	3.40
6—MIDWAY ROAD		15.40	9.00
1—SCRIMSHAW			4.00

$2 PICK THREE 10-8-9 PAID $652.40 $2 PICK FOUR 4-10-8-9 PAID $4,987.40
DAILY DOUBLE 8-9 PAID $30.40 $2 DAILY DOUBLE SPECIAL/PREAKNESS 3-9 PAID $18.80
$2 EXACTA 9-6 PAID $120.60 $2 HEAD2HEAD 7 VS. 9 (WINNER 9) PAID $3.80
$2 TRIFECTA 9-6-1 PAID $684.20 $2 SUPERFECTA 9-6-1-7 PAID $1,584.40

Ch. g., by Distorted Humor out of Belle's Good Cide, by Slewacide. Trainer: Barclay Tagg. Breeder: WinStar Farm (NY)

FUNNY CIDE brushed at start by New York Hero, stalked the pace in hand three wide, took over at the quarter pole, and drew away in a steady drive. MIDWAY ROAD settled inside, made a sharp move at the half-mile pole, brushed with Peace Rules at the sixteenth pole, up for second. SCRIMSHAW took a brief early lead on the inside, relinquished lead to Peace Rules on the first turn, came in to brush Peace Rules near the sixteenth pole, continued willingly. PEACE RULES battled for the early lead, rated on pace, brushed when in tight at the sixteenth pole, weakened. SENOR SWINGER devoid of early speed, very wide in stretch, made belated response. NEW YORK HERO broke outward and brushed Funny Cide, rated early in a wide trip, and came up empty. FOUFA'S WARRIOR hopped at start, was pinched back, on rail early, failed to respond. CHEROKEE'S BOY inside early, angled out at three-quarters, five-wide at quarter pole, faded. TEN CENTS A SHINE brushed by Midway Road at the start, well back early, lacked rally, eased late. KISSIN SAINT bobbled at start, in middle of pack early, three-wide in upper stretch, gave way.

Copyright © 2003 Equibase Co. LLC

2003 Belmont Stakes: Empire Strikes Back

Confidence dwelled in the light in his eyes, in the jauntiness of his swagger, and even in the stubble sprouting on his cheeks as he surveyed the early-morning rain pelting ever-bulging puddles with not the slightest care creasing his brow. Trainer Bobby Frankel was back in New York and ready to reclaim the spotlight. His stage is the racetrack, and in the roughly four decades since he circled the shedrows of Belmont Park as a hotwalker, he has earned the current starring role as North America's most successful trainer.

Yet, here he stood, only a few bedraggled reporters huddled around him and Juddmonte Farms' regally bred Empire Maker, the colt he had brazenly forecast could romp through the Triple Crown, at Belmont's Barn 2. Four barns away, Barclay Tagg, who had toiled in relative obscurity since saddling his first winner in 1972 at the old Liberty Bell Park, entertained throngs, although somewhat reluctantly, as he prepared storybook dual classic-winning gelding Funny Cide for the Belmont Stakes (G1) and an unprecedented coup in the Crown.

"After the race, I'll be in charge again," Frankel blurted in his characteristically blunt and blustery New York style. Two days later, his confidence transferred to a supremely composed Empire Maker and intensified through the laser focus of jockey Jerry Bailey, Frankel could proclaim, "I told you so." As the crowd of 101,864, second largest in Belmont history, gasped in sodden horror after enduring hours of rain while hoping

to catch a glimpse of the first Triple Crown winner in 25 years, Empire Maker loped past Funny Cide on the far turn and repelled a late run by Ten Most Wanted to triumph in the 135th running of the 1½-mile marathon.

Stunned fans booed as Bailey steered Empire Maker back to the winner's circle, reserving their applause for the gallant Funny Cide, who led most of the way before tiring to finish third, five lengths behind Empire Maker. Frankel just laughed and shrugged his shoulders. He had taken the ultimate bite of the Big Apple and broken through the classic barrier that had held him winless with 11 previous Triple Crown starters.

Confidence and hope had surrounded Empire Maker from the day he was born on April 27, 2000, at Khalid Abdullah's sprawling Juddmonte haven near Lexington. By the late 1990 Kentucky Derby (G1) winner Unbridled out of 2002 Broodmare of the Year and Grade 1 winner Toussaud, by El Gran Senor, Empire Maker surged with the blood and spirit of a potential champion.

Abdullah, about 50 friends and associates, and Frankel showed up in Louisville on the first Saturday in May daring to think that the Derby would be just the first of a trio of trips to the winner's circle in the demanding five-week classic season. But Funny Cide rebounded after losing the Wood Memorial Stakes (G1) to Empire Maker and galloped away from him down the stretch at Churchill Downs. Empire Maker just held off another Frankel runner, Peace Rules, and late-closing Atswhatimtalknbout for the runner-up spot.

After Empire Maker had bruised his foot in the Wood, Frankel eased off on his training so he would not be compromised for the Preakness Stakes (G1) and the Belmont, and he and Bailey now say that the combination of a lack of diligent work and the sore foot, as well as a wide trip, may have caused the Derby defeat. Afterward, Frankel opted to skip the Preakness and train Empire Maker up to the Belmont.

Only four runners were entered to take on Funny Cide and Empire Maker: Illinois Derby (G2) winner Ten Most Wanted, who labored home ninth of 16 in the Kentucky Derby after bumping with Scrimshaw after the break and hurting his back; lightly raced Lone Star Derby (G3) winner Dynever; Coolmore Lexington Stakes (G2) winner Scrimshaw, trained by four-time Belmont winner D. Wayne Lukas; and allowance winner Supervisor. Funny Cide drew the four post and was made the even-money program-line favorite; he started at those odds. Empire Maker, on the rail, was 6-to-5 in the program line and 2-to-1 at post time.

The Belmont backstretch buzzed when a keen

Owner-Breeder

Owned by Khalid Abdullah, a Saudi Arabian prince, **Juddmonte Farms** marked a milestone in 2003 when Empire Maker scored its 100th Grade 1 or Group 1 victory. Khalid bought his first horse in 1977 and established his first farm in England in 1981. The following year, he established his Juddmonte Farms in Kentucky, which now comprises 2,500 acres and approximately 300 horses. Known Fact, the 1980 Two Thousand Guineas (Eng-G1) winner, collected his first classic triumph, and through mid-June of 2003 the operation had won 14 classic races. The day after the Belmont, Juddmonte-bred Nebraska Tornado won the Prix de Diane (Fr-G1), the French Oaks. Juddmonte has raced three North American champions—Banks Hill (GB), Ryafan, and Wandesta (GB)—and the operation has been voted Eclipse Awards as outstanding owner in 1992 and outstanding breeder in 1995, 2001, and '02.

Trainer

Bobby Frankel, a Brooklyn native, turned a teenage interest in betting on horses into a Racing Hall of Fame career. He started as a hotwalker in the mid-1960s but by 1966 was training on his own. He registered his first winner in November 1966 at Aqueduct and soon began to develop a reputation as "king of the claimers." He moved to California in 1972, and that year scored a record 60 wins at Hollywood Park. In the 1980s, he began to upgrade his stable and in 1990 accepted horses from Juddmonte Farms, which became his principal client. Elected to the Racing Hall of Fame in 1993, he was voted Eclipse Awards as outstanding trainer in 1993, 2000, '01, and '02.

Funny Cide drilled five furlongs in :57.82 four days before the race. Exercise rider and assistant trainer Robin Smullen said she did everything she could think of to get the muscular gelding to relax—all to little avail. Back at the barn, her back ached from the effort. Meanwhile, Frankel kept smiling. He rankled some Funny Cide supporters when he contended that the early-morning workout had cooked Funny Cide.

When the starting gate clanged open, Empire Maker leapt out a full half-length in front of the field. But Funny Cide would have none of that; he pulled jockey Jose Santos to the lead before reaching the first turn. In a move that proved key to the race, Bailey and Empire Maker glided swiftly out from the rail, and took aim, as Santos feared, on Funny Cide's tail and just to his outside.

"When I turned up the backside, I knew I had Funny Cide," Bailey said. "He was pulling on Jose, and my horse was very relaxed, and that's the whole key going a mile and a half." Bailey cruised closer to the gelding, whose ears flicked back and forth as he tugged through fractions of :23.85, :48.70, and 1:13.51 for the first six furlongs on the sloppy surface.

Going around the far turn, Empire Maker ranged up effortlessly as Santos began to scrub, his visions of a Triple Crown crumbling as the Juddmonte colt began to leave him behind. Bailey flicked the whip lightly with his right wrist twice and Empire Maker opened up a lead as Ten Most Wanted, who had rated behind Empire Maker much of the way, also passed Funny Cide.

For a moment, it appeared the burly Ten Most Wanted would ramble past Empire Maker. But Bailey popped his colt once right-handed, which seemed to startle him as he switched abruptly to his left lead. Changing hands, Bailey hit him again, and the colt bounced back to his right lead and pulled away again, hitting the finish line three-quarters of a length in front in 2:28.26.

Santos and Tagg handled the defeat, which made Funny Cide the 17th horse to lose the Triple Crown in the Belmont, magnanimously. "I feel bad for everybody that was behind him, all the fans that were rooting for him," said Tagg. "I am proud of him no matter what," said Santos.

—*Michele MacDonald*

11TH RACE
Belmont
June 7, 2003

1½ MILES (2:24). 135th running of the Belmont Stakes. Purse $1,000,000. Grade 1. Three-year-olds.

Value of race $1,000,000; Winner $600,000; second $200,000; third $110,000; fourth $60,000; fifth $30,000.
Mutuel WPS Pool $21,283,153. Exacta Pool $11,308,960. Trifecta Pool $12,485,369. Daily Double Pool $513,341.

Horse	M/Eqt.	Wt.	PP	¼	½	1 mi.	1¼ mi.	Str.	Fin.	Jockey	Odds $1
Empire Maker	Lbc	126	1	3²	2¹	2¹½	1¹	1¹½	1¾	J. Bailey	2.00
Ten Most Wanted	Lf	126	6	4½	5⁵	4ʰᵈ	3⁴	2¹½	2⁴¼	P. Day	9.70
Funny Cide	L	126	4	1¹	1¹	1ʰᵈ	2¹	3⁵	3⁵¼	J. Santos	*1.00
Dynever	L	126	5	5⁴	4ʰᵈ	5⁷	4³	4¹⁰	4¹⁵¼	E. Prado	8.50
Supervisor	Lb	126	2	6	6	6	6	5¹	5⁴½	J. Velazquez	14.80
Scrimshaw	Lb	126	3	2¹½	3¹	3ʰᵈ	5⁴	6	6	G. Stevens	11.00

L=Lasix   b=blinkers   c=mud calks   f=front bandages

OFF AT 6:40 p.m. Start: Good for all. Weather: Rainy. Track: Sloppy.
Time: :23.85, :48.70, 1:13.51, 1:38.05, 2:02.62, 2:28.26.

$2 Mutuel Prices:	1—EMPIRE MAKER	6.00	3.70	2.80
	6—TEN MOST WANTED		5.80	3.20
	4—FUNNY CIDE			2.70

$2 EXACTA 1-6 PAID $44.00 $2 TRIFECTA 1-6-4 PAID $67.50
$2 DAILY DOUBLE 10-1 PAID $16.00 $2 DAILY DOUBLE (ACORN/BELMONT) 7-1 PAID $20.20
$2 PICK THREE 5-10-1 PAID $84.00 $2 PICK FOUR 2-5-10-1 PAID $271.00
$2 PICK SIX 5-6-2-5-10-1 PAID $900.00

Dk. b. or br. c., by Unbridled—Toussaud, by El Gran Senor. Trainer: Bobby Frankel. Breeder: Juddmonte Farms (Ky.)

EMPIRE MAKER angled out approaching the first turn, stalked the pace while four wide, drew alongside FUNNY CIDE on the final turn, took clear advantage early in stretch, dug in when challenged, and held off TEN MOST WANTED through the final sixteenth. TEN MOST WANTED brushed DYNEVER at the start, was five wide for much of the trip, made a bid on the outside in midstretch, but was second best. FUNNY CIDE broke slightly outward, set pace three wide while in hand on the backstretch, led into the stretch, and weakened in late stages. DYNEVER brushed at start with TEN MOST WANTED, raced between rivals, and came up empty in the stretch. SUPERVISOR broke slowly, raced wide, and posed no threat. SCRIMSHAW contested the early pace on rail, drifted very wide at the quarter pole, and tired.

Copyright © 2003 Equibase Co. LLC

BREEDERS' CUP
Breeders' Cup History

John R. Gaines, one of the central figures in the North American commercial breeding industry in the last quarter of the 20th century, is renowned for his creativity and his powers of persuasion. In the early 1980s, Gaines needed all his considerable talents to get a fractious industry lined up behind his concept, which he believed would help define the Thoroughbred industry and give it a centerpiece.

Gaines's creation was the Breeders' Cup. From the perspective of the 21st century, the Breeders' Cup stands as the most successful initiative of the Thoroughbred industry in the last half of the 20th century. Creation of the Breeders' Cup allowed the sport to hold a championship day of racing in late fall for the majority of age and sex divisions, an important element missing from a sport that had its major fall championship races scattered across the nation at a number of tracks.

Gaines conceived the idea in part out of anger and frustration. He was angered by a television program in the early 1980s that had depicted Thoroughbred racing as a haven of drug abuse. Indeed, permissive medication policies at racetracks had eroded confidence in the sport's integrity, and racing had continued its long, slow slide in popularity—a decline that began shortly after World War II. Even as the commercial bloodstock markets boomed in the early 1980s, race purses in real terms were shrinking.

The highly successful owner of Gainesway Farm in Lexington and an innovator in the stallion-station concept, Gaines developed the idea for a championship day of racing with multi-million-dollar purses to attract the world's best runners, with the races being broadcast nationally on a major television network. The day of racing, as important as it was, would not be an end unto itself. The event would be used to build racing's popularity, with the organization in charge of the event becoming a leader in marketing the sport.

Given the sport's propensity for self-destructive infighting, it is surprising the Breeders' Cup came into being in very much the form that Gaines first envisioned Thoroughbred racing's championship day. But it was not easy.

Gaines had to sell the concept to a skeptical industry in 1982, and he had to do it one person at a time. His first target was John W. Galbreath, owner of Darby Dan Farm and an influential sportsman in the United States and England. (At the time, Galbreath was the only person to have raced both a Kentucky Derby winner [Chateaugay] and an Epsom Derby victor [Roberto].)

Gaines flew to Columbus, Ohio, to meet with Galbreath, who initially thought little of the idea. But, as Gaines sketched out his idea in detail, Galbreath came on board. Moving quickly, Gaines lined up other supporters, including Spendthrift Farm's Leslie Combs II, Nelson Bunker Hunt, Windfields Farms' Charles Taylor, Will Farish, Racing Hall of Fame trainer John Nerud, Brereton C. Jones, John T. L. Jones Jr., and Seth Hancock, who a decade earlier had taken over management of his family's Claiborne Farm.

All great ideas have their moments, and Gaines's idea came at just the right time for the Thoroughbred industry. Commercial breeders, who would pay a big part of the program's cost by nominating their stallions and foals, were enjoying unprecedented prosperity as bloodstock

Where Championship Days Were Held

Churchill Downs (5): 1988, 1991, 1994, 1998, 2000
Hollywood Park (3): 1984, 1987, 1997
Belmont Park (3): 1990, 1995, 2001
Gulfstream Park (3): 1989, 1992, 1999
Santa Anita (2): 1986, 1993
Arlington Park (1): 2002
Aqueduct (1): 1985
Woodbine (1) 1996

Breeders' Cup Attendance and Betting Handle by Year

Year	Site	On-track attendance	On-track wagering*	Total wagering*
2002	Arlington	46,118	$12,143,114	$108,885,673
2001	Belmont	52,987	12,067,995	98,008,747
2000	Churchill	76,043	13,579,798	101,283,427
1999	Gulfstream	45,124	11,065,973	96,485,255
1998	Churchill	80,452	13,544,859	91,338,477
1997	Hollywood	51,161	8,191,459	71,639,333
1996	Woodbine	42,243	5,925,469	67,738,890
1995	Belmont	37,246	7,590,332	64,075,207
1994	Churchill	71,671	10,146,524	78,224,530
1993	Santa Anita	55,130	12,142,750	79,744,742
1992	Gulfstream	45,415	9,915,542	76,876,726
1991	Churchill	66,204	11,945,562	67,588,113
1990	Belmont	51,236	9,107,270	55,328,195
1989	Gulfstream	51,342	10,216,258	55,345,677
1988	Churchill	71,237	9,219,083	42,932,379
1987	Hollywood	57,734	10,202,252	31,864,457
1986	Santa Anita	69,155	12,510,109	31,984,490
1985	Aqueduct	42,568	7,200,175	26,941,288
1984	Hollywood	64,254	8,443,070	16,452,179

*Breeders' Cup races only

prices rose to record levels and stallion fees climbed.

At the same time, racing was perceived as a sport in trouble, and relatively low purse levels dissuaded some prospective owners from buying horses. Although overseas interests sent the bloodstock markets skyrocketing, many breeders realized the prices they received for their sale offerings and the stallion fees they charged were directly related to purses on the racetrack, which determined how much a sale purchase potentially could earn.

Gaines chose the sport's most prestigious event, the Kentucky Derby (G1), to announce his idea. He was honored at the Kentucky Derby Festival's "They're Off" luncheon on April 23, 1982, and there he outlined his idea, a $13-million afternoon featuring the world's best racehorses. Gaines named it the Breeders' Cup.

He moved quickly to name a board of directors and girded for the inevitable naysayers. New York racing interests were opposed because Gaines' proposal would diminish the importance of the New York Racing Association's fall races, which frequently decided year-end titles.

Smaller-scale breeders also voiced their opposition. Gaines said breeders could breed one more mare to a stallion to cover the cost of the stallion nomination fee each year. Such a strategy certainly would work for a breeder with barns filled with desirable stallions and whose books were filled, and Gaines was one of those breeders. But, for a small-scale breeder trying to fill the book of a less commercial stallion, the stallion nomination most likely would be paid out of the stallion owner's pocket.

Television Ratings for Breeders' Cup		
Date	**Racetrack**	**Rating/Share**
2002	Arlington Park	2.0/5
2001	Belmont Park	1.7/5
2000	Churchill Downs	1.8/5
1999	Gulfstream Park	1.9/5
1998	Churchill Downs	2.2/6
1997	Hollywood Park	2.2/6
1996	Woodbine	2.5/8
1995	Belmont Park	2.8/9
1994	Churchill Downs	2.7/8
1993	Santa Anita Park	3.4/9
1992	Gulfstream Park	3.0/8
1991	Churchill Downs	3.0/9
1990	Belmont Park	2.7/9
1989	Gulfstream Park	3.7/11
1988	Churchill Downs	4.0/11
1987	Hollywood Park	2.9/7
1986	Santa Anita Park	4.4/12
1985	Aqueduct	4.0/11
1984	Hollywood Park	5.1/13

Other breeders raised concerns that Gaines was putting all the money into one event, arguing that the money should be spread throughout the year to supplement purses of existing stakes races. On that point, a compromise was reached, with $10-million earmarked for the championship day and an equal portion going into Breeders' Cup-sponsored races around the country.

By the fall of 1982, the Breeders' Cup was beset with infighting, and Seth Hancock delivered an unexpected blow when he did not nominate Claiborne's stallions on grounds that the organization had not developed a clear game plan. Gaines realized he had become a lightning rod for opponents and resigned the presidency on October 22, becoming chairman. C. Gibson Downing Jr., a Lexington lawyer with a modest-sized stud farm and a reputation for consensus building, became Breeders' Cup president. Hancock signed up after a rules book was written on how the money would be spent, and smaller breeders followed his lead. D. G. Van Clief Jr. came on board that fall as executive director.

For several months, Gaines and Nerud traveled around the country, selling breeders and racetrack operators on the concept. By April 15, 1983, 1,083 stallions had been nominated to the program, and the Breeders' Cup was up and running. Nerud said in 1985 that a decision was made early to hold the first Breeders' Cup in a warm climate so television viewers would see racing in a pleasant setting. Marjorie Everett, chief executive of Hollywood Park, lobbied heavily for the first event, and on February 24, 1983, the Inglewood, California, track was named as host of the first Breeders' Cup, to be held on November 10, 1984. In a bow to New York interests, Aqueduct was host of the second Breeders' Cup in 1985.

At Nerud's suggestion, marketers Mike Letis and Mike Trager of Sports Marketing and Television International were brought in to negotiate a television deal, and a contract with NBC was signed on September 13, 1983. The show would run for four hours on a Saturday afternoon and would include all seven of the Breeders' Cup championship races. In January 1984, all seven races were granted Grade 1 status.

From the first race, won by Chief's Crown in the $1-million Breeders' Cup Juvenile (G1), the Breeders' Cup was an unprecedented success. That afternoon's races attracted a crowd of 64,254, and the day concluded with a breathtaking $3-million Breeders' Cup Classic (G1), in which supplemental entry Wild Again edged Gate Dancer and Slew o' Gold for the biggest race purse ever offered to that time.

An even larger crowd, 69,155, attended the third Breeders' Cup at Santa Anita Park in suburban Los Angeles, but that record lasted only two years until Churchill Downs hosted the fifth Breeders' Cup in 1988 before a crowd of 71,237. On a dreary, rainy, chilly day in Louisville, they were treated to one of the event's most exciting races when undefeated Personal Ensign closed relentlessly in the final yards and caught that year's Kentucky Derby winner, Winning Colors, at the finish line to win the Breeders' Cup Distaff (G1) by a nose. With that victory, Personal Ensign retired unbeaten in 13 starts.

The Breeders' Cup traveled to Florida for the first time in 1989, and Gulfstream Park was the scene for another monumental struggle in which Sunday Silence fought off the challenge of Easy Goer to win the Breeders' Cup Classic. The event reached its nadir the following year at Belmont Park, when Go for Wand sustained a fatal breakdown near the finish line of the Breeders' Cup Distaff and was humanely destroyed. Earlier on the card, a spill in the Breeders' Cup Sprint (G1) led to the deaths of Mr. Nickerson and Shaker Knit. Subsequently, Breeders' Cup Ltd. instituted prerace examinations to limit breakdowns.

Through the late 1980s and '90s, the Breeders' Cup grew in importance both to the racing industry, which began to regain its footing in that period, and to the sport's participants. The Breeders' Cup races often determine end-of-year titles, and such popular champions as Cigar sealed Horse of the Year honors with victories in the Breeders' Cup Classic.

As rich races became more common, especially internationally, Breeders' Cup Ltd. increased its championship day purses, raising the Classic to $4-million in 1996 and the Distaff to $2-million in '98. In 1999, a new race, the $1-million Filly and Mare Turf (G1), was added, raising the afternoon's total purses to $13-million. In 2001, the championship day was renamed the Breeders' Cup World Thoroughbred Championships. By 2003, the Breeders' Cup Stakes program had grown to 104 stakes races, with purses exceeding $18.5-million.—*Don Clippinger*

Breeders' Cup Trophy

The Breeders' Cup trophy is an authentic reproduction of the Torrie horse, created by Giovanni da Bologna in Florence, Italy, mostly likely in the late 1580s. The sculpture is known as an *ecorche* or flayed horse and shows the horse's muscles in great detail.

Although its original commission is not known, the sculpture may have been a study made for an equestrian statue of Duke Cosimo I, which was completed in 1591 and stands today in the Piazza della Signoria in Florence.

The sculptor's original *ecorche* in bronze was acquired

by Sir James Erskine of Torrie in the early 1800s. It was bequeathed to the University of Edinburgh in 1836 and today is housed in the university's Museum of Fine Arts in Scotland.

The Breeders' Cup trophy was cast from the original under supervision of University of Edinburgh curators, and the replica is owned by Breeders' Cup Ltd. Smaller replicas are presented to winners of each Breeders' Cup race, and winning breeders, trainers, and jockeys also are presented with replicas.

Breeders' Cup Purses

When John Gaines first proposed the Breeders' Cup in 1982, he envisioned a purse structure of $13-million for the championship day. As the concept was put into final form for the first championship day in 1984, purses and nominator fees totaled $10-million. Five of seven races had $1-million purses (Juvenile, Juvenile Fillies, Sprint, Distaff, Mile); the Turf had a $2-million purse, and the Classic was $3-million.

In 1996, the Classic was increased to $4-million, and the Distaff was raised to $2-million two years later. The addition of the Filly and Mare Turf in 1999 raised the day's total purse structure to $13-million.

A 1997 change in the rules for supplemental nominations has resulted in higher purses. Beginning in 1998, supplemental-nomination money is added to the total purse. Thus, the 1998 Breeders' Cup Classic, which contained supplemental nominees Gentlemen (Arg), Silver Charm, and Skip Away, raised the total purse ($4,689,920) and nominator fees above $5-million, then the biggest race purse ever.

In addition to purse money paid to the horse's owner or owners, the Breeders' Cup purse structure contains 5% awards for both the stallion nominator and the foal nominator. Here is the 2003 distribution for a $1-million race:

Finish	Purse	Owner	Stallion nominator	Foal nominator
1st	57.2%	$520,000	$26,000	$26,000
2nd	22.0%	200,000	10,000	10,000
3rd	13.2%	120,000	6,000	6,000
4th	5.6%	56,000		
5th	2.0%	20,000		
Total	**100.0%**	**$916,000**	**$42,000**	**$42,000**

Largest Breeders' Cup Purses

(Not including stallion and foal nominator fees)

Year	Race	Purse	Winner	Value to winner
1998	Classic	$4,689,920	Awesome Again	$2,662,400
2000	Classic	4,369,320	Tiznow	2,480,400
1997	Classic	4,030,400	Skip Away	2,288,000
2002	Classic	3,664,000	Volponi	2,080,000
2001	Classic	3,664,000	Tiznow	2,080,000
1999	Classic	3,664,000	Cat Thief	2,080,000
1996	Classic	3,664,000	Alphabet Soup	2,080,000
1995	Classic	2,798,000	Cigar	1,560,000
1994	Classic	2,748,000	Concern	1,560,000
1993	Classic	2,748,000	Arcangues	1,560,000
1992	Classic	2,748,000	A.P. Indy	1,560,000
1991	Classic	2,748,000	Black Tie Affair (Ire)	1,560,000

From 1984 through 1990, the Breeders' Cup Classic had a race purse of $2,739,000 and a winner's share of $1,350,000. The next highest purse was $2,271,680 in the 2000 Breeders' Cup Turf, won by Kalanisi (Ire).

Breeders' Cup Leaders

Leading Jockeys by Wins

13 Jerry Bailey (Orientate, 2002 Sprint; Squirtle Squirt, 2001 Sprint; Macho Uno, 2000 Juvenile; Perfect Sting, 2000 Filly and Mare Turf; Soaring Softly, 1999 Filly and Mare Turf; Cash Run, 1999 Juvenile Fillies; Answer Lively, 1998 Juvenile; Boston Harbor, 1996 Juvenile; Cigar, 1995 Classic; My Flag, 1995 Juvenile Fillies; Concern, 1994 Classic; Arcangues, 1993 Classic; Black Tie Affair [Ire], 1991 Classic)

12 Pat Day (Unbridled Elaine, 2001 Distaff; Cat Thief, 1999 Classic; Awesome Again, 1998 Classic; Favorite Trick, 1997 Juvenile; Timber Country, 1994 Juvenile; Flanders, 1994 Juvenile Fillies; Dance Smartly, 1991 Distaff; Unbridled, 1990 Classic; Theatrical (Ire), 1987 Turf; Epitome, 1987 Juvenile Fillies; Lady's Secret, 1986 Distaff; Wild Again, 1984 Classic)

10 Mike Smith (Azeri, 2002 Distaff; Vindication, 2002 Juvenile; Skip Away, 1997 Classic; Ajina, 1997 Distaff; Unbridled's Song, 1995 Juvenile; Inside Information, 1995 Distaff; Tikkanen, 1994 Turf; Cherokee Run, 1994 Sprint; Lure [twice], 1992, '93 Mile)

9 Chris McCarron (Tiznow [twice], 2000, '01 Classic; Alphabet Soup, 1996 Classic; Northern Spur [Ire], 1995 Turf; Paseana [Arg], 1992 Distaff; Gilded Time, 1992 Juvenile; Sunday Silence, 1989 Classic; Alysheba, 1988 Classic; Precisionist, 1985 Sprint)

8 Gary Stevens (War Chant, 2000 Mile; Anees, 1999 Juvenile; Escena, 1998 Distaff; Silverbulletday, 1998 Juvenile Fillies; Da Hoss, 1996 Mile; One Dreamer, 1994 Distaff; Brocco, 1993 Juvenile; In the Wings [GB], 1990 Turf)

7 Eddie Delahoussaye (Hollywood Wildcat, 1993 Distaff; Cardmania, 1993 Sprint; A.P. Indy, 1992 Classic; Thirty Slews, 1992 Sprint; Pleasant Stage, 1991 Juvenile Fillies; Prized, 1989 Turf; Princess Rooney, 1984 Distaff)

Laffit Pincay Jr. (Phone Chatter, 1993 Juvenile Fillies; Bayakoa [Arg], [twice], 1989, '90 Distaff; Is It True, 1988 Juvenile; Skywalker, 1986 Classic; Capote, 1986 Juvenile; Tasso, 1985 Juvenile)

Jose Santos (Volponi, 2002 Classic; Chief Bearhart, 1997 Turf; Fly So Free, 1990 Juvenile; Meadow Star, 1990 Juvenile Fillies; Steinlen [GB], 1989 Mile; Success Express, 1987 Juvenile; Manila, 1986 Turf)

6 Patrick Valenzuela (Fraise, 1992 Turf; Eliza, 1992 Juvenile Fillies; Arazi, 1991 Juvenile; Opening Verse, 1991 Mile; Very Subtle, 1987 Sprint; Brave Raj, 1986 Juvenile Fillies)

5 Corey Nakatani (Silic [Fr], 1999 Mile; Reraise, 1998 Sprint; Elmhurst, 1997 Sprint; Jewel Princess, 1996 Distaff; Lit de Justice, 1996 Sprint)

4 Angel Cordero Jr. (Dancing Spree, 1989 Sprint; Gulch, 1988 Sprint; Open Mind, 1988 Juvenile Fillies; Life's Magic, 1985 Distaff)

Craig Perret (Storm Song, 1996 Juvenile Fillies; Safely Kept, 1990 Sprint; Rhythm, 1989 Juvenile; Eillo, 1984 Sprint)

John Velazquez (Storm Flag Flying, 2002 Juvenile Fillies; Starine [Fr], 2002 Filly and Mare Turf; Caressing, 2000 Juvenile Fillies; Da Hoss, 1998 Mile)

Leading Trainers by Wins

17 D. Wayne Lukas (Orientate, 2002 Sprint; Spain, 2000 Distaff; Cat Thief, 1999; Classic; Cash Run, 1999 Juvenile Fillies; Boston Harbor, 1996 Juvenile; Timber Country, 1994 Juvenile; Flanders, 1994 Juvenile Fillies; Steinlen [GB], 1989 Mile; Is It True, 1988 Juvenile; Gulch, 1988 Sprint; Open Mind, 1988 Juvenile Fillies; Success Express, 1987 Juvenile; Sacahuista, 1987 Distaff; Capote, 1986 Juvenile; Lady's Secret, 1986 Distaff; Life's Magic, 1985 Distaff; Twilight Ridge, 1985 Juvenile Fillies)

8 Claude R. "Shug" McGaughey III (Storm Flag Flying, 2002 Juvenile Fillies; Inside Information, 1995 Distaff; My Flag, 1995 Juvenile Fillies; Lure [twice], 1992, '93 Mile; Rhythm, 1989 Juvenile; Dancing Spree, 1989 Sprint; Personal Ensign, 1988 Distaff)

6 Neil Drysdale (War Chant, 2000 Mile; Hollywood Wildcat, 1993 Distaff; A.P. Indy, 1992 Classic; Prized, 1989 Turf; Tasso, 1985 Juvenile; Princess Rooney, 1984 Distaff)

5 William I. Mott (Escena, 1998 Distaff; Ajina, 1997 Distaff; Cigar, 1995 Classic; Fraise, 1992 Turf; Theatrical [Ire], 1987 Turf)

4 Ron McAnally (Northern Spur [Ire], 1995 Turf; Paseana [Arg], 1992 Distaff; Bayakoa [Arg] [twice], 1989, '90 Distaff)

3 Bob Baffert (Vindication, 2002 Juvenile; Silverbulletday, 1998 Juvenile Fillies; Thirty Slews, 1992 Sprint)

Andre Fabre (Banks Hill [GB], 2001 Filly and Mare Turf; In the Wings [GB], 1990 Turf; Arcangues, 1993 Classic)

Francois Boutin (Arazi, 1991 Juvenile; Miesque [twice], 1987, '88 Mile)

Patrick Byrne (Awesome Again, 1998 Classic; Favorite Trick, 1997 Juvenile; Countess Diana, 1997 Juvenile Fillies)

Leading Owners by Wins

7 Allen E. Paulson (Escena, 1998 Distaff; Ajina, 1997 Distaff; Cigar, 1995 Classic; Eliza, 1992 Juvenile Fillies; Opening Verse, 1991 Mile; Arazi, 1991 Juvenile; Theatrical [Ire], 1987 Turf)

4 Flaxman Holdings (Domedriver [Ire], 2002 Mile; Spinning World, 1997 Mile; Miesque [twice], 1987, '88 Mile)

Eugene V. Klein (Is It True, 1988 Juvenile; Open Mind, 1988 Juvenile Fillies; Success Express, 1987 Juvenile; Twilight Ridge, 1985 Juvenile Fillies; Lady's Secret, 1986 Distaff)

3 Godolphin Racing (Fantastic Light, 2001 Turf; Tempera, 2001 Juvenile Fillies; Daylami [Ire], 1999 Turf)

Overbrook Farm (Cat Thief, 1999 Classic; Boston Harbor, 1996 Juvenile; Flanders, 1994 Juvenile Fillies)

Ogden Phipps (My Flag, 1995 Juvenile Fillies; Dancing Spree, 1989 Sprint; Personal Ensign, 1988 Distaff)

Ogden Mills Phipps (Storm Flag Flying, 2002 Juvenile Fillies; Inside Information, 1995 Distaff; Rhythm, 1989 Juvenile)

Stronach Stables (Macho Uno, 2000 Juvenile; Perfect Sting, 2000 Filly and Mare Turf; Awesome Again, 1998 Classic)

Sheikh Mohammed bin Rashid al Maktoum (Barathea [Ire], 1994 Mile; Pebbles [GB], 1985 Turf; In the Wings [GB], 1990 Turf)

Leading Breeders by Wins

6 **Allen E. Paulson** (Azeri, 2002 Distaff; Escena, 1998 Distaff; Ajina, 1997 Distaff; Cigar, 1995 Classic; Fraise, 1992 Turf; Eliza, 1992 Juvenile Fillies)

4 **Ogden Phipps** (Storm Flag Flying, 2002 Juvenile Fillies; My Flag, 1995 Juvenile Fillies; Dancing Spree, 1989 Sprint; Personal Ensign, 1988 Distaff)

3 **Aga Khan** (Kalanisi [Ire], 2000 Turf; Daylami [Ire], 1999 Turf; Lashkari [GB], 1984 Turf)

Flaxman Holdings (Spinning World, 1997 Mile; Miesque [twice], 1987, '88 Mile)

Overbrook Farm (Cat Thief, 1999 Classic; Boston Harbor, 1996 Juvenile; Flanders, 1994 Juvenile Fillies)

Frank Stronach (Macho Uno, 2000 Juvenile; Perfect Sting, 2000 Filly and Mare Turf; Awesome Again, 1998 Classic)

Leading Sires by Wins

5 **Danzig** (War Chant, 2000 Mile; Lure [twice], 1992, 1993 Mile; Dance Smartly, 1991 Distaff; Chief's Crown, 1984 Juvenile)

4 **Nureyev** (Spinning World, 1997 Mile; Miesque [twice], 1987, 1988 Mile; Theatrical [Ire], 1987 Turf)

Kris S. (Soaring Softly, 1999 Filly and Mare Turf; Brocco, 1993 Juvenile; Hollywood Wildcat, 1993 Distaff; Prized, 1989 Turf)

Sadler's Wells (High Chaparral [Ire], 2002 Turf; Northern Spur [Ire], 1995 Turf; Barathea [Ire], 1994 Mile; In the Wings [GB], 1990 Turf)

3 **Cox's Ridge** (Cardmania, 1993 Sprint; Twilight Ridge, 1985 Juvenile Fillies; Life's Magic, 1985 Distaff)

Deputy Minister (Awesome Again, 1999 Classic; Go for Wand, 1989 Juvenile Fillies; Open Mind, 1988 Juvenile Fillies)

Mr. Prospector (Rhythm, 1989 Juvenile; Gulch, 1988 Sprint; Eillo, 1984 Sprint)

Nijinsky II (Royal Academy, 1990 Mile; Dancing Spree, 1989 Sprint; Ferdinand, 1987 Classic)

Seattle Slew (Vindication, 2002 Juvenile; A.P. Indy, 1992 Classic; Capote, 1986 Juvenile)

Storm Cat (Storm Flag Flying, 2002 Juvenile Fillies; Cat Thief, 1999 Classic; Desert Stormer, 1995 Sprint)

Strawberry Road (Aus) (Escena, 1998 Distaff; Ajina, 1997 Distaff; Fraise, 1992 Turf)

Owners With Most Starts

Owner	Starts	Wins	Earnings
Juddmonte Farms	35	1	$3,269,200
Allen E. Paulson	32	6	7,570,000
Godolphin Racing	29	3	4,940,600
Overbrook Farm	27	3	4,387,000
The Thoroughbred Corp.	22	2	3,471,000
Sheikh Mohammed bin Rashid al Maktoum	21	2	3,564,160
Frank Stronach	21	3	5,378,000
Ogden Phipps	19	3	3,611,000
Daniel Wildenstein	19	2	3,917,000
Susan Magnier and Michael Tabor	18	2	3,240,320
Eugene V. Klein	17	4	2,593,000
Sam-Son Farms	16	2	2,878,000
Golden Eagle Farm	15	0	1,443,800
Peter M. Brant	14	2	1,198,000

Jockeys With Most Mounts

Jockey	Mounts	Wins	Earnings
Pat Day	107	12	$22,730,600
Chris McCarron	101	9	17,669,600
Gary Stevens	89	8	13,441,160
Jerry Bailey	82	13	15,768,120
Eddie Delahoussaye	68	7	7,775,000
Laffit Pincay Jr.	61	7	6,811,000
Jose Santos	55	7	7,948,200
Mike Smith	48	10	10,148,920

Trainers With Most Starts

Trainer	Starts	Wins	Earnings
D. Wayne Lukas	137	17	$18,608,400
Bobby Frankel	49	2	6,561,800
Claude R. McGaughey III	46	8	7,253,560
William I. Mott	40	5	8,492,560
Bob Baffert	36	3	4,921,800
Andre Fabre	34	3	6,435,400
Neil Drysdale	27	6	5,795,840
Ron McAnally	27	4	3,518,000

Most Starters on a Program, Owners

Starters	Owner	Year
8	Godolphin Racing	2001
7	Eugene V. Klein	1988
	Eugene V. Klein	1987
5	Allen E. Paulson	1997
	The Thoroughbred Corp.	1997
4	Susan Magnier & Michael Tabor	2001
	Stronach Stables	2000
	The Thoroughbred Corp.	2000
	Godolphin Racing	1996
	Overbrook Farm	1996
	Juddmonte Farms	1994
	Juddmonte Farms	1992
	Peter Brant	1986

Most Starters on a Program, Trainers

Starters	Trainer	Year
14	D. Wayne Lukas	1987
12	D. Wayne Lukas	1988
11	D. Wayne Lukas	1989
10	D. Wayne Lukas	1996
	D. Wayne Lukas	1985

Most Starters on a Program, Jockeys

Mounts	Jockey	Year
8	John Velazquez	2002
	Jerry Bailey	2001
	Jerry Bailey	2000
	Jerry Bailey	1999

Leading Jockeys by Purses Won

Jockey	Mounts	Wins	Earnings
Pat Day	107	12	$22,730,600
Chris McCarron	101	9	17,669,600
Jerry Bailey	82	13	15,768,120
Gary Stevens	88	8	13,441,160
Mike Smith	48	10	10,148,920
Jose Santos	55	7	7,948,200
Eddie Delahoussaye	68	7	7,775,000
Laffit Pincay Jr.	61	7	6,811,000
Corey Nakatani	45	5	6,500,280

Leading Trainers by Purses Won

Trainer	Starts	Wins	Earnings
D. Wayne Lukas	138	17	$18,608,400
William I. Mott	40	5	8,492,560
Claude R. McGaughey III	46	8	7,253,560
Bobby Frankel	49	2	6,561,800
Andre Fabre	33	3	6,435,400
Neil Drysdale	27	6	5,795,840
Jay Robbins	2	2	4,938,400
Bob Baffert	36	3	4,921,800
Charles Whittingham	24	2	4,298,000
Saeed bin Suroor	20	2	4,036,200
Aidan O'Brien	21	2	3,724,920
Patrick Byrne	6	3	3,718,000
Jack Van Berg	14	1	3,600,000
Ron McAnally	27	4	3,518,000
Sir Michael Stoute	24	2	3,135,400

Leading Owners by Purses Won

Owner	Starts	Wins	Earnings
Allen E. Paulson	32	6	$7,570,000
Frank Stronach	21	3	5,378,000
Godolphin Racing	26	3	4,940,600
Overbrook Farm	27	3	4,387,000
Daniel Wildenstein	19	2	3,917,000
Ogden Phipps	19	3	3,611,000
Sheikh Mohammed bin Rashid al Maktoum	21	2	3,564,160
The Thoroughbred Corp.	23	2	3,471,000
Robert and Beverly Lewis	10	1	2,556,800
Juddmonte Farms	32	1	3,269,200
Susan Magnier and Michael Tabor	17	2	3,240,320
Sam-Son Farm	16	2	2,878,000
Frances A. Genter	8	2	2,835,000

Leading Breeders by Purses Won

Breeder	Starts	Wins	Earnings
Allen E. Paulson	27	6	$7,734,800
Overbrook Farm	26	3	4,618,000
Cecilia Straub-Rubens	2	2	4,560,400
Frank Stronach	9	3	4,152,000
Ogden Phipps	18	4	4,131,000
Aga Khan	10	3	3,529,600
Juddmonte Farms	34	1	2,987,200
Oak Cliff Thoroughbreds	3	2	2,700,000
Flaxman Holdings Ltd.	20	4	2,620,400
Sheikh Mohammed bin Rashid al Maktoum	14	1	2,506,800
Allez France Stables	9	2	2,332,800
Anna Marie Barnhart	2	1	2,288,000
Bertram & Diana Firestone	13	1	2,240,000

Leading Sires by Purses Won

Sire	Starts	Wins	Earnings
Storm Cat	27	3	$5,947,000
Deputy Minister	24	3	5,355,400
Cee's Tizzy	3	2	5,360,400
Sadler's Wells	29	4	4,861,600
Alydar	19	1	4,495,000
Danzig	39	5	4,495,000
Seattle Slew	25	3	4,641,400
Cozzene	5	2	3,468,000
Mr. Prospector	41	3	3,421,680
Fappiano	15	2	3,316,000
Nijinsky II	12	3	3,283,000
Nureyev	19	4	3,280,000
Sovereign Dancer	11	0	3,053,000

Winners by Country and State Bred

Country	Starters	Winners
Ireland	117	11
Great Britain	99	7
Argentina	12	3
Canada	67	3
France	39	4
Kentucky	897	80
Florida	171	18
Maryland	23	3
Pennsylvania	18	3
California	55	2
Illinois	8	1
New Jersey	10	1
Oklahoma	3	1

Breeders' Cup Race Winners by Total Earnings

Horse	Breeders' Cup Victory	Total Earnings
Cigar	1995 Classic	$9,999,815
Skip Away	1997 Classic	9,616,360
Fantastic Light	2001 Turf	8,486,957
Alysheba	1988 Classic	6,679,242
Tiznow	2000, '01 Classic	6,427,830
Sunday Silence	1989 Classic	4,968,554
Daylami (Ire)	1999 Turf	4,614,762
Unbridled	1990 Classic	4,489,475
Awesome Again	1998 Classic	4,374,590
Pilsudski (Ire)	1996 Turf	4,080,297
Cat Thief	1999 Classic	3,951,012
Ferdinand	1987 Classic	3,777,978
High Chaparral (Ire)	2002 Turf	3,614,107
Precisionist	1985 Sprint	3,485,398
Chief Bearhart	1997 Turf	3,381,557
Black Tie Affair (Ire)	1991 Classic	3,370,694

Largest Winning Margins

Year	Winner	Race	Margin
1995	Inside Information	Distaff	13½
1997	Countess Diana	Juvenile Fillies	8½
1984	Princess Rooney	Distaff	7
1990	Bayakoa (Arg)	Distaff	6¾
2002	Volponi	Classic	6½
1985	Life's Magic	Distaff	6¼
1997	Skip Away	Classic	6
2001	Banks Hill (GB)	Filly and Mare Turf	5½
1997	Favorite Trick	Juvenile	5½
1986	Brave Raj	Juvenile Fillies	5½

Smallest Winning Margins

Year	Winner	Race	Margin
2001	Tiznow	Classic	nose
2000	Macho Uno	Juvenile	nose
1998	Escena	Distaff	nose
1996	Alphabet Soup	Classic	nose
1993	Hollywood Wildcat	Distaff	nose
1992	Fraise	Turf	nose
1988	Personal Ensign	Distaff	nose
1987	Ferdinand	Classic	nose
1987	Epitome	Juvenile Fillies	nose
1985	Tasso	Juvenile	nose
1984	Eillo	Sprint	nose

Nominations, Pre-Entries, Entries, and Starters by Year

Year	Foal nominations	Pre-Entries	Entries	Starters
2002	13,846	104	92	90
2001	15,020	109	98	94
2000	15,760	135	105	103
1999	15,191	128	102	101
1998	14,081	117	85	82
1997	12,751	94	77	76
1996	11,971	90	85	82
1995	10,543	101	84	81
1994	9,738	126	94	91
1993	9,564	103	82	81
1992	9,392	112	92	91
1991	10,056	116	91	90
1990	11,003	110	91	83
1989	11,734	101	89	80
1988	11,276	87	79	76
1987	12,183	106	91	84
1986	11,494	90	79	76
1985	10,907	110	90	82
1984	10,034	77	69	68
1983	7,839			
1982	9,260			

Pre-entries are number of individual horses made eligible. Owners may pre-enter a horse in up to two races.

Average Field Sizes

Race	Average field	Most starters	Fewest starters
Distaff	8.7	14	6
Juvenile Fillies	11.3	14	8
Mile	13.2	14	10
Sprint	13.1	14	9
Filly and Mare Turf	13.0	14	12
Juvenile	12.1	14	8
Turf	12.1	14	8
Classic	11.4	14	8

Most Pre-Entries for a Breeders' Cup Race

Year	Race	Pre-Entries
2000	Mile	29
1998	Mile	27
1999	Mile	25
1994	Sprint	25
1994	Turf	24
2002	Mile	24
1995	Mile	24
1998	Sprint	24
1994	Mile	23
1999	Sprint	23
1993	Sprint	23
1998	Juvenile	21
1997	Sprint	21
1995	Sprint	21
1994	Classic	20

Largest Breeders' Cup On-Track Attendance

Year	Site	On-Track Attendance
1998	Churchill Downs	80,452
2000	Churchill Downs	76,043
1994	Churchill Downs	71,671
1988	Churchill Downs	71,237
1986	Santa Anita Park	69,155
1991	Churchill Downs	66,204
1984	Hollywood Park	64,254
1987	Hollywood Park	57,734

Smallest Breeders' Cup On-Track Attendance

Year	Site	On-Track Attendance
1995	Belmont Park	37,246
1996	Woodbine	42,243
1985	Aqueduct	42,568
1999	Gulfstream Park	45,124
1992	Gulfstream Park	45,415
2002	Arlington Park	46,118

Largest Breeders' Cup On-Track Betting

Year	Site	On-Track Wagering
2000	Churchill Downs	$13,579,798
1998	Churchill Downs	13,544,859
1986	Santa Anita Park	12,510,109
2002	Arlington Park	12,143,114
1993	Santa Anita Park	12,142,750
2001	Belmont Park	12,067,995

Lowest Breeders' Cup On-Track Betting

Year	Site	On-Track Wagering
1996	Woodbine	$5,925,469
1985	Aqueduct	7,200,175
1995	Belmont Park	7,590,332
1997	Hollywood Park	8,191,459
1984	Hollywood Park	8,443,070
1990	Belmont Park	9,107,270

Average Pari-Mutuel Payout by Year

Year	Track	Average Payout ($2 bet)
1993	Santa Anita Park	$44.37
2000	Churchill Downs	35.30
1984	Hollywood Park	33.97
1991	Churchill Downs	32.71
1999	Gulfstream Park	27.40
1994	Churchill Downs	26.91
2002	Arlington Park	25.25
1986	Santa Anita Park	22.77
1987	Hollywood Park	19.20
1996	Woodbine	16.97
1992	Gulfstream Park	15.17
2001	Belmont Park	15.15
1989	Gulfstream Park	12.00
1988	Churchill Downs	11.17
1995	Belmont Park	10.79
1997	Hollywood Park	10.69
1998	Churchill Downs	10.63
1990	Belmont Park	9.49
1985	Aqueduct	8.63

Shortest-Priced Winners

Year	Horse	Race	Odds
1990	Meadow Star	Juvenile Fillies	.20-to-1
1985	Life's Magic	Distaff	.40-to-1*
1994	Flanders	Juvenile Fillies	.40-to-1*
1986	Lady's Secret	Distaff	.50-to-1*
1988	Personal Ensign	Distaff	.50-to-1
1991	Dance Smartly	Distaff	.50-to-1*
1985	Twilight Ridge	Juvenile Fillies	.60-to-1*
1984	Chief's Crown	Juvenile	.70-to-1
1984	Princess Rooney	Distaff	.70-to-1
1988	Open Mind	Juvenile Fillies	.70-to-1*
1989	Bayakoa (Arg)	Distaff	.70-to-1
1995	Cigar	Classic	.70-to-1

*Part of entry.

Longest-Priced Winners

Year	Horse	Race	Odds
1993	Arcangues	Classic	133.60-to-1
2000	Spain	Distaff	55.90-to-1
1984	Lashkari (GB)	Turf	53.40-to-1
1994	One Dreamer	Distaff	47.10-to-1
2000	Caressing	Juvenile Fillies	47.00-to-1

Year	Horse	Race	Odds
2002	Volponi	Classic	43.50-to-1
1986	Last Tycoon	Mile	35.90-to-1
1999	Cash Run	Juvenile Fillies	32.50-to-1
1984	Wild Again	Classic	31.30-to-1
1987	Epitome	Juvenile Fillies	30.40-to-1
1999	Anees	Juvenile	30.30-to-1

History of Breeders' Cup Races
Breeders' Cup Classic

America's classic distance is 1¼ miles on dirt, and the Breeders' Cup Classic (G1) has offered some classic, spine-tingling contests. The race has been the kingmaker among the eight Breeders' Cup races, producing nine Horses of the Year in its first 19 runnings.

Although the year's best horse does not always win the Breeders' Cup Classic, the race has been extremely well matched, with eight of the races decided by less than one length. The only two runaway victories were Volponi's 6½-length upset in the 2002 Classic at Arlington Park and Skip Trial's six-length triumph at Hollywood Park in 1997. The eventual champion older horse that year, Skip Away, won in 1:59.16, the fastest time ever for the Classic's 1¼ miles.

The series began with a classic finish in the 1984 Breeders' Cup at Hollywood Park, with three horses charging together through the final furlong. Longshot Wild Again set the pace and prevailed by a neck on the inside. Gate Dancer bore in on favorite Slew o' Gold nearing the wire, and jockey Angel Cordero Jr. restrained Slew o' Gold through the final yards to protect the eventual champion older male. Gate Dancer finished second, but Hollywood's stewards advanced Slew o' Gold to the second spot.

The race did not yield its first Horse of the Year until 1987, when the Breeders' Cup returned to Hollywood and '86 Kentucky Derby (G1) winner Ferdinand met '87 Derby victor Alysheba. They hooked up inside the sixteenth pole and fought to the wire, with even-money favorite Ferdinand prevailing by a nose under jockey Bill

Breeders' Cup Classic

Grade 1, $4-million, three-year-olds and up, 1¼ miles, dirt. Run October 26, 2002, at Arlington Park with gross value of $3,664,000. First run in 1984. Weights: Northern Hemisphere three-year-olds, 121 pounds, older, 126 pounds; Southern Hemisphere three-year-olds, 117 pounds, older, 126 pounds; fillies and mares allowed three pounds.

Year	Winner	Jockey	Second	Third	Site	Time	Track	1st purse
2002	Volponi, 4	J. Santos	Medaglia d'Oro	Milwaukee Brew	AP	2:01.39	ft	$2,080,000
2001	Tiznow, 4	C. McCarron	Sakhee	Albert the Great	Bel	2:00.62	ft	2,080,000
2000	Tiznow, 3	C. McCarron	Giant's Causeway	Captain Steve	CD	2:00.75	ft	2,480,400
1999	Cat Thief, 3	P. Day	Budroyale	Golden Missile	GP	1:59.52	ft	2,080,000
1998	Awesome Again, 4	P. Day	Silver Charm	Swain (Ire)	CD	2:02.16	ft	2,662,400
1997	Skip Away, 4	M. Smith	Deputy Commander	Dowty	Hol	1:59.16	ft	2,288,000
1996	Alphabet Soup, 5	C. McCarron	Louis Quatorze	Cigar	WO	2:01.00	ft	2,080,000
1995	Cigar, 5	J. Bailey	L'Carriere	Unaccounted For	Bel	1:59.58	my	1,560,000
1994	Concern, 3	J. Bailey	Tabasco Cat	Dramatic Gold	CD	2:02.41	ft	1,560,000
1993	Arcangues, 5	J. Bailey	Bertrando	Kissin Kris	SA	2:00.83	ft	1,560,000
1992	A.P. Indy, 3	E. Delahoussaye	Pleasant Tap	Jolypha	GP	2:00.20	ft	1,560,000
1991	Black Tie Affair (Ire), 5	J. Bailey	Twilight Agenda	Unbridled	CD	2:02.95	ft	1,560,000
1990	Unbridled, 3	P. Day	Ibn Bey (GB)	Thirty Six Red	Bel	2:02 1/5	ft	1,350,000
1989	Sunday Silence, 3	C. McCarron	Easy Goer	Blushing John	GP	2:00 1/5	ft	1,350,000
1988	Alysheba, 4	C. McCarron	Seeking the Gold	Waquoit	CD	2:04 4/5	my	1,350,000
1987	Ferdinand, 4	W. Shoemaker	Alysheba	Judge Angelucci	Hol	2:01 2/5	ft	1,350,000
1986	Skywalker, 4	L. Pincay Jr.	Turkoman	Precisionist	SA	2:00 2/5	ft	1,350,000
1985	Proud Truth, 3	J. Velasquez	Gate Dancer	Turkoman	Aqu	2:00 4/5	ft	1,350,000
1984	Wild Again, 4	P. Day	Slew o' Gold	Gate Dancer	Hol	2:03 2/5	ft	1,350,000

1997: Skip Away supplemental entry, Whiskey Wisdom disqualified from third to fourth; 1984: Gate Dancer disqualified from second to third

Shoemaker. Ferdinand was voted Horse of the Year and champion older male, while Alysheba was honored as champion three-year-old male. The following year, Alysheba won the Classic in near darkness at Churchill Downs's first Breeders' Cup and was voted Horse of the Year and champion older male.

The 1989 Breeders' Cup Classic reunited Triple Crown rivals Sunday Silence and Easy Goer, and they battled through deep stretch as they had in the Derby and Preakness Stakes (G1) that year. Sunday Silence, who had won both the Derby and Preakness, proved best and won by a neck over Belmont Stakes (G1) victor Easy Goer. Sunday Silence was voted champion three-year-old male and Horse of the Year. After a truncated four-year-old campaign, Sunday Silence was sold for stud duty in Japan, where he became that country's all-time leading sire.

Tiznow, the race's only two-time winner, provided two scintillating finishes, holding off Giant's Causeway in 2000 by a neck at Churchill and then coming back courageously to best Sakhee by a nose in '01 at Belmont Park.

Three-year-olds have done well in the Classic, winning seven of the first 19 runnings, and two three-year-old winners have become successful sires. The 1990 Classic winner, Derby victor Unbridled, sired winners of the Kentucky Derby and Preakness, as well as two Breeders' Cup Juvenile (G1) victors. A.P. Indy, the 1992 winner and Horse of the Year, regularly ranks among North America's leading sires and sired 2001 Juvenile Fillies (G1) winner Tempera. Tiznow was a three-year-old when he won in 2000 and was voted Horse of the Year.

While the Classic has yielded some classic contests, it also has produced its share of puzzles and one especially bizarre finish. Arcangues won in 1993 at 133.60-to-1, the longest price for any Breeders' Cup winner, and Volponi won at 43.50-to-1 in 2002. The unusual finish came in the 1998 Classic, which featured the best field ever assembled for a Breeders' Cup race. Silver Charm took the lead in the stretch but began to bear out in the final furlong. Swain (Ire), a leading European contender, followed Silver Charm to the far outside under left-handed whipping by his jockey, Frankie Dettori. Awesome Again dashed through the hole they created and won by three-quarters of a length over Silver Charm. Skip Away, the 1.90-to-1 favorite who finished sixth, was voted champion older male and Horse of the Year.

Jockeys by Wins

5   **Chris McCarron** (Alphabet Soup, Alysheba, Sunday Silence, Tiznow [twice])

4   **Jerry Bailey** (Arcangues, Black Tie Affair [Ire], Cigar, Concern), **Pat Day** (Awesome Again, Cat Thief, Unbridled, Wild Again)

1   **Eddie Delahoussaye** (A.P. Indy), **Laffit Pincay Jr.** (Skywalker), **Jose Santos** (Volponi), **Bill Shoemaker** (Ferdinand), **Mike Smith** (Skip Away), **Jorge Velasquez** (Proud Truth)

Trainers by Wins

2   **Jay Robbins** (Tiznow [twice]), **Charlie Whittingham** (Ferdinand, Sunday Silence)

1   **Patrick Byrne** (Awesome Again), **Neil Drysdale** (A.P. Indy), **Andre Fabre** (Arcangues), **Hubert "Sonny" Hine** (Skip Away), **P. G. Johnson** (Volponi), **David Hofmans** (Alphabet Soup), **D. Wayne Lukas** (Cat Thief), **Bill Mott** (Cigar), **Carl Nafzger** (Unbridled), **Ernie Poulos** (Black Tie Affair [Ire]), **Richard Small** (Concern), **Vincent Timphony** (Wild Again), **Jack Van Berg** (Alysheba), **John Veitch** (Proud Truth), **Mike Whittingham** (Skywalker)

Owners by Wins

1   **Amherst Stable and Spruce Pond Stable** (Volponi), **Black Chip Stable** (Wild Again), **Cee's Stable** (Tiznow), **Michael Cooper and Cecilia Straub-Rubens** (Tiznow), **Darby Dan Farm** (Proud Truth), **William S. Farish, Harold Goodman, William S. Kilroy, and Tomonori Tsurumaki** (A.P. Indy), **Frances Genter** (Unbridled), **Arthur Hancock III, Ernest Gaillard, and Charlie Whittingham** (Sunday Silence), **Carolyn Hine** (Skip Away), **Elizabeth Keck** (Ferdinand), **Robert Meyerhoff** (Concern), **Oak Cliff Stable** (Skywalker), **Overbrook Farm** (Cat Thief), **Allen E. Paulson** (Cigar), **Ridder Thoroughbred Stable** (Alphabet Soup), **Dorothy and Pamela Scharbauer** (Alysheba), **Stronach Stables** (Awesome Again), **Jeffrey Sullivan** (Black Tie Affair [Ire]), **Daniel Wildenstein** (Arcangues)

Breeders of Winners

2   **Oak Cliff Thoroughbreds** (Skywalker, Sunday Silence), **Cecilia Straub-Rubens** (Tiznow [twice])

1   **Allez France Stables** (Arcangues), **Amherst Stable** (Volponi), **Anna Marie Barnhart** (Skip Away), **William S. Farish and William S. Kilroy** (A.P. Indy), **Mrs. John W. Galbreath** (Proud Truth), **Howard B. Keck** (Ferdinand), **W. Paul Little** (Wild Again), **Preston Madden** (Alysheba), **Robert Meyerhoff** (Concern), **Overbrook Farm** (Cat Thief), **Allen E. Paulson** (Cigar), **Stephen Peskoff** (Black Tie Affair [Ire]), **Southeast Associates** (Alphabet Soup), **Frank L. Stronach** (Awesome Again), **Tartan Farms** (Unbridled)

Sires of Winners

2   **Cee's Tizzy** (Tiznow [twice])

1   **Alydar** (Alysheba), **Broad Brush** (Concern), **Cozzene** (Alphabet Soup), **Cryptoclearance** (Volponi), **Deputy Minister** (Awesome Again), **Fappiano** (Unbridled), **Graustark** (Proud Truth), **Halo** (Sunday Silence), **Icecapade** (Wild Again), **Miswaki** (Black Tie Affair [Ire]), **Nijinsky II** (Ferdinand), **Palace Music** (Cigar), **Relaunch** (Skywalker), **Sagace** (Arcangues), **Seattle Slew** (A.P. Indy), **Skip Trial** (Skip Away), **Storm Cat** (Cat Thief)

Winners by Place Where Bred

Locality	Winners	Locality	Winners
Kentucky	10	Pennsylvania	1
Maryland	2	Canada	1
California	2	Ireland	1
Florida	2		

Supplemental Entries

Year	Runner	Fee	Finish	Earnings
2001	**Tiznow**	$360,000	1	$2,080,000
	Gander	360,000	9	0
2000	**Tiznow**	360,000	1	2,480,400
	Captain Steve	360,000	3	562,800
	Gander	360,000	9	0
1998	Silver Charm	480,000	2	1,024,000
	Skip Away	480,000	6	0
	Gentlemen (Arg)	800,000	10	0
1997	**Skip Away**	480,000	1	2,288,000
1994	Best Pal	360,000	5	60,000
	Bertrando	360,000	6	0
1993	Bertrando	360,000	2	600,000
	Best Pal	360,000	10	0
1988	Waquoit	360,000	3	324,000
	Cutlass Reality	360,000	7	0
1985	Vanlandingham	360,000	7	0
1984	**Wild Again**	360,000	1	1,350,000

Champions from Race

Year	Runner	Finish	Title
2001	**Tiznow**	1	Older male
2000	**Tiznow**	1	HOY, 3yo male
	Lemon Drop Kid	5	Older male
1998	Skip Away	6	HOY, older male
1997	**Skip Away**	1	Older male
1996	Cigar	3	HOY, older male
1995	**Cigar**	1	HOY, older male
1993	Bertrando	2	Older male
1992	**A.P. Indy**	1	HOY, 3yo male
1991	**Black Tie Affair (Ire)**	1	HOY, older male
1990	**Unbridled**	1	3yo male
1989	**Sunday Silence**	1	HOY, 3yo male
1988	**Alysheba**	1	HOY, older male
1987	**Ferdinand**	1	HOY, older male
	Alysheba	2	3yo male
1986	Turkoman	2	Older male
1985	Vanlandingham	7	Older male
1984	Slew o' Gold	2	Older male

HOY = Horse of the Year

Largest Winning Margins

Year	Winner	Margin
2002	Volponi	6½
1997	Skip Away	6
1995	Cigar	2½
1993	Arcangues	2
1992	A.P. Indy	2

Smallest Winning Margins

Year	Winner	Margin
2001	Tiznow	nose
1996	Alphabet Soup	nose
1987	Ferdinand	nose
1985	Proud Truth	head
1984	Wild Again	head
2000	Tiznow	neck
1994	Concern	neck
1989	Sunday Silence	neck

Shortest-Priced Winners

Year	Horse	Odds
1995	Cigar	0.70-to-1
1987	Ferdinand	1.00-to-1
1988	Alysheba	1.50-to-1
1997	Skip Away	1.80-to-1

Longest-Priced Winners

Year	Horse	Odds
1993	Arcangues	133.60-to-1
2002	Volponi	43.50-to-1
1984	Wild Again	31.30-to-1
1996	Alphabet Soup	19.85-to-1
1999	Cat Thief	19.60-to-1

Fastest Winners

Year	Horse	Track	Time	Cond.
1997	Skip Away	Hol	1:59.16	fast
1999	Cat Thief	GP	1:59.52	fast
1995	Cigar	Bel	1:59.58	muddy
1992	A.P. Indy	GP	2:00.20	fast
1989	Sunday Silence	GP	2:00½	fast

Slowest Winners

Year	Horse	Track	Time	Cond.
1988	Alysheba	CD	2:04⅘	muddy
1984	Wild Again	Hol	2:03⅜	fast
1991	Black Tie Affair (Ire)	CD	2:02.95	fast
1994	Concern	CD	2:02.41	fast

Most Starters

Year	Track	Starters
1999	Gulfstream Park	14
1994	Churchill Downs	14
1992	Gulfstream Park	14
1990	Belmont Park	14

Fewest Starters

Year	Track	Starters
1989	Gulfstream Park	8
1985	Aqueduct	8
1984	Hollywood Park	8
1997	Gulfstream Park	9
1988	Churchill Downs	9

Winning Post Positions

Post	Starters	Winners	Percent
1	19	1	5.3%
2	19	2	10.3%
3	19	2	10.3%
4	19	1	5.3%
5	19	1	5.3%
6	19	3	15.8%
7	19	0	0.0%
8	19	2	10.3%
9	16	0	0.0%
10	14	2	14.3%
11	13	1	7.6%
12	10	3	30.0%
13	8	0	0.0%
14	4	1	25.0%

Changes in Classic

The only change in the Breeders' Cup Classic was an increase in the purse from $3-million to $4-million beginning in 1996.

Breeders' Cup Turf

The race conditions of the Breeders' Cup Turf (G1), 1½ miles on grass at weight for age, constitute the classic standard of European racing, and as a result, overseas runners have won a majority of the $2-million contests. But they have not been dominant, probably because running in late October or early November—sometimes in tropical conditions—is not part of the European schedule, which traditionally culminates for top horses in early October with the running of the Prix de l'Arc de Triomphe (Fr-G1).

In fact, American owners and trainers have fielded some outstanding grass runners, and they have defeated top-level European competitors over the years. At times, lesser American runners have prevailed because the Europeans were past their best form or did not adapt well to warm weather at the Florida or Southern California Breeders' Cup sites.

Because of its importance on the world racing calendar, the Breeders' Cup Turf has become the definitive North American championship race. In every year except 1984 (John Henry's last championship season) and '89 (when the male title went to Breeders' Cup Mile [G1] winner Steinlen [GB]), a North American turf champion has come out of the Turf.

In 1993, American-trained Kotashaan (Fr) dominated grass racing in Southern California and scored a half-length victory over fellow Californian Bien Bien in the Turf. With a weak handicap division that year and no dominant three-year-old coming out of the Triple Crown series, Kotashaan was voted both champion turf male and Horse of the Year. He remains the only Turf winner to earn the top North American honor.

Early in the Turf's history, European runners gave indications they would dominate the race. Unheralded Lashkari (GB) won the inaugural running at Hollywood Park in 1984 at 53.40-to-1, the longest winning odds in the race's history. Lashkari, who never duplicated that effort, was bred and owned by the Aga Khan, who also bred back-to-back Turf winners Daylami (Ire), who was leased to Godolphin Racing, and Kalanisi (Ire), also owned by the Aga Khan. In 2001, Godolphin's Fantastic Light won at 7-to-5.

Pebbles (GB) was supplemented to the race in 1985 and scored a hard-fought victory over Strawberry Road (Aus). The Turf in the following year at Santa Anita Park was expected to showcase Dancing Brave, the Arc winner whose only career defeat was a second-place finish in the Epsom Derby (Eng-G1). But Dancing Brave was clearly over the top and tired to finish fourth as Manila stormed to a neck victory over Theatrical (Ire), who would win the Turf the following year.

California-based runners Great Communicator and Prized won in 1988 and '89, respectively, and the American home-court advantage appeared to be an important factor in the Turf. But European runners won the following two years and subsequently have performed well. In 1996, overseas interests swept the top four spots as Pilsudski (Ire) finished ahead of Singspiel (Ire), Swain (Ire), and Shantou, and the top three spots in 2001 were swept by European invaders Fantastic Light, Milan (GB), and American-trained import Timboroa (GB).

Canada's only victory came in 1997 with Chief Bearhart. Europe failed to field a strong team the following year, and front-running Buck's Boy, an Illinois-bred, won. The pattern changed in 1999,

Breeders' Cup Turf

Grade 1, $2-million, three-year-olds and up, 1½ miles, turf. Run October 26, 2002, at Belmont Park with gross value of $2,216,720. First run in 1984. Weights: Northern Hemisphere three-year-olds, 121 pounds; older, 126 pounds; Southern Hemisphere three-year-olds, 116 pounds; older, 125 pounds; fillies and mares allowed three pounds.

Year	Winner	Jockey	Second	Third	Site	Time	Track	1st purse
2002	**High Chaparral (Ire)**	M. Kinane	With Anticipation	Falcon Flight (Fr)	AP	2:30.14	yl	$1,258,400
2001	**Fantastic Light**, 5	L. Dettori	Milan (GB)	Timboroa (GB)	Bel	2:24.36	fm	1,112,800
2000	**Kalinisi (Ire)**, 4	J. Murtagh	Quiet Resolve	John's Call	CD	2:26.96	fm	**1,289,600**
1999	**Daylami (Ire)**, 5	L. Dettori	Royal Anthem	Buck's Boy	GP	2:24.73	gd	1,040,000
1998	**Buck's Boy**, 5	S. Sellers	Yagli	Dushyantor	CD	2:28.74	fm	1,040,000
1997	**Chief Bearhart**, 4	J. Santos	Borgia (Ger)	Flag Down	Hol	**2:23.92**	fm	1,040,000
1996	**Pilsudski (Ire)**, 4	W. Swinburn	Singspiel (Ire)	Swain (Ire)	WO	2:30.20	gd	1,040,000
1995	**Northern Spur (Ire)**, 4	C. McCarron	Freedom Cry (GB)	Carnegie (Ire)	Bel	2:42.07	sf	1,040,000
1994	**Tikkanen**, 3	M. Smith	Hatoof	Paradise Creek	CD	2:26.50	fm	1,040,000
1993	**Kotashaan (Fr)**, 5	K. Desormeaux	Bien Bien	Luazur (Fr)	SA	2:25.16	fm	1,040,000
1992	**Fraise**, 4	P. Valenzuela	Sky Classic	Quest for Fame (GB)	GP	2:24.08	fm	1,040,000
1991	**Miss Alleged**, f, 4	E. Legrix	Itsallgreektome	Quest for Fame (GB)	CD	2:30.95	fm	1,040,000
1990	**In the Wings (GB)**, 4	G. Stevens	With Approval	El Senor	Bel	2:29⅗	gd	900,000
1989	**Prized**, 3	E. Delahoussaye	Sierra Roberta (Fr)	Star Lift (GB)	GP	2:28	gd	900,000
1988	**Great Communicatòr**, 5	R. Sibille	Sunshine Forever	Indian Skimmer	CD	2:35⅕	gd	900,000
1987	**Theatrical (Ire)**, 5	P. Day	Trempolino	Village Star (Fr)	Hol	2:24⅖	fm	900,000
1986	**Manila**, 3	J. Santos	Theatrical (Ire)	Estrapade	SA	2:25⅖	fm	900,000
1985	**Pebbles (GB)**, f, 4	P. Eddery	Strawberry Road (Aus)	Mourjane (Ire)	Aqu	2:27	fm	900,000
1984	**Lashkari (GB)**, 3	Y. Saint-Martin	All Along (Fr)	Raami (GB)	Hol	2:25⅕	fm	900,000

1985—Pebbles (GB) supplementary entry.

when Daylami bounced back from a poor Arc effort to win the Turf. In a race that usually is decided by a half-length or less, Daylami's 2½-length triumph remains the Turf's largest winning margin. In 2002, Aidan O'Brien-trained High Chaparral (Ire) continued the European domination into a fourth year, prevailing at 9-to-10, the shortest odds in the Turf's history.

Jockeys by Wins

2 Lanfranco Dettori (Daylami [Ire], Fantastic Light), Jose Santos (Chief Bearhart, Manila)

1 Pat Day (Theatrical [Ire]), Eddie Delahoussaye (Prized), Kent Desormeaux (Kotashaan [Fr]), Pat Eddery (Pebbles [GB]), Michael Kinane (High Chaparral [Ire]), Eric Legrix (Miss Alleged), Chris McCarron (Northern Spur [Ire]), John Murtagh (Kalanisi [Ire]), Yves Saint-Martin (Lashkari [GB]), Shane Sellers (Buck's Boy), Ray Sibille (Great Communicator), Mike Smith (Tikkanen), Gary Stevens (In the Wings [GB]), Walter Swinburn (Pilsudski [Ire]), Patrick Valenzuela (Fraise)

Trainers by Wins

2 William Mott (Fraise, Theatrical [Ire]), Sir Michael Stoute (Kalanisi [Ire], Pilsudski [Ire]), Saeed bin Suroor (Daylami [Ire], Fantastic Light)

1 Thad Ackel (Great Communicator), Pascal Bary (Miss Alleged), Clive Brittain (Pebbles [GB]), Neil Drysdale (Prized), Andre Fabre (In the Wings [GB]), Mark Frostad (Chief Bearhart), P. Noel Hickey (Buck's Boy), LeRoy Jolley (Manila), Richard Mandella (Kotashaan [Fr]), Ron McAnally (Northern Spur [Ire]), Aidan O'Brien (High Chaparral [Ire]), Jonathan Pease (Tikkanen), Alain de Royer-Dupre (Lashkari [GB])

Owners by Wins

2 Aga Khan (Kalanisi [Ire], Lashkari [GB]), Godolphin Racing (Daylami [Ire], Fantastic Light), Sheikh Mohammed bin Rashid al Maktoum (In the Wings [GB], Pebbles [GB])

1 Augustin Stables (Tikkanen), Charles Cella (Northern Spur [Ire]), Class Act Stable (Great Communicator), Clover Racing Stable and Meadowbrook Farm (Prized), Fares Farm (Miss Alleged), La Presle Farm (Kotashaan [Fr]), Susan Magnier and Michael Tabor (High Chaparral [Ire]), Allen Paulson (Theatrical [Ire]), Madeleine Paulson (Fraise), Quarter B Farm (Buck's Boy), Samson Farm (Chief Bearhart), Bradley M. "Mike" Shannon (Manila), Lord Arnold Weinstock and executors of Simon Weinstock (Pilsudski [Ire])

Breeders of Winners

3 Aga Khan (Daylami [Ire], Kalanisi [Ire], Lashkari [GB])

1 Ballymacoll Stud (Pilsudski [Ire]), Eduardo Cojuangco Jr. (Manila), Sean Coughlan (High Chaparral [Ire]), Bertram and Diana Firestone (Theatrical [Ire]), Carl M. Freeman (Miss Alleged), Gainsborough Farm (Fantastic Light), Irish Acres Farm (Buck's Boy), Sheikh Mohammed bin Rashid al Maktoum (In the Wings [GB]), Richard Maynard (Chief Bearhart), Meadowbrook Farm (Prized), Allen E. Paulson (Fraise), George M. Strawbridge

Jr. (Tikkanen), Swettenham Stud & Partners (Northern Spur [Ire]), Warren Hill Stud (Pebbles [GB]), James B. Watriss (Great Communicator), Wertheimer & Frere (Kotashaan [Fr])

Sires of Winners

3 Sadler's Wells (High Chaparral [Ire], In the Wings [GB], Northern Spur [Ire])

2 Doyoun (Daylami [Ire], Kalanisi [Ire])

1 Alleged (Miss Alleged), Bucksplasher (Buck's Boy), Chief's Crown (Chief Bearhart), Cozzene (Tikkanen), Darshaan (Kotashaan [Fr]), Key to the Kingdom (Great Communicator), Kris S. (Prized), Lyphard (Manila), Mill Reef (Lashkari [GB]), Nureyev (Theatrical [Ire]), Polish Precedent (Pilsudski [Ire]), Rahy (Fantastic Light), Sharpen Up (GB) (Pebbles [GB]), Strawberry Road (Aus) (Fraise)

Winners by Place Where Bred

Locality	Winners	Locality	Winners
Ireland	6	Florida	1
Kentucky	5	France	1
Great Britain	3	Illinois	1
Canada	1	Pennsylvania	1

Supplemental Entries

Year	Runner	Fee	Finish	Earnings
2002	High Chaparral (Ire)	$180,000	1	$1,258,400
	Falcon Flight (Fr)	180,000	3	290,400
2001	Timboroa (GB)	180,000	3	$256,800
2000	John's Call	240,000	3	297,600
	Montjeu (Ire)	180,000	7	0
	Subtle Power (Ire)	180,000	10	0
1986	Estrapade	240,000	3	216,000
1985	Pebbles (GB)	240,000	1	900,000
	Greinton (GB)	240,000	7	0

Champions from Race

Year	Runner	Finish	Title
2002	High Chaparral (Ire)	1	Turf male
2001	Fantastic Light	1	Turf male
2000	Kalanisi (Ire)	1	Turf male
1999	Daylami (Ire)	1	Turf male
1998	Buck's Boy	1	Turf male
1997	Chief Bearhart	1	Turf male
1996	Singspiel (Ire)	2	Turf male
1995	Northern Spur (Ire)	1	Turf male
1994	Paradise Creek	3	Turf male
1993	Kotashaan (Fr)	1	Horse of the Year, Turf male
1992	Sky Classic	2	Turf male
1991	Miss Alleged	1	Turf female
1988	Sunshine Forever	2	Turf male
1987	Theatrical (Ire)	1	Turf male
1986	Manila	1	Turf male
1985	Pebbles (GB)	1	Turf female

Largest Winning Margins

Year	Winner	Margin
1999	Daylami (Ire)	2½
1994	Tikkanen	1½
2002	High Chaparral (Ire)	1¼
1999	Buck's Boy	1¼
1996	Pilsudski (Ire)	1¼

Smallest Winning Margins

Year	Winner	Margin
1992	Fraise	nose
1989	Prized	head
1995	Northern Spur (Ire)	neck
1986	Manila	neck
1985	Pebbles (GB)	neck
1984	Lashkari (GB)	neck

Shortest-Priced Winners

Year	Horse	Odds
2002	High Chaparral (Ire)	0.90-to-1
2001	Fantastic Light	1.40-to-1
1993	Kotashaan (Fr)	1.50-to-1
1999	Daylami (Ire)	1.60-to-1
1987	Theatrical (Ire)	1.80-to-1
1997	Chief Bearhart	1.90-to-1
1990	In the Wings (GB)	1.90-to-1

Longest-Priced Winners

Year	Horse	Odds
1984	Lashkari (GB)	53.40-to-1
1991	Miss Alleged	42.10-to-1
1994	Tikkanen	16.60-to-1
1992	Fraise	14.00-to-1

Fastest Winners

Year	Horse	Track	Time	Cond.
1997	Chief Bearhart	Hol	2:23.92	firm
1992	Fraise	GP	2:24.08	firm
2001	Fantastic Light	Bel	2:24.36	firm
1987	Theatrical (Ire)	Hol	2:24⅗	firm
1999	Daylami (Ire)	GP	2:24.73	good

Slowest Winners

Year	Horse	Track	Time	Cond.
1995	Northern Spur (Ire)	Bel	2:42.07	soft
1988	Great Communicator	CD	2:35½	good
1991	Miss Alleged	CD	2:30.95	firm
1996	Pilsudski (Ire)	WO	2:30.20	good
2002	High Chaparral (Ire)	AP	2:30.14	yielding

Most Starters

Year	Track	Starters
1999	Gulfstream Park	14
1996	Woodbine	14
1994	Churchill Downs	14
1993	Santa Anita Park	14
1989	Gulfstream Park	14
1987	Hollywood Park	14
1985	Aqueduct	14

Fewest Starters

Year	Track	Starters
2002	Arlington Park	8
1986	Santa Anita Park	9
1992	Gulfstream Park	10
1988	Churchill Downs	10
2001	Belmont Park	11
1997	Hollywood Park	11
1990	Belmont Park	11
1984	Hollywood Park	11

Winning Post Positions

Post	Starters	Winners	Percent
1	19	2	10.5%
2	19	5	26.3%
3	19	1	5.3%
4	19	0	0.0%
5	19	2	10.5%
6	19	0	0.0%
7	19	1	5.3%
8	19	1	5.3%
9	18	2	11.1%
10	17	0	0.0%
11	15	0	0.0%
12	11	3	27.3%
13	10	2	20.0%
14	7	0	0.0%

Changes in Turf

No changes have been made in the 1½-mile distance or $2-million purse of the Breeders' Cup Turf since its inaugural running in 1984.

Breeders' Cup Juvenile

Until a winner of the Breeders' Cup Juvenile (G1) delivers a Kentucky Derby (G1) victory, the 1 1/16-mile race (run at 1⅛ miles in 2002, and at one mile in 1984, '85, and '87) will be regarded as a measure of two-year-old form—which it obviously is—rather than a reliable yardstick of classic potential.

The race has gone 19 years without fielding a Derby winner, and only one classic winner, 1995 Preakness Stakes (G1) victor Timber Country, has won the Juvenile.

With regularity, however, the Derby winner and other classic winners have been in the beaten Juvenile field, implying that classic winners were either not sufficiently precocious to win the Juvenile or found its distance to be too short for their best efforts.

The first Breeders' Cup Juvenile was won by Chief's Crown, who finished second or third in all of the following year's classics, won the Travers Stakes (G1) against three-year-olds, and took the Marlboro Cup Handicap (G1) against older horses. He had the three-year-old title and Horse of the Year honors in his sights until finishing fourth as the favorite in the 1985 Breeders' Cup Classic (G1).

Second to Chief's Crown in the 1984 Juvenile was Tank's Prospect, who won the following year's Preakness. Tiring to finish third, beaten only 1½ lengths, was Spend a Buck, the 1985 Derby winner who was voted three-year-old male champion and Horse of the Year.

The pattern would be repeated in subsequent editions of the Juvenile. Alysheba, third in 1986, won the following year's Derby and Preakness and was voted three-year-old male champion. Bet Twice, who conquered him in the Belmont Stakes (G1), finished fourth in the '86 Juvenile. Pine Bluff was seventh in the 1991 Juvenile but won the Preakness the following year. Sea Hero, also seventh in the 1992 Breeders' Cup race, won the following year's Derby. Finishing third to Brocco in the 1993

Juvenile was Tabasco Cat, who would become a dual classic winner in '94 for D. Wayne Lukas, the leading trainer of Juvenile winners. Seven years later, Point Given came off a close second-place finish in the Juvenile to win the 2001 Preakness, Belmont, and Travers. Retired with an injury after the Travers, he was voted 2001 Horse of the Year and champion three-year-old male.

Losing an equally close decision was the best sire of the late 1990s, Storm Cat, who just failed to last the one-mile distance of the Juvenile at Aqueduct in '85. Capote, winner of the '86 Juvenile, never won again but became a successful sire, getting '96 Juvenile winner Boston Harbor.

Perhaps the most memorable running of the Juvenile occurred at Churchill Downs in '91, when French-trained Arazi broke from the outside post position, blew by the field on the final turn, and romped to a five-length victory. Voted two-year-old male champion off that one North American start, Arazi was hampered by knee problems early in his three-year-old season. He finished eighth as the favorite in the '92 Derby.

Another disappointment was Favorite Trick, who was voted '97 Horse of the Year after an overwhelming victory in the Juvenile. His contemporaries caught up to him at age three, and he finished eighth in the Derby.

Jockeys by Wins

3 **Jerry Bailey** (Macho Uno, Answer Lively, Boston Harbor), **Laffit Pincay Jr.** (Is It True, Capote, Tasso)

2 **Pat Day** (Favorite Trick, Timber Country), **Jose Santos** (Fly So Free, Success Express), **Mike Smith** (Vindication, Unbridled's Song), **Gary Stevens** (Anees, Brocco)

1 **Michael Kinane** (Johannesburg), **Don MacBeth** (Chief's Crown), **Chris McCarron** (Gilded Time), **Craig Perret** (Rhythm), **Patrick Valenzuela** (Arazi)

Trainers by Wins

5 **D. Wayne Lukas** (Boston Harbor, Timber Country, Is It True, Success Express, Capote)

1 **Bob Baffert** (Vindication), **Bobby Barnett** (Answer Lively), **Francois Boutin** (Arazi), **Patrick Byrne** (Favorite Trick), **Neil Drysdale** (Tasso), **Alex Hassinger Jr.** (Anees), **Roger Laurin** (Chief's Crown), **Claude R. "Shug" McGaughey III** (Rhythm), **Aidan O'Brien** (Johannesburg), **Joseph Orseno** (Macho Uno), **James Ryerson** (Unbridled's Song), **Flint S. "Scotty" Schulhofer** (Fly So Free), **Darrell Vienna** (Gilded Time), **Randy Winick** (Brocco)

Owners by Wins

1 **Barry A. Beal, Lloyd R. "Bob" French Jr., Eugene V. Klein** (Capote), **Mr. and Mrs. Albert Broccoli** (Brocco), **John Franks** (Answer Lively), **Gainesway Stable, Overbrook Farm, Robert and Beverly Lewis** (Timber Country), **Eugene V. Klein** (Is It True, Success Express), **Joseph LaCombe** (Favorite Trick), **David Milch, Jack and Mark Silverman** (Gilded Time), **Overbrook Farm** (Boston Harbor), **Padua Stables** (Vindication), **Paraneck Stable** (Unbridled's Song), **Allen E. Paulson, Sheikh Mohammed bin Rashid al Maktoum** (Arazi), **Ogden Mills Phipps** (Rhythm), **Gerald Robins** (Tasso), **Stronach Stables** (Macho Uno), **Star Crown Stable** (Chief's Crown), **Michael Tabor and Susan Magnier** (Johannesburg), **The Thoroughbred Corp.** (Anees), **Thomas Valando** (Fly So Free)

Breeders of Winners

1 **Adena Springs** (Macho Uno), **Farfellow Farms** (Anees), **John Franks** (Answer Lively), **Bruce Hundley and Wayne Garrison** (Fly So Free), **Warner L. Jones** (Is It True), **Wayne G. Lyster III and Jayeff B Stables** (Johannesburg), **Lowquest Ltd.** (Timber Country), **Mandysland Farm** (Unbridled's Song), **Mr. and Mrs. Harry T. Mangurian Jr.** (Gilded Time), **Meadowbrook Farms** (Brocco), **North Ridge Farm** (Capote), **Overbrook Farm** (Boston Harbor), **Ogden Mills Phipps** (Rhythm), **Payson Stud** (Vindication), **Gerald L. Robins and Timothy H. Sams** (Tasso),

Breeders' Cup Juvenile

Grade 1, $1-million, two-year-old colts and geldings, 1 1/16 miles, dirt. Run on October 26, 2002, at Arlington Park with gross value of $980,120. First run in 1984. Weights: 122 pounds.

Year	Winner	Jockey	Second	Third	Site	Time	Track	1st purse
2002	Vindication	M. Smith	Kafwain	Hold That Tiger	AP	149.61	ft	$556,400
2001	Johannesburg	M. Kinane	Repent	Siphonic	Bel	1:42.27	ft	520,000
2000	Macho Uno	J. Bailey	Point Given	Street Cry (Ire)	CD	1:42.05	ft	556,400
1999	Anees	G. Stevens	Chief Seattle	High Yield	GP	1:42.29	ft	556,400
1998	Answer Lively	J. Bailey	Aly's Alley	Cat Thief	CD	1:44	ft	520,000
1997	Favorite Trick	P. Day	Dawson's Legacy	Nationalore	Hol	1:41.47	ft	520,000
1996	Boston Harbor	J. Bailey	Acceptable	Ordway	WO	1:43.40	ft	520,000
1995	Unbridled's Song	M. Smith	Hennessy	Editor's Note	Bel	1:41.60	my	520,000
1994	Timber Country	P. Day	Eltish	Tejano Run	CD	1:44.55	ft	520,000
1993	Brocco	G. Stevens	Blumin Affair	Tabasco Cat	SA	1:42.99	ft	520,000
1992	Gilded Time	C. McCarron	It'sali'lknownfact	River Special	GP	1:43.43	ft	520,000
1991	Arazi	P. Valenzuela	Bertrando	Snappy Landing	CD	1:44.78	ft	520,000
1990	Fly So Free	J. Santos	Take Me Out	Lost Mountain	Bel	1:43 3/5	ft	450,000
1989	Rhythm	C. Perret	Grand Canyon	Slavic	GP	1:43 3/5	ft	450,000
1988	Is It True	L. Pincay Jr.	Easy Goer	Tagel	CD	1:46 3/5	my	450,000
1987	Success Express	J. Santos	Regal Classic	Tejano	Hol	1:35 2/5	ft	450,000
1986	Capote	L. Pincay Jr.	Qualify	Alysheba	SA	1:43 2/5	ft	450,000
1985	Tasso	L. Pincay Jr.	Storm Cat	Scat Dancer	Aqu	1:36 1/5	ft	450,000
1984	Chief's Crown	D. MacBeth	Tank's Prospect	Spend a Buck	Hol	1:36 1/5	ft	450,000

1984-'85, 1987—run at one mile; 1985—Tasso supplementary entry.

Carl Rosen (Chief's Crown), Tri Star Stable (Success Express), Ralph Wilson Jr. (Arazi), Mr. and Mrs. M. L. Wood (Favorite Trick)

Sires of Winners

2 **Seattle Slew** (Capote, Vindication),**Unbridled** (Anees, Unbridled's Song)
1 **Blushing Groom (Fr)** (Arazi), **Capote** (Boston Harbor), **Danzig** (Chief's Crown), **Fappiano** (Tasso), **Hennessy** (Johannesburg), **Hold Your Peace** (Success Express), **Holy Bull** (Macho Uno), **Kris S.** (Brocco), **Lively One** (Answer Lively), **Mr. Prospector** (Rhythm), **Phone Trick** (Favorite Trick), **Raja Baba** (Is It True), **Time for a Change** (Fly So Free), **Timeless Moment** (Gilded Time), **Woodman** (Timber Country)

Winners by Place Where Bred

Locality	Winners
Kentucky	16
Florida	3

Supplemental Entries

Year	Runner	Fee	Finish	Earnings
2002	Whywhywhy	$90,000	10	$ 0
2001	Ibn Al Haitham (GB)	90,000	9	0
2000	Arabian Light	90,000	5	21,400
1999	Captain Steve	90,000	11	0
1992	Caponostro	120,000	6	0
1991	Bertrando	120,000	2	200,000
	Agincourt	120,000	5	20,000
1990	Best Pal	120,000	6	10,000
1985	**Tasso**	120,000	1	450,000
1984	Spend a Buck	120,000	3	108,000

Champions from Race

Year	Runner	Finish	Title
2002	**Vindication**	1	Juvenile male
001	**Johannesburg**	1	Juvenile male
2000	**Macho Uno**	1	Juvenile male
1999	**Anees**	1	Juvenile male
1998	**Answer Lively**	1	Juvenile male
1997	**Favorite Trick**	1	Horse of the Year, Juvenile male
1996	**Boston Harbor**	1	Juvenile male
1994	**Timber Country**	1	Juvenile male
1993	Dehere	8	Juvenile male
1992	**Gilded Time**	1	Juvenile male
1991	**Arazi**	1	Juvenile male
1990	**Fly So Free**	1	Juvenile male
1989	**Rhythm**	1	Juvenile male
1988	Easy Goer	2	Juvenile male
1986	**Capote**	1	Juvenile male
1985	**Tasso**	1	Juvenile male
1984	**Chief's Crown**	1	Juvenile male

Largest Winning Margins

Year	Winner	Margin
1997	Favorite Trick	5½
1993	Brocco	5
1991	Arazi	5
1990	Fly So Free	3

Smallest Winning Margins

Year	Winner	Margin
2000	Macho Uno	nose
1985	Tasso	nose
1998	Answer Lively	head
1996	Boston Harbor	neck
1995	Unbridled's Song	neck

Shortest-Priced Winners

Year	Horse	Odds
1984	Chief's Crown	0.70-to-1
1997	Favorite Trick	1.20-to-1
1990	Fly So Free	1.40-to-1
1992	Gilded Time	2.00-to-1

Longest-Priced Winners

Year	Horse	Odds
1999	Anees	30.30-to-1
1988	Is It True	9.20-to-1
2001	Johannesburg	7.20-to-1
2000	Macho Uno	6.30-to-1
1985	Tasso	5.60-to-1

Fastest Winners

Year	Horse	Track	Time	Cond.
1997	Favorite Trick	Hol	1:41.47	fast
1995	Unbridled's Song	Bel	1:41.60	muddy
2000	Macho Uno	CD	1:42.05	fast
2001	Johannesburg	Bel	1:42.27	fast
1999	Anees	GP	1:42.29	fast

Slowest Winners

Year	Horse	Track	Time	Cond.
1988	Is It True	CD	1:46⅗	muddy
1991	Arazi	CD	1:44.78	fast
1994	Timber Country	CD	1:44.55	fast
1998	Answer Lively	CD	1:44.00	fast

Most Starters

Year	Track	Starters
2000	Churchill Downs	14
1999	Gulfstream Park	14
1991	Churchill Downs	14

Fewest Starters

Year	Track	Starters
1997	Hollywood Park	8
1996	Woodbine	10
1988	Churchill Downs	10
1984	Hollywood Park	10

Winning Post Positions

Post	Starters	Winners	Percent
1	19	1	5.3%
2	19	1	5.3%
3	19	6	31.6%
4	19	2	10.5%
5	19	2	10.5%
6	19	1	5.3%
7	19	2	10.5%
8	19	1	5.3%
9	18	1	5.6%
10	18	0	0.0%
11	15	1	6.7%
12	13	0	0.0%
13	11	1	9%
14	3	1	33.3%

Changes in Juvenile

Originally contested at one mile, the Breeders' Cup Juvenile was run at 1⅟₁₆ miles at Santa Anita Park in 1986 to accommodate the track's layout. The distance was changed to 1⅟₁₆ miles in 1988. In 2002, it was run at 1⅛ miles to accommodate the configuration of Arlington Park.

Breeders' Cup Filly and Mare Turf

In July 1998, the Breeders' Cup board of directors voted to fill an obvious gap in its championship lineup by creating the $1-million Breeders' Cup Filly and Mare Turf. Until the first Filly and Mare Turf at Gulfstream Park in 1999, the female turf division had no definitive championship race, and distaffers were forced to race in open company in either the Breeders' Cup Turf (G1) at 1½ miles or the Breeders' Cup Mile (G1) at one mile.

The new race for fillies and mares, first run at 1⅜ miles because of Gulfstream's grass course configuration, fulfilled its intended function. Phillips Racing Partnership's Soaring Softly locked up an Eclipse Award as champion turf female with a three-quarter-length victory over Coretta (Ire) at Gulfstream in 1999. The following year, Stronach Stable's Perfect Sting won by the same margin over Tout Charmant at Churchill Downs. Perfect Sting was subsequently voted Eclipse Award winner as champion turf female. European interests broke through in 2001 when Juddmonte Farms' French-based Banks Hill (GB) won by 5½ lengths at Belmont Park. For the first time in 2001, the Filly and Mare Turf was run at 1¼ miles, its prescribed distance when turf-course configurations permit. The race also was run at that distance in 2002, when Starine (Fr) won at Arlington Park.

Jockeys by Wins

2 **Jerry Bailey** (Soaring Softly, Perfect Sting)
1 **Olivier Peslier** (Banks Hill [GB]), **John Velazquez** (Starine [Fr])

Trainers by Wins

1 **Andre Fabre** (Banks Hill [GB]), **Robert Frankel** (Starine [Fr]), **Joseph Orseno** (Perfect Sting), **James J. Toner** (Soaring Softly)

Owners by Wins

1 **Robert Frankel** (Starine [Fr]), **Juddmonte Farms** (Banks Hill [GB]), **Phillips Racing Partnership** (Soaring Softly), **Stronach Stables** (Perfect Sting)

Breeders of Winners

1 **Catherine Dubois** (Starine [Fr]), **Juddmonte Farms** (Banks Hill [GB]), **Frank Stronach** (Perfect Sting), **Galbreath-Phillips Racing Partnership** (Soaring Softly)

Sires of Winners

1 **Danehill** (Banks Hill [GB]), **Kris S.** (Soaring Softly), **Mendocino** (Starine [Fr]), **Red Ransom** (Perfect Sting)

Winners by Place Where Bred

Locality	Winners
Kentucky	2
France	1
Great Britain	1

Supplemental Entries

Year	Runner	Fee	Finish	Earnings
2002	Starine (Fr)	$90,000	1	$665,600
	Islington (Ire)	90,000	3	153,600
	Golden Apples (Ire)	90,000	4	71,680
	Kazzia (Ger)	90,000	6	0
	Turtle Bow (Fr)	90,000	9	0
2001	Spook Express (SAf)	200,000	2	278,000
	Kalypso Katie (Ire)	200,000	6	0
	Starine (Fr)	90,000	10	0
	England's Legend (Fr)	90,000	11	0
2000	Caffe Latte (Ire)	0	9	0
	Catella (Ger)	90,000	3	145,200
	Colstar	90,000	7	0
	Petrushka (Ire)	90,000	5	24,200
1999	Caffe Latte (Ire)	90,000	4	59,920

Champions from Race

Year	Runner	Finish	Title
2002	**Golden Apples (Ire)**	4	Turf female
2001	**Banks Hill (GB)**	1	Turf female
2000	**Perfect Sting**	1	Turf female
1999	**Soaring Softly**	1	Turf female

Odds of Winners

Year	Horse	Odds
2002	Starine (Fr)	13.20-to-1
2001	Banks Hill (GB)	6.00-to-1
2000	Perfect Sting	5.00-to-1
1999	Soaring Softly	3.60-to-1

Winning Times

Year	Horse	Track	Time	Cond.
2002	Starine (Fr)	AP	2:03.57	Yielding
2001	Banks Hill (GB)	Bel	2:00.36	Firm
2000	Perfect Sting	CD	2:13.07	Firm
1999	Soaring Softly	GP	2:13.89	Good

Breeders' Cup Filly and Mare Turf

Grade 1, $1-million, fillies and mares, three-year-olds and up, 1¼ miles, turf. Run October 26, 2002, at Arlington Park with gross value of $1,172,480. First run in 1999. Weights: Northern Hemisphere three-year-olds, 119 pounds; older, 123 pounds; Southern Hemisphere three-year-olds, 114 pounds; older, 123 pounds.

Year	Winner	Jockey	Second	Third	Site	Time	Track	1st purse
2002	Starine (Fr)	J. Velazquez	Banks Hill (GB)	Islington (GB)	AP	2:03.57	yl	$665,600
2001	Banks Hill (GB), 3	O. Peslier	Spook Express (SAf)	Spring Oak (GB)	Bel	2:00.36	fm	722,800
2000	Perfect Sting, 4	J. Bailey	Tout Charmant	Catella (Ger)	CD	2:13.07	fm	629,200
1999	Soaring Softly, 4	J. Bailey	Coretta (Ire)	Zomaradah (GB)	GP	2:13.89	gd	556,400

1999-2000, 1⅜ miles; 2001-'02, 1¼ miles

	Number of Starters	
Year	**Track**	**Starters**
2002	Arlington Park	12
2001	Belmont Park	12
2000	Churchill Downs	14
1999	Gulfstream Park	14

	Winning Post Positions		
Post	**Starters**	**Winners**	**Percent**
1	4	0	0.0%
2	4	0	0.0%
3	4	0	0.0%
4	4	0	0.0%
5	4	1	25.0%

Post	**Starters**	**Winners**	**Percent**
6	4	0	0.0%
7	4	0	0.0%
8	4	1	25.0%
9	4	0	0.0%
10	4	0	0.0%
11	4	1	25.0%
12	4	1	25.0%
13	2	0	0.0%
14	2	0	0.0%

Changes in Filly and Mare Turf

No changes in conditions or purse other than the distance have been made since the Breeders' Cup Filly and Mare Turf was inaugurated in 1999.

Breeders' Cup Sprint

Roughly half of all North American races are run at six furlongs, and thus the $1-million Breeders' Cup Sprint (G1) is the prototypical American race. The six-furlong dash has proved to be a competitive contest, principally among North American runners, and in many years it has been a nightmare for handicappers.

As a championship event, the Breeders' Cup Sprint has been especially decisive in years when no horse clearly dominated the division. In 12 of the 19 runnings of the Sprint, the Eclipse Award for champion sprinter has gone to the winner.

The first Breeders' Cup Sprint in 1984 set the tone for the series, with Eillo desperately holding off Commemorate to win by a nose. Seven runnings of the Breeders' Cup Sprint have been decided by a neck or less. Eillo was favored at 1.30-to-1, and no favorite would again win the Sprint for ten years, until Cherokee Run (2.80-to-1) in 1994. Lit de Justice was a lukewarm 4-to-1 favorite in 1996, Kona Gold won at 1.70-to-1 in 2000, and Orientate prevailed at 2.70-to-1 in 2002.

Between Eillo and Cherokee Run, the Sprint was won by two other champions, Precisionist (1985) and Gulch ('88), who could not be characterized as pure sprinters. Fred Hooper's home-bred Precisionist won the 1¼-mile Charles H. Strub Stakes (G1) the same year he was sprint champion, and Gulch was really best at one mile, winning the Metropolitan Handicap (G1) twice, 1987 and '88, the latter his championship year.

The Sprint in 1990 remains one of the most memorable in Breeders' Cup history. Safely Kept, the prior year's champion sprinter, fought a spirited, head-to-head battle with English invader Dayjur, the 2.40-to-1 favorite. Inside the furlong pole, Dayjur appeared to take command, but 40 yards from the wire he jumped the shadow of Belmont Park's grandstand and briefly lost his action. Those missteps proved sufficient for 12.20-to-1 Safely Kept to regain the lead and hold on for a neck victory.

Although Dayjur failed to become the first overseas horse to win the Sprint, the European contingent broke through the following year when Sheikh Albadou (GB) won at Churchill Downs. At 26.30-to-1, Sheikh Albadou remains the longest-priced winner of the Sprint. Average odds of Sprint winners over the first 19 years were a healthy 9.28-to-1.

Kona Gold, the 2000 winner, proved that top-quality sprinters could be durable as well as fast. Carefully managed by co-owner and trainer Bruce Headley, the Java Gold gelding ran third in 1998, second in '99, and finally won at age six. In winning at Churchill Downs, Kona Gold set a track record, 1:07.77, the fastest time ever for the Sprint. Kona Gold was the 7-to-2 favorite when seeking a second straight win in 2001 but finished seventh behind winner Squirtle Squirt. In 2002, his record fifth start in the race, he finished fourth.

Jockeys by Wins

3 **Corey Nakatani** (Reraise, Elmhurst, Lit de Justice)

2 **Angel Cordero Jr.** (Dancing Spree, Gulch), **Eddie Delahoussaye** (Cardmania, Thirty Slews), **Craig Perret** (Safely Kept, Eillo), **Jerry Bailey** (Squirtle Squirt, Orientate)

1 **Jorge Chavez** (Artax), **Kent Desormeaux** (Desert Stormer), **Pat Eddery** (Sheikh Albadou [GB]), **Chris McCarron** (Precisionist), **Mike Smith** (Cherokee Run), **Alex Solis** (Kona Gold), **Patrick Valenzuela** (Very Subtle), **Jacinto Vasquez** (Smile)

Trainers by Wins

2 **D. Wayne Lukas** (Gulch, Orientate), **Jenine Sahadi** (Elmhurst, Lit de Justice)

1 **Louis Albertrani** (Artax), **Frank Alexander** (Cherokee Run), **Bob Baffert** (Thirty Slews), **Craig Dollase** (Reraise), **Robert Frankel** (Squirtle Squirt), **Ross Fenstermaker** (Precisionist), **Alan Goldberg** (Safely Kept), **Bruce Headley** (Kona Gold), **Budd Lepman** (Eillo), **Frank Lyons** (Desert Stormer), **Claude R. "Shug" McGaughey III** (Dancing Spree), **Derek Meredith** (Cardmania), **Flint S. "Scotty" Schulhofer** (Smile), **Alexander Scott** (Sheikh Albadou [GB]), **Mel Stute** (Very Subtle)

Owners by Wins

1 **Peter M. Brant** (Gulch), **Jean Couvercelle** (Cardmania), **Crown Stable** (Eillo), **Mitch Degroot**,

Dutch Masters III, and Mike Pegram (Thirty Slews), Craig Dollase, Barry Fey, Moon Han, and Frank Sinatra (Reraise), Evergreen Farm (Lit de Justice), Evergreen Farm and Jenine Sahadi (Elmhurst), Frances Genter Stable (Smile), Fred Hooper (Precisionist), Bruce Headley, Irwin and Andrew Molasky, and High Tech Stable (Kona Gold), Jayeff B Stables and Barry Weisbord (Safely Kept), David J. Lanzman (Squirtle Squirt), Robert and Beverly Lewis (Orientate), Joanne Nor (Desert Stormer), Paraneck Stable (Artax), Ogden Phipps (Dancing Spree), Jill Robinson (Cherokee Run), Ben Rochelle (Very Subtle), Hilal Salem (Sheikh Albadou [GB])

Breeders of Winners

1 Peter M. Brant (Gulch), Calumet Farm (Elmhurst), Carondelet Farm and Vinery (Artax), Ollie A. Cohen (Eillo), Delta Thoroughbreds (Cardmania), Gainesway Thoroughbreds Ltd. (Orientate), Frances Genter Stable (Smile), Grousemont Farm (Thirty Slews), Mr. and Mrs. David Hayden (Safely Kept), Highclere Stud (Sheikh Albadou [GB]) Fred Hooper (Precisionist), John Howard King (Very Subtle), Audrey Narducci, M.D., (Squirtle Squirt), Joanne Nor (Desert Stormer), George Onett (Cherokee Run), Carlos Perez (Kona Gold), Ogden Phipps (Dancing Spree), Swettenham Stud (Lit de Justice), Willard Sergent (Reraise)

Sires of Winners

2 Marquetry (Artax, Squirtle Squirt), Mr. Prospector (Eillo, Gulch)

1 Cox's Ridge (Cardmania), Crozier (Precisionist), Danzatore (Reraise), El Gran Senor (Lit de Justice), Green Desert (Sheikh Albadou [GB]), Hoist the Silver (Very Subtle), Horatius (Safely Kept), In Reality (Smile), Java Gold (Kona Gold), Mt. Livermore (Orientate), Nijinsky II (Dancing Spree), Runaway Groom (Cherokee Run), Slewpy (Thirty Slews), Storm Cat (Desert Stormer), Wild Again (Elmhurst)

Winners by Place Where Bred

Locality	Winners
Kentucky	13
Florida	4
Maryland	1
Great Britain	1

Supplemental Entries

Year	Runner	Fee	Finish	Earnings
2002	Disturbingthepeace	$90,000	7	$ 0
	Bonapaw	90,000	10	0
1999	Son of a Pistol	120,000	13	0
	Enjoy the Moment	120,000	14	0
1998	Reraise	120,000	1	572,000
1997	Men's Exclusive	200,000	6	0
1996	Criollito (Arg)	200,000	12	0
1994	Cherokee Run	120,000	1	520,000
	Soviet Problem	120,000	2	200,000
	Exclusive Praline	120,000	9	0
1989	Sewickley	120,000	5	50,000
1987	Zabaleta	120,000	4	70,000
	Zany Tactics	120,000	9	0
1985	Committed	200,000	7	0
1984	Pac Mania	200,000	9	0

Champions from Race

Year	Runner	Finish	Title
2002	Orientate	1	Sprinter
2001	Squirtle Squirt	1	Sprinter
	Xtra Heat	2	3yo filly
2000	Kona Gold	1	Sprinter
1999	Artax	1	Sprinter
1998	Reraise	1	Sprinter
1996	Lit de Justice	1	Sprinter
1995	Not Surprising	4	Sprinter
1994	Cherokee Run	1	Sprinter
1993	Cardmania	1	Sprinter
1992	Rubiano	3	Sprinter
1991	Housebuster	9	Sprinter
1989	Safely Kept	2	Sprinter
1988	Gulch	1	Sprinter
1987	Groovy	2	Sprinter
1986	Smile	1	Sprinter
1985	Precisionist	1	Sprinter
1984	Eillo	1	Sprinter

Breeders' Cup Sprint

Grade 1, $1-million, three-year-olds and up, 6 furlongs. Held on October 26, 2002, at Arlington Park with gross value of $1,044,240. First run in 1984. Weights: Northern Hemisphere three-year-olds, 123 pounds; older, 126 pounds; Southern Hemisphere three-year-olds, 122 pounds; older, 126 pounds; fillies and mares allowed three pounds.

Year	Winner	Jockey	Second	Third	Site	Time	Track	1st purse
2002	Orientate	J. Bailey	Thunderello	Crafty C. T.	AP	1:08.89	ft	$592,800
2001	Squirtle Squirt, 3	J. Bailey	Xtra Heat	Caller One	Bel	1:08.41	ft	520,000
2000	Kona Gold, 6	A. Solis	Honest Lady	Bet On Sunshine	CD	1:07.77	ft	520,000
1999	Artax, 4	J. Chavez	Kona Gold	Big Jag	GP	1:07.89	ft	624,000
1998	Reraise, 3	C. Nakatani	Grand Slam	Kona Gold	CD	1:09.07	ft	572,000
1997	Elmhurst, 7	C. Nakatani	Hesabull	Bet On Sunshine	Hol	1:08.01	ft	613,600
1996	Lit de Justice, 6	C. Nakatani	Paying Dues	Honour and Glory	WO	1:08.60	ft	520,000
1995	Desert Stormer, f, 5	K. Desormeaux	Mr. Greeley	Lit de Justice	Bel	1:09.14	my	520,000
1994	Cherokee Run, 4	M. Smith	Soviet Problem	Cardmania	CD	1:09.54	ft	520,000
1993	Cardmania, 7	E. Delahoussaye	Meafara	Gilded Time	SA	1:08.76	ft	520,000
1992	Thirty Slews, 5	E. Delahoussaye	Meafara	Rubiano	GP	1:08.21	ft	520,000
1991	Sheikh Albadou (GB), 3	P. Eddery	Pleasant Tap	Robyn Dancer	CD	1:09.36	ft	520,000
1990	Safely Kept, f, 4	C. Perret	Dayjur	Black Tie Affair (Ire)	Bel	1:09 3/5	ft	450,000
1989	Dancing Spree, 4	A. Cordero Jr.	Safely Kept	Dispersal	GP	1:09	ft	450,000
1988	Gulch, 4	A. Cordero Jr.	Play the King	Afleet	CD	1:10 2/5	sy	450,000
1987	Very Subtle, f, 3	P. Valenzuela	Groovy	Exclusive Enough	Hol	1:08 4/5	ft	450,000
1986	Smile, 4	J. Vasquez	Pine Tree Lane	Beside Promise	SA	1:08 2/5	ft	450,000
1985	Precisionist, 4	C. McCarron	Smile	Mt. Livermore	Aqu	1:08 2/5	ft	450,000
1984	Eillo, 4	C. Perret	Commemorate	Fighting Fit	Hol	1:10 1/5	ft	450,000

Largest Winning Margins

Year	Winner	Margin
1987	Very Subtle	4
1991	Sheikh Albadou (GB)	3
1998	Reraise	2
1996	Lit de Justice	1¼
1986	Smile	1¼

Smallest Winning Margins

Year	Winner	Margin
1984	Eillo	nose
1994	Cherokee Run	head
1995	Desert Stormer	neck
1993	Cardmania	neck
1992	Thirty Slews	neck
1990	Safely Kept	neck
1989	Dancing Spree	neck

Shortest-Priced Winners

Year	Horse	Odds
1984	Eillo	1.30-to-1
2000	Kona Gold	1.70-to-1
2002	Orientate	2.70-to-1
1994	Cherokee Run	2.80-to-1
1985	Precisionist	3.40-to-1
1999	Artax	3.70-to-1
1998	Reraise	3.80-to-1

Longest-Priced Winners

Year	Horse	Odds
1991	Sheikh Albadou (GB)	26.30-to-1
1992	Thirty Slews	18.70-to-1
1997	Elmhurst	16.60-to-1
1989	Dancing Spree	16.60-to-1
1987	Very Subtle	16.40-to-1
1995	Desert Stormer	14.50-to-1**
1990	Safely Kept	12.20-to-1
1986	Smile	11.00-to-1

** pari-mutuel field

Fastest Winners

Year	Horse	Track	Time	Cond.
2000	Kona Gold	CD	1:07.77	Fast
1999	Artax	GP	1:07.89	Fast
1997	Elmhurst	Hol	1:08.01	Fast
1992	Thirty Slews	GP	1:08.21	Fast
1986	Smile	SA	1:08⅗	Fast
1985	Precisionist	Aqu	1:08⅖	Fast

Slowest Winners

Year	Horse	Track	Time	Cond.
1988	Gulch	CD	1:10⅖	Sloppy
1984	Eillo	Hol	1:10⅕	Fast
1990	Safely Kept	Bel	1:09⅗	Fast
1994	Cherokee Run	CD	1:09.54	Fast

Most Starters

Year	Track	Starters
2001	Belmont Park	14
2000	Churchill	14
1999	Gulfstream Park	14
1998	Churchill Downs	14
1997	Hollywood Park	14
1994	Churchill Downs	14
1993	Santa Anita Park	14
1992	Gulfstream Park	14
1990	Belmont Park	14
1985	Aqueduct	14

Fewest Starters

Year	Track	Starters
1986	Santa Anita Park	9
1991	Churchill Downs	11
1984	Hollywood Park	11

Winning Post Positions

Post	Starters	Winners	Percent
1	19	1	5.3%
2	19	2	10.5%
3	19	2	10.5%
4	19	2	10.5%
5	19	5	26.3%
6	19	0	0.0%
7	19	0	0.0%
8	19	1	5.3%
9	19	1	5.3%
10	18	3	16.7%
11	18	2	11.1%
12	16	0	0.0%
13	16	0	0.0%
14	10	0	0.0%

Changes in Sprint

No changes have been made in the conditions or purse of the Breeders' Cup Sprint since its first running in 1984.

Breeders' Cup Mile

In the Breeders' Cup Mile, good things have come in twos. Only three Breeders' Cup races have had repeat winners, and the Breeders' Cup Mile has had three horses who have posted two victories each. (Bayakoa [Arg] won the Breeders' Cup Distaff in 1989 and '90, and Tiznow won the Classic in 2000 and '01.)

Miesque, bred by owner Stavros Niarchos's Flaxman Holdings Ltd., sparkled in the Mile on turf at Hollywood Park in 1987 and conquered a significantly slower surface at Churchill Downs the following year. The remarkable Francois Boutin-trained filly won by 3½ lengths in California and by four lengths in Kentucky—the largest winning margins in the race's history. On the strength of her single North American victories, Miesque was voted champion grass female in 1987 and '88. The Niarchos family also campaigned Spinning World (1997) and Domedriver (Ire) in the name of Flaxman Holdings.

Claiborne Farm's homebred Lure, arguably one of the most accomplished horses never to win an end-of-year championship, also scored two daylight victories, winning by three lengths at Gulfstream Park in 1992 and by 2¼ lengths the following year at Santa Anita Park for trainer Claude R. "Shug" McGaughey III.

Although not necessarily possessing talent to equal Miesque or Lure, Da Hoss became a two-time Mile winner by virtue of his courage and the innovative training regimen of Michael Dickinson. In 1996, Dickinson had his assistant, Joan

Wakefield, test the Woodbine turf course in high heels to determine the best path for the Gone West gelding, who won by 1½ lengths. Da Hoss missed the entire following season due to injury and came back to run in the 1998 Mile with only one start in two years. He rallied on a firm Churchill turf course to overtake Hawksley Hill (Ire) and win by a head.

European-based horses have had consistent success in the Mile. Eight of the first 19 winners were based with European trainers prior to their wins.

Most remarkable about the Mile has been the domination of the Northern Dancer sire line. Although the great Windfields Farm stallion did not sire a winner himself, six of his sons and two of his grandsons have sired winners, accounting for 12 victories in the first 19 years. His sons Danzig and Nureyev have each sired three winners.

Jockeys by Wins

2 **Freddie Head** (Miesque, 1987 and '88), **Mike Smith** (Lure, twice), **Gary Stevens** (Da Hoss, War Chant)

1 **Cash Asmussen** (Spinning World), **Lanfranco Dettori** (Barathea [Ire]), **Walter Guerra** (Cozzene), **John Murtagh** (Ridgewood Pearl [GB]), **Corey Nakatani** (Silic [Fr]), **Lester Piggott** (Royal Academy), **Yves Saint-Martin** (Last Tycoon [Ire]), **Jose Santos** (Steinlen [GB]), **Thierry Thulliez** (Domedriver [Ire]), **Fernando Toro** (Royal Heroine [Ire]), **Jose Valdivia Jr.** (Val Royal [Fr]), **John Velazquez** (Da Hoss), **Patrick Valenzuela** (Opening Verse)

Trainers by Wins

2 **Francois Boutin** (Miesque, 1987 and '88), **Julio Canani** (Silic [Fr], Val Royal [Fr]), **Michael Dickinson** (Da Hoss, 1996 and '98), **Claude R. "Shug" McGaughey III** (Lure, 1992 and '93)

1 **Pascal Bary** (Domedriver [Ire]), **Robert Collet** (Last Tycoon [Ire]), **Luca Cumani** (Barathea [Ire]), **Neil Drysdale** (War Chant), **John Gosden** (Royal Heroine [Ire]), **D. Wayne Lukas** (Steinlen [GB]), **Richard Lundy** (Opening Verse), **Jan Nerud** (Cozzene), **Vincent O'Brien** (Royal Academy), **John Oxx** (Ridgewood Pearl [GB]), **Jonathan Pease** (Spinning World)

Owners by Wins

2 **Claiborne Farm** (Lure, 1992 and '93), **Flaxman Holdings Ltd.** (Domedriver [Ire], Spinning World), **Stavros Niarchos** (Miesque, twice), **Prestonwood Farm and Wall Street Stable** (Da Hoss, 1996 and '98)

1 **Classic Thoroughbreds PLC** (Royal Academy), **Anne Coughlan** (Ridgewood Pearl [GB]), **Marjorie and Irving Cowan** (War Chant), **J. Terrence Lanni, Bernard Schiappa, Kenneth Poslosky, et al.** (Silic [Fr]), **David S. Milch** (Val Royal [Fr]), **Sheikh Mohammed bin Rashid al Maktoum and Gerald Leigh** (Barathea [Ire]), **John Nerud** (Cozzene), **Allen E. Paulson** (Opening Verse), **Richard C. Strauss** (Last Tycoon [Ire]), **Robert Sangster** (Royal Heroine [Ire]), **Wildenstein Stable** (Steinlen [GB])

Breeders of Winners

3 **Flaxman Holdings Ltd.** (Miesque, 1987 and '88, Spinning World)

2 **Claiborne Farm and Gamely Corp.** (Lure, 1992 and '93), **Fares Farm** (Da Hoss, 1996 and '98)

1 **Allez France Stables Ltd.** (Steinlen [GB]), **Tom Gentry** (Royal Academy), **Sean Coughlan** (Ridgewood Pearl [GB]), **Marjorie and Irving Cowan** (War Chant), **M. Armenio Simoes de Almeida** (Silic [Fr]), **Jean-Luc Lagardere** (Val Royal [Fr]), **Gerald Leigh** (Barathea [Ire]), **John Nerud** (Cozzene), **Niarchos Family** (Domedriver [Ire]), **Jacques D. Wimpfheimer** (Opening Verse), **Kilfrush Stud Ltd.** (Last Tycoon [Ire]), **B. L. Ryan** (Royal Heroine [Ire])

Breeders' Cup Mile

Grade 1, $1-million, three-year-olds and up, 1 mile, turf. Run October 26, 2002, at Belmont Park with gross value of $980,200. First run in 1984. Weights: Northern Hemisphere three-year-olds, 123 pounds; older, 126 pounds; Southern Hemisphere three-year-olds, 120 pounds; older, 126 pounds; fillies and mares allowed three pounds.

Year	Winner	Jockey	Second	Third	Site	Time	Track	1st purse
2002	**Domedriver (Ire)**	T. Thulliez	Rock of Gibraltar (Ire)	Good Journey	AP	1:36.92	yl	$556,400
2001	**Val Royal (Fr)**, 5	J. Valdivia Jr.	Forbidden Apple	Bach (Ire)	Bel	**1:32.05**	fm	592,800
2000	**War Chant**, 3	G. Stevens	North East Bound	Dansili (GB)	CD	1:34.67	fm	608,400
1999	**Silic (Fr)**, 4	C. Nakatani	Tuzla (Fr)	Docksider	GP	1:34.26	gd	520,000
1998	**Da Hoss**, 6	J. Velazquez	Hawksley Hill (Ire)	Labeeb (GB)	CD	1:35.27	fm	520,000
1997	**Spinning World**, 4	C. Asmussen	Geri	Decorated Hero (GB)	Hol	1:32.77	fm	572,000
1996	**Da Hoss**, 4	G. Stevens	Spinning World	Same Old Wish	WO	1:35.80	gd	520,000
1995	**Ridgewood Pearl (GB)**, f, 3	J. Murtagh	Fastness (Ire)	Sayyedati (GB)	Bel	1:43.65	sf	520,000
1994	**Barathea (Ire)**, 4	L. Dettori	Johann Quatz (Fr)	Unfinished Symph	CD	1:34.50	fm	520,000
1993	**Lure**, 4	M. Smith	Ski Paradise	Fourstars Allstar	SA	1:33.58	fm	520,000
1992	**Lure**, 3	M. Smith	Paradise Creek	Brief Truce	GP	1:32.90	fm	520,000
1991	**Opening Verse**, 5	P. Valenzuela	Val des Bois (Fr)	Star of Cozzene	CD	1:37.59	fm	520,000
1990	**Royal Academy**, 3	L. Piggott	Itsallgreektome	Priolo	Bel	1:35⅕	gd	450,000
1989	**Steinlen (GB)**, 6	J. Santos	Sabona	Most Welcome (GB)	GP	1:37⅕	gd	450,000
1988	**Miesque**, f, 4	F. Head	Steinlen (GB)	Simply Majestic	CD	1:38⅗	gd	450,000
1987	**Miesque**, f, 3	F. Head	Show Dancer	Sonic Lady	Hol	1:32⅘	fm	450,000
1986	**Last Tycoon (Ire)**, 3	Y. Saint-Martin	Palace Music	Fred Astaire	SA	1:35⅕	fm	450,000
1985	**Cozzene**, 5	W. Guerra	Al Mamoon	Shadeed	Aqu	1:35	fm	450,000
1984	**Royal Heroine (Ire)**, f, 4	F. Toro	Star Choice	Cozzene	Hol	1:32⅗	fm	450,000

1985—Palace Music disqualified from second to ninth.

Sires of Winners

3 **Danzig** (Lure, 1992 and '93, War Chant), **Nureyev** (Miesque, 1987 and '88, Spinning World)

2 **Gone West** (Da Hoss, 1996 and '98), **Indian Ridge** (Domedriver [Ire], Ridgewood Pearl [GB])

1 **Caro (Ire)** (Cozzene), **Habitat** (Steinlen [GB]), **Lypheor (GB)** (Royal Heroine [Ire]), **Nijinsky II** (Royal Academy), **Royal Academy** (ValRoyal [Fr]), **Sadler's Wells** (Barathea [Ire]), **Sillery** (Silic [Fr]), **The Minstrel** (Opening Verse), **Try My Best** (Last Tycoon [Ire])

Winners by Place Where Bred

Locality	Winners
Kentucky	10
Ireland	4
France	2
Great Britain	2
Florida	1

Supplemental Entries

Year	Runner	Fee	Finish	Earnings
2002	Landseer (GB)	$ 90,000	DNF	$ 0
2001	**Val Royal (Fr)**	90,000	1	592,800
	Express Tour	90,000	10	0
2000	Ladies Din	120,000	8	0
	Indian Lodge (Ire)	90,000	13	0
1997	Lucky Coin	120,000	4	61,600
1992	Bistro Garden	120,000	14	0
1991	Star of Cozzene	120,000	3	120,000
1986	Hatim	120,000	13	0
	Truce Maker	120,000	14	0
1985	Rousillon	120,000	9	0
1984	Night Mover	120,000	8	0

DNF Did not finish

Champions from Race

Year	Runner	Finish	Title
1993	Flawlessly	9	Turf female
1991	Tight Spot	9	Turf male
1990	Itsallgreektome	2	Turf male
1989	**Steinlen (GB)**	1	Turf male
1988	**Miesque**	1	Turf female
1987	**Miesque**	1	Turf female
1985	**Cozzene**	1	Turf male
1984	**Royal Heroine (Ire)**	1	Turf female

Largest Winning Margins

Year	Winner	Margin
1988	Miesque	4
1987	Miesque	3½
1994	Barathea (Ire)	3
1992	Lure	3

Smallest Winning Margins

Year	Winner	Margin
1998	Da Hoss	head
1986	Last Tycoon (Ire)	head
2000	War Chant	neck
1999	Silic (Fr)	neck
1990	Royal Academy	neck

Shortest-Priced Winners

Year	Horse	Odds
1993	Lure	1.30-to-1
1984	Royal Heroine (Ire)	1.70-to-1*
1989	Steinlen (GB)	1.80-to-1
1988	Miesque	2.00-to-1*

*Part of entry

Longest-Priced Winners

Year	Horse	Odds
1986	Last Tycoon (Ire)	35.90-to-1
1991	Opening Verse	26.70-to-1
2002	Domedriver (Ire)	26.00-to-1
1998	Da Hoss	11.60-to-1
1994	Barathea (Ire)	10.40-to-1

Fastest Winners

Year	Horse	Track	Time	Cond.
2001	Val Royal (Fr)	Bel	1:32.05	Firm
1984	Royal Heroine (Ire)	Hol	1:32⅗	Firm
1997	Spinning World	Hol	1:32.77	Firm
1987	Miesque	Hol	1:32⅘	Firm
1992	Lure	GP	1:32.90	Firm

Slowest Winners

Year	Horse	Track	Time	Cond.
1995	Ridgewood Pearl (GB)	Bel	1:43.65	Soft
1988	Miesque	CD	1:38⅗	Good
1991	Opening Verse	CD	1:37.59	Firm
1989	Steinlen (GB)	GP	1:37⅕	Good

Most Starters

Year	Track	Starters
2002	Arlington Park	14
2000	Churchill Downs`	14
1999	Gulfstream Park	14
1998	Churchill Downs	14
1996	Woodbine	14
1994	Churchill Downs	14
1992	Gulfstream Park	14
1991	Churchill Downs	14
1987	Hollywood Park	14
1986	Santa Anita	14
1985	Aqueduct	14

Fewest Starters

Year	Track	Starters
1984	Hollywood Park	10
1989	Gulfstream Park	11
2001	Belmont Park	12
1997	Hollywood Park	12
1988	Churchill Downs	12

Winning Post Positions

Post	Starters	Winners	Percent
1	19	3	15.8%
2	19	3	15.8%
3	19	1	5.3%
4	19	2	10.5%
5	19	1	5.3%
6	19	2	10.5%
7	19	1	5.3%
8	19	1	5.3%
9	19	0	0.0%
10	19	1	5.3%
11	18	2	11.1%
12	17	2	11.8%
13	14	0	0.0%
14	11	0	0.0%

Changes in Mile

No changes have been made in the conditions or purse of the Breeders' Cup Mile since its inauguration.

Breeders' Cup Juvenile Fillies

One of the most all-American of the Breeders' Cup races, the Breeders' Cup Juvenile Fillies (G1) has produced the most champions in year-end Eclipse Award balloting among Breeders' Cup races. Sixteen of the first 19 winners were subsequently voted year-end champions.

The first Breeders' Cup Juvenile Fillies, the second race on the inaugural card in 1984, produced the afternoon's first bit of controversy. In making a winning move at the top of the stretch, Fran's Valentine knocked Pirate's Glow off stride and pushed her into Canadian star Bessarabian. Fran's Valentine held off Outstandingly to reach the finish line first, but stewards disqualified Fran's Valentine to tenth for causing interference. After Outstandingly followed with a win in the Hollywood Starlet Stakes, she was voted an Eclipse Award as champion two-year-old filly, a title that would be earned by all but three of the succeeding Juvenile Fillies winners.

The Juvenile Fillies at Aqueduct in 1985 launched a dominating run by D. Wayne Lukas, who took the first two spots that year with Twilight Ridge and Family Style. Lukas saddled the top three finishers in 1988, with Open Mind the winner. In 1994, he sent out Flanders and Serena's Song to finish one-two. Flanders pulled up lame after the race and subsequently was retired. Serena's Song, second by a head, was champion three-year-old filly the following year and retired as North America's then-leading female earner with $3,283,388. Lukas also won in 1999 with longshot Cash Run.

In addition to Open Mind, who was voted champion at two and three, Juvenile Fillies winners who earned two championship titles were Go for Wand and Silverbulletday. Go for Wand took the two-year-old title with a triumph at Gulfstream Park in 1989 and won an Eclipse Award as champion three-year-old filly posthumously after a fatal breakdown in the 1990 Breeders' Cup Distaff (G1). Silverbulletday scored a half-length victory over stablemate Excellent Meeting in the 1998 Juvenile Fillies and won four Grade 1 races the following year to wrap up the three-year-old filly title.

Through 2002, only 11 overseas-based fillies have competed in the Fillies, with their best finishes a pair of fourths in 1993 and '94. Godolphin Racing won in 2001 with Tempera, who was trained in the United States by Eoin Harty.

Jockeys by Wins

2 **Jerry Bailey** (My Flag, Cash Run); **Pat Day** (Epitome, Flanders), **John Velazquez** (Caressing, Storm Flag Flying)**Patrick Valenzuela** (Brave Raj, Eliza)

1 **Angel Cordero Jr.** (Open Mind), **Eddie Delahoussaye** (Pleasant Stage), **David Flores** (Tempera), **Walter Guerra** (Outstandingly), **Laffit Pincay Jr.** (Phone Chatter), **Craig Perret** (Storm Song), **Randy Romero** (Go for Wand), **Jose Santos** (Meadow Star), **Shane Sellers** (Countess Diana), **Gary Stevens** (Silverbulletday), **Jorge Velasquez** (Twilight Ridge)

Trainers by Wins

4 **D. Wayne Lukas** (Twilight Ridge, Open Mind, Flanders, Cash Run)

3 **Claude R. "Shug" McGaughey III** (My Flag, Storm Flag Flying)

1 **William Badgett** (Go for Wand), **Bob Baffert** (Silverbulletday), **Patrick Byrne** (Countess Diana), **Eoin Harty** (Tempera), **Alex Hassinger Jr.** (Eliza), **Philip Hauswald** (Epitome), **LeRoy Jolley** (Meadow Star), **Richard Mandella** (Phone Chatter), **Frank Martin** (Outstandingly), **Christopher Speckert**

Breeders' Cup Juvenile Fillies

Grade 1, $1-million, two-year-old fillies, 1⅛ miles, dirt. Run October 26, 2002, at Arlington Park with gross value of $916,000. First run in 1984. Weights: 119 pounds.

Year	Winner	Jockey	Second	Third	Site	Time	Track	1st purse
2002	**Storm Flag Flying**	J. Velaquez	Composure	Santa Catarina	AP	1:49.60	gd	$520,000
2001	**Tempera**	D. Flores	Imperial Gesture	Bella Bellucci	Bel	1:41.49	ft	520,000
2000	**Caressing**	J. Velazquez	Platinum Tiara	She's a Devil Due	CD	1:42.77	ft	**592,800**
1999	**Cash Run**	J. Bailey	Chilukki	Surfside	GP	1:43.31	ft	520,000
1998	**Silverbulletday**	G. Stevens	Excellent Meeting	Three Ring	CD	1:43.68	ft	520,000
1997	**Countess Diana**	S. Sellers	Career Collection	Primaly	Hol	**1:42.11**	ft	535,600
1996	**Storm Song**	C. Perret	Love That Jazz	Critical Factor	WO	1:43.60	ft	520,000
1995	**My Flag**	J. Bailey	Cara Rafaela	Golden Attraction	Bel	1:42.55	my	520,000
1994	**Flanders**	P. Day	Serena's Song	Stormy Blues	CD	1:45.28	ft	520,000
1993	**Phone Chatter**	L. Pincay	Sardula	Heavenly Prize	SA	1:43.08	ft	520,000
1992	**Eliza**	P. Valenzuela	Educated Risk	Boots 'n Jackie	GP	1:42.93	ft	520,000
1991	**Pleasant Stage**	E. Delahoussaye	La Spia	Cadillac Women	CD	1:46.48	ft	520,000
1990	**Meadow Star**	J. Santos	Private Treasure	Dance Smartly	Bel	1:44	ft	450,000
1989	**Go for Wand**	R. Romero	Sweet Roberta	Stella Madrid	GP	1:44⅕	ft	450,000
1988	**Open Mind**	A. Cordero Jr.	Darby Shuffle	Lea Lucinda	CD	1:46⅗	my	450,000
1987	**Epitome**	P. Day	Jeanne Jones	Dream Team	Hol	1:36⅖	ft	450,000
1986	**Brave Raj**	P. Valenzuela	Tappiano	Saros Brig	SA	1:43⅕	ft	450,000
1985	**Twilight Ridge**	J. Velasquez	Family Style	Steal a Kiss	Aqu	1:35⅘	ft	450,000
1984	**Outstandingly**	W. Guerra	Dusty Heart	Fine Spirit	Hol	1:37⅘	ft	450,000

1984-'85, '87—run at one mile; 1984—Fran's Valentine disqualified from first to tenth.

(Pleasant Stage), **Mel Stute** (Brave Raj), **David Vance** (Caressing), **Nick P. Zito** (Storm Song)

Owners by Wins

2 **Eugene V. Klein** (Twilight Ridge, Open Mind)
1 **John A. Bell III** (Epitome), **Buckland Farm** (Pleasant Stage), **Christiana Stable** (Go for Wand), **Dogwood Stable** (Storm Song), **Dolly Green** (Brave Raj), **Godolphin Racing** (Tempera), **Harbor View Farm** (Outstandingly), **Richard A. Kaster, Nancy R. Kaster, Nancy A. Kaster**, and **Donald Propson** (Countess Diana), **Carl Icahn** (Meadow Star), **Overbrook Farm** (Flanders), **Padua Stables** (Cash Run), **Allen E. Paulson** (Eliza), **Mike Pegram** (Silverbulletday), **Ogden Phipps** (My Flag), **Ogden Mills Phipps** (Storm Flag Flying), **Carl F. Pollard** (Caressing), **Herman Sarkowsky** (Phone Chatter)

Breeders of Winners

2 **Ogden Phipps** (My Flag, Storm Flag Flying)
1 **Thomas E. Burrow** (Twilight Ridge), **Jaime S. Carrion** (Meadow Star), **Christiana Stable** (Go for Wand), **Darley Stud Management** (Tempera), **Due Process Stable** (Open Mind), **Robert S. Evans** (Cash Run), **Mrs. Thomas M. Evans** (Pleasant Stage), **William S. Farish and Ogden Mills Phipps** (Storm Song), **Harbor View Farm** (Outstandingly), **Highclere Inc. and Clear Creek** (Silverbulletday), **Brereton C. Jones** (Caressing), **Richard A. and Nancy R. Kaster** (Countess Diana), **Wallace S. Karutz** (Brave Raj), **Jessica Bell Nicholson and H. Bennett Bell** (Epitome), **Overbrook Farm** (Flanders), **Allen E. Paulson** (Eliza), **Herman Sarkowsky** (Phone Chatter)

Sires of Winners

2 **Deputy Minister** (Open Mind, Go for Wand), **Seeking the Gold** (Flanders, Cash Run)
1 **A.P. Indy** (Tempera), **Cox's Ridge** (Twilight Ridge), **Deerhound** (Countess Diana), **Easy Goer** (My Flag), **Exclusive Native** (Outstandingly), **Honour and Glory** (Caressing), **Meadowlake** (Meadow Star), **Mt. Livermore** (Eliza), **Phone Trick** (Phone Chatter), **Pleasant Colony** (Pleasant Stage), **Rajab** (Brave Raj), **Silver Deputy** (Silverbulletday), **Storm Cat** (Storm Flag Flying), **Summer Squall** (Storm Song), **Summing** (Epitome)

Winners by Place Where Bred

Locality	Winners
Kentucky	14
Florida	3
New Jersey	1
Pennsylvania	1

Supplemental Entries

Year	Runner	Fee	Finish	Earnings
2000	Cindy's Hero	$ 90,000	4	$63,840
	Out of Sync	90,000	9	0
1995	Tipically Irish	120,000	6	0
1994	Post It	120,000	6	0

Champions from Race

Year	Runner	Finish	Title
2002	**Storm Flag Flying**	1	Juvenile filly
2001	**Tempera**	· 1	Juvenile filly
2000	**Caressing**	1	Juvenile filly

Year	Runner	Finish	Title
1999	Chilukki	2	Juvenile filly
1998	**Silverbulletday**	1	Juvenile filly
1997	**Countess Diana**	1	Juvenile filly
1996	**Storm Song**	1	Juvenile filly
1995	Golden Attraction	3	Juvenile filly
1994	**Flanders**	1	Juvenile filly
1993	**Phone Chatter**	1	Juvenile filly
1992	**Eliza**	1	Juvenile filly
1991	**Pleasant Stage**	1	Juvenile filly
1990	**Meadow Star**	1	Juvenile filly
1989	**Go for Wand**	1	Juvenile filly
1988	**Open Mind**	1	Juvenile filly
1987	**Epitome**	1	Juvenile filly
1986	**Brave Raj**	1	Juvenile filly
1985	Family Style	2	Juvenile filly
1984	**Outstandingly**	1	Juvenile filly

Largest Winning Margins

Year	Winner	Margin
1997	Countess Diana	8½
1986	Brave Raj	5½
1990	Meadow Star	5
1996	Storm Song	4½

Smallest Winning Margins

Year	Winner	Margin
1987	Epitome	nose
1994	Flanders	head
1993	Phone Chatter	head
1991	Pleasant Stage	head

Shortest-Priced Winners

Year	Winner	Odds
1990	Meadow Star	.20-to-1
1994	Flanders	.40-to-1*
1985	Twilight Ridge	.60-to-1*
1988	Open Mind	.70-to-1*
2002	Storm Flag Flying	.80-to-1
1998	Silverbulletday	.80-to-1

*Part of entry

Longest-Priced Winners

Year	Horse	Odds
2000	Caressing	47.00-to-1
1999	Cash Run	32.50-to-1
1987	Epitome	30.40-to-1
1984	Outstandingly	22.80-to-1

Odds-On Beaten Favorites

Year	Horse	Odds
2001	You	0.95-to-1

Fastest Winners at 1¹⁄₁₆ Miles

Year	Horse	Track	Time	Cond.
2001	Tempera	Bel	1:41.49	Fast
1997	Countess Diana	Hol	1:42.11	Fast
1995	My Flag	Bel	1:42.55	Muddy
2000	Caressing	CD	1:42.77	Fast
1992	Eliza	GP	1:42.93	Fast

Slowest Winners at 1¹⁄₁₆ Miles

Year	Horse	Track	Time	Cond.
1988	Open Mind	CD	1:46⅗	Muddy
1991	Pleasant Stage	CD	1:46.48	Fast
1994	Flanders	CD	1:45.28	Fast
1989	Go for Wand	GP	1:44⅕	Fast

Most Starters

Year	Track	Starters
1997	Hollywood Park	14
1991	Churchill Downs	14
1994	Churchill Downs	13
1990	Belmont Park	13

Fewest Starters

Year	Track	Starters
1995	Belmont Park	8
1993	Santa Anita Park	8
2001	Belmont Park	9
1999	Gulfstream Park	9

Winning Post Positions

Post	Starters	Winners	Percent
1	19	1	5.3%
2	19	1	5.3%
3	19	1	5.3%
4	19	3	15.8%
5	19	1	5.3%
6	19	3	15.8%
7	19	0	0.0%
8	19	4	21.1%
9	17	3	17.7%
10	15	0	0.0%
11	13	1	7.7%
12	12	0	0.0%
13	4	0	0.0%
14	2	1	50.0%

Changes in Juvenile Fillies

The only change to the Juvenile Fillies over the years has been the distance. Originally at one mile for the 1984 and '85 runnings, the distance was changed to 1 1/16 miles for 1986 to accommodate the Santa Anita Park track configuration. The distance reverted to one mile for the 1987 edition at Hollywood Park but returned to 1 1/16 miles for '88 and thereafter. For 2002, the distance was increased to 1 1/8 miles to accommodate the configuration of Arlington Park's main track.

Breeders' Cup Distaff

Although the Breeders' Cup Distaff (G1) has produced two of the four highest-priced winners in the event's history, the race for fillies and mares has in fact been one of the most consistent and predictable of the original seven races.

That record of consistency began with the inaugural Breeders' Cup Distaff at Hollywood Park in 1984. Princess Rooney, winner of the Vanity Handicap (G1) and Spinster Stakes (G1) in prior starts, went off as the 7-to-10 favorite and rolled to a seven-length victory.

In subsequent editions, the Distaff generally was characterized by dominant winners scoring by open lengths. In fact, Inside Information's 13 1/2-length win in 1995 remains the series' largest winning margin. Azeri waltzed away to a five-length victory in 2002 to lock up a Horse of the Year title, and Lady's Secret won by 2 1/2 lengths in 1986, her Horse of the Year season. Odds-on favorites have won the race seven times.

In 1988, Breeders' Cup Ltd. shortened the Distaff's distance from 1 1/4 miles to 1 1/8 miles with no effect on the quality of the race. Indeed, the 1988 running remains one of the most memorable of all Breeders' Cup races. Undefeated Personal Ensign, seemingly beaten at the sixteenth pole, closed relentlessly on Winning Colors, that year's Kentucky Derby winner, and put her nose in front at the wire to close out her career undefeated with 13 victories.

At year's end, Personal Ensign won the Eclipse Award for champion older female, and Winning Colors received an Eclipse as champion three-year-old filly. Dance Smartly, the 1991 Distaff winner, won an Eclipse Award as champion three-year-old filly and Canada's Horse of the Year after sweeping the Canadian Triple Crown. In 14 of 19 years, both the champion three-year-old filly and older female have competed in the Distaff.

Supplemental entries, principally top-quality mares from South America, have had excellent success in the Distaff. Bayakoa (Arg), supplemented for $200,000 in 1989 and '90, won both years. The latter year was the darkest day in Breeders' Cup history, when Go for Wand broke down fatally while battling Bayakoa for the lead deep in Belmont Park's stretch. Paseana (Arg), supplemented in 1992 and '93, won in her first try and finished second by a nose to Hollywood Wildcat in '93.

The biggest upset in Distaff history occurred in 2000, when dominant West Coast mare Riboletta (Brz) went off as the 2-to-5 favorite but did not handle the hard Churchill Downs track and finished seventh. Spain, at 55.90-to-1, won the race.

Racing Hall of Fame members who have contested the race are Princess Rooney, Lady's Secret, Personal Ensign, Winning Colors, Bayakoa, Go for Wand, Dance Smartly, Paseana, and Serena's Song.

Jockeys by Wins

3 **Pat Day** (Dance Smartly, Lady's Secret, Unbridled Elaine)
Mike Smith (Azeri, Ajina, Inside Information)
2 **Eddie Delahoussaye** (Hollywood Wildcat, Princess Rooney), **Laffit Pincay Jr.** (Bayakoa [Arg], twice), **Randy Romero** (Personal Ensign, Sacahuista), **Gary Stevens** (Escena, One Dreamer)
1 **Jorge Chavez** (Beautiful Pleasure), **Angel Cordero** (Life's Magic), **Victor Espinoza** (Spain), **Chris McCarron** (Paseana [Arg]), **Corey Nakatani** (Jewel Princess)

Trainers by Wins

4 **D. Wayne Lukas** (Lady's Secret, Life's Magic, Sacahuista, Spain)

3 **Ron McAnally** (Bayakoa [Arg], twice, Paseana [Arg])
2 **Neil Drysdale** (Hollywood Wildcat, Princess Rooney), **Claude R. "Shug" McGaughey III** (Inside Information, Personal Ensign), **William I. Mott** (Ajina, Escena)
1 **James Day** (Dance Smartly), **Laura de Seroux** (Azeri), **Wallace Dollase** (Jewel Princess), **Tom Proctor** (One Dreamer), **Dallas Stewart** (Unbridled Elaine), **John T. Ward Jr.** (Beautiful Pleasure)

Owners by Wins

2 **Allen E. Paulson** (Ajina, Escena), **Frank and Janis Whitham** (Bayakoa [Arg], twice)
1 **Barry A. Beal and L. R. French Jr.** (Sacahuista), **Irving and Marjorie Cowan** (Hollywood Wildcat), **Sidney Craig** (Paseana [Arg]), **Roger J. Devenport** (Unbridled Elaine), **Glen Hill Farm** (One Dreamer), **Mel Hatley and Eugene V. Klein** (Life's Magic), **Mr. and Mrs. Eugene V. Klein** (Lady's Secret), **John Oxley** (Beautiful Pleasure), **Allen E. Paulson Living Trust** (Azeri), **Ogden Phipps** (Personal Ensign), **Ogden Mills Phipps** (Inside Information), **Sam-Son Farms** (Dance Smartly), **The Thoroughbred Corp. and Martha and Richard Stephen** (Jewel Princess), **The Thoroughbred Corp.** (Spain), **Paula Tucker** (Princess Rooney)

Breeders of Winners

3 **Allen E. Paulson** (Ajina, Azeri, Escena)
2 **Farnsworth Farms** (Beautiful Pleasure, Jewel Princess), **Haras Principal** (Bayakoa [Arg], twice)
1 **Irving and Marjorie Cowan** (Hollywood Wildcat), **Glen Hill Farm** (One Dreamer), **Golden Orb Farm and K. David Schwartz** (Unbridled Elaine), **Haras Vacacion** (Paseana [Arg]), **G. Watts Humphrey and William S. Farish** (Sacahuista), **Mr. and Mrs. Douglas Parrish and David Parrish III** (Life's Magic), **Ogden Phipps** (Personal Ensign), **Ogden Mills Phipps** (Inside Information), **Ben and Tom Roach** (Princess Rooney), **Sam-Son Farms** (Dance Smartly), **Robert H. Spreen** (Lady's Secret), **The Thoroughbred Corp.** (Spain)

Sires of Winners

2 **Consultant's Bid** (Bayakoa [Arg], twice), **Private Account** (Inside Information, Personal Ensign), **Strawberry Road (Aus)** (Ajina, Escena)
1 **Ahmad** (Paseana [Arg]), **Cox's Ridge** (Life's Magic), **Danzig** (Dance Smartly), Jade Hunter (Azeri), **Key to the Mint** (Jewel Princess), **Kris S.** (Hollywood Wildcat), **Maudlin** (Beautiful Pleasure), **Raja Baba** (Sacahuista), **Relaunch** (One Dreamer), **Secretariat** (Lady's Secret), **Thunder Gulch** (Spain), **Unbridled's Song** (Unbridled Elaine), **Verbatim** (Princess Rooney)

Winners by Place Where Bred

Locality	Winners
Kentucky	10
Florida	4
Argentina	3
Oklahoma	1
Ontario	1

Supplemental Entries

Year	Runner	Fee	Finish	Earnings
2001	Miss Linda (Arg)	$400,000	6	$ 0
2000	Riboletta (Brz)	400,000	7	0
1996	Different (Arg)	200,000	3	120,000
1993	Paseana (Arg)	200,000	2	200,000
1992	**Paseana (Arg)**	200,000	1	520,000
1990	**Bayakoa (Arg)**	200,000	1	450,000
1989	**Bayakoa (Arg)**	200,000	1	450,000
1986	Classy Cathy	120,000	4	70,000
1985	Dontstop Themusic	120,000	3	108,000
	Isayso	120,000	6	10,000

Champions from Race

Year	Runner	Finish	Title
2002	**Azeri**	1	Horse of the Year, Older female
	Farda Amiga	2	3yo filly
2000	Surfside	2	3yo filly
	Riboletta (Brz)	7	Older female

Breeders' Cup Distaff

Grade 1, $2-million, fillies and mares, three-year-olds and up, 1⅛ miles. Run October 26, 2002, at Arlington Park with gross value of $1,832,000. First run in 1984. Weights: Northern Hemisphere three-year-olds, 120 pounds; older, 123 pounds; Southern Hemisphere three-year-olds, 115 pounds; older, 123 pounds.

Year	Winner	Jockey	Second	Third	Site	Time	Track	1st purse
2002	**Azeri**	M. Smith	Farda Amiga	Imperial Gesture	AP	1:48.64	gd	$1,040,000
2001	**Unbridled Elaine**, 3	P. Day	Spain	Two Item Limit	Bel	1:49.21	ft	1,227,200
2000	**Spain**, 3	V. Espinoza	Surfside	Heritage of Gold	CD	1:47.66	ft	**1,227,200**
1999	**Beautiful Pleasure**, 4	J. Chavez	Banshee Breeze	Heritage of Gold	GP	1:47.56	ft	1,040,000
1998	**Escena**, 5	G. Stevens	Banshee Breeze	Keeper Hill	CD	1:49.89	ft	1,040,000
1997	**Ajina**, 3	M. Smith	Sharp Cat	Escena	Hol	1:47.20	ft	520,000
1996	**Jewel Princess**, 4	C. Nakatani	Serena's Song	Different (Arg)	WO	1:48.40	ft	520,000
1995	**Inside Information**, 4	M. Smith	Heavenly Prize	Lakeway	Bel	**1:46.15**	my	520,000
1994	**One Dreamer**, 6	G. Stevens	Heavenly Prize	Miss Dominique	CD	1:50.70	ft	520,000
1993	**Hollywood Wildcat**, 3	E. Delahoussaye	Paseana (Arg)	Re Toss (Arg)	SA	1:48.35	ft	520,000
1992	**Paseana (Arg)**, 5	C. McCarron	Versailles Treaty	Magical Maiden	GP	1:48.17	ft	520,000
1991	**Dance Smartly**, 3	P. Day	Versailles Treaty	Brought to Mind	CD	1:50.95	ft	520,000
1990	**Bayakoa (Arg)**, 6	L. Pincay Jr.	Colonial Waters	Valay Maid	Bel	1:49⅕	ft	450,000
1989	**Bayakoa (Arg)**, 5	L. Pincay Jr.	Gorgeous	Open Mind	GP	1:47⅖	ft	450,000
1988	**Personal Ensign**, 4	R. Romero	Winning Colors	Goodbye Halo	CD	1:52	my	450,000
1987	**Sacahuista**, 3	R. Romero	Clabber Girl	Oueee Bebe	Hol	2:02⅘	ft	450,000
1986	**Lady's Secret**, 4	P. Day	Fran's Valentine	Outstandingly	SA	**2:01⅕**	ft	450,000
1985	**Life's Magic**, 4	A. Cordero Jr.	Lady's Secret	Dontstop Themusic	Aqu	2:02	ft	450,000
1984	**Princess Rooney**, 4	E. Delahoussaye	Life's Magic	Adored	Hol	2:02⅖	ft	450,000

1984-'87—run at 1¼ miles; 1989 and '90—Bayakoa (Arg) supplementary entry; 1992—Paseana (Arg) supplemental entry.

Year	Runner	Finish	Title
1999	**Beautiful Pleasure**	1	Older female
	Silverbulletday	6	3yo filly
1998	**Escena**	1	Older female
	Banshee Breeze	2	3yo filly
1997	**Ajina**	1	3yo filly
	Hidden Lake	7	Older female
1996	**Jewel Princess**	1	Older female
1995	**Inside Information**	1	Older female
	Serena's Song	5	3yo filly
1994	Heavenly Prize	2	3yo filly
	Sky Beauty	9	Older female
1993	**Hollywood Wildcat**	1	3yo filly
	Paseana (Arg)	2	Older female
1992	**Paseana (Arg)**	1	Older female
	Saratoga Dew	12	3yo filly
1991	**Dance Smartly**	1	3yo filly
	Queena	5	Older female
1990	**Bayakoa (Arg)**	1	Older female
	Go for Wand	DNF	3yo filly
1989	**Bayakoa (Arg)**	1	Older female
	Open Mind	3	3yo female
1988	Personal Ensign	1	Older female
	Winning Colors	2	3yo filly
1987	**Sacahuista**	1	3yo filly
	North Sider	6	Older female
1986	**Lady's Secret**	1	Horse of the Year, Older female
1985	**Life's Magic**	1	Older female
1984	**Princess Rooney**	1	Older female
	Life's Magic	2	3yo filly

Largest Winning Margins

Year	Winner	Margin
1995	Inside Information	13½
1984	Princess Rooney	7
1990	Bayakoa (Arg)	6¾
1985	Life's Magic	6¼
2002	Azeri	5
1992	Paseana (Arg)	4

Smallest Winning Margins

Year	Winner	Margin
1998	Escena	nose
1993	Hollywood Wildcat	nose
1988	Personal Ensign	nose
1994	One Dreamer	neck

Shortest-Priced Winners

Year	Horse	Odds
1985	Life's Magic	.40-to-1*
1991	Dance Smartly	.50-to-1*
1988	Personal Ensign	.50-to-1
1986	Lady's Secret	.50-to-1*
1989	Bayakoa (Arg)	.70-to-1
1984	Princess Rooney	.70-to-1
1995	Inside Information	.80-to-1*

*Part of entry

Longest-Priced Winners

Year	Horse	Odds
2000	Spain	55.90-to-1
1994	One Dreamer	47.10-to-1
2001	Unbridled Elaine	12.30-to-1
1997	Ajina	4.80-to-1*
1999	Beautiful Pleasure	3-to-1
1998	Escena	3-to-1

*Part of entry

Odds-On Beaten Favorites

Year	Horse	Odds	Finish
2000	Riboletta (Brz)	.40-to-1	7
1998	Banshee Breeze	.80-to-1	2
1990	Go for Wand	.70-to-1	DNF
1987	Infinidad (Chi)	.70-to-1	4

Fastest Winners at 1⅛ Miles

Year	Horse	Track	Time	Cond.
1995	Inside Information	Bel	1:46.15	Muddy
1997	Ajina	Hol	1:47.20	Fast
1989	Bayakoa (Arg)	GP	1:47⅗	Fast
1999	Beautiful Pleasure	GP	1:47.56	Fast
2000	Spain	CD	1:47.66	Fast

Slowest Winners at 1⅛ Miles

Year	Horse	Track	Time	Cond.
1988	Personal Ensign	CD	1:52	Muddy
1991	Dance Smartly	CD	1:50.95	Fast
1994	One Dreamer	CD	1:50.70	Fast
1998	Escena	CD	1:49.89	Fast
1990	Bayakoa (Arg)	Bel	1:49⅕	Fast
2001	Unbridled Elaine	Bel	1:49.21	Fast

Most Starters

Year	Track	Starters
1992	Gulfstream Park	14
1991	Churchill Downs	13
2001	Belmont Park	11
1995	Belmont Park	10
1989	Gulfstream Park	10

Fewest Starters

Year	Track	Starters
1996	Woodbine	6
1987	Hollywood Park	6
1990	Belmont Park	7
1985	Aqueduct	7
1984	Hollywood Park	7

Winning Post Positions

Post	Starters	Winners	Percent
1	19	4	21.0%
2	19	0	0.0%
3	19	0	0.0%
4	19	5	26.3%
5	19	4	21.1%
6	19	3	15.8%
7	17	1	5.9%
8	14	0	0.0%
9	8	0	0.0%
10	5	1	20.0%
11	3	0	0.0%
12	2	0	0.0%
13	2	0	0.0%
14	1	1	100.0%

Changes in Distaff

Two significant changes have occurred in the conditions of the Breeders' Cup Distaff. For the 1988 running, the distance was shortened to 1⅛ miles from 1¼ miles, and in 1998 the purse was increased to $2-million from $1-million.

Classic: Sly Old Fox

In the weeks before the 2002 Breeders' Cup World Thoroughbred Championships, Mary Kay Johnson advised her husband, Racing Hall of Fame trainer P. G. Johnson, that it was time for him to slow down.

After all, he had turned 77 earlier in October, had suffered from prostate cancer—including surgery just 23 days before the 2002 event—and had found the demands of conditioning 36 racehorses wearying as never before. But her advice went unheeded. "He's tough; tough to live with, too," she said on October 26, one day before their 57th wedding anniversary.

They had planned no special celebration until Johnson tightened the girth around Volponi, the four-year-old son of Cryptoclearance whom he and his family bred and co-own, for the $4-million Breeders' Cup Classic (G1) at Arlington Park. But they had many reasons to celebrate after Volponi—the longest shot in the 12-horse field at 43.50-to-1—spurted away to an electrifying 6½-length victory.

With a dazzling move at the top of the stretch under Jose Santos, Volponi surged inside fading dual classic winner War Emblem and darted past 2.70-to-1 favorite Medaglia d'Oro, who had gained the lead. Volponi quickly jumped two lengths clear and went on to the largest winning

margin in 19 runnings of the Breeders' Cup Classic. Volponi ran the Classic's 1¼ miles in 2:01.39 on a drying-out track rated fast. Johnson related that the winner's name came from writer-handicapper Paul Volponi, who translates his family name as "sly old fox" in Italian. Volponi's triumph was a complete family affair for the Johnsons because daughters Kathy and Karen share ownership in Amherst Stable, which co-owns the colt with longtime partner Edward Baier, who operates Spruce Pond Stable. P. G. Johnson became the oldest trainer to win a Breeders' Cup race, supplanting the late Hall of Famer Charlie Whittingham, who was 76 when he sent out Sunday Silence to defeat Easy Goer in the 1989 Classic. P. G. and Mary Kay Johnson began their life together in Chicago, where both were born and where they met on a bench at the old Washington Park racetrack. He began training at the Chicago tracks at age 18 but moved to New York in 1962. There, the likable horseman carved out a career that culminated with his induction into the Racing Hall of Fame in 1997.

Volponi will be known for some time as the horse who broke up the Breeders' Cup Ultra Pick Six fix. If Medaglia d'Oro had won, the winnings from the wager would have been spread among many bettors, including the three admitted fixers. But they had the bad luck of having the only winning tickets for Volponi's longshot victory, and attention soon focused on how they had picked the first four races cold and then wheeled the fields of the Breeders' Cup Turf (G1) and the Classic.

Twelve horses started in the Classic, with much of the attention on the six three-year-olds in America's richest race. Kentucky Derby (G1) and Preakness Stakes (G1) winner War Emblem, Travers Stakes (G1) winner Medaglia d'Oro, Santa Anita Derby (G1) and Pacific Classic Stakes (G1) winner Came Home, and Coolmore's European-based multiple Group 1 winner Hawk Wing led the three-year-olds and the wagering. Only Jockey Club Gold Cup Stakes (G1) winner Evening Attire gained respect among the older runners as the 4.80-to-1 third choice.

When the gates opened, Jorge Chavez gunned Godolphin Racing's four-year-old E Dubai to the lead. Trainer Bob Baffert had promised that War Emblem would be sent to the front by Victor Espinoza, but the nearly black colt could only get to within about one length of E Dubai through testing fractions of :23.07, :46.63, and 1:10.20. Perfect Drift and Medaglia d'Oro stalked in third and fourth through much of the early going, with Santos content to wait in fifth aboard Volponi.

As Espinoza fruitlessly sought acceleration from War Emblem, who briefly assumed the lead

Co-Owner-Breeder

Amherst Stable is the family breeding operation of Racing Hall of Fame trainer P. G. Johnson and his wife, Mary Kay Johnson, of Rockville Centre, New York, and their daughters, Kathy Johnson and Karen Johnson. Amherst bred Volponi, and the Johnsons are co-owners of the colt with **Spruce Pond Stable**, the nom de course of certified public accountant and longtime partner Edward Baier of Floral Park, New York. Baier has owned 15 horses, all in partnership with the Johnsons, who regularly offer him shares in the horses they breed.

Trainer

Philip G. Johnson, popularly known as P. G. in the stable areas of New York's racetracks, returned to his native Chicago for the 2002 Breeders' Cup and came away with a winner in North America's richest race. He bought his first horse in 1942, paying $75 for Song Master. He began training at the Detroit Fair Grounds in 1943, moved to Arlington Park in 1948, and shifted his base to New York in 1962. His first notable runner was Naskra, a two-time stakes winner in 1970 who was among the leading sires in the early 1980s. Johnson upset Forego with Quiet Little Table in the 1977 Suburban Handicap (G1), and among his other stakes winners are Match the Hatch, Maplejinsky, Nasty and Bold, and Kiri's Crown. He was inducted into the Racing Hall of Fame in 1997.

after seven furlongs, Santos saw his opportunity opening up like a dream before him. E Dubai was dropping out of contention and Medaglia d'Oro was trying to find his best stride on his outside when Santos dispatched Volponi like a shot through the emerging gap toward the rail.

"As soon as [War Emblem] was drifting out, there was a huge hole, and I said to my horse, 'Here we go.' And he just kept going and going," Santos said.

Medaglia d'Oro held on to second place by a neck over Stronach Stable's Santa Anita Handicap (G1) winner Milwaukee Brew, who finished three lengths in front of Evening Attire.

Volponi won the 2001 Pegasus Handicap (G2)

on the main track at the Meadowlands and won the 2002 Poker Handicap (G3) on turf at Belmont Park. He also placed in four 2002 graded stakes, including the 1½-mile Sword Dancer Invitational Handicap (G1) on turf. But Johnson said he felt the colt was at his best at 1¼ miles and thus decided to take a shot at the Classic. In what both Santos and Johnson said was a key change in strategy, the trainer added blinkers to sharpen Volponi's concentration.

"I dreamed something like this might happen," Mary Kay Johnson said after the race, recalling she had objected to selling Volponi when an attractive offer tempted Kathy Johnson. "I guess I was right."—*Michele MacDonald*

TENTH RACE
Arlington Park
October 22, 2002

1¼ miles. 19th running of the Breeders' Cup Classic (G1). Purse $4,000,000. 3-year-olds and up. Weights (Northern Hemisphere): 3-year-olds, 122 lbs. Older, 126 lbs. (Southern Hemisphere): 3-year-olds, 117 lbs. Older, 126 lbs. Fillies and mares allowed 3 lbs.

Value of race: $3,664,000. Value to winner: $2,080,000; second: $800,000; third: $480,000; fourth: $224,000; fifth, $80,000. Mutuel Pool: $7,684,971.

Horse	Wt	M/Eqt	PP	¼	½	¾	1	Str.	Fin.	Jockey	Odds $1
Volponi	126	L	2	5^1	5^{hd}	5^1	$2^{1/2}$	$12^{1/2}$	$16^{1/2}$	J. Santos	43.50
Medaglia d'Oro	121	L	7	$4^{1/2}$	3^{hd}	$4^{1/2}$	1^{hd}	2^2	2^{nk}	J. Bailey	*2.70
Milwaukee Brew	126	L	12	$9^{1/2}$	9^{hd}	$10^{3/2}$	5^1	3^2	3^3	E. Prado	24.20
Evening Attire	126	Lb	8	11^2	11^2	11^2	11^2	$6^{1/2}$	$4^{1/2}$	S. Bridgmohan	4.80
Macho Uno	126	Lb	6	$7^{2/2}$	$7^{1/2}$	7^{hd}	6^1	4^1	5^{nk}	G. Stevens	19.80
Dollar Bill	126	Lb	4	12	12	12	12	$7^{1/2}$	6^7	P. Day	18.50
Hawk Wing	121	L	10	$10^{2/2}$	10^5	9^1	7^2	8^2	$7^{3/4}$	M. Kinane	6.00
War Emblem	121	L	3	2^1	$2^{1/2}$	2^1	$3^{1/2}$	$5^{1/2}$	8^8	V. Espinoza	4.00
Harlan's Holiday	121	L	9	8^1	$8^{2/2}$	$6^{1/2}$	$9^{1/2}$	$11^{1/2}$	$9^{3/4}$	J. Velazquez	14.40
Came Home	121	L	11	6^{hd}	6^1	8^{hd}	$10^{1/2}$	$9^{1/2}$	10^4	M. Smith	6.10
E Dubai	126	L	1	1^1	$1^{1/2}$	1^1	4^{hd}	10^2	11^{nk}	J. Chavez	28.30
Perfect Drift	121	Lb	5	3^{hd}	$4^{1/2}$	3^{hd}	8^1	12	12	R. Albarado	29.50

OFF AT 4:41. Start: Good. Winner: Awaited Room Turn. Weather: Cloudy. Track: Fast.
Time: :23.07, 46.63, 1:10.20, 1:35.59, 2:01.39.

$2 Mutuel Prices:

2—VOLPONI	89.00	26.80	12.40
7—MEDAGLIA D'ORO		4.60	3.80
12—MILWAUKEE BREW			9.60

PICK THREE 6-5-2 PAID $1,442.60   PICK FOUR 11-6-5-2 PAID $32,698.60
PICK SIX 5-10-11-6-5-2 (5 CORRECT) PAID $4,606.20, (6 CORRECT) PAID $428,392.00
DAILY DOUBLE 5-2 PAID $150.60   EXACTA 2-7 PAID $463.60
HEAD2HEAD 3VS10-WINNER-10 PAID $3.20   SUPERFECTA 2-7-12-8 PAID $57,207.80
TRIFECTA 2-7-12 PAID $8,466.20

B. c., by Cryptoclearance—Prom Knight, by Sir Harry Lewis. Trainer Philip G. Johnson. Bred by Amherst Stable (Ky.).

VOLPONI saved ground going into the first turn, moved between horses entering the backstretch, settled in good position for a mile, closed the gap leaving the far turn, waited briefly for room nearing the stretch, split rivals to get clear approaching the quarter pole, unleashed a powerful move to take charge in upper stretch, opened a commanding lead under right hand urging in midstretch then drew off under a vigorous hand ride. MEDAGLIO D'ORO moved up from outside going into the first turn, stalked the pace while four wide along the backstretch, closed the gap from outside leaving the three-eighths pole, made a run to challenge on the turn, was unable to match strides with the winner in upper stretch but continued on willingly to hold for the place. MILWAUKEE BREW dropped back soon after the start, saved ground while racing well back along the backstretch, swung out on the turn, launched a rally four wide between horses entering the stretch then closed late to narrowly miss for the place. EVENING ATTIRE broke a bit slowly, raced well back for a mile, circled four wide on the turn, angled wider in upper stretch then rallied belatedly in the middle of the track, MACHO UNO angled to the inside approaching the first turn, was reserved while between horses along the backstretch, angled five wide while gaining a bit on the turn then lacked a strong closing response. DOLLAR BILL trailed a good portion of the trip while saving ground then improved his position with a late run along the inside. HAWK WING raced well back after breaking slowly, lodged a mild rally while six wide on the turn then flattened out. WAR EMBLEM faltered in the stretch. HARLAN'S HOLIDAY failed to mount a serious rally. CAME HOME raced within striking distance while four wide for seven furlongs then steadily tired thereafter. E DUBAI sprinted clear in the early stages, set a brisk pace along the inside for a mile then gave way. PERFECT DRIFT raced up close along the inside for seven furlongs and tired.

Copyright 2002 Equibase Company LLC

Turf: A High Peak

Aidan O'Brien, the youthful trainer for the powerhouse Coolmore Stud/Michael Tabor partnership, arrived at Arlington Park from Ballydoyle stables in County Tipperary loaded with contenders, and it was not out of the question that he could walk away with three champions and a contender for Horse of the Year. But heavily favored Rock of Gibraltar (Ire) was beaten in the Breeders' Cup Mile (G1) and stablemate Landseer (GB) was euthanized after breaking his leg and forcing Rock of Gibraltar to alter course. When Hold

Owner

Michael Tabor became a significant investor in bloodstock after selling his Arthur Prince betting shops for more than $15-million in 1995. He had his first major success in the United States when Thunder Gulch won the 1995 Kentucky Derby (G1) and Belmont Stakes (G1). A client of Coolmore Stud, he has had considerable success with **Susan Magnier**, wife of Coolmore managing partner John Magnier and the daughter of legendary Irish horseman Vincent O'Brien. European classic winners who have run in Tabor's and Susan Magnier's names, either jointly or solely, include Entrepreneur, King of Kings (Ire), and Montjeu (Ire).

Breeder

Sean and Anne Coughlan reside in County Kildare, Ireland, a short distance from the Curragh. Sean Coughlan retired from his building and civil-engineering business in 1977 and sent out his first winner, a jumper named Fortune Cookie, in 1979. The Coughlans' biggest success came when homebred Ridgewood Pearl (GB) won the 1995 Breeders' Cup Mile (G1). After selling High Chaparral's dam to Coolmore in 2002, they have three broodmares, including Ridgewood Pearl.

Trainer

Although still in his mid-30s, **Aidan O'Brien** has trained successfully both over jumps and on the flat. The son of a small-scale trainer, O'Brien was an assistant to top Irish trainer Jim Bolger for three years before becoming the assistant to his future wife, Ann-Marie Crowley, who had assumed her father's training license in 1991 and was Ireland's leading jumps trainer in 1992-'93. After their marriage, she handed over the license to her 23-year-old husband, who won his first race at Tralee in June 1993. He was Ireland's leading steeplechase trainer for five years. Coolmore's John Magnier persuaded him to concentrate more on his flat stable, and he won his first Group 1 race in 1996. The following year, O'Brien won his first Irish training title, and he has been one of the sport's leaders ever since. In 2001, he won 23 Group 1 or Grade 1 races, a record, and in 2002 he trained champions Rock of Gibraltar (Ire) and High Chaparral (Ire).

That Tiger had a troubled trip in the Breeders' Cup Juvenile (G1), only High Chaparral (Ire) was left to deliver O'Brien to the winner's circle. No problem. The three-year-old classic winner by Sadler's Wells accomplished the job with one of the most impressive performances of the day.

In a race that demonstrated his class and versatility, High Chaparral overcame a dawdling pace and a game performance by Augustin Stables' seven-year-old gelding With Anticipation to win the $2,216,720 Breeders' Cup Turf (G1) by 1¼ lengths under Michael Kinane. It was another three-quarters of a length back to Gary Tanaka's Falcon Flight (Fr) in third.

In a year rich in three-year-old European talent—Rock of Gibraltar and Breeders' Cup Classic (G1) starter Hawk Wing also were three-year-olds—High Chaparral proved to be the best at Europe's classic distance of 1½ miles on grass. Winner of the Epsom Derby (Eng-G1) and Irish Derby (Ire-G1), High Chaparral ran the distance in 2:30.14 on Arlington's spacious turf course, which was yielding. He went off as the 9-to-10 favorite in the field of eight, the fewest starters ever in the race.

Out of the Darshaan mare Kasora, High Chaparral, who shares his name with an NBC Western series that ran from 1967 to '71, collected $1,258,400 for his victory and raised his career earnings to $3,614,107 for owners Michael Tabor and Susan Magnier. Winner of seven of nine career starts, High Chaparral was a 9% supplemental entry to the Breeders' Cup Turf, a $180,000 bet that he ranked with the world's best turf runners. The bet paid off handsomely.

After winning the Epsom Derby on June 8 and the Irish Derby 22 days later, High Chaparral, like much of the rest of O'Brien's stable, was stricken with a virus. High Chaparral returned to the races on October 6 with a game third in the Prix de l'Arc de Triomphe (Fr-G1). The about 1½-mile Arc, run over Longchamp ground rated as good, was High Chaparral's only loss of the year, but it provided a valuable comeback race prior to the Breeders' Cup Turf 20 days later. Facing seven other horses, one less than Manila in the 1986 Turf at Santa Anita Park, High Chaparral was tucked behind horses early in the race as Ralph and Aury Todd's homebred The Tin Man rushed to the lead from the outside post position. Ridden by Mike Smith, the Clement L. Hirsch Memorial Stakes (G1) winner set pedestrian fractions of :25.69, :51.36, 1:17.01, and 1:41.33 for the first mile. While The Tin Man loped along on the lead, jockey Pat Day rated With Anticipation behind High Chaparral, a tactic suggested by trainer Jonathan Sheppard.

Entering the final turn, Kinane told High Chaparral it was time to run. "He is lazy," Kinane said. "You really have to get after him. I figured I'd just stay in the pack because you really have to work to keep his attention. I thought we'd be going quicker." When Kinane spied With Anticipation and Day drawing alongside on the turn, "I knew it was really time to go to work," he said. Shaking his stick, Kinane urged High Chaparral toward The Tin Man, who surrendered the lead before the furlong marker. An eighth of a mile from the finish, High Chaparral and Kinane had a head lead on The Tin Man, while With Anticipation was another length farther back.

"He really let it go," Kinane said. "He's the kind of horse that has loads saved. He's so, so all class. He went to the front very easy. We just didn't have much luck with 'The Rock,' but this made up for it."

Day credited Sheppard's tactics for With Anticipation's solid second-place finish. "He said I should lay behind High Chaparral. He settled nicely for me, and Jonathan called it right," Day said.

Sheppard, a Racing Hall of Fame horseman who has trained several steeplechase champions, was pleased with the performance by Augustin's homebred gelding, who won three Grade 1 races— the United Nations and Sword Dancer Invitational Handicaps and the Man o' War Stakes. "He ran a tremendously courageous race," Sheppard said. "He ran the best race he possibly could. Our horse is a tremendous horse, but he's not an English Derby winner."

High Chaparral's performance proved to be sufficiently impressive that he was voted an Eclipse Award as the year's outstanding turf male despite making only the single North American start. He also collected honors in Europe although the top laurels went to his stablemate Rock of Gibraltar (Ire), who had finished second in the Breeders' Cup Mile after a record seven consecutive Group 1 victories. In the 2002 International Classifications, the Epsom Derby (Eng-G1) winner was rated as the highweight in the 11-13 furlong category on the English and Irish Free Handicaps.—*Dave Joseph*

NINTH RACE												

Arlington Park — October 26, 2002

1½ miles on turf. 19th running of the Breeders' Cup Turf (G1). Purse $2-million. 3-year-olds and up. Weights (Northern Hemisphere): 3-year-olds, 122 lbs. Older, 126 lbs. (Southern Hemisphere): 3-year-olds, 117 lbs. Older, 126 lbs. Fillies and mares allowed 3 lbs. Supplemental nominees (9%): Falcon Flight, Golan, High Chaparral.

Value of race $2,216,720; Winner $1,258,400; second $484,000; third $290,400; fourth $135,520; fifth $48,400. Mutuel Pool $4,257,829.

Horse	Wt	M/Eqt	PP	¼	½	1m	1¼	Str.	Fin.	Jockey	Odds $1
High Chaparral (Ire) (S)	121	L	5	4hd	5½	5½	3hd	1hd	11¼	M. Kinane	*0.90
With Anticipation	126	Lb	7	8	7½	71	4½	32	2¾	P. Day	8.70
Falcon Flight (Fr) (S)	126	L	3	5½	6½	6hd	61½	52½	31	P. Valenzuela	12.30
The Tin Man	126	L	8	12	1½	12	12	21	42¾	M. Smith	14.10
Denon	126	L	1	31½	3hd	3hd	51½	41½	5no	E. Prado	7.60
Golan (Ire) (S)	126	L	4	71½	8	8	73	78	62¾	K. Fallon	3.70
Ballingarry (Ire)	121	L	2	2½	2½	2½	21	6hd	711½	K. Desormeaux	9.40
Perfect Soul (Ire)	126	Lb	6	61½	4½	41	8	8	8	J. Velazquez	33.00

OFF AT 4:01. Start: Good. Weather: Cloudy. Turf: Yielding. Won: Split Horses Turn.
Time: :25.69, :51.36, 1:17.01, 1:41.33, 2:05.99, 2:30.14.

$2 Mutuel Prices:

5—HIGH CHAPARRAL (IRE)	3.80	3.00	2.60
7—WITH ANTICIPATION		5.20	4.20
3—FALCON FLIGHT (FR)			5.20

PICK THREE 11-6-5 PAID $498.40   EXACTA 5-7 PAID $34.80
HEAD2HEAD 3VS.10-WINNER-3 PAID $2.20   SUPERFECTA 5-7-3-8 PAID $1,561.00
TRIFECTA 5-7-3 PAID $233.20

B. c., by Sadler's Wells—Kasora, by Darshaan. Trainer Aidan O'Brien. Bred by S. Coughlan (Ire.).

HIGH CHAPARRAL (IRE) tucked in behind the early leaders, was rated between horses for a mile, waited patiently for room while between horses on the turn, split rivals while just inside WITH ANTICIPATION while launching his bid at the top of the stretch, surged to the front in midstretch then edged clear under brisk right hand urging. WITH ANTICIPATION taken in hand early, was unhurried for seven furlongs while four wide, continued wide while launching his bid on the turn then finished well from outside but could not overtake the winner. FALCON FLIGHT (FR) raced in the middle of the pack while saving ground along the backstretch, waited briefly for room along the inside through the turn, angled out to get clear in upper stretch then rallied belatedly. THE TIN MAN sprinted clear soon after the start, was shaken up while attempting to prop going under the wire the first time, set the pace along the inside to the top of the stretch, maintained a clear lead into upper stretch then weakened from his early efforts. DENON raced in close contention along the inside into upper stretch and lacked a strong closing bid. GOLAN (IRE) broke slowly, checked slightly along the inside entering the stretch the first time, trailed to the turn then lacked a strong closing response. BALLINGARRY (IRE) chased the pacesetter from outside to the top of the stretch and tired. PERFECT SOUL (IRE) moved into contention while four wide along the backstretch, raced within striking distance to the turn then faltered.

Copyright 2002 Equibase Company LLC

Juvenile: Padua's Vindication

After five years of investing lavishly in Thoroughbreds and a pristine Ocala farm, Satish and Anne Sanan were seeking some vindication for the multimillion-dollar expenditures, and their Padua Stables took an important step in that direction in 2002 with an expensive Seattle Slew colt named Vindication.

Beginning in 1997, the Sanans' five-year plan was to win classic races and Breeders' Cup events.

Owner

Padua Stables is the Florida racing and breeding operation owned by retired computer software executive Satish Sanan and his wife, Anne. The Sanans entered the sport in 1997 and quickly became major players in the world's leading yearling markets. Padua initially employed D. Wayne Lukas as its primary trainer and general manager but ended that relationship in 2001. Padua Stables, which stands five stallions at its base near Ocala, has campaigned 1999 Breeders' Cup Juvenile Fillies (G1) winner Cash Run and stakes winners Exchange Rate and Yes It's True, among others.

Breeder

A feature writer for *Sports Illustrated* for 26 years and the author of five books, **Virginia Kraft Payson** is no stranger to the Breeders' Cup. Vindication was one of two runners in this year's event who is a product of Payson's breeding operation. The other, Farda Amiga, second in the Breeders' Cup Distaff (G1), is a granddaughter of 1995 Broodmare of the Year Northern Sunset (Ire). Payson bred and campaigned 1995 Classic (G1) runner-up L'Carriere, along with Irish Derby (Ire-G1) winner St. Jovite and Grade 2 winners Salem Drive and Lac Ouimet.

Trainer

Bob Baffert grew up on an Arizona ranch and started out grooming and galloping horses owned by his father. After graduating from the University of Arizona's Race Track Industry Program, Baffert began training Quarter Horses full-time and in 1986 had champion Gold Coast Express. One of his clients, Mike Pegram, urged him to switch to Thoroughbreds. Vindication is his third Breeders' Cup winner—he won the Breeders' Cup Sprint (G1) with Thirty Slews in 1992 and the Juvenile Fillies in 1998 with Silverbulletday. He has enjoyed extraordinary success in the spring classics, taking three horses to the brink of the Triple Crown in six years. He swept the Kentucky Derby (G1) and Preakness Stakes (G1) with Silver Charm and Real Quiet in 1997 and 1998. In 2001, Baffert-trained Point Given won the Preakness and Belmont Stakes (G1), and in 2002 War Emblem won the Derby and Preakness. Baffert was voted three consecutive Eclipse Awards as outstanding trainer, 1997-'99.

The game plan changed slightly in recent years, particularly when the Sanans significantly reduced their expenditures at yearling sales, but Padua Stables had a champion and an early Triple Crown favorite when Vindication scored an emphatic victory over Kafwain and Irish invader Hold That Tiger in the $980,120 Breeders' Cup Juvenile (G1) on October 26 at Arlington Park.

Ridden by Mike Smith, Vindication battled on the lead with Bull Market throughout the 1⅛-mile Juvenile before drawing off to a stylish 2¾-length win in 1:49.61. Trainer Bob Baffert nearly swept the first three spots with Vindication, Kafwain, and Bull Market, but Hold That Tiger, who had a troubled trip, got up late for third.

"I've said it often enough that we got into this game about five years ago and we love this game," Satish Sanan said after Padua's second Breeders' Cup victory. (Cash Run won the 1999 Juvenile Fillies [G1] for trainer D. Wayne Lukas, who brought the Sanans into the top end of the sport.) "We have had some bad times, and in this game you've got to stick with it," Sanan said. "There were a lot of people second-guessing us, a lot of Monday-morning quarterbacks in this game. We stayed with it. We continued to invest, and we're going to continue to invest. Every now and then you need a big one, and this is the one and we do feel vindicated."

For a period after Vindication's impressive victory in the Kentucky Cup Juvenile Stakes (G3) on September 14 at Turfway Park, Sanan nearly was among the second-guessers. Vindication, purchased for $2.15-million at the 2001 Fasig-Tipton Saratoga selected yearling sale, started his career with two impressive six-furlong victories at Del Mar. Baffert opted to take the colt to Turfway, a place he described as off the beaten path but a good place to give an education. He had used the Kentucky Cup as a springboard for Point Given's bid for the Breeders' Cup Juvenile, in which he came up just a nose short in 2000 at Churchill Downs.

"There's actually nothing wrong with Turfway Park," Baffert said. "I've run most of my good horses there, and I consider it a very safe track. Horses learn things at Turfway Park because, if things are going to go wrong, they usually go wrong there."

Vindication overcame plenty of trouble in the Kentucky Cup and, after posting a six-length victory in his first start around two turns, appeared to be primed for such races as the Champagne Stakes (G1) or Norfolk Stakes (G2).

Baffert instead opted to train Vindication up to the Breeders' Cup. That decision puzzled Sanan somewhat, and the retired computer outsourcing and software-services executive got on the phone to ask Baffert why. "He said, 'Michael Jordan, you don't take him to pick-up games, you take him to the big ones.' "

Baffert came into the Juvenile with a strong hand and was almost certain to improve his record of just one on-the-board finish from nine previous starters. In addition to Vindication, Baffert had the Norfolk's winner and runner-up, The Thoroughbred Corp.'s Kafwain and James McIngvale's Bull Market. The Baffert trio faced a strong challenge from Irish conditioner Aidan O'Brien's three starters—Hold That Tiger, Van Nistelrooy, and Tomahawk—and Patrick Biancone's duo of Futurity Stakes (G1) winner Whywhywhy and Zavata. The task got somewhat easier when Hopeful Stakes (G1) winner Sky Mesa, the 3-to-1 program favorite, was withdrawn the day before the race due to swelling in his right front ankle.

Vindication's effort against some of the best members of his generation was outstanding, and also eerily similar to some of those turned in by his late sire, Seattle Slew, during his championship seasons. "He did it all well within himself," Smith said. "The only tough part was down the lane when he was gawking at the starting gate, so I had to stay busy on him. This horse is a freak. I said all along that I expected big things today and in the future, and you know what that means."

Vindication completed his juvenile season undefeated in four starts.

The Breeders' Cup Juvenile has never produced a Kentucky Derby (G1) winner, and the jinx continued through 2003. Vindication was knocked off the Triple Crown trail when he strained his left suspensory ligament during a routine gallop on February 4.—*Tom Law*

EIGHTH RACE
Arlington Park
October 22, 2002

1⅛ miles. 19th running of the Breeders' Cup Juvenile (G1). Purse $1-million. Colts and geldings, 2-year-olds. Weight: 122 lbs. Supplemental nominee (9%): Whywhywhy

Value of race: $980,120. Value to winner: $556,400; second: $214,000; third: $128,400; fourth: $59,920; fifth, $21,400. Mutuel Pool $4,534,496.

Horse	Wt.	M/Eqt	PP	St.	¼	½	¾	Str.	Fin.	Jockey	Odds $1
Vindication	122	L	6	1	1^{hd}	$1^{\frac{1}{2}}$	$2^{2\frac{1}{2}}$	$1^{2\frac{1}{2}}$	$1^{2\frac{3}{4}}$	M. Smith	4.10
Kafwain	122	Lb	2	10	7^{hd}	7^{2}	6^{1}	$3^{2\frac{1}{2}}$	$2^{2\frac{1}{4}}$	V. Espinoza	19.80
Hold That Tiger	122	L	3	13	13	13	7^{hd}	$4^{1\frac{1}{2}}$	$3^{1\frac{1}{4}}$	K. Fallon	5.50
Bull Market	122	L	5	2	$2^{1\frac{1}{2}}$	2^{hd}	1^{hd}	2^{2}	4^{3}	J. Bailey	12.30
Van Nistelrooy	122	L	7	11	11^{hd}	10^{hd}	10^{hd}	7^{1}	5^{nk}	J. Velazquez	15.80
Most Feared	122	L b	11	5	$5^{1\frac{1}{2}}$	$5^{\frac{1}{2}}$	$3^{\frac{1}{2}}$	5^{2}	$6^{\frac{3}{4}}$	P. Valenzuela	28.30
Listen Indy	122	L	4	3	$8^{\frac{1}{2}}$	$8^{\frac{1}{2}}$	11^{2}	9^{1}	$7^{1\frac{3}{4}}$	A. Solis	13.20
Tomahawk	122	L	10	12	12^{4}	12^{2}	9^{2}	$6^{\frac{1}{2}}$	8^{4}	M. Kinane	17.20
Toccet	122	Lbf	13	6	6^{1}	6^{2}	8^{hd}	$10^{2\frac{1}{2}}$	$9^{\frac{1}{2}}$	J. Chavez	8.20
Whywhywhy (S)	122	Lb	1	9	4^{hd}	$4^{1\frac{1}{2}}$	$5^{1\frac{1}{2}}$	$8^{\frac{1}{2}}$	10^{4}	P. Day	*2.50
Lone Star Sky	122	L	8	7	9^{hd}	9^{hd}	12^{6}	12	$11^{1\frac{1}{2}}$	M. Guidry	30.70
Wando	122	L	12	4	3^{hd}	$3^{\frac{1}{2}}$	$4^{\frac{1}{2}}$	11^{2}	12	R. Migliore	36.40
Zavata	122	L	9	8	$10^{1\frac{1}{2}}$	$11^{\frac{1}{2}}$	13	13	13	G. Stevens	14.00
Sky Mesa Scratched											

OFF AT 3:25. Start: 3, 11. Weather: Cloudy. Track: Fast. Won: Steady Urging, Drifted.
Time: :23.29, :46.11, 1:09.98, 1:35.80, 1:49.61.

$2 Mutuel Prices:

6—VINDICATION	**10.20**	**6.20**	**4.00**
2—KAFWAIN		**16.00**	**8.40**
3—HOLD THAT TIGER			**4.60**

PICK THREE 10-11-6 PAID $1,137.40 **EXACTA 6-2 PAID $164.60**
SUPERFECTA 6-2-3-5 PAID $5,772.80 **TRIFECTA 6-2-3 PAID $1,131.20**

Dkb. c., by Seattle Slew—Strawberry Reason, by Strawberry Road (Aus). Trainer Bob Baffert. Bred by Payson Stud Inc. (Ky.).

VINDICATION rushed up from outside to contest the early pace, dueled heads apart along the backstretch, shook off BULL MARKET to get clear leaving the quarter pole, opened a clear advantage in upper stretch then held sway under steady right hand urging while drifting out of a bit through the final sixteenth. KAFWAIN was in a bit tight on the first turn, settled in the middle of the pack for six furlongs, closed the gap between horses on the turn then finished well from outside to clearly best the others. HOLD THAT TIGER was outrun for six furlongs after breaking in the air at the start, circled seven wide on the turn then rallied belatedly in the middle of the track. BULL MARKET rushed up along the rail to contest the early pace, alternated for the lead inside the winner to the turn then weakened from his early efforts. VAN NISTELROOY dropped back in the early stages, raced well back to the turn then failed to threaten while improving his position. MOST FEARED raced up close between horses to the top of the stretch and steadily tired thereafter. LISTEN INDY was caught in a bit tight between horses on the first turn, failed to mount a serious rally. TOMAHAWK broke in the air at the start and was never close thereafter. TOCCET faded after going five furlongs. WHYWHYWHY raced in close contention between horses to the turn and gave way. LONE STAR SKY was never a factor while racing between horses. WANDO stalked four wide to the far turn then faltered. ZAVATA was finished early and pulled up on the far turn.

Copyright 2002 Equibase Company LLC

2002 Filly and Mare Turf: All Frankel

The delight on Bobby Frankel's face was unmistakable as he walked to the Arlington Park winner's circle to greet Starine (Fr), the five-year-old mare he owned and trained, after she won the $1,172,480 Breeders' Cup Filly and Mare Turf (G1). With jockey John Velazquez aboard, Starine had just finished 1½ lengths in front of her more celebrated stablemate, defending champion Banks Hill (GB), and defeated several more of the world's most accomplished distaff turf runners.

The victory marked the second Breeders' Cup win for Frankel, who ended his well-documented Breeders' Cup drought in 2001 when he sent out Squirtle Squirt to win the Sprint (G1). One race later, Banks Hill, a homebred for Frankel's principal client, Khalid Abdullah's Juddmonte Farms, made her North American debut not for Frankel, but for trainer Andre Fabre. She blasted to a 5½-length victory to secure the Eclipse Award as champion turf female. Starine also was in that

Owner-Trainer

Robert Frankel began his racetrack career as a hotwalker and groom in the mid-1960s, but the Brooklyn native was on his own by 1966 and trained his first winner that November at Aqueduct. He became known as "king of the claimers" at the New York tracks and moved his operation to California in 1972. He won a record 60 races at Hollywood Park that year but upgraded his stable beginning in the 1980s with owners such as Edmund Gann, Jerome Moss, and Stavros Niarchos. In 1990, he accepted some horses from Khalid Abdullah's Juddmonte Farms, which in time became his principal client. Elected to the Racing Hall of Fame in 1993, he was voted Eclipse Awards as outstanding trainer in 1993, 2000, '01, and '02. He won his first Breeders' Cup race in 2001 with Squirtle Squirt. He had the best year of his career in 2002, racking up purses of $17.7-million, less than $100,000 short of D. Wayne Lukas's 1988 record. Frankel also had the most stakes winners, 31, and most graded stakes winners, 21. He has trained champions Bertrando, Possibly Perfect, Ryafan, Squirtle Squirt, and Wandesta (GB).

Breeder

Starine (Fr) began her career in 1999 in her native France racing for breeder **Catherine Dubois**. She won two races for Dubois before being claimed for about $35,000 in September of that year. Dubois, who resides in France in Maisons-Laffitte and Paris, owns only two mares, one of whom is Starine's dam, Grisonnante (Fr), a daughter of Kaldoun who was winless in six starts. Dubois's husband, Jacques, trains a stable of mostly jumpers, the most successful of which has been Bal Star, whom he bred and his wife raced.

race, finishing tenth.

In the spring of 2001, Frankel acquired Starine, who had won six of 22 races and earned $114,302 in France. That May, the daughter of Mendocino made her North American debut with a second-place finish in the Gallorette Handicap (G3) at Pimlico Race Course. In November, after competing against the sport's top turf females, she won Hollywood Park's Matriarch Stakes (G1). Starine began her 2002 campaign with a second behind Filly and Mare Turf favorite Golden Apples (Ire) in the Santa Ana Handicap (G2) at Santa Anita Park. In her next start, in May, she was second behind Astra in Hollywood's Gamely Breeders' Cup Handicap (G1).

In July, Starine's career appeared to be over. Frankel was reported to have retired the mare because she had not fared well physically after her first two races of the season. One month later, however, she was back in training. Frankel sent her to New York, where she finished fourth behind North American newcomers Kazzia (Ger) and Turtle Bow (Fr) in the Flower Bowl Invitational Stakes (G1) on September 28. Carried three wide around both turns in the 1¼-mile race over a soft turf course, Starine impressed Frankel enough to return her to the Filly and Mare Turf. "Starine is an absolute freak in the soft going," he said.

With rain falling in the Chicago area during the days leading up to the Breeders' Cup on October 26, Frankel was confident Starine would love a soft Arlington turf course, but he was more reserved about Banks Hill's chances because the champion preferred a firmer surface.

Banks Hill had returned to the United States after a four-race European campaign. She was entered in the Flower Bowl but was scratched when the course came up soft. She was flown to California for Santa Anita's Yellow Ribbon Stakes (G1) on October 5 and finished third behind Golden Apples, who previously had won Arlington's Beverly D. Stakes (G1).

"I didn't really expect her to do much in [the Yellow Ribbon] with all of the shipping she did," Frankel said. "Her training was interrupted and she got put in a bad spot where she couldn't run when she wanted to. Obviously, [the other jockeys] were all looking for her; they all wanted to trap her."

When the gates opened in the 1¼-mile Filly and Mare Turf on a course labeled yielding, dual English classic winner Kazzia in the 12 post veered out, then took the lead from her 11 rivals and set comfortable fractions of :24.42, :49.15, and 1:13.45 for six furlongs. Jerry Bailey on Banks Hill raced to the inside from the five post, while Velazquez waited patiently on Starine in fourth place. Near the eighth pole, Velazquez moved past a fading Kazzia and Turtle Bow and drew away to victory while Banks Hill finished a neck in front of Islington (Ire), who had recovered well after encountering traffic around the far turn and top of the stretch.

Starine's time was 2:03.57. "I couldn't have asked for a more perfect trip," said Velazquez. "She broke good and got right into the perfect spot. They came to her coming off the backside. I was able to just sit on her until we turned for home, and she just did her own thing when I let her go."

Bailey could tell Banks Hill would have preferred a firmer surface. "The ground just wasn't in her favor," Frankel said, "but she tried real hard."

Ten days after the Breeders' Cup, Starine was sold at the Keeneland November breeding stock sale in Lexington. German billionaire Klaus Jacobs purchased the mare for $1-million to join the broodmare band at his Newsells Park Stud in England.

Following the first three runnings of the Filly and Mare Turf, the Eclipse Award went to the race winner, but that precedent was broken in 2002 when voters chose Golden Apples (Ire) over Starine. Golden Apples was forced to steady repeatedly in the early going of her Breeders' Cup race, made a six-wide move on Arlington's final turn to reach a contending position, and rallied belatedly to finish fourth, beaten two lengths by Starine.—*Amy Owens*

SEVENTH RACE

Belmont Park
October 26, 2002

1¼ miles on turf. 4th running of the Breeders' Cup Filly and Mare Turf (G1). Purse $1-million. Fillies and mares 3-year-olds and up. Weights (Northern Hemisphere): 3-year-olds, 119 lbs. Older, 123 lbs. (Southern Hemisphere): 3-year-olds, 114 lbs. Older, 123 lbs. Supplemental nominees (9%): Golden Apples, Islington, Kazzia, and Turtle Bow. Supplemental nominee (9%) with credit: Starine.

Value of race: $1,172,480. Value to winner: $665,600; second: $256,000; third: $153,600; fourth: $71,680; fifth, $25,600. Mutuel Pool $4,218,999.

Horse	Wt	M/Eqt	PP	¼	½	¾	1	Str.	Fin.	Jockey	Odds $1
Starine (Fr) (S)	123	Lb	11	4¹	4¹½	4¹	3ʰᵈ	1½	1¹½	J. Velazquez	13.20
Banks Hill (GB)	123	L	5	5¹½	5¹½	5½	5ʰᵈ	4ʰᵈ	2ⁿᵏ	J. Bailey	3.80
Islington (Ire) (S)	118		2	8ʰᵈ	9ʰᵈ	7ʰᵈ	8ʰᵈ	6ʰᵈ	3ⁿᵏ	K. Fallon	4.00
Golden Apples (Ire) (S)	123	L	6	11¹¹½	11¹¹	11ʰᵈ	11¹¹½	7¹½	4ⁿᵏ	P. Valenzuela	*2.80
Gossamer (GB)	118	L	7	6½	6ʰᵈ	6¹½	6ʰᵈ	5½	5½	J. Spencer	11.40
Kazzia (Ger) (S)	118	L	12	1²	1²	1²	1²	2½	6ⁿᵒ	J. Chavez	10.20
Riskaverse	118	L	1	10½	10¹	9ʰᵈ	7ʰᵈ	8½	7½	M. Guidry	27.30
Zenda (GB)	118	L	8	1²	1²	1²	10¹	9¹	8½	R. Hughes	28.40
Turtle Bow (Fr) (S)	118		3	3²	3³	3ʰᵈ	4ʰᵈ	3½	9⁴	C. Soumillon	14.30
Dublino	118	L	4	7¹½	7¹½	8½	9½	11³	10ʰᵈ	K. Desormeaux	9.10
Chopinina	123	Lb	9	2³	2²	2³½	2½	10½	11¾	E. Ramsammy	41.70
Owsley	123	L	10	9ʰᵈ	8ʰᵈ	10¹	12	12	12	E. Prado	21.10

OFF AT 2:49. Start: Good for all but Zenda. Weather: Cloudy. Turf: Yielding. Winner: Well Placed, Clear.
Time: :24.42, :49.15, 1:13.45, 1:38.54, 2:03.57.

$2 Mutuel Prices:			
11—STARINE (FR)	28.40	10.00	8.40
5—BANKS HILL (GB)		5.60	4.40
2—ISLINGTON (IRE)			4.80

PICK THREE 5-10-11 PAID $4,651.20   EXACTA 11-5 PAID $156.60
HEAD2HEAD 2VS6-WINNER-2 $4.00   SUPERFECTA 11-5-2-6 PAID $2,638.40
TRIFECTA 11-5-2 PAID $1,060.40

Gr. or ro. m., by Mendocino—Grisonnante, by Kaldoun. Trainer Bobby Frankel. Bred by Catherine Dubois (Fr.).

STARINE (FR) broke inward bumping with OWSLEY at the start, settled in good position along the backstretch, rapidly closed the gap while three wide on the turn, charged to the front in upper stretch, extended her lead inside the furlong marker, then held off BANKS HILL (GB) under steady right hand encouragement. BANKS HILL was rated just off the early pace, raced just behind the winner to the turn, launched a rally four wide entering the stretch, then finished well from outside to hold the place. ISLINGTON (IRE) broke slowly, steadied repeatedly in the early stages, moved between horses on the first turn, raced well back for six furlongs, swung four wide for clear sailing on the turn, then finished strongly to narrowly miss the place. GOLDEN APPLES (IRE) steadied sharply in the early stages, was outrun for seven furlongs, circled six wide while launching her move on the turn, then rallied belatedly in the middle of the track. GOSSAMER (GB) saved ground while working her way forward on the turn, angled between horses at the top of the stretch, made a run to reach contention in midstretch, then improved her position with a mild late rally. KAZZIA (GER) sprinted clear in the early stages, set the pace along the rail into upper stretch, then faltered. RISKAVERSE was outrun for a mile while saving ground, rallied along the inside in upper stretch, checked in traffic inside the furlong marker and failed to threaten thereafter. ZENDA (GB) broke in the air at the start, steadied sharply in the early stages, closed the gap between horses on the turn, steadied in traffic in midstretch, then failed to menace thereafter. TURTLE BOW (FR) saved ground while just off the pace into upper stretch, then checked along the rail while tiring in the final eighth. DUBLINO steadied in traffic in the early stages, then failed to threaten while racing wide. CHOPININA chased the early leader from outside, lodged a mild bid on the turn, then faltered. OWSLEY was never a factor after being bumped in the start.

Copyright 2002 Equibase Company LLC

Sprint: First Win for Lewises

Standing with his wife, Beverly, in Arlington Park's paddock before the $1-million Breeders' Cup Sprint (G1) on October 26, Bob Lewis was asked about the evolution of their four-year-old colt Orientate from 2001 Breeders' Cup Classic (G1) also-ran to the favorite in the 2002 Sprint under the masterful handling of Racing Hall of Fame trainer D. Wayne Lukas. "I really have to say that Wayne Lukas just constantly comes up with these surprises," Lewis said.

Fifteen minutes later, the only surprise was which horse Orientate had to run down to win the 13-horse Sprint by a half-length: 48.70-to-1 longshot Thunderello.

Owner

Bob and Beverly Lewis have made a substantial impact on the sport since buying their first horse in 1990. They were co-owners of 1994 Breeders' Cup Juvenile (G1) winner Timber Country and also raced '95 champion three-year-old filly Serena's Song, who became the richest North American female of all time. They raced dual Kentucky Derby (G1) and Preakness Stakes (G1) victors Silver Charm (1997) and Charismatic ('99). The Lewises were awarded an Eclipse Award of Merit in 1997.

Breeder

Gainesway Thoroughbreds Ltd. was begun in 1989 by South African industrialist Graham Beck and succeeded his buying Stud Ltd. That year, Beck purchased Gainesway Farm in Lexington from John R. Gaines. His son, Antony, manages the farm. Beck, who also owns Highland Stud in South Africa, acquired most of his wealth from coal mining, and added Graham Beck Wines to his holdings in 1983. Gainesway was a co-owner of 1994 Breeders' Cup Juvenile (G1) winner Timber Country with Bob and Beverly Lewis and Overbrook Farm.

Trainer

In many ways, **D. Wayne Lukas** revolutionized the business of Thoroughbred horse racing. When he burst on the scene in the late 1970s, most trainers had no more than 40 horses, usually based at one or two tracks. The former basketball coach and Quarter Horse trainer broke all the norms and many unwritten rules, establishing a national racing stable with hundreds of horses based at major racetracks across the country. He also broke many of the sport's records, including highest earnings in a year ($17.8-million in 1988), most Breeders' Cup wins (17 through 2002), most champions (24), and highest career earnings (more than $210-million and counting). Lukas has won 13 classic races, four Eclipse Awards as outstanding trainer—1985, '86, '87, and '94—and was elected to the Racing Hall of Fame in 1999.

"I knew I had my work cut out, but I never thought I wouldn't get him," jockey Jerry Bailey said.

When Orientate won, he gave Bailey his leading 13th Breeders' Cup career victory and Lukas his 17th, nine ahead of Claude R. "Shug" McGaughey III in second. Lukas saddled just two horses in the 19th Breeders' Cup: Orientate and Day Trader in the Sprint. "We only had one chance, and we wanted to make the most of it," Lukas said.

Orientate indeed made the most of his opportunity, posting his fifth consecutive victory and sixth straight dirt win, all in stakes, off a 55-day layoff. Not bad for a horse who was beaten 29¾ lengths one year earlier by Tiznow in the Breeders' Cup Classic.

Orientate is not the first horse to run in the Classic and then win the Sprint. Precisionist followed a seventh in the 1984 Classic by taking the '85 Sprint. In 1987, Peter Brant's Gulch finished ninth in the Classic under the care of trainer LeRoy Jolley and was then turned over to Lukas. At the end of 1988, Gulch won the Sprint under Angel Cordero Jr.

"I got [Gulch] right after his three-year-old year, and I had him the entire year going right up to the Sprint," Lukas said. "I ran him a mile and [an eighth in the Philip H. Iselin Handicap (G1)] before the Sprint, and I remember Peter saying, 'You're crazy. You've taken all the speed away,' and we got into quite a discussion. But in training, if a horse has natural speed, the easiest thing in the world to do is shorten him up and get him to run six furlongs."

Lukas already had a top sprinter in his barn, Snow Ridge, but he was sidelined with a sesamoid injury after romping by 7¾ lengths in the Maryland Breeders' Cup Handicap (G3) at Pimlico. So Lukas turned to Orientate. The son of Mt. Livermore out of Dream Team, by Cox's Ridge, was purchased for $250,000 at the 1999 Keeneland September yearling sale. He followed the 2001 Classic by winning the Sir Beaufort Stakes on turf. He then returned to dirt, running second in the San Fernando Breeders' Cup Stakes (G2) and sixth in the Strub Stakes (G2) before winning the seven-furlong Commonwealth Breeders' Cup Stakes (G2) at Keeneland Race Course on April 14 by 1¼ lengths on a sloppy track.

Orientate's next two starts were on grass: ninth in the Aegon Turf Sprint Stakes (G3) and fourth in the Shoemaker Breeders' Cup Mile Stakes (G1). "I mismanaged him for a little while," Lukas said. "Then, when Snow Ridge was injured, we said, 'Let's let him do what he does best.'"

Orientate went undefeated for the rest of the year, ripping off victories in the Aristides Handicap (G3) by 4½ lengths, the Smile Sprint Handicap by six lengths, and the A.G. Vanderbilt Handicap (G2) by two lengths with Bailey back in the irons. He then stamped himself as the nation's best sprinter when he defeated Squirtle Squirt in the Forego Handicap (G1) at Saratoga Race Course on September 1.

In the Breeders' Cup Sprint, 2.70-to-1 favorite Orientate faced an accomplished group of opponents ranging in age from three to eight, including Xtra Heat, 2001's champion three-year-old filly, who had finished second to Squirtle Squirt in that year's Breeders' Cup Sprint. Kona Gold, an eight-year-old gelding, was making a record fifth start in the Breeders' Cup. He finished third in the 1998 Sprint, second in '99, first in 2000, and seventh in '01.

Thunderello put away the three-year-old filly Carson Hollow after completing the first quarter-mile in :21.53 and the half in :43.91. Xtra Heat could not keep up, but Bailey maneuvered Orientate into perfect striking position, one length off the longshot leader at the top of the stretch. It took the length of the stretch for Orientate to wear down Thunderello. Crafty C.T. finished a half-length behind Thunderello in third. Orientate's winning time was 1:08.89.

Within weeks of his Arlington victory, Orientate was sold to Graham Beck's Gainesway Farm and John Messara of Arrowfield Stud in Australia. The Mt. Livermore horse stood his first season for a $25,000 fee at Gainesway in Lexington and was scheduled to shuttle to Arrowfield for the Southern Hemisphere season.—*Bill Heller*

	SIXTH RACE		6 furlongs. 19th running of the Breeders' Cup Sprint (G1). Purse $1-million. 3-year-olds and up. Weights

Arlington Park
October 26, 2002

(Northern Hemisphere): 3-year-olds, 124 lbs. Older, 126 lbs. (Southern Hemisphere): 3-year-olds, 122 lbs. Older, 126 lbs. Fillies and mares allowed 3 lbs. Supplemental nominees (9%): Bonapaw and Disturbingthepeace.

Value of race $1,044,240; Winner $592,800; second $228,000; third $136,800; fourth $63,840; fifth $22,800. Mutuel Pool $4,197,468.

Horse	Wt.	M/Eqt	PP	St.	¼	½	Str.	Fin.	Jockey	Odds $1
Orientate	126	L	10	2	4½	2¹	2²	1½	J. Bailey	*2.70
Thunderello	123	Lf	1	5	1hd	1¹	1¹	2½	E. Prado	48.70
Crafty C. T.	126	L	11	10	7hd	4½	3½	32¼	P. Valenzuela	16.50
Kona Gold	126	L	9	7	11hd	9½	6½	6½	A. Solis	7.30
Kalookan Queen	123	L	2	6	82½	5hd	4hd	51¼	M. Smith	12.30
Xtra Heat	123	L	6	4	3½	3½	5½	6½	H. Vega	6.40
Disturbingthepeace (S)	126	Lb	3	9	9½	8hd	7hd	7¹	V. Espinoza	12.60
Swept Overboard	126	L	12	13	13	11²	8½	8¾	C. Nakatani	5.40
Touch Tone	126	L	5	8	6 hd	7½	9²	9³	J. Chavez	35.30
Bonapaw (S)	126	Lf	8	11	10²	10¹	11²	10no	G. Melancon	4.60
Day Trader	123	Lb	13	1	5hd	6½	10 hd	11½	P. Day	30.90
Wake At Noon	126	Lbf	7	12	12¹	13	1220	1245	E. Ramsammy	78.20
Carson Hollow	120	L	4	3	2¹	12½	13	13	J. Velazquez	18.40

OFF AT 2:12. Start: Good. Weather: Cloudy. Track: Fast. Won: 4 Wide, Up Late.
Time: :21.53, :43.91, :56.09, 1:08.89.

	10—ORIENTATE	7.40	5.00	3.80
$2 Mutuel Prices:	1—THUNDERELLO		33.00	13.00
	11—CRAFTY C. T.			9.00

PICK THREE 2/4-5-10 PAID $500.80   **EXACTA 10-1 PAID $312.00**
HEAD2HEAD 6VS12-WINNER-6 PAID $3.40   **SUPERFECTA 10-1-11-9 PAID $47,327.40**
TRIFECTA 10-1-11 PAID $4,683.40

Dk. b. c., by Mt. Livermore—Dream Team, by Cox's Ridge. Trainer D. Wayne Lukas. Bred by Gainesway Thoroughbreds Ltd. (Ky.).

ORIENTATE broke inward at the start, stalked four wide along the backstretch, edged closer on the turn, gradually gained inside the furlong marker, then wore down THUNDERELLO in the final twenty yards. THUNDERELLO dueled early along the inside, shook loose on the turn, maintained a clear advantage into midstretch, continued on the front into deep stretch, then yielded grudgingly. CRAFTY C. T. was unhurried along the backstretch, closed the gap while four wide on the turn then finished willingly to gain a share. KONA GOLD was outrun early after being bumped at the start, rallied six wide leaving the turn, closed the gap to reach contention in midstretch, then flattened out a bit in the final sixteenth. KALOOKAN QUEEN reserved early rallied along the inside to reach contention in upper stretch but could not sustain his bid. XTRA HEAT chased the leaders along the inside to the top of the stretch and steadily tired thereafter. DISTURBINGTHEPEACE saved ground to the turn after breaking a bit slowly, then lacked a strong, closing bid. SWEPT OVERBOARD failed to threaten while wide throughout. TOUCH TONE raced five wide while in the middle of the pack for a half, then lacked a further response. BONAPAW was bumped, then pinched back at the start and failed to threaten thereafter. DAY TRADER checked slightly at the start, raced within striking distance while four wide for a half, then faded in the stretch. WAKE AT NOON was never a factor after being bumped at the start. CARSON HOLLOW dueled for the lead from outside for three furlongs, then checked while giving way on the turn.

Copyright 2002 Equibase Company LLC

Mile: Domedriver's Inside Job

In the days preceding the 19th Breeders' Cup championship, Rock of Gibraltar (Ire) galloped around Arlington Park enveloped in an aura of invincibility. Winning a record seven consecutive Group 1 races will do that for you. The corona of accomplishment and hype surrounding the colt was so overwhelming that it seemed the only way he could lose the $980,120 Breeders' Cup Mile would be for him to give it away, to suffer bad luck during the race, or for someone else to steal it.

In a very real sense, all three happened on October 26. The Niarchos family's lightly regarded (26-to-1) Domedriver (Ire) benefited from a rail-hugging ride by Thierry Thulliez, stealing through an opening inside Good Journey in midstretch and then holding off the Rock's belated bid to win by three-quarters of a length. Good Journey, also bred and partly owned by the Niarchos family, finished third, a nose farther back.

Owner-Breeder

Maria Niarchos-Gouazé, daughter of Stavros Niarchos, manages the bloodstock holdings of her late father's children, including his sons Phillip, Spyros, and Constantine. International shipping magnate Stavros Niarchos founded the family's bloodstock empire in the 1950s, left the industry in the '60s, and returned in the '70s to build the family's current holdings. He died in 1996. The family breeds and races in Europe under the name of **Famille Niarchos** and in the United States under the name of **Flaxman Holdings Ltd.** The family owns Haras de Fresnay-le-Buffard near Falaise, France, and Oak Tree Farm, which is leased by Lane's End, near Lexington. The family bred and owned previous Breeders' Cup Mile (G1) winners Miesque (1987, '88) and Spinning World ('97), as well as many international champions, including Hernando (Fr), East of the Moon, Machiavellian, and Coup de Genie.

Trainer

Pascal Bary made his second trip to the Breeders' Cup winner's circle, following the victory of Miss Alleged in the 1991 Breeders' Cup Turf (G1) at 42.10-to-1 odds at Churchill Downs. Bary worked for Sir Mark Prescott at Newmarket in 1975 and after a year returned to France to be an assistant to the great trainer Francois Boutin, with whom he remained for four years. He took out his trainer's license in 1981 and has been based for more than 20 years at Chantilly. He has won the Prix du Jockey-Club (Fr-G1), the French Derby, four times, in 1994 with Celtic Arms (Fr), in '96 with Ragmar, in '98 with Dream Well (Fr), and in 2002 with Sulamani. He also trained Six Perfections, Europe's leading two-year-old filly in 2002.

"Before the race, I think we have a very good number [post position] with number five," said trainer Pascal Bary. "I just tell Thierry Thulliez to turn the rail, keeping a bit behind. We are not the favorite, so he can take any risk to keep on the rail and save the maximum ground, and he has done the job that I gave him. I think it is very important to save ground on this track."

In fact, Thulliez rode a brilliant race. The winner broke with the pack and encountered only one anxious moment, when he had to check while bending into the crowded first turn as Thulliez maneuvered him toward the rail. Once into the back straight, Domedriver settled into a snug position in the wake of Jerry Bailey, a good man to follow, on 6.50-to-1 Beat Hollow (GB).

When the field spread out at the top of the short Arlington home straight, a gap appeared between the unresponsive Beat Hollow and leader Good Journey. Domedriver accelerated and shot through the hole.

While Thulliez and Domedriver were stealing a march, Rock of Gibraltar gave away valuable ground at the start and then had to change course turning into the stretch when his stable companion, Landseer (GB), broke down.

"Both," Rock of Gibraltar's jockey, Michael Kinane, answered when asked which problem hurt the 4-to-5 favorite the most. "I had lovely momentum going when I had to switch course, and then I had to regroup and go again. It was tough to find the momentum again, because I was flying before I had to change direction. At the start, he was a bit fractious at the gate, and it just left me in that position that I had to be patient." The Rock accelerated sharply down the stretch, but his rally fell three-quarters of a length short.

Domedriver was bred in Ireland and races in the name of Flaxman Holdings Ltd., the corporate breeding entity established by the late Stavros Niarchos. He is the fourth winner of the Mile for the Niarchos family, following the great Miesque, who doubled in 1987 and '88, and Spinning World. Domedriver is the second Mile winner for his sire, Indian Ridge, following Ridgewood Pearl (GB) in 1995.

The Mile was marred by the horrific breakdown of Landseer as the field curved into the homestretch. He was in the midst of a menacing-looking move toward the leaders when he shattered his right front cannon bone.

The stricken horse careened to his left, then to his right, as jockey Edgar Prado tried desperately to pull him up. His swerve to the left caused Rock of Gibraltar to check and alter course; his slalom back outside put late-runners Touch of the Blues (GB) and Nuclear Debate out of the race.

Landseer was stopped by an outrider at the outside rail of the turf course near the sixteenth pole and moved onto the horse ambulance after a canvas screen was erected. He was euthanized on the ambulance.

The 2002 Mile will long be remembered as the race that Rock of Gibraltar lost rather than the race that Domedriver won. The glamour horse of the 2002 Breeders' Cup was unlucky but created some of his own misfortune with his inattention at the start. Whether he could still have won had he not been hampered by Landseer's breakdown is debatable, though he did make an eye-catching run.

As many other European horses have proved in previous years, the Rock was vulnerable because he had won his races with a superb change of pace, finishing his races faster than he began them, which is not how American races generally are won.

Domedriver did not receive serious consideration for an Eclipse Award, though Rock of Gibraltar received several votes for champion grass male. In Europe, Rock of Gibraltar was 2002 Horse of the Year.—*John P. Sparkman*

FIFTH RACE
Arlington Park
October 26, 2002

1 mile on turf. 19th running of the Breeders' Cup Mile (G1). Purse $1-million. 3-year-olds and up. Weights (Northern Hemisphere): 3-year-olds, 123 lbs. Older, 126 lbs. (Southern Hemisphere): 3-year-olds, 120 lbs. Older, 126 lbs. Fillies and mares allowed 3 lbs. Supplemental nominee (9%): Landseer.

Value of race: $980,120. Value to winner: $556,400; second: $214,000; third: $128,400; fourth: $59,920; fifth, $21,400. Mutuel Pool: $4,004,761.

Horse	Wgt.	M/Eqt	PP	St.	¼	½	¾	Str.	Fin.	Jockey	Odds $1
Domedriver (Ire)	126		5	11	$9^{1\frac{1}{2}}$	7^{hd}	$9^{1\frac{1}{2}}$	$3^{\frac{1}{2}}$	$1^{\frac{3}{4}}$	T. Thulliez	26.00
Rock of Gilbraltar (Ire)	122	L	10	12	14	$13^{1\frac{1}{2}}$	13^{2}	$6^{\frac{1}{2}}$	2no	M. Kinane	*0.80
Good Journey	126	L	4	2	$2^{\frac{1}{2}}$	2^{1}	1^{hd}	1^{1}	$3^{1\frac{1}{2}}$	P. Day	5.40
Forbidden Apple	126	L	1	4	3^{hd}	3^{hd}	5^{hd}	2^{hd}	$4^{1\frac{1}{2}}$	C. Nakatani	15.10
Green Fee	126	L	6	14	13^{hd}	12^{1}	$12^{1\frac{1}{2}}$	$7^{\frac{1}{2}}$	$5^{1\frac{3}{4}}$	J. Velazquez	45.00
Beat Hollow (GB)	126	L	2	6	5^{hd}	$5^{\frac{1}{2}}$	$6^{\frac{1}{2}}$	5^{1}	6no	J. Bailey	6.50
Del Mar Show	126	L	8	3	4^{1}	4^{hd}	3^{hd}	4^{12}	7^{hd}	P. Valenzuela	61.50
Dress to Thrill (Ire)	119	L	12	8	$10^{\frac{1}{2}}$	11^{1}	$11^{1\frac{1}{2}}$	$9^{2\frac{1}{2}}$	$8^{\frac{1}{2}}$	P. Smullen	32.30
Medecis (GB)	122		3	10	$11^{1\frac{1}{2}}$	10^{hd}	$10^{\frac{1}{2}}$	8^{hd}	$9^{5\frac{3}{4}}$	A. Solis	39.00
Touch of the Blues (Fr)	126	L	11	7	8^{hd}	$8^{\frac{1}{2}}$	$8^{\frac{1}{2}}$	10^{2}	$10^{1\frac{1}{4}}$	K. Desormeaux	33.90
Aldebaran	126	L	7	13	12^{1}	14	14	13	$11^{1\frac{1}{4}}$	J. Chavez	14.90
Nuclear Debate	126	L	14	9	7^{hd}	9^{1}	7^{hd}	$12^{2\frac{1}{2}}$	$12^{\frac{3}{4}}$	G. Stevens	53.20
Boston Common	122	L	9	1	1^{1}	1^{hd}	2^{hd}	11^{hd}	13	R. Douglas	69.10
Landseer (GB) (S)	122	L	13	5	6^{1}	6^{1}	$4^{\frac{1}{2}}$	14	14	E. Prado	14.30

OFF AT 1:37. Start Good. Weather: Cloudy. Turf: Yielding. Won: Checked First Turn.
Time, :23.86, :48.68, 1:12.96, 1:25.09, 1:36.92.

$2 Mutuel Prices:

5—DOMEDRIVER (IRE)	**54.00**	**18.20**	**5.80**
10—ROCK OF GIBRALTAR (GB)		**3.40**	**2.60**
4—GOOD JOURNEY			**3.60**

PICK THREE 4-2/4-5 PAID $361.60
EXACTA 5-10 PAID $152.60 HEAD2HEAD 2VS4-WINNER-4 PAID $3.20
SUPERFECTA 5-10-4-1 PAID $8,705.60 TRIFECTA 5-10-4 $984.00

Dk. b. or br. c., by Indian Ridge—Napoli, by Baillamont. Trainer Pascal Bary. Bred by the Niarchos Family (Ire.).

DOMEDRIVER (IRE) checked in tight between horses on the first turn, was unhurried while saving ground for five furlongs, launched a rally along the inside on the turn, split horses while gaining rapidly in upper stretch, accelerated to the front inside the furlong marker then edged clear in the final seventy yards. ROCK OF GIBRALTAR (IRE) outrun early after breaking a bit slowly, raced well back while four wide along the backstretch, closed the gap on the turn, checked inside LANDSEER at the top of the stretch then unleashed a strong late run in the mddle of the track but could not get up. GOOD JOURNEY forced the pace from outside for a half, surged to the front on the turn, opened a clear advantage in upper stretch, continued on the lead into deep stretch then yielded grudgingly. FORBIDDEN APPLE raced in close contention along inside the turn, dropped back slightly at the quarter pole then finished willingly along the inside. GREEN FEE was pinched back at the start, was outrun while saving ground for six furlongs then rallied belatedly. BEAT HOLLOW (GB) settled in good position between horses along the backstretch, raced within striking distance to the top of the stretch then lacked a strong closing bid. DEL MAR SHOW stalked the pace while four wide for six furlongs, made a run to threaten in upper stretch then flattened out. DRESS TO THRILL (IRE) failed to threaten while racing wide. MEDECIS (GB) was pinched back at the start then failed to threaten while saving ground. TOUCH OF THE BLUES (FR) raced in the middle of the pack between horses to the turn then steadied sharply when LANDSEER broke down at the top of the stretch. ALDEBARAN checked between horses on the first turn, was outrun for six furlongs then steadied sharply at the top of the stretch. NUCLEAR DEBATE raced six wide while in the middle of the pack for five furlongs, steadied sharply on the turn then faltered. BOSTON COMMON set the pace under pressure along the inside for five furlongs and faltered. LANDSEER (GB) raced in the middle of the pack for a half, closed the gap to threaten on the turn then broke down at the top of the stretch.

Copyright 2002 Equibase Company LLC

2002 Juvenile Fillies: A Phipps Tradition

If American Thoroughbred racing has a first family, that distinction certainly belongs to the Phipps clan, whose magnificent legacy now extends into a fourth generation. The dynasty began with the Wheatley Stable of Gladys Mills Phipps and her brother, Ogden Mills. Wheatley bred and raced, among others, Bold Ruler, a champion and the most influential sire of the 1960s.

Gladys Phipps's son Ogden bred such influential horses as Buckpasser, Private Account, and Easy Goer, again to name just a few. Ogden Phipps died on April 22, 2002, at age 93, and now his children, Ogden Mills "Dinny" Phipps and Cynthia Phipps, carry forward the family legacy, with the torch being passed to Dinny Phipps's

children.

At Arlington Park on October 26, Ogden Mills Phipps's Storm Flag Flying scored an impressive but quirky triumph in the $916,000 Breeders' Cup Juvenile Fillies (G1) and became the first third-generation winner of a Breeders' Cup race. Her grandam, Personal Ensign, retired without a defeat on her record with a breathtaking, come-from-behind victory in the 1988 Breeders' Cup Distaff (G1). Seven years later, Personal Ensign's daughter, My Flag, won the Juvenile Fillies. My Flag's daughter, Storm Flag Flying, the 4-to-5 favorite in the 2002 Juvenile Fillies, carried on that tradition with her fourth career victory without a defeat.

The Juvenile Fillies left no doubt about Storm Flag Flying's talent and perpetuated some questions about the temperament of the dark-coated Storm Cat filly. Her flighty personality took hold early in Arlington's stretch, when she assumed the lead and began gawking at the crowd in Arlington's temporary grandstands. Robert and Beverly Lewis's Composure loomed outside the Phipps filly and swept past her under Mike Smith. Storm Flag Flying appeared to be in trouble, but jockey John Velazquez merely moved her outside slightly so she could see Composure. With that, Storm Flag Flying kicked in again, quickly overtook Composure, and drew away to a half-length victory.

"She tried to pull herself up, but when the other filly came up on her she got back in the game," said Storm Flag Flying's trainer, Claude R. "Shug" McGaughey III, who collected his eighth Breeders' Cup victory.

Composure, the Oak Leaf Stakes (G2) winner who went off as the 7-to-2 second choice in the field of ten two-year-old fillies, easily held second over her 5.20-to-1 stablemate Santa Catarina, who finished 9¾ lengths farther back. Sea Jewel, third in the Oak Leaf, finished another two lengths back in fourth. The remainder of the field strung out behind her.

The Juvenile Fillies normally is run at 1¹⁄₁₆ miles, but the configuration of Arlington's track required it to be run for the first time at 1⅛ miles. Storm Flag Flying found the distance to be no challenge, completing the nine furlongs in 1:49.60 on a fast but wet track listed as good. Her time was almost identical to that of Vindication in the Juvenile (G1).

Storm Flag Flying's personality quirks, which included refusing to move or attempting to bolt, run in the genes. Personal Ensign was aggressive, McGaughey said, and My Flag had some temperament problems that she outgrew. Storm Flag Flying "has so much talent, but she can go ahead and do something dumb at any moment,"

Owner

Ogden Mills Phipps is chairman of the Jockey Club, a position he has held since 1983. His late father, Ogden Phipps, held the position before him, from 1964 to 1974. Known widely as "Dinny," the younger Phipps formerly served as chairman of the New York Racing Association and now is a director of the National Thoroughbred Racing Association. He owned two previous Breeders' Cup winners, both of whom he bred: Rhythm in the 1989 Juvenile (G1) and Inside Information in the 1995 Distaff (G1).

Breeder

Phipps Stable is the entity created by the late Ogden Phipps in the early 1990s to include the children of his son Ogden Mills Phipps in the Thoroughbred breeding business. All three generations were partners in the operation, which boards its broodmares and foals at Claiborne Farm in Kentucky. In his own name, Ogden Phipps bred three Breeders' Cup winners: Personal Ensign (1988 Distaff [G1]), Dancing Spree (1989 Sprint [G1]), and My Flag (1995 Juvenile Fillies [G1]).

Trainer

A Lexington native, **Claude R. "Shug" McGaughey III** became hooked on racing at Keeneland Race Course as a teenager. He attended the University of Mississippi but dropped out in his junior year to groom horses for trainer David Carr. He served as Carr's assistant and also as assistant to David Whiteley for five years before taking out his trainer's license in 1979. One of his first major clients was Loblolly Stable, for whom he trained his first champion, Vanlandingham. McGaughey agreed to be the Phipps family's private trainer on November 11, 1985. He had a breakthrough season in 1988, when he trained two champions, two-year-old male Easy Goer and older female Personal Ensign. That year, he was voted an Eclipse Award as outstanding trainer. In all, he has trained eight champions.

the trainer said.

McGaughey had waited until the final weeks of the Saratoga Race Course meet to unveil Storm Flag Flying, and she scored a one-length victory at 3.65-to-1 while racing greenly. Back at her home base, Belmont Park, the filly ran immaturely again but still won the one-mile Matron Stakes (G1) by 12¾ lengths as the 7-to-5 favorite. Her start before the Juvenile Fillies was Belmont's 1¹⁄₁₆-mile Frizette Stakes (G1). Storm Flag Flying went off as the 3-to-5 favorite and, showing more maturity, ran down Santa Catarina to win by two lengths on October 5.

To curb Storm Flag Flying's curiosity, McGaughey kept her in New York until two days before the Breeders' Cup.

When the starting gate opened for the Breeders' Cup Juvenile Fillies, Astarita Stakes (G2) winner Humorous Lady hurtled to the lead, with Storm Flag Flying in a stalking position. Santa Catarina took over at the half-mile pole, and Storm Flag Flying quickened, leaving the final turn to grab the advantage from the Frizette runner-up. She would not remain in front for long. Composure rolled past her and grabbed a half-length lead at the three-sixteenths pole, but Storm Flag Flying kicked in again when Velazquez hit her left-handed.

"We just ran into a champion and a half today," Smith said.

Storm Flag Flying was almost a unanimous choice as champion two-year-old filly, missing by just one vote. In the Experimental Free Handicap, she was the highweight at 123 pounds, two pounds more than Composure.

—Don Clippinger

FOURTH RACE
Arlington Park
October 26, 2002

1⅛ miles. 19th running of the Breeders' Cup Juvenile Fillies (G1). Purse $1-million. Fillies, 2-year-olds. Weight: 119 lbs.

Value of race, $916,000. Value to winner: $520,000; second: $200,000; third: $120,000; fourth: $56,000; fifth: $20,000. Mutuel Pool: $2,946,339.

Horse	Wt.	M/Eqt	PP	St	¼	½	¾	Str.	Fin.	Jockey	Odds $1
Storm Flag Flying	119	L	3	5	2^{hd}	3^{1}	$2^{1/2}$	2^{2}	$1^{1/2}$	J. Velazquez	*0.80
Composure	119	L	2	2	4^{hd}	$5^{1\frac{1}{2}}$	4^{1}	1^{hd}	$2^{9\frac{3}{4}}$	M. Smith	3.50
Santa Catarina	119	L	1	6	3^{1}	$2^{1/2}$	1^{1}	3^{4}	3^{2}	J. Bailey	5.20
Sea Jewel	119	Lb	6	8	$7^{1\frac{1}{2}}$	6^{1}	$6^{2\frac{1}{2}}$	4^{3}	$4^{4\frac{1}{2}}$	P. Valenzuela	27.00
Appleby Gardens	119	L	10	10	10	9^{hd}	7^{hd}	5^{1}	$5^{1\frac{1}{4}}$	R. Migliore	66.20
Westerly Breeze	119	L	9	7	6^{hd}	$7^{1\frac{1}{2}}$	8^{2}	7^{1}	6^{2}	R. Albarado	15.70
Buffythecenterfold	119	L	7	3	$5^{1\frac{1}{2}}$	4^{hd}	$5^{1\frac{1}{2}}$	6^{hd}	$7^{1\frac{1}{2}}$	M. Garcia	24.70
Humorous Lady	119	Lb	4	1	1^{2}	$1^{1\frac{1}{2}}$	3^{hd}	$8^{3\frac{1}{2}}$	$8^{1\frac{1}{2}}$	A. Solis	33.20
Atlantic Ocean	119	L	8	9	8^{1}	8^{hd}	$9^{2\frac{1}{2}}$	9^{2}	$9^{3/4}$	V. Espinoza	32.30
Ruby's Reception	119	L	5	4	9^{2}	10	10	10	10	T. Thompson	12.80

Ivanavinalot Scratched

OFF AT 12:56. Start Good. Winner: Headed, Very Game. Weather: Cloudy. Track: Good.
Time, :23.37, :46.28, 1:10.31, 1:35.86, 1:49.60.

$2 Mutuel Prices:

4—STORM FLAG FLYING	**3.60**	**2.60**	**2.20**
3—COMPOSURE		**3.40**	**2.80**
1—SANTA CATARINA			**3.00**

PICK THREE 3-4-2/4 PAID $50.80 DAILY DOUBLE 4-4 PAID $10.40
EXACTA 4-3 PAID $12.80 HEAD2HEAD 1VS10-Winner-1 PAID $2.20
SUPERFECTA 4-3-1-7 PAID $189.40 TRIFECTA 4-3-1 PAID $31.00

Dk. b. or br. f., by Storm Cat—My Flag, by Easy Goer. Trainer Claude McGaughey III. Bred by Phipps Stable (Ky.)

STORM FLAG FLYING settled just off the early pace, raced in good position between horses along the backstretch, launched her rally from outside on the turn, surged to the front nearing the three-sixteenths pole, relinquished the lead a furlong out then fought back gamely under strong handling to prevail in a long drive. COMPOSURE never far back, was rated just off the pace for six furlongs, closed the gap while inside the winner midway on the turn, dropped back slightly then altered her course to the outside approaching the quarter pole, moved past STORM FLAG FLYING to gain a brief lead in midstretch but could not hold off the winner through the final sixteenth. SANTA CATARINA stalked the pace from outside for five furlongs, accelerated to the front opening a clear advantage at the three-eighths pole, continued on the lead into upper stretch then weakened under pressure in the final sixteenth. SEA JEWEL was pinched back a bit after being bumped at the start, raced in the middle of the pack while angling out a bit along the backstretch, raced just behind the winner leaving the far turn, moved between horses on the turn then lacked a strong closing bid. APPLEBY GARDENS ducked out at the start, raced well back along the inside to the turn then failed to threaten while improving her position. WESTERLY BREEZE was never a factor while six wide throughout. BUFFYTHECENTERFOLD raced within striking distance while six wide to the turn then lacked a further response. HUMOROUS LADY sprinted clear soon after the start, set the pace along the inside for five furlongs then checked slightly while giving way on the turn. ATLANTIC OCEAN checked while being pinched back at the start then failed to threaten while racing wide throughout. RUBY'S RECEPTION bumped at the start, was never a factor.

2002 Distaff: Grand Tradition Continues

The legacy of Allen Paulson lives on in the Breeders' Cup World Thoroughbred Championships.

The winningest owner in Breeders' Cup history, Paulson died on July 19, 2000, his legacy of achievement in the Breeders' Cup encompassing 32 starters, a record six winners, and a record $7,570,000 in earnings. As a breeder, Paulson had a record five winners and leading earnings of $6,694,800 prior to the 2002 Breeders' Cup World Thoroughbred Championships. Well, you can keep adding to those totals.

More than two years after Paulson's death, he was at Arlington Park on October 26 in spirit, his influence palpable. Paulson homebred Azeri, a four-year-old filly who made her first career start more than 15 months after he died, made the 1⅛-mile, $1,832,000 Breeders' Cup Distaff (G1) her personal national showcase by trouncing seven other fillies and mares to win the race

by an impressive five lengths. Azeri is the third Distaff winner to carry the Paulson silks, following Ajina and Escena.

It was Azeri's eighth win in nine starts in 2002 and increased her season earnings to $2,181,540. The victory assured her the older female title, and it also put her squarely into the running for Horse of the Year honors in a topsy-turvy year in which there is no standout three-year-old or older male on dirt. In fact, in year-end voting announced on January 27, 2003, the victory earned her Horse of the Year honors. She is the first female to be voted Horse of the Year without defeating males in her championship season.

The chestnut daughter of Jade Hunter races in the name of Allen E. Paulson Living Trust, which is operated by his three sons, principally Michael Paulson, the youngest of the sons, who is the trustee. When Paulson died, he left massive holdings of Thoroughbreds, some 220 horses, even though he had sold off more than 100 horses from his prominent Brookside Farm earlier for estate-planning purposes. While mares and horses of racing age were being dispersed, a handful of horses remained in training for the trust. One was an unraced filly named Azeri.

In August 2001, Michael Paulson transferred Azeri and a handful of other horses to Laura de Seroux, a relative newcomer to training who had come up under Racing Hall of Fame trainer Charlie Whittingham. "The first time Laura worked her, she said we had something special," Michael Paulson said.

Azeri made her debut on November 1, 2001, at Santa Anita Park and won by six lengths under Mike Smith. Less than one year after her maiden score, Azeri won the Distaff, her seventh consecutive graded stakes victory—fifth in a Grade 1—to become the latest star to carry the familiar Paulson red, white, and blue silks. Like many of the Paulson horses, she is named for an aviation checkpoint. Azeri is a departure point from Kars, Turkey.

Unfortunately for the trust, the Ahonoora mare Zodiac Miss (Aus), dam of Azeri, was struck by lightning at Brookside Farm on July 21, 1999, and died at the age of ten. Also killed was her suckling daughter by Theatrical (Ire). Zodiac Miss is survived by just two foals—Azeri and an unraced horse.

Going into the Distaff, de Seroux was confident but did not boast of Azeri's near-perfect record or tout her as deserving to be an odds-on favorite. Maybe it was that, or that the filly was shipping from her familiar surroundings of Southern California to a deeper Midwest track, or because her trainer was not well known, or because she would be racing for the first time

---

Owner-breeder

Allen E. Paulson Living Trust is the legacy of Allen E. Paulson (April 22, 1922-July 19, 2000), founder of Gulfstream Aerospace Corp., which manufactured private jet planes. Paulson became involved in Thoroughbred racing in the late 1970s and built his Brookside Farm near Versailles, Kentucky, into one of the world's leading racing and breeding operations. Paulson campaigned more than 115 stakes winners, including two-time Horse of the Year Cigar and champions Theatrical (Ire), Blushing John, Arazi, Eliza, Escena, Ajina, and Estrapade. He is the leading owner of Eclipse Award winners, with eight. He campaigned Breeders' Cup winners Theatrical, Opening Verse, Eliza, Cigar, and Ajina, plus co-owned 1991 Juvenile (G1) winner Arazi. Paulson received an Eclipse Award as outstanding breeder in 1993 and Eclipse Awards as outstanding owner in both '95 and '96, the two years Cigar was Horse of the Year. The Allen E. Paulson Living Trust is managed by Paulson's son, Michael, of Las Vegas. Michael's two brothers are Richard and James.

Trainer

Although **Laura de Seroux** did not take out her trainer's license until 1999, her experience with top-level horsemen and horses spans 30 years. She spent 16 years galloping horses for Racing Hall of Fame trainer Charlie Whittingham. She also served as stable manager for Bruce McNall's Summa Stable in the early 1980s and was syndication manager for Nelson Bunker Hunt. She is married to Emmanuel de Seroux, owner of Narvick International, a bloodstock firm, and they are investors in San Luis Rey Downs, where de Seroux trains.

on a track other than fast. Whatever the reason, Azeri went off at 9-to-5 in the eight-horse field, generously high odds given her record. Her only defeat had occurred in her stakes debut in February 2002, the La Canada Stakes (G1), in which she had trouble at the start and finished second to Summer Colony.

On a track officially labeled good, upgraded from muddy as it dried out during the day, Azeri broke well from the fourth post position and took control of the race at the start. "She got away extremely well," said Smith. "It may have been the best she's ever broke. It was a good time to do it."

With Smith taking the fourth path off the rail, Azeri set comfortable fractions (for her) of :23.47, :46.20, and 1:09.70 for the opening three-quarters of a mile, with Imperial Gesture chasing her one length behind the entire way and the rest of the field strung out behind them.

When she came into the stretch, Azeri quickly kicked clear and opened up by two lengths in midstretch en route to her dominating win. Imperial Gesture showed the effects of her efforts and be- came leg weary in midstretch. From fourth charged Farda Amiga, the Kentucky Oaks (G1) winner, and the daughter of Broad Brush got up in the last several strides to nab second by a head from Imperial Gesture. Azeri's winning time was 1:48.64.

Azeri is expected to race in 2003, with the Breeders' Cup Classic (G1) a potential target.

"We considered it [this year]," Michael Paulson said. "I'm confident she would have put on a good show. But we'll consider it for next year."

A Los Angeles native, de Seroux had a break-out year in 2002. In addition to Azeri, she saddled graded stakes winners Astra, Dublino, and Little Treasure (Fr). De Seroux is the second woman to train a Breeders' Cup winner, following Jenine Sahadi, who saddled two Sprint (G1) winners, Lit de Justice and Elmhurst. Azeri's year ended in confusion, with her sale scheduled for the Barretts Equine Ltd. auction in March 2003 after Michael Paulson and trust executives agreed that all horses, including Azeri, would be sold. But a superceding agreement was reached in February 2003 that kept Azeri in de Seroux's stable and Paulson as owner.—*Mark Simon*

THIRD RACE **Arlington Park** October 26, 2002		1⅛ miles. 19th running of the Breeders' Cup Distaff (G1). Purse $2-million. Fillies and mares 3-year-olds and upward. Weights (Northern Hemisphere): 3-year-olds, 120 lbs. Older, 123 lbs. (Southern Hemisphere): 3-year-olds, 115 lbs. Older, 123 lbs.									

Value of race: $1,832,000. Value to winner: $1,040,000; second: $400,000; third: $240,000; fourth: $112,000; fifth, $40,000. Mutuel Pool $3,144,483.

Horse	Wt.	M/Eqt	PP	St.	¼	½	¾	Str.	Fin.	Jockey	Odds $1
Azeri	123	Lf	4	4	1^1	1^1	1^1	1^2	1^5	M. Smith	*1.80
Farda Amiga	119	L	3	1	$4^{1/2}$	4^{hd}	4^{hd}	3^2	2^{hd}	P. Day	4.90
Imperial Gesture	119	Lb	5	5	$2^{2 1/2}$	2^3	2^2	2^3	$3^{3 3/4}$	J. Bailey	4.10
Starrer	123	Lb	7	7	7^2	7^3	$7^{1 1/2}$	$5^{1/2}$	$4^{4 1/2}$	P. Valenzuela	41.60
Mandy's Gold	123	Lf	6	3	$5^{1/2}$	$6^{1/2}$	$5^{1 1/2}$	$6^{2 1/2}$	$5^{1/2}$	J. Santos	10.90
Take Charge Lady	119	L	8	2	3^2	$3^{1 1/2}$	3^2	4^{hd}	6no	E. Prado	3.20
Two Item Limit	123	Lb	1	8	8	8	8	7^2	$7^{7 1/2}$	R. Douglas	45.80
Summer Colony	123	L	2	6	$6^{1/2}$	$5^{1/2}$	$6^{1 1/2}$	8	8	J. Velazquez	7.00

OFF AT 12:22. Start: Good. Weather: Cloudy. Track: Good. Winner: Off Rail, Driving.
Time: :23.47, :46.20, 1:09.70, 1:35.32, 1:48.64.

$2 Mutuel Prices:	4—AZERI	5.60	3.60	2.60
	3—FARDA AMIGA		4.60	3.40
	5—IMPERIAL GESTURE			3.40

PICK THREE 1-3-4 PAID $45.00   EXACTA 4-3 PAID $35.00
HEAD2HEAD 3VS8-WINNER-3 PAID $4.40   SUPERFECTA 4-3-5-7 PAID $1,009.00
TRIFECTA 4-3-5 PAID $117.80

Ch. f., by Jade Hunter—Zodiac Miss (Aus), by Ahonoora. Trainer Laura De Seroux. Bred by Allen E. Paulson (Ky.).

AZERI outsprinted rivals for the early advantage, set the pace well off the rail along the backstretch, maintained a clear advantage to the top of the stretch, shook off IMPERIAL GESTURE in upper stretch, then drew off under a vigorous hand ride. FARDA AMIGA broke a bit awkwardly, was unhurried for a half while between horses, angled four wide while launching her bid on the turn, then finished willingly to edge IMPERIAL GESTURE for the place. IMPERIAL GESTURE broke a half-step slowly, moved up from outside to contest the early pace, forced the pace outside the winner into upper stretch, ducked in briefly nearing the furlong marker, then weakened from her early efforts. STARRER broke inward brushing with MANDY'S GOLD at the start, raced well back to the turn, lugged in slightly in upper stretch, then failed to threaten while improving her position. MANDY'S GOLD was bumped a bit at the start, raced five wide to the turn, then lacked the needed response when called upon. TAKE CHARGE LADY strung out six wide on the first turn, raced within striking distance along the backstretch, angled in on the turn, then steadily tired thereafter. TWO ITEM LIMIT checked slightly along the rail on the first turn, never reached contention. SUMMER COLONY raced in the middle of the pack while saving ground for six furlongs, then gave way leaving the turn.

Copyright 2002 Equibase Company LLC

RACING
Review of 2002 Racing Season

In many ways, the 2002 racing season was the year of the filly. Or, at least, the year of two highly notable fillies. A four-year-old filly, Azeri, so dominated her division that she was voted Horse of the Year by Eclipse Award balloters. Once she started rolling, after a second-place finish in the La Canada Stakes (G2) in February 2002, no one could come close to her for the remainder of the year.

Azeri was brilliant, setting the pace in most of her races, and she won by daylight each time. She won seven graded races in succession, including five Grade 1 races. She was so dominant that she was accorded the Horse of the Year title without ever racing against males, a departure from the precedent of All Along (Fr) in 1983 and Lady's Secret (1986), the only other females to be voted an Eclipse Award winner as Horse of the Year. Through a magical season, Azeri was professional, accomplished, and dazzling.

The other notable filly, two-year-old Storm Flag Flying, was not professional and not particularly accomplished, despite three Grade 1 victories in four starts, but she certainly was dazzling. She all but went to sleep in Arlington Park's stretch, gave away the lead, and then woke up long enough to come back and win the Breeders' Cup Juvenile Fillies (G1) going away.

Between them, Azeri and Storm Flag Flying drew only one dissenting vote in divisional balloting, and their dominance is a testament to their late breeders, Allen E. Paulson and Ogden Phipps, respectively. Paulson, who died in 2000, had won an Eclipse Award as outstanding breeder and two as outstanding owner, plus he bred and raced two-time Horse of the Year Cigar. He stood Azeri's sire, Jade Hunter, at his Brookside Farm near Versailles, Kentucky.

Storm Flag Flying represented three generations of Breeders' Cup winners—following her undefeated grandam, Personal Ensign, and her dam, My Flag. Phipps, who died in April 2002, bred them all and planned the mating of Storm Cat and My Flag that produced Storm Flag Flying.

The Payson Stud of Virginia Kraft Payson also had an extraordinary year, producing two champions, two-year-old male Vindication and three-year-old filly Farda Amiga.

To be sure, several other horses had very good seasons, but in general they did not dazzle at all times. While the two-year-old male division was promising, with three or four strong juvenile performers, the three-year-old male and older male divisions had no dominant horses.

War Emblem came out of nowhere to win the Kentucky Derby (G1) and Preakness Stakes (G1), but he stumbled out of contention for the Triple Crown in the Belmont Stakes (G1). He subsequently won the Haskell Invitational Handicap (G1), but that was his last win of the season. The older male division was set on its ear by Volponi's upset in the Breeders' Cup Classic (G1), but even before that race the handicap division was virtually leaderless.

While With Anticipation was game and won three Grade 1 grass races, he was bested in the Breeders' Cup Turf (G1) by High Chaparral (Ire), who in fact may not have been the best European runner in the Breeders' Cup World Thoroughbred Championships. Rock of Gibraltar (Ire) was a rock until he reached America's Midwest, but his much-discussed loss in the Breeders' Cup Mile (G1) was a case of too little too late. Indeed, the Danehill colt may well have been a bit past his best, which encompassed a record seven Group 1 wins in a row before his trip to America.

Older Female

Azeri, the unanimous choice as champion older female, added Horse of the Year to her laurels because—even though she never ran against males—she dominated her division. She was the third female Horse of the Year, after All Along in 1983 and Lady's Secret in 1986, since the Eclipse Awards were inaugurated in 1971. Azeri was brilliant from January through October and won her last seven starts, five Grade 1 stakes and two Grade 2 events, over five different tracks. She won convincingly, taking the last seven by a total of 21¾ lengths.

Bred by Paulson and owned by the Allen E. Paulson Living Trust, the chestnut four-year-old by Jade Hunter carried weight—125, 126, and 127 pounds, respectively, in her final 2002 handicap starts—and still won decisively in fast time. She saved her best for last, winning the Breeders' Cup Distaff (G1) by an authoritative five lengths.

Trained by Laura de Seroux, Azeri won her first start of the year, an $80,000 allowance/optional claiming race at Santa Anita Park, and then sustained her only defeat of 2002 when she finished second by a length to Summer Colony in Santa Anita's La Canada Stakes (G2) for four-year-old fillies. After that race, though, Azeri was dominant and unbeatable. She scored her first stakes victory in the Santa Margarita Handicap (G1) at Santa Anita, defeating Spain by three lengths.

Azeri then strung together victories in the Apple Blossom Handicap (G1) at Oaklawn Park and the Milady Breeders' Cup (G1) and Vanity (G1) Handicaps at Hollywood Park, leaving Janis Whitham's Affluent as the runner-up on all three occasions. After those Grade 1 wins, she scored victories in the Clement L. Hirsch Handicap (G2) at Del Mar and the Lady's Secret Breeders' Cup Handicap (G2) at Santa Anita before her appearance in the Breeders' Cup Distaff (G1) at Arlington Park. She dominated her field, going to the lead, setting fast fractions (1:09.70 for six furlongs), and winning by five lengths over Farda Amiga, the eventual three-year-old filly champion. At season's end, Azeri's career earnings totaled $2,227,740, with all but $46,200 earned in 2002.

Summer Colony, the only horse to beat Azeri in 2002, had an outstanding season through August, winning the Delaware Handicap (G3) and Saratoga Race Course's Personal Ensign Handicap (G1). But she finished third behind three-year-old Imperial Gesture in the Beldame Stakes (G1) and never was a factor in the Breeders' Cup Distaff, finishing eighth, 21 lengths behind Azeri.

The Thoroughbred Corp.'s homebred Spain was no match for Azeri in their two meetings, but she came back to win the Louisville Breeders' Cup (G2) and Fleur de Lis (G2) Handicaps at Churchill Downs and retired as North America's all-time leading female money-winner with $3,540,542. Other females had their moments in the spotlight. Canadian champion Dancethruthedawn captured the Go for Wand Handicap (G1) at Saratoga, Raging Fever won the Ogden Phipps Handicap (G1) at Belmont, Shine Again annexed the Ballerina Handicap (G1) at Saratoga, Favorite Funtime accounted for the Santa Maria Handicap (G1) at Santa Anita, and Mandy's Gold won Belmont's Ruffian Handicap (G1).—*Steve Schuelein*

Older Male

Results of 2002 Grade 1 races for older horses testify to the competitiveness of the older male division. Ten Grade 1 races were run at a mile or longer on dirt during the year, and ten different horses went to the winner's circle. (Only one of those Grade 1 races was won by a three-year-old, Came Home, in the Pacific Classic Stakes.) At season's end, six horses had received Eclipse Award votes for champion older male.

The nod went to Michael Tabor's Left Bank in a split decision, with the National Thoroughbred Racing Association voters narrowly favoring Volponi, who won the Breeders' Cup Classic (G1), his only stakes victory of the year, at 43.50-to-1. The decisive factor for Left Bank may not have been his race record, which showed three wins in four 2002 starts, but his track records, in which he scorched the strips at Belmont Park and Saratoga Race Course.

On the East Coast, Mongoose won the division's first Grade 1 race, the Donn Handicap, but finished second to Hal's Hope in the Gulfstream

Park Handicap (G1), w[ ] race in 2003. Out West, the winter's major event icap (G1), on March 2. Hollywood Park's Califor[ ] did not return to the win[ ] mainder of the year. In l... March, Godolphin Racing's Street Cry (Ire) made clear that he would be a factor in the 2002 season with a 4¼-length victory in the Dubai World Cup (UAE-G1), and he won Churchill Downs's Stephen Foster Handicap (G1) in June.

Left Bank, a five-year-old French Deputy horse, had closed out his 2001 season with a victory in the Cigar Mile Handicap (G1), and he returned with a win in Aqueduct's Bold Ruler Handicap (G3) on May 11. He was not competitive in the Metropolitan Handicap (G1), finishing 13 lengths behind winner Swept Overboard in fifth place. He then won Belmont's seven-furlong Tom Fool Handicap (G2) by 6¼ lengths in a track-record 1:20.17. Trainer Todd Pletcher sent him to Saratoga's 1⅛-mile Whitney Handicap (G1) on August 3 to face one of the year's toughest fields. Left Bank won by 1¼ lengths over Street Cry, with Lido Palace (Chi) finishing third. Left Bank's time, 1:47.04, equaled the track record. It would be his last race; he colicked, underwent surgery, and died from surgical complications.

Lido Palace (Chi), who like Milwaukee Brew was trained by Bobby Frankel, won Belmont's Woodward Handicap (G1) on September 7 but finished second by 2¾ lengths to Evening Attire in the Jockey Club Gold Cup Stakes (G1). He closed out the season with victories in a Belmont allowance and Churchill Downs's Clark Handicap (G2). Evening Attire's only misstep in the last five months of the season was a fourth-place finish in the Breeders' Cup Classic; he came back to win the Red Smith Handicap (G3) by eight lengths. Also emerging late in the year was Congaree, who won the Cigar Mile.

—*Ed DeRosa*

Three-Year-Old Male

While Kentucky Derby (G1) candidates turned in eye-catching performances at the usual proving grounds in Florida, California, and New York in 2002, eventual champion three-year-old male War Emblem failed to hit the board in his first two races of the year at Fair Grounds before easily winning an allowance race on St. Patrick's Day at Sportsman's Park.

The nearly black Our Emblem colt returned on April 6 to score a front-running, 6½-length victory in the Illinois Derby (G2), defeating Louisiana Derby (G2) winner Repent but turning few heads. However, he caught the attention of The Thoroughbred Corp.'s Ahmed bin Salman, who purchased 90% of War Emblem from Rus-

...an for $900,000 plus expenses and ...d the colt to trainer Bob Baffert.

...Emblem thrived in the four weeks lead-...up to the Derby and scored a front-running, ...ur-length victory over Proud Citizen in the Derby at 20.50-to-1 under jockey Victor Espinoza. Two weeks later, War Emblem delivered a similar effort in the Preakness Stakes (G1), notching a three-quarter-length victory over Magic Weisner, a Maryland-based 45.70-to-1 longshot bred, owned, and trained by Nancy Alberts. The 29th horse to win the Derby and the Preakness, War Emblem stumbled at the start of the Belmont Stakes (G1) and lost all chance of becoming racing's 12th Triple Crown winner. While he struggled, Sarava pulled off the biggest upset in the race's history, scoring at odds of 70.25-to-1 for trainer Ken McPeek, who in the previous weeks had had the 6-to-1 Derby favorite, Harlan's Holiday, taken from his stable. Winner of the Florida Derby (G1) and Blue Grass Stakes (G1), Harlan's Holiday had finished seventh in the Derby and fourth in the Preakness.

War Emblem scored a front-running victory in Monmouth Park's Haskell Invitational Handicap (G1) before off-the-board finishes in the Pacific Classic Stakes (G1) at Del Mar and the Breeders' Cup Classic (G1) at Arlington Park. After Salman's death in the summer, the Yoshida family's Shadai Stallion Station purchased War Emblem for stud duty for $17-million.

By no means was War Emblem the year's only notable three-year-old. Came Home, a Gone West colt bred by John Toffan and Trudy McCaffery, did not lose a race in California. He won the Santa Anita Derby (G1) in the spring and defeated older horses in winning the Pacific Classic on August 25 at Del Mar. Came Home also won the Swaps Stakes (G2) and the Affirmed Handicap (G3) at Hollywood Park after finishing sixth in the Derby. Although trained by California-based Bobby Frankel, Medaglia d'Oro stole the show on the East Coast. Second to Buddha in the Wood Memorial Stakes (G1), he finished fourth in the Derby and eighth in the Preakness. In the Belmont, he lost by a half-length to Sarava. At Saratoga Race Course, Medaglia d'Oro won the Jim Dandy Stakes (G2) by 13¾ lengths and the Travers Stakes (G1) by a half-length over Repent. The El Prado (Ire) colt was favored in the Breeders' Cup Classic but finished second to longshot Volponi.—*Frank Angst*

Three-Year-Old Filly

Just as the 2002 season for three-year-old fillies entered the crucial spring-summer period, the division sustained a significant loss with the death of Tempera, Godolphin Racing's champion, who had sparkled in the Breeders' Cup Juvenile Fillies (G1) a few months earlier. After spending the winter in Dubai, the daughter of A.P. Indy returned to the United States in mid-April to prepare for the Kentucky Oaks (G1). She developed a fever on April 26, and her condition deteriorated rapidly with the onset of colitis and laminitis. She was euthanized on April 28.

The division continued to be an emotional roller coaster at Churchill Downs five days later when Farda Amiga closed powerfully to score a 20-to-1 upset win over favored Take Charge Lady in the Kentucky Oaks (G1), setting off a lively winner's circle celebration by her Brazilian connections. The mood was anything but celebratory just hours later when trainer Paulo Lobo discovered that Farda Amiga's white blood cell count had dropped alarmingly. "She had an infection, and it was serious for a few days," said co-owner Jose de Camargo.

Farda Amiga recovered slowly, and Lobo decided to bring her along gradually for a return in the Alabama Stakes (G1) at Saratoga Race Course on August 17. In her absence, You reeled off victories in the Acorn Stakes (G1) at Belmont Park and the Test Stakes (G1) at Saratoga, prompting trainer Bobby Frankel to aim Edmund Gann's daughter of You and I at the Alabama.

You went off as the favorite in the 1¼-mile Alabama and sat in prime position at the rail behind front-runner Allamerican Bertie heading into the far turn. But Farda Amiga closed strongly from near the back of the pack, took the lead inside the furlong pole, and won by three-quarters of a length, with Allamerican Bertie second and You third.

Lobo again charted a conservative course following the Alabama, opting to train Farda Amiga up to the Breeders' Cup Distaff (G1) in late October. In the meantime, Imperial Gesture—Godolphin's second-place finisher in the 2001 Breeders' Cup Juvenile Fillies—asserted herself with victories in Belmont's Gazelle Handicap (G1) and Beldame Stakes (G1). Select Stable's Take Charge Lady re-entered the picture with a second-place finish in the Gazelle and a victory in the Overbrook Spinster Stakes (G1) at Keeneland Race Course.

But Farda Amiga stood out among her peers in the Distaff, making another late run to finish second behind eventual Horse of the Year Azeri. The performance cemented Farda Amiga's divisional honors, but it also brought a premature end to her career when she came away from the race with bone chips in an ankle.—*Jeff Lowe*

Two-Year-Old Male

Only a few weeks had elapsed in 2003 when it became known that the hex on the two-year-old male champion would continue. On February 6, juvenile male champion Vindication was found to have a strained suspensory ligament, and trainer Bob Baffert declared him from the Triple Crown. The last juvenile male champion to win the Kentucky Derby (G1) was Spectacular Bid in 1979. Vindication won his Eclipse Award with an undefeated streak over three months, culminating with his victory in the Breeders' Cup Juvenile (G1) at Arlington Park. Four other two-year-old colts—Sky Mesa, Kafwain, Whywhywhy, and Toccet—also stood out during the 2002 season.

John C. Oxley's Sky Mesa had the shortest campaign of the group, encompassing three wins in three starts. After a maiden victory at Saratoga Race Course, the Pulpit colt won the Hopeful Stakes (G1) and Keeneland Race Course's Lane's End Breeders' Futurity (G2). An ankle injury discovered the day before the Breeders' Cup Juvenile kept him out of that race, in which he probably would have been favored.

Kafwain, owned by The Thoroughbred Corp. and trained by Baffert, earned his maiden victory at Hollywood Park and, after finishing fourth in the Hollywood Juvenile Championship Stakes (G3), took Del Mar's Best Pal Stakes (G3). The Cherokee Run colt finished second to Baffert-trained Icecoldbeeratreds in the Del Mar Futurity (G2) but came back to win the Norfolk Stakes (G2) at Santa Anita Park as his Breeders' Cup tune-up.

With all the talent in Baffert's barn, he did not have the Breeders' Cup Juvenile favorite. That distinction fell to Whywhywhy, trained and partly owned by Patrick Biancone, who nearly two decades earlier had charmed America with 1983 Horse of the Year All Along (Fr). Whywhywhy scored his maiden victory in Belmont Park's Flash Stakes (G3) and then scored daylight victories in Saratoga's Sanford Stakes (G2) and Belmont's Futurity Stakes (G1). Favored at 5-to-2, he never was a factor in the Breeders' Cup Juvenile and finished tenth.

Vindication, owned by Padua Stables, did everything right for Baffert, but the trainer's conservative strategy all but assured that the Seattle Slew colt would not be favored at Arlington. He won twice at Del Mar but not impressively, and Baffert then shipped him to Turfway Park for the Kentucky Cup Juvenile (G3), which he won by six lengths. Always near the pace in the Breeders' Cup Juvenile, Vindication cruised to a 2¾-length victory under Mike Smith to lock up his title.

Daniel Borislow, the owner of Toccet, believed that his colt's ninth-place finish in the Breeders' Cup race was not the true bill. The Awesome Again colt had won Belmont's Champagne Stakes (G1) over Icecoldbeeratreds, and he came back after the Arlington race to win the Laurel Futurity (G3) and Aqueduct's Remsen Stakes (G2).

Borislow then challenged Baffert to run Vindication in the Hollywood Futurity (G1), an invitation that the trainer declined because Padua's likely champion had been geared down to light exercise. Toccet went on to win the Hollywood race, but ankle soreness delayed the start of his 2003 season.—*Don Clippinger*

Two-Year-Old Filly

At season's end, Storm Flag Flying clearly dominated the two-year-old filly division, and the only question was how good really was Ogden Mills Phipps's daughter of Storm Cat and My Flag. Although undefeated in four starts, the flashy but flighty filly still had not run a truly mature race. She was by no means the only talent in the division, which was diminished by injuries to early bloomers. Still, no other juvenile filly measured up to the brilliance of Storm Flag Flying, the near-unanimous (one dissenting vote) Eclipse Award winner.

The early proving grounds for two-year-olds are Saratoga Race Course and Del Mar, and two fillies flourished there. At Saratoga, Awesome Humor proved to be awesomely brilliant for WinStar Farm, which purchased the Distorted Humor filly after her victory in Churchill Downs's Debutante Stakes (G3) and transferred her to W. Elliott Walden, WinStar's private trainer. With Pat Day in the saddle, Awesome Humor cut all fractions to win Saratoga's Adirondack Stakes (G2) by 1¼ lengths and the Spinaway Stakes (G1) by 2¾ lengths. The Spinaway would be her final 2002 start. Bone chips were found in both ankles, and she underwent surgery in early October to remove them. Her brilliance, though, earned her one Eclipse Award vote. Storm Flag Flying won her maiden victory at Saratoga, but her quality would not become clear until racing shifted to Belmont Park after Labor Day.

In California, Buffythecenterfold grabbed the interest of Frank Stronach when she won Hollywood Park's Landaluce Stakes (G3), and he purchased 70% of her for approximately $1-million. She won Del Mar's Sorrento Stakes (G2) in Stronach's silks, but the Capote filly proved to be no match for Miss Houdini in the Del Mar Debutante (G1), in which she dueled for the early lead and faded to seventh. Misfortune befell Miss Houdini, who sustained a ruptured tendon shortly after the Debutante.

After the Labor Day holiday, the division began to take on a new look. At Calder Race Course, Gilbert G. Campbell's homebred Ivanavinalot ran her winning streak to three with a triumph in the My Dear Girl Stakes, part of the Florida Stallion Stakes series. But Campbell and trainer Kathleen O'Connell decided against a run in the Breeders' Cup Juvenile Fillies (G1) at Arlington Park on October 26. At the same time, trainer

Bob Baffert was loading up for the $1-million race. Most significantly, Robert and Beverly Lewis's Composure won the Oak Leaf Stakes (G2) at Santa Anita Park. At Keeneland, Carl Nafzger-trained Westerly Breeze won the Walmac Int'l Alcibiades Stakes (G2) on October 4.

By then, however, it was clear that every challenger would be shooting at Storm Flag Flying, granddaughter of undefeated Personal Ensign. At Belmont, she crushed her opponents in the Matron (G1) and Frizette (G1) Stakes while still running greenly. Favored in the Breeders' Cup, she lost interest when she made the lead, gave up the advantage to Composure in midstretch, but fought back to win by a half-length over Composure and lock up her title.—*Don Clippinger*

Turf Male

As is often the case with the North American turf males, the division spent much of the year looking for a leader, and when it finally found one, he could not quite close the deal. The winter and early-spring turf races in California and Florida ultimately proved little, though they did reveal two potential stars. Old stalwart Cetewayo flashed a spark of brilliance to win the division's first Grade 1 of the year, the Gulfstream Park Breeders' Cup Handicap (G1) in February, but that was the last time his eight-year-old legs could carry him that fast. The real early stars were stabled in California, where Beat Hollow (GB) and Sarafan embarked on a year-long rivalry.

Beat Hollow, a Juddmonte Farms homebred, began the year with an easy allowance victory at Santa Anita Park, but Gary Tanaka's Sarafan upset him with a late run in the Explosive Bid Handicap (G2) at Fair Grounds in March. The Sadler's Wells five-year-old rebounded by winning Churchill Downs's Woodford Reserve Turf Classic Stakes (G1) in impressive style from With Anticipation and the Manhattan Handicap (G1) from Forbidden Apple, putting him at the head of the division.

Beat Hollow was unlucky when he failed to catch Sarafan by 1¼ lengths after a poorly judged ride in Del Mar's Eddie Read Handicap (G1), but he gained his revenge on Sarafan by holding off his rival by a head in the Arlington Million Stakes (G1). The championship was his for the taking, but his connections chose the Breeders' Cup Mile (G1) instead of the Breeders' Cup Turf (G1) as his objective, and Beat Hollow simply was not fast enough for that assignment, finishing third in the Shadwell Keeneland Turf Mile Stakes (G1) and sixth in the Mile itself.

Another old warrior, George Strawbridge Jr.'s With Anticipation, had appeared to be the best American turf horse of 2001 before his abject display in the 2001 Turf, and, following losses to Beat Hollow in the Woodford Reserve and

Manhattan, he reeled off consecutive victories in the United Nations Handicap (G1), the Sword Dancer Invitational Handicap (G1), and the Man o' War Stakes (G1) to put himself back at the top of the division. The seven-year-old gray gelding threw in a clinker in the Turf Classic Invitational Stakes (G1) behind Denon but redeemed himself with a courageous second to invader High Chaparral (Ire) in the Breeders' Cup Turf. That, however, was not quite enough to sway Eclipse Award voters, who gave the championship to High Chaparral.—*John P. Sparkman*

Turf Female

Golden Apples (Ire) broke a short-lived tradition in 2002 when she became the first champion turf female not to win the Breeders' Cup Filly and Mare Turf (G1) since the race was inaugurated in 1999. The first three winners of the $1-million race—Soaring Softly (1999), Perfect Sting (2000), and Banks Hill (GB) ('01)—all had a Breeders' Cup win on their resumés to present to Eclipse Awards voters.

Golden Apples was favored at 2.80-to-1 in the Filly and Mare Turf and, after overcoming early traffic problems and racing wide, she finished fourth, two lengths behind Bobby Frankel's Starine (Fr). Despite not winning the division's most lucrative event, Golden Apples was its most consistent and convincing performer, finishing first or second in six Grade 1 or Grade 2 events from March until December.

A daughter of the exceptional English sprinter Pivotal, sire of another top 2002 female turf runner in Michael Bello's Megahertz (GB), Golden Apples was purchased by owner Gary A. Tanaka during the summer of 2001 and transferred to Southern California-based conditioner Ben Cecil, for whom she became a Grade 1 winner. She began her 2002 campaign in the Santa Ana Handicap (G2) and avenged her loss to Starine in the 2001 Matriarch Stakes (G1) by rallying from last to defeat her rival by 1¼ lengths. In her next start, Golden Apples encountered trouble in the Santa Barbara Handicap (G2) and finished two lengths behind Astra.

The Santa Barbara began a three-race win streak for Astra, a daughter of Theatrical (Ire) who raced for the Allen Paulson Living Trust and was trained by Laura de Seroux—the connections of Horse of the Year Azeri. Astra next defeated Starine in the Gamely Breeders' Cup Handicap (G1) and won the Beverly Hills Handicap (G1), both at Hollywood Park.

Meanwhile, Golden Apples was recovering from surgery to remove a cyst in her throat that was detected after the Santa Barbara. In her return race, she finished a neck behind Janis Whitham's Affluent in Del Mar's John C. Mabee Ramona Handicap (G1) in July. Cecil then sent

Golden Apples to Arlington for the Beverly D. Stakes (G1) and a rematch with Astra. She won by three-quarters of a length from Astra, who was retired because of a respiratory infection.

Back at Santa Anita, Golden Apples next won the Yellow Ribbon Stakes (G1), defeating Green Hills Farm's Grade 2 winner Voodoo Dancer and Juddmonte Farms' Banks Hill, who was making her 2002 North American debut. When Golden Apples and Banks Hill met again in the Breeders' Cup, the reigning champion's less-heralded stablemate, Starine, charged over Arlington's soft turf to defeat Banks Hill and give trainer Frankel a one-two finish in the race.

That was Starine's lone win of 2002 and her final race. The daughter of Mendocino was sold for $1-million at the Keeneland November breeding stock sale to Klaus Jacobs's Newsells Park Stud. Banks Hill also was retired. By the end of the year, Golden Apples had undergone arthroscopic surgery to remove bone chips from her ankles but was expected to race again.

—Amy Owens

Sprint

From the first day of 2002 to the Breeders' Cup nearly 11 months later, the sprint division played out as a relay race for Racing Hall of Fame trainer D. Wayne Lukas's stable. One four-year-old colt did all he could and then, when injured, passed the baton to his four-year-old stablemate, who finished the job in spectacular fashion.

Overbrook Farm's Snow Ridge did not waste a day bidding for the leadership of the division, taking Santa Anita Park's El Conejo Handicap (G3) on January 1 by 3½ lengths. He then defeated 2001 sprint champion Squirtle Squirt by four lengths in the Palos Verdes Handicap (G2) and added the San Carlos Handicap (G1). But in the Carter Handicap (G1) at Aqueduct on April 13, Snow Ridge tired to ninth, 13¾ lengths behind Affirmed Success.

Snow Ridge finished first by a neck in the Churchill Downs Handicap (G2) on May 4 but was disqualified to second because his jockey, Mike Smith, had struck second-finisher D'wildcat with his whip. In Pimlico Race Course's Maryland Breeders' Cup Handicap (G3) on May 18, Snow Ridge dominated, winning by 7¾ lengths. But he came out of the race with a sesamoid injury and did not race again.

Lukas turned to Bob and Beverly Lewis's Orientate, who had won just one of his first five starts in 2002, the Commonwealth Breeders' Cup Stakes (G2) on a sloppy Keeneland Race Course track on April 14. At Churchill on June 29, Orientate won the Aristides Handicap (G3) by 4¼ lengths. He was even more impressive in taking Calder Race Course's $400,000 Smile Sprint Handicap by six lengths on July 13.

Orientate stamped himself as the divisional leader at Saratoga Race Course. After coasting to a two-length victory in the A. G. Vanderbilt Handicap (G2), Orientate went head to head with Squirtle Squirt through a :44.36 half-mile in the Forego Handicap (G1) before spurting clear and winning by 2½ lengths on September 1. Orientate ran the Forego's 6½ furlongs in an impressive 1:15.68.

Lukas decided to train Orientate up to the Breeders' Cup Sprint (G1) at Arlington Park on October 26. The Lewises' colt faced a tough field that included 2001 champion three-year-old filly Xtra Heat, who had finished second in the 2001 Breeders' Cup Sprint to Squirtle Squirt, and 2000 Breeders' Cup Sprint winner and champion Kona Gold. Also in the field were Disturbingthepeace, whose six-race win streak included Grade 2 victories in the Triple Bend Breeders' Cup Handicap, Bing Crosby Breeders' Cup Handicap, and Pat O'Brien Handicap, and Bonapaw, who capped a three-race winning streak with a 2¼-length triumph in the Belmont Park's Vosburgh Stakes (G1) on September 21. But the horse whom Orientate had to overhaul in deep stretch was 48.70-to-1 longshot front-runner Thunderello. Orientate won by a half-length and was retired. The Mt. Livermore colt won his final five starts and his final six dirt races, all but one of them a graded stakes, at five different racetracks. His 2002 earnings totaled $1,412,970.—*Bill Heller*

Steeplechase

Some steeplechase championships are decided early in the year, as occurred in 2001 when the brilliant runner Pompeyo (Chi) locked up the title before the season was three months old. The 2002 season followed a more familiar pattern, though, with the title decided in the last major races of the year. Nancy Gerry's Flat Top won the 1998 title with end-of-season victories in the Breeders' Cup Grand National Steeplechase Hurdle Stakes and the Marion duPont Scott Colonial Cup Hurdle Stakes. Four years later, the Alleged gelding used victories in those same two races to claim his second championship after more than two years without a victory.

Flat Top was the American jump sport's predominant runner by year's end, but he reached that pre-eminent position because few older horses could put together consistent seasons as the steeplechase game completed its journey from Camden, South Carolina, in the early spring to Camden again in late fall. The year started with Lord Zada finishing first in the Carolina Cup Hurdle Stakes but being disqualified to third for interfering with Canta Ke Brave, who was placed first, and Al Skywalker. Pinkie Swear won the Atlanta Steeplechase in early April but was badly beaten in his only other start of the year.

Although steeplechasing long has been regarded as an East Coast sport, the Midwest now offers some of the richest purses each spring. The spring season's richest race, Keeneland Race Course's $175,000 Royal Chase for the Sport of Kings Hurdle Stakes, was won by William Pape's veteran It's a Giggle, who subsequently won the A. P. Smithwick Memorial Steeplechase Stakes at Saratoga Race Course but did not finish in the New York Turf Writers Steeplechase Handicap. The Northern Baby gelding succumbed to colic in December. In May, trainer F. Bruce Miller sent out 2000 champion All Gong (GB) for a victory in the Iroquois Hurdle Stakes at Nashville, home course of owner Calvin Houghland.

An emerging star among novices—jumpers in their first seasons of competition—was Michael Moran's McDynamo, a Dynaformer gelding who won the Hard Scuffle Hurdle Stakes at Churchill Downs in May and closed out the year with victories in the Foxbrook Supreme Hurdle Stakes in New Jersey and the U.S. Championship Supreme Hurdle Stakes in Georgia. Another emerging star was Zabenz (NZ), who invaded from Australia and won the New York Turf Writers impressively. He fell in the Breeders' Cup Steeplechase on October 19 and lost all chance for the title.

By then, trainer Janet Elliot had dealt with Flat Top's stall-walking problem—by shipping him directly to his starts without a layover—and the gelding prospered in the fall weather. He made all the pace in the Breeders' Cup Steeplechase, just as he had done four years earlier, and won by three lengths over Tres Touche. Jockey Rob Massey put him on the lead in the Colonial Cup and he won by 6¼ lengths over Tres Touche to lock up his second title.—*Don Clippinger*

Daily Racing Form/NTRA National Handicapping Championship

Steve Wolfson Jr., a Florida high school teacher with a formidable Thoroughbred-industry pedigree, won the fourth annual *Daily Racing Form*/NTRA National Handicapping Championship and the $100,000 first prize at Bally's Casino in Las Vegas on January 18, 2003.

The handicapping champion, then 35, is the grandson of Louis Wolfson, whose Harbor View Farm campaigned 1978 Triple Crown winner Affirmed. His father, Steve Wolfson Sr., has been involved in the Thoroughbred industry as a breeder and owner. His uncle Marty Wolfson is a trainer on the South Florida circuit.

Wolfson, who teaches social studies and coaches cross-country in Port Orange, took the top spot among 213 handicapping championship finalists, including his father, in the two-day event. His total from 30 $2 win and $2 place bets spread over eight tracks was $279.60. More than 45,000 players participated in 81 qualifying tournaments, held at 48 tracks and off-track facilities during 2002.

The winner is presented an Eclipse Award as the champion handicapper during the Eclipse Awards dinner.

Year	Winner	Residence	Winning Total
2003	Steve Wolfson Jr.	Port Orange, FL	$279.60
2002	Herman Miller	Oakland, CA	205.30
2001	Judy Wagner	New Orleans, LA	237.70
2000	Steve Walker	Lincoln, NE	305.40

Richest North American Races of 2002

Race (Grade)	Purse	Value to winner	Track	Dist.	Winner
Breeders' Cup Classic (G1)	$3,664,000	$2,080,000	Arlington Park	1¼	Volponi
Breeders' Cup Turf (G1)	2,216,720	1,258,400	Arlington Park	1½	High Chaparral (Ire)
Kentucky Derby (G1)	2,175,000	1,875,000	Churchill Downs	1¼	War Emblem
Breeders' Cup Distaff (G1)	1,832,000	1,040,000	Arlington Park	1⅛	Azeri
Canadian International S. (Can-G1)	1,500,000	900,000	Woodbine	1½	Ballingarry (Ire)
Breeders' Cup Filly & Mare Turf (G1)	1,172,480	665,600	Arlington Park	1¼	Starine (Fr)
Breeders' Cup Sprint (G1)	1,044,240	592,800	Arlington Park	6f	Orientate
Arlington Million S. (G1)	1,000,000	600,000	Arlington Park	1¼	Beat Hollow (GB)
Atto Mile (Can-G1)	1,000,000	600,000	Woodbine	1	Good Journey
Belmont S. (G1)	1,000,000	600,000	Belmont Park	1½	Sarava
Florida Derby (G1)	1,000,000	600,000	Gulfstream Park	1⅛	Harlan's Holiday
Jockey Club Gold Cup S. (G1)	1,000,000	600,000	Belmont Park	1¼	Evening Attire
Pacific Classic S. (G1)	1,000,000	600,000	Del Mar	1¼	Came Home
Preakness S. (G1)	1,000,000	650,000	Pimlico	1³⁄₁₆	War Emblem
Queen's Plate S.	1,000,000	600,000	Woodbine	1¼	T J's Lucky Moon
Santa Anita H. (G1)	1,000,000	600,000	Santa Anita Park	1¼	Milwaukee Brew
Travers S. (G1)	1,000,000	600,000	Saratoga	1¼	Medaglia d'Oro
Haskell Invitational H. (G1)	990,000	600,000	Monmouth Park	1⅛	War Emblem
Breeders' Cup Juvenile (G1)	980,120	556,400	Arlington Park	1⅛	Vindication
Breeders' Cup Mile (G1)	980,120	556,400	Arlington Park	1	Domedriver (Ire)

Race (Grade)	Purse	Value to winner	Track	Dist.	Winner
Breeders' Cup Juvenile Fillies (G1)	$916,000	$520,000	Arlington Park	1⅛	Storm Flag Flying
Stephen Foster H. (G1)	833,250	516,615	Churchill Downs	1⅛	Street Cry (Ire)
Alabama S. (G1)	750,000	450,000	Saratoga	1¼	Farda Amiga
Beldame S. (G1)	750,000	450,000	Belmont Park	1⅛	Imperial Gesture
Blue Grass S. (G1)	750,000	465,000	Keeneland	1⅛	Harlan's Holiday
E. P. Taylor S. (Can-G1)	750,000	502,650	Woodbine	1¼	Fraulein (GB)
Flower Bowl Invitational H. (G1)	750,000	450,000	Belmont Park	1¼	Kazzia (Ger)
Hollywood Gold Cup S. (G1)	750,000	450,000	Hollywood Park	1¼	Sky Jack
Louisiana Derby (G2)	750,000	450,000	Fair Grounds	1 1/16	Repent
Metropolitan H. (G1)	750,000	450,000	Belmont Park	1	Swept Overboard
Santa Anita Derby (G1)	750,000	450,000	Santa Anita Park	1⅛	Came Home
Turf Classic Invitational S. (G1)	750,000	450,000	Belmont Park	1½	Denon
Whitney H. (G1)	750,000	450,000	Saratoga	1⅛	Left Bank
Wood Memorial S. (G1)	750,000	450,000	Aqueduct	1⅛	Buddha
Beverly D. S. (G1)	700,000	420,000	Arlington Park	1 3/16	Golden Apples (Ire)
Explosive Bid H. (G2)	700,000	420,000	Fair Grounds	1⅛	Sarafan
Delaware H. (G3)	601,200	360,000	Delaware Park	1¼	Summer Colony
Shadwell Keeneland Turf Mile (G1)	600,000	372,000	Keeneland	1	Landseer (GB)
West Virginia Derby (G3)	600,000	360,000	Mountaineer Park	1⅛	Wiseman's Ferry
Kentucky Oaks (G1)	562,100	348,502	Churchill Downs	1⅛	Farda Amiga
Ashland S. (G1)	557,750	345,805	Keeneland	1 1/16	Take Charge Lady
Overbrook Spinster S. (G1)	546,000	338,520	Keeneland	1⅛	Take Charge Lady
WinStar Galaxy S. (G2)	544,500	337,590	Keeneland	1 3/16	Owsley
American Invitational Oaks	500,000	300,000	Hollywood Park	1¼	Megahertz (GB)
Apple Blossom H. (G1)	500,000	300,000	Oaklawn Park	1 1/16	Azeri
Arkansas Derby (G2)	500,000	300,000	Oaklawn Park	1⅛	Private Emblem
Breeders' S.	500,000	300,000	Woodbine	1½	Portcullis
Californian S. (G2)	500,000	300,000	Hollywood Park	1⅛	Milwaukee Brew
Champagne S. (G1)	500,000	300,000	Belmont Park	1 1/16	Toccet
Citation H. (G2)	500,000	300,000	Hollywood Park	1 1/16	Good Journey
Delta Jackpot S.	500,000	300,000	Delta Downs	1	Outta Here
Diana H. (G2)	500,000	300,000	Saratoga	1⅛	Tates Creek
Donn H. (G1)	500,000	300,000	Gulfstream Park	1⅛	Mongoose
Frizette S. (G1)	500,000	300,000	Belmont Park	1 1/16	Storm Flag Flying
Goodwood Breeders' Cup H. (G2)	500,000	300,000	Santa Anita Park	1⅛	Pleasantly Perfect
Hawthorne Gold Cup H. (G2)	500,000	300,000	Hawthorne	1¼	Hail The Chief (GB)
Hollywood Derby (G1)	500,000	300,000	Hollywood Park	1⅛	Johar
Illinois Derby (G2)	500,000	300,000	Sportsman's Park	1⅛	War Emblem
Jim Dandy S. (G2)	500,000	300,000	Saratoga	1⅛	Medaglia d'Oro
Lane's End Spiral S. (G2)	500,000	300,000	Turfway Park	1⅛	Perfect Drift
Lone Star Derby (G3)	500,000	277,500	Lone Star Park	1⅛	Wiseman's Ferry
Man o' War S. (G1)	500,000	300,000	Belmont Park	1⅜	With Anticipation
Massachusetts H. (G2)	500,000	300,000	Suffolk Downs	1⅛	Macho Uno
Matriarch S. (G1)	500,000	300,000	Hollywood Park	1⅛	Dress To Thrill (Ire)
New Orleans H. (G2)	500,000	300,000	Fair Grounds	1⅛	Parade Leader
Oaklawn H. (G1)	500,000	300,000	Oaklawn Park	1⅛	Kudos
Pennsylvania Derby (G3)	500,000	300,000	Philadelphia Park	1⅛	Harlan's Holiday
Prince of Wales S.	500,000	300,000	Fort Erie	1 3/16	Le Cinquieme Essai
Queen Elizabeth II Challenge Cup S. (G1)	500,000	310,000	Keeneland	1⅛	Riskaverse
Suburban H. (G2)	500,000	300,000	Belmont Park	1¼	E Dubai
Super Derby (G2)	500,000	300,000	Louisiana Downs	1⅛	Essence of Dubai
Swaps S. (G2)	500,000	300,000	Hollywood Park	1⅛	Came Home
Sword Dancer Invitational H. (G1)	500,000	300,000	Saratoga	1½	With Anticipation
United Nations H. (G1)	500,000	300,000	Monmouth Park	1⅜	With Anticipation
Virginia Derby	500,000	300,000	Colonial Downs	1¼	Orchard Park
Woodbine Oaks	500,000	300,000	Woodbine	1⅛	Ginger Gold
Woodward S. (G1)	500,000	300,000	Belmont Park	1⅛	Lido Palace (Chi)
Yellow Ribbon S. (G1)	500,000	300,000	Santa Anita Park	1¼	Golden Apples (Ire)
Gamely Breeders' Cup H. (G1)	474,000	300,000	Hollywood Park	1⅛	Astra
Clark H. (G2)	457,200	283,464	Churchill Downs	1⅛	Lido Palace (Chi)
Turf Classic S. (G1)	452,500	280,550	Churchill Downs	1⅛	Beat Hollow (GB)
Walmac Int'l Alcibiades S. (G2)	445,200	276,024	Keeneland	1 1/16	Westerly Breeze
Lane's End Breeders' Futurity (G2)	434,800	269,576	Keeneland	1 1/16	Sky Mesa
Indiana Derby (G3)	414,700	248,820	Hoosier Park	1 1/16	Perfect Drift
Hollywood Futurity (G1)	409,500	243,900	Hollywood Park	1 1/16	Toccet
Shoemaker Breeders' Cup Mile S. (G1)	408,000	240,000	Hollywood Park	1	Ladies Din

2002 Stakes Races

Academy Road S. (1st Div.), Santa Anita Park, March 14, $79,100, 3yo, 1mT, 1:35.49, MOUNTAIN RAGE, Greenhills (GB), National Park (GB) (DQ from 2nd), 7 started.

Academy Road S. (2nd Div.), Santa Anita Park, March 14, $80,100, 3yo, 1mT, 1:35.64, ROYAL GEM, Stormy Forever, Don't Holler, 9 started.

Achievement H. (R), Woodbine, March 31, $164,700, 3yo, Canadian-bred, 6f, 1:10.98, RARE FRIENDS, Wild Whiskey, Shaws Creek, 7 started.

ACK ACK H.-G3, Churchill Downs, Oct. 27, $112,700, 3&up, 7½f, 1:29.39, TWILIGHT ROAD, Mountain General, Binthebest, 9 started.

A. C. Kemp H., The Downs at Albuquerque, Sept. 18, $33,100, 2yo, 7f, 1:25.85, LATENITE TRICK, Ubi's General, Double Intrigue, 10 started.

ACORN S.-G1, Belmont Park, June 7, $250,000, 3yo, f, 1m, 1:34.05, YOU, Willa On the Move, Bella Bellucci, 5 started.

Adena Springs Matchmaker S., Remington Park, Sept. 8, $30,000, 3&up, f&m, 5fT, :58.12, SUPREME DISCOVERY, Darlin Dixie, Idadidit, 6 started.

Adena Springs Matchmaker S., Fort Erie, June 11, $89,600, 3&up, f&m, 5fT, :58.42, AMERICAN IN PARIS, Bubbi Trap, Guysmarlene, 10 started.

Adios H., Yellowstone Downs, Sept. 22, $3,550, 3&up, a7f, 1:26.60, FRUIT RAPPORT, Hollister Slew, Staged Reality, 5 started.

ADIRONDACK S.-G2, Saratoga Race Course, Aug. 12, $150,000, 2yo, f, 6½f, 1:17.75, AWESOME HUMOR, Stellar, Holiday Runner, 6 started.

AEGON TURF SPRINT S.-G3, Churchill Downs, May 3, $121,300, 3&up, 5fT, :57.39, TESTIFY, Texas Glitter, Gone Fishin, 10 started.

AFFECTIONATELY H.-G3, Aqueduct, Jan. 12, $113,400, 3&up, f&m, 1 1/16m, 1:42.58, ZONK, People's Princess, Search Party, 10 started.

AFFIRMED H.-G3, Hollywood Park, June 23, $107,500, 3yo, 1 1/16m, 1:41.99, CAME HOME, Tracemark, Calkins Road, 6 started.

Affirmed S. (R), Calder Race Course, Aug. 31, $125,000, 2yo, progeny of eligible Florida stallions, 7f, 1:24.56, LAWBOOK, Supah Blitz, The Name's Bond, 8 started.

Afleet S. (R), Woodbine, June 22, $106,000, 3yo, Canadian-bred, 6f, 1:10.75, RARE FRIENDS, Akbar, Dillinger, 6 started.

African Prince S. (R), Suffolk Downs, April 15, $30,000, 3yo, Massachusetts-bred, 6f, 1:14.75, JEREMIAH'S JUDGE, Storm Lad, Maximum Reward, 7 started.

Agassiz S. (R), Assiniboia Downs, Sept. 2, $30,000, 3&up, Manitoba-bred, 1m, 1:41.40, SPEEDY TREAT, Gus Again, Certified Coin, 7 started.

A GLEAM H.-G2, Hollywood Park, July 14, $200,000, 3&up, f&m, 7f, 1:22.50, IRGUNS ANGEL, Secret Liaison, Kalookan Queen, 10 started.

A. G. VANDERBILT H.-G2, Saratoga Race Course, Aug. 11, $200,000, 3&up, 6f, 1:09.72, ORIENTATE, Say Florida Sandy, Multiple Choice, 6 started.

Ahwatukee Express S., Turf Paradise, Sept. 29, $30,000, 3yo, f, 6f, 1:10.42, NO TURBULENCE, Supreme Discovery, Aspen Hill, 5 started.

Airline S., Louisiana Downs, July 28, $40,000, 3yo, 6f, 1:10.59, ELECTRODE, Remember the Party, Walk in the Snow, 9 started.

ALABAMA S.-G1, Saratoga Race Course, Aug. 17, $750,000, 3yo, f, 1¼m, 2:04.68, FARDA AMIGA, Allamerican Bertie, You, 6 started.

Alameda County Fillies and Mares H., Pleasanton, July 6, $50,550, 3&up, f&m, 1 1/16m, 1:41.68, DE GODDAUGHTER, Lindsay Jean, Bold Roberta, 5 started.

Alamedan H., Pleasanton, July 7, $51,100, 3&up, 1 1/16m, 1:42.70, HOOVERGETTHEKEYS, Takin It Deep, Boss Ego, 10 started.

Albany H., Golden Gate Fields, Nov. 9, $63,650, 3&up, 6f, 1:09.42, HALO CAT, San Nicolas, Radar Contact, 8 started.

Albany H. (R), Saratoga Race Course, Aug. 21, $181,284, 3yo, New York-bred, 1⅛m, 1:52.45, PRIVATE EMBLEM, Trial Prep, No Parole, 6 started.

Alberta-Bred S. (R), Lethbridge, Sept. 15, $9,050, 3&up, f&m, Alberta-bred, a6f, 1:10.40, FIGHTING SONG, Ragtime Miss, A Tempting Light, 7 started.

Alberta-Bred S. (R), Lethbridge, Sept. 15, $9,200, 3&up, Alberta-bred, a6f, 1:11, ARCTIC HORIZON, Native Gambler, Three Johns, 8 started.

Alberta-Bred S. (R), Lethbridge, Sept. 15, $9,050, 3yo, Alberta-bred, a6f, 1:10.60, IRISH INTRIGUE, Arnchew Gorgeous, Tyrus Creek, 7 started.

Alberta Breeders' H. (R), Northlands Park, Sept. 21, $50,000, 3&up, Alberta-bred, 1 1/16m, 1:45, TURBO CHARGER, Miki Bleu Eyes, Captain Creek, 7 started.

ALBERTA DERBY (Can-G3), Stampede Park, June 15, $100,000, 3yo, 1 1/16m, 1:46.20, LORD SHOGUN, Regal Rebel, Silent Shoes, 11 started.

Alberta Oaks (R), Northlands Park, Sept. 21, $40,000, 3yo, f, Alberta-bred, 1m, 1:39.20, CODE'S DECREE, S. L. Charmer, Slewpy Time, 7 started.

Alberta Premier's Futurity (R), Northlands Park, Sept. 21, $40,000, 2yo, Alberta-bred, 1m, 1:40.40, JIFFYJIMMYGEE, Bet the Breeze, Katahaula Myst, 6 started.

Albuquerque Derby, The Downs at Albuquerque, Sept. 15, $31,600, 3yo, 1 1/16m, 1:42.99, SNEAKER MIKE, Nino Alegre, Stormy Forever, 4 started.

Albuquerque Derby, The Downs at Albuquerque, June 17, $42,100, 3yo, 1 1/16m, 1:45.29, STORMY FOREVER, Nino Alegre, Shilukwa, 7 started.

Alex M. Robb H. (R), Aqueduct, Dec. 29, $85,500, 3&up, New York-bred, 1 1/16m, 1:42.92, TOM'S THUNDER, John Paul Too, Mount Intrepid, 10 started.

Algoma S. (R), Woodbine, Sept. 2, $104,450, 3&up, f&m, Canadian-bred, 1 1/16m, 1:45.14, SMALL PROMISES, Mulrainy, Night Edition, 6 started.

ALL ALONG BREEDERS' CUP S.-G3, Colonial Downs, July 13, $144,500, 3&up, f&m, 1⅛mT, 1:50.76, SECRET RIVER, Golden Corona, Cayman Sunset (Ire), 6 started.

ALL AMERICAN H.-G3, Bay Meadows, June 8, $150,000, 3&up, 1 1/16m, 1:42.31, PALMEIRO, Moonlight Meeting, Prodigious, 9 started.

All Brandy S. (R), Pimlico, June 8, $75,000, 3&up, f&m, Maryland-bred, 1⅛mT, 1:50.30, SNEAKS, Take It Off, Cruise Along, 11 started.

Allen Bogan Memorial S. (R), Lone Star Park, June 29, $100,000, 3&up, f&m, Texas-bred, 1m, 1:39.20, COASTALOTA, Miss Photogenic, Secret Brick, 11 started.

Allen E. Paulson H. (R), Gulfstream Park, Feb. 24, $75,000, 3&up, f&m, progeny of stallion seasons donated to the Georgia Thoroughbred Owners and Breeders stallion season auction, a1m 70y, 1:42.19, DE BERTIE, Bay Street Gal, Binalegend, 6 started.

Alliance H., Louisiana Downs, Oct. 26, $30,000, 3&up, 1 1/16mT, 1:45.63, REBRIDLED, Candid Glen, Paco Loco, 7 started.

All Sold Out S. (R), Fairmount Park, Oct. 1, $36,000, 2yo, f, Illinois-bred, 6f, 1:13.60, CASH THE FLASH, Cashmere Miss, She's Fantastic, 10 started.

Alma North S. (R), Timonium, Aug. 31, $40,000, 3&up, f&m, Maryland-bred, 1 1/16m, 1:45.58, SHINY SHEET, Amber Comet, Steppedoutofadream, 6 started.

Al Swihart Memorial H., Fonner Park, May 4, $25,000, 3&up, f&m, 6½f, 1:18, GIN N GINGER, Burning Memories, Supreme Discovery, 8 started.

Althea S., Oaklawn Park, April 13, $50,000, 3yo, f, 1m, 1:37.71, SWEET SIXTEEN, Sarah Jade, Bedanken, 9 started.

Alydar S., Hollywood Park, May 23, $77,200, 3yo, 1⅛m, 1:50.37, LIKE A HERO, World Light, Wheels N Wings, 5 started.

Alysheba Breeders' Cup S., Lone Star Park, July 3, $100,000, 3yo, 7f, 1:23.06, PREMEDITATION, Padlock, De Real Deal, 8 started.

Alysheba S., The Meadowlands, Sept. 13, $50,000, 3&up, 1 1/16m, 1:43.25, BURNING ROMA, Pickupspeed, Beknown to Me, 5 started.

Alyssa H. (R), Beulah Park, May 4, $30,000, 3&up, f&m, starters at Beulah Park in 2002, 6f, 1:11.15, PUNY, Lil Bit of Country, Star On Tour, 8 started.

Alywow S., Woodbine, June 1, $108,800, 3yo, f, 6½fT, 1:16.42, LUSH SOLDIER, Amy's Falcon, Seventh Choice, 11 started.

Amadevil H. (R), Columbus, Aug. 17, $20,000, 3&up, Nebraska-bred, 6f, 1:11.20, IRISH FLYER, High Dice, Doug's Shadow, 8 started.

Ambassador of Luck H. (R), Philadelphia Park, Oct. 5, $50,000, 3&up, f&m, Pennsylvania-bred, 7f, 1:24.06, BETTY'S HAT, Golden Lake, Midnite Madness, 7 started.

Amelia Peabody S. (R), Suffolk Downs, Nov. 16, $30,000, 2yo, f, Massachusetts-bred, 6f, 1:14.12, JILL'S LAYUP, Glory Be Good, For Love of Matt, 6 started.

Americana H., Calder Race Course, July 4, $100,000, 3&up, 1⅛mT, 1:52.26, DANCING GUY, Sir Bear, Wertz, 7 started.

American Beauty S., Oaklawn Park, Feb. 9, $50,000, 4&up, f&m, 6f, 1:10.95, SPANISH GLITTER, Southern Tour, Sweet and Firm, 8 started.

AMERICAN DERBY-G2, Arlington Park, July 21, $225,000, 3yo, 1 3/16mT, 1:57.11, MANANAN MCLIR, Jazz Beat (Ire), Extra Check, 8 started.

AMERICAN H.-G2, Hollywood Park, July 4, $150,000, 3&up, 1⅛mT,

1:46.82, THE TIN MAN, Devine Wind, Kappa King, 7 started.
American Invitational Oaks, Hollywood Park, July 6, $500,000, 3yo, f, 1¼mT, 2:00.46, MEGAHERTZ (GB), Dublino, Alozaina (Ire), 14 started.
Amerilad S., Calder Race Course, Nov. 23, $40,110, 3yo, 1⅟₁₆mT, 1:42.69, PAH, Military Man, Class of Seventy, 12 started.
AMSTERDAM S.-G2, Saratoga Race Course, Aug. 3, $150,000, 3yo, 6f, 1:09.58, LISTEN HERE, Boston Common, Bold Truth, 8 started.
Anark Millwrighting/Mechanical S., Grand Prairie, July 28, $2,600, 3&up, 5½f, 1:06.40, STORM DEVIL, Aran Island, Candi Story, 6 started.
ANCIENT TITLE BREEDERS' CUP H.-G1, Santa Anita Park, Oct. 5, $207,875, 3&up, 6f, 1:08.26, KALOOKAN QUEEN, Crafty C. T, Mellow Fellow, 6 started.
Anderson Fowler S., Monmouth Park, July 20, $50,000, 3yo, 5fT, :55.98, LUNAR BOUNTY, B K Dodger, Numbers Man, 10 started.
Angenora S. (R), Thistledown, April 20, $40,000, 3&up, f&m, Ohio-bred, 6f, 1:10.26, EASTER BUTTER, Honey Bee Mine, Eye Slew the City, 11 started.
Angie C. S., Emerald Downs, July 7, $35,000, 2yo, f, 6f, 1:10.60, CALLDARA, Stage Plan, Miss Mariah, 10 started.
Angi Go S. (R), Les Bois Park, July 20, $12,225, 3yo, f, Idaho-bred, 7f, 1:26.42, TROPHY EDITION TOO, Golo, Proud Mary Turnen, 6 started.
Anna M. Fischer Debutante S., Ellis Park, Aug. 17, $100,000, 2yo, f, 7f, 1:24.24, RUBY'S RECEPTION, Jodys Deelite, Santa Fe Strip, 7 started.
Ann Arbor S. (R), Great Lakes Downs, Aug. 23, $45,000, 3yo, f, Michigan-bred, 1m, 1:41.96, SWEETWATER PROMISE, Part Magic, Bad Thing, 6 started.
ANNE ARUNDEL S.-G3, Laurel Park, Dec. 14, $100,000, 3yo, f, 1⅛m, 1:50.84, MARTHA'S MUSIC, Pass the Virtue, Shop Till You Drop, 11 started.
Annie Oakley H. (R), Thistledown, June 22, $50,000, 3yo, f, Ohio-bred, 1⅟₁₆m, 1:44.82, CRYPTO'S TWINJET, Joanies Bella, Kind of Fun, 10 started.
Ann Owens Distaff H. (R), Turf Paradise, April 27, $30,000, 3&up, f&m, Arizona-bred, 6f, 1:08.65, (DH) NIKKI'S ANGEL, (DH) KNOLL LAKE, Drag Time Gal, 6 started.
Anoakia S., Santa Anita Park, Oct. 20, $81,600, 2yo, f, 6f, 1:09.97, PUXA SACO, Forest Native, Ionia, 7 started.
Answer Do S. (R), Hollywood Park, July 13, $82,173, 3&up, California-bred, 5½fT, 1:02.22, FULL MOON MADNESS, McCordnskuba, Flying Rudolph, 4 started.
Anthony Fair Derby, Anthony Downs, July 20, $4,480, 3yo, 7f, 1:32.94, MILD EXPENSE, Heavenly Ruler, A. D.'s Dream, 4 started.
Anthony Fair H., Anthony Downs, July 21, $4,000, 3&up, a6½f, 1:22.06, AMEGO MEL, Honour and Fame, Hey Billy, 6 started.
Anthony Thoroughbred Futurity, Anthony Downs, July 21, $10,150, 2yo, 5f, 1:02.72, LAURA'S MOMENT, Stutz Dancer, Polegro, 6 started.
Anthony "Tony" DeSpirito S., Suffolk Downs, Nov. 9, $30,000, 2yo, 6f, 1:13.36, MR. MESO, Wellfleet, Comp, 7 started.
Apache County Thoroughbred Maiden S., Apache County Fair, Sept. 22, $3,112, 3&up, 6f, 1:14.40, VALDOSTANA, Patricio, Latin Elegance, 4 started.
Apelia S. (R), Woodbine, June 15, $105,000, 3yo, f, Canadian-bred, 6f, 1:10.79, MOUNTAIN ORCHID, Spanish Decree, Brass in Pocket, 5 started.
Aphrodite S., Belmont Park, July 20, $39,650, 3&up, f&m, a1½mT, 2:31.02, MARANI (GB), Frosty Welcome, Pasithea (Ire), 8 started.
A.P. Indy S., Keeneland, Oct. 5, $85,650, 3&up, f&m, 5½fT, 1:03.47, DIXIE TACTICS, Presumed Innocent, Fuse It, 10 started.
Appalachian S., Keeneland, April 19, $112,100, 3yo, f, 1mT, 1:36.62, STYLELISTICK, Lush Soldier, August Storm, 9 started.
APPLE BLOSSOM H.-G1, Oaklawn Park, April 6, $500,000, 4&up, f&m, 1⅟₁₆m, 1:42.75, AZERI, Affluent, Miss Linda (Arg), 5 started.
APPLETON H.-G2, Gulfstream Park, Jan. 5, $150,000, 3&up, 1mT, 1:39.41, PISCES, North East Bound, Capsized, 10 started.
Appleton S., Far Hills, Oct. 19, $48,500, 4&up, a2⅛mT, 4:29.09, AL SKYWALKER, Big Brush, Shamrock Isle, 6 started.
Appointment S., Delaware Park, June 3, $59,100, 3&up, 6f, 1:10.48, RUSTY SPUR, Confucius Say, Shore Breeze, 6 started.
Aprisa H., Fairplex Park, Sept. 18, $45,500, 3&up, 6f, 1:09.67, F J'S PACE, Mistakenly Special, Hyder, 4 started.
A. P. Smithwick Memorial Steeplechase H., Saratoga Race Course, Aug. 8, $79,950, 4&up, a2⅟₁₆mT, 3:37.56, IT'S A GIGGLE, Tres Touche, Indispensable, 6 started.
AQUEDUCT H.-G3, Aqueduct, Jan. 19, $109,200, 3&up, 1⅟₁₆m, 1:42.69, EVENING ATTIRE, Ground Storm, Tempest Fugit, 7 started.
Arapahoe Park H., Arapahoe Park, Sept. 1, $75,000, 3&up, 1⅛m, 1:49, MAYSVILLE SLEW, Personal Beau, Moro Grande, 12 started.
Arapahoe Park Sprint S., Arapahoe Park, June 16, $30,000, 3&up, 6f, 1:09, UNCLE PUNK, Don't Walk At Nite, Tangarae Tango, 7 started.
ARCADIA H.-G2, Santa Anita Park, April 6, $150,000, 4&up, 1⅛mT, 1:47.16, SEINNE (Chi), Irish Prize, Kerrygold (Fr), 9 started.
Arcadia S. (R), Louisiana Downs, July 6, $44,000, 3yo, Louisiana-bred, 6f, 1:10.92, WALK IN THE SNOW, Hail to Bag, Won Better, 6 started.
Arctic Queen H. (R), Finger Lakes, Aug. 10, $35,000, 3&up, f&m, New York-bred, 6f, 1:11.13, RUNAWAY TIGER, Belongs to Mony, Here's Ya Mama, 7 started.
ARISTIDES H.-G3, Churchill Downs, June 29, $107,500, 3&up, 6½f, 1:14.41, ORIENTATE, Binthebest, No Armistice, 5 started.
Arizona Breeders' Derby (R), Turf Paradise, April 27, $49,142, 3yo, Arizona-bred, 1⅟₁₆m, 1:44.79, ROAD GRADER, Willcox, Coach Endres, 8 started.
Arizona Breeders' Futurity (R), Turf Paradise, Nov. 30, $44,583, 2yo, c&g, Arizona-bred, 6f, 1:13.28, MOODY SLEW, Count Remains, Rockford, 12 started.
Arizona Breeders' Futurity (R), Turf Paradise, Nov. 30, $43,654, 2yo, f, Arizona-bred, 6f, 1:15.42, DESERT CRANK, First Snowbound, Lakesville, 12 started.
Arizona Juvenile S., Turf Paradise, Dec. 21, $50,000, 2yo, 6½f, 1:17.45, SIBERLAND, Jimmy O, Deputy Doc, 8 started.
Arizona Oaks, Turf Paradise, Feb. 2, $75,000, 3yo, f, 1⅟₁₆m, 1:43.31, BELLA CASH, Calce Clunes, Lady Continental, 6 started.
Arizona Stallion S. (R), Turf Paradise, May 19, $39,279, 3yo, progeny of stallions standing in Arizona, 7½fT, 1:30.26, WILLCOX, Coach Endres, Road Grader, 7 started.
ARKANSAS DERBY-G2, Oaklawn Park, April 13, $500,000, 3yo, 1⅛m, 1:52.20, PRIVATE EMBLEM, Wild Horses, (DH) Windward Passage, (DH) Bay Monster, 11 started.
Ark-La-Tex H., Louisiana Downs, Aug. 3, $50,000, 3&up, 1⅟₁₆m, 1:44.70, PRINCE IROQUOIS, Rebridled, Big Numbers, 7 started.
Arlene Anderson Memorial S., Turf Paradise, Nov. 29, $22,900, 2yo, f, 6½f, 1:18.14, HULA KAT, Stage Plan, Top Penny, 8 started.
ARLINGTON CLASSIC S.-G2, Arlington Park, June 29, $175,000, 3yo, 1⅟₁₆mT, 1:41.95, MR. MELLON, Doc Holiday (Ire), Seainsky, 9 started.
ARLINGTON H.-G3, Arlington Park, July 27, $225,000, 3&up, 1¼mT, 2:03.13, FALCON FLIGHT (Fr), Kappa King, Gretchen's Star, 10 started.
ARLINGTON MATRON H.-G3, Arlington Park, Sept. 2, $150,000, 3&up, f&m, 1⅛m, 1:50.78, LAKENHEATH, With Ability, Your Out, 5 started.
ARLINGTON MILLION S.-G1, Arlington Park, Aug. 17, $1,000,000, 3&up, 1¼mT, 2:02.94, BEAT HOLLOW (GB), Sarafan, Forbidden Apple, 9 started.
Arlington Sprint H., Arlington Park, Aug. 24, $100,000, 3&up, 6f, 1:09.13, BONAPAW, Secret Romeo, Tic N Tin, 5 started.
ARLINGTON-WASHINGTON FUTURITY-G3, Arlington Park, Sept. 28, $150,000, 2yo, 1m, 1:37.52, MOST FEARED, Anasheed, Unleash the Power, 10 started.
ARLINGTON-WASHINGTON LASSIE S.-G3, Arlington Park, Sept. 28, $100,000, 2yo, f, 1m, 1:37.82, MOONLIGHT SONATA, Parting, Souris, 13 started.
Artax H., Gulfstream Park, April 6, $100,000, 3&up, 7f, 1:22.72, HE'S A KNOCKOUT, Sea of Tranquility, Fappie's Notebook, 6 started.
Ascot Graduation Breeders' Cup H., Hastings Park Racecourse, Oct. 27, $139,827, 2yo, 1⅟₁₆m, 1:45.49, ILLUSIVE FORCE, Weepinbell, Taiaslew, 9 started.
ASCOT H.-G3, Bay Meadows, May 12, $100,000, 3yo, 1⅟₁₆mT, 1:41.78, VAN ROUGE, Doc Holiday (Ire), Hecandigit, 7 started.
ASHLAND S.-G1, Keeneland, April 6, $557,750, 3yo, f, 1⅟₁₆m, 1:43.29, TAKE CHARGE LADY, Take the Cake, Belterra, 8 started.
Ashley T. Cole H. (R), Belmont Park, Sept. 21, $83,825, 3&up, New York-bred, 1⅛mT, 1:49.13, I'M ALL YOURS, Haggs Castle, Celtic Sky, 9 started.
Aspen Cup H., Ruidoso Downs, June 22, $22,100, 3yo, f, 6f, 1:11.60, ESPEEDYTOO, Miss Hadley, Slim's Secret, 10 started.
Aspen H. (R), Arapahoe Park, July 20, $30,000, 3&up, Colorado-bred, 6f, 1:09.80, SIR DEBONAIRE, Tangarae Tango, Package, 6 started.
Aspidistra H., Calder Race Course, July 27, $75,000, 3&up, f&m, 1mT, 1:37, BANDERIA (Arg), Bay Street Gal, Bail Money, 9 started.
Aspirant S. (R), Finger Lakes, Aug. 17, $73,938, 2yo, New York-bred, 6f, 1:12.66, DIXIE COUNTRY, Hill Top Man, Tomorrows Banquet, 9 started.

Assault S. (R), Lone Star Park, June 29, $125,000, 3&up, Texas-bred, 1⅟₁₆m, 1:44.97, DESERT DARBY, Logans Leo, Lights On Broadway, 7 started.
Assiniboia Oaks, Assiniboia Downs, Sept. 8, $30,000, 3yo, f, 1⅟₁₆m, 1:45.60, BEAUSOX, Miss Noire, Top Stage Dancer, 5 started.
ASTARITA S.-G2, Belmont Park, Oct. 13, $150,000, 2yo, f, 6½f, 1:17.76, HUMOROUS LADY, Fast Cookie, Chimichurri, 7 started.
Astoria S., Belmont Park, June 30, $109,700, 2yo, f, 5½f, 1:03.99, MIKE'S WILDCAT, Beautiful Treasure, Collymore Hall, 8 started.
ATBA Fall Sales S. (R), Turf Paradise, Oct. 19, $56,970, 2yo, c&g, consigned to the 2001 ATBA sale, 6f, 1:09.27, JOHNNY IS BAD, Icy Tobin, West Saratoga, 11 started.
ATBA Fall Sales S. (R), Turf Paradise, Oct. 19, $64,202, 2yo, f, consigned to the 2001 ATBA sale, 6f, 1:10.86, FIRST SNOWBOUND, Slam Inn, Buenobambino, 11 started.
ATBA Spring Sales S. (R), Turf Paradise, May 19, $53,361, 2yo, consigned to the 2001 ATBA Sales, 5f, :58.30, SNOWBOUND BOB, Johnny Is Bad, Count Remains, 10 started.
Atchison Topeka and Santa Fe H., The Woodlands, Oct. 19, $20,000, 3&up, 6f, 1:12.20, TIC N TIN, Airiasaffair, Diamonice, 8 started.
ATHENIA H.-G3, Aqueduct, Nov. 9, $116,700, 3&up, f&m, 1⅟₁₆mT, 1:44.90, BABAE (Chi), Strawberry Blonde (Ire), Silver Rail, 12 started.
Atlanta Cup Hurdle S., Atlanta, April 13, $72,750, 4&up, a2⅜mT, 4:53.80, PINKIE SWEAR, Teb's Bend, Tres Touche, 7 started.
ATTO MILE (Can-G1), Woodbine, Sept. 8, $1,000,000, 3&up, a1mT, 1:33.27, GOOD JOURNEY, Chopinina, Nuclear Debate, 13 started.
Auburn S., Emerald Downs, May 4, $35,000, 3yo, c&g, 6f, 1:08.80, BOLD RANGER, Colony Lane, Melcapwalker, 7 started.
Audubon Oaks, Ellis Park, Aug. 3, $60,000, 3yo, f, 1mT, 1:36.19, CAT'S GLOW, Lotta Rhythm, Join, 9 started.
Auld Lang Syne S., Calder Race Course, Dec. 31, $38,955, 3yo, f, 6½f, 1:18.43, SLEWS FINAL ANSWER, Wish It Were, Tchula Miss, 8 started.
Au Revoir H., Les Bois Park, Aug. 11, $5,529, 3&up, 1¼m, 2:07.75, NORTHERN RICKY, Can Star, Midnight Demon, 4 started.
Au Revoir H., Sun Downs, May 5, $3,100, 3&up, 7f, 1:27.40, NORTHERN RICKY, Tuxedo Jr., Stregawood, 8 started.
Au Revoir S., Delta Downs, April 7, $23,280, 4&up, 1m, 1:37.82, SAMLOT, Two Punch Sonny, Sunup Sundown, 8 started.
Autotote Derby, Lethbridge, Oct. 27, $11,200, 3yo, 1⅟₁₆m, 1:47.40, CHIEF JOSEPH, Late Nite Cat, Posidonas, 6 started.
Autumn Classic S. (R), Remington Park, Dec. 15, $33,350, 3&up, Oklahoma-bred, 6f, 1:09.84, MEDIUM RARE, Coldiron Slew, Trickmeister, 6 started.
Autumn Leaves H., Mountaineer Park, Oct. 1, $77,300, 3&up, f&m, 1⅟₁₆m, 1:47.61, SEVEN FOUR SEVEN, Countess Marq, Totally Crafty, 6 started.
Autumn Leaves H., Bay Meadows, Oct. 6, $60,350, 3&up, f&m, 1m, 1:35.80, DE GODDAUGHTER, Aunt Sophie, Bullish Miss, 6 started.
Aventura S., Gulfstream Park, April 6, $250,000, 3yo, 1⅟₁₆m, 1:44.11, MARASCA, Equality, Legislator, 9 started.
AZALEA BREEDERS' CUP S.-G3, Calder Race Course, July 13, $196,750, 3yo, f, 6f, 1:10.86, BOLD WORLD, Willa On the Move, Tchula Miss, 10 started.
Aztec Oaks (R), SunRay Park, Nov. 18, $67,300, 3yo, f, New Mexico-bred, 6½f, 1:17.60, LORD IMAJONES, Espeedytoo, Gray Ryder, 7 started.
Baby Doe H., Arapahoe Park, July 14, $30,000, 3&up, f&m, 7f, 1:23.80, ORANGE GLOW, Molly Or Me, Just React, 12 started.
Bachman S., Fonner Park, Feb. 23, $15,725, 3yo, 4f, TONIGHT RAINBOW, Partager Valay, Vibod, 9 started.
Backstretch Chapel S. (R), Emerald Downs, Sept. 14, $25,000, 3yo, c&g, Washington-bred non-winners of $19,000 since April 19, 2002, 6½f, 1:15.20, SLEW OF THE NIGHT, Slew's Carousel, Aladin Sane, 5 started.
BALDWIN S.-G3, Santa Anita Park, Feb. 24, $114,400, 3yo, a6½fT, 1:13.30, SHUFFLING KID (GB), Red Briar (Ire), Dark Sorcerer (GB), 12 started.
Ballade S. (R), Woodbine, June 12, $127,125, 3&up, f&m, progeny of eligible Ontario stallions, 6f, 1:11.16, MYSTERIOUS AFFAIR, Ruby Park, Moonlight Affair, 5 started.
BALLERINA BREEDERS' CUP S. (Can-G3), Hastings Park Racecourse, Oct. 6, $143,506, 3&up, f&m, 1⅛m, 1:52.87, GRACE FOR YOU, Full Scream Ahead, Castle Mountain, 12 started.
BALLERINA H.-G1, Saratoga Race Course, Aug. 25, $250,000, 3&up, f&m, 7f, 1:22.26, SHINE AGAIN, Raging Fever, Mandy's Gold, 7 started.
Ballston Spa Breeders' Cup H., Saratoga Race Course, Aug. 24, $191,800, 3&up, f&m, 1⅛m, 1:52.29, SURYA, Shooting Party, Solvig, 3 started.
BALTIMORE BREEDERS' CUP H.-G3, Pimlico, June 15, $97,000, 3&up, 1⅛m, 1:49.65, GRUNDLEFOOT, Lyracist, Private Ryan, 5 started.
Bam's Penny S. (R), Bay Meadows, Nov. 2, $80,000, 2yo, f, California-bred, 6f, 1:11.20, GLOBAL FINANCE, Market Garden, Joyously, 10 started.
Bangles and Beads S., Fairplex Park, Sept. 24, $48,000, 3&up, f&m, 6½f, 1:17.61, POSADAS, Absolutism, Sister Patricia (Aus), 5 started.
Banshee Breeze S., Gulfstream Park, April 5, $75,000, 3&up, f&m, 1⅟₁₆m, 1:43.56, MYSTIC LADY, Happily Unbridled, Jostle, 6 started.
Bara Lass S. (R), Sam Houston Race Park, Nov. 16, $50,000, 2yo, f, Texas-bred, 7f, 1:25.17, HANNAH'S ROYALROCK, Lady Mallory, Hadif's Allstar, 11 started.
BARBARA FRITCHIE H.-G2, Laurel Park, Feb. 16, $200,000, 3&up, f&m, 7f, 1:22.70, XTRA HEAT, Prized Stamp, Kimbralata, 8 started.
Barbara Shinpoch S., Emerald Downs, Aug. 24, $75,000, 2yo, f, 1m, 1:36.80, CALLDARA, Valour Road, Bisbee's Prospect, 7 started.
Barksdale H., Louisiana Downs, Sept. 2, $50,000, 3&up, 1⅟₁₆mT, 1:41.69, REBRIDLED, Big Hubie, Big Numbers, 7 started.
Barona Cup S. (R), Del Mar, Aug. 22, $73,026, 3&up, non-winners of $3,000 twice other than maiden, claiming, or starter or non-winners of three races or for a claiming price of $62,500, 1⅜mT, 2:13.80, IRISH MINSTREL, Turkish Prize, Reef Diver (GB), 5 started.
Barretts Debutante S. (R), Fairplex Park, Sept. 21, $102,600, 2yo, f, sold by Barretts Equine Sales Ltd., 6½f, 1:18.28, LAST KISS, Sky's Snow, Ionia, 10 started.
Barretts Juvenile S. (R), Fairplex Park, Sept. 22, $90,665, 2yo, c&g, sold by Barretts Equine Sales Ltd., 6½f, 1:17.32, TALIANO, Elan, Charmer Baron, 5 started.
BASHFORD MANOR S.-G3, Churchill Downs, July 7, $136,250, 2yo, 6f, 1:09.68, LONE STAR SKY, Posse, Cooper Crossing, 7 started.
Bassinet S., River Downs, Aug. 31, $100,000, 2yo, f, 6f, 1:11.40, FABULOUS BRUSH, Moonlight Sonata, Only Heaven Knows, 9 started.
Battlefield S., Monmouth Park, Aug. 4, $65,000, 3&up, 1⅛mT, 1:50.66, AUTONOMY (Ire), Revved Up, Spruce Run, 9 started.
Battle of the Alamo S., Retama Park, Aug. 24, $30,000, 3yo, 7f, 1:24.41, PADLOCK, Front Nine, Son of a Lue, 5 started.
Battler Star H. (R), Fair Grounds, March 10, $75,000, 3yo, f, Louisiana-bred, 6f, 1:10.64, YOU'LLBEINMYHEART, C J's Star, Sunny Scarlett, 6 started.
Baxter S., Fonner Park, March 16, $16,330, 3yo, 6½f, 1:19.80, TONIGHT RAINBOW, Strawberry Kid, Dazzling J. R., 10 started.
BAYAKOA H.-G2, Hollywood Park, Dec. 15, $150,000, 3&up, f&m, 1⅟₁₆m, 1:41.74, STARRER, Cee's Elegance, Angel Gift, 6 started.
Bayakoa S., Oaklawn Park, April 5, $75,000, 4&up, f&m, 1⅟₁₆m, 1:44.21, DUE TO WIN, Red n'Gold, Caressing, 8 started.
BAY MEADOWS BREEDERS' CUP H.-G3, Bay Meadows, Sept. 21, $200,000, 3&up, 1⅛mT, 1:48.95, DAVID COPPERFIELD, Ninebanks, Little Ghazi, 5 started.
BAY MEADOWS BREEDERS' CUP SPRINT H.-G3, Bay Meadows, May 11, $198,750, 3&up, 6f, 1:08.35, MELLOW FELLOW, Explicit, Swept Overboard, 6 started.
BAY MEADOWS DERBY-G3, Bay Meadows, Nov. 3, $100,000, 3yo, a1⅛mT, 1:48.38, ROYAL GEM, Aly Bubba, Century City (Ire), 8 started.
Bay Meadows Oaks, Bay Meadows, May 26, $55,350, 3yo, f, 1⅟₁₆mT, 1:43.11, ETNORIAS, Doc's Lil' Angel, Lost At Sea, 5 started.
Bayou Breeders' Cup H., Fair Grounds, March 2, $144,500, 4&up, f&m, a1⅛mT, 1:50.67, KATY KAT, Pretty Gale, Temis (Chi), 6 started.
Bayou City S., Sam Houston Race Park, Jan. 26, $30,000, 3yo, f, 6f, 1:11.66, TRULY SUNLIT, French Lass, Sly Kona, 9 started.
Bayouland Sales S. (R), Evangeline Downs, Aug. 3, $35,000, 2yo, sold at a Louisiana Thoroughbred Breeders sale, 5f, 59.80, LEGS O'NEAL, Lamarche's Oro, Mr. King Rex, 11 started.
BAY SHORE S.-G3, Aqueduct, April 13, $150,000, 3yo, 7f, 1:22.21, ROMAN DANCER, Warners, Monthir, 10 started.
B Cup S., Lethbridge, Oct. 12, $8,750, 3yo, f, a6f, 1:12, IRISH INTRIGUE, March Snowflake, I Came to Play, 4 started.
B Cup S., Lethbridge, Oct. 12, $8,750, 2yo, 5½f, 1:11, FLYING LADY CUE, Thumpers Gold, Game Princess, 5 started.
B Cup S., Lethbridge, Oct. 12, $8,900, 3yo, c&g, a6f, 1:11.60, (DH) TYRUS CREEK, (DH) J. J. SUN SHINE, Faiths Hope, Ma's Last Fight, 4 started.
B Cup S., Lethbridge, Oct. 12, $9,050, 3&up, 7f, 1:25.60, MR. I R S, Polish Poppa, Last One Standing, 7 started.
B Cup S., Lethbridge, Oct. 12, $9,050, 3&up, f&m, 7f, 1:26, A TEMPTING LIGHT, Nindawayma, Royal Shyann, 7 started.
B Cup S., Lethbridge, Oct. 12, $11,200, 3&up, 1⅛m, 1:55.80, RUN

WITH WINDS, High Powered Mack, Sentosa, 8 started.

B Cup S., Lethbridge, Oct. 12, $9,050, 3&up, f&m, 5½f, 1:09, ROMAN REALITY, Glowbulette, Alibi Expert, 7 started.

B Cup S., Lethbridge, Oct. 12, $8,750, 3&up, 5½f, 1:07.40, SEATTLE CUE, Wise Dancer, Stag, 5 started.

Beacon Hill S. (R), Suffolk Downs, May 26, $30,000, 3yo, Massachusetts-bred, 1mT, 1:42.92, STYLISH SULTAN, Little Time, (DH) Maximum Reward, (DH) Miss Chieftain, 6 started.

Beau Brummel S., Fairplex Park, Sept. 17, $49,500, 2yo, c&g, 6½f, 1:16.85, JIMMY O, Hell Cat, Spensive, 8 started.

Beaufort S. (R), Northlands Park, Sept. 21, $40,000, 3yo, Alberta-bred, 1¹⁄₁₆m, 1:45.80, GO GO TOMMY JOE, Cat in a Bag, Crescent Remark, 10 started.

BEAUGAY H.-G3, Aqueduct, May 5, $113,200, 3&up, f&m, 1¹⁄₁₆mT, 1:43.10, VOODOO DANCER, Golden Corona, Babae (Chi), 10 started.

Beaulieu of America Novice Hurdle S., Atlanta, April 13, $50,000, 4&up, a2mT, 3:46, NAJJM, Mr. Fater, Ethical Actions, 7 started.

Beautiful Day H., Delaware Park, July 8, $60,400, 3&up, f&m, 1⅛mT, 1:49.15, SHAG, High Lady, Battenkill, 7 started.

Beaver State S., Portland Meadows, Jan. 20, $8,550, 3yo, 5½f, 1:07.25, FIT TO BET, Brass Halo, Ransome Road, 8 started.

BED O' ROSES BREEDERS' CUP H.-G3, Aqueduct, April 20, $158,300, 3&up, f&m, 1m, 1:34.96, RAGING FEVER, Atelier, Shiny Band, 6 started.

BELDAME S.-G1, Belmont Park, Oct. 5, $750,000, 3&up, f&m, 1⅛m, 1:50.63, IMPERIAL GESTURE, Mandy's Gold, Summer Colony, 7 started.

Belle Geste S. (R), Woodbine, Aug. 24, $107,000, 3&up, f&m, Canadian-bred, 1⅛mT, 1:47.27, NOBLE STRIKE, Soundtrack, Ariel's Melody, 7 started.

Belle Mahone S., Woodbine, Aug. 3, $105,000, 3&up, f&m, 1¹⁄₁₆m, 1:45.51, EXTEND, Catch the Ring, Ma Kitty, 5 started.

Belle Roberts H., Emerald Downs, Sept. 8, $60,000, 3&up, f&m, 1⅛m, 1:49.20, TOP BRACKET, Graceful Cat, Latter Day Paula, 5 started.

BELMONT BREEDERS' CUP H.-G2, Belmont Park, Sept. 14, $208,600, 3&up, 1⅛mT, 1:46.60, STARTAC, Volponi, Dr. Kashnikow, 6 started.

BELMONT S.-G1, Belmont Park, June 8, $1,000,000, 3yo, 1½m, 2:29.71, SARAVA, Medaglia d'Oro, Sunday Break (Jpn), 11 started.

BEN ALI S.-G3, Keeneland, April 21, $103,984, 4&up, 1⅛m, 1:50.18, DUCKHORN, Parade Leader, Connected, 4 started.

Benburb S. (R), Fort Erie, July 21, $66,900, 3&up, Canadian-bred, 1¹⁄₁₆mT, 1:43.23, YATSKO, Go Figure, Coastal Display, 7 started.

Ben Cohen S., Pimlico, May 25, $50,000, 3&up, 5fT, :56.10, SPLENDEED, Please Me Doc, Elberton, 12 started.

Benjamin Harrison S. (R), Hoosier Park, Oct. 26, $43,600, 3yo, c&g, Indiana-bred, 1¹⁄₁₆m, 1:45.95, PASS RUSH, If I Were You, Donnies Pick, 6 started.

Bergen County S., The Meadowlands, Sept. 7, $50,000, 3yo, 6f, 1:08.18, OUTSTANDER, Second Collection, Our Wildcat, 5 started.

BERKELEY H.-G3, Golden Gate Fields, March 30, $100,000, 3&up, 1m, 1:35.41, IRISHEYESAREFLYING, Boss Ego, Palmeiro, 11 started.

BERNARD BARUCH H.-G2, Saratoga Race Course, July 26, $150,000, 3&up, 1⅛mT, 1:48.51, DEL MAR SHOW, Volponi, Forbidden Apple, 7 started.

Bernie Dowd H. (R), Monmouth Park, July 14, $50,000, 3&up, New Jersey-bred, 6f, 1:09.90, SUMMER SWING, H. M. S. Jackson, Spectacular Slew, 8 started.

Bersid S., Turf Paradise, Dec. 29, $22,700, 3yo, f, 1m, 1:37.45, ASPEN HILL, She's Finding Time, Princess Forever, 5 started.

Bertram F. Bongard S. (R), Belmont Park, Sept. 29, $83,975, 2yo, New York-bred, 7f, 1:22.95, FUNNY CIDE, Spite the Devil, Infinite Justice, 10 started.

BESSARABIAN H. (Can-G3), Woodbine, Nov. 20, $175,300, 3&up, f&m, 7f, 1:22.98, SHEILA'S PROSPECT, Miss Sweep, Lightning Pace, 8 started.

Best of Ohio Distaff H. (R), Thistledown, Oct. 14, $75,000, 3&up, f&m, Ohio-bred, 1⅛m, 1:51.72, ASHWOOD C C, Kind of Fun, Crypto's Twinjet, 8 started.

Best of Ohio Endurance H. (R), Thistledown, Oct. 14, $100,000, 3&up, Ohio-bred, 1¼m, 2:04.52, MAJESTIC DINNER, Bad Little Fellow, Your Abc's, 9 started.

Best of Ohio Juvenile Fillies S. (R), Thistledown, Oct. 14, $75,000, 2yo, f, Ohio-bred, 1¹⁄₁₆m, 1:47.38, BOLARO, Kiosk, Lady Delphinus, 14 started.

Best of Ohio Juvenile S. (R), Thistledown, Oct. 14, $75,000, 2yo, Ohio-bred, 1¹⁄₁₆m, 1:45.40, FOREST PICNIC, Hackendiffy, Boxcar Cat, 9 started.

Best of Ohio Sprint S. (R), Thistledown, Oct. 14, $50,000, 3&up, Ohio-bred, 6f, 1:10.76, WAIST GUNNER JOHN, Scioto Bootski, Disappearance, 14 started.

BEST PAL S.-G3, Del Mar, Aug. 21, $150,000, 2yo, 6½f, 1:17, KAFWAIN, Chief Planner, Outta Here, 7 started.

Best Turn S., Aqueduct, Feb. 23, $82,950, 3yo, 6f, 1:10.76, SMOOTH JAZZ, Tank's Expectation, President Butler, 9 started.

Bettie Bullock Memorial Derby, Wyoming Downs, Aug. 18, $10,200, 3yo, 5½f, 1:05.61, LINDYS DANCER, Rapid Slew, Silver Pines, 7 started.

Bettor's Invitational H., Grants Pass, July 4, $5,550, 3&up, 6½f, 1:23.80, DRAGON SIX, Imus, Oh Molly, 4 started.

BEVERLY D. S.-G1, Arlington Park, Aug. 17, $700,000, 3&up, f&m, 1³⁄₁₆mT, 1:54.86, GOLDEN APPLES (Ire), Astra, England's Legend (Fr), 6 started.

BEVERLY HILLS H.-G1, Hollywood Park, June 29, $250,000, 3&up, f&m, 1¼mT, 1:58.56, ASTRA, Peu a Peu (Ger), Crazy Ensign (Arg), 8 started.

BEWITCH S.-G3, Keeneland, April 25, $110,700, 4&up, f&m, 1½mT, 2:31.97, SWEETEST THING, Lapuma, Lady Upstage (Ire), 9 started.

Bien Bien S. (R), Hollywood Park, Nov. 6, $73,450, 3yo, non-winners of $50,000 at one mile or over, 1mT, 1:34.31, MUSIC'S STORM, Golden Arrow, Rushin' to Altar, 9 started.

Bienvenidos S., Turf Paradise, Sept. 27, $21,900, 3&up, 1m, 1:37.74, PERSONAL BEAU, Milk Wood (GB), Spectacular Kisser, 9 started.

Big Jag H. (R), Bay Meadows, Sept. 8, $64,050, 3&up, California-bred non-winners of $3,000 other than maiden, claiming, or starter and have never won two races, 6f, 1:08.72, PROFOUND SECRET, El Dorado Shooter, Sirpa, 5 started.

Big Red Mile H. (R), Lincoln State Fair, May 27, $13,025, 3&up, Nebraska-bred, 1m, 1:41.20, TATE'S WAY, High Dice, Master Swinger, 5 started.

Bill Callihan H., Columbus, Sept. 1, $7,942, 3&up, f&m, 6½f, 1:17.60, IRISH FLYER, Be My Friend, Real Intrusion, 7 started.

Bill Thomas Memorial H., Sunland Park, March 9, $33,700, 3&up, 6½f, 1:15.15, BEEHAY, Incredible Bulk, Radar Trap, 10 started.

Bill Wineberg S. (R), Portland Meadows, Nov. 17, $14,120, 2yo, c&g, Oregon-bred, 6f, 1:13.22, YADA YADA YADA, Stately Jack Flash, Glad to Be Here, 8 started.

Billy the Kid Casino Starter H., Ruidoso Downs, Sept. 2, $14,000, 3&up, 1⅛m, 1:55.40, MYSTERY YEARS, March of Kings, Navy Class, 9 started.

BING CROSBY BREEDERS' CUP H.-G2, Del Mar, July 27, $169,000, 3&up, 6f, 1:09.21, DISTURBINGTHEPEACE, Mellow Fellow, Freespool, 9 started.

Birdcatcher S., Northlands Park, Sept. 2, $50,000, 2yo, c&g, 6½f, 1:17.20, TAIASLEW, Diablo Contento, Judge Ruckus, 6 started.

Birdie Belle S., Calder Race Course, Nov. 10, $38,290, 3yo, f, 6½f, 1:18.76, SLEWS FINAL ANSWER, Chispiski, Four Pennies, 8 started.

Bird of Pay S., Northlands Park, Aug. 31, $50,000, 2yo, f, 6½f, 1:18, RAYLENE, Dowhatuthinksright, Volunteer Annie, 7 started.

Birdonthewire S., Calder Race Course, Oct. 12, $75,000, 2yo, 6f, 1:10.29, SUPER FUSE, Hear No Evil, True Enough, 7 started.

Bison City S. (R), Fort Erie, July 1, $250,000, 3yo, f, Canadian-bred, 1¹⁄₁₆m, 1:44.10, SILVER NITHI, Ginger Gold, Alpha Heat, 7 started.

BLACK-EYED SUSAN S-G2, Pimlico, May 17, $200,000, 3yo, f, 1⅛m, 1:51.61, CHAMROUSSE, Shop Till You Drop, Autumn Creek, 6 started.

Black Gold H., Fair Grounds, Jan. 4, $75,000, 3yo, a7½fT, 1:31.45, PRIVATE EMBLEM, Royalton, Native Mark, 9 started.

Black Mesa S. (R), Remington Park, Dec. 8, $31,550, 3&up, f&m, Oklahoma-bred, 7f, 1:24.80, BAYAKOA'S IMAGE, Blonde Okie, Hallie Cat, 7 started.

Black Mountain H., Turf Paradise, March 9, $35,000, 3&up, 1¹⁄₁₆m, 1:41.83, IRONMAN DEHERE, Mistakenly Special, Eagleton, 7 started.

Black Swan S., Fairplex Park, Sept. 25, $50,000, 2yo, f, 1¹⁄₁₆m, 1:45.65, AMBER HILLS, Iza Beauty, Skippingtomontana, 9 started.

Black Tie Affair H., Arlington Park, Oct. 26, $100,000, 3&up, 1⅛m, 1:49.01, HERO'S TRIBUTE, Balto Star, Silver Zipper, 6 started.

Blair's Cove S. (R), Canterbury Park, July 4, $36,850, 3&up, c&g, Minnesota-bred, a1¹⁄₁₆mT, 1:44.36, ASHAR, Bleu Victoriate, Now Playing, 7 started.

Blazing Sevens S., Fort Erie, July 30, $78,600, 3&up, 6f, 1:10.44, KRZ RUCKUS, Deputy Chris C., Dreams Go Bye, 4 started.

Blazing Sword S., Calder Race Course, Aug. 24, $75,000, 3yo, 1¹⁄₁₆m, 1:46.93, GEMMA'S STAR, Susie's Poker, Say No Maw, 8 started.

Bloomfield H., SunRay Park, Oct. 20, $32,000, 3&up, 1m, 1:37.60, VERNON INVADER, Seattle Sunshine, March of Kings, 6 started.

BLUE GRASS S.-G1, Keeneland, April 13, $750,000, 3yo, 1⅛m, 1:51.51, HARLAN'S HOLIDAY, Booklet, Ocean Sound (Ire), 6 started.

Blue Hen S., Delaware Park, Oct. 19, $101,500, 2yo, f, 1m, 1:41.79, HEIRLOOM DIAMOND, Lets Just Do It, Ladyecho, 10 started.

Blue Mountain Juvenile S. (R), Penn National Race Course, Nov. 15, $63,700, 2yo, f, Pennsylvania-bred, 6f, 1:12.91, A VISION IN GRAY, Always Devilish, Love for Ali, 10 started.

Blue Norther S., Santa Anita Park, Jan. 9, $76,300, 3yo, f, 1mT, 1:35.74, MEGAHERTZ (GB), Nunatall (GB), La Martina (GB), 8 started.

Blue Ridge S. (R), Charles Town, April 20, $36,550, 3&up, West Virginia-bred, 4½f, 52.56, CONFUCIUS SAY, Turbotaxman, Minnies Adam Ant, 6 started.

Bobbie Bricker Memorial H. (R), Beulah Park, Oct. 27, $45,000, 3&up, f&m, Ohio-bred, 1 1/16m, 1:45.06, LADY CHERIE, Come Hither, Shamrock Slew, 9 started.

Bob Bryant S. (R), Prairie Meadows, May 25, $67,390, 3yo, f, Iowa-bred, 6f, 1:10.21, ONE FINE SHWEETIE, True Tear Drops, Only At Night, 6 started.

Bob Feller S., Prairie Meadows, May 4, $50,000, 3&up, 5½f, 1:03.14, SAND RIDGE, Expert, Beverly Greedy, 7 started.

Bob Harding S., Monmouth Park, Aug. 31, $50,000, 3&up, 1mT, 1:37.95, NIGHT CALLER, Tempest Fugit, Bail Out the King, 5 started.

Bob Johnson Memorial S., Lone Star Park, July 14, $75,000, 3&up, 1m, 1:35.57, MOUNTAIN GENERAL, Compendium, Big Numbers, 8 started.

Boeing H., Emerald Downs, July 21, $40,000, 3&up, f&m, 1 1/16m, 1:42.80, TOP BRACKET, Latter Day Paula, Always a Dixie, 8 started.

BOILING SPRINGS BREEDERS' CUP H.-G3, The Meadowlands, Sept. 6, $194,000, 3yo, f, 1 1/16mT, 1:42.27, SHOWLADY, Dreamers Glory, With Patience, 9 started.

Boise River Festival Derby, Les Bois Park, June 22, 3yo, 1m, 1:39.71, DOWN THE CANYON, Cool Papa Rick, A Midnight Sheik, 5 started.

Bold Accent H., Fonner Park, Feb. 9, $15,970, 3&up, f&m, 4f, LADY J, Miss Musical Coin, Run Around Sue, 8 started.

Bold Ego H., Sunland Park, Jan. 5, $28,800, 3&up, f&m, 5½f, 1:04.64, STURGE WEBER, Quite Spender, Miss Einstein, 12 started.

Bold Ruckus S. (R), Woodbine, June 5, $129,875, 3yo, progeny of eligible Ontario stallions, 6fT, 1:12, MIGHTY QUINN, Dillinger, Akbar, 6 started.

BOLD RULER H.-G3, Belmont Park, May 11, $102,900, 3&up, 6f, 1:09.30, LEFT BANK, Silky Sweep, Say Florida Sandy, 4 started.

Bold Venture S., Woodbine, July 20, $133,375, 3&up, 6½f, 1:16.06, SAMBUCA ON ICE, Saratoga Prince, Wake At Noon, 5 started.

Bonnie Heath S. (R), Gulfstream Park, Feb. 24, $60,000, 3yo, progeny of eligible Georgia stallions, 6f, 1:11.21, SMOOTH LOVER, Mister Michael, Powder Keg, 10 started.

Bonnie Heath Turf Cup H. (R), Calder Race Course, Nov. 16, $150,000, 3&up, Florida-bred, 1⅛mT, 1:48.33, MIESQUE'S APPROVAL, Sir Brian's Sword, Stay Forever, 7 started.

BONNIE MISS S.-G2, Gulfstream Park, March 15, $250,000, 3yo, f, 1⅛m, 1:49.67, DUST ME OFF, Belterra, Nonsuch Bay, 6 started.

Boo La Boo S. (R), Santa Anita Park, Feb. 16, $107,400, 3yo, f, California-bred, 6f, 1:10.25, LADY GEORGE, Icantgoforthat, Super High, 6 started.

Boomer S. (R), Fair Meadows at Tulsa, June 14, $42,550, 3&up, f&m, Oklahoma-bred, 5½f, 1:06.60, LADY J, Tulsa World, Here Comes Kari, 8 started.

Border Cup S. (R), Fort Erie, July 21, $66,000, 3&up, f&m, Canadian-bred, 1 1/16mT, 1:44.38, PROSPECTIVE GAL, Rainy Mel, Orientalspringhope, 7 started.

Borderland Derby, Sunland Park, March 3, $32,900, 3yo, 1m, 1:36.16, PREMEDITATION, Mon Ouimet, Star Smasher, 8 started.

Bossier City H., Louisiana Downs, July 20, $50,000, 3yo, 1 1/16mT, 1:44.51, APRIL'S LUCKY BOY, Kamolia, Nocturnal Vision, 8 started.

Boston Common S. (R), Suffolk Downs, May 18, $30,000, 3yo, f, Massachusetts-bred, 1mT, 1:42.56, LITTLE TIME, African Princess, Judge Nancy, 7 started.

Bourbonette Breeders' Cup S., Turfway Park, March 23, $150,000, 3yo, f, 1m, 1:37.06, COLONIAL GLITTER, Southey, Madame X Ski, 9 started.

Bouwerie S. (R), Belmont Park, May 19, $85,025, 3yo, f, New York-bred, 7f, 1:23.62, CARSON HOLLOW, Message Red, Shawklit Mint, 11 started.

Bowl Game S., Arlington Park, July 7, $46,950, 3&up, 1 1/16mT, 1:42.09, GALIC BOY, Just Like Jimmy, Promise of War, 6 started.

BOWLING GREEN H.-G2, Belmont Park, July 13, $150,000, 3&up, 1⅜mT, 2:13.43, WHITMORE'S CONN, Staging Post, Moon Solitaire (Ire), 9 started.

Brandywine S., Delaware Park, June 29, $100,600, 3&up, 1m, 1:37.36, HE'S A KNOCKOUT, Marciano, Beau's Surprise, 7 started.

Brave Raj S., Calder Race Course, Sept. 21, $100,000, 2yo, f, 1m 70y, 1:45.04, IVANAVINALOT, Dakota Light, Puxa Saco, 8 started.

BREEDERS' CUP CLASSIC-G1, Arlington Park, Oct. 26, $3,664,000, 3&up, 1¼m, 2:01.39, VOLPONI, Medaglia d'Oro, Milwaukee Brew, 12 started.

BREEDERS' CUP DISTAFF-G1, Arlington Park, Oct. 26, $1,832,000, 3&up, f&m, 1⅛m, 1:48.64, AZERI, Farda Amiga, Imperial Gesture, 8 started.

BREEDERS' CUP FILLY & MARE TURF-G1, Arlington Park, Oct. 26, $1,172,480, 3&up, f&m, 1¼mT, 2:03.57, STARINE (Fr), Banks Hill (GB), Islington (Ire), 11 started.

BREEDERS' CUP JUVENILE-G1, Arlington Park, Oct. 26, $980,120, 2yo, c&g, 1⅛m, 1:49.61, VINDICATION, Kafwain, Hold That Tiger, 13 started.

BREEDERS' CUP JUVENILE FILLIES-G1, Arlington Park, Oct. 26, $916,000, 2yo, f, 1⅛m, 1:49.60, STORM FLAG FLYING, Composure, Santa Catarina, 10 started.

BREEDERS' CUP MILE-G1, Arlington Park, Oct. 26, $980,120, 3&up, 1mT, 1:36.92, DOMEDRIVER (Ire), Rock of Gibraltar (Ire), Good Journey, 14 started.

BREEDERS' CUP SPRINT-G1, Arlington Park, Oct. 26, $1,044,240, 3&up, 6f, 1:08.89, ORIENTATE, Thunderello, Crafty C. T, 13 started.

Breeders' Cup Steeplechase S., Far Hills, Oct. 19, $235,000, 4&up, a2⅝mT, 5:19.40, FLAT TOP, Tres Touche, All Gong (GB), 8 started.

BREEDERS' CUP TURF-G1, Arlington Park, Oct. 26, $2,216,720, 3&up, 1½mT, 2:30.14, HIGH CHAPARRAL (Ire), With Anticipation, Falcon Flight (Fr), 8 started.

Breeders' S. (R), Woodbine, Aug. 10, $500,000, 3yo, Canadian-bred, 1½mT, 2:29.80, PORTCULLIS, El Soprano, Mountain Beacon, 10 started.

Brent's Princess S. (R), Thistledown, May 25, $40,000, 3&up, f&m, Ohio-bred, 6f, 1:11.72, LADY CHERIE, Prissy Linda, Left Lane Lorrain, 7 started.

Briartic H., Woodbine, March 23, $101,800, 4&up, 5f, WAKE AT NOON, Balancethebudget, Mr. Epperson, 5 started.

Brickyard S. (R), Hoosier Park, Oct. 20, $44,500, 3&up, c&g, Indiana-bred, 6f, 1:10.41, JOANIES NO PHONY, Gravano, Red's Honor, 12 started.

Bridgeburg S., Fort Erie, Oct. 14, $72,300, 3&up, 1 1/16m, 1:43.58, DIVINE LUCK, Go Figure, Northernprospector, 11 started.

Brighouse Belles H., Hastings Park Racecourse, July 6, $37,173, 3&up, f&m, 1⅛m, 1:50.22, GREY TOBE FREE, Inish Glora, Watershed Park, 5 started.

BRITISH COLUMBIA BREEDERS' CUP OAKS (Can-G3), Hastings Park Racecourse, Sept. 7, $139,156, 3yo, f, 1⅛m, 1:51.67, ELANA D'AMOUR, Sweet Monarch, Grace for You, 10 started.

British Columbia Cup Classic H. (R), Hastings Park Racecourse, Aug. 5, $72,267, 3&up, British Columbia-bred, 1⅛m, 1:50.72, VERNON INVADER, Lord Nelson, Prodigious, 7 started.

British Columbia Cup Debutante S. (R), Hastings Park Racecourse, Aug. 5, $54,264, 2yo, f, British Columbia-bred, 6½f, 1:20.45, DANCEWITHAVIXEN, Lil' Irish Annie, My Miss Emily, 9 started.

British Columbia Cup Distaff H. (R), Hastings Park Racecourse, Aug. 5, $55,590, 3&up, f&m, British Columbia-bred, 1⅛m, 1:52.05, GREY TOBE FREE, Always a Dixie, Catahoula Rose, 7 started.

British Columbia Cup Nursery S. (R), Hastings Park Racecourse, Aug. 5, $54,140, 2yo, British Columbia-bred, 6½f, 1:19.86, DON'T PALI ME, Jay Ar Jay, Hammersmith, 11 started.

British Columbia Cup Sprint H. (R), Hastings Park Racecourse, Aug. 5, $55,590, 3&up, British Columbia-bred, 6½f, 1:17.13, KING JEREMY, Captain Des, Let's Go Rusty, 6 started.

British Columbia Cup Stallion S. (R), Hastings Park Racecourse, Aug. 5, $55,330, 3yo, c&g, British Columbia-bred, 1 1/16m, 1:45.11, SILVER DONN, The Jones Boy, No Time Flat, 9 started.

British Columbia Cup Stallion S. (R), Hastings Park Racecourse, Aug. 5, $55,590, 3yo, f, British Columbia-bred, 1 1/16m, 1:45.53, GRACE FOR YOU, Elana d'Amour, Lady Vye, 7 started.

BRITISH COLUMBIA DERBY (Can-G2), Hastings Park Racecourse, Sept. 21, $217,237, 3yo, 1⅛m, 1:50.49, CRUISING KAT, Blowin in the Wind, Silver Donn, 12 started.

British Columbia Lottery H., Kamloops, Aug. 18, $11,650, 3&up, 1m, 1:40.20, VICTOR'S HONOR, Miller's Legend, Shoo Fly Willie, 9 started.

British Columbia Lottery Support H., Kin Park, July 21, $2,800, 3&up, a7f, 1:22.80, SOUTHERN CROSS SKY, Start the Music, Similkameen Dancer, 5 started.

Broadway H. (R), Aqueduct, April 7, $82,650, 3&up, f&m, New York-bred, 7f, 1:22.81, WE'LL SEA YA, Maddie May, Dat You Miz Blue, 8 started.

BROOKLYN H.-G2, Belmont Park, June 15, $250,000, 3&up, 1⅛m, 1:46.35, SEEKING DAYLIGHT, Country Be Gold, Griffinite, 8 started.

Brookmeade S. (R), Colonial Downs, July 14, $40,000, 3&up, f&m, Virginia-bred, 1¹⁄₁₆mT, 1:47.58, LAURIE BEGONE, Key Wi Miss, Blue Hills, 9 started.

Brooks Fields S., Canterbury Park, June 15, $40,000, 3&up, 7½fT, 1:29.20, AL'S DEARLY BRED, Promise of War, Trinity River, 9 started.

Brother Brown S., Remington Park, Oct. 6, $30,750, 3&up, 5fT, :56.77, JEB'S HONOR, Abbi's Choice, Tonight Rainbow, 8 started.

BROWN BESS H.-G3, Golden Gate Fields, Feb. 2, $100,000, 4&up, f&m, 1¹⁄₁₆mT, 1:44.14, JANET (GB), Impeachable, Alexine (Arg), 5 started.

Bruce G. Smith Memorial S., Suffolk Downs, Oct. 5, $30,000, 3&up, a1¹⁄₁₆mT, 1:47.65, TOM MAIOR (Brz), Silent Thunder, Leo and Mike, 10 started.

Brumbeau S., Turf Paradise, April 16, $22,700, 3&up, f&m, 6f, 1:09.33, NOTHINBUTFASTNRED, Cove Point, Crown Connection, 7 started.

B. Thoughtful S. (R), Hollywood Park, April 28, $150,000, 4&up, f&m, California bred, 7f, 1:22.40, FAVORITE FUNTIME, Song of Summer, Warren's Whistle, 7 started.

Bucharest S., Sam Houston Race Park, Feb. 2, $30,000, 3yo, 6f, 1:10.86, FRONT NINE, Gone Off, Balkan, 7 started.

Buckeye Native S. (R), River Downs, Aug. 11, $45,000, 3&up, Ohio-bred, 1¹⁄₁₆mT, 1:42.60, WAIST GUNNER JOHN, Deadline Dude, Dinkers Millennium, 7 started.

Buckland S., Colonial Downs, July 6, $40,000, 3&up, f&m, 5fT, :57.29, MERRY PRINCESS, Maypole Dance, Lip Sing's Affair, 5 started.

Buckpasser H., Fairmount Park, Oct. 19, $26,000, 2yo, c&g, 6f, 1:12.60, SMALL CHARGER, Ww Conquistador, Cherokee Junction, 10 started.

Budweiser Mile S., Rillito Park, March 3, $3,827, 3&up, 1¹⁄₁₆m, 1:45.40, JUNK BOND KID, Cop Out, Rough, 7 started.

BUENA VISTA H.-G2, Santa Anita Park, Feb. 18, $150,000, 4&up, f&m, 1mT, 1:35.54, BLUE MOON (Fr), Old Money (Aus), Queen of Wilshire, 7 started.

Bueno S., Turf Paradise, Dec. 22, $22,700, 2yo, f, 6½f, 1:17.49, ALMOST FOOLED, Silk N Diamonds, Hula Kat, 6 started.

Buffalo Bayou S., Sam Houston Race Park, Nov. 9, $30,000, 3&up, 1¹⁄₁₆mT, 1:46.34, KRIS HAVINGFUNNOW, Rasby, Thunder Fish, 7 started.

Buffalo S. (R), Assiniboia Downs, Sept. 15, $35,000, 2yo, Manitoba-bred, 1m, 1:46, WILD RULER, Fancy Bru, Cabernet, 10 started.

Bull Dog S. (R), Fresno, Oct. 13, $48,440, 3&up, California-bred, 6f, 1:08.51, CON QUIXOTE, Men's Exclusive, Menacing Dennis, 4 started.

Bull Page S. (R), Woodbine, July 28, $132,875, 2yo, c&g, progeny of stallions standing in Ontario, 6f, 1:11.25, BIDDY'S LAD, Magic Jack, Godin, 8 started.

Bungalow H. (R), Fairmount Park, Oct. 1, $35,800, 3&up, f&m, Illinois-bred, 1m, 1:40, DENTONS RUBY, Erin G., Out of Options, 8 started.

Bunty Lawless S. (R), Woodbine, Oct. 19, $140,125, 3&up, progeny of eligible Ontario stallions, 1mT, 1:37.38, STEADY RUCKUS, Devil Valentine, Inish Glora, 12 started.

Burnaby Breeders' Cup H., Hastings Park Racecourse, June 29, $62,987, 3yo, 1¹⁄₁₆m, 1:44.32, SILVER DONN, Blowin in the Wind, Commodore Craig, 10 started.

Busanda S., Aqueduct, Jan. 27, $84,900, 3yo, f, 1m 70y, 1:43.40, TOTALY WILD, Madame X Ski, Sideways, 11 started.

Busher S., Aqueduct, March 2, $80,875, 3yo, f, 1¹⁄₁₆m, 1:45.99, BEMA, Sideways, Cobblestone Road, 5 started.

Bustles and Bows S., Fairplex Park, Sept. 19, $48,000, 2yo, f, 6½f, 1:18.42, ZAM ZAM, My Honey Bunny, Margaret's Fancy (Ire), 5 started.

Buttons and Bows S., Sun Downs, April 14, $3,150, 3&up, f&m, 4f, ALEX MARIE, O' Gata Yolanda, See Sea Lady, 5 started.

Caballos del Sol H., Turf Paradise, Oct. 12, $30,000, 3&up, 6f, 1:09.34, BEYOND BRILLIANT, Duddly Doo Run, Ex Kay E, 7 started.

Cacapon S. (R), Charles Town, May 11, $36,750, 3&up, f&m, West Virginia-bred, 4½f, 53.34, POWER PHAN, Sweet Annuity, She's a Spy Too, 10 started.

Cactus Cup H., Turf Paradise, March 2, $30,000, 3yo, f, 6½f, 1:17.03, BELLA CASH, Queen Marge, Bully's Del Mar, 7 started.

Cactus Flower H., Turf Paradise, March 9, $50,000, 3&up, f&m, 6f, 1:09.59, WIN A FEU, Ode to Elaine, Top Bracket, 10 started.

Caesar Rodney H., Delaware Park, Aug. 24, $200,900, 3&up, 1⅛mT, 1:51.02, REVVED UP, Rochester, Spruce Run, 8 started.

Caesar's Wish S. (R), Pimlico, April 20, $75,000, 3yo, f, Maryland-bred, 1¹⁄₁₆m, 1:44.91, MADAME X SKI, Tamayo, True Sensation, 6 started.

Cajun S. (R), Louisiana Downs, Oct. 19, $40,000, 3&up, Louisiana-bred, 6f, 1:10.85, BET ME BEST, Doctor Mike, Donna's Mailbag, 11 started.

Calder Breeders' Cup H., Calder Race Course, May 25, $105,000, 3&up, f&m, 1¹⁄₁₆mT, 1:42.45, SEPTIETTA, Wander Mom, Platinum Tiara, 10 started.

CALDER DERBY-G3, Calder Race Course, Oct. 12, $200,000, 3yo, 1⅛mT, 1:47.76, UNION PLACE, Miesque's Approval, The Judge Sez Who, 11 started.

Calder Oaks, Calder Race Course, Oct. 12, $200,000, 3yo, f, 1⅛mT, 1:48.85, CELLARS SHIRAZ, Maliziosa, Something Ventured, 9 started.

Calder Turf Sprint H., Calder Race Course, Oct. 12, $100,000, 3&up, 5fT, 54.89, TEXAS GLITTER, Ghostly Numbers, Petrina Above, 7 started.

Calgary Sun Marathon S., Lethbridge, Oct. 6, $9,200, 3&up, 1¹⁄₁₆m, 1:44.20, STAGE DOOR JADE, Arctic Horizon, High Powered Mack, 8 started.

Calgary Sun Marathon Series S., Lethbridge, Oct. 26, $9,050, 3&up, 1⅛m, 1:53, CANDID REMARK, Arctic Horizon, Joe T Bailey, 8 started.

California Breeders' Champion S. (R), Santa Anita Park, Dec. 26, $125,000, 2yo, c&g, California-bred, 7f, 1:22.62, EXCESSIVEPLEASURE, Martinblestme, Judge Swiss, 8 started.

California Breeders' Champion S. (R), Santa Anita Park, Dec. 27, $125,000, 2yo, f, California-bred, 7f, 1:23.16, POCKETFULLOFPESOS, Long Term Wish, Denali Cat, 10 started.

California Cup Classic H. (R), Santa Anita Park, Nov. 2, $250,000, 3&up, California-bred, 1⅛m, 1:49.16, CALKINS ROAD, Continental Red, Slippery When Bet, 9 started.

California Cup Distaff H. (R), Santa Anita Park, Nov. 2, $150,000, 3&up, f&m, California-bred, a6½fT, 1:13.36, LIL SISTER STICH, Party Pirate, Top of Our Game, 13 started.

California Cup Juvenile Fillies S. (R), Santa Anita Park, Nov. 2, $125,000, 2yo, f, California-bred, 1¹⁄₁₆m, 1:44.38, SUMMER WIND DANCER, Be Brite Over, Tizalovelylady, 12 started.

California Cup Juvenile S. (R), Santa Anita Park, Nov. 2, $125,000, 2yo, c&g, California-bred, 1¹⁄₁₆m, 1:43.82, CRACKUP, Excessive Barb, Hair Jordan, 8 started.

California Cup Matron H. (R), Santa Anita Park, Nov. 2, $150,000, 3&up, f&m, California-bred, 1¹⁄₁₆m, 1:42.64, SUPER HIGH, Broke the Slump, Elaine's Angel, 7 started.

California Cup Sprint H. (R), Santa Anita Park, Nov. 2, $50,000, 3&up, California-bred, 6f, 1:08.85, GIOVANNETTI, Affairintheforest, Coconut Mango, 10 started.

California Cup Starter H. (R), Santa Anita Park, Nov. 2, $50,000, 3&up, California-bred starters for a claiming price of $40,000 or less in 2002, 1½mT, 2:28.69, NOBLE KINSMAN, Fade to Blue, Windy's Halo, 7 started.

California Derby, Bay Meadows, April 13, $150,000, 3yo, 1⅛m, 1:47.93, TRACEMARK, Cappuchino, Captain Squire, 8 started.

CALIFORNIAN S.-G2, Hollywood Park, June 15, $500,000, 3&up, 1⅛m, 1:48.06, MILWAUKEE BREW, Bosque Redondo, Momentum, 8 started.

California Oaks, Golden Gate Fields, Feb. 18, $55,700, 3yo, f, 1¹⁄₁₆m, 1:47.16, LA MARTINA (GB), Redmond, Runaway Ab, 6 started.

California Sire S. (R), Hollywood Park, May 31, $100,000, 3yo, f, progeny of stallions standing in California, 1¹⁄₁₆mT, 1:42.45, SUPER HIGH, Kingdom Bound, Shalini, 6 started.

California Sire S. (R), Hollywood Park, May 30, $100,000, 3yo, c&g, progeny of stallions standing in California, 1¹⁄₁₆mT, 1:42.13, GOBI DAN, Sterling Wisdom, Kith, 5 started.

California Sprint Championship H. (R), Bay Meadows, Oct. 5, $100,000, 3&up, California-bred, 6f, 1:08.44, STONEY, El Dorado Shooter, Radar Contact, 5 started.

California Thoroughbred Breeders Association S. (R), Del Mar, July 26, $125,000, 2yo, f, California-bred, 5½f, 1:04.76, HUMOROUS LADY, Golden K K, Souvenir Crown, 9 started.

California Turf Championship H. (R), Bay Meadows, Sept. 2, $100,000, 3&up, California-bred, 1mT, 1:35.05, NINEBANKS, Surprise Halo, Spinelessjellyfish, 8 started.

Caltech H., Gulfstream Park, March 31, $75,000, 3yo, a1⅛mT, 1:51.43, LORD JUBAN, Mystic Salse (GB), Fuzzy Star, 7 started.

Camilla Urso H., Golden Gate Fields, Nov. 10, $60,600, 3&up, f&m, 6f, 1:09.96, ONSLAUGHT, Fertile, Bullish Miss, 7 started.

Camino Real Mile S., The Downs at Albuquerque, May 26, $42,800, 3&up, 1m, 1:37.82, LESTERS BOY, Musical Chairs, Darn Tootin, 8

started.
Canada Day H., Assiniboia Downs, July 1, $30,000, 3&up, f&m, 1m, 1:40.20, CATHY'S STAR, Miss Sandy Dee, Maui Money, 6 started.
Canad Construction S., Grand Prairie, July 5, $3,370, 3&up, f&m, 6f, 1:15, JAR OF BUTTONS, Bonjour, Sweet N Brassy, 5 started.
CANADIAN DERBY (Can-G3), Northlands Park, Aug. 24, $150,000, 3yo, 1⅜m, 2:19.40, LADY SHARI, Sweet Monarch, No Time Flat, 10 started.
CANADIAN H. (Can-G2), Woodbine, Sept. 8, $284,250, 3&up, f&m, a1⅛mT, 1:45.04, CALISTA (GB), Diadella, Lush Soldier, 8 started.
CANADIAN INTERNATIONAL S. (Can-G1), Woodbine, Sept. 29, $1,500,000, 3&up, 1½mT, 2:31.68, BALLINGARRY (Ire), Falcon Flight (Fr), Yavana's Pace (Ire), 8 started.
Canadian Juvenile S., Northlands Park, Oct. 14, $75,000, 2yo, 1¹⁄₁₆m, 1:45.20, TAIASLEW, Marjan, Jiffyjimmygee, 7 started.
Canadian Turf H., Gulfstream Park, Feb. 23, $145,500, 3&up, 1¹⁄₁₆m, 1:44.01, NORTH EAST BOUND, Capsized, Flying Avie, 4 started.
Candy Eclair S., Monmouth Park, July 27, $50,000, 3yo, f, 5fT, :56.43, TANGIER SOUND, Melody of Colors, Libby's Halo, 10 started.
Canterbury Park Breeders' Cup Derby, Canterbury Park, June 9, $94,500, 3yo, 1mT, 1:37.97, AFLEET BUCK, Montana Rush, Awol Soldier, 5 started.
Canterbury Park Juvenile S., Canterbury Park, July 13, $50,000, 2yo, 5½f, 1:04.65, K'S PATTON, Bold America, Giant Slam, 9 started.
Canterbury Park Oaks, Canterbury Park, June 16, $40,000, 3yo, f, 1¹⁄₁₆mT, 1:42.19, SARAH JADE, Gist, Don't Countess Out, 7 started.
Cape Henlopen H. (1st Div.), Delaware Park, July 21, $60,900, 3&up, 1½mT, 2:29.81, ROCHESTER, Dawn of the Condor, Phi Beta Doc, 9 started.
Cape Henlopen S. (2nd Div.), Delaware Park, July 21, $62,100, 3&up, 1½mT, 2:28.24, CRAIGSTEEL (GB), Man From Wicklow, Regal Dynasty, 10 started.
Capital City H. (R), Penn National Race Course, Aug. 30, $30,575, 3&up, Pennsylvania-bred, 1¹⁄₁₆mT, 1:41.66, WATCHMAN'S WARNING, Watching, Nordagus, 7 started.
Capitol City Futurity, Lincoln State Fair, July 14, $10,800, 2yo, 4½f, ROCKET CHARGE, Sundayblummer, Grayglen, 8 started.
Captain Condo S. (R), Emerald Downs, June 15, $35,000, 2yo, c&g, Washington-bred, 5f, :58.20, BUB, Knightsbridge Road, Devil's Bro, 8 started.
Captain My Captain S. (R), Philadelphia Park, Sept. 2, $53,850, 3&up, Pennsylvania-bred, 5f, :57.21, THE MACCABEE, Sleetwood Mac, Classic Verse, 6 started.
Captain Stanley Harrison H., Marquis Downs, June 28, $5,000, 3yo, f, 6f, 1:14.31, ROYAL FRACTIONS, Royal Brittany, Top Stage Dancer, 5 started.
Cardinal H. (R), Arlington Park, June 22, $90,450, 3&up, Illinois-conceived and/or -foaled, 1¹⁄₁₆mT, 1:42.21, MYSTERY GIVER, Just Like Jimmy, G All Day, 14 started.
CARDINAL H.-G3, Churchill Downs, Nov. 23, $173,100, 3&up, f&m, 1⅛mT, 1:51.08, QUICK TIP, Evil Woman, Bien Nicole, 10 started.
Carl 'Cub' Klahr H., Les Bois Park, June 23, $5,200, 3&up, 7f, 1:25.20, NORTHERN RICKY, Erhard, San Diego Pete, 9 started.
CARLETON F. BURKE H.-G3, Santa Anita Park, Oct. 27, $150,000, 3&up, 1½mT, 2:28.47, SPECIAL MATTER, Alyzig, Dance Dreamer, 5 started.
Carl G. Rose Classic H. (R), Calder Race Course, Nov. 16, $200,000, 3&up, Florida-bred, 1⅛m, 1:51.87, BEST OF THE REST, The Judge Sez Who, Dancing Guy, 6 started.
Carlos Salazar S. (R), The Downs at Albuquerque, May 19, $33,000, 3&up, f&m, New Mexico-bred, 7f, 1:23.65, FRITZIE'S PROSPECT, Sandy Sage, Dayvonna Express, 7 started.
Carmel H., Bay Meadows, Sept. 14, $61,250, 3yo, f, 1¹⁄₁₆mT, 1:42.75, ETNORIAS, Dancing (GB), Sentimental Value, 8 started.
Carolina First Carolina Cup Hurdle S., Camden, March 30, $97,000, 4&up, a 2¼mT, 4:20.40, CANTA KE BRAVE, Al Skywalker, Lord Zada, 5 started.
Carotene S. (R), Woodbine, Oct. 14, $161,250, 3yo, f, Canadian-bred, a1⅛mT, 1:46.75, FIRST QUARTER, Atlantic Fury, Silver Nithi, 6 started.
Carousel Breeders' Cup S., Oaklawn Park, April 7, $96,000, 4&up, f&m, 6f, 1:10.58, SOUTHERN TOUR, Spanish Glitter, Powder, 4 started.
Carousel S., Laurel Park, Dec. 29, $50,000, 3&up, f&m, 1¹⁄₁₆m, 1:44.57, SVEA DAHL, Hunka Hunka Lori Z, Runnin Wonder, 5 started.
Carris Memorial H., Remington Park, Aug. 11, $30,450, 3&up, f&m, 1¹⁄₁₆mT, 1:42.83, STRAWBAILEY, Devout Sinner, Darlin Dixie, 6 started.
Carry Back S., Calder Race Course, July 13, $250,000, 3yo, 6f, 1:10.73, ROYAL LAD, Captain Squire, Friendly Frolic, 9 started.
CARTER H.-G1, Aqueduct, April 13, $350,000, 3&up, 7f, 1:21.84, AFFIRMED SUCCESS, Voodoo, Burning Roma, 10 started.
Carterista H., Calder Race Course, May 18, $73,950, 3&up, 1¹⁄₁₆mT, 1:46.49, WERTZ, Lavender's Lad, Tour of the Cat, 4 started.
Carter McGregor Jr. Memorial S. (R), Lone Star Park, May 27, $50,000, 3&up, Texas-bred, 6f, 1:10.55, ST. MARTIN'S CLOAK, R. B Spirit, Kentucky Bay, 9 started.
Cascapedia S., Santa Anita Park, Oct. 31, $82,250, 3&up, f&m, 6f, 1:09.31, MADAME PIETRA, Harvest Girl, Brisquette, 8 started.
Casey Darnell S. (R), The Downs at Albuquerque, June 9, $52,100, 3yo, New Mexico-bred, 7f, 1:21.01, STAR SMASHER, Hooliea, Jacks Romeo, 6 started.
Casino Regina Derby, Queensbury Downs, Oct. 18, $2,500, 3yo, a1⅛m, 2:00.43, EVER QUEST, Fastasiwannabe, Minimuffin, 5 started.
Cassidy S., Calder Race Course, Oct. 12, $75,000, 2yo, f, 6f, 1:12.17, HUMMEL, Marnesia Light, Running Debate, 7 started.
Cat's Cradle H. (R), Hollywood Park, Nov. 24, $107,400, 3&up, f&m, California-bred, 7½f, 1:29.32, CEE'S ELEGANCE, Castling, Elaine's Angel, 6 started.
Cavonnier S. (R), Santa Anita Park, Oct. 4, $81,900, 2yo, c&g, California-bred, 7f, 1:22.97, EXCESSIVE BARB, Unfurl the Flag, Crackup, 8 started.
C. Edmund O'Brien S., Pimlico, May 27, $50,000, 3&up, 1¹⁄₁₆mT, 1:41.96, MUS-IF (GB), Cynics Beware, Trooper Red, 5 started.
Centennial H., Remington Park, Sept. 2, $31,050, 3&up, 7f, 1:21.13, MR ROSS, That Tat, Medium Rare, 6 started.
Central Iowa S., Prairie Meadows, Aug. 17, $55,000, 3&up, f&m, 1¹⁄₁₆m, 1:43.37, DELRAY DEW, Sharky's Review, Persimmon Ridge, 6 started.
Centre Stage Anne S. (R), Fort Erie, July 1, $65,700, 3&up, f&m, Canadian-bred, 6f, 1:10.90, CALLENDARS, Ready I Am, Orientalspringhope, 7 started.
CERF S. (R), Del Mar, Sept. 11, $75,000, 3&up, f&m, non-winners of $50,000 other than closed, claiming, or starter in 2002, 6f, 1:09.98, PALMAROLA (Arg), Fancee Bargain, Wild Tickle, 6 started.
CFCN Futurity, Lethbridge, Oct. 27, $9,200, 2yo, a6f, 1:12, FLYING LADY CUE, Game Princess, Feudal Lady, 8 started.
Challedon S. (R), Laurel Park, Dec. 28, $60,000, 3&up, Maryland-bred, 7f, 1:22.43, P DAY, Aggadan, Hay Getoutofmyway, 8 started.
Challenger S., Tampa Bay Downs, March 23, $50,000, 3yo, 1mT, 1:36.16, CLASSIC CASE, Red Masque, Awol Soldier, 12 started.
Chamisa H., The Downs at Albuquerque, May 5, $32,100, 3&up, f&m, 7f, 1:21.29, ODE TO ELAINE, Kham Beau, Tellme Truly, 5 started.
CHAMPAGNE S.-G1, Belmont Park, Oct. 5, $500,000, 2yo, 1¹⁄₁₆m, 1:44.45, TOCCET, Icecoldbeeratreds, Erinsouthernman, 9 started.
Chandler H., Turf Paradise, Nov. 9, $30,000, 3yo, f, 7½fT, 1:29.61, PINA COLADA (GB), Princess Forever, No Turbulence, 9 started.
Chantilly S., Assiniboia Downs, June 16, $30,000, 3yo, f, 6f, 1:12.20, SANDS FURY, Sassy Shonda, Torquilla, 9 started.
Chapel Belle S., Louisiana Downs, July 27, $50,000, 3yo, f, a1¹⁄₁₆mT, 1:42.94, JUST SCARLET, Distinctive Code, Sheza Nasty Lady, 9 started.
CHAPOSA SPRINGS H.-G3, Calder Race Course, Dec. 7, $100,000, 3&up, f&m, 7f, 1:25.14, CHISPISKI, Abundantly Blessed, Away, 8 started.
Chariot Chaser H., Northlands Park, July 1, $39,200, 3yo, f, 6½f, 1:19.60, FANCY PRANCER, Sister Patsy Ellen, Big Babe, 4 started.
Charles H. Russell H., Bay Meadows, Oct. 20, $60,850, 3&up, f&m, 6f, 1:09.10, BULLISH MISS, Onslaught, Gifted Daughter, 6 started.
Charles Town Dash Invitational H., Charles Town, July 4, $100,000, 3&up, 4½f, :52.23, SHERYAR SPECIAL, Wise Dusty, Blazing Count, 10 started.
CHARLES WHITTINGHAM MEMORIAL H.-G1, Hollywood Park, June 15, $350,000, 3&up, 1¼mT, 2:01.47, DENON, Night Patrol, Skipping (GB), 9 started.
Charlie Barley S., Woodbine, June 23, $110,000, 3yo, 1mT, 1:33.92, PORTCULLIS, Classic Case, Funny Soldier, 10 started.
Charlie Iles Throughbred Derby, The Downs at Albuquerque, May 11, $39,151, 3yo, 1m, 1:38.59, MON OUIMET, Royal de Hope, Always in Action, 9 started.
Charlie Palmer H., Ferndale, Aug. 10, $7,860, 3&up, f&m, 6½f, 1:19.51, LILLIE'S STAR, Missy Muffet, Get the Moneyhoney, 6 started.
Charon S. (R), Gulfstream Park, March 22, $76,387, 3yo, f, Florida-bred, 7f, 1:23.78, BOLD WORLD, Afnan, Miss Dixie Chick, 4 started.
Chenery S., Colonial Downs, July 23, $40,000, 2yo, 5½fT, 1:06.26, MY BOY KYLE, Maxwelsilverhammer, Mountain Coyote, 11 started.
CHICAGO BREEDERS' CUP H.-G3, Arlington Park, June 8, $164,440,

3&up, f&m, 7f, 1:22.86, MANDY'S GOLD, Cat and the Hat, Caressing, 6 started.
Chicagoland H. (R), Sportsman's Park, March 30, $85,600, 4&up, Illinois-conceived and/or -foaled, 6f, 1:09.73, MAGIC DOE, Classic Appeal, Freeway Ticket, 7 started.
Chick Lang Jr. Memorial H., Retama Park, Sept. 14, $30,000, 3&up, 1m, 1:37.98, COMPENDIUM, Arctic Boy, Ski Bum, 6 started.
Chief Bearhart S., Woodbine, Sept. 29, $109,000, 3&up, 1¼mT, 2:06.08, STAGE CLASSIC, Queensgate, Sky Chariot, 9 started.
Chief Narbona S. (R), The Downs at Albuquerque, May 19, $31,020, 3yo, f, New Mexico-bred, 6f, 1:10.47, ESPEEDYTOO, Quickkey, Dancing Promise, 9 started.
CHINESE CULTURAL CENTER S. (Can-G2), Woodbine, July 21, $336,300, 3&up, 1⅜mT, 2:13.16, STRIKE SMARTLY, Quiet Resolve, Muntej (GB), 9 started.
Chippewa Downs Open Thoroughbred Derby, Chippewa Downs, June 30, $6,200, 3yo, 6½f, 1:23.20, EVER QUEST, Icewater Veins, Ta Smalley, 6 started.
Chippewa Downs Open Thoroughbred Futurity, Chippewa Downs, June 22, $4,750, 2yo, 4½f, DAWN CRUSADER, Ll Fast Play, Perkins Punch, 5 started.
Chippewa Downs Open Thoroughbred S., Chippewa Downs, June 29, $5,150, 4&up, 6½f, 1:22, FLUID GOLD, Recall, Highway Home, 7 started.
Choice S., Monmouth Park, June 23, $50,000, 3yo, 1⅛mT, 1:47.15, KRIS'S PRAYER, Alphabetical, Emergency Status, 7 started.
Chou Croute H., Fair Grounds, Feb. 23, $150,000, 4&up, f&m, 1¹⁄₁₆m, 1:42.90, DESCAPATE, Mimi's Tizzy, Gal On the Go, 10 started.
Chris Christian S., Les Bois Park, June 30, $26,965, 2yo, 5f, SLEWBY'S SECRET, Hair Jordan, Frisky Are We, 9 started.
Christiana S., Delaware Park, Sept. 21, $101,200, 3yo, f, 1⅛mT, 1:50.31, KATZEN, Affirmed Dancer, Infinite Spirit, 9 started.
Christmas H., Mountaineer Park, Dec. 26, $77,650, 3&up, 6f, 1:11.85, MEETYOUATHEBRIG, Golden Oldie, Tonto Gusto, 5 started.
Christmas Past S., Gulfstream Park, April 21, $75,000, 3yo, f, 1¹⁄₁₆m, 1:45.73, CHARITABLEDONATION, Stormy Frolic, French Satin, 6 started.
Chuck Taliaferro Memorial S., Remington Park, Aug. 10, $30,750, 3&up, 6f, 1:10.17, MEDIUM RARE, Joyful Tune, Temperence Time, 5 started.
Chuckwagon Special S., Lethbridge, June 16, $7,200, 3&up, 7f, 1:26.20, SAGREENO, Island Slew, Mr. I R S, 7 started.
CHURCHILL DOWNS DISTAFF H.-G2, Churchill Downs, Nov. 9, $223,600, 3&up, f&m, 1m, 1:35.07, SOFTLY, Bare Necessities, Victory Ride, 9 started.
CHURCHILL DOWNS H.-G2, Churchill Downs, May 4, $171,450, 4&up, 7f, 1:22.37, D'WILDCAT, Snow Ridge, Binthebest, 10 started.
CICADA S.-G3, Aqueduct, March 23, $108,600, 3yo, f, 7f, 1:23.32, PROPER GAMBLE, Short Note, Forest Heiress, 6 started.
Cicero H., Sportsman's Park, March 16, $100,000, 4&up, f&m, 6f, 1:12.52, WIRED TO FLY, Adam's Time, Hattiesburg, 8 started.
CIGAR MILE H.-G1, Aqueduct, Nov. 30, $350,000, 3&up, 1m, 1:33.11, CONGAREE, Crafty C. T, Aldebaran, 8 started.
Cigar S., Arlington Park, Aug. 17, $62,750, 3&up, 1m, 1:33.76, THERE'S ZEALOUS, Slider, Mountain General, 5 started.
Cimarron S., Remington Park, Nov. 24, $30,775, 2yo, f, 6½f, 1:20.26, TULUPAI, Strolling Kris, Heart of the Cat, 12 started.
Cincinnatian S. (R), River Downs, July 7, $50,000, 3yo, f, Ohio-bred, 1¹⁄₁₆mT, 1:44.20, JOANIES BELLA, Come Hither, Wars Done, 8 started.
Cincinnati Trophy S., Turfway Park, Jan. 19, $50,000, 3yo, f, 6½f, 1:18.07, ART FAIR, Timeless Love, Honest Deceiver, 9 started.
Cinderella S., Hollywood Park, June 2, $98,775, 2yo, f, 5½f, 1:04.60, MAGIC SMOKE, Little Bit a Swiss, My Honey Bunny, 10 started.
CINEMA BREEDERS' CUP H.-G3, Hollywood Park, June 30, $182,600, 3yo, 1⅛mT, 1:47.63, INESPERADO (Fr), Regiment, Johar, 7 started.
CITATION H.-G2, Hollywood Park, Nov. 30, $500,000, 3&up, 1¹⁄₁₆mT, 1:41.45, GOOD JOURNEY, Seinne (Chi), White Heart (GB), 10 started.
CITGO DISTAFF TURF MILE S.-G3, Churchill Downs, May 4, $115,200, 3&up, f&m, 1mT, 1:35.72, STYLISH, La Recherche, Dianehill (Ire), 10 started.
City Centre Bingo H., Marquis Downs, July 20, $5,000, 3&up, f&m, 1m, 1:41.45, MS. LADY ROSE, Blue Camay, Princess Briartic, 7 started.
City of Anderson S. (R), Hoosier Park, Oct. 4, $33,650, 2yo, f, Indiana bred, 5½f, 1:07.42, HURRICANE HEBE, Money Mover, Miss Dakota, 9 started.
City of Bridges Sophomore S. (R), Marquis Downs, Sept. 14, $7,535, 3yo, c&g, Saskatchewan-bred, 1¹⁄₁₆m, 1:46.28, BRITTS XPRESS, Good Old Sprite, Persistent Heart, 5 started.
City of Phoenix H., Turf Paradise, Oct. 5, $30,000, 3&up, f&m, 6f, 1:10.23, CHANNING WAY, Miss Pixie, Cove Point, 9 started.
City of Sunland Park H. (R), Sunland Park, Dec. 26, $79,800, 3&up, New Mexico-bred, 1¹⁄₁₆m, 1:44.16, STAR SMASHER, Ciento, Runmore Mema, 12 started.
City of Vancouver H. (R), Hastings Park Racecourse, May 5, $38,010, 3yo, British Columbia-bred, 6½f, 1:17.95, COMMODORE CRAIG, Regal Rebel, Cruising Kat, 7 started.
C. J. Hindley Humboldt County Marathon H., Ferndale, Aug. 18, $12,690, 3&up, 1⅝m, 2:48, ROGER ROGER, Ironman Dehere, Justin's Halo, 5 started.
Claiming Crown Emerald S. (R), Philadelphia Park, Aug. 31, $118,750, 3&up, starters for a claiming price of $20,000 or less since July 31, 2001, 1¹⁄₁₆mT, 1:46.66, NOWRASS (GB), Grade One, Taylorman (NZ), 9 started.
Claiming Crown Express S. (R), Philadelphia Park, Aug. 31, $47,000, 3&up, starters for a claiming price of $7,500 or less since July 31, 2001, 6f, 1:09.29, TALKNOW, Danny E, Wise Sweep, 8 started.
Claiming Crown Glass Slipper S. (R), Philadelphia Park, Aug. 31, $71,500, 3&up, f&m, starters for a claiming price of $12,500 or less since July 31, 2001, 6½f, 1:17.01, WON MORO, Dandy Dulce, Playmera, 9 started.
Claiming Crown Iron Horse S. (R), Philadelphia Park, Aug. 31, $46,500, 3&up, starters for a claiming price of $5,000 or less since July 31, 2001, 1¹⁄₁₆m, 1:45.37, RUSKIN, Regal Tour, Entrepreneurship, 7 started.
Claiming Crown Jewel S. (R), Philadelphia Park, Aug. 31, $145,500, 3&up, starters for a claiming price of $25,000 or less since July 31, 2001, 1⅛m, 1:50.39, TRULY A JUDGE, Quiet Mike, Prince Iroquois, 9 started.
Claiming Crown Rapid Transit S. (R), Philadelphia Park, Aug. 31, $94,000, 3&up, starters for a claiming price of $16,000 or less since July 31, 2001, 6½f, 1:16.10, RISEN WARRIOR, Yavapai, Largeandincharge, 9 started.
Clarendon S. (R), Woodbine, June 29, $164,550, 2yo, Canadian-bred, 5½f, 1:05.26, FRANKIEFOURFINGERS, Lucky Larue, Magic Jack, 8 started.
CLARK H.-G2, Churchill Downs, Nov. 29, $457,200, 3&up, 1⅛m, 1:49.13, LIDO PALACE (Chi), Crafty Shaw, Hero's Tribute, 11 started.
Classy 'n Smart S. (R), Woodbine, Nov. 20, $127,250, 3&up, f&m, progeny of eligible Ontario stallions, 1¹⁄₁₆m, 1:43.21, BRASS IN POCKET, Inish Glora, Night Edition, 5 started.
CLEMENT L. HIRSCH H.-G2, Del Mar, Aug. 11, $300,000, 3&up, f&m, 1¹⁄₁₆m, 1:42.66, AZERI, Angel Gift, Se Me Acabo (Chi), 5 started.
CLEMENT L. HIRSCH MEMORIAL TURF CHAMPIONSHIP S.-G1, Santa Anita Park, Oct. 6, $300,000, 3&up, 1¼mT, 1:58.93, THE TIN MAN, Sarafan, Blue Steller (Ire), 6 started.
Cleveland Gold Cup H. (R), Thistledown, July 4, $100,000, 3yo, Ohio-bred, 1⅛m, 1:54.24, BAD LITTLE FELLOW, Truth Matters, Dinkers Millennium, 8 started.
Cleveland Kindergarten S. (R), Thistledown, July 6, $40,000, 2yo, Ohio-bred, 5½f, 1:05.64, HACKENDIFFY, Bolaro, Kiosk, 6 started.
Clever Trevor S., Remington Park, Nov. 10, $30,775, 2yo, 6½f, 1:17.62, MICK, Kickin Kountry, Mav Cat, 8 started.
Cliff Hanger H., The Meadowlands, Oct. 11, $145,500, 3&up, 1¹⁄₁₆m, 1:42.40, SAINT VERRE, Pinky Pizwaanski, Spruce Run, 4 started.
Clint Essential H., Calder Race Course, Aug. 27, $38,300, 3&up, 5f, :59.15, PLEASE ME DOC, Concorde's Appeal, Bog Hunter, 5 started.
Club House Special S., Columbus, Aug. 18, $8,199, 2yo, 6f, 1:14.20, DARK CAPE, Intervene, High Tech Racing, 10 started.
Cluff Sprint S., Western Montana Fair, July 27, $3,700, 3&up, 5f, :59.80, SEATTLE CUE, Fruit Rapport, Fire Ball John, 8 started.
COACHING CLUB AMERICAN OAKS-G1, Belmont Park, July 20, $350,000, 3yo, f, 1½m, 2:31.48, JILBAB, Tarnished Lady, Shop Till You Drop, 7 started.
Col. E. R. Bradley H., Fair Grounds, Jan. 5, $75,000, 4&up, a1¹⁄₁₆mT, 1:46.03, NORTHCOTE ROAD, Candid Glen, Red Mountain, 6 started.
Colin S., Woodbine, July 14, $133,625, 2yo, 6f, 1:11.51, RIGHTS RESERVED, Tackling Stress, Skeet, 5 started.
Colleen S., Monmouth Park, Aug. 3, $50,000, 2yo, f, 5½fT, 1:03.12, FOREVER PARTNERS, Grand Natalie Rose, Skipper's Mate, 7 started.
Collegian S., Suffolk Downs, Feb. 2, $30,000, 3yo, 6f, 1:15.04, STYLISH SULTAN, Storm Lad, Crypto Dixie, 7 started.
Colonel Power H., Fair Grounds, Jan. 12, $75,000, 4&up, 6f, 1:09.35, BONAPAW, Abajo, Crucible, 7 started.
Colonel Power S., Hawthorne Race Course, Dec. 28, $44,200, 3&up,

6½f, 1:15.07, TALKNOW, Classic Appeal, Silver Bid, 10 started.

Colonial Cup Hurdle S., Camden, Nov. 17, $100,000, 4&up, a2¾mT, 5:25.20, FLAT TOP, Tres Touche, All Gong (GB), 7 started.

Colorado Derby, Arapahoe Park, Aug. 4, $75,000, 3yo, 1 1/16m, 1:47, RAISE A BOOGER, Wishingitwas, Sneaker Mike, 7 started.

COL. R. S. MCLAUGHLIN S. (Can-G3), Woodbine, Sept. 14, $164,700, 3yo, 1⅛m, 1:52.19, EARLY WISDOM, Mark One, Shaws Creek, 8 started.

Columbia River S., Portland Meadows, Dec. 1, $10,000, 2yo, 6f, 1:12.11, STATELY JACK FLASH, Knightsbridge Road, Right You Are, 6 started.

Columbia S. (R), Tampa Bay Downs, May 4, $50,000, 3&up, Florida-bred, a1⅛mT, 1:48.12, GUARDIANOFTHEGATE, Fun n' Gun, Viva Pentelicus, 12 started.

Columbine H., Arapahoe Park, Aug. 18, $30,000, 3&up, f&m, 1 1/16m, 1:45, FOOL'S MATE, Just React, Devilinbluedenim, 8 started.

Columbus Day S., Suffolk Downs, Oct. 14, $30,000, 3&up, f&m, 6f, 1:12.84, CRESCENT COAST, Favorite Ending, Yacht to Pay For, 10 started.

Columbus Laddie S. (R), Columbus, Sept. 8, $10,400, 2yo, c&g, Nebarska-bred, 6f, 1:15, GRAYGLEN, High Tech Racing, Intervene, 6 started.

Columbus Lassie S., Columbus, Sept. 8, $10,450, 2yo, f, 6f, 1:15.60, DEVOTED FAN, Sundayblummer, Shania's Shadow, 7 started.

COMELY S.-G3, Aqueduct, April 14, $108,200, 3yo, f, 1m, 1:35.50, BELLA BELLUCCI, Short Note, Nonsuch Bay, 5 started.

Comet S., Calder Race Course, July 13, $50,000, 3&up, 5f, :57.74, GROOMSTICK STOCK'S, True Love's Secret, Handsome Smile, 7 started.

Comet S., The Meadowlands, Sept. 2, $45,500, 2yo, 6f, 1:10.03, RUN PRODUCTION, Down Play, Overpass, 3 started.

Commencement S., Great Lakes Downs, Oct. 29, $20,000, 2yo, c&g, 6f, 1:16.12, JUDGMATIC, Run for You, Smart Tale, 6 started.

COMMONWEALTH BREEDERS' CUP S.-G2, Keeneland, April 14, $272,000, 3&up, 7f, 1:21.54, ORIENTATE, Aldebaran, Twilight Road, 7 started.

Concord S., Rockingham Park, Sept. 22, $25,000, 2yo, f, 6f, 1:11.47, SWEET SAMANTHA, Jill's Layup, Ritzy Dame, 12 started.

Con Jackson Claiming H., The Downs at Albuquerque, Sept. 22, $12,500, 3&up, 1 13/16m, 3:06.31, GOOD ACTOR, Masked Rider, Speed Shifter, 9 started.

CONNAUGHT CUP S. (Can-G3), Woodbine, May 25, $178,500, 4&up, 1 1/16mT, 1:40.88, QUIET RESOLVE, No Comprende, Gone Fishin, 13 started.

Conniver S. (R), Laurel Park, March 9, $60,000, 4&up, f&m, Maryland bred, 7f, 1:23.18, WINTER LEAF, Your Out, Case of the Blues, 8 started.

Conroe S., Sam Houston Race Park, Nov. 30, $30,000, 3yo, 6f, 1:10.54, MY FRIEND DON, Agrivating General, Flash Forward, 6 started.

Continental Mile S., Monmouth Park, Aug. 18, $50,000, 2yo, 1mT, 1:38.06, MOST FEARED, My Boy Kyle, Stong, 8 started.

Convenience S. (R), Calder Race Course, Aug. 3, $50,000, 3yo, f, progeny of eligible Florida stallions, 1 1/16mT, 1:42.79, CELLARS SHIRAZ, Company B, Cagey Move, 8 started.

Cool Air H., Calder Race Course, June 3, $38,325, 3&up, f&m, 5fT, :57.34, ROCKY NORTH, Pageant Baby, Cinderella Story, 6 started.

COOLMORE LEXINGTON S.-G2, Keeneland, April 20, $364,650, 3yo, 1 1/16m, 1:44.58, PROUD CITIZEN, Crimson Hero, Easyfromthegitgo, 8 started.

Cool Reception S. (R), Fort Erie, Aug. 5, $65,200, 3&up, Canadian-bred, 1 1/16m, 1:43.82, YATSKO, Go Figure, Le Vainqueur, 6 started.

Coors Starter H. (R), Fonner Park, May 11, $10,650, 3&up, starters for a claiming price of $5,000 or less in 2001-'02, 1⅛m, 1:57.40, AMERICAN PACE, Harry's Mr. Bob, Timing's the Key, 10 started.

Copper Top Futurity (R), Sunland Park, April 7, $152,241, 2yo, New Mexico-bred, 4½f, STORMY LANE, Out of Focus, Quote This, 10 started.

Cordially S., Delaware Park, July 29, $59,700, 3yo, f, 1mT, 1:35.12, WITH PATIENCE, Smart Grace, Peace River Lady, 7 started.

Cormorant S. (R), Aqueduct, Nov. 10, $100,000, 3&up, c&g, New York-bred, 1mT, 1:39.54, HAGGS CASTLE, No White Flags, Chasin' Wimmin, 12 started.

Corona H., Hollywood Park, Dec. 8, $73,210, 3&up, f&m, 6f, 1:09.17, MADAME PIETRA, Habibti, Wild Tickle, 6 started.

Coronation Futurity (R), Woodbine, Nov. 2, $250,000, 2yo, Canadian-bred, 1⅛m, 1:53.75, ARCO'S GOLD, Mobil, Peef, 7 started.

Correction H., Aqueduct, Feb. 2, $82,775, 3&up, f&m, 6f, 1:11.59, CITY FAIR, Outstanding Info, Look of the Lynx, 8 started.

Corte Madera S., Golden Gate Fields, Dec. 28, $60,650, 2yo, f, 1m, 1:35.78, MADDIE'S CHARM, Tale of a Dream, Viansa Ossidiana, 6 started.

COTILLION H.-G2, Philadelphia Park, Oct. 5, $250,000, 3yo, f, 1 1/16m, 1:44.27, SMOK'N FROLIC, Pupil, Jilbab, 9 started.

Count Fleet S., Aqueduct, Jan. 5, $83,300, 3yo, 1m 70y, 1:41.67, IRON DEPUTY, D' Coach, No Parole, 9 started.

COUNT FLEET SPRINT H.-G3, Oaklawn Park, April 11, $150,000, 4&up, 6f, 1:08.60, EXPLICIT, Entepreneur, Junior Deputy, 5 started.

Count Latham H., Northlands Park, Aug. 3, $40,000, 3yo, 1 5/16m, 2:14.60, SIR DEUCES, Go Go Tommy Joe, Thundering Herd, 7 started.

Courtship S., Bay Meadows, Sept. 15, $67,250, 2yo, f, 5½f, 1:04.14, TALE OF A DREAM, Global Finance, Western Dame, 6 started.

Cover Gal S. (R), Santa Anita Park, Oct. 3, $81,975, 2yo, f, California-bred, 7f, 1:22.98, SUMMER WIND DANCER, Miss Nicolie, Small Town Girl, 8 started.

Cover Girl H., Hastings Park Racecourse, Sept. 7, $36,886, 3&up, f&m, 6½f, 1:17.41, LILSISTERLIGHTNING, Castle Mountain, Catahoula Rose, 7 started.

COWDIN S.-G3, Belmont Park, Oct. 13, $103,700, 2yo, 6½f, 1:16.37, BOSTON BULL, Roaring Fever, Wacky for Love, 4 started.

Coyote H., Turf Paradise, Feb. 16, $50,000, 4&up, 6f, 1:09.15, QUINTON'S GOLD, Nancy's Joker, Top Hit, 7 started.

Cradle S., River Downs, Sept. 2, $200,000, 2yo, 1 1/16m, 1:46.80, LONE STAR SKY, Christmas Away, Payforaday, 9 started.

Crafty Drone S., Hawthorne Race Course, Nov. 16, $44,200, 3&up, 5fT, MY GIRL LISA, Only You, Man o' Rhythm, 10 started.

Crank It Up S., Monmouth Park, June 9, $50,000, 3yo, 5fT, :57.29, RUNAWAY CHOICE, Lord Abounding, Stormy Day, 9 started.

CREME FRAICHE H.-G3, Gulfstream Park, March 10, $100,000, 3&up, 1 1/16m, 1:42.40, HAL'S HOPE, American Halo, Windsor Castle, 9 started.

Crescent City Derby (R), Fair Grounds, Jan. 19, $75,000, 3yo, Louisiana-bred, 1 1/16m, 1:47.40, SCREEN IDOL, Xtreme Monique, Doeny Rain, 8 started.

Crescent S., Lone Star Park, May 4, $72,750, 3&up, 6½f, 1:14.93, BEAU'S TOWN, Boots On Sunday, Exemplary, 4 started.

Criterium S., Calder Race Course, July 6, $100,000, 2yo, 5½f, 1:06.02, HEAR NO EVIL, Supah Blitz, Lex Luthier, 9 started.

CROWN ROYAL AMERICAN TURF S.-G3, Churchill Downs, May 3, $116,300, 3yo, 1 1/16mT, 1:44.43, LEGISLATOR, Stage Call (Ire), Orchard Park, 10 started.

Crystal Water H. (R), Santa Anita Park, March 24, $139,125, 4&up, California-bred, 1mT, 1:34.39, HUGH HEFNER, Spinelessjellyfish, Native Desert, 8 started.

CTBA Breeders' Oaks (R), Arapahoe Park, Aug. 10, $30,000, 3yo, f, Colorado-bred, 1m, 1:42, SHE'S FINDING TIME, Make the Deposit, Holly Dolly, 7 started.

CTBA Derby (R), Arapahoe Park, Aug. 25, $30,000, 3yo, Colorado-bred, 1 1/16m, 1:46.20, BEAU RAE ME, Phat Daddy, Gone With the Win, 11 started.

CTBA Futurity (R), Arapahoe Park, Aug. 3, $30,000, 2yo, Colorado-bred, 6f, 1:12, FANCY TAL ONE, Sara Margaret, Double Milion, 12 started.

CTBA Lassie S. (R), Arapahoe Park, Aug. 31, $30,000, 2yo, f, Colorado-bred, 6f, 1:12.40, TRICKY TRANSACTION, Lil Rhett's Vet, Rare Charm, 11 started.

CTBA Marian S. (R), Fairplex Park, Sept. 23, $50,000, 3yo, f, California-bred, 1 1/16m, 1:45.54, BOB'S LADY, Excessive Angi, Surprisingly, 8 started.

CTHS Sales S. (R), Hastings Park Racecourse, Sept. 8, $66,552, 2yo, c&g, Canadian-bred sold at a CTHS sale, 6½f, 1:19.28, HAMMERSMITH, Steady Smiler, Mike's Pick, 8 started.

CTHS Sales S. (R), Assiniboia Downs, Sept. 2, $30,000, 2yo, c&g, passed through the ring at a CTHS (Manitoba Div.) sale, 6f, 1:16.60, CABERNET, Bold Lover, Hopetobeastar, 8 started.

CTHS Sales S. (R), Northlands Park, Aug. 17, $50,000, 2yo, c&g, Canadian-bred sold at a CTHS sale, 6½f, 1:19, JIFFYJIMMYGEE, Rokeby's Speedster, Katahaula Myst, 8 started.

CTHS Sales S. (R), Hastings Park Racecourse, Sept. 8, $66,708, 2yo, f, Canadian-bred sold at a CTHS sale, 6½f, 1:19.37, SEARCHIN SOUTH, Handy N Candid, Proactive, 7 started.

CTHS Sales S. (R), Assiniboia Downs, Sept. 2, $30,000, 2yo, f, passed through the ring at a CTHS (Manitoba Div.) sale, 6f, 1:14.80, AIR DRIVER, New Release, Regal Dancer, 7 started.

CTHS Sales S. (R), Northlands Park, Aug. 17, $50,000, 2yo, f, Canadian-bred sold at a CTHS sale, 6½f, 1:20, DOWHATUTHINKSRIGHT, Grand Slam Gal, Brassy Nancy, 10 started.

CTT and Thoroughbred Owners of California H., Del Mar, Sept. 5,

$76,050, 3&up, f&m, 1⅜mT, 2:13.69, CANZONE (Brz), Nepenthe, Tropical Lady (Brz), 8 started.

Cup and Saucer S. (R), Woodbine, Oct. 12, $250,000, 2yo, Canadian-bred, 1 1/16mT, 1:42.33, MOBIL, Shoal Water, Gavro, 14 started.

Curribot H., Sunland Park, Feb. 9, $33,800, 3&up, 1 1/16m, 1:45.06, BREW, Vernon Invader, Alyou, 12 started.

Cut the Charm S., Calder Race Course, May 17, $36,960, 3yo, f, 1m, 1:40.24, FOUR PENNIES, Chit Chatter, Stormy Frolic, 5 started.

C. W. "Doc" Pardee Starter S. (R), Turf Paradise, April 27, $15,000, 3&up, f&m, Arizona-bred starters for a claming price of $8,000 or less since September 27, 2001, 1m, 1:38.49, CITY LOOT, Lil Lucia, Diamond Jill, 8 started.

Cyclones H. (R), Prairie Meadows, June 29, $76,930, 3&up, c&g, Iowa-bred, 1 1/16m, 1:43.44, COWBOY STUFF, Take Me Up, Sure Shot Biscuit, 5 started.

Cy-Fair S., Sam Houston Race Park, Dec. 7, $30,000, 3yo, f, 6f, 1:10, FLEETA DIF, Piniante, Cielo Girl, 7 started.

Czaria H., Sunland Park, Feb. 10, $33,900, 3&up, f&m, 6f, 1:09.47, ODE TO ELAINE, Good Timin Brook, Quite Spender, 11 started.

Dade Turf Classic S., Ellis Park, Aug. 31, $59,500, 3&up, f&m, 1⅛mT, 1:46.43, KISS THE DEVIL, Evil Woman, De Aar, 8 started.

DAHLIA H.-G2, Hollywood Park, Dec. 21, $150,000, 3&up, f&m, 1 1/16mT, 1:44.55, (DH) SURYA, (DH) TOUT CHARMANT, Honestly Darling, 9 started.

Da Hoss S., Colonial Downs, June 29, $40,000, 3&up, 1m, 1:35.90, LA REINE'S TERMS, Jubileo, Elberton, 10 started.

Daily Courier Inaugural H., Grants Pass, May 18, $4,075, 3&up, 5½f, 1:05.20, L. CAPONE, Imus, Victor Lehman, 8 started.

Dallas Turf Cup H., Lone Star Park, June 15, $250,000, 3&up, 1⅛mT, 1:49.09, SUANCES (GB), Our Main Man, Candid Glen, 8 started.

Dame Mysterieuse S., Gulfstream Park, Feb. 18, $71,000, 3yo, f, 5f, 57.05, BOLD WORLD, Awol, Castelli Miss, 7 started.

Damitrius S., Delaware Park, May 11, $75,300, 3&up, 6f, 1:10.51, STORMIN OEDY, Wild Current, Chief J Strongbow, 6 started.

Damon Runyon S. (R), Aqueduct, Dec. 15, $82,625, 2yo, New York-bred, 1 1/16m, 1:44.25, GREY COMET, Unswept, Go Rockin' Robin, 8 started.

DANCE SMARTLY S. (Can-G3), Woodbine, July 6, $210,100, 3&up, f&m, 1⅛mT, 1:45.72, SWEETEST THING, Mountain Angel, Rosthern, 7 started.

Dancing Count S., Laurel Park, Jan. 1, $40,000, 3yo, 6f, 1:12.20, PRESIDENT BUTLER, Southern Livin, Coach Knight, 7 started.

Daniel's Boy H., Calder Race Course, Sept. 1, $38,185, 3&up, 1 1/16m, 1:45.13, PAY THE PREACHER, Ballado's Devil, High Ideal, 6 started.

Daniel Van Clief S. (R), Colonial Downs, July 21, $40,000, 3&up, Virginia-bred, 1 1/16mT, 1:44.98, SMASHING BEAU, Cherokeeinthehills, Purple Sand, 9 started.

Danville H., Golden Gate Fields, March 24, $61,125, 3&up, 6f, 1:08.66, MELLOW FELLOW, Tony's Royalty, Today a Star, 5 started.

Danzig S. (R), Penn National Race Course, May 10, $30,625, 3yo, Pennsylvania-bred, 6f, 1:10.76, OSWAYO, Midnite Coach, R B's Boy, 7 started.

Dartsum S., Calder Race Course, Aug. 6, $43,955, 3yo, 1 1/16m, 1:45.79, RUSSIAN HAND, Sebastian Light, Class of Seventy, 9 started.

Dave Feldman S., Gulfstream Park, Jan. 14, $73,800, 3yo, 1 1/16mT, 1:43.62, WORLDLY VICTOR, Charming Colony, Lord Juban, 11 started.

Dave Lewis Memorial S., Grand Prairie, July 26, $4,315, 3&up, 7f, POLISH POPPA, Wise Dancer, Island Slew, 6 started.

Dave's Friend S., Laurel Park, Aug. 3, $50,000, 3&up, 6f, 1:09.34, SASSY HOUND, Deer Run, Rusty Spur, 5 started.

David L. 'Zeke' Ferguson Memorial S., Colonial Downs, July 13, $50,000, 4&up, a2¼mT, 4:09.75, INVEST WEST, Tres Touche, P. C. Plod, 7 started.

DAVONA DALE S.-G2, Gulfstream Park, Feb. 24, $100,000, 3yo, f, 1 1/16m, 1:45.14, MS BROOKSKI, Colonial Glitter, French Satin, 9 started.

Dayjur H., Hollywood Park, Dec. 22, $85,970, 3&up, 5½fT, 1:02.74, ECHO EDDIE, Rocky Bar, Slew of the Night, 5 started.

Dearly Precious S., Monmouth Park, June 30, $48,500, 3yo, f, 6f, 1:09.68, WISH IT WERE, Haunted Lass, School for Scandal, 4 started.

Dearly Precious S., Aqueduct, Feb. 16, $80,750, 3yo, f, 6f, 1:11.01, PROPER GAMBLE, Dancing Blues, Lost Expectations, 5 started.

Debutante S., Assiniboia Downs, July 20, $30,000, 2yo, f, 5½f, 1:07.80, TUCKY'S GIRL, Angels R Watching, Private Navy, 8 started.

DEBUTANTE S.-G3, Churchill Downs, July 6, $109,500, 2yo, f, 5½f, 1:03.45, AWESOME HUMOR, Vibs, Attemptress, 7 started.

Decoration Day H., Mountaineer Park, May 27, $79,100, 3&up, f&m, 7½fT, 1:28.75, FLASHING LIL, Elaine's Booboo, Knight Dancer, 11 started.

DE LA ROSE H.-G3, Gulfstream Park, Jan. 25, $100,000, 3&up, f&m, 1 1/16mT, 1:42.06, VEIL OF AVALON, Snow Dance, Wander Mom, 12 started.

DELAWARE H.-G3, Delaware Park, July 21, $601,200, 3&up, f&m, 1¼m, 2:04.52, SUMMER COLONY, Your Out, Two Item Limit, 9 started.

DELAWARE OAKS-G3, Delaware Park, July 20, $250,300, 3yo, f, 1 1/16m, 1:43.81, ALLAMERICAN BERTIE, Alternate, Pass the Virtue, 6 started.

Delaware Park-NATC Sorority (R), Delaware Park, Aug. 31, $201,800, 2yo, f, graduate of a two-year-olds in training sale and consigned by an NATC member and contributor to its ad fund, 6f, 1:13.21, COLLYMORE HALL, Niclie, Heirloom Diamond, 11 started.

Delicada S., Louisiana Downs, July 21, $39,200, 3&up, f&m, 1 1/16m, 1:46.12, DUE TO WIN, Blue Guru, McKinney, 5 started.

DEL MAR BREEDERS' CUP H.-G2, Del Mar, Sept. 2, $250,000, 3&up, 1m, 1:36.34, CONGAREE, Kela, Reba's Gold, 6 started.

DEL MAR DEBUTANTE S.-G1, Del Mar, Aug. 31, $250,000, 2yo, f, 7f, 1:23.43, MISS HOUDINI, Santa Catarina, Indy Groove, 8 started.

DEL MAR DERBY-G2, Del Mar, Sept. 7, $300,000, 3yo, 1⅛mT, 1:47.49, INESPERADO (Fr), Johar, Rock Opera, 9 started.

DEL MAR FUTURITY-G2, Del Mar, Sept. 11, $250,000, 2yo, 7f, 1:22.94, ICECOLDBEERATREDS, Kafwain, Chief Planner, 8 started.

DEL MAR H.-G2, Del Mar, Sept. 1, $250,000, 3&up, 1⅜mT, 2:12.15, DELTA FORM (Aus), The Tin Man, Blue Steller (Ire), 10 started.

DEL MAR OAKS-G1, Del Mar, Aug. 24, $300,000, 3yo, f, 1⅛mT, 1:47.16, DUBLINO, Megahertz (GB), Alozaina (Ire), 6 started.

Delta Colleen H., Hastings Park Racecourse, Sept. 22, $38,507, 3&up, f&m, 1 1/16m, 1:45.06, FULL SCREAM AHEAD, Catahoula Rose, Four Anne Affair, 8 started.

Delta Jackpot S., Delta Downs, Dec. 21, $500,000, 2yo, 1m, 1:37.77, OUTTA HERE, Comic Truth, Cherokee's Boy, 10 started.

Delta Miss S., Louisiana Downs, Sept. 29, $30,000, 2yo, f, 6½f, 1:17.99, MEKKO HOKTE, Hadif's Allstar, Obligatory, 6 started.

Delta Princess S., Delta Downs, Dec. 20, $250,000, 2yo, f, 1m, 1:39.54, MY TRUSTY CAT, Souris, Miss Mary Apples, 8 started.

Demetri's Boy S. (R), Hawthorne Race Course, Dec. 7, $43,400, 3yo, Illinois-conceived and/or-foaled, 1 1/16m, 1:46.54, COLORFUL TOUR, Happiness, Garesche, 8 started.

DEMOISELLE S.-G2, Aqueduct, Nov. 30, $200,000, 2yo, f, 1⅛m, 1:51.43, ROAR EMOTION, Savedbythelight, Feisty Step, 10 started.

Denise Rhudy Memorial S., Delaware Park, Aug. 31, $72,750, 3yo, f, 1 1/16mT, 1:45.38, HIGH MAINTENANCE (GB), Garden Dance, Behind the Bluff, 4 started.

Deputed Testamony S. (R), Laurel Park, March 2, $75,000, 3yo, Maryland-bred, 1 1/16m, 1:44.81, MAGIC WEISNER, Invent, Root With Style, 5 started.

DEPUTY MINISTER H.-G3, Gulfstream Park, Feb. 10, $100,000, 3&up, 6½f, 1:16.19, FAPPIE'S NOTEBOOK, Twilight Road, Binthebest, 7 started.

Deputy Minister S. (R), Woodbine, Oct. 16, $131,250, 3yo, progeny of eligible Ontario stallions, 7f, 1:22.96, MULLIGAN THE GREAT, Mister Coop, Sophia's Prince, 6 started.

Derby Day H., Blue Ribbon Downs, May 4, $13,675, 3&up, 6f, 1:10.69, CANROCK, Tricky Hawaiian, Proper Mariner, 9 started.

Derby Day H., Eureka Downs, May 4, $4,900, 3&up, 4f, R C MR HAY BOY, Maggierah, Brother Huz, 9 started.

Derby Trial S., Fairplex Park, Sept. 16, $49,500, 3yo, 1 1/16m, 1:43.38, BOLD MANGO, Lou's Expectation, National Park (GB), 7 started.

Derby Trial S., Assiniboia Downs, July 14, $30,000, 3yo, 1 1/16m, 1:47.40, EKATI, Winaferd, Portan, 5 started.

DERBY TRIAL S.-G3, Churchill Downs, April 27, $112,800, 3yo, 1m, 1:36.87, SKY TERRACE, Cashel Castle, Ide Be Spencers, 6 started.

DESERT STORMER H.-G3, Hollywood Park, June 7, $107,100, 3&up, f&m, 6f, 1:09.57, SLEWSBOX, Kalookan Queen, Rolly Polly (Ire), 6 started.

Desert Vixen S. (R), Calder Race Course, Aug. 10, $75,000, 2yo, f, progeny of eligible Florida stallions, 6f, 1:11.72, FORTUNATE CARD, Heavenly Miss, Running Debate, 10 started.

Dessie & Fern Sawyer Futurity (R), The Downs at Albuquerque, Sept. 22, $59,182, 2yo, f, New Mexico-bred, 6f, 1:10.58, MISS TRIXIE, Shemoveslikeaghost, Out of Focus, 11 started.

Devil's Honor H. (R), Philadelphia Park, Oct. 5, $50,000, 3&up, Pennsylvania-bred, 7f, 1:23.24, DOCENT, Wild Current, Beau's Surprise, 5 started.

Diamond 'A' USA S., Lone Star Park, May 27, $200,000, 3yo, 1 1/16mT, 1:44.75, REGIMENT, Diamond Hope, Kamolia, 6 started.

Diamond Trail S., Prairie Meadows, May 18, $50,000, 3&up, f&m, 1m 70y, 1:40.28, MINISTER'S BABY, Bold Bluff, Delray Dew, 6 started.

DIANA H.-G2, Saratoga Race Course, July 27, $500,000, 3&up, f&m, 1⅛mT, 1:48, TATES CREEK, Voodoo Dancer, Snow Dance, 9 started.

Diane Kem H., Portland Meadows, Nov. 10, $10,000, 3&up, f&m, 6f, 1:12.91, ICICLE ANGEL, Maria Kay, Stareaux, 9 started.

Dine S. (R), SunRay Park, Nov. 18, $66,500, 3yo, c&g, New Mexico-bred, 6½f, 1:18, URLACHER, J J Mystique, Stanton Street, 5 started.

Diplomat Way H., Fair Grounds, Jan. 20, $75,000, 4&up, 1 1/16m, 1:44.42, CRAFTY SHAW, Drewman, Tahkodha Hills, 9 started.

DISCOVERY H.-G3, Aqueduct, Oct. 23, $114,000, 3yo, 1⅛m, 1:49.13, SAINT MARDEN, Regency Park, No Parole, 10 started.

Display S., Woodbine, Nov. 20, $135,625, 2yo, 1 1/16m, 1:43.04, GIGAWATT, Chad's Hope, Tackling Stress, 5 started.

Distaff Bettor's Invitational H., Grants Pass, June 23, $5,525, 3&up, f&m, 6½f, 1:21.60, MISSY MUFFET, Oh Molly, Carey's Blue Mon, 4 started.

DISTAFF BREEDERS' CUP H.-G2, Aqueduct, March 30, $142,300, 3&up, f&m, 7f, 1:21.78, RAGING FEVER, Prized Stamp, La Galerie (Arg), 6 started.

Distaff S. (R), Assiniboia Downs, Sept. 2, $30,000, 3&up, f&m, Manitoba-bred, 1m, 1:41.80, DAWN EDITION, Complete Edition, Cayenne Pepper, 6 started.

Dixie Belle, Oaklawn Park, Jan. 25, $50,000, 3yo, f, 6f, 1:12.45, BEDANKEN, Born to Dance, For Rubies, 8 started.

Dixie Miss S., Louisiana Downs, Aug. 10, $40,000, 3yo, f, 6f, 1:11.43, TAYLOR'S QUEEN, Cielo Girl, Highhopesemilyluck, 6 started.

Dixie Poker Ace H. (R), Fair Grounds, March 3, $75,000, 4&up, Louisiana-bred, a7½fT, 1:35.69, COACH RAGS, Pink Duck, Doctor Mike, 9 started.

DIXIE S.-G2, Pimlico, May 18, $200,000, 3&up, 1⅛mT, 1:51.70, STRUT THE STAGE, Slew the Red, Del Mar Show, 7 started.

Dr. A. B. Leggio Memorial H., Fair Grounds, Dec. 7, $60,000, 3&up, f&m, a5½fT, 1:04.61, LESLIE'S LOVE, Lady of Peace, Presumed Innocent, 7 started.

Dr. O. G. Fischer Memorial H., SunRay Park, Oct. 11, $33,100, 3&up, f&m, 7f, 1:22.60, HAVA PEER, Foolish Megan, Okanagan Invader, 9 started.

DOGWOOD S.-G3, Churchill Downs, May 25, $109,500, 3yo, f, 1 1/16m, 1:42.73, TAKE CHARGE LADY, Charmed Gift, Allamerican Bertie, 7 started.

DOMINION DAY S. (Can-G3), Woodbine, July 1, $219,800, 3&up, 1¼m, 2:03.01, BONUS PACK, Attest, Win City, 7 started.

Donald LeVine Memorial S., Philadelphia Park, Aug. 17, $75,000, 3&up, 7f, 1:22.80, NIGHT CALLER, Ticket to Freedom, Sea of Green, 7 started.

Donald Valpredo California Cup Sprint H. (R), Santa Anita Park, Nov. 2, $150,000, 3&up, California-bred, 6f, 1:08.35, UNLIMITED VALUE, Treasured Note, Con Quixote, 8 started.

Don Bernhardt S., Ellis Park, July 27, $59,000, 3&up, 6½f, 1:15.97, DASH FOR DAYLIGHT, Better Road, Bet On Sunshine, 8 started.

Don B. S. (R), Bay Meadows, Nov. 2, $80,500, 2yo, California-bred, 6f, 1:11.01, SAILINWITHCAPTAIN, Timely Jeff, Novel T Dreamer, 5 started.

Don Juan De Onate S. (R), The Downs at Albuquerque, May 19, $33,000, 3yo, c&g, New Mexico-bred, 6f, 1:09.70, URLACHER, B. G. Tiger, Bulletman Jack, 8 started.

Donna Reed S. (R), Prairie Meadows, Aug. 31, $81,600, 4&up, f&m, Iowa-bred, 1m 70y, 1:43.15, SHARKY'S REVIEW, Pj's Halo, Scenic Won, 11 started.

DONN H.-G1, Gulfstream Park, Feb. 9, $500,000, 3&up, 1⅛m, 1:49.63, MONGOOSE, Kiss a Native, Rize, 14 started.

Donnie Wilhite Memorial S., Louisiana Downs, Sept. 21, $40,000, 3yo, 1/16mT, 1:43.17, DE REAL DEAL, Royal Win, Mooring Sand, 10 started.

Doubledogdare S., Keeneland, April 18, $107,600, 4&up, f&m, 1 1/16m, 1:42.92, DANCETHRUTHEDAWN, Maltese Superb, De Bertie, 5 started.

Double Your Flavor S. (R), Sam Houston Race Park, March 30, $30,000, 4&up, f&m, Texas-bred, 7f, 1:23.60, COASTALOTA, Tip the Man, June Spender, 8 started.

Dover S., Delaware Park, Oct. 26, $101,500, 2yo, 1m, 1:40.12, MT. CARSON, Valenzo, Cape Good Hope, 10 started.

Dowager S., Keeneland, Oct. 13, $112,200, 3&up, f&m, 1½mT, 2:35.17, LAPUMA, Evil Woman, Volga (Ire), 9 started.

Dowd Mile H., Fonner Park, April 6, $36,960, 3&up, 1m, 1:38.60, TATE'S WAY, Battle Mountain, King's Verse, 8 started.

Dowling S. (R), Great Lakes Downs, Aug. 24, $45,000, 3yo, c&g, Michigan-bred, 1m, 1:42.61, SPRING WINDS, Equi Power, Clinton County, 8 started.

Dr. Ernest Benner S. (R), Charles Town, Sept. 21, $31,550, 2yo, nominated to the West Virginia Breeders' Classic, 6½f, 1:21.80, LONGFIELD SPUD, Don't You Tell, Straight Star, 10 started.

Dr. Fager S. (R), Calder Race Course, Aug. 10, $75,000, 2yo, progeny of eligible Florida stallions, 6f, 1:11.28, LAWBOOK, Trust N Luck, Supah Blitz, 10 started.

Dr. James Penny Memorial H., Philadelphia Park, June 29, $100,000, 3&up, f&m, 1 1/16mT, 1:46.86, BABAE (Chi), Rhum, Watch, 5 started.

D. S. 'Shine' Young Memorial Futurity (R), Evangeline Downs, July 4, $100,000, 2yo, Louisiana-bred, 5f, 59.40, ONE TOUGH RAISER, Ruthy Red, Justlikejessejames, 12 started.

DTHA Owners Day H. (R), Delaware Park, Sept. 7, $100,900, 3&up, starters at Delaware Park in a non-stake in 2002, 1⅛m, 1:51.37, RUNSPASTUM, American Prince, Confucius Say, 8 started.

Duchess of York S., Stampede Park, June 8, $40,000, 3&up, f&m, 1 1/16m, 1:47.40, CATAHOULA ROSE, Slewability, Toppers Happy, 9 started.

DUCHESS S. (Can-G3), Woodbine, Aug. 10, $210,850, 3yo, f, 7f, 1:23.98, MULRAINY, For Rubies, Spanish Decree, 8 started.

Duncan Hopeful S., Greenelee County Fair, March 24, $4,842, 3&up, 5½f, 1:05.40, RISING ROYALITY, Ging, Bank Burglar, 6 started.

DURHAM CUP S. (Can-G3), Woodbine, Oct. 5, $164,850, 3&up, 1⅛m, 1:52.45, DREAM LAUNCHER, Parose, A Fleets Dancer, 8 started.

Dust Commander S., Turfway Park, Feb. 16, $50,000, 4&up, 1m, 1:36.66, GOLDEN OLDIE, Mail Call, Winning Connection, 9 started.

Dwight D. Patterson H. (R), Turf Paradise, April 27, $30,000, 3&up, Arizona-bred, 1 1/16mT, 1:42.86, LAKE GARDA, C. D. Haj, Four Fifteen, 9 started.

DWYER S.-G2, Belmont Park, July 7, $150,000, 3yo, 1 1/16m, 1:42.59, GYGISTAR, Nothing Flat, American Style, 6 started.

Earlene McCabe Derby (R), Sacramento, Aug. 25, $50,110, 3yo, California-bred, 6f, 1:08.40, MENACING DENNIS, Duddly Doo Run, Four Checker, 6 started.

EARLY TIMES MINT JULEP H.-G3, Churchill Downs, May 18, $112,900, 4&up, f&m, 1 1/16mT, 1:42.87, MEGANS BLUFF, Cozy Island, Solvig, 8 started.

East View S. (R), Aqueduct, Dec. 8, $80,775, 2yo, f, New York-bred, 1 1/16m, 1:46.64, MARC'S RAINBOW, Combanchera, Beautiful America, 6 started.

EATONTOWN H.-G3, Monmouth Park, Aug. 4, $100,000, 3&up, f&m, 1 1/16mT, 1:44.02, CLEARLY A QUEEN, Laurica, Presumed Innocent, 9 started.

E. B. Johnston S., Fairplex Park, Sept. 15, $49,000, 3&up, f&m, 1 1/16m, 1:43.96, SPUNKY GAL, Lookn Mighty Fine, Chastity Belle, 6 started.

ECLIPSE S. (Can-G3), Woodbine, May 11, $161,400, 4&up, 1 1/16m, 1:44.45, LIL PERSONALITEE, A Fleets Dancer, Dream Launcher, 6 started.

EDDIE READ H.-G1, Del Mar, July 28, $400,000, 3&up, 1⅛mT, 1:46.77, SARAFAN, Beat Hollow (GB), Redattore (Brz), 6 started.

Edgewood S., Churchill Downs, May 3, $115,800, 3yo, f, 1mT, 1:37.65, MALIZIOSA, Cellars Shiraz, Traci's Wild, 10 started.

Edmonton Distaff, Northlands Park, Aug. 24, $75,000, 3&up, f&m, 1 1/16m, 1:46, C D COOL, Full Scream Ahead, Toppers Happy, 7 started.

Edmonton Juvenile S., Northlands Park, July 26, $40,000, 2yo, c&g, 6f, 1:11.80, TAIASLEW, Judge Ruckus, Diablo Contento, 6 started.

Edward Babst Memorial S. (R), Beulah Park, April 6, $40,000, 3&up, Ohio-bred, 6f, 1:12.12, DISAPPEARANCE, Rollin Me Out, Down Thepike Mike, 9 started.

Edward J. DeBartolo Sr. Memorial Breeders' Cup H., Remington Park, Sept. 29, $147,750, 3&up, 1⅛mT, 1:49.42, BIEN NICOLE, Candid Glen, Maysville Slew, 9 started.

Egret S., The Meadowlands, Sept. 21, $50,000, 3yo, f, 5fT, AUGUST STORM, Dovetail, Storm Dancer, 12 started.

Eight Thirty S., Delaware Park, Sept. 24, $59,900, 3&up, 1⅛m, 1:51.65, TEMPEST FUGIT, Full Brush, Jakey D, 8 started.

E. K. Rolfson Senior Memorial Thoroughbred S. (R), Chippewa Downs, June 16, $9,375, 4&up, North Dakota-bred, 1m, 1:45.60, STILAFERD, Northern Cheyenne, Energy Plus, 6 started.

El Cajon S. (R), Del Mar, Sept. 6, $92,750, 3yo, non-winners of $60,000 at one mile or over in 2002, 1m, 1:36.94, JOEY FRANCO, Taste of Paradise, Paxtecum, 7 started.

EL CAMINO REAL DERBY-G3, Golden Gate Fields, March 9, $200,000, 3yo, 1 1/16m, 1:43.48, YOUGOTTAWANNA, Danthebluegrassman, Lusty Latin, 10 started.

EL CONEJO H.-G3, Santa Anita Park, Jan. 1, $109,500, 4&up, 5½f, 1:03.05, SNOW RIDGE, Explicit, Rio Oro, 8 started.

Eleanora Sears S. (R), Suffolk Downs, Nov. 2, $30,000, 3&up, f&m,

Massachusetts-bred, 6f, 1:14.83, BIG MISS, Conlua, Sunlit Ridge, 6 started.

EL ENCINO S.-G2, Santa Anita Park, Jan. 20, $150,000, 4yo, f, 1 1/16m, 1:42.60, AFFLUENT, Royally Chosen, Sea Reel, 6 started.

Eleven North H. (R), Monmouth Park, Aug. 28, $50,000, 3&up, f&m, New Jersey-bred, 6f, 1:10.32, GOLDEN MADE, Mary's Nickle, Silent Serenade, 5 started.

Elge Rasberry Memorial S. (R), Fair Grounds, Jan. 3, $22,750, 3yo, f, Louisiana-bred, 6f, 1:12.07, C J'S STAR, Monumental Upset, Ike and Fannie, 3 started.

Elgin S. (R), Woodbine, Sept. 2, $104,650, 3&up, c&g, Canadian-bred, 1 1/16m, 1:44.80, FOREVER GRAND, Cool N Collective, Barbeau Ruckus, 8 started.

El Gran Fernando H., Calder Race Course, July 28, $44,725, 3&up, 5fT, 56.62, TRUE LOVE'S SECRET, Sunny Approval, Roy's Ruckus, 10 started.

Elie Destruel H., Santa Rosa, Aug. 5, $50,990, 3&up, f&m, 6f, 1:09.45, CHANNING WAY, Onslaught, Party Pirate, 5 started.

Elite Jeblar H., Calder Race Course, Aug. 12, $41,020, 3&up, 1m, 1:37.94, JUNIOR DEPUTY, Pay the Preacher, Doowaley (Ire), 7 started.

Eliza S., Arlington Park, Oct. 27, $100,000, 2yo, f, 7f, 1:24.56, ALLSPICE, Jodys Deelite, Diamonds to Me, 6 started.

El Joven S., Retama Park, Aug. 31, $100,000, 2yo, c&g, 1mT, 1:37.81, ZYDECO AFFAIR, Leo's Last Hurrahy, Alpler, 11 started.

ELKHORN S.-G3, Keeneland, April 24, $150,000, 4&up, 1½mT, 2:32.49, KIM LOVES BUCKY, Rochester, Cetewayo, 10 started.

Elko Thoroughbred Derby, Elko County Fair, Sept. 2, $8,420, 3yo, 7f, HEYSHE'SATRADER, Crooked Monkey, Inside Trader, 6 started.

Elko Throroughbred Futurity, Elko County Fair, Sept. 2, $13,100, 2yo, 5½f, 1:12.20, SPARKS A FLYIN, Two Star Story, Buckaroot, 6 started.

Ellis Park Breeders' Cup H., Ellis Park, Aug. 10, $129,700, 3&up, f&m, 6f, 1:10.64, INTEREST ONLY, Hattiesburg, Juke, 7 started.

Elmer Heubeck Distaff H. (R), Calder Race Course, Nov. 16, $200,000, 3&up, f&m, Florida-bred, 1 1/16m, 1:46.29, COOLBYTHEPOOL, Sara's Success, Cellars Shiraz, 7 started.

El Paso Times H., Sunland Park, March 16, $32,900, 3yo, f, 6f, 1:11.94, AFTER THE BEEP, Sky Sprite, Excellently, 9 started.

Emerald Breeders' Cup Distaff, Emerald Downs, Aug. 25, $84,375, 3&up, f&m, 1m, 1:35, ALWAYS A DIXIE, Graceful Cat, Whatdidshesay, 9 started.

Emerald Downs Breeders' Cup Derby, Emerald Downs, Sept. 2, $123,125, 3yo, 1⅛m, 1:45.40, FLYING NOTES, World Light, Blowin in the Wind, 6 started.

Emerald Downs H., Hastings Park Racecourse, June 30, $38,010, 3yo, f, 6½f, 1:17.46, ELANA D'AMOUR, R C Gangster, Shelby Madison, 7 started.

Emerald Express S., Emerald Downs, July 13, $35,000, 2yo, c&g, 6f, 1:09.40, KNIGHTSBRIDGE ROAD, Bub, Grandpa Chan, 7 started.

Emerald H., Emerald Downs, June 16, $75,000, 3&up, 1m, 1:33.40, SECRET LAUNCH, Crowning Meeting, Jade Green, 8 started.

Emerald Necklace S. (R), Thistledown, Sept. 21, $30,000, 2yo, f, Ohio-bred, 6f, 1:12.20, IFUFEELFROGGYLEAP, Dinkers Pride, Gazelle Belle, 5 started.

Emeryville S., Golden Gate Fields, March 31, $55,700, 3yo, f, 6f, 1:09.48, HALO TYRA, Respectful, Rich Musique, 9 started.

Empire Classic H. (R), Belmont Park, Oct. 19, $250,000, 3&up, New York-bred, 1⅛m, 1:48.95, GANDER, Compelling World, Lord Ofthe Thunder, 12 started.

Endeavour S., Tampa Bay Downs, Feb. 9, $75,000, 4&up, f&m, a1⅛mT, 1:50.40, CHAUSSON POIRE, Kelly Bag, Golden Antigua, 11 started.

ENDINE S.-G3, Delaware Park, Sept. 7, $150,000, 3&up, f&m, 6f, 1:10.91, XTRA HEAT, Outstanding Info, Urban Dancer, 5 started.

Endless Surprise S., Laurel Park, March 17, $50,000, 4&up, 6f, 1:09.94, RUSTY SPUR, Deer Run, Trounce, 6 started.

E. P. TAYLOR S. (Can-G1), Woodbine, Sept. 29, $750,000, 3&up, f&m, 1¼mT, 2:10.03, FRAULEIN (GB), Alasha (Ire), Volga (Ire), 6 started.

Equalize S. (R), Gulfstream Park, March 16, $143,100, 3&up, Florida-bred, 1m, 1:33.40, UNITE'S BIG RED, Honorable Pic, Stokosky, 8 started.

Ernest Finley H., Santa Rosa, July 27, $50,770, 3&up, 6f, 1:08.22, SEMPAI, Profound Secret, Mistakenly Special, 7 started.

Escaped H. (R), The Meadowlands, Sept. 28, $50,000, 3&up, New Jersey-bred, 1m 70y, 1:40.97, BRUCKER'S BROTHER, Horrible Evening, Beknown to Me, 7 started.

Escena S., Gulfstream Park, Jan. 11, $75,400, 3&up, f&m, 1 1/16m, 1:45.60, DE BERTIE, Sara's Success, Lily's Affair, 13 started.

Escondido H. (R), Del Mar, Aug. 7, $78,650, 3&up, non-winners of $60,000 at one mile or over in 2002, 1⅜mT, 2:12.86, DANCE DREAMER, Little Ghazi, Homeland (Fr), 5 started.

ESSEX H.-G3, Oaklawn Park, Feb. 23, $75,000, 4&up, 1 1/16m, 1:43.14, CRAFTY SHAW, Kiss of Lion (Arg), Remington Rock, 6 started.

Estrapade H., Arlington Park, Oct. 25, $100,000, 3&up, f&m, 1 1/16mT, 1:44.52, BIEN NICOLE, Verruma (Brz), Kiss the Devil, 10 started.

Eternal Search S. (R), Woodbine, July 31, $127,125, 3yo, f, Canadian-bred, 1 1/16m, 1:45.67, BRASS IN POCKET, Bright Knight, Heyahohowdy, 5 started.

E.T. Springer S. (R), The Downs at Albuquerque, Sept. 7, $32,500, 3&up, New Mexico-bred, 7f, 1:21.73, BULLETMAN JACK, Romeos Wilson, Live Show, 8 started.

Eureka Downs Derby Final S., Eureka Downs, June 2, $13,220, 3&up, 6f, 1:18.12, DE GOLD STUFF, Cast of Gold, Mild Expense, 7 started.

Eureka Downs Distance H., Eureka Downs, July 4, $5,207, 3&up, 1 1/16m, 1:53.98, JUST A ECLIPSE, Moscows Quick Trip, Noble Dreamer, 5 started.

Eureka Downs Thoroughbred Futurity S., Eureka Downs, June 23, $15,500, 2yo, 4f, .91, NOBLE DELIGHT, Enemy Number Two, Snoopin for Gold, 7 started.

Evangeline Downs Sprint Championship, Evangeline Downs, June 22, $30,000, 3&up, 6f, 1:10, OAK HALL, No Its Not, Samlot, 7 started.

Evangeline Mile H., Evangeline Downs, Aug. 17, $75,000, 3&up, 1m, 1:39, OAK HALL, Compendium, L. A. Spider Legs, 7 started.

Evan Shipman H. (R), Belmont Park, July 21, $81,475, 3&up, New York-bred, 1 1/16m, 1:42.71, SHERPA GUIDE, Turnofthecentury, Mount Intrepid, 6 started.

Evanston Derby, Wyoming Downs, July 13, $3,600, 3yo, 6f, 1:12.87, PROMENADE, R Easy Money, Weavemesomefreedom, 6 started.

Evanston Speed H., Wyoming Downs, July 13, $3,550, 3&up, 4½f, FIRE BALL JOHN, Synapse, Hulibid, 9 started.

Evansville S. (R), Hoosier Park, Oct. 25, $44,700, 3yo, f, Indiana-bred, 1 1/16m, 1:49.56, JUST EMMA, Connies Travels, Thesullivanfive, 12 started.

Everett Nevin Alameda County Futurity (R), Pleasanton, July 5, $53,340, 2yo, California-bred, 5f, 57.49, TARAVAL, Standard Setter, Bang, 9 started.

Excalibur S., Louisiana Downs, Nov. 2, $30,000, 3yo, 7f, 1:22.29, DONNA'S MAILBAG, Ruling Star, Richest Half, 6 started.

EXCELSIOR BREEDERS' CUP H.-G3, Aqueduct, April 6, $200,000, 3&up, 1⅛m, 1:49.25, JOHN LITTLE, Windsor Castle, Ground Storm, 6 started.

Excess Energy S., Turf Paradise, May 11, $22,900, 3&up, f&m, 6f, 1:09.37, (DH) WIN A FEU, (DH) NIKKI'S ANGEL, Crown Connection, 9 started.

Exclusive Praline H., Calder Race Course, June 18, $43,195, 3&up, 6f, 1:10.17, TOUR OF THE CAT, Built Up, Uncle Rocco, 7 started.

EXPLOSIVE BID H.-G2, Fair Grounds, March 24, $700,000, 4&up, a1⅛mT, 1:48.88, SARAFAN, Beat Hollow (GB), Even the Score, 14 started.

Explosive Darling H., Arlington Park, Oct. 19, $42,000, 3&up, 1 1/16mT, 1:44.82, SMILIN' SLEW, Major Omansky, Buster Bailey, 9 started.

Express H., The Downs at Albuquerque, May 4, $32,400, 3&up, 5½f, 1:02.72, SILVER MATT, Dr. Holiday, Musical Chairs, 8 started.

Express Star H., Calder Race Course, Dec. 9, $43,080, 3&up, f&m, 1 1/16m, 1:46.36, REDOUBLED MISS, Multiplicity, Tonight's Wager, 8 started.

Fabulous Frolic S., Calder Race Course, May 5, $37,905, 3yo, 1 1/16mT, 1:42.06, LORD JUBAN, Class of Seventy, Bernie B, 7 started.

Fairfield S., Solano County Fair, July 20, $46,980, 3yo, f, 6f, 1:09.07, ERICA'S SMILE, Benefit Party, Summer Lite, 6 started.

Fair Grounds Breeders' Cup H., Fair Grounds, Feb. 2, $147,000, 4&up, a1⅛mT, 1:50.13, MYSTERY GIVER, Even the Score, Candid Glen, 13 started.

FAIR GROUNDS OAKS-G2, Fair Grounds, March 9, $350,000, 3yo, f, 1 1/16m, 1:43.30, TAKE CHARGE LADY, Lake Lady, Chamrousse, 8 started.

Fair Grounds Sales S. (R), Fair Grounds, Feb. 3, $80,000, 3yo, passed through the ring at the Fair Grounds Sale Co. two-year-olds in training sale, 1m, 1:39.94, KID TRISTAN, Toi Fund, Landrwillbeastar, 7 started.

Fair Lady S. (R), Hastings Park Racecourse, April 20, $38,010, 3yo, f, British Columbia-bred, 6½f, 1:18.70, ELANA D'AMOUR, Grace for You, Shelby Madison, 7 started.

Fair Queen H., The Downs at Albuquerque, Sept. 13, $32,900, 3yo, f, 6½f, 1:18.49, AFTER THE BEEP, Slim's Secret, My Little Luxury, 9 started.

Fairway Fun S., Turfway Park, March 30, $50,000, 4&up, f&m, 1⅟₁₆m, 1:43.36, BECKY VIRTUE, Gal On the Go, Seven Four Seven, 10 started.

Fall Classic Distaff S. (R), Northlands Park, Sept. 21, $50,000, 3&up, f&m, Alberta-bred, 1⅟₁₆m, 1:44.80, A RAY OF MAGIC, Northern Neechitoo, This Cat Can, 6 started.

Fall H., Mountaineer Park, Sept. 24, $77,800, 3&up, 1⅛m, 1:51.27, X COUNTRY, E Z Glory, Tour the Hive, 7 started.

FALL HIGHWEIGHT H.-G3, Aqueduct, Nov. 28, $111,600, 3&up, 6f, 1:09.62, TRUE DIRECTION, Gold I. D., Crossing Point, 9 started.

Falls Amiss H. (R), Lincoln State Fair, July 6, $22,500, 3&up, f&m, Nebraska-bred, 1m 70y, 1:41, IRISH FLYER, Oglala Sue, Chocolate Cowgirl, 9 started.

FALLS CITY H.-G2, Churchill Downs, Nov. 28, $270,000, 3&up, f&m, 1⅛m, 1:49.60, ALLAMERICAN BERTIE, Softly, Take Charge Lady, 6 started.

Fall Sprint S., Lethbridge, Aug. 31, $9,200, 3&up, 5½f, 1:09.40, WISE DANCER, Stag, Seattle Cue, 8 started.

Faneuil Hall S., Calder Race Course, Aug. 19, $42,985, 3yo, f, 1⅟₁₆mT, 1:43.63, COMPANY B, Tasso Run, Cagey Move, 6 started.

Fanfreluche S. (R), Woodbine, Oct. 20, $163,500, 2yo, f, Canadian-bred, 6f, 1:11.41, MISS CRISSY, Buffalo Jump, Elusive Thought, 7 started.

Fantasia S. (R), Louisiana Downs, July 7, $42,800, 3yo, f, Louisiana-bred, 6f, 1:10.48, HIGHHOPESEMILYLUCK, Taylor's Queen, Deal With Her, 7 started.

Fantastic Girl S., Del Mar, Aug. 3, $78,385, 3&up, f&m, 6f, 1:09.75, WARREN'S WHISTLE, Madame Pietra, Kona Queen, 6 started.

FANTASY S.-G2, Oaklawn Park, April 12, $200,000, 3yo, f, 1⅟₁₆m, 1:43.80, SEE HOW SHE RUNS, Lake Lady, Chamrousse, 6 started.

Fantasy S., Hastings Park Racecourse, Oct. 13, $43,245, 2yo, f, 1⅟₁₆m, 1:46.26, CHORUS DANCER, Brave Miss, Aquita, 11 started.

Farer Belle Lee H. (R), Great Lakes Downs, Sept. 13, $45,000, 3&up, f&m, Michigan-bred, 1⅟₁₆m, 1:52.99, EMPRESS LIVIA, Sefas Rose, My City Girl, 10 started.

Fashion S., Belmont Park, June 6, $81,050, 2yo, f, 5f, 58.26, HOLIDAY RUNNER, Miss Mary Apples, Milliondollarlady, 6 started.

FAYETTE S.-G3, Keeneland, Oct. 26, $156,122, 3&up, 1⅛m, 1:51.17, TENPINS, X Country, Crafty Shaw, 4 started.

Federal Way H., Emerald Downs, May 12, $40,462, 3yo, f, 6½f, 1:15.40, LASTING CODE, Strong Credentials, Double Quack, Midnight Lightning, 7 started.

Federico Tesio S., Pimlico, April 20, $107,250, 3yo, 1⅛m, 1:50.33, SMOKED EM, Magic Weisner, Heir D' Twine, 6 started.

Fern Sawyer H., Ruidoso Downs, June 30, $21,800, 3&up, f&m, 1m, 1:41.20, RUBIN'S GIRL, Hava Peer, Waveband, 9 started.

Fiesta Mile S. (R), Retama Park, Oct. 12, $30,000, 3&up, f&m, Texas-bred, 1mT, 1:34.83, EAGLE LAKE, Peppy Priscilla, Marfa's Taxes, 9 started.

Fifth Avenue S. (R), Aqueduct, Nov. 10, $125,000, 2yo, f, New York-bred, 6f, 1:10.41, BEAUTIFUL AMERICA, Hanselina, The Name Was Gone, 9 started.

Fillies and Mares Open S., Les Bois Park, Aug. 11, $5,800, 3&up, f&m, 5f, CONSTANTLY, Myths and Legends, Patience Is Mine, 8 started.

Fillies and Mares Spring S., Lethbridge, May 26, $8,700, 3&up, f&m, a6f, 1:20, A TEMPTING LIGHT, Da Ebony, Special Sweetpea, 8 started.

Find H. (R), Laurel Park, Aug. 11, $75,000, 3&up, Maryland-bred, 1⅛mT, 1:46.04, LA REINE'S TERMS, Purple Sand, Pinky Pizwaanski, 8 started.

Finger Lakes Juvenile S. (R), Finger Lakes, Oct. 12, $35,000, 2yo, New York-bred, 6f, 1:13.80, ABBYS SILVERDREAM, Hill Top Man, Real Saucy, 8 started.

Finlandia Cup H., Del Mar, Aug. 25, $76,050, 3yo, f, 1mT, 1:34.42, RAGIN T REX, Sentimental Value, Nobilissime (GB), 7 started.

FIRECRACKER BREEDERS' CUP H.-G2, Churchill Downs, July 4, $292,500, 3&up, 1mT, 1:34.83, GOOD JOURNEY, Morluc, Even the Score, 9 started.

Firecracker H., Mountaineer Park, July 2, $79,650, 3&up, f&m, 1mT, 1:36.41, CAUGHT OUT, The Goddess Athird, Media Access, 11 started.

Fire Plug S., Pimlico, April 13, $50,000, 3&up, 6f, 1:10.94, DEER RUN, Stormin Oedy, Wild Current, 5 started.

First Episode S. (R), Suffolk Downs, April 13, $30,000, 3&up, f&m, Massachusetts-bred, 1⅟₁₆m, 1:50.07, BIG MISS, Sunlit Ridge, She's a Trip, 6 started.

FIRST FLIGHT H.-G2, Aqueduct, Oct. 26, $150,000, 3&up, f&m, 7f, 1:23.75, SHINE AGAIN, Redhead Riot, Raging Fever, 5 started.

First Lady H., Ruidoso Downs, July 13, $21,200, 3&up, f&m, 6f, 1:11.60, GIMME A CLUE, Rubin's Girl, Hava Peer, 6 started.

FIRST LADY H.-G3, Gulfstream Park, Jan. 18, $100,000, 3&up, f&m, 6f, 1:10.36, RAGING FEVER, Cat Cay, Mandy's Gold, 7 started.

Flaming Page S., Woodbine, Aug. 31, $107,000, 3&up, f&m, 1½mT, 2:27.17, SAFFRON DANCER (Ire), Libretto, Catch the Ring, 6 started.

FLASH S.-G3, Belmont Park, June 7, $109,100, 2yo, 5f, 57.10, WHYWHYWHY, Presence, Down Play, 7 started.

Flawlessly S., Hollywood Park, July 5, $110,000, 3yo, f, 1mT, 1:35.51, SUPER HIGH, Carinae, Kirtle (GB), 8 started.

Flawlessly S., Arlington Park, June 9, $47,100, 3yo, f, a1⅟₁₆mT, 1:45.66, GUANA (Fr), Haylie's Dawn, Strikes No Spares, 7 started.

Fleet Treat S. (R), Del Mar, July 28, $100,000, 3yo, f, California-bred, 7f, 1:22.72, BEAR FAN, Nicole's Pursuit, The Parties Over, 7 started.

Fleur de Lis H., Churchill Downs, June 15, $329,400, 3&up, f&m, 1⅛m, 1:49.64, SPAIN, With Ability, Dancethruthedawn, 6 started.

FLORAL PARK H.-G3, Belmont Park, Sept. 14, $103,400, 3&up, f&m, 6f, 1:10.25, CARSON HOLLOW, Gold Mover, Shiny Band, 4 started.

Florida Breeders Distaff S., Ocala Training Center, March 18, $35,000, 3&up, f&m, 1⅟₁₆m, 1:46.60, FLAMING LIGHT, Laurel Light, Sea Mist, 10 started.

FLORIDA DERBY-G1, Gulfstream Park, March 16, $1,000,000, 3yo, 1⅛m, 1:48.80, HARLAN'S HOLIDAY, Blue Burner, Peekskill, 11 started.

FLORIDA OAKS-G3, Tampa Bay Downs, March 17, $150,000, 3yo, f, 1⅟₁₆m, 1:45.49, FRENCH SATIN, Romancin Dixie, Ciudad de Carson, 10 started.

Florida Thoroughbred Charities S. (R), Ocala Training Center, March 18, $35,000, 3&up, progeny of stallions whose seasons have been offered in the Florida Thoroughbred Charities Auction, 5f, HANDSOME SMILE, Fantastic Finish, Raysin Thunder, 8 started.

FLOWER BOWL INVITATIONAL H.-G1, Belmont Park, Sept. 28, $750,000, 3&up, f&m, 1¼mT, 2:05.22, KAZZIA (Ger), Turtle Bow (Fr), Mot Juste (GB), 7 started.

Floyd Duncan Memorial S., Rockingham Park, Sept. 14, $25,000, 2yo, c&g, 6f, 1:13.01, FARMER INTHE DELL, Jewels Rocket, Rare Tower, 7 started.

Floyd Duncan S., Suffolk Downs, Jan. 19, $30,000, 4&up, f&m, 6f, 1:12.97, RIPPLING RETURN, Guess, Valid Miss Chain, 8 started.

Flying Lark S., Portland Meadows, Feb. 10, $8,675, 3yo, 6f, 1:13.25, MANITO GENTLEMAN, Fit to Bet, Brass Halo, 9 started.

Flying Pidgeon H., Calder Race Course, Oct. 19, $100,000, 3&up, 1⅛mT, 1:49.50, BAND IS PASSING, Link to Jimmy, Marquette, 9 started.

Foggy Road S., Delaware Park, Nov. 2, $61,100, 3&up, 6f, 1:10.34, RED BULLET, Rusty Spur, Marciano, 8 started.

Folklore H., Louisiana Downs, Aug. 18, $40,000, 3&up, 6½f, 1:15.95, THAT TAT, Honor Me, Unrullah Bull, 6 started.

Fonner Park Special S. (R), Fonner Park, April 14, $31,275, 3yo, c&g, Nebraska-bred, 6f, 1:13, STRAWBERRY KID, Ottis P Coaltrain, Mr Clearwater, 9 started.

Fonner Park Special S. (R), Fonner Park, April 13, $31,200, 3yo, f, Nebraska-bred, 6f, 1:13.20, CUBE'S CUB, Flaming Night, Talk Too, 8 started.

Foolish Pleasure S., Calder Race Course, Sept. 21, $100,000, 2yo, 1m 70y, 1:45.02, SUPER FROLIC, Trust N Luck, Unbridels King, 8 started.

Foothill S., Fairplex Park, Sept. 13, $50,000, 3yo, 6½f, 1:16.33, LAFFIT, From A to Z, Crooked Key, 9 started.

Forego H., Fairmount Park, Sept. 17, $25,600, 3&up, c&g, 1m 70y, 1:42.80, CRACK THE VAULT, Regimental Flag, Tindell, 6 started.

Forego H., Turfway Park, Jan. 26, $49,500, 4&up, 6½f, 1:17.38, SENSE OF DUTY, Golden Oldie, Personal First, 10 started.

FOREGO H.-G1, Saratoga Race Course, Sept. 1, $250,000, 3&up, 6½f, 1:15.68, ORIENTATE, Aldebaran, Multiple Choice, 8 started.

Forerunner S., Keeneland, April 17, $111,000, 3yo, 1⅛mT, 1:49.15, RED MASQUE, Why Cross the Road, Royal Gem, 6 started.

FOREST HILLS H.-G2, Belmont Park, Oct. 6, $250,000, 3&up, 6f, 1:11, AVANZADO (Arg), Dash for Daylight, Esteemed Friend, 7 started.

FORT MARCY H.-G3, Aqueduct, April 27, $112,100, 3&up, 1⅟₁₆mT, 1:44.53, PYRUS, Proud Man, Capsized, 8 started.

Fort Wayne S. (R), Hoosier Park, Oct. 5, $43,750, 3yo, c&g, Indiana-bred, 6f, 1:12.49, PEMAQUID POINT, Saint Golddigger, Cowboy's Limelite, 9 started.

Forty Niner H., Golden Gate Fields, Nov. 29, $100,000, 3&up, 1⅟₁₆m, 1:40.67, JIMMY Z, Ninebanks, Mercenary, 7 started.

Forty One Carats H., Calder Race Course, May 19, $37,835, 3&up,

7f, 1:25.58, BALLADO'S DEVIL, Notebook Computer, Callie and Jake, 6 started.

FORWARD GAL S.-G3, Gulfstream Park, Jan. 27, $100,000, 3yo, f, 7f, 1:25.47, TAKE THE CAKE, Cherokee Girl, A New Twist, 7 started.

Forward Pass S., Arlington Park, Aug. 17, $63,500, 3yo, 7f, 1:22.79, TONYSPAL CRAIG, Attack the Books, Richest Half, 6 started.

Foster City H., Bay Meadows, May 25, $67,513, 3&up, 1⅟₁₆mT, 1:42.64, NATIVE DESERT, Cat Flight, R McLennen, 8 started.

Foundation Plan H., Calder Race Course, Sept. 29, $44,605, 3&up, 1⅟₁₆m, 1:47.01, BOG HUNTER, Steady Sammy, Sajon, 5 started.

FOUNTAIN OF YOUTH S.-G1, Gulfstream Park, Feb. 16, $200,000, 3yo, 1⅟₁₆m, 1:44.49, BOOKLET, Blue Burner, Harlan's Holiday, 8 started.

FOURSTARDAVE H.-G3, Saratoga Race Course, Aug. 24, $200,000, 3&up, 1⅛m, 1:50.90, CAPSIZED, Pure Prize, Pyrus, 5 started.

Foxbrook Supreme Hurdle S., Far Hills, Oct. 19, $75,000, 4&up, a2½mT, 5:10.79, MCDYNAMO, Mr Perkolater, Trebizond (Ire), 9 started.

Fox Sports Net H., Emerald Downs, May 19, $35,000, 3&up, 6½f, 1:13.80, CROWNING MEETING, Profound Secret, Secret Launch, 8 started.

Foxy J. G. S. (R), Philadelphia Park, July 6, $54,000, 3yo, f, Pennsylvania-bred, 7f, 1:24.60, CHEEKSANDPEANUTS, Marquee Kelly, Watsup, 10 started.

Frances A. Genter S., Calder Race Course, Dec. 21, $100,000, 3yo, f, 7½fT, 1:29.45, CELLARS SHIRAZ, Madeira Mist (Ire), May Gator, 12 started.

Frances Genter S. (R), Canterbury Park, June 29, $43,348, 3yo, f, Minnesota-bred, 6f, 1:10.84, DEMIPARFAIT, Lakeville, Susie Blues, 12 started.

Frances Slocum S. (R), Hoosier Park, Nov. 24, $44,100, 3&up, f&m, Indiana-bred, 1⅟₁₆m, 1:48.74, SENORITA ZIGGY, Cadillac Mountain, Winning Glory, 9 started.

Francis 'Jock' LaBelle Memorial S., Delaware Park, May 18, $75,300, 3yo, 1m 70y, 1:42.99, NOTHING FLAT, Outstander, Devil's Zone, 6 started.

Frank Arnason Sire S. (R), Assiniboia Downs, June 22, $30,000, 2yo, Canadian-bred, 5f, 1:02.20, BO DIPPITY, New Release, Pippy Dance, 7 started.

FRANK E. KILROE MILE H.-G2, Santa Anita Park, March 2, $300,000, 4&up, 1mT, 1:34.04, DECARCHY, Sarafan, Designed for Luck, 11 started.

Frank Figueroa Claiming S., Santa Cruz County Fair, April 28, $3,832, 3&up, 6f, 1:12.80, CHIRICAHUA CHIEF, Real Dancer, Cop Out, 8 started.

FRANK J. DE FRANCIS MEMORIAL DASH S.-G1, Laurel Park, Nov. 16, $300,000, 3&up, 6f, 1:10.81, D'WILDCAT, Deer Run, Sassy Hound, 8 started.

Fran's Valentine S. (R), Hollywood Park, April 28, $175,000, 4&up, f&m, California bred, 1⅟₁₆mT, 1:41.94, SMOKIN' CHARLOTTE, Stetson Lady, Super Tuesday, 8 started.

Fred 'Cappy' Capossela S., Aqueduct, Jan. 21, $79,650, 3yo, 6f, 1:10.31, SPIN ZONE, President Butler, War Native, 5 started.

Fred Mendel Memorial H., Marquis Downs, Aug. 24, $5,000, 3&up, 1⅛m, 1:53.49, BEAU RING, Victorious Type, Smokin Six Pack, 5 started.

FRED W. HOOPER H.-G3, Calder Race Course, Dec. 28, $100,000, 3&up, 1⅛m, 1:50.53, THE JUDGE SEZ WHO, Best of the Rest, Dancing Guy, 8 started.

Freedom of the City S. (R), Northlands Park, Oct. 12, $40,000, 2yo, f, Canadian-bred, 1m, 1:41.40, RAYLENE, I'm Quicksilver, Jadebquick, 9 started.

Free Press S., Assiniboia Downs, June 23, $30,000, 3&up, 6f, 1:10.80, KALFAARI, Kenyawin, Gus Again, 6 started.

Free Spirits H., Ruidoso Downs, June 23, $21,700, 3&up, 6f, 1:10.80, GEE WALLY, J W Jet, Live Show, 8 started.

Free Vacation H. (R), Hastings Park Racecourse, Aug. 24, $55,720, 3yo, f, Canadian-bred, 1⅟₁₆m, 1:45.21, ELANA D'AMOUR, Lady Vye, Regal Heir, 6 started.

Friendly Lover H. (R), Monmouth Park, Aug. 29, $50,000, 3&up, New Jersey-bred, 6f, 1:09.85, DIXIE TWO THOUSAND, H. M. S. Jackson, Summer Swing, 5 started.

Friendship S. (R), Louisiana Downs, Sept. 14, $63,911, 2yo, c&g, Louisiana-bred, 6f, 1:13.10, SCREEN PASS, Action Tonight, Father Martin, 5 started.

Friendship S. (R), Louisiana Downs, Sept. 15, $90,189, 2yo, f, Louisiana-bred, 6f, 1:10.80, HANNAH'S ROYALROCK, Parting, Hadif's Allstar, 8 started.

Frisk Me Now S., Monmouth Park, May 26, $50,000, 3&up, 1m, 1:38.40, SEA OF TRANQUILITY, Tempest Fugit, Summer Swing, 8 started.

FRIZETTE S.-G1, Belmont Park, Oct. 5, $500,000, 2yo, f, 1⅟₁₆m, 1:44.20, STORM FLAG FLYING, Santa Catarina, Appleby Gardens, 7 started.

Frontier H. (R), Great Lakes Downs, Sept. 17, $45,000, 3&up, Michigan-bred, 1⅛m, 1:54.59, SECRET ROMEO, That Gift, Above the Wind, 8 started.

Front Range H., Arapahoe Park, July 4, $30,000, 3&up, 7f, 1:23, UNCLE PUNK, Cheris' Pride, Mucho Daniero, 9 started.

Frost King S. (R), Woodbine, Oct. 9, $133,125, 2yo, progeny of eligible Ontario stallions, 7f, 1:25.10, SNAKE PIT, El Gran Maestro, Timeform, 6 started.

Fruitport S., Great Lakes Downs, Oct. 19, $20,000, 3yo, f, 1m, 1:43.28, EMERALD ISLE, Circle the Globe, Rock a Lot, 6 started.

FSIN S., Queensbury Downs, Oct. 18, $3,200, 3&up, a5f, 1:02.55, CARRFORTHECOURSE, Paniolo Road, Triple Great, 7 started.

FSIN Thoroughbred S., Queensbury Downs, Oct. 19, $3,150, 3&up, a1⅛m, 1:59.05, PRIZE OF TEXAS, Helabhai, Senor Markos, 6 started.

FT. LAUDERDALE H.-G3, Gulfstream Park, Jan. 26, $100,000, 3&up, 1⅟₁₆mT, 1:41.54, DEL MAR SHOW, North East Bound, Tv Sports Director, 7 started.

Furl Sail H., Fair Grounds, Dec. 27, $75,000, 3&up, f&m, a1mT, 1:38.43, HISTOIRE SAINTE (Fr), Quick Tip, Old Money (Aus), 10 started.

Fury S. (R), Woodbine, May 5, $163,500, 3yo, f, Canadian-bred, 7f, 1:22.86, GONETOFARR, Tacky Affair, Ginger Gold, 7 started.

FUTURITY S.-G1, Belmont Park, Sept. 15, $200,000, 2yo, 1m, 1:36.33, WHYWHYWHY, Pretty Wild, Truckle Feature, 7 started.

F. W. Gaudin Memorial H., Fair Grounds, Dec. 22, $75,000, 3&up, 6f, 1:09.38, KAZOO, Cojet, Gracie's Dancer, 6 started.

Gaily Gaily S., Gulfstream Park, March 1, $72,200, 3yo, f, 1⅛mT, 1:51.78, CELLARS SHIRAZ, She's Vested, Bells for Marlin, 7 started.

GALLANT BLOOM H.-G2, Belmont Park, Oct. 6, $150,000, 3&up, f&m, 6½f, 1:17.89, NASTY STORM, Raging Fever, Shine Again, 6 started.

Gallant Bob H., Philadelphia Park, Oct. 5, $150,000, 3yo, 6f, 1:09.83, THUNDERELLO, Boston Common, Calends, 5 started.

GALLANT FOX H.-G3, Aqueduct, Dec. 28, $112,200, 3&up, 1⅝m, 2:43.54, COYOTE LAKES, Pleasant Breeze, Fisher Pond, 10 started.

GALLORETTE H.-G3, Pimlico, May 18, $100,000, 3&up, f&m, 1⅟₁₆mT, 1:46.73, QUIDNASKRA, De Aar, Step With Style, 7 started.

GAMELY BREEDERS' CUP H.-G1, Hollywood Park, May 27, $474,000, 3&up, f&m, 1⅛mT, 1:46.93, ASTRA, Starine (Fr), Voodoo Dancer, 6 started.

GARDEN CITY BREEDERS' CUP H.-G1, Belmont Park, Sept. 8, $233,000, 3yo, f, 1⅛mT, 1:47.33, WONDER AGAIN, Riskaverse, Pertuisane (GB), 10 started.

Gardenia S. (R), Delta Downs, Dec. 14, $50,000, 3&up, f&m, Louisiana-bred, 5f, FUSE IT, Mike's Sister, Mamaleen, 8 started.

GARDENIA S.-G3, Ellis Park, Aug. 10, $200,000, 3&up, f&m, 1⅛m, 1:49.73, MINISTER'S BABY, Lakenheath, Softly, 8 started.

Garland of Roses H., Aqueduct, Dec. 14, $81,650, 3&up, f&m, 6f, 1:10.10, DAT YOU MIZ BLUE, Xtra Heat, Belle Artiste, 5 started.

Gasparilla S. (R), Tampa Bay Downs, Feb. 2, $50,000, 3yo, f, Florida-bred, 7f, 1:24.95, AFNAN, Rebecca's Charm, Expected Roll, 12 started.

Gateway to Glory S., Fairplex Park, Sept. 26, $49,500, 2yo, 1⅟₁₆m, 1:44.08, MANHATTAN EXPRESS, Jimmy O, Hair Jordan, 7 started.

GAZELLE H.-G1, Belmont Park, Sept. 7, $250,000, 3yo, f, 1⅛m, 1:47.12, IMPERIAL GESTURE, Take Charge Lady, Bella Bellucci, 7 started.

Geisha H. (R), Pimlico, April 20, $100,000, 3&up, f&m, Maryland-bred, 1⅟₁₆m, 1:44.56, SHINY SHEET, Stanza, Winter Leaf, 9 started.

Gen. Douglas MacArthur H. (R), Belmont Park, Sept. 6, $84,425, 3&up, New York-bred, 7f, 1:22, WELL FANCIED, Chasin' Wimmin, Impeachthepro, 10 started.

Gene Francis & Assoc. H. (1st Div.), Anthony Downs, July 20, $4,130, 3&up, a1⅟₁₆m, 1:55.27, MOSCOWS QUICK TRIP, Coupdeville Jack, Nalee's Knight, 4 started.

Gene Francis & Assoc. H. (2nd Div.), Anthony Downs, July 20, $4,130, 3&up, a1⅟₁₆m, 1:52.80, C'MON CHROMIE, Gettin' Overtime, Moscow Gold Bar, 4 started.

GENERAL GEORGE H.-G2, Laurel Park, Feb. 18, $200,000, 3&up, 7f, 1:22.53, WRANGLER, Rusty Spur, Affirmed Success, 8 started.

Generous Portion S. (R), Del Mar, Sept. 4, $100,000, 2yo, f, California-bred non-winners of $35,000, 6f, 1:11.24, MISS NICOLIE, Amber Hills, Summer Wind Dancer, 9 started.

GENEROUS S.-G3, Hollywood Park, Nov. 30, $200,000, 2yo, 1mT, 1:35.49, PEACE RULES, Lismore Knight, Outta Here, 9 started.

Genesee Valley Breeders' H. (R), Finger Lakes, Aug. 3, $40,000, 3&up, New York-bred, 1⅛m, 1:45.44, J'S WILD SLEW, Personal Pro, Impeachthepro, 8 started.

Genesis S., Delta Downs, Dec. 28, $40,000, 2yo, f, 5f, HADIF'S ALL-STAR, Ritzy Dame, Fantasy On Fire, 8 started.

Gentilly H. (R), Fair Grounds, March 23, $100,000, 3yo, Louisiana-bred, a1mT, 1:39.83, YOU'LLBEINMYHEART, Silent Goodbye, Ruff Flight, 11 started.

GENUINE RISK H-G2, Belmont Park, May 12, $150,000, 3&up, f&m, 6f, 1:10.24, XTRA HEAT, La Galerie (Arg), Shine Again, 6 started.

GEORGE C. HENDRIE S. (Can-G3), Woodbine, May 12, $169,450, 4&up, f&m, 6½f, 1:16.86, EL PRADO ESSENCE, Feathers, Quiet, 6 started.

George Lewis Memorial S. (R), Thistledown, July 28, $50,000, 3&up, Ohio-bred, 1⅛m, 1:51.30, MAJESTIC DINNER, Blame It On Ruby, Devil Time, 12 started.

George Maloof Futurity (R), The Downs at Albuquerque, Sept. 22, $61,163, 2yo, c&g, New Mexico-bred, 6f, 1:09.21, BUBBA HYDE, Hasty Gus, Geiger Tiger, 11 started.

George Rosenberger Memorial S. (R), Delaware Park, Sept. 7, $101,800, 3&up, f&m, starters at Delaware Park in 2002 in a non-stake, 1⅛mT, 1:42.50, HIGH LADY, Bloomy, Starry De, 11 started.

George Royal S., Hastings Park Racecourse, April 28, $37,125, 3&up, 6½f, 1:17.54, LORD NELSON, Danzilation, Diglett, 6 started.

George W. Barker S. (R), Finger Lakes, May 27, $35,000, 3&up, New York-bred, 6f, 1:10.47, STRIKE THE BRASS, Impeachthepro, Roman Sea, 9 started.

Georgia On My Mind H. (R), Calder Race Course, July 6, $50,000, 3&up, f&m, progeny of eligible stallions, 1¹⁄₁₆mT, 1:45.74, COOLBYTHEPOOL, Sea Mist, Bay Street Gal, 6 started.

Gilded Time S., Arlington Park, Oct. 25, $100,000, 2yo, 7f, 1:23.01, CAT GENIUS, Desert Warrior, Omega Code, 5 started.

Gillespie County Fair Association Texas-Bred S. (R), Gillespie County Downs, Aug. 25, $17,000, 3&up, Texas-bred, 7f, 1:26.53, ST. MARTIN'S CLOAK, Happy Smile, Touchoville, 6 started.

Ginger Welch S., Les Bois Park, July 6, $6,550, 3&up, f&m, 1m, 1:39.32, TROPHY EDITION TOO, Infantry Liz, Joanne Apple, 9 started.

Glacial Princess S. (R), Beulah Park, Dec. 7, $40,000, 2yo, f, Ohio-bred, 1⅛m, 1:48.79, MERCER U., Tnt Mill, Dinkers Pride, 8 started.

Gladstone Hurdle S., Far Hills, Oct. 19, $48,500, 3&up, a2⅛mT, 4:25.48, PALS PRIDE, Bubble Economy, Coal Dust, 8 started.

Glassy Dip S., Hawthorne Race Course, June 1, $75,000, 4&up, 5fT, DISTINCTIVE MR. B, Aloha Bold, Grey Cart, 9 started.

Gleaming S., Delaware Park, June 11, $59,300, 3yo, 1⅛mT, 1:41.38, EQUALITY, Coco's Madness, Cohoma, 7 started.

Glendale H., Turf Paradise, Feb. 9, $50,000, 4&up, f&m, 1¹⁄₁₆mT, 1:43.30, CATZ (Ire), So Wistfullee, Glorious Linda (Fr), 9 started.

GLENS FALLS H-G3, Saratoga Race Course, Aug. 26, $113,500, 3&up, f&m, 1⅜mT, 2:15.99, OWSLEY, Sunstone (GB), Mot Juste (GB), 10 started.

Glorious Song S., Woodbine, Nov. 10, $164,750, 2yo, f, 7f, 1:24.22, BUFFALO JUMP, Dolly Dynamite, Smart Angel, 6 started.

GO FOR WAND H-G1, Saratoga Race Course, July 28, $250,000, 3&up, f&m, 1⅛m, 1:50.21, DANCETHRUTHEDAWN, Transcendental, Too Scarlet, 7 started.

Go For Wand S., Delaware Park, May 4, $75,600, 3yo, f, 1¹⁄₁₆m, 1:46.35, ALTERNATE, Spelling, Sideways, 7 started.

Going Up S., Calder Race Course, Dec. 30, $39,900, 3&up, f&m, 1¹⁄₁₆mT, 1:40.55, STRAWBERRY BLONDE (Ire), Libretto, Shouldn't We All, 8 started.

Goldarama S., Calder Race Course, April 29, $37,835, 3&up, f&m, 6f, 1:12.64, SUGAR N SPICE, Dream Wish, Fly Me Crazy, 7 started.

Gold Breeders' Cup S., Assiniboia Downs, Sept. 29, $36,250, 3&up, 1⅛m, 1:53.80, SIR PUCKER, Beau Ring, Rim Dancer, 8 started.

Golden Bear S., Golden Gate Fields, Nov. 24, $65,600, 2yo, 6f, 1:10.64, BUDDY GIL, Natural Balance, Bases Are Loaded, 5 started.

Golden Boy S., Assiniboia Downs, June 9, $30,000, 3yo, 6f, 1:12.20, REGAL LEGACY, Jakes Wildindian, Ness Gadoll, 4 started.

Golden Circle S., Prairie Meadows, April 27, $50,000, 3yo, 6f, 1:10.07, PRIVATE HORDE, Vito Corleone, Lott, 7 started.

GOLDEN GATE BREEDERS' CUP H.-G3, Golden Gate Fields, March 16, $155,000, 3&up, 1⅛mT, 1:49.41, NO SLIP (Fr), Sumitas (Ger), Kerrygold (Fr), 5 started.

GOLDEN GATE DERBY-G3, Golden Gate Fields, Jan. 12, $125,000, 3yo, 1¹⁄₁₆m, 1:43.87, DANTHEBLUEGRASSMAN, Cappuchino, U S S Tinosa, 8 started.

Golden Gull Chris Brown Memorial S. (R), Charles Town, Sept. 21, $31,250, 2yo, f, nominated to the West Virginia Breeders Classic,

4½f, X TRA BRASSY, Hushaby Babe, Courageous Valor, 10 started.

Golden Horsehoe S. (R), Fort Erie, Aug. 13, $65,900, 3&up, f&m, Canadian-bred, a7fT, 1:24.02, BRANKSOME HALL, Oriental-springhope, Callendars, 6 started.

Golden Or H., Calder Race Course, Aug. 11, $42,310, 3&up, f&m, 1¹⁄₁₆m, 1:45.24, COOLBYTHEPOOL, Castlebrook, Multiplicity, 5 started.

Golden Poppy H., Bay Meadows, Oct. 27, $60,550, 3&up, f&m, 1¹⁄₁₆m, 1:41.47, ANGEL GIFT, Lindsay Jean, Erica's Smile, 7 started.

GOLDEN ROD S.-G2, Churchill Downs, Nov. 30, $219,600, 2yo, f, 1¹⁄₁₆m, 1:45, MY BOSTON GAL, Holiday Lady, My Trusty Cat, 7 started.

Golden State Mile S., Golden Gate Fields, Feb. 10, $59,100, 3yo, 1m, 1:35.57, CAPPUCHINO, Yougottawanna, Arsen, 8 started.

Golden Sylvia H., Mountaineer Park, June 18, $78,150, 3&up, f&m, 1m, 1:36.81, TAX AFFAIR, Seven Four Seven, Night of Delight, 8 started.

Golden Triangle S., Delta Downs, Dec. 7, $50,000, 3&up, f&m, 6½f, 1:20.20, RAYMOND'S DREAM, Lake Charles, Long Leg Lou, 6 started.

Goldfinch S., Prairie Meadows, April 26, $50,000, 3yo, f, 6f, 1:10.13, FOR RUBIES, Don't Countess Out, Freddie's Folly, 7 started.

Gold Rush Futurity, Arapahoe Park, Sept. 2, $88,650, 2yo, 6f, 1:09.80, DONNY BOY, Latenite Trick, Nycity, 12 started.

Gold Rush S., Golden Gate Fields, Dec. 14, $81,075, 2yo, 1m, 1:38.32, SPENSIVE, Always Remember, Natural Balance, 6 started.

Good Intentions S., Calder Race Course, Nov. 9, $38,465, 3yo, f, 1¹⁄₁₆mT, 1:40.47, MADEIRA MIST (Ire), Maliziosa, Shrimp Tempura, 7 started.

GOODWOOD BREEDERS' CUP H.-G2, Santa Anita Park, Oct. 6, $500,000, 3&up, 1⅛m, 1:46.80, PLEASANTLY PERFECT, Momentum, Reba's Gold, 9 started.

Goss L. Stryker S. (R), Laurel Park, Feb. 9, $60,000, 3yo, Maryland-bred, 7f, 1:24.92, MAGIC WEISNER, Majestic Sir, Radio One, 6 started.

GOTHAM S.-G3, Aqueduct, March 17, $200,000, 3yo, 1m, 1:34.90, MAYAKOVSKY, Saarland, Parade of Music, 7 started.

Gottstein Futurity, Emerald Downs, Sept. 15, $100,000, 2yo, 1¹⁄₁₆m, 1:45, CONDOTIERRI, Valour Road, Bub, 11 started.

Gourmet Girl S. (R), Hollywood Park, April 28, $60,000, 3&up, f&m, California-bred, a6½f, 1:17.37, BEAR FAN, Flying Heart, Kingdom Bound, 12 started.

Governor's Buckeye Cup S. (R), River Downs, Sept. 1, $75,000, 3&up, Ohio-bred, 1¼m, 2:07, MAJESTIC DINNER, Devil Time, Panta Ellinas, 8 started.

Governor's Cup H., Wyoming Downs, July 13, $3,725, 3&up, 1m, 1:39.14, BELGRAVIA (GB), Forrie's Courage, Fadski, 7 started.

Governor's Cup H., Fairplex Park, Sept. 29, $49,500, 3&up, 6½f, 1:16.45, PROFOUND SECRET, El Curioso, McCordnskuba, 7 started.

Governors Cup H., Les Bois Park, Aug. 3, $5,900, 3&up, 1m, 1:38.58, NORTHERN RICKY, Erhard, Unshackled, 5 started.

Governor's H., Sacramento, Aug. 24, $40,400, 3&up, 1½m, 1:48.60, TAKIN IT DEEP, Rio's Chase, Capt. Fly Hook, 4 started.

Governor's H., Ruidoso Downs, July 20, $21,800, 3&up, 7½f, 1:31.80, TAHOE AFFAIR, Sneaker Mike, J W Jet, 8 started.

Governor's H., Emerald Downs, Aug. 4, $60,000, 3&up, 6½f, 1:14.60, COLTERKIND, Road Afleet, Jumron Won, 7 started.

Governor's H., Ellis Park, Aug. 24, $75,000, 3&up, 1m, 1:37.35, DASH FOR DAYLIGHT, Frazee's Folly, Robin Zee, 7 started.

Governor's Lady H. (R), Sportsman's Park, March 30, $88,750, 4&up, f&m, Illinois-conceived and/or -foaled, 6f, 1:10.71, DARLING L, Island Riffle Cat, Little Mo, 10 started.

Gowell S., Turfway Park, Dec. 28, $43,000, 2yo, f, 6f, 1:12.30, WILDCAT ANNIE, Golden Marlin, Jenny's Prospector, 12 started.

Graceful Klinchit Distaff H., Marquis Downs, Aug. 23, $5,000, 3&up, f&m, 1⅛m, 1:48.53, TRULY REMARKABLE, Ms. Lady Rose, Red Vil Do, 5 started.

Graduation S., Delta Downs, Feb. 9, $50,280, 3yo, 5f, BELIEVE IM SPECIAL, Bold Glare, Dexcavate, 9 started.

Graduation S., Assiniboia Downs, July 6, $30,000, 2yo, 5½f, 1:06.60, NEW MEDIA, Sand Rush, Mr Don, 7 started.

Graduation S. (R), Del Mar, July 31, $125,000, 2yo, California-bred, 5½f, 1:03.27, ICECOLDBEERATREDS, Jury Box, Expression, 9 started.

Grand Canyon H. (R), Turf Paradise, April 27, $35,000, 3&up, Arizona-bred, 6f, 1:08.35, KOMAX, G Malleah, Exs Post Facto, 6 started.

Grand Prairie Turf Challenge S., Lone Star Park, April 6, $100,000, 3yo, 1mT, 1:41.17, NATIONAL PARK (GB), Victory Dawn, Dazzlin-

personality, 11 started.
Grasmick H., Fonner Park, Feb. 16, $15,975, 3&up, 4f, 45.80, R C MR HAY BOY, April Sunshine, Leaping Plum, 10 started.
Gravelines S. (R), Gulfstream Park, March 29, $82,050, 3yo, Florida-bred, 1⅛mT, 1:49.16, ORCHARD PARK, Emergency Status, Bernie B, 7 started.
GRAVESEND H.-G3, Aqueduct, Dec. 29, $109,200, 3&up, 6f, 1:09.26, MULTIPLE CHOICE, Sing Me Back Home, Gold I. D., 7 started.
Gray's Lake S. (R), Prairie Meadows, May 27, $66,823, 3yo, c&g, Iowa-bred, 6f, 1:09.49, COWBOY STUFF, Country Warrior, Cornpatch Road, 6 started.
Great Lady M. H., Hollywood Park, July 7, $91,925, 3&up, f&m, 5½fT, 1:01.99, GO GO, Dyna's Club, Brocky's Dream (Aut), 7 started.
Great White Way S. (R), Aqueduct, Nov. 10, $125,000, 2yo, c&g, New York-bred, 6f, 1:11.01, GREY COMET, Ruby's Pro, Polish Jewel, 10 started.
Green Carpet H. (R), River Downs, June 1, $50,000, 3yo, Ohio-bred, 1$\frac{1}{16}$mT, 1:48, TRUTH MATTERS, All Out Springs, Elm Grove, 10 started.
Green River S., Keeneland, Oct. 24, $111,500, 2yo, f, 1$\frac{1}{16}$mT, 1:44.30, OCEAN DRIVE, Sand Springs, Moonlight Sonata, 8 started.
Greenwood Cup H., Philadelphia Park, June 8, $100,000, 3&up, 1½mT, 2:35.01, CETEWAYO, Serial Bride, Dawn of the Condor, 8 started.
GREY BREEDERS' CUP S. (Can-G2), Woodbine, Oct. 6, $265,250, 2yo, 1$\frac{1}{16}$m, 1:45.10, WANDO, Gigawatt, Grand (Ire), 6 started.
Groomstick H., Calder Race Course, Aug. 17, $75,000, 3&up, 6½f, 1:15.99, TOUR OF THE CAT, Built Up, Groomstick Stock's, 10 started.
Groovy S. (R), Sam Houston Race Park, Nov. 16, $50,000, 2yo, Texas-bred, 7f, 1:24.12, CATALISSA, Call Me Lefty, Seneca Rock, 12 started.
GULFSTREAM PARK BREEDERS' CUP H.-G1, Gulfstream Park, Feb. 16, $200,000, 3&up, 1⅜mT, 2:17.44, CETEWAYO, Profit Option, Band Is Passing, 12 started.
GULFSTREAM PARK BREEDERS' CUP SPRINT CHAMPIONSHIP H.-G2, Gulfstream Park, March 9, $197,000, 3&up, 7f, 1:22.30, DREAM RUN, Binthebest, Burning Roma, 8 started.
GULFSTREAM PARK H.-G1, Gulfstream Park, March 30, $300,000, 3&up, 1¼m, 2:02.91, HAL'S HOPE, Mongoose, Sir Bear, 5 started.
Gus Fonner H., Fonner Park, April 27, $100,000, 3&up, 1$\frac{1}{16}$m, 1:48.80, MINER'S PRIZE, Fight for Ally, Rub, 9 started.
Gus Grissom S. (R), Hoosier Park, Nov. 10, $43,100, 3&up, c&g, Indiana-bred, 1$\frac{1}{16}$m, 1:48.38, IMAGEOFHOPE, J D's Diamond, Patriot's Key, 8 started.
Haggin S., Hollywood Park, June 16, $91,950, 2yo, 5½f, 1:05.01, OBERWALD, Royal Place, Crowned Dancer, 6 started.
H. A. Hindmarsh S. (R), Fort Erie, Sept. 24, $61,600, 3&up, f&m, sold at a CTHS or a CBS sale, 1$\frac{1}{16}$m, 1:43.62, SMALL PROMISES, Devastating, Royal Dalliance, 6 started.
Hail Emperor S., Laurel Park, Nov. 16, $50,000, 3&up, 1$\frac{1}{16}$m, 1:45.12, POLISH PRIDE, Pickupspeed, Marciano, 5 started.
Hail the Ruckus Dating Game S., Lethbridge, Oct. 25, $9,200, 3&up, f&m, 7f, 1:25.20, GUILTYBYSUPISCION, Irish Intrigue, A Tempting Light, 8 started.
Half Moon Bay H., Bay Meadows, Sept. 22, $68,450, 3yo, 1$\frac{1}{16}$mT, 1:42.57, WORLD LIGHT, Marcutio, Surprized, 11 started.
Half Moon S., The Meadowlands, Oct. 11, $50,000, 3yo, f, 6f, 1:09.76, WILZADA, Slews Final Answer, Mooji Moo, 7 started.
Hallandale Beach H., Gulfstream Park, April 20, $75,000, 3yo, 7f, 1:22.28, GYGISTAR, Juggernaut, Danielles Magic, 6 started.
Halton S. (R), Woodbine, Sept. 2, $104,650, 3&up, Canadian-bred, a1⅛mT, 1:46.25, STEADY RUCKUS, Mighty Quinn, Byzantine, 6 started.
Hancock County H., Mountaineer Park, May 14, $78,350, 3&up, f&m, 5f, 57.75, ISLAND RIFFLE CAT, Persian Silver, French Teacher, 8 started.
Hank Mills Memorial H., Wyoming Downs, Aug. 17, $5,200, 3&up, f&m, 5f, MYTHS AND LEGENDS, Boomer Bust, Tomencino, 8 started.
Hannah Dustin S., Suffolk Downs, Feb. 16, $30,000, 4&up, f&m, 1m 70y, 1:46.11, RODEO SPRINGS, Weekend Kaper, Big Miss, 7 started.
Hansel S., Turfway Park, March 23, $58,000, 3yo, 6f, 1:10.95, STORM COMMANDER, World Champion, World Trade, 6 started.
HANSHIN CUP H.-G3, Arlington Park, July 20, $100,000, 3&up, 1m, 1:34, BONAPAW, Slider, Discreet Hero, 7 started.
Hard Scuffle Hurdle S. (R), Churchill Downs, May 2, $102,141, 4&up, non-winners over hurdles prior to March 1, 2001, a2$\frac{1}{16}$mT, 3:48, MCDYNAMO, Najjm, Miles Ahead, 8 started.
Harold C. Ramser Sr. H. (1st Div.), Santa Anita Park, Oct. 14, $83,300, 3yo, f, 1mT, 1:33.73, KITHIRA (GB), Super High, Crousille (Fr), 7 started.
Harold C. Ramser Sr. H. (2nd Div.), Santa Anita Park, Oct. 14, $84,300, 3yo, f, 1mT, 1:33.98, SENTIMENTAL VALUE, Company B, Dancing (GB), 8 started.
Harold V. Goodman Memorial S. (R), Lone Star Park, June 29, $50,000, 3yo, Texas-bred, 6f, 1:10.70, FRONT NINE, Nuclear Assembly, Son of a Lue, 8 started.
Harper County H., Anthony Downs, July 14, $4,000, 3&up, a5f, 1:03.12, MOSCOWS QUICK TRIP, U Lover U, Whisper Whiz, 5 started.
Harper County H., Anthony Downs, July 14, $4,090, 3&up, a5f, 1:03.09, AMEGO MEL, Santero, Kings Own, 5 started.
Harrison E. Johnson Memorial S., Laurel Park, March 16, $50,000, 4&up, 1⅛m, 1:49.35, FIRST AMENDMENT, P Day, Lyracist, 7 started.
Harry F. Brubaker H. (R), Del Mar, Aug. 23, $76,125, 3&up, non-winners of $45,000 other than closed, claiming, or starter at one mile or over since March 1, 1$\frac{1}{16}$mT, 1:40.57, KACHAMANDI (Chi), Nicobar (GB), Fateful Dream, 8 started.
Harry Henson S., Hollywood Park, April 24, $77,925, 3yo, 5½fT, 1:02.97, LINE RIDER, Ecstatic, Void Floyd, 10 started.
Harry J. Addison H. (R), Fort Erie, Sept. 24, $57,600, 3&up, c&g, sold at a CTHS or a CBS sale, 1$\frac{1}{16}$m, 1:45.03, FOREVER GRAND, Le Vainqueur, Riddell's Creek, 4 started.
Harry Jeffreys S., Assiniboia Downs, Aug. 24, $30,000, 3yo, 1⅛m, 1:54.60, EKATI, Crescent Remark, Silver Greek, 7 started.
Harry W. Henson H., Sunland Park, April 6, $62,700, 3&up, f&m, 1m, 1:35.88, MCKINNEY, Ode to Elaine, Tellme Truly, 8 started.
Harvest H., The Downs at Albuquerque, April 6, $31,700, 3yo, 5½f, 1:02.51, RAISE A BOOGER, Trippy Lark, Mon Ouimet, 5 started.
Harvey Arneault Memorial H., Mountaineer Park, Aug. 10, $88,000, 3&up, 6f, 1:10.05, SECRET ROMEO, Mo Mon, Meetyouathebrig, 7 started.
HASKELL INVITATIONAL H.-G1, Monmouth Park, Aug. 4, $990,000, 3yo, 1⅛m, 1:48.21, WAR EMBLEM, Magic Weisner, Like a Hero, 5 started.
Hasta La Vista H., Turf Paradise, May 19, $50,000, 3&up, 1⅞mT, 3:11.52, WITHOUT DOUBT (Ire), Bristolville, Paladin Power, 11 started.
Hastings Park H., Emerald Downs, May 5, $35,000, 3&up, f&m, 6½f, 1:15.60, NEON QUEEN, Silky Secret, Rollette, 6 started.
Hastings Park Speed H., Hastings Park Racecourse, Aug. 18, $36,355, 3&up, 6½f, 1:15.74, DANZILATION, I'm Free, King Jeremy, 6 started.
Hatoof S., Arlington Park, Oct. 23, $48,750, 3yo, f, a1mT, 1:35.88, ATTICO, Beret, Delicatessa, 7 started.
Hawkeyes H. (R), Prairie Meadows, June 28, $79,900, 3&up, f&m, Iowa-bred, 1$\frac{1}{16}$m, 1:44.35, SHARKY'S REVIEW, Scarlet Glory, Sumthintotalkabout, 7 started.
HAWTHORNE DERBY-G3, Hawthorne Race Course, May 11, $250,000, 3yo, 1⅛mT, 1:58.88, SCOOTER ROACH, Quest Star, Colorful Tour, 7 started.
HAWTHORNE GOLD CUP H.-G2, Hawthorne Race Course, May 18, $500,000, 3&up, 1¼m, 2:02.80, HAIL THE CHIEF (GB), Dollar Bill, Parade Leader, 5 started.
HAWTHORNE H.-G3, Hollywood Park, April 27, $106,100, 3&up, f&m, 1$\frac{1}{16}$m, 1:43.16, QUEEN OF WILSHIRE, Alexine (Arg), Verruma (Brz), 5 started.
HBPA Almost Heaven S., Charles Town, July 14, $42,200, 3&up, f&m, 4½f, 52.23, TRICKY ACCOUNT, Who's Ya Mama, Miss Ruth, 9 started.
HBPA Au Revoir H., Grants Pass, July 7, $3,785, 3&up, 1$\frac{1}{16}$m, 1:50.20, JEWELS TOGO, Victor Lehman, Carey's Blue Mon, 6 started.
HBPA City of Charles Town S., Charles Town, Oct. 11, $51,950, 3&up, f&m, 1⅛m, 1:53.70, GOLDEN PHOEBE, Tamayo, Real Women, 9 started.
HBPA City of Ranson S., Charles Town, Oct. 11, $51,550, 3&up, 7f, 1:25.70, SARATOGA GAMES, Notably Frosty, Polish Music, 7 started.
HBPA Governor's Cup S., Charles Town, Oct. 11, $51,750, 3&up, 4½f, :51.58, BABY SHARK, The Maccabee, Periscope, 8 started.
HBPA H., Ellis Park, July 13, $100,000, 3&up, f&m, 1m, 1:38.19, HAPPILY UNBRIDLED, Gal On the Go, Red n'Gold, 8 started.
HBPA Jefferson County S., Charles Town, July 14, $42,050, 3&up, 1⅛m, 1:53.40, NOTABLY FROSTY, Confucius Say, Rebellious Dreamer, 9 started.
HBPA Opequon S., Charles Town, July 14, $42,000, 3&up, 4½f, :51.82, PERISCOPE, Brooklyn Bridge, Wise Dusty, 9 started.
HBPA S., Grants Pass, June 2, $3,590, 3yo, 5½f, 1:05.20, ROUX THEN GUMBO, Stately Key, Heza Hottie, 5 started.
HBPA/Sagebrush Downs Derby, Kamloops, Aug. 25, $5,250, 3&up,

1m, 1:43.20, BRASS ROBIN, Nonameit, Babybeef, 5 started.

HBPA West Virginia Oaks S., Charles Town, July 14, $42,400, 3&up, f&m, 7f, 1:27.74, NASTY SABRINA, Carson City Sham, Winter Leaf, 10 started.

Heavenly Cause S. (R), Laurel Park, Oct. 14, $60,000, 2yo, f, Maryland-bred, 7f, 1:26.19, KITTY KNIGHT, Mark Aim Fire, Butiwillflysomeday, 8 started.

Helen Anthony Memorial S., Yavapai Downs, June 1, $7,500, 3yo, f, 6f, 1:10.51, PETERS PUNKIN, Italian Diva, A Girl Like You, 4 started.

Helena S., Suffolk Downs, April 27, $30,000, 3yo, f, 1m, 1:42.67, AFRICAN PRINCESS, Conwiss, Lyd's a Winnah, 8 started.

Henry S. Clark S., Pimlico, May 4, $50,000, 3&up, 1mT, 1:36.33, MUSIF (GB), Great Woods, Banner Boy, 11 started.

Herald Gold Plate H., Stampede Park, June 9, $50,000, 3&up, 1⅟₁₆m, 1:46, RANCOUR, They Call Me Cody, Sixthirtyjoe, 7 started.

HERECOMESTHEBRIDE S.-G3, Gulfstream Park, Feb. 3, $100,000, 3yo, f, 1⅟₁₆mT, 1:43.21, CELLARS SHIRAZ, August Storm, She's Vested, 10 started.

Hidden Light S. (R), Santa Anita Park, Oct. 25, $51,000, 2yo, f, nonwinners of $40,000 other than closed or claiming at one mile or over, 1mT, 1:37.10, GOTDREAM (Fr), Chope Mockery (Fr), Major Idea, 6 started.

HIGHLANDER S. (Can-G3), Woodbine, Sept. 29, $160,800, 3&up, 6f, 1:09.72, WAKE AT NOON, Cheap Talk, Krz Ruckus, 5 started.

Highland Happening S., Suffolk Downs, Sept. 28, $30,000, 3&up, f&m, 1⅟₁₆mT, 1:44.81, TIP THE SCALE, Ayres Hall, Weekend Kaper, 8 started.

Hildene S. (R), Delaware Park, Nov. 9, $42,000, 2yo, f, Virginia-bred, 6f, 1:12.10, MAKIN HEAT, Charmie's Secret, Little Miss Pamela, 5 started.

HILL PRINCE S.-G3, Belmont Park, June 15, $109,300, 3yo, 1⅛mT, 1:54.42, VAN MINISTER, Miesque's Approval, Westcliffe, 5 started.

Hill Rise S., Santa Anita Park, Dec. 28, $76,350, 2yo, 1mT, 1:35.44, PEACE RULES, Outtake, Bis Repetitas, 5 started.

Hill Rise S., Santa Anita Park, Jan. 6, $76,850, 3yo, 1mT, 1:36.56, MOUNTAIN RAGE, Night Passion (GB), Leah's Candy, 10 started.

Hillsborough H., Bay Meadows, Sept. 28, $61,100, 3&up, f&m, 1⅟₁₆mT, 1:43.05, I'M THE BUSINESS (NZ), Crazy Ensign (Arg), Reine de Romance (Ire), 10 started.

Hillsborough S., Tampa Bay Downs, March 17, $100,000, 4&up, f&m, 1⅟₁₆mT, 1:41.34, PLATINUM TIARA, Ioya Two, Step With Style, 11 started.

Hillsdale S. (R), Hoosier Park, Oct. 5, $34,300, 2yo, c&g, Indiana-bred, 5½f, 1:06.10, GO DOCTOR MO, Jessica's Best, Louie Gold, 10 started.

Hilltop S., Pimlico, May 11, $50,000, 3yo, f, 1⅟₁₆mT, 1:42.20, NTOMBI, Smart Grace, Restraining Order, 12 started.

Hirsch Jacobs S., Pimlico, May 18, $76,500, 3yo, 6f, 1:10.90, TRUE DIRECTION, Listen Here, It's a Monster, 8 started.

Hoist Her Flag S., Canterbury Park, June 22, $35,000, 3&up, f&m, 6f, 1:09.23, EXTENDED VIEW, Feminine Fury, Kimme a Star, 7 started.

Holiday Inaugural S., Turfway Park, Dec. 7, $50,000, 3&up, f&m, 6f, 1:11.72, EMILY RING, Freefourracing, Don't Countess Out, 9 started.

Hollie Hughes H. (R), Aqueduct, Feb. 17, $77,725, 3&up, New York-bred, 6f, 1:11.10, VODKA, Kashatreya, Strike the Brass, 4 started.

HOLLYWOOD BREEDERS' CUP OAKS-G2, Hollywood Park, June 15, $266,800, 3yo, f, 1⅟₁₆m, 1:43.73, ADORATION, Sister Girl Blues, Saint Bernadette, 7 started.

HOLLYWOOD DERBY-G1, Hollywood Park, Dec. 1, $500,000, 3yo, 1⅛mT, 1:48.70, JOHAR, Mananan McLir, Royal Gem, 9 started.

HOLLYWOOD FUTURITY-G1, Hollywood Park, Dec. 21, $409,500, 2yo, 1⅟₁₆m, 1:41.26, TOCCET, Domestic Dispute, Golden Kiss, 6 started.

HOLLYWOOD GOLD CUP S.-G1, Hollywood Park, July 14, $750,000, 3&up, 1¼m, 2:01.73, SKY JACK, Momentum, Milwaukee Brew, 6 started.

HOLLYWOOD JUVENILE CHAMPIONSHIP S.-G3, Hollywood Park, July 20, $108,300, 2yo, 6f, 1:10.10, CROWNED DANCER, Outta Here, Chief Planner, 7 started.

Hollywood Park Allowance S. (R), Hollywood Park, April 28, $70,000, 3&up, California breds which have not won $3,000 other than maiden, claiming or starter or have never won two races, 7f, 1:23.60, AFFAIRINTHEFOREST, La Bandera, Ride and Shine, 9 started.

HOLLYWOOD PREVUE S.-G3, Hollywood Park, Nov. 23, $125,000, 2yo, 7f, 1:22.68, ROLL HENNESSY ROLL, Red Apache, Hell Cat, 7 started.

HOLLYWOOD STARLET S.-G1, Hollywood Park, Dec. 14, $366,500, 2yo, f, 1⅟₁₆m, 1:42.88, ELLOLUV, Composure, Summer Wind Dancer, 7 started.

HOLLYWOOD TURF CUP S.-G1, Hollywood Park, Nov. 23, $250,000, 3&up, 1½mT, 2:27.22, SLIGO BAY (Ire), Grammarian, Delta Form (Aus), 11 started.

HOLLYWOOD TURF EXPRESS H.-G3, Hollywood Park, Nov. 29, $200,000, 3&up, 5½fT, 1:01.52, TEXAS GLITTER, Rocky Bar, Malabar Gold, 5 started.

Hollywood Wildcat S., Calder Race Course, Nov. 30, $100,000, 2yo, f, 1⅟₁₆mT, 1:42.73, SWEETTRICKYDANCER, Askforaraise, Running Debate, 12 started.

HOLY BULL S.-G3, Gulfstream Park, Jan. 19, $100,000, 3yo, 1⅟₁₆m, 1:46.16, BOOKLET, Harlan's Holiday, Thiscannonsloaded, 7 started.

HONEYBEE S.-G3, Oaklawn Park, March 9, $75,000, 3yo, f, 1⅟₁₆m, 1:46.41, BEDANKEN, Cozy Susie, Sarah Jade, 6 started.

HONEY FOX H.-G3, Gulfstream Park, Jan. 4, $100,000, 3&up, f&m, a1⅟₁₆mT, 1:49.32, BATIQUE, My Sweet Westly, Silver Bandana, 8 started.

Honey Jay H. (R), Beulah Park, Sept. 14, $40,000, 3&up, Ohio-bred, 6f, 1:11.17, SCIOTO BOOTSKI, J. R.'s Town, Truth Matters, 9 started.

HONEYMOON BREEDERS' CUP H.-G2, Hollywood Park, June 8, $164,050, 3yo, f, 1⅛mT, 1:51.97, MEGAHERTZ (GB), Arabic Song (Ire), High Society (Ire), 7 started.

Honeymoon S., Louisiana Downs, June 29, $50,000, 3&up, f&m, a1mT, 1:36.50, DUE TO WIN AGAIN, Golden Rhythm, Eagle Lake, 9 started.

Hong Kong Jockey Club H., Hastings Park Racecourse, July 20, $38,593, 3&up, 1⅟₁₆m, 1:43.99, WORK VISA, King Jeremy, Jazzy Yacht, 8 started.

Honky Star S., Delaware Park, Oct. 12, $58,700, 3&up, f&m, 6f, 1:10.87, OZILDA'S KAREN, Bernie's Gold, Outstanding Info, 6 started.

HONORABLE MISS H.-G3, Saratoga Race Course, Aug. 2, $108,500, 3&up, f&m, 6f, 1:09.24, MANDY'S GOLD, Shine Again, Dat You Miz Blue, 6 started.

Honor the Hero S., Turf Paradise, Dec. 17, $22,700, 3&up, 6½f, 1:15.41, FLYING SUPERCON, Irish Cream Taffy, Iza Redhead, 5 started.

Honor the Hero S., Canterbury Park, May 27, $35,000, 3&up, 5fT, MY GIRL LISA, Freeway Ticket, Honor Me, 6 started.

Hoofprint On My Heart S., Stampede Park, May 26, $40,000, 3yo, 1m, 1:38.60, INTACT, Dark Fuse, Exclusive Banker, 10 started.

Hoosier Debutante S., Hoosier Park, Nov. 9, $103,700, 2yo, f, 6f, 1:11.50, JENNY'S PROSPECTOR, Hurry Home, Wildcat Annie, 7 started.

Hoosier Juvenile S., Hoosier Park, Nov. 23, $103,950, 2yo, c&g, 6f, 1:11.47, COACH JIMI LEE, Mr. Whitestone, Private Gold, 9 started.

Hoover S. (R), River Downs, Aug. 3, $40,000, 2yo, Ohio-bred, 6f, 1:12.80, HACKENDIFFY, Mercer's Cool Cat, Buckeye Teddy, 6 started.

Hoover S., Laurel Park, Jan. 26, $50,000, 4&up, 6f, 1:09.31, ADAM CAT, Rusty Spur, Jorgie Stover, 9 started.

HOPEFUL S.-G1, Saratoga Race Course, Aug. 31, $200,000, 2yo, 7f, 1:23.08, SKY MESA, Pretty Wild, Zavata, 6 started.

Hopemont S., Keeneland, Oct. 25, $115,000, 2yo, 1⅟₁₆mT, 1:46.45, RAPID PROOF, Zydeco Affair, Collateral Damage, 10 started.

Horatius S., Laurel Park, March 24, $40,000, 3yo, 7f, 1:24.01, OUTSTANDER, President Butler, Jo Jo Dancer, 6 started.

Horizon S. (R), River Downs, July 21, $50,000, 3yo, Ohio-bred, 1⅟₁₆mT, 1:44.40, DINKERS MILLENNIUM, Count On My Word, Nate's Rib, 9 started.

Hot Springs S., Oaklawn Park, March 29, $50,000, 4&up, 6f, 1:09.14, (DH) BEAU'S TOWN, (DH) KINGS COMMAND, Chindi, 6 started.

Howard B. Noonan S. (R), Beulah Park, March 23, $40,000, 3yo, Ohio-bred, 6f, 1:11.68, ALL OUT SPRINGS, Beaver Cat, Elm Grove, 7 started.

HPO Breeders' Derby (R), Horsemen's Park, July 21, $27,500, 3yo, Nebraska-bred, 1m, 1:39, MR CLEARWATER, Brown Whiskey, Keylargo Lady, 5 started.

Hudson H. (R), Belmont Park, Oct. 19, $125,000, 3&up, New York-bred, 6f, 1:09.82, WELL FANCIED, Tom's Thunder, Vodka, 13 started.

HUMANA DISTAFF H.-G1, Churchill Downs, May 4, $228,000, 4&up, f&m, 7f, 1:22.98, CELTIC MELODY, Gold Mover, Hattiesburg, 9 started.

Humphrey S. Finney S. (R), Laurel Park, Nov. 9, $60,000, 3yo, Maryland-bred, 1⅛mT, 1:51.68, BOCA FLYER, Hay Getoutofmyway, War Native, 5 started.

Huntington S., Aqueduct, Nov. 17, $82,475, 2yo, 6f, 1:10.40, SUPER FUSE, American Mon, First Blush, 8 started.

Hurricane Bertie S., Gulfstream Park, March 17, $100,000, 3&up, f&m,

6½f, 1:15.38, GOLD MOVER, Celtic Melody, Mandy's Gold, 5 started.
Hurricane Viv H., Calder Race Course, June 23, $42,345, 3&up, f&m, 1⅙m, 1:45.94, CASTLEBROOK, Banderia (Arg), Sea Mist, 6 started.
Huskerette Purse S. (R), Horsemen's Park, July 19, $29,500, 3&up, f&m, Nebraska-bred, 1m, 1:39.40, OGLALA SUE, Irish Flyer, Gary's Speedy Miss, 9 started.
HUTCHESON S.-G2, Gulfstream Park, Feb. 2, $150,000, 3yo, 7f, 1:26.07, SHOWMEITALL, Monthir, Royal Lad, 6 started.
Hyperactive S., Calder Race Course, Sept. 22, $44,760, 3yo, f, 1⅙mT, 1:43.30, CAGEY MOVE, Shrimp Tempura, Stormy Frolic, 12 started.
Idaho Cup Claiming S. (R), Les Bois Park, Aug. 11, $8,694, 3&up, Idaho-bred starters for a claiming price of $4,000 or less in 2001, 7f, 1:27.39, LUCKY REALITY, Mast Dancer, Dats Y, 7 started.
Idaho Cup Classic S. (R), Les Bois Park, Aug. 10, $31,936, 4&up, c&g, Idaho-bred, 1m, 1:38.63, SAN DIEGO PETE, Quiet Syns, La Fontaine, 5 started.
Idaho Cup Derby (R), Les Bois Park, Aug. 11, $35,946, 3yo, Idaho-bred, 1m, 1:39.23, MR MOTION, Rift, Our Megabucks, 10 started.
Idaho Cup Distaff Derby (R), Les Bois Park, Aug. 10, $32,058, 3yo, f, Idaho-bred, 1m, 1:40, TROPHY EDITION TOO, Bogus Plan, Letthelittlegirlgo, 5 started.
Idaho Cup Distaff Maturity (R), Les Bois Park, Aug. 10, $31,693, 4&up, f&m, Idaho-bred, 1m, 1:41.87, INFANTRY LIZ, Somer Wonders, Eyes Sucha Delight, 8 started.
Idaho Cup Juvenile Championship S. (R), Les Bois Park, Aug. 11, $41,130, 2yo, Idaho-bred, 5f, 59.62, ROYAL INFANTRY, Frisky Are We, Two Star Story, 8 started.
Idaho Cup Sprint S. (R), Les Bois Park, Aug. 10, $11,511, 3&up, Idaho-bred, 5f, BAYLEY BOPP, Northern Tide, Regal Edition, 7 started.
Illini Princess S. (R), Hawthorne Race Course, Nov. 9, $97,925, 3&up, f&m, Illinois-bred, 1⅙m, 1:48.60, VIBES, Out of Options, Ellie's Rose, 11 started.
Illinois Breeders' Debutante S. (R), Hawthorne Race Course, Dec. 14, $111,550, 2yo, f, Illinois-bred, 1⅙m, 1:49.66, JULIE'S PRIZE, Invader, Cashmere Miss, 12 started.
Illinois Coronet S. (R), Hawthorne Race Course, Nov. 9, $95,700, 3&up, Illinois-bred, 1⅙m, 1:46.85, CHINKAPIN, Colorful Tour, Saquache, 12 started.
ILLINOIS DERBY-G2, Sportsman's Park, April 6, $500,000, 3yo, 1⅛m, 1:49.92, WAR EMBLEM, Repent, Fonz's, 9 started.
I'm Smokin S. (R), Del Mar, Sept. 9, $100,000, 2yo, California-bred, 6f, 1:10.25, SIBERLAND, Martinblestme, Excessive Barb, 7 started.
Inaugural H., SunRay Park, Sept. 21, $32,100, 3&up, 6½f, 1:18.20, DEBATABLE, La Fontaine, Risen Ruler, 6 started.
Inaugural H., Wyoming Downs, June 22, $4,200, 3&up, 6f, 1:10.23, FIRE BALL JOHN, Testhaven, Fadski, 12 started.
Inaugural H., Yavapai Downs, May 25, $20,000, 3&up, 6f, 1:09, JO-MAX, Chevlon Canyon, Irish Cream Taffy, 11 started.
Inaugural H., Les Bois Park, May 4, $6,400, 3&up, 6½f, 1:18.24, BETTER CHOICE, San Diego Pete, Erhard, 7 started.
Inaugural H., Evangeline Downs, April 13, $30,000, 3yo, 6f, 1:11, HAIL TO BAG, Believe Im Special, Sky High Bag, 9 started.
Inaugural H., Portland Meadows, Oct. 19, $10,000, 3&up, 6f, 1:12.15, PROUD LOUIE, Bob Stories, Aint No Connection, 10 started.
Inaugural S., Columbus, July 26, $7,811, 3yo, f, 6f, 1:15.60, MAGIC TRUMP, Softly Played, Hawaiian Lullaby, 5 started.
Inaugural S., Tampa Bay Downs, Dec. 17, $50,000, 2yo, 6f, 1:11.99, AWESOME OF COURSE, Run for You, Penthouse Promise, 13 started.
Inaugural S., Arapahoe Park, June 9, $30,000, 3yo, 6f, 1:09, GONE WITH THE WIN, Jetson, Raise a Booger, 9 started.
Independence Breeders' Cup H., Louisiana Downs, July 4, $100,000, 3&up, 1⅙mT, 1:43.08, MAYSVILLE SLEW, Candid Glen, Rebridled, 9 started.
Independence Day H., Emerald Downs, July 4, $40,000, 3&up, 1⅙m, 1:41.40, MOONLIGHT MEETING, Sabertooth, Diglett, 5 started.
Independence Day H., Mountaineer Park, July 2, $79,250, 3&up, 1mT, 1:36.20, (DH) ON TO RICHMOND, (DH) BUENOS DIAS, Jake the Flake, 8 started.
INDIANA BREEDERS' CUP OAKS-G3, Hoosier Park, Oct. 4, $306,400, 3yo, f, 1⅙m, 1:45.83, BARE NECESSITIES, Erica's Smile, Tarnished Lady, 9 started.
INDIANA DERBY-G3, Hoosier Park, Oct. 5, $414,700, 3yo, 1⅙m, 1:43.50, PERFECT DRIFT, Easyfromthegitgo, Premeditation, 12 started.
Indiana Futurity (R), Hoosier Park, Nov. 16, $74,000, 2yo, c&g, Indiana-bred, 6f, 1:11.98, K K AVEY, Groovy Zone, Tin Man Commin, 11 started.
Indiana Stallion S. (R), Hoosier Park, Nov. 29, $44,400, 2yo, f, Indiana-bred, 6f, 1:13.35, SHEZA PRETTY GAL, Cattle Kate, Diplomatic Lady, 11 started.
INGLEWOOD H.-G3, Hollywood Park, May 5, $109,700, 3&up, 1⅙mT, 1:39.35, NIGHT PATROL, Redattore (Brz), Seinne (Chi), 7 started.
Ingrid Knotts H. (R), Arapahoe Park, June 8, $30,000, 3&up, f&m, Colorado-bred, 6f, 1:11.60, CRAFTY CINDY, Music Lover, Black Sea, 8 started.
In Reality S. (R), Calder Race Course, Oct. 12, $400,000, 2yo, progeny of eligible Florida stallions, 1⅙m, 1:46.52, TRUST N LUCK, The Name's Bond, Patriotic Flame, 14 started.
Interborough H., Aqueduct, Jan. 1, $81,925, 3&up, f&m, 6f, 1:11.10, XTRA HEAT, City Fair, Look of the Lynx, 6 started.
Interior Futurity, Kamloops, Sept. 8, $3,225, 2yo, 6½f, 1:20.80, MISTER MANE MAN, Devil Rock, Paul's Part, 9 started.
International Gold Cup S., Great Meadows, Oct. 19, $41,850, 4&up, a3⅛mT, 7:47.80, STAGE RADIANCE, Shimmer Shimmer, Sovereign Storm, 6 started.
Iowa Breeders' Derby (R), Prairie Meadows, Aug. 31, $75,210, 3yo, c&g, Iowa-bred, 1⅙m, 1:44.20, COWBOY STUFF, Cornpatch Road, Yoyo Jabo, 12 started.
Iowa Breeders' Oaks (R), Prairie Meadows, Aug. 31, $76,370, 3yo, f, Iowa-bred, 1m 70y, 1:42.81, DAZZLING CRYPTO, True Tear Drops, Stormin Sassy, 12 started.
Iowa Cradle S. (R), Prairie Meadows, Aug. 31, $74,910, 2yo, c&g, Iowa-bred, 6f, 1:10.63, EL SADDLER, Darkly Noon, Invaderfromtheeast, 9 started.
Iowa Derby, Prairie Meadows, July 5, $245,000, 3yo, 1⅙m, 1:42.59, EASYFROMTHEGITGO, Pass Rush, Thunderpumper, 5 started.
Iowa Distaff S., Prairie Meadows, July 6, $127,500, 3&up, f&m, 1⅙m, 1:41.98, MINISTER'S BABY, Caressing, Netherland (Arg), 10 started.
Iowa Oaks, Prairie Meadows, July 3, $150,000, 3yo, f, 1⅙m, 1:42.27, LOST AT SEA, See How She Runs, Don't Ruffle Me, 6 started.
Iowa Sorority S. (R), Prairie Meadows, Aug. 31, $72,750, 2yo, f, Iowa-bred, 6f, 1:11.84, CODING, Eolica, Lovesmegold, 6 started.
Iowa Sprint H., Prairie Meadows, July 4, $142,500, 3&up, 6f, 1:08.64, SAND RIDGE, Boots On Sunday, Men's Exclusive, 4 started.
Iowa Stallion Futurity (R), Prairie Meadows, Sept. 13, $103,820, 2yo, progeny of stallions standing in Iowa, 6f, 1:11.67, TRIAGE, Cmego, Invaderfromtheeast, 11 started.
Iowa Stallion S. (R), Prairie Meadows, July 27, $62,856, 3yo, progeny of stallions standing in Iowa, 1m 70y, 1:44.25, LADY SUNDARI, Sly Guy's Up, Yoyo Jabo, 5 started.
Iowa State Fair S., Prairie Meadows, Aug. 3, $46,600, 3&up, f&m, 6f, 1:08.27, DON'T COUNTESS OUT, Sharky's Review, Trisha Runs, 5 started.
Ioya Two H., Arlington Park, Oct. 20, $42,000, 3&up, f&m, 1⅙mT, 1:44.11, ELLIE'S ROSE, Out of Options, Soccory, 6 started.
Irish Day H., Emerald Downs, June 30, $40,000, 3yo, f, 1⅙m, 1:43.80, LASTING CODE, Premo Copy, Ashbecca, 9 started.
Irish O'Brien S. (R), Santa Anita Park, March 17, $107,000, 4&up, f&m, California-bred, a6½fT, 1:13.16, ABOVE PERFECTION, Jeweled Pirate, Song of the Moment, 6 started.
Irish Sonnet H., Calder Race Course, Aug. 25, $42,730, 3&up, f&m, 6f, 1:11.80, SUGAR N SPICE, Dema Dema Dancer, Vague Memory, 6 started.
Irish Sonnet S., Delaware Park, Sept. 23, $58,300, 2yo, f, 6f, 1:13.69, LETS JUST DO IT, Makin Heat, Stormy La Reine, 5 started.
Irish Vol H., Calder Race Course, Aug. 13, $43,220, 3&up, f&m, 5fT, :56.26, PETRINA ABOVE, Flying Birdie, Pageant Baby, 8 started.
Iroquois H. (R), Philadelphia Park, July 27, $52,950, 3&up, Pennsylvania-bred, 1⅙m, 1:45.04, DOCENT, Sumerset, Wild Over Ian, 7 started.
Iroquois H. (R), Belmont Park, Oct. 19, $125,000, 3&up, f&m, New York-bred, 7f, 1:22.84, DAT YOU MIZ BLUE, Princess Dixie, Maddie May, 10 started.
Iroquois Hurdle S., Percy Warner, May 11, $100,000, 4&up, a3mT, 5:32.40, ALL GONG (GB), Flat Top, Praise the Prince (NZ), 7 started.
IROQUOIS S.-G3, Churchill Downs, Nov. 3, $114,200, 2yo, 1m, 1:37.06, CHAMPALI, Alke, What a Bad Day, 10 started.
Irving Distaff (1st Div.), Lone Star Park, April 13, $75,000, 3&up, f&m, 7½fT, 1:34.20, PLEASANT STATE, Solo Attack, Mysia Jo, 6 started.
Irving Distaff S. (2nd Div.), Lone Star Park, April 13, $75,000, 3&up, f&m, 7½fT, 1:33.59, LA RECHERCHE, Golden Rhythm, Euryanthe (Ire), 9 started.
Isaac Murphy H. (R), Arlington Park, June 22, $85,450, 3&up, f&m, Illinois-conceived and/or -foaled, 6f, 1:10.64, COME SEPTEMBER, Faccia Bella, Darling L, 8 started.
Isadorable S. (R), Suffolk Downs, March 16, $29,400, 3&up, f&m,

Massachusetts-bred, 6f, 1:11.98, DR. DESAI, Sunlit Ridge, Big Miss, 5 started.
Isi Newborn Memorial S., Thistledown, July 20, $35,000, 3&up, 6f, 1:09.84, SECRET ROMEO, Tour the Hive, Waist Gunner John, 8 started.
Islander H., Fonner Park, March 9, $16,595, 3yo, f, 6f, 1:14.40, FLAMING NIGHT, Talk to Cathy, Aggies Style, T J Casey, 9 started.
Island Whirl H., Louisiana Downs, Sept. 28, $30,000, 3&up, 7f, 1:22.53, DOCTOR MIKE, That Tat, Yuma, 8 started.
Izvestia S. (R), Woodbine, July 20, $106,000, 3&up, Canadian-bred, 1⅟₁₆m, 1:44.45, PAROSE, Win City, Queensgate, 5 started.
Jack Betta Be Rite S. (R), Finger Lakes, Aug. 24, $40,000, 3&up, f&m, New York-bred, 1⅟₁₆m, 1:45.18, ALONG CAME MARY, Miss Ivy Hilton, Miss Royal Ibis, 10 started.
Jack Diamond Futurity (R), Hastings Park Racecourse, Sept. 28, $106,421, 2yo, c&g, Canadian-bred, 6½f, 1:18.30, ILLUSIVE FORCE, Native Judge, Bullseye Bill, 9 started.
Jack Dudley Sprint H. (R), Calder Race Course, Nov. 16, $150,000, 3&up, Florida-bred, 6f, 1:10.18, TOUR OF THE CAT, My Cousin Matt, Built Up, 8 started.
Jack Hardy S., Assiniboia Downs, Aug. 5, $30,000, 3yo, f, 1m, 1:43, BEAUSOX, Bitdaboss, Cool Cinder, 7 started.
Jackie Wackie H., Calder Race Course, April 28, $33,220, 3&up, 1mT, 1:34.48, MR. LIVINGSTON, Tour of the Cat, Unite's Big Red, 5 started.
Jack Price Juvenile S. (R), Calder Race Course, Nov. 16, $150,000, 2yo, Florida-bred, 7f, 1:24.76, SUPAH BLITZ, Hear No Evil, Unleash the Power, 8 started.
Jacques Cartier S., Woodbine, April 7, $132,625, 4&up, 6f, 1:10.26, WAKE AT NOON, Olympian, Hunter Todd, 5 started.
JAIPUR H.-G3, Belmont Park, May 27, $111,900, 3&up, 7fT, 1:20.08, SHIBBOLETH, Malabar Gold, Cozzy Corner, 7 started.
JAMAICA H.-G2, Belmont Park, Sept. 22, $200,000, 3yo, 1⅛m, 1:46.66, FINALITY, Union Place, Chiselling, 9 started.
Jameela S. (R), Laurel Park, Feb. 2, $60,000, 3yo, f, Maryland-bred, 7f, 1:27.04, BRONZE ABE, Phyxius, Nanden, 6 started.
James B. Moseley Breeders' Cup H., Suffolk Downs, June 1, $150,000, 3&up, 6f, 1:10.68, STORMIN OEDY, Southland Blues, Valiant Halory, 6 started.
James C. Ellis Juvenile S., Ellis Park, Aug. 17, $100,000, 2yo, 7f, 1:24.44, PRIVATE GOLD, Echeverria, Captain Amour, 12 started.
James F. Lyttle Memorial H., Santa Rosa, Aug. 2, $43,760, 3yo, 1⅟₁₆m, 1:42.95, FEDERAL HIGHWAY, Blue Slew's Shoes, Duddly Doo Run, 6 started.
James Leakos Sophomore S. (R), Marquis Downs, July 12, $7,670, 3yo, f, Saskatchewan-bred, 1m, 1:42.42, TOP STAGE DANCER, Royal Brittany, P J's Choice, 5 started.
Jammed Lovely S. (R), Woodbine, Nov. 3, $165,750, 3yo, f, Canadian-bred, 7f, 1:24.52, SPANISH DECREE, Mountain Orchid, Mulrainy, 8 started.
Jane Driggers Debutante S. (R), Portland Meadows, Dec. 14, $10,000, 2yo, f, Oregon-bred, 6f, 1:13.22, CARLYN ROAD, Our Lucky Kiss, Mismeridia, 5 started.
Janet Wineberg S. (R), Portland Meadows, Nov. 16, $15,780, 2yo, f, Oregon-bred, 6f, 1:13.57, OUR LUCKY KISS, Roada Ghost, Slew Falls, 5 started.
Japan Racing Association S., Laurel Park, July 28, $50,000, 3yo, 1⅛mT, 1:53.03, FAGER'S ISLAND, Fashion Award, Boca Flyer, 5 started.
Jean Lafitte Futurity, Delta Downs, April 7, $101,430, 2yo, 4f, 47.63, KNIGHT OF THE MT, Pancho's Karma, Amazing Glace, 10 started.
Jean Lafitte S., Delta Downs, Nov. 24, $75,000, 2yo, 7f, 1:25.35, COMIC TRUTH, Decatur, Gentlemen J J, 9 started.
JEFFERSON CUP S.-G3, Churchill Downs, June 8, $277,500, 3yo, 1⅛mT, 1:48.53, ORCHARD PARK, Mr. Mellon, Quest Star, 8 started.
JEH Stallion Station S. (R), Lone Star Park, May 27, $50,000, 3&up, f&m, Texas-bred, 6½f, 1:18.99, COASTALOTA, Suzie Sunshine, Princess Liza, 13 started.
Jennings H. (R), Pimlico, April 20, $100,000, 3&up, Maryland-bred, 1⅛m, 1:49.97, INCLUDE, Lightning Paces, First Amendment, 7 started.
Jenny Wade H., Penn National Race Course, Aug. 2, $50,000, 3&up, f&m, 5fT, :55.58, SCOOTIN' GIRL, Maypole Dance, Orage d'Hiver, 9 started.
JENNY WILEY S.-G3, Keeneland, April 11, $113,600, 4&up, f&m, 1⅟₁₆mT, 1:42.27, TATES CREEK, Snow Dance, Step With Style, 10 started.
JEROME H.-G2, Belmont Park, Sept. 14, $150,000, 3yo, 1m, 1:36.12, BOSTON COMMON, Vinemeister, No Parole, 7 started.
Jerry and Eileen Towslee Memorial H., Tillamook County Fair, Aug. 10, $3,686, 3&up, a5f, 1:04, HANDY MAN JEFF, Capable Quest, Haande Cap Her, 5 started.
Jersey Breeders' H. (R), Monmouth Park, June 16, $50,000, 3&up, New Jersey-bred, 1m, 1:36.82, SEA OF TRANQUILITY, Thistyranthasclass, Red Weasel, 6 started.
JERSEY DERBY-G3, Monmouth Park, May 27, $100,000, 3yo, 1⅟₁₆mT, 1:42.26, EMERGENCY STATUS, Kris's Prayer, Rapadash (Ire), 10 started.
Jersey Jumper S., The Meadowlands, Sept. 14, $48,500, 2yo, f, 6f, 1:10.50, CHIMICHURRI, Carson Cove, Hope for Love, 4 started.
Jersey Lilly S., Sam Houston Race Park, Feb. 23, $50,000, 4&up, f&m, 1⅟₁₆mT, 1:44.29, PLEASANT STATE, Zamba Canuta, Solo Attack, 11 started.
JERSEY SHORE BREEDERS' CUP S.-G3, Monmouth Park, July 4, $100,000, 3yo, 6f, 1:09.35, BOSTON COMMON, Listen Here, It's a Monster, 6 started.
Jersey Village S. (R), Sam Houston Race Park, Feb. 16, $30,000, 4&up, Texas-bred, 1⅟₁₆m, 1:44.70, CAPTAIN COUNTDOWN, Smiling Prince, Frankly Tee Riffic, 6 started.
Jiffy Lube S., Sam Houston Race Park, Nov. 2, $30,000, 3&up, f&m, 1⅟₁₆mT, 1:45.52, ASHEVILLE, Pleasant State, Lisa's Approval, 7 started.
Jim Bowie S., Retama Park, Sept. 7, $29,100, 3yo, 1⅟₁₆mT, 1:46.47, PADLOCK, Royal Win, S'more Smoke, 4 started.
Jim Coleman Province H., Hastings Park Racecourse, July 21, $38,731, 3yo, 1⅟₁₆m, 1:44.65, SHACANE, No Time Flat, Commodore Craig, 9 started.
JIM DANDY S.-G2, Saratoga Race Course, Aug. 4, $500,000, 3yo, 1⅛m, 1:47.82, MEDAGLIA D'ORO, Gold Dollar, Essence of Dubai, 9 started.
Jim Edgar Illinois Futurity (R), Hawthorne Race Course, Dec. 21, $109,775, 2yo, c&g, Illinois-bred and/or -conceived, 1⅟₁₆m, 1:47.17, ROY'S TRIGGER, He's Hammered, Fax Dance, 11 started.
Jim Murray Memorial H. (R), Hollywood Park, May 19, $80,175, 3&up, non-winners of $60,000 at one mile or over in 2002, 1½mT, 2:26.23, SKIPPING (GB), Startac, Our Main Man, 7 started.
J J'sdream S., Calder Race Course, June 29, $100,000, 2yo, f, 5½f, 1:06.07, HEAVENLY MISS, Crimson and Roses, Formal Miss, 9 started.
JOCKEY CLUB GOLD CUP S.-G1, Belmont Park, Sept. 28, $1,000,000, 3&up, 1¼m, 1:59.58, EVENING ATTIRE, Lido Palace (Chi), Harlan's Holiday, 8 started.
Joe Aitcheson Hurdle S. (R), Pimlico, May 17, $106,800, 4&up, non-winners over hurdles prior to March 1, 2001, a2⅛mT, 3:41.74, ANOFFERUCANTREFUSE, McDynamo, Ethical Actions, 10 started.
Joe Barroetabena & Karry Freeman Memorial H., Les Bois Park, Aug. 10, $5,800, 3&up, 1m, 1:39.27, RENO BOUND, Northern Land, Screaming Willy, 6 started.
Joe O'Farrell Juvenile Fillies S. (R), Calder Race Course, Nov. 16, $150,000, 2yo, f, Florida-bred, 7f, 1:25.11, ELEGANT DESIGNER, Running Debate, Crimson and Roses, 12 started.
John A. D'Amico S. (R), Gulfstream Park, Feb. 24, $60,000, 3yo, f, progeny of eligible Georgia stallions, 6f, 1:11.02, CHEROKEE GIRL, Pharmstar, Afnan, 6 started.
John Battaglia Memorial S., Turfway Park, March 2, $100,000, 3yo, 1⅟₁₆m, 1:43.08, REQUEST FOR PAROLE, Perfect Drift, Thunder On Land, 8 started.
John B. Campbell H., Laurel Park, Feb. 17, $100,000, 4&up, 1⅛m, 1:50.10, LYRACIST, Private Ryan, Top Official, 8 started.
John B. Connally Breeders' Cup Turf H., Sam Houston Race Park, Feb. 23, $222,000, 3&up, 1⅛mT, 1:50.38, CANDID GLEN, Nat's Big Party, El Gran Papa, 4 started.
John C. Mabee California Cup Mile H. (R), Santa Anita Park, Nov. 2, $175,000, 3&up, California-bred, 1mT, 1:34.82, TURKISH PRIZE, Spinelessjellyfish, Adminniestrator, 13 started.
JOHN C. MABEE RAMONA H.-G1, Del Mar, July 27, $400,000, 3&up, f&m, 1⅛mT, 1:48.37, AFFLUENT, Golden Apples (Ire), Janet (GB), 7 started.
John D. Marsh S. (R), Colonial Downs, June 23, $40,000, 3yo, Virginia-bred, 1⅟₁₆mT, 1:44.95, WILD GOOSE, Charles, Chain, 6 started.
John D. Schapiro Memorial Breeders' Cup S., Laurel Park, Oct. 12, $145,500, 3&up, 1⅛mT, 1:49, CERTANTEE, Polish Miner, Full Brush, 5 started.
John Henry H., Arlington Park, Oct. 25, $100,000, 3&up, 1³⁄₁₆mT, 1:59.83, RIDDLESDOWN (Ire), Tap the Admiral, National Anthem (GB), 7 started.
John Henry S., The Meadowlands, Sept. 20, $50,000, 3&up, 1m 70yT, 1:39.16, RIVER RUSH, American Freedom, Megantic, 7 started.

Johnie L. Jamison H. (R), Sunland Park, Dec. 8, $132,200, 3&up, New Mexico-bred, 6½f, 1:17.21, CIENTO, Star Smasher, Runmore Mema, 12 started.
John J. Reilly H. (R), Monmouth Park, May 12, $50,000, 3&up, New Jersey-bred, 6f, 1:11.07, SUMMER SWING, Sea of Tranquility, Red Weasel, 11 started.
John J. Shumaker H. (R), Penn National Race Course, Aug. 2, $30,500, 3&up, Pennsylvania-bred, 6f, 1:08.99, SLEETWOOD MAC, Tonto Gusto, Kelly's K. C., 6 started.
John Kirby S. (R), Suffolk Downs, Dec. 21, $30,000, 3&up, Massachusetts-bred, 1⅟₁₆m, 1:52.86, JINI'S JET, Papa Ho Ho, Puddle Time, 8 started.
John & Kitty Fletcher S. (R), Emerald Downs, Sept. 1, $24,375, 3yo, f, Washington-bred non-winners of $19,000 since April 19, 2002, 6½f, 1:15.40, PREMO COPY, Bubble's Girl, Ippodamia, 4 started.
John Longden '6000' H., Hastings Park Racecourse, June 9, $42,499, 3&up, 1⅟₁₆m, 1:43.47, KID KATABATIC, Diglett, King Jeremy, 6 started.
John McSorley S., Monmouth Park, July 7, $50,000, 3&up, 5fT, :55.44, RUDIRUDY, Joe's Son Joey, Manofglory, 8 started.
John Patrick H., Northlands Park, July 19, $40,000, 3&up, f&m, 1m, 1:41, FULL SCREAM AHEAD, Little Lolitta, C D Cool, 9 started.
John R. Macomber S. (R), Suffolk Downs, Oct. 12, $30,000, 3&up, Massachusetts-bred, 6f, 1:13.27, JINI'S JET, Diggin' for Fun, Naushon, 7 started.
John Wayne S. (R), Prairie Meadows, June 8, $64,200, 3&up, Iowa-bred, 6f, 1:09.42, REUBEN, Sure Shot Biscuit, Le Numerous, 6 started.
John W. Galbreath Memorial S. (R), Beulah Park, Nov. 3, $50,000, 2yo, f, Ohio-bred, 1⅟₁₆m, 1:49.12, WHITEWATER WAY, Platinum Hope, Mercer U., 9 started.
Joseph A. Gimma S. (R), Belmont Park, Sept. 29, $84,475, 2yo, f, New York-bred, 7f, 1:25.28, BEAUTIFUL AMERICA, Doc's Doll, Behrnik, 10 started.
Josephine County S., Grants Pass, June 9, $3,710, 3yo, f, 5½f, 1:06.20, HURRICANE HARBOUR, Coy Miss, Carey's Blue Mon, 6 started.
Joseph T. Grace H., Santa Rosa, Aug. 3, $100,990, 3&up, 1⅟₁₆m, 1:42.80, TAKIN IT DEEP, San Nicolas, Hoovergetthekeys, 9 started.
Journal H., Northlands Park, June 22, $40,000, 3&up, 6½f, 1:17.60, SIXTHIRTYJOE, Fussy's Kid, Vying Road, 5 started.
Journal Star S., Lincoln State Fair, May 25, $10,720, 3yo, 6f, 1:14.60, MR CLEARWATER, Dazzling J. R., Kansas Pioneer, 6 started.
J. R. Straus Memorial S., Retama Park, Aug. 2, $30,000, 3&up, 6f, 1:10.26, BOOTS ON SUNDAY, Ski Bum, Two Punch Sonny, 8 started.
Juan Gonzalez Memorial S., Pleasanton, June 30, $49,450, 2yo, f, 5f, :57.49, MY HONEY BUNNY, Frisco Belle, Phoenixledo, 6 started.
Judy's Red Shoes S., Calder Race Course, Sept. 7, $50,000, 3yo, f, 1⅟₁₆m, 1:45.66, REDOUBLED MISS, Stormy Frolic, Tasso Run, 6 started.
Julie Snellings S., Delaware Park, Sept. 4, $61,100, 3&up, f&m, 5fT, SAUVIGNON, Libby's Halo, Wingover, 9 started.
Junior Champion S., Monmouth Park, Sept. 1, $50,000, 2yo, f, 1mT, 1:41.08, FINAL ROUND, Paisley Park, Golden Number, 8 started.
JUST A GAME BREEDERS' CUP H.-G3, Belmont Park, June 8, $147,200, 3&up, f&m, a1mT, 1:34.57, BABAE (Chi), Tates Creek, Stylish, 8 started.
Justakiss S., Delaware Park, July 22, $59,900, 3&up, f&m, 1⅟₁₆m, 1:45.26, SHINY SHEET, Lily's Affair, Regal Countess, 7 started.
Juvenile S. (R), Fort Erie, Sept. 24, $64,300, 2yo, f, sold at a CTHS or a CBS sale, 6f, 1:13.39, ORDINARY PAULA, Touriga, Patient Patty, 9 started.
Juvenile S. (R), Fort Erie, Sept. 24, $60,500, 2yo, c&g, sold at a CTHS or a CBS sale, 6f, 1:13.58, RIGHT ON THE LINE, Frankiefourfingers, Walter Star, 5 started.
Juvenile S. (R), Thistledown, Sept. 8, $75,000, 2yo, Ohio-bred, 1⅟₁₆m, 1:45.80, HACKENDIFFY, Forest Picnic, Clever Jimmy C, 9 started.
J. W. Sifton S. (R), Assiniboia Downs, Sept. 21, $35,000, 3yo, Manitoba-bred, 1⅛m, 1:57.80, BEAU PIP, Portan, Rare Deputy, 7 started.
Kachina H., Turf Paradise, Dec. 28, $30,000, 3&up, f&m, 1m, 1:36.88, DAZZLING DIAMONDS, T. C. Lu, No Turbulence, 10 started.
Kachina S., Ruidoso Downs, July 28, $49,916, 2yo, f, 6f, 1:13, CHEROKEE'S DISCO, Sa Moken, Freeze Em Out, 7 started.
Kamar S. (R), Woodbine, July 14, $105,000, 3&up, f&m, Canadian-bred, 7f, 1:22.46, DEVASTATING, Mysterious Affair, Royal Dalliance, 4 started.
Kansas Oaks, The Woodlands, Oct. 31, $30,000, 3yo, f, 1m 70y, 1:50.60, RUMOR HAD IT, Pnutbutterandjolie, B T's Birthday, 6 started.
Kansas Thoroughbred Derby, The Woodlands, Oct. 12, $20,467, 3yo, f, 1m 70y, 1:50.40, WIND CHYMES, Dancing Bride, Doitdoitdoit, 4 started.
Kansas Thoroughbred Derby, The Woodlands, Oct. 13, $17,819, 3yo, c&g, 1m 70y, 1:48.20, RAISE A BOOGER, A Boy Named Luke, Axtell G R, 4 started.
Kansas Thoroughbred Futurity, The Woodlands, Oct. 4, $14,417, 2yo, f, 5½f, 1:10.60, MISSY CAN DO, Temptatious, Fine Ridge, 8 started.
Kansas Thoroughbred Futurity, The Woodlands, Oct. 5, $23,608, 2yo, c&g, 5½f, 1:09.60, EVANGLIE, Snoopin for Gold, Valiant Splash, 7 started.
Katy S. (R), Sam Houston Race Park, Feb. 23, $30,000, 3yo, f, Texas-bred, 7f, 1:25.37, SLY KONA, Bonus Bid, Wayne's Princess, 9 started.
Keeseecoose First Nation Classic S., Queensbury Downs, Oct. 11, $3,200, 3&up, 1⅟₁₆m, 1:50.75, HELABHAI, Zatz Mr. Cool, Back Twacking, 6 started.
Keith Brodkin Memorial S., Suffolk Downs, June 1, $30,000, 3&up, a5fT, CONCURRENT, Consider the Night, Duke Ora, 10 started.
KELSO H.-G2, Belmont Park, Oct. 5, $350,000, 3&up, 1mT, 1:33.83, GREEN FEE, Forbidden Apple, Moon Solitaire (Ire), 7 started.
Kelso S., Delaware Park, Oct. 5, $100,000, 3&up, 1³⁄₁₆m, 1:57.51, JARF, Acrolect, Full Brush, 5 started.
Ken Kendrick Memorial S., SunRay Park, Oct. 27, $41,739, 2yo, f, 6½f, 1:19.40, SA MOKEN, Manzotti Queen, Flying Cobra, 7 started.
Ken Maddy Sprint H. (R), Golden Gate Fields, Feb. 23, $100,000, 3&up, California-bred, 6f, 1:08.61, ECHO EDDIE, Gibson County, Radar Contact, 5 started.
Kennedy Road S., Woodbine, Nov. 30, $137,500, 3&up, 6f, 1:09.50, CHEAP TALK, Wake At Noon, Krz Ruckus, 7 started.
Kenneth L. Graf Memorial H., Rockingham Park, Sept. 2, $25,000, 3&up, f&m, 1⅟₁₆mT, 1:48.96, KIMSTER, Sword Princess, Sunlit Ridge, 8 started.
Kenny Noe Jr. H., Calder Race Course, Dec. 7, $100,000, 3&up, 7f, 1:23.30, BUILT UP, Tour of the Cat, Sea of Tranquility, 6 started.
Kenora S. (R), Woodbine, Sept. 2, $104,250, 3&up, Canadian-bred, 6f, 1:11.05, MULLIGAN THE GREAT, Rare Friends, Perlong, 7 started.
Ken Pearson Memorial H., Stampede Park, May 20, $40,000, 3&up, f&m, 1m, 1:37.60, SLEWABILITY, Little Lolitta, C D Cool, 7 started.
KENT BREEDERS' CUP S.-G3, Delaware Park, July 21, $247,900, 3yo, 1⅛mT, 1:48.81, MIESQUE'S APPROVAL, Regal Sanction, Quest Star, Coco's Madness, 8 started.
Kent H., Emerald Downs, June 2, $35,738, 3yo, f, 1m, 1:35.60, DOLLY'S HIT LADY, Miss Ballard, Mimi La Rue, 8 started.
KENTUCKY BREEDERS' CUP S.-G3, Churchill Downs, May 27, $160,000, 2yo, 5½f, 1:03.73, POSSE, Del Diablo, Blackjack Boy, 8 started.
KENTUCKY CUP CLASSIC H.-G2, Turfway Park, Sept. 14, $400,000, 3&up, 1⅛m, 1:51.24, PURE PRIZE, Dollar Bill, Hero's Tribute, 8 started.
Kentucky Cup Juvenile Fillies S., Turfway Park, Sept. 14, $83,750, 2yo, f, 1m, 1:40.39, ATLANTIC OCEAN, Ruby's Reception, Jodys Deelite, 8 started.
KENTUCKY CUP JUVENILE S.-G3, Turfway Park, Sept. 14, $100,000, 2yo, 1⅟₁₆m, 1:46.70, VINDICATION, Private Gold, Tito's Beau, 8 started.
Kentucky Cup Ladies Turf S., Kentucky Downs, Sept. 21, $100,000, 3&up, f&m, 1mT, 1:42.55, EVIL WOMAN, Doubly Fun, Sluice, 10 started.
Kentucky Cup Mile H., Kentucky Downs, Sept. 21, $200,000, 3&up, 1mT, 1:40.86, JAKE THE FLAKE, Glick, Pyrus, 8 started.
KENTUCKY CUP SPRINT S.-G3, Turfway Park, Sept. 14, $150,000, 3yo, 6f, 1:10.01, DAY TRADER, Premier Performer, Ecstatic, 11 started.
Kentucky Cup Turf Dash H., Kentucky Downs, Sept. 21, $100,000, 3&up, 6fT, 1:14.90, RED LIGHTNING, Aloha Bold, Mighty Beau, 8 started.
KENTUCKY CUP TURF H.-G3, Kentucky Downs, Sept. 21, $300,000, 3&up, 1½mT, 2:38.28, ROCHESTER, Nowrass (GB), Continental Red, 11 started.
KENTUCKY DERBY-G1, Churchill Downs, May 4, $2,175,000, 3yo, 1¼m, 2:01.13, WAR EMBLEM, Proud Citizen, Perfect Drift, 18 started.
KENTUCKY JOCKEY CLUB S.-G2, Churchill Downs, Nov. 30, $231,200, 2yo, 1⅟₁₆m, 1:44.67, SOTO, Ten Cents a Shine, Most Feared, 12 started.
KENTUCKY OAKS-G1, Churchill Downs, May 3, $562,100, 3yo, f, 1⅛m, 1:50.41, FARDA AMIGA, Take Charge Lady, Habibti, 9 started.
Kevin McHugh Memorial H., Rockingham Park, Aug. 18, $25,000, 3yo, 1⅟₁₆mT, 1:47.02, ALL LINE, Slippery Gator, O'Malley, 8 started.

Kimberlite Pipe S., Kentucky Downs, Sept. 22, $45,000, 2yo, 6fT, 1:13.79, RISKY CAT, Big Stone Gap, Mr. Whitestone, 9 started.
Kindergarten S., Philadelphia Park, Sept. 14, $75,000, 2yo, f, 6f, 1:11.39, BIG SCORE, Eliza's Cat, Manny's Gold Maker, 5 started.
Kindergarten S., Grants Pass, June 30, $3,805, 2yo, 4½f, CAN'T BE AN ANGEL, In Gold We Trust, Perks First Knight, 7 started.
Kingarvie S. (R), Woodbine, Dec. 1, $134,750, 2yo, progeny of eligible Ontario stallions, 1⅙m, 1:47.27, TIMEFORM, El Gran Maestro, Majestic Wisdom, 8 started.
King Cotton S., Oaklawn Park, Feb. 2, $50,000, 4&up, 6f, 1:09.30, KINGS COMMAND, Boots On Sunday, Bidis, 8 started.
King County H., Emerald Downs, June 22, $40,000, 3&up, f&m, 1m, 1:36, ALWAYS A DIXIE, Neon Queen, Graceful Cat, 11 started.
KING EDWARD BREEDERS' CUP H. (Can-G2), Woodbine, June 16, $324,700, 3&up, 1⅛mT, 1:50.26, MOON SOLITAIRE (Ire), Quiet Resolve, No Comprende, 8 started.
KING'S BISHOP S.-G1, Saratoga Race Course, Aug. 24, $200,000, 3yo, 7f, 1:22.85, GYGISTAR, Boston Common, Thunder Days, 8 started.
Kings Court S., Louisiana Downs, June 28, $50,000, 3&up, 6f, 1:09.40, HALO CAT, Beau's Town, Ski Bum, 7 started.
Kings Point H. (1st Div.) (R), Aqueduct, April 28, $81,200, 3&up, New York-bred, 1⅛m, 1:51.92, MOUNT INTREPID, Gander, Deputy Shaker, 5 started.
Kings Point H. (2nd Div.) (R), Aqueduct, April 28, $81,175, 3&up, New York-bred, 1⅛m, 1:52.27, COMPELLING WORLD, Tom's Thunder, Ahpo Here, 6 started.
Kingston H. (R), Belmont Park, May 26, $85,575, 3&up, New York-bred, 1⅛mT, 1:47.03, CELTIC SKY, Reluctant Groom, I'm All Yours, 10 started.
Kissin Kris S., Calder Race Course, June 8, $38,440, 3&up, 1⅛mT, 1:50.16, MARQUETTE, Zloty, Dillonmyboy, 8 started.
KLAQ H., Sunland Park, Nov. 23, $55,400, 3&up, 5½f, 1:03.32, AMERICAN PASTIME, Abajo, Reflecting Colors, 12 started.
Klassy Briefcase S., Monmouth Park, July 28, $50,000, 3&up, f&m, 5fT, :55.92, AMBER'S WAY, Slewgenes, Cloud City, 8 started.
Klondike H., Northlands Park, July 27, $40,000, 3&up, 1⅙m, 1:47, SIXTHIRTYJOE, Highland Leader, Rancour, 6 started.
Klondike H., Hastings Park Racecourse, June 2, $37,741, 3yo, 6½f, 1:16.86, SALT GRINDER, Commodore Craig, Test Drive, 6 started.
KNICKERBOCKER H.-G2, Aqueduct, Nov. 2, $150,000, 3&up, 1⅛mT, 1:52.54, DAWN OF THE CONDOR, Serial Bride, Polish Miner, 9 started.
Kobuk King S. (R), Del Mar, July 25, $65,050, 3&up, non-winners of $30,000 twice other than maiden, claiming or starter or non-winners of three races or starters for a claiming price of $62,500, 1⅜mT, 2:12.32, ARBITER, Sumati (GB), Komistar (GB), 7 started.
Kokopelli H., Turf Paradise, Jan. 5, $30,000, 4&up, 1mT, 1:35.96, COME BACK RONNIE, Bristolville, Eagleton, 9 started.
Kudzu Juvenile S. (R), Fair Grounds, Dec. 13, $35,000, 2yo, Alabama-bred, 5½f, 1:06.51, LAUNCH SPOT, Comalagold, Sun Block, 12 started.
Ky Alta H., Northlands Park, July 13, $40,000, 3yo, 1⅙m, 1:46.20, LORD SHOGUN, Dark Fuse, Go Go Tommy Joe, 10 started.
Labatts Derby, Grand Prairie, July 28, 3yo, 6f, 1:13.40, J. J. SUN SHINE, Brass Robin, Happy Blaze, 5 started.
Labeeb S., Woodbine, Nov. 3, $115,000, 3&up, 1mT, 1:37.72, RED SEA (GB), Silver Spear, Academic, 14 started.
Labor Day H., Mountaineer Park, Sept. 2, $77,800, 3&up, 1mT, 1:33.49, LA REINE'S TERMS, Magical Madness, Tin Smithen, 7 started.
Labor Day H., Columbus, Sept. 2, $7,892, 3&up, 6½f, 1:17.40, HIGH DICE, Valid Sunrise, Doug's Shadow, 6 started.
Labor Day Special-Invitational Handicap, Yellowstone Downs, Sept. 2, $2,850, 3&up, 5¼f, 1:02.20, KING OF ADVENTURE, Fruit Rapport, Peter Habit, 7 started.
LA BREA S.-G1, Santa Anita Park, Dec. 28, $200,000, 3yo, f, 7f, 1:22.57, GOT KOKO, Spring Meadow, Erica's Smile, 10 started.
LA CANADA S.-G2, Santa Anita Park, Feb. 9, $200,000, 4yo, f, 1⅛m, 1:49.26, SUMMER COLONY, Azeri, Ask Me No Secrets, 6 started.
La Coneja H. (R), Sunland Park, Dec. 22, $130,900, 3yo, f, New Mexico-bred, 5½f, 1:03.05, ESPEEDYTOO, Stormy Brie, Gray Ryder, 8 started.
LADIES H.-G3, Aqueduct, Dec. 21, $107,400, 3&up, f&m, 1¼m, 2:04.19, CRITICAL EYE, Ellie's Moment, With Ability, 6 started.
Ladnesian S., Hastings Park Racecourse, July 14, $38,080, 2yo, c&g, 6½f, 1:19.04, DON'T PALI ME, Johnny's Cache, Astral Lightning, 6 started.
Lady Angela S. (R), Woodbine, April 21, $134,375, 3yo, f, progeny of eligible Ontario stallions, 7f, 1:25.57, SPANISH DECREE, Oh Livia D., Matter of Law, 9 started.
Lady Baltimore S., Pimlico, Oct. 5, $50,000, 3&up, f&m, 1⅛mT, 1:48.93, SECRET RIVER, Lady Linda, Lady of the Future, 7 started.
Lady Finger S. (R), Finger Lakes, Aug. 17, $73,613, 2yo, f, New York-bred, 6f, 1:12.79, QUIET ROSE, Majorannouncement, Distinctive Kitten, 7 started.
Lady Hallie H., Sportsman's Park, April 14, $100,000, 3&up, f&m, 1⅙m, 1:45.99, PRETTY GALE, Lunar Star, Harlan Ash, 8 started.
Lady Morvich H., Bay Meadows Fair, Aug. 17, $42,720, 3&up, f&m, 1⅙mT, 1:43.06, ETNORIAS, Lindsay Jean, Monrow, 7 started.
Lady Razorback Futurity (R), Louisiana Downs, Nov. 3, $25,000, 2yo, f, Arkansas-bred, 6f, 1:12.82, IMPETUOUS MOLLY, Ashleys Paige, Sunny Divine, 10 started.
Lady Slipper S. (R), Canterbury Park, May 19, $36,900, 3&up, f&m, Minnesota-bred, 6f, 1:10.33, BLUMIN BAUBLE, Nidari, Burn the Legacy, 8 started.
Lady Sonata S., Calder Race Course, June 21, $42,310, 3yo, f, 6f, 1:12.62, SEA SPAN, Tchula Miss, Miss Dixie Chick, 6 started.
LADY'S SECRET BREEDERS' CUP H.-G2, Santa Anita Park, Oct. 2, $217,500, 3&up, f&m, 1⅙m, 1:41.10, AZERI, Starrer, Mystic Lady, 7 started.
Lady's Secret H., Fairmount Park, Sept. 10, $25,700, 3&up, f&m, 1m 70y, 1:44.20, OUT OF OPTIONS, Dentons Ruby, Genteel Lady, 6 started.
Lady's Secret H., Les Bois Park, May 25, $6,600, 3&up, f&m, 7½f, 1:31.53, BOOMER BUST, Honor by the Bay, Eyes Sucha Delight, 8 started.
Lady's Secret S., Remington Park, Nov. 17, $30,000, 3&up, f&m, 7f, 1:23, PRINCESS JEN, Cherylville Slew, Burning Memories, 11 started.
Lafayette H., Golden Gate Fields, Jan. 1, $100,000, 4&up, 1mT, 1:35.89, I'MADRIFTER, Poker Brad, Hoovergetthekeys, 7 started.
Lafayette S., Evangeline Downs, Sept. 2, $50,000, 2yo, 6f, 1:10.40, COMIC TRUTH, Justlikejessejames, Mighty Merlin, 11 started.
LAFAYETTE S.-G3, Keeneland, April 7, $111,300, 3yo, 7f, 1:24.47, CASHEL CASTLE, Sharp Flash, Sky Terrace, 6 started.
La Fiesta H., The Downs at Albuquerque, April 13, $32,700, 3yo, f, 5½f, 1:03.55, QUICKKEY, Espeedytoo, Devious Ways, 8 started.
La Habra S., Santa Anita Park, March 1, $113,150, 3yo, f, a6½fT, 1:12.96, HIGH SOCIETY (Ire), Ayzal (GB), Fun House, 11 started.
LA JOLLA H.-G3, Del Mar, Aug. 17, $147,000, 3yo, 1⅙mT, 1:43.92, INESPERADO (Fr), Regiment, Mountain Rage, 4 started.
LAKE GEORGE S.-G3, Saratoga Race Course, July 29, $115,000, 3yo, f, 1⅙mT, 1:40.71, NUNATALL (GB), Guana (Fr), Mariensky, 11 started.
LAKE PLACID H.-G2, Saratoga Race Course, Aug. 18, $150,000, 3yo, f, 1⅛mT, 1:49.24, WONDER AGAIN, Riskaverse, Miss Marcia, 9 started.
Lakeview Thoroughbred Farms S. (R), Hollywood Park, April 28, $70,000, 3&up, f&m, California-bred non-winners of $3,000 other than maiden, claiming, or starter and have never won two races, 7f, 1:23.72, THERESA'S YEAR, Free Shot, Geana Dawn, 11 started.
Lakeway S., Retama Park, Aug. 17, $30,000, 3yo, f, 7f, 1:23.88, MISS RITZ, Goodness, Sly Kona, 7 started.
La Lorgnette S., Woodbine, Sept. 28, $184,375, 3yo, f, 1⅙m, 1:44.04, MULRAINY, Winning Chance, Lady Shari, 7 started.
Lamplighter S., Monmouth Park, Aug. 4, $65,000, 3yo, 1⅙mT, 1:45.07, ENTITLEMENT, Jeb's Wild, Alphabetical, 8 started.
LANDALUCE S.-G3, Hollywood Park, July 4, $110,600, 2yo, f, 6f, 1:10.51, BUFFYTHECENTERFOLD, Tricks Her, Little Bit a Swiss, 9 started.
Land of Enchantment H. (R), Ruidoso Downs, July 14, $41,600, 3&up, New Mexico-bred, 7½f, 1:32.20, LIVE SHOW, Ciento, Romeos Wilson, 8 started.
Land of Jazz S., Ferndale, Aug. 16, $6,885, 3&up, 7f, 1:24.43, FIGHT FOR SILVER, Cee's Dude, Gentleman John, 4 started.
Land of Lincoln S. (R), Sportsman's Park, March 30, $87,700, 3yo, Illinois-conceived and/or -foaled, 6f, 1:10.59, COLORFUL TOUR, Nikobe, Pocket Taj, 11 started.
LANE'S END BREEDERS' FUTURITY-G2, Keeneland, Oct. 5, $434,800, 2yo, 1⅙m, 1:46.78, SKY MESA, Lone Star Sky, Truckle Feature, 6 started.
LANE'S END SPIRAL S.-G2, Turfway Park, March 23, $500,000, 3yo, 1⅛m, 1:48.83, PERFECT DRIFT, Azillion (Ire), Request for Parole, 8 started.
Lansing S. (R), Great Lakes Downs, June 14, $45,000, 3yo, c&g, Michigan-bred, 6f, 1:15.85, SPRING WINDS, Lite Ruckus, Equi Power, 10 started.
LA PREVOYANTE H.-G2, Calder Race Course, Dec. 28, $200,000,

3&up, f&m, 1½mT, 2:28.55, NEW ECONOMY, Septietta, Tweedside, 12 started.

La Prevoyante S. (R), Woodbine, Sept. 15, $129,625, 3yo, f, progeny of eligible Ontario stallions, 1mT, 1:40.59, HEYAHOHOWDY, Spanish Decree, Ariel's Melody, 6 started.

La Puente S. (R), Santa Anita Park, April 14, $82,050, 3yo, non-winners of a race worth $50,000 to the winner at one mile or over in 2002, 1mT, 1:34.84, MOUNTAIN RAGE, Doc Holiday (Ire), Stormy Forever, 8 started.

Larkspur H. (R), Great Lakes Downs, May 24, $45,000, 3&up, f&m, Michigan-bred, 6f, 1:13.72, SEFAS ROSE, Born to Dance, Double Hat Trick, 10 started.

Larry R. Riviello President's Cup, Philadelphia Park, Aug. 17, $100,000, 3yo, 1m 70y, 1:42.05, CITY SHARPSTER, Trump Marina, Foolish Gamble, 5 started.

LAS CIENEGAS H.-G3, Santa Anita Park, April 7, $108,500, 4&up, f&m, a6½fT, 1:12.55, ROLLY POLLY (Ire), Penny Marie, Twin Set (Ger), 7 started.

La Senora H. (R), Sunland Park, Jan. 26, $103,700, 3yo, f, New Mexico-bred, 6f, 1:10.93, GRAY RYDER, Quickkey, Dancing Promise, 11 started.

La Senorita S., Retama Park, Aug. 31, $100,000, 2yo, f, 1mT, 1:37.06, SEA BLOOM, Prom Date, Amiga, 12 started.

LAS FLORES H.-G3, Santa Anita Park, Feb. 23, $128,375, 4&up, f&m, 6f, 1:08.65, ABOVE PERFECTION, Kalookan Queen, Enchanted Woods, 4 started.

Las Madrinas H., Fairplex Park, Sept. 27, $99,000, 3&up, f&m, 1 1/16m, 1:43.78, LOOKN MIGHTY FINE, Hazen, Warren's Whistle, 7 started.

LAS PALMAS H.-G2, Santa Anita Park, Nov. 3, $200,000, 3&up, f&m, 1⅛mT, 1:47.69, TATES CREEK, Voodoo Dancer, Magic Mission (GB), 8 started.

Lassie H., Hastings Park Racecourse, Aug. 25, $37,312, 2yo, f, 6½f, 1:19.01, SPARKLIN KAT, My Miss Emily, Brave Miss, 11 started.

Lassie S., Portland Meadows, Nov. 30, $10,000, 2yo, f, 6f, 1:13.41, BACK STREET GAL, Our Lucky Kiss, Roada Ghost, 7 started.

Last Chance Derby, Turf Paradise, Dec. 31, $22,800, 3yo, 1 1/16mT, 1:43.06, PALMERTON, Lou's Expectation, Mr. Greedy, 8 started.

LAS VIRGENES S.-G1, Santa Anita Park, Feb. 10, $200,000, 3yo, f, 1m, 1:36.84, YOU, Habibti, Tali'sluckybusride, 6 started.

Late Bloomer S., Delaware Park, June 25, $63,100, 3&up, f&m, 6f, 1:10.83, URBAN DANCER, Divine Line, Outstanding Info, 11 started.

LA TROIENNE S.-G3, Churchill Downs, May 2, $112,600, 3yo, f, 7f, 1:24.83, CASHIER'S DREAM, Shameful, Colonial Glitter, 5 started.

LAUREL FUTURITY-G3, Laurel Park, Nov. 16, $100,000, 2yo, 1 1/16m, 1:46.10, TOCCET, Ironton, Cherokee's Boy, 7 started.

Laurel Lane S. (R), Louisiana Downs, Oct. 20, $39,300, 2yo, f, Louisiana-bred, 6f, 1:13.50, BELIEVE IT IS SO, Rubies N Roses, Kool K. J., 9 started.

Lauries Dancer S. (R), Fort Erie, Aug. 5, $64,700, 3&up, f&m, Canadian-bred, 1 1/16m, 1:44.90, WIRY WILLIE, Orientalspringhope, Roman Romance, 6 started.

La Voyageuse H., Woodbine, March 29, $102,800, 4&up, f&m, 5f, :57, MADAME ROAR, Mysterious Affair, Dreams Go Bye, 5 started.

Lawrence Realization H., Belmont Park, Oct. 12, $150,000, 3yo, 1½m, 2:30.34, FISHER POND, Irish Colonial, Extra Check, 5 started.

LAZARO BARRERA MEMORIAL S.-G2, Hollywood Park, May 27, $150,000, 3yo, 7f, 1:21.95, CAPTAIN SQUIRE, Fonz's, Kamsack, 5 started.

Lazer Show S., Arlington Park, Oct. 13, $50,750, 3&up, f&m, 5fT, :57.84, MY GIRL LISA, Feminine Fury, Shy Dory (Arg), 11 started.

Leader of the Band S., Delaware Park, Sept. 16, $60,100, 3&up, a1 1/16mT, 1:43.52, SIR BRIAN'S SWORD, Jubileo, Mus-If (GB), 7 started.

Lecomte H., Fair Grounds, Jan. 26, $100,000, 3yo, 1m, 1:37.98, EASYFROMTHEGITGO, Sky Terrace, It'sallinthechase, 11 started.

Legacy Chase Hurdle S., Shawan Downs, Sept. 28, $30,000, 4&up, a2⅜mT, 5:02.80, TRES TOUCHE, Pelagos (Fr), All Gong (GB), 8 started.

Legal Light S., Delaware Park, May 25, $75,600, 3yo, 6f, 1:11.13, RUNNING TIDE, Boston Common, Calends, 7 started.

Lenta S., Calder Race Course, May 4, $38,150, 3yo, f, 1 1/16mT, 1:42.44, ALWAYS COUNTRY, Miss Marcia, Tasso Run, 8 started.

LEONARD RICHARDS S.-G3, Delaware Park, June 8, $250,900, 3yo, 1 1/16m, 1:45.10, RUNNING TIDE, Nothing Flat, The Sewickley Kid, 8 started.

Les Bois Park Open Juvenile S., Les Bois Park, Aug. 10, $5,800, 2yo, 5f, 1:02.13, ROCK SEASONS, Summer Applause, Collateral Deposit, 6 started.

Les Mackin H., Yavapai Downs, June 24, $10,000, 3&up, 1 1/16m, 1:42.63, GUSTO FORZADO, C. D. Haj, Seventeen Candles, 7 started.

Les Mademoiselle S., Ferndale, Aug. 17, $10,700, 3&up, f&m, 1 1/16m, 1:47.08, MELT AWAY, Bold Victoress, Hello Lila, 6 started.

Lexington Park S., Laurel Park, Aug. 4, $50,000, 3&up, 1⅛m, 1:50.52, GRUNDLEFOOT, Cool N Collective, Ewer All Wet, 5 started.

LEXINGTON S.-G3, Belmont Park, July 14, $150,000, 3yo, 1¼mT, 2:00.42, CHISELLING, Finality, Irish Colonial, 8 started.

Liberation H. (R), Hastings Park Racecourse, June 16, $37,698, 3yo, f, British Columbia-bred, 1 1/16m, 1:45.71, ELANA D'AMOUR, Lady Vye, Fast and Free, 9 started.

Light Hearted S., Delaware Park, July 21, $75,600, 3&up, f&m, 6f, 1:11.55, BRUANNA, Haunted Lass, Urban Dancer, 7 started.

Lightning Jet S. (R), Hawthorne Race Course, Nov. 9, $108,350, 3&up, Illinois-bred, 6f, 1:11.18, TOO MANY BUCKS, Tic N Tin, Classic Appeal, 9 started.

Likely Exchange S., Turfway Park, Feb. 9, $50,000, 4&up, f&m, 1m, 1:37.18, MISS PICKUMS, Seven Four Seven, Growth Stock, 11 started.

Lilac S., Stampede Park, June 1, $40,000, 3yo, f, 1m, 1:38.80, SWEET MONARCH, Fancy Prancer, Brass to Diamonds, 7 started.

Lil E Tee S. (R), Philadelphia Park, Oct. 5, $50,000, 3yo, c&g, Pennsylvania-bred, 1 1/16m, 1:45.51, CAROUSE, Senor Charismatic, Fugitivo, 6 started.

Lincoln H. (R), Ruidoso Downs, July 14, $42,000, 4&up, f&m, New Mexico-bred, 6f, 1:11.40, WAMPUS WHO, Fritzie's Prospect, Festival Legs, 10 started.

Lincoln Heritage H. (R), Arlington Park, June 22, $87,150, 3&up, f&m, Illinois-conceived and/or -foaled, 1 1/16mT, 1:42.86, ELLIE'S ROSE, M and M Machine, Soccory, 10 started.

Lincroft H. (R), Monmouth Park, Aug. 11, $50,000, 3&up, New Jersey-bred, 1mT, 1:36.10, AMERICAN FREEDOM, Catechol, Red Weasel, 11 started.

Lineage Day Thoroughbred Claiming S. (R), The Downs at Albuquerque, May 19, $11,150, 3&up, New Mexico-bred, 6f, 1:10.47, BOBBY TOLD, Mr Silver Spade, Coronado Del, 8 started.

Lineage S. (R), The Downs at Albuquerque, May 19, $33,000, 3&up, New Mexico-bred, 1 1/16m, 1:44.20, CIENTO, Bobby Blurr, Ben Told, 9 started.

Linear H., Calder Race Course, June 1, $38,615, 3&up, 5f, TRUE LOVE'S SECRET, Uncle Rocco, Handsome Smile, 8 started.

Lite the Fuse S., Laurel Park, Oct. 19, $50,000, 3&up, 6f, 1:09.14, OUTSTANDER, Sassy Hound, Deer Run, 5 started.

Little Brother S., Hawthorne Race Course, Dec. 15, $42,800, 2yo, 6f, 1:13.15, DR. SPELLBINDER, Ww Conquistador, Judgmatic, 7 started.

Little Everglades Hurdle S., Little Everglades, March 10, $38,800, 4&up, a2⅛mT, 3:39.80, TRES TOUCHE, Electron, Cold Cat, 5 started.

Little Ones S. (R), Great Lakes Downs, Aug. 17, $45,000, 2yo, c&g, Michigan-bred, 6f, 1:15.18, BEAU CLASSIC, Elusive Hour, Hola C Bright, 10 started.

Little Silver S., Monmouth Park, May 18, $45,500, 3yo, f, 6f, 1:11.70, BOLD WORLD, Intent, Cherokee Girl, 3 started.

Little Sister S., Calder Race Course, Aug. 5, $37,730, 3&up, f&m, 6½f, 1:18.44, ABUELA ESTHER (Uru), Sugar N Spice, Vague Memory, 7 started.

Live the Dream H., Del Mar, Sept. 11, $76,425, 3&up, 1mT, 1:34.09, D'WILDCAT, Devine Wind, Kachamandi (Chi), 6 started.

Local Thriller S., Delaware Park, July 27, $60,300, 3&up, f&m, 5fT, :56.16, MUJADO (Ire), Oh Say Vicki, Merry Princess, 8 started.

LOCUST GROVE H.-G3, Churchill Downs, June 22, $168,900, 3&up, f&m, 1⅛mT, 1:46.91, VOODOO DANCER, Blue Moon (Fr), Solvig, 9 started.

LONE STAR DERBY-G3, Lone Star Park, May 11, $500,000, 3yo, 1⅛m, 1:49.92, WISEMAN'S FERRY, Tracemark, Peekskill, 14 started.

LONE STAR PARK H.-G3, Lone Star Park, May 27, $300,000, 3&up, 1 1/16m, 1:42.96, CONGAREE, Prince Iroquois, Mercenary, 12 started.

LONGACRES MILE H.-G3, Emerald Downs, Aug. 25, $250,000, 3&up, 1m, 1:34.60, SABERTOOTH, Moonlight Meeting, San Nicolas, 12 started.

LONG BRANCH BREEDERS' CUP S.-G3, Monmouth Park, July 13, $100,000, 3yo, 1 1/16m, 1:44.35, PUCK, Shah Jehan, Stephentown, 6 started.

Longfellow S., Monmouth Park, June 16, $50,000, 3&up, 6f, 1:09.53, IMPEACHTHEPRO, Esteemed Friend, Ticket to Freedom, 7 started.

Longhorn H. (R), Retama Park, Oct. 12, $30,000, 3&up, Texas-bred, 6f, 1:10.06, FITZROYAL, Term Sheet, Won C C, 5 started.

LONG ISLAND H.-G2, Aqueduct, Nov. 16, $150,000, 3&up, f&m, 1½mT, 2:42.48, URIAH (Ger), Sunstone (GB), Mot Juste (GB), 11 started.

LOS ANGELES H.-G3, Hollywood Park, June 2, $107,500, 3&up, 6f, 1:08.72, KONA GOLD, No Armistice, Komax, 6 started.

Los Ninos S., Ruidoso Downs, July 28, $36,227, 2yo, c&g, 6f, 1:11.60, ROLL HENNESSY ROLL, Star Status, Really Who, 9 started.

Lost Code H., Sportsman's Park, March 9, $100,000, 4&up, 6f, 1:11.96, SECRET ROMEO, Tic N Tin, Bet On Joe, 7 started.

Louise Kimball Distaff Championship S. (R), Suffolk Downs, Dec. 14, $30,000, 3&up, f&m, Massachusetts-bred, 1⅟₁₆m, 1:52.47, LITTLE TIME, Big Miss, Little Carbon, 7 started.

Louisiana Breeders' Derby (R), Louisiana Downs, Oct. 19, $65,100, 3yo, Louisiana-bred, 1⅟₁₆m, 1:46.37, WALK IN THE SNOW, Crescent Chief, Rapide, 8 started.

Louisiana Breeders' Oaks (R), Louisiana Downs, Oct. 20, $65,400, 3yo, f, Louisiana-bred, 1⅟₁₆m, 1:47.21, SUNNY SCARLETT, Highhopesemilyluck, Messinger, 9 started.

Louisiana Champions Day Classic S. (R), Fair Grounds, Dec. 14, $150,000, 3&up, Louisiana-bred, 1⅛m, 1:51.53, WALK IN THE SNOW, Prince Slew, Samlot, 5 started.

Louisiana Champions Day Franks Farm Ladies H. (R), Fair Grounds, Dec. 14, $100,000, 3&up, f&m, Louisiana-bred, 1⅟₁₆m, 1:46.41, PRIZED AMBERPRO, Wild Squaw, Autobesarah, 8 started.

Louisiana Champions Day Juvenile S. (R), Fair Grounds, Dec. 14, $100,000, 2yo, c&g, Louisiana-bred, 6f, 1:11.23, METEOR IMPACT, Witt Ante, Lighter Knot, 14 started.

Louisiana Champions Day Lassie S. (R), Fair Grounds, Dec. 14, $100,000, 2yo, f, Louisiana-bred, 6f, 1:12.16, KOOL K. J., Little Miss Deb, Itsmybag, 10 started.

Louisiana Champions Day Sprint H. (R), Fair Grounds, Dec. 14, $100,000, 3&up, Louisiana-bred, 6f, 1:10.23, ZARB'S LUCK, Noinbetweeners, Sunny Brick, 10 started.

Louisiana Champions Day Starter H. (R), Fair Grounds, Dec. 14, $50,000, 3&up, Louisiana-bred starters for a claiming price of $20,000 or less in 2002, 1⅟₁₆m, 1:46.01, SILKY ZARB, Paw Paw's Pride, Allie's Excavator, 10 started.

Louisiana Champions Day Turf S. (R), Fair Grounds, Dec. 14, $100,000, 3&up, Louisiana-bred, a1⅟₁₆mT, 1:44.26, ONE BRICK SHY, Coach Rags, Mr. Sulu, 8 started.

LOUISIANA DERBY-G2, Fair Grounds, March 10, $750,000, 3yo, 1⅟₁₆m, 1:43.86, REPENT, Easyfromthegitgo, It'sallinthechase, 7 started.

Louisiana Downs H., Louisiana Downs, Sept. 22, $100,000, 3&up, 1⅟₁₆mT, 1:42.21, BIG HUBIE, Dynameaux, Rebridled, 7 started.

Louisiana Futurity (R), Fair Grounds, Dec. 27, $85,795, 2yo, c&g, Louisiana-bred, 6f, 1:11.20, WITT ANTE, Orni's Big Hit, Spritely Walker, 8 started.

Louisiana Futurity (R), Fair Grounds, Dec. 26, $56,300, 2yo, f, Louisiana-bred, 6f, 1:12.18, FORTY DOLLS, Rubies N Roses, Kilt Lilt, 9 started.

Louisiana Premier Day Championship S. (R), Delta Downs, Nov. 16, $100,000, 3&up, Louisiana-bred, 1⅟₁₆m, 1:46.15, WALK IN THE SNOW, Oak Hall, One Brick Shy, 6 started.

Louisiana Premier Day Distaff S. (R), Delta Downs, Nov. 16, $75,000, 3&up, f&m, Louisiana-bred, 1m, 1:41.26, PRIZED AMBERPRO, Eastern Sun, Autobesarah, 7 started.

Louisiana Premier Day Juvenile S. (R), Delta Downs, Nov. 16, $50,000, 2yo, Louisiana-bred, 5f, 1:00.34, MIGHTY MERLIN, Justlikejessejames, One Tough Raiser, 5 started.

Louisiana Premier Day Sprint S. (R), Delta Downs, Nov. 16, $50,000, 3&up, Louisiana-bred, 5f, ZARB'S LUCK, Believe Im Special, Sixty Stars, 7 started.

Louisiana Premier Day Starlet S. (R), Delta Downs, Nov. 16, $50,000, 2yo, f, Louisiana-bred, 5f, 1:00.92, ITSMYBAG, Kool K. J., Believe It Is So, 8 started.

LOUISVILLE BREEDERS' CUP H.-G2, Churchill Downs, May 3, $334,200, 3&up, f&m, 1⅟₁₆m, 1:43.93, SPAIN, Mystic Lady, De Bertie, 6 started.

LOUISVILLE H.-G3, Churchill Downs, June 1, $115,500, 3&up, 1⅜mT, 2:15.82, CLASSIC PAR, PISCES, Red Mountain, 9 started.

Lou Smith Memorial H., Rockingham Park, July 28, $25,000, 3&up, 1⅟₁₆m, 1:46, DHAFFIR (Chi), Jini's Jet, Basil's Rhythm, 7 started.

Loyalty S. (R), Thistledown, Aug. 17, $30,000, 2yo, Ohio-bred, 6f, 1:13.24, IFUFEELFROGGYLEAP, Mercer's Cool Cat, Buckeye Teddy, 8 started.

LT. GOVERNOR'S H. (Can-G3), Hastings Park Racecourse, July 1, $80,870, 3&up, 1⅛m, 1:50.28, LORD NELSON, Jazzy Yacht, Kid Katabatic, 7 started.

Lure S., Pimlico, Sept. 7, $50,000, 3&up, 1mT, 1:36.37, BUENOS DIAS, Controls Free, Broadway Snowman, 6 started.

Luther Burbank H., Santa Rosa, July 28, $43,140, 3&up, f&m, 1⅟₁₆m, 1:43.49, DE GODDAUGHTER, Miss Terasita, Pheiffer, 7 started.

Lyman Sprint Championship S. (R), Philadelphia Park, June 15, $54,300, 3&up, Pennsylvania-bred, 7f, 1:23.32, BEAU'S SURPRISE, Wild Current, Docent, 7 started.

Lyrique H., Louisiana Downs, Sept. 1, $50,000, 3yo, f, 1⅟₁₆mT, 1:42.91, SHEZA NASTY LADY, Chula, Just Scarlet, 8 started.

MAC DIARMIDA H.-G3, Gulfstream Park, Jan. 20, $100,000, 3&up, 1⅜mT, 2:16.27, CRASH COURSE, Unite's Big Red, Eltawaasul, 12 started.

Mack Hall Starter H. (R), Turf Paradise, Oct. 19, $15,000, 3&up, consigned to and have passed through the sale ring at any ATBA sale and have started for a claiming price of $8,000 or less since September 27, 2001, 6½f, 1:17.06, BLAINE COUNTY HIGH, Lady's Lil' Ringer, Kensington Park, 7 started.

Mackinac H. (R), Great Lakes Downs, Sept. 16, $45,000, 3yo, c&g, Michigan-bred, 1⅟₁₆m, 1:51.07, EQUI POWER, Accountable Guy, Goldinrunner, 7 started.

Madamoiselle H., Northlands Park, Aug. 9, $40,000, 3&up, f&m, 1⅟₁₆m, 1:46, FULL SCREAM AHEAD, Confident, Toppers Happy, 6 started.

Madison County S. (R), Hoosier Park, Sept. 28, $43,300, 3&up, f&m, Indiana-bred, 6f, 1:12.53, MAGGIE'S DREAM, Amanda's Crown, One Eyed Jackie, 7 started.

Madison S., Keeneland, April 10, $111,300, 4&up, f&m, 7f, 1:23.70, VICTORY RIDE, Celtic Melody, Away, 7 started.

Mae de Vol Sprint, Bay Meadows, Aug. 31, $74,150, 3&up, f&m, 6f, 1:10.31, CHANNING WAY, Onslaught, More Mascara, 6 started.

Magic City Classic S. (R), River Downs, June 15, $35,000, 3&up, Alabama-bred, 6f, 1:12.60, NELL'S NINER, Azooma, Owen's Way, 12 started.

Magnolia S., Sam Houston Race Park, Dec. 14, $30,000, 3yo, 1m 70y, 1:41.56, AGRIVATING GENERAL, Doc Dopey, Faxamillion, 8 started.

Magnolia S., Delta Downs, April 6, $23,280, 3&up, f&m, 6½f, 1:19.82, RAYMOND'S DREAM, Sara Sweet, Prized Amberpro, 8 started.

Magnolia State H. (R), Fair Grounds, March 25, $14,100, 3&up, Mississippi-owned, 6f, 1:10.94, IT'S ME MARGARET, Superpave, Little Joe Tubb, 9 started.

Maid of the Mist S. (R), Belmont Park, Oct. 19, $100,000, 2yo, f, New York-bred, 1m, 1:37.61, BEAUTIFUL AMERICA, Combanchera, Shesasmokin, 9 started.

Majorette H., Louisiana Downs, Oct. 5, $30,000, 3&up, f&m, 7f, 1:22.93, PRINCESS JEN, Cielo Girl, Prized Amberpro, 8 started.

MAKER'S MARK MILE S.-G2, Keeneland, April 12, $200,000, 4&up, 1mT, 1:35.02, TOUCH OF THE BLUES (Fr), Pisces, Boastful, 10 started.

Malcolm Anderson S., Bay Meadows, Sept. 29, $70,800, 2yo, 6f, 1:09.01, ONLY THE BEST, Gray Jag, Tactical Strike, 5 started.

Malcolm Anderson S., Bay Meadows, June 16, $69,575, 2yo, 5f, :57.77, TARAVAL, Standard Setter, Banshee King, 7 started.

MALIBU S.-G1, Santa Anita Park, Dec. 26, $200,000, 3yo, 7f, 1:22.40, DEBONAIR JOE, Total Limit, American System, 11 started.

Mamie Eisenhower S. (R), Prairie Meadows, June 7, $64,200, 3&up, f&m, Iowa-bred, 6f, 1:09.51, SHARKY'S REVIEW, Sumthintotalkabout, Nut N Better, 6 started.

Mamzelle S., Churchill Downs, May 2, $114,000, 3&up, f&m, 5fT, :58.19, REPOSITORY, Island Echo, Dyna's Club, 8 started.

Manatee S., Tampa Bay Downs, Jan. 26, $50,000, 4&up, f&m, 7f, 1:24.37, LITTLE WON, Flashing Lil, Alley Ball, 12 started.

Manchester H., Rockingham Park, Aug. 31, $25,000, 3&up, 6f, 1:11.39, METHOD MAN, Gold I. D., Northend, 6 started.

Manhattan Beach S., Hollywood Park, June 9, $77,250, 3yo, f, 5½fT, 1:02.99, RAGIN T REX, Carinae, Partytime (Ire), 8 started.

MANHATTAN H.-G1, Belmont Park, June 8, $400,000, 3&up, 1¼mT, 2:01.29, BEAT HOLLOW (GB), Forbidden Apple, Strut the Stage, 8 started.

Manhattan H. (R), The Woodlands, Oct. 6, $25,000, 3&up, f&m, Kansas-bred, 6f, 1:15.20, DISCREETLY IRISH, Dunham's Social, Dancin Regiment, 7 started.

Manila S., Arlington Park, Oct. 12, $75,000, 2yo, 1mT, 1:38.53, ZYDECO AFFAIR, Larry B, Dr. Phil, 11 started.

Manila S., The Meadowlands, Oct. 4, $50,000, 3&up, 1⅜mT, 2:18.44, SERIAL BRIDE, Punkin Head, Stokosky, 10 started.

MANITOBA DERBY (Can-G3), Assiniboia Downs, Aug. 5, $100,000, 3yo, 1⅛m, 1:54.20, LORD SHOGUN, Silver Greek, Ekati, 7 started.

Manitoba Maturity S. (R), Assiniboia Downs, July 13, $35,000, 4yo, Manitoba-bred, 1⅟₁₆m, 1:48.40, SPEEDY TREAT, Cayenne Pepper, G and L Special, 5 started.

Manitoba S. (R), Assiniboia Downs, June 30, $30,000, 3yo, c&g, Manitoba-bred, 1m, 1:43.20, BEAU PIP, Palapeine, Hoist a Coin, 10

started.
Manor Downs ATB Distaff S. (R), Manor Downs, April 28, $30,000, 3&up, f&m, Texas-bred, 6f, 1:11.40, DISCOS PEARL, Bricketta, Touchoville, 9 started.
MAN O' WAR S.-G1, Belmont Park, Sept. 7, $500,000, 3&up, 1⅜mT, 2:15.05, WITH ANTICIPATION, Balto Star, Man From Wicklow, 8 started.
Manzano Mile & a Half Claiming H., The Downs at Albuquerque, June 17, $12,500, 3&up, 1½m, 2:35.99, EXCLUSIVE DANCER, Gold Bidder, Texastraveler, 6 started.
MAPLE LEAF S. (Can-G3), Woodbine, Nov. 2, $213,250, 3&up, f&m, 1¼m, 2:06.22, LADY SHARI, Small Promises, Silver Nithi, 9 started.
Marathon Series Final Invitational S., Turf Paradise, Feb. 10, $24,400, 4&up, 1⅝m, 2:44.40, MASKED RIDER, Belgravia (GB), Mystical Empire, 11 started.
Marcellus Frost Hurdle S., Percy Warner, May 11, $46,500, 4&up, a2mT, 3:54.60, PELAGOS (Fr), Golden Rule (GB), Brown Lad (Fr), 4 started.
Marco Bay S., Calder Race Course, May 26, $33,150, 3yo, 6½f, 1:17.82, KINGMAKER, Royal Lad, Barnacle Steve, 7 started.
Mardi Gras H., Fair Grounds, Feb. 12, $75,000, 4&up, a7½fT, 1:31.57, WHERE'S TAYLOR, King Slayer (GB), Northcote Road, 6 started.
Marfa S., Turfway Park, Sept. 21, $72,000, 3&up, 6½f, 1:16.75, MOUNTAIN GENERAL, Sea of Tranquility, Slider, 7 started.
Margarita Breeders' Cup H., Retama Park, Aug. 3, $48,500, 3&up, f&m, 1 1/16mT, 1:41.18, BIEN NICOLE, Wolfnik, Golden Rhythm, 11 started.
Marie P. DeBartolo Oaks, Louisiana Downs, Sept. 21, $50,000, 3yo, f, 1 1/16mT, 1:42.39, BEDANKEN, Chula, Sheza Nasty Lady, 10 started.
MARINE S. (Can-G3), Woodbine, May 18, $162,750, 3yo, 1 1/16m, 1:44.03, ANGLIAN PRINCE, Tails of the Crypt, Ford Every Stream, 5 started.
Marluel's Troy S. (R), Fairmount Park, Oct. 1, $36,000, 2yo, Illinois-bred, 6f, 1:11.40, WIGGINS, Dr. Spellbinder, Small Charger, 10 started.
Marshland S., Delta Downs, Nov. 30, $50,000, 3&up, 7f, 1:26.12, NO ITS NOT, Two Punch Sonny, Screen Idol, 7 started.
Marshua S., Laurel Park, Jan. 5, $44,000, 3yo, f, 6f, 1:11.63, TWO TIMES A LADY, Phyxius, Note Taker, 7 started.
Marshua's River S., Gulfstream Park, April 14, $75,000, 3&up, f&m, 5fT, :56.38, FLYING BIRDIE, Elvi Gamble, Fair Apache, 10 started.
Martanza H. (R), Sam Houston Race Park, Nov. 16, $75,000, 3&up, f&m, Texas-bred, 1m, 1:40.15, MANZOTTINA, Khazi, Lucky M, 10 started.
Martha Washington Breeders' Cup S., Laurel Park, July 27, $145,500, 3yo, f, 1 1/16m, 1:45.62, MARTHA'S MUSIC, Restraining Order, Bells for Marlin, 4 started.
Martha Washington S., Oaklawn Park, Feb. 18, $50,000, 3yo, f, 6f, 1:11.21, MISS CITY HALO, For Rubies, Gilded Wings, 8 started.
MARYLAND BREEDERS' CUP H.-G3, Pimlico, May 18, $200,000, 3&up, 6f, 1:10.06, SNOW RIDGE, Smile My Lord, Clever Gem, 7 started.
Maryland Hunt Cup S., Glyndon, April 27, $65,000, 5yo's & up, a4mT, 8:25.60, YOUNG DUBLINER (Ire), Swayo, Stone Buster, 6 started.
Maryland Juvenile Championship S. (R), Laurel Park, Dec. 31, $100,000, 2yo, Maryland-bred, 1⅛m, 1:52.23, FOUFA'S WARRIOR, Ironton, Cheverly Gold, 6 started.
Maryland Juvenile Filly Championship S. (R), Laurel Park, Dec. 31, $100,000, 2yo, f, Maryland-bred, 1⅛m, 1:51.77, COQUETTISH, Grace Bay, Angel Punch, 8 started.
Maryland Million Classic S. (R), Pimlico, Sept. 21, $190,000, 3&up, progeny of stallions standing in Maryland, 1 3/16m, 1:56.85, DOCENT, Hay Getoutofmyway, Concerned Minister, 9 started.
Maryland Million Distaff H. (R), Pimlico, Sept. 21, $95,000, 3&up, f&m, progeny of stallions standing in Maryland, 6f, 1:11.28, BLINDED BY LOVE, Case of the Blues, Gracefulciti, 11 started.
Maryland Million Distaff Starter H. (R), Pimlico, Sept. 21, $47,500, 3&up, f&m, progeny of stallions standing in Maryland who have started for a claming price of $16,000 or less since October 13, 2001, 1 1/16m, 1:45.78, MOJO GAL, Suzy Wrong, Valley Parking, 12 started.
Maryland Million Ladies S. (R), Pimlico, Sept. 21, $95,000, 3&up, f&m, prgoeny of stallions standing in Maryland, 1⅛mT, 1:48.61, SHOPPING FOR LOVE, Breezy Bri, Twilights Prayer, 14 started.
Maryland Million Lassie S. (R), Pimlico, Sept. 21, $95,000, 2yo, f, progeny of stallions standing in Maryland, 6f, 1:13.72, OBJECT OF VERTUE, Rachelle's Numbers, Butiwillflysomeday, 12 started.
Maryland Million Nursery S. (R), Pimlico, Sept. 21, $95,000, 2yo, progeny of stallions standing in Maryland, 6f, 1:11.21, CHEROKEE'S BOY, Ironton, Bridge Out Again, 11 started.
Maryland Million Oaks (R), Pimlico, Sept. 21, $95,000, 3yo, f, progeny of stallions standing in Maryland, 1 1/16m, 1:43.90, UNDERCOVER, Tamayo, Carnie's Dancer, 6 started.
Maryland Million Sprint H. (R), Pimlico, Sept. 21, $95,000, 3&up, progeny of stallions standing in Maryland, 6f, 1:10.60, DEER RUN, Smile My Lord, Summer Swing, 12 started.
Maryland Million Starter H. (R), Pimlico, Sept. 21, $47,500, 3&up, progeny of stallions standing in Maryland who have started for a claiming price of $16,000 or less since October 13, 2001, 1⅛m, 1:51.32, TOP OF THE NEWS, Ken Doll, Star Slugger, 3 started.
Maryland Million Turf S. (R), Pimlico, Sept. 21, $95,000, 3&up, progeny of stallions standing in Maryland, 1⅛m, 1:49.28, LA REINE'S TERMS, Elberton, Watchman's Warning, 11 started.
Maryland Racing Media H., Laurel Park, Feb. 23, $50,000, 4&up, f&m, 1⅛m, 1:50.32, IRVING'S BABY, Maria, Double Trick, 5 started.
Mason Houghland Memorial Timber S., Percy Warner, May 11, $46,500, 4&up, a3mT, 6:23, SAM SULLIVAN, Northern Task, Dr. Ramsey, 6 started.
Massachusetts Derby (R), Suffolk Downs, Nov. 30, $29,400, 3yo, Massachusetts-bred, 1 1/16m, 1:47.91, JILL'S JUMPSHOT, Little Time, Polar Express, 5 started.
MASSACHUSETTS H.-G2, Suffolk Downs, June 1, $500,000, 3&up, 1⅛m, 1:50.52, MACHO UNO, Evening Attire, Include, 9 started.
Massachusetts Oaks (R), Suffolk Downs, Nov. 23, $30,000, 3yo, f, Massachusetts-bred, 1 1/16m, 1:50.85, LITTLE TIME, African Princess, Judge Nancy, 6 started.
Massachusetts Thoroughbred Breeders' S. (R), Suffolk Downs, May 4, $30,000, 3&up, Massachusetts-bred, 1 1/16m, 1:47.50, PAPA HO HO, Jini's Jet, Dawn's First Light, 8 started.
MATCHMAKER H.-G3, Monmouth Park, July 7, $100,000, 3&up, f&m, 1⅛mT, 1:47.76, CLEARLY A QUEEN, Siringas (Ire), Platinum Tiara, 7 started.
Matchmaker H. (R), Lincoln State Fair, June 16, $13,125, 3&up, f&m, Nebraska-bred, 1m, 1:38.40, DOUBLE DREAMIN DEB, Gary's Speedy Miss, Sandpit Dancer, 7 started.
Matiara S., Hollywood Park, Nov. 9, $125,000, 3yo, f, 1⅛mT, 1:52.12, SENTIMENTAL VALUE, Secret Garden (Ire), Company B, 6 started.
MATRIARCH S.-G1, Hollywood Park, Dec. 1, $500,000, 3&up, f&m, 1⅛mT, 1:48.31, DRESS TO THRILL (Ire), Golden Apples (Ire), Magic Mission (GB), 6 started.
Matron Breeders' Cup S., Assiniboia Downs, Sept. 22, $52,500, 3&up, f&m, 1⅛m, 1:55.80, MISS NOIRE, Top Stage Dancer, Dawn Edition, 8 started.
Matron H., Marquis Downs, July 5, $5,000, 3&up, f&m, a7f, 1:26.28, MS. LADY ROSE, Truly Remarkable, Princess Briartic, 6 started.
Matron H., Evangeline Downs, Aug. 10, $30,000, 3&up, f&m, 6f, 1:11.60, PRIZED AMBERPRO, Raymond's Dream, Steppen Up, 7 started.
MATRON S.-G1, Belmont Park, Sept. 15, $200,000, 2yo, f, 1m, 1:38.52, STORM FLAG FLYING, Wild Snitch, Fircroft, 7 started.
Matt Scudder S., The Meadowlands, Sept. 27, $50,000, 3yo, 6f, 1:08.97, GOLD I. D., Smokieisabandit, Our Wildcat, 5 started.
Matt Winn S., Churchill Downs, May 11, $109,600, 3yo, 6f, 1:09.43, DAY TRADER, Medlin Road, Still Be Smokin', 7 started.
Maxine M. Piggott S. (R), Turf Paradise, April 27, $30,000, 3yo, f, Arizona-bred, 6½f, 1:17.25, KAVEENA, Hawley Lake, Our Columbine, 8 started.
Maxxam Gold Cup H., Sam Houston Race Park, Jan. 19, $100,000, 4&up, 1⅛m, 1:49.94, MR ROSS, Arctic Boy, Halo Kris, 7 started.
MAZARINE BREEDERS' CUP S. (Can-G2), Woodbine, Sept. 21, $272,000, 2yo, f, 1 1/16m, 1:45.33, BRUSQUE, Handpainted, Mountain Dawn, 8 started.
Meadow Brook Hurdle S. (R), Belmont Park, June 6, $101,947, 4&up, non-winners over hurdles prior to March 1, 2001, 2½mT, 4:37.32, SHARP FACE, Anofferucantrefuse, Najjm, 10 started.
MEADOWLANDS CUP H.-G2, The Meadowlands, Oct. 4, $400,000, 3&up, 1⅛m, 1:48.95, BURNING ROMA, Volponi, Windsor Castle, 9 started.
Meafara S., Arlington Park, Aug. 17, $63,500, 3&up, f&m, 6f, 1:10.18, SMOKE CHASER, Feminine Fury, Soul Onarazorsedge, 7 started.
Mecke S., Calder Race Course, Nov. 30, $100,000, 2yo, 1 1/16mT, 1:42.43, MILLENNIUM STORM, Kick In, Our Finale, 12 started.
Melair S. (R), Hollywood Park, April 28, $200,000, 3yo, f, California-bred, 1 1/16m, 1:44.88, LADYLORE, Super High, Calzada Kid, 8 started.
Memorial Day H., Mountaineer Park, May 27, $79,350, 3&up, 7½fT, 1:27.48, MAGICAL MADNESS, Irish Silence, Talkmeister, 11 started.
MEMORIAL DAY H.-G3, Calder Race Course, May 27, $97,000, 3&up, 1 1/16m, 1:44.75, BEST OF THE REST, High Ideal, Hal's Hope, 4 started.

Memorial S., Fort Erie, Oct. 14, $62,850, 3&up, f&m, 1⅟₁₆m, 1:45.48, LA PRINCESSE JOLIE, Foolish Kiss, Amber's Glow, 8 started.

Memories of Silver S. (R), Aqueduct, Nov. 27, $66,100, 3&up, f&m, non-winners of a stake at one mile or over in 2002, 1m, 1:38.48, VESPERS, Shooting Party, Cozzy Corner, 6 started.

Merrillville S. (R), Hoosier Park, Oct. 12, $43,750, 3&up, f&m, Indiana-bred, 6f, 1:11.01, MAGGIE'S DREAM, Senorita Ziggy, Winning Glory, 9 started.

Merry Times S. (R), Thistledown, June 8, $50,000, 3&up, f&m, Ohio-bred, 1⅟₁₆m, 1:45.34, EYE SLEW THE CITY, Lady Cherie, Ashwood C C, 8 started.

MERVYN LEROY H.-G2, Hollywood Park, May 12, $150,000, 3&up, 1⅟₁₆m, 1:41.36, SKY JACK, Bosque Redondo, Devine Wind, 6 started.

Mesa H., Turf Paradise, Oct. 26, $30,000, 3&up, f&m, 6½f, 1:14.88, KNOLL LAKE, Supreme Discovery, Cove Point, 5 started.

METROPOLITAN H.-G1, Belmont Park, May 27, $750,000, 3&up, 1m, 1:33.34, SWEPT OVERBOARD, Aldebaran, Crafty C. T, 10 started.

MIAMI MILE BREEDERS' CUP H.-G3, Calder Race Course, Sept. 2, $141,750, 3&up, 1m, 1:37.78, BAND IS PASSING, Pisces, Doowaley (Ire), 8 started.

Michael G. Schaefer Mile S., Hoosier Park, Nov. 16, $103,600, 3&up, 1m, 1:35.69, CRAFTY SHAW, M B Sea, Cool N Collective, 6 started.

Michigan Breeders' Governor's Cup H. (R), Great Lakes Downs, Aug. 6, $45,000, 3&up, Michigan-bred, 1⅟₁₆m, 1:47.43, ABOVE THE WIND, That Gift, Catch the Dew, 8 started.

Michigan Futurity (R), Great Lakes Downs, Oct. 25, $60,075, 2yo, c&g, Michigan-bred, 7f, 1:26.89, AKATSAKAT, Beau Classic, Jaguar Joe, 6 started.

Michigan Juvenile Fillies S. (R), Great Lakes Downs, Oct. 26, $68,125, 2yo, f, Michigan-bred, 7f, 1:27.78, MAGNA CUM LAUDE, Mercedees Red, Jean's Way, 10 started.

Michigan Oaks (R), Great Lakes Downs, Sept. 14, $45,000, 3yo, f, Michigan-bred, 1⅟₁₆m, 1:52.17, SWEETWATER PROMISE, Bad Thing, Born to Dance, 6 started.

Michigan Sire S. (R), Great Lakes Downs, Oct. 5, $149,012, 2yo, Michigan-bred, 6f, 1:14.97, MONETARY STAR, Damon T, Bar U Anio, 9 started.

Michigan Sire S. (R), Great Lakes Downs, Oct. 5, $148,012, 2yo, f, Michigan-bred, 6f, 1:15.47, SAILING SAL, Flaming Money, Ranchipur, 8 started.

Michigan Sire S. (R), Great Lakes Downs, Oct. 5, $149,112, 3yo, Michigan-bred, 1⅟₁₆m, 1:49.56, AMERICAN DEPUTY, Goldinrunner, That Final Answer, 9 started.

Michigan Sire S. (R), Great Lakes Downs, Oct. 5, $149,312, 3yo, f, Michigan-bred, 1⅟₁₆m, 1:49.90, SWEETWATER PROMISE, Circle the Globe, A Chance for More, 9 started.

Michigan Sire S. (R), Great Lakes Downs, Oct. 5, $150,112, 4&up, Michigan-bred, 1⅛m, 1:56.30, SECRET ROMEO, Smooth Roller, Catch the Dew, 10 started.

Michigan Sire S. (R), Great Lakes Downs, Oct. 5, $147,912, 4&up, f&m, Michigan-bred, 1⅛m, 1:56.68, SEFAS ROSE, Ruff Arrival, Empress Livia, 8 started.

Middleground Breeders' Cup S., Lone Star Park, July 13, $71,850, 2yo, c&g, 6f, 1:10.62, ACTION TONIGHT, Farma Boy, Flag Dancer, 8 started.

Mid-Peninsula S. (R), Bay Meadows Fair, Aug. 11, $50,660, 2yo, f, California-bred, 5½f, 1:02.72, HUMOROUS LADY, Her Emminence, Market Garden, 6 started.

MIESQUE S.-G3, Hollywood Park, Nov. 29, $200,000, 2yo, f, 1mT, 1:34.63, ATLANTIC OCEAN, Tangle (Ire), Major Idea, 8 started.

Migrating Moon S., Calder Race Course, July 5, $42,310, 3yo, 1⅟₁₆m, 1:45.76, THE JUDGE SEZ WHO, Thiscannonsloaded, Say No Maw, 6 started.

Mike Lee S. (R), Belmont Park, June 29, $122,034, 3yo, New York-bred, 7f, 1:22.60, NO PAROLE, Trial Prep, Private Emblem, 10 started.

MILADY BREEDERS' CUP H.-G1, Hollywood Park, May 25, $211,400, 3&up, f&m, 1⅟₁₆m, 1:42.02, AZERI, Affluent, Collect Call, 6 started.

Mile Hi H., Yavapai Downs, Aug. 27, $20,000, 3&up, 1⅟₁₆m, 1:42.81, GUSTO FORZADO, Seventeen Candles, C. D. Haj, 9 started.

Miles Valentine Memorial Hurdle S., Fair Hill, May 27, $30,000, 4&up, a2¼mT, 4:18.80, P. C. PLOD, Indispensable, Invest West, 6 started.

Millard Harrell S. (R), Charles Town, Sept. 14, $31,250, 3yo, West Virginia-bred, 7f, 1:27.65, TORI'S THUNDER, Adams Tribe, Social Mix, 9 started.

Millarville Derby, Millarville, July 1, $4,100, 3&up, 1⅛m, 1:55.20, SMART FIGURE, Sagreeno, Runaway Don, 5 started.

Miller Lite S., Lone Star Park, June 22, $75,000, 3&up, f&m, 5fT, :56.72, LESLIE'S LOVE, Asheville, Southern Tour, 7 started.

Milwaukee Avenue H. (R), Sportsman's Park, March 30, $84,950, 3&up, Illinois-conceived and/or -foaled, 1⅟₁₆m, 1:44.31, BAKER ROAD, R. Little Redhead, Paddy's Spy, 9 started.

Minaret S., Tampa Bay Downs, Jan. 5, $50,000, 4&up, f&m, 6f, 1:11.47, AWAY, Little Won, Flashing Lil, 12 started.

Mingus Mountain H., Yavapai Downs, July 15, $8,600, 3&up, 1m, 1:36.23, GUSTO FORZADO, C. D. Haj, Seventeen Candles, 5 started.

Minneapolis S., Canterbury Park, Aug. 11, $40,000, 3&up, f&m, 1⅟₁₆mT, 1:44.63, BE MY FRIEND, Sarah Jade, Picnic Spread, 7 started.

Minnesota Classic Championship S. (R), Canterbury Park, Aug. 25, $44,100, 3&up, Minnesota-bred, 1⅟₁₆m, 1:43.97, J. P. JET, Ashar, Now Playing, 6 started.

Minnesota Derby (R), Canterbury Park, Aug. 3, $58,028, 3yo, c&g, Minnesota-bred, 1m 70y, 1:40.26, J. P. JET, One Trick Ata Time, Double Duces, 9 started.

Minnesota Distaff Classic Championship S. (R), Canterbury Park, Aug. 25, $45,100, 3&up, f&m, Minnesota-bred, 1⅟₁₆m, 1:45.37, LAKEVILLE, Aashu, Susie Blues, 8 started.

Minnesota Distaff Sprint Championship S. (R), Canterbury Park, Aug. 25, $38,050, 3&up, f&m, Minnesota-bred, 6f, 1:11.69, FANCY FOR SARAH, Micro Tyme, Burn the Legacy, 5 started.

Minnesota HBPA Mile S., Canterbury Park, July 6, $35,000, 3&up, f&m, a1mT, 1:38.37, HAM AND EGGS, Picnic Spread, Moonlit Maddie, 10 started.

Minnesota HBPA Sprint S., Canterbury Park, July 6, $35,000, 3&up, 6½f, 1:15.66, EXPERT, Big Daddy Tee, Medium Rare, 5 started.

Minnesota Juvenile Sprint S. (R), Canterbury Park, Aug. 4, $36,650, 2yo, Minnesota-bred, 5½f, 1:06.02, CARR DELICIOUS, Sumthing for Alex, Joy Shannon, 6 started.

Minnesota Oaks, Canterbury Park, Aug. 3, $57,180, 3yo, f, 1m 70y, 1:41.66, SUSIE BLUES, Lakeville, Demiparfait, 10 started.

Minnesota Sprint Championship S. (R), Canterbury Park, Aug. 25, $37,850, 3&up, Minnesota-bred, 6f, 1:09.31, CROCROCK, Timberwolf Power, Tushar, 5 started.

Minstrel S., Louisiana Downs, Oct. 6, $29,400, 2yo, 6½f, 1:18.02, CROWNED KING, Whippee, Imperial Editor, 5 started.

Miss America H., Bay Meadows, April 7, $100,000, 3&up, f&m, 1mT, 1:34.72, CRAZY ENSIGN (Arg), Queen of Wilshire, Dispersed Reward, 6 started.

Mrs. Penny S., Philadelphia Park, Oct. 5, $50,000, 3&up, f&m, 1⅟₁₆mT, 1:45.34, CAUGHT IN THE RAIN, Run for Joy, Garden Dance, 9 started.

Miss Gibson County H., Calder Race Course, June 16, $42,495, 3&up, f&m, 6f, 1:11.79, VAGUE MEMORY, Fly Me Crazy, Sugar N Spice, 6 started.

Miss Gibson County S., Turf Paradise, Nov. 5, $22,800, 2yo, f, 6f, 1:10.23, SILK N DIAMONDS, Hula Kat, Buenobambino, 7 started.

Miss Grillo S., Aqueduct, Oct. 27, $84,000, 2yo, f, 1⅛mT, 1:49.79, FIRCROFT, Marc's Rainbow, One and Twenty, 6 started.

Miss Houston S., Sam Houston Race Park, Nov. 23, $30,000, 2yo, f, 7f, 1:25.58, MISS LISTO, Race to Glory, No Betta Cat, 6 started.

Miss Indiana S. (R), Hoosier Park, Nov. 15, $73,650, 2yo, f, Indiana-bred, 6f, 1:15.32, INDY FIRE, Miss Dakota, Cattle Kate, 9 started.

Miss Indy Anna S., Suffolk Downs, May 25, $30,000, 3&up, f&m, 6f, 1:13.08, GUESS, Folly Dollar, Demaloot's Girl, 8 started.

Mississippi Futurity (R), Fair Grounds, Dec. 6, $34,675, 2yo, Mississippi-owned, 6f, 1:12.35, G. W.'S SKIPPIE, Sam'n Sarah's Star, Kirby's Brogue, 10 started.

Miss Kansas City H., The Woodlands, Oct. 20, $30,000, 3&up, f&m, 1⅟₁₆m, 1:49.60, FAIR KATE, Brighton Way, Ucandoittoo, 9 started.

Miss Liberty S., The Meadowlands, Sept. 27, $50,000, 3yo, f, 1m, 1:38.02, SAM EYE AM, Hallowed, Smokeumifyougotem, 6 started.

Miss Moneypenny S. (R), Fort Erie, Sept. 2, $70,800, 3&up, f&m, starters at Fort Erie at least twice in 2002, 1⅟₁₆mT, 1:42.75, POWDERJAY, Branksome Hall, My Gabrielle, 12 started.

Miss Ohio S. (R), Thistledown, Aug. 24, $40,000, 2yo, f, Ohio-bred, 6f, 1:12.10, BOLARO, Pyrite Dance, Orangeberry, 8 started.

MISS PREAKNESS S.-G3, Pimlico, May 16, $100,000, 3yo, f, 6f, 1:10.25, VESTA, Willa On the Move, Shameful, 6 started.

Miss Woodford S., Monmouth Park, Aug. 31, $50,000, 3yo, f, 6f, 1:10.39, MARESHA, Miss Marni, Al Max Diner, 5 started.

Missy Good S. (R), Penn National Race Course, July 12, $30,700, 3&up, f&m, Pennsylvania-bred, 6f, 1:10.10, RUN FOR JOY, Malvern Rose, Golden Lake, 8 started.

Mister Diz S. (R), Laurel Park, Aug. 18, $50,000, 3&up, Maryland-bred, 5½fT, 1:03.10, GHOSTLY NUMBERS, Access Agenda, Elberton, 9 started.

Mo Bay S., Delaware Park, July 13, $61,300, 3&up, a5fT, GOVER-

NOR'S PRIDE, Splendeed, Grangeville, 8 started.

Moccasin S., Hollywood Park, Nov. 16, $100,000, 2yo, f, 7f, 1:21.84, PUXA SACO, Watching You, Atlantic Ocean, 5 started.

MODESTY H.-G3, Arlington Park, July 27, $150,000, 3&up, f&m, 1¹⁄₁₆mT, 1:55.69, ENGLAND'S LEGEND (Fr), Quick Tip, Innit (Ire), 8 started.

Mohawk H. (R), Belmont Park, Oct. 19, $150,000, 3&up, New York-bred, 1¹⁄₈mT, 1:55.16, QUIET RULER, Whitmore's Conn, Chasin' Wimmin, 11 started.

Molly Brown H., Arapahoe Park, June 23, $30,000, 3&up, f&m, 6f, 1:09.60, MOLLY OR ME, Orange Glow, Nothinbutfastnred, 9 started.

MOLLY PITCHER BREEDERS' CUP H.-G2, Monmouth Park, June 29, $300,000, 3&up, f&m, 1¹⁄₁₆m, 1:48.63, ATELIER, Summer Colony, Spain, 5 started.

Mom's Command S., Suffolk Downs, Oct. 19, $30,000, 2yo, f, 6f, 1:12.76, JILL'S LAYUP, Ritzy Dame, Island Melody, 7 started.

Monique Rene H., Louisiana Downs, Aug. 24, $50,000, 3&up, f&m, 6f, 1:10.51, CIELO GIRL, Miss Photogenic, Mike's Sister, 8 started.

Monmouth Beach S., Monmouth Park, May 27, $50,000, 3&up, f&m, 1m, 1:39.27, SOUTHERN FICTION, Unrestrained, Away, 6 started.

MONMOUTH BREEDERS' CUP OAKS-G2, Monmouth Park, Aug. 17, $239,000, 3yo, f, 1¹⁄₈m, 1:51.17, MAGIC STORM, Alternate, Bronze Autumn, 5 started.

MONROVIA H.-G3, Santa Anita Park, Dec. 31, $114,700, 3&up, f&m, a6¹⁄₂fT, 1:13.81, LIL SISTER STICH, Pina Colada (GB), I'm the Business (NZ), 12 started.

Montauk H. (R), Aqueduct, Dec. 1, $82,550, 3&up, f&m, New York-bred, 1¹⁄₈m, 1:52.36, Princess Dixie, Textbook Method, ALONG CAME MARY, 8 started.

Montclair H., Golden Gate Fields, Jan. 19, $61,937, 4&up, 6f, 1:09.19, MELLOW FELLOW, Radar Contact, Gibson County, 9 started.

Moonbeam H. (R), Great Lakes Downs, Aug. 5, $45,000, 3&up, f&m, Michigan-bred, 1¹⁄₁₆m, 1:47.83, I MATCH TOO, Tank Grrrl, Empress Livia, 8 started.

Morvich H., Santa Anita Park, Nov. 3, $111,700, 3&up, a6¹⁄₂fT, 1:12.26, MASTER BELT (NZ), I Love Silver, Kachamandi (Chi), 10 started.

MORVICH H.-G3, Santa Anita Park, Nov. 3, $111,700, 3&up, a6¹⁄₂fT, 1:12.26, MASTER BELT (NZ), I Love Silver, Kachamandi (Chi), 10 started.

MOTHER GOOSE S.-G1, Belmont Park, June 29, $242,500, 3yo, f, 1¹⁄₈m, 1:49.09, NONSUCH BAY, Chamrousse, Seba (GB), 4 started.

Mountaineer HBPA S. (R), Mountaineer Park, Oct. 15, $77,700, 3&up, starters at least three times at Mountaineer in 2002, 6f, 1:10.70, TOUR THE HIVE, Meetyouathebrig, Tonto Gusto, 8 started.

Mountaineer Mile H., Mountaineer Park, Nov. 16, $102,900, 3&up, 1m, 1:38.32, DOCENT, Tour the Hive, Smashing Beau, 5 started.

Mountaineer Park HBPA S. (R), Mountaineer Park, Oct. 22, $77,900, 3&up, starters at least three times at Mountaineer Park in 2002, 6f, 1:12.48, ABUNDANTLY BLESSED, Malvern Rose, Keepondealing, 9 started.

Mountain State H., Mountaineer Park, July 2, $78,000, 3&up, 6f, 1:08.77, DASH FOR DAYLIGHT, Jeanies Rob, High Flying Bid, 7 started.

Mountain Valley S., Oaklawn Park, Jan. 26, $50,000, 3yo, 6f, 1:11.81, RICHEST HALF, Cojet, Red and Rare, 12 started.

Mount Elbert H. (R), Arapahoe Park, Aug. 11, $30,000, 3&up, c&g, Colorado-bred, 1¹⁄₁₆m, 1:44.40, PERSONAL BEAU, Moro Grande, Socko, 9 started.

Mount Royal S., Stampede Park, May 12, $40,000, 3yo, f, 6f, 1:10.80, FANCY PRANCER, Brass to Diamonds, Sly Lady, 9 started.

Mount Vernon H. (R), Belmont Park, June 23, $84,125, 3&up, f&m, New York-bred, 1¹⁄₁₆m, 1:46.55, EVENTAIL, Lovely Amanda, Longingtobeme, 10 started.

Mount Vernon H. (R), Belmont Park, June 23, $83,850, 3&up, f&m, New York-bred, 1¹⁄₁₆m, 1:46.80, SHOPPING FOR LOVE, Indy Mood for Luv, Blue Iris, 10 started.

M. R. Jenkins Memorial H., Stampede Park, May 5, $40,000, 4&up, f&m, 6f, 1:11.60, LITTLE LOLITTA, Slewability, A Ray of Magic, 7 started.

MR. PROSPECTOR H.-G3, Gulfstream Park, Jan. 13, $100,000, 3&up, 6f, 1:09.69, HOOK AND LADDER, Kipperscope, Red's Honor, 8 started.

MRS. REVERE S.-G2, Churchill Downs, Nov. 16, $173,700, 3yo, f, 1¹⁄₁₆mT, 1:46.25, CAUGHT IN THE RAIN, Glia, Bedanken, 11 started.

Ms. Southern Ohio S. (R), River Downs, Aug. 4, $45,000, 3&up, f&m, Ohio-bred, 1¹⁄₁₆mT, 1:41.80, DOUBLY FUN, Cabot Cove, Lady Cherie, 8 started.

MTA Stallion Auction Lassie S. (R), Canterbury Park, July 14, $36,813, 3yo, f, progeny of a stallion whose service was sold at the MTA auc-

tion, 6¹⁄₂f, 1:18.04, LAKEVILLE, Wa Sarah, Micro Tyme, 10 started.

MTA Stallion Auction S. (R), Canterbury Park, July 14, $37,745, 3yo, progeny of a stallion whose service was sold at the MTA auction, 6¹⁄₂f, 1:17.63, FROSTY PRINCE, Aran Narayan, Lighting Jay, 12 started.

MTOBA Stallion Service Auction S. (R), Great Lakes Downs, July 27, $19,962, 3yo, progeny of a stallion whose service was sold at the MTOBA Stallion Service Auction, 7f, 1:28.31, QUEEN AT HEART, American Deputy, Goldinrunner, 6 started.

Mt. Rainier Breeders' Cup H., Emerald Downs, July 28, $90,000, 3&up, 1¹⁄₈m, 1:47, MOONLIGHT MEETING, Sabertooth, Hoodoo Peak, 7 started.

Mt. Sassafras S. (R), Woodbine, Oct. 27, $105,000, 3&up, Canadian-bred, 7f, 1:22.35, KRZ RUCKUS, Runaway Love, Dawn Watcher, 5 started.

M. Tyson Gilpin S. (R), Delaware Park, Nov. 9, $43,200, 2yo, Virginia-bred, 6f, 1:11.76, OVERPASS, Secret Look, Flash Can Dance, 7 started.

Muscogee (Creek) Nation S., Fair Meadows at Tulsa, Aug. 3, $33,300, 3&up, f&m, 6¹⁄₂f, 1:18.20, PEYVON, Blonde Okie, Here Comes Kari, 8 started.

Muskoka S. (R), Woodbine, Sept. 2, $105,550, 2yo, f, Canadian-bred, 7f, 1:26.19, SANTERRA, La Petite Justice, Kabeeb, 10 started.

MY CHARMER H.-G3, Calder Race Course, Dec. 7, $100,000, 3&up, f&m, 1¹⁄₈mT, 1:48.43, WANDER MOM, Strawberry Blonde (Ire), Babae (Chi), 10 started.

My Charmer S., Turfway Park, Dec. 31, $50,000, 3&up, f&m, 1¹⁄₁₆m, 1:46.04, TOWN QUEEN, Suddenly Gone, Gal On the Go, 10 started.

My Dear Girl S. (R), Calder Race Course, Oct. 12, $400,000, 2yo, f, progeny of eligible Florida stallions, 1¹⁄₁₆m, 1:45.92, IVANAVINALOT, Stars Go Blue, Dakota Light, 8 started.

My Dear S., Woodbine, June 22, $136,125, 2yo, f, 5f, HANDPAINTED, Short Shadow, Sensible, 5 started.

My Fair Lady S., Suffolk Downs, May 11, $30,000, 3&up, f&m, a1m 70yT, 1:45.87, RODEO SPRINGS, Big Miss, Sunlit Ridge, 8 started.

My Friend Russ S., Delaware Park, Sept. 14, $59,100, 3yo, a1mT, 1:36.17, COHOMA, Lord Abounding, Seeking Greatness, 6 started.

My Juliet S., Philadelphia Park, May 25, $75,000, 3&up, f&m, 6f, 1:09.59, MANDY'S GOLD, Nash's Prospect, Seasonal Change, 9 started.

My Mac H., Calder Race Course, Sept. 20, $37,695, 3&up, 1¹⁄₁₆m, 1:44.85, HIGH IDEAL, Pay the Preacher, Dancing Guy, 7 started.

My Own True Love H., Calder Race Course, July 14, $37,835, 3&up, f&m, 1¹⁄₁₆m, 1:46.85, BANDERIA (Arg), Multiplicity, Castlebrook, 6 started.

Mystery Jet S. (R), Suffolk Downs, March 30, $29,400, 3yo, f, Massachusetts-bred, 6f, 1:13.20, AFRICAN PRINCESS, Little Time, Judge Nancy, 5 started.

Naked Greed S. (R), Calder Race Course, June 9, $37,765, 3&up, non-winners of $35,000 since January 1, 6¹⁄₂f, 1:16.58, TOUR OF THE CAT, Sweeping Smoke, Notebook Computer, 7 started.

Nanaimo H., Hastings Park Racecourse, July 20, $38,200, 3yo, f, 1¹⁄₁₆m, 1:45.83, GRACE FOR YOU, Lady Vye, Classic Action, 10 started.

Nancy's Glitter H., Calder Race Course, May 11, $75,000, 3&up, f&m, 1¹⁄₈m, 1:48.47, COOLBYTHEPOOL, Bay Street Gal, Castlebrook, 5 started.

Nandi S. (R), Woodbine, July 27, $129,125, 2yo, f, progeny of stallions standing in Ontario, 6f, 1:11.58, BOLDEST OF ALL, Dressed for Action, Santerra, 5 started.

NASHUA S.-G3, Aqueduct, Nov. 2, $109,700, 2yo, 1m, 1:36.77, ADDED EDGE, Outer Reef, Boston Bull, 7 started.

NASSAU COUNTY BREEDERS' CUP S.-G2, Belmont Park, May 11, $200,000, 3yo, f, 7f, 1:23.90, NONSUCH BAY, Wopping, Wilzada, 8 started.

NASSAU S. (Can-G2), Woodbine, June 2, $281,600, 3&up, f&m, 1¹⁄₄mT, 1:41.01, SIRINGAS (Ire), Rosthern, Mountain Angel, 7 started.

Nastique S., Delaware Park, June 1, $97,000, 3&up, f&m, 1¹⁄₁₆m, 1:45.92, LILY'S AFFAIR, Border Fire, Quiet Lake, 4 started.

NATALMA S. (Can-G3) (1st Div.), Woodbine, Sept. 7, $179,200, 2yo, f, 1mT, 1:35.03, ONE AND TWENTY, Swift of Flight, Sand Springs, 10 started.

NATALMA S. (Can-G3) (2nd Div.), Woodbine, Sept. 7, $176,200, 2yo, f, 1mT, 1:36.54, FORTUITOUS, Sweet Storm Creek, Wawota, 11 started.

NATC Futurity (R), Delaware Park, Aug. 31, $202,100, 2yo, passed through the sales ring during 2002, 6f, 1:12.15, CRAFTY GUY, Mister Deux, Cape Good Hope, 12 started.

NATIONAL JOCKEY CLUB H.-G3, Sportsman's Park, April 20, $200,000, 4&up, 1⅛m, 1:51.72, HAIL THE CHIEF (GB), E Z Glory, Ubiquity, 7 started.

National Jockey Club Oaks, Sportsman's Park, April 27, $100,000, 3yo, f, 1 1/16m, 1:47.14, EMERALDFORAJUDGE, Summer Delight, Persimmon Ridge, 7 started.

NATIONAL MUSEUM OF RACING HALL OF FAME H.-G2, Saratoga Race Course, Aug. 5, $150,000, 3yo, 1⅛mT, 1:49.66, QUEST STAR, Union Place, Patrol, 5 started.

Native Dancer H., Laurel Park, Jan. 21, $50,000, 4&up, 1⅛m, 1:49.02, PRIVATE RYAN, Cowboy Magic, P Day, 6 started.

NATIVE DIVER H.-G3, Hollywood Park, Dec. 14, $100,000, 3&up, 1⅛m, 1:48.43, PIENSA SONANDO (Chi), Fleetstreet Dancer, Nose The Trade (GB), 8 started.

Navajo Princess S., The Meadowlands, Oct. 12, $45,500, 3&up, f&m, 1¼m, 2:03.08, FOREST PRINCESS, Tap Dance, Festive Madam, 3 started.

NEARCTIC S. (Can-G2), Woodbine, June 23, $292,250, 3&up, 6fT, 1:07.86, NUCLEAR DEBATE, Joe's Son Joey, Texas Glitter, 14 started.

Nebraska Breeders' Sophomore Fillies S., Columbus, Aug. 4, $14,250, 3yo, f, 1m 70y, 1:46.80, SWEETIEGUNZALLUS, Keylargo Lady, Mayihavethisdance, 6 started.

Nebraska Breeders' Sophomore S., Columbus, Aug. 4, $14,250, 3yo, 1 1/16m, 1:48.60, HE'SA LITTLETURKEY, Strawberry Kid, Mr Clearwater, 6 started.

Nebraska Derby, Fonner Park, May 5, $30,000, 3yo, 1m, 1:40.20, TEAGUE, Montana Rush, Tonight Rainbow, 9 started.

Nebraskaland H. (R), Horsemen's Park, July 20, $29,500, 4&up, Nebraska-bred, 1m, 1:37, HIGH DICE, Tate's Way, Harvey Bengal, 9 started.

Needles S., Calder Race Course, Sept. 14, $50,000, 3yo, 1 1/16mT, 1:46.60, GEMMA'S STAR, Susie's Poker, Bog Hunter, 8 started.

Nellie Morse S., Laurel Park, Jan. 20, $67,750, 4&up, f&m, 1 1/16m, 1:43.84, CASE OF THE BLUES, Irving's Baby, Your Out, 10 started.

New Braunfels S., Retama Park, Sept. 21, $30,000, 3&up, f&m, 6f, 1:10.97, GOODNESS, Miss Ritz, Nobody's Fool, 9 started.

New Castle H., Delaware Park, June 24, $100,300, 3&up, f&m, 1⅛mT, 1:48.92, LADY OF THE FUTURE, Calista (GB), Salty You, 6 started.

NEW HAMPSHIRE SWEEPSTAKES H.-G3, Rockingham Park, June 22, $200,000, 3&up, a1⅛mT, 1:47.51, DEL MAR SHOW, Mus-If (GB), Dr. Kashnikow, 9 started.

New Jersey Futurity (R), The Meadowlands, Nov. 23, $113,050, 2yo, New Jersey-bred, 6f, 1:10.90, KAW LIGA SIOUX, Something Smith, Trueamericanspirit, 7 started.

New Jersey Hunt Cup S., Far Hills, Oct. 19, $48,500, 4&up, a3¼mT, 7:39.23, MAIPO, Charlie's Dewan, Pleasant Parcel, 5 started.

New Mexico Breeder's Association H. (R), SunRay Park, Oct. 7, $64,500, 3&up, New Mexico-bred, 1m, 1:36.40, CIENTO, Romeos Wilson, Runmore Mema, 6 started.

New Mexico Distaff H. (R), SunRay Park, Sept. 22, $65,500, 3&up, f&m, New Mexico-bred, 6½f, 1:18.40, ESPEEDYTOO, Charlotte's Ego, Me a Spirit Too, 9 started.

New Mexico State Fair H., The Downs at Albuquerque, Sept. 22, $38,950, 3&up, 1⅛m, 1:48.92, VERNON INVADER, Tahoe Affair, Moro Grande, 7 started.

New Mexico State Fair Thoroughbred Breeders' Derby (R), The Downs at Albuquerque, Sept. 21, $46,712, 3yo, New Mexico-bred, 1 1/16m, 1:43.97, BULLETMAN JACK, Jacks Romeo, Dancing Promise, 7 started.

New Mexico State Racing Commission H. (R), Sunland Park, Nov. 24, $132,700, 3&up, f&m, New Mexico-bred, 6f, 1:11.66, ESPEEDYTOO, Fritzie's Prospect, Gollygot, 12 started.

New Mexico State University S. (R), Sunland Park, Feb. 3, $103,700, 4&up, New Mexico-bred, 1m, 1:38.79, RUNMORE MEMA, I'm Not Bluffin, Ciento, 11 started.

NEW ORLEANS H.-G2, Fair Grounds, March 3, $500,000, 4&up, 1⅛m, 1:50.44, PARADE LEADER, Keats, Graeme Hall, 9 started.

New Providence S. (R), Woodbine, May 19, $130,500, 3&up, progeny of eligible Ontario stallions, 6f, 1:10.76, SAMBUCA ON ICE, Mysterious Affair, Krz Ruckus, 6 started.

New Westminster H., Hastings Park Racecourse, Aug. 24, $38,822, 2yo, 6½f, 1:18.67, BULLSEYE BILL, Native Judge, Steady Smiler, 8 started.

New Year's Eve H., Mountaineer Park, Dec. 30, $78,400, 3&up, f&m, 6f, 1:11.30, EMILY RING, Miss Atticus, Malvern Rose, 9 started.

New York Breeders' Futurity (R), Finger Lakes, Sept. 2, $149,225, 2yo, New York-bred, 6f, 1:10.86, INFINITE JUSTICE, Tomorrows Banquet, Beautiful America, 10 started.

New York Derby (R), Finger Lakes, July 27, $143,733, 3yo, New York-bred, 1 1/16m, 1:45.18, TRIAL PREP, Private Emblem, No Parole, 5 started.

NEW YORK H.-G2, Belmont Park, July 4, $250,000, 3&up, f&m, 1¼mT, 1:59.81, OWSLEY, Volga (Ire), Janet (GB), 7 started.

New York Oaks (R), Finger Lakes, Sept. 2, $60,000, 3yo, f, New York-bred, 1 1/16m, 1:45.56, PRINCESS DIXIE, Drama Queen, Pretty Brassy, 6 started.

New York Turf Writers Cup Steeplechase H., Saratoga Race Course, Aug. 29, $109,600, 4&up, a2⅝mT, 4:28.04, ZABENZ (NZ), Double Leaf (GB), Flat Top, 8 started.

NEXT MOVE H.-G3, Aqueduct, March 29, $108,600, 3&up, f&m, 1⅛m, 1:49.88, WITH ABILITY, Irving's Baby, Diversa, 7 started.

NIAGARA BREEDERS' CUP H. (Can-G1), Woodbine, Aug. 31, $324,400, 3&up, 1½mT, 2:26.18, FULL OF WONDER, Perfect Soul (Ire), Muntej (GB), 9 started.

Niagara S. (R), Finger Lakes, July 20, $35,000, 3yo, f, New York-bred, 6f, 1:12.03, PRINCESS DIXIE, J's Happy Holiday, Ice Carnival, 8 started.

Nick Shuk Memorial S., Delaware Park, July 1, $75,000, 3yo, 1 1/16mT, 1:41.59, PATROL, Coco's Madness, Cohoma, 5 started.

Nicole S., Hawthorne Race Course, May 5, $50,000, 4&up, f&m, 1 1/16mT, 1:41.78, GOLDEN ANTIGUA, Ioya Two, Lady Angharad (Ire), 10 started.

NOBLE DAMSEL H.-G3, Belmont Park, Sept. 21, $114,400, 3&up, f&m, 1mT, 1:32.79, TATES CREEK, Amonita (GB), Dat You Miz Blue, 8 started.

Noble Royalty H., Calder Race Course, Sept. 28, $50,000, 3&up, f&m, 1 1/16mT, 1:44.75, STAY FOREVER, Pembroke Palace, Abuela Esther (Uru), 8 started.

Noel Laing Hurdle S., Montpelier, Nov. 2, $29,100, 4&up, a2½mT, 52:12, TRES TOUCHE, Turkish Corner, Hendler, 8 started.

No Le Hace S., Retama Park, Oct. 26, $30,000, 3&up, 1m, 1:38.97, DYNAMEAUX, Chauffe Au Rouge, Tedro, 8 started.

NORFOLK S.-G2, Santa Anita Park, Oct. 5, $200,000, 2yo, 1 1/16m, 1:42.75, KAFWAIN, Bull Market, Listen Indy, 7 started.

Norgor Derby, Ruidoso Downs, Aug. 10, $22,200, 3yo, 6f, 1:11.40, NINETY NINE JACK, Devious Ways, Smoke Dancer, 11 started.

Norman Hall S. (R), Suffolk Downs, Dec. 7, $30,000, 2yo, Massachusetts-bred, 6f, 1:16.61, MR. MESO, Glory Be Good, Dustins Mozart, 6 started.

Northampton S. (R), Northampton Fair, Sept. 15, $15,750, 3&up, Massachusetts-bred, a6½f, 1:22.85, DISTINCTLY CAROTIC, Gun Is Set, Woodside, 7 started.

North Dakota-Bred Thoroughbred Derby (R), Chippewa Downs, June 23, $9,100, 3yo, North Dakota-bred, 6½f, 1:24.40, YO DAN, Schaefer's Choice, Twilight Ladd, 4 started.

North Dakota-Bred Thoroughbred Futurity (R), Chippewa Downs, June 29, $9,100, 2yo, North Dakota-bred, 4½f, ROAD RUNNER JR., Baby Wallys Joy, Hey Vic'turr, 4 started.

North Dakota Derby (R), Assiniboia Downs, July 7, $20,000, 3yo, North Dakota-bred, 1m, 1:42, WINAFERD, Big R, Rennaissance Man, 7 started.

North Dakota Futurity, Assiniboia Downs, Sept. 1, $30,000, 2yo, 6f, 1:13.20, SUNTANA, Mistiff, My Friend Frank, 7 started.

North Dakota Stallion S. (R), Assiniboia Downs, Aug. 18, $30,000, 2yo, North Dakota-bred, 6f, 1:13.60, SUNTANA, Lady Della Rayne, My Friend Frank, 7 started.

North Dakota Stallion S. (R), Assiniboia Downs, Aug. 3, $20,000, 3yo, progeny of eligible North Dakota stallions, 1 1/16m, 1:50.20, HOIST A COIN, Big R, It's Stormin, 5 started.

Northern Dancer S. (R), Laurel Park, Nov. 30, $75,000, 3yo, Maryland-bred, 1⅛m, 1:51.05, AGGADAN, This Guns for Hire, Tamayno, 8 started.

Northern Dancer S., Churchill Downs, June 15, $109,500, 3yo, 1m, 1:35.04, DANTHEBLUEGRASSMAN, Stephentown, Sky Terrace, 7 started.

Northern Lights Debutante S. (R), Canterbury Park, Aug. 25, $56,605, 2yo, f, Minnesota-bred, 6f, 1:12.47, TRISA, Traffic Belle, Maywood's Jill, 10 started.

Northern Lights Futurity (R), Canterbury Park, Aug. 25, $52,450, 2yo, c&g, Minnesota-bred, 6f, 1:13.25, MAYWOOD'S JACK, Ima Smarty Boy, Imagery, 7 started.

Northern Spur S., Oaklawn Park, April 10, $75,000, 3yo, c&g, 1m, 1:38.32, SCREEN IDOL, Missme, Thunderpumper, 10 started.

Northlands Oaks, Northlands Park, July 20, $40,000, 3yo, f, 1m, 1:43, CODE'S DECREE, Sweet Monarch, O Howrude, 9 started.

North Randall S. (R), Thistledown, Aug. 10, $40,000, 3yo, Ohio-bred, 6f, 1:11.06, TRUTH MATTERS, Final Endeavor, Icy Star, 8 started.

Northwest Stallion S. (R), Emerald Downs, Aug. 3, $45,000, 2yo, c&g, progeny of eligible stallions, 6½f, 1:16.60, BUB, Knightsbridge Road, Personal Plan, 6 started.

Northwest Stallion S. (R), Emerald Downs, July 27, $42,300, 2yo, f, progeny of eligible stallions, 6½f, 1:18.20, GOLD THUNDER, C G Regency, Stage Plan, 9 started.

Norton Shores S., Great Lakes Downs, Oct. 21, $20,000, 3yo, c&g, 1m, 1:44.05, EQUI POWER, American Deputy, Accountable Guy, 7 started.

NTRA Great State Challenge Classic S. (R), Sam Houston Race Park, Dec. 7, $210,500, 3&up, limited to jurisdictions in which the official state horsemens association is an NTRA member, 1⅛m, 1:49.34, CONTINENTAL RED, Pass Rush, Pickupspeed, 6 started.

NTRA Great State Challenge Invitational Distaff S. (R), Sam Houston Race Park, Dec. 7, $206,000, 3&up, f&m, limited to jurisdictions in which the official state horsemens association is an NTRA member, 1$^1/_{16}$m, 1:44.40, TAKE CHARGE LADY, Mystic Lady, Coastalota, 4 started.

NTRA Great State Challenge Invitational Juvenile Fillies S. (R), Sam Houston Race Park, Dec. 7, $214,000, 2yo, f, limited to jurisdictions in which the official state horsemens association is an NTRA member, 7f, 1:23.48, ELEGANT DESIGNER, Souris, Midnight Cry, 9 started.

NTRA Great State Challenge Invitational Sprint S. (R), Sam Houston Race Park, Dec. 7, $240,000, 3&up, limited to jurisdictions in which the official state horsemens association is an NTRA member, 6f, 1:09.06, MY COUSIN MATT, Dash for Daylight, Deer Run, 8 started.

NTRA Great State Challenge Invitational Turf S. (R), Sam Houston Race Park, Dec. 7, $262,000, 3&up, limited to jurisdictions in which the official state horsemens association is an NTRA member, 1⅛mT, 1:51.61, LA REINE'S TERMS, Mystery Giver, Forbidden Apple, 9 started.

NTRA Great State Challenge Juvenile S. (R), Sam Houston Race Park, Dec. 7, $263,500, 2yo, c&g, limited to jurisdictions in which the official state horsemens association is an NTRA member, 7f, 1:22.73, CRACKUP, Supah Blitz, Cherokee's Boy, 10 started.

Nuit D'Amour S., Delaware Park, May 20, $58,700, 3yo, f, 6f, 1:11.50, HAUNTED LASS, Note Taker, Blue Creek, 6 started.

Nureyev S., Keeneland, Oct. 4, $84,450, 3&up, 5½fT, 1:03.99, MANOFGLORY, Mighty Beau, Brown Eyed Major, 10 started.

Nursery S., Hollywood Park, May 11, $85,580, 2yo, f, 5f, :58.78, GLOBAL FINANCE, Magic Smoke, Forthelifeofme, 6 started.

Oakland H., Golden Gate Fields, Dec. 7, $72,200, 3&up, 6f, 1:08.26, EL DORADO SHOOTER, Halo Cat, Profound Secret, 13 started.

OAKLAWN BREEDERS' CUP S.-G3, Oaklawn Park, March 16, $200,000, 3&up, f&m, 1$^1/_{16}$m, 1:44.56, ASK ME NO SECRETS, Red n'Gold, Descapate, 5 started.

OAKLAWN H.-G1, Oaklawn Park, April 6, $500,000, 4&up, 1⅛m, 1:48.34, KUDOS, Bowman's Band, Dollar Bill, 8 started.

OAK LEAF S.-G2, Santa Anita Park, Oct. 6, $200,000, 2yo, f, 1$^1/_{16}$m, 1:42.65, COMPOSURE, Buffythecenterfold, Sea Jewel, 6 started.

Oakley S. (R), Colonial Downs, June 30, $40,000, 3yo, f, Virginia-bred, 1$^1/_{16}$mT, 1:44.67, WITH PATIENCE, Midnite Deelite, Thunder and Rain, 9 started.

OAK TREE BREEDERS' CUP MILE S.-G2, Santa Anita Park, Oct. 5, $234,000, 3&up, 1mT, 1:32.93, NIGHT PATROL, Kachamandi (Chi), Nicobar (GB), 8 started.

OAK TREE DERBY-G2, Santa Anita Park, Oct. 13, $150,000, 3yo, 1⅛mT, 1:46, JOHAR, Rock Opera, Mananan McLir, 8 started.

Obeah S., Delaware Park, June 22, $101,200, 3&up, f&m, 1⅛m, 1:52.54, YOUR OUT, Quiet Lake, Shag, 9 started.

OBS Championship S. (R), Ocala Training Center, March 18, $100,000, 3yo, sold at an OBS sale, 1$^1/_{16}$m, 1:46.60, MOUNTAIN FORUM, Quest Star, Forum Bells, 6 started.

OBS Championship S. (R), Ocala Training Center, March 18, $100,000, 3yo, f, sold at an OBS sale, 1$^1/_{16}$m, 1:46.80, BRONZE AUTUMN, Salem Willow, Hi Tech Honeycomb, 12 started.

OBS Sprint S. (R), Ocala Training Center, March 18, $50,000, 3yo, sold at an OBS sale, 6f, 1:09.60, ROYAL LAD, Warners, Barnacle Steve, 8 started.

OBS Sprint S. (R), Ocala Training Center, March 18, $50,000, 3yo, f, sold at an OBS sale, 6f, 1:09.20, BOLD WORLD, Sea Span, Forum Search, 7 started.

Ocean Bay S., Turf Paradise, April 13, $22,900, 3&up, f&m, 1mT, 1:36.58, BALBOA PARK, Hazen, Win a Feu, 8 started.

Ocean Hotel S., Monmouth Park, June 8, $48,500, 3yo, f, 5fT, :56.73, BOLD WORLD, Little Out, Miss Atticus, 4 started.

Oceanport H., Monmouth Park, June 15, $91,000, 3&up, 1$^1/_{16}$m, 1:42.72, TEMPEST FUGIT, Runspastum, One Eyed Joker, 3 started.

Oceanside S. (1st Div.) (R), Del Mar, July 24, $82,800, 3yo, non-winners of a race worth $50,000 in 2002, 1mT, 1:34.14, ROCK OPERA, Mountain Rage, Johar, 6 started.

Oceanside S. (2nd Div.) (R), Del Mar, July 24, $84,300, 3yo, non-winners of a race worth $50,000 in 2002, 1mT, 1:34.52, TRUE PHENOMENON, Diamond Hope, Dream Machine (Fr), 8 started.

Office Queen S., Calder Race Course, June 15, $100,000, 3yo, f, 1$^1/_{16}$m, 1:47.49, CELLARS SHIRAZ, Four Pennies, Tasso Run, 6 started.

Office Wife S., Arlington Park, July 28, $63,000, 3yo, f, 1$^1/_{16}$mT, 1:42.89, TRANSITION TIME, Attico, Bee My Honey, 6 started.

Ogataul H. (R), Fonner Park, March 9, $25,700, 3&up, Nebraska-bred, 6f, 1:12.80, TATE'S WAY, Yankee Ruler, Harvey Bengal, 7 started.

OGDEN PHIPPS H.-G1, Belmont Park, June 22, $300,000, 3&up, f&m, 1$^1/_{16}$m, 1:41.75, RAGING FEVER, Transcendental, Two Item Limit, 9 started.

Ohio Debutante H. (R), Thistledown, Aug. 31, $40,000, 3yo, f, Ohio-bred, 6f, 1:10.68, CRYPTO'S TWINJET, Asinaway, Kind of Fun, 8 started.

OHIO DERBY-G2, Thistledown, July 20, $300,000, 3yo, 1⅛m, 1:49.96, MAGIC WEISNER, Wiseman's Ferry, The Judge Sez Who, 4 started.

Ohio Freshman S. (R), Beulah Park, Nov. 17, $40,000, 2yo, Ohio-bred, 1$^1/_{16}$m, 1:49.84, MERCER'S COOL CAT, Invincible Flight, Speedy Gazelle, 7 started.

Ohio Valley H., Mountaineer Park, May 28, $78,450, 3&up, f&m, 6f, 1:11.10, FRENCH TEACHER, Keepondealing, Rude Coyote, 8 started.

Oh Say S., Delaware Park, June 10, $57,700, 3yo, 6f, 1:09.80, IT'S A MONSTER, Kentucky Maid, Boston Common, 5 started.

Oklahoma Classics Day Classic S. (R), Remington Park, Oct. 27, $75,000, 3&up, Oklahoma-bred, 1$^1/_{16}$m, 1:44.34, ZEE OH SIX, Expensive Risk, Coldiron Slew, 6 started.

Oklahoma Classics Day Distaff S. (R), Remington Park, Oct. 27, $50,000, 3&up, f&m, Oklahoma-bred, 1m 70y, 1:44.42, BAYAKOA'S IMAGE, Fastybutnasty, Hallie Cat, 7 started.

Oklahoma Classics Day Filly & Mare Turf S. (R), Remington Park, Oct. 27, $50,000, 3&up, f&m, Oklahoma-bred, 7½fT, 1:34.88, RHYELIZ, Blonde Okie, Slew Ann, 10 started.

Oklahoma Classics Day Juvenile S. (R), Remington Park, Oct. 27, $50,000, 2yo, Oklahoma-bred, 6f, 1:11.83, NOTABLE OKIE, Saddle a Dream, Laura's Moment, 8 started.

Oklahoma Classics Day Lassie S. (R), Remington Park, Oct. 27, $50,000, 2yo, f, Oklahoma-bred, 6f, 1:12.06, TULUPAI, Reluctant Lady, No Betta Cat, 9 started.

Oklahoma Classics Day Sprint S., Remington Park, Oct. 27, $50,000, 3&up, 6f, 1:10.75, MEDIUM RARE, Trickmeister, Dance and Dazzle, 7 started.

Oklahoma Classics Day Turf S. (R), Remington Park, Oct. 27, $50,000, 3&up, Oklahoma-bred, 1mT, 1:40.65, HALO ENCLOSED, Mahal, Gambler's Share, 11 started.

OKLAHOMA DERBY-G3, Remington Park, Aug. 25, $295,000, 3yo, 1⅛m, 1:49.34, THE JUDGE SEZ WHO, Easyfromthegitgo, A. P. Five Hundred, 9 started.

Oklahoma Thoroughbred S., Fair Meadows at Tulsa, Aug. 2, $43,025, 3&up, 5½f, 1:05, DANCE AND DAZZLE, Abbi's Choice, Marlukin, 10 started.

Old Hat S., Gulfstream Park, Jan. 6, $100,000, 3yo, f, 6f, 1:10.61, A NEW TWIST, Forest Heiress, French Satin, 7 started.

Old Ironsides S., Suffolk Downs, June 1, $30,000, 3&up, a1m 70yT, 1:46.15, UP FRONT, Northwest Hill, River Image, 10 started.

Old Line Policy S., Turf Paradise, April 12, $22,000, 3yo, 1m, 1:36.82, JETSON, Nabatean, Road Grader, 8 started.

Old South H., Louisiana Downs, Oct. 12, $30,000, 3&up, f&m, 1$^1/_{16}$mT, 1:44.95, GOLDEN RHYTHM, Cocoa Creek, Chula, 9 started.

Omaha H., Horsemen's Park, July 21, $100,000, 3&up, 1m, 1:39.20, CATNIRO, Baker Road, Miner's Prize, 7 started.

Omnibus S., Monmouth Park, Sept. 1, $48,500, 3&up, f&m, 1mT, 1:38.08, VICTORY RIDE, Tap Dance, Cocktailsandreams, 4 started.

One Dreamer S. (R), Gulfstream Park, March 16, $145,100, 3&up, f&m, Florida-bred, 1mT, 1:33.81, BAY STREET GAL, Company Storm, Clearly a Queen, 9 started.

Ontario Colleen S., Woodbine, Aug. 25, $156,625, 3yo, f, 1mT, 1:34.59, STRAIT FROM TEXAS, Hot Talent, Lush Soldier, 9 started.

Ontario County S. (R), Finger Lakes, July 13, $35,000, 3yo, New York-bred, 6f, 1:11.93, SMOKIEISABANDIT, One N Three, J's Wild Slew, 7 started.

Ontario Damsel S. (R), Woodbine, June 30, $166,950, 3yo, f,

Canadian-bred, 6½fT, 1:15.70, CAVALIER BILLIE, Fleet of Foot, Spanish Decree, 9 started.

Ontario Debutante S., Woodbine, Aug. 11, $149,625, 2yo, f, 6f, 1:12.34, HANDPAINTED, Buffalo Jump, Curiosity, 7 started.

Ontario Fashion S., Woodbine, Oct. 26, $142,625, 3&up, f&m, 6f, 1:10.82, FEATHERS, Sheila's Prospect, Miss Sweep, 10 started.

Ontario Jockey Club S. (R), Woodbine, July 28, $105,000, 3&up, Canadian-bred, 7f, 1:22.06, STEADY RUCKUS, Dawn Watcher, Legal Heir, 5 started.

Ontario Lassie S. (R), Woodbine, Nov. 24, $160,200, 2yo, f, Canadian-bred, 1⅟₁₆m, 1:47.80, BRATTOTHECORE, Deputy Cures Blues, Kabul, 6 started.

Ontario Matron S., Woodbine, June 9, $179,874, 3&up, f&m, 1⅟₁₆m, 1:43.67, EXTEND, Devastating, Catch the Ring, 6 started.

On Trust H. (R), Hollywood Park, Nov. 23, $107,700, 3&up, California-bred, 7½f, 1:28.27, HOT MARKET, Grey Memo, Spinelessjellyfish, 6 started.

Open Fire S., Delaware Park, Aug. 10, $75,000, 3&up, f&m, 1⅛m, 1:53.27, UNRESTRAINED, Regal Countess, Shiny Sheet, 5 started.

Open Mind H. (R), Monmouth Park, May 11, $50,000, 3&up, f&m, New Jersey-bred, 6f, 1:10.73, SILENT SERENADE, Misspent, Now Listen Sister, 9 started.

Open S., Lethbridge, Sept. 1, $9,200, 3&up, 7f, 1:30.40, POLISH POPPA, One Hot Knight, Neighborhood Bully, 8 started.

Opera Diva S., Calder Race Course, Nov. 24, $44,525, 3yo, f, 1⅟₁₆mT, 1:42.54, MALIZIOSA, Something Ventured, Tasso Run, 9 started.

ORCHID H.-G2, Gulfstream Park, March 24, $200,000, 3&up, f&m, 1½mT, 2:25.89, JULIE JALOUSE, Sweetest Thing, Refugee, 9 started.

Oregon Hers S. (R), Portland Meadows, Dec. 14, $10,000, 3yo, f, Oregon-bred, 1m, 1:40.63, NICHOLE'S DELIGHT, Callie Mae, Stately's Choice, 8 started.

Oregon His S. (R), Portland Meadows, Dec. 14, $10,000, 3yo, c&g, Oregon-bred, 1⅟₁₆m, 1:46.90, AKA REMY, Badcopnodonut, Fit to Bet, 7 started.

Oregon Sprint S. (R), Portland Meadows, Dec. 14, $10,000, 3&up, Oregon-bred, 6f, 1:12.12, ROSE CITY SPECIAL, Lovers Son, Yesss, 9 started.

Orinda H., Golden Gate Fields, Jan. 21, $67,100, 4&up, f&m, 6f, 1:09.09, ABOVE PERFECTION, Bullish Miss, Phaenna, 8 started.

Orphan Kist H. (R), Fonner Park, March 10, $25,700, 3&up, f&m, Nebraska-bred, 6f, 1:14.20, SANDPIT DANCER, Run Around Sue, Double Dreamin Deb, 7 started.

Osiris Plate S., Assiniboia Downs, Sept. 29, $30,000, 2yo, 1m, 1:43.40, SUNTANA, Sovereign Creek, Mr Don, 5 started.

Osunitas H. (R), Del Mar, Aug. 14, $81,475, 3&up, f&m, non-winners of $60,000 at one mile or over in 2002, 1⅟₁₆mT, 1:42.82, DYNA'S CLUB, Four Plus Four, Tropical Lady (Brz), 9 started.

Os West Oregon Futurity (R), Portland Meadows, Dec. 14, $27,715, 2yo, Oregon-bred, 1m, 1:42.24, GLAD TO BE HERE, Stately Jack Flash, Yada Yada Yada, 8 started.

OTBA Sales S. (R), Portland Meadows, Nov. 2, $7,250, 2yo, sold at an OTBA sale, 6f, 1:14.55, RIGHT YOU ARE, Our Lucky Kiss, Dance With Pride, 7 started.

OTBA Stallion S. (R), Portland Meadows, Jan. 5, $10,000, 3yo, Oregon-bred, 6f, 1:12.88, RANSOME ROAD, Lammy, Maloya's Sun, 6 started.

Overage S., Hawthorne Race Course, May 18, $49,750, 4&up, 1⅟₁₆mT, 1:45.91, FOUR ON THE FLOOR, Ivars Big Peaceful, Smilin' Slew, 8 started.

OVERBROOK SPINSTER S.-G1, Keeneland, Oct. 6, $546,000, 3&up, f&m, 1⅛m, 1:49.90, TAKE CHARGE LADY, You, Printemps (Chi), 7 started.

Overlander S., Kamloops, June 9, $2,650, 3&up, 6½f, 1:18.80, WISE DANCER, Miller's Legend, R Ruby Rae, 6 started.

Overskate S. (R), Woodbine, July 3, $136,875, 3&up, progeny of stallions standing in Ontario, 7f, 1:23.56, KRZ RUCKUS, Mighty Quinn, Devil Valentine, 9 started.

Ozark Hills H., Blue Ribbon Downs, March 17, $8,150, 3&up, 4f, RUMORS FLY, Open for Business, Freds Valentine, 10 started.

Pacifica H., Bay Meadows, Oct. 26, $60,200, 3&up, 1⅟₁₆m, 1:43.59, SIRPA, San Nicolas, Rio's Chase, 4 started.

PACIFIC CLASSIC S.-G1, Del Mar, Aug. 25, $1,000,000, 3&up, 1¼m, 2:01.45, CAME HOME, Momentum, Milwaukee Brew, 14 started.

Pago Hop S., Fair Grounds, Dec. 21, $100,000, 3yo, f, a1mT, 1:36.96, BEDANKEN, Dynamic Lady, Lush Soldier, 12 started.

PALM BEACH S.-G3, Gulfstream Park, Feb. 22, $100,000, 3yo, 1⅛mT, 1:49.80, ORCHARD PARK, Lord Juban, Red's Top Gun, 12 started.

Palo Alto H., Bay Meadows, Oct. 19, $60,650, 3yo, f, 1m, 1:35.13, HALO TYRA, Etnorias, Ponche de Leona, 7 started.

Palo Alto H., Bay Meadows, May 27, $59,613, 3&up, f&m, 1⅟₁₆mT, 1:42.80, LINDSAY JEAN, Kabylia (Ire), Mimi's Cafe, 9 started.

PALOMAR H.-G2, Del Mar, Sept. 8, $150,000, 3&up, f&m, 1⅟₁₆mT, 1:41.56, VOODOO DANCER, I'm the Business (NZ), Skywriting, 7 started.

PALOS VERDES H.-G2, Santa Anita Park, Jan. 27, $150,000, 4&up, 6f, 1:07.70, SNOW RIDGE, Squirtle Squirt, Ceeband, 7 started.

Palo Verde H., Turf Paradise, Feb. 23, $30,000, 3yo, 6½f, 1:16.30, FLYING SUPERCON, Duddly Doo Run, Jetson, 9 started.

PAN AMERICAN H.-G2, Gulfstream Park, March 23, $200,000, 3&up, 1½mT, 2:24.14, DEELITEFUL IRVING, Cetewayo, Mr. Livingston, 9 started.

Panhandle H., Mountaineer Park, May 4, $78,450, 3&up, 5f, JEANIES ROB, Mo Mon, Ultimate Warrior, 8 started.

Panthers S., Prairie Meadows, June 14, $62,400, 3yo, f, 1m, 1:37.46, HI TECH HONEYCOMB, For Rubies, One Fine Shweetie, 6 started.

Pan Zareta H., Fair Grounds, Feb. 9, $72,750, 4&up, f&m, 6f, 1:10.40, MY BRENT'S DIAMOND, Hallowed Dreams, Hattiesburg, 4 started.

Paradise Creek S., Arlington Park, Oct. 24, $48,250, 3yo, a1⅛mT, 1:51.08, MAJOR RHYTHM, Stormy Impact, Macaw (Ire), 6 started.

Paradise Mile H., Turf Paradise, Dec. 14, $50,000, 3&up, 1mT, 1:36.57, CAMACHO (NZ), Milk Wood (GB), Nell's Bells, 8 started.

Paradise Valley H., Turf Paradise, Nov. 16, $30,000, 3yo, 7½fT, 1:29.22, LOU'S EXPECTATION, Duddly Doo Run, Playing It Cool, 10 started.

Paragon H., Emerald Downs, July 20, $40,000, 3yo, f, 1⅟₁₆m, 1:42.60, LASTING CODE, Dolly's Hit Lady, Blue Moon Special, 9 started.

Park Avenue S. (R), Aqueduct, April 21, $100,000, 3yo, f, New York-bred, 1m, 1:38.43, LIVEITUPNOW, Multiple Wins, Princess Dixie, 11 started.

Parkland Heritage S. (R), Marquis Downs, Aug. 17, $11,800, 3yo, f, Saskatchewan-bred, 1⅟₁₆m, 1:46.63, TOP STAGE DANCER, Royal Brittany, Silver Missile, 5 started.

Parnitha S. (R), Fort Erie, July 4, $65,700, 3&up, Canadian-bred, 6f, 1:11.71, R J'S GAME, Rotsa Ruckus, Best of the Duck, 7 started.

Pasco S., Tampa Bay Downs, Jan. 19, $50,000, 3yo, 7f, 1:24.53, MAJOR FOCUS, Expected Hour, Ran South, 12 started.

Passing Mood S. (R), Woodbine, July 17, $130,375, 3yo, f, progeny of stallions standing in Ontario, 7fT, 1:22.39, HEYAHOHOWDY, Spanish Decree, Oh Livia D., 5 started.

Paterson S., The Meadowlands, Sept. 2, $50,000, 3yo, 1⅟₁₆m, 1:42.45, TRUMP MARINA, Mazoolian Ghost, Foolish Gamble, 6 started.

PAT O'BRIEN H.-G2, Del Mar, Aug. 18, $150,000, 3&up, 7f, 1:21.89, DISTURBINGTHEPEACE, Hot Market, I Love Silver, 5 started.

Patrick Wood S. (R), Great Lakes Downs, Sept. 14, $45,000, 2yo, c&g, Michigan-bred, 6f, 1:15.61, BEAU CLASSIC, Hola C Bright, Jaguar Joe, 6 started.

Paul Cacci Eel River Sprint S., Ferndale, Aug. 11, $8,120, 3&up, 5f, FIGHT FOR SILVER, Irish Ruhl, Ironman Dehere, 7 started.

Paumonok H., Aqueduct, Jan. 26, $80,725, 3&up, 6f, 1:09.07, WRANGLER, Run Kush Run, Late Carson, 5 started.

Peach Blossom S., Delaware Park, April 27, $75,900, 3yo, f, 6f, 1:10.51, MS WELL, Haunted Lass, Cherokee Girl, 8 started.

Peach of It H. (R), Sportsman's Park, March 30, $97,150, 3&up, f&m, Illinois-conceived and/or -foaled, 1m, 1:39.29, OUT OF OPTIONS, Tap Your Feet, Ballado's Baby, 8 started.

Pearl Necklace S. (R), Laurel Park, Aug. 17, $60,000, 3yo, f, Maryland-bred, 1⅟₁₆mT, 1:42.97, SUPPOSEDLY, Quoit Quick, No Halos Here, 5 started.

Pebbles H., Belmont Park, Oct. 14, $114,300, 3yo, f, 1⅛m, 1:49.68, GLIA, Nonsuch Bay, Delta Princess, 5 started.

PEGASUS H.-G2, The Meadowlands, Sept. 27, $350,000, 3yo, 1⅛m, 1:49.87, REGAL SANCTION, No Parole, This Guns for Hire, 6 started.

Pelican S., Tampa Bay Downs, Dec. 28, $50,000, 3&up, 6f, 1:10.87, SECRET ROMEO, Tour the Hive, Winnie's Pooh Bear, 11 started.

Pelican State S. (R), Louisiana Downs, Nov. 10, $32,100, 2yo, Louisiana-bred, 6f, 1:11.38, MR. KING REX, Witt Ante, Sevenforbish, 7 started.

Pelleteri Breeders' Cup H., Fair Grounds, March 17, $150,000, 3&up, 6f, 1:09.25, EXPLICIT, Entepreneur, Crucible, 8 started.

Peninsula S. (R), Fort Erie, Aug. 25, $68,000, 3&up, Canadian-bred starters at Fort Erie at least twice in 2002, 6½f, 1:17.56, GO FIGURE, Osmanbek, Yatsko, 6 started.

PENNSYLVANIA DERBY-G3, Philadelphia Park, Sept. 2, $500,000, 3yo, 1⅛m, 1:51.10, HARLAN'S HOLIDAY, Essence of Dubai, Make the Bend, 5 started.

Pennsylvania Governor's Cup H., Penn National Race Course, Aug. 3, $50,000, 3&up, 5fT, :54.61, BOP, Sport d'Hiver, Manofglory, 11 started.
Pennsylvania Hunt Cup S., Unionville, Oct. 27, $26,400, 5 yo's & up, a4mT, DR. RAMSEY, Young Dubliner (Ire), Bruno Castelli, 5 started.
Pennsylvania Nursery S. (R), Philadelphia Park, Nov. 16, $60,600, 2yo, c&g, Pennsylvania-bred, 7f, 1:25.33, YO, Senor Cielo Two, Valleyman, 9 started.
Pennsylvania Oaks, Philadelphia Park, Sept. 2, $75,000, 3yo, f, 1m 70y, 1:42.31, WILLIE'S LUV, Pupil, Pass the Virtue, 9 started.
Penny Ridge S., Stampede Park, June 16, $40,000, 3yo, f, 1⅟₁₆m, 1:44.60, SLY LADY, Slewpy Time, Brass to Diamonds, 5 started.
Pepper Oaks Farm S. (R), Hollywood Park, April 28, $60,000, 3&up, c&g, California-bred, a6½f, 1:16.51, PUBLIC DOMAIN, The Mobile Man, Lil Cooper, 8 started.
Peppy Addy S. (R), Philadelphia Park, June 1, $54,050, 3yo, Pennsylvania-bred, 7f, 1:24.64, FINAL TABLE, R B's Boy, Pal's Partner, 8 started.
Pepsi Cola H. (R), Sunland Park, Jan. 20, $103,600, 3yo, New Mexico-bred, 6f, 1:09.56, STAR SMASHER, Ninety Nine Jack, Bulletman Jack, 11 started.
Pepsi-Cola H., Emerald Downs, May 27, $45,000, 3yo, c&g, 6½f, 1:13.80, BOLD RANGER, Flying Notes, All in One, 5 started.
Perfect Arc S. (R), Aqueduct, Nov. 10, $100,000, 3&up, f&m, New York-bred, 1mT, 1:40.48, LOVELY AMANDA, Wootie, Dat You Miz Blue, 9 started.
Perryville S., Keeneland, Oct. 11, $84,075, 3yo, a7f, 1:26, NAJRAN, Flying Free, Premier Performer, 9 started.
PERSONAL ENSIGN H.-G1, Saratoga Race Course, Aug. 23, $400,000, 3&up, f&m, 1¼m, 2:03.15, SUMMER COLONY, Transcendental, Dancethruthedawn, 6 started.
Pete Axthelm H., Calder Race Course, Dec. 21, $100,000, 3yo, 7½fT, 1:29.28, STORMY ROMAN, Swift Replica, Miesque's Approval, 12 started.
Pete Condellone H. (R), Fairmount Park, Oct. 1, $35,700, 3&up, Illinois-bred, 1m, 1:38.20, BAKER ROAD, Moe B Dick, Multiple Metal, 6 started.
PETER PAN S.-G2, Belmont Park, May 25, $200,000, 3yo, 1⅛m, 1:48.10, SUNDAY BREAK (Jpn), Puzzlement, Deputy Dash, 7 started.
Phantom on Tour H., Calder Race Course, May 4, $38,255, 3&up, 1⅟₁₆m, 1:45.90, BEST OF THE REST, High Ideal, Dancing Guy, 7 started.
PHILADELPHIA PARK BREEDERS' CUP H.-G3, Philadelphia Park, July 6, $183,000, 3&up, 6f, 1:10.72, TRUE PASSION, Late Carson, Really Irish, 7 started.
Phil D. Shepherd S., Fairplex Park, Sept. 14, $49,500, 3&up, 1⅟₁₆m, 1:41.80, SIGFRETO, Most Likely (Arg), J. T.'s Song, 7 started.
PHILIP H. ISELIN H.-G2, Monmouth Park, Aug. 18, $350,000, 3&up, 1⅛m, 1:49.10, CAT'S AT HOME, Bowman's Band, Runspastum, 7 started.
PHOENIX BREEDERS' CUP S.-G3, Keeneland, Oct. 5, $250,000, 3&up, 6f, 1:10.13, XTRA HEAT, Day Trader, Touch Tone, 5 started.
Phoenix Gold Cup S., Turf Paradise, March 9, $100,000, 3&up, 6f, 1:08.39, QUINTON'S GOLD, Profound Secret, Rio Oro, 10 started.
Phoenix Leisure Thoroughbred Championship, Wyoming Downs, Aug. 18, $4,900, 3&up, 1m, 1:40.93, SHOTMO, Kalolo, Fadski, 6 started.
Phoenix S., The Meadowlands, Sept. 6, $50,000, 3&up, f&m, 5fT, :56.66, MERRY PRINCESS, Broad Victory, To Marquet, 10 started.
Piedmont S., Golden Gate Fields, Nov. 23, $71,000, 2yo, f, 6f, 1:10.52, GLOBAL FINANCE, Ain't It Sweep, Viansa Ossidiana, 7 started.
Piedra Foundation H. (R), Del Mar, Aug. 30, $75,625, 3&up, f&m, non-winners of $45,000 other than closed, claiming, or starter at one mile or over since February 1, 1m, 1:36.78, NETHERLAND (Arg), Printemps (Chi), Se Me Acabo (Chi), 5 started.
Pierce County H. (R), Emerald Downs, June 9, $35,000, 2yo, f, Washington-bred, 5f, FREEDOM MARCH, Marva Jean, Miss Mariah, 9 started.
Pilgrim S., Aqueduct, Oct. 27, $82,950, 2yo, 1⅛mT, 1:51, ONE COLONY, Celtic Memories, Blakelock, 5 started.
PIMLICO BREEDERS' CUP DISTAFF H.-G3, Pimlico, May 17, $148,500, 3&up, f&m, 1⅟₁₆m, 1:42.90, SUMMER COLONY, Dancethruthedawn, Happily Unbridled, 7 started.
Pinjara S. (R), Santa Anita Park, Oct. 24, $52,300, 2yo, non-winners of $40,000 other than closed or claiming at one mile or over, 1mT, 1:34.64, MAN AMONG MEN, Peace Rules, Gohalo, 8 started.
Pinon H. (R), The Downs at Albuquerque, April 7, $52,700, 3&up, f&m, New Mexico-bred, 6½f, 1:19.31, WAMPUS WHO, Fritzie's Prospect, Kham Beau, 8 started.
Pioneer S., Louisiana Downs, Aug. 11, $40,000, 2yo, 6f, 1:11.60, COMIC TRUTH, Crowned King, Imperial Editor, 6 started.
Pio Pico S. (R), Fairplex Park, Sept. 20, $50,000, 3&up, f&m, California-bred, 6½f, 1:16.86, WARREN'S WHISTLE, Always the Lady, Cinnful Bride, 8 started.
Pippin S., Oaklawn Park, Feb. 16, $50,000, 4&up, f&m, 1⅟₁₆m, 1:44.68, RED N'GOLD, Victory At Sea, Please Sign In, 7 started.
Pirate's Bounty S. (R), Del Mar, Sept. 7, $75,075, 3&up, non-winners of $50,000 since May 15, 6f, 1:09.26, AVANZADO (Arg), Rio Oro, Top Hit, 6 started.
Pistol Packer H. (R), Philadelphia Park, Aug. 17, $50,000, 3&up, f&m, Pennsylvania-bred, 7f, 1:23.68, BETTY'S HAT, Run for Joy, Golden Lake, 7 started.
Plate Trial S. (R), Woodbine, June 1, $170,400, 3yo, Canadian-bred, 1⅛m, 1:52.38, SHAWS CREEK, Classic Mike, Anglian Prince, 11 started.
PLAY THE KING H. (Can-G3), Woodbine, Aug. 17, $173,100, 3&up, 7fT, 1:20.42, ZONE JUDGE, Waltzin' Storm, Gone Fishin, 10 started.
Pleasanton S., Pleasanton, July 3, $45,240, 3yo, 1⅟₁₆m, 1:41.97, RIO'S CHASE, Bold Mango, Court's in Session, 6 started.
Pleasant Temper S. (1st Div.), Kentucky Downs, Sept. 14, $45,000, 3&up, f&m, 1mT, 1:36.92, ROSA'S DELAWARE, Verruma (Brz), Naturally Wild, 9 started.
Pleasant Temper S. (2nd Div.), Kentucky Downs, Sept. 14, $45,000, 3&up, f&m, 1mT, 1:36.72, ORNATE, Presumed Innocent, Pure Glitter, 10 started.
Plymouth S. (R), Great Lakes Downs, July 6, $45,000, 3yo, f, Michigan-bred, 7f, 1:26.92, BORN TO DANCE, Bad Thing, Baklava, 7 started.
Pocahontas S., Churchill Downs, Nov. 2, $111,100, 2yo, f, 1m, 1:36.52, BELLE OF PERINTOWN, Star of Atticus, Souris, 8 started.
POKER H.-G3, Belmont Park, July 5, $111,200, 3&up, 1mT, 1:32.24, VOLPONI, Saint Verre, Navesink, 7 started.
Politely S. (R), Laurel Park, Nov. 2, $60,000, 3yo, f, Maryland-bred, 7f, 1:22.62, WILLA ON THE MOVE, Gazillion, Phyxius, 7 started.
Politely S., Monmouth Park, June 9, $50,000, 3&up, f&m, 1mT, 1:37.11, CAUGHT OUT, Sluice, Clearly a Queen, 7 started.
Polly's Jet S., Delaware Park, July 15, $59,700, 3yo, f, a5fT, :57.69, LIBBY'S HALO, No Halos Here, Miss Atticus, 7 started.
Pomona Derby, Fairplex Park, Sept. 28, $100,000, 3yo, a1⅛m, 1:50.12, ASONG FOR BILLY, Splendid Times, Sunkosi, 10 started.
Ponca City S., Remington Park, Aug. 18, $30,450, 3yo, f, 6f, 1:10.60, SUPREME DISCOVERY, Frilly Fun, Idadidit, 8 started.
Ponche H., Calder Race Course, April 27, $75,000, 3&up, 6f, 1:11.12, FAPPIE'S NOTEBOOK, Notebook Computer, Callie and Jake, 6 started.
Pony Express S. (R), The Downs at Albuquerque, May 19, $33,000, 3&up, New Mexico-bred, 5½f, 1:03.94, RUNMORE MEMA, Thatsaknife, Wild Bill R, 7 started.
Possibly Perfect S., Arlington Park, July 4, $47,250, 3&up, f&m, a1⅛mT, 1:50.90, LADY OF PEACE, Applesolutely, Golden Antigua, 7 started.
Post Deb S., Monmouth Park, Aug. 18, $65,000, 3yo, f, 1⅟₁₆mT, 1:44.94, CAT ROCKET, Smart Grace, Smokeumifyougotem, 9 started.
POTRERO GRANDE BREEDERS' CUP H.-G2, Santa Anita Park, March 30, $197,700, 4&up, 6½f, 1:15.31, KALOOKAN QUEEN, Ceeband, Elaborate, 8 started.
Powder Break S. (1st Div.), Calder Race Course, April 26, $34,025, 3&up, f&m, 1⅟₁₆mT, 1:42.86, GUILLOTINE, Kelly Bag, Tiffish, 7 started.
Powder Break S. (2nd Div.), Calder Race Course, April 26, $37,905, 3&up, f&m, 1⅟₁₆mT, 1:42.15, SEPTIETTA, Wander Mom, Platinum Tiara, 7 started.
Powerless S. (R), Hawthorne Race Course, Nov. 9, $96,200, 3&up, f&m, Illinois-bred, 6f, 1:12.11, TEJANO HONEY, Win Won, Come September, 11 started.
Prairie Bayou H., Turfway Park, Dec. 21, $41,500, 3&up, 1⅛m, 1:52.81, HORRIBLE EVENING, Dumaani of Course, Mail Call, 6 started.
Prairie Gold Juvenile S., Prairie Meadows, July 4, $60,000, 2yo, 5f, :57.35, BLACKJACK BOY, Fly Honor Fly, Ruby's Reception, 9 started.
Prairie Gold Lassie S., Prairie Meadows, July 3, $60,000, 2yo, f, 5f, :57.49, ADOPTED DAUGHTER, Goldleafed Mirror, Magical Tabitha, 8 started.
Prairie Lily Sales S. (R), Marquis Downs, Aug. 31, $30,996, 2yo,

sold at a CTHS sale, a7f, 1:29.25, PICTURE THE ANSWER, Stop the Act, She's Nifty, 8 started.

PRAIRIE MEADOWS CORNHUSKER BREEDERS' CUP H.-G3, Prairie Meadows, July 6, $400,000, 3&up, 1⅛m, 1:47.97, MR. JOHN, Unshaded, Fajardo, 10 started.

Prairie Meadows Debutante S., Prairie Meadows, Sept. 27, $52,500, 2yo, f, 6f, 1:10.68, TULUPAI, Onda Ray, Coding, 9 started.

Prairie Meadows Derby, Prairie Meadows, Sept. 21, $82,500, 3yo, 1⅛m, 1:48.42, ROBIN ZEE, Cowboy Stuff, Windward Passage, 10 started.

Prairie Meadows Freshman S., Prairie Meadows, Sept. 28, $51,250, 2yo, 6f, 1:10.42, SHANDY, Oneofthebirdboys, Jack Black and Ice, 8 started.

Prairie Meadows H., Prairie Meadows, Aug. 10, $110,000, 3&up, 1⅛m, 1:48.82, WOODMOON, Take Me Up, Halo Kris, 6 started.

Prairie Meadows Oaks, Prairie Meadows, Sept. 2, $75,000, 3yo, f, 1¹⁄₁₆m, 1:45.75, ULUVITNUNOIT, See How She Runs, Tejano Honey, 6 started.

Prairie Meadows Sprint S., Prairie Meadows, Sept. 14, $44,000, 3&up, 6f, 1:09.52, SAND RIDGE, Le Numerous, Majorbigtimesheet, 7 started.

Prairie Mile S., Prairie Meadows, June 15, $62,400, 3yo, 1m, 1:37.43, MISSME, Vito Corleone, Cowboy Stuff, 6 started.

Prairie Rose S., Prairie Meadows, May 11, $61,375, 3&up, f&m, 6f, 1:09.54, TRISHA RUNS, Princess Jen, Soul Onarazorsedge, 6 started.

PREAKNESS S.-G1, Pimlico, May 18, $1,000,000, 3yo, 1³⁄₁₆m, 1:56.36, WAR EMBLEM, Magic Weisner, Proud Citizen, 13 started.

Precisionist H., Prairie Meadows, June 1, $100,000, 3&up, 1¹⁄₁₆m, 1:41.65, MC MAHON, E Z Glory, Halo Kris, 6 started.

Prelude S., Louisiana Downs, Aug. 31, $50,000, 3yo, 1¹⁄₁₆m, 1:45.17, GLITZI'S CLASSIC, Walk in the Snow, De Real Deal, 10 started.

Premiere S. (R), Lone Star Park, April 4, $50,000, 3&up, Texas-bred, 1m, 1:38.25, LIGHTS ON BROADWAY, Won C C, Captain Countdown, 6 started.

Premier S., Arapahoe Park, July 7, $30,000, 3yo, 7f, 1:24, RAISE A BOOGER, Gone With the Win, Jetson, 6 started.

PREMIER'S H. (Can-G3), Hastings Park Racecourse, Oct. 20, $108,235, 3&up, 1⅜m, 2:16.92, SHACANE, Futural, Rim Dancer, 6 started.

President's Cup H., Lincoln State Fair, June 9, $10,480, 3&up, 6f, 1:10.80, TY MAN, Sturmovik, High Dice, 6 started.

Primal S., Calder Race Course, May 21, $38,080, 3yo, a1¹⁄₁₆m, 1:46.50, ROCKER, Puck, Juggernaut, 6 started.

Primer S., Laurel Park, Dec. 7, $40,000, 2yo, 6f, 1:08.98, CRAFTY GUY, Gators N Bears, Gimmeawink, 8 started.

Primonetta S., Pimlico, April 6, $50,000, 3&up, f&m, 6f, 1:11.57, ARIANNA'S PASSION, Lip Sing's Affair, Kimbralata, 6 started.

Prince of Wales S. (R), Fort Erie, July 21, $500,000, 3yo, Canadian-bred, 1³⁄₁₆m, 1:56.53, LE CINQUIEME ESSAI, Bravely, Anglian Prince, 12 started.

Princess Elaine S. (R), Canterbury Park, July 7, $36,875, 3&up, f&m, Minnesota-bred, a1¹⁄₁₆mT, 1:47.42, CLASSIC NIX, Pickin the Pace, Aashu, 8 started.

Princess Elizabeth S. (R), Woodbine, Oct. 13, $250,000, 2yo, f, Canadian-bred, 1¹⁄₁₆m, 1:49.49, KABEEB, Mountain Dawn, Santerra, 8 started.

Princess Margaret S., Northlands Park, Aug. 2, $40,000, 2yo, f, 6f, 1:12, RAYLENE, Whataweekend, Grand Slam Gal, 9 started.

Princess of Palms H., Turf Paradise, Jan. 19, $30,000, 4&up, f&m, 6f, 1:09.35, DIANEHILL (Ire), Crown Connection, Purls Ledgend, 8 started.

PRINCESS ROONEY H.-G2, Calder Race Course, July 13, $400,000, 3&up, f&m, 6f, 1:10.21, GOLD MOVER, Xtra Heat, Fly Me Crazy, 6 started.

Princess S., Sunland Park, Nov. 22, $54,450, 2yo, f, 6f, 1:11.54, VALID PULPIT, Miss Trixie, Silk N Diamonds, 10 started.

Princess S., Lincoln State Fair, May 18, $10,320, 3yo, f, 6f, 1:12, MAGIC TRUMP, Flaming Night, Hawaiian Lullaby, 6 started.

Princeton S., The Meadowlands, Oct. 4, $50,000, 3yo, 1mT, 1:37.04, THEFULL CIRCLE, Political Attack, Cohoma, 10 started.

PRIORESS S.-G1, Belmont Park, July 6, $200,000, 3yo, f, 6f, 1:08.79, CARSON HOLLOW, Spring Meadow, Proper Gamble, 7 started.

Prismatical S., The Meadowlands, Sept. 2, $50,000, 3&up, f&m, 1m 70y, 1:41.09, UNRESTRAINED, Run for Joy, Lily's Affair, 7 started.

Private Terms S., Suffolk Downs, Jan. 26, $30,000, 4&up, 6f, 1:13.14, GOODBAR, Esteemed Friend, Yasou a Team, 8 started.

Private Terms S., Laurel Park, March 30, $50,000, 3yo, 1⅛m, 1:51.15, MAGIC WEISNER, The Sewickley Kid, Root With Style, 5 started.

Pro or Con H. (R), Santa Anita Park, Feb. 2, $125,000, 4&up, f&m, California-bred, 1mT, 1:35.89, TA TA BE TRUE, Super Tuesday, Stetson Lady, 7 started.

Proud Puppy H., Finger Lakes, July 6, $35,000, 3&up, f&m, 6f, 1:11.38, FOLLY DOLLAR, Double the Debt, Belongs to Mony, 8 started.

Providencia S. (R), Santa Anita Park, April 13, $82,500, 3yo, f, non-winners of a race worth $50,000 to the winner at one mile or over in 2002, 1⅛mT, 1:47.34, MEGAHERTZ (GB), La Martina (GB), Ayzal (GB), 7 started.

PUCKER UP S.-G3, Arlington Park, Sept. 14, $150,000, 3yo, f, 1⅛mT, 1:49.92, LITTLE TREASURE (Fr), Cellars Shiraz, Kathy K D, 11 started.

Punch Line S. (R), Colonial Downs, June 22, $40,000, 3&up, Virginia-bred, 5fT, :55.85, BOP, Scootin' Girl, Kim, 10 started.

Purple Violet S. (R), Arlington Park, June 22, $86,750, 3yo, f, Illinois bred, 1m, 1:36.19, SUMMER MIS, Tejano Honey, Westend Tapper, 11 started.

Puss N Boots S. (R), Fort Erie, Sept. 2, $67,600, 3&up, starters at Fort Erie at least twice in 2002, 1¹⁄₁₆mT, 1:41.85, GET DOWN WOLFIE, Divine Luck, Private Oasis, 12 started.

Queen City Oaks (R), River Downs, July 27, $100,000, 3yo, f, Ohio-bred, 1⅛m, 1:55.40, KIND OF FUN, Come Hither, Crypto's Twinjet, 8 started.

QUEEN ELIZABETH II CHALLENGE CUP S.-G1 (R), Keeneland, Oct. 12, $500,000, 3yo, f, by invitation, 1⅛mT, 1:49.84, RISKAVERSE, Zenda (GB), Lush Soldier, 9 started.

Queen of the Green H., Turf Paradise, Nov. 23, $50,000, 3&up, f&m, 1mT, 1:37.07, DOUBLE CAT, Polaire (Ire), Moonlit Maddie, 10 started.

Queen S., Turfway Park, March 23, $53,500, 4&up, f&m, 6f, 1:10.78, SENORITA ZIGGY, Enchanted Woods, City Fair, 10 started.

QUEENS COUNTY H.-G3, Aqueduct, Dec. 7, $110,000, 3&up, 1³⁄₁₆m, 1:56.84, SNAKE MOUNTAIN, Docent, Cat's At Home, 7 started.

Queen's H., Horsemen's Park, July 20, $30,000, 3&up, f&m, 6f, 1:11.20, MISS GUTS, Nancybdancing, Iknowhowtodance, 5 started.

Queen's Plate S. (R), Woodbine, June 23, $1,000,000, 3yo, Canadian-bred, 1¼m, 2:06.88, T J'S LUCKY MOON, Anglian Prince, Forever Grand, 13 started.

Queenston S. (R), Woodbine, May 4, $168,150, 3yo, Canadian-bred, 7f, 1:23.46, SHAWS CREEK, Embattle, Rare Friends, 10 started.

Quicken Tree S. (R), Hollywood Park, April 28, $100,000, 4&up, California-bred, 1½mT, 2:26.66, ADMINNIESTRATOR, Turkish Prize, Our Main Man, 8 started.

Quick Step H. (R), Thistledown, May 11, $40,000, 3&up, Ohio-bred, 6f, 1:10.34, WAIST GUNNER JOHN, Down Thepike Mike, Count On My Word, 8 started.

Quill S., Delaware Park, Aug. 27, $60,300, 3&up, f&m, 1mT, 1:37.01, LADY OF THE FUTURE, Shag, Sandra's Song, 7 started.

Racino Inaugural S., Delta Downs, Nov. 7, $40,000, 3&up, 5f, :58.71, BELIEVE IM SPECIAL, Front Nine, Gracie's Dancer, 7 started.

Ragaey Island S., Ellis Park, July 20, $60,000, 3yo, 1¹⁄₁₆mT, 1:44.97, MISSME, Entitlement, Minerveeni, 8 started.

RAILBIRD S.-G3, Hollywood Park, May 18, $106,300, 3yo, f, 7f, 1:22.95, SEPTEMBER SECRET, Affairs of State, Fun House, 5 started.

Rainbow Connection S. (R), Fort Erie, July 16, $125,000, 3&up, f&m, progeny of eligible Ontario stallions, 5fT, BUBBI TRAP, Sports Flashy, Guysmarlene, 8 started.

Rainbow Miss S. (R), Oaklawn Park, March 30, $58,000, 3yo, f, Arkansas-bred, 6f, 1:12.26, SUPREME DISCOVERY, Humble Billie, Magical Miss, 8 started.

Rainbow S. (R), Oaklawn Park, March 30, $61,000, 3yo, c&g, Arkansas-bred, 6f, 1:12.06, PERFECT FANTASY, Snowball King, My Good Trick, 11 started.

Ralph Hayes H. (R), Prairie Meadows, Aug. 31, $81,200, 4&up, c&g, Iowa-bred, 1¹⁄₁₆m, 1:44.21, TAKE ME UP, Le Numerous, D. W. Wheels, 10 started.

Ralph M. Hinds Pomona Invitational H., Fairplex Park, Sept. 29, $100,000, 3&up, a1⅛m, 1:49.82, REBA'S GOLD, Nates Colony, Sigfreto, 8 started.

RAMPART H.-G2, Gulfstream Park, March 2, $200,000, 3&up, f&m, 1⅛m, 1:49.83, FOREST SECRETS, Summer Colony, Happily Unbridled, 6 started.

RANCHO BERNARDO H.-G3, Del Mar, Aug. 25, $150,000, 3&up, f&m, 6½f, 1:16.40, KALOOKAN QUEEN, Warren's Whistle, Fancee Bargain, 5 started.

RARE TREAT H.-G3, Aqueduct, Feb. 18, $108,600, 3&up, f&m, 1⅛m, 1:49.94, PEOPLE'S PRINCESS, Pocus Hocus, A. O. L. Hayes, 7 started.

Rattlesnake S., Turf Paradise, Jan. 13, $30,000, 3yo, 1m, 1:36.52, LUSTY LATIN, Jetson, Mr. Greedy, 10 started.
RAVEN RUN S.-G3, Keeneland, Oct. 9, $171,900, 3yo, f, 7f, 1:23.98, SIGHTSEEK, Miss Lodi, Respectful, 12 started.
Raymond Ambulance Spring Sprint S., Lethbridge, May 25, $8,550, 3&up, 5½f, 1:11.40, SAGREENO, Stag, Obby Be Good, 7 started.
Raymond G. Woolfe Memorial Hurdle S., Camden, Nov. 17, $25,000, 3yo, a2mT, 4:14.20, COAL DUST, Astaires Tipallade, Pals Pride, 7 started.
Razorback Futurity (R), Louisiana Downs, Nov. 3, $25,000, 2yo, c&g, Arkansas-bred, 6f, 1:13.20, QUOTE ME LATER, Redcuda, Humble Bob, 11 started.
RAZORBACK H.-G3, Oaklawn Park, March 16, $100,000, 4&up, 1 1/16m, 1:44.13, MR ROSS, Remington Rock, Big Numbers, 8 started.
R. C. Anderson S. (R), Assiniboia Downs, July 5, $30,000, 3yo, f, Canadian-bred, 1m, 1:42.40, BASHFUL DANCER, What Four, Dar You Go, 8 started.
Real Delight S., Arlington Park, July 20, $63,500, 3yo, f, 7f, 1:22.13, FOR RUBIES, Smoke Chaser, Cordoba, 6 started.
Real Good Deal S. (R), Del Mar, Aug. 12, $100,000, 3yo, California-bred non-winners of $50,000 twice, 7f, 1:22.44, HOT WAR, Black Bart, Modernist, 8 started.
Rebel S., Louisiana Downs, Aug. 4, $40,000, 2yo, f, 6f, 1:12.35, HADIF'S ALLSTAR, Princess Birdeye, Rubies N Roses, 6 started.
REBEL S.-G3, Oaklawn Park, March 23, $100,000, 3yo, 1 1/16m, 1:45.06, WINDWARD PASSAGE, Ocean Sound (Ire), Dusty Spike, 8 started.
Reb's Policy S., Santa Anita Park, Feb. 27, $84,100, 4&up, a6½fT, 1:12.40, CASEY GRIFFIN, Devine Wind, Lake William, 9 started.
Record Dash H., Calder Race Course, Oct. 20, $42,345, 3&up, 6f, 1:11.18, ROYAL LAD, Sweeping Smoke, Notebook Computer, 6 started.
RED BANK H.-G3, Monmouth Park, May 25, $100,000, 3&up, 1mT, 1:35.92, KEY LORY, Sardaukar (GB), Spruce Run, 8 started.
Red Bud H., Blue Ribbon Downs, April 28, $7,750, 3&up, f&m, 5½f, 1:04.68, BLONDE OKIE, Kyle's Cruiser, Dat's Afterburner, 9 started.
Red Camelia H. (R), Fair Grounds, March 25, $100,000, 4&up, f&m, Louisiana-bred, a1mT, 1:38.21, MYSIA JO, Eastern Sun, Autobesarah, 13 started.
Red Diamond Express S. (R), Northlands Park, Sept. 21, $40,000, 3&up, Alberta-bred, 6½f, 1:16.60, TYKO TYCOON, Timely Ruckus, Sixthirtyjoe, 7 started.
Red Dog S., Delaware Park, Aug. 20, $57,900, 3&up, 1 1/16m, 1:44.87, CONFUCIUS SAY, Marciano, Jarf, 5 started.
Red Earth Derby (R), Remington Park, Sept. 28, $30,000, 3yo, Oklahoma-bred, 1mT, 1:37.06, RED HAWKEYE, Blazin Sunrise, Coldiron Slew, 10 started.
Red Hedeman Mile S. (R), Sunland Park, Nov. 30, $131,250, 2yo, New Mexico-bred, 1m, 1:39.83, TORNADOS JACK, Lendl's Ghost, Stormy Lane, 10 started.
RED SMITH H.-G3, Aqueduct, Nov. 23, $150,000, 3&up, 1 3/8m, 2:14.81, EVENING ATTIRE, Fisher Pond, Pleasant Breeze, 6 started.
Redwood Empire S., Santa Rosa, Aug. 4, $46,990, 2yo, 5½f, 1:03.55, MR. TECHNIQUE, Taraval, Bang, 7 started.
Regal Rumor S., Hawthorne Race Course, Nov. 30, $44,200, 3&up, f&m, 6f, 1:12.06, WIN WON, Abba Gold, Sharky's Review, 10 started.
Regions Bank Imperial Cup Hurdle S., Aiken, March 23, $23,400, 4&up, a2¼mT, 4:20.20, P. C. PLOD, Devil's Reach, Electron, 3 started.
Regret S., Monmouth Park, Aug. 18, $65,000, 3&up, f&m, 6f, 1:09.63, TO MARQUET, Mary's Nickle, City Fair, 8 started.
REGRET S.-G3, Churchill Downs, June 15, $169,050, 3yo, f, 1 1/16mT, 1:42.71, DISTANT VALLEY (GB), Peace River Lady, Stylelistick, 9 started.
Regret S. (R), Great Lakes Downs, June 15, $45,000, 3yo, f, Michigan-bred, 6f, 1:13.57, BORN TO DANCE, Bad Thing, Sweetwater Promise, 7 started.
Reign Dance H., Calder Race Course, Sept. 9, $43,675, 3&up, f&m, 5f, :57.79, FLYING BIRDIE, Sara's Success, Alleycat Coat, 8 started.
Relaunch S. (R), Del Mar, Aug. 16, $67,900, 3yo, non-winners of $3,000 twice other than maiden, claiming, or starter or for a claiming price of $80,000, 1mT, 1:35.57, DELL PLACE, Ridley (Ire), Dream Machine (Fr), 8 started.
Reloy H., Santa Anita Park, Feb. 1, $79,100, 4&up, f&m, 1¼mT, 2:00.42, DESIRAES MY CANDY, Dispersed Reward, Tropical Lady (Brz), 7 started.
Reluctant Guest S., Arlington Park, Aug. 16, $63,750, 3&up, f&m, a1 1/16mT, 1:45.02, LADY OF PEACE, Curious Conundrum, Histoire Sainte (Fr), 7 started.
Remington Green S., Remington Park, Nov. 16, $30,775, 3&up, 1 1/16mT, 1:44.26, ZEE OH SIX, Amazon Ace, Jeb's Honor, 8 started.
Remington MEC Mile S., Remington Park, Dec. 1, $75,000, 2yo, 1m, 1:39.23, SHAWKLIT MAN, Skamper, Kickin Kountry, 9 started.
REMSEN S.-G2, Aqueduct, Nov. 30, $200,000, 2yo, 1⅛m, 1:50.40, TOCCET, Bham, Empire Maker, 8 started.
Retama Turf Cup H., Retama Park, Aug. 10, $50,000, 3&up, 1 1/16mT, 1:44.61, CHAUFFE AU ROUGE, Rasby, Kris Havingfunnow, 11 started.
Revidere S., Monmouth Park, May 25, $50,000, 3yo, f, 1mT, 1:37.30, ONCE AROUND, Affirmed Dancer, Midnite Deelite, 8 started.
Rhododendron S., Charles Town, June 22, $37,300, 3yo, f, 7f, 1:28.06, PASS THE VIRTUE, Shesanothergrump, Simon Slew, 10 started.
Richard King H. (R), Sam Houston Race Park, Nov. 16, $50,000, 3&up, Texas-bred, 1⅛mT, 1:54.29, STAR OF CAVEAT, Paco Loco, D C Storm, 9 started.
Richmond Derby Trial H., Hastings Park Racecourse, Sept. 1, $39,049, 3yo, 1 1/16m, 1:45.54, SHACANE, Silver Donn, Bold 'n Keen, 5 started.
Richmond H., Golden Gate Fields, Feb. 16, $59,163, 3&up, f&m, 6f, 1:09.48, HALL OF GOLD, Bullish Miss, Selector, 7 started.
Richmond S. (R), Hoosier Park, Nov. 10, $42,500, 3&up, f&m, Indiana-bred, 1 1/16m, 1:47.56, MAGGIE'S DREAM, Amanda's Crown, Bette, 6 started.
Ricks Memorial S., Remington Park, Sept. 15, $30,450, 3&up, f&m, 1mT, 1:38.24, STRAWBAILEY, Devout Sinner, Islay Mist (GB), 10 started.
Riley Allison Derby, Sunland Park, March 31, $77,100, 3yo, 1 1/16m, 1:42.64, FORTY NINE DEEDS, Star Smasher, Army General, 6 started.
Riley Allison Futurity, Sunland Park, Dec. 29, $161,761, 2yo, 6½f, 1:15.43, SUM TRICK, Double Intrigue, Seneca Prowler, 9 started.
Rio Grande Senor Futurity (R), Ruidoso Downs, July 14, $79,149, 2yo, c&g, New Mexico-bred, 5½f, 1:04.20, QUOTE THIS, Tornados Jack, Jackberun, 10 started.
Rio Grande Senorita Futurity (R), Ruidoso Downs, July 14, $80,539, 2yo, f, New Mexico-bred, 5½f, 1:05.80, SHEMOVESLIKEAGHOST, Out of Focus, Sweet Share, 10 started.
Rise Jim S. (R), Suffolk Downs, April 6, $30,000, 3&up, Massachusetts-bred, 6f, 1:13.66, JINI'S JET, Al Bark, Dawn's First Light, 7 started.
RISEN STAR S.-G3, Fair Grounds, Feb. 17, $150,000, 3yo, 1 1/16m, 1:43.17, REPENT, Bob's Image, Easyfromthegitgo, 9 started.
RIVA RIDGE S.-G2, Belmont Park, June 8, $190,000, 3yo, 7f, 1:22.61, GYGISTAR, Draw Play, True Direction, 9 started.
River Cities Breeders' Cup S., Louisiana Downs, Sept. 7, $131,250, 3&up, f&m, a1 1/16mT, 1:42.65, BIEN NICOLE, Due to Win Again, Wild Squaw, 7 started.
RIVER CITY H.-G3, Churchill Downs, Nov. 17, $175,650, 3&up, 1⅛mT, 1:51.44, DR. KASHNIKOW, Foster's Landing, Roxinho (Brz), 11 started.
River Memories S., Woodbine, Nov. 3, $114,000, 3&up, f&m, 1mT, 1:36.89, BYZANTINE, Strait From Texas, Love Kiss, 13 started.
R. J. Speers S., Assiniboia Downs, Sept. 14, $30,000, 3&up, 1 1/16m, 1:46.60, SIR PUCKER, Deputy Country, Victorious Type, 8 started.
Road Runner H. (R), Ruidoso Downs, July 14, $42,000, 3yo, New Mexico-bred, 5½f, 1:04, STAR SMASHER, How Bout Now, Hot Shot Hoolie, 10 started.
Roamin Rachel S., Calder Race Course, Sept. 5, $42,310, 3yo, f, 6½f, 1:17.94, CHISPISKI, Sea Span, Eltisha, 6 started.
ROBERT F. CAREY MEMORIAL H.-G3, Hawthorne Race Course, Nov. 2, $150,000, 3&up, 1mT, 1:35.94, KIMBERLITE PIPE, Aslaaf, Major Omansky, 10 started.
Robert G. Dick Memorial Breeders' Cup S., Delaware Park, July 20, $146,000, 3&up, f&m, 1⅜mT, 2:17.78, NEW ECONOMY, Rhum, Septietta, 10 started.
Robert G. Leavitt Memorial S. (R), Charles Town, Aug. 10, $36,300, 3yo, West Virginia-bred, 7f, 1:28.39, ADAMS TRIBE, Shesanothergrump, Shark Eye, 7 started.
Robert K. Kerlan Memorial S., Hollywood Park, June 19, $75,600, 3&up, 5½fT, 1:01.37, BLU AIR FORCE (Ire), Astonished (GB), Rocky Bar, 6 started.
Robert R. Hilton Memorial S. (R), Charles Town, Sept. 14, $31,100, 3&up, nominated to the West Virginia Breeders' Classic, 7f, 1:27.07, TURBOTAXMAN, Rebellious Dreamer, Coolmars, 10 started.
Rocket Man S., Calder Race Course, July 13, $50,000, 2&up, 2f, :20.81, BABY SHARK, Kelly's Hero, Roy's Ruckus, 8 started.
Rocking Chair Derby, Lethbridge, Oct. 14, $4,550, 3&up, 5½f, 1:07.80, IT'S ALL A BLURR, Bad Toda Bone, Don Coronaige, 7 started.
Rocking Chair S., Grants Pass, July 4, $3,040, 8 yo's & up, 6½f, 1:23.80, LEFTY MCSLEW, Mr One Ring, Wanham, 4 started.

Rockingham Breeders' Cup H., Rockingham Park, July 4, $75,000, 3&up, f&m, 1 1/16mT, 1:44.93, STYLISH, Sword Princess, Step With Style, 6 started.
Rockingham Park Derby, Rockingham Park, July 7, $25,000, 3yo, 1 1/16m, 1:46.14, DEVIL'S ZONE, Slippery Gator, All Line, 7 started.
Rockingham Park Distaff H., Rockingham Park, July 6, $25,000, 3&up, f&m, 6f, 1:12.51, LUCKY PAWS, Guess, Houston Pro, 8 started.
Rockingham Park Oaks, Rockingham Park, June 29, $25,000, 3yo, f, 1 1/16mT, 1:46.12, HIGH MAINTENANCE (GB), Nannie's Sword, Little Time, 8 started.
Rockingham Park Sprint H., Rockingham Park, July 20, $25,000, 3&up, 6f, 1:09.78, ESTEEMED FRIEND, Danielles Magic, Method Man, 6 started.
Rocky Mountain Futurity, Wyoming Downs, Aug. 17, $9,050, 2yo, 5f,.68, APPEALING WAYZ, Te Dusty Prospect, T E Prospect Creek, 6 started.
Roger Van Hoozer Memorial S. (R), Charles Town, Sept. 14, $31,000, 3&up, f&m, nominated to the West Virginia Breeders' Classic, 7f, 1:27.21, SWEET ANNUITY, Spanishinquisition, Longfield Star, 8 started.
Rollicking S. (R), Laurel Park, Oct. 14, $60,000, 2yo, Maryland-bred, 7f, 1:24.19, BRIDGE OUT AGAIN, Cherokee's Boy, Pud, 5 started.
Rollin On Over S. (R), Beulah Park, April 13, $40,000, 3yo, Ohio-bred, 6f, 1:09.76, COUNT ON MY WORD, Nate's Rib, T J My Man, 10 started.
Roman Brother S. (R), Calder Race Course, July 20, $50,000, 3yo, progeny of eligible Florida stallions, 1 1/16mT, 1:46.01, ISLAND SKIPPER, Sebastian Light, Thiscannonsloaded, 8 started.
Roman Colonel S., Fairmount Park, July 4, $25,600, 3yo, c&g, 6f, 1:12.20, BULLDOG GEORGE, Canyon de Oro, Little Joe Tubb, 5 started.
Ron and Jasmine Cloud Memorial S., Fresno, Oct. 5, $102,990, 2yo, 6f, 1:07.70, OMEGA CODE, Smokin Mike, Seemore Seemore, 9 started.
Ropersandwranglers S., Emerald Downs, April 19, $24,999, 4&up, f&m, 6f, 1:09.20, ROLLETTE, Whatdidshesay, Silky Secret, 10 started.
Rose DeBartolo Memorial S. (R), Thistledown, July 20, $75,000, 3&up, f&m, Ohio-bred, 1 1/8m, 1:53.36, ASHWOOD C C, Lady Cherie, Crypto Cream, 6 started.
Rosenna S., Delaware Park, June 8, $76,500, 3&up, f&m, 1 1/16mT, 1:42.78, RHUM, Morena Park (GB), De Aar, 10 started.
Round Table H., Bay Meadows, June 9, $56,988, 3yo, 1mT, 1:35.24, CAPPUCHINO, Mananan McLir, Blue Slew's Shoes, 6 started.
Round Table S., Arlington Park, July 27, $100,000, 3yo, 1 1/8m, 1:48.98, COWBOY STUFF, Pass Rush, A. P. Five Hundred, 9 started.
Route 66 S. (R), Fair Meadows at Tulsa, June 29, $42,875, 3&up, Oklahoma-bred, 6 1/2f, 1:18, DANCE AND DAZZLE, Hedorunrun, College Dean, 8 started.
Royal Chase for the Sport of Kings S., Keeneland, April 26, $169,958, 4&up, a2 1/2mT, 4:39.42, IT'S A GIGGLE, Al Skywalker, Flat Top, 7 started.
ROYAL HEROINE S.-G3, Hollywood Park, July 6, $114,800, 3&up, f&m, 1mT, 1:34.73, SURYA, Angel Gift, Reine de Romance (Ire), 12 started.
ROYAL NORTH S. (Can-G3), Woodbine, Aug. 3, $164,550, 3&up, f&m, 6fT, 1:09.53, QUICK BLUE, Mysterious Affair, Marisa Go, 6 started.
Royal North S. (R), Beulah Park, April 7, $40,000, 3yo, f, Ohio-bred, 6f, 1:13.73, R NURSE C, Saratoga Set, Ya Lateefah, 9 started.
R. R. M. Carpenter Jr. Memorial S., Delaware Park, July 20, $100,600, 3&up, 1 1/16m, 1:42.97, BOWMAN'S BAND, Grundlefoot, Runspastum, 7 started.
Rudy Baez S., Suffolk Downs, March 23, $30,000, 3yo, 1m, 1:39.43, STYLISH SULTAN, Method Man, B. W. Beetle, 8 started.
RUFFIAN H.-G1, Belmont Park, Sept. 14, $300,000, 3&up, f&m, 1 1/16m, 1:42.57, MANDY'S GOLD, You, Shine Again, 5 started.
Ruffian S., Arapahoe Park, July 21, $30,000, 3yo, f, 7f, 1:24, DEVILINBLUEDENIM, Russian Olive, Fool's Mate, 10 started.
Ruffian S., Fairmount Park, July 6, $24,480, 3yo, f, 6f, 1:12.80, TEJANO HONEY, Tricky Surprise, Jiroga Lite, 4 started.
Ruff/Kirchberg Memorial H. (R), Beulah Park, Nov. 23, $45,000, 3&up, Ohio-bred, 1 1/4m, 2:08.33, SCOUT ME, Lady Cherie, Heat Seeker, 6 started.
Ruidoso Derby, Ruidoso Downs, Sept. 1, $27,200, 3yo, 1 1/16m, 1:46, SNEAKER MIKE, Co Twining Niner, Stormy Forever, 11 started.
Ruidoso Mile H., Ruidoso Downs, Aug. 11, $26,400, 3&up, 1m, 1:39, CALIBAN, Tahoe Affair, Lesters Boy, 7 started.
Ruidoso Oaks, Ruidoso Downs, July 27, $24,500, 3yo, f, 6f, 1:12.20, DEVIOUS WAYS, Prairie Fire, Scifi Flick, 10 started.
Ruidoso Thoroughbred Championship, Ruidoso Downs, Sept. 2, $36,600, 3&up, 1 1/16m, 1:45.60, TAHOE AFFAIR, Caliban, Mr. Excitement, 8 started.
Ruidoso Thoroughbred Futurity, Ruidoso Downs, Sept. 2, $64,885, 2yo, 6f, 1:10.80, ROLL HENNESSY ROLL, Double Intrigue, Sa Moken, 8 started.
Rumson S., Monmouth Park, Aug. 18, $65,000, 3yo, 6f, 1:09.35, OUR WILDCAT, Outstander, Calends, 7 started.
Runza H., Fonner Park, March 30, $16,570, 3&up, f&m, 6f, 1:13.40, LADY J, Burning Memories, Irish Flyer, 10 started.
Rushaway S., Turfway Park, March 23, $98,000, 3yo, 1 1/16m, 1:42.90, MR. MELLON, Wild Horses, Derby Drive, 8 started.
Rushing Man S., The Meadowlands, Sept. 13, $100,000, 3yo, 1 1/16mT, 1:39.60, PATROL, Thefull Circle, Entitlement, 8 started.
Rustic Ruler S., Hawthorne Race Course, May 31, $47,750, 3yo, 6 1/2f, 1:17.50, GOLD TAKER, Medlin Road, Robin Zee, 5 started.
Ruth C. Funkhouser S. (R), Charles Town, Sept. 21, $30,900, 3yo, f, nominated to the West Virginia Breeders' Classic, 7f, 1:28.92, CONFEDERATECHATTER, Shesanothergrump, Keys for Chris, 7 started.
Ruthless S., Aqueduct, Jan. 6, $76,945, 3yo, f, 6f, 1:10.82, NICE BOOTS BABY, Proper Gamble, Al Max Diner, 4 started.
SABIN H.-G3, Gulfstream Park, Feb. 8, $100,000, 3&up, f&m, 1 1/16m, 1:42.61, MISS LINDA (Arg), Forest Secrets, Tap Dance, 12 started.
Sacramento H., Golden Gate Fields, March 2, $55,750, 3&up, f&m, 1m, 1:36.01, SECRET LIAISON, De Goddaughter, Princess Vye, 11 started.
Sadie Diamond Futurity (R), Hastings Park Racecourse, Sept. 28, $106,135, 2yo, f, Canadian-bred, 6 1/2f, 1:18.67, AQUITA, Dee's Love, Chorus Dancer, 11 started.
Sadie Hawkins S. (R), Charles Town, Aug. 17, $36,800, 3&up, f&m, West Virginia-bred, 7f, 1:27.36, WHO'S YA MAMA, Spanishinquisition, Shesanothergrump, 10 started.
Safely Kept H., Fairmount Park, July 12, $25,700, 4&up, f&m, 6f, 1:12.80, DENTONS RUBY, Feminine Fury, Little Mo, 6 started.
Safely Kept H., Arlington Park, Oct. 26, $100,000, 3&up, f&m, 7f, 1:22.70, GOLD MOVER, Oglala Sue, Victory At Sea, 5 started.
Safely Kept H., Hollywood Park, Nov. 17, $76,970, 3&up, f&m, 5 1/2fT, 1:03.01, ROLLY POLLY (Ire), Wild Tickle, Harvest Girl, 5 started.
SAFELY KEPT S.-G3, Pimlico, Sept. 14, $100,000, 3yo, f, 6f, 1:11.20, MISS LODI, For Rubies, Wilzada, 8 started.
Saguaro S., Turf Paradise, Sept. 28, $30,000, 3yo, 6f, 1:10.41, DUDDLY DOO RUN, Four Corners, Rich Musique, 7 started.
Sail On By S., Turf Paradise, Nov. 6, $22,700, 2yo, 6f, 1:09.52, DEPUTY DOC, Icy Tobin, Aye Chihuahua, 6 started.
Salem County S., The Meadowlands, Oct. 4, $50,000, 2yo, f, 1mT, 1:38.52, OCEAN DRIVE, Little Miss Pamela, Civility Cat, 11 started.
SALVATOR MILE H.-G3, Monmouth Park, July 27, $100,000, 3&up, 1m, 1:36.12, SEA OF TRANQUILITY, Free of Love, First Lieutenant, 8 started.
Sam F. Davis S. (R), Tampa Bay Downs, Feb. 23, $50,000, 3yo, Florida-bred, 1 1/16m, 1:49.86, BUNK N TED, Tails of the Crypt, Raymond Springs, 7 started.
Sam Houston Distaff H., Sam Houston Race Park, Jan. 12, $50,000, 4&up, f&m, 1 1/16m, 1:45.51, DEVOUT SINNER, Slapstick, Coastalota, 9 started.
Sam Houston Oaks, Sam Houston Race Park, March 9, $30,000, 3yo, f, 1m, 1:40.27, SLY KONA, Tomokas Outrageous, Bonus Bid, 10 started.
Sam Houston Sprint H., Sam Houston Race Park, Jan. 5, $50,000, 4&up, 7f, 1:23.98, OAK HALL, Boots On Sunday, Aloha Bold, 11 started.
Sam Houston Texan Juvenile S., Sam Houston Race Park, Nov. 16, $150,000, 2yo, 1 1/16m, 1:45.90, LEO'S LAST HURRAHY, Farma Boy, Zydeco Affair, 9 started.
Sam Houston Turf Sprint Cup H., Sam Houston Race Park, Feb. 23, $50,000, 4&up, 5fT, BOOTS ON SUNDAY, Morluc, Kentucky Bay, 7 started.
Sam J. Whiting Memorial H., Pleasanton, June 29, $50,880, 3&up, 6f, 1:09.15, PROFOUND SECRET, Texas Chili, Today a Star, 8 started.
Sam McCracken Memorial H., Rockingham Park, Sept. 1, $25,000, 3&up, 1 1/16mT, 1:46.39, TOM MAIOR (Brz), Slippery Gator, Mike's Pastry, 8 started.
Samuel H. (R), Beulah Park, Dec. 21, $26,000, 3&up, starters at Beulah Park since September 14, 2002, 6f, 1:12.44, DISAPPEARANCE, Expected Program, Mark's Green Coat, 12 started.

SAN ANTONIO H.-G2, Santa Anita Park, Feb. 3, $250,000, 4&up, 1⅛m, 1:48.66, REDATTORE (Brz), Euchre, Irisheyesareflying, 7 started.

San Antonio Oaks, Retama Park, Oct. 25, $30,000, 3yo, f, 1¹⁄₁₆mT, 1:47.58, VERY GERI, Manzottina, Sheza Nasty Lady, 7 started.

SAN BERNARDINO H.-G2, Santa Anita Park, April 6, $150,000, 4&up, 1⅛m, 1:49.11, BOSQUE REDONDO, Mysterious Cat, Freedom Crest, 6 started.

SAN CARLOS H.-G1, Santa Anita Park, March 3, $150,000, 4&up, 7f, 1:22.02, SNOW RIDGE, Alyzig, Grey Memo, 6 started.

San Carlos H., Bay Meadows, April 28, $57,038, 3&up, 1m, 1:34.79, BOSS EGO, Out of Mind (Brz), Moonlight Meeting, 8 started.

SAN CLEMENTE H.-G2, Del Mar, Aug. 3, $150,000, 3yo, f, 1mT, 1:33.97, LITTLE TREASURE (Fr), Pina Colada (GB), Arabic Song (Ire), 9 started.

Sandia H., The Downs at Albuquerque, Sept. 14, $32,200, 3&up, 5½f, 1:03.10, PACER, Ex Kay E, Smart Score, 7 started.

SAN DIEGO H.-G2, Del Mar, Aug. 4, $250,000, 3&up, 1¹⁄₁₆m, 1:43.48, GREY MEMO, Euchre, Congaree, 8 started.

Sandpiper S., Tampa Bay Downs, Jan. 12, $50,000, 3yo, f, 6f, 1:11.42, REBECCA'S CHARM, Forum Search, Expected Roll, 10 started.

SANDS POINT S.-G3, Belmont Park, June 16, $116,100, 3yo, f, 1⅛mT, 1:51.63, RISKAVERSE, Cyclorama, She's Vested, 11 started.

Sandy Blue S., Del Mar, Aug. 4, $64,800, 3yo, f, 1¹⁄₁₆mT, 1:42.71, RISTRA, Fair Bianca, Got Koko, 6 started.

San Felipe S., Sam Houston Race Park, Dec. 7, $30,000, 3&up, f&m, 6f, 1:10.55, GOODNESS, Discos Pearl, McKinney, 5 started.

SAN FELIPE S.-G2, Santa Anita Park, March 17, $250,000, 3yo, 1¹⁄₁₆m, 1:41.95, MEDAGLIA D'ORO, U S S Tinosa, Siphonic, 6 started.

SAN FERNANDO BREEDERS' CUP S.-G2, Santa Anita Park, Jan. 12, $214,200, 4yo, 1¹⁄₁₆m, 1:41.30, WESTERN PRIDE, Orientate, Fancy As, 10 started.

SANFORD S.-G2, Saratoga Race Course, July 25, $150,000, 2yo, 6f, 1:10.40, WHYWHYWHY, Wildcat Heir, Spite the Devil, 9 started.

SAN FRANCISCO BREEDERS' CUP MILE-G2, Bay Meadows, April 27, $216,250, 3&up, 1mT, 1:35.19, SUANCES (GB), Decarchy, The Tin Man, 4 started.

SAN GABRIEL H.-G2, Santa Anita Park, Dec. 29, $150,000, 3&up, 1⅛mT, 1:48.12, GRAMMARIAN, David Copperfield, Decarchy, 9 started.

SAN GORGONIO H.-G2, Santa Anita Park, Jan. 13, $150,000, 4&up, f&m, 1⅛mT, 1:47.22, TOUT CHARMANT, Janet (GB), Vencera (Fr), 8 started.

Sangue H., Louisiana Downs, Aug. 17, $50,000, 3&up, f&m, 1¹⁄₁₆mT, 1:44.61, DUE TO WIN, Due to Win Again, Wild Squaw, 6 started.

San Jacinto S. (R), Sam Houston Race Park, Nov. 16, $50,000, 3&up, f&m, Texas-bred, 1¹⁄₁₆mT, 1:45.53, EAGLE LAKE, Nanie's Dinner, Peppy Priscilla, 7 started.

San Jose S., Bay Meadows, April 20, $55,912, 3yo, f, 1m, 1:36, LOST AT SEA, Genteel World, Yourfinalanswer, 5 started.

SAN JUAN CAPISTRANO INVITATIONAL H.-G1, Santa Anita Park, April 21, $400,000, 4&up, a1¾mT, 2:44.49, RINGASKIDDY, Staging Post, Continental Red, 8 started.

San Juan County Commissioners H., SunRay Park, Nov. 17, $53,100, 3&up, 1⅛m, 1:51.20, MORO GRANDE, Personal Beau, Texastraveler, 10 started.

SAN LUIS OBISPO H.-G2, Santa Anita Park, Feb. 16, $200,000, 4&up, 1½mT, 2:26.09, NAZIRALI (Ire), Continental Red, Bonapartiste (Fr), 7 started.

SAN LUIS REY H.-G2, Santa Anita Park, March 16, $250,000, 4&up, 1½mT, 2:26.81, CONTINENTAL RED, Keemoon (Fr), Speedy Pick, 8 started.

SAN MARCOS S.-G2, Santa Anita Park, Jan. 21, $150,000, 4&up, 1¼mT, 2:01.27, IRISH PRIZE, Continental Red, Cagney (Brz), 6 started.

San Marino H. (R), Santa Anita Park, Feb. 17, $82,575, 4&up, non-winners of a race worth $50,000 to the winner at a mile or over in 2001-02, 1¼mT, 2:02.33, KUDOS, Lord Jim (Arg), National Anthem (GB), 6 started.

San Matean H., Bay Meadows Fair, Aug. 18, $49,500, 3&up, 1¹⁄₁₆mT, 1:42.10, NINEBANKS, Suspicious Minds, Dr. Park, 5 started.

San Mateo S., Bay Meadows, Sept. 1, $62,150, 2yo, 5½f, 1:04.66, MR. TECHNIQUE, Hawaiian Lyon, Bases Are Loaded, 5 started.

SAN MIGUEL S.-G3, Santa Anita Park, Jan. 13, $107,900, 3yo, 6f, 1:09, POPULAR, Roman Dancer, Royal Moro, 5 started.

SAN PASQUAL H.-G2, Santa Anita Park, Jan. 5, $200,000, 4&up, 1¹⁄₁₆m, 1:41.83, WOODEN PHONE, Euchre, Red Eye, 7 started.

San Pedro S., Santa Anita Park, March 23, $79,275, 3yo, 6½f, 1:16.36, ROMAN DANCER, Werblin, Saturday Hero, 5 started.

SAN RAFAEL S.-G2, Santa Anita Park, March 2, $200,000, 3yo, 1m, 1:36.24, CAME HOME, Easy Grades, Werblin, 7 started.

SAN SIMEON H.-G3, Santa Anita Park, April 21, $138,125, 4&up, a6½fT, 1:11.73, MALABAR GOLD, Astonished (GB), Nuclear Debate, 9 started.

SANTA ANA H.-G2, Santa Anita Park, March 23, $150,000, 4&up, f&m, 1⅛mT, 1:47.05, GOLDEN APPLES (Ire), Starine (Fr), Astra, 9 started.

SANTA ANITA DERBY-G1, Santa Anita Park, April 6, $750,000, 3yo, 1⅛m, 1:50.02, CAME HOME, Easy Grades, Lusty Latin, 8 started.

SANTA ANITA H.-G1, Santa Anita Park, March 2, $1,000,000, 4&up, 1¼m, 2:01.02, MILWAUKEE BREW, Western Pride, Kudos, 14 started.

SANTA ANITA OAKS-G1, Santa Anita Park, March 9, $300,000, 3yo, f, 1¹⁄₁₆m, 1:42.70, YOU, Habibti, Ile de France, 9 started.

SANTA BARBARA H.-G2, Santa Anita Park, April 20, $250,000, 4&up, f&m, 1¼mT, 2:01.48, ASTRA, Golden Apples (Ire), Polaire (Ire), 6 started.

SANTA CATALINA S.-G2, Santa Anita Park, Jan. 19, $150,000, 3yo, 1¹⁄₁₆m, 1:42.50, LABAMTA BABE, Siphonic, Cascade Cowboy, 6 started.

Santa Clara H., Bay Meadows, May 5, $61,175, 3&up, f&m, 1m, 1:35.19, MY FIRST LADY, Rosanda, Bold Roberta, 6 started.

Santa Lucia H. (R), Santa Anita Park, March 31, $82,725, 4&up, f&m, non-winners of a race worth $50,000 to the winner at one mile or over other than claiming or starter in 2002, 1¹⁄₁₆m, 1:42.52, ALEXINE (Arg), Cashmina, De Goddaughter, 7 started.

SANTA MARGARITA INVITATIONAL H.-G1, Santa Anita Park, March 10, $300,000, 4&up, f&m, 1⅛m, 1:49.01, AZERI, Spain, Printemps (Chi), 7 started.

SANTA MARIA H.-G1, Santa Anita Park, Feb. 17, $200,000, 4&up, f&m, 1¹⁄₁₆m, 1:44.15, FAVORITE FUNTIME, Verruma (Brz), Printemps (Chi), 7 started.

SANTA MONICA H.-G1, Santa Anita Park, Jan. 26, $200,000, 4&up, f&m, 7f, 1:22.37, KALOOKAN QUEEN, Leading Light, Spain, 5 started.

Santa Paula S., Santa Anita Park, March 24, $80,925, 3yo, f, 6½f, 1:16.36, BELLA BELLUCCI, Shameful, Spring Meadow, 5 started.

Santa Teresa H., Sunland Park, March 10, $33,700, 3&up, f&m, 6½f, 1:15.64, I GOT SILVER, K J Lucky Seven, Gollygot, 12 started.

SANTA YNEZ S.-G2, Santa Anita Park, Jan. 21, $150,000, 3yo, f, 7f, 1:23.07, DANCING (GB), Respectful, Lady George, 8 started.

SANTA YSABEL S.-G3, Santa Anita Park, Jan. 6, $105,000, 3yo, f, 1¹⁄₁₆m, 1:44.14, BELLA BELLA BELLA, Tamarack Bay, No Turbulence, 4 started.

Santo Lalomia H. (R), Monmouth Park, June 15, $50,000, 3&up, f&m, New Jersey-bred, 1m, 1:37.59, WILLIE'S LUV, Firecard, Gaelic Bay, 5 started.

SAN VICENTE S.-G2, Santa Anita Park, Feb. 2, $150,000, 3yo, 7f, 1:21.92, CAME HOME, Jack's Silver, Werblin, 6 started.

SAPLING S.-G3, Monmouth Park, Aug. 10, $100,000, 2yo, 6f, 1:09.88, VALID VIDEO, Farno, Boston Park, 8 started.

SARANAC H.-G3, Saratoga Race Course, Sept. 2, $111,500, 3yo, 1³⁄₁₆mT, 1:55.30, IBN AL HAITHAM (GB), Finality, Irish Colonial, 9 started.

SARATOGA BREEDERS' CUP H.-G2, Saratoga Race Course, Aug. 17, $300,000, 3&up, 1¼m, 2:02.95, EVENING ATTIRE, Abreeze, Dollar Bill, 10 started.

Saratoga H., Bay Meadows, June 1, $68,437, 3&up, 6f, 1:08.32, FULL MOON MADNESS, Echo Eddie, Beyond Brilliant, 7 started.

SARATOGA SPECIAL S.-G2, Saratoga Race Course, Aug. 14, $150,000, 2yo, 6½f, 1:17.65, ZAVATA, Lone Star Sky, Spite the Devil, 5 started.

Saskatchewan Derby, Marquis Downs, Aug. 3, $15,000, 3yo, 1¹⁄₁₆m, 1:46.28, REGAL RANDY, Monarch Brass, Kanha, 7 started.

Saskatchewan Futurity (R), Marquis Downs, July 27, $8,925, 2yo, c&g, Saskatchewan-bred, 6f, 1:17.31, EXTENDED CREDIT, Sifting Sand, Quiz the Wizard, 4 started.

Saskatchewan Futurity (R), Marquis Downs, July 27, $9,425, 2yo, f, Saskatchewan-bred, 6f, 1:16.45, SHE'S NIFTY, Picture the Answer, Royal Empress, 7 started.

Saskatoon H., Marquis Downs, June 29, $5,000, 3yo, 6f, 1:14.26, SOUTH ON CLARENCE, Good Old Sprite, Britts Xpress, 6 started.

Saylorville S., Prairie Meadows, July 5, $135,000, 3&up, f&m, 6f, 1:09.89, SWEET NANETTE, Trisha Runs, Miss Seffens, 6 started.

Scannapieco H., Calder Race Course, Dec. 8, $44,210, 3&up, 5fT, :55.51, WERTZ, Sam's Concorde, Termination Dust, Zoning (GB), 10 started.

Scarlet and Gray H. (R), Beulah Park, Nov. 10, $40,000, 3&up, f&m,

Ohio-bred, 6f, 1:10.77, DRAMA'S WAY, Scioto Bootski, Prizes, 11 started.

Schenectady H. (R), Belmont Park, Sept. 22, $81,275, 3&up, f&m, New York-bred, 6f, 1:11.01, MADDIE MAY, We'll Sea Ya, Shawklit Mint, 6 started.

SCHUYLERVILLE S.-G2, Saratoga Race Course, July 24, $150,000, 2yo, f, 6fT, 1:12.14, FREEDOM'S DAUGHTER, Miss Mary Apples, Mymich, 7 started.

Scissortail S., Blue Ribbon Downs, April 6, $7,425, 3yo, 6f, 1:10.23, PROPER MARINER, Carters Boy, Quick Claim, 8 started.

Scottsdale H., Turf Paradise, March 23, $35,000, 3yo, f, 1mT, 1:38.49, (DH) ACURE FOR GERI, (DH) LADY LOU, Lady Continental, 9 started.

Seagram Cup S., Woodbine, Aug. 7, $136,875, 3&up, 1⅟₁₆m, 1:44.51, LUCKY MOLAR, Attest, Win City, 7 started.

Sea O Erin Breeders' Cup Mile H., Arlington Park, Sept. 29, $168,400, 3&up, 1mT, 1:38.17, MYSTERY GIVER, Buenos Dias, Al's Dearly Bred, 8 started.

Seattle H., Emerald Downs, April 28, $35,000, 3&up, 6f, 1:07.80, CROWNING MEETING, Road Afleet, Jumron Won, 5 started.

Seattle Slew H., Emerald Downs, June 23, $42,750, 3yo, c&g, 1m, 1:35.20, FLYING NOTES, Salt Grinder, Vernon Lodge, 7 started.

Seaway S., Woodbine, Sept. 1, $136,500, 3&up, f&m, 7f, 1:24.48, EL PRADO ESSENCE, Hattiesburg, Feathers, 5 started.

Second Episode Stallion S. (R), Suffolk Downs, Nov. 11, $30,000, 3&up, Massachusetts-bred and -sired, 6f, 1:13.50, SUNLIT RIDGE, Stylish Sultan, Diggin' for Fun, 11 started.

SECRETARIAT S.-G1, Arlington Park, Aug. 17, $400,000, 3yo, 1¼mT, 2:04.16, CHISELLING, Jazz Beat (Ire), Extra Check, 7 started.

SELENE S. (Can-G1), Woodbine, May 20, $280,250, 3yo, f, 1⅟₁₆m, 1:45.49, SEE HOW SHE RUNS, Ginger Gold, Mulrainy, 8 started.

Selima S., Laurel Park, Nov. 16, $100,000, 2yo, f, 1⅟₁₆m, 1:47.60, MAKIN HEAT, Lets Just Do It, Heirloom Diamond, 10 started.

Selma S. (R), Retama Park, Oct. 12, $30,000, 3yo, f, Texas-bred, 5fT, :56.44, BONUS BID, Miss Ritz, Fleeta Dif, 10 started.

Senate Appointee H., Hastings Park Racecourse, Aug. 25, $38,010, 3&up, f&m, 1⅟₁₆m, 1:44.54, GREY TOBE FREE, Catahoula Rose, Adelle, 4 started.

SENATOR KEN MADDY H.-G3, Santa Anita Park, Oct. 12, $114,100, 3&up, f&m, a6½fT, 1:12.86, ROLLY POLLY (Ire), I'm the Business (NZ), Nanogram, 12 started.

Senorita S., Louisiana Downs, Oct. 27, $30,000, 3yo, f, 7f, 1:24.02, GIGI'S SKYFLYER, Cielo Girl, Khazi, 6 started.

SENORITA S.-G3, Hollywood Park, May 4, $107,300, 3yo, f, 1mT, 1:34.91, ADORATION, High Society (Ire), Nunatall (GB), 6 started.

Sensational Star H. (R), Santa Anita Park, Jan. 12, $108,000, 4&up, California-bred non-winners of $50,000 twice other than closed or claiming since March 1, a6½fT, 1:12.40, MACWARD, Echo Eddie, Love That Lion, 7 started.

Serena's Song S., Monmouth Park, June 22, $50,000, 3yo, f, 1m 70y, 1:42.25, SIXTYONE MARGAUX, Dubai Fall (Ire), Maresha, 6 started.

SHADWELL KEENELAND TURF MILE-G1, Keeneland, Oct. 6, $600,000, 3&up, 1mT, 1:35.55, LANDSEER (GB), Touch of the Blues (Fr), Beat Hollow (GB), 8 started.

Shady Well S. (R), Woodbine, July 7, $165,450, 2yo, f, Canadian-bred, 5½f, 1:05.93, APPLEBY GARDENS, Mountain Dawn, Rhiannon's Wish, 8 started.

Shakertown S., Keeneland, April 13, $85,050, 3&up, 5½fT, 1:03.25, MORLUC, Mighty Beau, Grangeville, 10 started.

Shakopee S., Canterbury Park, Aug. 10, $35,000, 3&up, 1m 70y, 1:40.27, SILVER ZIPPER, Tahkodha Hills, Top Secret Affair, 5 started.

Sham S. (R), Santa Anita Park, Feb. 8, $78,650, 3yo, non-winners of $50,000 at one mile or over, 1⅛m, 1:49.11, U S S TINOSA, Porto Bonus, Hot Contest, 6 started.

Shecky Greene S., Fairmount Park, July 19, $25,600, 3&up, c&g, 6f, 1:11.60, TIC N TIN, Two Thumbs Up, Too Many Bucks, 6 started.

Shecky Greene S., Delaware Park, June 17, $57,900, 3&up, 1⅟₁₆m, 1:45.42, FIRST AMENDMENT, Pechito, Lightning Paces, 5 started.

SHEEPSHEAD BAY H.-G2, Belmont Park, June 1, $150,000, 3&up, f&m, 1⅜mT, 2:13.63, TWEEDSIDE, Sweetest Thing, Golden Corona, 10 started.

Shenandoah S., Charles Town, June 8, $36,850, 3yo, 7f, 1:27.14, JO JO DANCER, Adams Tribe, Saints Go Marching, 7 started.

Shepperton S. (R), Woodbine, Aug. 24, $126,000, 3&up, progeny of eligible Ontario stallions, 6½f, 1:16.97, RUNAWAY LOVE, Krz Ruckus, Sambuca On Ice, 4 started.

SHIRLEY JONES H.-G3, Gulfstream Park, Feb. 15, $100,000, 3&up, f&m, 7f, 1:22.31, CAT CAY, Raging Fever, Vague Memory, 7 started.

Shiskabob S. (R), Louisiana Downs, Oct. 19, $67,600, 3&up, Louisiana-bred, 1⅟₁₆mT, 1:46.25, OAK HALL, White Star, One Brick Shy, 10 started.

Shocker T. H., Calder Race Course, Oct. 12, $100,000, 3&up, f&m, 1⅟₁₆m, 1:45.97, CASTLEBROOK, Banderia (Arg), Coolbythepool, 7 started.

SHOEMAKER BREEDERS' CUP MILE S.-G1, Hollywood Park, May 27, $408,000, 3&up, 1mT, 1:33.39, LADIES DIN, Redattore (Brz), Spinelessjellyfish, 10 started.

Shortgrass Heritage S. (R), Marquis Downs, Aug. 17, $11,800, 3yo, c&g, Saskatchewan-bred, 1⅟₁₆m, 1:48.25, GOOD OLD SPRITE, Britts Xpress, Makemeorbreakme, 6 started.

Showtime Deb S. (R), Hawthorne Race Course, Nov. 9, $109,350, 2yo, f, Illinois-bred, 6f, 1:13.27, SHE'S FANTASTIC, Invader, Julie's Prize, 12 started.

Shuvee H., Fairmount Park, Oct. 18, $25,700, 2yo, f, 6f, 1:13.40, MOON SHINE TIME, Unsprung, She's Fantastic, 7 started.

SHUVEE H.-G2, Belmont Park, May 18, $200,000, 3&up, f&m, 1m, 1:34.95, SHINY BAND, Raging Fever, Victory Ride, 5 started.

Sickle's Image S. (R), Great Lakes Downs, Sept. 13, $45,000, 2yo, f, Michigan-bred, 6f, 1:17.20, JEAN'S WAY, Cantouchis, Magna Cum Laude, 8 started.

Sierra Starlet S. (R), Ruidoso Downs, July 14, $42,000, 3yo, f, New Mexico-bred, 5½f, 1:05, ESPEEDYTOO, Lord Imajones, Quickkey, 10 started.

Silky Sullivan H. (R), Golden Gate Fields, March 17, $59,563, 3&up, starters for a claiming price of $40,000 or less in 2001-02, 1⅟₁₆mT, 1:42.53, BIG SHOT (Arg), Anstar (GB), Ninebanks, 6 started.

Silverado H. (R), The Downs at Albuquerque, April 21, $52,900, 3&up, New Mexico-bred, 6f, 1:08.98, RUNMORE MEMA, Wild Bill R, Star Smasher, 8 started.

Silver Bells S., Calder Race Course, Dec. 23, $43,300, 2yo, f, 6f, 1:11.43, JUST BILL ME, City Fire, Lavender Lass, 7 started.

SILVERBULLETDAY S.-G3, Fair Grounds, Feb. 16, $150,000, 3yo, f, 1⅟₁₆m, 1:42.09, TAKE CHARGE LADY, Charmed Gift, Chamrousse, 5 started.

Silver Deputy S., Woodbine, Sept. 1, $107,000, 2yo, 6½f, 1:19.39, ADDED EDGE, Snappy Tim, Makin Headlines, 7 started.

Silver Season H., Calder Race Course, May 6, $37,695, 3yo, 6f, 1:11.42, ROYAL LAD, Juggernaut, Danielles Magic, 6 started.

Silver Spur Breeders' Cup S., Lone Star Park, July 14, $84,450, 2yo, f, 6f, 1:11.02, CONFIDING WINNER, Sea Bloom, Parting, 11 started.

Simcoe S. (R), Woodbine, Sept. 2, $105,050, 2yo, c&g, Canadian-bred, 7f, 1:25.59, MOBIL, Timeform, Sircharlesschnabel, 7 started.

Simply Majestic S., Calder Race Course, June 1, $75,000, 3yo, 1⅟₁₆mT, 1:45.23, LORD JUBAN, Noble Jester, Erv's Creek, 10 started.

SINGAPORE PLATE S.-G3, Arlington Park, Aug. 10, $100,000, 3yo, f, 1⅛m, 1:50.58, LOST AT SEA, See How She Runs, Strikes No Spares, 7 started.

Sir Barton S. (R), Woodbine, Nov. 23, $128,625, 3yo, c&g, progeny of eligible Ontario stallions, 1⅟₁₆m, 1:44.47, BARBEAU RUCKUS, El Habanero, Twice Bid, 6 started.

Sir Barton S., Pimlico, May 18, $79,250, 3yo, 1⅟₁₆m, 1:44.11, SARAVA, Shah Jehan, No Pressure, 6 started.

Sir Beaufort S., Santa Anita Park, Dec. 26, $78,050, 3yo, 1mT, 1:35.82, INESPERADO (Fr), Music's Storm, Golden Arrow, 8 started.

Sir Winston Churchill H., Hastings Park Racecourse, Sept. 29, $36,407, 3&up, 1⅛m, 1:50.36, LORD NELSON, Futural, American Justice, 4 started.

SIXTY SAILS H.-G3, Sportsman's Park, April 28, $300,000, 3&up, f&m, 1⅛m, 1:51.37, WITH ABILITY, Lakenheath, Katy Kat, 7 started.

Sixty Sails H., Fair Grounds, Jan. 13, $75,000, 4&up, f&m, a1⅟₁₆mT, 1:44.97, HISTOIRE SAINTE (Fr), Tabianka, Lady of Peace, 13 started.

Skipat S., Pimlico, June 1, $50,000, 3&up, f&m, 6f, 1:11.31, MADAME ROAR, Prized Stamp, Karaoke Dancer, 5 started.

SKIP AWAY H.-G3, Gulfstream Park, Jan. 12, $100,000, 3&up, 1⅟₁₆m, 1:43.98, SIR BEAR, Red Bullet, Hal's Hope, 8 started.

Skip Away S., Monmouth Park, June 30, $50,000, 3&up, 1⅟₁₆m, 1:42.78, CAT'S AT HOME, Sea of Tranquility, Twilight Prince, 6 started.

Skip Trial S., The Meadowlands, Oct. 5, $50,000, 3&up, 6f, 1:10.74, FETCH DINNER, Rich in Glory, Unreal Party, 6 started.

Ski Roundtop Cup S., Shawan Downs, Sept. 28, $19,500, 4&up, a3½mT, 7:41.40, SOVEREIGN STORM, Lil Starvin Marvin, Maipo, 7 started.

SKY CLASSIC S. (Can-G2), Woodbine, Oct. 27, $279,500, 3&up, 1⅜mT, 2:19.33, STRUT THE STAGE, Cetewayo, Man From Wicklow, 9 started.

Sleepy Hollow S. (R), Belmont Park, Oct. 19, $100,000, 2yo, New York-bred, 1m, 1:36.76, FUNNY CIDE, Spite the Devil, Go Rockin' Robin, 6 started.

Slight in the Rear S. (R), Fairmount Park, Oct. 1, $35,800, 3yo, f, Illinois-bred, 6f, 1:11.20, TEJANO HONEY, Jiroga Lite, The Jeckle, 8 started.

Slipton Fell H., Mountaineer Park, June 8, $78,750, 3&up, 1m 70y, 1:40.62, X COUNTRY, Mo Mon, Tour the Hive, 9 started.

Smart Halo S., Pimlico, April 27, $41,400, 3yo, f, 6f, 1:10.27, VESTA, Fresh Tracks, Gracefulciti, 5 started.

Smile H., Arlington Park, Oct. 27, $100,000, 3&up, 5½fT, 1:03.53, ABDERIAN (Ire), Mighty Beau, Miners Gamble, 9 started.

Smile Sprint H., Calder Race Course, July 13, $400,000, 3&up, 6f, 1:09.98, ORIENTATE, Echo Eddie, Crafty C. T, 7 started.

Snazzle Dazzle H. (R), Calder Race Course, Dec. 15, $40,320, 3&up, f&m, non-winners of a stakes of $35,000 at one mile or over since March 15, 1mT, 1:36.29, AMONITA (GB), Laurica, Notable Craft, 10 started.

Snow Chief S. (R), Hollywood Park, April 28, $250,000, 3yo, California-bred, 1⅛m, 1:51.07, CALKINS ROAD, Menacing Dennis, Highly Suspect, 12 started.

Snow White S., Charles Town, Dec. 21, $42,300, 2yo, f, 7f, 1:28.26, SUCH A FLIRT, Home Run Hitter, Lets Just Do It, 10 started.

Sober Jig H. (R), Calder Race Course, Dec. 29, $37,800, 3&up, f&m, non-winners of a stakes of $50,000 since June 1, 6½f, 1:17.04, FOREST HEIRESS, Fly Me Crazy, Gentille Alouette, 5 started.

Solana Beach H. (R), Del Mar, Sept. 2, $125,000, 3&up, f&m, California-bred, 1mT, 1:33.65, SUPER HIGH, Stetson Lady, Elaine's Angel, 10 started.

Solano County Juvenile Filly S. (R), Solano County Fair, July 21, $53,030, 2yo, f, California-bred, 5½f, 1:04.81, MARKET GARDEN, Smokin Tempo, Her Emminence, 8 started.

Solo Haina S., Calder Race Course, Nov. 2, $45,705, 3&up, f&m, 1¹⁄₁₆mT, 1:41.48, STAY FOREVER, Pembroke Palace, Banderia (Arg), 12 started.

Some Sensation S., Santa Anita Park, March 15, $79,800, 3yo, f, 1mT, 1:35.44, MEGAHERTZ (GB), Simone's Show, Redmond, 8 started.

Somethingroyal S. (R), Colonial Downs, July 7, $40,000, 3&up, f&m, Virginia-bred, 5½fT, 1:03.90, BROAD VICTORY, Kim, All That Glitters, 10 started.

Sonny Hine S., Pimlico, Sept. 28, $50,000, 3yo, 6f, 1:11.57, MOE'S MON, Outstander, Private Opening, 6 started.

Sonoma H., Northlands Park, Aug. 10, $75,000, 3yo, f, 1¹⁄₁₆m, 1:45, SWEET MONARCH, Classic Action, Code's Decree, 8 started.

Sophomore Sprint Championship S., Mountaineer Park, Nov. 26, $77,800, 3yo, 6f, 1:11.70, TOMMY CAT, Still Be Smokin', Ran South, 8 started.

SORORITY S.-G3, Monmouth Park, Aug. 25, $100,000, 2yo, f, 6f, 1:11.09, WILD SNITCH, Grand Natalie Rose, The Bride Is Arose, 6 started.

SORRENTO S.-G2, Del Mar, Aug. 10, $150,000, 2yo, f, 6½f, 1:17.39, BUFFYTHECENTERFOLD, Tricks Her, Indy Groove, 8 started.

Southern Belle H., Grants Pass, May 26, $4,000, 3&up, f&m, 5½f, 1:04.20, MISSY MUFFET, Oh Molly, Da Leprechaun, 8 started.

Southern Belle S. (R), Louisiana Downs, Nov. 9, $30,870, 2yo, f, Louisiana-bred, 6f, 1:12.18, QUEEN KELLY, Rubies N Roses, Itsmybag, 5 started.

South Mississippi Owners and Breeders S. (R), Fair Grounds, Feb. 8, $30,200, 3yo, Mississippi-owned, 6f, 1:12.73, LITTLE JOE TUBB, Thats Our Queen, Frozen Chrome, 9 started.

South Ocean S. (R), Woodbine, Oct. 30, $132,625, 2yo, f, progeny of eligible Ontario stallions, 1¹⁄₁₆m, 1:47.23, SANTERRA, Deputy Cures Blues, Fancy Drinks, 8 started.

Southwest H., Blue Ribbon Downs, March 31, $8,250, 3&up, 7f, 1:27, YULE BE BLUE, Mighty Rick, Taxauditor, 9 started.

Southwest S. (1st Div.), Oaklawn Park, March 2, $75,000, 3yo, 1m, 1:40.29, PRIVATE EMBLEM, Dusty Spike, Clergy, 8 started.

Southwest S. (2nd Div.), Oaklawn Park, March 2, $75,000, 3yo, 1m, 1:41.70, PALOMA PARILLA, Cope With an Image, Windward Passage, 8 started.

Soviet Problem H., Golden Gate Fields, March 23, $60,550, 3&up, f&m, 6f, 1:09.21, MADAME PIETRA, Fancee Bargain, Bullish Miss, 8 started.

Spangled Jimmy H., Northlands Park, July 6, $40,000, 3&up, 1m, 1:38.20, SIXTHIRTYJOE, Highland Leader, Rancour, 7 started.

Spartan S. (R), Great Lakes Downs, July 5, $45,000, 3yo, c&g, Michigan-bred, 7f, 1:29.34, ACCOUNTABLE GUY, Equi Power, Pito, 9 started.

Spectacular Bid S., Arlington Park, Sept. 7, $75,000, 2yo, 6f, 1:10.29, SHARP IMPACT, Wiggins, Unleash the Power, 8 started.

SPECTACULAR BID S.-G3, Gulfstream Park, Jan. 3, $100,000, 3yo, 6f, 1:12.19, MAYBRY'S BOY, Showmeitall, Harmony Hall, 8 started.

SPEED TO SPARE CHAMPIONSHIP S. (Can-G3), Northlands Park, Sept. 7, $100,000, 3&up, 1⅜m, 2:17.40, BUBBLEGUM KID, Miki Bleu Eyes, Scotman, 7 started.

Spend a Buck H., Calder Race Course, Oct. 12, $100,000, 3&up, 1¹⁄₁₆m, 1:44.91, PAY THE PREACHER, Best of the Rest, Built Up, 8 started.

Spend a Buck S., Fairmount Park, Sept. 2, $25,500, 3yo, c&g, 1m 70y, 1:43, BULLDOG GEORGE, Canyon de Oro, My Lord's Majesty, 5 started.

Spend a Buck S., Monmouth Park, Aug. 24, $50,000, 3yo, 1mT, 1:36.07, JEB'S WILD, May Expectations, Lord Abounding, 6 started.

Spicy H. (R), Arapahoe Park, Sept. 2, $30,000, 3&up, f&m, Colorado-bred, 1¹⁄₁₆m, 1:46, BLACK SEA, Slewannavan, Just React, 7 started.

Spicy Living Sweepstakes, Rockingham Park, Aug. 4, $100,000, 3&up, f&m, 1⅛mT, 1:48.62, CALISTA (GB), Stylish, De Aar, 6 started.

SPINAWAY S.-G1, Saratoga Race Course, Aug. 30, $200,000, 2yo, f, 7f, 1:24.36, AWESOME HUMOR, Midnight Cry, Forever Partners, 12 started.

Spindletop S. (R), Sam Houston Race Park, March 2, $30,000, 3yo, Texas-bred, 7f, 1:26.20, FAXAMILLION, Kristys Excellent, Waggaman Road, 9 started.

Spirit of Texas S. (R), Sam Houston Race Park, Nov. 16, $50,000, 3&up, Texas-bred, 6f, 1:10.14, WON C C, Alamo Expense, Term Sheet, 10 started.

SPORT PAGE H.-G3, Aqueduct, Oct. 26, $111,400, 3&up, 7f, 1:23.28, MULTIPLE CHOICE, Bowman's Band, Sing Me Back Home, 8 started.

Sportsman's Park Breeders' Cup H., Sportsman's Park, March 24, $104,450, 3&up, 1m, 1:38.07, MC MAHON, Chicago Six, Kombat Kat, 8 started.

Spring Championship H., Grants Pass, June 16, $3,615, 3&up, 4½f, KINGSVIEW, Shotsfired, L. Capone, 5 started.

Spring Fever S., Oaklawn Park, March 10, $50,000, 4&up, f&m, 5½f, 1:03.74, POWDER, Spanish Glitter, Southern Tour, 5 started.

Springfield S. (R), Arlington Park, June 22, $83,250, 3yo, Illinois-bred, 1m, 1:36.21, COLORFUL TOUR, Medlin Road, Coping, 7 started.

Spring S. (R), Sam Houston Race Park, March 23, $30,000, 4&up, Texas-bred, 7f, 1:23.61, WON C C, Happy Smile, Kentucky Bay, 9 started.

Spring Sprint H., Hastings Park Racecourse, May 18, $37,464, 3&up, 6½f, 1:16.66, KID KATABATIC, Diglett, King Jeremy, 5 started.

Sprint H., Fonner Park, March 23, $30,000, 3&up, 6½f, 1:18.60, RUB, Leaping Plum, Abbi's Choice, 9 started.

Spruce Fir H. (R), Monmouth Park, Aug. 10, $50,000, 3&up, f&m, New Jersey-bred, 1mT, 1:36.28, TWILIGHTS PRAYER, Willie's Luv, Gaelic Bay, 11 started.

Squan Song S. (R), Laurel Park, Dec. 26, $50,000, 3&up, f&m, Maryland-bred, 7f, 1:23.06, GAZILLION, Tamayo, Darnestown, 10 started.

Stage Door Betty H., Calder Race Course, Dec. 28, $100,000, 3&up, f&m, 1¹⁄₁₆m, 1:44.08, STORMY FROLIC, Small Promises, Redoubled Miss, 7 started.

Stampede Park Sprint Championship, Stampede Park, May 4, $40,000, 4&up, 6f, 1:12.40, SIXTHIRTYJOE, Timely Ruckus, They Call Me Cody, 6 started.

Star Ball H., Golden Gate Fields, Nov. 30, $60,600, 3&up, f&m, 1¹⁄₁₆m, 1:41.71, LACIE GIRL, Erica's Smile, Lindsay Jean, 8 started.

Star de Naskra S. (R), Pimlico, April 20, $60,000, 3yo, Maryland-bred, 6f, 1:10.73, NO PRESSURE, Quarter Ton of Fun, Captain Chessie, 7 started.

Stardust S. (R), Louisiana Downs, Oct. 19, $41,100, 2yo, Louisiana-bred, 6f, 1:12.78, WITT ANTE, Sanctuary's Omooni, Mr. King Rex, 14 started.

Star of Texas S. (R), Sam Houston Race Park, Nov. 16, $100,000, 3&up, Texas-bred, 1¹⁄₁₆m, 1:44.95, RARE CURE, Crook, Faxamillion, 7 started.

STARS AND STRIPES BREEDERS' CUP TURF H.-G3, Arlington Park, July 6, $224,625, 3&up, 1½mT, 2:27.50, CETEWAYO, Private Son, Pisces, 9 started.

Stars and Stripes H., Les Bois Park, July 4, $5,000, 3&up, 7½f, 1:29.95, ERHARD, Northern Ricky, Reno Bound, 7 started.

Star Shoot S., Woodbine, April 6, $140,750, 3&up, f, 6f, 1:10.60, PLATEL, Miss City Halo, Lady Shari, 7 started.

State Fair Derby, Lincoln State Fair, June 22, $12,600, 3yo, 1m, 1:37.20, GEORGE TAYLOR, Kansas Pioneer, Strawberry Kid, 6 started.

State Fair Futurity (R), Lincoln State Fair, June 30, $13,275, 2yo, Nebraska-bred, 4½f, ROCKET CHARGE, Sundayblummer, This, 10 started.

Steady Growth S. (R), Woodbine, May 29, $142,125, 3&up, progeny of eligible Ontario stallions, 1⅟₁₆m, 1:44.67, RUNAWAY LOVE, Ice Water, Geraint, 12 started.

Stefanita S., Laurel Park, Nov. 16, $50,000, 3&up, f&m, 7f, 1:24.85, HUNKA HUNKA LORI Z, Belle Artiste, Abundantly Blessed, 8 started.

Steinlen H., Arlington Park, Oct. 26, $100,000, 3&up, 1⅟₁₆mT, 1:43.87, CAPSIZED, One More Round, Al's Dearly Bred, 8 started.

Steinlen H., Hollywood Park, Nov. 10, $72,850, 3&up, 1⅟₁₆mT, 1:44.77, REBA'S GOLD, Mercenary, Seinne (Chi), 7 started.

STEPHEN FOSTER H.-G1, Churchill Downs, June 15, $833,250, 3&up, 1⅛m, 1:47.84, STREET CRY (Ire), Dollar Bill, Tenpins, 8 started.

Stevens H. (R), Columbus, Sept. 15, $15,375, 3yo, Nebraska-bred, 6½f, 1:21.20, KINDA GOTTA WANNA, Keylargo Lady, What About David, 5 started.

Steve Van Buren H., Philadelphia Park, Sept. 2, $75,000, 3&up, f&m, 7f, 1:23.17, BELLE ARTISTE, Tugger, Vikki Slew, 6 started.

St. Nick S., Charles Town, Dec. 7, $42,450, 2yo, 7f, 1:27.15, JUST SWELL, Creative's Dream, Dan's Advantage, 8 started.

STONERSIDE BEAUMONT S.-G2, Keeneland, April 26, $250,000, 3yo, f, a7f, 1:28.79, PROPER GAMBLE, Respectful, Vicki Vallencourt, 7 started.

Stonerside S., Lone Star Park, May 25, $150,000, 3yo, f, 7f, 1:23.79, SPRING MEADOW, Gilded Wings, Savorthetime, 8 started.

Storm Cat S. (R), Philadelphia Park, Oct. 5, $50,000, 2yo, Pennsylvania-bred, 6f, 1:12.27, YO, Two Minute Warning, Valleyman, 8 started.

Storm Cat S., Keeneland, Oct. 6, $83,925, 3yo, 1mT, 1:36.52, FEBRUARY STORM, Honor in War, Gentle Bien, 8 started.

St. Paul S., Canterbury Park, May 25, $35,000, 3yo, 6f, 1:09.67, VITO CORLEONE, Montana Rush, Strawberry Kid, 7 started.

Straight Deal Breeders' Cup S., Laurel Park, Aug. 10, $122,000, 3&up, f&m, 7f, 1:23.06, XTRA HEAT, Outstanding Info, Winter Leaf, 5 started.

Stravinsky S., Keeneland, April 20, $84,900, 3&up, f&m, 5½fT, 1:03.41, DIANEHILL (Ire), Senorita Ziggy, Ioya Two, 9 started.

Strawberry Morn S., Hastings Park Racecourse, May 11, $35,324, 3&up, f&m, 6½f, 1:17.65, INISH GLORA, Grooms Derby, Always a Dixie, 8 started.

STRUB S.-G2, Santa Anita Park, Feb. 2, $400,000, 4yo, 1⅛m, 1:47.25, MIZZEN MAST, Giant Gentleman, Fancy As, 11 started.

Sturgeon River S. (R), Northlands Park, Sept. 21, $40,000, 2yo, f, Alberta-bred, 1m, 1:41.40, DOWHATUTHINKSRIGHT, Audio Express, Shady Classic, 9 started.

STUYVESANT H.-G3, Aqueduct, Nov. 5, $113,400, 3&up, 1⅛m, 1:50.56, SNAKE MOUNTAIN, Windsor Castle, Docent, 10 started.

STYMIE H.-G3, Aqueduct, March 9, $109,200, 3&up, 1⅛m, 1:48.89, GROUND STORM, Duckhorn, Pleasant Divorce, 7 started.

Subtle Dancer H., Calder Race Course, Nov. 17, $44,105, 3&up, f&m, 6½f, 1:18.85, GENTILLE ALOUETTE, Rule Brittania, Sugar N Spice, 10 started.

SUBURBAN H.-G2, Belmont Park, July 6, $500,000, 3&up, 1¼m, 2:00.95, E DUBAI, Lido Palace (Chi), Macho Uno, 7 started.

Sugar Bowl S., Fair Grounds, Dec. 29, $75,000, 2yo, 6f, 1:10.38, SAINTLY LOOK, Broke Again, Crowned King, 7 started.

Summer Finale H., Mountaineer Park, Sept. 2, $78,950, 3&up, f&m, 1mT, 1:34.72, LA RECHERCHE, Media Access, Eesee's Lass, 10 started.

Summer King S., Delaware Park, May 21, $59,100, 3&up, f&m, 1m 70y, 1:44.62, YOUR OUT, Kiss a Miss, Lily's Affair, 7 started.

SUMMER S. (Can-G2), Woodbine, Sept. 8, $291,250, 2yo, 1mT, 1:35.33, LISMORE KNIGHT, Wando, Walls of Jericho, 11 started.

Summertime Promise Breeders' Cup S., Hawthorne Race Course, May 25, $100,000, 3yo, f, 1⅟₁₆mT, 1:44.40, MALIZIOSA, Strikes No Spares, Sarah Jade, 6 started.

Summit S., The Meadowlands, Sept. 21, $50,000, 3yo, f, 1m 70y, 1:42.37, TARNISHED LADY, Cat Rocket, Whoop's Ah Daisy, 7 started.

Summit Silver Cup H. (R), Thistledown, May 4, $50,000, 3yo, Ohio-bred, 1⅟₁₆m, 1:45.32, ALL OUT SPRINGS, Elm Grove, Mary's Lord, 6 started.

Sun City H., Turf Paradise, May 4, $35,000, 3&up, f&m, 1mT, 1:36.39, COLOR ME FAST, Jocko Miss, Hazen, 9 started.

Suncoast S. (R), Tampa Bay Downs, Feb. 23, $50,000, 3yo, f, Florida-bred, 1⅟₁₆m, 1:50.03, ROMANCIN DIXIE, Ease Ahead, Quick Bird, 12 started.

Sun Devil S., Turf Paradise, Jan. 12, $30,000, 3yo, f, 1m, 1:37.33, KENDRICK PEAK, Calce Clunes, Bella Cash, 9 started.

Sunflower H. (R), The Woodlands, Oct. 14, $20,000, 3&up, c&g, Kansas-bred, 6f, 1:13.80, MR AMMO, Polar Barron, Scarlet Lad, 5 started.

Sun H., Hastings Park Racecourse, June 15, $36,075, 3&up, f&m, 1⅟₁₆m, 1:43.81, LAPIN REGALE, Inish Glora, Grooms Derby, 4 started.

Sunland Park H., Sunland Park, April 6, $78,200, 3&up, 1⅟₁₆m, 1:42.52, ACCOMODATOR, Big Numbers, Golden Tangle, 9 started.

Sunland Park Oaks, Sunland Park, March 30, $77,700, 3yo, f, 1m, 1:38.11, NO TURBULENCE, After the Beep, Gray Ryder, 8 started.

Sunland Park Yuletide Derby, Sunland Park, Dec. 7, $53,950, 3yo, 6½f, 1:16.01, PREMEDITATION, Lou's Expectation, Pacer, 8 started.

Sunny's Halo S. (R), Woodbine, Nov. 20, $108,000, 2yo, Canadian-bred, 6½f, 1:15.77, QUIET DARE, Shipman, Sonofawac, 7 started.

Sunny Slope S., Santa Anita Park, Oct. 19, $96,600, 2yo, 6f, 1:09.12, ONLY THE BEST, Domestic Dispute, Roll Hennessy Roll, 9 started.

Sunnyvale H., Bay Meadows, June 2, $60,600, 3&up, f&m, 6f, 1:08.86, IRGUNS ANGEL, Channing Way, Halo Tyra, 9 started.

Sun Power S. (R), Hawthorne Race Course, Nov. 9, $105,975, 2yo, c&g, Illinois-bred, 6f, 1:12.05, WHATASHOT, Bold America, Shandy, 10 started.

SunRay Park & Casino H., SunRay Park, Sept. 23, $32,600, 3yo, 6½f, 1:18, CO TWINING NINER, Smart Score, Steves Eldorado, 8 started.

SUNSET H.-G2, Hollywood Park, July 21, $250,000, 3&up, 1½mT, 2:26.59, GRAMMARIAN, Continental Red, Lord Flasheart, 7 started.

Sun Sprint S., Northlands Park, Aug. 5, $50,000, 3&up, 6½f, 1:17.40, TYKO TYCOON, Sixthirtyjoe, Fussy's Kid, 6 started.

SUPER DERBY-G2, Louisiana Downs, Sept. 21, $500,000, 3yo, 1⅛m, 1:49.43, ESSENCE OF DUBAI, Walk in the Snow, A. P. Five Hundred, 8 started.

Supernaturel H., Hastings Park Racecourse, May 18, $37,520, 3yo, f, 6½f, 1:18.76, REGAL HEIR, Classic Action, Fast and Free, 5 started.

Super S., Tampa Bay Downs, Jan. 22, $50,000, 4&up, 7f, 1:22.62, SECRET ROMEO, Tour of the Cat, Mountain Top, 9 started.

Survive S. (R), Santa Anita Park, Jan. 2, $112,600, 4&up, f&m, California-bred non-winners of a race worth $50,000 twice other than closed or claiming since March 1, 2001, 5½f, 1:03.38, PHAENNA, Song of Summer, Song of the Moment, 9 started.

Susan B. Anthony H. (R), Finger Lakes, June 22, $35,000, 3&up, f&m, New York-bred, 6f, 1:11.60, DOUBLE THE DEBT, Shesastonecoldfox, Belongs to Mony, 9 started.

Susan's Girl Breeders' Cup S., Delaware Park, June 29, $175,300, 3yo, f, 1⅟₁₆m, 1:46.24, PASS THE VIRTUE, Alternate, Shop Till You Drop, 6 started.

Susan's Girl S. (R), Calder Race Course, Aug. 31, $125,000, 2yo, f, progeny of eligible Florida stallions, 7f, 1:24.41, IVANAVINALOT, Heavenly Miss, Fortunate Card, 8 started.

Sussex H., Delaware Park, Aug. 3, $100,600, 3&up, 1⅟₁₆mT, 1:42.17, SYNCLINE, Dr. Kashnikow, Sardaukar (GB), 7 started.

Suthern Accent S., Louisiana Downs, July 13, $40,000, 3&up, f&m, 6f, 1:11, FUSE IT, Princess Jen, Raymond's Dream, 7 started.

SUWANNEE RIVER H.-G3, Gulfstream Park, March 3, $100,000, 3&up, f&m, 1⅛mT, 1:49.04, SNOW DANCE, Windsong, Step With Style, 6 started.

SWALE S.-G3, Gulfstream Park, March 16, $150,000, 3yo, 7f, 1:22.29, ETHAN MAN, Listen Here, Sharp Flash, 5 started.

SWAPS S.-G2, Hollywood Park, July 14, $500,000, 3yo, 1⅛m, 1:48.28, CAME HOME, Like a Hero, Fonz's, 7 started.

Sweet and Sassy S., Delaware Park, July 6, $100,600, 3&up, f&m, 6f, 1:11.21, MANDY'S GOLD, Madame Roar, Outstanding Info, 7 started.

Sweet Briar Too S., Woodbine, June 23, $107,000, 3&up, f&m, 7f, 1:22.75, DEVASTATING, El Prado Essence, Lightning Pace, 5 started.

Sweetest Chant S., Arlington Park, Oct. 14, $48,500, 3&up, f&m, 1⅛m, 1:52.49, SOFTLY, Giving Noreen, Sharky's Review, 7 started.

Swift S., Turf Paradise, Jan. 26, $30,000, 4&up, 5½f, 1:01.99, HANGONSLEWPYHANGON, Quinton's Gold, Valid Sunrise, 7 started.

SWORD DANCER INVITATIONAL H.-G1, Saratoga Race Course, Aug. 10, $500,000, 3&up, 1½mT, 2:24.06, WITH ANTICIPATION, Denon, Volponi, 11 started.

S. W. Randall Plate H., Hastings Park Racecourse, Sept. 2, $37,804, 3&up, 1⅛m, 1:50.61, KID KATABATIC, Work Visa, Mt. Ouray, 5 started.

Swynford S., Woodbine, Sept. 22, $133,250, 2yo, 7f, 1:23.33, ADDED EDGE, Canasta, Whispered Warning, 4 started.

Sycamore Breeders' Cup S., Keeneland, Oct. 6, $154,400, 3&up, 1½mT, 2:30.48, ROCHESTER, Roxinho (Brz), Lord Flasheart, 7 started.

Sydney Gendelman Memorial H. (R), River Downs, June 23, $50,000, 3&up, Ohio-bred, 1/16mT, 1:41.40, DEVIL TIME, Blame It On Ruby, Panta Ellinas, 11 started.
Tacoma H., Emerald Downs, July 14, $40,000, 3yo, c&g, 1/16m, 1:41.40, FLYING NOTES, Salt Grinder, Vernon Lodge, 6 started.
Tah Dah S. (R), River Downs, July 19, $40,000, 2yo, f, Ohio-bred, 5½f, 1:07.60, IFUFEELFROGGYLEAP, Da Dance, Notyourunofthemill, 13 started.
Taking Risks S. (R), Timonium, Sept. 2, $40,000, 3&up, Maryland-bred, 1/16m, 1:45.84, FULL BRUSH, Get the Picture, P Day, 5 started.
Tampa Bay Breeders' Cup S., Tampa Bay Downs, Feb. 16, $78,000, 3&up, 1/16mT, 1:40.95, BOASTFUL, Dog Tags, Tour of the Cat, 11 started.
TAMPA BAY DERBY-G3, Tampa Bay Downs, March 17, $200,000, 3yo, 1/16m, 1:43.66, EQUALITY, Tails of the Crypt, Political Attack, 9 started.
TANFORAN H.-G3, Golden Gate Fields, Feb. 9, $100,000, 4&up, 1/16mT, 1:44.25, DECARCHY, Ninebanks, Poker Brad, 9 started.
Ta Wee S., Laurel Park, Oct. 26, $50,000, 3&up, f&m, 6f, 1:09.53, WINTER LEAF, Blinded by Love, A Barry Good Act, 7 started.
Taylor's Special H., Fair Grounds, Feb. 24, $100,000, 4&up, 6f, 1:09.32, BONAPAW, Crucible, Abajo, 5 started.
Taylor's Special S., Arlington Park, Oct. 6, $49,500, 3&up, a5fT, :58.86, MAN O' RHYTHM, Justice for Auston, Bold Pilot, 9 started.
Teddy Drone S., Monmouth Park, Aug. 4, $65,000, 3&up, 6f, 1:08.84, SUMMER SWING, True Passion, Ticket to Freedom, 7 started.
Teeworth Plate H., Stampede Park, May 19, $40,000, 3&up, 1m, 1:37.80, SIXTHIRTYJOE, Rancour, Tyko Tycoon, 9 started.
Tejano Run S., Turfway Park, March 16, $50,000, 4&up, 1⅛m, 1:50.72, DOUBLE AFFAIR, Frazee's Folly, Two Point Two Mill, 10 started.
Tejas S. (R), Retama Park, Oct. 12, $30,000, 3yo, Texas-bred, 5fT, :56.57, SON OF A LUE, Sharpenupjoe, Royal Honey, 9 started.
Tellike H., Evangeline Downs, June 1, $30,000, 3&up, f&m, 6f, 1:11.40, HIGHHOPESEMILYLUCK, Raymond's Dream, Sofia So Fine, 11 started.
Tempe H., Turf Paradise, March 16, $35,000, 3yo, 1mT, 1:36.94, PLAYING IT COOL, Malone, Touring England, 12 started.
Temple Gwathmey Steeplechase H., Middleburg, April 20, $48,500, 4&up, a2½mT, 5:20.80, PRAISE THE PRINCE (NZ), P. C. Plod, Pelagos (Fr), 6 started.
TEMPTED S.-G3, Aqueduct, Nov. 3, $110,400, 2yo, f, 1m, 1:37.52, CHIMICHURRI, Reheat, Bonay, 8 started.
Temptress S. (R), Great Lakes Downs, Aug. 16, $45,000, 2yo, f, Michigan-bred, 6f, 1:17.05, MISS THE KISS, Magna Cum Laude, Jean's Way, 7 started.
Tenacious H., Fair Grounds, Dec. 8, $75,000, 3&up, 1/16m, 1:42.98, ROCK SLIDE, Discreet Hero, Connected, 10 started.
Ten Thousand Lakes S. (R), Canterbury Park, May 18, $36,900, 3&up, c&g, Minnesota-bred, 6fT, 1:09.97, CROCROCK, Ashar, This Little Piggy, 8 started.
Terre Haute S. (R), Hoosier Park, Nov. 29, $32,700, 2yo, f, Indiana-bred, 1m, 1:42.21, MISS DAKOTA, Pleasant Point, Indy Fire, 7 started.
Territorial Fair S. (R), The Downs at Albuquerque, May 19, $31,020, 3yo, New Mexico-bred, 1/16m, 1:44.52, STAR SMASHER, Jacks Romeo, Mister Slinky, 5 started.
TEST S.-G1, Saratoga Race Course, July 27, $250,000, 3yo, f, 7f, 1:22.84, YOU, Spring Meadow, Carson Hollow, 7 started.
Testum S. (R), Les Bois Park, July 20, $12,135, 3yo, c&g, Idaho-bred, 7f, 1:23.93, MR MOTION, Cool Papa Rick, Jazzing Jack, 8 started.
Texas Heritage S., Sam Houston Race Park, March 16, $30,000, 3yo, 1m, 1:38.71, STORM ALARM, Revered Soldier, Padlock, 9 started.
Texas Horse Racing Hall of Fame S. (R), Retama Park, Oct. 12, $100,000, 3&up, Texas-bred, 1/16mT, 1:42.48, DESERT DARBY, Rare Cure, D C Storm, 8 started.
TEXAS MILE S.-G3, Lone Star Park, April 27, $300,000, 3&up, 1m, 1:37.78, UNRULLAH BULL, Reba's Gold, Compendium, 9 started.
Texas Stallion Consolation S. (R), Lone Star Park, June 29, $52,500, 2yo, nominated and eligible to the Texas Stallion Stakes Series, 5½f, 1:04.66, FATHER MARTIN, Capitol H, Timber, 12 started.
Texas Stallion S. (R), Sam Houston Race Park, Dec. 7, $42,831, 3&up, f&m, nominated and eligible to the Texas Stallion Stakes Series, 1m, 1:38.39, EAGLE LAKE, Pancho's Affair, Khazi, 7 started.
Texas Stallion S. (R), Retama Park, Oct. 12, $125,000, 2yo, c&g, nominated and eligible to the Texas Stallion Stakes Series, 6f, 1:10.58, LEO'S LAST HURRAHY, Call Me Lefty, Screen Pass, 13 started.
Texas Stallion S. (R), Retama Park, Oct. 12, $125,000, 2yo, f, nominated and eligible to the Texas Stallion Stakes Series, 6f, 1:10.93, PARTING, Lady Mallory, Hay Allison, 9 started.
Texas Stallion S. (R), Sam Houston Race Park, Dec. 7, $43,839, 3&up, nominated and eligible to the Texas Stallion Stakes Series, 1m, 1:38.98, FITZROYAL, Star of Caveat, Lord Zotti, 7 started.
Texas Stallion S. (R), Retama Park, Sept. 28, $55,065, 3yo, c&g, nominated and eligible to the Texas Stallion Stakes Series, 6f, 1:10.70, FITZROYAL, Onlynurimagination, Royal Honey, 7 started.
Texas Stallion S. (R), Retama Park, Sept. 28, $54,157, 3yo, f, nominated and eligible to the Texas Stallion Stakes Series, 6f, 1:12.41, DANCING DREAMS, Pancho's Affair, Wings Alight, 7 started.
Texas Stallion S. (R), Lone Star Park, June 29, $122,500, 2yo, c&g, nominated and eligible to the Texas Stallion Stakes Series, 5½f, 1:04.76, ACTION TONIGHT, Leo's Last Hurrahy, Seneca Rock, 11 started.
Texas Stallion S. (R), Sam Houston Race Park, Dec. 28, $125,000, 2yo, f, nominated and eligible to the Texas Stallion Stakes Series, 1m, 1:40.28, SHOWMETOTHEVILLA, Hay Allison, Lady Mallory, 8 started.
Texas Stallion S. (R), Lone Star Park, June 29, $122,500, 2yo, f, nominated and eligible to the Texas Stallion Stakes Series, 5½f, 1:05.56, TIFFANY JENNIFER, Parting, Hay Allison, Bedif, 11 started.
Texas Stallion S. (R), Sam Houston Race Park, Dec. 28, $125,000, 2yo, nominated and eligible to the Texas Stallion Stakes Series, 1m, 1:38.87, CALL ME LEFTY, Lasttorun, Hasit, 8 started.
Texas Throughbred Breeders' S., Gillespie County Downs, July 20, $6,000, 3&up, 6f, 1:13.73, TOUCHOVILLE, Happy Smile, Crafty Loom, 5 started.
Tex's Zing S. (R), Fairmount Park, Oct. 1, $35,900, 3yo, c&g, Illinois-bred, 6f, 1:11.60, BULLDOG GEORGE, Char's Bob'n Robin, Inod, 8 started.
Thanksgiving Day Starter H. (R), Calder Race Course, Nov. 28, $32,800, 3&up, starters for a claiming price of $25,000 or less since January 1, 2001, 1¼m, 2:06.66, STRIKE THREE, Sea Leon, Watch Your Pennies, 7 started.
Thanksgiving H., Fair Grounds, Nov. 28, $75,000, 3&up, 6f, 1:08.03, MOUNTAIN GENERAL, Wild Summer, Aloha Bold, 7 started.
That's Our Buck S. (R), Calder Race Course, Dec. 22, $38,150, 3yo, non-winners of a stakes or $50,000 since March 15, 2002, 6½f, 1:17.21, HARMONY HALL, Longford Arms, Fire and Glory, 7 started.
The Bart S., Arlington Park, Aug. 18, $64,500, 3&up, 1/16mT, 1:43.53, PRIVATE SON, Just Like Jimmy, Smilin' Slew, 8 started.
The Downs at Albuquerque H., The Downs at Albuquerque, June 16, $109,500, 3&up, 1⅛m, 1:50.13, Darn Tootin, NATES COLONY, Reflecting Colors, 9 started.
Thelma S., Fair Grounds, Jan. 6, $75,000, 3yo, f, 6f, 1:11.12, LAKE LADY, Land Yachting, Vicki Vallencourt, 10 started.
THE VERY ONE H.-G3, Gulfstream Park, Feb. 17, $100,000, 3&up, f&m, a1⅜mT, 2:18.38, MOON QUEEN (Ire), Sweetest Thing, Septietta, 6 started.
The Very One S., Pimlico, May 17, $55,000, 3&up, f&m, 5fT, :56.67, MERRY PRINCESS, Maypole Dance, Scootin' Girl, 12 started.
Thirty Eight Go Go S., Laurel Park, Nov. 16, $50,000, 3&up, f&m, 1⅛m, 1:53.50, PASS THE VIRTUE, Lily's Affair, Golden Phoebe, 5 started.
Thomas Edison S., The Meadowlands, Sept. 2, $100,000, 3&up, 5f, :56.05, BOP, Rudirudy, Texas Glitter, 7 started.
Thomas F. Moran S. (R), Suffolk Downs, June 8, $29,400, 3&up, Massachusetts-bred, 1/16mT, 1:46.70, JINI'S JET, Papa Ho Ho, Dawn's First Light, 5 started.
Thomas J. Malley S., Monmouth Park, May 26, $50,000, 3&up, f&m, 5fT, :56.44, SPARKLING NUMBER, Merry Princess, Maypole Dance, 10 started.
Thoroughbred Claiming S., Gila County Fair, Oct. 5, $2,528, 3&up, 5½f, 1:06.60, REVENUE, Littlefield, Brooksbobnbucky, 6 started.
Thoroughbred Claiming S., Graham County Fair, April 7, $2,257, 3&up, 1m, 1:46, THREE TOMS, Hitaway Jay, Personal Pride, 7 started.
Thoroughbred Claiming S., Mohave County Fair, May 11, $3,095, 3&up, 1⅛m, 1:53.80, COP OUT, Mood Blue, Oil Man, 5 started.
Thoroughbred Claming S., Gila County Fair, Oct. 6, $2,328, 3&up, 1/16m, 1:50.80, TOOTIES TEDDY, Hiawatha Limited, Critter, 8 started.
THOROUGHBRED CLUB OF AMERICA S.-G3, Keeneland, Oct.

20, $125,000, 3&up, f&m, 6f, 1:09.75, FRENCH RIVIERA, Don't Countess Out, Away, 10 started.
Thoroughbred Maiden Derby, Les Bois Park, July 4, $15,800, 3yo, 6½f, 1:19.70, BUCKIES EXCLUSIVE, Chico's Gold, Spud Man, 9 started.
Thoroughbred Starter S., Les Bois Park, Aug. 10, $5,825, 3&up, 7½f, 1:33.37, BARGAINING CHIP, Skirl, Patticat, 8 started.
Three Chimneys Juvenile S., Churchill Downs, May 4, $121,400, 2yo, 5f, :57.71, HOLIDAY RUNNER, Zavata, Posse, 13 started.
Three Ring S., Calder Race Course, Dec. 14, $100,000, 2yo, f, 1$\frac{1}{16}$m, 1:47.54, DAKOTA LIGHT, Never Fail, Bird Town, 8 started.
Ticonderoga H. (R), Belmont Park, Oct. 19, $150,000, 3&up, f&m, New York-bred, 1⅛mT, 1:53.40, RHUM, Shopping for Love, Mandalay Bay, 11 started.
Tiffany Lass S., Fair Grounds, Jan. 27, $100,000, 3yo, f, 1m, 1:38.17, LAKE LADY, Charmed Gift, Emeraldforajudge, 7 started.
Timber Music S. (R), Hastings Park Racecourse, July 13, $38,080, 2yo, f, British Columbia-bred and/or -owned, 6½f, 1:19.46, MY MISS EMILY, Dancewithavixen, Rainbows Forever, 6 started.
Times Square S. (R), Aqueduct, April 21, $100,000, 3yo, c&g, New York-bred, 1m, 1:37.15, TRIAL PREP, Beyond Chance, Levendis, 5 started.
Time To Leave S., Bay Meadows, Oct. 13, $65,900, 2yo, f, 6f, 1:09.98, VIANSA OSSIDIANA, Hostility, Tale of a Dream, 6 started.
Time To Leave S., Bay Meadows, June 15, $69,675, 2yo, f, 5f, :58.07, HOSTILITY, Solo Singer, Proactive, 7 started.
Tippett S., Colonial Downs, July 20, $40,000, 2yo, f, 5½fT, 1:04.79, LITTLE MISS PAMELA, Raise the Level, City Fire, 8 started.
Toboggan H., Aqueduct, March 16, $108,200, 3&up, 7f, 1:22.87, AFFIRMED SUCCESS, Multiple Choice, Vodka, 6 started.
Tokyo City H., Santa Anita Park, March 9, $79,350, 4&up, 1m, 1:35.54, BOSQUE REDONDO, Reba's Gold, Discreet Hero, 5 started.
Tomball S. (R), Sam Houston Race Park, Feb. 9, $30,000, 4&up, f&m, Texas-bred, 1$\frac{1}{16}$m, 1:45, COASTALOTA, Madison Grace, Princess Liza, 9 started.
Tom Bane Starter Allowance S. (R), Turf Paradise, April 27, $15,000, 3&up, Arizona-bred starters for a claming price of $8,000 or less since September 27, 2001, 6f, 1:09.05, RED HOT ROCKET, Poco Stampede, Dunson, 9 started.
Tomboy S. (R), River Downs, May 18, $50,000, 3yo, f, Ohio-bred, 1$\frac{1}{16}$mT, 1:49.60, CRYPTO'S TWINJET, Saratoga Set, Come Hither, 13 started.
TOM FOOL H.-G2, Belmont Park, July 4, $150,000, 3&up, 7f, 1:20.17, LEFT BANK, Affirmed Success, Summer Note, 6 started.
To Much Coffee S. (R), Hoosier Park, Nov. 24, $44,350, 3&up, Indiana-bred, 1$\frac{1}{16}$m, 1:46.80, FIGHT FOR ALLY, Hail to Wild Again, Donnies Pick, 10 started.
Tondi H., Fonner Park, April 20, $25,800, 3&up, 6f, 1:12, MEDIUM RARE, Yankee Ruler, Buzz Bar, 8 started.
Toon's Mile H., Marquis Downs, July 19, $5,000, 3&up, 1m, 1:41.42, PANIOLO GOLD, Beau Ring, Arctic Pat, 6 started.
TOP FLIGHT H.-G2, Aqueduct, Nov. 29, $150,000, 3&up, f&m, 1m, 1:35.46, SIGHTSEEK, Nasty Storm, Zonk, 9 started.
Top Flight S., Arlington Park, Aug. 31, $75,000, 2yo, f, 6f, 1:11.08, SOURIS, Christmas Time, You Glitter Girl, 5 started.
Topsider S., Suffolk Downs, Oct. 26, $30,000, 3&up, 6f, 1:10.70, FIRST SHOT, Method Man, Chilling Sweep, 7 started.
TORONTO CUP S. (Can-G3), Woodbine, July 13, $163,050, 3yo, 1⅛mT, 1:47.98, PORTCULLIS, El Soprano, Funny Soldier, 5 started.
Torrey Pines S. (R), Del Mar, Sept. 8, $82,050, 3yo, f, non-winners of $60,000 at one mile or over in 2002, 1m, 1:37, GOT KOKO, Ragin T Rex, Bare Necessities, 9 started.
Totah Futurity (R), SunRay Park, Nov. 15, $81,939, 2yo, New Mexico-bred, 6½f, 1:20.80, HASTY GUS, Catch Simon, Spider Dash, 9 started.
Tougaloo S. (R), Thistledown, April 28, $40,000, 3yo, f, Ohio-bred, 6f, 1:13.10, COME HITHER, R Nurse C, Tisourturn, 9 started.
Transylvania S., Keeneland, April 5, $100,000, 3yo, 1mT, 1:35.69, FLYING DASH (Ger), Back Packer, Political Attack, 8 started.
TRAVERS S.-G1, Saratoga Race Course, Aug. 24, $1,000,000, 3yo, 1¼m, 2:02.53, MEDAGLIA D'ORO, Repent, Nothing Flat, 9 started.
TREMONT S.-G3, Belmont Park, June 29, $106,600, 2yo, 5½f, 1:02.66, ZAVATA, Hussar, Desert Warrior, 5 started.
Trend Home Improvements-Hart Home S., Grand Prairie, July 14, $3,325, 3&up, f&m, 6½f, 1:23.80, JAR OF BUTTONS, Sweet N Brassy, Bonjour, 5 started.
Tres Rios Juvenile S., SunRay Park, Nov. 2, $45,667, 2yo, c&g, 6½f, 1:19, NET FORCE, Star Status, Regal Punch, 9 started.
TRIPLE BEND BREEDERS' CUP INVITATIONAL H.-G2, Hollywood Park, July 6, $300,000, 3&up, 7f, 1:21.09, DISTURBINGTHEPEACE, D'wildcat, Mellow Fellow, 9 started.
Triple Crown H., Blue Ribbon Downs, June 8, $7,525, 3&up, 7½f, 1:32.58, MAGIC SHOT, Tedro, Taxauditor, 7 started.
Triple Crown Nutrition Breeders' Classic S. (R), Charles Town, Oct. 12, $67,500, 2yo, f, West Virginia-bred, -sired, or -raised, 4½f, 52.70, X TRA BRASSY, Hushaby Babe, Courageous Valor, 9 started.
Tri-State Futurity (R), Charles Town, Oct. 26, $80,875, 2yo, Maryland-bred, Virginia-bred, or West Virginia-bred, 7f, 1:26.76, CHEROKEE'S BOY, Forever Joe, Straight Star, 8 started.
Tri-State H., Ellis Park, Sept. 2, $58,750, 3&up, 1⅛mT, 1:45.39, ROXINHO (Brz), Red Mountain, X Country, 8 started.
TROPICAL PARK DERBY-G3, Calder Race Course, Jan. 1, $100,000, 3yo, 1⅛m, 1:51.71, POLITICAL ATTACK, The Judge Sez Who, Deeliteful Guy, 8 started.
Tropical Park Oaks, Calder Race Course, Jan. 1, $100,000, 3yo, f, 1$\frac{1}{16}$mT, 1:45.44, STORMY FROLIC, Ciudad de Carson, Bema, 8 started.
TROPICAL TURF H.-G3, Calder Race Course, Dec. 7, $100,000, 3&up, 1⅛mT, 1:47.02, KRIEGER, Stokosky, Serial Bride, 12 started.
TRUE NORTH H.-G2, Belmont Park, June 8, $250,000, 3&up, 6f, 1:09.98, EXPLICIT, Entepreneur, Late Carson, 7 started.
TTA Sales Futurity (R), Lone Star Park, June 8, $150,580, 2yo, c&g, sold at a TTA sale, 5f, 58.61, LEO'S LAST HURRAHY, Action Tonight, Sockitaway, 10 started.
TTA Sales Futurity (R), Lone Star Park, June 8, $142,040, 2yo, f, sold at a TTA sale, 5f, 59.29, JAZZ LADY, Kristys Gold Star, Afternoon Dreams, 11 started.
Tulsa Dash S., Fair Meadows at Tulsa, June 13, $33,090, 3&up, 4f, HOOKED ON EXPRESSO, Blazing Count, Here Comes Rebel, 10 started.
Tulsa Sprint S. (R), Fair Meadows at Tulsa, July 20, $42,650, 3&up, Oklahoma-bred, 4f, :45, ABBI'S CHOICE, Fashion Lover, Sam's Country Blue, 10 started.
TURF CLASSIC INVITATIONAL S.-G1, Belmont Park, Sept. 29, $750,000, 3&up, 1½mT, 2:28.47, DENON, Delta Form (Aus), Blazing Fury, 8 started.
Turf Distance Starters S., Turf Paradise, May 4, $41,850, 3&up, 1⅜mT, 2:16.30, DAVID'S DREAM, Belgravia (GB), Why Stop Now, 12 started.
Turf Monster H., Philadelphia Park, May 27, $100,000, 3&up, 5fT, :57.73, JOE'S SON JOEY, Texas Glitter, Rudirudy, 9 started.
Turf Paradise Breeders' Cup H., Turf Paradise, Feb. 2, $142,500, 3&up, 1$\frac{1}{16}$mT, 1:43.31, AUCTION HOUSE, Devine Wind, Casey Griffin, 6 started.
Turf Paradise Derby, Turf Paradise, Feb. 2, $100,000, 3yo, 1$\frac{1}{16}$m, 1:41.76, CAPTAIN SQUIRE, National Park (GB), Lusty Latin, 6 started.
Turf Sprint S., Lone Star Park, May 27, $100,000, 3&up, 5fT, :55.74, NUCLEAR DEBATE, Joyful Tune, Boots On Sunday, 7 started.
TURFWAY BREEDERS' CUP S.-G3, Turfway Park, Sept. 14, $200,000, 3&up, f&m, 1$\frac{1}{16}$m, 1:43.01, TRIP, Mystic Lady, Red n'Gold, 9 started.
TURFWAY PARK FALL CHAMPIONSHIP S.-G3, Turfway Park, Sept. 28, $100,000, 3&up, 1⅛m, 1:52.29, CRAFTY SHAW, Rock Slide, Deferred Comp, 7 started.
Turfway Prevue S., Turfway Park, Jan. 5, $47,500, 3yo, 6½f, 1:18.15, PERFECT DRIFT, Thunder On Land, World Champion, 7 started.
TURNBACK THE ALARM H.-G3, Aqueduct, Nov. 3, $108,000, 3&up, f&m, 1⅛m, 1:50.42, SVEA DAHL, Mystic Lady, Critical Eye, 5 started.
TVG California Cup Distance H. (R), Santa Anita Park, Nov. 2, $100,000, 3&up, f&m, California-bred, 1¼mT, 2:01.93, NICOLE'S PURSUIT, Shalini, Barely Daylight, 11 started.
TVG Khaled S. (R), Hollywood Park, April 28, $175,000, 4&up, California-bred, 1$\frac{1}{16}$mT, 1:41.87, NATIVE DESERT, Hugh Hefner, Visual Energy, 7 started.
Twilight Oilfield S., Grand Prairie, July 27, $3,715, 3&up, f&m, 6½f, 1:21.60, ALIBI EXPERT, Jar of Buttons, Sweet N Brassy, 7 started.
Twin Lights S., Monmouth Park, July 6, $50,000, 3yo, f, 1⅛mT, 1:48.34, BELLS FOR MARLIN, Once Around, Weepnomoremylady, 7 started.
Twixt S. (R), Laurel Park, Nov. 23, $75,000, 3yo, f, Maryland-bred, 1⅛m, 1:54.09, TRUE SENSATION, Tamayo, Ribbon Cane, 6 started.
Twixtslusive S. (1st Div.), Delaware Park, Sept. 15, $59,700, 3&up, f&m, a1$\frac{1}{16}$mT, 1:43.54, CRUISE ALONG, Langoureuse, Laurica, 7 started.
Twixtslusive S. (2nd Div.), Delaware Park, Sept. 15, $59,100, 3&up,

f&m, a1¹⁄₁₆mT, 1:44.56, LAPUMA, Decencia (Arg), Lady Linda, 6 started.

Tyro S., Monmouth Park, July 20, $50,000, 2yo, 5¹⁄₂f, 1:05.01, FARNO, Down Play, Max a Million, 6 started.

U Can Do It H., Calder Race Course, Oct. 5, $75,000, 3&up, f&m, 6¹⁄₂f, 1:18.54, CHISPISKI, Fly Me Crazy, Rule Brittania, 6 started.

Unbridled H. (R), Gulfstream Park, April 12, $80,500, 3&up, Florida-bred, 1¹⁄₁₆m, 1:43.83, BEST OF THE REST, Groomstick Stock's, Dancing Guy, 7 started.

Unbridled S., Calder Race Course, June 22, $100,000, 3yo, 1¹⁄₁₆m, 1:44.84, PUCK, The Judge Sez Who, Rocker, 8 started.

UNITED NATIONS H.-G1, Monmouth Park, July 6, $500,000, 3&up, 1³⁄₈mT, 2:12.81, WITH ANTICIPATION, Denon, Sarafan, 7 started.

United Tote Dash for Cash Breeders' Classic S. (R), Charles Town, Oct. 12, $67,500, 3&up, West Virginia-bred, -sired, or -raised, 4¹⁄₂f, 51.93, DOUBLEDAR DIAMOND, Not for Sam, Bandi's Boy, 8 started.

U. S. Bank S., Emerald Downs, April 21, $35,000, 3yo, f, 6f, 1:08.80, LASTING CODE, Strong Credentials, Double Quack, 8 started.

U. S. Championship Supreme Hurdle S. (R), Pine Mountain, Calloway Garden, Nov. 2, $100,000, 4&up, non-winners over hurdles prior to September 1, 2001, a2³⁄₄mT, 3:50, MCDYNAMO, Gallant Turk, Mr Perkolater, 4 started.

Vacaville H., Solano County Fair, July 13, $50,770, 3&up, f&m, 6f, 1:09.38, CHANNING WAY, Hadl, Fancee Bargain, 7 started.

VAGRANCY H.-G2, Belmont Park, June 9, $150,000, 3&up, f&m, 6¹⁄₂f, 1:16.44, XTRA HEAT, Gold Mover, Shine Again, 5 started.

Valdale S., Turfway Park, Feb. 23, $49,000, 3yo, f, 1m, 1:38.95, IDEVETER, Art Fair, Raise a Roar, 10 started.

Valedictory S., Woodbine, Dec. 1, $147,000, 3&up, 1³⁄₄m, 3:03.83, LUCKY MOLAR, Defenman, Malmaison, 14 started.

Valiant Pete H. (R), Santa Anita Park, April 19, $102,704, 4&up, California-bred, 6f, 1:09.01, FULL MOON MADNESS, Men's Exclusive, Ride and Shine, 4 started.

Valid Appeal S. (R), Gulfstream Park, April 19, $80,600, 2yo, Florida-bred, 3f, :33.02, SWEET PROMISES, Supah Blitz, Lucky Magus, 6 started.

Valid Expectations S., Lone Star Park, May 27, $100,000, 3&up, f&m, 6f, 1:10.56, PRIZED AMBERPRO, Hattiesburg, Hallowed Dreams, 5 started.

Valkyr H. (R), Hollywood Park, July 19, $76,875, 3&up, f&m, California-bred non-winners of three races other than maiden, claiming, or starter, 1mT, 1:35.57, CASTLING, Mind for Gold, Exclusiveandcatty, 6 started.

Vallejo S., Golden Gate Fields, Feb. 17, $57,925, 3yo, f, 6f, 1:10.03, FERTILE, That's Our Tricky, Lil' Awesome Annie, 5 started.

VALLEY STREAM S.-G3, Aqueduct, Nov. 24, $111,300, 2yo, f, 6f, 1:09.46, RANDAROO, House Party, Fast Cookie, 8 started.

VALLEY VIEW S.-G3, Keeneland, Oct. 19, $115,700, 3yo, f, 1¹⁄₁₆mT, 1:44.24, BEDANKEN, Mariensky, High Maintenance (GB), 10 started.

Valor Farm S. (R), Lone Star Park, June 29, $50,000, 3yo, f, Texas-bred, 6f, 1:10.43, MISS RITZ, Sly Kona, Lucky M, 6 started.

Vance Davenport & Ralph Taylor Claiming S., Les Bois Park, July 2¼, $3,700, 3&up, f&m, 7f, 1:26.14, HIT THE PRESS, Lady of Lights, Run N Honey, 7 started.

Vandal S. (R), Woodbine, Aug. 18, $164,550, 2yo, Canadian-bred, 6f, 1:11.90, WANDO, Snake Pit, Shipman, 4 started.

VANITY H.-G1, Hollywood Park, June 22, $250,000, 3&up, f&m, 1¹⁄₈m, 1:48.88, AZERI, Affluent, Collect Call, Starrer, 5 started.

Vector Communications S., Grand Prairie, Aug. 2, $2,600, 3&up, 6f, 1:13.60, DON CORONAIGE, Island Slew, Sceptical Diamonds, 6 started.

Veiled Look S., Delaware Park, Aug. 26, $59,100, 3&up, f&m, 6f, 1:10.61, BRUANNA, Urban Dancer, Border Fire, 6 started.

VERNON O. UNDERWOOD S.-G3, Hollywood Park, Dec. 7, $100,000, 3&up, 6f, 1:09.17, DEBONAIR JOE, F J's Pace, American System, 9 started.

Very Subtle Overnight S., Ruidoso Downs, Aug. 31, $15,000, 3&up, f&m, 6f, 1:11.60, RUBIN'S GIRL, Festival Legs, Hava Peer, 7 started.

Via Borghese S., Gulfstream Park, April 7, $75,000, 3yo, f, 1¹⁄₈m, 1:48.41, CELLARS SHIRAZ, Dame Sylvieguilhem, Kathy K D, 7 started.

Vice Regent S. (R), Woodbine, Aug. 7, $135,125, 3yo, progeny of eligible Ontario stallions, 1mT, 1:37.34, MIGHTY QUINN, Mulligan the Great, Dillinger, 8 started.

Victoria Day S., Assiniboia Downs, May 20, $29,400, 3&up, f&m, 5¹⁄₂f, 1:05.60, MISS SANDY DEE, Cathy's Star, Dawn Edition, 5 started.

Victoria H. (R), Louisiana Downs, Oct. 20, $38,350, 3&up, f&m, Louisiana-bred, 6f, 1:11.57, PRIZED AMBERPRO, Mike's Sister, Taylor's Queen, 7 started.

Victoria Lass S., Fair Grounds, March 16, $125,000, 4&up, f&m, 6f, 1:10.11, SERENA'S TUNE, Sweet Nanette, Dominica, 7 started.

Victoriana S. (R), Woodbine, Aug. 5, $129,625, 3&up, f&m, progeny of eligible Ontario stallions, 1¹⁄₁₆mT, 1:43.52, ARIEL'S MELODY, Peek a Boo Sara, Night Edition, 6 started.

Victorian Queen S. (R), Woodbine, Oct. 2, $127,500, 2yo, f, progeny of eligible Ontario stallions, 6f, 1:11.70, MISS CRISSY, Deputy Cures Blues, Dressed for Action, 6 started.

Victoria Park S., Woodbine, June 8, $135,500, 3yo, 1¹⁄₈m, 1:50.36, TAILS OF THE CRYPT, Forever Grand, Barbeau Ruckus, 6 started.

Victoria S., Woodbine, June 15, $134,375, 2yo, 5f, EL RULLER, Skeet, Biddy's Lad, 5 started.

Victor S. Myers Jr. S. (R), Canterbury Park, June 29, $42,120, 3yo, c&g, Minnesota-bred, 6f, 1:09.46, J. P. JET, Semi Sweet Dr, Frosty Prince, 9 started.

VIGIL S. (Can-G3), Woodbine, April 27, $165,000, 4&up, 7f, 1:23.13, WAKE AT NOON, Exciting Story, Geraint, 8 started.

Vincennes S. (R), Hoosier Park, Oct. 4, $44,350, 3yo, f, Indiana-bred, 6f, 1:13.15, AMANDA'S CROWN, Connies Travels, Demi Paige, 10 started.

Vincent A. Moscarelli Memorial S., Delaware Park, Aug. 17, $75,300, 3yo, 1¹⁄₈m, 1:54.88, MAKE THE BEND, Mazoolian Ghost, Boca Flyer, 6 started.

VIOLET H.-G3, The Meadowlands, Sept. 20, $150,000, 3&up, f&m, 1¹⁄₁₆mT, 1:41.17, BABAE (Chi), Platinum Tiara, Stylish, 10 started.

Violet S. (R), Sportsman's Park, March 30, $83,000, 3yo, f, Illinois-conceived and/or-foaled, 6f, 1:11.36, GRACILITY, Scarlet O'Hara, Tejano Honey, 10 started.

Virginia Derby, Colonial Downs, July 13, $500,000, 3yo, 1¹⁄₄mT, 2:03.10, ORCHARD PARK, Flying Dash (Ger), Touring England, 6 started.

Virginia Gold Cup Timber S., Great Meadows, May 4, $50,000, 5 yo's & up, a4mT, 8:27.40, MAKE ME A CHAMP, Ironfist, Company Eight, 10 started.

Vivace S., Calder Race Course, May 20, $38,115, 3&up, f&m, 6¹⁄₂f, 1:18.60, FLY ME CRAZY, Vague Memory, Lark's Impression, 7 started.

Vivacious H. (R), River Downs, Aug. 18, $50,000, 3&up, f&m, Ohio-bred, 1¹⁄₁₆mT, 1:47.60, LADY CHERIE, Ashwood C C, Prizes, 8 started.

VOSBURGH S.-G1, Belmont Park, Sept. 21, $300,000, 3&up, 7f, 1:22.34, BONAPAW, Aldebaran, Voodoo, 6 started.

Vulcan S. (R), Fair Grounds, March 22, $35,000, 3yo, Alabama-bred, 6f, 1:12.10, NELL'S NINER, The Rejected Stone, Kidontheblock, 8 started.

Wadsworth Memorial H., Finger Lakes, Sept. 7, $35,000, 3&up, 1¹⁄₈m, 1:51.48, TODDLER, Gigabyte, Makem Hagar, 7 started.

Wafare Farm S., Lone Star Park, April 20, $75,000, 3yo, f, 6f, 1:10.57, MISS RITZ, Gilded Wings, Truly Sunlit, 6 started.

Walmac Farm Matchmaker H. (R), Louisiana Downs, Oct. 20, $63,050, 3&up, f&m, Louisiana-bred, 1¹⁄₁₆mT, 1:47.56, MRS. MAC, Wild Squaw, Autobesarah, 8 started.

WALMAC INT'L. ALCIBIADES S.-G2, Keeneland, Oct. 4, $445,200, 2yo, f, 1¹⁄₁₆m, 1:46.90, WESTERLY BREEZE, Final Round, Ruby's Reception, 9 started.

Walmac Lone Star Oaks, Lone Star Park, July 4, $125,000, 3yo, f, 1¹⁄₁₆mT, 1:48.91, LA MARTINA (GB), Dyna Penny, Academic Angel, 8 started.

Walter Haight H., Laurel Park, Dec. 21, $50,000, 3&up, 1¹⁄₈m, 1:49.96, DADDY COOL, Full Brush, All Things French, 5 started.

Walter R. Cluer Memorial H., Turf Paradise, Nov. 2, $30,000, 3&up, 7¹⁄₂fT, 1:29.59, EAGLETON, Milk Wood (GB), Kolob, 9 started.

Waquoit S., Suffolk Downs, Feb. 23, $30,000, 4&up, 1¹⁄₈m, 1:48.82, COYOTE LAKES, Storm Wreck, Basil's Rhythm, 12 started.

Washington Breeders' Cup Oaks, Emerald Downs, Aug. 18, $94,375, 3yo, f, 1¹⁄₈m, 1:49.60, ERICA'S SMILE, Premo Copy, Blue Moon Special, 6 started.

Washington Championship H. (R), Emerald Downs, Sept. 16, $60,000, 3&up, Washington-bred, 1¹⁄₁₆m, 1:41.40, SABERTOOTH, Road Afleet, Alfurune, 7 started.

Washington Owners Breeders' Cup H., Emerald Downs, Aug. 11, $63,375, 3yo, c&g, 1¹⁄₁₆m, 1:40.60, SALT GRINDER, Flying Notes, Melcapwalker, 4 started.

WASHINGTON PARK H.-G2, Arlington Park, Sept. 29, $400,000, 3&up, 1³⁄₁₆m, 1:55.07, TENPINS, Generous Rosi (GB), Bonus Pack,

5 started.

Washington State Legislators H., Emerald Downs, May 26, $35,000, 3&up, f&m, 6½f, 1:15.20, ALWAYS A DIXIE, Neon Queen, Grey Tobe Free, 11 started.

Washington Thoroughbred Breeders' Association Lads, Emerald Downs, Aug. 24, $40,000, 2yo, c&g, 1m, 1:36.40, BUB, Knightsbridge Road, Condotierri, 6 started.

Waterford Park H., Mountaineer Park, May 18, $78,050, 3&up, 6f, 1:10.03, HIGH FLYING BID, Mo Mon, Meandmyloveman, 7 started.

Waya H., Hollywood Park, Nov. 28, $72,900, 3&up, f&m, 1½mT, 2:26.38, VIERNES (Brz), Julie Jalouse, Snowflake (Ire), 9 started.

Waya S., Laurel Park, Oct. 26, $50,000, 3&up, f&m, 1 1/16mT, 1:43.98, LILY'S AFFAIR, Your Out, Weekend Kaper, 6 started.

Wayme H., Calder Race Course, Sept. 15, $44,305, 3&up, 5f, :58.86, STRAIGHT A, Please Me Doc, Termination Dust, 7 started.

Wayward Lass S. (R), Tampa Bay Downs, March 2, $50,000, 4&up, f&m, Florida-bred, 1 1/16m, 1:45.20, TECHNICAL KEY, Coolbythepool, Pearly White, 9 started.

WEBN Frog S., Turfway Park, Feb. 2, $49,500, 3yo, 1m, 1:36.92, REQUEST FOR PAROLE, Perfect Drift, Thunder On Land, 10 started.

Wedding Jitters H., Calder Race Course, Dec. 1, $46,275, 3&up, f&m, 5fT, :56.32, PETRINA ABOVE, Mujado (Ire), Flying Birdie, 11 started.

Weekend Delight S., Turfway Park, Sept. 7, $75,000, 3&up, f&m, 6f, 1:10.44, DON'T COUNTESS OUT, Silent Stream, Nasty Storm, 9 started.

Wende S., Turf Paradise, May 18, $23,000, 3&up, f&m, 7½fT, 1:29.77, MOONLIT MADDIE, Jocko Miss, Hazen, 9 started.

WESTCHESTER H.-G3, Belmont Park, May 8, $112,500, 3&up, 1m, 1:35.56, FREE OF LOVE, Dayton Flyer, Country Be Gold, 9 started.

Western Canada H., Northlands Park, June 29, $40,000, 3yo, 6½f, 1:19.20, DARK FUSE, Exclusive Banker, My Birthday Boy, 9 started.

Westerner H., Northlands Park, Aug. 16, $40,000, 3&up, 1 3/16m, 2:13.20, MIKI BLEU EYES, Scotman, Hergesheimer, 7 started.

Western Heritage S. (R), Marquis Downs, Aug. 17, $12,100, 2yo, c&g, Saskatchewan-bred, 6½f, 1:22.64, QUIZ THE WIZARD, Sifting Sand, Stop the Act, 6 started.

West Long Branch S., Monmouth Park, July 5, $50,000, 3&up, f&m, 6f, 1:11.08, BELLE ARTISTE, True Rose, Superfines Luvey, 6 started.

West Mesa H., The Downs at Albuquerque, Sept. 20, $32,200, 3&up, f&m, 7f, 1:23.27, WAVEBAND, Kham Beau, T. C. Lu, 7 started.

West Point H. (R), Saratoga Race Course, Aug. 9, $82,900, 3&up, New York-bred, 1⅛mT, 1:48.05, CELTIC SKY, Reluctant Groom, Chasin' Wimmin, 7 started.

West Virginia Breeders' Classic S. (R), Charles Town, Oct. 12, $225,000, 3&up, West Virginia-bred, -sired, or -raised, 1⅛m, 1:50.93, CONFUCIUS SAY, Social Mix, Neal's Rodeo, 8 started.

West Virginia Cavada Breeders Classic S., Charles Town, Oct. 12, $135,000, 3&up, f&m, 7f, 1:26.19, SWEET MUSIC, Longfield Star, Spanishinquisition, 10 started.

WEST VIRGINIA DERBY-G3, Mountaineer Park, Aug. 10, $600,000, 3yo, 1⅛m, 1:49.63, WISEMAN'S FERRY, The Judge Sez Who, Captain Squire, 9 started.

West Virginia Division of Tourism Breeders Classic (R), Charles Town, Oct. 12, $67,500, 3yo, f, West Virginia-bred, -sired, or -raised, 7f, 1:25.80, SHESANOTHERGRUMP, Simon Slew, Confederatechatter, 7 started.

West Virginia Futurity (2nd Div.) (R), Charles Town, Nov. 16, $35,888, 2yo, West Virginia-bred, 7f, 1:28.29, COURAGEOUS VALOR, Straight Star, Very Eloquent, 6 started.

West Virginia Futurity (1st Div.) (R), Charles Town, Nov. 16, $35,038, 2yo, West Virginia-bred, 7f, 1:29.06, LONGFIELD SPUD, Aye a Hot Shot, Hushaby Babe, 5 started.

West Virginia Governor's H., Mountaineer Park, Aug. 10, $88,500, 3&up, 1 1/16m, 1:42.24, DOCENT, Burning Roma, X Country, 7 started.

West Virginia House of Delegates 'Speaker's Cup' S., Mountaineer Park, Aug. 10, $89,500, 3&up, 1mT, 1:33.57, ROYAL SPY, Buenos Dias, Magical Madness, 11 started.

West Virginia Legislature 'Chairman's Cup' S., Mountaineer Park, Aug. 10, $89,250, 3&up, 4½f,.67, SHERYAR SPECIAL, Abajo, Blazing Count, 12 started.

West Virginia Lottery Breeders' Classic S. (R), Charles Town, Oct. 12, $67,500, 3yo, West Virginia-bred, -sired, or -raised, 7f, 1:26.05, ADAMS TRIBE, Tori's Thunder, One More Storm, 9 started.

West Virginia 'Onion Juice' Breeders Classic S. (R), Charles Town, Oct. 12, $67,500, 3&up, c&g, West Virginia-bred, -sired, or -raised, 7f, 1:25.61, TURBOTAXMAN, Hot Ziggity, Aye Trouble, 9 started.

West Virginia 'Secretary of State' S., Mountaineer Park, Aug. 10, $88,250, 3&up, f&m, 6f, 1:10.32, URBAN DANCER, Night of Delight, Keepondealing, 8 started.

West Virginia Senate 'President's Cup' S., Mountaineer Park, Aug. 10, $89,350, 3&up, f&m, 1mT, 1:35.14, PERSIAN SILVER, Cayman Sunset (Ire), Media Access, 9 started.

West Virginia Vincent Moscarelli Memorial Breeders' Classic S. (R), Charles Town, Oct. 12, $67,500, 2yo, West Virginia-bred, -sired, or -raised, 6½f, 1:19.99, FOREVER JOE, Straight Star, Weshes Pearl, 8 started.

What a Pleasure S., Calder Race Course, Dec. 14, $100,000, 2yo, 1 1/16m, 1:44.07, TRUST N LUCK, Patriotic Flame, Super Frolic, 7 started.

What a Summer S., Laurel Park, Jan. 12, $50,000, 4&up, f&m, 6f, 1:10.34, OUTSTANDING INFO, Bedside Manner, Prized Stamp, 7 started.

Wheat City H., Assiniboia Downs, Aug. 5, $30,000, 3&up, 1m, 1:40.60, KALFAARI, Sir Pucker, Our Best Man, 12 started.

Whimsical S., Woodbine, April 13, $147,355, 4&up, f&m, 6f, 1:10.54, MYSTERIOUS AFFAIR, El Prado Essence, Devastating, 8 started.

Whirlaway H., Fair Grounds, Feb. 10, $125,000, 4&up, 1 1/16m, 1:42.94, VALHOL, Parade Leader, Fight for Ally, 10 started.

Whirlaway S., Aqueduct, Feb. 9, $82,525, 3yo, 1 1/16m, 1:44.93, SARATOGA BLUES, Smoked Em, D' Coach, 7 started.

White Lace S., Great Lakes Downs, Oct. 28, $20,000, 2yo, f, 6f, 1:16.19, OZILDA'S NANCY LEE, Satin Storm, Simply Tricky, 7 started.

White Oak H. (R), Arlington Park, June 22, $84,400, 3&up, Illinois bred, 6f, 1:09.95, TIC N TIN, Too Many Bucks, Classic Appeal, 8 started.

WHITNEY H.-G1, Saratoga Race Course, Aug. 3, $750,000, 3&up, 1⅛m, 1:47.04, LEFT BANK, Street Cry (Ire), Lido Palace (Chi), 6 started.

Who Doctor Who H. (R), Lincoln State Fair, July 7, $22,500, 3&up, Nebraska-bred, 1 1/16m, 1:47.20, HIGH DICE, Tate's Way, King's Verse, 6 started.

Wickerr H., Del Mar, Aug. 2, $77,075, 3&up, 1mT, 1:32.72, SPECIAL RING, Touch of the Blues (Fr), Fateful Dream, 10 started.

Wide Country S., Laurel Park, March 10, $42,200, 3yo, f, 1 1/16m, 1:46.82, SHOP TILL YOU DROP, Spelling, True Sensation, 6 started.

Wild and Wonderful S. (R), Charles Town, April 27, $36,550, 3yo, f, West Virginia-bred, 7f, 1:30.46, SIMON SLEW, Shesanothergrump, Tricky Mirage, 10 started.

Wildcat H., Turf Paradise, April 28, $35,000, 3&up, 1⅜mT, 2:16.62, EAGLETON, Bristolville, Venturesome Beau, 8 started.

Wilderness Song S., Woodbine, July 13, $107,000, 3yo, f, 1 1/16m, 1:45.01, JEALOUS FORUM, Winning Chance, Mulrainy, 7 started.

Wild Rose H., Northlands Park, June 28, $40,000, 3&up, f&m, 6½f, 1:19.40, VIVA RUCKUS, Slewability, Little Lolitta, 6 started.

Wild Rose H., Prairie Meadows, June 22, $60,000, 3&up, f&m, 1 1/16m, 1:42.97, DELRAY DEW, Rodeo Fan, Harlan Ash, 6 started.

Willard L. Proctor Memorial S. (R), Hollywood Park, May 26, $69,530, 2yo, non-winners of two races, 5f, :57.86, CROWNED DANCER, Skipping Stars, Fabulous World, 7 started.

William Almy Jr. S, Suffolk Downs, April 20, $30,000, 3&up, 6f, 1:11.62, ESTEEMED FRIEND, Personal Moon, Flex Jet, 7 started.

WILLIAM DONALD SCHAEFER H.-G2, Pimlico, May 18, $100,000, 3&up, 1⅛m, 1:50.20, TENPINS, Bowman's Band, Tactical Side, 7 started.

William Henry Harrison S. (R), Hoosier Park, Oct. 6, $42,450, 3&up, c&g, Indiana-bred and/or -sired, 6f, 1:11.74, RESTITUTION, J D's Diamond, Indy Energy, 6 started.

William Kyne H., Portland Meadows, Jan. 27, $8,450, 4&up, 1⅛m, 1:54.04, YESSS, Chinquapin Charlie, Fly Buddy Fly, 7 started.

William Livingston S., The Meadowlands, Sept. 27, $50,000, 3&up, 5fT, 56.93, GHOSTLY NUMBERS, Rudirudy, Sea of Green, 5 started.

Willow Lake H., Yavapai Downs, Aug. 3, $15,000, 3&up, f&m, 1m, 1:44.60, PETES TOMBOY, City Loot, Midnite Edition, 6 started.

WILL ROGERS S.-G3, Hollywood Park, June 1, $106,500, 3yo, 1mT, 1:34.64, DOC HOLIDAY (Ire), Johar, Golden Arrow, 5 started.

Willy Fiddle S. (R), Les Bois Park, July 24, $11,595, 3&up, Idaho-bred, 7½f, 1:30.52, QUIET SYNS, San Diego Pete, La Fontaine, 7 started.

Wilmington H., Delaware Park, June 15, $100,900, 3&up, 6f, 1:09.81, TRUE PASSION, Sing Me Back Home, Clever Gem, 8 started.

WILSHIRE H.-G3, Hollywood Park, April 26, $106,600, 3&up, f&m, 1mT, 1:34.31, EUROLINK RAINDANCE (Ire), Crazy Ensign (Arg), Impeachable, 5 started.

Wine Country H. (R), Finger Lakes, July 4, $35,000, 3&up, New York-bred, 6f, 1:10.74, STRIKE THE BRASS, As Wicked, Impeachthepro, 6 started.

Win For Jim Rocking Chair Claiming S., Grand Prairie, July 28, $2,735, 8 yo's & up, 7f, 1:26.80, CARSONS DREAM, Don Coronaige, Sir Brass, 6 started.

Winning Colors S. (R), Les Bois Park, June 15, $11,573, 3&up, f&m, Idaho-bred, 7f, 1:26.69, INFANTRY LIZ, Eyes Sucha Delight, Riband, 8 started.

Winnipeg Futurity, Assiniboia Downs, Aug. 5, $40,000, 2yo, 6f, 1:11.80, ONEOFTHEBIRDBOYS, Giant Slam, Judge Ruckus, 9 started.

Winnipeg Sun S., Assiniboia Downs, Aug. 4, $30,000, 3&up, f&m, 1$\frac{1}{16}$m, 1:47.40, CATHY'S STAR, Dawn Edition, Northern Tuscanny, 8 started.

Winsham Lad H., Sunland Park, Jan. 12, $29,100, 3&up, 1m, 1:36.74, BEEHAY, Vernon Invader, Major Caleb, 11 started.

WinStar Distaff H., Lone Star Park, May 27, $200,000, 3&up, f&m, 1mT, 1:38.96, QUEEN OF WILSHIRE, Pleasant State, Blushing Bride (GB), 12 started.

WINSTAR GALAXY S.-G2, Keeneland, Oct. 4, $544,500, 3&up, f&m, 1$\frac{3}{16}$mT, 1:56.72, OWSLEY, Snow Dance, Surya, 6 started.

Winter Solstice H., Santa Anita Park, March 7, $82,450, 4&up, f&m, a6½fT, 1:13.20, PENNY MARIE, Twin Set (Ger), La Ronge, 9 started.

Winter Solstice S., Sam Houston Race Park, Dec. 21, $30,000, 3yo, f, 1m 70y, 1:41.38, IFYOUPREFERSILVER, White Scarf, Bayakoa's Image, 8 started.

Wishing Well S., Turfway Park, Jan. 12, $42,500, 4&up, f&m, 6f, 1:11.92, KEEPONDEALING, Soul Onarazorsedge, Platinum Streak, 8 started.

Wistful H. (R), The Meadowlands, Oct. 5, $50,000, 3&up, f&m, New Jersey-bred, 1m 70y, 1:44.70, GOLDEN MADE, Sea Femma, Gaelic Bay, 7 started.

With Approval S. (R), Woodbine, Aug. 17, $106,000, 3&up, Canadian-bred, 1⅛mT, 1:47.30, SKY CHARIOT, Follow the Piper, Steady Ruckus, 5 started.

WITHERS S.-G3, Aqueduct, May 4, $150,000, 3yo, 1m, 1:36.41, FAST DECISION, Shah Jehan, Listen Here, 5 started.

W. L. MCKNIGHT H.-G2, Calder Race Course, Dec. 28, $200,000, 3&up, 1½mT, 2:28.05, MAN FROM WICKLOW, Serial Bride, Rochester, 12 started.

W. Meredith Bailes Memorial S. (R), Colonial Downs, July 4, $36,400, 3&up, Virginia-bred, 6f, 1:10.49, NATIVE HEIR, Robbie's Prince, Artistic Design, 3 started.

WNBC S. (R), Belmont Park, June 8, $66,150, 4&up, f&m, non-winners of a stakes worth $20,000, 1m, 1:37.13, TOO SCARLET, Ellie's Moment, Belle Artiste, 10 started.

Wolf Hill S., Monmouth Park, June 1, $50,000, 3&up, 5fT, RIDEOUTS PATTON, Rudirudy, Red Weasel, 9 started.

Wolverine S. (R), Great Lakes Downs, May 25, $45,000, 3&up, Michigan-bred, 6f, 1:13.19, SECRET ROMEO, O. B. Quiet, That Gift, 10 started.

Wonders Delight S. (R), Penn National Race Course, June 7, $30,725, 3yo, f, Pennsylvania-bred, 6f, 1:11.18, CHEEKSANDPEANUTS, Marquee Kelly, Watsup, 9 started.

Wonder Where S. (R), Woodbine, Aug. 5, $250,000, 3yo, f, Canadian-bred, 1¼mT, 2:02.27, HOT TALENT, Silver Nithi, Ginger Gold, 9 started.

Woodbine Oaks (R), Woodbine, June 8, $500,000, 3yo, f, Canadian-bred, 1⅛m, 1:51.56, GINGER GOLD, Silver Nithi, Alpha Heat, 10 started.

WOODBINE SLOTS CUP (Can-G3), Woodbine, Nov. 9, $167,700, 3&up, 1$\frac{1}{16}$m, 1:45.10, PAROSE, Attest, Divine Luck, 9 started.

Woodchopper H., Fair Grounds, Dec. 28, $100,000, 3yo, a1$\frac{1}{16}$mT, 1:45.25, SKATE AWAY, Seainsky, Runaway Choice, 11 started.

WOODFORD RESERVE TURF CLASSIC S.-G1, Churchill Downs, May 4, $452,500, 3&up, 1⅛mT, 1:47.35, BEAT HOLLOW (GB), With Anticipation, Hap, 10 started.

Woodland Heritage S. (R), Marquis Downs, Aug. 17, $12,100, 2yo, f, Saskatchewan-bred, 6½f, 1:24.25, SIMMERDOWN NOW, Star Pegasus, Picture the Answer, 7 started.

Woodlands Derby, The Woodlands, Oct. 26, $20,000, 3yo, 1$\frac{1}{16}$m, 1:49.40, CANYON DE ORO, Raise a Booger, A Boy Named Luke, 8 started.

Woodlands H., The Woodlands, Nov. 3, $20,000, 3&up, 1$\frac{1}{16}$m, 1:50.60, SADDLESPUR, Amazon Ace, Getaway in Style, 7 started.

Woodlands Juvenile S., The Woodlands, Nov. 2, $15,000, 2yo, 6f, 1:16.80, VENTURE CAT, Maddies Blues, Our Lady Punch, 9 started.

Woodlawn S., Pimlico, May 18, $75,750, 3yo, 1$\frac{1}{16}$mT, 1:46.01, MR. O'BRIEN, Regal Sanction, February Storm, 8 started.

WOOD MEMORIAL S.-G1, Aqueduct, April 13, $750,000, 3yo, 1⅛m, 1:48.61, BUDDHA, Medaglia d'Oro, Sunday Break (Jpn), 8 started.

Woodside H., Bay Meadows, May 4, $65,813, 3&up, f&m, 6f, 1:09.60, FANCEE BARGAIN, Slewsbox, Fertile, 7 started.

Woodstock S., Woodbine, April 20, $136,750, 3yo, 6f, 1:10.62, WILD WHISKEY, Anglian Prince, Rare Friends, 7 started.

WOODWARD S.-G1, Belmont Park, Sept. 7, $500,000, 3&up, 1⅛m, 1:47.75, LIDO PALACE (Chi), Gander, Express Tour, 6 started.

Work the Crowd H. (R), Golden Gate Fields, Jan. 5, $100,000, 4&up, f&m, California-bred, 1mT, 1:40.35, SUPER TUESDAY, Yes We Do, Muschi, 7 started.

World Appeal S., The Meadowlands, Sept. 27, $50,000, 2yo, 1m 70yT, 1:42.56, TITLE CONTENDER, Stong, Dr. Phil, 8 started.

Yaddo H. (R), Saratoga Race Course, Aug. 16, $84,775, 3&up, f&m, New York-bred, 1⅛mT, 1:51.42, TEXTBOOK METHOD, Indy Mood for Luv, Shopping for Love, 8 started.

Yankee Affair S. (R), Philadelphia Park, Oct. 5, $50,000, 3&up, c&g, Pennsylvania-bred, 1$\frac{1}{16}$mT, 1:44.66, SIR ECHO, Watchman's Warning, Sand and Water, 7 started.

Yankee Affair S., Gulfstream Park, April 13, $75,000, 3&up, 5fT, :55.68, TEXAS GLITTER, Joe's Son Joey, True Love's Secret, 6 started.

Yankee Fashion S., Suffolk Downs, Feb. 9, $30,000, 3yo, f, 6f, 1:15.73, MRSCOPPOLASKITCHEN, For Love of Darby, Maggie's Song, 10 started.

Yaqthan S., Kentucky Downs, Sept. 15, $45,000, 3&up, 1mT, 1:36.16, PROMISE OF WAR, Dernier Croise (Fr), Tin Smithen, 11 started.

Yavapai Classic H., Yavapai Downs, June 16, $15,000, 3&up, f&m, 6f, 1:09.20, MISS PIXIE, Petes Tomboy, Cove Point, 10 started.

Yavapai County Arizona Breeders' Futurity (R), Yavapai Downs, June 23, $24,677, 2yo, Arizona-bred, 5f, FIRST SNOWBOUND, Fast Force, Ripley, 7 started.

Yavapai Distance Series S., Yavapai Downs, July 15, $12,200, 3&up, 1¼m, 2:05.85, ABSENCE OF ORDER, Oil Man, Herb's Birthday, 9 started.

Yavapai Downs Derby, Yavapai Downs, Aug. 25, $14,200, 3yo, 1$\frac{1}{16}$m, 1:45.18, ROAD GRADER, Cool Friday, Sensational Jake, 6 started.

Yavapai Downs Futurity, Yavapai Downs, Sept. 3, $27,700, 2yo, 6f, 1:08.92, FIRST SNOWBOUND, Deputy Doc, Kate's Flame, 11 started.

Yavapai Downs H., Yavapai Downs, Aug. 24, $15,000, 3&up, 6f, 1:08.85, STORMY AMBITION, Bungalow Bud, Merits Dublin, 6 started.

Yavapai Sprint Series S., Yavapai Downs, July 15, $12,125, 3&up, 6f, 1:10.42, FOOL HEARTED MAN, Signal This, Welo, 11 started.

Ye Derby, Yellowstone Downs, Sept. 22, $8,800, 3yo, 1m 70y, 1:49, MISS WITH IT, I the Messiah, Silent Lane, 7 started.

YELLOW RIBBON S.-G1, Santa Anita Park, Oct. 5, $500,000, 3&up, f&m, 1¼mT, 1:59.72, GOLDEN APPLES (Ire), Voodoo Dancer, Banks Hill (GB), 6 started.

Yellow Rose S. (R), Sam Houston Race Park, Nov. 16, $50,000, 3&up, f&m, Texas-bred, 6f, 1:11.14, FLEETA DIF, Fasole, Bien Sur, 11 started.

Yellowstone Downs Futurity, Yellowstone Downs, Sept. 22, $10,905, 2yo, a7f, 1:29.60, DEMONFLIES, Rene's Last, Nightly Delusions, 8 started.

YERBA BUENA BREEDERS' CUP H.-G3, Bay Meadows, May 18, $108,750, 3&up, f&m, 1⅜mT, 2:16.39, PEU A PEU (Ger), Janet (GB), Racene, 6 started.

Zadracarta S. (R), Woodbine, June 29, $108,000, 3&up, f&m, Canadian-bred, 6fT, 1:08.73, MARISA GO, Healing Knowledge, Mysterious Affair, 7 started.

Zany Tactics S., Turf Paradise, April 26, $22,700, 3&up, 6f, 1:09.55, IZA REDHEAD, Stormy Ambition, Iza Tornado, 6 started.

Zany Tactics S. (R), Santa Anita Park, April 7, $106,800, 3yo, California-bred, 6½f, 1:15.71, OFFICER, Hot War, Duddly Doo Run, 6 started.

Zydeco S., Delta Downs, Nov. 9, $40,000, 3&up, f&m, 5f, :59.07, RAYMOND'S DREAM, Mike's Sister, Fuse It, 10 started.

How American Races Are Graded

At the urging of European racing officials who in 1972 had created the pattern race system to identify and grade the best-quality races in Europe, the Thoroughbred Breeders and Owners Association created the North American Graded Stakes Committee and implemented a similar grading system for the '73 racing season. The gradings were principally designed to assist bloodstock buyers by identifying the North American races that in the recent past had consistently attracted the highest levels of competition. Grade 1 would be the highest level, followed by Grade 2 and Grade 3, the latter being the lowest level of stakes race accorded a grade.

The first North American gradings, totaling 330 races, were announced in January 1974, and the English Jockey Club immediately accepted them. Fasig-Tipton Co. began to publish the gradings in its catalogs in 1975, and Keeneland Association followed in '76. In 1998, Canadian racing authorities began to grade that nation's races, and the name of the TOBA-led organization was changed to the American Graded Stakes Committee and dealt only with United States stakes races.

Grades of all of America's best races are reviewed annually by the American Graded Stakes Committee because stakes programs are dynamic and ever-changing products of conditions. The quality of any race's contestants may differ markedly from one year to the next. When a trend in the quality of the field of a race is established, be it improving or deteriorating, the race is re-evaluated for grading. Members have said that they take a five-year view of each race when considering the gradings.

Committee

The committee has ten voting members: five TOBA members serving five-year terms and five racing official members elected by the TOBA committee members and serving three-year terms. In addition, the committee's grading sessions have guest observers and invited guests. To be considered for membership on the committee, a candidate must have served as a guest observer for at least one grading session.

Seven votes are required to raise any grading, and six votes are needed to downgrade a race.

Members of the committee for the November 25-26, 2002, sessions at which 2003 gradings were determined:

TOBA: C. Steven Duncker (chairman), Rollin W. Baugh, Gary E. Biszantz, Dell Hancock, and Barry K. Schwartz.

Racing official members: Larry Craft, Frank C. Gabriel Jr., Michael S. Lakow, Thomas S. Robbins, and Robert D. Umphrey.

Guest observers: Sam Abbey, Reynolds Bell, Ben Huffman, and John Phillips.

Invited guests: W. B. Rogers Beasley, Doug Bredar, Hiroshi Ito, Bryan Krantz, and Geoffrey Russell.

Criteria

To be eligible for grading, a race must meet several criteria for being graded and for retaining the status. Among the criteria are:

Purse: The race must have a minimum purse, excluding state-bred supplements, of: $200,000 for Grade 1, $150,000 for Grade 2, and $100,000 for Grade 3.

Continuity: In general, a race must have two prior runnings under essentially the same conditions to be graded, although in rare circumstances Grade 1 status has been accorded

2003 Graded Stakes by Racetrack

Track	Gr. 1	Gr. 2	Gr. 3	Total
Santa Anita	22	30	12	64
Belmont Park	23	20	15	58
Hollywood Park	12	14	21	47
Aqueduct	3	8	24	35
Churchill Downs	5	10	19	34
Gulfstream Park	4	9	20	33
Saratoga	13	12	5	30
Keeneland	5	7	13	25
Del Mar	5	12	2	19
Arlington Park	3	3	10	16
Calder Race Course	0	3	12	15
Monmouth Park	2	2	11	15
Pimlico	2	2	7	11
Oaklawn Park	1	3	5	9
Fair Grounds	0	5	3	8
Bay Meadows	0	1	5	6
Hialeah	0	2	4	6
Laurel Park	1	2	3	6
Meadowlands	0	1	5	6
Turfway Park	0	2	4	6
Delaware Park	0	1	4	5
Golden Gate	0	0	5	5
Lone Star Park	0	0	4	4
Hawthorne	0	1	2	3
Philadelphia Park	0	1	2	3
Sportman's Park	0	1	2	3
Hoosier Park	0	0	2	2
Tampa Bay	0	0	2	2
Colonial Downs	0	0	1	1
Ellis Park	0	0	1	1
Emerald Downs	0	0	1	1
Kentucky Downs	0	0	1	1
Louisiana Downs	0	1	0	1
Mountaineer Park	0	0	1	1
Prairie Meadows	0	0	1	1
Remington Park	0	0	1	1
Rockingham Park	0	0	1	1
Suffolk Downs	0	1	0	1
Thistledown	0	1	0	1
Totals	**101**	**155**	**231**	**487**

Purse Comparison

	Grade/Group 1		Grade/Group 2		Grade/Group 3		Total	
	Races	Average 1st money	Races	Average 1st money	Races	Average 1st money	Races	Average 1st money
2001 season								
Canada	6	$625,000	10	$200,000	25	$132,000	41	$220,732
Ireland	10	281,507	4	79,860	23	49,913	37	115,743
Great Britain	27	264,092	29	82,646	55	40,604	111	105,914
France	26	153,789	27	45,856	54	29,770	107	63,964
Italy	8	148,306	7	63,741	10	40,968	25	81,692
Germany	7	185,048	14	58,385	23	37,479	44	67,607
North America	98	348,722	157	148,464	207	87,649	462	163,695
2000 season								
*Canada	6	$375,000	10	$118,500	26	$75,577	42	$128,571
Ireland	10	228,638	3	59,307	23	36,624	36	91,852
Great Britain	27	283,545	29	88,603	54	43,463	110	114,293
France	26	157,590	26	51,320	55	34,535	107	68,515
Italy	8	106,628	7	53,600	10	35,492	25	63,277
Germany	6	204,231	15	64,654	22	38,328	43	70,660
U.S.	96	353,839	152	141,999	225	87,286	473	158,968
1999 season								
*Canada	6	360,000	11	94,091	24	105,000	41	139,390
Ireland	10	251,170	3	66,600	23	41,073	36	101,560
Great Britain	26	259,006	30	82,257	53	38,885	109	103,328
France	25	172,240	27	58,650	55	39,145	107	75,165
Italy	8	79,246	7	40,662	10	27,429	25	47,716
Germany	6	166,363	15	78,613	21	43,101	42	73,392
U.S.	92	328,714	146	141,382	212	84,577	450	152,920

*Canada listed in Canadian dollars.

immediately to races of special note, such as the Breeders' Cup races. Races with restrictions other than sex or age are not eligible.

In addition, if track management changes a graded race from dirt to grass, or vice versa, or changes the race's distance by more than one-quarter mile or from less than one mile to more than one mile, or vice versa, the race will be considered a new race and ineligible for grading until it has been run twice under the same conditions. If a race's place on the calendar is changed substantially, such as from July to January, the race's grading may be reviewed.

In determining a grading, the committee considers the quality of its field over the prior five years as measured by several statistical yardsticks. Among the considerations are:

- Points based on number of in-the-money finishes in unrestricted black-type races;
- Percentage of graded stakes winners in the field;
- Quality points assigned to the race based on the number of graded stakes winners in the field; and
- Ratings of the North American Rating Committee, a panel composed of racing secretaries that each week assigns a hypothetical weight to every horse running in American black-type races.

Beginning in 1999, graded turf races moved to the main track because of course conditions were automatically downgraded one grade, although the American Graded Stakes Committee reviews each such race within five days of the running and can restore the original grading. The change in grading affects only that year's running and is not considered in the grading process.

For 2003, the American Graded Stakes Committee dropped its practice of deferring grade reductions for races run before May 1 into the following year. For instance, the committee in 2001 decided to downgrade the Gulfstream Park Handicap from Grade 1 to Grade 2, but the change did not take effect until 2003 because the race traditionally is run before May 1. Beginning with the 2003 gradings, any changes take effect immediately.

The American Graded Stakes Committee notifies racetracks with races in the lowest echelons of their respective gradings that the races may be downgraded, but the race will not be considered for downgrading until it has been run another time.

For 2002, 487 American stakes races were graded, with 101 Grade 1 races, 155 Grade 2 races, and 231 Grade 3 races. The number of Grade 1 and Grade 2 races was unchanged from 2001, while one Grade 3 races was added.

More graded stakes are offered in the United

States than all group races throughout Europe, which has evoked criticism among some Europeans who contend that American black type is cheapened by the plentiful graded races. However, less than 1% of all American races are graded, a smaller percentage than Ireland, Great Britain, or France. In 2001, for example, 0.8% of all United States races were graded, while 2.7% of French races were group races, and in Ireland the percentage was 4.7%.

For 2003, three races were raised from Grade 2 to Grade 1 level: the Diana Handicap on grass at Saratoga Race Course, the Suburban Handicap at Belmont Park, and the Triple Bend Breeders' Cup Handicap at Hollywood Park. See chart for other changes.

2003 Graded Stakes by State

State	Gr. 1	Gr. 2	Gr. 3	Total
California	39	57	45	141
New York	39	40	44	123
Kentucky	10	19	38	67
Florida	4	14	38	56
Illinois	3	5	14	22
New Jersey	2	3	16	21
Maryland	3	4	10	17
Arkansas	1	3	5	9
Louisiana	0	6	3	9
Delaware	0	1	4	5
Texas	0	0	4	4
Pennsylvania	0	1	2	3
Indiana	0	0	2	2
Iowa	0	0	1	1
Massachusetts	0	1	0	1
New Hampshire	0	0	1	1
Ohio	0	1	0	1
Oklahoma	0	0	1	1
Virginia	0	0	1	1
Washington	0	0	1	1
West Virginia	0	0	1	1
Totals	**101**	**155**	**231**	**487**

Summary of Grade Changes

	No.	Graded stakes	Change from 2002
Grade 1	101	20.7%	No change
Grade 2	155	31.8%	No change
Grade 3	231	47.4%	+0.4%

2003 Graded Stakes Changes

Upgrades

Grade 2 to Grade 1: Diana H. (Saratoga Race Course), Suburban H. (Belmont Park), Triple Bend Breeders' Cup H. (Hollywood Park)

Grade 3 to Grade 2: Best Pal S. (Del Mar), Delaware H. (Delaware Park), Silverbulletday S. (Fair Grounds)

Ungraded to Grade 3: Carry Back S. (Calder Race Course), Lecomte S. (Fair Grounds), Shakertown S. (Keeneland Race Course), Smile Sprint H. (Calder), Spend a Buck H. (Calder), Sycamore Breeders' Cup S. (Keeneland), Toboggan H. (Aqueduct), Transylvania S. (Keeneland), Whirlaway H. (Fair Grounds), WinStar Distaff H. (Lone Star Park)

Downgrades

Grade 1 to Grade 2: Beverly Hills H. (Hollywood Park), Gulfstream Park H. (Gulfstream Park), Oaklawn H. (Oaklawn Park)

Grade 2 to Grade 3: Pegasus Handicap (Meadowlands), San Bernardino H. (Santa Anita)

Grade 3 to ungraded: Ascot H. (Bay Meadows Race Course), Cowdin S. (Belmont Park), Gallant Fox H. (Aqueduct), Honeybee S. (Oaklawn Park), Rare Treat H. (Aqueduct), Rebel S. (Oaklawn), Stymie H. (Aqueduct), Tanforan H. (Golden Gate Fields)

Not eligible for grading: Laurel Dash S. (Laurel Park)

Graded Stakes History

Ack Ack Handicap

Grade 3, Churchill Downs, three-year-olds and up, 7½ furlongs, dirt. Held October 27, 2002, with a gross value of $112,700. First held in 1991. Graded since 1997. Stakes record 1:28.63 (2001 Illusioned).

Year	Winner	Jockey	Second	Third	Strs	Time	1st Purse
2002	Twilight Road, 5, 113	P. Day	Mountain General, 4	Binthebest, 4	9	1:29.39	$69,874
2001	Illusioned, 3, 118	P. Day	Strawberry Affair, 3	Fappie's Notebook, 3	11	**1:28.63**	$70,866
2000	Chindi, 6, 113	T. T. Doocy	Smolderin Heart, 5	Millencolin, 5	10	1:29.30	$70,494
1999	Littlebitlively, 5, 119	C. H. Borel	Run Johnny, 7	Tactical Cat, 7	11	1:28.97	$71,672
1998	Distorted Humor, 5, 120	C. H. Borel	Crafty Friend, 5	Chindi, 5	6	1:29.61	$68,262
1997	Cat's Career, 4, 108	W. Martinez	Rare Rock, 4	Victor Cooley, 4	6	1:32.06	$69,130
1996	Western Trader, 5, 113	C. H. Borel	Top Account, 4	Strategic Intent, 4	8	1:29.84	$70,308
1995	Mystery Storm, 3, 112	C. Gonzalez	I'm Very Irish, 4	Tarzans Blade, 4	10	1:29.10	$75,660
1994	Lost Pan, 4, 114	D. M. Barton	Sir Vixen, 6	Groovy Jett, 6	8	1:30.27	$54,795

Named for 1971 Horse of the Year Ack Ack (1966-'90, c. by Battle Joined). 1992-'93 not held. 1995 equaled track record; 2001 new track record.

Acorn Stakes

Grade 1, Belmont Park, three-year-olds, fillies, 1 mile, dirt. Held June 7, 2002, with a gross value of $250,000. First held in 1931. Graded since 1973. Stakes record 1:34.20 (1982 Cupecoy's Joy).

Year	Winner	Jockey	Second	Third	Strs	Time	1st Purse
2002	You, 3, 121	J. D. Bailey	Willa On the Move, 3	Bella Bellucci, 3	5	1:34.05	$150,000
2001	Forest Secrets, 3, 121	C. J. McCarron	Victory Ride, 3	Real Cozzy, 3	8	1:34.92	$120,000
2000	Finder's Fee, 3, 121	J. R. Velazquez	C'Est L' Amour, 3	Roxelana, 3	10	1:37.38	$120,000
1999	Three Ring, 3, 121	J. D. Bailey	Better Than Honour, 3	Madison's Charm, 3	8	1:36.16	$120,000
1998	Jersey Girl, 3, 121	M. E. Smith	Santaria, 3	Brave Deed, 3	10	1:36.32	$90,000

1997 **Sharp Cat**, 3, 121	G. L. Stevens	Dixie Flag, 3	Ajina, 3	7	1:34.41	$90,000
1996 **Star de Lady Ann**, 3, 121	M. E. Smith	Yanks Music, 3	Stop Traffic, 3	12	1:34.62	$90,000
1995 **Cat's Cradle**, 3, 121	C. W. Antley	Country Cat, 3	Lucky Lavender Gal, 3	7	1:37.53	$90,000
1994 **Inside Information**, 3, 121	M. E. Smith	Cinnamon Sugar (Ire), 3	Sovereign Kitty, 3	5	1:34.26	$90,000
1993 **Sky Beauty**, 3, 121	M. E. Smith	Educated Risk, 3	In Her Glory, 3	6	1:35.50	$90,000
1992 **Prospectors Delite**, 3, 121	P. Day	Pleasant Stage, 3	Turnback the Alarm, 3	12	1:35.10	$113,400

Named for the phrase "Great oaks from little acorns grow," the Acorn once had been run immediately preceding the Coaching Club American Oaks. 1960-'67, 1969-'75 held at Aqueduct.

Adirondack Stakes

Grade 2, Saratoga Race Course, two-year-olds, fillies, 6½ furlongs, dirt. Held August 12, 2002, with a gross value of $150,000. First held in 1901. Graded since 1973. Stakes record 1:15.16 (2001 You).

Year	Winner	Jockey	Second	Third	Strs	Time	1st Purse
2002	**Awesome Humor**, 2, 122	P. Day	Stellar, 2	Holiday Runner, 2	6	1:17.75	$90,000
2001	**You**, 2, 115	E. S. Prado	Cashier's Dream, 2	Magic Storm, 2	7	**1:15.16**	$90,000
2000	**Raging Fever**, 2, 122	J. D. Bailey	Two Item Limit, 2	Secret Lover, 2	6	1:17.47	$90,000
1999	**Regally Appealing**, 2, 114	E. S. Prado	Miss Wineshine, 2	Trump My Heart, 2	6	1:16.86	$90,000
1998	**Things Change**, 2, 114	J. A. Santos	Extended Applause, 2	Brittons Hill, 2	9	1:18.14	$90,000
1997	**Salty Perfume**, 2, 114	S. J. Sellers	Brac Drifter, 2	Joustabout, 2	6	1:17.94	$90,000
1996	**Storm Song**, 2, 113	P. Day	Last Two States, 2	(DH) Exclusive Hold, 2 (DH) Larkwhistle, 2	9	1:17.60	$84,075
1995	**Flat Fleet Feet**, 2, 113	M. E. Smith	Steady Cat, 2	Western Dreamer, 2	7	1:16.74	$65,760
1994	**Seeking Regina**, 2, 114	J. D. Bailey	Changing Ways, 2	Phone Bird, 2	7	1:18.51	$66,600
1993	**Astas Foxy Lady**, 2, 119	R. P. Romero	Footing, 2	Casa Eire, 2	6	1:10.11	$68,520
1992	**Sky Beauty**, 2, 116	E. Maple	Missed the Storm, 2	Distinct Habit, 2	7	1:10.16	$70,560

Named for the Adirondack mountain region of New York. 1901-'45 Adirondack H. 1975-'83 Grade 3. 1943-'45 held at Belmont; 1953-'54 Jamaica. 1901-'45, 1962-'93 6 furlongs; 1953-'55 5½ furlongs. 1901-'29 both sexes. 1996 dead heat for third.

(Aegon) Turf Sprint Stakes

Grade 3, Churchill Downs, three-year-olds and up, 5 furlongs, turf. Held May 3, 2002, with a gross value of $100,000. First held in 1995. Graded since 2001. Stakes record :56.09 (1996 Danjur).

Year	Winner	Jockey	Second	Third	Strs	Time	1st Purse
2002	**Testify**, 5, 119	E. J. Delahoussaye	Texas Glitter, 6	Gone Fishin, 6	10	:57.39	$75,206
2001	**Morluc**, 5, 122	R. Albarado	Testify, 4	Texas Glitter, 5	9	:56.60	$70,494
2000	**Bold Fact**, 5, 120	R. Migliore	Howbaddouwantit, 5	Fantastic Finish, 4	12	:56.37	$75,330
1999	**Howbaddouwantit**, 4, 123	M. E. Smith	Mr Festus, 4	Three Card Willie, 4	11	:57.03	$71,486
1998	**Indian Rocket (GB)**, 4, 116	G. L. Stevens	G H's Pleasure, 6	Claire's Honor, 4	12	:57.32	$75,950
1997	**Sandtrap**, 4, 123	A. O. Solis	Appealing Skier, 4	G H's Pleasure, 5	11	:56.51	$71,734
1996	**Danjur**, 4, 114	J. D. Bailey	Hello Paradise, 5	Linear, 6	10	**:56.09**	$57,281
1995	**Long Suit**, 4, 114	W. Martinez	Bold n' Flashy, 6	Scottish Fantasy, 7	11	:56.90	$57,086

Named for sponsor Aegon Insurance. 1995-'98 Churchill Downs Turf Sprint S. 1995 established course record; 1996 course record.

Affectionately Handicap

Grade 3, Aqueduct, three-year-olds and up, fillies and mares, 1¹⁄₁₆ miles, dirt. Held January 11, 2003, with a gross value of $109,600. First held in 1976. Graded since 1977. Stakes record 1:41.87 (1998 Sweetzie).

Year	Winner	Jockey	Second	Third	Strs	Time	1st Purse
2003	**Zonk**, 5, 118	C. C. Lopez	Wishful Splendor, 4	Kiss a Miss, 5	7	1:44.58	$65,760
2002	**Zonk**, 4, 116	C. C. Lopez	People's Princess, 6	Search Party, 6	10	1:42.58	$68,040
2001	**Pentatonic**, 6, 117	A. T. Gryder	Strolling Belle, 5	Pompeii, 5	8	1:43.17	$66,300
2000	**Theresa the Teacha**, 5, 114	H. Castillo Jr.	Roaring Twenties, 4	Two Fer Boston, 4	10	1:46.42	$51,855
1999	**Biding Time**, 5, 118	A. T. Gryder	Shoop, 8	Daily Reflection, 8	9	1:44.62	$50,220
1998	**Sweetzie**, 6, 113	J. M. Pezua	Shoop, 7	Gold Colony, 7	10	**1:41.87**	$50,700
1997	**Mil Kilates**, 4, 113	J. F. Chavez	Whaleneck, 4	Shoop, 4	8	1:44.63	$39,996
1996	**Lotta Dancing**, 5, 120	H. Castillo Jr.	Winner's Edge, 4	Vinista, 4	6	1:42.43	$39,024
1995	**Sea Ditty**, 4, 113	A. Madrid Jr.	Beloved Bea, 5	Acting Proud, 5	9	1:46.93	$50,190
1994	**Poolesta (Ire)**, 5, 115	F. Lovato Jr.	Hey Baba Lulu, 4	Groovy Feeling, 6	7	1:44.80	$49,425
1993	**Hilbys Brite Flite**, 4, 111	J. R. Velazquez	My Treasure, 6	Lady Lear, 6	8	1:44.64	$52,470
1992	**Get Lucky**, 4, 113	M. E. Smith	My Treasure, 5	Haunting, 6	7	1:46.00	$52,650

Named for Hirsch Jacob's champion Affectionately (1960-'79, f. by Swaps). 1976 one mile.

Affirmed Handicap

Grade 3, Hollywood Park, three-year-olds, 1¹⁄₁₆ miles, dirt. Held June 23, 2002, with a gross value of $107,500. First held in 1973. Graded since 1973. Stakes record 1:40.83 (1999 General Challenge).

Year	Winner	Jockey	Second	Third	Strs	Time	1st Purse
2002	**Came Home**, 3, 124	C. J. McCarron	Tracemark, 3	Calkins Road, 3	6	1:41.99	$64,500
2001	**Until Sundown**, 3, 117	G. L. Stevens	Top Hit, 3	Bayou the Moon, 3	5	1:43.10	$60,000
2000	**Tiznow**, 3, 117	V. Espinoza	Dixie Union, 3	Millencolin, 3	6	1:42.35	$80,550
1999	**General Challenge**, 3, 124	D. R. Flores	Desert Hero, 3	Crowning Storm, 3	5	**1:40.83**	$75,000
1998	**Old Trieste**, 3, 118	C. J. McCarron	Old Topper, 4	Kraal, 3	4	1:41.84	$62,340
1997	**Deputy Commander**, 3, 116	C. S. Nakatani	Hello (Ire), 3	Holzmeister, 3	6	1:42.89	$61,500

1996	**Hesabull**, 3, 117	E. J. Delahoussaye	Benton Creek, 3	Semoran, 3	7	1:43.25	$61,050
1995	**Mr Purple**, 3, 120	C. S. Nakatani	Pumpkin House, 3	Oncefortheroad, 3	6	1:42.37	$77,050
1994	**R Friar Tuck**, 3, 113	J. D. Bailey	Pollock's Luck, 3	Wild Invader, 3	8	1:49.08	$96,100
1993	**Codified**, 3, 117	G. L. Stevens	Roman Image, 3	Future Storm, 3	7	1:48.85	$94,100
1992	**Natural Nine**, 3, 117	L. A. Pincay Jr.	Prospect for Four, 3	Never Round, 3	8	1:49.42	$95,500

Named for two-time Horse of the Year and Triple Crown winner Affirmed (1975-2001, c. by Exclusive Native). Formerly named Argonaut H. 1973-'78. Formerly named Silver Screen Handicap, for Hollywood's film industry, 1979-'92. 1973-'89 Grade 2. 1979-'84,1987-'94 1⅛ miles; 1985-'86 1 mile. 1986 three-year-olds and up.

A Gleam Handicap

Grade 2, Hollywood Park, three-year-olds and up, fillies and mares, 7 furlongs, dirt. Held July 14, 2002, with a gross value of $200,000. First held in 1941. Graded since 1986. Stakes record 1:20.53 (1998 A. P. Assay).

Year	Winner	Jockey	Second	Third	Strs	Time	1st Purse
2002	**Irguns Angel**, 4, 116	E. J. Delahoussaye	Secret Liaison, 4	Kalookan Queen, 4	10	1:22.50	$120,000
2001	**Go Go**, 4, 124	E. J. Delahoussaye	Kitty On the Track, 4	Nany's Sweep, 4	5	1:22.19	$120,000
2000	**Honest Lady**, 4, 121	K. J. Desormeaux	Seth's Choice, 4	Hookedonthefeelin, 4	5	1:21.47	$120,000
1999	**Enjoy the Moment**, 4, 116	D. R. Flores	Snowberg, 4	Woodman's Dancer, 4	6	1:21.35	$120,000
1998	**A. P. Assay**, 4, 116	E. J. Delahoussaye	Exotic Wood, 6	Closed Escrow, 6	7	1:20.53	$150,000
1997	**Toga Toga Toga**, 5, 119	G. L. Stevens	Our Summer Bid, 5	Radu Cool, 5	5	1:22.75	$65,040
1996	**Igotrhythm**, 4, 116	E. J. Delahoussaye	Klassy Kim, 5	Cat's Cradle, 5	5	1:21.54	$63,840
1995	**Angi Go**, 5, 117	G. L. Stevens	Desert Stormer, 5	Dancing Mirage, 5	6	1:21.45	$62,700
1994	**Golden Klair (GB)**, 4, 117	C. J. McCarron	Cargo, 5	Minidar, 5	4	1:22.00	$60,400
1993	**Bold Windy**, 4, 115	G. L. Stevens	La Spia, 4	Bountiful Native, 4	9	1:21.62	$65,700
1992	**Forest Fealty**, 5, 116	M. A. Pedroza	Brought to Mind, 5	Devil's Orchid, 5	8	1:22.13	$64,800

Named for 1952 Hollywood Oaks winner A Gleam (1949-'74, f. by *Blenheim II). Formerly named for California's redwood, the sequoia. 1942-'43,1947-'58 not held. 1959-'78 Sequoia H. 1986-'89 Grade 3. 1944,1959-'82 6 furlongs. 1944 two-year-olds. 1998 equaled track record.

A. G. Vanderbilt Handicap

Grade 2, Saratoga Race Course, three-year-olds and up, 6 furlongs, dirt. Held August 11, 2002, with a gross value of $200,000. First held in 1985. Graded since 1990. Stakes record 1:08.29 (1996 Prospect Bay).

Year	Winner	Jockey	Second	Third	Strs	Time	1st Purse
2002	**Orientate**, 4, 121	J. D. Bailey	Say Florida Sandy, 8	Multiple Choice, 8	6	1:09.72	$120,000
2001	**Five Star Day**, 5, 117	G. K. Gomez	Delaware Township, 5	Bonapaw, 5	7	1:08.57	$120,000
2000	**Successful Appeal**, 4, 118	E. S. Prado	Intidab, 7	Chasin' Wimmin, 7	8	1:09.21	$120,000
1999	**Intidab**, 6, 113	R. G. Davis	Artax, 4	Yes It's True, 4	7	1:09.03	$90,000
1998	**Kelly Kip**, 4, 122	J-L. Samyn	Trafalger, 4	Receiver, 4	7	1:09.60	$82,545
1997	**Royal Haven**, 5, 116	R. Migliore	Cold Execution, 6	Punch Line, 6	7	1:09.65	$65,220
1996	**Prospect Bay**, 4, 113	J. D. Bailey	Honour and Glory, 3	Lite the Fuse, 3	7	1:08.29	$65,760
1995	**Not Surprising**, 5, 115	R. G. Davis	Chimes Band, 4	Mining Burrah, 4	10	1:09.60	$67,140
1994	**Boundary**, 4, 117	J. R. Velazquez	Cherokee Run, 4	I Can't Believe, 4	7	1:08.61	$65,880
1993	**Gold Spring (Arg)**, 5, 119	P. Day	Friendly Lover, 5	Detox, 5	5	1:09.31	$70,680
1992	**For Really**, 5, 115	P. Day	Burn Fair, 5	Drummond Lane, 5	9	1:08.68	$71,520

Named for Alfred Gwynne Vanderbilt (1912-'99), chairman of NYRA, president of Belmont and Pimlico. Formerly named for G1 sprinter A Phenomenon, who broke down while leading the Forego H. 1985-'93,1996-'97 A Phenomenon S.; 1994-'95, 1998-'99 A Phenomenon H. 1992-'94 Grade 3. 2000 Intidab finished first, DQ to second.

Alabama Stakes

Grade 1, Saratoga Race Course, three-year-olds, fillies, 1¼ miles, dirt. Held August 17, 2002, with a gross value of $750,000. First held in 1872. Graded since 1973. Stakes record 2:00.80 (1990 Go for Wand).

Year	Winner	Jockey	Second	Third	Strs	Time	1st Purse
2002	**Farda Amiga**, 3, 121	P. Day	Allamerican Bertie, 3	You, 3	6	2:04.68	$450,000
2001	**Flute**, 3, 121	E. S. Prado	Exogenous, 3	Two Item Limit, 3	7	2:01.88	$450,000
2000	**Jostle**, 3, 121	M. E. Smith	Secret Status, 3	Spain, 3	8	2:04.72	$450,000
1999	**Silverbulletday**, 3, 121	J. D. Bailey	Strolling Belle, 3	Gandria, 3	7	2:02.71	$240,000
1998	**Banshee Breeze**, 3, 121	J. D. Bailey	Lu Ravi, 3	Manistique, 3	6	2:03.41	$150,000
1997	**Runup the Colors**, 3, 121	J. D. Bailey	Ajina, 3	Tomisue's Delight, 3	6	2:02.28	$150,000
1996	**Yanks Music**, 3, 121	J. R. Velazquez	Escena, 3	My Flag, 3	7	2:03.06	$150,000
1995	**Pretty Discreet**, 3, 121	M. E. Smith	Friendly Beauty, 3	Rogues Walk, 3	9	2:02.14	$120,000
1994	**Heavenly Prize**, 3, 121	M. E. Smith	Lakeway, 3	Sovereign Kitty, 3	7	2:03.25	$120,000
1993	**Sky Beauty**, 3, 121	M. E. Smith	Future Pretense, 3	Silky Feather, 3	8	2:03.49	$120,000
1992	**November Snow**, 3, 121	C. W. Antley	Saratoga Dew, 3	Pacific Squall, 3	7	2:02.75	$120,000

Named for the home state of Confederate Capt. Cottrill of Mobile, the race's originator. 1893-'96,1898-1900,1911-'12 not held. 1943-'45 held at Belmont. 1872-'96,1904,1906-'16 1⅛ miles; 1901-'03 1⅟₁₆ miles; 1905 1⁵⁄₁₆ miles.

All Along Breeders' Cup Stakes

Grade 3, Colonial Downs, three-year-olds and up, fillies and mares, 1⅛ miles, turf. Held July 13, 2002, with a gross value of $144,500. First held in 1988. Graded since 1990. Stakes record 1:47.34 (1994 Alice Springs).

Year	Winner	Jockey	Second	Third	Strs	Time	1st Purse
2002	**Secret River**, 5, 117	H. Karamanos	Golden Corona, 4	Cayman Sunset (Ire), 4	6	1:50.76	$90,000

2001 **Colstar**, 5, 121	J. K. Court	Lucky Lune (Fr), 4	Crystal Sea, 4	8	1:47.53	$75,000
2000 **Idle Rich**, 5, 115	A. T. Gryder	Emanating, 4	Orange Sunset (Ire), 4	11	1:55.95	$60,000
1999 **Tampico**, 6, 122	E. S. Prado	Heavenly Advice, 5	Absolutely Queenie, 5	10	1:47.63	$60,000
1998 **Bursting Forth**, 4, 122	E. S. Prado	The Unforgiven, 4	Be Elusive, 4	8	1:48.01	$60,000
1997 **Beyrouth**, 5, 115	D. S. Rice	Hero's Pride (Fr), 4	Palliser Bay, 4	10	1:49.27	$67,830
1996 **Another Legend**, 4, 115	C. O. Klinger	Brushing Gloom, 4	Short Time, 4	7	1:58.80	$60,000
1994 **Alice Springs**, 4, 120	R. R. Douglas	Via Borghese, 5	Mz. Zill Bear, 5	6	**1:47.34**	$150,000
1993 **Lady Blessington (Fr)**, 5, 116	C. A. Black	Via Borghese, 4	Logan's Mist, 4	5	1:51.58	$150,000
1992 **Marble Maiden (GB)**, 3, 114	T. Jarnet	Wedding Ring (Ire), 3	Sheba Dancer (Fr), 3	7	1:49.89	$180,000

Named for 1983 Horse of the Year All Along (Fr) (1979, f. by Targowice). 1995 not held. 1988-'94,1996-2000 All Along S. 1988-'94,1996 held at Laurel Park; 1997 held at Delaware Park; 1999 held at Pimlico. 1990-'97 Grade 2. 2000 1³/₁₆ miles. 2001 equaled course record.

All-American Handicap

Grade 3, Bay Meadows, three-year-olds and up, 1¹/₁₆ miles, dirt. Held June 8, 2002, with a gross value of $150,000. First held in 1968. Graded since 1985. Stakes record 1:40.62 (1999 Worldly Ways [GB]).

Year Winner	Jockey	Second	Third	Strs	Time	1st Purse
2002 **Palmeiro**, 4, 115	J. P. Lumpkins	Moonlight Meeting, 7	Prodigious, 7	9	1:42.31	$82,500
2001 **Euchre**, 5, 118	J. P. Lumpkins	Irisheyesareflying, 5	Moonlight Charger, 5	8	1:41.69	$82,500
2000 **Peach Flat**, 6, 114	J. Valdivia Jr.	Boss Ego, 4	Casey Griffin, 4	5	1:42.48	$75,000
1999 **Worldly Ways (GB)**, 5, 116	R. A. Baze	Barter Town, 4	(DH) Scooter Brown, 4 (DH) Highland Gold, 4	8	**1:40.62**	$60,000
1998 **Wild Wonder**, 4, 121	R. A. Baze	Crypto Star, 4	General Royal, 4	6	1:41.33	$60,000
1997 **Mister Fire Eyes (Ire)**, 5, 115	R. J. Warren Jr.	Region, 8	Tolemeo, 8	6	1:41.28	$60,000
1996 **Tzar Rodney (Fr)**, 4, 114	T. M. Chapman	Joy of Glory, 7	Opera Score, 7	6	1:49.74	$60,000
1995 **Bluegrass Prince (Ire)**, 4, 114	T. M. Chapman	Lord Shirldor (SAf), 6	Kinema Red, 6	7	1:49.01	$68,750
1994 **Slew of Damascus**, 6, 122	T. M. Chapman	Fast Cure, 5	The Tender Track, 5	6	1:43.75	$55,000
1993 **Never Black**, 6, 115	C. S. Nakatani	Stark South, 5	Daros (GB), 5	6	1:42.53	$55,000
1992 **Gum**, 6, 112	G. Boulanger	Forty Niner Days, 5	Prudent Manner (Ire), 5	7	1:41.73	$55,000

Traditionally held on Memorial Day weekend. 1968-2000 held at Golden Gate. 1968-'74 6 furlongs; 1975-'78 5 furlongs; 1979-'86 7¹/₂ furlongs; 1987 1 mile; 1995-'96 1¹/₁₆ miles. 1975-'96 turf. 1999 dead heat for third.

American Derby

Grade 2, Arlington Park, three-year-olds, 1³/₁₆ miles, turf. Held July 21, 2002, with a gross value of $225,000. First held in 1884. Graded since 1973. Stakes record 1:54.60 (1955 Swaps).

Year Winner	Jockey	Second	Third	Strs	Time	1st Purse
2002 **Mananan McLir**, 3, 116	R. R. Douglas	Jazz Beat (Ire), 3	Extra Check, 3	8	1:57.11	$135,000
2001 **Fan Club's Mister**, 3, 121	R. A. Meier	Monsieur Cat, 3	Royal Spy, 3	7	2:03.27	$150,000
2000 **Pine Dance**, 3, 114	E. Ahern	Hymn (Ire), 3	Del Mar Show, 3	4	1:55.46	$120,000
1997 **Honor Glide**, 3, 120	G. K. Gomez	Worldly Ways (GB), 3	Daylight Savings, 3	8	1:55.94	$120,000
1996 **Jaunatxo**, 3, 114	J. L. Diaz	Trail City, 3	Marlin, 3	12	1:55.82	$180,000
1995 **Gold and Steel (Fr)**, 3, 114	A. T. Gryder	Torrential, 3	Unanimous Vote (Ire), 3	7	1:55.02	$180,000
1994 (DH) **Vaudeville**, 3, 114 (DH) **Overbury (Ire)**, 3	A. D. Lopez		Star Campaigner, 3	10	1:55.29	$120,000
1993 **Explosive Red**, 3, 120	S. J. Sellers	Earl of Barking (Ire), 3	Newton's Law (Ire), 3	9	1:59.92	$180,000
1992 **The Name's Jimmy**, 3, 120	P. Day	Standiford, 3	May I Inquire, 3	14	1:59.41	$180,000

1895-'97,1899,1905-'15,1917-'25,1936,1938-'39,1988,1998-'99 not held. 1973-'74,1981-'89 Grade 1. 1884-1904,1926-'27,1929-'57 held at Washington Park; 1916 Hawthorne. 1884-1904,1926-'27 1¹/₂ miles; 1916,1928-'51,1962-'65,1977-'91 1¹/₄ miles; 1952-'54,1958-'61,1966-'74,1976 1¹/₈ miles; 1975 1¹/₁₆ miles. 1884-1954,1958-'69,1977-'91 dirt. 1994 dead heat for first. 1996 Trail City finished first, DQ to second.

American Handicap

Grade 2, Hollywood Park, three-year-olds and up, 1¹/₈ miles, turf. Held July 4, 2002, with a gross value of $150,000. First held in 1938. Graded since 1973. Stakes record 1:45.60 (1987 Clever Song).

Year Winner	Jockey	Second	Third	Strs	Time	1st Purse
2002 **The Tin Man**, 4, 115	M. E. Smith	Devine Wind, 6	Kappa King, 6	7	1:46.82	$90,000
2001 **Takarian (Ire)**, 6, 114	G. K. Gomez	Fighting Falcon, 5	Fateful Dream, 5	7	1:48.19	$90,000
2000 **Dark Moondancer (GB)**, 5, 122	C. J. McCarron	Sardaukar (GB), 4	Sunshine Street, 4	6	1:46.74	$90,000
1999 **Takarian (Ire)**, 4, 114	G. K. Gomez	Montemiro (Fr), 5	Special Quest (Fr), 5	8	1:47.37	$90,000
1998 **Magellan**, 5, 116	G. L. Stevens	Bonapartiste (Fr), 4	Sharekann (Ire), 4	8	1:47.05	$90,000
1997 **El Angelo**, 5, 114	A. O. Solis	Naninja, 4	Wavy Run (Ire), 4	6	1:46.99	$96,360
1996 **Labeeb (GB)**, 4, 119	E. J. Delahoussaye	Gold and Steel (Fr), 4	Earl of Barking (Ire), 4	5	1:45.78	$66,120
1995 **Silver Wizard**, 5, 118	G. L. Stevens	Romarin (Brz), 5	Savinio, 5	5	1:46.02	$91,900
1994 **Blues Traveller (Ire)**, 4, 115	C. W. Antley	Gothland (Fr), 5	Johann Quatz (Fr), 5	7	1:46.50	$128,000
1993 †**Toussaud**, 4, 114	K. J. Desormeaux	Man From Eldorado, 5	Journalism, 5	6	1:46.87	$126,000
1992 **Man From Eldorado**, 4, 114	K. J. Desormeaux	Bold Russian (GB), 5	Golden Pheasant, 5	4	1:47.11	$122,000

Traditionally held during the July 4th holiday. 1942-'43 not held. 1949 held at Santa Anita. 1945-'46,1986 1¹/₁₆ miles; 1950 1¹/₄ miles; 1995-'96 about 1¹/₈ miles. 1938-'67 dirt. 1945 four-year-olds and up. †denotes female.

Amsterdam Stakes

Grade 2, Saratoga Race Course, three-year-olds, 6 furlongs, dirt. Held August 3, 2002, with a gross value of $150,000. First held in 1901. Graded since 1998. Stakes record 1:09.13 (1996 Distorted Humor).

Year	Winner	Jockey	Second	Third	Strs	Time	1st Purse
2002	Listen Here, 3, 121	P. Day	Boston Common, 3	Bold Truth, 3	8	1:09.58	$90,000
2001	City Zip, 3, 123	J. F. Chavez	Speightstown, 3	Smile My Lord, 3	6	1:11.03	$81,420
2000	Personal First, 3, 120	P. Day	Disco Rico, 3	Trippi, 3	6	1:09.33	$66,000
1999	Successful Appeal, 3, 122	E. S. Prado	Lion Hearted, 3	Silver Season, 3	9	1:10.25	$50,340
1998	(DH) Secret Firm, 3, 117	E. S. Prado		Southern Bostonion, 3	8	1:10.28	$33,060
	(DH) Mint, 3						
1997	Oro de Mexico, 3, 117	C. W. Antley	Trafalger, 3	Kelly Kip, 3	7	1:10.58	$49,275
1996	Distorted Humor, 3, 115	P. Day	Gold Fever, 3	Stu's Choice, 3	7	1:09.13	$32,820
1995	Kings Fiction, 3, 112	P. Day	Lord Carson, 3	Ft. Stockton, 3	5	1:09.75	$32,250
1994	Chimes Band, 3, 117	J. D. Bailey	Ledford, 3	Halo's Image, 3	6	1:09.90	$32,325
	Mr. Shawklit, 3, 115	W. H. McCauley	Scarlet Rage, 3	Groovy Jett, 3	5	1:10.89	$32,325
1993	Evil Bear, 3, 117	J. A. Santos	Punch Line, 3	Digging In, 3	5	1:22.09	$28,800

Named for Amsterdam, New York, located in Montgomery County. Formerly named for G2 SW Screen King (1976, c. by Silent Screen). 1993-'97 Screen King S. 1911-'12,1924-'92 not held. 1998-2000 Grade 3. 1993 held at Belmont Park. 1901-'23 1 mile; 1993 7 furlongs. 1901-'23 three-year-olds and up. 1994 two divisions. 1998 dead heat for first.

Ancient Title Breeders' Cup Handicap

Grade 1, Santa Anita Park, three-year-olds and up, 6 furlongs, dirt. Held October 5, 2002, with a gross value of $207,875. First held in 1985. Graded since 1990. Stakes record 1:07.67 (2001 Swept Overboard).

Year	Winner	Jockey	Second	Third	Strs	Time	1st Purse
2002	†Kalookan Queen, 6, 119	A. O. Solis	Crafty C. T., 4	Mellow Fellow, 4	6	1:08.26	$125,625
2001	Swept Overboard, 4, 116	E. J. Delahoussaye	Kona Gold, 7	I Love Silver, 7	6	1:07.67	$124,260
2000	Kona Gold, 6, 124	A. O. Solis	Regal Thunder, 6	Elaborate, 6	4	1:08.11	$123,060
1999	Lexicon, 4, 116	K. J. Desormeaux	Kona Gold, 5	Regal Thunder, 5	8	1:07.84	$125,400
1998	Gold Land, 7, 117	K. J. Desormeaux	†A. P. Assay, 4	Swiss Yodeler, 4	8	1:08.50	$94,020
1997	Elmhurst, 7, 114	C. S. Nakatani	Swiss Yodeler, 3	Larry the Legend, 3	7	1:08.82	$95,000
1996	Lakota Brave, 7, 117	E. J. Delahoussaye	Letthebighossroll, 8	Paying Dues, 8	5	1:08.16	$93,700
1995	†Track Gal, 4, 116	G. L. Stevens	Siphon (Brz), 4	Forest Gazelle, 4	6	1:08.32	$59,150
1994	Saratoga Gambler, 6, 113	M. A. Pedroza	Uncaged Fury, 3	Concept Win, 3	8	1:08.87	$62,500
1993	Cardmania, 7, 116	E. J. Delahoussaye	Music Merci, 7	Bahatur, 7	8	1:08.04	$61,975
1992	Gray Slewpy, 4, 118	K. J. Desormeaux	Trick Me, 4	Light of Morn, 4	9	1:08.48	$59,372

Named for multiple G1 stakes winner Ancient Title (1970-'81, g. by Gummo). 1985-'89 Ancient Title H. 1990-'98 Grade 3; 1999-2000 Grade 2. 1996 Criollito (Arg) finished third, DQ to fourth. 2001 new track record. †denotes female.

Anne Arundel Stakes

Grade 3, Laurel Park, three-year-olds, fillies, 1⅛ miles, dirt. Held December 14, 2002, with a gross value of $100,000. First held in 1974. Graded since 1996. Stakes record 1:49.34 (1999 Undermine).

Year	Winner	Jockey	Second	Third	Strs	Time	1st Purse
2002	Martha's Music, 3, 122	S. Elliott	Pass the Virtue, 3	Shop Till You Drop, 3	11	1:50.84	$60,000
2000	Gin Talking, 3, 122	R. A. Dominguez	Tax Affair, 3	A. O. L. Hayes, 3	9	1:50.21	$60,000
1999	Undermine, 3, 115	L. Melancon	Gold From the West, 3	Batique, 3	9	1:49.34	$60,000
1998	Merengue, 3, 122	M. T. Johnston	Queen of Oz, 3	Manoa, 3	9	1:51.97	$60,000
1997	G. O'Keefe, 3, 115	M. T. Johnston	Snit, 3	Cotton Carnival, 3	9	1:51.20	$60,000
1996	Hay Let's Dance, 3, 115	S. B. Martinez	Double Stake, 3	Mesabi Maiden, 3	7	1:50.82	$45,000
1995	Blue Sky Princess, 3, 122	M. G. Pino	Substantial, 3	Blonde Actress, 3	11	1:51.46	$45,000
1994	Miss Slewpy, 3, 114	L. C. Reynolds	Cherokee Wonder, 3	Churchbell Chimes, 3	6	1:51.11	$45,000
1993	By Your Leave, 3, 114	M. G. Pino	Tennis Lady, 3	Double Sixes, 3	5	1:52.58	$33,030
1992	Avian Assembly, 3, 112	L. C. Reynolds	Gammy's Alden, 3	Singing Ring, 3	11	1:50.77	$30,000

Named for Lady Anne Arundell (1615-'49), wife of Thomas Arundell, the founder of Maryland colony. 1975-'92 Anne Arundel H. 1918-'73, 2001 not held. 1911-'17 1⅛ miles; 1974-'87 1 mile; 1991 7 furlongs. 1911-'17 three-year-olds and up. 1911-'17 both sexes.

Apple Blossom Handicap

Grade 1, Oaklawn Park, four-year-olds and up, fillies and mares, 1¹⁄₁₆ miles, dirt. Held April 5, 2003, with a gross value of $500,000. First held in 1974. Graded since 1977. Stakes record 1:40.20 (1984 Heatherten).

Year	Winner	Jockey	Second	Third	Strs	Time	1st Purse
2003	Azeri, 5, 123	M. E. Smith	Take Charge Lady, 4	Mandy's Gold, 5	7	1:43.00	$300,000
2002	Azeri, 4, 117	M. E. Smith	Affluent, 4	Miss Linda (Arg), 4	5	1:42.75	$300,000
2001	Gourmet Girl, 6, 113	C. H. Borel	Lu Ravi, 6	Lazy Slusan, 6	11	1:42.15	$300,000
2000	Heritage of Gold, 5, 118	S. J. Sellers	Lu Ravi, 5	Bordelaise (Arg), 5	7	1:42.22	$300,000
1999	Banshee Breeze, 4, 122	J. D. Bailey	Sister Act, 4	Silent Eskimo, 4	6	1:44.000	$300,000
1998	Escena, 5, 117	J. D. Bailey	Glitter Woman, 4	Toda Una Dama (Arg), 4	7	1:40.95	$300,000
1997	Halo America, 7, 117	C. H. Borel	Jewel Princess, 5	Different (Arg), 5	8	1:41.65	$300,000
1996	Twice the Vice, 5, 117	C. J. McCarron	Halo America, 6	Serena's Song, 6	7	1:41.71	$300,000
1995	Heavenly Prize, 4, 120	P. Day	Halo America, 5	Paseana (Arg), 5	6	1:42.76	$300,000
1994	Nine Keys, 4, 116	M. E. Smith	Mamselle Bebette, 4	Re Toss (Arg), 4	10	1:42.15	$300,000
1993	Paseana (Arg), 6, 124	C. J. McCarron	Looie Capote, 4	Luv Me Luv Me Not, 4	9	1:41.80	$300,000

| 1992 | Paseana (Arg), 5, 124 | C. J. McCarron | Fit for a Queen, 6 | Slide Out Front, 6 | 8 | 1:42.13 | $300,000 |

Named for the apple trees typically in bloom during the Oaklawn meet. 1977 Grade 3; 1978-'81,1990-'91 Grade 2. 1974 6 furlongs; 1975-'79 1 mile 70 yards. 1974 three-year-olds and up.

Appleton Handicap

Grade 2, Gulfstream Park, three-year-olds and up, 1 mile, turf. Held January 4, 2003, with a gross value of $150,000. First held in 1952. Graded since 1973. Stakes record 1:33.69 (2001 Associate).

Year	Winner	Jockey	Second	Third	Strs	Time	1st Purse
2003	Point Prince, 4, 115	M. R. Cruz	Kreiger, 5	Red Sea (GB), 7	9	1:37.84	$90,000
2002	Pisces, 5, 113	R. I. Velez	North East Bound, 6	Capsized, 6	10	1:39.41	$90,000
2001	Associate, 6, 114	J. F. Chavez	Band Is Passing, 5	El Mirasol, 5	12	1:33.69	$90,000
2000	Band Is Passing, 4, 115	E. Coa	Hibernian Rhapsody (Ire), 5	Shamrock City, 5	11	1:40.11	$60,000
1999	Behaviour (GB), 7, 113	S. J. Sellers	Notoriety, 6	Legs Galore, 6	6	1:45.77	$60,000
1998	Sir Cat, 5, 119	J. D. Bailey	Wild Event, 5	Kingcanrunallday, 5	5	1:42.69	$60,000
1997	Montjoy, 5, 116	M. E. Smith	Mighty Forum (GB), 6	Elite Jeblar, 6	12	1:39.88	$60,000
1996	The Vid, 6, 122	W. H. McCauley	Dove Hunt, 5	Montreal Red, 5	11	1:41.79	$60,000
1995	Dusty Screen, 7, 116	W. H. McCauley	The Vid, 5	Dove Hunt, 5	7	1:42.72	$60,000
1994	Paradise Creek, 5, 121	M. E. Smith	Fourstars Allstar, 6	Elite Jeblar, 6	8	1:40.57	$60,000
1993	Cigar Toss (Arg), 6, 112	B. G. Moore	Bidding Proud, 4	Archies Laughter, 4	9	1:43.55	$60,000
1992	Royal Ninja, 6, 112	J. D. Bailey	Archies Laughter, 4	Native Boundary, 4	12	1:42.49	$60,000

Named in honor of Arthur I. Appleton, owner of Bridlewood Farm in Florida. 1975-'84 not graded; 1973-'74,1985-'97,1999 Grade 3. 1952,1992-2000 1 1/16 miles; 1953-'64 1 1/8 miles; 1965-'66,1972,1983 7 furlongs; 1991 1 mile 70 yards. 1952-'66,1972-'73,1983,1991,1993,1995,1998-'99 dirt.

Aqueduct Handicap

Grade 3, Aqueduct, three-year-olds and up, 1 1/16 miles, dirt. Held January 18, 2003, with a gross value of $107,400. First held in 1902. Graded since 1985. Stakes record 1:41.13 (1995 Danzig's Dance).

Year	Winner	Jockey	Second	Third	Strs	Time	1st Purse
2003	Snake Mountain, 5, 120	M. J. Luzzi	Ground Storm, 7	Cat's At Home, 6	5	1:44.17	$64,440
2002	Evening Attire, 4, 116	S. Bridgmohan	Ground Storm, 7	Tempest Fugit, 6	7	1:42.69	$65,520
2001	Liberty Gold, 7, 115	J. Bravo	Coyote Lakes, 7	Talk's Cheap, 7	7	1:42.20	$66,300
2000	Sky Approval, 6, 115	C. H. Velasquez	Parental Pressure, 9	Phone the King, 9	8	1:44.45	$49,770
1999	Mr. Sinatra, 5, 118	A. T. Gryder	Brushing Up, 6	Wouldn't We All, 6	5	1:43.11	$49,335
1998	Star of Valor, 5, 113	A. T. Gryder	Christian Soldier, 4	Mr. Sinatra, 4	8	1:42.48	$49,725
1997	Pacific Fleet, 5, 112	J. F. Chavez	More to Tell, 6	Admiralty, 6	8	1:43.45	$39,924
1996	Mighty Magee, 4, 118	M. J. Luzzi	May I Inquire, 7	More to Tell, 7	8	1:43.89	$39,780
1995	Danzig's Dance, 6, 111	J. F. Chavez	Key Contender, 7	Golden Larch, 7	8	1:41.13	$50,010
1994	As Indicated, 4, 121	R. G. Davis	Primitive Hall, 5	Jacksonport, 5	6	1:45.77	$48,690
1993	Shots Are Ringing, 6, 118	J. R. Velazquez	A Call to Rise, 5	Federal Funds, 5	6	1:44.44	$52,650
1992	Formal Dinner, 4, 112	A. Cordero Jr.	Shots Are Ringing, 5	Island Edition, 5	6	1:43.60	$51,750

1962-'65,1967-'68 Aqueduct S. 1910-'16,1924,1956-'58,1969-'72,1974-'75,1979 not held. 1961 held at Belmont. 1917-'19,1926-'32,1961-'73 1 1/8 miles; 1920-'23 1 5/16 miles; 1959-'60,1976 1 mile. 1904 two-year-olds and up; 1973 two-year-olds. 1995 equaled track record. 1992 Shots Are Ringing finished first, DQ to second.

Arcadia Handicap

Grade 2, Santa Anita Park, four-year-olds and up, 1 1/8 miles, turf. Held April 6, 2003, with a gross value of $150,000. First held in 1988. Graded since 1990. Stakes record 1:47.16 (2002 Seinne [Chi]).

Year	Winner	Jockey	Second	Third	Strs	Time	1st Purse
2003	Century City (Ire), 4, 114	J. Valdivia Jr.	Gondolieri (Chi), 4	Sunday Break (Jpn), 4	9	1:47.84	$90,000
2002	Seinne (Chi), 5, 115	C. J. McCarron	Irish Prize, 6	Kerrygold (Fr), 6	9	1:47.16	$90,000
2001	Lazy Lode (Arg), 7, 121	L. A. Pincay Jr.	Night Patrol, 5	Wake the Tiger, 5	5	1:49.74	$90,000
2000	Falcon Flight (Fr), 4, 114	B. Blanc	Bonapartiste (Fr), 6	Otavalo (Ire), 6	7	1:47.88	$97,950
1999	Commitisize, 4, 117	D. R. Flores	Majorien (GB), 5	Ladies Din, 5	7	1:48.25	$90,000
1998	Hawksley Hill (Ire), 5, 117	G. L. Stevens	Precious Ring, 5	Kirkwall (GB), 5	8	1:49.96	$100,410
1997	Labeeb (GB), 5, 120	E. J. Delahoussaye	Talloires, 7	Pinfloron (Fr), 7	5	1:35.96	$80,100
1996	Tychonic (GB), 6, 118	G. L. Stevens	Debutant Trick, 6	Savinio, 6	6	1:35.84	$80,300
1995	Savinio, 5, 116	C. J. McCarron	River Flyer, 4	Romarin (Brz), 4	7	1:34.74	$91,800
1994	Norwich (GB), 7, 117	P. A. Valenzuela	Megan's Interco, 5	Gothland (Fr), 5	5	1:34.14	$75,850
1993	Val des Bois (Fr), 7, 118	P. A. Valenzuela	Star of Cozzene, 5	C. Sam Maggio, 5	7	1:35.07	$77,750
1992	Exbourne, 6, 122	G. L. Stevens	Repriced, 4	Madjaristan, 4	6	1:33.21	$95,000

Named for Arcadia, California, city in which Santa Anita is located. Formerly named for two land grants named Rancho El Rincon. 1990-'94 Grade 3. 1988-2000 El Rincon H. 1988-'97 1 mile.

Aristides Handicap

Grade 3, Churchill Downs, three-year-olds and up, 6 1/2 furlongs, dirt. Held June 29, 2002, with a gross value of $107,500. First held in 1989. Graded since 1999. Stakes record 1:14.41 (2002 Orientate).

Year	Winner	Jockey	Second	Third	Strs	Time	1st Purse
2002	Orientate, 4, 118	R. Albarado	Binthebest, 5	No Armistice, 5	5	1:14.41	$66,650
2001	Bet On Sunshine, 9, 120	C. H. Borel	Alannan, 5	Dash for Daylight, 5	6	1:14.79	$67,208
2000	Bet On Sunshine, 8, 119	F. C. Torres	Proven Cure, 6	Sun Bull, 6	7	1:15.11	$68,014

1999	**Run Johnny**, 7, 116	P. Day	Squall Valley, 4	Neon Shadow, 4	8	1:16.27	$68,572
1998	**Thisnearlywasmine**, 4, 115	S. J. Sellers	Partner's Hero, 4	El Amante, 4	7	1:15.72	$67,518
1997	**High Stakes Player**, 5, 119	S. J. Sellers	Trafalger, 3	Bet On Sunshine, 3	7	1:15.85	$67,580
1996	**Lord Carson**, 4, 115	D. M. Barton	Criollito (Arg), 5	Bet On Sunshine, 5	5	1:15.94	$70,525
1995	**Boone's Mill**, 3, 106	D. M. Barton	Ojai, 6	Hot Jaws, 6	7	1:15.90	$69,924
1994	**Never Wavering**, 5, 116	S. J. Sellers	Demaloot Demashoot, 4	American Chance, 4	8	1:16.55	$53,479
1993	**Gold Spring (Arg)**, 5, 115	F. A. Arguello Jr.	Take Me Out, 5	In the Zone, 5	6	1:16.43	$35,718
1992	**Tricky Fun**, 4, 113	P. Day	Guns of Cielo, 5	Richman, 5	6	1:16.35	$44,720

Named for the first winner of the Kentucky Derby, Aristides (1872-'93, c. by *Leamington). 1989-'95 Aristides Breeders' Cup H. 2000 track record.

Arkansas Derby

Grade 2, Oaklawn Park, three-year-olds, 1 1/8 miles, dirt. Held April 12, 2003, with a gross value of $500,000. First held in 1936. Graded since 1973. Stakes record 1:46.80 (1984 Althea).

Year	Winner	Jockey	Second	Third	Strs	Time	1st Purse
2003	**Sir Cherokee**, 3, 118	T. J. Thompson	Eugene's Third Son, 3	Christine's Outlaw, 3	12	1:48.39	$300,000
2002	**Private Emblem**, 3, 122	D. J. Meche	Wild Horses, 3	(DH) Bay Monster, 3	11	1:50.20	$300,000
				(DH) Windward Passage, 3			
2001	**Balto Star**, 3, 122	M. Guidry	Jamaican Rum, 3	Son of Rocket, 3	11	1:49.04	$300,000
2000	**Graeme Hall**, 3, 118	R. Albarado	Snuck In, 3	Impeachment, 3	14	1:49.08	$300,000
1999	**Certain**, 3, 122	K. J. Desormeaux	Torrid Sand, 3	Ecton Park, 3	7	1:49.30	$300,000
1998	**Victory Gallop**, 3, 122	A. O. Solis	Hanuman Highway (Ire), 3	Favorite Trick, 3	9	1:49.86	$300,000
1997	**Crypto Star**, 3, 122	P. Day	Phantom On Tour, 3	Pacificbounty, 3	11	1:49.34	$300,000
1996	**Zarb's Magic**, 3, 122	R. D. Ardoin	Grindstone, 3	Halo Sunshine, 3	12	1:49.21	$300,000
1995	**Dazzling Falls**, 3, 122	G. K. Gomez	Flitch, 3	On Target, 3	8	1:50.60	$300,000
1994	**Concern**, 3, 118	G. K. Gomez	Blumin Affair, 3	Silver Goblin, 3	9	1:48.16	$300,000
1993	**Rockamundo**, 3, 118	C. H. Borel	Kissin Kris, 3	Foxtrail, 3	10	1:48.17	$300,000
1992	**Pine Bluff**, 3, 122	J. D. Bailey	Lil E. Tee, 3	Desert Force, 3	6	1:49.49	$300,000

1936 Arkansas Centennial Derby. 1945 not held. 1981-'88 Grade 1. 1999 Valhol finished first, DQ to seventh. 2002 dead heat for third.

Arlington Classic Stakes

Grade 2, Arlington Park, three-year-olds, 1 1/16 miles, turf. Held June 29, 2002, with a gross value of $175,000. First held in 1929. Graded since 1973. Stakes record 1:41.95 (2002 Mr. Mellon).

Year	Winner	Jockey	Second	Third	Strs	Time	1st Purse
2002	**Mr. Mellon**, 3, 121	R. R. Douglas	Doc Holiday (Ire), 3	Seainsky, 3	9	**1:41.95**	$105,000
2001	**Baptize**, 3, 121	M. Guidry	Indygo Shiner, 3	Cherokee Kim, 3	6	1:48.80	$120,000
2000	**King Cugat**, 3, 123	R. Albarado	Boyum, 3	El Ballezano, 3	5	1:48.16	$90,000
1997	**Honor Glide**, 3, 114	G. K. Gomez	Brave Act (GB), 3	Daylight Savings, 3	8	1:47.59	$75,000
1996	**Trail City**, 3, 114	P. Day	More Royal, 3	Winter Quarters, 3	5	1:48.61	$120,000
1995	**Hawk Attack**, 3, 114	P. Day	Via Lombardia (Ire), 3	Bryntirion, 3	10	1:48.04	$120,000
1994	**Eagle Eyed**, 3, 120	C. S. Nakatani	Mr. Angel, 3	Star Campaigner, 3	11	1:48.46	$180,000
1993	**Boundlessly**, 3, 120	P. Day	Hegar, 3	Williamstown, 3	13	1:49.89	$180,000
1992	**Saint Ballado**, 3, 120	J. A. Krone	Desert Force, 3	Star Recruit, 3	6	1:46.82	$180,000

1929-'45 Classic S.; 1971-'73 Pontiac Grand Prix S. 1974-'76,1988,1998-'99 not held. 1981-'89 Grade 1; 1977 not graded. 1943-'45 held at Washington Park. 1929-'51,1977-'79 1 1/4 miles; 1952-'72 1 mile; 1980-2001 1 1/8 miles. 1929-'93 dirt. 1977 three-year-olds and up. 1997 equaled course record.

Arlington Handicap

Grade 3, Arlington Park, three-year-olds and up, 1 1/4 miles, turf. Held July 27, 2002, with a gross value of $225,000. First held in 1929. Graded since 1973. Stakes record 2:00.40 (1985 Pass the Line).

Year	Winner	Jockey	Second	Third	Strs	Time	1st Purse
2002	**Falcon Flight (Fr)**, 6, 115	R. R. Douglas	Kappa King, 5	Gretchen's Star, 5	10	2:03.13	$135,000
2001	**Make No Mistake (Ire)**, 6, 116	R. Albarado	Takarian (Ire), 6	El Gran Papa, 6	7	2:02.53	$150,000
2000	**Northern Quest (Fr)**, 5, 113	R. Albarado	Profit Option, 5	Where's Taylor, 5	11	2:02.13	$90,000
1997	**Wild Event**, 4, 114	M. Guidry	Storm Trooper, 4	Chorwon, 4	8	2:01.52	$90,000
1996	**Torch Rouge (GB)**, 5, 116	M. Guidry	Sentimental Moi, 6	Volochine (Ire), 6	6	2:03.32	$120,000
1995	**Manilaman**, 4, 114	R. P. Romero	Snake Eyes, 5	Bluegrass Prince (Ire), 5	7	2:02.82	$120,000
1994	**Fanmore**, 6, 114	P. Day	Marastani, 4	Split Run, 4	7	2:01.72	$150,000
1993	**Evanescent**, 6, 114	A. T. Gryder	Split Run, 5	Magesterial Cheer, 5	9	2:00.93	$150,000
1992	**Sky Classic**, 5, 125	P. Day	Duckaroo, 6	Glity, 6	9	2:00.62	$150,000

1963,1972,1974 Arlington Park H. 1940,1969-'71,1988,1998-'99 not held. 1943-'45 held at Washington Park; 1985 held at Hawthorne. 1973-'80,1990-'97 Grade 2; 1981-'89 Grade 1. 1929,1952,1965 1 1/8 miles; 1941,1953-'62,1964,1973-'76 1 3/16 miles; 1963,1966-'67 1 mile; 1968 7 furlongs; 1972,1977-'83 1 1/2 miles. 1929-'39,1942-'53,1963,1965-'72,1975 dirt. 1992 Plate Dancer finished second, DQ to fifth.

Arlington Matron Handicap

Grade 3, Arlington Park, three-year-olds and up, fillies and mares, 1 1/8 miles, dirt. Held September 2, 2002, with a gross value of $150,000. First held in 1930. Graded since 1973. Stakes record 1:48.40 (1986 Queen Alexandra).

Year	Winner	Jockey	Second	Third	Strs	Time	1st Purse
2002	**Lakenheath**, 4, 115	C. A. Emigh	With Ability, 4	Your Out, 4	5	1:50.78	$90,000
2001	**Humble Clerk**, 4, 114	L. Melancon	Maltese Superb, 4	Lakenheath, 3	7	1:51.53	$90,000

					Strs	Time	1st Purse
2000	**Megans Bluff**, 3, 111	C. R. Woods Jr.	On a Soapbox, 4	Tutorial, 4	8	1:51.41	$90,000
1997	**Omi**, 4, 114	M. Guidry	Gold Memory, 4	Trick Attack, 4	6	1:51.93	$60,000
1996	**Belle of Cozzene**, 4, 115	D. R. Pettinger	War Thief, 4	Your Ladyship, 4	9	1:49.34	$75,000
1995	**Mariah's Storm**, 4, 117	R. N. Lester	Mysteriously, 4	Minority Dater, 4	9	1:50.98	$60,000
1994	**Hey Hazel**, 4, 115	M. G. Pino	Passing Vice, 4	Pennyhill Park, 4	8	1:49.58	$60,000
1993	**Erica's Dream**, 5, 115	W. Martinez	Pleasant Jolie, 5	Meafara, 5	6	1:50.09	$60,000
1992	**Lemhi Go**, 4, 114	E. Fires	Beth Believes, 4	Diamond City, 6	8	1:49.67	$45,000

Matron races are traditionally held for older fillies and mares. 1933-'36,1988,1998-'99 not held. 1964-'83 Matron H. 1973-'89 Grade 2. 1943-'45 held at Washington Park; 1985 Hawthorne. 1930-'57 1 mile; 1980-'85 1 1/4 miles. 1966-'74,1976-'79 turf. 1952 three-year-olds, fillies.

Arlington Million Stakes

Grade 1, Arlington Park, three-year-olds and up, 1 1/4 miles, turf. Held August 17, 2002, with a gross value of $1,000,000. First held in 1981. Graded since 1983. Stakes record 1:58.69 (1995 Awad).

Year	Winner	Jockey	Second	Third	Strs	Time	1st Purse
2002	**Beat Hollow (GB)**, 5, 126	J. D. Bailey	Sarafan, 5	Forbidden Apple, 5	9	2:02.94	$600,000
2001	**Silvano (Ger)**, 5, 126	A. Suborics	Hap, 5	Redattore (Brz), 5	12	2:02.64	$600,000
2000	**Chester House**, 5, 126	J. D. Bailey	Manndar (Ire), 4	Mula Gula, 4	7	2:01.37	$1,200,000
1997	**Marlin**, 4, 126	G. L. Stevens	Sandpit (Brz), 8	Percutant (GB), 8	8	2:02.54	$600,000
1996	**Mecke**, 4, 126	R. G. Davis	Awad, 6	Sandpit (Brz), 6	9	2:00.49	$600,000
1995	**Awad**, 5, 126	E. Maple	Sandpit (Brz), 6	The Vid, 6	11	**1:58.69**	$600,000
1994	**Paradise Creek**, 5, 126	P. Day	Fanmore, 6	Muhtarram, 6	14	1:59.78	$600,000
1993	**Star of Cozzene**, 5, 126	J. A. Santos	Evanescent, 6	Johann Quatz (Fr), 6	8	2:07.50	$600,000
1992	**Dear Doctor (Fr)**, 5, 126	C. B. Asmussen	Sky Classic, 5	Golden Pheasant, 5	12	1:59.84	$600,000

First million-dollar Thoroughbred race in North America. Formerly named for sponsor Anheuser-Busch's Budweiser beer. 1998-'99 not held. 1981 Arlington Million Invitational S.; 1982-'84 Budweiser Million S.; 1985-'87 Budweiser-Arlington Million S. 1989 held at Woodbine. 1995 course record.

Arlington-Washington Futurity

Grade 3, Arlington Park, two-year-olds, 1 mile, dirt. Held September 28, 2002, with a gross value of $150,000. First held in 1927. Graded since 1973. Stakes record 1:35.80 (1989 Secret Hello).

Year	Winner	Jockey	Second	Third	Strs	Time	1st Purse
2002	**Most Feared**, 2, 122	M. Guidry	Anasheed, 2	Unleash the Power, 2	10	1:37.52	$90,000
2001	**Publication**, 2, 122	R. A. Meier	It'sallinthechase, 2	Dubai Squire, 2	7	1:38.78	$90,000
2000	**Trailthefox**, 2, 121	S. J. Sellers	Starbury, 2	Blame It On Ruby, 2	11	1:37.25	$90,000
1997	**Cowboy Dan**, 2, 121	D. Kutz	Captain Maestri, 2	Fiamma, 2	9	1:37.68	$90,000
1996	**Night in Reno**, 2, 121	M. Guidry	Flying With Eagles, 2	Thisnearlywasmine, 2	8	1:36.67	$120,000
1994	**Evansville Slew**, 2, 121	P. Compton	Valid Wager, 2	Mr Purple, 2	9	1:37.84	$120,000
1993	**Polar Expedition**, 2, 121	C. C. Bourque	Gimme Glory, 2	Delicate Cure, 2	6	1:39.28	$120,000
1992	**Gilded Time**, 2, 121	C. J. McCarron	Boundlessly, 2	Rockamundo, 2	6	1:37.84	$200,580

Merged with old Washington Park Futurity, renamed after closure of Washington Park. 1929-'31,1970,1988,1995,1998-'99 not held. 1927-'28 American National Futurity; 1932-'61 Arlington Futurity. 1973-'89 Grade 1; 1990-2001 Grade 2. 1943-'45 held at Washington Park; 1985 Hawthorne. 1927-'61,1971-'73 6 furlongs; 1962-'69,1979-'83 7 furlongs; 1974-'78,1985 6 1/2 furlongs. 1973-'74,1976-'83 colts and geldings.

Arlington-Washington Lassie Stakes

Grade 3, Arlington Park, two-year-olds, fillies, 1 mile, dirt. Held September 28, 2002, with a gross value of $100,000. First held in 1929. Graded since 1973. Stakes record 1:36.58 (1991 Speed Dialer).

Year	Winner	Jockey	Second	Third	Strs	Time	1st Purse
2002	**Moonlight Sonata**, 2, 121	S. Laviolette	Parting, 2	Souris, 2	13	1:37.82	$60,000
2001	**Joanies Bella**, 2, 121	M. St. Julien	Brief Bliss, 2	First Again, 2	9	1:39.34	$60,000
2000	**Thunder Bertie**, 2, 119	J. Beasley	Caressing, 2	Zahwah, 2	10	1:36.91	$60,000
1997	**Silver Maiden**, 2, 119	S. Laviolette	Arctic Lady, 2	So Generous, 2	6	1:37.54	$60,000
1996	**Southern Playgirl**, 2, 119	R. P. Romero	Leo's Gypsy Dancer, 2	Broad Dynamite, 2	7	1:38.27	$90,000
1994	**Shining Light**, 2, 119	J. L. Diaz	She's a Lively One, 2	Alltheway Bertie, 2	5	1:41.70	$90,000
1993	**Mariah's Storm**, 2, 119	R. N. Lester	Shapely Scrapper, 2	Minority Dater, 2	14	1:38.95	$90,000
1992	**Eliza**, 2, 119	P. A. Valenzuela	Banshee Winds, 2	Tourney, 2	6	1:39.58	$134,850

Merged with old Washington Park Lassie, renamed after closure of Washington Park. 1970-'71,1988,1995,1998-'99 not held. 1929-'31 Lassie S.; 1932-'62 Arlington Lassie S. 1976-'80,1990-'97 Grade 2; 1981-'89 Grade 1. 1943-'45 held at Washington Park. 1929-'31 5 1/2 furlongs; 1932,1980-'84,1986-'87 7 furlongs; 1933-'61,1972-'79 6 furlongs; 1962-'69,1985 6 1/2 furlongs.

Ashland Stakes

Grade 1, Keeneland, three-year-olds, fillies, 1 1/16 miles, dirt. Held April 5, 2003, with a gross value of $551,750. First held in 1879. Graded since 1973. Stakes record 1:41.72 (1999 Silverbulletday).

Year	Winner	Jockey	Second	Third	Strs	Time	1st Purse
2003	**Elloluv**, 3, 120	R. Albarado	Lady Tak, 3	Holiday Lady, 3	7	1:43.58	$342,085
2002	**Take Charge Lady**, 3, 123	A. J. D'Amico	Take the Cake, 3	Belterra, 3	8	1:43.29	$345,805
2001	**Fleet Renee**, 3, 116	J. R. Velazquez	Golden Ballet, 3	Latour, 3	11	1:43.77	$357,275
2000	**Rings a Chime**, 3, 116	S. J. Sellers	Zoftig, 3	Circle of Life, 3	6	1:44.43	$341,155
1999	**Silverbulletday**, 3, 123	J. D. Bailey	Marley Vale, 3	Gold From the West, 3	6	**1:41.72**	$337,280

1998	**Well Chosen**, 3, 115	C. R. Woods Jr.	Let, 3	Banshee Breeze, 3	7	1:43.00	$344,410
1997	**Glitter Woman**, 3, 121	M. E. Smith	Anklet, 3	Storm Song, 3	6	1:43.98	$337,125
1996	**My Flag**, 3, 121	J. D. Bailey	Cara Rafaela, 3	Mackie, 3	5	1:42.69	$335,265
1995	**Urbane**, 3, 115	E. Delahoussaye	Conquistadoress, 3	Post It, 3	6	1:43.41	$207,483
1994	**Inside Information**, 3, 121	M. E. Smith	Bunting, 3	Private Status, 3	6	1:46.99	$171,198
1993	**Lunar Spook**, 3, 121	S. J. Sellers	Avie's Shadow, 3	Roamin Rachel, 3	7	1:43.43	$171,973
1992	**Prospectors Delite**, 3, 121	C. Perret	Spinning Round, 3	Luv Me Luv Me Not, 3	10	1:42.65	$186,063

Named for home of Henry Clay ("Ashland") located in Lexington, Kentucky. Ashland oil company has sponsored the race since 1986. 1897-1911,1933-'35,1938-'39 not held. 1879-1932 Ashland Oaks. 1973-'78 Grade 3; 1979-'85 Grade 2. 1879-1932 held at Kentucky Association; 1943-'45 Churchill Downs. 1879-'82 1½ miles; 1883-'89 1¼ miles; 1890-1926 1 mile; 1932 1 mile 70 yards; 1940-'73 6 furlongs; 1974-'80 about 7 furlongs. 1936-'37 three-year-olds and up, fillies and mares.

Astarita Stakes

Grade 2, Belmont Park, two-year-olds, fillies, 6½ furlongs, dirt. Held October 13, 2002, with a gross value of $150,000. First held in 1946. Graded since 1973. Stakes record 1:16.40 (1974 Stulcer).

Year	Winner	Jockey	Second	Third	Strs	Time	1st Purse
2002	**Humorous Lady**, 2, 117	J. D. Bailey	Fast Cookie, 2	Chimichurri, 2	7	1:17.76	$90,000
2001	**Bella Bellucci**, 2, 117	G. L. Stevens	Forest Heiress, 2	Speed to Burn, 2	4	1:16.67	$63,955
2000	**Xtra Heat**, 2, 117	M. T. Johnston	Gold Mover, 2	Major Wager, 2	8	1:16.71	$66,060
1999	**Silentlea**, 2, 119	R. G. Davis	Valerie's Dream, 2	Lucky Livi, 2	10	1:17.44	$67,620
1998	**Paved in Gold**, 2, 119	J. F. Chavez	Blushing Deed, 2	Paula's Girl, 2	5	1:18.86	$63,780
1997	**Ninth Inning**, 2, 119	R. G. Davis	Salty Perfume, 2	Madam Fireplace, 2	5	1:17.44	$64,680
1996	**Broad Dynamite**, 2, 119	D. W. Cordova	Glitter Woman, 2	Biding Time, 2	4	1:24.02	$63,960
1995	**Top Secret**, 2, 119	M. E. Smith	Plum Country, 2	Mesabi Maiden, 2	8	1:36.79	$69,480
1994	**Miss Golden Circle**, 2, 119	J. A. Krone	Golden Bri, 2	Mistress S., 2	6	1:23.67	$64,740
1993	**Shapely Scrapper**, 2, 119	J. Bravo	Brighter Course, 2	Fashion Maven, 2	4	1:24.02	$67,560
1992	**Missed the Storm**, 2, 119	M. E. Smith	Dispute, 2	Statuette, 2	6	1:24.90	$67,920

Named for Astarita (1900, f. by *Bathampton), first winner of the Astoria Stakes at Gravesend Park in 1902. 1958-'60 not held. 1995 New York City Astarita S. 1973-'80 Grade 3. 1946-'55,1962-'67,1991-'94,1996-'97 held at Aqueduct. 1946-'56 6 furlongs; 1957-'71,1991-'94,1996 7 furlongs; 1995 1 mile.

Athenia Handicap

Grade 3, Aqueduct, three-year-olds and up, fillies and mares, 1¹⁄₁₆ miles, turf. Held November 9, 2002, with a gross value of $116,700. First held in 1978. Graded since 1980. Stakes record 1:40.53 (2001 Babae [Chi] [2nd Div.]).

Year	Winner	Jockey	Second	Third	Strs	Time	1st Purse
2002	**Babae (Chi)**, 6, 120	J. F. Chavez	Strawberry Blonde (Ire), 4	Silver Rail, 4	12	1:44.90	$70,020
2001	**Verruma (Brz)**, 5, 114	J. R. Velazquez	Siringas (Ire), 3	Freefourracing, 3	8	1:42.09	$82,725
	Babae (Chi), 5, 116	J. F. Chavez	Batique, 5	Sweet Prospect (GB), 5	8	**1:40.53**	$82,725
2000	**Wild Heart Dancing**, 4, 115	J. F. Chavez	Fickle Friends, 4	Silken (GB), 4	8	1:43.40	$67,500
1999	**Antoniette**, 4, 119	J. F. Chavez	Dominique's Joy, 4	Prospectress, 4	8	1:41.89	$66,840
1998	**Tampico**, 5, 114	J. Bravo	Irish Daisy, 5	Rumpipumpy (GB), 5	10	1:42.90	$51,210
1997	**Rapid Selection**, 4, 113	J. Bravo	Dynasty, 4	Preachersnightmare, 4	6	1:47.11	$65,940
1996	**Sixieme Sens**, 4, 116	J. D. Bailey	Rapunzel Runz, 5	Fashion Star, 5	7	1:37.92	$66,660
1995	**Caress**, 4, 114	R. G. Davis	Manila Lila, 5	Vinista, 5	6	1:54.18	$68,340
1994	**Lady Affirmed**, 3, 111	J. F. Chavez	Irving's Girl, 4	Cox Orange, 4	11	1:48.66	$52,245
1993	**Trampoli**, 4, 117	M. E. Smith	Kirov Premiere (GB), 3	Dahlia's Dreamer, 3	8	2:17.16	$54,000
1992	**Fairy Garden**, 4, 112	J. A. Krone	Passagere du Soir (GB), 5	Seewillo, 5	5	2:13.62	$52,020

Named for Hal Price Headley's Athenia (1943, f. by *Pharamond II), winner of the 1946 Ladies H. 1978-'81,1983-'93,1996-'97, 2001 held at Belmont. 2001 two divisions. 1978-'81 1¼ miles; 1982-'93 1⅜ miles; 1994-'95,1997 1¹⁄₈ miles; 1996 1 mile. 1979,1990,1995 dirt. 1978-'83 three-year-olds, fillies.

Azalea Breeders' Cup Stakes

Grade 3, Calder Race Course, three-year-olds, fillies, 6 furlongs, dirt. Held July 13, 2002, with a gross value of $196,750. First held in 1972. Graded since 1996. Stakes record 1:10.86 (2002 Bold World).

Year	Winner	Jockey	Second	Third	Strs	Time	1st Purse
2002	**Bold World**, 3, 118	C. H. Borel	Willa On the Move, 3	Tchula Miss, 3	10	**1:10.86**	$105,000
2001	**Hattiesburg**, 3, 116	M. Guidry	Southern Tour, 3	Spanish Glitter, 3	11	1:11.81	$150,000
2000	**Swept Away**, 3, 116	P. Day	Precious Feather, 3	Watchfull, 3	8	1:11.53	$120,000
1999	**Show Me the Stage**, 3, 116	R. J. Courville	Could Be, 3	Exact, 3	9	1:11.91	$75,000
1998	**Cassidy**, 3, 114	J. A. Rivera II	Holy Capote, 3	Fantasy Angel, 3	8	1:11.93	$75,000
1997	**Little Sister**, 3, 116	F. Lovato Jr.	Princess Pietrina, 3	Maggie Auxier, 3	7	1:13.08	$120,000
1996	**J J'sdream**, 3, 118	H. Castillo Jr.	Supah Avalanche, 3	Race Artist, 3	7	1:23.87	$65,100
1995	**Lucky Lavender Gal**, 3, 116	R. R. Douglas	Chaposa Springs, 3	Dancin Renee, 3	6	1:23.50	$60,000
1994	**Cut the Charm**, 3, 115	H. Castillo Jr.	Just a Little Kiss, 3	Tasso Bee, 3	11	1:25.51	$60,000
1993	**Kimscountrydiamond**, 3, 115	J. Vasquez	Nijivision, 3	Hollywood Wildcat, 3	10	1:23.44	$60,000
1992	**C. C.'s Return**, 3, 113	R. J. Thibeau Jr.	Fortune Forty Four, 3	Subtle Dancer, 3	7	1:25.33	$30,000

Named for the azalea, a rhododendron common to South Florida. 1973-'74 not held. 1972,1992-'93 Azalea H.; 1975-'95 Azalea S. 1972 1¹⁄₁₆ miles; 1978-'79,1981-'90,1992-'96 7 furlongs. 1972 three-year-olds and up, fillies and mares.

Baldwin Stakes

Grade 3, Santa Anita Park, three-year-olds, about 6½ furlongs, turf. Held February 23, 2003, with a gross value of $114,550.
First held in 1968. Graded since 1973. Stakes record 1:12.56 (2003 Buddy Gil).

Year	Winner	Jockey	Second	Third	Strs	Time	1st Purse
2003	Buddy Gil, 3, 117	G. L. Stevens	King Robyn, 3	Flirt With Fortune, 3	11	1:12.56	$68,730
2002	Shuffling Kid (GB), 3, 117	P. A. Valenzuela	Red Briar (Ire), 3	Dark Sorcerer (GB), 3	12	1:13.30	$68,640
2001	Skip to the Stone, 3, 117	C. S. Nakatani	Trailthefox, 3	Bills Paid, 3	6	1:16.29	$66,000
2000	Fortifier, 3, 114	B. Blanc	Performing Magic, 3	Joopy Doopy, 3	8	1:16.79	$66,870
1999	American Spirit, 3, 114	E. Ramsammy	Chomper (Ire), 3	Impressive Grades, 3	13	1:13.93	$69,300
1998	Wrekin Pilot (GB), 3, 116	E. J. Delahoussaye	Commitisize, 3	Tenbyssimo (Ire), 3	8	1:13.32	$66,240
1997	Latin Dancer, 3, 116	C. A. Black	King of Swing, 3	Swiss Yodeler, 3	11	1:14.48	$67,850
1996	Sandtrap, 3, 114	C. S. Nakatani	Strangelove, 3	Benton Creek, 3	6	1:15.03	$64,300
1995	Sierra Diablo, 3, 116	E. J. Delahoussaye	Raji, 3	Huge Gator, 3	6	1:15.36	$47,300
1994	Silver Music, 3, 114	C. W. Antley	Eagle Eyed, 3	Makinanhonestbuck, 3	8	1:13.76	$48,375
1993	Future Storm, 3, 117	K. J. Desormeaux	Concept Win, 3	Siebe, 3	11	1:15.02	$51,550
1992	Reckless Ruckus, 3, 116	P. A. Valenzuela	Fabulous Champ, 3	Slerp, 3	8	1:17.28	$49,850

Named for Elias J. "Lucky" Baldwin, builder of the original Santa Anita Park. 1975-'94 not graded. 1979,1982-'83,1986,1991-'92,1995,2000-'01 6½ furlongs. 1979,1982-'83,1986,1991-'92,1995,2000-'01 dirt. 1978-'87 colts and geldings.

Ballerina Handicap

Grade 1, Saratoga Race Course, three-year-olds and up, fillies and mares, 7 furlongs, dirt. Held August 25, 2002, with a gross value of $250,000. First held in 1979. Graded since 1981. Stakes record 1:21.22 (1992 Serape).

Year	Winner	Jockey	Second	Third	Strs	Time	1st Purse
2002	Shine Again, 5, 116	J-L. Samyn	Raging Fever, 4	Mandy's Gold, 4	7	1:22.26	$150,000
2001	Shine Again, 4, 113	J-L. Samyn	Country Hideaway, 5	Dream Supreme, 5	5	1:22.33	$150,000
2000	Dream Supreme, 3, 113	P. Day	Country Hideaway, 4	Bourbon Belle, 4	9	1:22.97	$150,000
1999	Furlough, 5, 114	M. E. Smith	Bourbon Belle, 4	(DH) Hurricane Bertie, 4 (DH) Catinca, 4	10	1:23.04	$120,000
1998	Stop Traffic, 5, 118	S. J. Sellers	Runup the Colors, 4	U Can Do It, 4	6	1:22.23	$120,000
1997	Pearl City, 3, 110	J. Bravo	Ashboro, 4	Flashy n Smart, 4	5	1:22.39	$90,000
1996	Chaposa Springs, 4, 120	S. J. Sellers	Capote Belle, 3	Broad Smile, 3	6	1:21.88	$90,000
1995	Classy Mirage, 5, 119	J. A. Krone	Inside Information, 4	Laura's Pistolette, 4	6	1:22.55	$90,000
1994	Roamin Rachel, 4, 118	P. Day	Classy Mirage, 4	Twist Afleet, 4	6	1:21.85	$65,040
1993	Spinning Round, 4, 119	J. F. Chavez	November Snow, 4	Apelia, 4	7	1:21.49	$69,120
1992	Serape, 4, 116	C. W. Antley	Harbour Club, 5	Nanneri, 5	9	1:21.22	$71,160

Named for Howell E. Jackson's Ballerina (1950-'65, f. by Rosemont), first winner of the Maskette Stakes. 1979-'93 Ballerina S. 1981-'83 Grade 3; 1984-'87 Grade 2. 1999 dead heat for third.

Ballston Spa Breeders' Cup Handicap

Graded 3, Saratoga Race Course, three-year-olds and up, fillies and mares, 1⅛ miles, dirt (lost graded status in 2002 when taken off turf). Held August 24, 2002, with a gross value of $191,800. First held in 1989. Graded since 1995. Stakes record 1:52.29 (2002 Surya).

Year	Winner	Jockey	Second	Third	Strs	Time	1st Purse
2002	Surya, 4, 114	J. D. Bailey	Shooting Party, 4	Solvig, 4	3	1:52.29	$126,409
2001	Penny's Gold, 4, 118	J. D. Bailey	Babae (Chi), 5	Chaste, 5	6	1:40.69	$126,120
2000	License Fee, 5, 116	P. Day	Pico Teneriffe, 4	Hello Soso (Ire), 4	7	1:43.53	$125,700
1999	Pleasant Temper, 5, 118	J. D. Bailey	Cuanto Es, 4	Lets Get Cozzy, 4	5	1:41.84	$124,680
1998	Memories of Silver, 5, 122	J. D. Bailey	Witchful Thinking, 4	Ashford Castle, 4	7	1:40.93	$126,600
1997	Valor Lady, 5, 112	J. R. Velazquez	Antespend, 4	Rumpipumpy (GB), 4	6	1:39.47	$130,200
1996	Danish (Ire), 5, 115	J. A. Santos	Apolda, 5	(DH) Upper Noosh, 5 (DH) Caress, 5	8	1:41.50	$126,360
1995	Weekend Madness (Ire), 5, 117	S. J. Sellers	Irish Linnet, 7	Allez Les Trois, 7	7	1:40.34	$93,300
1994	Weekend Madness (Ire), 4, 115	S. J. Sellers	You'd Be Surprised, 5	Heed, 5	8	1:43.77	$93,510
1993	One Dreamer, 5, 116	E. Fires	Eenie Meenie Miney, 4	Irish Linnet, 4	10	1:39.38	$94,440
1992	Aurora, 4, 114	C. Perret	Olden Rijn, 4	Irish Linnet, 4	7	1:36.94	$93,870

Named for Ballston Spa, New York, located to the south of Saratoga Springs. 1989-'93 Aqueduct Breeders' Cup H.; 1994-'95 Saratoga Budweiser Breeders' Cup H.; 1996 Saratoga Breeders' Cup H. 1995-2001 Grade 3. 1992-'93 held at Aqueduct. 1989-'93 1 mile; 1994-2001 1⅛ miles. 1990-2001 turf. 1996 dead heat for third.

Baltimore Breeders' Cup Handicap

Grade 3, Pimlico, three-year-olds and up, 1⅛ miles, dirt. Held April 19, 2003, with a gross value of $95,000. First held in 1911. Graded since 1988. Stakes record 1:47.63 (1996 Pyramid Peak).

Year	Winner	Jockey	Second	Third	Strs	Time	1st Purse
2003	P Day, 8, 118	R. Fogelsonger	Changeintheweather, 4	Full Brush, 8	7	1:48.94	$45,000
2002	Grundlefoot, 5, 116	M. G. Pino	Lyracist, 6	Private Ryan, 6	5	1:49.65	$60,000
2001	Lightning Paces, 4, 114	G. W. Hutton	Milwaukee Brew, 4	Grundlefoot, 4	5	1:50.52	$60,000
2000	Leave It to Beezer, 7, 115	T. L. Dunkelberger	Eastern Daydream, 5	Thunder Flash, 5	6	1:49.02	$60,000
1999	Testafly, 5, 114	G. W. Hutton	Rod and Staff, 6	Willing, 6	7	1:49.80	$60,000

1998 **Testafly**, 4, 115	G. W. Hutton	Hot Brush, 4	Proud and True, 4	7	1:49.86	$60,000
1997 **Pyramid Peak**, 5, 118	P. Day	Wild Deputy, 4	Tam's Armada, 4	7	1:48.83	$125,520
1996 **Pyramid Peak**, 4, 122	W. H. McCauley	Coup D' Argent, 4	Personal Merit, 4	4	**1:47.63**	$124,350
1995 **Poor But Honest**, 5, 109	D. P. Butler	Mary's Buckaroo, 4	Rugged Bugger, 4	5	1:49.01	$126,120
1994 **Taking Risks**, 4, 117	M. T. Johnston	Conte Di Savoya, 5	Frottage, 5	7	1:49.21	$65,880
1993 **Sunny Sunrise**, 6, 120	M. T. Johnston	Snappy Landing, 4	Baron Mathew, 4	6	1:48.97	$108,750
1992 **Excellent Tipper**, 4, 112	E. S. Prado	Sunny Sunrise, 5	Out of Place, 5	10	1:47.64	$105,000

Named for the city of Baltimore, Maryland. In 2001, temporarily named for the Baltimore Ravens Super Bowl champion football team. 1919-'26 not held. 1911-'18,1927-'34 Baltimore H; 1935-'40 run twice a year as Baltimore Spring H. and Baltimore Autumn H.; 1941-'57 Baltimore Spring H.; 1986-'95 Baltimore Budweiser Breeders' Cup H.; 2001 Baltimore Ravens Breeders' Cup H. 1911-'18,1992-'97 held at Laurel Park. 1911-'18,1932,1986-'88 1¹/₁₆ miles; 1927-'30 1 mile 70 yards; 1933-'49,1957 6 furlongs; 1953-'56 5¹/₂ furlongs. 1927-'34 two-year-olds and up; 1935-'40 two-year-olds and up (Baltimore Autumn H.). 1992 new track record; 1996 equaled track record.

Barbara Fritchie Handicap

Grade 2, Laurel Park, three-year-olds and up, fillies and mares, 7 furlongs, dirt. Held February 22, 2003, with a gross value of $200,000. First held in 1952. Graded since 1973. Stakes record 1:21.40 (1989 Tappiano).

Year	Winner	Jockey	Second	Third	Strs	Time	1st Purse
2003	**Xtra Heat**, 5, 125	R. Wilson	Carson Hollow, 4	Spelling, 4	7	1:24.76	$120,000
2002	**Xtra Heat**, 4, 128	H. Vega	Prized Stamp, 5	Kimbralata, 5	8	1:22.70	$120,000
2001	**Prized Stamp**, 4, 113	T. L. Dunkelberger	Superduper Miss, 5	Tax Affair, 5	6	1:23.74	$120,000
2000	**Tap to Music**, 5, 115	J. Bravo	Her She Kisses, 4	Di's Time, 4	13	1:24.75	$120,000
1999	**Passeggiata (Arg)**, 6, 113	M. G. Pino	Catinca, 4	Nothing Special, 4	8	1:23.55	$150,000
1998	**J J'sdream**, 5, 115	L. C. Reynolds	Palette Knife, 5	Stylish Encore, 5	10	1:24.21	$150,000
1997	**Miss Golden Circle**, 5, 118	R. Migliore	Lottsa Talc, 7	Whaleneck, 7	12	1:23.05	$120,000
1996	**Lottsa Talc**, 6, 117	F. T. Alvarado	Up an Eighth, 5	Evil's Pic, 5	14	1:22.61	$120,000
1995	**Smart 'N Noble**, 4, 117	M. G. Pino	Dust Bucket, 4	Gooni Goo Hoo, 4	10	1:24.13	$120,000
1994	**Mixed Appeal**, 6, 111	A. C. Salazar	Known as Nancy, 4	Winka, 4	12	1:23.31	$120,000
1993	**Moon Mist**, 4, 112	T. G. Turner	Ritchie Trail, 5	Femma, 5	9	1:23.50	$120,000
1992	**Wood So**, 5, 113	M. G. Pino	Wide Country, 4	Wait for the Lady, 4	7	1:24.56	$120,000

Named for Barbara Fritchie, a 95-year-old woman who, according to legend, waved her Union flag as Confederate General Thomas "Stonewall" Jackson passed through Frederick, Maryland. 1960,1972 not held. 1952-'58 Barbara Frietchie H. 1973-'91 Grade 3. 1952-'84 held at Bowie. 1952-'54 1¹/₁₆ miles; 1957-'59,1963 6 furlongs; 1961 1 mile.

Bashford Manor Stakes

Grade 3, Churchill Downs, two-year-olds, 6 furlongs, dirt. Held July 7, 2002, with a gross value of $136,250. First held in 1902. Graded since 1991. Stakes record 1:09.68 (2002 Lone Star Sky).

Year	Winner	Jockey	Second	Third	Strs	Time	1st Purse
2002	**Lone Star Sky**, 2, 115	M. Guidry	Posse, 2	Cooper Crossing, 2	7	**1:09.68**	$84,475
2001	**Lunar Bounty**, 2, 115	F. Lovato Jr.	Binyamin, 2	Storm Passage, 2	5	1:09.90	$82,925
2000	**Duality**, 2, 115	C. H. Borel	Strait Cat, 2	Take Arms, 2	9	1:10.09	$86,258
1999	**Dance Master**, 2, 115	B. D. Peck	Sky Dweller, 2	Snuck In, 2	8	1:10.38	$89,280
1998	**Time Bandit**, 2, 115	C. R. Woods Jr.	Yes It's True, 2	Haus of Dehere, 2	8	1:10.78	$68,262
1997	**Favorite Trick**, 2, 121	P. Day	Double Honor, 2	Cowboy Dan, 2	8	1:09.92	$68,696
1996	**Boston Harbor**, 2, 115	M. J. Luzzi	Prairie Junction, 2	Nobel Talent, 2	8	1:09.96	$72,150
1995	**A. V. Eight**, 2, 115	A. J. Trosclair	Aggie Southpaw, 2	Seeker's Reward, 2	8	1:11.40	$71,630
1994	**Hyroglyphic**, 2, 116	G. K. Gomez	Boone's Mill, 2	Hobgoblin, 2	13	1:10.25	$75,660
1993	**†Miss Ra He Ra**, 2, 113	W. Martinez	Ramblin Guy, 2	Riverinn, 2	13	1:12.98	$76,180
1992	**Mountain Cat**, 2, 116	C. R. Woods Jr.	Tempered Halo, 2	Storm Flight, 2	7	1:10.62	$53,869

Named for an old Louisville-area plantation and neighborhood, Bashford Manor. 1999-2001 Grade 2. 1902-'25 4¹/₂ furlongs; 1926-'81 5 furlongs; 1982-'85 5¹/₂ furlongs. 1940-'81 colts and geldings. †denotes female.

Bayakoa Handicap

Grade 2, Hollywood Park, three-year-olds and up, fillies and mares, 1¹/₁₆ miles, dirt. Held December 15, 2002, with a gross value of $150,000. First held in 1981. Graded since 1983. Stakes record 1:41.20 (1993 Golden Klair [GB]).

Year	Winner	Jockey	Second	Third	Strs	Time	1st Purse
2002	**Starrer**, 4, 118	P. A. Valenzuela	Cee's Elegance, 5	Angel Gift, 5	7	1:41.74	$90,000
2001	**Starrer**, 3, 118	J. D. Bailey	Queenie Belle, 4	Tropical Lady (Brz), 4	7	1:42.52	$90,000
2000	**Feverish**, 5, 119	E. J. Delahoussaye	Gourmet Girl, 5	Lazy Slusan, 5	9	1:42.26	$90,000
1999	**Manistique**, 4, 124	C. S. Nakatani	Snowberg, 4	Riboletta (Brz), 4	7	1:43.16	$90,000
1998	**Manistique**, 3, 119	G. L. Stevens	India Divina (Chi), 4	Numero Uno, 4	4	1:42.51	$60,000
1997	**Sharp Cat**, 3, 121	A. O. Solis			1	1:42.68	$60,000
1996	**Listening**, 3, 120	C. J. McCarron	Cat's Cradle, 4	Belle's Flag, 4	7	1:42.66	$64,920
1995	**Pirate's Revenge**, 4, 119	C. W. Antley	Urbane, 3	Ashtabula, 3	5	1:41.80	$61,900
1994	**Thirst for Peace**, 5, 115	A. O. Solis	Glass Ceiling, 4	Dancing Mirage, 4	7	1:42.28	$63,500
1993	**Golden Klair (GB)**, 3, 115	C. J. McCarron	Pacific Squall, 4	Cargo, 4	7	**1:41.20**	$63,500
1992	**Brought to Mind**, 5, 120	P. A. Valenzuela	Re Toss (Arg), 5	Interactive, 5	8	1:42.62	$65,200

Named for 1989, '90 champion older female Bayakoa (Arg) (1984-'97, f. by Consultant's Bid). 1987 not held. 1981-'93 Silver Belles H. 1983-'85 Grade 3. 1981-'89 1¹/₈ miles. 1997 won in a walkover.

Bay Meadows Breeders' Cup Handicap

Grade 3, Bay Meadows, three-year-olds and up, 1⅛ miles, turf. Held September 21, 2002, with a gross value of $200,000. First held in 1934. Graded since 1981. Stakes record 1:45.91 (1993 Slew of Damascus).

Year	Winner	Jockey	Second	Third	Strs	Time	1st Purse
2002	David Copperfield, 5, 117	J. P. Lumpkins	Ninebanks, 4	Little Ghazi, 4	5	1:48.95	$110,000
2001	Super Quercus (Fr), 5, 117	R. A. Baze	Most Likely (Arg), 5	Sign of Hope (GB), 5	6	1:47.50	$55,000
2000	Devine Wind, 4, 114	G. K. Gomez	Irish Prize, 4	Deploy Venture (GB), 4	6	1:47.19	$110,000
1999	Kirkwall (GB), 5, 114	V. Espinoza	Special Quest (Fr), 4	Game Ploy (Pol), 4	8	1:47.13	$110,000
1998	Hawksley Hill (Ire), 5, 120	A. O. Solis	Magellan, 5	Floriselli, 5	5	1:45.49	$110,000
1997	El Angelo, 5, 119	A. O. Solis	Via Lombardia (Ire), 5	Dreamer, 5	5	1:45.47	$110,000
1996	Gentlemen (Arg), 4, 117	C. S. Nakatani	Party Season (GB), 5	Petit Poucet (GB), 5	5	1:45.90	$110,000
1995	Caesour, 5, 115	R. A. Baze	Johann Quatz (Fr), 6	Canaska Dancer (Ire), 6	6	1:45.45	$110,000
1994	Blues Traveller (Ire), 4, 116	G. L. Stevens	Fastness (Ire), 4	Wharf, 4	6	1:46.03	$110,000
1993	Slew of Damascus, 5, 114	T. M. Chapman	Fast Cure, 4	Lissitki (Fr), 4	7	1:45.91	$110,000
1992	Forty Niner Days, 5, 115	C. S. Nakatani	Bistro Garden, 4	Luthier Enchanteur, 4	8	1:46.58	$137,500

1934-2000 Bay Meadows H. 1982-'84,1986-'95 Grade 2; 1985 not graded. 1936-'37,1939,1954-'58,1960,1962-'69,1973-'77 1¹/₁₆ miles; 1952 1¼ miles; 1984 1⅜ miles; 1988,1990-'92,1994-2001 about 1⅛ miles. 1934-'77,1980 dirt. 1935-'40,1942,1947-'50,1953 two-year-olds and up. 1993,1995 new course record.

Bay Meadows Breeders' Cup Sprint Handicap

Grade 3, Bay Meadows, three-year-olds and up, 6 furlongs, dirt. Held May 11, 2002, with a gross value of $198,750. First held in 1986. Graded since 2000. Stakes record 1:07.94 (2001 Lexicon).

Year	Winner	Jockey	Second	Third	Strs	Time	1st Purse
2002	Mellow Fellow, 7, 119	R. A. Baze	Explicit, 5	Swept Overboard, 5	6	1:08.35	$110,000
2001	Lexicon, 6, 117	R. A. Baze	Swept Overboard, 4	You and You Alone, 4	4	1:07.94	$82,500
2000	Lexicon, 5, 115	R. A. Baze	Men's Exclusive, 7	Dixie Dot Com, 7	5	1:09.19	$110,000
1999	Big Jag, 6, 118	J. Valdivia Jr.	Men's Exclusive, 6	Lexicon, 6	6	1:08.87	$110,000
1998	Musafi, 4, 116	D. R. Flores	(DH) Mr. Doubledown, 4 (DH) The Barking Shark, 4		7	1:08.59	$110,000
1997	Tres Paraiso, 5, 116	C. S. Nakatani	Mashaka's Pride, 4	Boundless Moment, 4	5	1:07.98	$110,000
1996	Boundless Moment, 4, 116	K. J. Desormeaux	Concept Win, 6	Paying Dues, 6	11	1:08.81	$110,000
1995	Lucky Forever, 6, 116	G. F. Almeida	Wild Gold, 5	Uncaged Fury, 5	6	1:08.71	$117,700
1994	†Soviet Problem, 4, 120	R. A. Baze	Wild Gold, 4	Concept Win, 4	6	1:08.58	$31,200
1993	Lucky Forever, 4, 116	A. L. Castanon	Cardmania, 7	Scherando, 7	9	1:08.98	$87,750
1992	Superstrike (GB), 3, 114	D. Sorenson	Anjiz, 4	Naevus Star, 4	7	1:08.83	$86,950

1986-'95 Bay Meadows Budweiser Breeders' Cup H. 1986,1988-'89 1¹/₁₆ miles; 1987 1⅛ miles. 1998 dead heat for second. †denotes female.

Bay Meadows Derby

Grade 3, Bay Meadows, three-year-olds, about 1⅛ miles, turf. Held November 3, 2002, with a gross value of $100,000. First held in 1954. Graded since 1983. Stakes record 1:45.20 (1978 Quip).

Year	Winner	Jockey	Second	Third	Strs	Time	1st Purse
2002	Royal Gem, 3, 119	R. A. Baze	Aly Bubba, 3	Century City (Ire), 3	8	1:48.38	$55,000
2001	Blue Steller (Ire), 3, 119	A. O. Solis	Sir Alfred, 3	Sea to See, 3	8	1:46.81	$55,000
2000	Walkslikeaduck, 3, 122	E. J. Delahoussaye	Jokerman, 3	Calamari, 3	5	1:46.57	$82,500
1999	Mula Gula, 3, 117	R. Q. Meza	†Miss Chryss (Ire), 3	Fighting Falcon, 3	10	1:45.34	$82,500
1998	Takarian (Ire), 3, 116	C. A. Black	I. M. Bzy, 3	Prevalence (GB), 3	8	1:46.80	$82,500
1997	Shellbacks, 3, 113	R. Q. Meza	Brave Act (GB), 3	Zippersup, 3	7	1:49.01	$82,500
1996	†Ocean Queen, 3, 110	J. A. Garcia	Mateo, 3	Mystic Knight (GB), 3	8	1:47.80	$110,000
1995	Virginia Carnival, 3, 115	R. J. Warren Jr.	Helmsman, 3	Tabor, 3	10	1:46.17	$55,000
1994	Marvin's Faith (Ire), 3, 116	M. Castaneda	Western Trader, 3	Turbo Fan, 3	8	1:48.88	$55,000
1993	Ranger (Fr), 3, 114	G. Boulanger	El Atroz, 3	Guide (Fr), 3	9	1:48.90	$55,000
1992	Star Recruit, 3, 116	R. D. Hansen	Siberian Summer, 3	Fax News, 3	6	1:49.13	$55,000

1955-'56,1958-'77 not held. 1996-2000 Bay Meadows Breeders' Cup Derby. 1954,1985,1987,1992-'93,1996 1⅛ miles; 1957,1978-'82 1¹/₁₆ miles. 1992 dirt. †denotes female.

Bay Shore Stakes

Grade 3, Aqueduct, three-year-olds, 7 furlongs, dirt. Held April 12, 2003, with a gross value of $150,000. First held in 1925. Graded since 1973. Stakes record 1:20.54 (1998 Limit Out).

Year	Winner	Jockey	Second	Third	Strs	Time	1st Purse
2003	Halo Homewrecker, 3, 116	J. A. Santos	Don Six, 3	Stanislavsky, 3	11	1:23.19	$90,000
2002	Roman Dancer, 3, 120	K. J. Desormeaux	Warners, 3	Monthir, 3	10	1:22.21	$90,000
2001	Skip to the Stone, 3, 120	V. Espinoza	Multiple Choice, 3	Friday's a Comin', 3	8	1:22.46	$90,000
2000	Precise End, 3, 116	J. F. Chavez	Turnofthecentury, 3	Port Herman, 3	7	1:22.27	$66,000
1999	Perfect Score, 3, 118	E. S. Prado	Royal Ruby, 3	Prince Monty, 3	8	1:22.98	$66,120
1998	Limit Out, 3, 115	J-L. Samyn	Good and Tough, 3	Diamond Studs, 3	6	1:20.54	$65,460
1997	Hawks Landing, 3, 114	R. Migliore	Adverse, 3	Standing On Edge, 3	7	1:22.13	$66,480
1996	Jamies First Punch, 3, 115	J. R. Velazquez	Gold Fever, 3	Firey Jennifer, 3	9	1:22.13	$67,200
1995	Blissful State, 3, 118	M. J. Luzzi	Northern Ensign, 3	Pat n Jac, 3	6	1:23.92	$64,680

| 1994 | **Prank Call**, 3, 113 | J. R. Velazquez | Mr. Shawklit, 3 | Popol's Gold, 3 | 7 | 1:09.84 | $65,940 |
| 1992 | **Three Peat**, 3, 114 | C. W. Antley | Goldwater, 3 | Best Decorated, 3 | 10 | 1:21.68 | $75,600 |

Named for Bay Shore, a resort community located on Long Island, New York. 1910-'24,1956-'59,1993 not held. 1894-1909 Bayshore S.; 1925-'62,1979-'80 Bay Shore H. 1985-'92 Grade 2. 1894-1909 held at Gravesend. 1894 1¹/₁₆ miles; 1895,1933,1960-'63 1 mile; 1896-'98,1934-'35,1977-'78,1984,1994 6 furlongs; 1899-1909 about 6 furlongs; 1936-'39 6¹/₂ furlongs. 1894-1960 three-year-olds and up.

Beaugay Handicap

Grade 3, Aqueduct, three-year-olds and up, fillies and mares, 1¹/₁₆ miles, turf. Held May 5, 2002, with a gross value of $113,200. First held in 1978. Graded since 1986. Stakes record 1:40.16 (1991 Summer Secretary).

Year	Winner	Jockey	Second	Third	Strs	Time	1st Purse
2002	**Voodoo Dancer**, 4, 119	J. D. Bailey	Golden Corona, 4	Babae (Chi), 4	10	1:43.10	$67,920
2001	**Gaviola**, 4, 120	J. D. Bailey	Truebreadpudding, 6	Efficient Frontier, 6	6	1:41.74	$65,940
2000	**Perfect Sting**, 4, 119	J. D. Bailey	License Fee, 5	Fictitious (GB), 5	7	1:42.30	$65,820
1999	**Tampico**, 6, 114	J. R. Velazquez	U R Unforgetable, 5	Shashobegon, 5	7	1:44.32	$67,020
1998	**National Treasure**, 5, 117	R. Migliore	Aspiring, 5	Dixie Ghost, 5	7	1:37.94	$67,740
1997	**Careless Heiress**, 4, 116	J. Bravo	Song of Africa, 4	Gastronomical, 4	6	1:46.28	$65,760
1996	**Christmas Gift**, 4, 118	J. D. Bailey	Caress, 5	Aucilla, 5	9	1:42.89	$50,805
1995	**Caress**, 4, 113	R. G. Davis	Shir Dar (Fr), 5	Statuette, 5	8	1:42.06	$49,905
1994	**Cox Orange**, 4, 112	J. D. Bailey	Irish Linnet, 6	Statuette, 6	5	1:43.32	$49,395
1993	**McKaymackenna**, 4, 113	J. Velasquez	Aurora, 5	Chinese Empress, 5	10	1:44.80	$57,240
1992	**Christiecat**, 5, 116	J-L. Samyn	Metamorphose, 4	Navarra, 4	10	1:46.84	$56,520

Named for Maine Chance Farm's 1945 champion two-year-old filly Beaugay (1943, f. by Stimulus). 1983-'92 held at Belmont Park. 1998 1 mile. 1978-'82,1998 dirt.

Bed o' Roses Breeders' Cup Handicap

Grade 3, Aqueduct, three-year-olds and up, fillies and mares, 1 mile, dirt. Held April 19, 2003, with a gross value of $155,100. First held in 1957. Graded since 1973. Stakes record 1:33.60 (1998 Dixie Flag).

Year	Winner	Jockey	Second	Third	Strs	Time	1st Purse
2003	**Raging Fever**, 5, 119	A. T. Gryder	Smok'n Frolic, 4	Nonsuch Bay, 4	5	1:34.86	$93,960
2002	**Raging Fever**, 4, 121	J. R. Velazquez	Atelier, 5	Shiny Band, 5	6	1:34.96	$94,980
2001	**Country Hideaway**, 5, 117	J. R. Velazquez	Critical Eye, 4	Jostle, 4	7	1:34.98	$95,520
2000	**Ruby Rubles**, 5, 113	C. C. Lopez	Up We Go, 4	Go to the Ink, 4	7	1:36.96	$65,580
1999	**Catinca**, 4, 120	R. Migliore	Foil, 4	License Fee, 4	6	1:34.95	$94,620
1998	**Dixie Flag**, 4, 117	M. J. Luzzi	Hidden Reserve, 4	U Can Do It, 4	9	**1:33.60**	$96,780
1997	**Flat Fleet Feet**, 4, 121	M. E. Smith	Mama Dean, 4	Ashboro, 4	6	1:34.07	$95,940
1996	**Punkin Pie**, 6, 110	J. C. Trejo	Incinerate, 6	Lottsa Talc, 6	6	1:35.13	$65,220
1995	**Incinerate**, 5, 114	F. Leon	Imah, 5	Beckys Shirt, 5	5	1:35.86	$63,960
1994	**Classy Mirage**, 4, 117	R. G. Davis	For all Seasons, 4	Dispute, 4	6	1:34.00	$64,680
1993	**Lady d'Accord**, 6, 111	J. F. Chavez	Missy's Mirage, 5	Buck Some Belle, 5	5	1:36.76	$67,320
1992	**Nannerl**, 5, 115	J. A. Krone	English Charm, 6	Spy Leader Lady, 6	7	1:37.27	$68,100
	Lady d'Accord, 5, 114	J. F. Chavez	My Treasure, 5	Crystal Vous, 5	7	1:37.86	$68,580

Named for Alfred G. Vanderbilt's 1949 champion two-year-old filly and 1951 champion handicap mare Bed o' Roses (1947-'53, f. by Rosemont). 1957-'95 Bed o' Roses H. 1973-'74,1988-'96 Grade 2. 1957-'59 held at Jamaica. 1957-'59,1977-'78 1¹/₁₆ miles; 1984 1 mile 70 yards. 1992 two divisions.

Bel Air Handicap

Grade 2, Hollywood Park, three-year-olds and up, 1¹/₁₆ miles, dirt. Held July 7, 2001, with a gross value of $100,000. First held in 1939. Graded since 1975. Stakes record 1:40.12 (1997 Crafty Friend).

Year	Winner	Jockey	Second	Third	Strs	Time	1st Purse
2001	**Smile Again**, 6, 116	L. A. Pincay Jr.	Freedom Crest, 5	Dig for It, 5	6	1:41.74	$60,000
2000	**Euchre**, 4, 116	A. O. Solis	Sultry Substitute, 5	River Keen (Ire), 5	7	1:41.76	$90,000
1999	**River Keen (Ire)**, 7, 115	C. W. Antley	Barter Town, 4	Quake, 4	7	1:40.69	$75,000
1998	**Free House**, 4, 124	C. J. McCarron	Wild Wonder, 4	Albaha, 4	5	1:41.66	$63,660
1997	**Crafty Friend**, 4, 115	A. O. Solis	Hesabull, 4	Arrivederci Baby, 4	6	**1:40.12**	$64,380
1996	**Cleante (Arg)**, 7, 115	C. J. McCarron	Dare and Go, 5	Dernier Empereur, 5	4	1:41.01	$62,940
1995	**Soul of the Matter**, 4, 121	G. L. Stevens	Cleante (Arg), 6	Luthier Fever, 6	5	1:41.10	$76,200
1994	**Region**, 5, 117	G. L. Stevens	Tinners Way, 4	Williamstown, 4	6	1:40.21	$92,800
1993	**Marquetry**, 6, 119	K. J. Desormeaux	Memo (Chi), 6	Desert Sun (GB), 6	6	1:40.94	$92,800
1992	**Renegotiable**, 4, 113	A. O. Solis	Digression, 5	Missionary Ridge (GB), 5	5	1:41.95	$91,900

Named for Bel Air, California, famous as residential area of the stars. 1940-'67,1980-'82,2002 not held. 1969-'72 Bel Air Claiming S. 1983-'84 not graded; 1985-'86 Grade 3. 1939 7 furlongs; 1968 6 furlongs; 1969-'72,1974-'79,1985-'86 1¹/₈ miles; 1989-'90 1 mile. 1969-'73 turf. 1969-'72 four-year-olds and up. 1968-'72 fillies and mares. 1997 equaled track record.

Beldame Stakes

Grade 1, Belmont Park, three-year-olds and up, fillies and mares, 1¹/₈ miles, dirt. Held October 5, 2002, with a gross value of $750,000. First held in 1905. Graded since 1973. Stakes record 1:45.80 (1990 Go for Wand).

Year	Winner	Jockey	Second	Third	Strs	Time	1st Purse
2002	**Imperial Gesture**, 3, 120	J. D. Bailey	Mandy's Gold, 4	Summer Colony, 4	7	1:50.63	$450,000
2001	**Exogenous**, 3, 120	J. Castellano	Flute, 3	Spain, 3	8	1:49.20	$450,000

2000	Riboletta (Brz), 5, 123	C. J. McCarron	Beautiful Pleasure, 5	Pentatonic, 5	5	1:46.14	$450,000
1999	Beautiful Pleasure, 4, 123	J. F. Chavez	Silverbulletday, 3	Catinca, 3	5	1:47.74	$300,000
1998	Sharp Cat, 4, 123	C. S. Nakatani	Tomisue's Delight, 4	Pocho's Dream Girl, 4	7	1:46.20	$240,000
1997	Hidden Lake, 4, 123	R. Migliore	Ajina, 3	Jewel Princess, 3	8	1:48.26	$240,000
1996	Yanks Music, 3, 119	J. R. Velazquez	Serena's Song, 4	Clear Mandate, 4	6	1:47.02	$240,000
1995	Serena's Song, 3, 119	G. L. Stevens	Heavenly Prize, 4	Lakeway, 4	5	1:48.75	$150,000
1994	Heavenly Prize, 3, 119	P. Day	Educated Risk, 4	Classy Mirage, 4	4	1:48.86	$150,000
1993	Dispute, 3, 119	J. D. Bailey	Shared Interest, 5	Vivano, 5	6	1:47.22	$150,000
1992	Saratoga Dew, 3, 119	W. H. McCauley	Versailles Treaty, 4	Coxwold, 4	5	1:46.99	$150,000

Named for August Belmont II's consensus champion racemare Beldame (1901-'23, f. by Octagon). 1908,1910-'16,1933-'38 not held. 1905-'59 Beldame H. 1905-'56,1959,1962-'68 held at Aqueduct. 1905-'32 5 furlongs; 1939 1¹⁄₁₆ miles; 1977-'89 1¹⁄₄ miles. 1905-'32 two-year-olds. 1905-'32 fillies.

Belmont Breeders' Cup Handicap

Grade 2, Belmont Park, three-year-olds and up, 1¹⁄₈ miles, turf. Held September 14, 2002, with a gross value of $208,600. First held in 1986. Graded since 1988. Stakes record 1:45.90 (1998 Subordination).

Year	Winner	Jockey	Second	Third	Strs	Time	1st Purse
2002	Startac, 4, 116	J. D. Bailey	Volponi, 4	Dr. Kashnikow, 4	6	1:46.60	$125,160
2000	Forbidden Apple, 5, 114	J. A. Santos	Val's Prince, 8	Altibr, 8	6	1:51.73	$126,000
1999	With the Flow, 4, 114	J. A. Santos	Comic Strip, 4	Wised Up, 4	9	1:49.39	$127,620
1998	Subordination, 4, 121	D. R. Flores	Yagli, 5	Bomfim, 5	9	1:45.90	$127,020
1997	Fortitude, 4, 112	R. G. Davis	Green Means Go, 5	Boyce, 5	8	1:38.53	$126,600
1996	Gentleman Beau, 4, 114	J. A. Santos	Volochine (Ire), 5	Kiri's Clown, 5	7	1:41.18	$127,140
1995	Dove Hunt, 4, 121	P. Day	Fly Cry, 4	Unfinished Symph, 4	6	1:40.18	$92,970
1994	A in Sociology, 4, 116	J-L. Samyn	Fourstars Allstar, 6	Home of the Free, 6	10	1:40.19	$34,290
1993	Fourstars Allstar, 5, 116	J. A. Santos	Lech, 5	Cleone, 5	6	1:39.88	$92,880
1992	Roman Envoy, 4, 113	C. Perret	Lotus Pool, 5	Daarik (Ire), 5	10	1:41.50	$34,800

2001 not held due to World Trade Center attack. 1986-'93 Saratoga Budweiser Breeders' Cup H.; 1994-'95 Belmont Budweiser Breeders' Cup H. 1988-'97 Grade 3. 1986-'93 held at Saratoga. 1986-'97 1¹⁄₁₆ miles. 1996 Kiri's Clown finished first, DQ to third. 1997 new course record.

Belmont Stakes

(See Triple Crown section for complete history of the Belmont Stakes)

Grade 1, Belmont Park, three-year-olds, 1¹⁄₂ miles, dirt. Held June 7, 2003, with a gross value of $1,000,000. First held in 1867. Graded since 1973. Stakes record 2:24 (1973 Secretariat [new and current world record]).

Year	Winner	Jockey	Second	Third	Strs	Time	1st Purse
2003	Empire Maker, 3, 126	J.D. Bailey	Ten Most Wanted, 3	Funny Cide, 3	6	2:28.26	$600,000
2002	Sarava, 3, 126	E. S. Prado	Medaglia d'Oro, 3	Sunday Break (Jpn), 3	11	2:29.71	$600,000
2001	Point Given, 3, 126	G. L. Stevens	A P Valentine, 3	Monarchos, 3	9	2:26.56	$600,000
2000	Commendable, 3, 126	P. Day	Aptitude, 3	Unshaded, 3	11	2:31.19	$600,000
1999	Lemon Drop Kid, 3, 126	J. A. Santos	Vision and Verse, 3	Charismatic, 3	12	2:27.88	$600,000
1998	Victory Gallop, 3, 126	G. L. Stevens	Real Quiet, 3	Thomas Jo, 3	11	2:29.16	$600,000
1997	Touch Gold, 3, 126	C. J. McCarron	Silver Charm, 3	Free House, 3	7	2:28.82	$432,600
1996	Editor's Note, 3, 126	R. R. Douglas	Skip Away, 3	†My Flag, 3	14	2:28.96	$437,880
1995	Thunder Gulch, 3, 126	G. L. Stevens	Star Standard, 3	Citadeed, 3	11	2:32.02	$415,440
1994	Tabasco Cat, 3, 126	P. Day	Go for Gin, 3	Strodes Creek, 3	6	2:26.82	$392,280
1993	Colonial Affair, 3, 126	J. A. Krone	Kissin Kris, 3	Wild Gale, 3	13	2:29.97	$444,540
1992	A.P. Indy, 3, 126	E. J. Delahoussaye	My Memoirs (GB), 3	Pine Bluff, 3	11	2:26.13	$458,880

Named for August Belmont I (1816-'90), president of Jerome Park. 1911-'12 not held. 1895,1913 Belmont H. 1867-'89 held at Jerome Park; 1890-1904 Morris Park; 1963-'67 Aqueduct. 1867-'73 1⅝ miles; 1890-'92,1895,1904-'05 1¹⁄₄ miles; 1893-'94 1¹⁄₈ miles; 1896-1903,1906-'25 1³⁄₈ miles. †denotes female.

Ben Ali Stakes

Grade 3, Keeneland, four-year-olds and up, 1¹⁄₈ miles, dirt. Held April 25, 2003, with a gross value of $106,991. First held in 1917. Graded since 1973. Stakes record 1:48.16 (1999 Jazz Club).

Year	Winner	Jockey	Second	Third	Strs	Time	1st Purse
2003	Mineshaft, 4, 120	R. Albarado	American Style, 4	Metatron, 4	4	1:48.52	$68,386
2002	Duckhorn, 5, 116	J. F. Chavez	Parade Leader, 5	Connected, 5	5	1:50.18	$66,464
2001	Broken Vow, 4, 116	E. S. Prado	Perfect Cat, 4	Jadada, 4	5	1:48.47	$66,216
2000	Midway Magistrate, 6, 116	S. J. Sellers	Liberty Gold, 5	Early Warning, 6	6	1:49.15	$67,518
1999	Jazz Club, 4, 115	P. Day	Smile Again, 4	Early Warning, 4	6	1:48.16	$67,456
1998	Storm Broker, 4, 114	R. Albarado	Delay of Game, 5	Gator Dancer, 5	6	1:48.23	$67,208
1997	Louis Quatorze, 4, 119	P. Day	Knockadoon, 5	King James, 5	6	1:49.73	$66,526
1996	Knockadoon, 4, 112	J. D. Bailey	Halo's Image, 5	Thorny Crown, 5	4	1:48.92	$66,216
1995	Wildly Joyous, 4, 114	M. Walls	Danville, 4	Powerful Punch, 4	7	1:49.68	$50,406
1994	Pistols and Roses, 5, 123	M. E. Smith	Sunny Sunrise, 7	Compadre, 7	4	1:51.77	$50,251
1993	Sunny Sunrise, 6, 119	R. Wilson	Conte Di Savoya, 4	Prize Fight, 4	8	1:48.90	$50,933
1992	(DH) Profit Key, 5, 113	S. J. Sellers	Out of Place, 4	Out of Place, 4	6	1:49.95	$34,213
	(DH) Loach, 4	P. A. Valenzuela					

Named for James Ben Ali Haggin (1821-1914), native Kentuckian and owner of Elmendorf Farm, and his Kentucky Derby winner Ben Ali (1883, c. by Virgil). 1923-'27,1932-'36 not held. 1917-'89 Ben Ali H. 1917-'31 held at Kentucky Association; 1943-'45 Churchill Downs. 1917-'30,1937-'53,1963-'78 1¹⁄₁₆ miles; 1931 about 6 furlongs; 1954-'62 about 7 furlongs. 1917-'85 three-year-olds and up. 1992 dead heat for first.

Berkeley Handicap

Grade 3, Golden Gate Fields, three-year-olds and up, 1 mile, dirt. Held March 29, 2003, with a gross value of $100,000. First held in 1933. Graded since 2000. Stakes record 1:34.18 (2001 Blade Prospector [Brz]).

Year	Winner	Jockey	Second	Third	Strs	Time	1st Purse
2003	I'madrifter, 5, 115	R. M. Gonzalez	Palmeiro, 5	Skip to the Stone, 5	6	1:35.13	$55,000
2002	Irisheyesareflying, 6, 120	J. Valdivia Jr.	Boss Ego, 6	Palmeiro, 6	11	1:35.41	$55,000
2001	Blade Prospector (Brz), 6, 116	O. A. Berrio	Dixie Dot Com, 6	Milk Wood (GB), 6	6	1:34.18	$55,000
2000	Voice of Destiny, 4, 113	R. Q. Meza	Mr. Doubledown, 6	Twilight Affair, 6	8	1:35.67	$75,000
1999	Hal's Pal (GB), 6, 117	B. Blanc	Wild Wonder, 5	Worldly Ways (GB), 5	7	1:34.96	$75,000
1998	Wild Wonder, 4, 115	R. A. Baze	General Royal, 4	March of Kings, 4	7	1:35.19	$51,450
1996	Houston Fleet M D, 2, 118	D. Carr	Slewp'a Doop, 2	Big Find, 2	5	1:36.67	$26,600
1995	Double Jab, 4, 115	R. A. Baze	Corslew, 5	Cleante (Arg), 5	8	1:35.18	$49,725
1994	River Special, 4, 115	T. M. Chapman	He's Illustrious, 7	Misty Wind (Ire), 7	8	1:34.33	$32,600
1993	Infamous Deed, 5, 115	R. J. Warren Jr.	Misty Wind (Ire), 5	J. F. Williams, 5	7	1:35.67	$25,960
1992	Music Prospector, 5, 118	R. D. Hansen	Michael's Flyer, 6	Flying Continental, 6	5	1:35.29	$31,450

Named for Berkeley, California, located near San Francisco. 1934-'37,1939-'47,1961-'62,1980,1997 not held. 1948 Berkeley S. 1933 held at Tanforan; 1938 Bay Meadows. 1933 about 6 furlongs; 1938-'50,1952-'55,1957-'59 6 furlongs, 1960-'63,1965,1972-'75,1981 1 1/16 miles; 1966-'70 1 1/4 miles; 1971 1 1/8 miles. 1972-'74,1976 turf. 1933 two-year-olds and up; 1948,1957,1996 two-year-olds; 1949-'56,1958-'65 three-year-olds; 1968 four-year-olds and up. 1948 colts and geldings; 1956-'58,1964 fillies. 1992 non-winners of a race worth $35,000 to the winner at one mile or over in 1991-'92.

Bernard Baruch Handicap

Grade 2, Saratoga Race Course, three-year-olds and up, 1 1/8 miles, turf. Held July 26, 2002, with a gross value of $150,000. First held in 1959. Graded since 1973. Stakes record 1:45.40 (1973 Tentam).

Year	Winner	Jockey	Second	Third	Strs	Time	1st Purse
2002	Del Mar Show, 5, 120	J. D. Bailey	Volponi, 4	Forbidden Apple, 4	7	1:48.51	$90,000
2001	Hap, 5, 121	J. D. Bailey	Royal Strand (Ire), 7	Dr. Kashnikow, 7	7	1:47.06	$90,000
2000	Hap, 4, 115	J. D. Bailey	Inexplicable, 5	Draw Shot, 5	13	1:45.82	$90,000
1999	Middlesex Drive, 4, 117	S. J. Sellers	Tangazi, 4	Comic Strip, 4	8	1:46.55	$90,000
1998	Yagli, 5, 121	J. D. Bailey	Tamhid, 5	Jambalaya Jazz, 5	9	1:46.22	$85,380
1997	Sentimental Moi, 7, 112	C. P. DeCarlo	Jambalaya Jazz, 5	Boyce, 5	8	1:46.11	$66,480
1996	Volochine (Ire), 5, 113	P. Day	Green Means Go, 4	Compadre, 4	10	1:47.58	$68,700
1995	Fourstars Allstar, 7, 120	J. A. Santos	Turk Passer, 5	Compadre, 5	7	1:47.67	$66,240
1994	Lure, 5, 125	M. E. Smith	Paradise Creek, 5	Fourstardave, 5	5	1:46.10	$64,920
1993	Furiously, 4, 119	J. D. Bailey	Star of Cozzene, 5	Royal Mountain Inn, 5	5	1:45.46	$70,320
1992	Fourstars Allstar, 4, 113	M. E. Smith	Lotus Pool, 5	Maxigroom, 5	6	1:46.06	$70,680

Named for Bernard Baruch (1870-1965), avid racing fan known as adviser to presidents. 1959-'60 Bernard Baruch S. 1973-'82 Grade 3; 1988-'89 Grade 1. 1962-'71 1 1/16 miles; 1980 1 3/8 miles. 1959-'60,1979 dirt. 1959-'60 three-year-olds. 1993 equaled course record.

Best Pal Stakes

Grade 3, Del Mar, two-year-olds, 6 1/2 furlongs, dirt. Held August 21, 2002, with a gross value of $150,000. First held in 1972. Graded since 1983. Stakes record 1:15.08 (2001 Officer).

Year	Winner	Jockey	Second	Third	Strs	Time	1st Purse
2002	Kafwain, 2, 117	V. Espinoza	Chief Planner, 2	Outta Here, 2	7	1:17.00	$90,000
2001	Officer, 2, 121	V. Espinoza	Metatron, 2	Essence of Dubai, 2	3	1:15.08	$90,000
2000	Flame Thrower, 2, 117	C. S. Nakatani	Trailthefox, 2	Legendary Weave, 2	7	1:16.51	$90,000
1999	Dixie Union, 2, 121	A. O. Solis	Exchange Rate, 2	Captain Steve, 2	5	1:16.40	$90,000
1998	Worldly Manner, 2, 117	G. L. Stevens	Domination, 2	Waki American, 2	8	1:16.78	$65,580
1997	Old Topper, 2, 117	A. O. Solis	King of the Wild, 2	Souvenir Copy, 2	8	1:16.57	$68,825
1996	Swiss Yodeler, 2, 121	A. O. Solis	Golden Bronze, 2	Deeds Not Words, 2	8	1:16.12	$65,550
1995	Cobra King, 2, 117	R. A. Baze	Northern Afleet, 2	Desert Native, 2	8	1:15.89	$60,350
1994	Timber Country, 2, 117	A. O. Solis	Desert Mirage, 2	Supremo, 2	6	1:16.60	$46,575
1993	Creston, 2, 117	C. A. Black	Troyalty, 2	Flying Sensation, 2	6	1:16.35	$45,900
1992	Devil Diamond, 2, 117	K. J. Desormeaux	Wheeler Oil, 2	Crafty, 2	6	1:22.60	$45,900

Named for Golden Eagle Farm's one-time leading California-bred earner Best Pal (1988-'98, g. by *Habitony). Formerly named for Vasco Nuñez de Balboa, first European to see the Pacific Ocean. 1972-'95 Balboa S. 1972-'73 about 7 1/2 furlongs; 1974-'85 1 mile; 1986-'92 7 furlongs. 1972-'73 turf.

Beverly D. Stakes

Grade 1, Arlington Park, three-year-olds and up, fillies and mares, 1 3/16 miles, turf. Held August 17, 2002, with a gross value of $700,000. First held in 1987. Graded since 1991. Stakes record 1:53.20 (1990 Reluctant Guest).

Year	Winner	Jockey	Second	Third	Strs	Time	1st Purse
2002	Golden Apples (Ire), 4, 123	P. A. Valenzuela	Astra, 6	England's Legend (Fr), 5	6	1:54.86	$420,000
2001	England's Legend (Fr), 4, 123	C. S. Nakatani	The Seven Seas, 5	Spook Express (SAf), 5	9	1:56.75	$420,000
2000	Snow Polina, 5, 123	J. D. Bailey	Happyanunoit (NZ), 5	Country Garden (GB), 5	10	1:55.87	$300,000
1997	Memories of Silver, 4, 123	J. D. Bailey	Maxzene, 4	Dance Design (Ire), 4	6	1:54.38	$300,000
1996	Timarida (Ire), 4, 123	J. P. Murtagh	Perfect Arc, 4	Alpride (Ire), 4	11	1:54.06	$300,000
1995	Possibly Perfect, 5, 123	C. S. Nakatani	Alice Springs, 5	Alpride (Ire), 5	7	1:54.95	$300,000

1994 Hatoof, 5, 123	W. R. Swinburn	Flawlessly, 6	Potridee (Arg), 6	8	1:55.59	$300,000
1993 Flawlessly, 5, 123	C. J. McCarron	Via Borghese, 4	Let's Elope (NZ), 4	7	1:55.61	$300,000
1992 Kostroma (Ire), 6, 123	K. J. Desormeaux	Ruby Tiger (Ire), 5	Dance Smartly, 5	13	1:54.10	$300,000

Named for the late wife of Arlington Park Chairman Richard Duchossois, Beverly Duchossois. 1988,1998-'99 not held. 1987 1¹⁄₁₆ miles. 1993 Let's Elope (NZ) finished first, DQ to third.

Beverly Hills Handicap

Grade 1, Hollywood Park, three-year-olds and up, fillies and mares, 1¼ miles, turf. Held June 29, 2002, with a gross value of $250,000. First held in 1938. Graded since 1973. Stakes record 1:58.56 (2002 Astra).

Year	Winner	Jockey	Second	Third	Strs	Time	1st Purse
2002	Astra, 6, 124	K. J. Desormeaux	Peu a Peu (Ger), 4	Crazy Ensign (Arg), 4	8	**1:58.56**	$150,000
2001	Astra, 5, 121	K. J. Desormeaux	Happyanunoit (NZ), 6	Kalypso Katie (Ire), 6	5	1:59.61	$120,000
2000	Happyanunoit (NZ), 5, 121	B. Blanc	Sweet Life, 4	Polaire (Ire), 4	5	1:59.32	$150,000
1999	Virginie (Brz), 5, 118	L. A. Pincay Jr.	Tranquility Lake, 4	Keeper Hill, 4	6	2:00.21	$150,000
1998	Squeak (GB), 4, 115	G. L. Stevens	Sixy Saint, 4	Freeport Flight, 4	7	2:01.56	$180,000
1997	Windsharp, 6, 122	C. S. Nakatani	Different (Arg), 5	Donna Viola (GB), 5	6	2:00.72	$180,000
1996	Different (Arg), 4, 117	C. J. McCarron	Bail Out Becky, 4	Flagbird, 4	8	2:00.74	$163,800
1995	Alpride (Ire), 4, 115	C. J. McCarron	Possibly Perfect, 5	Wandesta (GB), 5	6	1:46.67	$185,000
1994	Corrazona, 4, 119	G. L. Stevens	Hollywood Wildcat, 4	Flawlessly, 4	7	1:47.40	$188,400
1993	Flawlessly, 5, 123	C. J. McCarron	Jolypha, 4	Party Cited, 4	4	1:47.00	$180,200
1992	Flawlessly, 4, 122	C. J. McCarron	Kostroma (Ire), 6	Alcando (Ire), 6	5	1:47.13	$184,000

Named for Beverly Hills, California. 1940-'67 not held. 1938 1¹⁄₁₆ miles; 1939 1 mile; 1968-'75 1³⁄₈ miles; 1976-'85,1987-'95 1¹⁄₈ miles. 1938-'39 dirt. 1939 three-year-olds. 1938-'39 California-breds. 1939 both sexes.

Bewitch Stakes

Grade 3, Keeneland, four-year-olds and up, fillies and mares, 1½ miles, turf. Held April 24, 2003, with a gross value of $112,100. First held in 1962. Graded since 1982. Stakes record 2:27.54 (1999 Bursting Forth).

Year	Winner	Jockey	Second	Third	Strs	Time	1st Purse
2003	Lilac Queen (Ger), 5, 116	J. D. Bailey	Beyond the Waves, 6	San Dare, 5	10	2:29.70	$69,503
2002	Sweetest Thing, 4, 120	M. Guidry	Lapuma, 5	Lady Upstage (Ire), 5	9	2:31.97	$68,634
2001	Keemoon (Fr), 5, 120	J. D. Bailey	Playact (Ire), 4	Krisada, 4	8	2:30.28	$124,000
2000	The Seven Seas, 4, 116	A. O. Solis	Innuendo (Ire), 5	Hollywood Baldcat, 5	10	2:29.31	$70,122
1999	Bursting Forth, 5, 114	J. F. Chavez	Moments of Magic, 4	Pinafore Park, 4	9	**2:27.54**	$68,758
1998	Maxzene, 5, 113	J. A. Santos	Cuando, 4	Gastronomical, 4	8	2:30.50	$69,626
1997	Cymbala (Fr), 4, 113	P. Day	Noble Cause, 4	Last Approach, 4	10	2:28.87	$69,130
1996	Memories (Ire), 5, 117	S. J. Sellers	Future Act, 4	Curtain Raiser, 4	5	2:30.14	$66,030
1995	Market Booster, 6, 119	P. Day	Memories (Ire), 4	Abigailthewife, 4	7	2:29.33	$50,732
1994	Freewheel, 5, 114	P. Day	Key Chance, 4	Amal Hayati, 5	6	1:50.24	$50,871
1993	Miss Lenora, 4, 112	J. A. Krone	Hero's Love, 5	Radiant Ring, 5	8	1:50.60	$51,367
1992	La Gueriere, 4, 114	B. D. Peck	Indian Fashion, 5´	Plenty of Grace, 5	10	1:48.37	$54,438

Named for Calumet Farm's 1947 champion two-year-old filly and 1949 champion handicap mare Bewitch (1945-'59, f. by Bull Lea). 1962-'64 about 4 furlongs; 1965-'78 4¹⁄₂ furlongs; 1979-'85 1¹⁄₁₆ miles; 1986-'94 1¹⁄₈ miles. 1962-'85 dirt. 1962-'78 two-year-olds; 1980-'85 three-year-olds. 1962-'78 fillies.

Bing Crosby Breeders' Cup Handicap

Grade 2, Del Mar, three-year-olds and up, 6 furlongs, dirt. Held July 27, 2002, with a gross value of $169,000. First held in 1946. Graded since 1985. Stakes record 1:07.80 (1962 Crazy Kid; 1968 Prelense; 1969 Kissin' George; 1978 Bad 'n Big).

Year	Winner	Jockey	Second	Third	Strs	Time	1st Purse
2002	Disturbingthepeace, 4, 116	V. Espinoza	Freespool, 6	Mellow Fellow, 6	9	1:09.21	$90,000
2001	Kona Gold, 7, 126	A. O. Solis	Caller One, 4	Swept Overboard, 4	4	1:08.22	$120,000
2000	Kona Gold, 6, 123	A. O. Solis	Love That Red, 4	Lexicon, 4	6	1:08.50	$124,200
1999	Christmas Boy, 6, 114	C. S. Nakatani	Son of a Pistol, 7	Expressionist, 7	6	1:08.11	$96,360
1998	Son of a Pistol, 6, 120	A. O. Solis	Gold Land, 6	Boundless Moment, 7	7	1:08.10	$97,200
1997	First Intent, 8, 115	R. R. Douglas	Boundless Moment, 5	High Stakes Player, 5	7	1:08.80	$102,000
1996	Lit de Justice, 6, 121	C. S. Nakatani	Concept Win, 6	Gold Land, 6	6	1:08.19	$126,750
1995	Gold Land, 4, 116	E. J. Delahoussaye	Lucky Forever, 6	G Malleah, 6	6	1:08.07	$89,300
1994	King's Blade, 3, 112	C. S. Nakatani	Memo (Chi), 7	Gundaghia, 7	8	1:08.64	$62,400
1993	The Wicked North, 4, 116	C. A. Black	Thirty Slews, 6	Black Jack Road, 6	6	1:08.52	$61,200
1992	Thirty Slews, 5, 116	E. J. Delahoussaye	Slerp, 3	Anjiz, 3	10	1:08.20	$64,900

Named for movie star and singer H. L. "Bing" Crosby (1903-'77), first president of Del Mar Turf Club. 1946-'95 Bing Crosby H. 1985-'98 Grade 3. 1970 about 7¹⁄₂ furlongs. 1970 turf.

Black-Eyed Susan Stakes

Grade 2, Pimlico, three-year-olds, fillies, 1¹⁄₈ miles, dirt. Held May 16, 2003, with a gross value of $200,000. First held in 1919. Graded since 1973. Stakes record 1:47.83 (1999 Silverbulletday).

Year	Winner	Jockey	Second	Third	Strs	Time	1st Purse
2003	Roar Emotion, 3, 122	J. R. Velazquez	Fircroft, 3	Santa Catarina, 3	8	1:52.33	$120,000
2002	Chamrousse, 3, 115	J. D. Bailey	Shop Till You Drop, 3	Autumn Creek, 3	6	1:51.61	$120,000
2001	Two Item Limit, 3, 122	R. Migliore	Indy Glory, 3	Tap Dance, 3	5	1:50.84	$120,000

				Strs	Time	
2000	Jostle, 3, 122	K. J. Desormeaux	March Magic, 3	Impending Bear, 3	7	1:52.56	$120,000
1999	Silverbulletday, 3, 122	G. L. Stevens	Dreams Gallore, 3	Vee Vee Star, 3	7	1:47.83	$120,000
1998	Added Gold, 3, 115	J. R. Velazquez	Tappin' Ginger, 3	Hansel's Girl, 3	8	1:49.75	$120,000
1997	Salt It, 3, 117	C. H. Marquez Jr.	Buckeye Search, 3	Holiday Ball, 3	7	1:50.52	$120,000
1996	Mesabi Maiden, 3, 115	M. E. Smith	Cara Rafaela, 3	Ginny Lynn, 3	8	1:51.00	$120,000
1995	Serena's Song, 3, 122	G. L. Stevens	Conquistadoress, 3	Rare Opportunity, 3	7	1:48.45	$120,000
1994	Calipha, 3, 114	R. Wilson	Bunting, 3	Golden Braids, 3	13	1:51.12	$120,000
1993	Aztec Hill, 3, 122	M. E. Smith	Traverse City, 3	Jacody, 3	10	1:49.78	$120,000
1992	Miss Legality, 3, 122	C. J. McCarron	Known Feminist, 3	Diamond Duo, 3	8	1:51.11	$150,000

Named for the Maryland state flower. 1932-'36,1950 not held. 1919-'31,1937-'49 Pimlico Oaks; 1951 Black-Eyed Susan H. 1973-'75 Grade 3. 1919-'29,1931,1937-'49,1953-'88 1 1/16 miles; 1930 1 mile 70 yards; 1951 1 3/16 miles.

Blue Grass Stakes

Grade 1, Keeneland, three-year-olds, 1 1/8 miles, dirt. Held April 12, 2003, with a gross value of $750,000. First held in 1911. Graded since 1973. Stakes record 1:47.29 (1996 Skip Away).

Year	Winner	Jockey	Second	Third	Strs	Time	1st Purse
2003	Peace Rules, 3, 123	E. S. Prado	Brancusi, 3	Offlee Wild, 3	9	1:51.73	$465,000
2002	Harlan's Holiday, 3, 123	E. S. Prado	Booklet, 3	Ocean Sound (Ire), 3	6	1:51.51	$465,000
2001	Millennium Wind, 3, 123	L. A. Pincay Jr.	Songandaprayer, 3	Dollar Bill, 3	7	1:48.32	$465,000
2000	High Yield, 3, 123	P. Day	More Than Ready, 3	Wheelaway, 3	8	1:48.79	$465,000
1999	Menifee, 3, 123	P. Day	Cat Thief, 3	Vicar, 3	8	1:48.66	$465,000
1998	Halory Hunter, 3, 123	G. L. Stevens	Lil's Lad, 3	Cape Town, 3	5	1:47.98	$434,000
1997	Pulpit, 3, 121	S. J. Sellers	Acceptable, 3	Stolen Gold, 3	7	1:49.91	$434,000
1996	Skip Away, 3, 121	S. J. Sellers	Louis Quatorze, 3	Editor's Note, 3	7	1:47.29	$434,000
1995	Wild Syn, 3, 121	R. P. Romero	Suave Prospect, 3	Tejano Run, 3	6	1:49.31	$310,000
1994	Holy Bull, 3, 121	M. E. Smith	Valiant Nature, 3	Mahogany Hall, 3	7	1:50.02	$310,000
1993	Prairie Bayou, 3, 121	M. E. Smith	Wallenda, 3	Dixieland Heat, 3	9	1:49.62	$310,000
1992	Pistols and Roses, 3, 121	J. Vasquez	Conte Di Savoya, 3	Ecstatic Ride, 3	11	1:49.19	$325,000

Named for the Bluegrass region of Kentucky. Since 1996 sponsored by Toyota Motor Manufacturing. 1915-'18,1927-'36 not held. 1911-'95 Blue Grass S. 1990-'98 Grade 2. 1911-'26 held at Kentucky Association; 1943-'45 Churchill Downs. 1964 6 furlongs.

Boiling Springs Breeders' Cup Handicap

Grade 3, Meadowlands, three-year-olds, fillies, 1 1/16 miles, turf. Held September 6, 2002, with a gross value of $194,000. First held in 1977. Graded since 1980. Stakes record 1:40.09 (1998 Mysterious Moll).

Year	Winner	Jockey	Second	Third	Strs	Time	1st Purse
2002	Showlady, 3, 114	R. Migliore	Dreamers Glory, 3	With Patience, 3	9	1:42.27	$120,000
2001	Mystic Lady, 3, 120	E. Coa	Shooting Party, 3	Plunderthepeasants, 3	4	1:42.63	$120,000
2000	Storm Dream (Ire), 3, 116	J-L. Samyn	Watch, 3	Lady Dora, 3	11	1:47.09	$60,000
1999	Wild Heart Dancing, 3, 116	J. F. Chavez	Confessional, 3	Petunia, 3	8	1:43.08	$120,000
1998	Mysterious Moll, 3, 116	J. L. Espinoza	Who Did It and Run, 3	Thunder Kitten, 3	12	1:40.09	$120,000
1997	Victory Chime, 3, 114	M. E. Smith	Miss Pop Carn, 3	Colonial Play, 3	9	1:41.99	$60,000
1997	Stoneleigh, 3, 114	J. A. Santos	Majestic Sunlight, 3	Dancing Water, 3	6	1:41.13	$60,000
1996	Careless Heiress, 3, 118	C. Perret	Briarcliff, 3	Dathuil (Ire), 3	9	1:50.54	$60,000
1995	Class Kris, 3, 118	R. Wilson	Twilight Encounter, 3	Appointed One, 3	5	1:43.27	$48,000
1995	Christmas Gift, 3, 116	W. H. McCauley	Ring by Spring, 3	Transient Trend, 3	7	1:43.49	$48,000
1994	Avie's Fancy, 3, 119	J. C. Ferrer	Teasing Charm, 3	Knocknock, 3	7	1:41.41	$45,000
1993	Tribulation, 3, 110	J-L. Samyn	Exotic Sea, 3	Bright Penny, 3	11	1:42.70	$45,000
1992	Captive Miss, 3, 120	J. Bravo	Logan's Mist, 3	Aquilegia, 3	9	1:40.78	$45,000

Named for former name of East Rutherford, New Jersey, Boiling Springs. 1977-'78,1981-'97 Boiling Springs H.; 1979-'80 Boiling Springs S. 2001 not graded. 1995,1997 two divisions. 1988, 2001 dirt.

Bold Ruler Handicap

Grade 3, Belmont Park, three-year-olds and up, 6 furlongs, dirt. Held May 11, 2002, with a gross value of $102,900. First held in 1976. Graded since 1982. Stakes record 1:07.54 (1999 Kelly Kip).

Year	Winner	Jockey	Second	Third	Strs	Time	1st Purse
2002	Left Bank, 5, 121	J. R. Velazquez	Silky Sweep, 6	Say Florida Sandy, 6	4	1:09.30	$63,646
2001	Say Florida Sandy, 7, 117	J. Bravo	Delaware Township, 5	Lake Pontchartrain, 5	7	1:08.67	$65,520
2000	Brutally Frank, 6, 115	S. Bridgmohan	Kelly Kip, 6	Kashatreya, 6	7	1:08.64	$65,880
1999	Kelly Kip, 5, 123	J-L. Samyn	Artax, 4	Brushed On, 4	5	1:07.54	$64,440
1998	Kelly Kip, 4, 117	J-L. Samyn	Say Florida Sandy, 4	Johnny Legit, 4	8	1:07.61	$66,120
1997	Punch Line, 7, 122	R. G. Davis	Golden Tent, 8	Blissful State, 8	6	1:08.80	$64,980
1996	Lite the Fuse, 5, 119	J. A. Krone	Cold Execution, 5	Splendid Sprinter, 5	5	1:09.51	$64,500
1995	Rizzi, 4, 112	D. V. Beckner	Lite the Fuse, 4	Evil Bear, 4	6	1:08.91	$64,560
1994	Chief Desire, 4, 117	J. R. Velazquez	Boom Towner, 6	Won Song, 6	8	1:08.76	$66,300
1993	Slerp, 4, 119	J. A. Santos	Argyle Lake, 7	Big Jewel, 7	8	1:09.17	$70,200
1992	Jolies Appeal, 4, 119	W. H. McCauley	Reappeal, 6	Fiercely, 6	5	1:09.29	$67,560

Named for 1957 Horse of the Year and eight-time leading sire Bold Ruler (1954-'71, c. by *Nasrullah). 1979-'93 Bold Ruler S. 1985-'89 Grade 2. 1976-2001 held at Aqueduct. 1998,1999 new track record.

Bonnie Miss Stakes

Grade 2, Gulfstream Park, three-year-olds, fillies, 1⅛ miles, dirt. Held March 14, 2003, with a gross value of $200,000. First held in 1971. Graded since 1982. Stakes record 1:49.67 (2002 Dust Me Off).

Year	Winner	Jockey	Second	Third	Strs	Time	1st Purse
2003	**Ivanavinalot**, 3, 122	J. R. Velazquez	My Boston Gal, 3	Holiday Lady, 3	7	1:50.72	$120,000
2002	**Dust Me Off**, 3, 116	M. Guidry	Nonsuch Bay, 3	Belterra, 3	6	**1:49.67**	$150,000
2001	**Tap Dance**, 3, 114	J. D. Bailey	Halo Reality, 3	Unbridled Lassie, 3	7	1:52.05	$150,000
2000	**Cash Run**, 3, 119	J. D. Bailey	Deed I Do, 3	Bejoyfulandrejoyce, 3	6	1:44.11	$120,000
1999	**Three Ring**, 3, 122	J. R. Velazquez	Olympic Charmer, 3	Marley Vale, 3	5	1:43.75	$120,000
1998	**Banshee Breeze**, 3, 114	R. P. Romero	Santaria, 3	Cotton House Bay, 3	8	1:46.57	$120,000
1997	**Glitter Woman**, 3, 117	M. E. Smith	Southern Playgirl, 3	Dixie Flag, 3	5	1:43.25	$120,000
1996	**My Flag**, 3, 117	J. D. Bailey	Escena, 3	La Rosa, 3	5	1:45.77	$120,000
1995	**Mia's Hope**, 3, 117	K. L. Chapman	Minister Wife, 3	Incredible Blues, 3	9	1:44.85	$120,000
1994	**Inside Information**, 3, 114	M. E. Smith	Cinnamon Sugar (Ire), 3	Jade Flush, 3	10	1:42.94	$120,000
1993	**Dispute**, 3, 114	J. D. Bailey	Sky Beauty, 3	Lunar Spook, 3	6	1:43.67	$120,000
1992	**Spectacular Sue**, 3, 114	W. S. Ramos	Spinning Round, 3	Tricky Cinderella, 3	6	1:44.14	$120,000

Named for James Donn Jr.'s daughter, Bonnie. 1976 Bonnie Miss H. 1982-'87 Grade 3. 1971 about 1¹⁄₁₆ miles; 1972,1974,1977-'80 7 furlongs; 1973,1975-'76,1981-2000 1¹⁄₁₆ miles. 1971,1975-'76 turf. 1971,1973,1975-'76 three-year-olds and up, fillies and mares.

Bowling Green Handicap

Grade 2, Belmont Park, three-year-olds and up, 1⅜ miles, turf. Held July 13, 2002, with a gross value of $150,000. First held in 1958. Graded since 1973. Stakes record 2:10.20 (1990 With Approval).

Year	Winner	Jockey	Second	Third	Strs	Time	1st Purse
2002	**Whitmore's Conn**, 4, 112	S. Bridgmohan	Staging Post, 4	Moon Solitaire (Ire), 4	9	2:13.43	$90,000
2001	**King Cugat**, 4, 119	J. D. Bailey	Slew Valley, 4	Man From Wicklow, 4	7	2:10.62	$90,000
2000	**Elhayq (Ire)**, 5, 113	S. Bridgmohan	Yankee Dollar, 4	Carpenter's Halo, 4	9	2:13.81	$90,000
1999	**Honor Glide**, 5, 114	J. A. Santos	Parade Ground, 4	Fahris (Ire), 5	6	2:11.07	$90,000
1998	**Cetewayo**, 4, 112	J. R. Velazquez	Officious, 5	Chief Bearhart, 5	6	2:13.45	$90,000
1997	**Influent**, 6, 120	J-L. Samyn	Flag Down, 7	Notoriety, 7	8	2:11.06	$90,000
1996	**Flag Down**, 6, 118	J. A. Santos	Broadway Flyer, 5	Diplomatic Jet, 4	9	2:13.29	$90,000
1995	**Sentimental Moi**, 5, 111	R. B. Perez	Awad, 5	Proceeded, 4	8	2:15.48	$90,000
1994	**Turk Passer**, 4, 110	J. R. Velazquez	Sea Hero, 4	Fraise, 6	6	2:13.25	$90,000
1993	**Dr. Kiernan**, 4, 114	C. W. Antley	Spectacular Tide, 4	Lomitas (GB), 4	9	2:17.70	$90,000
1992	**Wall Street Dancer**, 4, 114	P. Day	Fraise, 4	Libor, 4	7	2:12.92	$120,000

Named for the lower tip of Manhattan Island, where there was once a green for lawn bowling. 1983-'89 Grade 1. 1963-'67 held at Aqueduct. 1960-'62,1968-'76 1½ miles; 1963-'67 1⅝ miles; 1977 1¼ miles. 1997 new course record. 1999 Federal Trial finished third, DQ to fourth.

Breeders' Cup Classic

Grade 1, Arlington Park, three-year-olds and up, 1¼ miles, dirt. Held October 26, 2002, with a gross value of $4,000,000. First held in 1984. Graded since 1984. Stakes record 1:59.16 (1997 Skip Away).

Year	Winner	Jockey	Second	Third	Strs	Time	1st Purse
2002	**Volponi**, 4, 126	J. A. Santos	Medaglia d'Oro, 3	Milwaukee Brew, 3	12	2:01.39	$2,080,000
2001	**Tiznow**, 4, 126	C. J. McCarron	Sakhee, 4	Albert the Great, 4	13	2:00.62	$2,080,000
2000	**Tiznow**, 3, 122	C. J. McCarron	Giant's Causeway, 3	Captain Steve, 3	13	2:00.75	$2,480,400
1999	**Cat Thief**, 3, 122	P. Day	Budroyale, 6	Golden Missile, 6	14	1:59.52	$2,080,000
1998	**Awesome Again**, 4, 126	P. Day	Silver Charm, 4	Swain (Ire), 4	10	2:02.16	$2,662,400
1997	**Skip Away**, 4, 126	M. E. Smith	Deputy Commander, 3	Dowty, 3	9	**1:59.16**	$2,288,000
1996	**Alphabet Soup**, 5, 126	C. J. McCarron	Louis Quatorze, 3	Cigar, 3	13	2:01.00	$2,080,000
1995	**Cigar**, 5, 126	J. D. Bailey	L'Carriere, 4	Unaccounted For, 4	11	1:59.58	$1,560,000
1994	**Concern**, 3, 122	J. D. Bailey	Tabasco Cat, 3	Dramatic Gold, 3	14	2:02.41	$1,560,000
1993	**Arcangues**, 5, 126	J. D. Bailey	Bertrando, 4	Kissin Kris, 4	13	2:00.83	$1,560,000
1992	**A.P. Indy**, 3, 121	E. J. Delahoussaye	Pleasant Tap, 5	†Jolypha, 5	14	2:00.20	$1,560,000

1984,1987,1997 held at Hollywood; 1985 Aqueduct; 1986,1993 Santa Anita; 1988,1991,1994,1998, 2000 Churchill Downs; 1989,1992,1999 Gulfstream; 1990,1995, 2001 Belmont; 1996 Woodbine. 1996 new track record. 1997 Whiskey Wisdom finished third, DQ to fourth. †denotes female.

Breeders' Cup Distaff

Grade 1, Arlington Park, three-year-olds and up, fillies and mares, 1⅛ miles, dirt. Held October 26, 2002, with a gross value of $2,000,000. First held in 1984. Graded since 1984. Stakes record 1:46.15 (1995 Inside Information).

Year	Winner	Jockey	Second	Third	Strs	Time	1st Purse
2002	**Azeri**, 4, 123	M. E. Smith	Farda Amiga, 3	Imperial Gesture, 3	8	1:48.64	$1,040,000
2001	**Unbridled Elaine**, 3, 120	P. Day	Spain, 4	Two Item Limit, 3	11	1:49.21	$1,227,200
2000	**Spain**, 3, 120	V. Espinoza	Surfside, 3	Heritage of Gold, 5	9	1:47.66	$1,227,200
1999	**Beautiful Pleasure**, 4, 123	J. F. Chavez	Banshee Breeze, 4	Heritage of Gold, 4	8	1:45.56	$1,040,000
1998	**Escena**, 5, 123	G. L. Stevens	Banshee Breeze, 3	Keeper Hill, 3	8	1:49.89	$1,040,000
1997	**Ajina**, 3, 120	M. E. Smith	Sharp Cat, 3	Escena, 4	8	1:47.30	$520,000
1996	**Jewel Princess**, 4, 123	C. S. Nakatani	Serena's Song, 4	Different (Arg), 4	6	1:48.40	$520,000
1995	**Inside Information**, 4, 123	M. E. Smith	Heavenly Prize, 4	Lakeway, 4	10	**1:46.15**	$520,000

1994	**One Dreamer**, 6, 123	G. L. Stevens	Heavenly Prize, 3	Miss Dominique, 5	9	1:50.70 $520,000
1993	**Hollywood Wildcat**, 3, 120	E. J. Delahoussaye	Paseana (Arg), 6	Re Toss (Arg), 6	8	1:48.35 $520,000
1992	**Paseana (Arg)**, 5, 123	C. J. McCarron	Versailles Treaty, 4	Magical Maiden, 3	14	1:48.17 $520,000

1984,1987,1997 held at Hollywood; 1985 Aqueduct; 1986,1993 Santa Anita; 1988,1991,1994,1998, 2000 Churchill Downs; 1989,1992,1999 Gulfstream; 1990,1995,2001 Belmont; 1996 Woodbine. 1984-'87 1¼ miles.

Breeders' Cup Filly and Mare Turf

Grade 1, Arlington Park, three-year-olds and up, fillies and mares, 1¼ miles, turf. Held October 26, 2002, with a gross value of $1,280,000. First held in 1999. Graded since 1999. Stakes record 2:00.36 (2001 Banks Hill [GB]).

Year	Winner	Jockey	Second	Third	Strs	Time	1st Purse
2002	Starine (Fr), 5, 123	J. R. Velazquez	Banks Hill (GB), 4	Islington (Ire), 4	12	2:03.57	$665,600
2001	Banks Hill (GB), 3, 119	O. Peslier	Spook Express (SAf), 7	Spring Oak (GB), 7	12	**2:00.36**	$722,800
2000	Perfect Sting, 4, 123	J. D. Bailey	Tout Charmant, 4	Catella (Ger), 4	14	2:13.07	$629,200
1999	Soaring Softly, 4, 123	J. D. Bailey	Coretta (Ire), 5	Zomaradah (GB), 5	14	2:13.89	$556,400

1999 held at Gulfstream; 2000 Churchill Downs; 2001 Belmont. 1999-2000 1⅜ miles.

Breeders' Cup Juvenile

Grade 1, Arlington Park, two-year-olds, colts and geldings, 1⅟₁₆ miles, dirt. Held October 26, 2002, with a gross value of $1,070,000. First held in 1984. Graded since 1984. Stakes record 1:49.61 (2002 Vindication).

Year	Winner	Jockey	Second	Third	Strs	Time	1st Purse
2002	Vindication, 2, 122	M. E. Smith	Kafwain, 2	Hold That Tiger, 2	13	**1:49.61**	$556,400
2001	Johannesburg, 2, 122	M. J. Kinane	Repent, 2	Siphonic, 2	12	1:42.27	$520,000
2000	Macho Uno, 2, 122	J. D. Bailey	Point Given, 2	Street Cry (Ire), 2	14	1:42.05	$556,400
1999	Anees, 2, 122	G. L. Stevens	Chief Seattle, 2	High Yield, 2	14	1:42.29	$556,400
1998	Answer Lively, 2, 122	J. D. Bailey	Aly's Alley, 2	Cat Thief, 2	13	1:44.00	$520,000
1997	Favorite Trick, 2, 122	P. Day	Dawson's Legacy, 2	Nationalore, 2	8	1:41.47	$520,000
1996	Boston Harbor, 2, 122	J. D. Bailey	Acceptable, 2	Ordway, 2	10	1:43.40	$520,000
1995	Unbridled's Song, 2, 122	M. E. Smith	Hennessy, 2	Editor's Note, 2	13	1:41.60	$520,000
1994	Timber Country, 2, 122	P. Day	Eltish, 2	Tejano Run, 2	13	1:44.55	$520,000
1993	Brocco, 2, 122	G. L. Stevens	Blumin Affair, 2	Tabasco Cat, 2	11	1:42.99	$520,000
1992	Gilded Time, 2, 122	C. J. McCarron	It'sali'lknownfact, 2	River Special, 2	13	1:43.43	$520,000

In 2000-'02 sponsored by Bessemer Trust. 1984,1987,1997 held at Hollywood; 1985 Aqueduct; 1986,1993 Santa Anita; 1988,1991,1994,1998, 2000 Churchill Downs; 1989,1992,1999 Gulfstream; 1990,1995, 2001 Belmont; 1996 Woodbine. 1984-'85,1987 1 mile; 1986,1988-2001 1⅟₁₆ miles.

Breeders' Cup Juvenile Fillies

Grade 1, Arlington Park, two-year-olds, fillies, 1⅟₁₆ miles, dirt. Held October 26, 2002, with a gross value of $1,000,000. First held in 1984. Graded since 1984. Stakes record 1:49.60 (2002 Storm Flag Flying).

Year	Winner	Jockey	Second	Third	Strs	Time	1st Purse
2002	Storm Flag Flying, 2, 119	J. R. Velazquez	Composure, 2	Santa Catarina, 2	10	**1:49.60**	$520,000
2001	Tempera, 2, 119	D. R. Flores	Imperial Gesture, 2	Bella Bellucci, 2	9	1:41.49	$520,000
2000	Caressing, 2, 119	J. R. Velazquez	Platinum Tiara, 2	She's a Devil Due, 2	12	1:42.77	$592,800
1999	Cash Run, 2, 119	J. D. Bailey	Chilukki, 2	Surfside, 2	9	1:43.31	$520,000
1998	Silverbulletday, 2, 119	G. L. Stevens	Excellent Meeting, 2	Three Ring, 2	10	1:43.68	$520,000
1997	Countess Diana, 2, 119	S. J. Sellers	Career Collection, 2	Primaly, 2	14	1:42.11	$535,600
1996	Storm Song, 2, 119	C. Perret	Love That Jazz, 2	Critical Factor, 2	12	1:43.60	$520,000
1995	My Flag, 2, 119	J. D. Bailey	Cara Rafaela, 2	Golden Attraction, 2	8	1:42.55	$520,000
1994	Flanders, 2, 119	P. Day	Serena's Song, 2	Stormy Blues, 2	13	1:45.28	$520,000
1993	Phone Chatter, 2, 119	L. A. Pincay Jr.	Sardula, 2	Heavenly Prize, 2	8	1:43.08	$520,000
1992	Eliza, 2, 119	P. A. Valenzuela	Educated Risk, 2	Boots 'n Jackie, 2	12	1:42.93	$520,000

In 2002 sponsored by Long John Silver's. 1984,1987,1997 held at Hollywood; 1985 Aqueduct; 1986,1993 Santa Anita; 1988,1991,1994,1998, 2000 Churchill Downs; 1989,1992,1999 Gulfstream; 1990,1995,2001 Belmont; 1996 Woodbine. 1984-'85,1987 1 mile; 1986,1988-2001 1⅟₁₆ miles.

Breeders' Cup Mile

Grade 1, Arlington Park, three-year-olds and up, 1 mile, turf. Held October 26, 2002, with a gross value of $1,070,000. First held in 1984. Graded since 1984. Stakes record 1:32.05 (2001 Val Royal [Fr]).

Year	Winner	Jockey	Second	Third	Strs	Time	1st Purse
2002	Domedriver (Ire), 4, 126	T. Thulliez	Rock of Gibraltar (Ire), 3	Good Journey, 3	14	1:36.92	$556,400
2001	Val Royal (Fr), 5, 126	J. Valdivia Jr.	Forbidden Apple, 6	Bach (Ire), 6	12	**1:32.05**	$592,800
2000	War Chant, 3, 126	G. L. Stevens	North East Bound, 4	Dansili (GB), 4	14	1:34.67	$608,400
1999	Silic (Fr), 4, 126	C. S. Nakatani	†Tuzla (Fr), 5	Docksider, 5	14	1:34.26	$520,000
1998	Da Hoss, 6, 126	J. R. Velazquez	Hawksley Hill (Ire), 5	Labeeb (GB), 5	14	1:35.27	$520,000
1997	Spinning World, 4, 126	C. B. Asmussen	Geri, 5	Decorated Hero (GB), 5	12	1:32.77	$572,000
1996	Da Hoss, 4, 126	G. L. Stevens	Spinning World, 3	Same Old Wish, 3	14	1:35.80	$520,000
1995	†Ridgewood Pearl (GB), 3, 119	J. P. Murtagh	Fastness (Ire), 5	†Sayyedati (GB), 5	13	1:43.65	$520,000
1994	Barathea (Ire), 4, 126	L. Dettori	Johann Quatz (Fr), 5	Unfinished Symph, 5	14	1:34.50	$520,000
1993	Lure, 4, 126	M. E. Smith	†Ski Paradise, 3	Fourstars Allstar, 3	13	1:33.58	$520,000
1992	Lure, 3, 122	M. E. Smith	Paradise Creek, 3	Brief Truce, 3	14	1:32.90	$520,000

In 2002 sponsored by NetJets. 1984,1987,1997 held at Hollywood; 1985 Aqueduct; 1986,1993 Santa Anita;

1988,1991,1994,1998, 2000 Churchill Downs; 1989,1992,1999 Gulfstream; 1990,1995, 2001 Belmont; 1996 Woodbine. 1992,1994 new course record. †denotes female.

Breeders' Cup Sprint

Grade 1, Arlington Park, three-year-olds and up, 6 furlongs, dirt. Held October 26, 2002, with a gross value of $1,140,000. First held in 1984. Graded since 1984. Stakes record 1:07.77 (2000 Kona Gold).

Year	Winner	Jockey	Second	Third	Strs	Time	1st Purse
2002	**Orientate**, 4, 126	J. D. Bailey	Thunderello, 3	Crafty C. T., 3	13	1:08.89	$592,800
2001	**Squirtle Squirt**, 3, 124	J. D. Bailey	†Xtra Heat, 3	Caller One, 3	14	1:08.41	$520,000
2000	**Kona Gold**, 6, 126	A. O. Solis	†Honest Lady, 4	Bet On Sunshine, 4	14	**1:07.77**	$520,000
1999	**Artax**, 4, 126	J. F. Chavez	Kona Gold, 5	Big Jag, 5	14	1:07.89	$624,000
1998	**Reraise**, 3, 124	C. S. Nakatani	Grand Slam, 3	Kona Gold, 3	14	1:09.07	$572,000
1997	**Elmhurst**, 7, 126	C. S. Nakatani	Hesabull, 4	Bet On Sunshine, 4	14	1:08.01	$613,600
1996	**Lit de Justice**, 6, 126	C. S. Nakatani	Paying Dues, 4	Honour and Glory, 4	13	1:08.60	$520,000
1995	**†Desert Stormer**, 5, 123	K. J. Desormeaux	Mr. Greeley, 3	Lit de Justice, 3	13	1:09.14	$520,000
1994	**Cherokee Run**, 4, 126	M. E. Smith	†Soviet Problem, 4	Cardmania, 4	14	1:09.54	$520,000
1993	**Cardmania**, 7, 126	E. J. Delahoussaye	†Meafara, 4	Gilded Time, 4	14	1:08.76	$520,000
1992	**Thirty Slews**, 5, 126	E. J. Delahoussaye	†Meafara, 3	Rubiano, 3	14	1:08.21	$520,000

In 2002 sponsored by NAPA Auto Parts; in 2001 sponsored by Penske Auto Center. 1992,1999 held at Gulfstream; 1993 Santa Anita; 1994,1998, 2000 Churchill Downs; 1995, 2001 Belmont; 1996 Woodbine; 1997 Hollywood. 1996,1999 equaled track record; 2000 new track record. †denotes female.

Breeders' Cup Turf

Grade 1, Arlington Park, three-year-olds and up, 1½ miles, turf. Held October 26, 2002, with a gross value of $2,420,000. First held in 1984. Graded since 1984. Stakes record 2:23.92 (1997 Chief Bearhart).

Year	Winner	Jockey	Second	Third	Strs	Time	1st Purse
2002	**High Chaparral (Ire)**, 3, 121	M. J. Kinane	With Anticipation, 7	Falcon Flight (Fr), 7	8	2:30.14	$1,258,400
2001	**Fantastic Light**, 5, 126	L. Dettori	Milan (GB), 3	Timboroa (GB), 3	11	2:24.36	$2,112,800
2000	**Kalanisi (Ire)**, 4, 126	J. P. Murtagh	Quiet Resolve, 5	John's Call, 5	13	2:26.96	$1,289,600
1999	**Daylami (Ire)**, 5, 126	L. Dettori	Royal Anthem, 4	Buck's Boy, 4	14	2:24.73	$2,040,000
1998	**Buck's Boy**, 5, 126	S. J. Sellers	Yagli, 5	Dushyantor, 5	13	2:28.74	$1,040,000
1997	**Chief Bearhart**, 4, 126	J. A. Santos	†Borgia (Ger), 3	Flag Down, 3	11	**2:23.92**	$1,040,000
1996	**Pilsudski (Ire)**, 4, 126	W. R. Swinburn	Singspiel (Ire), 4	Swain (Ire), 4	14	2:30.20	$1,040,000
1995	**Northern Spur (Ire)**, 4, 126	C. J. McCarron	Freedom Cry (GB), 4	Carnegie (Ire), 4	13	2:42.07	$1,040,000
1994	**Tikkanen**, 3, 122	M. E. Smith	†Hatoof, 5	Paradise Creek, 5	14	2:26.50	$1,040,000
1993	**Kotashaan (Fr)**, 5, 126	K. J. Desormeaux	Bien Bien, 4	Luazur (Fr), 4	14	2:25.16	$1,040,000
1992	**Fraise**, 4, 126	P. A. Valenzuela	Sky Classic, 5	Quest for Fame (GB), 5	10	2:24.08	$1,040,000

In 2002 sponsored by John Deere. 1984,1987,1997 held at Hollywood; 1985 Aqueduct; 1986,1993 Santa Anita; 1988,1991,1994,1998, 2000 Churchill Downs; 1989,1992,1999 Gulfstream ; 1990,1995, 2001 Belmont; 1996 Woodbine. 1992 new course record. †denotes female.

Brooklyn Handicap

Grade 2, Belmont Park, three-year-olds and up, 1⅛ miles, dirt. Held June 15, 2002, with a gross value of $250,000. First held in 1887. Graded since 1973. Stakes record 1:46.21 (1997 Formal Gold).

Year	Winner	Jockey	Second	Third	Strs	Time	1st Purse
2002	**Seeking Daylight**, 4, 113	E. S. Prado	Country Be Gold, 5	Griffinite, 5	8	1:46.35	$150,000
2001	**Albert the Great**, 4, 122	J. F. Chavez	Perfect Cat, 4	Top Official, 6	7	1:47.41	$150,000
2000	**Lemon Drop Kid**, 4, 120	E. S. Prado	Lager, 6	Down the Aisle, 7	7	1:49.93	$150,000
1999	**Running Stag**, 5, 117	S. J. Sellers	Deputy Diamond, 4	Sir Bear, 6	8	1:46.39	$210,000
1998	**Subordination**, 4, 114	E. Coa	Sir Bear, 5	Mr. Sinatra, 4	11	1:46.64	$180,000
1997	**Formal Gold**, 4, 119	J. D. Bailey	Stephanotis, 4	Circle of Light, 4	8	**1:46.21**	$180,000
1996	**Wekiva Springs**, 5, 120	M. E. Smith	Mahogany Hall, 5	Admiralty, 4	7	1:46.78	$180,000
1995	**You and I**, 4, 115	J. F. Chavez	Key Contender, 7	Slick Horn, 5	9	1:49.02	$150,000
1994	**Devil His Due**, 5, 120	M. E. Smith	Wallenda, 4	Sea Hero, 4	7	1:46.71	$150,000
1993	**Living Vicariously**, 3, 111	R. G. Davis	Michelle Can Pass, 5	Jacksonport, 4	8	2:17.80	$150,000
1992	**Chief Honcho**, 5, 117	R. P. Romero	Valley Crossing, 4	Lost Mountain, 4	11	2:16.91	$210,000

Named for the Brooklyn borough of New York City. 1911-'12 not held. 1973-'92 Grade 1. 1887-1910 held at Gravesend; 1914-'44,1946-'55,1960-'74,1991-'93 Aqueduct; 1956-'59 Jamaica. 1887-1914,1940-'55,1960-'71,1975-'76 1¼ miles; 1956-'59,1972-'74 1⁹⁄₁₆ miles; 1991-'93 1⅛ miles; 1977-'90 1½ miles. 1992 Lost Mountain finished second, DQ to third.

Brown Bess Handicap

Grade 3, Golden Gate Fields, four-year-olds and up, fillies and mares, 1¹⁄₁₆ miles, turf. Held February 1, 2003, with a gross value of $100,000. First held in 1991. Graded since 1998. Stakes record 1:41.50 (1995 Work the Crowd).

Year	Winner	Jockey	Second	Third	Strs	Time	1st Purse
2003	**Lindsay Jean**, 5, 116	C. P. Schvaneveldt	Bush Triumph, 5	Crazy Ensign (Arg), 7	9	1:44.35	$55,000
2002	**Janet (GB)**, 5, 123	D. R. Flores	Impeachable, 5	Alexine (Arg), 5	5	1:44.14	$55,000
2001	**Out of Reach (GB)**, 4, 115	R. A. Baze	Miss of Wales (Chi), 6	Keld (Ire), 6	12	1:46.87	$55,000
2000	**Guinevere**, 5, 115	J. Matias	Royal Terminal, 5	Blending Element (Ire), 7	12	1:47.75	$55,000

Year	Winner	Jockey	Second	Third	Strs	Time	1st Purse
1999	Call Me (GB), 6, 115	R. Q. Meza	Curitiba, 5	Plus (Chi), 6	9	1:49.16	$50,475
1998	Traces of Gold, 6, 118	R. A. Baze	Taurus Forus, 5	La Soberbia (Arg), 6	6	1:43.14	$55,000
1997	Traces of Gold, 5, 115	R. A. Baze	Notagoldbrick, 4	Princess Kali, 6	7	1:44.52	$55,000
1996	Traces of Gold, 4, 115	R. A. Baze	Luzette (Brz), 6	Just a Wish, 4	7	1:42.15	$55,000
1995	Work the Crowd, 4, 118	R. A. Baze	Watch Rachel, 5	Zoonaqua, 5	7	1:41.50	$32,450
1994	Watch Rachel, 4, 115	R. J. Warren Jr.	Wendy's Daughter, 4	Wende, 4	7	1:42.21	$29,550
1993	Splashing Wave, 4, 113	R. Q. Meza	Peterhof's Patea, 5	Darling Dame, 4	7	1:44.92	$29,625
1992	La Paz, 4, 113	R. Q. Meza	Peterhof's Patea, 4	Paula Revere, 4	6	1:43.20	$29,475

Named for Calbourne Farm's 1989 champion turf female Brown Bess (1982, f. by *Petrone). 1991-'95 Brown Bess Breeders' Cup H. 1991-2000 held at Bay Meadows. 1996,1998 dirt. 1991-'94 three-year-olds and up.

Buena Vista Handicap

Grade 2, Santa Anita Park, four-year-olds and up, fillies and mares, 1 mile, turf. Held February 17, 2003, with a gross value of $150,000. First held in 1988. Graded since 1990. Stakes record 1:33.48 (1992 Gold Fleece [1st Div.]; 1997 Media Nox [GB]).

Year	Winner	Jockey	Second	Third	Strs	Time	1st Purse
2003	Final Destination (NZ), 5, 115	V. Espinoza	Gardenin the Rain (Fr), 6	Embassy Belle (Ire), 5	6	1:35.99	$90,000
2002	Blue Moon (Fr), 5, 115	B. Blanc	Queen of Wilshire, 6	Old Money (AUS), 6	7	1:35.54	$90,000
2001	Rare Charmer, 6, 115	L. A. Pincay Jr.	Elegant Ridge (Ire), 6	Uncharted Haven (GB), 4	11	1:36.67	$90,000
2000	Lexa (Fr), 6, 115	B. Blanc	Here's to You, 4	Sierra Virgen, 5	6	1:36.17	$97,290
1999	Tuzla (Fr), 5, 120	C. S. Nakatani	Supercilious, 6	Green Jewel (GB), 5	5	1:35.79	$90,000
1998	Dance Parade, 4, 116	K. J. Desormeaux	Shake the Yoke (GB), 5	Donna Viola (GB), 6	10	1:36.03	$101,520
1997	Media Nox (GB), 4, 116	C. S. Nakatani	Traces of Gold, 5	Grafin, 6	12	1:33.48	$85,250
1996	Matiara, 4, 119	G. L. Stevens	Real Connection, 5	Dirca (Ire), 4	8	1:35.74	$81,800
1995	Lyin to the Moon, 6, 116	K. J. Desormeaux	Jacodra's Devil, 4	Exchange, 7	5	1:36.77	$61,700
1994	Skimble, 5, 118	C. S. Nakatani	Hero's Love, 6	Possibly Perfect, 4	9	1:34.85	$66,300
1993	Marble Maiden (GB), 4, 118	K. J. Desormeaux	Suivi, 4	Party Cited, 4	7	1:36.23	$65,000
1992	Gold Fleece, 4, 114	A. O. Solis	Elegance, 5	Danzante, 4	9	1:33.48	$52,100
	Appealing Missy, 5, 117	C. J. McCarron	Exchange, 4	Re Toss (Arg), 5	9	1:34.25	$52,100

Named for two 19th century California ranchos named Buena Vista Rancho; buena vista means "good view." 1990-'94 Grade 3. 1992 two divisions. 1994 Lady Blessington (Fr) finished first, DQ to ninth.

Calder Derby

Grade 3, Calder Race Course, three-year-olds, 1⅛ miles, turf. Held October 12, 2002, with a gross value of $200,000. First held in 1972. Graded since 1996. Stakes record 1:47.70 (1998 Crowd Pleaser).

Year	Winner	Jockey	Second	Third	Strs	Time	1st Purse
2002	Union Place, 3, 115	E. Coa	Miesque's Approval, 3	The Judge Sez Who, 3	11	1:47.76	$120,000
2001	Western Pride, 3, 122	D. G. Whitney	Tour of the Cat, 3	Built Up, 3	10	1:51.12	$120,000
2000	Whata Brainstorm, 3, 122	R. B. Homeister Jr.	Muntej (GB), 3	Womble, 3	12	1:47.80	$120,000
1999	Isaypete, 3, 122	J. C. Ferrer	Rhythmean, 3	Phi Beta Doc, 3	12	1:50.01	$120,000
1998	Crowd Pleaser, 3, 122	J-L. Samyn	Stay Sound, 3	The Kaiser, 3	10	1:47.70	$120,000
1997	Blazing Sword, 3, 117	G. Boulanger	(DH) Topaz Runner, 3 (DH) Royal Tuneup, 3		10	1:53.15	$90,000
1996	Laughing Dan, 3, 117	P. A. Rodriguez	Sea Horse, 3	Flying Concert, 3	11	1:50.75	$66,300
1995	Pineing Patty, 3, 122	L. Melancon	Sea Emperor, 3	Mucha Mosca, 3	9	1:51.40	$60,000
1994	Halo's Image, 3, 117	G. Boulanger	Honest Colors, 3	Rocky's Halo, 3	10	1:52.38	$90,000
1993	Medieval Mac, 3, 113	M. Russ	Raise an Alarm, 3	Fight for Love, 3	9	1:41.79	$30,000
1992	Birdonthewire, 3, 112	M. T. Hunter	Shahpour, 3	Ponche, 3	7	1:44.36	$30,000

Formerly named for Hollywood, Florida, hometown of real-estate developer Stephen Calder, who built the track. 1972-'81,1984,1987-'93 Hollywood H.; 1982-'83,1985-'86 Hollywood S.; 1996 Calder Breeders' Cup Derby. 1998-'99 not graded. 1972-'73 7 furlongs; 1974-'78,1982-'92 1¹/₁₆ miles; 1993 1 mile 70 yards. 1972-'74,1976,1979-'97,2001 dirt. 1972-'81,1984 three-year-olds and up. 1997 dead heat for second. 1993 new track record.

Californian Stakes

Grade 2, Hollywood Park, three-year-olds and up, 1⅛ miles, dirt. Held June 15, 2002, with a gross value of $500,000. First held in 1954. Graded since 1973. Stakes record 1:45.80 (1980 Spectacular Bid).

Year	Winner	Jockey	Second	Third	Strs	Time	1st Purse
2002	Milwaukee Brew, 5, 122	K. J. Desormeaux	Bosque Redondo, 5	Momentum, 4	8	1:48.06	$300,000
2001	Skimming, 5, 116	G. K. Gomez	Futural, 5	Aptitude, 4	8	1:48.12	$300,000
2000	Big Ten (Chi), 5, 116	A. O. Solis	Early Pioneer, 5	Mojave Moon, 4	5	1:49.22	$150,000
1999	Old Trieste, 4, 116	C. J. McCarron	Budroyale, 6	Puerto Madero (Chi), 5	7	1:46.55	$180,000
1998	Mud Route, 4, 116	C. J. McCarron	Deputy Commander, 4	Worldly Ways (GB), 4	6	1:48.15	$150,000
1997	River Keen (Ire), 5, 117	K. J. Desormeaux	Hesabull, 4	Benchmark, 6	6	1:47.38	$150,000
1996	Tinners Way, 6, 116	E. J. Delahoussaye	Helmsman, 4	Mr Purple, 4	4	1:46.60	$151,980
1995	Concern, 4, 122	M. E. Smith	Tossofthecoin, 5	Tinners Way, 5	8	1:47.74	$160,900
1994	The Wicked North, 5, 120	K. J. Desormeaux	Kingdom Found, 4	Slew of Damascus, 6	7	1:46.68	$165,000
1993	Latin American, 5, 116	G. L. Stevens	Missionary Ridge (GB), 6	Memo (Chi), 6	7	1:46.92	$220,000
1992	Another Review, 4, 119	K. J. Desormeaux	Defensive Play, 5	Ibero (Arg), 5	7	1:48.11	$119,400

1973-'96 Grade 1. 1954-'79 1¹/₁₆ miles.

Canadian Turf Handicap

Grade 3, Gulfstream Park, three-year-olds and up, 1¹⁄₁₆ miles, turf. Held March 9, 2003, with a gross value of $100,000. First held in 1967. Graded since 1973. Stakes record 1:39.43 (2001 Inexplicable).

Year	Winner	Jockey	Second	Third	Strs	Time	1st Purse
2003	Political Attack, 4, 114	M. Guidry	Miesque's Approval, 4	Strategic Partner, 5	7	1:40.43	$60,000
2002	North East Bound, 6, 116	J. A. Velez Jr.	Capsized, 6	Flying Avie, 6	4	1:44.01	$90,000
2001	Inexplicable, 6, 115	J. A. Santos	Band Is Passing, 5	David Copperfield, 4	8	1:39.43	$90,000
2000	Shamrock City, 5, 114	E. S. Prado	Rhythmean, 4	Sharp Appeal, 7	10	1:47.15	$60,000
1999	Federal Trial, 4, 114	R. G. Davis	Deep Dive, 4	Unite's Big Red, 5	11	1:47.90	$60,000
1998	Subordination, 4, 112	J. D. Bailey	Cimarron Secret, 7	Tour's Big Red, 5	7	1:50.87	$60,000
1997	Devil's Cup, 4, 114	R. Wilson	Da Bull, 5	Green Means Go, 5	12	1:47.01	$60,000
1996	The Vid, 6, 124	W. H. McCauley	Gone for Real, 5	Warning Glance, 5	5	1:47.05	$60,000
1995	The Vid, 5, 117	J. D. Bailey	Star of Manila, 4	Country Coy, 5	9	1:47.19	$60,000
1994	Paradise Creek, 5, 123	M. E. Smith	Glenfiddich Lad, 5	Nijinsky's Gold, 5	8	1:47.84	$60,000
1993	Stagecraft (GB), 6, 112	J. D. Bailey	Roman Envoy, 5	Carterista, 4	10	1:47.80	$60,000
1992	Buckhar, 4, 113	J. Cruguet	Tin Can Ali, 4	Archies Laughter, 4	13	1:48.49	$60,000

Named in honor of the numerous Canadian tourists who visit South Florida. 1991 Canadian Club Turf H. 1985-'97 Grade 2. 1983 about 1¹⁄₁₆ miles; 1992-2000 1¹⁄₈ miles. 1967-'71,1973-'89,1991-'97,1999-2001 turf. 1992 new course record.

Cardinal Handicap

Grade 3, Churchill Downs, three-year-olds and up, fillies and mares, 1¹⁄₈ miles, turf. Held November 23, 2002, with a gross value of $150,000. First held in 1974. Graded since 1995. Stakes record 1:47.81 (1996 Bail Out Becky [DQ to second]).

Year	Winner	Jockey	Second	Third	Strs	Time	1st Purse
2002	Quick Tip, 4, 114	R. Albarado	San Dare, 4	Bien Nicole, 4	10	1:51.08	$107,322
2001	Watch, 4, 114	C. Perret	Sitka, 4	Gino's Spirits (GB), 5	9	1:49.12	$104,997
2000	Illiquidity, 4, 115	J. K. Court	License Fee, 5	Miss of Wales (Chi), 5	12	1:49.72	$109,182
1999	Pratella, 4, 114	B. D. Peck	Mingling Glances, 5	Uanme, 4	9	1:48.88	$106,299
1998	B. A. Valentine, 5, 115	J. F. Chavez	Mingling Glances, 4	Cuando, 4	13	1:48.62	$111,693
1997	Colcon, 4, 114	J. D. Bailey	Dance Clear (Ire), 4	Sagar Pride (Ire), 4	12	1:51.89	$108,903
1996	Miss Caerleona (Fr), 4, 114	L. Melancon	Bail Out Becky, 4	Striesen, 4	12	1:47.81	$72,850
1995	Apolda, 4, 114	P. Day	Alive With Hope, 4	Lady Reiko (Ire), 4	11	1:49.59	$75,530
1994	Bold Ruritana, 4, 116	P. Day	Eternal Reve, 3	Monaassabaat, 3	11	1:48.25	$76,375
1993	River Ball (Arg), 7, 109	J. Parsley	Marshua's River, 6	Logan's Mist, 4	9	1:55.79	$74,945
1992	Auto Dial, 4, 113	S. J. Sellers	Radiant Ring, 4	Red Journey, 4	5	1:52.04	$71,500

Named for Kentucky's state bird. 1974-'75,1983-'85 Kentucky Cardinal S.; 1976-'82 Kentucky Cardinal H.; 1986 Cardinal S. 1974-'75,1983-'87 1¹⁄₁₆ miles; 1976-'81 7 furlongs; 1982 1 mile. 1974-'86,1988,1992 dirt. 1974-'75 three-year-olds. 1974-'75 both sexes. 1996 Bail Out Becky finished first, DQ to second.

Carleton F. Burke Handicap

Grade 3, Santa Anita Park, three-year-olds and up, 1½ miles, turf. Held October 27, 2002, with a gross value of $150,000. First held in 1969. Graded since 1973. Stakes record 2:24.24 (1996 Dernier Empereur).

Year	Winner	Jockey	Second	Third	Strs	Time	1st Purse
2002	Special Matter, 4, 110	T. Baze	Alyzig, 5	Dance Dreamer, 5	5	2:28.47	$90,000
2001	Cagney (Brz), 4, 116	M. E. Smith	Kerrygold (Fr), 5	Northern Quest (Fr), 6	9	2:26.10	$90,000
2000	Timboroa (GB), 4, 114	D. R. Flores	(DH) Res Judicata (GB), 5		9	2:27.91	$84,990
			(DH) Kerrygold (Fr), 4				
1999	Public Purse, 5, 119	A. O. Solis	Star Performance, 6	Achilles (GB), 4	8	2:25.83	$90,000
1998	Perim (Fr), 5, 113	B. Blanc	Single Empire (Ire), 4	Rate Cut, 4	9	2:29.29	$75,000
1997	Prussian Blue, 5, 117	K. J. Desormeaux	Embraceable You (Fr), 4	Kessem Power (NZ), 5	7	2:31.37	$75,000
1996	Dernier Empereur, 6, 118	C. J. McCarron	Bon Point (GB), 6	Party Season (GB), 5	8	2:24.24	$98,750
1995	Varadavour (Ire), 6, 115	A. O. Solis	Patio de Naranjos (Chi), 4	Raintrap (GB), 5	7	2:30.27	$90,350
1994	Savinio, 4, 114	C. J. McCarron	Square Cut, 5	Sir Mark Sykes (Ire), 5	8	2:02.69	$95,700
1993	Know Heights (Ire), 4, 117	K. J. Desormeaux	Fanmore, 5	Myrakalu (Fr), 5	7	2:00.07	$96,000
1992	Missionary Ridge (GB), 5, 117	K. J. Desormeaux	Carnival Baby, 4	Myrakalu (Fr), 4	9	2:00.89	$98,000

Named for Carleton F. Burke (1882-1962), first chairman of the California Horse Racing Board. 1969-'70 Carleton F. Burke Invitational H. 1973-'84, 1990-'97 Grade 2; 1985-'89 Grade 1. 1969-'94 1¹⁄₄ miles; 2000 about 1½ miles. 2000 dead heat for second.

Carter Handicap

Grade 1, Aqueduct, three-year-olds and up, 7 furlongs, dirt. Held April 12, 2003, with a gross value of $350,000. First held in 1895. Graded since 1973. Stakes record 1:20.04 (1999 Artax).

Year	Winner	Jockey	Second	Third	Strs	Time	1st Purse
2003	Congaree, 5, 122	G. L. Stevens	Aldebaran, 5	Peeping Tom, 6	5	1:21.48	$210,000
2002	Affirmed Success, 8, 119	R. Migliore	Voodoo, 4	Burning Roma, 4	10	1:21.84	$210,000
2001	Peeping Tom, 4, 118	S. Bridgmohan	Say Florida Sandy, 7	Hook and Ladder, 4	7	1:21.33	$180,000
2000	Brutally Frank, 6, 116	S. Bridgmohan	Western Expression, 4	Affirmed Success, 6	7	1:21.66	$120,000
1999	Artax, 4, 114	J. F. Chavez	Affirmed Success, 5	Western Borders, 5	9	1:20.04	$120,000
1998	Wild Rush, 4, 117	K. J. Desormeaux	Banker's Gold, 4	Western Borders, 4	10	1:21.16	$120,000

Year	Winner	Jockey	Second		Third		Strs	Time	1st Purse
1997	Langfuhr, 5, 122	J. F. Chavez	Stalwart Member, 4		Western Winter, 5		9	1:22.99	$90,000
1996	Lite the Fuse, 5, 121	J. A. Krone	Flying Chevron, 4		Placid Fund, 4		10	1:20.92	$90,000
1995	Lite the Fuse, 4, 111	R. B. Perez	Our Emblem, 4		You and I, 4		9	1:21.48	$90,000
1994	Virginia Rapids, 4, 118	J-L. Samyn	Punch Line, 4		Cherokee Run, 4		11	1:21.45	$90,000
1993	Alydeed, 4, 122	C. Perret	Loach, 5		Argyle Lake, 7		10	1:22.70	$90,000
1992	Rubiano, 5, 118	J. A. Santos	Kid Russell, 6		In Excess (Ire), 5		9	1:21.41	$120,000

Named for Capt. William Carter of Brooklyn, who contributed $500 of the first $600 purse. 1909,1911-'13 not held. 1933-'34 held as a purse race. 1973-'87 Grade 2. 1946,1956-'59,1968-'69,1972-'74,1986,1994-'96 held at Belmont. 1895 1¼ miles; 1896 1⅛ miles; 1897 1¹/₁₆ miles; 1898 about 7 furlongs; 1899-1902 6½ furlongs. 1999 new track record.

Champagne Stakes

Grade 1, Belmont Park, two-year-olds, 1¹/₁₆ miles, dirt. Held October 5, 2002, with a gross value of $500,000. First held in 1867. Graded since 1973. Stakes record 1:40.59 (1997 Grand Slam).

Year	Winner	Jockey	Second	Third	Strs	Time	1st Purse
2002	Toccet, 2, 122	J. F. Chavez	Icecoldbeeratreds, 2	Erinsouthernman, 2	9	1:44.45	$300,000
2001	Officer, 2, 122	V. Espinoza	Jump Start, 2	Heavyweight Champ, 2	5	1:43.39	$300,000
2000	A P Valentine, 2, 122	J. F. Chavez	Point Given, 2	Yonaguska, 2	10	1:41.45	$300,000
1999	Greenwood Lake, 2, 122	J. F. Chavez	Chief Seattle, 2	High Yield, 2	7	1:43.70	$240,000
1998	The Groom Is Red, 2, 122	C. S. Nakatani	Lemon Drop Kid, 2	Weekend Money, 2	7	1:42.91	$240,000
1997	Grand Slam, 2, 122	G. L. Stevens	Lil's Lad, 2	Halory Hunter, 2	8	**1:40.59**	$240,000
1996	Ordway, 2, 122	J. R. Velazquez	Traitor, 2	Gold Tribute, 2	12	1:42.09	$240,000
1995	Maria's Mon, 2, 122	R. G. Davis	Diligence, 2	Devil's Honor, 2	8	1:42.39	$300,000
1994	Timber Country, 2, 122	P. Day	Sierra Diablo, 2	On Target, 2	11	1:44.01	$300,000
1993	Dehere, 2, 122	C. J. McCarron	Crary, 2	Amathos, 2	6	1:35.91	$300,000
1992	Sea Hero, 2, 122	J. D. Bailey	Secret Odds, 2	Press Card, 2	10	1:34.87	$300,000

Named after the Champagne Stakes in England, held at Doncaster. From 1994-'97 sponsored by Moet & Chandon Champagne. 1910-'13,1956 not held. 1867-'89 held at Jerome Park; 1890-1904 Morris Park; 1959,1961,1963-'67,1984 Aqueduct. 1867-'70,1890,1940-'83,1985-'93 1 mile; 1871-'89 6 furlongs; 1891-1904 7 furlongs; 1905-'32 about 7 furlongs; 1933-'39 6½ furlongs; 1984 1⅛ miles.

Chaposa Springs Handicap

Grade 3, Calder Race Course, three-year-olds and up, fillies and mares, 7 furlongs, dirt. Held December 7, 2002, with a gross value of $100,000. First held in 1983. Graded since 1992. Stakes record 1:23.09 (1994 Educated Risk).

Year	Winner	Jockey	Second	Third	Strs	Time	1st Purse
2002	Chispiski, 3, 115	J. A. Garcia	Abundantly Blessed, 3	Away, 3	8	1:25.14	$60,000
2001	Vague Memory, 4, 113	J. A. Garcia	Gold Mover, 3	Platinum Tiara, 3	10	1:24.15	$60,000
2000	England's Rose, 3, 112	J. R. Velazquez	Swept Away, 3	Sugar N Spice, 5	6	1:24.82	$60,000
	Could Be, 4, 115	P. Day	Extended Applause, 4	Class On Class, 5	8	1:24.97	$60,000
1998	Openstock, 6, 113	J. A. Garcia	Lily O'Gold, 3	U Can Do It, 5	7	1:24.84	$60,000
1997	Flashy n Smart, 4, 118	P. Day	U Can Do It, 4	Special Request, 4	11	1:26.67	$60,000
1996	Race Artist, 3, 112	G. Boulanger	La Nina de Orumila, 4	Flat Fleet Feet, 3	7	1:25.21	$60,000
1995	Chaposa Springs, 3, 119	J. D. Bailey	Investalot, 4	Easter Doll, 4	7	1:25.32	$60,000
1994	Educated Risk, 4, 122	M. E. Smith	Goldarama, 4	Floramera, 4	6	**1:23.09**	$60,000
1993	Lady Sonata, 4, 114	R. D. Lopez	Ophidian, 3	Capture the Crown, 4	11	1:24.47	$45,000
	Maggies Pistol, 4, 112	J. A. Bracho	My Own True Love, 5	Luv Me Luv Me Not, 4	11	1:23.97	$45,000
1992	Magal, 5, 115	R. Hernandez	Gene Propp's Dream, 5	My Own True Love, 4	12	1:24.37	$51,675

Named for multiple Grade 1 stakes winner Chaposa Springs (1992, f. by Baldski), who won the race when it was the Virginia H. 1987,1989,1991,1999 not held. 1988,1990, 2000 held in January and December. 1993 two divisions. 1983-'97 Virginia H. 1996 Chaposa Springs finished first, DQ to sixth.

Charles Whittingham Memorial Handicap

Grade 1, Hollywood Park, three-year-olds and up, 1¼ miles, turf. Held June 15, 2002, with a gross value of $350,000. First held in 1969. Graded since 1973. Stakes record 1:57.75 (1993 Bien Bien).

Year	Winner	Jockey	Second	Third	Strs	Time	1st Purse
2002	Denon, 4, 116	G. K. Gomez	Night Patrol, 6	Skipping (GB), 6	9	2:01.47	$210,000
2001	Bienamado, 5, 124	C. J. McCarron	Senure, 5	Timboroa (GB), 5	9	1:59.34	$210,000
2000	White Heart (GB), 5, 117	K. J. Desormeaux	Self Feeder (Ire), 5	Deploy Venture (GB), 4	6	2:00.83	$180,000
1999	River Bay, 6, 119	A. O. Solis	Majorien (GB), 5	Alvo Certo (Brz), 6	9	2:00.06	$240,000
1998	Storm Trooper, 5, 117	K. J. Desormeaux	River Bay, 5	Prize Giving (GB), 5	7	2:03.05	$240,000
1997	Rainbow Dancer (Fr), 6, 116	A. O. Solis	Sunshack (GB), 6	Marlin, 6	6	2:00.09	$240,000
1996	Sandpit (Brz), 7, 120	C. S. Nakatani	Northern Spur (Ire), 5	Awad, 6	6	1:59.52	$300,000
1995	Earl of Barking (Ire), 5, 115	G. F. Almeida	Sandpit (Brz), 5	Savinio, 6	10	1:59.78	$275,000
1994	Grand Flotilla, 7, 116	G. L. Stevens	Bien Bien, 5	Blues Traveller (Ire), 5	8	1:59.26	$275,000
1993	Bien Bien, 4, 119	C. J. McCarron	Best Pal, 5	Leger Cat (Arg), 5	8	**1:57.75**	$275,000
1992	Quest for Fame (GB), 5, 122	G. L. Stevens	Classic Fame, 6	River Traffic, 6	9	1:58.99	$275,000

Named for Racing Hall of Fame trainer Charles Whittingham (1913-'99). 1969-'70,1972 Hollywood Park Invitational Turf H.; 1971 Ford Pinto Invitational Turf H.; 1973-'88 Hollywood Invitational H.; 1989-'98 Hollywood Turf H.; 1999-2001 Charles Whittingham H. 1969-'87 1½ miles. 1993 new course record

Chicago Breeders' Cup Handicap

Grade 3, Arlington Park, three-year-olds and up, fillies and mares, 7 furlongs, dirt. Held June 8, 2002, with a gross value of $164,440. First held in 1986. Graded since 1992. Stakes record 1:21.24 (1992 Withallprobability).

Year	Winner	Jockey	Second	Third	Strs	Time	1st Purse
2002	Mandy's Gold, 4, 116	R. R. Douglas	Cat and the Hat, 4	Caressing, 4	6	1:22.86	$98,664
2001	Trip, 4, 114	C. Perret	Hidden Assets, 4	Rose of Zollern (Ire), 5	7	1:22.18	$99,312
2000	Saoirse, 4, 118	D. Clark	The Happy Hopper, 4	Dif a Dot, 5	7	1:23.09	$102,195
1997	J J'sdream, 4, 118	M. Guidry	Capote Belle, 4	Eseni, 4	7	1:22.25	$101,625
1996	Bunbeg, 4, 114	M. Walls	Morris Code, 4	Rhapsodic, 5	8	1:23.86	$102,990
1995	Low Key Affair, 4, 113	A. T. Gryder	Morning Meadow, 5	Marina Park (GB), 5	9	1:24.64	$93,840
1994	Minidar, 4, 116	V. Belvoir	Spinning Round, 5	Traverse City, 4	10	1:22.49	$93,960
1993	Meafara, 4, 121	J. L. Diaz	Shared Interest, 5	Real Display, 4	11	1:22.12	$93,870
1992	Withallprobability, 4, 115	G. K. Gomez	Fit for a Queen, 6	Madam Bear, 4	9	1:21.24	$93,450

1988,1998-'99 not held. 1986-'95 Chicago Budweiser Breeders' Cup H.

Churchill Downs Distaff Handicap

Grade 2, Churchill Downs, three-year-olds and up, fillies and mares, 1 mile, dirt. Held November 9, 2002, with a gross value of $200,000. First held in 1986. Graded since 1988. Stakes record 1:33.57 (2000 Chilukki).

Year	Winner	Jockey	Second	Third	Strs	Time	1st Purse
2002	Softly, 4, 114	J. K. Court	Bare Necessities, 3	Victory Ride, 4	9	1:35.07	$138,632
2001	Nasty Storm, 3, 115	P. Day	Forest Secrets, 3	Trip, 4	8	1:35.30	$137,764
2000	Chilukki, 3, 116	G. L. Stevens	Reciclada (Chi), 5	Rose of Zollern (Ire), 4	10	1:33.57	$154,008
1999	Let, 4, 113	C. H. Borel	Roza Robata, 4	Dif a Dot, 4	9	1:34.41	$138,880
1998	Dream Scheme, 5, 113	C. H. Borel	Sister Act, 3	Beautiful Pleasure, 3	9	1:34.41	$139,624
1997	Feasibility Study, 5, 120	R. Albarado	J J'sdream, 4	Mama's Pro, 4	14	1:37.61	$146,196
1996	Fast Catch, 4, 109	W. Martinez	Serena's Song, 4	Bedroom Blues, 5	9	1:36.55	$139,624
1995	Lakeway, 4, 122	K. J. Desormeaux	Alcovy, 4	Laura's Pistolette, 4	8	1:35.94	$137,280
1994	Educated Risk, 4, 118	P. Day	Pennyhill Park, 4	Alcovy, 4	8	1:35.74	$138,125
1993	Miss Indy Anna, 3, 111	P. Day	One Dreamer, 5	Deputation, 4	13	1:37.72	$141,960
1992	Wilderness Song, 4, 120	C. Perret	Miss Jealski, 3	Dance Colony, 5	11	1:36.22	$102,440

1986-'95 Churchill Downs Budweiser Breeders' Cup H. 1988-'91 Grade 3. 1986 7 furlongs. 2000 new track record.

Churchill Downs Handicap

Grade 2, Churchill Downs, four-year-olds and up, 7 furlongs, dirt. Held May 4, 2002, with a gross value of $171,450. First held in 1911. Graded since 1992. Stakes record 1:20.50 (2001 Alannan).

Year	Winner	Jockey	Second	Third	Strs	Time	1st Purse
2002	D'wildcat, 4, 115	K. J. Desormeaux	Snow Ridge, 4	Binthebest, 5	10	1:22.37	$106,299
2001	Alannan, 5, 116	E. S. Prado	Bonapaw, 5	Exchange Rate, 4	10	1:20.50	$111,321
2000	Straight Man, 4, 112	J. F. Chavez	Mula Gula, 4	Patience Game, 4	7	1:21.53	$104,904
1999	Rock and Roll, 4, 112	P. Day	Liberty Gold, 5	Run Johnny, 5	7	1:22.81	$103,137
1998	Distorted Humor, 5, 119	G. L. Stevens	Gold Land, 7	El Amante, 7	7	1:21.18	$103,509
1997	Diligence, 4, 114	M. E. Smith	Victor Cooley, 4	Criollito (Arg), 4	9	1:22.37	$70,432
1996	Criollito (Arg), 5, 115	C. J. McCarron	Forty Won, 5	Powis Castle, 5	9	1:22.01	$74,260
1995	Goldseeker Bud, 4, 109	W. Martinez	Level Sands, 4	Go for Gin, 4	11	1:21.75	$75,205
1994	Honor the Hero, 6, 116	G. K. Gomez	Memo (Chi), 7	Saratoga Gambler, 7	8	1:23.05	$71,370
1993	Callide Valley, 5, 116	G. L. Stevens	Furiously, 4	Ojai, 4	11	1:22.01	$56,063
1992	Pleasant Tap, 5, 120	E. Delahoussaye	Take Me Out, 4	Cantrell Road, 4	9	1:22.32	$55,526

Formerly named for sponsor W. S. Farish's Lane's End, located in Versailles, Kentucky. 1914-'37 not held. 1911-'99 Churchill Downs H.; 2000 Winnercomm H.; 2001 Lane's End Churchill Downs H. 1992-'97 Grade 3. 1911-'13 1⅛ miles. 1911-'13,1938-'43,1947-'88 three-year-olds and up. 1998,2001 new track record.

Cicada Stakes

Grade 3, Aqueduct, three-year-olds, fillies, 7 furlongs, dirt. Held March 22, 2003, with a gross value of $108,300. First held in 1975. Graded since 1996. Stakes record 1:22.38 (1994 Our Royal Blue).

Year	Winner	Jockey	Second	Third	Strs	Time	1st Purse
2003	Cyber Secret, 3, 122	S. Bridgmohan	Roar Emotion, 3	Boxer Girl, 3	6	1:22.55	$64,980
2002	Proper Gamble, 3, 122	J. Castellano	Short Note, 3	Forest Heiress, 3	6	1:23.32	$65,160
2001	Xtra Heat, 3, 122	R. Wilson	Erin Moor, 3	Chasm, 3	4	1:23.39	$63,770
2000	Finder's Fee, 3, 118	J. D. Bailey	Apollo Cat, 3	Southern Sandra, 3	6	1:23.07	$65,100
1999	Potomac Bend, 3, 118	M. T. Johnston	Carleaville, 3	Jane, 3	7	1:23.18	$48,915
1998	Jersey Girl, 3, 116	R. Migliore	Vienna Blues, 3	Babai Danzig, 3	9	1:22.95	$50,175
1997	Vegas Prospector, 3, 116	M. J. McCarthy	Ormsby County, 3	Valid Affect, 3	6	1:26.23	$48,375
1996	J J'sdream, 3, 121	G. Boulanger	Dahl, 3	Mystic Rhythms, 3	9	1:23.44	$50,310
1995	Lucky Lavender Gal, 3, 114	R. G. Davis	Stormy Blues, 3	Dancin Renee, 3	7	1:23.45	$48,870
1994	Our Royal Blue, 3, 114	R. Wilson	Sovereign Kitty, 3	Princess Joanne, 3	5	1:22.38	$48,375
1993	Personal Bid, 3, 118	J. A. Santos	Sheila's Revenge, 3	In Excelcis Deo, 3	4	1:23.52	$31,800

Named for Meadow Stable's 1961 champion two-year-old filly, three-year-old filly, '62 and '63 champion handicap mare Cicada (1959-'81, f. by Bryan G.). 1984-'87,1989-'92 not held. 1983,1993 held at Belmont Park. 1975-'82,1988 6 furlongs; 1983 1¹/₁₆ miles. 1975 two-year-olds, fillies; 1983 three-year-olds and up, fillies and mares.

Cigar Mile Handicap

Grade 1, Aqueduct, three-year-olds and up, 1 mile, dirt. Held November 30, 2002, with a gross value of $350,000. First held in 1988. Graded since 1990. Stakes record 1:32.80 (1989 Dispersal; 1990 Quiet American).

Year	Winner	Jockey	Second	Third	Strs	Time	1st Purse
2002	Congaree, 4, 119	J. D. Bailey	Aldebaran, 4	Crafty C. T., 4	8	1:33.11	$210,000
2001	Left Bank, 4, 120	J. R. Velazquez	Graeme Hall, 4	Red Bullet, 4	9	1:33.35	$210,000
2000	El Corredor, 3, 116	J. D. Bailey	Peeping Tom, 3	Affirmed Success, 6	11	1:34.68	$210,000
1999	Affirmed Success, 5, 118	J. F. Chavez	Adonis, 5	Honorifico (Arg), 5	9	1:34.18	$210,000
1998	Sir Bear, 5, 116	J. D. Bailey	Affirmed Success, 4	Distorted Humor, 5	8	1:34.05	$180,000
1997	Devious Course, 5, 112	J. F. Chavez	Lucayan Prince, 4	Basquelan, 6	12	1:34.98	$150,000
1996	Gold Fever, 3, 115	M. E. Smith	Diligence, 3	Top Account, 3	14	1:34.98	$150,000
1995	Flying Chevron, 3, 112	R. G. Davis	Wekiva Springs, 4	Dramatic Gold, 4	13	1:34.57	$150,000
1994	Cigar, 4, 111	J. D. Bailey	Devil His Due, 5	Punch Line, 5	12	1:36.10	$150,000
1992	Ibero (Arg), 5, 117	L. A. Pincay Jr.	Irish Swap, 5	Nines Wild, 5	7	1:33.97	$300,000

Named for 1995, '96 Horse of the Year Cigar (1990, c. by Palace Music). Formerly named for the New York Racing Association. 1993 not held. 1988-'96 NYRA Mile H.

Cinema Breeders' Cup Handicap

Grade 3, Hollywood Park, three-year-olds and up, 1⅛ miles, turf. Held June 30, 2002, with a gross value of $200,000. First held in 1946. Graded since 1973. Stakes record 1:46.56 (1994 Unfinished Symph).

Year	Winner	Jockey	Second	Third	Strs	Time	1st Purse
2002	Inesperado (Fr), 3, 116	K. J. Desormeaux	Regiment, 3	Johar, 3	7	1:47.63	$97,560
2001	Sligo Bay (Ire), 3, 118	L. A. Pincay Jr.	Learing At Kathy, 3	Marine (GB), 3	7	1:48.40	$65,160
2000	David Copperfield, 3, 116	V. Espinoza	Duke of Green (GB), 3	Silver Axe, 3	6	1:47.73	$64,560
1999	Fighting Falcon, 3, 119	B. Blanc	Eagleton, 3	Major Hero, 3	8	1:48.06	$66,000
1998	Commitisize, 3, 118	D. R. Flores	Killer Image, 3	Lord Smith (GB), 3	7	1:48.03	$65,220
1997	Worldly Ways (GB), 3, 115	C. S. Nakatani	P. T. Indy, 3	Brave Act (GB), 3	9	1:48.43	$66,180
1996	Let Bob Do It, 3, 120	K. J. Desormeaux	Dr. Sardonica, 3	Winter Quarters, 3	8	1:47.58	$81,660
1995	Via Lombardia (Ire), 3, 119	E. J. Delahoussaye	Bryntirion, 3	Oncefortheroad, 3	9	1:47.22	$65,400
1994	Unfinished Symph, 3, 118	G. Baze	Vaudeville, 3	Furno Di Londra (Ire), 3	7	1:46.56	$63,100
1993	Earl of Barking (Ire), 3, 121	C. J. McCarron	Manny's Prospect, 3	Minks Law, 3	5	1:47.45	$61,100
1992	Bien Bien, 3, 113	C. J. McCarron	Fax News, 3	Prospect for Four, 3	8	1:47.10	$65,600

Named for Los Angeles's area's best-known industry. 1974 not held. 1946-2001 Cinema H. 1973-'93 Grade 2. 1949 held at Santa Anita. 1946-'49,1951-'55,1981-'84 1¹⁄₁₆ miles; 1950 1 mile. 1946-'67 dirt.

Citation Handicap

Grade 2, Hollywood Park, three-year-olds and up, 1¹⁄₁₆ miles, turf. Held November 30, 2002, with a gross value of $500,000. First held in 1977. Graded since 1979. Stakes record 1:39.69 (1999 Brave Act [GB]).

Year	Winner	Jockey	Second	Third	Strs	Time	1st Purse
2002	Good Journey, 6, 123	P. Day	Seinne (Chi), 5	White Heart (GB), 5	10	1:41.45	$300,000
2001	Good Journey, 5, 115	C. J. McCarron	Decarchy, 4	Irish Prize, 5	8	1:44.30	$300,000
2000	Charge d'Affaires (GB), 5, 116	J. A. Santos	Ladies Din, 5	Native Desert, 7	10	1:40.30	$300,000
1999	Brave Act (GB), 5, 119	A. O. Solis	Native Desert, 6	Bouccaneer (Fr), 4	11	1:39.69	$300,000
1998	Military, 4, 118	G. K. Gomez	Mr Lightfoot (Ire), 4	Worldly Ways (GB), 4	8	1:50.58	$180,000
1997	Geri, 5, 121	J. D. Bailey	Mufattish, 4	Martiniquais (Ire), 4	6	1:48.35	$180,000
1996	Gentlemen (Arg), 4, 119	G. L. Stevens	Smooth Runner, 5	Via Lombardia (Ire), 4	7	1:45.55	$180,000
1995	Fastness (Ire), 5, 120	G. L. Stevens	Earl of Barking (Ire), 5	Silver Wizard, 5	7	1:44.78	$165,000
1994	Southern Wish, 5, 115	C. S. Nakatani	Square Cut, 5	Jeune Homme, 4	7	2:00.20	$137,500
1993	Jeune Homme, 3, 114	T. Jarnet	Paradise Creek, 4	Johann Quatz (Fr), 4	8	1:45.84	$137,500
1992	Leger Cat (Arg), 6, 114	C. S. Nakatani	†Trishyde, 3	Luthier Enchanteur, 5	8	1:46.48	$137,500

Named for Calumet Farm's 1948 Horse of the Year and Triple Crown winner Citation (1945-'70, c. by Bull Lea). 1979-'80,1984-'86 Grade 3; 1981-'83 not graded. 1980 1 mile; 1981,1983-'84,1986-'93,1995-'98 1⅛ miles; 1985 about 1⅛ miles; 1994 1¼ miles. 1977-'82,1984 dirt. 1995 new course record. †denotes female.

(Citgo) Distaff Turf Mile Stakes

Grade 3, Churchill Downs, three-year-olds and up, fillies and mares, 1 mile, turf. Held May 4, 2002, with a gross value of $100,000. First held in 1983. Graded since 1997. Stakes record 1:34.64 (1995 Bold Ruritana).

Year	Winner	Jockey	Second	Third	Strs	Time	1st Purse
2002	Stylish, 4, 116	J. D. Bailey	La Recherche, 4	Dianehill (Ire), 4	10	1:35.72	$71,424
2001	Iftiraas (GB), 4, 118	J. D. Bailey	Gino's Spirits (GB), 5	Solvig, 4	7	1:36.69	$70,432
2000	Don't Be Silly, 5, 116	J. F. Chavez	Really Polish, 5	Pricearose, 4	8	1:34.78	$71,548
1999	Shires Ende, 4, 118	J. R. Velazquez	Ashford Castle, 5	Sophie My Love, 4	9	1:35.43	$74,152
1998	Witchful Thinking, 4, 120	S. J. Sellers	Colcon, 5	Swearingen, 4	10	1:37.23	$74,896
1997	B. A. Valentine, 4, 114	S. J. Sellers	Striesen, 5	Romy, 6	10	1:36.98	$71,796
1996	Apolda, 5, 123	J. D. Bailey	Country Cat, 4	Bold Ruritana, 6	8	1:36.50	$55,283
1995	Bold Ruritana, 5, 123	P. Day	Icy Warning, 5	Rapunzel Runz, 4	10	1:34.64	$56,111
1994	Weekend Madness (Ire), 4, 123	C. R. Woods Jr.	Russian Bride, 4	Suspect Terrain, 5	9	1:38.58	$55,770
1993	Lady Blessington (Fr), 5, 120	P. Day	You'd Be Surprised, 4	Wassifa (GB), 4	9	1:34.96	$37,570
1992	Quilma (Chi), 5, 120	E. J. Delahoussaye	Behaving Dancer, 5	Radiant Ring, 4	10	1:35.36	$38,285

Named for sponsor Citgo. 1984-'86 not held. 1983-'87 Twin Spires S.; 1988 Capital Holding Twin Spires S.; 1989 Capital Holding Twin Spires H.; 1990-'91,1993-'94 Capital Holding Mile S.; 1992 Capital Holding S.; 1995-'97 Providian Mile S.;

1998 Aegon Mile S. 1999 Ashland Mile S.; 2000 Churchill Downs Distaff Turf Mile S. 1983,1989 1⅛ miles; 1987-'88 1¹/₁₆ miles. 1983-'89 dirt. 1983-'88 three-year-olds, both sexes. 1992 equaled course record; 1993 new course record.

Clark Handicap

Grade 2, Churchill Downs, three-year-olds and up, 1⅛ miles, dirt. Held November 29, 2002, with a gross value of $400,000. First held in 1975. Graded since 1973. Stakes record 1:48.26 (2001 Ubiquity).

Year	Winner	Jockey	Second	Third	Strs	Time	1st Purse
2002	Lido Palace (Chi), 5, 121	J. F. Chavez	Crafty Shaw, 4	Hero's Tribute, 4	11	1:49.13	$283,464
2001	Ubiquity, 4, 113	C. Perret	Include, 4	Mr Ross, 6	10	**1:48.26**	$280,240
2000	†Surfside, 3, 113	P. Day	Guided Tour, 4	Maysville Slew, 4	9	1:48.75	$276,272
1999	Littlebitlively, 5, 118	C. H. Borel	Pleasant Breeze, 4	Nite Dreamer, 4	12	1:50.88	$284,456
1998	Silver Charm, 4, 124	G. L. Stevens	Littlebitlively, 4	Wild Rush, 4	8	1:49.07	$275,776
1997	Concerto, 3, 113	J. D. Bailey	Terremoto, 6	Rod and Staff, 4	11	1:49.72	$284,704
1996	Isitingood, 5, 120	D. R. Flores	Savinio, 6	Coup D' Argent, 4	9	1:48.99	$174,220
1995	Judge T C, 4, 115	J. M. Johnson	Tyus, 5	Alphabet Soup, 4	14	1:49.82	$153,140
1994	Sir Vixen, 6, 112	D. Kutz	Danville, 3	Prize Fight, 5	7	1:51.36	$143,130
1993	Mi Cielo, 3, 117	M. E. Smith	Take Me Out, 5	Forry Cow How, 5	13	1:51.43	$150,540
1992	Zeeruler, 4, 113	G. K. Gomez	Flying Continental, 6	Echelon's Ice Man, 4	13	1:50.11	$76,050

Named for Meriwether Lewis Clark (1846-'99), founder of the Kentucky Derby. 1875-1901 Clark S. 1973-'97 Grade 3. 1875-'80 2 miles; 1881-'95 1¼ miles; 1902-'21,1925-'54 1¹/₁₆ miles. 1875-1901 three-year-olds. †denotes female.

Clement L. Hirsch Handicap

Grade 2, Del Mar, three-year-olds and up, fillies and mares, 1¹/₁₆ miles, dirt. Held August 11, 2002, with a gross value of $300,000. First held in 1937. Graded since 1983. Stakes record 1:40 (1982 Matching).

Year	Winner	Jockey	Second	Third	Strs	Time	1st Purse
2002	Azeri, 4, 126	M. E. Smith	Angel Gift, 4	Se Me Acabo (Chi), 4	5	1:42.66	$180,000
2001	Tranquility Lake, 6, 120	E. J. Delahoussaye	Gourmet Girl, 6	Nany's Sweep, 6	4	1:41.78	$180,000
2000	Riboletta (Brz), 5, 125	C. J. McCarron	Bordelaise (Arg), 5	Gourmet Girl, 5	6	1:42.06	$180,000
1999	A Lady From Dixie, 4, 116	C. W. Antley	Manistique, 4	Yolo Lady, 4	5	1:43.58	$180,000
1998	Sharp Cat, 4, 124	C. S. Nakatani	Supercilious, 5	Numero Uno, 5	4	1:42.16	$180,000
1997	Radu Cool, 5, 117	C. J. McCarron	Supercilious, 4	Swoon River, 4	6	1:42.66	$180,000
1996	Different (Arg), 4, 120	C. J. McCarron	Top Rung, 5	Borodislew, 5	4	1:42.48	$189,200
1995	Borodislew, 5, 118	C. J. McCarron	Lakeway, 4	Golden Klair (GB), 4	6	1:41.87	$178,100
1994	Paseana (Arg), 7, 123	C. J. McCarron	Exchange, 6	Magical Maiden, 6	4	1:40.59	$117,100
1993	Magical Maiden, 4, 120	G. L. Stevens	Vieille Vigne (Fr), 6	Party Cited, 6	8	1:42.68	$123,600
1992	Exchange, 4, 120	L. A. Pincay Jr.	Fowda, 4	Brought to Mind, 4	8	1:42.00	$123,100

Named for Clement L. Hirsch (1914-2000), an original Del Mar director. 1938-'66,1968-'72 not held. 1937-'99 Chula Vista H. 1983-'85 Grade 3. 1937 5½ furlongs; 1967,1974-'75 1 mile; 1973 1⅛ miles; 1976-'80 7½ furlongs. 1973,1976-'80 turf. 1937 California-bred two-year-olds; 1973-'80 both sexes.

Clement L. Hirsch Memorial Turf Championship Stakes

Grade 1, Santa Anita Park, three-year-olds and up, 1¼ miles, turf. Held October 6, 2002, with a gross value of $300,000. First held in 1969. Graded since 1973. Stakes record 1:58.48 (1996 Bon Point [GB] [DQ to fifth]).

Year	Winner	Jockey	Second	Third	Strs	Time	1st Purse
2002	The Tin Man, 4, 124	M. E. Smith	Sarafan, 5	Blue Steller (Ire), 5	6	1:58.93	$180,000
2001	Senure, 5, 124	A. O. Solis	White Heart (GB), 6	Cagney (Brz), 4	6	1:59.47	$180,000
2000	Mash One (Chi), 6, 124	D. R. Flores	Boatman, 4	Asidero (Arg), 4	6	2:00.67	$180,000
1999	Mash One (Chi), 5, 124	D. R. Flores	Lazy Lode (Arg), 5	Bonapartiste (Fr), 5	6	1:59.07	$180,000
1998	Military, 4, 124	C. S. Nakatani	Bonapartiste (Fr), 4	River Bay, 4	5	2:02.04	$180,000
1997	Rainbow Dancer (Fr), 6, 124	A. O. Solis	Lord Jain (Arg), 5	Sandpit (Brz), 5	5	2:01.94	$180,000
1996	†Admise (Fr), 4, 121	K. J. Desormeaux	Khoraz, 6	Golden Post, 6	5	**1:58.48**	$180,000
1995	Northern Spur (Ire), 4, 124	C. J. McCarron	Sandpit (Brz), 6	Royal Chariot, 6	8	2:02.37	$180,000
1994	Sandpit (Brz), 5, 124	C. S. Nakatani	Grand Flotilla, 7	Approach the Bench (Ire), 75	2:25.12	$180,000
1993	Kotashaan (Fr), 5, 124	K. J. Desormeaux	Luazur (Fr), 4	†Let's Elope (NZ), 4	4	2:25.06	$180,000
1992	Navarone, 4, 126	P. A. Valenzuela	Defensive Play, 5	Daros (Brz), 5	6	2:24.29	$240,000

Named for Clement L. Hirsch (1914-2000), co-founder and president of Oak Tree Racing Association. 1969-'70 Oak Tree S.; 1971-'95 Oak Tree Invitational; 1996-'99 Oak Tree Turf Championship; 2000 Clement L. Hirsch Turf Championship. 1969-'94 1½ miles. 1996 Bon Point (GB) finished first, DQ to fifth. †denotes female.

Cliff Hanger Handicap

Scheduled as a Grade 3 on the turf, Meadowlands, three-year-olds and up, 1¹/₁₆ miles, dirt. Held October 11, 2002, with a gross value of $145,500. First held in 1977. Graded since 1985. Stakes record 1:39.40 (1988 Wanderkin).

Year	Winner	Jockey	Second	Third	Strs	Time	1st Purse
2002	Saint Verre, 4, 113	J-L. Samyn	Pinky Pizwaanski, 4	Spruce Run, 4	4	1:42.40	$90,000
2001	Crash Course, 5, 114	R. Wilson	Solitary Dancer, 5	Union One, 4	10	1:43.14	$90,000
2000	North East Bound, 4, 118	J. A. Velez Jr.	Johnny Dollar, 4	Swamp, 4	11	1:41.78	$90,000
1999	Virginia Carnival, 7, 114	J-L. Samyn	Star Connection, 5	Grapeshot, 5	12	1:42.44	$90,000
1998	Mi Narrow, 4, 111	J. Bravo	Treat Me Doc, 4	Boyce, 7	6	1:43.58	$60,000
1997	Dixie Bayou, 4, 114	J. R. Velazquez	Brave Note (Ire), 6	Joker, 5	10	1:39.45	$60,000
1996	Thorny Crown, 5, 115	M. J. Luzzi	Ihtiraz (GB), 6	Winnetou, 6	5	1:44.71	$60,000
1995	Mighty Forum (GB), 4, 114	W. H. McCauley	Joker, 3	Fourstars Allstar, 7	7	1:41.09	$60,000

1994	**Binary Light**, 5, 112	J.-L. Samyn	Brazany, 4	Burst of Applause, 5	5	1:41.41	$45,000
1993	**Excellent Tipper**, 5, 117	C. Perret	Rinka Das, 5	First and Only, 6	6	1:43.69	$45,000
1992	**Roman Envoy**, 4, 116	C. Perret	Futurist, 4	Royal Ninja, 8	8	1:39.92	$45,000

Named to honor the early movie industry in New Jersey, referring to suspenseful silent film serials. 1982 Cliff Hanger S. 1985-2001 Grade 3. 1977,1982-'84, 1986, 1988-'92,1994-'95,1997,1999-2001 turf. 1997 equaled course record. 1995 Joker finished first, DQ to second.

Coaching Club American Oaks

Grade 1, Belmont Park, three-year-olds, fillies, 1½ miles, dirt. Held July 20, 2002, with a gross value of $350,000. First held in 1917. Graded since 1973. Stakes record 2:27.80 (1973 Magazine; 1975 Ruffian).

Year	Winner	Jockey	Second	Third	Strs	Time	1st Purse
2002	**Jilbab**, 3, 121	M. J. Luzzi	Tarnished Lady, 3	Shop Till You Drop, 3	7	2:31.48	$210,000
2001	**Tweedside**, 3, 121	J. R. Velazquez	Exogenous, 3	Unbridled Lassie, 3	8	2:30.70	$210,000
2000	**Jostle**, 3, 121	M. E. Smith	Resort, 3	Secret Status, 3	7	2:29.99	$210,000
1999	**On a Soapbox**, 3, 121	J. D. Bailey	Dreams Gallore, 3	Strolling Belle, 3	8	2:29.31	$210,000
1998	**Banshee Breeze**, 3, 121	J. D. Bailey	Keeper Hill, 3	Best Friend Stro, 3	6	2:31.56	$180,000
1997	**Ajina**, 3, 121	M. E. Smith	Tomisue's Delight, 3	Key Hunter, 3	5	2:00.45	$150,000
1996	**My Flag**, 3, 121	J. D. Bailey	Gold n Delicious, 3	Weekend in Seattle, 3	7	2:04.64	$150,000
1995	**Golden Bri**, 3, 121	J. A. Santos	Serena's Song, 3	Change Fora Dollar, 3	6	2:03.86	$150,000
1994	**Two Altazano**, 3, 121	J. A. Santos	Plenty of Sugar, 3	Sovereign Kitty, 3	7	2:02.88	$150,000
1993	**Sky Beauty**, 3, 121	J. A. Santos	Future Pretense, 3	Silky Feather, 3	5	2:01.56	$150,000
1992	**Turnback the Alarm**, 3, 121	C. W. Antley	Easy Now, 3	Pleasant Stage, 3	6	2:03.53	$150,000

Named in honor of the Coaching Club of America. 1917-'27 Coaching Club American Oaks H. 1963-'67 held at Aqueduct. 1917 1⅛ miles; 1918,1959-'70,1990-'97 1¼ miles; 1919-'41,1944-'58 1⅜ miles.

Comely Stakes

Grade 3, Aqueduct, three-year-olds, fillies, 1 mile, dirt. Held April 18, 2003, with a gross value of $107,900. First held in 1945. Graded since 1973. Stakes record 1:35.50 (2002 Bella Bellucci).

Year	Winner	Jockey	Second	Third	Strs	Time	1st Purse
2003	**Cyber Secret**, 3, 122	S. Bridgmohan	Storm Flag Flying, 3	Bonay, 3	5	1:35.97	$64,740
2002	**Bella Bellucci**, 3, 122	G. L. Stevens	Short Note, 3	Nonsuch Bay, 3	5	**1:35.50**	$64,920
2001	**Two Item Limit**, 3, 122	R. Migliore	Mandy's Gold, 3	It All Adds Up, 3	7	1:36.17	$66,060
2000	**March Magic**, 3, 114	R. Migliore	Jostle, 3	Finder's Fee, 3	6	1:36.79	$65,460
1999	**Madison's Charm**, 3, 112	J.-L. Samyn	Better Than Honour, 3	Oh What a Windfall, 3	7	1:35.54	$65,520
1998	**Fantasy Angel**, 3, 114	J. F. Chavez	Hansel's Girl, 3	Best Friend Stro, 3	12	1:37.44	$69,300
1997	**Dixie Flag**, 3, 114	J.-L. Samyn	Global Star, 3	How About Now, 3	7	1:36.96	$66,120
1996	**Little Miss Fast**, 3, 118	J. F. Chavez	J J'sdream, 3	Stop Traffic, 3	6	1:36.58	$65,940
1995	**Nappelon**, 3, 112	J. F. Chavez	Stormy Blues, 3	Incredible Blues, 3	6	1:36.26	$64,440
1994	**Dixie Luck**, 3, 116	F. Leon	Penny's Reshoot, 3	Our Royal Blue, 3	7	1:37.02	$66,240
1993	**Private Light**, 3, 112	R. G. Davis	Russian Bride, 3	True Affair, 3	6	1:44.19	$68,280
1992	**Saratoga Dew**, 3, 114	W. H. McCauley	City Dance, 3	Looking for a Win, 3	7	1:37.22	$69,480

Named for James Butler's Comely (1912, f. by Disguise); Butler was the owner of Empire City, where the race originated. 1954-'58 not held. 1945-'53 Comely H. 1988-'95 Grade 2. 1945-'51,1959 held at Jamaica; 1952-'53 Empire City; 1976,1981,1984-'85 Belmont Park. 1945-'53,1993 1¹⁄₁₆ miles; 1959 5 furlongs; 1960-'90 7 furlongs. 1945-'53 three-year-olds and up, fillies and mares; 1959 two-year-olds, both sexes. 2001 Mandy's Gold finished first, DQ to second.

Commonwealth Breeders' Cup Stakes

Grade 2, Keeneland, three-year-olds and up, 7 furlongs, dirt. Held April 13, 2003, with a gross value of $273,750. First held in 1987. Graded since 1990. Stakes record 1:20.50 (1998 Distorted Humor).

Year	Winner	Jockey	Second	Third	Strs	Time	1st Purse
2003	**Smooth Jazz**, 4, 118	E. S. Prado	Crafty C. T., 5	Multiple Choice, 5	7	1:21.73	$169,725
2002	**Orientate**, 4, 120	P. Day	Aldebaran, 4	Twilight Road, 4	7	1:21.54	$168,640
2001	**Alannan**, 5, 118	E. S. Prado	Valiant Halory, 4	Liberty Gold, 7	8	1:22.39	$170,965
2000	**Richter Scale**, 6, 121	R. Migliore	Son's Corona, 5	Deep Gold, 4	6	1:21.07	$128,836
1999	**Good and Tough**, 4, 115	S. J. Sellers	Purple Passion, 5	Crucible, 4	5	1:22.09	$127,906
1998	**Distorted Humor**, 5, 119	G. L. Stevens	El Amante, 4	Partner's Hero, 4	8	**1:20.50**	$130,820
1997	**Victor Cooley**, 4, 114	E. M. Martin Jr.	Western Winter, 5	Appealing Skier, 4	7	1:22.46	$129,332
1996	**Afternoon Deelites**, 4, 124	K. J. Desormeaux	Western Winter, 4	Our Emblem, 5	6	1:21.12	$131,068
1995	**Golden Gear**, 4, 118	C. Perret	Turkomatic, 4	Lit de Justice, 5	8	1:22.06	$130,758
1994	**Memo (Chi)**, 7, 118	P. Atkinson	American Chance, 5	British Banker, 6	10	1:22.32	$69,378
1993	**Alydeed**, 4, 115	C. Perret	Binalong, 4	Senor Speedy, 6	6	1:21.43	$113,057
1992	**Pleasant Tap**, 5, 116	E. J. Delahoussaye	To Freedom, 4	Run On the Bank, 5	6	1:22.40	$118,138

Named for the Commonwealth of Kentucky. 1989 Commonwealth Breeders' Cup H. 1990-'93 Grade 3. 1987-'88 6 furlongs.

(Coolmore) Lexington Stakes

Grade 2, Keeneland, three-year-olds, 1¹⁄₁₆ miles, dirt. Held April 19, 2003, with a gross value of $363,675. First held in 1936. Graded since 1986. Stakes record 1:41.06 (1999 Charismatic).

Year	Winner	Jockey	Second	Third	Strs	Time	1st Purse
2003	**Scrimshaw**, 3, 116	E. S. Prado	Eye of the Tiger, 3	Domestic Dispute, 3	7	1:45.47	$225,479
2002	**Proud Citizen**, 3, 116	M. E. Smith	Crimson Hero, 3	Easyfromthegitgo, 3	8	1:44.58	$226,083
2001	**Keats**, 3, 116	L. Melancon	Griffinite, 3	Bay Eagle, 3	10	1:43.54	$230,315
2000	**Unshaded**, 3, 116	S. J. Sellers	Globalize, 3	Harlan Traveler, 3	8	1:43.72	$221,588
1999	**Charismatic**, 3, 115	J. D. Bailey	Yankee Victor, 3	Finder's Gold, 3	12	**1:41.06**	$234,794

1998	**Classic Cat**, 3, 114	R. Albarado	Voyamerican, 3	Grand Slam, 3	8	1:42.85	$228,300
1997	**Touch Gold**, 3, 115	G. L. Stevens	Smoke Glacken, 3	Deeds Not Words, 3	5	1:43.27	$116,963
1996	**City by Night**, 3, 113	S. J. Sellers	Prince of Thieves, 3	Roar, 3	11	1:42.39	$123,473
1995	**Star Standard**, 3, 115	P. Day	Royal Mitch, 3	Guadalcanal, 3	5	1:45.02	$99,882
1994	**Southern Rhythm**, 3, 118	G. K. Gomez	Soul of the Matter, 3	Ulises, 3	8	1:45.72	$85,095
1993	**Grand Jewel**, 3, 118	J. D. Bailey	El Bakan, 3	Truth of It All, 3	9	1:43.61	$87,219
1992	**My Luck Runs North**, 3, 115	R. D. Lopez	Lure, 3	Agincourt, 3	5	1:44.06	$89,083

Named for the city of Lexington, Kentucky. Since 1998 named for sponsor Coolmore Stud in Ireland. 1938-'83 not held. 1936-'97 Lexington S. 1986-'87 Grade 3. 1936-'37 6 furlongs. 1936-'37 two-year-olds. 2001 Mr. John finished second, DQ to eighth.

Cotillion Handicap

Grade 2, Philadelphia Park, three-year-olds, fillies, 1¹⁄₁₆ miles, dirt. Held October 5, 2002, with a gross value of $250,000. First held in 1969. Graded since 1973. Stakes record 1:42.54 (2000 Jostle).

Year	Winner	Jockey	Second	Third	Strs	Time	1st Purse
2002	**Smok'n Frolic**, 3, 118	J. A. Velez Jr.	Pupil, 3	Jilbab, 3	9	1:44.27	$150,000
2001	**Mystic Lady**, 3, 121	E. Coa	Zonk, 3	Celtic Melody, 3	8	1:43.86	$150,000
2000	**Jostle**, 3, 124	M. E. Smith	Gold for My Gal, 3	Prized Stamp, 3	7	**1:42.54**	$120,000
1999	**Skipping Around**, 3, 114	M. J. McCarthy	Strolling Belle, 3	Waltz, 3	10	1:43.45	$120,000
1998	**Lu Ravi**, 3, 121	W. Martinez	Sister Act, 3	Let, 3	8	1:43.55	$90,000
1997	**Snit**, 3, 114	R. E. Colton	Proud Run, 3	Salt It, 3	9	1:43.91	$90,000
1996	**Double Dee's**, 3, 111	F. Leon	Ginny Lynn, 3	Princess Eloise, 3	5	1:44.69	$90,000
1995	**Clear Mandate**, 3, 113	J. C. Ferrer	Blue Sky Princess, 3	Country Cat, 3	11	1:42.87	$98,730
1994	**Sovereign Kitty**, 3, 118	W. H. McCauley	Cinnamon Sugar (Ire), 3	Cavada, 3	8	1:43.52	$97,440
1993	**Jacody**, 3, 118	T. G. Turner	Aztec Hill, 3	Cearas Dancer, 3	6	1:43.22	$95,520
1992	**Star Minister**, 3, 117	A. J. Seefeldt	Diamond Duo, 3	Squirm, 3	7	1:44.06	$80,760

A "cotillion" is a traditional society dance for young ladies. 1991 not held. 1975-'84 Cotillion S. 1973-'74 Grade 1; 1981-'88 Grade 3. 1969-'74 held at Liberty Bell; 1975-'84 Keystone.

Count Fleet Sprint Handicap

Grade 3, Oaklawn Park, four-year-olds and up, 6 furlongs, dirt. Held April 10, 2003, with a gross value of $150,000. First held in 1974. Graded since 1986. Stakes record 1:08.18 (2001 Bonapaw).

Year	Winner	Jockey	Second	Third	Strs	Time	1st Purse
2003	**Beau's Town**, 5, 122	J. Theriot	Honor Me, 5	Sand Ridge, 8	6	1:09.01	$90,000
2002	**Explicit**, 5, 116	L. Meche	Entepreneur, 5	Junior Deputy, 5	5	1:08.60	$90,000
2001	**Bonapaw**, 5, 118	G. Melancon	Chindi, 7	Bidis, 4	7	**1:08.18**	$75,000
2000	†**Show Me the Stage**, 4, 116	D. R. Flores	Smolderin Heart, 5	Vinnie's Boy, 4	6	1:09.62	$75,000
1999	**Reraise**, 4, 122	C. S. Nakatani	Run Johnny, 7	E J Harley, 7	6	1:08.59	$75,000
1998	**Chindi**, 4, 113	D. R. Pettinger	E J Harley, 6	Western Fame, 6	8	1:09.77	$75,000
1997	**High Stakes Player**, 5, 120	K. J. Desormeaux	†Capote Belle, 4	Victor Avenue, 4	8	1:08.86	$90,000
1996	**Concept Win**, 6, 116	G. L. Stevens	Roythelittleone, 4	Spiritbound, 4	7	1:09.06	$90,000
1995	**Hot Jaws**, 5, 113	C. H. Borel	Demaloot Demashoot, 5	Mr. Cooperative, 4	9	1:09.49	$90,000
1994	**Demaloot Demashoot**, 4, 115	M. E. Smith	Honor the Hero, 6	Sir Hutch, 4	8	1:08.39	$90,000
1993	**Approach**, 6, 116	P. Day	Ponche, 4	Never Wavering, 4	13	1:09.64	$90,000
1992	**Gray Slewpy**, 4, 117	K. J. Desormeaux	Potentiality, 6	Hidden Tomahawk, 4	7	1:08.97	$60,000

Named for 1943 Horse of the Year and Triple Crown winner Count Fleet (1940-'73, c. by Reigh Count). 1974-'82 Count Fleet H. 1988-'89 Grade 2. 1974-'75 three-year-olds and up. †denotes female.

(Crown Royal) American Turf Stakes

Grade 3, Churchill Downs, three-year-olds, 1¹⁄₁₆ miles, turf. Held May 3, 2002, with a gross value of $116,300. First held in 1992. Graded since 1998. Stakes record 1:40.93 (1997 Royal Strand [Ire]).

Year	Winner	Jockey	Second	Third	Strs	Time	1st Purse
2002	**Legislator**, 3, 116	E. S. Prado	Stage Call (Ire), 3	Orchard Park, 3	10	1:44.43	$72,106
2001	**Strategic Partner**, 3, 116	J. R. Velazquez	Baptize, 3	Dynameaux, 3	6	1:42.89	$73,098
2000	**King Cugat**, 3, 123	J. D. Bailey	Lendell Ray, 3	Go Lib Go, 3	11	1:41.25	$73,222
1999	**Air Rocket**, 3, 120	J. D. Bailey	Haus of Dehere, 3	Conserve, 3	10	1:42.65	$71,548
1998	**Dernier Croise (Fr)**, 3, 116	G. L. Stevens	Tenbyssimo (Ire), 3	Silver Lord, 3	10	1:44.28	$78,120
1997	**Royal Strand (Ire)**, 3, 116	P. Day	Rob 'n Gin, 3	Deputy Commander, 3	10	**1:40.93**	$71,796
1996	**Broadway Beau**, 3, 114	C. J. McCarron	Trail City, 3	Gotcha, 3	10	1:41.87	$76,375
1995	**Unanimous Vote (Ire)**, 3, 120	G. L. Stevens	Nostra, 3	Native Regent, 3	12	1:42.07	$76,700
1994	**Jaggery John**, 3, 123	M. E. Smith	Milt's Overture, 3	Zuno Star, 3	10	1:45.05	$56,453
1993	**Desert Waves**, 3, 118	S. J. Sellers	Compadre, 3	Super Snazzie, 3	5	1:42.64	$36,628
1992	**Senor Tomas**, 3, 118	M. E. Smith	Coaxing Matt, 3	Black Question, 3	8	1:43.10	$37,440

Named for sponsor Seagram's Crown Royal whiskey. 1992-'94 American Turf S. 1997 equaled course record. 1993 Compadre finished first, DQ to second.

Dahlia Handicap

Grade 2, Hollywood Park, three-year-olds and up, fillies and mares, 1¹⁄₁₆ miles, turf. Held December 21, 2002, with a gross value of $150,000. First held in 1982. Graded since 1984. Stakes record 1:40.40 (1989 [DH] Stylish Star/Saros Brig).

Year	Winner	Jockey	Second	Third	Strs	Time	1st Purse
2002	**(DH) Surya**, 4, 118	P. A. Valenzuela		Honestly Darling, 4	9	1:44.55	$60,000
	(DH) Tout Charmant, 6	A. O. Solis					

2001 Verruma (Brz), 5, 115	G. K. Gomez	Vencera (Fr), 4	Heads Will Roll (GB), 4	8	1:43.24	$90,000
2000 Follow the Money, 4, 115	V. Espinoza	Smooth Player, 4	Beautiful Noise, 4	7	1:40.71	$90,000
1999 Lady At Peace, 3, 113	G. K. Gomez	Cyrillic, 4	Country Garden (GB), 4	5	1:41.50	$90,000
1998 Tuzla (Fr), 4, 119	C. S. Nakatani	Sonja's Faith (Ire), 4	Curitiba, 4	5	1:41.75	$60,000
1997 Golden Arches (Fr), 3, 117	C. J. McCarron	Sonja's Faith (Ire), 3	Traces of Gold, 5	8	1:41.09	$60,000
1996 Sixieme Sens, 4, 116	C. S. Nakatani	Admise (Fr), 4		8	1:42.37	$66,600
1995 Didina (GB), 3, 115	E. J. Delahoussaye	Dirca (Ire), 3	Rapunzel Runz, 4	10	1:45.20	$68,300
1994 Skimble, 5, 118	E. J. Delahoussaye	Queens Court Queen, 5	Shir Dar (Fr), 4	8	1:42.33	$66,000
1993 Kalita Melody (GB), 5, 115	C. A. Black	Vinista, 3	Gumpher, 5	7	1:44.73	$64,500
1992 Kostroma (Ire), 6, 124	G. L. Stevens	Vijaya, 5	Guiza, 5	8	1:41.40	$66,500

Named for 1973, '74 English Horse of the Year and 1974 champion turf horse Dahlia (1970-2001, f. by *Vaguely Noble). 1984-'89 Grade 3. 2002 dead heat for first.

Davona Dale Stakes

Grade 2, Gulfstream Park, three-year-olds, fillies, 1 1/16 miles, dirt. Held February 23, 2003, with a gross value of $150,000. First held in 1988. Graded since 1993. Stakes record 1:44.96 (2003 Yell).

Year Winner	Jockey	Second	Third	Strs	Time	1st Purse
2003 Yell, 3, 117	J. R. Velazquez	Ivanavinalot, 3	Gold Player, 3	5	**1:44.96**	$90,000
2002 Ms Brookski, 3, 121	R. B. Homeister Jr.	Colonial Glitter, 3	French Satin, 3	9	1:45.14	$60,000
2001 Latour, 3, 112	J. R. Velazquez	Gold Mover, 3	Courageous Maiden, 3	7	1:45.51	$60,000
2000 Cash Run, 3, 118	J. D. Bailey	Regally Appealing, 3	Secret Status, 3	9	1:40.37	$60,000
1999 Three Ring, 3, 118	J. R. Velazquez	Golden Temper, 3	Gold From the West, 3	5	1:41.53	$60,000
1998 Diamond On the Run, 3, 112	P. Day	Uanme, 3	Dixie Melody, 3	10	1:42.65	$60,000
1997 Glitter Woman, 3, 114	M. E. Smith	City Band, 3	Southern Playgirl, 3	6	1:39.31	$60,000
1996 Plum Country, 3, 118	P. Day	My Flag, 3	La Rosa, 3	9	1:42.08	$60,000
1995 Mia's Hope, 3, 114	K. L. Chapman	Minister Wife, 3	Culver City, 3	6	1:43.26	$60,000
1994 Cut the Charm, 3, 118	J. D. Bailey	She Rides Tonite, 3	Delightful Bet, 3	8	1:41.44	$60,000
1993 Lunar Spook, 3, 118	M. Guidry	Boots 'n Jackie, 3	In Her Glory, 3	7	1:42.09	$30,000
1992 Miss Legality, 3, 116	J. A. Krone	November Snow, 3	Spectacular Sue, 3	8	1:42.00	$30,000

Named for Calumet Farm's 1979 champion three-year-old filly and filly triple crown winner Davona Dale (1976, f. by Best Turn). 1988 Davona Dale H.; 1989,1991 Davona Dale Breeders' Cup S. 1993-'97 Grade 3. 1988-'90 7 furlongs; 1991-2000 1 mile 70 yards. 1988 four-year-olds and up, fillies and mares; 1989 three-year-olds and up, fillies and mares. 1996 Rare Blend finished second, DQ to sixth.

Debutante Stakes

Grade 3, Churchill Downs, two-year-olds, fillies, 5 1/2 furlongs, dirt. Held July 6, 2002, with a gross value of $100,000. First held in 1889. Graded since 1996. Stakes record 1:02.52 (2001 Cashier's Dream).

Year Winner	Jockey	Second	Third	Strs	Time	1st Purse
2002 Awesome Humor, 2, 115	C. H. Borel	Vibs, 2	Attemptress, 2	7	1:03.45	$67,890
2001 Cashier's Dream, 2, 118	D. J. Meche	Lakeside Cup, 2	Colonial Glitter, 2	8	**1:02.52**	$68,510
2000 Gold Mover, 2, 121	C. Perret	Princess Belle, 2	Tricky Elaine, 2	9	1:03.79	$69,626
1999 Chilukki, 2, 121	W. Martinez	Miss Wineshine, 2	Cecilia's Crown, 2	9	1:03.66	$69,998
1998 Silverbulletday, 2, 115	W. Martinez	The Happy Hopper, 2	Mancari's Rose, 2	9	1:04.70	$69,502
1997 Love Lock, 2, 115	P. Day	Countess Diana, 2	Quick Lap, 2	13	1:03.84	$72,478
1996 Move, 2, 121	P. Day	Sarah's Prospector, 2	Live Your Best, 2	10	1:05.66	$73,840
1995 Golden Attraction, 2, 115	D. M. Barton	Western Dreamer, 2	Tipically Irish, 2	9	1:04.19	$70,948
1994 Chargedupsycamore, 2, 121	P. Day	Phone Bird, 2	Our Gem, 2	9	1:05.24	$54,405
1993 Fly Love, 2, 116	B. E. Bartram	Miss Ra He Ra, 2	Astas Foxy Lady, 2	11	1:05.23	$37,635
1992 Hollywood Wildcat, 2, 116	F. A. Arguello Jr.	Cosmic Speed Queen, 2	Dixie Band, 2	14	1:06.02	$38,480

Young women making their first formal appearance in society are known as "debutantes." 1932-'37 not held. 1928 Churchill Downs Debutante S. 1895-1922 4 furlongs; 1923-'25 4 1/2 furlongs; 1926-'81 5 furlongs; 1986-'90 6 furlongs. 1997,1999 equaled track record; 2001 new track record.

De La Rose Handicap

Grade 3, Gulfstream Park, three-year-olds and up, fillies and mares, 1 1/16 miles, turf. Held January 25, 2002, with a gross value of $100,000. First held in 1988. Graded since 1990. Stakes record 1:39.50 (1992 Grab the Green).

Year Winner	Jockey	Second	Third	Strs	Time	1st Purse
2002 Veil of Avalon, 5, 116	E. S. Prado	Snow Dance, 4	Wander Mom, 4	12	1:42.06	$60,000
2000 Fictitious (GB), 4, 113	J. A. Santos	Tres Coronas, 4	Dyna Two, 6	7	1:40.87	$45,000
1999 Lovers Knot (GB), 4, 114	J. D. Bailey	Pleasant Music, 5	Zinfandoll, 5	8	1:42.28	$45,000
1998 Dispersion, 5, 113	E. M. Jurado	Mistress Fletcher, 6	Bursting Forth, 4	5	1:48.28	$45,000
1997 Romy, 6, 115	F. C. Torres	Elusive, 5	Careless Heiress, 4	10	1:43.56	$60,000
1996 Class Kris, 4, 117	P. Day	Danish (Ire), 5	Logan's Mist, 7	5	1:42.51	$60,000
1995 Cox Orange, 5, 118	J. D. Bailey	Weekend Madness (Ire), 5	Ma Guerre, 5	11	1:43.47	$60,000
1994 Marshua's River, 7, 115	J. A. Santos	Sheila's Revenge, 4	Tango Charlie, 5	7	1:39.54	$60,000
1993 Quilma (Chi), 6, 113	J. A. Santos	Lemhi Go, 5	Palomelle (Fr), 5	8	1:43.88	$76,380
1992 Grab the Green, 4, 119	J. A. Santos	Christiecat, 5	Julie La Rousse (Ire), 4	10	**1:39.50**	$75,930

Named for Henryk de Kwiatkowski's 1981 champion turf female De La Rose (1978-2001, f. by Nijinsky II). 2001 not held. 1988-'96 Buckram Oak H. 1993,1998 dirt. 1992 new course record.

Delaware Handicap

Grade 3, Delaware Park, three-year-olds and up, fillies and mares, 1¼ miles, dirt. Held July 21, 2002, with a gross value of $600,000. First held in 1937. Graded since 1973. Stakes record 1:59.80 (1987 Coup de Fusil).

Year	Winner	Jockey	Second	Third	Strs	Time	1st Purse
2002	Summer Colony, 4, 118	J. R. Velazquez	Your Out, 4	Two Item Limit, 4	9	2:04.52	$360,000
2001	Irving's Baby, 4, 113	R. A. Dominguez	Under the Rug, 6	Lazy Slusan, 6	6	2:05.21	$360,000
2000	Lu Ravi, 5, 117	P. Day	Tap to Music, 5	Silverbulletday, 4	8	2:02.21	$360,000
1999	Tap to Music, 4, 116	P. Day	Keeper Hill, 4	Unbridled Hope, 5	13	2:02.15	$300,000
1998	Amarillo, 4, 110	J. A. Krone	Tuxedo Junction, 5	Timely Broad, 4	9	2:04.37	$300,000
1997	Power Play, 5, 114	L. C. Reynolds	Gold n Delicious, 4	Effectiveness, 4	11	2:03.53	$210,000
1996	Urbane, 4, 117	A. O. Solis	Alcovy, 6	Shoop, 5	13	2:01.89	$180,000
1995	Night Fax, 4, 108	J. D. Carle	Cavada, 4	It's Personal, 5	8	2:02.98	$95,070
1994	With a Wink, 4, 114	R. Migliore	Passing Vice, 4	Alphabulous, 5	9	2:03.37	$95,130
1993	Green Darlin, 4, 113	M. J. Luzzi	Girl On a Mission, 4	Starry Val, 4	11	2:03.76	$96,300
1992	Brilliant Brass, 5, 117	E. S. Prado	Train Robbery, 5	Risen Colony, 4	6	2:03.11	$93,780

1943 not held. 1937-'54 New Castle H. 1973-'89 Grade 1; 1990-'95 Grade 2. 1983-'85 held at Saratoga. 1937-'50 1¹⁄₁₆ miles.

Delaware Oaks

Grade 3, Delaware Park, three-year-olds, fillies, 1¹⁄₁₆ miles, dirt. Held July 20, 2002, with a gross value of $250,000. First held in 1938. Graded since 1973. Stakes record 1:42.81 (1998 Nickel Classic).

Year	Winner	Jockey	Second	Third	Strs	Time	1st Purse
2002	Allamerican Bertie, 3, 115	L. Melancon	Alternate, 3	Pass the Virtue, 3	6	1:43.81	$150,000
2001	Zonk, 3, 115	M. J. McCarthy	Mystic Lady, 3	Lady Andromeda, 3	11	1:45.27	$151,000
2000	Sincerely, 3, 117	M. J. McCarthy	Trip, 3	Valleydar, 3	5	1:43.83	$150,000
1999	Brushed Halory, 3, 115	E. M. Martin Jr.	Gold From the West, 3	Queen's Word, 3	5	1:43.42	$150,000
1998	Nickel Classic, 3, 119	C. H. Borel	Lu Ravi, 3	Taffy Davenport, 3	8	1:42.81	$120,000
1997	Runup the Colors, 3, 116	P. Day	Timely Broad, 3	City Band, 3	10	1:44.27	$90,000
1996	Like a Hawk, 3, 114	R. E. Colton	Mercedes Song, 3	Winter Melody, 3	10	1:37.01	$30,000

1943,1983-'95 not held. 1973-'80 Grade 1; 1981-'82 Grade 2; 1996-'98 not graded. 1938-'82 1¹⁄₈ miles; 1996 1 mile. 1996 turf.

Del Mar Breeders' Cup Handicap

Grade 2, Del Mar, three-year-olds and up, 1 mile, dirt. Held September 2, 2002, with a gross value of $250,000. First held in 1987. Graded since 1989. Stakes record 1:33.40 (1989 On the Line).

Year	Winner	Jockey	Second	Third	Strs	Time	1st Purse
2002	Congaree, 4, 119	M. E. Smith	Kela, 4	Reba's Gold, 5	6	1:36.34	$150,000
2001	El Corredor, 4, 121	V. Espinoza	Figlio Mio, 4	Performing Magic, 4	6	1:35.24	$150,000
2000	El Corredor, 3, 111	V. Espinoza	Cliquot, 4	Literal Prowler, 6	8	1:35.05	$158,160
1999	Hollycombe, 5, 116	G. L. Stevens	Flying With Eagles, 5	Old Trieste, 4	8	1:35.46	$126,060
1998	Old Trieste, 3, 116	C. J. McCarron	Grajagan (Arg), 4	Stalwart Tsu, 4	4	1:35.35	$123,172
1997	Benchmark, 6, 117	E. J. Delahoussaye	Crafty Friend, 4	Northern Afleet, 4	5	1:35.57	$126,700
1996	Dramatic Gold, 5, 118	K. J. Desormeaux	Alphabet Soup, 5	Savinio, 6	5	1:34.78	$125,650
1995	Alphabet Soup, 4, 115	C. J. McCarron	Lykatill Hil, 5	Luthier Fever, 4	9	1:34.33	$117,150
1994	Lykatill Hil, 4, 118	E. J. Delahoussaye	D'Hallevant, 4	Stuka, 4	6	1:34.01	$62,200
1993	Region, 4, 115	C. S. Nakatani	Lottery Winner, 4	L'Express (Chi), 4	10	1:34.98	$122,100
1992	Reign Road, 4, 114	D. R. Flores	Sir Beaufort, 5	Charmonnier, 4	10	1:35.29	$122,000

1987-'95 Del Mar Budweiser Breeders' Cup H. 1989 Grade 3.

Del Mar Debutante Stakes

Grade 1, Del Mar, two-year-olds, fillies, 7 furlongs, dirt. Held August 31, 2002, with a gross value of $250,000. First held in 1951. Graded since 1973. Stakes record 1:21.45 (1994 Call Now).

Year	Winner	Jockey	Second	Third	Strs	Time	1st Purse
2002	Miss Houdini, 2, 116	G. L. Stevens	Santa Catarina, 2	Indy Groove, 2	8	1:23.43	$150,000
2001	Habibti, 2, 115	V. Espinoza	Who Loves Aleyna, 2	Tempera, 2	5	1:22.22	$150,000
2000	Cindy's Hero, 2, 114	G. K. Gomez	Notable Career, 2	Euro Empire, 2	5	1:22.61	$150,000
1999	Chilukki, 2, 121	D. R. Flores	Spain, 2	She's Classy, 2	7	1:23.54	$150,000
1998	Excellent Meeting, 2, 115	K. J. Desormeaux	Antahkarana, 2	Colorado Song, 2	9	1:22.34	$150,000
1997	Vivid Angel, 2, 115	K. J. Desormeaux	Griselle, 2	Czarina, 2	8	1:24.26	$150,000
1996	Sharp Cat, 2, 115	R. R. Douglas	Desert Digger, 2	Broad Dynamite, 2	10	1:23.98	$150,000
1995	Batroyale, 2, 119	M. A. Pedroza	Proud Dixie, 2	General Idea, 2	12	1:22.55	$137,500
1994	Call Now, 2, 115	A. O. Solis	How So Oiseau, 2	Ski Dancer, 2	9	1:21.45	$137,500
1993	Sardula, 2, 115	E. J. Delahoussaye	Phone Chatter, 2	Ballerina Gal, 2	8	1:21.61	$137,500
1992	Beal Street Blues, 2, 116	G. L. Stevens	Fit n Fappy, 2	Zoonaqua, 2	10	1:37.17	$137,500

Young women making their first formal appearance in society are known as "debutantes." 1999 Vinery Del Mar Debutante S. 1973-'98 Grade 2. 1951-'73 6 furlongs. 1974-'92 1 mile.

Del Mar Derby

Grade 2, Del Mar, three-year-olds, 1¹⁄₈ miles, turf. Held September 7, 2002, with a gross value of $300,000. First held in 1945. Graded since 1973. Stakes record 1:46.60 (1968 [DH] Prince Hemp/Glory Hallelujah).

Year	Winner	Jockey	Second	Third	Strs	Time	1st Purse
2002	Inesperado (Fr), 3, 121	C. S. Nakatani	Johar, 3	Rock Opera, 3	9	1:47.49	$180,000
2001	Romanceishope, 3, 121	C. J. McCarron	Indygo Shiner, 3	Blue Steller (Ire), 3	10	1:47.93	$180,000

2000	**Walkslikeaduck**, 3, 121	E. J. Delahoussaye	Purely Cozzene, 3	New Story, 3	10	1:46.66	$180,000
1999	**Val Royal (Fr)**, 3, 121	C. S. Nakatani	Fighting Falcon, 3	In Frank's Honor, 3	10	1:48.53	$180,000
1998	**Ladies Din**, 3, 121	K. J. Desormeaux	Expressionist, 3	Scooter Brown, 3	9	1:48.59	$180,000
1997	**Anet**, 3, 121	G. L. Stevens	Brave Act (GB), 3	Worldly Ways (GB), 3	7	1:48.42	$180,000
1996	**Rainbow Blues (Ire)**, 3, 122	C. S. Nakatani	The Barking Shark, 3	Mateo, 3	9	1:50.01	$180,000
1995	**Da Hoss**, 3, 122	R. R. Douglas	Lake George, 3	Tabor, 3	9	1:48.08	$165,000
1994	**Ocean Crest**, 3, 122	L. A. Pincay Jr.	Unfinished Symph, 3	Powis Castle, 3	10	1:48.74	$165,000
1993	**Guide (Fr)**, 3, 122	K. J. Desormeaux	Future Storm, 3	The Real Vaslav, 3	12	1:49.73	$165,000
1992	**Daros (GB)**, 3, 122	E. J. Delahoussaye	Smiling and Dancin, 3	Major Impact, 3	12	1:48.80	$165,000

1945-'47 Quigley Memorial H.; 1991-'96 Del Mar Invitational Derby. 1973-'80 Grade 3. 1945-'48 1¹⁄₁₆ miles. 1945-'69 dirt. 2000 equaled course record. 1994 Eagle Eyed finished third, DQ to seventh.

Del Mar Futurity

Grade 2, Del Mar, two-year-olds, 7 furlongs, dirt. Held September 11, 2002, with a gross value of $250,000. First held in 1948. Graded since 1973. Stakes record 1:21.67 (1999 Forest Camp).

Year	Winner	Jockey	Second	Third	Strs	Time	1st Purse
2002	**Icecoldbeeratreds**, 2, 119	D. R. Flores	Kafwain, 2	Chief Planner, 2	8	1:22.94	$150,000
2001	**Officer**, 2, 121	V. Espinoza	Kamsack, 2	Metatron, 2	5	1:22.33	$150,000
2000	**Flame Thrower**, 2, 119	J. D. Bailey	Street Cry (Ire), 2	Arabian Light, 2	8	1:22.00	$150,000
1999	**Forest Camp**, 2, 116	D. R. Flores	Dixie Union, 2	Captain Steve, 2	5	1:21.67	$150,000
1998	**Worldly Manner**, 2, 119	K. J. Desormeaux	Daring General, 2	Waki American, 2	7	1:23.05	$150,000
1997	**Souvenir Copy**, 2, 115	C. J. McCarron	Old Topper, 2	Commitisize, 2	8	1:23.10	$150,000
1996	**Silver Charm**, 2, 116	D. R. Flores	Gold Tribute, 2	Swiss Yodeler, 2	7	1:22.88	$150,000
1995	**Future Quest**, 2, 115	K. J. Desormeaux	Othello, 2	Cavonnier, 2	8	1:21.81	$137,500
1994	**On Target**, 2, 115	A. O. Solis	Supremo, 2	Timber Country, 2	9	1:22.37	$137,500
1993	**Winning Pact**, 2, 115	C. S. Nakatani	Ramblin Guy, 2	Ferrara, 2	7	1:22.04	$137,500
1992	**River Special**, 2, 115	C. J. McCarron	Sudden Hush, 2	Seattle Sleet, 2	7	1:36.64	$137,500

1984-'89 Grade 1. 1948-'70 6 furlongs; 1971-'73 7½ furlongs; 1974-'92 1 mile. 1971-'73 turf.

Del Mar Handicap

Grade 2, Del Mar, three-year-olds and up, 1³⁄₈ miles, turf. Held September 1, 2002, with a gross value of $250,000. First held in 1937. Graded since 1973. Stakes record 2:12.15 (2002 Delta Form [Aus]).

Year	Winner	Jockey	Second	Third	Strs	Time	1st Purse
2002	**Delta Form (Aus)**, 6, 115	G. F. Almeida	The Tin Man, 4	Blue Steller (Ire), 4	10	**2:12.15**	$150,000
2001	**Timboroa (GB)**, 5, 118	L. A. Pincay Jr.	Northern Quest (Fr), 6	Super Quercus (Fr), 5	7	2:12.59	$150,000
2000	**Northern Quest (Fr)**, 5, 116	C. J. McCarron	Perssonet (Chi), 5	Alvo Certo (Brz), 7	8	2:12.65	$150,000
1999	**Sayarshan (Fr)**, 4, 115	B. Blanc	Dancing Place (Chi), 6	Ladies Din, 4	8	2:14.35	$150,000
1998	**Bonapartiste (Fr)**, 4, 115	C. J. McCarron	River Bay, 5	Military, 4	6	2:14.18	$150,000
1997	**Rainbow Dancer (Fr)**, 6, 118	A. O. Solis	Dowty, 5	Lord Jain (Arg), 5	8	2:13.68	$150,000
1996	**Dernier Empereur**, 6, 116	P. A. Valenzuela	Talloires, 6	Party Season (GB), 5	7	2:13.89	$150,000
1995	**Royal Chariot**, 5, 117	L. A. Pincay Jr.	River Rhythm, 8	Party Season (GB), 4	10	2:13.78	$137,500
1994	**Navarone**, 6, 117	P. A. Valenzuela	Approach the Bench (IRE, 6	Sir Mark Sykes (Ire), 5	8	2:14.37	$137,500
1993	**Luazur (Fr)**, 4, 116	P. Day	Kotashaan (Fr), 5	Myrakalu (Fr), 5	7	2:15.11	$137,500
1992	**Navarone**, 4, 117	P. A. Valenzuela	Qathif, 5	Stark South, 4	8	2:15.17	$137,500

1942-'44 not held. 1973,1975-'87,1989-'96 Del Mar Invitational H. 1937-'48 1¹⁄₁₆ miles; 1949-'69 1¹⁄₈ miles; 1971 1³⁄₄ miles; 1976-'85 about 1¹⁄₄ miles. 1937-'69,1976-'85 dirt. 2000 Alvo Certo (Brz) finished second, DQ to third.

Del Mar Oaks

Grade 1, Del Mar, three-year-olds, fillies, 1¹⁄₈ miles, turf. Held August 24, 2002, with a gross value of $300,000. First held in 1957. Graded since 1973. Stakes record 1:47.16 (2002 Dublino).

Year	Winner	Jockey	Second	Third	Strs	Time	1st Purse
2002	**Dublino**, 3, 121	K. J. Desormeaux	Megahertz (GB), 3	Alozaina (Ire), 3	6	**1:47.16**	$180,000
2001	**Golden Apples (Ire)**, 3, 121	G. K. Gomez	Affluent, 3	Reine de Romance (Ire), 3	8	1:47.98	$180,000
2000	**No Matter What**, 3, 121	V. Espinoza	Theoretically, 3	Premiere Creation (Fr), 3	9	1:50.02	$150,000
1999	**Tout Charmant**, 3, 121	D. R. Flores	Smooth Player, 3	Sweet Ludy (Ire), 3	10	1:48.64	$150,000
1998	**Sicy d'Alsace (Fr)**, 3, 121	C. S. Nakatani	Adel, 3	Tranquility Lake, 3	10	1:48.26	$150,000
1997	**Famous Digger**, 3, 121	B. Blanc	Golden Arches (Fr), 3	See You Soon (Fr), 3	10	1:49.14	$150,000
1996	**Antespend**, 3, 120	C. W. Antley	Gastronomical, 3	True Flare, 3	8	1:48.93	$150,000
1995	**Bail Out Becky**, 3, 120	S. J. Sellers	Sleep Easy, 3	Top Ruhl, 3	9	1:49.72	$137,500
1994	**Twice the Vice**, 3, 120	G. L. Stevens	Malli Star, 3	Pharma, 3	6	1:47.73	$96,250
1993	**Hollywood Wildcat**, 3, 120	E. J. Delahoussaye	Possibly Perfect, 3	Miami Sands (Ire), 3	10	1:48.31	$96,250
1992	**Suivi**, 3, 120	A. O. Solis	Race the Wild Wind, 3	Alysbelle, 3	8	1:48.60	$96,250

1992-'94,1996 Del Mar Invitational Oaks. 1973-'78,1988-'91 Grade 3; 1979-'87,1992-'93 Grade 2. 1957-'64 1 mile. 1957-'64 dirt. 1998 Tranquility Lake finished second, DQ to third.

Demoiselle Stakes

Grade 2, Aqueduct, two-year-olds, fillies, 1¹⁄₈ miles, dirt. Held November 30, 2002, with a gross value of $200,000. First held in 1908. Graded since 1973. Stakes record 1:50 (1978 Plankton).

Year	Winner	Jockey	Second	Third	Strs	Time	1st Purse
2002	**Roar Emotion**, 2, 115	J. R. Velazquez	Savedbythelight, 2	Feisty Step, 2	10	1:51.43	$120,000
2001	**Smok'n Frolic**, 2, 121	J. R. Velazquez	Lady Shari, 2	Proxy Statement, 2	7	1:50.57	$120,000
2000	**Two Item Limit**, 2, 122	R. Migliore	Sweep Dreams, 2	Kingsland, 2	8	1:52.25	$120,000

				Strs	Time	1st Purse
1999 **Jostle**, 2, 121	S. Elliott	March Magic, 2	Shawnee Country, 2	8	1:51.51	$120,000
1998 **Better Than Honour**, 2, 113	R. Migliore	Waltz On By, 2	Oh What a Windfall, 2	9	1:52.70	$120,000
1997 **Clark Street**, 2, 121	M. E. Smith	Soft Senorita, 2	Mercy Me, 2	8	1:53.98	$120,000
1996 **Ajina**, 2, 121	P. Day	Hidden Reserve, 2	Biding Time, 2	9	1:53.74	$120,000
1995 **La Rosa**, 2, 114	J. A. Krone	Quiet Dance, 2	Escena, 2	7	1:50.92	$120,000
1994 **Minister Wife**, 2, 121	J. D. Bailey	Miss Golden Circle, 2	Special Broad, 2	9	1:53.48	$120,000
1993 **Strategic Maneuver**, 2, 116	J. D. Bailey	Sovereign Kitty, 2	Princess Tru, 2	6	1:53.62	$120,000
1992 **Fortunate Faith**, 2, 112	A. Madrid Jr.	True Affair, 2	Our Tomboy, 2	8	1:53.59	$120,000

Demoiselle in French means "young female." 1909,1911-'13,1933-'35,1954-'57,1960-'62 not held. 1973-'75 Grade 3; 1981-'89 Grade 1. 1908-'14,1917-'42 held at Empire City; 1915-'16,1958 Belmont; 1944-'53 Jamaica. 1908-'32 5½ furlongs; 1936-'42 5¾ furlongs; 1943-'47 6 furlongs; 1948-'53 1¹⁄₁₆ miles; 1958-'59 7 furlongs; 1963-'74 1 mile. 1998 Tutorial finished first, DQ to fifth.

Deputy Minister Handicap

Grade 3, Gulfstream Park, three-year-olds and up, 6½ furlongs, dirt. Held February 9, 2003, with a gross value of $100,000. First held in 1990. Graded since 2000. Stakes record 1:15.17 (2003 Native Heir).

Year Winner	Jockey	Second	Third	Strs	Time	1st Purse
2003 **Native Heir**, 5, 114	C. H. Velasquez	Binthebest, 6	Fire and Glory, 4	8	**1:15.17**	$60,000
2002 **Fappie's Notebook**, 5, 116	J. F. Chavez	Twilight Road, 5	Binthebest, 5	8	1:16.19	$60,000
2001 **Istintaj**, 5, 118	J. D. Bailey	Fappie's Notebook, 4	Fantastic Finish, 5	8	1:16.08	$60,000
2000 **Deep Gold**, 4, 112	J. R. Velazquez	Forty One Carats, 4	Klabin's Gold, 5	8	1:15.89	$60,000
1999 **Good and Tough**, 4, 115	S. J. Sellers	Western Borders, 5	Mint, 4	7	1:21.63	$60,000
1998 **Irish Conquest**, 5, 113	E. Coa	Frisk Me Now, 4	Oro de Mexico, 4	10	1:22.54	$60,000
1997 **Templado (Ven)**, 4, 113	J. D. Bailey	Sea Emperor, 5	Punch Line, 7	6	1:09.69	$45,000
1996 **Jess C's Whirl**, 6, 115	J. A. Krone	Buffalo Dan, 5	Patton, 5	6	1:10.67	$30,000
1995 **Chimes Band**, 4, 120	J. D. Bailey	Distinct Reality, 4	Ponche, 6	6	1:09.16	$30,000
1994 **I Can't Believe**, 6, 113	E. Maple	Demaloot Demashoot, 4	Devil On Ice, 5	7	1:08.12	$30,000
1993 **Loach**, 5, 114	J. A. Santos	Hidden Tomahawk, 5	British Banker, 5	6	1:22.51	$30,000
1992 **Take Me Out**, 4, 118	J. D. Bailey	Drummond Lane, 5	Frozen Runway, 5	9	1:22.78	$30,000

Named for 1981 Canadian Horse of the Year, champion North American two-year-old male, and 1997, '98 leading sire Deputy Minister (1979, c. by Vice Regent). 1990-'93,1998-'99 7 furlongs; 1994-'97 6 furlongs.

Derby Trial Stakes

Grade 3, Churchill Downs, three-year-olds, 1 mile, dirt. Held April 26, 2003, with a gross value of $167,400. First held in 1938. Graded since 1985. Stakes record 1:34.40 (1969 Ack Ack).

Year Winner	Jockey	Second	Third	Strs	Time	1st Purse
2003 **Midas Eyes**, 3, 122	J. D. Bailey	Champali, 3	Desert Warrior, 3	6	1:36.22	$103,788
2002 **Sky Terrace**, 3, 114	C. Perret	Cashel Castle, 3	Ide Be Spencers, 3	6	1:36.87	$69,936
2001 **Meetyouathebrig**, 3, 122	R. Albarado	Dream Run, 3	One by the Knows, 3	11	1:36.44	$72,602
2000 **Performing Magic**, 3, 114	P. Day	Sun Cat, 3	Valiant Halory, 3	8	1:35.99	$70,680
1999 **Patience Game**, 3, 116	C. S. Nakatani	Prime Directive, 3	Straight Man, 3	9	1:37.86	$71,176
1998 **Souvenir Copy**, 3, 122	D. R. Flores	Yarrow Brae, 3	Black Cash, 3	8	1:35.80	$70,246
1997 **Richter Scale**, 3, 114	S. J. Sellers	Trafalger, 3	Precocity, 3	8	1:36.17	$70,122
1996 **Valid Expectations**, 3, 119	D. R. Pettinger	Great Southern, 3	Storm Creek, 3	10	1:36.81	$77,025
1995 **Peaks and Valleys**, 3, 122	P. Day	Our Gatsby, 3	Strategic Intent, 3	7	1:36.53	$73,515
1994 **Numerous**, 3, 115	C. J. McCarron	Dynamic Asset, 3	Exclusive Praline, 3	6	1:37.34	$72,540
1993 **Cherokee Run**, 3, 122	P. Day	Darien Deacon, 3	Ground Force, 3	9	1:37.57	$56,355
1992 **Alydeed**, 3, 119	C. Perret	Binalong, 3	Dignitas, 3	9	1:36.26	$56,209

Traditionally the final prep race before the Kentucky Derby. 1977-'81 7 furlongs.

Desert Stormer Handicap

Grade 3, Hollywood Park, three-year-olds and up, fillies and mares, 6 furlongs, dirt. Held June 7, 2002, with a gross value of $100,000. First held in 1997. Graded since 2001. Stakes record 1:08.09 (2001 Go Go).

Year Winner	Jockey	Second	Third	Strs	Time	1st Purse
2002 **Slewsbox**, 5, 117	L. A. Pincay Jr.	Kalookan Queen, 6	Rolly Polly (Ire), 6	6	1:09.57	$64,260
2001 **Go Go**, 4, 122	E. J. Delahoussaye	Kalookan Queen, 5	Wired to Fly, 4	5	**1:08.09**	$63,600
2000 **Theresa's Tizzy**, 6, 118	L. A. Pincay Jr.	Hookedonthefeelin, 4	Seth's Choice, 4	7	1:09.30	$64,980
1999 **A. P. Assay**, 5, 122	E. J. Delahoussaye	Woodman's Dancer, 5	Corona Lake, 5	5	1:08.69	$63,600
1998 **Corona Lake**, 4, 118	E. J. Delahoussaye	Lavender, 4	Grab the Prize, 6	5	1:14.71	$64,020
1997 **Advancing Star**, 4, 119	K. J. Desormeaux	Stop Traffic, 4	Tiffany Diamond, 4	5	1:14.21	$60,000

Named for 1995 Breeders' Cup Sprint (G1) winner Desert Stormer (1990, f. by Storm Cat). 1997-'98 6½ furlongs.

Diana Handicap

Grade 2, Saratoga Race Course, three-year-olds and up, fillies and mares, 1¹⁄₈ miles, turf. Held July 27, 2002, with a gross value of $500,000. First held in 1939. Graded since 1973. Stakes record 1:45.40 (1978 Waya [Fr]).

Year Winner	Jockey	Second	Third	Strs	Time	1st Purse
2002 **Tates Creek**, 4, 117	J. D. Bailey	Voodoo Dancer, 4	Snow Dance, 4	9	1:48.00	$300,000
2001 **Starine (Fr)**, 4, 114	J. R. Velazquez	Babae (Chi), 5	Penny's Gold, 4	9	1:46.17	$300,000
2000 **Perfect Sting**, 4, 123	J. D. Bailey	License Fee, 5	Hello Soso (Ire), 4	7	1:47.01	$300,000
1999 **Heritage of Gold**, 4, 115	S. J. Sellers	Khumba Mela (Ire), 4	Mossflower, 5	9	1:45.93	$180,000
1998 **Memories of Silver**, 5, 123	J. D. Bailey	B. A. Valentine, 5	Auntie Mame, 4	8	1:46.14	$180,000
1997 **Rumpipumpy (GB)**, 4, 114	J. A. Santos	B. A. Valentine, 4	Antespend, 4	12	1:48.59	$120,000
1996 **Electric Society (Ire)**, 5, 117	M. E. Smith	Powder Bowl, 4	Upper Noosh, 4	9	1:46.56	$120,000
1995 **Perfect Arc**, 3, 113	J. R. Velazquez	Danish (Ire), 4	Tiffany's Taylor, 6	9	1:46.85	$85,125

1994	**Via Borghese**, 5, 115	J. A. Santos	Blazing Kadie, 4	Coronation Cup, 3	7	1:52.01	$83,010
1993	**Ratings**, 5, 110	J. A. Krone	Lady Blessington (Fr), 5	Garendare (GB), 4	8	1:49.80	$72,240
1992	**Plenty of Grace**, 5, 114	W. H. McCauley	Ratings, 4	Highland Crystal, 4	12	1:46.66	$75,960

Named for the mythological goddess of the hunt, Diana. 1943-'45 held at Belmont. 1939-'72 dirt.

Discovery Handicap

Grade 3, Aqueduct, three-year-olds, 1⅛ miles, dirt. Held October 23, 2002, with a gross value of $100,000. First held in 1945. Graded since 1974. Stakes record 1:47.20 (1973 Forego).

Year	Winner	Jockey	Second	Third	Strs	Time	1st Purse
2002	**Saint Marden**, 3, 117	J. D. Bailey	Regency Park, 3	No Parole, 3	10	1:49.13	$68,400
2001	**Evening Attire**, 3, 111	S. Bridgmohan	Street Cry (Ire), 3	Free of Love, 3	7	1:48.62	$65,580
2000	**Left Bank**, 3, 119	J. R. Velazquez	Perfect Cat, 3	Open Sesame, 3	4	1:47.30	$64,020
1999	**Adonis**, 3, 118	J. R. Velazquez	Best of Luck, 3	Waddaan, 3	6	1:50.11	$64,980
1998	**Early Warning**, 3, 115	J. F. Chavez	Deputy Diamond, 4	Gulliver, 3	8	1:48.94	$50,010
1997	**Mr. Sinatra**, 3, 116	M. E. Smith	Concerto, 3	Twin Spires, 3	5	1:49.55	$64,626
1996	**Gold Fever**, 3, 121	M. E. Smith	Crafty Friend, 3	Early Echoes, 3	9	1:49.01	$66,720
1995	**Michael's Star**, 3, 112	J. A. Krone	Hunting Hard, 3	Reality Road, 3	10	1:50.34	$67,380
1994	**Serious Spender**, 3, 113	J. F. Chavez	Unaccounted For, 3	Malmo, 3	4	1:51.24	$63,540
1993	**Prospector's Flag**, 3, 114	J. F. Chavez	Virginia Rapids, 3	Living Vicariously, 3	8	1:52.30	$70,320
1992	**New Deal**, 3, 111	R. G. Davis	Offbeat, 3	Dodsworth, 3	11	1:48.08	$74,880

Named for Alfred G. Vanderbilt's 1935 Horse of the Year Discovery (1931-'58, c. by Display). 1988-'89 Grade 2. 1945-'58, 1960-'61, 1968-'70 held at Belmont.

Distaff Breeders' Cup Handicap

Grade 2, Aqueduct, three-year-olds and up, fillies and mares, 7 furlongs, dirt. Held March 29, 2003, with a gross value of $152,400. First held in 1954. Graded since 1973. Stakes record 1:21.18 (1991 Devil's Orchid).

Year	Winner	Jockey	Second	Third	Strs	Time	1st Purse
2003	**Carson Hollow**, 4, 120	M. J. Luzzi	Raging Fever, 5	Bonefide Reason, 5	6	1:22.42	$94,740
2002	**Raging Fever**, 4, 120	J. R. Velazquez	Prized Stamp, 5	La Galerie (Arg), 6	6	1:21.78	$94,680
2001	**Dream Supreme**, 4, 119	A. T. Gryder	Folly Dollar, 4	Country Hideaway, 5	5	1:23.66	$108,960
2000	**Honest Lady**, 4, 117	B. Blanc	Her She Kisses, 4	Tap to Music, 5	8	1:22.10	$111,300
1999	**Furlough**, 5, 115	H. Castillo Jr.	Catinca, 4	Tomorrows Sunshine, 5	9	1:23.23	$112,260
1998	**Parlay**, 4, 114	R. Migliore	Lucky Marty, 5	Green Light, 4	9	1:24.10	$67,260
1997	**Miss Golden Circle**, 5, 120	R. Migliore	Inquisitive Look, 4	Punkin Pie, 7	6	1:24.47	$65,400
1996	**Lottsa Talc**, 6, 120	F. T. Alvarado	Traverse City, 6	Dust Bucket, 5	7	1:24.04	$75,820
1995	**Recognizable**, 4, 120	M. E. Smith	Beckys Shirt, 4	Kurofune Mystery, 5	8	1:22.94	$66,540
1994	**Classy Mirage**, 4, 114	R. G. Davis	Jill Miner, 4	Air Port Won, 4	8	1:11.37	$66,480
1992	**Nannerl**, 5, 112	M. E. Smith	Missy's Mirage, 4	Withallprobability, 4	6	1:24.68	$68,880

Races for females are typically referred to as "distaff" races. 1993 not held. 1954-'98 Distaff H. 1973-'88 Grade 3. 1956-'59 held at Belmont. 1977-'79, 1984, 1994 6 furlongs.

Dixie Stakes

Grade 2, Pimlico, three-year-olds and up, 1⅛ miles, turf. Held May 17, 2003, with a gross value of $200,000. First held in 1870. Graded since 1973. Stakes record 1:47.04 (1991 Double Booked).

Year	Winner	Jockey	Second	Third	Strs	Time	1st Purse
2003	**Dr. Brendler**, 5, 117	R. A. Dominguez	Perfect Soul (Ire), 5	Sardaukar (GB), 7	6	1:57.74	$120,000
2002	**Strut the Stage**, 4, 117	R. Albarado	Del Mar Show, 5	Slew the Red, 5	7	1:51.70	$120,000
2001	**Hap**, 5, 119	J. D. Bailey	Make No Mistake (Ire), 6	Cynics Beware, 7	8	1:48.56	$120,000
2000	**Quiet Resolve**, 5, 117	R. Albarado	Haami, 5	Holditholditholdit, 4	9	1:50.42	$120,000
1999	**Middlesex Drive**, 4, 115	P. Day	Sky Colony, 6	Divide and Conquer, 5	10	1:48.64	$120,000
1998	**Yagli**, 5, 121	J. D. Bailey	Sky Colony, 5	Blazing Sword, 4	12	1:51.01	$120,000
1997	**Ops Smile**, 5, 115	E. S. Prado	Brave Note (Ire), 6	Sharp Appeal, 4	8	1:48.20	$120,000
1995	**The Vid**, 5, 119	J. D. Bailey	Pennine Ridge, 4	Blues Traveller (Ire), 4	6	1:52.25	$120,000
1996	**Gold and Steel (Fr)**, 4, 121	A. O. Solis	Same Old Wish, 6	Comstock Lode, 4	9	1:52.80	$120,000
1994	**Paradise Creek**, 5, 124	P. Day	Lure, 5	Astudillo (Ire), 4	5	1:48.51	$90,000
1993	**Lure**, 4, 124	M. E. Smith	Star of Cozzene, 4	Binary Light, 4	8	1:47.60	$90,000
1992	**Sky Classic**, 5, 122	P. Day	Fourstars Allstar, 4	Social Retiree, 5	10	1:47.83	$90,000

Named for Maj. Barak G. Thomas's mare Dixie (1859, f. by *Sovereign). 1889-1901, 1905-'23 not held. 1870 Dinner Party S.; 1871, 1902-'04, 1925-'90 Dixie H.; 1872-'88 Reunion S.; 1991-'94, 1996 Early Times Dixie H.; 1995 Early Times Dixie S. 1990-'93 Grade 3. 1902-'04 held at Benning, Washington D.C. 1870-'88 2 miles; 1902-'04 1¾ miles; 1924 1⁹/₁₆ miles; 1955-'59 1⅛ miles; 1960-'90 1½ miles; 1988 1⅝ miles; 1870-1954, 1988 dirt. 1870-1904 three-year-olds.

Dogwood Stakes

Grade 3, Churchill Downs, three-year-olds, fillies, 1¹/₁₆ miles, dirt. Held May 25, 2002, with a gross value of $100,000. First held in 1975. Graded since 1998. Stakes record 1:42.73 (2002 Take Charge Lady).

Year	Winner	Jockey	Second	Third	Strs	Time	1st Purse
2002	**Take Charge Lady**, 3, 121	A. J. D'Amico	Charmed Gift, 3	Allamerican Bertie, 3	7	**1:42.73**	$67,890
2001	**Nasty Storm**, 3, 114	L. Meche	Love At Noon, 3	Golly Greeley, 3	7	1:43.41	$68,014
2000	**Welcome Surprise**, 3, 112	F. C. Torres	Lady Melesi, 3	Vivid Sunset, 3	7	1:46.80	$68,014
1999	**Golden Temper**, 3, 116	S. J. Sellers	Boom Town Girl, 3	Honey Hill Lil, 3	8	1:43.73	$69,068
1998	**Really Polish**, 3, 116	P. Day	Beat the Play, 3	Victorica, 3	5	1:44.78	$67,642

Year	Winner	Jockey	Second	Third	Strs	Time	1st Purse
1997	Leo's Gypsy Dancer, 3, 116	P. Day	Buckeye Search, 3	Flying Lauren, 3	7	1:44.95	$69,006
1996	Ginny Lynn, 3, 121	L. Melancon	Everhope, 3	Hidden Lake, 3	7	1:43.22	$53,576
1995	Gal in a Ruckus, 3, 121	W. H. McCauley	Country Cat, 3	Naskra Colors, 3	7	1:43.88	$53,528
1994	Briar Road, 3, 114	L. Melancon	Stella Cielo, 3	Shadow Miss, 3	6	1:44.78	$53,186
1993	With a Wink, 3, 114	C. R. Woods Jr.	Lovat's Lady, 3	Unlaced, 3	8	1:44.21	$36,010
1992	Hitch, 3, 121	B. E. Bartram	Bionic Soul, 3	Secretly, 3	8	1:47.68	$36,075

Named for the dogwood tree, plentiful in Kentucky. 1975-'81 7 furlongs; 1983-'85 1¹⁄₁₆ miles.

Donn Handicap

Grade 1, Gulfstream Park, three-year-olds and up, 1¹⁄₈ miles, dirt. Held February 22, 2003, with a gross value of $500,000. First held in 1959. Graded since 1973. Stakes record 1:46.40 (1979 Jumping Hill).

Year	Winner	Jockey	Second	Third	Strs	Time	1st Purse
2003	Harlan's Holiday, 4, 120	J. R. Velazquez	Hero's Tribute, 5	Puzzlement, 4	11	1:49.17	$300,000
2002	Mongoose, 4, 114	E. S. Prado	Kiss a Native, 5	Rize, 5	14	1:49.63	$300,000
2001	Captain Steve, 4, 120	J. D. Bailey	Albert the Great, 4	Gander, 5	7	1:48.95	$300,000
2000	Stephen Got Even, 4, 115	S. J. Sellers	Golden Missile, 5	Behrens, 6	10	1:48.50	$300,000
1999	Puerto Madero (Chi), 5, 120	K. J. Desormeaux	Behrens, 5	Silver Charm, 5	12	1:48.34	$300,000
1998	Skip Away, 5, 126	J. D. Bailey	Unruled, 5	Sir Bear, 5	10	1:50.17	$180,000
1997	Formal Gold, 4, 113	J. Bravo	Skip Away, 4	Mecke, 5	10	1:47.49	$180,000
1996	Cigar, 6, 128	J. D. Bailey	Wekiva Springs, 5	†Heavenly Prize, 5	8	1:49.12	$180,000
1995	Cigar, 5, 115	J. D. Bailey	Primitive Hall, 6	Bonus Money (GB), 4	9	1:49.68	$180,000
1994	Pistols and Roses, 5, 113	H. Castillo Jr.	Eequalsmcsquared, 5	Wallenda, 4	11	1:50.67	$180,000
1993	Pistols and Roses, 4, 112	H. Castillo Jr.	Irish Swap, 6	Missionary Ridge (GB), 6	9	1:50.10	$240,000
1992	Sea Cadet, 4, 115	A. O. Solis	Out of Place, 5	Sunny Sunrise, 5	8	1:48.17	$300,000

Named to honor James Donn Sr., founder of modern Gulfstream Park. 1973-'74 Grade 3; 1975-'87 Grade 2. 1959-'64 1¹⁄₂ miles; 1976 7 furlongs; 1978 1¹⁄₁₆ miles. 1959-'64 turf. †denotes female.

Dwyer Stakes

Grade 2, Belmont Park, three-year-olds, 1¹⁄₁₆ miles, dirt. Held July 7, 2002, with a gross value of $150,000. First held in 1887. Graded since 1973. Stakes record 1:40.38 (2001 E Dubai).

Year	Winner	Jockey	Second	Third	Strs	Time	1st Purse
2002	Gygistar, 3, 121	J. R. Velazquez	Nothing Flat, 3	American Style, 3	6	1:42.59	$90,000
2001	E Dubai, 3, 121	J. D. Bailey	Windsor Castle, 3	Hero's Tribute, 3	4	1:40.38	$90,000
2000	Albert the Great, 3, 115	R. Migliore	More Than Ready, 3	Red Bullet, 3	4	1:42.62	$90,000
1999	Forestry, 3, 122	J. D. Bailey	Doneraile Court, 3	Successful Appeal, 3	6	1:41.00	$90,000
1998	Coronado's Quest, 3, 124	M. E. Smith	Ian's Thunder, 3	Scatmandu, 3	5	1:42.49	$90,000
1997	Behrens, 3, 117	J. D. Bailey	Glitman, 3	Banker's Gold, 3	6	1:42.26	$90,000
1996	Victory Speech, 3, 117	J. D. Bailey	Gold Fever, 3	Robb, 3	6	1:41.53	$99,000
1995	Hoolie, 3, 117	R. G. Davis	Reality Road, 3	Western Larla, 3	6	1:42.74	$90,000
1994	Holy Bull, 3, 124	M. E. Smith	Twining, 3	Bay Street Star, 3	4	1:41.15	$90,000
1993	Cherokee Run, 3, 123	P. Day	Miner's Mark, 3	Silver of Silver, 3	6	1:47.62	$120,000
1992	Agincourt, 3, 119	J. F. Chavez	Three Peat, 3	Windundermywings, 3	6	1:47.84	$120,000

Named in honor of leading 19th century owners the Dwyer brothers, Mike and Phil. 1911-'12 not held. 1887-1917 Brooklyn Derby; 1956-'78 Dwyer H. 1983-'88 Grade 1. 1887-1910 held at Gravesend Park; 1914-'55,1960-'74,1976 Aqueduct; 1956,1959 Jamaica. 1887,1898-1909 1¹⁄₂ miles; 1888-'97,1915-'24,1935-'39,1975-'93 1¹⁄₈ miles; 1910-'14,1940-'55,1960-'74 1¹⁄₄ miles; 1925 1⁵⁄₁₆ miles; 1926-'34 1¹⁄₂ miles; 1956-'59 1³⁄₁₆ miles. 1992 Three Peat finished first, DQ to 2nd.

Eatontown Handicap

Grade 3, Monmouth Park, three-year-olds and up, fillies and mares, 1¹⁄₁₆ miles, turf. Held August 4, 2002, with a gross value of $100,000. First held in 1971. Graded since 1996. Stakes record 1:40.40 (1996 Gail's Brush).

Year	Winner	Jockey	Second	Third	Strs	Time	1st Purse
2002	Clearly a Queen, 5, 119	E. Coa	Laurica, 5	Presumed Innocent, 5	9	1:44.02	$60,000
2001	Cousin Gigi, 4, 115	R. Wilson	Quidnaskra, 6	Crystal Sea, 4	8	1:47.50	$60,000
2000	Reciclada (Chi), 5, 115	A. O. Solis	Mumtaz (Fr), 4	Dominique's Joy, 5	8	1:44.34	$60,000
1999	Formal Tango, 4, 113	J. D. Bailey	Proud Owner, 4	Natalie Too, 5	7	1:42.62	$60,000
1998	Gastronomical, 5, 115	G. L. Stevens	Tampico, 5	(DH) Dance Clear (Ire), 5	10	1:43.39	$41,400
				(DH) Poopsie, 4			
1997	B. A. Valentine, 4, 122	C. J. McCarron	Everhope, 4	Vashon, 4	11	1:41.32	$41,460
1996	Gail's Brush, 5, 116	G. Boulanger	Plenty of Sugar, 5	Lady Affirmed, 5	7	1:40.40	$45,000
1995	Symphony Lady, 5, 119	J. Bravo	Cox Orange, 5	Grafin, 4	6	1:43.64	$30,000
1994	Verbal Volley, 5, 119	R. E. Colton	Irving's Girl, 4	Uptown Show, 5	8	1:44.71	$24,000
1993	Topsa, 6, 113	L. R. Rivera Jr.	Naked Royalty, 4	Suspect Terrain, 4	8	1:46.39	$21,000
1992	Red Journey, 4, 115	N. Santagata	Hot Times Are Here, 4	Flashing Eyes, 4	7	1:45.06	$21,000

Named for Eatontown, New Jersey, located in Monmouth County. 1991-'95,1997-2000 Eatontown S. 1988-'90, 2001 1¹⁄₈ miles. 1974,1977 dirt. 1998 dead heat for third.

Eddie Read Handicap

Grade 1, Del Mar, three-year-olds and up, 1¹⁄₈ miles, turf. Held July 28, 2002, with a gross value of $400,000. First held in 1974. Graded since 1980. Stakes record 1:46.60 (1986 Al Mamoon).

Year	Winner	Jockey	Second	Third	Strs	Time	1st Purse
2002	Sarafan, 5, 117	C. S. Nakatani	Beat Hollow (GB), 5	Redattore (Brz), 5	6	1:46.77	$240,000
2001	Redattore (Brz), 6, 115	A. O. Solis	Native Desert, 8	Super Quercus (Fr), 5	7	1:47.16	$240,000
2000	Ladies Din, 5, 120	K. J. Desormeaux	Chester House, 5	Gold Nugget, 5	8	1:48.64	$240,000

1999	**Joe Who (Brz)**, 6, 116	C. W. Antley	Ladies Din, 4	Bouccaneer (Fr), 4	10	1:48.75	$240,000
1998	**Subordination**, 4, 117	D. R. Flores	Bonapartiste (Fr), 4	Hawksley Hill (Ire), 5	5	1:47.49	$180,000
1997	**Expelled**, 5, 113	J. A. Garcia	El Angelo, 5	Marlin, 4	7	1:48.60	$180,000
1996	**Fastness (Ire)**, 6, 124	C. S. Nakatani	Smooth Runner, 5	Gold and Steel (Fr), 4	6	1:47.05	$193,000
1995	**Fastness (Ire)**, 5, 115	G. L. Stevens	Romarin (Brz), 5	Northern Spur (Ire), 4	8	1:48.42	$182,600
1994	**Approach the Bench (IRE**, 6, 113	C. S. Nakatani	Fastness (Ire), 4	Johann Quatz (Fr), 5	7	1:48.83	$187,250
1993	**Kotashaan (Fr)**, 5, 122	K. J. Desormeaux	Leger Cat (Arg), 7	Rainbow Corner (GB), 4	6	1:48.45	$183,750
1992	**Marquetry**, 5, 118	D. R. Flores	Luthier Enchanteur, 5	Leger Cat (Arg), 6	7	1:47.20	$187,250

Named in honor of long-time Del Mar publicity director Eddie Read. 1980-'81 Grade 3; 1982-'87 Grade 2.

El Camino Real Derby

Grade 3, Golden Gate Fields, three-year-olds, 1¹/₁₆ miles, dirt. Held March 8, 2003, with a gross value of $200,000. First held in 1982. Graded since 1986. Stakes record 1:39.40 (1988 Ruhlmann).

Year	Winner	Jockey	Second	Third	Strs	Time	1st Purse
2003	**Ocean Terrace**, 3, 115	M. E. Smith	Ministers Wild Cat, 3	Ten Most Wanted, 3	10	1:42.26	$110,000
2002	**Yougottawanna**, 3, 120	J. P. Lumpkins	Danthebluegrassman, 3	Lusty Latin, 3	10	1:43.48	$110,000
2001	**Hoovergetthekeys**, 3, 120	R. J. Warren Jr.	Startac, 3	Mo Mon, 3	8	1:40.85	$110,000
2000	**Remember Sheikh**, 3, 117	F. T. Alvarado	True Confidence, 3	Country Coast, 3	14	1:43.47	$110,000
1999	**Cliquot**, 3, 115	D. R. Flores	Charismatic, 3	No Cal Bread, 3	7	1:43.29	$110,000
1998	**Event of the Year**, 3, 115	R. A. Baze	Post a Note, 3	Clover Hunter, 3	5	1:40.27	$110,000
1997	**Pacificbounty**, 3, 120	K. J. Desormeaux	Wild Wonder, 3	Carmen's Baby, 3	6	1:41.85	$110,000
1996	**Cavonnier**, 3, 115	M. A. Pedroza	Sergeant Stroh, 3	E C's Dream, 3	9	1:43.41	$110,000
1995	**Jumron (GB)**, 3, 113	G. F. Almeida	Snow Kidd'n, 3	American Day, 3	8	1:43.73	$110,000
1994	**Tabasco Cat**, 3, 113	P. Day	Flying Sensation, 3	Robannier, 3	7	1:42.78	$110,000
1993	**El Atroz**, 3, 117	R. Q. Meza	Offshore Pirate, 3	Lykatill Hil, 3	9	1:43.77	$110,000
1992	**Casual Lies**, 3, 117	A. Patterson	Seahawk Gold, 3	Silver Ray, 3	11	1:42.00	$165,000

Named for the El Camino Real, "the Royal Road" through the California frontier. 1982-2000 held at Bay Meadows.

El Conejo Handicap

Grade 3, Santa Anita Park, four-year-olds and up, 5¹/₂ furlongs, dirt. Held January 1, 2003, with a gross value of $108,800. First held in 1981. Graded since 2000. Stakes record 1:01.74 (1999 Kona Gold).

Year	Winner	Jockey	Second	Third	Strs	Time	1st Purse
2003	**Kona Gold**, 9, 123	A. O. Solis	Radiata, 6	No Armistice, 6	7	1:02.63	$65,280
2002	**Snow Ridge**, 4, 114	M. E. Smith	Explicit, 5	Rio Oro, 5	8	1:03.05	$65,700
2000	**Freespool**, 4, 115	C. J. McCarron	Men's Exclusive, 7	Lexicon, 5	7	1:02.50	$65,220
	Freespool, 4, 114	C. J. McCarron	Mellow Fellow, 5	Old Topper, 5	6	1:03.33	$64,200
1999	**Kona Gold**, 5, 119	A. O. Solis	Big Jag, 6	Mr. Doubledown, 5	6	**1:01.74**	$64,380
1998	**The Exeter Man**, 6, 114	G. K. Gomez	Tower Full, 6	Red, 4	5	1:02.23	$64,020
1997	**High Stakes Player**, 5, 115	C. S. Nakatani	Kern Ridge, 6	Subtle Trouble, 6	5	1:02.89	$63,850
1996	**Lit de Justice**, 6, 119	C. S. Nakatani	A. J. Jett, 4	Fu Man Slew, 5	6	1:01.85	$64,250
1995	**Phone Roberto**, 6, 114	C. J. McCarron	Lost Pan, 5	Rotsaluck, 4	8	1:02.34	$65,000
1994	**Gundaghla**, 7, 116	E. J. Delahoussaye	Sir Hutch, 4	Davy Be Good, 6	8	1:02.01	$64,800
1993	**Fabulous Champ**, 4, 113	C. J. McCarron	Arrowtown, 5	Slerp, 4	7	1:02.66	$63,800
1992	**Gray Slewpy**, 4, 114	K. J. Desormeaux	Frost Free, 7	Cardmania, 6	5	1:02.01	$61,275

Named for Rancho El Conejo, located in Ventura; conejo means "rabbit." 1987, 2001 not held. 2000 held in January and December. 2000 (January) not graded. 1992,1996,1999 new track record. 1992-2000 four-year-olds and up. 1995 Lit de Justice finished second, DQ to sixth.

El Encino Stakes

Grade 2, Santa Anita Park, four-year-olds, fillies, 1¹/₁₆ miles, dirt. Held January 19, 2003, with a gross value of $150,000. First held in 1954. Graded since 1980. Stakes record 1:41.20 (1980 It's In the Air; 1982 Edge; 1983 Beautiful Glass; 1990 Akinemod).

Year	Winner	Jockey	Second	Third	Strs	Time	1st Purse
2003	**Got Koko**, 4, 119	A. O. Solis	Bella Bellucci, 4	Bare Necessities, 4	8	1:42.25	$90,000
2002	**Affluent**, 4, 119	E. J. Delahoussaye	Royally Chosen, 4	Sea Reel, 4	6	1:42.60	$90,000
2001	**Chilukki**, 4, 119	G. L. Stevens	Spain, 4	Queenie Belle, 4	4	1:42.55	$90,000
2000	**Olympic Charmer**, 4, 119	C. J. McCarron	Her She Kisses, 4	Smooth Player, 4	7	1:42.71	$97,470
1999	**Manistique**, 4, 119	G. L. Stevens	Gourmet Girl, 4	Magical Allure, 4	3	1:43.10	$90,000
1998	**Fleet Lady**, 4, 117	G. K. Gomez	Minister's Melody, 4	I Ain't Bluffing, 4	6	1:43.04	$96,840
1997	**Belle's Flag**, 4, 119	C. S. Nakatani	Housa Dancer (Fr), 4	Listening, 4	9	1:41.61	$82,650
1996	**Jewel Princess**, 4, 117	A. O. Solis	Sleep Easy, 4	Urbane, 4	4	1:41.94	$78,800
1995	**Klassy Kim**, 4, 117	K. J. Desormeaux	Twice the Vice, 4	Crissy Aya, 4	5	1:42.43	$61,400
1994	**Supah Gem**, 4, 117	C. S. Nakatani	Sensational Eyes, 4	Stalcreek, 4	8	1:41.33	$64,500
1993	**Pacific Squall**, 4, 119	C. J. McCarron	Avian Assembly, 4	Magical Maiden, 4	7	1:45.67	$63,900
1992	**Exchange**, 4, 117	L. A. Pincay Jr.	Grand Girlfriend, 4	Damewood, 4	10	1:43.32	$67,000

Named for Rancho El Encino, one of the original Spanish ranchos located in western Los Angeles County. 1958-'67,1970 not held. 1954-'57,1974-'75 El Encino H.; 1968-'73 El Encino Claiming S. 1980-'89 Grade 3. 1955-'57 1¹/₄ miles; 1974-'75 1¹/₈ miles. 1955-'57 turf. 1954-'75 four-year-olds and up, both sexes. 1998 I Ain't Bluffing finished first, DQ to third.

Elkhorn Stakes

Grade 3, Keeneland, four-year-olds and up, 1¹/₂ miles, turf. Held April 23, 2003, with a gross value of $150,000. First held in 1986. Graded since 1988. Stakes record 2:27.84 (1999 African Dancer).

Year	Winner	Jockey	Second	Third	Strs	Time	1st Purse
2003	**Kim Loves Bucky**, 6, 117	K. J. Desormeaux	Man From Wicklow, 6	Williams News, 8	10	2:29.39	$93,000

2002	Kim Loves Bucky, 5, 116	J. F. Chavez	Rochester, 6	Cetewayo, 6	10	2:32.49	$93,000
2001	Williams News, 6, 116	R. Albarado	Gritty Sandie, 5	Craigsteel (GB), 6	9	2:29.13	$70,308
2000	Drama Critic, 4, 116	J. D. Bailey	Craigsteel (GB), 5	Dixie's Crown, 4	10	2:28.03	$69,750
1999	African Dancer, 7, 114	J. D. Bailey	Magest, 4	Chorwon, 6	8	2:27.84	$68,138
1998	African Dancer, 6, 114	J. D. Bailey	Chief Bearhart, 5	Chorwon, 5	5	2:31.71	$66,712
1997	Chief Bearhart, 4, 114	J. A. Santos	Snake Eyes, 7	Lassigny, 6	8	2:28.43	$68,324
1996	Vladivostok, 6, 112	P. Day	Penn Fifty Three, 4	Party Season (GB), 5	7	2:30.83	$68,262
1995	Marvin's Faith (Ire), 4, 123	C. Perret	Hasten To Add, 5	Opera Score, 4	10	1:47.10	$70,680
1994	Lure, 5, 123	M. E. Smith	Buckhar, 6	Pride of Summer, 6	5	1:53.76	$66,526
1993	Coaxing Matt, 4, 118	P. Day	Cleone, 4	Maxigroom, 5	9	1:47.64	$68,603
1992	Fourstars Allstar, 4, 113	J. D. Bailey	Slew the Slewor, 5	Rainbows for Life, 4	10	1:47.66	$72,995

Named for a large local creek, the Elkhorn, long used as a water source by Bluegrass farms. 1990-'95 Grade 2. 1986-'95 1 1/8 miles. 1995,1999 new course record.

Endine Stakes

Grade 3, Delaware Park, three-year-olds and up, fillies and mares, 6 furlongs, dirt. Held September 7, 2002, with a gross value of $150,000. First held in 1971. Graded since 2001. Stakes record 1:08.75 (1999 Hurricane Bertie).

Year	Winner	Jockey	Second	Third	Strs	Time	1st Purse
2002	Xtra Heat, 4, 121	H. Vega	Outstanding Info, 4	Urban Dancer, 4	5	1:10.91	$90,000
2001	Xtra Heat, 3, 118	R. Wilson	Ivy's Jewel, 4	Big Bambu, 4	5	1:09.64	$90,000
2000	Superduper Miss, 4, 114	T. G. Turner	Debby d'Or, 5	Cassidy, 5	7	1:10.22	$60,000
1999	Hurricane Bertie, 4, 117	P. Day	Little Sister, 5	Bourbon Belle, 4	4	1:08.75	$60,000
1998	Soverign Lady, 4, 115	M. E. Smith	Weather Vane, 4	Little Sister, 4	8	1:09.43	$45,000
1997	Dancin Renee, 5, 122	J. A. Velez Jr.	Two Punch Lil, 5	Ana Belen (Chi), 4	6	1:10.04	$30,000
1996	Hay Hanne, 4, 114	J. A. Velez Jr.	Know B's, 4	Ayrial Delight, 4	8	1:10.30	$22,770

Named for two-time Delaware H. winner Endine (1954, f. by *Rico Monte). 1983-'95 not held. 1971-'82 Endine H.

Essex Handicap

Grade 3, Oaklawn Park, four-year-olds and up, 1 1/16 miles, dirt. Held February 22, 2003, with a gross value of $100,000. First held in 1976. Graded since 1985. Stakes record 1:41 (1976 Navajo; 1987 Sun Master).

Year	Winner	Jockey	Second	Third	Strs	Time	1st Purse
2003	Colorful Tour, 4, 116	L. S. Quinonez	Ask the Lord, 6	Premeditation, 4	10	1:46.62	$60,000
2002	Crafty Shaw, 4, 116	J. Lopez	Kiss of Lion (Arg), 7	Remington Rock, 7	6	1:43.14	$45,000
2001	Mr Ross, 6, 117	D. R. Pettinger	Remington Rock, 7	Maysville Slew, 5	7	1:43.59	$45,000
2000	Maysville Slew, 4, 115	L. S. Quinonez	Sand Ridge, 5	Mr Ross, 7	7	1:44.12	$45,000
1999	Brush With Pride, 7, 116	T. T. Doocy	Littlebitlively, 5	Treat Me Doc, 5	7	1:43.26	$45,000
1998	Relic Reward, 4, 113	C. H. Borel	Phantom On Tour, 4	Brush With Pride, 6	7	1:43.92	$45,000
1997	No Spend No Glow, 5, 113	R. N. Lester	Illesam, 5	Auggie My Dad, 6	8	1:45.94	$45,000
1996	Classic Fit, 6, 114	C. Gonzalez	Judge T C, 5	Juliannus, 7	4	1:42.98	$47,700
1995	Silver Goblin, 4, 122	D. W. Cordova	Prince of the Mt., 4	Golden Gear, 4	7	1:42.10	$33,150
1994	Greatsilverfleet, 4, 116	G. K. Gomez	Prize Fight, 5	All Gone, 4	5	1:42.08	$32,250
1993	Delafield, 4, 113	P. Day	Famed Devil, 5	Yukon Robbery, 4	8	1:42.11	$33,900
1992	Allijeba, 6, 118	P. Day	On the Edge, 5	Bedeviled, 5	10	1:43.95	$34,500

Named for old Essex Park in Hot Springs. 1976-'86 1 mile 70 yards.

Excelsior Breeders' Cup Handicap

Grade 3, Aqueduct, three-year-olds and up, 1 1/8 miles, dirt. Held April 5, 2003, with a gross value of $170,000. First held in 1903. Graded since 1973. Stakes record 1:47.69 (1997 Ormsby).

Year	Winner	Jockey	Second	Third	Strs	Time	1st Purse
2003	Classic Endeavor, 5, 113	C. C. Lopez	Balto Star, 5	Tempest Fugit, 6	5	1:48.10	$90,000
2002	John Little, 4, 111	N. Arroyo Jr.	Windsor Castle, 4	Ground Storm, 4	6	1:49.25	$120,000
2001	Cat's At Home, 4, 115	F. Leon	Top Official, 6	Boston Party, 5	8	1:48.92	$120,000
2000	Lager, 6, 113	H. Castillo Jr.	Best of Luck, 4	Chester House, 5	9	1:49.76	$120,000
1999	Smart Coupons, 6, 114	R. R. Douglas	Archers Bay, 4	Pasay, 4	9	1:49.71	$120,000
1998	Sir Bear, 5, 117	E. M. Jurado	K. J's Appeal, 4	Accelerator, 4	8	1:49.24	$120,000
1997	Ormsby, 5, 116	C. C. Lopez	Greatsilverfleet, 7	Circle of Light, 4	9	1:47.69	$120,000
1996	May I Inquire, 7, 111	J. Bravo	Personal Merit, 5	Ormsby, 4	8	1:50.67	$120,000
1995	Iron Gavel, 5, 111	J. R. Martinez Jr.	Electrojet, 6	Danzig's Dance, 6	7	1:49.28	$90,000
1994	Colonial Affair, 4, 121	J. A. Santos	Contract Court, 4	West by West, 5	6	1:49.82	$90,000
1993	Devil His Due, 4, 117	M. E. Smith	Exotic Slew, 6	Bill Of Rights, 4	10	2:03.05	$72,120
1992	Defensive Play, 5, 117	D. R. Flores	Alyten, 4	Will to Reign, 5	5	2:01.95	$102,780

Named for the state motto of New York, "Excelsior," meaning "upward, ever upward." 1909,1911-'12,1914,1933,1967 not held. 1903-'95 Excelsior H. 1973-'97 Grade 2. 1903-'10,1915-'59 held at Jamaica. 1903-'59 1 1/4 miles; 1960 1 mile; 1979-'93 1 1/4 miles.

Explosive Bid Handicap

Grade 2, Fair Grounds, four-year-olds and up, about 1 1/8 miles, turf. Held March 23, 2003, with a gross value of $650,000. First held in 1992. Graded since 1996. Stakes record 1:48.88 (2002 Sarafan).

Year	Winner	Jockey	Second	Third	Strs	Time	1st Purse
2003	Candid Glen, 6, 114	E. J. Perrodin	Rouvres (Fr), 4	Freefourinternet, 5	11	1:51.15	$390,000
2002	Sarafan, 5, 116	C. S. Nakatani	Beat Hollow (GB), 5	Even the Score, 5	14	1:48.88	$420,000
2001	Tijiyr (Ire), 5, 110	R. Albarado	Northcote Road, 6	King Cugat, 4	13	1:50.72	$360,000
2000	Brave Act (GB), 6, 121	C. B. Asmussen	Where's Taylor, 4	Chester House, 5	13	1:48.98	$360,000
1999	Lord Smith (GB), 4, 117	G. K. Gomez	Hawksley Hill (Ire), 6	Chorwon, 6	12	1:51.27	$398,160

1998 **Joyeux Danseur**, 5, 121	R. Albarado	Martiniquais (Ire), 5	Hollie's Chief, 7	9	1:49.30	$223,980
1997 **Always a Classic**, 4, 114	E. M. Martin Jr.	Rainbow Blues (Ire), 4	Snake Eyes, 7	7	1:54.83	$131,970
1996 **Kazabaiyn**, 6, 113	K. J. Desormeaux	Party Season (GB), 5	Coaxing Matt, 7	10	1:50.80	$93,195
1995 **Earl of Barking (Ire)**, 5, 115	G. F. Almeida	Kazabaiyn, 5	Coaxing Matt, 6	11	1:52.01	$93,375
1994 **Snake Eyes**, 4, 115	B. E. Bartram	Yukon Robbery, 5	(DH) Dipotamos, 6	8	1:49.41	$76,305
			(DH) Cozzene's Prince, 7			
Pride of Summer, 6, 113	R. King Jr.	Alpine Choice, 6	Empire Pool (GB), 4	10	1:49.59	$76,425
1993 **Coaxing Matt**, 4, 114	E. M. Martin Jr.	Dixie Poker Ace, 6	Spending Record, 6	12	1:50.80	$47,010
1992 **Slick Groom**, 4, 112	K. P. LeBlanc	Little Bro Lantis, 4	Brownsboro, 8	10	1:52.60	$31,590

Named for 1984 Louisiana H. winner Explosive Bid (1978-'90, c. by Exploded). 1992-'94 Explosive Bid S. 1996-2000 Grade 3. 1994 two divisions. 1994 dead heat for third (2nd Div.). 1992 City Ballet finished first, DQ to sixth.

Fair Grounds Oaks
Grade 2, Fair Grounds, three-year-olds, fillies, 1¹/₁₆ miles, dirt. Held March 8, 2003, with a gross value of $350,000. First held in 1966. Graded since 1982. Stakes record 1:42.38 (1997 Blushing K. D.).

Year	Winner	Jockey	Second	Third	Strs	Time	1st Purse
2003	**Lady Tak**, 3, 121	D. J. Meche	Atlantic Ocean, 3	Belle of Perintown, 3	6	1:44.36	$210,000
2002	**Take Charge Lady**, 3, 121	A. J. D'Amico	Lake Lady, 3	Chamrousse, 3	8	1:43.30	$210,000
2001	**Real Cozzy**, 3, 121	E. M. Martin Jr.	Mystic Lady, 3	She's a Devil Due, 3	9	1:44.58	$210,000
2000	**Shawnee Country**, 3, 121	D. J. Meche	Eden Lodge, 3	Zoftig, 3	9	1:44.81	$210,000
1999	**Silverbulletday**, 3, 121	G. L. Stevens	Runaway Venus, 3	Brushed Halory, 3	7	1:44.99	$223,740
1998	**Lu Ravi**, 3, 121	W. Martinez	Well Chosen, 3	Silent Eskimo, 3	6	1:43.70	$180,000
1997	**Blushing K. D.**, 3, 121	L. Meche	Tomisue's Delight, 3	Cozy Blues, 3	5	1:42.38	$105,000
1996	**Bright Time**, 3, 112	L. F. Diaz	Mackie, 3	Proper Dance, 3	6	1:45.98	$94,530
1995	**Brushing Gloom**, 3, 112	J. Brown	Kuda, 3	Legendary Priness, 3	9	1:45.12	$90,000
1994	**Two Altazano**, 3, 112	K. P. LeBlanc	Tricky Code, 3	Minority Dater, 3	6	1:42.50	$93,840
1993	**Silky Feather**, 3, 112	E. J. Perrodin	She's a Little Shy, 3	Sum Runner, 3	7	1:44.60	$64,080
1992	**Prospectors Delite**, 3, 118	P. Day	Glitzi Bj, 3	Desert Radiance, 3	7	1:44.20	$63,990

1979 not held. 1989-'90 Coca-Cola Fair Grounds Oaks. 1982-2000 Grade 3. 1977-'78 1¹/₈ miles. 1978 three- and four-year-old fillies. 1994 equaled track record.

Fall Highweight Handicap
Grade 3, Aqueduct, three-year-olds and up, 6 furlongs, dirt. Held November 28, 2002, with a gross value of $100,000. First held in 1914. Graded since 1973. Stakes record 1:08.40 (1944 Ariel Lad; 1952 Hitex).

Year	Winner	Jockey	Second	Third	Strs	Time	1st Purse
2002	**True Direction**, 3, 134	J. Castellano	Crossing Point, 5	Gold I. D., 3	9	1:09.62	$66,960
2001	**Yonaguska**, 3, 131	J. A. Santos	Big E E, 4	Voodoo, 3	8	1:09.60	$67,320
2000	**Kashatreya**, 6, 131	O. Vergara	Exciting Story, 3	Oro de Mexico, 6	8	1:11.03	$67,140
1999	**Richter Scale**, 5, 134	J. F. Chavez	Aristotle, 3	Bought in Dixie, 3	5	1:09.05	$66,060
1998	**Punch Line**, 8, 136	J. F. Chavez	American Champ, 4	Golden Tent, 9	9	1:10.07	$66,840
1997	**Royal Haven**, 5, 136	R. Migliore	King Roller, 6	Kelly Kip, 3	7	1:10.68	$65,820
1996	**Victor Avenue**, 3, 127	J. F. Chavez	Splendid Sprinter, 4	Stalwart Member, 3	10	1:09.24	$67,440
1995	**Jess C's Mint**, 3, 131	J. F. Chavez	†Classy Mirage, 5	Demaloot Demashoot, 5	8	1:09.87	$66,180
1994	**Chimes Band**, 3, 135	J. D. Bailey	Golden Pro, 4	Boom Towner, 6	6	1:11.37	$65,940
1993	**Fly So Free**, 5, 137	J. D. Bailey	Demaloot Demashoot, 3	Take Me Out, 5	10	1:09.41	$72,360
1992	**Salt Lake**, 3, 128	M. E. Smith	Burn Fair, 5	Belong to Me, 3	6	1:09.07	$68,520

Traditionally held during the fall season originally with a mandatory top weight of 140 pounds. 1914-'20 Autumn Highweight H. 1976-2001 Grade 2. 1914-'59,1961,1969-'93 held at Belmont. 1914-'58 two-year-olds and up. †denotes female.

Falls City Handicap
Grade 2, Churchill Downs, three-year-olds and up, fillies and mares, 1¹/₈ miles, dirt. Held November 28, 2002, with a gross value of $250,000. First held in 1875. Graded since 1973. Stakes record 1:48.85 (1999 Silent Eskimo).

Year	Winner	Jockey	Second	Third	Strs	Time	1st Purse
2002	**Allamerican Bertie**, 3, 117	P. Day	Take Charge Lady, 3	Softly, 3	6	1:49.60	$167,400
2001	**Forest Secrets**, 3, 113	C. Perret	Printemps (Chi), 4	Unbridled Elaine, 3	7	1:49.49	$169,570
2000	**Bordelaise (Arg)**, 5, 117	P. Day	Spain, 3	On a Soapbox, 4	5	1:50.01	$168,020
1999	**Silent Eskimo**, 4, 117	C. H. Borel	Let, 4	Pleasant Temper, 5	8	1:48.85	$171,585
1998	**Tomisue's Delight**, 4, 121	S. J. Sellers	Top Secret, 5	Silent Eskimo, 3	8	1:51.05	$171,740
1997	**Feasibility Study**, 5, 122	M. E. Smith	Omi, 4	Naskra Colors, 5	8	1:50.65	$170,345
1996	**Halo America**, 6, 118	C. H. Borel	Bedroom Blues, 5	Debit My Account, 4	8	1:49.08	$171,120
1995	**Mariah's Storm**, 4, 120	R. N. Lester	Alcovy, 5	Heavenliness, 5	7	1:51.37	$143,390
1994	**Alcovy**, 4, 114	S. E. Miller	Pennyhill Park, 4	Hey Hazel, 5	7	1:51.16	$141,440
1993	**Gray Cashmere**, 4, 120	P. Day	Avie's Shadow, 3	Princess Polonia, 5	7	1:50.96	$142,090
1992	**Bungalow**, 5, 118	P. Day	Wilderness Song, 4	Auto Dial, 4	6	1:52.03	$70,915

Named for the early nickname of Louisville, "Falls City." 1878-'81,1885-'91,1893-1909,1928-'40 not held. 1973-2001 Grade 3. 1875-'77,1892,1941-'75 1 mile; 1882-'83 1½ miles; 1884,1919,1976-'81 1¹/₁₆ miles; 1910,1912-'18 6 furlongs. 1875-'77 three-year-olds, both sexes. 1882-'92 two-year-olds and up, both sexes. 1910-'26 both sexes.

Fantasy Stakes
Grade 2, Oaklawn Park, three-year-olds, fillies, 1¹/₁₆ miles, dirt. Held April 11, 2003, with a gross value of $200,000. First held in 1974. Graded since 1975. Stakes record 1:41.20 (1984 My Darling One).

Year	Winner	Jockey	Second	Third	Strs	Time	1st Purse
2003	**Ruby's Reception**, 3, 121	T. J. Thompson	Harbor Blues, 3	Go for Glamour, 3	6	1:44.61	$120,000

2002	**See How She Runs**, 3, 117	D. R. Pettinger	Lake Lady, 3	Chamrousse, 3	6	1:43.80	$120,000
2001	**Mystic Lady**, 3, 121	E. Coa	Collect Call, 3	Mysia Jo, 3	10	1:43.32	$120,000
2000	**Classy Cara**, 3, 121	I. Puglisi	Eden Lodge, 3	Gold for My Gal, 3	8	1:43.95	$120,000
1999	**Excellent Meeting**, 3, 121	K. J. Desormeaux	The Happy Hopper, 3	Dreams Gallore, 3	6	1:42.73	$150,000
1998	**Silent Eskimo**, 3, 117	C. Gonzalez	Misty Hour, 3	Came Unwound, 3	8	1:43.84	$150,000
1997	**Blushing K. D.**, 3, 121	L. Meche	Valid Bonnet, 3	Ajina, 3	5	1:42.61	$150,000
1996	**Escena**, 3, 117	P. Day	Antespend, 3	Ski Trail, 3	7	1:43.93	$150,000
1995	**Cat's Cradle**, 3, 121	C. W. Antley	Forever Cherokee, 3	Humble Eight, 3	8	1:44.29	$150,000
1994	**Two Altazano**, 3, 121	K. P. LeBlanc	Slide Show, 3	Flying in the Lane, 3	11	1:43.64	$150,000
1993	**Aztec Hill**, 3, 121	M. E. Smith	Adorydar, 3	Stalcreek, 3	7	1:44.33	$150,000
1992	**Race the Wild Wind**, 3, 117	C. J. McCarron	Golden Treat, 3	Now Dance, 3	8	1:43.74	$150,000

1978-'89 Grade 1. 1973 1 mile 70 yards.

Fastness Handicap

Grade 3, Hollywood Park, three-year-olds and up, 1¹⁄₈ miles, turf. Held May 13, 2001, with a gross value of $100,000. First held in 1997. Graded since 2000. Stakes record 1:46.50 (1999 Bonapartiste [Fr]).

Year	Winner	Jockey	Second	Third	Strs	Time	1st Purse
2001	**Irish Prize**, 5, 119	G. L. Stevens	Timboroa (GB), 5	City West (Arg), 5	8	1:50.01	$66,240
2000	**Senure**, 4, 114	B. Blanc	Bonapartiste (Fr), 6	Hook Call (Brz), 5	5	1:47.00	$64,020
1999	**Bonapartiste (Fr)**, 5, 121	C. J. McCarron	Alvo Certo (Brz), 6	Native Desert, 6	6	**1:46.50**	$45,990
1998	**Vetheuil**, 6, 113	B. Blanc	Via Lombardia (Ire), 6	Flick (GB), 6	9	1:34.52	$43,620
1997	**Helmsman**, 5, 123	C. J. McCarron	Smooth Runner, 6	Khoraz, 7	4	1:34.69	$42,800

Named for 1995 Citation H. (G2) winner Fastness (Ire) (1990, c. by Rousillon). 2002 not held. 1997-'98 1 mile.

Fayette Stakes

Grade 3, Keeneland, three-year-olds and up, 1¹⁄₈ miles, dirt. Held October 26, 2002, with a gross value of $150,000. First held in 1959. Graded since 1979. Stakes record 1:46.80 (1987 Good Command).

Year	Winner	Jockey	Second	Third	Strs	Time	1st Purse
2002	**Tenpins**, 4, 123	C. Perret	X Country, 4	Crafty Shaw, 4	4	1:51.17	$99,789
2001	**Connected**, 4, 119	M. St. Julien	Broken Vow, 4	Outofthebox, 3	9	1:50.05	$103,509
2000	**Jadada**, 5, 118	S. J. Sellers	Mojave Moon, 4	Get Away With It (Ire), 7	5	1:54.92	$133,176
1999	**Social Charter**, 4, 120	M. St. Julien	Master O Foxhounds, 4	Early Warning, 4	4	1:55.28	$135,904
1998	**Arch**, 3, 123	S. J. Sellers	Touch Gold, 4	Wild Tempest, 4	4	1:53.87	$98,394
1997	**Whiskey Wisdom**, 4, 115	W. Martinez	City by Night, 4	Pyramid Peak, 5	6	1:48.64	$101,184
1996	**Isitingood**, 5, 120	D. R. Flores	Distorted Humor, 3	Strawberry Wine, 4	8	1:50.42	$120,110
1995	**Judge T C**, 4, 114	J. M. Johnson	Powerful Punch, 6	Sir Vixen, 7	9	1:49.05	$104,625
1994	**Sunny Sunrise**, 7, 120	J. D. Carle	Key Contender, 6	Powerful Punch, 5	7	1:50.18	$67,766
1993	**Grand Jewel**, 3, 120	J. D. Bailey	Split Run, 5	Secreto's Hideaway, 4	8	1:46.87	$68,634
1992	**Barkerville**, 4, 114	S. J. Sellers	Medium Cool, 4	Majesterian, 4	11	1:48.43	$70,680

Named for Fayette County, Kentucky, in which Keeneland is located. 1959-'91 Fayette H.; 1999-2000 Fayette Breeders' Cup S. 1987-'96 Grade 2. 1963-'78 1¹⁄₁₆ miles; 1998-2000 1³⁄₁₆ miles. 1985 turf. 1993 equaled track record; 1998 new track record.

Fifth Season Stakes

Grade 3, Oaklawn Park, four-year-olds and up, 1¹⁄₁₆ miles, dirt. Held April 9, 2003, with a gross value of $100,000. First held in 1988. Graded since 1999. Stakes record 1:40.30 (1991 Hang on Slewpy).

Year	Winner	Jockey	Second	Third	Strs	Time	1st Purse
2003	**Patton's Victory**, 5, 117	A. Birzer	Colorful Tour, 4	Makors Mark, 6	7	1:43.26	$60,000
2001	**Remington Rock**, 7, 114	D. E. Simington	Kombat Kat, 4	Da Devil, 4	7	1:43.13	$45,000
2000	**Mr Ross**, 5, 115	E. C. Perner	Relic Reward, 6	Crimson Classic, 6	7	1:42.93	$60,000
1999	**Truluck**, 4, 114	L. Melancon	Slide to the Left, 4	Rock and Roll, 4	8	1:42.28	$60,000
1998	**Acceptable**, 4, 117	A. O. Solis	Littlebitlively, 4	Brush With Pride, 6	8	1:42.50	$60,000
1997	**Krigeorj's Gold**, 4, 119	J. M. Johnson	Bucks Nephew, 7	Prince of the Mt., 6	9	1:43.35	$49,050
1996	**No Spend No Glow**, 4, 117	R. N. Lester	Bucks Nephew, 6	Groovy Jett, 5	7	1:42.96	$47,880
1995	**Tyus**, 5, 114	C. H. Borel	Prince of the Mt., 4	Joseph's Robe, 4	7	1:42.98	$26,760
1994	**Nelson**, 7, 117	S. P. Romero	Punch Line, 4	Senor Tomas, 5	6	1:43.16	$41,640
1993	**Delafield**, 4, 117	J. A. Santos	Far Out Wadleigh, 5	Lanyons Star, 5	11	1:42.43	$43,080
1992	**Medium Cool**, 4, 117	C. S. Nakatani	On the Edge, 5	Hayes G., 5	10	1:43.35	$40,500

Named for Hot Springs, Arkansas's "fifth season," the Oaklawn Park meet. 2002 not held. 1989-2001 Fifth Season Breeders' Cup S. 1989-2001 three-year-olds and up.

Firecracker Breeders' Cup Handicap

Grade 2, Churchill Downs, three-year-olds and up, 1 mile, turf. Held July 4, 2002, with a gross value of $250,000. First held in 1983. Graded since 1995. Stakes record 1:33.78 (1995 Jaggery John).

Year	Winner	Jockey	Second	Third	Strs	Time	1st Purse
2002	**Good Journey**, 6, 118	P. Day	Morluc, 6	Even the Score, 4	9	1:34.83	$181,350
2001	**Irish Prize**, 5, 122	G. L. Stevens	Aly's Alley, 5	Where's Taylor, 5	7	1:34.68	$175,770
2000	**Conserve**, 4, 116	S. J. Sellers	Riviera (Fr), 6	King Slayer (GB), 5	8	1:35.12	$177,940
1999	**Joe Who (Brz)**, 6, 113	R. Albarado	Middlesex Drive, 4	Wild Event, 6	9	1:36.78	$132,680
1998	**Claire's Honor**, 4, 109	A. J. D'Amico	Soviet Line (Ire), 8	Optic Nerve, 5	9	1:35.93	$177,630
1997	**Soviet Line (Ire)**, 7, 114	P. Day	Volochine (Ire), 6	Same Old Wish, 7	10	1:37.67	$126,077

Year	Winner	Jockey	Second	Third	Strs	Time	1st Purse
1996	**Rare Reason**, 5, 115	P. A. Johnson	Artema (Ire), 5	Wavy Run (Ire), 5	9	1:33.81	$131,950
1995	**Jaggery John**, 4, 113	D. Kutz	Rare Reason, 4	Fly Cry, 4	10	**1:33.78**	$74,360
1994	**First and Only**, 7, 118	T. J. Hebert	†Weekend Madness (Ire), 4	Avid Affection, 5	8	1:35.33	$73,580
1993	**Cleone**, 4, 115	C. Perret	Magesterial Cheer, 5	Harlan, 4	9	1:35.90	$74,815

Traditionally held during the July 4th holiday. 1986-'92 not held. 1983-'95 Firecracker H. 1995-'99 Grade 3. 1983-'85 7 furlongs. 1983-'85 dirt. 1995 new course record. 2001 Where's Taylor finished second, DQ to third. †denotes female.

First Flight Handicap

Grade 2, Aqueduct, three-year-olds and up, fillies and mares, 7 furlongs, dirt. Held October 26, 2002, with a gross value of $150,000. First held in 1978. Graded since 1982. Stakes record 1:20.65 (1992 Shared Interest).

Year	Winner	Jockey	Second	Third	Strs	Time	1st Purse
2002	**Shine Again**, 5, 117	J-L. Samyn	Redhead Riot, 3	Raging Fever, 3	5	1:23.75	$90,000
2001	**Shine Again**, 4, 116	J-L. Samyn	Dream Supreme, 4	Kalookan Queen, 5	6	1:23.21	$90,000
2000	**Country Hideaway**, 4, 117	J. L. Espinoza	Go to the Ink, 4	Cat Cay, 3	7	1:22.60	$90,000
1999	**Country Hideaway**, 3, 114	H. Castillo Jr.	Harpia, 5	Anklet, 5	8	1:23.00	$90,000
1998	**Catinca**, 3, 116	R. Migliore	Glitter Woman, 4	Blue Begonia, 5	7	1:22.14	$82,260
1997	**Dixie Flag**, 3, 113	M. J. Luzzi	Silent City, 3	Aldiza, 3	4	1:22.84	$64,800
1996	**Thunder Achiever**, 3, 112	R. G. Davis	Miss Golden Circle, 4	Call Account, 4	10	1:21.59	$81,864
1995	**Twist Afleet**, 4, 121	G. L. Stevens	Igotrhythm, 3	Lottsa Talc, 5	5	1:22.95	$66,780
1994	**Twist Afleet**, 3, 117	J. D. Bailey	Ann Dear, 4	Incinerate, 4	8	1:23.02	$66,120
1993	**Raise Heck**, 5, 114	R. I. Velez	Regal Victress, 6	Shared Interest, 5	6	1:23.51	$69,000
1992	**Shared Interest**, 4, 111	J. D. Bailey	Missy's Mirage, 4	Nannerl, 5	5	**1:20.65**	$120,000

Named for C. V. Whitney's 1946 champion two-year-old filly First Flight (1944-'75, f. by *Mahmoud). 1995 I Love New York First Flight H. 1982-'89 Grade 3. 1990,1992,1995, 2001 held at Belmont.

First Lady Handicap

Grade 3, Gulfstream Park, three-year-olds and up, fillies and mares, 6 furlongs, dirt. Held January 12, 2003, with a gross value of $100,000. First held in 1981. Graded since 1993. Stakes record 1:09.60 (1999 Scotzanna).

Year	Winner	Jockey	Second	Third	Strs	Time	1st Purse
2003	**Harmony Lodge**, 5, 113	J. R. Velazquez	Fly Me Crazy, 5	Haunted Lass, 4	7	1:10.31	$60,000
2002	**Raging Fever**, 4, 118	J. R. Velazquez	Cat Cay, 5	Mandy's Gold, 4	7	1:10.36	$60,000
2001	**Another**, 4, 113	E. S. Prado	Curious Treasures, 4	Dynamite Diablo, 4	11	1:10.41	$60,000
2000	**Hurricane Bertie**, 5, 118	P. Day	Marley Vale, 4	Cassidy, 5	7	1:10.22	$45,000
1999	**Scotzanna**, 7, 114	R. Migliore	U Can Do It, 6	Foil, 4	8	**1:09.60**	$45,000
1998	**U Can Do It**, 5, 115	S. J. Sellers	Start At Once, 5	Vivace, 5	10	1:09.86	$45,000
1997	**Chip**, 4, 113	J. Bravo	Phone the Doctor, 5	Surprising Fact, 4	10	1:09.76	$45,000
1996	**Chaposa Springs**, 4, 122	J. D. Bailey	Phone the Doctor, 4	Market Slide, 5	9	1:10.23	$45,000
1995	**Recognizable**, 4, 113	M. E. Smith	Insight to Cope, 5	Maison de Reve, 5	10	1:09.74	$30,000
1994	**Santa Catalina**, 6, 114	J. D. Bailey	Insight to Cope, 4	Capture the Crown, 5	11	1:11.26	$30,000
1993	**Si Si Sezyou**, 5, 112	R. Hernandez	Illeria, 6	Jeano, 5	11	1:10.06	$30,000
1992	**Withallprobability**, 4, 118	C. Perret	Christina Czarina, 4	Spirit of Fighter, 9	14	1:11.14	$30,000

Named for either the United States president's wife or as an apt name for a race for fillies and mares. 1982,1984 not held. 1990 First Lady Breeders' Cup H.

Flash Stakes

Grade 3, Belmont Park, two-year-olds, 5 furlongs, dirt. Held June 7, 2002, with a gross value of $100,000. First held in 1869. Graded since 2001. Stakes record :56.93 (2001 Buster's Daydream).

Year	Winner	Jockey	Second	Third	Strs	Time	1st Purse
2002	**Whywhywhy**, 2, 114	E. S. Prado	Presence, 2	Down Play, 2	7	:57.10	$65,460
2001	**Buster's Daydream**, 2, 115	E. S. Prado	Harmony Hall, 2	Huber Woods, 2	8	**:56.93**	$49,365
2000	**Yonaguska**, 2, 115	J. D. Bailey	The Goo, 2	City Zip, 2	7	:57.86	$49,470
1999	**More Than Ready**, 2, 119	J. R. Velazquez	Diablo's Addition, 2	Bevo, 2	6	:57.10	$49,245

1896,1898-1900,1911-'12,1960,1972-'80,1983-'98 not held. 1869-1942,1946-'71 held at Saratoga. 1869-'97 4 furlongs; 1902-'68,1981-'82 5½ furlongs; 1969-'76 6 furlongs. 1981-'82 colts and geldings.

Fleur de Lis Handicap

Grade 2, Churchill Downs, three-year-olds and up, fillies and mares, 1⅛ miles, dirt. Held June 15, 2002, with a gross value of $300,000. First held in 1975. Graded since 1988. Stakes record 1:48.26 (2000 Heritage of Gold).

Year	Winner	Jockey	Second	Third	Strs	Time	1st Purse
2002	**Spain**, 5, 121	J. F. Chavez	With Ability, 4	Dancethruthedawn, 4	6	1:49.64	$204,228
2001	**Saudi Poetry**, 4, 114	V. Espinoza	Secret Status, 4	Asher, 4	8	1:49.27	$206,460
2000	**Heritage of Gold**, 5, 121	S. J. Sellers	Silverbulletday, 4	Roza Robata, 5	5	**1:48.26**	$201,252
1999	**Banshee Breeze**, 4, 124	R. Albarado	Silent Eskimo, 4	Meadow Vista, 4	4	1:50.02	$197,718
1998	**Escena**, 5, 123	S. J. Sellers	One Rich Lady, 4	Tomisue's Delight, 4	5	1:50.19	$199,020
1997	**Gold n Delicious**, 4, 113	C. H. Borel	Effectiveness, 4	Everhope, 4	10	1:52.87	$104,718
1996	**Serena's Song**, 4, 124	G. L. Stevens	Halo America, 6	Alcovy, 6	9	1:50.30	$109,493
1995	**Fit to Lead**, 5, 115	S. J. Sellers	Pennyhill Park, 4	Low Key Affair, 4	7	1:51.59	$107,055
1994	**Trishyde**, 5, 117	C. J. McCarron	Eskimo's Angel, 5	Ma Guerre, 4	8	1:51.34	$107,315
1993	**Quilma (Chi)**, 6, 117	R. P. Romero	Fappies Cosy Miss, 5	Hitch, 4	6	1:50.80	$71,240

| 1992 | Bungalow, 5, 114 | F. C. Torres | Til Forbid, 4 | Beth Believes, 6 | 12 | 1:50.87 | $74,815 |

Named for the fleur de lis (the lily), symbol of the city of Louisville. 1988-2001 Grade 3. 1975-'76 1 mile; 1977-'82 1 1/16 miles. 1983-'85,1987-'89 four-year-olds and up.

Floral Park Handicap

Grade 3, Belmont Park, three-year-olds and up, fillies and mares, 6 furlongs, dirt. Held September 14, 2002, with a gross value of $100,000. First held in 1995. Graded since 2002. Stakes record 1:09.20 (1995 Twist Afleet).

Year	Winner	Jockey	Second	Third	Strs	Time	1st Purse
2002	Carson Hollow, 3, 117	J. R. Velazquez	Gold Mover, 4	Shiny Band, 4	4	1:10.25	$63,955
2001	Gold Mover, 3, 114	E. S. Prado	Dat You Miz Blue, 4	Finder's Fee, 4	6	1:10.03	$65,040
2000	Big Bambu, 3, 114	R. G. Davis	Tropical Punch, 4	Cash Run, 3	5	1:09.81	$64,620
1999	Positive Gal, 3, 113	J. D. Bailey	Final Proposal, 4	Flamingo Way, 5	7	1:09.23	$49,125
1998	Blue Begonia, 5, 114	J. F. Chavez	Dixie Flag, 4	Soverign Lady, 4	5	1:10.30	$48,570
1997	Creamy Dreamy, 4, 118	J. F. Chavez	Silent City, 3	Secret Prospect, 4	5	1:10.56	$47,835
1996	Lottsa Talc, 6, 119	F. T. Alvarado	Fresa, 4	Culver City, 4	5	1:09.81	$38,736
1995	Twist Afleet, 4, 120	G. L. Stevens	For all Seasons, 5	Regal Solution, 5	6	1:09.20	$32,490

Named after a community in Nassau County, Long Island, near Belmont Park.

Florida Derby

Grade 1, Gulfstream Park, three-year-olds, 1 1/8 miles, dirt. Held March 15, 2003, with a gross value of $1,000,000. First held in 1952. Graded since 1973. Stakes record 1:46.80 (1957 Gen. Duke).

Year	Winner	Jockey	Second	Third	Strs	Time	1st Purse
2003	Empire Maker, 3, 122	J. D. Bailey	Trust N Luck, 3	Indy Dancer, 3	7	1:49.05	$600,000
2002	Harlan's Holiday, 3, 122	E. S. Prado	Blue Burner, 3	Peekskill, 3	11	1:48.80	$600,000
2001	Monarchos, 3, 122	J. F. Chavez	Outofthebox, 3	Invisible Ink, 3	13	1:49.95	$600,000
2000	Hal's Hope, 3, 122	R. I. Velez	High Yield, 3	Tahkodha Hills, 3	10	1:51.49	$450,000
1999	Vicar, 3, 122	S. J. Sellers	Wondertross, 3	Cat Thief, 3	10	1:50.83	$450,000
1998	Cape Town, 3, 122	S. J. Sellers	Lil's Lad, 3	Halory Hunter, 3	6	1:49.21	$450,000
1997	Captain Bodgit, 3, 122	A. O. Solis	Pulpit, 3	Frisk Me Now, 3	8	1:50.74	$300,000
1996	Unbridled's Song, 3, 122	M. E. Smith	Editor's Note, 3	Skip Away, 3	9	1:47.85	$300,000
1995	Thunder Gulch, 3, 122	M. E. Smith	Suave Prospect, 3	Mecke, 3	10	1:49.70	$300,000
1994	Holy Bull, 3, 122	M. E. Smith	Ride the Rails, 3	Halo's Image, 3	14	1:47.66	$300,000
1993	Bull Inthe Heather, 3, 122	W. S. Ramos	Storm Tower, 3	Wallenda, 3	13	1:51.38	$300,000
1992	Technology, 3, 122	J. D. Bailey	Dance Floor, 3	Pistols and Roses, 3	12	1:50.72	$300,000

1998 Lil's Lad finished first, DQ to second.

Florida Oaks

Grade 3, Tampa Bay Downs, three-year-olds, fillies, 1 1/16 miles, dirt. Held March 16, 2003, with a gross value of $150,000. First held in 1984. Graded since 1996. Stakes record 1:44.60 (1986 Noranc).

Year	Winner	Jockey	Second	Third	Strs	Time	1st Purse
2003	Ebony Breeze, 3, 120	M. Guidry	Dakota Light, 3	Crimson and Roses, 3	6	1:45.20	$90,000
2002	French Satin, 3, 118	R. A. Dominguez	Romancin Dixie, 3	Ciudad de Carson, 3	11	1:45.49	$90,000
2001	Quick Tip, 3, 116	R. Migliore	Southern Fiction, 3	Emery Board, 3	9	1:45.36	$90,000
2000	Secret Status, 3, 118	P. Day	March Magic, 3	Musical, 3	8	1:45.05	$75,000
1999	Crown Jewel, 3, 118	L. J. Martinez	Madison's Charm, 3	Here I Go, 3	8	1:46.69	$60,000
1998	Pantufla, 3, 114	P. Day	Puddlejump, 3	Try N Sue, 3	11	1:45.40	$60,000
1997	Anklet, 3, 118	S. J. Sellers	Global Star, 3	Screamer, 3	10	1:45.60	$60,000
1996	Mindy Gayle, 3, 118	J. A. Guerra	Plum Country, 3	Weekend in Seattle, 3	7	1:45.80	$60,000
1995	Sneaky Quiet, 3, 121	M. E. Smith	Commando Dancer, 3	Smooth Quest, 3	6	1:45.40	$60,000
1994	Cavada, 3, 118	K. Whitley	Come On Joy, 3	Strategic Maneuver, 3	7	1:46.40	$60,000
1993	Star Jolie, 3, 111	E. O. Nunez	Hollywood Wildcat, 3	Jacody, 3	11	1:45.60	$60,000
1992	Luv Me Luv Me Not, 3, 121	W. Martinez	Now Dance, 3	Foxy Persuasion, 3	8	1:45.60	$60,000

1984 7 furlongs.

Flower Bowl Invitational Stakes

Grade 1, Belmont Park, three-year-olds and up, fillies and mares, 1 1/4 miles, turf. Held September 28, 2002, with a gross value of $750,000. First held in 1978. Graded since 1980. Stakes record 1:59.33 (1998 Auntie Mame).

Year	Winner	Jockey	Second	Third	Strs	Time	1st Purse
2002	Kazzia (Ger), 3, 118	J. F. Chavez	Turtle Bow (Fr), 3	Mot Juste (GB), 3	7	2:05.22	$450,000
2001	Lailani (GB), 3, 118	J. D. Bailey	England's Legend (Fr), 4	Starine (Fr), 4	6	2:01.88	$450,000
2000	Colstar, 4, 116	J-L. Samyn	Snow Polina, 5	Pico Teneriffe, 5	5	2:01.78	$450,000
1999	Soaring Softly, 4, 118	J. D. Bailey	Coretta (Ire), 5	Mossflower, 5	7	2:01.41	$300,000
1998	Auntie Mame, 4, 121	J. R. Velazquez	B. A. Valentine, 4	Bahr (GB), 5	5	1:59.33	$240,000
1997	Yashmak, 3, 114	C. S. Nakatani	Maxzene, 4	Memories of Silver, 4	8	1:59.73	$240,000
1996	Chelsey Flower, 5, 115	R. G. Davis	Powder Bowl, 4	Electric Society (Ire), 4	10	2:05.96	$210,000
1995	Northern Emerald, 5, 113	R. B. Perez	Danish (Ire), 4	Duda, 4	10	2:06.68	$120,000
1994	Dahlia's Dreamer, 5, 112	J. F. Chavez	Alywow, 3	Danish (Ire), 3	12	2:05.52	$120,000
1993	Far Out Beast, 6, 111	J-L. Samyn	Dahlia's Dreamer, 4	Lady Blessington (Fr), 4	10	2:03.88	$90,000
1992	Christiecat, 5, 116	J-L. Samyn	Ratings, 4	Plenty of Grace, 4	9	2:01.06	$120,000

Named for Brookmeade Stable's 1956 Ladies H. winner Flower Bowl (1952-'68, f. by *Alibhai), dam of champion Bowl of Flowers and sires Graustark and His Majesty. 1978-'93 Flower Bowl H. 1980-'81 Grade 2. 1987 dirt.

Forego Handicap

Grade 1, Saratoga Race Course, three-year-olds and up, 6½ furlongs, dirt. Held September 1, 2002, with a gross value of $250,000. First held in 1980. Graded since 1983. Stakes record 1:15 (2000 Shadow Caster).

Year	Winner	Jockey	Second	Third	Strs	Time	1st Purse
2002	Orientate, 4, 122	J. D. Bailey	Aldebaran, 4	Multiple Choice, 4	8	1:15.68	$150,000
2001	Delaware Township, 5, 116	J. D. Bailey	Left Bank, 4	Alannan, 5	9	1:15.53	$150,000
2000	Shadow Caster, 4, 113	J. F. Chavez	Intidab, 7	Successful Appeal, 4	10	**1:15.00**	$150,000
1999	Crafty Friend, 6, 119	G. L. Stevens	Affirmed Success, 5	Sir Bear, 6	9	1:21.32	$150,000
1998	Affirmed Success, 4, 115	J. F. Chavez	Receiver, 5	Purple Passion, 4	4	1:21.98	$120,000
1997	Score a Birdie, 6, 113	W. H. McCauley	Victor Cooley, 4	Royal Haven, 5	8	1:22.47	$120,000
1996	Langfuhr, 4, 110	J. F. Chavez	Top Account, 4	Lite the Fuse, 5	7	1:21.90	$90,000
1995	Not Surprising, 5, 121	R. G. Davis	Our Emblem, 4	Lite the Fuse, 4	4	1:21.91	$64,200
1994	American Chance, 5, 113	P. Day	Evil Bear, 4	Go for Gin, 3	7	1:22.74	$66,000
1993	Birdonthewire, 4, 117	M. E. Smith	Harlan, 4	Senor Speedy, 6	9	1:21.88	$73,080
1992	Rubiano, 5, 124	J. A. Krone	Drummond Lane, 5	Diablo, 5	8	1:22.54	$70,080

Named for 1974, '75, '76 Horse of the Year Forego (1970-'97, g. by *Forli). 1983 Grade 3; 1984-2000 Grade 2. 1980-'81 held at Belmont. 1980-'81 1 mile; 1982-'99 7 furlongs.

Forest Hills Handicap

Grade 2, Belmont Park, three-year-olds and up, 6 furlongs, dirt. Held October 6, 2002, with a gross value of $250,000. First held in 1975. Graded since 1984. Stakes record 1:07.66 (1999 Artax).

Year	Winner	Jockey	Second	Third	Strs	Time	1st Purse
2002	Avanzado (Arg), 5, 116	T. Baze	Dash for Daylight, 5	Esteemed Friend, 5	7	1:11.00	$150,000
2001	Delaware Township, 5, 118	E. Coa	Hook and Ladder, 4	Yonaguska, 3	5	1:09.49	$150,000
2000	Delaware Township, 4, 114	P. Day	Bevo, 3	Valiant Halory, 3	7	1:08.56	$150,000
1999	Artax, 4, 120	J. F. Chavez	Good and Tough, 4	Intidab, 6	7	**1:07.66**	$150,000
1998	Punch Line, 8, 118	J. F. Chavez	King Roller, 7	Johnny Legit, 4	7	1:09.67	$120,000
1997	Kelly Kip, 3, 111	J-L. Samyn	Crafty Friend, 4	Royal Haven, 5	11	1:08.83	$120,000
1996	Lord Carson, 4, 116	S. J. Sellers	Honour and Glory, 3	Splendid Sprinter, 4	9	1:08.72	$105,000
1995	Friendly Lover, 7, 118	R. Wilson	Lite the Fuse, 4	Mining Burrah, 5	11	1:10.13	$86,100
1994	Meritocrat, 3, 113	M. E. Smith	Birdonthewire, 5	Lite the Fuse, 3	8	1:09.03	$83,025
1993	Boom Towner, 5, 113	F. Lovato Jr.	Take Me Out, 5	Thelastcrusade, 4	7	1:09.29	$69,360
1992	Belong to Me, 3, 112	M. E. Smith	Diablo, 5	Fast Turn, 5	9	1:10.05	$71,280

Named for a neighborhood in Queens, New York. 1975-'96 Boojum H. 1984-'93 Grade 3. 1992-'93 held at Aqueduct. 1999 new track record.

Fort Marcy Handicap

Grade 3, Aqueduct, three-year-olds and up, 1 mile (originally scheduled at 1¹⁄₁₆ miles on the turf), dirt. Held April 26, 2003, with a gross value of $117,500. First held in 1975. Graded since 1980. Stakes record 1:40.88 (2000 Spindrift [Ire]).

Year	Winner	Jockey	Second	Third	Strs	Time	1st Purse
2003	Saint Verre, 5, 117	J. L. Espinoza	Windsor Castle, 5	Judge's Case, 6	8	1:33.77	$70,500
2002	Pyrus, 4, 113	E. S. Prado	Proud Man, 4	Capsized, 4	8	1:44.53	$67,260
2001	Strategic Mission, 6, 118	R. Migliore	Pine Dance, 4	Legal Jousting (Ire), 4	9	1:41.62	$67,740
2000	Spindrift (Ire), 5, 115	J-L. Samyn	Middlesex Drive, 6	Wised Up, 5	9	**1:40.88**	$67,680
1999	Wised Up, 4, 112	M. J. Luzzi	N B Forrest, 7	La-Faah (Ire), 4	11	1:45.03	$69,660
1998	Subordination, 4, 118	J. F. Chavez	Fortitude, 5	Crimson Guard, 6	6	1:35.24	$67,620
1997	Influent, 6, 117	J-L. Samyn	Slicious (GB), 5	Montjoy, 5	8	1:47.59	$67,440
1996	Warning Glance, 5, 119	M. E. Smith	Shahid (GB), 4	Grand Continental, 5	10	1:42.48	$51,450
1995	Fourstars Allstar, 7, 118	J. A. Santos	Chief Master, 5	A in Sociology, 5	8	1:41.69	$50,250
1994	Adam Smith (GB), 6, 118	M. E. Smith	Halissee, 4	Nijinsky's Gold, 5	7	1:42.49	$49,650
1993	Adam Smith (GB), 5, 112	J-L. Samyn	Kiri's Clown, 4	Casino Magistrate, 4	11	1:42.30	$55,260
1992	Maxigroom, 4, 111	J. A. Krone	Colchis Island (Ire), 7	Buchman, 5	6	1:42.66	$53,460

Named for Rokeby Stable's 1970 Horse of the Year Fort Marcy (1964-'91, g. by *Amerigo). 1976-'77 not held. 1975, 1981, 1987-'88 held at Belmont. 1975 7 furlongs; 1998 1 mile. 1998 dirt.

Fountain of Youth Stakes

Grade 1, Gulfstream Park, three-year-olds, 1¹⁄₁₆ miles, dirt. Held February 15, 2003, with a gross value of $200,000. First held in 1945. Graded since 1973. Stakes record 1:41 (1978 Sensitive Prince).

Year	Winner	Jockey	Second	Third	Strs	Time	1st Purse
2003	Trust N Luck, 3, 122	C. H. Velasquez	Supah Blitz, 3	Midway Cat, 3	8	1:43.33	$120,000
2002	Booklet, 3, 122	J. F. Chavez	Harlan's Holiday, 3	Blue Burner, 3	8	1:44.49	$120,000
2001	Songandaprayer, 3, 117	E. S. Prado	Outofthebox, 3	City Zip, 3	11	1:43.48	$120,000
2000	High Yield, 3, 117	P. Day	Hal's Hope, 3	Elite Mercedes, 3	11	1:42.56	$120,000
1999	Vicar, 3, 114	S. J. Sellers	Cat Thief, 3	Certain, 3	10	1:45.64	$120,000
1998	Lil's Lad, 3, 112	J. D. Bailey	Coronado's Quest, 3	Halory Hunter, 3	4	1:42.63	$120,000
1997	Pulpit, 3, 112	S. J. Sellers	Blazing Sword, 3	Captain Bodgit, 3	9	1:41.86	$120,000
1996	Built for Pleasure, 3, 112	G. Boulanger	Unbridled's Song, 3	Victory Speech, 3	9	1:43.64	$120,000
1995	Thunder Gulch, 3, 119	M. E. Smith	Suave Prospect, 3	Jambalaya Jazz, 3	12	1:43.21	$120,000

1994	Dehere, 3, 119	C. Perret	Go for Gin, 3	Ride the Rails, 3	6	1:44.70	$120,000
1993	Duc d'Sligovil, 3, 112	J. A. Krone	Bull Inthe Heather, 3	Silver of Silver, 3	9	1:45.16	$113,094
	Storm Tower, 3, 113	R. Wilson	Great Navigator, 3	Kissin Kris, 3	9	1:44.98	$113,094
1992	Dance Floor, 3, 122	C. W. Antley	Pistols and Roses, 3	Tiger Tiger, 3	11	1:45.32	$150,258

Named for the mythical spring sought by Spanish explorer Ponce de Leon in Florida. 1946,1948,1952 not held. 1947 held twice. 1947-'56,1958 Fountain of Youth H. 1973-'81 Grade 3; 1982-'98 Grade 2. 1945,1947 1 mile 70 yards; 1947 6 furlongs. 1945-'47 two-year-olds. 1993 two divisions. 1992 Careful Gesture finished second, DQ to fifth.

Fourstardave Handicap

Grade 3, Saratoga Race Course, three-year-olds and up, 1 1/8 miles, dirt. Held August 24, 2002, with a gross value of $200,000. First held in 1985. Graded since 1988. Stakes record 1:50.90 (2002 Capsized).

Year	Winner	Jockey	Second	Third	Strs	Time	1st Purse
2002	Capsized, 6, 115	J. A. Santos	Pure Prize, 4	Pyrus, 4	5	1:50.90	$120,000
2001	Dr. Kashnikow, 4, 113	J. R. Velazquez	Tubrok, 4	Aly's Alley, 5	12	1:39.30	$120,000
2000	Hap, 4, 118	J. D. Bailey	Altibr, 5	Weatherbird, 5	11	1:40.24	$120,000
1999	Comic Strip, 4, 115	P. Day	Divide and Conquer, 5	Bornfim, 6	11	1:41.76	$90,000
1998	Wild Event, 5, 116	M. Guidry	Bornfim, 5	Rob 'n Gin, 4	11	1:39.25	$68,940
1997	Soviet Line (Ire), 7, 118	P. Day	Val's Prince, 4	Outta My Way Man, 5	7	1:39.99	$67,500
1996	Da Hoss, 4, 113	J. R. Velazquez	Green Means Go, 4	Rare Reason, 5	13	1:40.54	$71,100
1995	Pride of Summer, 7, 115	E. Maple	Fourstars Allstar, 7	Jaggery John, 4	8	1:40.85	$69,240
1994	A in Sociology, 4, 115	J-L. Samyn	Namaqualand, 4	Fourstars Allstar, 6	9	1:41.23	$68,340
1993	Lure, 4, 122	M. E. Smith	Fourstardave, 8	Scott the Great, 7	6	1:40.84	$72,120
1992	Now Listen, 5, 119	J. R. Velazquez	Crackedbell, 7	Cold Hoist, 4	5	1:36.64	$71,640

Named for multiple graded stakes winner and local favorite Fourstardave (1985-2002, g. by Compliance), who won a race at Saratoga for eight consecutive years. 1985-'93,1995 Daryl's Joy S.; 1994 Daryl's Joy H.; 1996-'97 Fourstardave S. 1988-'99 Grade 3. 1985-'91,1993-2001 1 1/16 miles; 1992 1 mile. 1985-'91,1993-2001 turf.

Frank E. Kilroe Mile Handicap

Grade 2, Santa Anita Park, four-year-olds and up, 1 mile, turf. Held March 1, 2003, with a gross value of $400,000. First held in 1955. Graded since 1973. Stakes record 1:31.89 (1997 Atticus [new course and world record]).

Year	Winner	Jockey	Second	Third	Strs	Time	1st Purse
2003	Redattore (Brz), 8, 120	A. O. Solis	Good Journey, 7	Decarchy, 6	11	1:34.94	$240,000
2002	Decarchy, 5, 119	K. J. Desormeaux	Sarafan, 5	Designed for Luck, 5	11	1:34.04	$180,000
2001	Road to Slew, 6, 117	L. A. Pincay Jr.	Val Royal (Fr), 5	(DH) Exchange Rate, 5	10	1:35.96	$240,000
				(DH) Hawksley Hill (Ire), 8			
2000	Commitisize, 5, 112	V. Espinoza	Chullo (Arg), 6	Sultry Substitute, 6	6	1:36.61	$120,000
1999	Lord Smith (GB), 4, 116	G. K. Gomez	Hawksley Hill (Ire), 6	Ladies Din, 6	6	1:34.53	$90,000
1998	Hawksley Hill (Ire), 5, 115	P. Day	Via Lombardia (Ire), 6	A Magicman (Fr), 6	10	1:34.84	$101,190
1997	Atticus, 5, 117	C. S. Nakatani	Pinfloron (Fr), 5	Rainbow Blues (Ire), 5	6	1:31.89	$97,400
1996	Tychonic (GB), 6, 116	G. L. Stevens	Debutant Trick, 6	Silver Wizard, 6	8	1:35.52	$99,400
1995	College Town, 4, 117	L. A. Pincay Jr.	Romarin (Brz), 5	Finder's Fortune, 5	5	1:40.62	$63,800
1994	Megan's Interco, 5, 118	C. A. Black	Tinners Way, 4	Ibero (Arg), 4	7	1:33.86	$64,400
1993	Leger Cat (Arg), 7, 114	C. S. Nakatani	Luthier Enchanteur, 6	The Name's Jimmy, 6	12	1:34.19	$70,800
1992	Fly Till Dawn, 6, 120	L. A. Pincay Jr.	Itsallgreektome, 5	Qathif, 5	11	1:34.69	$100,200

Named in honor of Frank E. "Jimmy" Kilroe, longtime racing secretary and handicapper at Santa Anita. 1955-'59 Camino Real H.; 1960-2000 Arcadia H. 1973-'83,1990-'94, 2000 Grade 3. 1955-'71,1973-'86 1 1/4 miles. 1972 about 1 1/4 miles. 1975-'76,1978,1983,1995, 2000 dirt. 1955-'61 three-year-olds and up. 2001 dead heat for third. 1997 new course and world record.

Frank J. De Francis Memorial Dash Stakes

Grade 1, Laurel Park, three-year-olds and up, 6 furlongs, dirt. Held November 16, 2002, with a gross value of $300,000. First held in 1990. Graded since 1992. Stakes record 1:07.95 (2000 Richter Scale).

Year	Winner	Jockey	Second	Third	Strs	Time	1st Purse
2002	D'wildcat, 4, 122	J. F. Chavez	Deer Run, 5	Sassy Hound, 5	8	1:10.81	$180,000
2001	Delaware Township, 5, 125	J. D. Bailey	Early Flyer, 3	†Xtra Heat, 3	7	1:09.00	$180,000
2000	Richter Scale, 6, 123	R. Migliore	Just Call Me Carl, 5	Falkenburg, 5	4	1:07.95	$180,000
1999	Yes It's True, 3, 114	J. D. Bailey	Good and Tough, 4	Storm Punch, 4	6	1:08.67	$180,000
1998	Kelly Kip, 4, 121	J-L. Samyn	Affirmed Success, 4	Partner's Hero, 4	6	1:08.50	$180,000
1997	Smoke Glacken, 3, 113	C. Perret	Wise Dusty, 4	†Capote Belle, 4	7	1:09.54	$180,000
1996	Lite the Fuse, 5, 117	J. A. Krone	Meadow Monster, 5	Prospect Bay, 4	7	1:08.81	$180,000
1995	Lite the Fuse, 4, 119	J. A. Krone	Crafty Dude, 6	Hot Jaws, 5	7	1:08.89	$180,000
1994	Cherokee Run, 4, 114	C. Perret	Boom Towner, 6	Fu Man Slew, 3	11	1:08.92	$180,000
1993	Montbrook, 3, 112	C. J. Ladner III	Lion Cavern, 4	Flaming Emperor, 7	9	1:08.71	$180,000
1992	Superstrike (GB), 3, 112	D. Sorenson	Parisian Flight, 4	King Corrie, 4	12	1:09.90	$180,000

Named in honor of Frank J. De Francis (1927-'89), president and chairman of Laurel Park and Pimlico Race Course. 1992-'93 Grade 3; 1994-'98 Grade 2. 1990 held at Pimlico. 2000 new track record.

Fred W. Hooper Handicap

Grade 3, Calder Race Course, three-year-olds and up, 1 1/8 miles, dirt. Held December 28, 2002, with a gross value of $100,000. First held in 1938. Graded since 1992. Stakes record 1:50.53 (2002 The Judge Sez Who).

Year	Winner	Jockey	Second	Third	Strs	Time	1st Purse
2002	The Judge Sez Who, 3, 116	C. H. Velasquez	Best of the Rest, 7	Dancing Guy, 7	8	1:50.53	$60,000

2001	Kiss a Native, 4, 116	C. H. Velasquez	Hal's Hope, 4	Groomstick Stock's, 4	8	1:51.05	$60,000
2000	American Halo, 4, 111	C. Hunt	General Grant, 3	Sir Bear, 7	8	1:51.68	$60,000
1999	Dancing Guy, 4, 120	J. C. Ferrer	Wicapi, 7	Loon, 4	8	1:50.83	$60,000
1998	Wicapi, 6, 113	J. Bravo	Smuggler's Prize, 4	Best of the Rest, 3	5	1:52.15	$60,000
1997	Shrike, 4, 113	J. D. Bailey	Wicapi, 5	Sir Bear, 4	11	1:51.50	$60,000
1996	Cimarron Secret, 5, 115	J. A. Velez Jr.	Laughing Dan, 3	Wicapi, 4	8	1:52.70	$60,000
1995	Bound by Honor, 4, 112	J. A. Krone	Bay Street Star, 4	Halo's Image, 4	10	1:51.81	$60,000
1994	Halo's Image, 3, 117	G. Boulanger	Fight for Love, 4	Migrating Moon, 4	7	1:51.44	$60,000
	Take Me Out, 6, 115	M. E. Smith	Migrating Moon, 4	Meena, 6	11	1:51.80	$60,000
1993	Barkerville, 5, 114	R. P. Romero	Pistols and Roses, 4	Count the Time, 4	7	1:52.47	$45,000
1992	Classic Seven, 4, 110	C. E. Lopez Sr.	Honest Ensign, 4	Le Merle Blanc, 4	13	1:53.01	$102,960

Named in honor of Fred W. Hooper (1898-2000), longtime Florida breeder. 1943,1945,1948,1951,1972-'85,1991 not held. 1938-'40,1942-'58 Tropical H.; 1941, 1959-'96 Tropical Park H. 1938-'71 held at Tropical Park. 1938-'41,1946-'49 1¹/₁₆ miles; 1987 1³/₁₆ miles; 1988 1¹/₄ miles. 1986 turf. 1944 three-year-olds; 1949,1992 four-year-olds and up. 1994 held in January and December.

Frizette Stakes

Grade 1, Belmont Park, two-year-olds, fillies, 1¹/₁₆ miles, dirt. Held October 5, 2002, with a gross value of $500,000. First held in 1945. Graded since 1973. Stakes record 1:42.47 (1996 Storm Song).

Year	Winner	Jockey	Second	Third	Strs	Time	1st Purse
2002	Storm Flag Flying, 2, 120	J. R. Velazquez	Santa Catarina, 2	Appleby Gardens, 2	7	1:44.20	$300,000
2001	You, 2, 120	E. S. Prado	Cashier's Dream, 2	Riskaverse, 2	5	1:43.94	$300,000
2000	Raging Fever, 2, 120	J. D. Bailey	Out of Sync, 2	Western Justice, 2	10	1:43.57	$300,000
1999	Surfside, 2, 119	P. Day	Darling My Darling, 2	March Magic, 2	5	1:43.18	$240,000
1998	Confessional, 2, 119	J. D. Bailey	Things Change, 2	Pico Teneriffe, 2	5	1:42.88	$240,000
1997	Silver Maiden, 2, 119	J. D. Bailey	Diamond On the Run, 2	Brac Drifter, 2	6	1:42.74	$240,000
1996	Storm Song, 2, 119	C. Perret	Sharp Cat, 2	Aldiza, 2	7	**1:42.47**	$240,000
1995	Golden Attraction, 2, 119	G. L. Stevens	My Flag, 2	Flat Fleet Feet, 2	5	1:42.95	$150,000
1994	Flanders, 2, 119	P. Day	Change Fora Dollar, 2	Pretty Discreet, 2	4	1:43.94	$150,000
1993	Heavenly Prize, 2, 119	M. E. Smith	Facts of Love, 2	Footing, 2	7	1:35.46	$150,000
1992	Educated Risk, 2, 119	J. D. Bailey	Standard Equipment, 2	Beal Street Blues, 2	8	1:36.62	$150,000

Named for James R. Keene's stakes winner and foundation mare Frizette (1905, f. by Hamburg). 1949-'51 not held. 1945-'58 held at Jamaica; 1959-'61,1963-'67 Aqueduct. 1945-'47,1952-'53 6 furlongs; 1948 5 furlongs; 1959-'93 1 mile.

Ft. Lauderdale Handicap

Grade 3, Gulfstream Park, three-year-olds and up, 1¹/₁₆ miles, turf. Held January 26, 2002, with a gross value of $100,000. First held in 1947. Graded since 1995. Stakes record 1:39.30 (1994 Paradise Creek).

Year	Winner	Jockey	Second	Third	Strs	Time	1st Purse
2002	Del Mar Show, 5, 119	J. D. Bailey	North East Bound, 6	Tv Sports Director, 6	7	1:41.54	$60,000
2000	Beckon the King, 4, 114	J. D. Bailey	Kettle Won, 4	Missionary, 4	8	1:40.36	$60,000
1999	Garbu, 5, 113	J. D. Bailey	Wild Event, 6	Sharp Appeal, 6	8	1:39.33	$60,000
1998	Statesmanship, 4, 114	J. A. Santos	Subordination, 4	Donthelumbertrader, 5	9	1:40.46	$60,000
1997	Doublethebetwice, 4, 116	J. D. Bailey	Donthelumbertrader, 4	Volochine (Ire), 6	8	1:42.61	$60,000
1996	Winged Victory, 6, 114	J. D. Bailey	Warning Glance, 5	Marcie's Ensign, 4	12	1:41.94	$60,000
1995	The Vid, 5, 120	J. D. Bailey	Flying American, 6	D J's Rainbow, 5	12	1:41.12	$60,000
1994	Paradise Creek, 5, 125	M. E. Smith	Bidding Proud, 5	Social Retiree, 7	9	**1:39.30**	$60,000
1993	Archies Laughter, 5, 114	J. A. Santos	Pidgeon's Promise, 4	May I Inquire, 4	5	1:44.13	$60,000
1992	Now Listen, 5, 114	J. A. Santos	Slew the Slewor, 5	Stage Colony, 5	12	1:40.44	$60,000

Named for the seaside community of Ft. Lauderdale, Florida, located near Hallandale, home of Gulfstream Park. 1948,1951,1958-'65,1972,1974-'75,1977,1981, 2001 not held. 1980-'83,1985-'86 7 furlongs. 1947,1956-'57,1976-'83,1985-'87,1989,1993 dirt. 1994 equaled course record.

Futurity Stakes

Grade 1, Belmont Park, two-year-olds, 1 mile, dirt. Held September 15, 2002, with a gross value of $200,000. First held in 1888. Graded since 1973. Stakes record 1:35.12 (1995 Maria's Mon).

Year	Winner	Jockey	Second	Third	Strs	Time	1st Purse
2002	Whywhywhy, 2, 120	E. S. Prado	Pretty Wild, 2	Truckle Feature, 2	7	1:36.33	$120,000
2000	Burning Roma, 2, 122	R. Wilson	City Zip, 2	Scorpion, 2	9	1:37.90	$120,000
1999	Bevo, 2, 122	J. Bravo	Greenwood Lake, 2	More Than Ready, 2	8	1:36.16	$90,000
1998	Lemon Drop Kid, 2, 122	J. R. Velazquez	Yes It's True, 2	Medievil Hero, 2	5	1:37.50	$90,000
1997	Grand Slam, 2, 122	G. L. Stevens	K. O. Punch, 2	Devil's Pride, 2	10	1:35.69	$90,000
1996	Traitor, 2, 122	J. R. Velazquez	Night in Reno, 2	Harley Tune, 2	9	1:35.29	$90,000
1995	Maria's Mon, 2, 122	R. G. Davis	Louis Quatorze, 2	Honour and Glory, 2	7	**1:35.12**	$90,000
1994	Montreal Red, 2, 122	J. A. Santos	Northern Ensign, 2	Wild Escapade, 2	6	1:36.22	$66,180
1993	Holy Bull, 2, 122	M. E. Smith	Dehere, 2	Prenup, 2	6	1:23.31	$69,360
1992	Strolling Along, 2, 122	C. W. Antley	Fight for Love, 2	Caponostro, 2	9	1:23.67	$72,120

Named for the early nominations, sometimes before the foal was born, of early futurity races. 1911-'12 not held; 2001 not held due to World Trade Center attack. 1888-1909 held at Sheepshead Bay; 1910-'14 Saratoga; 1959-'60,1963-'67 Aqueduct. 1888-'91,1902-'09 6 furlongs; 1892-1901 about 6 furlongs; 1910-'24,1934-'75 6¹/₂ furlongs; 1925-'33 about 7 furlongs; 1976-'93 7 furlongs. 1944 colts and fillies; 1977 colts and geldings. 2000 City Zip finished first, DQ to 2nd.

Gallant Bloom Handicap

Grade 2, Belmont Park, three-year-olds and up, fillies and mares, 6½ furlongs, dirt. Held October 6, 2002, with a gross value of $150,000. First held in 1994. Graded since 1997. Stakes record 1:15.60 (1998 Catinca).

Year	Winner	Jockey	Second	Third	Strs	Time	1st Purse
2002	Nasty Storm, 4, 114	J. A. Santos	Raging Fever, 4	Shine Again, 4	6	1:17.89	$90,000
2001	Finder's Fee, 4, 113	J. R. Velazquez	Cedar Knolls, 4	Gold Mover, 3	4	1:17.60	$79,928
2000	Dream Supreme, 3, 118	P. Day	Finder's Fee, 3	Tropical Punch, 4	5	1:15.86	$64,380
1999	Positive Gal, 3, 116	J. D. Bailey	Flamingo Way, 5	Torch, 6	6	1:16.86	$65,820
1998	Catinca, 3, 114	R. Migliore	Dixie Flag, 4	Crab Grass, 4	9	1:15.60	$50,595
1997	Top Secret, 4, 120	J. R. Velazquez	Aldiza, 3	Dixie Flag, 3	7	1:16.00	$49,260
1996	Miss Golden Circle, 4, 115	R. Migliore	J J'sdream, 3	Nappelon, 4	9	1:16.26	$50,040
1995	Classy Mirage, 5, 123	J. D. Bailey	Dust Bucket, 4	Fantastic Women, 3	5	1:17.34	$48,375
1994	Vivano, 5, 116	W. H. McCauley	Ann Dear, 4	Strategic Reward, 5	5	1:10.93	$48,255

Named for 1968 champion two-year-old filly and '69 champion three-year-old filly and older female Gallant Bloom (1966-'91, f. by *Gallant Man). 1997-2000 Grade 3. 1994 6 furlongs.

Gallorette Handicap

Grade 3, Pimlico, three-year-olds and up, fillies and mares, 1¹/₁₆ miles, turf. Held May 18, 2002, with a gross value of $125,000. First held in 1952. Graded since 1973. Stakes record 1:41.60 (1985 La Reine Elaine).

Year	Winner	Jockey	Second	Third	Strs	Time	1st Purse
2002	Quidnaskra, 7, 116	C. J. McCarron	De Aar, 5	Step With Style, 5	7	1:46.73	$60,000
2001	License Fee, 6, 118	P. Day	Starine (Fr), 4	Crystal Sea, 4	8	1:42.81	$60,000
2000	Colstar, 4, 120	A. Delgado	Melody Queen (GB), 4	Terreavigne, 5	10	1:43.60	$60,000
1999	Winfama, 6, 114	E. S. Prado	Pleasant Temper, 5	Earth to Jackie, 5	8	1:43.31	$60,000
1998	Tresoriere, 4, 113	J. A. Santos	Bursting Forth, 4	Starry Dreamer, 4	7	1:45.35	$60,000
1997	Palliser Bay, 5, 111	C. H. Marquez Jr.	Elusive, 5	Sangria, 4	8	1:43.81	$60,000
1996	Aucilla, 5, 114	M. E. Smith	Julie's Brilliance, 4	Brushing Gloom, 4	4	1:44.96	$60,000
1995	It's Personal, 5, 112	J. A. Krone	Churchbell Chimes, 4	Open Toe, 5	6	1:43.72	$60,000
1994	Tribulation, 4, 117	J-L. Samyn	McKaymackenna, 5	Fleet Broad, 4	6	1:41.66	$60,000
1993	You'd Be Surprised, 4, 113	J. D. Bailey	Captive Miss, 4	Dior's Angel, 4	12	1:43.54	$60,000
1992	Brilliant Brass, 5, 113	E. S. Prado	Spanish Dior, 5	Stem the Tide, 4	6	1:44.81	$60,000

Named for 1946 champion older female Gallorette (1942-'59, f. by *Challenger II). 1952-'66 Gallorette S. 1952-'66 1⅛ miles. 1952-'72,1979-'80,1984,1986-'87,1995-'96 dirt.

Gamely Breeders' Cup Handicap

Grade 1, Hollywood Park, three-year-olds and up, fillies and mares, 1⅛ miles, turf. Held May 27, 2002, with a gross value of $474,000. First held in 1939. Graded since 1977. Stakes record 1:45.07 (1993 Toussaud).

Year	Winner	Jockey	Second	Third	Strs	Time	1st Purse
2002	Astra, 6, 123	K. J. Desormeaux	Starine (Fr), 5	Voodoo Dancer, 5	6	1:46.93	$300,000
2001	Happyanunoit (NZ), 6, 121	B. Blanc	Tranquility Lake, 6	Beautiful Noise, 5	7	1:47.34	$115,710
2000	Astra, 4, 117	K. J. Desormeaux	Happyanunoit (NZ), 5	Tout Charmant, 4	5	1:45.81	$157,170
1999	Tranquility Lake, 4, 119	E. J. Delahoussaye	Midnight Line, 4	Green Jewel (GB), 5	5	1:46.04	$157,800
1998	Fiji (GB), 4, 123	K. J. Desormeaux	Kool Kat Katie (Ire), 4	Squeak (GB), 4	6	1:47.42	$158,880
1997	Donna Viola (GB), 5, 121	G. L. Stevens	Real Connection, 6	Different (Arg), 6	7	1:45.56	$120,000
1996	Auriette (Ire), 4, 118	K. J. Desormeaux	Flagbird, 5	Didina (GB), 5	6	1:46.59	$128,760
1995	Possibly Perfect, 5, 123	K. J. Desormeaux	Lady Affirmed, 4	Don't Read My Lips, 4	6	1:46.99	$92,900
1994	Hollywood Wildcat, 4, 122	E. J. Delahoussaye	Mz. Zill Bear, 5	Flawlessly, 5	6	1:46.55	$92,900
1993	Toussaud, 4, 116	K. J. Desormeaux	Gold Fleece, 5	Bel's Starlet, 5	9	1:45.07	$97,700
1992	Metamorphose, 4, 114	G. L. Stevens	Guiza, 5	Silvered, 5	6	1:46.56	$93,300

Named for William Haggin Perry's 1967 champion three-year-old filly and 1968, '69 champion handicap mare Gamely (1964-'75, f. by Bold Ruler). 1940-'67 not held. 1939-'75 Long Beach H.; 1976-'97 Gamely H. 1973-'75, 1977-'82 Grade 2; 1976 not graded. 1939,1969 1 mile; 1968,1970-'72 1¹/₁₆ miles. 1939-'68,1978 dirt. 1968 both sexes.

Garden City Breeders' Cup Handicap

Grade 1, Belmont Park, three-year-olds, fillies, 1 mile, dirt. Held September 9, 2002, with a gross value of $233,000. First held in 1904. Graded since 1985. Stakes record 1:47.10 (1998 Pharatta [Ire]).

Year	Winner	Jockey	Second	Third	Strs	Time	1st Purse
2002	Wonder Again, 3, 119	E. S. Prado	Riskaverse, 3	Pertuisane (GB), 3	10	1:47.33	$150,000
2001	Voodoo Dancer, 3, 120	C. S. Nakatani	Shooting Party, 3	Wander Mom, 3	10	1:47.69	$150,000
2000	Gaviola, 3, 123	J. D. Bailey	Flawly (GB), 3	Millie's Quest, 3	8	1:48.89	$150,000
1999	Perfect Sting, 3, 120	P. Day	Nordican Inch (GB), 3	Ronda (GB), 3	12	1:49.41	$129,900
1998	Pharatta (Ire), 3, 120	C. S. Nakatani	Tenski, 3	Pratella, 3	12	1:47.10	$129,720
1997	Auntie Mame, 3, 122	J. D. Bailey	Parade Queen, 3	Swearingen, 3	9	1:48.49	$128,040
1996	True Flare, 3, 121	G. L. Stevens	Henlopen, 3	Zephyr, 3	9	1:42.58	$128,460
1995	Perfect Arc, 3, 123	J. R. Velazquez	Bail Out Becky, 4	Christmas Gift, 3	5	1:42.35	$101,070
1994	Jade Flush, 3, 111	R. G. Davis	Lady Affirmed, 4	Sexuality, 3	8	1:46.79	$67,140
1993	Sky Beauty, 3, 124	M. E. Smith	Fadetta, 3	For all Seasons, 3	6	1:35.76	$68,400
1992	November Snow, 3, 124	C. W. Antley	Vivano, 3	Easy Now, 3	4	1:35.91	$66,480

Named for the community of Garden City, located in the heart of Nassau County, Long Island. 1908,1910-'12,1914,1933-'78 not held. 1904-'13 Garden City S.; 1915-'32 Garden City Selling S.; 1979-'95 Rare Perfume S.; 1996-'97 Rare Perfume Breeders' Cup H. 1985-'86 Grade 3; 1987-'98 Grade 2. 1904-'79,1994-'96 1¹/₁₆ miles; 1984 1 mile 70 yards. 1904-'93 dirt. 1904-'32 three-year-olds and up.

Gardenia Handicap

Grade 3, Ellis Park, three-year-olds and up, fillies and mares, 1⅛ miles, dirt. Held August 10, 2002, with a gross value of $200,000. First held in 1982. Graded since 1988. Stakes record 1:47.60 (1988 Lt. Lao).

Year	Winner	Jockey	Second	Third	Strs	Time	1st Purse
2002	Minister's Baby, 4, 117	C. Perret	Lakenheath, 4	Softly, 4	8	1:49.73	$120,000
2001	Asher, 4, 115	M. Guidry	Zenith, 4	Royal Fair, 5	8	1:50.16	$120,000
2000	Silent Eskimo, 5, 116	J. Lopez	Roza Robata, 5	Tap to Music, 5	7	1:50.56	$120,000
1999	Lines of Beauty, 4, 112	F. C. Torres	Roza Robata, 4	Castle Blaze, 6	10	1:49.60	$120,000
1998	Meter Maid, 4, 119	P. A. Johnson	Proper Banner, 4	Three Fanfares, 5	7	1:51.00	$120,000
1997	Three Fanfares, 4, 113	F. A. Arguello Jr.	Gold n Delicious, 4	Birr, 4	7	1:49.00	$120,000
1996	Country Cat, 4, 115	D. M. Barton	Bedroom Blues, 5	Alcovy, 6	8	1:49.60	$120,000
1995	Laura's Pistolette, 4, 115	E. M. Martin Jr.	Sadie's Dream, 5	Cat Appeal, 3	9	1:50.80	$120,000
1994	Alphabulous, 5, 112	Otto Thorwarth	Added Asset, 4	Hey Hazel, 4	10	1:50.00	$120,000
1993	Erica's Dream, 5, 113	W. Martinez	Fappies Cosy Miss, 5	Hitch, 4	8	1:49.80	$120,000
1992	Bungalow, 5, 118	F. C. Torres	Forever Fond, 4	Fappies Cosy Miss, 4	11	1:48.60	$120,000

Named for the flower used in the winner's garland. 1982-'84 Stroh's H.; 1985 Coca Cola Summer Festival H.; 1986 Coca Cola Centennial H.; 1990,1997-'98 Gardenia S.

Gazelle Handicap

Grade 1, Belmont Park, three-year-olds, fillies, 1⅛ miles, dirt. Held September 7, 2002, with a gross value of $250,000. First held in 1887. Graded since 1973. Stakes record 1:46.80 (1974 Maud Muller).

Year	Winner	Jockey	Second	Third	Strs	Time	1st Purse
2002	Imperial Gesture, 3, 117	J. A. Santos	Take Charge Lady, 3	Bella Bellucci, 3	7	1:47.12	$150,000
2001	Exogenous, 3, 118	J. Castellano	Two Item Limit, 3	Fleet Renee, 3	8	1:47.68	$150,000
2000	Critical Eye, 3, 115	M. E. Smith	Plenty of Light, 3	Resort, 3	8	1:48.54	$120,000
1999	Silverbulletday, 3, 124	J. D. Bailey	Queen's Word, 3	Awful Smart, 3	6	1:47.71	$120,000
1998	Tap to Music, 3, 112	P. Day	Keeper Hill, 3	French Braids, 3	7	1:49.72	$120,000
1997	Royal Indy, 3, 113	P. Day	Starry Dreamer, 3	Pearl City, 3	7	1:49.11	$120,000
1996	My Flag, 3, 121	J. D. Bailey	Escena, 3	Top Secret, 3	6	1:48.08	$120,000
1995	Serena's Song, 3, 124	G. L. Stevens	Miss Golden Circle, 3	Golden Bri, 3	6	1:47.29	$90,000
1994	Heavenly Prize, 3, 123	M. E. Smith	Cinnamon Sugar (Ire), 3	Sovereign Kitty, 3	5	1:47.20	$90,000
1993	Dispute, 3, 120	J. D. Bailey	Silky Feather, 3	In Her Glory, 3	8	1:47.20	$90,000
1992	Saratoga Dew, 3, 120	W. H. McCauley	Vivano, 3	Tiney Toast, 3	6	1:47.63	$103,140

Named for the speedy hooved mammal, the gazelle. 1911-'16,1933-'35 not held. 1887-1921,1923-'55 Gazelle S. 1973-'83 Grade 2. 1887-1909 held at Gravesend; 1910-'55,1960,1963-'68 Aqueduct. 1900-'58 1 1/16 miles; 1959-'60 1 mile. 1917-'20 fillies and mares, three-year-olds and up.

General George Handicap

Grade 2, Laurel Park, three-year-olds and up, 7 furlongs, dirt. Held February 22, 2003, with a gross value of $200,000. First held in 1973. Graded since 1991. Stakes record 1:21.96 (1992 Senor Speedy).

Year	Winner	Jockey	Second	Third	Strs	Time	1st Purse
2003	My Cousin Matt, 4, 113	R. A. Dominguez	Peeping Tom, 6	Disturbingthepeace, 5	11	1:22.12	$120,000
2002	Wrangler, 4, 115	A. T. Gryder	Rusty Spur, 4	Affirmed Success, 8	8	1:22.53	$120,000
2001	Peeping Tom, 4, 114	S. Bridgmohan	Delaware Township, 5	Disco Rico, 4	7	1:22.00	$120,000
2000	Affirmed Success, 6, 121	J. F. Chavez	Young At Heart, 6	Badge, 4	9	1:22.02	$120,000
1999	Esteemed Friend, 5, 116	M. J. Luzzi	Star of Valor, 6	Purple Passion, 5	9	1:22.54	$150,000
1998	Royal Haven, 6, 122	R. Migliore	Purple Passion, 4	Wire Me Collect, 5	9	1:23.04	$150,000
1997	Why Change, 4, 113	M. Guidry	Appealing Skier, 4	Le Grande Pos, 6	10	1:22.41	$120,000
1996	Meadow Monster, 5, 120	R. Wilson	Splendid Sprinter, 4	Cat Be Nimble, 4	9	1:22.11	$120,000
1995	Who Wouldn't, 6, 119	J. Rocco	Storm Tower, 5	Powis Castle, 4	8	1:22.08	$120,000
1994	Blushing Julian, 4, 118	R. E. Colton	Chief Desire, 4	Who Wouldn't, 5	12	1:22.91	$120,000
1993	Majesty's Turn, 4, 118	A. Delgado	Senor Speedy, 6	Ameri Valay, 4	7	1:22.66	$120,000
1992	Senor Speedy, 5, 126	J. F. Chavez	Sunny Sunrise, 5	Formal Dinner, 4	12	1:21.96	$120,000

Named for General George Washington (1731-'99), first president of the United States. 1979,1982-'83 not held. 1973-'94 General George S. 1973-'84 held at Bowie; 1986 Pimlico. 1973-'78,1984,1986-'87 1 1/16 miles; 1985 1 mile. 1973-'88 three-year-olds.

Generous Stakes

Grade 3, Hollywood Park, two-year-olds, 1 mile, turf. Held November 30, 2002, with a gross value of $200,000. First held in 1982. Graded since 1986. Stakes record 1:34.49 (1992 Earl of Barking [Ire]).

Year	Winner	Jockey	Second	Third	Strs	Time	1st Purse
2002	Peace Rules, 2, 118	V. Espinoza	Lismore Knight, 2	Outta Here, 2	9	1:35.49	$120,000
2001	Mountain Rage, 2, 116	D. R. Flores	Miesque's Approval, 2	National Park (GB), 2	8	1:40.31	$120,000
2000	Startac, 2, 118	A. O. Solis	Broadway Moon, 2	Deeliteful Irving, 2	9	1:34.76	$120,000
1999	Jokerman, 2, 118	P. Day	Purely Cozzene, 2	Kleofus, 2	8	1:35.23	$120,000
1998	Incurable Optimist, 2, 121	J. R. Velazquez	Company Approval, 2	Brave Gun, 2	8	1:37.72	$150,000
1997	Mantles Star (GB), 2, 114	C. J. McCarron	F J's Pace, 2	Commitisize, 2	8	1:36.73	$150,000
1996	Hello (Ire), 2, 121	C. J. McCarron	Steel Ruhlr, 2	Divine Insight, 2	12	1:34.77	$150,000
1995	Old Chapel, 2, 121	G. L. Stevens	Ayrton S, 2	Heza Gone West, 2	10	1:35.11	$137,500
1994	Native Regent, 2, 121	D. Penna	Dangerous Scenario, 2	Claudius, 2	9	1:37.15	$137,500
1993	Delineator, 2, 118	R. A. Baze	Devon Port (Fr), 2	Ferrara, 2	8	1:34.73	$137,500

| 1992 | Earl of Barking (Ire), 2, 114 | A. O. Solis | Devil's Rock, 2 | Corby, 2 | 8 | 1:34.49 | $137,500 |

Named for 1991 Irish Horse of the Year and dual classic winner Generous (1988, c. by Caerleon [Ire]). Previously named for champion Hoist the Flag (1968-'80, c. by Tom Rolfe). 1982-'92 Hoist the Flag S. 1988-'89 Grade 2. 1984,1986 1¹/₁₆ miles. 1985,1988 dirt.

Genuine Risk Handicap

Grade 2, Belmont Park, three-year-olds and up, fillies and mares, 6 furlongs, dirt. Held May 12, 2002, with a gross value of $150,000. First held in 1984. Graded since 1986. Stakes record 1:08.40 (1996 Exotic Wood).

Year	Winner	Jockey	Second	Third	Strs	Time	1st Purse
2002	Xtra Heat, 4, 126	H. Vega	Shine Again, 5	La Galerie (Arg), 6	6	1:10.24	$90,000
2001	Katz Me If You Can, 4, 113	J. Bravo	Lucky Livi, 4	Shine Again, 4	10	1:09.55	$90,000
2000	Imperfect World, 4, 113	R. G. Davis	Gold Princess, 5	Tropical Punch, 4	7	1:10.00	$90,000
1999	Foil, 4, 114	J-L. Samyn	Harpia, 5	Gold Princess, 4	9	1:10.43	$90,000
1998	J J'sdream, 5, 118	L. C. Reynolds	Tate, 4	Capote Belle, 5	8	1:10.28	$83,310
1997	Miss Golden Circle, 5, 120	R. Migliore	Start At Once, 4	Nappelon, 5	6	1:09.49	$65,040
1996	Exotic Wood, 4, 119	M. E. Smith	Lottsa Talc, 6	Miss Golden Circle, 4	6	1:08.40	$65,100
1995	Classy Mirage, 5, 122	J. A. Krone	Through the Door, 5	Lottsa Talc, 5	4	1:11.25	$64,080
1994	Apelia, 5, 119	L. Attard	Spinning Round, 5	Ann Dear, 4	6	1:09.01	$64,680
1993	Apelia, 4, 119	L. Attard	Santa Catalina, 5	Reach for Clever, 6	7	1:10.18	$69,600
1992	Parisian Flight, 4, 117	J. A. Santos	Serape, 4	Devil's Orchid, 5	6	1:09.18	$70,680

Named for 1980 champion three-year-old filly and Kentucky Derby winner Genuine Risk (1977, f. by Exclusive Native). 1984-'94 Genuine Risk S. 1986-'88 Grade 3.

Glens Falls Handicap

Grade 3, Saratoga Race Course, three-year-olds and up, fillies and mares, 1³/₈ miles, turf. Held August 26, 2002, with a gross value of $100,000. First held in 1996. Graded since 1999. Stakes record 2:07.41 (2000 I'm Indy Mood).

Year	Winner	Jockey	Second	Third	Strs	Time	1st Purse
2002	Owsley, 4, 116	E. S. Prado	Mot Juste (GB), 4	Sunstone (GB), 4	10	2:15.99	$68,100
2001	Irving's Baby, 4, 126	J. D. Bailey	New Assembly (Ire), 4	Caveat's Shot, 6	4	2:07.56	$65,995
2000	I'm Indy Mood, 5, 116	H. Castillo Jr.	Idle Rich, 5	Cybil, 4	6	2:07.41	$66,120
1999	Idle Rich, 4, 115	J. D. Bailey	Adrian, 5	Bundling, 5	7	2:12.81	$65,760
1998	Auntie Mame, 4, 120	J. R. Velazquez	Yvecrique (Fr), 4	Makethemostofit, 4	6	2:13.15	$66,000
1997	Shemozzle (Ire), 4, 115	J. D. Bailey	Picture Hat, 5	Last Approach, 5	5	2:12.89	$64,740
1996	Ampulla, 5, 113	S. J. Sellers	Look Daggers, 4	Electric Society (Ire), 5	8	2:16.49	$67,500

Named for Glens Falls, a town about 15 miles north of Saratoga Springs, New York. 1996-'97 Glens Falls S. 2001 not graded. 2000-'01 1¹/₄ miles. 2000-'01 dirt.

Go for Wand Handicap

Grade 1, Saratoga Race Course, three-year-olds and up, fillies and mares, 1¹/₈ miles, dirt. Held July 28, 2002, with a gross value of $250,000. First held in 1954. Graded since 1973. Stakes record 1:49.44 (1996 Exotic Wood).

Year	Winner	Jockey	Second	Third	Strs	Time	1st Purse
2002	Dancethruthedawn, 4, 118	J. D. Bailey	Transcendental, 4	Too Scarlet, 4	7	1:50.21	$150,000
2001	Serra Lake, 4, 113	E. S. Prado	Pompeii, 4	March Magic, 4	8	1:49.62	$150,000
2000	Heritage of Gold, 5, 123	S. J. Sellers	Beautiful Pleasure, 5	Roza Robata, 5	5	1:49.84	$150,000
1999	Banshee Breeze, 4, 124	J. D. Bailey	Beautiful Pleasure, 4	Heritage of Gold, 4	5	1:49.95	$150,000
1998	Aldiza, 4, 114	M. E. Smith	Escena, 5	Tomisue's Delight, 4	7	1:49.88	$150,000
1997	Hidden Lake, 4, 123	R. Migliore	Flat Fleet Feet, 4	Clear Mandate, 4	7	1:49.64	$150,000
1996	Exotic Wood, 4, 115	C. J. McCarron	Shoop, 5	Frolic, 5	8	1:49.44	$105,000
1995	Heavenly Prize, 4, 123	P. Day	Forcing Bid, 4	Little Buckles, 4	5	1:49.90	$105,000
1994	Sky Beauty, 4, 123	M. E. Smith	Link River, 4	Life Is Delicious, 4	5	1:49.47	$90,000
1993	Turnback the Alarm, 4, 123	C. W. Antley	Nannerl, 6	November Snow, 6	4	1:36.02	$120,000
1992	Easy Now, 3, 111	J. D. Bailey	Train Robbery, 5	Wide Country, 5	5	1:36.13	$120,000

Named for Christiana Stable's 1989 champion two-year-old filly and 1990 champion three-year-old filly Go for Wand (1987-'90, f. by Deputy Minister). Go for Wand is buried in Saratoga's infield. Formerly named for champion Maskette (1906, f. by Disguise). 1954-'78 Maskette H.; 1979-'91 Maskette S.; 1992-'97 Go for Wand S. 1954-'58,1961,1969-'93 held at Belmont; 1959-'60,1962-'68 Aqueduct. 1954-'93 1 mile. 1992 Nannerl finished second, DQ to fifth.

Golden Gate Breeders' Cup Handicap

Grade 3, Golden Gate Fields, three-year-olds and up, 1¹/₈ miles, turf. Held March 16, 2003, with a gross value of $136,250. First held in 1947. Graded since 1975. Stakes record 1:48.21 (1993 Val de Bois [Fr]).

Year	Winner	Jockey	Second	Third	Strs	Time	1st Purse
2003	Ninebanks, 5, 116	R. J. Warren Jr.	Surprise Halo, 5	Royal Gem, 4	4	1:50.07	$82,500
2002	No Slip (Fr), 4, 117	K. J. Desormeaux	Kerrygold (Fr), 6	Sumitas (Ger), 6	5	1:49.41	$82,500
2001	Northern Quest (Fr), 6, 118	V. Espinoza	Eagleton, 5	Entorchado (Fr), 6	6	1:58.58	$137,500
2000	Deploy Venture (GB), 4, 115	R. A. Baze	Single Empire (Ire), 6	Bonapartiste (Fr), 6	8	2:19.12	$120,000
1999	Sayarshan (Fr), 4, 112	B. Blanc	Alvo Certo (Brz), 6	Pllick (Ire), 4	8	2:15.56	$120,000
1998	Dushyantor, 5, 118	C. S. Nakatani	Eternity Range, 5	Star Performance, 5	6	2:15.06	$150,000
1997	Irish Wings (Ire), 5, 114	D. Carr	Savinio, 7	Mufattish, 4	7	1:49.68	$120,000
1996	Time Star, 5, 116	C. A. Black	Sand Reef (GB), 5	Bon Point (GB), 6	5	2:16.37	$120,000
1995	Special Price, 6, 122	E. J. Delahoussaye	Bluegrass Prince (Ire), 4	Sans Ecocide (GB), 4	6	2:15.14	$110,000

1994	Alex the Great (GB), 5, 118	P. A. Valenzuela	Fanmore, 6	Emerald Jig, 5	8	2:15.11	$165,000
1993	Val des Bois (Fr), 7, 119	P. A. Valenzuela	Norwich (GB), 6	Never Black, 6	5	1:48.21	$165,000
1992	Algenib (Arg), 5, 120	L. A. Pincay Jr.	Missionary Ridge (GB), 5	Never Black, 5	7	2:13.96	$220,000

1947-2000 Golden Gate H. 1985-'96 Grade 2. 1947-'50,1952,1955,1959-'61 1¼ miles; 1953 1³/₁₆ miles; 1962-'64,1968-'73,1975-'82 1¹/₁₆ miles; 1974 1½ miles; 1983-'92,1994-'96,1998-2000 1³/₈ miles. 1947-'71,1982 dirt. 1993 equaled course record.

Golden Gate Derby

Grade 3, Golden Gate Fields, three-year-olds, 1¹/₁₆ miles, dirt. Held January 11, 2003, with a gross value of $100,000. First held in 1947. Graded since 1999. Stakes record 1:42.20 (1959 Mr. Eiffel).

Year	Winner	Jockey	Second	Third	Strs	Time	1st Purse
2003	Standard Setter, 3, 120	R. M. Gonzalez	Ozzie Cat, 3	Pine for Java, 3	10	1:43.76	$55,000
2002	Danthebluegrassman, 3, 120	J. J. Steiner	Cappuchino, 3	U S S Tinosa, 3	6	1:43.87	$68,750
2001	Hoovergetthekeys, 3, 120	R. J. Warren Jr.	High Cascade, 3	Media Mogul (GB), 3	7	1:42.88	$82,500
2000	New Advantage, 3, 120	A. D. Lopez	Nurdlinger, 3	Shake Loose, 3	9	1:42.66	$90,000
1999	Epic Honor, 3, 120	L. Meche	Blue Tune, 3	Brave Gun, 3	8	1:43.58	$90,000
1998	Clover Hunter, 3, 120	R. A. Baze	Mantles Star (GB), 3	Allen's Oop, 3	8	1:43.33	$120,000
1997	Pacificbounty, 3, 118	K. J. Desormeaux	Dancer's Kolo, 3	Esteemed Friend, 3	12	1:43.08	$120,000

1951,1953-'54,1956-'57,1960-'96 not held. 1947 1³/₁₆ miles; 1948-'55 1¹/₈ miles.

Golden Rod Stakes

Grade 2, Churchill Downs, two-year-olds, fillies, 1¹/₁₆ miles, dirt. Held November 30, 2002, with a gross value of $200,000. First held in 1910. Graded since 1973. Stakes record 1:43.82 (2001 Belterra).

Year	Winner	Jockey	Second	Third	Strs	Time	1st Purse
2002	My Boston Gal, 2, 117	C. H. Borel	Holiday Lady, 2	My Trusty Cat, 2	7	1:45.00	$136,152
2001	Belterra, 2, 117	J. K. Court	Take Charge Lady, 2	Lotta Rhythm, 2	5	1:43.82	$133,424
2000	Miss Pickums, 2, 122	J. J. Vitek	Nasty Storm, 2	My White Corvette, 2	9	1:48.84	$138,384
1999	Humble Clerk, 2, 119	J. K. Court	Cash Run, 2	Secret Status, 2	9	1:45.26	$138,880
1998	Silverbulletday, 2, 122	G. L. Stevens	Here I Go, 2	Lefty's Dollbaby, 2	6	1:43.87	$134,292
1997	Love Lock, 2, 119	R. Albarado	Barefoot Dyana, 2	Grechelle, 2	9	1:44.49	$139,996
1996	City Band, 2, 122	S. J. Sellers	Glitter Woman, 2	Water Street, 2	10	1:46.82	$139,996
1995	Gold Sunrise, 2, 113	W. Martinez	Birr, 2	Solana, 2	11	1:45.46	$97,500
1994	Lilly Capote, 2, 113	D. M. Barton	Morris Code, 2	Cat Appeal, 2	8	1:46.66	$97,500
1993	At the Half, 2, 122	P. Day	Spiritofpocahontas, 2	Mystic Union, 2	9	1:46.83	$97,500
1992	Boots 'n Jackie, 2, 120	M. A. Lee	Mollie Creek, 2	Dance Account, 2	6	1:47.29	$97,500

Named for the state flower of Kentucky, the goldenrod. 1928-'61 not held. 1973-'82,1989-'99 Grade 3; 1983-'88 not graded. 1910-'18 6 furlongs; 1919 1 mile; 1920-'27,1962-'79 7 furlongs.

Goodwood Breeders' Cup Handicap

Grade 2, Santa Anita Park, three-year-olds and up, 1¹/₈ miles, dirt. Held October 6, 2002, with a gross value of $500,000. First held in 1982. Graded since 1982. Stakes record 1:46.72 (1994 Bertrando).

Year	Winner	Jockey	Second	Third	Strs	Time	1st Purse
2002	Pleasantly Perfect, 4, 115	A. O. Solis	Momentum, 4	Reba's Gold, 5	9	1:46.80	$300,000
2001	Freedom Crest, 5, 116	K. J. Desormeaux	Skimming, 5	Tiznow, 4	6	1:48.86	$300,000
2000	Tiznow, 3, 116	C. J. McCarron	Captain Steve, 3	Euchre, 4	7	1:47.38	$240,000
1999	Budroyale, 6, 119	G. K. Gomez	General Challenge, 3	Old Trieste, 4	6	1:48.31	$300,000
1998	Silver Charm, 4, 124	G. L. Stevens	Free House, 4	Score Quick, 6	6	1:47.21	$262,800
1997	Benchmark, 6, 118	E. J. Delahoussaye	Score Quick, 5	Hesabull, 4	5	1:47.60	$158,700
1996	Savinio, 6, 117	C. S. Nakatani	Dare and Go, 5	Alphabet Soup, 5	4	1:47.88	$189,300
1995	Soul of the Matter, 4, 121	K. J. Desormeaux	Tinners Way, 5	Alphabet Soup, 4	5	1:47.54	$144,450
1994	Bertrando, 5, 120	G. L. Stevens	Dramatic Gold, 3	Tossofthecoin, 4	6	1:46.72	$124,400
1993	Lottery Winner, 4, 115	K. J. Desormeaux	Region, 4	Pleasant Tango, 3	7	1:47.71	$127,200
1992	Reign Road, 4, 116	K. J. Desormeaux	Sir Beaufort, 5	Marquetry, 5	6	1:48.36	$125,200

Named for Goodwood Race Course in England, the Oak Tree Racing Association's sister track. 1982-'95 Goodwood H. 1982,1985-'89 Grade 3; 1983-'84 not graded. 1982-'84,1986 1¹/₁₆ miles. 1996 Alphabet Soup finished first, DQ to third.

Gotham Stakes

Grade 3, Aqueduct, three-year-olds, 1 mile 70 yards, dirt. Held March 16, 2003, with a gross value of $200,000. First held in 1953. Graded since 1973. Stakes record 1:40.40 (1984 Bear Hunt).

Year	Winner	Jockey	Second	Third	Strs	Time	1st Purse
2003	Alysweep, 3, 120	R. Migliore	Grey Comet, 3	Spite the Devil, 3	9	1:40.60	$120,000
2002	Mayakovsky, 3, 116	E. S. Prado	Saarland, 3	Parade of Music, 3	7	1:34.90	$120,000
2001	Richly Blended, 3, 116	R. Wilson	Mr. John, 3	Voodoo, 3	8	1:35.14	$120,000
2000	Red Bullet, 3, 113	A. O. Solis	Aptitude, 3	Performing Magic, 3	9	1:34.27	$120,000
1999	Badge, 3, 120	S. Bridgmohan	Apremont, 3	Robin Goodfellow, 3	11	1:34.72	$90,000
1998	Wasatch, 3, 117	J. D. Bailey	Dr J, 3	Late Edition, 3	10	1:36.56	$90,000
1997	Smokin Mel, 3, 112	J. R. Velazquez	Ordway, 3	Wild Wonder, 3	11	1:34.38	$120,000
1996	Romano Gucci, 3, 119	J. A. Krone	Tiger Talk, 3	Feather Box, 3	10	1:34.40	$120,000
1995	Talkin Man, 3, 122	M. E. Smith	Da Hoss, 3	Devious Course, 3	11	1:36.82	$150,000

1994 **Irgun**, 3, 114	J. D. Bailey	Bit of Puddin, 3	Jesse F, 3	12	1:36.27	$150,000
1993 **As Indicated**, 3, 114	C. V. Bisono	Itaka, 3	Strolling Along, 3	8	1:36.24	$120,000
1992 **(DH) Lure**, 3, 114	M. E. Smith		Best Decorated, 3	8	1:35.63	$102,500
(DH) Devil His Due, 3	W. H. McCauley					

Named for the unofficial nickname of New York City, "Gotham." 1973-'97 Grade 2. 1953-'59 held at Jamaica. 1953-'59,1977,1979 1¹/₁₆ miles; 1984 1 mile 70 yards. 1958 four-year-olds and up. 1992 dead heat for first.

Gravesend Handicap

Grade 3, Aqueduct, three-year-olds and up, 6 furlongs, dirt. Held December 29, 2002, with a gross value of $109,200. First held in 1959. Graded since 1988. Stakes record 1:08.60 (1973 Petrograd).

Year Winner	Jockey	Second	Third	Strs	Time	1st Purse
2002 **Multiple Choice**, 4, 118	V. Carrero	Sing Me Back Home, 4	Gold I. D., 3	7	1:09.26	$65,520
2001 **Here's Zealous**, 4, 114	E. S. Prado	Peeping Tom, 4	Say Florida Sandy, 7	6	1:10.37	$64,740
2000 **Say Florida Sandy**, 6, 116	J. Bravo	Liberty Gold, 6	Lake Pontchartrain, 5	11	1:09.80	$51,450
1999 **Cowboy Cop**, 5, 115	A. T. Gryder	Brushed On, 4	Power by Far, 4	9	1:09.41	$50,370
1998 **Say Florida Sandy**, 4, 117	S. Bridgmohan	Esteemed Friend, 4	Home On the Ridge, 4	8	1:11.17	$50,220
1997 **(DH) Stalwart Member**, 4, 118	A. T. Gryder		Laredo, 4	7	1:10.08	$32,670
(DH) Royal Haven, 5	R. Migliore					
1996 **Victor Avenue**, 3, 119	J. F. Chavez	Royal Haven, 4	Stalwart Member, 3	9	1:09.25	$50,325
1995 **Cold Execution**, 4, 116	J. M. Pezua	Crafty Alfel, 7	Golden Tent, 6	10	1:09.50	$50,820
1994 **Mining Burrah**, 4, 111	J. R. Velazquez	Golden Pro, 4	Won Song, 4	9	1:10.85	$51,270
1993 **Astudillo (Ire)**, 3, 108	F. A. Arguello Jr.	Fabersham, 5	Ferociously, 3	6	1:11.91	$51,300
1992 **Hidden Tomahawk**, 4, 111	J. F. Chavez	Smart Alec, 4	Miner's Dream, 5	8	1:08.65	$52,920

Named for old Gravesend Park, a racetrack located in the Coney Island section of Brooklyn. 1959-'60 held at Jamaica; 1974-'75 Belmont. 1962 7 furlongs. 1992 equaled track record. 1997 dead heat for first. 1999 Unreal Madness finished third, DQ to ninth.

Gulfstream Park Breeders' Cup Handicap

Grade 1, Gulfstream Park, three-year-olds and up, 1³/₈ miles, turf. Held February 16, 2003, with a gross value of $194,000. First held in 1986. Graded since 1990. Stakes record 2:10.73 (1999 Yagli).

Year Winner	Jockey	Second	Third	Strs	Time	1st Purse
2003 **Man From Wicklow**, 6, 119	J. D. Bailey	Just Listen, 7	Sardaukar (GB), 7	10	2:11.62	$120,000
2002 **Cetewayo**, 8, 115	C. H. Velasquez	Band Is Passing, 6	Profit Option, 7	12	2:17.44	$120,000
2001 **Subtle Power (Ire)**, 4, 113	P. Day	Whata Brainstorm, 4	Stokosky, 5	9	2:13.50	$60,000
2000 **Royal Anthem**, 5, 121	J. D. Bailey	Thesaurus, 6	Band Is Passing, 4	7	2:11.34	$120,000
1999 **Yagli**, 6, 121	J. D. Bailey	Wild Event, 6	Unite's Big Red, 5	6	2:10.73	$120,000
1998 **Flag Down**, 8, 120	J. A. Santos	Buck's Boy, 5	Copy Editor, 6	12	2:12.59	$120,000
1997 **Lassigny**, 6, 116	J. D. Bailey	Flag Down, 7	Awad, 7	11	2:11.33	$102,840
1996 **Celtic Arms (Fr)**, 5, 114	M. E. Smith	Broadway Flyer, 5	Flag Down, 6	11	2:13.90	$101,880
1995 **Misil**, 7, 119	J. A. Santos	Myrmidon, 6	Star of Manila, 4	11	2:12.41	$94,200
1994 **Strolling Along**, 4, 117	J. D. Bailey	Conveyor, 6	Awad, 4	6	2:05.01	$93,150
1993 **Stagecraft (GB)**, 6, 115	J. D. Bailey	Social Retiree, 6	Futurist, 5	8	2:13.24	$93,600
1992 †**Passagere du Soir (GB)**, 5, 114	J. D. Bailey	Colchis Island (Ire), 7	Crystal Moment, 7	14	2:15:71	$95,130

1987-'95 Gulfstream Park Budweiser Breeders' Cup H. 1990-'91 Grade 3; 1992-'98 Grade 2. 1986-'90 1¹/₁₆ miles; 1991 about 1³/₈ miles; 1994 1¹/₄ miles. 1987,1994 dirt. 1993,1999 new course record; 1997 equaled course record. †denotes female.

Gulfstream Park Handicap

Grade 2, Gulfstream Park, three-year-olds and up, 1¹/₄ miles, dirt. Held March 29, 2003, with a gross value of $300,000. First held in 1946. Graded since 1973. Stakes record 1:59 (1984 Mat-Boy [Arg]).

Year Winner	Jockey	Second	Third	Strs	Time	1st Purse
2003 **Hero's Tribute**, 5, 115	E. S. Prado	Aeneas, 4	Puzzlement, 4	8	2:02.24	$180,000
2002 **Hal's Hope**, 5, 113	R. I. Velez	Mongoose, 4	Sir Bear, 9	5	2:02.91	$180,000
2001 **Sir Bear**, 8, 116	E. Coa	Pleasant Breeze, 6	Broken Vow, 4	9	2:02.96	$120,000
2000 **Behrens**, 6, 120	J. F. Chavez	Adonis, 4	With Anticipation, 5	6	2:01.79	$210,000
1999 **Behrens**, 5, 114	J. F. Chavez	Archers Bay, 4	Sir Bear, 6	6	2:01.91	$210,000
1998 **Skip Away**, 5, 127	J. D. Bailey	Unruled, 5	Behrens, 4	6	2:03.21	$300,000
1997 **Mt. Sassafras**, 5, 113	J. D. Bailey	Skip Away, 4	Tejano Run, 5	6	2:02.39	$300,000
1996 **Wekiva Springs**, 5, 117	J. D. Bailey	Star Standard, 4	Powerful Punch, 7	8	2:03.18	$300,000
1995 **Cigar**, 5, 118	J. D. Bailey	Pride of Burkaan, 5	Mahogany Hall, 4	11	2:02.95	$300,000
1994 **Scuffleburg**, 5, 113	C. Perret	Migrating Moon, 4	Wallenda, 4	10	2:00.46	$300,000
1993 **Devil His Due**, 4, 113	W. H. McCauley	Offbeat, 4	Pistols and Roses, 4	9	2:01.33	$300,000
1992 **Sea Cadet**, 4, 119	A. O. Solis	Strike the Gold, 4	Sunny Sunrise, 5	6	2:01.79	$180,000

1949-'51 purse race. 1946,1968 Gulfstream H. 1975-2002 Grade 1. 1946 four-year-olds and up.

Hal's Hope Handicap

Grade 3, Gulfstream Park, three-year-olds and up, 1¹/₁₆ miles, dirt. Held January 11, 2003, with a gross value of $100,000. First held in 1990. Graded since 1993. Stakes record 1:41.49 (1996 Geri).

Year Winner	Jockey	Second	Third	Strs	Time	1st Purse
2003 **Windsor Castle**, 5, 115	E. Coa	Saint Verre, 5	Najran, 4	8	1:42.33	$60,000
2002 **Hal's Hope**, 5, 112	R. I. Velez	American Halo, 6	Windsor Castle, 6	9	1:42.40	$60,000
2000 **Dancing Guy**, 5, 120	J. D. Bailey	Yankee Victor, 4	Midway Magistrate, 6	8	1:44.94	$45,000

1999	**Jazz Club**, 4, 114	P. Day	Rock and Roll, 4	Hanarsaan, 6	7	1:42.76	$45,000
1998	**K. J.'s Appeal**, 4, 114	J. R. Velazquez	Powerful Goer, 4	Tour's Big Red, 5	8	1:42.34	$45,000
1997	**Louis Quatorze**, 4, 121	P. Day	Strawberry Wine, 5	Exalto, 6	5	1:43.43	$45,000
1996	**Geri**, 4, 114	J. D. Bailey	Halo's Image, 5	Second Childhood, 4	6	1:41.49	$45,000
1995	**Warm Wayne**, 4, 112	J. D. Bailey	Meadow Monster, 4	Silent Lake, 5	9	1:43.11	$45,000
1994	**Forever Whirl**, 4, 113	W. H. McCauley	Northern Trend, 6	Royal n Gold, 5	10	1:41.81	$45,000
1993	**Classic Sense**, 5, 116	C. E. Lopez Sr.	Devil On Ice, 4	Keratoid, 4	10	1:43.49	$60,000
1992	**Peanut Butter Onit**, 6, 114	J. A. Santos	Sunny Sunrise, 5	Honest Ensign, 4	7	1:43.78	$45,000

Named for Hal Rose's 2000 Florida Derby (G1) winner Hal's Hope (1997-2002, c. by Jolie's Halo). Formerly named for classic winner Creme Fraiche (1982, g. by Rich Cream). 2001 not held. 1990 Creme Fraiche S.; 1991-2002 Creme Fraiche H. 1990 7 furlongs. 1990 four-year-olds and up.

Hanshin Cup Handicap

Grade 3, Arlington Park, three-year-olds and up, 1 mile, dirt. Held July 20, 2002, with a gross value of $100,000. First held in 1941. Graded since 1983. Stakes record 1:33.20 (1965 Pia Star; 1966 Hedevar; 1979 Bask).

Year	Winner	Jockey	Second	Third	Strs	Time	1st Purse
2002	**Bonapaw**, 6, 121	G. Melancon	Slider, 4	Discreet Hero, 4	7	1:34.00	$60,000
2001	**Bright Valour**, 5, 119	R. Albarado	Apt to Be, 4	Castlewood, 4	8	1:36.21	$60,000
2000	**Bright Valour**, 4, 114	J. Campbell	Desert Demon, 4	Battle Mountain, 6	5	1:34.97	$60,000
1997	**Announce**, 5, 116	C. C. Bourque	Victor Cooley, 4	Hunk of Class, 4	7	1:36.95	$60,000
1996	**Golden Gear**, 5, 122	M. Guidry	Exclusive Garth, 4	Prospect for Love, 4	10	1:36.13	$105,000
1995	**Tarzans Blade**, 4, 115	P. Day	Swank, 4	Come On Flip, 4	9	1:35.64	$45,000
1994	**Slerp**, 5, 117	E. Fires	Seattle Morn, 4	Dancing Jon, 6	5	1:35.43	$60,000
1993	**Split Run**, 5, 114	E. Fires	Gee Can He Dance, 4	Danc'n Jake, 4	11	1:34.46	$60,000
1992	**Katahaula County**, 4, 114	C. C. Bourque	The Great Carl, 5	Stalwars, 7	9	1:37.27	$45,000

Named in honor of the Japan Racing Association, which conducts a race in honor of Arlington Park. Formerly named for two-time Horse of the Year Equipoise (1928-'38, c. by Pennant). 1970-'78,1988,1998-'99 not held. 1941-'97 Equipoise Mile H.; 2000 Hanshin H. 1943-'45 held at Washington Park. 2000 Yankee Victor finished first, DQ to fifth.

Haskell Invitational Handicap

Grade 1, Monmouth Park, three-year-olds, 1 1/8 miles, dirt. Held August 4, 2002, with a gross value of $1,000,000. First held in 1885. Graded since 1973. Stakes record 1:47 (1976 Majestic Light; 1987 Bet Twice).

Year	Winner	Jockey	Second	Third	Strs	Time	1st Purse
2002	**War Emblem**, 3, 124	V. Espinoza	Magic Weisner, 3	Like a Hero, 3	5	1:48.21	$600,000
2001	**Point Given**, 3, 124	G. L. Stevens	Touch Tone, 3	Burning Roma, 3	6	1:49.77	$900,000
2000	**Dixie Union**, 3, 117	A. O. Solis	Captain Steve, 3	Milwaukee Brew, 3	9	1:50.00	$600,000
1999	**Menifee**, 3, 124	P. Day	Cat Thief, 3	Forestry, 3	7	1:48.06	$600,000
1998	**Coronado's Quest**, 3, 124	M. E. Smith	Victory Gallop, 3	Grand Slam, 3	6	1:48.60	$600,000
1997	**Touch Gold**, 3, 125	C. J. McCarron	Anet, 3	Free House, 3	5	1:47.62	$850,000
1996	**Skip Away**, 3, 124	J. A. Santos	Dr. Caton, 3	Victory Speech, 3	7	1:47.73	$450,000
1995	**†Serena's Song**, 3, 118	G. L. Stevens	Pyramid Peak, 3	Citadeed, 3	11	1:48.94	$300,000
1994	**Holy Bull**, 3, 126	M. E. Smith	Meadow Flight, 3	Concern, 3	6	1:48.36	$300,000
1993	**Kissin Kris**, 3, 118	J. A. Santos	Storm Tower, 3	Dry Bean, 3	7	1:49.58	$300,000
1992	**Technology**, 3, 120	J. D. Bailey	Nines Wild, 3	Scudan, 3	9	1:48.78	$300,000

Named for Amory L. Haskell (1894-1966), former president of Monmouth Park. 1893-1945 not held. 1885-'92,1946-'67 Choice S.; 1968-'80 Monmouth Invitational H.; 1996-'98 Buick Haskell Invitational H. 1885-'92 1 1/2 miles; 1946-'52 1 1/4 miles; 1958-'67 1 1/16 miles. †denotes female.

Hawthorne Derby

Grade 3, Hawthorne Race Course, three-year-olds, 1 1/8 miles, turf. Held May 11, 2002, with a gross value of $250,000. First held in 1965. Graded since 1973. Stakes record 1:44.70 (1991 Rainbows for Life).

Year	Winner	Jockey	Second	Third	Strs	Time	1st Purse
2002	**Scooter Roach**, 3, 115	J. Campbell	Quest Star, 3	Colorful Tour, 3	7	1:58.88	$150,000
2001	**Kalu**, 3, 119	J. A. Santos	Proud Man, 3	Rahy's Secret, 3	5	1:50.49	$150,000
2000	**(DH) Hymn (Ire)**, 3, 115	L. A. Pincay Jr.		Lonely Place (Ire), 3	10	1:53.79	$100,000
	(DH) Rumsonontheriver, 3, 115	J. Juarez Jr.					
1999	**Minor Wisdom**, 3, 115	R. Zimmerman	Air Rocket, 3	Fred of Gold, 3	12	1:49.06	$150,000
1998	**Stay Sound**, 3, 115	A. J. D'Amico	El Mirasol, 3	Yankee Brass, 3	11	1:47.54	$150,000
1997	**River Squall**, 3, 119	C. Perret	Honor Glide, 3	Blazing Sword, 3	6	1:48.20	$120,000
1996	**Jaunatxo**, 3, 122	J. L. Diaz	Trail City, 3	Canyon Run, 3	11	1:47.18	$120,000
1995	**Cuzzin Jeb**, 3, 117	C. C. Lopez	Hawk Attack, 3	Seven n Seven, 3	9	1:48.90	$90,000
1994	**Chrysalis House**, 3, 115	M. Guidry	Unfinished Symph, 3	Marvin's Faith (Ire), 3	11	1:51.88	$90,000
1993	**Snake Eyes**, 3, 122	G. K. Gomez	Lt. Pinkerton, 3	Ft. Bent, 3	12	1:50.28	$90,000
1992	**Bantan**, 3, 117	C. C. Bourque	†Words of War, 3	Gee Can He Dance, 3	11	1:48.05	$60,000

1965-'68 Hawthorne Diamond Jubilee H.; 1969-'75 Hawthorne Derby H. 1979 held at Sportsman's. 1965-'74,1976-'84 1 1/16 miles; 1985-'87 1 3/16 miles. 1965-'83 dirt. 2000 dead heat for first. †denotes female.

Hawthorne Gold Cup Handicap

Grade 2, Hawthorne Race Course, three-year-olds and up, 1 1/4 miles, dirt. Held May 18, 2002, with a gross value of $500,000. First held in 1928. Graded since 1973. Stakes record 1:58.80 (1970 Gladwin; 1974 Group Plan).

Year	Winner	Jockey	Second	Third	Strs	Time	1st Purse
2002	**Hail The Chief (GB)**, 5, 114	J. F. Chavez	Dollar Bill, 4	Parade Leader, 5	5	2:02.80	$300,000

2001	Duckhorn, 4, 112	R. A. Meier	Lido Palace (Chi), 4	Guided Tour, 5	7	2:01.61	$300,000
2000	Dust On the Bottle, 5, 112	T. T. Doocy	Guided Tour, 4	Golden Missile, 5	8	2:03.09	$300,000
1999	Supreme Sound (GB), 5, 112	R. A. Meier	Golden Missile, 4	Beboppin Baby, 6	8	2:01.19	$300,000
1998	Awesome Again, 4, 123	P. Day	Unruled, 5	Muchacho Fino, 4	8	2:02.71	$240,000
1997	Buck's Boy, 4, 114	M. Guidry	Cairo Express, 5	Beboppin Baby, 4	7	2:00.54	$180,000
1996	Come On Flip, 5, 113	C. A. Emigh	Michael's Star, 4	Mt. Sassafras, 4	10	2:03.40	$180,000
1995	Yourmissinthepoint, 4, 113	M. Guidry	Basquelan, 4	Sky Carr, 5	9	2:01.00	$150,000
1994	Recoup the Cash, 4, 117	J. L. Diaz	Run Softly, 3	Kissin Kris, 4	11	2:01.99	$240,000
1993	Evanescent, 6, 115	A. T. Gryder	Marquetry, 6	Valley Crossing, 5	8	2:02.19	$240,000
1992	Irish Swap, 5, 115	B. E. Poyadou	Sea Cadet, 4	Evanescent, 5	8	2:01.12	$240,000

1934,1936,1940-'45,1978 not held. 1928-'35 Hawthorne Gold Cup S.; 1985-'86,1988-'91 Budweiser-Hawthorne Gold Cup H.; 1987,1992 Hawthorne Budweiser Gold Cup H. 1997-2000 Grade 3. 1979 held at Sportsman's. 1979 1⅛ miles.

Hawthorne Handicap

Grade 3, Hollywood Park, three-year-olds and up, fillies and mares, 1¹/₁₆ miles, dirt. Held April 25, 2003, with a gross value of $103,292. First held in 1974. Graded since 1982. Stakes record 1:41.12 (1993 Freedom Cry).

Year	Winner	Jockey	Second	Third	Strs	Time	1st Purse
2003	Keys to the Heart, 4, 115	J. Valdivia Jr.	Rhiana, 6	Alexine (Arg), 7	4	1:42.97	$63,240
2002	Queen of Wilshire, 6, 115	P. A. Valenzuela	Alexine (Arg), 6	Verruma (Brz), 6	5	1:43.16	$63,660
2001	Printemps (Chi), 4, 116	C. J. McCarron	Feverish, 6	Brianda (Ire), 4	4	1:43.21	$90,000
2000	Riboletta (Brz), 5, 117	C. J. McCarron	Excellent Meeting, 4	Speaking of Time, 4	5	1:42.33	$90,000
1999	Victory Stripes (Arg), 5, 115	C. J. McCarron	Magical Allure, 4	Housa Dancer (Fr), 6	4	1:41.73	$90,000
1998	I Ain't Bluffing, 4, 118	C. J. McCarron	Fun in Excess, 4	Tomorrows Sunshine, 4	5	1:41.49	$63,720
1997	Twice the Vice, 6, 120	C. J. McCarron	Chile Chatte, 4	Listening, 4	7	1:42.72	$64,860
1996	Borodislew, 6, 118	C. S. Nakatani	Jewel Princess, 4	Urbane, 4	6	1:41.28	$64,200
1995	Paseana (Arg), 8, 122	C. J. McCarron	Pirate's Revenge, 4	Top Rung, 4	7	1:42.40	$63,300
1994	Golden Klair (GB), 4, 118	K. J. Desormeaux	Likeable Style, 4	Andestine, 4	4	1:41.41	$60,000
1993	Freedom Cry, 5, 117	A. O. Solis	Vieille Vigne (Fr), 6	Miss High Blade, 5	11	1:41.12	$67,600
1992	Sacramentada (Chi), 6, 117	K. J. Desormeaux	Brought to Mind, 5	Re Toss (Arg), 5	5	1:43.04	$61,600

Named for the nearby town of Hawthorne, California. 1983-2001 Grade 2. 1974-'75 7 furlongs; 1985-'90 1 mile. 1976-'80 turf.

Herecomesthebride Stakes

Grade 3, Gulfstream Park, three-year-olds, fillies, 1¹/₁₆ miles, turf. Held February 1, 2003, with a gross value of $100,000. First held in 1984. Graded since 1998. Stakes record 1:42 (1984 Delta Mary [1st Div.]).

Year	Winner	Jockey	Second	Third	Strs	Time	1st Purse
2003	Gal O Gal, 3, 117	C. P. DeCarlo	Formal Miss, 3	Devil At the Wire, 3	8	1:42.38	$60,000
2002	Cellars Shiraz, 3, 117	C. H. Velasquez	August Storm, 3	She's Vested, 3	10	1:43.21	$60,000
2001	Mystic Lady, 3, 116	J. D. Bailey	Open Minded, 3	Ruff, 3	7	1:46.73	$60,000
2000	Gaviola, 3, 114	J. D. Bailey	Solvig, 3	Are You Up, 3	8	1:47.28	$45,000
1999	Pico Teneriffe, 3, 118	J. D. Bailey	European Rose, 3	Wild Heart Dancing, 3	8	1:48.82	$45,000
1998	Rashas Warning, 3, 118	M. E. Smith	Quick Lap, 3	Runaway Dream, 3	7	1:51.44	$45,000
1997	Auntie Mame, 3, 114	J. D. Bailey	Witchful Thinking, 3	Classic Approval, 3	7	1:46.49	$45,000
1996	Lulu's Ransom, 3, 116	J. D. Bailey	Cymbala (Fr), 3	Vashon, 3	9	1:47.55	$30,000
1995	Clever Thing, 3, 114	C. Perret	Transient Trend, 3	Palliser Bay, 3	6	1:53.06	$30,000
1994	Cut the Charm, 3, 116	W. S. Ramos	Mynameispanama, 3	Tambien Me Voy, 3	11	1:43.72	$30,000
1993	Sigrun, 3, 116	R. R. Douglas	So Say all of Us, 3	Supah Gem, 3	8	1:45.79	$30,000
1992	Morrision Belle, 3, 118	D. Penna	Snazzle Dazzle, 3	Miss Jealski, 3	11	1:42.23	$30,000

Named for 1977 Bonnie Miss S. winner Herecomesthebride (1974, f. by Al Hattab). 1990-'91 not held. 1995-'97,1999-2000 1¹/₈ miles; 1998 about 1¹/₈ miles. 1993-'95,2001 dirt. 1997 equaled course record.

Hill Prince Stakes

Grade 3, Belmont Park, three-year-olds, turf. Held June 15, 2002, with a gross value of $100,000. First held in 1975. Graded since 1981. Stakes record 1:45.69 (1997 Subordination).

Year	Winner	Jockey	Second	Third	Strs	Time	1st Purse
2002	Van Minister, 3, 114	M. J. Luzzi	Miesque's Approval, 3	Westcliffe, 3	5	1:54.42	$65,580
2001	Proud Man, 3, 122	R. R. Douglas	Package Store, 3	Navesink, 3	10	1:48.25	$68,760
2000	Promontory Gold, 3, 119	E. S. Prado	Rob's Spirit, 3	Avezzano (GB), 3	7	1:49.15	$66,540
1999	Time Off, 3, 113	J-L. Samyn	Hoyle, 3	Lenny's Ransom, 3	8	1:47.48	$66,720
1998	Recommended List, 3, 119	J. F. Chavez	Daniel My Brother, 3	Availability, 3	5	1:49.28	$67,800
1997	Subordination, 3, 113	J. R. Velazquez	Rob 'n Gin, 3	Tekken (Ire), 3	6	1:45.69	$67,200
1996	Optic Nerve, 3, 114	J. A. Santos	Fortitude, 3	Allied Forces, 3	7	1:39.70	$66,420
1995	Green Means Go, 3, 117	J. D. Bailey	Smells and Bells, 3	Debonair Dan, 3	10	1:40.33	$68,160
1994	Pennine Ridge, 3, 112	J. D. Bailey	Check Ride, 3	Add the Gold, 3	9	1:39.87	$50,925
1993	Halissee, 3, 121	J. A. Krone	Proud Shot, 3	Logroller, 3	5	1:40.91	$52,020
1992	Free At Last, 3, 126	J. D. Bailey	Casino Magistrate, 3	Kiri's Clown, 3	8	1:41.05	$53,190

Named for Christopher T. Chenery's 1950 Horse of the Year Hill Prince (1947-'70, c. by *Princequillo). 1975-'80 Hill Prince H. 1979-'80,1982 held at Aqueduct. 1975 1⅜ miles; 1976,1979-'96 1¹/₁₆ miles; 1977-'78 1 mile. 1998 dirt. 1997 new course record. 1992 Casino Magistrate finished first, DQ to second.

Hollywood Breeders' Cup Oaks

Grade 2, Hollywood Park, three-year-olds, fillies, 1¹/₁₆ miles, dirt. Held June 15, 2002, with a gross value of $250,000. First held in 1946. Graded since 1973. Stakes record 1:46.93 (1994 Lakeway).

Year	Winner	Jockey	Second	Third	Strs	Time	1st Purse
2002	Adoration, 3, 115	G. K. Gomez	Sister Girl Blues, 3	Saint Bernadette, 3	7	1:43.73	$160,080
2001	Affluent, 3, 116	E. J. Delahoussaye	Collect Call, 3	Secret of Mecca, 3	5	1:49.20	$90,000
2000	Kumari Continent, 3, 117	K. J. Desormeaux	Queenie Belle, 3	Saudi Poetry, 3	5	1:49.13	$90,000
1999	Smooth Player, 3, 117	E. J. Delahoussaye	Excellent Meeting, 3	Nany's Sweep, 3	5	1:48.17	$90,000
1998	Manistique, 3, 115	G. L. Stevens	Sweet and Ready, 3	Yolo Lady, 3	5	1:48.46	$120,000
1997	Sharp Cat, 3, 121	A. O. Solis	Freeport Flight, 3	Really Happy, 3	5	1:49.64	$120,000
1996	Listening, 3, 121	C. J. McCarron	Antespend, 3	Ocean View, 3	4	1:48.70	$110,640
1995	Sleep Easy, 3, 121	C. S. Nakatani	Bello Cielo, 3	Carsona, 3	5	1:50.24	$122,400
1994	Lakeway, 3, 121	K. J. Desormeaux	Sardula, 3	Fancy 'n Fabulous, 3	4	**1:46.93**	$120,000
1993	Hollywood Wildcat, 3, 121	E. J. Delahoussaye	Fit to Lead, 3	Adorydar, 3	9	1:48.48	$130,400
1992	Pacific Squall, 3, 121	K. J. Desormeaux	Race the Wild Wind, 3	Alysbelle, 3	7	1:48.07	$127,200

1946-2001 Hollywood Oaks. 1979-'96 Grade 1. 1949 held at Santa Anita. 1946,1948-'50 1 mile; 1947 7 furlongs; 1954-2001 1¹/₈ miles.

Hollywood Derby

Grade 1, Hollywood Park, three-year-olds, 1¹/₈ miles, turf. Held December 1, 2002, with a gross value of $500,000. First held in 1938. Graded since 1973. Stakes record 1:45.82 (1999 Super Quercus [Fr]).

Year	Winner	Jockey	Second	Third	Strs	Time	1st Purse
2002	Johar, 3, 122	A. O. Solis	Mananan McLir, 3	Royal Gem, 3	9	1:48.70	$300,000
2001	Denon, 3, 122	C. J. McCarron	Sligo Bay (Ire), 3	Aldebaran, 3	12	1:49.28	$300,000
2000	Brahms, 3, 122	P. Day	David Copperfield, 3	Zentsov Street, 3	12	1:46.73	$300,000
1999	Super Quercus (Fr), 3, 122	A. O. Solis	Manndar (Ire), 3	Fighting Falcon, 3	14	**1:45.82**	$300,000
1998	Vergennes, 3, 122	J. R. Velazquez	Dixie Dot Com, 3	$Lone Bid (Fr), 3	10	1:49.44	$300,000
1997	Subordination, 3, 122	J. D. Bailey	Lasting Approval, 3	Blazing Sword, 3	13	1:50.12	$300,000
1996	Marlin, 3, 122	J. R. Velazquez	Rainbow Blues (Ire), 3	Devil's Cup, 3	14	1:46.08	$300,000
1995	Labeeb (GB), 3, 122	E. J. Delahoussaye	Helmsman, 3	Da Hoss, 3	13	1:46.42	$220,000
1994	River Flyer, 3, 122	C. W. Antley	Dare and Go, 3	Fadeyev, 3	13	1:47.48	$220,000
1993	Explosive Red, 3, 122	C. S. Nakatani	Jeune Homme, 3	Earl of Barking (Ire), 3	14	1:46.88	$220,000
1992	Paradise Creek, 3, 122	P. Day	Bien Bien, 3	Kitwood, 3	12	1:47.36	$220,000

1942-'44 not held. 1948-'58 Westerner S.; 1995-'96 Crown Royal Hollywood Derby; 1998-2000 Early Times Hollywood Derby. 1949 held at Santa Anita. 1938-'41,1946-'49,1951-'72 1¹/₄ miles; 1973-'75 1¹/₂ miles. 1938-'72,1976-'80 dirt. 2000 Designed for Luck finished first, DQ to fifth.

Hollywood Futurity

Grade 1, Hollywood Park, two-year-olds, 1¹/₁₆ miles, dirt. Held December 21, 2002, with a gross value of $200,000. First held in 1981. Graded since 1983. Stakes record 1:40.74 (1994 Afternoon Deelites).

Year	Winner	Jockey	Second	Third	Strs	Time	1st Purse
2001	Siphonic, 2, 121	J. D. Bailey	Fonz's, 2	Officer, 2	8	1:42.09	$274,050
2000	Point Given, 2, 121	G. L. Stevens	Millennium Wind, 2	Golden Ticket, 2	4	1:42.21	$204,300
1999	Captain Steve, 2, 121	R. Albarado	High Yield, 2	Cosine, 2	6	1:43.27	$251,400
1998	Tactical Cat, 2, 121	L. A. Pincay Jr.	Prime Timber, 2	Premier Property, 2	5	1:42.63	$235,800
1997	Real Quiet, 2, 121	K. J. Desormeaux	Artax, 2	Nationalore, 2	11	1:41.34	$282,120
1996	Swiss Yodeler, 2, 121	A. O. Solis	Stolen Gold, 2	In Excessive Bull, 2	13	1:42.70	$348,510
1995	Matty G, 2, 121	A. O. Solis	Odyle, 2	Ayrton S, 2	7	1:41.75	$275,000
1994	Afternoon Deelites, 2, 121	K. J. Desormeaux	Thunder Gulch, 2	A. J. Jett, 2	5	**1:40.74**	$275,000
1993	Valiant Nature, 2, 121	L. A. Pincay Jr.	Brocco, 2	Flying Sensation, 2	6	1:40.78	$275,000
1992	River Special, 2, 121	L. A. Pincay Jr.	Stuka, 2	Earl of Barking (Ire), 2	6	1:43.27	$275,000

1985-'90 1 mile.

Hollywood Gold Cup Stakes

Grade 1, Hollywood Park, three-year-olds and up, 1¹/₄ miles, dirt. Held July 14, 2002, with a gross value of $750,000. First held in 1938. Graded since 1973. Stakes record 1:58.20 (1972 Quack).

Year	Winner	Jockey	Second	Third	Strs	Time	1st Purse
2002	Sky Jack, 6, 124	L. A. Pincay Jr.	Momentum, 4	Milwaukee Brew, 5	6	2:01.73	$450,000
2001	Aptitude, 4, 124	L. A. Pincay Jr.	Skimming, 5	Futural, 5	5	2:01.79	$450,000
2000	Early Pioneer, 5, 124	V. Espinoza	General Challenge, 4	David, 4	9	2:01.40	$600,000
1999	Real Quiet, 4, 124	J. D. Bailey	Budroyale, 6	Malek (Chi), 6	4	1:59.67	$600,000
1998	Skip Away, 5, 124	J. D. Bailey	Puerto Madero (Chi), 4	Gentlemen (Arg), 6	8	2:00.16	$600,000
1997	Gentlemen (Arg), 5, 124	G. L. Stevens	Siphon (Brz), 6	Sandpit (Brz), 8	8	1:59.26	$600,000
1996	Siphon (Brz), 5, 117	D. R. Flores	Geri, 4	Helmsman, 4	8	2:00.50	$600,000
1995	Cigar, 5, 126	J. D. Bailey	Tinners Way, 5	Tossofthecoin, 5	8	1:59.46	$550,000
1994	Slew of Damascus, 6, 117	G. L. Stevens	Fanmore, 6	Del Mar Dennis, 4	5	2:00.76	$412,500
1993	Best Pal, 5, 121	C. A. Black	Bertrando, 4	Major Impact, 4	10	2:00.17	$412,500
1992	Sultry Song, 4, 113	J. D. Bailey	Marquetry, 5	Another Review, 4	6	2:00.23	$550,000

1942-'43 not held. 1938-'71,1973,1976-'96 Hollywood Gold Cup H.; 1972,1974-'75 Hollywood Gold Cup Invitational H.; 2000 Sempra Energy Hollywood Gold Cup S. 1949 held at Santa Anita. 2001 Futural finished first, DQ to third.

Hollywood Juvenile Championship Stakes

Grade 3, Hollywood Park, two-year-olds, 6 furlongs, dirt. Held July 20, 2002, with a gross value of $100,000. First held in 1938. Graded since 1973. Stakes record 1:08.60 (1974 Dimaggio).

Year	Winner	Jockey	Second	Third	Strs	Time	1st Purse
2002	Crowned Dancer, 2, 120	A. O. Solis	Outta Here, 2	Chief Planner, 2	7	1:10.10	$64,980
2001	Came Home, 2, 117	C. J. McCarron	Metatron, 2	A Major Pleasure, 2	6	1:09.20	$64,440
2000	Squirtle Squirt, 2, 120	L. A. Pincay Jr.	Legendary Weave, 2	Drumcliff, 2	5	1:09.98	$63,540
1999	Dixie Union, 2, 117	A. O. Solis	Exchange Rate, 2	High Yield, 2	5	1:09.95	$63,780
1998	Yes It's True, 2, 120	J. D. Bailey	O'Rey Fantasma, 2	Worldly Manner, 2	7	1:09.58	$61,620
1997	K. O. Punch, 2, 120	G. L. Stevens	Old Topper, 2	Majorbigtimesheet, 2	9	1:09.95	$66,120
1996	Swiss Yodeler, 2, 120	A. O. Solis	Red, 2	Vermilion, 2	5	1:09.77	$61,740
1995	Hennessy, 2, 117	G. L. Stevens	Reef Reef, 2	Desert Native, 2	7	1:09.85	$57,400
1994	Mr Purple, 2, 117	C. J. McCarron	†Serena's Song, 2	Cyrano, 2	7	1:10.16	$57,600
1993	Ramblin Guy, 2, 117	E. J. Delahoussaye	Swift Walker, 2	Individual Style, 2	8	1:09.99	$57,600
1992	Altazarr, 2, 117	E. J. Delahoussaye	Tatum Canyon, 2	Just Sid, 2	6	1:10.01	$58,700

1942-'43 not held. 1938-'39 Starlet Sweepstakes; 1940-'58 Starlet S. 1973-'96 Grade 2. 1949 held at Santa Anita. 1938 5¹/₂ furlongs; 1944 7 furlongs; 1950 1¹/₁₆ miles. †denotes female.

Hollywood Prevue Stakes

Grade 3, Hollywood Park, two-year-olds, 7 furlongs, dirt. Held November 23, 2002, with a gross value of $125,000. First held in 1981. Graded since 1985. Stakes record 1:20.98 (1994 Afternoon Deelites).

Year	Winner	Jockey	Second	Third	Strs	Time	1st Purse
2002	Roll Hennessy Roll, 2, 119	A. O. Solis	Red Apache, 2	Hell Cat, 2	7	1:22.68	$75,000
2001	Fonz's, 2, 117	L. A. Pincay Jr.	Popular, 2	Labamta Babe, 2	7	1:22.03	$60,000
2000	Proud Tower, 2, 122	V. Espinoza	Chinook Cat, 2	Yonaguska, 2	8	1:23.01	$60,000
1999	Grey Memo, 2, 115	M. S. Garcia	Magical Dragon, 2	Cameron Pass, 2	6	1:24.44	$60,000
1998	Premier Property, 2, 119	D. R. Flores	Select Few, 2	American Spirit, 2	7	1:23.29	$60,000
1997	Commitisize, 2, 113	D. R. Flores	Buttons N Moes, 2	Search Me, 2	6	1:21.64	$60,000
1996	In Excessive Bull, 2, 115	C. S. Nakatani	Thisnearlywasmine, 2	Constant Demand, 2	5	1:21.54	$61,020
1995	Cobra King, 2, 121	C. J. McCarron	Hennessy, 2	Exetera, 2	6	1:21.25	$58,800
1994	Afternoon Deelites, 2, 115	K. J. Desormeaux	Valid Wager, 2	Hunt for Missouri, 2	4	1:20.98	$57,500
1993	Individual Style, 2, 121	C. W. Antley	Egayant, 2	Soul of the Matter, 2	6	1:21.17	$46,100
1992	Stuka, 2, 115	P. A. Valenzuela	Codified, 2	Altazarr, 2	8	1:21.94	$62,350

Traditionally used as a prep race for the Hollywood Futurity. 1987 not held. 1990-'95 Hollywood Prevue Breeders' Cup S.

Hollywood Starlet Stakes

Grade 1, Hollywood Park, two-year-olds, fillies, 1¹/₁₆ miles, dirt. Held December 14, 2002, with a gross value of $356,500. First held in 1981. Graded since 1983. Stakes record 1:41.96 (1994 Serena's Song).

Year	Winner	Jockey	Second	Third	Strs	Time	1st Purse
2002	Elloluv, 2, 120	P. A. Valenzuela	Composure, 2	Summer Wind Dancer, 2	7	1:42.88	$213,900
2001	Habibti, 2, 120	V. Espinoza	You, 2	Tali'sluckybusride, 2	5	1:43.12	$214,800
2000	I Believe In You, 2, 120	A. O. Solis	Jetin Excess, 2	Whoopddoo, 2	6	1:43.57	$205,050
1999	Surfside, 2, 120	P. Day	She's Classy, 2	Abby Girl, 2	5	1:43.51	$228,150
1998	Excellent Meeting, 2, 120	K. J. Desormeaux	Lacquaria, 2	Perfect Six, 2	6	1:42.14	$240,000
1997	Love Lock, 2, 120	K. J. Desormeaux	Career Collection, 2	Snowberg, 2	6	1:42.17	$168,600
1996	Sharp Cat, 2, 120	C. S. Nakatani	City Band, 2	High Heeled Hope, 2	8	1:44.69	$165,600
1995	Cara Rafaela, 2, 120	C. S. Nakatani	Advancing Star, 2	Chile Chatte, 2	5	1:43.10	$137,500
1994	Serena's Song, 2, 120	C. S. Nakatani	Urbane, 2	Ski Dancer, 2	5	1:41.96	$137,500
1993	Sardula, 2, 120	E. J. Delahoussaye	Princess Mitterand, 2	Viz, 2	5	1:42.34	$139,095
1992	Creaking Board (GB), 2, 120	C. S. Nakatani	Passing Vice, 2	Madame l'Enjoleur, 2	9	1:43.73	$137,500

Young actresses in old Hollywood were traditionally known as "starlets" before reaching full star status. 1985-'90 1 mile.

Hollywood Turf Cup Stakes

Grade 1, Hollywood Park, three-year-olds and up, 1¹/₂ miles, turf. Held November 23, 2002, with a gross value of $250,000. First held in 1981. Graded since 1983. Stakes record 2:24.80 (1990 Itsallgreektome).

Year	Winner	Jockey	Second	Third	Strs	Time	1st Purse
2002	Sligo Bay (Ire), 4, 126	L. A. Pincay Jr.	Grammarian, 4	Delta Form (Aus), 6	11	2:27.22	$150,000
2001	Super Quercus (Fr), 5, 126	A. O. Solis	Bonapartiste (Fr), 7	Blazing Fury, 3	9	2:29.86	$150,000
2000	Bienamado, 4, 126	C. J. McCarron	Northern Quest (Fr), 5	Lazy Lode (Arg), 6	8	2:25.98	$240,000
1999	Lazy Lode (Arg), 5, 126	L. A. Pincay Jr.	Public Purse, 5	Single Empire (Ire), 5	7	2:25.85	$240,000
1998	Lazy Lode (Arg), 4, 126	C. S. Nakatani	Yagli, 5	Ferrari (Ger), 4	10	2:28.36	$300,000
1997	River Bay, 4, 126	A. O. Solis	Awad, 7	Flag Down, 7	12	2:26.47	$300,000
1996	Running Flame (Fr), 4, 126	C. J. McCarron	Marlin, 3	Talloires, 6	10	2:28.53	$300,000
1995	Royal Chariot, 5, 126	A. O. Solis	Talloires, 5	Earl of Barking (Ire), 5	14	2:25.18	$275,000
1994	Frenchpark (GB), 4, 126	C. A. Black	Dare and Go, 3	Regency (GB), 4	11	2:25.66	$275,000
1993	Fraise, 5, 126	C. J. McCarron	Know Heights (Ire), 4	Explosive Red, 3	6	2:32.34	$275,000
1992	Bien Bien, 3, 122	C. J. McCarron	Fraise, 4	†Trishyde, 3	6	2:31.28	$275,000

1981-'85,1988,1990 Hollywood Turf Cup H.; 1986-'87 Hollywood Turf Cup Invitational H. 1982-'84 1³/₈ miles. 1992 Fraise finished first, DQ to second. †denotes female.

Hollywood Turf Express Handicap

Grade 3, Hollywood Park, three-year-olds and up, 5½ furlongs, turf. Held November 29, 2002, with a gross value of $200,000. First held in 1985. Graded since 1994. Stakes record 1:01.40 (1991 Gundaghia [1st Div.]; 1991 Answer Do [2nd Div.]).

Year	Winner	Jockey	Second	Third	Strs	Time	1st Purse
2002	**Texas Glitter**, 6, 119	J. R. Velazquez	Rocky Bar, 4	Malabar Gold, 5	5	1:01.52	$120,000
2001	**Swept Overboard**, 4, 122	E. J. Delahoussaye	Speak in Passing, 4	Blu Air Force (Ire), 4	10	1:01.86	$120,000
2000	**El Cielo**, 6, 122	C. S. Nakatani	Texas Glitter, 4	Full Moon Madness, 5	7	1:01.73	$120,000
1999	**Mr. Doubledown**, 5, 115	V. Espinoza	Howbaddouwantit, 4	Champ's Star, 4	8	1:01.98	$120,000
1998	**Soldier Field**, 3, 117	R. Wilson	Surachai, 5	Bodyguard (GB), 3	10	1:02.19	$120,000
1997	**Advancing Star**, 4, 119	K. J. Desormeaux	Latin Dancer, 3	Surachai, 4	9	1:02.68	$120,000
1996	**Sandtrap**, 3, 114	A. O. Solis	Cyrano Storme (Ire), 6	Suggest, 4	8	1:01.46	$120,000
1995	**Cyrano Storme (Ire)**, 5, 116	R. R. Douglas	Lakota Brave, 6	Pembroke, 5	9	1:01.64	$110,000
1994	**Rotsaluck**, 3, 118	F. H. Valenzuela	†Marina Park (GB), 4	D'Hallevant, 4	11	1:02.27	$82,500
1993	**Wild Harmony**, 4, 117	C. J. McCarron	Robin des Pins, 5	Monde Bleu (GB), 5	8	1:01.88	$110,000
1992	**Answer Do**, 6, 121	E. J. Delahoussaye	Repriced, 4	Gundaghia, 5	11	1:02.14	$110,000

1985 Hollywood Turf Sprint Championship. 1985-'90 6 furlongs. 1985,1988 dirt. †denotes female.

Holy Bull Stakes

Grade 3, Gulfstream Park, three-year-olds, 1¹⁄₁₆ miles, dirt. Held January 18, 2003, with a gross value of $100,000. First held in 1972. Graded since 1995. Stakes record 1:41.62 (1994 Go for Gin).

Year	Winner	Jockey	Second	Third	Strs	Time	1st Purse
2003	**Offlee Wild**, 3, 116	M. Guidry	Powerful Touch, 3	Bham, 3	13	1:43.00	$60,000
2002	**Booklet**, 3, 122	E. Coa	Harlan's Holiday, 3	Thiscannonsloaded, 3	7	1:46.16	$60,000
2001	**Radical Riley**, 3, 119	E. O. Nunez	Buckle Down Ben, 3	Cee Dee, 3	8	1:46.06	$60,000
2000	**Hal's Hope**, 3, 112	R. I. Velez	Personal First, 3	Megacles, 3	11	1:44.52	$60,000
1999	**Grits'n Hard Toast**, 3, 114	R. G. Davis	Doneraile Court, 3	Mountain Range, 3	7	1:45.32	$60,000
1998	**Cape Town**, 3, 119	J. D. Bailey	Comic Strip, 3	Sweetsouthernsaint, 3	7	1:44.15	$60,000
1997	**Arthur L.**, 3, 122	J. R. Velazquez	Acceptable, 3	Captain Bodgit, 3	9	1:42.93	$60,000
1996	**Cobra King**, 3, 117	C. J. McCarron	Editor's Note, 3	Tilden, 3	7	1:43.42	$45,000
1995	**Royal Mitch**, 3, 115	R. G. Davis	Private Rite, 3	Wild Syn, 3	7	1:43.16	$30,405
	Suave Prospect, 3, 119	J. D. Bailey	Bullet Trained, 3	Rush Dancer, 3	8	1:44.03	$45,000
1994	**Go for Gin**, 3, 119	J. D. Bailey	Halo's Image, 3	Senor Conquistador, 3	6	1:41.62	$45,000
1993	**Pride of Burkaan**, 3, 112	J. D. Bailey	Kassec, 3	Jetting Along, 3	8	1:44.74	$45,000
1992	**Waki Warrior**, 3, 114	E. Fires	Scream Machine, 3	Careful Gesture, 3	13	1:44.32	$78,258

Named for 1994 Horse of the Year Holy Bull (1991, c. by Great Above). 1973,1975-'76,1978,1980-'89 not held. 1995 two divisions. 1972-'95 Preview S.; 1972-'79 6 furlongs; 1990 1¹⁄₈ miles.

Honey Bee Handicap

Grade 3, Meadowlands, three-year-olds, fillies, 1¹⁄₁₆ miles, dirt. Held November 2, 2001, with a gross value of $200,000. First held in 1977. Graded since 1985. Stakes record 1:40.60 (1984 Squan Song).

Year	Winner	Jockey	Second	Third	Strs	Time	1st Purse
2001	**Mystic Lady**, 3, 122	E. Coa	Latour, 3	Shiny Band, 3	4	1:42.29	$120,000
2000	**Critical Eye**, 3, 121	M. E. Smith	Eventail, 3	Rosie Dooley, 3	7	1:41.90	$120,000
1999	**Belle Cherie**, 3, 115	J. A. Velez Jr.	Gaelic Bay, 3	Boom Town Girl, 3	11	1:42.19	$90,000
1998	**Thunder Kitten**, 3, 112	S. J. Sellers	Salty Lady, 3	Patty's Positive, 3	7	1:41.24	$60,000
1997	**Fancy Freda**, 3, 114	W. H. McCauley	Alarming Prospect, 3	Key Hunter, 3	9	1:41.12	$60,000
1996	**Proper Angel**, 3, 115	M. G. Pino	Gold n Delicious, 3	Plum Country, 3	6	1:44.62	$30,000
1995	**Rogues Walk**, 3, 120	J. R. Velazquez	Full and Fancy, 3	Transient Trend, 3	7	1:42.77	$30,000
1994	**Sterling Pound**, 3, 114	M. E. Smith	Footing, 3	Perfect Night, 3	6	1:42.68	$30,000
1993	**Nine Keys**, 3, 113	M. E. Smith	Aztec Hill, 3	Broad Gains, 3	6	1:43.00	$30,000
1992	**Vivano**, 3, 121	M. E. Smith	Caged Heart, 3	Dior's Angel, 3	5	1:43.98	$30,000

Named for New Jersey's state insect, the honey bee. 2002 not held. 1996 Novotel Meadowlands Honey Bee H.; 1997 Honey Bee Breeders' Cup H. 1977 three-year-olds and up. 1977 fillies and mares.

Honey Fox Handicap

Grade 3, Gulfstream Park, three-year-olds and up, fillies and mares, about 1¹⁄₁₆ miles, turf. Held January 5, 2003, with a gross value of $100,000. First held in 1985. Graded since 1994. Stakes record 1:46.19 (2003 San Dare).

Year	Winner	Jockey	Second	Third	Strs	Time	1st Purse
2003	**San Dare**, 5, 115	M. Guidry	Calista (GB), 5	Laurica, 6	10	**1:46.19**	$60,000
2002	**Batique**, 6, 117	J. F. Chavez	My Sweet Westly, 6	Silver Bandana, 6	8	1:49.32	$60,000
2001	**Spook Express (SAf)**, 7, 115	M. E. Smith	Please Sign In, 5	Lady Dora, 4	12	1:35.60	$60,000
2000	**Dominique's Joy**, 5, 113	J. D. Bailey	Circus Charmer, 5	Pico Teneriffe, 4	7	1:39.91	$45,000
1999	**Colcon**, 6, 119	J. D. Bailey	Lovers Knot (GB), 4	Tampico, 6	10	1:41.71	$45,000
1998	**Parade Queen**, 4, 118	P. Day	Dispersion, 5	Dance Clear (Ire), 5	12	1:42.10	$45,000
1997	**Rare Blend**, 4, 118	J. D. Bailey	Queen Tutta, 5	Hurricane Viv, 4	6	1:44.28	$45,000
1996	**Apolda**, 5, 116	J. D. Bailey	Class Kris, 4	Alice Springs, 6	11	1:41.55	$45,000
1995	**Regal Joy**, 4, 113	D. Penna	Sambacarioca, 6	Sovereign Kitty, 4	6	1:44.79	$36,000
1994	**Sambacarioca**, 5, 121	J. D. Bailey	Tiney Toast, 5	Marshua's River, 7	6	1:43.41	$36,000
1993	**Hero's Love**, 5, 113	E. Fires	Quilma (Chi), 6	Lady Blessington (Fr), 5	14	1:42.90	$30,000
1992	**Explosive Kate**, 5, 113	D. Penna	Indian Fashion, 5	Belleofbasinstreet, 4	14	1:43.37	$30,000

Named for 1981 Orchid H. (G2) winner Honey Fox (1977, f. by Minnesota Mac). Formerly named for NFL Hall of Fame quarterback Joe Namath. 1985-2000 Joe Namath H. 1985,1987-'89,2001 1 mile; 1986 7 furlongs; 1990 about one mile; 1991 1 mile 70 yards; 1992-2000 1¹⁄₁₆ miles. 1986,1991,1994-'95,1997 dirt. 1985 three-year-olds. 1985 fillies.

Honeymoon Breeders' Cup Handicap

Grade 2, Hollywood Park, three-year-olds, fillies, 1¹⁄₈ miles, turf. Held June 8, 2002, with a gross value of $200,000. First held in 1952. Graded since 1976. Stakes record 1:51.97 (2002 Megahertz [GB]).

Year	Winner	Jockey	Second	Third	Strs	Time	1st Purse
2002	Megahertz (GB), 3, 120	P. A. Valenzuela	Arabic Song (Ire), 3	High Society (Ire), 3	7	**1:51.97**	$97,830
2001	Innit (Ire), 3, 117	C. J. McCarron	Live Your Dreams, 3	Beefeater Baby, 3	9	2:01.28	$120,000
2000	Classy Cara, 3, 122	I. Puglisi	Kumari Continent, 3	Minor Details, 3	9	1:48.05	$90,000
1999	Sweet Ludy (Ire), 3, 116	G. L. Stevens	Tout Charmant, 3	Aviate, 3	7	1:48.05	$65,160
1998	Country Garden (GB), 3, 120	K. J. Desormeaux	Janine Rose, 3	Chenille (Ire), 3	6	1:48.74	$64,080
1997	Famous Digger, 3, 116	B. Blanc	Freeport Flight, 3	Kentucky Kaper, 3	8	1:47.68	$65,460
1996	Antespend, 3, 122	C. W. Antley	Clamorosa, 3	Najecam, 3	8	1:47.50	$82,410
1995	Auriette (Ire), 3, 117	E. J. Delahoussaye	Artica, 3	Top Shape (Fr), 3	6	1:41.68	$62,100
1994	Work the Crowd, 3, 117	C. J. McCarron	Malli Star, 3	Fancy 'n Fabulous, 3	8	1:39.68	$64,700
1993	Likeable Style, 3, 122	E. J. Delahoussaye	Adorydar, 3	Vinista, 3	5	1:46.29	$62,200
1992	Pacific Squall, 3, 115	K. J. Desormeaux	Miss Turkana, 3	Morriston Belle, 3	10	1:41.02	$67,100

Named for multiple California stakes winner Honeymoon (1943, f. by *Beau Pere), once the leading California-bred distaff earner. 1952-'55 Sea Breeze S.; 1956-'74 Honeymoon S.; 1975-2000 Honeymoon H.; 2001 Honeymoon Breeders' Cup Invitational H. 1976-'80,1983-'97 Grade 3. 1952-'53 6 furlongs; 1954 7 furlongs; 1955-'67, 1970 1 mile; 1968-'69, 1971-'95 1¹⁄₁₆ miles; 2001 1¹⁄₄ miles. 1952-'72,1993 dirt.

Honorable Miss Handicap

Grade 3, Saratoga Race Course, three-year-olds and up, fillies and mares, 6 furlongs, dirt. Held August 2, 2002, with a gross value of $100,000. First held in 1992. Graded since 1996. Stakes record 1:08.93 (2000 Bourbon Belle [2nd Div.]).

Year	Winner	Jockey	Second	Third	Strs	Time	1st Purse
2002	Mandy's Gold, 4, 116	E. S. Prado	Shine Again, 5	Dat You Miz Blue, 5	6	1:09.24	$65,100
2001	Big Bambu, 4, 118	J. D. Bailey	Country Hideaway, 5	Dat You Miz Blue, 4	4	1:09.64	$63,708
2000	Debby d'Or, 5, 114	S. J. Sellers	Tropical Punch, 4	Katz Me If You Can, 3	9	1:10.11	$66,450
	Bourbon Belle, 5, 116	W. Martinez	Cassidy, 5	Go to the Ink, 4	8	**1:08.93**	$65,850
1999	Bourbon Belle, 4, 116	P. A. Johnson	Gold Princess, 4	License Fee, 4	10	1:09.53	$67,560
1998	Furlough, 4, 113	M. E. Smith	Angel's Tearlet, 5	Dixie Flag, 4	6	1:11.32	$48,765
1997	Dancin Renee, 5, 116	R. Migliore	Ashboro, 4	Vivace, 4	6	1:09.16	$48,465
1996	Twist Afleet, 5, 119	M. E. Smith	Broad Smile, 4	In Conference, 4	8	1:09.91	$49,005
1995	Low Key Affair, 4, 115	P. Day	Classy Mirage, 5	Twist Afleet, 4	5	1:09.67	$48,195
1994	Classy Mirage, 4, 122	J. A. Krone	Spinning Round, 5	For all Seasons, 4	6	1:09.72	$48,675
1993	Nannerl, 6, 117	J. D. Bailey	Vivano, 4	Via Dei Portici, 4	6	1:15.19	$29,040
1992	Nice Assay, 4, 115	C. J. McCarron	Madam Bear, 4	Real Irish Hope, 5	5	1:08.97	$31,620

Named for Pen-Y-Bryn Farm's 1975, '76 Fall Highweight H. (G2) winner Honorable Miss (1970-'87, f. by Damascus). 1992-'97 Honorable Miss S. 1993 6¹⁄₂ furlongs. 2000 two divisions.

Hopeful Stakes

Grade 1, Saratoga Race Course, two-year-olds, 7 furlongs, dirt. Held August 31, 2002, with a gross value of $200,000. First held in 1903. Graded since 1973. Stakes record 1:21.94 (2001 Came Home).

Year	Winner	Jockey	Second	Third	Strs	Time	1st Purse
2002	Sky Mesa, 2, 122	E. S. Prado	Pretty Wild, 2	Zavata, 2	6	1:23.08	$120,000
2001	Came Home, 2, 122	C. J. McCarron	Mayakovsky, 2	Thunder Days, 2	7	**1:21.94**	$120,000
2000	(DH) City Zip, 2, 122	J. A. Santos		Macho Uno, 2	11	1:24.52	$80,000
	(DH) Yonaguska, 2, 122	J. D. Bailey					
1999	High Yield, 2, 122	J. D. Bailey	Settlement, 2	Exciting Story, 2	9	1:22.85	$120,000
1998	Lucky Roberto, 2, 122	R. G. Davis	Tactical Cat, 2	Time Bandit, 2	7	1:23.81	$120,000
1997	Favorite Trick, 2, 122	P. Day	K. O. Punch, 2	Jess M, 2	7	1:23.87	$120,000
1996	Smoke Glacken, 2, 122	C. Perret	Ordway, 2	Gun Fight, 2	8	1:23.63	$120,000
1995	Hennessy, 2, 122	G. L. Stevens	Louis Quatorze, 2	Maria's Mon, 2	7	1:23.44	$120,000
1994	Wild Escapade, 2, 122	J. F. Chavez	Montreal Red, 2	Law of the Sea, 2	6	1:23.24	$120,000
1993	Dehere, 2, 122	C. J. McCarron	Slew Gin Fizz, 2	Whitney Tower, 2	7	1:15.97	$120,000
1992	Great Navigator, 2, 122	A. T. Gryder	Strolling Along, 2	England Expects, 2	8	1:15.71	$120,000

As the first major two-year-old race longer than 6 furlongs, owners are "hopeful" that their horses will be able to go a classic distance. 1911-'12 not held. 1943-'45 held at Belmont. 1903-'09 6 furlongs; 1910-'93 6¹⁄₂ furlongs. 2000 dead heat for first.

(Humana) Distaff Handicap

Grade 1, Churchill Downs, four-year-olds and up, fillies and mares, 7 furlongs, dirt. Held May 4, 2002, with a gross value of $228,000. First held in 1987. Graded since 1990. Stakes record 1:20.70 (2001 Dream Supreme).

Year	Winner	Jockey	Second	Third	Strs	Time	1st Purse
2002	Celtic Melody, 4, 114	M. Guidry	Gold Mover, 4	Hattiesburg, 4	9	1:22.98	$141,360
2001	Dream Supreme, 4, 120	P. Day	La Feminn, 5	Nany's Sweep, 5	5	**1:20.70**	$102,300
2000	Ruby Surprise, 5, 114	J. C. Judice	Honest Lady, 4	Cassidy, 5	7	1:21.25	$102,951
1999	Zuppardo Ardo, 5, 114	S. J. Sellers	French Braids, 4	Prospector's Song, 4	9	1:23.40	$105,183

1998	Colonial Minstrel, 4, 115	J. R. Velazquez	Stop Traffic, 5	Meter Maid, 4	11	1:22.12	$71,300
1997	Capote Belle, 4, 118	J. R. Velazquez	Hidden Lake, 4	J J'sdream, 4	8	1:22.38	$70,060
1996	In Conference, 4, 113	M. E. Smith	Supah Jess, 4	Morris Code, 4	8	1:23.30	$72,930
1995	Laura's Pistolette, 4, 114	C. S. Nakatani	Morning Meadow, 5	Traverse City, 5	10	1:22.24	$74,425
1994	Roamin Rachel, 4, 118	M. E. Smith	Arches of Gold, 5	Glory's Ghost, 5	7	1:23.83	$72,345
1993	Court Hostess, 5, 115	C. J. McCarron	Santa Catalina, 5	Ifyoucouldseemenow, 5	12	1:23.18	$56,550
1992	Ifyoucouldseemenow, 4, 120	C. Perret	Madam Bear, 4	Magal, 4	10	1:22.22	$56,599

Named for sponsor Humana Inc., headquartered in Louisville, Kentucky. 1987 Brown & Williamson S.; 1988-'94 Brown & Williamson H. 1990-'98 Grade 3; 1999-2001 Grade 2.

Hutcheson Stakes

Grade 2, Gulfstream Park, three-year-olds, 7 furlongs, dirt. Held February 15, 2003, with a gross value of $150,000. First held in 1955. Graded since 1973. Stakes record 1:20.80 (1978 Sensitive Prince).

Year	Winner	Jockey	Second	Third	Strs	Time	1st Purse
2003	Lion Tamer, 3, 118	J. R. Velazquez	Strength Within, 3	Crafty Guy, 3	6	1:22.60	$90,000
2002	Showmeitall, 3, 118	J. F. Chavez	Monthir, 3	Royal Lad, 3	8	1:26.07	$90,000
2001	Yonaguska, 3, 119	J. D. Bailey	City Zip, 3	Sparkling Sabre, 3	11	1:22.63	$90,000
2000	(DH) Summer Note, 3, 113	S. J. Sellers		American Bullet, 3	8	1:21.76	$60,000
	(DH) More Than Ready, 3	J. R. Velazquez					
1999	Bet Me Best, 3, 122	J. D. Bailey	Texas Glitter, 3	Cat Thief, 3	7	1:22.33	$90,000
1998	Time Limit, 3, 119	J. D. Bailey	Coronado's Quest, 3	Zippy Zeal, 3	5	1:22.53	$60,000
1997	Frisk Me Now, 3, 112	E. L. King Jr.	Confide, 3	Crown Ambassador, 3	8	1:22.51	$60,000
1996	Appealing Skier, 3, 119	R. Wilson	Unbridled's Song, 3	Gold Fever, 3	5	1:24.72	$45,000
1995	Valid Wager, 3, 119	M. A. Pedroza	Mr. Greeley, 3	Don Juan A, 3	7	1:23.51	$45,000
1994	Holy Bull, 3, 122	M. E. Smith	Patton, 3	You and I, 3	5	1:21.23	$45,000
1993	Hidden Trick, 3, 114	R. P. Romero	Great Navigator, 3	Forever Whirl, 3	9	1:23.61	$54,108
1992	My Luck Runs North, 3, 113	R. D. Lopez	Sneaky Solicitor, 3	Frosted Spy, 3	9	1:24.95	$55,008

Named for labor leader William Levi Hutcheson, who served as a member of the Gulfstream Park Advisory Board. 1954 held as a purse race. 1955,1984 Hutcheson H.; 1997 Danka Hutcheson S. 1955-'60 6½ furlongs. 1993 Demaloot Demashoot finished second, DQ to fourth. 2000 dead head for first.

Illinois Derby

Grade 2, Hawthorne Race Course, three-year-olds, 1⅛ miles, dirt. Held April 5, 2003, with a gross value of $500,000. First held in 1923. Graded since 1973. Stakes record 1:47.51 (1997 Wild Rush).

Year	Winner	Jockey	Second	Third	Strs	Time	1st Purse
2003	Ten Most Wanted, 3, 114	P. Day	Fund of Funds, 3	Foufa's Warrior, 3	10	1:51.47	$300,000
2002	War Emblem, 3, 114	L. J. Sterling Jr.	Repent, 3	Fonz's, 3	9	1:49.92	$300,000
2001	Distilled, 3, 114	M. E. Smith	Saint Damien, 3	Dream Run, 3	8	1:51.37	$300,000
2000	Performing Magic, 3, 119	S. J. Sellers	Country Only, 3	Country Coast, 3	9	1:50.86	$300,000
1999	Vision and Verse, 3, 114	H. Castillo Jr.	Prime Directive, 3	Pineaff, 3	10	1:48.47	$300,000
1998	Yarrow Brae, 3, 114	W. Martinez	One Bold Stroke, 3	Orville N Wilbur's, 3	10	1:51.21	$300,000
1997	Wild Rush, 3, 117	K. J. Desormeaux	Anet, 3	Saratoga Sunrise, 3	8	1:47.51	$300,000
1996	Natural Selection, 3, 114	R. P. Romero	El Amante, 3	Irish Conquest, 3	13	1:48.60	$300,000
1995	Peaks and Valleys, 3, 124	J. A. Krone	Da Hoss, 3	Western Echo, 3	13	1:48.99	$300,000
1994	Rustic Light, 3, 117	E. Fires	Amathos, 3	Seminole Wind, 3	7	1:51.89	$300,000
1993	Antrim Rd., 3, 114	A. T. Gryder	Seattle Morn, 3	Secret Negotiator, 3	13	1:48.68	$300,000
1992	Dignitas, 3, 117	J. D. Bailey	American Chance, 3	Straight to Bed, 3	13	1:49.09	$320,100

1924-'32,1939-'62,1970-'71 not held. 1973-'87 Grade 3. 1924-'32,1939-'98,2000-'02 held at Sportsman's Park; 1933-'38 Aurora. 1923 1¼ miles. 1997 new track record.

Indiana Breeders' Cup Oaks

Grade 3, Hoosier Park, three-year-olds, fillies, 1⅟₁₆ miles, dirt. Held October 4, 2002, with a gross value of $250,000. First held in 1995. Graded since 2001. Stakes record 1:42.40 (2000 Humble Clerk).

Year	Winner	Jockey	Second	Third	Strs	Time	1st Purse
2002	Bare Necessities, 3, 118	J. Valdivia Jr.	Erica's Smile, 3	Tarnished Lady, 3	9	1:45.83	$183,840
2001	Scoop, 3, 121	R. Albarado	Gold Huntress, 3	Caressing, 3	9	1:44.06	$123,480
2000	Humble Clerk, 3, 114	L. Melancon	Megans Bluff, 3	Miss Seffens, 3	5	1:42.40	$92,580
1999	Brushed Halory, 3, 121	E. M. Martin Jr.	The Happy Hopper, 3	Chelsie's House, 3	10	1:44.64	$123,330
1998	French Braids, 3, 116	W. Martinez	Remember Ike, 3	Barefoot Dyana, 3	7	1:43.11	$124,080
1997	Cotton Carnival, 3, 121	E. M. Martin Jr.	Sheepscot, 3	Valid Bonnet, 3	9	1:43.30	$64,440
1996	Princess Eloise, 3, 118	S. T. Saito	Talking Tower, 3	Shuffle Again, 3	6	1:37.00	$33,540
1995	Niner's Home, 3, 121	T. J. Hebert	Alltheway Bertie, 3	Graceful Minister, 3	6	1:37.00	$24,480

1995-'97 Indiana Oaks. 1995-'96 1 mile.

Indiana Derby

Grade 3, Hoosier Park, three-year-olds, 1⅟₁₆ miles, dirt. Held October 5, 2002, with a gross value of $400,000. First held in 1995. Graded since 2002. Stakes record 1:41.40 (1996 Canyon Run).

Year	Winner	Jockey	Second	Third	Strs	Time	1st Purse
2002	Perfect Drift, 3, 124	J. K. Court	Easyfromthegitgo, 3	Premeditation, 3	12	1:43.50	$248,820
2001	Orientate, 3, 115	R. Albarado	Saratoga Games, 3	Trion Georgia, 3	11	1:42.22	$188,460
2000	Mister Deville, 3, 119	L. S. Quinonez	Performing Magic, 3	One Call Close, 3	5	1:41.80	$184,500
1999	Forty One Carats, 3, 115	J. F. Chavez	Zanetti, 3	First American, 3	12	1:42.24	$188,100

1998	**One Bold Stroke**, 3, 122	R. Albarado	Dixie Dot Com, 3	Da Devil, 3	11	1:43.14	$188,700
1997	**Dubai Dust**, 3, 113	S. P. LeJeune Jr.	Frisk Me Now, 3	Tansit, 3	8	1:44.00	$127,440
1996	**Canyon Run**, 3, 115	F. C. Torres	Broadway Bit, 3	Hunk of Class, 3	10	**1:41.40**	$64,560
1995	**Peruvian**, 3, 117	D. Kutz	I Still Believe, 3	Mine Inspector, 3	11	1:43.00	$66,900

Inglewood Handicap

Grade 3, Hollywood Park, three-year-olds and up, 1¹⁄₁₆ miles, turf. Held May 5, 2002, with a gross value of $100,000. First held in 1938. Graded since 1973. Stakes record 1:38.77 (1998 Fantastic Fellow).

Year	Winner	Jockey	Second	Third	Strs	Time	1st Purse
2002	**Night Patrol**, 6, 113	V. Espinoza	Redattore (Brz), 7	Seinne (Chi), 5	7	1:39.35	$65,820
2001	**Fateful Dream**, 4, 114	D. R. Flores	National Anthem (GB), 5	Casino King (Ire), 6	5	1:41.65	$64,260
2000	**Montemiro (Fr)**, 6, 113	V. Espinoza	Bonapartiste (Fr), 6	Takarian (Ire), 5	6	1:40.71	$66,300
1999	**Brave Act (GB)**, 5, 120	G. F. Almeida	Lord Smith (GB), 4	Expressionist, 4	8	1:39.13	$66,420
1998	**Fantastic Fellow**, 4, 118	C. S. Nakatani	Via Lombardia (Ire), 6	Sharekann (Ire), 6	6	**1:38.77**	$64,740
1997	**El Angelo**, 5, 115	C. S. Nakatani	Irish Wings (Ire), 5	Tychonic (GB), 7	5	1:40.29	$63,900
1996	**Fastness (Ire)**, 6, 122	C. S. Nakatani	Helmsman, 4	Tychonic (GB), 5	5	1:39.54	$79,470
1995	**Blaze O'Brien**, 8, 116	C. A. Black	Savinio, 5	Stoller, 4	7	1:39.53	$79,800
1994	**Gothland (Fr)**, 5, 117	C. S. Nakatani	Rapan Boy (AUS), 6	Johann Quatz (Fr), 5	4	1:39.60	$60,700
1993	**The Tender Track**, 6, 116	E. J. Delahoussaye	Journalism, 5	Johann Quatz (Fr), 4	6	1:40.00	$62,500
1992	**Golden Pheasant**, 6, 121	G. L. Stevens	Blaze O'Brien, 5	Native Boundary, 4	7	1:39.86	$64,900

Named for the city of Inglewood, California, location of Hollywood Park. 1942-'44 not held. 1938-'39 Inglewood Mile H.; 1972 Miller High Life Inglewood H. 1973-'74,1987-'94 Grade 2; 1975-'81 not graded. 1949 held at Santa Anita. 1938-'39 1 mile; 1945-'47,1973 7 furlongs; 1948 6 furlongs; 1950,1968-'72,1986 1¹⁄₈ miles; 1974 6¹⁄₂ furlongs. 1938-'66,1968-'74 dirt. 1973-'74 three-year-olds. 1998 new course record.

Iroquois Stakes

Grade 3, Churchill Downs, two-year-olds, 1 mile, dirt. Held November 3, 2002, with a gross value of $100,000. First held in 1982. Graded since 1990. Stakes record 1:35.01 (2001 Harlan's Holiday).

Year	Winner	Jockey	Second	Third	Strs	Time	1st Purse
2002	**Champali**, 2, 118	P. Day	Alke, 2	What a Bad Day, 2	10	1:37.06	$70,804
2001	**Harlan's Holiday**, 2, 121	A. J. D'Amico	Request for Parole, 2	Gold Dollar, 2	10	**1:35.01**	$70,184
2000	**Meetyouathebrig**, 2, 118	G. L. Stevens	Hero's Tribute, 2	Keats, 2	13	1:35.24	$77,066
1999	**Mighty**, 2, 112	M. St. Julien	Ifitstobeitsuptome, 2	Nature, 2	8	1:35.88	$68,758
1998	**Exploit**, 2, 115	C. J. McCarron	Crowning Storm, 2	Olympic Journey, 2	8	1:36.26	$71,114
1997	**Keene Dancer**, 2, 121	P. Day	Yarrow Brae, 2	Dawn Exodus, 2	7	1:37.84	$68,882
1996	**Global View**, 2, 112	K. Bourque	Partner's Hero, 2	Haint, 2	6	1:36.49	$68,200
1995	**Ide**, 2, 121	C. Perret	El Amante, 2	City by Night, 2	8	1:36.89	$73,645
1994	**Peruvian**, 2, 121	J. A. Santos	Our Gatsby, 2	Super Jeblar, 2	11	1:36.68	$77,025
1993	**Tarzans Blade**, 2, 121	B. E. Bartram	Dove Hunt, 2	Amathos, 2	11	1:37.00	$74,945
1992	**Shoal Creek**, 2, 114	B. E. Bartram	Saw Mill, 2	Demaloot Demashoot, 2	13	1:37.51	$76,375

Named for the Iroquois Park area of the city of Louisville. 1982 colts and geldings.

Jaipur Handicap

Grade 3, Belmont Park, three-year-olds and up, 7 furlongs, turf. Held May 27, 2002, with a gross value of $100,000. First held in 1984. Graded since 1986. Stakes record 1:20.06 (1994 Nijinsky's Gold [1st Div.]).

Year	Winner	Jockey	Second	Third	Strs	Time	1st Purse
2002	**Shibboleth**, 5, 121	J. D. Bailey	Malabar Gold, 5	Cozzy Corner, 4	7	1:20.08	$67,140
2001	**Affirmed Success**, 7, 123	J. D. Bailey	Texas Glitter, 5	Bought in Dixie, 5	3	1:21.69	$66,475
2000	**Gone Fishin**, 4, 114	J. R. Velazquez	Weatherbird, 5	French Envoy, 4	12	1:21.73	$52,290
1999	**Notoriety**, 6, 115	J. L. Espinoza	Optic Nerve, 6	Cryptic Rascal, 4	12	1:21.35	$52,335
1998	**Elusive Quality**, 5, 115	J. D. Bailey	Bristling, 6	Optic Nerve, 5	11	1:20.99	$51,750
1997	**Atraf (GB)**, 5, 114	J. R. Velazquez	Mighty Forum (GB), 5	Play Smart, 5	4	1:23.64	$49,635
1996	**Grand Continental**, 5, 114	R. Migliore	Inside the Beltway, 5	Goldmine (Fr), 5	10	1:23.78	$51,720
1995	**Inside the Beltway**, 4, 114	J. F. Chavez	Gabr (GB), 5	Golden Cloud, 5	5	1:21.23	$49,245
	Mighty Forum (GB), 4, 117	G. L. Stevens	Dominant Prospect, 5	City Nights (Ire), 5	9	1:21.12	$49,995
1994	**Nijinsky's Gold**, 5, 114	J. A. Santos	Dominant Prospect, 4	Home of the Free, 4	7	**1:20.06**	$34,905
	A in Sociology, 4, 119	E. Maple	Roman Envoy, 6	Halissee, 6	7	1:20.38	$34,905
1993	**Home of the Free**, 5, 117	J. D. Bailey	Wind Symbol (GB), 4	Fourstardave, 8	8	1:20.69	$55,080
1992	**To Freedom**, 4, 117	J. A. Krone	Fourstardave, 7	Smart Alec, 7	5	1:22.83	$55,710

Named for George D. Widener's 1962 champion three-year-old male Jaipur (1959-'87, c. by *Nasrullah). 1984-'95 Jaipur S. 1990-'91,2001 not graded. 1984-'85 6 furlongs. 1984-'86,1992,1997,2001 dirt. 1994,1995 two divisions. 1993,1994 (1st Div.) new course record.

Jamaica Handicap

Grade 2, Belmont Park, three-year-olds, 1¹⁄₈ miles, turf. Held September 22, 2002, with a gross value of $200,000. First held in 1929. Graded since 1978. Stakes record 1:49 (1997 Subordination).

Year	Winner	Jockey	Second	Third	Strs	Time	1st Purse
2002	**Finality**, 3, 116	J. R. Velazquez	Union Place, 3	Chiselling, 3	9	1:46.66	$120,000
2001	**Navesink**, 3, 118	E. S. Prado	Strategic Partner, 3	Baptize, 3	7	1:51.53	$120,000
2000	**King Cugat**, 3, 123	J. D. Bailey	Mandarin Marsh, 3	Parade Leader, 3	8	1:49.63	$120,000

1999 **Monarch's Maze**, 3, 117	J. Bravo	Killer Joe, 3	Monkey Puzzle, 3	8	1:51.66	$90,000
1998 **Vergennes**, 3, 115	J. R. Velazquez	Tangazi, 3	Middlesex Drive, 3	10	1:50.42	$90,000
1997 **Subordination**, 3, 120	J. F. Chavez	Premier Krischief, 3	Skybound, 3	12	**1:49.00**	$90,000
1996 **Allied Forces**, 3, 119	R. Migliore	Cliptomania, 3	Lite Approval, 3	11	1:40.91	$86,325
1994 **Pennine Ridge**, 3, 118	J. R. Velazquez	Holy Mountain, 3	I'm Very Irish, 3	7	1:35.13	$66,540
1993 **Mi Cielo**, 3, 116	M. E. Smith	Prospector's Flag, 3	Cherokee Run, 3	8	1:35.20	$70,440
1992 **West by West**, 3, 112	J-L. Samyn	Offbeat, 3	Portroe, 3	7	1:34.27	$70,320

Named for the Jamaica neighborhood of Queens. Jamaica Racetrack was located there until it was closed in 1959. 1933-'35,1955-'56,1961-'74,1995 not held. 1978-'87 Grade 3. 1929-'59 held at Jamaica; 1960-'77,1979-'81,1987 Aqueduct. 1929-'53,1957-'60 6 furlongs; 1975-'94 1 mile; 1996 1 1/16 miles. 1929-'93 dirt. 1929-'44,1949-'54,1960 three-year-olds and up. 1975 fillies.

Jefferson Cup Stakes

Grade 3, Churchill Downs, three-year-olds, 1 1/8 miles, turf. Held June 8, 2002, with a gross value of $250,000. First held in 1977. Graded since 2001. Stakes record 1:47.27 (2000 King Cugat).

Year	Winner	Jockey	Second	Third	Strs	Time	1st Purse
2002	**Orchard Park**, 3, 119	M. Guidry	Mr. Mellon, 3	Quest Star, 3	8	1:48.53	$172,050
2001	**Indygo Shiner**, 3, 113	L. Meche	Strategic Partner, 3	Fast City, 3	9	1:48.81	$175,150
2000	**King Cugat**, 3, 122	R. Albarado	Four On the Floor, 3	Field Cat, 3	10	**1:47.27**	$177,940
1999	**Special Coach**, 3, 122	C. H. Velasquez	Silver Chadra, 3	Air Rocket, 3	12	1:49.82	$180,110
1998	**Buff**, 3, 122	C. H. Borel	Keene Dancer, 3	Ladies Din, 3	7	1:50.80	$175,770
1997	**Greed Is Good**, 3, 115	W. Martinez	Royal Strand (Ire), 3	Crimson Classic, 3	5	1:49.47	$69,068
1996	**Unruled**, 3, 119	C. Perret	Broadway Beau, 3	Trail City, 3	6	1:50.07	$54,210
1995	**Ago**, 3, 115	S. J. Sellers	Michael's Star, 3	Lemon Drop, 3	11	1:49.48	$56,550
1994	**Milt's Overture**, 3, 112	P. Day	Jaggery John, 3	Camptown Dancer, 3	6	1:48.21	$53,528
1993	**Lt. Pinkerton**, 3, 115	T. J. Hebert	Snake Eyes, 3	Mi Cielo, 3	6	1:48.27	$35,555
1992	**Senor Tomas**, 3, 122	P. Day	Coaxing Matt, 3	Black Question, 3	7	1:49.80	$35,945

Named for Jefferson County, Kentucky, in which Churchill Downs is located. 1977-'81 5 1/2 furlongs; 1982 1 1/16 miles. 1977-'87 dirt. 1977-'81 two-year-olds.

Jenny Wiley Stakes

Grade 3, Keeneland, four-year-olds and up, fillies and mares, 1 1/16 miles, turf. Held April 13, 2003, with a gross value of $113,300. First held in 1989. Graded since 1995. Stakes record 1:40.78 (1996 Apolda).

Year	Winner	Jockey	Second	Third	Strs	Time	1st Purse
2003	**Sea of Showers**, 4, 116	J. D. Bailey	Magic Mission (GB), 5	Snow Dance, 5	10	1:41.89	$70,246
2002	**Tates Creek**, 4, 116	K. J. Desormeaux	Snow Dance, 4	Step With Style, 5	10	1:42.27	$70,432
2001	**Penny's Gold**, 4, 116	J. A. Santos	License Fee, 6	Solvig, 4	9	1:40.93	$70,618
2000	**Astra**, 4, 116	C. S. Nakatani	Pratella, 5	Ronda (GB), 4	8	1:42.48	$69,688
1999	**Pleasant Temper**, 5, 117	J. D. Bailey	Mingling Glances, 5	Red Cat, 4	8	1:40.93	$70,246
1998	**Maxzene**, 5, 114	J. A. Santos	Parade Queen, 4	Rumpipumpy (GB), 5	7	1:42.82	$69,192
1997	**Thrilling Day (GB)**, 4, 115	W. Martinez	Romy, 6	Gastronomical, 4	7	1:41.16	$68,634
1996	**Apolda**, 5, 121	J. D. Bailey	Mediation (Ire), 4	Luzette (Brz), 6	9	**1:40.78**	$69,006
1995	**Romy**, 4, 118	F. C. Torres	Weekend Madness (Ire), 5	Bold Ruritana, 5	9	1:43.32	$52,173
1994	**Misspitch**, 4, 118	M. E. Smith	Park Dream (Ire), 5	Sh Bang, 5	10	1:43.83	$34,658
1993	**Lady Blessington (Fr)**, 5, 118	P. Day	Radiant Ring, 5	Super Fan, 6	6	1:42.59	$34,844
1992	**Indian Fashion**, 5, 115	J. A. Santos	Spanish Parade, 4	Radiant Ring, 4	10	1:41.26	$36,514

Named for eastern Kentucky heroine Jenny Wiley (1760-1831), a pioneer woman who was captured by Indians and escaped to return to her family. 1991 about 1 1/16 miles. 1992,1996 new course record.

Jerome Handicap

Grade 2, Belmont Park, three-year-olds, 1 mile, dirt. Held September 14, 2002, with a gross value of $150,000. First held in 1866. Graded since 1973. Stakes record 1:33.20 (1981 Noble Nashua).

Year	Winner	Jockey	Second	Third	Strs	Time	1st Purse
2002	**Boston Common**, 3, 118	J. F. Chavez	Vinemeister, 3	No Parole, 3	7	1:36.12	$90,000
2001	**Express Tour**, 3, 115	J. R. Velazquez	Illusioned, 3	Burning Roma, 3	5	1:34.57	$90,000
2000	**Fusaichi Pegasus**, 3, 124	K. J. Desormeaux	El Corredor, 3	Albert the Great, 3	6	1:34.07	$90,000
1999	**Doneraile Court**, 3, 117	C. W. Antley	Vicar, 3	Badger Gold, 3	7	1:35.63	$90,000
1998	**Limit Out**, 3, 117	J-L. Samyn	Grand Slam, 3	Scatmandu, 3	5	1:36.22	$90,000
1997	**Richter Scale**, 3, 118	S. J. Sellers	Trafalger, 3	Smokin Mel, 3	8	1:35.88	$90,000
1996	**Why Change**, 3, 112	C. C. Lopez	Distorted Humor, 3	Diligence, 3	10	1:34.22	$90,000
1995	**French Deputy**, 3, 113	G. L. Stevens	Mr. Greeley, 3	Top Account, 3	6	1:33.53	$120,000
1994	**Prenup**, 3, 113	J. D. Bailey	Ulises, 3	End Sweep, 3	8	1:34.59	$120,000
1993	**Schossberg**, 3, 113	J. D. Bailey	Williamstown, 3	Mi Cielo, 3	5	1:35.53	$120,000
1992	**Furiously**, 3, 113	J. D. Bailey	Colony Light, 3	Dixie Brass, 3	6	1:34.20	$120,000

Named for Leonard Jerome (1817-'91), builder of Jerome Park and president of Coney Island Jockey Club. Jerome was also the maternal grandfather of Sir Winston Churchill. 1910-'13 not held; 2001 not held due to World Trade Center attack. 1984-'94 Grade 1. 1866,1872-'92 Jerome S.; 1867-'71 Champion S. 1866-'89 held at Jerome Park; 1890-1904 Morris Park; 1960,1962-'67,1972-'74 Aqueduct. 1866-'70 one mile heats; 1871-'77 2 miles; 1878-'89 1 3/4 miles; 1890-'91,1903-'09 1 5/16 miles; 1892 1 1/2 miles; 1893-'94,1896,1914 1 1/4 miles; 1895 1 1/8 miles.

Jersey Derby

Grade 3, Monmouth Park, three-year-olds, 1¹/₁₆ miles, turf. Held May 27, 2002, with a gross value of $100,000. First held in 1864. Graded since 1973. Stakes record 1:40.80 (1997 Rob 'n Gin).

Year	Winner	Jockey	Second	Third	Strs	Time	1st Purse
2002	Emergency Status, 3, 122	R. Alvarado Jr.	Kris's Prayer, 3	Rapadash (Ire), 3	10	1:42.26	$60,000
2001	†Mystic Lady, 3, 114	F. Leon	Sir Brian's Sword, 3	What's Your Wish, 3	6	1:44.31	$60,000
2000	Lendell Ray, 3, 114	A. T. Gryder	Powerful Appeal, 3	Cogburn, 3	8	1:42.96	$60,000
1999	Swamp, 3, 124	R. Migliore	Crash Course, 3	Good Skate, 3	7	1:40.94	$90,000
1998	†Who Did It and Run, 3, 116	F. L. Ortiz	Essential, 3	Cryptic Rascal, 3	8	1:41.37	$90,000
1997	Rob 'n Gin, 3, 119	J. D. Bailey	Tekken (Ire), 3	Keep It Strait, 3	9	**1:40.80**	$90,000
1996	More Royal, 3, 123	J. A. Krone	Optic Nerve, 3	Value Investor, 3	10	1:42.46	$90,000
1995	Da Hoss, 3, 119	J. A. Krone	Claudius, 3	Crimson Guard, 3	10	1:43.01	$90,000
1994	Zuno Star, 3, 116	M. E. Smith	Seattle Rob, 3	(DH) Warn Me (GB), 3	10	1:43.86	$90,000
				(DH) Mr. Angel, 3			
1993	Llandaff, 3, 116	J. A. Krone	Logroller, 3	Forest Wind, 3	11	1:42.50	$90,000
1992	American Chance, 3, 126	P. Day	Majestic Sweep, 3	Palace Line, 3	9	1:50.86	$180,000

1865-1941,1978-'80 not held. 1942-'47,1951 Jersey H.; 1948-'50,1952-'59 Jersey S. 1973-'77 Grade 1; 1981-'82 not graded; 1986-'99 Grade 2. 1864 held at Paterson; 1942-'76,1985-'98 Garden State; 1977-'84 Atlantic City. 1864 1¹/₂ miles; 1942-'47,1953-'84,1991-'92 1¹/₈ miles; 1948-'52,1985-'90 1¹/₄ miles. 1864,1942-'92,2001 dirt. 1864 colts and fillies. 1997,1999 equaled course record. 1994 dead heat for third. †denotes female.

Jersey Shore Breeders' Cup Stakes

Grade 3, Monmouth Park, three-year-olds, 6 furlongs, dirt. Held July 4, 2002, with a gross value of $100,000. First held in 1992. Graded since 1994. Stakes record 1:08.53 (1997 Smoke Glacken).

Year	Winner	Jockey	Second	Third	Strs	Time	1st Purse
2002	Boston Common, 3, 117	E. M. Martin Jr.	Listen Here, 3	It's a Monster, 3	6	1:09.35	$60,000
2001	City Zip, 3, 119	J. C. Ferrer	Sea of Green, 3	Songandaprayer, 3	5	1:09.02	$60,000
2000	Disco Rico, 3, 115	J. Bravo	Max's Pal, 3	Stormin Oedy, 3	6	1:09.05	$60,000
1999	Yes It's True, 3, 122	J. D. Bailey	Erlton, 3	Flying Griffoni, 3	4	1:08.59	$60,000
1998	Good and Tough, 3, 115	W. H. McCauley	Klabin's Gold, 3	El Mirasol, 3	6	1:10.01	$45,000
1997	Smoke Glacken, 3, 122	C. Perret	Partner's Hero, 3	King Buck, 3	4	**1:08.53**	$30,000
1996	Swing and Miss, 3, 112	T. G. Turner	Seacliff, 3	Dixie Connection, 3	6	1:10.00	$60,000
1995	Ft. Stockton, 3, 115	J. Bravo	Jealous Crusader, 3	Gala Knockout, 3	9	1:22.64	$64,050
1994	End Sweep, 3, 115	M. E. Smith	Meadow Flight, 3	Foxie G, 3	5	1:21.20	$63,450
1993	Montbrook, 3, 122	C. J. Ladnier	Evil Bear, 3	Shu Fellow, 3	7	1:21.04	$63,420
1992	Surely Six, 3, 115	R. Wilson	Superstrike (GB), 3	Salt Lake, 3	8	1:21.94	$64,230

Monmouth Park is located on the coast of New Jersey. 1992-'95 Jersey Shore Budweiser Breeders' Cup S. 1992-'96 held at Atlantic City. 1992-'95 7 furlongs.

Jim Dandy Stakes

Grade 2, Saratoga Race Course, three-year-olds, 1¹/₈ miles, dirt. Held August 4, 2002, with a gross value of $500,000. First held in 1964. Graded since 1973. Stakes record 1:47.26 (1996 Louis Quatorze).

Year	Winner	Jockey	Second	Third	Strs	Time	1st Purse
2002	Medaglia d'Oro, 3, 121	J. D. Bailey	Gold Dollar, 3	Essence of Dubai, 3	9	1:47.82	$300,000
2001	Scorpion, 3, 114	J. D. Bailey	Free of Love, 3	Congaree, 3	6	1:48.90	$360,000
2000	Graeme Hall, 3, 120	J. D. Bailey	Curule, 3	Unshaded, 3	7	1:48.95	$240,000
1999	Ecton Park, 3, 116	A. O. Solis	Lemon Drop Kid, 3	Badger Gold, 3	7	1:49.52	$180,000
1998	Favorite Trick, 3, 119	P. Day	Deputy Diamond, 3	Raffie's Majesty, 3	5	1:50.00	$150,000
1997	Awesome Again, 3, 116	M. E. Smith	Glitman, 3	Affirmed Success, 3	9	1:51.16	$150,000
1996	Louis Quatorze, 3, 124	P. Day	Will's Way, 3	Secreto de Estado, 3	8	**1:47.26**	$90,000
1995	Composer, 3, 112	J. D. Bailey	Malthus, 3	Pat n Jac, 3	7	1:51.13	$82,575
1994	Unaccounted For, 3, 112	J. A. Santos	Tabasco Cat, 3	Ulises, 3	5	1:49.69	$80,820
1993	Miner's Mark, 3, 117	C. J. McCarron	Virginia Rapids, 3	Colonial Affair, 3	6	1:49.01	$90,000
1992	Thunder Rumble, 3, 117	W. H. McCauley	Dixie Brass, 3	Devil His Due, 3	8	1:47.53	$108,000

Named for 100-to-1 1930 Travers S. winner Jim Dandy (1927, g. by Jim Gaffney), who upset heavily favored rivals Gallant Fox and Whichone in the 1930 edition. 1973-'83 Grade 3; 2001 Grade 1. 1964-'70 1 mile; 1971 7 furlongs.

Jockey Club Gold Cup

Grade 1, Belmont Park, three-year-olds and up, 1¹/₄ miles, dirt. Held September 28, 2002, with a gross value of $1,000,000. First held in 1919. Graded since 1973. Stakes record 1:58.89 (1997 Skip Away).

Year	Winner	Jockey	Second	Third	Strs	Time	1st Purse
2002	Evening Attire, 4, 126	S. Bridgmohan	Lido Palace (Chi), 5	Harlan's Holiday, 3	8	1:59.58	$600,000
2001	Aptitude, 4, 126	J. D. Bailey	Generous Rosi (GB), 6	Country Be Gold, 4	7	2:01.49	$600,000
2000	Albert the Great, 3, 122	J. F. Chavez	Gander, 4	Vision and Verse, 4	7	1:59.24	$600,000
1999	River Keen (Ire), 7, 126	C. W. Antley	Behrens, 5	Almutawakel (GB), 4	8	2:01.40	$600,000
1998	Wagon Limit, 4, 126	R. G. Davis	Gentlemen (Arg), 6	Skip Away, 5	6	2:00.62	$600,000
1997	Skip Away, 4, 126	J. D. Bailey	Instant Friendship, 4	Wagon Limit, 3	7	**1:58.89**	$600,000
1996	Skip Away, 3, 121	S. J. Sellers	Cigar, 6	Louis Quatorze, 3	6	2:00.70	$600,000
1995	Cigar, 5, 126	J. D. Bailey	Unaccounted For, 4	Star Standard, 3	7	2:01.29	$450,000

1994 **Colonial Affair**, 4, 126	J. A. Santos	Devil His Due, 5	Flag Down, 4	8	2:02.19	$450,000
1993 **Miner's Mark**, 3, 121	C. J. McCarron	Colonial Affair, 3	Brunswick, 4	5	2:02.79	$510,000
1992 **Pleasant Tap**, 5, 126	G. L. Stevens	Strike the Gold, 4	A.P. Indy, 3	7	1:58.95	$510,000

Named for the Jockey Club, keeper of the *American Stud Book*, and once the arbiter of American racing. 1919-'20 Jockey Club S. 1959-'61,1963-'67,1969-'74 held at Aqueduct. 1919-'20,1976-'89 1½ miles; 1921-'75 2 miles. 1944 colts and fillies.

John C. Mabee Ramona Handicap

Grade 1, Del Mar, three-year-olds and up, fillies and mares, 1⅛ miles, turf. Held July 27, 2002, with a gross value of $400,000. First held in 1945. Graded since 1973. Stakes record 1:47 (1969 Greta [2nd Div.]).

Year	Winner	Jockey	Second	Third	Strs	Time	1st Purse
2001	**Janet (GB)**, 4, 116	D. R. Flores	Tranquility Lake, 6	Minor Details, 4	6	1:48.20	$240,000
2000	**Caffe Latte (Ire)**, 4, 117	B. Blanc	Tout Charmant, 4	Alexine (Arg), 4	7	1:47.16	$240,000
1999	**Tuzla (Fr)**, 5, 121	D. R. Flores	Happyanunoit (NZ), 4	Spanish Fern, 4	10	1:47.66	$240,000
1998	**See You Soon (Fr)**, 4, 114	C. S. Nakatani	Sonja's Faith (Ire), 4	Fiji (GB), 4	8	1:47.43	$180,000
1997	**Escena**, 4, 115	P. Day	Real Connection, 6	Different (Arg), 5	7	1:49.80	$180,000
1996	**Matiara**, 4, 118	C. S. Nakatani	Alpride (Ire), 5	Pourquoi Pas (Ire), 4	6	1:49.28	$193,500
1995	**Possibly Perfect**, 5, 123	C. S. Nakatani	Morgana, 4	Yearly Tour, 4	7	1:49.98	$180,600
1994	**Flawlessly**, 6, 124	C. J. McCarron	Hollywood Wildcat, 4	Skimble, 5	5	1:48.25	$181,000
1993	**Flawlessly**, 5, 125	C. J. McCarron	Heart of Joy, 6	Let's Elope (NZ), 6	7	1:48.38	$186,500
1992	**Flawlessly**, 4, 123	C. J. McCarron	Re Toss (Arg), 5	Polemic, 4	7	1:50.00	$187,500

Named for the town of Ramona, California; since 2002 also named for John C. Mabee (1921-2002), owner of Golden Eagle Farm, located in Ramona, and long-time chairman of Del Mar Thoroughbred Club. 1946-'58 not held. 1945-2001 Ramona H. 1973-'79 Grade 3; 1980-'83 Grade 2. 1945 1 mile. 1945-'69 dirt.

Just a Game Breeders' Cup Handicap

Grade 3, Belmont Park, three-year-olds and up, fillies and mares, 1 mile, turf. Held June 8, 2002, with a gross value of $200,000. First held in 1994. Graded since 1997. Stakes record 1:32.53 (1995 Caress).

Year	Winner	Jockey	Second	Third	Strs	Time	1st Purse
2002	**Babae (Chi)**, 6, 115	J. F. Chavez	Tates Creek, 4	Stylish, 4	8	1:34.57	$67,920
2001	**License Fee**, 6, 118	P. Day	Shopping for Love, 4	Veil of Avalon, 4	11	1:32.62	$114,780
2000	**Perfect Sting**, 4, 121	J. D. Bailey	Ronda (GB), 4	Snow Polina, 5	7	1:34.48	$111,180
1999	**Cozy Blues**, 5, 112	J. F. Chavez	U R Unforgettable, 5	Mysterious Moll, 4	7	1:33.33	$94,620
1998	**Witchful Thinking**, 4, 118	C. J. McCarron	Sopran Mariduff (GB), 4	Dixie Ghost, 4	9	1:33.45	$95,745
1997	**Memories of Silver**, 4, 120	J. D. Bailey	Dynasty, 4	Elusive, 5	7	1:32.90	$95,370
1996	**Caress**, 5, 117	R. G. Davis	Class Kris, 4	Upper Noosh, 4	7	1:33.30	$94,890
1995	**Caress**, 4, 119	R. G. Davis	Coronation Cup, 4	Grafin, 4	5	1:32.53	$49,320
1994	**Elizabeth Bay**, 4, 114	M. E. Smith	Tiffany's Taylor, 5	Statuette, 5	5	1:32.85	$33,330

Named for 1980 champion turf female Just a Game (Ire) (1976-'93, f. by Tarboosh). 1994-'95 Just a Game II S. 1995 equaled course record. 1996 Class Kris finished first, DQ to second.

Kelso Handicap

Grade 2, Belmont Park, three-year-olds and up, 1 mile, turf. Held October 5, 2002, with a gross value of $350,000. First held in 1980. Graded since 1984. Stakes record 1:32.40 (1990 Expensive Decision).

Year	Winner	Jockey	Second	Third	Strs	Time	1st Purse
2002	**Green Fee**, 6, 113	J. R. Velazquez	Forbidden Apple, 7	Moon Solitaire (Ire), 5	7	1:33.83	$210,000
2001	**Forbidden Apple**, 6, 118	J. A. Santos	Sarafan, 4	City Zip, 3	9	1:36.77	$150,000
2000	**Forbidden Apple**, 5, 116	J-L. Samyn	Affirmed Success, 6	Johnny Dollar, 4	9	1:34.39	$150,000
1999	**Middlesex Drive**, 4, 117	S. J. Sellers	Divide and Conquer, 5	Wised Up, 4	10	1:35.45	$150,000
1998	**Dixie Bayou**, 5, 112	J. F. Chavez	Sahm, 4	Let Goodtimes Roll, 5	6	1:36.21	$120,000
1997	**Lucky Coin**, 4, 119	R. G. Davis	Hawksley Hill (Ire), 4	†Colcon, 4	12	1:33.72	$120,000
1996	**Same Old Wish**, 6, 113	S. J. Sellers	Da Hoss, 4	Volochine (Ire), 5	10	1:34.42	$105,000
1995	**Mighty Forum (GB)**, 4, 115	E. J. Delahoussaye	Fastness (Ire), 5	Dowty, 3	14	1:39.58	$120,000
1994	**Nijinsky's Gold**, 5, 114	J. A. Santos	Lure, 6	A in Sociology, 4	7	1:34.18	$120,000
1993	**Lure**, 4, 125	M. E. Smith	Paradise Creek, 4	Daarik (Ire), 6	10	1:35.86	$120,000
1992	**Roman Envoy**, 4, 117	C. Perret	Lure, 3	Val des Bois (Fr), 6	9	1:36.39	$120,000

Named for 1960-'64 Horse of the Year Kelso (1957-'83, g. by Your Host), only five-time Horse of the Year. 1983 not held. 1984-'96 Grade 3. 1980-'82 held at Aqueduct. 1980-'82 2 miles; 1984-'87 1¼ miles. 1980-'82 dirt. †denotes female.

Kent Breeders' Cup Stakes

Grade 3, Delaware Park, three-year-olds, 1⅛ miles, turf. Held July 21, 2002, with a gross value of $247,900. First held in 1937. Graded since 1999. Stakes record 1:48.01 (1997 Royal Strand [Ire]).

Year	Winner	Jockey	Second	Third	Strs	Time	1st Purse
2002	**Miesque's Approval**, 3, 115	J. D. Bailey	Regal Sanction, 3	Quest Star, 3	8	1:48.81	$150,000
2001	**Navesink**, 3, 115	R. A. Dominguez	Bowman Mill, 3	Harrisand (Fr), 3	10	1:49.98	$151,000
2000	**Three Wonders**, 3, 115	P. Day	Field Cat, 3	Dawn of the Condor, 3	8	1:48.95	$150,000
1999	**North East Bound**, 3, 114	J. A. Velez Jr.	Courtside, 3	Swamp, 3	8	1:51.93	$150,000

1998	**Keene Dancer**, 3, 117	P. Day	Red Reef, 3	Danielle's Gray, 3	11	1:50.65	$120,000
1997	**Royal Strand (Ire)**, 3, 122	P. Day	Subordination, 3	Broad Choice, 3	7	**1:48.01**	$90,000
1996	**Sir Cat**, 3, 113	J. D. Bailey	Optic Nerve, 3	Fortitude, 3	5	1:52.93	$60,000

Named for Kent County, Delaware. 1943,1977-'78,1980-'81,1983-'95 not held. 1937-'41 Kent H.; 1942-'82 Kent S. 1937-'68,1979,1982 1^1/₁₆ miles; 1969-'76 1 mile. 1937-'68 dirt. 1997 new course record.

Kentucky Breeders' Cup Stakes

Grade 3, Churchill Downs, two-year-olds, 5½ furlongs, dirt. Held May 27, 2002, with a gross value of $150,000. First held in 1988. Graded since 1999. Stakes record 1:03.11 (2001 Leelanau).

Year	Winner	Jockey	Second	Third	Strs	Time	1st Purse
2002	**Posse**, 2, 115	D. J. Meche	Del Diablo, 2	Blackjack Boy, 2	8	1:03.73	$102,300
2001	**Leelanau**, 2, 115	J. K. Court	Gygistar, 2	†Lakeside Cup, 2	6	**1:03.11**	$100,812
2000	†**Gold Mover**, 2, 113	C. Perret	City Zip, 2	Unbridled Time, 2	6	1:03.67	$101,091
1999	†**Chilukki**, 2, 112	R. Albarado	Barrier, 2	Sky Dweller, 2	7	1:04.01	$106,485
1998	**Yes It's True**, 2, 121	S. J. Sellers	Tactical Cat, 2	Alannan, 2	8	1:03.61	$85,948
1997	**Favorite Trick**, 2, 121	P. Day	Jess M, 2	†Cutie Luttie, 2	8	1:04.80	$68,882
1996	†**Move**, 2, 113	S. J. Sellers	Prairie Junction, 2	†Live Your Best, 2	7	1:05.74	$71,175
1995	†**Miraloma**, 2, 112	D. M. Barton	Great Southern, 2	A.V. Eight, 2	9	1:04.04	$68,933
1994	**My My**, 2, 116	S. J. Sellers	Wise Affair, 2	Hyroglyphic, 2	11	1:05.96	$37,310
1993	†**Astas Foxy Lady**, 2, 118	T. J. Herbert	Dish It Out, 2	Riverinn, 2	9	1:05.51	$68,738
1992	**Tempered Halo**, 2, 121	P. A. Johnson	Mountain Cat, 2	†Secret Bundle, 2	7	1:05.39	$50,326

1988-'95 Kentucky Budweiser Breeders' Cup S. 1998,2001 new track record. †denotes female.

Kentucky Cup Classic Handicap

Grade 2, Turfway Park, three-year-olds and up, 1^1/₈ miles, dirt. Held September 14, 2002, with a gross value of $400,000. First held in 1994. Graded since 1996. Stakes record 1:47.43 (1996 Atticus).

Year	Winner	Jockey	Second	Third	Strs	Time	1st Purse
2002	**Pure Prize**, 4, 115	M. E. Smith	Dollar Bill, 4	Hero's Tribute, 4	8	1:51.24	$254,000
2001	**Guided Tour**, 5, 119	L. Melancon	Balto Star, 3	A Fleets Dancer, 6	6	1:47.90	$254,000
2000	**Captain Steve**, 3, 115	S. J. Sellers	Golden Missile, 5	Early Pioneer, 5	6	1:49.95	$314,500
1999	**Da Devil**, 4, 112	C. H. Borel	Social Charter, 4	Cat Thief, 3	8	1:50.54	$314,500
1998	**(DH) Wild Rush**, 4, 117	P. Day		Acceptable, 4	5	1:47.48	$271,000
	(DH) Silver Charm, 4, 123	G. L. Stevens					
1997	**Semoran**, 4, 116	K. J. Desormeaux	Distorted Humor, 4	Coup D' Argent, 5	8	1:48.08	$217,000
1996	**Atticus**, 4, 115	C. S. Nakatani	Judge T C, 5	Isitingood, 5	10	**1:47.43**	$325,000
1995	**Thunder Gulch**, 3, 121	G. L. Stevens	Judge T C, 4	Bound by Honor, 4	6	1:49.42	$260,000
1994	**Tabasco Cat**, 3, 120	P. Day	Mighty Avanti, 4	Best Pal, 4	6	1:50.32	$260,000

1994 Kentucky Cup Classic S. 1996-'98 Grade 3. 1998 dead heat for first.

Kentucky Cup Juvenile Stakes

Grade 3, Turfway Park, two-year-olds, 1^1/₁₆ miles, dirt. Held September 14, 2002, with a gross value of $100,000. First held in 1986. Graded since 1989. Stakes record 1:42.89 (1996 Boston Harbor).

Year	Winner	Jockey	Second	Third	Strs	Time	1st Purse
2002	**Vindication**, 2, 116	M. E. Smith	Private Gold, 2	Tito's Beau, 2	8	1:46.70	$62,750
2001	**Repent**, 2, 114	A. J. D'Amico	French Assault, 2	Gold Dollar, 2	7	1:43.78	$62,750
2000	**Point Given**, 2, 114	S. J. Sellers	Holiday Thunder, 2	The Goo, 2	11	1:47.01	$62,600
1999	**Millencolin**, 2, 114	P. Day	Personal First, 2	Deputy Warlock, 2	10	1:47.02	$62,600
1998	**Aly's Alley**, 2, 118	P. A. Johnson	Time Bandit, 2	Mac's Rule, 2	9	1:45.63	$62,600
1997	**Laydown**, 2, 114	M. E. Smith	Time Limit, 2	Da Devil, 2	7	1:43.17	$62,600
1996	**Boston Harbor**, 2, 120	D. M. Barton	Play Waki for Me, 2	Dr. Spine, 2	8	**1:42.89**	$65,000
1995	**Editor's Note**, 2, 115	G. L. Stevens	Devil's Honor, 2	Never to Squander, 2	8	1:45.07	$65,000
1994	**Tejano Run**, 2, 120	J. D. Bailey	Gold Miner, 2	Bick, 2	7	1:46.10	$65,000
1993	**Bibury Court**, 2, 120	S. T. Saito	Moving Van, 2	Durham, 2	11	1:47.75	$81,250
1992	**Mountain Cat**, 2, 120	C. R. Woods Jr.	Saw Mill, 2	Shoal Creek, 2	10	1:43.50	$97,500

1986-'88 In Memoriam S.; 1989-'93 Alysheba S.; 1998 Gallery Furniture Kentucky Cup Juvenile S. 1986-'87 1 mile.

Kentucky Cup Sprint Stakes

Grade 3, Turfway Park, three-year-olds and up, 6 furlongs, dirt. Held September 14, 2002, with a gross value of $150,000. First held in 1994. Graded since 1996. Stakes record 1:08.24 (1996 Appealing Skier).

Year	Winner	Jockey	Second	Third	Strs	Time	1st Purse
2002	**Day Trader**, 3, 118	P. Day	Premier Performer, 3	Ecstatic, 3	11	1:10.01	$94,500
2001	**Snow Ridge**, 3, 114	P. Day	City Zip, 3	Dream Run, 3	5	1:09.22	$94,500
2000	**Caller One**, 3, 120	K. J. Desormeaux	Millencolin, 3	Kings Command, 3	6	1:09.46	$93,750
1999	**Successful Appeal**, 3, 122	E. S. Prado	Five Star Day, 3	American Spirit, 3	6	1:09.42	$74,400
1998	**Reraise**, 3, 116	C. S. Nakatani	Copelan Too, 3	Mr Bert, 3	7	1:08.50	$93,900
1997	**Partner's Hero**, 3, 114	P. Day	Oro de Mexico, 3	Prosong, 3	6	1:09.02	$74,400
1996	**Appealing Skier**, 3, 118	M. E. Smith	†Capote Belle, 3	Delay of Game, 3	9	**1:08.24**	$97,500

1995 **Lord Carson**, 3, 116	M. E. Smith	Ft. Stockton, 3	Evansville Slew, 3	10	1:08.60	$97,500
1994 **End Sweep**, 3, 120	C. J. McCarron	Exclusive Praline, 3	Chimes Band, 3	7	1:09.99	$97,500

1996-2001 Grade 2. 1995 equaled track record. †denotes female.

Kentucky Cup Turf Handicap

Grade 3, Kentucky Downs, three-year-olds and up, 1½ miles, turf. Held September 21, 2002, with a gross value of $300,000. First held in 1998. Graded since 2001. Stakes record 2:27.60 (1998 Yaqthan [Ire]).

Year	Winner	Jockey	Second	Third	Strs	Time	1st Purse
2002	**Rochester**, 6, 115	E. M. Martin Jr.	Nowrass (GB), 6	Continental Red, 6	11	2:38.28	$186,000
2001	**Chorwon**, 8, 113	J. K. Court	The Knight Sky, 5	Man From Wicklow, 4	7	2:28.68	$186,000
2000	**Down the Aisle**, 7, 117	R. Albarado	Crowd Pleaser, 5	Royal Strand (Ire), 6	8	2:27.70	$186,000
1999	**Fahris (Ire)**, 5, 116	S. J. Sellers	Yaqthan (Ire), 9	Royal Strand (Ire), 5	12	2:29.60	$186,000
1998	**Yaqthan (Ire)**, 8, 115	B. D. Peck	Perim (Fr), 5	Chorwon, 5	8	**2:27.60**	$186,000

1998 established course record.

Kentucky Derby

(See Triple Crown section for complete history of the Kentucky Derby)

Grade 1, Churchill Downs, three-year-olds, 1¼ miles, dirt. Held May 3, 2003, with a gross value of $1,000,000. First held in 1875. Graded since 1973. Stakes record 1:59.40 (1973 Secretariat).

Year	Winner	Jockey	Second	Third	Strs	Time	1st Purse
2003	**Funny Cide**, 3, 126	J. Santos	Empire Maker, 3	Peace Rules, 3	16	2:01.19	$800,200
2002	**War Emblem**, 3, 126	V. Espinoza	Proud Citizen, 3	Perfect Drift, 3	18	2:01.13	$1,875,000
2001	**Monarchos**, 3, 126	J. F. Chavez	Invisible Ink, 3	Congaree, 3	17	1:59.97	$812,000
2000	**Fusaichi Pegasus**, 3, 126	K. J. Desormeaux	Aptitude, 3	Impeachment, 3	19	2:01.12	$1,038,400
1999	**Charismatic**, 3, 126	C. W. Antley	Menifee, 3	Cat Thief, 3	19	2:03.29	$886,200
1998	**Real Quiet**, 3, 126	K. J. Desormeaux	Victory Gallop, 3	Indian Charlie, 3	15	2:02.38	$738,800
1997	**Silver Charm**, 3, 126	G. L. Stevens	Captain Bodgit, 3	Free House, 3	13	2:02.44	$700,000
1996	**Grindstone**, 3, 126	J. D. Bailey	Cavonnier, 3	Prince of Thieves, 3	19	2:01.06	$869,800
1995	**Thunder Gulch**, 3, 126	G. L. Stevens	Tejano Run, 3	Timber Country, 3	19	2:01.27	$707,400
1994	**Go for Gin**, 3, 126	C. J. McCarron	Strodes Creek, 3	Blumin Affair, 3	14	2:03.72	$628,800
1993	**Sea Hero**, 3, 126	J. D. Bailey	Prairie Bayou, 3	Wild Gale, 3	19	2:02.42	$735,900
1992	**Lil E. Tee**, 3, 126	P. Day	Casual Lies, 3	Dance Floor, 3	18	2:03.04	$724,800

The Kentucky Derby was named for the Epsom Derby in England, its predecessor and model. 1875-'95 1½ miles.

Kentucky Jockey Club Stakes

Grade 2, Churchill Downs, two-year-olds, 1¹⁄₁₆ miles, dirt. Held November 30, 2002, with a gross value of $200,000. First held in 1920. Graded since 1973. Stakes record 1:43.14 (1999 Captain Steve).

Year	Winner	Jockey	Second	Third	Strs	Time	1st Purse
2002	**Soto**, 2, 117	L. Melancon	Ten Cents a Shine, 2	Most Feared, 2	12	1:44.67	$143,344
2001	**Repent**, 2, 122	A. J. D'Amico	Request for Parole, 2	High Star, 2	6	1:44.42	$134,540
2000	**Dollar Bill**, 2, 113	C. H. Borel	Holiday Thunder, 2	Gift of the Eagle, 2	6	1:47.18	$135,656
1999	**Captain Steve**, 2, 122	R. Albarado	Mighty, 2	Personal First, 2	12	**1:43.14**	$143,840
1998	**Exploit**, 2, 122	C. J. McCarron	Vicar, 2	Grits'n Hard Toast, 2	11	1:44.16	$140,740
1997	**Cape Town**, 2, 113	W. Martinez	Time Limit, 2	Real Quiet, 2	11	1:43.97	$142,228
1996	**Concerto**, 2, 119	C. H. Marquez Jr.	Celtic Warrior, 2	Carmen's Baby, 2	11	1:46.91	$142,104
1995	**Ide**, 2, 122	C. Perret	Editor's Note, 2	El Amante, 2	5	1:44.31	$97,500
1994	**Jambalaya Jazz**, 2, 113	S. Maple	You're the One, 2	Peaks and Valleys, 2	7	1:46.46	$97,500
1993	**War Deputy**, 2, 112	G. K. Gomez	Tarzans Blade, 2	Rustic Light, 2	11	1:46.75	$97,500
1992	**Wild Gale**, 2, 116	S. J. Sellers	Mi Cielo, 2	Shoal Creek, 2	11	1:45.64	$105,918

Formerly sponsored by Brown & Williamson Tobacco Corp. 1939-'45 not held. 1987-'93,1996-2000 Brown & Williamson Kentucky Jockey Club S. 1973-'82,1984-'86,1989-'97 Grade 3; 1983 not graded. 1931-'33 held at Old Latonia. 1920-'79 1 mile.

Kentucky Oaks

Grade 1, Churchill Downs, three-year-olds, fillies, 1¹⁄₈ miles, dirt. Held May 3, 2002, with a gross value of $500,000. First held in 1875. Graded since 1973. Stakes record 1:48.83 (1991 Lite Light).

Year	Winner	Jockey	Second	Third	Strs	Time	1st Purse
2002	**Farda Amiga**, 3, 121	C. J. McCarron	Take Charge Lady, 3	Habibti, 3	9	1:50.41	$348,502
2001	**Flute**, 3, 121	J. D. Bailey	Real Cozzy, 3	Collect Call, 3	13	1:48.85	$377,704
2000	**Secret Status**, 3, 121	P. Day	Rings a Chime, 3	Classy Cara, 3	14	1:50.30	$378,696
1999	**Silverbulletday**, 3, 121	G. L. Stevens	Dreams Gallore, 3	Sweeping Story, 3	7	1:49.92	$341,620
1998	**Keeper Hill**, 3, 121	D. R. Flores	Banshee Breeze, 3	Really Polish, 3	13	1:52.06	$375,410
1997	**Blushing K. D.**, 3, 121	L. Meche	Tomisue's Delight, 3	Storm Song, 3	9	1:50.29	$362,514
1996	**Pike Place Dancer**, 3, 121	C. S. Nakatani	Escena, 3	Cara Rafaela, 3	9	1:49.88	$325,000
1995	**Gal in a Ruckus**, 3, 121	W. H. McCauley	Urbane, 3	Sneaky Quiet, 3	8	1:50.09	$235,040
1994	**Sardula**, 3, 121	E. J. Delahoussaye	Lakeway, 3	Dianes Halo, 3	7	1:51.16	$184,340
1993	**Dispute**, 3, 121	P. Day	Eliza, 3	Quinpool, 3	11	1:52.47	$191,230
1992	**Luv Me Luv Me Not**, 3, 121	F. A. Arguello Jr.	Pleasant Stage, 3	Prospectors Delite, 3	6	1:51.41	$182,455

Named for the Epsom Oaks, its prototype in England. 1973-'77 Grade 2. 1875-'90 1½ miles; 1891-'95 1¼ miles; 1896-1919,1942-'81 1¹⁄₁₆ miles. 1997 Sharp Cat finished third, DQ to eighth.

King's Bishop Stakes

Grade 1, Saratoga Race Course, three-year-olds, 7 furlongs, dirt. Held August 24, 2002, with a gross value of $200,000. First held in 1984. Graded since 1986. Stakes record 1:21 (1999 Forestry).

Year	Winner	Jockey	Second	Third	Strs	Time	1st Purse
2002	Gygistar, 3, 124	J. R. Velazquez	Boston Common, 3	Thunder Days, 3	8	1:22.85	$120,000
2001	Squirtle Squirt, 3, 121	J. D. Bailey	Illusioned, 3	City Zip, 3	8	1:21.97	$120,000
2000	More Than Ready, 3, 124	P. Day	Valiant Halory, 3	Millencolin, 3	6	1:22.49	$120,000
1999	Forestry, 3, 124	C. W. Antley	Five Star Day, 3	Successful Appeal, 3	12	1:21.00	$120,000
1998	Secret Firm, 3, 121	E. S. Prado	Mint, 3	Scatmandu, 3	8	1:22.78	$120,000
1997	Tale of the Cat, 3, 114	J. A. Krone	Oro de Mexico, 3	Trafalger, 3	6	1:21.71	$90,000
1996	Honour and Glory, 3, 123	J. A. Santos	Elusive Quality, 3	Distorted Humor, 3	6	1:21.78	$64,920
1995	Top Account, 3, 112	P. Day	Ft. Stockton, 3	Excelerate, 3	10	1:22.50	$68,100
1994	Chimes Band, 3, 117	J. D. Bailey	End Sweep, 3	Halo's Image, 3	7	1:21.82	$65,700
1993	Mi Cielo, 3, 115	M. E. Smith	Williamstown, 3	Schossberg, 3	11	1:21.73	$74,280
1992	Salt Lake, 3, 117	M. E. Smith	Binalong, 3	Agincourt, 3	10	1:21.53	$73,440

Named for 1973 Carter H. (G2) winner King's Bishop (1969-'81, c. by Round Table). 1986 not held. 1987-'91 Grade 3; 1992-'98 Grade 2.

Knickerbocker Handicap

Grade 2, Aqueduct, three-year-olds and up, 1⅛ miles, turf. Held November 2, 2002, with a gross value of $150,000. First held in 1960. Graded since 1973. Stakes record 1:52.54 (2002 Dawn of the Condor).

Year	Winner	Jockey	Second	Third	Strs	Time	1st Purse
2002	Dawn of the Condor, 5, 114	J. F. Chavez	Serial Bride, 5	Polish Miner, 5	9	1:52.54	$90,000
2001	Sumitas (Ger), 5, 115	E. S. Prado	Manndar (Ire), 5	Crash Course, 5	11	2:02.55	$90,000
2000	Charge d'Affaires (GB), 5, 115	J. A. Santos	Devine Wind, 4	Understood, 4	7	1:49.01	$90,000
1999	Charge d'Affaires (GB), 4, 114	J. A. Santos	Comic Strip, 4	Nat's Big Party, 5	7	1:49.06	$66,480
1998	Sahm, 4, 116	J. R. Velazquez	Glok, 4	Let Goodtimes Roll, 5	8	1:48.69	$67,440
1997	Sir Cat, 4, 115	M. E. Smith	Tamhid, 4	Outta My Way Man, 5	5	1:50.02	$69,060
1996	Mr. Bluebird, 5, 113	M. E. Smith	Devil's Cup, 3	Ops Smile, 4	12	1:49.21	$69,660
1995	Diplomatic Jet, 3, 113	M. E. Smith	Flag Down, 5	Easy Miner, 4	11	2:04.97	$87,870
1994	Kiri's Clown, 5, 114	M. J. Luzzi	River Majesty, 5	Red Earth, 3	12	1:49.38	$52,335
1993	River Majesty, 4, 115	M. E. Smith	Daarik (Ire), 5	Home of the Free, 5	6	1:54.54	$52,920
1992	Binary Light, 3, 111	J. Cruguet	Share the Glory, 4	Turkey Point, 7	7	1:52.70	$56,160

Named for a Washington Irving fictional character, Diedrich Knickerbocker; in the 19th century, New Yorkers were often called "Knickerbockers." 1973-'97 Grade 3. 1962,1975,1995,2001 held at Belmont Park. 1960-'61,1970-'74 1⅛ miles; 1962,1975-'76,1978-'86 1⅜ miles; 1963-'69 1⁷⁄₁₆ miles; 1977,1995,2001 1¼ miles. 1977,1992,1997 dirt.

La Brea Stakes

Grade 1, Santa Anita Park, three-year-olds, fillies, 7 furlongs, dirt. Held December 28, 2002, with a gross value of $200,000. First held in 1974. Graded since 1983. Stakes record 1:20.45 (1993 Mamselle Bebette).

Year	Winner	Jockey	Second	Third	Strs	Time	1st Purse
2002	Got Koko, 3, 117	A. O. Solis	Spring Meadow, 3	Erica's Smile, 3	10	1:22.57	$120,000
2001	Affluent, 3, 121	E. J. Delahoussaye	Royally Chosen, 3	Love At Noon, 3	12	1:21.29	$120,000
2000	Spain, 3, 123	V. Espinoza	Cover Gal, 3	Serenita (Arg), 3	6	1:22.27	$120,000
1999	Hookedonthefeelin, 3, 119	D. R. Flores	Olympic Charmer, 3	Kalookan Queen, 3	8	1:21.84	$120,000
1998	Magical Allure, 3, 121	G. L. Stevens	Gourmet Girl, 3	Tranquility Lake, 3	7	1:22.06	$120,000
1997	I Ain't Bluffing, 3, 119	E. J. Delahoussaye	Minister's Melody, 3	Praviana (Chi), 3	9	1:21.23	$99,540
1996	Hidden Lake, 3, 115	C. J. McCarron	Belle's Flag, 3	Tiffany Diamond, 3	7	1:22.00	$80,900
1995	Exotic Wood, 3, 119	C. J. McCarron	Evil's Pic, 3	Jewel Princess, 3	6	1:21.57	$80,250
1994	Top Rung, 3, 117	G. L. Stevens	Klassy Kim, 3	Twice the Vice, 3	7	1:21.84	$63,700
1993	Mamselle Bebette, 3, 115	C. S. Nakatani	Desert Stormer, 3	Island Orchid, 3	9	1:20.45	$65,900
1992	Arches of Gold, 3, 115	E. J. Delahoussaye	Race the Wild Wind, 3	Terre Haute, 3	8	1:21.28	$64,800

Named for Rancho La Brea in Los Angeles County; brea means "tar." 1977,1984,1986 not held. 1983-'93 Grade 3; 1994-'96 Grade 2. 1974-'76 1¹⁄₁₆ miles. 1974,1975 (January),1978-'81,1982 (January),1985 (January),1987-'89,1990 (January) four-year-olds. 1974-'76 both sexes.

La Cañada Stakes

Grade 2, Santa Anita Park, four-year-olds, fillies, 1⅛ miles, dirt. Held February 8, 2003, with a gross value of $200,000. First held in 1975. Graded since 1977. Stakes record 1:47.60 (1980 Glorious Song; 1982 Safe Play).

Year	Winner	Jockey	Second	Third	Strs	Time	1st Purse
2003	Got Koko, 4, 121	A. O. Solis	Sightseek, 4	Bella Bellucci, 4	5	1:48.41	$120,000
2002	Summer Colony, 4, 119	G. L. Stevens	Azeri, 4	Ask Me No Secrets, 4	6	1:49.26	$120,000
2001	Spain, 4, 122	V. Espinoza	Chilukki, 4	Letter of Intent, 4	5	1:49.74	$120,000
2000	Scholars Studio, 4, 116	C. S. Nakatani	Smooth Player, 4	The Seven Seas, 4	5	1:49.14	$120,000
1999	Manistique, 4, 119	G. L. Stevens	Magical Allure, 4	Gourmet Girl, 4	7	1:48.81	$120,000
1998	Fleet Lady, 4, 119	G. K. Gomez	Minister's Melody, 4	I Ain't Bluffing, 4	7	1:48.59	$120,000
1997	Belle's Flag, 4, 119	C. S. Nakatani	Chile Chatte, 4	Housa Dancer (Fr), 4	8	1:48.26	$133,200
1996	Jewel Princess, 4, 119	A. O. Solis	Dixie Pearl, 4	Privity, 4	6	1:49.42	$129,900

1995	**Dianes Halo**, 4, 115	C. S. Nakatani	Twice the Vice, 4	Klassy Kim, 4	6	1:49.35	$123,800
1994	**Stalcreek**, 4, 119	G. L. Stevens	Alyshena, 4	Hollywood Wildcat, 4	4	1:48.85	$120,000
1993	**Alysbelle**, 4, 116	E. J. Delahoussaye	Pacific Squall, 4	Interactive, 4	9	1:49.85	$130,850
1992	**Exchange**, 4, 119	L. A. Pincay Jr.	Winglet, 4	Damewood, 4	8	1:49.96	$128,250

Named for Rancho La Cañada where the city of La Crescenta is located; cañada means "glen" or "dell." 1978-'89 Grade 1. 1975 1¹⁄₁₆ miles.

Ladies Handicap

Grade 3, Aqueduct, three-year-olds and up, fillies and mares, 1¹⁄₄ miles, dirt. Held December 21, 2002, with a gross value of $107,400. First held in 1868. Graded since 1973. Stakes record 2:01.40 (1976 *Bastonera II).

Year	Winner	Jockey	Second	Third	Strs	Time	1st Purse
2002	**Critical Eye**, 5, 116	M. J. Luzzi	Ellie's Moment, 4	With Ability, 4	6	2:04.19	$64,440
2001	**Summer Colony**, 3, 114	J. R. Velazquez	Stop for Schnapps, 3	Strolling Belle, 5	9	2:05.80	$66,660
2000	**Strolling Belle**, 4, 120	H. Castillo Jr.	Pentatonic, 5	Reine Amandine (Fr), 5	7	2:06.60	$66,000
1999	**Strolling Belle**, 3, 116	H. Castillo Jr.	Maiden Fair, 5	Sazarac Jazz, 4	7	2:04.72	$65,640
1998	**Unbridled Hope**, 4, 114	R. Migliore	Manoa, 3	Sazarac Jazz, 3	11	2:03.44	$51,150
1997	**Prophet's Warning**, 4, 112	J. F. Chavez	Mil Kilates, 4	Biogio's Rose, 3	10	2:06.25	$67,620
1996	**Miss Slewpy**, 5, 120	L. C. Reynolds	Hooded Dancer, 6	Very True, 4	9	2:03.31	$66,600
1995	**Transient Trend**, 3, 110	J-L. Samyn	Lotta Dancing, 4	Manila Lila, 5	10	2:01.53	$67,800
1994	**Tara Roma**, 4, 114	F. T. Alvarado	Beloved Bea, 4	Dancer's Gate, 4	10	2:06.77	$84,300
1993	**Groovy Feeling**, 4, 112	W. H. McCauley	Turnback the Alarm, 4	Avie's Daisy, 5	9	2:05.88	$120,000
1992	**Brilliant Brass**, 5, 120	E. S. Prado	Low Tolerance, 3	Lady Lear, 5	10	2:03.55	$150,000

1895,1911-'12 not held. 1973-'89 Grade 1; 1990-'97 Grade 2. 1868-'89 held at Jerome Park; 1890-1904 Morris Park; 1905-'58 Belmont. 1868-'73 1⁵⁄₈ miles; 1874-'85,1940-'58,1960,1963-'64 1¹⁄₈ miles; 1889,1892 1¹⁄₈ miles; 1890-'91 about 6¹⁄₄ furlongs; 1893-'94 1¹⁄₁₆ miles; 1896-1939 1 mile; 1959,1961-'62 1⁵⁄₁₆ miles. 1868-1910 three-year-olds; 1913-'39 two-year-olds and up.1868-1910 fillies. 1995 new track record. 2000 Pentatonic finished first, DQ to second.

Lady's Secret Breeders' Cup Handicap

Grade 2, Santa Anita Park, three-year-olds and up, fillies and mares, 1¹⁄₁₆ miles, dirt. Held October 2, 2002, with a gross value of $200,000. First held in 1993. Graded since 1995. Stakes record 1:40.61 (1994 Hollywood Wildcat).

Year	Winner	Jockey	Second	Third	Strs	Time	1st Purse
2002	**Azeri**, 4, 127	M. E. Smith	Starrer, 4	Mystic Lady, 4	7	1:41.10	$130,500
2001	**Queenie Belle**, 4, 116	B. Blanc	Letter of Intent, 4	Nany's Sweep, 5	6	1:43.64	$126,240
2000	**Smooth Player**, 4, 116	E. J. Delahoussaye	Speaking of Time, 4	Bordelaise (Arg), 5	6	1:42.27	$126,360
1999	**Manistique**, 4, 123	C. S. Nakatani	Cookin Vickie, 4	Kalosca (Fr), 5	5	1:42.39	$125,100
1998	**Magical Allure**, 3, 116	D. R. Flores	Victory Stripes (Arg), 4	Housa Dancer (Fr), 5	8	1:42.55	$110,280
1997	**Sharp Cat**, 3, 117	A. O. Solis	Twice the Vice, 6	Minister's Melody, 3	5	1:41.45	$109,400
1996	**Top Rung**, 5, 116	E. Fires	Jewel Princess, 4	Sleep Easy, 4	5	1:41.84	$109,450
1995	**Borodislew**, 5, 120	G. L. Stevens	Top Rung, 4	Golden Klair (GB), 5	6	1:41.61	$74,000
1994	**Hollywood Wildcat**, 4, 124	E. J. Delahoussaye	Exchange, 4	Dancing Mirage, 3	5	**1:40.61**	$61,400
1993	**Hollywood Wildcat**, 3, 117	E. J. Delahoussaye	Re Toss (Arg), 6	Wedding Ring (Ire), 4	5	1:41.05	$61,700

Named for 1986 Horse of the Year Lady's Secret (1982-2003, f. by Secretariat). 1993-'95 Lady's Secret H. 1995 Grade 3.

Lafayette Stakes

Grade 3, Keeneland, three-year-olds, 7 furlongs, dirt. Held April 6, 2003, with a gross value of $107,900. First held in 1937. Graded since 1990. Stakes record 1:21.25 (1993 Cherokee Run).

Year	Winner	Jockey	Second	Third	Strs	Time	1st Purse
2003	**Posse**, 3, 118	C. J. Lanerie	Roll Hennessy Roll, 3	Bossanova, 3	6	1:23.14	$66,898
2002	**Cashel Castle**, 3, 116	P. Day	Governor Hickel, 3	Sky Terrace, 3	6	1:24.47	$69,006
2001	**Griffinite**, 3, 116	J. A. Santos	Sam Lord's Castle, 3	Yonaguska, 3	7	1:22.61	$68,820
1999	**Yes It's True**, 3, 123	J. D. Bailey	Trickey Crew, 3	Fort La Roca, 3	5	1:22.15	$66,340
1998	**Dontletthebigonego**, 3, 114	W. Martinez	Flashing Tammany, 3	Swear by Dixie, 3	6	1:23.15	$67,394
1997	**Trafalger**, 3, 113	J. D. Bailey	Open Forum, 3	Muchacho Fino, 3	6	1:21.68	$67,456
1996	**Wire Me Collect**, 3, 112	K. L. Chapman	Appealing Skier, 3	Irish Conquest, 3	9	1:21.82	$69,192
1995	**Mr. Greeley**, 3, 121	J. A. Krone	Peaks and Valleys, 3	Tethra, 3	7	1:21.43	$51,429
1994	**Exclusive Praline**, 3, 121	J. A. Santos	Dynamic Asset, 3	End Sweep, 3	5	1:23.82	$49,321
1993	**Cherokee Run**, 3, 118	P. Day	Poverty Slew, 3	Williamstown, 3	8	**1:21.25**	$52,297
1992	**American Chance**, 3, 118	P. Day	Capitalimprovement, 3	Mon Capitan, 3	7	1:22.16	$53,365

Named for the Marquis de Lafayette, French hero of the American Revolutionary War. 1945 not held. 1943-'44 held at Churchill Downs. 1937-'42,1946-'64 about 4 furlongs; 1943-'44,1965-'81 4¹⁄₂ furlongs; 1982-'85 6 furlongs. 1937-'78 colts and geldings. 1993 equaled track record.

La Jolla Handicap

Grade 3, Del Mar, three-year-olds, 1¹⁄₁₆ miles, turf. Held August 17, 2002, with a gross value of $150,000. First held in 1937. Graded since 1973. Stakes record 1:41.50 (2000 Purely Cozzene).

Year	Winner	Jockey	Second	Third	Strs	Time	1st Purse
2002	**Inesperado (Fr)**, 3, 118	E. J. Delahoussaye	Regiment, 3	Mountain Rage, 3	4	1:43.92	$90,000
2001	**Marine (GB)**, 3, 117	C. S. Nakatani	Romanceishope, 3	Mister Approval, 3	8	1:41.72	$90,000
2000	**Purely Cozzene**, 3, 120	D. R. Flores	Duke of Green (GB), 3	Sign of Hope (GB), 3	9	**1:41.50**	$90,000
1999	**Eagleton**, 3, 119	I. D. Enriquez	In Frank's Honor, 3	Zanetti, 3	9	1:41.89	$90,000

1998 **Ladies Din**, 3, 120	G. L. Stevens	Success and Glory (Ire), 3	Lucayan Indian (Ire), 3	7	1:41.94	$81,810
1997 **Fantastic Fellow**, 3, 118	A. O. Solis	Worldly Ways (GB), 3	Falkenham (GB), 3	7	1:43.43	$85,450
1996 **Ambivalent**, 3, 116	R. R. Douglas	The Barking Shark, 3	Caribbean Pirate, 3	10	1:43.34	$82,850
1995 **Petionville**, 3, 120	C. S. Nakatani	Private Interview, 3	Beau Temps (GB), 3	7	1:44.26	$74,600
1994 **Marvin's Faith (Ire)**, 3, 114	C. W. Antley	Unfinished Symph, 3	Ocean Crest, 3	7	1:42.38	$62,800
1993 **Manny's Prospect**, 3, 115	C. J. McCarron	Golden Slewpy, 3	Hawk Spell, 3	9	1:42.12	$64,700
1992 **Blacksburg**, 3, 119	K. J. Desormeaux	Free At Last, 3	Fax News, 3	9	1:41.60	$64,700

Named for the resort community of La Jolla, California, located in the San Diego area. 1939,1942-'44 not held. 1937-'65,1982-'86 La Jolla Mile H.; 1977-'81 La Jolla Mile S. 1938-'86 1 mile. 1937-'74 dirt. 1937-'38,1945-'46,1949-'50 three-year-olds and up.

Lake George Stakes

Grade 3, Saratoga Race Course, three-year-olds, fillies, 1¹/₁₆ miles, turf. Held July 29, 2002, with a gross value of $100,000. First held in 1996. Graded since 1998. Stakes record 1:40.11 (1999 Nani Rose).

Year	Winner	Jockey	Second	Third	Strs	Time	1st Purse
2002	**Nunatall (GB)**, 3, 115	J. F. Chavez	Guana (Fr), 3	Mariensky, 3	11	1:40.71	$69,000
2001	**Voodoo Dancer**, 3, 122	J. D. Bailey	Sadler's Sarah, 3	O K to Dance, 3	9	1:41.45	$67,350
	Light Dancer, 3, 117	M. Guidry	Owsley, 3	Cozzy Corner, 3	9	1:41.06	$67,050
2000	**Millie's Quest**, 3, 114	J. R. Velazquez	Shopping for Love, 3	Battenkill, 3	9	1:44.52	$70,080
1999	**Nani Rose**, 3, 122	S. J. Sellers	Perfect Sting, 3	Intrigued, 3	8	**1:40.11**	$67,680
1998	**Caveat Competor**, 3, 116	J. R. Velazquez	Mysterious Moll, 3	Recording, 3	10	1:41.05	$50,760
	Tenski, 3, 114	R. Migliore	Pratella, 3	Camella, 3	8	1:40.86	$50,070
1997	**Auntie Mame**, 3, 121	J. D. Bailey	Crab Grass, 3	Innovate, 3	9	1:42.80	$51,120
1996	**Dynasty**, 3, 112	J. D. Bailey	River Antoine, 3	Vashon, 3	8	1:42.26	$33,630
	Memories of Silver, 3, 112	J. D. Bailey	Clamorosa, 3	Captive Number, 3	10	1:42.98	$33,780

Named for a favorite summertime resort in upstate New York, located north of Saratoga Springs. 1999 Lake George H. 1996,1998, 2001 two divisions.

Lake Placid Handicap

Grade 2, Saratoga Race Course, three-year-olds, fillies, 1¹/₈ miles, turf. Held August 18, 2002, with a gross value of $150,000. First held in 1984. Graded since 1986. Stakes record 1:46.33 (1998 Tenski).

Year	Winner	Jockey	Second	Third	Strs	Time	1st Purse
2002	**Wonder Again**, 3, 114	E. S. Prado	Riskaverse, 3	Miss Marcia, 3	9	1:49.24	$90,000
2001	**Snow Dance**, 3, 116	R. Migliore	Wander Mom, 3	Mystic Lady, 3	12	1:47.42	$90,000
2000	**Gaviola**, 3, 122	J. D. Bailey	Good Game, 3	Millie's Quest, 3	11	1:48.04	$90,000
1999	**Badouizm**, 3, 113	R. G. Davis	Confessional, 3	Emanating, 3	8	1:46.44	$90,000
1998	**Tenski**, 3, 119	R. Migliore	Naskra's de Light, 3	Caveat Competor, 3	12	**1:46.33**	$90,000
1997	**Witchful Thinking**, 3, 123	S. J. Sellers	Miss Huff n' Puff, 3	Majestic Sunlight, 3	12	1:47.65	$90,000
1996	**Memories of Silver**, 3, 115	J. D. Bailey	Unify, 3	Henlopen, 3	9	1:47.80	$68,640
1995	**Bail Out Becky**, 3, 115	S. J. Sellers	Fashion Star, 3	Grand Charmer, 3	9	1:41.87	$67,680
	Class Kris, 3, 112	P. Day	In a Daydream, 3	Shocking Pleasure, 3	9	1:40.90	$67,380
1994	**Alywow**, 3, 121	M. E. Smith	Irish Forever, 3	Knocknock, 3	9	1:43.81	$66,660
	Coronation Cup, 3, 114	J. D. Bailey	Stretch Drive, 3	Golden Tajniak (Ire), 3	7	1:43.88	$65,760
1993	**Statuette**, 3, 114	M. E. Smith	Icy Warning, 3	Dispute, 3	8	1:41.58	$55,980
	Amal Hayati, 3, 121	J. D. Bailey	Eloquent Silver, 3	Irving's Girl, 3	10	1:40.97	$56,940
1992	**Heed**, 3, 114	M. E. Smith	Captive Miss, 3	Mystic Hawk, 3	10	1:40.98	$72,420
	Shannkara (Ire), 3, 114	M. E. Smith	Tiney Toast, 3	Favored Lady, 3	11	1:41.84	$73,380

Named for the popular Adirondack mountain resort that has hosted the Winter Olympics twice. 1984-'97 Nijana S. 1991-'98 Grade 3. 1984-'89,1991-'95 1¹/₁₆ miles. 1990 dirt. 1992-'95 two divisions.

Landaluce Stakes

Grade 3, Hollywood Park, two-year-olds, fillies, 6 furlongs, dirt. Held July 4, 2002, with a gross value of $100,000. First held in 1945. Graded since 1973. Stakes record 1:08 (1982 Landaluce).

Year	Winner	Jockey	Second	Third	Strs	Time	1st Purse
2002	**Buffythecenterfold**, 2, 116	M. S. Garcia	Tricks Her, 2	Little Bit a Swiss, 2	9	1:10.51	$66,360
2001	**Georgia's Storm**, 2, 119	C. J. McCarron	Respectful, 2	Who Loves Aleyna, 2	7	1:10.45	$65,040
2000	**Notable Career**, 2, 116	C. S. Nakatani	Sea Reel, 2	Starrer, 2	7	1:11.10	$65,040
1999	**Magicalmysterycat**, 2, 119	C. W. Antley	She's Classy, 2	Princes Melissa, 2	4	1:11.01	$63,120
1998	**Hookedonthefeelin**, 2, 119	G. L. Stevens	Box Office Girl, 2	Excellent Meeting, 2	11	1:09.60	$62,820
1997	**Career Collection**, 2, 116	C. S. Nakatani	Bent Creek City, 2	Unreal Squeal, 2	7	1:10.41	$62,820
1996	**Starry Ice**, 2, 119	E. J. Delahoussaye	Trav n' Kris, 2	Montecito, 2	6	1:11.13	$62,160
1995	**Raw Gold**, 2, 116	A. O. Solis	Wasmi Song, 2	Liberty Nite, 2	10	1:10.64	$59,600
1994	**Serena's Song**, 2, 116	G. L. Stevens	Embroidered, 2	Cat's Cradle, 2	10	1:10.11	$66,800
1993	**Rhapsodic**, 2, 116	E. J. Delahoussaye	Miss Gibson County, 2	Becky's Appeal, 2	9	1:10.59	$59,800
1992	**Zealous Connection**, 2, 116	M. A. Pedroza	Medici Bells, 2	Sweet Mama, 2	8	1:09.86	$58,500

Named for 1982 champion two-year-old filly Landaluce (1980-'82, f. by Seattle Slew). 1945-'82 Hollywood Lassie S. 1983,1991-'99 Grade 2. 1947-'49,1951-'68 5¹/₂ furlongs.

(Lane's End) Breeders' Futurity

Grade 2, Keeneland, two-year-olds, 1¹/₁₆ miles, dirt. Held October 5, 2002, with a gross value of $434,800. First held in 1910. Graded since 1973. Stakes record 1:42.23 (1993 Polar Expedition).

Year	Winner	Jockey	Second	Third	Strs	Time	1st Purse
2002	Sky Mesa, 2, 121	E. S. Prado	Lone Star Sky, 2	Truckle Feature, 2	6	1:46.78	$269,576
2001	Siphonic, 2, 121	C. J. McCarron	Harlan's Holiday, 2	Metatron, 2	11	1:43.79	$281,728
2000	Arabian Light, 2, 121	S. J. Sellers	Dollar Bill, 2	Holiday Thunder, 2	10	1:43.18	$279,744
1999	Captain Steve, 2, 121	G. K. Gomez	Graeme Hall, 2	Millencolin, 2	8	1:42.59	$274,040
1998	Cat Thief, 2, 121	P. Day	Answer Lively, 2	Yes It's True, 2	8	1:44.17	$272,552
1997	Favorite Trick, 2, 121	P. Day	Time Limit, 2	Laydown, 2	5	1:43.36	$265,112
1996	Boston Harbor, 2, 121	J. D. Bailey	Blazing Sword, 2	Haint, 2	5	1:45.31	$1,166,005
1995	Honour and Glory, 2, 121	P. Day	City by Night, 2	Blushing Jim, 2	10	1:43.33	$139,252
1994	Tejano Run, 2, 121	J. D. Bailey	Cinch, 2	Gold Miner, 2	11	1:44.71	$71,548
1993	Polar Expedition, 2, 121	C. C. Bourque	Goodbye Doeny, 2	Solly's Honor, 2	8	1:42.23	$122,200
1992	Mountain Cat, 2, 121	P. Day	Living Vicariously, 2	Boundlessly, 2	4	1:45.42	$1,122,200

Sponsored by W. S. Farish's Lane's End, located in Versailles, and in honor of Kentucky breeders. 1934-'37 not held. 1910-'96 Breeders' Futurity. 1910-'30 held at Kentucky Association; 1931-'33 Old Latonia; 1943-'45 Churchill Downs. 1910-'11 4 furlongs; 1912 4¹/₂ furlongs; 1913-'16 5 furlongs; 1917-'33 about 6 furlongs; 1938-'49 6 furlongs; 1950-'55 7 furlongs; 1956-'80 about 7 furlongs. 1992,1996 winner's purse includes $1,000,000 bonus from the KTDF.

Lane's End Stakes

Grade 2, Turfway Park, three-year-olds, 1¹/₈ miles, dirt. Held March 22, 2003, with a gross value of $500,000. First held in 1972. Graded since 1984. Stakes record 1:46.70 (1991 Hansel).

Year	Winner	Jockey	Second	Third	Strs	Time	1st Purse
2003	New York Hero, 3, 121	N. Arroyo Jr.	Eugene's Third Son, 3	Champali, 3	9	1:50.68	$300,000
2002	Perfect Drift, 3, 121	E. J. Delahoussaye	Azillion (Ire), 3	Request for Parole, 3	8	1:48.83	$300,000
2001	Balto Star, 3, 121	M. Guidry	Halo's Stride, 3	Mongoose, 3	9	1:47.23	$360,000
2000	Globalize, 3, 121	F. C. Torres	Elite Mercedes, 3	Rollin With Nolan, 3	10	1:49.16	$360,000
1999	Stephen Got Even, 3, 121	S. J. Sellers	K One King, 3	Epic Honor, 3	8	1:49.03	$450,000
1998	Event of the Year, 3, 121	R. A. Baze	Yarrow Brae, 3	Truluck, 3	10	1:47.12	$360,000
1997	Concerto, 3, 121	C. H. Marquez Jr.	Jack Flash, 3	Shammy Davis, 3	10	1:48.23	$360,000
1996	Roar, 3, 121	M. E. Smith	Ensign Ray, 3	Victory Speech, 3	9	1:49.70	$360,000
1995	†Serena's Song, 3, 116	C. S. Nakatani	Tejano Run, 3	Mecke, 3	8	1:49.65	$360,000
1994	Polar Expedition, 3, 121	C. C. Bourque	Powis Castle, 3	Chimes Band, 3	11	1:49.03	$360,000
1993	Prairie Bayou, 3, 121	C. J. McCarron	Proudest Romeo, 3	Miner's Mark, 3	9	1:50.97	$360,000
1992	Lil E. Tee, 3, 121	P. Day	Vying Victor, 3	Treekster, 3	11	1:53.44	$300,000

Named for sponsor W. S. Farish's Lane's End, located in Versailles, Kentucky. 1972-'81 Spiral S.; 1982-'83 Jim Beam Spiral S.; 1984-'98 Jim Beam S.; 1999 Gallery Furniture.com S.; 2000-'01 Turfway Spiral S.; 2002 Lane's End Spiral S. 1972-'85 held at Latonia Race Course. 1972-'81 1 mile; 1982-'87 1¹/₁₆ miles. †denotes female.

La Prevoyante Handicap

Grade 2, Calder Race Course, three-year-olds and up, fillies and mares, 1¹/₂ miles, turf. Held December 28, 2002, with a gross value of $200,000. First held in 1976. Graded since 1982. Stakes record 2:25.20 (1988 Singular Bequest).

Year	Winner	Jockey	Second	Third	Strs	Time	1st Purse
2002	New Economy, 4, 113	R. B. Homeister Jr.	Jennasietta, 4	Tweedside, 4	12	2:28.55	$120,000
2001	Krisada, 5, 115	P. Day	Sweetest Thing, 3	Great Fever (Fr), 4	10	2:26.63	$90,000
2000	Prospectress, 5, 114	J. D. Bailey	Innuendo (Ire), 5	Orange Sunset (Ire), 4	10	2:26.97	$90,000
1999	Coretta (Ire), 5, 120	J. A. Santos	Idle Rich, 4	St. Bernadette (Per), 3	8	2:27.27	$90,000
1998	Coretta (Ire), 4, 117	J. A. Santos	Starry Dreamer, 4	(DH) Tedarshana (GB), 4	12	2:26.67	$90,000
				(DH) Cuando, 4			
1997	Last Approach, 5, 110	J. A. Krone	Flying Concert, 4	Grey Way, 4	6	2:39.13	$90,000
1996	Ampulla, 5, 122	S. J. Sellers	Miss Caerleona (Fr), 4	Electric Society (Ire), 5	8	2:27.50	$90,000
1995	Interim (GB), 4, 116	C. S. Nakatani	Northern Emerald, 5	Caromana, 4	10	2:26.38	$90,000
1994	Abigailthewife, 5, 114	J. A. Santos	Trampoli, 5	Market Booster, 5	14	2:28.91	$90,000
	Trampoli, 5, 120	M. E. Smith	Putthepowdertoit, 4	Adoryphar, 5	14	2:28.14	$90,000
1993	Lemhi Go, 5, 112	M. A. Gonzalez	Indian Chris (Brz), 6	Silvered, 6	6	2:37.53	$60,000
1992	Sardaniya (Ire), 4, 113	J. Cruguet	Flaming Torch (Ire), 5	Expensiveness, 5	9	2:29.62	$90,000

Named for 1972 Canadian Horse of the Year and North American champion two-year-old filly La Prevoyante (1970-'74, f. by Buckpasser). 1977 not held. 1986-'93 La Prevoyante Invitational H. 1982-'87 Grade 3. 1976 1¹/₁₆ miles; 1978-'79,1981-'83 about 1¹/₈ miles; 1980 1¹/₈ miles; 1992 about 1¹/₂ miles; 1980,1987,1990,1993,1997 dirt. 1994 held in January and December.

Las Cienegas Handicap

Grade 3, Santa Anita Park, four-year-olds and up, fillies and mares, about 6¹/₂ furlongs, turf. Held April 5, 2003, with a gross value of $110,000. First held in 1974. Graded since 1992. Stakes record 1:12.50 (1997 Advancing Star).

Year	Winner	Jockey	Second	Third	Strs	Time	1st Purse
2003	Heat Haze (GB), 4, 114	J. Valdivia Jr.	Icantgoforthat, 4	Paga (Arg), 6	8	1:13.11	$66,000
2002	Rolly Polly (Ire), 4, 119	K. J. Desormeaux	Penny Marie, 6	Twin Set (Ger), 5	7	1:12.55	$65,100
2001	Go Go, 4, 118	E. J. Delahoussaye	Separata (Chi), 5	Dianehill (Ire), 5	8	1:13.54	$65,700

2000	**Evening Promise (GB)**, 4, 114	D. Sorenson	La Madame (Chi), 5	Reciclada (Chi), 5	5	1:13.66	$63,840
1999	**Desert Lady (Ire)**, 4, 118	C. S. Nakatani	Hula Queen, 5	Bella Chiarra, 4	7	1:13.55	$65,640
1998	**Dance Parade**, 4, 119	K. J. Desormeaux	Advancing Star, 5	Imroz, 4	6	1:13.60	$64,800
1997	**Advancing Star**, 4, 116	G. L. Stevens	Ski Dancer, 5	Grab the Prize, 5	6	**1:12.50**	$96,550
1996	**Ski Dancer**, 4, 117	G. L. Stevens	Klassy Kim, 5	Igotrhythm, 4	6	1:14.59	$64,300
1995	**Marina Park (GB)**, 5, 119	A. O. Solis	Pirate's Revenge, 4	Rabiadella, 4	9	1:13.77	$63,175
1994	**Mamselle Bebette**, 4, 120	C. J. McCarron	Cool Air, 4	Bel's Starlet, 4	5	1:13.05	$45,975
1993	**Glen Kate (Ire)**, 6, 121	C. A. Black	Heart of Joy, 6	Worldly Possession, 6	6	1:12.71	$61,225
1992	**Heart of Joy**, 5, 123	C. J. McCarron	Sheltered View, 4	Crystal Gazing, 4	9	1:12.72	$63,475

Named for Rancho Las Cienegas in southwestern Los Angeles County; las cienegas means "the swamps." 1975 not held. 1976 Las Cienegas S.; 1992-'95 Las Cienegas Breeders' Cup H. 1976 6 furlongs; 1979,1982-'83,1986 6½ furlongs. 1976,1979,1982-'83,1986 dirt. 1976 three-year-olds. 1974-'76 both sexes.

Las Flores Handicap

Grade 3, Santa Anita Park, four-year-olds and up, fillies and mares, 6 furlongs, dirt. Held February 22, 2003, with a gross value of $135,500. First held in 1951. Graded since 1973. Stakes record 1:08.20 (1990 Stormy But Valid).

Year	Winner	Jockey	Second	Third	Strs	Time	1st Purse
2003	**Spring Meadow**, 4, 117	C. S. Nakatani	Brisquette, 5	(DH) September Secret, 4	6	1:10.20	$81,300
				(DH) Wild Tickle, 5			
2002	**Above Perfection**, 4, 117	C. S. Nakatani	Kalookan Queen, 6	Enchanted Woods, 5	4	1:08.65	$78,642
2001	**Go Go**, 4, 116	E. J. Delahoussaye	La Feminn, 5	Cover Gal, 4	6	1:08.83	$80,400
2000	**Show Me the Stage**, 4, 118	K. J. Desormeaux	Theresa's Tizzy, 6	Woodman's Dancer, 6	6	1:08.54	$79,440
1999	**Enjoy the Moment**, 4, 117	L. A. Pincay Jr.	Tomorrows Sunshine, 5	Closed Escrow, 6	5	1:08.55	$78,720
1998	**Funallover**, 4, 114	A. O. Solis	Advancing Star, 5	Zenda's Diablo, 4	7	1:09.10	$79,800
1997	**Our Summer Bid**, 5, 114	J. Silva	Track Gal, 6	Advancing Star, 4	6	1:09.15	$80,100
1996	**Igotrhythm**, 4, 115	C. S. Nakatani	Miss L Attack, 6	Little Blue Sheep, 4	4	1:08.88	$81,100
1995	**Desert Stormer**, 5, 117	K. J. Desormeaux	Velvet Tulip, 5	Flying in the Lane, 5	5	1:08.49	$59,725
1994	**Mamselle Bebette**, 5, 118	C. S. Nakatani	Arches of Gold, 5	Aspasante, 5	7	1:08.32	$47,475
1993	**Bountiful Native**, 5, 121	P. A. Valenzuela	Freedom Cry, 5	Forest Fealty, 5	6	1:09.42	$60,325
1992	**Forest Fealty**, 5, 116	M. A. Pedroza	Middlefork Rapids, 4	Phil's Illusion, 4	9	1:08.87	$49,350

Named for the 1844 land grant Rancho Las Flores, located in Tehama County; flores means "flowers." 1953,1969,1971,1974,1980,1988 not held. 1990-'95 Las Flores Breeders' Cup H. 1975-'84 not graded. 1951-'52,1956-'68,1970,1977 (December),1978,1987 (December) three-year-olds and up; 1972 (December),1973, 1983 two-year-olds and up.

Las Palmas Handicap

Grade 2, Santa Anita Park, three-year-olds and up, fillies and mares, 1⅛ miles, turf. Held November 3, 2002, with a gross value of $200,000. First held in 1969. Graded since 1973. Stakes record 1:43.92 (1991 Kostroma [Ire] [new and current world record]).

Year	Winner	Jockey	Second	Third	Strs	Time	1st Purse
2002	**Tates Creek**, 4, 120	J. D. Bailey	Voodoo Dancer, 4	Magic Mission (GB), 4	8	1:47.69	$120,000
2001	**Golden Apples (Ire)**, 3, 115	G. K. Gomez	Dancingonice, 5	Janet (GB), 4	9	1:46.61	$150,000
2000	**Smooth Player**, 4, 117	E. J. Delahoussaye	Beautiful Noise, 4	Happyanunoit (NZ), 4	10	1:46.99	$105,000
1999	**Sapphire Ring (GB)**, 4, 118	G. L. Stevens	Cyrillic, 4	Country Garden (GB), 4	11	1:48.20	$150,000
1998	**Sonja's Faith (Ire)**, 4, 115	E. Ramsammy	See You Soon (Fr), 4	Idealistic Cause, 4	6	1:48.92	$90,000
1997	**Real Connection**, 6, 115	G. F. Almeida	Toda Una Dama (Arg), 4	Luna Wells (Ire), 5	9	1:47.76	$75,000
1996	**Wandesta (GB)**, 5, 120	C. S. Nakatani	Real Connection, 5	Alpride (Ire), 5	7	1:46.72	$79,700
1995	**Onceinabluemamoon**, 4, 116	B. Blanc	Yearly Tour, 4	Don't Read My Lips, 4	9	1:50.34	$76,400
1994	**Aube Indienne (Fr)**, 4, 115	K. J. Desormeaux	Queens Court Queen, 5	Skimble, 5	5	1:49.62	$61,300
1993	**Miatuschka**, 5, 114	C. A. Black	Skimble, 4	Potridee (Arg), 4	4	1:47.98	$62,600
1992	**Super Staff**, 4, 116	K. J. Desormeaux	Flawlessly, 4	Re Toss (Arg), 5	7	1:46.89	$77,750

Named for Las Palmas, winner of the first race run at Santa Anita on December 25, 1934. 1973-'82 Grade 3. 1969,1982 1¹⁄₁₆ miles. 1969,1979 dirt.

Las Virgenes Stakes

Grade 1, Santa Anita Park, three-year-olds, fillies, 1 mile, dirt. Held February 9, 2003, with a gross value of $200,000. First held in 1983. Graded since 1985. Stakes record 1:35.14 (1994 Lakeway).

Year	Winner	Jockey	Second	Third	Strs	Time	1st Purse
2003	**Composure**, 3, 120	J. D. Bailey	Elloluv, 3	Watching You, 3	6	1:36.13	$120,000
2002	**You**, 3, 122	J. D. Bailey	Habibti, 3	Tali'sluckybusride, 3	6	1:36.84	$120,000
2001	**Golden Ballet**, 3, 122	C. J. McCarron	Two Item Limit, 3	Affluent, 3	7	1:36.89	$120,000
2000	**Surfside**, 3, 122	P. Day	Spain, 3	Rings a Chime, 3	4	1:37.00	$120,000
1999	**Excellent Meeting**, 3, 122	K. J. Desormeaux	Tout Charmant, 3	Weekend Squall, 3	5	1:35.35	$120,000
1998	**Keeper Hill**, 3, 114	D. R. Flores	Star of Broadway, 3	Occhi Verdi (Ire), 3	9	1:36.94	$120,000
1997	**Sharp Cat**, 3, 122	C. S. Nakatani	High Heeled Hope, 3	Demon Acquire, 3	8	1:35.52	$98,800
1996	**Antespend**, 3, 120	C. W. Antley	Cara Rafaela, 3	Hidden Lake, 3	8	1:36.45	$96,900
1995	**Serena's Song**, 3, 122	C. S. Nakatani	Cat's Cradle, 3	Urbane, 3	7	1:35.46	$92,700
1994	**Lakeway**, 3, 117	K. J. Desormeaux	Fancy 'n Fabulous, 3	Princess Mitterand, 3	8	**1:35.14**	$93,600
1993	**Likeable Style**, 3, 117	G. L. Stevens	Incindress, 3	Blue Moonlight, 3	6	1:36.67	$91,000
1992	**Magical Maiden**, 3, 121	G. L. Stevens	Golden Treat, 3	Red Bandana, 3	10	1:36.23	$96,800

Named for Rancho Las Virgenes, an 1837 land grant located in Los Angeles County. 1985-'86 Grade 3; 1987 Grade 2.

La Troienne Stakes

Grade 3, Churchill Downs, three-year-olds, fillies, 7 furlongs, dirt. Held May 2, 2002, with a gross value of $100,000. First held in 1956. Graded since 1998. Stakes record 1:21.97 (2000 Roxelana).

Year	Winner	Jockey	Second	Third	Strs	Time	1st Purse
2002	Cashier's Dream, 3, 121	D. J. Meche	Shameful, 3	Colonial Glitter, 3	5	1:24.83	$69,812
2001	Caressing, 3, 121	P. Day	Sweet Nanette, 3	Golly Greeley, 3	9	1:22.90	$75,020
2000	Roxelana, 3, 116	L. Melancon	Magicalmysterycat, 3	Watchfull, 3	7	1:21.97	$70,308
1999	Sapphire n' Silk, 3, 113	P. Day	English Bay, 3	Grand Deed, 3	6	1:23.85	$69,936
1998	Sister Act, 3, 113	C. H. Borel	Bourbon Belle, 3	Marie J, 3	6	1:24.46	$69,874
1997	Star of Goshen, 3, 115	A. O. Solis	Pearl City, 3	Flying Lauren, 3	8	1:22.75	$70,370
1996	Rare Blend, 3, 121	P. Day	Ruby Baby, 3	Prissy One, 3	8	1:23.75	$55,624
1995	Dixieland Gold, 3, 121	D. Penna	Daylight Ridge, 3	Ivorilla, 3	7	1:22.74	$55,088
1994	Packet, 3, 113	J. M. Johnson	Golden Braids, 3	Miss Ra He Ra, 3	10	1:24.14	$55,770
1993	Traverse City, 3, 116	J. A. Krone	Added Asset, 3	Bellewood, 3	10	1:24.38	$38,025
1992	Bell Witch, 3, 111	J. A. Krone	Take the Cure, 3	Meadow Storm, 3	6	1:24.35	$36,497

Named for great foundation mare *La Troienne (1926-'54, f. by *Teddy). 1956-'66 Oaks Prep S. 1956-'60 6 furlongs.

Laurel Futurity

Grade 3, Laurel Park, two-year-olds, 1¹/₁₆ miles, dirt. Held November 16, 2002, with a gross value of $100,000. First held in 1921. Graded since 1973. Stakes record 1:46.10 (2002 Toccet).

Year	Winner	Jockey	Second	Third	Strs	Time	1st Purse
2002	Toccet, 2, 122	J. F. Chavez	Ironton, 2	Cherokee's Boy, 2	7	1:46.10	$60,000
2000	Buckle Down Ben, 2, 122	M. J. McCarthy	Gift of the Eagle, 2	Niner's Echo, 2	8	1:51.93	$60,000
1999	Scottish Halo, 2, 122	T. G. Turner	Un Fino Vino, 2	Grundlefoot, 2	8	1:49.35	$60,000
1998	Millions, 2, 122	E. S. Prado	Raire Standard, 2	More Better, 2	8	1:51.52	$60,000
1997	Fight for M'lady, 2, 122	C. H. Marquez Jr.	Victory Gallop, 2	Essential, 2	6	1:53.63	$60,000
1996	Captain Bodgit, 2, 122	F. G. Douglas	Concerto, 2	Carrolls Favorite, 2	10	1:49.53	$60,000
1995	Appealing Skier, 2, 122	R. Wilson	Liberty Road, 2	Pirate Performer, 2	8	1:30.70	$60,000
1994	Western Echo, 2, 122	E. S. Prado	Old Tascosa, 2	Shimmering Prince, 2	10	1:30.82	$60,000
1993	Dove Hunt, 2, 122	R. G. Davis	Lotsa Chile, 2	Thrilla in Manila, 2	8	1:49.03	$81,000
1992	Lord of the Bay, 2, 122	R. Wilson	Glorieux Dancer (Fr), 2	Halissee, 2	11	1:45.54	$120,000

1933-'34, 2001 not held. 1921-'66 Pimlico Futurity; 1967-'71 Pimlico-Laurel Futurity. 1973-'88 Grade 1; 1989 Grade 2. 1921-'65,1979 held at Pimlico. 1921-'28 1 mile; 1994-'95 7½ furlongs; 1996-2000 1¹/₈ miles. 1987-'88,1990-'93 turf. 1993 Linkatariat finished third, DQ to fourth.

Lawrence Realization Handicap

Originally scheduled as a Grade 3 on the turf, Belmont Park, three-year-olds, 1½ miles, dirt. Held October 12, 2002, with a gross value of $150,000. First held in 1889. Graded since 1973. Stakes record 2:25.94 (1998 Parade Ground).

Year	Winner	Jockey	Second	Third	Strs	Time	1st Purse
2002	Fisher Pond, 3, 116	J. R. Velazquez	Irish Colonial, 3	Extra Check, 3	5	2:30.34	$90,000
2001	Sharp Performance, 3, 120	J. R. Velazquez	Tiger Trap, 3	Whitmore's Conn, 3	6	2:27.04	$90,000
2000	Ciro, 3, 123	J. A. Santos	Whata Brainstorm, 3	Lodge Hill, 3	10	2:31.48	$90,000
1999	Gritty Sandie, 3, 114	M. E. Smith	Monkey Puzzle, 3	Just Listen, 3	14	2:28.60	$90,000
1998	Parade Ground, 3, 121	P. Day	Pay Zone, 3	Vergennes, 3	8	2:25.94	$83,595
1997	Renewed, 3, 112	F. Leon	Devonwood, 3	Belgravia (GB), 3	10	2:27.21	$67,320
1996	Da Dean, 3, 113	R. Migliore	Senor Senor, 3	Value Investor, 3	12	2:39.06	$68,880
1995	Flitch, 3, 117	M. E. Smith	Look Daggers, 3	Diplomatic Jet, 3	11	2:34.40	$69,300
1994	Personal Merit, 3, 113	J. F. Chavez	Kristen's Baby, 3	Holy Mountain, 3	8	2:29.30	$67,260
1993	Strolling Along, 3, 114	C. J. McCarron	Scattered Steps, 3	Noble Sheba, 3	12	2:32.70	$75,480
1992	Timber Cat, 3, 114	R. G. Davis	Tomorrow's Spirit, 3	Gainzer, 3	13	2:28.87	$76,560

Named for James G. K. Lawrence, originator of the Futurity Stakes at Sheepshead Bay. 1911-'12,1914-'15 not held. 1889-'98 Realization S.; 1899-1993 Lawrence Realization S. 1973-'88 Grade 2; 1989-2001 Grade 3. 1889-1910 held at Sheepshead Bay; 1959,1961,1963-'67 Aqueduct. 1889-1913,1918-'69 1⅝ miles. 1889-1969,1977,1985,1987,1994 dirt. 1944 colts and fillies.

Lazaro Barrera Memorial Stakes

Grade 2, Hollywood Park, three-year-olds, 7 furlongs, dirt. Held May 27, 2002, with a gross value of $150,000. First held in 1953. Graded since 2001. Stakes record 1:20.42 (2001 Early Flyer).

Year	Winner	Jockey	Second	Third	Strs	Time	1st Purse
2002	Captain Squire, 3, 123	C. J. Rollins	Fonz's, 3	Kamsack, 3	5	1:21.95	$90,000
2001	Early Flyer, 3, 123	C. J. McCarron	Squirtle Squirt, 3	Top Hit, 3	7	1:20.42	$65,160
2000	Caller One, 3, 122	C. S. Nakatani	Dixie Union, 3	Swept Overboard, 3	4	1:21.10	$60,960
1999	Love That Red, 3, 122	G. K. Gomez	Apremont, 3	O'Rey Fantasma, 3	4	1:20.81	$56,910
1998	Reraise, 3, 116	E. Delahoussaye	Souvenir Copy, 3	Full Moon Madness, 3	6	1:08.51	$39,930
1996	Future Quest, 3, 122	K. J. Desormeaux	Slews Royal Son	Tiger Talk	8	1:15.17	$35,100
1995	Flying Standby, 3, 115	C. W. Antley	Desert Pirate	Boundless Moment	6	1:08.09	$40,200

Named for Racing Hall of Fame and Eclipse Award-winning trainer Lazaro Barrera (1924-'91), trainer of Triple Crown winner Affirmed. 1953-'54,1995-'96,1998 Playa Del Rey S. 1955-'94,1997 not held. 2001 Grade 3. 1954,1995,1998 6 furlongs; 1996 6½ furlongs.

Lecomte Stakes

Grade 3, Fair Grounds, three-year-olds, 1 mile, dirt. Held January 25, 2003, with a gross value of $100,000. First held in 1943. Graded since 2003. Stakes record 1:37.60 (1993 Dixieland Heat).

Year	Winner	Jockey	Second	Third	Strs	Time	1st Purse
2003	Saintly Look, 3, 122	S. J. Sellers	Call Me Lefty, 3	Winning Fans, 3	11	1:37.62	$60,000
2002	Easyfromthegitgo, 3, 114	D. J. Meche	Sky Terrace, 3	It'sallinthechase, 3	11	1:37.98	$60,000
2001	Sam Lord's Castle, 3, 122	R. Albarado	Wild Hits, 3	Mc Mahon, 3	10	1:37.98	$60,000
2000	Noble Ruler, 3, 114	L. Melancon	Mighty, 3	Peninsula, 3	10	1:39.00	$60,000
1999	Some Actor, 3, 114	E. Martin Jr.	Desert Demon, 3	Silver Chadra, 3	14	1:38.40	$60,000
1998	Western City, 3, 112	R. Albarado	Captain Maestri, 3	Slick Report, 3	6	1:37.84	$60,000
1997	Cash Deposit, 3, 120	R. Ardoin	Stroke, 3	Kalispell, 3	5	1:37.97	$36,000
1996	Boomerang, 3, 116	E. Martin Jr.	Commanders Palace, 3	Playing To Win, 3	8	1:39.49	$25,845
1995	Moonlight Dancer, 3, 112	L. Melancon	Beavers Nose, 3	Timeless Honor, 3	8	1:40.13	$25,725
1994	Fly Cry, 3, 119	R. Ardoin	Smilin Singin Sam, 3	Sweet Wager, 3	12	1:39.29	$19,905
1993	Dixieland Heat, 3, 116	E. J. Perrodin	Apprentice, 3	Masters Windfall, 3	13	1:36.60	$19,995
1992	Line In The Sand, 3, 112	S. P. Romero	Greinton's Dancer, 3	Best Boy's Jade, 3	7	1:39.80	$19,215

Named for Lecomte (1850-'56, c. by Boston); Lecomte was the only horse to defeat Lexington, in a match race at Metairie Race Course in New Orleans.

Leonard Richards Stakes

Grade 3, Delaware Park, three-year-olds, 1¹/₁₆ miles, dirt. Held June 8, 2002, with a gross value of $250,900. First held in 1937. Graded since 1973. Stakes record 1:42.41 (2001 Burning Roma).

Year	Winner	Jockey	Second	Third	Strs	Time	1st Purse
2002	Running Tide, 3, 115	R. A. Dominguez	Nothing Flat, 3	The Sewickley Kid, 3	8	1:45.10	$150,000
2001	Burning Roma, 3, 122	R. Wilson	Marciano, 3	Bay Eagle, 3	5	1:42.41	$120,000
2000	Grundlefoot, 3, 113	T. L. Dunkelberger	Perfect Cat, 3	Mercaldo, 3	8	1:44.04	$120,000
1999	Stellar Brush, 3, 114	M. J. McCarthy	Smart Guy, 3	Successful Appeal, 3	8	1:42.78	$120,000
1998	Scatmandu, 3, 114	R. Migliore	Hot Wells, 3	True Silver, 3	7	1:42.43	$90,000
1997	Leestown, 3, 116	J. A. Velez Jr.	Universe, 3	Bleu Madura, 3	8	1:43.46	$90,000

Named for Leonard P. Richards, second chairman of the Delaware Racing Commission. 1943,1983-'96 not held. 1937-'47 Diamond State S. 1973-'74 Grade 2; 1980-'82,1997-2001 not graded. 1937-'68,1979-'82 1¹/₈ miles. 1970-'80 turf.

Lexington Stakes

Grade 3, Belmont Park, three-year-olds, 1¹/₄ miles, turf. Held July 14, 2002, with a gross value of $150,000. First held in 1961. Graded since 1973. Stakes record 1:58.93 (2001 Sharp Performance).

Year	Winner	Jockey	Second	Third	Strs	Time	1st Purse
2002	Chiselling, 3, 114	J. D. Bailey	Finality, 3	Irish Colonial, 3	8	2:00.42	$90,000
2001	Sharp Performance, 3, 114	J. R. Velazquez	Package Store, 3	Whitmore's Conn, 3	8	1:58.93	$90,000
2000	Rob's Spirit, 3, 113	J. D. Bailey	Plato, 3	Rumsonontheriver, 3	6	2:02.87	$90,000
1999	Mythical Gem, 3, 117	J. F. Chavez	Monkey Puzzle, 3	Bugatti, 3	11	2:01.21	$90,000
1998	Parade Ground, 3, 117	M. E. Smith	Ay Rouge, 3	La Reine's Terms, 3	8	2:00.55	$84,060
1997	Private Buck Trout, 3, 119	J. F. Chavez	Red Castle, 3	Renewed, 3	10	2:01.29	$90,000
1996	Ok by Me, 3, 122	J. F. Chavez	Value Investor, 3	Alzeus (Ire), 3	10	2:03.58	$68,160
1995	Green Means Go, 3, 119	J. D. Bailey	Nostra, 3	Flitch, 3	9	2:01.69	$66,960
1994	Holy Mountain, 3, 112	J. R. Velazquez	Islefaxyou, 3	Check Ride, 3	10	1:59.74	$50,850
1993	Llandaff, 3, 123	J. A. Krone	Strolling Along, 3	Eastern Memories (Ire), 3	7	2:02.93	$52,380
1992	Spectacular Tide, 3, 114	J. A. Krone	Preferences, 3	Casino Magistrate, 3	6	2:02.20	$69,120

Named for champion and leading sire Lexington (1850-'75, c. by Boston). 1961-'80 Lexington H. 1973-'89 Grade 2. 1961-'76 held at Aqueduct. 1961 1⁵/₈ miles; 1962 1 mile; 1963-'70,1977-'78 1¹/₁₆ miles; 1971-'74 1³/₁₆ miles; 1976 1¹/₈ miles. 1962 dirt.

Locust Grove Handicap

Grade 3, Churchill Downs, three-year-olds and up, fillies and mares, 1¹/₈ miles, turf. Held June 22, 2002, with a gross value of $150,000. First held in 1982. Graded since 1998. Stakes record 1:46.91 (2002 Voodoo Dancer).

Year	Winner	Jockey	Second	Third	Strs	Time	1st Purse
2002	Voodoo Dancer, 4, 120	J. A. Santos	Blue Moon (Fr), 5	Solvig, 5	9	1:46.91	$104,718
2001	Colstar, 5, 121	J. K. Court	Solvig, 4	Megans Bluff, 4	11	1:48.79	$107,136
2000	Colstar, 4, 121	A. Delgado	Pricearose, 4	Histoire Sainte (Fr), 4	6	1:47.44	$102,300
1999	Shires Ende, 4, 117	W. Martinez	Formal Tango, 4	Uanme, 4	11	1:49.11	$107,508
1998	Colcon, 5, 118	S. J. Sellers	Leo's Gypsy Dancer, 4	Mingling Glances, 4	6	1:48.53	$103,974
1997	Romy, 6, 121	F. C. Torres	Yokama, 4	Cymbala (Fr), 4	6	1:48.89	$68,634
1996	Bail Out Becky, 4, 121	C. Perret	Ms. Isadora, 4	Memories (Ire), 4	6	1:47.38	$72,670
1995	Memories (Ire), 4, 114	S. J. Sellers	Market Booster, 6	Thread, 4	7	1:47.48	$71,760
1994	Life Is Delicious, 4, 113	J. R. Martinez Jr.	Eurostorm, 4	Obtain, 4	4	1:53.87	$70,850
1993	Lady Blessington (Fr), 5, 121	C. A. Black	Gone Seeking, 4	Crusie, 4	8	1:50.16	$74,425

| 1992 | Behaving Dancer, 5, 117 | D. L. Howard | Firm Stance, 4 | Olden Rijn, 4 | 10 | 1:47.27 | $74,750 |

Named for the National Historic Landmark, Locust Grove, a house once owned by the brother-in-law and surveying partner of George Rogers Clark. 1982-'85,1988 Locust Grove S. 1982 1 mile; 1983-'86,1988-'89 1¹/₁₆ miles; 1990 about 1¹/₈ miles. 1982-'86,1994 dirt. 1983-'89 four-year-olds and up.

Lone Star Derby

Grade 3, Lone Star Park, three-year-olds, 1¹/₈ miles, dirt. Held May 11, 2002, with a gross value of $500,000. First held in 1997. Graded since 2002. Stakes record 1:49.92 (2002 Wiseman's Ferry).

Year	Winner	Jockey	Second	Third	Strs	Time	1st Purse
2002	Wiseman's Ferry, 3, 122	J. F. Chavez	Tracemark, 3	Peekskill, 3	14	**1:49.92**	$277,500
2001	Percy Hope, 3, 122	J. K. Court	Fifty Stars, 3	Gift of the Eagle, 3	8	1:50.27	$292,500
2000	Tahkodha Hills, 3, 122	E. Coa	Jeblar Sez Who, 3	Big Numbers, 3	7	1:44.05	$180,000
1999	T. B. Track Star, 3, 122	E. M. Martin Jr.	Desert Demon, 3	Congratulate, 3	11	1:42.92	$165,000
1998	Smolderin Heart, 3, 122	T. T. Doocy	Shot of Gold, 3	Troy's Play, 3	8	1:46.29	$145,000
1997	Anet, 3, 122	D. R. Flores	Frisk Me Now, 3	Holzmeister, 3	9	1:40.88	$140,000

1997-2000 1¹/₁₆ miles.

Lone Star Park Handicap

Grade 3, Lone Star Park, three-year-olds and up, 1¹/₁₆ miles, dirt. Held May 27, 2002, with a gross value of $300,000. First held in 1997. Graded since 2000. Stakes record 1:40.53 (2001 Dixie Dot Com).

Year	Winner	Jockey	Second	Third	Strs	Time	1st Purse
2002	Congaree, 4, 119	P. Day	Prince Iroquois, 5	Mercenary, 4	12	1:42.96	$180,000
2001	Dixie Dot Com, 6, 118	D. R. Flores	Fan the Flame, 4	Big Numbers, 4	8	**1:40.53**	$180,000
2000	Luftikus, 4, 114	D. R. Flores	Nite Dreamer, 5	Sultry Substitute, 5	11	1:40.87	$180,000
1999	Mocha Express, 5, 116	M. St. Julien	Littlebitlively, 5	Nite Dreamer, 4	7	1:43.36	$183,300
1998	Mocha Express, 4, 114	M. St. Julien	Prince of the Mt., 7	Dickey Rickey, 5	5	1:42.17	$123,000
1997	Connecting Terms, 4, 112	L. Melancon	Humble Seven, 5	Isitingood, 6	7	1:41.97	$120,000

2000 equaled track record; 2001 new track record.

Longacres Mile Handicap

Grade 3, Emerald Downs, three-year-olds and up, 1 mile, dirt. Held August 25, 2002, with a gross value of $250,000. First held in 1935. Graded since 1975. Stakes record 1:33.20 (1998 Wild Wonder; 2000 Edneator).

Year	Winner	Jockey	Second	Third	Strs	Time	1st Purse
2002	Sabertooth, 4, 114	N. J. Chaves	Moonlight Meeting, 7	San Nicolas, 4	12	1:34.60	$137,500
2001	Irisheyesareflying, 5, 117	I. Puglisi	Handy N Bold, 6	Makors Mark, 4	10	1:35.40	$137,500
2000	Edneator, 4, 111	G. V. Mitchell	Big Ten (Chi), 5	Crafty Boy, 5	11	**1:33.20**	$137,500
1999	Budroyale, 6, 119	G. K. Gomez	Mike K, 5	Kid Katabatic, 6	8	1:34.60	$137,500
1998	Wild Wonder, 4, 121	E. J. Delahoussaye	Mocha Express, 4	Hal's Pal (GB), 5	9	**1:33.20**	$110,000
1997	Kid Katabatic, 4, 113	C. Loseth	Hesabull, 4	Liberty Road, 4	7	1:34.20	$110,000
1996	Isitingood, 5, 117	D. R. Flores	Cleante (Arg), 7	Humpty's Hoedown, 6	10	1:35.60	$110,000
1995	L. J. Express, 5, 119	M. Allen	Funboy, 4	Secret Damascus, 5	10	1:34.60	$50,350
1994	Want a Winner, 4, 119	V. Belvoir	Sneakin Jake, 7	Forgotten Days, 8	8	1:35.20	$48,250
1993	Adventuresome Love, 7, 117	G. Baze	Sneakin Jake, 6	For the Children, 3	8	1:34.60	$48,050
1992	Bolulight, 4, 121	R. D. Hansen	Ibero (Arg), 5	Charmonnier, 4	12	1:34.00	$181,300

Named for Longacres Park in Renton, Washington; Longacres closed in 1992. 1943 not held. 1991 Rainier Mile H.; 1993,1995 Budweiser Mile H.; 1994 Emerald Mile H. 1982-'89 Grade 2. 1935-'92 held at Longacres; 1993-'95 Yakima Meadows. 1970 four-year-olds and up. 1996 established track record; 1998 new track record; 2000 equaled track record.

Long Branch Breeders' Cup Stakes

Grade 3, Monmouth Park, three-year-olds, 1¹/₁₆ miles, dirt. Held July 13, 2002, with a gross value of $100,000. First held in 1878. Graded since 1973. Stakes record 1:41 (1956 Skipper Bill).

Year	Winner	Jockey	Second	Third	Strs	Time	1st Purse
2002	Puck, 3, 122	M. Aguilar	Shah Jehan, 3	Stephentown, 3	6	1:44.35	$60,000
2001	Burning Roma, 3, 122	R. Wilson	This Fleet Is Due, 3	Thunder Blitz, 3	7	1:43.28	$60,000
2000	Thistyranthasclass, 3, 114	J. A. Velez Jr.	Graeme Hall, 3	Summinitup, 3	9	1:43.60	$60,000
1999	Ghost Story, 3, 112	R. G. Davis	Unbridled Jet, 3	Clever Gem, 3	6	1:42.64	$60,000
1998	Favorite Trick, 3, 116	P. Day	Tomorrows Cat, 3	Arctic Sweep, 3	6	1:43.10	$60,000
1997	Jules, 3, 114	A. T. Gryder	Leestown, 3	Capture the Gold, 3	4	1:42.48	$60,000
1996	Dr. Caton, 3, 112	J. Bravo	Devil's Honor, 3	Clash by Night, 3	5	1:41.89	$45,000
1995	Pyramid Peak, 3, 120	W. H. McCauley	Suave Prospect, 3	Mighty Magee, 3	5	1:44.09	$47,250
1994	Meadow Flight, 3, 120	J. Bravo	Red Tazz, 3	Don's Sho, 3	5	1:43.92	$47,370
1993	Bert's Bubbleator, 3, 120	E. L. King Jr.	P. J. Higgins, 3	Signoir Valery, 3	5	1:45.92	$32,310
1992	Scudan, 3, 114	N. Santagata	Pistols and Roses, 3	Munch n' Nosh, 3	8	1:42.18	$39,300

Named for a popular seaside resort of the 1880s, Long Branch; Long Branch is near Oceanport, Monmouth's current location. 1894-1946,1959-'62 not held. 1878-1958 Long Branch H.; 1963-'91,1996-'97 Long Branch S. 1989-2001 not graded. 1878-'93 1¹/₄ miles; 1963 6 furlongs; 1964-'70,1972-'89 1 mile. 1963-'69,1971-'74,1976,1978-'82,1984,1986,1988-'89 turf. 1947-'58 three-year-olds and up.

Long Island Handicap

Grade 2, Aqueduct, three-year-olds and up, fillies and mares, 1½ miles, turf. Held November 16, 2002, with a gross value of $150,000. First held in 1956. Graded since 1973. Stakes record 2:29.04 (1992 Villandry).

Year	Winner	Jockey	Second	Third	Strs	Time	1st Purse
2002	Uriah (Ger), 3, 112	N. Arroyo Jr.	Sunstone (GB), 4	Mot Juste (GB), 4	11	2:42.48	$90,000
2001	Queue, 4, 115	J. L. Espinoza	Sweetest Thing, 3	Lady Dora, 4	13	2:29.36	$90,000
2000	Moonlady (Ger), 3, 114	C. P. DeCarlo	Playact (Ire), 3	La Ville Rouge, 4	11	2:17.94	$90,000
1999	Midnight Line, 4, 120	J. D. Bailey	Win for Us (Ger), 3	Horatia (Ire), 3	10	2:29.67	$90,000
1998	Coretta (Ire), 4, 114	J. A. Santos	Starry Dreamer, 4	Dixie Ghost, 4	11	2:29.73	$60,000
	Yokama, 5, 120	J. D. Bailey	Moments of Magic, 3	Bristol Channel (GB), 3	11	2:31.03	$60,000
1997	Sweetzie, 5, 115	J. F. Chavez	Sweet Sondra, 4	Scenic Point, 4	6	2:16.66	$90,000
1996	Ampulla, 5, 121	S. J. Sellers	Wandering Star, 3	Beyrouth, 4	12	2:30.70	$87,270
1995	Yenda (GB), 4, 114	C. S. Nakatani	Windsharp, 4	Market Booster, 6	10	2:37.15	$86,400
1994	Market Booster, 5, 115	M. J. Luzzi	Tiffany's Taylor, 5	Lady Affirmed, 3	12	2:31.95	$87,495
1993	Trampoli, 4, 119	M. E. Smith	Bright Generation (Ire), 3	Northern Emerald, 3	5	2:31.57	$68,760
1992	Villandry, 4, 115	M. E. Smith	Ratings, 4	Gina Romantica, 4	8	**2:29.04**	$71,160

Named for the largest island in the continental United States, Long Island; Aqueduct is located on Long Island. 1956-'58 Grade 3. 1956-'58 held at Jamaica; 1960,1962,1968-'69,1975-'76,1990-'93,1995 Belmont Park. 1956-'58 1⅝ miles; 1959,1961,1963-'67,1970-'71 1³/₁₆ miles; 1960,1962,1968-'69,2000 1⅜ miles; 1972 1 mile; 1973-'77 1¹/₁₆ miles. 1956-'58,1961,1972,1975,1989,1997,2000 dirt. 1972-'76 three-year-olds. 1956-'71 both sexes; 1972-'76 fillies. 1998 two divisions.

Los Angeles Handicap

Grade 3, Hollywood Park, three-year-olds and up, 6 furlongs, dirt. Held June 2, 2002, with a gross value of $100,000. First held in 1938. Graded since 1973. Stakes record 1:07.90 (1995 Forest Gazelle).

Year	Winner	Jockey	Second	Third	Strs	Time	1st Purse
2002	Kona Gold, 8, 125	A. O. Solis	No Armistice, 5	Komax, 4	6	1:08.72	$64,500
2001	Caller One, 4, 124	C. S. Nakatani	Stormy Jack, 4	Rapidough, 6	6	1:08.35	$64,380
2000	Highland Gold, 5, 115	C. J. McCarron	Mellow Fellow, 5	Your Halo, 5	6	1:09.11	$64,260
1999	Son of a Pistol, 7, 122	A. O. Solis	Men's Exclusive, 6	Ray of Sunshine (Ire), 4	4	1:08.17	$63,300
1998	Gold Land, 7, 116	K. J. Desormeaux	Mr. Doubledown, 4	The Exeter Man, 6	7	1:08.06	$64,800
1997	Men's Exclusive, 4, 117	L. A. Pincay Jr.	First Intent, 8	Gold Land, 6	7	1:08.97	$80,970
1996	(DH) Paying Dues, 4, 115	C. W. Antley		Score Quick, 4	6	1:08.33	$53,480
	(DH) Abaginone, 5, 119	G. L. Stevens					
1995	Forest Gazelle, 4, 117	K. J. Desormeaux	Lucky Forever, 6	Cardmania, 9	10	**1:07.90**	$83,650
1994	J. F. Williams, 5, 115	C. J. McCarron	Gundaghia, 7	Thirty Slews, 7	6	1:09.03	$61,900
1993	Star of the Crop, 4, 119	G. L. Stevens	Fabulous Champ, 4	Wild Harmony, 4	7	1:08.78	$63,300
1992	Cardmania, 6, 118	E. J. Delahoussaye	Gray Slewpy, 4	Robyn Dancer, 5	5	1:08.73	$61,200

Named for the city of Los Angeles, California. 1940-'54 not held. 1973-'79 Grade 2. 1938-'39 1¹/₁₆ miles; 1957-'78 7 furlongs. 1995 new track record. 1996 dead heat for first. 1997 Surachai finished second, DQ to sixth.

Louisiana Derby

Grade 2, Fair Grounds, three-year-olds, 1¹/₁₆ miles, dirt. Held March 9, 2003, with a gross value of $750,000. First held in 1894. Graded since 1973. Stakes record 1:42.60 (1997 Crypto Star).

Year	Winner	Jockey	Second	Third	Strs	Time	1st Purse
2003	Peace Rules, 3, 122	E. S. Prado	Funny Cide, 3	Lone Star Sky, 3	10	1:42.67	$450,000
2002	Repent, 3, 122	J. D. Bailey	Easyfromthegitgo, 3	It'sallinthechase, 3	7	1:43.86	$450,000
2001	Fifty Stars, 3, 122	D. J. Meche	Millennium Wind, 3	Hero's Tribute, 3	9	1:44.78	$450,000
2000	Mighty, 3, 122	S. J. Sellers	More Than Ready, 3	Captain Steve, 3	10	1:43.29	$450,000
1999	Kimberlite Pipe, 3, 122	R. Albarado	Answer Lively, 3	Ecton Park, 3	8	1:43.56	$384,000
1998	Comic Strip, 3, 122	S. J. Sellers	Nite Dreamer, 3	Captain Maestri, 3	10	1:43.36	$300,000
1997	Crypto Star, 3, 118	P. Day	Stop Watch, 3	Smoke Glacken, 3	9	**1:42.60**	$240,000
1996	Grindstone, 3, 118	J. D. Bailey	Zarb's Magic, 3	Commanders Palace, 3	8	1:42.79	$222,000
1995	Petionville, 3, 122	C. W. Antley	In Character (GB), 3	Moonlight Dancer, 3	11	1:42.96	$210,000
1994	Kandaly, 3, 118	C. Perret	Game Coin, 3	Argolid, 3	10	1:42.86	$195,750
1993	Dixieland Heat, 3, 117	R. P. Romero	Offshore Pirate, 3	Tossofthecoin, 3	13	1:44.55	$180,000
1992	Line In The Sand, 3, 117	P. Day	Hill Pass, 3	Colony Light, 3	9	1:43.40	$120,000

1895-'97,1909-'19,1921-'22,1940-'42,1945 not held. 1985-'98 Grade 3. 1894-1908 held at Crescent City; 1920-'31 Jefferson Park. 1894 1 mile; 1898-1987 1⅛ miles. 1992 Colony Light finished first, DQ to third.

Louisville Breeders' Cup Handicap

Grade 2, Churchill Downs, three-year-olds and up, fillies and mares, 1¹/₁₆ miles, dirt. Held May 3, 2002, with a gross value of $300,000. First held in 1986. Graded since 1988. Stakes record 1:42.50 (1996 Jewel Princess).

Year	Winner	Jockey	Second	Third	Strs	Time	1st Purse
2002	Spain, 5, 118	J. D. Bailey	Mystic Lady, 4	De Bertie, 5	6	1:43.93	$206,274
2001	Saudi Poetry, 4, 112	V. Espinoza	Royal Fair, 5	Dreams Gallore, 5	8	1:42.53	$172,980
1999	Silent Eskimo, 4, 113	C. H. Borel	Lu Ravi, 4	Leo's Gypsy Dancer, 5	6	1:43.82	$169,415
1998	Escena, 5, 119	J. D. Bailey	One Rich Lady, 4	Three Fanfares, 5	10	1:44.84	$178,405
1997	Halo America, 7, 120	C. H. Borel	Escena, 4	Rare Blend, 4	7	1:42.78	$138,012
1996	Jewel Princess, 4, 118	C. J. McCarron	Serena's Song, 4	Naskra Colors, 4	6	**1:42.50**	$143,000
1995	Fit to Lead, 5, 113	K. J. Desormeaux	Jade Flush, 4	Teewinot, 4	9	1:43.46	$138,125

1994	**One Dreamer**, 6, 115	G. L. Stevens	Kalita Melody (GB), 6	Added Asset, 6	7	1:43.73	$136,630
1993	**Quilma (Chi)**, 6, 113	J. A. Santos	Looie Capote, 4	Hitch, 4	12	1:44.61	$37,570
1992	**Fowda**, 4, 117	P. A. Valenzuela	Dance Colony, 5	Fit for a Queen, 5	7	1:44.16	$100,750

Named for the city of Louisville, Kentucky, home of Churchill Downs. 1987-'95 Louisville Budweiser Breeders' Cup H. 1988-'89 Grade 3. 1986 1⅛ miles. 1986 both sexes.

Louisville Handicap

Grade 3, Churchill Downs, three-year-olds and up, 1⅜ miles, turf. Held June 1, 2002, with a gross value of $100,000. First held in 1895. Graded since 2002. Stakes record 2:14.15 (1999 Chorwon).

Year	Winner	Jockey	Second	Third	Strs	Time	1st Purse
2002	**Classic Par**, 4, 114	D. J. Meche	Pisces, 5	Red Mountain, 5	9	2:15.82	$47,355
2001	**With Anticipation**, 6, 112	J. K. Court	Profit Option, 6	Gritty Sandie, 5	6	2:16.28	$68,138
2000	**Buff**, 5, 113	F. C. Torres	Williams News, 5	Royal Strand (Ire), 6	11	2:14.31	$71,734
1999	**Chorwon**, 6, 114	C. H. Borel	Buff, 4	Keats and Yeats, 5	8	**2:14.15**	$69,812
1998	**Chorwon**, 5, 114	P. Day	African Dancer, 6	Thesaurus, 4	5	2:17.10	$67,890
1997	**Chorwon**, 4, 113	C. H. Borel	Down the Aisle, 4	Snake Eyes, 7	5	2:19.45	$67,952
1996	**Nash Terrace (Ire)**, 4, 105	D. M. Barton	Vladivostok, 6	Hawkeye Bay, 5	6	2:18.82	$71,760
1995	**Lindon Lime**, 5, 114	C. Perret	Caesour, 5	Snake Eyes, 5	8	1:48.12	$72,800
1994	**L'Hermine (GB)**, 5, 110	L. Melancon	Llandaff, 4	Snake Eyes, 4	5	1:48.36	$70,525
1993	**Stark South**, 5, 116	R. P. Romero	Cleone, 4	Coaxing Matt, 4	5	1:48.88	$71,955
1992	**Lotus Pool**, 5, 115	C. R. Woods Jr.	Buchman, 5	Magesterial Cheer, 4	8	1:47.69	$74,230

Named for the city of Louisville, Kentucky. 1897,1900-'06,1914-'37,1939-'45,1953-'56 not held. 1946 Churchill Downs Special; 1982-'86 Louisville S. 1895-'99,1938,1957-'81,1986 1¹⁄₁₆ miles; 1907-'13 6 furlongs; 1946-'52,1982-'85,1988-'95 1⅛ miles; 1987 1 mile. 1895-1986 dirt. 1986-'87 four-year-olds and up

Mac Diarmida Handicap

Grade 3, Gulfstream Park, three-year-olds and up, 1⅜ miles, turf. Held January 19, 2003, with a gross value of $100,000. First held in 1995. Graded since 1997. Stakes record 2:12.14 (2000 Unite's Big Red).

Year	Winner	Jockey	Second	Third	Strs	Time	1st Purse
2002	**Crash Course**, 6, 114	J. D. Bailey	Unite's Big Red, 8	Eltawaasul, 6	12	2:16.27	$60,000
2000	**Unite's Big Red**, 6, 113	J. F. Chavez	Thesaurus, 6	Carpenter's Halo, 4	8	**2:12.14**	$60,000
1999	**Panama City**, 5, 114	J. D. Bailey	The Kaiser, 4	Notoriety, 6	5	2:20.65	$60,000
1998	**Copy Editor**, 6, 114	J. D. Bailey	Inkatha (Fr), 4	Lafitte the Pirate (GB), 5	12	2:16.72	$60,000
1997	**Mecke**, 5, 123	J. D. Bailey	Fabulous Frolic, 6	Spicilege, 5	4	2:05.80	$45,000
1996	**A Real Zipper**, 3, 114	A. T. Gryder	Tour's Big Red, 3	Shananie's Finale, 3	12	1:42.66	$30,000
1995	**Kings Fiction**, 3, 112	R. G. Davis	Ops Smile, 3	Mecke, 3	10	1:43.12	$30,000

Named for 1978 champion turf horse Mac Diarmida (1975-'93, c. by Minnesota Mac). 2001 not held. 1995-'96 Mac Diarmida S. 1995 1 mile 70 yards; 1996 1¹⁄₁₆ miles; 1997 1¼ miles; 1999 about 1⅜ miles. 1995-'96 three-year-olds. 1995,1997 dirt.

Maker's Mark Mile Stakes

Grade 2, Keeneland, four-year-olds and up, 1 mile, turf. Held April 11, 2003, with a gross value of $200,000. First held in 1989. Graded since 1991. Stakes record 1:34.44 (2001 North East Bound).

Year	Winner	Jockey	Second	Third	Strs	Time	1st Purse
2003	**Royal Spy**, 5, 118	R. Albarado	Miesque's Approval, 4	Touch of the Blues (Fr), 6	9	1:35.82	$124,000
2002	**Touch of the Blues (Fr)**, 5, 116	K. J. Desormeaux	Pisces, 5	Boastful, 4	10	1:35.02	$124,000
2001	**North East Bound**, 5, 120	J. A. Velez Jr.	Brahms, 4	Strategic Mission, 6	8	**1:34.44**	$140,492
2000	**Conserve**, 4, 116	S. J. Sellers	Marquette, 4	Inkatha (Fr), 6	9	1:35.08	$105,927
1999	**Soviet Line (Ire)**, 9, 115	J. R. Velazquez	Trail City, 6	Rob 'n Gin, 5	8	1:35.37	$68,696
1998	**Lasting Approval**, 4, 122	R. Albarado	Soviet Line (Ire), 8	Same Old Wish, 8	10	1:35.57	$70,060
1997	**Influent**, 6, 116	J-L. Samyn	Chief Bearhart, 4	Foolish Pole, 4	9	1:34.59	$69,936
1996	**Tejano Run**, 4, 113	J. D. Bailey	Sandpit (Brz), 7	Dove Hunt, 7	10	1:35.03	$70,618
1995	**Dove Hunt**, 4, 113	J. A. Santos	Road of War, 5	Night Silence, 5	10	1:35.95	$53,196
1994	**First and Only**, 7, 116	T. J. Hebert	The Name's Jimmy, 5	Pride of Summer, 5	7	1:36.63	$50,685
1993	**Ganges**, 5, 113	J. D. Bailey	Bidding Proud, 4	Rocket Fuel, 4	10	1:35.40	$52,731
1992	**Shudanz**, 4, 114	C. Perret	To Freedom, 4	Cudas, 4	9	1:36.52	$55,283

Named for sponsor Maker's Mark Distillery, located in Loretto, Kentucky. Formerly named for Fort Harrod, the first permanent settlement west of the Alleghenies. 1989-'96 Fort Harrod S. 1991-'99 Grade 3. 1989 about 1¹⁄₁₆ miles.

Malibu Stakes

Grade 1, Santa Anita Park, three-year-olds, 7 furlongs, dirt. Held December 26, 2002, with a gross value of $200,000. First held in 1952. Graded since 1973. Stakes record 1:20 (1980 Spectacular Bid).

Year	Winner	Jockey	Second	Third	Strs	Time	1st Purse
2002	**Debonair Joe**, 3, 119	J. A. Krone	Total Limit, 3	American System, 3	11	1:22.40	$120,000
2001	**Mizzen Mast**, 3, 117	K. J. Desormeaux	Giant Gentleman, 3	I Love Silver, 3	13	1:22.13	$120,000
2000	**Dixie Union**, 3, 121	A. O. Solis	Caller One, 3	Wooden Phone, 3	6	1:21.62	$120,000
1999	**Love That Red**, 3, 119	G. K. Gomez	Straight Man, 3	Cat Thief, 3	7	1:22.06	$120,000
1998	**Run Man Run**, 3, 115	M. J. Luzzi	Artax, 3	Event of the Year, 3	10	1:21.51	$120,000

1997	Lord Grillo (Arg), 3, 119	E. J. Delahoussaye	Silver Charm, 3	Swiss Yodeler, 3	9	1:21.46	$120,000
1996	King of the Heap, 3, 116	K. J. Desormeaux	Hesabull, 3	Northern Afleet, 3	9	1:21.84	$134,300
1995	Afternoon Deelites, 3, 120	K. J. Desormeaux	Score Quick, 3	High Stakes Player, 3	9	1:21.73	$100,000
1994	Powis Castle, 3, 117	P. A. Valenzuela	Ferrara, 3	Numerous, 3	8	1:20.96	$64,300
1993	Diazo, 3, 120	L. A. Pincay Jr.	Concept Win, 3	Mister Jolie, 3	8	1:21.17	$64,700
1992	Star of the Crop, 3, 118	G. L. Stevens	The Wicked North, 3	Bertrando, 3	11	1:20.67	$67,850

Named for Topanga Malibu Sequit Rancho in Los Angeles County. 1959,1964,1967,1970 not held. 1973-'94 Grade 2. 1955 (January),1960 (January),1965,1966 (January),1968-'75,1977-'83,1984 (January) four-year-olds; 1976 four-year-olds and up.

Manhattan Handicap

Grade 1, Belmont Park, three-year-olds and up, 1¼ miles, turf. Held June 8, 2002, with a gross value of $400,000. First held in 1896. Graded since 1973. Stakes record 1:57.79 (1994 Paradise Creek).

Year	Winner	Jockey	Second	Third	Strs	Time	1st Purse
2002	Beat Hollow (GB), 5, 118	A. O. Solis	Forbidden Apple, 7	Strut the Stage, 4	8	2:01.29	$240,000
2001	Forbidden Apple, 6, 117	C. S. Nakatani	King Cugat, 4	Tijiyr (Ire), 5	10	2:00.77	$240,000
2000	Manndar (Ire), 4, 117	C. S. Nakatani	Boatman, 4	Spindrift (Ire), 5	8	1:59.61	$240,000
1999	Yagli, 6, 122	J. D. Bailey	Federal Trial, 4	Middlesex Drive, 4	10	1:58.48	$180,000
1998	Chief Bearhart, 5, 122	J. A. Santos	Devonwood, 4	Buck's Boy, 5	9	1:58.25	$150,000
1997	Ops Smile, 5, 116	R. G. Davis	Flag Down, 7	Always a Classic, 4	8	1:59.08	$120,000
1996	Diplomatic Jet, 4, 117	J. F. Chavez	Flag Down, 6	Kiri's Clown, 6	12	2:00.14	$120,000
1995	Awad, 5, 121	E. Maple	Blues Traveller (Ire), 5	Kiri's Clown, 6	12	1:58.57	$120,000
1994	Paradise Creek, 5, 124	P. Day	Solar Splendor, 7	River Majesty, 7	7	**1:57.79**	$275,000
1993	Star of Cozzene, 5, 118	J. A. Santos	Lure, 4	Solar Splendor, 4	8	1:58.99	$190,000
1992	Sky Classic, 5, 123	P. Day	Roman Envoy, 4	Leger Cat (Arg), 4	11	2:02.42	$252,860

Named for the borough of Manhattan, principal borough of New York City. 1897,1909-'13 not held. 1991-'92 Early Times Manhattan H.; 1993-'96 Early Times Manhattan S. 1973-'83,1990-'93 Grade 2. 1896-1904 held at Morris Park; 1959,1961,1963-'67 Aqueduct. 1898-1908 6 furlongs; 1914-'15 7 furlongs; 1916-'32 1 mile; 1933-'58,1960,1962-'64,1968-'69,1977 1½ miles; 1959,1965-'67 1⅝ miles; 1961 1⁵⁄₁₆ miles; 1970-'76 1³⁄₈ miles. 1896-1969,1975,1977,1988 dirt. 1994 new course record.

Man o' War Stakes

Grade 1, Belmont Park, three-year-olds and up, 1⅜ miles, turf. Held September 7, 2002, with a gross value of $500,000. First held in 1959. Graded since 1973. Stakes record 2:11.69 (1997 Influent).

Year	Winner	Jockey	Second	Third	Strs	Time	1st Purse
2002	With Anticipation, 7, 126	P. Day	Balto Star, 4	Man From Wicklow, 5	8	2:15.05	$300,000
2001	With Anticipation, 6, 126	P. Day	Silvano (Ger), 5	†Ela Athena (GB), 5	8	2:15.11	$300,000
2000	Fantastic Light, 4, 126	J. D. Bailey	†Ela Athena (GB), 4	Drama Critic, 4	8	2:17.44	$300,000
1999	Val's Prince, 7, 126	J. F. Chavez	Single Empire (Ire), 5	Federal Trial, 4	7	2:16.69	$300,000
1998	Daylami (Ire), 4, 126	J. D. Bailey	Buck's Boy, 5	Indy Vidual, 4	9	2:13.18	$240,000
1997	Influent, 6, 126	J. D. Bailey	Val's Prince, 5	Awad, 7	10	**2:11.69**	$240,000
1996	Diplomatic Jet, 4, 126	J. F. Chavez	Mecke, 4	Marlin, 3	8	2:14.37	$240,000
1995	Millkom (GB), 4, 126	G. L. Stevens	Kaldounevees (Fr), 4	Signal Tap, 4	12	2:12.80	$240,000
1994	Royal Mountain Inn, 5, 126	J. A. Krone	Flag Down, 4	Fraise, 6	9	2:11.75	$240,000
1993	Star of Cozzene, 5, 126	J. A. Santos	Serrant, 5	Dr. Kiernan, 4	8	2:23.14	$240,000
1992	Solar Splendor, 5, 126	W. H. McCauley	Dear Doctor (Fr), 5	Spinning (Ire), 5	8	2:12.45	$240,000

Named for the great Man o' War (1917-'47, c. by Fair Play), champion and leading sire. 1959,1961 Man o' War H. 1959,1961,1963-'67,1987 held at Aqueduct. 1959-'60,1962,1968-'77 1½ miles; 1961,1963-'67 1⅝ miles. †denotes female.

Martha Washington Breeders' Cup Stakes

Originally scheduled as a Grade 3 on the turf, Laurel Park, three-year-olds, fillies, 1¹⁄₁₆ miles, dirt. Held July 27, 2002, with a gross value of $145,500. First held in 1982. Graded since 1988. Stakes record 1:42.21 (2000 Tippity Witch).

Year	Winner	Jockey	Second	Third	Strs	Time	1st Purse
2002	Martha's Music, 3, 115	H. Vega	Bells for Marlin, 3	Restraining Order, 3	4	1:45.62	$90,000
2000	Tippity Witch, 3, 115	J. L. Espinoza	Senza Paura, 3	Windsong, 3	8	**1:42.21**	$60,000
1999	Colstar, 3, 119	A. Delgado	Polaire (Ire), 3	Jazz, 3	9	1:45.64	$60,000
1998	Mysterious Moll, 3, 118	R. Wilson	Wolfer, 3	Proud Owner, 3	9	1:42.31	$90,000
1997	Cotton Carnival, 3, 122	M. G. Pino	Romantic Notions, 3	Bursting Forth, 3	8	1:46.27	$60,000
1996	Silent Greeting, 3, 119	L. C. Reynolds	Rare Blend, 3	Stop That Broad, 3	9	1:43.41	$60,000
1995	Strawberry Reason, 3, 117	E. S. Prado	Blue Sky Princess, 3	Rosebud (GB), 3	6	1:44.62	$60,000
1994	Tee Kay, 3, 115	R. Wilson	Avie's Fancy, 3	Lady Ellen, 3	8	1:45.37	$60,000
1993	Tennis Lady, 3, 113	A. J. Seefeldt	Putthepowdertoit, 3	Missymooiloveyou, 3	12	1:42.83	$45,000
1992	Mz. Zill Bear, 3, 112	S. D. Hamilton	Star Minister, 3	Toosie, 3	10	1:48.75	$45,000

Named for America's initial First Lady, Martha Washington (1731-1802). 1983, 2001 not held. 1982-'92 Martha Washington H.; 1993-'97,1999-2000 Martha Washington S. 1991-'92 1⅛ miles. 1988-'94,1998-2000 turf.

Maryland Breeders' Cup Handicap

Grade 3, Pimlico, three-year-olds and up, 6 furlongs, dirt. Held May 18, 2002, with a gross value of $200,000. First held in 1987. Graded since 1994. Stakes record 1:09.07 (1996 Forest Wildcat).

Year	Winner	Jockey	Second	Third	Strs	Time	1st Purse
2002	Snow Ridge, 4, 120	M. E. Smith	Smile My Lord, 4	Clever Gem, 6	7	1:10.06	$120,000
2001	Disco Rico, 4, 118	H. Vega	Flame Thrower, 3	Istintaj, 5	6	1:10.40	$120,000
2000	Dr. Max, 4, 113	S. J. Sellers	Moon Over Prospect, 4	Crucible, 5	7	1:10.91	$60,000
1999	Yes It's True, 3, 113	J. D. Bailey	The Trader's Echo, 5	Purple Passion, 5	8	1:09.20	$120,000
1998	Richter Scale, 4, 117	J. D. Bailey	Trafalger, 4	Original Gray, 4	7	1:09.45	$120,000
1997	Cat Be Nimble, 5, 118	J. Rocco	Political Whit, 4	Excelerate, 5	7	1:10.12	$127,560
1996	Forest Wildcat, 5, 109	J. Bravo	Kayrawan, 4	Demaloot Demashoot, 6	9	1:09.07	$129,720
1995	Commanche Trail, 4, 113	M. E. Smith	Goldminer's Dream, 6	Marry Me Do, 6	6	1:09.35	$92,850
1994	Secret Odds, 4, 119	E. S. Prado	Honor the Hero, 6	Linear, 6	10	1:10.38	$93,615
1993	Senor Speedy, 6, 117	J. D. Bailey	He Is Risen, 5	Who Wouldn't, 5	7	1:09.69	$93,390
1992	Potentiality, 6, 117	P. Day	Smart Alec, 4	Boom Tonwer, 4	9	1:10.25	$93,300

1987-'95 Maryland Budweiser Breeders' Cup H. 1987 held at Laurel Park. 1987 7 furlongs.

Massachusetts Handicap

Grade 2, Suffolk Downs, three-year-olds and up, 1⅛ miles, dirt. Held June 1, 2002, with a gross value of $500,000. First held in 1935. Graded since 1973. Stakes record 1:47.27 (1998 Skip Away).

Year	Winner	Jockey	Second	Third	Strs	Time	1st Purse
2002	Macho Uno, 4, 117	G. L. Stevens	Evening Attire, 4	Include, 5	9	1:50.52	$300,000
2001	Include, 4, 118	J. D. Bailey	Sir Bear, 8	Broken Vow, 4	7	1:48.61	$300,000
2000	Running Stag, 6, 116	J. R. Velazquez	Out of Mind (Brz), 5	David, 4	6	1:49.45	$400,000
1999	Behrens, 5, 118	J. F. Chavez	Running Stag, 5	Real Quiet, 4	6	1:49.14	$400,000
1998	Skip Away, 5, 130	J. D. Bailey	Puerto Madero (Chi), 4	K. J.'s Appeal, 4	5	1:47.27	$500,000
1997	Skip Away, 4, 119	S. J. Sellers	Formal Gold, 4	Will's Way, 4	6	1:47.92	$500,000
1996	Cigar, 6, 130	J. D. Bailey	Personal Merit, 5	Prolanzier, 6	6	1:49.63	$400,000
1995	Cigar, 5, 124	J. D. Bailey	Poor But Honest, 5	Double Calvados, 5	6	1:48.74	$650,000

1990-'94 not held. 1980-'82,1997-'98 Grade 3; 1995-'96 not graded. 1948-'69 1¼ miles; 1970-'71 about 1½ miles. 1970-'71 turf. 1998 new track record.

Matchmaker Handicap

Grade 3, Monmouth Park, three-year-olds and up, fillies and mares, 1⅛ miles, turf. Held July 7, 2002, with a gross value of $100,000. First held in 1967. Graded since 1973. Stakes record 1:46.19 (2001 Batique).

Year	Winner	Jockey	Second	Third	Strs	Time	1st Purse
2002	Clearly a Queen, 5, 115	E. Coa	Siringas (Ire), 4	Platinum Tiara, 4	7	1:47.76	$60,000
2001	Batique, 5, 113	J. C. Ferrer	Melody Queen (GB), 5	Lucky Lune (Fr), 4	8	1:46.19	$60,000
2000	Horatia (Ire), 4, 114	J. A. Santos	Camella, 5	Champagne Royal, 6	11	1:47.52	$60,000
1999	Natalie Too, 5, 116	J. Bravo	Saralea (Fr), 4	U R Unforgetable, 5	6	1:46.81	$60,000
1998	Bursting Forth, 4, 116	M. E. Verge	French Buster, 4	Gastronomical, 5	8	1:48.46	$60,000
1997	Fleur de Nuit, 4, 113	J. A. Krone	Flame Valley, 4	Overcharger, 4	8	1:48.91	$60,000
1996	Powder Bowl, 4, 113	D. S. Rice	Class Kris, 4	Turkish Tryst, 5	6	1:54.71	$60,000
1995	Avie's Fancy, 4, 113	W. H. McCauley	Plenty of Sugar, 4	Northern Emerald, 4	8	1:54.19	$60,000
1994	Alice Springs, 4, 123	J. A. Krone	Hero's Love, 6	Cox Orange, 6	8	1:55.21	$60,000
1993	Fairy Garden, 5, 120	M. E. Smith	Saratoga Source, 4	Logan's Mist, 4	8	1:57.81	$60,000
1992	Radiant Ring, 4, 115	R. E. Colton	Highland Crystal, 4	La Gueriere, 4	8	1:55.92	$60,000

The first three finishers of this race are awarded future breeding seasons; named for "matchmaking" between stallions and mares. 1967-'95 Matchmaker S.; 1996,1998-2001 Vinery Matchmaker S.; 1997 Gainesway Matchmaker S. 1973-'79 Grade 1; 1980-'96 Grade 2. 1967-'96 held at Atlantic City. 1967-'96 1 9/16 miles. 1967-'78,1983 dirt. 2001 new course record.

Matriarch Stakes

Grade 1, Hollywood Park, three-year-olds and up, fillies and mares, 1⅛ miles, turf. Held December 1, 2002, with a gross value of $500,000. First held in 1981. Graded since 1983. Stakes record 1:46.06 (2000 Tout Charmant).

Year	Winner	Jockey	Second	Third	Strs	Time	1st Purse
2002	Dress To Thrill (Ire), 3, 120	Pat Smullen	Golden Apples (Ire), 4	Magic Mission (GB), 4	6	1:48.31	$300,000
2001	Starine (Fr), 4, 123	J. R. Velazquez	Lethals Lady (GB), 3	Golden Apples (Ire), 3	12	1:50.16	$300,000
2000	Tout Charmant, 4, 123	C. J. McCarron	Tranquility Lake, 6	Happyanunoit (NZ), 5	9	1:46.06	$300,000
1999	Happyanunoit (NZ), 4, 123	B. Blanc	Tuzla (Fr), 5	Spanish Fern, 4	8	1:46.30	$300,000
1998	Squeak (GB), 4, 123	A. O. Solis	Real Connection, 7	Green Jewel (GB), 4	8	2:05.08	$420,000
1997	Ryafan, 3, 120	A. O. Solis	Maxzene, 4	Yokama, 4	8	2:05.90	$420,000
1996	Wandesta (GB), 5, 123	C. S. Nakatani	Windsharp, 5	Memories of Silver, 3	12	2:00.14	$420,000
1995	Duda, 4, 123	J. D. Bailey	Angel in My Heart (Fr), 3	Wandesta (GB), 4	14	2:00.37	$385,000
1994	Exchange, 6, 123	L. A. Pincay Jr.	Aube Indienne (Fr), 4	Wandesta (GB), 3	8	1:49.42	$220,000
1993	Flawlessly, 5, 123	C. J. McCarron	Toussaud, 3	Skimble, 4	8	1:46.78	$220,000
1992	Flawlessly, 4, 123	C. J. McCarron	Super Staff, 4	Kostroma (Ire), 6	9	1:46.14	$220,000

Older women are sometimes known as "matriarchs." 1983-'87 Matriarch Invitational S. 1995-'98 1¼ miles.

Matron Stakes

Grade 1, Belmont Park, two-year-olds, fillies, 1 mile, dirt. Held September 15, 2002, with a gross value of $200,000. First held in 1892. Graded since 1973. Stakes record 1:35.16 (1994 Stormy Blues).

Year	Winner	Jockey	Second	Third	Strs	Time	1st Purse
2002	Storm Flag Flying, 2, 119	J. R. Velazquez	Wild Snitch, 2	Fircroft, 2	7	1:38.52	$120,000
2000	Raging Fever, 2, 120	J. D. Bailey	Dancinginmydreams, 2	Ilusoria, 2	5	1:38.20	$120,000
1999	Finder's Fee, 2, 119	H. Castillo Jr.	Darling My Darling, 2	Circle of Life, 2	7	1:36.68	$90,000
1998	Oh What a Windfall, 2, 119	S. J. Sellers	Arrested Dreams, 2	Marley Vale, 2	6	1:39.29	$90,000
1997	Beautiful Pleasure, 2, 119	J. D. Bailey	Diamond On the Run, 2	Carrielle, 2	11	1:35.71	$90,000
1996	Sharp Cat, 2, 119	J. D. Bailey	Storm Song, 2	Fabulously Fast, 2	6	1:36.19	$90,000
1995	Golden Attraction, 2, 119	G. L. Stevens	Cara Rafaela, 2	My Flag, 2	8	1:36.33	$90,000
1994	Stormy Blues, 2, 119	J. A. Santos	Pretty Discreet, 2	Phone Caller, 2	6	1:35.16	$64,740
1993	Strategic Maneuver, 2, 119	J. A. Santos	Astas Foxy Lady, 2	Sovereign Kitty, 2	8	1:23.84	$70,680
1992	Sky Beauty, 2, 119	E. Maple	Educated Risk, 2	Family Enterprize, 2	9	1:23.32	$72,480

1895-'98,1911-'13,1915-'22 not held; 2001 not held due to World Trade Center attack. 1892-1904 held at Morris Park; 1910 Pimlico; 1960,1964-'68 Aqueduct. 1892-1971 6 furlongs; 1973-'93 7 furlongs. 1892-1901 colts and fillies; 1902-'14 colt and filly divisions. 1994 Flanders finished first, DQ to sixth.

Meadowlands Cup Handicap

Grade 2, Meadowlands, three-year-olds and up, 1⅛ miles, dirt. Held October 4, 2002, with a gross value of $400,000. First held in 1977. Graded since 1979. Stakes record 1:46.06 (1998 K. J.'s Appeal).

Year	Winner	Jockey	Second	Third	Strs	Time	1st Purse
2002	Burning Roma, 4, 115	E. Coa	Volponi, 4	Windsor Castle, 4	9	1:48.95	$240,000
2001	Gander, 5, 114	J. R. Velazquez	Broken Vow, 4	Include, 4	5	1:47.11	$300,000
2000	North East Bound, 4, 116	J. A. Velez Jr.	Lord Sterling, 4	Where's Taylor, 4	10	1:48.84	$240,000
1999	Pleasant Breeze, 4, 110	J. F. Chavez	Jazz Club, 4	Vision and Verse, 3	8	1:47.17	$300,000
1998	K. J.'s Appeal, 4, 112	J. R. Velazquez	Hal's Pal (GB), 5	Sir Bear, 5	8	1:46.06	$300,000
1996	Dramatic Gold, 5, 119	K. J. Desormeaux	Formal Gold, 3	Mt. Sassafras, 4	11	1:48.02	$450,000
1995	Peaks and Valleys, 3, 116	J. A. Krone	Poor But Honest, 5	Concern, 4	6	1:48.07	$300,000
1994	Conveyor, 6, 113	M. E. Smith	Personal Merit, 3	Bruce's Mill, 3	11	1:47.96	$300,000
1993	Marquetry, 6, 120	K. J. Desormeaux	Michelle Can Pass, 5	Northern Trend, 5	9	1:47.21	$300,000
1992	Sea Cadet, 4, 120	A. O. Solis	Valley Crossing, 4	American Chance, 3	10	1:48.19	$300,000

1997 not held. 1996 Buick Meadowlands Cup H. 1983-'98 Grade 1. 1977-'89 1¼ miles. 1998 new track record.

Memorial Day Handicap

Grade 3, Calder Race Course, three-year-olds and up, 1¹⁄₁₆ miles, dirt. Held May 27, 2002, with a gross value of $100,000. First held in 1971. Graded since 2002. Stakes record 1:45.20 (1972 Willmar).

Year	Winner	Jockey	Second	Third	Strs	Time	1st Purse
2002	Best of the Rest, 7, 123	C. H. Velasquez	High Ideal, 4	Hal's Hope, 5	4	1:44.75	$60,000
2001	Hal's Hope, 4, 115	R. I. Velez	American Halo, 5	Tahkodha Hills, 4	7	1:45.81	$45,000
2000	Dancing Guy, 5, 121	J. C. Ferrer	Reporter, 5	Groomstick Stock's, 4	9	1:46.28	$45,000
1999	Wicapi, 7, 116	E. Coa	Dancing Guy, 4	Golf Game, 4	8	1:46.79	$45,000
1998	Born Mighty, 4, 114	J. A. Rivera II	Hard Rock Ridge, 5	Auroral, 6	7	1:40.96	$30,000
1997	Vilhelm, 5, 114	J. C. Ferrer	Sir Bear, 4	Donthelumbertrader, 4	9	1:40.91	$30,000
1996	Marcie's Ensign, 4, 115	E. Coa	Derivative, 6	Halo Bird (Arg), 5	9	1:50.02	$30,000
1995	Mr. Light Tres (Arg), 6, 113	K. L. Chapman	Fabulous Frolic, 4	Flying American, 6	11	1:47.17	$30,000
1994	Final Sunrise, 4, 113	P. A. Rodriguez	Crucial Trial, 4	Bill Mooney, 4	4	1:51.86	$30,000
1993	Boots 'n Buck, 4, 116	M. Russ	Yankee Axe, 6	Darian's Reason, 5	10	1:53.82	$30,000
1992	Jodi's Sweetie, 4, 114	J. C. Duarte	Scottish Ice, 4	Bidding Proud, 3	9	1:44.21	$30,000

Traditionally held on Memorial Day weekend. 1981,1984,1986-'87 not held. 1971 1 mile; 1976,1978,1993-'96 1⅛ miles; 1977,1992 about 1⅛ miles. 1977,1989,1992,1995,1997-'98 turf.

Mervyn LeRoy Handicap

Grade 2, Hollywood Park, three-year-olds and up, 1¹⁄₁₆ miles, dirt. Held May 12, 2002, with a gross value of $150,000. First held in 1980. Graded since 1980. Stakes record 1:40.20 (1989 Ruhlmann).

Year	Winner	Jockey	Second	Third	Strs	Time	1st Purse
2002	Sky Jack, 6, 117	L. A. Pincay Jr.	Bosque Redondo, 5	Devine Wind, 6	6	1:41.36	$90,000
2001	Futural, 5, 117	C. J. McCarron	Skimming, 5	Moonlight Charger, 6	5	1:42.02	$90,000
2000	Out of Mind (Brz), 5, 116	E. J. Delahoussaye	Early Pioneer, 5	Skimming, 4	7	1:41.82	$90,000
1999	Budroyale, 6, 118	G. K. Gomez	Moore's Flat, 5	Wild Wonder, 5	6	1:42.12	$90,000
1998	Wild Wonder, 4, 116	E. Delahoussaye	Budroyale,5	Flick (GB), 5	7	1:40.92	$64,320
1997	Hesabull, 4, 116	G. F. Almeida	Region, 8	Kingdom Found, 7	5	1:41.30	$63,720
1996	Siphon (Brz), 5, 117	D. R. Flores	Del Mar Dennis, 6	Dramatic Gold, 5	4	1:40.44	$61,500
1995	Tossofthecoin, 5, 118	C. S. Nakatani	Ferrara, 4	Polar Route, 5	8	1:40.70	$64,600
1994	Del Mar Dennis, 4, 115	S. Gonzalez Jr.	Tinners Way, 4	Hill Pass, 5	6	1:40.48	$93,300
1993	Marquetry, 6, 117	K. J. Desormeaux	Potrillon (Arg), 5	Lottery Winner, 4	6	1:49.10	$92,800

1992 **Another Review**, 4, 116   K. J. Desormeaux   Sir Beaufort, 5   Marquetry, 5   5   1:41.38 $87,900

Named for Mervyn LeRoy, one of the organizers of Hollywood Park and its president until 1985; LeRoy was a leading Hollywood producer and director. 1988-'91 Grade 1. 1981-'87 1 mile; 1993 1¹⁄₁₆ miles. †denotes female.

Metropolitan Handicap

Grade 1, Belmont Park, three-year-olds and up, 1 mile, dirt. Held May 27, 2002, with a gross value of $750,000. First held in 1891. Graded since 1973. Stakes record 1:32.81 (1996 Honour and Glory).

Year	Winner	Jockey	Second	Third	Strs	Time	1st Purse
2002	**Swept Overboard**, 5, 117	J. F. Chavez	Aldebaran, 4	Crafty C. T., 4	10	1:33.34	$450,000
2001	**Exciting Story**, 4, 115	P. Husbands	Peeping Tom, 4	Alannan, 5	10	1:37.14	$450,000
2000	**Yankee Victor**, 4, 117	H. Castillo Jr.	†Honest Lady, 4	Sir Bear, 7	8	1:34.64	$450,000
1999	**Sir Bear**, 6, 117	J. R. Velazquez	Crafty Friend, 6	Liberty Gold, 5	8	1:34.55	$300,000
1998	**Wild Rush**, 4, 119	J. D. Bailey	Banker's Gold, 4	Accelerator, 4	9	1:33.50	$300,000
1997	**Langfuhr**, 5, 122	J. F. Chavez	Western Winter, 5	Northern Afleet, 4	10	1:33.11	$240,000
1996	**Honour and Glory**, 3, 110	J. R. Velazquez	(DH) Lite the Fuse, 5		9	**1:32.81**	$240,000
			(DH) Afternoon Deelites, 4				
1995	**You and I**, 4, 112	J. F. Chavez	Lite the Fuse, 4	Our Emblem, 4	9	1:34.63	$300,000
1994	**Holy Bull**, 3, 112	M. E. Smith	Cherokee Run, 4	Devil His Due, 5	10	1:33.98	$300,000
1993	**Ibero** (Arg), 6, 119	L. A. Pincay Jr.	Bertrando, 4	Alydeed, 4	9	1:34.29	$300,000
1992	**Dixie Brass**, 3, 107	J. M. Pezua	Pleasant Tap, 5	In Excess (Ire), 5	11	1:33.68	$300,000

1895,1911-'12 not held. 1891-1904 held at Morris Park; 1960-'67,1969,1975 Aqueduct. 1891-'96 1¹⁄₈ miles. 1996 dead heat for second. †denotes female.

Miami Mile Breeders' Cup Handicap

Grade 3, Calder Race Course, three-year-olds and up, 1 mile, turf. Held September 2, 2002, with a gross value of $150,000. First held in 1987. Graded since 1989. Stakes record 1:33.75 (2001 Mr. Livingston).

Year	Winner	Jockey	Second	Third	Strs	Time	1st Purse
2002	**Band Is Passing**, 6, 117	C. H. Velasquez	Pisces, 5	Doowaley (Ire), 6	8	1:37.78	$90,000
2001	**Mr. Livingston**, 4, 115	A. Castellano Jr.	Honorable Pic, 4	Pisces, 4	8	**1:33.75**	$90,000
2000	**Band Is Passing**, 4, 120	E. Coa	Hurrahy, 7	Tiger Shark, 4	9	1:37.28	$90,000
1999	**Sharp Appeal**, 6, 114	J. Castellano	Shamrock City, 4	Hurrahy, 6	10	1:35.70	$135,000
1998	**Unite's Big Red**, 4, 115	E. O. Nunez	Fig Fest, 5	Ensign Ray, 5	10	1:36.62	$120,000
1997	**Vilhelm**, 5, 114	J. C. Ferrer	Marcie's Ensign, 5	Elite Jeblar, 7	11	1:36.67	$120,000
1996	**Satellite Nealski**, 3, 112	J. C. Ferrer	Marcie's Ensign, 4	Copy Editor, 4	10	1:47.63	$95,805
1995	**Elite Jeblar**, 5, 113	E. Fires	Myrmidon, 4	Fabulous Frolic, 4	10	1:47.67	$94,200
1994	**The Vid**, 4, 114	R. R. Douglas	Mr. Angel, 3	Carterista, 5	9	1:48.28	$94,350
1993	**Carterista**, 4, 117	M. A. Lee	Wild Forest, 4	Mr. Explosive, 5	13	1:47.51	$95,610
1992	**Jodi's Sweetie**, 4, 115	J. D. Bailey	Walkie Talker, 3	Futurist, 4	10	1:43.94	$94,140

Named for the city of Miami, Florida. 1987-'95 Miami Budweiser Breeders' Cup H.; 1996-'98 Miami Breeders' Cup H. 1987-'89,1992-'93 about 1¹⁄₈ miles; 1990-'91,1994-'96 1¹⁄₁₆ miles. 1990-'91 dirt.

Miesque Stakes

Grade 3, Hollywood Park, two-year-olds, fillies, 1 mile, turf. Held November 29, 2002, with a gross value of $200,000. First held in 1990. Graded since 1995. Stakes record 1:34.30 (1995 Antespend).

Year	Winner	Jockey	Second	Third	Strs	Time	1st Purse
2002	**Atlantic Ocean**, 2, 121	D. R. Flores	Tangle (Ire), 2	Major Idea, 2	8	1:34.63	$120,000
2001	**Forty On Line** (GB), 2, 117	C. S. Nakatani	Riskaverse, 2	Daisyago, 2	10	1:36.38	$120,000
2000	**Fantastic Filly** (Fr), 2, 116	G. K. Gomez	Smart Timing, 2	Eminent, 2	11	1:35.11	$120,000
1999	**Prairie Princess**, 2, 116	A. O. Solis	She's Classy, 2	Mary Kies, 2	6	1:37.30	$120,000
1998	**Here's to You**, 2, 116	E. J. Delahoussaye	Sweet Ludy (Ire), 2	Nausicaa, 2	7	1:36.57	$120,000
1997	**Star's Proud Penny**, 2, 116	G. K. Gomez	Superlative, 2	Ransom the Dreamer, 2	9	1:37.42	$120,000
1996	**Ascutney**, 2, 116	E. J. Delahoussaye	Wealthy, 2	Clever Pilot, 2	8	1:35.16	$120,000
1995	**Antespend**, 2, 121	C. W. Antley	Wheatly Special, 2	Platinum Blonde, 2	10	**1:34.30**	$110,000
1994	**Bail Out Becky**, 2, 121	K. J. Desormeaux	Miss Union Avenue, 2	Makin Whopee (Fr), 2	10	1:37.26	$110,000
1993	**Tricky Code**, 2, 116	C. S. Nakatani	Irish Forever, 2	Roget's Fact, 2	6	1:35.15	$137,500
1992	**Creaking Board** (GB), 2, 115	K. J. Desormeaux	Ask Anita, 2	Zoonaqua, 2	10	1:35.62	$137,500

Named for 1987, '88 champion turf female, Europeon champion and prominent broodmare Miesque (1984, f. by Nureyev). 1990 1¹⁄₁₆ miles. 1990 three-year-olds.

Milady Breeders' Cup Handicap

Grade 1, Hollywood Park, three-year-olds and up, fillies and mares, 1¹⁄₁₆ miles, dirt. Held May 25, 2002, with a gross value of $200,000. First held in 1952. Graded since 1973. Stakes record 1:40.20 (1980 Image of Reality).

Year	Winner	Jockey	Second	Third	Strs	Time	1st Purse
2002	**Azeri**, 4, 122	M. E. Smith	Affluent, 4	Collect Call, 4	6	1:42.02	$126,840
2001	**Lazy Slusan**, 6, 119	V. Espinoza	Lady Melesi, 4	Feverish, 6	6	1:42.25	$157,980
2000	**Riboletta** (Brz), 5, 120	C. J. McCarron	Bordelaise (Arg), 5	Excellent Meeting, 4	6	1:42.01	$112,860
1999	**Gourmet Girl**, 4, 115	E. J. Delahoussaye	Yolo Lady, 4	Victory Stripes (Arg), 5	5	1:40.97	$112,440
1998	**I Ain't Bluffing**, 4, 120	C. J. McCarron	Fleet Lady, 4	Real Connection, 7	6	1:42.16	$158,640
1997	**Listening**, 4, 116	A. O. Solis	Chile Chatte, 4	Exotic Wood, 4	5	1:41.37	$95,220
1996	**Twice the Vice**, 5, 120	C. J. McCarron	Jewel Princess, 4	Urbane, 4	5	1:40.96	$110,100

1995 **Pirate's Revenge**, 4, 116	C. W. Antley	Paseana (Arg), 8	Private Persuasion, 8	5	1:41.57	$91,000
1994 **Andestine**, 4, 116	C. J. McCarron	Golden Klair (GB), 4,	Zarani Sidi Anna, 4	7	1:41.40	$94,900
1993 **Paseana (Arg)**, 6, 125	C. J. McCarron	Bold Windy, 4	Re Toss (Arg), 6	7	1:41.67	$94,500
1992 **Paseana (Arg)**, 5, 125	C. J. McCarron	Re Toss (Arg), 5	Fowda, 5	7	1:41.46	$94,200

1952-'95 Milady H. 1952-'53 7 furlongs; 1954,1958-'66,1970-'72,1985 1 mile; 1955-'57 6 furlongs; 1986-'87 1⅛ miles.

Mint Julep Handicap

Grade 3, Churchill Downs, four-year-olds and up, fillies and mares, 1¼ miles, turf. Held May 18, 2002, with a gross value of $112,900. First held in 1977. Graded since 2001. Stakes record 1:40.98 (1994 Words of War).

Year	Winner	Jockey	Second	Third	Strs	Time	1st Purse
2002	**Megans Bluff**, 5, 118	C. Perret	Cozy Island, 4	Solvig, 5	8	1:42.87	$69,998
2001	**Megans Bluff**, 4, 118	C. Perret	Sitka, 4	Good Game, 4	10	1:42.88	$70,432
2000	**Pratella**, 5, 118	L. Melancon	Silver Comic, 4	Histoire Sainte (Fr), 4	8	1:43.08	$69,378
1999	**Mingling Glances**, 5, 113	L. Melancon	Formal Tango, 4	Red Cat, 4	11	1:42.59	$70,928
1998	**B. A. Valentine**, 5, 116	F. C. Torres	Lordy Lordy, 5	Mingling Glances, 5	9	1:41.42	$70,804
1997	**Valor Lady**, 5, 114	R. Albarado	My Secret, 5	Everhope, 5	11	1:41.20	$71,238
1996	**Ball Out Becky**, 4, 118	C. Perret	Country Cat, 4	Fluffkins, 4	8	1:41.86	$54,698
1995	**Romy**, 4, 118	J. L. Diaz	Olden Lek, 5	Memories (Ire), 4	6	1:42.69	$54,941
1994	**Words of War**, 5, 117	C. H. Marquez Jr.	Freewheel, 5	Eurostorm, 5	10	1:40.98	$55,673
1993	**Classic Reign**, 4, 115	F. A. Arguello Jr.	Tap Routine, 4	Liz Cee, 4	10	1:42.84	$37,375
1992	**Lady Shirl**, 5, 123	P. A. Johnson	Topsa, 5	Behaving Dancer, 5	10	1:41.41	$37,083

Named for the traditional bourbon drink served at the Kentucky Derby. 1977-'81,1988-'94,1997,1999-2000 Mint Julep H.; 1982-'87,1995-'96,1998 Mint Julep S. 1977-'82 7 furlongs; 1983-'87 1 mile; 1988-'89 1⅛ miles. 1977-'84,1988 three-year-olds and up. 1992,1994 new course record. 1997 Romy finished first, DQ to fourth.

Miss Preakness Stakes

Grade 3, Pimlico, three-year-olds, fillies, 6 furlongs, dirt. Held May 16, 2002, with a gross value of $100,000. First held in 1986. Graded since 2002. Stakes record 1:10 (2000 Lucky Livi).

Year	Winner	Jockey	Second	Third	Strs	Time	1st Purse
2002	**Vesta**, 3, 117	M. G. Pino	Willa On the Move, 3	Shameful, 3	6	1:10.25	$60,000
2001	**Kimbralata**, 3, 117	T. L. Dunkelberger	Carafe, 3	Stormy Pick, 3	5	1:11.20	$60,000
2000	**Lucky Livi**, 3, 119	R. Wilson	Big Bambu, 3	Swept Away, 3	5	1:10.00	$60,000
1999	**Hookedonthefeelin**, 3, 122	G. L. Stevens	Silent Valay, 3	Paula's Girl, 3	4	1:11.26	$60,000
1998	**Storm Beauty**, 3, 119	C. R. Woods Jr.	Brac Drifter, 3	Hair Spray, 3	5	1:10.81	$45,000
1997	**Weather Vane**, 3, 122	M. G. Pino	Move, 3	Cayman Sunset, 3	8	1:11.94	$64,740
1996	**Nic's Halo**, 3, 117	R. Wilson	Palette Knife, 3	Crafty But Sweet, 3	4	1:11.75	$32,655
1995	**Lilly Capote**, 3, 122	G. L. Stevens	Broad Smile, 3	Norstep, 3	7	1:10.90	$32,640
1994	**Foolish Kisses**, 3, 113	E. S. Prado	Aly's Conquest, 3	Platinum Punch, 3	8	1:12.45	$32,730
1993	**My Rosa**, 3, 113	E. S. Prado	Fighting Jet, 3	Code Blum, 3	5	1:11.33	$32,175
1992	**Toots La Mae**, 3, 113	J. Bravo	Missy White Oak, 3	Jazzy One, 3	6	1:11.97	$26,505

Modesty Handicap

Grade 3, Arlington Park, three-year-olds and up, fillies and mares, 1³⁄₁₆ miles, turf. Held July 27, 2002, with a gross value of $150,000. First held in 1942. Graded since 1985. Stakes record 1:55.31 (1993 Hero's Love).

Year	Winner	Jockey	Second	Third	Strs	Time	1st Purse
2002	**England's Legend (Fr)**, 5, 121	R. R. Douglas	Quick Tip, 4	Innit (Ire), 4	8	1:55.69	$90,000
2001	**Ioya Two**, 6, 115	M. Guidry	Megans Bluff, 4	Solvig, 4	11	1:55.47	$90,000
2000	**Wade for Me**, 5, 116	C. A. Emigh	Candleinthedark, 5	Wild Heart Dancing, 4	10	1:57.06	$60,000
1997	**War Thief**, 5, 116	S. J. Sellers	My Secret, 5	Bog Wild, 4	8	1:57.47	$60,000
1996	**Belle of Cozzene**, 4, 114	D. R. Pettinger	Trick Attack, 5	Naskra Colors, 4	6	1:58.24	$60,000
1994	**Assert Oneself**, 4, 115	F. H. Valenzuela	One Dreamer, 6	Seventies, 4	9	1:56.01	$60,000
1993	**Hero's Love**, 5, 120	E. Fires	Villandry, 5	Silvered, 6	10	1:55.31	$60,000
1992	**Tango Charlie**, 3, 114	A. G. Sorrows Jr.	Alcando (Ire), 6	Hero's Love, 4	13	1:58.79	$45,000

Named for Modesty (1881, f. by War Dance), first female winner of the American Derby. 1969-'79,1988,1995,1998-'99 not held. 1942-'50,1991-'93 Modesty S. 1942-'45,1958-'61 held at Washington Park; 1985 Hawthorne. 1942,1944-'46,1952,1966 1 mile; 1943,1963-'65 7 furlongs; 1947-'51,1953-'54,1959-'62 6 furlongs; 1955-'58,1967-'68 1¹⁄₁₆ miles; 1987 1⅛ miles. 1942-'54,1959-'65,1996 dirt. 1942 three-year-olds. 1994 Aube Indienne (Fr) finished first, DQ to seventh.

Molly Pitcher Breeders' Cup Handicap

Grade 2, Monmouth Park, three-year-olds and up, fillies and mares, 1⅛ miles, dirt. Held June 29, 2002, with a gross value of $300,000. First held in 1946. Graded since 1973. Stakes record 1:41.20 (1983 Ambassador of Luck; 1986 Lady's Secret).

Year	Winner	Jockey	Second	Third	Strs	Time	1st Purse
2002	**Atelier**, 5, 115	E. Coa	Summer Colony, 4	Spain, 5	5	1:48.63	$180,000
2001	**March Magic**, 4, 113	M. J. Luzzi	Vivid Sunset, 4	Shine Again, 4	7	1:43.79	$180,000
2000	**Lu Ravi**, 5, 116	P. Day	Silverbulletday, 4	Bella Chiarra, 5	7	1:43.17	$180,000
1999	**Heritage of Gold**, 4, 114	C. T. Lambert	Harpia, 5	Tap to Music, 5	6	1:41.76	$180,000
1998	**Relaxing Rhythm**, 4, 116	P. Day	Minister's Melody, 4	Glitter Woman, 4	6	1:42.30	$120,000
1997	**Rare Blend**, 4, 116	M. E. Smith	Top Secret, 4	Chip, 4	5	1:43.60	$120,000
1996	**Halo America**, 6, 117	P. Day	Rogues Walk, 4	Why Be Normal, 8	6	1:41.75	$120,000
1995	**Inside Information**, 4, 124	M. E. Smith	Jade Flush, 4	Halo America, 4	5	1:43.81	$90,000
1994	**Hey Hazel**, 4, 114	R. C. Landry	Ann Dear, 4	Future of Gold, 4	6	1:46.41	$120,000

1993	**Wilderness Song**, 5, 119	D. Clark	Quilma (Chi), 6	Looie Capote, 6	6	1:44.79	$90,000
1992	**Versailles Treaty**, 4, 120	M. E. Smith	Quick Mischief, 6	Cozzene's Wish, 6	6	1:43.18	$90,000

Named for Molly Pitcher, a woman who supposedly handled a cannon during the Battle of Monmouth in the Revolutionary War. 1946-'95 Molly Pitcher H.

Monmouth Breeders' Cup Oaks

Grade 2, Monmouth Park, three-year-olds, fillies, 1⅛ miles, dirt. Held August 17, 2002, with a gross value of $250,000. First held in 1871. Graded since 1973. Stakes record 1:48 (1985 Golden Horde; 1987 Without Feathers).

Year	Winner	Jockey	Second	Third	Strs	Time	1st Purse
2002	**Magic Storm**, 3, 112	E. L. King Jr.	Alternate, 3	Bronze Autumn, 3	5	1:51.17	$150,000
2001	**Unbridled Elaine**, 3, 121	E. Coa	Unrestrained, 3	Indy Glory, 3	7	1:51.02	$150,000
2000	**Spain**, 3, 114	J. A. Velez Jr.	North Lake Jane, 3	Prized Stamp, 3	7	1:42.78	$150,000
1999	**Silverbulletday**, 3, 121	J. D. Bailey	Boom Town Girl, 3	Bag Lady Jane, 3	4	1:43.03	$150,000
1998	**Kirby's Song**, 3, 121	T. Kabel	Santaria, 3	Brave Deed, 3	6	1:43.31	$120,000
1997	**Blushing K. D.**, 3, 121	L. Meche	Holiday Ball, 3	Snowy Apparition, 3	7	1:41.92	$120,000
1996	**Top Secret**, 3, 114	J. Bravo	Yanks Music, 3	Mesabi Maiden, 3	5	1:42.33	$120,000
1995	**Kathie's Colleen**, 3, 112	J. S. McAleney	Gal in a Ruckus, 3	Country Cat, 3	5	1:51.50	$90,000
1994	**Two Altazano**, 3, 121	C. Perret	Stellarina, 3	Cavada, 3	5	1:52.19	$90,000
1993	**Jacody**, 3, 121	T. G. Turner	Deputy Jane West, 3	Sheila's Revenge, 3	5	1:50.77	$90,000
1992	**Diamond Duo**, 3, 121	T. G. Turner	(DH) Secretly, 3	C. C.'s Return, 3	8	1:51.40	$90,000
			(DH) C. C.'s Return, 3				

1878,1894-1945 not held. 1871-'75,1977-'95 Monmouth Oaks; 1976 Monmouth Bicentennial Oaks. 1891 held at Jerome Park. 1871-'77 1½ miles; 1879-'93 1¼ miles; 1946-'52,1996-2000 1¹⁄₁₆ miles. 1992 dead heat for second.

Monrovia Handicap

Grade 3, Santa Anita Park, three-year-olds and up, fillies and mares, about 6½ furlongs, turf. Held December 31, 2002, with a gross value of $114,700. First held in 1968. Graded since 1973. Stakes record 1:12.40 (1981 Kilijaro [Ire]).

Year	Winner	Jockey	Second	Third	Strs	Time	1st Purse
2002	**Lil Sister Stich**, 5, 117	L. A. Pincay Jr.	Pina Colada (GB), 3	I'm the Business (NZ), 5	12	1:13.81	$68,820
2001	**Paga (Arg)**, 4, 117	M. E. Smith	Twin Set (Ger), 4	Impeachable, 4	13	1:15.09	$70,890
2000	**Evening Promise (GB)**, 4, 120	K. J. Desormeaux	Squall Linda, 4	New Heaven (Arg), 6	12	1:12.62	$68,640
1999	**Show Me the Stage**, 3, 117	K. J. Desormeaux	Chichim, 4	Honest Lady, 3	4	1:15.14	$64,140
	Desert Lady (Ire), 4, 116	C. S. Nakatani	Sweet Mazarine (Ire), 5	Supercilious, 6	7	1:14.59	$65,100
1998	**Madame Pandit**, 5, 118	E. J. Delahoussaye	Ski Dancer, 6	Dixie Pearl, 6	7	1:15.80	$65,700
1997	**Grab the Prize**, 5, 116	A. O. Solis	Finite E. F., 4	Evil's Pic, 5	7	1:16.89	$66,900
1996	**Klassy Kim**, 5, 116	G. F. Almeida	Ski Dancer, 4	Baby Diamonds, 5	8	1:14.48	$65,650
1995	**Rabiadella**, 4, 117	P. A. Valenzuela	Dezibelle's Star, 4	Las Meninas (Ire), 4	5	1:14.92	$47,450
1994	**Mamselle Bebette**, 4, 117	C. S. Nakatani	Shuggleswon, 4	Kalita Melody (GB), 6	6	1:15.35	$49,650
1993	**Glen Kate (Ire)**, 6, 118	C. A. Black	Bel's Starlet, 6	Heart of Joy, 6	7	1:12.89	$48,650
1992	**Middlefork Rapids**, 4, 116	P. A. Valenzuela	Remarkably Easy, 4	Crystal Gazing, 4	11	1:12.55	$51,150

Named for railroad pioneer W. N. Monroe (1841-1935), founder of the city of Monrovia, California. 1975-'89 not graded. 1969-'70,1976,1978,1980,1989,1994,1997-'99 6½ furlongs. 1969-'70,1976,1978,1980,1989,1994,1997-'99 dirt. 1968-'98,1999 (January) four-year-olds and up. 1999 held in January and December.

Morvich Handicap

Grade 3, Santa Anita Park, three-year-olds and up, about 6½ furlongs, turf. Held November 3, 2002, with a gross value of $100,000. First held in 1974. Graded since 1999. Stakes record 1:11.47 (2001 El Cielo).

Year	Winner	Jockey	Second	Third	Strs	Time	1st Purse
2002	**Master Belt (NZ)**, 4, 114	T. Baze	I Love Silver, 4	Kachamandi (Chi), 5	10	1:12.26	$67,020
2001	**El Cielo**, 7, 123	J. Valdivia Jr.	Speak in Passing, 4	Islander, 6	6	**1:11.46**	$64,680
2000	**El Cielo**, 6, 119	J. Valdivia Jr.	Kahal (GB), 6	Montemiro (Fr), 6	10	1:12.00	$67,020
1999	**Riviera (Fr)**, 5, 118	B. Blanc	Kahal (GB), 5	Howbaddouwantit, 4	10	1:12.99	$66,840
1998	**Musafi**, 4, 117	G. K. Gomez	Fabulous Guy (Ire), 4	Expelled, 6	8	1:14.54	$60,000
1997	**Reality Road**, 5, 115	C. S. Nakatani	Latin Dancer, 3	Torch Rouge (GB), 6	7	1:13.60	$60,000
1996	**Comininalittlehot**, 5, 117	K. J. Desormeaux	Wild Zone, 6	Wavy Run (Ire), 5	7	1:11.57	$65,100
1995	**Score Quick**, 3, 113	G. F. Almeida	Dramatic Gold, 4	Fu Man Slew, 4	7	1:14.64	$60,700
1994	**Rotsaluck**, 3, 115	F. H. Valenzuela	D'Hallevant, 4	Didyme, 4	7	1:13.66	$47,925
1993	**Western Approach**, 4, 115	K. J. Desormeaux	Yousefia, 4	Exemplary Leader, 7	6	1:12.12	$47,025
1992	**Regal Groom**, 5, 118	M. A. Pedroza	Bailarin, 5	Repriced, 4	4	1:16.88	$45,150

Named for Morvich (1919, c. by Runnymede), first California-bred winner of the Kentucky Derby. 1983,1992,1995 6½ furlongs. 1983,1992,1995 dirt. 1974-'92 two-year-olds and up.

Mother Goose Stakes

Grade 1, Belmont Park, three-year-olds, fillies, 1⅛ miles, dirt. Held June 29, 2002, with a gross value of $250,000. First held in 1957. Graded since 1973. Stakes record 1:46.58 (1994 Lakeway).

Year	Winner	Jockey	Second	Third	Strs	Time	1st Purse
2002	**Nonsuch Bay**, 3, 121	J. D. Bailey	Chamrousse, 3	Seba (GB), 3	4	1:49.09	$150,000
2001	**Fleet Renee**, 3, 121	J. R. Velazquez	Real Cozzy, 3	Exogenous, 3	10	1:47.19	$150,000
2000	**Secret Status**, 3, 121	P. Day	Jostle, 3	Finder's Fee, 3	7	1:48.03	$150,000

1999	Dreams Gallore, 3, 121	R. Albarado	Oh What a Windfall, 3	Better Than Honour, 3	6	1:48.69	$150,000
1998	Jersey Girl, 3, 121	M. E. Smith	Keeper Hill, 3	Banshee Breeze, 3	11	1:47.77	$120,000
1997	Ajina, 3, 121	M. E. Smith	Sharp Cat, 3	Tomisue's Delight, 3	6	1:48.56	$120,000
1996	Yanks Music, 3, 121	J. R. Velazquez	Escena, 3	Cara Rafaela, 3	7	1:47.90	$120,000
1995	Serena's Song, 3, 121	G. L. Stevens	Golden Bri, 3	Forested, 3	6	1:50.37	$120,000
1994	Lakeway, 3, 121	K. J. Desormeaux	Cinnamon Sugar (Ire), 3	Inside Information, 3	6	**1:46.58**	$120,000
1993	Sky Beauty, 3, 121	M. E. Smith	Dispute, 3	Silky Feather, 3	4	1:49.69	$120,000
1992	Turnback the Alarm, 3, 121	C. W. Antley	Easy Now, 3	Queen of Triumph, 3	7	1:48.80	$120,000

Named for Harry Payne Whitney's consensus 1924 champion two-year-old filly Mother Goose (1922, f. by *Chicle). 1963-'67,1969,1975 held at Aqueduct. 1957-'58 1 1/16 miles.

Mr. Prospector Handicap

Grade 3, Gulfstream Park, three-year-olds and up, 6 furlongs, dirt. Held January 4, 2003, with a gross value of $100,000. First held in 1946. Graded since 1999. Stakes record 1:08.45 (1997 Punch Line).

Year	Winner	Jockey	Second	Third	Strs	Time	1st Purse
2003	Baileys Edge, 6, 114	G. Boulanger	Friendly Frolic, 4	Out of Fashion, 7	6	1:09.95	$60,000
2002	Hook and Ladder, 5, 116	J. R. Velazquez	Kipperscope, 5	Red's Honor, 5	8	1:09.69	$60,000
2001	Istintaj, 5, 116	J. D. Bailey	Miners Gamble, 5	Smokin Pete, 4	13	1:09.63	$60,000
2000	Mountain Top, 5, 115	J. A. Santos	Lifeisawhirl, 4	Silver Season, 4	6	1:10.80	$45,000
1999	Cowboy Cop, 5, 114	P. Day	Good and Tough, 4	Mint, 4	6	1:08.80	$45,000
1998	Rare Rock, 5, 116	P. Day	Heckofaralph, 5	Banjo, 4	8	1:08.67	$45,000
1997	Punch Line, 7, 116	P. Day	Appealing Skier, 4	Constant Escort, 5	8	**1:08.45**	$45,000
1996	Meadow Monster, 5, 114	R. Wilson	Lord Carson, 4	Ponche, 7	8	1:09.47	$30,000
1995	Sweet Beast, 5, 118	M. E. Smith	Exclusive Praline, 4	Distinct Reality, 4	5	1:09.36	$30,000
1994	Binalong, 5, 116	J. D. Bailey	I Can't Believe, 6	Golden Pro, 4	12	1:09.68	$30,000
1993	Surely Six, 4, 113	R. Wilson	Groomstick, 7	Poulain d'Or, 4	9	1:21.85	$30,000
1992	Take Me Out, 4, 115	J. D. Bailey	Gizmo's Fortune, 4	Ocala Flame, 4	8	1:23.75	$30,000

Named for 1987, '88 leading sire Mr. Prospector (1970-'99, c. by Raise a Native), who set six-furlong track record at Gulfstream in 1973. Formerly named for Hallandale, Florida, location of Gulfstream. 1949,1957-'77,1979,1981 not held. 1950-'55 held as an allowance race. 1946-2000 Hallandale H. 1946,1984 1 1/16 miles; 1947-'56 1 1/8 miles; 1978 about 2 miles; 1980,1982 1 1/2 miles; 1987,1990-'93 7 furlongs. 1978-'82 turf. 1946,1984 three-year-olds; 1947 four-year-olds and up.

Mrs. Revere Stakes

Grade 2, Churchill Downs, three-year-olds, fillies, 1 1/16 miles, turf. Held November 16, 2002, with a gross value of $150,000. First held in 1991. Graded since 1995. Stakes record 1:42.86 (2001 Snow Dance).

Year	Winner	Jockey	Second	Third	Strs	Time	1st Purse
2002	Caught in the Rain, 3, 119	E. L. King Jr.	Glia, 3	Bedanken, 3	11	1:46.25	$107,694
2001	Snow Dance, 3, 122	C. Perret	Stylish, 3	Cozy Island, 3	10	**1:42.86**	$106,950
2000	Megans Bluff, 3, 122	M. Guidry	Uncharted Haven (GB), 3	Impending Bear, 3	12	1:43.37	$107,973
1999	Silver Comic, 3, 115	L. Melancon	St Clair Ridge (Ire), 3	Circle of Gold (Ire), 3	12	1:45.13	$108,345
1998	Anguilla, 3, 119	P. Day	Darling Alice, 3	White Beauty, 3	11	1:45.67	$107,601
1997	Parade Queen, 3, 122	P. Day	Mystery Code, 3	Starry Dreamer, 3	11	1:45.46	$108,624
1996	Maxzene, 3, 117	J. A. Krone	Fasta, 3	Turkappeal, 3	12	1:43.78	$72,354
1995	Petrouchka, 3, 122	D. Penna	Christmas Gift, 3	Ms. Isadora, 3	11	1:44.20	$75,725
1994	Mariah's Storm, 3, 122	R. N. Lester	Avie's Fancy, 3	Bear Truth, 3	10	1:43.99	$75,400
1993	Weekend Madness (Ire), 3, 117	C. R. Woods Jr.	Flower Circle, 3	Amal Hayati, 3	10	1:46.32	$74,685
1992	McKaymackenna, 3, 119	J. Velasquez	Spinning Round, 3	Aquilegia, 3	10	1:45.04	$56,209

Named for 1984 Dogwood, Edgewood, and Regret Stakes winner Mrs. Revere (1981, f. by Silver Series). 1995-'97 Grade 3.

My Charmer Handicap

Grade 3, Calder Race Course, three-year-olds and up, fillies and mares, 1 1/8 miles, turf. Held December 7, 2002, with a gross value of $100,000. First held in 1984. Graded since 1998. Stakes record 1:46.40 (1995 Danish [Ire]).

Year	Winner	Jockey	Second	Third	Strs	Time	1st Purse
2002	Wander Mom, 4, 114	E. Coa	Strawberry Blonde (Ire), 4	Babae (Chi), 6	10	1:48.43	$60,000
2001	Batique, 5, 116	J. F. Chavez	Please Sign In, 5	Wander Mom, 3	12	1:49.85	$60,000
2000	Wild Heart Dancing, 4, 116	J. F. Chavez	Megans Bluff, 3	Orange Sunset (Ire), 4	12	1:47.58	$60,000
1999	Crystal Symphony, 3, 114	C. H. Velasquez	Winfama, 6	Khumba Mela (Ire), 4	12	1:47.65	$60,000
1998	Colcon, 5, 118	J. D. Bailey	Cuando, 4	Winfama, 6	12	1:50.51	$60,000
1997	Overcharger, 5, 116	J. A. Rivera II	Dance Clear (Ire), 4	Hero's Pride (Fr), 4	12	1:48.18	$60,000
1996	Romy, 5, 114	F. C. Torres	Delta Love, 3	Ms. Mostly, 3	7	1:47.33	$60,000
1995	Danish (Ire), 4, 116	J. A. Santos	Cox Orange, 5	Alice Springs, 5	11	**1:46.40**	$60,000
1994	Caress, 3, 114	R. G. Davis	Putthepowdertoit, 4	Cox Orange, 4	10	1:50.63	$60,000
1993	Chickasha, 4, 115	R. D. Lopez	Marshua's River, 6	Always Nettie, 4	14	1:47.36	$30,000
1992	Julie La Rousse (Ire), 4, 120	J. D. Bailey	Marshua's River, 5	Highland Crystal, 4	10	1:45.78	$30,000
	Explosive Kate, 5, 118	D. Penna	Mia Bird Too, 3	Kiwi Mint, 4	9	1:46.58	$30,000
	Lady Shirl, 5, 120	E. Fires	Ratings, 4	Seaquay, 6	11	1:44.74	$51,150

Named for My Charmer (1969-'93, f. by Poker), dam of Horse of the Year and Triple Crown winner Seattle Slew. 1987,1991 not held. 1992 held Apr., Dec. (two divisions). 1984-'85,1988-'93 about 1 1/8 miles; 1986 dirt.

Nashua Stakes

Grade 3, Aqueduct, two-year-olds, 1 mile, dirt. Held November 2, 2002, with a gross value of $100,000. First held in 1975. Graded since 1982. Stakes record 1:35.40 (1977 Quadratic).

Year	Winner	Jockey	Second	Third	Strs	Time	1st Purse
2002	Added Edge, 2, 122	P. Husbands	Outer Reef, 2	Boston Bull, 2	7	1:36.77	$65,820
2001	Listen Here, 2, 117	J. D. Bailey	Monthir, 2	Thunder Days, 2	6	1:37.61	$65,580
2000	Ommadon, 2, 115	A. T. Gryder	Windsor Castle, 2	Griffinite, 2	10	1:36.74	$67,920
1999	Mass Market, 2, 117	M. E. Smith	Polish Miner, 2	Parade Leader, 2	9	1:38.60	$67,020
1998	Doneraile Court, 2, 115	J. D. Bailey	Successful Appeal, 2	Exiled Groom, 2	8	1:36.17	$66,600
1997	Coronado's Quest, 2, 122	M. E. Smith	Not Tricky, 2	Dice Dancer, 2	5	1:37.06	$65,100
1996	Jules, 2, 114	J. A. Santos	Shammy Davis, 2	Sal's Driver, 2	9	1:36.89	$68,340
1994	Devious Course, 2, 114	F. T. Alvarado	Mighty Magee, 2	Old Tascosa, 2	7	1:37.50	$65,580
1993	Popol's Gold, 2, 114	W. H. McCauley	Personal Merit, 2	Sonny's Bruno, 2	11	1:46.68	$74,400
1992	Dalhart, 2, 114	M. E. Smith	Rohwer, 2	Peace Baby, 2	11	1:44.60	$74,640

Named for Belair Stud's 1955 Horse of the Year Nashua (1952-'82, c. by *Nasrullah). 1995 not held. 1986-'88 Grade 2. 2001 held at Belmont Park. 1985 1 mile 70 yards; 1986-'93 1 1/16 miles.

Nassau County Breeders' Cup Stakes

Grade 2, Belmont Park, three-year-olds, fillies, 7 furlongs, dirt. Held May 11, 2002, with a gross value of $200,000. First held in 1996. Graded since 1998. Stakes record 1:22.19 (1996 Star de Lady Ann).

Year	Winner	Jockey	Second	Third	Strs	Time	1st Purse
2002	Nonsuch Bay, 3, 116	J. Castellano	Wopping, 3	Wilzada, 3	8	1:23.90	$120,000
2001	Cat Chat, 3, 114	J. R. Velazquez	Xtra Heat, 3	Shooting Party, 3	6	1:23.02	$90,000
2000	C'Est L' Amour, 3, 115	E. S. Prado	Tugger, 3	Miss Inquisitive, 3	6	1:23.46	$90,000
1999	Oh What a Windfall, 3, 118	M. E. Smith	Paved in Gold, 3	Things Change, 3	8	1:23.59	$66,480
1998	Jersey Girl, 3, 121	M. E. Smith	Countess Diana, 3	Foil, 3	4	1:22.63	$48,831
1997	Alyssum, 3, 116	J. A. Santos	Screamer, 3	Sinclara, 3	7	1:22.90	$49,065
1996	Star de Lady Ann, 3, 114	J. F. Chavez	Stop Traffic, 3	J J'sdream, 3	8	1:22.19	$49,590

Named for Nassau County, Long Island, New York; Belmont Park is located in Nassau County. 1996-2001 Nassau County S. 1998-99 Grade 3.

National Jockey Club Handicap

Grade 3, Hawthorne Race Course, three-year-olds and up, 1 1/8 miles, dirt. Held April 19, 2003, with a gross value of $250,000. First held in 1956. Graded since 1984. Stakes record 1:47.60 (1999 Baytown).

Year	Winner	Jockey	Second	Third	Strs	Time	1st Purse
2003	Fight for Ally, 6, 116	E. Razo Jr.	Colonial Colony, 5	Parrott Bay, 6	8	1:53.46	$150,000
2002	Hail The Chief (GB), 5, 114	J. F. Chavez	E Z Glory, 5	Ubiquity, 5	7	1:51.72	$120,000
2001	Chicago Six, 6, 117	A. J. Juarez Jr.	Guided Tour, 5	Glacial, 6	5	1:48.28	$120,000
2000	Take Note of Me, 6, 120	R. Albarado	Glacial, 5	Nite Dreamer, 5	8	1:49.91	$120,000
1999	Baytown, 5, 114	M. Guidry	Precocity, 5	Fred Bear Claw, 5	7	1:47.60	$120,000
1998	Polar Expedition, 7, 117	M. Guidry	Bucks Nephew, 8	Shed Some Light, 5	9	1:49.91	$120,000
1997	Bucks Nephew, 7, 118	G. K. Gomez	Natural Selection, 4	Gotha, 5	8	1:49.87	$120,000
1996	Prory, 4, 113	C. H. Silva	Polar Expedition, 5	Shed Some Light, 4	9	1:50.83	$150,000
1995	Dusty Screen, 7, 116	E. Maple	Come On Flip, 4	Adhocracy, 5	8	1:51.57	$150,000
1994	Recoup the Cash, 4, 113	J. L. Diaz	Dread Me Not, 4	Danc'n Jake, 5	7	1:49.03	$150,000
1993	Stalwars, 8, 113	J. L. Diaz	Count the Time, 4	Richman, 5	8	1:49.46	$150,000
1992	Stalwars, 7, 115	M. Guidry	Richman, 4	Sunny Prince, 5	6	1:48.15	$156,300

Named for the National Jockey Club, parent company of Sportsman's Park until 2002, when it allied with Hawthorne Race Course to become Hawthorne National LLC. 1956-'98, 2000-'02 held at Sportsman's. 1956-'71,1974-'76,1979-'80 1 1/16 miles; 1972 6 1/2 furlongs; 1973,1977-'78 1 mile. 1984-2002 four-year-olds and up. 1992,1993 new track record. 1996 Bucks Nephew finished first, DQ to fourth.

National Museum of Racing Hall of Fame Handicap

Grade 2, Saratoga Race Course, three-year-olds, 1 1/8 miles, turf. Held August 5, 2002, with a gross value of $150,000. First held in 1985. Graded since 1987. Stakes record 1:46.65 (1992 Paradise Creek).

Year	Winner	Jockey	Second	Third	Strs	Time	1st Purse
2002	Quest Star, 3, 117	P. Day	Union Place, 3	Patrol, 3	5	1:49.66	$90,000
2001	Baptize, 3, 122	J. D. Bailey	Strategic Partner, 3	Saint Verre, 3	7	1:47.94	$90,000
2000	Turnofthecentury, 3, 118	A. T. Gryder	Aldo, 3	Polish Miner, 3	5	1:52.35	$90,000
1999	Marquette, 3, 119	J. D. Bailey	Phi Beta Doc, 3	Good Night, 3	13	1:49.33	$90,000
1998	Parade Ground, 3, 120	S. J. Sellers	Vergennes, 3	Stay Sound, 3	8	1:47.82	$90,000
1997	Rob 'n Gin, 3, 120	J. D. Bailey	River Squall, 3	Subordination, 3	6	1:42.09	$66,000
1996	Sir Cat, 3, 113	J. D. Bailey	Fortitude, 3	Optic Nerve, 3	9	1:40.46	$68,340
1995	Flitch, 3, 113	M. E. Smith	Diplomatic Jet, 3	Nostra, 3 (DH) Lahint, 3	8	1:48.08	$83,700
1994	Islefaxyou, 3, 113	E. Maple	Jaggery John, 3	(DH) Mr. Impatience, 3	13	1:48.61	$70,200
1993	A in Sociology, 3, 115	C. W. Antley	Strolling Along, 3	Palashall, 3	10	1:48.81	$73,080
1992	Paradise Creek, 3, 115	M. E. Smith	Smiling and Dancin, 3	Spectacular Tide, 3	8	1:46.65	$72,600

Named for the National Museum of Racing and Hall of Fame located in Saratoga Springs, New York. 1985-'91 Gallant Man S.; 1992-'97 National Museum of Racing Hall of Fame S. 1991 1 3/16 miles; 1996-'97 1 1/16 miles. 2000 dirt. 1991 three-year-olds and up. 1991 fillies and mares.

Native Diver Handicap

Grade 3, Hollywood Park, three-year-olds and up, 1⅛ miles, dirt. Held December 14, 2002, with a gross value of $100,000. First held in 1979. Graded since 1979. Stakes record 1:45.35 (1996 Gentlemen [Arg]).

Year	Winner	Jockey	Second	Third	Strs	Time	1st Purse
2002	Piensa Sonando (Chi), 4, 117	L. A. Pincay Jr.	Fleetstreet Dancer, 4	Nose The Trade (GB), 4	8	1:48.43	$60,000
2001	Momentum, 3, 117	C. S. Nakatani	Euchre, 5	Last Parade (Arg), 5	7	1:48.24	$60,000
2000	Sky Jack, 4, 118	L. A. Pincay Jr.	Lethal Instrument, 4	Grey Memo, 3	8	1:46.81	$60,000
1999	General Challenge, 3, 123	C. J. McCarron	Moore's Flat, 5	Koslanin (Arg), 5	6	1:49.07	$60,000
1998	Puerto Madero (Chi), 4, 121	K. J. Desormeaux	Musical Gambler, 4	River Keen (Ire), 6	5	1:48.43	$60,000
1997	Refinado Tom (Arg), 4, 119	G. L. Stevens	Steel Ruhlr, 3	Boggle, 5	8	1:47.84	$60,000
1996	Gentlemen (Arg), 4, 121	G. L. Stevens	Dramatic Gold, 5	Don't Blame Rio, 3	5	1:45.35	$63,840
1995	Alphabet Soup, 4, 117	C. W. Antley	El Florista (Arg), 5	Regal Rowdy, 6	5	1:47.03	$61,400
1994	Best Pal, 6, 121	C. J. McCarron	Tossofthecoin, 4	Royal Chariot, 4	7	1:48.44	$64,000
1993	Slew of Damascus, 5, 118	C. S. Nakatani	Lottery Winner, 4	L'Express (Chi), 4	7	1:47.46	$63,300
1992	Sir Beaufort, 5, 119	C. J. McCarron	Memo (Chi), 5	Berillon (GB), 5	4	1:47.88	$61,700

Named for three-time Hollywood Gold Cup winner Native Diver (1959-'67, g. by Imbros); Native Diver won 33 stakes, second only to Exterminator. 1979 Grade 2. 1979-'81,1984-'85 1 mile; 1982-'83 1¹⁄₁₆ miles.

New Hampshire Sweepstakes Handicap

Grade 3, Rockingham Park, three-year-olds and up, about 1⅛ miles, turf. Held June 22, 2002, with a gross value of $200,000. First held in 1964. Graded since 1986. Stakes record 1:45.04 (2000 Inexplicable).

Year	Winner	Jockey	Second	Third	Strs	Time	1st Purse
2002	Del Mar Show, 5, 120	J. D. Bailey	Mus-If (GB), 6	Dr. Kashnikow, 5	9	1:47.51	$120,000
2001	Hap, 5, 123	J. R. Velazquez	Gander, 5	Flash of Joy, 6	7	1:46.32	$120,000
2000	Inexplicable, 5, 114	J. A. Santos	Where's Taylor, 4	Distant Mirage (Ire), 5	10	1:45.04	$120,000
1999	Adcat, 4, 113	J. F. Hampshire Jr.	Hurrahy, 6	Hibernian Rhapsody (Ire), 4	8	1:46.29	$120,000
1998	Statesmanship, 4, 118	J. A. Santos	Long War, 4	Daylight Savings, 4	7	1:48.49	$120,000
1997	Ok by Me, 4, 114	J. Bravo	Influent, 6	Diplomatic Jet, 5	8	1:47.14	$120,000
1996	Brave Note (Ire), 5, 112	R. E. Colton	Darnay (GB), 5	My Mogul, 6	9	1:47.64	$120,000
1995	Kiri's Clown, 6, 116	M. J. Luzzi	Pennine Ridge, 4	Torch Rouge (GB), 4	12	1:45.70	$120,000
1994	Kiri's Clown, 5, 113	M. J. Luzzi	River Majesty, 5	Fourstars Allstar, 6	8	1:46.76	$120,000
1993	Fourstars Allstar, 5, 115	J. A. Santos	Futurist, 5	Eternal Orage, 6	10	1:47.17	$120,000
1992	Rainbows for Life, 4, 119	D. Penna	Now Listen, 5	Buckhar, 4	12	1:46.83	$150,000

1968-'83 not held. 1984-'85,1988 New Hampshire H. 1964 1³⁄₁₆ miles; 1965 about 1¹⁄₄ miles; 1966-'67 1¹⁄₄ miles; 1984-'87 1⅛ miles. 1964-'86 dirt. 1964-'67 three-year-olds. 1992,1994,1995, 2000 new course record. 1993 dead heat for first. 1993 Idle Son finished first, DQ to sixth.

New Orleans Handicap

Grade 2, Fair Grounds, four-year-olds and up, 1⅛ miles, dirt. Held March 2, 2003, with a gross value of $500,000. First held in 1918. Graded since 1973. Stakes record 1:48.13 (1998 Phantom On Tour).

Year	Winner	Jockey	Second	Third	Strs	Time	1st Purse
2003	Mineshaft, 4, 115	R. Albarado	Olmodavor, 4	Strive, 4	11	1:48.92	$300,000
2002	Parade Leader, 5, 115	C. J. Lanerie	Graeme Hall, 5	Keats, 4	9	1:50.44	$300,000
2001	Include, 4, 114	J. D. Bailey	Nite Dreamer, 6	Valhol, 5	5	1:49.18	$300,000
2000	Allen's Oop, 5, 112	W. Martinez	Take Note of Me, 6	Ecton Park, 4	8	1:48.80	$300,000
1999	Precocity, 5, 118	E. M. Martin Jr.	Real Quiet, 4	Allen's Oop, 4	6	1:49.17	$320,640
1998	Phantom On Tour, 4, 114	L. Melancon	Precocity, 4	Lord Cromby (Ire), 4	8	1:48.13	$300,000
1997	Isitingood, 6, 121	D. R. Flores	Western Trader, 6	Scott's Scoundrel, 5	7	1:48.43	$180,000
1996	Scott's Scoundrel, 4, 116	R. D. Ardoin	Knockadoon, 4	Patio de Naranjos (Chi), 5	9	1:49.97	$162,540
1995	Concern, 4, 125	M. E. Smith	Fly Cry, 4	Tossofthecoin, 5	7	1:49.40	$120,000
1994	Brother Brown, 4, 118	P. Day	Far Out Wadleigh, 6	Eequalsmcsquared, 5	10	1:48.83	$120,000
1993	Latin American, 5, 112	G. K. Gomez	Delafield, 4	West by West, 4	12	1:49.20	$90,000
1992	Jarraar, 5, 112	B. J. Walker Jr.	Irish Swap, 5	Bayou Reality, 4	8	1:48.80	$60,000

Named for the city of New Orleans, Louisiana, home of Fair Grounds. 1919-'23,1941-'42,1945 not held. 1973-'80,1990-2000 Grade 3. 1918,1925-'31,1933,1936,1938-'39,1943-'53,1975 1¹⁄₁₆ miles; 1924,1935,1937 1 mile; 1940 1 mile 70 yards; 1978-'86 1¹⁄₄ miles. 1918-'36,1939-'78 three-year-olds and up; 1937-'38 three-year-olds. 1992,1994 equaled track record; 1997,1998 new track record.

New York Handicap

Grade 2, Belmont Park, three-year-olds and up, fillies and mares, 1¹⁄₄ miles, turf. Held July 4, 2002, with a gross value of $250,000. First held in 1940. Graded since 1977. Stakes record 1:58.40 (1990 Capades).

Year	Winner	Jockey	Second	Third	Strs	Time	1st Purse
2002	Owsley, 4, 114	E. S. Prado	Volga (Ire), 4	Janet (GB), 5	7	1:59.81	$150,000
2001	England's Legend (Fr), 4, 115	C. S. Nakatani	Gaviola, 4	Spook Express (SAf), 7	4	1:59.63	$150,000
2000	Perfect Sting, 4, 122	J. D. Bailey	Snow Polina, 5	Pico Teneriffe, 4	8	2:05.36	$150,000
1999	Soaring Softly, 4, 117	M. E. Smith	Tampico, 6	Anguilla, 4	6	2:02.25	$150,000
1998	Auntie Mame, 4, 118	J. R. Velazquez	Tresoriere, 4	Cuando, 4	8	1:59.50	$120,000
1997	Maxzene, 4, 120	M. E. Smith	Memories of Silver, 4	Shemozzle (Ire), 4	6	1:59.91	$120,000
1996	Electric Society (Ire), 5, 115	J. F. Chavez	Danish (Ire), 5	Chelsey Flower, 5	7	2:03.79	$90,000

1995	Irish Linnet, 7, 118	J. R. Velazquez	Danish (Ire), 4	Market Booster, 6	6	1:59.92	$65,520
1994	You'd Be Surprised, 5, 118	J. D. Bailey	Dahlia's Dreamer, 5	Aquilegia, 5	6	1:59.69	$65,340
1993	Aquilegia, 4, 114	J. A. Krone	Via Borghese, 4	Ginny Dare, 5	11	1:59.05	$74,760
1992	Plenty of Grace, 5, 111	J. A. Krone	Dancing Devlette, 5	Flaming Torch (Ire), 5	9	2:00.74	$72,720

Named for New York City, New York. 1957,1973-'75 not held. 1977-'82 Grade 3. 1940-'60,1963-'72 held at Aqueduct. 1940-'50 2¼ miles; 1951-'54,1959-'60 1⅛ miles; 1955-'58,1961 1⅜ miles; 1963,1968-'71 1³/₁₆ miles; 1965-'67,1977-'79 1¹/₁₆ miles; 1972 7 furlongs. 1940-'54,1972 dirt. 1972 three-year-olds. 1940-'62 both sexes; 1972 fillies.

Next Move Handicap

Grade 3, Aqueduct, three-year-olds and up, fillies and mares, 1⅛ miles, dirt. Held March 23, 2003, with a gross value of $108,000. First held in 1975. Graded since 1977. Stakes record 1:48.96 (1999 Diggins).

Year	Winner	Jockey	Second	Third	Strs	Time	1st Purse
2003	Smok'n Frolic, 4, 120	J. R. Velazquez	Ellie's Moment, 5	Pupil, 4	6	1:49.11	$64,800
2002	With Ability, 4, 113	J. Castellano	Irving's Baby, 5	Diversa, 4	7	1:49.88	$65,160
2001	Atelier, 4, 117	E. S. Prado	Pompeii, 4	Tax Affair, 4	4	1:50.65	$64,264
2000	Biogio's Rose, 6, 117	N. Arroyo Jr.	Up We Go, 4	Perlinda (Arg), 5	7	1:51.32	$49,875
1999	Diggins, 5, 113	J. L. Espinoza	Biogio's Rose, 5	Powerful Nation, 5	7	1:48.96	$48,915
1998	Panama Canal, 4, 113	S. Bridgmohan	Endowment, 4	Dewars Rocks, 4	8	1:51.37	$49,455
1997	Full and Fancy, 5, 115	R. Migliore	Shoop, 6	Prophet's Warning, 4	8	1:51.12	$49,500
1996	Madame Adolphe, 4, 110	F. Leon	Shoop, 5	Lotta Dancing, 5	7	1:51.39	$49,080
1995	Restored Hope, 4, 118	M. J. Luzzi	Cherokee Wonder, 4	Sterling Pound, 4	6	1:52.26	$48,975
1994	Groovy Feeling, 5, 123	M. J. Luzzi	Broad Gains, 4	Megaroux, 4	7	1:59.79	$63,735
1993	Low Tolerance, 4, 114	M. E. Smith	Hilbys Brite Flite, 4	Lady Lear, 4	8	1:55.93	$67,470
1992	Spy Leader Lady, 4, 112	M. E. Smith	Haunting, 4	Grecian Pass, 4	6	2:00.26	$67,560

Named for Alfred G. Vanderbilt's1950 champion three-year-old filly and 1952 champion handicap mare Next Move (1947-'68, f. by Bull Lea). 1990-'95 Next Move Breeders' Cup H. 1975 1 mile; 1984-'94 1³/₁₆ miles. 1975 three-year-olds. 1975 fillies.

Noble Damsel Handicap

Grade 3, Belmont Park, three-year-olds and up, fillies and mares, 1 mile, turf. Held September 21, 2002, with a gross value of $100,000. First held in 1988. Graded since 1988. Stakes record 1:32.80 (1997 Colcon; 1998 Oh Nellie).

Year	Winner	Jockey	Second	Third	Strs	Time	1st Purse
2002	Tates Creek, 4, 119	J. D. Bailey	Amonita (GB), 4	Dat You Miz Blue, 5	8	1:32.79	$68,640
2001	Tugger, 4, 119	J. D. Bailey	Shine Again, 4	Tippity Witch, 4	6	1:35.18	$68,280
2000	Gino's Spirits (GB), 4, 114	E. S. Prado	La Ville Rouge, 4	Solar Bound, 4	8	1:36.61	$66,720
1999	Khumba Mela (Ire), 4, 118	J. A. Santos	Uanme, 4	Cyrillic, 4	8	1:34.50	$67,740
1998	Oh Nellie, 4, 116	J. R. Velazquez	Heaven's Command (GB), 4	Irish Daisy, 5	7	1:32.80	$50,400
1997	Colcon, 4, 113	J. D. Bailey	Antespend, 4	Tiffany's Taylor, 8	11	1:32.80	$69,360
1996	Perfect Arc, 4, 125	J. R. Velazquez	Fashion Star, 4	Tough Broad, 4	7	1:42.41	$60,160
1995	Irish Linnet, 7, 121	J. R. Velazquez	Caress, 4	Weekend Madness (Ire), 5	7	1:40.67	$60,048
1994	Irish Linnet, 6, 117	J. R. Velazquez	Statuette, 4	Cox Orange, 4	10	1:39.59	$50,790
1993	McKaymackenna, 4, 120	C. W. Antley	La Piaf (Fr), 4	Heed, 4	10	1:43.74	$55,620
1992	Miss Otis, 5, 115	A. Madrid Jr.	Big Big Affair, 5	Tiney Toast, 3	4	1:43.64	$53,460

Named for G. Watts Humphrey's 1982 New York H. (G3) winner Noble Damsel (1978, f. by *Vaguely Noble). 1988 Leixable S.; 1989-'93 Noble Damsel S. 1988-'96 1¹/₁₆ miles. 1992,2001 dirt.

Norfolk Stakes

Grade 2, Santa Anita Park, two-year-olds, 1¹/₁₆ miles, dirt. Held October 5, 2002, with a gross value of $200,000. First held in 1970. Graded since 1973. Stakes record 1:34.86 (2000 Flame Thrower).

Year	Winner	Jockey	Second	Third	Strs	Time	1st Purse
2002	Kafwain, 2, 120	V. Espinoza	Bull Market, 2	Listen Indy, 2	7	1:42.75	$120,000
2001	Essence of Dubai, 2, 118	A. O. Solis	Ibn Al Haitham (GB), 2	Ecstatic, 2	6	1:37.16	$150,000
2000	Flame Thrower, 2, 118	V. Espinoza	Street Cry (Ire), 2	Mr Freckles, 2	8	1:34.86	$120,000
1999	Dixie Union, 2, 118	A. O. Solis	Forest Camp, 2	Anees, 2	6	1:35.79	$120,000
1998	Buck Trout, 2, 118	E. J. Delahoussaye	Eagleton, 2	Daring General, 2	9	1:37.55	$120,000
1997	Souvenir Copy, 2, 118	G. L. Stevens	Old Trieste, 2	Double Honor, 2	7	1:36.00	$120,000
1996	Free House, 2, 118	K. J. Desormeaux	Zippersup, 2	Swiss Yodeler, 2	7	1:43.54	$120,000
1995	Future Quest, 2, 118	K. J. Desormeaux	Odyle, 2	Exetera, 2	8	1:43.31	$120,000
1994	Supremo, 2, 118	G. L. Stevens	Desert Mirage, 2	Strong Ally, 2	9	1:43.48	$120,000
1993	Shepherd's Field, 2, 118	C. J. McCarron	Ramblin Guy, 2	Ferrara, 2	7	1:43.11	$120,000
1992	River Special, 2, 118	K. J. Desormeaux	Imperial Ridge, 2	Devil Diamond, 2	5	1:43.58	$120,000

Named for Theodore Winter's undefeated Norfolk (1861-'90, c. by Lexington), member of the great "triumvirate" of Lexington sons, with Asteroid and Kentucky. 1980-'92 Grade 1. 1997-2001 1 mile.

Oaklawn Breeders' Cup Stakes

Grade 3, Oaklawn Park, three-year-olds and up, fillies and mares, 1¹/₁₆ miles, dirt. Held March 15, 2003, with a gross value of $200,000. First held in 1987. Graded since 1990. Stakes record 1:42.01 (1999 Sister Act).

Year	Winner	Jockey	Second	Third	Strs	Time	1st Purse
2003	Bien Nicole, 5, 122	D. R. Pettinger	Red n'Gold, 5	Mandy's Gold, 5	9	1:44.19	$120,000
2002	Ask Me No Secrets, 4, 116	M. E. Smith	Red n'Gold, 4	Descapate, 4	5	1:44.56	$120,000
2001	Heritage of Gold, 6, 116	R. Albarado	Lu Ravi, 6	Ive Gota Bad Liver, 4	8	1:44.30	$120,000

Year	Winner	Jockey	Second	Third	Strs	Time	1st Purse
2000	**Heritage of Gold**, 5, 112	S. J. Sellers	Lu Ravi, 5	Light Line, 5	4	1:44.15	$120,000
1999	**Sister Act**, 4, 113	C. H. Borel	Glitter Woman, 5	Mil Kilates, 6	6	**1:42.01**	$60,000
1998	**Turn to the Queen**, 5, 112	T. T. Doocy	Danzalert, 4	Leo's Gypsy Dancer, 4	7	1:44.76	$90,000
1997	**Halo America**, 7, 118	C. H. Borel	Gold n Delicious, 4	Capote Belle, 4	6	1:42.18	$90,000
1996	**Belle of Cozzene**, 4, 113	D. R. Pettinger	Halo America, 6	Little May, 6	5	1:43.32	$94,350
1995	**Halo America**, 5, 115	W. T. Cloninger Jr.	Heavenly Prize, 4	Biolage, 4	6	1:42.59	$92,700
1994	**Morning Meadow**, 4, 116	S. P. Romero	Gravette, 4	Her Valentine, 4	10	1:44.60	$94,650
1993	**Guiza**, 6, 118	C. S. Nakatani	Teddy's Top Ten, 4	Fappies Cosy Miss, 4	8	1:44.79	$93,600
1992	**Cuddles**, 4, 118	D. Guillory	Rare Guest, 5	Dixie Splash, 5	10	1:43.82	$94,500

1987-'95 Oaklawn Budweiser Breeders' Cup H. 1995-'99 not graded.

Oaklawn Handicap

Grade 2, Oaklawn Park, four-year-olds and up, dirt. Held April 5, 2003, with a gross value of $500,000. First held in 1946. Graded since 1973. Stakes record 1:46.60 (1987 Snow Chief).

Year	Winner	Jockey	Second	Third	Strs	Time	1st Purse
2003	**Medaglia d'Oro**, 4, 122	J. D. Bailey	Slider, 5	Kudos, 6	5	1:47.66	$300,000
2002	**Kudos**, 5, 117	E. J. Delahoussaye	Bowman's Band, 4	Dollar Bill, 4	8	1:48.34	$300,000
2001	**Traditionally**, 4, 112	P. Day	Mr Ross, 6	Wooden Phone, 4	7	1:48.15	$360,000
2000	**K One King**, 4, 113	C. H. Borel	Almutawakel (GB), 5	Cat Thief, 4	6	1:48.02	$360,000
1999	**Behrens**, 5, 116	J. F. Chavez	Littlebitlively, 5	Precocity, 5	7	1:47.77	$450,000
1998	**Precocity**, 4, 114	C. Gonzalez	Frisk Me Now, 4	Phantom On Tour, 4	7	1:48.28	$450,000
1997	**Atticus**, 5, 114	S. J. Sellers	Isitingood, 6	Tejano Run, 5	8	1:48.22	$450,000
1996	**Geri**, 4, 115	J. D. Bailey	Wekiva Springs, 5	Scott's Scoundrel, 4	7	1:47.52	$450,000
1995	**Cigar**, 5, 120	J. D. Bailey	Silver Goblin, 4	Concern, 4	7	1:47.22	$450,000
1994	**The Wicked North**, 5, 119	K. J. Desormeaux	Devil His Due, 5	Brother Brown, 4	12	1:47.86	$450,000
1993	**Jovial (GB)**, 6, 117	E. J. Delahoussaye	Lil E. Tee, 4	Best Pal, 5	10	1:48.63	$450,000
1992	**Best Pal**, 4, 125	K. J. Desormeaux	Sea Cadet, 4	Twilight Agenda, 6	7	1:48.10	$300,000

1955-'62 not held. 1973-'76 Grade 3; 1988-2002 Grade 1. 1946-'83 1 1/16 miles. 1946-'76 three-year-olds and up.

Oak Leaf Stakes

Grade 2, Santa Anita Park, two-year-olds, fillies, 1 1/16 miles, dirt. Held October 6, 2002, with a gross value of $200,000. First held in 1969. Graded since 1973. Stakes record 1:41.20 (1978 It's In the Air).

Year	Winner	Jockey	Second	Third	Strs	Time	1st Purse
2002	**Composure**, 2, 119	M. E. Smith	Buffythecenterfold, 2	Sea Jewel, 2	6	1:42.65	$120,000
2001	**Tali'sluckybusride**, 2, 117	J. Valdivia Jr.	Imperial Gesture, 2	Ms Louisett, 2	6	1:37.77	$150,000
2000	**Notable Career**, 2, 118	D. R. Flores	Euro Empire, 2	Cindy's Hero, 2	7	1:36.34	$120,000
1999	**Chilukki**, 2, 118	D. R. Flores	Abby Girl, 2	Spain, 2	5	1:36.12	$120,000
1998	**Excellent Meeting**, 2, 115	K. J. Desormeaux	Antahkarana, 2	Stylish Talent, 2	7	1:37.71	$120,000
1997	**Vivid Angel**, 2, 116	E. J. Delahoussaye	Love Lock, 2	Balisian Beauty, 2	9	1:37.33	$120,000
1996	**City Band**, 2, 115	J. A. Garcia	Clever Pilot, 2	Wealthy, 2	8	1:44.57	$120,000
1995	**Tipically Irish**, 2, 117	L. A. Pincay Jr.	Ocean View, 2	Gastronomical, 2	7	1:42.60	$120,000
1994	**Serena's Song**, 2, 115	C. S. Nakatani	Call Now, 2	Mama Mucci, 2	5	1:41.83	$120,000
1993	**Phone Chatter**, 2, 117	L. A. Pincay Jr.	Sardula, 2	Tricky Code, 2	6	1:41.78	$120,000
1992	**Zoonaqua**, 2, 115	C. J. McCarron	Turkstand, 2	Madame l'Enjoleur, 2	10	1:43.91	$120,000

Run at Santa Anita's fall Oak Tree Racing Association meeting. 1980-'89,1992-2001 Grade 1. 1997-2001 1 mile.

Oak Tree Breeders' Cup Mile Stakes

Grade 2, Santa Anita Park, three-year-olds and up, 1 mile, turf. Held October 5, 2002, with a gross value of $250,000. First held in 1986. Graded since 1989. Stakes record 1:32.44 (1996 Urgent Request [Ire]).

Year	Winner	Jockey	Second	Third	Strs	Time	1st Purse
2002	**Night Patrol**, 6, 119	J. Valdivia Jr.	Kachamandi (Chi), 5	Nicobar (GB), 5	8	1:32.93	$150,000
2001	**Val Royal (Fr)**, 5, 119	J. Valdivia Jr.	Thady Quill, 4	I've Decided, 4	7	1:33.21	$120,000
2000	**War Chant**, 3, 117	G. L. Stevens	Road to Slew, 5	Sharan (GB), 5	8	1:33.75	$150,000
1999	**Silic (Fr)**, 4, 121	C. S. Nakatani	Bouccaneer (Fr), 4	Brave Act (GB), 5	7	1:33.76	$150,000
1998	**Hawksley Hill (Ire)**, 5, 123	A. O. Solis	Mr Lightfoot (Ire), 4	Magellan, 5	5	1:36.72	$166,200
1997	**Fantastic Fellow**, 3, 115	A. O. Solis	Magellan, 4	Taiki Blizzard, 4	8	1:36.23	$165,000
1996	**Urgent Request (Ire)**, 6, 115	C. J. McCarron	Megan's Interco, 7	Felon (Ire), 4	6	**1:32.44**	$110,300
1995	**Ventiquattrofogli (Ire)**, 5, 116	G. F. Almeida	Megan's Interco, 6	Debutant Trick, 5	8	1:35.30	$76,850
1994	**Bon Point (GB)**, 4, 116	E. J. Delahoussaye	Journalism, 6	Johann Quatz (Fr), 5	5	1:33.86	$62,050
1993	**Johann Quatz (Fr)**, 4, 119	E. J. Delahoussaye	Myrakalu (Fr), 5	The Tender Track, 6	5	1:36.28	$62,350
1992	**Twilight Agenda**, 6, 120	C. J. McCarron	Luthier Enchanteur, 5	Bourgogne (GB), 4	8	1:33.36	$65,300

Run at Santa Anita's fall Oak Tree Racing Association meeting. 1986-'95 Col. F. W. Koester H.; 1996-'98 Oak Tree Breeders' Cup Mile H. 1989,1996-'99 Grade 3. 1996 new course record.

Oak Tree Derby

Grade 2, Santa Anita Park, three-year-olds, 1 1/8 miles, turf. Held October 13, 2002, with a gross value of $150,000. First held in 1969. Graded since 1974. Stakes record 1:46.56 (2001 No Slip [Fr]).

Year	Winner	Jockey	Second	Third	Strs	Time	1st Purse
2002	**Johar**, 3, 118	A. O. Solis	Rock Opera, 3	Mananan McLir, 3	8	1:46.00	$90,000
2001	**No Slip (Fr)**, 3, 118	K. J. Desormeaux	Sligo Bay (Ire), 3	Romanceishope, 3	9	**1:46.56**	$90,000
2000	**Sign of Hope (GB)**, 3, 118	A. O. Solis	David Copperfield, 3	El Gran Papa, 3	5	1:47.71	$150,000

1999 **Mula Gula**, 3, 118	G. L. Stevens	Eagleton, 3	Super Quercus (Fr), 3	9	1:46.67	$150,000
1998 **Ladies Din**, 3, 120	G. L. Stevens	Dr Fong, 3	Bouccaneer (Fr), 3	7	1:50.24	$150,000
1997 **Lasting Approval**, 3, 118	A. O. Solis	Voyagers Quest, 3	Early Colony, 3	7	1:50.84	$150,000
1996 **Odyle**, 3, 117	C. J. McCarron	Lago, 3	Rainbow Blues (Ire), 3	6	1:46.83	$80,250
1995 **Helmsman**, 3, 115	C. J. McCarron	Virginia Carnival, 3	Mr Purple, 3	8	1:48.98	$75,650
1994 **Run Softly**, 3, 115	L. A. Pincay Jr.	Alphabet Soup, 3	Powis Castle, 3	8	1:49.96	$64,800
1993 **Eastern Memories (Ire)**, 3, 113	J. D. Bailey	Cigar, 3	Snake Eyes, 3	9	1:48.03	$66,800
1992 **Blacksburg**, 3, 118	A. O. Solis	Siberian Summer, 3	Star Recruit, 3	10	1:48.12	$67,700

Run at Santa Anita's fall Oak Tree Racing Association meeting. 1973 not held. 1969-'96 Volante H. 1974-'87,1990-'95 Grade 3.

Oceanport Handicap

Originally scheduled as a Grade 3 on the turf, Monmouth Park, three-year-olds and up, 1¹/₁₆ miles, dirt. Held June 15, 2002, with a gross value of $100,000. First held in 1947. Graded since 1973. Stakes record 1:39.40 (1999 Mi Narrow).

Year Winner	Jockey	Second	Third	Strs	Time	1st Purse
2002 **Tempest Fugit**, 5, 115	J. A. Velez Jr.	Runspastum, 5	One Eyed Joker, 4	3	1:42.72	$60,000
2001 **Key Lory**, 7, 111	C. C. Lopez	North East Bound, 5	Crash Course, 5	13	1:40.39	$60,000
2000 **North East Bound**, 4, 114	J. A. Velez Jr.	Rize, 4	Selective, 7	6	1:44.70	$60,000
1999 **Mi Narrow**, 5, 113	J. Bravo	Hurrahy, 6	Forbidden Apple, 4	8	**1:39.40**	$60,000
1998 **Daylight Savings**, 4, 115	H. Castillo Jr.	Mi Narrow, 4	Rob 'n Gin, 4	8	1:42.31	$60,000
1997 **Boyce**, 6, 118	J. A. Krone	Foolish Pole, 4	Jambalaya Jazz, 5	7	1:40.28	$60,000
1995 **Boyce**, 4, 114	A. S. Black	Myrmidon, 4	Rocket City, 4	9	1:40.91	$45,000
1994 **Nijinsky's Gold**, 5, 120	R. G. Davis	Winnetou, 4	Marco Bay, 4	5	1:41.66	$45,000
1993 **Furiously**, 4, 119	J. D. Bailey	Adam Smith (GB), 5	Rocket Fuel, 6	5	1:39.60	$45,000
1992 **Maxigroom**, 4, 113	R. G. Davis	Rocket Fuel, 5	Go Dutch, 5	9	1:41.77	$45,000

Monmouth Park is located in Oceanport, New Jersey. 1996 not held. 1984-2001 Grade 3. 1947-'63 6 furlongs; 1964-'67 5 furlongs; 1968-'72,1979 1 mile. 1964-'69,1971,1973-'83,1985-'89,1992-'99,2001 turf. 1993,1999 new course record.

Ogden Phipps Handicap

Grade 1, Belmont Park, three-year-olds and up, fillies and mares, 1¹/₁₆ miles, dirt. Held June 22, 2002, with a gross value of $300,000. First held in 1961. Graded since 1973. Stakes record 1:38.90 (1998 Mossflower).

Year Winner	Jockey	Second	Third	Strs	Time	1st Purse
2002 **Raging Fever**, 4, 120	J. R. Velazquez	Transcendental, 4	Two Item Limit, 4	9	1:41.75	$180,000
2001 **Critical Eye**, 4, 115	M. J. Luzzi	Jostle, 4	Apple of Kent, 5	7	1:42.18	$150,000
2000 **Beautiful Pleasure**, 5, 124	J. F. Chavez	Pentatonic, 5	Roza Robata, 5	6	1:41.54	$150,000
1999 **Sister Act**, 4, 117	P. Day	Beautiful Pleasure, 4	Catinca, 4	6	1:40.79	$150,000
1998 **Mossflower**, 4, 114	R. G. Davis	Glitter Woman, 4	Colonial Minstrel, 4	6	**1:39.90**	$150,000
1997 **Hidden Lake**, 4, 117	R. Migliore	Twice the Vice, 6	Jewel Princess, 5	9	1:40.87	$150,000
1996 **Serena's Song**, 4, 125	J. D. Bailey	Shoop, 5	Restored Hope, 5	8	1:41.63	$120,000
1995 **Heavenly Prize**, 4, 122	P. Day	Little Buckles, 4	Sky Beauty, 4	4	1:43.37	$90,000
1994 **Sky Beauty**, 4, 128	M. E. Smith	You'd Be Surprised, 5	Schway Baby Sway, 4	5	1:47.48	$90,000
1993 **Turnback the Alarm**, 4, 119	C. W. Antley	Deputation, 4	You'd Be Surprised, 4	6	1:48.14	$90,000
1992 **Missy's Mirage**, 4, 118	E. Maple	Harbour Club, 5	Versailles Treaty, 4	6	1:47.03	$120,000

Named for Ogden Phipps (1908-2002), former chairman of the Jockey Club and New York Racing Association. Formerly named for Hempstead, New York, located in Nassau County. 1910-'60,1962-'69 not held. 1904-'09 Hempstead S.; 1961-2001 Hempstead H. 1973-'83 Grade 2. 1904-'09 held at Jamaica; 1973-'74 Aqueduct. 1904-'09,1970,'71 6 furlongs; 1961 1¹/₂ miles; 1972-'94 1¹/₈ miles. 1904-'09 two-year-olds. 1904-'09,1961 both sexes.

Ohio Derby

Grade 2, Thistledown, three-year-olds, 1¹/₈ miles, dirt. Held July 20, 2002, with a gross value of $300,000. First held in 1876. Graded since 1973. Stakes record 1:47.40 (1979 Smarten).

Year Winner	Jockey	Second	Third	Strs	Time	1st Purse
2002 **Magic Weisner**, 3, 116	R. Migliore	Wiseman's Ferry, 3	The Judge Sez Who, 3	4	1:49.96	$195,000
2001 **Western Pride**, 3, 119	D. G. Whitney	Woodmoon, 3	Macho Uno, 3	6	1:48.66	$180,000
2000 **Milwaukee Brew**, 3, 116	M. J. McCarthy	Brave Quest, 3	Kiss a Native, 3	10	1:50.58	$180,000
1999 **Stellar Brush**, 3, 119	M. J. McCarthy	Ecton Park, 3	Valhol, 3	13	1:49.22	$180,000
1998 **Classic Cat**, 3, 122	S. J. Sellers	One Bold Stroke, 3	Hot Wells, 3	10	1:49.92	$180,000
1997 **Frisk Me Now**, 3, 122	E. L. King Jr.	Anet, 3	Mr. Groush, 3	7	1:48.28	$180,000
1996 **Skip Away**, 3, 122	J. A. Santos	Victory Speech, 3	Clash by Night, 3	10	1:47.86	$180,000
1995 **Petionville**, 3, 122	P. Day	Dazzling Falls, 3	Is Sveikatas, 3	6	1:48.93	$180,000
1994 **Exclusive Praline**, 3, 118	W. Martinez	Concern, 3	Smilin Singin Sam, 3	8	1:48.54	$180,000
1993 **Forever Whirl**, 3, 122	A. Toribio	Boundlessly, 3	Mighty Avanti, 3	10	1:49.44	$180,000
1992 **Majestic Sweep**, 3, 117	E. Fires	Technology, 3	Always Silver, 3	8	1:50.07	$180,000

1884-1923,1927,1933-'34,1936-'51 not held. 1876-'83 held at Chester Park; 1924-'26 Maple Heights; 1928-'35 Bainbridge Park; 1952 Cranwood Park; 1961-'62 Randall Park. 1876-'83 1¹/₂ miles; 1960-'64 1¹/₁₆ miles.

Oklahoma Derby

Grade 3, Remington Park, three-year-olds, 1¹/₈ miles, dirt. Held August 25, 2002, with a gross value of $250,000. First held in 1989. Graded since 1999. Stakes record 1:48 (1998 Classic Cat).

Year Winner	Jockey	Second	Third	Strs	Time	1st Purse
2002 **The Judge Sez Who**, 3, 115	C. H. Velasquez	Easyfromthegitgo, 3	A. P. Five Hundred, 3	9	1:49.34	$177,000
2001 **Top Hit**, 3, 114	G. K. Gomez	Unbridled Time, 3	Compendium, 3	6	1:49.79	$180,000

2000	**Performing Magic**, 3, 124	S. J. Sellers	Mister Deville, 3	Del Mar Danny, 3	9	1:50.36	$180,000
1999	**Temperence Time**, 3, 119	T. T. Doocy	Answer Lively, 3	Stellar Brush, 3	8	1:49.40	$180,000
1998	**Classic Cat**, 3, 124	S. J. Sellers	Leave a Legacy, 3	Sir Tiff, 3	8	**1:48.00**	$180,000
1997	**Wild Rush**, 3, 121	G. L. Stevens	Blazing Sword, 3	Precocity, 3	9	1:53.60	$180,000
1996	**Semoran**, 3, 122	R. A. Baze	Connecting Terms, 3	Devil's Honor, 3	5	1:46.60	$180,000
1995	**Dazzling Falls**, 3, 122	G. K. Gomez	Our Gatsby, 3	Capote's Promise, 3	7	1:42.80	$180,000
1994	**Smilin Singin Sam**, 3, 122	L. Melancon	Blumin Affair, 3	Silver Goblin, 3	8	1:43.20	$180,000
1993	**Marked Tree**, 3, 122	G. K. Gomez	Brother Brown, 3	Ragtime Rebel, 3	9	1:43.80	$180,000
1992	**Vying Victor**, 3, 122	R. D. Hansen	Ecstatic Ride, 3	Capitalimprovement, 3	10	1:43.60	$150,000

1989-2000 Remington Park Derby. 1989-'96 1¹⁄₁₆ miles; 1997 1³⁄₁₆ miles. 1992,1995,1998 new track record; 1994 equaled track record.

Orchid Handicap

Grade 2, Gulfstream Park, three-year-olds and up, fillies and mares, 1¹⁄₂ miles, dirt (originally scheduled on the turf). Held March 23, 2003, with a gross value of $200,000. First held in 1954. Graded since 1973. Stakes record 2:24.20 (1990 Coolawin).

Year	Winner	Jockey	Second	Third	Strs	Time	1st Purse
2003	**Tweedside**, 5, 116	R. R. Douglas	San Dare, 5	Hi Tech Honeycomb, 4	7	2:32.36	$120,000
2002	**Julie Jalouse**, 4, 114	J. A. Santos	Sweetest Thing, 4	Refugee, 4	9	2:25.89	$120,000
2001	**Innuendo (Ire)**, 6, 116	J. D. Bailey	Windsong, 4	Aiglonne, 4	4	2:25.24	$120,000
2000	**Lisieux Rose (Ire)**, 5, 114	J. A. Santos	Champagne Royal, 6	Fly for Avie, 5	10	2:25.64	$120,000
1999	**Coretta (Ire)**, 5, 118	J. A. Santos	Delilah (Ire), 5	Almost Skint (Ire), 5	11	2:23.85	$120,000
1998	**Colonial Play**, 4, 113	R. G. Davis	Almost Skint (Ire), 4	Gastronomical, 5	11	2:24.75	$120,000
1997	**Golden Pond (Ire)**, 4, 116	W. H. McCauley	Tocopilla (Arg), 7	Miss Caerleona (Fr), 5	11	2:26.84	$120,000
1996	**Memories (Ire)**, 5, 114	J. A. Santos	Caromana, 5	Curtain Raiser, 4	11	2:31.51	$120,000
1995	**Exchange**, 7, 120	L. A. Pincay Jr.	Market Booster, 6	Northern Emerald, 5	10	2:29.02	$120,000
1994	**Trampoli**, 5, 121	M. E. Smith	Good Morning Smile, 6	Northern Emerald, 4	7	2:25.42	$120,000
1993	**Fairy Garden**, 5, 115	W. S. Ramos	Rougeur, 4	Trampoli, 4	14	2:25.79	$120,000
1992	**Crockadore**, 5, 115	M. E. Smith	Indian Fashion, 5	Sardaniya (Ire), 4	10	2:28.32	$120,000

James Donn Sr., Gulfstream Park founder, was a world-renowned florist who developed a special breed of orchid in honor of his wife. 1955-'64 not held. 1954-'66 Orchid S. 1973-'80 Grade 3. 1954 6 furlongs; 1965-'66,1969-'85 1¹⁄₁₆ miles; 1967-'68 1 mile; 1992 about 1¹⁄₂ miles. 1954-'66,1983-'84 dirt. 1954-'66 three-year-olds. 1954-'66 fillies. 1992 new course record.

Overbrook Spinster Stakes

Grade 1, Keeneland, three-year-olds and up, fillies and mares, 1¹⁄₈ miles, dirt. Held October 6, 2002, with a gross value of $500,000. First held in 1956. Graded since 1973. Stakes record 1:47 (1990 Bayakoa [Arg]).

Year	Winner	Jockey	Second	Third	Strs	Time	1st Purse
2002	**Take Charge Lady**, 3, 120	E. S. Prado	You, 3	Printemps (Chi), 5	7	1:49.90	$338,520
2001	**Miss Linda (Arg)**, 4, 123	R. Migliore	Starrer, 3	Printemps (Chi), 4	10	1:49.79	$348,440
2000	**Plenty of Light**, 3, 120	G. K. Gomez	Spain, 3	Roza Robata, 5	6	1:48.18	$336,970
1999	**Keeper Hill**, 4, 123	K. J. Desormeaux	Banshee Breeze, 4	A Lady From Dixie, 4	9	1:47.19	$344,410
1998	**Banshee Breeze**, 3, 119	R. Albarado	Runup the Colors, 4	Aldiza, 4	8	1:47.04	$341,930
1997	**Clear Mandate**, 5, 123	P. Day	Feasibility Study, 5	Naskra Colors, 5	7	1:50.47	$336,350
1996	**Different (Arg)**, 4, 123	C. J. McCarron	Top Secret, 3	Belle of Cozzene, 4	6	1:49.74	$336,040
1995	**Inside Information**, 4, 123	M. E. Smith	Jade Flush, 4	Mariah's Storm, 4	4	1:50.01	$198,276
1994	**Dispute**, 4, 123	P. Day	Lets Be Alert, 3	Miss Dominique, 5	8	1:48.91	$204,414
1993	**Paseana (Arg)**, 6, 123	C. J. McCarron	Gray Cashmere, 4	Jacody, 3	9	1:48.46	$205,902
1992	**Fowda**, 4, 123	P. A. Valenzuela	Paseana (Arg), 5	Meadow Star, 4	10	1:49.91	$209,994

A "spinster" is an unmarried woman beyond the traditional marriage age, hence an appropriate name for a race for females still racing in the fall. Sponsored by W. T. Young's Overbrook Farm, located in Lexington, Kentucky. Formerly sponsored by Robert N. Clay's Three Chimneys Farm, in Midway. 1956-'95 Spinster S.; 1996-2000 Three Chimneys Spinster S. 1956-'63 three, four, and five-year-olds.

Pacific Classic Stakes

Grade 1, Del Mar, three-year-olds and up, 1¹⁄₄ miles, dirt. Held August 25, 2002, with a gross value of $1,000,000. First held in 1991. Graded since 1993. Stakes record 1:59.43 (1994 Tinners Way).

Year	Winner	Jockey	Second	Third	Strs	Time	1st Purse
2002	**Came Home**, 3, 117	M. E. Smith	Momentum, 4	Milwaukee Brew, 5	14	2:01.45	$600,000
2001	**Skimming**, 5, 124	G. K. Gomez	Dixie Dot Com, 6	Dig for It, 6	6	1:59.96	$600,000
2000	**Skimming**, 4, 124	G. K. Gomez	Tiznow, 3	Ecton Park, 4	7	2:01.22	$600,000
1999	**General Challenge**, 3, 117	D. R. Flores	River Keen (Ire), 7	Barter Town, 4	8	2:00.57	$700,000
1998	**Free House**, 4, 124	C. J. McCarron	Gentlemen (Arg), 6	Pacificbounty, 4	9	2:00.29	$600,000
1997	**Gentlemen (Arg)**, 5, 124	G. L. Stevens	Siphon (Brz), 6	Crafty Friend, 4	5	2:00.56	$850,000
1996	**Dare and Go**, 5, 124	A. O. Solis	Cigar, 6	Siphon (Brz), 5	6	1:59.85	$600,000
1995	**Tinners Way**, 5, 124	E. J. Delahoussaye	Soul of the Matter, 4	Blumin Affair, 4	6	1:59.63	$550,000
1994	**Tinners Way**, 4, 124	E. J. Delahoussaye	Best Pal, 6	Dramatic Gold, 3	9	**1:59.43**	$550,000
1993	**Bertrando**, 4, 124	G. L. Stevens	Missionary Ridge (GB), 6	Best Pal, 5	7	1:59.55	$550,000
1992	**Missionary Ridge (GB)**, 5, 124	K. J. Desormeaux	Defensive Play, 5	Claret (Ire), 4	7	2:00.87	$550,000

Named for the Pacific Ocean, where Del Mar's "turf meets the surf." 1993,1994 new track record.

Palm Beach Stakes

Grade 3, Gulfstream Park, three-year-olds, 1¹⁄₈ miles, turf. Held February 21, 2003, with a gross value of $100,000. First held in 1987. Graded since 1990. Stakes record 1:47.32 (1997 Unite's Big Red).

Year	Winner	Jockey	Second	Third	Strs	Time	1st Purse
2003	Nothing to Lose, 3, 122	J. D. Bailey	White Cat, 3	Imitation, 3	12	1:48.28	$60,000
2002	Orchard Park, 3, 118	J. D. Bailey	Lord Juban, 3	Red's Top Gun, 3	12	1:49.80	$60,000
2001	Proud Man, 3, 119	R. R. Douglas	One Eyed Joker, 3	Strategic Partner, 3	12	1:48.32	$90,000
2000	Mr. Livingston, 3, 114	S. J. Sellers	Powerful Appeal, 3	Gateman (GB), 3	11	1:48.04	$45,000
1999	Swamp, 3, 114	R. Migliore	Marquette, 3	Valid Reprized, 3	12	1:48.38	$45,000
1998	Cryptic Rascal, 3, 119	M. E. Smith	The Kaiser, 3	American Odyssey, 3	8	1:55.01	$45,000
1997	Unite's Big Red, 3, 117	R. Hernandez	Trample, 3	Tekken (Ire), 3	7	1:47.32	$45,000
1996	Harrowman, 3, 114	M. E. Smith	A Real Zipper, 3	Ok by Me, 3	6	1:49.22	$45,000
1995	Admiralty, 3, 114	J. A. Krone	Nostra, 3	Smells and Bells, 3	4	1:51.03	$30,000
1994	Mr. Angel, 3, 112	W. H. McCauley	Clint Essential, 3	Fabulous Frolic, 3	9	1:44.66	$30,000
1993	Kissin Kris, 3, 112	D. Penna	Pride Prevails, 3	Awad, 3	10	1:46.41	$38,760
1992	Preferences, 3, 114	J. C. Duarte	Doo You, 3	Stress Buster, 3	12	1:42.64	$38,940

Named in honor of the residents of West Palm Beach and Palm Beach County, Florida. 1987 Palm Beach H. 1987-'89 1 mile; 1990 7 furlongs; 1991-'93 1¹⁄₁₆ miles; 1994 about 1¹⁄₁₆ miles; 1998 about 1¹⁄₈ miles. 1990,1993,1995 dirt. 1987 three-year-olds and up.

Palomar Handicap

Grade 2, Del Mar, three-year-olds and up, fillies and mares, 1¹⁄₁₆ miles, turf. Held September 8, 2002, with a gross value of $150,000. First held in 1945. Graded since 1981. Stakes record 1:41.01 (2000 Tranquility Lake).

Year	Winner	Jockey	Second	Third	Strs	Time	1st Purse
2002	Voodoo Dancer, 4, 120	K. J. Desormeaux	I'm the Business (NZ), 5	Skywriting, 4	7	1:41.56	$90,000
2001	Tranquility Lake, 6, 123	E. J. Delahoussaye	La Ronge, 4	Al Desima (GB), 4	6	1:41.94	$90,000
2000	Tranquility Lake, 5, 121	E. J. Delahoussaye	Tout Charmant, 4	Miss of Wales (Chi), 5	7	1:41.01	$82,170
1999	Happyanunoit (NZ), 4, 113	B. Blanc	Tuzla (Fr), 5	Isle de France, 4	6	1:41.28	$80,520
1998	Tuzla (Fr), 4, 117	C. S. Nakatani	Ecoute, 5	Call Me (GB), 5	7	1:42.28	$80,970
1997	Blushing Heiress, 5, 117	C. J. McCarron	Traces of Gold, 5	Listening, 4	6	1:43.32	$83,200
1996	Yearly Tour, 5, 116	C. J. McCarron	Slewvera, 4	Real Connection, 5	8	1:42.56	$81,350
1995	Morgana, 4, 118	G. L. Stevens	Yearly Tour, 4	Lady Affirmed, 4	7	1:42.41	$74,450
1994	Shir Dar (Fr), 4, 114	C. S. Nakatani	Baby Diamonds, 3	Prying (Arg), 6	7	1:42.95	$63,600
1993	Heart of Joy, 6, 119	D. R. Flores	Kalita Melody (GB), 4	Amal Hayati, 3	8	1:42.07	$63,000
1992	Super Staff, 4, 114	C. J. McCarron	Odalea (Arg), 6	Only Yours (GB), 4	10	1:42.20	$64,900

Named for Palomar and Mt. Palomar, California, located near San Diego; Mt. Palomar was once the site of the world's largest telescope. 1981-'84,1997-2000 Grade 3. 1945-'69 6 furlongs; 1970-'76 7¹⁄₂ furlongs; 1977-'87 1 mile. 1945-'69 dirt.

Palos Verdes Handicap

Grade 2, Santa Anita Park, four-year-olds and up, 6 furlongs, dirt. Held January 26, 2003, with a gross value of $150,000. First held in 1951. Graded since 1973. Stakes record 1:07.20 (1989 Sunny Blossom).

Year	Winner	Jockey	Second	Third	Strs	Time	1st Purse
2003	Avanzado (Arg), 6, 116	T. Baze	Mellow Fellow, 8	Disturbingthepeace, 5	6	1:07.85	$90,000
2002	Snow Ridge, 4, 116	M. E. Smith	Squirtle Squirt, 4	Ceeband, 5	7	1:07.70	$90,000
2001	Men's Exclusive, 8, 116	L. A. Pincay Jr.	Big Jag, 8	Freespool, 5	6	1:08.33	$120,000
2000	Kona Gold, 6, 121	A. O. Solis	Big Jag, 7	Freespool, 4	5	1:08.55	$120,000
1999	Big Jag, 6, 116	J. Valdivia Jr.	Kona Gold, 5	Swiss Yodeler, 5	5	1:08.05	$120,000
1998	Funontherun, 4, 113	G. F. Almeida	Red, 4	Elmhurst, 8	9	1:08.93	$120,000
1997	High Stakes Player, 5, 118	C. S. Nakatani	Rotsaluck, 6	Larry the Legend, 5	7	1:08.44	$131,600
1996	Lit de Justice, 6, 122	E. J. Delahoussaye	Siphon (Brz), 5	Lakota Brave, 7	9	1:08.88	$135,100
1995	D'Hallevant, 5, 117	C. S. Nakatani	Cardmania, 9	Subtle Trouble, 4	10	1:08.44	$94,400
1994	Concept Win, 4, 115	G. L. Stevens	J. F. Williams, 5	Scherando, 5	6	1:07.71	$62,100
1993	Music Merci, 7, 114	D. R. Flores	Star of the Crop, 4	Cardmania, 7	7	1:08.82	$63,700
1992	Individualist, 5, 117	L. A. Pincay Jr.	High Energy, 5	Rushmore, 5	9	1:08.66	$65,600

Named for the 1824 land grant named Los Palos Verdes Ranchos; it means "green trees." 1969-'70,1991 not held. 1973-'74,1988-'97 Grade 3. 1951-'66,1971 (January) three-year-olds and up; 1967-'68,1971 (December),1972-'89 two-year-olds and up.

Pan American Handicap

Grade 2, Gulfstream Park, three-year-olds and up, about 1¹⁄₂ miles, turf. Held March 22, 2003, with a gross value of $200,000. First held in 1962. Graded since 1973. Stakes record 2:23.15 (1999 Unite's Big Red).

Year	Winner	Jockey	Second	Third	Strs	Time	1st Purse
2003	Quest Star, 4, 113	E. S. Prado	Man From Wicklow, 6	Reduit (GB), 5	9	2:28.45	$120,000
2002	Deeliteful Irving, 4, 113	C. P. DeCarlo	Ceteways, 6	Mr. Livingston, 5	9	2:24.14	$120,000
2001	Whata Brainstorm, 4, 114	J. R. Velazquez	Subtle Power (Ire), 4	Craigsteel (GB), 6	7	2:23.75	$150,000
2000	Buck's Boy, 7, 120	E. S. Prado	Thesaurus, 6	Epistolaire (Ire), 5	7	2:24.80	$150,000
1999	Unite's Big Red, 5, 114	M. E. Smith	African Dancer, 7	Panama City, 5	7	2:23.15	$150,000
1998	Buck's Boy, 5, 115	E. Fires	African Dancer, 6	Royal Strand (Ire), 4	9	2:23.43	$150,000
1997	Flag Down, 7, 117	J. A. Santos	Lassigny, 6	Awad, 7	6	2:27.08	$180,000
1996	Celtic Arms (Fr), 5, 115	M. E. Smith	Broadway Flyer, 5	Flag Down, 5	7	2:25.71	$180,000

1995	**Awad**, 5, 114	E. Maple	Misil, 7	Frenchpark (GB), 5	9	2:29.44	$180,000
1994	**Fraise**, 6, 124	M. E. Smith	Summer Ensign, 5	Fairy Garden, 6	10	2:24.65	$180,000
1993	**Fraise**, 5, 124	P. A. Valenzuela	Stagecraft (GB), 6	Futurist, 5	8	2:32.86	$180,000
1992	**Wall Street Dancer**, 4, 114	J. Velasquez	†Passagere du Soir (GB), 5	Missionary Ridge (GB), 5	14	2:25.53	$210,000

Named in honor of the multicultural heritage of South Florida's residents. 1996 Crown Royal Pan American H. 1983-'89 Grade 1. 1962-'64 1⅛ miles; 1989 1¼ miles; 1993 about 1½ miles. 1962-'64,1975,1989 dirt. 1999 new course record. 2000 Beautiful Dancer finished third, DQ to sixth. †denotes female.

Pat O'Brien Handicap

Grade 2, Del Mar, three-year-olds and up, 7 furlongs, dirt. Held August 18, 2002, with a gross value of $150,000. First held in 1986. Graded since 1994. Stakes record 1:20.06 (1995 Lit de Justice).

Year	Winner	Jockey	Second	Third	Strs	Time	1st Purse
2002	**Disturbingthepeace**, 4, 119	V. Espinoza	Hot Market, 4	I Love Silver, 4	5	1:21.89	$90,000
2001	**El Corredor**, 4, 119	V. Espinoza	Swept Overboard, 4	Ceeband, 4	7	1:20.42	$90,000
2000	**Love That Red**, 4, 118	C. S. Nakatani	Cliquot, 4	Son of a Pistol, 8	5	1:21.89	$90,000
1999	**Regal Thunder**, 5, 116	C. W. Antley	Christmas Boy, 6	Bet On Sunshine, 7	9	1:21.13	$90,000
1998	**Old Topper**, 3, 116	E. J. Delahoussaye	Son of a Pistol, 6	Uncaged Fury, 7	5	1:21.51	$95,220
1997	**Tres Paraiso**, 5, 115	G. L. Stevens	High Stakes Player, 5	Gold Land, 6	7	1:21.45	$68,200
1996	**Alphabet Soup**, 5, 118	C. W. Antley	Boundless Moment, 4	Lit de Justice, 6	8	1:20.79	$65,450
1995	**Lit de Justice**, 5, 118	C. S. Nakatani	D'Hallevant, 5	Pembroke, 5	7	**1:20.06**	$60,400
1994	**D'Hallevant**, 4, 115	C. S. Nakatani	Minjinsky, 4	J. F. Williams, 5	5	1:20.25	$59,725
1993	**Slerp**, 4, 117	A. D. Lopez	Portoferraio (Arg), 5	Cardmania, 7	7	1:21.36	$47,850
1992	**Light of Morn**, 6, 116	E. J. Delahoussaye	Three Peat, 3	Slerp, 3	12	1:20.65	$66,025

Named in honor of Pat O'Brien, co-founder with Bing Crosby of the Del Mar Turf Club. 1990-'95 Pat O'Brien Breeders' Cup H. 1994-'98 Grade 3. 1995 equaled track record.

Pebbles Handicap

Originally scheduled as Grade 3 on the turf, Belmont Park, three-year-olds, fillies, 1⅛ miles, dirt. Held October 14, 2002, with a gross value of $100,000. First held in 1993. Graded since 1999. Stakes record 1:47.50 (2001 Love n' Kiss S. [2nd Div.]).

Year	Winner	Jockey	Second	Third	Strs	Time	1st Purse
2002	**Glia**, 3, 113	J. Castellano	Nonsuch Bay, 3	Delta Princess, 3	5	1:49.68	$68,580
2001	**Heads Will Roll (GB)**, 3, 115	E. S. Prado	New Economy, 3	Salty You, 3	8	1:47.75	$66,060
	Love n' Kiss S., 3, 114	J. A. Santos	Calista (GB), 3	Shooting Party, 3	8	**1:47.50**	$66,360
2000	**Lady Dora**, 3, 114	J. R. Velazquez	De Aar, 3	Tippity Witch, 3	11	1:48.76	$52,245
1999	**Eze**, 3, 113	R. G. Davis	Colstar, 3	Jazz, 3	6	1:52.96	$49,950
1998	**Sophie My Love**, 3, 118	J. R. Velazquez	Appealing Kris, 3	Proud Owner, 3	9	1:52.23	$51,150
1997	**Heaven's Command (GB)**, 3, 116	J. A. Santos	Wollastina, 3	Colonial Minstrel, 3	10	1:42.81	$51,375
1996	**Rare Blend**, 3, 115	G. L. Stevens	Polish Spring (Ire), 3	Inner Circle, 3	9	1:44.47	$52,110
1995	**Queen Tutta**, 3, 115	G. L. Stevens	Transient Trend, 3	Nappelon, 3	10	1:43.27	$53,820
1994	**Saxuality**, 3, 114	J. A. Krone	Lady Affirmed, 3	Tensie's Pro, 3	11	1:34.13	$41,580
1993	**Statuette**, 3, 121	M. E. Smith	Tricky Princess (Fr), 3	Belle Nuit, 3	11	1:40.68	$45,060

Named for 1985 champion turf female and English champion Pebbles (GB) (1981, f. by Sharpen Up [GB]). 1993-'95 Pebbles S. 1999-2001 Grade 3. 1993,1995-'97 1¹⁄₁₆ miles; 1994 1 mile. 1995, 2002 dirt. 2001 two divisions.

Pegasus Handicap

Grade 2, Meadowlands, three-year-olds, 1⅛ miles, dirt. Held September 27, 2002, with a gross value of $350,000. First held in 1980. Graded since 1983. Stakes record 1:45.50 (1999 Forty One Carats).

Year	Winner	Jockey	Second	Third	Strs	Time	1st Purse
2002	**Regal Sanction**, 3, 115	J. A. Santos	No Parole, 3	This Guns for Hire, 3	6	1:49.87	$210,000
2001	**Volponi**, 3, 114	S. Bridgmohan	Burning Roma, 3	Giant Gentleman, 3	6	1:46.55	$150,000
2000	**Kiss a Native**, 3, 119	M. Walls	Cool N Collective, 3	Pine Dance, 3	7	1:48.33	$150,000
1999	**Forty One Carats**, 3, 120	J. F. Chavez	Unbridled Jet, 3	Talk's Cheap, 3	6	**1:45.50**	$240,000
1998	**Tomorrows Cat**, 3, 113	J. Bravo	Limit Out, 3	Comic Strip, 3	6	1:46.95	$300,000
1997	**Behrens**, 3, 117	J. D. Bailey	Anet, 3	Frisk Me Now, 3	4	1:46.61	$600,000
1996	**Allied Forces**, 3, 116	R. Migliore	Lite Approval, 3	Defacto, 3	9	1:47.19	$120,000
1995	**Flying Chevron**, 3, 112	R. G. Davis	Da Hoss, 3	Ghostly Moves, 3	4	1:40.27	$120,000
1994	**Brass Scale**, 3, 114	E. S. Prado	Hello Chicago, 3	Serious Spender, 3	9	1:49.27	$120,000
1993	**Diazo**, 3, 117	L. A. Pincay Jr.	Press Card, 3	Schossberg, 3	7	1:47.18	$150,000
1992	**Scuffleburg**, 3, 111	J. A. Krone	Nines Wild, 3	Agincourt, 3	11	1:49.09	$300,000

Named for the winged horse of Greek mythology. 1980 Pegasus S.; 1996 Pegasus Breeders' Cup H.; 1997-'98 Buick Pegasus H. 1987-'93 Grade 1. 1980 6 furlongs; 1995-'96 1¹⁄₁₆ miles. 1996 turf. 1999 new track record.

Pennsylvania Derby

Grade 3, Philadelphia Park, three-year-olds, 1⅛ miles, dirt. Held September 2, 2002, with a gross value of $500,000. First held in 1979. Graded since 1981. Stakes record 1:47.60 (1989 Western Playboy).

Year	Winner	Jockey	Second	Third	Strs	Time	1st Purse
2002	**Harlan's Holiday**, 3, 122	E. S. Prado	Essence of Dubai, 3	Make the Bend, 3	5	1:51.10	$300,000
2001	**Macho Uno**, 3, 116	G. L. Stevens	†Unbridled Elaine, 3	Touch Tone, 3	6	1:49.69	$300,000

2000 **Pine Dance**, 3, 122	M. J. McCarthy	Mass Market, 3	Cherokeeinthehills, 3	10	1:49.03	$180,000
1999 **Smart Guy**, 3, 119	R. E. Colton	Ghost Ring, 3	Pineaff, 3	10	1:49.40	$180,000
1998 **Rock and Roll**, 3, 114	H. Castillo Jr.	Tomorrows Cat, 3	Black Blade, 3	11	1:47.69	$150,000
1997 **Frisk Me Now**, 3, 122	E. L. King Jr.	Envy of the Crown, 3	Christian Soldier, 3	8	1:48.14	$120,000
1996 **Devil's Honor**, 3, 122	A. S. Black	Formal Gold, 3	Clash by Night, 3	7	1:48.58	$120,000
1995 **Pineing Patty**, 3, 122	L. Melancon	Royal Haven, 3	Tenants Harbor, 3	12	1:48.05	$120,000
1994 **Meadow Flight**, 3, 122	J. Bravo	Red Tazz, 3	Kandaly, 3	9	1:49.08	$120,000
1993 **Wallenda**, 3, 114	W. H. McCauley	Press Card, 3	Saintly Prospector, 3	9	1:49.33	$120,000
1992 **Thelastcrusade**, 3, 114	V. H. Molina	Ecstatic Ride, 3	Nines Wild, 3	10	1:49.47	$90,000

1985-'95 Grade 2. †denotes female.

Personal Ensign Handicap

Grade 1, Saratoga Race Course, three-year-olds and up, fillies and mares, 1¼ miles, dirt. Held August 23, 2002, with a gross value of $400,000. First held in 1948. Graded since 1973. Stakes record 2:02.57 (1999 Beautiful Pleasure).

Year	Winner	Jockey	Second	Third	Strs	Time	1st Purse
2002	**Summer Colony**, 4, 120	J. R. Velazquez	Transcendental, 4	Dancethruthedawn, 4	6	2:03.15	$240,000
2001	**Pompeii**, 4, 117	R. Migliore	Beautiful Pleasure, 6	Irving's Baby, 4	7	2:04.60	$240,000
2000	**Beautiful Pleasure**, 5, 124	J. F. Chavez	Heritage of Gold, 5	Pentatonic, 5	5	2:03.77	$240,000
1999	**Beautiful Pleasure**, 4, 113	J. F. Chavez	Banshee Breeze, 4	Keeper Hill, 4	6	**2:02.57**	$240,000
1998	**Tomisue's Delight**, 4, 115	P. Day	Tuzia, 4	One Rich Lady, 4	8	2:04.08	$240,000
1997	**Clear Mandate**, 5, 115	M. E. Smith	Shoop, 6	Power Play, 5	6	2:03.71	$210,000
1996	**Urbane**, 4, 119	A. O. Solis	Shoop, 5	Frolic, 4	8	2:03.05	$180,000
1995	**Heavenly Prize**, 4, 127	P. Day	Forcing Bid, 4	Cinnamon Sugar (Ire), 4	8	2:04.16	$120,000
1994	**Link River**, 4, 114	J. A. Krone	You'd Be Surprised, 5	Dispute, 4	7	1:50.46	$120,000
1993	**You'd Be Surprised**, 4, 115	J. D. Bailey	Avian Assembly, 4	Gray Cashmere, 4	8	1:48.59	$90,000
1992	**Quick Mischief**, 6, 113	C. Perret	Versailles Treaty, 4	Shared Interest, 4	7	1:47.96	$120,000

Named for Ogden Phipps's undefeated 1988 champion older female and 1996 Broodmare of the Year Personal Ensign (1984, f. by Private Account). 1948-'85 Firenze H.; 1986-'97 John A. Morris H. 1983-'86 Grade 2. 1948-'57 held at Jamaica; 1958-'74,1976-'85 Aqueduct; 1975 Belmont. 1948-'51,1958 1¹⁄₁₆ miles; 1952-'57,1959,1962-'74,1976-'94 1¹⁄₈ miles; 1960-'61 1 mile; 1975 1³⁄₈ miles. 1972-'75 turf.

Peter Pan Stakes

Grade 2, Belmont Park, three-year-olds, 1¹⁄₈ miles, dirt. Held May 25, 2002, with a gross value of $200,000. First held in 1940. Graded since 1978. Stakes record 1:46.80 (1983 Slew o' Gold).

Year	Winner	Jockey	Second	Third	Strs	Time	1st Purse
2002	**Sunday Break (Jpn)**, 3, 121	G. L. Stevens	Puzzlement, 3	Deputy Dash, 3	7	1:48.10	$120,000
2001	**Hero's Tribute**, 3, 117	J. F. Chavez	E Dubai, 3	Dayton Flyer, 3	7	1:47.47	$120,000
2000	**Postponed**, 3, 113	E. S. Prado	Unshaded, 3	Globalize, 3	9	1:49.71	$120,000
1999	**Best of Luck**, 3, 113	J-L. Samyn	Treasure Island, 3	Lemon Drop Kid, 3	9	1:47.94	$90,000
1998	**Grand Slam**, 3, 120	J. D. Bailey	Rubiyat, 3	Parade Ground, 3	7	1:49.14	$90,000
1997	**Banker's Gold**, 3, 113	E. Maple	Zede, 3	Prince Guistino, 3	4	1:48.79	$90,000
1996	**Jamies First Punch**, 3, 118	J. R. Velazquez	Unbridled's Song, 3	Diligence, 3	5	1:47.32	$90,000
1995	**Citadeed**, 3, 112	E. Maple	Pat n Jac, 3	Treasurer (GB), 3	10	1:50.03	$90,000
1994	**Twining**, 3, 122	J. A. Santos	Lahint, 3	Gash, 3	5	1:49.11	$90,000
1993	**Virginia Rapids**, 3, 114	E. Maple	Colonial Affair, 3	Itaka, 3	6	1:48.48	$90,000
1992	**A.P. Indy**, 3, 126	E. J. Delahoussaye	Colony Light, 3	Berkley Fitz, 3	7	1:47.49	$106,380

Named for James R. Keene's 1907 Belmont S. winner and champion Peter Pan (1904-'33, c. by Commando). 1961-'74 not held. 1940-'60 Peter Pan H. 1978-'82 Grade 3; 1984-'86 Grade 1. 1940-'43,1945-'49,1952-'55,1958-'60,1975 held at Aqueduct. 1975-'76 1 mile. 1979 three-year-olds and up.

Philadelphia Park Breeders' Cup Handicap

Grade 3, Philadelphia Park, three-year-olds and up, 6 furlongs, dirt. Held July 6, 2002, with a gross value of $183,000. First held in 1986. Graded since 1988. Stakes record 1:07.89 (2000 Iron Punch).

Year	Winner	Jockey	Second	Third	Strs	Time	1st Purse
2001	**Say Florida Sandy**, 7, 118	A. T. Gryder	Wake At Noon, 4	Max's Pal, 4	4	1:08.51	$120,000
2000	**Iron Punch**, 6, 114	C. M. Cruz	Say Florida Sandy, 6	Just Call Me Carl, 5	7	**1:07.89**	$60,000
1999	**Loaded Gun**, 4, 114	J. L. Flores	Artax, 4	Power by Far, 4	9	1:08.52	$60,000
1998	**Buffalo Dan**, 7, 117	S. Elliott	Western Fame, 6	Inajam, 4	9	1:08.82	$120,000
1997	**Cat Be Nimble**, 5, 122	J. Rocco	Wire Me Collect, 4	Score a Birdie, 6	6	1:09.33	$90,000
1996	**Friendly Lover**, 8, 118	W. H. McCauley	Elajud, 4	Goldminer's Dream, 7	10	1:09.51	$90,000
1995	**Friendly Lover**, 7, 122	R. Wilson	Buffalo Dan, 4	Goldminer's Dream, 6	9	1:08.45	$93,420
1994	**King Ruckus**, 4, 122	T. Kabel	Friendly Lover, 6	Demaloot Demashoot, 4	6	1:09.07	$92,580
1993	**Blushing Julian**, 3, 111	R. E. Colton	Thelastcrusade, 4	Brukabookie, 6	7	1:09.77	$92,640
1992	**Smart Alec**, 4, 113	M. G. Pino	Megas Vukefalos, 4	Arrowtown, 4	7	1:09.69	$92,820

1986-'95 Philadelphia Park Budweiser Breeders' Cup H. 1986-'88 7 furlongs. 1998 Thunder Breeze finished third, DQ to eighth. 2000 new track record.

Philip H. Iselin Handicap

Grade 2, Monmouth Park, three-year-olds and up, 1¹⁄₈ miles, dirt. Held August 18, 2002, with a gross value of $350,000. First held in 1884. Graded since 1973. Stakes record 1:46.80 (1985 Spend a Buck; 1992 Jolie's Halo).

Year	Winner	Jockey	Second	Third	Strs	Time	1st Purse
2002	**Cat's At Home**, 5, 116	J. A. Velez Jr.	Bowman's Band, 4	Runspastum, 5	7	1:49.10	$210,000

2001	Broken Vow, 4, 119	R. A. Dominguez	First Lieutenant, 4	Sir Bear, 8	5	1:49.55	$210,000
2000	Rize, 4, 112	J. C. Ferrer	Sir Bear, 7	Talk's Cheap, 4	6	1:48.42	$210,000
1999	Frisk Me Now, 5, 117	E. L. King Jr.	Call Me Mr. Vain, 5	Black Cash, 4	6	1:49.00	$210,000
1998	Skip Away, 5, 131	J. D. Bailey	Stormin Fever, 4	Devil's Fire, 6	7	1:47.33	$300,000
1997	Formal Gold, 4, 121	K. J. Desormeaux	Skip Away, 4	Distorted Humor, 4	4	1:40.20	$250,000
1996	Smart Strike, 4, 115	C. Perret	Eltish, 4	†Serena's Song, 4	7	1:41.59	$180,000
1995	Schossberg, 5, 118	D. Penna	Poor But Honest, 5	Mickeray, 4	10	1:49.22	$180,000
1994	Taking Risks, 4, 115	M. T. Johnston	Valley Crossing, 6	Proud Shot, 4	9	1:48.33	$150,000
1993	Valley Crossing, 5, 113	C. W. Antley	Devil His Due, 4	Bertrando, 4	8	1:49.20	$300,000
1992	Jolie's Halo, 5, 116	E. S. Prado	Out of Place, 5	Valley Crossing, 4	11	**1:46.80**	$300,000

Named for Philip H. Iselin (1902-'76), president and chairman of the board of Monmouth Park (1966-'77). 1894-1945 not held. 1884-'93,1946-'66,1981-'85 Monmouth H.; 1967-'80 Amory L. Haskell H. 1973-'96 Grade 1. 1884-'93 1½ miles; 1956-'78 1¼ miles; 1996-'97 1¹⁄₁₆ miles. 1884-'86 two-year-olds and up. 1998 Testafly finished third, DQ to seventh. 1992 equaled track record. †denotes female.

Phoenix Breeders' Cup Stakes

Grade 3, Keeneland, three-year-olds and up, 6 furlongs, dirt. Held October 5, 2002, with a gross value of $250,000. First held in 1831. Graded since 2000. Stakes record 1:07.78 (1993 Anjiz).

Year	Winner	Jockey	Second	Third	Strs	Time	1st Purse
2002	Xtra Heat, 4, 123	H. Vega	Day Trader, 3	Touch Tone, 4	5	1:10.13	$155,000
2001	Bet On Sunshine, 9, 123	C. H. Borel	Robin de Nest, 4	Eriton, 5	5	1:09.65	$166,470
2000	Five Star Day, 4, 119	G. K. Gomez	Istintaj, 4	Bet On Sunshine, 8	5	1:07.90	$167,245
1999	Richter Scale, 5, 117	K. J. Desormeaux	Bet On Sunshine, 7	Vicar, 3	6	1:08.40	$166,780
1998	Partner's Hero, 4, 117	C. H. Borel	Pyramid Peak, 6	High Stakes Player, 6	6	1:09.25	$100,533
1997	Bet On Sunshine, 5, 123	F. C. Torres	Receiver, 4	Valid Expectations, 4	5	1:08.70	$97,464
1996	Forest Wildcat, 5, 121	J. Bravo	Valid Expectations, 3	Bet On Sunshine, 4	10	1:09.57	$101,246
1995	Golden Gear, 4, 124	C. Perret	Hello Paradise, 4	Mississippi Chat, 3	6	1:08.96	$67,456
1994	Lost Pan, 4, 114	D. M. Barton	Pacific West, 4	Fort Chaffee, 4	5	1:09.45	$33,728
1993	Anjiz, 5, 114	D. A. Miller Jr.	Gold Spring (Arg), 5	Friendly Lover, 5	9	**1:07.78**	$50,251
1992	British Banker, 4, 114	D. Kutz	Megas Vukefalos, 4	Binalong, 3	6	1:09.20	$49,693

Named for the old Phoenix Hotel in Lexington, Kentucky; oldest recognized race in North America. The race has also been known as the Brennan, Chiles, Phoenix, Association, Phoenix Hotel S. and Phoenix H. 1898-1904; 1906-'10,1914-'16,1929,1931-'36 not held. 1937-'89 Phoenix H.; 1990-'91 Phoenix Breeders' Cup H.; 1994-'95 Phoenix S. 1831-1930 held at Kentucky Association; 1943-'45 Churchill Downs. 1831-'77 held as a heat race. 1993 new track record.

Pimlico Breeders' Cup Distaff Handicap

Grade 3, Pimlico, three-year-olds and up, fillies and mares, 1¹⁄₁₆ miles, dirt. Held May 17, 2002, with a gross value of $148,500. First held in 1992. Graded since 1994. Stakes record 1:42.90 (2002 Summer Colony).

Year	Winner	Jockey	Second	Third	Strs	Time	1st Purse
2002	Summer Colony, 4, 121	J. R. Velazquez	Dancethruthedawn, 4	Happily Unbridled, 4	7	**1:42.90**	$90,000
2001	Serra Lake, 4, 112	P. Day	Jostle, 4	Prized Stamp, 4	6	1:50.22	$120,000
2000	Roza Robata, 5, 114	P. Day	Bella Chiarra, 5	On a Soapbox, 4	8	1:49.82	$120,000
1999	Mil Kilates, 6, 113	S. J. Sellers	Merengue, 4	Unbridled Hope, 5	8	1:49.05	$120,000
1998	Ajina, 4, 120	J. D. Bailey	Naskra Colors, 6	Pocho's Dream Girl, 4	8	1:48.70	$120,000
1997	Rare Blend, 4, 114	J. D. Bailey	Scenic Point, 4	Aileen's Countess, 5	5	1:51.51	$120,000
1996	Serena's Song, 4, 123	G. L. Stevens	Shoop, 5	Churchbell Chimes, 5	4	1:49.75	$120,000
1995	Pennyhill Park, 5, 115	M. E. Smith	Halo America, 5	Calipha, 4	6	1:49.32	$120,000
1994	Double Sixes, 4, 112	E. S. Prado	Broad Gains, 4	Mz. Zill Bear, 5	6	1:51.19	$120,000
1993	Deputation, 4, 114	C. W. Antley	D. Theatrical Gal, 4	Low Tolerance, 4	6	1:49.12	$120,000
1992	Wilderness Song, 4, 121	C. Perret	Harbour Club, 5	Brilliant Brass, 5	7	1:49.06	$150,000

1992-'01 1⅛ miles.

Pimlico Special Handicap

Grade 1, Pimlico, three-year-olds and up, 1³⁄₁₆ miles, dirt. Held May 16, 2003, with a gross value of $600,000. First held in 1937. Graded since 1990. Stakes record 1:53 (1990 Criminal Type).

Year	Winner	Jockey	Second	Third	Strs	Time	1st Purse
2003	Mineshaft, 4, 121	R. Albarado	Western Pride, 5	Judge's Case, 6	9	1:56.16	$400,000
2001	Include, 4, 114	J. D. Bailey	Albert the Great, 4	Pleasant Breeze, 6	6	1:55.61	$500,000
2000	Golden Missile, 5, 116	K. J. Desormeaux	Pleasant Breeze, 5	Lemon Drop Kid, 4	8	1:54.65	$450,000
1999	Real Quiet, 4, 120	G. L. Stevens	Free House, 5	Fred Bear Claw, 5	5	1:54.31	$300,000
1998	Skip Away, 5, 128	J. D. Bailey	Precocity, 4	Hot Brush, 4	5	1:54.26	$450,000
1997	Gentlemen (Arg), 5, 122	G. L. Stevens	Skip Away, 4	Tejano Run, 5	8	1:53.03	$360,000
1996	Star Standard, 4, 111	P. Day	Key of Luck, 5	Geri, 4	6	1:54.46	$360,000
1995	Cigar, 5, 122	J. D. Bailey	Devil His Due, 6	Concern, 4	6	1:53.72	$360,000
1994	As Indicated, 4, 120	R. G. Davis	Devil His Due, 5	Valley Crossing, 5	5	1:55.08	$360,000
1993	Devil His Due, 4, 120	W. H. McCauley	Valley Crossing, 5	Pistols and Roses, 4	6	1:55.53	$510,000
1992	Strike the Gold, 4, 114	C. Perret	Fly So Free, 4	Twilight Agenda, 6	7	1:54.86	$420,000

In the past, "special" races were winner take all. 1959-'87, 2002 not held. 1937,1954 three-year-olds; 1988-'97 four-year-olds and up. 1993 winner's share includes mid-series bonus of $150,000 from ACRS.

Poker Handicap

Grade 3, Belmont Park, three-year-olds and up, 1 mile, turf. Held July 5, 2002, with a gross value of $100,000. First held in 1985. Graded since 1988. Stakes record 1:31.63 (1998 Elusive Quality [new and current world record]).

Year	Winner	Jockey	Second	Third	Strs	Time	1st Purse
2002	Volponi, 4, 115	S. Bridgmohan	Saint Verre, 4	Navesink, 4	7	1:32.24	$66,720
2001	Affirmed Success, 7, 121	J. D. Bailey	In Frank's Honor, 5	Union One, 4	6	1:34.60	$66,240
2000	Affirmed Success, 6, 117	J. F. Chavez	Rabi (Ire), 4	Weatherbird, 5	10	1:34.06	$68,280
1999	Rob 'n Gin, 5, 118	J. F. Chavez	Bomfim, 6	Wised Up, 4	8	1:32.81	$69,120
1998	Elusive Quality, 5, 117	J. D. Bailey	Za-Im (GB), 4	Fortitude, 5	9	**1:31.63**	$51,240
1997	Draw Shot, 4, 118	C. W. Antley	Val's Prince, 5	Fortitude, 4	10	1:33.08	$51,345
1996	Smooth Runner, 5, 113	J. A. Krone	Mighty Forum (GB), 5	Da Hoss, 4	10	1:33.62	$51,600
1995	Caress, 4, 117	R. G. Davis	Fourstars Allstar, 7	Pennine Ridge, 4	9	1:34.35	$51,030
1994	Dominant Prospect, 4, 114	J. F. Chavez	Fourstardave, 9	Nijinsky's Gold, 5	8	1:32.69	$49,905
1993	Fourstardave, 8, 117	R. Migliore	Adam Smith (GB), 5	Lech, 5	7	1:33.02	$53,190
1992	Scott the Great, 6, 117	J-L. Samyn	Kate's Valentine, 7	Cigar Toss (Arg), 5	7	1:33.27	$54,810

Named for 1967 Bowling Green H. winner Poker (1963-'86, c. by Round Table), broodmare sire of Seattle Slew and Silver Charm. 1985-'95 Poker S.

Potrero Grande Breeders' Cup Handicap

Grade 2, Santa Anita Park, four-year-olds and up, 6½ furlongs, dirt. Held March 29, 2003, with a gross value of $134,000. First held in 1983. Graded since 1988. Stakes record 1:13.71 (1998 Son of a Pistol).

Year	Winner	Jockey	Second	Third	Strs	Time	1st Purse
2003	Bluesthestandard, 6, 115	M. E. Smith	Joey Franco, 4	Kona Gold, 9	7	1:14.86	$72,000
2002	†Kalookan Queen, 6, 116	A. O. Solis	Ceeband, 5	Elaborate, 7	8	1:15.31	$130,620
2001	Kona Gold, 7, 126	A. O. Solis	(DH) Hollycombe, 7		4	1:15.03	$123,000
			(DH) Explicit, 4				
2000	Kona Gold, 6, 122	A. O. Solis	Old Topper, 5	Your Halo, 5	5	1:14.75	$123,060
1999	Big Jag, 6, 119	J. Valdivia Jr.	Gold Land, 8	Son of a Pistol, 7	5	1:15.09	$123,720
1998	Son of a Pistol, 6, 114	G. K. Gomez	White Bronco, 4	Gold Land, 7	9	**1:13.71**	$66,420
1997	First Intent, 8, 114	R. R. Douglas	Hesabull, 4	Northern Afleet, 4	6	1:14.75	$64,250
1996	Abaginone, 5, 115	G. L. Stevens	Dramatic Gold, 5	Kingdom Found, 6	6	1:14.59	$124,400
1995	Lit de Justice, 5, 115	C. S. Nakatani	Cardmania, 9	Phone Roberto, 9	6	1:14.65	$63,000
1994	Sir Hutch, 4, 117	P. A. Valenzuela	Concept Win, 4	Furiously, 4	5	1:14.48	$61,100
1993	Gray Slewpy, 5, 118	K. J. Desormeaux	Cardmania, 7	Star of the Crop, 7	8	1:14.91	$64,700
1992	Cardmania, 6, 117	E. Delahoussaye	Frost Free, 7	Answer Do, 7	4	1:17.16	$60,200

Named for Potrero Grande Rancho, near present-day El Monte; potrero grande means "big pasture." 1983-'95 Potrero Grande H. 1988-'96 Grade 3. 1998 new track record. 1999 Early Pioneer finished second, DQ to fourth. 2001 dead heat for second.

Prairie Meadows Cornhusker Breeders' Cup Handicap

Grade 3, Prairie Meadows, three-year-olds and up, 1⅛ miles, dirt. Held July 6, 2002, with a gross value of $400,000. First held in 1966. Graded since 1973. Stakes record 1:46.62 (1998 Beboppin Baby).

Year	Winner	Jockey	Second	Third	Strs	Time	1st Purse
2002	Mr. John, 4, 114	M. Guidry	Unshaded, 5	Fajardo, 5	10	1:47.97	$240,000
2001	Euchre, 5, 116	G. K. Gomez	Dixie Dot Com, 6	Sure Shot Biscuit, 5	7	1:47.72	$240,000
2000	Sir Bear, 7, 116	E. Coa	Skimming, 4	Ecton Park, 4	5	1:48.49	$240,000
1999	Nite Dreamer, 4, 113	R. Albarado	Mocha Express, 5	Worldly Ways (GB), 5	7	1:48.85	$231,000
1998	Beboppin Baby, 5, 114	J. Campbell	Acceptable, 4	Pacificbounty, 4	8	**1:46.62**	$150,000
1997	Semoran, 4, 117	D. R. Flores	Mister Fire Eyes (Ire), 6	Come On Flip, 6	9	1:48.47	$120,000
1995	Powerful Punch, 6, 115	C. C. Bourque	All Gone, 5	Glaring, 5	8	1:49.80	$90,000
1994	Zeeruler, 6, 116	R. N. Lester	Powerful Punch, 5	Dancing Jon, 6	8	1:50.20	$75,000
1993	Link, 5, 114	Ronald Ardoin	Rapid World, 5	Flying Continental, 7	9	1:50.40	$75,000
1992	Irish Swap, 5, 117	B. E. Poyadou	Zeeruler, 4	Stalwars, 7	11	1:47.80	$75,000

The Cornhusker Handicap was formerly held at AKsarben in Nebraska, the "Cornhusker State." 1996 not held. 1966-'72,1985-'95 Cornhusker H.; 1973-'84 Ak-Sar-Ben Cornhusker H.; 1997 Prairie Meadows Cornhusker H. 1966-'95 held at AKsarben. 1966-'73 1¹⁄₁₆ miles. 1998 new track record.

Preakness Stakes

(See Triple Crown section for complete history of the Preakness Stakes)

Grade 1, Pimlico, three-year-olds, 1³⁄₁₆ miles, dirt. Held May 17, 2003, with a gross value of $1,000,000. First held in 1873. Graded since 1973. Stakes record 1:53 ²⁄₅ (1985 Tank's Prospect, Louis Quatorze, 1:53.43).

Year	Winner	Jockey	Second	Third	Strs	Time	1st Purse
2003	Funny Cide, 3, 126	J. Santos	Midway Road, 3	Scrimshaw, 3	10	1:55.61	$650,000
2002	War Emblem, 3, 126	V. Espinoza	Magic Weisner, 3	Proud Citizen, 3	13	1:56.36	$650,000
2001	Point Given, 3, 126	G. L. Stevens	A P Valentine, 3	Congaree, 3	11	1:55.51	$650,000
2000	Red Bullet, 3, 126	J. D. Bailey	Fusaichi Pegasus, 3	Impeachment, 3	8	1:56.04	$650,000
1999	Charismatic, 3, 126	C. W. Antley	Menifee, 3	Badge, 3	13	1:55.32	$650,000
1998	Real Quiet, 3, 126	K. J. Desormeaux	Victory Gallop, 3	Classic Cat, 3	10	1:54.75	$650,000
1997	Silver Charm, 3, 126	G. L. Stevens	Free House, 3	Captain Bodgit, 3	10	1:54.84	$488,150
1996	Louis Quatorze, 3, 126	P. Day	Skip Away, 3	Editor's Note, 3	12	1:53.43	$458,120

1995	**Timber Country**, 3, 126	P. Day	Oliver's Twist, 3	Thunder Gulch, 3	11	1:54.45	$446,810
1994	**Tabasco Cat**, 3, 126	P. Day	Go for Gin, 3	Concern, 3	10	1:56.47	$447,720
1993	**Prairie Bayou**, 3, 126	M. E. Smith	Cherokee Run, 3	El Bakan, 3	12	1:56.61	$471,835
1992	**Pine Bluff**, 3, 126	C. J. McCarron	Alydeed, 3	Casual Lies, 3	14	1:55.60	$484,120

Named for Preakness (1867-'81, c. by Lexington), first winner of the Dinner Party S. (now the Dixie S.) at Pimlico. 1891-'93 not held. 1894 1½ miles; 1889 1¼ miles; 1894-1900,1908 1¹⁄₁₆ miles; 1901-'07 1 mile 70 yards; 1909-'10 1 mile; 1911-'24 1¹⁄₈ miles. 1890 held at Morris Park; 1894-1908 Gravesend Park. Dancer's Image finished third, DQ to eighth.

Princess Rooney Handicap

Grade 2, Calder Race Course, three-year-olds and up, fillies and mares, 6 furlongs, dirt. Held July 13, 2002, with a gross value of $400,000. First held in 1985. Graded since 1999. Stakes record 1:10.12 (1998 U Can Do It).

Year	Winner	Jockey	Second	Third	Strs	Time	1st Purse
2002	**Gold Mover**, 4, 115	J. D. Bailey	Xtra Heat, 4	Fly Me Crazy, 4	6	1:10.21	$240,000
2001	**Dream Supreme**, 4, 122	P. Day	Hidden Assets, 4	Sugar N Spice, 6	9	1:10.48	$240,000
2000	**Hurricane Bertie**, 5, 117	P. Day	Bourbon Belle, 5	Cassidy, 5	7	1:11.43	$240,000
1999	**Princess Pietrina**, 5, 114	R. B. Homeister Jr.	Hurricane Bertie, 4	U Can Do It, 6	8	1:10.49	$180,000
1998	**U Can Do It**, 5, 118	E. Coa	Closed Escrow, 5	Colonial Minstrel, 4	9	**1:10.12**	$150,000
1997	**Vivace**, 4, 117	R. P. Romero	Ashboro, 4	Special Request, 4	9	1:10.94	$150,000
1996	**Chaposa Springs**, 4, 126	L. A. Pincay Jr.	Reign Dance, 4	Supah Jess, 4	6	1:23.54	$60,000
1995	**Miss Gibson County**, 4, 115	G. Boulanger	Goldarama, 5	Sigrun, 5	7	1:23.18	$60,000
1994	**Roamin Rachel**, 4, 119	W. S. Ramos	Sigrun, 4	Goldarama, 4	10	1:24.01	$60,000
1993	**Lady Sonata**, 4, 115	M. A. Lee	Fortune Forty Four, 4	Treasured, 6	5	1:23.00	$30,000
1992	**Magal**, 5, 117	R. Hernandez	Fortune Forty Four, 3	My Own True Love, 4	8	1:23.60	$30,000

Named for 1984 champion older female Princess Rooney (1980, f. by Verbatim). 1999-2001 Grade 3. 1985-'96 7 furlongs.

Princess Stakes

Grade 2, Hollywood Park, three-year-olds, fillies, 1¹⁄₁₆ miles, dirt. Held June 16, 2001, with a gross value of $100,000. First held in 1966. Graded since 1973. Stakes record 1:41.27 (1992 Race the Wild Wind).

Year	Winner	Jockey	Second	Third	Strs	Time	1st Purse
2001	**Starrer**, 3, 115	C. J. McCarron	Love At Noon, 3	Affluent, 3	6	1:41.90	$60,000
2000	**Queenie Belle**, 3, 116	B. Blanc	Saudi Poetry, 3	Cash Run, 3	6	1:43.57	$90,000
1999	**Excellent Meeting**, 3, 122	K. J. Desormeaux	Colorado Song, 3	Dianehill (Ire), 3	6	1:41.73	$75,000
1998	**Sweet and Ready**, 3, 116	C. J. McCarron	Brulay, 3	Visible Slew, 3	4	1:42.52	$90,000
1997	**Freeport Flight**, 3, 115	E. J. Delahoussaye	Really Happy, 3	Desert Digger, 3	6	1:43.99	$64,440
1996	**Listening**, 3, 115	C. J. McCarron	Najecam, 3	Pike Place Dancer, 3	5	1:42.96	$63,660
1995	**Favored One**, 3, 119	A. O. Solis	Our Summer Bid, 3	Sleep Easy, 3	8	1:43.98	$64,100
1994	**Sardula**, 3, 119	E. J. Delahoussaye	Fancy 'n Fabulous, 3	Pirate's Revenge, 3	4	1:42.57	$60,200
1993	**Fit to Lead**, 3, 117	E. J. Delahoussaye	Swazi's Moment, 3	Passing Vice, 3	5	1:42.52	$61,000
1992	**Race the Wild Wind**, 3, 119	C. J. McCarron	Magical Maiden, 3	Looie Capote, 3	5	**1:41.27**	$61,800

2002 not held. 1973-'86 Grade 3. 1985-'86 1 mile. 1968-'73 turf.

Prioress Stakes

Grade 1, Belmont Park, three-year-olds, fillies, 6 furlongs, dirt. Held July 6, 2002, with a gross value of $200,000. First held in 1948. Graded since 1973. Stakes record 1:08.26 (2001 Xtra Heat).

Year	Winner	Jockey	Second	Third	Strs	Time	1st Purse
2002	**Carson Hollow**, 3, 114	J. R. Velazquez	Spring Meadow, 3	Proper Gamble, 3	7	1:08.79	$120,000
2001	**Xtra Heat**, 3, 121	R. Wilson	Above Perfection, 3	Harmony Lodge, 3	7	**1:08.26**	$120,000
2000	**I'm Brassy**, 3, 113	M. J. Luzzi	Dat You Miz Blue, 3	Lucky Livi, 3	9	1:09.53	$90,000
1999	**Sapphire n' Silk**, 3, 121	P. Day	Marley Vale, 3	Confessional, 3	8	1:09.55	$90,000
1998	**Hurricane Bertie**, 3, 121	P. Day	Catinca, 3	Foil, 3	11	1:08.85	$68,220
1997	**Pearl City**, 3, 118	J. D. Bailey	Alyssum, 3	Vegas Prospector, 3	5	1:09.40	$64,680
1996	**Capote Belle**, 3, 112	J. R. Velazquez	Flat Fleet Feet, 3	Miss Maggie, 3	10	1:08.81	$67,200
1995	**Scotzanna**, 3, 121	R. Platts	Culver City, 3	Miss Golden Circle, 3	9	1:10.61	$66,840
1994	**Penny's Reshoot**, 3, 116	J. R. Velazquez	Heavenly Prize, 3	Beckys Shirt, 3	6	1:09.07	$64,500
1993	**Classy Mirage**, 3, 114	J. A. Krone	Missed the Storm, 3	Educated Risk, 3	5	1:08.89	$67,680
1992	**American Royale**, 3, 118	J. A. Santos	Debra's Victory, 3	Preach, 3	6	1:09.36	$68,280

Named for the first American Thoroughbred to ever win a race in England, Prioress (1853, by *Sovereign). 1973-'74,1985-'87 Grade 3; 1975-'84 not graded; 1988-2000 Grade 2. 1948-'59 held at Jamaica; 1960-'86 Aqueduct.

Pucker Up Stakes

Grade 3, Arlington Park, three-year-olds, fillies, 1¹⁄₈ miles, turf. Held September 14, 2002, with a gross value of $150,000. First held in 1961. Graded since 1973. Stakes record 1:47.58 (1991 Jinski's World).

Year	Winner	Jockey	Second	Third	Strs	Time	1st Purse
2002	**Little Treasure (Fr)**, 3, 122	R. R. Douglas	Cellars Shiraz, 3	Kathy K D, 3	11	1:49.92	$90,000
2001	**Snow Dance**, 3, 122	C. Perret	Kiss the Devil, 3	Twilite Tryst, 3	12	1:47.93	$90,000
2000	**Solvig**, 3, 121	P. Day	Zoftig, 3	Impending Bear, 3	6	1:52.40	$90,000
1997	**Witchful Thinking**, 3, 121	G. K. Gomez	Swearingen, 3	Cozy Blues, 3	8	1:48.88	$75,000
1996	**Ms. Mostly**, 3, 114	R. P. Romero	Mountain Affair, 3	Clamorosa, 3	9	1:51.18	$90,000

1995	Grand Charmer, 3, 116	P. Day	Upper Noosh, 3	Set Me Straight, 3	8	1:49.59	$60,000
1994	Work the Crowd, 3, 118	A. T. Gryder	Irish Forever, 3	Looking for Heaven, 3	14	1:49.32	$60,000
1993	Amal Hayati, 3, 113	W. S. Ramos	Warside, 3	Future Starlet, 3	11	1:53.39	$60,000
1992	Ziggy's Act, 3, 116	G. Boulanger	Bernique, 3	Luv Me Luv Me Not, 3	10	1:48.79	$60,000

Named for 1957 champion handicap mare Pucker Up (1953-'75, f. by Olympia). 1988,1998-'99 not held. 1961,1963-'73 Pucker Up H. 1979 not graded; 1996-'97 Grade 2. 1985 held at Hawthorne. 1961,1966-'73 1 mile; 1962-'65,1974-'75,1986 1¹/₁₆ miles; 1979 1³/₁₆ miles. 1961-'74,1976 dirt.

Queen Elizabeth II Challenge Cup Stakes

Grade 1, Keeneland, three-year-olds, fillies, 1¹/₈ miles, turf. Held October 12, 2002, with a gross value of $500,000. First held in 1984. Graded since 1986. Stakes record 1:45.81 (1996 Memories of Silver).

Year	Winner	Jockey	Second	Third	Strs	Time	1st Purse
2002	Riskaverse, 3, 121	M. Guidry	Zenda (GB), 3	Lush Soldier, 3	9	1:49.84	$310,000
2001	Affluent, 3, 121	E. J. Delahoussaye	Golden Apples (Ire), 3	Snow Dance, 3	10	1:50.03	$310,000
2000	Collect the Cash, 3, 121	S. J. Sellers	Blue Moon (Fr), 3	Theoretically, 3	9	1:47.94	$310,000
1999	Perfect Sting, 3, 121	P. Day	Tout Charmant, 3	Wannabe Grand (Ire), 3	9	1:50.66	$310,000
1998	Tenski, 3, 121	R. Migliore	Shires Ende, 3	Sierra Virgen, 3	9	1:48.54	$248,000
1997	Ryafan, 3, 121	A. O. Solis	Auntie Mame, 3	Golden Arches (Fr), 3	8	1:46.64	$248,000
1996	Memories of Silver, 3, 121	R. G. Davis	Shake the Yoke (GB), 3	Antespend, 3	10	**1:45.81**	$248,000
1995	Perfect Arc, 3, 121	J. R. Velazquez	Auriette (Ire), 3	Country Cat, 3	8	1:49.84	$155,000
1994	Danish (Ire), 3, 121	J. A. Krone	Eternal Reve, 3	Avie's Fancy, 3	10	1:48.89	$124,000
1993	Tribulation, 3, 121	J-L. Samyn	Miami Sands (Ire), 3	Possibly Perfect, 3	9	1:53.62	$124,000
1992	Captive Miss, 3, 121	J. A. Krone	Suivi, 3	Trampoli, 3	10	1:48.66	$124,000

Named in honor of the 1984 visit of Queen Elizabeth II of England to Central Kentucky; she presented the first winner's trophy. 1986-'87 Grade 3; 1988-'90 Grade 2. 1987 1¹/₁₆ miles. 1984-'86 dirt.

Queens County Handicap

Grade 3, Aqueduct, three-year-olds and up, 1³/₁₆ miles, dirt. Held December 7, 2002, with a gross value of $100,000. First held in 1902. Graded since 1973. Stakes record 1:54.40 (1972 Sunny and Mild).

Year	Winner	Jockey	Second	Third	Strs	Time	1st Purse
2002	Snake Mountain, 4, 117	J. A. Santos	Docent, 4	Cat's At Home, 5	7	1:56.84	$66,000
2001	Evening Attire, 3, 113	S. Bridgmohan	Balto Star, 3	Top Official, 6	8	1:55.08	$67,140
2000	Boston Party, 4, 114	N. Arroyo Jr.	Talk's Cheap, 4	Turnofthecentury, 3	9	1:56.32	$50,340
1999	Early Warning, 4, 116	J. F. Chavez	Doc Martin, 4	Yankee Victor, 3	7	1:55.03	$49,230
1998	Fire King, 5, 113	F. Lovato Jr.	Las Vegas Ernie, 4	Mr. Sinatra, 4	7	1:56.88	$49,140
1997	Mr. Sinatra, 3, 115	R. Migliore	Delay of Game, 4	Draw, 4	8	1:55.68	$49,725
1996	Topsy Robsy, 4, 111	P. Keim-Bruno	More to Tell, 5	Colonial Secretary, 4	5	1:55.30	$48,705
1995	Aztec Empire, 5, 113	J-L. Samyn	Mighty Magee, 3	More to Tell, 4	9	1:55.56	$50,340
1994	Federal Funds, 5, 112	D. Carr	Jacksonport, 5	Contract Court, 4	8	1:56.42	$49,665
1993	Repletion, 4, 111	M. E. Smith	Dibbs n' Dubbs, 4	Primitive Hall, 4	8	1:44.35	$53,010
1992	Shots Are Ringing, 5, 117	J. R. Velazquez	A Call to Rise, 4	Jacksonport, 4	6	1:54.90	$51,120

Named for Queens County, New York, in which Aqueduct is located. 1909,1911-'13 not held. 1973-'74 Grade 2; 1980 not graded. 1946 held at Belmont Park; 1956-'58 Jamaica. 1902-'03 1 mile 70 yards; 1904-'39,1959-'62 1 mile; 1940-'58,1993 1¹/₁₆ miles; 1963-'71 1¹/₈ miles.

Railbird Stakes

Grade 3, Hollywood Park, three-year-olds, fillies, 7 furlongs, dirt. Held May 18, 2002, with a gross value of $100,000. First held in 1963. Graded since 1973. Stakes record 1:20.60 (1979 Eloquent).

Year	Winner	Jockey	Second	Third	Strs	Time	1st Purse
2002	September Secret, 3, 118	P. A. Valenzuela	Affairs of State, 3	Fun House, 3	5	1:22.95	$63,780
2001	Golden Ballet, 3, 123	C. J. McCarron	Starrer, 3	Pretty 'n Smart, 3	6	1:21.57	$90,000
2000	Cover Gal, 3, 122	L. A. Pincay Jr.	Wired to Fly, 3	Classic Olympio, 3	5	1:22.57	$90,000
1999	Olympic Charmer, 3, 115	C. J. McCarron	Dianehill (Ire), 3	Fee Fi Foe, 3	9	1:21.18	$90,000
1998	Brulay, 3, 115	G. L. Stevens	Gourmet Girl, 3	Unreal Squeal, 3	5	1:20.84	$64,260
1997	I Ain't Bluffing, 3, 118	E. J. Delahoussaye	Really Happy, 3	Montecito, 3	7	1:22.77	$66,840
1996	Supercilious, 3, 121	C. S. Nakatani	Tiffany Diamond, 3	Raw Gold, 3	6	1:22.55	$64,260
1995	Sleep Easy, 3, 113	C. S. Nakatani	Texinadress, 3	Laguna Seca, 3	6	1:22.42	$64,600
1994	Sportful Snob, 3, 118	P. A. Valenzuela	Pirate's Revenge, 3	Accountable Lady, 3	5	1:21.94	$61,400
1993	Afto, 3, 114	P. Atkinson	Fit to Lead, 3	Nijivision, 3	8	1:22.48	$64,500
1992	She's Tops, 3, 114	K. J. Desormeaux	Race the Wild Wind, 3	Magical Maiden, 3	9	1:22.78	$66,500

Named for racing fans who watch races from along the rail, known as "railbirds." 1963-'64 Railbird H. 1988,1991-2001 Grade 2. 1963 both sexes. 2001 Abby Girl finished first, DQ to fifth.

Rampart Handicap

Grade 2, Gulfstream Park, three-year-olds and up, fillies and mares, 1¹/₈ miles, dirt. Held March 1, 2003, with a gross value of $200,000. First held in 1976. Graded since 1986. Stakes record 1:47.92 (2003 Allamerican Bertie).

Year	Winner	Jockey	Second	Third	Strs	Time	1st Purse
2003	Allamerican Bertie, 4, 122	J. R. Velazquez	Smok'n Frolic, 4	Softly, 5	6	**1:47.92**	$120,000
2002	Forest Secrets, 4, 117	P. Day	Summer Colony, 4	Happily Unbridled, 4	6	1:49.83	$120,000
2001	De Bertie, 4, 116	J. F. Chavez	Apple of Kent, 5	Scratch Pad, 4	7	1:50.04	$120,000
2000	Bella Chiarra, 5, 116	S. J. Sellers	Lines of Beauty, 5	Up We Go, 4	8	1:43.27	$120,000

1999	Banshee Breeze, 4, 122	J. D. Bailey	Glitter Woman, 5	Timely Broad, 5	5	1:42.83	$120,000
1998	Dance for Thee, 4, 113	J. Bravo	Escena, 5	Glitter Woman, 4	6	1:44.73	$120,000
1997	Chip, 4, 114	J. Bravo	Rare Blend, 4	Hurricane Viv, 4	9	1:42.51	$120,000
1996	Investalot, 5, 114	S. J. Sellers	Queen Tutta, 4	Alcovy, 6	9	1:43.99	$120,000
1995	Educated Risk, 5, 126	M. E. Smith	Recognizable, 4	Jade Flush, 4	5	1:43.09	$120,000
1994	Nine Keys, 4, 113	M. E. Smith	Educated Risk, 4	Traverse City, 4	6	1:42.12	$120,000
1993	Girl On a Mission, 4, 112	J. D. Bailey	Luv Me Luv Me Not, 4	Haunting, 5	8	1:45.47	$120,000
1992	Fit for a Queen, 6, 119	J. D. Bailey	Firm Stance, 4	Nannerl, 5	12	1:43.66	$120,000

Named for Rampart (1942, f. by Trace Call), first distaff winner of the Gulfstream Park H. in 1948. 1977-'80 not held. 1989-'90 Johnnie Walker Black Classic H. 1986-'87 Grade 3. 1976 7 furlongs; 1981-2000 1¹⁄₁₆ miles. 1993 Now Dance finished second, DQ to fifth.

Rancho Bernardo Handicap

Grade 3, Del Mar, three-year-olds and up, fillies and mares, 6¹⁄₂ furlongs, dirt. Held August 25, 2002, with a gross value of $150,000. First held in 1967. Graded since 1988. Stakes record 1:14.28 (1995 Track Gal).

Year	Winner	Jockey	Second	Third	Strs	Time	1st Purse
2002	Kalookan Queen, 6, 123	A. O. Solis	Warren's Whistle, 4	Fancee Bargain, 6	5	1:16.40	$90,000
2001	Kalookan Queen, 5, 119	A. O. Solis	Go Go, 4	Warren's Whistle, 3	6	1:15.52	$90,000
2000	Theresa's Tizzy, 6, 117	L. A. Pincay Jr.	Nany's Sweep, 4	Hookedonthefeelin, 4	6	1:16.23	$90,000
1999	Enjoy the Moment, 4, 119	D. R. Flores	Snowberg, 4	Stop Traffic, 6	6	1:15.97	$90,000
1998	Advancing Star, 5, 120	C. J. McCarron	Closed Escrow, 5	Tiffany Diamond, 5	4	1:14.64	$64,140
1997	Track Gal, 6, 120	G. L. Stevens	Madame Pandit, 4	Advancing Star, 4	8	1:15.64	$69,125
1996	Track Gal, 5, 122	C. J. McCarron	Tricky Code, 5	Evil's Pic, 4	5	1:14.64	$63,550
1995	Track Gal, 4, 118	C. J. McCarron	Desert Stormer, 5	Lakeway, 4	5	1:14.28	$58,650
1994	Desert Stormer, 4, 116	E. J. Delahoussaye	Magical Maiden, 5	Booklore, 4	9	1:14.81	$62,800
1993	Knight Prospector, 4, 119	K. J. Desormeaux	Interactive, 4	Bountiful Native, 5	5	1:16.14	$45,675
1992	Bountiful Native, 4, 117	P. A. Valenzuela	Devil's Orchid, 5	She's Tops, 3	9	1:15.30	$63,400

Named for Rancho Bernardo, California. 1968-'72 not held. 1990-'95 Rancho Bernardo Breeders' Cup H. 1967 1 mile; 1973 1¹⁄₁₆ miles; 1974-'85 6 furlongs. 1973 turf. 1967-'73 both sexes.

Raven Run Stakes

Grade 3, Keeneland, three-year-olds, fillies, 7 furlongs, dirt. Held October 9, 2002, with a gross value of $150,000. First held in 1999. Graded since 2002. Stakes record 1:20.88 (2000 Darling My Darling).

Year	Winner	Jockey	Second	Third	Strs	Time	1st Purse
2002	Sightseek, 3, 117	J. D. Bailey	Miss Lodi, 3	Respectful, 3	12	1:23.98	$106,578
2001	Nasty Storm, 3, 123	P. Day	Hattiesburg, 3	Forest Secrets, 3	7	1:23.30	$68,138
2000	Darling My Darling, 3, 117	M. E. Smith	Surfside, 3	Cat Cay, 3	6	1:20.88	$51,104
1999	Dreamy Maiden, 3, 117	P. Day	Golden Illusion, 3	Cosmic Wing, 3	6	1:22.64	$37,076

Named for the Raven Run nature sanctuary located outside Lexington, Kentucky.

Razorback Handicap

Grade 3, Oaklawn Park, four-year-olds and up, 1¹⁄₁₆ miles, dirt. Held March 16, 2003, with a gross value of $100,000. First held in 1976. Graded since 1978. Stakes record 1:40.40 (1988 Lost Code).

Year	Winner	Jockey	Second	Third	Strs	Time	1st Purse
2003	Colorful Tour, 4, 118	L. S. Quinonez	Crafty Shaw, 5	Windward Passage, 4	7	1:43.53	$60,000
2002	Mr Ross, 7, 120	D. R. Pettinger	Remington Rock, 8	Big Numbers, 5	8	1:44.13	$60,000
2001	Mr Ross, 6, 119	D. R. Pettinger	Graeme Hall, 4	Maysville Slew, 5	9	1:42.60	$75,000
2000	Well Noted, 5, 112	T. T. Doocy	Crimson Classic, 6	Mr Ross, 5	7	1:43.21	$75,000
1999	Desert Air, 4, 113	C. J. Lanerie	Magnify, 6	Black Tie Dinner, 6	7	1:44.75	$75,000
1998	Brush With Pride, 6, 115	T. T. Doocy	Littlebitlively, 4	Krigeorj's Gold, 5	8	1:43.55	$75,000
1997	No Spend No Glow, 5, 115	R. N. Lester	Illesam, 5	Come On Flip, 6	8	1:43.38	$90,000
1996	Juliannus, 7, 113	R. Albarado	Judge T C, 5	Dazzling Falls, 4	5	1:43.37	$90,000
1995	Silver Goblin, 4, 124	D. W. Cordova	Joseph's Robe, 4	Wooden Ticket, 5	6	1:42.79	$120,000
1994	Prize Fight, 5, 113	P. A. Johnson	Brother Brown, 4	Country Store, 4	8	1:43.70	$90,000
1993	Lil E. Tee, 4, 123	P. Day	Zeeruler, 5	Senor Tomas, 4	7	1:41.55	$90,000
1992	Tokatee, 6, 115	G. K. Gomez	On the Edge, 5	Total Assets, 7	9	1:42.87	$90,000

Named for the unofficial state animal and University of Arkansas mascot, the razorback pig. 1985-'96 Grade 2.

Red Bank Handicap

Grade 3, Monmouth Park, three-year-olds and up, 1 mile, turf. Held May 25, 2002, with a gross value of $100,000. First held in 1974. Graded since 1986. Stakes record 1:33.34 (1991 Double Booked).

Year	Winner	Jockey	Second	Third	Strs	Time	1st Purse
2002	Key Lory, 8, 117	H. Vega	Sardaukar (GB), 6	Spruce Run, 4	8	1:35.92	$60,000
2001	Pavillon (Brz), 7, 112	J. Bravo	Western Summer, 4	Runspastum, 4	10	1:36.38	$90,000
2000	Mi Narrow, 6, 114	C. H. Velasquez	Deep Gold, 4	Inkatha (Fr), 6	9	1:34.84	$90,000
1999	Inkatha (Fr), 5, 114	H. Castillo Jr.	Rob 'n Gin, 5	Soviet Line (Ire), 9	8	1:33.95	$90,000
1998	Statesmanship, 4, 117	J. A. Santos	Rob 'n Gin, 4	Bomfim, 5	11	1:35.00	$60,000
1997	Basqueian, 6, 118	R. Wilson	Wild Night Out, 5	Jambalaya Jazz, 5	6	1:35.37	$60,000
1996	Joker, 4, 113	J. A. Velez Jr.	Rare Reason, 4	Diplomatic Jet, 4	8	1:35.90	$60,000
1995	Dove Hunt, 4, 118	W. H. McCauley	Rare Reason, 4	Winnetou, 5	9	1:33.95	$45,000

1994	**Adam Smith (GB)**, 6, 120	J. A. Krone	Discernment, 5	Fourstardave, 9	8	1:34.43	$45,000
1993	**Adam Smith (GB)**, 5, 116	J-L. Samyn	Fourstars Allstar, 5	Rinka Das, 5	8	1:34.39	$45,000
1992	**Daarik (Ire)**, 5, 114	L. Saumell	Leger Cat (Arg), 6	Kate's Valentine, 7	8	1:34.07	$45,000

Named for the town of Red Bank, New Jersey. 1974 Red Bank S. 1974-'75,1977-'79 1 1/16 miles; 1976 1 mile 70 yards. 1974-'78,1982,1987,1990,1997 dirt. 1974 two-year-olds. 1975-'79 fillies and mares. 1999 new course record.

Red Smith Handicap

Grade 3, Aqueduct, three-year-olds and up, 1 3/8 miles, dirt. Held November 23, 2002, with a gross value of $150,000. First held in 1960. Graded since 1973. Stakes record 2:14.44 (1999 Monarch's Maze).

Year	Winner	Jockey	Second	Third	Strs	Time	1st Purse
2002	**Evening Attire**, 4, 126	S. Bridgmohan	Fisher Pond, 3	Pleasant Breeze, 7	6	2:14.81	$90,000
2001	**Mr. Pleasentfar (Brz)**, 4, 115	J. A. Santos	Eltawaasul, 5	Regal Dynasty, 5	12	2:16.94	$90,000
2000	**Cetewayo**, 6, 114	R. Migliore	Understood, 4	Val's Prince, 8	13	2:17.93	$90,000
1999	**Monarch's Maze**, 3, 113	J. Bravo	Williams News, 4	Gritty Sandie, 3	14	2:14.44	$90,000
1998	**Musical Ghost**, 6, 115	J. R. Velazquez	Rice, 6	Plato's Love, 3	12	2:15.53	$90,000
1997	**Instant Friendship**, 4, 123	J. R. Velazquez	Demi's Bret, 4	Trample, 3	5	2:17.08	$90,000
1996	**Mr. Bluebird**, 5, 116	M. E. Smith	Ops Smile, 4	Raintrap (GB), 6	13	2:15.35	$87,750
1995	**Flag Down**, 5, 114	J. A. Santos	Party Season (GB), 4	Proceeded, 4	11	2:22.03	$69,900
1994	**Franchise Player**, 5, 109	D. V. Beckner	Red Bishop, 6	Same Old Wish, 4	14	2:20.53	$72,120
1993	**Royal Mountain Inn**, 4, 110	J. A. Krone	Spectacular Tide, 4	Share the Glory, 5	8	1:59.82	$71,760
1992	**Montserrat**, 4, 118	J. A. Krone	Preferences, 3	First Rate (Ire), 7	7	2:00.32	$70,920

Named in honor of Walter "Red" Smith, Pulitzer Prize-winning sports columnist. 1979 not held. 1960-'73,1976-'81,1974-'75 Edgemere S. 1981-2001 Grade 2. 1960-'62,1968-'78,1980-'93 held at Belmont. 1963-'67 1 3/16 miles; 1972-'76,1978,1980-'93 1 1/4 miles; 1977 1 1/16 miles. 1965-'83,1985-'96,1998-2001 turf.

Regret Stakes

Grade 3, Churchill Downs, three-year-olds, fillies, 1 1/16 miles, turf. Held June 15, 2002, with a gross value of $150,000. First held in 1970. Graded since 1999. Stakes record 1:42.06 (1992 Tiney Toast).

Year	Winner	Jockey	Second	Third	Strs	Time	1st Purse
2002	**Distant Valley (GB)**, 3, 119	J. D. Bailey	Peace River Lady, 3	Stylelistick, 3	9	1:42.71	$104,811
2001	**Casual Feat**, 3, 115	L. Melancon	Amaretta, 3	La Vida Loca (Ire), 3	9	1:42.75	$103,695
2000	**Solvig**, 3, 122	P. Day	Trip, 3	Miss Chief, 3	9	1:42.95	$104,439
1999	**Nani Rose**, 3, 115	S. J. Sellers	Solar Bound, 3	Suffragette, 3	8	1:42.40	$104,439
1998	**Formal Tango**, 3, 115	C. R. Woods Jr.	Adel, 3	Pratella, 3	10	1:43.73	$105,927
1997	**Starry Dreamer**, 3, 122	W. Martinez	Cozy Blues, 3	Swearingen, 3	8	1:42.77	$69,378
1996	**Daylight Come**, 3, 117	C. C. Bourque	Fleur de Nuit, 3	Esquive (GB), 3	9	1:45.72	$55,526
1995	**Christmas Gift**, 3, 122	C. R. Woods Jr.	Bail Out Becky, 3	Grand Charmer, 3	7	1:45.00	$54,210
1994	**Packet**, 3, 117	J. M. Johnson	Thread, 3	Slew Kitty Slew, 3	7	1:42.14	$54,551
1993	**Lovat's Lady**, 3, 112	B. D. Peck	Warside, 3	Mari's Key, 3	8	1:42.95	$36,595
1992	**Tiney Toast**, 3, 122	S. P. Payton	Shes Just Super, 3	Riverjinsky, 3	10	1:42.06	$37,440

Named for H. P. Whitney's Regret (1912-'34, f. by Broomstick), first female winner of the Kentucky Derby in 1915. 1970-'81 6 furlongs; 1982-'87 1 mile. 1970-'86 dirt.

Remsen Stakes

Grade 2, Aqueduct, two-year-olds, 1 1/8 miles, dirt. Held November 30, 2002, with a gross value of $200,000. First held in 1904. Graded since 1973. Stakes record 1:47.80 (1977 Believe It).

Year	Winner	Jockey	Second	Third	Strs	Time	1st Purse
2002	**Toccet**, 2, 122	J. F. Chavez	Bham, 2	Empire Maker, 2	8	1:50.40	$120,000
2001	**Saarland**, 2, 116	J. R. Velazquez	Nokoma, 2	Silent Fred, 2	9	1:51.28	$120,000
2000	**Windsor Castle**, 2, 116	R. G. Davis	Ommadon, 2	Buckle Down Ben, 2	8	1:51.92	$120,000
1999	**Greenwood Lake**, 2, 122	J-L. Samyn	Un Fino Vino, 2	Polish Miner, 2	8	1:50.63	$120,000
1998	**Comeonmom**, 2, 113	J. Bravo	Millions, 2	Wondertross, 2	9	1:49.84	$120,000
1997	**Coronado's Quest**, 2, 122	M. E. Smith	Halory Hunter, 2	Brooklyn Nick, 2	7	1:52.27	$120,000
1996	**The Silver Move**, 2, 114	R. Migliore	Jules, 2	Accelerator, 2	8	1:53.54	$120,000
1995	**Tropicool**, 2, 112	J. F. Chavez	Skip Away, 2	Crafty Friend, 2	11	1:50.30	$170,000
1994	**Thunder Gulch**, 2, 115	G. L. Stevens	Western Echo, 2	Mighty Magee, 2	10	1:53.80	$120,000
1993	**Go for Gin**, 2, 117	J. D. Bailey	Arrovente, 2	Linkatariat, 2	7	1:52.79	$120,000
1992	**Silver of Silver**, 2, 122	J. Vasquez	Dalhart, 2	Wild Gale, 2	11	1:50.25	$120,000

Named for Col. Joremus Remsen (1735-'90), leader of the Revolutionary forces at the battle of Long Island. 1908,1910-'17,1951 not held. 1904-'53 Remsen H. 1981-'88 Grade 1. 1904-'58 held at Jamaica. 1904-'09 5 1/2 furlongs; 1918-'45,1949-'50 6 furlongs; 1946-'47,1952-'58 1 1/16 miles; 1948 5 furlongs; 1959-'72 1 mile. 1954-'57 colts only; 1958-'60 colts and geldings.

Richter Scale Breeders' Cup Handicap

Grade 2, Gulfstream Park, three-year-olds and up, 7 furlongs, dirt. Held March 8, 2003, with a gross value of $200,000. First held in 1972. Graded since 1996. Stakes record 1:21.15 (2003 Tour of the Cat).

Year	Winner	Jockey	Second	Third	Strs	Time	1st Purse
2003	**Tour of the Cat**, 5, 116	A. Cabassa Jr.	Burning Roma, 5	Highway Prospector, 6	8	1:21.15	$120,000

2002	Dream Run, 4, 113	P. Day	Binthebest, 5	Burning Roma, 4	8	1:22.30	$120,000
2001	Hook and Ladder, 4, 115	R. Migliore	Trippi, 4	Rollin With Nolan, 4	6	1:21.85	$120,000
2000	Richter Scale, 6, 118	R. Migliore	Forty One Carats, 4	Kelly Kip, 6	10	1:23.30	$120,000
1999	Frisk Me Now, 5, 117	E. L. King Jr.	Young At Heart, 5	Good and Tough, 4	6	1:22.86	$60,000
1998	Rare Rock, 5, 117	P. Day	Irish Conquest, 5	Frisco View, 5	7	1:22.00	$120,000
1997	Frisco View, 4, 116	J. D. Bailey	El Amante, 4	Templado (Ven), 4	7	1:23.14	$98,160
1996	Patton, 5, 113	R. G. Davis	Forty Won, 5	Our Emblem, 5	10	1:21.81	$100,140
1995	Cherokee Run, 5, 122	M. E. Smith	Waldoboro, 4	Evil Bear, 5	6	1:21.70	$60,000
1994	I Can't Believe, 6, 113	E. Maple	American Chance, 5	British Banker, 6	8	1:22.55	$60,000
1993	Binalong, 4, 112	J. D. Bailey	Loach, 5	Richman, 5	6	1:22.35	$60,000
1992	Groomstick, 6, 112	W. S. Ramos	Ocala Flame, 4	Cold Digger, 5	9	1:23.98	$60,000

Named for Frank J. De Francis Memorial S. (G1) winner Richter Scale (1994, c. by *Habitony), who won the race named for him when it was called the Gulfstream Park Breeders' Cup Sprint Championship H. 1973,1975-'76,1978-'80,1982 not held. 1972,1974,1977,1981 Sprint Championship H.; 1983-'90 Gulfstream Sprint Championship H.; 1991-'93 Gulfstream Park Sprint Championship H.; 1994-'85 Gulfstream Park Sprint H.; 1996-2002 Gulfstream Park Breeders' Cup Sprint Championship H. 1996-'98 Grade 3. 1987,1990 6 furlongs.

Risen Star Stakes

Grade 3, Fair Grounds, three-year-olds, 1¹⁄₁₆ miles, dirt. Held February 16, 2003, with a gross value of $150,000. First held in 1973. Graded since 2002. Stakes record 1:42.98 (1996 Zarb's Magic).

Year	Winner	Jockey	Second	Third	Strs	Time	1st Purse
2003	Badge of Silver, 3, 116	R. Albarado	Lone Stary Sky, 3	Defrere's Vixen, 3	12	1:42.99	$90,000
2002	Repent, 3, 122	A. J. D'Amico	Bob's Image, 3	Easyfromthegitgo, 3	9	1:43.17	$90,000
2001	Dollar Bill, 3, 122	C. J. McCarron	Gracie's Dancer, 3	Rahy's Secret, 3	10	1:43.45	$75,000
2000	Exchange Rate, 3, 119	C. S. Nakatani	Mighty, 3	Ifitstobeitsuptome, 3	8	1:44.25	$75,000
1999	Ecton Park, 3, 114	S. J. Sellers	Answer Lively, 3	Kimberlite Pipe, 3	12	1:44.83	$75,000
1998	Comic Strip, 3, 119	S. J. Sellers	Captain Maestri, 3	Time Limit, 3	7	1:44.27	$75,000
1997	Open Forum, 3, 117	D. M. Barton	Crypto Star, 3	Cash Deposit, 3	5	1:44.37	$60,000
1996	Zarb's Magic, 3, 122	E. J. Perrodin	Imminent First, 3	Palikar, 3	9	1:42.98	$37,950
1995	Beavers Nose, 3, 117	K. Bourque	Moonlight Dancer, 3	Fuzzy Me, 3	8	1:45.22	$31,792
	Knockadoon, 3, 114	W. Martinez	Key to Malagra, 3	Scott's Scoundrel, 3	9	1:45.44	$31,882
1994	Fly Cry, 3, 122	R. D. Ardoin	Smilin Singin Sam, 3	Little Jazz Boy, 3	7	1:43.02	$31,155
1993	Dry Bean, 3, 117	A. T. Gryder	Apprentice, 3	Grand Jewel, 3	6	1:43.80	$16,020
	Dixieland Heat, 3, 119	R. P. Romero	O'Star, 3	Gold Angle, 3	7	1:43.20	$16,080
1992	Line In The Sand, 3, 119	S. P. Romero	Hill Pass, 3	Sheik to Sheik, 3	11	1:45.00	$19,635

Named for Louisiana-owned 1988 champion three-year-old male Risen Star (1985-'98, c. by Secretariat). 1973-'88 Louisiana Derby Trial S. 1973-'74,1988-'90 1 mile 40 yards. 1993, 1995 two divisions.

Riva Ridge Stakes

Grade 2, Belmont Park, three-year-olds, 7 furlongs, dirt. Held June 8, 2002, with a gross value of $190,000. First held in 1985. Graded since 1988. Stakes record 1:20.33 (1994 You and I).

Year	Winner	Jockey	Second	Third	Strs	Time	1st Purse
2002	Gygistar, 3, 119	P. Day	Draw Play, 3	True Direction, 3	9	1:22.61	$120,000
2001	Put It Back, 3, 120	N. A. Wynter	Flame Thrower, 3	Touch Tone, 3	6	1:21.76	$90,000
2000	Trippi, 3, 123	J. D. Bailey	Bevo, 3	Sun Cat, 3	6	1:23.68	$90,000
1999	Yes It's True, 3, 123	J. D. Bailey	Lion Hearted, 3	Silver Season, 3	8	1:22.35	$90,000
1998	Coronado's Quest, 3, 123	M. E. Smith	Mellow Roll, 3	Flashing Tammany, 3	7	1:22.50	$82,050
1997	Smoke Glacken, 3, 123	C. Perret	Trafalger, 3	Wild Wonder, 3	6	1:20.98	$66,060
1996	Gold Fever, 3, 118	M. E. Smith	Gameel, 3	Bright Launch, 3	9	1:23.30	$67,620
1995	Western Larla, 3, 119	G. L. Stevens	Mr. Greeley, 3	Blu Tusmani, 3	8	1:24.24	$66,960
1994	You and I, 3, 122	C. J. McCarron	End Sweep, 3	Slew Gin Fizz, 3	9	1:20.33	$67,080
1993	Montbrook, 3, 117	C. J. Ladner III	As Indicated, 3	Forever Whirl, 3	10	1:23.34	$74,160
1992	Superstrike (GB), 3, 115	J. A. Santos	Three Peat, 3	Windundermywings, 3	7	1:22.41	$70,560

Named for Meadow Stable's 1971 champion two-year-old male and 1973 champion older male Riva Ridge (1969-'85, c. by First Landing). 1988-'97 Grade 3. 1994 new track record.

River City Handicap

Grade 3, Churchill Downs, three-year-olds and up, 1¹⁄₈ miles, turf. Held November 17, 2002, with a gross value of $150,000. First held in 1978. Graded since 1996. Stakes record 1:47.90 (2001 Dr. Kashnikow).

Year	Winner	Jockey	Second	Third	Strs	Time	1st Purse
2002	Dr. Kashnikow, 5, 116	R. Albarado	Foster's Landing, 4	Roxinho (Brz), 4	11	1:51.44	$108,903
2001	Dr. Kashnikow, 4, 116	R. Albarado	Tijiyr (Ire), 6	Strategic Mission, 6	8	1:47.90	$109,926
2000	Brahms, 3, 112	P. Day	Vergennes, 5	Super Quercus (Fr), 4	9	1:48.09	$111,879
1999	Comic Strip, 4, 119	P. Day	Keats and Yeats, 5	Aboriginal Apex, 6	10	1:50.71	$106,113
1998	Wild Event, 5, 116	S. J. Sellers	Buff, 3	Floriselli, 4	13	1:49.69	$116,436
1997	Same Old Wish, 7, 117	S. J. Sellers	Aboriginal Apex, 4	Joyeux Danseur, 4	9	1:50.90	$106,578
1996	Same Old Wish, 6, 119	S. J. Sellers	Jet Freighter, 5	Franchise Player, 7	7	1:49.21	$70,122
1995	Homing Pigeon, 5, 113	R. P. Romero	Hawk Attack, 3	Dusty Asher, 5	8	1:51.00	$73,320
1994	Lindon Lime, 4, 113	S. J. Sellers	Torch Rouge (GB), 3	Jaggery John, 3	11	1:49.30	$75,660

1993	**Secreto's Hideaway**, 4, 110	W. Martinez	Little Bro Lantis, 5	Ganges, 5	5	1:53.83	$72,670
1992	**Cozzene's Prince**, 5, 117	D. Penna	Lotus Pool, 5	Stagecraft (GB), 5	8	1:49.31	$73,060

Named for one of the nicknames of Louisville, Kentucky, "River City." 1983-'86 River City S. 1978-'81 6 furlongs; 1982-'86 1 mile; 1987 1¹⁄₁₆ miles. 1978-'86,1988,1993 dirt.

Robert F. Carey Memorial Handicap

Grade 3, Hawthorne Race Course, three-year-olds and up, 1 mile, turf. Held November 2, 2002, with a gross value of $150,000. First held in 1983. Graded since 1986. Stakes record 1:33.40 (1998 Soviet Line [Ire]).

Year	Winner	Jockey	Second	Third	Strs	Time	1st Purse
2002	Kimberlite Pipe, 6, 115	C. A. Emigh	Aslaaf, 4	Major Omansky, 6	10	1:35.94	$90,000
2001	Galic Boy, 6, 115	R. Sibille	Where's Taylor, 5	Good Journey, 5	10	1:35.10	$90,000
2000	Where's Taylor, 4, 117	C. J. Lanerie	Dernier Croise (Fr), 5	Associate, 5	11	1:36.31	$90,000
1999	Ray's Approval, 6, 114	E. Fires	Stay Sound, 4	Inkatha (Fr), 5	9	1:37.01	$90,000
1998	Soviet Line (Ire), 8, 115	S. J. Sellers	Fun to Run, 5	Wild Event, 5	10	**1:33.40**	$90,000
1997	Trail City, 4, 119	J. D. Bailey	Power of Opinion, 4	Da Bull, 5	8	1:36.04	$90,000
1996	Homing Pigeon, 6, 114	R. Albarado	Joker, 4	Why Change, 3	12	1:36.58	$90,000
1995	Homing Pigeon, 5, 114	R. Albarado	Gilder, 4	Rare Reason, 4	9	1:38.09	$60,000
1994	Recoup the Cash, 4, 119	J. L. Diaz	Road of War, 4	Glenfiddich Lad, 5	7	1:40.91	$60,000
1993	High Habitation, 5, 114	G. C. Retana	Beau Fasa, 7	Glenfiddich Lad, 4	12	1:35.33	$60,000
1992	Double Booked, 7, 115	J. C. Ferrer	Evanescent, 5	That's Sunny, 7	11	1:39.82	$60,000

Named for Robert F. Carey (1904-1980), managing director of Hawthorne Race Course (1947-'80). 1984-'85 Robert F. Carey H.; 1995 United Airlines Robert F. Carey Memorial H. 1990-'97 not graded. 1983 1³⁄₁₆ miles; 1984-'87 1¹⁄₄ miles; 1988-'89 1¹⁄₈ miles; 1994 1 mile 70 yards. 1985,1994 dirt.

Royal Heroine Stakes

Grade 3, Hollywood Park, three-year-olds and up, fillies and mares, 1 mile, turf. Held July 6, 2002, with a gross value of $100,000. First held in 1986. Graded since 2001. Stakes record 1:33.98 (2000 Tranquility Lake).

Year	Winner	Jockey	Second	Third	Strs	Time	1st Purse
2002	Surya, 4, 117	K. J. Desormeaux	Angel Gift, 4	Reine de Romance (Ire), 4	12	1:34.73	$68,880
2001	Kalatiara (Aus), 4, 114	C. J. McCarron	Dianehill (Ire), 5	Al Desima (GB), 4	7	1:34.41	$65,940
2000	Tranquility Lake, 5, 121	E. J. Delahoussaye	Dianehill (Ire), 4	Reciclada (Chi), 5	6	**1:33.98**	$46,590
1999	Tuzla (Fr), 5, 123	C. S. Nakatani	Isle de France, 4	Chime After Chime, 4	5	1:34.32	$42,240
1998	Tuzla (Fr), 4, 115	C. S. Nakatani	Sonja's Faith (Ire), 4	Plus (Chi), 5	6	1:34.33	$42,990

Named for 1984 champion turf female Royal Heroine (Ire) (1980, f. by Lypheor [GB]). 1986 1¹⁄₁₆ miles.

Ruffian Handicap

Grade 1, Belmont Park, three-year-olds and up, fillies and mares, 1¹⁄₁₆ miles, dirt. Held September 14, 2002, with a gross value of $300,000. First held in 1976. Graded since 1976. Stakes record 1:40.35 (2000 Riboletta [Brz]).

Year	Winner	Jockey	Second	Third	Strs	Time	1st Purse
2002	Mandy's Gold, 4, 116	J. A. Santos	You, 3	Shine Again, 5	5	1:42.57	$180,000
2000	Riboletta (Brz), 5, 125	C. J. McCarron	Gourmet Girl, 5	Country Hideaway, 4	7	**1:40.35**	$150,000
1999	Catinca, 4, 119	J. D. Bailey	Furlough, 5	Keeper Hill, 4	5	1:41.94	$150,000
1998	Sharp Cat, 4, 124	C. S. Nakatani	Furlough, 4	Stop Traffic, 5	8	1:42.48	$150,000
1997	Tomisue's Delight, 3, 113	J. D. Bailey	Clear Mandate, 5	Mil Kilates, 4	9	1:44.43	$150,000
1996	Yanks Music, 3, 116	J. R. Velazquez	Serena's Song, 4	Head East, 4	6	1:41.84	$150,000
1995	Inside Information, 4, 125	M. E. Smith	Unlawful Behavior, 5	Incinerate, 5	5	1:40.98	$120,000
1994	Sky Beauty, 4, 130	M. E. Smith	Dispute, 4	Educated Risk, 4	5	1:41.79	$120,000
1993	Shared Interest, 5, 114	R. G. Davis	Dispute, 4	Turnback the Alarm, 4	5	1:41.92	$120,000
1992	Versailles Treaty, 4, 120	M. E. Smith	Quick Mischief, 6	Nannerl, 5	6	1:41.41	$120,000

Named for 1974 champion two-year-old filly and 1975 champion three-year-old filly Ruffian (1972-'75, f. by Reviewer); Ruffian is buried in the Belmont infield. 2001 not held due to World Trade Center attack. 1976 Ruffian S. 1976 1¹⁄₄ miles; 1977-'89 1¹⁄₈ miles.

Sabin Handicap

Grade 3, Gulfstream Park, three-year-olds and up, fillies and mares, 1¹⁄₁₆ miles, dirt. Held February 8, 2003, with a gross value of $100,000. First held in 1991. Graded since 1994. Stakes record 1:42.49 (2003 Allamerican Bertie).

Year	Winner	Jockey	Second	Third	Strs	Time	1st Purse
2003	Allamerican Bertie, 4, 120	J. D. Bailey	Small Promises, 5	Redoubled Miss, 4	11	**1:42.49**	$60,000
2002	Miss Linda (Arg), 5, 119	R. Migliore	Forest Secrets, 4	Tap Dance, 4	12	1:42.61	$60,000
2001	De Bertie, 4, 115	J. F. Chavez	Royal Fair, 5	Frankly My Dear, 4	8	1:44.74	$60,000
2000	Brushed Halory, 4, 115	M. E. Smith	Roza Robata, 4	Mop Squeezer, 4	5	1:41.84	$45,000
1999	Timely Broad, 5, 115	N. J. Petro	Highfalutin, 5	Mudslinger, 4	9	1:42.50	$45,000
1998	Radiant Megan, 5, 113	J. A. Krone	Escena, 5	Biding Time, 4	7	1:41.25	$45,000
1997	Rare Blend, 4, 120	J. D. Bailey	Golden Gale, 4	Termly, 4	7	1:41.28	$45,000
1996	Lindsay Frolic, 4, 117	P. Day	Investalot, 5	Queen Tutta, 4	8	1:43.70	$45,000
1995	Recognizable, 4, 115	M. E. Smith	Jade Flush, 4	Sambacarioca, 6	8	1:42.50	$45,000
1994	Hunzinga, 5, 113	J. E. Felix	Nine Keys, 4	Pleasant Jolie, 6	9	1:39.57	$45,000

| 1993 **Now Dance**, 4, 113 | M. Guidry | Spinning Round, 4 | Luv Me Luv Me Not, 4 | 10 | 1:41.68 | $30,000 |
| 1992 **Lemhi Go**, 4, 113 | R. N. Lester | Trumpet's Blare, 5 | Tappanzee, 4 | 8 | 1:44.79 | $45,000 |

Named for Henryk de Kwiatkowski's 1984 Orchid H. (G2) winner Sabin (1980, f. by Lyphard). 1993-2000 1 mile 70 yards.

Safely Kept Stakes

Grade 3, Pimlico, three-year-olds, fillies, 6 furlongs, dirt. Held September 14, 2002, with a gross value of $100,000. First held in 1988. Graded since 1990. Stakes record 1:09.21 (1999 Godmother).

Year	Winner	Jockey	Second	Third	Strs	Time	1st Purse
2002	**Miss Lodi**, 3, 117	R. Fogelsonger	For Rubies, 3	Wilzada, 3	8	1:11.20	$60,000
2000	**Swept Away**, 3, 122	J. Beasley	Another, 3	Cat Cay, 3	8	1:09.51	$60,000
1999	**Godmother**, 3, 117	M. G. Pino	Superduper Miss, 3	Rills, 3	7	**1:09.21**	$60,000
1998	**Hair Spray**, 3, 117	J. A. Velez Jr.	Expensive Issue, 3	Ninth Inning, 3	8	1:10.67	$66,390
1997	**Weather Vane**, 3, 119	M. G. Pino	Vegas Prospector, 3	Requesting More, 3	7	1:10.21	$64,800
1996	**J J'sdream**, 3, 122	M. G. Pino	Flat Fleet Feet, 3	Rare Blend, 3	5	1:09.45	$60,000
1995	**Broad Smile**, 3, 117	J. Brown	Scotzanna, 3	Shebatim's Trick, 3	7	1:10.30	$60,000
1994	**Twist Afleet**, 3, 117	D. Carr	Penny's Reshoot, 3	Our Royal Blue, 3	7	1:10.88	$60,000
1993	**Miss Indy Anna**, 3, 113	D. B. Thomas	Ann Dear, 3	Lily of the North, 3	7	1:10.12	$60,000
1992	**Meafara**, 3, 119	B. Swatuk	Squirm, 3	Super Doer, 3	6	1:10.55	$60,000

Named for Jayeff B Stables' and Barry Weisbord's 1989 champion sprinter Safely Kept (1986, f. by Horatius). 2001 not held. 1988-'95 Columbia S. 1988,1990,1998-2000 held at Laurel Park; 1997 Colonial Downs. 1988 6½ furlongs.

Salvator Mile Handicap

Grade 3, Monmouth Park, three-year-olds and up, 1 mile, dirt. Held July 27, 2002, with a gross value of $100,000. First held in 1948. Graded since 1973. Stakes record 1:34.46 (1991 Peanut Butter Onit).

Year	Winner	Jockey	Second	Third	Strs	Time	1st Purse
2002	**Sea of Tranquility**, 6, 120	J. C. Ferrer	Free of Love, 4	First Lieutenant, 5	8	1:36.12	$60,000
2001	**Sea of Tranquility**, 5, 115	J. C. Ferrer	Knock Again, 4	Hal's Hope, 4	7	1:36.74	$90,000
2000	**Leave It to Beezer**, 7, 120	R. Alvarado Jr.	Delaware Township, 4	Prime Directive, 4	5	1:37.29	$90,000
1999	**Truluck**, 4, 115	J. Bravo	Rock and Roll, 4	Siftaway, 4	6	1:35.18	$90,000
1998	**El Amante**, 5, 119	J. A. Krone	Stormin Fever, 4	Gold Token, 5	8	1:34.95	$60,000
1997	**Distorted Humor**, 4, 114	J. A. Krone	Wild Deputy, 4	Smooth the Loot, 4	4	1:36.03	$60,000
1996	**Smart Strike**, 4, 113	S. Hawley	Cozy Drive, 4	November Sunset, 4	10	1:36.28	$60,000
1995	**Schossberg**, 5, 116	D. Penna	Cast Iron, 4	Relentless Star, 5	9	1:35.86	$45,000
1994	**Storm Tower**, 4, 119	R. Wilson	Cold Digger, 7	Koluctoo Jimmy Al, 4	6	1:36.26	$45,000
1993	**Dusty Screen**, 5, 117	E. L. King Jr.	Count New York, 4	Root Boy, 5	8	1:35.86	$45,000
1992	**Peanut Butter Onit**, 6, 120	A. T. Gryder	Root Boy, 4	He Is Risen, 4	7	1:36.21	$45,000

Named for James Ben Ali Haggin's great racehorse Salvator (1886-1909, c. by *Prince Charlie), who set an American record for one mile at Monmouth Park in 1890; the mark stood for 28 years.

San Antonio Handicap

Grade 2, Santa Anita Park, four-year-olds and up, 1⅛ miles, dirt. Held February 2, 2003, with a gross value of $250,000. First held in 1935. Graded since 1973. Stakes record 1:46.20 (1978 Vigors).

Year	Winner	Jockey	Second	Third	Strs	Time	1st Purse
2003	**Congaree**, 5, 123	J. D. Bailey	Milwaukee Brew, 6	Pleasantly Perfect, 5	6	1:47.60	$150,000
2002	**Redattore (Brz)**, 7, 116	A. O. Solis	Euchre, 6	Irisheyesareflying, 6	7	1:48.66	$150,000
2001	**Guided Tour**, 5, 115	L. Melancon	Lethal Instrument, 5	Moonlight Charger, 6	8	1:48.26	$180,000
2000	**Budroyale**, 7, 121	G. K. Gomez	Cat Thief, 4	Elaborate, 5	5	1:48.70	$180,000
1999	**Free House**, 5, 123	C. J. McCarron	Malek (Chi), 6	Dramatic Gold, 8	4	1:48.54	$180,000
1998	**Gentlemen (Arg)**, 6, 124	G. L. Stevens	Da Bull, 6	Refinado Tom (Arg), 5	5	1:47.60	$180,000
1997	**Gentlemen (Arg)**, 5, 122	G. L. Stevens	Alphabet Soup, 6	Kingdom Found, 7	5	1:47.38	$180,300
1996	**Alphabet Soup**, 5, 119	C. W. Antley	Soul of the Matter, 5	Dare and Go, 5	5	1:49.96	$184,900
1995	**Best Pal**, 7, 121	C. J. McCarron	Slew of Damascus, 7	Tossofthecoin, 5	10	1:47.43	$148,500
1994	**The Wicked North**, 5, 116	K. J. Desormeaux	Region, 5	Hill Pass, 5	9	1:47.48	$155,500
1993	**Marquetry**, 6, 117	E. J. Delahoussaye	Sir Beaufort, 6	Reign Road, 5	6	1:48.96	$155,500
1992	**Ibero (Arg)**, 5, 115	A. O. Solis	In Excess (Ire), 5	Cobra Classic, 5	8	1:47.05	$189,750

Named for seven land grants called Rancho San Antonio; two were in Los Angeles County, one is now Beverly Hills. 1941-'45 not held. 1968-'82 San Antonio S. 1983-'89 Grade 1. 1940 1¹⁄₁₆ miles. 1946,1948,1950-'52,1956,1958,1960 three-year-olds and up. 1994 Hill Pass finished second, DQ to third.

San Bernardino Handicap

Grade 3, Santa Anita Park, four-year-olds and up, 1⅛ miles, dirt. Held April 5, 2003, with a gross value of $150,000. First held in 1957. Graded since 1973. Stakes record 1:45.80 (1979 Star Spangled).

Year	Winner	Jockey	Second	Third	Strs	Time	1st Purse
2003	**Western Pride**, 5, 116	P. A. Valenzuela	Total Impact (Chi), 5	Fleetstreet Dancer, 5	8	1:48.56	$90,000
2002	**Bosque Redondo**, 5, 114	C. J. McCarron	Mysterious Cat, 4	Freedom Crest, 6	6	1:49.11	$90,000
2001	**Futural**, 5, 115	G. K. Gomez	Irisheyesareflying, 5	Tribunal, 4	5	1:47.87	$90,000
2000	**Early Pioneer**, 5, 113	M. S. Garcia	David, 4	General Challenge, 4	5	1:49.08	$95,490
1999	**Classic Cat**, 4, 122	G. L. Stevens	Budroyale, 6	Klinsman (Ire), 5	4	1:47.77	$90,000

1998	Budroyale, 5, 112	M. S. Garcia	Don't Blame Rio, 5	Bagshot, 4	10	1:48.48	$100,530
1997	Benchmark, 6, 114	C. J. McCarron	Kingdom Found, 7	Private Song, 4	7	1:48.26	$97,650
1996	Del Mar Dennis, 6, 118	K. J. Desormeaux	Just Java, 5	Regal Rowdy, 7	6	1:48.37	$96,650
1995	Del Mar Dennis, 5, 117	C. W. Antley	Wharf, 5	Stoller, 4	8	1:47.27	$130,000
1994	Del Mar Dennis, 4, 112	S. Gonzalez Jr.	Hill Pass, 5	Tinners Way, 4	8	1:48.36	$129,400
1993	Memo (Chi), 6, 114	P. Atkinson	Charmonnier, 5	Marquetry, 6	7	1:47.49	$125,800
1992	Another Review, 4, 114	K. J. Desormeaux	Defensive Play, 5	Loach, 4	11	1:47.33	$163,100

Named for Rancho San Bernardino, location of the present-day city of San Bernardino. 1978 not graded; 1973-'77,1979-2002 Grade 2. 1957-'66,1974 1¹⁄₁₆ miles. 1957-'72,1974-'78 turf. 1957 three-year-olds; 1958-'67 three-year-olds and up.

San Carlos Handicap

Grade 1, Santa Anita Park, four-year-olds and up, 7 furlongs, dirt. Held March 2, 2003, with a gross value of $200,000. First held in 1935. Graded since 1973. Stakes record 1:20.20 (1981 Flying Paster).

Year	Winner	Jockey	Second	Third	Strs	Time	1st Purse
2003	Aldebaran, 5, 116	J. Valdivia Jr.	Crafty C. T., 5	Grey Memo, 6	6	1:21.53	$120,000
2002	Snow Ridge, 4, 118	M. E. Smith	Alyzig, 5	Grey Memo, 5	6	1:22.02	$90,000
2001	Kona Gold, 7, 125	A. O. Solis	Blade Prospector (Brz), 6	Grey Memo, 4	7	1:21.35	$90,000
2000	Son of a Pistol, 8, 117	G. K. Gomez	Kona Gold, 6	Old Topper, 5	6	1:22.11	$96,930
1999	Big Jag, 6, 118	J. Valdivia Jr.	Kona Gold, 5	Dramatic Gold, 8	5	1:21.18	$90,000
1998	Reality Road, 6, 116	C. J. McCarron	Gold Land, 7	Son of a Pistol, 6	10	1:21.62	$100,530
1997	Northern Afleet, 4, 117	C. J. McCarron	Hesabull, 4	High Stakes Player, 5	7	1:21.45	$97,700
1996	Kingdom Found, 6, 116	C. J. McCarron	Lakota Brave, 7	Lit de Justice, 6	8	1:22.23	$98,850
1995	Softshoe Sure Shot, 9, 113	A. O. Solis	Ferrara, 4	Subtle Trouble, 4	5	1:21.46	$91,600
1994	Cardmania, 8, 122	E. J. Delahoussaye	The Wicked North, 5	Portoferraio (Arg), 6	7	1:21.23	$63,900
1993	Sir Beaufort, 6, 120	C. J. McCarron	Cardmania, 7	Excavate, 5	6	1:22.22	$62,900
1992	Answer Do, 6, 120	G. L. Stevens	Individualist, 5	Media Plan, 4	7	1:21.23	$63,700

Named for Rancho El Potrero de San Carlos in Monterey County, California. 1942-'45,1950 not held. 1973-2000 Grade 2. 1935-'39 1¹⁄₁₆ miles. 1946,1949-'52,1954-'59 three-year-olds and up.

San Clemente Handicap

Grade 2, Del Mar, three-year-olds, fillies, 1 mile, turf. Held August 3, 2002, with a gross value of $150,000. First held in 1950. Graded since 1994. Stakes record 1:34.88 (1991 Flawlessly; 2001 Reine de Romance [Ire]).

Year	Winner	Jockey	Second	Third	Strs	Time	1st Purse
2002	Little Treasure (Fr), 3, 117	K. J. Desormeaux	Pina Colada (GB), 3	Arabic Song (Ire), 3	9	1:33.97	$90,000
2001	Reine de Romance (Ire), 3, 116	E. J. Delahoussaye	Gabriellina Giof (GB), 3	La Vida Loca (Ire), 3	8	1:34.88	$90,000
2000	Uncharted Haven (GB), 3, 116	A. O. Solis	Automated, 3	Islay Mist (GB), 3	10	1:35.13	$90,000
1999	Sweet Ludy (Ire), 3, 118	C. S. Nakatani	Caffe Latte (Ire), 3	Sweet Life, 3	10	1:35.02	$90,000
1998	Sicy d'Alsace (Fr), 3, 115	C. S. Nakatani	Miss Hot Salsa, 3	Tranquility Lake, 3	10	1:34.97	$67,500
1997	Famous Digger, 3, 120	B. Blanc	Cozy Blues, 3	Really Happy, 3	10	1:36.00	$71,725
1996	True Flare, 3, 116	C. S. Nakatani	Gastronomical, 3	Najecam, 3	10	1:35.59	$67,200
1995	Jewel Princess, 3, 115	C. J. McCarron	Auriette (Ire), 3	Scratch Paper, 3	6	1:36.12	$59,650
1994	Work the Crowd, 3, 120	C. J. McCarron	Pharma, 3	Dancing Mirage, 3	8	1:36.07	$48,550
1993	Hollywood Wildcat, 3, 120	E. J. Delahoussaye	Miami Sands (Ire), 3	Beal Street Blues, 3	10	1:34.89	$49,950
1992	Golden Treat, 3, 121	K. J. Desormeaux	Morriston Belle, 3	Alysbelle, 3	8	1:35.20	$49,350

Named for San Clemente, California, located in Orange County. 1951-'69 not held. 1994-'95 Grade 3. 1950,1970-'87 1¹⁄₁₆ miles. 1950 dirt.

San Diego Handicap

Grade 2, Del Mar, three-year-olds and up, 1¹⁄₁₆ miles, dirt. Held August 4, 2002, with a gross value of $250,000. First held in 1937. Graded since 1983. Stakes record 1:40.20 (1978 Vic's Magic).

Year	Winner	Jockey	Second	Third	Strs	Time	1st Purse
2002	Grey Memo, 5, 116	E. J. Delahoussaye	Euchre, 6	Congaree, 4	8	1:43.48	$150,000
2001	Skimming, 5, 120	G. K. Gomez	Futural, 5	Captain Steve, 4	7	1:41.62	$150,000
2000	Skimming, 4, 112	G. K. Gomez	Prime Timber, 4	National Saint, 4	7	1:41.06	$150,000
1999	Mazel Trick, 4, 117	C. J. McCarron	River Keen (Ire), 7	Tibado, 5	4	1:40.68	$150,000
1998	Mud Route, 4, 117	C. J. McCarron	Hal's Pal (GB), 5	Benchmark, 7	5	1:41.11	$150,300
1997	Northern Afleet, 4, 118	C. J. McCarron	Benchmark, 6	New Century, 5	9	1:41.80	$100,300
1996	Savinio, 6, 116	C. W. Antley	Misnomer, 4	Nonproductiveasset, 6	6	1:40.82	$95,350
1995	Blumin Affair, 4, 116	C. J. McCarron	Rapan Boy (AUS), 7	Luthier Fever, 4	4	1:41.29	$87,200
1994	Kingdom Found, 4, 116	C. J. McCarron	Tossofthecoin, 4	Rapan Boy (AUS), 6	6	1:41.21	$75,850
1993	Fanatic Boy (Arg), 6, 115	C. J. McCarron	Memo (Chi), 6	Missionary Ridge (GB), 6	5	1:48.59	$74,450
1992	Another Review, 4, 120	L. A. Pincay Jr.	Claret (Ire), 4	Quintana, 4	6	1:47.00	$76,050

Named for the city of San Diego, California; Del Mar is located in the nearby town of Del Mar. 1939-'40,1942-'44 not held. 1983-2000 Grade 3. 1937,1945-'47 6 furlongs; 1941 1 mile; 1991-'93 1⅛ miles.

Sands Point Stakes

Grade 3, Belmont Park, three-year-olds, fillies, 1⅛ miles, turf. Held June 16, 2002, with a gross value of $100,000. First held in 1995. Graded since 1998. Stakes record 1:46.65 (1997 Auntie Mame).

Year	Winner	Jockey	Second	Third	Strs	Time	1st Purse
2002	Riskaverse, 3, 119	R. G. Davis	Cyclorama, 3	She's Vested, 3	11	1:51.63	$69,660

2001	Tweedside, 3, 119	R. Migliore	Owsley, 3	Platinum Tiara, 3	4	1:50.43	$66,674
2000	Gaviola, 3, 121	J. D. Bailey	Shopping for Love, 3	Millie's Quest, 3	8	1:47.77	$66,780
1999	Perfect Sting, 3, 118	P. Day	Pico Teneriffe, 3	Illiquidity, 3	6	1:46.99	$65,160
1998	Recording, 3, 113	J. F. Chavez	Royal Ransom, 3	Naskra's de Light, 3	11	1:48.93	$69,600
1997	Auntie Mame, 3, 121	J. D. Bailey	Hoochie Coochie, 3	Sagasious, 3	8	1:46.65	$66,720
1996	Merit Wings, 3, 120	R. G. Davis	Unify, 3	Turkappeal, 3	10	1:45.83	$51,885
1995	Perfect Arc, 3, 117	J. R. Velazquez	Miss Union Avenue, 3	Transient Trend, 3	5	1:43.14	$49,395

Named for the community of Sands Point, New York, located on Long Island. 1995-'97 Sands Point H. 2001 not graded. 1995-'96 1⅟₁₆ miles. 2001 dirt.

San Felipe Stakes

Grade 2, Santa Anita Park, three-year-olds, 1⅟₁₆ miles, dirt. Held March 16, 2003, with a gross value of $250,000. First held in 1935. Graded since 1973. Stakes record 1:41.20 (1979 Pole Position).

Year	Winner	Jockey	Second	Third	Strs	Time	1st Purse
2003	Buddy Gil, 3, 119	G. L. Stevens	Atswhatimtalknbout, 3	Brancusi, 3	10	1:43.64	$150,000
2002	Medaglia d'Oro, 3, 116	L. A. Pincay Jr.	U S S Tinosa, 3	Siphonic, 3	6	1:41.95	$150,000
2001	Point Given, 3, 122	G. L. Stevens	I Love Silver, 3	Jamaican Rum, 3	8	1:41.94	$150,000
2000	Fusaichi Pegasus, 3, 116	K. J. Desormeaux	The Deputy (Ire), 3	Anees, 3	7	1:42.66	$150,000
1999	Prime Timber, 3, 116	D. R. Flores	Exploit, 3	High Wire Act, 3	7	1:42.16	$150,000
1998	Artax, 3, 122	C. J. McCarron	Real Quiet, 3	Prosperous Bid, 3	5	1:41.73	$150,000
1997	Free House, 3, 119	D. R. Flores	Silver Charm, 3	King Crimson, 3	9	1:42.49	$152,400
1996	Odyle, 3, 116	C. S. Nakatani	Smithfield, 3	Cavonnier, 3	7	1:42.43	$152,400
1995	Afternoon Deelites, 3, 119	K. J. Desormeaux	Timber Country, 3	Lake George, 3	4	1:42.11	$117,200
1994	Soul of the Matter, 3, 116	K. J. Desormeaux	Brocco, 3	Valiant Nature, 3	5	1:44.68	$118,500
1993	Corby, 3, 116	C. J. McCarron	Personal Hope, 3	Devoted Brass, 3	6	1:42.11	$121,100
1992	Bertrando, 3, 122	A. O. Solis	Arp, 3	Hickman Creek, 3	6	1:42.76	$120,800

Named for the Rancho Valle de San Felipe located in present San Diego County, California. 1942-'44 not held. 1935-'41, 1952-'90 San Felipe H. 1984-'88 Grade 1. 1935-'36 1 mile; 1937, 1941, 1947-'51 7 furlongs; 1938-'40, 1945-'46 6 furlongs. 1935-'40 three-year-olds and up. 1935-'51 colts and geldings.

San Fernando Breeders' Cup Stakes

Grade 2, Santa Anita Park, four-year-olds, 1⅟₁₆ miles, dirt. Held January 11, 2003, with a gross value of $219,600. First held in 1952. Graded since 1973. Stakes record 1:40.80 (1955 *Poona II).

Year	Winner	Jockey	Second	Third	Strs	Time	1st Purse
2003	Pass Rush, 4, 116	C. S. Nakatani	Tracemark, 4	Tizbud, 4	8	1:42.37	$131,760
2002	Western Pride, 4, 122	G. K. Gomez	Orientate, 4	Fancy As, 4	10	1:41.30	$134,640
2001	Tiznow, 4, 122	C. J. McCarron	Walkslikeaduck, 4	Wooden Phone, 4	6	1:42.05	$98,880
2000	Saint's Honor, 4, 117	K. J. Desormeaux	Cat Thief, 4	Mr. Broad Blade, 4	7	1:41.94	$190,200
1999	Dixie Dot Com, 4, 116	D. R. Flores	Event of the Year, 4	Old Topper, 4	8	1:41.06	$190,800
1998	Silver Charm, 4, 122	G. L. Stevens	Mud Route, 4	Lord Grillo (Arg), 4	4	1:41.94	$125,520
1997	Northern Afleet, 4, 116	C. J. McCarron	Ambivalent, 4	Ready to Order, 4	9	1:48.59	$194,400
1996	Helmsman, 4, 118	C. J. McCarron	Gold and Steel (Fr), 4	The Key Rainbow (Ire), 4	9	1:48.87	$134,500
1995	Wekiva Springs, 4, 118	K. J. Desormeaux	Dramatic Gold, 4	Dare and Go, 4	7	1:48.59	$126,800
1994	Zignew, 4, 116	C. J. McCarron	Nonproductiveasset, 4	Pleasant Tango, 4	12	1:47.87	$135,400
1993	Bertrando, 4, 120	C. J. McCarron	Star Recruit, 4	The Wicked North, 4	8	1:51.22	$127,800
1992	Best Pal, 4, 122	K. J. Desormeaux	Olympio, 4	Dinard, 4	9	1:48.25	$130,000

Named for San Fernando, California, located west of Santa Anita. 1970 not held. 1952-'96 San Fernando S. 1981-'89 Grade 1. 1960-'97 1⅛ miles. 1981 four-year-olds and up.

Sanford Stakes

Grade 2, Saratoga Race Course, two-year-olds, 6 furlongs, dirt. Held July 25, 2002, with a gross value of $150,000. First held in 1913. Graded since 1973. Stakes record 1:09.60 (1977 Affirmed).

Year	Winner	Jockey	Second	Third	Strs	Time	1st Purse
2002	Whywhywhy, 2, 122	E. S. Prado	Wildcat Heir, 2	Spite the Devil, 2	9	1:10.40	$90,000
2001	Buster's Daydream, 2, 122	J. R. Velazquez	Seeking the Money, 2	Heavyweight Champ, 2	6	1:10.55	$64,680
2000	City Zip, 2, 119	J. A. Santos	Yonaguska, 2	Scorpion, 2	7	1:10.69	$65,220
1999	More Than Ready, 2, 122	J. R. Velazquez	Mighty, 2	Bulling, 2	5	1:09.65	$64,560
1998	Time Bandit, 2, 119	P. Day	Prime Directive, 2	Texas Glitter, 2	9	1:11.59	$66,480
1997	Polished Brass, 2, 116	P. Day	Double Honor, 2	Jigadee, 2	7	1:10.23	$65,520
1996	Kelly Kip, 2, 118	J-L. Samyn	Boston Harbor, 2	Say Florida Sandy, 2	8	1:10.31	$66,840
1995	Maria's Mon, 2, 115	R. G. Davis	Seeker's Reward, 2	Frozen Ice, 2	11	1:10.80	$68,340
1994	Montreal Red, 2, 115	J. A. Santos	Boone's Mill, 2	De Niro, 2	5	1:10.56	$64,620
1993	Dehere, 2, 122	C. J. McCarron	Prenup, 2	Distinct Reality, 2	6	1:10.48	$68,520
1992	Mountain Cat, 2, 119	P. Day	Satellite Signal, 2	Rule Sixteen, 2	10	1:10.62	$73,440

Named for the Sanford family, owners of the Hurricana Farm in Amsterdam, New York. 1961 not held. 1913-'26 Sanford Memorial S. 1990-'98 Grade 3. 1943-'45 held at Belmont. 1962-'68 5½ furlongs. 1992 Thirty Two Slew finished second, DQ to fourth.

San Francisco Breeders' Cup Mile Stakes

Grade 2, Bay Meadows, three-year-olds and up, 1 mile, turf. Held April 26, 2003, with a gross value of $177,500. First held in 1948. Graded since 1987. Stakes record 1:33.40 (1980 Don Alberto).

Year	Winner	Jockey	Second	Third	Strs	Time	1st Purse
2003	Ninebanks, 5, 117	R. J. Warren Jr.	Nicobar (GB), 6	National Anthem (GB), 7	8	1:37.20	$110,000
2002	Suances (GB), 5, 116	D. R. Flores	Decarchy, 5	The Tin Man, 4	4	1:35.19	$110,000
2001	Redattore (Brz), 6, 115	J. P. Lumpkins	Hawksley Hill (Ire), 8	Kerrygold (Fr), 5	9	1:35.14	$137,500
2000	Ladies Din, 5, 120	K. J. Desormeaux	Fighting Falcon, 4	Self Feeder (Ire), 6	10	1:35.46	$150,000
1999	†Tuzla (Fr), 5, 112	B. Blanc	Poteen, 5	Rob 'n Gin, 5	10	1:35.46	$180,000
1998	Hawksley Hill (Ire), 5, 119	G. L. Stevens	Fantastic Fellow, 4	Uncaged Fury, 4	6	1:34.33	$120,000
1997	Wavy Run (Ire), 6, 116	B. Blanc	Savinio, 7	Romarin (Brz), 7	7	1:37.11	$120,000
1996	Gold and Steel (Fr), 4, 114	A. O. Solis	Savinio, 6	Debutant Trick, 6	7	1:35.07	$120,000
1995	Unfinished Symph, 4, 118	C. W. Antley	Vaudeville, 4	Torch Rouge (GB), 4	9	1:34.14	$110,000
1994	Gothland (Fr), 5, 115	C. S. Nakatani	Emerald Jig, 5	The Tender Track, 5	11	1:35.46	$110,000
1993	Norwich (GB), 6, 114	K. J. Desormeaux	Qathif, 6	Luthier Enchanteur, 8	8	1:35.57	$137,500
1992	Tight Spot, 5, 125	L. A. Pincay Jr.	Notorious Pleasure, 6	Forty Niner Days, 6	9	1:35.57	$110,000

Named for the city of San Francisco, California. 1960,1976 not held. 1948-'98 San Francisco Mile H.; 1999-2002 San Francisco Breeders' Cup Mile H. 1987-'93 Grade 3. 1948-2000 held at Golden Gate. 1948-'65 dirt. 1968 four-year-olds and up. †denotes female.

San Gabriel Handicap

Grade 2, Santa Anita Park, three-year-olds and up, 1⅛ miles, turf. Held December 29, 2002, with a gross value of $150,000. First held in 1935. Graded since 1973. Stakes record 1:46.20 (1989 Wretham).

Year	Winner	Jockey	Second	Third	Strs	Time	1st Purse
2002	Grammarian, 4, 117	J. Valdivia Jr.	David Copperfield, 5	Decarchy, 5	9	1:48.12	$90,000
2001	Irish Prize, 5, 121	G. L. Stevens	Sligo Bay (Ire), 3	El Gran Papa, 4	11	1:50.56	$90,000
	Irish Prize, 5, 117	K. J. Desormeaux	Manndar (Ire), 5	Here Comes Big C, 6	8	1:47.88	$90,000
2000	Brave Act (GB), 6, 120	A. O. Solis	Native Desert, 7	Manndar (Ire), 4	6	1:49.25	$97,470
1998	Brave Act (GB), 4, 118	G. F. Almeida	Mash One (Chi), 4	Fabulous Guy (Ire), 4	8	1:46.78	$90,000
1997	Martiniquais (Ire), 4, 116	C. S. Nakatani	Bienvenido (Arg), 4	Da Bull, 5	8	1:48.42	$99,180
	Rainbow Blues (Ire), 4, 119	G. L. Stevens	River Deep, 6	Via Lombardia (Ire), 5	7	1:46.89	$81,500
1996	Romarin (Brz), 6, 119	C. S. Nakatani	Virginia Carnival, 4	Silver Wizard, 6	8	1:49.69	$82,050
1995	Romarin (Brz), 5, 119	C. S. Nakatani	Inner City (Ire), 6	Ianomami (Ire), 5	6	1:49.36	$62,900
1994	Earl of Barking (Ire), 4, 118	C. J. McCarron	Fanmore, 6	Navarone, 6	8	1:48.64	$65,300
1993	Star of Cozzene, 5, 118	G. L. Stevens	Bistro Garden, 5	Leger Cat (Arg), 7	9	1:48.33	$66,100
1992	Classic Fame, 6, 118	E. J. Delahoussaye	Super May, 6	Defensive Play, 5	6	1:46.69	$64,300

Named for the nearby city of San Gabriel, California; the city was named for a mission. 1936,1939-'44,1947-'51,1970,1976,1982,1991,1999 not held. 1973-'93 Grade 3. 1997, 2001 held in January and December. 1935-'38 3 furlongs; 1945-'46 6 furlongs; 1952-'54 7 furlongs; 1955-'59 1¼ miles. 1935-'54,1965,1972,1974,1977,1987-'88 dirt. 1935-'38 two-year-olds; 1945-'46,1975-'77,1981,1988,1989-'90,1997-'98,2001-'02 three-year-olds and up; 1952-'54 three-year-olds.

San Gorgonio Handicap

Grade 2, Santa Anita Park, four-year-olds and up, fillies and mares, 1⅛ miles, turf. Held January 11, 2003, with a gross value of $150,000. First held in 1968. Graded since 1983. Stakes record 1:46.40 (1983 Castilla; 1990 Invited Guest).

Year	Winner	Jockey	Second	Third	Strs	Time	1st Purse
2003	Tates Creek, 5, 121	P. A. Valenzuela	Megahertz (GB), 4	Double Cat, 5	7	1:46.91	$90,000
2002	Tout Charmant, 6, 120	C. J. McCarron	Janet (GB), 4	Vencera (Fr), 5	8	1:47.22	$90,000
2001	Uncharted Haven (GB), 4, 115	A. O. Solis	Brianda (Ire), 4	Beautiful Noise, 5	12	1:50.02	$90,000
2000	Lady At Peace, 4, 115	G. K. Gomez	Spanish Fern, 5	Riboletta (Brz), 5	5	1:48.75	$90,000
1999	See You Soon (Fr), 5, 117	K. J. Desormeaux	Sonja's Faith (Ire), 5	Verinha (Brz), 5	6	1:49.14	$90,000
1998	Golden Arches (Fr), 4, 120	C. J. McCarron	Ecoute, 5	Real Connection, 7	6	1:49.42	$96,870
1997	Sixieme Sens, 5, 116	C. S. Nakatani	Alpride (Ire), 6	Grafin, 5	9	1:47.16	$82,950
1996	Wandesta (GB), 5, 119	C. S. Nakatani	Matiara, 4	Yearly Tour, 5	6	1:49.13	$80,550
1995	Queens Court Queen, 6, 117	C. S. Nakatani	Wende, 5	Vinista, 5	5	1:48.70	$62,000
1994	Hero's Love, 6, 119	L. A. Pincay Jr.	Skimble, 5	Miss Turkana, 5	10	1:47.65	$66,800
1993	Southern Truce, 5, 114	C. S. Nakatani	Laura Ly (Arg), 7	Lite Light, 5	5	1:51.28	$67,100
1992	Paseana (Arg), 5, 118	C. J. McCarron	Laura Ly (Arg), 6	Reluctant Guest, 6	4	1:53.88	$77,250

Named for San Gorgonio Mountain, highest mountain in Southern California. 1970,1978 not held. 1969-'75 San Gorgonio Claiming S. 1983-'84 Grade 3. 1968 6½ furlongs. 1969-'71,1973-'74,1977-'80,1982,1988-'89,1992-'93,1995 dirt. 1977 three-year-olds and up. 1968-'75 both sexes. 1998 Escabiosa (Arg) finished third, DQ to fourth.

San Juan Capistrano Handicap

Grade 1, Santa Anita Park, four-year-olds and up, about 1¾ miles, turf. Held April 20, 2003, with a gross value of $400,000. First held in 1935. Graded since 1973. Stakes record 2:42.96 (2001 Bienamado).

Year	Winner	Jockey	Second	Third	Strs	Time	1st Purse
2003	Passinetti, 7, 111	B. Blanc	All the Boys, 6	Champion Lodge (Ire), 9	2:46.97	$240,000
2002	Ringaskiddy, 6, 116	E. Delahoussaye	Staging Post, 4	Continental Red, 6	8	2:44.49	$240,000
2001	Bienamado, 5, 122	C. J. McCarron	Persianlux (GB), 5	Blueprint (Ire), 11	2:42.96	$240,000
2000	Sunshine Street, 5, 115	J. D. Bailey	Single Empire (Ire), 6	Chelsea Barracks (GB), 4	5	2:49.06	$240,000

1999	Single Empire (Ire), 5, 118	K. J. Desormeaux	Le Paillard (Ire), 5	Lucayan Indian (Ire), 4	9	2:45.93	$240,000
1998	Amerique, 4, 116	E. Delahoussaye	Star Performance, 5	Kessem Power (NZ), 6	10	2:47.08	$240,000
1997	Marlin, 4, 119	E. Delahoussaye	(DH) African Dancer, 5	Sunshack (GB), 6	7	2:44.56	$240,000
			(DH) Sunshack (GB), 6				
1996	Raintrap (GB), 6, 115	A. O. Solis	†Windsharp, 5	Awad, 6	7	2:48.40	$240,000
1995	Red Bishop, 7, 119	M. E. Smith	Special Price, 6	Liyoun (Ire), 7	8	2:48.02	$220,000
1994	Bien Bien, 5, 122	J. D. McCarron	Grand Flotilla, 7	Alex the Great (GB), 5	9	2:46.69	$220,000
1993	Kotashaan (Fr), 5, 121	K. J. Desormeaux	Bien Bien, 4	Fraise, 5	5	2:45.00	$220,000
1992	Fly Till Dawn, 6, 121	P. A. Valenzuela	†Miss Alleged, 5	Wall Street Dancer, 4	9	2:46.53	$275,000

Named for San Juan Capistrano, California, which took its name from the mission. 1942-'44,1947-'48 not held. 1965-2002 San Juan Capistrano Invitational H. 1935-'38 1⅛ miles; 1939,1941,1945-'46,1949,1954 1½ miles; 1940 1¼ miles; 1950-'53 1¾ miles. 1935-'53 dirt. 1935-'39,1941-'67 three-year-olds and up; 1940 three-year-olds. 1993, 2001 new course record. †denotes female.

San Luis Obispo Handicap

Grade 2, Santa Anita Park, four-year-olds and up, 1½ miles, turf. Held February 15, 2003, with a gross value of $200,000. First held in 1952. Graded since 1973. Stakes record 2:23.80 (1974 Captain Cee Jay).

Year	Winner	Jockey	Second	Third	Strs	Time	1st Purse
2003	The Tin Man, 5, 121	M. E. Smith	Special Matter, 5	Harrisand (Fr), 5	5	2:31.22	$120,000
2002	Nazirali (Ire), 5, 112	B. Blanc	Continental Red, 6	Bonapartiste (Fr), 8	7	2:26.09	$120,000
2001	Persianlux (GB), 5, 113	T. Baze	Devon Deputy, 5	Falcon Flight (Fr), 5	10	2:27.70	$120,000
2000	Dark Moondancer (GB), 5, 120	C. J. McCarron	The Fly (GB), 6	Casino King (Ire), 5	5	2:39.61	$120,000
1999	Kessem Power (NZ), 7, 115	G. L. Stevens	Brave Act (GB), 5	Lazy Lode (Arg), 5	5	2:28.02	$120,000
1998	Bienvenido (Arg), 5, 115	C. J. McCarron	Prize Giving (GB), 5	Callisthene (Fr), 6	6	2:29.34	$120,000
1997	Shanawi (Ire), 5, 111	B. Blanc	Rainbow Dancer (Fr), 6	Bon Point (GB), 7	7	2:24.51	$132,100
1996	†Windsharp, 5, 115	E. J. Delahoussaye	†Wandesta (GB), 5	Virginia Carnival, 4	6	2:30.33	$130,800
1995	Square Cut, 6, 114	C. W. Antley	Ianomami (Ire), 5	River Rhythm, 8	10	2:26.04	$133,200
1994	Fanmore, 6, 116	K. J. Desormeaux	Bien Bien, 5	Navire (Fr), 5	9	2:27.03	$131,400
1993	Kotashaan (Fr), 5, 114	K. J. Desormeaux	Carnival Baby, 5	The Name's Jimmy, 4	8	2:27.64	$129,600
1992	Quest for Fame (GB), 5, 121	G. L. Stevens	Cool Gold Mood, 5	†Miss Alleged, 5	9	2:28.79	$158,500

Named for St. Louis of Toulouse, a Franciscan bishop. 1963-'67 not held. 1952-'62 Washington's Birthday H. 1990-'91 Grade 3. 1952-'53 7 furlongs; 1954,1970 1¼ miles; 1968,1972 about 1½ miles. 1952-'53,1973,1980 dirt. †denotes female.

San Luis Rey Handicap

Grade 2, Santa Anita Park, four-year-olds and up, 1½ miles, turf. Held March 15, 2003, with a gross value of $250,000. First held in 1952. Graded since 1973. Stakes record 2:23 (1970 Fiddle Isle; 1980 John Henry).

Year	Winner	Jockey	Second	Third	Strs	Time	1st Purse
2003	Champion Lodge (Ire), 6, 116	A. O. Solis	Special Matter, 5	Adminniestrator, 6	7	2:33.48	$150,000
2002	Continental Red, 6, 116	P. A. Valenzuela	Keemoon, 6	Speedy Pick, 4	6	2:26.81	$150,000
2001	Blueprint (Ire), 6, 116	G. L. Stevens	Devon Deputy, 5	Kerrygold (Fr), 5	8	2:28.57	$150,000
2000	Dark Moondancer (GB), 5, 122	C. J. McCarron	single Empire (Ire), 6	Bonapartiste (Fr), 6	6	2:26.00	$150,000
1999	Single Empire (Ire), 5, 122	K. J. Desormeaux	Kessem Power (NZ), 7	Alvo Certo (Brz), 7	7	2:27.97	$150,000
1998	Kessem Power (NZ), 6, 122	L. Dettori	Storm Trooper, 5	Star Performance, 5	12	2:28.40	$150,000
1997	Marlin, 4, 122	C. J. McCarron	Sunshack (GB), 6	Peckinpah's Soul (Fr), 6	10	2:28.14	$166,600
1996	†Windsharp, 5, 117	E. Delahoussaye	†Wandesta (GB), 5	Silver Wizard, 5	7	2:27.91	$161,900
1995	Sandpit (Brz), 6, 124	C. S. Nakatani	River Rhythm, 8	Square Cut, 8	7	2:27.15	$155,000
1994	Bien Bien, 5, 124	C. J. McCarron	Navire (Fr), 5	Grand Flotilla, 5	5	2:26.65	$149,500
1993	Kotashaan (Fr), 5, 124	K. J. Desormeaux	Bien Bien, 4	Fast Cure, 4	4	2:23.91	$148,250
1992	Fly Till Dawn, 6, 124	L. A. Pincay Jr.	Provins, 4	Quest for Fame (GB), 5	6	2:27.26	$179,000

Named for the San Luis Rey Mission; the mission was named in honor of King and St. Louis IX of France. 1952-'53,1973-2000 San Luis Rey S. 1973-'96 Grade 1. 1952 7 furlongs; 1953 6 furlongs; 1954 1 mile. 1952-'54,1962,1975 dirt. 1958-'59 three-year-olds and up. 1952-'54 California-bred. †denotes female.

San Marcos Stakes

Grade 2, Santa Anita Park, four-year-olds and up, 1¼ miles, turf. Held January 20, 2003, with a gross value of $150,000. First held in 1952. Graded since 1973. Stakes record 1:58.02 (2003 Johar).

Year	Winner	Jockey	Second	Third	Strs	Time	1st Purse
2003	Johar, 4, 120	A. O. Solis	The Tin Man, 5	Grammarian, 5	7	1:57.92	$90,000
2002	Irish Prize, 6, 122	G. L. Stevens	Continental Red, 6	Cagney (Brz), 5	6	2:01.27	$90,000
2001	Bienamado, 5, 122	C. J. McCarron	Kerrygold (Fr), 5	Northern Quest (Fr), 6	7	2:02.75	$90,000
2000	Public Purse, 6	A. O. Solis	Dark Moondancer (GB), 5	The Fly (GB), 5	7	1:59.58	$98,280
1999	Brave Act (GB), 5	G. F. Almeida	Ferrari (Ger), 5	Native Desert, 5	7	2:04.25	$90,000
1998	Prize Giving (GB), 5	A. O. Solis	Bienvenido (Arg), 5	Martiniquais (Ire), 5	6	2:04.41	$97,380
1997	Sandpit (Brz), 8	C. S. Nakatani	River Deep, 6	Shanawi (Ire), 6	8	2:00.61	$99,000
1996	Urgent Request (Ire), 6	C. W. Antley	Bon Point (GB), 6	Virginia Carnival, 6	6	2:02.26	$97,000
1995	River Flyer, 4	C. W. Antley	Silver Wizard, 5	Savinio, 5	7	2:05.61	$92,200
1994	Bien Bien, 5	L. A. Pincay Jr.	Explosive Red, 4	Myrakalu (Fr), 4	6	2:00.55	$75,850
1993	Star of Cozzene, 5	G. L. Stevens	Kotashaan (Fr), 5	Carnival Baby, 5	7	2:01.71	$77,650
1992	Classic Fame, 6	E. Delahoussaye	Fly Till Dawn, 6	French Seventyfive, 6	6	1:58.02	$90,600

Named for Rancho San Marcos, which was located in Santa Barbara County. 1970 not held. 1952-2000 San Marcos H. 1973-'92 Grade 3. 1952-'53 1 mile; 1978 1⅛ miles. 1952-'53,1956,1962,1969,1973,1975,1978-'83,1996 dirt. 1955-'59 three-year-olds and up.

San Miguel Stakes

Grade 3, Santa Anita Park, three-year-olds, 6 furlongs, dirt. Held January 12, 2003, with a gross value of $107,800. First held in 1956. Graded since 1973. Stakes record 1:08.22 (1991 Prince Wild).

Year	Winner	Jockey	Second	Third	Strs	Time	1st Purse
2003	Omega Code, 3, 121	M. A. Pedroza	Only the Best, 3	Jimmy O, 3	5	1:08.65	$64,680
2002	Popular, 3, 114	V. Espinoza	Roman Dancer, 3	Royal Moro, 3	5	1:09.00	$64,740
2001	Lasersport, 3, 116	C. S. Nakatani	Early Flyer, 3	Bills Paid, 3	6	1:08.60	$64,500
2000	Swept Overboard, 3, 116	E. J. Delahoussaye	Forest Camp, 3	Joopy Doopy, 3	6	1:08.99	$64,320
1999	Cape Canaveral, 3, 118	D. R. Flores	Aristotle, 3	Actin Time, 3	4	1:09.15	$62,760
1998	Rio Oro, 3, 118	D. A. Lozoya	Iron Cat, 3	Cat Doctor, 3	9	1:08.60	$66,180
1997	Thisnearlywasmine, 3, 118	C. J. McCarron	Smokin Mel, 3	Renteria, 3	6	1:08.55	$64,350
1996	Honour and Glory, 3, 121	G. L. Stevens	Afleetaffair, 3	Valid Expectations, 3	6	1:08.93	$64,350
1995	Petionville, 3, 114	C. W. Antley	Regal Fighter, 3	Cold n Calculating, 3	4	1:09.16	$45,225
1994	Mr. Cooperative, 3, 114	M. A. Pedroza	Subtle Trouble, 3	Ramblin Guy, 3	8	1:09.53	$48,300
1993	Denmars Dream, 3, 114	A. O. Solis	Altazarr, 3	Boss Soss, 3	7	1:08.76	$47,475

Named for three California land grants called Rancho San Miguel. Home of the famous Mission San Miguel. 1959,1970,1992 not held. 1975-'98 not graded. 1956 7 furlongs; 1958-'63 6½ furlongs. 1985-'91 two-year-olds.

San Pasqual Handicap

Grade 2, Santa Anita Park, four-year-olds and up, 1 1/16 miles, dirt. Held January 4, 2003, with a gross value of $150,000. First held in 1935. Graded since 1973. Stakes record 1:40.20 (1978 Ancient Title; 1980 Valdez).

Year	Winner	Jockey	Second	Third	Strs	Time	1st Purse
2003	Congaree, 5, 121	J. D. Bailey	Kudos, 6	Hot Market, 5	9	1:41.04	$90,000
2002	Wooden Phone, 5, 119	D. R. Flores	Euchre, 6	Red Eye, 6	6	1:41.83	$120,000
2001	Freedom Crest, 5, 116	G. L. Stevens	Bosque Redondo, 4	Sultry Substitute, 6	8	1:41.94	$120,000
2000	Dixie Dot Com, 5, 118	P. A. Valenzuela	Budroyale, 7	Six Below, 5	6	1:40.95	$120,000
1999	Silver Charm, 5, 125	G. L. Stevens	Malek (Chi), 6	Crafty Friend, 6	5	1:41.78	$120,000
1998	Hal's Pal (GB), 5, 113	B. Blanc	Malek (Chi), 5	Flick (GB), 6	9	1:41.89	$120,000
1997	Kingdom Found, 7, 115	G. L. Stevens	Savinio, 7	Eltish, 5	4	1:40.74	$122,200
1996	Alphabet Soup, 5, 118	C. W. Antley	Luthier Fever, 5	Cezind, 6	9	1:41.66	$130,100
1995	Del Mar Dennis, 5, 118	A. O. Solis	Slew of Damascus, 7	Tossofthecoin, 5	5	1:41.23	$116,100
1994	Hill Pass, 5, 113	C. J. McCarron	Best Pal, 6	Lottery Winner, 5	7	1:41.00	$87,800
1993	Jovial (GB), 6, 115	M. Walls	Marquetry, 6	Provins, 5	7	1:41.94	$91,400
1992	Twilight Agenda, 6, 125	K. J. Desormeaux	Ibero (Arg), 5	Answer Do, 6	6	1:42.32	$89,000

Named for El Rancho San Pasqual, which encompassed almost all of what is now the Pasadena, California, area. 1942-'44 not held. 1935-'36 6 furlongs; 1938 7 furlongs; 1939-'41 1⅛ miles; 1955 1¼ miles. 1935-'36 three-year-olds; 1937-'53,1958 three-year-olds and up. 1993 Best Pal finished second, DQ to fifth.

San Rafael Stakes

Grade 2, Santa Anita Park, three-year-olds, 1 mile, dirt. Held March 1, 2003, with a gross value of $200,000. First held in 1975. Graded since 1983. Stakes record 1:34.40 (1982 Prince Spellbound).

Year	Winner	Jockey	Second	Third	Strs	Time	1st Purse
2003	Rojo Toro, 3, 115	J. D. Bailey	Spensive, 3	Crowned Dancer, 3	7	1:35.89	$120,000
2002	Came Home, 3, 118	C. J. McCarron	Easy Grades, 3	Werblin, 3	7	1:36.24	$120,000
2001	Crafty C. T., 3, 116	E. J. Delahoussaye	Palmeiro, 3	Early Flyer, 3	9	1:35.79	$120,000
2000	War Chant, 3, 116	K. J. Desormeaux	Archer City Slew, 3	Cocky, 3	6	1:36.45	$120,000
1999	Desert Hero, 3, 116	C. S. Nakatani	Prime Timber, 3	Capsized, 3	9	1:36.45	$120,000
1998	Orville N Wilbur's, 3, 115	C. S. Nakatani	Souvenir Copy, 3	Futuristic, 3	6	1:35.96	$120,000
1997	Funontherun, 3, 115	G. F. Almeida	Inexcessivelygood, 3	Hello (Ire), 3	10	1:36.01	$121,800
1996	Honour and Glory, 3, 121	G. L. Stevens	Halo Sunshine, 3	Matty G, 3	8	1:36.45	$122,000
1995	Larry the Legend, 3, 118	K. J. Desormeaux	Fandarel Dancer, 3	Timber Country, 3	5	1:37.61	$88,600
1994	Tabasco Cat, 3, 121	P. Day	Powis Castle, 3	Shepherd's Field, 3	5	1:36.39	$89,700
1993	Devoted Brass, 3, 115	K. J. Desormeaux	Union City, 3	Stuka, 3	5	1:35.13	$90,000
1992	A.P. Indy, 3, 121	E. J. Delahoussaye	Treekster, 3	Prince Wild, 3	6	1:35.41	$90,300

Named for Rancho San Rafael, a 1785 land grant where Burbank, Glendale, and Montrose, California, are currently located. 1977,1979-'80 not held. 1983 Grade 3. 1975 6 furlongs; 1976 1⅛ miles. 1976 turf. 1975-'78 four-year-olds and up. 1975-'78 fillies and mares.

San Simeon Handicap

Grade 3, Santa Anita Park, four-year-olds and up, about 6½ furlongs, turf. Held April 19, 2003, with a gross value of $137,500. First held in 1968. Graded since 1973. Stakes record 1:12.20 (1990 Coastal Voyage).

Year	Winner	Jockey	Second	Third	Strs	Time	1st Purse
2003	Speak in Passing, 6, 118	D. R. Flores	Spinelessjellyfish, 7	Rocky Bar, 5	8	1:12.87	$82,500
2002	Malabar Gold, 5, 117	C. J. McCarron	Astonished (GB), 6	Nuclear Debate, 7	9	1:11.73	$82,825
2001	Lake William, 5, 114	V. Espinoza	Macward, 5	Touch of the Blues (Fr), 4	6	1:12.34	$80,175
2000	El Cielo, 6, 117	J. Valdivia Jr.	King Slayer (GB), 5	Scooter Brown, 5	6	1:12.66	$79,440
1999	Naninja, 6, 115	C. J. McCarron	Expressionist, 4	Indian Rocket (GB), 5	7	1:13.32	$65,220

1998	**Labeeb (GB)**, 6, 120	K. J. Desormeaux	Surachai, 5	Captain Collins (Ire), 4	11	1:12.94	$67,860
1997	**Sandtrap**, 4, 117	A. O. Solis	Daggett Peak, 6	Tychonic (GB), 7	6	1:12.50	$96,850
1996	†**Ski Dancer**, 4, 114	G. L. Stevens	Daggett Peak, 5	Boulderdash Bay, 6	6	1:13.98	$64,200
1995	**Finder's Fortune**, 6, 117	P. A. Valenzuela	Rotsaluck, 4	Pembroke, 5	7	1:13.65	$64,550
1994	**Rapan Boy (Aus)**, 6, 114	G. L. Stevens	The Berkeley Man, 4	Artistic Reef (GB), 5	7	1:13.16	$63,100
1993	**Exemplary Leader**, 7, 113	M. A. Pedroza	Prince Ferdinand (GB), 4	Wild Harmony, 4	8	1:13.98	$64,300
1992	†**Heart of Joy**, 5, 119	C. J. McCarron	Regal Groom, 5	Time Gentlemen (GB), 4	10	1:13.94	$69,600

Named for Rancho San Simeon, originally attached to the San Miguel Mission. 1975-'83 not graded. 1968-'75,1977-'79 7 furlongs; 1976 1 mile; 1980-'85,1987-'90 6½ furlongs. 1968-'79,1981,1983,1988 dirt. 1997 Destiny's Venture finished second, DQ to fourth. †denotes female.

Santa Ana Handicap

Grade 2, Santa Anita Park, four-year-olds and up, fillies and mares, 1⅛ miles, turf. Held March 22, 2003, with a gross value of $150,000. First held in 1968. Graded since 1981. Stakes record 1:46.23 (1993 Exchange).

Year	Winner	Jockey	Second	Third	Strs	Time	1st Purse
2003	**Noches de Rosa (Chi)**, 5, 115	M. E. Smith	Garden in the Rain (Fr), 6	Megahertz (GB), 4	8	1:48.31	$90,000
2002	**Golden Apples (Ire)**, 4, 119	G. K. Gomez	Starine (Fr), 5	Astra, 6	9	1:47.05	$90,000
2001	**Beautiful Noise**, 5, 115	C. J. McCarron	High Walden, 4	Matiere Grise (Fr), 4	12	1:47.27	$90,000
2000	**See You Soon (Fr)**, 5, 119	V. Espinoza	Virginie (Brz), 6	Country Garden (GB), 5	7	1:49.30	$97,830
1999	**See You Soon (Fr)**, 5, 119	K. J. Desormeaux	Blending Element (Ire), 6	La Madame (Chi), 4	6	1:49.46	$90,000
1998	**Fiji (GB)**, 4, 115	K. J. Desormeaux	Shake the Yoke (GB), 5	Golden Arches (Fr), 4	6	1:49.85	$96,480
1997	**Windsharp**, 6, 121	E. J. Delahoussaye	Wheatly Special, 4	Donna Viola (GB), 5	7	1:49.47	$97,750
1996	**Pharma**, 5, 116	C. J. McCarron	Angel in My Heart (Fr), 4	Matiara, 4	5	1:49.14	$95,650
1995	**Wandesta (GB)**, 4, 115	C. S. Nakatani	Yearly Tour, 4	Aube Indienne (Fr), 5	7	1:50.18	$90,700
1994	**Possibly Perfect**, 4, 119	K. J. Desormeaux	Hero's Love, 6	Lady Blessington (Fr), 6	7	1:51.05	$91,000
1993	**Exchange**, 5, 120	L. A. Pincay Jr.	Party Cited, 4	Villandry, 5	5	**1:46.23**	$89,700
1992	**Gravieres (Fr)**, 4, 116	G. L. Stevens	Appealing Missy, 5	Explosive Ele, 5	8	1:47.75	$94,900

Named for the Rancho Santa Ana, located in what is now Ventura County, California. 1981 Grade 3; 1984-'96 Grade 1. 1971 1⅟₁₆ miles. 1981-'83,1986 dirt. 1994 Waitryst (NZ) finished third, DQ to last.

Santa Anita Derby

Grade 1, Santa Anita Park, three-year-olds, 1¼ miles, dirt. Held April 5, 2003, with a gross value of $750,000. First held in 1935. Graded since 1973. Stakes record 1:47 (1965 Lucky Debonair; 1973 Sham; 1998 Indian Charlie).

Year	Winner	Jockey	Second	Third	Strs	Time	1st Purse
2003	**Buddy Gil**, 3, 122	G. L. Stevens	Indian Express, 3	Kafwain, 3	9	1:49.36	$450,000
2002	**Came Home**, 3, 122	C. J. McCarron	Easy Grades, 3	Lusty Latin, 3	8	1:50.02	$450,000
2001	**Point Given**, 3, 122	G. L. Stevens	Crafty C. T., 3	I Love Silver, 3	6	1:47.77	$450,000
2000	**The Deputy (Ire)**, 3, 120	C. J. McCarron	War Chant, 3	Captain Steve, 3	8	1:49.08	$600,000
1999	**General Challenge**, 3, 120	G. L. Stevens	Prime Timber, 3	Desert Hero, 3	8	1:48.92	$450,000
1998	**Indian Charlie**, 3, 120	G. L. Stevens	Real Quiet, 3	Artax, 3	7	**1:47.00**	$450,000
1997	**Free House**, 3, 120	K. J. Desormeaux	Silver Charm, 3	Hello (Ire), 3	10	1:47.60	$450,000
1996	**Cavonnier**, 3, 120	C. J. McCarron	Honour and Glory, 3	Corker, 3	8	1:48.81	$600,000
1995	**Larry the Legend**, 3, 122	G. L. Stevens	Afternoon Deelites, 3	Jumron (GB), 3	8	1:47.99	$385,000
1994	**Brocco**, 3, 122	G. L. Stevens	Tabasco Cat, 3	Strodes Creek, 3	6	1:48.33	$275,000
1993	**Personal Hope**, 3, 122	G. L. Stevens	Union City, 3	†Eliza, 3	7	1:49.03	$275,000
1992	**A.P. Indy**, 3, 122	E. J. Delahoussaye	Bertrando, 3	Casual Lies, 3	7	1:49.25	$275,000

1942-'44 not held. 1935-'37 1⅟₁₆ miles; 1947 1¼ miles. 1996 Alyrob finished second, DQ to eighth. †denotes female.

Santa Anita Handicap

Grade 1, Santa Anita Park, four-year-olds and up, 1¼ miles, dirt. Held March 1, 2003, with a gross value of $1,000,000. First held in 1935. Graded since 1973. Stakes record 1:58.60 (1979 Affirmed).

Year	Winner	Jockey	Second	Third	Strs	Time	1st Purse
2003	**Milwaukee Brew**, 6, 119	E. S. Prado	Congaree, 5	Kudos, 6	6	1:59.80	$600,000
2002	**Milwaukee Brew**, 5, 115	K. J. Desormeaux	Western Pride, 4	Kudos, 5	14	2:01.02	$600,000
2001	**Tiznow**, 4, 122	C. J. McCarron	Wooden Phone, 4	Tribunal, 4	12	2:01.55	$600,000
2000	**General Challenge**, 4, 121	C. S. Nakatani	Budroyale, 7	Puerto Madero (Chi), 6	8	2:01.49	$600,000
1999	**Free House**, 5, 123	C. J. McCarron	Event of the Year, 4	Silver Charm, 5	6	2:00.67	$600,000
1998	**Malek (Chi)**, 5, 115	A. O. Solis	Bagshot, 4	Don't Blame Rio, 5	4	2:02.26	$600,000
1997	**Siphon (Brz)**, 6, 120	D. R. Flores	Sandpit (Brz), 8	Gentlemen (Arg), 5	11	2:00.23	$600,000
1996	**Mr Purple**, 4, 116	E. J. Delahoussaye	Luthier Fever, 5	Just Java, 5	11	2:02.04	$600,000
1995	**Urgent Request (Ire)**, 5, 116	G. L. Stevens	Best Pal, 7	Dare and Go, 4	10	1:59.25	$550,000
1994	**Stuka**, 4, 115	C. W. Antley	Bien Bien, 5	Myrakalu (Fr), 6	8	2:00.17	$550,000
1993	**Sir Beaufort**, 6, 119	P. A. Valenzuela	Star Recruit, 4	Major Impact, 4	11	2:00.55	$550,000
1992	**Best Pal**, 4, 124	K. J. Desormeaux	Twilight Agenda, 6	Defensive Play, 5	7	1:59.08	$550,000

The race and track are both named for Rancho Santa Anita, the name of the land when it was purchased by E. J. "Lucky" Baldwin. 1942-'44 not held. 1935-'68 three-year-olds and up. 1994 The Wicked North finished first, DQ to fourth.

Santa Anita Oaks

Grade 1, Santa Anita Park, three-year-olds, fillies, 1¹⁄₁₆ miles, dirt. Held March 8, 2003, with a gross value of $300,000. First held in 1935. Graded since 1973. Stakes record 1:41.20 (1980 Bold 'n Determined).

Year	Winner	Jockey	Second	Third	Strs	Time	1st Purse
2003	Composure, 3, 117	J. D. Bailey	Elloluv, 3	Go for Glamour, 3	5	1:43.34	$180,000
2002	You, 3, 117	J. D. Bailey	Habibti, 3	Ile de France, 3	9	1:42.70	$180,000
2001	Golden Ballet, 3, 117	C. J. McCarron	Flute, 3	Affluent, 3	8	1:41.83	$180,000
2000	Surfside, 3, 117	P. Day	Kumari Continent, 3	Classy Cara, 3	5	1:44.03	$180,000
1999	Excellent Meeting, 3, 117	K. J. Desormeaux	Tout Charmant, 3	Gleefully, 3	6	1:43.26	$150,000
1998	Hedonist, 3, 117	K. J. Desormeaux	Keeper Hill, 3	Nijinsky's Passion, 3	7	1:44.14	$150,000
1997	Sharp Cat, 3, 117	C. S. Nakatani	Queen of Money, 3	Double Park (Fr), 3	5	1:42.22	$128,800
1996	Antespend, 3, 117	C. W. Antley	Cara Rafaela, 3	Hidden Lake, 3	5	1:43.04	$128,600
1995	Serena's Song, 3, 117	C. S. Nakatani	Urbane, 3	Mari's Sheba, 3	5	1:42.71	$121,600
1994	Lakeway, 3, 117	K. J. Desormeaux	Dianes Halo, 3	Flying in the Lane, 3	6	1:41.66	$122,800
1993	Eliza, 3, 117	P. A. Valenzuela	Stalcreek, 3	Dance for Vanny, 3	9	1:42.97	$129,200
1992	Golden Treat, 3, 117	K. J. Desormeaux	Magical Maiden, 3	Queens Court Queen, 3	8	1:43.20	$129,300

1936,1942-'44,1955 not held. 1951-'85 Santa Susana S. 1973-'78 Grade 2. 1935 3 furlongs; 1937-'38,1946 6 furlongs; 1939-'45,1947-'51,1956 7 furlongs; 1954,1957 1 mile. 1935 two-year-olds.

Santa Barbara Handicap

Grade 2, Santa Anita Park, four-year-olds and up, fillies and mares, 1¼ miles, turf. Held April 19, 2003, with a gross value of $250,000. First held in 1935. Graded since 1973. Stakes record 1:57.50 (1991 Bequest).

Year	Winner	Jockey	Second	Third	Strs	Time	1st Purse
2003	Megahertz (GB), 4, 117	A. O. Solis	Trekking, 4	Noches de Rosa (Chi), 5	5	2:00.08	$150,000
2002	Astra, 6, 121	K. J. Desormeaux	Golden Apples (Ire), 4	Polaire (Ire), 6	6	2:01.48	$150,000
2001	Astra, 5, 118	K. J. Desormeaux	Beautiful Noise, 5	Uncharted Haven (GB), 4	7	2:01.33	$150,000
2000	Caffe Latte (Ire), 4, 116	C. S. Nakatani	Happyanunoit (NZ), 5	Country Garden (GB), 5	6	2:00.51	$150,000
1999	Tranquility Lake, 4, 116	E. J. Delahoussaye	Virginie (Brz), 5	Midnight Line, 4	7	2:01.06	$150,000
1998	Fiji (GB), 4, 119	K. J. Desormeaux	Pomona (GB), 5	Ecoute, 5	5	2:00.35	$150,000
1997	Donna Viola (GB), 5, 120	G. L. Stevens	Fanjica (Ire), 5	Windsharp, 6	8	1:59.85	$197,200
1996	Auriette (Ire), 4, 116	K. J. Desormeaux	Angel in My Heart (Fr), 4	Wandesta (GB), 5	5	2:02.10	$190,900
1995	Wandesta (GB), 4, 118	C. S. Nakatani	Yearly Tour, 4	Morgana, 4	7	2:01.77	$126,400
1994	Possibly Perfect, 4, 121	K. J. Desormeaux	Pracer, 4	Waitryst (NZ), 5	5	2:00.56	$122,800
1993	Exchange, 5, 121	L. A. Pincay Jr.	Trishyde, 4	Revasser, 4	4	2:02.26	$120,400
1992	Kostroma (Ire), 6, 121	K. J. Desormeaux	Miss Alleged, 5	Free At Last (GB), 5	6	1:59.63	$152,700

Named for Santa Barbara, California, where an 1841 tax was the first on racing wagers. 1939-'40,1942-'45,1947-'51,1959-'61 not held. 1973-'95 Grade 1. 1935-'41 3 furlongs; 1946-'52 7 furlongs; 1953-'54,1958 6 furlongs; 1955-'57 1¹⁄₁₆ miles; 1968 about 1¼ miles. 1935-'58,1973,1977,1982 dirt. 1937-'41 two-year-olds; 1952-'54 three-year-olds; 1955-'65 three-year-olds and up. 1935-'54 California-bred.

Santa Catalina Stakes

Grade 2, Santa Anita Park, three-year-olds, 1¹⁄₁₆ miles, dirt. Held January 18, 2003, with a gross value of $150,000. First held in 1935. Graded since 1998. Stakes record 1:41.40 (1981 Stancharry).

Year	Winner	Jockey	Second	Third	Strs	Time	1st Purse
2003	Domestic Dispute, 3, 113	D. R. Flores	Our Bobby V., 3	Scrimshaw, 3	8	1:42.20	$90,000
2002	Labamta Babe, 3, 115	K. J. Desormeaux	Siphonic, 3	Cottonwood Cowboy, 3	6	1:42.50	$90,000
2001	Millennium Wind, 3, 114	C. J. McCarron	Palmeiro, 3	Denied, 3	6	1:42.38	$64,620
2000	The Deputy (Ire), 3, 115	C. J. McCarron	High Yield, 3	Captain Steve, 3	6	1:43.04	$64,380
1999	General Challenge, 3, 117	G. L. Stevens	Buck Trout, 3	Brilliantly, 3	5	1:42.93	$63,900
1998	Artax, 3, 114	C. J. McCarron	Souvenir Copy, 3	Allen's Oop, 3	6	1:42.32	$64,320
1997	Hello (Ire), 3, 120	C. J. McCarron	Bagshot, 3	Carmen's Baby, 3	8	1:42.60	$65,950
1996	Prince of Thieves, 3, 113	G. L. Stevens	Smithfield, 3	Matty G, 3	6	1:42.94	$64,250
1995	Larry the Legend, 3, 117	K. J. Desormeaux	In Character (GB), 3	Awesome Thought, 3	5	1:42.93	$45,975
1994	Wekiva Springs, 3, 121	K. J. Desormeaux	Gracious Ghost, 3	Dream Trapp, 3	5	1:41.94	$45,900
1993	Art of Living, 3, 115	G. L. Stevens	Tossofthecoin, 3	Glowing Crown, 3	5	1:43.48	$45,900
1992	Vying Victor, 3, 115	C. A. Black	Turbulent Kris, 3	Al Sabin, 3	11	1:44.33	$51,000

Named for Rancho Santa Catalina Island, which occupied the entire south off the California coast. 1936,1942-'44 not held. 1935,1941-'63,1997 Santa Catalina H.; 1937-'39 Santa Catalina California-bred Championship; 1940 Santa Catalina Nursery S. 1998 Grade 3. 1935 1 mile; 1939,1947-'52,1954-'63 1¹⁄₁₆ miles; 1940 3 furlongs; 1970 7 furlongs. 1937-'38,1941-'46,1991 three-year-olds and up; 1940 two-year-olds; 1947-'63 four-year-olds and up. 1992 for non-winners of a race worth $25,000 to the winner.

Santa Margarita Handicap

Grade 1, Santa Anita Park, four-year-olds and up, fillies and mares, 1⅛ miles, dirt. Held March 9, 2003, with a gross value of $300,000. First held in 1935. Graded since 1973. Stakes record 1:47 (1954 Cerise Reine; 1986 Lady's Secret).

Year	Winner	Jockey	Second	Third	Strs	Time	1st Purse
2003	Starrer, 5, 121	P. A. Valenzuela	Sightseek, 4	Bella Bellucci, 4	5	1:48.20	$180,000
2002	Azeri, 4, 115	M. E. Smith	Spain, 5	Printemps (Chi), 5	7	1:49.01	$180,000
2001	Lazy Slusan, 6, 116	D. R. Flores	Spain, 4	Critikola (Arg), 6	7	1:48.59	$180,000

2000	**Riboletta (Brz)**, 5, 115	C. S. Nakatani	Bordelaise (Arg), 5	Snowberg, 5	5	1:50.40	$180,000
1999	**Manistique**, 4, 122	G. L. Stevens	Magical Allure, 4	India Divina (Chi), 4	4	1:48.31	$180,000
1998	**Toda Una Dama (Arg)**, 5, 114	G. F. Almeida	Exotic Wood, 6	Praviana (Chi), 4	10	1:48.87	$180,000
1997	**Jewel Princess**, 5, 125	C. S. Nakatani	Top Rung, 6	Hidden Lake, 4	6	1:49.30	$180,000
1996	**Twice the Vice**, 5, 117	C. J. McCarron	Sleep Easy, 4	Jewel Princess, 4	8	1:49.53	$180,000
1995	**Queens Court Queen**, 6, 120	C. S. Nakatani	Paseana (Arg), 8	Klassy Kim, 4	5	1:48.81	$180,000
1994	**Paseana (Arg)**, 7, 123	C. J. McCarron	Kalita Melody (GB), 6	Stalcreek, 4	9	1:49.12	$180,000
1993	**Southern Truce**, 5, 115	C. S. Nakatani	Paseana (Arg), 6	Guiza, 6	9	1:49.46	$180,000
1992	**Paseana (Arg)**, 5, 122	C. J. McCarron	Laramie Moon (Arg), 5	Colour Chart, 5	5	1:47.48	$180,000

Named for the 1841 land grant Rancho Santa Margarita y Las Flores. 1942-'44 not held. 1935-'67 Santa Margarita H. 1935-'36 7 furlongs; 1937 6 furlongs; 1938-'48,1953-'54 1 1/16 miles. 1935-'40,1945-'60 three-year-olds and up. 1935-'37 both sexes.

Santa Maria Handicap

Grade 1, Santa Anita Park, four-year-olds and up, fillies and mares, 1 1/16 miles, dirt. Held February 16, 2003, with a gross value of $200,000. First held in 1934. Graded since 1973. Stakes record 1:40.95 (1998 Exotic Wood).

Year	Winner	Jockey	Second	Third	Strs	Time	1st Purse
2003	**Starrer**, 5, 119	P. A. Valenzuela	You, 4	Rhiana, 6	5	1:42.75	$120,000
2002	**Favorite Funtime**, 5, 116	G. L. Stevens	Verruma (Brz), 6	Printemps (Chi), 5	7	1:44.15	$120,000
2001	**Lovellon (Arg)**, 5, 116	G. L. Stevens	Feverish, 6	Critikola (Arg), 5	5	1:43.37	$120,000
2000	**Manistique**, 5, 125	C. S. Nakatani	Snowberg, 5	Gourmet Girl, 5	8	1:42.60	$120,000
1999	**India Divina (Chi)**, 5, 114	G. K. Gomez	Victory Stripes (Arg), 5	Belle's Flag, 6	5	1:42.71	$120,000
1998	**Exotic Wood**, 6, 121	C. J. McCarron	Toda Una Dama (Arg), 5	Tuxedo Junction, 5	5	1:40.95	$120,000
1997	**Jewel Princess**, 5, 123	C. S. Nakatani	Cat's Cradle, 5	Top Rung, 6	7	1:41.72	$97,900
1996	**Serena's Song**, 4, 124	G. L. Stevens	Twice the Vice, 5	Real Connection, 5	5	1:42.21	$95,800
1995	**Queens Court Queen**, 6, 118	C. S. Nakatani	Paseana (Arg), 8	Key Phrase, 4	5	1:41.61	$89,300
1994	**Supah Gem**, 4, 116	C. S. Nakatani	Paseana (Arg), 7	Alysbelle, 5	7	1:41.83	$90,700
1993	**Race the Wild Wind**, 4, 117	K. J. Desormeaux	Paseana (Arg), 6	Southern Truce, 5	6	1:41.27	$90,550
1992	**Paseana (Arg)**, 5, 120	C. J. McCarron	Colour Chart, 5	Campagnarde (Arg), 5	5	1:41.94	$89,100

Named for the city of Santa Maria, California, located in Santa Barbara County. 1937,1942-'45,1948-'51 not held. 1934-'47 Santa Maria S. 1973-'89 Grade 2. 1934-'40 6 furlongs; 1941 3 furlongs; 1946-'53 1 mile; 1954-'56 7 furlongs. 1934-'35 two-year-olds and up; 1936-'40,1946-'47 three-year-olds; 1941 two-year-olds; 1952-'59 three-year-olds and up. 1936-'47 fillies. 1941 California-bred.

Santa Monica Handicap

Grade 1, Santa Anita Park, four-year-olds and up, fillies and mares, 7 furlongs, dirt. Held January 25, 2003, with a gross value of $200,000. First held in 1957. Graded since 1973. Stakes record 1:20.60 (1982 Past Forgetting).

Year	Winner	Jockey	Second	Third	Strs	Time	1st Purse
2003	**Affluent**, 5, 199	A. O. Solis	Sightseek, 4	Secret of Mecca, 5	7	1:22.17	$120,000
2002	**Kalookan Queen**, 6, 119	A. O. Solis	Leading Light, 7	Spain, 5	5	1:22.37	$120,000
2001	**Nany's Sweep**, 5, 117	K. J. Desormeaux	Serenita (Arg), 4	Surfside, 4	7	1:22.50	$120,000
2000	**Honest Lady**, 4, 114	C. S. Nakatani	Kalookan Queen, 4	Enjoy the Moment, 5	9	1:21.45	$132,840
1999	**Stop Traffic**, 6, 120	C. A. Black	Belle's Flag, 6	Closed Escrow, 6	8	1:22.17	$120,000
1998	**Exotic Wood**, 6, 121	C. J. McCarron	Madame Pandit, 5	Advancing Star, 5	8	1:21.07	$120,000
1997	**Toga Toga Toga**, 5, 114	J. A. Garcia	Ski Dancer, 5	Grab the Prize, 5	6	1:23.27	$96,750
1996	**Serena's Song**, 4, 123	G. L. Stevens	Exotic Wood, 4	Klassy Kim, 5	6	1:21.56	$96,800
1995	**Key Phrase**, 4, 116	C. W. Antley	Flying in the Lane, 4	Desert Stormer, 5	9	1:22.82	$93,100
1994	**Southern Truce**, 6, 116	G. L. Stevens	Arches of Gold, 5	Mamselle Bebette, 4	9	1:21.44	$93,100
1993	**Freedom Cry**, 5, 114	A. O. Solis	Devil's Orchid, 6	Mama Simba, 6	7	1:21.78	$91,200
1992	**Laramie Moon (Arg)**, 5, 116	E. J. Delahoussaye	D'Or Ruckus, 4	Ifyoucouldseemenow, 4	10	1:22.66	$94,700

Named for the city of Santa Monica, California. 1970 not held. 1973-'83,1988-'89 Grade 2; 1984-'87 Grade 3. 1957-'59 three-year-olds and up.

Santa Ynez Stakes

Grade 2, Santa Anita Park, three-year-olds, fillies, 7 furlongs, dirt. Held January 20, 2003, with a gross value of $150,000. First held in 1952. Graded since 1973. Stakes record 1:21.20 (1979 Terlingua).

Year	Winner	Jockey	Second	Third	Strs	Time	1st Purse
2003	**Elloluv**, 3, 121	P. A. Valenzuela	Watching You, 3	Himalayan, 3	5	1:23.03	$90,000
2002	**Dancing (GB)**, 3, 116	G. L. Stevens	Respectful, 3	Lady George, 3	8	1:23.07	$90,000
2001	**Golden Ballet**, 3, 123	C. J. McCarron	Affluent, 3	Warren's Whistle, 3	9	1:22.30	$90,000
2000	**Penny Blues**, 3, 118	E. J. Delahoussaye	Classic Olympio, 3	Mean Imogene, 3	5	1:23.38	$63,600
1999	**Honest Lady**, 3, 115	K. J. Desormeaux	Rayelle, 3	Controlled, 3	4	1:21.67	$63,240
1998	**Nijinsky's Passion**, 3, 121	C. A. Black	Well Chosen, 3	Vivid Angel, 3	7	1:23.15	$64,980
1997	**Queen of Money**, 3, 116	D. R. Flores	Goodnight Irene, 3	High Heeled Hope, 3	8	1:22.55	$65,650
1996	**Raw Gold**, 3, 121	C. W. Antley	Pareja, 3	Hidden Lake, 3	6	1:22.66	$64,550
1995	**Serena's Song**	C. S. Nakatani	Cat's Cradle	Call Now	5	1:21.45	$59,800
1994	**Tricky Code**	C. S. Nakatani	Fancy 'n Fabulous	Sophisticatedcielo	5	1:22.16	$59,575
1993	**Fit to Lead**	C. S. Nakatani	Nijivision	Booklore	8	1:22.55	$62,500
1992	**Looie Capote**	K. J. Desormeaux	Icy Eyes	Soviet Sojourn	7	1:23.42	$61,450

Named for the city of Santa Ynez, California, which takes its name from an 1804 mission. 1953 not held. 1990-'95 Santa Ynez Breeders' Cup S. 1975-'80,1984-'98 Grade 3. 1952,1956-'57 6 furlongs; 1958-'66 6 1/2 furlongs. 1952 (December) two-year-olds.

Santa Ysabel Stakes

Grade 3, Santa Anita Park, three-year-olds, fillies, 1¹⁄₁₆ miles, dirt. Held January 5, 2003, with a gross value of $110,900. First held in 1968. Graded since 1998. Stakes record 1:41.34 (1997 Sharp Cat).

Year	Winner	Jockey	Second	Third	Strs	Time	1st Purse
2003	Atlantic Ocean, 3, 120	D. R. Flores	Sea Jewel, 3	Summer Wind, 3	6	1:43.25	$66,540
2002	Bella Bella Bella, 3, 115	C. J. McCarron	Tamarack Bay, 3	No Turbulence, 3	4	1:44.14	$64,550
2001	Collect Call, 3, 115	A. O. Solis	Irguns Angel, 3	Eminent, 3	8	1:44.69	$65,580
2000	Surfside, 3, 123	P. Day	Rings a Chime, 3	She's Classy, 3	4	1:43.53	$62,880
1999	Holywood Picture, 3, 115	O. Vergara	Exbourne Free, 3	Gleefully, 3	7	1:43.48	$64,860
1998	Nonies Dancer Ali, 3, 114	G. K. Gomez	Mamaison Miss, 3	Continental Lea, 3	5	1:44.14	$63,660
1997	Sharp Cat, 3, 120	C. S. Nakatani	Clever Pilot, 3	Guthrie, 3	6	1:41.34	$64,300
1996	Antespend, 3, 120	C. W. Antley	Dancing Prism, 3	Rumpipumpy (GB), 3	6	1:43.87	$64,950
1995	Ski Dancer, 3, 115	K. J. Desormeaux	Dixie Pearl, 3	Wilga, 3	5	1:44.24	$45,750
1994	Princess Mitterand, 3, 119	C. J. McCarron	Dianes Halo, 3	Jacodra's Devil, 3	4	1:43.25	$44,925
1993	Likeable Style, 3, 115	G. L. Stevens	Fit to Lead, 3	Amandari, 3	5	1:44.74	$45,900
1992	Crownette, 3, 116	P. A. Valenzuela	Golden Treat, 3	Looie Capote, 3	9	1:44.33	$48,975

Named for two land grants called Rancho Santa Ysabel. Home of the Santa Ysabel mission. 1970 7 furlongs. 1992 for non-winners of a race worth $25,000 to the winner. 1996 Love Lock finished first, DQ to fifth.

San Vicente Stakes

Grade 2, Santa Anita Park, three-year-olds, 7 furlongs, dirt. Held February 1, 2003, with a gross value of $150,000. First held in 1935. Graded since 1973. Stakes record 1:21.07 (1997 Silver Charm).

Year	Winner	Jockey	Second	Third	Strs	Time	1st Purse
2003	Kafwain, 3, 123	V. Espinoza	Sum Trick, 3	Southern Image, 3	5	1:21.12	$90,000
2002	Came Home, 3, 123	C. J. McCarron	Jack's Silver, 3	Werblin, 3	6	1:21.92	$90,000
2001	Early Flyer, 3, 114	C. J. McCarron	Lasersport, 3	D'wildcat, 3	5	1:21.51	$90,000
2000	Archer City Slew, 3, 117	K. J. Desormeaux	Joopy Doopy, 3	Gibson County, 3	6	1:22.18	$90,000
1999	Exploit, 3, 123	C. J. McCarron	Aristotle, 3	Yes It's True, 3	3	1:22.00	$90,000
1998	Sea of Secrets, 3, 116	K. J. Desormeaux	Late Edition, 3	Pleasant Drive, 3	5	1:22.00	$64,080
1997	Silver Charm, 3, 120	C. J. McCarron	Free House, 3	Funontherun, 3	9	1:21.07	$66,400
1996	Afleetaffair, 3, 116	C. S. Nakatani	Honour and Glory, 3	Ready to Order, 3	5	1:22.28	$63,850
1995	Afternoon Deelites, 3, 120	K. J. Desoremeaux	Mr Purple, 3	Fandarel Dancer, 3	5	1:21.35	$59,725
1994	Fly'n J. Bryan, 3, 114	C. A. Black	Gracious Ghost, 3	Cois Na Tine (Ire), 3	6	1:22.32	$60,700
1993	Yappy, 3, 116	P. A. Valenzuela	Denmars Dream, 3	Devoted Brass, 3	3	1:22.33	$63,100
1992	Mineral Wells, 3, 116	P. A. Valenzuela	Star of the Crop, 3	Prince Wild, 3	7	1:21.28	$61,450

Named for El Rancho San Vicente; early horse races were held there on a mesa. 1942-'44,1949-'51,1970 not held. 1956-'66 San Vicente H.; 1990-'95 San Vicente Breeders' Cup S. 1973-'82,1984-'97 Grade 3. 1935-'36,1952-'54 6 furlongs; 1940-'46 1 mile; 1947-'48 1¹⁄₁₆ miles. 1935-'36 three-year-olds and up. 1935-'53 colts and geldings.

Sapling Stakes

Grade 3, Monmouth Park, two-year-olds, 6 furlongs, dirt. Held August 10, 2002, with a gross value of $100,000. First held in 1883. Graded since 1973. Stakes record 1:07.84 (1992 Gilded Time).

Year	Winner	Jockey	Second	Third	Strs	Time	1st Purse
2002	Valid Video, 2, 120	C. C. Lopez	Farno, 2	Boston Park, 2	8	1:09.88	$60,000
2001	Pure Precision, 2, 120	E. Coa	Truman's Raider, 2	Wild Navigator, 2	8	1:10.82	$90,000
2000	Shooter, 2, 119	J. Bravo	Snow Ridge, 2	T P Louie, 2	7	1:10.63	$120,000
1999	Dont Tell the Kids, 2, 122	J. E. Tejeira	Outrigger, 2	House Burner, 2	6	1:10.18	$120,000
1998	Yes It's True, 2, 122	S. J. Sellers	Erlton, 2	Heroofthegame, 2	7	1:10.09	$120,000
1997	Double Honor, 2, 122	J. Bravo	Jigadee, 2	E Z Line, 2	8	1:09.75	$120,000
1996	Smoke Glacken, 2, 122	C. Perret	Harley Tune, 2	Country Rainbow, 2	10	1:10.16	$120,000
1995	Hennessy, 2, 122	D. M. Barton	Built for Pleasure, 2	Cashier Coyote, 2	7	1:10.84	$120,000
1994	Boone's Mill, 2, 122	P. Day	Enlighten, 2	Western Echo, 2	6	1:10.46	$120,000
1993	Sacred Honour, 2, 122	C. E. Lopez Sr.	Meadow Flight, 2	Solly's Honor, 2	6	1:11.19	$120,000
1992	Gilded Time, 2, 122	C. J. McCarron	Wild Zone, 2	Great Navigator, 2	8	1:07.84	$120,000

1894-1945 not held. 1893 5½ furlongs. 1973-'83 Grade 1; 1984-'96 Grade 2. 1992 new track record.

Saranac Handicap

Grade 3, Saratoga Race Course, three-year-olds, 1³⁄₁₆ miles, turf. Held September 2, 2002, with a gross value of $100,000. First held in 1901. Graded since 1973. Stakes record 1:51.61 (1999 Phi Beta Doc).

Year	Winner	Jockey	Second	Third	Strs	Time	1st Purse
2002	Ibn Al Haitham (GB), 3, 114	R. Migliore	Finality, 3	Irish Colonial, 3	9	1:55.30	$66,900
2001	Blazing Fury, 3, 113	J. Castellano	Fast City, 3	Rapid Ryan, 3	9	1:54.88	$67,500
2000	Rob's Spirit, 3, 120	J. D. Bailey	Whata Brainstorm, 3	Dawn of the Condor, 3	9	1:55.47	$68,280
1999	Phi Beta Doc, 3, 118	R. A. Dominguez	Monarch's Maze, 3	Big Rascal, 3	8	1:51.61	$67,020
1998	Crowd Pleaser, 3, 115	J-L. Samyn	Parade Ground, 3	Reformer Rally, 3	7	1:53.42	$66,060
1997	River Squall, 3, 114	C. Perret	Daylight Savings, 3	Inkatha (Fr), 3	10	1:52.82	$68,460
1996	Harghar, 3, 113	P. Day	Sir Cat, 3	Defacto, 3	11	1:48.58	$69,180
1995	Debonair Dan, 3, 112	J. F. Chavez	Crimson Guard, 3	Treasurer (GB), 3	7	1:33.65	$50,400
1994	Casa Eire, 3, 114	J. Bravo	Warn Me (GB), 3	Presently, 3	8	1:34.67	$66,480

| 1993 | Halissee, 3, 114 | J. A. Krone | Forest Wind, 3 | Compadre, 3 | 9 | 1:34.34 | $74,280 |
| 1992 | Casino Magistrate, 3, 120 | E. Maple | Restless Doctor, 3 | Smiling and Dancin, 3 | 10 | 1:39.37 | $76,440 |

Named for an Adirondack mountain village in Clinton County, New York. 1911-'12,1944,1946-'47 not held. 1943,1945 allowance race. 1901-'97 Saranac S. 1973-'89 Grade 2. 1948-'56 held at Jamaica; 1957-'61,1963-'67,1972-'74,1976 Aqueduct; 1962,1968-'71,1975,1977-'95 Belmont. 1901-'08,1996-'97 1⅛ miles; 1909,1913-'42,1960-'95 1 mile; 1948-'59 1¹⁄₁₆ miles. 1901-'79 dirt.

Saratoga Breeders' Cup Handicap

Grade 2, Saratoga Race Course, three-year-olds and up, 1¼ miles, dirt. Held August 17, 2002, with a gross value of $300,000. First held in 1865. Graded since 1996. Stakes record 2:01.11 (1999 Running Stag).

Year	Winner	Jockey	Second	Third	Strs	Time	1st Purse
2002	Evening Attire, 4, 115	S. Bridgmohan	Abreeze, 7	Dollar Bill, 4	10	2:02.95	$180,000
2001	Aptitude, 4, 122	J. D. Bailey	Perfect Cat, 4	A Fleets Dancer, 6	7	2:01.55	$180,000
2000	Pleasant Breeze, 5, 116	J. F. Chavez	Catienus, 6	Gander, 4	7	2:02.17	$180,000
1999	Running Stag, 5, 122	S. J. Sellers	Catienus, 5	Golden Missile, 4	8	2:01.11	$180,000
1998	Awesome Again, 4, 120	P. Day	Concerto, 4	Early Warning, 3	7	2:03.14	$180,000
1997	Cairo Express, 5, 111	J-L. Samyn	Golden Larch, 6	Instant Friendship, 4	9	2:03.99	$180,000
1996	L'Carriere, 5, 114	J. F. Chavez	Peaks and Valleys, 4	Mahogany Hall, 5	8	2:01.67	$130,000
1995	L'Carriere, 4, 113	J. D. Bailey	Yourmissinthepoint, 4	Unaccounted For, 4	6	2:02.87	$120,000
1994	Thunder Rumble, 5, 112	R. Migliore	West by West, 5	Wallenda, 4	8	1:48.52	$150,000

1887-'90,1892-1900,1908,1911-'12,1956-'62,1964-'93 not held. 1865-'96 Saratoga Cup H. 1996-'97 Grade 3. 1943-'45 held at Belmont. 1865-'86 2¼ miles; 1891 2 miles; 1901,1963 1⅝ miles; 1902-'55 1¾ miles; 1994 1⅛ miles.

Saratoga Special Stakes

Grade 2, Saratoga Race Course, two-year-olds, 6½ furlongs, dirt. Held August 14, 2002, with a gross value of $150,000. First held in 1901. Graded since 1973. Stakes record 1:16.37 (1996 All Chatter).

Year	Winner	Jockey	Second	Third	Strs	Time	1st Purse
2002	Zavata, 2, 122	J. D. Bailey	Lone Star Sky, 2	Spite the Devil, 2	5	1:17.65	$90,000
2001	Jump Start, 2, 115	P. Day	Heavyweight Champ, 2	Booklet, 2	6	1:17.35	$90,000
2000	City Zip, 2, 122	J. A. Santos	Scorpion, 2	Standard Speed, 2	8	1:16.88	$90,000
1999	Bevo, 2, 117	E. S. Prado	Afternoon Affair, 2	Settlement, 2	6	1:17.78	$90,000
1998	Prime Directive, 2, 114	J. F. Chavez	Silk Broker, 2	Tactical Cat, 2	4	1:17.18	$90,000
1997	Favorite Trick, 2, 122	P. Day	Case Dismissed, 2	K. O. Punch, 2	5	1:17.15	$90,000
1996	All Chatter, 2, 113	J. F. Chavez	Gray Raider, 2	Just a Cat, 2	10	1:16.37	$84,375
1995	Bright Launch, 2, 112	J. A. Santos	Devil's Honor, 2	Severe Clear, 2	8	1:17.40	$66,540
1994	Montreal Red, 2, 122	J. A. Santos	Flitch, 2	Law of the Sea, 2	5	1:17.96	$64,800
1993	Dehere, 2, 117	E. Maple	Slew Gin Fizz, 2	Whitney Tower, 2	9	1:09.92	$71,760
1992	Tactical Advantage, 2, 117	J. A. Krone	Strolling Along, 2	Mi Cielo, 2	10	1:10.59	$72,600

In the past, "special" races were winner-take-all. 1911-'12 not held. 1901-'58 Saratoga Special Sweepstakes. 1943-'45 held at Belmont. 1901-'05 5½ furlongs; 1906-'93 6 furlongs.

Schuylerville Stakes

Grade 2, Saratoga Race Course, two-year-olds, fillies, 6 furlongs, dirt. Held July 24, 2002, with a gross value of $150,000. First held in 1918. Graded since 1973. Stakes record 1:09.80 (1974 Laughing Bridge [2nd Div.]; 1988 Wonders Delight).

Year	Winner	Jockey	Second	Third	Strs	Time	1st Purse
2002	Freedom's Daughter, 2, 118	J. R. Velazquez	Miss Mary Apples, 2	Mymich, 2	7	1:12.14	$90,000
2001	Touch Love, 2, 118	J. F. Chavez	Lakeside Cup, 2	Lost Expectations, 2	6	1:11.12	$65,460
2000	Gold Mover, 2, 122	C. Perret	Seeking It All, 2	Miss Doolittle, 2	5	1:10.33	$64,920
1999	Magicalmysterycat, 2, 122	P. Day	Circle of Life, 2	Regally Appealing, 2	7	1:10.91	$65,700
1998	Call Me Up, 2, 117	J. F. Chavez	Brittons Hill, 2	Fantasy Lake, 2	8	1:12.89	$66,060
1997	Countess Diana, 2, 116	S. J. Sellers	Love Lock, 2	Sequence, 2	6	1:10.39	$64,800
1996	How About Now, 2, 115	R. Migliore	Exclusive Hold, 2	City College, 2	11	1:12.37	$68,220
1995	Golden Attraction, 2, 121	D. M. Barton	Daylight Come, 2	Western Dreamer, 2	8	1:10.84	$65,940
1994	Changing Ways, 2, 114	M. E. Smith	Unacceptable, 2	Artic Experience, 2	10	1:12.66	$67,980
1993	Strategic Maneuver, 2, 114	J. A. Santos	Astas Foxy Lady, 2	She Rides Tonite, 2	11	1:11.15	$73,560
1992	Distinct Habit, 2, 119	J. D. Bailey	Tourney, 2	Lily La Belle, 2	9	1:11.03	$72,480

Named for a town located 12 miles east of Saratoga Springs in upstate New York. 1975-'86 Grade 3. 1943-'45 held at Belmont; 1952 Jamaica. 1918-'59,1962-'68 5½ furlongs.

Secretariat Stakes

Grade 1, Arlington Park, three-year-olds, 1¼ miles, turf. Held August 17, 2002, with a gross value of $400,000. First held in 1974. Graded since 1975. Stakes record 2:00.17 (1995 Hawk Attack).

Year	Winner	Jockey	Second	Third	Strs	Time	1st Purse
2002	Chiselling, 3, 121	K. J. Desormeaux	Jazz Beat (Ire), 3	Extra Check, 3	7	2:04.16	$240,000
2001	Startac, 3, 121	A. O. Solis	Strut the Stage, 3	Sharp Performance, 3	11	2:04.91	$240,000
2000	Ciro, 3, 120	M. J. Kinane	King Cugat, 3	Guillamou City (Fr), 3	8	2:01.64	$240,000
1997	Honor Glide, 3, 123	G. K. Gomez	Casey Tibbs (Ire), 3	Glok, 3	9	2:02.74	$240,000
1996	Marlin, 3, 114	S. J. Sellers	Trail City, 3	Dancing Fred, 3	10	2:01.09	$300,000
1995	Hawk Attack, 3, 120	P. Day	Mecke, 3	Petit Poucet (GB), 3	10	2:00.17	$240,000

1994	**Vaudeville**, 3, 123	G. L. Stevens	Dare and Go, 3	Jaggery John, 3	13	2:01.11	$240,000
1993	**Awad**, 3, 120	J. Velasquez	Explosive Red, 3	Brazany, 3	14	2:08.74	$240,000
1992	**Ghazi**, 3, 114	R. G. Davis	Paradise Creek, 3	Tango Charlie, 3	10	2:01.18	$180,000

Named for the 1972, '73 Horse of the Year and 1973 Triple Crown winner Secretariat (1970-'89, c. by Bold Ruler); he made his first start after the Belmont S. in a stakes race at Arlington Park. 1988,1998-'99 not held. 1975-'83 Grade 2. 1985 held at Hawthorne. 1974,1977 1¹⁄₁₆ miles; 1975-'76 1⅛ miles; 1978-'84 1½ miles. 1977 dirt.

Senator Ken Maddy Handicap

Grade 3, Santa Anita Park, three-year-olds and up, fillies and mares, about 6½ furlongs, turf. Held October 12, 2002, with a gross value of $100,000. First held in 1969. Graded since 1998. Stakes record 1:11.63 (1992 Bel's Starlet).

Year	Winner	Jockey	Second	Third	Strs	Time	1st Purse
2002	**Rolly Polly (Ire)**, 4, 119	P. A. Valenzuela	I'm the Business (NZ), 5	Nanogram, 5	12	1:12.86	$68,460
2001	**A La Reine**, 4, 115	A. O. Solis	Nanogram, 4	Global, 4	8	1:13.27	$66,240
2000	**Evening Promise (GB)**, 4, 118	K. J. Desormeaux	Strawberry Way, 5	Southern House (Ire), 4	10	1:13.05	$67,020
1999	**Hula Queen**, 5, 116	A. O. Solis	Desert Lady (Ire), 4	Ecudienne, 5	11	1:13.05	$67,740
1998	**Dance Parade**, 4, 120	K. J. Desormeaux	Advancing Star, 5	Green Jewel (GB), 4	8	1:13.87	$60,000
1997	**Madame Pandit**, 4, 118	E. J. Delahoussaye	Advancing Star, 4	Highest Dream (Ire), 4	10	1:13.82	$60,000
1996	**Dixie Pearl**, 4, 116	E. J. Delahoussaye	Ski Dancer, 4	Cat's Cradle, 4	5	1:12.33	$66,400
1995	**Denim Yenem**, 3, 115	C. J. McCarron	Miss L Attack, 5	Jacodra's Devil, 4	7	1:14.92	$60,400
1994	**Starolamo**, 5, 117	K. J. Desormeaux	Sophisticatedcielo, 3	Beautiful Gem, 3	6	1:16.07	$47,475
1993	**Toussaud**, 4, 122	K. J. Desormeaux	Best Dress, 3	Yousefia, 4	6	1:14.32	$46,950
1992	**Bel's Starlet**, 5, 120	K. J. Desormeaux	Glen Kate (Ire), 5	Brisa de Mar, 4	9	**1:11.63**	$49,575

Named for California state Sen. Kenneth L. Maddy (1935-2000), a longtime racing enthusiast. 1969 Autumn Days S.; 1970-'98 Autumn Days H. 1983,1994 6½ furlongs. 1983,1994 dirt. 1988-'89 two-year-olds and up. 1969-'70 both sexes.

Senorita Stakes

Grade 3, Hollywood Park, three-year-olds, fillies, 1 mile, turf. Held May 17, 2003, with a gross value of $113,500. First held in 1968. Graded since 1990. Stakes record 1:33.66 (1992 Charme a Gendarme).

Year	Winner	Jockey	Second	Third	Strs	Time	1st Purse
2003	**Makeup Artist**, 3, 117	V. Espinoza	Rutters Revenge, 3	Shapes and Shadows, 3	7	1:36.54	$68,100
2002	**Adoration**, 3, 117	G. K. Gomez	High Society (Ire), 3	Nunatall (GB), 3	6	1:34.91	$64,380
2001	**Fantastic Filly (Fr)**, 3, 123	G. K. Gomez	Innit (Ire), 3	Blushing Bride (GB), 3	8	1:35.13	$65,880
2000	**Islay Mist (GB)**, 3, 116	D. R. Flores	Fire Sale Queen, 3	Miss Pixie, 3	10	1:34.16	$67,080
1999	**Coracle**, 3, 116	K. J. Desormeaux	Aviate, 3	Dianehill (Ire), 3	11	1:34.04	$67,740
1998	**Dancing Rhythm**, 3, 117	K. J. Desormeaux	Phone Alex (Ire), 3	Star's Proud Penny, 3	7	1:35.39	$64,920
1997	**Kentucky Kaper**, 3, 114	R. R. Douglas	Ascutney, 3	Ava Knowsthecode, 3	10	1:34.74	$66,780
1996	**To B. Super**, 3, 118	C. W. Antley	Gastronomical, 3	Ribot's Secret (Ire), 3	13	1:34.36	$68,940
1995	**Top Shape (Fr)**, 3, 114	C. S. Nakatani	Artica, 3	Auriette (Ire), 3	10	1:34.79	$63,900
1994	**Rabiadella**, 3, 118	L. A. Pincay Jr.	Magical Avie, 3	Fancy 'n Fabulous, 3	6	1:34.84	$60,800
1993	**Likeable Style**, 3, 121	K. J. Desormeaux	Adorydar, 3	Icy Warning, 3	7	1:34.56	$61,250
1992	**Charm a Gendarme**, 3, 116	R. Q. Meza	Moonlight Elegance, 3	Morriston Belle, 3	13	**1:33.66**	$67,250

1974 not held. 1992-'95 Senorita Breeders' Cup S. 1973,1986 1¹⁄₁₆ miles. 1973 dirt.

Shadwell Keeneland Turf Mile Stakes

Grade 1, Keeneland, three-year-olds and up, 1 mile, turf. Held October 6, 2002, with a gross value of $600,000. First held in 1986. Graded since 1988. Stakes record 1:33.72 (2000 Altibr).

Year	Winner	Jockey	Second	Third	Strs	Time	1st Purse
2002	**Landseer (GB)**, 3, 123	E. S. Prado	Touch of the Blues (Fr), 5	Beat Hollow (GB), 5	8	1:35.55	$372,000
2001	**Hap**, 5, 126	J. D. Bailey	Where's Taylor, 5	Aly's Alley, 5	9	1:35.98	$346,270
2000	**Altibr**, 5, 126	R. Migliore	Strategic Mission, 5	Quiet Resolve, 5	9	**1:33.72**	$279,744
1999	**Kirkwall (GB)**, 5, 126	V. Espinoza	Delay of Game, 6	Ladies Din, 4	10	1:37.96	$281,232
1998	**Favorite Trick**, 3, 123	P. Day	Soviet Line (Ire), 8	Wild Event, 5	5	1:35.00	$168,795
1997	**Wild Event**, 4, 126	M. Guidry	Trail City, 4	Soviet Line (Ire), 7	10	1:34.66	$134,075
1996	**Dumaani**, 5, 126	J. A. Krone	Desert Waves, 6	Dove Hunt, 5	9	1:35.68	$133,843
1995	**Dumaani**, 4, 126	J. A. Krone	Holy Mountain, 4	Mr Purple, 3	10	1:38.78	$116,514
1994	**†Weekend Madness (Ire)**, 4, 123	S. J. Sellers	†Words of War, 5	Pennine Ridge, 3	10	1:38.73	$116,328
1993	**Coaxing Matt**, 4, 126	E. M. Martin Jr.	Adam Smith (GB), 5	Mr. Light Tres (Arg), 4	9	1:53.16	$116,421
1992	**Lotus Pool**, 5, 126	C. R. Woods Jr.	Thunder Regent, 5	Chenin Blanc, 6	6	1:48.36	$114,902

Sponsored by Sheikh Hamdan bin Rashid al Maktoum's Shadwell Farm, located a short distance from Keeneland. 1991-'95 Keeneland Breeders' Cup S.; 1996-'98 Keeneland Breeders' Cup Mile S. 1991-'97 Grade 3; 1998-2001 Grade 2. 1991-'93 1⅛ miles. †denotes female.

Shakertown Stakes

Grade 3, Keeneland, three-year-olds and up, 5½ furlongs, turf. Held April 12, 2003, with a gross value of $113,700. First held in 1997. Graded since 2003. Stakes record 1:02.35 (1998 Sesaro).

Year	Winner	Jockey	Second	Third	Strs	Time	1st Purse
2003	**No Jacket Required**, 6, 118	B. Blanc	Testify, 6	Abderian (Ire), 6	10	1:03.25	$70,494
2002	**Morluc**, 6, 118	R. Albarado	Mighty Beau, 3	Grangeville, 7	10	1:03.25	$52,731

2001	**Airbourne Command**, 6, 118	J. F. Chavez	Final Row (GB), 4	Grangeville, 6	10	1:02.71	$52,824
2000	**Bold Fact**, 5, 115	R. Migliore	Howbaddouwantit, 5	Claire's Honor, 6	10	1:02.61	$46,800
1999	**Prankster**, 6, 115	S. J. Sellers	Tyaskin, 6	Howbaddouwantit, 4	10	1:02.43	$43,850
1998	**Sesaro**, 6, 123	S. J. Sellers	Brave Pancho, 4	Claire's Honor, 4	9	**1:02.35**	$43,850
1997	**G. H.'s Pleasure**, 5, 114	J. A. Santos	Louie the Lucky, 6	Parklo, 5	10	1:03.00	$34,410

Named for Shakertown, a Shaker village located at Pleasant Hill, Kentucky, near Harrodsburg. 1997 The Minstrel S. 1997,1998 new course record.

Sheepshead Bay Handicap

Grade 2, Belmont Park, three-year-olds and up, fillies and mares, 1⅜ miles, turf. Held June 1, 2002, with a gross value of $150,000. First held in 1959. Graded since 1973. Stakes record 2:11.57 (1997 Maxzene).

Year	Winner	Jockey	Second	Third	Strs	Time	1st Purse
2002	**Tweedside**, 4, 114	J. R. Velazquez	Sweetest Thing, 4	Golden Corona, 4	10	2:13.63	$90,000
2001	**Critical Eye**, 4, 122	M. J. Luzzi	Playact (Ire), 4	Janet (GB), 4	5	2:18.18	$90,000
2000	**Lisieux Rose (Ire)**, 5, 116	J. A. Santos	Melody Queen (GB), 4	La Ville Rouge, 4	7	2:14.16	$90,000
1999	**Soaring Softly**, 4, 114	M. E. Smith	Starry Dreamer, 5	Pinafore Park, 4	6	2:15.11	$90,000
1998	**Maxzene**, 5, 121	J. A. Santos	Sweetzie, 6	Colonial Play, 4	6	2:14.17	$90,000
1997	**Maxzene**, 4, 117	M. E. Smith	Fanjica (Ire), 5	Future Act, 5	8	**2:11.57**	$90,000
1996	**Chelsey Flower**, 5, 114	R. G. Davis	Look Daggers, 4	Transient Trend, 4	10	2:12.64	$67,320
1995	**Duda**, 4, 112	J. D. Bailey	Danish (Ire), 4	Chelsey Flower, 4	7	2:13.69	$65,700
1994	**Market Booster**, 5, 114	J. A. Santos	Irish Linnet, 6	Fairy Garden, 6	9	2:11.69	$66,960
1993	**Trampoli**, 4, 116	M. E. Smith	Aquilegia, 4	Revasser, 4	4	2:14.08	$67,680
1992	**Ratings**, 4, 112	J. Cruguet	Ristna (GB), 4	Dancing Devlette, 5	12	2:15.14	$75,000

Named for the old Brooklyn racetrack, Sheepshead Bay, which closed in 1911 with the ban of racing in New York and never reopened. 1991-'94 Grade 3. 1959 held at Jamaica; 1960-'74,1976 Aqueduct. 1959,1963-'64 1¹⁄₁₆ miles; 1960-'61,1976 1⅛ miles; 1962 1 mile; 1965-'74 1³⁄₁₆ miles; 1975,1977-'79 1¼ miles. 1959,1962,1974,1990,2001 dirt. 1959-'61 both sexes. 1997 new course record.

Shirley Jones Handicap

Grade 3, Gulfstream Park, three-year-olds and up, fillies and mares, 7 furlongs, dirt. Held February 14, 2003, with a gross value of $100,000. First held in 1976. Graded since 1988. Stakes record 1:21.94 (1994 Santa Catalina).

Year	Winner	Jockey	Second	Third	Strs	Time	1st Purse
2003	**Harmony Lodge**, 5, 114	J. R. Velazquez	Gold Mover, 5	Nonsuch Bay, 4	6	1:22.35	$60,000
2002	**Cat Cay**, 5, 118	P. Day	Raging Fever, 4	Vague Memory, 5	7	1:22.31	$60,000
2001	**Hidden Assets**, 4, 114	J. D. Bailey	Another, 4	Dream Supreme, 4	6	1:22.40	$60,000
2000	**Marley Vale**, 4, 118	J. R. Velazquez	Cassidy, 5	Class On Class, 5	8	1:22.24	$60,000
1999	**Harpia**, 5, 118	R. Migliore	Scotzanna, 7	Memories of Gold, 4	5	1:22.17	$60,000
1998	**U Can Do It**, 5, 116	S. J. Sellers	Glitter Woman, 4	Flashy n Smart, 5	5	1:23.33	$60,000
1997	**Chip**, 4, 114	J. Bravo	Steady Cat, 4	Flat Fleet Feet, 4	7	1:22.24	$60,000
1996	**Dust Bucket**, 5, 112	R. G. Davis	Russian Flight (Ire), 4	Culver City, 4	5	1:25.97	$60,000
1995	**Educated Risk**, 5, 125	M. E. Smith	Elizabeth Bay, 5	Clever Act, 4	5	1:22.94	$60,000
1994	**Santa Catalina**, 6, 115	P. Day	Jeano, 6	Traverse City, 4	11	**1:21.94**	$60,000
1993	**Jeano**, 5, 113	S. J. Sellers	Santa Catalina, 5	Miss Jealski, 4	13	1:23.56	$39,060
1992	**Nannerl**, 5, 111	J. A. Krone	Withallprobability, 4	Fit for a Queen, 6	10	1:23.23	$36,600

Named for 1959 Test S. winner Shirley Jones (1956-'78, f. by Double Jay); Shirley Jones, the horse, was named for the actress. 1977-'78,1980 not held. 1976 1¹⁄₁₆ miles; 1979 6 furlongs.

Shoemaker Breeders' Cup Mile Stakes

Grade 1, Hollywood Park, three-year-olds and up, 1 mile, turf. Held May 27, 2002, with a gross value of $408,000. First held in 1938. Graded since 1973. Stakes record 1:32.64 (1994 Megan's Interco).

Year	Winner	Jockey	Second	Third	Strs	Time	1st Purse
2002	**Ladies Din**, 7, 124	P. A. Valenzuela	Redattore (Brz), 7	Spinelessjellyfish, 6	10	1:33.39	$240,000
2001	**Irish Prize**, 5, 124	G. L. Stevens	Touch of the Blues (Fr), 4	Brahms, 4	9	1:33.68	$285,000
2000	**Silic (Fr)**, 5, 124	C. S. Nakatani	Ladies Din, 5	Sharan (GB), 5	11	1:33.36	$304,800
1999	**Silic (Fr)**, 4, 124	C. S. Nakatani	Ladies Din, 4	Hawksley Hill (Ire), 6	8	1:32.95	$280,000
1998	**Labeeb (GB)**, 6, 124	K. J. Desormeaux	Fantastic Fellow, 4	Hawksley Hill (Ire), 5	7	1:33.29	$319,200
1997	**Pinfloron (Fr)**, 5, 124	D. R. Flores	Surachai, 4	Helmsman, 5	14	1:34.46	$353,400
1996	**Fastness (Ire)**, 6, 124	C. S. Nakatani	Romarin (Brz), 6	Atticus, 4	7	1:32.74	$420,000
1995	**Unfinished Symph**, 4, 121	C. W. Antley	Rapan Boy (AUS), 7	Journalism, 7	9	1:33.14	$98,400
1994	**Megan's Interco**, 5, 119	C. A. Black	Furiously, 5	Rapan Boy (Aus), 5	6	**1:32.64**	$63,200
1993	**Journalism**, 5, 114	A. O. Solis	Lomitas (GB), 5	Brief Truce, 4	7	1:32.89	$63,800

Named for Racing Hall of Fame jockey William Shoemaker (1931-), who retired as leading rider by number of wins. 1942-'43,1948,1981-'83,1992 not held. 1938-'63 Hollywood Premiere H.; 1964-'70,1972-'80,1984-'89 Premiere H.; 1971 Miller High Life Premiere H.; 1990-'95 Shoemaker H. 1973-'74,1987-'89 Grade 3; 1975-'86 not graded; 1990-'99 Grade 2. 1949 held at Santa Anita. 1938-'49,1951-'77 6 furlongs; 1950 7 furlongs; 1978-'80,1986-'87 1¹⁄₁₆ miles. 1938-'80 dirt. 1944 two-year-olds and up. 1993,1996 equaled course record; 1994 new course record.

Shuvee Handicap

Grade 2, Belmont Park, three-year-olds and up, fillies and mares, 1 mile, dirt. Held May 17, 2003, with a gross value of $200,000. First held in 1976. Graded since 1978. Stakes record 1:34.38 (1999 Catinca).

Year	Winner	Jockey	Second	Third	Strs	Time	1st Purse
2003	Wild Spirit (Chi), 4, 115	J. Castellano	Smok'n Frolic, 4	You, 4	6	1:34.51	$120,000
2002	Shiny Band, 4, 113	R. G. Davis	Raging Fever, 4	Victory Ride, 4	5	1:34.95	$120,000
2001	Apple of Kent, 5, 114	R. Migliore	March Magic, 4	Country Hideaway, 5	5	1:35.16	$120,000
2000	Beautiful Pleasure, 5, 122	J. F. Chavez	Biogio's Rose, 6	Up We Go, 4	5	1:35.65	$120,000
1999	Catinca, 4, 121	R. Migliore	Sister Act, 4	Tap to Music, 4	6	**1:34.38**	$90,000
1998	Colonial Minstrel, 4, 117	J. R. Velazquez	Dixie Flag, 4	Hidden Reserve, 4	5	1:36.20	$90,000
1997	Hidden Lake, 4, 115	R. Migliore	Flat Fleet Feet, 4	Escena, 4	9	1:35.27	$90,000
1996	Clear Mandate, 4, 111	J. A. Krone	Smooth Charmer, 4	Restored Hope, 5	7	1:35.01	$90,000
1995	Inside Information, 4, 119	J. A. Santos	Sky Beauty, 5	Restored Hope, 4	4	1:35.10	$80,220
1994	Sky Beauty, 4, 125	M. E. Smith	For all Seasons, 4	Looie Capote, 5	4	1:40.60	$90,000
1993	Turnback the Alarm, 4, 117	C. W. Antley	Shared Interest, 5	Vivano, 4	9	1:43.11	$90,000
1992	Missy's Mirage, 4, 116	E. Maple	Harbour Club, 5	Versailles Treaty, 4	6	1:40.74	$102,960

Named for Morven Stud's 1970, '71 champion handicap mare Shuvee (1966-'86, f. by Nashua). 1986-'96 Grade 1. 1977-'94 1¹⁄₁₆ miles.

Silverbulletday Stakes

Grade 2, Fair Grounds, three-year-olds, fillies, 1¹⁄₁₆ miles, dirt. Held February 15, 2003, with a gross value of $150,000. First held in 1982. Graded since 1999. Stakes record 1:42.48 (1997 Blushing K. D.).

Year	Winner	Jockey	Second	Third	Strs	Time	1st Purse
2002	Take Charge Lady, 3, 122	J. K. Court	Charmed Gift, 3	Chamrousse, 3	5	1:42.09	$90,000
2001	Lakenheath, 3, 119	C. J. Lanerie	Morning Sun, 3	Beloved by All, 3	5	1:46.09	$75,000
2000	Shawnee Country, 3, 122	D. J. Meche	Chilukki, 3	Humble Clerk, 3	9	1:45.11	$75,000
1999	Silverbulletday, 3, 122	G. L. Stevens	Brushed Halory, 3	On a Soapbox, 3	8	1:44.36	$75,000
1998	Cool Dixie, 3, 122	R. Ardoin	Lu Ravi, 3	Silent Eskimo, 3	9	1:43.38	$75,000
1997	Blushing K. D., 3, 122	L. Meche	Tomisue's Delight, 3	Morelia, 3	6	**1:42.48**	$60,000
1996	Up Dip, 3, 114	C. C. Bourque	Brush With Tequila, 3	Not Likely, 3	8	1:44.61	$37,635
1995	Legendary Priness, 3, 113	C. A. Emigh	Broad Smile, 3	Hero's Valor, 3	9	1:44.42	$25,875
1994	Playcaller, 3, 119	R. Ardoin	Two Altazano, 3	Briar Road, 3	7	1:44.31	$31,095
1993	Bright Penny, 3, 114	R. Ardoin	She's a Little Shy, 3	Wakerup, 3	7	1:44.80	$19,095
1992	Prospectors Delite, 3, 117	B. J. Walker Jr.	Royal Med, 3	Glitzi Bj, 3	7	1:43.80	$19,020

Named for Mike Pegram's 1998 champion two-year-old filly and '99 champion three-year-old filly Silverbulletday (1996, f. by Silver Deputy). Formerly named for Calumet Farm's champion Davona Dale (1976, f. by Best Turn). 1982-2000 Davona Dale S. 1982-'84 1 mile 40 yards.

Singapore Plate Stakes

Grade 3, Arlington Park, three-year-olds, fillies, 1¹⁄₈ miles, dirt. Held August 10, 2002, with a gross value of $100,000. First held in 1930. Graded since 1982. Stakes record 1:48.20 (1983 Choose a Partner).

Year	Winner	Jockey	Second	Third	Strs	Time	1st Purse
2002	Lost At Sea, 3, 122	R. R. Douglas	See How She Runs, 3	Strikes No Spares, 3	7	1:50.58	$60,000
2001	Caressing, 3, 120	R. R. Douglas	Gal On the Go, 3	Scoop, 3	8	1:50.74	$75,000
2000	Megans Bluff, 3, 114	M. Guidry	Instinct, 3	My Turn Kissin, 3	6	1:50.22	$75,000
1997	Minister's Melody, 3, 112	G. K. Gomez	Lady of Blue	Dawn's Black Tie	9	1:51.32	$60,000
1996	Cuando Puede, 3, 113	R. Albarado	Ginny Lynn	Effectiveness	8	1:51.33	$75,000
1995	Niner's Home, 3, 111	T. J. Hebert	A Goodlookin Broad	Strawberry Reason	4	1:52.15	$45,000
1994	Mariah's Storm, 3, 118	R. N. Lester	Stellarina	Minority Dater	7	1:49.63	$60,000
1993	Added Asset, 3, 116	S. J. Sellers	Dream Mary	Princess Polonia	9	1:50.19	$60,000
1992	Pleasant Baby, 3, 111	G. K. Gomez	Low Tolerance	Pleasureconnection	4	1:55.18	$45,000

Named in honor of the Singapore Turf Club, sponsor of the race. 1933-'79,1988,1998-'99 not held. 1930-'32,1980-'91 Arlington Oaks; 1992-'97 Arlington Heights Oaks. 1985 held at Hawthorne.

Sixty Sails Handicap

Grade 3, Hawthorne Race Course, three-year-olds and up, fillies and mares, 1¹⁄₈ miles, dirt. Held April 26, 2003, with a gross value of $250,000. First held in 1976. Graded since 1984. Stakes record 1:46.69 (1999 Crafty Oak).

Year	Winner	Jockey	Second	Third	Strs	Time	1st Purse
2003	Bare Necessities, 4, 118	R. R. Douglas	Jaramar Rain, 4	Lakenheath, 5	9	1:52.84	$150,000
2002	With Ability, 4, 115	J. Castellano	Lakenheath, 4	Katy Kat, 4	7	1:51.37	$180,000
2001	License Fee, 6, 116	L. Melancon	Lady Melesi, 4	Megans Bluff, 4	8	1:49.11	$180,000
2000	Lu Ravi, 5, 116	P. Day	Tap to Music, 5	Batuka, 4	8	1:49.15	$180,000
1999	Crafty Oak, 5, 114	R. Sibille	Highfalutin, 5	Lines of Beauty, 4	7	**1:46.69**	$180,000
1998	Glitter Woman, 4, 118	G. L. Stevens	Top Secret, 5	(DH) Im Out First, 5 (DH) Tuxedo Junction, 5	7	1:50.49	$180,000
1997	Top Secret, 4, 115	C. Perret	Hurricane Viv, 4	Gold n Delicious, 4	9	1:49.71	$180,000
1996	Alcovy, 6, 119	W. Martinez	Shoop, 5	Lotta Dancing, 5	13	1:50.70	$180,000
1995	Eskimo's Angel, 6, 114	M. Guidry	Little Buckles, 4	Norfolk Lavender, 4	13	1:51.53	$180,000
1994	Princess Polonia, 4, 113	W. S. Ramos	Eskimo's Angel, 5	Joyous Melody, 4	8	1:51.88	$180,000

| 1993 | **Pleasant Baby**, 4, 112 | J. L. Diaz | Miss Jealski, 4 | Steff Graf (Brz), 5 | 9 | 1:49.30 | $180,000 |
| 1992 | **Peach of It**, 6, 114 | E. T. Baird | Bungalow, 5 | Zend to Aiken, 4 | 13 | 1:51.28 | $162,090 |

Named for 1974, '75 Matron H. (G2) winner Sixty Sails (1970-'90, f. by Creme dela Creme). 1976-'98,2000-'02 held at Sportsman's Park. 1976-'81 1 mile; 1982-'84 1¹⁄₁₆ miles. 1984-'87 four-year-olds and up. 1993 new track record; 1999 equaled track record. 1998 dead heat for third.

Skip Away Handicap

Grade 3, Gulfstream Park, three-year-olds and up, 1¹⁄₁₆ miles, dirt. Held April 20, 2003, with a gross value of $100,000. First held in 1987. Graded since 1992. Stakes record 1:42.31 (2001 American Halo).

Year	Winner	Jockey	Second	Third	Strs	Time	1st Purse
2003	**Best of the Rest**, 8, 121	E. Coa	Consistency, 4	Roger E, 4	5	1:42.72	$60,000
2002	**Sir Bear**, 9, 116	E. S. Prado	Red Bullet, 5	Hal's Hope, 5	8	1:43.98	$60,000
2001	**American Halo**, 5, 114	R. G. Davis	Vision and Verse, 5	Pleasant Breeze, 6	10	**1:42.31**	$60,000
2000	**Horse Chestnut (SAF)**, 5, 117	M. E. Smith	Isaypete, 4	Rock and Roll, 5	6	1:42.78	$60,000
1999	**Sir Bear**, 6, 119	J. D. Bailey	Behrens, 5	Hanarsaan, 6	8	1:43.66	$60,000
1998	**Sir Bear**, 5, 112	E. M. Jurado	Black Forest, 4	Kiridashi, 6	7	1:43.27	$60,000
1997	**Crafty Friend**, 4, 114	M. E. Smith	Diligence, 4	Ghostly Moves, 5	8	1:42.27	$45,000
1996	**Halo's Image**, 5, 119	P. Day	Wekiva Springs, 5	Flying Chevron, 4	7	1:42.71	$45,000
1995	**Fight for Love**, 5, 113	J. D. Bailey	Danville, 4	Pride of Burkaan, 5	7	1:43.98	$45,000
1994	**Devil His Due**, 5, 121	M. E. Smith	Migrating Moon, 4	Northern Trend, 6	8	1:43.17	$45,000
1993	**Technology**, 4, 118	J. D. Bailey	Barkerville, 5	Bidding Proud, 4	8	1:42.47	$45,000
1992	**Honest Ensign**, 4, 109	J. Cruguet	Peanut Butter Onit, 6	Strike the Gold, 4	7	1:49.41	$45,000

Named for Carolyn Hine's 1998 Horse of the Year Skip Away (1993, c. by Skip Trial). Formerly named for Broward County, Florida, location of Gulfstream. 1987-2000 Broward H. 1991-'92 1¹⁄₈ miles. 1987 turf. 1987 three-year-olds. 1995 Northern Trend finished second, DQ to fifth.

Smile Sprint Handicap

Grade 3, Calder Race Course, three-year-olds and up, 6 furlongs, dirt. Held July 13, 2002, with a gross value of $400,000. First held in 1984. First graded in 2003. Stakes record 1:08.95 (2000 Forty One Carats).

Year	Winner	Jockey	Second	Third	Strs	Time	1st Purse
2002	**Orientate**, 4, 119	M. E. Smith	Echo Eddie, 5	Crafty C. T., 4	7	1:09.98	$240,000
2001	**Fappie's Notebook**, 4, 116	J. F. Chavez	Thrillin Discovery, 6	Salty Glance, 6	12	1:09.89	$120,000
2000	**Forty One Carats**, 4, 116	J. Castellano	Personal First, 3	Alice's Notebook, 4	7	**1:08.95**	$180,000
1999	**Silver Season**, 3, 112	E. Coa	Son of a Pistol, 7	My Jeff's Mombo, 5	7	1:10.03	$180,000
1998	**Heckofaralph**, 5, 115	W. Ramos	Thunder Breeze, 4	Nicholas Ds, 4	13	1:11.40	$180,000
1997	†**Vivace**, 4, 114	R. P. Romero	Score a Birdie, 6	Valid Expectations, 4	9	1:10.60	$150,000
1996	**Constant Escort**, 4, 114	E. O. Nunez	Honest Colors, 5	Excelerate, 4	10	1:21.80	$60,000
1995	**Request a Star**, 4, 113	A. Toribio	Thats Our Buck, 5	Halo's Image, 4	11	1:23.60	$60,000
1994	**Exclusive Praline**, 3, 117	W. Ramos	Migrating Moon, 4	Fortunate Joe, 3	10	1:22.20	$60,000
1993	**Song of Ambition**, 4, 116	R. Lopez	Coolin It, 4	Daniel's Boy, 5	12	1:22.40	$45,000
1992	**My Luck Runs North**, 3, 114	R. Lopez	Groomstick, 6	Cigar Toss (Arg), 5	9	1:17.40	$45,000

Named for Frances A. Genter's 1986 champion sprinter Smile (1982-'97, c. by In Reality). 1984-'93 Miami Beach H.; 1994-'98 Miami Beach Sprint H. 1985-'88,1990-'91,1993-'96 7 furlongs; 1992 6½ furlongs.

Sorority Stakes

Grade 3, Monmouth Park, two-year-olds, fillies, 6 furlongs, dirt. Held August 25, 2002, with a gross value of $100,000. First held in 1956. Graded since 1973. Stakes record 1:09 (1974 Ruffian).

Year	Winner	Jockey	Second	Third	Strs	Time	1st Purse
2002	**Wild Snitch**, 2, 119	E. Coa	Grand Natalie Rose, 2	Runaway Chanel, 2	6	1:11.09	$60,000
2001	**Forest Heiress**, 2, 119	D. V. Beckner	Haunted Lass, 2	Divine Angel, 2	6	1:11.61	$90,000
2000	**Stormy Pick**, 2, 119	J. C. Ferrer	Zonk, 2	With Ability, 2	7	1:10.96	$90,000
1999	**Sister Fiona**, 2, 119	J. Bravo	Katz Me If You Can, 2	Mycatcandance, 2	5	1:09.66	$90,000
1998	**Appealing Phylly**, 2, 119	C. C. Lopez	Paved in Gold, 2	Betty's Star, 2	8	1:10.84	$90,000
1997	**Unky and Ally**, 2, 119	J. R. Martinez Jr.	Tipperary Melody, 2	Love in the Hills, 2	9	1:11.47	$90,000
1996	**Annie Cake**, 2, 119	W. H. McCauley	Corporate Vision, 2	Little Sister, 2	7	1:11.62	$90,000
1995	**Crafty But Sweet**, 2, 119	N. Santagata	Golden Attraction, 2	Careless Heiress, 2	6	1:10.98	$120,000
1994	**Stormy Blues**, 2, 119	J. A. Krone	Cat Appeal, 2	A Real Eye Opener, 2	9	1:11.03	$120,000
1993	**Cat Attack**, 2, 119	R. G. Davis	Shapely Scrapper, 2	At the Half, 2	10	1:11.41	$120,000
1992	**Hollywood Wildcat**, 2, 119	F. A. Arguello Jr.	Family Enterprize, 2	D'Accordress, 2	6	1:10.84	$120,000

1973-'83 Grade 1; 1984-'88 Grade 2.

Sorrento Stakes

Grade 2, Del Mar, two-year-olds, fillies, 6½ furlongs, dirt. Held August 10, 2002, with a gross value of $150,000. First held in 1967. Graded since 1986. Stakes record 1:15.26 (1995 Batroyale).

Year	Winner	Jockey	Second	Third	Strs	Time	1st Purse
2002	**Buffythecenterfold**, 2, 121	M. S. Garcia	Tricks Her, 2	Indy Groove, 2	8	1:17.39	$90,000
2001	**Tempera**, 2, 117	D. R. Flores	Respectful, 2	Roaring Blaze, 2	8	1:16.13	$90,000

2000	**Give Praise**, 2, 116	L. A. Pincay Jr.	Sea Reel, 2	Fort Lauderdale, 2	7	1:17.88	$90,000
1999	**Chilukki**, 2, 121	D. R. Flores	November Slew, 2	She's Classy, 2	6	1:16.40	$90,000
1998	**Silverbulletday**, 2, 121	G. L. Stevens	Excellent Meeting, 2	Colorado Song, 2	7	1:17.56	$64,980
1997	**Career Collection**, 2, 121	C. S. Nakatani	Griselle, 2	Bent Creek City, 2	7	1:17.83	$67,825
1996	**Desert Digger**, 2, 116	E. J. Delahoussaye	Silken Magic, 2	Montecito, 2	9	1:16.03	$65,950
1995	**Batroyale**, 2, 119	G. L. Stevens	Cosmic Fire, 2	Waycross, 2	6	**1:15.26**	$59,200
1994	**How So Oiseau**, 2, 117	P. A. Valenzuela	Ski Dancer, 2	Serena's Song, 2	8	1:15.89	$47,100
1993	**Phone Chatter**, 2, 117	L. A. Pincay Jr.	Rhapsodic, 2	Noassemblyrequired, 2	6	1:16.23	$45,900
1992	**Zoonaqua**, 2, 117	E. J. Delahoussaye	Eliza, 2	Medici Bells, 2	11	1:22.67	$49,125

Named for Sorrento, California, and the Sorrento Valley region. 1968-'69 not held. 1986-'93 Grade 3. 1967 about 7½ furlongs; 1970-'73 6 furlongs; 1974-'85 1 mile; 1986-'92 7 furlongs. 1967 turf.

Spectacular Bid Stakes

Grade 3, Gulfstream Park, three-year-olds, 6 furlongs, dirt. Held January 3, 2003, with a gross value of $100,000. First held in 1981. Graded since 1995. Stakes record 1:09.40 (1999 Texas Glitter).

Year	Winner	Jockey	Second	Third	Strs	Time	1st Purse
2003	**First Blush**, 3, 116	J. F. Chavez	Crafty Guy, 3	Silver Squire, 3	9	1:10.97	$60,000
2002	**Maybry's Boy**, 3, 116	J. R. Velazquez	Showmeitall, 3	Harmony Hall, 3	8	1:12.19	$60,000
2001	**Icanseetherain**, 3, 114	J. A. Santos	Diablo's Choice, 3	American Century, 3	10	1:11.04	$60,000
2000	**B L's Appeal**, 3, 114	M. E. Smith	American Bullet, 3	Tour the Hive, 3	8	1:10.68	$45,000
1999	**Texas Glitter**, 3, 117	J. R. Velazquez	Valid Trefaire, 3	Lifeisawhirl, 3	9	**1:09.40**	$45,000
1998	**Time Limit**, 3, 117	J. D. Bailey	Sejm Run, 3	Governor Hicks, 3	8	1:10.56	$45,000
1997	**Confide**, 3, 114	M. E. Smith	Kelly Kip, 3	Crown Ambassador, 3	9	1:09.87	$45,000
1996	**Seacliff**, 3, 122	R. R. Douglas	Built for Pleasure, 3	Gomtuu, 3	8	1:11.92	$45,000
1995	**Mr. Greeley**, 3, 112	J. A. Krone	Make Me, 3	Sea Emperor, 3	7	1:10.76	$44,823
1994	**Halo's Image**, 3, 114	J. Vasquez	Distinct Reality, 3	Senor Conquistador, 3	8	1:10.39	$44,811
1993	**Great Navigator**, 3, 119	J. A. Santos	Demaloot Demashoot, 3	Hidden Trick, 3	8	1:09.53	$45,078
1992	**Return to Quarters**, 3, 114	W. S. Ramos	Scream Machine, 3	Majestic Sweep, 3	8	1:10.10	$45,048

Named for Hawksworth Farm's 1980 Horse of the Year Spectacular Bid (1976-2003, c. by Bold Bidder). 1991-'95 Spectacular Bid Breeders' Cup S. 1982,1984 1¹⁄₁₆ miles; 1987 1 mile. 1982,1984,1987 turf.

Spend a Buck Handicap

Not graded, Calder Race Course, three-year-olds and up, 1¹⁄₁₆ miles, dirt. Held October 12, 2002, with a gross value of $100,000. First held in 1991. First graded in 2003. Stakes record 1:42.59 (2001 Best of the Rest).

Year	Winner	Jockey	Second	Third	Strs	Time	1st Purse
2002	**Pay the Preacher**, 4, 114	C. H. Velasquez	Best of the Rest, 7	Built Up, 4	8	1:44.91	$60,000
2001	**Best of the Rest**, 6, 116	E. Coa	Dancing Guy, 6	Sir Bear, 8	7	**1:42.59**	$60,000
2000	**Groomstick Stock's**, 4, 111	R. B. Homeister Jr.	Reporter, 5	Broadway Tune, 4	8	1:44.82	$60,000
1999	**Best of the Rest**, 4, 114	E. Coa	Dancing Guy, 4	High Security (VEN), 4	10	1:44.67	$60,000
1998	**Unruled**, 5, 116	G. Boulanger	Sir Bear, 5	Laughing Dan, 5	6	1:45.68	$60,000
1997	**Derivative**, 6, 116	J. C. Ferrer	Shan's Ready, 6	Sur Irish's Secret, 4	8	1:45.65	$30,000
1996	**King Rex**, 4, 116	R. D. Lopez	Derivative, 5	Leave'm Inthedark, 4	6	1:52.92	$48,945
1995	**Pride of Burkaan**, 5, 119	R. R. Douglas	Crafty Chris, 5	Dauntless Gem, 5	10	1:51.96	$60,000
1994	**Daniel's Boy**, 6, 111	P. A. Rodriguez	It'sali'lknownfact, 4	Aggressive Chief, 4	8	1:52.68	$60,000

Named for 1985 Horse of the Year Spend a Buck (1982-2002, c. by Buckaroo). 1993 not held. 1992 held as an overnight handicap. 1996 Spend a Buck Breeders' Cup H. 1994-'96 1⅛ miles. 1991 three-year-olds.

Spinaway Stakes

Grade 1, Saratoga Race Course, two-year-olds, fillies, 7 furlongs, dirt. Held August 30, 2002, with a gross value of $200,000. First held in 1881. Graded since 1973. Stakes record 1:23.18 (1994 Flanders).

Year	Winner	Jockey	Second	Third	Strs	Time	1st Purse
2002	**Awesome Humor**, 2, 121	P. Day	Forever Partners, 2	Midnight Cry, 2	12	1:24.36	$120,000
2001	**Cashier's Dream**, 2, 121	D. J. Meche	Smok'n Frolic, 2	Magic Storm, 2	7	1:23.47	$120,000
2000	**Stormy Pick**, 2, 121	J. C. Ferrer	Nasty Storm, 2	Seeking It All, 2	9	1:24.33	$120,000
1999	**Circle of Life**, 2, 121	J. R. Velazquez	Surfside, 2	Miss Wineshine, 2	6	1:23.25	$120,000
1998	**Things Change**, 2, 121	J. A. Santos	Extended Applause, 2	Miss Jennifer Lynn, 2	7	1:24.82	$120,000
1997	**Countess Diana**, 2, 121	S. J. Sellers	Brac Drifter, 2	Aunt Anne, 2	5	1:24.17	$120,000
1996	**Oath**, 2, 121	S. J. Sellers	Pearl City, 2	Fabulously Fast, 2	9	1:23.71	$120,000
1995	**Golden Attraction**, 2, 121	G. L. Stevens	Flat Fleet Feet, 2	Western Dreamer, 2	8	1:23.85	$120,000
1994	**Flanders**, 2, 119	P. Day	Sea Breezer, 2	Stormy Blues, 2	6	**1:23.18**	$120,000
1993	**Strategic Maneuver**, 2, 119	J. A. Santos	Astas Foxy Lady, 2	Delta Lady, 2	5	1:10.34	$120,000
1992	**Family Enterprize**, 2, 119	P. Day	Standard Equipment, 2	Sky Beauty, 2	5	1:09.82	$120,000

Named for 1880 consensus champion two-year-old filly Spinaway (1878, f. by *Leamington). 1892-1900,1911-'12 not held. 1943-'45 held at Belmont. 1881-'91 5 furlongs; 1901-'22 5½ furlongs; 1923-'93 6 furlongs.

Sport Page Handicap

Grade 3, Aqueduct, three-year-olds and up, 7 furlongs, dirt. Held October 26, 2002, with a gross value of $100,000. First held in 1953. Graded since 1984. Stakes record 1:21.49 (1998 Stormin Fever).

Year	Winner	Jockey	Second	Third	Strs	Time	1st Purse
2002	**Multiple Choice**, 4, 113	V. Carrero	Bowman's Band, 4	Sing Me Back Home, 4	8	1:23.28	$66,840

2001	Yonaguska, 3, 116	C. J. McCarron	Silky Sweep, 5	Big E E, 4	6	1:15.54	$65,640
2000	Stalwart Member, 7, 117	N. Arroyo Jr.	Istintaj, 4	Mister Tricky (GB), 5	6	1:21.97	$48,690
1999	Scatmandu, 4, 115	A. T. Gryder	Aristotle, 3	Watchman's Warning, 4	8	1:22.68	$50,250
1998	Stormin Fever, 4, 120	R. Migliore	Olympic Cat, 4	Adverse, 4	9	1:21.49	$50,115
1997	Stalwart Member, 4, 114	A. T. Gryder	Basqueian, 6	Why Change, 4	10	1:22.15	$68,640
1996	Valid Expectations, 3, 117	C. B. Asmussen	Diligence, 3	Blissful State, 4	8	1:21.80	$68,040
1995	Siphon (Brz), 4, 117	K. J. Desormeaux	In Case, 5	Ft. Stockton, 3	13	1:22.08	$71,460
1994	Man's Hero, 4, 111	M. J. Luzzi	Itaka, 4	Storm Tower, 4	10	1:22.10	$51,045
1993	Boom Towner, 5, 117	F. Lovato Jr.	Raise Heck, 5	Fabersham, 5	9	1:10.62	$53,730
1992	R. D. Wild Whirl, 4, 114	R. G. Davis	Senor Speedy, 5	Burn Fair, 5	6	1:09.93	$51,570

Named for Royce Martin's 1948 East View S. winner Sport Page (1946-'72, c. by Our Boots). 1953-'58 held at Jamaica; 1968,1971,1995,2001 Belmont. 1953-'93 6 furlongs; 2001 6½ furlongs. 1953-'58 two-year-olds and up.

Stars and Stripes Breeders' Cup Turf Handicap

Grade 3, Arlington Park, three-year-olds and up, 1½ miles, turf. Held July 6, 2002, with a gross value of $224,625. First held in 1929. Graded since 1973. Stakes record 2:27.50 (2002 Cetewayo).

Year	Winner	Jockey	Second	Third	Strs	Time	1st Purse
2002	Cetewayo, 8, 118	R. R. Douglas	Private Son, 4	Pisces, 5	9	2:27.50	$137,475
2001	Falcon Flight (Fr), 5, 114	R. R. Douglas	Langston, 4	Williams News, 6	11	2:27.86	$96,300
2000	Williams News, 5, 115	R. Albarado	Profit Option, 5	Buff, 5	12	2:31.22	$148,425
1997	Lakeshore Road, 4, 114	C. H. Borel	Chief Bearhart, 4	Awad, 7	9	2:29.57	$140,025
1996	Vladivostok, 6, 116	C. Perret	Raintrap (GB), 6	Special Price, 7	8	2:30.23	$138,075
1995	Snake Eyes, 5, 116	R. Albarado	Coaxing Matt, 6	Bucks Nephew, 5	7	1:56.46	$45,000
1994	Marastani, 4, 113	A. T. Gryder	Snake Eyes, 4	The Vid, 4	12	1:54.64	$60,000
1993	Little Bro Lantis, 5, 114	C. C. Bourque	Stark South, 5	Coaxing Matt, 4	12	1:56.92	$60,000
1992	Plate Dancer, 7, 114	E. Fires	Little Bro Lantis, 4	Stark South, 4	9	1:55.00	$60,000

Traditionally held during the July 4th holiday celebrating the birth of the United States and its flag. 1988,1998-'99 not held. 1929-'95 Stars and Stripes H.; 2000-'01 Stars and Stripes Breeders' Cup H. 1973-'89 Grade 2. 1943-'45,1958-'59 held at Washington Park. 1929-'41,1943-'72,1974-'75,1986 1⅛ miles; 1942,1987-'95 1³⁄₁₆ miles; 1973 1 mile; 1976-'85 1¹⁄₁₆ miles. 1929-'49,1956-'58,1960-'64,1968-'74 dirt. 1958 three-year-olds.

Stephen Foster Handicap

Grade 1, Churchill Downs, three-year-olds and up, 1⅛ miles, dirt. Held June 15, 2002, with a gross value of $750,000. First held in 1982. Graded since 1988. Stakes record 1:47.28 (1999 Victory Gallop).

Year	Winner	Jockey	Second	Third	Strs	Time	1st Purse
2002	Street Cry (Ire), 4, 120	J. D. Bailey	Dollar Bill, 4	Tenpins, 4	8	1:47.84	$516,615
2001	Guided Tour, 5, 113	L. Melancon	Captain Steve, 4	Brahms, 4	8	1:47.74	$515,220
2000	Golden Missile, 5, 118	K. J. Desormeaux	Ecton Park, 4	Cat Thief, 4	6	1:49.56	$502,200
1999	Victory Gallop, 4, 120	J. D. Bailey	Nite Dreamer, 4	Littlebitlively, 5	7	1:47.28	$512,895
1998	Awesome Again, 4, 113	P. Day	Silver Charm, 4	Semoran, 5	7	1:48.61	$495,690
1997	City by Night, 4, 113	S. J. Sellers	Victor Cooley, 4	Semoran, 4	6	1:50.52	$101,649
1996	Tenants Harbor, 4, 112	F. C. Torres	Pleasant Tango, 6	Mt. Sassafras, 4	8	1:49.94	$107,933
1995	Recoup the Cash, 5, 119	A. T. Gryder	Tyus, 5	Powerful Punch, 6	9	1:49.39	$109,298
1994	Recoup the Cash, 4, 112	J. L. Diaz	Taking Risks, 4	Dignitas, 5	7	1:49.46	$106,275
1993	Root Boy, 5, 113	T. G. Turner	Discover, 5	Flying Continental, 7	11	1:50.80	$74,100
1992	Discover, 4, 116	B. E. Bartram	Barkerville, 4	Classic Seven, 4	13	1:50.14	$75,335

Named for composer Stephen Foster (1826-'64), who wrote Kentucky's state song, "My Old Kentucky Home." 1988-'94 Grade 3; 1995-2001 Grade 2. 1983,1985-'87 four-year-olds and up. 1999 new track record.

(Stonerside) Beaumont Stakes

Grade 2, Keeneland, three-year-olds, fillies, about 7 furlongs, dirt. Held April 10, 2003, with a gross value of $250,000. First held in 1986. Graded since 1986. Stakes record 1:25.61 (1999 Swingin On Ice).

Year	Winner	Jockey	Second	Third	Strs	Time	1st Purse
2003	My Boston Gal, 3, 120	P. Day	Bird Town, 3	Midnight Cry, 3	9	1:26.87	$155,000
2002	Proper Gamble, 3, 118	J. Castellano	Respectful, 3	Vicki Vallencourt, 3	8	1:28.79	$155,000
2001	Xtra Heat, 3, 120	R. Wilson	Mountain Bird, 3	Raging Fever, 3	5	1:27.86	$155,000
2000	Sahara Gold, 3, 123	J. D. Bailey	Swept Away, 3	Darling My Darling, 3	6	1:26.58	$84,847
1999	Swingin On Ice, 3, 115	R. Albarado	Secret Hills, 3	Appealing Phylly, 3	7	1:25.61	$83,917
1998	Star of Broadway, 3, 119	P. Day	Santaria, 3	Bourbon Belle, 3	12	1:26.67	$91,140
1997	(DH) Make Haste, 3, 112	P. Day		Move, 3	7	1:28.08	$57,042
	(DH) Screamer, 3, 112	R. Albarado					
1996	Golden Gale, 3, 115	M. E. Smith	Birr, 3	Bright Time, 3	7	1:26.10	$84,398
1995	Dixieland Gold, 3, 118	D. Penna	Niner's Home, 3	Conquistadoress, 3	10	1:27.42	$69,874
1994	Her Temper, 3, 112	P. Day	Lotta Dancing, 3	Term Limits, 3	6	1:28.41	$67,456
1993	Roamin Rachel, 3, 122	C. W. Antley	Added Asset, 3	Fit to Lead, 3	10	1:26.48	$69,998
1992	Fluttery Danseur, 3, 122	S. J. Sellers	Miss Iron Smoke, 3	Spinning Round, 3	8	1:27.46	$53,918

Named for Hal Price Headley's Beaumont Farm, one of Keeneland's founders and the track's first president. Beginning in 2000 sponsored by Janice and Robert McNair's Stonerside Stable of Paris, Kentucky. 1986-'99 Beaumont S. 1990-'92 Grade 3. 1997 dead heat for first.

(Stonerside) Forward Gal Stakes

Grade 3, Gulfstream Park, three-year-olds, fillies, 7 furlongs, dirt. Held March 14, 2003, with a gross value of $100,000. First held in 1981. Graded since 1986. Stakes record 1:21.76 (1997 Glitter Woman).

Year	Winner	Jockey	Second	Third	Strs	Time	1st Purse
2003	Midnight Cry, 3, 117	E. S. Prado	Final Round, 3	Chimichurri, 3	8	1:22.55	$60,000
2002	Take the Cake, 3, 117	R. R. Douglas	A New Twist, 3	Cherokee Girl, 3	7	1:25.47	$60,000
2001	Gold Mover, 3, 121	J. D. Bailey	Hazino, 3	Thunder Bertie, 3	5	1:22.43	$60,000
2000	Miss Inquistive, 3, 114	T. G. Turner	Swept Away, 3	Regally Appealing, 3	9	1:22.25	$45,000
1999	China Storm, 3, 114	P. Day	Three Ring, 3	Extended Applause, 3	5	1:23.69	$45,000
1998	Uanme, 3, 113	S. J. Sellers	Diamond On the Run, 3	Holy Capote, 3	7	1:24.56	$45,000
1997	Glitter Woman, 3, 114	M. E. Smith	City Band, 3	Southern Playgirl, 3	6	**1:21.76**	$45,000
1996	Mindy Gayle, 3, 112	J. A. Krone	Marfa's Finale, 3	Supah Jen, 3	7	1:24.54	$45,000
1995	Chaposa Springs, 3, 114	H. Castillo Jr.	Culver City, 3	Mackenzie Slew, 3	7	1:24.18	$44,580
1994	Mynameispanama, 3, 113	M. Castaneda	Frigid Coed, 3	Wonderlan, 3	9	1:22.97	$45,960
1993	Sum Runner, 3, 118	R. P. Romero	Boots 'n Jackie, 3	Lunar Spook, 3	9	1:23.67	$45,270
1992	Spinning Round, 3, 118	J. A. Santos	Patty's Princess, 3	Super Doer, 3	5	1:24.85	$44,550

Named for 1970 champion two-year-old filly Forward Gal (1968-'84, f. by Native Charger). Beginning in 2003, sponsored by Janice and Robert McNair's Stonerside Stable of Paris, Kentucky. 1991-'95 Forward Gal Breeders' Cup S.; 1996-2002 Forward Gal S. 1991-'96 Grade 2.

Strub Stakes

Grade 2, Santa Anita Park, four-year-olds, 1⅛ miles, dirt. Held February 1, 2003, with a gross value of $400,000. First held in 1948. Graded since 1973. Stakes record 1:47.25 (2002 Mizzen Mast).

Year	Winner	Jockey	Second	Third	Strs	Time	1st Purse
2003	Medaglia d'Oro, 4, 123	J. D. Bailey	Olmodavor, 4	Tracemark, 4	6	1:48.04	$240,000
2002	Mizzen Mast, 4, 121	K. J. Desormeaux	Giant Gentleman, 4	Fancy As, 4	11	**1:47.25**	$240,000
2001	Wooden Phone, 4, 117	C. S. Nakatani	Tiznow, 4	Jimmy Z, 4	6	1:48.43	$300,000
2000	General Challenge, 4, 123	C. S. Nakatani	Luftikus, 4	Saint's Honor, 4	4	1:48.81	$300,000
1999	Event of the Year, 4, 119	C. S. Nakatani	Dr Fong, 4	Hanuman Highway (Ire), 4	7	1:47.65	$300,000
1998	Silver Charm, 4, 123	G. L. Stevens	Mud Route, 4	Bagshot, 4	6	1:47.27	$300,000
1997	Victory Speech, 4, 124	J. D. Bailey	The Barking Shark, 4	Ambivalent, 4	9	2:01.50	$300,000
1996	Helmsman, 4, 122	C. J. McCarron	Afternoon Deelites, 4	Mr Purple, 4	9	2:02.76	$300,000
1995	Dare and Go, 4, 118	A. O. Solis	Dramatic Gold, 4	Wekiva Springs, 4	5	2:00.15	$275,000
1994	Dlazo, 4, 120	L. A. Pincay Jr.	Nonproductiveasset, 4	Stuka, 4	11	2:00.33	$275,000
1993	Siberian Summer, 4, 118	C. S. Nakatani	Bertrando, 4	Major Impact, 4	8	2:00.78	$275,000
1992	Best Pal, 4, 124	K. J. Desormeaux	Dinard, 4	Reign Road, 4	8	1:59.95	$275,000

Named for Charles H. Strub (1884-1958), founder of modern Santa Anita Park. Race name shortened in 1993 to also honor Robert P. Strub (1919-1993), his son and former track president. 1948-'62 Santa Anita Maturity; 1963-'93 Charles H. Strub S. 1973-'97 Grade 1. 1948-'69,1971-'97 1¼ miles.

Stuyvesant Handicap

Grade 3, Aqueduct, three-year-olds and up, 1⅛ miles, dirt. Held November 5, 2002, with a gross value of $100,000. First held in 1916. Graded since 1973. Stakes record 1:47 (1973 Riva Ridge).

Year	Winner	Jockey	Second	Third	Strs	Time	1st Purse
2002	Snake Mountain, 4, 114	J. A. Santos	Windsor Castle, 4	Docent, 4	10	1:50.56	$68,040
2001	Graeme Hall, 4, 119	J. R. Velazquez	Country Be Gold, 4	Cat's At Home, 4	6	1:47.95	$64,620
2000	Lager, 6, 116	H. Castillo Jr.	Top Official, 5	Fire King, 7	6	1:50.03	$64,860
1999	Best of Luck, 3, 114	M. E. Smith	Wild Imagination, 5	Durmiente (Chi), 5	9	1:49.77	$67,200
1998	Mr. Sinatra, 4, 115	A. T. Gryder	Rock and Roll, 3	Accelerator, 4	5	1:48.16	$65,280
1997	Delay of Game, 4, 114	J-L. Samyn	Concerto, 3	Mr. Sinatra, 3	8	1:47.72	$66,060
1996	Poor But Honest, 6, 116	J. F. Chavez	Flitch, 4	Admiralty, 4	8	1:49.44	$66,480
1995	Silver Fox, 4, 113	M. E. Smith	Yourmissinthepoint, 4	Earth Colony, 4	7	1:48.03	$68,940
1994	Wallenda, 4, 118	W. H. McCauley	Lost Soldier, 4	Pistols and Roses, 5	6	1:50.69	$64,560
1993	Michelle Can Pass, 5, 115	J. R. Velazquez	Key Contender, 5	Primitive Hall, 4	8	1:51.07	$70,200
1992	Shots Are Ringing, 5, 114	J. R. Velazquez	Key Contender, 4	Timely Warning, 7	7	1:49.36	$69,120

Named for the Bedford-Stuyvesant neighborhood in the borough of Brooklyn, New York. 1925-'36,1940-'62 not held. 1916-'24,1937-'39 held at Jamaica; 1990,1995,2001 Belmont. 1916-'17 6 furlongs; 1919-'24,1965-'72,1988 1 mile. 1916-'24 three-year-olds.

Suburban Handicap

Grade 2, Belmont Park, three-year-olds and up, 1¼ miles, dirt. Held July 6, 2002, with a gross value of $500,000. First held in 1884. Graded since 1973. Stakes record 1:58.33 (1991 In Excess [Ire]).

Year	Winner	Jockey	Second	Third	Strs	Time	1st Purse
2002	E Dubai, 4, 116	J. R. Velazquez	Lido Palace (Chi), 5	Macho Uno, 4	7	2:00.95	$300,000
2001	Albert the Great, 4, 123	J. F. Chavez	Lido Palace (Chi), 4	Include, 4	6	2:00.39	$300,000
2000	Lemon Drop Kid, 4, 122	E. S. Prado	Behrens, 6	Lager, 6	6	1:58.97	$300,000
1999	Behrens, 5, 121	J. F. Chavez	Catienus, 6	Social Charter, 4	8	2:01.06	$240,000
1998	Frisk Me Now, 4, 118	E. L. King Jr.	Ordway, 4	Sir Bear, 5	8	2:00.45	$210,000
1997	Skip Away, 4, 122	S. J. Sellers	Will's Way, 4	Formal Gold, 4	6	2:02.39	$210,000
1996	Wekiva Springs, 5, 122	M. E. Smith	Mahogany Hall, 5	L'Carriere, 5	5	2:02.78	$300,000
1995	Key Contender, 7, 115	J. D. Bailey	Kissin Kris, 5	Federal Funds, 6	10	2:02.30	$210,000

1994	**Devil His Due**, 5, 124	M. E. Smith	Valley Crossing, 6	Federal Funds, 5	5	2:02.52	$210,000
1993	**Devil His Due**, 4, 121	W. H. McCauley	Pure Rumor, 4	West by West, 4	8	2:01.25	$180,000
1992	**Pleasant Tap**, 5, 119	E. J. Delahoussaye	Strike the Gold, 4	Defensive Play, 5	7	2:00.33	$337,500

Named after the City and Suburban Handicap in England, won by Parole, one of the first American horses to win a major English stakes race. 1911-'12,1914 not held. 1973-'96 Grade 1. 1884-1910 held at Sheepshead Bay; 1961-'74,1976 Aqueduct. 1975 1½ miles; 1976 1$^{3}/_{16}$ miles.

Sunset Handicap

Grade 2, Hollywood Park, three-year-olds and up, 1½ miles, turf. Held July 21, 2002, with a gross value of $250,000. First held in 1938. Graded since 1973. Stakes record 2:23.55 (1996 Talloires).

Year	Winner	Jockey	Second	Third	Strs	Time	1st Purse
2002	**Grammarian**, 4, 112	B. Blanc	Continental Red, 6	Lord Flasheart, 5	7	2:26.59	$150,000
2001	**Blueprint (Ire)**, 6, 116	G. L. Stevens	Kudos, 4	Northern Quest (Fr), 6	5	2:26.16	$120,000
2000	**Bienamado**, 4, 122	C. J. McCarron	Deploy Venture (GB), 4	Single Empire (Ire), 6	5	2:25.06	$150,000
1999	**Plicck (Ire)**, 4, 116	D. R. Flores	River Bay, 6	Lazy Lode (Arg), 5	8	2:26.97	$150,000
1998	**River Bay**, 5, 121	A. O. Solis	Lazy Lode (Arg), 4	Devonwood, 4	6	2:27.40	$210,000
1997	**Marlin**, 4, 120	D. R. Flores	Flyway (Fr), 4	Percutant (GB), 6	6	2:25.39	$240,000
1996	**Talloires**, 6, 116	K. J. Desormeaux	Awad, 6	Sandpit (Brz), 7	7	**2:23.55**	$420,000
1995	**Sandpit (Brz)**, 6, 124	C. S. Nakatani	Special Price, 6	Liyoun (Ire), 7	5	2:25.50	$464,700
1994	**Grand Flotilla**, 7, 119	G. L. Stevens	Semillon (GB), 4	Emerald Jig, 5	7	2:26.35	$158,000
1993	**Bien Bien**, 4, 122	C. J. McCarron	Emerald Jig, 4	Beyton, 4	6	2:25.69	$154,300
1992	**Qathif**, 5, 114	A. O. Solis	Seven Rivers, 6	Stark South, 4	5	2:26.72	$153,600

The Sunset is traditionally one of the last races run at the Hollywood Park spring meeting. Formerly named for sponsor Caesars International's hotel, Caesars Palace. 1942-'45 not held. 1938-'39 Aloha H.; 1995-'96 Caesars Palace Turf Championship H. 1973-'89 Grade 1. 1949 held at Santa Anita. 1938,1950 1⅛ miles; 1941-'49,1952,1955-'59,1961-'66 1⅝ miles; 1969-'72 2 miles. 1938-'66 dirt. 1996 new course record.

Super Derby

Grade 2, Louisiana Downs, three-year-olds, 1⅛ miles, dirt. Held September 21, 2002, with a gross value of $500,000. First held in 1980. Graded since 1982. Stakes record 1:49.43 (2002 Essence of Dubai).

Year	Winner	Jockey	Second	Third	Strs	Time	1st Purse
2002	**Essence of Dubai**, 3, 124	J. F. Chavez	Walk in the Snow, 3	A. P. Five Hundred, 3	8	**1:49.43**	$300,000
2001	**Outofthebox**, 3, 124	L. Meche	E Dubai, 3	Quadrophonic Sound, 3	9	2:06.20	$300,000
2000	**Tiznow**, 3, 124	C. J. McCarron	Commendable, 3	Mass Market, 3	6	1:59.84	$300,000
1999	**Ecton Park**, 3, 126	A. O. Solis	Menifee, 3	Pineaff, 3	8	2:00.59	$300,000
1998	**Arch**, 3, 126	C. S. Nakatani	Classic Cat, 3	Sir Tiff, 3	7	2:01.51	$300,000
1997	**Deputy Commander**, 3, 126	C. J. McCarron	Precocity, 3	Blazing Sword, 3	6	2:00.92	$300,000
1996	**Editor's Note**, 3, 126	G. L. Stevens	The Barking Shark, 3	Devil's Honor, 3	11	2:02.37	$450,000
1995	**Mecke**, 3, 126	J. D. Bailey	Pineing Patty, 3	Scott's Scoundrel, 3	12	2:00.34	$450,000
1994	**Soul of the Matter**, 3, 126	K. J. Desormeaux	Concern, 3	Bay Street Star, 3	6	2:03.57	$450,000
1993	**Wallenda**, 3, 126	W. H. McCauley	Saintly Prospector, 3	Peteski, 3	12	2:02.71	$450,000
1992	**Senor Tomas**, 3, 126	A. T. Gryder	Count the Time, 3	Orbit's Revenge, 3	14	2:04.09	$450,000

1980-'86 Super Derby Invitational; 1995 Isle of Capri Super Derby; 1996 Isle of Capri Casino Super Derby. 1983-2001 Grade 1. 1980-2001 1¼ miles.

Suwannee River Handicap

Grade 3, Gulfstream Park, three-year-olds and up, fillies and mares, 1⅛ miles, turf. Held March 2, 2003, with a gross value of $100,000. First held in 1947. Graded since 1973. Stakes record 1:46.68 (1994 Marshua's River).

Year	Winner	Jockey	Second	Third	Strs	Time	1st Purse
2003	**Amonita (GB)**, 5, 117	J-L. Samyn	What a Price, 5	Calista (GB), 5	9	1:47.90	$60,000
2002	**Snow Dance**, 4, 119	P. Day	Step With Style, 5	Windsong, 5	6	1:49.04	$60,000
2001	**Spook Express (SAF)**, 7, 116	M. E. Smith	Gaviola, 4	Windsong, 4	8	1:47.28	$60,000
2000	**Pico Teneriffe**, 4, 115	J. F. Chavez	Dominique's Joy, 5	Crystal Symphony, 4	8	1:47.83	$45,000
1999	**Winfama**, 6, 114	R. Migliore	Circus Charmer, 4	Colcon, 6	10	1:52.38	$45,000
1998	**Seebe**, 4, 114	D. S. Rice	Colcon, 5	Parade Queen, 4	10	1:47.58	$45,000
1997	**Golden Pond (Ire)**, 4, 115	J. D. Bailey	Rumpipumpy (GB), 4	Elusive, 5	11	1:47.87	$45,000
1996	**Class Kris**, 4, 116	P. Day	Apolda, 5	Majestic Dy, 4	5	1:49.17	$45,000
1995	**Cox Orange**, 5, 116	J. D. Bailey	Irving's Girl, 5	Alice Springs, 5	7	1:47.43	$45,000
1994	**Marshua's River**, 7, 114	J. A. Santos	Sheila's Revenge, 4	Icy Warning, 4	12	**1:46.68**	$45,000
1993	**Via Borghese**, 4, 116	J. D. Bailey	Marshua's River, 6	Blue Daisy, 5	14	1:48.22	$40,230
1992	**Julie La Rousse (Ire)**, 4, 115	J. D. Bailey	Christiecat, 5	Grab the Green, 4	11	1:48.48	$38,670

Named for Stephen Foster's song "Old Folks at Home (Suwannee River)," Florida's state song. 1949 not held. 1950-'52 held as an overnight handicap. 1979-'81 not graded. 1947,1961-'66,1977,1983 (2 divs.) 7 furlongs; 1948 6 furlongs; 1953-'60,1967-'68,1986-'91 1$^{1}/_{16}$ miles; 1969-'76,1978-'79,1981-'82,1983 (1 div.),1984-'85 1 mile; 1999 about 1⅛ miles. 1965-'66,1977,1983 (2 divs.),1986,1991 dirt. 1994 four-year-olds and up. 1992 equaled course record.

Swale Stakes

Grade 3, Gulfstream Park, three-year-olds, 7 furlongs, dirt. Held March 15, 2003, with a gross value of $150,000. First held in 1985. Graded since 1990. Stakes record 1:21.06 (2003 Midas Eyes).

Year	Winner	Jockey	Second	Third	Strs	Time	1st Purse
2003	**Midas Eyes**, 3, 116	J. D. Bailey	Posse, 3	Whywhywhy, 3	8	**1:21.06**	$90,000
2002	**Ethan Man**, 3, 116	P. Day	Listen Here, 3	Governor Hickel, 3	5	1:22.29	$90,000

2001	D'wildcat, 3, 116	C. S. Nakatani	Tarek, 3	Yonaguska, 3	6	1:22.25	$90,000
2000	Trippi, 3, 113	J. D. Bailey	Ultimate Warrior, 3	Harlan Traveler, 3	8	1:23.43	$60,000
1999	Yes It's True, 3, 122	J. D. Bailey	Texas Glitter, 3	Lucky Roberto, 3	5	1:22.29	$60,000
1998	Favorite Trick, 3, 122	P. Day	Good and Tough, 3	Dice Dancer, 3	9	1:22.86	$60,000
1997	Confide, 3, 117	M. E. Smith	Country Rainbow, 3	The Silver Move, 3	9	1:23.35	$45,000
1996	Roar, 3, 113	M. E. Smith	Gomtuu, 3	Dixie Connection, 3	6	1:22.46	$45,000
1995	Mr. Greeley, 3, 114	J. A. Krone	Devious Course, 3	Pyramid Peak, 3	6	1:22.18	$45,000
1994	Arrival Time, 3, 115	C. J. McCarron	Senor Conquistador, 3	Meadow Monster, 3	7	1:22.53	$45,000
1993	Premier Explosion, 3, 114	D. Penna	Demaloot Demashoot, 3	Cherokee Run, 3	8	1:23.23	$53,520
1992	D. J. Cat, 3, 114	J. D. Bailey	Binalong, 3	Always Silver, 3	10	1:23.39	$71,250

Named for Claiborne Farm's 1984 champion three-year-old male Swale (1981-'84, c. by Seattle Slew).

Swaps Stakes

Grade 2, Hollywood Park, three-year-olds, 1⅛ miles, dirt. Held July 14, 2002, with a gross value of $500,000. First held in 1974. Graded since 1975. Stakes record 1:45.96 (1997 Free House).

Year	Winner	Jockey	Second	Third	Strs	Time	1st Purse
2002	Came Home, 3, 122	M. E. Smith	Like a Hero, 3	Fonz's, 3	7	1:48.24	$300,000
2001	Congaree, 3, 122	G. L. Stevens	Until Sundown, 3	Jamaican Rum, 3	6	1:48.61	$300,000
2000	Captain Steve, 3, 120	C. S. Nakatani	Tiznow, 3	Spacelink, 3	6	1:48.01	$300,000
1999	Cat Thief, 3, 120	P. Day	General Challenge, 3	Walk That Walk, 3	4	1:47.87	$300,000
1998	Old Trieste, 3, 118	C. J. McCarron	Grand Slam, 3	Old Topper, 3	6	1:47.06	$300,000
1997	Free House, 3, 122	K. J. Desormeaux	Deputy Commander, 3	Wild Rush, 3	6	**1:45.96**	$300,000
1996	Victory Speech, 3, 118	J. D. Bailey	Prince of Thieves, 3	Hesabull, 3	5	1:48.28	$300,000
1995	Thunder Gulch, 3, 126	G. L. Stevens	Da Hoss, 3	Petionville, 3	7	1:49.09	$275,000
1994	Silver Music, 3, 119	C. W. Antley	Dramatic Gold, 3	Valiant Nature, 3	6	2:00.76	$123,800
1993	Devoted Brass, 3, 123	L. A. Pincay Jr.	Future Storm, 3	Codified, 3	6	2:00.64	$124,000
1992	Bien Bien, 3, 119	C. J. McCarron	Treekster, 3	Sevengreenpairs, 3	5	2:02.91	$123,400

Named for Rex Ellsworth's 1956 Horse of the Year Swaps (1952-'72, c. by *Khaled). 1975-'88,1999-2001 Grade 1. 1974-'94 1¼ miles.

Sword Dancer Invitational Handicap

Grade 1, Saratoga Race Course, three-year-olds and up, 1½ miles, turf. Held August 10, 2002, with a gross value of $500,000. First held in 1975. Graded since 1981. Stakes record 2:23.20 (1997 Awad).

Year	Winner	Jockey	Second	Third	Strs	Time	1st Purse
2002	With Anticipation, 7, 120	P. Day	Denon, 4	Volponi, 4	11	2:24.06	$300,000
2001	With Anticipation, 6, 114	P. Day	King Cugat, 4	Slew Valley, 4	9	2:26.41	$300,000
2000	John's Call, 9, 114	J-L. Samyn	Aly's Alley, 4	Single Empire (Ire), 6	8	2:32.17	$300,000
1999	Honor Glide, 5, 116	J. A. Santos	Val's Prince, 7	Chorwon, 6	7	2:28.23	$240,000
1998	Cetewayo, 4, 115	J. R. Velazquez	Val's Prince, 6	Dushyanter, 5	6	2:29.56	$180,000
1997	Awad, 7, 117	P. Day	Fahim (GB), 4	Val's Prince, 5	10	**2:23.20**	$150,000
1996	Broadway Flyer, 5, 118	M. E. Smith	Kiri's Clown, 7	Flag Down, 6	9	2:32.08	$150,000
1995	Kiri's Clown, 6, 114	M. J. Luzzi	Awad, 5	King's Theatre (Ire), 4	13	2:25.45	$150,000
1994	Alex the Great (GB), 5, 118	P. A. Valenzuela	Kiri's Clown, 5	L'Hermine (GB), 5	10	2:28.66	$150,000
1993	Spectacular Tide, 4, 112	J. A. Krone	Square Cut, 4	Dr. Kiernan, 4	9	2:30.39	$120,000
1992	Fraise, 4, 113	J. D. Bailey	Wall Street Dancer, 4	Montserrat, 4	8	2:25.88	$150,000

Named for Brookmeade Stable's 1959 Horse of the Year Sword Dancer (1956-'84, c. by Sunglow). 1975-'78,1983-'93 Sword Dancer H.; 1979-'82 Sword Dancer S. 1981 Grade 3; 1982-'83 Grade 2. 1975-'76 held at Aqueduct; 1977-'91 Belmont. 1975-'76 6 furlongs; 1977-'79 1¹⁄₁₆ miles. 1975-'76 dirt. 1975-'76 three-year-olds.

Sycamore Breeders' Cup Stakes

Grade 3, Keeneland, three-year-olds and up, 1½ miles, turf. Held October 6, 2002, with a gross value of $150,000. First held in 1995. First graded in 2003. Stakes record 2:30.48 (2002 Rochester).

Year	Winner	Jockey	Second	Third	Strs	Time	1st Purse
2002	Rochester, 6, 125	P. Day	Roxinho (Brz), 4	Lord Flasheart, 5	7	**2:30.48**	$101,928
2001	Rochester, 5, 119	P. Day	Chorwon, 8	Regal Dynasty, 5	7	2:31.29	$103,044
2000	Crowd Pleaser, 5, 118	C. H. Borel	Dixie's Crown, 4	Kim Loves Bucky, 3	7	2:44.00	$44,439
1999	Royal Strand (Ire), 5, 117	P. Day	Arizona Storm, 4	Majest, 4	6	2:38.60	$42,315
1998	Royal Strand (Ire), 4, 116	S. Sellers	Thesaurus, 4	Lakeshore Road, 5	5	2:41.80	$33,015
1997	Gleaming Key, 5, 116	S. Sellers	Double Leaf, 4	Seattle Blossom, 4	5	2:45.80	$33,015
1996	Gleaming Key, 4, 114	R. Albarado	Nash Terrace (Ire), 4	Hawkeye Bay, 5	4	2:44.40	$32,860
1995	Lindon Lime, 5, 123	C. Perret	Hyper Shu, 5	Lordly Prospect, 6	9	2:42.60	$39,098

Named for the sycamore tree at the entrance to Keeneland's walking ring. 1995-2000 Sycamore S.

Tampa Bay Derby

Grade 3, Tampa Bay Downs, three-year-olds, 1¹⁄₁₆ miles, dirt. Held March 16, 2003, with a gross value of $250,000. First held in 1981. Graded since 1984. Stakes record 1:43.66 (2002 Equality).

Year	Winner	Jockey	Second	Third	Strs	Time	1st Purse
2003	Region of Merit, 3, 120	E. Coa	Aristocat, 3	Hear No Evil, 3	8	1:44.61	$150,000
2002	Equality, 3, 118	R. A. Dominguez	Tails of the Crypt, 3	Political Attack, 3	9	**1:43.66**	$120,000
2001	Burning Roma, 3, 123	R. Migliore	American Prince, 3	Paging, 3	11	1:44.30	$120,000
2000	Wheelaway, 3, 116	R. Migliore	Impeachment, 3	Perfect Cat, 3	10	1:43.90	$90,000
1999	Pineaff, 3, 122	J. A. Santos	Menifee, 3	Doneraile Court, 3	6	1:45.33	$90,000

1998	**Parade Ground**, 3, 118	P. Day	Middlesex Drive, 3	Rock and Roll, 3	8	1:44.20	$90,000
1997	**Zede**, 3, 118	J. D. Bailey	Brisco Jack, 3	Favorable Regard, 3	12	1:44.80	$90,000
1996	**Thundering Storm**, 3, 118	J. A. Guerra	El Amante, 3	Natural Selection, 3	10	1:43.80	$90,000
1995	**Gadzook**, 3, 116	G. Boulanger	Composer, 3	Bet Your Bucks, 3	10	1:45.20	$90,000
1994	**Prix de Crouton**, 3, 120	M. Walls	Able Buck, 3	Parental Pressure, 3	7	1:46.60	$90,000
1993	**Marco Bay**, 3, 120	R. D. Allen Jr.	Thriller Chiller, 3	Tunecke Charlie, 3	12	1:44.40	$90,000
1992	**Careful Gesture**, 3, 118	R. N. Lester	Chief Speaker, 3	Clipper Won, 3	12	1:45.93	$120,000

1981-'86 Budweiser-Tampa Bay Derby. 1990-2001 not graded.

Tempted Stakes

Grade 3, Aqueduct, two-year-olds, fillies, 1 mile. Held November 3, 2002, with a gross value of $100,000. First held in 1975. Graded since 1980. Stakes record 1:35.40 (1975 Secret Lanvin).

Year	Winner	Jockey	Second	Third	Strs	Time	1st Purse
2002	**Chimichurri**, 2, 119	J. R. Velazquez	Reheat, 2	Bonay, 2	8	1:37.52	$66,240
2001	**Smok'n Frolic**, 2, 119	J. R. Velazquez	Saintly Action, 2	Wopping, 2	8	1:37.77	$66,900
2000	**Two Item Limit**, 2, 117	R. Migliore	Celtic Melody, 2	Twining Star, 2	6	1:38.53	$65,520
1999	**Shawnee Country**, 2, 116	J. F. Chavez	To Marquet, 2	Marigalante, 2	5	1:38.60	$65,460
1998	**Oh What a Windfall**, 2, 121	J. D. Bailey	La Ville Rouge, 2	Honour a Bull, 2	8	1:39.84	$66,120
1997	**Dancing With Ruth**, 2, 118	T. G. Turner	Soft Senorita, 2	Aunt Anne, 2	6	1:37.55	$65,340
1996	**Ajina**, 2, 112	J. D. Bailey	Glitter Woman, 2	Aldiza, 2	7	1:36.59	$66,240
1994	**Special Broad**, 2, 114	J. A. Krone	Carson Creek, 2	Golden Bri, 2	7	1:37.20	$66,000
1993	**Sovereign Kitty**, 2, 112	J. R. Velazquez	Seeking the Circle, 2	Her Temper, 2	8	1:46.84	$69,720
1992	**True Affair**, 2, 121	J. Bravo	Broad Gains, 2	Touch of Love, 2	6	1:47.48	$68,520

Named for Mrs. Philip duPont's 1959 champion handicap mare Tempted (1955, f. by *Half Crown). 1995 not held. 1981-'82,1988 Grade 2. 2001 held at Belmont. 1984-'93 1 1/16 miles.

Test Stakes

Grade 1, Saratoga Race Course, three-year-olds, fillies, 7 furlongs, dirt. Held July 27, 2002, with a gross value of $250,000. First held in 1922. Graded since 1973. Stakes record 1:21 (1987 Very Subtle; 1990 Go for Wand).

Year	Winner	Jockey	Second	Third	Strs	Time	1st Purse
2002	**You**, 3, 123	J. D. Bailey	Carson Hollow, 3	Spring Meadow, 3	7	1:22.84	$150,000
2001	**Victory Ride**, 3, 116	E. S. Prado	Xtra Heat, 3	Nasty Storm, 3	8	1:21.72	$150,000
2000	**Dream Supreme**, 3, 115	P. Day	Big Bambu, 3	Finder's Fee, 3	11	1:22.66	$150,000
1999	**Marley Vale**, 3, 116	J. R. Velazquez	Awful Smart, 3	Emanating, 3	11	1:22.77	$150,000
1998	**Jersey Girl**, 3, 123	M. E. Smith	Brave Deed, 3	Catinca, 3	11	1:23.02	$120,000
1997	**Fabulously Fast**, 3, 114	J. D. Bailey	Aldiza, 3	Pearl City, 3	9	1:21.65	$90,000
1996	**Capote Belle**, 3, 115	J. R. Velazquez	Flat Fleet Feet, 3	J J'sdream, 3	8	1:21.08	$90,000
1995	**Chaposa Springs**, 3, 120	J. D. Bailey	Miss Golden Circle, 3	Daijin, 3	9	1:21.81	$90,000
1994	**Twist Afleet**, 3, 114	J. D. Bailey	Penny's Reshoot, 3	Heavenly Prize, 3	8	1:22.08	$90,000
1993	**Missed the Storm**, 3, 114	M. E. Smith	Miss Indy Anna, 3	Educated Risk, 3	5	1:22.12	$90,000
1992	**November Snow**, 3, 116	C. W. Antley	Meafara, 3	Preach, 3	8	1:21.33	$105,480

Sometimes used as a prep or "test" race for the Alabama Stakes later in the meet. 1923-'25,1961 not held. 1973-'74,1979-'87 Grade 2; 1975-'78 Grade 3. 1943-'45 held at Belmont. 1922 1 1/4 miles.

Texas Mile Stakes

Grade 3, Lone Star Park, three-year-olds and up, 1 mile, dirt. Held April 26, 2003, with a gross value of $300,000. First held in 1997. Graded since 1999. Stakes record 1:34.44 (1997 Isitingood).

Year	Winner	Jockey	Second	Third	Strs	Time	1st Purse
2003	**Bluesthestandard**, 6, 120	M. A. Pedroza	Bonapaw, 7	Compendium, 5	9	1:35.68	$170,000
2002	**Unrullah Bull**, 5, 116	A. J. Lovato	Reba's Gold, 5	Compendium, 4	9	1:37.78	$170,000
2001	**Dixie Dot Com**, 6, 116	D. R. Flores	Mr Ross, 6	Five Straight, 4	7	1:34.72	$180,000
2000	**Sir Bear**, 7, 116	E. Coa	Lexington Park, 4	Luftikus, 4	9	1:35.98	$170,000
1999	**Littlebitlively**, 5, 116	C. Gonzalez	Real Quiet, 4	Allen's Oop, 4	8	1:35.65	$145,000
1998	**Littlebitlively**, 4, 118	C. Gonzalez	Anet, 4	Scott's Scoundrel, 6	5	1:37.07	$160,000
1997	**Isitingood**, 6, 123	D. R. Flores	Spiritbound, 5	Skip Away, 4	7	**1:34.44**	$150,000

The Very One Handicap

Grade 3, Gulfstream Park, three-year-olds and up, fillies and mares, 1 3/8 miles, turf. Held February 8, 2003, with a gross value of $100,000. First held in 1987. Graded since 1996. Stakes record 2:13.45 (1999 Delilah [Ire]).

Year	Winner	Jockey	Second	Third	Strs	Time	1st Purse
2003	**San Dare**, 5, 116	M. Guidry	Tweedside, 5	Hi Tech Honeycomb, 4	12	2:13.76	$60,000
2002	**Moon Queen (Ire)**, 4, 118	J. D. Bailey	Jennasietta, 4	Sweetest Thing, 4	6	2:18.38	$60,000
2001	**Innuendo (Ire)**, 6, 115	J. D. Bailey	Lucky Lune (Fr), 4	Silver Bandana, 5	10	2:13.62	$60,000
2000	**My Sweet Westly**, 4, 110	P. Day	I'm Indy Mood, 5	Manoa, 5	6	2:06.79	$45,000
1999	**Delilah (Ire)**, 5, 116	J. D. Bailey	Starry Dreamer, 5	Justenuffheart, 4	8	**2:13.45**	$45,000
1998	**Shemozzle (Ire)**, 5, 114	J. R. Velazquez	Turkappeal, 5	Yokama, 5	8	2:19.06	$45,000
1997	**Tocopilla (Arg)**, 7, 114	B. D. Peck	Ampulla, 6	Beyrouth, 5	6	2:14.35	$45,000
1996	**Electric Society (Ire)**, 5, 113	M. E. Smith	Northern Emerald, 6	Chelsey Flower, 5	13	2:15.23	$30,000
1995	**P J Floral**, 6, 113	S. J. Sellers	Trampoli, 5	Memories (Ire), 4	6	2:14.44	$30,000
1994	**Russian Tango**, 4, 112	J. D. Bailey	Maxamount, 6	Camiunch, 5	6	2:02.58	$30,000

| 1993 | Fairy Garden, 5, 113 | W. S. Ramos | Trampoli, 4 | Tango Charlie, 4 | 11 | 2:14.67 | $30,000 |
| 1992 | Bungalow, 5, 112 | S. J. Sellers | Raffinierte (Ire), 4 | Lover's Quest, 4 | 7 | 2:05.79 | $30,000 |

Named for 1981 Santa Barbara H. (G1) winner The Very One (1975-'92, f. by One for All). 1988-'89 not held. 2000 not graded. 1987 1 mile; 1990 7 furlongs; 1992,1994,2000 1¼ miles; 1998,2002 about 1⅜ miles. 1990,1992,1994,2000 dirt. 1996 four-year-olds and up.

Thoroughbred Club of America Stakes

Grade 3, Keeneland, three-year-olds and up, fillies and mares, 6 furlongs, dirt. Held October 20, 2002, with a gross value of $125,000. First held in 1981. Graded since 1988. Stakes record 1:08.70 (1998 Bourbon Belle).

Year	Winner	Jockey	Second	Third	Strs	Time	1st Purse
2002	French Riviera, 3, 116	D. J. Meche	Don't Countess Out, 3	Away, 5	10	1:09.75	$77,500
2001	Cat Cay, 4, 118	P. Day	Spanish Glitter, 3	Another, 4	7	1:09.24	$67,580
2000	Katz Me If You Can, 3, 115	J. F. Chavez	Hurricane Bertie, 5	My Alibi, 4	6	1:09.42	$67,394
1999	Cinemine, 4, 120	E. M. Martin Jr.	Bourbon Belle, 4	Lucky Again, 3	5	1:08.86	$62,000
1998	Bourbon Belle, 3, 111	W. Martinez	J J'sdream, 5	Meter Maid, 4	8	1:08.70	$62,000
1997	Sky Blue Pink, 3, 111	P. Day	Bluffing Girl, 3	Mama's Pro, 4	7	1:10.06	$62,000
1996	Surprising Fact, 3, 110	P. Day	Morris Code, 4	Mama's Pro, 3	9	1:10.14	$62,000
1995	Cat Appeal, 3, 116	D. M. Barton	Russian Flight (Ire), 3	Traverse City, 5	9	1:10.02	$46,500
1994	Tenacious Tiffany, 4, 113	C. Perret	Roamin Rachel, 4	Jeano, 6	7	1:11.00	$46,500
1993	Jeano, 5, 120	P. Day	Apelia, 4	Fluttery Danseur, 4	6	1:09.39	$46,500
1992	Ifyoucouldseemenow, 4, 120	C. Perret	Harbour Club, 5	Madam Bear, 4	8	1:09.67	$48,750

Named for the Thoroughbred Club of America, whose headquarters building is a short distance from Keeneland. 1981-'82 Thoroughbred Club Dinner S. Bourbon Belle finished first, DQ to second.

Toboggan Handicap

Grade 3, Aqueduct, three-year-olds and up, 6 furlongs, dirt. Held March 15, 2003, with a gross value of $109,100. First held in 1890. Graded since 1973. Stakes record 1:08.40 (1956 Nance's Lad; 1957 Decimal).

Year	Winner	Jockey	Second	Third	Strs	Time	1st Purse
2003	Affirmed Success, 9, 118	R. Migliore	Peeping Tom, 6	Captain Red, 6	6	1:09.09	$65,460
2002	Affirmed Success, 8, 119	R. Migliore	Vodka, 5	Multiple Choice, 4	6	1:22.87	$64,920
2001	Peeping Tom, 4, 118	S. Bridgmohan	Say Florida Sandy, 7	Lake Pontchartrain, 6	6	1:21.25	$64,380
2000	Brutally Frank, 6, 114	S. Bridgmohan	Master O Foxhounds, 5	Watchman's Warning, 5	8	1:20.77	$49,410
1999	Wouldn't We All, 5, 114	R. Migliore	Brushed On, 4	Esteemed Friend, 5	7	1:20.95	$48,900
1998	Home On the Ridge, 4, 114	W. H. McCauley	Wire Me Collect, 5	King Roller, 7	7	1:23.01	$49,650
1997	Royal Haven, 5, 115	R. Migliore	Jamies First Punch, 4	Cold Execution, 6	6	1:22.47	$48,600
1996	Placid Fund, 4, 112	J. F. Chavez	Valid Wager, 4	Pat n Jac, 4	12	1:22.92	$51,480
1995	Boom Towner, 7, 117	F. Lovato Jr.	Virginia Rapids, 5	Won Song, 5	6	1:23.77	$49,080
1994	Blare of Trumpets, 5, 112	D. Carr	Preporant, 5	Fabersham, 6	6	1:09.70	$49,200
1993	Argyle Lake, 7, 109	D. Carr	The Great M. B., 4	Regal Conquest, 5	12	1:10.11	$55,530
1992	Boom Towner, 4, 115	D. Nelson	Real Minx, 5	Gallant Step, 5	8	1:10.03	$52,740

Originally the Toboggan Slide H., held on the downhill course at Old Morris Park in the Bronx. 1891,1895,1911-'12 not held. 1890-'94 Toboggan Slide H. 1975-'83,1996-2002 not graded. 1890-'94 held at Morris Park; 1896-'61 Belmont. 1995-2002 7 furlongs.

Tom Fool Handicap

Grade 2, Belmont Park, three-year-olds and up, 7 furlongs, dirt. Held July 4, 2002, with a gross value of $150,000. First held in 1975. Graded since 1981. Stakes record 1:20.17 (2002 Left Bank).

Year	Winner	Jockey	Second	Third	Strs	Time	1st Purse
2002	Left Bank, 5, 121	J. R. Velazquez	Affirmed Success, 8	Summer Note, 5	6	1:20.17	$90,000
2001	Exchange Rate, 4, 114	J. D. Bailey	Say Florida Sandy, 7	Here's Zealous, 4	5	1:21.24	$90,000
2000	Trippi, 3, 112	J. D. Bailey	Cornish Snow, 7	Sailor's Warning, 4	6	1:21.69	$90,000
1999	Crafty Friend, 6, 116	R. Migliore	Affirmed Success, 5	Artax, 4	5	1:20.62	$90,000
1998	Banker's Gold, 4, 115	J. F. Chavez	Boundless Moment, 6	Partner's Hero, 4	6	1:21.04	$90,000
1997	Diligence, 4, 116	J. A. Santos	Royal Haven, 5	Elusive Quality, 4	7	1:22.40	$90,000
1996	Kayraван, 4, 113	R. Migliore	Cold Execution, 5	Lite the Fuse, 5	5	1:22.95	$64,860
1995	Lite the Fuse, 4, 117	J. A. Krone	Our Emblem, 4	Evil Bear, 4	6	1:21.72	$65,220
1994	Virginia Rapids, 4, 124	J-L. Samyn	Cherokee Run, 4	Boundary, 4	5	1:22.27	$64,380
1993	Birdonthewire, 4, 119	C. Perret	Fly So Free, 5	Take Me Out, 5	5	1:20.93	$67,680
1992	Rubiano, 5, 126	J. A. Krone	Take Me Out, 4	Arrowtown, 4	8	1:21.70	$70,920

Named for Greentree Stable's 1953 Horse of the Year and handicap triple crown winner Tom Fool (1949-'76, c. by Menow). 1979-'95 Tom Fool S. 1981 Grade 3. 1975-'76 held at Aqueduct.

Top Flight Handicap

Grade 2, Aqueduct, three-year-olds and up, fillies and mares, 1 mile, dirt. Held November 29, 2002, with a gross value of $150,000. First held in 1940. Graded since 1973. Stakes record 1:34.96 (1994 Educated Risk).

Year	Winner	Jockey	Second	Third	Strs	Time	1st Purse
2002	Sightseek, 3, 113	J. D. Bailey	Zonk, 4	Nasty Storm, 4	9	1:35.46	$90,000

2001	Cat Cay, 4, 117	J. R. Velazquez	Tugger, 4	Atelier, 4	9	1:35.45	$90,000
2000	Reciclada (Chi), 5, 116	J. D. Bailey	Country Hideaway, 4	Critical Eye, 4	8	1:35.54	$90,000
1999	Belle Cherie, 3, 113	J. R. Velazquez	(DH) Harpia, 5		7	1:35.46	$90,000
			(DH) Furlough, 5				
1998	Catinca, 3, 119	R. Migliore	Furlough, 4	Glitter Woman, 4	5	1:35.81	$90,000
1997	Dixie Flag, 3, 117	M. J. Luzzi	Aldiza, 3	Mil Kilates, 4	9	1:35.34	$90,000
1996	Flat Fleet Feet, 3, 116	M. E. Smith	Queen Tutta, 4	Miss Golden Circle, 4	9	1:37.00	$90,000
1995	Twist Afleet, 4, 123	M. E. Smith	Chaposa Springs, 3	Lotta Dancing, 4	8	1:35.26	$90,000
1994	Educated Risk, 4, 120	M. E. Smith	Triumph At Dawn, 4	Imah, 4	8	1:34.96	$90,000
1993	You'd Be Surprised, 4, 112	J. D. Bailey	Looie Capote, 4	Shared Interest, 5	7	1:48.82	$90,000
1992	Firm Stance, 4, 114	P. Day	Haunting, 4	Lady d'Accord, 5	14	1:50.55	$120,000

Named for C. V. Whitney's 1931 champion two-year-old filly and '32 champion three-year-old filly Top Flight (1929-'49, f. by *Dis Donc). 1996-2000 Delta Air Lines Top Flight H. 1973-'96 Grade 1. 1940-'61,1993 held at Belmont. 1940-'60 1¹⁄₁₆ miles; 1961-'93 1⅛ miles. 1988,1990 four-year-olds and up. 1999 dead heat for second.

Transylvania Stakes

Grade 3, Keeneland, three-year-olds, 1 mile, turf. Held April 4, 2003, with a gross value of $100,000. First held in 1989. First graded in 2003. Stakes record 1:34.65 (1998 Dog Watch [GB]).

Year	Winner	Jockey	Second	Third	Strs	Time	1st Purse
2003	White Cat, 3, 116	S. J. Sellers	Deep Shadow, 3	Christmas Away, 3	9	1:34.98	$62,000
2002	Flying Dash (Ger), 3, 116	J. D. Bailey	Back Packer, 3	Political Attack, 3	8	1:35.69	$62,000
2001	Baptize, 3, 120	J. D. Bailey	Dynameaux, 3	Act of Reform, 3	9	1:35.28	$70,556
2000	Field Cat, 3, 116	M. E. Smith	Lendell Ray, 3	Go Lib Go, 3	9	1:35.19	$70,618
1999	Good Night, 3, 114	S. J. Sellers	Air Rocket, 3	Make Your Mark, 3	10	1:35.00	$70,308
1998	Dog Watch (GB), 3, 116	R. G. Davis	Reformer Rally, 3	American Odyssey, 3	10	1:34.65	$45,781
1997	Near the Bank, 3, 118	P. Day	Daylight Savings, 3	Song for James, 3	6	1:36.53	$44,249
1996	More Royal, 3, 112	J. A. Krone	Defacto, 3	Rough Opening, 3	5	1:35.92	$43,202
1995	Crimson Guard, 3, 118	M. E. Smith	Dixie Dynasty, 3	Nostra, 3	9	1:44.04	$42,259
1994	Star of Manila, 3, 121	S. J. Sellers	Prix de Crouton, 3	Carpet, 3	6	1:42.87	$33,635
1993	Proud Shot, 3, 118	W. H. McCauley	Explosive Red, 3	Awad, 3	7	1:44.17	$34,364
1992	Casino Magistrate, 3, 121	R. D. Lopez	Coaxing Matt, 3	Trans Caribbean, 3	7	1:46.62	$35,636

Named for Transylvania University, the oldest college west of the Allegheny Mountains, founded in 1780 in Lexington, Kentucky. 1989-'95 1¹⁄₁₆ miles.

Travers Stakes

Grade 1, Saratoga Race Course, three-year-olds, 1¼ miles, dirt. Held August 24, 2002, with a gross value of $1,000,000. First held in 1864. Graded since 1973. Stakes record 2:00 (1979 General Assembly).

Year	Winner	Jockey	Second	Third	Strs	Time	1st Purse
2002	Medaglia d'Oro, 3, 126	J. D. Bailey	Repent, 3	Nothing Flat, 3	9	2:02.53	$600,000
2001	Point Given, 3, 126	G. L. Stevens	E Dubai, 3	Dollar Bill, 3	9	2:01.40	$600,000
2000	Unshaded, 3, 126	S. J. Sellers	Albert the Great, 3	Commendable, 3	9	2:02.59	$600,000
1999	Lemon Drop Kid, 3, 126	J. A. Santos	Vision and Verse, 3	Menifee, 3	8	2:02.19	$600,000
1998	Coronado's Quest, 3, 126	M. E. Smith	Victory Gallop, 3	Raffie's Majesty, 3	7	2:03.40	$450,000
1997	Deputy Commander, 3, 126	C. J. McCarron	Behrens, 3	Awesome Again, 3	8	2:04.08	$450,000
1996	Will's Way, 3, 126	J. F. Chavez	Louis Quatorze, 3	Skip Away, 3	7	2:02.55	$450,000
1995	Thunder Gulch, 3, 126	G. L. Stevens	Pyramid Peak, 3	Malthus, 3	7	2:03.70	$450,000
1994	Holy Bull, 3, 126	M. E. Smith	Concern, 3	Tabasco Cat, 3	5	2:02.03	$450,000
1993	Sea Hero, 3, 126	J. D. Bailey	Kissin Kris, 3	Miner's Mark, 3	11	2:01.95	$600,000
1992	Thunder Rumble, 3, 126	W. H. McCauley	Devil His Due, 3	Dance Floor, 3	10	2:00.99	$600,000

Named for the first president of Saratoga Race Course, William R. Travers; he won the inaugural running with Kentucky. 1896,1898,1900,1911-'12 not held. 1927-'32 Travers Midsummer Derby. 1943-'45 held at Belmont. 1864-'89 1¾ miles; 1890-'92 1½ miles; 1895,1901-'03 1⅛ miles.

Tremont Stakes

Grade 3, Belmont Park, two-year-olds, 5½ furlongs, dirt. Held June 29, 2002, with a gross value of $106,600. First held in 1887. Graded since 1973. Stakes record 1:02.56 (1999 More Than Ready).

Year	Winner	Jockey	Second	Third	Strs	Time	1st Purse
2002	Zavata, 2, 114	J. D. Bailey	Hussar, 2	Desert Warrior, 2	5	1:02.66	$63,960
2001	Buster's Daydream, 2, 120	J. R. Velazquez	Draw Play, 2	Day Trader, 2	5	1:03.96	$63,780
2000	City Zip, 2, 116	J. A. Santos	The Goo, 2	Scorpion, 2	5	1:03.81	$64,320
1999	More Than Ready, 2, 119	J. R. Velazquez	Afternoon Affair, 2	King Kokand, 2	6	1:02.56	$65,040
1998	Tactical Cat, 2, 115	J. D. Bailey	Lucky Roberto, 2	King's Crown, 2	9	1:03.33	$50,440
1997	Time Limit, 2, 114	J. Bravo	Torgan, 2	El Mirasol, 2	5	1:06.65	$32,100
1996	Kelly Kip, 2, 114	J-L. Samyn	Say Florida Sandy, 2	Leestown, 2	7	1:04.60	$33,210
1995	†Rosie O'Greta, 2, 115	J. A. Santos	Busheta Buck	Victory Speech	6	1:07.32	$32,400
1994	De Niro, 2, 114	E. Maple	Jump the Shadow	Mane Ingredient	6	1:05.05	$63,240

1993	**Distinct Reality**, 2, 115	J. D. Bailey	Gusto Z	Slew Gin Fizz	7	1:04.76	$67,470
1992	**England Expects**, 2, 115	J. D. Bailey	Peace Baby	Linear	10	1:03.20	$69,900

Named for undefeated 1886 two-year-old male Tremont (1884-1901, c. by Virgil). 1911-'13,1933-'35 not held. 1990-'95 Tremont Breeders' Cup S. 1975-'80,1990-'95,1997-'98 not graded. 1887-1910 held at Gravesend Park; 1914-'55,1960-'74,1976 Aqueduct; 1956,1958 Jamaica. 1887-1900,1914-'32,1974-'88 6 furlongs; 1901-'10 about 6 furlongs; 1936-'39 5 furlongs. 1997 Jigadee finished third, DQ to fourth. 1999 new track record. †denotes female.

Triple Bend Breeders' Cup Invitational Handicap

Grade 2, Hollywood Park, three-year-olds and up, 7 furlongs, dirt. Held July 6, 2002, with a gross value of $300,000. First held in 1952. Graded since 1988. Stakes record 1:19.40 (1980 Rich Cream).

Year	Winner	Jockey	Second	Third	Strs	Time	1st Purse
2002	**Disturbingthepeace**, 4, 113	V. Espinoza	D'wildcat, 4	Mellow Fellow, 7	9	1:21.09	$180,000
2001	**Ceeband**, 4, 110	M. S. Garcia	Squirtle Squirt, 3	Elaborate, 6	10	1:21.17	$150,000
2000	**Elaborate**, 5, 114	V. Espinoza	Cliquot, 4	Lexicon, 5	10	1:21.19	$180,000
1999	**Mazel Trick**, 4, 115	C. J. McCarron	Christmas Boy, 6	Regal Thunder, 5	8	1:19.97	$180,000
1998	**Son of a Pistol**, 6, 118	A. O. Solis	The Exeter Man, 6	Benchmark, 6	11	1:20.81	$120,000
1997	**Score Quick**, 5, 113	G. F. Almeida	Elmhurst, 7	First Intent, 7	11	1:21.01	$100,980
1996	**Letthebighossroll**, 8, 116	C. J. McCarron	Score Quick, 4	Comininalittlehot, 4	7	1:21.43	$125,460
1995	**Concept Win**, 5, 118	P. A. Valenzuela	Gold Land, 4	Lucky Forever, 4	6	1:21.09	$63,100
1994	**Memo (Chi)**, 7, 120	P. Atkinson	Minjinsky, 4	Slerp, 4	6	1:20.52	$62,400
1993	**Now Listen**, 6, 116	K. J. Desormeaux	Cardmania, 7	Star of the Crop, 7	10	1:20.83	$66,400
1992	**Slew the Surgeon**, 4, 111	M. G. Linares	Softshoe Sure Shot, 6	Record Boom, 6	8	1:21.44	$64,600

Named for 1972 Los Angeles H. winner Triple Bend (1968-'95, c. by Never Bend). 1952-'78 Lakes and Flowers H.; 1979-'95 Triple Bend H.; 1996-'97 Triple Bend Breeders' Cup H.; 1998 Triple Bend Invitational Breeders' Cup H. 1988-'97 Grade 3. 1956-'72 6 furlongs. 1993 equaled track record; 1994,1999 new track record.

Tropical Park Derby

Grade 3, Calder Race Course, three-year-olds, 1⅛ miles, turf. Held January 1, 2003, with a gross value of $100,000. First held in 1976. Graded since 1978. Stakes record 1:46.60 (2000 Go Lib Go).

Year	Winner	Jockey	Second	Third	Strs	Time	1st Purse
2003	**Nothing to Lose**, 3, 115	J. D. Bailey	Millennium Storm, 3	Supah Blitz, 3	12	1:50.45	$60,000
2002	**Political Attack**, 3, 119	M. Guidry	The Judge Sez Who, 3	Deeliteful Guy, 3	8	1:51.71	$60,000
2001	**Proud Man**, 3, 115	R. R. Douglas	Mr Notebook, 3	Cee Dee, 3	11	1:47.95	$60,000
2000	**Go Lib Go**, 3, 119	J. A. Santos	Mr. Livingston, 3	Granting, 3	12	**1:46.60**	$60,000
1999	**Valid Reprized**, 3, 115	J. Castellano	Mr. Roark, 3	Wertz, 3	12	1:53.58	$60,000
1998	**Draw Again**, 3, 117	J. Bravo	Buddha's Delight, 3	Daddy's Dream, 3	11	1:51.28	$60,000
1997	**Arthur L.**, 3, 119	E. Coa	Unite's Big Red, 3	Keep It Strait, 3	12	1:46.93	$60,000
1996	**Ok by Me**, 3, 117	J. D. Bailey	Darn That Erica, 3	Tour's Big Red, 3	12	1:47.25	$60,000
1995	**Mecke**, 3, 117	H. Castillo Jr.	Val's Prince, 3	Claudius, 3	14	1:51.12	$60,000
1994	**Fabulous Frolic**, 3, 112	J. Cruguet	Wake Up Alarm, 3	Gator Back, 3	14	1:46.99	$60,000
1993	**Summer Set**, 3, 112	M. A. Gonzalez	Duc d'Sligovil, 3	Silver of Silver, 3	10	1:53.87	$60,000
1992	**Technology**, 3, 119	J. D. Bailey	Majestic Sweep, 3	Always Silver, 3	10	1:53.01	$134,160

Named for the old Tropical Park racetrack in Miami; it closed in 1972. 1983-'89 Grade 2. 1976-'85 1 1/16 miles; 1994 about 1⅛ miles. 1978-'93,2002 dirt.

Tropical Turf Handicap

Grade 3, Calder Race Course, three-year-olds and up, 1⅛ miles, turf. Held December 7, 2002, with a gross value of $100,000. First held in 1972. Graded since 1981. Stakes record 1:44.95 (1993 Carterista).

Year	Winner	Jockey	Second	Third	Strs	Time	1st Purse
2002	**Krieger**, 4, 113	E. Coa	Stokosky, 6	Serial Bride, 5	12	1:47.02	$60,000
2001	**Band Is Passing**, 5, 118	C. Gonzalez	Crash Course, 5	Groomstick Stock's, 5	12	1:46.90	$60,000
2000	**Stokosky**, 4, 114	C. A. Hernandez	(DH) Special Coach, 4 (DH) Band Is Passing, 4		11	1:48.77	$60,000
1999	**Hibernian Rhapsody (Ire)**, 4, 114	R. R. Douglas	Garbu, 5	Shamrock City, 4	12	1:46.17	$60,000
1998	**Unite's Big Red**, 4, 115	E. O. Nunez	N B Forrest, 6	Glok, 4	8	1:48.96	$60,000
1997	**Sir Cat**, 4, 116	J. A. Rivera II	Foolish Pole, 4	Written Approval, 5	6	1:54.08	$60,000
1996	**Mecke**, 4, 124	R. G. Davis	Satellite Nealski, 3	Elite Jeblar, 6	10	1:46.51	$60,000
1995	**The Vid**, 5, 120	W. H. McCauley	Elite Jeblar, 5	Scannapieco, 5	12	1:44.99	$60,000
1994	**The Vid**, 4, 116	R. R. Douglas	Country Coy, 4	Gone for Real, 3	10	1:49.06	$60,000
1993	**Carterista**, 4, 121	W. S. Ramos	Rinka Das, 5	Daarik (Ire), 6	12	**1:44.95**	$45,000
1992	**Bidding Proud**, 3, 115	J. A. Santos	Buckhar, 4	Plate Dancer, 7	7	1:46.02	$30,000
	Carterista, 3, 112	M. A. Lee	Rinka Das, 4	Pidgeon's Promise, 3	11	1:46.35	$30,000

Named for the old Tropical Park racetrack in Miami; it closed in 1972. Formerly run on or about December 25. 1976-'78,1987,1991 not held. 1972-'92 Christmas Day H. 1972-'75 1 1/16 miles; 1988-'93 about 1⅛ miles. 1972-'86,1997 dirt. 1975 two-year-olds. 1992 two divisions. 2000 dead heat for second.

True North Handicap

Grade 2, Belmont Park, three-year-olds and up, 6 furlongs, dirt. Held June 8, 2002, with a gross value of $250,000. First held in 1979. Graded since 1983. Stakes record 1:07.80 (1987 Groovy).

Year	Winner	Jockey	Second	Third	Strs	Time	1st Purse
2002	Explicit, 5, 119	L. Meche	Entepreneur, 5	Late Carson, 6	7	1:09.98	$150,000
2001	Say Florida Sandy, 7, 116	A. T. Gryder	Wake At Noon, 4	Explicit, 4	8	1:08.77	$90,000
2000	Intidab, 7, 117	R. G. Davis	Brutally Frank, 6	Oro de Mexico, 6	7	1:10.22	$90,000
1999	Kashatreya, 5, 110	J-L. Samyn	Artax, 4	The Trader's Echo, 5	9	1:09.63	$90,000
1998	Richter Scale, 4, 119	J. D. Bailey	Trafalger, 4	Kelly Kip, 4	8	1:08.83	$83,160
1997	Punch Line, 7, 122	R. G. Davis	Cold Execution, 6	Jamies First Punch, 4	7	1:08.96	$66,180
1996	Not Surprising, 6, 121	R. G. Davis	Prospect Bay, 4	Forest Wildcat, 5	8	1:09.17	$66,720
1995	Waldoboro, 4, 112	E. Maple	Corma Ray, 5	Mining Burrah, 5	8	1:09.62	$66,300
1994	Friendly Lover, 6, 114	R. Wilson	Boundary, 4	Birdonthewire, 5	9	1:09.65	$67,380
1993	Lion Cavern, 4, 116	J. A. Krone	Arrowtown, 5	Codys Key, 4	7	1:10.33	$69,120
1992	Shining Bid, 4, 112	E. Maple	Arrowtown, 4	To Freedom, 4	9	1:08.28	$71,880

Named for 1945 Fall Highweight H. winner True North (1940, g. by Only One). 1983-'84 Grade 3.

Turf Classic Invitational Stakes

Grade 1, Belmont Park, three-year-olds and up, 1½ miles, turf. Held September 29, 2002, with a gross value of $750,000. First held in 1977. Graded since 1979. Stakes record 2:24.50 (1992 Sky Classic).

Year	Winner	Jockey	Second	Third	Strs	Time	1st Purse
2002	Denon, 4, 126	E. S. Prado	Blazing Fury, 4	Delta Form (Aus), 6	8	2:28.47	$450,000
2001	Timboroa (GB), 5, 126	E. S. Prado	King Cugat, 4	Cetewayo, 7	6	2:29.43	$450,000
2000	John's Call, 9, 126	J-L. Samyn	Craigsteel (GB), 5	†Ela Athena (GB), 4	12	2:28.58	$450,000
1999	Val's Prince, 7, 126	J. F. Chavez	Dream Well (Fr), 4	Fahris (Ire), 5	7	2:28.63	$360,000
1998	Buck's Boy, 5, 126	S. J. Sellers	Cetewayo, 4	Lazy Lode (Arg), 4	6	2:33.25	$300,000
1997	Val's Prince, 5, 126	M. E. Smith	Flag Down, 7	Ops Smile, 5	5	2:28.92	$300,000
1996	Diplomatic Jet, 4, 126	J. F. Chavez	Awad, 6	Marlin, 3	10	2:27.51	$300,000
1995	Turk Passer, 5, 126	J. R. Velazquez	Hernando (Fr), 5	Celtic Arms (Fr), 4	4	2:36.63	$300,000
1994	Tikkanen, 3, 121	C. B. Asmussen	Vaudeville, 3	Yenda (GB), 3	5	2:25.88	$300,000
1993	Apple Tree (Fr), 4, 126	M. E. Smith	Solar Splendor, 6	George Augustus, 5	5	2:28.31	$300,000
1992	Sky Classic, 5, 126	P. Day	Fraise, 4	Solar Splendor, 5	6	**2:24.50**	$300,000

1977-'79,1981-'83 held at Aqueduct. 1992 new course record. †denotes female.

Turfway Breeders' Cup Stakes

Grade 3, Turfway Park, three-year-olds and up, fillies and mares, 1¹⁄₁₆ miles, dirt. Held September 14, 2002, with a gross value of $200,000. First held in 1986. Graded since 1990. Stakes record 1:41.67 (1995 Mariah's Storm).

Year	Winner	Jockey	Second	Third	Strs	Time	1st Purse
2002	Trip, 5, 116	P. Day	Mystic Lady, 4	Red n'Gold, 4	9	1:43.01	$125,500
2001	Trip, 4, 118	C. Perret	Precious Feather, 4	Spain, 4	7	1:42.47	$125,500
2000	Spain, 3, 118	P. Day	Ruby Surprise, 5	Undermine, 4	9	1:44.85	$156,500
1999	Ruby Surprise, 4, 118	W. Martinez	Let, 4	French Braids, 4	8	1:44.95	$162,886
1998	Biding Time, 4, 117	C. S. Nakatani	Meter Maid, 4	Dancing Gulch, 4	7	1:43.13	$162,266
1997	Feasibility Study, 5, 119	M. E. Smith	City Band, 3	Gold n Delicious, 4	8	1:42.50	$161,522
1996	Golden Attraction, 3, 114	G. L. Stevens	Bedroom Blues, 5	Betty Van, 4	8	1:42.53	$205,920
1995	Mariah's Storm, 4, 117	R. N. Lester	Serena's Song, 3	Alcovy, 5	5	**1:41.67**	$116,415
1994	Pennyhill Park, 4, 123	C. J. McCarron	Roamin Rachel, 4	Hey Hazel, 4	10	1:44.20	$118,073
1993	Gray Cashmere, 4, 117	D. Kutz	Deputation, 4	November Snow, 4	8	1:43.39	$117,130
1992	Fit for a Queen, 6, 123	R. D. Lopez	Auto Dial, 4	Hitch, 3	9	1:43.30	$117,975

1986 Latonia Breeders' Cup S.; 1987-'88,1991-'95 Turfway Park Budweiser Breeders' Cup S.; 1989-'90 Turfway Park Breeders' Cup H.; 1992-'98 Grade 2. 1986 held at Latonia.

Turfway Park Fall Championship Stakes

Grade 3, Turfway Park, three-year-olds and up, 1⅛ miles, dirt. Held September 28, 2002, with a gross value of $100,000. First held in 1919. Graded since 1997. Stakes record 1:48.67 (1992 Flying Continental).

Year	Winner	Jockey	Second	Third	Strs	Time	1st Purse
2002	Crafty Shaw, 4, 117	J. Lopez	Rock Slide, 4	Deferred Comp, 4	7	1:52.29	$62,750
2001	Generous Rosi (GB), 6, 115	L. Meche	Storm Day, 4	Jadada, 6	6	1:49.83	$46,500
2000	Mount Lemon, 6, 117	R. Albarado	Unloosened, 5	Phil the Grip, 6	7	1:51.14	$62,600
1999	Phil the Grip, 5, 112	R. Albarado	Part the Waters, 5	Metatonia, 4	5	1:52.15	$49,600
1998	Acceptable, 4, 116	C. Perret	Magnify, 5	Muchacho Fino, 4	6	1:51.95	$62,600
1997	Tejano Run, 5, 122	W. Martinez	Short Stay, 5	Thesaurus, 3	7	1:49.44	$46,950
1996	Strawberry Wine, 4, 114	B. D. Peck	Kiridashi, 4	Prospect for Love, 4	8	1:50.15	$65,000
1995	Bound by Honor, 4, 113	R. P. Romero	Lord Gordon, 5	Lordly Prospect, 6	6	1:51.54	$48,750
1994	Meena, 6, 114	W. Martinez	Powerful Punch, 5	It'sall'lkownfact, 4	4	1:52.92	$27,284
1993	Powerful Punch, 4, 116	C. C. Bourque	Medium Cool, 5	Benburb, 4	5	1:50.51	$41,048
1992	Flying Continental, 6, 122	J. Velasquez	Alyten, 4	Regal Affair, 6	5	**1:48.67**	$27,511

1934-'63,1972 not held. 1919-'33,1964-'86 Latonia Championship S.; 1987-'90 Turfway Championship S.; 1991-'95,1997 Turfway Championship H.; 1996,1998-'99 Kentucky Cup Classic Preview H.; 2000 Turfway Park Fall Championship H. 1919-'33 held at Old Latonia; 1964-'86 Latonia. 1919-'33 1¾ miles; 1964-'87 1¹⁄₁₆ miles. 1919-'33 three-year-olds.

Turnback the Alarm Handicap

Grade 3, Aqueduct, three-year-olds and up, fillies and mares, 1⅛ miles, dirt. Held November 3, 2002, with a gross value of $100,000. First held in 1995. Graded since 1999. Stakes record 1:48.89 (1995 Incinerate).

Year	Winner	Jockey	Second	Third	Strs	Time	1st Purse
2002	Svea Dahl, 5, 114	R. Migliore	Mystic Lady, 4	Critical Eye, 5	5	1:50.42	$64,800
2001	Rochelle's Terms, 4, 113	R. G. Davis	Resort, 4	Strolling Belle, 5	6	1:51.19	$65,100
2000	Atelier, 3, 113	E. S. Prado	Tap to Music, 5	Pentatonic, 5	10	1:48.95	$67,920
1999	Belle Cherie, 3, 112	J. R. Velazquez	Brushed Halory, 3	Sweet Misty, 5	8	1:50.03	$66,000
1998	Snit, 4, 117	J. R. Velazquez	Manoa, 3	Shoop, 7	8	1:51.30	$49,740
1997	Mil Kilates, 4, 116	J. Bravo	Radiant Megan, 4	Shoop, 6	5	1:49.40	$48,330
1996	Shoop, 5, 121	J. D. Bailey	Queen Tutta, 4	Madame Adolphe, 4	4	1:51.35	$48,420
1995	Incinerate, 5, 115	F. Leon	Lotta Dancing, 4	Pretty Discreet, 3	7	1:48.89	$49,005

Named for 1992 Coaching Club American Oaks (G1) and Mother Goose S. (G1) winner Turnback the Alarm (1989, f. by Darn That Alarm).

United Nations Handicap

Grade 1, Monmouth Park, three-year-olds and up, 1⅜ miles, turf. Held July 6, 2002, with a gross value of $500,000. First held in 1953. Graded since 1973. Stakes record 2:12.81 (2002 With Anticipation).

Year	Winner	Jockey	Second	Third	Strs	Time	1st Purse
2002	With Anticipation, 7, 119	P. Day	Denon, 4	Sarafan, 5	7	2:12.81	$300,000
2001	Senure, 5, 116	R. G. Davis	With Anticipation, 6	Gritty Sandie, 5	8	2:13.56	$300,000
2000	Down the Aisle, 7, 114	R. G. Davis	Aly's Alley, 4	Honor Glide, 6	7	2:13.63	$210,000
1999	Yagli, 6, 124	J. D. Bailey	Supreme Sound (GB), 5	Amerique, 5	6	2:16.02	$150,000
1997	Influent, 6, 117	J-L. Samyn	Geri, 5	Flag Down, 5	4	1:53.72	$240,000
1996	Sandpit (Brz), 7, 122	C. S. Nakatani	Diplomatic Jet, 4	Northern Spur (Ire), 4	8	1:55.71	$300,000
1995	Sandpit (Brz), 6, 122	C. S. Nakatani	Celtic Arms (Fr), 4	Alice Springs, 4	9	1:57.25	$300,000
1994	Lure, 5, 123	M. E. Smith	Fourstars Allstar, 6	Star of Cozzene, 6	5	1:52.66	$300,000
1993	Star of Cozzene, 5, 120	J. A. Santos	Lure, 4	Finder's Choice, 4	7	1:53.22	$300,000
1992	Sky Classic, 5, 123	P. Day	Chenin Blanc, 6	Lotus Pool, 6	9	1:52.53	$300,000

Named for the United Nations, headquartered in New York City. 1998 not held. 1953-'81 United Nations Invitational H. 1990-'97 Caesars International H. 1990-'93 Grade 2. 1953-'97 held at Atlantic City. 1953-'97 1¾6 miles. 1969,1975 dirt. 1999 equaled course record; 2000 new course record. 2001 With Anticipation finished first, DQ to second.

Vagrancy Handicap

Grade 2, Belmont Park, three-year-olds and up, fillies and mares, 6½ furlongs, dirt. Held June 9, 2002, with a gross value of $150,000. First held in 1948. Graded since 1973. Stakes record 1:15.32 (2001 Dat You Miz Blue).

Year	Winner	Jockey	Second	Third	Strs	Time	1st Purse
2002	Xtra Heat, 4, 127	H. Vega	Gold Mover, 4	Shine Again, 5	5	1:16.44	$90,000
2001	Dat You Miz Blue, 4, 116	J. R. Velazquez	Dream Supreme, 4	Katz Me If You Can, 4	5	1:15.32	$64,080
2000	Country Hideaway, 4, 117	J. D. Bailey	Hurricane Bertie, 5	Imperfect World, 4	7	1:17.05	$65,640
1999	Gold Princess, 4, 114	J. R. Velazquez	Hurricane Bertie, 4	Delta Music, 4	5	1:16.57	$63,840
1998	Chip, 5, 115	J. Bravo	Furlough, 4	Parlay, 4	6	1:15.69	$48,945
1997	Inquisitive Look, 4, 111	J. F. Chavez	Flat Fleet Feet, 4	Mama Dean, 4	6	1:22.07	$64,800
1996	Twist Afleet, 5, 122	J. A. Krone	Smooth Charmer, 4	Lottsa Talc, 6	4	1:20.94	$66,300
1995	Sky Beauty, 5, 125	M. E. Smith	Aly's Conquest, 4	Through the Door, 5	4	1:21.56	$47,865
1994	Sky Beauty, 4, 122	M. E. Smith	For all Seasons, 4	Pamzig, 4	6	1:21.67	$48,855
1993	Spinning Round, 4, 112	J. F. Chavez	Reach for Clever, 6	Nannerl, 6	4	1:24.52	$52,740
1992	Nannerl, 5, 116	J. A. Santos	Serape, 4	Makin Faces, 4	6	1:22.55	$51,210

Named for Belair Stud's 1942 champion three-year-old filly and handicap mare Vagrancy (1939-'64, f. by *Sir Gallahad III). 1949-'51 not held. 1948-'55,1960,1963-'67,1975,1977-'86,1997 held at Aqueduct. 1948-'52 1¼6 miles; 1953-'97 7 furlongs. 1999 Hurricane Bertie finished first, DQ to second

Valley Stream Stakes

Grade 3, Aqueduct, two-year-olds, fillies, 6 furlongs, dirt. Held November 24, 2002, with a gross value of $100,000. First held in 1995. Graded since 2001. Stakes record 1:08.66 (2001 Forest Heiress).

Year	Winner	Jockey	Second	Third	Strs	Time	1st Purse
2002	Randaroo, 2, 116	J. R. Velazquez	House Party, 2	Fast Cookie, 2	8	1:09.46	$66,780
2001	Forest Heiress, 2, 122	R. Migliore	A New Twist, 2	On Parade, 2	6	1:08.66	$48,465
2000	Astrapi, 2, 116	D. Nelson	Major Wager, 2	Look of the Lynx, 2	5	1:10.66	$48,570
1999	Magicalmysterycat, 2, 121	M. E. Smith	Sahara Gold, 2	Silentlea, 2	8	1:10.53	$49,815
1998	Paula's Girl, 2, 116	J. R. Velazquez	President's Girl, 2	Godmother, 2	5	1:11.99	$38,700
1997	Cotton House Bay, 2, 114	J. F. Chavez	Foil, 2	Kate Again, 2	10	1:10.11	$33,990
1996	Dixie Flag, 2, 116	J-L. Samyn	Alyssum, 2	Nimble Tread, 2	6	1:10.13	$32,490
1995	Oxford Scholar, 2, 112	J. D. Bailey	Zee Lady, 2	Stormy Krissy, 2	5	1:12.13	$32,430

Named for a town in Long Island's Nassau County. 1995 held at Belmont.

Valley View Stakes

Grade 3, Keeneland, three-year-olds, fillies, 1¾6 miles, turf. Held October 19, 2002, with a gross value of $100,000. First held in 1991. Graded since 1999. Stakes record 1:41.51 (1992 Spinning Round).

Year	Winner	Jockey	Second	Third	Strs	Time	1st Purse
2002	Bedanken, 3, 119	D. R. Pettinger	Mariensky, 3	High Maintenance (GB), 3	10	1:44.24	$71,114

2001	**(DH) Cozzy Corner**, 3, 119	L. Meche		Quick Tip, 3	10	1:42.93	$46,576
	(DH) Chausson Poire, 3, 119	R. W. Woolsey					
2000	**Good Game**, 3, 119	P. Day	Impending Bear, 3	Soccory, 3	10	1:45.69	$71,176
1999	**Gimmeakissee**, 3, 115	P. J. Cooksey	The Happy Hopper, 3	Celestialbutterfly, 3	9	1:42.05	$70,122
1998	**White Beauty**, 3, 113	C. H. Borel	Shires Ende, 3	Leaveemlaughing, 3	8	1:43.09	$52,406
1997	**Mingling Glances**, 3, 117	J. Bravo	Majestic Sunlight, 3	Fluid Move, 3	9	1:44.51	$52,592
1996	**Turkappeal**, 3, 117	D. M. Barton	Inner Circle, 3	Mariuka, 3	9	1:46.10	$52,126
1995	**Country Cat**, 3, 121	D. M. Barton	Appointed One, 3	Petrouchka, 3	10	1:44.88	$51,150
1994	**Pharma**, 3, 121	C. W. Antley	Mariah's Storm, 3	Thread, 3	9	1:42.48	$50,747
1993	**Weekend Madness (Ire)**, 3, 121	C. R. Woods Jr.	Life Is Delicious, 3	Augusta Springs, 3	10	1:43.06	$23,870
1992	**Spinning Round**, 3, 121	F. A. Arguello Jr.	Shes Just Super, 3	Enticed, 3	9	**1:41.51**	$23,870

Named for the Valley View ferry, Kentucky's oldest recorded commercial business. 1994-'95 Valley View Breeders' Cup S. 2001 dead heat for first.

Vanity Handicap

Grade 1, Hollywood Park, three-year-olds and up, fillies and mares, 1⅛ miles, dirt. Held June 22, 2002, with a gross value of $250,000. First held in 1940. Graded since 1973. Stakes record 1:46.20 (1984 Princess Rooney).

Year	Winner	Jockey	Second	Third	Strs	Time	1st Purse
2002	**Azeri**, 4, 125	M. E. Smith	Affluent, 4	Collect Call, 4	5	1:48.88	$150,000
2001	**Gourmet Girl**, 6, 119	G. L. Stevens	Lazy Slusan, 6	Setareh, 4	5	1:49.21	$150,000
2000	**Riboletta (Brz)**, 5, 123	C. J. McCarron	Speaking of Time, 4	Excellent Meeting, 4	6	1:48.54	$180,000
1999	**Manistique**, 4, 122	C. J. McCarron	Yolo Lady, 4	Bella Chiarra, 4	6	1:48.06	$240,000
1998	**Escena**, 5, 124	J. D. Bailey	Housa Dancer (Fr), 5	Different (Arg), 5	7	1:48.13	$210,000
1997	**Twice the Vice**, 6, 121	K. J. Desormeaux	Real Connection, 6	Jewel Princess, 5	5	1:46.41	$240,000
1996	**Jewel Princess**, 4, 120	C. S. Nakatani	Serena's Song, 4	Top Rung, 4	6	1:47.17	$150,000
1995	**Private Persuasion**, 4, 114	G. L. Stevens	Top Rung, 4	Wandesta (GB), 4	7	1:48.30	$165,000
1994	**Potridee (Arg)**, 5, 114	A. O. Solis	Exchange, 6	Golden Klair (GB), 6	8	1:48.08	$165,000
1993	**Re Toss (Arg)**, 6, 116	E. J. Delahoussaye	Paseana (Arg), 6	Guiza, 6	8	1:47.92	$165,000
1992	**Paseana (Arg)**, 5, 127	C. J. McCarron	Fowda, 4	Re Toss (Arg), 5	6	1:48.06	$165,000

1942-'43 not held. 1981-'96,1998 Vanity Invitational H. 1949 held at Santa Anita. 1940 1 mile; 1941-'53 1⅛ miles; 1986-'87 1¼ miles.

Vernon O. Underwood Stakes

Grade 3, Hollywood Park, three-year-olds and up, 6 furlongs, dirt. Held December 7, 2002, with a gross value of $100,000. First held in 1981. Graded since 1984. Stakes record 1:08.17 (1997 Tower Full).

Year	Winner	Jockey	Second	Third	Strs	Time	1st Purse
2002	**Debonair Joe**, 3, 112	J. A. Krone	F J's Pace, 7	American System, 3	9	1:09.17	$60,000
2001	**Men's Exclusive**, 8, 120	L. A. Pincay Jr.	Tavasco, 4	Caller One, 4	7	1:09.04	$60,000
2000	**Men's Exclusive**, 7, 116	L. A. Pincay Jr.	Love All the Way, 5	Lexicon, 5	7	1:09.02	$60,000
1999	**Five Star Day**, 3, 120	A. O. Solis	Your Halo, 4	Son of a Pistol, 7	5	1:09.91	$60,000
1998	**Love That Jazz**, 4, 117	K. J. Desormeaux	Peyrano (Arg), 6	Swiss Yodeler, 4	8	1:08.79	$60,000
1997	**Tower Full**, 5, 118	C. S. Nakatani	Trafalger, 3	Swiss Yodeler, 3	4	**1:08.17**	$60,000
1996	**Paying Dues**, 4, 124	P. Day	Men's Exclusive, 3	Kern Ridge, 5	7	1:08.24	$64,860
1995	**Powis Castle**, 4, 114	G. L. Stevens	Lucky Forever, 6	Plenty Zloty, 5	8	1:08.40	$62,300
1994	**Wekiva Springs**, 3, 118	K. J. Desormeaux	Cardmania, 8	Gundaghia, 7	9	1:08.37	$63,750
1993	**†Meafara**, 4, 119	G. L. Stevens	†Arches of Gold, 4	Davy Be Good, 5	6	1:10.01	$60,900
1992	**Gundaghia**, 5, 116	G. L. Stevens	Gray Slewpy, 4	Cardmania, 6	5	1:09.33	$61,300

Named for Vernon O. Underwood, chief executive officer and chairman of the board of Hollywood Park (1972-'85). 1981-'89 National Sprint Championship S.; 1993-'95 Vernon O. Underwood Breeders' Cup S. †denotes female.

Violet Handicap

Grade 3, Meadowlands, three-year-olds and up, fillies and mares, 1¹⁄₁₆ miles, turf. Held September 20, 2002, with a gross value of $150,000. First held in 1977. Graded since 1983. Stakes record 1:39.60 (1989 Gather the Clan).

Year	Winner	Jockey	Second	Third	Strs	Time	1st Purse
2002	**Babae (Chi)**, 6, 119	J. F. Chavez	Platinum Tiara, 4	Stylish, 4	10	1:41.17	$90,000
2001	**Clearly a Queen**, 4, 115	J. F. Chavez	Queue, 4	Paga (Arg), 4	12	1:43.56	$115,000
2000	**Follow the Money**, 4, 116	C. J. McCarron	Melody Queen (GB), 4	Fickle Friends, 4	7	1:42.65	$90,000
1999	**Tookin Down**, 4, 113	E. S. Prado	Proud Run, 5	Darling Alice, 4	7	1:42.39	$90,000
1998	**Heaven's Command (GB)**, 4, 115	R. Migliore	Maxzene, 5	Oh Nellie, 4	7	1:40.71	$60,000
1997	**Sangria**, 4, 114	R. Wilson	Fasta, 4	Shemozzle (Ire), 4	8	1:42.02	$60,000
1996	**Plenty of Sugar**, 5, 117	R. E. Colton	Brushing Gloom, 4	Hello Mom, 4	6	1:48.62	$60,000
1995	**Symphony Lady**, 5, 116	J. Bravo	Kira's Dancer, 6	Irish Linnet, 7	8	1:45.48	$60,000
1994	**It's Personal**, 4, 111	J. R. Velazquez	Carezza, 5	Artful Pleasure, 4	11	1:42.61	$45,000
1993	**Mz. Zill Bear**, 4, 113	E. S. Prado	Vivano, 4	Topsa, 6	4	1:44.55	$45,000
1992	**Highland Crystal**, 4, 116	E. S. Prado	Irish Actress, 5	Navarra, 4	7	1:41.26	$45,000

Named for New Jersey's state flower, the common violet. 1995 Sheraton Meadowlands Violet H. 1977,1993,1999 dirt.

Vosburgh Stakes

Grade 1, Belmont Park, three-year-olds and up, 7 furlongs, dirt. Held September 21, 2002, with a gross value of $300,000. First held in 1940. Graded since 1973. Stakes record 1:20.20 (1968 Dr. Fager).

Year	Winner	Jockey	Second	Third	Strs	Time	1st Purse
2002	Bonapaw, 6, 126	G. Melancon	Aldebaran, 4	Voodoo, 4	6	1:22.34	$180,000
2001	Left Bank, 4, 126	J. R. Velazquez	Squirtle Squirt, 3	Big E E, 4	6	1:20.73	$180,000
2000	Trippi, 3, 123	J. D. Bailey	More Than Ready, 3	One Way Love, 5	10	1:21.66	$180,000
1999	Artax, 4, 126	J. F. Chavez	Stormin Fever, 5	Mountain Top, 4	6	1:21.65	$150,000
1998	Affirmed Success, 4, 126	J. F. Chavez	Stormin Fever, 4	Tale of the Cat, 4	7	1:21.99	$150,000
1997	Victor Cooley, 4, 126	J. F. Chavez	Score a Birdie, 6	Tale of the Cat, 3	12	1:22.05	$150,000
1996	Langfuhr, 4, 126	J. F. Chavez	Honour and Glory, 3	Lite the Fuse, 5	8	1:21.25	$120,000
1995	Not Surprising, 5, 126	R. G. Davis	You and I, 4	Our Emblem, 4	13	1:22.48	$120,000
1994	Harlan, 5, 126	J. D. Bailey	American Chance, 5	Cherokee Run, 4	10	1:21.82	$120,000
1993	Birdonthewire, 4, 126	M. E. Smith	Take Me Out, 5	Lion Cavern, 4	6	1:22.28	$120,000
1992	Rubiano, 5, 126	J. A. Krone	Sheikh Albadou (GB), 4	Salt Lake, 3	8	1:22.80	$120,000

Named for Walter S. Vosburgh (1855-1938), official handicapper for the Jockey Club and various racing associations. 1940-'78 Vosburgh H. 1973-'79 Grade 2. 1959,1961-'74,1976-'77,1979-'83,1985-'86 held at Aqueduct. 1940-'57 two-year-olds and up.

(Walmac Int'l.) Alcibiades Stakes

Grade 2, Keeneland, two-year-olds, fillies, 1¹⁄₁₆ miles, dirt. Held October 4, 2002, with a gross value of $400,000. First held in 1952. Graded since 1973. Stakes record 1:42.24 (1998 Silverbulletday).

Year	Winner	Jockey	Second	Third	Strs	Time	1st Purse
2002	Westerly Breeze, 2, 118	R. Albarado	Ruby's Reception, 2	Final Round, 2	9	1:46.90	$276,024
2001	Take Charge Lady, 2, 118	A. J. D'Amico	Never Out, 2	Cunning Play, 2	11	1:46.23	$280,736
2000	She's a Devil Due, 2, 118	M. Guidry	Nasty Storm, 2	Cash Deal, 2	7	1:44.86	$270,320
1999	Scratch Pad, 2, 118	W. Martinez	Rare Beauty, 2	Cash Run, 2	8	1:44.16	$274,288
1998	Silverbulletday, 2, 118	G. L. Stevens	Extended Applause, 2	Grand Deed, 2	11	1:42.24	$281,976
1997	Countess Diana, 2, 118	S. J. Sellers	Lily O'Gold, 2	Beautiful Pleasure, 2	6	1:45.39	$266,600
1996	Southern Playgirl, 2, 118	R. P. Romero	Screamer, 2	Private Pursuit, 2	7	1:46.94	$168,330
1995	Cara Rafaela, 2, 118	P. Day	Birr, 2	Gold Sunrise, 2	10	1:44.43	$139,252
1994	Post It, 2, 118	S. Maple	Morris Code, 2	Cat Appeal, 2	5	1:46.33	$66,650
1993	Stellar Cat, 2, 118	S. J. Sellers	Slew Kitty Slew, 2	Beau Blush, 2	6	1:44.68	$122,200
1992	Eliza, 2, 118	P. A. Valenzuela	Avie's Shadow, 2	True Affair, 2	6	1:43.30	$122,200

Named for Hal Price Headley's 1929 consensus champion two-year-old filly and champion three-year-old filly Alcibiades (1927-'57, f. by Supremus). Since 1997, sponsored by Walmac Int'l. of Lexington, Kentucky. 1952-'96 Alcibiades S. 1973-'75 Grade 3. 1952-'80 about 7 furlongs. 1996 Private Pursuit finished second, DQ to third.

Washington Park Handicap

Grade 2, Arlington Park, three-year-olds and up, 1³⁄₁₆ miles, dirt. Held September 29, 2002, with a gross value of $400,000. First held in 1926. Graded since 1973. Stakes record 1:55.07 (2002 Tenpins).

Year	Winner	Jockey	Second	Third	Strs	Time	1st Purse
2002	Tenpins, 4, 116	R. Albarado	Generous Rosi (GB), 7	Bonus Pack, 4	5	1:55.07	$240,000
2001	Guided Tour, 5, 116	L. Melancon	A Fleets Dancer, 6	Duckhorn, 4	5	2:00.76	$240,000
2000	Blazing Sword, 6, 113	J. A. Rivera II	Mula Gula, 4	Nite Dreamer, 5	8	1:50.59	$150,000
1997	Beboppin Baby, 4, 112	G. K. Gomez	City by Night, 4	Stephanotis, 4	5	1:49.03	$90,000
1996	Polar Expedition, 5, 115	M. Guidry	Knockadoon, 4	Tejano Run, 4	8	1:49.97	$120,000
1994	Brother Brown, 4, 117	P. Day	Eequalsmcsquared, 5	Antrim Rd., 4	11	1:49.77	$120,000
1993	Powerful Punch, 4, 114	C. C. Bourque	Memo (Chi), 6	Northern Trend, 5	13	1:50.19	$120,000
1992	Irish Swap, 5, 118	B. E. Poyadou	Clever Trevor, 6	Barkerville, 4	7	1:47.83	$90,000

Named for the old Washington Park racetrack near Chicago. 1928,1937,1986,1988,1995,1998-'99 not held. 1964 Washingtor. H. 1973-'81 Grade 3. 1926-'57 held at Washington Park. 1926,1935-'36,1940-'50,1973-'74,2001 1¼ miles; 1927-34,1938 6 furlongs; 1939,1951-'58,1960-'62,1965-'72 1 mile; 1959,1963-'64,1975-2000 1⅛ miles. 1977-'79 turf.

Westchester Handicap

Grade 3, Belmont Park, three-year-olds and up, 1 mile, dirt. Held May 8, 2002, with a gross value of $100,000. First held in 1918. Graded since 1973. Stakes record 1:33.60 (2001 Cat's At Home).

Year	Winner	Jockey	Second	Third	Strs	Time	1st Purse
2002	Free of Love, 4, 114	J. D. Bailey	Dayton Flyer, 4	Country Be Gold, 5	9	1:35.56	$67,500
2001	Cat's At Home, 4, 114	F. Leon	Little Hans, 4	Milwaukee Brew, 4	6	1:33.60	$64,920
2000	Yankee Victor, 4, 115	H. Castillo Jr.	Golden Missile, 5	Watchman's Warning, 5	7	1:34.37	$66,000
1999	Mr. Sinatra, 5, 116	C. C. Lopez	Laredo, 6	Brushing Up, 6	4	1:35.04	$64,202
1998	Wagon Limit, 4, 114	J-L. Samyn	Draw, 5	Lucayan Prince, 4	8	1:34.06	$66,420
1997	Pacific Fleet, 5, 114	F. T. Alvarado	Circle of Light, 4	Stalwart Member, 4	7	1:33.88	$65,940
1996	Valid Wager, 4, 115	J. M. Pezua	Pat n Jac, 4	More to Tell, 5	7	1:34.74	$66,240
1995	Mr. Shawklit, 4, 112	M. J. Luzzi	Devil His Due, 6	Our Emblem, 4	6	1:34.66	$65,760
1994	Virginia Rapids, 4, 116	J-L. Samyn	Colonial Affair, 4	Cherokee Run, 4	7	1:34.52	$65,640
1993	Bill Of Rights, 4, 110	J-L. Samyn	Fly So Free, 5	Loach, 5	10	1:34.69	$72,720

1992	**Rubiano**, 5, 117	J. A. Santos	Out of Place, 5	Wild Away, 5	6	1:34.83	$68,880

Named for Westchester County, New York, located to the north of the Bronx. 1932-'33,1954-'58 not held. 1918,1920-'39 Yorktown H.; 1919 Victory H.; 1953-'71 Westchester S. 1973-'79 Grade 2. 1918-'42 held at Empire City; 1943-'59 Jamaica; 1960-2001 Aqueduct. 1918,1922-'39,1951-'53 1⅛ miles; 1919-'21 1¼ miles; 1940-'50 1³⁄₁₆ miles; 1977-'79 1¹⁄₁₆ miles; 1984 1 mile 70 yards. 1959-'71 four-year-olds and up.

West Virginia Derby

Grade 3, Mountaineer Park, three-year-olds, 1⅛ miles, dirt. Held August 10, 2002, with a gross value of $600,000. First held in 1958. Graded since 2002. Stakes record 1:47.20 (2001 Western Pride).

Year	Winner	Jockey	Second	Third	Strs	Time	1st Purse
2002	**Wiseman's Ferry**, 3, 122	J. F. Chavez	The Judge Sez Who, 3	Captain Squire, 3	9	1:49.63	$360,000
2001	**Western Pride**, 3, 113	D. G. Whitney	Saratoga Games, 3	Thunder Blitz, 3	9	**1:47.20**	$300,000
2000	**Mass Market**, 3, 115	R. Wilson	Hal's Hope, 3	Bet On Red, 3	10	1:49.94	$180,000
1999	**Stellar Brush**, 3, 122	J. Stokes	American Spirit, 3	Harry's Halo, 3	11	1:49.02	$150,000
1998	**Da Devil**, 3, 113	J. K. Court	One Bold Stroke, 3	Jess M, 3	12	1:48.84	$120,000

1960,1962,1982-'87,1991-'97 not held. 1958-'61 held at Wheeling Downs; 1963-'81 Waterford Park. 2001 new track record.

Whirlaway Handicap

Grade 3, Fair Grounds, four-year-olds and up, 1¹⁄₁₆ miles, dirt. Held February 9, 2003, with a gross value of $125,000. First held in 1973. First graded in 2003. Stakes record 1:42.55 (1994 Cool Quaker).

Year	Winner	Jockey	Second	Third	Strs	Time	1st Purse
2003	**Balto Star**,5,118	E. M. Martin Jr.	Mineshaft, 4	Bonapaw, 7	8	1:43.74	$75,000
2002	**Valhol**, 6, 115	R. Albarado	Parade Leader, 5	Fight for Ally, 5	10	1:42.94	$75,000
2001	**Include**, 4, 112	L. Meche	Connected, 4	Kombat Kat, 4	8	1:44.01	$75,000
2000	**Take Note of Me**, 6, 118	R. Albarado	Crimson Classic, 6	Nite Dreamer, 5	6	1:42.94	$75,000
1999	**Precocity**, 5, 117	E. M. Martin Jr.	Prory, 7	Take Note of Me, 5	5	1:43.42	$75,000
1998	**Moonlight Dancer**, 6, 114	C. C. Bourque	Precocity, 4	Hot Brush, 4	7	1:44.34	$75,000
1997	**Byars**, 4, 114	C. C. Bourque	Bucks Nephew, 7	Clash by Night, 4	7	1:44.47	$60,000
1996	**Bucks Nephew**, 6, 116	C. Perret	Prory, 4	Vast Joy, 4	9	1:43.40	$38,025
1995	**Adhocracy**, 5, 112	L. Melancon	Dynamic Brush, 5	Cool Quaker, 6	7	1:43.10	$31,530
1994	**Cool Quaker**, 5, 114	E. M. Martin Jr.	Dixie Poker Ace, 7	Dixieland Heat, 4	6	**1:42.55**	$31,005
1993	**West by West**, 4, 117	J-L. Samyn	Place Dancer, 4	Genuine Meaning, 6	5	1:43.80	$18,885
1992	**Irish Swap**, 5, 118	B. E. Poyadou	Jarraar, 5	Wild and Tingley, 5	6	1:43.00	$18,975

Named for Calumet Farm's 1941, '42 Horse of the Year and Triple Crown winner Whirlaway (1938-'53, c. by *Blenheim II). 1978-'80,1982-'84,1986-'91 not held. 1992,1997-'99 Whirlaway S. 1973-'81 1 mile 40 yards.

Whitney Handicap

Grade 1, Saratoga Race Course, three-year-olds and up, 1⅛ miles, dirt. Held August 3, 2002, with a gross value of $750,000. First held in 1928. Graded since 1973. Stakes record 1:47 (1974 Tri Jet).

Year	Winner	Jockey	Second	Third	Strs	Time	1st Purse
2002	**Left Bank**, 5, 118	J. R. Velazquez	Street Cry (Ire), 4	Lido Palace (Chi), 5	6	1:47.04	$450,000
2001	**Lido Palace (Chi)**, 4, 115	J. D. Bailey	Albert the Great, 4	Gander, 5	7	1:47.94	$540,000
2000	**Lemon Drop Kid**, 4, 123	E. S. Prado	Cat Thief, 4	Behrens, 6	6	1:48.30	$680,000
1999	**Victory Gallop**, 4, 123	J. D. Bailey	Behrens, 5	Catienus, 5	8	1:48.66	$360,000
1998	**Awesome Again**, 4, 117	P. Day	Tale of the Cat, 4	Crypto Star, 4	8	1:49.71	$240,000
1997	**Will's Way**, 4, 117	J. D. Bailey	Formal Gold, 4	Skip Away, 4	6	1:48.37	$210,000
1996	**Mahogany Hall**, 5, 113	J. A. Santos	†Serena's Song, 4	Peaks and Valleys, 4	9	1:48.65	$210,000
1995	**Unaccounted For**, 4, 114	P. Day	L'Carriere, 4	Silver Fox, 4	9	1:49.29	$210,000
1994	**Colonial Affair**, 4, 117	J. A. Santos	Devil His Due, 5	West by West, 5	7	1:48.61	$210,000
1993	**Brunswick**, 4, 112	M. E. Smith	West by West, 4	Devil His Due, 4	7	1:47.41	$150,000
1992	**Sultry Song**, 4, 115	J. D. Bailey	Out of Place, 5	Chief Honcho, 5	9	1:47.29	$150,000

Named for the Whitney family, one of the most important families in 20th century American racing. 1928-'53,1955-'59,1961-'65,1967-'75,1978-'80 Whitney S. 1973-'80 Grade 2. 1943-'45 held at Belmont. 1928-'54 1¼ miles. 1957-'69 four-year-olds and up. 1928-'40 colts and fillies. †denotes female.

William Donald Schaefer Handicap

Grade 3, Pimlico, three-year-olds and up, 1⅛ miles, dirt. Held May 18, 2002, with a gross value of $100,000. First held in 1994. Graded since 2001. Stakes record 1:48.19 (1995 Tidal Surge).

Year	Winner	Jockey	Second	Third	Strs	Time	1st Purse
2002	**Tenpins**, 4, 114	R. Albarado	Bowman's Band, 4	Tactical Side, 5	7	1:50.20	$60,000
2001	**Perfect Cat**, 4, 115	J. D. Bailey	Rize, 5	Judge's Case, 4	8	1:49.55	$60,000
2000	**Ecton Park**, 4, 116	P. Day	The Groom Is Red, 4	Crosspatch, 6	4	1:49.21	$60,000
1999	**Perfect to a Tee**, 7, 112	A. C. Cortez	Allen's Oop, 4	Smile Again, 4	7	1:49.20	$60,000
1998	**Acceptable**, 4, 118	J. D. Bailey	Littlebitlively, 4	Testafly, 4	8	1:48.76	$60,000
1997	**Western Echo**, 5, 116	E. S. Prado	Suave Prospect, 5	Mary's Buckaroo, 6	5	1:49.41	$60,000
1996	**Canaveral**, 5, 115	S. J. Sellers	Michael's Star, 4	Rugged Bugger, 5	7	1:49.03	$45,000
1995	**Tidal Surge**, 5, 112	J. D. Carle	Mary's Buckaroo, 4	Ameri Valay, 6	5	**1:48.19**	$60,000

1994 **Taking Risks**, 4, 117   M. T. Johnston   Frottage, 5   Super Memory, 4   6   1:49.53 $45,000
Named for William Donald Schaefer, governor of Maryland (1987-'95) and mayor of Baltimore (1971-'86).

Will Rogers Stakes

Grade 3, Hollywood Park, three-year-olds, 1 mile, turf. Held June 1, 2002, with a gross value of $100,000. First held in 1938. Graded since 1973. Stakes record 1:33.98 (1998 Magical [GB]).

Year	Winner	Jockey	Second	Third	Strs	Time	1st Purse
2002	Doc Holiday (Ire), 3, 116	D. R. Flores	Johar, 3	Golden Arrow, 3	5	1:34.64	$63,900
2001	(DH) Media Mogul (GB), 3, 116	A. O. Solis		Learing At Kathy, 3	8	1:35.10	$43,920
	(DH) Dr. Park, 3, 117	T. Baze					
2000	Purely Cozzene, 3, 120	V. Espinoza	Duke of Green (GB), 3	Silver Axe, 3	8	1:34.67	$66,000
1999	Eagleton, 3, 118	C. A. Black	Hidden Magic (GB), 3	Mr. Reignmaker, 3	11	1:34.38	$67,800
1998	Magical (GB), 3, 114	R. R. Douglas	Commitisize, 3	Son's Corona, 3	8	1:33.98	$65,820
1997	Brave Act (GB), 3, 117	C. J. McCarron	P. T. Indy, 3	Without Doubt (Ire), 3	12	1:34.01	$68,520
1996	Let Bob Do It, 3, 118	K. J. Desormeaux	Nightcapper, 3	Dr. Sardonica, 3	10	1:34.05	$67,140
1994	Unfinished Symph, 3, 116	G. Baze	Silver Music, 3	Valiant Nature, 3	8	1:40.60	$64,600
1993	Future Storm, 3, 116	K. J. Desormeaux	Lykatill Hil, 3	Earl of Barking (Ire), 3	12	1:40.01	$68,900
1992	The Name's Jimmy, 3, 116	D. Sorenson	Bold Assert, 3	Prospect for Four, 3	7	1:40.99	$63,600

Named for actor and American humorist Will Rogers (1879-1935); Rogers was killed in an Alaska plane crash. 1942-'43,1950 not held. 1938-'40 Will Rogers Memorial H.; 1941-'51,1973-'94,1996-2000 Will Rogers H.; 1995 Will Rogers Breeders' Cup H. 1973-'82,1988-'89 Grade 2. 1949 held at Santa Anita. 1938-'44,1946-'47 7 furlongs; 1948-'54 6 furlongs; 1974-'94 1⅛ miles. 1938-'68 dirt. 1938,1944 three-year-olds and up. 1953-'73 colts and geldings. 2001 dead heat for first.

Wilshire Handicap

Grade 3, Hollywood Park, three-year-olds and up, fillies and mares, 1 mile, turf. Held April 27, 2003, with a gross value of $111,000. First held in 1953. Graded since 1975. Stakes record 1:33.62 (2003 Dublino).

Year	Winner	Jockey	Second	Third	Strs	Time	1st Purse
2003	Dublino, 4, 120	K. J. Desormeaux	Southern Oasis, 5	Final Destination (NZ), 5	9	1:33.62	$66,600
2002	Eurolink Raindance (Ire), 5, 115	C. J. McCarron	Crazy Ensign (Arg), 6	Impeachable, 5	5	1:34.31	$63,960
2001	Tranquility Lake, 6, 123	E. J. Delahoussaye	Dianehill (Ire), 5	Out of Reach (GB), 4	7	1:34.69	$65,160
2000	Tout Charmant, 4, 121	C. J. McCarron	Penny Marie, 4	Perfect Copy, 4	6	1:33.86	$64,740
1999	Sapphire Ring (GB), 4, 119	G. L. Stevens	Bella Chiarra, 4	Green Jewel (GB), 5	7	1:33.86	$65,160
1998	Shake the Yoke (GB), 5, 118	E. J. Delahoussaye	Traces of Gold, 6	Cozy Blues, 4	9	1:34.10	$66,240
1997	Blushing Heiress, 5, 115	C. J. McCarron	Real Connection, 6	De Puntillas (GB), 5	7	1:40.95	$65,040
1996	Pharma, 5, 118	C. S. Nakatani	Didina (GB), 4	Matiara, 4	5	1:40.96	$79,770
1994	Skimble, 5, 118	E. J. Delahoussaye	Bel's Starlet, 7	Miami Sands (Ire), 4	6	1:41.39	$62,800
1993	Toussaud, 4, 116	K. J. Desormeaux	Visible Gold, 5	Wedding Ring (Ire), 4	7	1:40.14	$63,500
1992	Kostroma (Ire), 6, 123	K. J. Desormeaux	Danzante, 4	Appealing Missy, 5	5	1:41.35	$62,600

Named for Wilshire, California, a historic district of Los Angeles. 1954-'62 not held. 1953,1970-'72 Wilshire S. 1983-'97 Grade 2. 1963-'69 7 furlongs; 1970-'78 1⅛ miles; 1979-'97 1⅛ miles. 1953-'69,1983 dirt. 1953,1970 three-year-olds; 1971-'72 four-year-olds and up. 1953,1970 fillies.

(WinStar) Distaff Handicap

Grade 3, Lone Star Park, three-year-olds and up, fillies and mares, 1 mile, turf. Held May 27, 2002, with a gross value of $200,000. First held in 1999. First graded in 2003. Stakes record 1:37.28 (2000 Mumtaz [Fr]).

Year	Winner	Jockey	Second	Third	Strs	Time	1st Purse
2002	Queen of Wilshire, 6, 117	D. R. Flores	Pleasant State, 7	Blushing Bride (GB), 4	12	1:38:96	$120,000
2001	Voladora, 6, 114	M. C. Berry	Dyna Likes Bingo, 6	Iftiraas (GB), 4	10	1:42:23	$120,000
2000	Mumtaz (Fr), 4, 113	V. Espinoza	Evening Promise (GB), 4	Really Polish, 5	9	1:37.28	$120,000
1999	Heritage of Gold, 4, 114	C. T. Lambert	Red Cat, 4	Nalynn, 5	10	1:37:75	$90,000

Named for sponsor WinStar Farm of Versailles, Kentucky. Formerly named for Prestonwood Farm, previous name of WinStar Farm. 1999 Prestonwood Distaff H.

(WinStar) Galaxy Stakes

Grade 2, Keeneland, three-year-olds and up, fillies and mares, 1⅜ miles, turf. Held October 4, 2002, with a gross value of $500,000. First held in 1998. Graded since 2000. Stakes record 1:53.91 (1999 Happyanunoit [NZ]).

Year	Winner	Jockey	Second	Third	Strs	Time	1st Purse
2002	Owsley, 4, 122	E. S. Prado	Snow Dance, 4	Surya, 4	6	1:56.72	$337,590
2001	Spook Express (SAf), 7, 120	M. E. Smith	Solvig, 4	Veil of Avalon, 4	9	1:54.70	$349,370
2000	Tout Charmant, 4, 117	C. J. McCarron	Perfect Sting, 4	License Fee, 5	7	1:54.74	$343,480
1999	Happyanunoit (NZ), 4, 119	B. Blanc	Pleasant Temper, 5	Fiji (GB), 5	9	1:53.91	$346,270
1998	Witchful Thinking, 4, 115	C. J. McCarron	Memories of Silver, 5	Starry Dreamer, 4	6	1:54.24	$169,415

Named for sponsor WinStar Farm of Versailles, Kentucky. Formerly named for sponsor Vinery of Lexington, Kentucky. 1998-'99 Vinery First Lady S. 2000 Grade 3.

Withers Stakes

Grade 3, Aqueduct, three-year-olds, 1 mile, dirt. Held May 4, 2002, with a gross value of $150,000. First held in 1874. Graded since 1973. Stakes record 1:32.79 (1993 Williamstown).

Year	Winner	Jockey	Second	Third	Strs	Time	1st Purse
2002	**Fast Decision**, 3, 116	J. A. Santos	Shah Jehan, 3	Listen Here, 3	5	1:36.41	$90,000
2001	**Richly Blended**, 3, 123	R. Wilson	Le Grande Danseur, 3	Telescarn, 3	7	1:35.66	$90,000
2000	**Big E E**, 3, 116	H. Castillo Jr.	Precise End, 3	Port Herman, 3	8	1:35.69	$90,000
1999	**Successful Appeal**, 3, 120	J. L. Espinoza	Best of Luck, 3	Treasure Island, 3	8	1:35.18	$90,000
1998	**Dice Dancer**, 3, 123	J. F. Chavez	Rubiyat, 3	Limit Out, 3	7	1:34.48	$90,000
1997	**Statesmanship**, 3, 123	W. H. McCauley	Cryp Too, 3	Stormin Fever, 3	7	1:35.30	$67,140
1996	**Appealing Skier**, 3, 123	R. Wilson	Jamies First Punch, 3	Roar, 3	5	1:35.02	$66,120
1995	**Blu Tusmani**, 3, 123	J. A. Santos	Pat n Jac, 3	Slice of Reality, 3	9	1:35.19	$67,260
1994	**Twining**, 3, 123	J. A. Santos	Able Buck, 3	Presently, 3	8	1:34.75	$67,140
1993	**Williamstown**, 3, 124	C. Perret	Virginia Rapids, 3	Farmonthefreeway, 3	12	**1:32.79**	$76,800
1992	**Dixie Brass**, 3, 126	J. M. Pezua	Big Sur, 3	Superstrike (GB), 3	8	1:33.71	$73,080

Named for David Dunham Withers (1821-'72), one of the founders of Jerome Park and president of Monmouth Park. 1911-'12 not held. 1973-'99 Grade 2. 1874-'89 held at Jerome Park; 1890-1904 Morris Park; 1905-'55,1957-'59,1972-'74,1976,1981,1984-'85,1987-'96 Belmont; 1956 Jamaica. 1956 1⅛ miles. 1944 colts and fillies. 1993 new track record.

W. L. McKnight Handicap

Grade 2, Calder Race Course, three-year-olds and up, 1½ miles, turf. Held December 28, 2002, with a gross value of $200,000. First held in 1973. Graded since 1975. Stakes record 2:24.11 (1995 Flag Down).

Year	Winner	Jockey	Second	Third	Strs	Time	1st Purse
2002	**Man From Wicklow**, 5, 118	J. D. Bailey	Serial Bride, 5	Rochester, 6	12	2:28.05	$120,000
2001	**Profit Option**, 6, 115	M. Guidry	Deeliteful Irving, 3	Eltawaasul, 5	12	2:27.95	$90,000
2000	**A Little Luck**, 6, 114	M. E. Smith	Stokosky, 4	Whata Brainstorm, 3	12	2:29.01	$90,000
1999	**Wicapi**, 7, 114	C. H. Velasquez	Special Coach, 3	King's Jewel, 3	12	2:26.28	$90,000
1998	**Wild Event**, 5, 116	S. J. Sellers	N B Forrest, 6	Glok, 4	8	2:26.93	$90,000
1997	**Panama City**, 3, 117	P. Day	Slicious (GB), 5	Skillington, 4	12	2:27.19	$90,000
1996	**Diplomatic Jet**, 4, 123	J. F. Chavez	Marcie's Ensign, 4	(DH) Identity, 4	12	2:24.20	$90,000
				(DH) Lassigny, 5			
1995	**Flag Down**, 5, 116	J. A. Santos	Mecke, 3	Green Means Go, 3	12	**2:24.11**	$90,000
1994	**Star of Manila**, 3, 116	C. Perret	Spectacular Tide, 5	Kissin Kris, 4	13	2:28.43	$90,000
	Cobblestone Road, 5, 113	J. C. Ferrer	Daarik (Ire), 7	Fraise, 6	12	2:27.89	$90,000
1993	**Antartic Wings**, 5, 113	R. R. Douglas	Cigar Toss (Arg), 6	Luv U. Jodi, 6	9	2:33.44	$60,000
1992	**Bye Union Ave.**, 6, 113	R. R. Douglas	†Crockadore, 5	Skate On Thin Ice, 5	9	2:27.23	$90,000

Named for William L. McKnight (1881-1978), co-founder of Calder Race Course and founder of Tartan Farms. 1986-'93 W. L. McKnight Invitational H. 1976-'81 Grade 3. 1973-'75,1977-'80 1⅛ miles; 1976 about 1⅛ miles. 1993 dirt. 1996 dead heat for third. 1994 held in January and December. †denotes female.

(Woodford Reserve) Turf Classic Stakes

Grade 1, Churchill Downs, three-year-olds and up, 1⅛ miles, turf. Held May 4, 2002, with a gross value of $400,000. First held in 1987. Graded since 1989. Stakes record 1:46.34 (1993 Lure).

Year	Winner	Jockey	Second	Third	Strs	Time	1st Purse
2002	**Beat Hollow (GB)**, 5, 115	A. O. Solis	With Anticipation, 7	Hap, 6	10	1:47.35	$280,550
2001	**White Heart (GB)**, 6, 116	G. L. Stevens	King Cugat, 4	Brahms, 4	8	1:48.75	$216,938
2000	**Manndar (Ire)**, 4, 114	C. S. Nakatani	Falcon Flight (Fr), 4	Yagli, 7	8	1:47.91	$217,310
1999	**Wild Event**, 6, 120	S. J. Sellers	Garbu, 5	Hawksley Hill (Ire), 5	7	1:47.25	$206,646
1998	**Joyeux Danseur**, 5, 123	R. Albarado	Lasting Approval, 4	Hawksley Hill (Ire), 4	8	1:48.14	$174,282
1997	**Always a Classic**, 4, 120	J. D. Bailey	Labeeb (GB), 5	Down the Aisle, 5	8	1:49.29	$145,328
1996	**Mecke**, 4, 123	P. Day	Petit Poucet (GB), 4	Winged Victory, 4	11	1:49.48	$165,230
1995	**Romarin (Brz)**, 5, 118	C. S. Nakatani	Blues Traveller (Ire), 5	Hasten To Add, 5	12	1:46.86	$160,095
1994	**Paradise Creek**, 5, 118	P. Day	Lure, 5	Yukon Robbery, 5	7	1:48.34	$152,068
1993	**Lure**, 4, 123	M. E. Smith	Star of Cozzene, 5	Cleone, 5	8	**1:46.34**	$117,683
1992	**Cudas**, 4, 117	P. A. Valenzuela	Sky Classic, 5	Fourstars Allstar, 5	12	1:46.56	$124,703

Named for sponsor Woodford Reserve Distillery. Previously named for sponsor Early Times Distillery. 1987-'99 Early Times Turf Classic S. 1989-'93 Grade 3; 1994-'95 Grade 2. 1987-'91 four-year-olds and up. 1992,1993 new course record.

Wood Memorial Stakes

Grade 1, Aqueduct, three-year-olds, 1⅛ miles, dirt. Held April 12, 2003, with a gross value of $750,000. First held in 1925. Graded since 1973. Stakes record 1:47.20 (1988 Private Terms).

Year	Winner	Jockey	Second	Third	Strs	Time	1st Purse
2003	**Empire Maker**, 3, 123	J. D. Bailey	Funny Cide, 3	Kissin Saint, 3	8	1:48.70	$450,000
2002	**Buddha**, 3, 123	P. Day	Medaglia d'Oro, 3	Sunday Break (JPN), 3	8	1:48.61	$450,000
2001	**Congaree**, 3, 123	V. Espinoza	Monarchos, 3	Richly Blended, 3	6	1:47.96	$450,000
2000	**Fusaichi Pegasus**, 3, 123	K. J. Desormeaux	Red Bullet, 3	Aptitude, 3	12	1:47.92	$450,000

1999	**Adonis**, 3, 123	J. F. Chavez	Best of Luck, 3	Cliquot, 3	11	1:47.71	$360,000
1998	**Coronado's Quest**, 3, 123	R. G. Davis	Dice Dancer, 3	Parade Ground, 3	11	1:47.47	$300,000
1997	**Captain Bodgit**, 3, 123	A. O. Solis	Accelerator, 3	Smokin Mel, 3	10	1:48.39	$300,000
1996	**Unbridled's Song**, 3, 123	M. E. Smith	In Contention, 3	Romano Gucci, 3	6	1:49.80	$300,000
1995	**Talkin Man**, 3, 123	S. J. Sellers	Is Sveikatas, 3	Candy Cone, 3	8	1:49.24	$300,000
1994	**Irgun**, 3, 123	G. L. Stevens	Go for Gin, 3	Shiprock, 3	9	1:49.07	$300,000
1993	**Storm Tower**, 3, 126	R. Wilson	Tossofthecoin, 3	Marked Tree, 3	12	1:48.50	$300,000
1992	**Devil His Due**, 3, 126	M. E. Smith	West by West, 3	Rokeby (GB), 3	12	1:49.32	$300,000

Named for Eugene D. Wood (died 1924), one of the founders of Jamaica racetrack. 1925-'26 Wood S. 1984-'93 Wood Memorial Invitational S. 1995-2001 Grade 2. 1925-'59 held at Jamaica. 1925-'39 1 mile 70 yards; 1940-'51 1 1/16 miles.

Woodward Stakes

Grade 1, Belmont Park, three-year-olds and up, 1⅛ miles, dirt. Held September 7, 2002, with a gross value of $500,000. First held in 1954. Graded since 1973. Stakes record 1:45.80 (1976 Forego; 1990 Dispersal).

Year	Winner	Jockey	Second	Third	Strs	Time	1st Purse
2002	**Lido Palace (Chi)**, 5, 126	J. F. Chavez	Gander, 6	Express Tour, 4	6	1:47.75	$300,000
2001	**Lido Palace (Chi)**, 4, 126	J. D. Bailey	Albert the Great, 4	Tiznow, 4	5	1:47.42	$300,000
2000	**Lemon Drop Kid**, 4, 126	E. S. Prado	Behrens, 6	Gander, 4	5	1:50.53	$300,000
1999	**River Keen (Ire)**, 7, 126	C. W. Antley	Almutawakel (GB), 4	Stephen Got Even, 3	7	1:46.85	$300,000
1998	**Skip Away**, 5, 126	J. D. Bailey	Gentlemen (Arg), 6	Running Stag, 4	5	1:47.80	$300,000
1997	**Formal Gold**, 4, 126	K. J. Desormeaux	Skip Away, 4	Will's Way, 4	5	1:47.51	$300,000
1996	**Cigar**, 6, 126	J. D. Bailey	L'Carriere, 5	Golden Larch, 5	5	1:47.06	$300,000
1995	**Cigar**, 5, 126	J. D. Bailey	Star Standard, 3	Golden Larch, 4	6	1:47.07	$300,000
1994	**Holy Bull**, 3, 121	M. E. Smith	Devil His Due, 5	Colonial Affair, 4	8	1:46.89	$300,000
1993	**Bertrando**, 4, 126	G. L. Stevens	Devil His Due, 4	Valley Crossing, 5	6	1:47.00	$525,000
1992	**Sultry Song**, 4, 126	J. D. Bailey	Pleasant Tap, 5	Out of Place, 5	8	1:47.05	$300,000

Named for William Woodward (1876-1953), chairman of the Jockey Club from 1930-'50; owned Belair Stud. 1955,1976-'77,1988-'90 Woodward H. 1959-'60,1962-'67 held at Aqueduct. 1954 1 mile; 1956-'71 1978-'80 ,1988-'891¼ miles; 1972-'75 1½ miles.

Yellow Ribbon Stakes

Grade 1, Santa Anita Park, three-year-olds and up, fillies and mares, 1¼ miles, turf. Held October 5, 2002, with a gross value of $500,000. First held in 1977. Graded since 1979. Stakes record 1:57.60 (1989 Brown Bess).

Year	Winner	Jockey	Second	Third	Strs	Time	1st Purse
2002	**Golden Apples (Ire)**, 4, 123	P. A. Valenzuela	Voodoo Dancer, 4	Banks Hill (GB), 4	6	1:59.72	$300,000
2001	**Janet (GB)**, 4, 123	D. R. Flores	Tranquility Lake, 6	Al Desima (GB), 4	8	1:58.64	$300,000
2000	**Tranquility Lake**, 5, 123	E. J. Delahoussaye	Spanish Fern, 5	Polaire (Ire), 4	6	2:02.98	$300,000
1999	**Spanish Fern**, 4, 123	C. J. McCarron	Caffe Latte (Ire), 3	Shabby Chic, 3	7	1:59.52	$300,000
1998	**Fiji (GB)**, 4, 122	K. J. Desormeaux	Sonja's Faith (Ire), 4	Pomona (GB), 5	10	2:05.23	$300,000
1997	**Ryafan**, 3, 118	A. O. Solis	Fanjica (Ire), 5	Memories of Silver, 4	8	2:03.89	$300,000
1996	**Donna Viola (GB)**, 4, 122	G. L. Stevens	Real Connection, 5	Dixie Pearl, 4	8	2:00.62	$360,000
1995	**Alpride (Ire)**, 4, 122	C. J. McCarron	Angel in My Heart (Fr), 3	Bold Ruritana, 5	12	2:01.68	$360,000
1994	**Aube Indienne (Fr)**, 4, 122	K. J. Desormeaux	Fondly Remembered, 4	Zoonaqua, 4	11	2:02.32	$240,000
1993	**Possibly Perfect**, 3, 118	C. S. Nakatani	Tribulation, 3	Miatuschka, 5	13	2:02.91	$240,000
1992	**Super Staff**, 4, 123	K. J. Desormeaux	Flawlessly, 4	Campagnarde (Arg), 5	9	1:59.36	$240,000

Named for the song, "Tie a Yellow Ribbon," which refers to tying a ribbon around the "old oak tree." The Yellow Ribbon is run at the Oak Tree Racing Association meeting. 1979-'87,1989-'94 Yellow Ribbon Invitational S.

Yerba Buena Breeders' Cup Handicap

Grade 3, Bay Meadows, three-year-olds and up, fillies and mares, 1⅜ miles, turf. Held May 18, 2002, with a gross value of $150,000. First held in 1973. Graded since 1978. Stakes record 2:13.60 (1978 *Star Ball).

Year	Winner	Jockey	Second	Third	Strs	Time	1st Purse
2002	**Peu a Peu (Ger)**, 4, 115	R. A. Baze	Janet (GB), 5	Racene, 5	6	2:16.39	$55,000
2001	**Janet (GB)**, 4, 115	D. R. Flores	Keemoon (Fr), 5	Alexine (Arg), 5	4	2:17.09	$82,500
2000	**Gleefully**, 4, 113	R. Q. Meza	Country Garden (GB), 5	Marie de Bayeux (Fr), 4	8	2:15.99	$120,000
1999	**Blending Element (Ire)**, 6, 117	G. K. Gomez	Queen Douna (Fr), 6	Midnight Line, 4	6	2:17.26	$120,000
1998	**Miss Universal (Ire)**, 5, 114	P. Mercado	Proud Fillie (Fr), 4	Squeak (GB), 4	12	2:15.72	$75,000
1997	**De Puntillas (GB)**, 5, 116	V. Espinoza	Dynatar, 5	Tricky Code, 6	11	1:46.71	$60,000
1996	**Fanjica (Ire)**, 4, 114	D. Carr	Nimble Mind, 4	Dynatar, 4	8	2:17.42	$60,000
1995	**Work the Crowd**, 4, 123	R. A. Baze	Late Sailing, 5	Ask Anita, 5	5	1:49.27	$68,750
1994	**Ask Anita**, 4, 116	V. Belvoir	Miami Sands (Ire), 4	Oxava (Fr), 4	7	2:15.55	$55,000
1993	**Party Cited**, 4, 117	R. J. Warren Jr.	Silvered, 6	Rougeur, 4	6	2:15.11	$55,000
1992	**Flaming Torch (Ire)**, 5, 114	R. A. Baze	Indian Chris (Brz), 5	Silvered, 5	8	2:16.26	$82,500

Named for Yerba Buena Island in San Francisco Bay; Yerba Buena was once known as Goat Island, for the herd of wild goats living there. 1979 not held. 1973-'98 Yerba Buena H. 1982-'83 Grade 2; 1990-'92 not graded. 1973-2000 held at Golden Gate. 1974,1983-'87 1½ miles; 1995 1⅛ miles; 1997 1 1/16 miles. 1975 dirt.

Oldest Stakes Races

Although horse racing in North America dates from the Colonial period, stakes races did not become popular until the mid-1800s.

The oldest continually run stakes in North America—meaning that it has been run every year since its inception—is the Queen's Plate Stakes at Woodbine. First run in 1860, the race was named for Queen Victoria, then in the 23rd year of her 64-year reign, and was for horses of all ages foaled in the province of Ontario. The winner of that first Queen's Plate was Don Juan, a five-year-old Sir Tatton Sykes gelding. (Another Queen's Plate, restricted to horses foaled in Quebec, dated from 1836 and was discontinued after World War II.) From 1902 through '51, the race was known as the King's Plate, for a succession of English male monarchs.

North America's oldest stakes race still in existence is the Phoenix Breeders' Cup Stakes (G3), first run in 1831 at the Kentucky Association track in Lexington. Known at various times as the Phoenix Hotel S., Phoenix S., Brennan S., Chiles S., Association S., and the Phoenix H., the race was discontinued in 1930. It was revived with the first spring race meeting of Keeneland Race Course in 1937.

Oldest Continually Run Stakes

Race	Track	First running	First winner
Queen's Plate	Woodbine	1860	Don Juan
Kentucky Derby	Churchill	1875	Aristides
Kentucky Oaks	Churchill	1875	Vinaigrette
Clark H.	Churchill	1875	Voltigeur
Bashford Manor S.	Churchill	1902	Von Rouse
Fall Highweight H.	Aqueduct	1914	Comely
Coaching Club American Oaks	Belmont	1917	Wistful
Schuylerville S.	Saratoga	1918	Tuscaloosa
Jockey Club Gold Cup S.	Belmont	1919	Purchase
Cowdin S.	Belmont	1923	Mr. Mutt
Wood Memorial S.	Aqueduct	1925	Backbone
Selima S.	Laurel	1926	Fair Star
Whitney H.	Saratoga	1928	Black Maria
Canadian Derby	Northlands	1930	Jack Whittier

Oldest Stakes Races

Race	Track	First running	First winner

PHOENIX BREEDERS' CUP S. Keeneland 1831 McDonough
1831-'77, run as a heat race; 1898-1904,1906-'10, 1914-'16, 1929, 1931-'36, not run; before 1937, held at the Kentucky Association track; 1943-'45, held at Churchill Downs; 1972, 1981, run in two divisions; before 1989, held during the spring meeting; inaugurated in 1831 as the Phoenix Hotel S.; has also been run as Brennan S., Chiles S., Phoenix S., Association S., and Phoenix H.

QUEEN'S PLATE S. Woodbine 1860 Don Juan
Before 1887, run at 1½ miles; 1924-'56, run at 1⅛ miles; before 1938, for three-year-olds and up; 1938, for three- and four-year-olds; 1902-'51, run as the King's Plate; before 1956, held at Old Woodbine; before 1959, for three-year-olds bred and owned in Canada

TRAVERS S. Saratoga 1864 Kentucky
1943, 1944, 1945, held at Belmont Park; 1896, 1898, 1899, 1900, 1911, 1912, not run; before 1890, run at 1¾ miles; 1890-'92, run at 1½ miles; 1895, 1901-'03, run at 1⅛ miles; 1927-'32, run as the Travers Midsummer Derby

JEROME H. Belmont 1866 Watson
1866-'89, held at Jerome Park; 1890-1905, held at Morris Park; 1960, 1962-'67, held at Aqueduct; 1910-'13, not run; 1866-'70, run in two divisions; 1871-'77, run at 2 miles; 1878-'89, run at 1¾ miles; 1890, 1891, 1903, run at 1⁵⁄₁₆ miles; 1892, run at 1½ miles; 1893, 1894, 1896-1909, run at 1¼ miles; 1895, run at 1⅛ miles

Race	Track	First running	First winner

BELMONT S. Belmont 1867 Ruthless
1867-'89, held at Jerome Park; 1890-1904, held at Morris Park; 1963-'67, held at Aqueduct; 1911-'12, not run; 1867-'73, run at 1⅝ miles; 1890-'92, 1895, 1904-'05, run at 1¼ miles; 1893-'94, run at 1⅛ miles; 1896-1903, 1906-'25, run at 1⅜ miles; 1895, 1913, run as a handicap stakes

CHAMPAGNE S. Belmont 1867 Sarah B.
Before 1890, held at Jerome Park; 1890-1905, held at Morris Park; 1959, 1963-'67, 1984, held at Aqueduct; 1910-'13, 1956, not run; 1871-'80, run at six furlongs; 1891-1904, run at seven furlongs; 1905-'32, run on the Widener course (165 feet less than seven furlongs); 1933-'39, run on the Widener course at 6½ furlongs; 1940-'83, 1985-'93, run at one mile; 1984, run at 1⅛ miles; 1973, run in two divisions

LADIES H. Aqueduct 1868 Bonnie Braes
Before 1913, for three-year-old fillies; 1931-'34, 1940-2001, for fillies and mares all ages, three-year-olds and up; before 1890, held at Jerome Park; 1890-1904, held at Morris Park; 1950-'58, 1960, held at Belmont Park; 1895, 1911, 1912, not run; before 1874, run at 1⅝ miles; 1889, 1892, run at 1⅛ miles; 1890, 1891, run at 1,400 yards; 1893, 1894, run at 1¹⁄₁₆ miles; 1896-1939, run at one mile; 1961, 1962, run at 1⁵⁄₁₆ miles; 1874-'85, 1940-'58, 1960, 1963, 1964, run at 1½ miles.

FLASH S. Belmont 1869 Remorseless
1869-1942, 1946-'71, held at Saratoga; 1943-'45, held at Belmont Park on the Widener course; 1981, 1982, held at Belmont Park; 1896, 1898-1900, 1911, 1912, 1960, 1972-'80, 1983-'98, not run; before 1901, run at four furlongs, 1901, run at five furlongs; 1969-'71, run at six furlongs; 1981, 1982, run at 5½ furlongs

DIXIE S. Pimlico 1870 Preakness
1870, run as Dinner Party S.; 1871, run as Reunion S.; 1903-'04, held at Benning, Washington, D.C., at 1¾ miles for three-year-olds; 1870-'88, run at two miles for three-year-olds; 1924-'52, run at 1³⁄₁₆ miles; 1960-'87, 1989, 1990, run at 1½ miles; 1955-'59, run at 1⅜ miles; 1988, run at 1⅝ miles; before 1955, 1988, run on dirt; 1889-1901, 1905-'23, not run; 1965-'78, run in two divisions

MONMOUTH PARK BREEDERS' CUP OAKS Monmouth 1871 Salina
1871-'77, run at 1½ miles; 1879-'93, run at 1¼ miles; 1946-'52, 1996-2001, run at 1¹⁄₁₆ miles; 1953-'95, run at 1⅛ miles; 1891, held at Jerome Park; 1878, 1894-1945, not run; 1976, run as Monmouth Bicentennial Oaks

ALABAMA S. Saratoga 1872 Woodbine
1943-'45, held at Belmont Park; 1893-'96, 1898-1900, 1911, 1912, not run; before 1901, 1904, 1906-'16, run at

		First				First	
Race	Track	running	First winner	Race	Track	running	First winner

1⅛ miles; 1901-'03, run at 1¹⁄₁₆ miles; 1903, run on turf; 1905, run at 1⁵⁄₁₆ miles

CALIFORNIA DERBY Bay Meadows **1873** Camilla Urso
  1897-1909, run at 1¼ miles; 1923, run at 1½ miles; 1936-'48, 1976-'81, run at 1¹⁄₁₆ miles; 1874, 1891-'96, 1900, 1911-'22, 1924-'34, 1939, 1940, 1942, 1943, 1945, 1947, 1949-'53, 1957, not run; 1873-1959, 1962, held at Tanforan; 1961, 1964-2000, held at Golden Gate Fields

PREAKNESS S. Pimlico **1873** Survivor
  Before 1894, run at 1½ miles; 1889, run at 1¼ miles; 1894-1900, 1908, run at 1¹⁄₁₆ miles; 1901-'07, run at one mile and 70 yards; 1909, 1910, run at one mile; 1911-'24, run at 1⅛ miles; 1891-'93, not run; 1890, for three-year-olds and up; 1890, held at Morris Park, New York; 1894-1908, held at Gravesend, New York; 1918, run in

two divisions

WITHERS S. Aqueduct **1874** Dublin
  1847-'89, held at Jerome Park; 1890-1904, held at Morris Park; 1956, held at Jamaica; 1984-'96, held at Belmont Park; 1911, 1912, not run; 1956, run at 1¹⁄₁₆ miles

CLARK H. Churchill **1875** Voltigeur
  1875-1901, run as three-year-old stakes; 1902-2001, run as a handicap for three-year-olds and up; 1875-'80, run at two divisions; 1881-'95, run at 1¼ miles; 1902-'21, 1925-'54, run at 1¹⁄₁₆ miles; 1953, run in two divisions

KENTUCKY DERBY Churchill **1875** Aristides
  Before 1896, run at 1½ miles

KENTUCKY OAKS Churchill **1875** Vinaigrette
  1875-'90, run at 1½ miles; 1891-'95, run at 1¼ miles; 1896-1919, 1942-'81, run at 1¹⁄₁₆ miles

Fastest Race Times of 2002

Distance	Time	Winner, age	Track	Date
2f	:20.81	Baby Shark	Calder Race Course	07-13
2½f	:31.60	LI Fast Play	Chippewa Downs	06-08
		Zula Bay	Chippewa Downs	06-30
3f	:32.99	Sports Banquet	Gulfstream Park	04-05
3½f	:39.20	Misty River	Northlands Park	09-18
		Nu Chance to Dance	Northlands Park	09-22
		Ole' Olay	Northlands Park	09-01
		Tychonic Lady	Stampede Park	05-26
4f	:43.60	Iza Twister	Mohave County Fair	05-12
4½f	:50.00	Mr Clearwater	Lincoln State Fair	06-09
		Wondrous Zeal	SunRay Park	10-11
4½fT	:50.44	Twin Meteors	Mountaineer Park	06-11
5f	:56.00	Nycity	Arapahoe Park	07-13
5fT	::54.61	Bop	Penn National Race Course	08-03
5¼f	1:01.60	King of Adventure	Yellowstone Downs	09-15
5½f	1:01.40	Salt Grinder	Emerald Downs	04-20
5½fT	1:00.52	Bettybird	Ellis Park	08-21
6f	1:07.60	Blue Tejano	Emerald Downs	06-07
6fT	1:07.86	Nuclear Debate	Woodbine	06-23
6½f	1:13.80	Bold Ranger	Emerald Downs	05-27
		Crowning Meeting	Emerald Downs	05-19
6½fT	1:15.15	Irish Line	Woodbine	08-21
a6½fT	1:11.73	Malabar Gold	Santa Anita Park	04-21
7f	1:20.17	Left Bank	Belmont Park	07-04
7fT	1:20.08	Shibboleth	Belmont Park	05-27
7½f	1:27.98	Lethal Instrument	Hollywood Park	05-01
7½fT	1:27.48	Magical Madness	Mountaineer Park	05-27
1m	1:33.11	Congaree	Aqueduct	11-30
1mT	1:32.24	Volponi	Belmont Park	07-05
1m 40y	1:38.97	Mineshaft	Fair Grounds	12-20
1m 70y	1:38.58	Hourly Storm	Meadowlands	09-05
1m 70yT	1:38.98	Calling Again	Penn National Race Course	08-16
1¹⁄₁₆m	1:40.11	Wild Years	Belmont Park	06-07
1¹⁄₁₆mT	1:39.17	Balto Star	Saratoga Race Course	08-11
1⅛m	1:45.40	Flying Notes	Emerald Downs	09-02
1⅛mT	1:45.39	Roxinho (Brz)	Ellis Park	09-02
1³⁄₁₆m	1:55.07	Tenpins	Arlington Park	09-29
1³⁄₁₆mT	1:53.97	Blazing Fury	Saratoga Race Course	07-27
1¼m	1:59.58	Evening Attire	Belmont Park	09-28
1¼mT	1:58.56	Astra	Hollywood Park	06-29
1⁵⁄₁₆m	2:13.20	Miki Bleu Eyes	Northlands Park	08-16
1⅜m	2:13.42	Golden Ticket	Hollywood Park	12-21
1⅜mT	2:12.15	Delta Form (Aus)	Del Mar	09-01
1⁷⁄₁₆m	2:28.40	Paw Paw's Pride	Evangeline Downs	07-19
1½m	2:29.71	Sarava	Belmont Park	06-08

Distance	Time	Winner, age	Track	Date
1½mT	2:24.06	With Anticipation	Saratoga Race Course	08-10
1⁹⁄₁₆m	2:47.99	Dr. Robbie	Hoosier Park	10-25
1⅝m	2:43.54	Coyote Lakes	Aqueduct	12-28
1¾m	2:59.86	Gist of Art	Fort Erie	10-01
1¹³⁄₁₆m	3:06.31	Good Actor	Downs at Albuquerque	09-22
1⅞m	3:17.43	Disappeared	Woodbine	12-01
1⅞mT	3:09.06	Landiland	Mountaineer Park	09-02
2m	3:27.83	A Storm Is Brewing	Churchill Downs	11-30
2m 70y	3:38.92	Ace of Suedes	Fort Erie	11-05
2¹⁄₁₆m	3:40.05	Pete's Skianno	Mountaineer Park	12-29

North American Dirt and Turf Records

Distance	Time	Winner, age	Track	Date
2f	:20.80	Big Racket, 4	Hippodromo, Mexico	2-5-1945
2½f	:26.53	Yes He Will, 4	Lone Star Park	11-7-1997
3f	:31.20	Raisable Adversary, 11	Remington Park	8-29-1999
3½f	:38.00	Primero Del Anno, 5	Flagstaff	7-4-1998
4f	:43.10	Slewofrainbows, 7	Mohave County Fair	5-23-1999
4fT	:46.60	Fine Tassles, 5	Rillito	1-30-1994
4½f	:49.20	Valiant Pete, 4	Los Alamitos	8-11-1990
4½fT	:50.00	Cake n' Steak, 8	Mountaineer Race Track	8-9-1993
5f	:55.20	Chinook Pass, 3	Longacres	9-17-1982
5fT	:54.60	General Express, 5	Monmouth Park	7-8-2000
5½f	1:01.10	Plenty Zloty, 5	Turf Paradise	4-18-1998
5½fT	1:00.46	Pembroke, 5	Hollywood Park	7-15-1995
6f	1:06.60	G Malleah, 4	Turf Paradise	4-8-1995
6fT	1:07.00	Answer Do, 4	Hollywood Park	12-15-1990
6¼f	1:15.80	Montanic, 4	Washington Park	7-20-1901
6½f	1:13.24	Lucky Forever, 6	Hollywood Park	5-20-1995
6½fT	1:14.20	Key Twenty Two, 6	Woodbine	6-4-1992
about 6½fT	1:11.45	Cayoke, 6	Santa Anita Park	1-16-2003
7f	1:19.40	Rich Cream, 5	Hollywood Park	5-28-1980
		Time to Explode, 3	Hollywood Park	6-26-1982
7fT	1:19.88	Officialpermission, 6	Belmont Park	7-23-2000
7½f	1:26.26	Awesome Daze, 5	Hollywood Park	11-23-1997
7½fT	1:26.54	Court Lark, 6	Calder Race Course	7-16-1994
1m	1:32⅕	Dr. Fager, 4	Arlington Park	8-24-1968
	1:32.24	Najran, 4	Belmont Park	5-7-2003
1mT	1:31.63	Elusive Quality, 5	Belmont Park	7-4-1998
1m 20y	1:39.00	Froglegs, 4	Churchill Downs	5-13-1913
1m 40y	1:38.20	Zafarrancho, 5	Rockingham	6-19-1987
1m 40yT	1:38.08	Castaneto (Arg), 7	Atlantic City	6-28-1991
1m 55y	1:40.80	Terrain, 3	Bay Meadows Race Course	11-13-1934
1m 60y	1:41.00	Brush Hook, 5	Tropical Park	3-16-1938
1m 70y	1:38.20	Majestic Nasr, 6	Pleasanton	7-11-1993
1m 70yT	1:37.20	Aborigine, 6	Penn National	8-20-1978
1m 100y	1:43.80	Old Honesty, 3	Empire City	8-20-1907
1¹⁄₁₆m	1:38.40	Hoedown's Day, 5	Bay Meadows Race Course	10-23-1983
1¹⁄₁₆mT	1:38.00	Told, 4	Penn National	9-14-1980
1⅛m	1:45.00	Simply Majestic, 4	Golden Gate Fields	4-2-1988
1⅛mT	1:43.92	Kostroma (Ire), 5	Santa Anita Park	10-20-1991
1³⁄₁₆m	1:52.40	Riva Ridge, 4	Aqueduct	7-4-1973
1³⁄₁₆mT	1:51.40	Toonerville, 4	Hialeah Park	2-7-1976
1¼m	1:57.80	Spectacular Bid, 4	Santa Anita Park	2-3-1980
1¼mT	1:57.40	Double Discount, 4	Santa Anita Park	10-9-1977
1⁵⁄₁₆m	2:07.32	Gold Star Deputy, 5	Aqueduct	4-10-1999
1⁵⁄₁₆mT	2:06.00	Ruff Mack, 5	Mountaineer Race Track	8-25-1962
1⅜m	2:12.31	Demi's Bret, 4	Aqueduct	10-26-1997
1⅜mT	2:10.20	With Approval, 4	Belmont Park	6-17-1990
1⁷⁄₁₆m	2:23.00	Who's In Command, 5	Hastings Park	8-10-1987
1⁷⁄₁₆mT	2:25.00	Dina's Playmate, 11	River Downs	8-30-1969
1½m	2:24.00	Secretariat, 3	Belmont Park	6-9-1973
1½mT	2:22.80	Hawkster, 3	Santa Anita Park	10-14-1989

Distance	Time	Winner, age	Track	Date
1⁹⁄₁₆m	2:35.77	Well Lit, 5	Sportsman's Park	4-25-1992
1⁹⁄₁₆mT	2:40.26	To the Floor, 7	Fair Grounds	3-29-1999
1⁵⁄₈m	2:38.20	Swaps, 4	Hollywood Park	7-25-1956
1⁵⁄₈mT	2:37.00	Tom Swift, 5	Saratoga Race Course	8-23-1978
1¾m	2:52.60	Major Pots, 5	Woodbine	12-8-1994
1¾mT	2:56.40	Desperado Dan, 4	Woodbine	7-22-1984
1⅞m	3:11.56	Asserche, 6	Laurel Park	3-20-1994
1⅞mT	3:08.23	Code's Best, 6	Mountaineer Race Track	9-4-2000
2m	3:19.20	Kelso, 7	Aqueduct	10-31-1964
2mT	3:18.00	Petrone, 5	Hollywood Park	7-23-1969
2¼m	3:47.00	Fenelon, 4	Belmont Park	10-4-1941
2¼mT	3:48.40	Buteo, 6	River Downs	9-3-1990
2½m	4:14.60	*Miss Grillo, 6	Pimlico Race Course	11-12-1948

Leading Earners of All Time

North America

Because of the paucity and unreliability of published records of Thoroughbred racing before the Civil War, the earliest leading North American earner whose record can be reliably verified is the great American Eclipse, who became an American popular hero in the 1820s. More than 20 years later, the baton was handed on to the giant filly Peytona, who collected the largest purse on the continent to that date, $41,000, for her victory in the Peyton Stakes at Nashville, Tennessee, in 1843. Her owner promptly changed her name from the unwieldy Glumdalclitch and named her after her most famous win.

The pace of change on the leading earner list has quickened since antebellum days. Perhaps the most exciting exchange occurred in 1947, when Racing Hall of Fame members Assault, Armed, and Stymie batted Whirlaway's previous record around like a badminton shuttlecock. Stymie's durability finally outlasted the other two, and he ended his career with earnings of $918,485. Citation, who became the leading earner in 1950, moved the mark above $1-million the following year.

The great two-year-old and epochal sire Domino held the torch for the longest period, 27 years, from 1893 until supplanted by Man o' War in 1920. Assault and Stymie each held the title for the shortest period, seven days, during their duel in 1947. The only stallion to sire two leading North American money earners is Bull Lea. Peytona and Miss Woodford are the only females to hold the title.

International racing has always complicated the issue. Parole's record earnings include about $20,000 earned on his sojourn in England in 1879-'80. Cigar's earnings similarly include the $2.4-million earned in his Dubai World Cup victory.

As the following list shows, the title of leading North American earner has been held by 27 horses, down to current leader Cigar, who took the title from Alysheba during his 16-race win streak in 1996. As shown in the following worldwide list, the earnings of Japanese-based T.M.Opera O have already far surpassed Cigar's total.

Chronology of Leading American Money Winners

1823—American Eclipse, 1814 ch. h., Duroc—Millers Damsel, by Messenger. 8-8-0-0, **$56,700.**

1845—Peytona, 1839 ch. f., *Glencoe—Giantess, by *Leviathan. 8-6-1-0, **$62,400.**

1861—Planet, 1855 ch. h., Revenue—Nina, by Boston. 31-27-4-0, **$69,700.**

1881—Hindoo, 1878 b. h., Virgil—Florence, by Lexington. 35-30-3-2, **$71,875.**

1881—Parole, 1873 br. h., *Leamington—Maiden, by Lexington. 129-59-22-16, **$82,816.**

1885—Miss Woodford, 1880 br. f., *Billet—Fancy Jane, by Neil Robinson. 48-37-7-2, **$118,270.**

1889—Hanover, 1884 ch. h., Hindoo—Bourbon Belle, by *Bonnie Scotland. 50-32-14-2, **$118,887.**

1892—Kingston, 1884 dk. b. or br. h., Spendthrift—*Kapanga, by Victorious. 138-89-33-12, **$138,917.**

1893—Domino, 1891 br. h., Himyar—Mannie Gray, by Enquirer. 25-19-3-1, **$193,550.**

1920—Man o' War, 1917 ch. h., Fair Play—Mahubah, by *Rock Sand. 21-20-1-0, **$249,465.**

1923—Zev, 1920 dk. b. or br. h., Finn—Miss Kearney, by *Planudes. 43-23-8-5, **$313,639.**

1930—Gallant Fox, 1927 b. h., *Sir Gallahad III—Marguerite, by Celt. 17-11-3-2, **$328,165.**

1931—Sun Beau, 1925 b. h., *Sun Briar—Beautiful Lady, by Fair Play. 74-33-12-10, **$376,744.**

1940—Seabiscuit, 1933 b. h., Hard Tack—Swing On, by Whisk Broom II. 89-33-15-13, **$437,730.**

1942—Whirlaway, 1938 ch. h., *Blenheim II—Dustwhirl, by Sweep. 60-32-15-9, **$561,161.**

1947 (June 21)—Assault, 1943 ch. h., Bold Venture—Igual, by Equipoise. 42-18-6-7, **$576,670.**

1947 (July 5)—Stymie, 1941 ch. h., Equestrian—Stop Watch, by On Watch. 131-35-33-28, **$595,510.**

1947 (July 12)—Assault, $613,370 (career $675,470).

1947 (July 19)—Stymie, $678,510.

1947 (October 9)—Armed, 1941 dk. b. or br. g., Bull Lea—Armful, by Chance Shot. 81-41-20-10, **$761,500 (career $817,475).**

1947 (October 25)—Stymie $816,060 (career $918,485).

1950—Citation, 1945 b. h., Bull Lea—*Hydroplane II, by Hyperion. 45-32-10-2, **$1,085,760.**

1956—Nashua, 1952 b. h., *Nasrullah—Segula, by Johnstown. 30-22-4-1, **$1,288,565.**

1958—Round Table, 1954 b. h., *Princequillo—*Knight's Daughter, by Sir Cosmo. 66-43-8-5, **$1,749,869.**

1965—Kelso, 1957 dk. b. or br. g., Your Host—Maid of Flight, by Count Fleet. 63-39-12-2, **$1,977,896.**

1979—Affirmed, 1975 ch. h., Exclusive Native—Won't Tell You, by Crafty Admiral. 29-22-5-1, **$2,393,818.**

1980—Spectacular Bid, 1976 gr. h., Bold Bidder—Spectacular, by Promised Land. 30-26-2-1, **$2,781,608.**

1981—John Henry, 1975 b. g., Ole Bob Bowers—Once Double, by Double Jay. 83-39-15-9, **$6,591,860.**

1988—Alysheba, 1984 b. h., Alydar—Bel Sheba, by Lt. Stevens. 26-11-8-2, **$6,679,242.**

1996—Cigar, 1990 b. h., Palace Music—Solar Slew, by Seattle Slew. 33-19-4-5, **$9,999,815.**

International

In the 20th century, America became so accustomed to being the home of the world's leading money-winning racehorse that it did not even notice when Japanese-bred and -trained Oguri Cap soared past American leader Alysheba in 1990.

Since organized Thoroughbred racing originated in England in the early 18th century, it is obvious that the earliest leading earners must have resided there as well. Determining the first world's richest Thoroughbred is all but impossible because early records are nonexistent or unclear on purse awards.

English record-keepers recorded that in 1889 Donovan broke the record previously held by the French-bred Gladiateur. In turn, Gladiateur had broken the previous record of England's The Flying Dutchman.

The earliest horse who can reliably be accorded the palm of world's leading earner is the undefeated Highflyer, who was foaled in 1774. Based on the exchange rate of $5 to £1 that prevailed in the 19th century (America was still a British colony in 1774), Highflyer earned the equivalent of $38,395 by winning all 12 of his races.

By that standard, American Eclipse surpassed Highflyer, but 1830 Epsom Derby winner *Priam earned more money by the same exchange rate.

The title remained in Europe until 1923, when Zev's victory over *Papyrus propelled him past Isinglass, who remained England's leading earner for more than 60 years.

Zev began a 67-year reign for American horses at the same time the American economy began to dominate the world. Only the huge increases in Japanese purses beginning in the 1980s changed that equation. As shown by the accompanying list of the world's current leading earners, the earnings of T.M.Opera O far exceed any American horse.

Chronology of Leading International Money Winners

1780—Highflyer, 1774 b. h., Herod—Rachel, by Blank. 12-12-0-0, **$38,395.**

1823—American Eclipse, 1814 ch. h., Duroc—Miller's Damsel, by *Messenger. 8-8-0- 0, **$56,700.**

1830—*Priam, 1827 br. h., Emilius—Cressida, by Whiskey. 16-14-1-1, **$65,100.**

1850—The Flying Dutchman, 1846 b. h., Bay Middleton—Barbelle, by Sandbeck. 15-14-1-0, **$93,900.**

1865—Gladiateur, 1862 b. h., Monarque—Miss Gladiator, by Gladiator. 19-16-0-1, **$236,537.**

1889—Donovan, 1886 b. h., Galopin—Mowerina, by The Scottish Chief. 21-18-2-1, **$275,775.**

1895—Isinglass, 1890 b. h., Isonomy—Dead Lock, by Wenlock. 12-11-1-0, **$287,275.**

1923—Zev, 1920 dk. b. or br. h., The Finn—Miss Kearney, by *Planudes. 43-23-8-5, **$313,639.**

1930—Gallant Fox, 1927 b. h., *Sir Gallahad III—Marguerite, by Celt. 17-11-3-2, **$328,165.**

1931—Sun Beau, 1925 b. h., *Sun Briar—Beautiful Lady, by Fair Play. 74-33-12-10, **$376,744.**

1940—Seabiscuit, 1933 b. h., Hard Tack—Swing On, by Whisk Broom II. 89-33-15-13, **$437,730.**

1942—Whirlaway, 1938 ch. h., *Blenheim II—Dustwhirl, by Sweep. 60-32-15-9, **$561,161.**

1947 (June 21)—Assault, 1943 ch. h., Bold Venture—Igual, by Equipoise. 42-18-6-7, **$576,670.**

1947 (July 5)—Stymie, 1941 ch. h., Equestrian—Stop Watch, by On Watch. 131-35-33-28, **$595,510.**

1947 (July 12)—Assault, $613,370 (career $675,470).

1947 (July 19)—Stymie, $678,510.

1947 (October 9)—Armed, 1941 dk. b. or br. g., Bull Lea—Armful, by Chance Shot. 81-41-20-10, **$761,500 (career $817,475).**

1947 (October 25)—Stymie $816,060 (career $918,485).

1950—Citation, 1945 b. h., Bull Lea—*Hydroplane II, by Hyperion. 45-32-10-2, **$1,085,760.**

1956—Nashua, 1952 b. h., *Nasrullah—Segula, by Johnstown. 30-22-4-1, **$1,288,565.**

1958—Round Table, 1954 b. h., *Princequillo—*Knight's Daughter, by Sir Cosmo. 66-43-8-5, **$1,749,869.**

1965—Kelso, 1957 dk. b. or br. g., Your Host—Maid of Flight, by Count Fleet. 63-39-12-2, **$1,977,896.**

1979—Affirmed, 1975 ch. h., Exclusive Native—Won't Tell You, by Crafty Admiral. 29-22-5-1, **$2,393,818.**

1980—Spectacular Bid, 1976 gr. h., Bold Bidder—Spectacular, by Promised Land. 30-26-2-1, **$2,781,608.**
1981—John Henry, 1975 b. g., Ole Bob Bowers—Once Double, by Double Jay 83-39-15-9, **$6,591,860.**
1988—Alysheba, 1984 b. h., Alydar—Bel Sheba, by Lt. Stevens 26-11-8-2, **$6,679,242.**
1990—Oguri Cap, 1985 gr. h., Dancing Cap—White Narubi, by *Silver Shark. 32-22-6-1, **$6,919,201.**

1993—Mejiro McQueen, 1987 gr. h., Mejiro Titan—Mejiro Aurola, by Remand. 14-9-3-0, **$7,618,803.**
1995—Narita Brian, 1991 dk b. or br. h., Brian's Time—Pacificus, by Northern Dancer. 21-12-3-1, **$9,296,552.**
1996—Cigar, 1990 b. h., Palace Music—Solar Slew, by Seattle Slew. 33-19-4-5, **$9,999,815.**
2000—T.M.Opera O, 1996 ch. h., Opera House (GB)—Once Wed, by Blushing Groom (Fr). 26-14-6-3, **$16,200,337.**

World's Leading Earners
Through May 19, 2003

Rank	Horse	YOB, Pedigree	Country	Earnings (in dollars)
1.	T.M.Opera O	1996 ch. c., Opera House (GB)-Once Wed, by Blushing Groom (Fr)	Jpn	$16,200,337
2.	Cigar	1990 b. c., Palace Music-Solar Slew, by Seattle Slew	USA	9,999,815
3.	Skip Away	1993 gr. c., Skip Trial-Ingot Way, by Diplomat Way	USA	9,616,360
4.	Special Week	1995 dk. b. or br. c., Sunday Silence-Campaign Girl, by Maruzensky	Jpn	9,346,435
5.	Narita Brian	1991 b. or br. c., Brian's Time-Pacificus, by Northern Dancer	Jpn	9,296,552
6.	Stay Gold	1994 dk. b. or br. c., Sunday Silence-Golden Sash, by Dictus	Jpn	8,682,142
7.	Fantastic Light	1996 b. c., Rahy-Jood, by Nijinsky II	GB	8,486,957
8.	Narita Top Road	1996 ch. c., Soccer Boy-Floral Magic, by Affirmed	Jpn	8,389,594
9.	Hokuto Vega	1990 b. f., Nagurski-Takeno Falcon, by Philip of Spain	Jpn	8,300,301
10.	Meisho Doto	1996 b. c., Bigstone (Ire)-Princess Reema, by Affirmed	Jpn	8,088,202
11.	Mejiro Mc Queen	1987 gr. c., Mejiro Titan-Mejiro Aurola, by Remand	Jpn	7,618,803
12.	Biwa Hayahide	1990 gr. c., Sharrood-Pacificus, by Northern Dancer	Jpn	7,555,480
13.	Mayano Top Gun	1992 ch. c., Brian's Time-Alp Me Please, by Blushing Groom (Fr)	Jpn	7,463,557
14.	Eishin Preston	1997 dk. b/br. c., Green Dancer-Warranty Applied, by Monteverdi (Ire)	Jpn	7,077,800
15.	Agnes Digital	1997 ch. c., Crafty Prospector-Chancey Squaw, by Chief's Crown	Jpn	7,068,806
16.	Hishi Amazon	1991 dk. b. or br. f., Theatrical (Ire)-Katies (Ire), by Nonoalco	Jpn	6,981,102
17.	Silver Charm	1994 gr. c., Silver Buck-Bonnie's Poker, by Poker	USA	6,944,369
18.	Oguri Cap	1985 gr. c., Dancing Cap-White Narubi, by *Silver Shark	Jpn	6,919,201
19.	Mejiro Bright	1994 b. c., Mejiro Ryan-Reru du Temps, by Maruzensky	Jpn	6,848,423
20.	Air Groove	1993 b. f., Tony Bin-Dyna Carle, by Northern Taste	Jpn	6,832,242
21.	Captain Steve	1997 ch. c., Fly So Free-Sparkling Delite, by Vice Regent	USA	6,828,356
22.	Alysheba	1984 b. c., Alydar-Bel Sheba, by Lt. Stevens	USA	6,679,242
23.	Sunline	1995 b. f., Desert Sun-Songline, by Western Symphony	NZ	6,625,105
24.	John Henry	1975 b. g., Ole Bob Bowers-Once Double, by Double Jay	USA	6,591,860
25.	Tiznow	1997 b. c., Cee's Tizzy-Cee's Song, by Seattle Song	USA	6,427,830
26.	Wing Arrow	1995 b. c., Assatis-Sanyo Arrow, by Mr C B	Jpn	6,273,733
27.	Mejiro Dober	1994 b. f., Mejiro Ryan-Mejiro Beauty, by Partholon	Jpn	6,240,681
28.	Rice Shower	1989 dk. b. or br. c., Real Shadai-Lilac Point, by Maruzensky	Jpn	6,070,429
29.	Grass Wonder	1995 ch. c., Silver Hawk-Ameriflora, by Danzig	Jpn	5,987,405
30.	Dance Partner	1992 b. f., Sunday Silence-Dancing Key, by Nijinsky II	Jpn	5,973,652
31.	Singspiel (Ire)	1992 b. c., In the Wings (GB)-Glorious Song, by Halo	GB	5,952,825
32.	Fast Friend	1994 ch. f., Ines Fujin-The Last Word, by Northern Taste	Jpn	5,896,693
33.	Jungle Pocket	1998 b. c., Tony Bin-Dance Charmer, by Nureyev	Jpn	5,788,198
34.	Sakura Laurel	1991 b. c., Rainbow Quest-Lola Lola, by Saint Cyrien	Jpn	5,751,390
35.	Black Hawk (GB)	1994 b. c., Nureyev-Silver Lane, by Silver Hawk	Jpn	5,750,386
36.	Best Pal	1988 b. g., *Habitony-Ubetshedid, by King Pellinore	USA	5,668,245
37.	Kyoto City	1991 b. c., Soccer Boy-Mountain Queen, by Nizon	Jpn	5,622,437
38.	Taiki Blizzard	1991 dk. b/br. c., Seattle Slew-Tree of Knowledge (Ire), by Sassafras (Fr)	Jpn	5,523,549
39.	Genuine	1992 dk. b. or br. c., Sunday Silence-Croupier Lady, by What Luck	Jpn	5,455,575
40.	Marvelous Sunday	1992 ch. c., Sunday Silence-Momiji Dancer, by Viceregal	Jpn	5,305,340
41.	To the Victory	1996 b. f., Sunday Silence-Fairy Doll, by Habitony	Jpn	5,303,281
42.	Nice Nature	1988 b. c., Nice Dancer-Urakawa Miyuki, by *Habitony	Jpn	5,232,135
43.	Daiwa Texas	1993 ch. c., Tolomeo (Ire)-Robe Decollete, by No Attention	Jpn	5,200,877
44.	Sakura Chitose O	1990 b. c., Tony Bin-Sakura Clare, by Northern Taste	Jpn	5,178,760
45.	Street Cry (Ire)	1998 dk. b. or br. c., Machiavellian-Helen Street (GB), by Troy	USA	5,150,837

Leading North American Earners by Year
North American Racing Only

Year	Horse, YOB Sex, Pedigree	Earnings
2002	War Emblem, 1999, c., Our Emblem—Sweetest Lady, by Lord At War (Arg)	$3,455,000
2001	Point Given, 1998 c., Thunder Gulch—Turko's Turn, by Turkoman	3,350,000
2000	Tiznow, 1997 c., Cee's Tizzy—Cee's Song, by Seattle Song	3,445,950
1999	Cat Thief, 1996 c., Storm Cat—Train Robbery, by Alydar	3,020,500
1998	Awesome Again, 1994 c., Deputy Minister—Primal Force, by Blushing Groom (Fr)	3,845,990
1997	Skip Away, 1993 c., Skip Trial—Ingot Way, by Diplomat Way	4,089,000
1996	Skip Away, 1993 c., Skip Trial—Ingot Way, by Diplomat Way	2,699,280
1995	Cigar, 1990 h., Palace Music—Solar Slew, by Seattle Slew	4,819,800
1994	Concern, 1991 c., Broad Brush—Fara's Team, by Tunerup	2,541,670
1993	Sea Hero, 1990 c., Polish Navy—Glowing Tribute, by Graustark	2,484,190
1992	A.P. Indy, 1989 c., Seattle Slew—Weekend Surprise, by Secretariat	2,622,560
1991	Dance Smartly, 1988 f., Danzig—Classy 'n Smart, by Smarten	2,876,821
1990	Unbridled, 1987 c., Fappiano—Gana Facil, by *Le Fabuleux	3,718,149
1989	Sunday Silence, 1986 c., Halo—Wishing Well, by Understanding	4,578,454
1988	Alysheba, 1984 c., Alydar—Bel Sheba, by Lt. Stevens	3,808,600
1987	Alysheba, 1984 c., Alydar—Bel Sheba, by Lt. Stevens	2,511,156
1986	Snow Chief, 1983 c., Reflected Glory—Miss Snowflake, by *Snow Sporting	1,875,200
1985	Spend a Buck, 1982 c., Buckaroo—Belle de Jour, by Speak John	3,552,704
1984	Slew o' Gold, 1980 c., Seattle Slew—Alluvial, by Buckpasser	2,627,944
1983	Sunny's Halo, 1980 c., Halo—Mostly Sunny, by Sunny	1,011,962
1982	Perrault (GB), 1977 h., Djakao—Innocent Air, by *Court Martial	1,197,400
1981	John Henry, 1975 g., Ole Bob Bowers—Once Double, by Double Jay	1,798,030
1980	Temperence Hill, 1977 c., Stop the Music—Sister Shannon, by Etonian	1,130,452
1979	Spectacular Bid, 1976 c., Bold Bidder—Spectacular, by Promised Land	1,279,334
1978	Affirmed, 1975 c., Exclusive Native—Won't Tell You, by Crafty Admiral	901,541
1977	Seattle Slew, 1974 c., Bold Reasoning—My Charmer, by Poker	641,370
1976	Forego, 1970 g., *Forli—Lady Golconda, by Hasty Road	491,701
1975	Foolish Pleasure, 1972 c., What a Pleasure—Fool-Me-Not, by Tom Fool	716,278
1974	Chris Evert, 1971 f., Swoon's Son—Miss Carmie, by T. V. Lark	551,063
1973	Secretariat, 1970 c., Bold Ruler—Somethingroyal, by *Princequillo	860,404
1972	Droll Role, 1968 c., Tom Rolfe—*Pradella, by Preciptic	471,633
1971	Riva Ridge, 1969 c., First Landing—Iberia, by *Heliopolis	503,263
1970	Personality, 1967 c., Hail to Reason—Affectionately, by Swaps	444,049
1969	Arts and Letters, 1966 c., *Ribot—All Beautiful, by Battlefield	555,604
1968	Forward Pass, 1965 c., On-and-On—Princess Turia, by *Heliopolis	546,674
1967	Damascus, 1964 c., Sword Dancer—Kerala, by *My Babu	817,941
1966	Buckpasser, 1963 c., Tom Fool—Busanda, by War Admiral	669,078
1965	Buckpasser, 1963 c., Tom Fool—Busanda, by War Admiral	568,096
1964	Gun Bow, 1960 c., Gun Shot—Ribbons and Bows, by War Admiral	580,100
1963	Candy Spots, 1960 c., *Nigromante—Candy Dish, by *Khaled	604,481
1962	Never Bend, 1960 c., *Nasrullah—Lalun, by *Djeddah	402,969
1961	Carry Back, 1958 c., Saggy—Joppy, by Star Blen	565,349
1960	Bally Ache, 1957 c., *Ballydam—Celestial Blue, by Supremus	455,045
1959	Sword Dancer, 1956 c., Sunglow—Highland Fling, by By Jimminy	537,004
1958	Round Table, 1954 c., *Princequillo—*Knight's Daughter, by Sir Cosmo	662,780
1957	Round Table, 1954 c., *Princequillo—*Knight's Daughter, by Sir Cosmo	600,383
1956	Needles, 1953 c., Ponder—Noodle Soup, by Jack High	440,850
1955	Nashua, 1952 c., *Nasrullah—Segula, by Johnstown	752,550
1954	Determine, 1951 c., *Alibhai—Koubis, by *Mahmoud	328,700
1953	Native Dancer, 1950 c., Polynesian—Geisha, by Discovery	513,425
1952	Crafty Admiral, 1948 c., Fighting Fox—Admiral's Lady, by War Admiral	277,225
1951	Counterpoint, 1948 c., Count Fleet—Jabot, by *Sickle	250,525
1950	*Noor, 1945 h., *Nasrullah—Queen of Baghdad , by *Bahram	346,940
1949	Ponder, 1946 c., Pensive—Miss Rushin, by *Blenheim II	321,825
1948	Citation, 1945 c., Bull Lea—*Hydroplane II, by Hyperion	709,470
1947	Armed, 1941 g., Bull Lea—Armful, by Chance Shot	376,325
1946	Assault, 1943 c., Bold Venture—Igual, by Equipoise	424,195
1945	Busher, 1942 f., War Admiral—Baby League, by Bubbling Over	273,735
1944	Pavot, 1942 c., Case Ace—Coquelicot, by Man o' War	179,040
1943	Count Fleet, 1940 c., Reigh Count—Quickly, by Haste	174,055
1942	Shut Out, 1939 c., Equipoise—Goose Egg, by *Chicle	238,972
1941	Whirlaway, 1938 c., *Blenheim II—Dustwhirl, by Sweep	272,386
1940	Bimelech, 1937 c., Black Toney—*La Troienne, by *Teddy	110,005
1939	Challedon, 1936 c., *Challenger II—Laura Gal, by *Sir Gallahad III	184,535
1938	Stagehand, 1935 c., *Sickle—Stagecraft, by Fair Play	189,710
1937	Seabiscuit, 1933 c., Hard Tack—Swing On, by Whisk Broom II	168,580
1936	Granville, 1933 c., Gallant Fox—Gravita, by *Sarmatian	110,295
1935	Omaha, 1932 c., Gallant Fox—Flambino, by *Wrack	142,255
1934	Cavalcade, 1931 c., *Lancegaye—*Hastily, by Hurry On	111,235
1933	Singing Wood, 1931 c., *Royal Minstrel—Glade, by Touch Me Not	88,050
1932	Gusto, 1929 c., American Flag—Daylight Saving, by *Star Shoot	145,940
1931	Top Flight, 1929 f., *Dis Donc—Flyatit, by Peter Pan	219,000
1930	Gallant Fox, 1927 c., *Sir Gallahad III—Marguerite, by Celt	308,275

Following are leaders for racing in North America only.

Leading Earners in North America

Horse, YOB, Sex	Wins	SWs	Earnings
Skip Away, 1993, h., by Skip Trial	18	16	$9,616,360
Cigar, 1990, h., by Palace Music	18	14	7,599,815
Alysheba, 1984, h., by Alydar	11	10	6,679,242
John Henry, 1975, g., by Ole Bob Bowers	39	30	6,591,860
Tiznow, 1997, h., by Cee's Tizzy	8	7	6,427,830
Best Pal, 1988, g., by *Habitony	18	17	5,668,245
Sunday Silence, 1986, h., by Halo	9	7	4,968,554
Easy Goer, 1986, h., by Alydar	14	12	4,873,770
Unbridled, 1987, h., by Fappiano	8	5	4,489,475
Silver Charm, 1994, h., by Silver Buck	11	10	4,444,369
Awesome Again, 1994, h., by Deputy Minister	9	7	4,374,590
Spend a Buck, 1982, h., by Buckaroo	10	7	4,220,689
Creme Fraiche, 1982, h., by Rich Cream	17	14	4,024,727
Point Given, 1998, h., by Thunder Gulch	9	8	3,968,500
Cat Thief, 1996, h., by Storm Cat	4	3	3,951,012
Devil His Due, 1989, h., by Devil's Bag	11	9	3,920,405
Ferdinand, 1983, h., by Nijinsky II	8	7	3,777,978
Spain, 1997, m., by Thunder Gulch	9	7	3,540,542
Slew o' Gold, 1980, h., by Seattle Slew	12	8	3,533,534
War Emblem, 1999, c., by Our Emblem	7	4	3,491,000
Precisionist, 1981, h., by Crozier	20	17	3,485,398
Strike the Gold, 1988, h., by Alydar	6	4	3,457,026
Snow Chief, 1983, h., by Reflected Glory	13	12	3,383,210
Cryptoclearance, 1984, h., by Fappiano	12	9	3,376,327
Gentlemen (Arg), 1992, h., by Robin des Bois	9	8	3,374,890
Black Tie Affair (Ire), 1986, h., by Miswaki	18	13	3,370,694
Sky Classic, 1987, h., by Nijinsky II	15	13	3,320,398
Bet Twice, 1984, h., by Sportin' Life	10	7	3,308,599
Serena's Song, 1992, m., by Rahy	18	17	3,283,388
Real Quiet, 1995, h., by Quiet American	6	5	3,271,802
Dance Smartly, 1988, m., by Danzig	12	10	3,263,835
Lemon Drop Kid, 1996, h., by Kingmambo	10	7	3,245,370
Behrens, 1994, h., by Pleasant Colony	9	7	3,243,500
Steinlen (GB), 1983, h., by Habitat	16	14	3,229,752
Captain Steve, 1997, h., by Fly So Free	8	7	3,228,356
Chief Bearhart, 1993, h., by Chief's Crown	12	9	3,219,017
Bertrando, 1989, h., by Skywalker	9	8	3,185,610
Free House, 1994, h., by Smokester	9	8	3,178,971
Sandpit (Brz), 1989, h., by Baynoun (Ire)	9	8	3,147,973
Paseana (Arg), 1987, m., by Ahmad	14	14	3,111,292
Gulch, 1984, h., by Mr. Prospector	13	11	3,095,521
Silverbulletday, 1996, m., by Silver Deputy	15	14	3,093,207
Concern, 1991, h., by Broad Brush	7	4	3,079,350
Lady's Secret, 1982, m., by Secretariat	25	22	3,021,325
Albert the Great, 1997, h., by Go for Gin	8	5	3,012,490
Victory Gallop, 1995, h., by Cryptoclearance	9	7	3,005,895
Alphabet Soup, 1991, h., by Cozzene	10	7	2,990,270
A.P. Indy, 1989, h., by Seattle Slew	8	6	2,979,815
Escena, 1993, m., by Strawberry Road (Aus)	11	7	2,962,639
Awad, 1990, h., by Caveat	14	11	2,949,179
Hansel, 1988, h., by Woodman	7	6	2,936,586
Sea Hero, 1990, h., by Polish Navy	6	3	2,929,869
Great Communicator, 1983, h., by Key to the Kingdom	14	9	2,922,615
Thunder Gulch, 1992, h., by Gulch	9	8	2,915,086
Farma Way, 1987, h., by Marfa	8	6	2,897,175
General Challenge, 1996, g., by General Meeting	9	8	2,876,018
With Approval, 1986, h., by Caro (Ire)	13	9	2,863,540
Marquetry, 1987, h., by Conquistador Cielo	9	7	2,844,942
Budroyale, 1993, g., by Cee's Tizzy	17	7	2,840,810
Theatrical (Ire), 1982, h., by Nureyev	7	7	2,840,500
Bayakoa (Arg), 1984, m., by Consultant's Bid	18	16	2,785,259
Banshee Breeze, 1995, m., by Unbridled	10	8	2,784,798
Spectacular Bid, 1976, h., by Bold Bidder	26	23	2,781,608
Buck's Boy, 1993, g., by Bucksplasher	16	9	2,750,148
Volponi, 1998, h., by Cryptoclearance	7	4	2,748,976
Beautiful Pleasure, 1995, m., by Maudlin	10	7	2,734,078
Forty Niner, 1985, h., by Mr. Prospector	11	9	2,726,000
Pleasant Tap, 1987, h., by Pleasant Colony	9	6	2,721,169

North American Leaders by Graded Stakes Earnings

Horse, year of birth, sex, sire	Years raced	Graded Stakes Wins	Graded Stakes Earnings
Skip Away, 1993, h., by Skip Trial	4	16	$9,548,100
Alysheba, 1984 h., by Alydar	3	10	6,616,417
Tiznow, 1997 h., by Cee's Tizzy	2	7	6,382,830
Cigar, 1990 h., by Palace Music	4	14	5,695,000
John Henry, 1975 g., by Ole Bob Bowers	8	30	4,953,417
Sunday Silence, 1986 h., by Halo	3	7	4,929,254
Easy Goer, 1986 h., by Alydar	3	12	4,775,280
Best Pal, 1988 g., by *Habitony	7	17	4,713,795
Silver Charm, 1994 h., by Silver Buck	4	10	4,416,619
Unbridled, 1987 h., by Fappiano	3	5	4,105,529
Awesome Again, 1994 h., by Deputy Minister	2	7	4,065,590
Point Given, 1998 h., by Thunder Gulch	2	8	3,930,900
Cat Thief, 1996 h., by Storm Cat	3	3	3,909,952
Devil His Due, 1989 h., by Devil's Bag	4	9	3,895,265
Spend a Buck, 1982 h., by Buckaroo	2	7	3,809,004
Creme Fraiche, 1982 h., by Rich Cream	6	14	3,689,091
Ferdinand, 1983 h., by Nijinsky II	4	7	3,619,978
Spain, 1997 m., by Thunder Gulch	4	7	3,490,307
Slew o' Gold, 1980 h., by Seattle Slew	3	8	3,454,694
War Emblem, 1999 c., by Our Emblem	2	4	3,425,000
Strike the Gold, 1988 h., by Alydar	4	4	3,391,210
Gentlemen (Arg), 1992 h., by Robin des Bois	3	8	3,324,140
Serena's Song, 1992 m., by Rahy	3	17	3,260,353
Behrens, 1994 h., by Pleasant Colony	4	7	3,204,500
Real Quiet, 1995 h., by Quiet American	3	5	3,195,740
Lemon Drop Kid, 1996 h., by Kingmambo	3	7	3,168,900
Cryptoclearance, 1984 h., by Fappiano	4	9	3,162,157
Snow Chief, 1983 h., by Reflected Glory	3	12	3,162,110
Free House, 1994 h., by Smokester	4	8	3,153,021
Precisionist, 1981 h., by Crozier	5	17	3,136,608
Black Tie Affair (Ire), 1986 h., by Miswaki	4	13	3,132,547
Bertrando, 1989 h., by Skywalker	5	8	3,131,320
Paseana (Arg), 1987 m., by Ahmad	5	14	3,074,292
Sandpit (Brz), 1989 h., by Baynoun (Ire)	4	8	3,066,480
Captain Steve, 1997 h., by Fly So Free	3	7	3,050,756
Gulch, 1984 h., by Mr. Prospector	3	11	3,049,671
Concern, 1991 h., by Broad Brush	3	4	3,004,530
Silverbulletday, 1996 m., by Silver Deputy	3	14	2,998,073
A.P. Indy, 1989 h., by Seattle Slew	2	6	2,952,340
Sky Classic, 1987 h., by Nijinsky II	4	13	2,942,152
Steinlen (GB), 1983 h., by Habitat	4	14	2,935,042
Hansel, 1988 h., by Woodman	2	6	2,926,986
Albert the Great, 1997 h., by Go for Gin	2	5	2,913,620
Escena, 1993 m., by Strawberry Road (Aus)	4	7	2,884,039
Victory Gallop, 1995 h., by Cryptoclearance	3	7	2,874,615
Alphabet Soup, 1991 h., by Cozzene	4	7	2,858,560

North American Leaders by Grade 1 Earnings

Horse, year of birth, sex, sire	Years raced	Grade 1 Stakes Wins	Grade 1 Stakes Earnings
Skip Away, 1993 h., by Skip Trial	4	16	$7,310,920
Alysheba, 1984 h., by Alydar	3	10	6,230,506
Tiznow, 1997 h., by Cee's Tizzy	2	7	5,815,400
Cigar, 1990 h., by Palace Music	4	14	5,660,000
Sunday Silence, 1986 h., by Halo	3	7	4,757,454
Easy Goer, 1986 h., by Alydar	3	12	4,606,980
John Henry, 1975 h., by Ole Bob Bowers	8	30	4,125,680
Unbridled, 1987 h., by Fappiano	3	5	4,039,360
Best Pal, 1988 g., by *Habitony	7	17	3,841,870
Point Given, 1998 h., by Thunder Gulch	2	8	3,718,300
Devil His Due, 1989 h., by Devil's Bag	4	9	3,466,000
Slew o' Gold, 1980 h., by Seattle Slew	3	8	3,420,314
Cat Thief, 1996 h., by Storm Cat	3	3	3,366,500
Ferdinand, 1983 h., by Nijinsky II	4	7	3,326,678
War Emblem, 1999 c., by Our Emblem	2	4	3,125,000
Awesome Again, 1994 h., by Deputy Minister	2	7	2,999,900
Real Quiet, 1995 h., by Quiet American	3	5	2,920,920
Creme Fraiche, 1982 h., by Rich Cream	6	14	2,897,068
Strike the Gold, 1988 h., by Alydar	4	4	2,800,876

Horse, year of birth, sex, sire	Years raced	Stakes Wins	Grade 1 Stakes Earnings
Paseana (Arg), 1987 m., by Ahmad	5	14	$2,753,942
A.P. Indy, 1989 h., by Seattle Slew	2	6	2,725,660
Theatrical (Ire), 1982 h., by Nureyev	3	7	2,724,040
Silver Charm, 1994 h., by Silver Buck	4	10	2,716,350
Gulch, 1984 h., by Mr. Prospector	3	11	2,683,496
Sea Hero, 1990 h., by Polish Navy	3	3	2,635,960
Lemon Drop Kid, 1996 h., by Kingmambo	3	7	2,630,400
Gentlemen (Arg), 1992 h., by Robin des Bois	3	8	2,610,000
Bet Twice, 1984 h., by Sportin' Life	3	7	2,573,337
Bertrando, 1989 h., by Skywalker	5	8	2,554,820
Fantastic Light, 1996 h., by Rahy	2	2	2,507,400
Spain, 1997 m., by Thunder Gulch	4	7	2,499,900
Beautiful Pleasure, 1995 m., by Maudlin	5	7	2,467,500
Sandpit (Brz), 1989 h., by Baynoun (Ire)	4	8	2,396,000
Concern, 1991 h., by Broad Brush	3	4	2,375,780
Bayakoa (Arg), 1984 m., by Consultant's Bid	4	16	2,345,509
Farma Way, 1987 h., by Marfa	3	6	2,340,000
Chief Bearhart, 1993 h., by Chief's Crown	4	9	2,321,000
Cryptoclearance, 1984 h., by Fappiano	4	9	2,317,732
Lady's Secret, 1982 m., by Secretariat	4	22	2,314,731
Banshee Breeze, 1995 m., by Unbridled	3	8	2,311,680
Daylami (Ire), 1994 h., by Doyoun	2	2	2,280,000
Serena's Song, 1992 m., by Rahy	3	17	2,244,400
Albert the Great, 1997 h., by Go for Gin	2	5	2,237,120
With Anticipation, 1995 g., by Relaunch	6	8	2,233,500
Free House, 1994 h., by Smokester	4	8	2,229,361
Hansel, 1988 h., by Woodman	2	6	2,226,466
Precisionist, 1981 h., by Crozier	5	17	2,207,810
Snow Chief, 1983 h., by Reflected Glory	3	12	2,181,590
Escena, 1993 m., by Strawberry Road (Aus)	4	7	2,172,000
Great Communicator, 1983 h., by Key to the Kingdom	6	9	2,162,000
Affirmed, 1975 h., by Exclusive Native	3	19	2,158,031
Volponi, 1998 h., by Cryptoclearance	3	4	2,156,000
Gate Dancer, 1981 h., by Sovereign Dancer	4	4	2,137,245

North American Leading Males by Turf Earnings

Horse, year of birth, sex, sire	Years raced	Stakes Wins	Turf Earnings
John Henry, 1975 g., by Ole Bob Bowers	8	30	$5,269,212
Steinlen (GB), 1983 h., by Habitat	5	16	3,229,752
Sky Classic, 1987 h., by Nijinsky II	4	13	3,176,638
Chief Bearhart, 1993 h., by Chief's Crown	4	9	3,164,509
Great Communicator, 1983 h., by Key to the Kingdom	6	9	2,908,485
Awad, 1990 h., by Caveat	7	11	2,871,645
Theatrical (Ire), 1982 h., by Nureyev	4	7	2,840,500
Sandpit (Brz), 1989 h., by Baynoun (Ire)	7	9	2,752,973
Manila, 1983 h., by Lyphard	3	10	2,676,299
Paradise Creek, 1989 h., by Irish River (Fr)	4	10	2,675,514
Fraise, 1988 h., by Strawberry Road (Aus)	4	6	2,613,105
Fantastic Light, 1996 h., by Rahy	4	8	2,507,400
Buck's Boy, 1993 g., by Bucksplasher	5	9	2,493,520
Lure, 1989 h., by Danzig	4	10	2,348,839
Quiet Resolve, 1995 g., by Affirmed	5	5	2,346,768
With Anticipation, 1995 g., by Relaunch	6	8	2,313,173
Daylami (Ire), 1994 h., by Doyoun	4	8	2,280,000
Marlin, 1993 h., by Sword Dance (Ire)	3	6	2,262,255
With Approval, 1986 h., by Caro (Ire)	3	9	2,254,760
Yankee Affair, 1982 h., by Northern Fling	5	15	2,204,524
Sunshine Forever, 1985 h., by Roberto	3	5	2,083,700
Kotashaan (Fr), 1988 h., by Darshaan	4	8	2,017,050
Star of Cozzene, 1988 h., by Cozzene	5	9	2,015,039
Bien Bien, 1989 h., by Manila	3	8	1,998,725
Majesty's Prince, 1979 h., by His Majesty	4	9	1,942,922
Ladies Din, 1995 g., by Din's Dancer	6	9	1,883,460
Itsallgreektome, 1987 g., by Sovereign Dancer	5	7	1,821,893
El Senor, 1984 h., by Valdez	5	6	1,767,245
Yagli, 1993 h., by Jade Hunter	5	6	1,702,121
Good Journey, 1996 h., by Nureyev	4	4	1,642,965
Val's Prince, 1992 g., by Eternal Prince	7	4	1,585,940
Da Hoss, 1992 g., by Gone West	4	8	1,559,780
John's Call, 1991 g., by Lord At War (Arg)	7	6	1,542,130
Fly Till Dawn, 1986 h., by Swing Till Dawn	5	7	1,536,150
Mecke, 1992 h., by Maudlin	4	9	1,522,080

North American Leading Females by Turf Earnings

Horse, year of birth, sex, sire	Years raced	Stakes Wins	Turf Earnings
Flawlessly, 1988 m., by Affirmed	5	15	$2,459,250
Perfect Sting, 1996 m., by Red Ransom	4	11	2,163,673
Estrapade, 1980 m., by *Vaguely Noble	4	10	1,789,600
Tout Charmant, 1996 m., by Slewvescent	5	7	1,607,219
Golden Apples (Ire), 1998 m., by Pivotal	2	5	1,601,680
Starine (Fr), 1997 m., by Mendocino	4	4	1,560,189
Miss Alleged, 1987 m., by Alleged	3	4	1,532,500
Happyanunoit (NZ), 1995 m., by Yachtie	4	5	1,481,892
Memories of Silver, 1993 m., by Silver Hawk	3	8	1,435,140
Tranquility Lake, 1995 m., by Rahy	4	9	1,420,770
Dance Smartly, 1988 m., by Danzig	3	10	1,412,650
Astra, 1996 m., by Theatrical (Ire)	4	8	1,378,424
Possibly Perfect, 1990 m., by Northern Baby	4	8	1,367,050
All Along (Fr), 1979 m., by Targowice	4	7	1,337,146
Tuzla (Fr), 1994 m., by Panoramic (GB)	4	8	1,266,079
Carotene, 1983 m., by Great Nephew	4	8	1,242,126
Brown Bess, 1982 m., by *Petrone	6	11	1,224,265
Soaring Softly, 1995 m., by Kris S.	3	5	1,193,450
Irish Linnet, 1988 m., by Seattle Song	6	13	1,191,980
Windsharp, 1991 m., by Lear Fan	4	6	1,191,600
Fieldy (Ire), 1983 m., by Northfields	6	14	1,182,530
Wandesta (GB), 1991 m., by Nashwan	4	6	1,170,650
Royal Heroine (Ire), 1980 m., by Lypheor (GB)	3	8	1,110,900
Bold Ruritana, 1990 m., by Bold Ruckus	6	10	1,102,790
Kostroma (Ire), 1986 m., by Caerleon	4	7	1,093,275
Banks Hill (GB), 1998 m., by Danehill	3	3	1,068,800
Maxzene, 1993 m., by Cozzene	3	7	1,067,587
Colstar, 1996 m., by Opening Verse	4	7	1,053,056
Janet (GB), 1997 m., by Emperor Jones	4	5	1,004,585

North American Leading Two-Year-Old Male Earners

Horse, year of birth, sex, sire	Starts	Wins	Stakes Wins	Earnings
Boston Harbor, 1994 h., by Capote	7	6	5	$1,928,605
Mountain Cat, 1990 h., by Storm Cat	8	6	5	1,460,627
Favorite Trick, 1995 h., by Phone Trick	8	8	7	1,231,998
Tejano, 1985 h., by Caro (Ire)	10	5	4	1,177,189
Best Pal, 1988 g., by *Habitony	8	6	5	1,026,195
Grand Canyon, 1987 h., by Fappiano	8	4	3	1,019,540
Snow Chief, 1983 h., by Reflected Glory	9	5	4	935,740
Timber Country, 1992 h., by Woodman	7	4	3	928,590
Chief's Crown, 1982 h., by Danzig	9	6	5	920,890
Fly So Free, 1988 h., by Time for a Change	6	4	2	872,580
Gilded Time, 1990 h., by Timeless Moment	4	4	3	855,980
Regal Classic, 1985 h., by Vice Regent	8	4	4	812,500
Roving Boy, 1980 h., by Olden Times	7	5	4	800,425
Macho Uno, 1998 h., by Holy Bull	4	3	2	768,803
Tasso, 1983 h., by Fappiano	7	5	3	761,534
Toccet, 2000 c., by Awesome Again	8	6	4	755,610
Fali Time, 1981 h., by Faliraki (Ire)	7	3	2	748,829
Captain Steve, 1997 h., by Fly So Free	8	4	3	744,880
Officer, 1999 c., by Bertrando	8	5	4	740,010
Success Express, 1985 h., by Hold Your Peace	8	4	3	737,207
Siphonic, 1999 c., by Siphon (Brz)	4	3	2	703,978
Easy Goer, 1986 h., by Alydar	6	4	2	697,500
Answer Lively, 1996 h., by Lively One	7	4	2	695,296
Bet Twice, 1984 h., by Sportin' Life	7	5	3	690,565
Vindication, 2000 c., by Seattle Slew	4	4	2	680,950
Spend a Buck, 1982 h., by Buckaroo	8	5	2	667,985
River Special, 1990 h., by Riverman	6	3	3	663,900
Capote, 1984 h., by Seattle Slew	4	3	2	654,680
Brocco, 1991 h., by Kris S.	4	3	1	653,550
Stephan's Odyssey, 1982 h., by Danzig	4	3	1	651,100
King Glorious, 1986 h., by Naevus	5	5	4	646,100
Forty Niner, 1985 h., by Mr. Prospector	6	5	4	634,908
Point Given, 1998 h., by Thunder Gulch	6	3	2	618,500
Swiss Yodeler, 1994 h., by Eastern Echo	9	6	5	617,200
Rhythm, 1987 h., by Mr. Prospector	5	3	1	612,920
Anees, 1997 h., by Unbridled	4	2	1	609,200
Music Merci, 1986 g., by Stop the Music	9	5	3	607,220
Is It True, 1986 h., by Raja Baba	6	2	1	605,342

North American Leading Two-Year-Old Female Earners

Horse, year of birth, sex, sire	Starts	Wins	Stakes Wins	Earnings
Silverbulletday, 1996 m., by Silver Deputy	7	6	5	$1,114,110
Countess Diana, 1995 m., by Deerhound	6	5	4	1,019,785
Meadow Star, 1988 m., by Meadowlake	7	7	6	992,250
Storm Flag Flying, 2000 f., by Storm Cat	4	4	3	967,000
Brave Raj, 1984 m., by Rajab	9	6	5	933,650
Storm Song, 1994 m., by Summer Squall	7	4	3	898,205
Outstandingly, 1982 m., by Exclusive Native	6	3	2	867,872
Eliza, 1990 m., by Mt. Livermore	5	4	3	808,00U
Family Style, 1983 m., by State Dinner	10	4	3	805,809
Flanders, 1992 m., by Seeking the Gold	5	4	3	805,000
Excellent Meeting, 1996 m., by General Meeting	8	4	3	773,824
Chilukki, 1997 m., by Cherokee Run	7	6	5	762,723
Phone Chatter, 1991 m., by Phone Trick	6	4	3	753,500
Open Mind, 1986 m., by Deputy Minister	6	4	3	724,064
Althea, 1981 m., by Alydar	9	5	4	692,625
Caressing, 1998 m., by Honour and Glory	5	3	2	690,642
Pleasant Stage, 1989 m., by Pleasant Colony	4	2	2	687,240
Surfside, 1997 m., by Seattle Slew	6	4	2	677,350
Golden Attraction, 1993 m., by Mr. Prospector	8	6	5	675,588
Tempera, 1999 f., by A.P. Indy	5	3	2	670,240
Cash Run, 1997 m., by Seeking the Gold	6	3	1	653,352
Twilight Ridge, 1983 m., by Cox's Ridge	5	3	2	617,808
My Flag, 1993 m., by Easy Goer	6	2	1	614,614
Raging Fever, 1998 m., by Storm Cat	6	5	4	598,500
Serena's Song, 1992 m., by Rahy	10	4	3	597,335
Boots 'n Jackie, 1990 m., by Major Moran	12	4	3	579,820
Tappiano, 1984 m., by Fappiano	5	4	3	572,820
Sacahuista, 1984 m., by Raja Baba	9	4	3	564,965
I'm Splendid, 1983 m., by Our Native	7	4	3	560,857
Go for Wand, 1987 m., by Deputy Minister	4	3	1	548,390
Cara Rafaela, 1993 m., by Quiet American	9	3	2	546,962
You, 1999 f., by You and I	6	3	2	540,440
Life's Magic, 1981 m., by Cox's Ridge	7	2	1	537,259
Epitome, 1985 m., by Summing	8	3	2	534,805
Sardula, 1991 m., by Storm Cat	5	3	2	532,545
Stella Madrid, 1987 m., by Alydar	7	4	3	519,096
Sharp Cat, 1994 m., by Storm Cat	7	4	3	505,950
Lost Kitty, 1985 m., by Magesterial	11	4	3	499,038
She's a Devil Due, 1998 m., by Devil His Due	5	4	2	495,320
Love Lock, 1995 m., by Silver Ghost	9	4	3	483,122
Career Collection, 1995 m., by General Meeting	8	4	3	482,005
Arewehavingfunyet, 1983 m., by Sham	9	5	5	475,730
Nancy's Glitter, 1995 m., by Glitterman	8	5	4	464,460
Lea Lucinda, 1986 m., by Secreto	9	3	2	459,962
Three Ring, 1996 m., by Notebook	5	3	2	458,440
Private Treasure, 1988 m., by Explodent	8	3	2	457,242
Tiltalating, 1982 m., by Tilt Up	10	4	3	454,944
Numbered Account, 1969 m., by Buckpasser	10	8	7	446,594
Ruling Angel, 1984 m., by Vice Regent	9	6	5	433,952
Goodbye Halo, 1985 m., by Halo	4	3	2	431,585
Composure, 2000 f., by Touch Gold	6	2	1	431,300
La Spia, 1989 m., by Capote	7	2	1	428,008
Stocks Up, 1986 m., by Kris S.	6	3	2	418,751
Ivanavinalot, 2000 f., by West Acre	6	5	3	418,300
La Prevoyante, 1970 m., by Buckpasser	12	12	10	417,109

North American Leading Three-Year-Old Male Earners in Single Season

Horse, year of birth, sex, sire	Starts	Wins	Stakes Wins	Earnings
Sunday Silence, 1986 h., by Halo	9	7	6	$4,578,454
Easy Goer, 1986 h., by Alydar	11	8	8	3,837,150
Unbridled, 1987 h., by Fappiano	11	4	3	3,718,149
Spend a Buck, 1982 h., by Buckaroo	7	5	5	3,552,704
War Emblem, 1999 c., by Our Emblem	10	5	4	3,455,000
Tiznow, 1997 h., by Cee's Tizzy	9	5	4	3,445,950
Point Given, 1998 h., by Thunder Gulch	7	6	6	3,350,000
Cat Thief, 1996 h., by Storm Cat	13	2	2	3,020,500
Skip Away, 1993 h., by Skip Trial	12	6	6	2,699,280
Thunder Gulch, 1992 h., by Gulch	10	7	7	2,644,080

Horse, year of birth, sex, sire	Starts	Wins	Stakes Wins	Earnings
A.P. Indy, 1989 h., by Seattle Slew	7	5	5	$2,622,560
Hansel, 1988 h., by Woodman	9	4	4	2,565,680
Concern, 1991 h., by Broad Brush	14	3	2	2,541,670
Alysheba, 1984 h., by Alydar	10	3	3	2,511,156
Izvestia, 1987 h., by Icecapade	11	8	8	2,486,667
Sea Hero, 1990 h., by Polish Navy	9	2	2	2,484,190
Medaglia d'Oro, 1999 c., by El Prado (Ire)	9	4	3	2,260,600
Tabasco Cat, 1991 h., by Storm Cat	12	5	5	2,164,334
Seeking the Gold, 1985 h., by Mr. Prospector	12	4	4	2,145,620
Holy Bull, 1991 h., by Great Above	10	8	8	2,095,000
Forty Niner, 1985 h., by Mr. Prospector	13	6	5	2,091,092
Sunshine Forever, 1985 h., by Roberto	12	8	5	2,032,636
Charismatic, 1996 h., by Summer Squall	10	4	3	2,007,404
Fusaichi Pegasus, 1997 h., by Mr. Prospector	8	6	4	1,987,800
Victory Gallop, 1995 h., by Cryptoclearance	8	3	3	1,981,720
Pine Bluff, 1989 h., by Danzig	6	3	3	1,970,896
Risen Star, 1985 h., by Secretariat	8	6	5	1,958,368
Proud Truth, 1982 h., by Graustark	11	7	5	1,926,327
Bet Twice, 1984 h., by Sportin' Life	9	3	3	1,922,642
Prized, 1986 h., by Kris S.	7	4	4	1,888,705
Captain Steve, 1997 h., by Fly So Free	11	3	3	1,882,276
Snow Chief, 1983 h., by Reflected Glory	9	6	6	1,875,200
Louis Quatorze, 1993 h., by Sovereign Dancer	12	4	2	1,854,908
Deputy Commander, 1994 h., by Deputy Minister	10	4	3	1,849,440
Manila, 1983 h., by Lyphard	10	8	6	1,814,729
Real Quiet, 1995 h., by Quiet American	6	2	2	1,788,800
With Approval, 1986 h., by Caro (Ire)	10	6	5	1,772,150
Coronado's Quest, 1995 h., by Forty Niner	11	5	5	1,739,950
Monarchos, 1998 h., by Maria's Mon	7	4	2	1,711,600
Menifee, 1996 h., by Harlan	9	3	2	1,695,400
General Challenge, 1996 g., by General Meeting	11	6	6	1,658,100
Silver Charm, 1994 h., by Silver Buck	7	3	3	1,638,750
Came Home, 1999 c., by Gone West	8	6	6	1,624,500
Java Gold, 1984 h., by Key to the Mint	8	6	4	1,621,300
Harlan's Holiday, 1999 c., by Harlan	10	3	3	1,606,000
Touch Gold, 1994 h., by Deputy Minister	7	4	3	1,522,313

North American Leading Three-Year-Old Female Earners in Single Season

Horse, year of birth, sex, sire	Starts	Wins	Stakes Wins	Earnings
Dance Smartly, 1988, m, by Danzig	8	8	8	$2,876,821
Spain, 1997, m, by Thunder Gulch	13	5	4	1,979,500
Silverbulletday, 1996, m, by Silver Deputy	11	8	8	1,707,640
Unbridled Elaine, 1998, m, by Unbridled's Song	8	4	3	1,663,175
Serena's Song, 1992, m, by Rahy	13	9	9	1,524,920
Banshee Breeze, 1995, m, by Unbridled	10	6	4	1,425,980
Take Charge Lady, 1999, f, by Dehere	10	6	6	1,388,635
Winning Colors, 1985, m, by Caro (Ire)	10	4	4	1,347,746
Farda Amiga, 1999, f, by Broad Brush	6	3	2	1,248,902
Surfside, 1997, m, by Seattle Slew	7	4	4	1,147,637
Open Mind, 1986, m, by Deputy Minister	11	8	8	1,120,308
Flute, 1998, m, by Seattle Slew	7	4	2	1,094,104
Dancethruthedawn, 1998, m, by Mr. Prospector	6	3	2	1,045,039
Xtra Heat, 1998, m, by Dixieland Heat	13	9	9	1,012,040
Lady's Secret, 1982, m, by Secretariat	17	10	10	994,349
Ajina, 1994, m, by Strawberry Road (Aus)	9	3	3	979,175
Jostle, 1997, m, by Brocco	9	4	4	975,570
Ryafan, 1994, m, by Lear Fan	3	3	3	968,000
Keeper Hill, 1995, m, by Deputy Minister	8	3	2	949,410
Very Subtle, 1984, m, by Hoist the Silver	12	6	4	947,135
My Flag, 1993, m, by Easy Goer	10	4	4	933,043
Sharp Cat, 1994, m, by Storm Cat	11	7	7	911,300
Exogenous, 1998, m, by Unbridled	7	4	4	901,500
Hollywood Wildcat, 1990, m, by Kris S.	9	5	5	893,330
You, 1999, f, by You and I	9	4	4	883,805
Life's Magic, 1981, m, by Cox's Ridge	12	4	4	873,956
Imperial Gesture, 1999, f, by Langfuhr	5	3	2	873,600
Blushing K. D., 1994, m, by Blushing John	8	6	6	845,040
Secret Status, 1997, m, by A.P. Indy	9	5	3	842,796
Go for Wand, 1987, m, by Deputy Minister	9	7	7	824,948
Life At the Top, 1983, m, by Seattle Slew	18	6	7	821,349
Lite Light, 1988, m, by Majestic Light	9	5	5	804,685

North American Leading Males Single-Season Earners at Age Four or Older

Horse, year of birth, sex, sire	Age	Starts	Wins	Stakes Wins	Earnings
Cigar, 1990 h., by Palace Music	5	10	10	9	$4,819,800
Skip Away, 1993 h., by Skip Trial	4	11	4	4	4,089,000
Awesome Again, 1994 h., by Deputy Minister	4	6	6	5	3,845,990
Alysheba, 1984 h., by Alydar	4	9	7	7	3,808,600
Tiznow, 1997 h., by Cee's Tizzy	4	6	3	3	2,981,880
Skip Away, 1993 h., by Skip Trial	5	9	7	7	2,740,000
Slew o' Gold, 1980 h., by Seattle Slew	4	6	5	4	2,627,944
Farma Way, 1987 h., by Marfa	4	11	5	5	2,598,350
Alphabet Soup, 1991 h., by Cozzene	5	7	4	4	2,536,450
Cigar, 1990 h., by Palace Music	6	7	4	4	2,510,000
Black Tie Affair (Ire), 1986 h., by Miswaki	5	10	7	7	2,483,540
Volponi, 1998 h., by Cryptoclearance	4	8	3	2	2,389,200
John Henry, 1975 g., by Ole Bob Bowers	9	9	6	6	2,336,650
Silver Charm, 1994 h., by Silver Buck	4	8	5	5	2,296,506
Criminal Type, 1985 h., by Alydar	5	11	7	6	2,270,290
Theatrical (Ire), 1982 h., by Nureyev	5	9	7	7	2,235,500
Bertrando, 1989 h., by Skywalker	4	9	3	3	2,217,800
Ferdinand, 1983 h., by Nijinsky II	4	10	4	4	2,185,150
Gentlemen (Arg), 1992 h., by Robin des Bois	5	6	4	4	2,125,300
Fantastic Light, 1996 h., by Rahy	5	1	1	1	2,112,800
Wild Again, 1980 h., by Icecapade	4	16	6	4	2,054,409
Daylami (Ire), 1994 h., by Doyoun	5	1	1	1	2,040,000
Great Communicator, 1983 h., by Key to the Kingdom	5	11	6	6	2,017,950
Chief Bearhart, 1993 h., by Chief's Crown	4	7	5	5	2,011,259
Festin (Arg), 1986 h., by Mat-Boy (Arg)	5	11	3	3	2,003,250
Kotashaan (Fr), 1988 h., by Darshaan	5	9	6	6	1,984,100
Pleasant Tap, 1987 h., by Pleasant Colony	5	10	4	4	1,959,914
Devil His Due, 1989 h., by Devil's Bag	4	11	4	4	1,939,120
Paradise Creek, 1989 h., by Irish River (Fr)	5	10	8	8	1,920,872
Strike the Gold, 1988 h., by Alydar	4	13	2	2	1,920,176
Buck's Boy, 1993 g., by Bucksplasher	5	10	6	6	1,874,020
Skywalker, 1982 h., by Relaunch	4	9	4	4	1,811,400
John Henry, 1975 g., by Ole Bob Bowers	6	10	8	8	1,798,030
Albert the Great, 1997 h., by Go for Gin	4	9	3	3	1,740,000
Budroyale, 1993 g., by Cee's Tizzy	6	11	4	4	1,735,640
Sky Classic, 1987 h., by Nijinsky II	5	9	5	5	1,735,482
Behrens, 1994 h., by Pleasant Colony	5	9	4	4	1,735,000
Lemon Drop Kid, 1996 h., by Kingmambo	4	9	5	4	1,673,900
Best Pal, 1988 g., by *Habitony	4	5	4	4	1,672,000
Star of Cozzene, 1988 h., by Cozzene	5	11	6	6	1,620,744

North American Leading Females Single-Season Earners at Age Four or Older

Horse, year of birth, sex, sire	Age	Starts	Wins	Stakes Wins	Earnings
Azeri, 1998 m., by Jade Hunter	4	9	8	7	$2,181,540
Escena, 1993 m., by Strawberry Road (Aus)	5	9	5	5	2,032,425
Lady's Secret, 1982 m., by Secretariat	4	15	10	10	1,871,053
Beautiful Pleasure, 1995 m., by Maudlin	4	7	4	3	1,716,404
Paseana (Arg), 1987 m., by Ahmad	5	9	7	7	1,518,290
Bayakoa (Arg), 1984 m., by Consultant's Bid	5	11	9	8	1,406,403
Riboletta (Brz), 1995 m., by Roi Normand	5	11	7	7	1,384,860
Perfect Sting, 1996 m., by Red Ransom	4	6	5	5	1,367,000
Banshee Breeze, 1995 m., by Unbridled	4	7	4	4	1,358,818
Miss Alleged, 1987 m., by Alleged	4	3	2	2	1,345,000
Heritage of Gold, 1995 m., by Gold Legend	5	8	5	5	1,332,282
Bayakoa (Arg), 1984 m., by Consultant's Bid	6	10	7	7	1,234,406
Personal Ensign, 1984 m., by Private Account	4	7	7	7	1,202,640
Soaring Softly, 1995 m., by Kris S.	4	8	7	5	1,193,450
Estrapade, 1980 m., by *Vaguely Noble	6	9	3	3	1,184,800
Serena's Song, 1992 m., by Rahy	4	15	5	5	1,161,133
Inside Information, 1991 m., by Private Account	4	8	7	6	1,160,408
Jewel Princess, 1992 m., by Key to the Mint	4	9	5	5	1,150,800
Golden Apples (Ire), 1998 m., by Pivotal	4	7	3	3	1,111,680
Tout Charmant, 1996 m., by Slewvescent	4	7	3	3	1,089,044
Royal Heroine (Ire), 1980 m., by Lypheor (GB)	4	8	4	4	1,023,500
Summer Colony, 1998 m., by Summer Squall	4	8	4	4	992,500

Horse, year of birth, sex, sire	Age	Starts	Wins	Stakes Wins	Earnings
Safely Kept, 1986 m., by Horatius	4	10	8	7	$959,280
Paseana (Arg), 1987 m., by Ahmad	6	8	3	3	950,402
Manistique, 1995 m., by Unbridled	4	9	6	6	935,100
Lu Ravi, 1995 m., by A.P. Indy	5	8	3	3	918,200
Pebbles (GB), 1981 m., by Sharpen Up (GB)	4	1	1	1	900,000
Heavenly Prize, 1991 m., by Seeking the Gold	4	7	4	4	895,900
Tuzla (Fr), 1994 m., by Panoramic (GB)	5	8	4	4	889,080
Flawlessly, 1988 m., by Affirmed	5	5	4	4	886,700
Spook Express (SAf), 1994 m., by Comic Blush	7	8	3	3	866,870
Happyanunoit (NZ), 1995 m., by Yachtie	4	8	4	3	862,792
Princess Rooney, 1980 m., by Verbatim	4	9	6	5	854,791
Heritage of Gold, 1995 m., by Gold Legend	4	10	6	5	853,680
North Sider, 1982 m., by Topsider	5	17	7	6	847,107
Life's Magic, 1981 m., by Cox's Ridge	4	13	2	2	844,003
Different (Arg), 1992 m., by Candy Stripes	5	4	3	3	839,290
One Dreamer, 1988 m., by Relaunch	6	8	4	4	837,730
Spain, 1997 m., by Thunder Gulch	4	9	1	1	837,705
Starine (Fr), 1997 m., by Mendocino	5	4	1	1	820,600
All Along (Fr), 1979 m., by Targowice	4	3	3	3	813,631
Fiji (GB), 1994 m., by Rainbow Quest	4	7	6	4	805,560
Claire Marine (Ire), 1985 m., by What A Guest	4	12	7	6	801,565

Leading Winners of Stakes Races in North America

Horse, Sex, YOB	Wins	Graded SWs	SWs	Earnings
Exterminator, g., 1915	50	0	34	$221,227
Native Diver, h., 1959	37	0	33	1,026,500
Kelso, g., 1957	39	0	31	1,977,896
Round Table, h., 1954	43	0	31	1,749,869
John Henry, g., 1975	39	25	30	6,591,860
Who Doctor Who, g., 1983	33	1	26	813,870
Little Bold John, g., 1982	38	5	25	1,956,406
Stymie, h., 1941	35	0	25	918,485
Forego, g., 1970	34	23	24	1,938,957
Susan's Girl, m., 1969	29	13	24	1,251,668
Spectacular Bid, h., 1976	26	21	23	2,781,608
Xtra Heat, m., 1998	24	10	23	2,039,635
Citation, h., 1945	32	3	22	1,085,760
Curribot, g., 1977	37	0	22	491,527
Lady's Secret, m., 1982	25	15	22	3,021,325
Royal Harmony, h., 1964	38	0	22	587,164
Safely Kept, m., 1986	24	12	22	2,194,206
Swoon's Son, h., 1953	30	0	22	970,605
Buckpasser, h., 1963	25	0	21	1,462,014
Frost King, h., 1978	26	2	21	1,033,260
Rosy Way, g., 1989	28	0	21	97,389
Special Hank, h., 1977	13	0	21	81,435
Amadevil, h., 1974	33	0	20	653,534
Ancient Title, h., 1970	24	17	20	1,252,791
Chilcoton Blaze, h., 1980	31	0	20	490,862
Hidden Treasure, h., 1957	24	0	20	187,734
Judy's Red Shoes, m., 1983	25	1	20	1,085,668
Affirmed, h., 1975	22	18	19	2,393,818
Armed, g., 1941	41	0	19	817,475
Delta Colleen, m., 1985	23	0	19	810,798
Nashua, h., 1952	22	2	19	1,288,565
Police Inspector, h., 1977	25	1	19	713,707
Rapido Dom, h., 1978	25	0	19	466,974
Scott's Scoundrel, h., 1992	22	2	19	1,270,052
Spirit of Fighter, m., 1983	33	0	19	847,454
Affectionately, m., 1960	28	0	18	546,659
Arctic Laur, h., 1988	21	0	18	634,809
Cicada, m., 1959	23	2	18	783,674
Copper Case, g., 1977	33	0	18	365,374
Decathlon, h., 1953	25	0	18	269,530
Dixie Poker Ace, g., 1987	27	0	18	850,126
Energetic King, h., 1979	35	0	18	765,776
Fantango Lady, m., 1994	22	0	18	279,295
In Rem, g., 1975	21	0	18	307,742
Orphan Kist, m., 1984	28	0	18	631,997
Overskate, h., 1975	24	3	18	791,634
Say Florida Sandy, h., 1994	31	5	18	1,988,806
Timely Ruckus, g., 1993	24	0	18	589,964
Twixt, m., 1969	26	7	18	619,141

North American Leading Runners by Most Stakes Placings

Horse, sex, YOB	Wins	Stakes Wins	Stakes Placings	Earnings
Find, g., 1950	22	13	38	$803,615
Stymie, h., 1941	35	25	38	918,485
Pampas Host, h., 1972	19	13	32	310,922
Major Presto, g., 1963	24	12	30	125,694
Tick Tock, g., 1953	20	10	30	386,951
Alerted, h., 1948	20	12	29	440,485
Orphan Kist, m., 1984	28	18	28	631,997
Talent Show, g., 1955	16	7	28	507,038
Gene's Lady, m., 1981	14	10	27	946,190
Royal Harmony, h., 1964	38	22	27	587,164
Ruhe, g., 1948	11	6	27	294,490
Gallorette, m., 1942	21	13	26	445,535
Love Your Host, h., 1966	22	16	26	160,683
*Grey Monarch, h., 1955	13	7	25	216,146
Creme Fraiche, h., 1982	17	14	25	4,024,727
Delegate, g., 1944	31	15	25	277,530
Delta Colleen, m., 1985	23	19	25	810,798
Military Hawk, g., 1987	18	12	25	686,128
Nostalgia's Star, h., 1982	9	7	25	2,154,827
Special Intent, h., 1981	30	17	25	438,558
Stranglehold, g., 1949	25	9	25	289,190
Fiftieth Star, h., 1972	19	6	24	167,035
Armed, g., 1941	41	19	23	817,475
Double B Express, g., 1975	31	13	23	246,013
Eddie Schmidt, h., 1953	20	12	23	526,292
Fourstardave, g., 1985	21	13	23	1,636,737
In the Curl, m., 1984	26	10	23	749,891
Ky Alta, h., 1977	14	9	23	313,885
On Trust, h., 1944	23	11	23	554,145
Straight Deal, m., 1962	21	13	23	733,020
Arctic Laur, h., 1988	21	18	22	634,809
Buzfuz, g., 1942	35	11	22	286,740
Chompion, h., 1965	14	10	22	604,401
Foncier, h., 1976	29	17	22	323,515
Homebuilder, h., 1984	11	8	22	1,172,153
Honor Medal, h., 1981	19	9	22	1,347,073
Judy's Red Shoes, m., 1983	25	20	22	1,085,668
Lucky Salvation, h., 1980	22	5	22	467,891
Ruler's Whirl, h., 1966	27	8	22	116,354
Sir Bear, g., 1993	19	11	22	2,538,422
Susan's Girl, m., 1969	29	24	22	1,251,668
Adventuresome Love, h., 1986	16	9	21	436,244
Bye and Near, h., 1963	21	10	21	202,040
Charlie Chalmers, g., 1985	9	6	21	378,715
Dixie Poker Ace, g., 1987	27	18	21	850,126
First Fiddle, h., 1939	23	10	21	398,610
Fort Marcy, g., 1964	21	16	21	1,109,791
Kent Green, g., 1983	13	8	21	395,469
King's Swan, h., 1980	31	12	21	1,924,845
Pongo Boy, g., 1992	22	12	21	776,184
Say Florida Sandy, h., 1994	31	18	21	1,988,806

Leading Winners of Grade 1 Races in North America

Horse, Sex, YOB	Grade 1 Wins	SWs	SWs	Earnings
John Henry, g., 1975	39	16	30	$6,591,860
Affirmed, h., 1975	22	14	19	2,393,818
Forego, g., 1970	34	14	24	1,938,957
Spectacular Bid, h., 1976	26	13	23	2,781,608
Bayakoa (Arg), m., 1984	18	12	16	2,785,259
Cigar, h., 1990	18	11	14	7,599,815
Lady's Secret, m., 1982	25	11	22	3,021,325
Serena's Song, m., 1992	18	11	17	3,283,388
Paseana (Arg), m., 1987	14	10	14	3,111,292
Skip Away, h., 1993	18	10	16	9,616,360
Alysheba, h., 1984	11	9	10	6,679,242
Easy Goer, h., 1986	14	9	12	4,873,770
Flawlessly, m., 1988	16	9	15	2,572,536
Sky Beauty, m., 1990	15	9	13	1,336,000

Horse, Sex, YOB	Grade 1 Wins	SWs	SWs	Earnings
Susan's Girl, m., 1969	29	8	24	$1,251,668
Chief's Crown, h., 1982	12	8	10	2,191,168
Heavenly Prize, m., 1991	9	8	8	1,825,940
Personal Ensign, m., 1984	13	8	10	1,679,880
Seattle Slew, h., 1974	14	8	9	1,208,726
Creme Fraiche, h., 1982	17	7	14	4,024,727
Exceller, h., 1973	8	7	8	1,125,772
Foolish Pleasure, h., 1972	16	7	12	1,216,705
Go for Wand, m., 1987	10	7	8	1,373,338
Goodbye Halo, m., 1985	11	7	10	1,706,702
Gulch, h., 1984	13	7	11	3,095,521
Honest Pleasure, h., 1973	12	7	9	839,997
Open Mind, m., 1986	12	7	11	1,844,372
Sharp Cat, m., 1994	15	7	14	2,032,575
Slew o' Gold, h., 1980	12	7	8	3,533,534
Alydar, h., 1975	14	6	11	957,195
Beautiful Pleasure, m., 1995	10	6	7	2,734,078
Best Pal, g., 1988	18	6	17	5,668,245
Bold 'n Determined, m., 1977	16	6	11	949,599
Desert Vixen, m., 1970	13	6	9	421,538
Holy Bull, h., 1991	13	6	11	2,481,760
Inside Information, m., 1991	14	6	9	1,641,806
Meadow Star, m., 1988	11	6	10	1,445,740
Miss Oceana, m., 1981	11	6	9	1,010,385
Optimistic Gal, m., 1973	13	6	10	686,861
Point Given, h., 1998	9	6	8	3,968,500
Possibly Perfect, m., 1990	11	6	8	1,367,050
Precisionist, h., 1981	20	6	17	3,485,398
Snow Chief, h., 1983	13	6	12	3,383,210
Sunday Silence, h., 1986	9	6	7	4,968,554
Theatrical (Ire), h., 1982	7	6	7	2,840,500

Leading Winners of Graded Stakes in North America

Horse, Sex, YOB	Graded Wins	SWs	SWs	Earnings
John Henry, g., 1975	39	25	30	$6,591,860
Forego, g., 1970	34	23	24	1,938,957
Spectacular Bid, h., 1976	26	21	23	2,781,608
Affirmed, h., 1975	22	18	19	2,393,818
Ancient Title, h., 1970	24	17	20	1,252,791
Serena's Song, m., 1992	18	17	17	3,283,388
Skip Away, h., 1993	18	16	16	9,616,360
Bayakoa (Arg), m., 1984	18	15	16	2,785,259
Lady's Secret, m., 1982	25	15	22	3,021,325
Paseana (Arg), m., 1987	14	14	14	3,111,292
Flawlessly, m., 1988	16	13	15	2,572,536
Precisionist, h., 1981	20	13	17	3,485,398
Silverbulletday, m., 1996	15	13	14	3,093,207
Sky Beauty, m., 1990	15	13	13	1,336,000
Best Pal, g., 1988	18	12	17	5,668,245
Sabin, m., 1980	18	12	14	1,098,341
Safely Kept, m., 1986	24	12	22	2,194,206
Sharp Cat, m., 1994	15	12	14	2,032,575
Steinlen (GB), h., 1983	16	12	14	3,229,752
Susan's Girl, m., 1969	29	12	24	1,251,668
Black Tie Affair (Ire), h., 1986	18	11	13	3,370,694
Cigar, h., 1990	18	11	14	7,599,815
Creme Fraiche, h., 1982	17	11	14	4,024,727
Foolish Pleasure, h., 1972	16	11	12	1,216,705
Gulch, h., 1984	13	11	11	3,095,521
Housebuster, h., 1987	15	11	14	1,229,696
Royal Glint, h., 1970	21	11	15	1,004,816
Alysheba, h., 1984	11	10	10	6,679,242
Easy Goer, h., 1986	14	10	12	4,873,770
Goodbye Halo, m., 1985	11	10	10	1,706,702
King's Swan, h., 1980	31	10	12	1,924,845
Lure, h., 1989	14	10	10	2,515,289
Optimistic Gal, m., 1973	13	10	10	686,861
Personal Ensign, m., 1984	13	10	10	1,679,880
Silver Charm, h., 1994	11	10	10	4,444,369
Sir Bear, g., 1993	19	10	11	2,538,422
Xtra Heat, m., 1998	24	10	23	2,039,635

North American Leading Runners by Most Stakes Placings Without a Stakes Win

Horse, year of birth, sex, sire	Years Raced	Starts	Wins	Stakes Plcgs	Earnings
Stunning Native, 1978, m, by Our Native	3	35	3	13	$155,312
Grand Galop, 1962, g, by Victoria Park	7	119	20	12	115,744
Blue Trumpeter, 1949, h, by Thumbs Up	6	106	15	11	120,912
Gat's Girl, 1975, m, by Lurullah	5	70	6	11	119,242
Mistress Fletcher, 1992, m, by Sovereign Don	6	71	9	11	260,638
Aces Court, 1981, m, by Know Your Aces	6	75	8	10	112,740
Behind the Scenes, 1984, m, by Hurry Up Blue	4	41	7	10	331,045
Big Numbers, 1997, h, by Numerous	4	37	5	10	305,939
Dance Play, 1988, m, by Sovereign Dancer	3	42	4	10	168,431
Distinctive Moon, 1979, m, by Distinctive	3	36	4	10	124,086
Hold the Reins, 1977, h, by Northern Fling	10	186	18	10	175,528
Ladies Agreement, 1970, m, by Royal Union	5	68	14	10	295,193
Little Buckles, 1991, m, by Buckley Boy	5	43	9	10	466,755
Lonny's Secret, 1966, h, by Terrang	4	38	6	10	107,542
Lotta Tike, 1974, m, by Skin Head	5	58	10	10	91,760
March of Kings, 1993, g, by River of Kings (Ire)	8	90	15	10	486,258
Patti L., 1987, m, by Lyphard's Wish (Fr)	5	55	9	10	211,995
Rebridled, 1994, g, by Unbridled	6	60	11	10	424,690
Rule by Reason, 1967, h, by Hail to Reason	5	91	15	10	263,547
Sweets, 1985, g, by Mr. Redoy	8	85	8	10	196,524
Vaunted Vamp, 1992, m, by Racing Star	6	78	21	10	419,641

Winningest Horses of All Time
Through 2002

Horse, year of birth, sex, sire	Starts	Wins	Earnings
Kingston, 1884, h, by Spendthrift	138	89	$140,195
Bankrupt, 1883, g, by Spendthrift	348	86	41,260
King Crab, 1885, g, by Kingfisher	310	85	55,682
Little Minch, 1880, h, by Glenelg	222	85	58,225
Hiblaze, 1935, h, by Blazes	406	79	32,647
Tippity Witchet, 1915, g, by Broomstick	265	78	88,241
Pan Zareta, 1910, m, by Abe Frank	151	76	39,082
Badge, 1885, h, by *Ill-Used	167	70	73,253
Raceland, 1885, g, by *Billet	130	70	116,391
Care Free, 1918, g, by Colin	227	67	59,873
Welsh Lad, 1934, g, by Prince of Wales	329	67	25,317
Shot One, 1941, g, by Shoeless Joe	360	65	29,982
Worthowning, 1935, g, by *Longworth	339	63	41,830
Back Bay, 1908, g, by Rubicon	289	62	40,377
Banquet, 1887, g, by *Rayon d'Or	166	62	118,872
Ed R., 1948, g, by Donnay	248	62	63,552
Imp, 1894, f, by *Wagner	171	62	70,069
Leochares, 1910, g, by Broomstick	175	62	68,867
Seth's Hope, 1924, h, by Seth	327	62	74,341
Vantime, 1939, g, by Playtime	295	62	46,290
Brandon Prince, 1929, h, by *Axenstein	280	61	47,287
Irene's Bob, 1929, h, by The Turk	237	61	58,010
Kenilworth, 1898, h., by *Sir Modred	163	61	31,270
Molasses Bill, 1933, g, by *Challenger II	262	61	50,699
Mucho Gusto, 1932, h, by Marvin May	217	61	101,880
Shuchor, 1910, g, by Haste	261	61	33,607
Vantryst, 1936, h, by Tryster	334	61	31,971
Frank Fogarty, 1918, g, by Wrack	270	60	47,651
George de Mar, 1922, h, by *Colonel Vennie	333	60	69,091
Indiantown, 1930, h, by Trojan	224	60	55,455
Lewis A. D., 1947, h, by Galway	212	60	65,482
Noah's Pride, 1929, g, by Noah	317	60	41,507
Parole, 1873, g, by Leamington	127	59	82,111
Strathmeath, 1888, g, by Strathmore	133	59	114,958
Charlie Boy, 1955, h, by Graphic	241	58	207,642
Flag Bearer, 1926, h, by *Porte Drapeau	222	58	37,683
Golden Arrow, 1961, h, by Fort Salonga	176	58	167,264
Top o' the Morning, 1912, c, by Peep o'Day	217	58	48,120
Columcille, 1948, h, by Alaking	182	57	89,665
El Puma, 1929, h, by *Spanish Prince II	242	57	44,807
End of Street, 1963, h, by Bunty's Flight	202	57	67,686

Horse, year of birth, sex, sire	Starts	Wins	Earnings
Bulwark, 1933, h, by *Bull Dog	252	56	$65,125
Matchup, 1936, h, by Misstep	229	55	58,528
Tommy Whelan, 1936, g, by Enoch	233	55	33,279
Vote Boy, 1932, g, by Torchilla	304	55	39,240
Argos, 1937, g, by *Happy Argo	215	54	37,507
Bee Golly, 1942, m, by Bee Line	183	53	54,544
Crying for More, 1965, h, by I'm For More	192	53	183,685
Door Prize, 1952, g, by Eight Thirty	131	53	109,920
Hamburger Jim, 1928, h, by Whiskaway	212	53	24,383
Onus, 1933, g, by Jack High	344	53	32,039
Post War Style, 1941, m, by Burgoo King	179	53	52,600
Agrarian-U, 1942, g, by Agrarian	236	52	199,345
Alviso, 1932, h, by *Hand Grenade	193	52	41,898
Billy Brier, 1953, g, by Bunty Lawless	231	52	83,168
Cloudy Weather, 1934, g, by Mud	294	52	53,487
Fleet Argo, 1947, g, by *Happy Argo	243	52	149,000
Float Away, 1936, g, by Whiskaway	265	52	61,365
My Blaze, 1930, h, by Big Blaze	338	52	32,707
Old Kickapoo, 1924, h, by Runnymede	217	52	35,827
Port Conway Lane, 1969, h, by Bold Commander	242	52	431,593
Air Patrol, 1941, h, by Sun Teddy	146	51	163,100
Blenweed, 1938, g, by *Blenheim II	202	51	105,415
Commendable, 1935, g, by Insco	163	51	30,583
Dr. Johnson, 1940, h, by *Boswell	256	51	54,422
Estin, 1923, g, by Westy Hogan	205	51	46,901
Gay Parisian, 1924, g, by *Parisian Diamond	209	51	49,197
Sagely, 1970, h, by Sage and Sand	124	51	116,196
Small Change, 1930, h, by Aromatic	200	51	18,495
Talked About, 1934, h, by The Porter	235	51	49,447

Most Consecutive Victories

Camarero, an unfamiliar name to almost all racing fans, holds the record for the most consecutive victories by a Thoroughbred. His 56 straight wins were not registered in the sport's sometimes murky and poorly documented distant past, however. He raced in the 1950s, going undefeated until his 57th career start. All of his races were in Puerto Rico and were against other Puerto Rican-bred horses. Camarero broke the win mark set by undefeated Kincsem, a Hungarian-bred mare who raced in the late 19th century. Boston made the list of most consecutive wins twice, with 19 wins from 1839-'42 and 17 straight wins from 1836-'38.

Citation and Cigar share the modern record for most consecutive victories, 16, along with Louisiana-bred mare Hallowed Dreams, who won many of her races against overmatched state-breds. Citation and Cigar competed at the highest level of the sport in North America while compiling their win skeins.

Cons. Wins	Horse	Year of Birth	Where Raced
56	Camarero	1951	Puerto Rico
54	Kincsem	1874	Europe, England
39	Galgo Jr.	1928	Puerto Rico
23	Leviathan	1793	United States
22	Miss Petty	1981	Australia
	Pooker T.	1957	Puerto Rico
21	Bond's First Consul	1798	United States
	Lottery	1803	United States
	Meteor	1783	England
	Picnic in the Park	1979	Australia
20	Filch	1773	Ireland

	Fashion	1837	United States
	Kentucky	1861	United States
19	Boston	1833	United States
	Skiff	1821	Scotland
18	Hindoo	1878	United States
	Karayel	1970	Turkey
17	Alice Hawthorn	1838	England
	Beeswing	1835	United States
	Boston	1833	United States
	Careless	1751	England
	Dudley	1914	England
	Gradisco	1957	Venezuela
	Harkaway	1834	Ireland
	Hanover	1884	United States
	Mainbrace	1947	New Zealand
	Sir Ken	1947	England
16	Cigar	1990	United States
	Citation	1945	United States
	Hallowed Dreams	1997	United States
	Luke Blackburn	1877	United States
	Master Bagot	1787	Ireland
	Minimo	1968	Turkey
	Miss Woodford	1880	United States
	Mister Frisky	1987	Puerto Rico, United States
	*Ormonde	1883	England
	Prestige	1903	France
	*Ribot	1952	Europe, England
	The Bard	1883	England
15	Bayardo	1906	England
	*Bernborough	1939	Australia
	Brigadier Gerard	1968	England
	Buckpasser	1963	United States
	Carbine	1885	New Zealand, Australia
	Colin	1905	United States
	Macon	1922	Argentina
	Pretty Polly	1901	England, France
	Rattler	1816	United States
	Squanderer	1973	India
	Thebais	1878	England
	Vander Pool	1928	United States
14	Friponnier	1864	England
	Harry Bassett	1868	United States
	Lucifer	1813	Scotland
	Man o' War	1917	United States
	Nearco	1935	Europe
	*Phar Lap	1926	New Zealand, Australia, Mexico
	*Prince Charlie	1869	England
	Springfield	1873	England
13	Dungannon	1780	England
	Effie Deans	1815	England
	Grano de Oro	1937	Ireland, Venezuela
	Hippolitus	1767	Ireland
	Kingston	1884	United States
	Limerick	1923	New Zealand, Australia
	Personal Ensign	1984	United States
	Phenomenom	1780	England
	Planet	1855	United States
	Polar Star	1904	England
	Rockingham	1781	England
	Sweet Wall	1925	Ireland
	The Flying Dutchman	1846	England
	Timoleon	1814	United States
	Tremont	1884	United States
	Weimar	1968	Italy

Leading Unbeaten Racehorses

A rare breed indeed is the racehorse that completes its career without a defeat on its record. No modern horse can ever expect to equal the

record of Kincsem, who went unbeaten in 54 starts over five racing seasons in Hungary. Although her pedigree was largely English, she was bred in Hungary; her name derives from the Magyar "kincs," which means treasure or jewel. The word itself means "my treasure," and she indeed was a jewel.

The most recent jewel to rival Kincsem's luminescence was Ogden Phipps's Personal Ensign, who retired with a perfect record in 13 starts after refusing to be beaten by Winning Colors in the 1988 Breeders' Cup Distaff (G1) at Churchill Downs.

Following are some of the best-known horses who have retired unbeaten after careers at the top levels of their divisions. Eclipse's record, in particular, is worth noting because 18th-century records are unreliable. He is attributed in various sources with anywhere from ten to 18 victories. In this listing, he is assigned the highest number, and the one fact for certain is that he never was beaten.

54 Kincsem, 1874 m., Cambuscan—Waternymph, by Cotswold

18 Eclipse, 1764 h., Marske—Spiletta, by Regulus

16 *Ormonde, 1883 h., Bend Or—Lily Agnes, by Macaroni

   *Ribot, 1952 h., Tenerani—Romanella, by El Greco

15 Colin, 1905 h., Commando—*Pastorella, by Springfield

14 Nearco, 1935 h., Pharos—Nogara, by Havresac II

13 Personal Ensign, 1984 m., Private Account—Grecian Banner, by Hoist the Flag

   Tremont, 1884 h., Virgil—Ann Fief, by Alarm

12 Asteroid, 1861 h., Lexington—Nebula, by *Glencoe

   Barcaldine, 1878 h., Solon—Ballyroe, by Belladrum

   Crucifix, 1837 m., *Priam—Octaviana, by Octavian

9 *Bahram, 1932 h., Blandford—Friar's Daughter, by Friar Marcus

   St. Simon, 1881 h., Galopin—St. Angela, by King Tom

8 American Eclipse, 1814 h., Duroc—Millers Damsel, by *Messenger

   Rare Brick, 1983 h., Rare Performer—Windy Brick, by Mr. Brick

   Sensation, 1877, h., *Leamington—Susan Beane, by Lexington

7 El Rio Rey, 1887 h., Norfolk—Marian, by Malcolm

   Regulus, 1739 h., Godolphin Arabian—Grey Robinson, by Bald Galloway

   The Tetrarch, 1911 h., Roi Herode—Vahren, by Bona Vista

5 Ajax, 1901 h., Flying Fox—Amie, by Clamart

   Bay Middleton, 1833 h., Sultan—Cobweb, by Phantom

   Landaluce, 1980 f., Seattle Slew—Strip Poker, by Bold Bidder

   Norfolk, 1861 h., Lexington—Novice, by *Glencoe

4   **Golden Fleece,** 1979 h., Nijinsky II—Exotic Treat,
     by *Vaguely Noble
     Lammtarra, 1992 h., Nijinsky II—Snow Bride, by
     Blushing Groom (Fr)
     Raise a Native, 1961 h., Native Dancer—Raise
     You, by Case Ace

Losingest Horses
of All Time
(Without a Win)

Thrust, a chestnut gelding by Bold Salute
out of Stitching, by Sting, had very little thrust
and lost 105 consecutive races before retiring
from the field of battle in 1956.

Thrust finished second five times and was
third on seven occasions, with career earnings
of $8,180.

Zippy Chippy, a foal of 1991, for now is notable
only for the length of time he has tried and failed.
He began his tenth racing season in 2003, a longer
career than any other horse with more than 58
defeats. Following is a list of the sport's leading
losers since 1930 through May 2003.

Through 2002

Losses	Horse, YOB	Raced	Earnings
105	Thrust, 1950	5	$8,180
97	Zippy Chippy, 1991	10	30,034
92	Star Time, 1943	5	7,215
89	Good Get, 1940	5	2,805
86	Fagrace, 1943	5	6,200
85	Maker of Trouble, 1922	4	565
84	Western Holiday, 1929	5	620
83	City Limit, 1934	5	1,105
82	Giant's Heel, 1943	6	1,560
82	Master Mark, 1941	6	290
81	Jibberty Bell, 1955	4	4,802
79	Omashane, 1942	5	1,475
79	Arvella, 1957	4	2,531
77	Fred Whitham, 1925	7	1,100
77	Space, 1942	5	3,070
76	Prima Whisk, 1936	4	670
76	Sure Its Legal, 1988	5	9,772
75	War Bull, 1980	4	10,568
73	Gray Leaves, 1961	4	1,424

Losses	Horse, YOB	Raced	Earnings
73	Judgaville, 1981	3	12,965
72	Winnie's Pride, 1988	6	6,790
72	Lattanzio, 1991	5	19,163
71	Ninon, 1923	3	1,360
71	Roman Sandal, 1924	4	990
71	Stark Mad, 1946	4	2,950
71	Lady Jule, 1925	3	1,095
70	Red Alley Cat, 1990	6	7,610
69	Tuff Nuggets, 1980	4	8,120
69	Buddugie, 1920	4	1,865
68	Lucky Change, 1941	4	3,930
68	Right Chief, 1961	4	3,689
68	Buck Flares, 1955	4	6,100
67	Jimmy What, 1987	6	14,036
67	Bengal Dancer, 1954	4	5,240
67	Tchadar, 1924	6	480
66	Doug's Dame, 1965	4	3,558
66	Filly Gumbo, 1970	3	4,667
66	Unclebuck, 1939	7	730
66	Rosette, 1926	4	243
66	Really Rushing, 1995	5	17,184
66	Dominate'em, 1978	4	5,860
65	Tarbucket, 1932	3	945
65	Sam's Tip, 1975	4	14,344
65	Brill Lon, 1956	4	1,420
65	Amarushka, 1981	5	24,336
65	Petulant, 1928	4	690
65	Goodyear, 1927	5	20
65	Flashy Lark, 1981	5	14,510
65	Icy Ethel, 1948	5	3,215
65	Alpha's Star, 1990	6	12,530
65	Jacinto's Arky, 1980	4	4,536
64	Clay K., 1965	6	2,570
64	Dawn's Debbie, 1982	3	7,292
64	Truckin, 1936	5	865
64	Gosport, 1936	5	465
64	Able Archer, 1957	3	1,847
64	Junior T., 1948	4	1,160
64	Pacific Star, 1946	7	1,000
63	Ruby's Crystal, 1980	4	5,575
63	Dusky Boy, 1928	5	1,310
63	Mail Plane, 1948	3	1,805
63	Sweet Bernice, 1935	8	995
63	Castle Rock, 1927	4	625
63	Bell's Luck, 1961	4	867
62	Indiana Spa, 1935	5	635
62	Suspended Star, 1954	3	3,040
62	Kitty Leon, 1939	7	595
62	War O'Gold, 1966	3	4,313
62	Rebel Girl, 1951	4	4,005
62	Navy Bean Soup, 1952	4	3,705
62	White Hoops, 1928	6	350
62	Colonel Titus, 1939	9	605

Leading Horses of All Time By Starts

Horse, sex, year of birth, sire	Years raced	Starts	Wins	2nds	3rds	Stakes Wins	Earnings
Hiblaze, h., 1935, Blazes	14	406	79	73	52	0	$32,647
*Galley Sweep, g., 1933, Aga Khan	14	399	19	34	46	0	10,677
Shot One, g., 1941, Shoeless Joe	13	360	65	65	68	0	29,982
Uno, m., 1939, Boot to Boot	12	348	35	54	50	0	N/A
Onus, g., 1933, Jack High	15	344	53	58	63	0	32,039
Worthowning, g., 1935, *Longworth	14	339	63	62	64	0	41,830
Agreed, g., 1950, Revoked	14	338	39	50	49	0	68,004
My Blaze, h., 1930, Big Blaze	11	338	52	35	51	0	32,707
Marabou, h., 1925, *Hourless	10	337	41	61	44	0	27,458
Vantryst, h., 1936, Tryster	13	334	61	78	48	0	31,971
George de Mar, h., 1922, *Colonel Vennie	13	333	60	54	64	0	69,091
Buffoon, h., 1937, St. Brideaux	10	329	37	36	45	0	11,538
Welsh Lad, g., 1934, Prince of Wales	13	329	67	54	49	0	25,317
Panjab, g., 1937, *Kiev	11	327	21	32	44	0	17,929
Seth's Hope, h., 1924, Seth	11	327	62	51	50	0	74,341
Copin, h., 1937, Mate	13	323	42	40	53	0	27,926
Commission, h., 1935, Banstar	13	319	41	36	39	0	25,626

All-time Leading Earners by Deflated Dollars

Comparing horses of different eras is always an entertaining exercise. Was Secretariat a better racehorse than Citation? That question will never be answered definitively because they never met on the track, so comparing horses of one era to another is subjective.

Earnings are one measure of performance, though that yardstick also has its drawbacks because the purses of yesteryear do not compare to the purses of today. There is a way to use earnings as a measure of productivity, however, by deflating the earnings; that is, adjusting earnings to account for the effects of inflation.

In the tables presented on this page and the following two pages are deflated earnings of the all-time leaders in Thoroughbred racing since 1929. Considered for inclusion on the list is any horse that started at least once in North America. Horses that raced at least once in North America and also raced overseas have all their earnings included, all being converted

to United States dollars and then deflated by racing year.

All-time leading money winner adjusted for inflation is two-time Horse of the Year John Henry, who raced 83 times from 1977 through '84. The durable gelding won the first $1-million Thoroughbred race in the U.S., the 1981 Arlington Million Stakes (G1), and his career ended the year in which the Breeders' Cup was inaugurated. Second on the list is two-time Horse of the Year Cigar, the all-time leading earner in North America in current dollars.

The deflator used to convert all earnings is the Gross Domestic Product implicit price deflator published by the U.S. Bureau of Economic Analysis.

On the first two pages are the all-time leaders by deflated dollars regardless of sex. On the third page is a list of the all-time leading female earners by deflated dollars. Statistics are through December 31, 2002.

All-time Leading Earners by Deflated Dollars

Horse, sex, year of birth, sire	Yrs raced	Starts	1st	2nd	3rd	Nominal earnings	Deflated earnings
John Henry, g, 1975, by Ole Bob Bowers	8	83	39	15	9	$6,591,860	$11,293,455
Cigar, h, 1990, by Palace Music	4	33	19	4	5	9,999,815	11,182,699
Skip Away, h, 1993, by Skip Trial	4	38	18	10	6	9,616,360	10,461,908
Kelso, g, 1957, by Your Host	8	63	39	12	2	1,977,896	9,600,229
Alysheba, h, 1984, by Alydar	3	26	11	8	2	6,679,242	9,363,675
Round Table, h, 1954, by *Princequillo	4	66	43	8	5	1,749,869	9,020,329
Fantastic Light, h, 1996, by Rahy	4	25	12	5	3	8,486,957	8,706,111
Silver Charm, h, 1994, by Silver Buck	4	24	12	7	2	6,944,369	7,466,654
Nashua, h, 1952, by *Nasrullah	3	30	22	4	1	1,288,565	7,164,651
Captain Steve, h, 1997, by Fly So Free	3	25	9	3	7	6,828,356	6,984,444
Citation, h, 1945, by Bull Lea	4	45	32	10	2	1,085,760	6,932,745
Best Pal, g, 1988, by *Habitony	7	47	18	11	4	5,668,245	6,848,727
Stymie, h, 1941, by Equestrian	7	131	35	33	28	918,485	6,820,935
Buckpasser, h, 1963, by Tom Fool	3	31	25	4	1	1,462,014	6,657,933
Sunday Silence, h, 1986, by Halo	3	14	9	5	0	4,968,554	6,584,998
Tiznow, h, 1997, by Cee's Tizzy	2	15	8	4	2	6,427,830	6,582,769
Singspiel (Ire), h, 1992, by In the Wings (GB)	4	20	9	8	0	5,952,825	6,530,856
Easy Goer, h, 1986, by Alydar	3	20	14	5	1	4,873,770	6,494,731
Spend a Buck, h, 1982, by Buckaroo	2	15	10	3	2	4,220,689	6,369,167
Taiki Blizzard, h, 1991, by Seattle Slew	4	23	6	8	2	5,523,549	6,154,190
Carry Back, h, 1958, by Saggy	4	62	21	11	11	1,241,165	6,107,074
Armed, g, 1941, by Bull Lea	7	81	41	20	10	817,475	5,880,265
Creme Fraiche, h, 1982, by Rich Cream	6	64	17	12	13	4,024,727	5,863,384
Spectacular Bid, h, 1976, by Bold Bidder	3	30	26	2	1	2,781,608	5,759,941
Unbridled, h, 1987, by Fappiano	3	24	8	6	6	4,489,475	5,723,969
Whirlaway, h, 1938, by *Blenheim II	4	60	32	15	9	561,161	5,528,091
Slew o' Gold, h, 1980, by Seattle Slew	3	21	12	5	1	3,533,534	5,526,770
Forego, g, 1970, by *Forli	6	57	34	9	7	1,938,957	5,437,350
Ferdinand, h, 1983, by Nijinsky II	4	29	8	9	6	3,777,978	5,423,899
Affirmed, h, 1975, by Exclusive Native	3	29	22	5	1	2,393,818	5,345,631
Swoon's Son, h, 1953, by The Doge	4	51	30	10	3	970,605	5,197,611
Precisionist, h, 1981, by Crozier	5	46	20	10	4	3,485,398	5,180,035
Jim and Tonic (Fr), g, 1994, by Double Bed (Fr)	7	39	13	13	4	4,975,807	5,166,486
Street Cry (Ire), h, 1998, by Machiavellian	3	12	5	6	1	5,150,837	5,166,274
Damascus, h, 1964, by Sword Dancer	3	32	21	7	3	1,176,781	5,108,097

Horse, sex, year of birth, sire	Yrs raced	Starts	1st	2nd	3rd	Nominal earnings	Deflated earnings
Snow Chief, h, 1983, by Reflected Glory	3	24	13	3	5	3,383,210	4,976,331
Daylami (Ire), h, 1994, by Doyoun	4	21	11	3	4	4,614,762	4,901,706
Assault, h, 1943, by Bold Venture	6	42	18	6	7	675,470	4,888,768
Behrens, h, 1994, by Pleasant Colony	4	27	9	8	3	4,563,500	4,812,995
Native Diver, h, 1959, by Imbros	7	81	37	7	12	1,026,500	4,729,604
Bet Twice, h, 1984, by Sportin' Life	3	26	10	6	4	3,308,599	4,716,169
Awesome Again, h, 1994, by Deputy Minister	2	12	9	0	2	4,374,590	4,697,234
Swaps, h, 1952, by *Khaled	3	25	19	2	2	848,900	4,675,763
Cryptoclearance, h, 1984, by Fappiano	4	44	12	10	7	3,376,327	4,670,851
Seabiscuit, h, 1933, by Hard Tack	6	89	33	15	13	437,730	4,653,205
Devil His Due, h, 1989, by Devil's Bag	4	41	11	12	3	3,920,405	4,597,162
Dahlia, m, 1970, by *Vaguely Noble	5	48	15	3	7	1,489,105	4,540,781
Native Dancer, h, 1950, by Polynesian	3	22	21	1	0	785,240	4,529,083
T. V. Lark, h, 1957, by *Indian Hemp	4	72	19	13	6	902,194	4,488,889
Lady's Secret, m, 1982, by Secretariat	4	45	25	9	3	3,021,325	4,475,769
Fort Marcy, g, 1964, by *Amerigo	6	75	21	18	14	1,109,791	4,475,594
Pilsudski (Ire), h, 1992, by Polish Precedent	4	22	10	6	2	4,080,297	4,467,585
Roman Brother, g, 1961, by Third Brother	4	42	16	10	5	943,473	4,464,814
Secretariat, h, 1970, by Bold Ruler	2	21	16	3	1	1,316,808	4,420,452
Steinlen (GB), h, 1983, by Habitat	5	45	20	10	7	3,297,169	4,384,245
Trinycarol (Ven), m, 1979, by Velvet Cap	4	29	18	3	1	2,644,392	4,373,434
Gulch, h, 1984, by Mr. Prospector	3	32	13	8	4	3,095,521	4,370,200
Seeking the Pearl, m, 1994, by Seeking the Gold	4	21	8	2	3	4,021,716	4,349,820
Dr. Fager, h, 1964, by Rough'n Tumble	3	22	18	2	1	1,002,642	4,342,290
Find, g, 1950, by Discovery	8	110	22	27	27	803,615	4,322,064
Sandpit (Brz), h, 1989, by Baynoun (Ire)	7	40	14	11	6	3,812,597	4,249,379
Symboli Rudolf (Jpn), h, 1981, by Partholon	4	16	13	1	1	2,764,980	4,229,714
Theatrical (Ire), h, 1982, by Nureyev	4	22	10	4	2	2,940,036	4,226,274
Black Tie Affair (Ire), h, 1986, by Miswaki	4	45	18	9	6	3,370,694	4,212,579
Strike the Gold, h, 1988, by Alydar	4	31	6	8	5	3,457,026	4,206,414
Sword Dancer, h, 1956, by Sunglow	3	39	15	7	4	829,610	4,182,291
Cat Thief, h, 1996, by Storm Cat	3	30	4	9	8	3,951,012	4,171,806
Swain (Ire), h, 1992, by Nashwan	4	22	10	4	6	3,797,566	4,121,471
*Cougar II, h, 1966, by Tale of Two Cities	6	50	20	7	17	1,172,625	4,104,253
Sky Classic, h, 1987, by Nijinsky II	4	29	15	6	1	3,320,398	4,089,447
Susan's Girl, m, 1969, by Quadrangle	5	63	29	14	11	1,251,668	4,032,840
Dance Smartly, m, 1988, by Danzig	3	17	12	2	3	3,263,835	4,031,860
Point Given, h, 1998, by Thunder Gulch	2	13	9	3	0	3,968,500	4,028,080
Great Communicator, h, 1983, by Key to the Kingdom	6	56	14	10	7	2,922,615	4,022,727
Bold Ruler, h, 1954, by *Nasrullah	3	33	23	4	2	764,204	4,000,033
Exceller, h, 1973, by *Vaguely Noble	5	33	15	5	6	1,674,587	3,997,932
Candy Spots, h, 1960, by *Nigromante	3	22	12	5	1	824,718	3,967,024
Paradise Creek, h, 1989, by Irish River (Fr)	4	25	14	7	1	3,401,416	3,957,218
Paseana (Arg), m, 1987, by Ahmad	6	36	19	10	2	3,317,427	3,951,798
First Landing, h, 1956, by *Turn-to	3	37	19	9	2	779,577	3,944,899
Mongo, h, 1959, by *Royal Charger	4	46	22	10	4	820,766	3,939,443
Lando (Ger), h, 1990, by Acatenango	4	24	10	3	1	3,438,727	3,934,640
Gentlemen (Arg), h, 1992, by Robin des Bois	5	24	13	4	2	3,608,558	3,923,708
Manila, h, 1983, by Lyphard	3	18	12	5	0	2,692,799	3,919,361
Allez France, h, 1970, by *Sea-Bird	4	21	13	3	1	1,262,801	3,916,191
Riva Ridge, h, 1969, by First Landing	3	30	17	3	1	1,111,497	3,900,445
Crimson Satan, h, 1959, by Spy Song	4	58	18	9	9	796,077	3,871,318
Broad Brush, h, 1983, by Ack Ack	3	27	14	5	5	2,656,793	3,853,087
Almutawakel (GB), h, 1995, by Machiavellian	4	19	4	4	1	3,643,021	3,849,386
Cicada, m, 1959, by Bryan G.	4	42	23	8	6	783,674	3,832,893
Gate Dancer, h, 1981, by Sovereign Dancer	4	28	7	8	7	2,501,705	3,810,373
Bally Ache, h, 1957, by *Ballydam	2	31	16	9	4	758,522	3,803,690
Forty Niner, h, 1985, by Mr. Prospector	2	19	11	5	0	2,726,000	3,790,145
Bertrando, h, 1989, by Skywalker	5	24	9	6	2	3,185,610	3,783,606
Gun Bow, h, 1960, by Gun Shot	3	42	17	8	4	798,722	3,774,083
Social Outcast, g, 1950, by Shut Out	5	58	18	9	6	668,300	3,758,141
With Approval, h, 1986, by Caro (Ire)	3	23	13	5	1	2,863,540	3,755,518
Bayakoa (Arg), m, 1984, by Consultant's Bid	6	39	21	9	0	2,861,701	3,746,384

Female All-time Earners by Deflated Dollars

Horse, sex, year of birth, sire	Yrs raced	Starts	1st	2nd	3rd	Nominal earnings	Deflated earnings
Dahlia, m, 1970, by *Vaguely Noble	5	48	15	3	7	$1,489,105	$4,540,781
Lady's Secret, m, 1982, by Secretariat	4	45	25	9	3	3,021,325	4,475,769
Trinycarol (Ven), m, 1979, by Velvet Cap	4	29	18	3	1	2,644,392	4,373,434
Seeking the Pearl, m, 1994, by Seeking the Gold	4	21	8	2	3	4,021,716	4,349,820
Susan's Girl, m, 1969, by Quadrangle	5	63	29	14	11	1,251,668	4,032,840
Dance Smartly, m, 1988, by Danzig	3	17	12	2	3	3,263,835	4,031,860
Paseana (Arg), m, 1987, by Ahmad	6	36	19	10	2	3,317,427	3,951,798
Allez France, m, 1970, by *Sea-Bird	4	21	13	3	1	1,262,801	3,916,197
Cicada, m, 1959, by Bryan G.	4	42	23	8	6	783,674	3,832,893
Bayakoa (Arg), m, 1984, by Consultant's Bid	6	39	21	9	0	2,861,701	3,746,384
Serena's Song, m, 1992, by Rahy	3	38	18	11	3	3,283,388	3,693,254
Spain, m, 1997, by Thunder Gulch	4	35	9	9	7	3,540,542	3,628,427
Shuvee, m, 1966, by Nashua	4	44	16	10	6	890,445	3,507,622
Life's Magic, m, 1981, by Cox's Ridge	3	32	8	11	6	2,255,218	3,484,117
All Along (Fr), m, 1979, by Targowice	4	21	9	4	2	2,125,809	3,403,743
Triptych, m, 1982, by Riverman	5	41	14	5	11	2,318,946	3,337,534
Silverbulletday, m, 1996, by Silver Deputy	3	23	15	3	1	3,093,207	3,280,403
Straight Deal, m, 1962, by Hail to Reason	6	99	21	21	9	733,020	3,269,726
Gallorette, m, 1942, by *Challenger II	5	72	21	20	13	445,535	3,265,469
Escena, m, 1993, by Strawberry Road (Aus)	4	29	11	9	3	2,962,639	3,200,580
Let's Elope (NZ), m, 1987, by Nassipour	5	26	11	0	5	2,528,902	3,110,384
Flawlessly, m, 1988, by Affirmed	5	28	16	4	3	2,572,536	3,083,313
Bewitch, m, 1945, by Bull Lea	5	55	20	10	11	462,605	3,003,098
Banshee Breeze, m, 1995, by Unbridled	3	18	10	5	2	2,784,798	2,965,078
Miesque, m, 1984, by Nureyev	3	16	12	3	1	2,070,163	2,923,583
Top Flight, m, 1929, by *Dis Donc	2	16	12	0	0	275,900	2,881,868
Estrapade, m, 1980, by *Vaguely Noble	4	30	12	5	5	1,937,142	2,881,241
Tosmah, m, 1961, by Tim Tam	4	39	23	6	2	612,588	2,876,423
Beautiful Pleasure, m, 1995, by Maudlin	5	25	10	5	2	2,734,078	2,874,978
Safely Kept, m, 1986, by Horatius	4	31	24	2	3	2,194,206	2,830,033
Busher, m, 1942, by War Admiral	3	21	15	3	1	334,035	2,820,338
Honeymoon, m, 1943, by *Beau Pere	6	78	20	14	9	387,760	2,772,597
Old Hat, m, 1959, by Boston Doge	6	80	35	18	9	556,401	2,614,918
Affectionately, m, 1960, by Swaps	4	52	28	8	6	546,659	2,604,569
Open Mind, m, 1986, by Deputy Minister	3	19	12	2	2	1,844,372	2,487,480
Heritage of Gold, m, 1995, by Gold Legend	4	28	16	2	4	2,381,762	2,484,092
Next Move, m, 1947, by Bull Lea	4	46	17	11	3	398,550	2,460,554
Sickle's Image, m, 1948, by Sickletoy	5	73	27	13	16	413,275	2,425,555
Gamely, m, 1964, by Bold Ruler	3	41	16	9	6	574,961	2,406,247
Bed o' Roses, m, 1947, by Rosemont	4	46	18	8	6	383,925	2,386,660
Politely, m, 1963, by *Amerigo	4	49	21	9	5	552,972	2,378,469
Goodbye Halo, m, 1985, by Halo	3	24	11	5	4	1,706,702	2,349,932
Personal Ensign, m, 1984, by Private Account	3	13	13	0	0	1,679,880	2,347,168
Perfect Sting, m, 1996, by Red Ransom	4	21	14	3	0	2,202,042	2,293,494
Very Subtle, m, 1984, by Hoist the Silver	4	29	12	6	4	1,608,360	2,287,821
Family Style, m, 1983, by State Dinner	3	35	10	8	7	1,537,118	2,270,093
Xtra Heat, m, 1998, by Dixieland Heat	3	33	24	5	2	2,239,635	2,260,283
Azeri, m, 1998, by Jade Hunter	2	11	10	1	0	2,227,740	2,228,261
Convenience, m, 1968, by Fleet Nasrullah	4	35	15	9	4	648,933	2,216,946
Sharp Cat, m, 1994, by Storm Cat	3	22	15	3	0	2,032,575	2,208,660
Gallant Bloom, m, 1966, by *Gallant Man	3	22	16	1	1	535,739	2,177,334
Numbered Account, m, 1969, by Buckpasser	3	22	14	3	2	607,048	2,172,524
Miss Alleged, m, 1987, by Alleged	3	15	5	4	3	1,757,342	2,170,577
Hatoof, m, 1989, by Irish River (Fr)	4	21	9	4	1	1,841,070	2,167,418
Trillion, m, 1974, by Hail to Reason	3	32	9	14	3	957,413	2,157,916
The Very One, m, 1975, by One for All	5	71	22	12	9	1,104,623	2,147,415
Pebbles (GB), m, 1981, by Sharpen Up (GB)	3	15	8	4	0	1,419,632	2,145,860
Outstandingly, m, 1982, by Exclusive Native	4	28	10	4	3	1,412,206	2,145,295
Princess Rooney, m, 1980, by Verbatim	3	21	17	2	1	1,343,339	2,123,112
Royal Native, m, 1956, by *Royal Charger	4	49	18	13	8	422,769	2,116,595
User Friendly (GB), m, 1989, by Slip Anchor	3	16	8	1	2	1,764,938	2,114,998
Jewel Princess, m, 1992, by Key to the Mint	4	29	13	4	7	1,904,060	2,102,288
Winning Colors, m, 1985, by Caro (Ire)	3	19	8	3	1	1,526,837	2,100,185
Heavenly Prize, m, 1991, by Seeking the Gold	4	18	9	6	3	1,825,940	2,087,732

Leading Earners by Foal Crop in North America
Worldwide Racing Through 2002

Year	MALE, YOB, Sire	Yrs Raced	Strts	Wins	St. Wins	Earnings	FEMALE, YOB, Sire	Yrs Raced	Strts	Wins	St. Wins	Earnings
1930	Ladysman, h., Pompey	5	22	8	5	$134,310	Swivel, m., *Swift and Sure	2	24	5	0	$74,955
1931	Top Row, h., Peanuts	5	42	14	0	213,870	Mata Hari, m., Peter Hastings	2	16	7	0	66,699
1932	Rosemont, h., The Porter	4	23	7	1	168,750	Esposa, m., Espino	7	96	19	0	132,055
1933	Seabiscuit, h., Hard Tack	6	89	33	1	437,730	Columbiana, m., Petee-Wrack	4	28	11	0	60,925
1934	War Admiral, h., Man o' War	4	26	21	15	273,240	Dawn Play, m., Clock Tower	2	14	4	3	50,800
1935	Stagehand, h., *Sickle	3	25	9	0	200,110	Jacola, m., *Jacopo	3	25	11	0	70,060
1936	Challedon, h., *Challenger II	5	44	20	9	334,660	Loveday, m., Petee-Wrack	6	85	17	0	56,225
1937	Bimelech, h., Black Toney	3	15	11	4	248,745	Fairy Chant, m., Chance Shot	4	42	10	4	81,985
1938	Whirlaway, h., *Blenheim II	4	60	32	18	561,161	Moon Maiden, m., *Challenger II	6	109	19	1	76,780
1939	First Fiddle, h., *Royal Minstrel	6	95	23	10	398,610	Vagrancy, m., *Sir Gallahad III	3	42	15	9	102,480
1940	Count Fleet, h., Reigh Count	2	21	16	9	250,300	Happy Issue, m., Bow to Me	9	157	27	2	225,424
1941	Stymie, h., Equestrian	7	131	35	25	918,485	Twilight Tear, m., Bull Lea	3	24	18	10	202,165
1942	Pavot, h., Case Ace	4	32	14	5	373,365	Gallorette, m., *Challenger II	5	72	21	13	445,535
1943	Assault, h., Bold Venture	6	42	18	15	675,470	Honeymoon, m., *Beau Pere	6	78	20	12	387,760
1944	On Trust, h., *Alibhai	7	88	23	11	554,145	But Why Not, m., Blue Larkspur	5	46	12	8	295,155
1945	Citation, h., Bull Lea	4	45	32	22	1,085,760	Bewitch, m., Bull Lea	5	55	20	15	462,605
1946	Ponder, h., Pensive	4	41	14	11	541,275	Two Lea, m., Bull Lea	4	26	15	9	309,250
1947	Oil Capitol, h., *Mahmoud	5	80	19	14	580,756	Next Move, m., Bull Lea	4	46	17	12	398,550
1948	Crafty Admiral, h., Fighting Fox	4	39	18	12	499,200	Sickle's Image, m., Sickletoy	5	73	27	10	413,275
1949	Mark-Ye-Well, h., Bull Lea	4	40	14	11	581,910	Real Delight, m., Bull Lea	2	15	12	10	261,822
1950	Find, g., Discovery	8	110	22	13	803,615	Grecian Queen, m., *Heliopolis	4	53	12	9	323,575
1951	Determine, h., *Alibhai	3	44	18	16	573,360	Queen Hopeful, m., Roman	5	65	18	10	365,044
1952	Nashua, h., *Nasrullah	3	30	22	19	1,288,565	High Voltage, m., *Ambiorix	3	45	13	10	362,240
1953	Swoon's Son, h., The Doge	4	51	30	22	970,605	Dotted Line, m., *Princequillo	5	67	11	5	324,159
1954	Round Table, h., *Princequillo	4	66	43	31	1,749,869	Endine, m., *Rico Monte	3	45	10	4	306,547
1955	Bald Eagle, h., *Nasrullah	4	29	12	12	692,946	Idun, m., *Royal Charger	3	30	17	9	392,490
1956	Sword Dancer, h., Sunglow	3	39	15	10	829,610	Royal Native, m., *Royal Charger	4	49	18	11	422,769
1957	Kelso, g., Your Host	8	63	39	31	1,977,896	Airmans Guide, m., One Count	3	20	13	8	315,673
1958	Carry Back, h., Saggy	4	62	21	14	1,241,165	Bowl of Flowers, m., Sailor	2	16	10	6	398,504
1959	Native Diver, h., Imbros	7	81	37	33	1,026,500	Cicada, m., Bryan G.	4	42	23	18	783,674
1960	Candy Spots, h., *Nigromante	3	22	12	9	824,718	Affectionately, m., Swaps	4	52	28	18	546,659
1961	Roman Brother, g., Third Brother	4	42	16	10	943,473	Tosmah, m., Tim Tam	4	39	23	16	612,588
1962	Tom Rolfe, h., *Ribot	3	32	16	9	671,297	Straight Deal, m., Hail to Reason	5	99	21	13	733,020
1963	Buckpasser, h., Tom Fool	3	31	25	21	1,462,014	Politely, m., *Amerigo	4	49	21	13	552,972
1964	Damascus, h., Sword Dancer	3	32	21	17	1,176,781	Gamely, m., Bold Ruler	3	41	16	13	574,961
1965	Nodouble, h., *Noholme II	4	42	13	9	846,749	Gay Matelda, m., Sir Gaylord	3	37	9	5	409,945
1966	Ack Ack, h., Battle Joined	4	27	19	13	636,641	Shuvee, m., Nashua	4	44	16	15	890,445
1967	Loud, g., *Herbager	7	88	12	3	527,779	Saturnina, m., *Ballydonnell	5	107	47	8	392,195
1968	Run the Gantlet, h., Tom Rolfe	3	21	9	7	559,079	Convenience, m., Fleet Nasrullah	4	35	15	8	648,933
1969	Riva Ridge, h., First Landing	3	30	17	13	1,111,497	Susan's Girl, m., Quadrangle	5	63	29	24	1,251,668
1970	Forego, g., *Forli	6	57	34	24	1,938,957	Dahlia, m., *Vaguely Noble	5	48	15	14	1,489,105
1971	Sharp Gary, g., Carry Back	7	115	16	8	535,198	Chris Evert, m., Swoon's Son	3	15	10	7	679,475
1972	Foolish Pleasure, h., What a Pleasure	3	26	16	12	1,216,705	Ivanjica, m., Sir Ivor	3	15	6	5	626,682
1973	Exceller, h., *Vaguely Noble	5	33	15	13	1,674,587	Optimistic Gal, m., Sir Ivor	2	21	13	10	686,861
1974	Seattle Slew, h., Bold Reasoning	3	17	14	9	1,208,726	Trillion, m., Hail to Reason	3	32	9	8	957,413
1975	John Henry, g., Ole Bob Bowers	8	83	39	30	6,591,860	The Very One, m., One for All	5	71	22	13	1,104,623
1976	Spectacular Bid, h., Bold Bidder	3	30	26	23	2,781,608	Track Robbery, m., No Robbery	6	59	22	13	1,098,537
1977	Temperence Hill, h., Stop the Music	3	31	11	9	1,567,650	Bold 'n Determined, m., Bold and Brave	3	20	16	11	949,599
1978	Silveyville, h., *Petrone	8	56	19	14	1,282,880	Sintrillium, m., Sinister Purpose	5	46	14	9	743,602
1979	Majesty's Prince, h., His Majesty	4	43	12	9	2,077,796	Sefa's Beauty, m., Lt. Stevens	5	52	25	17	1,171,628
1980	Slew o' Gold, h., Seattle Slew	3	21	12	8	3,533,534	Estrapade, m., *Vaguely Noble	4	30	12	10	1,937,142
1981	Precisionist, h., Crozier	5	46	20	17	3,485,398	Life's Magic, m., Cox's Ridge	3	32	8	7	2,255,218
1982	Spend a Buck, h., Buckaroo	2	15	10	7	4,220,689	Lady's Secret, m., Secretariat	4	45	25	22	3,021,325
1983	Ferdinand, h., Nijinsky II	4	29	8	7	3,777,978	Family Style, m., State Dinner	3	35	10	9	1,537,118
1984	Alysheba, h., Alydar	3	26	11	10	6,679,242	Miesque, m., Nureyev	3	16	12	11	2,070,163
1985	Forty Niner, h., Mr. Prospector	2	19	11	9	2,726,000	Goodbye Halo, m., Halo	3	24	11	10	1,706,702
1986	Sunday Silence, h., Halo	3	14	9	7	4,968,554	Safely Kept, m., Horatius	4	31	24	22	2,194,206
1987	Unbridled, h., Fappiano	3	24	8	5	4,489,475	Miss Alleged, m., Alleged	3	15	5	4	1,757,342
1988	Best Pal, h., *Habitony	7	47	18	17	5,668,245	Dance Smartly, m., Danzig	3	17	12	10	3,263,835
1989	Devil His Due, h., Devil's Bag	4	41	11	9	3,920,405	Hatoof, m., Irish River (Fr)	4	21	9	8	1,841,070
1990	Cigar, h., Palace Music	4	33	19	15	9,999,815	Ski Paradise, m., Lyphard	3	20	6	5	1,470,588
1991	Taiki Blizzard, h., Seattle Slew	4	23	6	3	5,523,549	Heavenly Prize, m., Seeking the Gold	4	18	9	8	1,825,940
1992	Thunder Gulch, h., Gulch	2	16	9	8	2,915,086	Serena's Song, m., Rahy	3	38	18	17	3,283,388
1993	Skip Away, h., Skip Trial	4	38	18	16	9,616,360	Escena, m., Strawberry Road (Aus)	4	29	11	7	2,962,639
1994	Silver Charm, h., Silver Buck	4	24	12	11	6,944,369	Seeking the Pearl, m., Seeking the Gold	4	21	8	7	4,021,716
1995	Victory Gallop, h., Cryptoclearance	3	17	9	7	3,505,895	Banshee Breeze, m., Unbridled	3	18	10	8	2,784,798
1996	Fantastic Light, h., Rahy	4	25	12	8	8,486,957	Silverbulletday, m., Silver Deputy	3	23	15	14	3,093,207
1997	Captain Steve, h., Fly So Free	3	25	9	8	6,828,356	Spain, m., Thunder Gulch	4	35	9	7	3,540,542
1998	Point Given, h., Thunder Gulch	2	13	9	8	3,968,500	Xtra Heat, m., Dixieland Heat	4	33	24	23	2,239,635
1999	War Emblem, c., Our Emblem	2	13	7	4	3,491,000	Take Charge Lady, f., Dehere	3	15	9	7	1,760,351
2000	Toccet, c., Awesome Again	1	8	6	4	755,610	Storm Flag Flying, f., Storm Cat	2	4	4	3	967,000

All-Time Leading Earners by State Where Bred 1954-2002

State	MALE, YOB, Sire	Strts	Wins	Earnings	FEMALE, YOB, Sire	Strts	Wins	Earnings
Alabama	Winonly, 1957, Olympia	64	21	$326,264	My Portrait, 1958, Olympia	94	17	$261,275
Alaska	Austin Texas, 1988, Tom Tulle	76	9	27,778	Ice Blue Moon, 1979, *Hard Water	60	4	15,146
Arizona	Coyote Lakes, 1994, Society Max	61	20	724,977	Monrow, 1996, Fool the Experts	41	17	287,344
Arkansas	Nodouble, 1965, *Noholme II	42	13	846,749	Humble Clerk, 1997, Humble Eleven	17	6	503,545
California	Tiznow, 1997, Cee's Tizzy	15	8	6,427,830	Fran's Valentine, 1982, Saros (GB)	34	13	1,375,465
Colorado	To Erin, 1976, Epic Journey	104	28	392,707	Prairie Maiden, 1993, Badger Land	30	10	294,784
Connecticut	Fast Smile, 1970, Fast Gun	105	32	142,795	Skipat, 1974, Jungle Cove	45	26	614,215
Delaware	Baitman, 1961, Assemblyman	113	27	298,198	Pokey Lady, 1984, Georgeandthedragon	74	20	155,275
Florida	Skip Away, 1993, Skip Trial	38	18	9,616,360	Beautiful Pleasure, 1995, Maudlin	25	10	2,734,078
Georgia	Maybe Jack, 1993, Classic Account	102	29	450,345	Vivace, 1993, Shot Gun Scott	40	20	1,037,671
Hawaii	Hawaii Boy, 1970, Kaaba	87	17	46,817	Mapu, 1964, Hauli	99	9	19,078
Idaho	Gratteau, 1995, Synastry	46	14	366,282	Angi Go, 1990, Idaho's Majesty	36	15	437,493
Illinois	Buck's Boy, 1993, Bucksplasher	30	16	2,750,148	Two Item Limit, 1998, Twining	28	7	1,060,585
Indiana	Hillsdale, 1955, Take Away	41	23	646,935	Honky Star, 1971, Bupers	39	18	353,012
Iowa	Sure Shot Biscuit, 1996, Miracle Heights	49	23	1,008,019	Nut N Better, 1997, Miracle Heights	28	14	572,828
Kansas	I Dancer, 1995, I Enclose	55	15	256,787	Sunnie Do It, 1994, Do It Again Dan	60	16	314,911
Kentucky	Fantastic Light, 1996, Rahy	25	12	8,486,957	Spain, 1997, Thunder Gulch	35	9	3,540,542
Louisiana	Scott's Scoundrel, 1992, L'Enjoleur	50	22	1,270,052	Sarah Lane's Oates, 1994, Sunshine Forever	77	21	888,296
Maine	Seboomook, 1976, Sunny South	96	22	124,837	North of Boston, 1972, Midland Man	25	4	40,693
Maryland	Cigar, 1990, Palace Music	33	19	9,999,815	Safely Kept, 1986, Horatius	31	24	2,194,206
Massachusetts	Rise Jim, 1976, Jim J.	52	27	528,789	Isadorable, 1983, Moleolus	39	19	415,018
Michigan	Pongo Boy, 1992, Matchlite	87	22	776,184	Peppen, 1994, Pep Up	37	15	623,417
Minnesota	Blair's Cove, 1985, Bucksplasher	58	17	533,528	Courtly Kathy, 1991, Lost Code	89	18	277,950
Mississippi	American Cowboy, 1994, Gold Crest	56	9	174,867	Real Irish Hope, 1987, Tilt Up	49	15	433,190
Missouri	Carjack, 1981, Cojak	72	20	469,181	Peaceful River, 1979, Peaceful Tom	72	14	250,990
Montana	Payday Mackee, 1990, Black Mackee	79	17	214,668	Hallelujah Angel, 1991, Dance Centre	55	12	197,496
Nebraska	Dazzling Falls, 1992, Taylor's Falls	20	9	904,622	Orphan Kist, 1984, Fort Prevel	100	28	631,997
Nevada	Y Flash, 1960, Flash o' Night	28	6	226,635	Wood and Wine, 1975, Fleet Allied	54	18	261,119
New Hampshire	Road to Rock, 1963, Ross Sea	187	36	248,113	Lite Ft., 1981, Last Dance	71	15	137,000
New Jersey	Friendly Lover, 1988, Cutlass	66	22	1,247,670	Open Mind, 1986, Deputy Minister	19	12	1,844,372
New Mexico	Run Johnny, 1992, Johnny Blade	52	14	518,790	Yulla Yulla, 1995, Look See	27	21	443,022
New York	Say Florida Sandy, 1994, Personal Flag	92	31	1,988,806	Grecian Flight, 1984, Cormorant	40	21	1,320,215
North Carolina	Bold Circle, 1986, Circle Home	55	11	372,488	Top Socialite, 1982, Topsider	34	10	521,944
North Dakota	Dakota Prospect, 1997, Slewdledo	48	8	130,004	Hoist Her Flag, 1982, Aferd	43	19	290,849
Ohio	Harlan's Holiday, 1999, c., Harlan	16	7	1,947,564	Tougaloo, 1983, Lot o' Gold	33	13	583,030
Oklahoma	Clever Trevor, 1986, Slewacide	30	15	1,388,841	Lady's Secret, 1982, Secretariat	45	25	3,021,325
Oregon	Polynesian Flyer, 1982, Flying Lark	54	14	346,525	Revillew Slew, 1996, Can't Be Slew	41	12	366,284
Pennsylvania	Alphabet Soup, 1991, Cozzene	24	10	2,990,270	Go for Wand, 1987, Deputy Minister	13	10	1,373,338
Rhode Island	Beau Britches, 1975, Oxford Accent	89	8	121,145	Good Musical, 1977, Rock Talk	45	12	155,580
South Carolina	Big Rut, 1993, Kokand	79	18	543,582	Double Stake, 1993, Kokand	37	11	343,480
South Dakota	Little Bro Lantis, 1988, Lost Atlantis	120	23	719,866	Reen Aferd, 1985, Aferd	78	13	96,107
Tennessee	Slew of Damascus, 1988, Slewacide	48	16	1,420,350	Fancy Naskra, 1978, Naskra	26	8	291,769
Texas	Groovy, 1983, Norcliffe	26	12	1,346,956	Two Altazano, 1991, Manzotti	20	9	709,725
Utah	Pharaoh's Heart, 1990, Persevered	67	10	340,470	Jones Time Machine, 1979, Current Concept	28	13	329,500
Vermont	Peter Orbit, 1971, Big Pete	90	17	43,953	Snowshoes, 1961, *North Carolina	107	16	29,685
Virginia	Paradise Creek, 1989, Irish River (Fr)	25	14	3,401,416	Seeking the Pearl, 1994, Seeking the Gold	21	8	4,021,716
Washington	Saratoga Passage, 1985, Pirateer	22	6	800,212	Peterhof's Patea, 1988, Peterhof	52	16	623,367
West Virginia	Soul of the Matter, 1991, Private Terms	16	7	2,302,818	Evil's Pic, 1992, Piccolino	31	10	437,877
Wisconsin	Chad's Boy, 1965, Disdainful	106	13	73,871	Cheetah Chick, 1977, Captain Seaweed	36	10	43,882
Wyoming	Peter Glory, 1956, New World	197	35	81,319	Zip Pouch, 1990, Destroyer (SAf)	16	7	48,981

Leading 2002 Earners by State Where Bred

State	MALE, YOB, Sire	Strts	Wins	Earnings	FEMALE, YOB, Sire	Strts	Wins	Earnings
Alabama	Leading Ruler, 1997, Double Leader	15	2	$27,515	Nell's Niner, 1999, Royal Empire	7	2	$43,930
Arizona	Coyote Lakes, 1994, Society Max	7	4	152,920	Monrow, 1996, Fool the Experts	13	4	118,265
Arkansas	Talknow, 1997, Pick Up the Phone	13	9	181,853	Supreme Discovery, 1999, Supremo	12	7	156,250
California	Grey Memo, 1997, Memo (Chi)	10	2	808,000	Super High, 1999, High Brite	11	5	410,748
Colorado	Personal Beau, 1996, Personal Flag	10	3	78,834	She's Finding Time, 1999, Ragtime Rascal	9	3	43,705
Connecticut	Nantucketeer, 1998, Departing Prints	14	5	76,658	Simply Striking, 1999, Skywalker	4	1	19,680
Delaware					Dog's Last Dance, 1999, Dog Watch	3	0	4,160
Florida	Orchard Park, 1999, Hennessy	7	5	613,310	Cellars Shiraz, 1999, Kissin Kris	13	7	513,320
Georgia	Bluesthestandard, 1997, American Standard	14	7	148,810	Southern Treasure, 1999, Bold Smoocher	12	2	40,270
Idaho	L'Effaceur, 1997, Jestic	3	3	117,600	Lookn Mighty Fine, 1997, Peterhof	10	2	113,980
Illinois	Mystery Giver, 1998, Dynaformer	9	3	302,060	Tejano Honey, 1999, Tejano Run	9	6	201,590
Indiana	Pass Rush, 1999, Crown Ambassador	10	3	199,540	Senorita Ziggy, 1998, Senor Speedy	12	5	133,095
Iowa	Cowboy Stuff, 1999, Evansville Slew	10	6	264,820	Sharky's Review, 1998, Sharkey	13	4	215,983
Kansas	Raise a Booger, 1999, Gold Ruler	10	4	111,956	Swinging Janie Gal, 1997, A. M. Swinger	5	2	33,414
Kentucky	War Emblem, 1999, Our Emblem	10	5	3,455,000	Azeri, 1998, Jade Hunter	9	8	2,181,540
Louisiana	Walk in the Snow, 1999, In a Walk	8	4	331,380	Prized Amberpro, 1997, Aspro	16	8	291,778
Maryland	Magic Weisner, 1999, Ameri Valay	8	4	791,000	Shine Again, 1997, Wild Again	10	4	425,500
Massachusetts	Jini's Jet, 1998, A. P Jet	11	5	99,790	Little Time, 1999, Scarlet Ibis	14	5	92,084
Michigan	Tenpins, 1998, Smart Strike	7	5	560,629	Sweetwater Promise, 1999, Service Stripe	12	5	172,110
Minnesota	J. P. Jet, 1999, A. P Jet	6	4	100,436	Lakeville, 1999, Evansville Slew	6	2	73,374
Mississippi	Question of Gold, 1994, Gold Angle	8	2	12,717	Lil' Nancy Dickens, 2000, Blushing Star	1	1	13,200
Missouri	Fort Metfield, 1994, Metfield	15	4	49,098	Dazzling Dana, 1998, Flying Victor	12	4	22,094

State	MALE, YOB, Sire	Strts	Wins	Earnings	FEMALE, YOB, Sire	Strts	Wins	Earnings
Montana	Ryan On Broadway, 1998, Fleet Sudan	12	3	29,668	Jocko Miss, 1997, Black Mackee	12	4	49,984
Nebraska	Mr Clearwater, 1999, Gourami	8	5	56,849	Oglala Sue, 1998, Verzy	9	4	99,480
Nevada	Debonair Kennedy, 1995, Highland Park	16	1	6,968				
New Hampshire	Alybull, 1997, Alyfoe	7	1	14,250	A Wish for Abby, 1993, Maudlin's Pleasure	1	0	204
New Jersey	Sea of Tranquility, 1996, Heff	11	4	188,312	Willie's Luv, 1999, Williamstown	7	3	124,005
New Mexico	Star Smasher, 1999, Full Choke	9	5	227,360	Espeedytoo, 1999, Ghost Ranch	16	9	321,094
New York	Private Emblem, 1999, Our Emblem	8	4	550,940	Carson Hollow, 1999, Carson City	7	5	335,370
North Carolina	Jason's Love, 1999, Above Normal	17	4	40,350	Lark's Impression, 1998, Above Normal	16	4	87,978
North Dakota	Suntana, 2000, Sun Man	6	4	57,587	Duffel's Macrena, 1996, Storada	8	2	10,476
Ohio	Harlan's Holiday, 1999, Harlan	10	3	1,606,000	Ashwood C C, 1998, Cryptoclearance	11	5	156,179
Oklahoma	Mr Ross, 1995, Slewacide	4	3	138,750	Tulupai, 2000, Coordinator	6	4	101,935
Oregon	Lethal Grande, 1999, Corslew	13	2	62,080	Absolutism, 1999, Abstract	10	3	65,175
Pennsylvania	With Anticipation, 1995, Relaunch	8	3	1,507,700	Caught in the Rain, 1999, Petionville	8	4	195,506
Rhode Island					Fracas, 1998, Chenin Blanc	10	2	14,760
South Carolina	American Prince, 1998, Miner	8	3	114,190	Sparky Diamond, 1997, All of a Sudden	12	6	71,060
South Dakota	Prairie Runner, 1998, Proud Northern	9	2	12,368	Lu's Luck, 1995, Rushing Raj	10	1	9,300
Tennessee	Clever Crawford, 1999, El Prado (Ire)	8	1	17,230	Southern Sweet, 1998, Tethra	6	2	54,795
Texas	Leo's Last Hurrahy, 2000, Leo Castelli	7	5	326,848	Got Koko, 1999, Signal Tap	8	4	242,946
Utah	Chory Four, 1999, Four Seasons (GB)	13	3	61,950	Lovehermadly, 1997, Regal Groom	9	3	23,247
Vermont	Pocantico, 1998, Slew the Knight	5	2	14,880				
Virginia	Bop, 1997, Rahy	7	5	170,983	Mandy's Gold, 1998, Gilded Time	13	5	715,404
Washington	Sabertooth, 1998, Petersburg	7	2	194,725	No Turbulence, 1999, Skywalker	12	2	109,566
West Virginia	Confucius Say, 1998, Eastover Court	8	5	243,540	Shesanothergrump, 1999, Weshaam	14	5	114,474
Wisconsin	Auat, 1998, Armed Truce	13	3	27,440	Jami Pari, 1996, Bold James	19	1	6,251

Performance Rates for 2002

Performance Rates are an objective measurement of racetrack performance developed by the Jockey Club Information Systems. Performance Rates were originally developed by the Jockey Club and first published in *The Thoroughbred Record* in the 1960s. Performance Rates assign a rate to horses based on beaten lengths—who beat whom and by how much—with some adjustments made to standardize beaten distances to account for horses that were not pressed or were eased in large fields. Races in which individual horses did not finish are not counted for those horses.

Time is not a factor in Performance Rates, which are based on every start by every horse in North America in 2002. Performance Rates are expressed in lengths around a theoretical mean of zero. The average performance of the best horses in a given year are generally about 30 lengths better than an average performance of the average horse.

Performance Rates give the premium to large winning margins, and Travers Stakes (G1) victor Medaglia d'Oro ranked atop the three-year-old males partly on the strength of his 13¾-length victory in Saratoga Race Course's Jim Dandy Stakes (G2). Medaglia d'Oro won the Travers, also at Saratoga, by a half-length. Second among

the three-year-olds was Buddha, runaway winner of a Gulfstream Park allowance race before narrowly winning the Wood Memorial Stakes (G1), his last start of the year, over Medaglia d'Oro. Eclipse Award winner War Emblem, victor of the Kentucky Derby (G1) and Preakness Stakes (G1), ranked fifth.

The only champion to head a Performance Rates category was Storm Flag Flying, the undefeated two-year-old filly. Medaglia d'Oro and Take Charge Lady, who led Performance Rates' three-year-old filly category, were Eclipse nominees. Azeri, voted Horse of the Year, was seventh in her division behind leader Dancethruthedawn.

Funny Cide, a two-time winner of New York-bred races by open lengths, was the leading two-year-old male in the 2002 Performance Rates, narrowly ahead of undefeated Hopeful Stakes (G1) victor Sky Mesa. Vindication, the Eclipse Award winner as champion two-year-old male, ranked seventh. Funny Cide won the 2003 Kentucky Derby (G1) and Preakness Stakes (G1).

To be included in Performance Rates, a horse must have made a minimum of three starts in North America in 2002. Following are the 100 leading Performance Rates runners by category in 2002.

Two-Year-Old Males

	Horse	Starts	Rating
1.	Funny Cide	3	26.40
2.	Sky Mesa	3	26.36
3.	Soto	3	25.68
4.	Zavata	5	24.76
5.	Trust N Luck	7	24.49
6.	Toccet	8	24.45
7.	Vindication	4	24.06
8.	Valid Video	3	23.88
9.	Alke	3	23.44
10.	Cat Genius	3	23.40
11.	Pretty Wild	6	22.94
12.	Whywhywhy	5	22.91
13.	Bham	6	22.77
14.	Cherokee's Boy	8	22.69
15.	Arco's Gold	3	22.50
16.	Crackup	5	22.34
17.	Icecoldbeeratreds	5	22.29
18.	Marry Me Monece	3	22.13
19.	Torre and Zim	3	21.80
20.	Taiaslew	5	21.39
21.	Boston Bull	4	21.37
22.	Siberland	5	21.13
23.	Unleash the Power	6	21.04
24.	Super Fuse	5	20.99
25.	Call Me Lefty	6	20.98
26.	Lone Star Sky	6	20.92
27.	Crafty Guy	4	20.87
28.	Grey Comet	3	20.78
29.	Bull Market	4	20.75
30.	Kafwain	8	20.68
31.	Change Course	3	20.62
32.	Catalissa	3	20.57
33.	Champali	4	20.53
34.	Outta Here	7	20.44
35.	Wiggins	4	20.38
36.	Ironton	5	20.37
37.	Canaan Land	4	20.36
38.	Hear No Evil	9	20.34
	Sharp Impact	3	20.34
40.	Outer Reef	6	20.26
41.	Quote This	4	20.17
42.	Run Production	5	20.14
43.	Spite the Devil	7	20.12

	Horse	Starts	Rating
	Forest Picnic	4	20.12
45.	Comic Truth	9	20.09
46.	Most Feared	7	19.98
47.	Shawklit Man	3	19.96
48.	Cape Good Hope	6	19.83
49.	Supah Blitz	10	19.79
50.	Donny Boy	3	19.76
51.	Coach Jimi Lee	3	19.66
52.	Hackendiffy	6	19.56
	Unswept	4	19.56
54.	Midway Road	4	19.55
55.	Kissin' Jack	4	19.34
56.	Witt Ante	3	19.17
57.	Nothing to Lose	4	19.09
58.	Mr. Makah	3	19.00
59.	Posse	7	18.93
60.	Excessive Barb	4	18.92
61.	Choctaw Charlie	3	18.86
62.	Roll Hennessy Roll	6	18.72
63.	Added Edge	4	18.66
64.	Peace Rules	6	18.59
65.	Meteor Impact	3	18.45
	Farno	5	18.45
67.	First Blush	5	18.43
68.	Storm Cadet	3	18.36
69.	Private Gold	7	18.32
70.	Infinite Justice	3	18.30
71.	Stong	6	18.19
72.	Ozzie Cat	7	18.13
	Roaring Fever	4	18.13
74.	Untold Tale	4	18.09
75.	Collateral Damage	5	18.03
76.	Conservation	3	18.00
	Doc Robbins	3	18.00
78.	Mt. Carson	6	17.91
79.	Listen Indy	5	17.84
80.	Echeverria	5	17.71
81.	Leo's Last Hurrahy	7	17.69
82.	Skamper	6	17.66
83.	Gators N Bears	3	17.60
84.	Bluegrass Spirit	4	17.55
85.	Boston Park	9	17.47
	Sevenforbish	4	17.47
87.	Lawbook	10	17.46
88.	Patacon	5	17.44
89.	Affable	3	17.41
	Formal Attire	3	17.41
	Christmas Away	4	17.41
92.	Title Contender	7	17.37
	Super Frolic	6	17.37
94.	True Enough	4	17.33
95.	Whispered Warning	5	17.23
96.	Gimmeawink	5	17.14
97.	H. M. S. Hollywood	5	17.13
98.	Cooper Crossing	3	17.12
99.	The Lady's Groom	3	17.08
100.	Patriotic Flame	7	17.07

Two-Year-Old Fillies

	Horse	Starts	Rating
1.	Storm Flag Flying	4	31.50
2.	Roar Emotion	3	27.89
3.	Ivanavinalot	6	27.33
4.	Awesome Humor	4	26.92
5.	Stellar	3	26.24
6.	Sweet Samantha	3	24.92
7.	Caucus	3	24.41
8.	Souris	6	24.20
9.	Santa Catarina	3	23.94
10.	Feisty Step	3	23.87
11.	Chimichurri	5	23.01
12.	Forever Partners	3	22.80
13.	Final Round	4	22.76
14.	Bird Town	3	22.64
15.	My Boston Gal	3	22.60
16.	Beautiful America	4	22.32
17.	Combanchera	4	21.67
18.	Wild Snitch	3	21.48
	Puxa Saco	5	21.48
20.	My Trusty Cat	6	21.39
21.	Westerly Breeze	5	21.27

	Horse	Starts	Rating
22.	Ruby's Reception	7	21.23
23.	House Party	4	21.16
24.	Fast Cookie	7	21.01
25.	Star of Atticus	4	20.74
26.	Holiday Lady	6	20.71
27.	Christmas Time	3	20.67
	Shesasmokin	5	20.67
29.	Savedbythelight	4	20.62
30.	Midnight Cry	6	20.09
31.	Ocean Drive	4	19.95
32.	Composure	6	19.87
33.	Mymich	6	19.30
34.	Hope for Love	4	19.28
35.	Moonlight Sonata	6	19.24
36.	Just Bill Me	3	19.21
37.	Cyber Secret	3	19.20
38.	Doc's Doll	5	19.17
39.	Fircroft	5	19.15
40.	Sea Jewel	4	19.07
41.	Appleby Gardens	4	19.02
42.	Allspice	3	18.97
43.	Reheat	4	18.91
44.	Perfect Story	3	18.87
45.	Angel Punch	4	18.84
46.	Parting	7	18.83
47.	Watching You	3	18.75
48.	Tulupai	6	18.71
49.	Receivership	5	18.69
50.	Heavenly Miss	9	18.68
51.	Ebony Breeze	5	18.65
52.	Vibs	7	18.43
53.	Explosive Beauty	7	18.39
54.	Wildcat Annie	6	18.38
55.	Dakota Light	6	18.31
56.	Cherokee Lite	6	18.29
57.	Coquettish	4	18.25
58.	Glorious Miss	5	18.23
59.	Just Call Me Angel	4	18.21
60.	Dreamy Song	3	18.16
61.	Civility Cat	4	18.03
62.	Jodys Deelite	6	17.94
	U K Trick	7	17.94
64.	Elloluv	3	17.93
65.	Spinning Wind	5	17.87
66.	Roses for Sonja	3	17.86
67.	Crimson and Roses	7	17.83
68.	Oyster Bay	3	17.79
69.	Crystal Dancer	3	17.77
70.	Summer Wind Dancer	5	17.71
71.	Behrnik	6	17.70
	Hadif's Allstar	6	17.70
73.	Blink Twice	3	17.62
74.	Tricks Her	3	17.55
75.	Tale of the Ticker	4	17.45
76.	Silk N Diamonds	4	17.39
77.	Red Cell	4	17.37
	Sweet Davia	3	17.37
79.	Fabulous Brush	6	17.34
80.	Elegant Designer	7	17.30
81.	Race to Glory	3	17.27
82.	Onda Ray	3	17.25
83.	Mischievously	5	17.12
84.	Lady Stars	6	17.08
	Throne	7	17.08
86.	Lets Just Do It	10	17.05
87.	Heirloom Diamond	6	17.03
88.	Buffythecenterfold	6	17.02
89.	Fortunate Card	5	16.99
	Sunny Victory	5	16.99
91.	Holiday Runner	5	16.98
92.	Bonay	7	16.97
93.	Hannah's Royalrock	6	16.94
94.	Ladyecho	6	16.90
95.	D' Nile	4	16.86
96.	Atlantic Ocean	8	16.85
97.	Princess Birdeye	3	16.82
98.	Home Run Hitter	5	16.81
99.	Running Debate	8	16.72
100.	Marc's Rainbow	5	16.71

Three-Year-Old Males

	Horse	Starts	Rating
1.	Medaglia d'Oro	9	32.25
2.	Buddha	3	31.81
3.	Proud Citizen	5	29.27
4.	Sarava	4	29.07
5.	War Emblem	10	28.36
6.	Repent	5	28.00
7.	Gygistar	5	27.36
8.	Harlan's Holiday	10	26.82
9.	Blueformer	3	25.87
10.	Onthedeanslist	3	25.78
11.	Essence of Dubai	5	25.64
12.	Magic Weisner	8	25.29
13.	Blue Burner	5	24.96
14.	Yankee Gentleman	5	24.32
15.	Request for Parole	5	23.71
16.	Najran	7	23.38
17.	Saarland	4	23.34
18.	Easyfromthegitgo	11	23.12
19.	Sunday Break (Jpn)	7	22.75
20.	Cashel Castle	3	22.61
21.	Quest	7	22.43
22.	Greatness	3	22.33
23.	Strive	8	22.28
24.	Flying Notes	7	22.27
25.	Deputy Dash	5	22.04
26.	Regency Park	5	21.98
27.	Like a Hero	9	21.94
28.	Booklet	7	21.88
29.	Came Home	8	21.85
30.	Police Alert	4	21.80
31.	Thunderello	4	21.79
32.	Puzzlement	9	21.75
33.	Equality	6	21.74
34.	Speed Hunter	5	21.55
35.	The Judge Sez Who	11	21.51
36.	Volkonsky	6	21.33
37.	Youghal Bay	8	21.00
38.	Perfect Drift	8	20.92
39.	Puck	9	20.87
40.	Straight Gin	6	20.75
41.	Pass Rush	10	20.70
42.	Nothing Flat	11	20.67
	Marasca	4	20.67
44.	Saint Marden	7	20.60
45.	Fisher Pond	9	20.47
46.	A. P. Five Hundred	6	20.44
47.	Ole Faunty	3	20.31
48.	Jeremiah Jack	5	20.00
49.	Flatter	4	19.84
50.	No Parole	10	19.80
51.	True Direction	8	19.73
52.	Running Tide	3	19.71
53.	Private Emblem	8	19.68
54.	U S S Tinosa	6	19.59
55.	Trump Marina	6	19.52
56.	Warners	4	19.50
	Bulldog George	8	19.50
58.	Smokin' John	3	19.49
59.	Legislator	5	19.32
60.	Regal Sanction	8	19.30
61.	This Guns for Hire	11	19.27
62.	Peekskill	12	19.26
63.	Draw Play	3	19.25
64.	Essayons	11	19.20
65.	Ethan Man	3	19.15
66.	Pleasant Hall	3	19.12
67.	Sonic West	3	19.04
68.	Quest Star	13	19.03
69.	Kasparov	3	18.99
70.	Monthir	6	18.96
71.	Thebigapple	10	18.87
72.	Political Attack	8	18.83
73.	Burnt Ember	3	18.65
74.	Star Smasher	9	18.63
75.	Miesque's Approval	7	18.59
76.	In Halo's Image	7	18.52
77.	Thunderpumper	7	18.50
78.	Quantis	3	18.47
79.	M B Sea	13	18.44
80.	Harbor Star	5	18.40
81.	Listen Here	6	18.33
82.	Walk in the Snow	8	18.33

83.	Patrol	6	18.29
84.	Crimson Hero	8	18.25
85.	Colorful Tour	8	18.21
86.	Premeditation	9	18.18
87.	Bunk N Ted	9	18.12
	Wiseman's Ferry	8	18.12
89.	Tracemark	8	18.05
90.	Salt Grinder	7	18.00
91.	Rubino	4	17.99
92.	Finality	6	17.96
93.	Fast Decision	7	17.89
94.	Mayakovsky	4	17.88
95.	Lusty Latin	5	17.85
	Jazz Beat (Ire)	3	17.85
97.	Missme	11	17.84
98.	Bag of Mischief	12	17.82
99.	Super X One	5	17.76
100.	Honor in War	5	17.75

Three-Year-Old Fillies

	Horse	Starts	Rating
1.	Take Charge Lady	10	29.16
2.	You	9	26.41
3.	Jilbab	5	25.87
4.	Allamerican Bertie	11	25.77
5.	Sightseek	5	25.74
6.	Alternate	8	25.54
7.	Imperial Gesture	5	25.01
8.	Tricky Indy	3	24.69
9.	Bella Bellucci	6	23.89
10.	Willa On the Move	7	23.76
11.	Alchemilla	5	23.07
12.	Belterra	3	22.84
13.	Farda Amiga	6	22.81
14.	See How She Runs	4	22.69
15.	Chamrousse	7	22.66
16.	Pupil	7	22.57
17.	Shop Till You Drop	8	22.45
18.	Sixtyone Margaux	8	22.40
19.	Bema	3	22.20
20.	Lake Lady	5	22.16
21.	Cheeksandpeanuts	4	22.04
22.	To the Queen	9	22.01
23.	Bedanken	7	21.88
24.	Slews Final Answer	7	21.79
25.	Sweet Sixteen	5	21.61
26.	My Golden Girl	6	21.45
	Miss Lodi	7	21.45
28.	Nonsuch Bay	10	21.38
29.	Delmonico Cat	4	21.12
30.	Tomokas Outrageous	4	20.89
31.	Proper Gamble	6	20.81
32.	Wishful Splendor	12	20.79
33.	Bold World	9	20.75
34.	Spelling	10	20.74
35.	Grab Bag	4	20.50
36.	Martha's Music	10	20.45
37.	Wilzada	10	20.42
38.	Charmed Gift	7	20.38
39.	Zawzooth	7	20.31
40.	Amazing Lady	9	20.25
41.	Clear Destiny	5	20.24
42.	Cades Cove	3	20.21
43.	Ribbon Cane	5	20.12
44.	Honorville	4	20.00
45.	Maresha	6	19.89
46.	Jester Rahab	12	19.85
	Strike the Sky	4	19.85
48.	Lady Liberty	5	19.84
49.	Gazillion	9	19.82
50.	Pass the Virtue	12	19.77
51.	Sarah Jade	8	19.58
52.	Riskaverse	7	19.57
53.	Dublino	3	19.46
54.	Delta Princess	3	19.44
55.	Cellars Shiraz	13	19.41
56.	Fly Borboleta	9	19.35
57.	Election Star	6	19.34
58.	Ginger Gold	5	19.27
59.	Desert Gold	7	19.20
60.	Silver Sonnet	8	19.16
61.	Pass the Pepper	5	19.15

62.	Cash Tyme	7	19.13
	Summer Mis	4	19.13
64.	Dreamers Glory	8	19.07
	Redoubled Miss	11	19.07
66.	French Riviera	4	19.05
67.	Bear Fan	3	19.02
68.	Quiet Delight	6	18.97
69.	Megahertz (GB)	7	18.95
70.	Dignified Diva	3	18.92
71.	Darnestown	4	18.89
72.	Habibti	7	18.87
73.	Consort Music	4	18.84
74.	Princess Dixie	6	18.83
75.	Swinging Gate	11	18.55
76.	Hear This	3	18.50
	French Satin	6	18.50
78.	Take the Cake	7	18.45
79.	Tarnished Lady	14	18.44
80.	Bare Necessities	8	18.42
81.	Glorious Cat	5	18.41
82.	Charitabledonation	6	18.38
83.	Undercover	8	18.36
84.	Vesta	6	18.29
85.	So Much More	4	18.27
	Cyclorama	5	18.27
	Knocking	12	18.27
88.	Spring Meadow	13	18.22
89.	Hi Tech Honeycomb	9	18.20
90.	Litany	6	18.19
91.	For Rubies	12	18.13
92.	Copper Belle	5	18.04
	Arabis	9	18.04
	Shawklit Mint	15	18.04
95.	Smok'n Frolic	5	18.02
96.	September Secret	3	18.01
97.	Affirmed Dancer	4	17.96
	A New Twist	5	17.96
99.	Lady Adare	6	17.95
100.	Chase Gap	5	17.94
	Devilish Look	3	17.94

Males, Four-Year-Olds and Older

	Horse	Starts	Rating
1.	Wild Years	3	28.12
2.	Evening Attire	9	25.62
3.	Kudos	3	25.27
4.	Tenpins	7	24.61
5.	Macho Uno	6	24.44
6.	Lido Palace (Chi)	7	24.28
7.	Hail The Chief (GB)	6	24.21
8.	Unbridling	3	24.20
9.	Milwaukee Brew	7	24.07
10.	Abreeze	7	23.57
11.	Dollar Bill	9	23.43
12.	Left Bank	4	23.19
13.	Mr. John	4	23.12
14.	Chicago Six	3	22.93
15.	Learned	3	22.78
16.	Rock Slide	5	22.26
17.	Volponi	8	22.10
18.	Bowman's Band	9	22.09
19.	Rize	3	22.00
20.	Orientate	10	21.75
21.	Unbridled Vision	4	21.64
22.	Best of the Rest	9	21.13
	Affirmed Success	6	21.13
24.	Mongoose	4	21.08
25.	X Country	10	21.01
26.	Parade Leader	7	20.99
27.	Docent	10	20.95
28.	Snake Mountain	10	20.89
29.	Momentum	6	20.77
30.	Mc Mahon	6	20.63
31.	Crafty C. T.	7	20.61
32.	Crossing Point	5	20.58
33.	High Commissioner	9	20.50
34.	Good Journey	5	20.47
35.	Fancy As	3	20.38
36.	Cat's At Home	8	20.33
37.	Include	4	20.32
38.	Ground Storm	10	20.23
	Ciento	8	20.23
40.	Western Pride	3	20.22

41.	Hero's Tribute	7	20.17
	Grundlefoot	5	20.17
43.	Aldebaran	8	20.12
44.	Crafty Shaw	10	20.10
45.	Pure Prize	7	20.08
	Nowrass (GB)	6	20.08
47.	Congaree	6	20.07
48.	Cat Tracker	5	20.06
	Graeme Hall	3	20.06
50.	Windsor Castle	11	19.98
51.	Falcon Flight (Fr)	4	19.97
52.	Lavender's Lad	4	19.90
53.	Hal's Hope	6	19.83
54.	Free of Love	7	19.76
55.	Sea of Tranquility	11	19.66
56.	Mister Business	5	19.63
57.	Red Bullet	5	19.58
	Oak Hall	8	19.58
59.	E Z Glory	8	19.56
60.	Neon Shadow	5	19.47
	Seeking Daylight	5	19.47
62.	Confucius Say	8	19.45
63.	Pleasant Breeze	11	19.43
64.	Bonapaw	8	19.37
65.	Coyote Lakes	7	19.29
66.	This Fleet Is Due	4	19.18
67.	Pleasantly Perfect	8	19.14
68.	River Rush	6	19.12
69.	Horrible Evening	7	19.09
	Tailfromthecrypt	8	19.09
	Swept Overboard	5	19.09
72.	Smashing Beau	13	19.02
73.	Twilight Road	11	18.99
74.	First Lieutenant	4	18.96
75.	No Armistice	3	18.93
	Alotta Numbers	4	18.93
77.	Krieger	5	18.92
78.	La Reine's Terms	4	18.89
79.	Kona Gold	3	18.83
80.	Private Ryan	5	18.80
81.	Runspastum	12	18.79
82.	Esperence	3	18.72
83.	Forbidden Apple	6	18.69
84.	Jackpot	4	18.64
85.	Compelling World	9	18.59
86.	Seattle Chief	4	18.56
	Reba's Gold	10	18.56
88.	Secret Romeo	13	18.52
89.	Express Tour	4	18.50
90.	Song Dancer	5	18.47
91.	Jake the Flake	10	18.38
92.	Saquache	9	18.31
93.	Amjaad	5	18.30
94.	Unshaded	7	18.28
95.	Compendium	6	18.19
96.	Yaeger	15	18.12
97.	Talknow	13	18.09
	Dash for Daylight	5	18.09
99.	Sardaukar (GB)	6	17.95
100.	Buenos Dias	5	17.94

Females, Four-Year-Olds and Older

	Horse	Starts	Rating
1.	Dancethruthedawn	6	27.81
2.	Transcendental	6	26.08
3.	Regal Countess	7	25.60
4.	Miss Linda (Arg)	3	25.21
5.	Summer Colony	8	25.15
6.	Irving's Baby	3	24.47
7.	Azeri	9	24.20
8.	Descapate	3	24.13
9.	Minister's Baby	8	23.77
10.	Too Scarlet	4	23.63
11.	Ellie's Moment	6	23.43
12.	Shine Again	10	22.86
13.	Xtra Heat	10	22.85
14.	Pocus Hocus	4	22.32
15.	Mandy's Gold	13	22.21
16.	Sound of the West	3	22.13
17.	Gold Mover	9	22.03
18.	Raging Fever	10	21.86
19.	Forest Secrets	5	21.84
20.	Surya	6	21.50

#	Horse	Starts	Rating
21.	Ashwood C C	11	21.34
22.	Southern Fiction	5	21.20
23.	Lady Upstage (Ire)	3	21.19
24.	With Ability	11	20.94
25.	Starrer	6	20.92
26.	Quiet Lake	7	20.83
27.	Victory Ride	5	20.76
28.	Softly	12	20.74
29.	Printemps (Chi)	5	20.69
30.	Lady Cherie	10	20.64
31.	Strawberry Blonde (Ire)	4	20.60
32.	Babae (Chi)	8	20.58
33.	Your Out	9	20.35
	Ask Me No Secrets	4	20.35
35.	Celtic Melody	5	20.32
36.	Shiny Sheet	11	20.27
37.	Sweetest Thing	5	20.25
38.	Spain	7	20.23
39.	Roxelana	3	20.20
40.	Starine (Fr)	4	20.19
41.	Search Party	3	20.16
42.	Amonita (GB)	3	20.13
43.	Caressing	5	19.97
44.	Golden Apples (Ire)	7	19.92
45.	Voodoo Dancer	7	19.72
46.	Nasty Storm	8	19.53
47.	Affluent	8	19.45
48.	Astra	5	19.40
49.	Binalegend	3	19.34
50.	Crossing Denali	3	19.33
51.	Cozy Island	7	19.31
52.	Snow Dance	7	19.25
53.	Owsley	8	19.05
54.	Calista (GB)	4	18.94
55.	Banks Hill (GB)	3	18.87
56.	Tap Dance	10	18.85
57.	Miss Kristy	5	18.83
58.	Critical Eye	12	18.77
59.	Kalookan Queen	8	18.69
60.	De Bertie	5	18.66
61.	Secret Liaison	4	18.59
62.	Quick Tip	9	18.51
63.	Harmony Lodge	3	18.47
	Tates Creek	8	18.47
65.	Pompeii	4	18.45
66.	Dat You Miz Blue	12	18.43
	Bien Nicole	10	18.43
68.	Crowd Teaser	5	18.41
69.	Atelier	6	18.37
70.	Freefourracing	7	18.33
71.	Zonk	6	18.32
	Tweedside	6	18.32
73.	San Dare	14	18.22
74.	Gal On the Go	11	18.14
75.	Lady Linda	4	18.06
76.	Diversa	7	18.05
	Pleasant County	5	18.05
78.	Run for Joy	14	17.97
79.	Happily Unbridled	9	17.90
80.	Belle Artiste	11	17.83
81.	Banderia (Arg)	12	17.82
82.	Banished Lover	3	17.78
83.	Annatoga	9	17.77
84.	Along Came Mary	5	17.76
85.	Emery Board	3	17.74
86.	Volga (Ire)	6	17.71
87.	Monabella	4	17.67
88.	Tippity Witch	9	17.66
89.	Emily Ring	9	17.65
90.	Away	9	17.63
91.	Siringas (Ire)	5	17.60
92.	Lapuma	8	17.59
93.	Silent Stream	8	17.53
94.	Dania Bay	7	17.51
95.	La Galerie (Arg)	7	17.50
96.	Chopinina	4	17.47
97.	Cashmina	3	17.45
98.	Blue Moon (Fr)	4	17.40
99.	Montelena	3	17.39
100.	Watch	6	17.35
	Silver Rail	10	17.35

Turf Males, Three and Older

#	Horse	Starts	Rating
1.	Nowrass (GB)	5	21.20
2.	Good Journey	5	20.47
3.	Coco's Madness	4	20.22
4.	Falcon Flight (Fr)	4	19.97
5.	Volponi	4	19.38
6.	Legislator	3	19.31
7.	Back Packer	3	19.24
8.	River Rush	6	19.12
9.	Quest Star	7	19.05
10.	Krieger	5	18.92
11.	La Reine's Terms	6	18.89
12.	Tam's Terms	3	18.86
13.	Esperence	3	18.72
14.	Forbidden Apple	6	18.69
15.	Ibn Al Haitham (GB)	3	18.63
16.	Miesque's Approval	7	18.59
17.	Political Attack	4	18.58
18.	Jake the Flake	10	18.38
19.	Patrol	6	18.29
20.	Coahoma	7	18.13
21.	Jubileo	5	18.03
22.	Finality	6	17.96
23.	Sardaukar (GB)	6	17.95
24.	Buenos Dias	6	17.94
25.	Jazz Beat (Ire)	3	17.85
26.	Beat Hollow (GB)	8	17.84
27.	Stage Show	3	17.71
28.	Green Fee	6	17.67
29.	Rochester	10	17.66
30.	With Anticipation	8	17.62
31.	Skate Away	3	17.46
32.	Denon	7	17.40
33.	Del Mar Show	6	17.39
34.	Youghal Bay	3	17.29
35.	Ladies Din	3	17.25
36.	Union Place	10	17.21
37.	Mr. Mellon	3	17.10
38.	Boastful	9	17.08
39.	Lucky Scarab	3	16.98
40.	Strut the Stage	8	16.92
41.	Schaumburg	3	16.91
42.	Continental Red	6	16.84
43.	Morluc	5	16.83
44.	Sarafan	10	16.82
45.	Decarchy	6	16.78
46.	Quiet Resolve	7	16.65
47.	Suances (GB)	4	16.64
48.	Man From Wicklow	6	16.62
49.	L. A. Albert	3	16.61
	Guardianofthegate	4	16.61
	Portcullis	10	16.61
52.	Package Store	4	16.59
53.	Entitlement	5	16.57
54.	Honor in War	4	16.54
55.	Nat's Big Party	5	16.52
56.	Nobodys Listening	3	16.51
57.	Designed for Luck	3	16.50
58.	Northcote Road	4	16.49
59.	Dr. Kashnikow	8	16.46
60.	Cetewayo	6	16.42
61.	Orchard Park	6	16.41
62.	White Heart (GB)	5	16.35
63.	Grammarian	9	16.31
64.	Haggs Castle	4	16.27
65.	Four On the Floor	4	16.23
66.	Skipping (GB)	4	16.18
67.	Band Is Passing	4	16.16
68.	Foster's Landing	6	16.12
	Mountain Beacon	4	16.12
	Rock Opera	7	16.12
71.	Baptize	5	16.10
72.	Pisces	10	16.09
73.	Polish Miner	6	16.05
74.	Shibboleth	4	16.03
75.	Aslaaf	7	16.02
76.	The Tin Man	9	16.01
77.	Redattore (Brz)	3	16.00
	Everything to Gain	6	16.00
79.	Insperado (Fr)	6	15.99
80.	Glick	7	15.92
81.	Astrologist	4	15.88
	Royal Spy	4	15.88
83.	Artax Too	4	15.85
84.	Le Cinquieme Essai	3	15.85
85.	Kris Havingfunnow	7	15.84
86.	Classic Par	7	15.83
87.	Regal Sanction	4	15.82
	Lord Juban	5	15.82
89.	He's Crafty	4	15.81
	Al's Dearly Bred	9	15.81
91.	Even the Score	9	15.75
	Scooter Roach	4	15.75
93.	Red Mountain	8	15.74
	David Copperfield	3	15.74
95.	Kamolia	5	15.64
	Startac	6	15.64
97.	Root With Style	3	15.62
98.	Moon Solitaire (Ire)	6	15.61
99.	Bristolville	5	15.58
100.	Ringaskiddy	7	15.56

Turf Females, Three and Older

#	Horse	Starts	Rating
1.	Bedanken	4	22.55
2.	Lady Upstage (Ire)	3	21.19
3.	Strawberry Blonde (Ire)	4	20.60
4.	Babae (Chi)	8	20.58
5.	Sweetest Thing	5	20.25
6.	Starine (Fr)	4	20.19
7.	Amonita (GB)	3	20.13
8.	Golden Apples (Ire)	7	19.92
9.	Voodoo Dancer	7	19.72
10.	Fighting Duchess	3	19.58
11.	Riskaverse	7	19.57
12.	Dublino	3	19.46
13.	Astra	5	19.40
14.	Snow Dance	7	19.25
15.	With Patience	6	19.16
16.	Owsley	8	19.05
17.	Megahertz (GB)	7	18.95
18.	Calista (GB)	4	18.94
19.	Caught in the Rain	4	18.89
20.	Banks Hill (GB)	3	18.87
21.	Voodoo Lady	4	18.66
22.	Cellars Shiraz	9	18.54
23.	Dreamers Glory	3	18.52
24.	Quick Tip	9	18.51
25.	Tates Creek	8	18.47
26.	Bien Nicole	10	18.43
27.	Mountain Angel	3	18.40
28.	Tweedside	6	18.32
29.	Cyclorama	5	18.27
30.	Cozy Island	5	18.21
31.	Sadler's Sarah	4	18.14
32.	Surya	5	18.07
33.	Lady Linda	4	18.06
34.	Hi Tech Honeycomb	6	17.99
35.	Affirmed Dancer	4	17.96
36.	San Dare	9	17.87
37.	Wonder Again	6	17.84
	Alozaina (Ire)	6	17.84
39.	Mariensky	4	17.83
40.	Volga (Ire)	6	17.71
41.	Hot Talent	6	17.68
42.	Monabella	4	17.67
43.	Siringas (Ire)	5	17.60
44.	Lapuma	8	17.59
45.	Eagle Lake	5	17.51
46.	Chopinina	4	17.47
47.	Silver Nithi	3	17.42
48.	Blue Moon (Fr)	4	17.40
49.	Coney Kitty (Ire)	7	17.38
50.	Silver Rail	10	17.35
	Watch	6	17.35
52.	Rhum	7	17.28
53.	Manhattan Skyline	4	17.25
	Tarnished Lady	6	17.25
55.	Maliziosa	11	17.21
56.	Stylish	7	17.19
	Secret River	3	17.19
58.	Tippity Witch	7	17.17
	Crowd Teaser	3	17.17

	Horse	Starts	Rating
60.	Party Queen	3	17.15
61.	High Maintenance (GB)	8	17.08
62.	Mot Juste (GB)	7	17.07
63.	Sarah Jade	4	17.03
64.	De Aar	8	16.99
65.	Peanut Gallery	7	16.91
66.	Dame Sylvieguilhem	3	16.90
67.	Smart Grace	5	16.87
	May Gator		16.87
69.	Dat You Miz Blue	4	16.85
70.	Sunstone (GB)	9	16.85
71.	Affluent	3	16.83
72.	Beret	4	16.81
73.	Heyahohowdy	6	16.80
74.	Unbridled Vice	6	16.78
75.	Magic Mission (GB)	6	16.77
76.	Megans Bluff	6	16.76
	Eventail	5	16.76
78.	New Economy	7	16.73
79.	Lady of the Future	6	16.72
80.	Wander Mom	11	16.71
	Brandala	10	16.71
82.	Guana (Fr)	6	16.68
83.	Kiss the Devil	8	16.65
84.	Take It Off	5	16.64
85.	Love n' Kiss S.	5	16.59
86.	Lovely Lady	3	16.58
87.	When I Grow Up	5	16.53
88.	A B Noodle	6	16.50
89.	Sluice	10	16.49
	Platinum Tiara	6	16.49
	Salty Farma	8	16.49
92.	Picture Palace	7	16.47
93.	Sobrina Del Rey (Chi)	3	16.46
94.	Silent Stream	4	16.45
95.	Bloomy	5	16.37
	Clearly a Queen	6	16.37
97.	Lush Soldier	12	16.35
98.	Salty You	7	16.32
	Special County	3	16.32
100.	She's Vested	8	16.30

Sprint Males, Three and Older

	Horse	Starts	Rating
1.	Gygistar	4	27.78
2.	Najran	4	22.97
3.	Orientate	7	22.47
4.	Greatness	3	22.33
5.	Thunderello	4	21.79
6.	Speed Hunter	3	20.79
7.	Crossing Point	5	20.58
8.	Affirmed Success	4	20.32
9.	Aldebaran	5	20.30
10.	Secret Romeo	9	19.82
11.	True Direction	8	19.73
12.	No Parole	4	19.68
13.	Unbridled Trick	5	19.64
14.	Crafty C. T.	5	19.57
15.	Warners	4	19.50
16.	Windsor Castle	3	19.45
17.	Out of Fashion	4	19.41
18.	Boston Common	8	19.37
19.	Draw Play	3	19.25
	Twilight Road	10	19.25
21.	No Armistice	3	18.93
22.	Bonapaw	6	18.88
23.	Listen Here	5	18.84
24.	Kona Gold	3	18.83
25.	Disturbingthepeace	7	18.64
	Reflecting Colors	5	18.64
27.	Fast Decision	4	18.63
	In Halo's Image	4	18.63
29.	Clergy	3	18.60
30.	My Cousin Matt	8	18.53
31.	Quantis	3	18.47
32.	Liberty Run	5	18.44
33.	Premier Performer	9	18.31
34.	Amjaad	5	18.30
35.	Bulldog George	5	18.23
36.	Talknow	8	18.09
37.	Hay Getoutofmyway	3	18.05
38.	Mountain General	7	17.94
39.	Halo's Tiger	3	17.86
	Kings Command	3	17.86
41.	Premeditation	3	17.81
42.	One N Three	7	17.79
43.	Snow Ridge	6	17.76
44.	Bird Valley	3	17.69
45.	Pop Rocks	4	17.66
46.	Sea of Tranquility	6	17.58
	Gold Dollar	3	17.58
48.	Flying Notes	3	17.54
49.	Fappie's Notebook	4	17.52
50.	Matanzas Creek	6	17.51
51.	Aggadan	8	17.50
	D'wildcat	6	17.50
53.	Stoney	6	17.43
54.	Dash for Daylight	6	17.34
55.	Smile n Wildcat	3	17.32
56.	Halo Cat	9	17.28
57.	Tour of the Cat	8	17.18
58.	Song Dancer	4	17.16
59.	Beau's Town	6	17.14
60.	Past Tence	3	17.13
61.	Say Florida Sandy	12	17.11
62.	Personable Pete	6	17.10
63.	Confucius Say	4	17.07
64.	Sterling Gold	5	17.06
65.	Heavenly Search	4	17.04
66.	Kentucky Maid	5	17.02
67.	Ciento	4	16.86
68.	Le Bourget	6	16.76
	Top Shoter	4	16.76
70.	Folkestone Park	6	16.75
71.	Soaring Free	5	16.71
	Hudson Street	9	16.71
73.	Sharp Gold	5	16.69
74.	Summer Note	3	16.67
75.	Sassy Hound	8	16.62
76.	Multiple Choice	11	16.59
77.	Spin Time	5	16.58
78.	Boots On Sunday	10	16.54
79.	Entepreneur	5	16.51
	This Guns for Hire	5	16.51
81.	Restage	4	16.49
	Big Talkin Man	3	16.49
83.	Star Smasher	5	16.46
84.	Parade of Music	3	16.45
85.	Bold Truth	6	16.44
86.	Sing Me Back Home	12	16.43
	Ceeband	4	16.43
	Swept Overboard	4	16.43
89.	Cojet	8	16.42
90.	Flying Free	7	16.38
91.	Medlin Road	4	16.37
92.	Big E E	4	16.34
93.	Voodoo	6	16.30
94.	Car Keys	6	16.29
95.	Juggernaut	4	16.25
	Meetyouathebrig	6	16.25
97.	Plazas Lil Waki	3	16.23
98.	Marching Orders	3	16.22
99.	American System	7	16.21
100.	Mr Bassett	4	16.18

Sprint Females, Three and Older

	Horse	Starts	Rating
1.	Nonsuch Bay	3	26.24
2.	Tricky Indy	3	24.69
3.	Willa On the Move	5	23.76
4.	Raging Fever	6	22.86
5.	Xtra Heat	10	22.85
6.	Shine Again	9	22.63
7.	Spelling	3	22.20
8.	Cheeksandpeanuts	4	22.04
9.	Gold Mover	9	22.03
10.	Slews Final Answer	7	21.79
11.	Miss Lodi	7	21.45
12.	Mandy's Gold	9	21.19
13.	Freefourracing	3	21.06
14.	Proper Gamble	6	20.81
15.	Bold World	3	20.75
16.	Grab Bag	4	20.50
17.	Sweet Sixteen	3	20.49
18.	To the Queen	3	20.44
19.	Wilzada	10	20.42
20.	Celtic Melody	5	20.32
21.	Zawzooth	7	20.31
22.	Cades Cove	3	20.21
23.	Roxelana	3	20.20
24.	Gazillion	9	19.82
25.	Dreamers Glory	3	19.45
26.	Spring Meadow	10	19.28
27.	Respectful	7	19.19
28.	Dat You Miz Blue	9	19.18
29.	Silver Sonnet	8	19.16
30.	Pass the Pepper	5	19.15
31.	French Riviera	4	19.05
32.	Bear Fan	3	19.02
33.	Dignified Diva	3	18.92
34.	Allamerican Bertie	3	18.84
35.	Cash Tyme	5	18.81
36.	Got Koko	3	18.74
37.	Kalookan Queen	8	18.69
38.	Nasty Storm	7	18.66
39.	Whiletheiron'shot	4	18.63
40.	Hear This	3	18.50
41.	Harmony Lodge	3	18.47
42.	Irguns Angel	3	18.37
	Quiet Delight	4	18.37
44.	Amazing Lady	5	18.31
45.	Vesta	6	18.29
46.	Secret Liaison	3	18.28
47.	For Rubies	11	18.25
48.	Don't Countess Out	8	18.17
	Miss Dixie Chick	5	18.17
50.	Cosmah Star	3	18.08
51.	Tchula Miss	8	18.06
52.	Shawklit Mint	15	18.04
	Copper Belle	5	18.04
54.	September Secret	3	18.01
55.	Away	7	18.00
56.	Belle Artiste	7	17.99
57.	School for Scandal	6	17.98
58.	A New Twist	5	17.96
59.	Speed to Burn	5	17.93
60.	Forest Heiress	5	17.79
	Betty's Hat	4	17.79
62.	Born to Dance	6	17.70
63.	Elana d'Amour	3	17.65
	Emily Ring	9	17.65
65.	Desert Gold	4	17.63
66.	Princess Dixie	3	17.62
67.	La Galerie (Arg)	7	17.50
68.	Boozin' Susan	10	17.47
69.	Prized Stamp	5	17.42
70.	Vicki Vallencourt	3	17.41
71.	Icantgoforthat	4	17.39
72.	Miss N Texas	4	17.25
73.	Chispiski	12	17.20
74.	Reason to Talk	3	17.19
75.	Honorable Peace	4	17.16
76.	Hattiesburg	7	17.15
77.	She's Got the Beat	5	17.13
78.	Barbara O'Brien	3	17.11
79.	Arabis	7	17.03
80.	Raymond's Dream	8	16.98
81.	Driana	4	16.96
82.	Blinded by Love	6	16.95
83.	Bel Baie	6	16.93
84.	Interest Only	7	16.90
85.	Fancy Prancer	3	16.88
86.	Little Out	5	16.85
87.	Silent Stream	6	16.83
88.	Cherokee Girl	6	16.79
89.	Drippingindiamonds	4	16.75
90.	Saint Bernadette	4	16.70
91.	Savorthetime	9	16.68
92.	Cat Cay	6	16.63
93.	Four Pennies	7	16.62
94.	Dynamite Miss	12	16.58
	Netherland (Arg)	3	16.58
96.	Maddie May	8	16.56
97.	Littelfuse	3	16.55
98.	Haunted Lass	5	16.53
99.	Southern Tour	8	16.52
100.	Princess Jen	9	16.48

Experimental Free Handicap

The Experimental Free Handicap, published annually by the Jockey Club, is based on a hypothetical 1⅛-mile race for two-year-olds on dirt. Walter S. Vosburgh, the legendary Jockey Club handicapper, compiled the first Experimental Free Handicap in 1933. He placed Sanford Stakes winner First Minstrel atop his list at 126 pounds, although the filly Mata Hari at 122 pounds effectively was the highweight when considering the five-pound sex allowance then in effect. The 126-pound high weight became the standard impost for a champion of average accomplishment.

Vosburgh, who had been the racing secretary at New York tracks since 1894, retired in 1934, and no Experimental Free Handicap was prepared for that year. John B. Campbell assumed the task in 1935 and continued to compile the list until his death in '54.

Campbell, also racing secretary at the New York tracks, wrote in a 1943 letter that his Experimental Free Handicap was intended primarily as a forecast of how the horses would perform as three-year-olds. The Experimental, he wrote, "is based mainly upon my opinion of what the two-year-olds will accomplish as three-year-olds and at distances of a mile and a furlong or greater."

Following Campbell's death, Frank E. "Jimmy" Kilroe

assigned the weights through 1960. Thomas Trotter, who compiled the list through 1972, followed him.

Starting in 1969, at the behest of the Jockey Club, the thrust of the Experimental was changed from a prediction of future performance to a measure of accomplishment during the two-year-old season exclusively.

Kenneth Noe Jr. prepared the Experimental Free Handicap from 1972 through '75, and Trotter resumed the task in 1976. Beginning in 1979, a committee of three racing secretaries was chosen to establish the Experimental weights. In 1985, for the first time, separate lists were compiled for males and fillies. The 2002 Experimental Free Handicap was prepared by Frank Gabriel of Arlington Park, Mike Lakow of the New York Racing Association, and Tom Robbins of Del Mar.

The highest Experimental weight ever assigned was 132 pounds to Count Fleet in 1942; the following year, he won the Triple Crown. However, 1946 Triple Crown winner Assault was not among the Experimental highweights despite winning the '45 Flash Stakes. All Triple Crown winners since Assault have also been Experimental highweights: Citation (126 pounds), Secretariat (129), Seattle Slew (126), and Affirmed (126).

Past Experimental Free Handicap Highweights

Year	Male	Female	Year	Male	Female
2002	Vindication (126)	Storm Flag Flying (123)	1966	Successor (126)	Regal Gleam (116)
2001	Johannesburg (126)	Tempera (123)	1965	Buckpasser (126)	Moccasin (120)
2000	Macho Uno (126)	Caressing (123)	1964	Bold Lad (130)	Queen Empress (118)
1999	Anees (126)	Cash Run (123)	1963	Raise a Native (126)	Castle Forbes (115)
		Chilukki (123)			Tosmah (115)
		Surfside (123)	1962	Never Bend (126)	Affectionately (115)
1998	Answer Lively (126)	Silverbulletday (123)			Smart Deb (115)
1997	Favorite Trick (128)	Countess Diana (125)	1961	Crimson Satan (126)	Cicada (118)
1996	Boston Harbor (126)	Storm Song (124)	1960	Hail to Reason (126)	Bowl of Flowers (120)
1995	Maria's Mon (126)	My Flag (123)	1959	Warfare (126)	My Dear Girl (117)
	Unbridled's Song (126)		1958	First Landing (126)	Quill (117)
1994	Timber Country (126)	Flanders (124)	1957	Jewel's Reward (126)	Idun (120)
1993	Brocco (126)	Phone Chatter (123)	1956	Barbizon (126)	Alanesian (117)
	Dehere (126)		1955	Career Boy (126)	Doubledogdare (116)
1992	Gilded Time (126)	Eliza (123)			Nasrina (116)
1991	Arazi (130)	Pleasant Stage (123)	1954	Summer Tan (128)	High Voltage (117)
1990	Fly So Free (126)	Meadow Star (123)	1953	Porterhouse (126)	Evening Out (118)
1989	Rhythm (126)	Go for Wand (123)		*Turn-to (126)	
1988	Easy Goer (126)	Open Mind (123)	1952	Native Dancer (130)	Bubbley (116)
1987	Forty Niner (126)	Epitome (123)			Sweet Patootie (116)
		Over All (123)	1951	Tom Fool (126)	Rose Jet (115)
1986	Capote (126)	Brave Raj (123)	1950	Uncle Miltie (126)	Aunt Jinny (115)
1985†	Ogygian (126)	I'm Splendid (123)			How (115)
	Tasso (126)		1949	Middleground (126)	Bed o' Roses (119)
1984	Chief's Crown (126)	Outstandingly (118)	1948	Blue Peter (126)	Myrtle Charm (121)
1983	Devil's Bag (128)	Miss Oceana (120)	1947	Citation (126)	Bewitch (121)
1982	Copelan (126)	Landaluce (121)	1946	Cosmic Bomb (126)	First Flight (126)
	Roving Boy (126)	Princess Rooney (121)		Double Jay (126)	
1981	Deputy Minister (126)	Before Dawn (120)	1945	Lord Boswell (128)	Beaugay (121)
	Timely Writer (126)		1944	Free for All (126)	Busher (119)
1980	Lord Avie (126)	Heavenly Cause (120)		Pavot (126)	
1979	Rockhill Native (126)	Smart Angle (120)	1943	Pukka Gin (126)	Durazna (121)
1978	Spectacular Bid (126)	Candy Eclair (119)			Miss Keeneland (121)
		It's in the Air (119)	1942	Count Fleet (132)	Askmenow (119)
1977	Affirmed (126)	Lakeville Miss (119)			Good Morning (119)
1976	Seattle Slew (126)	Sensational (119)	1941	Alsab (130)	Chiquita Mia (115)
1975	Honest Pleasure (126)	Dearly Precious (119)			Ficklebush (115)
		Optimistic Gal (119)	1940	Whirlaway (126)	Level Best (121)
1974	Foolish Pleasure (127)	Ruffian (122)	1939	Bimelech (130)	Now What (119)
1973	Protagonist (126)	Talking Picture (121)	1938	El Chico (126)	Inscoelda (116)
1972	Secretariat (129)	La Prevoyante (121)	1937	Menow (126)	Jacola (116)
1971	Riva Ridge (126)	Numbered Account (119)	1936	Brooklyn (126)	Rifted Clouds (115)
1970	Hoist the Flag (126)	Forward Gal (118)	1935	Red Rain (126)	Forever Yours (116)
1969	Silent Screen (128)	Fast Attack (116)	1933	First Minstrel (126)	Mata Hari (122)
1968	Top Knight (126)	Gallant Bloom (118)			
		Process Shot (118)	†Starting in 1985, fillies were separately.		
1967	Vitriolic (126)	Queen of the Stage (117)	No weights assigned in 1934		

2002 Experimental Free Handicap Colts and Geldings

Wt.	Horse	Sire—Dam, Broodmare sire (State)	Sts	1st	2nd	3rd	Earnings
126	Vindication	Seattle Slew—Strawberry Reason, by Strawberry Road (Aus)	4	4	0	0	$680,950
124	Toccet	Awesome Again—Cozzene's Angel, by Cozzene	8	6	0	1	755,610
122	Kafwain	Cherokee Run—Swazi's Moment, by Moment of Hope	8	3	2	1	535,848
	Sky Mesa	Pulpit—Caress by Storm Cat	3	3	0	0	416,576
119	Hold That Tiger	Storm Cat—Beware of the Cat, by Caveat	5	3	0	1	380,907
	Icecoldbeeratreds	In Excess (Ire)—Guilded Times, by Crafty Prospector	5	3	1	0	353,800
	Whywhywhy	Mr. Greeley—Thorough Fair, by Quiet American	5	3	1	0	284,060
117	Bull Market	Holy Bull—Capote Miss, by Capote	4	1	1	0	128,120
116	Listen Indy	A.P. Indy—Ecoute, by Manila	5	1	1	2	70,660
	Zavata	Phone Trick—Pert Lady, by Cox's Ridge	6	3	1	1	226,040
115	Added Edge	Smart Strike—Sweet Nostalgia, by Mr. Redoy	4	4	0	0	250,328
	Domestic Dispute	Unbridled's Song—Majestical Moment, by Magesterial	6	1	2	1	134,320
	Pretty Wild	Wild Again—Pretty Discreet, by Private Account	6	1	2	2	145,260
114	Lone Star Sky	Conquistador Cielo—Ministrada, by Deputy Minister	6	3	2	0	338,235
113	Most Feared	Commanchero—Visual, by Avata	7	3	0	2	166,020
	Soto	Dehere—Subtle Fragrance, by Crafty Prospector	3	3	0	0	192,964
112	Champali	Glitterman—Radioactivity, by Dixieland Band	4	3	0	0	125,874
	Chief Planner	General Meeting—Flag of Freedom, by Fappiano	5	1	2	2	107,396
	Peace Rules	Jules—Hold to Fashion, by Hold Your Peace	6	3	1	1	209,990
	Truckle Feature	Saint Ballado—Magic Gleam, by Danzig	6	2	0	2	125,300
111	Erinsouthernman	Eltish—Southern Swing, by Dixieland Band	2	1	0	1	82,000
	Lismore Knight	Woodman—Lismore Lady, by Ogygian	5	2	1	0	246,800
110	Boston Bull	Boston Harbor—Delicacy, by Pleasant Colony	4	2	1	1	112,208
	Man Among Men	Gentlemen (Arg)—La Favorita (Fr), by Nikos (GB)	4	2	0	0	74,040
	Posse	Silver Deputy—Raska, by Rahy	7	2	1	1	184,415
	Roll Hennessy Roll	Hennessy—Roll Over Baby, by Rollin On Over	6	4	0	1	148,158
	Ten Cents a Shine	Devil His Due—Aunt Mottz, by Honey Jay	2	1	1	0	66,080
	Valid Video	Valid Wager—Miss Video, by Star Gallant	3	2	0	0	91,200
109	Bham	Boston Harbor—Best in the West, by Gone West	6	2	2	0	98,000
	Tito's Beau	Beau Genius—Frigidette, by It's Freezing	5	1	0	1	48,660
108	Coax Kid	Kissin Kris—Wreath of Gold, by Lucky North	5	1	1	2	89,640
	Outta Here	Dehere—Just Out, by Forty Niner	7	2	2	2	404,260
	Super Fuse	Lite the Fuse—Season's Flair, by D'Accord	5	4	0	0	106,485
107	Anasheed	A.P. Indy—Flagbird, by Nureyev	4	1	2	0	56,400
	Cat Genius	Western Cat—Vidaca, by Strawberry Road (Aus)	4	3	0	0	90,586
	Super Frolic	Pine Bluff—Lindsay Frolic, by Mt. Livermore	6	3	0	1	114,044
	What a Bad Day	Dehere—Native Scent, by Native Charger	4	2	0	1	59,219
106	Alke	Grand Slam—Pasampsi, by Crow (Fr)	3	1	2	0	58,985
	Boston Park	Boston Harbor—Maple Creek, by Forty Niner	9	2	0	1	75,902
	Empire Maker	Unbridled—Toussaud, by El Gran Senor	2	1	0	1	49,600
	Farno	Tactical Advantage—Concorde's Info, by Concorde Bound	5	1	3	0	64,700
	Only the Best	Smokester—Mesquite Miss, by Mehmet	6	3	0	0	140,764
	Private Gold	Seeking the Gold—Temper the Wind, by Elocutionist	7	2	2	1	132,395
	Wildcat Heir	Forest Wildcat—Penniless Heiress, by Pentelicus	2	1	1	0	49,200
	Zydeco Affair	Islefaxyou—Affirmed Affair, by Affirmed	8	3	1	2	157,733
105	Action Tonight	Hadif—Sudden Attraction, by Rare Performer	9	2	3	0	162,029
	Coach Jimi Lee	Roar—Princess Lili, by My Gallant	3	2	1	0	87,270
	Comic Truth	Proudest Romeo—Comic Wish, by Lyphard's Ridge	9	4	2	1	224,240
	Crackup	Distorted Humor—Lightly Go Lightly, by *Habitony	5	3	1	1	274,828
	Echeverria	Awesome Again—Evil's Pic, by Piccolino	5	2	1	0	56,970
	Friendly Mike	Honour and Glory—Majestic Number, by Polish Numbers	2	1	0	0	43,200
	Ironton	Not For Love—Baccata, by Baederwood	5	1	3	0	83,100
	Leo's Last Hurrahy	Leo Castelli—Kate's Hurrahy, by Rahy	7	5	2	0	326,848
	Millennium Storm	Future Storm—Jolie Boutique, by Northern Jove	10	3	1	2	99,740
	Rapid Proof	Fast Play—Hard Evidence, by Alleged	6	2	1	1	102,622
	Red Apache	End Sweep—Mepache, by Iron Constitution	6	2	2	0	95,400
	Trust N Luck	Montbrook—Bold Burst, by Dahar	8	4	2	0	382,800
	Unleash the Power	Unbridled—My Working Gal, by Seattle Slew	6	1	0	5	68,655
104	Outer Reef	Pulpit—Flippers, by Coastal	6	1	3	0	79,540
	Roaring Fever	Storm Cat—Pennant Fever, by Seattle Slew	4	1	1	0	60,966
	Royal Siphon	Siphon (Brz)—Royal Herat, by Herat	2	1	0	0	30,700
	Sharp Impact	Siphon (Brz)—Fast and Early, by Carson City	3	2	0	0	64,800
	Sir Cherokee	Cherokee Run—La Cucina (Ire), by Last Tycoon (Ire)	6	1	3	0	62,775

2002 Experimental Free Handicap Fillies

Wt.	Horse	Sire—Dam, Broodmare sire (State)	Sts	1st	2nd	3rd	Earnings
123	Storm Flag Flying	Storm Cat—My Flag, by Easy Goer	4	4	0	0	$967,000
121	Composure	Touch Gold—Party Cited, by Alleged	6	2	3	0	431,300
119	Elloluv	Gilded Time—Currency Quest, by Cryptoclearance	3	2	0	1	242,700
118	Awesome Humor	Distorted Humor—Horns Gray, by Pass the Tab	4	4	0	0	309,115
117	Miss Houdini	Belong to Me—Magical Maiden, by Lord Avie	2	2	0	0	175,800
	Santa Catarina	Unbridled—Purrfectly, by Storm Cat	5	1	2	1	302,580
115	Buffythecenterfold	Capote—Augusta Springs, by Nijinsky II	6	3	1	0	222,160
113	Freedom's Daughter	Saint Ballado—Carezza, by Caro (Ire)	2	2	0	0	109,200
	My Boston Gal	Boston Harbor—Western League, by Forty Niner	3	3	0	0	194,537
	Westerly Breeze	Gone West—On the Brink, by Cox's Ridge	5	2	0	0	302,804
112	Atlantic Ocean	Stormy Atlantic—Super Chef, by Seattle Slew	8	3	0	1	234,780
111	Roar Emotion	Roar—Emotional Outburst, by Capote	3	2	1	0	156,600
	Ruby's Reception	Rubiano—Court Reception, by A.P. Indy	7	3	2	1	209,230
110	Chimichurri	Elusive Quality—Hard Knocker, by Raja Baba	5	3	1	1	148,340
	Forever Partners	Not For Love—My New Pal, by Saratoga Six	3	2	1	0	91,660
	Ivanavinalot	West Acre—Beaty Sark, by Deputy Minister	6	5	0	0	418,300
	Puxa Saco	Dehere—Salty Sal, by Cox's Ridge	5	4	0	1	150,890
	Randaroo	Gold Case—Validated, by Valid Appeal	2	2	0	0	90,180
	Sea Jewel	Sea Hero—Set Them Free, by Stop the Music	4	1	0	1	123,200
109	Wild Snitch	Forest Wildcat—Infomint, by Key to the Mint	3	2	1	0	119,200
108	Humorous Lady	Distorted Humor—My Glamorous One, by It's the One	7	4	0	1	211,970
	Miss Mary Apples	Clever Trick—Sacred Sue, by Holy Bull	7	1	2	2	109,155
	Ocean Drive	Belong to Me—Clever But Costly, by Clever Trick	4	3	0	0	138,730
	Summer Wind Dancer	Siberian Summer—Native Wind Dancer, by Incinderator	5	3	0	2	207,165
107	Fast Cookie	Deputy Minister—Fleet Lady, by Avenue of Flags	7	1	3	1	90,123
	Holiday Runner	Meadowlake—Dixie Holiday, by Dixieland Band	5	3	0	1	171,623
	Tricks Her	Favorite Trick—Pudding Pop, by It's Freezing	4	0	3	0	60,720
106	Major Idea	Cherokee Run—Ciencia, by El Gran Senor	6	2	1	2	98,320
	Midnight Cry	Smart Strike—Mythical Ruler, by Sovereign Dancer	6	2	1	1	128,152
	Mike's Wildcat	Forest Wildcat—Old Flame, by Black Tie Affair (Ire)	4	2	0	0	87,600
	Moonlight Sonata	Carson City—Wheatly Way, by Wheatly Hall	6	1	2	3	105,220
	One and Twenty	Honour and Glory—Smuggle, by Lord Avie	6	2	0	1	173,520
	Savedbythelight	Saint Ballado—Wild Royal, by Wild Again	4	1	2	0	83,424
	Stellar	Grand Slam—Starr County, by Ogygian	3	1	1	0	69,000
105	Indy Groove	A.P. Indy—Niner's Home, by Forty Niner	3	1	0	2	67,800
	Makin Heat	Makin—Warmedbythesun, by Lobsang (Ire)	11	4	5	0	147,002
	Souris	Defrere—Meet Hunca Munca, by Northern Prospect	6	2	1	3	159,410
104	Allspice	Coronado's Quest—Music House, by Sadler's Wells	3	2	0	0	76,800
	Elegant Designer	Suave Prospect—Rosana's Design, by Dr. Carter	7	5	1	0	273,670
	Espy	Mt. Livermore—Locate, by Cox's Ridge	3	1	1	0	50,600
	Final Round	Storm Cat—Profit Column, by Private Account	4	2	0	1	110,120
	Holiday Lady	Deputy Commander—Olatha, by Miswaki	6	1	2	1	89,655
	Little Bit a Swiss	Swiss Yodeler—Lots of Stingers, by Drone	5	1	1	1	71,837
	Marc's Rainbow	Summer Squall—Marc's Lark, by Miner's Mark	5	3	1	0	120,465
	My Trusty Cat	Tale of the Cat—Entrusted, by Private Account	6	2	3	1	228,025
	Sweettrickydancer	Green Dancer—My Sweet Talker, by Phone Trick	6	3	1	1	92,110
	Tangle (Ire)	Bob Back—Tertia (Ire), by Polish Patriot	2	1	1	0	50,134
103	Appleby Gardens	A.P. Indy—Larkswhistle, by Silver Deputy	4	1	0	1	174,270
	Belle of Perintown	Dehere—Hot Match, by Mr. Prospector	7	2	2	1	124,075
	Fabulous Brush	Cobra King—Brush With Reality, by Broad Brush	6	2	0	1	93,355
	Feisty Step	Coronado's Quest—Miss Turlington, by Seattle Slew	3	1	0	1	50,950
	Fircroft	A.P. Indy—Pemaquid, by Deputy Minister	5	2	0	1	105,400
	House Party	French Deputy—Bill Back, by Relaunch	4	1	2	1	63,210
	Parting	Hay Halo—Pocasset, by Damascus	7	2	3	1	162,229
	Red Cell	Geri—Red Bandana, by Fred Astaire	4	1	0	0	32,661
	Watching You	Coronado's Quest—Dodie Mae, by Capote	3	1	1	0	66,590

Scale of Weights

The scale of weights provides a guideline to the weights that horses carry at different ages and over different distances. As in many standards in Thoroughbred racing, the current scale of weights evolved over time.

The earliest Thoroughbred races in the 17th century were run at catch weights—whatever the rider, usually the owner, weighed. As racing became more sophisticated, various methods were tried to make contests more fair as well as more competitive, including assigning different weights according to the height of the horse, known as "give-and-take" weights.

That concept eventually evolved into assigning different weights to horses of differing perceived abilities. The first recorded handicap race was the Subscription Handicap Plate at Newmarket in 1785.

In 1740, the English Parliament established minimum weights for horses of different ages. Those weights were not meant to be assigned to horses of different ages in the same race, however.

In the mid-19th century, Admiral Henry Rous, British racing's de facto dictator, applied and expanded the concept to horses of different ages in the same race. Rous published the world's first weight-for-age scale in his 1850 book *On the Laws and Practice of Horse Racing*. Rous's scale also recognized that Thoroughbreds mature steadily from ages two through four; he assigned different weights at different distances for every month of the year.

All subsequent scales essentially have been refinements of Rous's work. The first official scale of weights was published in the *Racing Calendar* in 1880. In the modern scale of weights, the differences between weights for three-year-olds and older horses are much smaller than in Rous's day due to the increased early maturity of the modern Thoroughbred.

The scale of weights listed below is the official scale used by American racing secretaries.

Distance and Age	Jan.	Feb.	Mar.	Apr.	May	June	July	Aug.	Sept.	Oct.	Nov.	Dec.
Half mile												
2 years	x	x	x	x	x	x	x	105	108	111	114	114
3 years	117	117	119	119	121	123	125	126	127	128	129	129
4 years	130	130	130	130	130	130	130	130	130	130	130	130
5 years & up	130	130	130	130	130	130	130	130	130	130	130	130
6 furlongs												
2 years	x	x	x	x	x	x	x	102	105	108	111	111
3 years	114	114	117	117	119	121	123	125	126	127	128	128
4 years	129	129	130	130	130	130	130	130	130	130	130	130
5 years & up	130	130	130	130	130	130	130	130	130	130	130	130
1 mile												
2 years	x	x	x	x	x	x	x	x	96	99	102	102
3 years	107	107	111	111	113	115	117	119	121	122	123	123
4 years	127	127	128	128	127	126	126	126	126	126	126	126
5 years & up	128	128	128	128	127	126	126	126	126	126	126	126
1¼ miles												
2 years	x	x	x	x	x	x	x	x	x	x	x	x
3 years	101	101	107	107	111	113	116	118	120	121	122	122
4 years	125	125	127	127	127	126	126	126	126	126	126	126
5 years & up	127	127	127	127	127	126	126	126	126	126	126	126
1½ miles												
2 years	x	x	x	x	x	x	x	x	x	x	x	x
3 years	98	98	104	104	108	111	114	117	119	121	122	122
4 years	124	124	126	126	126	126	126	126	126	126	126	126
5 years & up	126	126	126	126	126	126	126	126	126	126	126	126
2 miles												
3 years	96	96	102	102	106	109	112	114	117	119	120	120
4 years	124	124	126	126	126	126	126	125	125	124	124	124
5 years & up	126	126	126	126	126	126	126	125	125	124	124	124

(a) In races of intermediate lengths, the weights for the shorter distance are carried.

(b) In races exclusively for three-year-olds or four-year-olds, the weight is 126 lbs., and in races exclusively for two-year-olds, it is 122 lbs.

(c) In all races except handicaps and races where the conditions expressly state to the contrary, the scale of weights is less, by the following: for two-year-old fillies, 3 lbs.; for three-year-old and up fillies and mares, 5 lbs. before September 1, and 3 lbs. thereafter.

(d) In all handicaps that close more than 72 hours prior to the race the top weight shall not be less than 126 lbs., except in handicaps for fillies and mares, the top weight shall not be less than 126 lbs. less the sex allowance at the time of the race.

American Match Races

Match races, a prominent part of American Thoroughbred racing through the mid-1970s, slowed to a trickle after Ruffian's fatal showdown with Foolish Pleasure at Belmont Park on July 6, 1975. Of all the match races in North America during the 20th century, very few were contested after the undefeated filly shattered her right front ankle and was euthanized the next day. Only nine of those 13 were in the United States, and none of them commanded the national attention given the Ruffian–Foolish Pleasure match and such earlier match races as Seabiscuit–War Admiral and Nashua–Swaps.

Match races in America were mostly winner take all and trace back to the early 1820s, when American Eclipse engaged in and won two matches. Similarly, the great sire Lexington won twice in head-to-head competition in the 1850s. Since Domino defeated Clifford by three-quarters of a length in a one-mile match race at Sheepshead Bay Racetrack in New York on September 6, 1894, 15 match races have contained at least one starter who was recognized officially or unofficially as a champion. (*Daily Racing Form* first designated champions in 1936.) Thirteen of the 15 races offered wagering, and favorites lost nine of them. None was more noteworthy than War Admiral's loss to Seabiscuit in 1938, and none was more one-sided than Miss Musket's 50-length loss to Chris Evert on July 20, 1974, at Hollywood Park.

To appreciate America's greatest match races, it is necessary to understand the hype and expectations heading into them. For more than a year, racing fans had clamored for a match-up of Seabiscuit and War Admiral, the two dominant horses of the late 1930s. When the two finally met, they were the only two entrants in the 1³⁄₁₆-mile Pimlico Special Stakes on November 1, 1938. A record crowd of 40,000 turned out to see Seabiscuit, a five-year-old grandson of Man o' War, take on War Admiral, a four-year-old son of Man o' War who had won the 1937 Triple Crown and 16 of 17 starts prior to the match.

Seabiscuit, breaking from the second post position, was sent off at 2.20-to-1 under George Woolf; War Admiral, thought to be the quicker from the gate, was 0.25-to-1 under Charley Kurtsinger. War Admiral was expected to lead at the start, but Seabiscuit outbroke him. Seabiscuit had been on the lead in just one of his previous 13 starts.

War Admiral made several moves at his opponent and once drew within a nose, but Seabiscuit had plenty left and won by four lengths in track-record time of 1:56.60.

Nearly 17 years later, Kentucky Derby winner Swaps went off as the 3-to-10 favorite against Preakness and Belmont Stakes winner Nashua in the $100,000 Washington Park Match Race at 1¼ miles on August 31, 1955. Swaps was undefeated as a three-year-old and ownerbreeder Rex Ellsworth had returned him to California after he defeated Nashua by 1½ lengths in the 1955 Derby. Nashua's only loss in 11 starts had been in the Derby. Swaps was the favorite under Bill Shoemaker, while Nashua was 6-to-5 with Eddie Arcaro. Nashua won by 6½ lengths, leading from start to finish.

The race that effectively ended top-level match races pitted Foolish Pleasure, 1995 Kentucky Derby winner, against undefeated Ruffian, a three-year-old filly who never had been headed in ten career starts, all against other fillies. Jacinto Vasquez was the regular rider of both horses and chose to ride Frank Whiteley-trained Ruffian in the nationally televised race. Ruffian went off at 0.40-to-1; Foolish Pleasure was 0.90-to-1.

Ruffian broke from the rail and narrowly led Foolish Pleasure through a blazing first quarter-mile in :22⅖ on Belmont's deep 1¼-mile chute. Shortly after they entered the main track, however, Ruffian broke down and swerved to the outside. Foolish Pleasure finished the race under Braulio Baeza. Ruffian, who fought her handlers when coming out of anesthetic after surgery, reinjured her leg, and was euthanized early on July 7. Match races since then never have been the same.—*Bill Heller*

Match Races, 1930 to 2002

Winner, age, sex	Opponent, age, sex	Race	Date	Track	Distance	Final Time
Soviet Problem, 4, f	Mamselle Bebette, 4, f	Match Race	08-21-1994	Del Mar	5fT	:56.58
Soviet Problem, 4, f	Lazor, 4, g	Match Race	05-12-1994	Golden Gate Fields	6f	1:08.55
Who Doctor Who, 5, g	Explosive Girl, 4, f	Match Race	07-23-1988	Ak-Sar-Ben	8f 70y	1:42.00
Foolish Pleasure, 3, c	Ruffian, 3, f	Great Match Race	07-06-1975	Belmont Park	1 1/4m	2:02.80
Chris Evert, 3, f	Miss Musket, 3, f	Hollywood Special S.	07-20-1974	Hollywood Park	1 1/14m	2:02.00
Jovial John, 4, g	Blunt Man, 9, h	Match Race	11-16-1972	Cahokia Downs	5f	1:00.80
Convenience, 4, f	Typecast, 6, m	Hollywood Park Match Race	06-17-1972	Hollywood Park	1 1/18m	1:47.60
Nasharco, 4, c	Nancycee, 4, f	Match Race	04-10-1966	Turf Paradise	5 1/2f	1:10.20
Nancycee, 4, f	Nasharco, 4, c	Match Race	03-20-1966	Turf Paradise	5f	:56.20
Short Nail, 2, c	Florida Cracker, 2, c	Match Race	12-04-1962	Garden State	1:13.40	1:13.40
Cesca, 2, f	Aim n Fire, 2, c	Match Race	07-07-1962	Woodbine	5 1/2f	1:04.60
Wichita Maid, 4, f	Gilhooley, 5, m	Australian Welcome Inv. Match Race	08-19-1961	Centennial	5 1/2f	1:04.40
Routeen, 2, f	Modest Step, 2, f	Latonia Match Race	10-01-1960	Latonia	6f	1:13.60
Roman Colonel, 4, c	Benedicto, 5, g	Special Match Race	06-11-1960	Detroit Race Course	6f	1:10.40
Lori Lynn, 4, f	*Salmon Peter, 9, g	Inv. Match Race	08-22-1959	Centennial	1 1/4m	2:05.00
Wildoath, 3, c	War Marshal, 4, c	Special Match Race	10-12-1957	Fresno	1 1/16m	1:43.60
Noorahge, 4, c	Early Bull, 7, h	Dapper Dan Match Race	09-14-1957	Wheeling Downs	6 1/2f	1:24.00
Queen Doris, 3, f	Molly Darling, 4, f	Inv. Match Race	07-28-1956	Centennial	5 1/2f	1:05.60
Nashua, 3, c	Swaps, 3, c	Washington Park Match Race	08-31-1955	Washington Park	1 1/4m	2:04.20
Virginia Fair, 2, f	Virden, 2, c	Inv. Match Race	08-15-1952	Edmonton	abt. 5f	1:00.40
Capot, 3, c	Coaltown, 4, c	Pimlico Special	10-28-1949	Pimlico	1 3/16m	1:56.80
Armed, 6, g	Assault, 4, c	The Special	09-27-1947	Belmont Park	1 1/4m	2:02.80
Busher, 3, f	Durazna, 4, f	Match Race	08-29-1945	Washington Park	1m	1:37.80
Alsab, 3, c	Whirlaway, 4, c	Narragansett Championship	09-19-1942	Narragansett	1 3/16m	1:56.40
Lavengro, 7, g	*Sir Winsome, 4, c	Pacific Coast Sprint Championship	08-16-1942	Longacres	3f	1:10.00
Wise Moss, 3, f	Sweet Willow, 4, f	New Hampshire Special	11-22-1941	Rockingham	6f	1:11.20
Alsab, 2, c	Requested, 2, c	Match Race	09-23-1941	Belmont Park	6 1/2f	1:16.00
Unerring, 3, f	Flying Lill, 3, f	Match Race	08-31-1939	Washington Park	1m	1:37.80
Seabiscuit, 5, h	War Admiral, 4, c	Pimlico Special	11-01-1938	Pimlico	1 3/16m	1:56.60
Seabiscuit, 5, h	*Ligaroti, 6, h	Special Stake Race	08-12-1938	Del Mar	1 1/8m	1:49.00
Myrtlewood, 4, f	Miss Merriment, 5, m	Special Sweepstakes	10-24-1936	Keeneland	6f	1:11.80
Clang, 3, g	Myrtlewood, 3, f	Match Race	10-12-1935	Coney Island	6f	1:09.20
Myrtlewood, 3, f	Clang, 3, g	Match Race	09-25-1935	Hawthorne	6f	1:10.80

Notable Walkovers since 1930

Walkovers are rare in Thoroughbred racing if only because competition is at the heart of the sport. The most recent walkover occurred in 1997 when Sharp Cat's two opponents, Alzora and Toda Una Dama (Arg) were scratched from the Bayakoa Handicap (G2) after December rains turned Hollywood Park's track muddy. Prior to that, champion Spectacular Bid walked over when Winter's Tale, Temperence Hill, and Dr. Patches were scratched from the 1980 Woodward Stakes (G1).

In consecutive years, Calumet Farm champions Coaltown and Citation walked over in Maryland races. Coaltown was unopposed in the 1949 Edward Burke Handicap at Havre de Grace, and Citation had no opponents entered against him in the 1948 Pimlico Special.

Although walkovers usually involve only one horse, two horses with the same owner may walk over if they are entered in a race and no horses oppose them. Here are several of the most important walkovers since 1930.

Walkovers, 1930 to 2002

Horse, age, sex	Race(Grade)	Date	Track	Distance	Final Time
Sharp Cat, 3, f	Bayakoa H. (G2)	12-07-1997	Hollywood Park	1 1/16m	1:42.68
Spectacular Bid, 4, c	Woodward S. (G1)	09-20-1980	Belmont Park	1 1/4m	2:02.40
Coaltown, 4, c	Edward Burke H.	04-23-1949	Havre De Grace	1 1/16m	1:52.20
Citation, 3, c	Pimlico Special	10-29-1948	Pimlico	1 3/16m	1:59.80
Stymie, 5, h	Saratoga Cup	08-31-1946	Saratoga Race Course	1 3/4m	3:07.40

The Claiming Game

Claiming races are the heart of almost every racing meet in America. In 2002, nearly two-thirds of all races (65.9%) were either straight claiming or maiden claiming. The horses that populate those races are an eclectic band of warriors whose common bond is their owners' willingness to lose them for a specified price as soon as the race is over.

The claimers are typified by such horses as Creme de La Fete, a chestnut gelding who went to post with a price on his head in all but 20 of his 151 career starts in the late 1970s and early '80s. His claiming prices ranged from $7,000 to $72,500.

Creme de La Fete was so well known that he was saluted in a ceremony at Aqueduct. The National Horsemen's Benevolent and Protective Association annually selects a claimer of the year, and the Claiming Crown held each summer has given more attention to the sport's foot soldiers.

But publicity for claimers is rare, accorded usually to horses that were claimed early in their careers and developed into champions, as Stymie did in the 1940s. Or, the attention goes to horses that ran in claiming races but were not taken, such as two-time Horse of the Year John Henry or 1999 Horse of the Year Charismatic.

Most claimers toil in anonymity, week after week, start after start, battling their infirmities as much as the competition. Most males are geldings and race well past their prime.

Claiming races have been a part of Thoroughbred racing for more than three centuries, though they began in England in a much different fashion and were called selling races.

In a story in the January 1972 issue of *The Thoroughbred of California*, Barry H. Irwin uncovered the original set of horse racing rules used in England in 1698, '99, and 1700 for races "at Thettford in the Countys of Norfolke and Suffolke" for the last Friday in September of each year. Eight noblemen and 11 commoners wrote 15 conditions for the races. One was that every owner would sell every horse entered for "Thirty Guineys" and that the "Contributors present shall throw dice" and that "the Purchaser will be he who throwes most at three."

More than 300 years later, if more than one claim is entered on a particular horse, the winner is determined by lot by the stewards. Getting to that point took several revisions once racing became established in the United States.

According to the Jockey Club's 1828 *Racing Calendar*, the owner of the second-place finisher in a selling race was entitled to purchase the winner for a specified sum. That rule was modified to allow all losing owners in a race to buy the winner, with the option to purchase determined by the order of finish. If the owner of the second-place horse did not want the winner, the option to buy passed to the third-place finisher.

In the early 1900s, Canadian racetracks introduced the concept of sealed bids for the winner being submitted within 15 minutes after the race. A similar rule was approved by the Kentucky Association on September 1, 1916, and used at the 1917 spring race meeting in Lexington.

On opening day that spring, April 28, the Kentucky Association approved a Claiming Race Rule that allowed all horses in a claiming race to be purchased, and it set down the chilling reality for the person making a claim. The purchaser would become the owner of the horse "whether he be alive or dead, sound or unsound, or injured during the race or after it." To this day, the claim takes effect as soon as the starting gate opens. If a claimed horse dies during the race, the person who claimed it must not only buy the horse but also pay to remove the horse from the track and pay its burial fees.

Claiming races were well received and soon spread to East Coast tracks in the 1920s. However, selling races remained a part of the Jockey Club's rules of racing to the 1950s. By the 1940s, the selling race had become a variation of a claiming race in which only the winner was auctioned off for at the least the offering price. All other horses in the race were eligible to be claimed for the stated claiming price.

Claiming rules today vary modestly from one racing jurisdiction to another, but two basic concepts apply in almost all of them. First, any licensed trainer or owner who has had at least one starter at a race meeting may claim any horse at that meeting, although an owner or trainer who lost the last horse of his stable on a claim at the previous meeting is eligible to make a claim. Second, for a period of 30 days, the horse must race for at least 25% more than the price for which it was claimed. For example, a horse claimed for $10,000 cannot start in a claiming race for less than $12,500 for 30 days. Under those restrictions, the horse is frequently referred to as being "in jail," ostensibly because the new owner does not have the freedom to place him at any claiming price. Some racing jurisdictions have experimented with eliminating jail time. In addition, the claimed horse cannot be sold privately to another party in the 30-day period, and the horse cannot race at another track until the end of the race meet at which it was claimed.

For every claimer, there is a claiming trainer, and, like their horses, some have risen to prominence. Hirsch Jacobs, who led the nation in victories 11 times between 1933 and '44, may have been the first great claiming trainer. Jacobs claimed Stymie from a maiden claimer for $1,500 on June 8, 1943, and Stymie rewarded him by winning more than $900,000.

On the West Coast, one of the most prominent claiming trainers was R. H. "Red" McDaniel, who led the nation in victories from 1950 through 1954. In 1955, McDaniel saddled a winner at Golden Gate Fields and a few minutes later jumped to his death from the San Francisco Bay Bridge.

Claimers have been an integral part of the success of father-son Racing Hall of Fame members Marion and Jack Van Berg. Jack Van Berg led

the nation's trainers in victories nine times, including a still-record 496 wins in 1976. Only Steve Asmussen (407 in 2002) and Scott Lake (with 407 in 2001) also have won more than 400 races in one year.

Frank "Pancho" Martin won 11 New York training titles, the first in 1971 and then ten straight from 1973 through 1982. The Cuban-born Martin explained his training philosophy in a 1972 magazine article: "The most important thing to remember is to treat your cheapest horse as good as your best," Martin said. "Give a claimer the same care you give a stakes horse, and he'll win for you in his own class. If you improve a horse, move him up in company, but never ask him to do the impossible."

Three of Martin's greatest claimers were Manassa Mauler, a $12,800 claim who won the 1959 Wood Memorial Stakes and earned $359,171; Autobiography, a $29,000 claim who won the '72 Jockey Club Gold Cup over Key to the Mint and Riva Ridge; and *Big Shot II, a $25,000 claim who won a $100,000 stakes, the '71 Century Handicap.

Though Bobby Frankel shifted his base of operations to California in 1972, he had considerable success with claimers in his six New York seasons before heading west. In that period, Frankel developed claimers Barometer, Baitman, and Pataha Prince into stakes winners. Barometer, claimed for $15,000, won the 1970 Suburban Handicap and earned $174,584. Baitman, who was seven years old when Frankel claimed him for $15,000, earned more than $150,000 after the claim. In California, Frankel claimed Wickerr for $50,000 and then won the 1981 and '82 Eddie Read Handicaps (G1) with him. Wickerr also won the 1981 Del Mar Handicap (G2).

West Virginia-based Dale Baird led the nation's trainers in victories 15 times from 1971 through '99, almost exclusively with claimers. He was displaced as America's top trainer by victories in 2000 and '01 by Lake, who races simultaneously at several tracks in the Northeast. Asmussen was the 2002 leader by wins.

Fifty-two years after Stymie was claimed for $1,500, a first-time starter at Hollywood Park named Budroyale was claimed in a maiden race for $32,000 by trainer Dan Hendricks for Decourcy W. Graham. Budroyale was subsequently claimed twice more for $40,000 and for $50,000 before he matured to win several graded stakes, finish second in the 1999 Breeders' Cup Classic (G1), and earn more than $2.8-million, most of it for small-scale owner Jeffrey Sengara. Such horses as Stymie and Budroyale are the exceptions, but the hope of finding a diamond in the rough keeps many owners and trainers in the claiming game.

—Bill Heller

North American Claiming Races in 2002

Created by the National Horsemen's Benevolent and Protective Association, the six-race, $550,000 Claiming Crown was scheduled to have its fifth running at Canterbury Park near Minneapolis on July 19, 2003. The series rewards the hard-working claiming horses, and those runners certainly deserve credit for their tireless labors and contributions to the sport. In many ways, they are the underpinning of Thoroughbred racing in North America, accounting for roughly two of every three races. In all, claimers accounted for 336,861 North American starts in 2002, or 68% of all runners in all races.

The claimers are a significant economic force in the industry. In 2002, the total value of all horses claimed in the United States was $180.2-million, up from $174.5-million in 2001. When the percentage of claims is considered, 4.6% of all claiming starters were claimed in 2002, the total value of all claimers in all U.S. races was $39.2-billion. Canadian trainers also were active at the claims box, with a 5.5% claiming rate from 31,728 starts. (Because of the different values of the U.S. and Canadian currencies, their claiming programs are looked at separately.)

California and New York, which have high-quality racing programs, had the highest dollar volume of claims. California had 2,266 horses claimed for a total of $42.3-million in 2002, and New York had 748 claims for a total of $20.9-million.

Claims by Category at United States Tracks in 2002

Claiming Price Range	No. of Starts	No. Claims	% Claimed	% of All of Claims	Total Value Of Claims	Average Claim Price
Less than $1,000	1	0	0.0%	0.0%	0	-
$1,000 to $2,499	1,583	29	1.8%	0.2%	$53,650	$1,850
$2,500 to $4,999	86,286	2,947	3.4%	20.8%	10,425,350	3,538
$5,000 to $7,499	56,281	2,942	5.2%	20.8%	15,781,500	5,364
7,500 to $9,999	35,360	1,472	4.2%	10.4%	11,381,500	7,732
$10,000 to $14,999	50,847	2,623	5.2%	18.5%	29,679,500	11,315
$15,000 to $19,999	22,185	1,243	5.6%	8.8%	19,903,500	16,012
$20,000 to $29,999	27,861	1,591	5.7%	11.2%	37,151,500	23,351
$30,000 to $39,999	11,649	567	4.9%	4.0%	18,441,000	32,524
$40,000 to $49,999	5,489	284	5.2%	2.0%	11,500,000	40,493
$50,000 to $74,999	6,106	408	6.7%	2.9%	21,735,000	53,272
$75,000 and up	1,485	52	3.5%	0.4%	4,185,000	80,481
TOTALS	**305,133**	**14,158**	**4.6%**	**100.0%**	**$180,237,500**	**$12,730**

Claims by Category at Canadian Tracks in 2002

Claiming Price Range	No. of Starts	No. Claims	% Claimed	% of All of Claims	Total Value Of Claims	Average Claim Price
Less than $1,000	0	0	0	0.0%	0	-
$1,000 to $2,499	940	13	1.4%	0.7%	$26,000	$2,000
$2,500 to $4,999	4,481	195	4.4%	11.1%	724,850	3,717
$5,000 to $7,499	7,449	301	4.0%	17.2%	1,646,500	5,470
7,500 to $9,999	3,834	208	5.4%	11.9%	1,665,875	8,009
$10,000 to $14,999	4,304	282	6.6%	16.1%	3,173,000	11,252
$15,000 to $19,999	3,317	188	5.7%	10.7%	2,980,000	15,851
$20,000 to $29,999	3,737	303	8.1%	17.3%	6,824,000	22,521
$30,000 to $39,999	1,630	124	7.6%	7.1%	4,002,500	32,278
$40,000 to $49,999	907	80	8.8%	4.6%	3,280,000	41,000
$50,000 to $74,999	916	52	5.7%	3.0%	2,812,500	54,087
$75,000 and up	213	5	2.3%	0.3%	397,500	79,500
TOTALS	**31,728**	**1,751**	**5.5%**	**100.0%**	**$27,532,725**	**$15,724**

United States Claiming Activity by Track and State for 2002

	No. of Horses Claimed	Total Value of Claims	Avg. Price of Claim
Arizona			
Flagstaff	1	$2,000	$2,000
Greenelee County Fair	1	1,500	1,500
Mohave County Fair	2	3,750	1,875
Turf Paradise	485	2,841,450	5,859
Yavapai Downs	57	190,450	3,341
Total Arizona	**546**	**3,039,150**	**5,566**

	No. of Horses Claimed	Total Value of Claims	Avg. Price of Claim
Arkansas			
Oaklawn Park	191	$3,030,500	$15,866
Total Arkansas	**191**	**3,030,500**	**15,866**
California			
Bay Meadows	356	$4,400,600	$12,361
Bay Meadows Fair	21	250,950	11,950
Del Mar	275	7,670,500	27,893
Fairplex Park	80	923,250	11,541
Fresno	16	81,350	5,084
Golden Gate Fields	408	4,915,700	12,048

	No. of Horses Claimed	Total Value of Claims	Avg. Price of Claim
Hollywood Park	361	9,285,000	25,720
Los Alamitos	163	563,000	3,454
Pleasanton	28	268,900	9,604
Sacramento	18	109,450	6,081
Santa Anita Park	470	13,318,000	28,336
Santa Rosa	32	249,500	7,797
Solano County Fair	22	195,600	8,891
Stockton	16	90,450	5,653
Total California	**2,266**	**42,322,250**	**18,677**

Colorado

Arapahoe Park	48	$242,800	$5,058
Total Colorado	**48**	**242,800**	**5,058**

Delaware

Delaware Park	820	$12,880,750	$15,708
Total Delaware	**820**	**12,880,750**	**15,708**

Florida

Calder Race Course	312	$5,205,000	$16,683
Gulfstream Park	315	7,831,500	24,862
Tampa Bay Downs	190	1,526,500	8,034
Total Florida	**817**	**14,563,000**	**17,825**

Idaho

Les Bois Park	19	$58,200	$3,063
Total Idaho	**19**	**58,200**	**3,063**

Illinois

Arlington Park	487	$8,221,500	$16,882
Fairmount Park	131	683,600	5,218
Hawthorne Race Course	241	2,380,000	9,876
Sportsman's Park	152	1,953,750	12,854
Total Illinois	**1,011**	**13,238,850**	**13,095**

Indiana

Hoosier Park	150	$766,000	$5,107
Total Indiana	**150**	**766,000**	**5,107**

Iowa

Prairie Meadows	96	$1,025,250	$10,680
Total Iowa	**96**	**1,025,250**	**10,680**

Kansas

Anthony Downs	1	$3,500	$3,500
Eureka Downs	1	5,000	5,000
The Woodlands	1	5,000	5,000
Total Kansas	**3**	**13,500**	**4,500**

Kentucky

Churchill Downs	343	$7,416,000	$21,621
Ellis Park	101	1,094,000	10,832
Keeneland Race Course	46	947,500	20,598
Kentucky Downs	1	10,000	10,000
Turfway Park	213	2,119,000	9,948
Total Kentucky	**704**	**11,586,500**	**16,458**

Louisiana

Delta Downs	159	$940,500	$5,915
Evangeline Downs	151	777,000	5,146
Fair Grounds	342	5,702,000	16,673
Louisiana Downs	121	1,275,250	10,539
Total Louisiana	**773**	**8,694,750**	**11,248**

Maryland

	No. of Horses Claimed	Total Value of Claims	Avg. Price of Claim
Laurel Park	499	$7,579,000	$15,188
Pimlico Race Course	223	3,388,500	15,195
Timonium	11	94,500	8,591
Total Maryland	**733**	**11,062,000**	**15,091**

Massachusetts

Suffolk Downs	251	$1,797,250	$7,160
Total Massachusetts	**251**	**1,797,250**	**7,160**

Michigan

Great Lakes Downs	26	$145,000	$5,577
Total Michigan	**26**	**145,000**	**5,577**

Minnesota

Canterbury Park	76	$530,000	$6,974
Total Minnesota	**76**	**530,000**	**6,974**

Montana

Yellowstone Downs	2	$4,100	$2,050
Total Montana	**2**	**4,100**	**2,050**

Nebraska

Atokad Park	1	$3,000	$3,000
Columbus	9	32,500	3,611
Fonner Park	21	85,500	4,071
Horsemen's Park	3	23,500	7,833
Lincoln State Fair	21	74,750	3,560
Total Nebraska	**55**	**219,250**	**3,986**

Nevada

Elko County Fair	1	$2,500	$2,500
Total Nevada	**1**	**2,500**	**2,500**

New Hampshire

Rockingham Park	105	$789,250	$7,517
Total New Hampshire	**105**	**789,250**	**7,517**

New Jersey

Monmouth Park	137	$2,330,250	$17,009
The Meadowlands	99	1,186,500	11,985
Total New Jersey	**236**	**3,516,750**	**14,901**

New Mexico

Ruidoso Downs	37	$217,800	$5,886
Sunland Park	107	646,300	6,040
SunRay Park	21	107,400	5,114
The Downs at Albuquerque	32	174,900	5,466
Total New Mexico	**197**	**1,146,400**	**5,819**

New York

Aqueduct	397	$11,239,000	$28,310
Belmont Park	160	5,562,000	34,763
Finger Lakes	103	662,750	6,434
Saratoga Race Course	88	3,440,000	39,091
Total New York	**748**	**20,903,750**	**27,946**

Ohio

Beulah Park	73	$353,250	$4,839
River Downs	107	592,750	5,540
Thistledown	184	799,500	4,345
Total Ohio	**364**	**1,745,500**	**4,795**

Oklahoma

	No. of Horses Claimed	Total Value of Claims	Avg. Price of Claim
Blue Ribbon Downs	6	$22,000	$3,667
Fair Meadows at Tulsa	13	57,000	4,385
Remington Park	42	253,500	6,036
Total Oklahoma	**61**	**332,500**	**5,451**

Oregon

Eastern Oregon Livestock Show	1	$2,500	$2,500
Grants Pass	8	21,700	2,713
Portland Meadows	54	197,750	3,662
Total Oregon	**63**	**221,950**	**3,523**

Pennsylvania

Penn National Race Course	242	$1,492,750	$6,168
Philadelphia Park	516	4,860,750	9,420
Total Pennsylvania	**758**	**6,353,500**	**8,382**

Texas

Lone Star Park	267	$3,641,250	$13,638
Retama Park	62	440,000	7,097
Sam Houston Race Park	115	1,052,500	9,152
Total Texas	**444**	**5,133,750**	**11,563**

Virginia

Colonial Downs	17	$236,500	$13,912
Total Virginia	**17**	**236,500**	**13,912**

Washington

Emerald Downs	214	$1,916,800	$8,957
Total Washington	**214**	**1,916,800**	**8,957**

West Virginia

	No. of Horses Claimed	Total Value of Claims	Avg. Price of Claim
Charles Town Races	1498	$7,410,750	$4,947
Mountaineer Park	860	5,276,500	6,135
Total West Virginia	**2358**	**12,687,250**	**5,381**

Canadian Claiming Activity by Track and Province in 2002

Alberta

Lethbridge	9	$19,500	$2,167
Northlands Park	191	1,808,250	9,467
Stampede Park	133	1,433,500	10,778
Total Alberta	**333**	**3,261,250**	**9,794**

British Columbia

Hastings Park	216	$2,653,500	$12,285
Kamloops	1	2,000	2,000
Total British Columbia	**217**	**2,655,500**	**12,237**

Manitoba

Assiniboia Downs	124	$584,000	$4,710
Total Manitoba	**124**	**584,000**	**4,710**

Ontario

Fort Erie	441	$3,745,500	$8,493
Woodbine	625	17,255,000	27,608
Total Ontario	**1066**	**21,000,500**	**19,700**

Saskatchewan

Marquis Downs	10	$27,100	$2,710
Queensbury Downs	1	4,375	4,375
Total Saskatchewan	**11**	**31,475**	**2,861**

Horses Claimed the Most Times in 2002

No. Times Claimed	Horse, YOB sex, sire	Average Claim Price	Tracks Where Claimed	2002 Race Record
10	Mapeb, 1997 h., Wallenda	3,050	CT	19-4-7-5, $38,574
9	Stone Mill Maiden, 1997 m., Boone's Mill	4,667	CT	11-0-4-4, $16,201
9	Palace Heroine, 1996 m., Fort Chaffee	5,000	CT	13-4-2-4, $44,547
9	Old Lodge, 1996 h., Lure	3,722	CT	17-0-6-2, $15,515
9	Baby Spice, 1996 h., Kitwood	4,778	CT	20-2-3-3, $29,720
8	Harper Valley, 1996 h., Harperstown	18,375	AP, FG, HAW, SPT	12-2-0-3, $48,964
8	T Time Music, 1998 m., Prospector's Music	7,781	CT, LRL, PIM	20-4-5-3, $38,934
8	Deporte Total (CHI) 1997 h., Laxey Bay (Ire)	10,438	DEL, LRL, PIM	17-3-1-6, $32,740
8	Thanks Amy, 1994 m., Compliance	4,563	MNR	15-2-2-3, $36,509
8	Last Supper, 1997 m., De Niro	4,250	MNR	13-4-1-2, $41,259
8	Chicago's Hope, 1997 h., Personal Hope	4,625	MNR	13-3-1-0, $40,120
8	Kerri's Best, 1997 m., Horatius	3,063	CT	21-3-5-2, $27,785
7	Governor Joe, 1997 h., Jeblar	6,750	CT, LRL	16-3-5-2, $41,475
7	My Friend Lumpy, 1997 h., Chaka	19,000	GG, HOL, SA	12-7-0-1, $106,540
7	Cien Seas, 1997 h., Cien Fuegos	10,714	HOU, LS	18-4-5-2, $38,228
7	Mr. Sundancer, 1995 g., Allen's Prospect	4,143	MNR	8-3-0-2, $24,654
7	Bam, 1995 m., Marine Brass	3,214	CT, LRL	20-2-6-5, $24,345
7	Chief Rainbow, 1996 g., Chief Honcho	5,714	MNR	15-5-1-2, $72,091
7	Fight Forever, 1998 m., Fit to Fight	11,429	HOU, MNR	15-3-6-3, $70,566
7	Pell Mell, 1998 h., Press Card	3,214	CT	12-3-1-4, $20,354
7	Harbor of Grace, 1996 h., Deputed Testamony	12,857	MNR	15-8-1-1, $137,136
7	Bandit d'Or, 1996 g., Tour d'Or	10,429	SUF	16-3-1-2, $27,220
7	Gather the Roses 1996 h., Danzatore	6,429	CT	19-5-4-3, $59,301
7	Executioness, 1997 m., Lordhyexecutioner	2,786	CT	19-5-3-2, $32,221

Horses with Highest Earnings After First Claim in 2002

Horse, YOB sex, sire	Claiming Price	Wins After Claim	Earnings After Claim
Turkish Prize, 1995 h., Prized	$50,000	4	$257,856
Svea Dahl, 1997 m., Honor Grades	32,000	6	246,780
Debonair Joe, 1999 c., Ole'	12,500	4	225,795
My Cousin Matt, 1999 c., Matty G	85,000	2	209,400
Chinkapin, 1996 h., Personal Flag	35,000	5	199,848
Vany's Forum, 1999 g., Open Forum	16,000	5	180,348
Stoney, 1998 h., Bold Badgett	20,000	4	175,060
Nates Colony, 1997 h., Pleasant Colony	32,000	2	174,940
Expected Flirt, 1999 g., Valid Expectations	40,000	4	174,845
Special Matter, 1998 h., River Special	16,000	3	169,065
Real Paranoide, 1998 m., Paranoide (Arg)	25,000	5	164,048
Shake the Dice, 1998 h., Boundary	25,000	5	163,600
Rich Assertion, 1999 f., Rizzi	20,000	4	159,900
Ozilda's Karen, 1998 m., Piccolino	25,000	4	157,179
Bonus Pay Day, 1998 h., Bonus Money (GB)	16,000	3	156,416
Prince Iroquois, 1997 h., Iroquois Park	25,000	3	156,360
Esteemed Friend, 1994 g., Gulch	35,000	5	155,000
Run for Joy, 1996 m., Geiger Counter	40,000	8	154,350
Delray Dew, 1998 m., Devil His Due	45,000	4	153,500
Air Cool, 1994 h., Cool Groom	25,000	5	152,070

Horses with Most Wins After First Claim in 2002

Horse, YOB sex, sire	Claiming Price	Wins After Claim	Earnings After Claim
Tejano Couture, 1994 h., Tejano	$4,000	10	$64,375
Run for Joy, 1996 m., Geiger Counter	40,000	8	154,350
Gamblin Town, 1998 m., Town Caper	16,000	8	72,760
Onasilverplatter, 1998 h., Ide	12,500	8	60,063
Harbor of Grace, 1996 h., Deputed Testamony	10,000	7	119,060
Tahoe Affair, 1997 g., Black Tie Affair (Ire)	4,000	7	93,398
No Its Not, 1998 h., Is It True	15,000	7	89,285
Playmera, 1997 m., Emerald Jig	4,000	7	75,688
Country Joe, 1996 g., Country Pine	6,500	7	57,956
Heat of the Night, 1995 h., Dynaformer	5,000	7	54,100
Hunters Halo, 1998 g., Winter Halo	5,000	7	50,460
Mana Torpedoes, 1997 h., Crafty Mana	3,500	7	49,952
Donald's Tomorrow, 1997 g., Sabona	5,000	7	48,675
Island Getaway, 1996 m., Island Whirl	4,000	7	41,495

Horses Claimed the Most Consecutive Times in 2002

Cons Claims	Horse, YOB sex, sire	Starts	Wins	Earnings
7	Mr. Sundancer, 1995 g., Allen's Prospect	8	3	24,654
7	Mapeb, 1997 h., Wallenda	19	4	38,574
6	Cien Seas, 1997 h., Cien Fuegos	18	4	38,228
6	Remission, 1997 m., Superbity	9	3	30,935
6	Pell Mell, 1998 h., Press Card	12	3	20,354
6	Tenfortynine, 1998 h., Ide	13	5	50,070
6	Parlay Cory, 1995 g., Parlay Me	12	1	14,532

Horses Claimed Most Consecutive Times, 1991-2002

Horse, YOB sex, sire	Consec Claims	Initial Claim Price	Date of 1st Claim	Wins After 1st Claim	Earnings During Claim Period
I Wood Be a Winner, 1995 g., by Knight Skiing	9	$6,250	1998-11-21	17	$251,039
Adjustable Note, 1993 g., by Native Prospector	8	5,000	1998-08-07	2	22,230
Silver Mystery, 1994 m., by Norquestor	7	16,000	1999-02-21	8	126,247
Mapeb, 1997 h., by Wallenda	7	3,500	2001-06-21	7	64,298
Mr. Sundancer, 1995 g., by Allen's Prospect	7	17,500	1999-06-04	10	96,513
Foyt Sparkler, 1988 g., by Foyt	6	12,500	1996-07-30	6	59,342
Nasty Newt, 1989 g., by Nasty and Bold	6	10,000	1994-02-19	9	53,691
Sox On Top, 1995 g., by Black Moonshine	6	35,000	1998-11-29	7	184,678
Where's Sally, 1996 m., by Mi Cielo	6	12,500	1998-12-08	8	86,994
Tenfortynine, 1998 h., by Ide	6	4,000	2002-09-01	3	29,544
Lambourne, 1995 g., by Exbourne	6	12,500	2001-05-05	3	36,303
Cien Seas, 1997 h., by Cien Fuegos	6	7,500	2001-08-23	4	41,938

Horse, YOB sex, sire	Consec Claims	Initial Claim Price	Date of 1st Claim	Wins After 1st Claim	Earnings During Claim Period
Catch If You Can, 1990 g., by Big Burn	6	8,000	1994-12-01	11	57,238
Remission, 1997 m., by Superbity	6	8,000	2002-05-19	3	27,416
Tender Hearted, 1995 m., by Bello	6	20,000	1999-05-07	2	87,268
Sound System, 1993 g., by Waquoit	6	18,500	1996-09-15	26	261,930
Parlay Cory, 1995 g., by Parlay Me	6	5,500	2001-08-04	4	28,161
Pell Mell, 1998 h., by Press Card	6	2,500	2002-04-19	2	16,274
Crijinsky, 1989 g., by Sir Jinsky	6	8,000	1995-09-07	7	53,330

Horses with Most Claiming Wins in 2002

Horse, YOB sex, sire	Starts	Cl Wins	Cl Earnings
Gamblin Town, 1998 m., by Town Caper	17	10	$91,980
Tejano Couture, 1994 h., by Tejano	26	8	47,830
Crystal Appeal, 1998 m., by World Appeal	17	8	51,854
Donald's Tomorrow, 1997 g., by Sabona	23	8	51,314
Harbor of Grace, 1996 h., by Deputed Testamony	15	8	137,136
Avalancher, 1992 g., by Frosty the Snowman	19	8	43,570

Runners Claimed Most Times, 1991-2002

No Times Claimed	Horse, YOB sex, sire	Aggregate Claim Price	Average Claim Price	Starts	Wins	Earnings
22	Sound System, 1993 g., by Waquoit	$170,000	$7,727	104	28	$306,101
20	Game Skipper, 1992 g., by Skip Trial	165,000	8,250	122	18	232,126
19	Above the Crowd, 1993 g., by Housebuster	531,500	27,974	80	21	440,711
18	Nauset Flash, 1987 g., by Parfaitement	204,000	11,333	164	20	299,579
18	North Salem, 1994 h., by Badger Land	239,500	13,306	82	15	265,733
18	Out for Gold, 1990 g., by Gold Crest	171,500	9,528	181	33	313,536
18	Sharp n Strong, 1992 m., by Stalwart	226,000	12,556	86	14	290,071
17	Shot On Stage, 1991 g., by Gold Stage	154,000	9,059	129	12	184,274
17	Imua Keoki, 1991 g., by Qui Native	178,500	10,500	86	17	201,224
17	Takeitlikeaman, 1991 g., by Exuberant	148,000	8,706	111	14	291,699
17	Halos Wonder, 1993 m., by Hay Halo	109,750	6,456	77	18	140,509
16	Erhard, 1996 h., by Gallant Prospector	149,000	9,313	65	12	97,155
16	Unreal Mot, 1989 g., by Unreal Zeal	376,000	23,500	92	21	368,800
16	Palace Heroine, 1996 m., by Fort Chaffee	89,000	5,563	62	9	154,172
16	Carny Princess, 1996 m., by Carnivalay	121,250	7,578	63	10	85,502
16	Rich Kelle, 1992 m., by Brio Cielo	73,500	4,594	92	23	160,291
16	Set On Cruise, 1991 g., by Wavering Monarch	376,500	23,531	77	16	388,600
16	Sandtucker, 1991 g., by Irish Open	118,000	7,375	89	12	107,683
16	Victoriously Bold, 1987 g., by Cool Victor	222,700	13,919	105	29	519,422
16	Brisa, 1995 m., by Prince of Fame	78,500	4,906	73	8	115,411
16	Baby Spice, 1996 h., by Kitwood	81,000	5,063	74	10	122,045
15	Bold Lancer, 1993 g., by Private Key	76,750	5,117	73	12	66,972
15	Jump Buck n' Go, 1992 m., by Buckley Boy	148,000	9,867	100	17	226,963
15	Raising Havoc, 1992 g., by Temperence Hill	270,500	18,033	84	23	375,019
15	Is It Possible, 1992 g., by Premiership	186,500	12,433	110	12	187,139
15	Organic, 1994 g., by Sunny's Halo	270,500	18,033	102	16	348,770
15	Captivator, 1993 g., by Irish Tower	161,750	10,783	120	26	240,554
15	Masked Wolf, 1992 m., by Northern Wolf	207,750	13,850	105	21	267,436
15	Batten Island, 1994 g., by Pentelicus	222,250	14,817	83	13	158,178
15	Mr. C I Prospector, 1990 g., by Native Prospector	209,000	13,933	78	11	242,444
15	Seattle's Spirit, 1992 g., by Gold Meridian	126,250	8,417	84	15	115,405
15	Slicker, 1993 g., by Northern Jove	145,500	9,700	75	9	171,106
15	Seven Salutes, 1986 g., by Salutely	183,000	12,200	177	34	332,296
15	Shoe Shine Man, 1991 g., by Northern Symphony	69,500	4,633	93	15	94,194

Horses With Most Wins After First Claim, 1991-2002

Horse, YOB sex, sire	Initial Claim Price	Date of Claim	Starts After Claim	Wins After Claim	Earnings After Claim
Sawmill Run, 1988 g., by It's Freezing	$4,000	1992-06-28	125	35	$224,514
Mankato, 1988 g., by Meadowlake	15,000	1992-03-17	145	34	330,856
Oh So Fabulous, 1992 g., by Singular	6,250	1997-02-21	96	33	229,216
It's the Wind, 1989 g., by Contare	5,000	1992-03-01	123	32	202,300
The Mighty Zip, 1988 g., by Fire Dancer	5,000	1992-10-05	121	32	223,453
Meine Empress, 1989 m., by Rex Imperator	14,000	1992-09-12	75	32	145,190
Out for Gold, 1990 g., by Gold Crest	35,000	1993-01-06	173	30	284,351

Horse, YOB sex, sire	Initial Claim Price	Date of Claim	Starts After Claim	Wins After Claim	Earnings After Claim
Belle's Ruckus, 1985 g., by Bold Ruckus	5,000	1992-07-11	106	30	156,856
Arromanches, 1993 h., by Relaunch	12,500	1996-06-24	75	30	800,224
Adorable Racer, 1992 g., by Two's a Plenty	3,500	1996-02-13	102	30	333,151
Sgt. Ivor, 1990 g., by Ivor Street	5,000	1994-01-28	157	30	165,012
Secret Service Man, 1992 g., by Shot Gun Scott	18,000	1996-08-02	98	29	290,043
Mahrally, 1991 g., by Ballydoyle	6,250	1994-08-01	134	29	144,603
Cope With Peace, 1988 h., by Copelan	10,000	1992-02-20	109	29	182,749
Bell Buzzer, 1990 g., by Sauce Boat	4,000	1994-11-17	101	29	111,630
Spacemaker, 1988 g., by Sunny Clime	5,000	1992-10-11	83	28	148,711
Victory Tower, 1990 g., by Singular	10,000	1993-08-20	151	28	151,654
Gold Digs, 1987 g., by Regal and Royal	4,000	1992-04-05	103	28	150,206
Boca Ratony, 1988 g., by Boca Rio	14,000	1993-07-31	103	28	75,934
Tate Express, 1992 g., by Naevus	12,500	1995-12-29	110	27	216,090
Maybe Jack, 1993 g., by Classic Account	15,000	1997-04-18	87	27	428,025
Fit for Royalty, 1988 g., by Fighting Fit	9,000	1993-04-09	135	27	206,439
Rosy Way, 1989 g., by Lord Avie	20,000	1993-08-22	46	27	88,779
Win Man, 1985 g., by Con Man	8,250	1992-02-23	66	27	262,792
Exuberant's Tip, 1990 g., by Exuberant	30,000	1992-06-26	87	27	116,315

Horses with Most Claiming Wins Since 1991

No. Claiming Wins	Horse,YOB, Sex, Sire	Claiming Starts	Claiming Earnings	Total Earnings
36	Boca Ratony, 1988 g., by Boca Rio	117	$107,020	$123,587
34	Best Boy's Jade, 1989 g., by Raja's Best Boy	134	170,982	223,983
32	Mankato, 1988 g., by Meadowlake	139	299,146	381,821
32	Spacemaker, 1988 g., by Sunny Clime	91	145,020	174,097
31	Sawmill Run, 1988 g., by It's Freezing	123	195,437	251,404
31	Smart Graustark, 1990 h., by Special Graustark	85	46,897	48,327
30	Dundee Maverick, 1989 g., by Implore	110	112,638	125,220
30	Gold Digs, 1987 g., by Regal and Royal	107	151,805	182,566
30	Halo Round My Head, 1988 m., by Gregorian	97	112,852	130,383
29	Thar He Blows, 1988 g., by Dewan Keys	143	75,020	80,867
29	The Mighty Zip, 1988 g., by Fire Dancer	114	183,953	265,341
28	Inspector Moomaw, 1987 g., by Entropy	128	184,689	207,948
28	It's the Wind, 1989 g., by Contare	102	163,627	207,100
28	Sgt. Ivor, 1990 g., by Ivor Street	151	143,856	173,316
28	Son Coming, 1986 g., by Son of Briartic	130	128,806	136,579
28	Two the Twist, 1987 g., by Two's a Plenty	141	292,975	496,488
28	Wilowy's Image, 1989 m., by Mongo's Image	70	130,208	154,698
27	Elegant Bo, 1987 g., by Swelegant	121	153,132	199,284
27	Monsignor K., 1987 g., by Gala Harry	158	130,434	138,286
27	Northern Broadway, 1988 g., by Northern Magus	156	116,592	124,476
27	Oh So Fabulous, 1992 g., by Singular	87	172,895	286,153
27	Out for Gold, 1990 g., by Gold Crest	163	253,569	313,536
27	Primetime Pirate, 1991 g., by Word Pirate	107	64,305	69,968
27	Regal Peace, 1988 m., by Peace for Peace	112	113,460	115,383
27	Sheila K., 1988 m., by Family Doctor	127	117,413	117,833

Leading Earners After Being Claimed, 1991-2002

Horse,YOB Sex, Sire	Claiming Price	Date of Claim	Starts After Claim	Wins After Claim	Total Earnings
Budroyale, 1993 g., by Cee's Tizzy	$32,000	1995-12-09	52	17	$2,837,610
Ladies Din, 1995 g., by Din's Dancer	32,000	1997-07-30	33	11	1,885,604
Native Desert, 1993 g., by Desert Classic	32,000	1996-10-10	64	20	1,741,561
Say Florida Sandy, 1994 h., by Personal Flag	70,000	1997-09-14	79	25	1,678,146
River Keen (Ire), 1992 h., by Keen	100,000	1998-12-04	16	3	1,338,880
Lazy Slusan, 1995 m., by Slewvescent	20,000	1997-10-22	45	11	1,142,196
Recoup the Cash, 1990 g., by Copelan	15,000	1993-06-03	67	22	1,090,713
License Fee, 1995 m., by Black Tie Affair (Ire)	75,000	1998-09-02	34	13	1,084,276
Early Pioneer, 1995 g., by Rahy	62,500	1998-10-25	22	7	1,068,815
Elated Guy, 1989 g., by Brave Shot (GB)	40,000	1991-08-22	63	9	941,904
One Way Love, 1995 h., by Regal Classic	50,000	1997-11-01	37	14	937,095
Full Moon Madness, 1995 g., by Half a Year	32,000	1997-06-25	33	14	919,105
Shoop, 1991 m., by Double Sonic	25,000	1995-08-26	70	11	911,515
Royal Haven, 1992 g., by Hail Emperor	75,000	1995-08-06	37	16	847,161
Beboppin Baby, 1993 g., by Hatchet Man	32,000	1996-07-13	63	13	830,990

Horse, YOB sex, sire	Initial Claim Price	Date of Claim	Starts After Claim	Wins After Claim	Earnings After Claim
Mr. Epperson, 1995 g., by Cabrini Green	50,000	1998-07-10	45	13	827,175
Judge T C, 1991 h., by Judge Smells	30,000	1993-06-11	27	11	825,960
Arromanches, 1993 h., by Relaunch	12,500	1996-06-24	75	30	800,224
Peeping Tom, 1997 g., by Eagle Eyed	40,000	2000-03-24	28	9	791,033
Dancing Guy, 1995 g., by Robyn Dancer	18,000	1997-11-25	73	19	774,853
Coyote Lakes, 1994 g., by Society Max	12,500	1996-10-26	57	19	720,977
Sharp Appeal, 1993 h., by World Appeal	50,000	1995-07-14	39	12	712,346
Irisheyesareflying, 1996 h., by Flying Continental	12,500	1999-02-20	32	8	706,956
Same Old Wish, 1990 g., by Lyphard's Wish (Fr)	35,000	1994-08-04	49	5	675,935
Chicago Six, 1995 h., by Wild Again	18,000	1999-09-02	29	15	675,147
Golden Tent, 1989 g., by Shelter Half	50,000	1994-05-15	105	17	673,903
Mr. Sinatra, 1994 h., by Mining	75,000	1997-08-22	53	10	667,205
Boom Towner, 1988 g., by Obligato	50,000	1993-09-01	56	16	663,070
Wicapi, 1992 g., by Waquoit	20,000	1996-01-11	54	17	651,601
Iron Gavel, 1990 g., by Time for a Change	15,500	1993-11-18	77	24	646,408
Esteemed Friend, 1994 g., by Gulch	50,000	1997-08-21	48	16	644,297
Parose, 1994 g., by Parlay Me	15,000	1998-07-22	52	13	641,332
Oro de Mexico, 1994 g., by Well Decorated	80,000	1997-03-14	60	9	638,950
Freedom Crest, 1996 h., by To Freedom	32,000	1999-06-10	25	7	636,560
Theresa's Tizzy, 1994 m., by Cee's Tizzy	20,000	1997-07-25	31	13	612,171
Morluc, 1996 h., by Housebuster	50,000	1999-01-15	31	10	605,028
Fit for a King, 1993 g., by General Meeting	16,000	1996-11-09	29	15	598,618
Greatsilverfleet, 1990 g., by On to Glory	62,500	1993-05-12	69	15	593,637
Back Ring Al, 1992 g., by Allen's Prospect	25,000	1995-01-15	104	25	590,679
Slerp, 1989 h., by Slewpy	40,000	1992-01-17	31	9	588,842
Nappelon, 1992 m., by Bold Revenue	35,000	1995-02-09	58	14	584,720
Countess Steffi, 1989 m., by Geiger Counter	25,000	1991-08-16	33	11	580,835
Poor But Honest, 1990 g., by Nasty and Bold	17,500	1994-05-18	28	11	579,230
Fabersham, 1988 g., by Nepal	35,000	1992-11-28	78	18	574,268
King Roller, 1991 g., by Silent King	35,000	1997-04-23	53	11	572,465
Perfect to a Tee, 1992 g., by Parfaitement	14,500	1995-12-01	59	13	570,010
Brutally Frank, 1994 g., by Groovy	25,000	1998-01-31	48	10	565,500
K. J.'s Appeal, 1994 h., by Valid Appeal	32,000	1996-07-21	19	6	554,780
Federal Funds, 1989 h., by Settlement Day	50,000	1992-01-04	134	10	552,220
Jacksonport, 1989 h., by Vigors	35,000	1992-01-09	93	7	551,239
Tic N Tin, 1995 h., by Lac Ouimet	25,000	1999-10-02	52	20	551,100
Rocking Josh, 1989 g., by Whitesburg	12,500	1992-09-12	101	22	547,605
Echo Eddie, 1997 g., by Restless Con	20,000	1999-11-20	19	7	544,584
Taking Risks, 1990 g., by Two Punch	11,500	1993-07-27	20	12	540,945
Ringaskiddy, 1996 g., by Slewvescent	50,000	1999-03-13	40	4	540,111
McKaymackenna, 1989 m., by Ends Well	35,000	1992-05-16	29	13	538,542

Some of the Best Claimers

Following are some of the most prominent horses who either were claimed prior to outstanding careers on the racetrack or at stud or started in claiming races but went unclaimed:

ASPIDISTRA—1954 b. m., Better Self—Tilly Rose, by Bull Brier. 14-2-2-2, $5,115. Bred by King Ranch, Aspidistra was purchased by William L. McKnight's Minnesota Mining & Manufacturing Co. employees as a 70th birthday gift in 1957. Aspidistra, named for a hardy house plant, then was in the midst of a nondescript racing career that did not improve after her purchase. For McKnight, she raced for a $6,500 claiming tag. Retired after one racing season at age three, she became the foundation of McKnight's Tartan Farms in Florida, producing 1968 Horse of the Year Dr. Fager and champion sprinter Ta Wee.

BOOM TOWNER—1988 b. g., Obligato—Perfect Profile, by Stop the Music. 82-29-16-14, $962,391. Boom Towner began his eight-year career in a $5,000 maiden claimer at Rockingham Park, winning by 10¾ lengths. He won the 1992 Toboggan Handicap (G3) and was claimed the following year for $50,000 by

trainer Mike Hushion for Barry Schwartz. In Hushion's care, Boom Towner won the 1993 Boojum (G3) and Sport Page (G3) Handicaps, both at Aqueduct. He won the Toboggan again in 1995.

BROWN BESS—1982 dk. b. or br. m., *Petrone—Chickadee, by Windy Sands. 36-16-8-6, $1,300,920. Brown Bess's owner-breeder, Calbourne Farm, put her at risk only once, for $50,000 in a Bay Meadows Race Course claimer on September 28, 1986. It was her first start on grass, and she finished second by a nose. Brown Bess would thrive on the grass, winning the 1989 Yellow Ribbon Invitational Stakes (G1) and the Ramona Handicap (G1) on her way to an Eclipse Award as champion female grass horse.

BUDROYALE—1993 b. g., Cee's Tizzy—Cee's Song, by Seattle Song. 52-17-12-2, $2,840,810. First-time starter Budroyale was taken for $32,000 by trainer Dan Hendricks from breeder/co-owner Cecilia Straub-Rubens on December 9, 1995, at Hollywood Park. Budroyale was subsequently claimed for $40,000 by trainer Nick Canani on August 17, 1997, and for $50,000 by trainer Ted West for Jeffrey Sengara on February 15,

1998. He won the 1998 San Bernardino Handicap (G2) and in '99 scored victories in the Goodwood Breeders' Cup Handicap (G2), the Mervyn LeRoy Handicap (G2), and the Longacres Mile Handicap (G3). He was second five times, including the Breeders' Cup Classic (G1). In 2000, Budroyale won the San Antonio Handicap (G2) the same year his full brother Tiznow won the first of his two Breeders' Cup Classics.

CHARISMATIC—1996 ch. h., Summer Squall—Bail Babe, by Drone. 17-5-2-4, $2,038,064. Charismatic won only one of his first 13 starts and raced four more times in his career. Trained by D. Wayne Lukas and owned by Robert and Beverly Lewis, Charismatic was placed first in a $62,500 claimer at Santa Anita Park on February 11, 1999. After finishing second in the El Camino Real Derby (G3) at Bay Meadows Race Course, Charismatic was a soundly beaten fourth in the Santa Anita Derby (G1). He subsequently won the Coolmore Lexington Stakes (G2), the Kentucky Derby (G1), and the Preakness Stakes (G1) before finishing third in the Belmont Stakes (G1), in which he sustained two fractures of his right foreleg. He was voted 1999 champion three-year-old male and Horse of the Year.

CREME DE LA FETE—1976 ch. g., Creme Dela Creme—Bridge Day, by *Tudor Minstrel. 151-40-27-16, $460,350. After winning his career debut by a nose at a two-year-old at Keeneland Race Course in 1978, Creme de La Fete finished fifth of six in the Bashford Manor Stakes at Churchill Downs. Unlike many two-year-olds that faded from the racing scene, Creme de La Fete would make 149 more starts. His two best years were in 1981, when he won 12 of 26 starts and $123,180, and in '83, when he won nine of 30 starts and earned $127,240. In his final start, Creme de La Fete was second in a $7,000 claimer at Garden State Park, the 12th racetrack at which he had raced, in June 1985.

DEPUTED TESTAMONY—1980 b. h., Traffic Cop—Proof Requested, by Prove It. 20-11-3-0, $674,329. Owned by Francis Sears and trained by J. William Boniface, Deputed Testamony was not competitive in his first start, finishing sixth by 12¾ lengths in a $25,000 maiden claimer at Bowie Race Course on September 21, 1982. In his next start, the colt won a $22,500 maiden claimer at Keystone Race Track, and Boniface put him at risk once more, in a $40,000 open claimer at the Meadowlands. Deputed Testamony won by three lengths and was not claimed. The following year, he won the Preakness Stakes (G1) and Monmouth Park's Haskell Invitational Handicap (G1). He won his two 1984 starts, including a track-record effort in the City of Baltimore Handicap, before retiring to stud at Boniface's Bonita Farm, the place of his birth.

GAIL'S BRUSH—1991 b. m., Broad Brush—Parade of Roses, by Blues Parade. 39-11-5-4, $250,701. Claimed by John E. Salzman Jr. on November 25, 1995, for $25,000, Gail's Brush made only two starts for the Maryland trainer before she was picked up by owner-trainer Edwin T. Broome from a $40,000 claimer on grass at Gulfstream Park in early 1996. Gail's Brush, whose performance had improved dramatically when switched to grass, made only six starts for Broome, but they included consecutive victories in the 1996 Columbiana Handicap, Politely Stakes, Eatontown Handicap (G3), and Rumson Stakes.

GOLDEN TENT—1989 dk. b. or br. g., Shelter Half—Jump for Gold, by Search for Gold. 114-21-27-17, $732,793. By the standards of racing in the new century, Golden Tent is made of iron. He started once at three and then made 113 starts through 2001.

Golden Tent was claimed seven times, four within a little more than four months in 1999 at the age of ten. Trainer Mike Hushion claimed Golden Tent three times for Barry Schwartz, for whom the gelding finished second in the 1998 Bold Ruler Handicap (G3) and third in the Fall Highweight Handicap (G2) that year.

JEWEL PRINCESS—1992 b. m., Key to the Mint—Jewel Ridge, by Melyno (Ire). 29-13-4-7, $1,904,060. An Eclipse Award winner as outstanding older female after winning the 1996 Breeders' Cup Distaff (G1), Jewel Princess began her career with a third-place finish in a $20,000 maiden claimer at Calder Race Course on October 27, 1994. She won her next start in a $30,000 maiden claimer and never looked back. In the care of Wally Dollase, Jewel Princess won the 1996 Vanity Invitational Handicap (G1) in addition to the Distaff, and in '97 she won the Santa Maria (G1) and Santa Margarita Invitational (G1) Handicaps. At the 2000 Keeneland November breeding stock sale, she was sold for $4.9-million to Coolmore Stud principal owner John Magnier.

JOHN HENRY—1975 b. g., Old Bob Bowers—Once Double, by Double Jay. 83-39-15-9, $6,591,860. John Henry raced five times in claiming races in 1978 but was not claimed. Purchased privately for $27,500 by Sam Rubin in 1978, he made his final claiming start for Sam and Dorothy Rubin's Dotsam Stable at $35,000 on June 28, 1978, at Belmont Park and won by 14 lengths. Trained by Robert Donato, Victor "Lefty" Nickerson, and Ron McAnally, he was Horse of the Year in 1981 and '84 as well as a four-time champion turf male and once champion older male. He retired as the richest North American Thoroughbred of all time. After his final claiming start, he compiled a record of 64-36-13-6 with earnings of $6,527,882.

KING COMMANDER—1949 dk. b. or br. g., Brown King—Guinea Egg, by *Cohort. 67-17-15-9, $100,295. King Commander made 27 of his first 31 starts in claimers although he was claimed only once, for $5,000 at Aqueduct in 1952. Converted to steeplechasing after winning three of 32 starts on the flat, King Commander won 14 of 35 starts over fences and was voted champion steeplechase horse in 1954.

KING'S SWAN—1980 b. h., King's Bishop—Royal Cygnet, by *Sea-Bird. 107-31-19-18, $1,924,845. King's Swan already had won 11 of 44 starts and $212,350 when he was claimed in 1985 for $80,000 by trainer Richard Dutrow. The following year, King's Swan won eight of 15 starts, including the Vosburgh Stakes (G1) and Boojum Handicap (G3), and earned $451,207. At seven, he won three Grade 3 stakes in 12 starts and earned $477,218. He was even better at eight, winning five graded stakes, including the Bold Ruler (G2) and Tom Fool (G2) Stakes in 14 starts and banking $539,681.

KOBUK KING—1966 dk. b. or br. h., One-Eyed King—Winby, by Crafty Admiral. 68-12-10-11, $173,921. After showing considerable promise as a two-year-old in 1968, winning three of 13 starts and finishing second in the El Camino Stakes at Bay Meadows Race Course, Kobuk King went zero-for-three as a three-year-old and zero-for-19 at four. Claimed for $15,000 in 1971, Kobuk King found himself and scored consecutive victories in the Cabrillo Handicap at Del Mar, the Tanforan Handicap at Bay Meadows, and Santa Anita Park's Carleton F. Burke Invitational Handicap for co-owners Allegre Stable and Ron McAnally, who trained the horse. He won eight of 18 starts in 1971 but only one of 15 races in his final two years, a division of the '73 Arcadia Handicap (G3) at Santa Anita.

LADY MARYLAND—1934 gr. m., Sir Greysteel—Palestra, by *Prince Palatine. 82-18-14-14, $31,067. The 1939 champion handicap mare, Lady Maryland made 19 of her 82 starts in claimers and was taken for $2,500 in her 28th career start by B. B. Archer. Her final start in a claimer was as a four-year-old for $4,500 at Havre de Grace. She was not claimed and quickly improved in her five-year-old season, winning the Carroll and Ritchie Handicaps at Pimlico Race Course.

LAKEVILLE MISS—1975 dk. b. or br. m., Rainy Lake—Hew, by Blue Prince. 14-7-4-1, $371,582. While Affirmed and Alydar slugged it out for two-year-old male honors in 1977, the juvenile filly championship was taken by the strapping Lakeville Miss, who possessed a blue-collar pedigree and started her career as a $25,000 maiden claimer for owner-breeder Randolph Weinsier. She won a 5½-furlong claiming race at Belmont Park by four lengths on June 30 and never started again for a claiming tag. Trained by Jose Martin, Lakeville Miss won the Matron (G1) and Frizette (G1) Stakes at Belmont and the Selima Stakes (G1) at Laurel Race Course. She concluded her career with a four-length win in the 1978 Coaching Club American Oaks (G1).

LEAVE IT TO BEEZER—1993 b. g., Henbane—Blue Shocker, by Copelan. 75-22-11-13, $587,086. Although he had lost ten straight races, six-year-old Leave It to Beezer was claimed for $32,000 by trainer Scott Lake for Leo Gaspari Racing Stable on December 22, 1999. His third-place finish that day extended his losing streak to 11. Lake backed off on the gelding's training regimen, and Leave It to Beezer responded by winning nine of 15 starts, including the Salvator Mile Handicap (G3) at Monmouth Park and the Baltimore Breeders' Cup Handicap (G3) at Pimlico on the way to earning $350,830 in 2000.

McKAYMACKENNA—1989 b. m., Ends Well—Amuse, by Secretariat. 38-15-6-2, $581,322. R Kay Stable claimed McKaymackenna for $35,000 from a Belmont Park race in which she was beaten by more than 35 lengths. Sloppy tracks like the one she encountered at Belmont on May 16, 1992, were not to her liking; turf racing was her game. After trainer Gary Sciacca claimed her, she won seven grass stakes, including the 1993 Beaugay Handicap (G3) and Noble Damsel Stakes (G3).

PARKA—1958 br. g., *Arctic Prince—Manchon, by *Blenheim II. 93-27-14-18, $446,236. Bred by Marion duPont Scott and unraced at two, Parka was claimed for $10,000 in his 11th career start by Warren A. "Jimmy" Croll Jr. for client Rachel Carpenter. Parka won that Atlantic City Race Course race by a head, and Croll entered him in a $13,000 claimer 15 days later. He won that race by eight lengths and never raced in a claimer again. He was 1965 champion grass horse off victories in the Bougainvillea Handicap at Hialeah Park, the Kelly-Olympic and United Nations Handicaps at Atlantic City, and Aqueduct's Long Island Handicap in his final career start.

PEAT MOSS—1975 b. g., *Herbager—Moss, by Round Table. 55-15-7-9, $635,517. A little more than one year after winning a $10,000 claimer, Claiborne Farm-bred Peat Moss came within a head of upsetting John Henry in the 1981 Jockey Club Gold Cup (G1). Owned and trained by Murray Garren, Peat Moss loved to go a distance, winning the 1980 Display Handicap (G3) at 2¼ miles and the 1980 and '81 Kelso Handicap at two miles. In his first 1981 start, he set an Aqueduct track record for 2⅛ miles when winning a handicap by 6½ lengths in 3:40⅘.

PORT CONWAY LANE—1969 gr. h., Bold Com-mander—*Grey Taffety, by Grey Sovereign. 242-52-39-36, $431,593. Port Conway Lane spent most of his lengthy career in claimers, although he started his career in allowance and stakes races, including a second-place finish in the 1971 Marlboro Nursery Stakes. He won Pimlico Race Course's City of Baltimore Handicap twice, in 1974 and '75, as well as Bowie Race Course's '74 Bowie Handicap and '75 Terrapin Handicap. By the end of 1976, however, he was racing principally in claimers and continued to do so through '83.

*PRINCEQUILLO—1940 b. h., by Prince Rose—*Cosquilla, by *Papyrus. 33-12-5-7, $96,550. Exported from England in 1941, *Princequillo was offered for a $2,500 claiming price by owner Anthony Pelleteri on August 20, 1942. Taking him for Boone Hall Stable was Horatio Luro, who would develop *Princequillo into a multiple stakes winner during World War II. At Claiborne Farm, he proved to be an outstanding stallion, leading the general sire list in 1957 and '58 and topping the broodmare sire list eight times in North America and once in England.

SEABISCUIT—1933 b. h., Hard Tack—Swing On, by Whisk Broom II. 89-33-15-13, $437,730. Long before he became a top handicap horse, Seabiscuit lost the first 17 races of his career, including three defeats in $2,500 claimers and a loss in a $4,000 claimer at Havre de Grace in April 1935. Nobody took him, and later Wheatley Stable sold him to Charles Howard. Under the care of Racing Hall of Fame trainer Tom Smith, Seabiscuit went on to spectacular success, including a seven-stakes win streak in 1937, when he was champion handicap horse. The following year, he was voted Horse of the Year and handicap champion.

STYMIE—1941 ch. h., Equestrian—Stop Watch, by On Watch. 131-35-33-28, $918,485. Taken in his third lifetime start for $1,500 by Hirsch Jacobs, Stymie became the richest Thoroughbred of all time by his retirement in 1949, a record that only lasted until Citation moved past him in 1950. In his prime from ages four through seven, he won 28 of 69 starts, including the Saratoga Cup Stakes and the Gallant Fox, Metropolitan, Grey Lag, Aqueduct, and Sussex Handicaps twice each.

TIMELY WRITER—1979 b., c., Staff Writer—Timely Roman, by Sette Bello. 15-9-1-2, $605,491. A $13,000 yearling purchase owned by Peter and Francis Martin and trained by Dominic Imprescia, Timely Writer made his debut with an eight-length victory in a $30,000 maiden claimer at Monmouth Park. He subsequently won Saratoga Race Course's Hopeful Stakes (G1) and the Champagne Stakes (G1) at Belmont Park, earning him co-highweight with Eclipse Award champion Deputy Minister on the 1981 Experimental Free Handicap. At three, he won the Flamingo Stakes (G1) and Florida Derby (G1), but surgery for an intestinal blockage knocked him out of the Triple Crown races. He returned in the fall but sustained a fatal breakdown in the Jockey Club Gold Cup (G1).

VIDEOGENIC—1982 b. m., Caucasus—Video Babe, by T.V. Commercial. 73-20-9-10, $1,154,360. Trainer Gasper Moschera convinced owner Albert Davis to claim Videogenic for $100,000 on May 24, 1985. She was not much to look at, but she could run, winning 11 stakes races after the claim, including the 1985 Ladies Handicap (G1) at Aqueduct and the 1986 Santa Ana Handicap (G1) at Santa Anita Park. She won more than $1-million for Davis on the racetrack and was sold as a broodmare prospect for $625,000 at the 1988 Keeneland November breeding stock sale.

Racetracks of North America

Arizona

Apache County Fair

Location: 825 W. 4th St. North, Saint Johns, AZ 85936-0357
Phone: (520) 337-4364
Fax: (520) 337-2783
Abbreviation: SJ

Racing Dates
2002: September 14-September 22
2003: September 15-September 22, 4 days

Leaders
Recent meeting, leading jockey: Fernando Manuel Gamez, 4, 2002
Recent meeting, leading trainer: Steve R. Irlando, 4, 2002

Fastest Times of 2002 (Dirt)
4 furlongs: Whatsrightisright, :44.40, September 21
5 1/2 furlongs: Minnesota Mackee, 1:07.40, September 21; Revenue, 1:07.40, September 22
6 furlongs: Mr. Fine Fine, 1:13.80, September 21
7 furlongs: Private Award, 1:26.40, September 22
1 mile: Mymomisaprincess, 1:49.40, September 14

Cochise County Fair

Location: 3677 N. Leslie Canyon Rd., Douglas, AZ 85607-6304
Phone: (520) 432-9454
Abbreviation: DG

Racing Dates
2002: April 13-April 21
2003: April 12-April 20, 4 days

Leaders
Recent meeting, leading jockey: Richard C. Gamez, 3, 2002
Recent meeting, leading trainer: Adalberto G. Romero, 1, 2002, Alex Quiroga, 1, 2002, Alex Villa Jr., 1, 2002, Jaykie Betancourt, 1, 2002, Joe G. Candelaria, 1, 2002, Lowell N. Bunyard, 1, 2002, Lyndel G. Rutherford, 1, 2002, Wiley Aker, 1, 2002

Fastest Times of 2002 (Dirt)
About 3 furlongs: My Man Vincent, :37.80, April 21; Whatsrightisright, :37.80, April 14
5 1/2 furlongs: Manzanola, 1:05.00, April 21
6 furlongs: North Northwest, 1:12.00, April 21
7 furlongs: Cop Out, 1:25.20, April 13

Coconino County Fair

Location: HC 30 Box 3A, Flagstaff, AZ 86001
Phone: (928) 774-5139
Fax: (928) 774-2572
Abbreviation: Flg
Acreage: 400
Number of stalls: 320
Seating capacity: 3,500

Officers
General Manager: Linda Kellogg
Racing Secretary: Hank Denonby
Director of Operations: Linda Kellogg
Director of Finance: Kelly Burkhart
Director of Marketing: Jennifer Hartin

Stewards: Gerry Howard, Rita Fresquez, Violet Smith
Track Announcer: Craig Willis
Track Photographer: Double B Photography
Track Superintendent: Dave Stewart

Racing Dates
2002: July 4-July 7, 4 days
2003: July 4-July 7, 4 days
2004: July 4-July 7, 4 Days

Track Layout
Main circumference: 5/8 Mile
Main width: 75 Feet

Attendance
Average daily recent meeting: 1,800
Highest single day record: 2,600
Highest single meet record: 12,000
Lowest single day record: 800
Total attendance recent meeting: 8,000

Gila County Fair

Location: P.O. Box 2193, Globe, AZ 85502-2193
Phone: (520) 473-3521
Fax: (520) 473-4122
Abbreviation: GCF

Racing Dates
2002: September 28-October 6
2003: September 28-October 6, 4 days

Leaders
Recent meeting, leading jockey: Don Lee French, 3, 2002, Fernando Manuel Gamez, 3, 2002
Recent meeting, leading trainer: Butch Clinton, 2, 2002

Fastest Times of 2002 (Dirt)
3 furlongs: Whatsrightisright, :34.60, October 6
5 furlongs: Wahines Reality, 1:01.60, October 6
5 1/2 furlongs: Revenue, 1:06.60, October 5
6 furlongs: Revenue, 1:13.00, September 28
7 furlongs: Tooties Teddy, 1:31.00, September 29
1 1/16 miles: Tooties Teddy, 1:50.80, October 6

Graham County Fair

Location: 527 E. Armory Rd., Safford, AZ 85546-2231
Phone: (928) 428-7180
Fax: (928) 348-0023
Year founded: 1965
Inaugural meeting: 1965
Abbreviation: SAF
Acreage: 220

Officers
President: Phil Curtis
Vice President: Jon Haralson
General Manager: Casey Faunce
Director of Racing: Casey Faunce
Racing Secretary: Tom Figueroa
Secretary: Jessie Hines
Director of Operations: Larry Jensen
Director of Mutuels: Jerome Doolittle
Horsemen's Liaison: Robert Pledge
Stewards: Bob Clink, Roy Snedigar, Violet Smith
Track Announcer: Red Davis
Track Photographer: Double D
Track Superintendent: Jim Gutierrez

Racing Dates
2002: March 30-April 7, 4 days
2003: March 29-April 6, 4 days

Leaders
Recent meeting, leading jockey: Robert Boyce, 5, 2002
Recent meeting, leading trainer: Wiley Aker, 3, 2002

Track Records, Main Dirt
4 furlongs: In the Military, :44 2/5
5 1/2 furlongs: Dusty Orchid, 1:05 2/5
6 furlongs: Bendabout's Trump, 1:11 1/5
7 furlongs: Hum Dewey Slew, 1:26 3/5
1 1/16 miles: Cop Out, 1:46 3/5, March 31, 2001

Fastest Times of 2002 (Dirt)
3 furlongs: Broadside, :34.40, March 30
4 furlongs: My Man Vincent, :47.00, March 31
5 1/2 furlongs: High Riser, 1:07.00, April 6
6 furlongs: Tooties Teddy, 1:12.40, March 31
7 furlongs: Three Toms, 1:27.00, March 31
1 mile: Three Toms, 1:46.00, April 7

Greenelee County Fair

Location: P.O. Box 123, Duncan, AZ 85534-0123
Phone: (928) 359-2032
Fax: (928) 359-2721

Officers
Racing Secretary: Tom Figueroa
Director of Mutuels: Jerry Doolittle
Director of Publicity: Douglas Barlow
Stewards: Roy Snedigar, Violet Smith
Track Announcer: Tom Figueroa

Racing Dates
2002: March 16-March 24
2003: March 15-March 23, 4 days

Leaders
Recent meeting, leading jockey: Fernando Manuel Gamez, 4, 2002
Recent meeting, leading trainer: Audrey Lyman, 1, 2002, Clay Brinson, 1, 2002, Clyde England, 1, 2002, Ernesto Alcoverde, 1, 2002, Jim Crotts, 1, 2002, Joe G. Candelaria, 1, 2002, Lowell N. Bunyard, 1, 2002, Pablo E. Figueroa Jr., 1, 2002, Randall Vasey, 1, 2002, S. Eugene Johnson, 1, 2002, Wiley Aker, 1, 2002

Track Records, Main Dirt
5 1/2 furlongs: Fire In the Hole, 1:05 1/5
5 furlongs: Ack Like A Dancer, 1:00, March 26, 2000
6 furlongs: Please Explain, 1:11 1/5, March 25, 2000
7 furlongs: Saros Irish Luck, 1:24 1/5
1 1/16 miles: Sunburst, 1:47 4/5

Fastest Times of 2002 (Dirt)
5 furlongs: Zambonus, 1:00.80, March 24
5 1/2 furlongs: Real Dancer, 1:05.00, March 24
About 6 furlongs: Desert Best, 1:12.20, March 17; Tooties Teddy, 1:12.20, March 16
7 furlongs: Personal Pride, 1:26.80, March 23

Mohave County Fair

Location: 2600 Fairgrounds Blvd., Kingman, AZ 86401-4169
Phone: (928) 753-2636
Fax: (928) 753-8383
Abbreviation: MOF

Officers
Chairman: Mike Burton

Racing Dates
2002: May 11-May 19
2003: May 10-May 18, 4 days

Leaders
Recent meeting, leading jockey: Anna M. Barrio, 6, 2002
Recent meeting, leading trainer: Dennis Swenson, 2, 2002, Lowell N. Bunyard, 2, 2002, W. R. Whitehouse, 2, 2002

Fastest Times of 2002 (Dirt)
4 furlongs: Iza Twister, :43.60, May 12
5 1/2 furlongs: Manzanola, 1:06.60, May 19
6 furlongs: Cop Out, 1:13.80, May 18
6 1/2 furlongs: Samak, 1:19.20, May 12
7 furlongs: Orphaned, 1:26.00, May 19
1 1/8 miles: Cop Out, 1:53.80, May 11

Rillito Park

Location: 4502 N. 1st Ave., Tucson, AZ 85718
Phone: (520) 293-5011
Fax: (520) 293-1287

Officers
Vice President: Tim Kelly
General Manager: Patricia White
Director of Racing: Patricia White
Racing Secretary: Josie Stavens
Secretary: Patricia White
Treasurer: Patricia White
Director of Operations: Tim Kelly
Director of Finance: Patricia White
Director of Marketing: Jim Collins
Director of Mutuels: Tim Kelly
Director of Publicity: Jim Collins
Director of Admissions: Lisa Pina
Horsemen's Liaison: Doreen Rawls
Steward: Jim Dreyer
Track Announcer: Craig Willis
Track Photographer: Coady Photography
Track Superintendent: John King
Other officials: Jock Room Custodian: Tuck Miller

Racing Dates
2002: February 2-March 3
2003: January 18-March 2
2004: January 17-February 29

Attendance
Average daily recent meeting: 2,562
Highest single day record: 3,449, January 18, 2003
Total attendance recent meeting: 35,872, 14 Days

Handle
Average all sources recent meeting: $94,821
Average on-track recent meeting: $76,724
Single day on-track handle: $101,263
Single day total handle all sources: $120,337
Total all sources recent meeting: $1,327,497

Mutuel Records
Highest win: $2,032

Leaders
Recent meeting, leading jockey: Floyd Campbell, 9, 2001
Recent meeting, leading trainer: Eddie Tellez, 4, 2001, Gene K. Wilson, 4, 2001, Santiago Lowe, 4, 2001

Fastest Times of 2002 (Dirt)
4 furlongs: Docs Gotta Wish, :44.60, February 9
5 1/2 furlongs: Real Dancer, 1:04.80, February 9
6 furlongs: Fresh Victor, 1:11.60, February 3
6 1/2 furlongs: Shuga Shaq, 1:18.40, February 17

7 furlongs: Cop Out, 1:25.00, February 9
1 1/16 miles: Junk Bond Kid, 1:45.40, March 3

Santa Cruz County Fair

Location: P.O. Box 85, Sonoita, AZ 85637-0085
Phone: (520) 455-5553
Fax: (520) 455-5330
Abbreviation: Son
Acreage: 36.5
Number of stalls: 180
Seating capacity: 2,200

Officers
President: Scott McDaniel
General Manager: Marilyn Parker

Racing Dates
2002: April 27-May 5
2003: April 26-May 4, 4 days

Track Layout
Main circumference: 4 furlongs

Leaders
Recent meeting, leading jockey: Robert W. Johnson, 5, 2002
Recent meeting, leading trainer: Wiley Aker, 4, 2002

Fastest Times of 2002 (Dirt)
5 furlongs: Littlefield, :59.40, April 27
5 1/2 furlongs: R. Scrapper, 1:07.20, May 4
6 furlongs: Babyletsrocknroll, 1:12.20, May 4
7 furlongs: Solo Pal, 1:31.80, April 27
1 1/16 miles: Oil Man, 1:53.60, April 2

Turf Paradise

A Phoenix tradition for nearly a half-century, Turf Paradise has survived several ownership changes and the dramatic reshaping of Thoroughbred racing to remain a vital part of the winter racing scene.

Turf Paradise was the vision of businessman Walter Cluer, who purchased 1,400 acres of desert land in 1954 and transformed it into a racetrack, which opened its doors on January 7, 1956. Cluer owned the track until 1980. The track's next two owners, Herb Owens and Robert Walker, added a turf course and off-track betting, respectively.

Hollywood Park purchased the track in 1994 and weathered an influx of Native American casino gambling in Arizona before selling the track to Phoenix developer Jerry Simms in June 2000. Simms's reign as owner was troubled; in October 2001, the Arizona Department of Racing stripped him of his license, citing his involvement in a California bribery scandal and alleged organized-crime ties, but in late 2002 the Arizona Racing Commission voted 3-2 to restore his license. The track suffered a further setback in November 2002 when Arizona voters rejected slot machines at the state's racetracks and approved more machines at Native American casinos.

Location: 1501 W. Bell Rd., Phoenix, AZ 85023-3411
Phone: (602) 942-1101
Fax: (602) 942-8659
E-mail: webmaster@turfparadise.net
Web site: http://www.turfparadise.com
Year founded: 1955
Inaugural meeting: January 7, 1956

Abbreviation: TuP
Acreage: 1,400
Number of stalls: 1,700
Seating capacity: 7,284

Officers
President: Randy Fozzard
Vice President: Dave Johnson
General Manager: Randy Fozzard
Director of Racing: Shawn Swartz
Racing Secretary: Shawn Swartz
Director of Operations: Brian Whitman
Director of Communications: Vincent Francia
Director of Marketing: Vince Francia
Director of Mutuels: Jack Mullins
Director of Publicity: Vincent Francia
Director of Simulcasting: Jack Mullen
Horsemen's Liaison: Debbie Zimmerman
Steward: Jerry Nicodemus
Track Announcer: Luke Kruytbosch
Track Photographer: Coady Photography
Track Superintendent: Terry Brown

Racing Dates
2002: September 28, 2001-May 19, 2002, 164 days
2003: September 27, 2002-May 18, 2003, 169 days

Track Layout
Main circumference: 1 mile
Main track chute: 3 furlongs, 6 1/2 furlongs
Main width: 80 feet
Main turf circumference: 7 furlongs
Main turf chute: 1/8 mile
Main turf length of stretch: 999 Feet
Main turf width: 73 Feet

Mutuel Records
Highest Daily Double: $5,355, April 24, 1985
Highest Exacta: $17,092.20, May 8, 1988
Highest Pick 6: $137,372, March 3, 1986
Highest Trifecta: $42,774, October 18, 1987
Highest win: $287.60, Gaye Rest, May 23, 1974

Attendance
Highest single day record: 16,000 est., March 18, 1984

Leaders
Career, leading jockey by titles: Sam Powell, 16
Career, leading owner by titles: Dennis Weir, 10
Career, leading trainer by titles: Richard Hazelton, 27

Records
Single day jockey wins: Marty Wentz, Ray York, 7
Single meet, leading jockey by wins: Pat Steinberg, 225
Single meet, leading trainer by wins: Bart Hone, 88

Track Records, Main Dirt
4 1/2 furlongs: Kathryn's Doll, :50 2/5, April 9, 1967
5 furlongs: Zip Pocket, :55 2/5, April 22, 1967
5 1/2 furlongs: Plenty Zloty, 1:01.10, April 18, 1995
6 furlongs: G Malleah, 1:06.60, April 8, 1995
6 1/2 furlongs: G Malleah, 1:13.80, December 3, 1994
7 furlongs: Free Duty, 1:26 1/5, January 23, 1985
1 mile: Mr. Pappion, 1:33.20, January 30, 1993
1 1/16 miles: Down the Isle, 1:39 1/5, February 11, 1987
1 1/8 miles: Our Forbes, 1:47.60, November 29, 1996
1 1/4 miles: Truly a Pleasure, 2:01.40, March 26, 1995
1 3/8 miles: Bloom n Character, 2:15 2/5, April 12, 1980
1 5/8 miles: Masked Rider, 2:44.40, February 10, 2002
1 3/4 miles: Arsenal, 2:55 2/5, February 7, 1971
2 miles: Vermejo, 3:24, April 20, 1969
Other: 2 furlongs, Wandering Boy, :21 1/5, December 5, 1965;
3 furlongs, Never Shamed, :31.60, April 1, 1996

Course Records, Main Turf
5 furlongs: Honor the Hero, :56.20, February 5, 1995
7 furlongs: Lord Pleasant, 1:22.80, October 12, 1992
7 1/2 furlongs: Bristolville, 1:28.71, November 3, 2001
1 mile: Prose (Ire), 1:34.83, March 27, 2001
1 1/16 miles: Caesour, 1:40.40, February 5, 1995
1 1/8 miles: Narghile, 1:48, February 1, 1987
1 3/8 miles: Turk Flyer, 2:16.11, April 14, 2001
1 1/2 miles: Senator McGuire, 2:29 3/5, May 22, 1988
Other: 1 7/8 miles, Shadows Fall, 3:09 2/5, May 17, 1987

Major Races
$100,000 Phoenix Gold Cup, $100,000 Turf Paradise Derby,
$150,000 Turf Paradise Breeders' Cup

Fastest Times of 2002 (Dirt)
4 1/2 furlongs: Johnny Is Bad, :50.54, May 3
5 furlongs: Rotsaluck, :57.48, January 15
5 1/2 furlongs: Regal Edition, 1:01.98, December 13
6 furlongs: Nancy's Joker, 1:08.20, March 24
6 1/2 furlongs: Knoll Lake, 1:14.88, October 26
About 6 1/2 furlongs: Joe Holiday, 1:17.51, October 18
1 mile: Formal Meeting, 1:34.85, February 12
1 1/16 miles: Captain Squire, 1:41.76, February 2
1 1/8 miles: Long Term Investor, 1:50.70, May 19
1 1/4 miles: Vince, 2:03.41, January 22
1 5/8 miles: Masked Rider, 2:44.40, February 10

Fastest Times of 2002 (Turf)
5 furlongs: Amersham, :56.29, February 2
7 1/2 furlongs: Bristolville, 1:29.03, March 26
1 mile: Jelly On Top, 1:35.31, April 22
1 1/16 miles: Lake Garda, 1:42.86, April 27
1 1/8 miles: Bristolville, 1:48.73, April 9
1 3/8 miles: David's Dream, 2:16.30, May 4
1 7/8 miles: Without Doubt (Ire), 3:11.52, May 19

Yavapai Downs

The story of Yavapai Downs is the story of two tracks, not one. Located in Arizona's Prescott Valley region, Yavapai opened its doors in 2001 and replaced Prescott Downs, a half-mile oval that had been in operation since 1913.

While Prescott was known for its rustic atmosphere and occasionally wild bullring racing, Yavapai quickly established a reputation as a more refined track, with modern amenities and a one-mile oval. The $23-million facility was completed in 13 months, almost one year ahead of schedule, allowing it to open in May 2001.

The physical plant features a three-story clubhouse and grandstand with Arizona's Mingus Mountains as a backdrop. The backstretch offers stabling for 1,200 horses. During its first two meets, average purses exceeded $30,000 per day.

Prescott, Arizona's summer racing home for the better part of nine decades, was the site of Racing Hall of Fame jockey Pat Day's first riding victory.

Location: P.O. Box 26557, Prescott Valley, AZ 86312
Phone: (928) 775-8000
Fax: (928) 445-0408
Web site: *http://www.yavapaidownsatpv.com*
Year founded: 2001
Inaugural meeting: May-September, 2001
Abbreviation: Yav
Acreage: 200
Number of stalls: 1,500
Seating capacity: 5,000

Officers
President: Lew Rees
Vice President: Bob Gray

General Manager: Jim Grundy
Director of Racing: Hank Demoney
Racing Secretary: Hank Demoney
Secretary: James Pickering
Director of Sales: Jim Grundy
Director of Finance: Sharon Fischer
Director of Admissions: Janet Howard
Director of Marketing: Janet Howard
Director of Mutuels: Bob Chisholm
Director of Publicity: Janet Howard
Director of Simulcasting: Don Rogers
Stewards: Gerry Howard, Rita Fesquez, Violet Smith
Track Announcer: Greg Wry
Track Photographer: Coady Photography
Track Superintendent: Aaron O'Brien
Treasurer: Jean Knight

Racing Dates
2002: May 25-September 3
2003: May 24-September 2
2004: May 28-September 7

Track Layout
Main circumference: 1 mile
Main track chute: 1/4 mile, 6 furlongs
Main width: 75 feet
Main length of stretch: 1,280 feet

Attendance
Average daily recent meeting: 1,500, 2002

Handle
Average all sources recent meeting: $789,000, 2002
Total all sources recent meeting: $44,200,000, 2002

Leaders
Recent meeting, leading jockey: Estaban Angel Gomez, 90, 2002
Recent meeting, leading owner: Blackjack Stables, 12, 2002
Recent meeting, leading trainer: Justin Evans, 39, 2002

Course Records, Main Dirt
4 1/2 furlongs: Galloping Christos, :52.67, May 29, 2002
5 1/2 furlongs: Buzz's Dancer, 1:02.90, May 29, 2001
5 furlongs: Highway One O One, :56.67, September 4, 2001
6 furlongs: Miss Pixie, 1:08.12, August 24, 2002
1 mile: Heightenedinterest, 1:35.01, June 3, 2002
1 1/16 miles: Gusto Forzado, 1:42.63, June 24, 2002
1 1/8 miles: Moonray, 1:49.40, June 25, 2002
1 1/4 miles: Absence of Order, 2:05.85, July 15, 2002

Fastest Times of 2002 (Dirt)
4 1/2 furlongs: Enduring Image, :52.60, June 30
5 furlongs: First Snowbound, :56.60, June 23
5 1/2 furlongs: Scaffold Man Two, 1:02.36, September 3
6 furlongs: Miss Pixie, 1:08.12, August 24
1 mile: Heightenedinterest, 1:35.01, June 3
1 1/16 miles: Gusto Forzado, 1:42.63, June 24
1 1/8 miles: Moonray, 1:49.40, June 25
1 1/4 miles: Absence of Order, 2:05.85, July 15

Arkansas

Oaklawn Park

Arkansas's leading tourist attraction is Oaklawn Park in the resort community of Hot Springs. The track first opened in 1905 but closed two years later due to political problems in the state. The track reopened in 1916 under the ownership of Louis Cella, whose great-nephew Charles Cella is the track's current president and board chairman. Oaklawn, which offers live racing from January to mid-April, annually attracts runners from across the United States for its Racing Festival of the South. The festival features at least one stakes race each day on the final seven days of the meet, ending with the $500,000 Arkansas Derby (G2), which was first run in 1936. Although a major stepping stone to the Triple Crown, only one winner of the Arkansas Derby (G2), Sunny's Halo in 1983, has won the Kentucky Derby (G1). Other major races include the Apple Blossom Handicap (G1) for fillies and mares, and the $500,000-guaranteed Oaklawn Handicap (G2) for older horses.

Location: 2705 Central Ave., Hot Springs, AR 71902
Phone: (501) 623-4411
Fax: (501) 624-4950
E-mail: winning@oaklawn.com
Web site: http://www.oaklawn.com
Year founded: 1904
Inaugural meeting: February 24, 1905
Acreage: 120
Number of stalls: 1,600
Seating capacity: 26,200

Officers

President: Charles J. Cella
General Manager: R. Eric Jackson
Racing Secretary: Patrick J. Pope
Director of Operations: Craig Holtz
Director of Mutuels: Bobby Geiger
Director of Publicity: Terry Wallace
Director of Simulcasting: Bobby Geiger
Horsemen's Liaison: Debbie Keene
Stewards: John Ferrara Jr., Johnnie Johnson, Larry Snyder
Track Announcer: Terry Wallace
Track Photographer: Jeff Coady
Track Superintendent: Donnie Ellison
Other officials: Kim Burge-Baron, Director of Guest Relations, Ray Russell, Director of Maintenance

Racing Dates

2002: January 25-April 13, 54 days
2003: January 24-April 12, 55 days

Track Layout

Main circumference: 1 mile
Main track chute: 6 furlongs
Main width: 70 feet
Main length of stretch: 1,155 feet

Attendance

Average daily recent meeting: 11,980, 2002
Highest single day record: 71,203, April 19, 1986
Highest single meet record: 1,419,650, 1984
Record daily average for single meet: 23,272, 1983
Total attendance recent meeting: 622,983, 2002

Handle

Average all sources recent meeting: $5,288,620, 2002
Record daily average for single meet: $5,288,620, 2002
Single day on-track handle: $15,133,537, April 15, 2000
Single day total handle all sources: $15,133,537, April 15, 2000
Total all sources recent meeting: $275,010,311, 2002

Mutuel Records

Highest Exacta: $3,915.20, April 8, 1994
Highest Pick Three: $36,686.80, February 17, 1996
Highest Pick Six: $818,693.40, February 15, 1995
Highest Trifecta: $46,395, March 12, 1998
Highest win: $350.80, Phaltup, March 7, 1950

Leaders

Career, leading jockey by titles: Pat Day, 12
Career, leading trainer by titles: Henry Forest, 11
Recent meeting, leading jockey: James Lopez, 59, 2002
Recent meeting, leading owner: Hiway 1 Racing Stable, 17, 2002
Recent meeting, leading trainer: Cole Norman, 45, 2002

Records

Single day jockey wins: Larry Snyder, 6, April 1, 1969, Pat Day, 6, February 17, 1986, Pat Day, 6, February 20, 1995, Pat Day, 6, March 11, 1993
Single meet, leading jockey by wins: Pat Day, 137, 1986
Single meet, leading trainer by wins: David Vance, 50, 1974

Track Records, Main Dirt

4 1/2 furlongs: Montague, :53, March 29, 1937
4 furlongs: Crimson Saint, :44 4/5, April 1, 1971
5 1/2 furlongs: Sis Pleasure Fager, 1:02 3/5, February 15, 1984
5 furlongs: Miss Brendy, :57 3/5, February 22, 1966
6 furlongs: Karen's Tom, 1:07 4/5, April 16, 1990
1 mile: Whitebrush, 1:34 2/5, March 10, 1984
1 mile 70 yards: Win Stat, 1:38 2/5, March 7, 1984
1 3/8 miles: Homeplace, 2:20 3/5, March 29, 1961
1 3/4 miles: Flag Carrier, 2:58, April 18, 1987
1 3/16 miles: Brassy, 1:57 2/5, March 29, 1952
1 1/8 miles: Snow Chief, 1:46 3/5, April 17, 1987
1 1/4 miles: Out of Fire, 2:04, March 31, 1937
1 1/2 miles: Dapper, 2:31 3/5, March 30, 1957
1 1/16 miles: Heatherten, 1:40 1/5, April 18, 1984
Other: 2 miles 70 yds, Turntable, 3:34, March 27, 1942

Fastest Times of 2002

5 1/2 furlongs: Powder, 1:03.74, March 10
6 furlongs: Explicit, 1:08.60, April 11
1 mile: Song Dancer, 1:36.98, March 28
1 1/16 miles: Azeri, 1:42.75, April 6
1 1/8 miles: Kudos, 1:48.34, April 6
1 3/4 miles: Goodtime Rocket, 3:02.84, April 13

California

Bay Meadows Race Course

Located 20 miles south of San Francisco in San Mateo, Bay Meadows Race Course was founded in 1934 by the innovative William P. Kyne, who helped to bring about the legalization of pari-mutuel wagering in California that year. At Bay Meadows, Kyne introduced the totalizator system, photo-finish camera, and the still-popular daily double wager. Bay Meadows also was the site of the first all-enclosed starting gate in America in 1939 and, on October 27, 1945, the destination point of the first equine air passenger when El Lobo, a Thoroughbred, was flown from Los Angeles to an airstrip adjacent to Bay Meadows.

Bay Meadows was the only California racetrack allowed to operate during World War II as Kyne pledged all profits to various war relief projects. In 1951, Coaltown captured the Children's Hospital Handicap, another charity fundraiser.

Bay Meadows introduced the El Camino Real Derby (G3) in 1982 as a prep for the Kentucky Derby (G1), and 17 years later Charismatic finished second by a head in the race (to Cliquot) before winning the Derby and Preakness Stakes (G1). The race was shifted to Golden Gate Fields in 2001.

In November 2000, Magna Entertainment Corp. purchased the track's operating license for $24.1-million, and the property is expected to be developed, with Bay Meadows's dates being run at Magna-owned Golden Gate or at a new track to replace both properties.

Location: 2600 S. Delaware St., San Mateo, CA 94403
Phone: (650) 574-7223
Fax: (650) 345-6826
E-mail: help@baymeadows.com
Web site: http://www.baymeadows.com
Year founded: 1934
Inaugural meeting: November 3, 1934
Acreage: 100
Seating capacity: 9,500
Number of stalls: 900

Officers

President: F. Jack Liebau
Vice President: Michael A. Scalzo
Director of Racing: Thomas S. Robbins
Racing Secretary: C. Gregory Brent Jr.
Director of Sales: Dyan Grealish
Director of Mutuels: Bernice Thurman
Director of Publicity: Tom Ferrall
Director of Simulcasting: Kay Webb
Stewards: Darrell McHargue, Dennis Nevin, John Herbuveaux
Track Announcer: Tony Calo
Track Photographer: William Vassar
Track Superintendent: Robert Turman

Racing Dates

2002: April 3-June 16, 55 days, August 30-November 11, 49 days
2003: April 2-June 15, August 29-November 2

Track Layout

Main circumference: 1 mile
Main track chutes: 1 1/4 miles, 6 furlongs
Main length of stretch: 990 feet
Main turf circumference: 7 furlongs 32 feet
Main turf chute: 1 1/8 miles
Main turf width: 75 feet

Attendance

Highest single day record: 29,300, April 17, 1948

Handle

Single day on-track handle: $8,660,396, November 6, 1999

Mutuel Records

Highest Daily Double: $5,231
Highest Exacta: $2,108
Highest Other Exotics: $1,298.80, Quinella, $347,970.40, Pick Nine
Highest Pick Six: $1,132,466
Highest win: $599.80

Leaders

Career, leading jockey by titles: Russell Baze, 19
Recent meeting, leading jockey: Russell Baze, 109, Fall-2002, Russell Baze, 99, Spring-2002
Recent meeting, leading trainer: Jerry Hollendorfer, 48, Fall-2002, Jerry Hollendorfer, 54, Spring-2002

Records

Single day jockey wins: Bill Shoemaker, 6, October 13, 1950; John Adams, 6, April 7, 1938; John Longden, 6, November 22, 1947; Ralph Neves, 6, October 24, 1961; Russell Baze, 6, January 31, 1999; Russell Baze, 6, September 1, 1984; William Harmatz, 6, September 23, 1954

Track Records, Main Dirt

4 furlongs: Ima Dear, :46 2/5, April 2, 1935
4 1/2 furlongs: My Jasmine, :50.63, August 13, 1997
5 furlongs: Mr. Doubledown, :56.44, March 9, 2000
5 1/2 furlongs: Arches of Gold, 1:01:69, November 23, 1994

6 furlongs: Black Jack Road, 1:07 1/5, October 28, 1990
7 1/2 furlongs: Lookabout, 1:30 2/5, November 26, 1936
1 mile: Aristocratical, 1:33 3/5, November 10, 1983
1 mile 70 yards: Redress, 1:41 3/5, December 10, 1934
1 1/16 miles: Hoedown's Day, 1:38 2/5, October 23, 1983
1 1/8 miles: Super Moment, 1:46 1/5, December 13, 1980
1 3/16 miles: Force of Reason, 1:52 4/5, November 5, 1983
1 1/4 miles: Ask Father, 2:00 2/5, November 28, 1968
1 1/2 miles: Cattle Creek, 2:27 3/5, December 8, 1979
1 5/8 miles: Rag King, 2:43 1/5, December 15, 1990
1 3/4 miles: Tornillo, 2:57 3/5, November 21, 1936
Other: 3 1/2 furlongs, Harrogate, :40 4/5, March 16, 1935

Course Records, Main Turf

4 1/2 furlongs: Salta's Pride, :50.41, September 15, 1994
7 furlongs: First Flyer, 1:24.23, September 25, 1997
7 1/2 furlongs: Hegemony (Ire), 1:28 4/5, October 12, 1984
1 mile: Position's Best, 1:34 3/5, September 6, 1987
1 1/16 miles: Dreamer, 1:40.21, August 17, 1997
1 1/8 miles: Ocean Queen, 1:47.80, October 12, 1996
1 3/8 miles: Golden Doc Ray, 2:16 2/5, October 6, 1979
1 1/2 miles: Swiss Conviction, 2:31.46, October 12, 1998
2 miles: Lighting Star, 3:28.39, March 23, 1997

Fastest Times of 2002 (Dirt)

2 furlongs: Royalette, :21.11, April 12
4 1/2 furlongs: Bang, :51.34, May 2
5 furlongs: Banshee King, :56.85, May 27
5 1/2 furlongs: A Bunch of Maniacs, 1:01.89, September 4
6 furlongs: Full Moon Madness, 1:08.32, June 1
1 mile: How Bout Jose, 1:34.26, May 24
1 1/16 miles: Angel Gift, 1:41.47, October 27
1 1/8 miles: Tracemark, 1:47.93, April 13

Fastest Times of 2002 (Turf)

4 1/2 furlongs: Sarigor (Ire), :50.57, May 1
7 1/2 furlongs: Hooked On Niners, 1:30.95, September 26
1 mile: Crazy Ensign (Arg), 1:34.72, April 7
1 1/16 miles: R McLennen, 1:41.65, April 6
1 1/8 miles: David Copperfield, 1:48.95, September 21
About 1 1/8 miles: Prized Friend, 1:46.21, April 28
1 3/8 miles: Peu a Peu (Ger), 2:16.39, May 18

Bay Meadows Fair

Location: 2495 S. Delaware St., San Mateo, CA 94403-1902
Phone: (650) 574-7223
Fax: (650) 345-6826
Web site: http://www.calfairs.com
Number of stalls: 1,535

Officers

President: Tom Mack
Vice President: Carol Conroy
General Manager: John S. Root
Director of Racing: Hiro Higashi
Racing Secretary: C. Gregory Brent Jr.
Director of Publicity: Tom Ferrall
Stewards: Darrell McHargue, John Herbuveaux, Pam Berg

Racing Dates

2002: August 7-August 19, 12 days
2003: August 6-August 18, 12 days

Track Layout

Main circumference: 1 mile
Main track chutes: 1 1/4 mile, 6 furlongs
Main length of stretch: 990 feet
Main turf circumference: 7 furlongs

Attendance

Average daily recent meeting: 2,457, 2002
Total attendance recent meeting: 29,481, 2002

Handle
Average all sources recent meeting: $2,535,123, 2002
Average on-track recent meeting: $610,858, 2002
Total all sources recent meeting: $30,421,478, 2002
Total on-track recent meeting: $7,330,295, 2002

Leaders
Recent meeting, leading jockey: Francisco Duran, 16, 2002
Recent meeting, leading trainer: Jerry Hollendorfer, 8, 2002

Fastest Times of 2002 (Dirt)
4 1/2 furlongs: Urgently, :51.39, August 16
5 furlongs: Can I Do It, :57.29, August 11
5 1/2 furlongs: Hurricane Smoke, 1:01.87, August 9
6 furlongs: A Bunch of Maniacs, 1:08.92, August 17
1 mile: Sky Strider, 1:35.05, August 8

Fastest Times of 2002 (Turf)
4 1/2 furlongs: Colonel Kelly, :51.41, August 17
1 mile: Capt. Fly Hook, 1:36.34, August 11
1 1/16 miles: Ninebanks, 1:42.10, August 18

Del Mar

Known as the track "where the surf meets the turf," Del Mar is renowned for its laid-back environment and rich purses. The Del Mar style is a legacy of the film stars who helped build it, principally Bing Crosby and Pat O'Brien. But the track's beginnings were rocky. In the mid-1930s, the 22nd District Agricultural Association began to build a fair grounds with a one-mile racetrack and grandstand north of San Diego, and Crosby formed the Del Mar Turf Club to lease the facility for ten years. But the agricultural district soon ran out of money, and Crosby and O'Brien borrowed almost $600,000 to complete the project. The track opened on July 3, 1937, with Crosby greeting the first patron through the turnstiles. The following year, the crooner wrote "Where the Surf Meets the Turf" and sang it on opening day; it still is played every day at the track.

Del Mar was closed during World War II, serving as a Marine training center and an assembly center for B-17 wing ribs. It reopened in 1945, and the lease was extended through 1959. In 1970, a group of prominent California owners and breeders formed the Del Mar Thoroughbred Club and leased the facility for 20 years. The lease was extended for another 20 years in 1990. A rebuilt Del Mar grandstand and clubhouse costing $80-million were completed in 1993, two years after the first running of the track's signature event, the Pacific Classic Stakes (G1).

Location: 2260 Jimmy Durante Blvd., Del Mar, CA 92014-0700
Phone: (858) 755-1141
Fax: (858) 792-1477
E-mail: marys@dmtc.com
Web site: http://www.delmarracing.com
Year founded: 1937
Inaugural meeting: July 3-31, 1937
Acreage: 350
Number of stalls: 2,100
Seating capacity: 14,304

Officers
President: Joe Harper
Vice President: Craig R. Fravel
General Manager: Joe Harper

Director of Racing: Tom Robbins
Racing Secretary: Tom Robbins
Director of Sales: Josh Rubinstein
Director of Operations: Tim Read
Director of Finance: Michael R. Ernst
Director of Marketing: Daniel G. Smith
Director of Mutuels: Bill Navarro
Director of Publicity: Daniel G. Smith
Director of Simulcasting: T. Pat Stubbs
Horsemen's Liaison: Lisa Iaria
Stewards: David Samuel, George Slender, Ingrid Fermin
Track Announcer: Trevor Denman
Track Photographer: Benoit & Associates
Track Superintendent: Steve Wood

Racing Dates
2002: July 24-September 11, 43 days
2003: July 23-September 10, 43 days

Track Layout
Main circumference: 1 mile
Main track chutes: 1 1/4 miles, 7 furlongs
Main width: 80 feet
Main length of stretch: 919 feet
Main turf circumference: 7 1/2 furlongs
Main turf chute: 1 1/8 miles diagonal
Main turf width: 63 feet
Main turf length of stretch: 761 feet
Training track: 1/2 mile

Attendance
Average daily recent meeting: 15,518, 2002
Highest single day record: 44,181, August 10, 1996
Highest single meet record: 709,760, 1990
Record daily average for single meet: 19,776, 1985
Total attendance recent meeting: 667,280, 2002

Handle
Single day on-track handle: $5,657,840, August 15, 1998
Single day total handle all sources: $22,857,785, August 15, 1998
Average all sources recent meeting: $12,361,942, 2002
Average on-track recent meeting: $2,298,684, 2002
Record daily average for single meet: $3,861,247, 1987
Total all sources recent meeting: $531,563,512, 2002
Total on-track recent meeting: $98,843,419, 2002

Mutuel Records
Highest win: $130.70, *Cipria, September 1, 1955
Highest Exacta: $2,383, August 7, 1987
Highest Trifecta: $13,405.50, July 28, 1997
Highest Daily Double: $5,299.30, July 28, 1971
Highest Pick 3: $57,507.90, August 17, 1995
Highest Pick 6: $1,039,259.20, September 7, 1995
Highest Other Exotics: $133,013.40, Superfecta, September 6, 1998, Pick 4, $34,534.70, July 26, 2002

Leaders
Career, leading jockey by stakes wins: Chris McCarron, 134
Career, leading jockey by titles: Bill Shoemaker, 7
Career, leading jockey by wins: Laffit Pincay Jr., 1,011
Career, leading owner by titles: Golden Eagle Farm, 6
Career, leading trainer by stakes wins: Charles Whittingham, 74
Career, leading trainer by titles: Farrell W. Jones, 11
Career, leading trainer by wins: Ron McAnally, 400
Recent meeting, leading jockey: Patrick Valenzuela, 46, 2002
Recent meeting, leading owner: The Thoroughbred Corp., 8, 2002
Recent meeting, leading trainer: Bob Baffert, 30, 2002

Records
Single day jockey wins: Bill Shoemaker, 6, September 4, 1954, Laffit Pincay Jr., 6, July 28, 1976, Laffit Pincay Jr., 6, July 29, 1978, Rudy Rosales, 6, September 9, 1969
Single day trainer wins: Farrell W. Jones, 4, August 13,

1963, Jack Van Berg, 4, August 3, 1995, R. H. "Red" Mc-Daniel, 4, September 4, 1954, Ron McAnally, 4, August 20, 1989

Single meet, leading jockey by wins: Bill Shoemaker, 94, 1954

Single meet, leading trainer by wins: R. H. McDaniel, 47, 1954

Track Records, Main Dirt

5 furlongs: Soldier Girl, :56 2/5, August 13, 1964
5 1/2 furlongs: Ack Ack, 1:02 1/5, September 12, 1970; Lakeside Trail, 1:02 1/5, August 18, 1974; Little Mustard, 1:02 1/5, September 5, 1974; Brainstorming, 1:02 1/5, August 28, 1991
6 furlongs: King of Cricket, 1:07 3/5, August 22, 1973
6 1/2 furlongs: Native Paster, 1:13 3/5, September 4, 1988
7 furlongs: Solar Launch, 1:20, August 10, 1990
1 mile: Precisionist, 1:33 1/5, August 1, 1988
1 1/16 miles: Windy Sands, 1:40, August 4, 1962; Native Diver, 1:40, August 7, 1965; Matching, 1:40, August 18, 1982
1 1/8 miles: Latin Touch, 1:46, September 1, 1979
1 3/16 miles: Four By Five, 1:56 2/5, August 16, 1954
1 1/4 miles: Bertrando, 1:59.55, August 21, 1993
1 1/2 miles: Spring Boy, 2:29 2/5, August 16, 1958
1 5/8 miles: Ormolu, 2:45, August 24, 1957
1 3/4 miles: Lurline B., 2:57 2/5, August 26, 1949
2 miles: Pilot Anne, 3:24 1/5, September 2, 1949

Course Records, Main Turf

7 1/2 furlongs: Syncopate, 1:27 4/5, August 24, 1981
1 mile: Special Ring, 1:32.72, August 2, 2002
1 1/16 miles: Ice Hot, 1:40, August 13, 1986
1 1/8 miles: Al Mamoon, 1:46 3/5, August 10, 1986
1 3/8 miles: Delta Form (Aus), 2:12.15, September 1, 2002

Fastest Times of 2002 (Dirt)

5 furlongs: Bull Market, :57.28, July 24
5 1/2 furlongs: Icecoldbeeratreds, 1:03.27, July 31
6 furlongs: Avanzado (Arg), 1:08.93, August 18
6 1/2 furlongs: Stoney, 1:15.14, August 10
7 furlongs: Disturbingthepeace, 1:21.89, August 18
1 mile: Eric Da Bomb, 1:34.97, August 5
1 1/16 miles: Azeri, 1:42.66, August 11
1 1/8 miles: Gentle Giant, 1:50.84, September 7
1 1/4 miles: Came Home, 2:01.45, August 25

Fastest Times of 2002 (Turf)

1 mile: Special Ring, 1:32.72, August 2
1 1/16 miles: Beautiful Balance, 1:40.35, September 11
1 1/8 miles: Sarafan, 1:46.77, July 28
1 3/8 miles: Delta Form (Aus), 2:12.15, September 1

Fairplex Park

For nearly 80 years, the Los Angeles County Fair Association has offered racing at Fairplex Park. In recent decades, the fair meet has given the major Southern California circuit a welcome break between the Del Mar and Oak Tree (at Santa Anita) meets in September. The inaugural Los Angeles County Fair was conducted in 1922, a five-day meet over a half-mile track. By the mid-1930s, after pari-mutuel wagering had been legalized in California, the fair was extended to a 17-day meeting. With minor changes over the years, the meet has remained essentially the same.

The track, with its five-furlong configuration, has been the scene of some wild racing over the years. It also has witnessed tragedy; in 1999, jockey J. C. Gonzalez was killed in a spill at the track. In May 2002, Fairplex agreed to move the dates to Santa Anita, but that proposal sparked considerable opposition and was shelved through at least 2003.

Location: 1101 W. McKinley Ave., Pomona, CA 91769
Phone: (909) 865-4545
Fax: (909) 623-8170
E-mail: info@fairplex.com
Web site: *http://www.fairplex.com*
Year founded: 1922
Inaugural meeting: 1922
Acreage: 487
Seating capacity: 10,000
Number of stalls: 1,306

Officers

President: James E. Henwood
General Manager: Michael Seder
Director of Racing: George Bradvica
Racing Secretary: Richard Wheeler
Director of Sales: John Buck
Director of Communications: Wendy Talarico
Director of Finance: Mike Seder
Director of Marketing: Scott Kelly
Stewards: David Samuel, Tom Ward, Will Meyers
Track Announcer: Trevor Denman
Track Photographer: Benoit & Asssociates
Track Superintendent: Steve Wood

Racing Dates

2002: September 13-September 29, 18 days
2003: September 12-September 28, 17 days

Track Layout

Main circumference: 5/8 mile
Main track chute: 1 1/8 miles, 1/4 mile
Main width: 75 feet
Main length of stretch: 660 feet

Attendance

Highest single meet record: 337,491, 1998
Record daily average for single meet: 18,749, 1998
Total attendance recent meeting: 121,497 est., 2001
Average daily recent meeting: 6,750 est., 2001
Highest single day record: 28,300, September 25, 1948

Handle

Average daily recent meeting: 6,750 est., 2001
Average on-track recent meeting: $713,010, 2000
Average all sources recent meeting: $5,750,000, 2001
Single day total handle all sources: $7,842,907, September 27, 1997
Total all sources recent meeting: $104-million, 2001

Mutuel Records

Highest win: $182.20, Uncle Fox, September 21, 1976
Highest Exacta: $5,645, September 13, 1986
Highest Trifecta: $29,278.80, September 30, 1996
Highest Daily Double: $4,362.40, September 17, 1990
Highest Pick 6: $199,346.60, September 13, 1999
Highest Other Exotics: $30,497, $1 Superfecta, September 19, 2000

Leaders

Career, leading jockey by wins: Martin Pedroza, 293
Recent meeting, leading trainer: Jeff Mullins, 11, 2001
Career, leading jockey by stakes wins: David Flores, 51
Career, leading trainer by stakes wins: Mel Stute, 41
Career, leading trainer by wins: Mel Stute, 164
Recent meeting, leading jockey: Martin Pedroza, 29, 2001

Records

Single day trainer wins: Gordon Campbell, 4, September 30, 1967; Jerry Fanning, 4, September 24, 1984
Single day jockey wins: David Flores, 6, September 20, 1992; David Flores, 6, September 30, 1992

Track Records, Main Dirt

4 furlongs: Nashua's Asset, :45.55, September 15, 2002
6 furlongs: Drouilly's Boy, 1:09 1/5, September 19, 1989
6 1/2 furlongs: Bundle of Iron, 1:15 1/5, September 23, 1986
7 furlongs: Best of Time, 1:22.66, September 16, 2000
1 1/16 miles: Monte Parnes (Arg), 1:41 3/5, September 29, 1990
1 1/8 miles: Dachi's Folly, 1:48 2/5, September 29, 1990
1 3/8 miles: Mummy's Pleasure, 2:15, September 28, 1986

Fastest Times of 2002
About 4 furlongs: Nashua's Asset, :45.55, September 15
6 furlongs: Bills Paid, 1:09.46, September 15
6 1/2 furlongs: Rico Fighter (Brz), 1:15.99, September 14
7 furlongs: Rico Fighter (Brz), 1:22.70, September 20
1 1/16 miles: Sigfreto, 1:41.80, September 14
About 1 1/8 miles: Reba's Gold, 1:49.82, September 29
1 3/8 miles: Fade to Blue, 2:16.79, September 29

Ferndale

Location: 1250 Fifth St., Ferndale, CA 95536
Phone: (707) 786-9525
Fax: (707) 786-9450
Web site: http://www.calfairs.com
Number of stalls: 258 permanent, 200 portable
Seating capacity: 2,200

Officers
President: Don Becker
Vice President: Bill Branstetter
Racing Secretary: Charlie Palmer
Director of Mutuels: George Vidak
Director of Publicity: Stuart Titus
Track Announcer: John McGary

Racing Dates
2002: August 8-August 18, 10 days
2003: August 7-August 17, 10 days

Track Layout
Main circumference: 1/2 mile
Main track chute: 5 furlongs, 7 furlongs
Main length of stretch: 530 feet

Handle
Average all sources recent meeting: $250,590, 2002
Average on-track recent meeting: $72,871, 2002
Total all sources recent meeting: $2,502,903, 2002
Total on-track recent meeting: $728,705, 2002

Leaders
Recent meeting, leading jockey: James E. Burns, 15, 2002
Recent meeting, leading trainer: Jim Bumgardner, 8, 2002

Fastest Times of 2002
5 furlongs: Fight for Silver, :57.18, August 11
6 1/2 furlongs: Lillie's Star, 1:19.51, August 10
7 furlongs: Fight for Silver, 1:24.43, August 16
1 1/16 miles: Melt Away, 1:47.08, August 17
1 5/8 miles: Roger Roger, 2:48.00, August 18

Fresno

Location: 1121 Chance Ave., Fresno, CA 93702
Phone: (559) 650-3331
Fax: (559) 650-3226
Web site: http://www.fresnofair.com

Officers
President: Andriana Majarian
Vice President: Dean Thonesen
Director of Communications: Kristi Brangle
Director of Marketing: Sheri Durham

Racing Dates
2002: October 2-October 13, 12 days
2003: October 1-October 13, 11 days

Handle
Average all sources recent meeting: $519,649, 2002
Average on-track recent meeting: $264,871, 2002
Total all sources recent meeting: $6,235,789, 2002
Total on-track recent meeting: $3,178,454, 2002

Leaders
Recent meeting, leading jockey: Ken S. Tohill, 15, 2002
Recent meeting, leading trainer: Wesley A. Ward, 6, 2002

Fastest Times of 2002
5 furlongs: Kindon, :56.75, October 3
5 1/2 furlongs: Fog City Willy, 1:02.10, October 4
6 furlongs: Omega Code, 1:07.70, October 5
1 mile: Book Review, 1:35.20, October 11
1 1/8 miles: Potus, 1:48.50, October 13

Golden Gate Fields

On April 29, 1949, a 19-year-old apprentice jockey from Texas named Bill Shoemaker rode Shafter V. to victory in the second race at Golden Gate Fields in Albany, California. That win marked the first of a then-record 8,833 victories for Shoemaker, a Racing Hall of Fame jockey. Several famous horses have raced at the San Francisco-area track, as well. Citation, the 1948 Triple Crown winner, defeated champion older male *Noor in the '50 Golden Gate Mile Handicap, setting a world record for one mile in the process. Silky Sullivan captured his first stakes victory in the 1957 Golden Gate Futurity and went on to win 12 of 27 career starts and earned more than $150,000.

In February 1941, entrepreneur Edward "Slip" Madigan opened the track, then known as the Albany Turf Club. The track closed after its first five days of racing due to flooding from heavy rains. During World War II, the United States Navy used Golden Gate as a landing base for amphibious craft. Racing resumed in 1947 after the water problem was resolved, and in '71 the track added a turf course. In 1989, Ladbroke Group purchased Golden Gate for $41-million. As it wound down its North American racing operations, Ladbroke sold the facility to Frank Stronach-led Magna Entertainment Corp. in 1999. The track's perennial leaders in recent years have been Racing Hall of Fame jockey Russell Baze and trainer Jerry Hollendorfer.

Location: 1100 Eastshore Hwy., Albany, CA 94710
Phone: (510) 559-7300
Fax: (510) 559-7467
E-mail: help@baymeadows.com
Web site: http://www.ggfields.com
Inaugural meeting: February 1, 1941, 33 days
Acreage: 225
Number of stalls: 1,425
Seating capacity: 14,750

Officers
President: Jack Liebau
General Manager: Michael A. Scalzo
Racing Secretary: C. Greg Brent
Secretary: Gary Cohn
Treasurer: Barbara Helm
Director of Operations: Calvin Rainey
Director of Marketing: Amanda Stifle
Director of Mutuels: Bryan Wayte
Director of Publicity: Tom Ferrall

Director of Sales: Dyan Grealish
Director of Simulcasting: Kay Webb
Stewards: Darrell McHargue, Dennis Nevin, John Herbuveaux
Horsemen's Liaison: Jenny Scullin
Track Announcer: Tony Calo
Track Photographer: William Vassar
Track Superintendent: Juan Meza

Racing Dates
2002: November 17, 2001 to March 31, 2002, 101 days
2003: November 6, 2002 to March 30, 2003, 105 days

Track Layout
Main circumference: 1 mile
Main width: 78 feet
Main length of stretch: 1,000 feet
Main turf circumference: 9/10 mile
Main turf chute: 3/16 mile
Main turf width: 65 feet

Mutuel Records
Highest win: $322.60, Pasadena Slim, October 28, 1957
Highest Exacta: $2,270.20, January 18, 1997
Highest Trifecta: $38,689.20, January 18, 1997
Highest Daily Double: $8,711.40, November 16, 1960
Highest Pick 3: $18,851, December 13, 1998
Highest Pick 6: $1,074,405.80, May 23, 1990
Highest Other Exotics: $63,954, Superfecta, March 2, 2002

Leaders
Career, leading jockey by titles: Russell Baze, 24
Career, leading trainer by titles: Jerry Hollendorfer, 22
Recent meeting, leading jockey: Russell Baze, 159, 2001/2002
Recent meeting, leading trainer: Jerry Hollendorfer, 83, 2001/2002

Records
Single day jockey wins: Russell Baze, 7, April 16, 1992
Single day trainer wins: Walter Greenman, 5, November 25, 1970; Ace Gibson, 5, February 24, 1971; Jerry Hollendorfer, 5, May 1, 1996; Jerry Hollendorfer, 5, January 23, 1997
Single meet, leading jockey by wins: Russell Baze, 178, 1992
Single meet, leading trainer by wins: Jerry Hollendorfer, 89, 1990

Track Records, Main Dirt
4 furlongs: Glenbar, :47, March 12, 1952, Giddy Up, :47, March 25, 1952
4 1/2 furlongs: Victory Found, :50.30, April 30, 1992
5 furlongs: Contradiction, :56.12, January 1, 2003
5 1/2 furlongs: Proudest Hour, 1:02, May 30, 1986
6 furlongs: El Dorado Shooter, 1:07.55, January 20, 2001
1 mile: Caros Love, 1:33, February 13, 1988
1 1/16 miles: Restless Con, 1:39.50, June 24, 1991
1 1/8 miles: Simply Majestic, 1:45, April 2, 1988
1 3/16 miles: Fleet Bird, 1:52 3/5, October 24, 1953
1 1/4 miles: *Noor, 1:58 1/5, June 24, 1950
1 3/8 miles: Forin Sea, 2:18 3/5, October 3, 1959
1 1/2 miles: Bo Donna, 2:29 2/5, June 8, 1979
1 3/4 miles: Sirmark, 2:57 1/5, October 16, 1948
2 miles: Mantourist, 3:25 4/5, October 23, 1948
Other: 2 furlongs, The Money Doctor, :21 4/5, February 21, 1975

Course Records, Main Turf
4 1/2 furlongs: Bonne Nuite, :50.58, May 22, 1994
5 furlongs: Black Tornado, :56, May 10, 1975; L'Natural, :56, May 28, 1977; Goldie's Goldian, :56, May 27, 1978
7 1/2 furlongs: Struttin' George, 1:28, May 5, 1979; His Honor, 1:28, April 25, 1981; Clever Song, 1:28, May 25, 1986
1 mile: Don Alberto, 1:33 2/5, March 22, 1980
1 1/16 miles: Announcer, 1:40 2/5, April 16, 1977
1 1/8 miles: Blues Traveller (Ire), 1:47.71, May 14, 1994
1 3/8 miles: John Henry, 2:13, May 6, 1984
1 1/2 miles: Silveyville, 2:27 2/5, June 10, 1984; Kings Island

(Ire), 2:27 2/5, June 9, 1985; Val Danseur, 2:27 2/5, June 8, 1986
2 miles: Never-Rust, 3:25 3/5, June 26, 1988
Other: 2 3/8 miles, Situada (Chi), 4:10 4/5, June 25, 1990

Fastest Times of 2002 (Dirt)
2 furlongs: Souvenir's Lad, :21.92, March 28
5 furlongs: Fancy High, :56.94, March 23
5 1/2 furlongs: Granger Express, 1:02.84, December 8
6 furlongs: Actin Like a Pro, 1:08.21, December 26
1 mile: Fleet Coord, 1:35.24, December 26
1 1/16 miles: Jimmy Z, 1:40.67, November 29
1 1/8 miles: Johnny Show, 1:47.98, December 29
1 1/4 miles: The Chang, 2:04.79, January 6

Fastest Times of 2002 (Turf)
4 1/2 furlongs: Always Game, :50.91, December 1
1 mile: Super Tuesday, 1:36.78, March 15
1 1/16 miles: Suspicious Minds, 1:43.03, March 2
1 1/8 miles: No Slip (Fr), 1:49.41, March 16
1 3/8 miles: Cantil, 2:18.52, March 16

Hollywood Park

Hollywood Park sprung to life in 1938 when the Hollywood Turf Club was formed with Warner Brothers executive Jack L. Warner as its chairman. Several Hollywood power brokers, including actors (Ralph Bellamy), singers (Bing Crosby), and studio executives (Walt Disney, Darryl Zanuck) were among the original shareholders in the Inglewood, California, track.

Not everything has had a Hollywood ending at Hollywood Park, however. A fire in 1949 destroyed the club's physical plant and forced racing over to Santa Anita Park for one year. But the track reopened in time for a typical Hollywood fairy-tale finish when Citation won the 1951 Hollywood Gold Cup to become racing's first equine millionaire. Hollywood again was the backdrop of history 28 years later when Affirmed won the Hollywood Gold Cup (G1) to break racing's $2-million barrier. In 1983, John Henry became the first $4-million earner when he won the Hollywood Turf Cup (G1).

The first Breeders' Cup championship day was staged at Hollywood in 1984. The event returned in 1987 and again in '97.

Hollywood has not been immune from controversy. An expensive rebuilding of the track—including an extension of the track to 1⅛ miles and construction of a new clubhouse structure, the Pavilion of the Stars—preceded the first Breeders' Cup, and fans resented the moving of the finish line toward the new facility. A bitter fight for control of the track raged in the late 1980s and early '90s, and the struggle was resolved in February '91 when R. D. Hubbard wrested control from longtime executive Marjorie Lindheimer Everett in a proxy fight. Hubbard immediately launched a multi-million-dollar renovation program that spruced up the track and transformed the clubhouse pavilion into a card-club casino. As a part of that project, the finish line was returned to its original location. Through the 1980s and '90s, the Inglewood neighborhood deteriorated and was touched by the '92 Los Angeles riots.

In 1999, Churchill Downs Inc. bought Hollywood Park for $140-million. On December 10, 1999, Laffit Pincay Jr. became the winningest rider in racing history with a triumph at Hollywood, surpassing the record of 8,833 wins long held by Bill Shoemaker. History and dramatic events have a way of maintaining their grip on the track that the film industry built.

Location: 1050 S. Prairie Ave., Inglewood, CA 90306-0369
Phone: (310) 419-1500
Fax: (310) 672-4664
Web site: *http://www.hollywoodpark.com*
Year founded: 1938
Inaugural meeting: June 10, 1938
Acreage: 240
Seating capacity: 10,000
Number of stalls: 1,958

Officers
President: Rick Baedeker
Vice President: Don R. Richardson
General Manager: Eual Wyatt Jr.
Director of Racing: Martin Panza
Racing Secretary: Martin Panza
Director of Operations: Rick Baedeker
Director of Communications: Michael Mooney
Director of Marketing: Christy Tucker
Director of Publicity: Michael Mooney
Horsemen's Liaison: Diana Hudak
Stewards: George Slender, Pete Pedersen, Thomas Ward
Track Announcer: Vic Stauffer
Track Photographer: Benoit & Associates
Track Superintendent: Dennis Moore

Racing Dates
2002: April 24-July 21, 65 days; November 6-December 22
2003: April 23-July 20, 65 days; November 11-December 21

Track Layout
Main circumference: 1 1/8 miles
Main track chute: 7 1/2 furlongs
Main width: 92 feet
Main length of stretch: 991 feet
Main turf circumference: 1 mile
Main turf width: 64 feet
Main turf length of stretch: 990 feet
Training track: 1/2 mile

Attendance
Average daily recent meeting: 6,458, Fall-2002; 9,130, Spring/Summer-2002
Highest single meet record: 2,398,528, Spring/Summer-1980
Record daily average for single meet: 34,516, Spring/Summer-1965
Highest single day record: 80,348, May 4, 1980
Total attendance recent meeting: 226,033, Fall-2002; 593,441, Spring/Summer-2002

Handle
Record daily average for single meet: $5,486,172, 1985
Average all sources recent meeting: $11,136,784, Spring/Summer-2002; $9,661,600, Fall-2002
Average on-track recent meeting: $1,444,595, Fall-2002; $1,900,000, Spring/Summer-2002
Single day on-track handle: $13,002,176, November 21, 1987
Single day total handle all sources: $67,096,242, November 2, 1997
Total all sources recent meeting: $338,156,025, Fall-2002

Mutuel Records
Highest win: $361.80, Family Flair, June 29, 1989
Highest Exacta: $6,989.40, May 11, 1991
Highest Trifecta: $28,294, July 17, 1997
Highest Daily Double: $6,141.60, July 10, 1962
Highest Pick 3: $137,200.20, December 17, 1993
Highest Pick 6: $774,014, June 27, 1997
Highest Other Exotics: $190,769.80, Superfecta, November 11, 1994

Leaders
Career, leading jockey by wins: Laffit Pincay Jr., 3,000 (through June 8, 2002)
Career, leading owner by titles: Juddmonte Farms, 6
Career, leading trainer by titles: Robert Frankel, 12
Career, leading trainer by wins: Charlie Whittingham, 859
Recent meeting, leading jockey: Alex Solis, 34, Fall-2002, Patrick Valenzuela, 74, Spring/Summer-2002, Victor Espinoza, 34, Fall-2002
Recent meeting, leading trainer: Doug O'Neill, 16, Fall-2002, Robert Frankel, 23, Spring/Summer-2002
Career, leading jockey by stakes wins: Laffit Pincay Jr., 285 (through June 7, 2002)
Career, leading jockey by titles: Bill Shoemaker, 18

Records
Single day jockey wins: Bill Shoemaker, 6, June 20, 1953; Laffit Pincay Jr., 6, May 27, 1968; Bill Shoemaker, 6, June 24, 1970; Kent Desormeaux, 6, July 3, 1992
Single day trainer wins: Allen Drumheller Sr., 5, July 4, 1955
Single meet, leading jockey by wins: Laffit Pincay Jr., 148
Single meet, leading trainer by wins: Robert Frankel, 60

Track Records, Main Dirt
4 1/2 furlongs: Bridge of Royalty, :50.59, May 4, 1995
5 furlongs: Magical Mile, :56 2/5, May 18, 1989; Goodtimesinexcess, :56.25, July 3, 1999
5 1/2 furlongs: Hombre Rapido, 1:01.67, December 20, 2002
6 furlongs: Apalachee Ridge, 1:07.52, December 12, 1997
6 1/2 furlongs: Lucky Forever, 1:13.24, May 20, 1995
7 furlongs: Mazel Trick, 1:19.97, June 27, 1999
7 1/2 furlongs: Awesome Daze, 1:26.26, November 23, 1997
1 mile: Greinton (GB), 1:32 3/5, June 9, 1985
1 1/16 miles: Power Forward, 1:40, December 19, 1987; Crafty Friend, 1:40, July 12, 1997; New Journey, 1:40, November 27, 1997
1 1/8 miles: Gentlemen (Arg), 1:45.35, December 22, 1996
1 3/16 miles: Shorten Sail, 1:55.36, June 7, 1998
1 1/4 miles: Greinton (GB), 1:58 2/5, June 23, 1985
1 3/8 miles: Lovely One (Arg), 2:14.42, May 7, 1994
1 5/8 miles: Ol' Henry, 2:42.50, June 27, 1997
1 3/4 miles: Roman Cuzzin, 2:56.77, July 21, 1997

Course Records, Main Turf
5 1/2 furlongs: Pembroke, 1:00.46, July 15, 1995
6 furlongs: Answer Do, 1:07, December 15, 1990
1 mile: Megan's Interco, 1:32.64, May 22, 1994
1 1/16 miles: Fantastic Fellow, 1:38.77, April 26, 1998
1 1/8 miles: Fastness (Ire), 1:44.78, November 25, 1995
1 3/16 miles: Kudos, 1:51.99, April 25, 2001
1 1/4 miles: Bien Bien, 1:57.75, May 31, 1993
1 1/2 miles: Talloires, 2:23.55, July 21, 1996

Fastest Times of 2002 (Dirt)
4 1/2 furlongs: Expression, :51.36, May 8
5 furlongs: Kafwain, :57.50, June 22
5 1/2 furlongs: Hombre Rapido, 1:01.67, December 20
6 furlongs: Mighty David, 1:08.27, July 10
6 1/2 furlongs: Rough R. N., 1:14.69, December 20
7 furlongs: Disturbingthepeace, 1:21.09, July 6
7 1/2 furlongs: Lethal Instrument, 1:27.98, May 1
1 1/16 miles: George Bailey, 1:40.83, December 20
1 1/8 miles: Milwaukee Brew, 1:48.06, June 15
1 1/4 miles: Sky Jack, 2:01.73, July 14
1 3/8 miles: Golden Ticket, 2:13.42, December 21

Fastest Times of 2002 (Turf)
5 1/2 furlongs: Always Game, 1:01.06, April 27
1 mile: Special Ring, 1:32.91, July 7
1 1/16 miles: Night Patrol, 1:39.35, May 5
1 1/8 miles: The Tin Man, 1:46.82, July 4
1 1/4 miles: Astra, 1:58.56, June 29
1 1/2 miles: Skipping (GB), 2:26.23, May 19

Los Alamitos Race Course

Thoroughbreds have competed at Los Alamitos Race Course in Cypress, California, since 1994, when the track received permission to begin offering races for the breed. Los Alamitos primarily had been known as a Quarter Horse track since 1947, when nonpari-mutuel racing debuted at the track built by Frank Vessels on his ranch. In 1951, Los Alamitos received approval to begin holding pari-mutuel racing. After Vessels's death in 1963, his son Frank Vessels Jr. took over operation of the track, which five years later began offering night racing. After Vessels Jr.'s death in 1974, his wife, Millie, assumed the track's presidency and became one of the first women to hold a leadership position in Thoroughbred racing. In 1984, Los Alamitos was sold to Hollywood Park and entered a period of decline. Five years later, businessmen and harness-racing enthusiasts Lloyd Arnold and Chris Bardis bought the facility. Edward C. Allred, a physician and the all-time leading breeder of Quarter Horses by earnings, then purchased a majority interest in Los Alamitos and today is sole owner of the track, which also offers Paint, Appaloosa, and Arabian racing.

Location: 4961 Katella Ave., Los Alamitos, CA 90720
Phone: (714) 995-1234
Fax: (714) 995-6276
E-mail: larace@losalamitos.com
Web site: http://www.losalamitos.com
Year founded: 1951
Inaugural meeting: 1951
Number of stalls: 1,400
Seating capacity: 13,000

Officers
President: Edward C. Allred
General Manager: Jeff True
Director of Racing: Ron Church
Racing Secretary: Ron Church
Secretary: G. Michael Lyon
Treasurer: Kathleen Chavez
Director of Operations: Howard Knuchell
Director of Marketing: Jeff True
Director of Mutuels: Bob DiGiovanni
Director of Publicity: Orlando Gutieriez
Director of Sales: Vandi Ekins
Director of Simulcasting: Melodie Knuchell
Horsemen's Liaison: Vandi Ekins
Stewards: Albert Christensen, Merlin Volske
Track Announcer: Ed Burgart
Track Photographer: Scott Martinez
Track Superintendent: Frank Sabato

Racing Dates
2002: January 4-December 29
2003: January 4-December 29

Track Layout
Main circumference: 5 furlongs
Main track chute: 550 yards
Main length of stretch: 1/8 mile
Inner circumference: 5 furlongs
Inner track chute: 550 yards
Training track: 5 furlongs

Attendance
Highest single day record: 19,970, May 6, 1983
Highest single meet record: 1,046,158, 1994
Record daily average for single meet: 9,492, 1970

Handle
Average all sources recent meeting: $1,137,971, 2001/2002
Record daily average for single meet: $1,276,936, 2000
Single day on-track handle: $2,127,758, June 30, 1995
Total all sources recent meeting: $231,000,000+, 2001/2002

Mutuel
Highest Daily Double: $2,107.90, June 12, 1997
Highest Exacta: $8,650.30, August 30, 1996
Highest Other Exotics: Superfecta, $21,198, July 12, 1997
Highest Pick 3: $12,017.60, August 21, 1991
Highest Trifecta: $27,386.10, July 27, 1996

Leaders
Career, leading jockey by titles: Jorge Bordieu, Ramon Guce, Alex Bautista, 2 each
Career, leading trainer by titles: Charles S. Treece, 6 (1996-2001)
Career, leading jockey by wins: Alex Bautista, 308
Career, leading trainer by wins: Charles S. Treece, 194
Recent meeting, leading jockey: Ramon Guce, 63, 2002
Recent meeting, leading owner: Zvi Kriple, 14, 2002
Recent meeting, leading trainer: Jesus Nunez, 33, 2002

Interesting Facts
Achievements/milestones: Los Alamitos is the home of the richest horse race of any breed in California—the $1.3-million Los Alamitos Million

Track Records, Main Dirt
4 1/2 furlongs: Valiant Pete, :49 2/5, August 11, 1990

Fastest Times of 2002
4 1/2 furlongs: Cielo Canosa, :50.70, February 17; Oh to Win, :50.70, May 5

Oak Tree at Santa Anita

In 1968, Southern California horsemen Clement Hirsch, Jack K. Robbins, and Louis R. Rowan approached Santa Anita Park President Robert P. Strub with a proposal for a brief, high-quality fall meet at the Arcadia track. Except for the brief Fairplex Park meet, the Southern California racing calendar was empty between the close of Del Mar in September and the opening of Santa Anita's winter-spring meet each December 26. (Hollywood Park then had only a spring-summer meet.) Strub initially resisted, but Santa Anita officials finally agreed to try a fall meet under the auspices of the Oak Tree Racing Association, headed by Hirsch, in October 1969. In case the idea flopped, Oak Tree's directors had to guarantee the first day's purses. The initial 20-day fall meet was a success, and Oak Tree has become an important part of the racing scene in Southern California and nationally.

Oak Tree secured rights to stage the third Breeders' Cup championship day in 1986, and the event attracted an on-track crowd of 69,155, the largest crowd to that point. Oak Tree also played host to the championship day in 1993. In addition, Oak Tree's stakes serve as leading prep races for the Breeders' Cup championship events. Oak Tree was scheduled to host the Breeders' Cup championship again in 2000 and '02, but construction projects of the track's new owner, Frank Stronach-controlled Magna Entertainment Corp., forced shifts to other sites. Oak Tree, which now runs a 32-day meet, was the host for the 2003 Breeders' Cup championship. Hirsch died in 2000 and was succeeded as Oak Tree president by Robbins.

Location: 285 W. Huntington St., Arcadia, CA 91007-3439
Phone: (626) 574-6352
Fax: (626) 446-5803
Web site: http://www.santaanita.com
Inaugural meeting: October 7, 1969

Officers
Executive Vice President: Sherwood Chillingworth
General Manager: F. Jack Liebau
Director of Racing: Michael J. Harlow
Racing Secretary: Michael J. Harlow
Director of Marketing: Stuart Zanville
Director of Publicity: Stuart Zanville
Track Photographer: Benoit & Associates

Racing Dates
2002: October 2-November 3
2003: September 28-November 9

Attendance
Total attendance recent meeting: 263,504, 2002
Record daily average for single meet: 30,469, 1993
Average daily recent meeting: 10,135, 2002
Highest single day record: 69,155, November 1, 1986
Highest single meet record: 858,652, 1985

Handle
Single day on-track handle: $15,410,409, November 1,1986
Average all sources recent meeting: $10,647,917, 2002
Record daily average for single meet: $10,237,220, 1998
Single day total handle all sources: $36,264,799, November 6,1993
Total all sources recent meeting: $276,845,846, 2002

Mutuel Records
Highest win: $269.20, Arcangues, November 6,1993
Highest Exacta: $1,834.60, October 19, 1997
Highest Trifecta: $15,805.40, October 19, 1997
Highest Daily Double: $5,000, October 13,1990
Highest Pick 3: $174,331.80, October 18,1991
Highest Pick 6: $1,010,221.20, October 19,1994
Highest Other Exotics: $51,713.70, Superfecta, November 6, 1998

Leaders
Career, leading jockey by stakes wins: Chris McCarron, 72
Career, leading jockey by wins: Laffit Pincay Jr., 611
Career, leading trainer by stakes wins: Charles Whittingham, 68
Career, leading trainer by wins: Ronald McAnally, 225
Recent meeting, leading jockey: Laffit Pincay Jr., 31, 2001
Recent meeting, leading owner: Juddmonte Farms, 4, 2001
Recent meeting, leading trainer: William Spawr, 11, 2001

Records
Single day jockey wins: Steve Valdez, 6, October 15,1973; Darrell McHargue, 6, October 25, 1979; Patrick Valenzuela, 6, October 21,1988; Martin Pedroza, 6, October 31, 1992

Track Records, Main Dirt
5 furlongs: Zero Henry, :57.78, October 23, 1996
5 1/2 furlongs: Davy Be Good, 1:02.17, November 14, 1993
6 furlongs: Beira, 1:07 4/5, October 13, 1974; Grenzen, 1:07 4/5, October 7, 1978; Hawkin's Special, 1:07 4/5, October 27, 1978
6 1/2 furlongs: Enjoy the Moment, 1:14.15, October 8, 1998
7 furlongs: Ancient Title, 1:20 4/5, October 18, 1972
1 mile: Salud y Pesetas, 1:33 4/5, October 7, 1987
1 1/16 miles: Cajun Prince, 1:40 1/5, October 9, 1982
1 1/8 miles: My Sonny Boy, 1:46, November 3, 1990
1 1/4 miles: King Pellinore, 2:00, November 6, 1976
1 1/2 miles: Whisk Spree, 2:29.17, October 16, 1993

Course Records, Main Turf
6 1/2 furlongs: Comininalittlehot, 1:11.57, October 27, 1996
1 mile: Urgent Request (Ire), 1:32.44, October 5, 1996
1 1/16 miles: Manistique, 1:42.39, October 10, 1999
1 1/8 miles: Kostroma (Ire), 1:43.92, October 20, 1991
1 1/4 miles: Double Discount, 1:57 2/5, October 9, 1977
1 1/2 miles: Hawkster, 2:22 4/5, October 14, 1989

Fastest Times of 2002 (Dirt)
5 1/2 furlongs: U U Star, 1:02.83, October 3
6 furlongs: Kalookan Queen, 1:08.26, October 5
6 1/2 furlongs: American System, 1:15.35, October 27
7 furlongs: Resolve, 1:21.22, October 2
1 mile: Piensa Sonando (Chi), 1:34.63, October 24
1 1/16 miles: Azeri, 1:41.10, October 2
1 1/8 miles: Pleasantly Perfect, 1:46.80, October 6

Fastest Times of 2002 (Turf)
About 6 1/2 furlongs: Master Belt (NZ), 1:12.26, November 3
1 mile: Night Patrol, 1:32.93, October 5
1 1/8 miles: Johar, 1:46.00, October 13
1 1/4 miles: The Tin Man, 1:58.93, October 6
1 1/2 miles: Special Matter, 2:26.21, October 14

Pleasanton

Location: 4501 Pleasanton Ave., Pleasanton, CA 94566
Phone: (925) 426-7519
Fax: (925) 426-7599
Web site: http://www.calfairs.com
Number of stalls: 700
Seating capacity: 6,608

Officers
President: Tim Koopman
Vice President: Tony Macchiano
General Manager: Rick K. Pickering
Racing Secretary: Greg Brent
Director of Finance: Ted Holder
Director of Marketing: April Chase
Director of Mutuels: Brian Wayte
Director of Racing: Greg Brent
Director of Simulcasting: Jeanne Wasserman
Track Superintendent: Paul Wayt

Racing Dates
2002: June 26-July 7, 12 days
2003: June 25-July 6, 11 days

Track Layout
Main circumference: 1 mile
Main length of stretch: 1,085 feet
Main track chutes: 2 furlongs, 6 furlongs
Main width: 60 feet

Handle
Average on-track recent meeting: $2,969,184, 2002
Average all sources recent meeting: $2,721,752, 2002
Total all sources recent meeting: $32,661,026, 2002
Total on-track recent meeting: $6,801,437, 2002

Leaders
Recent meeting, leading jockey: Russell Baze, 17, 2002
Recent meeting, leading trainer: Jerry Hollendorfer, 8, 2002

Fastest Times of 2002
4 1/2 furlongs: Tuff Ray, :52.24, June 27
5 furlongs: My Honey Bunny, :57.49, June 30; Taraval, :57.49, July 5
5 1/2 furlongs: Too Excessive, 1:03.12, June 30
6 furlongs: Federal Highway, 1:08.60, July 1
1 mile 70 yards: Funny Bone, 1:40.12, July 3
1 1/16 miles: De Goddaughter, 1:41.68, July 6

Sacramento

Location: 1600 Exposition Blvd., Sacramento, CA 95815
Phone: (916) 263-4677
Fax: (916) 263-3198
Web site: http://www.calfairs.com
Seating capacity: 7,100
Number of stalls: 1,000

Officers

General Manager: Norb Bartosik
Director of Racing: David Elliott
Racing Secretary: Grant Baker
Director of Mutuels: George Vidak
Director of Publicity: David Elliott
Track Announcer: Joe Alto
Track Superintendent: Steve Wood

Racing Dates

2002: August 21-September 2, 12 days
2003: August 20-September 1, 12 days

Track Layout

Main circumference: 1 mile
Main track chutes: 1 1/4 miles, 6 furlongs
Main length of stretch: 990 feet

Attendance:

Average daily recent meeting: 5,808, 2002
Total attendance recent meeting: 69,701, 2002

Handle

Average all sources recent meeting: $1,824,171, 2002
Average on-track recent meeting: $298,219, 2002
Total all sources recent meeting: $21,890,053, 2002
Total on-track recent meeting: $3,578,627, 2002

Leaders

Recent meeting, leading jockey: Paul Atkinson, 14, 2002
Recent meeting, leading trainer: Garland McAlester, 8, 2002

Fastest Times of 2002

5 furlongs: Lovely Ticket, :57.59, August 29
5 1/2 furlongs: Valid Redress, 1:02.00, August 28
6 furlongs: Menacing Dennis, 1:08.40, August 25
1 mile: Gifted Athlete, 1:36.00, August 23
1 1/16 miles: How Great Thou Art, 1:44.40, August 28
1 1/8 miles: Takin It Deep, 1:48.60, August 24
1 1/4 miles: Eldorado Gold, 2:05.34, September 2

Santa Anita Park

With the San Bernardino Mountains as a backdrop, an undulating downhill turf course, and an abundance of quality racing, Santa Anita Park symbolizes racing's possibilities. On a big race day, with a sizable crowd in the stands and quality Thoroughbreds on the track, the Arcadia, California, track is one of the world's finest facilities.

The story of Santa Anita is told in two parts. The first part is the original track, the dream of early 20th century California entrepreneur E. J. "Lucky" Baldwin. Opened in 1907, the track gave Los Angeles racing fans a tantalizing glimpse of racing as an opulent spectacle. But Baldwin's death two years later and the lack of legal pari-mutuel wagering in California postponed the Santa Anita dream until the 1930s.

When pari-mutuel wagering was legalized in 1933, the Los Angeles Turf Club was organized, and it built a $1-million facility near the site of Baldwin's track.

Opened in 1934, the track's inaugural 1934-'35 racing season featured two races that immediately had an impact on the national racing calendar, the Santa Anita Handicap and the Santa Anita Derby. Now Grade 1 races, they continue to have an important place on the spring schedule.

With a $100,000 purse for its inaugural running, the Big 'Cap immediately became one of America's best-known races. The race and its $1-million purse today draw some of the best handicap runners from around North America. The Santa Anita Derby is one of the top Kentucky Derby (G1) prep races and has been utilized by recent Derby winners Silver Charm, Real Quiet, and Charismatic.

Legendary jockey Bill Shoemaker rode in his final race at Santa Anita in February 1990. And the track hosts the noted Oak Tree Racing Association meet each fall. Not all of the action has revolved around the track, however. Canadian industrialist Frank Stronach purchased the track in December 1998, the first purchase in what would become Magna Entertainment Corp.'s chain of racetracks. Stronach, Magna's chairman, has undertaken some controversial improvements and has unveiled plans to expand the track to include an entertainment center.

Location: 285 W. Huntington St., Arcadia, CA 91007-3439
Phone: (626) 574-7223
Fax: (626) 446-1456
E-mail: info@santaanita.com
Web site: http://www.santaanita.com
Year founded: 1907
Inaugural meeting: December 25, 1934
Acreage: 323
Number of stalls: 2,000
Seating capacity: 19,249

Officers

President: F. Jack Liebau
Vice Presidents: Craig Dado, Mike Scalzo
General Manager: Brant Latta
Director of Racing: Michael J. Harlow
Director of Marketing: Stuart A. Zanville
Track Announcer: Trevor Denman

Racing Dates

2002: December 26, 2001 to April 21, 2002, 85 days
2003: December 26, 2002 to April 20 2003, 85 days

Track Layout

Main circumference: 1 mile
Main track chutes: 1 1/4 miles, 7 furlongs
Main width: 85 feet
Main length of stretch: 900 feet
Main turf chute: about 1 3/4 miles
Main turf length of stretch: 1,408 feet

Attendance

Average daily recent meeting: 8,842, 2002-2003
Highest single day record: 85,527, March 3, 1985
Highest single meet record: 2,936,086, 1983/1984
Record daily average for single meet: 35,247, 1946/1947

Handle

Record daily average for single meet: $11,949,188, 1999/2000
Total all sources recent meeting: $1.0-billion, 2002-2003
Single day total handle all sources: $36,264,799, November 6, 1993
Single day on-track handle: $15,410,409, November 1, 1986
Average all sources recent meeting: $11.8-million, 2002-2003

Mutuel Records

Highest win: $673.40, Playmay, February 4, 1938
Highest Exacta: $5,208.80, December 26, 1995
Highest Trifecta: $80,883.40, December 26, 1995
Highest Daily Double: $5,000, October 3, 1990
Highest Pick 3: $73,527.30, February 16, 1997
Highest Pick 6: $1,020,221.20, October 16, 1994
Highest Other Exotics: $151,713.70, Superfecta, November 6, 1998

Leaders

Career, leading jockey by stakes wins: William Shoemaker, 260
Career, leading jockey by wins: Laffit Pincay Jr., 2,669
Career, leading trainer by stakes wins: Charles Whittingham, 204
Career, leading trainer by wins: Charles Whittingham, 869
Recent meeting, leading jockey: Laffit Pincay Jr., 73, 2000-2001
Recent meeting, leading owner: The Thoroughbred Corp., 12, 2000-2001
Recent meeting, leading trainer: Bob Baffert, 44, 2000-2001

Records

Single day jockey wins: Laffit Pincay Jr., 7, March 14, 1987
Single day trainer wins: Clyde Van Dusen, 4, February 6, 1941; Farrell Jones, 4, January 5, 1962; M. E. "Buster" Millerick, 4, December 29, 1965; Charles Whittingham, 4, February 9, 1967; Bobby Frankel, 4, January 3, 1976; Bobby Frankel, 4, March 26, 1981; Richard Mandella, 4, November 6, 1993 (all stakes); Mike Mitchell, 4, January 13, 1995

Track Records, Main Dirt

4 furlongs: Valiant Pete, :44 1/5, April 20, 1991
4 1/2 furlongs: Willy Float, :51 2/5, March 23, 1972
5 furlongs: Zero Henry, :57.78, October 23, 1996
5 1/2 furlongs: Kona Gold, 1:01.74, January 3, 1999
6 furlongs: Sunny Blossom, 1:07 1/5, December 30, 1989
6 1/2 furlongs: Son of a Pistol, 1:13.71, April 4, 1998
7 furlongs: Spectacular Bid, 1:20, January 5, 1980
1 mile: Ruhlmann, 1:33 2/5, March 5, 1989
1 1/16 miles: Efervescente (Arg), 1:39.18, January 6, 1993
1 1/8 miles: Star Spangled, 1:45 4/5, March 24, 1979
1 1/4 miles: Spectacular Bid, 1:57 4/5, February 8, 1980
1 3/8 miles: Be Faithful, 2:15 1/5, February 9, 1946
1 1/2 miles: Queen's Hustler, 2:27 1/5, February 19, 1973
1 5/8 miles: Ace Admiral, 2:39 4/5, July 23, 1949
1 3/4 miles: *Noor, 2:52 4/5, March 4, 1950
2 miles: Durango, 3:26 1/5, February 2, 1935; Fuego, 3:26 1/5, June 30, 1945; Jimmy John, 3:26 1/5, March 9, 1946
Other: 2 furlongs, Beautiful Moment, :21, April 3, 1996; 3 furlongs, King Rhymer, :32, February 27, 1947; 2 1/4 miles, English Harry, 3:55 3/5, February 16, 1940; 2 1/2 miles, Big Ed, 4:22, February 23, 1940; 3 miles, 5:20 1/5, English Harry, March 1, 1940

Course Records, Main Turf

About 6 1/2 furlongs: El Cielo, 1:11.46, November 11, 2001
1 mile: Atticus, 1:31.89, March 1, 1997
1 1/8 miles: Kostroma (Ire), 1:43.92, October 20, 1991
1 1/4 miles: Double Discount, 1:57 2/5, October 9, 1977; Bequest, 1:57.50, March 31, 1991
1 1/2 miles: Hawkster, 2:22 4/5, October 14, 1989
1 3/4 miles: Marlin, 2:44.56, April 20, 1997

Fastest Times of 2002 (Dirt)

2 furlongs: Mr. Elusive, :21.18, April 12
5 1/2 furlongs: Snow Ridge, 1:03.05, January 1
6 furlongs: Snow Ridge, 1:07.70, January 27
6 1/2 furlongs: Primerica, 1:15.01, February 16; Southern Image, 1:15.01, December 26
7 furlongs: Wild and Wise, 1:21.33, January 13
1 mile: Reba's Gold, 1:35.39, February 9
1 1/16 miles: Western Pride, 1:41.30, January 12
1 1/8 miles: Mizzen Mast, 1:47.25, February 2
1 1/4 miles: Milwaukee Brew, 2:01.02, March 2

Fastest Times of 2002 (Turf)

About 6 1/2 furlongs: Malabar Gold, 1:11.73, April 21
1 mile: Climate, 1:32.98, March 22
1 1/8 miles: Toqueville, 1:46.83, March 13
1 1/4 miles: Our Main Man, 2:00.27, January 25
1 1/2 miles: Tiger Trap, 2:25.96, April 4
About 1 3/4 miles: Ringaskiddy, 2:44.49, April 21

Santa Rosa

Location: 1350 Bennett Valley Rd., Santa Rosa, CA 95403
Phone: (707) 545-6206
Fax: (707) 573-9342
Web site: http://www.sonomacountyfair.com
Number of stalls: 1,022

Officers

President: Changes Annually
General Manager: G. James Moore
Racing Secretary: C. Gregory Brent Jr.
Director of Finance: Roger Hayes
Director of Mutuels: George Vidak
Director of Publicity: Mary Cilley
Track Announcer: Vic Stauffer

Racing Dates

2002: July 24-August 5, 12 days
2003: July 23-August 4, 12 days

Track Layout

Main circumference: 1 mile
Main track chutes: 1 1/4 miles, 6 furlongs
Main length of stretch: 1,145.8 feet

Handle

Average all sources recent meeting: $3,062,611, 2002
Average on-track recent meeting: $504,945, 2002
Total all sources recent meeting: $36,751,334, 2002
Total on-track recent meeting: $6,059,342, 2002

Leaders

Recent meeting, leading jockey: Russell A. Baze, 14, 2002
Recent meeting, leading trainer: Greg Gilchrist, 7, 2002

Fastest Times of 2002

4 1/2 furlongs: Never Ready, :51.22, July 25
5 furlongs: Truckee River, :56.59, August 1
5 1/2 furlongs: Smokin' Freddy, 1:03.06, July 31
6 furlongs: Sempai, 1:08.22, July 27
1 mile: Withholding Info, 1:35.82, July 31
1 1/16 miles: Takin It Deep, 1:42.80, August 3

Stockton

Location: 1658 Airport Wy., Sherman, CA 95205
Phone: (209) 466-5041
Fax: (209) 466-5739
Web site: http://www.calfairs.com
Inaugural meeting: August 1934
Number of stalls: 800

Officers

President: Karylene Mann
Vice President: Eddie Rishwain
General Manager: Forrest J. White
Director of Racing: Forrest J. White
Racing Secretary: Robert Moreno
Director of Mutuels: George Vidak
Director of Publicity: Lea Isetti
Track Announcer: John McGary

Racing Dates
2002: June 12-June 23, 10 days
2003: June 11-June 22
2004: June 16-June 27

Track Layout
Main circumference: 1 mile
Main track chute: 1 1/4 miles, 6 furlongs
Main width: 80 feet

Handle
Average all sources recent meeting: $1,494,502, 2002
Average on-track recent meeting: $226,833, 2002
Total all sources recent meeting: $14,945,022, 2002
Total on-track recent meeting: $2,268,334, 2002

Leaders
Recent meeting, leading jockey: Francisco Duran, 7, 2002, Paul Atkinson, 7, 2002
Recent meeting, leading trainer: Garland McAlester, 5, 2002

Fastest Times of 2002
4 1/2 furlongs: Danger, :51.69, June 21
5 1/2 furlongs: Flight Zone, 1:04.17, June 19
6 furlongs: Johnny Be Good, 1:10.18, June 13
1 mile: Nickle Oakie, 1:37.03, June 19

Vallejo

Location: 900 Fairgrounds Dr., Vallejo, CA 94589
Phone: (707) 644-4455
Fax: (707) 642-7947
E-mail: pskelton@scfair.org
Web site: http://www.scfair.com
Year founded: 1950
Abbreviation: SOL
Number of stalls: 884

Officers
President: Richard Martinez
Vice President: Michael Freese
General Manager: Kim Myrman
Director of Racing: Greg Brent
Racing Secretary: Greg Brent
Treasurer: William Luiz
Director of Mutuels: George Vidak
Track Announcer: John McGary

Racing Dates
2002: July 10-July 21, 11 days
2003: July 9-July 20, 10 days

Track Layout
Main circumference: 7 furlongs
Main track chute: 6 furlongs
Main length of stretch: 1,085 feet

Handle
Average all sources recent meeting: $2,673,365, 2002
Average on-track recent meeting: $269,540, 2002
Total all sources recent meeting: $29,407,019, 2002
Total on-track recent meeting: $2,965,941, 2002

Leaders
Recent meeting, leading jockey: Francisco Duran, 18, 2002
Recent meeting, leading trainer: Jerry Hollendorfer, 5, 2002

Fastest Times of 2002
4 1/2 furlongs: Genuine Sparky, :51.38, July 20
5 furlongs: Onebadshark, :56.73, July 14
5 1/2 furlongs: One Troy Ounce, 1:02.51, July 14
6 furlongs: Winner's Code, 1:08.41, July 20
1 mile: Suspicious Minds, 1:35.37, July 14
1 1/16 miles: Future Article, 1:46.10, July 13
1 1/8 miles: Weatherbug, 1:50.93, July 20

Colorado

Arapahoe Park

One of racing's quiet survivors, Denver-area Arapahoe Park has survived a disastrous launch, increased gambling competition, and disputes with horsemen to remain a summer racing fixture in the Rocky Mountains region.

The track opened in the mid-1980s, replacing longtime Denver track Centennial Park. But its location southeast of Denver was far from any interstate highways; interest in the track was negligible, and it was closed for several years after its opening.

The track reopened in the early 1990s but has struggled to develop a fan base amid competition from a state lottery and Native American casinos, which were legalized in the early '90s. A dispute between the track's current owner, Wembley USA, and horsemen over racing dates nearly forced the cancellation of the 2000 race meet.

The future may be brighter for Arapahoe, however. In August 2001, new Wembley USA chief executive officer Ty Howard said he planned to develop some of the nonracing real estate around the track to increase revenue and to attract more people to its rural location. He also has lobbied for video lottery terminals.

Location: 26000 E. Quincy Ave., Aurora, CO 80016
Phone: (303) 690-2400
Fax: (303) 690-6730
E-mail: Arapahoe@Wembleyusa.com
Web site: http://www.wembleyusa.com/arapahoe
Abbreviation: ArP
Acreage: 297
Number of stalls: 1,495
Seating capacity: 8,400

Officers
President: Ty Howard
General Manager: Bruce Seymore
Director of Racing: Bill Powers
Racing Secretary: Bill Powers
Director of Operations: Frank Borowitz
Director of Marketing: Jessica Costello
Director of Mutuels: Kathy Keeley
Director of Simulcasting: Bill Powers
Track Announcer: Peter Berry
Track Superintendent: Paul Guerrieri

Racing Dates
2002: June 7-September 2, 41 days
2003: June 7-August 17, 41 days

Track Layout
Main circumference: 1 mile
Main track chutes: 1 5/16 miles, 6 furlongs, 7 furlongs
Main width: 90 feet
Main length of stretch: 1,029 feet

Leaders
Recent meeting, leading jockey: Frank Gonzalves, 51, 2002
Recent meeting, leading owner: Tangarae Farms LLP, 11, 2002
Recent meeting, leading trainer: Kenneth Gleason, 31, 2002

Track Records, Main Dirt
4 furlongs: Pleasant Harmony, :46.40, June 25, 1995
4 1/2 furlongs: V G's Catch, :50.40, June 23, 2002
5 furlongs: Nycity, :56.00, July 13, 2002

5 1/2 furlongs: Ribot Line, 1:02.20, June 30, 2002
6 furlongs: Jumbled Pete, 1:08.80, August 23, 1993
6 1/2 furlongs: Pray for Booger, 1:18.60, August 25, 1995
7 furlongs: Debatable, 1:21.80, July 13, 2002
1 mile: Honor Bright, 1:35.20, August 7, 1993
1 mile 70 yards: Naskra's Advocate, 1:38.20, July 23, 1993
1 1/16 miles: I'm A Gene, 1:43, July 25, 1992
1 1/8 miles: Maysville Slew, 1:49.00, September 1, 2002
1 1/4 miles: Builder's Boy, 2:05.40, June 26, 1992; Elegant Beau, 2:05.40, July 28, 2002
1 1/2 miles: Luedke, 2:35.80, July 30, 1994
2 miles: Little Reeves, 3:28.40, August 27, 1994

Fastest Times of 2002

4 1/2 furlongs: V G's Catch, :50.40, June 23
5 furlongs: Nycity, :56.00, July 13
5 1/2 furlongs: Ribot Line, 1:02.20, June 30
6 furlongs: All Night Long (Ire), 1:09.00, June 23; Gone With the Win, 1:09.00, June 9; Tank Two, 1:09.00, July 12; Uncle Punk, 1:09.00, June 16
7 furlongs: Debatable, 1:21.80, July 13
1 mile: Mr. Vic, 1:36.60, June 23
1 1/16 miles: Cheris' Pride, 1:44.40, July 28; Personal Beau, 1:44.40, August 11
1 1/8 miles: Maysville Slew, 1:49.00, September 1
1 1/4 miles: Elegant Beau, 2:05.40, July 28
1 3/4 miles: Salem Malone, 3:02.20, September 2

Delaware

Delaware Park

Competition from racetracks in neighboring Pennsylvania and New Jersey forced the closure of historic Delaware Park in Stanton, Delaware, near Wilmington in September 1982. In late 1983, Maryland developer William Rickman Sr. acquired Delaware Park in partnership with Maryland horseman William Christmas, and the track ran abbreviated meets in the spring and fall of '84. Rickman's son, William Rickman Jr., managed track operations and in 1994 helped to secure state approval for installing slot machines in the track. Delaware's slots facility opened in December 1995, and revenues from the slots have more than tripled purses.

The track, which today also offers Arabian racing, was designed by banker and horseman William duPont Jr. and became a haven for summer racing fans throughout the Mid-Atlantic region. The track's richest race, the Delaware Handicap (G2), debuted in 1937 as the New Castle Handicap and has been won by some of the sport's leading fillies and mares.

Location: 777 Delaware Park Blvd., Stanton, DE 19804
Phone: (302) 994-2521
Fax: (302) 998-1216
E-mail: programs@delpark.com
Web site: http://www.delpark.com
Year founded: 1936
Inaugural meeting: June 26, 1937
Abbreviation: Del

Officers

President: William M. Rickman Jr.
General Manager: Andrew Gentile
Director of Racing: Greg Pettciewicz
Racing Secretary: Sam Abbey
Director of Operations: James Hartman
Director of Communications: Mike McGinnis
Director of Finance: Joseph Lofink
Director of Marketing: Pam Cunningham

Director of Mutuels: Richard Sobocinski
Director of Publicity: Chris Sobocinski
Director of Simulcasting: Dave Lermond
Horsemen's Liaison: Joe'Lyn Rigione
Stewards: Fritz Burkhardt, Jack Houghton, Lisa Comer
Track Announcer: John Curran
Track Photographer: Hoofprints Inc.
Track Superintendent: Ed Lyons
Other officials: Joe DeFrancesco, CEO and Director of Slots; William Fasy, Chief Operating Officer; William M. Rickman Sr., Chairman, Ray Spera, Senior Vice President of Operations

Racing Dates

2002: April 27-November 17, 139 days
2003: April 26-November 9, 142 days

Track Layout

Main circumference: 1 mile
Main track chutes: 1 1/4 miles, 6 furlongs
Main width: 100 feet
Main length of stretch: 995 feet
Main turf circumference: 7 furlongs
Main turf chute: 1/8 mile

Attendance

Highest single day record: 35,473, July 5, 1954

Handle

All sources average recent meeting: $2,033,706, 2002
Single day total handle all sources: $4,837,856, July 21, 2002
Single day on-track handle: $2,380,166, August 11, 1974
Total all sources recent meeting: $282,685,168, 2002

Mutuel Records

Highest win: $403.20, Gerabon, June 16, 1949
Lowest Win: $2.20, Spectacular Bid, August 26, 1979
Highest Exacta: $4,565.60, July 21, 1972
Lowest Exacta: $3.80, August 7, 1977; $3.80, August 26, 1979
Highest Trifecta: $50,870.80, May 25, 1974
Highest Daily Double: $5,507.80, July 4, 1941
Lowest Daily Double: $6.40, June 11, 1976
Highest Other Exotics: Quinella, $623.40, June 13, 1968
Lowest Other Exotics: Quinella, $5.40, July 1, 1968

Leaders

Career, leading jockey by titles: Mike McCarthy, 5
Career, leading trainer by titles: Grover "Bud" Delp, 11
Recent meeting, leading jockey: Michael J. McCarthy, 157, 2002
Recent meeting, leading owner: Mike Gill, 85, 2002
Recent meeting, leading trainer: Scott A. Lake, 84, 2002

Records

Single day jockey wins: Eldon Nelson, 6, June 20, 1958; George Cusimano, 6, July 16, 1968; Greg McCarron, 6, July 6, 1974; Jimmy Edwards, 6, May 28, 1984; Michael McCarthy, 6, November 2, 1997; Michael McCarthy, 6, May 20, 1998
Single meet, leading jockey by wins: Michael McCarthy, 218, 1997
Single meet, leading trainer by wins: Tim Ritchey, 87, 2001

Track Records, Main Dirt

4 furlongs: Star Event, :47, May 5, 1997
4 1/2 furlongs: Erlton, :51.80, May 5, 1998
5 furlongs: Milky Way Gal, :56.20, July 29, 1989
5 1/2 furlongs: Dontcloseyoureyes, 1:03, October 14, 1990
6 furlongs: Damitrius, 1:08.20, September 2, 1980
1 mile: Ashlar, 1:35.20, June 25, 1960
1 mile 70 yards: St. Bonaventure, 1:39.40, June 15, 1970
1 1/16 miles: Lies of Omission, 1:41.20, July 4, 1998
1 1/8 miles: Victoria Park, 1:47.40, June 18, 1960
1 3/16 miles: Gold Star Deputy, 1:56.72, October 31, 1999
1 1/4 miles: Coup de Fusil, 1:59.80, July 25, 1987

1 1/2 miles: Bam, 2:31, June 26, 1948
1 5/8 miles: Flying Restina Run, 2:45.40, September 4, 2000
1 3/4 miles: Cer Vantes, 2:56.40, June 27, 1951
2 miles: Dixies Act, 3:29.40, August 10, 1975
Other: 2 furlongs, Glitter River, :21.60, September 5, 2000; 2 miles 70 yds, Wolfe Tone, 3:34, November 7, 1993; 2 1/4 miles, 3:58.60, Sanguine Sword, July 2, 1986

Course Records, Main Turf
5 furlongs: Incredible Revent, :56, September 4, 1996
5 1/2 furlongs: Jumping to Joy, 1:08.21, October 11, 1994
1 mile: Hanover Hollywood, 1:34.74, August 3, 2002
1 1/16 miles: Charabanc, 1:40 1/5, July 20, 1963
1 1/8 miles: Royal Strand (Ire), 1:48, July 13, 1997
1 3/8 miles: Cool Prince, 2:12 2/5, July 3, 1965
1 1/2 miles: John's Call, 2:28, July 23, 2000
2 miles: Verdance, 3:24 2/5, September 21, 1986
Other: 1 7/8 miles, *El Moro, 3:11 4/5, July 22, 1963; 2 3/8 miles, Lively London, 4:09, July 25, 1986; 2 7/8 miles, Call Louis, 5:08 1/5, August 24, 1986

Fastest Times of 2002 (Dirt)
4 1/2 furlongs: Forever Partners, :53.29, May 19
5 furlongs: Absolute Jewel, :58.21, June 9
5 1/2 furlongs: Deep Meadows, 1:03.72, June 9
6 furlongs: Rich in Glory, 1:09.55, July 28
1 mile: Four Alert, 1:36.92, July 15
1 mile 70 yards: Saint Marden, 1:42.13, June 9
1 1/16 miles: Bowman's Band, 1:42.97, July 20
1 1/8 miles: Runspastum, 1:51.37, September 7
1 3/16 miles: Jarf, 1:57.51, October 5
1 1/4 miles: Summer Colony, 2:04.52, July 21

Fastest Times of 2002 (Turf)
5 furlongs: Mujado (Ire), :56.16, July 27
About 5 furlongs: Governor's Pride, :57.19, July 13
1 mile: Hanover Hollywood, 1:34.74, August 3
About 1 mile: Capazuri, 1:36.08, July 13
1 1/16 miles: Equality, 1:41.38, June 11
About 1 1/16 miles: Sir Brian's Sword, 1:43.52, September 16
1 1/8 miles: Tam's Terms, 1:48.73, June 25
About 1 1/8 miles: Blushing Rainbow, 1:51.39, September 14
1 3/8 miles: New Economy, 2:17.78, July 20
1 1/2 miles: Craigsteel (GB), 2:28.24, July 21

Florida

Calder Race Course

Calder Race Course, which offers racing from May through early January, is located in Miami next to Pro Player Stadium, home of the National Football League's Miami Dolphins. Built by real-estate businessman Stephen A. Calder, the track was granted summer racing dates for 1970. Because the track was under construction, those dates were run at Tropical Park. Calder officially opened on May 6, 1971, debuting an all-weather synthetic track surface designed by 3M that remained in place until 1992. In 1972, Tropical Park closed and began holding its meet at Calder; the last several weeks of each year's season are known as the Tropical Park meet. From 1980-'84, Calder underwent $10.5-million in improvements. In 1988, Thoroughbred owner-breeder Bertram R. Firestone bought Calder. Three years later, Kawasaki Leasing Inc. assumed control of the track. The track underwent a $1-million renovation of its first floor, and in 1995 it added full-card simulcasting. In 1999, Churchill Downs Inc. bought Calder for approximately $86-million. Today,

Calder features three successful racing events: the Florida Stallion Stakes, a series of races for offspring of Florida stallions; Festival of the Sun, seven stakes races highlighted by the finals of the Florida Stallion Stakes series; and Summit of Speed, five sprint stakes races with combined purses exceeding $1-million. The first national pick four was offered on the Summit of Speed in 2000.

Location: 21001 NW. 27th Ave., Miami, FL 33055-0808
Phone: (305) 625-1311
Fax: (305) 623-6695
E-mail: marketing@calderracecourse.com
Web site: http://www.calderracecourse.com
Year founded: 1970
Inaugural meeting: May 6, 1971
Abbreviation: Crc
Acreage: 220
Number of stalls: 1,850
Seating capacity: 15,575

Officers
President: C. Kenneth Dunn
Vice President: Randall E. Soth
General Manager: Randall E. Soth
Racing Secretary: Robert D. Umphrey
Secretary: Rebecca C. Reed
Treasurer: Michael Abes
Director of Sales: Tammy Gantt
Director of Operations: Mike Anifantis
Director of Admissions: Bill Keers
Director of Communications: Michele Blanco
Director of Marketing: Mike Cronin
Director of Mutuels: Ed Mackie
Director of Publicity: Michele Blanco
Director of Simulcasting: Diane Stoess
Horsemen's Liaison: Joanne Roberts
Stewards: Charles Camac, Jeff Noe, Walter Blum
Track Announcer: Phil Saltzman
Track Photographer: Jean Raftery
Track Superintendent: Steve Cross

Racing Dates
2002: April 26-November 3
2003: April 25-October 24, 128 days

Track Layout
Main circumference: 1 mile
Main track chutes: 1/4 mile, 7 furlongs
Main length of stretch: 990 feet
Main width: 80 feet
Main turf circumference: 7 furlongs
Main turf chute: 1/4 mile
Training track: 4 furlongs

Attendance
Average daily recent meeting: 4,872, 2002
Highest single day record: 23,103, May 4, 1985
Record daily average for single meet: 9,401, 1976
Total attendance recent meeting: 623,629, 2002

Handle
Total all sources recent meeting: $733,883,656, 2002
Single day total handle all sources: $9,461,604, December 29, 2001
Total on-track recent meeting: $54,554,352, 2002
Single day on-track handle: $2,954,162, May 7, 1988
Average all sources recent meeting: $5,733,466, 2002
Average on-track recent meeting: $426,206, 2002
Record daily average for single meet: $1,206,739, 1986

Mutuel Records
Highest win: $345.40, Lou Glory, September 12, 1991
Lowest Win: $2.10, Isle O'Style, June 12, 1974
Highest Exacta: $31,133.20, November 3, 1972
Lowest Exacta: $3.40, August 16, 1989

Highest Trifecta: $58,432.40, October 25, 1986
Lowest Trifecta: $10.40, July 31, 1994
Highest Daily Double: $2,671, July 2, 1976
Lowest Daily Double: $3.20, September 16, 1992
Highest Pick 3: $16,038.20, September 2, 1992
Lowest Pick 3: $9, September 12, 2000
Highest Other Exotics: $74,622, Superfecta, October 26, 1996
Lowest Other Exotics: $33.40, Superfecta, August 7, 1995

Leaders

Career, leading jockey by wins: Gene St. Leon, 1,310
Recent meeting, leading jockey: Cornelio Velasquez, 169, 2002
Recent meeting, leading owner: Michael Sherman, 38, 2002
Recent meeting, leading trainer: Bill White, 61, 2002
Career, leading jockey by stakes wins: Gene St. Leon, 73
Career, leading trainer by stakes wins: Frank Gomez, 87
Career, leading trainer by wins: Frank Gomez, 852

Records

Single day jockey wins: George Gomez, 6, May 12, 1977; Walter Guerra, 6, October 3, 1979; Rene Douglas, 6, July 15, 1995; Eibar Coa, 6, September 7, 1998
Single day trainer wins: Arnold N. Winick, 5, September 16, 1972; Stanley Hough, 5, May 12, 1977

Track Records, Main Dirt

4 1/2 furlongs: Imperial Action, :52.54, June 3, 1993
5 furlongs: Honest, :57.61, July 1, 1996
5 1/2 furlongs: Bernard's Candy, 1:04.2, August 9, 2002
6 furlongs: Forty One Carats, 1:08.95, October 7, 2000
6 1/2 furlongs: Tour of the Cat, 1:15.8, August 17, 2002
7 furlongs: Constant Escort, 1:21.82, September 28, 1996
1 mile: Cutandthrust, 1:37.47, September 19, 1993
1 mile 70 yards: Halo's Image, 1:41.78, October 31, 1995
1 1/16 miles: King Rex, 1:43.36, June 22, 1996
1 1/8 miles: Jumping Hill, 1:50, December 30, 1978
1 3/16 miles: Arctic Honeymoon, 1:59 3/5, January 3, 1987
1 1/4 miles: Wicapi, 2:05, June 25, 1996
1 1/2 miles: Lead'm Home, 2:32 3/5, December 31, 1977
1 5/8 miles: Timberlea Tune, 2:50 1/5, October 16, 1971
1 3/4 miles: *Detective II, 3:03 1/5, October 23, 1971
2 miles: *Detective II, 3:30 1/5, November 11, 1971
Other: 2 furlongs, Lifeisawhirl, :20.99, July 15, 2000

Course Records, Main Turf

5 furlongs: Heckofaralph, :54.96, August 1, 1998
7 furlongs: Carterista, 1:22.36, June 19, 1993
7 1/2 furlongs: Court Lark, 1:26.54, July 16, 1994
1 mile: Copy Editor, 1:33.68, August 2, 1998
1 1/16 miles: Spendable, 1:39.33, July 30, 1999
1 1/8 miles: The Vid, 1:44.99, November 25, 1995
1 3/8 miles: King's Design, 2:13, July 23, 1999
1 1/2 miles: Flag Down, 2:24, December 16, 1995
2 miles: Skate On Thin Ice, 3:21.89, January 2, 1996

Fastest Times of 2002 (Dirt)

2 furlongs: Baby Shark, :20.81, July 13
4 1/2 furlongs: Massive, :52.12, June 22
5 furlongs: Groomstick Stock's, :57.74, July 13
5 1/2 furlongs: Bernard's Candy, 1:04.39, August 9
6 furlongs: Orientate, 1:09.98, July 13
6 1/2 furlongs: Tour of the Cat, 1:15.99, August 17
7 furlongs: Jet Thrust, 1:24.00, August 13
1 mile: Pay the Preacher, 1:37.58, June 17
1 mile 70 yards: Super Frolic, 1:45.02, September 21
1 1/16 miles: Best of the Rest, 1:44.75, May 27
1 1/8 miles: Dancing Guy, 1:52.26, July 4
1 1/4 miles: Strike Three, 2:07.06, September 29

Fastest Times of 2002 (Turf)

5 furlongs: Texas Glitter, :54.89, October 12
7 1/2 furlongs: Stormy Pleasure, 1:28.07, May 4
1 mile: Creek's Shore, 1:34.48, May 13; Mr. Livingston, 1:34.48, April 28
1 1/16 miles: Tame Native, 1:41.02, May 13
1 1/8 miles: Union Place, 1:47.76, October 12

Gulfstream Park

Since the 1940s, Gulfstream Park, located north of Miami in Hallandale, Florida, has been a favorite winter destination for horsemen and annually offers high-quality winter racing. Gulfstream opened in February 1939 but went bankrupt and closed after four days of racing. In 1944, James Donn Sr., who owned a local floral shop and was a creditor of the track, reopened Gulfstream. In 1952, the Florida Derby (G1) debuted and became a major stop on the road to the Kentucky Derby (G1). Ten winners of the race, including Northern Dancer, Unbridled, Thunder Gulch, and, most recently, Monarchos, went on to win the Kentucky Derby. Gulfstream in 1989 held the first of the track's three Breeders' Cup championship days. In 1999, Frank Stronach-led Magna Entertainment Corp. purchased Gulfstream for $95-million. Stronach has announced plans for significant additions and improvements to the facility, and in October 2001 Magna broke ground on Palm Meadows, a 304-acre training facility located near Boynton Beach, approximately 35 miles north of the track. The training center, which opened in 2003, was to be fully operational in 2004.

Location: 901 S. Federal Hwy., Hallandale, FL 33009-7124
Phone: (954) 454-7000
Fax: (954) 457-6357
800 number: (800) 771-TURF
Web site: *http://www.gulfstreampark.com*
Year founded: 1938
Inaugural meeting: February 1-4, 1939
Number of stalls: 1,454
Seating capacity: 20,300
Acreage: 256

Officers

Chairman: Douglas Donn
President: Scott Savin
Vice Presidents: Don Amos, Graham Orr
General Manager: Scott Savin
Director of Racing: David Bailey
Racing Secretary: David Bailey
Director of Operations: Dennis Testa
Director of Admissions: David Lang
Director of Communications: Joe Tanenbaum
Director of Finance: Robert W. Zambreny Jr.
Director of Marketing: David Rovine
Director of Mutuels: Edward Mackie
Director of Publicity: Joe Tanenbaum
Director of Simulcasting: Mike Tanner
Horsemen's Liaison: Raina Chingos-Gunderson
Stewards: Charles Camac, Jeffrey Noe, Walter Blum
Track Announcer: Vic Stauffer
Track Photographer: Equi-Photo/Bill Denver
Track Superintendent: Dale Henricksen
Other officials: Chairman of the Board: Frank Stronach, Executive Vice Presidents: Graham Orr and Don Amos, Group Vice President: Corey Johnson

Racing Dates

2002: January 3-April 24, 90 days
2003: January 3-April 24, 89 days

Track Layout

Main circumference: 1 mile
Main track chutes: 3 furlongs, 7 furlongs
Main width: 80 feet
Main length of stretch: 952 feet, 2 inches
Main turf circumference: 7 furlongs
Main turf chute: 1 1/8 miles
Main turf width: 70 feet

Main turf length of stretch: 921 feet
Training track: Palm Meadows

Attendance
Highest single day record: 45,124, November 6, 1999
Average daily recent meeting: 9,359, 2002
Record daily average for single meet: 15,528, 1979
Highest single meet record: 1,096,404, 1991

Handle
Average all sources recent meeting: $10,642,046, 2001
Average on-track recent meeting: $2,053,846, 2001
Record daily average for single meet: $2,121,121, 1998
Highest single meet record: 1,096,404, 1991
Single day on-track handle: $7,993,485, March 12, 1994
Single day total handle all sources: $21,102,814, March 16, 1996
Total all sources recent meeting: 842,310, 2002

Mutuel Records
Highest win: $404, Concert Grand, February 14, 1993
Lowest Win: $2.10, Honest Pleasure, April 3, 1976; $2.10, Spectacular Bid, February 7, 1979; $2.10, Spectacular Bid, March 6, 1979
Highest Exacta: $8,948.80, March 13, 1987
Lowest Exacta: $3.80, March 6, 1979; $3.80, March 10, 1991
Highest Trifecta: $96,751.80, January 31, 1993
Lowest Trifecta: $9.60, March 6, 1979
Highest Daily Double: $6,683.60, January 28, 1972
Lowest Daily Double: $6, January 14, 1995
Highest Pick 3: $63,737.60, January 26, 1995
Lowest Pick 3: $9.80, February 22, 1994
Highest Pick 6: $301,585.80, February 24, 1996

Leaders
Career, leading jockey by stakes wins: Jerry Bailey
Career, leading jockey by titles: Jorge Chavez, 4
Career, leading trainer by titles: A. N. Winick, 12
Recent meeting, leading jockey: Edgar Prado, 82, 2002
Recent meeting, leading owner: Runnin Horse Farms, 14, 2002
Recent meeting, leading trainer: William I. Mott, 34, 2002

Records
Single meet, leading jockey by wins: Julio Pezua, 97, 1987; Wigberto Ramos, 97, 1991; Jerry Bailey, 97, 1996
Single meet, leading trainer by wins: William I. Mott, 39, 1996
Single day jockey wins: Jerry Bailey, 7, March 11, 1995

Track Records, Main Dirt
4 furlongs: Growing Up, :46 1/5, March 12, 1949; Piet, :46 1/5, April 3, 1947
4 1/2 furlongs: Iron Rail, :51 2/5, April 6, 1960
5 furlongs: Boston Brat, :56.35, January 17, 2003
5 1/2 furlongs: Rare Rock, 1:02.50, January 3, 1998
6 furlongs: Mr. Prospector, 1:07 4/5, March 31, 1973; Artax, 1:07.89, November 6, 1999
6 1/2 furlongs: Alydeed, 1:15, March 6, 1993; Federal Hill, 1:15, March 25, 1957
7 furlongs: Elusive Quality, 1:20, February 21, 1997
1 mile 70 yards: Blacksburg, 1:39, February 6, 1994
1 1/16 miles: Saxony Warrior, 1:40 1/5, March 6, 1973
1 1/8 miles: Jumping Hill, 1:46 2/5, February 3, 1979
1 3/16 miles: Michael's Choice, 1:56, March 23, 1960; Sal's Boat, 1:56, April 22, 1960
1 1/4 miles: Mat Boy (Arg), 1:59, March 24, 1984
1 3/8 miles: Blacktype, 2:15 2/5, March 17, 1956; Bayluc, 2:15 2/5, April 2, 1960
1 1/2 miles: Buffalo Lark, 2:27 3/5, April 12, 1975
1 5/8 miles: Toulouse, 2:43 2/5, April 7, 1956
1 3/4 miles: Tisbury, 2:57 2/5, April 20, 1953
2 miles: Undue Influence, 3:25.73, March 16, 1997
Other: 2 1/2 furlongs, Rich Coins, :28, March 31, 2000; 2 1/2 furlongs, Sonnyhero, :28, April 5, 2000; 3 furlongs, El Macho,

:32 1/5, February 26, 1974; 1 7/8 miles, Pharawell, 3:13 4/5, April 8, 1947; 2 miles 70 yds, Pharawell, 3:53 4/5, April 17, 1947

Course Records, Main Turf
5 furlongs: Heckofaralph, :56.25, April 8, 2000
1 mile: Lure, 1:32.90, October 31, 1992
1 1/16 miles: Garbu, 1:39.33, March 13, 1999
1 1/8 miles: Auntie Mame, 1:46.54, March 5, 1997
1 3/8 miles: Yagli, 2:10.73, February 6, 1999
1 1/2 miles: Unite's Big Red, 2:23, March 6, 1999
2 miles: Sabinus, 3:22 2/5, April 17, 1971

Interesting Facts
Trivia: Bill Shoemaker rode the last winner of his career (Beau Genius) in the 1990 Hallandale Handicap. Turf course opened in 1959.
Major Races: Sunshine Millions races, Florida Derby, Donn Handicap

Fastest Times of 2002 (Dirt)
3 furlongs: Sports Banquet, :32.99, April 5
5 furlongs: Bold World, :57.05, February 18
5 1/2 furlongs: Gators Get, 1:03.72, March 24
6 furlongs: Wopping, 1:09.33, April 11
6 1/2 furlongs: Gold Mover, 1:15.38, March 17
7 furlongs: He's a Knockout, 1:21.77, March 13
1 mile 70 yards: Macho Uno, 1:41.10, March 23
1 1/16 miles: Buddha, 1:42.29, March 16
1 1/8 miles: Harlan's Holiday, 1:48.80, March 16
1 1/4 miles: Hal's Hope, 2:02.91, March 30

Fastest Times of 2002 (Turf)
5 furlongs: Texas Glitter, :55.68, April 13
About 5 furlongs: Trouble In Love, :56.99, April 12
1 mile: Unite's Big Red, 1:33.40, March 16
About 1 mile: Broadway Snowman, 1:34.68, April 20
1 1/16 miles: Wertz, 1:41.31, March 29
About 1 1/16 miles: Wertz, 1:42.58, April 17
1 1/8 miles: Legislator, 1:48.03, March 24
About 1 1/8 miles: Serial Bride, 1:48.65, April 18
1 3/8 miles: Lodge Hill, 2:14.59, January 25
About 1 3/8 miles: Moon Queen (Ire), 2:18.38, February 17
1 1/2 miles: Deeliteful Irving, 2:24.14, March 23
About 1 1/2 miles: Big Hope, 2:29.84, April 17

Hialeah Park

The dowager queen of South Florida racetracks, Hialeah Park did not conduct any racing in 2002, the first year of Florida's latest bout of deregulation of Thoroughbred racing, or in 2003.

Holding its inaugural meeting in 1925, Hialeah was the first Thoroughbred racing operation in the Miami area. It blossomed after Philadelphia industrialist Joseph E. Widener purchased the track in 1931 and with his partners completely remodeled it. Widener gave the track its distinctive Renaissance Revival architecture and in 1931 imported the track's signature flock of flamingos from Cuba.

Into the 1970s, Hialeah Park held the prime midwinter dates and attracted the best stables from the North to its gentle climate and kind racing surface. Under its soaring palms and pines, such legends as Citation, Nashua, Bold Ruler, Never Bend, Northern Dancer, Seattle Slew, Alydar, and Spectacular Bid prepared for the classics with victories in the track's Flamingo Stakes. By 1979, when Spectacular Bid romped to a 12-length victory in that race, Hialeah had already begun its long decline. In 1978, the track lost exclusive control of the prime racing dates, and in the 1990s it lost the key dates to Gulfstream Park.

Location: 105 E. 21st St., Hialeah, FL 33011
Phone: (305) 885-8000
Fax: (305) 887-8006
Web site: *http://www.hialeahpark.com*
Inaugural meeting: January 25, 1925
Abbreviation: Hia
Acreage: 220
Year founded: 1924
Inaugural meeting: January 25, 1925
Number of stalls: 1,631
Seating capacity: 20,000

Officers
President: John Brunetti Jr.
General Manager: David Romanik
Director of Racing: Stephen Brunetti
Racing Secretary: J. Sam Abbey
Director of Operations: Sergio Lopez
Director of Finance: Rene Leoncio
Director of Marketing: Steve Bovo
Director of Mutuels: Ed Mackie
Director of Publicity: Joe Savage
Director of Simulcasting: Ed Mackie Jr.
Horsemen's Liaison: Rhonda Soth

Racing Dates
2001: March 17-May 22, 61 days

Track Layout
Main circumference: 1 1/8 miles
Main track chute: 3 furlongs, 7 furlongs
Main width: 80 feet
Main length of stretch: 1,410 feet
Main turf circumference: 7 1/2 furlongs
Main turf width: 90 feet
Main turf length of stretch: 975 feet

Attendance
Highest single day record: 42,366, February 18, 1956

Handle
Single day on-track handle: $4,822,601, February 28, 1987
Single day total handle all sources: $8,421,464, April 1, 1995

Mutuel Records
Highest win: $325.60, Robber, 1950
Lowest Win: $2.10, Coaltown, 1949; $2.10, Cure the Blues, March 26, 1981
Highest Exacta: $5,583.80, February 4, 1984
Lowest Exacta: $4, February 17, 1982
Highest Trifecta: $67,432, February 15, 1987
Lowest Trifecta: $8.20, April 22, 1989
Highest Daily Double: $5,919,20, January 25, 1987
Lowest Daily Double: $5.80, May 2, 1981
Highest Pick 3: $19,186, December 28, 1991
Lowest Pick 3: $16.20, March 20, 1995; $16.20, April 17, 1995
Highest Pick 6: $382,344.80, January 25, 1982

Leaders
Career, leading jockey by titles: Bobby Ussery, 5
Career, leading trainer by titles: H. A. "Jimmy" Jones, 7

Records
Single meet, leading trainer by wins: John Tammaro, 71, 1986
Single day jockey wins: Angel Cordero Jr., 6, February 28, 1968; Craig Perret, 6, March 9, 1989
Single day trainer wins: Ben A. Jones, 4, January 17, 1940; Dan Hurtak, 4, May 17, 1996
Single meet, leading jockey by wins: Jorge Chavez, 93, 1989

Track Records, Main Dirt
4 1/2 furlongs: Elvis On Velvet, :53.53, April 29, 2001
5 furlongs: Barnacle Jim, :56.54, May 16, 1997
5 1/2 furlongs: Lover's Trust, 1:02 3/5, May 6, 1989
6 furlongs: Earthmover, 1:08, March 7, 1985
7 furlongs: Seattle Slew, 1:20 3/5, March 9, 1977
1 1/16 miles: A P Valentine, 1:40.39, March 24, 2001
1 1/8 miles: Albert the Great, 1:45.52, March 24, 2001
1 3/16 miles: Swoon's Plume, 1:55 4/5, March 4, 1978
1 1/4 miles: Turkoman, 1:58 3/5, March 29, 1986
Other: 3 furlongs, Cherokee Road, :32, April 30, 2001

Course Records, Main Turf
5 1/2 furlongs: Glitterman, 1:01 3/5, May 20, 1989
1 1/16 miles: Judge Connelly, 1:38.78, April 2, 1995
1 1/8 miles: Signal Tap, 1:46, March 31, 1996
1 3/16 miles: Toonerville, 1:51 2/5, February 7, 1976
1 1/2 miles: Out of the Realm, 2:24.43, March 26, 1995

Ocala Training Center

Location: 1701 SW 60th Ave., Ocala, FL 34474
Phone: (352) 237-2154
Fax: (352) 237-3566
E-mail: obs@obssales.com
Web site: *http://www.obssales.com*

Racing Dates
2002: March 18
2003: March 17

Leaders
Recent meeting, leading jockey: John Velazquez, 2, 2002, Jorge Chavez, 2, 2002
Recent meeting, leading owner: Anstu Stables, 1, 2002, Cindy and Ron Stengel, 1, 2002, Hardacre Farm, 1, 2002, J D Farms, 1, 2002, James R. Lewis Jr., 1, 2002, Mike Polselli, H. Schmidt, and Charlotte Gershaw, 1, 2002
Recent meeting, leading trainer: David R. Brownlee, 1, 2002, Emanuel Tortora, 1, 2002, Ralph Ziadie, 1, 2002, Ronald James Taylor, 1, 2002, Ronald Spatz, 1, 2002, Todd Pletcher, 1, 2002

Fastest Times of 2002
5 furlongs: Handsome Smile, :58.20, March 18
6 furlongs: Royal Lad, 1:09.60, March 18
1 1/16 miles: Flaming Light, 1:46.60, March 18; Mountain Forum, 1:46.60, March 18

Tampa Bay Downs

Tampa Bay Downs, the only Thoroughbred track on Florida's west coast, opened on February 18, 1926, as Tampa Downs. The initial 39-day meet was orchestrated by Harvey Mayers, a businessman from Ohio, and Churchill Downs executive Col. Matt J. Winn.

Renamed Sunshine Park in 1947, it became known as the "Santa Anita of the South" in the '50s, a nickname provided by legendary sportswriters Grantland Rice, Red Smith, and Arthur Daley, who frequented the track while covering baseball spring training.

Following the sale of the track, its name was changed to Florida Downs in 1965 and to Tampa Bay Downs in 1980. On February 12, 1981, jockey Julie Krone scored the first victory of her Racing Hall of Fame career on Lord Farkle. In 1983, Tampa Bay Downs became the first track in the country to regularly schedule races for Arabians.

Tampa Bay Downs was sold again in 1986 and has since added a picnic area, year-round simulcasting, a seven-furlong turf course, a luxurious Sports Gallery featuring an extensive video racing library, an updated grandstand with private work stations, central air conditioning, and a renovated deli, bar, and pizza area. The track's two biggest races, the $250,000 Tampa Bay Derby (G3) and the $150,000 Florida Oaks (G3), are contested in mid-March for three-year-olds.

Location: 11225 Race Track Rd., Oldsmar, FL 34677
Phone: (813) 855-4401
Fax: (813) 854-3539
Web site: http://www.tampadowns.com
Year founded: 1926
Inaugural meeting: 1926 (39 days)
Abbreviation: Tam
Acreage: 450
Number of stalls: 1,462
Seating capacity: 6,000

Officers
President: Stella F. Thayer
Vice Presidents: Howell Ferguson, John E. Grady Jr., Peter Berube
General Manager: Peter Berube
Director of Racing: Robert Clark
Racing Secretary: Robert Clark
Secretary: Howell Ferguson
Treasurer: Stella F. Thayer
Director of Operations: Robert Cassanese
Director of Admissions: Judy Gittens
Director of Communications: Margo Flynn
Director of Finance: Greg Gelyon
Director of Marketing: Margo Flynn
Director of Mutuels: Lamarr Daughtry
Director of Publicity: Margo Flynn
Director of Sales: Nicole McGill
Director of Simulcasting: Cathy Dwyer
Horsemen's Liaison: Margo Flynn
Stewards: Art Pedregal, Charles Miranda, Dennis Lima
Track Announcer: Richard Grunder
Track Photographer: Tom Cooley
Track Superintendent: Tom McLaughlin
Other officials: Lorraine King, Vice President of Administration

Racing Dates
2002: December 15, 2001 to May 5, 2002, 93 days
2003: December 14, 2002 to May 4, 2003, 93 days

Track Layout
Main circumference: 1 mile
Main track chutes: 3 furlongs, 7 furlongs
Main width: 75 feet
Main length of stretch: 976 feet
Main turf circumference: 7 furlongs
Main turf chute: 1/4 mile
Main turf width: 80 feet

Attendance
Average daily recent meeting: 3,291, 2001/2002
Highest single day record: 9,765, April 8, 1990
Highest single meet record: 457,414, 1988/1989
Total attendance recent meeting: 306,042, 2001/2002

Handle
Single day on-track handle: $3,877,477, March 18, 2001
Average all sources recent meeting: $2,075,782, 2001/2002
Average on-track recent meeting: $253,767, 2001/2002
Record daily average for single meet: $1,788,733
Single day total handle all sources: $1,336,000, May 4, 2002
Total all sources recent meeting: $193,047,767, 2001/2002

Mutuel Records
Highest win: $249, March 23, 1988

Highest Trifecta: $50,617, January 26, 1999
Highest Daily Double: $3,320, January 17, 1950
Highest Pick 3: $12,913.40, January 9, 2001
Highest Other Exotics: $33,237.50, Superfecta, January 12, 1999; $9,754, Perfecta, February 8, 1973

Leaders
Career, leading jockey by titles: Bill Henry, 4
Career, leading trainer by titles: Don Rice, 5
Recent meeting, leading jockey: Manoel Cruz, 91, 2001/2002
Recent meeting, leading owner: Glen Hill Farm, 15, 2001/2002, L and D Farm, 15, 2001/2002
Recent meeting, leading trainer: Don Rice, 44, 2001/2002
Career, leading jockey by stakes wins: William Henry, 21
Career, leading owner by stakes wins: Harold Queen, 6
Career, leading trainer by stakes wins: Don Rice, 8

Records
Single day jockey wins: Richard DePass, 7, March 15, 1980
Single day owner wins: Christos Gatis, 3, April 10, 2001
Single day trainer wins: Don Rice, 3, February 13, 1997; Sam Cronk, 3, December 28, 1997; William Mitchell, 3, April 10, 2001; Duane Knipe, 3, April 24, 2001
Single meet, leading jockey by wins: Bill Henry, 123, 1992/1993; Willie Martinez, 123, 1991/1992
Single meet, leading trainer by wins: Don Rice, 44, 2001/2002

Track Records, Main Dirt
4 furlongs: Camp Izard, :46.80, May 1, 1993
4 1/2 furlongs: Geronimo J., :52 4/5, March 16, 1984
5 furlongs: Arion Fair, :57 1/5, March 20, 1982, Mr. Buffum, :57.28, March 17, 2002
5 1/2 furlongs: Schmoopy, 1:03.55, March 17, 2000
6 furlongs: Bootlegger's Pet, 1:09, January 26, 1974
7 furlongs: Oh So Striking, 1:22.60, April 5, 1997
7 1/2 furlongs: Secret Romeo, 1:22.62, January 22, 2002
1 mile: Double Prince, 1:42 3/5, February 8, 1966; Rianan, 1:42 3/5, February 11, 1966
1 mile 40 yards: Mistum, 1:41 1/5, March 21, 1981
1 mile 70 yards: Deep Thought, 1:41 4/5, January 21, 1956
1 1/16 miles: Sunny Prospector, 1:43 2/5, March 29, 1989
1 3/16 miles: Warning Flag, 1:59 3/5, January 25, 1986
1 1/4 miles: Finale Puer, 2:07 2/5, March 7, 1959
1 3/8 miles: Rugged Zeal, 2:20.68, April 23, 2002
1 1/2 miles: Royal Jacopo, 2:33, March 12, 1955
1 5/8 miles: Most Valiant, 2:48.20, March 29, 1997
1 3/4 miles: Our Day, 3:00 2/5, March 20, 1957
2 miles: Boss Man Jarett, 3:30.30, April 24, 1999
Other: 2 furlongs, Silver Dollar Boy, :21 4/5, January 18, 1980; 3 furlongs, Hot Star, :33 2/5, February 14, 1980; 1 7/8 miles, Best Hearted, 3:18 3/5, March 22, 1986; 2 miles 70 yds, Turkey Foot Road, 3:39 4/5, March 22, 1969; 2 1/16 miles, Mystic Fox, 3:37 3/5, March 27; 1988

Course Records, Main Turf
5 furlongs: Exclusive Pow Wow, :56.39, May 5, 2001
1 mile: Lucky J J, 1:33.79, February 12, 2000
1 1/16 miles: Legs Galore, 1:39.65, February 20, 1999
1 1/8 miles: Lilys Cousin, 1:46.34, May 6, 2000
1 3/8 miles: Fun n' Gun, 2:24.06, March 30, 2002
1 1/2 miles: Top Senor, 2:31.60, February 26, 2002

Interesting Facts
Previous names and dates: Florida Downs, 1965; Sunshine Park, 1947, Tampa Downs, 1926

Fastest Times of 2002 (Dirt)
3 furlongs: Reece and Heather, :35.00, April 28
5 furlongs: Mr. Buffum, :57.28, March 17
5 1/2 furlongs: Peter's Pond, 1:04.04, April 7
6 furlongs: Mr. Buffum, 1:10.38, January 26
7 furlongs: Secret Romeo, 1:22.62, January 22
1 1/16 miles: Equality, 1:43.66, March 17
1 1/8 miles: Royal Feast, 1:54.21, December 27

1 1/4 miles: Regal by Design, 2:08.40, January 19
1 3/8 miles: Rugged Zeal, 2:20.68, April 23
1 1/2 miles: Mr. Mularkey, 2:35.24, March 16

Fastest Times of 2002 (Turf)
5 furlongs: Chickamauga Trail, :57.72, May 5
1 mile: Staples N Stitches, 1:35.60, May 4
About 1 mile: Twisted Cord, 1:38.01, January 25
1 1/16 miles: Boastful, 1:40.95, February 16
About 1 1/16 miles: Warrant, 1:42.74, January 27
About 1 1/8 miles: Guardianofthegate, 1:48.12, May 4
About 1 3/8 miles: Fun n' Gun, 2:24.06, March 30
About 1 1/2 miles: Top Senor, 2:31.60, February 26

Tropical Park

Tropical Park no longer has a physical presence but remains alive as the late fall-early winter meeting at Calder Race Course in northwest Miami. The Tropical Park meet at Calder Race Course runs from late October until the first days of January, which approximates the traditional Tropical Park spot in the South Florida rotation. Starting in the late 1940s, Tropical operated from late November until mid-January.

Tropical Park first was a greyhound track and opened as a Thoroughbred track on December 26, 1931, in Coral Gables, a suburb southwest of Miami. The track was sold in 1941 and went through two ownership changes in the early 1950s. Tropical was host for the first Calder meeting in 1970 and for that season used an experimental, synthetic Tartan track, developed by Minnesota Mining and Manufacturing Co., inside the main, one-mile oval. Calder's investors, including 3M Chairman William L. McKnight, bought out Tropical with the intention of moving its dates to the new track. Tropical closed its gates for the last time on January 15, 1972, and was transformed into a municipal park. Several of Calder's graded stakes races are held in the Tropical Park meeting.

Tropical Park still maintains separate meet records from Calder for leading jockey, trainer, etc., though all track records are the same for both.

Location: 21001 NW. 27th Ave., Miami, FL 33055-0808
Phone: (305) 625-1311
Fax: (305) 620-2569
Seating capacity: 15,000
Number of stalls: 1,800

Officers
President: C. Kenneth Dunn
Vice President: Randall E. Soth
General Manager: Randall E. Soth

Racing Dates
2002: November 3, 2001 to January 2, 2002, 52 days
2003: October 25, 2003-January 2, 2004, 53 days

Track Layout
Main circumference: 1 mile
Main track chute: 1/4 mile, 7 furlongs
Main turf circumference: 7 furlongs
Main turf chute: 1/4 mile

Attendance
Highest single day record: 17,671, January 14, 1978
Highest single meet record: 514,496, 1979/1980
Record daily average for single meet: 10,324, 1975/1976
Total attendance recent meeting: 269,745, 2002/2003
Average daily recent meeting: 5,090, 2002/2003

Handle
Average all sources recent meeting: $5,955,875, 2002/2003
Average on-track recent meeting: $455,596, 2002/2003
Single day on-track handle: $2,793,767, January 1, 1989
Single day total handle all sources: $8,479,712, December 16, 1995
Total all sources recent meeting: $315,661,359, 2002/2003
Total on-track recent meeting: $24,146,568, 2002/2003

Mutuel Records
Highest win: $447.40, Skyline's Delight, December 23, 1986
Lowest Win: $2.20, Hold Your Peace, December 18, 1972
Highest Exacta: $10,837.20, December 18, 1988
Lowest Exacta: $4.80, December 18, 1972
Highest Trifecta: $52,398, January 6, 1979
Lowest Trifecta: $11.40, December 9, 1993
Highest Daily Double: $7,907.80, December 14, 1973
Lowest Daily Double: $6.40, April 18, 1992
Highest Pick 3: $28,275, December 21, 1993
Lowest Pick 3: $15.80, December 17, 1988
Highest Other Exotics: $68,684.20, Superfecta, November 16, 1996
Lowest Other Exotics: $37.80, Superfecta, November 16, 1995

Leaders
Career, leading jockey by stakes wins: Jacinto Vasquez, 23, Jose Santos, 23
Career, leading jockey by wins: Jacinto Vasquez, 456
Career, leading trainer by stakes wins: Luis Olivares, 18
Career, leading trainer by wins: Frank Gomez, 315
Recent meeting, leading jockey: Cornelio Velasquez, 84, 2002/2003
Recent meeting, leading owner: Michael Sherman, 26, 2002/2003
Recent meeting, leading trainer: Eddie Plesa Jr., 22, 2002/2003, Luis Olivares, 22, 2002/2003

Records
Single day jockey wins: Jacinto Vasquez, 6, December 22, 1990; Rene Douglas, 6, December 8, 1993; Javier Castellano, 6, December 31, 2000
Single meet, leading jockey by wins: Cornelio Velasquez, 84, 2002/2003

Fastest Times of 2002 (Dirt)
5 furlongs: Friendly Frolic, :58.03, December 16
5 1/2 furlongs: Misty Wager, 1:05.04, December 28
6 furlongs: Tour of the Cat, 1:10.18, November 16
6 1/2 furlongs: Forest Heiress, 1:17.04, December 29
7 furlongs: Built Up, 1:23.30, December 7
1 mile: High Ideal, 1:38.22, November 22
1 1/16 miles: Trust N Luck, 1:44.07, December 14
1 1/8 miles: The Judge Sez Who, 1:50.53, December 28
1 1/4 miles: Aeneas, 2:05.99, December 31

Fastest Times of 2002 (Turf)
5 furlongs: Wertz, :55.51, December 8
7 1/2 furlongs: Wander Mom, 1:27.82, November 9
1 mile: Stormy Pleasure, 1:34.61, October 31
1 1/16 miles: Madeira Mist (Ire), 1:40.47, November 9
1 1/8 miles: Krieger, 1:47.02, December 7
1 1/2 miles: Man From Wicklow, 2:28.05, December 28

Idaho

Les Bois Park

Located in Boise on the Western Idaho Fairgrounds, Les Bois Park is one of the largest racetracks in the Northwest and annually holds the Idaho Cup for state-bred Thoroughbreds, Quarter Horses, Paints, and Appaloosas. Operating since May 1970, Les Bois, which is French for "the woods," opened six years after pari-mutuel wagering was legalized in Idaho. The track had difficult times in the late 1980s, when a downturn in horse racing caused the track owners, the Ada County Commission, to put the Les Bois lease up for auction. A group of horsemen led by veterinarian Chris Christian won the lease for $100 per month and successfully lobbied for full-card simulcasting, which turned the track around and allowed it to increase its purses. In April 2002, the track was sold to former college and professional basketball player Arnell Jones and his wife, Lanae. The track races Thoroughbreds, Quarter Horses, Appaloosas, and Paints from early May to mid-August. Les Bois was the launching pad for Racing Hall of Fame jockey Gary Stevens, who scored his first career victory there aboard Little Star in 1979.

Location: 5610 Glenwood Rd., Boise, ID 83714
Phone: (208) 376-3991
Fax: (208) 378-4032
Web site: *http://www.lesboispark.org*
Inaugural meeting: May 1970
Year founded: 1970 (current location)
Abbreviation: Boi
Number of stalls: 864
Seating capacity: 4,100

Officers
President: Arnell Jones
Vice President: Lanae Jones
Director of Racing: Duayne Didericksen
Racing Secretary: Roger White
Director of Marketing: Kassie Cerami
Director of Simulcasting: Ron Andreoli
Director of Admissions: Billie Madison
Director of Mutuels: Diana Fairchild
Track Announcer: Greg Culver
Track Photographer: Paula Hoopes

Track Layout
Main circumference: 6 furlongs
Main length of stretch: 220 yards
Main track chute: 440 yards
Main width: 70 feet

Racing Dates
2002: May 4-August 11, 45 days
2003: May 3 to August 10, 46 days

Leaders
Recent meeting, leading jockey: Clark Jones, 59, 2002
Recent meeting, leading trainer: Keith Bennett, 37, 2002
Recent meeting, leading owner: Tawnja Elison, 7, 2002

Handle
Average all sources recent meeting: $98,402, 2002
Average on-track recent meeting: $43,564, 2002
Record daily average for single meet: $147,903
Single day on-track handle: $286,202
Total on-track recent meeting: $2,047,522, 2002

Fastest Times of 2002
2 furlongs: Mr. Rob, :23.93, May 18
4 1/2 furlongs: Twice Deceived, :52.98, May 27
5 furlongs: Top Arazi, :56.97, July 17
6 1/2 furlongs: Better Choice, 1:18.24, May 4
7 furlongs: Mr Motion, 1:23.93, July 20
7 1/2 furlongs: Erhard, 1:29.95, July 4
1 mile: Quiet Syns, 1:37.30, July 4
1 1/4 miles: Northern Ricky, 2:07.75, August 11

Pocatello Downs
Location: 10588 Fairgrounds Rd., Pocatello, ID 83204
Phone: (208) 238-1721
Fax: (208) 238-1763
Abbreviation: PoD

Racing Dates
2003: May 17-June 8, 9 days

Rupert Downs
Location: P.O. Box 263, Rupert, ID 83350
Abbreviation: Rup

Racing Dates
2003: June 28-July 6

Illinois

Arlington Park

Arlington Park first opened on October 13, 1927, and has been home to many firsts in Thoroughbred racing. Located northwest of Chicago in Arlington Heights, the track became the first in Illinois to offer turf races in 1934. In 1966, Laffit Pincay Jr. recorded his first United States victory there on his way to a place in the Racing Hall of Fame and a record 9,530 victories. In 1981, Arlington became the world's first track to host a million-dollar race for Thoroughbreds when it inaugurated the Arlington Million (G1). The first running was won by John Henry, who returned to win the race in 1984. Today, the Million is part of Arlington's International Festival of Racing, which also includes the Beverly D. (G1) and Secretariat (G1) Stakes. On July 31, 1985, fire destroyed Arlington's clubhouse, causing the track to shift most of its remaining races to Hawthorne Race Course. The exception was the Million, which was held on August 25 at Arlington, and more than 35,000 fans watched the race from tents and temporary facilities. Those efforts led to Arlington becoming the first racetrack to earn an Eclipse Award. Arlington was rebuilt lavishly by Chicago-area industrialist Richard Duchossois, who closed the track for two seasons—1998 and '99—due to unfavorable economic and regulatory conditions. Arlington reopened in 2000 and the Arlington Million was resumed. Also in 2000, Churchill Downs Inc. purchased the track and assumed about $80-million in loans, while Duchossis received close to 4-million shares of common stock in Churchill.

Location: 2200 W. Euclid Ave., Arlington Heights, IL 60004
Phone: (847) 385-7500
Fax: (847) 385-7251
Web site: *http://www.arlingtonpark.com*
Year founded: 1926
Inaugural meeting: October 13, 1927
Abbreviation: AP
Seating capacity: 35,000
Number of stalls: 2,140

Officers
Chairman: Richard Duchossois
President: Clifford Goodrich
Vice President of Racing and Operations: Frank Gabriel Jr.

Director of Racing: William A. Thayer Jr.
Racing Secretary: Frank Gabriel Jr.
Director of Operations: Gil Carmichael
Director of Admissions: Bill Adams
Director of Communications: Dan Leary
Director of Finance: Michael Cody
Director of Marketing: Keith Darby
Director of Mutuels: Jack Lisowski
Director of Publicity: Dan Leary
Director of Simulcasting: Marc Anderson
Track Announcer: John G. Dooley
Track Superintendent: Javier Barajas

Racing Dates

2002: June 5-October 27, 107 days
2003: May 9-September 27, 104 days

Track Layout

Main circumference: 1 1/8 miles
Main track chute: 1 mile
Main width: 90 feet
Main length of stretch: 1,049 feet
Main turf circumference: 1 mile
Main turf width: 150 feet
Main turf chute: 1 mile
Main turf length of stretch: 1,020 feet
Training track: 5 furlongs

Attendance

Average daily recent meeting: 6,663, 2002
Highest single day record: 50,638, July 4, 1938
Total attendance recent meeting: 712,952, 2002

Handle

Average all sources recent meeting: $3,909,831, 2002
Average on-track recent meeting: $578,079, 2002
Single day total handle all sources: $108,513,107, October 26, 2002
Single day on-track handle: $13,568,209, October 26, 2002
Total all sources recent meeting: $522,955,208, 2002
Total on-track recent meeting: $74,844,558, 2002

Mutuel Records

Highest Daily Double: $3,835.20, July 5, 1939
Highest Exacta: $6267, August 7, 1991
Highest Other Exotics: $16,349.30, Pick 5, October 26, 2002, $2,701, Quinella, September 3, 2000, $52,686, Superfecta, August 13, 1995
Highest Pick 3: $21,775.40, June 11, 1990
Highest Pick 6: $269,253.60, September 25, 1984
Highest Trifecta: $58,116.20, September 14, 2001
Highest win: $382, Ivalinda, August 12, 1963

Leaders

Recent meeting, leading trainer: Jerry Hollendorfer, 41, 2001
Career, leading jockey by titles: Earlie Fires, 6
Career, leading owner by titles: Calumet Farm, 9
Career, leading trainer by titles: Richard Hazelton, 8; William Hal Bishop, 8
Career, leading jockey by stakes wins: Earlie Fires, 100
Career, leading owner by stakes wins: Calumet Farm, 58
Career, leading trainer by stakes wins: Harry Trotsek, 45
Career, leading jockey by wins: Earlie Fires, 2,709
Career, leading trainer by wins: Richard Hazelton, 1,114
Recent meeting, leading jockey: Rene R. Douglas, 167, 2002
Recent meeting, leading owner: Frank Calabrese, 66, 2002
Recent meeting, leading trainer: Wayne M. Catalano, 64, 2002

Records

Single meet, leading jockey by wins: Shane Sellers, 219, 1991
Single meet, leading trainer by wins: Wayne Catalano, 64, 2002
Single meet, leading owner by wins: Frank Calabrese, 66, 2002
Single day jockey wins: Pat Day, 8, September 13, 1989

Track Records, Main Dirt

4 1/2 furlongs: Wheat Penny, :51.64, June 8, 2000, Bold America, :51.64, June 28, 2002
5 furlongs: Staunch Avenger, :57 1/5, June 29, 1970; Heisanative, :57 1/5, June 12, 1971; Shecky Greene, :57 1/5, June 15, 1972
5 1/2 furlongs: Hey That's Great, 1:02.60, June 27, 1992
6 furlongs: Taylor's Special, 1:08, August 22, 1986
6 1/2 furlongs: Pentelicus, 1:14 1/5, July 14, 1990
7 furlongs: Tumiga, 1:20 2/5, July 13, 1968
7 1/2 furlongs: I'll Raise You One, 1:28 4/5, August 3, 1987
1 mile: Dr. Fager, 1:32 1/5, August 24, 1968
1 mile 70 yards: Geo. Groom, 1:42 4/5, October 25, 1927
1 1/16 miles: Kindly Manner, 1:41 2/5, August 22, 1977; Mojave, 1:41 2/5, June 30, 1981
1 1/8 miles: Spectacular Bid, 1:46 1/5, July 19, 1980
1 3/16 miles: Royal Glint, 1:55 4/5, August 30, 1975
1 1/4 miles: Private Thoughts, 1:59 2/5, August 20, 1977
1 3/8 miles: Playdale, 2:15 2/5, July 19, 1932
1 1/2 miles: El Misterio, 2:15 2/5, September 5, 1960
1 5/8 miles: Fool's Robbery, 2:45 3/5, July 5, 1973
1 3/4 miles: *Deux-Moulins, 2:59 2/5, July 14, 1955
2 miles: Swede of Norfolk, 3:26 2/5, August 15, 1970
Other: 1 5/16 miles, Evanescent, 2:10, July 18, 1993; 1 5/16 miles, Rush Home, 2:10, August 7, 1971; 2 1/4 miles, *Djem, 4:05 3/5, July 30, 1953

Course Records, Main Turf

5 furlongs: Ghost Power, :56.37, October 8, 1993
5 1/2 furlongs: Chief Sun Dance, 1:02 3/5, July 6, 1970
1 mile: Gee Can He Dance, 1:34 2/5, September 4, 1995
1 mile 70 yards: Pass the Brandy, 1:38 4/5, July 25, 1970
1 1/16 miles: Zeeruler, 1:41, September 7, 1992
1 1/8 miles: Mr. Leader, 1:47 2/5, July 4, 1970; World Class Splash, 1:47.40, July 11, 1992
1 3/16 miles: Reluctant Guest, 1:53 1/5, September 1, 1990
1 1/4 miles: Awad, 1:58.69, August 27, 1995
1 1/2 miles: Cetewayo, 2:27.50, July 6, 2002
1 5/8 miles: Coincident, 2:45, July 26, 1951
1 3/4 miles: *Pennsburg, 3:02 3/5, July 5, 1941
2 miles: Penaway, 3:25 2/5, July 24, 1953
Other: 2 1/16 miles, *Deux-Moulins, 3:30 4/5, July 28, 1955; 2 1/8 miles, English Harry, 3:45, July 30, 1941

Interesting Facts

Previous name and dates: Arlington International Racecourse, 1989-2000
Achievements/milestones: July 31, 1985, destroyed by fire; June 28, 1989, reopened

Fastest Times of 2002 (Dirt)

4 1/2 furlongs: Bold America, :51.64, June 28
5 furlongs: Zarb's Magic, :57.31, September 7
5 1/2 furlongs: Aloha Bold, 1:02.80, July 21
6 furlongs: Orientate, 1:08.89, October 24
6 1/2 furlongs: Meadowmore, 1:15.38, August 23
7 furlongs: Talknow, 1:21.80, June 30
1 mile: There's Zealous, 1:33.76, August 17
1 1/8 miles: Azeri, 1:48.64, October 26
1 3/16 miles: Tenpins, 1:55.07, September 29
1 1/4 miles: Volponi, 2:01.39, October 26
1 1/2 miles: Tricky Mocha, 2:33.22, October 18

Fastest Times of 2002 (Turf)

5 furlongs: My Girl Lisa, :57.81, September 14
About 5 furlongs: Man o' Rhythm, :58.86, October 6
5 1/2 furlongs: Abderian (Ire), 1:03.53, October 27
1 mile: Al's Dearly Bred, 1:35.13, September 8
About 1 mile: Attico, 1:35.88, October 23; Purplest, 1:35.88, October 10
1 1/16 miles: Mr. Mellon, 1:41.95, June 29
About 1 1/16 miles: Go for Puddin, 1:42.85, October 11
1 1/8 miles: G All Day, 1:49.37, August 31
About 1 1/8 miles: Kiss the Devil, 1:50.11, August 8
1 3/16 miles: Golden Apples (Ire), 1:54.86, August 17
1 1/4 miles: Beat Hollow (GB), 2:02.94, August 17
1 1/2 miles: Cetewayo, 2:27.50, July 6
About 1 1/2 miles: Showing Your Stuff, 2:32.16, August 2

Fairmount Park

Fairmount Park, located in Collinsville, Illinois, about 30 minutes east of St. Louis, opened on September 26, 1925. The track was built to resemble a small Churchill Downs by Col. E. R. Bradley, who owned four Kentucky Derby winners, and Col. Matt Winn, who made the Kentucky Derby at Churchill a sporting institution. In 1947, Fairmount became the first one-mile oval racetrack in the world to provide lighting for night Thoroughbred racing. Fairmount's most famous horseman is jockey Dave Gall, who retired in 1999 with 7,396 wins, placing him among Thoroughbred racing's winningest jockeys. Fairmount, which has been owned since 1969 by Ogden Services Corp., has struggled to compete against riverboat gambling casinos throughout the St. Louis area.

Location: 9301 Collinsville Rd., Collinsville, IL 62234
Phone: (618) 345-4303
Fax: (618) 344-8218
E-mail: fmtpark@fairmountpark.com
Web site: http://www.fairmountpark.com
Inaugural meeting: September 26, 1925
Acreage: 190
Number of stalls: 1,080
Seating capacity: 3,420

Officers
General Manager: Brian F. Zander
Racing Secretary: Bobby Pace
Director of Mutuels: Mike Heidemann
Director of Publicity: John Slone
Director of Simulcasting: Greg Graves
Other officials: Linda Schwaegel, Group Sales Director

Racing Dates
2002: April 12-October 19, 110 days
2003: April 4-October 18

Track Layout
Main circumference: 1 mile
Main track chutes: 1 1/4 miles, 6 furlongs
Main width: 80 feet
Main length of stretch: 1,050 feet

Leaders
Recent meeting, leading jockey: Thomas L. Pompell, 129, 2002
Recent meeting, leading trainer: Ralph Martinez, 123, 2002

Track Records, Main Dirt
4 furlongs: Aledo, :45.60, June 2, 1994
4 1/2 furlongs: Vague Promise, :51 3/5, May 19, 1978
5 furlongs: Slight in the Rear, :56 4/5, July 25, 1989
5 1/2 furlongs: Sarof Jr., 1:03 2/5, June 5, 1980
6 furlongs: Ye Country, 1:08 3/5, November 26, 1977
1 mile: Dusty Appeal, 1:37.40, June 20, 1992
1 mile 70 yards: Dusty Appeal, 1:39 4/5, July 30, 1989
1 1/16 miles: Lt. Lao, 1:40 4/5, July 22, 1989
1 1/8 miles: Andover Man, 1:47 3/5, August 26, 1989
1 1/4 miles: Leaddrop, 2:03, July 2, 1989
1 1/2 miles: *Firth of Tay, 2:33, September 21, 1927
1 5/8 miles: Monthazar, 2:46, November 3, 1973
1 3/4 miles: Lightin Bill, 3:02 4/5, October 14, 1939
2 miles: East Royalty, 3:32.60, December 1, 1991
Other: 2 furlongs, Fantan Sam, :21 2/5, November 22, 1989; 2 miles 70 yds, King Boogie, 3:33 3/5, September 1, 1984; 2 1/16 miles, Tim Trefle, 3:38 4/5, September 10, 1983; 2 1/8 miles, Lucrest, 3:46 1/5, September 24, 1983; 2 1/4 miles, Baye Dawn, 4:00, October 8, 1983; 2 1/2 miles, Cat Walk, 4:29, October 22, 1983

Fastest Times of 2002
2 furlongs: Sammy the Champ, :21.40, April 12
4 furlongs: Glit, :45.80, April 13
4 1/2 furlongs: Irish Love, :52.80, May 21
5 furlongs: Tic N Tin, :58.20, April 12
5 1/2 furlongs: Tic N Tin, 1:03.60, May 21
6 furlongs: Silver Bid, 1:10.40, August 24
1 mile: Baker Road, 1:38.20, October 1; Nantucketeer, 1:38.20, October 5
1 mile 70 yards: Roberto Royale, 1:42.40, May 18
1 1/16 miles: Go Gavin Go, 1:46.60, June 11

Hawthorne Race Course

For nearly 100 years, members of the Carey family have overseen Hawthorne Race Course in the Chicago suburbs of Cicero and Stickney. In 1909, Thomas Carey bought the track from horseman and noted gambler Ed Corrigan, who had opened the track in 1891. Under Corrigan's ownership, Hawthorne closed when the state Senate banned racing in Chicago in 1905, and new owner Carey attempted over the next several years to revive racing. He finally was successful in 1922. In 1928, the track's most notable race, the Hawthorne Gold Cup (G2), debuted. Among the winners of the Hawthorne Gold Cup are five-time Horse of the Year Kelso, 1968 Horse of the Year Dr. Fager, and 1991 Horse of the Year Black Tie Affair (Ire). In 1977, a fire destroyed Hawthorne's grandstand, and the remainder of its meet was held at Sportsman's Park, located a block away. Racing returned to the track in 1980. Over the years, Hawthorne has conducted harness racing, and meets for Standardbreds were held in 2002 and 2003. Late in 2002, Hawthorne merged with Sportsman's, with Thomas F. Carey III becoming president of the new entity, Hawthorne National.

Location: 3501 S. Laramie Ave., Cicero, IL 60804
Phone: (708) 780-3700
Fax: (708) 780-3677
E-mail: thomas.carey3@mindspring.com
Web site: http://www.hawthorneracecourse.com
Year founded: 1890, by Edward Corrigan
Inaugural meeting: May 20, 1891
Acreage: 119
Number of stalls: 2,400
Seating capacity: 18,000

Officers
President: Thomas F. Carey
General Manager: Thomas F. Carey
Director of Racing: Gary M. Duch
Racing Secretary: Gary M. Duch
Director of Operations: Thomas F. Carey III
Director of Admissions: Mike Harris
Director of Communications: Jim Miller
Director of Marketing: Howie Fagan
Director of Mutuels: Michael P. Hart
Director of Publicity: Jim Miller
Director of Sales: Pam Dorr
Director of Simulcasting: Lorene Heninger
Horsemen's Liaison: Eric Viox
Stewards: Eddie Arroyo, Joe Lindeman, Larry Hill, Steve Morgan
Track Announcer: Peter Galassi
Track Photographer: Four Footed Fotos
Track Superintendents: Gregorio Cardenas, Roosevelt Lomax

Racing Dates
2002: May 5-June 4, 23 days; November 1-December 31, 43 days
2003: March 1-May 8, September 28-December 31

Track Layout

Main circumference: 1 mile
Main track chute: 6 1/2 furlongs
Main width: 75 feet
Main length of stretch: 1,320 feet
Main turf circumference: 7 furlongs 148 feet

Attendance

Highest single day record: 37,792, September 6, 1937

Handle

Average all sources recent meeting: $2,086,087, Spring-2002, $2,854,176, Fall-2002
Average on-track recent meeting: $232,527, Fall-2002, $245,800, Spring-2002
Record daily average for single meet: $3,575,861, 1996
Single day on-track handle: $10,300,640, May 5, 2001

Leaders

Career, leading jockey by wins: Earlie Fires, 1,117
Recent meeting, leading jockey: Chris Emigh, 46, Fall-2002, Shane Laviolette, 19, Spring-2002
Recent meeting, leading owner: Hondo Ranch, 8, Fall-2002, Lothenbach Stables, 5, Spring-2002, Louis O'Brien, 8, Fall-2002, Louis Roussel III, 5, Spring-2002
Recent meeting, leading trainer: Mike Reavis, 34, Fall-2002, Tom Tomillo, 13, Spring-2002

Records

Single day jockey wins: Johnny Heckman, 7, October 1, 1956
Single day trainer wins: Mike Reavis, 5, November 2, 2002
Single meet, leading trainer by wins: Richard Hazelton, 48, 1976

Track Records, Main Dirt

4 1/2 furlongs: Joanies Bella, :51.80, May 28, 2001
5 furlongs: De La Concorde, :57, November 11, 1992
5 1/2 furlongs: Marluel's Troy, 1:02 2/5, November 2, 1976
6 furlongs: Satan's Poppy, 1:08 1/5, October 21, 1978
6 1/2 furlongs: Dee Lance, 1:14 2/5, August 27, 1988
1 mile: Actuary, 1:37 1/5, July 17, 1923; Hopeless, 1:37 1/5, August 29, 1925
1 mile 70 yards: Soldat Bleu, 1:39 1/5, July 27, 1988
1 1/16 miles: Sensitive Prince, 1:39 3/5, September 23, 1978
1 1/8 miles: *Zografos, 1:46 3/5, October 9, 1974
3 1/16 miles: Lindy's Lad, 1:59 2/5, November 12, 1980
1 1/4 miles: Gladwin, 1:58 4/5, October 1, 1970; Group Plan, 1:58 4/5, October 19, 1974
1 1/2 miles: David, 2:29 3/5, October 1, 1969
1 5/8 miles: Viale (Uru), 2:47, December 10, 2000
1 3/4 miles: America Fore, 3:02 1/5, October 2, 1943
Other: 2 furlongs, Minty Flavors, :20.88, May 14, 1999; 1 13/16 miles, Stiffelio (Ire), 3:14.60, November 15, 1997; 2 miles 70 yds, Sun N Shine, 3:30 2/5, October 19, 1974

Course Records, Main Turf

5 furlongs: Sulemark, :56, October 25, 1992
7 furlongs: Glassy Dip, 1:22 3/5, May 30, 1977
7 1/2 furlongs: Joey Jr., 1:27 1/5, November 5, 1989
1 mile: Soviet Line (Ire), 1:33.40, July 25, 1998
1 1/16 miles: Bendecida, 1:40.53, September 6, 1999
1 1/8 miles: Rainbows for Life, 1:44 3/5, October 13, 1991
1 3/16 miles: Royal Glint, 1:54 2/5, September 28, 1974; Sari's Baba, 1:54 2/5, September 24, 1985
1 1/4 miles: Pass the Line, 2:00 2/5, August 10, 1985
1 3/8 miles: Shayzari (Ire), 2:15 1/5, September 3, 1988
1 1/2 miles: Lord Comet, 2:26.87, October 27, 1999
1 3/4 miles: Neverest, 2:58 4/5, August 31, 1973

Interesting Facts

Trivia: First major U.S. track to use an electric timer (1931). Track announcer Phil Georgeff entered the Guinness Book of World Records when he called his 85,000th race on August 13, 1988.

Fastest Times of 2002 (Dirt)

4 1/2 furlongs: Twitch N Shout, :52.83, May 19
6 furlongs: Lively Minister, 1:08.61, December 28
6 1/2 furlongs: Silver Bid, 1:14.87, November 27
1 mile 70 yards: Bella Villa, 1:40.24, November 27
1 1/16 miles: Wild Lies, 1:41.56, November 28
1 1/8 miles: Nosetothe, 1:51.98, December 6
1 3/16 miles: Alfayiz, 2:00.58, December 7
1 1/4 miles: Hail The Chief (GB), 2:02.80, May 18
1 5/8 miles: Alfayiz, 2:48.70, December 21

Fastest Times of 2002 (Turf)

5 furlongs: My Girl Lisa, :56.30, November 16
1 mile: Purplest, 1:34.37, June 1
1 1/16 miles: Crowd Watcher, 1:40.87, June 2
1 1/8 miles: Private Bound, 1:48.03, June 1
1 1/2 miles: Game Bird, 2:30.05, November 16

Sportsman's Park

Sportsman's Park closed its gates in 2002 after agreeing to a merger with nearby Hawthorne Race Course. The track fell victim to an ill-fated reconstruction as a joint-use auto and horse track, and the site was to be sold and developed. Located in Cicero, Sportsman's had a history as rich and raucous as the near-southwest Chicago suburb where it was located. Cicero, known for its bare-knuckles politics and mob connections, was the site of the Hawthorne Kennel Club, an illegal greyhound track controlled by the Al Capone mob in the early 1930s. Sportsman's opened as a horse track property on May 2, 1932, under the banner of the National Jockey Club. The track's first president was Edward J. O'Hare, a lawyer and Capone associate; O'Hare, who informed on Capone, was gunned down in 1939. Chicago's principal airport, was named for his son, an ace pilot killed in the Pacific in World War II.

Charles Bidwill Sr., owner of the Chicago Cardinals (now Arizona) football team, served as Sportsman's managing director until his death in 1947. His son Charles W. "Stormy" Bidwill Jr. became Sportsman's president in 1967, and the eldest Bidwill's grandson, Charles W. Bidwill III, became the track's president in '95. Sportsman's track, which had been extended to five furlongs in 1956, was further extended to seven furlongs in '92. The track's principal race was the Illinois Derby (G2) for three-year-olds, which was first run at Sportsman's in 1963. The race was won in 2002 by eventual Kentucky Derby (G1) winner War Emblem.

Location: 3301 S. Laramie Ave., Cicero, IL 60804
Phone: (773) 242-1121
Fax: (773) 242-0775
Web site: http://www.sportsmanspark.com
Year founded: 1932
Number of stalls: 1,900
Seating capacity: 65,000

Officers

President: Charles W. Bidwill III
Vice President: Terry Hart
General Manager: H. Eddie Arroyo
Racing Secretary: Allan Plever
Treasurer: Michael Bidwell
Director of Operations: Bill Duffy

Director of Communications: Christian Polzin
Stakes Coordinator: Dan Leary
Director of Finance: Jeff Kras
Director of Mutuels: Michael Hart
Director of Publicity: John Brokopp
Director of Sales: Sandy Reinhart
Director of Simulcasting: Rhonda Sosnowski
Horsemen's Liaison: P. J. Mudro
Stewards: Eddie Arroyo, Joseph Lindeman, Larry Hill, Steve Morgan
Track Announcer: John G. Dooley
Track Photographer: Four-Footed Fotos
Track Superintendent: Albert Jozwiak

Racing Dates
2002: March 1-May 4, 46 days
2003: March 1-May 8

Track Layout
Main circumference: 7 furlongs
Main length of stretch: 1,463 feet

Leaders
Career, leading jockey by titles: Tony Skoronski, 11
Career, leading jockey by wins: Randall Meier, 1,074
Career, leading trainer by titles: Richard Hazelton, 20
Recent meeting, leading jockey: Larry Sterling Jr., 57, 2002
Recent meeting, leading trainer: Mike Reavis, 36, 2002

Records
Single meet, leading jockey by wins: Mark Guidry, 134, 1992
Single meet, leading trainer by wins: Richard Hazelton, 59, 1981
Single day jockey wins: Chris Valovich, 4, March 11, 2001; Randall Meier, 4, April 1, 2001

Track Records, Main Dirt
5 furlongs: Hez Comin Thru, :58.06, March 3, 2001
5 1/2 furlongs: Faultless Appeal, 1:03.78, April 8, 2001
6 furlongs: Linear, 1:08.85, March 26, 1994
6 1/2 furlongs: Bold Favorite, 1:15 2/5, October 2, 1971
1 mile: Tabasco Cid, 1:36, March 30, 1994
1 1/16 miles: Humble Eight, 1:42.29, June 3, 1995
1 1/8 miles: Wild Rush, 1:47.51, May 10, 1997
1 3/8 miles: Skinny C., 2:17 3/5, May 27, 1974
1 5/8 miles: Ball Hawk, 2:48 2/5, October 24, 1956
2 miles: Tri for Charlie, 3:37 3/5, May 8, 1990
Other: 2 furlongs, Nervous Moment, :20.98, June 8, 1998; 1 7/16 miles, Theoretic, 2:24 1/5, October 15, 1973; 1 9/16 miles, Well Lit, 2:35.77, April 25, 1992

Fastest Times of 2002
5 furlongs: Uwana Prop, :58.23, March 2
5 1/2 furlongs: Gold Taker, 1:04.14, March 1
6 furlongs: Talknow, 1:09.56, April 5
1 mile: Talknow, 1:37.26, March 10
1 1/16 miles: Fact Not Fiction, 1:44.21, April 11
1 1/8 miles: War Emblem, 1:49.92, April 6

Indiana

Hoosier Park

In 1989, Indiana approved pari-mutuel wagering, and the state's first pari-mutuel racetrack, Hoosier Park, opened its inaugural season of Standardbred racing in 1994. Thoroughbred racing debuted at Hoosier in 1995. Located northeast of Indianapolis in Anderson, Indiana, the $10-million track was developed by majority owner Churchill Downs Inc. as the company's first racing interest outside Kentucky. Hoosier annually holds a Thoroughbred meet, which includes a limited number of Quarter Horse races, and a season for Standardbreds. For 2003, Hoosier hosted two graded stakes, the $300,000 Indiana Breeders' Cup Oaks (G3) and its richest event, the $400,000 Indiana Derby (G3). A competitor, Indiana Downs, opened on April 1, 2003, only 40 miles from its facility.

Location: 4500 Dan Patch Circle, Anderson, IN 46013
Phone: (765) 642-7223
Fax: (765) 644-0467
E-mail: info@hoosierpark.com
Web site: http://www.hoosierpark.com
Year founded: 1994
Inaugural meeting: September 1-October 28, 1995
Acreage: 105
Seating capacity: 15,000
Number of stalls: 980

Officers
President: Richard B. Moore
Vice President: Don R. Richardson
General Manager: Richard B. Moore
Director of Racing: Warren Groce
Racing Secretary: Warren Groce
Secretary: Rebecca C. Reed
Treasurer: Steven L. Wilkening
Director of Operations: Kevin Mack
Director of Admissions: Sue Walters
Director of Communications: Thomas F. Bannon
Director of Finance: Steven L. Wilkening
Director of Marketing: Donna Smith
Director of Mutuels: Randy Westerman
Director of Publicity: Tammy Knox
Director of Simulcasting: Joy Narducci
Horsemen's Liaison: Kitty Bonham
Stewards: Gary Wilfert, Mike Manganello
Track Announcer: Steve Cross
Track Photographer: Jim Linscott
Track Superintendent: John Betts
Other officials: Jim Garrett, Director of Group/Guest Services

Racing Dates
2002: August 29-December 1, 70 days
2003: August 29-December 4, 70 days

Track Layout
Main circumference: 7 furlongs
Main track chute: 6 furlongs
Main width: 90 feet
Main length of stretch: 1,255 feet

Attendance
Average daily recent meeting: 967, 2002
Highest single day record: 10,827, October 7, 2000
Highest single meet record: 95,468, 1995
Lowest single meet record: 65,750, 1996
Record daily average for single meet: 2,273, 1995
Total attendance recent meeting: 65,756, 2002

Handle
Single day on-track handle: $1,085,338, November 17, 1996
Average all sources recent meeting: $1,275,901, 2002
Average on-track recent meeting: $93,003, 2002
Record daily average for single meet: $1,221,931, 2000
Total all sources recent meeting: $86,761,283, 2002
Total on-track recent meeting: $6,324,204, 2002

Mutuel Records
Highest win: $200, Mandingo, September 26, 1997
Highest Exacta: $3,212.60, September 10, 2000
Highest Trifecta: $24,911.90, December 1, 2000
Highest Daily Double: $1,988.80, September 22, 1998

Highest Pick 3: $4,095.20, November 13, 1999
Highest Other Exotics: $13,584.40, Superfecta, October 15, 1999

Leaders

Career, leading trainer by titles: Stanley Roberts, 2
Career, leading jockey by stakes wins: Jon Court, 9
Career, leading jockey by titles: Jon Court, 3
Career, leading jockey by wins: Jon Court, 386
Career, leading owner by titles: Highway 1 Racing Stable, 2; Michael Bruder, 2
Career, leading owner by wins: Highway 1 Racing Stable, 66
Career, leading trainer by stakes wins: Dale Romans, 13
Career, leading trainer by wins: Stanley Roberts, 86
Recent meeting, leading jockey: Lester Knight, 84, 2002
Recent meeting, leading owner: Gary Patrick, 32, 2002
Recent meeting, leading trainer: Gary Patrick, 33, 2002

Records

Single day jockey wins: Jon Court, 6, September 24, 1998; Jon Court, 6, November 24, 1998; Mike Morgan, 6, December 5, 1999
Single day trainer wins: David Pate, 3, October 11, 1995; Bernie Flint, 3, November 4, 1995; Kathleen Cooper, 3, September 20, 1996; Stephen Dunn, 3, September 14, 1997; Stanley Roberts, 3, October 2, 1998; Barbara McBride, 3, September 14, 1999; Stanley Roberts, 3, October 29, 1999; Stanley Roberts, 3, September 22, 2000
Single meet, leading jockey by wins: Terry Thompson, 122, 2001
Single meet, leading owner by wins: Highway 1 Racing Stable, 29
Single meet, leading trainer by wins: Ray Stifano, 39, 2000

Track Records, Main Dirt

5 1/2 furlongs: Chukker Creek, 1:02.20, November 24, 1996; Moro Oro, 1:02.20, September 20, 1996
6 furlongs: Moro Oro, 1:07.40, November 16, 1996
1 mile: Vic's Rebel, 1:33.40, October 13, 1998
1 1/16 miles: Alydar's Rib, 1:41, November 1, 1996
1 5/8 miles: Open Space, 2:41.20, November 16, 1996
Other: 1 9/16 miles, Our Forbes, 2:39.20, November 7, 1997; 1 7/8 miles, Raw New, 3:16.20, December 1, 2000

Fastest Times of 2002

5 1/2 furlongs: Run Little Richie, 1:04.33, October 14
6 furlongs: Solingen, 1:10.18, September 30
1 mile: Crafty Shaw, 1:35.69, November 16
1 1/16 miles: Perfect Drift, 1:43.50, October 5
1 9/16 miles: Dr. Robbie, 2:47.99, October 25
1 5/8 miles: Brass Music, 2:52.77, November 8
1 7/8 miles: Forty Karats Jade, 3:22.80, November 22

Indiana Downs

Located in Shelbyville, about 40 miles southeast of Indianapolis, Indiana Downs held its inaugural Thoroughbred meet in 2003, operating from April 11 to May 26. Construction of the $35-million track was opposed vigorously by Hoosier Park, but the red-and-white grandstand facility opened on schedule for its inaugural 2002 Standardbred meet. The track owned by Oliver Racing LLC and LHT Capital LLC has battled back against Hoosier, which is managed by Churchill Downs Inc. Indiana Downs opened its first off-track betting facility in February 2003 in Evansville, near Churchill-owned Ellis Park, and in April 2003 proposed another OTB across the river from Louisville after Hoosier opposed an Indiana Downs OTB in Indianapolis. For 2003, Indiana Downs and Hoosier were to split the state subsidy generated by a tax on riverboat admissions.

Location: 4200 N. Michigan Road, Shelbyville, IN 46176
Phone: (317) 421-0000
Web site: http://www.indianadowns.com
Inaugural Meet: April 11-May 26, 2003

Officers

Vice President and General Manager: Jon Schuster

Track layout

Main track circumference: One mile
Turf course: 7 furlongs

Iowa

Prairie Meadows Racetrack

The Thoroughbred industry in Iowa received a boost when Prairie Meadows Racetrack in Altoona, not far from Des Moines, opened in 1989. But financial difficulties forced the track to file for bankruptcy in 1991 and to close for live racing in '92. The following year, Prairie Meadows became the property of Polk County, which today leases the facility to the nonprofit Racing Association of Central Iowa. The track's future was secured in 1995 when slot machines were installed, with a portion of revenues significantly increasing race purses. Today, Prairie Meadows's live racing schedule begins with a Thoroughbred meet that is followed by a mixed meet for Thoroughbreds and Quarter Horses, and concludes with a harness racing season. One of the track's most popular events is the Iowa Classic, a ten-race event for state-bred Thoroughbreds and Quarter Horses. Prairie Meadows's lone Thoroughbred graded stakes is the Prairie Meadows Cornhusker Breeders' Cup Handicap (G3), the track's richest race.

Location: 1 Prairie Meadows Dr., Altoona, IA 50009-0901
Phone: (515) 967-1000
Fax: (515) 967-1344
E-mail: racinginfo@prairiemeadows.com
Web site: http://www.prairiemeadows.com
Inaugural meeting: March 1, 1989-March 15, 1989
Year founded: July 19, 1984
Abbreviation: PrM
Acreage: 233
Seating capacity: 7,000
Number of stalls: 1,350

Officers

President: Robert A. Farinella
Vice President: Gary Palmer
General Manager: Robert A. Farinella
Director of Racing: Derron Heldt
Racing Secretary: Pat Pope
Director of Operations: Don McGlory, Gary Palmer
Director of Marketing: Tom Manning
Director of Mutuels: Dorine Lawrence
Director of Publicity: Mary Lou Day-Coady
Director of Simulcasting: Matt Kingdon
Horsemen's Liaison: Chuck Schott
Stewards: Dick Garrison, Johnnie Johnson, Ralph D'Amico
Track Announcer: Ken Miller
Track Photographer: Jack Coady Jr.
Track Superintendent: Robert Beaubien
Other officials: Ron Morden, Vice President of Finance

Racing Dates
2002: April 26-July 6, 53 days; July 15-September 28, 45 days
2003: April 25-July 4, July 5-September 13

Track Layout
Main circumference: 1 mile
Main track chutes: 2 furlongs, 6 furlongs
Main length of stretch: 990 feet
Main width: 90' homestretch, 60' backstretch
Training track: 5/8 mile

Attendance
Average daily recent meeting: 8,801, Spring 2002, 9,105, Fall 2002
Total attendance recent meeting: 409,736, Fall 2002, 466,442, Spring 2002

Handle
Average all sources recent meeting: $631,017, Summer-Fall 2002, $820,867, Spring 2002
Average on-track recent meeting: $62,136, Summer/Fall 2002, $81,609, Spring 2002
Single day on-track handle: $488,070, May 5, 1990
Record daily average for single meet: $580,430, Fall 2002
Total all sources recent meeting: $28,395,756, Summer/Fall 2002, $43,505,965, Spring-2002
Total on-track recent meeting: $2,796,120, Summer/Fall 2002, $4,325,273, Spring-2002

Mutuel Records
Highest win: $254, August 15, 1998
Lowest Win: $2.20, Who Doctor Who, April 22, 1989
Highest Exacta: $2,424.20, May 19, 1997
Lowest Exacta: $3.60, July 28, 1994
Highest Trifecta: $35,761.40, August 31, 2002
Lowest Trifecta: $11.20, May 4, 1998
Highest Daily Double: $2,216, September 24, 1998
Lowest Daily Double: $3.20, June 30, 1995

Leaders
Recent meeting, leading jockey: Cindy Noll, 42, Fall-2002, Glenn W. Corbett, 42, Fall-2002, Terry Thompson, 94, Spring-2002
Career, leading jockey by titles: Vicki Warhol, 3
Career, leading trainer by titles: Dick Clark, 9
Career, leading owner by titles: River Ridge Ranch, 6
Career, leading trainer by wins: Dick Clark, 337
Career, leading owner by wins: River Ridge Ranch, 119
Recent meeting, leading trainer: Dick R. Clark, 29, Fall-2002, Stanley Roberts, 35, Spring-2002
Recent meeting, leading owner: River Ridge Ranch, 22, Fall-2002

Records
Single meet, leading jockey by wins: Kelly Murray, 101, 1989
Single meet, leading owner by wins: River Ridge Ranch, 26, 1997 and 2001
Single meet, leading trainer by wins: Gary Ryan, 76, 1989

Major Races
Prairie Meadows Cornhusker Breeders' Cup Handicap (G3), Iowa Derby, Iowa Oaks, Iowa Sprint, Iowa Classic-10 all Iowa-bred.

Track Records, Main Dirt
4 furlongs: Straight Fever, :46.20, July 16, 1993
4 1/2 furlongs: Southern Alert, :51.24, May 7, 2002
5 furlongs: Dayjob, :56, May 1, 1999
5 1/2 furlongs: Leaping Plum, 1:02.50, August 5, 1997
6 furlongs: Don't Countess Out, 1:08.21, August 3, 2002
1 mile: Apak, 1:35.07, August 11, 1998
1 mile 70 yards: Makaha, 1:39.60, June 10, 2002
1 1/16 miles: Man the Shipp, 1:40.91, September 20, 1997
1 1/8 miles: Beboppin Baby, 1:46.62, July 4, 1998
1 1/4 miles: Famous Event, 2:02.60, June 23, 1995
1 1/2 miles: Famous Event, 2:32, July 9, 1995
1 5/8 miles: Sir Star, 2:44.3, May 12, 1989
2 miles: Gritti Marco, 3:26, July 28, 1995

Fastest Times of 2002
4 1/2 furlongs: Southern Alert, :51.24, May 7
5 furlongs: Blackjack Boy, :57.35, July 4
5 1/2 furlongs: Kidd Cat, 1:02.61, August 10
6 furlongs: Don't Countess Out, 1:08.27, August 3
1 mile: Halo Kris, 1:36.11, June 21
1 mile 70 yards: Makaha, 1:39.76, June 10
1 1/16 miles: Mc Mahon, 1:41.65, June 1
1 1/8 miles: Mr. John, 1:47.97, July 6

Kansas

Anthony Downs

Location: 521 E. Sherman, Anthony, KS 67003-0444
Phone: (316) 842-3796
Fax: (316) 842-3772
Web site: http://www.ohmygosh.com/anthonydowns/
Abbreviation: AnF

Officers
President: Dan Bird
Vice President: Joe Wilcox
Director of Racing: Frances Snell
Racing Secretary: Norris E. Gwin
Secretary: Terry Allen
Treasurer: Mel Kitts
Director of Publicity: Tommy Morris

Racing Dates
2002: July 12-July 21, 6 days
2003: July 11-July 20, 6 days

Track Layout
Main circumference: 4 furlongs

Leaders
Recent meeting, leading jockey: Dustin Williams, 2002
Recent meeting, leading trainer: James Sweet, 5, 2002, Zack Ashlock, 5, 2002

Fastest Times of 2002
About 4 1/2 furlongs: D D Dot Comm, :56.80, July 21
5 furlongs: U Lover U, 1:01.82, July 21
About 5 furlongs: Amego Mel, 1:03.09, July 14
About 6 1/2 furlongs: Amego Mel, 1:22.06, July 21
7 furlongs: Patch Conway, 1:29.14, July 13
About 1 1/16 miles: C'Mon Chromie, 1:52.80, July 20

Eureka Downs

Eureka Downs, located 60 miles east of Wichita in Eureka, runs a 20-day mixed horse meet on weekends and holidays from the first week of May through July 4. The five-furlong track, which dates back to 1872, raced Standardbreds in the late 1940s and was the site of Kansas's first pari-mutuel race for Thoroughbreds on September 3, 1988. The track closed in 1991 and re-opened in '93 with the Greenwood County Fair Association and the Kansas Quarter Horse Racing Association co-licensed as operators.

Eureka Downs races Thoroughbreds, Quarter Horses, Appaloosas, Paints, and mules. Nonbetting mule contests began in the late 1990s and proved so popular that they were added to the pari-mutuel menu. Simulcasting is conducted during live racing only.

Location: 210 N. Jefferson St., Eureka, KS 67405
Phone: (316) 583-5528

Fax: (316) 583-5381
E-mail: info@eurekadowns.com
Web site: *http://www.eurekadowns.com*

Officers
Director of Publicity: Coraley Farley

Racing Dates
2002: May 4-July 4, 20 days
2003: May 3-July 4

Leaders
Recent meeting, leading jockey: Richard M. Vasquez, 19, 2002
Recent meeting, leading trainer: Joe F. Thomas Sr., 15, 2002

Fastest Times of 2002
4 furlongs: R C Mr Hay Boy, :46.45, May 4
6 furlongs: Amego Mel, 1:15.65, July 4
7 furlongs: Noble Dreamer, 1:29.60, May 5
1 1/16 miles: Just a Eclipse, 1:53.98, July 4

The Woodlands

Opened in September 1989 for greyhound racing, The Woodlands began Thoroughbred racing on May 24, 1990. The track, located in the northwest corner of Kansas City, offers a 26-day mixed horse racing meet for Thoroughbreds and Quarter Horses in October and year-round greyhound racing on a separate track. The three types of racing have been conducted concurrently since 1990.

A typical day of horse racing at The Woodlands consists of ten races, with three races for Quarter Horses followed by seven for Thoroughbreds, although the mixture of Quarter Horse and Thoroughbred races varies.

The Woodlands set a single-day attendance record of 22,015 in its first year of Thoroughbred operation with a wallet giveaway. The track's then-parent company filed for bankruptcy protection from its creditors in 1996. The track was sold in 1998 to William M. Grace, principal owner of the St. Jo Frontier Casino in St. Joseph, Missouri. While advocating slot machines at the track, Grace received permission to buy the track's debt securities in 1997.

Location: 9700 Leavenworth Rd., Kansas City, KS 66112
Phone: (913) 299-9797
Fax: (913) 299-9804
E-mail: info@woodlandskc.com
Web site: *http://www.woodlandskc.com*
Inaugural meeting: 1990
Year founded: 1989
Abbreviation: Wds
Acreage: 700
Number of stalls: 1,250
Seating capacity: 5,000

Officers
President: William Grace
General Manager: James Gartland
Racing Secretary: Rick Bogdanovich
Director of Publicity: Connie Loesback
Director of Admissions: Kathy Schroll
Director of Finance: Charles Wheeler
Director of Mutuels: Carl Schroll
Director of Operations: Kathy Schroll
Director of Sales: Denise Souza
Director of Simulcasting: Jayme LaRocca
Track Announcer: Robert Fox
Track Superintendent: Dan Beckerdite

Racing Dates
2002: October 2-November 3, 26 days
2003: September 23-November 2, 30 days

Track Layout
Main circumference: 1 mile
Main length of stretch: 1,030 feet

Leaders
Recent meeting, leading trainer: Jose Ibara, 14, 2002
Recent meeting, leading jockey: Ken A. Shino, 65, 2002

Handle
Average all sources recent meeting: $111,545, 2002
Average on-track recent meeting: $55,557, 2002
Total all sources recent meeting: $2,900,174, 2002
Total on-track recent meeting: $1,444,487, 2002

Track Records, Main Dirt
4 1/2 furlongs: Lanyons Star, :51 2/5, June 29, 1990
5 furlongs: Jungle Merit, :57.40, October 29, 1993
5 1/2 furlongs: Axe Age, 1:03.20, August 15, 1993
6 furlongs: Great Immunity, 1:08.50, June 30, 1991
1 mile: French Fritter, 1:36, June 1, 1991
1 mile 70 yards: Holly's Wind, 1:40 2/5, June 24, 1990
1 1/16 miles: Axle Lode, 1:42.80, September 22, 1996
1 1/8 miles: Model Age, 1:49 4/5, July 18, 1990
1 3/16 miles: Lady Taneb, 1:59, September 7, 1994
1 1/4 miles: Midway Mail, 2:03.20, September 10, 1993
1 1/2 miles: He's A Valentine, 2:33.20, October 14, 1994
1 3/4 miles: Mark of Strength, 3:02, November 5, 1993

Fastest Times of 2002
4 furlongs: U Lover U, :48.20, October 23
5 furlongs: Double Milion, 1:03.00, October 5; Fine Ridge, 1:03.00, October 16; Snoopin for Gold, 1:03.00, October 14
5 1/2 furlongs: Honest Sparkler, 1:06.80, October 24
6 furlongs: Tic N Tin, 1:12.20, October 19
1 mile: Gun Runner, 1:43.00, October 14
1 mile 70 yards: Premiere Dancer, 1:46.80, October 26
1 1/16 miles: Canyon de Oro, 1:49.40, October 26; Honest Speed, 1:49.40, October 24
1 3/4 miles: Gun Runner, 3:11.20, November 3

Kentucky

Churchill Downs

Churchill Downs in Louisville is one of the world's best-known racetracks, and its premier event, the Kentucky Derby (G1), is widely recognized as the sport's most famous race. First staged in 1875, the Derby is one of America's oldest continually run races and annually attracts an on-track audience exceeding 140,000, the nation's largest crowd for a Thoroughbred race, as well as worldwide television viewership in the millions. The Derby has been held at Churchill since the track opened on its current site in 1875. Col. M. Lewis Clark, Jr., the track's founder, built the first grandstand on land he secured from uncles John and Henry Churchill. Churchill Downs had financial problems for the first 28 years of its existence, forcing its sale by Clark and subsequent owners until Col. Matt Winn and partners bought the track in 1902.

The track, whose famous Twin Spires date from 1895, today is owned by Churchill Downs Inc., which also owns Hollywood Park near Los Angeles, Arlington Park near Chicago, Calder Race Course in Miami, and Ellis Park in western Kentucky. It also is part-owner of Hoosier

Park in Indiana. Churchill has held five runnings of the Breeders' Cup, beginning in 1988 and most recently in 2000. In 2001, the track announced plans to embark on a $27-million renovation and expansion that includes creating premium suites overlooking the track. That work began in December 2002. The track was to undertake a $100-million rebuilding of the clubhouse area following the 2003 Derby.

Location: 700 Central Ave., Louisville, KY 40208-1200
Phone: (502) 636-4400
Fax: (502) 636-4479
Web site: http://www.churchilldowns.com
Year founded: 1875
Inaugural meeting: May 17, 1875
Acreage: 147
Number of stalls: 1,404
Seating capacity: 48,500

Officers
President: Steve Sexton
Director of Racing: Douglas Bredar
Racing Secretary: Douglas Bredar
Director of Operations: David Sweazy
Director of Communications: John Asher
Director of Marketing: Kevin Marie Nuss
Director of Sales: Tyrone Tubbs
Director of Mutuels: Rick Smith
Director of Publicity: Tony Terry
Director of Admissions: Ray Pait Jr.
Horsemen's Liaison: J. L. "Buck" Wheat
Stewards: Bernard J. Hettel, Jack Middleton, Richard S. Leigh
Track Announcer: Luke Kruytbosch
Track Photographer: Four Footed Fotos
Track Superintendent: Raymond "Butch" Lehr Jr.

Racing Dates
2002: April 27-July 7, 53 days; October 27-November 30, 30 days
2003: April 26-July 6, 53 days, October 26-November 29, 27 days

Track Layout
Main circumference: 1 mile
Main track chute: 1 mile
Main width: 80 feet
Main length of stretch: 1,234 1/2 feet
Main turf circumference: 7 furlongs
Main turf width: 80 feet

Attendance
Highest single meet record: 811,446, Spring 1988
Record daily average for single meet: 20,066, Spring 1944
Total attendance recent meeting: 202,059, Fall 2002, 677,876, Spring 2002
Average daily recent meeting: 13,036, Spring 2002; 6,735, Fall 2002
Highest single day record: 163,628, May 4, 1974

Handle
Average all sources recent meeting: $10,638,067, Spring 2002, $6,789,843, Fall 2002
Average on-track recent meeting: $1,772,571, Spring 2002, $969,854, Fall 2002
Record daily average for single meet: $2,054,901, Spring 1997
Total all sources recent meeting: $203,695,292, Fall 2002, $553,179,503, Spring 2002
Total on-track recent meeting: $29,095,615, Fall 2002, $92,173,678, Spring 2002
Single day on-track handle: $19,400,818, May 4, 2002
Single day total handle all sources: $123,233,111, May 4, 2002

Mutuel Records
Highest win: $495.60, Gold and Rubies, November 21, 1978
Highest Exacta: $8,062.40, November 13, 1984
Highest Trifecta: $55,902.40, November 10, 2000
Highest Daily Double: $6,818.20, October 29, 1984
Highest Pick 3: $114,156, November 4, 2000
Highest Pick 6: $417,389.80, May 10, 1995
Highest Other Exotics: $76,063.80, Superfecta, June 27, 1998

Leaders
Career, leading jockey by titles: Pat Day, 33
Recent meeting, leading trainer: Dale Romans, 23, Spring 2002, Ken McPeek, 15, Fall 2002, Tom Amoss, 23, Spring 2002
Recent meeting, leading owner: Kenneth and Sarah Ramsey, 19, Spring 2002, Kenneth and Sarah Ramsey, 7, Fall-2002
Career, leading trainer by stakes wins: Bill Mott, 65
Career, leading jockey by wins: Pat Day, 2,289
Career, leading owner by stakes wins: Calumet Farm, 32
Career, leading owner by titles: Calumet Farm, 8, T. Alie Grissom, 8
Career, leading trainer by wins: Bill Mott, 516
Recent meeting, leading jockey: Pat Day, 50, Fall 2002, Pat Day, 72, Spring 2002
Career, leading trainer by titles: D. Wayne Lukas, 11

Records
Single day jockey wins: Pat Day, 7, June 20, 1984
Single meet, leading jockey by wins: Pat Day, 169
Single meet, leading trainer by wins: William I. Mott, 54

Track Records, Main Dirt
4 furlongs: Fair Phantom, :46 3/5, May 7, 1921; Casey, :46 3/5, May 9, 1921; Miss Joy, :46 3/5, May 10, 1921
4 1/2 furlongs: Chilukki, :51, April 28, 1999
5 furlongs: D'Nile, :57.14, June 23, 2002
5 1/2 furlongs: Cashier's Dream, 1:02.52, July 7, 2002
6 furlongs: Kona Gold, 1:07.77, November 4, 2000
6 1/2 furlongs: Love At Noon, 1:14.34, May 5, 2001
7 furlongs: Alannan, 1:20.50, May 5, 2001
7 1/2 furlongs: Miss Lodi, 1:28.08, June 1, 2002
1 mile: Chilukki, 1:33.57, November 4, 2000
1 mile 70 yards: The Porter, 1:41 3/5, May 30, 1919
1 1/16 miles: Yes Sir, 1:41 3/5, November 25, 1970
1 1/8 miles: Victory Gallop, 1:47.28, June 12, 1999
1 3/16 miles: Bonnie Andrew, 1:58 3/5, November 14, 1942
1 1/4 miles: Secretariat, 1:59 2/5, May 5, 1973
1 3/8 miles: Elliott, 2:20 3/5, October 15, 1906
1 1/2 miles: Cascade Peaks, 2:32.04, June 6, 1999
1 5/8 miles: Tupolev (Arg), 2:49 2/5, July 23, 1983
1 3/4 miles: Caslon Bold, 2:59.64, July 4, 1995
2 miles: Libertarian, 3:22.26, November 28, 1998
Other: 1m 20 yds, Frog Legs, 1:39, May 13, 1913; 1m 50 yds, Hodge, 1:41 4/5, October 4, 1916; 1m 100 yds, The Caxton, 1:49 1/5, May 16, 1902; 2 1/16 miles, Hi Neighbor, 3:40 4/5, November 11, 1949; 2 1/4 miles, Raincoat, 3:53, October 7, 1915; 3 miles, Ten Broeck, 5:26 1/2, September 3, 1876; 4 miles, Sotemia, 7:10 4/5, October 7, 1912

Course Records, Main Turf
5 furlongs: Morluc, :55.73, June 15, 2002
1 mile: Jaggery John, 1:33.78, July 4, 1995
1 1/16 miles: Royal Strand (Ire), 1:40.93, May 2, 1997
1 1/8 miles: Lure, 1:46.34, April 30, 1993
1 3/8 miles: Snake Eyes, 2:13, May 22, 1997
1 1/2 miles: Tikkanen, 2:26.50, November 5, 1994

Fastest Times of 2002 (Dirt)
4 1/2 furlongs: Big Score, :51.18, June 2
5 furlongs: D' Nile, :57.14, June 23
5 1/2 furlongs: Slammed, 1:03.03, June 29
6 furlongs: Entepreneur, 1:08.67, May 4
6 1/2 furlongs: Orientate, 1:14.41, June 29
7 furlongs: Hero's Tribute, 1:21.72, June 2

7 1/2 furlongs: Miss Lodi, 1:28.08, June 1
1 mile: There's Zealous, 1:34.51, July 4
1 1/16 miles: Bonus Pack, 1:42.07, June 7
1 1/8 miles: Street Cry (Ire), 1:47.84, June 15
1 1/4 miles: War Emblem, 2:01.13, May 4
2 miles: A Storm Is Brewing, 3:27.83, November 30

Fastest Times of 2002 (Turf)

5 furlongs: Morluc, :55.73, June 15
1 mile: Good Journey, 1:34.58, June 15
1 1/16 miles: Jeremiah Jack, 1:41.09, May 31
1 1/8 miles: Voodoo Dancer, 1:46.91, June 22
1 3/8 miles: Pisces, 2:15.82, June 1
About 2 1/16 miles: McDynamo, 3:48.00, May 2

Ellis Park

Ellis Park near Henderson, Kentucky, holds the distinction of being the only racetrack where soybeans are grown in the infield. Built in 1922 and designed after Saratoga Race Course, the track located on an island in the Ohio River near Evansville, Indiana, was originally named Dade Park and intended for harness racing. Within one month of its opening, the track replaced harness racing with Thoroughbred racing. Ellis was plagued with financial problems and, in 1923 and '24, the only racing held was for race cars on Labor Day weekend. In 1924, James C. Ellis, who owned construction and oil enterprises, purchased the track for $35,100 and reopened it for racing in 1925. In 1954, two years before Ellis's death, the track's name was changed to James C. Ellis Park. In 1998, Churchill Downs Inc. purchased Ellis, and its purses have benefited from full-card simulcasting revenues. However, Churchill Downs Inc. announced in early 2003 that it had lost money on Ellis and intended to sell it. Ellis's richest race each year is the $200,000 Gardenia Stakes (G3) for fillies and mares.

Location: 3300 U.S. Hwy. 41 N, Henderson, KY 42419-0033
Phone: (812) 425-1456
Fax: (812) 425-3725
Web site: http://www.ellisparkracing.com
Year founded: 1922
Inaugural meeting: November 8, 1922
Acreage: 214
Number of stalls: 1,142
Seating capacity: 7,750

Officers

President: Steve Sexton
Vice President: Paul D. Kuerzi
General Manager: Paul D. Kuerzi
Director of Racing: Douglas Bredar
Racing Secretary: Douglas Bredar
Director of Operations: Robert A. Jackson
Director of Admissions: Marianne Wagner
Director of Marketing: B. Todd Mosby
Director of Mutuels: Jeff Hall
Director of Publicity: Luke Kruytbosch
Director of Simulcasting: Robert A. Jackson
Director of Finance: Tom Hattenbach
Horsemen's Liaison: Donna Porter
Stewards: Ronald Herbstreit, Steve Obrekaitis, Warren Croce
Track Announcer: Luke Kruytbosch
Track Photographer: Four Footed Photos
Track Superintendent: Glenn Thompson

Racing Dates

2002: July 10-September 2, 41 days
2003: July 9-September 1, 41 days

Track Layout

Main circumference: 1 1/8 miles
Main track chute: 1 mile, 7 furlongs
Main width: Homestretch: 100 feet; Backstretch: 85 feet
Main length of stretch: 1,175 feet
Main turf circumference: 1 mile

Attendance

Total attendance recent meeting: 123,688, 2002
Average daily recent meeting: 3,017, 2002
Highest single day record: 15,500 est., September 4, 1967

Handle

Total on-track recent meeting: $15,936,288, 2002
Total all sources recent meeting: $120,897,602, 2002
Average on-track recent meeting: $388,690, 2002
Average all sources recent meeting: $2,948,722, 2002

Leaders

Recent meeting, leading owner: Richard, Bertram, and Elaine Klein, 11, 2002
Recent meeting, leading trainer: Bernard S. Flint, 26, 2002
Recent meeting, leading jockey: Jon Court, 69, 2002
Career, leading jockey by titles: Leroy Tauzin, 7
Career, leading trainer by titles: Bernard S. Flint, 10
Single meet, leading jockey by wins: Mike McDowell, 89, 1986
Single meet, leading owner by wins: Tom Dorris, 20, 1978
Single meet, leading trainer by wins: Angel Montano, 34, 1976

Records

Single day trainer wins: Wayne Bearden, 5, August 7, 1997
Single meet, leading jockey by wins: Mike McDowell, 89
Single meet, leading trainer by wins: Angel Montano, 34
Single day jockey wins: Willie Martinez, 8

Track Records, Main Dirt

5 furlongs: White Image, :57 3/5, July 9, 1988
5 1/2 furlongs: Mount Forloon, 1:03 2/5, July 17, 1988
6 furlongs: Stubilem, 1:09, July 1, 1982
6 1/2 furlongs: American Chance, 1:15, July 16, 1994
7 furlongs: Sheena Native, 1:21 3/5, July 23, 1988
1 mile: Still Waving, 1:34 3/5, August 13, 1988
1 1/8 miles: Lt. Lao, 1:47 3/5, August 27, 1988
1 1/4 miles: Won Du Loup, 2:03, September 4, 1988
1 3/8 miles: Ramona Jay, 2:23, August 24, 1985
1 1/2 miles: Unaccountable, 2:29 3/5, July 23, 1988
1 5/8 miles: Sir Lightning, 2:45.80, August 9, 1992
1 3/4 miles: Bondi, 3:00, August 27, 1966
2 miles: Classic Deal, 3:25 3/5, August 21, 1988
Other: 2 1/4 miles, Bondi, 3:54, September 5, 1966

Course Records, Main Turf

5 1/2 furlongs: Bettybird, 1:00.52, August 21, 2002
1 mile: Slewper Imp, 1:32.60, July 16, 1995; Suffragette, 1:32.60, July 24, 1999
1 1/16 miles: Majestic Jove, 1:39.20, August 27, 1997
1 1/8 miles: Yaqthan (Ire), 1:44.60, September 2, 1996
1 1/4 miles: Ye Slew, 1:59.60, August 6, 1994
1 1/2 miles: Our Forbes, 2:25.40, August 10, 1994
2 miles: Irish Harbour, 3:20.20, September 2, 1996

Interesting Facts

Previous name: Dade Park

Fastest Times of 2002 (Dirt)

5 furlongs: Reason to Change, :59.11, August 2
5 1/2 furlongs: Relentless Seller, 1:03.37, August 16
6 furlongs: Nany's Forum, 1:10.34, August 3
6 1/2 furlongs: Dash for Daylight, 1:15.97, July 27
7 furlongs: Rock Slide, 1:22.44, August 14
1 mile: Dash for Daylight, 1:37.35, August 24
1 1/8 miles: Minister's Baby, 1:49.73, August 10
1 1/2 miles: Forty Karats Jade, 2:35.16, August 10

Fastest Times of 2002 (Turf)
5 1/2 furlongs: Bettybird, 1:00.52, August 21
1 mile: Tin Smithen, 1:32.95, July 25
1 1/16 miles: Dream Tripper, 1:39.23, July 24
1 1/8 miles: Roxinho (Brz), 1:45.39, September 2
1 1/4 miles: Ambenay, 2:06.96, August 3
1 1/2 miles: Thrym, 2:28.88, August 25

Keeneland Race Course

Some tracks offer nothing more than an endless procession of live and simulcast races. But a few American tracks offer a sense of history and a state of mind. Keeneland Race Course falls into the latter category.

Since its opening meeting in October 1936, the Lexington track has developed a unique identity. The stately facility offers two short, marquee meetings—including races such as the Blue Grass Stakes (G1) in the spring and Spinster Stakes (G1) in the fall—in a setting that screams atmosphere.

But Keeneland offers more than its race meets. Generating the cash for Keeneland's rich purses are the top-drawer sales that take place next to the track at the sales pavilion. Want to see a future Kentucky Derby (G1) winner? Keeneland's yearling sales often provide that opportunity.

The Keeneland Association was incorporated in 1935 and purchased 147½ acres of land, including an ornate training track, from J. O. "Jack" Keene to build the facility. Lexington, bereft of racing after the Kentucky Association track closed earlier in the 1930s, quickly embraced the new facility, and more than 25,000 people attended the inaugural nine-day meeting.

Crowds in excess of 25,000 on a single day now are common at Keeneland. In one of the few areas of the country where the Thoroughbred is truly king, the Keeneland meets have become one of the social events of the season, drawing a wide range of spectators, including veteran racegoers, local business executives, socialites, breeders, and college students.

Location: 4201 Versailles Rd., Lexington, KY 40592-1690
Phone: (859) 254-3412
Fax: (859) 288-4348
E-mail: keeneland@keeneland.com
Web site: http://www.keeneland.com
Year founded: 1935
Inaugural meeting: October 15-24, 1936
Abbreviation: Kee
Acreage: 907
Number of stalls: 1,845
Seating capacity: 7,000

Officers
President: Nick Nicholson
Vice President: Harvie B. Wilkinson
Director of Racing: W. B. Rogers Beasley
Racing Secretary: Ben Huffman
Treasurer: Harvie B. Wilkinson
Secretary: William T. Bishop III
Director of Operations: James A. Perry
Director of Auctions: Geoffrey Russell
Director of Communications: R. James Williams
Director of Finance: Jessica Green
Director of Marketing: Fran Taylor
Director of Mutuels: Robert Butcher
Director of Sales: Geoffrey Russell
Director of Simulcasting: Maggie Johnson

Horsemen's Liaison: Kathleen Torok
Stewards: Bernard J. Hettel, Jack Middleton III, R. Spencer Leigh III
Track Announcer: Kurt Becker
Track Photographer: Bill Straus, Patrick Lang
Track Superintendent: Mike Young
Other officials: James E. Bassett III, Chairman of the Board

Racing Dates
2002: April 5-April 26, 2002, 16 days; October 4-October 26, 2002, 17 days
2003: April 4-April 25, 15 days, October 3-October 25, 17 days

Track Layout
Main circumference: 1 1/16 miles
Main track chutes: 4 1/2 furlongs, 7 furlongs, 184 feet
Main length of stretch: 1,174 ft.
Main width: 77 feet
Main turf circumference: 7 1/2 furlongs
Main turf length of stretch: 1,190 ft.
Training track: 5 furlongs

Attendance
Record daily average for single meet: 14,649, Spring 2001
Total attendance recent meeting: 211,661, Fall-2002, 227,545, Spring-2002
Average daily recent meeting: 12,451, Fall-2002, 14,222, Spring-2002
Highest single day record: 29,687, April 15, 2000
Highest single meet record: 232,339, Spring 1988
Lowest single day record: 1,294, October 16, 1936

Handle
Average all sources recent meeting: $6,953,400, Fall 2002, $8,478,506, Spring 2002
Average on-track recent meeting: $1,493,794, Fall 2002, $1,701,013, Spring 2002
Record daily average for single meet: $1,695,948, Spring 2001
Single day on-track handle: $3,516,621, April 13, 2002
Single day total handle all sources: $17,076,993, April 14, 2001
Total all sources recent meeting: $118,207,807, Fall 2002, $135,656,102, Spring 2002
Total on-track recent meeting: $25,394,500, Fall 2002, $27,216,210, Spring 2002

Leaders
Career, leading jockey by stakes wins: Pat Day, 84
Career, leading trainer by stakes wins: D. Wayne Lukas, 45
Career, leading owner by stakes wins: Calumet Farm, 20, Claiborne Farm, 20
Career, leading jockey by wins: Pat Day, 841
Career, leading owner by wins: T. A. and J. E. Grissom, 171
Career, leading trainer by wins: D. Wayne Lukas, 235
Recent meeting, leading jockey: Pat Day, 24, Fall 2002, Robby Albarado, 26, Spring 2002
Recent meeting, leading owner: Kenneth and Sarah Ramsey, 4, Fall 2002, Kenneth and Sarah Ramsey, 7, Spring 2002, Sam-Son Farm, 7, Spring 2002, WinStar Farm, 4, Fall 2002
Recent meeting, leading trainer: D. Wayne Lukas, 11, Spring-2002, Dale Romans, 8, Fall-2002
Career, leading jockey by titles: Pat Day, 20
Career, leading trainer by titles: D. Wayne Lukas, 15
Career, leading owner by titles: T. A. and J. E. Grissom, 14

Records
Single meet, leading jockey by wins: Pat Day, 45
Single meet, leading trainer by wins: D. Wayne Lukas, 22
Single day trainer wins: 16 different trainers have saddled three winners in one day
Single day jockey wins: Craig Perret, 6, April 18, 1990; Randy Romero, 6, April 7, 1990

Interesting Facts

Achievements/milestones: Part of the film *Seabiscuit* was filmed at Keeneland in 2002.

Track Records, Main Dirt

4 1/2 furlongs: Quick Swoon, :51, April 20, 1966; Royality Note, :51, April 23, 1968; Bend the Times, :51, April 8, 1980
6 furlongs: Anjiz, 1:07.78, October 9, 1993
6 1/2 furlongs: Number One Sheikh, 1:14.70, October 11, 2000
7 furlongs: Binalong, 1:20.39, October 13, 1993
1 1/16 miles: Din's Dancer, 1:40 4/5, October 9, 1990
1 1/8 miles: Good Command, 1:46 4/5, October 10, 1987
1 3/16 miles: Arch, 1:53.87, October 11, 1998
1 1/4 miles: Political Fact, 2:02.21, October 15, 1993
1 5/8 miles: Put-in-Bay, 2:45, October 13,1967; Mr. Copy Chief, 2:45, October 20, 1971
Other: 7 furlongs 184 feet, Lamb Chop, 1:24 3/5, October 10, 1963

Course Records, Main Turf

5 1/2 furlongs: Chris's Thunder, 1:01.72, October 8, 2000
1 mile: Altibr, 1:33.72, October 7, 2000
1 1/16 miles: Quiet Resolve, 1:40.30, April 27, 2000
1 1/8 miles: Memories of Silver, 1:45.81, October 5, 1996
1 3/16 miles: Happyanunoit (NZ), 1:53.91, October 15, 1999
1 1/2 miles: Bursting Forth, 2:27.54, April 22, 1999
1 5/8 miles: Royal Strand (Ire), 2:38.68, October 24, 1999

Fastest Times of 2002 (Dirt)

4 1/2 furlongs: Posse, :51.43, April 10
6 furlongs: Storm Craft, 1:08.93, April 5
6 1/2 furlongs: Bold Truth, 1:16.44, April 13
7 furlongs: Orientate, 1:21.54, April 14
About 7 furlongs: Najran, 1:26.00, October 11
1 1/16 miles: Tenpins, 1:42.56, April 10
1 1/8 miles: Take Charge Lady, 1:49.90, October 6
1 3/16 miles: Law Review, 1:59.16, April 13
1 1/4 miles: Tubby Cat, 2:04.90, October 23
1 5/8 miles: Equinox, 2:50.07, October 18

Fastest Times of 2002 (Turf)

5 1/2 furlongs: Morluc, 1:03.25, April 13
1 mile: Touch of the Blues (Fr), 1:35.02, April 12
1 1/16 miles: Critical Battle, 1:41.71, April 17
1 1/8 miles: Beefeater Baby, 1:47.76, April 11
1 3/16 miles: Owsley, 1:56.72, October 4
1 1/2 miles: Rochester, 2:30.48, October 6
About 2 miles: Hotspur, 3:52.40, April 26
About 2 1/2 miles: It's a Giggle, 4:39.42, April 26

Kentucky Downs

Straddling the Kentucky-Tennessee state border adjacent to Interstate 65, Kentucky Downs has enjoyed a short, colorful history. Opened in 1990 as Dueling Grounds Race Course—the track site was reputed to be the scene of several 19th century duels—the turf-only racecourse was conceived as a simulcasting facility with one day of live racing a year.

That one day of racing featured steeplechase racing and was well-received by the steeplechase community. But ownership controversies dogged the facility until the late 1990s, when businessman Brad Kelley, Turfway Park, and Churchill Downs purchased the facility. Kelley owns 52%, and the tracks each hold 24%. Track officials have found ways to make Kentucky Downs's turf-only status pay off. The track now offers a series of turf stakes on the flat to coincide partly with the Kentucky Cup series of dirt-only races at Turfway Park in Florence, Kentucky.

Location: 5629 Nashville Rd., Franklin, KY 42135
Phone: (270) 586-7778
Fax: (270) 586-8080
Web site: *http://www.kentuckydowns.com*
Year founded: 1990
Inaugural meeting: April 22, 1990

Officers

General Manager: Ryan Driscoll
Racing Secretary: Richard Leigh
Director of Operations: Jon Goodman
Director of Mutuels: Shelley Spears
Simulcasting Director: Mary Troilo

Racing Dates

2002: September 14-September 23, 7 days
2003: September 13-September 23, 7 days

Track Layout

Main turf circumference: 1 5/16 miles

Leaders

Recent meeting, leading trainer: Tom Amoss, 3, 2002
Career, leading jockey by titles: Jon Court, 2
Recent meeting, leading jockey: Jon Court, 6, 2002

Records

Single meet, leading jockey by wins: Jon Court, 8

Course Records, Main Turf

6 furlongs: Morluc, 1:09.66, September 23, 2000
7 furlongs: Slew of Deuces, 1:22.77, September 18, 2000
1 mile: Rob 'n Gin, 1:35.00, September 19, 1998
1 1/2 miles: Yaqthan (Ire), 2:27.60, September 19, 1998

Interesting Facts

Previous name and dates: Dueling Grounds 1990-1996

Fastest Times of 2002 (Turf)

6 furlongs: Riverman's Tea, 1:10.10, September 17
7 furlongs: Konyak, 1:25.03, September 15
1 mile: Promise of War, 1:36.16, September 15
1 1/2 miles: Shannon the Cannon, 2:33.94, September 23

Turfway Park

Turfway Park is the Northern Kentucky successor to Old Latonia, a track that opened in the Latonia section of Covington in 1883 and shut down in 1939. In the late 1950s, an investor group built a new Latonia Race Course in Florence, approximately ten miles from the former site, and it opened on August 27, 1959. On April 9, 1986, Nashville real-estate developer Jerry Carroll and partners bought Latonia for $13.5-million and renamed it Turfway Park. Carroll undertook an extensive renovation program and raised the purse of the track's spring race for three-year-old Triple Crown prospects, the Jim Beam Stakes (G2), to $500,000 in 1987. The race's purse would peak at $750,000 when it lost its initial sponsor and became the Galleryfurniture.com Stakes (G2) for 1999 only. In 2002, the race became the Lane's End Spiral Stakes (G2), and in 2003 it was renamed the Lane's End Stakes (G2).

During Carroll's tenure, Turfway was a leader in offering intertrack wagering in Kentucky (1988) and in promoting legislation for full-card simulcasting in '94. Also in 1994, Turfway launched its Kentucky Cup Day of Champions, a September event featuring five stakes races. Carroll and partners sold the track to a partnership led by the Keeneland Association for $37-million on January 15, 1999.

Location: 7500 Turfway Rd., Florence, KY 41042
Phone: (859) 371-0200
Fax: (859) 371-0200
E-mail: turfway@turfway.com
Web site: *http://www.turfway.com*
Inaugural meeting: April 9, 1986 (Turfway), August 27, 1959 (Latonia)
Acreage: 197
Number of stalls: 1,200

Officers
President: Robert N. Elliston
Vice President: Clifford Reed
General Manager: Greg Schmitz
Director of Racing: Richard S. Leigh
Racing Secretary: Richard S. Leigh
Treasurer: Clifford Reed
Director of Operations: Greg Schmitz
Director of Admissions: Kenny Kramer
Director of Marketing: Brian Gardner
Director of Mutuels: Kenny Kramer
Director of Simulcasting: Mary Troilo
Horsemen's Liaison: Randy Wehrman
Stewards: Brooks Becraft III, Jack Middleton, Ron Herbstreit
Track Announcer: Mike Battaglia
Track Photographer: Pat Lang
Track Superintendent: Daniel Chapman
Other officials: Randy Wehrman, Stakes Coordinator; Robin Rodgers, Controller

Racing Dates
2002: November 25, 2001 to April 4, 2002, 92 days; September 4-October 3, 22 days
2003: December 1, 2002-April 3, 2003, 88 days; September 3-October 2, 22 days; November 30, 2003-April 1, 2004

Track Layout
Main circumference: 1 mile
Main track chutes: 1/4 mile, 6 1/2 furlongs
Main width: Backstretch: 50 feet; Homestretch: 90 feet
Main length of stretch: 970 feet

Attendance
Average daily recent meeting: 1,710, Winter/Spring, 2001/2002
Highest single day record: 22,480, March 25, 2000
Highest single meet record: 354,867, Spring 1988
Total attendance recent meeting: 104,306, Winter/Spring 2001/2002
Record daily average for single meet: 5,377, Spring 1988

Handle
Average all sources recent meeting: $3,595,362, Holiday 2002
Total on-track recent meeting: $7,328,698, Holiday 2002
Total all sources recent meeting: $224,483,000, Winter/Spring, 2001/2002; $67,478,042, Fall 2002
Average on-track recent meeting: $333,123, Holiday Meet 2002
Single day on-track handle: $3,223,778, April 2, 1994
Single day total handle all sources: $79,097,955, Holiday 2002

Mutuel Records
Highest Exacta: $6,777.20, January 29, 1988
Lowest Exacta: $3.20, September 26, 1998
Highest Trifecta: $101,694.80, February 21, 1996
Lowest Trifecta: $5.20, September 26, 1998
Highest Daily Double: $4,575.80, December 12, 1986
Lowest Daily Double: $5, September 24, 1994
Highest Pick 3: $24,752.40, December 16, 1993
Lowest Pick 3: $13.80, November 25, 1990
Highest Pick 6: $1,474,380, March 23, 1988
Highest Other Exotics: $56,375.20, Superfecta, January 5, 2000

Leaders
Career, leading jockey by stakes wins: Michael McDowell, 32 and Pat Day, 32
Career, leading jockey by titles: Willie Martinez, 9
Career, leading trainer by stakes wins: D. Wayne Lukas, 31
Career, leading trainer by titles: Bernard Flint, 16
Recent meeting, leading jockey: John McKee, 24, Fall 2002; Rodney Prescott, 21, Holiday 2002
Recent meeting, leading owner: Billy Hays, Fall 2002; WinStar Farm, Holiday 2002
Recent meeting, leading trainer: Bernard S. Flint, 11, Fall 2002; Bernard S. Flint, 11, Holiday Meet 2002

Records
Single day jockey wins: Kris Prather, 6, February 11, 2001
Single meet, leading trainer by wins: John Parisella, 40, Winter/Spring 1996
Single day trainer wins: D. Wayne Lukas, 4; Dennis Freking, 4; George Isaacs, 4; Harry Trotsek, 4; V. R. Wright, 4
Single meet, leading jockey by wins: Kris Prather, 109, Winter/Spring 2001

Track Records, Main Dirt
5 furlongs: Salutee, :56.98, February 23, 2002
5 1/2 furlongs: Da' White Judge, 1:03 4/5, September 29, 1979
6 furlongs: Appealing Skier, 1:08.24, September 21, 1996; Partner's Hero, 1:08.24, March 29, 1998
6 1/2 furlongs: Boone's Mill, 1:14.32, December 30, 1995
1 mile: Secreto's Hideaway, 1:34.12, March 5, 1994
1 mile 70 yards: Venture, 1:40 3/5, September 2, 1963
1 1/16 miles: Anet, 1:40.73, March 29, 1997
1 1/8 miles: Hansel, 1:46.70, March 30, 1991
1 3/16 miles: Roman Justice, 1:58 3/5, December 24, 1966
1 1/4 miles: Executor, 2:03.82, December 29, 2000
1 3/8 miles: Briarwick, 2:21, December 10, 1968
1 1/2 miles: Canive, 2:31 2/5, September 7, 1963
1 5/8 miles: Bluegrass Warrior, 2:46.61, February 23, 1991
1 3/4 miles: Bluegrass Warrior, 2:59, March 10, 1990
2 miles: Bluegrass Warrior, 3:23.90, March 30, 1991
Other: 2 furlongs, Kadabra, :21.25, March 31, 2001; 3 furlongs, Cut Glass, :34 3/5, March 27, 1976; 1 11/16 miles, Sestos, 2:56 1/5, January 1, 1969

Fastest Times of 2002
2 furlongs: Lady Wink, :22.08, March 30
5 furlongs: Salutee, :56.98, February 23
5 1/2 furlongs: Rojo Toro, 1:04.03, September 21
6 furlongs: Drippingindiamonds, 1:09.46, March 23
6 1/2 furlongs: Racing Nut, 1:16.65, April 3
1 mile: Ide Be Spencers, 1:36.08, March 23
1 1/16 miles: Mr. Mellon, 1:42.90, March 23
1 1/8 miles: Jarrett, 1:48.81, April 4
1 1/4 miles: Timber Wolf, 2:09.79, September 14
1 1/2 miles: Linda's Lad, 2:34.02, March 2

Louisiana

Delta Downs

Lee Berwick, a prominent Quarter Horse breeder and owner and a former president of the American Quarter Horse Association, opened the first Delta Downs as a nonpari-mutuel match track on his farm at St. Joseph, Louisiana, on the banks of the Mississippi River. He moved the operation to Vinton, Louisiana, two hours northeast of Houston, and opened Delta Downs in 1973. Berwick served as track president until 1997, when his daughter, Kathryn, succeeded him in the position. In 1999, the Berwicks sold Delta Downs for more than $10-million to Shaun Scott and Jinho Cho, who began renovating the facility in hopes of installing slot machines. In 2001, the track was again sold for $125-million to Las Vegas-based Boyd Gaming Corp., which owns casinos in Louisiana, Nevada, Illinois, and Mississippi. In October 2001, Boyd received approval from the Louisiana Gaming Control Board to operate 1,700 slot machines. Delta Downs offers racing for Thoroughbreds as well as a separate season for Quarter Horses and Paints. The slots have resulted in sizable increases in Thoroughbred purses, with the average daily distribution increasing 60% to $183,323 for the 2002-'03 season. Average purse for that meet was $18,287.

Location: 2717 Hwy. 3063, Vinton, LA 70668
Phone: (337) 589-7441
Fax: (337) 589-2399
E-mail: deltadownsalb@aol.com
Web site: http://www.deltadowns.com
Year founded: 1973
Abbreviation: DeD
Acreage: 240
Number of stalls: 1,200

Officers
President: William S. Boyd
Vice President: Jack Bernsmeier
General Manager: Jack Bernsmeier
Director of Racing: Chris Warren
Racing Secretary: Trent McIntosh
Director of Operations: Charles Sonnier (racing), Lenny Brondum
Director of Communications: Wynn Findley
Director of Finance: Toni Demahy
Director of Marketing: Adrian King
Director of Mutuels: Sylvia Rentz
Director of Publicity: Steve Nick
Director of Simulcasting: Chris Warren
Stewards: Aaron Emigh, Duane Domingue, Judy Dugas
Track Announcer: Chris Kotulak
Track Photographer: Coady Photography
Track Superintendent: Darald Wilfer
Other officials: Susan Ribio, Director of Human Resources

Racing Dates
2002: November 17, 2001-April 7, 2002, 82 days
2003: November 7, 2002-March 23, 2003, 80 days

Track Layout
Main circumference: 6 furlongs
Main track chutes: 1 1/16 miles, 5 furlongs
Main width: 70 feet
Main length of stretch: 660 feet

Track Records, Main Dirt
4 furlongs: Rock Afire, :46 1/5, December 10, 1994
4 1/2 furlongs: Road to Seattle, :52, January 15,1998
5 furlongs: Mollie McLash, :57.69, January 31, 2002
6 1/2 furlongs: Chief Okie Dokie, 1:18.76, February 8, 2002
7 furlongs: Norms Promise, 1:24 3/5, March 2, 1975
7 1/2 furlongs: Junior Gent, 1:33 1/5, March 14, 1974
1 mile: Freon Flier, 1:37.52, March 10, 2002
1 mile 70 yards: Thriller, 1:42 2/5, September 27, 1973
1 1/16 miles: Norms Promise, 1:43 1/5, March 23, 1975
1 1/8 miles: Lucky Silence, 1:55 2/5, February 18, 1994
1 3/16 miles: Ponderosa Lark, 2:03 3/5, October 31, 1975
1 1/4 miles: Shy Bull, 2:10 1/5, November 3, 1974
1 3/8 miles: Ponderosa Lark, 2:27 1/5, December 15, 1974
1 1/2 miles: Art Work, 2:41 1/5, December 11, 1974
2 miles: Can Em, 3:43 4/5, December 10, 1988
Other: 1 5/16 miles, Gentleman Mike, 2:17 3/5, December 1, 1974; 1 9/16 miles, Landing Officer, 2:51 4/5, December 15, 1989

Interesting Facts
Trivia: Three alligators live in the infield.

Major Races
Delta Jackpot for 2 year olds, $500,000

Fastest Times of 2002
4 furlongs: Pancho's Karma, :46.67, March 21
4 1/2 furlongs: Canrock, :52.20, March 10
5 furlongs: Mollie McLash, :57.69, January 31
6 1/2 furlongs: Chief Okie Dokie, 1:18.76, February 8
7 furlongs: Comic Truth, 1:25.35, November 24
7 1/2 furlongs: Kreems View, 1:33.94, December 20
1 mile: Freon Flier, 1:37.52, March 10
1 1/16 miles: Revered Soldier, 1:46.08, November 30
1 1/4 miles: Desiard, 2:10.89, March 25

Evangeline Downs

Located in Louisiana's colorful Cajun country, Evangeline Downs near Lafayette is known as the cradle of jockeys. Racing Hall of Fame member Eddie Delahoussaye, multiple Eclipse Award winner Kent Desormeaux, and leading jockeys Shane Sellers and Mark Guidry all won their first races at the track. Several nationally known horses also have competed at Evangeline. In 1977, a two-year-old named John Henry won two of three starts at Evangeline and scored his first stakes win in the Lafayette Futurity. From that beginning, John Henry went on to earn more than $6.5-million and was voted Horse of the Year in 1981 and '84. In 1999 and 2000, Louisiana-bred Hallowed Dreams won 16 consecutive races, including six at Evangeline. The track, which offers some Quarter Horse racing, conducts live racing from mid-April to early September. The track's future includes a new location and slot machines. Plans call for the track to move to nearby Opelousas to take advantage of a state law that permits slot machines at racetracks if authorized by local parishes (counties). Gaming devices were not approved in St. Landry Parish, where Evangeline is located. The new track would have a grandstand that seats nearly 6,000 fans, a one-mile dirt oval—increased from the current seven-furlong track—and a turf course inside the main track. The facility could eventually include an 18-hole golf course, water park, amusement park, civic center, and agricultural center.

Location: P.O. Box 90270, Lafayette, LA 70509-0270
Phone: (337) 896-7223
Fax: (337) 896-5445
E-mail: evdinfo@evangelinedowns.com
Web site: http://www.evangelinedowns.com
Year founded: 1966
Inaugural meeting: 1966
Abbreviation: EvD
Acreage: 133.7
Number of stalls: 960
Seating capacity: 4,200

Officers
President: Michael Luzich
General Manager: David A. Yount
Racing Secretary: David Frizzell
Director of Finance: Steve Orrbonne
Director of Marketing: Calzone & Associates
Director of Mutuels: Rachael Conway
Director of Publicity: Sean D. Beirne
Director of Simulcasting: Sean Beirne
Horsemen's Liaison: Chris Granger
Stewards: Brent Seward, E. J. Fayard, Larry Munster
Track Announcer: Sean Beirne
Track Photographer: S. C. I. Photography

Racing Dates
2002: April 13-September 2, 82 days
2003: April 4-September 1, 87 days

Track Layout
Main circumference: 7 furlongs
Main track chute: 1 3/16 miles, 6 furlongs
Main width: 70 feet
Main length of stretch: 1,020 feet

Attendance
Highest single day record: 8,218, July 4, 1975
Average daily recent meeting: 8,176, 2002
Total attendance recent meeting: 99,709, 2002

Handle
Single day total handle all sources: $2,052,653, July 1, 1999
Record daily average for single meet: $1,531,758, 2000
Average all sources recent meeting: $1,324,234, 2002
Average on-track recent meeting: $110,196, 2002
Total all sources recent meeting: $108,587,190, 2002
Total all sources recent meeting: $108,587,190, 2002

Mutuel Records
Highest win: $412.20, Princely Greek, April 26, 1987
Highest Exacta: $24,213.90, August 1, 1982
Highest Trifecta: $37,995, August 23, 1997

Leaders
Career, leading trainer by titles: Don Cormier Sr., 8 (consecutive 1992-1999)
Recent meeting, leading jockey: C. J. Woodley, 93, 2002
Recent meeting, leading owner: Francis E. Boustany Jr., 10, 2002; Kelly Huval, 10, 2002
Recent meeting, leading trainer: Dale Angelle, 74, 2002

Records
Single day jockey wins: Gerard Melancon, 6, 1984; Shane Sellers, 6, 1985; James Avant, 6, 1988; Curt Bourque, 6, 1989; Curt Bourque, 6, 1991; James Avant, 6, 1995; Kirk LeBlanc, 6, 1995
Single meet, leading jockey by wins: Curt Bourque, 141; Randy Romero, 141
Single meet, leading trainer by wins: Don Cormier Sr., 91, 1996

Track Records, Main Dirt
4 furlongs: Rare Trip, :46 3/5, May 20, 1977
4 1/2 furlongs: Bag in Hand, :51.60, August 28, 2000
5 furlongs: Hallowed Dreams, :57.40, July 3, 1999
5 1/2 furlongs: Hot Patriot, 1:04, June 6, 1997
6 furlongs: Rail, 1:09.20, July 22, 1995
7 1/2 furlongs: Top Silk, 1:31.40, June 2, 1991
1 mile: Selma's Boy, 1:36 3/5, July 12, 1981; Winning Connection, 1:36.60, August 19, 2000
1 mile 40 yards: Mr. D's Prank, 1:43 3/5, July 11, 1983
1 mile 70 yards: State Commander, 1:42, April 22, 1991
1 1/16 miles: Nin's Pick, 1:43 2/5, June 19, 1977
1 1/8 miles: Report to Glory, 1:50.80, August 9, 1993
1 3/16 miles: Beebe's Fair Eve, 2:00 4/5, September 13, 1968
1 1/4 miles: Nageire, 2:10 4/5, June 3, 1972
1 3/8 miles: Stubzy, 2:22 2/5, September 10, 1970
1 1/2 miles: Just for Charlie, 2:41 2/5, September 15, 1986
1 5/8 miles: Lucky Man, 2:49.60, August 4, 2000
2 miles: Gray Gardner, 3:31 3/5, August 27, 1990
Other: 1 7/16 miles, Red and Bold, 2:30 1/5, July 31, 1988; 1 7/8 miles, Concho County, 3:19.60, August 18, 2000

Fastest Times of 2002
4 1/2 furlongs: Word of Advice, :51.80, May 18
5 furlongs: Fly Harold, :58.40, July 6; Gulf Developer, :58.40, May 10; Lark's Lark, :58.40, June 1; Monday Nite Mac, :58.40, May 10
5 1/2 furlongs: Hunters Halo, 1:03.80, July 15
6 furlongs: Sunny Brick, 1:09.60, June 21

7 1/2 furlongs: Sutter's Sparkle, 1:32.00, May 4; Thrive, 1:32.00, June 7
1 mile: No Its Not, 1:38.40, May 20
1 mile 70 yards: Tough Gus, 1:43.80, July 5
1 1/16 miles: Guiness On Tap, 1:45.60, June 7
1 1/8 miles: Paw Paw's Pride, 1:52.80, July 5
1 7/16 miles: Paw Paw's Pride, 2:28.40, July 19
1 5/8 miles: Lucky Man, 2:48.20, August 2

Fair Grounds

Thoroughbred racing has been conducted at the site of Fair Grounds in New Orleans with few interruptions since 1853, when a racetrack named Union Course held its first Thoroughbred meeting. The track, which has been called Fair Grounds since the 1860s, served as a military camp during the Civil and Spanish-American Wars. At times, changing political climates have halted racing, and devastating fires destroyed the facility in 1919 and '93. Fair Grounds survived, and some of the sport's most famous racehorses have run there. Legendary distaffer Pan Zareta died of pneumonia at Fair Grounds in 1918 and was buried at the track. Kentucky Derby winner Black Gold, winner of the Louisiana Derby at Fair Grounds in 1924, was fatally injured in the Salome Handicap in '28 and was buried in the track's infield. Other noted horses who have raced at Fair Grounds include 1941 Triple Crown winner Whirlaway, winner of the inaugural Louisiana Handicap in '42; multiple Fair Grounds stakes winner Master Derby, who captured the '75 Preakness Stakes (G1); and Silverbulletday, who won two Fair Grounds stakes during her '99 championship season. Since 1990, Fair Grounds has been owned by the Krantz family, whose members have worked to strengthen the track in the face of competition from other forms of gaming. After the 1993 fire destroyed its grandstand, temporary structures were used during construction of a $34.5-million grandstand and clubhouse, which opened on November 27, 1997. Fair Grounds, which offers racing from late November through late March, plays host to Louisiana Champions Day, a $1-million event for state-bred Thoroughbreds and Quarter Horses, in December. The Louisiana Derby (G2) in March is a prep race for the Kentucky Derby (G1).

Location: 1751 Gentilly Blvd., New Orleans, LA 70119
Phone: (504) 944-5515
Fax: (504) 944-2511
E-mail: fgno@accesscom.net
Web site: http://www.fgno.com
Year founded: 1852
Inaugural meeting: April 13, 1872
Acreage: 145
Number of stalls: 1,950

Officers
President: Bryan G. Krantz
Vice President: Vickie L. Krantz
General Manager: Bryan G. Krantz
Director of Racing: Mervin Muniz Jr.
Racing Secretary: Mervin Muniz Jr.
Director of Admissions: George Graham
Director of Marketing: Lenny Vangilder
Director of Mutuels: Eddie Fenasci
Director of Publicity: Lenny Vangilder
Director of Simulcasting: Raymond Beard
Director of Sales: Karen Robicheaux
Stewards: Bill Hartack, Larry Munster, Peter Kosiba

Track Announcer: Frank Mirahmadi, Michael Wrona
Track Photographer: Louis Hodges Jr.
Track Superintendent: Paul Gregoire

Racing Dates
2002: November 22, 2001-March 25, 2002, 89 days
2003: November 28, 2002-March 31, 2003, 85 days

Track Layout
Main circumference: 1 mile
Main track chute: 2 furlongs
Main width: 75 feet
Main length of stretch: 1,346 feet
Main turf circumference: 7 furlongs

Attendance
Total attendance recent meeting: 196,151, 2001/2002
Average daily recent meeting: 2,204, 2001/2002
Highest single day record: 23,662, November 27, 1969

Handle
Single day on-track handle: $740,854, March 12, 2000
Single day total handle all sources: $9,080,419, March 12, 2000
Average all sources recent meeting: $4,501,143, 2001/2002
Average on-track recent meeting: $255,777, 2001/2002
Total all sources recent meeting: $400,601,717, 2001/2002
Total on-track recent meeting: $22,764,119, 2001/2002

Mutuel Records
Highest win: $500.60, Grey Hip, March 16, 1933
Lowest Win: $2.20, C J's Star, January 3, 2002
Highest Exacta: $2,626.20, January 2, 1999
Lowest Exacta: $2.20, January 3, 2002
Highest Daily Double: $2,917, January 5, 1971
Lowest Daily Double: $5.20, March 10, 2002
Highest Pick 3: $23,731.40, December 26, 1999
Lowest Pick 3: $14.60, December 4, 1998
Highest Pick 6: $108,848.20, March 29, 1999
Highest Other Exotics: $91,533, Superfecta, March 29, 1999
Lowest Other Exotics: $61.80, Superfecta, January 24, 1998

Leaders
Recent meeting, leading trainer: Steven M. Asmussen, 68, 2001/2002
Recent meeting, leading owner: Nelson Bunker Hunt, 21, 2001/2002
Recent meeting, leading jockey: Eddie Martin Jr., 120, 2001/2002
Career, leading jockey by titles: Ronald Ardoin, 6
Career, leading trainer by titles: Jack Van Berg, 10

Records
Single day trainer wins: Thomas Amoss, 4, January 19, 1995
Single day jockey wins: James P. Bowlds, 6, March 11, 1965; E. J. Perrodin, 6, November 18, 1979; Randy Romero, 6, February 8, 1984; V. L. "Billy" Smith, 6, March 15, 1990; Shane Romero, 6, February 10, 1991; Shane Romero, 6, February 24, 1991
Single meet, leading trainer by wins: Jack Van Berg, 92
Single meet, leading jockey by wins: Randy Romero, 181

Track Records, Main Dirt
4 furlongs: Blue Carbon, :46 1/5, March 18, 1967
4 1/2 furlongs: Debs Mini Bars, :52 1/5, March 8, 1971
5 furlongs: Foreign Pass, :57.50, November 27, 1998
5 1/2 furlongs: Chief Howcome, 1:03.26, February 11, 2000
6 furlongs: Mountain General, 1:08.03, November 28, 2002
7 furlongs: For Fair, 1:24 2/5, February 8, 1915
7 1/2 furlongs: Begue, 1:33 3/4, March 30, 1896
1 mile: Kitwe, 1:35.94, March 26, 1998
1 mile 40 yards: Total Rage, 1:38.52, March 23, 1997
1 mile 70 yards: Zevson, 1:41, November 26, 1936
1 1/16 miles: Pie in Your Eye, 1:42.02, March 19, 1994
1 1/8 miles: Phantom On Tour, 1:48.13, March 8, 1998
1 3/16 miles: Half Magic, 1:56 1/5, March 21, 1977
1 1/4 miles: It's the One, 2:01 4/5, March 21, 1982; Westheimer, 2:01 4/5, March 24, 1985; Herat, 2:01 4/5, March 16, 1986

1 3/8 miles: Carroll Road, 2:18 1/5, January 30, 1965; Tahuna, 2:18 1/5, March 6, 1965
1 1/2 miles: Tahuna, 2:32 2/5, March 13, 1965
1 5/8 miles: From Afar, 2:49 3/5, February 27, 1954; Major Mansir, 2:49 3/5, January 4, 1904
1 3/4 miles: Aladdin Prince, 3:01 2/5, April 5, 1981
2 miles: Bolster, 3:28 1/5, February 7, 1920
Other: 2 furlongs, Baloma, :21 4/5, February 14, 1952; 2 furlongs, Baloma, :21 4/5, January 26, 1952; 3 furlongs, Henry's Baby, :33 4/5, February 15, 1971; 3 furlongs, It's the Law, :33 4/5, February 18, 1976; 3 1/2 furlongs, Silver Finn, :41, February 24, 1925; 1 mile 20 yds, Grumpy, 1:40 3/5, February 5, 1916; 1 mile 20 yds, Lucky R., 1:40 3/5, January 11, 1916; 1 9/16 miles, Retintin, 2:42 4/5, March 28, 1970; 1 7/8 miles, Julius Caesar, 3:19, February 27, 1900; 2 miles 70 yds, Omar, 3:39 1/5, March 3, 1940; 2 1/16 miles, Quib's Bally, 3:47 1/5, March 6, 1948; 2 1/4 miles, Marvin Neal, 3:56, February 23, 1907; 3 miles, Colonist, 5:35, February 17, 1906; 4 miles, Major Mansir, 8:04 3/5, March 21, 1903

Course Records, Main Turf
5 1/2 furlongs: Beware Avalanche, 1:03.37, March 12, 2000
7 1/2 furlongs: Northcote Road, 1:29.26, March 7, 2000
1 mile: Rich and Ready, 1:35 4/5, January 17, 1982
1 1/16 miles: Dixie Poker Ace, 1:42, January 8, 1994
1 1/8 miles: Rich and Ready, 1:46 4/5, February 21, 1982
1 3/8 miles: Present the Colors, 2:17 1/5, April 4, 1982
1 1/2 miles: Palace Panther (Ire), 2:32, April 6, 1986
Other: 1 9/16 miles, To the Floor, 2:40.26, March 29, 1999

Fastest Times of 2002 (Dirt)
5 furlongs: Land of Dixie, :57.98, January 31
5 1/2 furlongs: Punching, 1:03.74, December 5
6 furlongs: Mountain General, 1:08.03, November 28
1 mile: Almuhathir, 1:37.16, November 30
1 mile 40 yards: Mineshaft, 1:38.97, December 20
1 1/16 miles: Take Charge Lady, 1:42.09, February 16
1 1/8 miles: Parade Leader, 1:50.44, March 3

Fastest Times of 2002 (Turf)
About 5 1/2 furlongs: Full Spectrum, 1:03.62, December 22
About 7 1/2 furlongs: Mercenary, 1:30.61, January 10
About 1 mile: Bedanken, 1:36.96, December 21
About 1 1/16 miles: Zamek, 1:43.69, March 25
About 1 1/8 miles: Sarafan, 1:48.88, March 24

Louisiana Downs

Louisiana Downs, located near Shreveport in Bossier City, opened in 1974. Built by the late shopping-center developer Edward DeBartolo Sr., the track introduced the Super Derby (G2) in 1980, and since then the fall race has attracted leading three-year-olds. The first running was won by Temperence Hill, winner of that year's Belmont Stakes (G1). The 1¼-mile race's purse initially was $500,000, then one of the biggest pots in the sport, and was increased to $1-million in 1987, when Kentucky Derby (G1) and Preakness Stakes (G1) victor Alysheba defeated Candi's Gold. In the late 1990s, however, it was reduced to its original $500,000 purse. Two three-year-olds—Sunday Silence in 1989 and Tiznow in 2000—used the Super Derby as a stepping stone to victory in the Breeders' Cup Classic (G1) and Horse of the Year honors in their respective years. DeBartolo's racetrack holdings were sold in the years following his death, and Louisiana Downs was acquired by his son-in-law, John York II. In November 2001, a group of investors headed by Shreveport lawyer Jim

Davis announced plans to buy Louisiana Downs. In 2002, Harrah's Entertainment Corp. acquired approximately 95% of Louisiana Downs and opened a casino with 905 slot machines in 2003, with expansion to about 1,500 machines in the future. Harrah's valued the purchase, including renovations, at $183.4-million.

Location: 8000 E. Texas St., Bossier City, LA 71171-5519
Phone: (318) 742-5555; (800) 551-2361
Fax: (318) 741-2591
E-mail: bburgess@ladowns.com
Web site: http://www.ladowns.com
Year founded: 1974
Inaugural meeting: October 30, 1974, to January 26, 1975
Abbreviation: LaD
Acreage: 350
Number of stalls: 1,360
Seating capacity: 17,240

Officers
Vice President: Ray A. Tromba
General Manager: Ray A. Tromba
Director of Racing: Patrick J. Pope
Racing Secretary: Patrick J. Pope
Director of Operations: Cliff D. Burge
Director of Communications: Jennifer Ray
Director of Admissions: Tom Stedman
Director of Finance: Kristi Holley
Director of Marketing: Jennifer Ray
Director of Mutuels: Holly Romain
Director of Publicity: Scott Jester
Director of Sales: Tom Showalter
Director of Simulcasting: Dick Pollack
Horsemen's Liaison: Patrick J. Pope
Stewards: Coleman Lloyd, Johnnie Johnson, Judy Dugas
Track Announcer: Frank Mirahmadi
Track Photographer: Reed Palmer Photography
Track Superintendent: George McDermott
Other officials: John C. York II, Chairman

Racing Dates
2002: June 28-September 22, 80 days
2003: June 27-November 9, 80 days

Track Layout
Main circumference: 1 mile
Main track chutes: 1 1/4 miles, 7 furlongs
Main width: 80 feet
Main length of stretch: 1,010 feet
Main turf circumference: 7 furlongs 50 feet
Main turf width: 70 feet
Main turf length of stretch: 940 feet

Attendance
Average daily recent meeting: 3,542, 2002
Highest single day record: 26,513, May 26, 1986
Total attendance recent meeting: 283,360, 2002

Handle
Total all sources recent meeting: $184,064,560, 2002
Total on-track recent meeting: $18,257,364, 2002
Average all sources recent meeting: $2,300,807, 2002
Average on-track recent meeting: $228,217, 2002
Single day total handle all sources: $6,763,853, October 2, 1999
Single day on-track handle: $4,371,781, September 27, 1987

Mutuel Records
Highest win: $249, B.J.'s Spruce, June 21, 1996
Lowest Win: $2.20, Appealing Breeze, 1989; $2.20, Richman, 1990; $2.20, Morning Meadow, 1993; $2.20, Runaway Venus, 1999; $2.20, Smart Ring, 1999
Highest Exacta: $2,780.80, May 1, 1994
Lowest Trifecta: $18.90, August 19, 1994
Highest Daily Double: $5,556.20, October 14, 1976
Highest Pick 3: $37,286.20, June 6, 1992

Lowest Pick 3: $11.80, September 12, 1994
Highest Pick 6: $555,287, May 25, 1991
Highest Other Exotics: $52,017.60, Superfecta, June 2, 1996

Leaders
Career, leading owner by stakes wins: John Franks, 144
Recent meeting, leading trainer: Cole Norman, 125, 2002
Career, leading owner by titles: John Franks, 18
Career, leading trainer by stakes wins: Frank Brothers
Career, leading trainer by wins: C. W. Walker, 820
Recent meeting, leading jockey: Gerard Melancon, 116, 2002
Recent meeting, leading owner: Kenneth W. Murphy, 27, 2002
Career, leading jockey by wins: Ronald Ardoin, 2,773
Career, leading trainer by titles: Frank Brothers, 7
Career, leading jockey by stakes wins: Ronald Ardoin
Career, leading jockey by titles: Larry Snyder, 6, Ronald Ardoin, 6

Records
Single day jockey wins: Ricky Frazier, 7, October 27, 1984
Single day trainer wins: Frank Brothers, 5, May 16, 1982; Frank Brothers, 5, September 3, 1984; Jack Van Berg, 5, December 5, 1976
Single meet, leading jockey by wins: Ronald Ardoin, 198
Single meet, leading owner by wins: John Franks, 65, 1983
Single meet, leading trainer by wins: Frank Brothers, 99, 1987

Track Records, Main Dirt
4 1/2 furlongs: Sondor, :51 3/5, May 16, 1984
5 furlongs: Oh Mar, :57.21, September 25, 2000
5 1/2 furlongs: Fighting K, 1:02.84, September 11, 1993
6 furlongs: Tangent, 1:08 4/5, April 28, 1984
6 1/2 furlongs: Prince of the Mt., 1:14.98, May 23, 1996
7 furlongs: Carrysport, 1:21 3/5, July 4, 1984
1 mile 70 yards: Country Jim, 1:39 2/5, July 4, 1982
1 1/16 miles: Nelson, 1:41.44, August 15, 1993
1 1/8 miles: Mocha Express, 1:48.14, July 24, 1999
1 3/16 miles: Jungle Pocket, 1:57 2/5, August 15, 1984
1 1/4 miles: Tiznow, 1:59.84, September 30, 2000
1 1/2 miles: Frankie's Pal, 2:31 4/5, September 3, 1990
1 3/4 miles: Frankie's Pal, 2:58 4/5, October 14, 1990
2 miles: Vain Lass, 3:35 1/5, November 16, 1975
Other: 1 13/16 miles, Stage Door Joey, 3:09.91, September 20, 1992

Course Records, Main Turf
5 furlongs: Mo Dinero, :55.40, September 26, 1999
7 1/2 furlongs: Chuck N Luck, 1:28 2/5, August 5, 1989
1 mile: Cherokee Circle, 1:34 1/5, July 24, 1983
1 1/16 miles: Clever Song, 1:40 1/5, August 11, 1985; Marastani, 1:40.29, May 28, 1994
1 1/4 miles: Tali Hai, 2:04.19, August 31, 1997
1 3/8 miles: Semillero (Chi), 2:13 1/5, October 21, 1985

Fastest Times of 2002 (Dirt)
5 furlongs: Joyful Tune, :56.90, September 7
5 1/2 furlongs: Gethomefirst, 1:03.62, June 30
6 furlongs: Halo Cat, 1:09.40, June 28
6 1/2 furlongs: That Tat, 1:15.95, August 18
7 furlongs: Donna's Mailbag, 1:22.29, November 2
1 mile 70 yards: Strike Reality, 1:41.42, July 18
1 1/16 miles: Classic Stag, 1:44.61, November 2
1 1/8 miles: Essence of Dubai, 1:49.43, September 21

Fastest Times of 2002 (Turf)
5 furlongs: Sunshine Classic, :55.79, August 31
About 5 furlongs: Go J. S. Go, :55.97, September 2
7 1/2 furlongs: Sherry's Cahill, 1:30.50, July 7
About 7 1/2 furlongs: Nelson's Magic, 1:28.47, September 27
1 mile: Prefer, 1:35.93, August 31
About 1 mile: Clooney, 1:34.88, September 28
1 1/16 miles: Rebridled, 1:41.69, September 2
About 1 1/16 miles: Steel Man, 1:41.59, August 2

Maryland

Laurel Park

Located in Laurel, midway between Baltimore and Washington, D.C., Laurel Park became a part of the Magna Entertainment Corp. family when the company headed by Frank Stronach bought a majority interest in the Maryland Jockey Club in 2002. Racing began at Laurel in 1911, and, three years later, New York City grocery entrepreneur James Butler acquired the track and hired Col. Matt Winn as the track's general manager. In 1947, the Maryland Jockey Club bought the track from Butler's estate, but the state's racing commission refused to permit Pimlico Race Course's dates to be moved to Laurel. Baltimore industrialist Morris Schapiro purchased the track in 1950 and put his youngest son, John D. Schapiro, in charge of the facility. Two years later, Laurel debuted the Washington, D.C., International, a turf stakes that was the first North American race to become a major annual target of European horses. Among the winners of the race was Racing Hall of Fame member Kelso in 1964. In 1984, Schapiro sold Laurel to a group of investors headed by Frank De Francis. In late 1986, De Francis and partners bought Pimlico, thus consolidating ownership of Maryland's major tracks. With the Breeders' Cup Turf (G1) and Mile (G1) attracting European and American turf horses, the International was suspended after the 1994 running. De Francis died in 1989 and was succeeded as president by his son, Joe, who remains a minority owner with his sister, Karin.

Location: P.O. Box 130, Laurel, MD 20725
Phone: (301) 725-0400
Fax: (301) 725-4561
E-mail: webmaster@marylandracing.com
Web site: http://www.marylandracing.com
Inaugural meeting: October 2, 1911
Abbreviation: Lrl
Acreage: 360
Number of stalls: 880
Seating capacity: 5,185

Officers
President: Joseph A. De Francis
General Counsel and Treasurer: Martin Jacobs
Senior Vice President of Public Relations and Marketing: Karin De Francis
Chief Operating Officer: Louis J. Raffetto
Executive Vice President: Timothy T. Capps
Chief Administrative Officer: Robert J. Di Pietro
Chief Financial Officer: Douglas J. Illig
Senior Vice President, Facilities and Courses: John Passero
Senior Vice President, Finance and Development: Antonio Cobuzzi
Racing Secretary: Georganne Hale
Director of Admissions: Ronald Louden
Director of Finance: Douglas J. Illig
Director of Facilities: John Olsen
Director of Communications: Mike Gathagan
Director of Marketing: Carrie L. Everly
Director of Mutuels: Elizabeth Quill
Director of Operations: Louis J. Raffetto Jr.
Director of Publicity: Mike Gathagan
Director of Sales: Keith Leacock

Director of Simulcasting: Dennis Smoter
Horsemen's Liaison: Phoebe Hayes
Stewards: Phillip E. Grove, William J. Passmore
Track Announcer: Dave Rodman
Track Photographer: James McCue
Track Superintendent: John Olsen

Racing Dates
2003: January 1-March 31; July 24-August 22; October 7-December 21

Track Layout
Main circumference: 1 1/8 miles
Main track chute: 7 furlongs
Main width: 75 feet
Main length of stretch: 1,344 feet
Main turf circumference: 1 mile
Main turf width: 70 feet
Main turf length of stretch: 990 feet

Attendance
Highest single day record: 40,276, November 11, 1958

Handle
Average all sources recent meeting: $2,893,886, Summer 2002
Average on-track recent meeting: $300,086, Summer 2002
Total all sources recent meeting: $63,665,495, Summer 2002
Total on-track recent meeting: $6,601,885, Summer 2002

Leaders
Career, leading trainer by titles: King T. Leatherbury, 25
Recent meeting, leading jockey: Horatio Karamanos, 31, Summer 2002
Recent meeting, leading trainer: Rodney Jenkins, 8, Summer 2002

Records
Single day jockey wins: Chuck Baltazar, 7, 1969, Horatio Karamanos, 7, October 26, 2002
Single meet, leading jockey by wins: Edgar Prado, 197, Winter 1998/1999
Single meet, leading trainer by wins: King T. Leatherbury, 86, Winter 1995

Track Records, Main Dirt
4 1/2 furlongs: Weighmaster, :52 2/5, April 13, 1964
5 furlongs: Dave's Friend, :57, November 21, 1980
5 1/2 furlongs: Wire Me Collect, 1:02.80, January 25, 1998
6 furlongs: Richter Scale, 1:07.95, July 15, 2000
6 1/2 furlongs: Ebonizer, 1:15 2/5, November 23, 1990
7 furlongs: Tappiano, 1:21 2/5, February 12, 1989
7 1/2 furlongs: Tidal Surge, 1:29.52, March 12, 1994
1 mile: Skipper's Friend, 1:34 2/5, December 6, 1980
1 1/16 miles: Willard Scott, 1:41 4/5, November 16, 1985
1 1/8 miles: Excellent Tipper, 1:47.64, July 5, 1992
1 3/16 miles: Testing, 1:54.51, October 21, 2000
1 1/4 miles: Richie the Coach, 1:59.96, November 23, 1996
1 3/8 miles: Amber Wave, 2:17 4/5, November 28, 1968
1 3/4 miles: Asserche, 2:58.51, February 13, 1994

Course Records, Main Turf
5 furlongs: Sikkim, :57 2/5, November 21, 1967
5 1/2 furlongs: Oops I Am, 1:02.20, June 14, 1994
6 furlongs: Texas Glitter, 1:08, October 28, 2000
1 mile: Portsmouth, 1:34, October 30, 1965
1 1/16 miles: Water Moccasin, 1:39 2/5, June 15, 1987
1 1/8 miles: Finder's Choice, 1:46.13, October 24, 1992
1 3/16 miles: Guilded Youth, 1:53.70, June 27, 1998
1 1/4 miles: Dynamic Trick 1:58.42, October 22, 2000
1 1/2 miles: Kelso, 2:23 4/5, November 11, 1964
2 miles: Summer Ensign, 3:23.64, June 15, 1993

Fastest Times of 2002 (Dirt)
5 1/2 furlongs: Crossing Point, 1:02.45, November 1
6 furlongs: Crafty Guy, 1:08.98, December 7
7 furlongs: P Day, 1:22.04, February 16
1 1/16 miles: Intensive Dancer, 1:42.57, December 27
1 1/8 miles: P Day, 1:48.76, March 29

Fastest Times of 2002 (Turf)
5 1/2 furlongs: Pal Joey, 1:02.96, August 11; Trip Charge, 1:02.96, August 4
1 mile: A Queen's Smile, 1:37.70, August 8
1 1/16 miles: Jeremiah's Story, 1:41.82, August 22
1 1/8 miles: La Reine's Terms, 1:46.04, August 11

Pimlico Race Course

The first horse to win a stakes race at Baltimore's Pimlico Race Course during the track's inaugural season in 1870 is the namesake of one of the world's most famous horse races. Preakness, a colt by legendary 19th-century sire Lexington, won the Dinner Party Stakes that year, and in 1873 the Preakness Stakes (G1) made its debut. The race was not run in 1891, '92, or '93, and then it was held in New York for 15 years before it was returned to Pimlico in 1909. The Preakness now is the middle jewel of the Triple Crown and is run on the third Saturday in May. The day before the Preakness, Pimlico runs the race's three-year-old filly counterpart, the Black-Eyed Susan Stakes (G2). Another of the track's most famous races is the Pimlico Special Handicap (G1), which in 1938 captured the attention of the nation when Seabiscuit defeated War Admiral in a two-horse race. Magna Entertainment Corp. purchased majority ownership of Pimlico and Laurel Park near Washington, D.C., for $50.6 million in 2002. The two tracks share host duties for the Maryland Million, a day of racing for state-breds. Pimlico long has been called "Old Hilltop," a nickname that dates from the era when a small rise in the infield was a favorite gathering place for trainers and racing fans. The hill was removed in 1938, but the nickname remained.

Location: 5200 Park Heights Ave., Baltimore, MD 21215
Phone: (410) 542-9400
Fax: (410) 466-2521
E-mail: webmaster@marylandracing.com
Web site: http://www.marylandracing.com
Year founded: 1743 (Maryland Jockey Club)
Inaugural meeting: October 25, 1870
Acreage: 140
Number of stalls: 800
Seating capacity: 13,047

Officers
President: Joseph A. De Francis
Senior Vice President of Public Relations and Marketing: Karin De Francis
Chief Operating Officer: Louis J. Raffetto
Executive Vice President: Timothy T. Capps
Chief Administrative Officer: Robert J. Di Pietro
Chief Financial Officer: Douglas J. Illig
Senior Vice President, Facilities and Courses: John Passero
Senior Vice President, Finance and Development: Antonio Cobuzzi
Racing Secretary: Georganne Hale
Director of Facilities: John Olsen
Director of Communications: Mike Gathagan
Director of Marketing: Carrie L. Everly
Director of Mutuels: Elizabeth Quill
Director of Sales: Keith Leacock

Director of Simulcasting: Dennis Smoter
Horsemen's Liaison: Phoebe Hayes
Stewards: Josette Edwards, Philip E. Grove, William J. Passmore
Track Announcer: Dave Rodman
Track Photographer: Double J Photos
Track Superintendent: John Olsen

Racing Dates
2003: April 2-June 8; September 3-October 4

Track Layout
Main circumference: 1 mile
Main track chutes: 1 1/4 miles, 6 furlongs
Main width: 70 feet
Main length of stretch: 1,152 feet
Main turf circumference: 7 furlongs

Attendance
Highest single day record: 104,454, May 19, 2001

Handle
Average on-track recent meeting: $374,871, Fall 2002, $535,102, Spring 2002
Average all sources recent meeting: $3,785,516, Fall 2002, $5,099,491, Spring 2002
Total on-track recent meeting: $28,895,509, Spring 2002, $7,497,422, Fall 2002
Total all sources recent meeting: $275,372,515, Spring 2002, $75,710,316, Fall 2002
Single day total handle all sources: $71,407,008, May 18, 2002

Mutuel Records
Highest win: $574, Cadeaux, May 7, 1913
Lowest Win: $2.10, War Admiral, November 3, 1937
Highest Exacta: $5,223.60, May 27, 1989
Lowest Exacta: $2.60, March 28, 1981
Highest Daily Double: $5,932.20, December 1, 1955
Highest Other Exotics: $414,243.90, Twin Trifecta

Leaders
Career, leading jockey by titles: Edgar Prado, 11
Career, leading trainer by titles: King T. Leatherbury, 25
Recent meeting, leading jockey: Mario Pino, 72, Spring 2002; Ryan Fogelsonger, 49, Summer/Fall 2002
Recent meeting, leading owner: Daniel Borislow, 6, Summer/Fall 2002; Michael Gill, 30, Spring 2002
Recent meeting, leading trainer: Dale Capuano, 12, Summer/Fall 2002; Dale Capuano, 28, Spring 2002

Records
Single meet, leading jockey by wins: Kent Desormeaux, 184, Summer-1989
Single meet, leading trainer by wins: King T. Leatherbury, 100, 1976

Track Records, Main Dirt
4 furlongs: Gavotte, :47 2/5, May 4, 1925
4 1/2 furlongs: Countess Diana, :51.50, June 6, 1997
5 furlongs: Goldminer's Dream, :56.80, May 20, 1993
5 1/2 furlongs: Higher Strata, 1:02.46, July 29, 1995
6 furlongs: Northern Wolf, 1:09, August 18, 1990
7 furlongs: Zeus, 1:26, May 3, 1921
1 mile: June Grass, 1:37 3/5, May 2, 1923
1 mile 70 yards: Sabotage, 1:41 2/5, December 17, 1958
1 1/16 miles: Deputed Testamony, 1:40 4/5, May 19, 1984
1 1/8 miles: Private Terms, 1:47 1/5, May 27, 1989
1 3/16 miles: Farma Way, 1:52.55, May 11, 1991
1 1/4 miles: Manzotti, 2:01 4/5, March 19, 1988
1 3/8 miles: Narwhal, 2:16 2/5, December 15, 1962
1 1/2 miles: War Trophy, 2:29 2/5, November 8, 1948
1 5/8 miles: Market Wise, 2:43 1/5, November 13, 1941
1 3/4 miles: Blue Hills, 2:55 2/5, October 25, 1949
2 miles: Everett, 3:25 3/5, October 31, 1920

Other: 1 11/16 miles, Post Morton, 2:57 4/5, December 7, 1957; 2 miles 70 yds, Filisteo, 3:30 4/5, October 31, 1941; 2 1/16 miles, Beau Diable, 3:35 3/5, December 10, 1960; 2 1/4 miles, Edith Cavell, 3:52 1/5, November 13, 1926; 2 1/2 miles, Miss Grillo, 4:14 3/5, November 12, 1948

Course Records, Main Turf
5 furlongs: Elberton, :56.11, September 15, 2001
7 furlongs: Lofty Peak, 1:23 1/5, May 14, 1956
1 mile: North East Bound, 1:33.42, May 7, 2000
1 1/16 miles: Air Attack, 1:40.33, May 27, 1991
1 1/8 miles: Double Booked, 1:47.04, May 17, 1991
1 3/16 miles: Bayard Park, 2:01, May 7, 1966
1 1/4 miles: Manzotti, 2:01 4/5, March 19, 1988
1 3/8 miles: Dunsinyne, 2:13.74, June 22, 1997
1 1/2 miles: Fort Marcy, 2:27 2/5, May 9, 1970
Other: 1 7/8 miles, Brightly, 3:17, December 1, 1955

Fastest Times of 2002 (Dirt)
4 1/2 furlongs: Renegade Warrior, :51.70, April 21
5 furlongs: Kentucky J B, :57.80, May 2
5 1/2 furlongs: Key West Kid, 1:05.11, May 8
6 furlongs: Storm Punch, 1:09.47, May 4
1 1/16 miles: Call Me Mr. Vain, 1:42.80, April 13
1 1/8 miles: Grundlefoot, 1:49.65, June 15
1 3/16 miles: War Emblem, 1:56.36, May 18

Fastest Times of 2002 (Turf)
5 furlongs: Splendeed, :56.10, May 25
1 mile: Buying Rain, 1:34.89, June 12
1 1/16 miles: Caught Out, 1:40.55, May 12
1 1/8 miles: Shopping for Love, 1:48.61, September 21
About 2 1/8 miles: Anofferucantrefuse, 3:41.74, May 17

Timonium

Although Timonium's annual live meeting lasts only a few days through Labor Day, in conjunction with the Maryland State Fair, it attracts more than a half-million fans every year to the community located near Baltimore's northern border. In 2001, Timonium lost two dates of its usual ten dates because of insufficient purses but still had a successful meet. In 2002, the track again ran eight dates, with an 11% reduction in average daily purses.

Timonium, which was struggling in the early 1990s until the addition of simulcasting both into and out of the track, is operated by the not-for-profit Maryland State Fair and Agricultural Society Inc., which directs all profits to the fair, 4-H Club awards, and improvements.

Racing at Timonium began in September 1887. Its five-eighths-mile track has a four-furlong chute and a 6½-furlong chute. A record crowd of 17,306 attended the races on September 4, 1967. Timonium's record handle of $2,452,514 was set on August 29, 1998. In the early 1980s, it raced as many as 42 dates, but its season was sharply reduced in 1985 when Maryland's mile tracks began running year-round.

Location: 2200 York Rd., Timonium, MD 21094
Phone: (410) 252-0200
Fax: (410) 561-5610
E-mail: msfair@msn.com
Web site: http://www.bcpl.lib.md.us/~mdstfair
Year founded: 1887
Acreage: 100
Number of stalls: 600
Seating capacity: 4,850

Officers
President: Howard M. Mosner Jr.
Vice President: Howard M. Mosner Jr.

General Manager: Howard M. Mosner Jr.
Racing Secretary: Georganne Hale
Secretary: John H. Mosner Jr.
Treasurer: John H. Mosner Jr.
Director of Mutuels: Richard Insley
Track Announcer: Richard Wooley
Track Photographer: Jerry Frutkoff
Track Superintendent: Don Denmyer

Racing Dates
2003: August 23-September 1, 10 days
2004: August 28-September 6, 10 days

Track Layout
Main circumference: 5/8 mile
Main track chutes: 4 furlongs, 6 1/2 furlongs
Main width: 70 feet
Main length of stretch: 700 feet

Attendance
Average daily recent meeting: 4,363, 2002
Highest single day record: 17,306, September 4, 1967
Total attendance recent meeting: 34,904, 2002

Handle
Single day on-track handle: $2,452,514, August 29, 1998
Total all sources recent meeting: $17,027,554, 2002
Total on-track recent meeting: $2,681,540, 2002
Average all sources recent meeting: $1,702,755, 2002
Average on-track recent meeting: $335,193, 2002

Leaders
Recent meeting, leading jockey: Ryan Fogelsonger, 22, 2002
Recent meeting, leading trainer: Dale Capuano, 7, 2002

Fastest Times of 2002
4 furlongs: Bill the Banker, :45.61, September 1
6 1/2 furlongs: Kenny N Billy, 1:18.35, August 29
About 6 1/2 furlongs: Huber Woods, 1:17.94, September 1
1 mile: Nimbus Twothousand, 1:42.20, August 28
1 1/16 miles: Shiny Sheet, 1:45.58, August 31

Massachusetts

Brockton Fair

Location: P.O. Box 6, Brockton, MA 02303-0006
Phone: (508) 586-8000
Fax: (508) 821-3239
E-mail: sue@brocktonfair.com
Web site: http://www.brocktonfair.com
Abbreviation: BF

Racing Dates
2002: June 29-August 17

Northampton Fair

Location: P.O. Box 305 Northampton MA 01061-0305
Phone: (413) 584-2237
Fax: (413) 586-1297
Web site: http://www.3countyfair.com
Year founded: 1818 (fair)
Inaugural meeting: 1942
Acreage: 50+
Seating capacity: 2,400
Number of stalls: 450

Officers
President: Dayne Tracy
Vice President: Frank Basile
General Manager: Bruce Shallcross

Director of Racing: Sandy Staniewski
Racing Secretary: Sam Siciliano
Treasurer: Norman Ray
Director of Operations: John Renaud
Director of Communications: Dayne Tracy
Director of Marketing: Sandy Staniewski
Director of Mutuels: Jack Kovalski
Director of Publicity: Sandy Staniewski
Director of Simulcasting: Sandy Staniewski
Horsemen's Liaison: Art Lyman
Stewards: Richard Tobin, William Keene
Track Announcer: Peter Kules
Track Photographer: CB Photo
Track Superintendent: Joe Jasinki

Racing Dates
2002: August 23-September 15
2003: August 29-September 14, 10 Days

Track Layout
Main circumference: 1/2 mile

Attendance
Average daily recent meeting: 2,000

Handle
Single day on-track handle: $351,000

Leaders
Recent meeting, leading jockey: Ivan Ortiz Jr., 15, 2002
Recent meeting, leading trainer: Anthony Tamburino, 9, 2002

Interesting Facts
Major Races: Mass-Bred Handicap Smirnoff and T.G.I.Friday's Fair Challenge

Fastest Times of 2002
About 5 furlongs: Shamrock Tune, :55.42, September 6
About 6 1/2 furlongs: Rajya Sabha, 1:21.64, September 7

Suffolk Downs

Built in just 62 days for $2-million by the Eastern Racing Association, Suffolk Downs opened before an estimated crowd of 35,000 in East Boston on July 10, 1935, as the nation's only racetrack with a concrete grandstand. Just one month later, 52,726 fans set an attendance record that still stands.

Suffolk's signature race, the Massachusetts Handicap (G2), was inaugurated in 1935, and it has been won by such champions as Seabiscuit in 1937 and two-time MassCap winners Cigar and Skip Away in the 1990s. To conserve purse money for a longer meet, the MassCap was canceled for 2003 only.

On June 4, 1966, a fan ran onto the homestretch during the Mayflower Stakes and was brushed by three horses but sustained no injuries. Legendary promoter Bill Veeck carded chariot races, livestock giveaways, and mock Indian battles in the infield during his tenure there in 1969 and '70. He also successfully sued the state to allow children to attend the races.

Following a two-year shutdown in 1990 and '91, James B. Moseley's and John Hall's Sterling Suffolk Racecourse Ltd. leased the track and Thoroughbred racing returned to Boston. In 1997, Suffolk Racecourse LLC bought Suffolk for $40-million. Suffolk received a major boost at the end of 2001 when the state legislature authorized $3-million in tax revenue and uncashed winning tickets to be used for purses.

Location: 111 Waldemar Ave., East Boston, MA 02128
Phone: (617) 567-3900
Fax: (617) 561-5100
E-mail: sufdowns@shore.net
Web site: *http://www.suffolkdowns.com*
Year founded: 1935
Inaugural meeting: July 10-August 10, 1935, 28 days
Acreage: 190
Number of stalls: 1,380
Seating capacity: 9,505

Officers
President: Patricia Moseley
Director of Racing: John H. Morrissey
Racing Secretary: John H. Morrissey
Director of Operations: Joseph Fatalo
Director of Marketing: JoEllen Gradowski
Director of Mutuels: James Alcott
Director of Publicity: Christian Teja
Stewards: James Gigliotti, Richard DeStasio, William Keen
Track Announcer: Larry Collmus

Racing Dates
2002: September 29, 2001-June 8, 2002, 152 days
2003: September 28, 2002-June 14, 2003

Track Layout
Main circumference: 1 mile
Main track chutes: 1 1/4 miles, 6 furlongs
Main width: 90 feet
Main length of stretch: 1,030 feet
Main turf circumference: 7 furlongs
Main turf width: 65 to 70 feet
Main turf length of stretch: 1,030 feet

Attendance
Highest single day record: 52,726, August 10, 1935
Record daily average for single meet: 18,388, 1945

Handle
Record daily average for single meet: $1,164,240, 1946
Single day on-track handle: $2,175,836, May 30, 1960
Single day total handle all sources: $5,867,414, May 31, 1997

Mutuel Records
Highest win: $445, Sue Harper, June 14, 1940
Highest Exacta: $9,923,80, January 13, 1985
Highest Trifecta: $51,778, January 13, 1985
Lowest Trifecta: $7.40
Highest Daily Double: $16,515, May 25, 1979
Lowest Daily Double: $3.60, May 30, 1998
Highest Pick 3: $10,515.40, December 26, 1992
Lowest Pick 3: $11, April 21, 1993
Highest Pick 6: $25,399, November 28, 1982
Highest Other Exotics: $23,079.40, Superfecta, March 27, 1996, $9,923.90, Perfecta, January 13, 1985
Lowest Other Exotics: $3.60, Perfecta, November 10, 1985

Leaders
Recent meeting, leading trainer: Ron Dandy, 28, Fall-2002
Recent meeting, leading jockey: Joe Hampshire, 75, Fall-2002

Records
Single day jockey wins: Leroy Moyers, 7, July 4, 1967
Single meet, leading jockey by wins: S. Elliott, 381, 1989
Single meet, leading trainer by wins: W. W. Perry, 140, 1989

Track Records, Main Dirt
4 furlongs: Crimson Streak, :45 2/5, April 6, 1970
4 1/2 furlongs: Lovely Gypsy, :51 4/5, May 7, 1965; Happy Voter, :51 4/5, May 16, 1966
5 furlongs: Rene Depot, :57 2/5, June 25, 1972
5 1/2 furlongs: Stage Trick, January 14, 2001, The Way Holme, March 20, 2002
6 furlongs: Canal, 1:08 1/5, May 14, 1966
1 mile: Back Bay Brave, 1:35 1/5, July 12, 1986

1 mile 70 yards: Half Breed, 1:40, May 23, 1964
1 1/16 miles: Talent Show, 1:41 4/5, May 12, 1962; Bear the Palm, 1:41 4/5, July 3, 1977
1 1/8 miles: Skip Away, 1:47.27, May 30, 1998
1 3/16 miles: Shut Out, 1:55 2/5, July 4, 1942
1 1/4 miles: Helioscope, 2:01, May 19, 1955
1 1/2 miles: Connie Rab, 2:30 3/5, May 15, 1954
1 5/8 miles: Count Fire, 2:45 2/5, June 23, 1962
1 3/4 miles: Toulouse, 2:58 2/5, June 16, 1956
2 miles: Hutch, 3:35 2/5, August 1, 1950
Other: 2 furlongs, Adriano's Girl, :21.94, June 4, 1997; 2 1/16 miles, Bold Fencer, 3:35 4/5, April 18, 1983; 2 miles 70 yds, On the Square, 3:39 4/5, April 16, 1973; 2 1/4 miles, Fundy Bay, 3:54 1/5, December 9, 1973

Course Records, Main Turf

5 furlongs: Bishop Ridley, :57 1/5, July 19, 1987
7 1/2 furlongs: Times Ahead, 1:32 2/5, September 3, 1988
1 mile: I'ma Handful, 1:39 2/5, September 4, 1983
1 mile 70 yards: Darn Special, 1:42.44, May 31, 1997
1 1/16 miles: Landing Court, 1:44.91, October 26, 1994
1 3/8 miles: Chompion, 2:20 4/5, July 18, 1970, Gaybrook Swan, 2:20 4/5, July 18, 1970
1 1/2 miles: *Akbar Khan, 2:30 3/5, June 17, 1957
2 miles: Jean-Pierre, 3:19 4/5, June 28, 1969
Other: 1 15/16 miles, Jamf, 3:11 1/5, July 4, 1975

Fastest Times of 2002 (Dirt)

5 furlongs: Baby Trend, :59.16, May 6
5 1/2 furlongs: The Way Holme, 1:04.74, March 20
6 furlongs: Starship Seminole (Ven), 1:09.92, February 12
1 mile: Soes Bandit, 1:38.77, March 19
1 mile 70 yards: Threepointer, 1:42.41, February 12; Tracethe Call, 1:42.41, May 20
1 1/16 miles: Northwest Hill, 1:44.28, May 20
1 1/8 miles: Macho Uno, 1:50.52, June 1
1 1/4 miles: Code Found, 2:09.49, March 13

Fastest Times of 2002 (Turf)

About 5 furlongs: Natalis (Ire), :58.65, October 11
About 1 mile: Likeable Irish, 1:39.90, June 3
About 1 mile 70 yards: Jokesonme, 1:45.14, May 25
About 1 1/16 miles: Spider Wire, 1:46.93, October 9

Michigan

Great Lakes Downs

One of America's newest racetracks, Great Lakes Downs was born in 1999 out of the necessity to preserve live racing in Michigan following the shuttering of Ladbroke-owned Detroit Race Course. Located at the site of a former Standardbred track in Muskegon, Great Lakes Downs came together quickly as a group of horse owners and racing enthusiasts raised the capital to renovate the facility and prepare for racing.

After an understated first meeting in 1999, the track gained national attention in the winter of 2000 when Frank Stronach-led Magna Entertainment Corp., in the midst of a track-buying spree, added Great Lakes Downs to its holdings. In early 2003, Magna reported that Great Lakes was losing money and that it might write down the book value of the track. Magna has received preliminary local approval for building a new track near Detroit.

Location: 4800 S. Harvey St., Muskegon, MI 49444
Phone: (231) 799-2400
Fax: (231) 798-3120
Web site: *http://www.greatlakesdowns.com*

Officers

General Manager: Chris Dragone
Racing Secretary: Allan Plever
Director of Publicity: Janie Goddard
Director of Finance: Marc McCurry
Director of Mutuels: Mashelle Ring
Director of Simulcasting: Amy MacNeil
Track Announcer: Matt Hook

Racing Dates

2002: April 29-October 29, 118 days
2003: April 26-October 28, 118 days

Track Layout

Main circumference: 5 furlongs
Main track chutes: 4 furlongs, 7 furlongs
Main length of stretch: 580 feet

Leaders

Recent meeting, leading trainer: Richard R. Rettele, 65, 2002
Recent meeting, leading jockey: T. D. Houghton, 175, 2002

Track Records, Main Dirt

4 furlongs: Dinner Band, :45.87, May 15, 2001
5 1/2 furlongs: Scent a Grade, 1:06.66, June 5, 2000
6 furlongs: Timely Factor, 1:13.15, October 16, 2001
6 1/2 furlongs: Touch of Power, 1:19.57, August 13, 2001
7 furlongs: Secret Romeo, 1:24.77, September 2, 2001
1 mile: Override Battle, 1:40.14, October 31, 2000; Secret Romeo, 1:40.14, October 29, 2001
1 mile 70 yards: Secret Romeo, 1:49.50, November 4, 2000
1 1/16 miles: That Monetary, 1:47.28, August 27, 2001
1 1/8 miles: The Bold Bruiser, 1:54.11, October 28, 2000
Other: 2 furlongs, Skirt in the Wind, :23.52, June 22, 1999

Fastest Times of 2002

4 furlongs: True Wisper, :46.13, September 24
5 1/2 furlongs: Deputy Stripe, 1:06.37, July 22
6 furlongs: Deputy Stripe, 1:12.57, August 27
6 1/2 furlongs: Native Ruck, 1:19.43, July 28
7 furlongs: Touch of Power, 1:26.56, May 29
1 mile: Poppa Corky, 1:40.84, August 23
1 1/16 miles: Above the Wind, 1:47.43, August 6
1 1/8 miles: Secret Romeo, 1:54.59, September 17

Mt. Pleasant Meadows

Location: 500 N. Mission Rd., Mount Pleasant, MI 48804-0220
Phone: (517) 773-0012
Fax: (517) 773-7616

Officers

Director of Publicity: Geoff Huntly

Racing Dates

2002: May 4-September 28
2003: May 3-September 28, 36 days

Track Layout

Main circumference: 4 furlongs
Main width: 60 feet

Leaders

Recent meeting, leading jockey: Colin Skinner, 19, 2002
Recent meeting, leading trainer: Scot D. Jensen, 12, 2002

Fastest Times of 2002

4 furlongs: Wild About Jackie, :48.50, June 2
4 1/2 furlongs: Up in Smoke, :54.15, June 29
5 furlongs: Grandpa Ed, 1:00.35, September 14
5 1/2 furlongs: Business Decision, 1:08.45, August 17
6 furlongs: Grandma Ruby, 1:18.00, July 28

Minnesota

Canterbury Park

Canterbury Park is located in Shakopee, southwest of Minneapolis and St. Paul. When the track first opened in 1985, three years after Minnesota legalized parimutuel wagering, it was known as Canterbury Downs, and its ownership group included the Santa Anita Operating Co. In 1990, the track was purchased by Ladbroke Racing Corp., but, due to declining business, closed in '92. One year later, Irwin Jacobs, a Twin Cities financier, purchased the track and sold it to businessman and breeder Curtis Sampson, Sampson's son, Randy, and partner Dale Schenian. Four months later, the owners held an initial public offering of the newly created Canterbury Park Holding Corp. The track, which reopened in 1995 as Canterbury Park, offers Thoroughbred racing and some Quarter Horse racing during its live racing season, which runs from mid-May through early September. In 1999, Canterbury held the first of three consecutive runnings of the Claiming Crown, which quickly became recognized as a major sporting event in Minnesota. In 2001, the 11-race event worth $550,000 drew claiming-level runners from across the United States. Canterbury is scheduled to host the event in odd-numbered years from 2003-'07. The Canterbury Card Club, Minnesota's first legal card club, opened in 2000 at the track, and its revenues supplement race purses. In 2003, Canterbury sought legislative approval for slot machines.

Location: 1100 Canterbury Rd., Shakopee, MN 55379
Phone: (952) 445-7223; (800) 340-6361
Fax: (952) 496-6480
E-mail: cbypark@canterburypark.com
Web site: http://www.canterburypark.com
Year founded: 1984
Inaugural meeting: June 26, 1985
Acreage: 355
Number of stalls: 1,620
Seating capacity: 22,830

Officers
President: Randall Sampson
General Manager: Randall Sampson
Director of Racing: Douglas Schoepf
Racing Secretary: Douglas Schoepf
Director of Operations: Nat Wess
Director of Finance: Judy Dahlke
Director of Marketing: Linda Erickson
Director of Mutuels: Eric Halstrom
Director of Simulcasting: Linda Arnoldi
Horsemen's Liaison: Mary Green
Track Announcer: Paul Allen
Track Photographer: Palmer/Malarkey Photography
Track Superintendent: Tony Caterina

Racing Dates
2002: May 17-September 2, 62 days
2003: May 16-September 1, 62 days

Track Layout
Main circumference: 1 mile
Main track chutes: 1 1/4 miles, 3 1/2 furlongs, 6 1/2 furlongs
Main turf circumference: 7 furlongs
Main turf chute: 1 1/16 miles

Attendance
Average daily recent meeting: 4,350, 2002
Total attendance recent meeting: 265,363, 2002
Highest single day record: 27,439, April 24, 1987

Handle
Single day on-track handle: $2,265,404, June 28, 1987
Average all sources recent meeting: $687,041, 2002
Average on-track recent meeting: $502,510, 2002
Total all sources recent meeting: $41,909,520, 2002
Total on-track recent meeting: $30,653,098, 2002

Leaders
Recent meeting, leading jockey: Seth Martinez, 93, 2002
Recent meeting, leading trainer: David Van Winkle, 40, 2002
Recent meeting, leading owner: Jer-Mar Stables, 14, 2002; Lothenbach Stables, 14, 2002

Interesting Facts
Previous names and dates: Canterbury Downs 1984-1994

Track Records, Main Dirt
4 1/2 furlongs: Gallapiat's Song, :51.27, June 23, 1991
5 furlongs: Feather in My Hat, :57 1/5, August 25, 1990
5 1/2 furlongs: Nickel Slot, 1:02 4/5, May 17, 1989
6 furlongs: So Long Seoul, 1:08 3/5, May 6, 1990; Iwazza Bad Boy, 1:08.60, August 18, 1996
6 1/2 furlongs: Don's Irish Melody, 1:14, June 12, 1988
1 mile: Minneapple, 1:35 1/5, September 27, 1987
1 mile 70 yards: Come Summer, 1:40 1/5, August 18, 1985
1 1/16 miles: Power Boat, 1:41 4/5, July 30, 1988
1 1/8 miles: Olympio, 1:46.47, July 7, 1991
1 1/4 miles: John Bullit, 2:04 3/5, July 25, 1986
1 1/2 miles: Loustros (GB), 2:32 3/5, August 28, 1987
1 3/4 miles: Luciole (Arg), 2:59 4/5, October 12, 1985
2 miles: My Tulles Free, 3:25 3/5, September 1, 1986
Other: 3 1/2 furlongs, In Moderation, :39.11, May 26, 1997

Course Records, Main Turf
5 furlongs: Thatsusintheolebean, :56.40, May 23, 1998
7 1/2 furlongs: Honor the Hero, 1:28, June 18, 1995
1 mile: Go Go Jack, 1:33.40, June 3, 1995
1 mile 70 yards: Numchuek, 1:39 1/5, July 6, 1988
1 1/16 miles: Little Bro Lantis, 1:40.20, June 17, 1995
1 1/8 miles: Fluffkins, 1:44, July 22, 1995
1 3/8 miles: Treizieme, 2:12 3/5, August 3, 1986
Other: 1 7/8 miles, John Bullit, 3:11 2/5, September 26, 1987

Fastest Times of 2002 (Dirt)
3 1/2 furlongs: Surf Liner, :39.37, June 2
5 furlongs: Giant Slam, :58.01, June 30
5 1/2 furlongs: Susie Blues, 1:03.41, May 17
6 furlongs: Expert, 1:08.92, June 16
6 1/2 furlongs: Expert, 1:15.66, July 6
1 mile: Bobby Naz, 1:37.32, May 24
1 mile 70 yards: J. P. Jet, 1:40.26, August 3
1 1/16 miles: J. P. Jet, 1:43.97, August 25

Fastest Times of 2002 (Turf)
5 furlongs: My Girl Lisa, :57.56, May 27
7 1/2 furlongs: Al's Dearly Bred, 1:29.20, June 15
About 7 1/2 furlongs: Awol Soldier, 1:29.58, July 13
1 mile: Gist, 1:36.03, May 31
About 1 mile: Premiere Dancer, 1:35.68, June 30
1 1/16 miles: Sarah Jade, 1:42.19, June 16
About 1 1/16 miles: Rich Vein (Ire), 1:41.83, June 1
1 3/8 miles: King's Verse, 2:14.51, September 2

Montana

Great Falls

Location: P.O. Box 442, Black Eagle, MT 59414
Phone: (406) 453-0080
Fax: (406) 453-0080
Abbreviation: GF

Racing Dates
2002: June 8-July 28
2003: July 4-August 2, 8 days

Leaders
Recent meeting, leading jockey: Shannon Wippert, 12, 2002
Recent meeting, leading trainer: Janis D. Schoepf, 5, 2002, Lyle Arthur, 5, 2002

Helena Downs

Location: P.O. Box 9706, Helena, MT 59604
Phone: (406) 457-9492

Western Montana Fair and Races

Location: 1101 South Ave. W., Missoula, MT 9801-7907
Phone: (406) 421-3247
Fax: (406) 728-7479
E-mail: fair@montana.com
Web site:: http://www.westernmontanafair.com
Year founded: 1879
Abbreviation: WMF
Acreage: 40
Number of stalls: 356
Seating capacity: 3000

Officers
General Manager: Scot Meader
Racing Secretary: Shorty Martin
Secretary: Toni Hinton
Director of Mutuels: Teri Lerch
Director of Operations: Scot Meader
Director of Publicity: Samuel Yewusika, Scot Meader
Director of Racing: Gary Keopplin
Director of Simulcasting: Montana Simulcast Partners
Stewards: John Ragen, Raleigh Swensrud, Walt Horning
Track Announcers: Phil Benson, Bruce Micklus

Racing Dates
2002: August 6-11, 6 days
2003: August 5-10, 6 days
2004: August 10-15, 6 days

Handle
Average on-track recent meeting: $61,938, 2002
Total on-track recent meeting: $617,397, 2002

Records
Single meet, leading jockey by wins: Mark Boaq, 2002
Single meet, leading trainer by wins: Mike Taylor, 2002

Track records, Main dirt
5 furlongs: Rejected Frenchman, 1:04, August 11, 1996
1 1/16 miles: Early Shove, 1:44.4, August 11, 1996
1 1/8 miles: Rulvic, 1:53.2, August 23, 1986

Fastest Time of 2002
About 5 furlongs: Merlot High, 1:04.80, July 27

Yellowstone Downs

Location: P.O. Box 1138, Billings, MT 59103
Phone: (406) 656-1619
Fax: (406) 633-2503

Officers
Director of Publicity: Ben Carlson

Racing Dates
2002: June 15-July 14, 6 days; August 24-September 22, 11 days
2003: August 23-September 21, 12 days

Handle
Average on-track recent meeting: $48,093, 2002
Total on-track recent meeting: $817,581, 2002

Leaders
Recent meeting, leading jockey: Russell David Kingrey, 21, 2002
Recent meeting, leading trainer: Dale Bagnell, 8, 2002

Fastest Times of 2002
5 1/2 furlongs: King of Adventure, 1:01.60, September 15
About 7 furlongs: Fruit Rapport, 1:25.60, September 15, Staged Reality, 1:25.60, September 2
7 furlongs: Second Addition, 1:27.00, June 23
1 mile 70 yards: Second Addition, 1:45.60, September 14

Nebraska

Horsemen's Atokad Downs

Live Thoroughbred racing in Nebraska did not die when Omaha's Ak-Sar-Ben closed in 1995 after 74 years. Ak-Sar-Ben, which was torn down in 1997, is Nebraska spelled backward. Atokad is Dakota spelled backward, and the track is located in Dakota County, in the state's northwest corner near the South Dakota border. The five-eighths-mile track in South Sioux City opened on September 20, 1956.

Atokad conducted a late-summer meeting in most years, though it did not race from 1998 through 2000. A single-day meet was resurrected in 2001 by Robert E. Lee, president of the Nebraska Horsemen's and Benevolent Protective Association. Eight races with total purses of $130,000 were held on September 22, 2001, and the track was to hold a one-day meet on July 19, 2003, to qualify for year-round simulcasting. A record crowd of 6,200 attended on October 18, 1958. The record handle of $483,486 was set on November 9, 1980.

Location: P.O. Box 518, South Sioux City, NE 68776
Phone: (402) 494-5869
Year founded: 1951
Inaugural meeting: September 20,1956
Acreage: 50
Seating capacity: 5,000
Number of stalls: 84 (120 overflow)

Officers
President: Bob Lee
Vice President: Bill Vannoy
General Manager: Tom Harris
Director of Racing: Tom Harris
Racing Secretary: Tom Harris
Secretary: Shelly Hosch
Treasurer: Thelma Carver
Director of Operations: Tom Harris
Director of Admissions: Sally Carver
Director of Auctions: Bob Lee
Director of Communications: Mike Fansler
Director of Finance: Mike Fansler
Director of Marketing: Mike Fansler
Director of Mutuels: Sean Bruillette
Director of Publicity: Mike Fansler
Director of Sales: Sally Carver

Director of Simulcasting: Tom Harris
Horsemen's Liaison: Bob Lee
Track Announcer: Charles Pernnell
Track Photographer: Coady Services
Track Superintendent: John Riney

Racing Dates
2002: September 21
2003: July 19

Track Layout
Main circumference: 5 furlongs
Main track chute: 6 furlongs and 50 yads
Main width: 70 feet
Main length of stretch: 660 feet

Attendance
Total attendance recent meeting: 5,000 est., 2001
Highest single day record: 6,200, October 18, 1958

Handle
Single day on-track handle: $483,486, November 9, 1980

Leaders
Recent meeting, leading jockey: Alejandro Granda, 2, 2002; D. Collins, 2, 2002
Recent meeting, leading trainer: D. Burns, 1, 2002; D. Burns, 1, 2002; Gary L. Kelley, 2, 2002; Gerald Big Hair, 1, 2002; Herb Riecken, 1, 2002; J. Ritter, 1, 2002; Ron Wise, 1, 2002; S. Sortino, 1, 2002
Recent meeting, leading owner: Dean and Julie Warwick, 1, 2002; Gary L. Kelley, 1, 2002; Herb Riecken, 1, 2002; Jack Breemes, 1, 2002; Leslie and Pearl Oerman, 1, 2002; Linda Parker, 1, 2002; Ron Wise, 1, 2002; Roger L. Boerkircher, 1, 2002.

Fastest Times of 2002
4 furlongs: Yokozuma, :46.40, September 21
About 6 furlongs: Solo Special, 1:17.00, September 21
1 mile: Schadow, 1:43.80, September 21
1 mile 70 yards: Full Response, 1:47.60, September 21; J. R. Honor, 1:47.60, September 21

Columbus Races

Opened in the 1950, Columbus Races in Columbus, 90 miles northwest of Lincoln, is operated on the Platte County Agricultural Society Fairgrounds. It was at Columbus that Racing Hall of Fame trainer Marion H. Van Berg and his son, Jack, also a Racing Hall of Fame member, began their careers. The elder Van Berg operated a sales barn—offering hogs, cattle, and horses—in addition to running his stable. Columbus usually runs a 25-day summer meet from mid-July through mid-September, racing on Fridays, Saturdays, and Sundays. Extensive simulcasting is also offered. The five-eighths-mile oval has a 6½-furlong chute. A record crowd of 8,856 attended on September 3, 1973. The record handle of $719,725 was set exactly 11 years later.

Location: 822 15th St., Columbus, NE 68601
Phone: (402) 564-0133
Fax: (402) 564-0990
E-mail: agpark@megavision.com
Web site: *http://www.agpark.com*
Year founded: June 2, 1941
Inaugural meeting: July 1942
Abbreviation: Cls
Acreage: 160
Seating capacity: 4,000
Number of stalls: 1,000

Officers
President: Lynn Anderson
Vice President: Eldon Engel
General Manager: Gary Bock
Racing Secretary: Dennis Kochevar
Secretary: Gary Kruse
Treasurer: Larry Hemmer
Director of Publicity: Gary Bock
Director of Finance: Gary Kruse
Director of Mutuels: Leon Ebel
Director of Racing: Dennis Kochever
Director of Simulcasting: Gary Bock
Stewards: Jim Heberland, Quient Schaeffer, Rol Shaal
Track Announcer: Keith Nelson
Track Photographer: Coady Photography
Track Superintendent: Bill Luesche

Racing Dates
2002: July 26-September 15, 25 days

Track Layout
Main circumference: 5 furlongs
Main length of stretch: 650 feet
Main track chutes: 4 furlongs-6 1/2 furlongs
Main width: 80 feet

Attendance
Average daily recent meeting: 1,850
Highest single day record: 8,856, September 3, 1973
Total attendance recent meeting: 48,000

Handle
Single day on-track record: $719,725, September 3, 1984

Leaders
Recent meeting, leading jockey: Armando Martinez, 44, 2002
Recent meeting, leading trainer: David C. Anderson, 14, 2002

Track records, Main dirt
4 furlongs: Kips Flyer, :39 4/5, August 11, 2000
6 furlongs: Eve's Choice, 1:10 2/5, August 27, 1994
6 1/2 furlongs: Jae Ranch, 1:17, August 12, 1984
1 mile 70 yards: Ilafan, 1:41.40, Swptember 9, 1984
1 1/16 miles: Foreign Intent, 1:44.40, September 21, 1974

Fastest Times of 2002
3 1/2 furlongs: Timetoprofit, :39.60, August 24
6 furlongs: Irish Flyer, 1:11.20, August 17; Luby Do, 1:11.20, September 2
6 1/2 furlongs: High Dice, 1:17.40, September 2
1 mile 70 yards: Dust Bag, 1:42.00, August 25
1 1/16 miles: Zavana, 1:46.00, August 16

Fonner Park

The closing of Omaha's Ak-Sar-Ben racecourse in 1995 dealt a serious blow to Nebraska racing. But Fonner Park in Grand Island has been one of the tracks to keep the flame flickering in the Cornhusker State with its down-home brand of racing.

The 280-acre facility staged its first race meet in 1954. Fonner Park is operated by a nonprofit organization, with the track's profits going to charitable and community activities in the Grand Island region. With the advent of telephone-account wagering in Nebraska in October 2001, Fonner officials sought to reach more of the state's bettors.

The five-furlong facility has never been known as a racing mecca, but some interesting horses have competed at Fonner. One of them is sprinter Leaping Plum, who in 2001 won his seventh consecutive renewal of the opening-week Grasmick Handicap. The gelding also won the Coca-Cola Sprint Handicap four consecutive times (1995-'98).

Human athletes have also been in the spotlight at Fonner, with jockey Ken Shino winning eight races there on April 1, 2001, including seven straight.

Location: 700 E. Stolley Park Rd., Grand Island, NE 68802
Phone: (308) 382-4515
Fax: (308) 384-2753
E-mail: fonnerpark@aol.com
Web site: http://www.fonnerpark.com
Year founded: 1953
Inaugural meeting: April 29, 1954
Acreage: 240
Number of stalls: 1,100
Seating capacity: 5,766

Officers
President: Frank Haack
Vice President: Doyle Hulme, Francis Gauthier, Gary Rosacker
General Manager: Hugh Miner Jr.
Director of Racing: Douglas Schoepf
Racing Secretary: Douglas Schoepf
Secretary: Barry Sandstrom
Treasurer: Jim Cannon
Director of Operations: Bruce A. Swihart
Director of Mutuels: William McConnell
Director of Simulcasting: Todd W. Otto
Track Announcer: Matt Hook
Track Photographer: Coady Photography
Track Superintendent: Rick Danburg

Racing Dates
2002: February 9-May 11, 40 days
2003: February 8-May 4, 38 days

Track Layout
Main circumference: 5/8 mile
Main track chute: 4 furlongs, 6 1/2 furlongs
Main width: 70 feet
Main length of stretch: 700 feet
Training track: 1/2 mile

Attendance
Highest single day record: 10,387, April 2, 1977

Handle
Single day on-track handle: $1,204,660, April 16, 1983

Mutuel Records
Highest Win: $520.40, Black Ticket, March 10, 1977
Lowest Win: $2.20, Ben's Whiz, March 30, 1974; $2.20, Real Style, March 30, 1974; I'ma Game Master, April 29, 1995, $2.20
Highest Exacta: $5,421, March 28, 1994
Lowest Exacta: $4, May 6, 2000
Highest Trifecta: $26,474.40, March 30, 1990
Lowest Trifecta: $14.60, March 15, 1998
Highest Daily Double: $5,451.20, March 18, 1977
Lowest Daily Double: $5, March 10, 1994; $5, April 21, 1995
Highest Pick 3: $13,800.80, February 27, 1988
Lowest Pick 3: $3.20, March 18, 2000
Highest Other Exotics: $17,526.60, Superfecta, March 23, 2001
Lowest Other Exotics: $271.40, Superfecta, March 4, 2001

Leaders
Career, leading jockey by titles: R. D. Williams, 9
Recent meeting, leading trainer: David C. Anderson, 26, 2002
Career, leading trainer by titles: Tim Gleason, 8
Recent meeting, leading jockey: Perry Compton, 72, 2002
Single meet, leading jockey by wins: Perry Compton, 85, 2000

Single meet, leading trainer by wins: Marvin Johnson, 50, 2000

Records
Single day jockey wins: Ken Shino, 8, April 2, 2000
Single day trainer wins: Tim Gleason, 5, February 18, 1989; Marvin Johnson, 5, February 26, 2000; Marvin Johnson, 5, April 2, 2000
Single meet, leading jockey by wins: Perry Compton, 85
Single meet, leading trainer by wins: Marvin Johnson, 50

Track Records, Main Dirt
4 furlongs: Leaping Plum, :44.20, February 17, 1996
5 1/2 furlongs: Little L.M., 1:04 2/5, April 12, 1975
6 furlongs: Orphan Kist, 1:10, April 8, 1989
6 1/2 furlongs: Majority of One, 1:17, March 18, 1989
1 mile: Brian's Star, 1:36 3/5, April 9, 1986; High On Laraka, 1:36 3/5, April 19, 1986
1 mile 70 yards: Advice, 1:40, April 25, 1987; Shamtastic, 1:40, April 26, 1986
1 1/16 miles: Sahara King, 1:43, April 27, 1996
1 1/8 miles: Potro, 1:51.40, April 25, 1993
1 3/8 miles: Meat Loaf, 2:22 2/5, April 29, 1970
Other: 1 7/16 miles, Wenga, 2:30 2/5, May 1, 1968

Fastest Times of 2002
4 furlongs: R C Mr Hay Boy, :45.80, February 16
6 furlongs: Medium Rare, 1:12.00, April 20
6 1/2 furlongs: Gin N Ginger, 1:18.00, May 4
1 mile: Timing's the Key, 1:38.40, April 20
1 mile 70 yards: Little Joe Lewis, 1:43.00, May 3
1 1/16 miles: Miner's Prize, 1:48.80, April 27
1 1/8 miles: American Pace, 1:57.40, May 11

Horsemen's Park

Boasting a simulcasting facility that offers wagering on 15 to 18 racetracks daily, Horsemen's Park opened on January 3, 1998, for simulcasting in south-central Omaha, four miles south of the former Ak-Sar-Ben site. Two live races were held each day on two consecutive days in July 1998 by the Nebraska Horsemen's Benevolent and Protective Association, which owns and operates the track.

The meet was expanded to three days in 2000, with more than $200,000 now offered in purses each year. The track is a five-eighths-mile oval with chutes for seven-furlong and 1⅛-mile races. The simulcasting facility offers seating for 2,800 and contains 600 closed-circuit monitors.

Location: 6303 Q St., Omaha, NE 68117
Phone: (402) 731-2900
Fax: (402) 731-5122
Seating capacity: 2,800

Officers
President: Robert E. Lee
General Manager: Dick Moore
Racing Secretary: Greg Hosch
Director of Mutuels: Mary Palais, Mary Snelling
Director of Simulcasting: Patricia Shefland
Track Superintendent: Tim Hurd

Racing Dates
2002: July 19-July 21, 3 days
2003: July 10-July 13, 3 days

Track Layout
Main circumference: 5 furlongs
Main width: 65 feet
Main length of stretch: 680 feet

Leaders
Recent meeting, leading jockey: Ken A. Shino, 3, 2002
Recent meeting, leading trainer: C. Stuart, 1, 2002; D. Anderson, 1, 2002; H. Robertson, 1, 2002; Herb Riecken, 1, 2002; J. Weedin, 1, 2002; Phil Cirian, 1, 2002; R. Morse, 1, 2002; Ray Tracy Jr., 1, 2002
Recent meeting, leading owner: Bluestem Farm, 1, 2002; Dennis S. Johnson, 1, 2002; Gordon Nicholas, 1, 2002; Herb Riecken, 1, 2002; Joseph L. Koziol, 1, 2002; Joseph L. Sola, 1, 2002; Lloyd DeBruycker, 1, 2002; Luann J. Kizer-Sirucek, 1, 2002

Fastest Times of 2002
6 furlongs: Luby Do, 1:10.40, July 20
1 mile: High Dice, 1:37.00, July 20
1 3/8 miles: Aly Aly Oxen Free, 2:18.00, July 21

Lincoln State Fair

Location: 27th St., P.O. Box 81223, Lincoln, NE 68501-1223
Phone: (402) 474-5371
Fax: (402) 473-4114
Web site: http://www.statefair.org

Officers
President: B. J. Meyer
General Manager: Pat Lloyd
Racing Secretary: Gregory C. Hosch
Director of Marketing: Chris Rasmussen
Director of Mutuels: Mark Jensen
Track Superintendent: Scott Yound
Track Announcer: Scott Yound

Racing Dates
2002: May 17-July 14, 34 days
2003: May 9-July 5, 34 days

Leaders
Recent meeting, leading jockey: Jerry Carkeek, 59, 2002
Recent meeting, leading trainer: David C. Anderson, 29, 2002

Fastest Times of 2002
4 furlongs: Poppys Grey Cat, :47.40, June 20
4 1/2 furlongs: Mr Clearwater, :50.00, June 9
6 furlongs: Genuine Lass, 1:10.20, June 20
1 mile: Sensitive Ghost, 1:36.00, July 14
1 mile 70 yards: Whats Gonna, 1:39.80, June 16
1 1/16 miles: Renato, 1:43.40, June 13
1 1/8 miles: Flashy Finale, 1:52.00, June 2
2 miles: Red Dirt Roughneck, 3:30.80, July 4

New Hampshire

Rockingham Park

Rockingham Park has survived a 25-year shutdown, a hurricane, and a horrific fire in its long history, but changing economics may have ended its tenure as a Thoroughbred track. In 2003, "The Rock" switched to all Standardbred racing, and its owners have said the facility may be sold and developed if the New Hampshire Legislature does not approve slot machines. Located in Salem, Rockingham opened on June 28, 1906, before a crowd of more than 10,000, thanks to the work of John "Bet-A-Million" Gates and August Belmont II. That initial 21-day meet had one fundamental problem: Betting on horses was illegal in New Hampshire. Pinker-

ton detectives closed the track, and it remained shuttered for 25 years, though it was used as a site for an aviation exposition, the Rockingham Fair, Grand Circuit harness racing (without betting), a bivouac during World War I, and auto racing when a wooden track was laid over the dirt track.

With some prodding by famed sportswriter Damon Runyon, New Hampshire legislators reconsidered the ban on pari-mutuel racing, and the track reopened in 1933 and subsequently attracted champions Discovery and Seabiscuit. In September 1938, a hurricane whipped across the track and blew track announcer Babe Rubenstein's box off the roof. Dr. Fager raced at Rockingham in 1967, winning the New Hampshire Sweepstakes Classic by 1¼ lengths over In Reality.

An early-morning fire on July 29, 1980, destroyed the grandstand and damaged the clubhouse. Rockingham reopened in 1984 under the ownership of Rockingham Venture Inc., headed by Joseph E. Carney Jr., who died in March 2003. In 1985, a turf course was added. A plush Sports Club and family picnic pavilion were added in 1991 after full-card, interstate simulcasting was approved.

Location: Rockingham Park Blvd., P.O. Box 47, Salem, NH 03079
Phone: (603) 898-2311
Fax: (603) 898-1424
Web site: http://www.rockinghampark.com
Year founded: 1906
Inaugural meeting: June 28, 1906
Acreage: 325
Number of stalls: 1,400
Seating capacity: 15,000

Officers
Vice Presidents: Edward J. Keelan, Edward M. Callahan
General Manager: Edward M. Callahan
Director of Racing: Bob DeStasio
Racing Secretary: L. J. Pambianchi Jr.
Secretary: Daniel Callaghan
Treasurer: Thomas F. Carney
Director of Admissions: Larry Murphy
Director of Communications: Lynne Snierson
Director of Marketing: Lynne Snierson
Director of Mutuels: Kathleen Brothers
Director of Publicity: Lynne Snierson
Director of Simulcasting: John Vitale
Steward: Thomas Smith
Track Announcer: John Vitale
Track Photographer: Louis Hodges Jr.
Track Superintendent: Ray Messina

Racing Dates
2002: June 9-September 22, 75 days

Track Layout
Main circumference: 1 mile
Main track chutes: 1 1/4 miles, 6 furlongs
Main width: 83 feet
Main turf circumference: 7 furlongs
Main turf chute: 1 1/8 miles

Attendance
Highest single day record: 41,509, September 6, 1965

Handle
Single day on-track handle: $2,669,721, September 2, 1968
Single day total handle all sources: $2,669,721, September 2, 1968

Leaders
Career, leading jockey by titles: Rudy Baez, 10
Recent meeting, leading jockey: Josi(J Hampshire Jr., 102, 2002
Recent meeting, leading owner: Hy-Hopes Farm, 38, 2002
Recent meeting, leading trainer: Ron Dandy, 67, 2002

Records
Single day jockey wins: Rudy Baez, 7, September 27, 1991; Willie Turnbull, 7, July 31, 1942
Single meet, leading jockey by wins: Harry Vega, 302, 1989

Track Records, Main Dirt
4 furlongs: Maria's Brown Eyes, :46 1/5, May 28, 1987
4 1/2 furlongs: Kipper Katz, :52.44, June 25, 1997
5 furlongs: Sneaky Pal, :56 4/5, July 8, 1974
5 1/2 furlongs: Bama Redd, 1:03 4/5, May 21, 1987
6 furlongs: Dandy Blitzen, 1:08 4/5, August 29, 1959
1 mile 40 yards: Zafarrancho (Arg), 1:38 1/5, June 19, 1987
1 1/16 miles: Herbalist, 1:42, August 19, 1972
1 1/8 miles: Dr. Fager, 1:48 1/5, July 15, 1967
1 1/4 miles: Dr. Fager, 1:59 4/5, September 2, 1967
1 1/2 miles: Girder, 2:29 3/5, October 10, 1953
Other: 2 miles 40 yds, Zagora, 3:34 2/5, September 2, 1985; 2 1/4 miles, Usable, 3:58 2/5, September 4, 1978; 2 1/2 miles, Bert Leo B., 4:23 3/5, July 5, 1978

Course Records, Main Turf
1 mile: Rode to Ankara, 1:37.19, June 24, 1993
1 1/16 miles: Simply Majestic, 1:42 3/5, June 18, 1989; Paris Opera, 1:42 3/5, July 4, 1990
1 1/8 miles: Statesmanship, 1:48.49, June 20, 1998
1 3/8 miles: Autonomo, 2:20.80, June 15, 1991
Other: 1 7/8 miles, Hypnotizer, 3:15 3/5, August 19, 1989

Interesting Facts
Trivia: Mentioned in the movie, *The Sting*

Fastest Times of 2002 (Dirt)
4 1/2 furlongs: Max a Million, :53.18, July 1
5 furlongs: Naushon, :58.07, June 9
5 1/2 furlongs: Jamie's Melody, 1:05.09, September 16
6 furlongs: Esteemed Friend, 1:09.78, July 20
1 mile 40 yards: Financial Diplomat, 1:40.86, September 22
1 1/16 miles: Dhaffir (Chi), 1:46.00, July 28
1 1/8 miles: Classic Time, 1:55.91, July 6
1 3/16 miles: Hankamer, 1:59.37, July 20
1 1/4 miles: Hankamer, 2:08.48, August 3

Fastest Times of 2002 (Turf)
1 mile: Sword Princess, 1:36.30, June 9
1 1/16 miles: Jackpot Jo, 1:43.65, June 9
1 1/8 miles: Calista (GB), 1:48.62, August 4
About 1 1/8 miles: Del Mar Show, 1:47.51, June 22

New Jersey

Atlantic City Race Course

When Atlantic City Race Course opened on July 22, 1946, its roster of stockholders read more like the A-list from a Hollywood party than investors in a racetrack in McKee City, 13 miles from the Jersey Shore resort. Bob Hope, Frank Sinatra, Harry James, Xavier Cugat, and Sammy Kaye were among the initial shareholders. John B. Kelly Sr., an Olympic gold-medal rower, brick magnate, and father of the late Princess Grace of Monaco, was Atlantic City's first president. Kelly was succeeded in 1960 by radio and television pioneer Dr. Leon Levy, whose son Robert succeeded him. An innovator who arranged the nation's first full-card simul-cast from Meadowlands racetrack in September 1983, the younger Levy also raced 1987 Belmont Stakes (G1) winner Bet Twice and champion sprinter Housebuster.

Crowds of more than 30,000 turned out to see such races as the United Nations Handicap (G1), first run in 1953, and such outstanding horses as Dr. Fager, Round Table, and Mongo. The disruption of the New Jersey circuit with the 1977 Garden State Park fire and the opening of Atlantic City's first casinos the following year hurt the track's business and led to a gradual reduction in its schedule. Atlantic City conducted a six-day, all-turf meet in 1999 and 2000, and it raced ten days in 2001 to qualify for year-round, full-card simulcasting. Atlantic City was sold to Greenwood Racing for $13-million in August 2001. Atlantic City runs a brief, all-turf meet at its McKee City plant as well as races at Monmouth Park.

Location: 4501 Black Horse Pike, Mays Landing, NJ 08330
Phone: (609) 641-2190
Fax: (609) 645-8309
Acreage: 250

Officers
President: Hal Handel
Vice President: Kathy D'Orsaneo
General Manager: Jim Miller
Racing Secretary: Sam Abbey
Secretary: Frank McDonnell
Treasurer: Anthony D. Ricci
Director of Racing: Sal Sinatra
Director of Publicity: Maureen Gallagher-Bugdon
Track Superintendent: William Gatto

Racing Dates
2002: May 3-May 14, 10 days
2003: May 9

Track Layout
Main circumference: 1 1/8 miles
Main width: 100 feet
Main length of stretch: 947.29 feet
Main turf circumference: 1 mile
Main turf width: 100 feet

Leaders
Recent meeting, leading trainer: Elizabeth M. Hendriks, 1, 2002; Keith C. Dickey, 1, 2002; Manuel Berrios, 1, 2002; Patricia Farro, 1, 2002; Paul Bonaventura, 1, 2002; Robert J. Durso, 1, 2002; Timothy C. Kreiser, 1, 2002
Recent meeting, leading jockey: Anibal Prado, 1, 2002; Eddie King Jr., 1, 2002; Eddie Martin Jr., 1, 2002; Gilbert Cappacetti, 1, 2002; Luis R. Rivera Jr., 1, 2002; Stewart Elliott, 1, 2002; Sunday Diaz, 1, 2002

Fastest Times of 2002 (Turf)
5 furlongs: B K Dodger, :58.76, May 10
5 1/2 furlongs: Open Zilzaling, 1:04.80, May 10
1 1/16 miles: Junk Yard Jerry, 1:44.10, May 10

Meadowlands

Meadowlands racetrack, located on former marshland in East Rutherford, New Jersey, has been the economic engine of the Meadowlands Sports Complex. Built by the New Jersey Sports and Exposition Authority for $340-million, the complex includes the Continental Airlines Arena, home of basketball's New Jersey Nets and hockey's New Jersey Devils, and Giants Stadium, where the New York Giants and Jets play football. Meadowlands, which held its first Thoroughbred meet in September 1977, has played host to a number of great moments in racing history. In 1978, Dr. Patches upset Seattle Slew in the Paterson Handicap. John Henry, once the all-time leading earner in the sport, closed his career with a stunning, come-from-behind victory in the Ballantine's Scotch Classic Handicap in 1984. Four years later, Alysheba set a 1¼-mile track record when he captured the Meadowlands Cup (G1) during his Horse of the Year campaign. Meadowlands, whose world-renowned Standardbred meet runs from December through August, conducts Thoroughbred racing in the fall. Its 2003 meet was shortened to 28 days in October and November.

Location: 50 Route 120, East Rutherford, NJ 07073
Phone: (201) 935-8500
Fax: (201) 460-4042
Web site: *http://www.thebigm.com*
Year founded: 1977
Inaugural meeting: September 6, 1977
Acreage: 220
Number of stalls: 1,760
Seating capacity: 4,650

Officers
President: George Zoffinger
Vice Presidents: Chris McErlean, Bob Kulina, Bruce Garland
General Manager: Chris McErlean
Racing Secretary: Sean Greely
Director of Admissions: Marianne Rotella
Director of Communications: Carol Hodes
Director of Finance: Jim Jemas
Director of Operations: Marcello Esposito
Director of Marketing: Glenn Cademartori
Director of Mutuels: Bob Halpin
Director of Publicity: Steve Schwartz
Director of Simulcasting: Carol Ciarco
Stewards: Joseph Piarulli, Richard Lawrenson, Samuel Boulmetis Sr.
Horsemen's Liaison: Mary Beth Yates
Track Announcers: Dave Johnson, Ken Warkentin, Sam McKee
Track Photographer: Equi-Photo
Track Superintendent: Bob Ashelman

Racing Dates
2002: May 15-May 16, 2 days; September 1-November 30, 64 days
2003: October 2-November 8, 28 days

Track Layout
Main circumference: 1 mile
Main track chutes: 1 1/4 miles, 6 furlongs
Main width: 90 feet
Main length of stretch: 990 feet
Main turf circumference: 7 furlongs

Attendance
Average daily recent meeting: 4,241, 2002
Highest single meet record: 1,772,209, 1977
Lowest single meet record: 260,172, 2000
Record daily average for single meet: 17,901, 1977
Highest single day record: 41,155
Total attendance recent meeting: 400,329, 2002

Handle
Record daily average for single meet: $2,619,909, 1994
Single day total handle all sources: $5,025,645, 1994
Total all sources recent meeting: $113,201,274, 2002
Total on-track recent meeting: $26,518,640, 2002
Average all sources recent meeting: $1,825,827, 2002
Average on-track recent meeting: $427,720, 2002

Mutuel Records
Highest win: $354.80, Great Normand, 1990
Lowest Win: $2.20, Spectacular Bid, 1979

Leaders
Career, leading jockey by titles: Joe Bravo, 8
Career, leading trainer by titles: John Forbes, 7
Career, leading jockey by stakes wins: Angel Cordero, 27; Jorge Velasquez, 27
Career, leading jockey by wins: Nick Santagata, 961
Career, leading trainer by stakes wins: Philip G. Johnson, 17
Career, leading trainer by wins: John H. Forbes, 590
Recent meeting, leading jockey: Eddie King Jr., 63, 2002
Recent meeting, leading owner: E & G Stables, 15, 2002
Recent meeting, leading trainer: John McCaslin, 19, 2002

Records
Single day trainer wins: John Forbes, 4, November 8, 1978
Single meet, leading jockey by wins: Joe Bravo, 142
Single meet, leading owner by wins: William C. Martucci, 34
Single meet, leading trainer by wins: John Forbes, 47; Joseph Pierce Jr., 47
Single day jockey wins: Julie Krone, 6, September 19, 1989

Track Records, Main Dirt
5 furlongs: Stu's Choice, :55.95, September 6, 1996
5 1/2 furlongs: King Bold Reality, 1:04 1/5, September 15, 1983
6 furlongs: Hay Cody, 1:07.81, September 6, 1996
1 mile: On the Tour, 1:34.43, November 10, 1999
1 mile 70 yards: Colonel Bart, 1:38.09, September 26, 1998
1 1/16 miles: Black Forest, 1:40.39, September 26, 1998
1 1/8 miles: Forty One Carats, 1:45.50, October 29, 1999
1 3/16 miles: Key Lory, 1:53.88, November 20, 1999
1 1/4 miles: Alysheba, 1:58 4/5, October 14, 1988

Course Records, Main Turf
5 furlongs: Special Occasion, :55.17, September 4, 2000
1 mile: True Diplomacy, 1:34, September 8, 1989
1 mile 70 yards: Cape Playhouse, 1:38, October 25, 1978
1 1/16 miles: Wanderkin, 1:39 2/5, September 30, 1988
1 3/8 miles: Rice, 2:12.02, September 25, 1998

Fastest Times of 2002 (Dirt)
5 furlongs: Bop, :56.05, September 2
5 1/2 furlongs: Luvinbillyiseasy, 1:02.55, October 17
6 furlongs: Outstander, 1:08.18, September 7
1 mile: Four Alert, 1:35.73, November 6
1 mile 70 yards: Hourly Storm, 1:38.58, September 5
1 1/16 miles: Saint Verre, 1:42.40, October 11
1 1/8 miles: Burning Roma, 1:48.95, October 4
1 1/4 miles: Forest Princess, 2:03.08, October 12

Fastest Times of 2002 (Turf)
5 furlongs: Sport d'Hiver, :55.88, September 14
About 5 furlongs: Tangier Sound, :59.05, November 4
1 mile: Access Agenda, 1:34.98, September 14
About 1 mile: Onasilverplatter, 1:38.96, October 23
1 mile 70 yards: River Rush, 1:39.16, September 20
About 1 mile 70 yards: Pyrite Search, 1:44.01, October 24
1 1/16 miles: Patrol, 1:39.60, September 13
1 3/8 miles: Royal Rapids, 2:14.64, September 13

Monmouth Park

The first Monmouth Park opened in July 1870 and was located three miles from Long Branch, New Jersey. The track's early years included performances by some of the era's most famous horses, including Longfellow and Miss Woodford, the first racehorse to earn $100,000. However, Monmouth fell victim to changing times, and it closed in 1893 after New Jersey outlawed wagering. Fifty years later, pari-mutuel wagering was legalized, and a group of investors led by Amory L. Haskell built a new Monmouth in 1946 at its current location in Oceanport. Since then, the track known for its seaside location has been a popular destination for some of the sport's leading Thoroughbreds. The track's richest race is the Haskell Invitational Handicap (G1), a $1-million race for three-year-olds and the first major East Coast event after the Triple Crown races. Monmouth also features the Philip H. Iselin Handicap (G2), named in honor of the former Monmouth president who became involved in the racetrack after it was constructed near his home. Among Iselin winners were two horses named Horse of the Year, Alysheba (1988) and Skip Away ('98). The Iselin formerly was known as the Monmouth Handicap, which was inaugurated in 1884.

Location: Oceanport Avenue, P.O. Box MP, Oceanport, NJ 07757-1298
Phone: (732) 222-5100
Fax: (732) 571-8658
E-mail: mpinfo@njsea.com
Web site: http://www.monmouthpark.com
Year founded: Original: 1870; Current Track: 1946
Inaugural meeting: July 30, 1870
Acreage: 500
Seating capacity: 18,000
Number of stalls: 1,600

Officers
President: George R. Zoffinger
General Manager: Robert J. Kulina
Racing Secretary: Sean Greely
Director of Operations: Horace Smith
Director of Admissions: Judi Gittins
Director of Finance: James Jemas
Director of Marketing: Peter Verdee
Director of Publicity: Bill Knauf
Director of Simulcasting: John S. Grasty
Horsemen's Liaison: Mary Beth Yates
Stewards: Harvey Wardell, Sam Boulmetis, Steve Pagano
Track Announcer: Larry Collmus
Track Photographer: Bill Denver
Track Superintendent: Dave Harrington
Other officials: Bill Knauf, Director of Media Relations

Racing Dates
2002: May 11-September 1, 76 days
2003: May 21-September 28, 92 days

Track Layout
Main circumference: 1 mile
Main track chutes: 1 1/4 miles, 6 furlongs
Main width: 100 feet
Main length of stretch: 985 feet
Main turf circumference: 7 furlongs
Main turf chute: 1 1/16 miles, 1 1/8 miles
Main turf width: 90 feet

Attendance
Highest single meet record: 1,150,658, 1981
Record daily average for single meet: 20,907, 1957
Average daily recent meeting: 9,838, 2002
Highest single day record: 43,591, August 4, 1962
Total attendance recent meeting: 767,424, 2002

Handle
Single day total handle all sources: $11,407,470, 1999
Average all sources recent meeting: $3,450,861, 2002
Average on-track recent meeting: $785,976, 2002
Single day on-track handle: $11,407,470, 1999
Record daily average for single meet: $1,997,807, 1970

Total all sources recent meeting: $269,167,260, 2002
Total on-track recent meeting: $61,306,166, 2002

Mutuel Records
Highest win: $229.20, July 15, 1951
Lowest Win: Skip Away, August 30, 1998, $2.10; Silverbulletday, July 10, 1999, $2.10
Highest Trifecta: $62,172, June 15, 1978
Lowest Trifecta: $17.60, July 29, 1985
Highest Daily Double: $3,962.50, July 19, 1952
Lowest Daily Double: $2.80, June 3, 1995

Leaders
Career, leading jockey by titles: Joe Bravo, 8
Career, leading trainer by titles: Budd Lepman, 5; John H. Forbes, 5; Juan Serey, 5
Recent meeting, leading jockey: Eibar Coa, 82, 2002
Recent meeting, leading owner: Mac Fehsenfeld, 15, 2002; Runnin Horse Farms, 15, 2002
Recent meeting, leading trainer: Tim Hills, 28, 2002

Records
Single meet, leading jockey by wins: Chris Antley, 171, 1984
Single meet, leading trainer by wins: J. Willard Thompson, 55, 1975; John Tammaro III, 55, 1974
Single day jockey wins: Walter Blum, 6, June 9, 1961; Chris Antley, 6, July 30, 1984; Julie Krone, 6, August 19, 1987; Joe Bravo, 6, August 31, 1994
Single day trainer wins: J. Willard Thompson, 4, November 8, 1975; Robert Klesaris, 4, July 10, 1987; John H. Forbes, 4, August 28, 1989

Track Records, Main Dirt
5 furlongs: Camden Harbor, :56.22, June 18, 1991
5 1/2 furlongs: American Royale, 1:02.96, July 21, 1991
6 furlongs: Gilded Time, 1:07.84, August 8, 1992
1 mile: Forty Niner, 1:33 4/5, July 16, 1988
1 mile 70 yards: Razzle Dazzle Rey, 1:39 1/5, May 13, 1978; Grecian Flight, 1:39 1/5, June 17, 1989; Back Bay Banquet, 1:39 1/5, July 10, 1989
1 1/16 miles: Formal Gold, 1:40.20, August 23, 1997
1 1/8 miles: Spend a Buck, 1:46 4/5, August 17, 1985; Jolie's Halo, 1:46.80, August 8, 1992
1 3/16 miles: Okamsel, 1:59 3/5, June 20, 1951
1 1/4 miles: Carry Back, 2:00 2/5, July 14, 1962; Majestic Light, 2:00 2/5, August 30, 1977
1 1/2 miles: Chappys Joy, 2:34 1/5, August 5, 1989
1 3/4 miles: *Halconero, 3:04 1/5, August 5, 1950

Course Records, Main Turf
5 furlongs: Klassy Briefcase, :54.97, June 8, 1991
1 mile: Double Booked, 1:33.34, June 2, 1991
1 1/16 miles: Mi Narrow, 1:39.40, July 11, 1999
1 1/8 miles: Horatia (Ire), 1:47.52, July 2, 2000
1 3/16 miles: *Dorienne, 2:01, June 30, 1953
1 1/4 miles: Muzzle, 2:08 2/5, July 10, 1953
1 3/8 miles: With Anticipation, 2:12.81, July 6, 2002
1 1/2 miles: Agacode, 2:29 2/5, June 14, 1985

Fastest Times of 2002 (Dirt)
5 furlongs: Bold World, :56.73, June 8
5 1/2 furlongs: Forever Partners, 1:03.12, August 3
6 furlongs: Summer Swing, 1:08.84, August 4
1 mile: Sea of Tranquility, 1:36.12, July 27
1 mile 70 yards: Tap Dance, 1:41.24, June 16
1 1/16 miles: Tempest Fugit, 1:42.72, June 15
1 1/8 miles: War Emblem, 1:48.21, August 4
1 1/4 miles: Personal Journey, 2:06.24, August 25

Fastest Times of 2002 (Turf)
5 furlongs: Sport d'Hiver, :55.39, July 21
1 mile: Autonomy (Ire), 1:34.80, June 22
1 1/16 miles: Personal Journey, 1:41.44, August 8
1 1/8 miles: Kris's Prayer, 1:47.15, June 23
1 3/8 miles: With Anticipation, 2:12.81, July 6
1 1/2 miles: White Hot (GB), 2:32.56, August 10

New Mexico

The Downs at Albuquerque

The Downs at Albuquerque, located on the New Mexico State Fairgrounds in Albuquerque, features Thoroughbred and Quarter Horse racing each spring and during the 17-day New Mexico State Fair in September. The fair dates from 1881, while its race meet, which opened October 1938, is the oldest in New Mexico. The New Mexico State Fair Futurity for Quarter Horses debuted in 1946 and is the oldest continuously run stakes race for the breed. One notable Thoroughbred horseman who competed at Albuquerque early in his career is jockey Mike Smith, a New Mexico native who became a Racing Hall of Fame member in 2003. In 1990, the track debuted The Lineage, a day of racing exclusively for state-bred Thoroughbreds and Quarter Horses. With assistance from its slots casino, which opened in 1999, the track has been able to solidify its business and increase purses.

Location: 201 California St. NE, Albuquerque, NM 87198
Phone: (505) 266-5555
Fax: (505) 268-1970
E-mail: downsatalb@aol.com
Web site: http://www.abqdowns.com
Year founded: 1938

Officers
Director of Racing: Don Cook
Racing Secretary: Rick Kloeppel
Director of Publicity: Mark Lezaurs

Racing Dates
2002: March 29-June 17, 48 days; September 6-September 22, 17 days

Track Records, Main Dirt
4 furlongs: Chipper J., :45.76, May 6, 2001
4 1/2 furlongs: Silver Matt, :51.22, June 17, 2000
5 furlongs: Scout Revolt, :56.35, December 12, 1998
5 1/2 furlongs: Yulla Yulla, 1:01.68, September 23, 2000
6 furlongs: Huggin the Rail, 1:08.44, September 29, 1996
6 1/2 furlongs: Shellerton, 1:14.92, May 18, 2001
1 mile: Dashing Forbes, 1:35.74, September 16, 1994
1 1/16 miles: Ciento, 1:40.60, September 22, 2001
1 1/8 miles: Brew, 1:48.47, June 3, 2001
1 3/16 miles: Savage Wind, 2:05 4/5, September 23, 1981
1 1/4 miles: Luedke, 2:03.69, April 14, 1996
1 1/2 miles: Luedke, 2:33.73, September 25, 1994
1 5/8 miles: Vikings Shield, 2:43 2/5, April 17, 1988
Other: 1 13/16 miles, Vermejo, 3:05 2/5, September 27, 1970

Fastest Times of 2002
5 furlongs: Full Command, :57.40, April 27; Tyger Smiles, :57.40, September 14
5 1/2 furlongs: Arthur's Dream, 1:02.45, May 11
6 furlongs: Sky Diver, 1:08.60, April 29
6 1/2 furlongs: Ben Told, 1:14.59, May 10
7 furlongs: Star Smasher, 1:21.01, June 9
1 mile: Lesters Boy, 1:35.74, April 27
1 1/16 miles: Sneaker Mike, 1:42.99, September 15
1 1/8 miles: Vernon Invader, 1:48.92, September 22
1 1/4 miles: Zapateo, 2:05.40, June 9
1 1/2 miles: Exclusive Dancer, 2:35.99, June 17
1 13/16 miles: Good Actor, :3:06.31, September 22

Ruidoso Downs

Located 7,000 feet above sea level in the pine-covered mountains of southeastern New Mexico, Ruidoso Downs long has been a popular destination for Southwestern horsemen and racing fans seeking to escape the summer heat. Since 1959, the track has held Quarter Horse racing's richest and most famous event, the All American Futurity, which in 1978 became the world's first million-dollar horse race. Leading trainers such as D. Wayne Lukas and Bob Baffert raced Quarter Horses at Ruidoso before switching to Thoroughbred racing. Thoroughbred racing also is a fixture at Ruidoso, where purses have increased significantly due to revenues from the Billy the Kid Casino that opened at the track in 1999. Ruidoso has a unique track configuration for the two breeds that compete there. A separate straightaway for Quarter Horses is located on the outside of the seven-furlong Thoroughbred oval.

Location: P.O. Box 449, Ruidoso Downs, NM 88346
Phone: (505) 378-4431
Fax: (505) 378-4631
E-mail: info@ruidownsracing.com
Web site: http://www.ruidownsracing.com
Inaugural meeting: July 1, 1947
Number of stalls: 2,000
Seating capacity: 7,000

Officers
President: Bruce Rimbo
Vice President: Edward Burger
General Manager: Rick Baugh
Racing Secretary: Rob Junk
Secretary: Edward Burger
Treasurer: Edward Burger
Director of Marketing: Neal Mullarky
Director of Mutuels: Deano McTeague
Director of Publicity: Kristian Lovelace
Director of Simulcasting: Kristian Lovelace
Stewards: Arnold Rael, Bobby Allison, Richard Bickel, Richard Lidberg
Track Announcer: Jim McAulay
Track Photographer: Bill Pitt Jr.
Track Superintendent: Dennis Moore
Other officials: R. D. Hubbard, Chairman

Racing Dates
2002: May 24-September 2, 61 days
2003: May 23-September 1, 61 days

Track Layout
Main circumference: 7 furlongs
Main track chutes: 1 1/8 miles, 6 furlongs
Main length of stretch: 656 feet

Attendance
Highest single day record: 17,009, September 2, 2002

Handle
Single day on-track handle: $1,432,897, September 2, 2002

Leaders
Recent meeting, leading jockey: Carlos Madeira, 36, 2002
Recent meeting, leading trainer: Ferd Danley, 17, 2002

Track Records, Main Dirt
4 1/2 furlongs: Bold Approach, :52 3/5, June 3, 1988
5 furlongs: King of Stars, :57.20, July 30, 1999
5 1/2 furlongs: Jack Wilson, 1:02.80, August 8, 1992
6 furlongs: Jack Wilson, 1:08.80, August 16, 1992
6 1/2 furlongs: Mr. Tattoo, 1:17 3/5, July 4, 1973

7 furlongs: Fill Mackis Cup, 1:24 2/5, July 15, 1984
7 1/2 furlongs: Last Don B., 1:31, May 29, 1993
1 mile: Set Records, 1:37, July 28, 1995
1 mile 70 yards: Brogander, 1:45 1/5, January 1, 1954
1 1/16 miles: Roythelittleone, 1:45.40, August 13, 1995
1 1/8 miles: Run John, 1:53.40, July 5, 1996
1 1/4 miles: Best Finish (GB), 2:08.20, September 7, 1998
1 3/8 miles: Start Jumpin, 2:24 1/5, August 18, 1990
1 1/2 miles: Decidedly Henry C., 2:37, August 19, 1989
1 5/8 miles: More Than Glory, 2:25.80, August 15, 1992

Fastest Times of 2002
5 furlongs: Nashville, :57.40, August 31
5 1/2 furlongs: Values of the Hunt, 1:03.20, August 16
6 furlongs: Live Show, 1:09.20, August 18
7 1/2 furlongs: Tahoe Affair, 1:31.80, July 20
1 mile: Kotuspeeding, 1:38.80, August 25
1 1/16 miles: Tahoe Affair, 1:45.60, September 2
1 1/8 miles: Mystery Years, 1:55.40, September 2

Sunland Park

Opened in 1959, Sunland Park was built just across the state line from El Paso, Texas, in New Mexico, which unlike its neighbor allowed pari-mutuel wagering. Sunland launched the career of several notable horsemen and horses. Jerry Bailey, one of Thoroughbred racing's all-time leading riders, began his career at the track in 1974. Bold Ego, who won Sunland's Riley Allison Futurity in 1980, captured the '81 Arkansas Derby (G1) and ran second in the Preakness Stakes (G1). In the mid-1990s, the track nearly closed because of competition from Native American casinos and pari-mutuel racing in Texas and Oklahoma. New Mexico horsemen and racetracks successfully lobbied for legalizing slot machines at tracks, and Sunland's casino opened in February 1999. With a portion of casino revenues earmarked to purses, the quality of racing improved significantly.

Location: P.O. Box 1, Sunland Park, NM 88063
Phone: (505) 874-5200
Fax: (505) 589-1518
E-mail: sunlandinfo@anchorgaming.com
Web site: http://www.sunland-park.com
Year founded: 1959
Inaugural meeting: October 9, 1959
Number of stalls: 1,600
Seating capacity: 5,710

Officers
President: Harold Payne
General Manager: Harold Payne
Director of Racing: Paul Ryneveld
Racing Secretary: Norm Amundson
Director of Operations: Paul Ryneveld
Director of Communications: Paul Ryneveld
Director of Finance: Charlie Casiano
Director of Marketing: Adeline Rogers
Director of Mutuels: Dustin Dix
Director of Publicity: Eric Alwan
Director of Sales: Connie Blevins
Director of Simulcasting: Charles Chrisman
Stewards: Bruce Brinkly, Richard Ladberg, Robert Allison
Horsemen's Liaison: Donna Martin
Track Announcer: Robert Geller
Track Photographer: Bill Pitt
Track Superintendent: Bob Patty
Other officials: Clerk of Scales: Joe Sherman, Starter: Albert Dominguez

Racing Dates
2002: November 20, 2001-April 7, 2002
2003: November 19, 2002-April 6, 2003, 80 days

Track Layout
Main circumference: 1 mile
Main track chute: 1 1/4 miles, 6 1/2 furlongs
Main width: 80 feet
Main length of stretch: 990 feet

Attendance
Highest single day record: 8,494

Handle
Total all sources recent meeting: $40,857,532, 2001/2002
Total on-track recent meeting: $7,112,636, 2001/2002
Average all sources recent meeting: $510,719, 2001/2002
Average on-track recent meeting: $88,908, 2001/2002
Record daily average for single meet: $495,093, 1991
Single day on-track handle: $610,572
Single day total handle all sources: $1,658,953, February 18, 2003

Leaders
Career, leading jockey by titles: Bobby Harmon, 8
Career, leading trainer by titles: Bob E. Arnett, 12
Recent meeting, leading jockey: Daryl Montoya, 51, 2001/2002
Recent meeting, leading trainer: Ramon Gonzalez, 37, 2001/2002

Records
Single meet, leading trainer by wins: Ramon Gonzalez, 37

Track Records, Main Dirt
4 furlongs: Tamran's Jet, :44 4/5, March 22, 1968
4 1/2 furlongs: Bold Liz, :50 2/5, March 25, 1972
5 furlongs: Draconic's Loom, :56 2/5, February 13, 1980; Tyger Smiles, :56.2, January 26, 2003
5 1/2 furlongs: Treasure Hunt, 1:02.1, January 28, 2003
6 furlongs: Pacer, 1:08.36, January 7, 2003
6 1/2 furlongs: Funny Meeting, 1:14.84
1 mile: Caliban, 1:35.42, February 16, 2003
1 1/16 miles: Winsham Lad, 1:42, April 22, 1962; Native Shuffle, 1:42, April 11, 1971; Brew, 1:42, April 7, 2001
1 1/8 miles: Winsham Lad, 1:48 1/5, January 8, 1961; Prenupcial, 1:48 1/5, April 28, 1962
1 3/16 miles: Mickey J., 1:58 1/5, November 14, 1970
1 1/4 miles: Curribot, 2:01 2/5, May 6, 1984
1 3/8 miles: Hot Deck, 2:19 2/5, January 10, 1970
1 5/8 miles: Rush Line, 2:47 3/5, April 6, 1969

Interesting Facts
Achievements/milestones: Casino opened February 2, 1999.

Fastest Times of 2002
4 furlongs: Gulchrunssweet, :45.81, April 6
4 1/2 furlongs: Quote This, :51.26, March 19
5 furlongs: Literary Justice, :56.84, March 17
5 1/2 furlongs: Wild Bill R, 1:02.69, March 5
6 furlongs: Potranca Muy Fria, 1:08.98, February 17
6 1/2 furlongs: Proud to Be Bold, 1:14.95, December 20
1 mile: McKinney, 1:35.88, April 6
1 1/16 miles: Accomodator, 1:42.52, April 6
1 1/8 miles: Verzy Man, 1:50.74, March 3
1 1/4 miles: Verzy Man, 2:04.97, April 7

SunRay Park

SunRay Park in Farmington, New Mexico, is located in an area called the Four Corners region, where northwestern New Mexico, northeastern Arizona, southeastern Utah, and southwestern Colorado meet. The racetrack, which offers Thoroughbred and Quarter

Horse racing, originally was known as San Juan Downs; it was built by San Juan County at the county fairgrounds and opened in 1984. Declining business forced the track to close after its 1993 season. SunRay Gaming of New Mexico LLC secured a ten-year option to operate the track, which was renamed SunRay Park and reopened in October 1999. SunRay Gaming's interest in reviving horse racing at the facility largely was based on its ability to operate a casino with slot machines. A portion of revenues from the slots enhances race purses.

Location: 39 Road 5568, Farmington, NM 87401-1466
Phone: (505) 566-1200
Fax: (505) 326-4292
Web site: *http://www.sunraygaming.com*
Inaugural meeting: September 1984
Year founded: 1984
Abbreviation: SRP
Number of stalls: 1,098
Seating capacity: 3,000

Officers
General Manager: Byron Cambell
Racing Secretary: Hank DeMoney
Director of Publicity: Sharron Freelove
Director of Finance: Keith Rodolf
Director of Mutuels: Natalie Swisher
Director of Operations: Toni Wright
Director of Racing: Hank DeMoney
Director of Simulcasting: Toni Wright
Track Announcer: Greg "Boomer" Wry
Track Photographer: Coady Photography
Track Superintendent: Everett Simons
Other officials: Clerk of Scales: Dell Jessup

Racing Dates
2002: September 21-November 18
2003: September 19-November 23

Leaders
Recent meeting, leading jockey: Adan Fuentes, Carl Mel Kutz, 23, 2002
Recent meeting, leading owner: Three H Racing
Recent meeting, leading trainer: Carlos Sedillo, Gary W. Cross, 16, 2002

Fastest Times of 2002 (Dirt)
4 furlongs: May Nard, :46.20, November 10
4 1/2 furlongs: Wondrous Zeal, :50.00, October 11
6 1/2 furlongs: Mr. Crimson, 1:17.20, October 8
7 furlongs: Hava Peer, 1:22.60, October 11
7 1/2 furlongs: Conference, 1:32.40, November 18
1 mile: Ciento, 1:36.40, October 7
1 1/8 miles: Moro Grande, 1:51.20, November 17

New York

Aqueduct

Offering roughly half of the New York Racing Association's year-round schedule, the track known as the Big A offers racing in winter, spring, and fall. Aqueduct opened as a six-furlong track in New York's Queens Borough on September 27, 1894. Site of the only triple dead heat in a stakes race—Brownie, Bossuet, and Wait a Bit hit the wire together in the Carter Handicap on June 10, 1944—Aqueduct was torn down in 1956 and completely rebuilt over three years. For four years, from 1964 through 1967, Aqueduct played host to the Belmont Stakes while Belmont Park was rebuilt. An all-time record crowd of 73,435 watched Gun Bow win the Metropolitan Handicap on Memorial Day, May 31, 1965.

In 1975, the one-mile inner dirt track was completed, allowing racing throughout the winter. Six years later, Aqueduct opened Equestris, a 300-foot-long, $7-million facility for 1,600 diners. A $3-million renovation in 1985 prior to its only hosting of the Breeders' Cup championship day expanded Aqueduct's paddock, grandstand, and back-yard seating. The renovation included the installation of mini-theaters. The spring meet's principal race is the Wood Memorial Stakes (G1), a Kentucky Derby (G1) prep, and the Cigar Mile Handicap (G1) is one of the fall features. The New York Legislature in 2001 authorized video-lottery terminals to be installed at the track, and a slot-machine contractor, MGM Mirage, was chosen in 2003.

Location: 11000 Rockaway Blvd., Jamaica, NY 11417
Phone: (718) 641-4700
Web site: *http://www.nyra.com/aqueduct/*
Year founded: 1894
Inaugural meeting: September 27, 1894
Acreage: 192
Number of stalls: 547
Seating capacity: 17,000

Officers
Chairman: Barry K. Schwartz
President: Terence J. Meyocks
Senior Vice President: William A. Nader
Racing Secretary: Michael S. Lakow
Treasurer: John Giombarrese
Director of Admissions: Jerry A. Davis Jr.
Director of Communications: Glen Mathes
Director of Finance: Alexander W. Ingle
Director of Marketing: William A. Nader
Director of Mutuels: Patrick Mahony
Horsemen's Liaison: Carmen Barrera
Stewards: Carmine Donofrio, David Hicks, Dr. Theodore Hill
Track Announcer: Tom Durkin
Track Photographers: Adam Coglianese, Bob Coglianese
Track Superintendent: Jerry Porcelli

Racing Dates
2002: October 31, 2001-May 5, 2002, 132 days
2003: January 1-May 5; October 29-December 31

Track Layout
Main circumference: 1 1/8 miles
Main width: 100 feet
Main length of stretch: 1,155.6 feet
Main turf circumference: 7 furlongs
Inner circumference: 1 mile

Attendance
Average daily recent meeting: 4,825, Fall-2002, 5,256, Winter/Spring-2002
Highest single day record: 73,435, May 31, 1965
Total attendance recent meeting: 217,144, Fall-2002, 457,247, Winter/Spring-2002

Handle
Single day on-track handle: $8,171,520, November 2, 1985
Total on-track recent meeting: $136,945,498, Winter/Spring-2002; $70,053,164, Fall-2002
Average all sources recent meeting: $9,236,441, Winter/Spring-2002; $9,342,922 Fall-2002
Average on-track recent meeting: $1,556,737, Fall-2002; $1,574,086, Winter/Spring-2002
Total all sources recent meeting: $420,431,468, Fall-2002; $803,570,338, Winter/Spring-2002

Leaders
Recent meeting, leading jockey: John Velazquez, 33, Winter/Spring-2002; Shaun Bridgmohan, 33, Winter/Spring-2002

Recent meeting, leading trainer: Richard Dutrow Jr., 15, Fall-2002; Richard Dutrow Jr., 16, Winter/Spring-2002; Richard Dutrow Jr., 16, Winter/Spring-2002

Mutuel Records
Highest win: $434, Markobob, September 3, 1943
Highest Pick 6: $767,998, April 9, 1990

Records
Single day jockey wins: Michael Venezia, 6, December 7, 1964; Rudy L. Turcotte, 6, December 2, 1969; Angel Cordero Jr., 6, March 12, 1975; Ron Turcotte, 6, March 5, 1976; Steve Cauthen, 6, January 22, 1977; Steve Cauthen, 6, April 7, 1977; Steve Cauthen, 6, November 29, 1977; Mike Smith, 6, January 13, 1992; Mike Smith, 6, January 30, 1992; Jorge Chavez, 6, February 18, 1996; Shaun Bridgmohan, 6, February 15, 1998

Track Records, Main Dirt
4 1/2 furlongs: About to Burst, :51 3/5, August 26, 1984
6 furlongs: Kelly Kip, 1:07.54, April 10, 1999
6 1/2 furlongs: Coronado's Quest, 1:14.35, October 26, 1997
7 furlongs: Artax, 1:20.04, May 2, 1999
1 mile: Easy Goer, 1:32 2/5, April 8, 1989
1 1/8 miles: Riva Ridge, 1:47, October 15, 1973
1 3/16 miles: Riva Ridge, 1:52 2/5, July 4, 1973
1 1/4 miles: Damascus, 1:59 1/5, July 20, 1968
1 3/8 miles: Demi's Bret, 2:12.31, October 26, 1997
1 1/2 miles: Going Abroad, 2:26 1/5, October 12, 1964
1 5/8 miles: Sharp Gary, 2:40 2/5, December 13, 1975
1 3/4 miles: Malmo, 2:53.73, March 30, 1996
2 miles: Kelso, 3:19 1/5, October 31, 1964
Other: 1 5/16 miles, Gold Star Deputy, 2:07.32, April 10, 1999; 1 7/8 miles, Erin Bright, 3:12 4/5, April 18, 1985; 2 1/4 miles, Paraje, 3:47 4/5, December 15, 1973

Course Records, Main Turf
1 mile: Tax Dodge, 1:34 3/5, November 1, 1985
1 1/16 miles: Spindrift (Ire), 1:40.88, May 6, 2000
1 1/8 miles: Slew the Dragon, 1:47, November 3, 1985
1 3/8 miles: Fluorescent Light, 2:14 1/5, November 7, 1978
1 1/2 miles: Pebbles (GB), 2:27, November 2, 1985
2 miles: Putting Green, 3:30 2/5, November 23, 1984

Track records, Inner dirt
4 1/2 furlongs: Call Me Up, :52.29, February 16, 1998
6 furlongs: Whirling Blade, 1:08.57, March 5, 1997
1 mile: Tejano Couture, 1:35.79, March 9, 2000
1 mile 70 yards: Carry My Colors, 1:38.92, February 5, 2000
1 1/16 miles: Autoroute, 1:41, December 19, 1992
1 1/8 miles: Conveyor, 1:47.33, March 6, 1993
1 3/16 miles: Victoriously, 1:54.42, January 25, 1998
1 1/4 miles: Transient Trend, 2:01.53, December 21, 1995
1 1/2 miles: Piling, 2:29 3/5, March 13, 1983
1 5/8 miles: Relaxing, 2:42 2/5, December 13, 1980
1 3/4 miles: Sophie's Friend, 2:56.73, February 10, 1996
2 miles: Charlie Coast, 3:24 4/5, February 21, 1979
Other: 2 1/16 miles, Rollix, 3:38 4/5, February 3, 1983; 2 1/8 miles, Peat Moss, 3:40 3/5, January 31, 1981; 2 1/4 miles, Field Cat, 3:51 4/5, December 31, 1981

Fastest Times of 2002 (Dirt)
4 1/2 furlongs: Look Out Evan, :53.03, May 2
6 furlongs: Say Florida Sandy, 1:08.92, November 8
6 1/2 furlongs: Profit, 1:15.69, October 27
7 furlongs: Raging Fever, 1:21.78, March 30
1 mile: Congaree, 1:33.11, November 30
1 mile 70 yards: Boston Party, 1:39.63, January 5
1 1/16 miles: Zonk, 1:42.58, January 12
1 1/8 miles: Buddha, 1:48.61, April 13
1 3/16 miles: Snake Mountain, 1:56.84, December 7
1 1/4 miles: Critical Eye, 2:04.19, December 21
1 3/8 miles: Evening Attire, 2:14.81, November 23
1 1/2 miles: Williamthenchanted, 2:34.48, January 27
1 5/8 miles: Coyote Lakes, 2:43.54, December 28

Fastest Times of 2002 (Turf)
1 mile: Island Guide, 1:36.76, April 14

1 1/16 miles: Voodoo Dancer, 1:43.10, May 5
1 1/8 miles: Trucking Baron, 1:51.04, April 13
1 3/8 miles: Quiet Ruler, 2:24.66, November 8
1 1/2 miles: Uriah (Ger), 2:42.48, November 16

Belmont Park

With a 1½-mile oval, Belmont Park on Long Island is the largest racetrack in North America, and its huge grandstand has a 90,000-person capacity. Built for $2.5-million and opened on May 4, 1905, Belmont is host to the third leg of the Triple Crown, the Belmont Stakes (G1), which was named for German-born financier August Belmont I. The first Belmont Stakes was run in 1867 at Jerome Park and was moved to Morris Park in 1890. Within a few years of Belmont's opening, antigambling legislation shut the track in 1911 and '12. The track reopened in 1913. The grandstand was rebuilt in 1920, raising seating capacity to 17,500. In 1963, deterioration of the grandstand forced a five-year closing while the current facility was constructed for $30.7-million. In those years, the Belmont and most of the track's dates were run at Aqueduct. Belmont has played host to three runnings of the Breeders' Cup World Thoroughbred Championships—in 1990, '95, and 2001. The most recent running of the championship event marked the first international sporting event to be held in the New York City area following the September 11, 2001, terrorist attack on the World Trade Center.

Location: 2150 Hempstead Pike, Elmont, NY 11003
Phone: (516) 488-6000
E-mail: nyra@nyra.com
Web site: http://www.nyra.com/belmont/
Year founded: 1895
Inaugural meeting: May 4, 1905
Acreage: 430
Number of stalls: 2,200
Seating capacity: 32,941

Officers
Chairman: Barry K. Schwartz
President: Terence B. Meyocks
Senior Vice President: William A. Nader
Racing Secretary: Michael S. Lakow
Treasurer: John Giombarrese
Director of Admissions: Jerry A. Davis Jr.
Director of Communications: Glen Mathes
Director of Mutuels: Patrick Mahony
Director of Simulcasting: Liz Bracken
Horsemen's Liaison: Carmen Barrera
Track Announcer: Tom Durkin
Track Photographers: Adam Coglianese, Bob Coglianese
Track Superintendent: Jerry Porcelli

Racing Dates
2002: May 8-July 21, 55 days; September 6-October 20, 33 days
2003: May 7-July 20, September 5-October 26

Track Layout
Main circumference: 1 1/2 miles
Main length of stretch: 1,097 feet
Main turf circumference: 1 5/16 miles
Inner turf circumference: 1 3/16 miles
Training track: 7 furlongs

Attendance
Total attendance recent meeting: 202,015, Fall-2002; 465,220, Spring/Summer-2002

Average daily recent meeting: 6,122, Fall-2002; 8,314, Spring/Summer-2002
Highest single day record: 103,222, June 8, 2002

Handle
Total all sources recent meeting: $368,528,262, Fall-2002; $657,789,165, Spring/Summer-2002
Total on-track recent meeting: $107,381,285, Spring/Summer-2002; $65,044,372, Fall-2002
Average on-track recent meeting: $1,711,694, Fall 2002; $1,952,387, Spring/Summer 2002
Single day on-track handle: $13,087,814, October 27, 2001
Single day total handle all sources: $95,423,752, June 8, 2002
Average all sources recent meeting: $10,686,231, Fall-2002; $11,959,803, Spring/Summer 2002

Mutuel Records
Highest Exacta: $5,454, June 1, 1985

Leaders
Recent meeting, leading trainer: Richard Dutrow Jr., 18, Fall-2002; Todd Pletcher, 18, Fall-2002; Todd Pletcher, 30, Spring/Summer-2002
Recent meeting, leading jockey: John Velazquez, 50, Fall-2002; John Velazquez, 58, Spring/Summer-2002
Recent meeting, leading owner: Sanford Goldfarb, 9, Spring/Summer-2002

Records
Single day jockey wins: Jorge Velasquez, 6, July 9, 1981

Track Records, Main Dirt
5 furlongs: Kelly Kip, :55.75, June 21, 1996
5 1/2 furlongs: More Than Ready, 1:02.56, July 4, 1999
6 furlongs: Artax, 1:07.66, October 16, 1999
6 1/2 furlongs: Confide, 1:14.51, October 16, 1997
7 furlongs: Left Bank, 1:20.17, July 4, 2002
1 mile: Williamstown, 1:32.79, May 5, 1993
1 1/16 miles: Rock and Roll, 1:39.51, June 13, 1998
1 1/8 miles: Secretariat, 1:45 2/5, September 15, 1973
1 3/16 miles: Lueders, 1:56, June 24, 1982
1 1/4 miles: In Excess (Ire), 1:58 1/5, July 4, 1991
1 3/8 miles: Victoriously, 2:14.72, October 16, 1997
1 1/2 miles: Secretariat, 2:24, June 9, 1973

Course Records, Main Turf
6 furlongs: Masterclass, 1:07.31, May 24, 1992
7 furlongs: Officialpermission, 1:19.88, July 23, 2000
1 mile: Elusive Quality, 1:31.63, July 4, 1998
1 1/16 miles: Fortitude, 1:38.53, September 6, 1997
1 3/8 miles: Influent, 2:11.06, July 13, 1997
1 1/2 miles: Sky Classic, 2:24.50, October 3, 1992
2 miles: King's General (GB), 3:20 2/5, July 4, 1983

Course Records Inner turf
1 1/16 miles: Roman Envoy, 1:39.38, May 23, 1992
1 1/8 miles: Subordination, 1:45.69, June 15, 1997
1 1/4 miles: Paradise Creek, 1:57.79, June 11, 1994
1 3/8 miles: With Approval, 2:10 1/5, June 17, 1990

Fastest Times of 2002 (Dirt)
5 furlongs: Whywhywhy, :57.10, June 7
5 1/2 furlongs: Zavata, 1:02.66, June 29
6 furlongs: Self Rising, 1:08.57, June 7
6 1/2 furlongs: Greatness, 1:14.65, June 15
7 furlongs: Left Bank, 1:20.17, July 4
1 mile: Swept Overboard, 1:33.34, May 27
1 1/16 miles: Wild Years, 1:40.11, June 7
1 1/8 miles: Seeking Daylight, 1:46.35, June 15
1 1/4 miles: Evening Attire, 1:59.58, September 28
1 3/8 miles: Ahpo Here, 2:15.55, June 15
1 1/2 miles: Sarava, 2:29.71, June 8

Fastest Times of 2002 (Turf)
6 furlongs: Lismore Knight, 1:09.74, July 20
7 furlongs: Shibboleth, 1:20.08, May 27

1 mile: Volponi, 1:32.24, July 5
1 1/16 miles: Lunar Sovereign, 1:39.57, September 8
1 1/8 miles: Madagascar (Arg), 1:46.02, June 22
1 1/4 miles: Nowrass (GB), 1:59.69, July 4
1 3/8 miles: J W Black, 2:12.73, June 2
1 1/2 miles: Bicentennial, 2:27.12, June 23
2 1/2 miles: Sharp Face, 4:37.32, June 6

Finger Lakes

In Native American lore, the Finger Lakes region of upstate New York was created when the Great Spirit placed his hand down on the land to create the series of long, thin lakes. Finger Lakes Race Track, which is located 20 miles from Rochester in Farmington, opened May 23, 1962, and offers racing from mid-April to early December. Owned by Finger Lakes Racing Association Inc., the track has featured Eclipse Award-winning sprinters Not Surprising, Groovy, and Safely Kept. Fio Rito shipped out of western New York to win the 1981 Whitney Handicap (G1) at Saratoga Race Course. In 2001, Shesastonecoldfox became the first horse based at Finger Lakes to compete in the Breeders' Cup World Thoroughbred Championships. The $125,000 New York Derby, which has been held at Finger Lakes since 1969, annually is the track's richest race.

Location: 5857 Route 96, Farmington, NY 14425
Phone: (716) 924-3232
Fax: (716) 924-3967
E-mail: smartin@fingerlakesracetrack.com
Web site: http://www.fingerlakesracetrack.com
Year founded: 1962
Inaugural meeting: May 23, 1962
Acreage: 400
Number of stalls: 1,214
Seating capacity: 6,000

Officers
President: Christian Riegle
General Manager: Christian Riegle
Racing Secretary: Daniel Doocy
Director of Admissions: Brenda Tarzia
Director of Finance: Stephen Richardson
Director of Marketing: Steven Martin
Director of Mutuels: Ann Blazey
Director of Publicity: Steven Martin
Director of Sales: Sally Berry
Director of Simulcasting: Patrick Placito
Horsemen's Liaison: Kim DeLong
Stewards: Rick Coyne
Track Announcer: Ross Morton
Track Photographer: Tom Cooley
Track Superintendent: Rick Brongo
Other officials: Arthur Green, Racing Coordinator

Racing Dates
2002: April 12-December 8, 161 days
2003: April 18-November 29, 162 days

Track Layout
Main circumference: 1 mile
Main track chute: 1 1/4 miles, 6 furlongs
Main width: 85 feet
Main length of stretch: 960 feet

Attendance
Average daily recent meeting: 1,225, 2002
Highest single meet record: 698,113, 1974
Lowest single meet record: 197,182, 2002
Record daily average for single meet: 5,032, 1962
Total attendance recent meeting: 197,182, 2002

Handle

Average all sources recent meeting: $934,428, 2002
Single day on-track handle: $765,580, September 24, 1978
Average on-track recent meeting: $96,986, 2002
Total all sources recent meeting: $150,443,046, 2002
Record daily average for single meet: $348,608, 1982
Total on-track recent meeting: $15,614,825, 2002

Mutuel Records

Highest Pick 6: $161,490, June 21, 2001

Leaders

Career, leading trainer by titles: Michael S. Ferraro, 17
Career, leading jockey by titles: Kevin Whitley, 9
Recent meeting, leading jockey: John Davila Jr., 139, 2002
Recent meeting, leading owner: Charlton A. Baker, 26, 2002
Recent meeting, leading trainer: Michael S. Ferraro, 85, 2002

Records

Single day jockey wins: Robert Messina, 6, November 23, 2001
Single meet, leading jockey by wins: John Grabowski, 233, 2000
Single meet, leading trainer by wins: Michael S. Ferraro, 107, 1977

Track Records, Main Dirt

4 1/2 furlongs: Top End, :50.60, April 8, 1998
5 furlongs: Wonderous Wise, :57 1/5, April 11, 1989; Bobby's Code, :57.20, April 8, 1998
5 1/2 furlongs: Hilary Star, 1:02 4/5, April 16, 1989; With It, 1:02.80, June 12, 1994; What a Rollick, 1:02.80, December 12, 1994
6 furlongs: Kelly Kip, 1:08.20, June 20, 1998
1 mile: Transact, 1:36.20, August 29, 1994; Fling n Roll, 1:36.20, November 28, 1995
1 mile 70 yards: C B Account, 1:40, July 6, 1997
1 1/16 miles: Fit for Royalty, 1:43, May 19, 1997
1 1/8 miles: Copper Mount, 1:48.80, August 27, 1994
1 3/16 miles: North Warning, 1:58.40, July 10, 1994
1 1/4 miles: Caramba, 2:05 1/5, July 11, 1987
1 1/2 miles: Brave Beast, 2:33.70, September 22, 1991
1 5/8 miles: North Warning, 2:46.60, September 4, 1994
Other: 2 furlongs, Broadway Blondie, :21.80, April 30, 1998

Interesting Facts

Achievements/milestones: 2001 marked 40th season of operation.

Fastest Times of 2002 (Dirt)

4 1/2 furlongs: Solomon's Seal, :52.37, April 14
5 furlongs: Stage Run, :58.82, October 6
5 1/2 furlongs: Strider's Comet, 1:04.34, August 3
6 furlongs: Pinky Floyd, 1:10.15, November 29
1 mile 70 yards: Native Coast, 1:42.72, September 20
1 1/16 miles: Along Came Mary, 1:45.18, August 24; Trial Prep, 1:45.18, July 27
1 1/8 miles: Toddler, 1:51.48, September 7
1 1/4 miles: L. A. Fitz, 2:07.18, August 31

Saratoga Race Course

An American landmark and one of the world's leading sports venues, Saratoga Race Course operates six weeks each year and draws huge crowds to the foothills of the Adirondack Mountains in historic Saratoga Springs, approximately 25 miles north of Albany. Saratoga again set wagering records in 2002, although its attendance slipped below one million after crossing that milestone for the first time in 2001.

Opened August 2, 1864, Saratoga Race Course is the oldest existing track in America. Major renovations of the facility occurred in 1902, '28, '40, '65, '85, and 2000, when $8-million was spent to remodel the track's three main entrances, construct state-of-the-art jockeys' quarters, and restore an elegant 19th-century fountain in front of the clubhouse gate.

Known as the "graveyard of champions," Saratoga has been host to many of Thoroughbred racing's greatest upsets, none more notable than Man o' War's early career loss to Upset in the 1919 Sanford Stakes; Gallant Fox's loss in the 1930 Travers Stakes to 100-to-1 longshot Jim Dandy; Onion's shocking victory over Secretariat in the 1973 Whitney Stakes (G2); and Runaway Groom's 1982 Travers Stakes (G1) upset of Conquistador Cielo. Racing at Saratoga is enhanced annually by the inductions at the National Museum of Racing and Hall of Fame, Fasig-Tipton's yearling sale, and the Jockey Club Round Table Conference.

Location: P.O. Box 564, Saratoga Springs, NY 12866
Phone: (518) 584-6200
Fax: (518) 587-4646
Web site: http://www.nyra.com/saratoga/
Inaugural meeting: August 3-6, 1863
Year founded: 1863
Acreage: 350
Number of stalls: 1,830
Seating capacity: 18,000

Officers

Chairman: Barry K. Schwartz
President: Terence J. Meyocks
Senior Vice President: William A. Nader
Racing Secretary: Michael S. Lakow
Treasurer: John Giombarrese
Director of Admissions: Jerry A. Davis Jr.
Director of Communications: Glen Mathes
Director of Marketing: William A. Nader
Director of Mutuels: Patrick Mahony
Horsemen's Liaison: Carmen Barrera
Stewards: Carmine Donofrio, David Hicks, Dr. Theodore Hill
Track Announcer: Tom Durkin
Track Photographers: Adam Coglianese, Bob Coglianese
Track Superintendent: Jerry Porcelli

Racing Dates

2002: July 24-September 2, 36 days
2003: July 23-September 1, 36 days

Track Layout

Main circumference: 1 1/8 miles
Main track chute: 7 furlongs
Main length of stretch: 1,144 feet
Main turf circumference: 1 mile
Main turf length of stretch: 1,144 feet
Inner turf circumference: 7 furlongs
Inner turf length of stretch: 1,164 feet
Training track: 1 mile, 7 furlongs turf

Attendance

Average daily recent meeting: 27,761, 2002
Highest single day record: 69,523, August 4, 2002
Highest single meet record: 1,011,669, 2001
Record daily average for single meet: 28,479, 1989
Total attendance recent meeting: 999,388, 2002

Handle

Average all sources recent meeting: $16,312,846, 2002
Single day on-track handle: $7,887,462, August 19, 1995
Record daily average for single meet: $3,742,773, 1993
Average on-track recent meeting: $3,475,241, 2002
Total all sources recent meeting: $587,262,467, 2002
Total on-track recent meeting: $125,108,665, 2002

Mutuel Records

Highest Trifecta: $63,624, August 22, 1974
Highest Daily Double: $4,313.90, August 27, 1945

Leaders

Career, leading trainer by titles: Bill Mott, 7
Recent meeting, leading jockey: Edgar Prado, 54, 2002
Recent meeting, leading owner: Eugene and Laura Melnyk, 6, 2002; Sanford Goldfarb, 6, 2002; WinStar Farm, 6, 2002
Recent meeting, leading trainer: Todd Pletcher, 19, 2002
Career, leading jockey by titles: Angel Cordero Jr., 13

Records

Single meet, leading jockey by wins: Jerry Bailey, 55, 2001
Single meet, leading trainer by wins: Bill Mott, 22, 2001
Single day jockey wins: John Velazquez, 6, September 3, 2001

Track Records, Main Dirt

5 furlongs: Fabulous Force, :56.71, August 18, 1993
5 1/2 furlongs: Mayakovsky, 1:03.32, July 25, 2001
6 furlongs: Spanish Riddle, 1:08, August 18, 1972
6 1/2 furlongs: Topsider, 1:14 2/5, August 1, 1979
7 furlongs: Darby Creek Road, 1:20 3/5, August 8, 1978
1 mile: Key Contender, 1:34.72, August 9, 1992
1 1/8 miles: Tri Jet, 1:47, August 3, 1974; Left Bank, 1:47.04, August 3, 2002
1 3/16 miles: Winter's Tale, 1:54 3/5, August 21, 1982
1 1/4 miles: General Assembly, 2:00, August 18, 1979
1 5/8 miles: Green Highlander, 2:43.57, August 15, 1991
2 miles: James Boswell, 3:26, August 11, 1983

Course Records, Main Turf

1 1/16 miles: Fourstardave, 1:38.91, July 29, 1991
1 1/8 miles: Tentam, 1:45 2/5, August 10, 1973
1 3/16 miles: Phi Beta Doc, 1:51.61, September 1, 1999
1 5/8 miles: Tom Swift, 2:37, August 23, 1978

Course Records Inner turf

1 mile: Bomfim, 1:33.78, August 1, 1999
1 1/16 miles: Roman Envoy, 1:39.99, August 3, 1992
1 1/8 miles: Amarettitorun, 1:46.22, July 26, 1997
1 3/8 miles: Babinda (GB), 2:12, July 26, 1997
1 1/2 miles: Awad, 2:23.20, August 9, 1997

Fastest Times of 2002 (Dirt)

5 furlongs: Hope for Love, :58.20, August 1
5 1/2 furlongs: Chimichurri, 1:04.38, July 25
6 furlongs: Mandy's Gold, 1:09.24, August 2
6 1/2 furlongs: Orientate, 1:15.68, September 1
7 furlongs: Voodoo, 1:21.48, August 3
1 1/8 miles: Left Bank, 1:47.04, August 3
1 1/4 miles: Medaglia d'Oro, 2:02.53, August 24

Fastest Times of 2002 (Turf)

1 mile: River Rush, 1:35.09, August 15
1 1/16 miles: Balto Star, 1:39.17, August 11
1 1/8 miles: Unbridled Vice, 1:47.56, July 29
1 3/16 miles: Blazing Fury, 1:53.97, July 27
1 3/8 miles: Ibn Al Haitham (GB), 2:14.35, August 7
1 1/2 miles: With Anticipation, 2:24.06, August 10

Ohio

Beulah Park

Ohio's oldest racetrack, Beulah Park is located in Grove City, south of Columbus. Operating since 1923, the track offered a spring meet that once was a popular stopping point for horses in transit from Florida to New York. Beulah was started by successful paving contractor Robert J. Deist. After Deist's death, ownership of the track passed to his son, Robert Y. Deist. In 1983, the younger Deist sold Beulah, which passed through a succession of owners and was known as Darby Downs from 1983 to '86. Current owner Charles Ruma restored the track's original name in 1986. Under Ruma's leadership, Beulah was the first Ohio track to offer simulcasting, phone wagering, and Internet wagering through its *http://www.winticket.com*. Along with Thistledown near Cleveland and River Downs near Cincinnati, Beulah shares host duties for the Best of Ohio day, which offers five stakes races for Ohiobreds.

Location: 3664 Grant Ave., Grove City, OH 43123
Phone: (614) 871-9600
Fax: (614) 871-0433
E-mail: mweiss@iwaynet.net
Web site: *http://www.beulahpark.com*
Seating capacity: 7,200
Number of stalls: 1,200

Officers

President: Charles J. Ruma
General Manager: Michael Weiss
Director of Racing: Ed Vomacka
Racing Secretary: Ed Vomacka
Director of Publicity: Vic Mason
Director of Operations: Holly Freking
Director of Simulcasting: Brian DeJong
Track Announcer: Bill Downes
Track Photographer: Harry Kaplan
Track Superintendent: Ernest Ratcliff

Racing Dates

2002: January 11-May 4, 66 days; September 14-December 22
2003: January 10-May 3, 70 days, September 13-December 21

Track Layout

Main circumference: 1 mile
Main length of stretch: 1,100 feet
Main turf circumference: 6 furlongs, less 223 feet

Leaders

Recent meeting, leading jockey: Huber Villa-Gomez, 54, Fall/Winter-2002
Recent meeting, leading trainer: Jake Radosevich, 24, Fall/Winter-2002

Track Records, Main Dirt

5 furlongs: Love Pappa Mucci, :56.75, February 11, 1994
5 1/2 furlongs: Jilsie's Gigalo, 1:03, May 4, 1991
6 furlongs: Whatta Brave, 1:08.50, October 29, 2000
1 mile: Appygolucky, 1:35.47, January 17, 2003
1 mile 70 yards: King's Wailea, 1:40.15, November 19, 1993
1 1/16 miles: Din's Dancer, 1:40 4/5, November 3, 1990
1 1/8 miles: Lord Try On, 1:48.96, September 26, 1992
1 3/16 miles: World of Magic, 1:55, September 21, 1991
1 1/4 miles: On the Scent, 2:00.22, October 19, 1991
1 1/2 miles: Doctor's Romance, 2:29.50, March 26, 1994
1 5/8 miles: Big Beans, 2:46, October 5, 1957
1 3/4 miles: Dot Your Eye, 2:57 3/5, October 20, 1971
Other: 2 furlongs, Go Chop, :21 3/5, May 7, 1989; 2 miles 70 yds, Benomen, 3:29.81, November 20, 1993; 2 1/16 miles, She Looks Great, 3:41 2/5, November 28, 1983; 2 1/8 miles, Second City, 3:48 4/5, November 25, 1984; 2 1/4 miles, Hallay's Pride, 3:48.90, May 4, 1991

Course Records, Main Turf

1 mile: Gaelic Cross, 1:35 2/5, September 23, 1987
1 mile 70 yards: Twin to Win, 1:41, October 24, 1986
1 3/8 miles: Syncospin, 2:12 3/5, September 25, 1987
1 5/8 miles: Nigilik, 2:48 1/5, October 24, 1986

Fastest Times of 2002

5 furlongs: Polly's Comet, :58.40, October 20
5 1/2 furlongs: Bad Boy Eric, 1:04.45, April 13
6 furlongs: Count On My Word, 1:09.76, April 13
1 mile: Acacian Song, 1:38.33, February 10
1 mile 70 yards: Western Heritage, 1:41.13, November 7
1 1/16 miles: Slew City Jay, 1:44.50, February 22
1 1/8 miles: Harvard Men, 1:53.30, September 28
1 3/16 miles: Exclusively Risque, 2:00.22, March 9
1 1/4 miles: Harvard Men, 2:02.09, October 26
1 1/2 miles: Private Change, 2:38.14, March 23
1 3/4 miles: Proper Blue, 3:09.10, April 6
2 miles: Round Rock, 3:39.48, December 21

River Downs

With the Ohio River serving as an attractive and sometimes destructive backdrop, River Downs has been part of the southern Ohio racing scene for more than 75 years. The track at Cincinnati's eastern edge opened in July 1925 as Coney Island racetrack. A crowd of 10,000 packed the facility for opening day, according to River Downs historians, and the track was off to a fast start.

But the floods of 1937 put a temporary stop to that. The track rebuilt following the flooding and reopened as River Downs. Sixty years later, the track again endured major Ohio River flooding, but once more the track was cleaned up and reopened. The track's grandstand had undergone an extensive rebuilding in the 1980s.

River Downs offers a pair of quality two-year-old stakes every year in the Cradle and the Bassinet (for fillies). The 1984 Cradle was won by Spend a Buck, who the next year won the Kentucky Derby (G1) and was named Horse of the Year. River Downs also was one of the first tracks at which Racing Hall of Fame jockey Steve Cauthen competed. After a one-year hiatus, River Downs in 2003 resumed its seven-and-seven racing format with Thistledown, in which each track runs seven alternating races. River Downs and Beulah Park had maintained the seven-and-seven format on a limited basis in 2002.

Location: 6301 Kellogg Ave., Cincinnati, OH 45230-0286
Phone: (513) 232-8000
Fax: (513) 232-1269
E-mail: turfclub@one.net
Web site: http://www.riverdowns.com
Year founded: 1925
Inaugural meeting: July 6, 1925
Number of stalls: 1,350
Seating capacity: 9,350

Officers

President: Dr. J. David Rutherford
General Manager: Jack Hanessian
Director of Racing: Ed Vomacka
Racing Secretary: Ed Vomacka
Director of Operations: Kathy Ewing
Director of Communications: John Engelhardt
Director of Marketing: Jolynn Johnston
Director of Mutuels: Larry Alexander
Director of Publicity: John Engelhardt
Director of Simulcasting: Vince Cyster
Stewards: Mike Manganelo, Philip Gour Jr., Tim Day
Track Announcer: Bill Downs
Track Photographer: Patrick Lang Photography
Track Superintendent: Jim Cornett
Other officials: John C. Hoover, Chairman of the Board

Racing Dates

2002: April 13-September 2
2003: April 12-September 1

Track Layout

Main circumference: 1 mile
Main track chutes: 3/4 mile, 1 1/4 miles
Main width: 80 feet
Main length of stretch: 1,117 feet
Main turf circumference: 7 furlongs

Leaders

Recent meeting, leading jockey: John McKee, 114, 2002
Recent meeting, leading trainer: Luis Albert Palacios, 29, 2002

Track Records, Main Dirt

4 1/2 furlongs: Sans Terre, :52 2/5, May 24, 1971
5 furlongs: Banker's Forbes, :57.60, June 7, 1994
5 1/2 furlongs: Tazua, 1:03, August 1, 1964
6 furlongs: Francine M., 1:08 3/5, July 4, 1969
1 mile: Alladin Rib, 1:36 1/5, August 8, 1988
1 mile 70 yards: South Dakota, 1:40, August 4, 1945
1 1/16 miles: Irish Dude, 1:41 4/5, July 5, 1969
1 1/8 miles: Brown Sugar, 1:49, September 2, 1925
1 1/4 miles: Crusader, 2:02, July 24, 1926
1 1/2 miles: South Dakota, 2:30 3/5, July 1, 1950
1 3/4 miles: Brigler, 2:59 3/5, October 19, 1940
2 miles: South Dakota, 3:21 2/5, July 8, 1950
Other: 1 11/16 miles, Distribute, 2:51 3/5, September 7, 1940; 1 7/8 miles, Shot Bills, 3:26 3/5, August 19, 1979; 2 miles 70 yds, Omar, 3:33 3/5, September 2, 1940; 2 1/4 miles, Almac, 3:54, October 31, 1936; 2 1/2 miles, Here Come Midge, 4:30 4/5, June 17, 1972; 3 miles 70 yds, Gloria Dream, 5:32 2/5, August 9, 1972

Course Records, Main Turf

4 1/2 furlongs: Adena, :50 4/5, April 26, 1977
5 furlongs: Hobbs, :56.30, September 1, 1991
7 1/2 furlongs: Stormy Deep, 1:28 2/5, August 15, 1990
1 mile: Bad News Blues, 1:34.20, July 23, 1994
1 1/16 miles: Franchise Player, 1:40.60, June 12, 1994
1 3/8 miles: Hi Rise, 2:15.60, August 15, 2000
1 1/2 miles: Rebel Thunder, 2:28, June 28, 1996
Other: 1 7/16 miles, Dina's Pl'ymate, 2:25, August 30, 1969

Interesting Facts

Previous name and dates: Coney Island 1925-1937
Major Race: $200,000 Cradle Stakes

Fastest Times of 2002 (Dirt)

4 1/2 furlongs: Tour D' Tiger, :52.40, May 3
5 furlongs: Sultan of Swat, :59.00, June 16; Tour D' Tiger, :59.00, July 25
5 1/2 furlongs: Benge B, 1:05.60, June 13
6 furlongs: Fabulous Brush, 1:11.40, August 31
1 mile: Vegas Rebels, 1:39.20, April 26
1 mile 70 yards: Groovy Add Vice, 1:44.60, May 27; Payforaday, 1:44.60, August 10
1 1/16 miles: Taylortwofeathers, 1:45.00, June 8
1 1/8 miles: Kind of Fun, 1:55.40, July 27
1 1/4 miles: Majestic Dinner, 2:07.00, September 1

Fastest Times of 2002 (Turf)

5 furlongs: Jimmy Jones, :56.60, July 14
7 1/2 furlongs: Casimir (Ire), 1:29.00, August 11
1 mile: Carol's Choice, 1:36.20, July 27; Trail, 1:36.20, July 26
1 1/16 miles: Devil Time, 1:41.40, June 23
1 3/8 miles: It's Slew to You, 2:16.60, June 23
1 1/2 miles: Check and Go, 2:31.20, July 21

Thistledown

Thistledown in suburban Cleveland is the home of Ohio's most important race, the $300,000 Ohio Derby (G2). Opened on July 20, 1925, Thistledown was owned and operated by the DeBartolo Corp. from 1959 through '99, when the track was purchased by Magna Entertainment Corp.

Thistledown has a full-color Diamond Vision infield display board, and inside the grandstand is its interactive Starting Gate educational museum, which features exhibits, weekly handicapping seminars, and information on racing in Ohio. The track also has two state-of-the-art simulcast theaters.

In the summer of 2000, Thistledown reconfigured the outdoor paddock area to allow fans to be closer to the racing experience. The newly landscaped paddock added more than 9,000 square feet and such amenities as picnic tables, television monitors, and mutuel windows. The North Randall track typically races from late March through the end of December. Starting in the 1990s, Thistledown conducted seven-and-seven programs—seven live races and seven simulcast races—with the state's two other Thoroughbred tracks. Thistledown halted that arrangement in 2002, but it was reinstituted for 2003.

Location: 21501 Emery Rd., North Randall, OH 44128
Phone: (216) 662-8600
Fax: (216) 662-5339
Web site: *http://www.thistledown.com*
Year founded: 1925
Inaugural meeting: July 20, 1925
Acreage: 128
Number of stalls: 1,560
Seating capacity: 3,800

Officers
President: Jim McAlpine
Vice President: William D. Murphy
General Manager: William D. Murphy
Director of Racing: William Couch
Director of Operations: Dave Ellsworth
Director of Finance: Ron Marinko
Director of Marketing: Brent Reitz
Director of Mutuels: Bob Hickey
Director of Publicity: Heather McColloch
Director of Simulcasting: Greg Davis
Horsemen's Liaison: Alan McKee
Stewards: Allen Fairbanks, Joel McCullar, Kim Sawyer
Track Announcer: Charles Pinnell
Track Photographer: Jeff Zamaiko
Track Superintendent: John Banno

Racing Dates
2002: March 29-December 23, 187 days
2003: March 15-December 15, 187 days

Track Layout
Main circumference: 1 mile
Main track chutes: 1 1/4 miles, 6 furlongs
Main width: 95 feet
Main length of stretch: 978 feet

Attendance
Highest single day record: 19,411, June 18, 1978
Average daily recent meeting: 3,438, 2002
Highest single meet record: 986,095 (191-day meet, 1979)
Record daily average for single meet: 7,049, 1954
Total attendance recent meeting: 642,918, 2002

Handle
Single day on-track handle: $3,851,575, July 24, 1999
Average all sources recent meeting: 1,175,264, 2002

Mutuel Records
Highest win: $500.20, Nobody's Secret, November 22, 1995
Highest Daily Double: $4,553.40, June 8, 1967
Highest Pick 6: $89,306.20, November 29, 1985

Leaders
Career, leading jockey by stakes wins: Julio Felix, 12
Career, leading jockey by titles: Michael Rowland, 28
Career, leading trainer by titles: Gary Johnson, 22
Recent meeting, leading jockey: Michael Rowland, 145, 2002
Recent meeting, leading owner: Pyrite Stables, 55, 2002
Recent meeting, leading trainer: Gary Johnson and Andrew Konkoly, 57, 2002

Records
Single meet, leading jockey by wins: Antonio Graell, 93, Summit Meet-1976
Single meet, leading trainer by wins: Gary Johnson, 40, Thistledown Meet-1998
Single day jockey wins: Buddy Haas, 6, August 28, 1933; John Adams, 6, September 2, 1942; Danny Weiler, 6, August 12, 1961; Anthony Rini, 6, June 12, 1970; Antonio Graell, 6, February 21, 1976; Benny Feliciano, 6, June 18, 1978; Antonio Graell, 6, November 14, 1980; Tom Ford, 6, December 13, 1982; Michael Rowland, 6, March 29, 1991; Brian Mills, 6, August 28, 1993; Michael Rowland, 6, October 19, 1999
Single day trainer wins: Gary Johnson, 6, November 27, 1999

Track Records, Main Dirt
4 furlongs: What About Quin, :45.40, June 5, 2002
4 1/2 furlongs: Onion Roll, :51.57, November 20, 1992
5 furlongs: Great Allegiance, :57.56, May 18, 1997
5 1/2 furlongs: Down Thepike Mike, 1:03.20, August 10, 1998
6 furlongs: Fancy Threat, 1:08 2/5, November 21, 1987
1 mile: Setting Limits, 1:35 3/5, November 17, 1989
1 mile 40 yards: Ifthisbe Britches, 1:38 3/5, December 8, 1989; North Island, 1:38 3/5, December 9, 1989
1 mile 70 yards: Wisdom Seeker, 1:40.92, July 22, 1995
1 1/16 miles: Entitled To Star, 1:41.32, November 25, 1995
1 1/8 miles: Smarten, 1:45 2/5, June 17, 1979
1 3/16 miles: Smoke Screen, 1:55 3/5, July 17, 1954
1 1/4 miles: Pert Near, 2:03, December 1, 1979
1 1/2 miles: Martha's Wave, 2:31 4/5, June 18, 1955
1 5/8 miles: Alsang, 2:46, August 8, 1936
1 3/4 miles: Mala Kee, 2:57 3/5, July 19, 1957
2 miles: Likely Advice, 3:27, December 15, 1980
Other: 2 furlongs, Onion Roll, :20.95, September 27, 1993; 1 9/16 miles, Military Girl, 2:44 1/5, June 13, 1942; 2 miles 40 yds, Winning Mark, 3:29 2/5, July 20, 1940; 2 1/16 miles, Bunker, 3:32 4/5, July 13, 1955; 2 1/8 miles, Lonely Cloud, 3:52.65, July 3, 1992; 2 1/4 miles, Son Richard, 3:54 3/5, August 27, 1938; 2 3/16 miles, Current Data, 3:54 3/5, December 5, 1981; 2 11/16 miles, Bea Beauty, 4:47 4/5, September 8, 1973; 3 miles 40 yds, Bea Beauty, 5:31 4/5, September 22, 1973; 3 5/8 miles, Eastern Promise, 6:49 3/5, October 6, 1973

Major Races
Ohio Derby (G2) for 3-year-olds, $300,000; Cleveland Gold Cup for 3-year-olds, $100,000

Fastest Times of 2002
2 furlongs: Cumberland Gap, :21.62, October 30
4 furlongs: What About Quin, :45.58, June 5
4 1/2 furlongs: Look At Al, :52.60, November 21
5 furlongs: Reoccurring Dream, :57.88, October 4
5 1/2 furlongs: Moonlight Gardens, 1:04.72, April 27
6 furlongs: Secret Romeo, 1:09.84, July 20
1 mile: Market Mover, 1:37.72, June 22
1 mile 40 yards: Taylortwofeathers, 1:40.92, May 20
1 mile 70 yards: Cardiogenic, 1:43.23, May 10

1 1/16 miles: Ashwood C C, 1:44.25, September 22
1 1/8 miles: Magic Weisner, 1:49.96, July 20
1 3/16 miles: Popular Host, 2:01.84, July 22
1 1/4 miles: Majestic Dinner, 2:04.52, October 14
1 1/2 miles: Silver Alarm, 2:35.40, June 16

Oklahoma

Blue Ribbon Downs

Blue Ribbon Downs, located near Sallisaw, Oklahoma, was developed by Blue Ribbon Ranch owner Bill Hedge on ranch property. It first offered racing in 1960 as a nonpari-mutuel racetrack, with all business operations based in Hedge's house. In 1973, Hedge sold the track to a group of investors. A decade later, Blue Ribbon was the first track to offer pari-mutuel racing in Oklahoma, but fire destroyed its grandstand two weeks before the 1983 meet was to open. Within one week, a new grandstand was erected. The track's richest Thoroughbred race is the Oklahoma-bred Thoroughbred Futurity for two-year-olds. The track races Thoroughbreds, Quarter Horses, Appaloosas, and Paints from mid-February to early December.

Location: 3700 W. Cherokee, Sallisaw, OK 74955
Phone: (918) 775-7771
Fax: (918) 775-5805
E-mail: brd@blueribbondowns.net
Web site: http://www.blueribbondowns.net
Abbreviation: BRD
Acreage: 165
Number of stalls: 1,064

Officers

President: Mary Watkins
General Manager: Don Essary
Assistant General Manager: Tonya Maxwell
Racing Secretary: Shirley Ellis
Secretary: Charles D. Whitsitt
Treasurer: Charles D. Whitsitt
Director of Admissions: Bob Vickery
Director of Finance: Jim Urban
Director of Marketing: Robin Akers
Director of Mutuels: Ladonna Perkins
Director of Publicity: Robin Akers
Director of Simulcasting: Tonya Maxwell
Stewards: Tom Clark, Bill Brown, Bill McNutt
Track Announcer: Fred Davis
Track Photographer: Gene Wilson and Associates
Track Superintendent: Gields Smith
Other officials: Jinx Blades, Horsemen's Bookeeper

Racing Dates

2002: February 2-November 24, 94 days
2003: February 1-November 23, 84 days

Track Layout

Main circumfrence: 7/8 mile oval
Main length of stretch: 845 feet

Leaders

Recent meeting, leading jockey: Fernando Camacho, 37, 2002
Recent meeting, leading trainer: Thomas Stephen Orr, 17, 2002

Track Records, Main Dirt

4 furlongs: Iwontbeback, :44.35, July 3, 1995
4 1/2 furlongs: Rebel's Jon, :50.35, June 29, 1996

5 furlongs: Pow Wow Al, :56.45, May 27, 1996
5 1/2 furlongs: Rebel's Jon, 1:02, October 1, 1995
6 furlongs: Rebel's Jon, 1:08.45, July 9, 1995
7 furlongs: Prententious Chief, 1:23, September 10, 1995
7 1/2 furlongs: Karate Kick, 1:29.35, September 17, 1994
1 mile: Staged Attraction, 1:36.15, June 10, 1989
1 1/16 miles: Just Ask Rudy, 1:43.15, April 6, 1996
1 1/8 miles: Long On Rowdy, 1:49.35, July 17, 1994
1 1/4 miles: Dare More, 2:03.35, August 28, 1994
1 3/8 miles: Say It All, 2:17.15, October 1, 1995
1 1/2 miles: Mr Sanhedrin, 2:32.35, November 14, 1993
1 5/8 miles: Sharp's Caliber, 2:47.15, December 11, 1994

Fastest Times of 2002

4 furlongs: Frisco Racer, :45.86, October 6
4 1/2 furlongs: Miss Shady Brook, :51.40, October 5
5 furlongs: Blonde Okie, :58.05, April 6
5 1/2 furlongs: Mighty Rick, 1:03.60, November 24
6 furlongs: Proper Mariner, 1:10.23, April 6
7 furlongs: Magic Shot, 1:25.40, April 6
7 1/2 furlongs: Directaccess, 1:31.80, October 5
1 mile: Quit Dodging, 1:38.84, June 1
1 1/16 miles: Magic Shot, 1:45.98, April 20
1 1/8 miles: Drysdale, 1:52.00, May 18

Fair Meadows at Tulsa

Offering nighttime Thoroughbred, Quarter Horse, Paint, and Appaloosa racing on its five-furlong oval, Fair Meadows at Tulsa is one of the entertainment facilities located at Expo Square, which hosts the Tulsa State Fair and some 400 other events each year. Fair Meadows, which has been holding live racing since 1989, is located on a former auto-racing oval and is next to the stadium of the Tulsa Drillers, the Class AA minor-league baseball team of the Texas Rangers. During racing season, a giant net between the stadium and Fair Meadows keeps foul balls from landing on the track's final turn. Expo Square includes an amusement park, water park, and hotel, and Fair Meadows offers a state-of-the-art simulcast facility that provides year-round racing action.

Location: 4145 E. 21st St., Tulsa, OK 74114
Phone: (918) 744-6999
Fax: (918) 746-3503
Web site: http://www.fairmeadows.com
Abbreviation: FMT
Inaugural meeting: 1988 (Summer)
Number of stalls: About 700
Seating capacity: 10,000

Officers

General Manager: Ron Shotts
Director of Racing: Ron Shotts
Director of Marketing: Richard Linihan
Director of Mutuels: Fred Davis
Director of Publicity: Richard Linihan
Director of Simulcasting: Kevin Jones
Horsemen's Liaison: Nina Parrish
Track Announcer: Fred Davis
Track Photographer: Gene Wilson & Associates
Track Superintendent: Jim Parrish

Racing Dates

2002: June 3-August 3, 33 days
2003: April 10-June 7, 36 days

Track Layout

Main circumference: 5/8 mile
Main track chute: 350 yards
Main length of stretch: 300 yards

Attendance
Average daily recent meeting: 1,701
Total attendance recent meeting: 56,129

Handle
Average on-track recent meeting: $143,137
Total on-track recent meeting: $4,723,536

Track Records, Main Dirt
4 furlongs: Only Cash, :44.40, May 30, 1997
5 1/2 furlongs: Visibility O, 1:04.60, July 5, 1998
6 furlongs: Carsoni, 1:10.80, August 3, 1995
6 1/2 furlongs: Assension Crozier, 1:16.80, August 20, 1994
1 mile: Judge North, 1:37, August 5, 1995
1 1/16 miles: Citation Rock, 1:46, September 11, 1991
1 1/8 miles: Demascus Slew, 1:51.78, May 30, 1998
1 3/8 miles: Second Avie, 2:20, August 5, 1995
1 5/8 miles: Phantom Cottage, 2:51.80, August 1, 1992

Interesting Facts
Trivia: Was formerly stockcar race track.

Fastest Times of 2002
4 furlongs: Rocky Ballado, :44.80, June 28
5 1/2 furlongs: Dance and Dazzle, 1:05.00, August 2; Real Pro, 1:05.00, July 25
6 furlongs: Baron Von Tom, 1:11.60, June 21
6 1/2 furlongs: Dance and Dazzle, 1:18.00, June 29
1 mile: Tedro, 1:39.40, August 2
1 1/16 miles: Fergie's Showtime, 1:47.00, June 29
1 1/8 miles: Pleasant Prince, 1:53.00, July 20
1 3/8 miles: Cryptotune, 2:22.20, August 3

Remington Park

Built by the late Edward J. DeBartolo, Remington Park opened its doors on September 1, 1988, and was purchased by Magna Entertainment Corp. in October 1999 after average attendance had plummeted from a high of 11,263 in 1989 to 2,517 in 1998.

The track began a new era in 2001 with the addition of lights, thus allowing evening racing. Thoroughbreds race during a summer-fall meet from mid-August to late November, and Quarter Horses are also featured in a spring meet. The track's feature Thoroughbred race is the $150,000 Oklahoma Derby (G3), which was to be run for the 15th time in 2003.

Customers have multiple choices for settings, including the Players Sports Bar, Club One with box seats, a nonsmoking section in the clubhouse, the Silks Restaurant, the Eclipse Restaurant, and luxurious private suites. Remington's decline continued in the 2002 season, and Magna reported that it wrote down the value of the track and Michigan's Great Lake Downs by a total of $17.5-million in 2002.

Location: 1 Remington Pl., Oklahoma City, OK 73111
Phone: (405) 424-1000
Fax: (405) 425-3297
E-mail: RMP IT@remingtonpark.com
Web site: http://www.remingtonpark.com
Inaugural meeting: September 1, 1988
Abbreviation: RP
Number of stalls: 1,312

Officers
President: Corey Johnson
Vice President: Jeff Greco
General Manager: R.D. Logan
Director of Racing: Fred Hutton
Racing Secretary: Fred Hutton

Director of Operations: Matt Vance
Director of Admissions: Diane Bynum
Director of Communications: Dale Day
Director of Finance: Julie Tillman
Director of Marketing: Dale Day
Director of Mutuels: Carrie Kluck
Director of Sales: Sharon Lair
Director of Simulcasting: Fred Hutton
Stewards: Charlie Cox, David Southard, Mike Corey, Norma Calhoun
Track Announcer: Don Stevens
Track Photographer: Reed Palmer
Track Superintendent: Mike Raidt

Racing Dates
2002: August 10-December 23, 76 days
2003: July 25-November 30, 69 days

Track Layout
Main circumference: 1 mile
Main track chutes: 1 3/8 miles, 7 furlongs
Main width: 100 feet
Main length of stretch: 990 feet
Main turf circumference: 7 furlongs
Main turf chute: 1 1/8 miles
Main turf width: 80 feet
Main turf length of stretch: 990 feet

Attendance
Highest single day record: 26,411, February 29, 1992
Record daily average for single meet: 11,128, 1988

Handle
Record daily average for single meet: $1,310,542, 1990
Single day on-track handle: $2,808,243, February 24, 1990

Mutuel Records
Highest win: $254.20, Cherokee County, October 28, 2001
Highest Exacta: $5,495.80, December 3, 1988
Highest Trifecta: $58,662.40, February 24, 1995
Highest Daily Double: $2,969.60, September 2, 2000
Highest Pick 3: $18,057.60, November 13, 1994
Highest Other Exotics: $38,968.80, Superfecta, December 1, 1996

Leaders
Career, leading jockey by stakes wins: Don Pettinger, 108
Career, leading jockey by titles: Pat Steinberg, 9
Career, leading trainer by titles: Donnie Von Hemel, 11
Career, leading jockey by wins: Don Pettinger, 1,266
Career, leading owner by stakes wins: Barbara and John Smicklas, 20
Career, leading trainer by stakes wins: Donnie Von Hemel, 115
Recent meeting, leading jockey: Cliff Berry, 108, 2002
Recent meeting, leading owner: C. R. Trout, 13, 2002
Recent meeting, leading trainer: Donnie Von Hemel, 36, 2002

Records
Single day trainer wins: Wade White, 5, November 17, 1993
Single day jockey wins: Cliff Berry, 6, September, 30, 2001; Tim Doocy, 6, December 5, 1993

Track Records, Main Dirt
4 1/2 furlongs: Payday Two, :52.20, February 26, 2000
5 furlongs: Highland Ice, :57.20, December 3, 1999
5 1/2 furlongs: Run Johnny, 1:02, September 26, 1997
6 furlongs: Smoke of Ages, 1:08, September 29, 1991
6 1/2 furlongs: Kangaroo King, 1:14.40, July 26, 1997
7 furlongs: Golden Gear, 1:20.40, March 18, 1995
1 mile: White Wheels, 1:35.40, August 17, 1997
1 mile 70 yards: Marked Tree, 1:39.60, March 13, 1993
1 1/16 miles: Valid Bonnet, 1:41.20, July 26, 1997
1 1/8 miles: Classic Cat, 1:48, August 30, 1998
1 3/16 miles: Wild Rush, 1:53.60, August 10, 1997
1 1/4 miles: Double Platinum, 2:03.40, October 10, 1999

1 3/8 miles: Wild and Comfy, 2:17.96, October 18, 2002
1 1/2 miles: Bid the Zeal, 2:31.40, October 24, 1998
Other: 3 furlongs, Raisable Adversary, :31.20, August 29, 1999

Course Records, Main Turf
5 furlongs: Otro Mambo, :55.85, October 5, 2001
7 1/2 furlongs: Finally Tops, 1:27.60, May 1, 1996
1 mile: No More Hard Times, 1:33.80, September 20, 1992
1 1/16 miles: Burbank, 1:39.20, August 30, 1997
1 1/8 miles: Gauntlett Boy, 1:47 4/5, November 5, 1989
1 3/8 miles: Vergennes, 2:13.00, September 3, 2000
2 miles: Big Notice, 3:29, November 20, 1993

Fastest Times of 2002 (Dirt)
3 furlongs: L. B. Long Gone, :33.71, August 11
5 furlongs: Quick Claim, :57.96, August 23
5 1/2 furlongs: Baron On Tom, 1:03.97, October 19
6 furlongs: Trickmeister, 1:09.75, November 8
6 1/2 furlongs: Slew Ann, 1:17.04, August 23
7 furlongs: Mr Ross, 1:21.13, September 2
1 mile: Dounome, 1:37.20, November 11
1 mile 70 yards: Luz de Esperanza, 1:41.49, August 25
1 1/16 miles: Zee Oh Six, 1:44.34, October 27
1 1/8 miles: The Judge Sez Who, 1:49.34, August 25
1 3/8 miles: Wild and Comfy, 2:17.96, October 18

Fastest Times of 2002 (Turf)
5 furlongs: Jeb's Honor, :56.34, August 17
7 1/2 furlongs: George Taylor, 1:29.38, August 24
1 mile: Eye Found It, 1:36.18, October 5
1 1/16 miles: Strawbailey, 1:42.83, August 11
1 1/8 miles: Bien Nicole, 1:49.42, September 29

Will Rogers Downs

Will Rogers Downs is located on 210 acres just east of Claremore and approximately 25 miles from downtown Tulsa. Live racing on Fridays, Saturdays, and Sundays in the spring of 2001 was reduced from 12 days to ten because of a shortage of horses. No racing was scheduled for 2003. The track is home to rodeos as well as Will Rogers County Jamborees every other Saturday night, presenting a family-oriented country show and concert.

Location: 20900 S. 4200 Rd., Claremore, OK 74018
Phone: (918) 343-5900
Fax: (918) 343-6399
Web site: *http://www.willrogersdowns.com*

Racing Dates
2002: November 1-November 24

Oregon

Grants Pass

Location: 1451 Fairgrounds Rd., Grants Pass, OR 97527
Phone: (541) 476-3215
Fax: (541) 476-0127

Officers
Director of Racing: Al Westoff
Racing Secretary: Jerry Kohls
Director of Operations: Wally Starner (backside)
Director of Publicity: Gary Davison

Racing Dates
2002: May 18-July 7
2003: May 17-July 6

Officers
Racing Secretary: Jerry Kohls
Director of Operations: Wally Starner (backside)
Director of Publicity: Gary Davison
Director of Racing: Al Westoff

Leaders
Recent meeting, leading jockey: Twyler Beckner, 29, 2002
Recent meeting, leading trainer: John McDevitt, 12, 2002

Fastest Times of 2002
4 1/2 furlongs: Torreon, :53.00, May 27; Touched by N Angel, :53.00, June 22
5 1/2 furlongs: Missy Muffet, 1:04.20, May 26; Natural Wonder, 1:04.20, May 25
6 1/2 furlongs: Mr One Ring, 1:20.20, May 27
1 1/16 miles: Jewels Togo, 1:50.00, June 23

Portland Meadows

Founded by Bay Meadows Race Course builder William Kyne, Portland Meadows has a rich history dating back to September 14, 1946, when a crowd of 10,000 watched the nation's first evening Thoroughbred racing card. General Electric Co., which devised the lighting system, boasted at the time: "This system, the first of its kind, has enough power to light a four-lane super highway from Portland to Salem (a distance of more than 40 miles)."

But Portland Meadows officials were powerless to fight the Vanport flood, which in 1948 canceled the track's season after just 13 cards and caused $250,000 in damage. The track was hit again in the early-morning hours of April 25, 1970, when a fire razed the grandstand. Portland Meadows was rebuilt, opening its 1971 season before a record crowd of 12,635.

Portland Meadows served as an early proving ground for Racing Hall of Fame jockey Gary Stevens, who won two riding titles there in the early 1980s. New Portland Meadows Inc. operated the track from 1991 until it leased the track to Magna Entertainment Corp. in mid-2001. In 2002, Magna purchased the long-term operating rights to Portland Meadows for an undisclosed price.

Location: 1001 N. Schmeer Rd., Portland, OR 97217
Phone: (503) 285-9144
Fax: (503) 285-1015
E-mail: tnpm@portlandmeadows.com
Web site: *http://www.portlandmeadows.com*

Officers
President: Arthur McFadden
General Manager: Jeff Grady
Director of Racing: Jerry Kohls
Racing Secretary: Jerry Kohls
Director of Operations: Woodrow Mitchell
Director of Marketing: Rod Whitesmith

Racing Dates
2002: October 20, 2001-February 10, 2002, 46 days
2003: October 19, 2002-April 27, 2003, 80 days

Fastest Times of 2002
4 1/2 furlongs: Strike the Chord, :52.22, December 20
5 furlongs: Strike the Chord, :59.45, November 11
5 1/2 furlongs: Strike the Chord, 1:06.09, October 25
6 furlongs: An Naabi, 1:10.88, December 15

1 mile: Thunder Zoot, 1:40.19, December 22
1 1/16 miles: Aka Remy, 1:46.90, December 14
1 1/8 miles: Yesss, 1:54.04, January 27

Pennsylvania

Penn National Race Course

Built by a group of Central Pennsylvania investors, Penn National Race Course is located 13 miles from the state capital, Harrisburg. It staged its first race meeting on August 30, 1972. The following year, Penn National bought the racing license of defunct Pitt Park and began an essentially year-round racing schedule. In 1978, Penn National built the state's first turf course.

Led by principal owner Peter D. Carlino, Penn National has been an innovator in Pennsylvania's racing industry. Philadelphia-area businessman Carlino bought one of the track's operating licenses in 1974 and the other in '83. With legalization of telephone betting in 1982, Penn National began the commonwealth's first account-wagering system, and the following year it began the first cable-television broadcast of its races. Following legislative approval of off-track wagering in 1989, Penn National built and operated six facilities in Central Pennsylvania.

In 1994, the track's parent company, Penn National Gaming Inc., held an initial public stock offering. With those proceeds and subsequent stock issues, Penn National has financed the acquisitions of Charles Town Races, a Thoroughbred track in West Virginia, and Pocono Downs, a Standardbred track near Williamsport, Pennsylvania, as well as casino properties. Penn National Gaming's chairman is Peter M. Carlino, son of the track's principal investor.

Location: Route 743, Grantville, PA 17028
Phone: (717) 469-2211
Fax: (717) 469-2910
E-mail: pnrc@pngaming.com
Web site: http://www.pnrc.com
Acreage: 600
Number of stalls: 1,200
Seating capacity: 9,570

Officers
President: Richard Orbann
Vice President: Richard T. Schnaars
General Manager: Richard T. Schnaars
Racing Secretary: Paul Jenkins
Director of Marketing: Frederick D. Lipkin
Director of Mutuels: Carole Kneasel
Director of Publicity: Frederick D. Lipkin
Director of Simulcasting: Chris Camplese
Stewards: Rodney Peters, Robert Campbell, Thomas Crouse
Track Announcer: John Bogar
Track Photographer: Gill's Positive Images
Track Superintendent: Robert Longenecker

Racing Dates
2002: January 1-December 31, 203 days
2003: January 2-December 30, 204 days

Track Layout
Main circumference: 1 mile
Main track chutes: 1 1/4 miles, 6 furlongs

Main length of stretch: 990 feet
Main turf circumference: 7 furlongs

Attendance
Highest single day record: 15,442, August 2, 1980

Handle
Single day on-track handle: $2,173,921, December 26, 1998

Leaders
Recent meeting, leading jockey: David Cora, 268, 2002
Recent meeting, leading owner: Danny Chen, 79, 2002
Recent meeting, leading trainer: Harry Thompson Jr., 176, 2002

Mutuel Records
Highest Exacta: $8,430, April 13, 1988
Highest Other Exotics: Twin Trifecta, $543,014, June 14, 1988
Highest Trifecta: $42,886.50, May 27, 1980
Highest win: $343.40, Busy Lady, December 20, 1977
Lowest Daily Double: $27,985.80, July 11, 1975

Track Records, Main Dirt
2 furlongs: Five Cousins, :21.00, February 27, 2003
4 furlongs: Gross, :46 1/5, April 13, 1973
4 1/2 furlongs: Rita's Best, :50.3, April 27, 2001
5 furlongs: On the Phone, :56.60, July 13, 1996
5 1/2 furlongs: Cortan, 1:03 1/5, May 29, 1978
6 furlongs: Jiva Coolit, 1:08 4/5, May 22, 1977
1 mile: Vambourine, 1:36 1/5, June 12, 1977
1 mile 70 yards: Wee Thunder, 1:39.60, July 13, 1996
1 1/16 miles: A Letter to Harry, 1:41 1/5, September 10, 1978
1 1/8 miles: Collection Agent, 1:49 4/5, August 22, 1987
1 3/16 miles: Bar Tab, 1:55 2/5, October 14, 1972
1 1/4 miles: Adda Nickell, 2:03 3/5, October 30, 1976
1 1/2 miles: Holly Holme, 2:31 2/5, September 29, 1973
1 3/4 miles: Chasqui, 3:00, June 21, 1980
2 miles: Finny Flyer, 3:28, May 25, 1974

Course Records, Main Turf
5 furlongs: Admiral Yi, :55.20, June 24, 1994
1 mile: The Very One, 1:33 1/5, July 15, 1979
1 mile 70 yards: Aborigine, 1:37 1/5, August 20, 1978
1 1/16 miles: Told, 1:38, September 14, 1980
1 1/2 miles: Coalitioncandidate, 2:27, May 27, 1991
1 5/8 miles: New Episode, 2:45, May 18, 2001

Fastest Times of 2002 (Dirt)
4 1/2 furlongs: Mana Torpedoes, :51.20, October 9
5 furlongs: Divisional Champ, :57.86, March 13
5 1/2 furlongs: Tanky Boy, 1:03.42, July 24
6 furlongs: Holiday Music, 1:08.89, May 4
1 mile: Sumerset, 1:36.82, August 14
1 mile 70 yards: Clever Gent, 1:41.68, August 28
1 1/16 miles: Fred Bear Claw, 1:43.98, June 29
1 1/8 miles: Pardner, 1:51.88, October 18
1 3/16 miles: Pardner, 1:59.69, December 29
1 1/4 miles: Colonial Mate, 2:05.89, April 17
2 miles: Service, 3:35.40, August 31

Fastest Times of 2002 (Turf)
5 furlongs: Bop, :54.61, August 3
1 mile: Glitter's Alone, 1:35.11, July 6
1 mile 70 yards: Calling Again, 1:38.98, August 16
1 1/16 miles: Watchman's Warning, 1:41.66, August 30

Philadelphia Park

Built reluctantly and inexpensively in the early 1970s, the track known as Philadelphia Park has had a difficult history. But, it has emerged as a leader in providing fan amenities and phone wagering in its region. When racing first arrived in Pennsylvania in the late 1960s, both Thoroughbred and Standardbred racing were conducted at Liberty Bell Park in Philadelphia's Northeast section. But with regional lawmakers insisting on a separate Thoroughbred facility, Keystone Race Track was built for $20-million approximately one mile north of Liberty Bell in Bensalem Township, across the city border in Bucks County. It opened in November 1974 with two ownership groups, which often feuded. Keystone inaugurated the track's signature race, the Pennsylvania Derby (G3), in 1979, and phone betting was authorized in 1982.

In 1984, Robert Brennan-controlled International Thoroughbred Breeders Inc. bought Keystone for $37.5-million to avoid competition for its Garden State Park, which opened in April 1985 (and closed in 2001). Brennan's company renamed the track Philadelphia Park and invested several million dollars into the grandstand and the racing surface, including the addition of a turf course. Financially failing International Thoroughbred Breeders sold the track to Greenwood Racing, headed by British bookmaking executives Robert Green and William Hogwood, for $67-million in 1990, the year in which the track opened the first of its five off-track betting facilities. In May 1999, Philadelphia Park completed an acclaimed, $4-million renovation of its first floor.

Location: 3001 Street Rd., Bensalem, PA 19020-2096
Phone: (215) 639-9000
Fax: (215) 639-0337
Web site: *http://www.philadelphiapark.com*
Year founded: 1969
Inaugural meeting: 1969
Acreage: 417
Number of stalls: 1,700
Seating capacity: 8,700

Officers
President: Robert W. Green
Chief Executive Officer: Harold G. Handel
Director of Racing: Salvatore Sinatra Jr.
Director of Marketing: James Milligan
Director of Mutuels: Bill Barnes
Director of Publicity: Keith Jones
Director of Simulcasting: Geri Mercer
Track Announcer: W. Keith Jones
Other officials: Andrew J. Green, Senior Vice President of Administration

Racing Dates
2002: January 1-December 31, 227 days
2003: January 1-December 31, 227 days

Track Layout
Main circumference: 1 mile
Main track chutes: 1 1/4 miles, 7 furlongs
Main width: 80 feet
Main length of stretch: 974 feet
Main turf circumference: 7 furlongs
Main turf chute: 1 1/8 miles

Leaders
Career, leading jockey by titles: Rick Wilson, 9
Recent meeting, leading jockey: Stewart Elliott, 236, 2002
Recent meeting, leading trainer: Scott Lake, 169, 2002
Recent meeting, leading owner: Plumstead Stables of Robert and Robin Seeger, 43, E&G Stables of Eric and Greg Fral, 43, 2002
Career, leading trainer by titles: Efrain T. Garcia, 5

Track Records, Main Dirt
4 furlongs: Heres a Tip, :45, June 11, 1982
4 1/2 furlongs: Distinctive Hat, :51.48, May 2, 1994
5 furlongs: My Favorite Grub, :56, September 7, 1998
5 1/2 furlongs: Saint Verre, 1:02.65, July 17, 2000
6 furlongs: Iron Punch, 1:07.89, July 29, 2000
6 1/2 furlongs: Tricky Mister, 1:14.40, June 21, 1998
7 furlongs: Flaming Bridle, 1:20.61, September 28, 1999
1 mile: Regal Count, 1:34 4/5, December 5, 1985
1 mile 70 yards: Tragedy, 1:38.70, December 12, 1995
1 1/16 miles: Cool Spring Park, 1:40 4/5, November 4, 1974
1 1/8 miles: Selari Spirit, 1:47, November 30, 1974
1 3/16 miles: Southern Shade, 1:56 2/5, October 20, 1984
1 1/4 miles: It's Always Archie, 2:02, November 23, 1974
1 1/2 miles: Laugh a Minute, 2:31, January 4, 1992
1 5/8 miles: River Wolf, 2:46 2/5, October 13, 1990
1 3/4 miles: Johnny's Silencer, 2:57 4/5, December 17, 1988
2 miles: Perfect to a Tee, 3:25.87, September 2, 1996
Other: 2 furlongs, Queen Millie, :21.32, January 30, 1994; 1 9/16 miles, Laugh a Minute, 2:40.85, January 18, 1992; 1 11/16 miles, Laugh a Minute, 2:53.20, December 21, 1991; 1 13/16 miles, Fire North, 3:04.80, March 14, 1992; 1 7/8 miles, Haberdasher, 3:13 3/5, October 17, 1987; 2 1/4 miles, Transfer Ticket, 3:56, December 31, 1988; 2 1/8 miles, Heavy Medal Man, 3:39.59, April 25, 1992; 2 1/2 miles, Half Chance, 4:24.15, May 25, 1992;

Course Records, Main Turf
5 furlongs: Lou's Bucks, :56, September 20, 1998
7 1/2 furlongs: Here Comes Scott, 1:30.85, September 10, 1994
1 mile: Lake Cecebe, 1:35 3/5, June 28, 1986
1 mile 70 yards: Rolfe's Ruby, 1:39 2/5, June 21, 1986; Marlish, 1:39 2/5, August 13, 1986
1 1/16 miles: Whatever For, 1:40 2/5, June 22, 1986
1 1/8 miles: Whatever For, 1:46 1/5, September 1, 1986
1 3/8 miles: Juanca (Arg), 2:16 2/5, September 1, 1986
1 1/2 miles: Lord Zada, 2:28.38, June 10, 2000
2 miles: Chippenham Park, 3:28 4/5, September 1, 1990

Interesting Facts
Previous names and dates: Keystone Race Track 1974-1984

Fastest Times of 2002 (Dirt)
4 1/2 furlongs: Lightningintheair, :52.48, June 29
5 furlongs: The Maccabee, :57.21, September 2
5 1/2 furlongs: All the Marbles, 1:03.04, July 22
6 furlongs: The Maccabee, 1:08.83, June 16
6 1/2 furlongs: Night Caller, 1:15.01, December 31
7 furlongs: Night Caller, 1:22.80, August 17
1 mile: Ruskin, 1:38.55, May 13
1 mile 70 yards: American Car, 1:40.69, January 8
1 1/16 miles: Quiet Mike, 1:43.00, July 20
1 1/8 miles: Truly a Judge, 1:50.39, August 31
1 1/4 miles: Mint to Kiss, 2:08.06, September 3

Fastest Times of 2002 (Turf)
5 furlongs: Trip Charge, :57.05, July 8
About 5 furlongs: Nun On the Run, :57.72, July 28
7 1/2 furlongs: False Evidence, 1:32.28, September 14; Start That Song, 1:32.28, September 22
About 7 1/2 furlongs: Feisty Vick, 1:34.33, July 29
1 mile: Great Will, 1:38.41, July 9
About 1 mile: Garden Dance, 1:39.79, July 21
1 mile 70 yards: Sugar Loaf Mint, 1:42.57, June 2
About 1 mile 70 yards: Stephan's Prize, 1:41.88, July 22
1 1/16 miles: Cyber Chat, 1:43.75, July 15
About 1 1/16 miles: Stephan's Prize, 1:44.49, August 11
1 1/8 miles: Bostic Hill, 1:52.42, July 6
About 1 1/8 miles: Demons and Devils, 1:53.66, July 27
1 3/8 miles: Make Your Own, 2:22.52, September 10
About 1 3/8 miles: Quality Affirmed, 2:18.89, July 30
1 1/2 miles: Cetewayo, 2:35.01, June 8
About 2 1/16 miles: Valay Pass, 3:42.54, October 7

Texas

Lone Star Park

One decade after Texas legalized pari-mutuel racing, Lone Star Park at Grand Prairie opened in 1997 and joined Sam Houston Race Park in Houston and Retama Park near San Antonio as the three major tracks in the state. Located in the Dallas-Fort Worth metropolitan area, Lone Star was built for $96-million by the Lone Star Jockey Club, a group headed by real estate moguls Trammell Crow and his son, Harlan, of Trammell Crow Co. The National Thoroughbred Racing Association All-Star Jockey Championship brings the nation's leading riders to the track for a ten-race competition. Texas-bred Thoroughbreds take center stage for the Stars of Texas Day. Lone Star is scheduled to host the Breeders' Cup World Thoroughbred Championships in 2004. The track's sale to Magna Entertainment Corp. for $99-million, including assumption of debt, was completed in 2002.

Location: 1000 Lone Star Pkwy., Grand Prairie, TX 75050
Phone: (972) 263-7223
Fax: (972) 237-1155
E-mail: bartl@lonestarpark.com
Web site: *http://www.lonestarpark.com*
Inaugural meeting: April 17, 1997
Acreage: 315
Number of stalls: 1,400
Seating capacity: 12,000

Officers
President: Corey S. Johnsen
Vice President: Jeffrey Greco
Director of Racing: Larry A. Craft
Racing Secretary: Larry A. Craft
Director of Marketing: G.W. Hail
Director of Mutuels: Don Fontenot
Director of Publicity: Darren Rogers
Director of Simulcasting: Mindy Hutchison
Track Announcer: Michael Wrona
Track Photographer: Reed Palmer
Track Superintendent: Ron Moore

Racing Dates
2002: April 4-July 14, 70 days
2003: April 3-July 13, 70 days

Track Layout
Main circumference: 1 mile
Main track chute: 7 furlongs
Main width: 90 feet
Main length of stretch: 930 feet
Main turf circumference: 7 furlongs
Main turf chute: 1 1/8 miles
Main turf width: 70 feet
Main turf length of stretch: 900 feet

Attendance
Highest single day record: 33,805, July 3, 2000
Average daily recent meeting: 9,025, 2002
Highest single meet record: 675,321, 2000
Total attendance recent meeting: 631,726, 2002

Handle
Single day on-track handle: $3,130,221, May 1, 1999
Average all sources recent meeting: $3,340,034, 2002
Single day total handle all sources: $7,218,982, May 1, 1999
Average on-track recent meeting: $1,291,535, 2002
Total all sources recent meeting: $233,802,356, 2002

Mutuel Records
Highest win: $201.40, Slightly Slew, June 26, 1997
Highest Exacta: $3,657.20, May 2, 1998
Highest Trifecta: $31,825.50, May 2, 1998
Highest Daily Double: $3,016.80, July 18, 1998
Highest Pick 3: $15,088.40, July 11, 1997
Highest Pick 6: $39,891.80, April 26, 1998
Highest Other Exotics: $35,640.60, Superfecta, June 27, 1998

Leaders
Career, leading owner by wins: Tom Durant, 17
Career, leading trainer by wins: Dallas Keen, 77
Recent meeting, leading jockey: Corey S. Lanerie, 92, 2002
Recent meeting, leading owner: Ken Murphy, 24, 2002
Recent meeting, leading trainer: Steve Asmussen, 95, 2002
Career, leading jockey by wins: Marlon St. Julien, 165

Records
Single day jockey wins: Ronald Ardoin, 6, July 17, 1997
Single day trainer wins: Steve Asmussen, 3, May 6, 1998; Jim Gaston, 3, June 11, 1998; Dallas Keen, 3, July 9, 1998

Track Records, Main Dirt
4 1/2 furlongs: Rayanegra, :51.39, May 22, 1997
5 furlongs: Joyful Tune, :56.25, May 5, 2002
5 1/2 furlongs: Term Sheet, 1:02.78, July 5, 2001
6 furlongs: Triple Card, 1:08.06, May 28, 2001
6 1/2 furlongs: Spiritbound, 1:14.16, May 3, 1997
7 furlongs: Clooney, 1:20.98, June 22, 2001
1 mile: Isitingood, 1:34.44, April 20, 1997
1 1/16 miles: Dixie Dot Com, 1:40.53, May 28, 2001
1 1/8 miles: Moosekabear, 1:49.69, April 19, 1997
1 3/16 miles: Moosekabear, 1:56.21, May 10, 1997
1 1/4 miles: Tali Hai, 2:04.68, June 14, 1997
1 1/2 miles: Tali Hai, 2:32.57, July 5, 1997
1 3/4 miles: Sir Moon Dancer, 3:00.46, July 19, 1998
Other: 2 1/2 furlongs, Yes He Will, :26.53, October 7, 1997

Course Records, Main Turf
5 furlongs: Icy Morn, :55.60, May 26, 1997
7 1/2 furlongs: Special Moments, 1:28.20, May 24, 1998
1 mile: Kiraday, 1:33.56, July 4, 1997
1 1/16 miles: Sharpest Image (Ire), 1:40.05, June 12, 1998
1 1/8 miles: Yaqthan (Ire), 1:45.54, May 25, 1998
1 3/8 miles: Rugged Bugger, 2:13.53, May 10, 1998
1 1/2 miles: Final Val, 2:28.20, July 4, 1998

Fastest Times of 2002 (Dirt)
4 1/2 furlongs: Lonely Concorde, :52.30, May 1
5 furlongs: Joyful Tune, :56.25, May 5
5 1/2 furlongs: Lake Charles, 1:03.84, July 14
6 furlongs: Peanutsinacoke, 1:09.45, July 13
6 1/2 furlongs: Beau's Town, 1:14.93, May 4
7 furlongs: Premeditation, 1:23.06, July 3
1 mile: Mountain General, 1:35.57, July 14
1 1/16 miles: Congaree, 1:42.96, May 27
1 1/8 miles: Wiseman's Ferry, 1:49.92, May 11

Fastest Times of 2002 (Turf)
5 furlongs: Nuclear Debate, :55.74, May 27
7 1/2 furlongs: Clooney, 1:29.01, July 7
1 mile: Lampedusa, 1:35.37, July 7
1 1/16 miles: Maysville Slew, 1:40.99, May 25
1 1/8 miles: Suances (GB), 1:49.09, June 15
1 3/8 miles: Wyconda, 2:18.73, June 1
1 1/2 miles: Corinthian (Ire), 2:34.39, July 14

Manor Downs

Thoroughbred racing debuted in 2002 at Manor Downs, a small racetrack near Austin, Texas, that long had offered only straightaway Quarter Horse and Paint racing. Ordered by the Texas Racing Commission to improve its racetrack to accommodate Thoroughbred racing, Manor spent more than $4-million to expand its oval to 7½ furlongs and to renovate the barn area and other sections. Manor, which is owned by Frances Tapp, was among the tracks in Texas's far-flung non-pari-mutuel circuit that flourished before legislation allowing pari-mutuel wagering was passed in 1987.

Location: 9211 Hill Lane, Manor, TX 78653
Phone: (512) 272-5581
Fax: (512) 278-1892
E-mail: manordowns@aol.com
Web site: http://www.manordowns.com

Officers
Chief Operating Officer: Howard Phillips
Racing Secretary: Sammy Burton
Director of Publicity: Brian Monshower
Track Superintendent: Allan Key

Racing Dates
2002: May 11-June 9, 10 days
2003: May 3-May 11, 4 days

Fastest Times of 2002 (Dirt)
4 furlongs: Fight Festival, :47.05, May 18
4 1/2 furlongs: Jakolby, :51.60, April 27
5 furlongs: Getting Old, :57.40, May 4
5 1/2 furlongs: Cousin Steve, 1:04.49, May 25
6 furlongs: Halo Cat, 1:08.49, May 26
7 1/2 furlongs: Inforcer, 1:31.40, April 28
1 mile: Milk Money, 1:37.92, May 19
1 1/16 miles: Double the Dose, 1:45.20, April 28

Retama Park

One of the country's newest racing facilities, Retama Park opened in April 1995 in Selma, Texas, 15 minutes northeast of San Antonio. The racetrack is both uniquely named—for the green-limbed deciduous tree or shrub native to south and west Texas—and uniquely designed, with its mission-style, five-tiered grandstand featuring arched entranceways, food courts, the Terrace Dining Room, the Race Book and Sports Bar, and the new Player's Club for Turf and Field Club members. The track's original investors hired well-known racing executive Robert J. Quigley to oversee construction of the $79-million plant and the track's opening, but the facility failed to meet even modest wagering projections. After failing to pay its bondholders, the track filed for bankruptcy protection in 1996 and was purchased by William Allen's Call Now Inc. Thomas Johnson took over as president and chief executive of Call Now on November 29, 2001.

Location: 1 Retama Pkwy., Selma, TX 78154
Phone: (210) 651-7000
Fax: (210) 651-7099
E-mail: run@retamapark.com
Web site: http://www.retamapark.com
Year founded: 1989
Inaugural meeting: April 7, 1995
Abbreviation: Ret

Acreage: 226
Number of stalls: 1,288
Seating capacity: 6,800

Officers
Chairman: Joe R. Straus Jr.
Chief Executive Officer: Bryan P. Brown
General Manager: Robert W. Pollock
Director of Racing: Larry A. Craft
Racing Secretary: Larry A. Craft
Director of Admissions: Steven M. Ross
Director of Finance: Lisa L. Medrano
Director of Marketing: Susan Rundell
Director of Mutuels: Jackie F. Hart
Director of Publicity: Douglas B. Vair
Director of Simulcasting: Steven M. Ross
Stewards: Chuck Nuber, Donnie Walker, John Ferrara
Track Announcer: Don Alexander
Track Photographer: Coady Photography
Track Superintendent: Jesse L. Cardenas

Racing Dates
2002: August 2-October 26, 51 days
2003: August 1-October 25, 51 days

Track Layout
Main circumference: 1 mile
Main track chute: 7 furlongs
Main width: 110 feet
Main length of stretch: 990 feet
Main turf circumference: 7 furlongs
Main turf chute: 1 1/8 miles
Main turf width: 90 feet

Attendance
Average daily recent meeting: 2,276, 2002
Highest single day record: 16,827, April 7, 1995
Highest single meet record: 452,421, 1995
Record daily average for single meet: 4,713, 1995
Total attendance recent meeting: 116,077, 2002

Handle
Average all sources recent meeting: $1,166,782, 2002
Average on-track recent meeting: $104,150, 2002
Record daily average for single meet: $429,562
Single day on-track handle: $705,712, April 7, 1995
Single day on-track handle: $705,712, April 7, 1995
Total all sources recent meeting: $59,505,875, 2002
Total on-track recent meeting: $5,311,626, 2002

Mutuel Records
Highest win: $136.40, Icy's Baba, August 15, 1999

Leaders
Recent meeting, leading jockey: Roman Chapa, 72, 2002
Recent meeting, leading owner: Leland Cook
Recent meeting, leading trainer: Danny Pish, 35, Fall-2002

Track Records, Main Dirt
4 1/2 furlongs: Raise a Tab, :51.06, August 1, 1998
5 furlongs: Teed Off, :56.20, August 20, 2000
5 1/2 furlongs: Bailando, 1:02.90, May 13, 1995
6 furlongs: Bucharest, 1:08.82, May 10, 1995
6 1/2 furlongs: Heavily Armed, 1:15.30, August 30, 1997
7 furlongs: Bucharest, 1:21.84, May 4, 1996
1 mile: Mr. Pappion, 1:36.90, May 11, 1995
1 1/16 miles: Heavily Armed, 1:43.20, September 20, 1997
1 1/8 miles: Fletcher's Pride, 1:51.43, August 14, 1998
1 1/4 miles: Call Me Wild, 2:04.01, September 3, 1995
1 3/8 miles: Slews Minister, 2:19.95, October 28, 2000
Other: 2 1/2 furlongs, Texas Hope, :28.20, June 28, 1998; 1 5/16 miles, Opening Remark, 2:13.99, September 5, 1996

Course Records, Main Turf
7 1/2 furlongs: Call Me Wild, 1:28.43, September 17, 1995
1 mile: Empire Pool (GB), 1:34.62, May 6, 1995
1 1/16 miles: Gold Nugget, 1:41.13, October 9, 1999

1 1/8 miles: Untraceable, 1:48.13, August 10, 1996
Other: 1 13/16 miles, Misting Rain, 3:13.22, September 28, 1996

Fastest Times of 2002 (Dirt)

4 1/2 furlongs: Smart Ring, :52.80, August 3
5 furlongs: Run Zeal Run, :58.43, October 11
5 1/2 furlongs: Strolling Kris, 1:04.28, October 18
6 furlongs: Fitzroyal, 1:10.06, October 12
6 1/2 furlongs: Coat of Armor, 1:16.41, October 18
7 furlongs: Miss Ritz, 1:23.88, August 17
1 mile: Compendium, 1:37.98, September 14
1 1/16 miles: Padlock, 1:46.47, September 7
1 1/8 miles: Muchtael, 1:53.76, October 11
1 5/16 miles: Guiness On Tap, 2:15.32, October 26

Fastest Times of 2002 (Turf)

5 furlongs: Major City, :56.39, August 4
About 5 furlongs: Mine Glow, :56.35, September 6
7 1/2 furlongs: Silver Chadra, 1:28.50, August 3
1 mile: Paco Loco, 1:34.66, September 13
1 1/16 miles: Bien Nicole, 1:41.18, August 3

Sam Houston Race Park

In April 1994, Sam Houston Race Park opened as the first Class I racetrack in Texas, which had outlawed pari-mutuel wagering for more than 50 years. Built for $85-million and named for one of the state's founding fathers, the racetrack in northwest Houston is a part of the Class I Texas racing circuit that includes Lone Star Park in the Dallas-Fort Worth metroplex and Retama Park near San Antonio. Sam Houston, which conducts nighttime racing, holds a fall-winter-spring Thoroughbred meet and races Quarter Horses in the summer. Although the track initially posted disappointing results, its fortunes have improved under the leadership of Robert Bork, a racetrack professional who joined the track in 1995 as senior vice president and general manager. The track's signature event is Texas Champions Day, which offers nine lucrative stakes races for state-breds. Sam Houston's majority owner is MAXXAM Inc., a Houston-based Fortune 500 company involved in aluminum, forest products, and real estate that is chaired by Texas native Charles Hurwitz. The track is the home of the Houston Equine Research Organization, a not-for-profit group that works to promote the welfare of racehorses through research and also offers a successful racehorse adoption program. In December 2002, Sam Houston was host to the first NTRA Great State Challenge.

Location: 7575 Sam Houston Pkwy., Houston, TX 77064
Phone: (281) 807-8700
Fax: (281) 807-8701
Web site: http://www.samhoustonracepark.com
Year founded: 1993
Inaugural meeting: April 29, 1994
Acreage: 230
Seating capacity: 18,000
Number of stalls: 1,250

Officers

President: Robert L. Bork
General Manager: Robert L. Bork
Racing Secretary: Eric Johnston
Director of Operations: Ann McGovern
Director of Admissions: Todd Duckett
Director of Communications: Martha Claussen
Director of Finance: Michael Vitek

Director of Marketing: Kerry Graves
Director of Mutuels: Kim Pomposelli
Director of Publicity: Martha Claussen
Director of Sales: Amber Fraser
Director of Simulcasting: Steve Hofmann
Horsemen's Liaison: Sherry Wolter
Stewards: Fred Winch, Pat Powell, Steve O'Malley
Track Announcer: Michael Chamberlain
Track Photographer: Jack Coady
Track Superintendent: Greg Johnson

Racing Dates

2002: November 2, 2001-March 30, 2002, 82 days; November 2-December 28
2003: January 2-March 30, 2003

Track Layout

Main circumference: 1 mile
Main track chutes: 1 1/4 miles, 7 furlongs
Main width: 90 feet
Main length of stretch: 966 feet
Main turf circumference: 7 furlongs
Main turf chute: 1 1/8 miles
Main turf width: 80 feet

Attendance

Average daily recent meeting: 3,131, 2001/2002
Highest single day record: 24,124, July 4, 2002
Total attendance recent meeting: 256,717, 2001/2002

Handle

Average all sources recent meeting: $2,551,562, 2001/2002
Single day on-track handle: $3,557,018, December 7, 2002
Single day total handle all sources: $5,083,692, December 7, 2002
Average on-track recent meeting: $154,226, 2001/2002
Total all sources recent meeting: $209,228,101, 2001/2002
Total on-track recent meeting: $12,646,526, 2001/2002

Leaders

Career, leading trainer by titles: Amos Laborde, 3
Career, leading trainer by wins: Amos Laborde, 200
Career, leading jockey by titles: Steve Bourque, 3
Career, leading owner by titles: Israel Flores, 2
Recent meeting, leading jockey: John Jacinto, 67, 2001/2002
Career, leading jockey by wins: Steve Bourque, 419
Career, leading owner by wins: Israel Flores, 59
Recent meeting, leading trainer: Steve Asmussen, 56, 2001/2002
Recent meeting, leading owner: Nelson Bunker Hunt, 14, 2001/2002, Shirley Miller and Jaime Castellano, 14, 2001/2002

Records

Single meet, leading trainer by wins: Steve Asmussen, 56, 2001/2002
Single day jockey wins: Austin Lovelace, 7, December 10, 1994
Single day trainer wins: Gilbert Ciavaglia, 5, February 23, 1997
Single meet, leading jockey by wins: Steve Bourque, 120, 2000/2001
Single meet, leading owner by wins: John Franks, 24, 1994/1995

Track Records, Main Dirt

4 1/2 furlongs: Angels Lady, :51.93, May 4, 1997
5 furlongs: Dixieland Gambler, :57.43, November 1, 1996
5 1/2 furlongs: Bucharest, 1:02.92, April 13, 1996
6 furlongs: Bucharest, 1:08.88, May 11, 1994
6 1/2 furlongs: Brass Jacks, 1:15.74, May 21, 1994
7 furlongs: Bucharest, 1:21.27, May 4, 1996
1 mile: Vindictive Silence, 1:36.51, December 26, 1995
1 mile 70 yards: Capt. Tiff's Beau, 1:40.52, October 24, 1998
1 1/16 miles: Desert Air, 1:42.74, February 13, 1999
1 1/8 miles: Lost Soldier, 1:48.75, May 3, 1997
1 1/4 miles: Sauvage Isn't Home, 2:04.75, December 29, 1995
1 1/2 miles: Final Val, 2:32.99, February 20, 1998

1 3/4 miles: Final Val, 3:01.50, March 13, 1998
2 miles: Final Val, 3:31.29, April 3, 1998

Course Records, Main Turf
5 furlongs: Go Scotty, :56.93, March 6, 1999
1 mile: Solo Attack, 1:36, March 17, 2001
1 1/16 miles: Luna Delight, 1:43.24, December 4, 1998
1 1/8 miles: Chorwon, 1:47.65, March 6, 1999
1 1/2 miles: Commander Calhoun, 2:32.56, October 3, 1996

Interesting Facts
Trivia: First Class 1 racetrack in Texas.

Fastest Times of 2002 (Dirt)
5 furlongs: Dimity, 1:00.00, January 5
5 1/2 furlongs: Triple Card, 1:03.38, December 26
6 furlongs: My Cousin Matt, 1:09.06, December 7
6 1/2 furlongs: Diplomatic Justice, 1:17.35, February 14
7 furlongs: Term Sheet, 1:22.67, December 18
1 mile: L. A. Spider Legs, 1:38.30, December 6
1 mile 70 yards: Ifyouprefersilver, 1:41.38, December 21
1 1/16 miles: Take Charge Lady, 1:44.40, December 7
1 1/8 miles: Continental Red, 1:49.34, December 7

Fastest Times of 2002 (Turf)
5 furlongs: Kentucky Bay, :57.60, January 26
1 mile: Bar B Drew, 1:37.08, March 29
1 1/16 miles: Popped Corn, 1:43.47, March 29
1 1/8 miles: Candid Glen, 1:50.38, February 23
1 1/2 miles: Fall Out, 2:33.24, March 23

Virginia

Colonial Downs

Colonial Downs has featured a high standard of racing since its opening in 1997, but the facility has been slow to build a strong local brand name or national following, and its owner has feuded with the Virginia Racing Commission.

Constructed in New Kent County approximately 24 miles from Richmond, the track is the only facility to open in Virginia since pari-mutuel wagering was legalized in 1993. The track features seating for 6,000 in an attractive setting. Colonial's ten-furlong dirt track is one of North America's largest, and its turf course has drawn praise for its quality.

But the track has suffered its share of controversy since its opening. Its operations run by the Maryland Jockey Club, the track endured several disputes over racing dates, an issue that has also drawn in Maryland's horsemen, who supply most of the track's runners. Colonial originally raced in late summer and early fall but switched to a 25-day, early summer meeting in 2001.

The 2001 meeting turned out to be Colonial's strongest to date. On-track daily attendance skyrocketed 61% to 1,940, while handle increased 21%. The gains continued into 2002, when wagering increased 12.5% and attendance grew by 13.6%. In mid-2001, Colonial Chief Executive Officer Jeffrey Jacobs bought out the track's shareholders and transformed Colonial into a private company.

Location: 10515 Colonial Downs Pkwy., New Kent, VA 23124
Phone: (804) 966-7223
Fax: (804) 966-1565

E-mail: cdwn@richmond.infi.net
Web site: *http://www.colonialdowns.com*
Year founded: 1997
Inaugural meeting: September 1-October 12, 1997
Abbreviation: Cnl
Acreage: 345
Number of stalls: 1,050
Seating capacity: 6,000

Officers
President: Ian Stewart
Vice President: Jerry Monahan
General Manager: John E. Mooney
Racing Secretary: Richard C. Beck
Director of Admissions: Tom Cade
Director of Communications: Darrell Wood
Director of Finance: Tom Hamilton
Director of Mutuels: Jeanna Boozer
Director of Sales: Teresa Harver
Director of Operations: Jack Howard
Director of Marketing: Darrell Wood
Director of Publicity: Darrell Wood
Director of Simulcasting: Darrell Wood/Jeanna Boozer
Stewards: Jean Chalk, Stan Bowker, William Passmore
Track Announcer: Dave Rodman
Track Photographer: Coady Photography
Track Superintendent: Wes Sheldon

Racing Dates
2002: June 21-July 23, 26 days
2003: June 13-July 22, 26 days

Track Layout
Main circumference: 1 1/4 miles
Main track chute: 1 1/8 miles
Main width: 80 feet
Main length of stretch: 1,290.50 feet
Main turf circumference: 7 1/2 furlongs
Main turf width: 180 feet
Main turf length of stretch: 1,123.62 feet

Attendance
Highest single day record: 13,468, September 1, 1997
Highest single meet record: 108,900, 1997
Record daily average for single meet: 3,630, 1997
Average daily recent meeting: 2,204, 2002

Handle
Record daily average for single meet: $191,212, 2002
Single day on-track handle: $508,199, September 1, 1997
Average all sources recent meeting: $1,193,669, 2002
Average on-track recent meeting: $191,212, 2002
Total on-track recent meeting: $4,971,500, 2002
Single day total handle all sources: $2,105,650, October 3, 1998
Total all sources recent meeting: $31,035,401, 2002

Leaders
Career, leading jockey by wins: Mario Pino, 184
Career, leading trainer by wins: A. Ferris Allen III, 76
Career, leading jockey by titles: Mario Pino, 3
Recent meeting, leading jockey: Horatio Karamanos, 57, 2002
Recent meeting, leading trainer: Hamilton Smith, 14, 2002
Career, leading trainer by titles: A. Ferris Allen III, 5

Records
Single day jockey wins: Mario Pino, 6, July 9, 2001
Single meet, leading jockey by wins: Edgar Prado, 59, 1997
Single meet, leading trainer by wins: A. Ferris Allen III, 25, 1997

Track Records, Main Dirt
5 furlongs: Band Performance, :56.66, September 4, 2000
5 1/2 furlongs: Ameri Prospect, 1:02.94, September 1, 1997
6 furlongs: Capture the Gold, 1:08.11, October 4, 1997

6 1/2 furlongs: Cool Ken Jane, 1:16.60, September 7, 1997
7 furlongs: Sky Watch, 1:20.87, September 1, 1997
1 mile: Assault John, 1:35.48, October 8, 1997
1 1/16 miles: Gold Token, 1:41.09, September 13, 1998
1 1/8 miles: Our Toby, 1:48.95, October 4, 1997
1 1/4 miles: Macgyver, 2:03.54, September 1, 1997
1 1/2 miles: Lord Mendelson, 2:30.13, September 4, 2000

Course Records, Main Turf
5 furlongs: Take Achance On Me, :56.56, July 27, 2001
5 1/2 furlongs: Devereux, 1:01.93, September 24, 1999
6 furlongs: Tyaskin, 1:08.11, September 20, 1998
1 1/16 miles: Lonesome Sound, 1:41.28, September 18, 1998
1 1/8 miles: Kerfoot Corner, 1:47.40, September 26, 1998
1 3/16 miles: Jacsonzac, 1:54.41, October 10, 1998
1 1/4 miles: Phi Beta Doc, 1:59.97, October 2, 1999
1 1/2 miles: Attention Mark, 2:31.76, September 11, 1998
1 5/8 miles: Beluga, 2:45.80, September 26, 1998

Course Records Inner Turf
5 furlongs: Smart Sunny, :56.02, September 8, 2000
5 1/2 furlongs: Smart Sunny, 1:02.94, September 13, 1998
1 mile: La Reine's Terms, 1:34.24, September 17, 1998
1 1/16 miles: Grass Roots, 1:41.01, October 8, 1999
1 1/8 miles: Steak Scam, 1:48.71, September 25, 1999
1 1/4 miles: Franc, 2:03.02, September 9, 2000
1 1/2 miles: Winsox, 2:27.04, September 28, 1998
1 5/8 miles: Our Game, 2:44.82, September 24, 1999

Fastest Times of 2002 (Dirt)
5 1/2 furlongs: Cobbley Six, 1:04.56, June 29
6 furlongs: Native Heir, 1:10.49, July 4
7 furlongs: Alberta Light, 1:24.41, July 1
1 mile: Captain Chessie, 1:36.26, June 30
1 1/16 miles: Freddie the Leader, 1:45.34, June 28

Fastest Times of 2002 (Turf)
5 furlongs: Bop, :55.85, June 22
5 1/2 furlongs: Bop, 1:02.95, July 16
1 mile: La Reine's Terms, 1:35.90, June 29
1 1/16 miles: Island Fever, 1:43.80, June 29
1 1/8 miles: Caique, 1:48.57, July 4
1 1/4 miles: Fager's Island, 2:02.70, July 5
About 2 miles: Tallow, 3:26.93, June 22
About 2 1/4 miles: Invest West, 4:09.75, July 13

Washington

Emerald Downs

Emerald Downs returned Thoroughbred racing to the Seattle area when it opened in 1996. Since the 1930s, the hub of Northwest racing had been Longacres, which was sold in '90 to aircraft manufacturer Boeing Co. After Longacres held its last season of racing in 1992, Yakima Meadows in Yakima became its short-term successor. A group of investors headed by Ron Crockett, who formerly was involved in an airline-related company, built Emerald for $83-million. The track, which offers racing from mid-April to mid-September, became the new host of the Northwest's most famous race when the Longacres Mile Handicap (G3) was first held at the track during its inaugural season. The Mile, which debuted at Longacres in 1935, was held at Yakima Meadows in 1993, '94, and '95.

Location: 2300 Emerald Downs Dr., Auburn, WA 98071-0617
Phone: (253) 288-7000
Fax: (253) 288-7750
Web site: *http://www.emdowns.com*
Inaugural meeting: June 20, 1996

Acreage: 167
Number of stalls: 1,276

Officers
President: Ron Crockett
Vice President: Jack E. Hodge Jr.
Director of Racing: Grant Holcomb
Racing Secretary: Grant Holcomb
Director of Operations: Bob Fraser
Director of Marketing: Susie Sourwine
Director of Mutuels: Gary Hallett
Director of Publicity: Susie Sourwine
Director of Sales: Don Campbell
Director of Simulcasting: Chuck Potter
Track Announcer: Robert Geller
Track Photographer: Reed Palmer
Track Superintendent: Wayne Damron
Other officials: Grant Clark, Media Relations

Racing Dates
2002: April 19-September 16, 91 days
2003: April 19-September 22, 92 days

Track Layout
Main circumference: 1 mile
Main track chutes: 1 1/4 miles, 6 1/2 furlongs
Main width: 90 feet
Main length of stretch: 1,033 feet

Handle
Single day on-track handle: $2,731,852, August 22, 1999
Average all sources recent meeting: $1,253,521, 2002
Average on-track recent meeting: $726,571, 2002
Total all sources recent meeting: $114,070,450, 2002
Total on-track recent meeting: $66,117,925, 2002

Mutuel Records
Highest win: $142, My Lady Boots, July 27, 1997
Lowest Win: $2.60, Sharp Cajun, October 5, 1996
Highest Exacta: $2,317.80, August 28, 1998
Lowest Exacta: $2.80, June 13, 1999
Highest Trifecta: $23,782.80, August 28, 1998
Lowest Trifecta: $11.80, August 28, 1999
Highest Daily Double: $1,464.80, July 5, 1999
Lowest Daily Double: $4.40, August 24, 1997
Highest Pick 3: $19,219.40, July 27, 1996
Lowest Pick 3: $4.70, May 8, 1997
Highest Pick 6: $217,140, June 8, 1997
Lowest Pick 6: $146.20, August 31, 1997
Highest Other Exotics: $14,423.10, Superfecta, July 25, 1999
Lowest Other Exotics: $75.20, Superfecta, May 22, 1999

Leaders
Recent meeting, leading jockey: Kevin Radke, 143, 2002
Recent meeting, leading owner: Ron Crockett Inc., 18, 2002
Recent meeting, leading trainer: Tim McCanna, 53, 2002
Career, leading jockey by stakes wins: Gallyn Mitchell, 22
Career, leading jockey by wins: Frank Gonsalves, 478
Career, leading owner by wins: Ron Crockett, 60
Career, leading trainer by wins: Tim McCanna, 228
Career, leading trainer by stakes wins: Bud Klokstad, 22

Records
Single day jockey wins: Frank Gonsalves, 5, September 26, 1996; Vann Belvoir, 5, October, 20, 1996; Pedro Alvarado, 5, May 22, 1998; Miguel Perez, 5, April 15, 2000
Single day trainer wins: Jim Penney, 5, September 6, 1998

Track Records, Main Dirt
4 1/2 furlongs: I. M. Adevil, :50.60, May 30, 1999; Pacificat, :50.60, May 21, 2000
5 furlongs: Jazzy Mac, :55.40, August 20, 2000
5 1/2 furlongs: Salt Grinder, 1:01.40, April 20, 2002
6 furlongs: Blue Tejano, 1:07.60, June 7, 2002
6 1/2 furlongs: Bold Ranger, 1:13.80, May 27, 2002; Crowning Meeting, 1:13.80, May 19, 2002

1 mile: Wild Wonder, 1:33.20, August 23, 1998; Edneator, 1:33.20, September 11, 2000
1 1/16 miles: Kid Katabatic, 1:39.60, July 26, 1998
1 1/8 miles: Flying Notes, 1:45.40, September 2, 2002
1 1/4 miles: Rapid Stream, 2:01.80, August 15, 1998
1 1/2 miles: Keen Line, 2:30.60, September 6, 1997
2 miles: Kavil, 3:26.80, November 1, 1996
Other: 2 furlongs, Midnight Cruiser, :21.40, May 4, 2000

Fastest Times of 2002

2 furlongs: Jumpingjupiter, :21.80, May 19
4 1/2 furlongs: Bub, :51.60, May 16; Knightsbridge Road, :51.60, June 2
5 furlongs: Makors Mark, :56.20, August 25
5 1/2 furlongs: Salt Grinder, 1:01.40, April 20
6 furlongs: Blue Tejano, 1:07.60, June 7
6 1/2 furlongs: Bold Ranger, 1:13.80, May 27; Crowning Meeting, 1:13.80, May 19
1 mile: Secret Launch, 1:33.40, June 16
1 1/16 miles: Salt Grinder, 1:40.60, August 11
1 1/8 miles: Flying Notes, 1:45.40, September 2
1 1/4 miles: Charlie Haan, 2:03.40, September 12
1 1/2 miles: Faithful Gal, 2:33.60, August 17

Playfair Park

An oasis for racing fans in eastern Washington for many years, the Spokane track has endured two closings over the past several years. With inadequate resources and a racing program that was not attractive to simulcast patrons, Playfair was shuttered for three years starting in 1997. The Lilac City Racing Association received a license to operate a three-month race meeting in 2000, but the meet finished with a 30% decline in handle over 1997, and the association finished the year with an $850,000 shortfall. The Washington Racing Commission subsequently revoked Lilac City's operating license

No racing was held in 2001 and 2002, but Nevada real estate broker Eric Nelson leased Playfair from owner Jack Pring and was granted a 40-date meet in 2003. Simulcasting operations began in February 2003, but Nelson shut down full-card wagering in May 2003 and canceled the live racing program. In June 2003, he asked the Washington Horse Racing Commission to rescind his license.

Location: 202 N. Altamont St., Spokane, WA 99220
Phone: (509) 534-0505
Fax: (509) 534-0101
Year founded: 1901
Number of stalls: 1,000+

Officers

President: Bruce Wagar
Vice President: Amy Haven
General Manager: Daniel McCanna
Director of Racing: Ted Martin
Racing Secretary: Mike Pfliger
Director of Marketing: Tom Blaine

Racing Dates

2003: None

Track Layout

Main circumference: 5 furlongs
Main length of stretch: 704 feet

Sun Downs

Location: Benton-Franklin County Fairgrounds, Kennewick, WA
Phone: (509) 582-5434
Fax: (509) 586-9780
Year founded: 1969
Abbreviation: SuD
Number of stalls: 400
Seating capacity: 6,000

Officers

President: Cliff Schellinger
Vice President: William Henderson
Racing Secretary: Shorty Martin
Treasurer: Nancy Ann Sorick
Director of Admissions: Helen Lizotte
Director of Marketing: Des Ritari
Director of Mutuels: Helen Lizotte
Director of Simulcasting: Helen Lizotte
Stewards: Charlie Landells, Frank O'Leary
Horsemen's Liaison: Dorothy Adams
Track Announcer: Zane Torester
Track Superintendent: Bill Harrison
Other officials: Nellie Schellinger, Richard Monahan, Abigail Kawananakoa

Racing Dates

2002: April 6-May 5
2003: April 5-May 4

Attendance

Average daily recent meeting: 2,000
Total attendance recent meeting: 20,000

Handle

Single day on-track handle: $76,445
Total on-track recent meeting: $418,600

Leaders

Recent meeting, leading jockey: Clark Jones, 2002
Recent meeting, leading trainer: Tracy Lebren, Jimmy McDonnell, and Lin Melton, 2002

Track Layout

Main circumference: 5/8 Mile
Main track chute: 440 Yards

Track Records, Main Dirt

4 furlongs: Trip Six, :45.00, April 19, 1994
6 furlongs: Rulo Auction, 1:13.00, May 4, 1991

Fastest Times of 2002

4 furlongs: Kingsview, :46.40, May 4
6 furlongs: Mast Dancer, 1:15.80, April 28
6 1/2 furlongs: W. W. Dixie, 1:22.20, May 4
7 furlongs: Northern Ricky, 1:27.40, May 5
1 1/16 miles: Northern Ricky, 1:52.20, April 27

Waitsburg Race Track

Location: P.O. Box 391, Waitsburg, WA 99361-0391
Phone: (509) 337-6623
Fax: (509) 337-6026
Abbreviation: Wts

Racing Dates

2002: May 18-May 19, 2 days
2003: May 17-May 18

Leaders

Recent meeting, leading jockey: Edgar Montehermoso, 1, 2002; Ty Dangerfield, 1, 2002
Recent meeting, leading trainer: Bill Hof, 2, 2002

Walla Walla

Location: Southeastern Washington Fairgrounds, Walla Walla, WA 99362
Phone: (509) 527-3247
Fax: (509) 527-3259
Number of stalls: 180
Seating capacity: 3,000

Officers
President: Dick Monahan
General Manager: Cory Hewitt
Racing Secretary: Dick Monahan
Director of Racing: Dick Monahan
Racing Secretary: Dick Monahan
Director of Publicity: Cory Hewitt
Stewards: Frank O'Leary, Robert Lightfoot
Track Announcer: Pete O'Laughlin
Track Photographer: Roger Neilsen

Racing Dates
2002: May 11-May 12, August 31-September 2
2003: May 10-May 11, August 30-September 1
2004: May 8-May 9, September 4-September 6

Attendance
Total attendance recent meeting: approx. 80,000 (included in fair attendance)

Handle
Total all sources recent meeting: $46,424, 2002

Leaders
Recent meeting, leading owner: Judy Yearout, 5, 2002
Recent meeting, leading trainer: Bill Hof, 7, 2002

Track Layout
Main circumference: 4 furlongs
Main length of stretch: 150 yards
Main track chute: 6 furlongs

West Virginia

Charles Town Races

Founded in 1933 by Albert Boyle, Charles Town Races in Charles Town, West Virginia, has been wholly owned by Penn National Gaming Inc. since 2000. The company also owns Penn National Race Course and Pocono Downs harness track in Pennsylvania as well as other gaming and resort facilities. Penn National Gaming bought a majority interest in Charles Town after local voters approved slot machines at the track in late 1996. Charles Town Races has seen its fortunes improve dramatically since the slot machines were installed. Purses for horse racing receive a portion of revenues on slot-machine play at Charles Town, which has more than 2,500 machines at the track. The track's marquee event is the West Virginia Breeders' Classic, a series of races that showcase runners bred, sired, or raised in the state, and is highlighted by the $250,000 West Virginia Breeders' Classic. Charles Town broke ground October 31, 2001, on a $45-million expansion project.

Location: U.S. Route 340, Charles Town, WV 25414
Phone: (304) 725-7001
Fax: (304) 724-4326
Web site: http://www.ctownraces.com
Year founded: 1933

Inaugural meeting: December 2, 1933
Number of stalls: 1,500
Seating capacity: 3,550

Officers
President: James Buchanan
Vice President: Roger Ramey
General Manager: Richard Moore
Director of Racing: James E. Hammond Jr.
Racing Secretary: James Hammond
Director of Mutuels: Joy Lushbaugh
Director of Publicity: Roger Ramey
Director of Sales: Ann Fortner
Stewards: Danny Wright, Ismael L. Trejo, L. Robert Lotts
Track Announcer: Jeff Cernik
Track Photographer: Mike Montgomery
Track Superintendent: Doug Bowling
Other officials: Frank Carulli, Simulcast Showhost

Racing Dates
2002: January 3-December 31
2003: January 1-December 31

Track Layout
Main circumference: 6 furlongs
Main track chutes: 1 5/16 miles, 4 1/2 furlongs
Main length of stretch: 660 feet

Attendance
Highest single day record: 21,480, September 17, 1981

Handle
Single day on-track handle: $1,168,055, March 19, 1977

Records
Single day jockey wins: Travis Dunkelberger, 7, March 30, 2000

Track Records, Main Dirt
4 1/2 furlongs: It's Only Money, :50.36, July 4, 1999
6 1/2 furlongs: Jet Appeal, 1:17, January 6, 1976
7 furlongs: Ohmylove, 1:24, January 7, 1976
1 1/16 miles: My Sister Pearl, 1:43.83, January 4, 2001
1 1/8 miles: A Huevo, 1:50.10, October 10, 1999
1 1/4 miles: Belle d'Amour, 2:05 3/5, June 28, 1941
1 1/2 miles: Guasave Breeze, 2:34, June 9, 1972

Fastest Times of 2002
4 furlongs: Make Mischief, :47.54, December 26
4 1/2 furlongs: Baby Shark, :51.58, October 11
6 1/2 furlongs: Judges' View, 1:18.11, May 2
7 furlongs: Big Becker, 1:25.05, August 2
1 1/16 miles: Pride of Benray, 1:46.42, May 15; Silver Fax, 1:46.42, May 15
1 1/8 miles: Confucius Say, 1:50.93, October 12

Mountaineer Race Track

Mountaineer Race Track in Chester, West Virginia, was recognized in 2001 as one of the top small businesses in the United States when *Forbes* magazine ranked MTR Gaming Group Inc., which owns the track, seventh among the top 200 such enterprises. Much of Mountaineer's success resulted from the legalization of slot machines in 1993, which increased revenues and enabled the track to offer higher purses. In 2003, the track received approval for 500 additional slot machines, enabling it to operate a maximum of 3,500 slot machines. MTR Gaming, headed by Edson "Ted" Arneault, also owns a golf course, hotel, spa, theater, and other entertainment facilities at the track's location. The track was known as Waterford Park when it was opened in 1951 by the Charles Town Jockey Club; the facility was renamed Mountaineer Park in '87 and Mountainer Race Track in 2001. Mountaineer offers year-round night racing four nights a week. The West Virginia Derby, whose purse was increased to $500,000 in 2001, is the richest race to be run in West Virginia history. It was granted Grade 3 status for its 2002 running. In 2003, MTR Gaming Group bought Scioto Downs, an Ohio harness track, and in late 2002 it received approval from the Pennsylvania Horse Racing Commission to build a $56-million Thoroughbred track, Presque Isle Downs, near Erie.

Location: Route 2, Chester, WV 26034
Phone: (304) 387-2400
Fax: (304) 378-3156
E-mail: info@mtrgaming.com
Web site: *http://www.mtrgaming.com*
Year founded: 1951
Inaugural meeting: May 16, 1951
Number of stalls: 1,164
Seating capacity: 7,400

Officers

President: Edson Arneault
Director of Operations: Patrick Arneault
Director of Racing: Rose Mary Williams
Racing Secretary: Joseph Narcavish
Director of Finance: Mary Jo Needham
Director of Marketing: Dorothy Welsh
Director of Mutuels: Gary Mackey
Director of Publicity: Tamara Petit
Director of Sales: Alan Selip
Director of Simulcasting: Deborah Howells
Horsemen's Liaison: Charles Bailey
Stewards: Jim O'Brien, Larry Dupuy, Steve Kourpas
Track Announcer: Jim Dolan
Track Photographer: Ethel Riser
Track Superintendent: Tom Trevor

Racing Dates

2002: January 1-December 31
2003: January 11-December 30, 211 days

Track Layout

Main circumference: 1 mile
Main track chutes: 1 1/4 miles, 6 furlongs
Main width: 80 feet
Main length of stretch: 905.31 feet
Main turf circumference: 7 furlongs

Attendance

Average daily recent meeting: 4,332, 2002
Highest single day record: 17,934, August 10, 2002
Total attendance recent meeting: 996,380, 2002 (through November 1)

Handle

Average all sources recent meeting: $1,121,870, December 21, 2002
Average on-track recent meeting: $70,588, December 31, 2002
Single day total handle all sources: $2,230,312, August 10, 2002
Single day on-track handle: $966,508, May 8, 1973
Total all sources recent meeting: $274,265,318, 2002
Total on-track recent meeting: $16,235,199, 2002

Leaders

Recent meeting, leading trainer: Dale Baird, 115, 2002
Recent meeting, leading jockey: Dana Whitney, 220, 2002

Track Records, Main Dirt

2 furlongs: Promised Cruise, :21, June 23,1990
4 1/2 furlongs: Fina Dur, :50.33, August 11, 2001
5 furlongs: Last At the Table, :56.16, April 1, 2000
5 1/2 furlongs: The Dancer, 1:02.24, December 29, 2000
6 furlongs: Hustler, 1:07.81, August 11, 2001
1 mile: Find the Mine, 1:33.86, July 4, 2000
1 mile 40 yards: Ski Sez, 1:39.83, March 9, 1996
1 mile 70 yards: Mort, 1:38.81, April 1, 2000
1 1/16 miles: It's Reality, 1:41.75, December 23, 2000
1 1/8 miles: Western Pride, 1:47.20, August 11, 2001
1 3/16 miles: No Spend No Glow, 1:56.95, May 19, 2001
1 1/4 miles: Georgie Porgie, 2:03.69, August 6, 1995
1 1/2 miles: Pete's Skianno, 2:31.43, June 10, 2000
1 5/8 miles: Prince Swivel, 2:45, September 8, 1973
1 3/4 miles: Chased Again, 2:58.58, July 18, 1959
2 miles: Sovereign M.D., 3:27.66, December 10, 2000
Other: 2 1/16 miles, Sovereign M.D., 3:28.40, December 30, 2000

Course Records, Main Turf

4 1/2 furlongs: Cake n' Steak, :50, August 9, 1993
5 furlongs: Fina Dur, :55.52, September 6, 1999
7 furlongs: On To Richmond, 1:21.40, June 16, 2002
7 1/2 furlongs: Magical Madness, 1:27.48, May 22, 2002
1 mile 70 yards: Fast and Friendly, 1:34, September 7, 1964; Poteau, 1:34, July 25, 1982
1 3/8 miles: Sunset Party, 2:13.23, September 26, 1999
1 1/2 miles: Guild Hall, 2:33.20, June 20, 1969
1 3/4 miles: Just Steady, 2:57.20, August 18, 1996
Other: 1 7/8 miles, Code's Best, 3:08.23, September 4, 2000

Interesting Facts

Previous names: Waterford Park, Mountaineer Park

Fastest Times of 2002 (Dirt)

4 1/2 furlongs: Mayor Steve, :50.87, July 26
5 furlongs: Tonto Gusto, :57.69, April 20
5 1/2 furlongs: Tonto Gusto, 1:03.13, September 2
6 furlongs: Dash for Daylight, 1:08.77, July 2
1 mile: Tax Affair, 1:36.81, June 18
1 mile 70 yards: King's Design, 1:39.36, July 7
1 1/16 miles: Docent, 1:42.24, August 10
1 1/8 miles: Wiseman's Ferry, 1:49.63, August 10
1 3/16 miles: Chief Gray Wolf, 1:59.70, May 18
1 1/4 miles: King's Design, 2:09.58, September 17
1 1/2 miles: World Beater, 2:38.08, June 8
1 3/4 miles: Ivars Big Peaceful, 3:05.48, November 24
2 miles: Clark Fork, 3:37.55, December 8
2 1/16 miles: Pete's Skianno, 3:40.05, December 29

Fastest Times of 2002 (Turf)

4 1/2 furlongs: Twin Meteors, :50.44, June 11
5 furlongs: Lou's Bucks, :55.82, May 27
7 furlongs: On to Richmond, 1:21.40, June 16
7 1/2 furlongs: Magical Madness, 1:27.48, May 27
1 mile: La Reine's Terms, 1:33.49, September 2
1 3/8 miles: Landiland, 2:16.18, August 3
1 7/8 miles: Landiland, 3:09.06, September 2

Wyoming

Wyoming Downs

Though it is one of North America's least-known Thoroughbred facilities, Wyoming Downs has been providing racing to southwestern Wyoming for nearly

20 years. Located just north of Evanston, Wyoming Downs offers Thoroughbred and Quarter Horse racing. Like Blue Ribbon Downs in Oklahoma, Wyoming Downs places the majority of its emphasis on the Quarter Horse program. The track's top races are Quarter Horse events, the Silver Dollar and Diamond Classic Futurities, each with estimated purses of $100,000.

For Thoroughbreds, the top event is the $5,000-added Rocky Mountain Futurity for two-year-olds and the $5,000 Bettie Bullock Memorial Derby for three-year-olds.

Wyoming Downs usually races during the summer. The track also operates a system of off-track betting facilities that offer simulcast wagering year-round.

Location: 10180 Hwy. 89 N., Evanston, WY 82931
Phone: (307) 789-0511
Fax: (307) 789-4614
E-mail: info@wydowns.com
Web site: http://www.wyomingdowns.com
Inaugural meeting: 1985
Year founded: 1985
Abbreviation: Wyo
Acreage: 200
Seating capacity: approx. 5,000

Officers
President: Eric Nelson
General Manager: Dale Parker
Racing Secretary: Dale Parker
Director of Operations: Joan Ramos
Director of Admissions: Ethellynn Sims
Director of Finance: Lorie Anderson Miller
Director of Marketing: Kortney Kettleson
Director of Mutuels: Jerome Doolittle
Director of Racing: Dale Parker
Director of Publicity: Nina Earll
Director of Simulcasting: Jodi Lopez
Track Photographer: Gene Wilson & Associates
Track Superintendent: Angel Lopez

Racing Dates
2002: June 22-August 18
2003: June 21-August 17

Track Layout
Main circumference: 7 furlongs
Main track chute: 550 yards

Attendance
Average daily recent meeting: 1,423, 2002
Total attendance recent meeting: 25,617, 2002

Handle
Average on-track recent meeting: $64,291, 2002

Leaders
Recent meeting, leading jockey: Justin Vanderwoude, 5, 2002; Melisa Marshall, 5, 2002
Recent meeting, leading trainer: Mike Taylor, 7, 2002

Fastest Times of 2002
4 1/2 furlongs: Fire Ball John, :51.53, July 13
5 furlongs: Fire Ball John, :57.39, August 18
5 1/2 furlongs: Santiam Storm Cat, 1:05.18, July 13
6 furlongs: Fire Ball John, 1:10.23, June 22
7 1/2 furlongs: Juan's Pepe, 1:33.55, August 10
1 mile: Belgravia (GB), 1:39.14, July 13

Canada
Alberta

Evergreen Park (Grand Prairie)

Location: Grand Prairie Fairgrounds, Grand Prairie, AB T8V 3A5
Phone: (780) 532-3279
Fax: (780) 539-0373
Abbreviation: GPR

Racing Dates
2002: July 5-August 4, 15 days
2003: July 4-August 3

Leaders
Recent meeting, leading jockey: Carl Hebert, 10, 2002
Recent meeting, leading trainer: Mel Berkram, 6, 2002

Fastest Times of 2002
4 furlongs: Plenty of Talk, :47.20, July 7
5 1/2 furlongs: Storm Devil, 1:06.40, July 28
6 furlongs: J. J. Sun Shine, 1:13.40, July 28; Sam George Hill, 1:13.40, July 6
6 1/2 furlongs: Sam George Hill, 1:21.20, August 4
7 furlongs: Ice Mine, 1:25.60, August 3
1 mile: Wise Dancer, 1:42.60, July 5
1 1/16 miles: Nalee's Classic, 1:50.20, July 14
1 1/8 miles: Kristopher Road, 1:54.80, August 4

Lethbridge (Whoop Up Downs)

Location: 3401 Parkside Dr., S Lethbridge, AB T1J 1G6
Phone: (403) 380-1905
Fax: (403) 380-1903
E-mail: racedot@telusplanet.net
Web site: http://www.countrytimes.com/whoopupdowns/index.htm
Seating capacity: 3,000
Number of stalls: 300

Officers
President: Max Gibb
Racing Secretary: Jim Ralph
Director of Marketing: Rose Rossi
Director of Publicity: Rose Rossi
Stewards: Don Hamilton, Gary Belecki, Peter Sebzda
Track Announcer: Murray Slough
Track Photographer: Coady Photo

Racing Dates
2002: May 4- June 16, 15 days; August 24-October 27, 25 days
2003: August 30-October 26, May 3-June 15

Leaders
Recent meeting, leading jockey: Terri Landaker, 29, Fall-2002
Recent meeting, leading trainer: Gene Starlin, 13, Fall-2002

Track Layout
Main circumference: 4 furlongs

Fastest Times of 2002
3 furlongs: X Rated Movie, :35.10, September 15
5 furlongs: Express Post, :59.20, September 13
5 1/2 furlongs: Speed Ruckus, 1:07.20, October 19
About 6 furlongs: Nite Talkin, 1:10.00, October 19
7 furlongs: Drive the Avenue, 1:24.60, October 20

1 1/16 miles: Stage Door Jade, 1:44.20, October 6
1 1/8 miles: Candid Remark, 1:53.00, October 26
1 3/16 miles: Crown Butte, 2:04.20, October 5

Northlands Park

Like many Canadian racetracks, Northlands Park in Edmonton races both Thoroughbreds and Standardbreds. Both breeds enjoy richer purses due to the arrival of slot machines. In late December 2001, Northlands received 250 additional machines to double its original total as part of a $42-million racing rehabilitation project under Alberta Premier Ralph Klein, an amateur harness driver, former TV reporter, and former Calgary mayor who now is in his third term as the province's chief executive. Opened in July 1925 as Edmonton Racetrack, the track was renamed Northlands Park in January 1964. Northlands conducts harness racing from early March through mid-June and Thoroughbred racing from late June through late October.

Location: Northlands Spectrum, Edmonton, AB T5J 2N5
Phone: (403) 471-7379
Fax: (403) 471-7134
E-mail: racing@northlands.com
Web site: www.northlands.com

Officers
President: Eric Young
General Manager: Les Butler
Racing Secretary: Alan Bott
Director of Communications: Jason Douziech
Director of Mutuels: Glen Weir
Director of Publicity: Jonathan Huntington
Director of Finance: Ken Baker
Director of Marketing: Stephanie Hughes
Director of Operations: Kevin Behm
Track Announcer: Mike Dimoff
Track Photographer: Ryan Haynes

Racing Dates
2002: June 21-October 19
2003: June 21-October 19

Track Layout
Main circumference: 5/8 mile
Main width: 70 feet
Main length of stretch: 567 feet

Leaders
Recent meeting, leading jockey: Quincy Welch, 2002
Recent meeting, leading trainer: Red Smith, 2002

Track Records, Main Dirt
5 1/2 furlongs: So Long Fellas, 1:04 2/5, August 16, 1975
6 1/2 furlongs: Timely Ruckus, 1:15.40, June 26, 1999
6 furlongs: Sageata, 1:09.80, July 22, 1984; Lynn's Dream, 1:09.80, July 6, 2000
1 mile: Bagfull, 1:35 4/5, May 16, 1981
1 1/16 miles: Chilcoton Blaze, 1:42 3/5, August 4, 1984
1 3/8 miles: Slyly Gifted, 2:15 4/5, August 30, 1986
1 5/8 miles: Racey Richard, 2:46, September 1, 1986
Other: 3 1/2 furlongs, Steel Penny Black, :38 1/5, June 14, 1984; 1 5/18 miles, Arctic Laur, 2:09, August 20, 1995

Fastest Times of 2002
3 1/2 furlongs: Misty River, :39.20, September 18; Nu Chance to Dance, :39.20, September 22; Ole' Olay, :39.20, September 1
5 1/2 furlongs: Raylene, 1:05.40, July 14; Taiaslew, 1:05.40, June 28
6 furlongs: James Logan, 1:10.40, October 19

6 1/2 furlongs: Dr. Sardonica, 1:16.20, October 18
1 mile: Popsicle Pete, 1:37.20, October 18
1 1/16 miles: Dr. Sardonica, 1:43.60, September 28
1 5/16 miles: Miki Bleu Eyes, 2:13.20, August 16
1 3/8 miles: Bubblegum Kid, 2:17.40, September 7
1 5/8 miles: Glance Remark, 2:48.40, September 27

Stampede Park

Though it is famous for its annual Calgary Stampede rodeo, Stampede Park is also a longtime part of the Thoroughbred racing scene in Alberta. Thoroughbred racing debuted at Stampede in 1974, with the facility offering racing on a five-furlong oval and stabling for 1,400 horses. Though the track's seating of 25,000 is snug during the Calgary Stampede, it has been more than adequate for racing; the track's record attendance is 6,167, set on August 15, 1981.

Stampede in recent years has dealt with uncertainty over the future of racing in Alberta. Track officials planned to halt racing after Resortport Development Corp. announced plans in 1998 to build a $100-million racetrack and resort facility in Calgary. But the plans fell apart, and Stampede Park is now looking at ways to upgrade its facility and maintain racing well into the 21st century. Stampede runs a spring Thoroughbred meet from early April through mid-June and a Standardbred meet in the summer and early fall. Its major Thoroughbred race is the $100,000 Alberta Derby (Can-G3) in mid-June.

Location: Box 1060, Station M, Calgary, AB T2P 2K8
Phone: (403) 261-0214
Fax: (403) 261-0526
E-mail: stpracing@calgarystampede.com
Web site: http://www.stampede-park.com/
Seating capacity: 25,000
Number of stalls: 1,400

Officers
President: Don Wilson
Vice President: Steve Allen
General Manager: Steve Edwards
Racing Secretary: Barry McGrath
Director of Racing: Gail Poole
Director of Mutuels: Sheri Holmes
Director of Publicity: Patti Hunt
Director of Simulcasting: Sheri Holmes
Stewards: Conrad Dick, Al Lennox, Scott Woodley
Track Announcer: Joe Carbury
Track Photographer: Coady Photo
Track Superintendent: Kevin Hannon

Racing Dates
2002: April 5-June 16, 43 days
2003: April 4-June 15, 43 days

Attendance
Average daily recent meeting: 2,000 Estimated
Total attendance recent meeting: 90,000 Estimated
Highest single day record: 6,167, August 15, 1981

Handle
Average all sources recent meeting: $272,048
Average on-track recent meeting: $124,652
Total all sources recent meeting: $11,698,099
Total on-track recent meeting: $5,360,056

Leaders
Recent meeting, leading jockey: Quincy Welch, 54, 2002
Recent meeting, leading trainer: Ron Grieves, 19, 2002

Fastest Times of 2002

3 1/2 furlongs: Tychonic Lady, :39.20, May 26
4 furlongs: Timely Ruckus, :44.20, April 6
6 furlongs: Tyko Tycoon, 1:10.60, April 20; Vying Road, 1:10.60, May 29
1 mile: Gray Aras, 1:36.60, May 26
1 1/16 miles: Sly Lady, 1:44.60, June 16

British Columbia

Hastings Park

For more than 80 years, the racing scene in the Canadian province of British Columbia has focused on the tract of land where Hastings Park currently stands.

From 1994 to 2002, the nonprofit Pacific Racing Association managed racing at Hastings, which conducts Thoroughbred racing at the five-furlong facility usually from April through November. Woodbine Entertainment Group bought the facility in 2002.

First opened in 1920, Hastings reached its peak as a racing facility in the early 1980s, when the track sometimes drew crowds of 20,000 or more. The track has also appealed to Vancouver's expanding Asian population by offering simulcast wagering from Hong Kong. Plans include building a new Thoroughbred-Standardbred facility to replace Hastings.

Location: Hastings Park Racecourse, Vancouver, BC V5K 3N8
Phone: (604) 254-1631
Fax: (604) 254-0411
Web site: http://www.hastingspark.com
Year founded: 1889
Inaugural meeting: 1920
Acreage: 45
Seating capacity: 5,600
Number of stalls: 1,000

Officers

President: Phil Heard
Vice President: Garth Essery
General Manager: Phil Heard
Director of Racing: Debbie Peebles
Racing Secretary: Debbie Peebles
Director of Operations: Dalbir Kanig
Director of Admissions: Michael Brown
Director of Communications: Pamela Newton
Director of Finance: Steven Keenan
Director of Marketing: Brenda Smith
Director of Mutuels: Colleen MacLeod
Director of Publicity: Pamela Newton
Director of Simulcasting: Colleen Macleod
Horsemen's Liaison: Debbie Peebles
Stewards: Keith Smith, Sten Matell, Wayne Russell
Track Announcer: Dan Jukich
Track Photographer: Larry Goulding
Track Superintendent: Ross Mansell

Racing Dates

2002: April 20-November 3, 89 days
2003: April 26-November 30, 69 days

Track Layout

Main track chute: 6 1/2 furlongs
Main width: 65 feet
Main length of stretch: 513 feet
Training track: 1/2 mile

Attendance

Highest single day record: 21,156, July 9, 1982

Handle

Average all sources recent meeting: $1,292,657, 2001
Average on-track recent meeting: $602,627, 2001
Single day on-track handle: $2,612,316, July 9, 1982
Total all sources recent meeting: $120,217,116, 2001
Total on-track recent meeting: $56,044,378, 2001

Mutuel Records

Highest win: $508.10, 1953
Highest Exacta: $4,092, 1962
Highest Trifecta: $21,806.20, 1982
Highest Daily Double: $4,863.10, 1995
Highest Pick 3: $11,474, 1993
Highest Other Exotics: $39,752, Superfecta, 1999; $63,326.70, Win 4, 1988; $920,411.70, Sweep 6, 1982

Leaders

Recent meeting, leading jockey: Pedro Alvarado, 121, 2002
Recent meeting, leading trainer: Harold Barroby, 50, 2002
Career, leading trainer by titles: Harold Barroby, 10
Career, leading trainer by wins: Harold Barroby, 454
Career, leading jockey by titles: Chris Loseth, 8
Career, leading jockey by wins: Chris Loseth, 3,441
Career, leading trainer by stakes wins: Harold Barroby, 148
Career, leading jockey by stakes wins: Chris Loseth

Records

Single day jockey wins: Chris Loseth, 8, 04/09/84
Single day trainer wins: George Cummings, 5, 11/08/92
Single meet, leading jockey by wins: Mark Patzer, 173, 1991
Single meet, leading trainer by wins: Lance Giesbrecht, 76, 1997

Track Records, Main Dirt

6 furlongs: Great Discretion, 1:10 4/5, May 10, 1969; Humphrey Lad, 1:10 4/5, April 13, 1988; Sir Khaled 1:10 4/5, April 15, 1988
6 1/2 furlongs: Torque Converter, 1:15, July 1, 1996
1 mile 70 yards: Westbury Road, 1:40 4/5, July 29, 1967
1 1/16 miles: Coral Isle, 1:42 2/5, July 28, 1973; No Time Flat, 1:42 2/5, August 12, 1987; Timely Stitch, 1:42.20, July 6, 1996
1 1/8 miles: Artic Son, 1:46.80, August 3, 1998
1 3/8 miles: Irish Bear, 2:14 4/5, October 17, 1987
1 1/2 miles: Lucky Son, 2:29, August 25, 1995
1 3/4 miles: Glen Glower, 2:59, August 25, 1987
Other: 3 1/2 furlongs, Smokin Finish, :39.79, July 2, 2000

Major Races

BC Cup (August 4) and BC Derby (Can-G2) (September 21)

Fastest Times of 2002

3 1/2 furlongs: Five Point Star, :39.81, September 15
About 3 1/2 furlongs: Free My Soul, :40.62, May 8
6 furlongs: Work Visa, 1:11.32, May 1
6 1/2 furlongs: Danzilation, 1:15.74, August 18
1 1/16 miles: Kid Katabatic, 1:43.47, June 9
1 1/8 miles: Eternal Secrecy, 1:49.08, December 1
1 3/8 miles: Shacane, 2:16.92, October 20
About 1 1/2 miles: Sensitive Issue, 2:32.00, September 14
1 3/4 miles: Timely Minister, 3:04.21, October 5

Kamloops

Location: 479 Chilcotin St., Kamloops, BC V2H 1G4
Phone: (250) 314-9645
Fax: (250) 828-0836
Number of stalls: 310
Seating capacity: 2000

Officers

President: Lugi Sale
Director of Racing: Lugi Sale
Track Announcer: Keith Reid

Racing Dates

2002: Fall: May 19-June 23; August 11-September 8
2003: August 10, 17, 24, 31, September 7, May 25, June 1, 8, 15, 22, 29

Attendance

Total attendance recent meeting: 800 daily

Leaders

Recent meeting, leading trainer: Fred Cooper, 3, Fall-2002; Terry Clyde, 3, Fall-2002
Recent meeting, leading jockey: Brooke Mellish, 9, Fall-2002

Fastest Times of 2002

3 1/2 furlongs: Aly's Martini, :41.00, September 1
About 4 1/2 furlongs: Perth Power, :50.60, August 18
6 1/2 furlongs: Wise Dancer, 1:18.80, June 9
7 furlongs: Nonameit, 1:27.60, September 8
1 mile: Victor's Honor, 1:39.80, September 8

Kin Park

Location: P.O. Box 682, Vernon, BC V1T 6M6
Phone: (250) 542-5759
Fax: (250) 542-9317

Racing Dates

2002: July 17-August 4
2003: July 13-August 10

Leaders

Recent meeting, leading jockey: Brooke Mellish, 4, 2002; Ronald Joseph Bilodeau, 4, 2002
Recent meeting, leading trainer: Barry R. Price, 2, 2002; Bob Honeyman, 2, 2002

Fastest Times of 2002

About 4 furlongs: I Am This Guy, :44.60, July 28
About 6 furlongs: Miller's Legend, 1:13.20, July 14
About 6 1/2 furlongs: Aint No Connection, 1:20.00, July 21
About 7 furlongs: Southern Cross Sky, 1:22.80, July 21

Manitoba

Assiniboia Downs

Assiniboia Downs continues a rich tradition of horse racing in Winnipeg, dating from the last quarter of the 19th century. Racing enthusiast and businessman Jack Hardy built Assiniboia, which opened in 1958 to replace Polo Park, a 30-year-old track located on property that became a shopping center. In 1974, Jim Wright bought the track and racing experienced a boom under his leadership. By the early 1990s, however, competition from other gambling forms made the track unprofitable. In 1993, Assiniboia was sold to its current owners, the Manitoba Jockey Club, a nonprofit organization that solidified its future by pouring profits from video lottery terminals and full-card simulcasting back into the facility. Assiniboia, which offers live racing from early May through September, was the first track in Canada to offer pick-six and telephone-account wagering. The track's richest race, the Manitoba Derby (Can-G3), has been run at Assiniboia since 1960. In 1970, Queen Elizabeth II and Prince Philip attended the race as part of Manitoba's centennial year. The winner was Fanfreluche, a daughter of Northern Dancer, who was that year's Canadian Horse of the Year as well as an Eclipse Award winner as North America's champion three-year-old filly. Her son L'Enjoleur won the Manitoba Derby in 1975, the year in which he earned his second Canadian Horse of the Year title.

Location: 3975 Portage Ave., Winnipeg, MB R3K 2E9
Phone: (204) 885-3330
Fax: (204) 831-5348
E-mail: info@assiniboiadowns.com
Web site: http://www.assiniboiadowns.com
Inaugural meeting: 1958
Number of stalls: 936
Seating capacity: 6,000

Officers

President: Harvey Warner
Vice President: Dr. Norm Elder
General Manager: Sharon Gulyas
Racing Secretary: Ray Miller
Director of Operations: Darren Dunn
Director of Finance: Kris Nancoo
Director of Mutuels: Glenn Passey
Director of Sales: Jamie Sullivan
Director of Publicity: Ernie Nairn
Director of Simulcasting: Glenn Passey
Stewards: Craig MacDonald, Larry Huber, Hazel Bochinski
Track Announcer: Darren Dunn
Track Photographer: Gerry Hart

Racing Dates

2002: May 4-September 29, 76 days
2003: May 4-September 28, 75 days

Track Layout

Main circumference: 1 3/16 miles
Main width: 80 feet
Main length of stretch: 990 feet
Training track: 1/2 mile

Attendance

Average daily recent meeting: 1,904, 2002
Highest single day record: 13,276, August 6, 1979
Total attendance recent meeting: 140,887, 2002

Handle

Total all sources recent meeting: $10,038,617, 2002
Single day on-track handle: $713,756, September 5, 1988
Average all sources recent meeting: $135,657, 2002
Average on-track recent meeting: $84,631, 2002
Total on-track recent meeting: $6,262,718, 2002

Mutuel Records

Highest win: $474.20, May 31, 1986
Highest Exacta: $3,514.80, May 16, 1998
Highest Trifecta: $40,026.60, May 18, 1981
Highest Daily Double: $4,235.50, July 23, 1971
Highest Pick 3: $3,269.40, June 28, 1998
Highest Other Exotics: $14,584.95, Pick 4, September 1, 1986

Leaders

Career, leading jockey by titles: Larry Bird, 29
Recent meeting, leading jockey: Jacques DesAutels, 99, 2002
Recent meeting, leading owner: Ardell Sayler, 41, 2002
Career, leading jockey by wins: Ken Hendricks, 1,501
Career, leading trainer by wins: Don Gray, 879
Recent meeting, leading trainer: Ardell Sayler, 41, 2002

Records

Single day jockey wins: Jim Sorenson, 7, June 23, 1976

Track records, Main dirt

4 furlongs: Northern Spike, :44.40, April 23, 1982
4 1/2 furlongs: Astral Moon, :50.80, May 1, 1982
5 furlongs: Northern Spike, :56.40, May 9, 1982
5 1/2 furlongs: Sunny Famous, 1:02.80, September 19, 1992
6 furlongs: Mr. Quill, 1:09, October 10, 1981; Nephrite, 1:09, October 8, 1989
7 furlongs: Victor's Pride, 1:23.20, August 16, 1978
1 1/16 miles: Goa, 1:41.60, July 23, 1988
1 1/4 miles: Nifty (Fr), 2:05, September 20, 1986; Northern Debut, 2:05, October 3, 1993
1 1/8 miles: Overskate, 1:47.60, September 9, 1978
1 mile: *Gladiatore II, 1:35.80, July 7, 1972; Tower of Shan, 1:35.80, June 24, 1990

Fastest Times of 2002

About 3 furlongs: Suntana, :29.80, June 22
4 1/2 furlongs: Heezatalknback, :55.00, July 1
5 furlongs: Kalfaari, :58.40, May 11
5 1/2 furlongs: Amersham, 1:05.60, May 20; Miss Sandy Dee, 1:05.60, May 20; Sterling Account, 1:05.60, May 18
6 furlongs: Kalfaari, 1:10.80, June 23
7 furlongs: Ekati, 1:25.80, June 23
1 mile: Star Survivor, 1:39.00, June 15
1 1/16 miles: Beausox, 1:45.60, September 8
1 1/8 miles: Sir Pucker, 1:53.80, September 29
1 1/4 miles: Jaboo, 2:09.80, September 28

Ontario

Fort Erie

Founded in 1897, Fort Erie is one of Canada's oldest racetracks. Located in southern Ontario across the border from Buffalo, New York, the track began its premier event, the Prince of Wales Stakes, in 1959 with the help of prominent Ontario horseman E. P. Taylor. The race for three-year-old Canadian-breds now has become the second leg of Canada's Triple Crown. Taylor-bred Northern Dancer made his career debut at Fort Erie in August 1963. The following year, the Nearctic colt became the first Canadian-bred to win the Kentucky Derby. The track now is owned by Nordic Gaming Corp., which consists of three business interests from southern Ontario and two foreign investors. It underwent $30-million in renovations in 1999 to prepare for 1,200 slot machines that help to support the racing operation.

Location: 230 Catherine St., Fort Erie, ON L2A 5N9
Phone: (905) 871-3200
Fax: (905) 994-36229
E-mail: femedia@forterieracetrack.com
Web site: http://www.forterieracing.com
Inaugural meeting: June 16, 1897
Seating capacity: 4,000
Number of stalls: 1,000

Officers

General Manager: Eddie Lynn
Treasurer: Bonnie Loubert
Director of Racing: Herb McGirr
Director of Finance: Bonnie Loubert
Director of Marketing: Herb McGirr
Director of Mutuels: Chad Gates
Director of Publicity: Brian Blessing
Director of Simulcasting: Chad Gates
Track Announcer: Daryl Wells
Track Superintendent: Ken Macsweyn

Racing Dates

2002: April 27-November 25, 118 days
2003: April 26-November 11, 117 days

Track Layout

Main circumference: 1 mile
Main width: 75 feet
Main length of stretch: 1,060 feet
Main turf circumference: 7 furlongs

Leaders

Recent meeting, leading jockey: Martin Ramirez, 127, 2002
Recent meeting, leading owner: Bruno Schickedanz, 32, 2002
Recent meeting, leading trainer: Layne S. Gilforte, 79, 2002

Track records, Main dirt

4 furlongs: Kirk's Dandy, :47 2/5, May 2, 1957
4 1/2 furlongs: Dawn Deluxe, :52, April 17, 1971; Dozen Dancer, :52, April 24, 1971; Trade Wagon, :52, May 8, 1968
5 furlongs: Cool Shot, :56.60, July 15, 1995
5 1/2 furlongs: Emotionally, 1:03.60, June 28, 1997; Just a Lord, 1:03.60, June 15, 1991
6 furlongs: Deputy Carson, 1:08.85, September 9, 2001
6 1/2 furlongs: Muzledick, 1:15, August 10, 1968
1 1/8 miles: Laurie's Dancer, 1:48, August 23, 1972
1 3/16 miles: Bruce's Mill, 1:53.20, July 31, 1994
1 mile 70 yards: Myrtle Irene, 1:39.80, August 26, 1994

Track records, Main turf

5 furlongs: Oh Mar, :56.99, September 9, 2002
7 furlongs: Native Vigil, 1:22.10, July 2, 1991
1 1/16 miles: Road of War, 1:40.80, June 19, 1994
1 mile: Fifth and a Jigger, 1:34.30, June 10, 1991

Fastest Times of 2002 (Dirt)

2 furlongs: Pembroke Hall, :21.87, September 8
5 furlongs: Winner's Bid, :57.53, November 2
5 1/2 furlongs: Migrating South, 1:04.46, September 1
6 furlongs: Callendars, 1:09.73, May 28
6 1/2 furlongs: Exclusive Run, 1:16.05, August 31
1 mile 70 yards: Centurian Man, 1:41.83, May 20
1 1/16 miles: Original One, 1:43.43, August 24
1 1/8 miles: Jubalani, 1:51.28, September 1
1 3/16 miles: Le Cinquieme Essai, 1:56.53, July 21
1 3/4 miles: Gist of Art, 2:59.86, October 1
2 miles 70 yards: Ace of Suedes, 3:38.92, November 5

Fastest Times of 2002 (Turf)

5 furlongs: Oh Mar, :56.99, September 9
About 5 furlongs: Dreams Go Bye, :57.32, July 6
About 7 furlongs: Lion Castle, 1:23.37, June 22
1 mile: Southern Heat, 1:36.88, June 25
About 1 mile: Ronaldo, 1:38.61, July 15
1 1/16 miles: Get Down Wolfie, 1:41.85, September 2
About 1 1/16 miles: Northernprospector, 1:44.73, July 7
About 1 3/8 miles: Liquid Courage, 2:23.07, August 31
About 1 1/2 miles: Winning Skier, 2:35.45, August 6

Woodbine

The addition of 1,700 slot machines in March 2000 substantially increased purses and made Canada's best-known racetrack into a financial success after years of operating under a burdensome debt load. After installing the slot machines, the organization that owns the track changed its name from the Ontario Jockey Club to the Woodbine Entertainment Group. Woodbine, located in the Toronto suburb of Rexdale, is home of the Queen's Plate Stakes, first run in 1860 and North America's oldest continually run stakes race. With a unique track arrangement on its 650 acres, Woodbine is the only track in North America to conduct Standardbred and Thoroughbred racing on the same day. Its 1½-mile grass course, the E. P. Taylor Turf Course, features the longest stretch run in North America, 1,440 feet. Inside the turf course is the one-mile dirt track, which was completely rebuilt in 1994. Inside the main dirt track is a seven-eighths-mile, 85-foot-wide harness track.

Woodbine's rich history extends back to 1874, when the track opened on what was then the eastern outskirts of Toronto, which is now Toronto's downtown. That track's name was changed to Old Woodbine in 1956 and then renamed Greenwood Raceway in 1963.

The present Woodbine opened on June 12, 1956. In 1996, Woodbine became the first Canadian track to host the Breeders' Cup, and it drew a record Woodbine crowd of 42,243. Besides the Queen's Plate, Woodbine hosts the $1.5-million Canadian International (Can-G1) and the $1-million Atto Mile (Can-G1), which has evolved into an important stakes for grass horses aiming for the Breeders' Cup Mile (G1).

Location: 555 Rexdale Blvd., Rexdale, ON M9W 5L2
Phone: (416) 675-6110
Fax: (416) 213-2104
E-mail: csd@woodbineentertainment.com
Web site: http://www.woodbineentertainment.com
Year founded: 1874
Inaugural meeting: June 12-July 14 1956; October 1-November 17, 1956
Acreage: 650
Number of stalls: 2,060
Seating capacity: 18,996

Officers

President: David S. Willmot
Vice President: Hugh M. Mitchell
Director of Racing: Chris Evans
Racing Secretary: Steve Lynn
Secretary: Robert Careless
Treasurer: Tom Valiquette
Director of Operations: Al Dymon
Director of Admissions: Steve Mitchell
Director of Communications: Glenn Crouter
Director of Finance: Tom Valiquette
Director of Marketing: Nick Eaves
Director of Mutuels: Sean Pinsonneault
Director of Publicity: John Siscos
Director of Sales: Joseph Araujo
Director of Simulcasting: Debbie Chomiak
Horsemen's Liaison: Tom Cosgrove
Stewards: Nelson Ham, Richard Grubb, William McMahon
Track Announcer: Dan Loiselle
Track Photographer: Michael Burns
Track Superintendent: Ron Aspden
Other officials: James W. Ormiston, Executive Vice President/CEO

Racing Dates

2002: March 23-December 1, 168 days
2003: March 22-November 30, 167 days

Track Layout

Main circumference: 1 mile
Main width: 85 feet
Main length of stretch: 975 feet
Main turf circumference: 1 1/2 miles
Main turf width: 100 feet
Main turf length of stretch: 1,440 feet

Attendance

Highest single day record: 42,243, October 26, 1996

Handle

Average all sources recent meeting: $2,191,447, 2002
Total all sources recent meeting: $363,780,210, 2002

Leaders

Career, leading jockey by titles: Sandy Hawley, 18
Career, leading trainer by titles: Frank Merrill, 30
Recent meeting, leading jockey: Patrick Husbands, 167, 2002
Recent meeting, leading owner: Stronach Stables, 58, 2002
Recent meeting, leading trainer: Mark Casse, 69, 2002

Records

Single day jockey wins: Richard Grubb, 7, May 16, 1967; Sandy Hawley, 7, May 22, 1972; Sandy Hawley, 7, October 10, 1974

Track Records, Main Dirt

4 1/2 furlongs: Hallmarked, :50.40, March 24, 1996; Written Approval, :50.40, March 24, 1996
5 furlongs: Tailor's Thread, :56.20, April 2, 1999
5 1/2 furlongs: Uncle Woger, 1:02.70, April 4, 1999
6 furlongs: Great Defender, 1:08.17, November 27, 1999
6 1/2 furlongs: Fair Juror, 1:14 3/5, October 17, 1961
7 furlongs: Oronero, 1:20.60, December 6, 1995
1 mile 70 yards: Regal Courser, 1:39 3/5, August 8, 1998
1 1/16 miles: Kiridashi, 1:40.80, August 17, 1996
1 1/8 miles: Glorious Song, 1:48, July 1, 1981
1 3/16 miles: Runnin Roman, 1:55 4/5, September 15, 1974
1 1/4 miles: Alphabet Soup, 2:01, October 26, 1996
1 3/8 miles: Lovely Sunrise, 2:17, October 26, 1974
1 1/2 miles: Norcliffe, 2:29 1/5, October 29, 1977
1 5/8 miles: *Eugenia II, 2:43 2/5, October 27, 1956
1 3/4 miles: Major Pots, 2:52.60, December 8, 1994
Other: 1 7/8 miles, Barnsboro, 3:16.80, December 14, 1996

Course Records, Main Turf

6 furlongs: Wild Zone, 1:07.60, July 7, 1996
6 1/2 furlongs: Always a Rainbow, 1:14.80, June 2, 1996
7 furlongs: Wild Zone, 1:20.20, July 30, 1995
1 mile: Lost Soldier, 1:32.80, July 24, 1996
1 1/16 miles: Jet Freighter, 1:39.20, June 4, 1995; Honolulu Gold, 1:39.20, July 11, 1996; Western Express, 1:39.20, July 12, 1998
1 1/8 miles: Bold Ruritana, 1:45.20, June 18, 1995
1 1/4 miles: Arbalest, 2:01, June 15, 1995; Set Ablaze, 2:01, July 5, 1996
1 3/8 miles: Dawson's Legacy, 2:13.05, September 26, 1999
1 1/2 miles: Raintrap (GB), 2:25.60, October 16, 1994

Course Records, Inner turf

5 furlongs: Deputy Regent, :58, July 4, 1982
1 mile: Charlie Barley, 1:34 4/5, May 28, 1989; Myrtle Irene, 1:34.80, September 19, 1993
1 1/16 miles: Overskate, 1:40 4/5, June 3, 1979; Seattle Sangue, 1:40 4/5, June 17, 1990
1 1/4 miles: Mill Native, 2:00, June 26, 1983
1 3/8 miles: Wayover, 2:19 1/5, June 26, 1985
1 1/2 miles: Great Stake, 2:34, July 5, 1985

Interesting Facts

Previous name and dates: Ontario Jockey Club 1881-2001
Achievements/milestones: Hosted Arlington Million in 1988, hosted Breeders' Cup in 1996

Fastest Times of 2002 (Dirt)

4 1/2 furlongs: El Ruller, :51.95, May 5
5 furlongs: Wake At Noon, :56.48, March 23
5 1/2 furlongs: Regal 'n Bold, 1:04.86, September 18
6 furlongs: Classic Manner, 1:09.42, June 1
6 1/2 furlongs: Quiet Dare, 1:15.77, November 20
7 furlongs: Raja Choice, 1:21.79, March 23
1 mile 70 yards: Ford Every Stream, 1:42.49, May 3

1 1/16 miles: Lucky Molar, 1:42.33, July 14
1 1/8 miles: Tails of the Crypt, 1:50.36, June 8
1 3/16 miles: Slim Dusty, 1:57.03, November 20
1 1/4 miles: Bonus Pack, 2:03.01, July 1
1 1/2 miles: Rhodesian Storm, 2:34.71, November 9
1 3/4 miles: Lucky Molar, 3:03.83, December 1
1 7/8 miles: Disappeared, 3:17.43, December 1

Fastest Times of 2002 (Turf)
6 furlongs: Nuclear Debate, 1:07.86, June 23
6 1/2 furlongs: Irish Line, 1:15.15, August 21
7 furlongs: Zone Judge, 1:17.19, August 17
1 mile: Good Journey, 1:33.27, September 8
1 1/16 miles: Waltzin' Storm, 1:39.74, September 2
1 1/8 miles: Sweetest Thing, 1:45.72, July 6
About 1 1/8 miles: Calista (GB), 1:45.04, September 8
1 1/4 miles: Full of Wonder, 2:01.46, July 1
About 1 1/4 miles: Lucky Molar, 2:03.43, August 25
1 3/8 miles: Strike Smartly, 2:13.16, July 21
1 1/2 miles: Full of Wonder, 2:26.18, August 31

Saskatchewan

Marquis Downs

Marquis Downs in Saskatoon has offered live racing since 1969. With a five-furlong track and a grandstand capacity of 4,500, Marquis is part of the Saskatoon Prairieland Exhibition, a multipurpose facility that includes meeting and exhibition halls and a casino. Racing annually takes place from May through September.

Location: 2326 Herman Ave., Saskatoon, SK S7K 4E4
Phone: (306) 242-6100
Fax: (306) 242-6907
Seating capacity: 4,500

Officers
Board Chair: Lynn Evans
President: Mark Regier
Vice President: Les Cannam
General Manager: Mark Regier
Director of Communications: Marlene Rochelle
Director of Marketing: Maurice Neault
Director of Publicity: Marlene Rochelle
Director of Simulcasting: Doug King
Track Announcer: Steve Tatarniuk

Racing Dates
2002: May 18-September 21
2003: May 23-September 13

Track Layout
Main circumference: 5 furlongs
Main length of stretch: 660 feet

Handle
Average on-track recent meeting: $19,820, 2002
Total on-track recent meeting: $634,240, 2002

Leaders
Recent meeting, leading jockey: Serge Rocheleau, 53, 2002
Recent meeting, leading trainer: Tom Gardipy Jr., 27, 2002

Interesting Facts
Trivia: Jockey Tim Moccasin rode 14 consecutive winners August 24 through September 1, 2001, believed to be a North American record.

Fastest Times of 2002
4 furlongs: Royal Empress, :46.44, June 29

6 furlongs: Pawhuska, 1:12.42, August 23
6 1/2 furlongs: Quiz the Wizard, 1:22.64, August 17
About 7 furlongs: Rouge Royale, 1:25.75, July 6
1 mile: Magik Step, 1:40.27, September 13
1 1/16 miles: Britts Xpress, 1:46.28, September 14; Regal Randy, 1:46.28, August 3
1 1/8 miles: Beau Ring, 1:53.49, August 24

Puerto Rico

El Comandante

El Comandante is all but synonymous with Bold Forbes and Mister Frisky, the two best-known horses to race at the Puerto Rico track. A dual-classic winner and 1976 champion three-year-old in the United States, Bold Forbes began his career at El Comandante. So did Mister Frisky, who started his unbeaten string there in 1989 before coming to the United States and going off as the favorite in the 1990 Kentucky Derby (G1), in which he finished eighth.

Located in Canovanas, El Comandante has been the island's racing outlet for many decades, and in recent years it has added a sophisticated network of off-track wagering outlets and a daily television racing report.

The track, owned by holding company El Comandante Credit Corp., has encountered financial problems, however. In early 2002, the corporation, whose parent company is Equus Gaming Co., announced it was in default on its mortgage notes for the third time in a year. The company made payments on the notes during the default period.

Location: P.O. Box 1675, Canovanas, PR 00729
Phone: (787) 641-6060
Fax: (787) 876-5170
E-mail: ecmc@comandantepr.com
Web site: *http://www.comandantepr.com*
Acreage: 257
Number of stalls: 1,500+

Officers
President: Juan M. Rivera
Vice President/General Manager: Alejandro Fuentes
Racing Secretary: Angel Agala
Director of Communications: Nidnal J. Adrover
Director of Mutuels: Wilma Curet
Director of Racing: Marcos Rivera Puga
Director of Operations: Richard C. Voorhies
Director of Marketing: Jessica Salgado
Director of Finance: Stanley J. Pinkerton
Track Photographer: Ivan Baella

Racing Dates
2002: January 1-December 31
2003: January 1-December 31

Track Layout
Main circumference: 1 mile
Main track chute: 7 furlongs

Leaders
Career, leading jockey by stakes wins: Wilfredo Rohena
Career, leading jockey by wins: Juan Carlos Diaz
Career, leading owner by titles: Villa Real
Career, leading trainer by titles: Maximo Gomez
Recent meeting, leading jockey: Ramon Vazquez
Recent meeting, leading owner: Villa Real
Recent meeting, leading trainer: Julio Diaz Jr.

North American Racetracks:

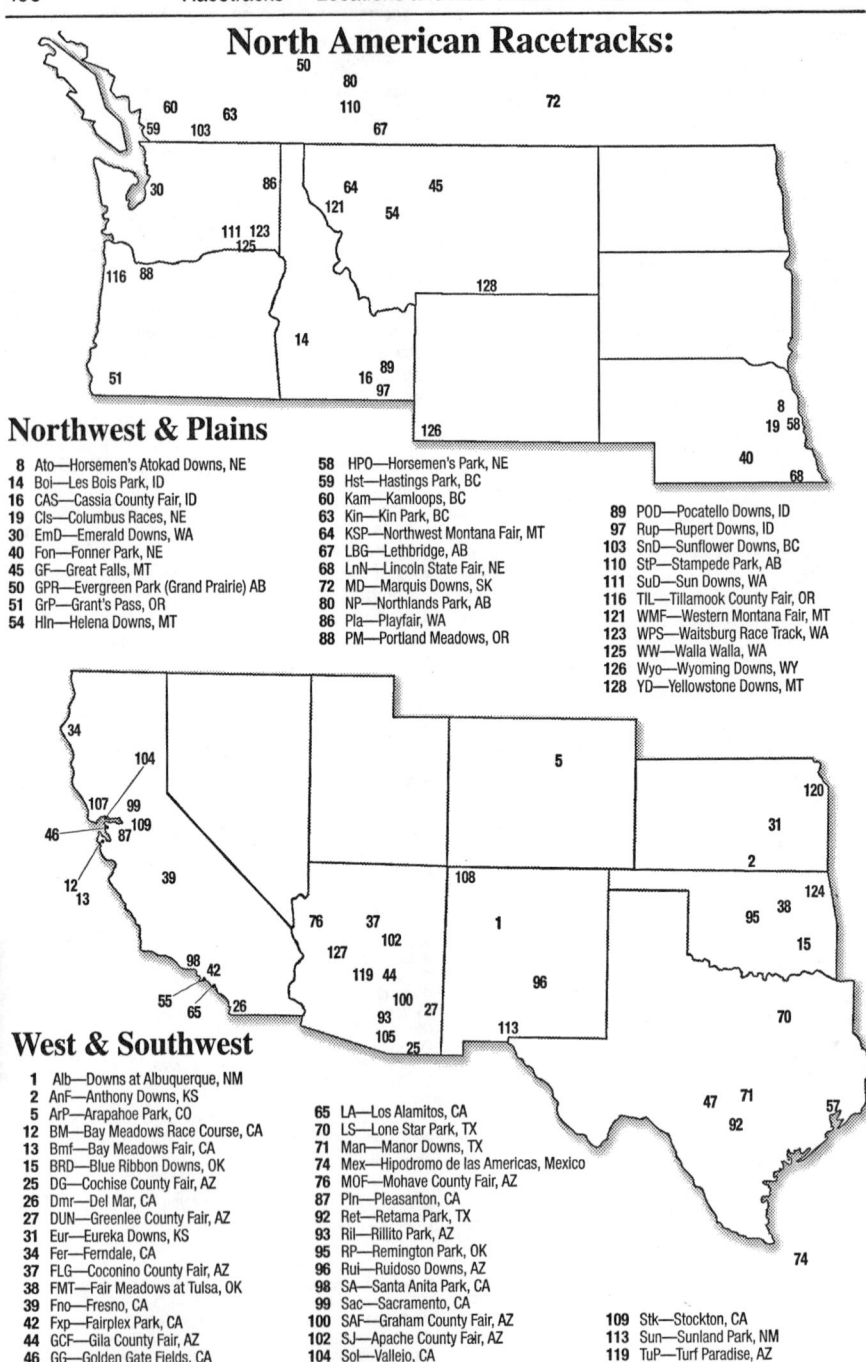

Northwest & Plains

8 Ato—Horsemen's Atokad Downs, NE	58 HPO—Horsemen's Park, NE
14 Boi—Les Bois Park, ID	59 Hst—Hastings Park, BC
16 CAS—Cassia County Fair, ID	60 Kam—Kamloops, BC
19 Cls—Columbus Races, NE	63 Kin—Kin Park, BC
30 EmD—Emerald Downs, WA	64 KSP—Northwest Montana Fair, MT
40 Fon—Fonner Park, NE	67 LBG—Lethbridge, AB
45 GF—Great Falls, MT	68 LnN—Lincoln State Fair, NE
50 GPR—Evergreen Park (Grand Prairie) AB	72 MD—Marquis Downs, SK
51 GrP—Grant's Pass, OR	80 NP—Northlands Park, AB
54 Hln—Helena Downs, MT	86 Pla—Playfair, WA
	88 PM—Portland Meadows, OR

89 POD—Pocatello Downs, ID
97 Rup—Rupert Downs, ID
103 SnD—Sunflower Downs, BC
110 StP—Stampede Park, AB
111 SuD—Sun Downs, WA
116 TIL—Tillamook County Fair, OR
121 WMF—Western Montana Fair, MT
123 WPS—Waitsburg Race Track, WA
125 WW—Walla Walla, WA
126 Wyo—Wyoming Downs, WY
128 YD—Yellowstone Downs, MT

West & Southwest

1 Alb—Downs at Albuquerque, NM	
2 AnF—Anthony Downs, KS	
5 ArP—Arapahoe Park, CO	65 LA—Los Alamitos, CA
12 BM—Bay Meadows Race Course, CA	70 LS—Lone Star Park, TX
13 Bmf—Bay Meadows Fair, CA	71 Man—Manor Downs, TX
15 BRD—Blue Ribbon Downs, OK	74 Mex—Hipodromo de las Americas, Mexico
25 DG—Cochise County Fair, AZ	76 MOF—Mohave County Fair, AZ
26 Dmr—Del Mar, CA	87 Pln—Pleasanton, CA
27 DUN—Greenlee County Fair, AZ	92 Ret—Retama Park, TX
31 Eur—Eureka Downs, KS	93 Ril—Rillito Park, AZ
34 Fer—Ferndale, CA	95 RP—Remington Park, OK
37 FLG—Coconino County Fair, AZ	96 Rui—Ruidoso Downs, AZ
38 FMT—Fair Meadows at Tulsa, OK	98 SA—Santa Anita Park, CA
39 Fno—Fresno, CA	99 Sac—Sacramento, CA
42 Fxp—Fairplex Park, CA	100 SAF—Graham County Fair, AZ
44 GCF—Gila County Fair, AZ	102 SJ—Apache County Fair, AZ
46 GG—Golden Gate Fields, CA	104 Sol—Vallejo, CA
47 Gil—Gillespie County Fair, TX	105 SON—Santa Cruz County Fair, AZ
55 Hol—Hollywood Park, CA	107 SR—Santa Rosa, CA
57 Hou—Sam Houston Race Park, TX	108 SRP—SunRay Park, NM

109 Stk—Stockton, CA
113 Sun—Sunland Park, NM
119 TuP—Turf Paradise, AZ
120 Wds—Woodlands, KS
124 WRD—Will Rogers Downs, OK
127 YAV—Yavapai Downs, AZ

Abbreviations and Locations

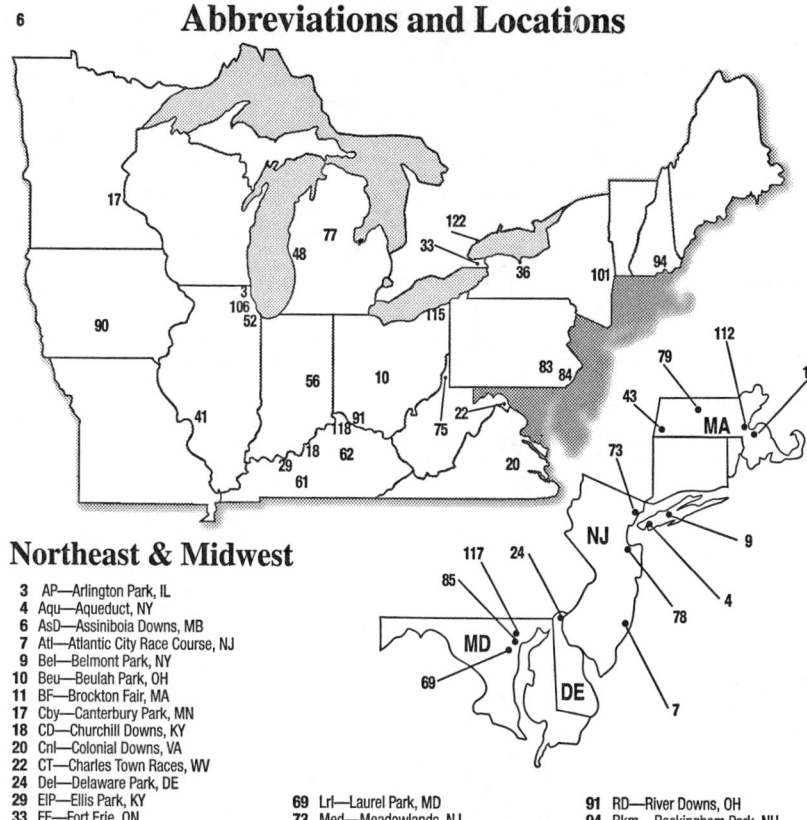

Northeast & Midwest

3 AP—Arlington Park, IL
4 Aqu—Aqueduct, NY
6 AsD—Assiniboia Downs, MB
7 Atl—Atlantic City Race Course, NJ
9 Bel—Belmont Park, NY
10 Beu—Beulah Park, OH
11 BF—Brockton Fair, MA
17 Cby—Canterbury Park, MN
18 CD—Churchill Downs, KY
20 Cnl—Colonial Downs, VA
22 CT—Charles Town Races, WV
24 Del—Delaware Park, DE
29 ElP—Ellis Park, KY
33 FE—Fort Erie, ON
36 FL—Finger Lakes, NY
41 FP—Fairmont Park, IL
43 GBF—Great Barrington Fair, MA
48 GLD—Great Lakes Downs, MI
52 Haw—Hawthorne Park, IL
56 Hoo—Hoosier Park, IN
61 KD—Kentucky Downs, KY
62 Kee—Keeneland Race Course, KY

69 Lrl—Laurel Park, MD
73 Med—Meadowlands, NJ
75 Mnr—Mountaineer Race Track, WV
77 MPM—Mt Pleasant Meadows, MI
78 Mth—Monmouth Park, NJ
79 Nmp—Northampton Fair, MA
83 Pen—Penn National Race Course, PA
84 Pha—Philadelphia Park, PA
85 Pim—Pimlico Race Course, MD
90 PrM—Prairie Meadows, IA

91 RD—River Downs, OH
94 Rkm—Rockingham Park, NH
101 Sar—Saratoga Race Course, NY
106 Spt—Sportsman's Park, IL
112 Suf—Suffolk Downs, MA
115 Tdn—Thistledown, OH
117 Tim—Timonium, MD
118 TP—Turfway Park, KY
122 WO—Woodbine, ON

Southeast

21 Crc—Calder Race Course, FL
23 DeD—Delta Downs, LA
28 ElC—El Comandante, PR
32 EvD—Evangeline Downs, LA
35 FG—Fair Grounds, LA
49 GP—Gulfstream Park, FL
53 Hia—Hialeah Park, FL
66 LaD—Louisiana Downs, LA
81 OP—Oaklawn Park, AR
82 OTC—Ocala Training Center, FL
114 Tam—Tampa Bay Downs, FL

North American Purse Distribution by Year

Year	No. of runners	No. of races	Total purses	Average purse	Per Runner Average	Median
2002	72,504	59,712	$1,170,169,267	$19,597	$16,139	$6,003
2001	70,942	60,538	1,146,337,367	18,936	16,159	6,010
2000	69,230	60,579	1,093,661,241	18,053	15,798	5,796
1999	68,435	60,118	1,008,162,608	16,770	14,732	5,310
1998	68,419	61,141	968,366,929	15,838	14,153	4,939
1997	69,067	63,491	888,667,752	13,997	12,867	4,425
1996	70,371	64,263	845,916,706	13,163	12,021	3,937
1995	72,316	68,197	815,987,125	11,965	11,283	3,702
1994	74,939	70,617	770,426,193	10,910	10,280	3,314
1993	78,763	72,224	748,415,925	10,362	9,502	2,850
1992	83,468	77,711	771,136,296	9,989	9,238	2,731
1991	86,483	78,671	761,446,198	9,679	8,805	2,433
1990	89,722	79,971	775,006,519	9,691	8,637	2,376
1989	91,436	82,726	771,421,230	9,325	8,437	2,218
1988	90,482	79,589	736,698,230	9,256	8,142	2,127
1987	89,504	80,376	704,372,435	8,763	7,870	2,101
1986	86,022	77,732	661,826,092	8,514	7,694	2,070
1985	82,548	75,687	641,658,553	8,478	7,773	2,158
1984	78,253	74,396	599,348,425	8,056	7,659	2,345
1983	74,540	71,034	544,260,167	7,662	7,302	2,435
1982	69,505	71,515	526,587,096	7,363	7,576	2,703
1981	65,797	70,881	507,007,953	7,153	7,706	2,865
1980	64,499	68,236	449,631,322	6,589	6,971	2,524
1979	63,728	69,406	414,629,063	5,974	6,506	2,440
1978	62,937	69,498	367,163,242	5,283	5,834	n/a
1977	61,960	68,826	335,720,312	4,878	5,418	2,189
1976	61,084	69,480	318,680,094	4,587	5,217	2,100
1975	58,818	68,203	291,194,571	4,270	4,951	2,058
1974	56,524	65,288	262,942,547	4,027	4,652	1,904
1973	54,812	62,264	233,662,724	3,753	4,263	1,764
1972	52,561	59,417	210,435,265	3,542	4,004	1,647

Data reflect all Thoroughbred purses distributed to racehorses in North America, excluding Mexico and Puerto Rico, from Jockey Club Information Systems data. Steeplechase races are excluded.

Top 25 North American Race Meetings by Average Attendance in 2002

Rank, Track	No. of Racing Days	Total Attendance	Average Attendance
1. Saratoga Race Course	36	999,388	27,761
2. Del Mar	43	667,280	15,518
3. Keeneland Race Course (Spring)	16	227,545	14,222
4. Churchill Downs (Spring)	53	677,876	13,036
5. Keeneland Race Course (Fall)	17	211,661	12,451
6. Oaklawn Park	52	622,983	11,980
7. Oak Tree at Santa Anita	26	263,504	10,135
8. Santa Anita Park	85	844,060	9,930
9. Monmouth Park	76	767,424	9,838
10. Gulfstream Park	90	842,310	9,359
11. Hollywood Park (Spring/Summer)	65	593,441	9,130
12. Lone Star Park	70	631,726	9,025
13. Belmont Park (Spring)	55	465,220	8,314
14. Churchill Downs (Fall)	30	202,059	6,735
15. Hollywood Park (Fall)	35	226,033	6,458
16. Arlington Park	107	712,952	*6,291
17. Belmont Park (Fall)	33	202,015	6,122
18. Aqueduct (Spring)	85	457,247	5,256
19. Tropical Park at Calder	52	262,918	5,056
20. Calder Race Course	128	623,629	4,872
21. Aqueduct (Fall)	51	217,144	4,825
22. Meadowlands	62	252,216	4,068
23. Fair Grounds	89	340,624	3,827
24. Tampa Bay Downs	93	306,042	3,291
25. Turfway (Fall)	22	41,553	·1,888

*Including Breeders' Cup World Thoroughbred Championships day

Top 25 North American Race Meetings by Average Handle in 2002

Rank, Track	Racing Dates	Total Handle	Average Handle
1. Saratoga Race Course	36	$ 587,262,467	$ 16,312,846
2. Santa Anita Park (Winter)	85	1,020,645,057	12,050,726
3. Belmont (Spring)	55	657,789,165	11,959,803
4. Belmont (Fall)	33	368,528,262	11,167,523
5. Oak Tree at Santa Anita	26	276,845,846	10,647,917
6. Churchill Downs (Spring)	53	538,945,956	10,168,791
7. Aqueduct (Spring)	85	803,570,338	9,453,768
8. Del Mar	43	379,324,725	8,821,505
9. Gulfstream Park	90	†789,600,000	†8,733,333
10. Hollywood Park (Spring/Summer)	65	538,094,001	8,278,369
11. Aqueduct (Fall)	51	420,431,468	8,243,754
12. Keeneland Race Course (Spring)	16	129,403,800	8,087,737
13. Hollywood Park (Fall)	35	255,211,111	7,291,746
14. Keeneland Race Course (Fall)	17	111,180,879	6,540,051
15. Churchill Downs (Fall)	30	196,970,485	6,565,682
16. Oaklawn Park	52	275,010,311	5,288,620
17. Arlington Park	107	*522,955,208	*4,887,431
18. Fair Grounds	89	400,601,717	4,501,142
19. Tropical Park at Calder	52	224,701,909	4,321,191
20. Calder Race Course	128	452,540,885	3,535,476
21. Monmouth Park	76	269,167,260	3,450,861
22. Lone Star Park	70	†233,802,380	†3,340,034
23. Pimlico (Spring)	54	177,278,793	3,282,940
24. Ellis Park	41	120,897,602	2,948,722
25. Hawthorne (Fall)	43	122,729,568	2,854,176

*Including Breeders' Cup World Championships day; †Estimated handle

Pari-Mutuel Takeout by State

Pari-mutuel takeout is the amount deducted from wagers before odds are calculated and payments are made to winning bettors. The money taken out from the wagers goes to state taxes, horsemen as purses, the racetrack operators, breed enhancement funds, and other funds. At most tracks, after the state and special allotments are deducted, the track and horsemen split the remainder equally.

ARIZONA—Up to 25% on win-place-show wagers; up to 30% on two-horse wagers; up to 35% on multiple-horse wagers.

ARKANSAS—17% on win-place-show wagers; 21% on multiple wagers.

CALIFORNIA—15.63% on win-place-show wagers; 20.38% on exotic wagers.

COLORADO—18.5% on win-place-show wagers; 25% on exotic wagers.

DELAWARE—17% on win-place-show wagers; 19% on daily doubles and exactas; 27% on all other exotic wagers.

FLORIDA—Individual tracks determine takeout rate.

IDAHO—20% on win-place-show wagers; 20.75% on exotic wagers.

ILLINOIS—17% on total handle; 20.5% on two-horse wagers; 25% on wagers involving three or more horses.

INDIANA—18% on win-place-show wagers; 21.5% on exotic wagers.

IOWA—Up to 18% on win-place-show wagers; up to 24% on two-horse wagers; up to 25% on all other wagers.

KANSAS—18% on win-place-show wagers; up to 22% on multiple wagers.

KENTUCKY—At tracks above $1,200,000 daily average: 16% on win-place-show wagers; 19% on exotic wagers. At tracks below $1,200,000 daily average: 17.5% on win-place-show wagers; 19% on exotic wagers.

LOUISIANA—17% on win-place-show wagers; 20.5% on two-horse wagers; 25% on three-horse wagers.

MARYLAND—18% on win-place-show wagers; 21% on two-horse multiple wagers; 25.75% on three-horse multiple wagers.

MASSACHUSETTS—19% on win-place-show wagers; 26% on exotic wagers (19% at fairs).

MICHIGAN—17% on win-place-show wagers; 20.5% on multiples; 25% on "special sweepstakes."

MINNESOTA—Up to 17% on win-place-show wagers; 23% on exotic wagers.

MONTANA—20% on win-place-show wagers; up to 25% on exotic wagers.

NEBRASKA—15% to 18% on win-place-show wagers; up to 24% on exotic wagers.

NEW HAMPSHIRE—19% on win-place-show wagers; 26% on multiple wagers.

NEW JERSEY—17% on win-place-show wagers; 19% on two-horse wagers; 25% on all other wagers.

NEW MEXICO—Class A tracks: 19% on win-place-show wagers; 21% to 25% on exotic wagers. Class B tracks: 18.75% to 25% on win-place-show wagers; 21% to 30% on exotic wagers.

NEW YORK—At NYRA racetracks, 15% on win-place-show wagers; 20% on multiple wagers; 25% on exotics and super exotics. At Finger Lakes, 18% on win-place-show wagers, 20% on multiple wagers, 25% on exotics and super exotics.

OHIO—18% on win-place-show wagers; 22.5% on exotic wagers.

OKLAHOMA—18% on win-place-show wagers; 20% on multiple-horse wagers; 20% on up to three-race wagers (such as Pick Three); 25% on multiple-race wagers (more than three races, such as Pick Six).

OREGON—19% on win-place-show wagers; 22% on multiple wagers. At fairs, up to 22% on all wagers.

PENNSYLVANIA—17% on regular wagering pools; 19% if average daily handle is less than $300,000; 20% on exactas, daily doubles and quinellas; 26% to 35% on trifectas.

TEXAS—18% on win-place-show wagers; up to 21% on two-horse wagers; up to 25% on three-horse wagers.

VIRGINIA—18% on win-place-show wagers; 22% on all other wagers.

WASHINGTON—16.1% on win-place-show wagers; 22.1% on all other wagers.

WEST VIRGINIA—17.25% on win-place-show wagers; 19% on two-horse wagers; 25% on three horses or more.

WYOMING—20.9% on win-place-show wagers; 25.9% on exotic wagers.

Revenues to States From Horse Racing

For a few decades, horse racing was the golden goose for producing revenue for state governments, as shown in the table of current-dollar revenues prepared by the Association of Racing Commissioners International. The revenue figures cover all forms of horse racing, but a substantial portion of the total is derived from Thoroughbred racing.

When the effects of inflation are removed from the figures using the United States Commerce Department's gross domestic product implicit price deflator, the peak period for state taxation of horse racing was from 1963 through 1979, when inflation-adjusted state revenues exceeded $1.3-billion annually. State revenues topped out in 1975 at almost $2-billion in deflated dollars.

In both current and inflation-adjusted dollars, state revenues began a sharp decline in the 1980s as states reduced their pari-mutuel tax rates. With one exception, 1990, revenues to states declined from the preceding year since 1988 in both current and deflated dollars.

Revenue to States from Horse Racing

Year	Current Dollars	Deflated Dollars
2000	$367,786,590	$344,082,731
1999	392,201,085	374,634,474
1998	431,722,361	418,319,407
1997	441,768,972	433,327,747
1996	443,882,538	443,882,538
1995	455,764,292	464,586,795
1994	451,546,549	470,326,694
1993	471,735,474	501,584,785
1992	491,259,606	534,884,811
1991	523,249,392	583,579,880
1990	623,839,806	721,093,715
1989	584,888,183	702,391,208
1988	596,202,319	743,264,666
1987	608,351,461	784,190,496
1986	587,357,677	779,878,478
1985	625,159,697	848,341,336
1984	650,262,852	910,260,582
1983	641,387,176	931,220,129
1982	652,888,463	985,447,396
1981	680,199,584	1,090,675,193
1980	712,727,523	1,249,478,495
1979	680,919,798	1,303,295,559
1978	673,063,831	1,395,616,213
1977	700,239,986	1,555,259,386
1976	714,629,120	1,689,350,669
1975	780,081,431	1,948,547,312
1974	645,980,984	1,764,059,597
1973	585,201,524	1,741,567,538
1972	531,404,550	1,670,085,641
1971	512,838,417	1,680,280,518
1970	486,403,097	1,673,961,858
1969	461,498,886	1,672,764,094
1968	426,856,448	1,623,275,205
1967	394,381,913	1,564,324,751
1966	388,452,125	1,588,436,414
1965	369,892,036	1,555,671,599
1964	350,095,928	1,499,982,554
1963	316,570,791	1,376,634,158
1962	287,930,030	1,266,016,049
1961	264,853,077	1,180,429,991
1960	258,039,385	1,162,863,384
1959	243,388,655	1,112,277,922
1958	222,049,651	1,026,297,148

Year	Current Dollars	Deflated Dollars
1957	$216,747,621	$1,025,684,370
1956	207,456,272	1,014,257,710
1955	186,989,588	945,490,155
1954	178,015,828	915,766,387
1953	167,426,465	869,883,436
1952	142,489,696	749,866,835
1951	117,250,564	626,840,759
1950	98,366,167	563,735,268
1949	95,327,053	552,364,428
1948	95,803,364	554,385,533
1947	97,926,984	598,978,433
1946	94,035,859	636,840,437
1945	65,265,405	495,523,537
1944	55,971,233	436,763,426
1943	38,194,727	304,874,896
1942	22,005,278	185,011,586
1941	21,128,173	191,586,625
1940	16,145,182	156,263,860
1939	10,369,807	101,804,506
1938	9,576,335	92,992,183
1937	8,434,792	79,491,019
1936	8,611,538	84,576,095
1935	8,386,255	83,312,686
1934	6,024,193	60,985,959

Minimum Age to Attend and Wager at U.S. Racetracks

State	Minimum Age	Legal Wagering Age
Arizona	None	21
Arkansas	Under 16 with adult	18
California	None	18
Colorado	None	18
Delaware	Under 18 with adult	18
Florida	Under 18 with adult	18
Idaho	None	18
Illinois	Under 17 with adult	17
Indiana	Under 17 with adult	18
Iowa	Under 18 with adult	21
Kansas	Under 18 with adult	18
Kentucky	None	18
Louisiana	6	21
Maryland	None	18
Massachusetts	None	18
Michigan	None	18
Minnesota	Under 18 with adult	18
Montana	None	18
Nebraska	Under 18 with adult	19
New Hampshire	Under 18 with adult	18
New Jersey	Under 18 with adult	18
New Mexico	Under 18 with adult	18
New York	Under 18 with adult	18
Ohio	Under 18 with adult	18
Oklahoma	6	18
Oregon	12 after 6 p.m.	18
Pennsylvania	None	18
Puerto Rico	None	18
Texas	Under 16 with adult	21
Virginia	None	18
Washington	None	18
West Virginia	None	18
Wyoming	None	19

PEOPLE

Leading Owners of 2002

Along with bettors, Thoroughbred owners are the primary source of the billions of dollars that make the Thoroughbred industry the living, breathing, wonderful thing that it is. Owners spend more than $1-billion annually purchasing Thoroughbreds of various descriptions at public auctions and by private contract, thus taking on the privilege and responsibility of paying further untold sums for their training, veterinary care, board, and other expenses. In return, owners in North America get a shot at more than $1.17-billion annually in purses.

Total purses are divided among thousands of owners but, in the natural order of things, some do better than others. The following lists rate the accomplishments of owners in 2002 according to various criteria. The annual THOROUGHBRED TIMES leading owners list ranks owners according to four equally weighted criteria: total earnings, average earnings per starter, percentage of stakes winners from starters, and percentage of graded stakes winners from starters. That weighted list purposely favors quality over quantity, rewarding owners with good percentages in the best races.

In 2002, quality certainly was rewarded, with California-based Edmund A. Gann rising to the top spot, with ten winners from 19 starters. Of the ten winners, five won graded stakes races, and one of them, Medaglia d'Oro, was a candidate for an Eclipse Award as champion three-year-old male.

Other lists included here rank the leading owners of 2002 by each of those criteria individually, as well as by number of wins, giving full credit to quantity as well as quality. It takes both to make a $1-billion game go.

Leading Owners by Purses Won
(North American Earnings)

Year	Name	Wins	Earnings
2002	Stronach Stable	122	$8,349,249
2001	Richard Englander	406	9,812,272
2000	Stronach Stable	163	11,198,225
1999	Stronach Stable	124	6,221,147
1998	Stronach Stable	91	7,221,416
1997	Allen Paulson	66	5,259,107
1996	Allen E. Paulson	69	9,086,865
1995	Allen E. Paulson	86	7,232,967
1994	John Franks	193	4,518,088

THOROUGHBRED TIMES Leading Owners of 2002

Rankings based on formula that gives equal weighting to four statistical categories for performance in 2002: 1) total earnings; 2) average earnings per starter; 3) percent stakes winners from starters; and 4) percent graded stakes winners from starters. A minimum of ten starters required to be considered for inclusion. Names of owners are of individual property lines as reported by the Jockey Club. No attempt was made to consolidate any names where an owner had more than one partnership or property line. Statistics are for North America only and for racing in 2002.

Rank	Owner	No. strs	No. wnrs	No. SWs	SWs/ strs	No. GSWs	GSWs/ strs	Total earnings	Average earnings/ starter	Leading earner	Earnings of leading earner
1	Edmund A. Gann	19	10	5	26.3%	5	26.3%	$4,015,522	$211,343	Medaglia d'Oro	$2,245,000
2	Juddmonte Farms	38	24	11	29.0%	7	18.4%	5,172,287	136,113	Beat Hollow (GB)	1,437,150
3	Gary A. Tanaka	35	12	8	22.9%	6	17.1%	4,078,701	116,534	Golden Apples (Ire)	1,111,680
4	Michael B. Tabor	17	11	6	35.3%	5	29.4%	1,894,775	111,457	Left Bank	626,146
5	The Thoroughbred Corp.	76	44	13	17.1%	9	11.8%	7,887,915	103,788	War Emblem	3,125,000
6	Edward P. Evans	56	26	10	17.9%	7	12.5%	4,472,047	79,858	Summer Colony	992,500
7	Sam-Son Farm	49	24	7	14.3%	6	12.2%	4,003,749	81,709	Portcullis	562,535
8	Amerman Racing Stables	25	12	4	16.0%	3	12.0%	2,118,553	84,742	Lido Palace (Chi)	1,015,764
9	Godolphin Racing	47	16	7	14.9%	6	12.8%	3,637,855	77,401	Imperial Gesture	873,600
10	John C. Oxley	24	11	4	16.7%	3	12.5%	1,712,076	71,337	Booklet	425,760
11	Starlight Stable	12	4	1	8.3%	1	8.3%	1,736,640	144,720	Harlan's Holiday	1,606,000
12	Anstu Stables	16	13	5	31.3%	1	6.3%	1,267,838	79,240	Tarnished Lady	225,150
11	James Cassels & Bob Zollars	16	10	2	12.5%	1	6.3%	1,500,720	93,795	Easyfromthegitgo	606,905
14	Bohemia Stable	13	10	3	23.1%	2	15.4%	1,007,568	77,505	Shine Again	425,500
15	John Paul Reddam	18	4	2	11.1%	2	11.1%	1,433,201	79,622	Momentum	526,888
16	Stonerside Stable	41	25	8	19.5%	2	4.9%	2,349,975	57,316	Congaree	570,000
17	Gary and Mary West	31	16	3	9.7%	2	6.5%	2,107,368	67,980	Dollar Bill	496,850
18	Ogden Mills Phipps, et al.	15	5	2	13.3%	2	13.3%	1,035,962	69,064	Storm Flag Flying	447,000
19	Susan and John Moore	11	7	3	27.3%	1	9.1%	875,210	79,565	Regal Sanction	318,400
20	Molinaro Stable	19	9	2	10.5%	1	5.3%	1,315,779	69,252	T J's Lucky Moon	644,212
21	Mr. & Mrs. Jerome Moss	35	20	5	14.3%	3	8.6%	1,799,978	51,428	Kudos	468,735
22	Joseph Allen	12	9	3	25.0%	2	16.7%	829,308	69,109	Volga (Ire)	208,720
23	Robert and Beverly Lewis	44	13	2	4.6%	2	4.6%	2,731,088	62,070	Orientate	1,412,970
24	Augustin Stables	68	25	6	8.8%	4	5.9%	3,330,669	48,980	With Anticipation	1,507,700
25	Richard, Bertram, & Elaine Klein	31	21	4	12.9%	1	3.2%	1,561,795	50,380	Allamerican Bertie	619,235

Rank	Owner	No. strs	No. wnrs	No. SWs	SWs/ strs	No. GSWs	GSWs/ strs	Total earnings	Average earnings/ starter	Leading earner	Earnings of leading earner
26	Arthur B. Hancock III	14	7	1	7.1%	1	7.1%	934,360	66,740	Owsley	593,870
27	Steeplechase Farm	11	5	1	9.1%	1	9.1%	818,854	74,441	Mandy's Gold	715,404
28	Dominion Bloodstock, Derek Ball, & Hugh Galbraith	22	12	2	9.1%	1	4.6%	1,190,518	54,114	Lady Shari	316,506
29	Albert Fried Jr.	10	7	2	20.0%	1	10.0%	674,781	67,478	Affirmed Success	383,120
30	Sondra D. Bender	30	14	7	23.3%	1	3.3%	1,360,223	45,341	La Reine's Terms	320,680
31	Janis R. Whitham	16	10	1	6.3%	1	6.3%	958,864	59,929	Affluent	560,615
32	Fog City Stable	23	9	3	13.0%	1	4.4%	1,123,902	48,865	D'wildcat	424,444
33	Stronach Stable	172	87	7	4.1%	4	2.3%	8,349,249	48,542	Milwaukee Brew	1,590,000
34	James B. Tafel	32	18	3	9.4%	2	6.3%	1,450,046	45,314	Softly	349,768
35	Ogden Mills Phipps	12	5	1	8.3%	1	8.3%	801,460	66,788	Storm Flag Flying	520,000
36	Fox Ridge Farm	12	3	2	16.7%	2	16.7%	674,221	56,185	Riskaverse	461,160
37	Roddy J. Valente	19	16	2	10.5%	2	10.5%	916,023	48,212	Jester Rahab	207,470
38	Frank D. DiGiulio Jr.	21	12	1	4.8%		0.0%	1,215,905	57,900	Brass in Pocket	299,155
39	Michael E. Pegram	27	12	3	11.1%	2	7.4%	1,145,570	42,429	Icecoldbeeratreds	353,800
40	Mohammed bin Rashid al Maktoum	21	13	2	9.5%	2	9.5%	951,750	45,321	Showlady	158,640
41	Herbert and Carol Schwartz	14	9	1	7.1%	1	7.1%	804,607	57,472	Critical Eye	228,771
42	Cynthia Knight	15	8	2	13.3%	1	6.7%	777,529	51,835	Dat You Miz Blue	287,671
43	Flaxman Holdings	10	7	1	10.0%	1	10.0%	615,595	61,560	Surya	237,930
44	Gainsborough Farm	17	6	2	11.8%	2	11.8%	798,779	46,987	Touch of the Blues (Fr)	288,625
45	Stan E. Fulton	17	10	6	35.3%	1	5.9%	754,799	44,400	Crackup	274,828
46	Pin Oak Stable	47	20	4	8.5%	2	4.3%	1,784,196	37,962	See How She Runs	403,550
47	Padua Stables	37	24	2	5.4%	2	5.4%	1,482,712	40,073	Vindication	680,950
48	Peter Vegso	17	7	1	5.9%	1	5.9%	815,342	47,961	Orchard Park	613,310
49	Mockingbird Farm	42	27	1	2.4%		0.0%	1,841,856	43,854	Open Concert	207,906
50	Sez Who Racing	17	4	1	5.9%	1	5.9%	811,936	47,761	The Judge Sez Who	558,186
51	Stonecrest Farm	11	5	1	9.1%	1	9.1%	587,546	53,413	Perfect Drift	446,300
52	William Currin and Al Eisman	11	3	2	18.2%		0.0%	604,551	54,959	Outta Here	404,260
53	New Farm	16	10	3	18.8%	1	6.3%	686,842	42,928	Wild Snitch	119,200
54	Theodore F. Burnett	13	7	2	15.4%		0.0%	670,173	51,552	Santerra	205,966
55	S. V. G. B. Stable	11	9	1	9.1%		0.0%	634,648	57,695	Heyahohowdy	278,571
56	James F. Edwards	13	8	2	15.4%		0.0%	665,542	51,196	Pretty Brassy	140,280
57	Overbrook Farm	63	28	4	6.4%	2	3.2%	2,215,500	35,167	Snow Ridge	399,990
58	Live Oak Plantation	38	18	3	7.9%	1	2.6%	1,424,330	37,482	Miesque's Approval	325,550
59	William L. Clifton Jr.	23	8	3	13.0%	2	8.7%	865,931	37,649	Pleasant Breeze	195,240
60	Peachtree Stable	20	13	1	5.0%	1	5.0%	854,717	42,736	Chimichurri	148,340
61	Maktoum bin Rashid al Maktoum	16	5	1	6.3%	1	6.3%	714,483	44,655	Magic Mission (GB)	163,400
62	C. T. Grether Inc.	11	5	1	9.1%		0.0%	600,645	54,604	Crafty C. T.	250,075
63	Joseph V. Shields Jr.	10	8		0.0%		0.0%	712,676	71,268	Puzzlement	157,140
64	Cam Allard	12	5	1	8.3%		0.0%	618,991	51,583	Tuff Chick	178,964
65	Red Baron's Barn	37	14	2	5.4%	2	5.4%	1,280,605	34,611	Suances (GB)	260,000
66	Daniel M. Borislow	30	18	1	3.3%	1	3.3%	1,155,867	38,529	Toccet	755,610
67	Gerald F. Sleeter	11	7	2	18.2%		0.0%	540,182	49,107	Summer Swing	129,000
68	Stubbs Investment Inc.	25	13	1	4.0%		0.0%	1,002,815	40,113	Passing Ships	142,255
69	Eugene and Laura Melnyk	79	35	5	6.3%	1	1.3%	2,633,260	33,332	Fisher Pond	183,462
70	Love 2 Win Stable	18	10		0.0%		0.0%	867,778	48,210	Chanceisalady	150,140
71	Aaron and Marie Jones	20	9	1	5.0%		0.0%	845,438	42,272	Kela	139,600
72	William A. Sorokolit	16	5	1	6.3%	1	6.3%	671,335	41,958	Union Place	224,600
73	Glen C. Warren	19	13	3	15.8%		0.0%	746,212	39,274	Candid Glen	303,240
74	Kinsman Stable	31	18	2	6.5%		0.0%	1,092,432	35,240	Blue Burner	256,100
75	Diamond A Racing Corp.	24	7	1	4.2%	1	4.2%	902,294	37,596	Pleasantly Perfect	479,880
76	David and Holly Wilson	28	17	3	10.7%		0.0%	963,652	34,416	Casey Griffin	98,837
77	Gilbert G. Campbell	25	15	2	8.0%		0.0%	909,717	36,389	Ivanavinalot	418,300
78	S J B Jr. Stable	27	15	4	14.8%		0.0%	914,515	33,871	Holiday Runner	171,623
79	Team Valor Stables	26	12	2	7.7%	2	7.7%	875,485	33,673	Windward Passage	169,750
80	Kristine and John Richter	13	7	2	15.4%		0.0%	556,910	42,839	Bien Nicole	340,610
81	Chester and Mary Broman	26	17	2	7.7%	1	3.9%	877,411	33,747	Beautiful America	241,363
82	Einar Paul Robsham	45	23	1	2.2%		0.0%	1,522,837	33,841	Trust N Luck	382,800
83	Claiborne Farm	31	18	2	6.5%	1	3.2%	1,026,153	33,102	Trip	195,955
84	Eastern Sky Unlimited Trust and Charles Cono	13	6	1	7.7%	1	7.7%	526,653	40,512	Crowned Dancer	122,858
85	K. K. Sangara	46	23	2	4.4%	1	2.2%	1,489,899	32,389	Sheila's Prospect	322,814
86	Russell L. Reineman Stable	37	22	3	8.1%	1	2.7%	1,175,437	31,769	War Emblem	330,000
87	Alpine Stable	42	27		0.0%		0.0%	1,457,372	34,699	Lightning Pace	223,658
88	Thunderhead Farms	10	6	1	10.0%		0.0%	483,598	48,360	Sand Ridge	205,480
89	Carl F. Pollard	15	6	2	13.3%		0.0%	577,809	38,521	My Trusty Cat	228,025
90	Lorraine and Rod Rodriguez	13	7	1	7.7%	1	7.7%	512,073	39,390	Roman Dancer	166,009

Leading Owners by Earnings in 2002

Owner	No. strs	No. wnrs	Total earnings
Stronach Stable	172	87	$8,349,249
The Thoroughbred Corp.	76	44	7,887,915
Richard A. Englander	298	167	7,515,562
Michael J. Gill	317	146	5,639,292
Juddmonte Farms	38	24	5,172,287
Edward P. Evans	56	26	4,472,047
Gary A. Tanaka	35	12	4,078,701
Edmund A. Gann	19	10	4,015,522
Sam-Son Farm	49	24	4,003,749
John Franks	186	85	3,905,246
Godolphin Racing	47	16	3,637,855
Augustin Stables	68	25	3,330,669
Robert and Beverly Lewis	44	13	2,731,088
Eugene and Laura Melnyk	79	35	2,633,260
Stonerside Stable	41	25	2,349,975
Nelson Bunker Hunt	87	54	2,288,909
Overbrook Farm	63	28	2,215,500
Bruno Schickedanz	133	66	2,199,915
Amerman Racing Stables	25	12	2,118,553
Gary L. and Mary E. West	31	16	2,107,368
Dale Baird	235	105	2,034,019
Rosendo G. Parra	139	66	1,971,880
Frank Carl Calabrese	117	68	1,957,182
Michael B. Tabor	17	11	1,894,775
Mockingbird Farm	42	27	1,841,856
Mr. and Mrs. Jerome Moss	35	20	1,799,978
Pin Oak Stable	47	20	1,784,196
Golden Eagle Farm	93	26	1,771,284
Starlight Stable	12	4	1,736,640
John C. Oxley	24	11	1,712,076
Kenneth and Sarah Ramsey	92	53	1,692,922
WinStar Farm	61	33	1,601,721
Richard, Bertram, & Elaine Klein	31	21	1,561,795
Michael H. Sherman	99	51	1,531,053
Einar Paul Robsham	45	23	1,522,837
Gumpster Stable	94	55	1,507,823
James Cassels and Bob Zollars	16	10	1,500,720
K. K. Sangara	46	23	1,489,899
Padua Stables	37	24	1,482,712
Alpine Stable	42	27	1,457,372
James B. Tafel	32	18	1,450,046

Leading Owners by Average Earnings per Starter in 2002

(Minimum of 10 starters)

Owner	No. strs	No. wnrs	Average earnings per starter
Edmund A. Gann	19	10	$211,343
Starlight Stable	12	4	144,720
Juddmonte Farms	38	24	136,113
Gary A. Tanaka	35	12	116,534
Michael B. Tabor	17	11	111,457
The Thoroughbred Corp.	76	44	103,788
James Cassels and Bob Zollars	16	10	93,795
Amerman Racing Stables	25	12	84,742
Sam-Son Farm	49	24	81,709
Edward P. Evans	56	26	79,858
John Paul Reddam	18	4	79,622
Susan and John Moore	11	7	79,565
Anstu Stables	16	13	79,240
Bohemia Stable	13	10	77,505

Owner	No. strs	No. wnrs	Average earnings per starter
Godolphin Racing	47	16	77,401
Steeplechase Farm	11	5	74,441
John C. Oxley	24	11	71,337
Joseph V. Shields Jr.	10	8	71,268
Molinaro Stable	19	9	69,252
Joseph Allen	12	9	69,109
Ogden Mills Phipps, et al.	15	5	69,064
Gary L. and Mary E. West	31	16	67,980
Albert Fried Jr.	10	7	67,478
Ogden Mills Phipps	12	5	66,788
Arthur B. Hancock III	14	7	66,740
Robert and Beverly Lewis	44	13	62,070
Flaxman Holdings	10	7	61,560
Janis R. Whitham	16	10	59,929
Frank D. DiGiulio Jr.	21	12	57,900
S. V. G. B. Stable	11	9	57,695
Herbert and Carol Schwartz	14	9	57,472
Stonerside Stable	41	25	57,316
Fox Ridge Farm Inc.	12	3	56,185
William Currin and Al Eisman	11	3	54,959
C. T. Grether Inc.	11	5	54,604
Dominion Bloodstock, Derek Ball, and Hugh Galbraith	22	12	54,114
Stonecrest Farm	11	5	53,413

Leading Owners by Number of Stakes Winners in 2002

Owner	No. strs	No. wnrs	No. SWs
The Thoroughbred Corp.	76	44	13
Juddmonte Farms	38	24	11
Edward P. Evans	56	26	10
Gary A. Tanaka	35	12	8
Richard A. Englander	298	167	8
Stonerside Stable	41	25	8
Sam-Son Farm	49	24	7
Sondra D. Bender	30	14	7
Stronach Stable	172	87	7
Godolphin Racing	47	16	7
Dennis E. Weir	52	30	7
Augustin Stables	68	25	6
Stan E. Fulton	17	10	6
Nelson Bunker Hunt	87	54	6
Heiligbrodt Racing Stable	60	30	6
Michael B. Tabor	17	11	6
Edmund A. Gann	19	10	5
Mr. and Mrs. Jerome Moss	35	20	5
John Franks	186	85	5
Anstu Stables	16	13	5
G. Watts Humphrey Jr.	50	20	5
Eugene and Laura Melnyk	79	35	5
Herb Riecken	27	18	5
Anthony W. Dutrow	15	11	5
Tangarae Farms	26	12	5
Overbrook Farm	63	28	4
Richard, Bertram, and Elaine Klein	31	21	4
Amerman Racing Stables	25	12	4
S J B Jr. Stable	27	15	4
Tom R. Durant	49	22	4
Michael J. Gill	317	146	4
Pin Oak Stable	47	20	4
M. Y. Stables Inc.	41	27	4
Keith A. Asmussen	18	10	4
John C. Oxley	24	11	4

Leading Owners by Percent
Stakes Winners from Starters
(Minimum of 10 starters)

Owner	No. strs	No. wnrs	No. SWs	SWs/ strs
Stan E. Fulton	17	10	6	35.3%
Michael B. Tabor	17	11	6	35.3%
Anthony W. Dutrow	15	11	5	33.3%
Anstu Stables	16	13	5	31.3%
Juddmonte Farms	38	24	11	29.0%
Susan and John Moore	11	7	3	27.3%
Edmund A. Gann	19	10	5	26.3%
Joseph Allen	12	9	3	25.0%
Linwood Stables	12	6	3	25.0%
Sondra D. Bender	30	14	7	23.3%
Bohemia Stable	13	10	3	23.1%
Auburn Express Inc.	13	7	3	23.1%
Gary A. Tanaka	35	12	8	22.9%
Keith A. Asmussen	18	10	4	22.2%
Albert Fried Jr.	10	7	2	20.0%
Allen Floyd	10	6	2	20.0%
David Beard	10	5	2	20.0%
Stonerside Stable	41	25	8	19.5%
Tangarae Farms	26	12	5	19.2%
New Farm	16	10	3	18.8%
Herb Riecken	27	18	5	18.5%
William Currin & Al Eisman	11	3	2	18.2%
Arcadia Stable	11	5	2	18.2%
Canyon Farms	11	7	2	18.2%
Stud El Aguila	11	5	2	18.2%
Team Canonie Stable	11	7	2	18.2%
Gerald F. Sleeter	11	7	2	18.2%
Heinz Steinmann	11	7	2	18.2%
Edward P. Evans	56	26	10	17.9%
The Thoroughbred Corp.	76	44	13	17.1%
Manfred Roos	18	11	3	16.7%
Ponderosa Pine Stable	12	8	2	16.7%
Fox Ridge Farm	12	3	2	16.7%
John C. Oxley	24	11	4	16.7%
Harlequin Ranches	12	4	2	16.7%
Mary L. Bonham	12	5	2	16.7%
Amerman Racing Stables	25	12	4	16.0%
Glen C. Warren	19	13	3	15.8%
James F. Edwards	13	8	2	15.4%
Barnett Stables	13	6	2	15.4%
Theodore F. Burnett	13	7	2	15.4%
Harry J. Aleo	13	9	2	15.4%
Kristine and John Richter	13	7	2	15.4%

Leading Owners by Number
of Graded Stakes Winners in 2002

Owner	No. strs	No. wnrs	No. GSWs	GSWs/ strs
The Thoroughbred Corp.	76	44	9	11.8%
Edward P. Evans	56	26	7	12.5%
Juddmonte Farms	38	24	7	18.4%
Gary A. Tanaka	35	12	6	17.1%
Sam-Son Farms	49	24	6	12.2%
Godolphin Racing	47	16	6	12.8%
Edmund A. Gann	19	10	5	26.3%
Michael B. Tabor	17	11	5	29.4%
Augustin Stables	68	25	4	5.9%
Stronach Stable	172	87	4	2.3%

Owner	No. strs	No. wnrs	No. GSWs	GSWs/ strs
Mr. & Mrs. Jerome Moss	35	20	3	8.6%
Dogwood Stable	56	25	3	5.4%
Amerman Racing Stables	25	12	3	12.0%
John C. Oxley	24	11	3	12.5%
Roddy J. Valente	19	16	2	10.5%
Michael E. Pegram	27	12	2	7.4%
Robert and Beverly Lewis	44	13	2	4.6%
Bohemia Stable	13	10	2	15.4%
Overbrook Farm	63	28	2	3.2%
James B. Tafel	32	18	2	6.3%
Ogden Mills Phipps, et al.	15	5	2	13.3%
Mohammed bin Rashid al Maktoum	21	13	2	9.5%
Nelson Bunker Hunt	87	54	2	2.3%
Padua Stables	37	24	2	5.4%
Tom R. Durant	49	22	2	4.1%
Mack Fehsenfeld	31	12	2	6.5%
Stonerside Stable	41	25	2	4.9%
John Paul Reddam	18	4	2	11.1%
Bradley Wayne Hughes	43	23	2	4.7%
Pin Oak Stable	47	20	2	4.3%
Fox Ridge Farm	12	3	2	16.7%
Gary L. and Mary West	31	16	2	6.5%
William L. Clifton Jr.	23	8	2	8.7%
Joseph Allen	12	9	2	16.7%
Team Valor Stables	26	12	2	7.7%
Red Baron's Barn	37	14	2	5.4%
Gainsborough Farm	17	6	2	11.8%

Leading Owners
by Number of Wins in 2002

Owner	No. strs	No. wnrs	No. wins
Richard A. Englander	298	167	278
Michael J. Gill	317	146	228
John Franks	186	85	150
Dale Baird	235	105	141
Louis D. O'Brien	111	69	136
Daniel J. Chen	97	63	126
Stronach Stable	172	87	122
Rosendo G. Parra	139	66	103
Bruno Schickedanz	133	66	99
Frank Carl Calabrese	117	68	99
Nelson Bunker Hunt	87	54	92
Gumpster Stable	94	55	90
Pyrite Stables	48	37	86
Monarch Stables	76	44	79
Lothenbach Stables	101	49	79
Michael H. Sherman	99	51	78
Kenneth and Sarah Ramsey	92	53	77
Mark Yagour Inc.	124	48	77
Highway 1 Racing Stable	76	39	76
E and G Stables	45	30	74
Kenneth W. Murphy	69	36	72
Turf Express Inc.	78	45	70
The Thoroughbred Corp.	76	44	69
Hy-Hopes Farm	39	27	65
Yasou Stable Trust	40	29	63
Home Team Stables	79	40	60
Billy Hays	74	37	60
Jerry Hollendorfer and George Todaro	69	34	60
Maggie Moss	63	31	57
Eugene and Laura Melnyk	79	35	56

Leading Breeders of 2002

Thoroughbred racing is played on an international stage, and so too is the exceedingly complex business of breeding Thoroughbreds for the racecourse. In 2002, the breeding game was a decidedly international enterprise, with the four top breeders in the THOROUGHBRED TIMES rankings based outside the United States.

Breeding operations commonly are built over decades, and the rankings also reflect longtime investments in the horse business. The four criteria used to determine the THOROUGHBRED TIMES rankings are total earnings, average earnings per starter, percentage of stakes winners from starters, and percentage of graded stakes winners from starters.

The criteria reward quality over quantity, and certainly high-quality Thoroughbreds were hallmarks of the year's leading breeders. Atop the 2002 list was Flaxman Holdings Ltd., an international operation begun by Greek shipping magnate Stavros Niarchos and continued since his 1996 death under the leadership of his daughter, Maria Niarchos-Gouazé. The Flaxman operation, with bases in France and Kentucky, had 13 winners from 25 North American starters and four graded stakes winners. It bred and raced Domedriver (Ire), winner of the 2002 Breeders' Cup Mile (G1).

Occupying second position for the second consecutive year was Juddmonte Farms, the international breeding and racing operation of Khalid Abdullah, a Saudi Arabian prince and London-based businessman. Juddmonte's operation is significantly larger than Flaxman, with 30 winners from 58 starters and 11 stakes winners. The international sweep of the top positions continued with Orpendale, which is associated with Coolmore Stud's John Magnier. The fourth position belonged to Sam-Son Farm, an Ontario-based operation begun by the late Ernie Samuel. The Phipps Stable, the highest-ranked United States-based operation on the list, again produced high quality from limited numbers, with three graded stakes winners from 20 starters, including champion two-year-old filly Storm Flag Flying. Mockingbird Farm was the year's leader by quantity, with more than $10.9-million in purse earnings, and led that category for the second straight year.

THOROUGHBRED TIMES Leading Breeders of 2002

Rankings based on formula that gives equal weighting to four statistical categories for performance in 2002: 1) total earnings; 2) average earnings per starter; 3) percent stakes winners from starters; and 4) percent graded stakes winners from starters. A minimum of ten starters required to be considered for inclusion. Names of breeders are of individual property lines as reported by the Jockey Club. No attempt was made to consolidate any names where a breeder had more than one partnership or property line. Statistics are for North America only and for racing in 2002.

Rank	Breeder	No. strs	No. wnrs	No. SWs	SWs/ strs	No. GSWs	GSWs/ strs	Total earnings	Average earnings/ starter	Leading earner	Earnings of leading earner
1	Flaxman Holdings Ltd.	25	13	5	20.0%	4	16.0%	$3,755,968	$150,239	Good Journey	$1,247,665
2	Juddmonte Farms	58	30	11	19.0%	7	12.1%	5,526,006	95,276	Beat Hollow (GB)	1,437,150
3	Orpendale	12	6	3	25.0%	3	25.0%	1,244,505	103,709	Ballingarry (Ire)	900,000
4	Sam-Son Farm	50	29	6	12.0%	5	10.0%	3,678,044	73,562	Portcullis	562,535
5	Phipps Stable	20	7	3	15.0%	3	15.0%	1,790,948	89,547	Storm Flag Flying	967,000
6	Dolphus C. Morrison	11	8	3	27.3%	1	9.1%	1,274,397	115,854	You	883,805
7	George Strawbridge Jr.	45	22	6	13.3%	4	8.9%	3,119,455	69,321	With Anticipation	1,507,700
8	Robert Spiegel	12	7	1	8.3%	1	8.3%	1,800,619	150,052	Milwaukee Brew	1,590,000
9	The Thoroughbred Corp.	38	25	6	15.8%	4	10.5%	2,545,546	66,988	Johar	582,215
10	Payson Stud	26	13	3	11.5%	2	7.7%	2,250,337	86,551	Farda Amiga	1,248,902
11	William Schettine	12	7	1	8.3%	1	8.3%	1,662,161	138,516	Take Charge Lady	1,388,635
12	Albert Fried Jr.	11	9	3	27.3%	2	18.2%	936,714	85,156	Affirmed Success	383,120
13	Taylor Made Farm	10	6	1	10.0%	1	10.0%	964,346	96,435	Repent	840,000
14	Edward P. Evans	122	66	12	9.8%	8	6.6%	6,115,347	50,126	Summer Colony	992,500
15	New Farm	13	9	4	30.8%	2	15.4%	916,342	70,488	D'wildcat	424,444
16	Mr. and Mrs. J. S. Moss	19	15	2	10.5%	2	10.5%	1,160,470	61,077	Kudos	468,735
17	Allen E. Paulson	139	82	12	8.6%	6	4.3%	7,011,714	50,444	Azeri	2,181,540
18	Mrs. Richard C. duPont	27	21	3	11.1%	2	7.4%	1,371,856	50,809	Shine Again	425,500
19	Timber Bay Farm	16	13	2	12.5%	1	6.3%	1,007,988	62,999	Sarava	665,040
20	Michael Edward Pegram	13	7	3	23.1%	1	7.7%	868,929	66,841	Icecoldbeeratreds	353,800
21	James Tafel	21	14	2	9.5%	2	9.5%	1,134,191	54,009	Softly	349,768
22	Dan Borislow	13	9	1	7.7%	1	7.7%	947,250	72,865	Toccet	755,610
23	Robert and Lawana Low	11	6	2	18.2%	2	18.2%	769,035	69,912	Green Fee	280,460
24	Sondra and Howard Bender	39	21	9	23.1%	1	2.6%	1,853,686	47,530	La Reine's Terms	320,680
25	Farfellow Farms	23	14	2	8.7%	1	4.4%	1,229,267	53,446	Buddha	489,600
26	Gainesway Thoroughbreds	44	21	2	4.6%	1	2.3%	2,448,343	55,644	Orientate	1,412,970
27	John Toffan & Trudy McCaffery	60	32	3	5.0%	2	3.3%	2,987,578	49,793	Came Home	1,624,500
28	Michael C. Byrne	34	24	4	11.8%		0.0%	1,780,143	52,357	Miss Crissy	212,160
29	Charles Nuckols Jr. & Sons	104	65	4	3.9%	1	1.0%	5,624,116	54,078	War Emblem	3,455,000
30	William Reed & Stonecrest Farm	16	10	1	6.3%	1	6.3%	945,032	59,065	Perfect Drift	695,120

Rank	Breeder	No. strs	No. wnrs	No. SWs	SWs/ strs	No. GSWs	GSWs/ strs	Total earnings	Average earnings/ starter	Leading earner	Earnings of leading earner
31	Beclawat Stable	21	12	3	14.3%	1	4.8%	$1,044,370	$49,732	True Direction	$228,620
32	Audley Farm	25	13	3	12.0%	1	4.0%	1,165,030	46,601	Mandy's Gold	715,404
33	Janis R. Whitham	20	12	1	5.0%	1	5.0%	1,080,669	54,033	Affluent	560,615
34	Herbert T. Schwartz	15	12	2	13.3%	1	6.7%	805,501	53,700	Critical Eye	229,071
35	Fox Ridge Farm	14	6	2	14.3%	2	14.3%	728,522	52,037	Riskaverse	461,160
36	North Wales LLC	12	7	2	16.7%	1	8.3%	680,921	56,743	Elloluv	242,700
37	Pin Oak Stud	65	37	5	7.7%	3	4.6%	2,533,094	38,971	See How She Runs	403,550
38	John and Barbara Smicklas	14	4	1	7.1%		0.0%	840,215	60,015	Momentum	526,888
39	Arthur B. Hancock III	74	41	7	9.5%	3	4.1%	2,616,906	35,364	Owsley	593,870
40	Cherokee Farms	14	9	3	21.4%	1	7.1%	685,230	48,945	Stormy Frolic	160,043
41	Hill 'n' Dale Farms	25	15	2	8.0%		0.0%	1,104,750	44,190	Steady Ruckus	263,129
42	Lance Robinson	26	15	3	11.5%	1	3.9%	1,035,850	39,840	Crafty Shaw	148,445
43	Sez Who Thoroughbreds	22	11	1	4.6%	1	4.6%	960,800	43,673	The Judge Sez Who	558,186
44	Sabine Stable	32	22	2	6.3%	2	6.3%	1,211,125	37,848	Nonsuch Bay	439,362
45	Wind Hill Farm	18	10	2	11.1%	2	11.1%	742,681	41,260	Starrer	310,000
46	Eaton Hall Farm	16	10	1	6.3%		0.0%	820,854	51,303	Buffalo Jump	224,820
47	William Sorokolit	20	10	1	5.0%	1	5.0%	848,643	42,432	Union Place	245,000
48	Stonerside Stable	66	43	6	9.1%	1	1.5%	2,306,751	34,951	Congaree	570,000
49	Darley Stud Management	10	5	1	10.0%	1	10.0%	540,895	54,090	Jilbab	319,300
50	Andrea Pollack RevocableTrust	10	4	2	20.0%		0.0%	586,296	58,630	Like a Hero	408,910
51	Moyglare Stud Farm	10	5	1	10.0%	1	10.0%	536,958	53,696	Dress To Thrill (Ire)	300,000
52	Lazy E Ranch.	33	22	2	6.1%	1	3.0%	1,200,680	36,384	Voodoo Dancer	562,638
53	The Aga Khans Studs S. C.	12	6	1	8.3%	1	8.3%	586,510	48,876	Nazirali (Ire)	158,400
54	Dr. and Mrs. R. Smiser West and Mr. and Mrs.Mackenzie Miller	16	9	2	12.5%	1	6.3%	668,582	41,786	Hero's Tribute	203,345
55	Gainsborough Stud Mgnt.	13	8	1	7.7%		0.0%	682,837	52,526	Nowrass (GB)	187,840
56	Dr. and Mrs. R. Smiser West	22	9	1	4.6%	1	4.6%	869,430	39,520	Kafwain	535,848
57	Adena Springs	280	150	11	3.9%	3	1.1%	9,360,102	33,429	Macho Uno	519,600
58	John W. Rooker	12	7	2	16.7%		0.0%	606,100	50,508	Bowman's Band	333,800
59	Centaur Farms	44	27	3	6.8%	1	2.3%	1,459,652	33,174	Classic Par	135,438
60	Prestonwood Farm	63	36	3	4.8%	2	3.2%	2,063,915	32,761	Regal Sanction	318,400
61	Asiel Stable	12	8	2	16.7%		0.0%	594,535	49,545	Chinkapin	218,888
62	James E. Day	20	14	2	10.0%		0.0%	801,176	40,059	Runaway Love	227,566
63	White Fox Farm	25	15	3	12.0%		0.0%	925,382	37,015	Extend	167,845
64	James T. Sabiston	18	14	1	5.6%		0.0%	770,463	42,804	High Flying Bid	148,819
65	Joanne H. Nor	11	7	1	9.1%	1	9.1%	524,825	47,711	Legislator	143,626
66	Double D Farm Corp.	68	34	2	2.9%	1	1.5%	2,324,296	34,181	Harlan's Holiday	1,606,000
67	Dark Hollow Farm	14	10	1	7.1%	1	7.1%	590,662	42,190	Sheila's Prospect	322,814
68	Bruno Schickedanz	38	24	1	2.6%	1	2.6%	1,325,625	34,885	Wake At Noon	463,011
69	Grousemont Farm	11	6	3	27.3%	2	18.2%	477,978	43,453	Nasty Storm	167,304
70	Gustav Schickedanz	41	13	3	7.3%	1	2.4%	1,315,855	32,094	Wando	362,377
71	Mockingbird Farm	327	236	6	1.8%		0.0%	10,876,022	33,260	Expected Flirt	208,495
72	Carolyn Sleeter	16	12	2	12.5%		0.0%	662,036	41,377	Summer Swing	129,000
73	Robert H. & Bea Roberts	94	62	6	6.4%	1	1.1%	2,951,716	31,401	Lady Shari	316,506
74	Joseph Allen	10	7	1	10.0%		0.0%	513,627	51,363	City Sharpster	148,180
75	Harris Farms Inc.	72	40	2	2.8%		0.0%	2,321,280	32,240	Super High	410,748
76	Landon Knight	17	10	1	5.9%	1	5.9%	634,932	37,349	Flat Top	237,831
77	Four Horsemen's Ranch	41	21	3	7.3%		0.0%	1,298,575	31,673	Thunderello	355,600
78	Lucy G. Bassett	15	5	1	6.7%	1	6.7%	571,144	38,076	Adoration	283,106
79	Kenneth & Sarah Ramsey	56	35	1	1.8%		0.0%	1,828,194	32,646	Private Lap	136,260
80	Brambly Lane Farm	13	10	1	7.7%		0.0%	550,396	42,338	Mountain Rage	179,736
81	Knob Hill Stable	34	17	1	2.9%		0.0%	1,113,570	32,752	Chopinina	292,280
82	Iron County Farms	35	18	2	5.7%	2	5.7%	1,056,107	30,174	Nuclear Debate	363,580
83	Ronald J. Whiting	19	13	1	5.3%	1	5.3%	653,708	34,406	Texas Glitter	313,408
84	J. V. Shields Jr.	24	14		0.0%		0.0%	876,338	36,514	Puzzlement	157,140
85	Robert E. Meyerhoff	45	29	1	2.2%		0.0%	1,427,454	31,721	Rosthern	177,966
86	Gallagher's Stud	21	15	2	9.5%		0.0%	705,509	33,596	Quiet Ruler	165,540
87	William Harris	18	11	1	5.6%		0.0%	667,771	37,098	Deer Run	262,220
88	La Quebrada	26	12	2	7.7%	2	7.7%	800,296	30,781	Avanzado (Arg)	229,125
89	Meadowbrook Farms	38	22	3	7.9%	1	2.6%	1,106,099	29,108	Ladies Din	285,600
90	Liberation Farm & Oratis T'breds.	25	17	2	8.0%		0.0%	802,752	32,110	Crafty Guy	167,100
91	Minshall Farms	43	21	1	2.3%		0.0%	1,339,056	31,141	Snake Pit	124,905
92	SLU Inc.	36	23	3	8.3%		0.0%	1,081,144	30,032	Bold Mango	144,155
93	CBF Corp.	25	14	2	8.0%		0.0%	798,587	31,943	Pretty Brassy	140,280
94	Josham Farms	11	8	2	18.2%		0.0%	458,381	41,671	Santerra	205,966
95	A. B. Hancock III & Stonerside	12	3	1	8.3%	1	8.3%	453,705	37,809	E Dubai	315,000
96	Windwoods Farm	11	7	1	9.1%		0.0%	462,163	42,015	Windsor Castle	167,275
97	Calumet Farm	51	32	4	7.8%	1	2.0%	1,392,892	27,312	Julie Jalouse	179,117
98	Kinsman Farm	46	30	3	6.5%		0.0%	1,323,502	28,772	Blue Burner	256,100
99	Gulf Coast Farms Bloodstock	26	11	1	3.9%	1	3.9%	806,372	31,014	Added Edge	250,328
100	Mt. Brilliant Farm	33	12	1	3.0%	1	3.0%	986,749	29,901	Snow Ridge	399,990

Leading Breeders by Earnings in 2002

Breeder	No. strs	No. wnrs	Total earnings
Mockingbird Farm	327	236	$10,876,022
Adena Springs	280	150	9,360,102
Farnsworth Farms	398	237	8,420,666
John Franks	378	201	8,296,050
Allen E. Paulson	139	82	7,011,714
Edward P. Evans	122	66	6,115,347
Mr. and Mrs. John Mabee	253	132	5,728,206
Charles Nuckols Jr. & Sons	104	65	5,624,116
Juddmonte Farms	58	30	5,526,006
Brereton C. Jones	254	131	4,222,359
Harry T. Mangurian	148	86	3,812,915
Flaxman Holdings Ltd.	25	13	3,755,968
Sam-Son Farm	50	29	3,678,110
Overbrook Farm	126	65	3,342,120
George Strawbridge Jr.	45	22	3,119,455
John Toffan and Trudy McCaffery	60	32	2,987,578
Robert and Bea Roberts	94	62	2,951,716
Arthur I. Appleton	130	79	2,904,785
Arthur B. Hancock III	74	41	2,616,906
Dr. D. W. Frazier	115	77	2,578,613
The Thoroughbred Corp.	38	25	2,545,546
Pin Oak Stud	65	37	2,533,094
Gilbert G. Campbell	124	69	2,508,192
Gainesway Thoroughbreds	44	21	2,448,343
Double D Farm Corp.	68	34	2,324,296
Harris Farms	72	40	2,321,280
Stonerside Stable	66	43	2,306,751
Live Oak Stud	88	42	2,282,790
Payson Stud	26	13	2,250,337
J D Farms	100	54	2,234,867
Prestonwood Farm	63	36	2,063,915
Mr. and Mrs. Martin Wygod	99	54	1,993,238
Everest Stables	89	51	1,989,691
Sondra and Howard Bender	39	21	1,853,686
Kenneth and Sarah Ramsey	56	35	1,828,194
Robert Spiegel	12	7	1,800,619
Phipps Stable	20	7	1,790,948
Michael C. Byrne	34	24	1,780,143
William Schettine	12	7	1,662,191
Hill 'n' Dale Farm	72	35	1,573,072
Donald R. Dizney	74	49	1,476,686
Centaur Farms	44	27	1,459,652
Robert E. Meyerhoff	45	29	1,427,454
Calumet Farm	51	32	1,392,892
Mrs. Richard C. duPont	27	21	1,371,856
Ocala Stud Farm	66	39	1,339,136
Minshall Farms	43	21	1,339,056
Claiborne Farm	58	27	1,326,021

Breeder	No. strs	No. wnrs	Average earnings per starter
Payson Stud	26	13	$86,551
Albert Fried Jr.	11	9	85,156
Sam-Son Farm	50	29	73,562
Dan Borislow	13	9	72,865
New Farm	13	9	70,488
Robert and Lawana Low	11	6	69,912
George Strawbridge Jr.	45	22	69,321
The Thoroughbred Corp.	38	25	66,988
Michael Edward Pegram	13	7	66,841
Timber Bay Farm	16	13	62,999
Mr. and Mrs. J. S. Moss	19	15	61,077
John and Barbara Smicklas	14	5	60,015
William Reed & Stonecrest Farm	16	10	59,065
Andrea Pollack RevocableTrust	10	4	58,630
North Wales LLC	12	7	56,743
Gainesway Thoroughbreds	44	21	55,644
Darley Stud Management	10	5	54,090
Charles Nuckols Jr. & Sons	104	65	54,078
Janis R. Whitham	20	12	54,033
James Tafel	21	14	54,009
Herbert T. Schwartz	15	12	53,700
Moyglare Stud Farm	10	5	53,696
Farfellow Farms	23	14	53,446
Gainsborough Stud Mgmt.	13	8	52,526
Michael C. Byrne	34	24	52,357
Fox Ridge Farm	14	6	52,037
Joseph Allen	10	7	51,363
Eaton Hall Farm	16	10	51,303
Mrs. Richard C. duPont	27	21	50,809

Leading Breeders by Number of Stakes Winners in 2002

Breeder	No. strs	No. wnrs	No. SWs
Allen E. Paulson	139	82	12
Edward P. Evans	122	66	12
Adena Springs	280	150	11
Juddmonte Farms	58	30	11
Farnsworth Farms	398	237	11
John Franks	378	201	9
Sondra and Howard M. Bender	39	21	9
Arthur B. Hancock III	74	41	7
Mr. and Mrs. John C. Mabee	253	132	7
Billingsley Creek Ranch	38	24	6
Mockingbird Farm	327	236	6
Robert H. & Bea Roberts	94	62	6
Sam-Son Farm	50	29	6
Stonerside Stable	66	43	6
The Thoroughbred Corp.	38	25	6
George Strawbridge Jr.	45	22	6
Triple AAA Ranch	60	39	6
Brereton C. Jones	254	131	5
Mr. and Mrs. Martin J. Wygod	99	54	5
Overbrook Farm	126	65	5
Pin Oak Stud	65	37	5
Dr. D. W. Frazier	115	77	5
Flaxman Holdings Ltd.	25	13	5
Calumet Farm	51	32	4
Charles Nuckols Jr. & Sons	104	65	4
Michael C. Byrne	34	24	4
New Farm	13	9	4
Foxwood Plantation	45	26	4
Willard Burbach	20	9	4
William F. and Annabel Murphy	15	8	4

Leading Breeders by Average Earnings per Starter in 2002

(Minimum of 10 starters)

Breeder	No. strs	No. wnrs	Average earnings per starter
Flaxman Holdings Ltd.	25	13	$150,239
Robert Spiegel	12	7	150,052
William Schettine	12	7	138,516
Dolphus C. Morrison	11	8	115,854
Orpendale	12	6	103,709
Taylor Made Farm	10	6	96,435
Juddmonte Farms	58	30	95,276
Phipps Stable	20	7	89,547

Breeder	No. strs	No. wnrs	No. SWs
Albert Fried Jr.	11	9	3
Arthur I. Appleton	130	79	3
Audley Farm	25	13	3
Beclawat Stable	21	12	3
Brylynn Farm	40	19	3
Centaur Farms	44	27	3
Cherokee Farms	14	9	3
Claiborne Farm	58	27	3
Lance Robinson	26	15	3
Live Oak Stud	88	42	3
Marshall Naify Revocable Trust	45	16	3
Marvin Malmuth	20	10	3
McDowell Farm	58	25	3
Meadowbrook Farms	38	22	3
Michael Edward Pegram	13	7	3
Mrs. Richard C. duPont	27	21	3
Orpendale	12	6	3
Patricia Generazio	42	25	3
Harry T. Mangurian	148	86	3
Herb Riecken	21	15	3

Breeder	No. strs	No. wnrs	No. GSWs	GSWs/ strs
Brylynn Farm	40	19	1	2.5%
Calumet Farm	51	32	1	2.0%
Canyon Farms	22	13	1	4.6%
Casey Seaman	34	21	1	2.9%
Centaur Farms	44	27	1	2.3%
C. E. S. Racing	16	9	1	6.3%
Charles Nuckols Jr. & Sons	104	65	1	1.0%
Cherokee Farms	14	9	1	7.1%
Claiborne Farm	58	27	1	1.7%
Dan Borislow	13	9	1	7.7%
Dark Hollow Farm	14	10	1	7.1%

Leading Breeders by Number of Wins in 2002

Breeder	No. strs	No. wnrs	No. wins
Mockingbird Farm	327	236	479
Farnsworth Farms	398	237	452
John Franks	378	201	371
Mr. and Mrs. John C. Mabee	253	132	245
Adena Springs	280	150	237
Brereton C. Jones	254	131	228
Harry T. Mangurian	148	86	175
Allen E. Paulson	139	82	151
Dr. D. W. Frazier	115	77	148
Arthur I. Appleton	130	79	141
Edward P. Evans	122	66	131
Charles Nuckols Jr. & Sons	104	65	117
Robert and Bea Roberts	94	62	113
Gilbert G. Campbell	124	69	112
Overbrook Farm	126	65	111
J D Farms	100	54	95
Mr. and Mrs. Martin J. Wygod	99	54	92
Harris Farms	72	40	89
Everest Stables	89	51	83
Stonerside Stable	66	43	82
Donald R. Dizney	74	49	82
Arthur B. Hancock III	74	41	76
Live Oak Stud	88	42	75
Ocala Stud Farm	66	39	72
Triple AAA Ranch	60	39	72
Kenneth and Sarah Ramsey	56	35	71
J. Adcock	101	44	70
Pin Oak Stud	65	37	70
Mr. & Mrs. R. J. Bennett	60	35	67
Highland Farms	69	34	67
Hargus & Sandra Sexton	68	37	65
Stanley Ersoff	69	40	65
Foxwood Plantation	45	26	63
Hidden Point Farm	56	30	62
Foxfield	60	36	61
Mr. and Mrs. Guy C. Roberts	49	28	60
Prestonwood Farm	63	36	60
Ron Gomez	67	32	59
Glen Hill Farm	54	34	59
John Toffan and Trudy McCaffery	60	32	58
Robert E. Meyerhoff	45	29	58
Hill 'n' Dale Farm	72	35	57
Sam-Son Farm	50	29	57
Bruno Schickedanz	38	24	56
Centaur Farms	44	27	56
Calumet Farm	51	32	55
McDowell Farm	58	25	54
Hart Farm	55	29	54

Leading Breeders by Number of Graded Stakes Winners in 2002

Breeder	No. strs	No. wnrs	No. GSWs	GSWs/ strs
Edward P. Evans	122	66	8	6.6%
Juddmonte Farms	58	30	7	12.1%
Allen E. Paulson	139	82	6	4.3%
Sam-Son Farm	50	29	5	10.0%
The Thoroughbred Corp.	38	25	4	10.5%
Flaxman Holdings Ltd.	25	13	4	16.0%
George Strawbridge Jr.	45	22	4	8.9%
Adena Springs	280	150	3	1.1%
Arthur B. Hancock III	74	41	3	4.1%
Orpendale	12	6	3	25.0%
Overbrook Farm	126	65	3	2.4%
John Franks	378	201	3	0.8%
Phipps Stable	20	7	3	15.0%
Pin Oak Stud	65	37	3	4.6%
Albert Fried Jr.	11	9	2	18.2%
La Quebrada	26	12	2	7.7%
Mr. and Mrs. John Mabee	253	132	2	0.8%
Mr. and Mrs. J. S. Moss	19	15	2	10.5%
Mrs. Richard C. duPont	27	21	2	7.4%
New Farm	13	9	2	15.4%
Iron County Farms	35	18	2	5.7%
James Tafel	21	14	2	9.5%
John Toffan & Trudy McCaffery	60	32	2	3.3%
Payson Stud	26	13	2	7.7%
Prestonwood Farm	63	36	2	3.2%
Robert & Lawana Low	11	6	2	18.2%
Sabine Stable	32	22	2	6.3%
Dennis Drazin	21	8	2	9.5%
Dr. D. W. Frazier	115	77	2	1.7%
Fox Ridge Farm	14	6	2	14.3%
Grousemont Farm	11	6	2	18.2%
William Lussky	37	22	2	5.4%
Wind Hill Farm	18	10	2	11.1%
A. B. Hancock III & Stonerside	12	3	1	8.3%
Arthur I. Appleton	130	79	1	0.8%
Audley Farm	25	13	1	4.0%
Beclawat Stable	21	12	1	4.8%
Brereton C. Jones	254	131	1	0.4%
Bruno Schickedanz	38	24	1	2.6%

Leading Trainers of 2002

Robert Frankel is beginning to make a habit of ranking atop the THOROUGHBRED TIMES listing of leading trainers. For the second consecutive year, he ranked first in the THOROUGHBRED TIMES rankings based on four criteria, three of which emphasize quality over quantity. The criteria are total purses, average earnings per starter, percentage of stakes winners from starters, and percentage of graded stakes winners from starters.

By any measure, the Racing Hall of Fame trainer had a fantastic season. In terms of quantity, his runners earned $17,748,340, less than $100,000 short of D. Wayne Lukas's record set in 1988. Frankel achieved his numbers with 480 starts, while Lukas had 1,500 starts in his record-setting season. In 2001, Frankel finally broke through with his first Breeders' Cup win when Squirtle Squirt upset the Breeders' Cup Sprint (G1) and subsequently was voted champion sprinter. In 2002, he owned and trained Starine (Fr), winner of the Breeders' Cup Filly and Mare Turf (G1). He also trained Edmund Gann's Medaglia d'Oro, a top three-year-old, and several graded stakes winners for Juddmonte Farms, his principal client.

Rich opportunities in the Breeders' Cup and other major races attract overseas interest, and the respective second- and third-leading trainers were Saeed bin Suroor of Godolphin Racing and Aidan O'Brien, who trains primarily for Ireland's Coolmore operation and its clients. O'Brien trained High Chaparral (Ire), the Breeders' Cup Turf (G1) winner, and Rock of Gibraltar (Ire), the European champion who finished second in the Breeders' Cup Mile (G1). Making the most of a relatively small stable was California-based Laura de Seroux, who trained 2002 Horse of the Year Azeri and other stakes winners for the Allen E. Paulson Living Trust.

In terms of sheer numbers, the leading trainer of 2002 by wins was Steve Asmussen, who had 407 victories to edge Scott Lake, who had 399 wins. Lake had been the 2001 leader with 406 wins.

Leading Trainers by Year
(Worldwide Purses)

Year	Name	Wins	Purses
2002	Robert Frankel	117	$17,748,340
2001	Bob Baffert	138	16,354,996
2000	Bob Baffert	146	11,831,605
1999	Bob Baffert	169	16,934,607
1998	Bob Baffert	139	15,000,870
1997	D. Wayne Lukas	175	10,351,397
1996	D. Wayne Lukas	192	14,967,608
1995	D. Wayne Lukas	194	12,842,865
1994	D. Wayne Lukas	147	9,247,457
1993	Robert Frankel	79	8,933,252
1992	D. Wayne Lukas	230	9,806,436
1991	D. Wayne Lukas	289	15,942,223
1990	D. Wayne Lukas	267	14,511,690
1989	D. Wayne Lukas	305	16,103,998

THOROUGHBRED TIMES Leading Trainers of 2002

Rankings based on formula that gives equal weighting to four statistical categories for performance in 2002: 1) total purses; 2) average earnings per starter; 3) percent stakes winners from starters; and 4) percent graded stakes winners from starters. A minimum of ten starters required to be considered for inclusion. Statistics are for North America only and for racing in 2002.

Rank	Trainer	No. strs	No. wnrs	No. SWs	SWs/ strs	No. GSWs	GSWs/ strs	Total purses	Average earnings/ starter	Leading earner	Earnings of leading earner
1	Robert J. Frankel	121	66	31	25.6%	23	19.0%	$17,748,340	$146,680	Medaglia d'Oro	$2,245,000
2	Saeed bin Suroor	26	10	6	23.1%	6	23.1%	3,352,275	128,934	Imperial Gesture	873,600
3	Aidan P. O'Brien	10	3	3	30.0%	3	30.0%	2,894,200	289,420	High Chaparral (Ire)	1,258,400
4	Laura de Seroux	41	14	6	14.6%	4	9.8%	3,894,900	94,998	Azeri	2,181,540
5	Mark R. Frostad	52	24	7	13.5%	6	11.5%	4,062,163	78,119	Portcullis	562,535
6	Wallace A. Dollase	22	15	4	18.2%	4	18.2%	2,647,045	120,320	Good Journey	1,247,665
7	James A. Jerkens	46	28	9	19.6%	5	10.9%	3,063,904	66,607	Regal Sanction	318,400
8	Bob Baffert	175	82	17	9.7%	11	6.3%	12,029,115	68,738	War Emblem	3,125,000
9	Claude McGaughey III	69	33	8	11.6%	6	8.7%	3,852,648	55,835	Storm Flag Flying	967,000
10	Neil D. Drysdale	62	19	7	11.3%	5	8.1%	3,752,896	60,531	Sarafan	1,089,252
11	Richard E. Mandella	75	29	8	10.7%	5	6.7%	4,442,267	59,230	The Tin Man	598,020
12	John T. Ward Jr.	30	15	5	16.7%	4	13.3%	2,033,377	67,779	Booklet	425,760
13	Todd A. Pletcher	191	94	24	12.6%	12	6.3%	8,702,228	45,561	Left Bank	626,146
14	Mark A. Hennig	112	47	12	10.7%	7	6.3%	5,814,441	51,915	Summer Colony	992,500
15	Christophe Clement	119	52	16	13.5%	8	6.7%	4,853,898	40,789	Voodoo Dancer	562,638
16	Kenneth G. McPeek	116	49	9	7.8%	6	5.2%	6,647,289	57,304	Take Charge Lady	1,388,635
17	D. Wayne Lukas	120	50	10	8.3%	6	5.0%	5,996,362	49,970	Orientate	1,412,970
18	Niall M. O'Callaghan	70	25	8	11.4%	4	5.7%	3,343,187	47,760	Wiseman's Ferry	766,552
19	W. Elliott Walden	102	55	11	10.8%	5	4.9%	4,087,995	40,078	Mr. John	325,382
20	H. James Bond	68	27	7	10.3%	4	5.9%	3,129,813	46,027	Buddha	489,600
21	William I. Mott	183	91	17	9.3%	8	4.4%	7,521,998	41,104	Orchard Park	613,310
22	Randy Schulhofer	35	17	3	8.6%	3	8.6%	2,060,744	58,878	Owsley	593,870
23	Juan "Paco" Gonzalez	31	9	2	6.5%	2	6.5%	2,355,016	75,968	Came Home	1,624,500
24	Ben D. A. Cecil	17	6	2	11.8%	2	11.8%	1,408,354	82,844	Golden Apples (Ire)	1,111,680

Rank	Trainer	No. strs	No. wnrs	No. SWs	SWs/strs	No. GSWs	GSWs/strs	Total purses	Average earnings/starter	Leading earner	Earnings of leading earner
25	Paulo H. Lobo	14	2	2	14.3%	1	7.1%	$1,376,423	98,316	Farda Amiga	$1,248,902
26	Darrell Vienna	86	30	7	8.1%	6	7.0%	3,312,442	38,517	Disturbingthepeace	452,640
27	Frank A. Alexander	31	16	4	12.9%	2	6.5%	1,703,084	54,938	Nonsuch Bay	439,362
28	H. Allen Jerkens	63	33	5	7.9%	3	4.8%	2,911,503	46,214	Shine Again	425,500
29	Patrick J. Kelly	38	6	2	5.3%	2	5.3%	2,441,141	64,241	Evening Attire	1,332,720
30	Carl A. Nafzger	69	33	4	5.8%	4	5.8%	3,239,876	46,955	Softly	349,768
31	Ronald L. McAnally	80	29	5	6.3%	4	5.0%	3,339,144	41,739	Affluent	560,615
32	Bruce Headley	48	24	3	6.3%	3	6.3%	2,273,578	47,366	Kalookan Queen	560,640
33	Roger L. Attfield	88	36	6	6.8%	1	1.1%	4,566,453	51,892	Perfect Soul (Ire)	280,020
34	John A. Ross	33	16	5	15.2%		0.0%	2,056,360	62,314	Shaws Creek	250,643
35	Robert P. Tiller	58	33	4	6.9%		0.0%	3,627,594	62,545	Cheap Talk	381,404
36	Kiaran P. McLaughlin	29	18	3	10.3%	2	6.9%	1,435,872	49,513	Abreeze	194,765
37	John A. Shirreffs	46	19	4	8.7%	3	6.5%	1,834,772	39,886	Calkins Road	374,100
38	Steven B. Flint	30	17	4	13.3%	1	3.3%	1,481,138	49,371	Allamerican Bertie	619,235
39	Neil J. Howard	34	19	3	8.8%	2	5.9%	1,533,260	45,096	Parade Leader	459,503
40	Craig Dollase	61	23	3	4.9%	2	3.3%	2,772,786	45,456	Momentum	526,888
41	Lawrence E. Murray	31	14	7	22.6%	1	3.2%	1,362,723	43,959	La Reine's Terms	320,680
42	Philip G. Johnson	38	17	1	2.6%	1	2.6%	3,268,350	86,009	Volponi	2,389,200
43	Milton W. Wolfson	23	13	3	13.0%	1	4.4%	1,239,738	53,902	The Judge Sez Who	558,186
44	Donnie K. Von Hemel	77	50	9	11.7%	3	3.9%	2,245,045	29,156	See How She Runs	403,550
45	Jonathan E. Sheppard	109	38	5	4.6%	4	3.7%	3,664,250	33,617	With Anticipation	1,507,700
46	Anthony W. Dutrow	75	53	12	16.0%	1	1.3%	2,296,689	30,623	Elegant Designer	238,200
47	James Mort Hardy	14	6	2	14.3%	1	7.1%	942,274	67,305	Anglian Prince	410,112
48	Warren Stute	37	18	5	13.5%	2	5.4%	1,261,973	34,107	Grey Memo	208,000
49	Jenine Sahadi	65	21	7	10.8%	3	4.6%	1,885,523	29,008	Delta Form (Aus)	274,980
50	Vito Armata	64	36	2	3.1%	1	1.6%	2,944,149	46,002	T J's Lucky Moon	644,212
51	Ian P. D. Jory	48	15	3	6.3%	2	4.2%	1,682,826	35,059	Continental Red	540,000
52	David Cotey	30	15	2	6.7%	1	3.3%	1,348,998	44,967	Lady Shari	316,506
53	John C. Kimmel	117	57	6	5.1%	2	1.7%	3,645,501	31,158	Marasca	179,740
54	Richard A. Violette Jr.	38	14	3	7.9%	3	7.9%	1,288,549	33,909	Man From Wicklow	247,865
55	Patrick L. Biancone	26	11	3	11.5%	3	11.5%	1,023,969	39,383	Whywhywhy	284,060
56	Ralph Ziadie	64	32	4	6.3%	1	1.6%	2,136,424	33,382	Trust N Luck	382,800
57	Abraham R. Katryan	64	35	2	3.1%	1	1.6%	2,552,178	39,878	Wake At Noon	463,011
58	Malcolm Pierce	46	25	2	4.4%		0.0%	2,030,046	44,131	Hot Talent	328,600
59	Lorne Richards	20	11	1	5.0%	1	5.0%	1,133,598	56,680	Sheila's Prospect	322,814
60	Audre Cappuccitti	57	23	3	5.3%	2	3.5%	1,831,054	32,124	El Prado Essence	254,932
61	C. Beau Greely	29	7	3	10.3%	2	6.9%	1,054,433	36,360	Like a Hero	408,910
62	H. Graham Motion	97	40	6	6.2%	2	2.1%	2,771,173	28,569	Your Out	269,850
63	Paul J. McGee	70	38	6	8.6%	2	2.9%	1,925,171	27,502	Colonial Glitter	195,205
64	Rita A. Schnitzler	24	14	2	8.3%		0.0%	1,207,963	50,332	Sambuca On Ice	249,965
65	Sid C. Attard	56	31	1	1.8%	1	1.8%	2,437,291	43,523	Ginger Gold	466,250
66	Michael E. Gorham	58	26	3	5.2%	1	1.7%	1,898,928	32,740	Mandy's Gold	715,404
67	Michael W. Dickinson	64	30	5	7.8%	2	3.1%	1,807,988	28,250	Cetewayo	443,375
68	Macdonald Benson	27	10	2	7.4%		0.0%	1,264,338	46,827	Mountain Orchid	206,154
69	Josie Carroll	58	24	3	5.2%		0.0%	1,977,616	34,097	Handpainted	256,210
70	Frank R. Springer	16	11	3	18.8%	1	6.3%	773,775	48,361	War Emblem	330,000
71	David R. Bell	69	19	2	2.9%		0.0%	2,453,234	35,554	Silver Nithi	432,153
72	Gene A. Cilio	70	31	5	7.1%	1	1.4%	2,004,836	28,640	Lakenheath	219,817
73	John E. Salzman	51	27	4	7.8%	1	2.0%	1,519,387	29,792	Xtra Heat	765,485
74	Joseph F. Orseno	53	19	3	5.7%	2	3.8%	1,549,571	29,237	Macho Uno	519,600
75	Nicholas P. Zito	118	55	3	2.5%		0.0%	3,713,208	31,468	Nothing Flat	345,900
76	Scott M. Schwartz	20	12	1	5.0%	1	5.0%	993,276	49,664	Critical Eye	229,071
77	Steven M. Asmussen	415	244	29	7.0%	4	1.0%	10,246,910	24,691	Easyfromthegitgo	606,905
78	David E. Hofmans	55	16	5	9.1%	2	3.6%	1,493,886	27,162	Adoration	283,106
79	Michael R. Matz	55	23	3	5.5%	2	3.6%	1,587,524	28,864	Bowman's Band	333,800
80	Richard E. Dutrow Jr.	144	72	6	4.2%	1	0.7%	4,060,544	28,198	Carson Hollow	335,370
81	George R. Arnold II	58	24	4	6.9%		0.0%	1,775,316	30,609	Belle Artiste	177,378
82	Patrick B. Byrne	45	20	4	8.9%	2	4.4%	1,272,839	28,285	Pass Rush	199,540
83	Eduardo Inda	32	11	3	9.4%		0.0%	1,178,537	36,829	Kela	139,600
84	John Cardella	32	16	1	3.1%	1	3.1%	1,274,300	39,822	Lil Personalitee	253,181
85	Dallas Stewart	95	34	4	4.2%	1	1.1%	2,685,946	28,273	Dollar Bill	496,850
86	Bruce N. Levine	84	42	2	2.4%	2	2.4%	2,389,730	28,449	Jester Rahab	207,470
87	Timothy F. Ritchey	103	51	7	6.8%		0.0%	2,621,473	25,451	Docent	327,974
88	James J. Toner	34	14	1	2.9%	1	2.9%	1,242,270	36,537	Wonder Again	323,840
89	Timothy A. Hills	82	48	5	6.1%		0.0%	2,183,529	26,628	Joe's Son Joey	143,450
90	Mark E. Casse	150	56	4	2.7%	1	0.7%	4,055,134	27,034	Added Edge	250,328
91	Doug O'Neill	133	60	6	4.5%	3	2.3%	3,245,798	24,404	Sky Jack	556,900
92	Rafael Becerra	42	18	4	9.5%	2	4.8%	1,126,414	26,819	Crackup	274,828
93	Ted H. West	38	18	2	5.3%		0.0%	1,268,968	33,394	Easy Grades	284,705
94	Benjamin Perkins Jr.	64	27	6	9.4%	1	1.6%	1,587,237	24,801	Wild Snitch	119,200
95	Rodney Jenkins	65	36	5	7.7%	1	1.5%	1,638,557	25,209	Willa On the Move	197,550

Leading Trainers by Earnings in 2002

Trainer	No. strs	No. wnrs	Total purses
Robert J. Frankel	121	66	$17,748,340
Bob Baffert	175	82	12,029,115
Steven M. Asmussen	415	244	10,246,910
Todd A. Pletcher	191	94	8,702,228
Scott A. Lake	446	228	8,292,547
William I. Mott	183	91	7,521,998
Kenneth G. McPeek	116	49	6,647,289
D. Wayne Lukas	120	50	5,996,362
Jerry Hollendorfer	274	161	5,909,710
Mark A. Hennig	112	47	5,814,441
Christophe Clement	119	52	4,853,898
Roger L. Attfield	88	36	4,566,453
Richard E. Mandella	75	29	4,442,267
Cole Norman	247	157	4,394,860
W. Elliott Walden	102	55	4,087,995
Mark R. Frostad	52	24	4,062,163
Richard E. Dutrow Jr.	144	72	4,060,544
Mark E. Casse	150	56	4,055,134
Laura de Seroux	41	14	3,894,906
Claude R. McGaughey III	69	33	3,852,648
Allen Iwinski	170	90	3,759,817
Neil D. Drysdale	62	19	3,752,896
Nicholas P. Zito	118	55	3,713,208
Jonathan E. Sheppard	109	38	3,664,250
John C. Kimmel	117	57	3,645,501
Robert P. Tiller	58	33	3,627,594
Thomas M. Amoss	151	80	3,611,011
Dale Capuano	215	118	3,569,335
Gary C. Contessa	170	76	3,524,675
Saeed bin Suroor	26	10	3,352,275
Niall M. O'Callaghan	70	25	3,343,187
Ronald L. McAnally	80	29	3,339,144
Darrell Vienna	86	30	3,312,442
Philip G. Johnson	38	17	3,268,350
Mark Shuman	200	73	3,262,725
Doug O'Neill	133	60	3,245,798
Carl A. Nafzger	69	33	3,239,876
H. James Bond	68	27	3,129,813
James A. Jerkens	46	28	3,063,904
Bernard S. Flint	124	70	2,948,950
Vito Armata	64	36	2,944,149
H. Allen Jerkens	63	33	2,911,503
Aidan P. O'Brien	10	3	2,894,200
Dale L. Romans	116	53	2,874,012
Craig Dollase	61	23	2,772,786

Leading Trainers by Average Earnings per Starter in 2002
(Minimum of 10 starters)

Trainer	No. strs	No. wnrs	Average earnings per starter
Aidan P. O'Brien	10	3	$289,420
Robert J. Frankel	121	66	146,680
Saeed bin Suroor	26	10	128,934
Wallace A. Dollase	22	15	120,320
Paulo H. Lobo	14	2	98,316
Laura de Seroux	41	14	94,998
Philip G. Johnson	38	17	86,009
Ben D. A. Cecil	17	6	82,844
Mark R. Frostad	52	24	78,119
Juan Paco Gonzalez	31	9	75,968
Bob Baffert	175	82	68,738
John T. Ward Jr.	30	15	67,779

Trainer	No. strs	No. wnrs	Average earnings per starter
James Mort Hardy	14	6	$67,305
James A. Jerkens	46	28	66,607
Patrick J. Kelly	38	6	64,241
Robert P. Tiller	58	33	62,545
John A. Ross	33	16	62,314
Neil D. Drysdale	62	19	60,531
Richard E. Mandella	75	29	59,230
Randy Schulhofer	35	17	58,878
Kenneth G. McPeek	116	49	57,304
Lorne Richards	20	11	56,680
Claude R. McGaughey III	69	33	55,835
William L. Currin	11	3	54,959
Frank A. Alexander	31	16	54,938
Milton W. Wolfson	23	13	53,902
Mark A. Hennig	112	47	51,915
Roger L. Attfield	88	36	51,892
Rita A. Schnitzler	24	14	50,332
D. Wayne Lukas	120	50	49,970
Scott M. Schwartz	20	12	49,664
Kiaran P. McLaughlin	29	18	49,513
Steven B. Flint	30	17	49,371
Frank R. Springer	16	11	48,361
Niall M. O'Callaghan	70	25	47,760
Bruce Headley	48	24	47,366
Carl A. Nafzger	69	33	46,955

Leading Trainers by Percent Stakes Winners from Starters
(Ten or More Starters)

Trainer	No. strs	No. wnrs	No. SWs	SWs/ strs
Aidan P. O'Brien	10	3	3	30.0%
Fred Costa	11	7	3	27.3%
Robert J. Frankel	121	66	31	25.6%
Saeed bin Suroor	26	10	6	23.1%
Lawrence E. Murray	31	14	7	22.6%
Johnie L. Jamison	33	15	7	21.2%
Todd W. Fincher	24	16	5	20.8%
John A. Casey	10	6	2	20.0%
Gene Starlin	10	8	2	20.0%
Robert J. Anderson	25	18	5	20.0%
Thomas A. Dodds	15	8	3	20.0%
Ron David	10	3	2	20.0%
James A. Jerkens	46	28	9	19.6%
Frank R. Springer	16	11	3	18.8%
Joseph E. Johnson	11	7	2	18.2%
Wallace A. Dollase	22	15	4	18.2%
Margaret Root	11	8	2	18.2%
Hubert Pilon	11	6	2	18.2%
William L. Currin	11	3	2	18.2%

Leading Trainers by Number of Stakes Winners in 2002

Trainer	No. strs	No. wnrs	No. SWs
Robert J. Frankel	121	66	31
Steven M. Asmussen	415	244	29
Todd A. Pletcher	191	94	24
Cole Norman	247	157	17
Bob Baffert	175	82	17
William I. Mott	183	91	17
Christophe Clement	119	52	16
Mark A. Hennig	112	47	12
Jerry Hollendorfer	274	161	12

Trainer	No. strs	No. wnrs	No. SWs
Anthony W. Dutrow	75	53	12
W. Elliott Walden	102	55	11
D. Wayne Lukas	120	50	10
Kenneth G. McPeek	116	49	9
Donnie K. Von Hemel	77	50	9
James A. Jerkens	46	28	9
Scott A. Lake	446	228	8
Niall M. O'Callaghan	70	25	8
Jeff Bonde	96	43	8
Richard E. Mandella	75	29	8
Claude R. McGaughey III	69	33	8
Bernard S. Flint	124	70	8
Neil D. Drysdale	62	19	7
H. James Bond	68	27	7
Lawrence E. Murray	31	14	7
Darrell Vienna	86	30	7
Martin D. Wolfson	51	21	7
Keith Bennett	49	36	7
Mark R. Frostad	52	24	7
Kenneth Gleason	52	26	7
Timothy F. Ritchey	103	51	7
Jenine Sahadi	65	21	7
Johnie L. Jamison	33	15	7
Saeed bin Suroor	26	10	6
Richard E. Dutrow Jr.	144	72	6
Laura de Seroux	41	14	6
H. Graham Motion	97	40	6
Paul J. McGee	70	38	6
Benjamin W. Perkins Jr.	64	27	6
Roger L. Attfield	88	36	6
Joel H. Marr	51	26	6
Thomas M. Amoss	151	80	6
Gerald S. Bennett	57	35	6
John C. Kimmel	117	57	6
Doug O'Neill	133	60	6
Emanuel Tortora	82	44	6

Leading Trainers by Number of Graded Stakes Winners in 2002

Trainer	No. strs	No. wnrs	No. GSWs	GSWs/ strs
Robert J. Frankel	121	66	23	19.0%
Todd A. Pletcher	191	94	12	6.3%
Bob Baffert	175	82	11	6.3%
William I. Mott	183	91	8	4.4%
Christophe Clement	119	52	8	6.7%
Mark A. Hennig	112	47	7	6.3%
Saeed bin Suroor	26	10	6	23.1%
Mark R. Frostad	52	24	6	11.5%
Claude R. McGaughey III	69	33	6	8.7%
Kenneth G. McPeek	116	49	6	5.2%
D. Wayne Lukas	120	50	6	5.0%
Darrell Vienna	86	30	6	7.0%
W. Elliott Walden	102	55	5	4.9%
Richard E. Mandella	75	29	5	6.7%
Neil D. Drysdale	62	19	5	8.1%
James A. Jerkens	46	28	5	10.9%
Laura de Seroux	41	14	4	9.8%
Steven M. Asmussen	415	244	4	1.0%
Ronald L. McAnally	80	29	4	5.0%
Wallace A. Dollase	22	15	4	18.2%
H. James Bond	68	27	4	5.9%
Carl A. Nafzger	69	33	4	5.8%
John T. Ward Jr.	30	15	4	13.3%
Jonathan E. Sheppard	109	38	4	3.7%

Trainer	No. strs	No. wnrs	No. GSWs	GSWs/ strs
Niall M. O'Callaghan	70	25	4	5.7%
F. Bruce Miller	34	13	3	8.8%
Richard A. Violette Jr.	38	14	3	7.9%
H. Allen Jerkens	63	33	3	4.8%
Bruce Headley	48	24	3	6.3%
Donnie K. Von Hemel	77	50	3	3.9%
Jenine Sahadi	65	21	3	4.6%
Aidan P. O'Brien	10	3	3	30.0%
John A. Shirreffs	46	19	3	6.5%
Patrick L. Biancone	26	11	3	11.5%
Randy Schulhofer	35	17	3	8.6%
Doug O'Neill	133	60	3	2.3%

Leading Trainers by Wins in 2002

Trainer	No. strs	No. wnrs	No. wins
Steven M. Asmussen	415	244	407
Scott A. Lake	446	228	399
Cole Norman	247	157	266
Jerry Hollendorfer	274	161	265
Harry F. Thompson Jr.	175	115	221
Dale Capuano	215	118	201
Bruce M. Kravets	211	99	170
Ronald J. Dandy	152	87	151
William I. Mott	183	91	149
Todd A. Pletcher	191	94	147
Dale Baird	249	109	146
Ralph Martinez	111	69	136
Allen Iwinski	170	90	136
Ronney W. Brown	207	89	136
Bob Baffert	175	82	133
John Charles Zimmerman	104	64	132
Gary L. Johnson	219	83	132
Keith L. Bourgeois	170	84	130
Armando Lage	226	97	127
Thomas M. Amoss	151	80	123
Richard E. Dutrow Jr.	144	72	120
Jeff C. Runco	204	91	119
Bernard S. Flint	124	70	119
Robert J. Frankel	121	66	117
Flint W. Stites	128	65	116
Mark Shuman	200	73	113
John S. McCaslin	85	54	112
Dale Angelle	76	49	111
Gary C. Contessa	170	76	108
Don J. Mills	99	61	103
Stanley W. Roberts	120	52	101
Danny Pish	135	64	101
A. Ferris Allen III	140	63	100
Doris Hebert	108	63	99
John J. Robb	187	68	96
William P. White	133	64	96
Wayne M. Catalano	114	65	95
Michael L. Reavis	127	68	94
Art Sherman	143	60	93
Layne S. Giliforte	109	50	93
Chris Tuttle	100	55	93
Donnie K. Von Hemel	77	50	91
Nicholas P. Zito	118	55	90
Michael V. Pino	141	65	88
W. Elliott Walden	102	55	87
Justin Evans	99	51	87
Michael S. Ferraro	50	38	86
Wesley A. Ward	126	56	85
M. Anthony Ferraro	69	38	85
Timothy F. Ritchey	103	51	84

Leading Jockeys of 2002

Among North America's leading jockeys, two patterns asserted themselves in 2002. First, Jerry Bailey was the leading jockey again, maintaining the top spot for the eighth consecutive year in the THOROUGHBRED TIMES rankings based on three criteria—number of wins, percentage of wins from total mounts, and average earnings per mount. Eclipse Award voters also noted his banner year, voting him outstanding jockey for the sixth time.

Bailey also established a record for worldwide purses won, with $22,871,814. His North American earnings were $19,271,814, with the difference being the $3.6-million winner's purse for Street Cry (Ire) in the Dubai World Cup (UAE-G1), a race that the Racing Hall of Fame jockey has won four times through 2003. He also won the 2002 Breeders' Cup Sprint (G1) with Orientate, his record 13th victory in the series, breaking a tie for most wins with Pat Day.

Overall, Bailey won with one of every four horses he rode. Only wins leader Russell Baze had a higher winning percentage, 28.6%. The Northern California jockey, also a Racing Hall of Fame member, again cracked the 400-victory mark, with 431 wins for the 2002 season.

Another familiar pattern re-established itself in 2002 when Day took the second spot in the THOROUGHBRED TIMES rankings. From 1998 through 2000, he was the runner-up to Bailey, but in 2001 John Velazquez displaced him from that spot. With considerable help from multiple graded stakes winner With Anticipation, Day stormed back into the second spot, with average earnings per mount of $13,770, fourth behind Bailey's $23,163 per mount. Velazquez, who had two winners on the Breeders' Cup program (Storm Flag Flying and Starine [Fr]), had 2002 earnings of $16,361,445, third behind Bailey and Day. Ranking fourth was Ramon Dominguez, who had been the wins leader in 2001 with 433 victories.

Leading Jockeys by Year
(Worldwide Purses)

Year	Name	Wins	Purses
2002	Jerry Bailey	213	$22,871,814
2001	Jerry Bailey	227	22,597,720
2000	Pat Day	267	17,479,838
1999	Pat Day	254	18,092,845
1998	Gary Stevens	178	19,358,840
1997	Jerry Bailey	273	18,320,743
1996	Jerry Bailey	300	19,214,409
1995	Jerry Bailey	287	16,308,230
1994	Mike Smith	317	15,979,820
1993	Mike Smith	343	14,024,815
1992	Kent Desormeaux	361	14,193,006
1991	Chris McCarron	265	14,441,083
1990	Gary Stevens	283	13,881,198
1989	Jose Santos	285	13,838,389

THOROUGHBRED TIMES Leading Jockeys of 2002

Rankings based on a formula that gives equal weighting to three statistical categories for performance in 2002: 1) total number of wins; 2) percent winners from mounts; and 3) average earnings per mount. A minimum of 100 starters is required to be considered for inclusion. Statistics are for North America only and for racing in 2002.

Rank	Jockey	No. mounts	No. wins	wins/ mounts	No. stakes wins	SWs/ mounts	No. graded st. wins	Total purses	Average earnings/ mount	Leading earner	Earnings of leading earner
1	Jerry D. Bailey	832	213	25.6%	67	8.1%	43	$19,271,814	$23,163	Medaglia d'Oro	$1,700,000
2	Pat Day	1,155	258	22.3%	40	3.5%	27	15,904,396	13,770	With Anticipation	1,498,500
3	John R. Velazquez	1,394	289	20.7%	46	3.3%	30	16,361,445	11,737	Storm Flag Flying	967,000
4	Ramon Dominguez	1,019	236	23.2%	24	2.4%	3	6,689,408	6,565	Your Out	233,100
5	Russell A. Baze	1,508	431	28.6%	21	1.4%	4	7,346,246	4,872	Mellow Fellow	191,400
6	Edgar S. Prado	1,527	289	18.9%	33	2.2%	25	18,024,429	11,804	Harlan's Holiday	1,415,000
7	Eibar Coa	1,367	287	21.0%	38	2.8%	9	8,774,284	6,419	Burning Roma	270,000
8	Robby Albarado	1,374	270	19.7%	21	1.5%	8	10,181,703	7,410	Tenpins	377,515
9	Alex O. Solis	1,123	217	19.3%	28	2.5%	15	12,027,315	10,710	Beat Hollow (GB)	777,150
10	Cornelio Velasquez	1,630	332	20.4%	28	1.7%	6	8,483,039	5,204	Cellars Shiraz	388,000
11	Jorge F. Chavez	1,196	223	18.7%	39	3.3%	27	13,721,254	11,473	Lido Palace (Chi)	900,764
12	Patrick Husbands	856	169	19.7%	13	1.5%	2	9,343,361	10,915	Added Edge	250,328
13	Todd Kabel	649	131	20.2%	19	2.9%	6	8,567,773	13,201	Hot Talent	328,600
14	Anthony S. Black	899	193	21.5%	8	0.9%	1	4,587,963	5,103	True Passion	273,262
15	Rene R. Douglas	1,208	231	19.1%	19	1.6%	9	7,712,389	6,384	Take the Cake	198,213
16	Gerard Melancon	1,170	249	21.3%	30	2.6%	2	5,047,836	4,314	Bonapaw	423,000
17	Jason P. Lumpkins	1,208	258	21.4%	23	1.9%	4	5,052,681	4,183	A B Noodle	125,360
18	Mario G. Pino	1,433	286	20.0%	25	1.7%	2	6,459,965	4,508	Deer Run	144,800
19	Ryan Fogelsonger	1,227	267	21.8%	7	0.6%	1	4,490,561	3,660	Cherokee's Boy	199,819
20	Patrick Valenzuela	1,297	221	17.0%	29	2.2%	12	12,544,098	9,672	Golden Apples (Ire)	891,680
21	Jeremy Rose	1,542	286	18.6%	19	1.2%		7,301,129	4,735	Docent	247,757
22	Laffit A. Pincay Jr.	1,189	205	17.2%	16	1.4%	7	9,568,457	8,047	Sky Jack	556,900
23	Horatio Karamanos	1,217	237	19.5%	18	1.5%	1	5,081,816	4,176	La Reine's Terms	274,000
24	Victor Espinoza	1,143	188	16.5%	24	2.1%	11	12,590,646	11,015	War Emblem	3,125,000
25	Michael J. McCarthy	947	172	18.2%	12	1.3%		5,309,747	5,607	Mandy's Gold	125,400

Rank	Jockey	No. mounts	No. wins	wins/ mounts	No. stakes wins	SWs/ mounts	No. graded st. wins	Total purses	Average earnings/ mount	Leading earner	Earnings of leading earner
26	David Flores	813	143	17.6%	22	2.7%	7	$7,314,619	$8,997	Icecoldbeeratreds	$328,000
27	Chantal Sutherland	754	135	17.9%	5	0.7%	1	5,923,820	7,857	Mulrainy	368,464
28	Kent Desormeaux	977	160	16.4%	38	3.9%	20	11,676,407	11,951	Milwaukee Brew	1,110,000
29	James McAleney	597	108	18.1%	10	1.7%	3	5,877,995	9,846	Anglian Prince	366,394
30	Travis Dunkelberger	1,256	249	19.8%	5	0.4%		4,046,073	3,221	Adams Tribe	78,428
31	Donald R. Pettinger	496	104	21.0%	15	3.0%	5	2,215,472	4,467	See How She Runs	403,550
32	Anthony J. Lovato	809	159	19.7%	10	1.2%	1	2,971,710	3,673	Unrullah Bull	183,350
33	Javier Castellano	1,243	194	15.6%	10	0.8%	7	8,819,053	7,095	With Ability	357,120
34	Jose Luis Flores	1,187	237	20.0%	4	0.3%		3,486,291	2,937	The Maccabee	151,890
35	Joe Bravo	170	38	22.4%	2	1.2%		1,100,939	6,476	Hudson Street	42,520
36	Chris J. McCarron	315	57	18.1%	15	4.8%	12	4,461,790	14,164	Came Home	724,500
37	Jose A. Santos	1,161	176	15.2%	29	2.5%	12	11,917,955	10,265	Volponi	2,176,720
38	Richard Migliore	1,016	157	15.5%	17	1.7%	7	8,646,376	8,510	Magic Weisner	455,000
39	Terry J. Thompson	1,197	213	17.8%	12	1.0%		4,067,703	3,398	My Trusty Cat	171,960
40	Clinton L. Potts	883	151	17.1%	6	0.7%		4,031,694	4,566	Ozilda's Karen	113,740
41	Larry J. Sterling Jr.	959	164	17.1%	9	0.9%	1	4,065,878	4,240	War Emblem	300,000
42	Josiah Hampshire Jr.	1,277	300	23.5%	9	0.7%		2,864,753	2,243	Calista (GB)	60,000
43	Corey J. Lanerie	1,240	197	15.9%	12	1.0%	1	5,316,050	4,287	Parade Leader	380,000
44	Pedro V. Alvarado	577	122	21.1%	9	1.6%	2	1,806,864	3,131	Elana d'Amour	182,076
45	Stewart Elliott	1,336	250	18.7%	4	0.3%	1	3,689,303	2,761	Pupil	98,200
46	Mark Guidry	1,030	156	15.2%	14	1.4%	9	6,933,474	6,732	Lone Star Sky	321,435
47	Mike E. Smith	741	112	15.1%	33	4.5%	22	10,807,977	14,586	Azeri	2,181,540
48	Edwin L. King Jr.	1,073	176	16.4%	12	1.1%	2	4,372,525	4,075	Caught in the Rain	167,694
49	Elvis Trujillo	669	118	17.6%	3	0.5%		2,765,141	4,133	Our Here Tiz	76,446
50	Manoel R. Cruz	1,485	258	17.4%	14	0.9%		4,271,654	2,877	Ivanavinalot	418,300
51	Glenn W. Corbett	1,116	202	18.1%	16	1.4%		3,036,224	2,721	Lusty Latin	148,000
52	Garrett K. Gomez	528	83	15.7%	12	2.3%	5	4,510,527	8,543	Momentum	422,400
53	Jon Kenton Court	1,335	200	15.0%	6	0.5%	3	6,078,225	4,553	Softly	320,668
54	Jorge M. Bourdieu	594	129	21.7%	8	1.4%		1,532,446	2,580	Runmore Mema	169,608
55	Donnie J. Meche	701	108	15.4%	21	3.0%	6	4,783,293	6,824	Easyfromthegitgo	547,905
56	Chad Schvaneveldt	773	134	17.3%	8	1.0%		2,676,340	3,462	Taraval	80,545
57	Emile Ramsammy	881	128	14.5%	11	1.3%	4	7,253,186	8,233	Wake At Noon	399,800
58	Jose A. Velez Jr.	626	97	15.5%	15	2.4%	3	3,727,027	5,954	Cat's At Home	210,000
59	Christopher Griffith	662	116	17.5%	3	0.5%		2,265,367	3,422	Yatsko	94,810
60	Constant Montpellier	662	99	15.0%	8	1.2%	3	5,337,760	8,063	Lady Shari	316,506
61	Julio A. Garcia	578	99	17.1%	12	2.1%	1	2,335,096	4,040	Coolbythepool	240,000
62	Charles C. Lopez	948	143	15.1%	7	0.7%	2	4,143,943	4,371	Zonk	104,556
63	Roman Chapa	999	177	17.7%	10	1.0%		2,565,226	2,568	Action Tonight	159,529
64	Roberto Alvarado Jr.	622	107	17.2%	1	0.2%	1	2,143,778	3,447	Heroofthegame	81,000
65	Shaun Bridgmohan	1,333	177	13.3%	10	0.8%	6	8,725,586	6,546	Evening Attire	1,332,720
66	Mark T. Johnston	1,282	189	14.7%	5	0.4%		4,674,682	3,646	Crafty Guy	167,100
67	Martin R. Ramirez	826	142	17.2%	1	0.1%		2,382,457	2,884	Judith Come Home	78,347
68	John McKee	1,006	182	18.1%	3	0.3%		2,373,638	2,359	Jenny's Prospector	78,871
69	Shane J. Sellers	243	41	16.9%	4	1.7%		1,281,232	5,273	Saintly Look	78,285
70	Calvin H. Borel	1,312	180	13.7%	11	0.8%	3	5,821,553	4,437	Jake the Flake	215,998
71	Eddie M. Martin Jr.	1,147	161	14.0%	9	0.8%	2	4,832,772	4,213	Rochester	201,000
72	Kirk Paul LeBlanc	1,150	179	15.6%	10	0.9%		3,352,297	2,915	Walk in the Snow	303,060
73	Craig Perret	372	55	14.8%	9	2.4%	4	3,322,058	8,930	Minister's Baby	195,000
74	Lorenzo Lezcano	341	54	15.8%		0.0%		1,693,062	4,965	Pocus Hocus	48,120
75	Quincy Welch	806	148	18.4%	10	1.2%	1	1,898,750	2,356	Jiffyjimmygee	76,063
76	Carlos M. Cruz	531	83	15.6%	6	1.1%		2,190,729	4,126	Autonomy (Ire)	61,200
77	Nicola Wright	555	104	18.7%	3	0.5%	1	1,402,500	2,527	Cruising Kat	157,422
78	Steven J. Bourque	967	204	21.1%	5	0.5%		1,826,925	1,889	Raymond's Dream	92,032
79	Harry Vega	803	114	14.2%	15	1.9%	6	3,660,153	4,558	Xtra Heat	749,155
80	Eddie Delahoussaye	495	67	13.5%	16	3.2%	9	5,687,776	11,490	Affluent	534,280
81	Miguel S. Fuentes	235	42	17.9%	15	6.4%		772,253	3,286	Star Smasher	227,360
82	David Clark	514	71	13.8%	5	1.0%		3,856,139	7,502	Brass in Pocket	162,285
83	Martin A. Pedroza	776	112	14.4%	6	0.8%		3,174,897	4,091	Nates Colony	181,660
84	T. D. Houghton	1,202	253	21.1%	12	1.0%		2,140,929	1,781	Secret Romeo	212,822
85	Jason R. Eads	919	154	16.8%		0.0%		2,261,485	2,461	Lord of Speed	49,703
86	Corey S. Nakatani	562	75	13.4%	9	1.6%	5	5,510,965	9,806	Sarafan	1,013,252
87	Francisco Duran	1,295	202	15.6%	2	0.2%		3,167,771	2,446	Motel Staff	87,467
88	Edward T. Baird	793	121	15.3%	4	0.5%		2,601,924	3,281	Smoke Chaser	102,800
89	Monte Clifton Berry	995	174	17.5%	10	1.0%		2,180,766	2,192	Tulupal	92,125
90	Kevin Radke	690	143	20.7%	8	1.2%		1,382,784	2,004	Flying Notes	103,750
91	Cory Clark	493	83	16.8%		0.0%		1,459,001	2,959	Native Brick	89,585
92	Chad K. Murphy	872	135	15.5%	2	0.2%		2,444,989	2,804	Cryptorouge	64,012
93	Joseph C. Judice	373	73	19.6%	6	1.6%		891,936	2,391	Sweetwater Promise	143,588
94	Winston Thompson	1,342	249	18.6%	11	0.8%		2,575,363	1,919	Little Time	60,700
95	Paul Albert Nicol Jr.	1,004	171	17.0%	4	0.4%		2,220,043	2,211	Social Mix	58,300

Leading Jockeys by Earnings in 2002

Jockey	No. mounts	No. wins	Total purses
Jerry D. Bailey	832	213	$19,271,814
Edgar S. Prado	1,527	289	18,024,429
John R. Velazquez	1,394	289	16,361,445
Pat Day	1,155	258	15,904,396
Jorge F. Chavez	1,196	223	13,721,254
Victor Espinoza	1,143	188	12,590,646
Patrick Valenzuela	1,297	221	12,544,098
Alex O. Solis	1,123	217	12,027,315
Jose A. Santos	1,161	176	11,917,955
Kent J. Desormeaux	977	160	11,676,407
Mike E. Smith	741	112	10,807,977
Robby Albarado	1,374	270	10,181,703
Laffit A. Pincay Jr.	1,189	205	9,568,457
Patrick Husbands	856	169	9,343,361
Javier Castellano	1,243	194	8,819,053
Eibar Coa	1,367	287	8,774,284
Shaun Bridgmohan	1,333	177	8,725,586
Richard Migliore	1,016	157	8,646,376
Todd Kabel	649	131	8,567,773
Cornelio Velasquez	1,630	332	8,483,039
Rene R. Douglas	1,208	231	7,712,389
Russell A. Baze	1,508	431	7,346,246
David Romero Flores	813	143	7,314,619
Jeremy Rose	1,542	286	7,301,129
Emile Ramsammy	881	128	7,253,186
Mark Guidry	1,030	156	6,933,474
Ramon A. Dominguez	1,019	236	6,689,408
Mario G. Pino	1,433	286	6,459,965
Jon Kenton Court	1,335	200	6,078,225
Chantal Sutherland	754	135	5,923,820
James McAleney	597	108	5,877,995
Calvin H. Borel	1,312	180	5,821,553
Eddie Delahoussaye	495	67	5,687,776
Michael J. Luzzi	1,066	119	5,685,956
Corey S. Nakatani	562	75	5,510,965

Leading Jockeys by Average Earnings Per Mount in 2002

Jockey	No. mounts	No. wins	Average earnings per mount
Jerry D. Bailey	832	213	$23,163
Mike E. Smith	741	112	14,586
Chris J. McCarron	315	57	14,164
Pat Day	1,155	258	13,770
Todd Kabel	649	131	13,201
Gary L. Stevens	339	45	12,321
Kent J. Desormeaux	977	160	11,951
Edgar S. Prado	1,527	289	11,804
John R. Velazquez	1,394	289	11,737
Eddie Delahoussaye	495	67	11,490
Jorge F. Chavez	1,196	223	11,473
Victor Espinoza	1,143	188	11,015
Patrick Husbands	856	169	10,915
Alex O. Solis	1,123	217	10,710
Jose A. Santos	1,161	176	10,265
James McAleney	597	108	9,846
Corey S. Nakatani	562	75	9,806
Patrick Valenzuela	1,297	221	9,672
David Romero Flores	813	143	8,997
Craig Perret	372	55	8,930
Garrett K. Gomez	528	83	8,543
Richard Migliore	1,016	157	8,510
Robert C. Landry	513	52	8,358
Emile Ramsammy	881	128	8,233
Constant Montpellier	662	99	8,063

Jockey	No. mounts	No. wins	Average earnings per mount
Laffit A. Pincay Jr.	1,189	205	$8,047
Mickey Walls	154	15	7,979
Chantal Sutherland	754	135	7,857
James McKnight	283	39	7,813
David Clark	514	71	7,502
Raymond Sabourin	479	64	7,437
Robby Albarado	1,374	270	7,410
Javier Castellano	1,243	194	7,095
Richard Dos Ramos	374	37	7,083
Larry Melancon	485	63	6,826
Donnie J. Meche	701	108	6,824
Mark Guidry	1,030	156	6,732
Slade Callaghan	522	57	6,714
Ramon A. Dominguez	1,019	236	6,565
Shaun Bridgmohan	1,333	177	6,546
Joe Bravo	170	38	6,476
Eibar Coa	1,367	287	6,419
Rene R. Douglas	1,208	231	6,384
Jean-Luc Samyn	492	57	6,190
Julie A. Krone	133	20	6,124

Leading Jockeys by Number of Stakes Wins in 2002

Jockey	No. mounts	No. wins	No. stakes wins
Jerry D. Bailey	832	213	67
John R. Velazquez	1,394	289	46
Pat Day	1,155	258	40
Jorge F. Chavez	1,196	223	39
Kent J. Desormeaux	977	160	38
Eibar Coa	1,367	287	38
Edgar S. Prado	1,527	289	33
Mike E. Smith	741	112	33
Gerard Melancon	1,170	249	30
Jose A. Santos	1,161	176	29
Patrick Valenzuela	1,297	221	29
Alex O. Solis	1,123	217	28
Cornelio H. Velasquez	1,630	332	28
Mario G. Pino	1,433	286	25
Victor Espinoza	1,143	188	24
Ramon A. Dominguez	1,019	236	24
Jason P. Lumpkins	1,208	258	23
David Romero Flores	813	143	22
Russell A. Baze	1,508	431	21
Donnie J. Meche	701	108	21
Robby Albarado	1,374	270	21
Todd Kabel	649	131	19
Rene R. Douglas	1,208	231	19
Jeremy Rose	1,542	286	19
Horatio Karamanos	1,217	237	18
Richard Migliore	1,016	157	17
Laffit A. Pincay Jr.	1,189	205	16
Eddie J. Delahoussaye	495	67	16
Glenn W. Corbett	1,116	202	16
Donald R. Pettinger	496	104	15
Chris J. McCarron	315	57	15
Harry Vega	803	114	15
Jose A. Velez Jr.	626	97	15
Miguel Sanchez Fuentes	235	42	15
Manoel R. Cruz	1,485	258	14
Mark Guidry	1,030	156	14
Miguel Gaeta Hernandez	1,115	160	14
Patrick Husbands	856	169	13
Seth B. Martinez	1,432	276	13

Leading Jockeys by Percent Stakes Winners from Mounts in 2002

Jockey	No. mounts	No. wins	No. stakes wins	Stakes wins/ mounts
Jerry D. Bailey	832	213	67	8.1%
Miguel Fuentes	235	42	15	6.4%
Chris J. McCarron	315	57	15	4.8%
Cammie Papineau	218	47	10	4.6%
Mike E. Smith	741	112	33	4.5%
Kent Desormeaux	977	160	38	3.9%
Pat Day	1,155	258	40	3.5%
John Velazquez	1,394	289	46	3.3%
Serge R. Rocheleau	214	53	7	3.3%
Jorge F. Chavez	1,196	223	39	3.3%
Gary L. Stevens	339	45	11	3.2%
Eddie Delahoussaye	495	67	16	3.2%
Ron W. Keckler	345	66	11	3.2%
Richard M. Vasquez	162	36	5	3.1%
Donald R. Pettinger	496	104	15	3.0%
Donnie J. Meche	701	108	21	3.0%
Todd Kabel	649	131	19	2.9%
Eibar Coa	1,367	287	38	2.8%
David Bentley	108	18	3	2.8%
David Romero Flores	813	143	22	2.7%
Abad Cabassa Jr.	188	22	5	2.7%
Carlos D. Madeira	416	71	11	2.6%
Gerard Melancon	1,170	249	30	2.6%
Jose A. Santos	1,161	176	29	2.5%
Alex O. Solis	1,123	217	28	2.5%
Craig Perret	372	55	9	2.4%
Jose A. Velez Jr.	626	97	15	2.4%
Ramon Dominguez	1,019	236	24	2.4%
Anderson Ward	213	24	5	2.4%

Leading Jockeys by Number of Wins in 2002

Jockey	No. mounts	No. wnrs	No. wins
Russell A. Baze	1,508	322	431
Cornelio H. Velasquez	1,630	259	332
Josiah F. Hampshire Jr.	1,277	217	300
David Cora	1,503	213	295
John R. Velazquez	1,394	226	289
Edgar S. Prado	1,527	232	289
Eibar Coa	1,367	239	287
Jeremy Rose	1,542	214	286
Mario G. Pino	1,433	224	286
Seth B. Martinez	1,432	211	276
Robby Albarado	1,374	228	270
Ryan Fogelsonger	1,227	216	267
Manoel R. Cruz	1,485	191	258
Jason P. Lumpkins	1,208	203	258
Pat Day	1,155	213	258
T. D. Houghton	1,202	194	253
Stewart Elliott	1,336	195	250
Winston Albert Thompson	1,342	162	249
Gerard Melancon	1,170	181	249
Travis L. Dunkelberger	1,256	205	249
Esteban Angel Gomez	1,257	161	241
Jose Luis Flores	1,187	183	237
Horatio Karamanos	1,217	182	237
Ramon A. Dominguez	1,019	203	236
Rene R. Douglas	1,208	188	231
Jorge F. Chavez	1,196	185	223
Patrick Valenzuela	1,297	184	221

Jockey	No. mounts	No. wnrs	No. wins
Dana G. Whitney	1,537	186	219
Alex O. Solis	1,123	166	217
Terry J. Thompson	1,197	169	213
Jerry D. Bailey	832	162	213
Laffit A. Pincay Jr.	1,189	145	205
Steven Joseph Bourque	967	154	204
Glenn W. Corbett	1,116	168	202
Francisco Duran	1,295	159	202
Thomas L. Pompell	1,190	159	200
Jon Kenton Court	1,335	164	200
Deshawn L. Parker	1,311	157	200
Corey J. Lanerie	1,240	170	197
Javier Castellano	1,243	160	194
Federico Mata	1,323	157	193
Anthony S. Black	899	146	193
Carl James Woodley	1,076	140	190
Mark T. Johnston	1,282	150	189
Manuel Aguilar	1,355	144	189
Gary A. Birzer	1,375	142	188
Victor Espinoza	1,143	153	188
Jamie Theriot	1,212	146	187
Luis Antonio Gonzalez	1,270	145	185
John McKee	1,006	154	182

Leading Jockeys by Number of Individual Winners in 2002

Jockey	No. mounts	No. wnrs
Russell A. Baze	1,508	322
Cornelio H. Velasquez	1,630	259
Eibar Coa	1,367	239
Edgar S. Prado	1,527	232
Robby Albarado	1,374	228
John R. Velazquez	1,394	226
Mario G. Pino	1,433	224
Josiah Francis Hampshire Jr.	1,277	217
Ryan Fogelsonger	1,227	216
Jeremy Rose	1,542	214
David Cora	1,503	213
Pat Day	1,155	213
Seth B. Martinez	1,432	211
Travis L. Dunkelberger	1,256	205
Ramon A. Dominguez	1,019	203
Jason P. Lumpkins	1,208	203
Stewart Elliott	1,336	195
T. D. Houghton	1,202	194
Manoel R. Cruz	1,485	191
Rene R. Douglas	1,208	188
Dana G. Whitney	1,537	186
Jorge F. Chavez	1,196	185
Patrick Angel Valenzuela	1,297	184
Jose Luis Flores	1,187	183
Horatio Karamanos	1,217	182
Gerard Melancon	1,170	181
Corey J. Lanerie	1,240	170
Terry J. Thompson	1,197	169
Glenn W. Corbett	1,116	168
Alex O. Solis	1,123	166
Jon Kenton Court	1,335	164
Jerry D. Bailey	832	162
Winston Albert Thompson	1,342	162
Esteban Angel Gomez	1,257	161
Javier Castellano	1,243	160
Thomas L. Pompell	1,190	159
Francisco Duran	1,295	159
Federico Mata	1,323	157
Deshawn L. Parker	1,311	157

Leading Jockeys by Number of Graded Stakes Wins in 2002

Jockey	No. mounts	No. wins	Graded stakes wins	Graded wins/ mounts
Jerry D. Bailey	832	213	43	5.2%
John R. Velazquez	1,394	289	30	2.2%
Jorge F. Chavez	1,196	223	27	2.3%
Pat Day	1,155	258	27	2.3%
Edgar S. Prado	1,527	289	25	1.6%
Mike E. Smith	741	112	22	3.0%
Kent J. Desormeaux	977	160	20	2.1%
Alex O. Solis	1,123	217	15	1.3%
Jose A. Santos	1,161	176	12	1.0%
Patrick Valenzuela	1,297	221	12	0.9%
Chris J. McCarron	315	57	12	3.8%
Victor Espinoza	1,143	188	11	1.0%
Eibar Coa	1,367	287	9	0.7%
Eddie Delahoussaye	495	67	9	1.8%
Rene R. Douglas	1,208	231	9	0.8%
Mark Guidry	1,030	156	9	0.9%
Robby Albarado	1,374	270	8	0.6%
Gary L. Stevens	339	45	8	2.4%
Laffit A. Pincay Jr.	1,189	205	7	0.6%
David Flores	813	143	7	0.9%
Richard Migliore	1,016	157	7	0.7%
Javier Castellano	1,243	194	7	0.6%

Leading Jockeys by Career Earnings

Jockey	Career earnings
1. Pat Day	$276,005,646 +
2. Chris McCarron	264,380,651
3. Jerry Bailey	258,357,133 +
4. Laffit Pincay Jr.	237,157,192
5. Gary Stevens	216,149,422 +
6. Eddie Delahoussaye	195,801,624
7. Kent Desormeaux	170,942,100 +
8. Angel Cordero Jr.	164,561,227
9. Alex Solis	160,879,229 +
10. Jose Santos	158,254,369 +
11. Mike Smith	154,719,757 +
12. Corey Nakatani	136,154,095 +
13. Jorge Chavez	133,813,165 +
14. Jorge Velasquez	125,544,379
15. Bill Shoemaker	123,375,524
16. Russell Baze	120,353,063 +
17. Richard Migliore	118,873,023 +
18. Edgar Prado	116,298,075 +
19. Robbie Davis	115,732,836 +
20. Pat Valenzuela	114,521,852 +
21. Shane Sellers	112,059,161 +
22. Craig Perret	110,124,037 +
23. John Velazquez	109,102,718 +
24. Eddie Maple	105,338,573
25. Chris Antley	92,203,341
26. Sandy Hawley	88,681,292
27. David Flores	88,136,386 +
28. Julie Krone	83,559,511 +
29. Jean-Luc Samyn	82,584,548 +
30. Earlie Fires	79,367,510 +
31. Mario Pino	78,874,454 +
32. Aaron Gryder	75,622,467 +
33. Randy Romero	75,264,198
34. Rick Wilson	74,437,043 +
35. Mark Guidry	74,434,462 +

*Active jockeys; statistics through April 8, 2003

Leading Jockeys by Career Wins

Jockey	Career wins
1. Laffit Pincay Jr.	9,530
2. Bill Shoemaker	8,833
3. Pat Day	8,437 +
4. Russell Baze	8,193 +
5. David Gall	7,396
6. Chris McCarron	7,139
7. Angel Cordero Jr.	7,057
8. Jorge Velasquez	6,795
9. Sandy Hawley	6,449
10. Larry Snyder	6,388
11. Eddie Delahoussaye	6,384
12. Carl Gambardella	6,349
13. Earlie Fires	6,210 +
14. John Longden	6,032
15. Jerry Bailey	5,430 +
16. Ronnie Ardoin	5,225 +
17. Mario Pino	5,118 +
18. Rudy Baez	4,875
19. Rick Wilson	4,810 +
20. Edgar Prado	4,794 +
21. Eddie Arcaro	4,779
22. Gary Stevens	4,771 +
23. Don Brumfield	4,573
24. Anthony Black	4,532 +
25. Mark Guidry	4,485 +
26. Steve Brooks	4,451
27. Eddie Maple	4,398
28. Walter Blum	4,382
29. Craig Perret	4,357 +
30. Ray Sibille	4,351 +
31. Kent Desormeaux	4,350 +
32. Randy Romero	4,294
33. Jeff Lloyd	4,276
34. Bill Hartack	4,272
35. Timothy Doocy	4,236 +
36. Perry Ouzts	4,227 +
37. Mike Smith	4,209 +
38. Avelino Gomez	4,081
39. Hugo Dittrach	4,000
40. Phil Grove	3,991
41. Robert Colton	3,971 +
42. Mike Rowland	3,862 +
43. Shane Sellers	3,835 +
44. Leslie Hulet	3,816
45. Ted Atkinson	3,795

+Active jockeys; statistics through April 8, 2003

Female Jockeys With More Than 1,000 Wins

	Wins	Active Years
Julie Krone	3,595	1981-2003
Patti Cooksey	2,136	1979-2003
Vicky Aragon Baze	1,769	1985-2001
Jill Jellison	1,701	1982-2003
Dodie Cartier Duys	1,669	1983-2003
Vicki Warhol	1,583	1979-2003
Rosemary Homeister Jr.	1,578	1977-2003
Cindy Noll	1,484	1990-2003
Lillian Kuykendall	1,419	1980-2001
Lori Wydick	1,289	1984-2000
Donna Barton	1,130	1987-1998
Patti Barton	1,085	1969-1984
Diane Nelson	1,076	1986-2003
Cynthia Herman Medina	1,024	1986-2003
Mary Randall Doser	1,004	1986-2003

Through April 10, 2003

Notable Names in Racing's Past

(Names of Racing Hall of Fame members are in boldface italics.)

As much as great horses are central to the sport, Thoroughbred racing and breeding would not exist without the important individuals of the past who worked to perfect the breed or sport and who performed with distinction within the industry. Here are outstanding individuals from racing's history, with members of the Racing Hall of Fame noted in boldface italics.

Adams, John H., 1914-'95. Jockey, trainer. Leading jockey 1937, '42, '43; inducted into Racing Hall of Fame in '65; George Woolf Memorial Jockey Award in '56. Rode 3,270 winners, including *Kayak II, Hasty Road. Trained J. O. Tobin. Won 1954 Preakness Stakes aboard Hasty Road.

Aga Khan III, Sultan Sir Mahomed Shah, 1877-1957. Ismaili Muslim leader. Owner of Gilltown, Sheshoon, Ballymany, Sallymount, and Ongar Studs in Ireland; Haras de la Coquenne, Haras de Marly-la-Ville, Haras de Saint-Crespin in France. Leading owner in England 13 times; leading breeder in England eight times. Bred *Bahram, *Nasrullah, *Tulyar, *Mahmoud, *Alibhai, *Khaled, *Masaka; owned Mumtaz Mahal, *Blenheim II. Grandfather of current Aga Khan.

Alexander, Alexander J., 1824-1902. Iron works, farming. Owner of Woodburn Stud, Kentucky. Stood leading sire Lexington. Leading breeder. Bred Duke of Magenta, Spendthrift, Tom Bowling, Tom Ochiltree, Harry Bassett, Joe Daniels, Fellowcraft, Fonso, etc. Brother of Robert A. S. C. Alexander.

Alexander, Robert A. S. C., 1819-'67. Iron works, farming. Founder of Woodburn Stud, Kentucky. Stood leading sire Lexington. Leading breeder. Bred Norfolk, Asteroid, Maiden, Virgil, Preakness, etc. Brother of Alexander J. Alexander.

Annenberg, Moses L., 1878-1942. Publisher. Published *Daily Racing Form* 1922-'42, *Morning Telegraph.* Founded Triangle Publications.

Annenberg, Walter, 1908-2002. Former publisher, *Daily Racing Form.* Took control of his family's Triangle Publications Inc. in 1940 and built largest private publishing empire in the country; ambassador to Great Britain 1968-'74. Sold publishing enterprises by late 1980s. Son of publisher Moses Annenberg.

Arcaro, Eddie, 1916-'97. Jockey. Inducted into Racing Hall of Fame in 1958; George Woolf Memorial Jockey Award in '53. Rode 4,779 winners, including Whirlaway, Citation, Bold Ruler, Nashua. Won two Triple Crowns, five Kentucky Derbys, six Preakness Stakes, and six Belmont Stakes.

Archer, Fred, 1857-'86. Jockey. Winner of 12 consecutive riding titles in England (1874-1885) and rode 2,748 career winners, a record that stood for 57 years. Won 21 classic races, including five Epsom Derbys with Silvio, Bend Or, Iroquois, Melton, *Ormonde.

Bacon, Mary, 1948-'91. Pioneer female jockey; rode 286 winners.

Baldwin, Elias J. "Lucky," 1828-1909. Mining, investments. Owned Rancho el Santa Anita, California. Bred and owned Emperor of Norfolk, Volante, Rey el Santa Anita, Americus. Built original Santa Anita Park racetrack.

Barbee, George, ca. 1855-1941. Jockey. Inducted into Racing Hall of Fame in 1996. Rode Saxon, Survivor, Shirley, Jacobus. Won the first Preakness Stakes aboard Survivor in 1873; won two other Preakness

Stakes and one Belmont Stakes.

Barrera, Lazaro, 1924-'91. Trainer. Eclipse Award trainer 1976-'79; leading trainer by money won 1977-'80; inducted into Racing Hall of Hall of Fame in 1979. Trained more than 140 stakes winners and six champions, including Affirmed, Bold Forbes. Only trainer to win four consecutive Eclipse Awards.

Bassett, Carroll K., 1905-'72. Jockey. Inducted into Racing Hall of Fame in 1972. Rode more than 100 steeplechase winners, including Battleship, Peacock, Night Retired, Passive, Sable Muff. Rode Battleship to victory in the American Grand National and two National Steeplechase Hunt Cups.

Beard, Louis A., 1888-1954. Farm manager, racing executive. Managed Greentree Stud 1927-'48. Co-founder and president, Keeneland Race Course; co-founder, American Thoroughbred Breeders' Association; co-founder, Grayson Foundation.

Bedwell, H. Guy, 1876-1951. Trainer. Leading trainer by races won in 1909, '12-'17; leading trainer by money won 1918-'19; inducted into Racing Hall of Fame in 1971. Trained 2,160 winners, including Sir Barton, Billy Kelly. First trainer to saddle a Triple Crown winner (Sir Barton in 1919); won 16 races in 14 days in 1910.

Belmont, August I, 1816-'90. Banker. President of American Jockey Club (Jerome Park) 1866-'86. Owner of Nursery Stud in New York and later in Kentucky. Leading owner. Bred and owned Woodbine, Potomac, Fides, Prince Royal; also owned Glenelg, Fenian, *The Ill-Used.

Belmont, August II, 1853-1924. Banker. First president of Belmont Park; chairman, the Jockey Club 1895-1924; chairman, Belmont Park. Owned Nursery Stud, Kentucky. Leading breeder. Bred Man o' War, Fair Play, Tracery, Beldame; also owned *Hourless, Henry of Navarre.

Bieber, Isidor, 1887-1974. Restaurateur, gambler. Co-owner of Bieber-Jacobs Stable, Stymie Manor, Maryland. Leading breeder 1964-'67; co-breeder of Hail to Reason, Allez France, Affectionately, Straight Deal; also co-owned Stymie, Searching.

Bobinski, Kazimierz, 1905-'69. Russian-born pedigree authority. In collaboration with Stefan Zamoyski, authored the *Family Tables of Racehorses, Volumes I & II,* which expanded on the work of Bruce Lowe and Hermann Goos.

Bostwick, George, 1909-'82. Jockey, trainer. Leading amateur steeplechase jockey 1928-'32, '41; leading steeplechase trainer 1940, '51, '55; inducted into Racing Hall of Fame in 1968. Rode 87 winners, including Chenango, Escapade, Sussex, Darkness. Trained Neji and Oedipus. Played on six United States championship polo teams.

Boussac, Marcel, 1889-1980. Textile tycoon. Leading French breeder 19 times, winner of the Prix du Jockey-Club (French Derby) 12 times. Bred notable racehorses or sires Tourbillon, Pharis, Djebel, *Goya II, and *Ambiorix. In 1950 became first foreign owner to lead English owners list, the year he won the Epsom Derby with Galcador. Also bred and owned two-time Prix de l'Arc de Triomphe winner Corrida.

Bowie, Oden, 1826-'94. Railways, politician. Maryland governor 1869-'72; first president of Pimlico Race Course in 1870. Owner of Fairview Plantation, Maryland. Bred Catesby, Crickmore.

Bradley, Edward R., 1859-1946. Gambler. Owner of Idle Hour Stock Farm, Kentucky. Bred and owned Blue Larkspur, Bimelech, Black Helen, Busher, Bubbling Over. Bred and owned four Kentucky Derby winners and imported foundation mare *La Troienne.

Brady, James Cox Jr., 1908-'71. Investments. Chairman of the Jockey Club 1961-'69; chairman of New York Racing Association 1961-'69. Owner of Dixiana Farm, Kentucky, and Hamilton Stable. Bred Long Look, War Plumage, Jungle Cove. Co-founder of Monmouth Park, American Horse Council; oversaw rebuilding of Belmont Park. Father of Nicholas J. Brady, United States treasury secretary 1988-'93.

Brooks, Steve, 1922-'79. Jockey. Leading jockey in 1949; inducted into Racing Hall of Fame in 1963; George Woolf Memorial Jockey Award in 1962. Rode 4,451 winners, including Two Lea, Citation, Round Table. Rode Ponder in 1949 Kentucky Derby.

Brown, Edward D. "Brown Dick," 1850-1906. Trainer, jockey. Inducted into Racing Hall of Fame in 1984. Trained Ben Brush, Plaudit, Spendthrift, Hindoo. Rode Asteroid to an undefeated 9-for-9 record in 1864-'65.

Brown, Harry D. "Curly," 1863-1930. Restaurateur, racetrack executive. Founder and first president of Arlington Park; built Laurel Park, Oriental Park. Owned Brown Shasta Farm, California.

Bruce, Benjamin G., 1827-'91. Publisher. Founder and editor of the *Livestock Record* 1875-'91 (predecessor of *The Thoroughbred Record*). Brother of Sanders D. Bruce.

Bruce, Sanders D., 1825-1902. Hotelier, publisher. Co-editor of *Turf, Field and Farm* 1865-1902. Compiler of first four volumes of *American Stud Book.* Brother of Benjamin G. Bruce.

Bull, Phil, 1910-1989. Handicapper, gambler, owner-breeder, publisher. In 1948 launched *Timeform,* a British Thoroughbred industry information service that annually assesses the individual merits of thousands of runners. Founded Hollins Stud; bred major stakes winner Romulus.

Burch, Preston, 1884-1978. Trainer, breeder, owner. Leading trainer in 1950; inducted into Racing Hall of Fame in 1963. Trained more than 70 stakes winners, including George Smith, Sailor, Flower Bowl, Bold. Bred Gallorette. Trained stakes winners in New York, Canada, Cuba, France, and Italy. Wrote influential book on training, *Training Thoroughbred Horses.* Son of William P. Burch; father of Racing Hall of Fame trainer J. Elliott Burch.

Burch, William P., 1846-1926. Trainer. Inducted into Racing Hall of Fame in 1955. Trained Grey Friar, My Own, Decanter. First of three generations of Hall of Fame trainers. Father of Preston Burch.

Burke, Carleton F., 1882-1962. Banker, farmer. First chairman of California Horse Racing Board 1933-'39.

Burlew, Fred, 1871-1927. Trainer. Inducted into Racing Hall of Fame in 1973. Trained 32 stakes winners and two champions, including Beldame, Morvich, Inchcape.

Burns, Tommy H., 1879-1913. Jockey. Leading jockey by races won in 1898-'99; inducted into Racing Hall of Fame in 1983. Rode 1,333 winners, including Broomstick, Imp, Caughnawaga. Set an American record in the 1¼-mile Brighton Beach Handicap aboard Broomstick.

Butler, James Sr., 1855-1934. Grocery-chain owner. Owner of Empire City racetrack. Owner of East View Farm, New York. Bred Questionnaire, Sting, Pebbles, Spur; owned Comely.

Butler, James II, 1891-1940. Grocery-chain owner. President of Empire City Racing Association. Owner of East View Farm, New York.

Butwell, James, 1896-1956. Jockey, racing official. Leading jockey in 1912; leading jockey by races won in '20; inducted into Racing Hall of Fame in '84. Rode 1,402 winners, including Roamer, Sweep, Hilarious, Maskette. Leading American jockey by number of wins at the time of his retirement.

Byers, J. Dallett "Dolly," 1898-1966. Jockey, trainer. Leading steeplechase jockey 1918, '21, '28; leading jockey by money won in '28; inducted into Racing Hall of Fame in '67. Rode 149 winners, including Jolly Roger, Fairmount. Trained Tea-Maker, Lovely Night, Invader. Won the Temple Gwathmey Steeplechase Handicap five years in a row.

Byrnes, Matthew, 1854-1933. Jockey, trainer. Rode *Glenelg, Kingfisher; trained Racing Hall of Fame members Parole, Salvator, Firenze.

Caldwell, Thomas, 1928-2001. Auctioneer. Auctioneer and director of auctions for the Keeneland Association 1975-2001. Owned Gavel Ranch, Oregon.

Campbell, John B., 1876-1954. Racing executive. Racing secretary and handicapper at New York tracks 1935-'54. Handicapped three-way dead heat in 1944 Carter Handicap.

Capossela, Fred, 1903-'91. Famed race caller at New York racetracks 1943-'71.

Cassidy, Mars, 1862-1929. Racing executive. Legendary starter at New York racetracks 1902-'29. Father of Marshall Cassidy.

Cassidy, Marshall, 1892-1968. Racing executive. Executive secretary of the Jockey Club. Developed first modern starting gate; developed modern photo-finish camera; instituted first film patrol and saliva tests; founded Jockey Club Round Table meetings. Son of Mars Cassidy.

Cella, Charles, 1875-1940. Hotelier, theater owner. Founder of Oaklawn Park; co-owner of Fort Erie racetrack.

Chenery, Christopher T., 1886-1973. Utilities. First president of Thoroughbred Owners and Breeders Association. Owner of Meadow Stud, Virginia. Bred Secretariat, Riva Ridge, Hill Prince, Cicada, First Landing, Sir Gaylord. Co-founder of New York Racing Association.

Childs, Frank E., 1886-1973. Trainer. Inducted into Racing Hall of Fame in 1968. Trained 23 stakes winners, including *Tomy Lee, Canina, Dinner Gong. Known for his ability to turn claiming horses into stakes winners.

Chinn, Philip T., 1874-1962. Horse trader. Owner of Himyar Stud, Kentucky. Bred 58 stakes winners, including Miss Merriment, Black Maria, In Memoriam, High Resolve. Leading consignor at Saratoga in 1920s; sold then-record $70,000 yearling in '27.

Clark, Henry S., 1904-'99. Trainer. Inducted into Racing Hall of Fame in 1982. Trained 37 stakes winners and one champion, including Tempted, Cyane, Endine, Obeah. Twice won back-to-back Delaware Handicaps.

Clark, John C., 1891-1974. Advertising executive. President of Hialeah Park 1940-'54; first president of Thoroughbred Racing Associations 1942-'43. Owned Sun Briar Court, New York. Bred Charlie McAdam, Accomplish.

Clark, John H. "Trader," 1919-'96. Horse trader, author. President, Thoroughbred Breeders of Kentucky. Author of *Trader Clark.*

Clark, Meriwether Lewis, 1846-'99. Racing executive. Founder and president of Louisville Jockey Club. Founder of Kentucky Derby in 1875. Established first uniform scale of weights in America.

Clay, Albert, (1917-2002). Farmer, burley warehousing. Breeder or co-breeder of at least 20 stakes winners, including Albert the Great, Seaside Attraction, Gorgeous, Pompeii, George Navonod; helped to found the American Horse Council and was instrumental in establishing the University of Kentucky's Maxwell H. Gluck Equine Research Center. Father of Three Chimneys Farm owner Robert Clay.

Clay, Ezekiel F., 1841-1920. Farmer, breeder. President, Kentucky Racing Association. Co-owner of Runnymede Farm, Kentucky. Chairman of Kentucky Racing Commission. Bred Hanover, Sir Dixon, Miss Woodford, Raceland.

Clay, Henry, 1777-1852. Lawyer, politician. Owner of Ashland Stud, Kentucky. Bred Heraldry. Father of John M. Clay.

Clay, John M., 1820-'87. Farmer, breeder. Owner of Ashland Stud, Kentucky. Bred Kentucky, Maggie B. B., Daniel Boone, Simon Kenton, Gilroy, Star Davis, Lodi, Day Star. Son of Henry Clay.

Cocks, W. Burling, 1915-'98. Trainer. Leading steeplechase trainer 1949, '65, '73, '80; inducted into Racing Hall of Fame in '85; F. Ambrose Clark Award in '73. Trained 49 stakes winners, including six American Grand National winners. Trained Zaccio, Down First.

Coe, William R., 1869-1955. Insurance, financier. Owner of Shoshone Farm, Kentucky. Bred and owned Pompey, Pompoon; owned Ladysman, Cleopatra, Black Maria, Pilate.

Cole, Ashley T., 1876-1965. New York industry leader. Chairman of the New York State Racing Commission 1945-'65; president of the National Association of State Racing Commissioners. Involved in organizing the not-for-profit New York Racing Association, in building the new Aqueduct Race Course, and in developing the New York breeders awards program.

Coltiletti, Frank, 1904-'87. Jockey, trainer, racing official. Inducted into Racing Hall of Fame in 1970. Rode 667 winners, including Mars, Crusader, Sun Beau. Won Preakness Stakes at age 17 aboard Broomspun in 1921.

Combs, Leslie II, 1901-'90. Breeder. Owner of Spendthrift Farm, Kentucky. Leading breeder in 1972. Chairman of Kentucky Racing Commission. Bred 247 stakes winners, including Majestic Prince, Myrtle Charm, Idun, Mr. Prospector. Originated modern stallion syndicates in 1950s.

Conway, James P., 1910-'84. Trainer. Inducted into Racing Hall of Fame in 1996. Trained 43 stakes winners and five champions, including Chateaugay, Primonetta, Grecian Queen. Won 1963 Kentucky Derby and Belmont Stakes with three-year-old champion colt Chateaugay.

Corrigan, Edward, 1854-1924. Railway investor. Founded Hawthorne Race Course. Raced *McGee.

Corum, M. W. "Bill", 1895-1958. President of Churchill Downs (1949-'58). Sports writer for the New York *Journal-American*. In 1925 coined the phrase "run for the roses" to describe the Kentucky Derby.

Cowdin, John E., 1859-1941. Silk merchant. President of Queens County Jockey Club (Aqueduct).

Crawford, Robert H. "Specs," 1897-1975. Jockey, trainer. Leading steeplechase jockey 1919-'20, '22, '26; inducted into Racing Hall of Fame in '73. Rode 139 winners, including Jolly Roger, Fairmount, Lytle, Erne II. Won four American Grand Nationals.

Croker, Richard "Boss," 1841-1922. Real estate, politician. Head of New York's Tammany Hall political machine. Owner of Glencairn Stud, Ireland. Bred Orby, Rhodora, Grand Parade.

Cromwell, Thomas B., 1871-1957. Publisher, bloodstock agent. Founded *The Blood-Horse*, Cromwell Bloodstock agency. Credited with refining past performance charts.

Crosby, H. L. "Bing," 1903-'77. Entertainer. First president of Del Mar Turf Club 1936-'46. Co-owner of Binglin Stock Farm, California. Owned *Meadow Court, *Ligaroti, *Don Bingo, *Blackie II.

Daingerfield, Algernon, 1867-1941. Racing executive. Executive secretary of the Jockey Club. Son of Foxhall Daingerfield.

Daingerfield, Elizabeth, 1870-1951. Farm manager. Owner of Haylands Farm. Managed Wickliffe Stud, Faraway Farm. Managed leading sires Man o' War, High Time. Daughter of Foxhall Daingerfield.

Daingerfield, Foxhall A., ca. 1840-1913. Farm manager. Managed stud careers of Domino, Commando, Ben Brush, Kingston at Castleton Stud, Kentucky. Father of Algernon and Elizabeth Daingerfield.

Daingerfield, J. Keene, 1910-'93. Racing executive, author. Kentucky state steward 1973-'85. Eclipse Award of Merit in 1989. Author of *Training for Fun and Profit (Maybe)*. Grandson of Foxhall Daingerfield.

Daly, William C. "Father Bill," 1837-1931. Trainer. Famous mentor of Racing Hall of Fame jockeys James McLaughlin, Snapper Garrison, Winnie O'Connor, Danny Maher.

Daly, Marcus, 1842-1900. Mining. Owner of Bitter Root Stock Farm, Montana. Bred *Ogden, Tammany; owned Hamburg.

De Bartolo, Edward J., 1909-'94. Real estate developer. Owned Louisiana Downs, Thistledown, Remington Park. Special Eclipse Award in 1988.

De Francis, Frank, 1927-'89. Lawyer, racing executive. Owner of King of Mardi Gras, Hail Emperor. Led groups to buy Laurel Park in 1984 and Pimlico Race Course in '86, thus consolidating ownership of Maryland racetracks.

de Kwiatkowski, Henryk, 1924-2003. Aviation. Owner of Calumet Farm, Kentucky; Kennelot Stable. Joe Palmer Award in 1993. Owned Conquistador Cielo, De La Rose, Danzig. Bought bankrupt Calumet Farm for $17-million at public auction in 1992.

DeLancey, James, 1732-1801. Real estate. Owner of Bouwerie Farm, New York. Bred Maria Slamerkin, Bashaw. Imported *DeLancey's Cub mare (great American foundation mare), *Lath, *Wildair.

Donn, James Sr., 1887-1972. Landscaping contractor, nursery owner. Chairman of Gulfstream Park 1944-'72. Grandfather of Gulfstream Park executive Douglas Donn.

Donoghue, Steve, 1884-1945. Jockey. Winner of ten consecutive riding titles in England (1914-'23). Rode six Epsom Derby winners: Humorist, Captain Cuttle, *Papyrus, Manna, Pommern, Gay Crusader. Rode 1,840 winners in a 33-year career.

Doswell, Thomas W., 1792-1890. Tobacco plantations. Owner of Bullfield Plantation. Bred Planet, Eolus, Algerine, Morello, Fanny Washington; owner of Knight of Ellerslie, Nina, Abd-el-Kader. Mentor and partner of Capt. Richard Hancock, who established Ellerslie Stud.

Drayton, Spencer, 1911-'94. FBI special agent who, upon recommendation of J. Edgar Hoover, in 1946 became the first head of the Thoroughbred Racing Protective Bureau. Served as TRPB president until his retirement in 1978. Inaugurated lip tattoos as a means of horse identification.

Duke, William, 1858-1926. Trainer. Inducted into Racing Hall of Fame in 1956. Trained Flying Ebony, Coventry. Won the 1924 French Derby with *Pot Au Feu; won '25 Kentucky Derby with Flying Ebony; won '25 Preakness Stakes with Coventry.

Dunn, Neville, 1904-'57. Publisher, editor. Editor of *The Thoroughbred Record* 1941-'57. Co-founder of Thoroughbred Club of America.

duPont, William Jr., 1897-1966. Banker. Owner of Walnut Hall Farm, Virginia. Bred and owned Parlo, Berlo, Rosemont, Fairy Chant, Ficklebush; owned Fair Star, Dauber. Founder of Delaware Park.

Duryea, Herman B., 1862-1916. Investments. Owner of Haras du Gazon, France. Leading owner in 1904, when leasing W. C. Whitney's horses. Bred and owned *Durbar II, Banshee, *Sweeper; also owned Irish Lad.

Dwyer, Michael F., 1847-1906. Meat processor. Leading owner. Owned or co-owned Hindoo, Hanover, Miss Woodford, Kingston, Luke Blackburn, Bramble, Ben Brush, Tremont, etc. Brother of Philip J. Dwyer.

Dwyer, Philip J., 1843-1917. Meat processor. President of Brooklyn Jockey Club (Gravesend), Queens County Jockey Club (Aqueduct). Leading owner. Co-owned Hindoo, Hanover, Miss Woodford, Kingston, Luke Blackburn, Bramble, Tremont, etc. Brother of Michael F. Dwyer.

Easton, William, ca. 1850-1909. Auctioneer. American representative of Tattersalls; auctioneer for Fasig-Tipton Co. First great American auctioneer.

Ellis, James C., 1872-1956. Oilman, banker, Thoroughbred breeder, racetrack owner. In 1925 he acquired Dade Park racetrack in Henderson, Kentucky, at court auction. Thirty years later the track's name was changed to James C. Ellis Park.

Ellsworth, Rex, 1907-'97. Rancher. Owner of Ellsworth Farm, California. Leading owner and breeder 1962-'63. Bred and owned Swaps, Candy Spots, Olden Times, Prove It; owned *Prince Royal II; imported *Khaled.

Engelhard, Charles W., 1917-'71. Precious metals. Owner of Cragwood Stable. Leading owner in England in 1970. Owned Nijinsky II, *Hawaii, Assagai, Ribocco, Ribero, Halo, Mr. Leader, Indiana.

Ensor, Lavelle "Buddy," 1900-'47. Jockey. Inducted into Racing Hall of Fame in 1962. Rode 411 winners, including Exterminator, Grey Lag, Hannibal. Rode 33 winners in 11 days, including five of six races on one of those days, in 1919.

Estes, Joseph A., 1902-'70. Journalist. Editor of *The Blood-Horse* 1930-'63. Devised Average Earnings Index; established Jockey Club Statistical Bureau.

Evans, Thomas Mellon, 1910-'97. Mergers and acquisitions. Owner of Buckland Farm. Bred and owned Pleasant Colony, Pleasant Tap, Pleasant Stage.

Fairbairn, Robert A., 1867-1951. Financier. Owner of Fairholme Farm, Kentucky. Bred Gallahadion, Hoop, Jr. Co-owner of *Sir Gallahad III, *Blenheim II.

Fasig, William B., 1846-1902. Auctioneer. Co-founder of Fasig-Tipton Co. in 1898. Conducted first equine auctions in Madison Square Garden.

Fator, Laverne, 1900-'36. Jockey. Leading jockey 1925-'26; inducted into Racing Hall of Fame in '55. Rode 1,075 winners, including Grey Lag, Black Maria, Pompey, Scapa Flow. Won consecutive runnings of Belmont Futurity and Carter and Gazelle Handicaps.

Feustel, Louis, 1884-1970. Trainer. Leading trainer in 1920; inducted into Racing Hall of Fame in '64. Trained two champions and Man o' War, Rock View, Ordinance, Ladkin. Won 20 of 21 races with Man o' War.

Field, Marshall W. III, 1893-1956. Publisher, retailer. Bred High Quest, High Strung, Escutcheon, Clang, Eclair; owned Nimba, Stimulus.

Fink, Jule, 1913-1990. Thoroughbred owner-breeder and noted handicapper. Known as one of the "Speed Boys," his gambling success resulted in the Jockey Club refusing to renew his owner's license in 1949. His subsequent suit against the Jockey Club led to a significant reduction in the club's power over racing, but the New York State Racing and Wagering Board continued the ban until 1967. He was a partner in 1966 Santa Anita Derby winner Boldnesian.

Finney, Humphrey S., 1903-'84. Auctioneer. Chairman of Fasig-Tipton Co. 1952-'84. Founded *Maryland Horse;* author of *A Stud Farm Diary, Fair Exchange.* Father of John M. S. Finney.

Finney, John M. S., 1934-'94. Auctioneer. President Fasig-Tipton Co. 1968-'89. Son of Humphrey Finney.

Fisher, Charles T., 1880-1964. Automobile manufacturer. Owner of Dixiana Farm, Kentucky. Bred Spy Song, Mata Hari, Sweep All, Star Reward.

Fitzsimmons, James E. "Sunny Jim," 1874-1966. Trainer. Leading trainer 1930, '32, '36, '39, '55; inducted into Racing Hall of Fame in '58. Trained 2,275 winners, 155 stakes winners, including Triple Crown winners Gallant Fox and Omaha, and eight champions, including Bold Ruler, Nashua, Granville.

Galbreath, John W., 1897-1988. Real estate developer. Owned Darby Dan Farm, Kentucky and Ohio. Eclipse Award, Man of the Year in 1972. Bred and owned Roberto, Chateaugay, Primonetta, Little Current, Graustark, His Majesty, Proud Truth, Proud Clarion. Instrumental in overseeing rebuilding of Belmont Park and Aqueduct.

Garner, J. Mack, 1900-'36. Jockey. Leading jockey by races won in 1915; leading jockey by money won in '29; inducted into Racing Hall of Fame in '69. Rode 1,346 winners, including Cavalcade, Blue Larkspur. Won 1934 Kentucky Derby on Cavalcade.

Garrison, Edward R. "Snapper," 1868-1930. Jockey, stable agent, trainer, racing official. Inducted into Racing Hall of Fame in 1955. By his estimate, rode more than 700 winners, including Firenze, Tammany. His come-from-behind style immortalized as "Garrison finish."

Gaver, John M., 1900-'82. Trainer. Leading trainer 1942, '51; inducted into Racing Hall of Fame in '66. Trained 73 stakes winners and four champions, including Tom Fool, Capot, Stage Door Johnny, Devil Diver. Won the handicap triple crown with Tom Fool in 1953.

Genter, Frances S., 1898-1992. Household appliances manufacturer. Owned Frances S. Genter Stable. Eclipse Award owner in 1990. Bred and owned In Reality, Smile; owned Unbridled, My Dear Girl, Rough'n Tumble.

Gentry, Olin B., 1900-'90. Farm manager. Managed Idle Hour Stock Farm, Darby Dan Farm. Planned matings for 188 stakes winners, 20 champions, five Kentucky Derby winners. Father of Kentucky breeder Tom Gentry.

Gluck, Maxwell F., 1899-1984. Apparel stores. Owner of Elmendorf Farm. Eclipse Award outstanding owner in 1977; leading owner '77, '81; leading breeder '73, '81. Bred and owned Protagonist, Talking Picture, Big Spruce, Hold Your Peace; owned Prince John. Donation endowed Maxwell F. Gluck Equine Research Center at University of Kentucky.

Gomez, Avelino, 1929-'80. Jockey. Leading Canadian jockey seven times; North American leading jockey in 1966; inducted into Racing Hall of Fame in '82. Rode 4,081 winners, including Ridan, Buckpasser, Affectionately.

Graham, Florence N. "Elizabeth Arden," 1885-1966. Cosmetics manufacturer. Owner of Maine Chance Farm, Kentucky. Leading owner in 1945. Bred Gun Bow, Jewel's Reward, Jet Action; owned Jet Pilot, Beaugay, Myrtle Charm, Star Pilot, Mr. Busher, Lord Boswell.

Grayson, Cary T., 1878-1938. Physician. Owner of Blue Ridge Farm, Virginia. Bred Insco, My Own, Happy Argo; also owned High Time. Co-founder of Grayson Foundation.

Griffin, Henry "Harry," 1876-1955. Jockey. Inducted into Racing Hall of Fame in 1956. Rode 569 winners, including The Butterflies, Henry of Navarre. One of the original investors in Hollywood Park.

Guerin, O. Eric, 1924-'93. Jockey. Leading apprentice jockey in 1942; inducted into Racing Hall of Fame in '72. Rode 2,712 winners, including Native Dancer, Bed o' Roses, Jet Pilot. Rode Native Dancer in 20 of his 21 victories (in 22 starts).

Guest, Raymond R., 1907-'91. Investments. Owner of Powhatan Plantation, Virginia; Ballygoran Stud, Ireland. Bred and owned Tom Rolfe, Chieftain; bred Cascapedia; owned Sir Ivor, Larkspur.

Guggenheim, Harry F., 1890-1971. Publisher, mining. Owner of Cain Hoy Stable. Leading breeder in England in 1963. Bred and owned Never Bend, Bald Eagle, Ack Ack, Cherokee Rose, Red God; bred Ragusa, Crafty Admiral; owned Dark Star, *Turn-to. Co-founder of New York Racing Association.

Haggin, James Ben Ali, 1821-1914. Lawyer, mining. Owner of Elmendorf Farm, Kentucky; Rancho del Paso, California. Bred Firenze, Africander, Tyrant, Waterboy, Tournament; owned Salvator, Ben Ali.

Haggin, Louis L. II, 1913-'80. Real estate. Chairman of Keeneland Association 1970-'80; president of Thoroughbred Racing Associations 1967-'68; co-founder of Thoroughbred Breeders of Kentucky. Bred and owned Himalayan, Harbor Springs, Tingle. Great-grandson of James Ben Ali Haggin.

Hagyard, Charles W., 1901-'95. Veterinarian. Owner of Hagyard Farm, Kentucky. Breeder of Rough'n Tumble, Rising Market. Stood Hail to Reason, Promised Land. Co-founder of Hagyard-Davidson-McGee equine clinic.

Hancock, Arthur B. Sr., 1875-1957. Breeder. President of Breeders' Sales Co. Founder and owner of Claiborne Farm, Kentucky; owner of Ellerslie Stud, Virginia. Leading breeder 1935-'37, '39, '43. Breeder of Johnstown, Beaugay, Cleopatra, St. James, Jacola, Nimba, Jet Pilot. Imported and syndicated *Sir Gallahad III, *Blenheim II. Son of Richard J. Hancock, father of Arthur B. "Bull" Hancock Jr.

Hancock, Arthur B. Jr. "Bull," 1910-'72. Breeder. President of American Thoroughbred Breeders' Association. Owner of Claiborne Farm, Kentucky, and Ellerslie Stud, Virginia. Leading breeder 1958-'59, '68-'69. Breeder of Round Table, Gamely, Apalachee, Moccasin, Doubledogdare, Bayou, Lamb Chop. Imported and syndicated *Nasrullah, *Ambiorix, *Herbager; stood Bold Ruler, Nijinsky II, *Princequillo, Round Table. Son of A. B. Hancock Sr.; father of Kentucky breeders Arthur B. Hancock III (Stone Farm) and Seth Hancock (Claiborne Farm).

Hancock, Richard J., 1838-1912. Breeder. Founder of Ellerslie Stud, Virginia. Bred Knight of Ellerslie, Elkwood, Eon, Eole, Eolist. Father of A. B. Hancock Sr.

Hanes, John W., 1892-1988. Textiles, investments. Co-founder and first chairman of New York Racing Association; president of National Museum of Racing and Hall of Fame. Bred Idun; owned Bold Bidder.

Harbut, Will, 1885-1947. Groom. Stud groom of Man o' War. Coined well-known phrase, "He was the mostest hoss."

Harding, William G., 1808-'86. Farming, railways. Owner of Belle Meade Stud, Tennessee. Bred Vandalite. Stood leading sires *Priam, Vandal, *Bonnie Scotland.

Harper, John, 1803-'74. Farmer. Owner of Nantura Stock Farm, Kentucky. Bred Longfellow, Ten Broeck, Rhynodyne, Fanny Holton.

Harriman, W. Averill, 1891-1986. Railways, politician. Owner of Arden Farm Stable. Owned Chance Play, Ladkin, Mary Jane. As governor of New York (1955-'59), aided formation of New York Racing Association in 1955.

Haskell, Amory L., 1894-1966. Automobiles, safety glass. President of Monmouth Park 1946-'66; president of Thoroughbred Racing Associations 1954-'55. Owner of Blue Sparkler. Aided campaign to legalize pari-mutuel wagering in New Jersey.

Hatton, Charles W., 1906-'75. Journalist. President, New York Turf Writers Association. Eclipse Special Award in 1974. Popularized concept of American Triple Crown.

Hawkins, Abe, Birthdate unknown-1867. Jockey. A slave when he rode Lecomte to victory over Lexington in an 1854 match race, was perhaps the first African-American professional athlete to gain national and international prominence.

Headley, Duval A., 1910-'87. Horseman. President, Keeneland Race Course; president, Thoroughbred Club of America. Owner of Manchester Farm, Kentucky. Breeder of Tom Fool, Dark Mirage, Aunt Ginny. Trained 23 stakes winners, including champions Menow, Apogee. Nephew of Hal Price Headley.

Headley, Hal Petit, 1856-1921. Timber interests. Founder of Beaumont Farm, Kentucky. Bred and owned Ornament. Father of Hal Price Headley.

Headley, Hal Price, 1888-1962. Timber, burley. First president of Keeneland Race Course. Owner of Beaumont Farm, Kentucky. Bred and owned Menow, Alcibiades, Askmenow, Handy Mandy, Chacolet. Co-founder of Keeneland Association; co-founder of American Thoroughbred Breeders' Association. Father of Kentucky breeder Alice Headley Chandler (Mill Ridge Farm).

Healey, Thomas J., 1866-1944. Trainer, racing official. Inducted into Racing Hall of Fame in 1955. Trained three champions, Equipoise, Top Flight, Campfire. Won five Preakness Stakes.

Helis, William G., 1887-1950. Oil exploration. Co-owner of Fair Grounds. Owner of Helis Stock Farm, New Jersey. Owned Cosmic Bomb, Rippey, Salmagundi.

Hern, Maj. William Richard "Dick," (1921-2002). Trainer. Four-time leading British trainer; won 17 classics, including Epsom Derby three times; trained once-beaten Brigadier Gerard; trained for Queen Elizabeth II.

Hernandez, Joe, 1909-'72. Race caller at Santa Anita Park 1935-'72 and Hollywood Park.

Hertz, John D., 1879-1961 and **Frances,** 1881-1963. Taxis and rental cars. Co-owner of Arlington Park. Owner of Stoner Creek Stud, Kentucky; Leona Farm, Illinois. Bred and owned Count Fleet, Anita Peabody, Prince John, Fleet Nasrullah, Blue Banner, Count of Honor; owned Reigh Count.

Hervey, John L., 1870-1947. Journalist. Racing historian and author under pen name of "Salvator." Author of *Racing in America,* Vols. 1, 2, 4.

Hildreth, Samuel, 1866-1929. Trainer, owner. Leading trainer by money won nine times; leading trainer by races won 1921, '27; leading owner by money won 1909-'10, '11; inducted into Racing Hall of Fame in '55. Trained Grey Lag, Zev. Trained ten champions, seven Belmont Stakes winners.

Hine, Hubert "Sonny", 1931-2000. Trainer. Elected to Racing Hall of Fame in 2003. Trained Skip Away, Guilty Conscience, Skip Trial, Technology.

Hirsch, Clement L., 1914-2000. Canned foods. Co-founder and president of Oak Tree Racing Association. Eclipse Award for distinguished service in 1999. Owner of *Figonero, June Darling, *Snow Sporting, Magical Mile, Magical Maiden.

Hirsch, Mary (Mrs. Charles McLennan), 1914-'63. Trainer. First licensed woman trainer in 1933. Owner (with Charles McLennan) of Cowpens Farm, Maryland. Trained stakes winner No Sir. Daughter of Max Hirsch.

Hirsch, Max, 1880-1969. Trainer, jockey, owner, breeder. Inducted into Racing Hall of Fame in 1959. Trained more than 100 stakes winners and six champions, including Assault, Sarazen, Middleground, Bold Venture, Gallant Bloom. Won 1946 Triple Crown with Assault. Father of William J. "Buddy" Hirsch, Mary Hirsch.

Hirsch, William J. "Buddy," 1909-'97. Trainer. Inducted into Racing Hall of Fame in 1982. Trained 56 stakes winners and one champion, Gallant Bloom. Owned stakes winner Columbiana. Son of Max Hirsch.

Hitchcock, Thomas, 1861-1941. Trainer. Inducted into Racing Hall of Fame in 1973. Trained three champions: Good and Plenty, Salvidere, Annibal. Captained America's first international polo team.

Hollingsworth, Kent, 1930-'99. Journalist. Editor of *The Blood-Horse* 1963-'87; president of Thoroughbred Club of America 1974-'75; president of National Museum of Racing Hall of Fame 1982-'86.

Hoomes, John, 1755-1805. Stagecoaches. Founder of Virginia Jockey Club. Imported *Diomed, *Spread Eagle, *Buzzard.

Hooper, Fred W., 1898-2000. Highway construction. Owner of Hooper Farm, Florida. Eclipse Award outstanding breeder 1975, '82; Eclipse Award of Merit in '92. Bred and owned Susan's Girl, Precisionist, Crozier, Tri Jet, Copelan; owned Hoop, Jr., Olympia, Education. Brought Racing Hall of Fame jockeys Braulio Baeza, Laffit Pincay Jr., and Jorge Velasquez to United States.

Howard, Charles S., 1881-1950. Automobile dealer, real estate. Leading owner 1937, '40. Owner of Seabiscuit, *Noor, *Kayak II.

Hughes, Hollie, 1888-1981. Trainer. Inducted into Racing Hall of Fame in 1973. Trained more than 20 stakes winners, including, *Tourist II. Trained 1916 Kentucky Derby winner George Smith.

Hunter, John, 1833-1914. Real estate. First chairman of the Jockey Club 1894-'95; co-founder of Saratoga Race Course. Owner of Annieswood Stud, New York. Owner of Kentucky, Sultana; bred and owned Alarm, Olitipa, Rhadamanthus.

Hyland, John J., Birthdate unknown-1913. Trainer. Inducted into Racing Hall of Fame in 1956. Trained six champions, including Beldame, Henry of Navarre, His Highness, The Butterflies.

Isaacs, Harry Z., 1904-'90. Clothing manufacturer. Owner of Brookfield Farm, Maryland. Bred and owned Intentionally, Intent, Itsabet.

Iselin, Philip H., 1902-'76. Clothing manufacturer. President of Monmouth Park 1966-'77. Instrumental in consolidation of year-end polls into Eclipse Awards.

Jackson, James, 1782-1840. Merchant. Owner of Forks of Cypress Farm, Alabama. Bred Peytona, Reel. Imported *Glencoe, *Galopade, *Leviathan.

Jacobs, Hirsch, 1904-'70. Owner-breeder, trainer. Leading breeder by money won 1964-'67; leading trainer by money won 1946, '60, '65; leading trainer by races won 1933-'39, '41-'44; inducted into Racing Hall of Fame in '58. Trained 3,596 winners and four champions. Bred Affectionately, Hail to Reason, Straight Deal, Personality. Co-owned and trained Hail to Reason, Stymie, Affectionately, Straight Deal.

Janney, Stuart S. Jr., 1907-'88. Lawyer, financier. Chairman, Maryland Racing Commission in 1947; president of Maryland Horse Breeders Association. Owner of Locust Hill Farm, Maryland. Bred and owned Ruffian, Icecapade, Buckfinder, Private Terms. Father of Maryland breeder Stuart S. Janney III.

Jeffords, Walter M. Sr., 1883-1960. Investments. President of Grayson Foundation; president of National Museum of Racing and Hall of Fame 1954-'60. Owner of Faraway Farm, Kentucky. Bred and owned One Count, Pavot, Bateau, Kiss Me Kate, Scapa Flow, Snow Goose.

Jerome, Leonard W., 1817-'91. Financier. Built Jerome Park in 1866; president of Coney Island Jockey Club (Sheepshead Bay racetrack). Owned Kentucky, Fleetwing, Decoursey.

Johnson, Albert, 1900-'66. Jockey, trainer. Leading jockey by money won in 1922; inducted into Racing Hall of Fame in '71. Rode 503 winners, including Exterminator, American Flag, Crusader. Rode two Kentucky Derby winners.

Johnson, William Ransom, 1782-1849. Trainer. Inducted into Racing Hall of Fame in 1986. Trained more than 20 champions, including Boston, Sir Archy. First great American trainer, called the "Napoleon of the Turf;" won 61 of 63 races during a two-year period.

Johnston, Elwood B., 1909-'81. California industry leader. Established Old English Rancho in the 1930s. Founder of the HBPA's California division. North America's leading breeder of stakes winners in 1972, with 13; co-leader in 1971 (nine). Breeder of more than 100 stakes winners, including Real Good Deal, Special Warmth, MacArthur Park, Impressive Style, June Darling, Fleet Treat, Admirably, Generous Portion. Bought and raced Fleet Nasrullah.

Jones, Ben A., 1882-1961. Trainer. Leading trainer by money won 1941, '43-'44, '52; inducted into Racing Hall of Fame in '58. Trained 11 champions, including Whirlaway, Lawrin, Bewitch, Twilight Tear, Armed. Won six record Kentucky Derbys. Father of Horace A. "Jimmy" Jones.

Jones, Horace A. "Jimmy," 1906-2001. Trainer. Leading trainer by money won 1947-'49, '57, '61; inducted into Racing Hall of Fame in '59. Trained 54 stakes winners and seven champions, including Citation, Armed, Coaltown, Tim Tam. First trainer to win more than $1-million in purses. Son of Ben Jones.

Jones, Warner L., 1916-'94. Distiller, breeder. Chairman of Churchill Downs 1984-'92; president of Thoroughbred Breeders of Kentucky. Owner of Hermitage Farm, Kentucky. Eclipse Award of Merit in 1990. Breeder of Dark Star, Lomond, Is It True, Seattle Dancer, Northern Trick, Woodman, King's Bishop. Sold world-record $13.1-million yearling in 1984; co-founder of the American Horse Council.

Joyner, Andrew Jackson, 1861-1943. Trainer. Leading trainer by races won in 1908; inducted into Racing Hall of Fame in '55. Trained five champions, including Ethelbert, St. James, Whisk Broom II.

Keck, Howard B., 1913-'96. Oil production. Bred Ferdinand; bred and owned Turkish Trousers, Bagdad, Fiddle Isle, Tell, etc.

Keene, Foxhall P., 1867-1941. Sportsman. Owner of Domino, Cap and Bells. Purchased Domino for $3,000 as a yearling. Son of James R. Keene.

Keene, James R., 1838-1913. Financier. Owner of Castleton Stud, Kentucky. Leading owner 1905-'08; leading breeder. Bred and owned Colin, Commando, Peter Pan, Sweep, Kingston, Sysonby, Cap and Bells; owned Domino, Spendthrift. Prime mover in formation of the Jockey Club in late 1893. Father of Foxhall P. Keene.

Kenner, Duncan F., 1813-'87. Sugar planter. President, Louisiana Jockey Club. Owner of Blue Bonnet. Owned slave jockey Abe Hawkins.

Kilmer, Willis Sharpe, 1868-1940. Patent-medicine distributor. Owner of Court Manor Stud, Virginia; Sun Briar Court, New York. Bred and owned Sun Beau, Sally's Alley, Chance Sun; owned Exterminator, *Sun Briar; bred Reigh Count.

Kilroe, Frank E. "Jimmy," 1912-'96. Racing executive. Racing secretary and handicapper at Santa Anita Park 1953-'90 and at New York tracks 1954-'59. Eclipse Award of Merit in 1979.

Kirkpatrick, Haden, 1911-'88. Publisher, journalist. Publisher, editor of *The Thoroughbred Record* 1941-'80.

Kleberg, Robert J., 1896-1974. Rancher, oilman. Owner of King Ranch, Kentucky and Texas. Leading owner in 1954. Bred and owned Assault, Middleground, Gallant Bloom, But Why Not, Bridal Flower, Dawn Play, Stymie, Miss Cavandish; owned High Gun.

Klein, Eugene V., 1921-'90. Automobile dealer. Leading owner 1985, '87; Eclipse Award owner 1985-'87. Owned Lady's Secret, Winning Colors, Capote, Life's Magic, Tank's Prospect, Open Mind, Family Style.

Knapp, Willie, 1888-1972. Jockey, trainer, racing official. Inducted into Racing Hall of Fame in 1969. Rode 649 winners, including Exterminator, Upset. Won 1919 Sanford Stakes aboard Upset, handing Man o' War his only loss.

Knight, Henry H., 1889-'59. Automobile dealer. Owner of Almahurst Farm and Coldstream Stud, Kentucky. Bred Almahmoud, Nail, Cosmah. Stood leading sires *Bull Dog, *Heliopolis.

Kummer, Clarence, 1899-1930. Jockey. Leading jockey by money won in 1920; inducted into Racing Hall of Fame in '72. Rode 464 winners, including Man o' War, Sir Barton, Exterminator, Sarazen. Defeated French champion *Epinard by a head aboard Ladkin in 1924 International Special.

Kurtsinger, Charles F., 1906-'46. Jockey. Leading jockey by money won 1931, '37; inducted into Racing Hall of Fame in '67. Rode 721 winners. Won 1931 Kentucky Derby with Twenty Grand; rode War Admiral to victory in 1937 Triple Crown.

Kyne, William P., 1887-1957. Racing executive. General manager of California Jockey Club (Bay Meadows Race Course) 1934-'57; owner of Portland Meadows racetrack 1946-'57. Promoted passage of California pari-mutuel law in 1933.

Lakeland, William, 1853-1914. Trainer. Trained Domino, Hamburg, *Ogden, Electioneer, Exile. Co-breeder and co-owner of Commando.

Laurin, Lucien, 1912-2000. Trainer, jockey. Eclipse Award trainer in 1972; inducted into Racing Hall of Fame in '77. Trained 36 stakes winners and three champions, including Secretariat, Quill, Riva Ridge. Trained 1972-'73 Horse of the Year Secretariat to Triple Crown.

LeRoy, Mervyn, 1900-'87. Movie producer. President of Hollywood Park 1951-'85. Co-bred and owned Honeymoon, Stepfather, Honey's Alibi.

Lewis, J. Howard, 1862-1947. Trainer. Inducted into Racing Hall of Fame in 1969. Trained 14 steeplechase champions, including Bushranger, Fairmount.

Lindheimer, Benjamin F., 1891-1960. Real-estate developer. Chairman of Arlington Park 1938-'60, Washington Park 1934-'60. Father of Marjorie Everett, former chief executive of Hollywood Park.

Loftus, Johnny, 1895-1976. Jockey, trainer. Leading jockey by money won in 1919; inducted into Racing Hall of Fame in '59. Rode 580 winners, including Man o' War, Sir Barton, Pan Zareta. First jockey to win the Triple Crown, aboard Sir Barton in 1919.

Longden, John, 1907-2003. Jockey, trainer. Leading jockey by races won in 1938, '47-'48; leading jockey by money won in 1943, '45; inducted into Racing Hall of Fame in '58; Special Eclipse Award in '94; George Woolf Memorial Jockey Award in '52; Avelino Gomez Memorial Award in '85. Rode then-record 6,032 winners, including Count Fleet, Busher, *Noor. Trained Majestic Prince, Jungle Savage, Baffle. Founded Jockeys' Guild with Eddie Arcaro and Sam Renick in 1940.

Lord Derby (Edward Stanley, 12th Earl of Derby), 1752-1834. A pillar of 18th-century British racing, he was responsible for founding the Epsom Oaks (1779) and Epsom Derby (1780), the latter bearing his family name after he won a coin toss with Sir Charles Bunbury. Won 1787 Derby with Sir Peter Teazle.

Lord Derby (Edward Stanley, 17th Earl of Derby), 1865-1948. Bred then-record 19 English classic winners, including Hyperion, Sansovino, Fairway, Swynford, Colorado, and *Watling Street. Also bred influential sires Phalaris, Pharos, *Sickle, and *Pharamond II. Generally acknowledged as one of the most successful owners-breeders in British Turf history.

Lorillard, George, 1843-'86. Tobacco sales. President of Monmouth Park. Owner of Westbrook Stable. Leading owner 1877-'80. Owned Tom Ochiltree, Spinaway, Duke of Magenta, Harold, Saunterer, Grenada.

Lorillard, Pierre, 1832-1901. Tobacco sales. Owner of Rancocas Stud, New Jersey. Bred and owned Wanda, Exile, Sibola, Dewdrop, Hiawasse; owned Iroquois, Parole, Saxon, Democrat. First American to win Epsom Derby, with Iroquois in 1881; inspired formation of the Board of Control (predecessor to the Jockey Club) in 1891.

Luro, Horatio, 1901-'91. Trainer. Inducted into Racing Hall of Fame in 1980. Trained 43 stakes winners, including Northern Dancer, *Kayak II, Decidedly, *Princequillo.

Mabee, John C., 1921-2002. Grocery chain owner. Chairman, Del Mar Thoroughbred Club. Co-owner with wife Betty of Golden Eagle Farm, California. Eclipse Award breeder 1991, '97, '98. Bred and owned Best Pal, Event of the Year, General Challenge, Jeanne Jones, Worldly Manner. Founding member of the board of directors of Breeders' Cup Ltd.; Del Mar's largest growth occurred under his leadership.

MacBeth, Don, 1949-'87. Jockey. George Woolf Memorial Jockey Award in 1987. Rode Chief's Crown, Temperence Hill, Silver Buck, Half Iced. Inspired formation of injured jockey's fund that bears his name.

Macomber, A. Kingsley, 1876-1955. Banker, oilman. Important owner-breeder in California and France. Worked in 1920s to bring big-time horse racing to California; founder of the New Pacific Coast Jockey Club; also owned Haras de Quesnay in France, Mira Monte Stock Farm in California. Owned Parth, Rose Prince; imported *North Star III.

Madden, John E., 1856-1929. Trainer, owner, breeder. Owner of Hamburg Place. Leading breeder 1917-'27; leading trainer 1901-'03; inducted into Racing Hall of Fame in '83. Trained at least 38 stakes winners and eight champions. Bred Grey Lag, Sir Barton, Old Rosebud; owned Hamburg; trained Hamburg, Plaudit, Sir Martin. Bred five Kentucky Derby winners.

Maher, Danny, 1881-1916. Jockey. Leading jockey in U.S. in 1898; leading jockey in England 1908, '13; inducted into Racing Hall of Fame in '55. Rode 1,771 winners, including Ethelbert, *Rock Sand, Banastar.

Maloney, James W., 1909-'84. Trainer. Inducted into Racing Hall of Fame in 1989. Trained 42 stakes winners and two champions, including Gamely, Lamb Chop, Princessnesian.

Markey, Lucille P. (Wright), 1897-1982. Investments. Owner of Calumet Farm, Kentucky. Leading breeder 1950-'57, '61; leading owner 1952, '56-'58, '61. Bred and owned Alydar, Fabius, Tim Tam, Our Mims, Forward Pass, Davona Dale, Iron Liege, Barbizon, Before Dawn.

Mars, Ethel V., 1884-1945. Confectioner. Owner of Milky Way Farm, Tennessee. Leading owner in 1936. Owned Gallahadion, Forever Yours, Sky Larking, Case Ace, Reaping Reward.

Mayer, Louis B., 1885-1957. Movie producer. Owner of Louis B. Mayer Stock Farm, California. Bred Honeymoon, Your Host, On Trust, Clem, Lurline B.; imported *Alibhai, *Beau Pere.

McAtee, J. Linus "Pony," 1897-1963. Jockey. Leading jockey in 1928; inducted into Racing Hall of Fame in '56. Rode 930 winners, including Exterminator, Twenty Grand, Jack High. Won 1927, '28 Kentucky Derby.

McCarthy, Clem, 1883-1962. Sportscaster. First radio broadcast of Kentucky Derby in 1928; broadcast Derby from 1928-'50.

McCreary, Conn, 1921-'79. Jockey, trainer. Inducted into Racing Hall of Fame in 1975. Rode 1,263 winners, including Racing Hall of Fame members Stymie, Twilight Tear, Armed, Searching. Trained three stakes winners.

McDaniel, Henry, 1867-1948. Trainer. Co-leading trainer by races won in 1922; inducted into Racing Hall of Fame in '56. Trained 1,041 recorded winners and four champions, including Exterminator, Reigh Count, Sun Beau.

McDaniel, Robert H. "Red," 1911-'55. Trainer. Leading trainer by races won 1950-'54. Trained *Poona II, Blue Reading.

McGrath, H. Price, 1814-'81. Tailor, bookmaker. Owner of McGrathiana Stud, Kentucky. Bred Aristides, Thora, Tom Bowling.

McKinney, Rigan, 1908-'85. Jockey, trainer, breeder. Leading amateur steeplechase jockey 1933-'34, '36, '38; inducted into Racing Hall of Fame in '68. Rode 138 winners, including Green Cheese, Beacon Hill, Annibal. Trained Navigate, Drift, The Heir. Won American Grand National aboard Green Cheese in 1931.

McKnight, William L., 1888-1978. Industrialist. Chairman, Minnesota Mining and Manufacturing Co. 1949-'66. Co-founder of Calder Race Course. Owner of Tartan Farms, Florida. Eclipse Award, Man of the Year, in 1974. Leading breeder in 1990. Bred and owned Dr. Fager, Ta Wee, Dr. Patches; bred Unbridled.

McLaughlin, James, 1861-1927. Jockey. Leading jockey 1884-'87; inducted into Racing Hall of Fame in 1955. Rode Hindoo, Tecumseh, Tremont, Firenze. Won 1881 Kentucky Derby on Hindoo; won '85 Preakness Stakes aboard Tecumseh; won six Belmont Stakes.

McLennan, Joseph, 1868-1933. Racing executive. Racing secretary at Hialeah Park, Arlington Park.

Meadors, Joel C. "Skeets," 1896-1967. Photographer.

Mellon, Paul, 1908-'99. Investments, banking. Owner of Rokeby Stud, Virginia. Eclipse Award owner-breeder in 1971; breeder in '86; Award of Merit in '93. Bred and owned Mill Reef, Arts and Letters, Key to the Mint, Fort Marcy, Sea Hero, Quadrangle, Run the Gantlet, Java Gold; owned Fit to Fight, Summer Guest, Blue Banner.

Miller, Walter, 1890-1959. Jockey. Leading jockey 1906-'07; inducted into Racing Hall of Fame in '55. Rode 1,904 winners, including Colin, Ballot, Peter Pan, Whimsical. Won 388 races in 1906 (at age 16), a record that stood until Racing Hall of Fame jockey William Shoemaker tied the mark 44 years later in 1950 and broke it in '52.

Mills, James P., 1909-'87, and **Alice**, 1912-2000. Aviation. Owner of Hickory Tree Farm, Virginia. Bred and owned Committed, Believe It, Terpsichorist, Hagley; owned Devil's Bag, Gone West.

Mills, Ogden, 1884-1937. Investments. Co-owner of Wheatley Stable. Bred Seabiscuit, Edelweiss; owned Dice, Diavolo, Dark Secret.

Molter, William, 1910-'60. Trainer. Leading trainer by races won 1946-'49; leading trainer by money won 1954, '56, '58, '59; inducted into Racing Hall of Fame in '60. Trained 2,158 winners and 48 stakes winners, including Round Table, Determine, T. V. Lark.

Mori, Eugene, 1898-1975. Banker, real-estate developer. Builder and president of Garden State Park 1942-'72; owned Hialeah Park 1954-'72. Owner of East Acres Farm, New Jersey. Bred Tosmah; owned Alma North, Cosmah. Promoted pari-mutuel wagering in New Jersey.

Morris, Francis, 1810-'86. Shipping. Owner of Morris Stud, New York. Bred and owned Ruthless, Relentless, Narragansett. Aided Leonard W. Jerome in founding of American Jockey Club and Jerome Park in 1866.

Morris, Green B., 1837-1920. Owner, trainer. Leading owner in 1902. Trained Apollo, Sir Dixon, Strathmeath, Star Ruby.

Morris, John A., 1892-1985. Financier. President of Thoroughbred Racing Associations, Jamaica Racetrack. Eclipse Award, Man of the Year, in 1975. Bred and owned Missile Belle, Proudest Roman, L'Heureux; owned Missile. Great-grandson of Francis Morris.

Morrissey, John, 1831-'78. Prizefighter, gambler, politician. Co-founder of Saratoga Race Course in 1863.

Mulholland, W. F. "Bert," 1884-1968. Trainer. Inducted into Racing Hall of Fame in 1967. Trained 832 winners, 57 stakes winners, and five champions, including Jaipur, Eight Thirty, Lucky Draw, Battlefield. Trained for George D. Widener for more than 40 years.

Munnings, Sir Alfred, 1878-1959. Painter. Greatest English painter of horses of 20th century.

Murphy, Isaac, 1860-'96. Jockey, trainer, owner. Inducted into Racing Hall of Fame in 1955. Rode 530 recorded winners, including Falsetto, Firenze, Salvator, Emperor of Norfolk. First jockey to win three Kentucky Derbys; first jockey elected to Racing Hall of Fame. Won with 44% of his mounts.

Neloy, Eddie, 1921-'71. Trainer. Leading trainer by money won 1966-'68; inducted into Racing Hall of Fame in '83. Trained 60 stakes winners and five champions, including Buckpasser, Bold Lad, Gun Bow.

Neves, Ralph, 1921-'95. Jockey. Inducted into Racing Hall of Fame in 1960; George Woolf Memorial Jockey Award in '54. Rode 3,771 winners, ranked sixth all-time by wins at retirement; rode 173 stakes winners, including Round Table, Native Diver. Rode five winners at Bay Meadows after track announcer declared him "deceased" following an accident the previous day.

Newman, Neil, 1886-1951. Journalist. Wrote under the pen name of "Roamer." Author of *Famous Horses of the American Turf* series 1930-'32.

Niarchos, Stavros, 1909-'96. Shipping. Owner of Haras de Fresnay-le-Buffard, France; Oak Tree Farm, Kentucky. Bred and owned Miesque, Spinning World, Kingmambo, Hernando (Fr), Hector Protector, Machiavellian; owned Nureyev.

Niccolls, Richard, 1624-72. Soldier, politician. Founded first American racecourse, Newmarket, at Salisbury Plain (near modern Hempstead), Long Island, New York.

Notter, Joe, 1890-1973. Jockey. Leading jockey by money won in 1908; inducted into Racing Hall of Fame in '63. Rode Regret, Whisk Broom II, Colin. First jockey to ride a filly, Regret, to victory in the Kentucky Derby (1915); first jockey to win handicap triple crown, on Whisk Broom II.

O'Connor, Winnie, 1884-1947. Jockey, trainer. Leading jockey in 1901; inducted into Racing Hall of Fame in '56. Rode 1,229 winners in United States and France, including Yankee, Reina. One of "Father Bill" Daly's "Five Aces."

Odom, George M., 1883-1964. Jockey, trainer. Inducted into Racing Hall of Fame in 1955. Rode 527 winners, including Broomstick, Delhi, Banastar. Trained Busher, Pasteurized. Won the Belmont Stakes as a jockey and later as a trainer.

O'Farrell, Joe, 1912-'82. Breeder. President, Florida Breeders' Sales Co. Owner of Ocala Stud, Florida. Bred Roman Brother, Office Queen, My Dear Girl. Stood Rough'n Tumble. Primary founder of Florida breeding industry.

Olin, John M., 1892-1982. Small-arms munitions. Bred and owned Cannonade; owned Bold Bidder, Northfields.

O'Neill, Frank, 1886-1960. Jockey. Inducted into Racing Hall of Fame in 1956. Rode Beldame, Roseben, *Prince Palatine. Also successful jockey in France and England.

Palmer, Joe H., 1904-'52. Journalist. Author of *This Was Racing, American Racehorses* series 1944-'51.

Parke, Burley, 1905-'77. Trainer. Inducted into Racing Hall of Fame in 1986. Trained 37 stakes winners

and two champions, including Roman Brother, *Noor, Raise a Native. *Noor beat Citation in four consecutive stakes races. Brother of Ivan Parke.

Parke, Ivan, 1908-'95. Jockey, trainer. Leading jockey by races won in 1923, '24 (his first two years of racing); leading jockey by money won in '24; inducted into Racing Hall of Fame in '78. Rode 419 winners, including Backbone. Trained 27 stakes winners, including Exclusive Native, Hoop, Jr. Brother of Burley Parke.

Patrick, Gilbert "Gilpatrick," 1812-ca. 1880. Jockey. Inducted into Racing Hall of Fame in 1970. Rode Ruthless, Boston, Kentucky, Lexington. Rode first Belmont Stakes winner, Ruthless, in 1867.

Paulson, Allen E., 1922-2000. Aviation. Owner of Brookside Farm, Kentucky. Eclipse Award breeder in 1993; owner '95 and '96. Owned and bred Cigar, Ajina, Escena, Fraise; owned Theatrical (Ire), Strawberry Road (Aus), Blushing John, Arazi, Paradise Creek; bred Azeri.

Payson, Mrs. Charles S. (Joan Whitney), 1903-'75. Publisher, investments. Co-owner of Greentree Stud. Leading owner in 1951. Owned and bred Stage Door Johnny, Capot, Bowl Game, Late Bloomer, The Axe II, Cohoes, Stop the Music; owned Tom Fool. Daughter of Mr. and Mrs. Payne Whitney; sister of John Hay Whitney.

Pelleteri, Anthony, 1893-1952. Trainer, racing executive. Won the 1941 Santa Anita Handicap with 90-to-1 Bay View, and developed stakes winners Bull Reigh and Andy K. In 1941 Pelleteri organized a partnership that saved the historic Fair Grounds racetrack in New Orleans from being auctioned and subdivided; served as the track's executive vice president until his death.

Penna, Angel, 1923-'92. Trainer. Leading trainer in Argentina in 1952; leading trainer in Venezuela in '54; leading trainer in France in '74; inducted into Racing Hall of Fame in '88. Trained more than 250 stakes winners, including Allez France, Relaxing, San San, Private Account.

Perry, William Haggin, 1911-'93. Investments. Owner of Waterford Farm, Virginia. Co-owned and co-bred Gamely, Lure, Revidere, Coastal, Lamb Chop, Boldnesian.

Phipps, Mrs. Henry C. (Gladys Mills), 1883-1970. Investments. Owner of Wheatley Stable. Leading owner in 1966. Bred and owned Bold Ruler, Bold Lad, Seabiscuit, High Voltage, Misty Morn, Queen Empress, Successor, Bold Bidder, Castle Forbes. Mother of leading owner-breeder Ogden Phipps; sister of Ogden Mills.

Phipps, Ogden, 1908-2002. Investments. Chairman, Jockey Club 1964-'74; former chairman New York Racing Association. Leading owner by money won 1988, '89; Eclipse Award breeder in '88; Eclipse Award owner 1988, '89; Mr. Fitz Award in '89. Bred and owned Buckpasser, Easy Goer, Private Account. Bred and raced Personal Ensign, who was unbeaten in 13 starts.

Piatt, Thomas, 1877-1965. Farmer, tobacco. First president of Thoroughbred Club of America; president, Breeders' Sales Co. Owner of Brookdale Farm, Kentucky. Bred Alsab, Donau. Father of Thomas Carr Piatt.

Piatt, Thomas Carr, 1900-'53. Farmer, tobacco. President, Breeders' Sales Co. 1949-'53. Owner of Crestwood Farm, Kentucky. Co-breeder of Occupation, Occupy, Errard. Son of Thomas Piatt.

Pincus, Jacob, 1838-1918. Trainer, jockey. Leading trainer in 1869; inducted into Racing Hall of Fame in '88. Trained Glenelg, Eagle, Richmond. Trained Iroquois, first American winner of the Epsom Derby.

Pollard, John "Red," 1909-1981. Canadian-born jockey. Rode his first Thoroughbred winner in 1926. In mid-1930s began association with C. S. Howard, owner of Seabiscuit, whom he rode to many important victories—although not in the famed 1938 match against War Admiral. Retired after injury-plagued 30-year career. Later inducted into the Canadian Racing Hall of Fame.

Porter, William T., 1809-'58. Publisher. Founded *Spirit of the Times* magazine in 1831.

Price, Jack, 1908-'95. Trainer. Trained 1961 Kentucky Derby and Preakness Stakes winner Carry Back, whom he bred out of a $265 mare, Joppy.

Purdy, Samuel, 1785-1836. Jockey. Inducted into Racing Hall of Fame in 1970. Semi-retired when pulled from the crowd to replace American Eclipse's jockey at the Union Course in 1823, winning the next two heats to win the match over Henry.

Reiff, John, 1885-1974. Jockey. Leading jockey in France in 1902; inducted into Racing Hall of Fame in '56. Rode 1,016 winners, including Orby, Tagalie, Retz, Moia. Among the top ten jockeys for ten seasons in France; won two Epsom Derbys and one French Derby.

Rice, Daniel, 1896-1975, and **Ada L.,** 1899-1977. Stock and grain broker. Co-owners of Arlington Park 1940-'68. Owners of Danada Farm, Kentucky. Bred and owned Lucky Debonair, Pucker Up, Proud Delta, Delta Judge, Advocator.

Rice, Grantland, 1880-1954. Journalist. Covered most major sports for the New York *Herald Tribune,* but horse racing was a favorite. Among the great racing events he covered was the 1938 Seabiscuit-War Admiral match.

Richards, A. Keene, 1827-'81. Sugar and cotton planter. Owner of Blue Grass Park Stud, Kentucky. Owned *Australian, Starke, War Dance. Bred Fenian, Target, Eliza Davis, Ulrica.

Richards, Sir Gordon, 1904-1986. Jockey. Champion British flat jockey 26 times in 34 seasons of racing. First to ride more than 4,000 winners, he retired in 1954 with a then-world record 4,870 career victories. In 1953 he became the first professional jockey to be knighted.

Richards, Leonard P., Birthdate and date of death unknown. Chemical manufacturer. Second chairman of the Delaware Racing Commission.

Riddle, Samuel D., 1862-1951. Textiles. Owner of Faraway Farm, Kentucky; Glen Riddle Stable. Leading owner in 1925. Owned Man o' War; bred and owned War Admiral, Crusader, American Flag, War Relic.

Riggs, William P., 1874-1936. Racetrack executive. Secretary of the Maryland Jockey Club; a driving force behind the revival of Pimlico Race Course and return of Preakness Stakes to Maryland in 1909.

Robertson, Alfred, 1911-'75. Jockey. Inducted into Racing Hall of Fame in '71; New York Turf Writers Association's best jockey in 1942. Rode 1,856 winners, including Top Flight, Whirlaway, Riverland, Sky Larking. Twice rode six winners in a single day.

Robertson, William H. P., 1920-'82. Journalist. Editor of *The Thoroughbred Record* 1962-'78. Author of *History of Thoroughbred Racing in America, Hoofprints of the Century.*

Roebling, Joseph M., 1909-'80. Building contractor. Owner of Harbourton Stud, New Jersey. Bred and owned Blue Peter, Fall Aspen, Rainy Lake.

Rogers, John W., ca. 1850-1908. Trainer. Inducted into Racing Hall of Fame in 1955. Trained 11 champions, including Artful, Modesty. Trained Artful to win the 1904 Belmont Futurity, giving Sysonby the only defeat of his career.

Rolapp, R. Richards, 1941-'93. Lawyer. President of American Horse Council 1978-'93.

Ross, John K. L., 1876-1951. Railways. Leading owner 1918-'19. Owned Sir Barton, Billy Kelly, Cudgel.

Rous, Adm. Henry J., 1795-1877. English Jockey Club steward, Turf reformer, handicapper. Published "Handbook on the Laws of Racing," which included the first standard scale of weights. Established and enforced strict standards and banned unsavory characters. Often referred to as the "Father of the Turf."

Rowan, Louis R., 1911-'88. Investments. Original shareholder in Santa Anita Racetrack; six-term president of the California Thoroughbred Breeders Association; conceived California Cup; founding director of Oak Tree Racing Association and Del Mar Thoroughbred Club. Founding chairman of the Winners Foundation.

Rowe, James Sr., 1857-1929. Trainer, jockey. Leading jockey 1871-'73; inducted into Racing Hall of Fame in '55. Trained 34 horses regarded as champions, more than any other Hall of Fame trainer. Trained Colin, Miss Woodford, Regret, Luke Blackburn, Hindoo.

Runyon, Damon, 1884-1946. Journalist, sports columnist, author, humorist. Many of his short stories had to do with gambling and horse racing. Most famous for writing *Guys and Dolls,* although probably best known in racing for the poem "Gimme a Handy Guy Like Sande," about jockey Earl Sande.

Salman, Ahmed bin, 1958-2002. Publisher, Saudi royal family. Owner of The Thoroughbred Corp. Bred and owned Point Given, Spain. Owned Sharp Cat, Jewel Princess, Oath, Anees, Royal Anthem, War Emblem.

Salmon, Walter J., ca. 1880-1953. Real estate. Owner of Mereworth Farm. Leading breeder in 1946. Bred Discovery, Display, Dr. Freeland, Battleship (first American-bred and -owned winner of England's Grand National Steeplechase), Free For All; owned Vigil.

Samuel, Ernest, 1930-2000. Steel distribution. Owner of Sam-Son Farm, Ontario and Florida. Eclipse Award owner in 1991; leading owner and breeder in '91. Bred and raced more than 100 stakes winners, including Dance Smartly, Sky Classic, Chief Bearhart.

Sande, Earl, 1899-1968. Jockey, trainer. Leading jockey 1921, '23, '27; leading trainer in '38; inducted into Racing Hall of Fame in '55. Rode 968 winners, including Gallant Fox, Zev, Man o' War. Trained Stagehand, Sceneshifter. Won three Kentucky Derbys, five Belmont Stakes, and five Jockey Club Gold Cups.

Sanford, John, 1851-1939. Carpet mills, politician. Owner of Hurricane Stud, New York. Bred and raced *Affection, *Snob II, Sir John Johnson, *Donnacona; owned George Smith. Son of Stephen Sanford.

Sanford, Milton H., 1812-1883. Cotton mills. Owner of Preakness Stud, New Jersey; North Elkhorn Farm, Kentucky. Bred Vagrant, Vigil; also owned Preakness, Virgil, Monarchist. Stood leading sire Glenelg.

Sanford, Stephen, 1826-1913. Carpet mills. Owner of Hurricane Stud, New York. Raced only homebreds, which he gave Indian names, including Caughnawaga, Chuctununda, and Mohawk II. Stood Clifford, *Voter. Father of John Sanford.

Schapiro, John, 1914-2002. President of Laurel Park racetrack in Maryland for 35 years; inaugurated the Washington, D. C., International at Laurel in 1952; *Sports Illustrated*'s Racing Man of the Year in 1960. Eclipse Award of Merit in 1980.

Scott, Marion duPont, 1891-1983. Investments. Owner of Montpelier Farm, Virginia. Bred more than 50 stakes winners, including Mongo, Parka, Neji, Soothsayer; owned Proud Delta, Battleship. Founded Carolina Cup Steeplechase in Camden, South Carolina. Member of syndicate that imported *Blenheim II.

Seagram, Joseph E., 1841-1919. Distiller. Member of Canadian Parliament. President of Ontario Jockey Club. Bred and raced Inferno, Belle Mahone. Won 15 King's (Queen's) Plates.

Shaffer, Charles B., 1859-1943. Oil production. Owner of Coldstream Stud, Kentucky. Bred Bull Lea, Occupation, Occupy, Star Pilot, Reaping Reward, Plucky Play. Stood leading sires *Bull Dog, *Heliopolis. Father of E. E. Dale Shaffer.

Shaffer, E. E. Dale, 1917-'74. Oil production. Founder of Detroit Race Course; chairman of Kentucky Racing Commission 1950-'51; president of Michigan Racing Association; president of Thoroughbred Racing Associations 1960-'61. Owner of Coldstream Stud, Kentucky. Leading breeder in 1945. Bred Sweet Patootie, Star Pilot, Johns Joy. Stood leading sires *Bull Dog, *Heliopolis. Son of Charles Shaffer.

Shilling, Carroll, 1882-1950. Jockey. Leading jockey in 1910; inducted into Racing Hall of Fame in '70. Rode 969 winners, including Colin, Sir Martin, Fitz Herbert, King James. Won 1912 Kentucky Derby aboard Worth.

Simms, Edward F., 1870-1938. Oil production. Owner of Xalapa Farm, Kentucky. Bred Coventry; owned Eternal, My Play.

Simms, Willie, 1870-1927. Jockey. Leading jockey in 1894; inducted into Racing Hall of Fame in 1977. Rode 1,125 winners, including Henry of Navarre, Ben Brush, Plaudit, Commanche. Won back-to-back Belmont Stakes (1893-'94) aboard Commanche and Henry of Navarre.

Sinclair, Harry F., 1876-1956. Oil production. Owner of Rancocas Stud, New Jersey. Bred and owned Mad Play, Ariel; owned Zev, Grey Lag, Mad Hatter.

Skinner, John S., 1788-1851. Publisher. Founded *American Turf Register* in 1830.

Sloan, James F. "Tod," 1874-1933. Jockey. Inducted into Racing Hall of Fame in 1955. Rode Hamburg, Clifford. Credited with popularizing the use of shortened stirrups in United States and England.

Sloane, Isabel Dodge, 1898-1962. Automobile heiress. Owner of Brookmeade Stud, Virginia. First female leading owner 1934, '50. Bred and owned Sword Dancer, Bowl of Flowers, Bold, Sailor, Greek Ship; owned Cavalcade, High Quest.

Smith, George "Pittsburgh Phil," 1862-1905. Gambler. Most successful gambler of Victorian era, died a millionaire.

Smith, Robert A., 1869-1942. Trainer, owner. Leading trainer 1933-'34; inducted into Racing Hall of Fame in '76. Trained more than 27 stakes winners and three champions, including 1934 Horse of the Year Cavalcade, High Quest. Owned Articulate. Won 1934 Kentucky Derby with Cavalcade.

Smith, Tom "Silent Tom," 1879-1957. Trainer. Leading trainer 1940, '45; inducted into Racing Hall of Fame in 2001. Trained 29 stakes winners and six champions, including Seabiscuit, Jet Pilot, *Kayak II. Trained 1947 Kentucky Derby winner Jet Pilot.

Smithwick, Alfred "Paddy," 1927-'73. Jockey. Leading steeplechase jockey by races won 1956-'58, '62; inducted into Racing Hall of Fame in '73. Rode 398 winners, including Neji, Bon Nouvel, Elkridge. Won two American Grand Nationals aboard Neji. Trained two stakes winners.

Sommer, Sigmund, 1917-'79. Real estate. Leading owner 1971-'72. Owned 29 stakes winners, including Autobiography, Sham, Never Bow.

Spreckels, Adolph, 1857-1924. Sugar merchant. President of Pacific Coast Jockey Club. Owner of Napa Stock Farm, California. Bred Morvich; bred and owned Runstar.

Stanford, Leland, 1824-'93. Politician. Governor of California 1861-1863; United States senator 1885-1893; founder of Stanford University. Developed Palo Alto Stock Farm. In 1872 hired photographer to prove that all of a horse's feet are off the ground at one point in the gallop.

Stephens, Woodford C. "Woody," 1913-'98. Trainer. Eclipse Award trainer in 1983; inducted into Racing Hall of Fame in '76. Trained 131 stakes winners and 11 champions, including Swale, Conquistador Cielo, Never Bend. Won five consecutive Belmont Stakes (1982-'86).

Stout, James, 1914-'76. Jockey, racing official. Inducted into Racing Hall of Fame in 1968. Rode Johnstown, Granville, Assault, Omaha, Stymie. Finished in the first triple win dead heat in a major stakes aboard Bousset in the 1944 Carter Handicap.

Strub, Charles H., 1884-1958. Baseball team owner, real estate, investments. Founder of Santa Anita Park. Father of Robert P. Strub.

Strub, Robert P., 1919-'93. Real estate. President of Los Angeles Turf Club (Santa Anita Park); chairman, Santa Anita Operating Co.; president of Thoroughbred Racing Associations 1963-'64. Eclipse Award of Merit in 1992. Son of Charles H. Strub.

Stull, Henry, 1851-1913. Noted American equine painter. First to accurately portray racehorses at a gallop. Owned Swarthmore.

Sutcliffe, Leonard S., 1880-1937. Photographer. Published photographic volumes *Thoroughbred Sires* and *Famous Mares in America.*

Swigert, Daniel, 1833-1912. Breeder. Founded Elmendorf Farm, Kentucky. Leading breeder. Bred Spendthrift, Hindoo, Salvator, Tremont, Baden-Baden. Managed Woodburn Stud. Father-in-law of Leslie Combs Sr.

Swinebroad, George W., 1901-'75. Auctioneer. Legendary auctioneer at Keeneland and Saratoga. Hammered down first $100,000 yearling in 1961.

Swope, Herbert Bayard, 1882-1958. Journalist, investments. Chairman of New York Racing Commission.

Taral, Fred, 1867-1925. Jockey, trainer. Inducted into Racing Hall of Fame in 1955. Rode 1,437 winners, including Domino, Henry of Navarre, Dr. Rice, Ramapo. Rode Domino to nine consecutive victories in 1893.

Tasker, Col. Benjamin Jr., 1720-'60. Planter. Prominent owner-breeder during Colonial era. Owner of Belair Stud, Maryland. Imported great racemare *Selima from England in 1750, notable sire *Othello; bred Pacolet, Selim.

Tayloe, John II, 1721-'79. Planter. Owner of Mount Airy Stud, Virginia. Bred Yorick, Ariel, Bellair; owned *Selima, Moreton's Traveller. Father of John Tayloe III.

Tayloe, John III, 1771-1828. Planter. Owner of Mount Airy Stud, Virginia. Bred American foundation sire Sir Archy, Lady Lightfoot, Grey Diomed, Calypso. Imported *Castianira, dam of Sir Archy. Son of John Tayloe II.

Taylor, Charles P. B., 1935-'97. Journalist. Investments. Owner of Windfields Farm, Canada and Maryland; chairman, Canadian Jockey Club; vice president, Breeders' Cup Inc. Son of Edward P. Taylor.

Taylor, Edward P., 1901-'89. Brewing. President, Ontario Jockey Club and Canadian Thoroughbred Horse Society. Owner of Windfields Farm, Canada and Maryland. Leading breeder 1974-'80. Bred and owned Northern Dancer, Nearctic, Victoria Park; bred Nijinsky II, El Gran Senor, Devil's Bag, The Minstrel, Secreto, Shareef Dancer, Storm Bird, Viceregal. Father of Charles P. B. Taylor.

Ten Broeck, Richard, 1809-'92. Gambler, sportsman. Owner of Metairie Race Course, Louisiana. Bred Umpire; owned Lexington, Lecomte, Prioress, *Eclipse, Starke. Conducted first successful invasion of England with American-breds in 1860s.

Tenney, Meshach, 1907-'93. Trainer. Leading trainer 1962-'63; inducted into Racing Hall of Fame in '91. Trained 36 stakes winners and one champion, including Swaps, Candy Spots, Olden Times, Prove It. Won 1955 Kentucky Derby with Swaps.

Tesio, Federico, 1869-1954. Breeder. Acclaimed Italian breeder of *Ribot, Nearco, Donatello II, Niccolo Dell'Arca. Bred and owned 20 Italian Derby winners. Author of *Breeding the Racehorse*.

Thomas, Barak G., 1826-1906. Planter, publisher. Noted owner-breeder in post-Civil War America. Founded Dixiana Farm, Kentucky. Bred and owned Himyar; bred Domino, Correction.

Thompson, Henry J. "Derby Dick," 1881-1937. Trainer. Inducted into Racing Hall of Fame in 1969. Trained 373 recorded winners and five champions, including Blue Larkspur, Burgoo King, Bubbling Over. First trainer to saddle four Kentucky Derby winners.

Tipton, Edward A., 1855-1930. Auctioneer. Co-founder of Fasig-Tipton Co. in 1898. Manager of Bitter Root Stud, Montana, 1896-1900. Sold company to E. J. Tranter.

Tranter, Enoch J., 1875-1938. Auctioneer. Owner of Fasig-Tipton Co. 1904-'38. Revolutionized Thoroughbred auction business in America. Launched annual yearling sale at Saratoga.

Travers, William R., 1819-'87. Stockbroker, raconteur. First president of Saratoga Association. Owned Kentucky, Alarm, Sultana.

Trotsek, Harry, 1912-'97. Trainer. Inducted into Racing Hall of Fame in 1984. Trained 96 stakes winners and two champions; trained Moccasin, Hasty Road, *Stan. Expert handler of imported horses; coached young jockeys at his jockey school in the 1940s.

Troye, Edward, 1808-'74. Painter. Prolific equine portraitist, his subjects included Lexington, Boston, and many of America's great mid-19th-century Thoroughbreds.

Tuckerman, Bayard J., 1889-1974. Jockey, breeder, owner. First president of Suffolk Downs. Inducted into Racing Hall of Fame in 1973. Rode Homestead. Bred Lavender Hill. Leading amateur jockey.

Turner, Nash, 1881-1937. Jockey, trainer, owner. Inducted into Racing Hall of Fame in 1955. Rode Imp, Flying Star, Goldsmith, Irish Lad. Rider of Imp, the first filly to win the Suburban Handicap in 1899; won 1906 Prix du Jockey-Club (French Derby).

Van Berg, Marion H., 1896-1971. Trainer, owner. Leading owner by money won 1965, '68-'70; leading owner by races won 1952, '54, '56, '60-'70; inducted into Racing Hall of Fame in '70. Trained more than 1,470 winners and six stakes winners, including *Estacion, Rose Bed. Father of Racing Hall of Fame trainer Jack Van Berg.

Vanderbilt, Alfred G., 1912-'99. Investments. Chairman, New York Racing Association; president, Belmont Park and Pimlico Race Course. Owner of Sagamore Farm, Maryland. Eclipse Award of Merit in 1994. Bred and owned Native Dancer, Next Move, Bed o' Roses, Now What, Petrify; owned Discovery; bred Conniver, Miss Disco.

Van Ranst, Cornelius W., Birthdate and date of death unknown. Owned American Eclipse, *Messenger.

Veitch, Sylvester, 1910-'96. Trainer. Inducted into Racing Hall of Fame in 1977. Trained 44 stakes winners and five champions, including Counterpoint, Career Boy. Trained Horse of the Year Counterpoint, who won the 1951 Belmont Stakes. Father of trainer John Veitch.

Vosburgh, Walter, 1855-1938. Handicapper, author. Racing secretary, Westchester Racing Association (Belmont Park) 1894-1934. Author of *Racing in America 1866-1921;* Turf editor of *Spirit of the Times.* Originated Experimental Free Handicap in 1933.

Waggoner, William T., 1852-1934. Oil production, rancher. Early 20th-century force in Texas racing. Owner of 3D's Stock Farm, Texas. Built Arlington Downs racetrack, Texas, in 1929.

Walden, R. Wyndham, Birthdate unknown-1905. Trainer. Inducted into Racing Hall of Fame in 1970. Trained 101 stakes winners, including Duke of Magenta, Grenada, Saunterer. Trained seven Preakness Stakes winners, five consecutively.

Walsh, Michael G., 1906-'93. Trainer. Leading steeplechase trainer by races won 1953-'55; leading steeplechase trainer by money won 1953-'54, '60; inducted into Racing Hall of Fame in '97; F. Ambrose Clark Award in '75. Trained 31 stakes winners, including champion King Commander, Independence, Rhythminhim. Founder of Stoneybrook Races in Southern Pines, North Carolina.

Ward, Sherrill, 1911-'84. Trainer. Eclipse Award trainer in 1974; inducted into Racing Hall of Fame in '78. Trained 20 stakes winners and two champions, including Forego, Summer Tan, Idun. Trained Forego to Horse of the Year honors in 1975 and '76.

Warfield, Elisha, 1781-1859. Physician. Co-founder of the Kentucky Association racetrack, Lexington. Owner of The Meadows Stud, Kentucky. Breeder of Lexington, Berthune, Alice Carneal. Known as the "father of the Kentucky Turf."

Welch, Aristides J., 1811-'90. Owner of Erdenheim Stud, Pennsylvania. Bred Iroquois, Parole, Sensation, Harold, Spinaway. Stood leading sire *Leamington.

Wells, Thomas J., 1803-'62. Sugar planter. President of Metairie Race Course. Bred Lecomte, Prioress; owned Reel.

Werblin, David A. "Sonny," 1910-'91. Entertainment and sports executive. First president of New Jersey Sports and Exposition Authority (originally the Meadowlands and now including Monmouth Park). Owner of Silent Screen, Process Shot.

Westrope, Jack, 1918-'58. Jockey. Leading jockey in 1933 at age 15, when he rode 301 winners. Inducted into Racing Hall of Fame in 2002.

Whitney, Cornelius V., 1899-1992. Investments. First president of National Museum of Racing Hall of Fame. Owner of C. V. Whitney Farm, Kentucky. Leading breeder 1933, '34, '38, '60; leading owner 1930-'33, '60. Bred more than 175 stakes winners. Bred and owned Counterpoint, Silver Spoon, Career Boy, First Flight; owned Equipoise, Top Flight. Son of Harry Payne Whitney.

Whitney, Harry Payne, 1872-1930. Investments. Owner of Brookdale Stud, New Jersey; Whitney Farm, Kentucky. Leading breeder 1926-'32; leading owner 1913, '20, '24, '26, '27, '29. Bred and owned Regret, Equipoise, First Flight, Whisk Broom II, Whichone, Whiskery, Pennant, Upset, John P. Grier, Prudery.

Whitney, Mrs. Payne (Helen Hay), 1876-1944. Investments. "First Lady of the American Turf." Owner of Greentree Stud, Kentucky. Leading owner and breeder in 1942. Bred and owned Twenty Grand, Shut Out, Devil Diver, First Minstrel. Mother of John Hay Whitney and Joan Whitney (Mrs. Charles S.) Payson.

Whitney, John Hay "Jock," 1904-'82. Investments, publisher. Co-founder of American Thoroughbred Breeders' Association. Co-owner of Greentree Stud, Kentucky; owner of Mare's Nest Farm, Kentucky. Leading owner in 1951. Bred and raced Stage Door Johnny, Capot, Late Bloomer, Bowl Game, The Axe II, Cohoes, Stop the Music; owned Tom Fool. Stood The Porter.

Whitney, W. Payne, 1875-1927. Investments. Owner of Greentree Stud, Kentucky. Son of William C. Whitney; brother of H. P. Whitney; father of John Hay Whitney and Joan Whitney (Mrs. Charles S.) Payson.

Whitney, William C., 1841-1904. Transportation, oil production. President of Saratoga Race Course. Owner of La Belle Stud, Kentucky. Leading owner 1901, '03. Owned Volodyovski, Plaudit, Artful, Endurance By Right, Nasturtium; bred Artful, Tanya. Father of Harry Payne and W. Payne Whitney.

Whittingham, Charles E., 1913-'99. Trainer. Leading trainer 1970-'73, '75, '81, '82; Eclipse Award trainer 1971, '82, '89; inducted into Racing Hall of Fame in '74. Trained 252 stakes winners and 11 champions, including Ack Ack, Sunday Silence, Ferdinand, Turkish Trousers. All-time leading trainer at Hollywood Park and Santa Anita Park; trained two Kentucky Derby winners.

Wickham, John, 1763-1839. Lawyer. Bred champion and leading sire Boston, Tuckahoe.

Widener, George D., 1889-1971. Investments. Chairman of the Jockey Club 1950-'64; president, National Museum of Racing; president, Belmont Park. Owner of Old Kenney Farm, Kentucky; Erdenheim Stud, Pennsylvania. Bred and owned more than 100 stakes winners, including Jaipur, Eight Thirty, What a Treat, Jamestown, High Fleet, Platter, Stefanita, Jester, Seven Thirty, Rare Treat. Nephew of Joseph E. Widener.

Widener, Joseph E., 1871-1943. Investments. President of Hialeah Park, Belmont Park. Owner of Elmendorf Farm, Kentucky. Leading breeder in 1940. Bred Polynesian, Peace Chance, Osmand; owned Chance Shot. Imported leading sire *Sickle. Father of P. A. B. Widener II; uncle of George D. Widener.

Widener, Peter A. B. II, 1896-1952. Investments. Owner of Elmendorf Farm, Kentucky. Son of Joseph E. Widener.

Williamson, Ansel, ca. 1806-81. Trainer. Inducted into Racing Hall of Fame in 1998. Trained Aristides, Tom Bowling, Brown Dick, Virgil. Trained first Kentucky Derby winner, Aristides.

Willmot, Donald G., 1917-'94. Brewer, investments. Owner of Kinghaven Farm, Ontario. Leading owner in 1990. Bred and owned With Approval, Izvestia, Steady Growth, Candle Bright, Bayford, Play the King, Carotene; co-owner of Deputy Minister.

Winfrey, B. Carey, 1885-1962. Trainer, owner. Inducted into Racing Hall of Fame in 1975. Trained 16 stakes winners and one champion, including Dedicate, Squared Away, Bulwark, Martyr. Stepfather of William C. Winfrey.

Winfrey, William C., 1916-'94. Trainer. Leading trainer in 1964; inducted into Racing Hall of Fame in '71. Trained 38 stakes winners and seven champions, including Native Dancer, Bed o' Roses, Next Move, Bold Lad. Trained Native Dancer, who retired in 1954 with 21 wins in 22 starts. Stepson of G. Carey Winfrey.

Winkfield, Jimmy, 1882-1974. Jockey. Won the 1901 and 1902 Kentucky Derbys aboard His Eminence and Alan-a-Dale, becoming the last African-American rider to capture the Louisville classic. In 1904 became a leading rider in Russia; later competed in Poland, Romania, Germany, and France.

Winn, Col. Matt. G., 1861-1949. Racing executive. President of Louisville Jockey Club. Legendary racetrack promoter, developed Kentucky Derby into world-class event.

Winters, Theodore, 1823-'94. Mining. Owner of Rancho del Rio, California; Rancho del Sierra, Nevada. Bred Emperor of Norfolk, Yo Tambien, El Rio Rey, Rey del Rey, Thad Stevens; owned Norfolk.

Withers, David D., 1821-1892. Banker. President, Monmouth Park. Owner of Brookdale Farm, New Jersey. Bred Requital, Laggard, Kinglike.

Woodford, Catesby, 1849-1923. President of Kentucky Racing Association. Owner of Raceland Farm, Kentucky. Co-owner of Runnymede Stud, Kentucky. Stood Hindoo, *Star Shoot. Co-breeder of Miss Woodford, Hanover, Sir Dixon.

Wood, Eugene D., Birthdate unknown-1924. Racing executive. Treasurer of the Metropolitan Jockey Club (Jamaica). Namesake of Wood Memorial Stakes.

Woodward, William Sr., 1876-1953. Banker. Chairman of the Jockey Club 1930-'50. Owner of Belair Stud, Maryland. Leading owner in 1939. Part of syndicate that imported *Sir Gallahad III. Bred and owned Gallant Fox, Omaha, Nashua, Granville, Vagrancy.

Woodward, William Jr., 1920-'55. Banker, sportsman. Owner of Belair Stud. Owned Nashua.

Woolf, George "The Iceman," 1910-'46. Jockey. Leading jockey by money won 1942, '44; inducted into Racing Hall of Fame in '55. Rode 721 winners, including Seabiscuit, Whirlaway, Challedon. Won the Belmont Futurity three straight years, the first running of the Santa Anita Derby, and the Preakness Stakes.

Workman, Raymond "Sonny," 1909-'66. Jockey. Leading jockey by races won 1930, '33, '35; leading jockey by money won 1930, '32; inducted into Racing Hall of Fame in '56. Rode 1,169 winners, including Equipoise, Top Flight, Discovery. Won two Kentucky Derbys, two Belmont Stakes, and the first three runnings of the Pimlico Futurity.

Wright, Warren, 1875-1950. Baking powder, investments. Owner of Calumet Farm, Kentucky. Leading breeder 1941, '44, '47-'50; leading owner 1941, '43-'44, '46-'49. Bred and owned Citation, Whirlaway, Pensive, Ponder, Coaltown, Bewitch, Hill Gail, Twilight Tear, Real Delight, Armed; owned Nellie Flag, Bull Lea. Stood leading sire Bull Lea, Sun Again, Chance Play.

Yoshida, Zenya, 1921-'93. Breeder. Owner of Shadai Farm, Japan; Fontainebleau Farm, Kentucky. Leading Japanese breeder 20 times. Bred Amber Shadai, Gallop Dyna, Dyna Gulliver, Vega; co-owned Wajima; stood Northern Taste, Sunday Silence.

Young, Col. Milton S., 1851-1918. Retail hardware, real estate. Chairman of Kentucky Racing Commission. Owner of McGrathiana Stud, Kentucky. Leading breeder in 1890. Bred Broomstick, Yankee; stood Hanover.

Contemporary Individuals in Racing and Breeding

(Names of Racing Hall of Fame members are in boldface italics.)

Abdullah, Khalid, 1942-. Investments. Owner of Juddmonte Farms, Kentucky and England. Eclipse Award breeder in 1995, 2001-'02; Eclipse Award owner in '92; P.A.B. Widener Trophy in '93; honorary member of Great Britain's Jockey Club in '83. Bred Ryafan, Wandesta (GB), Commander in Chief, Warning (GB), Banks Hill (GB). Owned Known Fact, Dancing Brave, Rainbow Quest. Member of the ruling family of Saudi Arabia; first Arab owner to win a British classic (Two Thousand Guineas [Eng-G1] with Known Fact in 1980).

Abercrombie, Josephine, 1926-. Oil production, boxing promoter. Owner of Pin Oak Farm, Kentucky. Bred and owned Laugh and Be Merry, Peaks and Valleys. Co-owned Maria's Mon. Bred Elocutionist, Touching Wood.

Adams, Frank D. "Dooley", 1927-. Jockey, trainer. Leading steeplechase jockey 1946, '49-'55; inducted into Racing Hall of Fame in '70. Rode 337 winners, including Neji, Elkridge, Oedipus, Refugio, and Floating Isle. Trained Subversive Chick. Operated Refugio Farm training center in Southern Pines, North Carolina, after retiring as a jockey.

Aga Khan IV, Karim, 1936-. Investments, Ismaili Muslim leader. Owner of Gilltown Stud, Sheshoon Stud in Ireland; Haras de Bonneval in France. Bred Shergar, Sinndar, Kahyasi, Daylami (Ire), Kalanisi (Ire). Built Aiglemont training facility near Chantilly, France, in 1977; continued breeding operations begun by his grandfather, Aga Khan III, and his father, Prince Aly Khan.

Aitcheson, Joe Jr., 1929-. Jockey. Leading steeplechase jockey 1961, '63-'64, '67-'70; inducted into Racing Hall of Fame in '78; first jockey to receive the F. Ambrose Clark Memorial Award, in '75. Rode 478 winners, including Amber Diver, Bon Nouvel, Tuscalee, Top Bid, Soothsayer, Inkslinger. Won eight Virginia Gold Cups, seven Carolina Cups, and two Colonial Cups.

Alexander, Helen, 1951-. Investments. President, Thoroughbred Club of America, 1989-'91. Owner of Middlebrook Farm, Kentucky. Bred Twining. Bred and owned Althea, Aishah, Aquilegia. Granddaughter of Robert J. Kleberg.

Allbritton, Joseph, 1924-. Publishing, banking, broadcasting, real estate. Owner of Lazy Lane Farms, Kentucky and Virginia. Owned Hansel, Secret Hello, Life At the Top, Kittiwake.

Anthony, John Ed, 1939-. Timber. Owner of Shortleaf Farm, Arkansas; president of Loblolly Stable. Bred and owned Temperence Hill, Vanlandingham, Prairie Bayou. Owned Cox's Ridge. Established the Exercise Induced Pulmonary Hemorrhage Fund after his Demons Begone bled during the 1987 Kentucky Derby (G1).

Appleton, Arthur, 1915-. Electrical manufacturing. Owner of Bridlewood Farm, Florida. Bred and owned Jolie's Halo, Wild Event. Owned Skip Trial. One of stockholders of *The Florida Horse*.

Asmussen, Cash, 1962-. Jockey. Leading jockey by money won in 1979; leading jockey in France 1985-'86, '88-'90; Eclipse Award as apprentice jockey in '79. Rode Suave Dancer, Hector Protector, Mill Native, Northern Trick. Won inaugural Japan Cup aboard Mairzy Doates in 1981; three times won five races on a single card in New York.

Asmussen, Steven, 1965-. Trainer. Leading trainer by wins in 2002. Brother of Cash Asmussen.

Atkinson, Ted F., 1916-. Jockey, racing official. Leading jockey by money won 1944, '46; leading jockey by races won 1944, '46; inducted into Racing Hall of Fame

in '57; George Woolf Memorial Jockey Award in '57. Rode 3,795 winners, including Tom Fool, Gallorette, Devil Diver. Rode 1953 Horse of the Year Tom Fool to handicap triple crown; first jockey whose mounts earned more than $1-million in one year (1946).

Bacharach, Burt, 1929-. Composer. Co-owner of Country Roads Farm, West Virginia. Thoroughbred Owners and Breeders Association Award for outstanding owner-breeder 1995-'96. Bred and owned Heartlight No. One, Afternoon Deelites, Soul of the Matter.

Baeza, Braulio, 1940-. Jockey, trainer. Leading jockey by money won 1965-'68, '75; Eclipse Award jockey 1972, '75; inducted into Racing Hall of Fame in '76; George Woolf Memorial Jockey Award in '68. Rode 3,140 winners, including Buckpasser, Dr. Fager, Ack Ack, Gallant Bloom, Affectionately, Chateaugay. Trained Double Zeus. Rode Buckpasser to one-mile record in 1966 and then lowered it aboard Dr. Fager in '68; first jockey to win more than $3-million in purses in a single year (1967).

Baffert, Bob, 1953-. Trainer. Leading trainer by money won, 1998-2001; Eclipse Award trainer 1997-'99; United Thoroughbred Trainers of America's Trainer of the Year in '98; Mr. Fitz Award in '97. Trained Chilukki, Real Quiet, Silverbulletday, Silver Charm, Point Given, War Emblem. Won a record 13 stakes at Del Mar in 2000; only trainer to win Kentucky Derby (G1) and Preakness Stakes (G1) in consecutive years (1997-'98).

Bailey, Jerry, 1957-. Jockey. President, Jockeys' Guild, 1990-'97. Leading jockey by money won 1995-'98, 2001, '02; inducted into Racing Hall of Fame in '95; Eclipse Award jockey 1995-'97, 2000-'02; George Woolf Memorial Jockey Award in '92; Mike Venezia Award in '93. Rode Cigar, Fit to Fight, Black Tie Affair (Ire), Sea Hero. In 1996, rode Cigar to his 16th consecutive win; rode seven winners on Florida Derby (G1) day program in '95; successfully lobbied for protective vests to be worn by all jockeys; won handicap triple crown with Fit to Fight in '84.

Baird, Dale, 1935-. Leading American trainer by annual winners 15 times. On July 22, 1999, became the first trainer to saddle more than 8,000 career winners. Inducted into National HBPA Hall of Fame in 2001. Based at Mountaineer Park in West Virginia.

Barton, Patti, 1945-. Helped break gender barrier when she became one of the first female jockeys in 1969. Retired in 1984 as world's winningest female rider, with 1,202 victories. Mother of jockey-television personality Donna Barton Brothers and trainer Jerry Barton.

Bassett, James E. "Ted" III, 1921-. Racing executive. Former chairman, Keeneland Association; former president, Breeders' Cup Ltd.; also served as chairman, Equibase Co.; president, Thoroughbred Racing Associations; chairman, Kentucky Horse Park; president, Thoroughbred Club of America. Co-owner of Lanark Farm, Kentucky. Eclipse Award of Merit in 1995; John W. Galbreath Award in '91; Turf and Field Club Award in '84; Joe Palmer Award in '86; John A. Morris Award in '97; Lord Derby Award in '98. Owned Falconese.

Baze, Russell, 1958-. Jockey. Leading jockey by races won 1992-'96, 2002; inducted into Racing Hall of Fame in '99; Special Eclipse Award in '95; Isaac Murphy Award 1995-2002; George Woolf Memorial Jockey Award in 2002. Rode Hawkster, Both Ends Burning, Itsallgreektome. Won 24 stakes races in 1998; won 400 races a year nine times.

Beck, Graham, 1929-. Mining, investments, vintner. Owner of Gainesway Farm, Kentucky; Silvercrest Farm, Kentucky; Midway Farm, Kentucky; Highlands Farm, South Africa; Maine Chance Farm, South Africa; Noreen Stud, South Africa. Bred Pompeii, Real Cozzy, Irish Prize. Co-owned Timber Country.

Bell, John A. III, 1918-. Owner, breeder, bloodstock agent. Director, Thoroughbred Owners and Breeders Association; president, Thoroughbred Club of America in 1954; former president, Farm Manager's Club. Owned Jonabell Farm, Kentucky. Bred Battlefield, Aglimmer, One for All, Never Say Die. Owned Epitome. Former president of *The Blood-Horse* magazine; acquired half interest in Cromwell Bloodstock Agency in 1950.

Bellocq, Pierre "Peb", 1926-. Caricaturist. Special Eclipse Award in 1980; John Hervey Award 1965-'66, '68; Knights of Arts and Letters Award in '90; Golden Horseshoe Award in '91. Achieved international acclaim as *Daily Racing Form*'s caricaturist; has murals at Aqueduct, Oaklawn Park, and Arlington Park; founded the Amateur Riders Club of the Americas with son Remi Bellocq.

Bellocq, Remi, 1961-. Marketing executive, organization executive. Former marketing director at Turf Paradise and Santa Anita Park. Became executive director of the National Horsemen's Benevolent and Protective Association in 2001. Son of Pierre Bellocq.

Berube, Paul, 1941-. President of the Thoroughbred Racing Protective Bureau since 1988. Background in military intelligence; TRPB agent and vice president 1965-'88. Serves on the National Thoroughbred Racing Association task force on computer security.

Biszantz, Gary, 1934-. Golf-club manufacturer. Chairman of Thoroughbred Owners and Breeders Association; serves on American Graded Stakes Committee, Integrity in Racing Committee. Jockey Club member; Breeders' Cup director. Owns 350-acre Cobra Farm in Lexington. Owned Old Trieste, Running Flame (Fr), Admise (Fr), Lord Grillo (Arg), homebred Cobra King. Co-founder of Cobra Golf, sold in 1996 to American Brands.

Blum, Walter, 1934-. Jockey, racing official. Former president, Jockeys' Guild. Leading jockey by races won 1963-'64; inducted into Racing Hall of Fame in '87; George Woolf Memorial Jockey Award in '65. Rode 4,382 winners, including Affectionately, Gun Bow, Forego, Mr. Prospector, Pass Catcher, Summer Scandal, Boldnesian, Priceless Gem, Lady Pitt.

Boulmetis, Sam Sr., 1927-. Jockey, racing official. Inducted into Racing Hall of Fame in 1973. Rode 2,783 winners. Rode Tosmah, Helioscope, Dedicate. Long-time steward at New Jersey tracks.

Brady, Nicholas J., 1930-. Financier. Chairman, Jockey Club, 1974-'82; United States treasury secretary 1988-'93; Co-owner of Mill House Stable. Bred and owned Sensational, Furiously, Meritus. Son of James Cox Brady Jr.

Bramlage, Larry, 1952-. Veterinarian. Vice president, American Association of Equine Practitioners in 2002. Jockey Club Gold Medal in 1994; British Equine Veterinary Association's Special Award of Merit in '98. Developed and improved ways to repair serious bone fractures.

Brumfield, Don, 1938-. Jockey, racing official. Inducted into Racing Hall of Fame in 1996; George Woolf Memorial Jockey Award in '88. Rode 4,573 winners, including Forward Pass, Alysheba, Gold Beauty, Our Mims, Old Hat. Retired in 1989 with the most wins in the history of Churchill Downs (925) and Keeneland Race Course (716).

Brunetti, John, 1931-. President and owner of Hialeah Park, which he purchased in 1978; track has not conducted racing since 2001. Owner of Red Oak Farm, Florida; owned Strolling Belle.

Burch, J. Elliott, 1922-. Trainer. Leading trainer by money won in 1969; inducted into Racing Hall of Fame in '80. Trained more than 30 stakes winners and six champions, including Sword Dancer, Fort Marcy, Arts and Letters, Bowl of Flowers, Run the Gantlet, Key to the Mint. Son of Racing Hall of Fame trainer Preston Burch; grandson of Racing Hall of Fame trainer William Burch.

Campbell, W. Cothran "Cot", 1927-. Advertising, racing syndicates. President of Dogwood Stable, South Carolina. John W. Galbreath Award in 1992. Owned Summer Squall, Storm Song, Dominion (GB). Popularized racing syndicates; wrote *Lightning in a Jar: Catching Racing Fever.*

Carey, Thomas, 1932-. Racing executive. President and general manager, Hawthorne Race Course. Inducted into Chicago Sports Hall of Fame in 1998. Instrumental in rebuilding Hawthorne after fire in 1978.

Cauthen, Steve, 1960-. Jockey. Leading jockey by races won in 1977; inducted into Racing Hall of Fame in '94; Eclipse Award apprentice jockey in '77; Eclipse Award jockey in '77; Eclipse Award of Merit in '77; George Woolf Memorial Jockey Award in '84. Rode 2,794 winners, including Affirmed, Oh So Sharp (Ire), Old Vic, Johnny D., Diminuendo, Indian Skimmer. Rode Affirmed to Triple Crown in 1978; only jockey to win the Kentucky, Epsom, Irish, French, and Italian Derbys; at 18, youngest jockey to win Kentucky Derby.

Cella, Charles, 1936-. Real estate, racing executive. President, Oaklawn Park; president, Thoroughbred Racing Associations 1975-'76. Became TRA's youngest president in 1975. Owned Northern Spur (Ire), Out of Hock.

Chandler, Alice Headley, 1927-. Farm owner. Chairman, Maxwell F. Gluck Equine Research Center; former chairman, Kentucky Racing Commission; president, Kentucky Thoroughbred Owners and Breeders Association; former president, Kentucky Thoroughbred Associaton; director, Keeneland Association. Owner of Mill Ridge Farm, Kentucky. Bred and owned Keeper Hill. Bred Sir Ivor, Secret Hello, Ciao, Flemensfirth.

Chavez, Jorge, 1961-. Jockey. Leading jockey in New York 1994-'99; Eclipse Award jockey in '99. Rode Monarchos, Artax, Beautiful Pleasure, A P Valentine, Affirmed Success. Rode six winners on single card at Gulfstream Park in 1999.

Chenery, Helen "Penny", 1931-. Investments. President, Thoroughbred Owners and Breeders Association, 1976-'84. Former owner of Meadow Stud and Meadow Stable, Virginia. Bred Alada. Owned Secretariat, Riva Ridge. First woman to head a major national racing organization; one of the first three women inducted into the Jockey Club, in 1983.

Chillingworth, Sherwood, 1926-. Executive vice president of Oak Tree Racing Association. Jockey Club board of stewards; board of NTRA Investments; ex-officio member of NTRA Thoroughbred Industry Council; vice chairman of Santa Anita Realty 1994-'96.

Clay, Robert N., 1946-. Farm owner. President, Thoroughbred Owners and Breeders Association, 1990-'93; president, National Thoroughbred Association; president, Thoroughbred Club of America. Co-owner of Three Chimneys Farm, Kentucky. John W. Galbreath Award in 1995. Bred and owned Hidden Lake, Gorgeous. Bred Seaside Attraction, Subordination.

Combs II, Brownell, 1933-. Former president and chairman of Spendthrift Farm; former Kentucky Racing Commission chairman. Son of Leslie Combs II, renowned commercial horse salesman, stallion syndicator, and founder of Spendthrift Farm in 1930s. Pleaded guilty in 2001 to federal income tax fraud charges.

Cooksey, Patricia, 1958-. Second all-time leading female jockey with more than 2,100 winners and purse earnings of $20-million. Captured four riding titles at Turfway Park. All-time leading female rider at Churchill Downs. In 1985 became first female to ride in the Preakness Stakes (G1) (sixth on Tajawa). Member of the Kentucky Athletic Hall of Fame.

Cordero, Angel Jr., 1942-. Jockey, trainer, jockey's agent. Leading jockey by money won 1976, '82-'83; leading jockey by races won in '68; inducted into Racing Hall of Fame in '88; Eclipse Award jockey 1982-'83; George Woolf Memorial Jockey Award in '72; Mike Venezia Award in '92. Rode 7,076 winners, including Seattle Slew, Slew o' Gold, All Along (Fr), Bold Forbes, Broad Brush. Won jockey's title at Saratoga 13 times, 11 consecutively.

Craig, Sidney, 1932- and **Craig, Jenny**, 1932-. Diet foods. Owners of Rancho del Rayo training center in California. Owned 1992-'93 champion older female Paseana (Arg), Exchange, Dr Devious (Ire), Alpride (Ire).

Croll, Warren A. "Jimmy" Jr., 1920-. Trainer. Inducted into Racing Hall of Fame in 1994; United Thoroughbred Trainers of America Outstanding Trainer Award in '94; Big Sport of Turfdom Award in '95; Mr. Fitz Award in '95. Owned and trained Holy Bull. Trained Mr. Prospector, Bet Twice, Parka, Forward Gal, Housebuster.

Day, Pat, 1953-. Jockey. President, Jockeys' Guild, 2000-'01. Leading jockey by races won 1982-'84, '86, '90-'91; inducted into Racing Hall of Fame in '91; Eclipse Award jockey in 1984, '86-'87, '91; George Woolf Memorial Jockey Award in '85; Mike Venezia Award in '95; Mr. Fitz Award in 2000. Rode Wild Again, Flanders, Lady's Secret, Easy Goer, Summer Squall, Tank's Prospect, Louis Quatorze, Lil E. Tee, Dance Smartly. All-time leader by earnings among jockeys and third-highest number of winners; set a record for most stakes won (60) in a single season in 1991; rode seven winners in one day at Churchill Downs in '84; won on eight of nine mounts at Arlington Park in '89.

De Francis, Joseph, 1955-. Racing executive, lawyer. President, Maryland Jockey Club; president, Pimlico Race Course and Laurel Park. Son of Frank De Francis.

Delahoussaye, Eddie, 1951-. Jockey. Leading jockey in 1978; inducted into Racing Hall of Fame in '93; George Woolf Memorial Jockey Award in '81. Rode A.P. Indy, Princess Rooney, Prized, Gato Del Sol, Sunny's Halo, Pleasant Stage, Thirty Slews, Gate Dancer. One of four jockeys to win consecutive Kentucky Derbys, in 1982-'83. Retired in early 2003.

Delp, Grover G. "Bud", 1932-. Trainer. Eclipse Award trainer in 1980. Inducted into Racing Hall of Fame in 2002. Trained Spectacular Bid, Include, Timeless Native, Aspro, Silent King.

Desormeaux, Kent, 1970-. Jockey. Leading jockey by races won 1987-'89; leading jockey by money won in '92; Eclipse Award apprentice jockey in '87; Eclipse Award jockey 1989, '92; George Woolf Memorial Jockey Award in '93. Rode Fusaichi Pegasus, Real Quiet, Kotashaan (Fr), Risen Star. Won record 598 races in 1989; won six races on a single card at Hollywood Park in 1992.

Dickinson, Michael, 1950-. Trainer. Owner of Tapeta Farm, Maryland. Trained Da Hoss, Fleet Renee, Cetewayo. Trained first five finishers in England's Cheltenham Gold Cup in 1983.

DiMauro, Steve Sr., 1932-. Trainer. Owner of DiMauro Farm, New York. Eclipse Award trainer in 1975. Bred Flip's Pleasure, Father Don Juan. Trained Wajima, Dearly Precious, Nagurski, Father Don Juan.

Dixon, F. Eugene, 1923-. Investments. Owner of Erdenheim Farm in Pennsylvania, formerly owned by his uncle George D. Widener. Member of the Jockey Club; former chairman of the Pennsylvania Horse Racing Commission. Former owner of Philadelphia 76ers basketball team.

Donn, Douglas, 1947-. President of Gulfstream Park racetrack 1978-2000; became chairman in 2000 after the track was purchased by Magna Entertainment Corp. Grandson of late Gulfstream owner James Donn Sr.

Dreyfus, Jack J. Jr., 1913-. Financier. Chairman, New York Racing Association, in 1969 and '75. Owner Hobeau Farm, Florida. Leading owner by money won in 1967; Eclipse Award of Merit in '76. Bred and owned Beau Purple, Duck Dance, Never Bow, Step Nicely. Exacta introduced in New York betting under his direction; his Beau Purple upset Kelso three times.

Drysdale, Neil, 1947-. Trainer. Inducted into Racing Hall of Fame in 2000. Trained A.P. Indy, Fusaichi Pegasus, Princess Rooney, Tasso, Hollywood Wildcat, Fiji (GB), Bold 'n Determined.

Duchossois, Richard L., 1921-. Industrialist. Chairman, Arlington Park. Owner of Hill 'N Dale Farm, Illinois. Special Eclipse Award in 1989; Special Sovereign Award in '88; Lord Derby Award in '88; Jockey Club Medal in '86; Jockey Agents' Benevolent Association's Man of the Year in '90. Bred Explosive Darling. Rebuilt Arlington Park after the track was destroyed by fire in 1985; under his leadership, Arlington received a Special Eclipse Award in '85, the first awarded to a racetrack.

duPont, Allaire (Mrs. Richard C.), 1913-. Investments. Owner of Woodstock Farm, Maryland; Bohemia Stable, Maryland. Thoroughbred Owners and Breeders Association award for Maryland in 1984. Bred and owned Politely, Believe the Queen. Bred and raced Kelso, only five-time Horse of the Year (1960-'64); one of the first three women inducted into the Jockey Club, in 1983.

Englander, Richard, 1959-. Investments. Eclipse Award owner in 2001, when he led the nation with stable earnings of $9,784,822, and in '02.

Evans, Edward P. "Ned", 1942-. Publishing. Owner of Spring Hill Farm, Virginia. Bred and owned Minstrella, Prenup, Raging Fever, Fairy Garden, Colonial Minstrel. Owned Withallprobability. Brother of Robert S. Evans; son of Thomas Mellon Evans.

Evans, Robert S. "Shel", 1944-. Manufacturing. Owner of Winter Haven Farm, Florida; Courtland Farm, Maryland. Bred and owned Sewickley, Shared Interest. Bred Forestry, Cash Run. Brother of Edward P. Evans; son of Thomas Mellon Evans.

Everett, Marjorie L., 1921-. Racing executive. Former chairman and chief executive officer, Hollywood Park; former owner, Arlington Park; former owner, Washington Park. Undertook major improvements at Hollywood Park, including expanding the circumference of the track, building the Cary Grant Pavilion, and improving the backstretch; successfully lobbied for inaugural Breeders' Cup to be held at Hollywood Park in 1984.

Fabre, Andre, 1945-. Champion French trainer 1987-2002. Began career as a jump jockey; trained steeplechasers before switching to the flat in 1980. Won five Prix de l'Arc de Triomphes (Fr-G1), three Breeders' Cup events—the 1993 Classic with 134-to-1 Arcangues; 1990 Turf with In the Wings (GB); and 2001 Filly and Mare Turf with Banks Hill (GB). Also trained Trempolino, Swain (Ire), Subotica (Fr), Sagamix (Fr), Zafonic.

Farish, William S., 1939-. Investments. Chairman, Churchill Downs, 1992-2001. President and owner of Lane's End, Kentucky. Eclipse Award breeder in 1992, '99; P.A.B. Widener Trophy in '92. Bred or co-bred A.P. Indy, Law Society, Lemon Drop Kid, Charismatic, Summer Squall, Prospectors Delite. Owned Bee Bee Bee, Miss Brio (Chi), Sweet Revenge. Former chairman of the Breeders' Cup executive committee; United States ambassador to Great Britain and Northern Ireland, 2001-. Nephew of Martha Gerry.

Fenwick Jr., Charles, 1948-. Auto dealer; steeplechase jockey, trainer. Trained and rode Dosdi to two National Steeplechase Association Timber Horse of the Year titles. In 1980 rode *Ben Nevis II to victory in England's Grand National Steeplechase. Trained 1987 Eclipse Award-winning steeplechaser Inlander (GB) and timber champions Buck Jakes, Free Throw, Sugar Bee.

Fires, Earlie, 1947-Jockey. Leading apprentice jockey in 1965; inducted into Racing Hall of Fame in 2001; George Woolf Memorial Jockey Award in '91. Rode In Reality, War Censor, Dike, Abe's Hope, Pattee Canyon, Woozem, Gallant Romeo. Won seven races from eight mounts in a single day at Arlington Park in 1983; won on all six mounts in one day at Hawthorne Race Course in '89.

Firestone, Bertram S., 1931- and **Firestone, Diana**, 1932-. Real estate, investments. Owner, Calder Race Course and Gulfstream Park 1988-'91. Owner of Catoctin Stud, Virginia. Eclipse Award owner in 1980. Owned Genuine Risk. Bred and owned Theatrical (Ire), Paradise Creek, April Run (Ire), Honest Pleasure, What a Summer.

Fishback, Jerry, 1947-. Jockey, bloodstock agent. Leading steeplechase jockey by races won 1971, '73-'75, '77; leading steeplechase jockey by money won in '85; inducted into Racing Hall of Fame in '92. Rode 301 winners, including Cafe Prince, Flatterer. Won the Temple Gwathmey Steeplechase Handicap six times; won four Carolina Cups and four International Gold Cups.

Foreman, Alan, 1950-. Lawyer. Chairman and chief executive officer, Thoroughbred Horsemen's Association. Creator of Mid-Atlantic Thoroughbred Championship (MATCH) series; general counsel for the Maryland Thoroughbred Horsemen's Association.

Forsythe, John, 1918-. Actor. Director, Hollywood Park. Owner of Big Train Farm. Eclipse Award of Merit in 1988. Owned Targa. Longtime Eclipse Awards dinner host.

Francis, Dick, 1920-. International best-selling author of 39 mystery novels. Owner of horse racing. England's champion steeplechase jockey of 1953-'54 when he rode for the Queen Mother. Published first novel—*Dead Cert*—in 1962 and last—*Shattered*—in 2000. Winner of three Edgar Allen Poe Awards for best mystery novel.

Frankel, Robert, 1941-. Trainer. Leading trainer by money won in 1993, 2002; inducted into Racing Hall of Fame in '95; Eclipse Award trainer in 1993, 2000-'02. Trained Bertrando, Possibly Perfect, Wandesta (GB), Marquetry, Squirtle Squirt. Once called the king of claimers for his ability to turn claiming horses into winners; won a record 60 races at Hollywood Park during his first year in California (1972).

Franks, John, 1925-. Oil production. Owner of Franks Farms, Louisiana; Louisiana Stallions, Louisiana; South-

land Farm, Florida. Co-owner of Heatherten Farm, Maryland. Leading owner by money won 1983-'84, '86, '93; leading owner by races won in 1983-'84, '86-'89; leading breeder by races won 1988-'93; leading owner by races won in '89; leading owner by money won in '93; Eclipse Award owner in 1983-'84, '93-'94. Bred and owned Answer Lively, Derby Wish, Kissin Kris. Bred Sharp Cat, Royal Anthem. Owned Heatherten, Dave's Friend, Top Avenger. Earned $3.1-million in 1984, then a single-season record for owners.

Fuller, Peter S., 1923-. Automobile dealer. John A. Morris Award in 1985. Bred and owned Dancer's Image, Mom's Command, Shananie, Donna's Time.

Gaines, John R., 1928-. Breeder. Former chairman, Breeders' Cup Ltd. Founder of Gainesway Farm, Kentucky. Eclipse Award of Merit in 1984; John W. Galbreath Award in '93. Bred Halo, Silent King, Time Limit. Owned Bold Bidder, Oil Royalty. Founder of Breeders' Cup, Kentucky Horse Park; assisted in developing the Maxwell H. Gluck Center for Equine Research at the University of Kentucky.

Gann, Edmund A., 1923-. Commercial fisheries, banking. Entered racing in 1960s when a fishing buddy offered him half-interest in a filly to settle a debt. Owned more than 35 stakes winners, including Pay the Butler, Al Mamoon, Medaglia d'Oro, Peace Rules, Midas Eyes, You.

Garland, Bruce, 1950-. Senior executive vice president of racing for New Jersey Sports and Exposition Authority; vice chairman of Harness Tracks of America; serves on board of the Thoroughbred Racing Associations and U.S. Trotting Association. In 2003 elected to the NTRA board representing independent Mid-Atlantic region racetracks; formerly executive director of New Jersey Racing Commission.

Gentry, Tom, 1937-. Bloodstock agent, breeder. Former owner of Tom Gentry Farm, Kentucky. Bred Royal Academy, Brazen, Marfa, Terlingua, Pancho Villa, Artichoke.

Gerry, Martha Farish, 1918-. Investments. Owner of Lazy F Ranch, Texas. Bred and owned Forego, Maid of France, Clef d'Argent, French Colonial. Bred and raced three-time Horse of the Year Forego, who earned nearly $2-million from 1973-'78. Aunt of William S. Farish.

Hancock, Arthur B. III, 1943-. Breeder. Owner of Stone Farm, Kentucky. Mr. Fitz Award in 1990. Bred and owned Sunday Silence, Gato Del Sol, Goodbye Halo. Co-bred Fusaichi Pegasus. Stood leading sire Halo. Brother of Seth Hancock; son of Arthur B. "Bull" Hancock Jr.

Hancock, Seth, 1949-. Breeder. Director, Churchill Downs; director, Keeneland Association. President of Claiborne Farm, Kentucky. Eclipse Award breeder 1979, '84. Bred and owned Swale, Forty Niner, Lure. Bred Wajima, Nureyev, Caerleon. Organized a syndicate to acquire Secretariat for more than $6-million. Stood Mr. Prospector, Unbridled, stands Danzig, Seeking the Gold,. Brother of Arthur B. Hancock III; son of Arthur B. "Bull" Hancock Jr.

Harper, Joseph, 1943-. President and chief executive officer of Del Mar Thoroughbred Club since 1990; elected president of Thoroughbred Racing Associations in 2003. Member of Jockey Club; former executive vice president and general manager of Oak Tree Racing Association; grandson of Cecil B. DeMille.

Harris, John C., 1943-. Breeder, agricultural products. President, California Thoroughbred Breeders Association; director, Thoroughbred Owners of California.

Owner of Harris Farms, California. Bred and owned Soviet Problem.

Handel, Harold G. "Hal", 1947-. Chief executive officer of Greenwood Racing Inc. operator of Philadelphia Park, since 1998. Former executive vice president of the New Jersey Sports and Exposition Authority, owner of the Meadowlands and Monmouth Park racetracks; former executive director and legal counsel for New Jersey Racing Commission.

Hartack, William J., 1932-. Jockey, racing official. Leading jockey by races won in 1955-'57, '60; leading jockey by money won in 1956-'57; inducted into Racing Hall of Fame in '59. Rode 4,272 winners, including Northern Dancer, Tim Tam, Majestic Prince. First jockey to earn $3-million in one year (1957); won five Kentucky Derbys (aboard Iron Liege in 1957, Venetian Way in '60, Decidedly in '62, Northern Dancer in '64, and Majestic Prince in '69).

Hawley, Sandy, 1949-. Jockey. Leading jockey by races won in 1970, '72-'73, '76; leading rider in Canada nine times; inducted into Racing Hall of Fame in '92; inducted into Canada's Hall of Fame in '86; Eclipse Award jockey in '76; George Woolf Memorial Jockey Award in '76; Sovereign Award in 1978, '88; Avelino Gomez Memorial Award in '86; Joe Palmer Award in '98. Rode 6,449 winners, including Youth, Desert Waves, Kiridashi, Smart Strike, Highland Vixen. First jockey to win more than 500 races in one season (1973).

Hettinger, John, 1933-. Investments, real estate. Director, Breeders' Cup Ltd. Owner of Akindale Farm, New York. Special Eclipse Award in 2000. Bred and owned Warfie, Yestday's Kisses, Chase the Dream, Genuine Regret. Instrumental in founding the Racehorse Adoption Referral Program; chairman of the Grayson-Jockey Club Research Foundation; major shareholder, Fasig-Tipton Co.

Hickey, Jay, 1944-. Lawyer, lobbyist. President, American Horse Council. Represented equine organizations, horse owners, and horse breeders during his time as a practicing lawyer.

Hirsch, Joe, 1929-. Journalist. Co-founder and first president of the National Turf Writers Association 1959-'60. Lord Derby Award in 1985; Jockey Club Medal in '89; Mr. Fitz Award in '98; Walter Haight Award in '84; Joe Palmer Award in '94; Eclipse Award of Merit in '92; Eclipse Award for outstanding newspaper writing in '79. Longtime executive columnist of *Daily Racing Form*.

Hollendorfer, Jerry, 1949-. All-time leading trainer in Northern California. Trained more than 3,500 winners through 2002. Won Bay Meadows Race Course training title 24 consecutive times; won Golden Gate Fields title 22 consecutive times. Trained Lite Light, King Glorious, Pike Place Dancer, Event of the Year.

Hubbard, R. D., 1935-. Glass manufacturing. Former chairman and chief executive officer, Hollywood Park; owner, Ruidoso Downs. Owner of Crystal Springs Farm, Kentucky; Frontera Farm, New Mexico. Owned Gentlemen (Arg), Talloires, Leger Cat (Arg), Fit to Lead, Invited Guest, Mistico (Chi). Co-founded the Shoemaker Foundation in 1990 to help horsemen suffering from catastrophic accidents or illnesses.

Humphrey, G. Watts Jr., 1944-. Investments, manufacturing. Director, Breeders' Cup; director, Keeneland Association. Owner of Shawnee Farm, Kentucky. Bred Creme Fraiche, Sacahuista. Owned Likely Exchange, Amherst Wayside, Noble Damsel, Sorbet.

Hunt, Nelson Bunker, 1926-. Oil production. Owned Bluegrass Farm, Kentucky. Eclipse Award breeder in 1976, '85, '87; P.A.B. Widener Trophy in '85-'87. Bred and owned Dahlia, Youth, Empery, Trillion, Estrapade. Owned *Vaguely Noble, Exceller, Glorious Song. Bred Dahlia, the first mare to earn more than $1-million.

Icahn, Carl, 1936-. Financier. Owner of Foxfield Thoroughbreds, Kentucky. John A. Morris Award in 1990. Bred Blushing K. D., Great Navigator, Vaudeville, Helmsman, Brave Tender. Owned Meadow Star, Rose's Cantina, Colonial Waters.

Janney, Stuart III, 1948-. Financier. Former chairman, Thoroughbred Owners and Breeders Association. Bred and owned Coronado's Quest, Warning Glance, Deputation, Mesabi Maiden. Aided in the formation of the National Thoroughbred Racing Association.

Jerkens, H. Allen, 1929-. Trainer. Leading trainer in New York in 1957, '62, '66, '69; inducted into Racing Hall of Fame in '75; Mr. Fitz Award in 2001; Eclipse Award trainer in '73. Trained 157 stakes winners, including Sky Beauty, Onion, Beau Purple, Duck Dance, Prove Out. Known as the "Giant Killer" for training horses who upset champions Secretariat, Kelso, Forego, and Buckpasser. Father of trainer Jimmy Jerkens.

Johnsen, Corey, 1955-. Racing executive. Magna Entertainment Corp. group vice president and president of Lone Star Park; former general manager, Remington Park; created the All-Star Jockey Championship in 1997; played a key role in the development, construction, and opening of Lone Star and Remington; produced Eclipse Award-winning television program while at Louisiana Downs.

Johnson, Phil G., 1925-. Trainer. Inducted into Racing Hall of Fame in 1997. Trained Quiet Little Table, *Amen II, Maplejinsky, Match the Hatch, Naskra, Nasty and Bold, Volponi.

Jolley, LeRoy, 1938-. Trainer. Inducted into Racing Hall of Fame in 1987. Trained Foolish Pleasure, Honest Pleasure, Genuine Risk, What a Summer, Manila, Meadow Star. Won the Kentucky Derby in 1980 with Genuine Risk, the first filly to compete in all three Triple Crown races. Son of trainer Moody Jolley.

Jones, Aaron U., 1921-. and **Jones, Marie**. Timber. Bred and owned Lemhi Gold, Western, Tiffany Lass. Owned Riboletta (Brz), Forestry, Plenty of Light.

Jones, Brereton, 1939-. Breeder, politician. Treasurer, Breeders' Cup Ltd.; president and director, Thoroughbred Club of America. Owner of Airdrie Stud, Kentucky. Bred Desert Wine, Southjet, Formidable Lady, Dansil. Owned By Land by Sea, Imp Society, Silver Medallion. Helped persuade Breeders' Cup to supplement purses at tracks around the country in addition to the Breeders' Cup day events in formative stage of the organization; inaugurated Kentucky Thoroughbred Development Fund while governor of Kentucky. Governor of Kentucky 1991-'95.

Jones, John T. L. Jr., 1935-. Breeder. Owner and general manager, Walmac International, Kentucky. One of the founding members of the Breeders' Cup Ltd.; stood Alleged, Nureyev, Phone Trick.

Kelly, Tommy J., 1919-. Trainer. Inducted into Racing Hall of Fame in 1993. Trained Plugged Nickle, Colonel Moran, Droll Role, Pet Bully, Globemaster. Co-owner of Evening Attire. Father of trainer Pat Kelly.

Krantz, Bryan, 1960-. Racing executive. President and general manager, Fair Grounds Race Course; owner, Jefferson Downs. Built new grandstand after a fire destroyed Fair Grounds's physical plant in 1993.

Krone, Julie, 1963-. Jockey. Inducted into Racing Hall of Fame in 2000. All-time leading female jockey with more than 3,500 victories. Major winners include Colonial Affair, Rubiano, Da Hoss, Maxzene, Clear Mandate. Won the Belmont Stakes (G1) in 1993, becoming the first woman to win a Triple Crown race; resumed riding career in November 2002 after 3½-year retirement.

Lewis, Robert, 1924- and **Lewis, Beverly**, 1927-. Beer distributor. Eclipse Award of Merit in 1997; Big Sport of Turfdom Award in '95. Owned Silver Charm, Charismatic, Serena's Song, Timber Country, Hennessy. Won two-thirds of the Triple Crown in 1997 and '99 (with Silver Charm and Charismatic, respectively).

Levy, Robert P., 1931-. Chemical storage. Former owner, Atlantic City Race Course; former president, Thoroughbred Racing Associations. Owner of Muirfield East, Maryland. Owned Housebuster, Smoke Glacken, Bet Twice. Inaugurated full-card simulcasting in 1983.

Liebau, F. Jack, 1938-. Lawyer, racetrack executive. President, Santa Anita Park; president, Bay Meadows Operating Co.; president, Bay Meadows Race Course; president, Golden Gate Fields. Owner of Valley Creek Farm, California. Owned Yashgan (GB), Boo La Boo, Forzando (GB), Kadial (Ire).

Little, Donald, 1934-. Financial management. Owner of Centennial Farms, Virginia. Owned Colonial Affair, Rubiano, King Cugat. President of the United States Polo Association; organizes racing syndicates with investors.

Lukas, D. Wayne, 1935-. Trainer. Leading trainer by money won in 1983-'92, '94-'97; leading trainer by races won in 1987-'90; leading trainer by stakes races won in 1985-'92; inducted into Racing Hall of Fame in '99; Eclipse Award trainer in 1985-'87, '94; John W. Galbreath Award in '98. Leading trainer of Eclipse Award winners. Trained Lady's Secret, Thunder Gulch, Timber Country, Gulch, Flanders, Tabasco Cat, Codex, Charismatic. First trainer to reach both $100-million and $200-million in earnings; first trainer to win two Breeders' Cup races in one day (in 1985) and three races in one day (in '88); transformed modern training with entrepreneurial methods.

Madden, Preston, 1934- and **Madden, Anita**, 1933-. Real estate development. Owner of Hamburg Place, Kentucky. Bred Alysheba, Pink Pigeon, Miss Carmie, Romeo, Kentuckian. Owned T. V. Lark. Stood leading sire T. V. Lark; Anita Madden was the first female member of the Kentucky State Racing Commission.

Magnier, John, 1948-. Farm owner. Owner of Coolmore Stud, Ireland; Coolmore Stud, Australia; Ashford Stud, Kentucky. Bred Galileo (Ire), Sadler's Wells, Dr Devious (Ire). Originated shuttle-stallion concept; expanded mare books; stood Sadler's Wells, Be My Guest, El Gran Senor, Woodman, Danehill.

Maktoum, Sheikh Hamdan bin Rashid al 1945-. Deputy ruler of Dubai; minister of finance and industry for United Arab Emirates; UAE representative to OPEC. Owns Shadwell Farm in Kentucky, Shadwell Estate, Nunnery Stud, England; Derrinstown Stud, Ireland. leading owner in England, 1995. Bred and owned Nashwan, Erhaab, Salsabil (Ire); partner with brothers Mohammed and Maktoum in Godolphin Racing.

Maktoum, Sheikh Maktoum bin Rashid al, 1943-. Ruler of Dubai; vice president and prime minister of United Arab Emirates. Owner of Gainsborough Farm, Kentucky and several farms in Europe. Owned Shareef Dancer, Touching Wood, Shadeed, Ma Biche. Partner in Godolphin Racing with brothers Mohammed and Hamdan.

Maktoum, Sheikh Mohammed bin Rashid al, 1949-. Crown prince of Dubai. Owner of Raceland Farm, Kentucky; Darley Stud, Kentucky; Dalham Hall Stud, England; Kildangan Stud, Ireland. Bred and owned Dubai Millennium, Intrepidity (GB), In the Wings (GB), Swain (Ire). Owned Oh So Sharp (GB), Daylami (Ire), Pebbles (GB). Created Godolphin Racing, Dubai World Cup.

Mandella, Richard, 1950-. Trainer. Inducted into Racing Hall of Fame in 2001. Trained Kotashaan (Fr), Phone Chatter, Dixie Union, Gentlemen (Arg), Wild Rush, and Dare and Go, who won the Pacific Classic (G1) in 1996, ending Cigar's 16-race winning streak.

Maple, Edward, 1948-. Jockey. Began riding in Ohio and West Virginia, moved to New Jersey in 1970 and New York in '71. Rode champions Conquistador Cielo, Devil's Bag; won the Belmont Stakes (G1) with Temperence Hill and Creme Fraiche. Won 4,398 races and earned more than $105-million; rode Secretariat in champion's last career start, 1973 Canadian International. George Woolf Memorial Jockey Award in 1995; retired from racing in 1998 immediately after receiving the Mike Venezia Award.

Martin, Frank "Pancho", 1925-. Trainer. Leading trainer by money won in 1974; leading trainer in New York in 1973-'82; inducted into Racing Hall of Fame in '81. Trained 51 stakes winners and two champions, including Autobiography, Outstandingly, Sham, Manassa Mauler, Rube the Great.

Marzelli, Alan, 1954-. President and chief operating officer of the Jockey Club since January 1, 2003; chairman of Equibase Co. LLC since 1996. Joined the Jockey Club in 1983 as chief financial officer and later became executive vice president.

McAnally, Ron, 1932-. Trainer. Inducted into Racing Hall of Fame in 1990; Eclipse Award trainer in 1981, '91-'92; Mr. Fitz Award in '92. Trained John Henry, Bayakoa (Arg), Tight Spot, Paseana (Arg), Northern Spur (Ire).

McCarron, Chris, 1955-. Jockey. Leading jockey by races won in 1974-'75, '80; leading jockey by money won in 1980-'81, '84, '91; inducted into Racing Hall of Fame in '89; Eclipse Award apprentice jockey in '74; Eclipse Award jockey in '80; George Woolf Memorial Jockey Award in '80; Mike Venezia Award in '91. Rode Alysheba, John Henry, Lady's Secret, Sunday Silence, Go for Gin. Retired in 2002 as leading earner among jockeys with $264-million; along with his wife, Judy, and comedian Tim Conway, created the Don MacBeth Memorial Fund for disabled jockeys. Became general manager of Santa Anita Park in 2003.

McGaughey, Claude R. "Shug" III, 1951-. Trainer. Eclipse Award trainer in 1988. Trained Easy Goer, Personal Ensign, Rhythm, Inside Information, Heavenly Prize, My Flag, Storm Flag Flying. Trained Personal Ensign, unbeaten in 13 races; won five graded stakes at Belmont Park on Breeders' Cup preview day in 1993.

McKathan, J. B., 1966- and **McKathan, Kevin**, 1968-. Bloodstock agents. Owners of McKathan Brothers Training Facility in Ocala; purchased for clients Silver Charm, Real Quiet, Silverbulletday, Captain Steve.

McKay, Jim (Jim McManus), 1921-. Broadcaster. President, Maryland Million Ltd. Eclipse Award of Merit in 2000; Big Sport of Turfdom Award in 1987; Joe Palmer Award in '00. Co-founder of Maryland Million; broadcast host of Triple Crown 1975-2000 on ABC.

McNair, Robert, 1937- and **McNair, Janice**, 1936-. Investments, NFL team owner. Owner of Stonerside Stable, Kentucky; training facilities in Aiken, South Carolina and Saratoga Springs, New York. Co-bred Fusaichi Pegasus; bred and owned Congaree. Owned Chilukki, Tuzla (Ire). Co-owned Coronado's Quest, Touch Gold.

Meeker, Thomas, 1943-. Racing executive. President, Churchill Downs Inc.; president, Thoroughbred Racing Associations, 1991-'92. John W. Galbreath Award in 1999. Beginning in 1984, implemented a $25-million, five-year improvement plan for Churchill, including a $3.6-million turf course and a $2.8-million paddock. Undertook $100-million renovation of Churchill Downs in 2002; oversaw expansion of Churchill Downs Inc. to encompass tracks from coast to coast.

Metzger, Dan, 1963-. President of Thoroughbred Owners and Breeders Association since 1999. Former director of marketing services and licensing for Breeders' Cup Ltd.

Meyerhoff, Robert, 1924-. Real estate development. Owner of Fitzhugh Farm, Maryland. Bred and owned Broad Brush, Concern, Include, Valley Crossing.

Meyocks, Terry, 1951-. President and chief operating officer of New York Racing Association since 1996. Former vice president of racing for NYRA; Former racing secretary at Calder Race Course, director of racing at Gulfstream Park. Member of American Graded Stakes Committee; NTRA board; Equibase Management Committee.

Miller, MacKenzie "Mack", 1921-. Trainer, breeder. Inducted into Racing Hall of Fame in 1987; Mr. Fitz Award in '96. Trained 72 stakes winners, including Leallah, Assagai, Hawaii, and *Snow Knight. Trained Fit to Fight to New York handicap triple crown in 1984; trained Sea Hero to Kentucky Derby victory in 1993. Bred De La Rose, Lite Light, Chilukki.

Moran, Elizabeth, 1932-. Investments. Owner of Brushwood Stable, Pennsylvania. Bred High Yield. Owned Creme Fraiche, Rich Cream, Family Style. Won American Grand National Steeplechase with McAdam in 1984; won English Grand National Steeplechase Handicap with Papillon in 2000.

Mott, William, 1953-. Trainer. Inducted into Racing Hall of Fame in 1998; Eclipse Award trainer in 1995-'96. Trained Cigar, Paradise Creek, Ajina, Theatrical (Ire), Geri, Escena, Wekiva Springs. Cigar won 16 consecutive races from 1994-'96, including the inaugural Dubai World Cup in '96.

Nafzger, Carl, 1941-. Trainer. Eclipse Award trainer in 1990; Big Sport of Turfdom Award in '90. Trained Unbridled, Banshee Breeze, Unshaded, Vicar, Solvig. Wrote *Traits of a Winner: The Formula for Developing Thoroughbred Racehorses* in '94.

Nerud, John A., 1913-. Trainer, breeder. President of Tartan Farms, Florida, 1959-'89. Inducted into Racing Hall of Fame in 1972. Trained 27 stakes winners and five champions, including Dr. Fager, Ta Wee, Delegate, Intentionally, Dr. Patches, *Gallant Man. Bred and owned Cozzene, Fappiano. Dr. Fager is the only horse to win four championships in one year.

Niarchos-Gouazé, Maria, Investments. Director, Breeders' Cup Ltd. Owner of Haras de Fresnay-le-Buffard, France. In partnership with her brothers, breeds under the name Flaxman Holdings Ltd. Bred and owned Dream Well, Sulamani. Daughter of shipping magnate Stavros Niarchos.

Nicholson, George "Nick", 1947-. Racing executive. President and chief executive officer, Keeneland Association; executive director, Jockey Club 1989-2000; former chief operating officer, National Thoroughbred Racing Association; president, Thoroughbred Club of America in '91. Jockey Club Gold Medal in 1998. Involved in the planning and development of the Kentucky Horse Park; played key role in formation of

Equibase racing and pedigree database; helped to pull industry together to support the National Thoroughbred Racing Association.

Noe, Kenny, 1928-. New York Racing Association chairman and chief executive officer 1995-2000. NYRA president, general manager 1994-'95. president, general manager of Calder Race Course 1979-'90. Served as racing secretary and steward at various racetracks.

Nuckols, Charles Jr., 1922-. Breeder. Former president, Thoroughbred Club of America; director, Keeneland Association. Owner of Nuckols Farm, Kentucky. Bred Hidden Lake, Habitat, Decathlon, Typecast. Co-bred War Emblem. Co-authored the Kentucky Thoroughbred Development Fund as a member of the Thoroughbred Breeders of Kentucky.

O'Brien, Aidan, 1969-. Trainer. Won a record 23 Grade or Group 1 races in 2001. Trains for Coolmore Stud and partners at Ballydoyle, Ireland. Won 2001-'02 Epsom Derby (Eng-G1) with Galileo (Ire) and High Chaparral (Ire). Trained Giant's Causeway, King of Kings (Ire), Milan (GB), Imagine (Ire), Stravinsky, Hawk Wing, Rock of Gibraltar (Ire), Ballingarry (Ire), Johannesburg.

O'Brien, Vincent, 1917-. Legendary Irish trainer. Founded Ballydoyle training center in Ireland; with John Magnier and Robert Sangster established Coolmore Stud in 1975. Trained winners of 27 Irish classics, 16 English classics, and in 1977 saddled then-record 22 Group 1 winners. Trained Nijinsky II, Roberto, Golden Fleece, Sir Ivor, The Minstrel, Alleged. In a 2003 *Racing Post* poll, he was voted the all-time most important figure in English racing.

O'Byrne, Dermot "Demi", 1944-. Bloodstock agent, veterinarian. Purchased Thunder Gulch, Honour and Glory, High Yield, Fasliyev, Stravinsky, King of Kings (Ire), Johannesburg. Chief talent spotter for Coolmore Stud-Michael Tabor partnerships.

O'Farrell, Michael, 1948-. Breeder. First vice president, Florida Thoroughbred Owners' and Breeders' Association. Owner of Ocala Stud Farm, Florida. Bred Bolshoi Boy, Proudest Duke, Queen Alexandra. Son of Joe O'Farrell.

Oxley, John C., 1937- and **Oxley, Debbie**, 1951-. Oil production. Owner of Fawn Leap Farm, Kentucky. Bred and owned Pyramid Peak. Owned Monarchos, Beautiful Pleasure, Sky Mesa.

Pape, William L., 1930-. Auto dealership. Former president, National Steeplechase Association. Co-bred champions Flatterer and Martie's Anger; owned champion Athenian Idol.

Payson, Virginia Kraft, 1930-. Investments. Owner of Payson Stud, Kentucky. Bred and owned St. Jovite, L'Carriere. Owned Carr de Naskra. Owner and operator of Payson Park training center in Florida.

Pegram, Mike, 1952-. Fast food franchises. Owned Real Quiet, Silverbulletday, Isitingood, Thirty Slews, Captain Steve.

Perret, Craig, 1951-. Jockey. Eclipse Award jockey in 1990; George Woolf Memorial Jockey Award in '98. Rode Unbridled, Housebuster, Safely Kept, Eillo, Rhythm, Alydeed, Bet Twice. Won a record-tying 57 stakes in 1990.

Phillips, John W., 1952-. Investments, lawyer. Managing partner of Darby Dan Farm, Kentucky. Bred and owned Memories of Silver, Sunshine Forever, Brian's Time, Soaring Softly. Won inaugural Breeders' Cup Filly and Mare Turf (G1) with Soaring Softly in 1999. Grandson of John W. Galbreath.

Phipps, Ogden Mills "Dinny", 1940-. Investments. Chairman, Jockey Club; former chairman, New York Racing Association; director, Grayson-Jockey Club Research Foundation. Eclipse Award of Merit in 1978. Bred and owned Inside Information, Rhythm, Educated Risk, Storm Flag Flying. Co-bred and owned Successor. Son of Ogden Phipps.

Piggott, Lester, 1936-. Champion English jockey 11 times. Won more than 5,300 races, including record 30 English classics. Winner of the Epsom Derby record nine times; Ascot Gold Cup 11 times; Irish Derby five times; and the 1990 Breeders' Cup Mile (G1) at age 54. Rode Nijinsky II, Sir Ivor, Roberto, The Minstrel, Alleged. Trained for a time during the 1980s; imprisoned a year for tax evasion 1987-'88 before resuming his riding career.

Pincay, Laffit Jr., 1946-. Jockey. Leading jockey by money won in 1970-'74, '79, '85; leading jockey by races won in '71; inducted into Racing Hall of Fame in '75 ; Eclipse Award jockey in 1971, '73-'74, '79, '85; Special Eclipse Award in '99; George Woolf Memorial Jockey Award in '70. Rode Affirmed, John Henry, Gamely, Susan's Girl, Desert Vixen, Genuine Risk. Broke Bill Shoemaker's lifetime win record on December 10, 1999, with his 8,834th victory; first jockey to win seven races on a single card at Santa Anita Park, in '87; first jockey to win more than 9,000 races. Retired on April 29, 2003, with a record 9,530 victories and purse earnings of $237-million.

Pollard, Carl, 1938-. Health care executive. Chairman, Churchill Downs Inc.; president, Kentucky Derby Museum. Owner of Hermitage Farm, Kentucky. Owned Caressing, Sheepscot, Duck Trap, Take Me Out.

Powell, Lonny, 1959-. President of Association of Racing Commissioners International. Former president of Santa Anita Park.

Rasmussen, Leon, 1915-. Journalist. "Bloodlines" columnist, *Daily Racing Form* 1950-'87. Walter Haight Award in 1987; Engelhard Award in '87. Bred and owned Apollo, Nanetta. Popularized Dr. Steven A. Roman's dosage system in his column.

Rickman, William Sr. Chairman of Delaware Park; owner-breeder. Bought Delaware Park in 1983, reopened it after a one-year shutdown, and turned it into profitable enterprise. Introduced slots in 1995. Son William Rickman Jr. is president and chief executive. Also owns Ocean Downs harness track and holds license to build a new track in Allegany County, Maryland.

Robertson, Walter, 1949-. Auctioneer. President, Fasig-Tipton Co.; former president, Thoroughbred Club of America. Auctioneer at the Calumet Farm sale in 1992.

Robbins, Jack K., D.V.M., 1921-. President, founding director of Oak Tree Racing Association; Jockey Club member; director of Grayson-Jockey Club Research Foundation; distinguished life member of American Association of Equine Practitioners; member of NTRA Drug Testing Task Force. Father of trainer Jay Robbins, Del Mar Director of Racing Tom Robbins, and former Hollywood Park President Don Robbins.

Romero, Randy, 1957-. Jockey. Father, Lloyd, was Quarter Horse trainer; film *Casey's Shadow* was based on his Louisiana family; won Breeders' Cup races with champions Sacahuista (1987 Distaff [G1]), Personal Ensign (1988 Distaff), and Go for Wand (1989 Juvenile Fillies [G1]). Sustained life-threatening burns in a 1983 accident in Oaklawn Park jockeys room. Won 4,285 races, earned more than $75-million.

Rotz, John L., 1934-. Jockey, racing official. Leading jockey by stakes winners in 1968-'69; inducted into Racing Hall of Fame in '83; George Woolf Memorial Jockey Award in '73. Rode 2,908 winners. Rode Gallant Bloom, Ta Wee, Carry Back, Dr. Fager, Silent Screen.

Sampson, Curtis, 1933-. Chairman of Canterbury Park Holding Corp. Previously established two successful telecommunications companies in Minnesota. Bought closed track in 1994 with partners and reopened it in 1995. Entered racing in 1987 as an owner; now among Minnesota's leading breeders.

Samuel-Balaz, Tammy, Investments. Co-owner of Sam-Son Farm, Canada and Florida. Bred and owned Dancethruthedawn, Scatter the Gold, Catch the Ring, Mountain Angel, Quiet Resolve. Daughter of Ernest Samuel.

Santos, Jose, 1961-. Jockey. Leading jockey by money won in 1986-'89; Eclipse Award jockey in '88; George Woolf Memorial Jockey Award in '99. Rode Lemon Drop Kid, Skip Away, Colonial Affair, Chief Bearhart, Volponi. Led all jockeys by money won with a then-record $14.86-million in 1988; rode 13 winners in three days at Aqueduct in '88. Won 2003 Kentucky Derby (G1) and Preakness Stakes (G1) on Funny Cide.

Santulli, Richard, 1944-. Aviation. Co-owner of Jayeff B Stable. Bred and owned Ciro. Owned Safely Kept, Banshee Breeze, Korveya.

Savin, Scott, 1960-. Owner, executive. President, Gulfstream Park; president, Florida Horsemen's Benevolent and Protective Association. Owned Big Bet, Cheshire Kitten. Grandson of A. I. "Butch" Savin, owner of Mr. Prospector.

Scherf, Christopher, 1951-. Executive vice president of Thoroughbred Racing Associations since 1988; president of TRA Enterprises. Serves on the American Horse Council's Racing and Government Affairs committees. Former sportswriter for the Louisville *Courier-Journal* and United Press International; director of press relations for the New York Racing Association (1978-'81).

Schulhofer, Flint W. "Scotty", 1926-. Trainer. Inducted into Racing Hall of Fame in 1992. Trained 80 stakes winners, including champions Ta Wee, Mac Diarmida, Smile, Fly So Free, Lemon Drop Kid, Rubiano; also trained Cryptoclearance. Began career as steeplechase jockey. Father of trainer Randy Schulhofer.

Schwartz, Barry, 1942-. Clothing executive. Chairman and chief executive officer, New York Racing Association. Owner of Stonewall Farm, New York. Bred and owned Beru, Patricia J. K. Owned Three Ring. Lowered New York's pari-mutuel takeout; mandated color-coded saddlecloths.

Sexton, Steve, 1959-. Racetrack executive. President of Churchill Downs. Former executive vice president of Arlington Park; executive vice president and general manager of Lone Star Park; general manager of Thistledown racetrack.

Sheppard, Jonathan, 1940-. Trainer, breeder. Owner of Ashwell Stables, Pennsylvania. Leading steeplechase trainer by money won in 1973-'90, '92-'95; inducted into Racing Hall of Fame in '90. Trained 119 stakes winners, including champions Cafe Prince, Flatterer, Athenian Idol, Martie's Anger, Jimmy Lorenzo (GB), Highland Bud. Also trained Storm Cat, With Anticipation. Co-bred Martie's Anger, Flatterer.

Sherman, Michael, 1940-. Breeder. Owner and president of Farnsworth Farms, Florida. Leading breeder by stakes winners in 1994-'95; Eclipse Award breeder in '96. Bred Beautiful Pleasure, Jewel Princess, Mecke, Frisk Me Now, Once Wild.

Shoemaker, William, 1931-. Jockey, trainer. President, Jockeys' Guild in 1975-'90. Leading jockey by money won in 1958-'64; inducted into Racing Hall of Fame in '58; Special Eclipse Award in '76; Eclipse Award jockey in '81; Eclipse Award of Merit in '81; George Woolf Memorial Jockey Award in '51; Mike Venezia Award in '90. Rode then-record 8,833 winners and 1,009 stakes winners, including Swaps, Spectacular Bid, Round Table, Ack Ack, Forego, John Henry, Prove It, Olden Times, Sword Dancer. Trained Fire the Groom, Alcando (Ire). First jockey to reach $100-million in earnings; mounts earned more than $123-million in purses. Paralyzed in single-car accident April 8, 1991.

Smith, Mike, 1965-. Jockey. Elected to Racing Hall of Fame in 2003. Leading jockey by races won in 1994; Eclipse Award jockey in 1993-'94; Mike Venezia Award in '94; George Woolf Memorial Jockey Award in 2000. Rode Holy Bull, Lure, Skip Away, Azeri, Unbridled's Song, Coronado's Quest, Vindication. Won record 66 stakes in 1994. Through 2002, won 4,169 races and earned more than $150-million.

Smith, Tim, 1948-. Racing executive. Commissioner, chief executive officer of National Thoroughbred Racing Association. Helped increase national television exposure for horse racing; formed partnership between NTRA and Television Games Network; initiated merger of NTRA and Breeders' Cup Ltd.

Smithwick, D. M. "Mike", 1929-. Trainer. Inducted into Racing Hall of Fame in 1971. Trained 52 stakes winners and six champions. Trained Neji, Bon Nouvel, Ancestor, Mako, Top Bid, Straight and True. Trained Neji to three championships in 1955, '57, and '58; trained the first two winners (Top Bid and Inkslinger) of the Colonial Cup. Brother of Racing Hall of Fame jockey Paddy Smithwick.

Sommer, Viola (Mrs. Sigmund), 1921-. Real estate. Leading owner in 1982; Eclipse Award owner in '82. Bred and owned Bottled Water. Owned Sham, Ten Below, Tom Swift.

Steinbrenner, George, 1930-. Shipping. Director, Florida Thoroughbred Breeders' and Owners' Association. Owner of Kinsman Farm, Florida. Bred and owned Concerto, Diligence, Eternal Prince. Purchased major interest in Florida Downs (later Tampa Bay Downs) in 1980. Managing partner, New York Yankees.

Stevens, Gary, 1963-. Jockey. President, Jockeys' Guild, 1995-2000. Leading jockey by money won in 1990; inducted into Racing Hall of Fame in '97; Eclipse Award jockey in '98; George Woolf Memorial Jockey Award in '96. Rode more than 4,500 winners, including Point Given, Silver Charm, Winning Colors, Thunder Gulch, Hennessy, Broad Brush. Youngest rider to earn more than $100-million in purses, in 1993; won inaugural NTRA All-Star Jockey Championship in '97.

Stoute, Sir Michael, 1945-. Five-time champion trainer in England. Trained Epsom Derby (Eng-G1) winners Shergar (1981) and Shahrastani (1986), and Unite (Ire), Sonic Lady, Shareef Dancer, Melodist, Ivor's Image, Ajdal, Saddlers' Hall, Northern Tempest, Marwell (Ire), Zilzal, Opera House (GB), Ezzoud (Ire), Russian Rhythm.

Strauss, Robert S., 1918-. Lawyer, diplomat. Chairman of Del Mar Thoroughbred Club since 2002; board member since 1988. Jockey Club member. Former FBI special agent; ambassador to the Soviet Union 1991-'92; President Carter's representative to the Middle East peace negotiations; winner of the Presidential Medal of Freedom 1981; chairman of the Democratic National Committee 1973-'76.

Strawbridge, George Jr., 1937-. Investments. President, National Steeplechase Association. Owner of Augustin Stables, Pennsylvania. F. Ambrose Clark Award in 1979. Bred and owned Tikkanen, Selkirk, Silver Fling, With Anticipation. Bred Treizieme, Turgeon. Owned Cafe Prince, Mo Bay.

Stronach, Frank, 1932-. Auto parts magnate. Chairman, Magna International Corp., Magna Entertainment Corp. Owner of Adena Springs Farm, Kentucky; Adena Springs North, Ontario; Adena Springs South, Florida. Owner of Stronach Stable. Eclipse Award owner in 1998-2000; Eclipse Award breeder in '00; seven Sovereign Awards as owner of year and four Sovereign Awards as breeder of year. Bred and owned Macho Uno, Perfect Sting. Co-owned Touch Gold, Glorious Song. Also bred and owned Awesome Again, richest Canadian-bred runner of all-time with $4,374,590. Through Magna Entertainment, purchased Santa Anita Park, Gulfstream Park, Thistledown, Golden Gate Fields, Remington Park, Great Lakes Downs, Portland Meadows, Lone Star Park; majority of Pimlico Race Course and Laurel Park; company operates Bay Meadows Race Course.

Stute, Melvin F., 1927-. Trainer. Won two Eclipse Awards in 1986 with Preakness Stakes (G1) winner Snow Chief and Breeders' Cup Juvenile Fillies (G1) winner Brave Raj. Also trained Very Subtle, winner of the 1987 Breeders' Cup Sprint (G1). Brother of trainer Warren Stute.

Suroor, Saeed bin, 1967-. Trainer. Leading trainer in England by money won in 1995. Trained Dubai Millennium, Fantastic Light, Swain (Ire), E Dubai, Lammtarra, Mark of Esteem (Ire). Head trainer for Godolphin Racing; won the Emirates World Series in 1999 with Daylami (Ire), Fantastic Light (2000-'01), and Grandera in 2002.

Switzer, David, 1945-. Executive director of Kentucky Thoroughbred Association. Board member of University of Kentucky-Gluck Research Foundation; Lexington Arts and Cultural Council, United Way of the Bluegrass; member of Kentucky Agriculture Resource Development Authority .

Tabor, Michael, 1941-. Former betting shop owner, investments. Owned or co-owned Thunder Gulch, Montjeu (Ire), Desert King, Honour and Glory, Johannesburg, Galileo (Ire), High Chaparral (Ire).

Tanaka, Gary, 1943-. Stockbroker, owner of Amerindo Investment Advisors Inc. Frequently buys proven horses in Europe and races them in California. Owned User Friendly (GB), Dernier Empereur, Donna Viola (GB), Dreams Gallore, Golden Apples (Ire).

Taylor, Duncan, 1956-. Farm owner. Co-owner (with brothers Frank, Ben, and Mark) of Taylor Made Farm and Sales Agency, Kentucky. Sold approximately $670-million total value of horses at public auctions since 1978.

Taylor, Mickey, 1940- and **Taylor, Karen**, 1940-. Timber. Owned and bred Slew o' Gold, Slewpy. Co-owned Seattle Slew, who won 14 of 17 starts, including the Triple Crown in 1977, and earned $1.2-million.

Turcotte, Ron, 1941-. Jockey. Leading jockey by stakes won in 1972-'73; inducted into Racing Hall of Fame in '79; George Woolf Memorial Jockey Award in

'79. Rode 3,032 winners, including Secretariat, Damascus, Northern Dancer, Riva Ridge, Shuvee, Dark Mirage, Fort Marcy. Won Triple Crown in 1973 aboard Secretariat. Paralyzed in 1978 spill.

Turner, William H. "Billy", 1941-. Trained Seattle Slew through his three-year-old season to become the only undefeated American Triple Crown winner. Also trained Czaravich. Rode in steeplechase races from 1958-'62; assistant to Racing Hall of Fame trainer W. Burling Cocks before going on his own in 1966.

Ussery, Robert N., 1935-. Jockey. Inducted into Racing Hall of Fame in 1980. Rode 3,611 winners, including Hail to Reason, Bally Ache, Bramalea, Never Bow. Ranked fifth by money won among jockeys at retirement; finished first in two consecutive Kentucky Derbys, aboard Proud Clarion and Dancer's Image.

Van Berg, Jack, 1936-. Trainer. Leading trainer by races won in 1968-'70, '72, '74, '76, '83-'84, '86; leading trainer by money won in '76; inducted into Racing Hall of Fame in '85; Eclipse Award trainer in '84; Big Sport of Turfdom Award in '87; Jockey Club Gold Medal in '87; Mr. Fitz Award in '88. Trained Alysheba, Gate Dancer. Holds record for most races won in a single year (496 in 1976); trained champion Alysheba, who retired with a then-record total earnings of $6,679,242; 6,000th career win in February 1995. Son of Racing Hall of Fame trainer Marion Van Berg.

Van Clief, Daniel G. Jr., 1948-. Racing executive. President, Breeders' Cup Ltd.; chairman, Fasig-Tipton Co.; former president, Thoroughbred Club of America. Co-owner of Nydrie Stud, Virginia. Eclipse Award of Merit in 1998; Jockey Club Medal in '84. Worked to put together Breeders' Cup day of championship races; key figure in development of the National Thoroughbred Racing Association.

Van de Kamp, John, 1936-. Lawyer, association executive. President and general counsel, Thoroughbred Owners of California; director, National Thoroughbred Racing Association. Gathered support in the TOC to pass account wagering bill; lobbied for horse industry tax relief measures in California.

Varola, Francesco, 1922-. Author, bloodstock advisor. Author of *Typology of the Racehorse*; added to the dosage theory by creating aptitudinal classes in which he categorized each *chef-de-race* stallion.

Vasquez, Jacinto, 1944-. Jockey, trainer. Inducted into Racing Hall of Fame in 1998. Rode 5,231 winners, including Ruffian, Genuine Risk, Princess Rooney, Forego. Nation's 15th all-time winning jockey at his retirement in 1996; rode Ruffian to victory in the New York filly triple crown in '75.

Veitch, John, 1945-. Trainer. Trained Davona Dale, Our Mims, Before Dawn, Proud Truth. Trained Alydar, who finished second behind Affirmed in all three Triple Crown races in 1978. Son of Racing Hall of Fame trainer Sylvester Veitch.

Velasquez, Jorge, 1946-. Jockey. Leading jockey by races won in 1967; leading jockey by money won in '69; leading jockey by stakes races won in '85; inducted into Racing Hall of Fame in '90; George Woolf Memorial Jockey Award in '86. Rode 6,795 winners, including Alydar, Chris Evert, Davona Dale, Lady's Secret, Shuvee, Fort Marcy. Won the New York filly triple crown with Chris Evert in 1974 and Davona Dale in '79; first jockey to win six of six races in New York, in '81.

Ward, John T. Jr., 1945-. Trainer. Owner of Sugar Grove Farm, Kentucky; John T. Ward Stables, Kentucky. Trained Monarchos, Beautiful Pleasure, Darling My Darling, Jambalaya Jazz, Pyramid Peak. Nephew of Racing Hall of Fame trainer Sherrill Ward.

Weber, Charlotte, 1942-. Investments. Owner of Live Oak Stud, Florida. Bred and owned Peaceful Union, Gnome Home, Medieval Man, Laser Light, Sultry Song, Sultry Sun.

Weisbord, Barry, 1950-. Publisher. Joe Palmer Award in 1992. Co-owned Safely Kept. Created the American Championship Racing Series in 1991; created the Matchmaker Breeders' Exchange, the first centralized market for stallion seasons and shares.

West, R. Smiser, Breeder. Owner of Waterford Farm, Kentucky. Bred Lite Light, De La Rose, Chilukki.

Whiteley, Frank Jr., 1915-. Trainer. Inducted into Racing Hall of Fame in 1978. Trained 35 stakes winners and four champions, including Damascus, Forego, Ruffian, Tom Rolfe.

Whitney, Marylou, 1926-. Investments. Owner of Whitney Farm, Kentucky; Blue Goose Stable, Kentucky. Bred and owned Silver Buck, Bird Town. Bred Silver Creamer, Dawn Mountain, Bird Cage. Long known for her Derby Eve parties and for her parties in Saratoga Springs, New York. Widow of C. V. Whitney; married to John Hendrickson.

Willmot, David, 1950-. Breeder, investments. President, Woodbine Entertainment Group, formerly Ontario Jockey Club. Owner of Kinghaven Farms, Canada. John W. Galbreath Award in 2001; Sovereign Award in 1998. Bred and owned Talkin Man, Poetically, Alywow, Play the King, Summer Mood, With Approval. Brought Ontario Jockey Club out of financial troubles; successfully lobbied for legislation to add slot machines at Woodbine racetrack; Kinghaven became the first Canadian stable to earn more than $2-million, in 1986. Son of Donald Willmot.

Wolfson, Louis, 1912-. **and Wolfson, Patrice.** Investments. Owner of Harbor View Farm, Florida. Leading breeder in 1970-'71. Bred and owned Affirmed, Flawlessly, Exclusive Native, It's In the Air, Outstandingly. Owned Raise a Native. Bred and raced two-time Horse of the Year Affirmed, winner of the Triple Crown in 1978. Patrice Wolfson is daughter of Racing Hall of Fame trainer Hirsch Jacobs.

Ycaza, Manuel, 1938-. Jockey. Inducted into Racing Hall of Fame in 1977. Rode 2,367 winners, including Ack Ack, Dr. Fager, Damascus, Sword Dancer, Gamely, Dark Mirage, Never Bend. Won first New York filly triple crown with Dark Mirage in 1968.

Yoshida, Teruya, 1947-. Owner, president of Shadai Farm, founded by his late father, Zenya Yoshida. With brothers Haruya and Katsumi, owns Shadai Stallion Station, home to Japan's leading sire in 20 of the last 21 years, including ten-time leader Northern Taste and eight-time leader Sunday Silence. Vice chairman of the Japanese Racing Horse Association.

Young, William T., 1918-. Foods, storage. Owner of Overbrook Farm, Kentucky. Eclipse Award breeder in 1994. Bred and owned Storm Cat, Tabasco Cat, Cat Thief, Boston Harbor, Flanders, Surfside, Golden Attraction. Owned Editor's Note, Grindstone.

Zilber, Maurice, 1926-. Trainer. Ten times leading trainer during the 1950s in his native Egypt; leading trainer in France. Trained Racing Hall of Fame members Dahlia and Exceller, and Trillion, Youth, Argument (Fr), Hippodamia.

Zito, Nick, 1948-. Trainer. Trained Go for Gin, Strike the Gold, Louis Quatorze, A P Valentine, Thirty Six Red.

Industry Awards

Eric Beitia Memorial Award

Awarded annually by the New York Racing Association to the leading apprentice jockey at the NYRA tracks. Named for the leading apprentice of 1980 who died November 28, 1983, at age 21 of a gunshot wound suffered a week earlier.

2002	Lorenzo Lezcano
2001	Lorenzo Lezcano
2000	Norberto Arroyo Jr.
1999	Ariel Smith
1998	Shaun Bridgmohan
1997	Phil Teator
1996	Jose Trejo
1995	Ramon Perez
1994	Dale Beckner
1993	Caesar Bisono
1992	Gerry Brocklebank
1991	Rafael Mojica Jr.
1990	Paul Toscano
1989	Jose Martinez
1988	Brian Peck
1987	David Nuesch
1986	David Nuesch, Edward Thomas Baird
1985	Wesley Ward
1984	Wesley Ward
1983	Declan Murphy

Big Sport of Turfdom Award

Sponsored by the Turf Publicists of America and awarded to the individual or individuals whose cooperation with the media enhances coverage and brings favorable attention to Thoroughbred racing.

2002	Ken and Sue McPeek
2001	Laura Hillenbrand
2000	Laffit Pincay Jr.
1999	D. Wayne Lukas
1998	Mike Pegram
1997	Bob Baffert
1996	Cigar, Allen Paulson, Bill Mott, Jerry Bailey
1995	Robert and Beverly Lewis
1994	Warren "Jimmy" Croll Jr.
1993	Chris McCarron
1992	Angel Cordero Jr.
1991	Hammer and Oaktown Stable
1990	Carl Nafzger
1989	Tim Conway
1988	Julie Krone
1987	Jack Van Berg
1986	Jim McKay
1985	Laffit Pincay Jr.
1984	John Henry
1983	Joe Hirsch
1982	Woody Stephens
1981	John Forsythe
1980	Jack Klugman
1979	Laz Barrera
1978	Ron Turcotte
1977	Steve Cauthen
1976	Telly Savalas
1975	Francis P. Dunne
1974	Eddie Arcaro
1973	Penny Chenery
1972	John Galbreath
1971	Burt Bacharach
1970	Saul Rosen
1969	Bill Shoemaker
1968	John Nerud
1967	Allaire duPont
1966	E. P. Taylor

F. Ambrose Clark Award

Presented periodically by the National Steeplechase Association to those who promote, improve, or encourage steeplechase racing. Named for steeplechase owner who hosted the Meadow Brook Cup at his Long Island estate from 1926 to '41.

2002	George A. Sloan
2001	John A. Wayt Jr.
1995	John T. von Stade
1991	Beverly Steinman
1988	William L. Pape
1982	Mrs. Miles Valentine
1980	Charles Fenwick Jr.
1979	George Strawbridge Jr.
1978	Morris H. Dixon
1977	Alfred M. Hunt
1976	Joseph Aitcheson Jr.
1975	Michael Walsh
1974	John Cooper
1973	W. Burling Cocks
1972	Russell M. Arundel
1971	Raymond G. Woolfe
1970	Raymond R. Guest
1969	Mrs. Odgen Phipps
1968	John W. Hanes
1967	S. Bryce Wing
1966	Crompton Smith Jr.
1965	Marion duPont Scott

Coman Humanitarian Award

Presented by Kentucky Thoroughbred Owners and Breeders for contributions to better human relations in the Thoroughbred industry. Named for KTOB Executive Director William C. Coman, who formulated the Kentucky Thoroughbred Development Fund breeders' incentive awards program.

2002	Alice Chandler
2001	Sheikh Mohammed bin Rashid al Maktoum
2000	Benjamin Roach, M.D.
1999	J. David Richardson, M.D.
1998	Gary Biszantz
1997	Dr. John T. Bryans
1996	Larry Weber
1995	Not awarded
1994	Paul Mellon
1993	John A. Bell III
1992	Charles Nuckols Jr.
1991	William T. Young
1990	Carl Icahn
1989	Tim Conway
1988	Jim and Linda Ryan
1987	Jay Spurrier
1986	James E. "Ted" Bassett III
1985	Drs. Charles Hagyard, Arthur Davidson, and William McGee
1984	Keene Daingerfield
1983	Brownell Combs
	Maxwell Gluck

Dogwood Dominion Award

Sponsored by Dogwood Stable and presented to the "unsung heroes" of racing, especially in the backstretch areas. Named for Dominion (GB), Dogwood's first graded stakes winner who raced from 1974 to '78.

2002	Jim Greene and Shirley Edwards
2001	Julian "Buck" Wheat
2000	Katherine Todd Smith
1999	Danny Perlsweig
1998	Donald "Peanut Butter" Brown

1997   Nick Caras
1996   Grace Belcuore
1995   Peggy Sprinkles
1994   Howard "Gelo" Hall
1993   H. W. "Salty" Roberts

Charles W. Engelhard Award

Presented by Kentucky Thoroughbred Owners and Breeders for outstanding media coverage of the Thoroughbred industry. Named for owner of champions Nijinsky II, *Hawaii, and Assagai.

2002   Television Games Network
2001   John Henderson ("Thoroughbred Week")
2000   Ray Paulick (*The Blood-Horse*)
1999   Maryjean Wall (Lexington *Herald-Leader*)
1998   David Heckerman (*The Blood-Horse*)
1997   Jim Bolus
1996   Kenny Rice (WTVQ-TV)
1995   Not awarded
1994   Jay Hovdey (*The Blood-Horse*)
        John Asher (WHAS Radio)
1993   Jennie Rees (Louisville *Courier-Journal*)
1992   Josh Pons (*Country Life Diary*)
1991   Cawood Ledford
1990   Jim McKay (ABC)
1989   Lewis Owens (Lexington *Herald-Leader*)
1988   Anheuser-Busch
1987   Jim Wilburn and Chris Lincoln
        (Winner Communications)
1986   Leon Rasmussen (*Daily Racing Form*)
1985   Dick Enberg (NBC)
1984   NBC Sports
1983   Cawood Ledford
1982   Tom Hammond
1981   *The Thoroughbred Record*
1980   Billy Reed (Louisville *Courier-Journal*)
1979   Logan Bailey (*Daily Racing Form*)
1978   Kent Hollingsworth (*The Blood-Horse*)
1977   Jim McKay (ABC)
1976   Heywood Hale Broun (CBS)
1975   Robert Wussler (CBS)
1974   Joe Hirsch (*Daily Racing Form*)
1973   Jack Whitaker (CBS)
1972   Hugh "Mickey" McGuire
        (*Daily Racing Form*)
1971   Red Smith (New York *Times*)
1970   Win Elliott (CBS Radio)

John W. Galbreath Award

Sponsored by the University of Louisville's Equine Industry Program, the award named for the Darby Dan Farm owner honors equine-industry entrepreneurs who have utilized creative business techniques in their enterprises.

2002   William S. Morris III
2001   David Willmot
2000   Denny Gentry
1999   Tom Meeker
1998   D. Wayne Lukas
1997   John M. Lyons
1996   B. Thomas Joy
1995   Robert Clay
1994   Ami Shinitzky
1993   John Gaines
1992   W. Cothran "Cot" Campbell
1991   James E. "Ted" Bassett III
1990   John A. Bell III

Avelino Gomez Memorial Award

Sponsored by Woodbine, the award named for jockey Avelino "El Perfecto" Gomez is presented to the Canadian-born, -raised, or -based jockey who has made a significant contribution to Thoroughbred racing. North America's leading rider in 1966, Gomez died of injuries suffered in a three-horse spill in the Canadian Oaks on June 21, 1980.

2002   Richard Dos Ramos
2001   Chris Loseth
2000   Jim McKnight
1999   David Clark
1998   Irwin Driedger
1997   Richard Grubb
1996   David Gall
1995   Don Seymour
1994   Not awarded
1993   Larry Attard
1992   Robin Platts
1991   Hugo Dittfach
1990   Lloyd Duffy
1989   Jeff Fell
1988   Chris Rogers
1987   Don MacBeth
1986   Sandy Hawley
1985   John Longden
1984   Ron Turcotte

John K. Goodman Alumni Award

University of Arizona Race Track Industry Program award for a program graduate who has achieved distinction in the racing industry. Named for one of the program's founders.

2002   Todd Pletcher
2001   Luke Kruytbosch
2000   Ann McGovern
1999   Lonny Powell
1998   Dan Fick
1997   Bob Baffert

Walter Haight Award

Presented by the National Turf Writers Association for excellence in Turf writing. Named for Washington *Post* racing columnist and handicapper known for his humorous style.

2002   Billy Reed
2001   Gary West (Dallas *Morning News*)
2000   Bill Christine (Los Angeles *Times*)
1999   Jennie Rees (Louisville *Courier Journal*)
1998   Andrew Beyer (Washington *Post*)
1997   Jim Bolus
1996   Ed Schuyler Jr. (Associated Press)
1995   Jay Hovdey
1994   Ed Bowen
1993   Jack Mann (New York *Herald-Tribune*)
1992   Mike Barry (*Kentucky Irish American*
        and The Louisville *Times*)
        Bill Nack (*Sports Illustrated*)
1991   Bob Harding (Newark *Star-Ledger*)
1990   Kent Hollingsworth (*The Blood-Horse*)
1989   William Leggett (THOROUGHBRED TIMES)
1988   Leon Rasmussen (*Daily Racing Form*)
1987   Si Burick (Dayton *Daily News*)
1986   Ed Comerford (*Newsday*)
1985   Sam McCracken (Boston *Globe*)
1984   Joe Hirsch (*Daily Racing Form*)
1983   Fred Russell (Nashville *Banner*)
1982   Joe Agrella (Chicago *Sun-Times*)
1981   Bill Robertson (*The Thoroughbred Record*)
1980   Joe Nichols (New York *Times*)
1979   Barney Nagler (*Daily Racing Form*)
1978   Nelson Fisher (San Diego *Union*)

1977	Red Smith (New York *Times*)
1976	Saul Rosen (*Daily Racing Form*)
1975	Don Fair (*Daily Racing Form*)
1974	Raleigh Burroughs (*Turf and Sport Digest*)
1973	George Ryall (*The New Yorker*)
1972	Jimmy Doyle (Cleveland *Plain Dealer*)

Hardboot Award

Sponsored by Kentucky Thoroughbred Owners and Breeders, award named for the prototypical Kentucky horseman honors individuals for their careers in horsemanship.

2002	Charles Nuckols Jr.
	Virginia Kraft Payson
2001	Robert Courtney Sr.
2000	Carlos Perez
1999	Dr. and Mrs. R. Smiser West
	Mr. and Mrs. MacKenzie Miller

Joe Hirsch Breeders' Cup Newspaper Writing Award

Sponsored by Breeders' Cup Ltd. and the National Thoroughbred Racing Association, award named for the longtime *Daily Racing Form* columnist honors excellence in newspaper coverage of the Breeders' Cup World Thoroughbred Championships.

2002	Pat Forde
2001	Jay Privman
2000	Pat Forde
1999	Robert Edmondson
1998	Dick Jerardi
1997	Jennie Rees
1996	Pat Forde
1995	Dick Jerardi
1994	Jay Posner

Jockey Club Medal of Honor

Awarded periodically by the Jockey Club for meritorious service to the Thoroughbred industry.

1998	Nick Nicholson and Alan Marzelli
1994	Larry Bramlage, D.V.M.
1993	Kenny Noe Jr.
1992	R. Richards Rolapp
1991	Dr. Manuel Gilman
1990	Dr. Charles Randall
1989	Joe Hirsch
1988	Dennis Swanson
1987	Jack Van Berg
1986	Richard Duchossois
1985	Jean Romanet
1984	D. G. Van Clief Jr.

Lavin Cup

Sponsored by the American Association of Equine Practitioners and awarded to a nonveterinary individual or organization that has demonstrated exceptional compassion for horses or has developed and enforced guidelines for horses' welfare. Named for Kentucky veterinarian A. Gary Lavin, AAEP president in 1994.

1999	Tom Dorrance
1998	Thoroughbred Retirement Foundation
1997	American Quarter Horse Association
1996	California Horse Racing Board

Bill Leggett Breeders' Cup Magazine Writing Award

Sponsored by Breeders' Cup Ltd. and the National Thoroughbred Racing Association, award named for the late *Sports Illustrated* and THOROUGHBRED TIMES writer honors excellence in magazine coverage of the Breeders' Cup World Thoroughbred Championships.

2002	Tom Law
2001	Billy Reed
2000	Tom Law

1999	Bill Heller
1998	Tom LaMarra
1997	Robbie Henwood
1996	Glenye Cain
1995	Jay Hovdey
1994	Jay Hovdey

William H. May Award

Awarded by Association of Racing Commissioners International for distinguished service to racing. Named for former president of National Association of State Racing Commissioners (now Association of Racing Commissioners International) and Kentucky Racing Commission chairman known for his problem-solving abilities.

2003	American Association of Equine Practitioners
2002	American Quarter Horse Association
2001	John R. Gaines
2000	R. D. Hubbard
1999	Bob and Beverly Lewis
1998	Fred Noe
1997	James E. "Ted" Bassett III
1996	Allen Paulson
1995	Paul Mellon
1994	Joe Hirsch
1993	Tony Chamblin
1992	Bill Shoemaker
1991	Jockey Club
1990	James P. Ryan
1989	Stanley Bergstein
1988	*Daily Racing Form*
1987	Breeders' Cup Ltd.
1986	Robert H. Strub

Mr. Fitz Award

Sponsored by National Turf Writers Association, award named for Racing Hall of Fame trainer James E. "Sunny Jim" Fitzsimmons honors individuals who typify the spirit of horse racing.

2002	Chris McCarron
2001	H. Allen Jerkens
2000	Pat Day
1999	Bob and Beverly Lewis
1998	Joe Hirsch
1997	Bob Baffert
1996	MacKenzie Miller
1995	Warren "Jimmy" Croll
1994	Jeff Lukas
1993	Angel Cordero Jr.
1992	Ron McAnally
1991	Frances Genter
1990	Arthur B. Hancock III
1989	Ogden Phipps
1988	Jack Van Berg
1987	Laffit Pincay Jr.
1986	Arlington Park management
1985	John Henry
1984	Penny Chenery
1983	Fred Hooper
1982	Bill Shoemaker, Woody Stephens
1981	Jack Klugman

Isaac Murphy Award

Named for 19th-century black jockey who won with 44% of his career mounts, National Turf Writers Association award honors jockey with highest winning percentage for the year with a minimum of 500 mounts.

2002	Russell Baze
2001	Russell Baze
2000	Russell Baze
1999	Russell Baze
1998	Russell Baze
1997	Russell Baze
1996	Russell Baze
1995	Russell Baze

Nikon Preakness Photography Award

Sponsored by Pimlico Race Course and Nikon, for best Preakness Stakes (G1) photo from previous year.

2003	Skip Dickstein (*The Blood-Horse*)
2002	Molly Riley (Reuters)

Old Hilltop Award

Presented by Pimlico Race Course for distinction in Thoroughbred racing reporting. Name derives from Pimlico's nickname.

2003	John Patti (WBAL-AM)
	Steve Haskins (*The Blood-Horse*)
2002	Stan Charles (Baltimore radio)
	Michele MacDonald (THOROUGHBRED TIMES)
2001	Keith Mills (WMAR-TV)
	Jennie Rees (Louisville *Courier-Journal*)
2000	Marty Bass (WJZ-TV)
	Joe Kelly (Turf historian)
1999	Harry Kakel (WMAR-TV)
	Pohla Smith (Pittsburgh *Post-Gazette*)
1998	Ed Kiernan (WBAL Radio)
	Vinnie Perrone (*Maryland Turf Writers*)
1997	Reid Cherner (*USA Today*)
	Chris Lincoln (ESPN)
1996	Dan Farley (*Racing Post*)
	George Michael (WRC-TV)
1995	Charlsie Cantey (ABC Sports)
	Neil Milbert (Chicago *Tribune*)
1994	Ed Schuyler Jr. (*Associated Press*)
	Jim West (WBAL Radio)
1993	Jim Bolus (free-lance journalist)
	John Buren (WJZ TV)
1992	Dave Johnson (ABC Sports)
	Maryjean Wall (Lexington *Herald-Leader*)
1991	Sam Lacy (Baltimore *Afro-American*)
	Demmie Stathopolos (*Sports Illustrated*)
1990	Bill Tanton (Baltimore *Evening Sun*)
	Shelby Whitfield (ABC Radio)
1989	Bill Christine (Los Angeles *Times*)
	John Steadman (Baltimore *Evening Sun*)
1988	Ed Bowen (*The Blood-Horse*)
	Bill Nack (*Sports Illustrated*)
1987	Jack Dawson (WMAR-TV)
	Dave Feldman (Chicago *Sun-Times*)
1986	Vince Bagli (WBAL-TV)
	Shirley Povich (Washington *Post*)
1985	Howard Cosell (ABC Sports)
	Sam McCracken (Boston *Globe*)
1984	Jim McKay (ABC Sports)
	Billy Reed (Louisville *Courier-Journal*)
1983	Jack Whitaker (ABC Sports)
	Dale Austin (Baltimore *Sun*)
1982	Russ Harris (New York *Daily News*)
	Kent Hollingsworth (*The Blood-Horse*)
1981	William Leggett (*Sports Illustrated*)
	Jack Mann (Baltimore *Evening Sun*)
1980	Edwin Pope (Miami *Herald*)
	Snowden Carter (*Maryland Horse*)
1979	Whitney Tower (*Sports Illustrated*)
	Joe Kelly (Washington *Star*)
	William C. Phillips (*Daily Racing Form*)
1978	Win Elliott (CBS)
	Joe Hirsch (*Daily Racing Form*)
	Bob Maisel (Baltimore *Sun*)
1977	William Boniface (Baltimore *Sun*)
	Barney Nagler (*Daily Racing Form*)

	Charles Lamb (*News American*)
1976	Red Smith (New York *Times*)
	Raoul Carlisle (Arkansas *Times Herald*)

Joe Palmer Award

National Turf Writers Association Award for meritorious service to racing. Named for New York *Herald Tribune* Turf writer known for his overall appreciation of the sport.

2002	Richard Duchossois, Eugene Melnyk
2001	Shirley Day Smith
2000	Jim McKay
1999	Kent Hollingsworth
1998	Sandy Hawley
1997	Jim Bolus
1996	Allen Paulson
1995	Mark Kaufman
1994	Joe Hirsch
1993	Henryk de Kwiatkowski
1992	Barry Weisbord
1991	Joe Burnham
1990	James P. Ryan
1989	Claude "Shug" McGaughey III
1988	Charlie Whittingham
1987	Alfred Vanderbilt
1986	James E. "Ted" Bassett III
1985	John Gaines
1984	E. P. Taylor
1983	David "Sonny" Werblin
1982	Frank "Jimmy" Kilroe
1981	Keene Daingerfield, Marion duPont Scott
1980	Chick Lang Sr., Leo O'Donnell
1979	Laz Barrera
1978	Steve Cauthen
1977	Nelson Bunker Hunt
1976	Fred Hooper
1975	I. J. Collins
1974	Secretariat
1973	John Galbreath
1972	Paul Mellon
1971	Bill Shoemaker
1970	Warner Jones Jr.
1969	Raymond Guest
1968	Marion Van Berg
1967	John Longden
1966	Marshall Cassidy
1965	John Schapiro
1964	Wathen Knebelkamp

Joan F. Pew Award

Sponsored by the Association of Racing Commissioners International and awarded to racing commissioner who demonstrates vision and vitality. Named for first woman member of Pennsylvania Horse Racing Commission and first woman president of National Association of State Racing Commissioners (now Association of Racing Commissioners International).

2003	Norman I. Barron
2002	Stan Sadinsky
2001	Basil Plasteras
2000	Timothy "Ted" Connors
1999	Robin Traywick Williams
1998	Jon McKinnie
1997	Arthur Khoury
1996	Not awarded
1995	Not awarded
1994	Gil Moutray
1993	Joe Neglia
1992	Joanne McAdam

1991 Dr. Glenn Blodgett
1990 Frank Drea
1989 Richard Corbisiero Jr.
1988 Dr. James Smith
1987 Eric Braun

Red Smith Award

Churchill Downs award for outstanding print coverage of the Kentucky Derby (G1) in four categories. Named for late New York *Times* columnist.

Feature story

2002 Jennie Rees (Louisville *Courier-Journal*)
2001 Bill Christine (Los Angeles *Times*)
2000 Jerry Izenberg (Newark *Star-Ledger*)
1999 Jay Privman (*Daily Racing Form*)
1998 Matt Graves (Albany *Times Union*)
1997 Jennie Rees (Louisville *Courier-Journal*)
1996 Dave Koerner
      (Louisville *Courier-Journal*)
1995 Bob Fortus (New Orleans *Times-Picayune*)
1994 Rick Bozich (Louisville *Courier-Journal*)
1993 Rick Bozich (Louisville *Courier-Journal*)
1992 Tom Archdeacon (Dayton *Daily News*)
1991 Dave Koerner (Louisville *Courier-Journal*)
1990 Jim Wells (St. Paul *Pioneer-Press*)
1989 Steve Crist (New York *Times*)
1988 Bill Christine (Los Angeles *Times*)
1987 Hubert Mizell (St. Petersburg *Times*)
1986 Bill Christine (Los Angeles *Times*)
1985 Dick Fenlon (Columbus *Dispatch*)
1984 Stan Hochman (Philadelphia *Daily News*)
1983 Jim Bolus (Louisville *Times*)

Advance story

2002 Rick Bozich (Louisville *Courier-Journal*)
2001 Mike Kane ([Schenectady] *Daily Gazette*)
2000 Rick Bozich (Louisville *Courier-Journal*)
1999 Rick Bozich (Louisville *Courier-Journal*)
1998 Vic Ziegel (New York *Daily News*)
1997 Matt Graves (Albany *Times Union*)
1996 Steve Haskin (*Daily Racing Form*)
1995 Blackie Sherrod (Dallas *Morning News*)
1994 Billy Reed (Lexington *Herald-Leader*)
1993 Rick Bozich (Louisville *Courier-Journal*)
1992 Vic Ziegel (New York *Daily News*)
1991 Steve Woodward (*USA Today*)
1990 Jerry Izenberg (New York *Post*)
1989 Rick Bozich (Louisville *Courier-Journal*)
1988 Billy Reed (Lexington *Herald-Leader*)
1987 Billy Reed (Lexington *Herald-Leader*)
1986 Bob Harding (Newark *Star-Ledger*)
1985 Jack Patterson (Akron *Beacon-Journal*)
1984 Bill Christine (Los Angeles *Times*)
1983 Peter Finney
      (New Orleans *Times-Picayune*)

Sunday wrap-up

2002 Mike Kane ([Schenectady] *Daily Gazette*)
2001 Jennie Rees (Louisville *Courier-Journal*)
2000 Mike Kane ([Schenectady] *Daily Gazette*)
1999 Mike Kane ([Schenectady] *Daily Gazette*)
1998 Jay Privman (New York *Times*)
1997 Jay Privman (New York *Times*)
1996 Billy Reed (Lexington *Herald-Leader*)
1995 Chuck Culpepper
      (Lexington *Herald-Leader*)
1994 Tom Archdeacon (Dayton *Daily News*)

1993 Jennie Rees (Louisville *Courier-Journal*)
1992 Bill Christine (Los Angeles *Times*)
1991 Tom Archdeacon (Dayton *Daily News*)
1990 Billy Reed (Lexington *Herald-Leader*)
1989 Jay Privman (Los Angeles *Daily News*)
1988 Jay Privman (Los Angeles *Daily News*)
1987 Bill Christine (Los Angeles *Times*)
1986 Paul Moran ([Long Island] *Newsday*)
1985 Tom McEwen (Tampa *Tribune*)
1984 Billy Reed (Louisville *Courier-Journal*)
1983 Billy Reed (Louisville *Courier-Journal*)

Monday wrap-up

2002 Lew Freedman (Chicago *Tribune*)
2001 John Harrell (THOROUGHBRED TIMES)
2000 Steve Haskin (*The Blood-Horse*)
1999 Steve Haskin (*The Blood-Horse*)
1998 Bill Nack (*Sports Illustrated*)
1997 Dick Jerardi (Philadelphia *Daily News*)
1996 Greg Boeck (*USA Today*)
1995 Bill Nack (*Sports Illustrated*)
1994 Chuck Culpepper
      (Lexington *Herald-Leader*)
1993 Jack Murray (Cincinnati *Enquirer*)
1992 Harry King (*Associated Press*)
1991 Dick Jerardi (Philadelphia *Daily News*)
1990 Rick Bozich (Louisville *Courier-Journal*)
1989 Tom Cushman (San Diego *Tribune*)
1988 Stan Hochman (Philadelphia *Daily News*)
1987 Dick Jerardi (Philadelphia *Daily News*)
1986 Stan Hochman (Philadelphia *Daily News*)
      Edwin Pope (Miami *Herald*)
1985 Stan Hochman (Philadelphia *Daily News*)
1984 Dave Anderson (New York *Times*)
1983 Tom Jackson (Washington *Times*)

UTTA Outstanding Trainer of the Year Award

Outstanding trainer among year's Trainer of the Month award winners as voted by United Thoroughbred Trainers of America officers.

2001 John T. Ward Jr.
2000 Bobby Frankel
1999 D. Wayne Lukas
1998 Bob Baffert
1997 Pat Byrne
1996 Hubert "Sonny" Hine
1995 Bill Mott
1994 Warren "Jimmy" Croll Jr.
1993 Claude R. "Shug" McGaughey III
1992 H. Allen Jerkens
1991 Frank Brothers

Clay Puett Award

Sponsored by the University of Arizona Race Track Industry Program, for long-term, multifaceted, or far-reaching contributions to the racing industry. Named for creator of modern starting gate.

2002 John and Betty Mabee and family
2001 Joe Hirsch
2000 John Gaines
1999 Vessels family
1998 Brady family
1997 Hancock family
1996 Phipps family
1995 Allen Paulson
1994 Clement Hirsch

University of Arizona Race Track Industry Program Distinguished Service Award

For outstanding service to the Race Track Industry Program and its students.

2002	Not awarded
2001	Bob Benoit
2000	Stan Bergstein
1999	*Daily Racing Form*
1998	Sherwood Chillingworth
1997	Bennett Liebman
	Ronald Sultemeier
1996	Joe Harper
1995	Lonny Powell
1994	Rukin Jelks
1993	John Goodman
	Dr. Darrel Metcalfe
	Vessels family
1992	Dan Fick

University of Arizona Race Track Industry Program Distinguished Senior Award

2002	Stacia Mumm
2001	Laura Plato
2000	Scot Waterman
1999	Sable Downs
1998	Mike Hummel
1997	Valora Kilby

Alfred Gwynne Vanderbilt Award

New York Turf Writers Association award for individual or group that did the most for racing. Named for owner-breeder of Native Dancer; formerly known as the John A. Morris Award.

2002	Hans Stahl
2001	Barry K. Schwartz
2000	Kenny Noe Jr.
1999	Alfred Gwynne Vanderbilt
1998	Carolyn and Hubert "Sonny" Hine
1997	Skip Away
1996	James "Ted" Bassett
1995	Cigar
1994	Holy Bull
1993	Paul Mellon
1992	Allen Gutterman
1991	Barry Weisbord, American Championship Racing Series
1990	Not awarded
1989	John Gaines
	Whitney Tower
1988	Linda and Jim Ryan
1987	David "Sonny" Werblin
1986	ESPN/Thoroughbred Sports Television
1985	Peter Fuller
	John Galbreath
	Fred Hooper
1984	John Nerud
1983	Allaire duPont
1982	Helen "Penny" Chenery
	Frank "Jimmy" Kilroe
1981	Sam Rubin
1980	Jack Klugman
1979	Louis and Patrice Wolfson
1978	Affirmed
	Alydar

1977	Ogden Mills Phipps
1976	Marion duPont Scott
1975	Eddie Arcaro
	Johnny Longden
	Warren Mehrtens
	William "Smokey" Saunders
	Ron Turcotte
	Jack Dreyfus Jr.
1974	Martha F. Gerry
1973	Secretariat
1972	John H. "Jack" Krumpe
	Arthur B. "Bull" Hancock Jr.
1971	Jacques D. Wimpfheimer
1970	Charles W. Engelhard
	Sen. Thomas Morton
1969	Raymond Guest
1968	John W. Hanes
1967	Robert J. Kleberg Jr.
1966	Jack Dreyfus
1965	James Cox Brady
1964	Allaire duPont
1963	Alfred Gwynne Vanderbilt
1962	Capt. Harry F. Guggenheim
1961	Francis Dunne
1960	Capt. Harry F. Guggenheim
1959	John W. Hanes
1958	Marshall Cassidy
1957	C. V. Whitney
1956	George Widener
1955	Not awarded
1954	Not awarded
1953	Walter Jeffords
1952	C. V. Whitney
1951	John Hay Whitney
1950	Saratoga Association
1949	Marshall Cassidy
	George Widener
1948	Lou Smith
1947	Dr. Charles H. Strub
1946	John Blanks Campbell
1945	Not awarded
1944	Harry Parr III
1943	Lincoln Plaut
1942	Herbert Bayard Swope
1941	Alfred Gwynne Vanderbilt
1940	Herbert Bayard Swope
1939	George H. Bull
1938	Alfred Gwynne Vanderbilt
1937	Mrs. Payne Whitney
1936	Alfred Gwynne Vanderbilt

P.A.B. Widener II Trophy

Sponsored by Kentucky Thoroughbred Owners and Breeders and presented to breeder whose Kentucky-bred horses have performed the best based on a point system. Named for owner-breeder who raced under Elmendorf Farm.

2002	Allen Paulson
2001	Juddmonte Farms
2000	Adena Springs
1999	Overbrook Farm
1998	Mr. and Mrs. John C. Mabee
1997	Juddmonte Farms
1996	Juddmonte Farms
1995	Juddmonte Farms
1994	Overbrook Farm
1993	Juddmonte Farms
1992	William S. Farish and partners
1991	Verne Winchell

1990	Calumet Farm
1989	Ogden Phipps
1988	Ogden Phipps
1987	Nelson Bunker Hunt
1986	Nelson Bunker Hunt
1985	Nelson Bunker Hunt
1984	Hancock family
1983	Hancock family
1982	Fred Hooper
1981	Verna Lehmann
1980	Verna Lehmann
1979	Hancock family
1978	Randolph Weinsier
1977	Ben Castleman
1976	Ogden Mills Phipps
1975	Hancock family
1974	John Galbreath
1973	Maxwell H. Gluck
1972	Leslie Combs

David F. Woods Memorial Award

Presented by Pimlico Race Course for best Preakness Stakes (G1) story from previous year. Named for longtime racetrack publicist and Baltimore *Evening Sun* columnist.

2003	Bill Finley (New York *Times*)
2002	Jay Privman (*Daily Racing Form*)
2001	Tom LaMarra (*The Blood-Horse*)
2000	Rick Snider (Washington *Times*)
1999	Bill Mooney (*The Backstretch*)
1998	Jay Hovdey (*Daily Racing Form*)
1997	Jay Hovdey (*Daily Racing Form*)
1996	Steve Haskin (*Daily Racing Form*)
1995	Bill Finley (New York *Daily News*)
1994	Jay Posner (San Diego *Union-Tribune*)
1993	Bill Mooney (*The Blood-Horse*)
1992	Jay Hovdey (*The Blood-Horse*)
1991	Bill Christine (Los Angeles *Times*)
1990	Bill Christine (Los Angeles *Times*)
1989	Larry Bortstein
	(Orange County *Register*)
1988	Don Clippinger
	(*The Thoroughbred Record*)
	Bob Roberts (Cleveland *Plain Dealer*)
1987	Billy Reed (Lexington *Herald-Leader*)
1986	Dave Kindred
	(Atlanta *Constitution-Journal*)
1985	George Vecsey (New York *Times*)
1984	Jack Murphy (Cincinnati *Enquirer*)
1983	John Schulian (Chicago *Sun-Times*)
1982	Billy Reed (Louisville *Courier-Journal*)

George Woolf Memorial Jockey Award

Sponsored by Santa Anita Park and awarded to jockey whose career and character earn esteem for themselves and Thoroughbred racing, based on a vote of their fellow jockeys. Named for Racing Hall of Fame jockey George "Iceman" Woolf, who died January 4, 1946, a day after suffering severe head injuries in a spill at Santa Anita.

2002	Edgar Prado
2001	Dean Kutz
2000	Mike Smith
1999	Jose Santos
1998	Craig Perret
1997	Alex Solis
1996	Gary Stevens
1995	Eddie Maple
1994	Phil Grove

1993	Kent Desormeaux
1992	Jerry Bailey
1991	Earlie Fires
1990	John Lively
1989	Larry Snyder
1988	Don Brumfield
1987	Don MacBeth
1986	Jorge Velasquez
1985	Pat Day
1984	Steve Cauthen
1983	Marco Castaneda
1982	Patrick Valenzuela
1981	Eddie Delahoussaye
1980	Chris McCarron
1979	Ron Turcotte
1978	Darrel McHargue
1977	Frank Olivares
1976	Sandy Hawley
1975	Fernando Toro
1974	Alvaro Pineda
1973	John Rotz
1972	Angel Cordero Jr.
1971	Jerry Lambert
1970	Laffit Pincay Jr.
1969	John Sellers
1968	Braulio Baeza
1967	Donald Pierce
1966	Alex Maese
1965	Walter Blum
1964	Manuel Ycaza
1963	Ismael Valenzuela
1962	Steve Brooks
1961	Peter Moreno
1960	Bill Harmatz
1959	Bill Boland
1958	Merlin Volzke
1957	Ted Atkinson
1956	John Adams
1955	Ray York
1954	Ralph Neves
1953	Eddie Arcaro
1952	John Longden
1951	Bill Shoemaker
1950	Gordon Glisson

Mike Venezia Memorial Award

Named for the popular New York jockey who was killed in an on-track accident on October 13, 1988, the Mike Venezia Memorial Award honors jockeys who exemplify extraordinary sportsmanship and citizenship. Created by the New York Racing Association, the winners are determined by a vote of fans, sports writers, and jockeys. Recipients receive a 13-inch bronze statuette, "The Jockey, A Champion," by Tom Lear.

2003	Richard Migliore
2002	Dean Kutz
2001	Mike Luzzi
2000	Jorge Chavez
1999	Gary Stevens
1998	Eddie Maple
1997	Robbie Davis
1996	Laffit Pincay Jr.
1995	Pat Day
1994	Mike Smith
1993	Jerry Bailey
1992	Angel Cordero Jr.
1991	Chris McCarron
1990	Bill Shoemaker
1989	Mike Venezia

BREEDING
Development of Breeding Industry

Because the English aristocracy developed the Thoroughbred, the first harbingers of anything remotely resembling a Thoroughbred breeding industry necessarily appeared in England. Kings James I, Charles I, and especially Charles II were crucially important in importing Arabian stallions and broodmares in the 17th century.

When Charles I was deposed and beheaded by the Puritans in 1649, his stud at Tutbury was inventoried and dispersed, thus providing some of the earliest written records on the foundations of many modern pedigrees. Principal beneficiaries of that dispersal were members of Yorkshire's Darcy family, whose head, James Darcy Sr., was appointed Master of the Horse to Charles II. The Darcys, whose principal stud farm was at Sedbury in northern Yorkshire, were closely connected by marriage to other prominent early Yorkshire breeders: the Wyvil, Gascoigne, Hutton, and Villiers (the Dukes of Buckingham) families.

The Yorkshire land holdings of those families centered the early English breeding industry in that county, but Charles II chose the more southerly Suffolk village of Newmarket in East Anglia as his racing headquarters and established Newmarket racecourse in the 1660s. Newmarket's Rowley Mile, the course over which the Two Thousand Guineas (Eng-G1) and One Thousand Guineas (Eng-G1) are run, is named after "Bonnie Prince Charlie," whose nickname in his more mature days was "Old Rowley."

The English lords who followed the royal family's lead in breeding racehorses owned estates all over the country, and each established their principal stud farms according to the location of their lands. For example, the various Earls of Derby's principal stud farms were at Knowsley, near Liverpool, while the Dukes of Newcastle's (and later Dukes of Portland's) stud was at Welbeck Abbey, near Newcastle. Newmarket's place as the headquarters of English racing eventually led to a cluster of breeding farms in the surrounding area, but English stud farms are still scattered throughout the country.

Printed Record

The early Yorkshire breeders often kept meticulous, handwritten records of their breeding activities in private stud books, some of which have survived. The earliest printed record that included pedigrees was John Cheney's *Racing Calendar*, an annual volume of race results that first appeared in 1727. After Cheney's death in 1751, competing calendars produced by John Pond, Reginald Heber, and William Pick appeared, and the competition continued until James Weatherby established his version of the *Racing Calendar* as the sole authority, beginning in 1773.

Although Cheney included pedigree information on prominent runners in his annual volumes, it was Heber who first requested pedigree information from breeders in a standardized

---

Jersey Act

America's Thoroughbred industry was nearly destroyed between 1908 and 1910 when antiwagering legislation swept the country—closing many racetracks, slashing purses to minuscule levels for those that remained open, and rendering American bloodstock all but worthless at home. Desperate breeders thus began looking abroad for racing opportunities and markets for their horses.

English breeders were disturbed by this sudden influx of foreign bloodstock onto European shores. They had long perceived themselves as the world's supplier of Thoroughbreds and feared that American horses for sale in great numbers would threaten the international demand for their own products. In 1913, England's Jockey Club, chaired by the seventh Earl of Jersey, sought to protect its breeders' interests by enacting a rule that effectively barred American bloodstock from the Thoroughbred canon.

Known as the Jersey Act, the rule designated as "half-bred" any horse that did not trace in every pedigree line "without flaw" to foundation stock recorded in the earliest volumes of England's *General Stud Book*, which much of the world accepted as an industry bible. The Jersey Act thus labeled as half-breds many American

Thoroughbreds whose distant ancestors had been lost in the chaos of revolution and civil war. Although the rule was not retroactive, after 1913 horses carrying the blood of Lexington, Hanover, Spendthrift, Ben Brush, and other influential American progenitors no longer were admitted into the *General Stud Book*.

This discriminatory rule ultimately worked to America's advantage. For more than three decades and through two world wars, Americans imported top English bloodstock to enrich their breeding programs, while England could not look to America to do the same. While America acquired horses like *Mahmoud, *Sir Gallahad III, and *Bull Dog, England had no access to Man o' War, Bull Lea, or Black Toney—halfbreds one and all under the Jersey Act.

In June 1949, the Jersey Act was quietly repealed. Lady Wentworth, a respected British pedigree authority and historian, applauded the action as long overdue and described the Jersey Act as "a mistake that made us look rather foolish." Under the revised rule, admission to the *General Stud Book* required only eight or nine proven crosses of pure blood and "such performances of its immediate family on the Turf as to warrant the belief in the purity of its blood."

format. But no one attempted to collect this information into a separate book until Weatherby published Volume 1 of the *General Stud Book* in 1791. Based largely on private stud books and the various *Racing Calendars*, especially Pick's reconstruction of pre-Cheney races and pedigrees, Volume 1 of the *General Stud Book* was revised five times, with the final edition published in 1891.

The *Racing Calendar* and the *General Stud Book* gave the nascent Thoroughbred industry the kind of documentation required for expansion to other countries. Although records of racing in America extend back almost to the earliest English colonization, the first Thoroughbred recorded as imported to the New World in the *American Stud Book* is *Bulle (or Bully) Rock, by Darley Arabian, listed as imported to Virginia, "before the Revolution."

Virginia and Maryland became the first centers for breeding racehorses in America, led by the Tayloe family of Virginia and the Tasker family in Maryland. Given the primitive conditions of Colonial America, it is little wonder that many early records of imported Thoroughbreds and their produce in America were lost, and other records were reconstructed or fabricated at later dates.

As in England, early racing in America was the province of aristocratic families, and further progress by American breeders did not occur until the disruption caused by the American Revolution had thoroughly passed. The importation of *Diomed in 1799 proved pivotal because he established the first enduring American sire line through his son Sir Archy, great-grandsire of Lexington.

Commercial Beginnings

It was Lexington who cemented the transfer of the breeding industry west across the Appalachian Mountains to Kentucky. If any one man is the founder of the American commercial breeding industry, that person is Robert A. S. C. Alexander, who purchased Lexington for his Woodburn Stud near the city of Lexington in 1855. Lexington's success as 16-time leading sire and the many top racehorses that Alexander and his brother

Alexander J. Alexander sold at Woodburn's annual yearling auctions enticed many other breeders to locate their breeding operations in the Bluegrass.

The Alexanders also were among the sponsors of what became the definitive *American Stud Book*, after several false starts. George W. Jeffreys published the *Virginia Stud Book* in 1828, but the first comprehensive attempt at an American Stud Book was Patrick Nisbett Edgar's *American Race-Turf Register, Sportsman's Herald, and General Stud Book*, published in 1833.

Unfortunately, Edgar's work included a stunning number of obvious inaccuracies, some of which remain in the official record. As in England, several competitors, including John S. Skinner and William T. Porter, published versions of Racing Calendars or Stud Books before Sanders D. Bruce's *American Stud Book, Volume 1*, appeared in 1868.

Although Bruce's book retained some of Edgar's errors and created some of its own, it was a considerable advance on previous offerings. It rapidly became the official record and was purchased by the American Jockey Club in May 1897 for $35,000. That purchase was the first step toward the Jockey Club's current position as the breed registry and the keeper of the sport's records.

Early American race results were recorded primarily by periodicals such as Porter's *Spirit of the Times* and Bruce's *Turf, Field, and Farm*. *Daily Racing Form* and the *Morning Telegraph* took over these functions in the late 19th century, and the *Racing Form* became the de facto newspaper of record by the 1920s. In 1991, the Jockey Club and the Thoroughbred Racing Associations formed Equibase Co. to develop the official database of the Thoroughbred industry, and in 1998 Equibase became the data provider to the *Racing Form* as well.

Key Figures

Key figures in the development of an American commercial breeding industry on the foundation laid by the Alexanders were John E. Madden, Arthur B. Hancock Sr. and his son Arthur B. "Bull" Hancock Jr., Leslie Combs II, and John R. Gaines. A hands-on horseman who bred and

---

Designating Imported Horses

In its earliest years, the *American Stud Book* designated horses imported to North America for racing or breeding with "Imported" or "Imp." before the horse's name.

This practice changed in 1906 with publication of the *American Stud Book*'s Volume 9. Its preface noted: "While the general features of this volume remain the same as Volume 8, it has been found necessary, in order to avoid a two-volume work, to condense the subject matter in every way possible, the most radical change being the substitution of an * in place of the word Imported wherever possible.

"The prefix Imported has been omitted from the

following horses, they having been foaled in the United States, viz.: Bel Demonio, Donald A., Dundee, Flax Spinner, Glenelg, Keene, Loiterer, Pontiac, Paladin, Uncommon and Victory."

The asterisk, which preceded such notable names in American breeding history as *Nasrullah and *Ribot, was eliminated in 1975. An introductory note to the *American Stud Book, Foals of 1981*, states: "The practice of designating imported horses with an asterisk (*) was discontinued in 1975, and from that time forward, the country of origin is reflected in the suffix attached to the name. The asterisk or suffix is omitted in the cases of horses which were imported in utero."

trained his own horses with a keen eye for profit, Madden bred five Kentucky Derby winners at Hamburg Place, named for his first great coup with the great racehorse and sire Hamburg.

Hancock Sr. founded Claiborne Farm near Paris, Kentucky, in 1908 and stood Celt, who became the first of 11 leading American sires who won 29 sire championships at Claiborne during the 20th century.

Combs modernized both the stallion-syndication process and yearling salesmanship at his Spendthrift Farm near Lexington. Combs stood leading sires Exclusive Native and Seattle Slew, but it was his recruitment of wealthy clients to the sales ring and the breeding industry that helped set the stage for the bloodstock boom of the 1970s and '80s.

Combs's success made clear that big money could be made by breeding and selling potential racehorses, but it was Gaines who developed the syndication of stallions into a highly lucrative enterprise. An innovative thinker, Gaines also created the concept of the Breeders' Cup, which came to fruition in 1984, and was one of the founders of the National Thoroughbred Association, which was quickly subsumed by the industry-backed National Thoroughbred Racing Association in 1998.

From its beginnings as a passionate pursuit of a few aristocratic Englishmen, Thoroughbred racing and breeding have developed into a worldwide, multibillion-dollar industry. Though still primarily a business for the wealthy, Thoroughbreds are now produced in every condition from the brick palaces of the Bluegrass and Newmarket to, quite literally, suburban back yards.—*John P. Sparkman*

Registration Rules for Breeding
Copyright © 2003 The Jockey Club

History of Registration

The Jockey Club, an organization dedicated to improving Thoroughbred breeding and racing, registers more than 30,000 Thoroughbred foals each year, introducing them to the *American Stud Book* following a disciplined process of initiation that began more than 300 years ago.

Early in the 17th century, three stallions brought to England—the Darley Arabian, the Godolphin Arabian, and the Byerly Turk—became the foundation sires of the Thoroughbred industry. In 1791, James Weatherby published the first stud book, the *General Stud Book*. It listed the pedigrees of 387 mares that could be traced to one of three descendants of the foundation sires: Eclipse, a direct descendant of the Darley Arabian; Matchem, a grandson of the Godolphin Arabian; and Herod, a great-great-grandson of the Byerly Turk.

In America, Patrick Edgar attempted to publish a national stud registry in 1833 but was unsuccessful. One year later, John Skinner reprinted the entire *General Stud Book* and added the existing pedigrees of American horses at the end. Following Skinner's effort, the pedigree section of *Mason's Farrier* was the only available resource until 1867, when John H. Wallace published *Wallace's American Stud Book*. Wallace soon abandoned the enterprise, which was a fiscal failure, and turned his attention to compiling the American Trotting Registry.

One year later, Col. Sanders D. Bruce published the *American Stud Book*. On May 17, 1897, the Jockey Club acquired the rights to Bruce's work. Now, more than 100 years later, the Jockey Club continues to maintain the *American Stud Book* to ensure the integrity of the breed.

Today, registering a Thoroughbred is as simple as logging onto the Internet. Through Jockey Club Interactive™ (*http://www.registry.jockeyclub. com*), owners and breeders can complete registration forms, submit digital photos, review a database of active names, and check the status of a registration. A goal of the Jockey Club is to provide a virtual foal certificate that will eliminate paper, which can be lost, destroyed, or illegally altered, while at the same time providing real-time access to all registry-related information.

How to Register

All requirements of the Principal Rules and Requirements of the *American Stud Book* must be met within one year of a foal's originally reported foaling date.

Step 1

For foals of 2001 and after, the foal's sire and dam must be DNA-typed. For foals of 2000 and earlier, the foal's sire and dam must be blood-typed.

Step 2

Report of Mares Bred (Deadline: August 1 each year)

Stallion owners must file a report of all Thoroughbred mares bred to a stallion in a breeding season (February-July).

Step 3

Live Foal/No Foal Report (Deadline: Within 30 days after foaling)

1. The owner of record in the Jockey Club files will receive a preprinted Live Foal/No Foal Report. Note: All changes of mare ownership should be reported to the Jockey Club immediately.

2. The Live Foal/No Foal Report must be filed within 30 days of the birth of a foal, or when it is determined that a mare will not have a foal. Note: The registration services department at the Jockey Club should be contacted if a preprinted Live Foal/No Foal Report is not received by the time the foal is born.

Step 4

DNA/Blood-Typing (Deadline: Within 45 days of receipt of DNA/blood kit)

1. Between four to seven months after the reported foaling date, a Registration DNA/Blood-typing Kit will be mailed to the address shown on the Live Foal/No Foal Report. Note: If DNA/blood kit is not used within 45 days, the DNA/blood-typing process may have to be restarted at an additional fee.

2. Mane hairs pulled/blood drawn from the foal must be mailed to the laboratory shown on the preprinted mailer.

Notes:

Helpful hints for taking a DNA sample:

• Clean the mane comb thoroughly before pulling the mane.

• Grasp the mane close to the neck to help ensure you get roots.

• Do not try to pull a sample if the mane is wet.

Helpful hints for drawing blood:

• If, for some reason, a syringe must be used to draw blood, insert needle through stopper and depress plunger on syringe slowly.

• Do not remove stoppers or chemicals from tubes.

• Do not shake tubes; turn them end over end.

• Refrigerate blood if not mailing the same day. (Do not put tubes in Styrofoam container during refrigeration, and do not freeze the sample).

• Do not mail samples on the weekend or immediately before a holiday. (If samples are untestable on receipt by laboratory, another kit will be mailed and the process must be repeated).

Step 5

Registration/DNA-Typing/Blood-Typing Form (Deadline: Send to the Jockey Club when DNA/blood sample is mailed to lab. Before sending to the Jockey Club, be certain that):

1. Both sides of form are completed, including:

i) Written description of markings, indicating:

• All white markings.

• All flesh-colored markings.

• All dark and chestnut markings on coronet.

• All head and neck cowlicks (except cowlick at the very top of forehead).

• Any other distinguishing characteristics.

ii) Signature by foal's owner or authorized agent.

iii) One to six name choices. (This could avoid additional naming fees).

2. A set of four color photos is enclosed, clearly showing color and all markings from the front, back, and both sides. Note: Do not take photographs until the foal has shed its "baby hair."

3. The Stallion Service Certificate (acquired from the stallion owner) is attached.

4. Fee payment is enclosed.

How to Name a Horse

A. A name may be claimed on the Registration Form, on a Name Claiming Form, or through Jockey Club Interactive™. Name selections should be listed in order of preference. Names will be assigned based upon availability and compliance with the naming rules as stated herein. Names may not be claimed or reserved by telephone. When a foreign language name is submitted, an English translation must be furnished to the Jockey Club. An explanation must accompany "coined" or "made-up" names that have no apparent meaning. Horses born in the United States, Puerto Rico, or Canada and currently residing in another country must be named by the Jockey Club through the Stud Book Authority of their country of residence.

B. If a valid attempt to name a foal is submitted to the Jockey Club by February 1 of the foal's two-year-old year and such a name is determined not eligible for use, no additional fee is required for a subsequent claim of name for that foal. If a valid attempt to name a foal is not submitted to the Jockey Club by February 1 of the foal's two-year-old year, a fee is required to claim a name for such a foal.

C. A reserved name must be used within one year (365 days) from the day it was reserved. Reserved names cannot be used until written notification requesting the assignment of the name to a specific horse is received by the Registry Office. If the reserved name is not used within one year (365 days) from its reservation, it will thereafter be available for any horse. A fee is required to reserve a name for a foal.

D. A foal's name may be changed at any time prior to starting in its first race. Ordinarily, no name change will be permitted after a horse has started in its first race or has been used for breeding purposes. However, in the event a name must be changed after a horse has started in its first race, both the old and new names must be used until the horse has raced three times following the name change. The prescribed fee and the Certificate of Foal Registration must accompany any request to the Registry Office for a change of name.

E. Names of horses more than ten years old may be eligible if they are not excluded under Rule 6(F) and have not been used during the preceding five years either in the stud or on the turf.

Names of both geldings and horses that never raced or were not used in the stud may be available five years from the date of their death as reported.

F. The following classes of names are not eligible for use:

1. Names consisting of more than 18 letters (spaces and punctuation marks count as letters).

2. Initials such as C.O.D., F.O.B., etc.

3. Names ending in "filly," "colt," "stud," "mare," "stallion," or any similar horse-related term.

4. Names consisting entirely of numbers, except numbers above 30 may be used if they are spelled out.

5. Names ending with a numerical designation

such as "2nd" or "3rd," whether or not such a designation is spelled out.

6. Names of persons unless written permission to use their name is on file with the Jockey Club.

7. Names of "famous" people no longer living unless approval is granted by the Board of Stewards of the Jockey Club.

8. Names of "notorious" people.

9. Names of racetracks or graded stakes races.

10. Recorded names such as assumed names or stable names.

11. Names clearly having commercial significance, such as trade names.

12. Copyrighted material, titles of books, plays, motion pictures, popular songs, etc., unless the applicant furnishes the Jockey Club with proof that the copyright has been abandoned or that such material has not been used within the past five years.

13. Names that are suggestive or have a vulgar or obscene meaning; names considered in poor taste; or names that may be offensive to religious, political, or ethnic groups.

14. Names that are currently active either in the stud or on the turf, and names similar in spelling or pronunciation to such names, see 6(E).

15. Permanent names and names similar in spelling or pronunciation to permanent names. The list of criteria to establish a permanent name is as follows:

a. Horses in the Racing Hall of Fame;

b. Horses that have been voted Horse of the Year;

c. Horses that have won an Eclipse Award;

d. Horses that have won a Sovereign Award (Canadian championship);

e. Annual leading sire and broodmare sire by progeny earnings;

f. Cumulative money winners of $2-million or more;

g. Horses that have won the Kentucky Derby (G1), Preakness Stakes (G1), Belmont Stakes (G1), Jockey Club Gold Cup (G1), Breeders' Cup Classic (G1), or Breeders' Cup Turf (G1);

h. Horses included in the International List of Protected Names.

G. In addition to the provisions of this Rule 6, the Registrar of the Jockey Club reserves the right of approval on all name-claiming requests.

Age Definitions

Foal: A young horse of either sex in its first year of life.

Suckling: A foal of any sex in its first year of life while it is still nursing.

Weanling: A foal of any sex in its first year of life after being separated from its dam.

Yearling: A colt, filly, or gelding in its second calendar year of life (beginning January 1 of the year following its birth).

Two-Year-Old: A colt, filly, or gelding in its third calendar year of life (beginning January 1 of the year following its yearling year).

Color Definitions

The following colors are recognized by the Jockey Club:

Bay: The entire coat of the horse may vary from a yellow-tan to a bright auburn. The mane, tail, and lower portion of the legs are always black, unless white markings are present.

Black: The entire coat of the horse is black, including the muzzle, the flanks, the mane, tail, and legs, unless white markings are present.

Chestnut: The entire coat of the horse may vary from a red-yellow to a golden-yellow. The mane, tail, and legs are usually variations of coat color, unless white markings are present.

Dark Bay or Brown: The entire coat of the horse will vary from a brown, with areas of tan on the shoulders, head, and flanks, to a dark brown, with tan areas seen only in the flanks and/or muzzle. The mane, tail, and lower portion of the legs are always black, unless white markings are present.

Gray or Roan: In order to reduce the number of corrections involving the colors gray and roan, the Jockey Club has combined these colors into one color category. This does not change the individual definitions of the colors for gray and roan and in no way impacts on the two-coat color inheritance principle as stated in (a previous rule).

Gray: The majority of the coat of the horse is a mixture of black and white hairs. The mane, tail, and legs may be either black or gray, unless white markings are present.

Roan: The majority of the coat of the horse is a mixture of red and white hairs or brown and white hairs. The mane, tail, and legs may be black, chestnut, or roan, unless white markings are present.

Breeding Terminology

Bred (Mated): Any filly or mare that has undergone the physical act of breeding (mating).

Bred (Area Foaled): The term "bred" is sometimes used to describe the location where a foal was born; i.e., Kentucky-bred, New York-bred, etc.

Breeder: The breeder of a foal is the owner of the dam at the time of foaling, unless the dam was under a lease or foal-sharing agreement at the time of foaling. In that case, the person(s) specified by the terms of the agreement is (are) the breeder of the foal.

Stallion: A male horse that is used to produce foals.

Sire: A male horse that has produced, or is producing, foals.

Broodmare: A filly or mare that has been bred (mated) and is used to produce foals.

Dam: A female horse that has produced, or is producing, foals.

Maiden: A filly or mare that has never been bred (mated).

In Foal (Pregnant) Broodmare: A filly or mare that was bred (mated), conceived, and is currently in foal (pregnant).

Aborted: A term used to describe a broodmare that has been pronounced in foal (pregnant) based on an examination of 42 days or more post breeding (mating) and lost her foal prematurely; or a broodmare from whom an aborted fetus has been observed.

Barren (Not Pregnant): A term used to describe a filly or mare, other than a maiden mare, that was bred (mated) and did not conceive during the last breeding season.

Breeding (Mating): The physical act of a stallion mounting a filly or mare with intromission and ejaculation of semen into the reproductive tract.

Sex Terminology

Colt: An entire male horse four years old or younger.

Horse: When reference is made to sex, a "horse" is an entire male five years old or older.

Ridgling ("rig"): A lay term used to describe either a monorchid or cryptorchid.

Cryptorchid: A male horse of any age that has no testes in his scrotum but was never gelded (the testes are undescended).

Monorchid: A male horse of any age that has only one testicle in his scrotum—the other testicle was either removed or is undescended.

Gelding: A male horse of any age that is unsexed—had both testicles removed.

Filly: A female horse four years old or younger.

Mare: A female horse five years old or older.

Deadlines

Report of Mares Bred (Stallion Reports): This report must be filed by August 1 of the breeding year.

Live Foal/No Foal Report (Mare Reports):
• Reporting live foal information. This report must be filed within 30 days after the foaling date.
• Reporting no foal information. This report must be filed within 30 days after the intended foaling date or in January if the mare was "not bred."

Foal registration: All requirements must be completed by one year from the foaling date, including DNA/blood typing.

Naming: Must be named by February 1 of two-year-old year to avoid paying a fee.

Death: Must be reported within 30 days of the death.

Foreign registration: Requirements must be met within 60 days of the horse's arrival to avoid paying an additional fee.

Export: Requirements must be met within 60 days of the horse's departure to avoid paying an additional fee.

Geldings and spayed females: Must be reported immediately.

Fees

Foal registration fees: If all requirements are completed within the one-year deadline (includes DNA/blood-typing of the foal and parentage verifications, as well as ownership transfers and corrections):

Foals of 1999: $175

Foals of 2000 or later: $200

If DNA/blood kit is used and foal is not registered: $80

By December 31 of yearling year: $525

By December 31 of two-year-old year: $775

Beyond December 31 of two-year-old year: $2,000

Reserved names: $50

Foal-naming fee: After February 1 of the foal's two-year-old year. (Before this date, no fee is required): $50

Name-change fee: $100

DNA/blood-typing fees:

DNA/blood-typing, entry into the Ownership Registry: $80

Restart/Reactivate DNA/blood-typing case: $80

Duplicate certificate fee: $150

Corrected certificate fee (six months after original certificates issued): $50

Certificate of exportation fees:

If all requirements are completed within 60 days of the horse's departure from the United States, Canada, or Puerto Rico: $150

If all requirements are completed after 60 days of the horse's departure from the United States, Canada, or Puerto Rico: $400

Certificate of foreign registration fees:

If all requirements are completed within 60 days of the horse's arrival in the United States, Canada, or Puerto Rico: $150

If all requirements are completed after 60 days and up until one year of the horse's arrival in the United States, Canada, or Puerto Rico: $400

If all requirements are not completed within one year of the horse's arrival in the United States, Canada, or Puerto Rico, and the horse is eligible for late registration: $750

American horses returning to the U.S.: $150

Thirty-day (foreign) racing permit fee: If applied for within 30 days of the horse's arrival in the United States, Canada, or Puerto Rico: $150

Express handling fee: $50

How to Contact the Jockey Club:

Address: The Jockey Club, 821 Corporate Drive, Lexington, KY 40503-2794

Telephone: (859) 224-2700

Registration Services: (800) 444-8521

Fax: (859) 224-2710

Web site: *http://home.jockeyclub.com*

Jockey Club Interactive™ Web site: *http://www.registry.jockeyclub.com*

Foal Registration

Foal registration for all Thoroughbreds in North America—the United States, Canada, and Puerto Rico—is performed by the Jockey Club, which was founded in 1894 and is a not-for-profit organization dedicated to improving the Thoroughbred breed. To be registered in the *American Stud Book*, which is maintained by the Jockey Club, the parentage of all foals must be verified, a process that today includes DNA typing of all stallions, broodmares, and foals.

Registration of American Thoroughbreds was started by Col. Sanders D. Bruce, a Kentuckian who spent a lifetime researching pedigrees of American Thoroughbreds. He published the first volume of the *American Stud Book* in 1868, and he produced six volumes of the registry. In 1897, the Jockey Club purchased all rights to the *American Stud Book*.

Foal Registration by State in North America in 2001

Alabama 64	Iowa............................480	New Hampshire..............7	Texas.......................1,919
Alaska...........................0	Kansas 100	New Jersey................332	Utah..............................66
Arizona 333	Kentucky..................9,786	New Mexico................536	Vermont...........................1
Arkansas 292	Louisiana..................1,364	New York 1,715	Virginia 500
California 3,647	Maine.............................3	North Carolina 46	Virgin Islands.................3
Colorado 219	Maryland...................1,098	North Dakota 38	Washington 844
Connecticut 3	Massachusetts 71	Ohio...........................641	West Virginia 353
Delaware 0	Michigan....................302	Oklahoma................1,032	Wisconsin 21
Florida 4,270	Minnesota..................208	Oregon.......................276	Wyoming.......................17
Georgia.........................56	Mississippi...................19	Pennsylvania..............901	**Total U.S. 33,757**
Hawaii............................0	Missouri........................39	Rhode Island 0	**Total Canada 2,509**
Idaho 204	Montana.....................114	South Carolina 72	**Total Puerto Rico.....583**
Illinois 957	Nebraska....................162	South Dakota...............55	
Indiana.......................536	Nevada 8	Tennessee 47	

Trend of Foal Registration in North America

Year	United States	Change	Canada	Change	Puerto Rico	Change	Total	Change
2002	32,235*	−4.5%	2,600*	3.6%	765*	31.2%	35,600*	−3.4%
2001	33,757	−2.5%	2,509	2.0%	583	3.9%	36,849	−2.1%
2000	34,605	2.4%	2,460	1.7%	561	−13.7%	37,626	2.1%
1999	33,782	2.6%	2,420	3.5%	650	−11.4%	36,862	2.4%
1998	32,936	2.6%	2,339	2.5%	734	−0.8%	36,009	2.5%
1997	32,114	−0.4%	2,284	−4.7%	740	1.9%	35,138	−0.6%
1996	32,238	1.1%	2,397	−2.0%	726	11.2%	35,361	1.1%
1995	31,879	−0.8%	2,445	−5.6%	653	3.3%	34,977	−1.0%
1994	32,117	−5.0%	2,591	−4.5%	632	4.5%	35,340	−4.8%
1993	33,818	−3.5%	2,713	−2.3%	605	−0.8%	37,136	−3.4%
1992	35,050	−8.1%	2,777	−8.2%	610	−2.9%	38,437	−8.0%
1991	38,149	−5.4%	3,024	−5.3%	628	1.8%	41,801	−5.3%
1990	40,333	−8.8%	3,193	−4.9%	617	−1.4%	44,143	−8.5%

*Estimated

Annual Foal Registration in North America

2003 ....37,000*	1981 38,669	1959 12,240	1937 5,535	1915 2,120
2002 ....35,600*	1980 35,679	1958 11,377	1936 5,042	1914 1,702
2001 36,849	1979 32,904	1957 10,832	1935 5,038	1913 1,722
2000 37,626	1978 31,510	1956 10,112	1934 4,924	1912 1,900
1999 36,862	1977 30,036	1955 9,610	1933 5,158	1911 2,040
1998 36,009	1976 28,809	1954 9,064	1932 5,256	1910 1,950
1997 35,138	1975 28,271	1953 9,040	1931 5,266	1909 2,340
1996 35,361	1974 27,586	1952 8,811	1930 5,137	1908 3,080
1995 34,977	1973 26,811	1951 8,944	1929 4,903	1907 3,780
1994 35,340	1972 25,726	1950 9,095	1928 4,503	1906 3,840
1993 37,136	1971 24,301	1949 8,770	1927 4,182	1905 3,800
1992 38,437	1970 24,361	1948 8,434	1926 3,632	1904 3,990
1991 41,801	1969 23,844	1947 7,705	1925 3,272	1903 3,440
1990 44,143	1968 22,910	1946 6,579	1924 2,921	1902 3,600
1989 48,235	1967 21,876	1945 5,819	1923 2,763	1901 3,784
1988 49,220	1966 20,228	1944 5,650	1922 2,352	1900 3,476
1987 50,917	1965 18,846	1943 5,923	1921 2,035	1899 3,080
1986 51,296	1964 17,343	1942 6,427	1920 1,833	1898 2,940
1985 50,433	1963 15,917	1941 6,805	1919 1,665	1897 2,992
1984 49,247	1962 14,870	1940 6,003	1918 1,950	1893–'96 ......5,940*
1983 47,237	1961 13,794	1939 6,316	1917 1,680	1803–'92 ......3,950*
1982 42,894	1960 12,901	1938 5,696	1916 2,128	*Estimated

Evolution of the Breed

In genetic terms, the Thoroughbred is a hybrid, created by crossing two or possibly more breeds of horses to produce an animal with specific characteristics. One of those breeds was the Arabian horse, but the exact identities of other contributors are considerably less clear.

Early records do not identify most of the mares mated to the many Arabian, Barb, and Turk (all are varieties of Arabians) stallions imported to England after the Markham Arabian's acquisition by King James I. Although the Markham Arabian was the first Arabian whose importation was noted by history, no doubt others, both males and females, were transported from the Middle East over several centuries, beginning with the Crusades of the 12th and 13th centuries. However, many horses called Arabians or Barbs in the *General Stud Book* were certainly not purebreds.

These imports were crossed with native English stock over many generations. By the time the modern Thoroughbred was created, there were two varieties of pony-sized English racehorses known as Hobbies and Galloways, and Oriental imports of the time were not much larger. Both English breeds certainly carried Oriental blood, but no one knows how much. Before the Puritan revolution in 1649, the royal stud of King James I and his ill-fated son King Charles I probably included mares of both mixed English and Oriental blood and pure-bred Arabians. These mares came to be called "royal mares" and now stand as the earliest known female ancestors of several modern female families.

The surge of importations that began with the restoration of King Charles II in 1660 included both males and females. With King Charles leading the way, the English nobility engaged in fierce competition to produce better, faster racehorses, and they quickly learned that the more Arabian blood their stock could claim, the better chance they had.

Estimated Relationships of Some Important Horses to Modern Thoroughbreds

Horse (year of birth)	Percentage relationship
Herod (1758)	17.2%
Eclipse (1764)	15.2%
Highflyer (1774)	12.8%
Godolphin Arabian (1724)	12.7%
Partner (1718)	11.4%
Regulus (1739)	9.4%
St. Simon (1881)	8.7%
Stockwell (1849)	8.7%
Curwen Bay Barb mare (1710)	8.4%
Birdcatcher (1833)	7.4%
Pocahontas (1837)	7.0%
Matchem (1748)	6.3%
Flying Childers (1715)	5.7%
Darley Arabian (ca. 1700)	5.3%
*Teddy (1913)	4.9%
Byerley Turk (ca. 1680)	4.6%
Curwen Bay Barb (ca. 1695)	4.4%
Hyperion (1930)	4.2%
*Nasrullah (1940)	4.2%
Bald Galloway (ca. 1700)	4.0%

Figures based on an unpublished statistical study. Percentages of horses born since about 1850 may change slightly.

Foundation Sires

The arrivals of the Byerley Turk, Place's White Turk, the Curwen Bay Barb, the Darley Arabian, and finally the Godolphin Arabian (around 1730) sharply accelerated the development of the breed. The Darley Arabian sired Flying Childers, generally recognized as the first great Thoroughbred, in 1714. Through Flying Childers's full brother Bartlett's Childers, the Darley Arabian established today's dominant male line, leading to Phalaris and his descendants.

The Godolphin Arabian was the most prepotent immediate influence among the three founding

The Darley Arabian

Of the Thoroughbred's three male-line foundation sires, only the Darley Arabian was almost certainly a pure-bred Arabian. The Godolphin Arabian was almost certainly a Turcoman-Arabian cross, while the Byerley Turk may have been born in England, sired by another Turcoman-Arabian cross horse whose identity is uncertain.

Probably born in what is now Syria in 1700, the Darley Arabian was purchased in Aleppo, then part of the Ottoman Empire, by English merchant Thomas Darley in 1704 and shipped to his brother Richard Darley at Aldby Park near York, England. The Darley Arabian was said to be of the "keheilan" or "manicca" breed, the subset of Arabians then most prized by Bedouins. Ottoman law forbade the sale of any pure-bred Arabian to a foreigner, but Darley's merchant connections in Aleppo allowed him to spirit the horse out of the country.

The Darley Arabian mostly covered his owner's broodmares, but one of the few outside mares bred to him was Leonard Childers's Betty Leedes, by Careless, who produced Flying Childers in 1714 and his full brother Bartlett's Childers in 1715. Flying Childers was unbeaten and considered by far the fastest horse until that time. Darley Arabian also sired the good racehorses Almanzor, Cupid, and Brisk.

Although Flying Childers was a successful sire, his brother Bartlett's Childers—unraced because he was a bleeder—carried on the line. He sired the good racehorse Squirt, who in turn sired Marske, sire of Eclipse (1764). Eclipse in turn founded the male lines that lead to the modern lines of Phalaris (Northern Dancer, Native Dancer), St. Simon (*Ribot and *Princequillo), Hyperion, Domino, *Teddy, and Blandford.

male-line sires, establishing the male line that leads to dual Breeders' Cup Classic (G1) winner Tiznow. Although the Godolphin Arabian male line is now far less prominent than that of the Darley Arabian, almost 13% of the genes of the modern Thoroughbred come from the Godolphin Arabian, according to modern statistical studies.

The male line tracing to the Byerley Turk achieved dominance in the late 18th century through his great-great-grandson Herod. By 1825, inbreeding to Herod had reached its limit, and his overall influence began to decline. Today, his male line appears to be headed for extinction, with tendrils hanging on in Europe through Ahonoora and in Australia through Century. Nevertheless, more than 17% of the genes of the modern Thoroughbred come from Herod.

Beneficiary of the intense early inbreeding to Godolphin Arabian and Herod was the Darley Arabian line. The line from Flying Childers was prominent for approximately 50 years, but descendants of his unraced full brother, the bleeder Bartlett's Childers, gained ascendance

through his great-grandson Eclipse, foaled in 1764. Eclipse was the greatest of the four-milers, and during his stud career a shift began from the four-mile heat racing that had been popular since King Charles's era to "dash" racing over shorter distances, exemplified by the Epsom Derby, founded in 1780 and contested at one mile that year.

Eclipse and Herod surpassed all other stallions of their time in producing the speedier, more brilliant horse necessary for dash racing. Added together, Herod, Godolphin Arabian, and Eclipse account for 45% of the genes of the modern Thoroughbred.

In the same time period that surviving male lines were being whittled down to three, female lines descending from approximately 100 foundation mares listed in Volume 1 of the *General Stud Book* were cut in half. That, of course, does not mean that those foundation mares and stallions had no influence on the development of the breed. Indeed, their names persist, sometimes with great influence, in the nether reaches of pedigrees.

Averages for the Breed

Averages for the Breed statistics are designed to provide a baseline to evaluate the performances of contemporary racehorses, sires, and dams. Statistics shown in the column on the left below reflect the worldwide performances of all named foals born in North America between 1985-'94. Statistics in the column on the right reflect the same data for foals by the top 1% of all sires by total earnings for the same decade. All statistics are based on data in the Jockey Club Information System's worldwide database. The Jockey Club database includes complete records for racing in United States, Canada, Puerto Rico, England, Ireland, France, Germany, Italy, Japan, Australia, Hong Kong, Saudi Arabia, Argentina, Brazil, and United Arab Emirates for some, but not all of the years covered by these statistics.

Statistics below are designed to give a snapshot of what an average "good" horse should accomplish.

	Foals of 1985-'94	Foals by top 1% of sires
Starters/foals	68.9%	84.9%
Winners/foals (starters)	45.1% (65.5%)	65.6% (77.3%)
Repeat winners/foals (starters)	33.6% (48.8%)	53.6% (63.1%)
Stakes winners/foals (starters)	3.2% (4.6%)	9.2% (10.9%)
Graded SW/foals (starters)	0.7% (1%)	3.6% (4.2%)
Grade 1 SW/foals (starters	0.20% (0.29%)	1.2% (1.4%)
Stakes-placed/foals (starters)	4.9% (7.2%)	12.0% (14.2%)
2-year-old starters/foals	33.5%	46.2%
2yo winners/foals (% 2yo starters)	11.1% (33%)	18.5% (40.1%)
2yo SW/foals (% 2yo starters)	0.96% (2.9%)	2.5% (5.3%)
3-year-old starters/foals	59%	76.7%
4-year-old starters/foals	44%	57.3%
5-year-old and up starters/foals	26.6%	36.2%
Average career starts/foal	14.8	19.2
Average career starts/starter	21.5	22.6
Average win distance in furlongs	6.82	7.24
Average win distance on turf	8.40	8.56
Average earnings/starter	$29,588	$72,633
Average earnings/starter male (female)	$34,788 ($24,109)	$89,409 ($54,927)
Average earnings/start	$1,376	$3,216
Average earnings/start male (female)	$1,422 ($1,313)	$3,221 ($3,206)
Average Racing Index (RI)	1.16	2.54

Exportation of the Thoroughbred to other countries, particularly to North America, Australia, and Argentina, inevitably resulted in the introduction of female lines not found in the *General Stud Book*. The chaotic circumstances of Colonial and Revolutionary America meant that records were lost on many legitimate members of the breed and invented for many who doubtless were not.

Such chaos inevitably led to controversy. When American racing collapsed early in the 20th century due to antigambling hysteria, England's Turf authority, the Jockey Club, essentially banned American-bred stock from the hallowed pages of the *General Stud Book* when American exports threatened to flood the market. Fortunately for the future of the breed, the Jersey Act of 1913 excluding American-breds included a provision that grandfathered in American-bred stock already included in earlier volumes.

Within 40 years, descendants of those acceptable American-breds—including such horses as Nearco and his son *Nasrullah—and descendants of French-bred Tourbillon (branded as a half-bred by the Jersey Act because of his American antecedents) dominated English racing, forcing repeal of the exclusionary rules.

Changing Conditions

The descendants of Eclipse's great-grandson Whalebone through his great-great-grandson Stockwell proved especially adaptable to the pattern of English racing established by the five classic races. Stockwell led the English sire list eight times and his great-grandson, unbeaten Triple Crown winner *Ormonde, is widely considered the best racehorse of the 19th century. The male line of *Ormonde lives on tenuously through the descendants of Damascus.

The inauguration of several valuable races outside the classic pattern in the 1890s changed the requirements of English racing at about the same time that an invasion of American jockeys changed race-riding. After American riders such as Tod Sloan and Danny Maher proved the virtues of setting a faster pace, male-line descendants of one stallion, Phalaris, gradually proved the most capable of adapting to the new conditions.

A top-class sprinter during World War I, Phalaris sired two sets of full brothers who established powerful male lines: Pharos and Fairway, and *Sickle and *Pharamond II. Pharos and his descendants generally sired heavier, more muscular horses with speed, while the Fairways tended toward taller, lighter individuals. Today the Fairway line hangs by the thread of Lord At War (Arg), while Pharos reigns supreme through descendants of his grandsons *Nasrullah, sire of Bold Ruler, and Nearctic, sire of Northern Dancer.

*Sickle led the U.S. sire list twice, and his brother *Pharamond II finished second to him in 1938. *Sickle's great-grandson Native Dancer, another heavy, powerful horse, established the second most powerful male line in modern pedigrees, that descending from his grandson Mr. Prospector.

In 300 years, the Thoroughbred breed has evolved from a small, relatively lightly made animal designed to gallop 3½ miles at a sedate pace and then sprint for a half-mile. It has become a much larger, heavier, shorter-legged animal designed primarily for high speeds from the start over distances up to 1¼ miles. Without much doubt, Flying Childers would hardly recognize his modern descendants.

—John P. Sparkman

Breeding Theories

Flying Childers was the first great racehorse who clearly could be defined as a Thoroughbred, and undoubtedly his breeder, Leonard Childers, had a theory to explain why his greatest creation was so fast. In the three centuries since Flying Childers first saw daylight in 1714, it is certain that most breeders were equally sure they knew why their latest champion could run a hole in the wind.

Over time, however, breeders' ideas about why one horse runs faster than another have coalesced into a remarkably small set of concepts. Breeding theories range from vaguely general precepts such as "breed the best to the best and hope for the best" to highly specific constructs such as the many varieties of dosage theory.

Breed the Best to the Best

The logic behind the broadest of these ideas—breed the best to the best—is obvious. If speed in the racehorse is determined to a degree by inheritance, then it is logical to assume that the fastest horses—both male and female—have the best chances to pass on their abilities to their offspring.

The history of the breed has shown irrefutably that this assumption is true. In general, the horses that turn out to be the best sires are almost always high-class racehorses themselves. The correlation between racecourse ability and sire success is, of course, far from guaranteed but undeniably positive.

The case for the female of the species is less clear but still undeniable. On average, the best racemares become more successful broodmares than those females that showed less ability on the racecourse. Thus, if a high-class racehorse is mated to a high-class racemare, the breeder theoretically increases the probability that another high-class racehorse will result.

Because probability is capricious, the odds are still against the breeder. The most successful stallions in history have sired only about 25% stakes winners. Individual broodmares may achieve higher percentages, but percentages based on the relatively small numbers of foals from those mares are meaningless in the larger picture.

So, breeding the best to the best certainly works, on average. However, it is far too general a precept to satisfy many Thoroughbred breeders—and of no use whatsoever to those who cannot afford to buy the best, most expensive racing prospects, both male and female.

Inbreeding

For the first 100 years or so of the Thoroughbred's existence as a distinct, definable breed, the number of horses bred each year was so small that inbreeding was inevitable.

Inbreeding, as most commonly used by Thoroughbred breeders, means the repetition of one or more names at least once on both the sire's and dam's side of a pedigree within the first four or five generations. In genetic terms, inbreeding reduces the number of different and distinct gene alleles available to appear in the genome of the new individual. Thus, it increases the chances that the offspring of that mating will display uniform and specific characteristics.

Inbreeding is therefore used in animal husbandry to fix type—that is, to create a more uniform subspecies, which is exactly what Thoroughbred breeders were doing in the 18th century.

The process of creating the Thoroughbred was largely one of inbreeding to certain prepotent stallions and mares—often very closely. For example, the third dam of Flying Childers is listed in the *General Stud Book*'s Volume 1—detailing the genesis of the Thoroughbred breed—as being by the excellent 17th-century racehorse and sire Spanker and out of Spanker's own dam, the Old Morocco mare. That's about as close as inbreeding can get.

The best racehorses of the 18th century and early 19th century were almost invariably closely inbred to a succession of great stallions, beginning with the Godolphin Arabian and continuing through Eclipse, Herod, and the latter's son Highflyer. By about 1825, the genes of those four stallions were so highly concentrated in the Thoroughbred that breeders were forced to seek outcrosses. Since that time, inbreeding has gone in and out of fashion, and a few great breeders, notably French breeder Marcel Boussac, have used its principles to create great racehorses, sires, and broodmares.

Inbreeding is described in contemporary industry texts by a shorthand method that denotes the name and location in the five-cross pedigree of the individual or individuals to which the subject horse is inbred. Thus "inbred 3x4 to Northern Dancer" means that the name of

Some Famous Inbred Horses

Horse (year of birth)	Inbreeding	Accomplishment
Spanker mare (ca 1690)	2x1 Old Morocco mare	Third dam of Flying Childers
Rachel (1763)	2x3 Godolphin Arabian	Dam of Highflyer, undefeated, 13-time leading sire
Eclipse (1764)	3x4 Snake mare	Unbeaten champion, sire line founder
Prunella (1788)	3x3 Blank	Dam of three classic winners, grandam of seven others
Sir Archy (1802)	3x4 Herod	American foundation sire
Boston (1833)	3x3 *Diomed	Greatest American four-miler
Lexington (1850)	3x4 Sir Archy	16-time leading American sire
Galopin (1872)	3x3 Voltaire	Epsom Derby winner, sire of St. Simon
Americus (1892)	3x3 Lexington	Key horse in pedigree of *Nasrullah
Flying Fox (1896)	3x2 Galopin	English Triple Crown, grandsire of *Teddy
Bromus (1905)	2x3 Springfield	Dam of Phalaris
Bayardo (1906)	4x2 Galopin	English champion, sire of two Triple Crown winners
Havresac II (1915)	2x3 St. Simon	Leading Italian sire, broodmare sire of Nearco
*Ksar (1918)	3x2 Omnium II	Prix de l'Arc de Triomphe winner, sire of Tourbillon
Pharos (1920)	4x3 St. Simon	Champion Stakes winner, sire of Nearco, Pharis
Hyperion (1930)	4x3 St. Simon	Epsom Derby winner, six-time leading sire
Coronation (1946)	2x2 Tourbillon	Prix de l'Arc de Triomphe winner
*Turn-to (1951)	3x3 Pharos	Sire of sires Hail to Reason, Sir Gaylord, Cyane, Best Turn
Broad Brush (1983)	3x3 *Turn-to	Leading sire of 1995

Northern Dancer appears in the third generation on the sire's side of the pedigree and in the fourth generation of the dam's side.

A more accurate method would be to calculate the inbreeding coefficient, or percentage of inbreeding, to that individual. By that method, the inbreeding coefficient of a horse inbred 3x4 to Northern Dancer would be 1.56%.

Nicks

Thoroughbred breeding is of necessity both a retrospective and a predictive art. Early Thoroughbred breeders could not help but notice the efficacy of inbreeding to certain stallions and mares, and the repeated success of combining certain sires and broodmares also became apparent. For reasons that are now obscure, this pattern of combining a specific sire and broodmares sired by another stallion became known as a nick.

Perhaps the best early example of a nick was the combination of the immortal racehorse and great sire Herod and mares by the even-greater sire Herod. This direct cross produced 1784 Epsom Derby winner Serjeant. The reverse cross of Herod on an Eclipse mare produced 1783 St. Leger Stakes winner Phenomenom, but the real gold mine for breeders was in the innumerable crosses of sons of Eclipse on mares by Herod or his sons, and sons of Herod on mares by Eclipse or his sons. That more generalized nick was preserved in the breed most notably through 1793 Derby winner Waxy (by Eclipse's son Pot8o's out of a Herod mare), tail-male ancestor of the Phalaris male line.

Phalaris, a foal of 1913, contributed to the most famous 20th-century nick. The four current male lines tracing to Phalaris all descend from sons out of Chaucer mares. *Sickle (Raise a Native line) and *Pharamond II (Buckpasser line) were both foaled by Selene, by Chaucer, while Pharos (*Nasrullah and Northern Dancer lines) and Fairway (Lord At War [Arg] line) were both sons of Scapa Flow, by Chaucer.

Contemporary advocates of nicking theory have compiled and marketed nicking information that evaluates various crosses according to percentage of stakes winners or graded winners produced by all exemplars of that cross. To accumulate sufficient numbers of exemplars of the cross to be statistically meaningful, these formulations frequently extend the concept to include grandsons or great-grandsons of a particular sire crossed on granddaughters or great-granddaughters of another sire.

At that point, such data are focusing on the hypothetical power of one individual in the third generation of a pedigree and another in the fourth while ignoring the rest of the pedigree. Even at the sire–broodmare sire level, statistical studies of some of the most famous nicks such as the *Nasrullah–*Princequillo cross have not been encouraging.

Still, the fact that certain crosses such as Phalaris-Chaucer have had extraordinary impact on the breed lends some credence to the concept.

Bruce Lowe Numbers

For the first 150 years of the Thoroughbred as a distinct breed, breeding theories focused almost entirely on the influence of stallions. Toward the end of the 19th century, however, an Australian, Bruce Lowe, and a German, Herman Goos, independently began to trace every mare in the *General Stud Book* back to the earliest female ancestor recorded in Volume 1. Both found that every mare traced to one of about 50 of approximately 100 original foundation mares recorded in Volume 1.

Goos published his results in *Family Tables of English Thoroughbred Stock*, a monumental work that was the foundation for the even more monumental *Family Tables of Racehorses* by Kazimierz Bobinski and Stefan Zamoyski in 1953. Goos noted that some female lines had been much more successful than others, but Lowe went several steps further. The Australian numbered each family according to the cumulative number of winners of the Epsom Derby, Epsom Oaks, and St. Leger Stakes each had produced up to his era. Thus, the female line tracing to Tregonwell's Natural Barb mare was named the Number 1 family, and that tracing to the Burton Barb mare was Number 2. In all, 49 families were numbered.

Based on their success rates, Lowe designated families 1 through 5 as his "running" families. He also designated families 3, 8, 11, 12, and 14 his "sire" families, based on his judgment that the highest number of successful sires occurred in those families. He called those family numbers "figures." He then developed several theories of breeding racehorses based on combinations of those families. His theories were published posthumously in 1895 in *Breeding Race Horses by the Figure System*.

Lowe's system ignored the fact that the primary reason families 1 through 5 produced the most classic winners was that they had produced the most foals in pretty much the same proportions. Numerical superiority, not innate hereditary superiority, accounted for the differences. His theories on breeding also ignored the fact that the original foundation mares were so many generations removed from contemporary horses that their genetic influences were statistically negligible.

Bruce Lowe's theories were promoted assiduously by his editor, English journalist and bloodstock agent William Allison. Lowe's theories were widely influential around the turn of the 20th century, especially in America, where Allison's purchases of broodmares formed the basis for James R. Keene's stud. Genetic science in the 20th century proved Lowe's theories were useless, but his numbering system of female lines has remained a valuable contribution.

Vuillier Dosage

The late 19th century was a remarkably fertile period for pedigree research. At about the same time Lowe and Goos were tracing their female lines, French cavalry officer Col. Jean-Joseph Vuillier overheard two men arguing over whether Eclipse or Herod was the more influential sire and set out to answer the question statistically. To do so, Vuillier compiled complete pedigrees of more than 650 high-class racehorses, mostly winners of the English classics that Lowe used.

Although he apparently had no knowledge of either theory, Vuillier correctly applied a modern Mendelian interpretation of Galton's Law of genetic inheritance, which states that each parent contributes 50% of the genetic material to their offspring on average. Extending his pedigrees to a minimum of 12 generations, he assigned a value of 1 to a name that appeared in the 12th generation, a value of 2 in the 11th, 4 in the tenth, 8 in the ninth, and on down to a value of 2,048 for first-generation parents.

To determine the percentage contribution of Eclipse and Herod, Vuillier added up the numbers for each occurrence in each generation. Vuillier found that when he averaged the results for his 650 pedigrees, Herod's average number was 750 while Eclipse's average was only 568. He also discovered that Herod's son Highflyer was almost as influential as Eclipse with an average of 543.

In pursuing his research over 15 years, Vuillier noticed that other, more recent ancestors also accumulated high numbers, and he compiled figures that he called "dosages" for 11 more stallions and one mare, Pocahontas. Vuillier's dosages are in fact remarkably accurate representations of the percentage of genetic influence on the classic Thoroughbred of the 15 horses in his classification.

Since classic winners were frequently the most successful sires of future generations, Vuillier reasoned that the breed as a whole

Vuillier Dosages

First Series

Horse	Dosage
Herod (1758)	750
Eclipse (1764)	568
Highflyer (1774)	543

Second Series

Birdcatcher (1833)	288
Touchstone (1831)	351
Pocahontas (1837)	313
Voltaire (1826)	186
Pantaloon (1824)	140
Melbourne (1834)	184
Bay Middleton (1833)	127
Gladiator (1833)	95

Third Series

Stockwell (1849)	340
Newminster (1848)	295

Fourth Series

St. Simon (1881)	420
Galopin (1872)	405
Isonomy (1875)	280
Hampton (1872)	260
Hermit (1864)	235
Bend Or (1877)	210

would and should move in the same direction as the classic pedigree. Thus, he concluded the object of a breeding program should be to produce pedigrees with the same dosages as his classic pedigrees.

To facilitate this process, Vuillier devised the *ecart* system. *Ecart* is a French word that translates loosely to mean mathematical difference. For any potential mating using Vuillier's system, the breeder could calculate the dosages of the prospective foal. The difference between the prospective dosages and the ideal is the *ecart*. The object of Vuillier's system was to reduce the ecart as much as possible.

Vuillier published his findings privately in volumes 1 and 2 of *Les Croisements Rationnels* (Rational Breeding) in 1903 and '27. The Aga Khan hired him to manage his stud in 1925, but Vuillier died shortly thereafter. His widow took over and arranged the Aga Khan's matings for more than 30 years. During that period, the Aga Khan was the most successful and influential breeder in the world, with his stud producing such great racehorses and sires as *Bahram, *Mahmoud, and *Nasrullah. The Vuillier system, privately modernized and updated, is still in use by the current Aga Khan.

Varola Dosage

Vuillier's method was not widely available and was difficult to execute because it required constructing 12-generation pedigrees and keeping track of mathematical data in an era long before computers. Italian journalist Francesco Varola built on Vuillier's work in his *Typology of the Racehorse,* published in 1974. Since Vuillier's published series of influential stallions extended only through the late 19th century, Varola updated and vastly expanded this list of influential stallions. His initial work identified 120 more horses, all born in the 20th century.

Unlike Vuillier, Varola did not utilize Galton's Law in his formulation, applying equal value to an appearance by a given stallion regardless of the generation of the pedigree in which he appeared. Recognizing that the modern Thoroughbred racehorse is much more specialized than in Vuillier's day, Varola divided his 120 stallions initially into five groups defined by his judgment of the type of influence they exerted on the breed.

His five categories—Brilliant, Intermediate, Classic, Stout, and Professional—were based partly on sociological concepts, partly on physical type and racecourse expression, and partly on inspiration. Varola eventually split the Brilliant group into Brilliant and Transbrilliant and Stout into Solid and Rough, but the original five categories quickly became associated in the public mind with varying degrees of stamina. Varola has consistently disavowed this interpretation.

Varola arranged the names of all his *"chefs-de-race"* in a "dosage diagram," dividing the names of each *chef-de-race* (chief of the breed) that occurs in a given pedigree into the five (or seven) categories and totaling the number of occurrences, regardless of generation. The resulting series of numbers offered breeders a thumbnail picture of the balance in a pedigree among all of Varola's different aptitudes.

Varola's chief contribution may be his insight into the increasing specialization of the Thoroughbred into sprinters, stayers, and middle-distance horses, among others, and his recognition that human sociology plays a role in determining the type of racehorse produced in different countries in different eras.

Roman Dosage

In the 1980s, Steve Roman, an American chemistry professor, developed a system combining some of the aspects of the Vuillier and Varola dosage systems. Considering only the first four generations of a pedigree, Roman assigned a numerical value of 16 to any *chef-de-race* that appeared in the first generation of a pedigree, eight to a second-generation *chef,* four for the third generation, and two for the fourth.

Roman interpreted Varola's five original categories strictly in terms of stamina, with Brilliant horses defined as those contributing extreme speed but little stamina, while Professional *chefs* contributed stamina but little speed. Applying the appropriate value according to generation for each occurrence of a *chef*'s name and adding those values up for each of Varola's five aptitudinal categories, Roman devised a "dosage profile" meant to give breeders insight into the relative stamina inherent in a given pedigree.

Roman invented the "dosage index," a single number that is calculated by dividing the total points in the Brilliant and Intermediate categories plus half the Classic points by the total of the points in the Stout and Professional categories plus the other half of the Classic points. The resultant figure is intended to predict a horse's ability to stay classic distances.

Applying his ideas to the history of the Kentucky Derby (G1), Roman found that almost all Derby winners since the 1930s had dosage indexes of 4.00 or less. Leon Rasmussen of *Daily Racing Form* popularized Roman's ideas in the 1980s and early '90s, and, though a number of Kentucky Derby winners have subsequently defied their Roman dosage, his theories remain popular.

Modern Genetics

The science of genetics, like the other physical sciences, made enormous strides during the 20th century. Though published earlier, Mendel's laws were virtually unknown at the turn of the 20th century, but early in the 21st century the complete human genome was mapped. Science had progressed from cross-breeding garden peas to cloning sheep and other large mammals.

None of this progress has significantly affected Thoroughbred breeding. An equine genome mapping project is under way, but even that should have no immediate effect on the breed because knowing the location of genes does not reveal the traits or characteristics that they control. Even coat-color genetics, once thought to be a relatively simple dominance series consisting of gray, bay (or brown), and chestnut alleles, proved to be not so simple because white Thoroughbreds began to appear about 30 years ago.

The problem is that the traits that produce a successful racehorse are not governed by single genes. Factors such as speed, stamina, temperament, and soundness are each dependent on thousands of different genes working together with the environment to create outstanding racehorses.—*John P. Sparkman*

SIRES
Leading Sires by Progeny Earnings
Worldwide in 2002

Worldwide earnings for stallions standing in North America or having last stood
in North America if pensioned or dead; or represented by 25 2002 starters in North America.

Sire, Where stands	Strs	Wnrs	SWs	Leading earner (earnings)	Progeny earnings
Dehere, Jpn	282	132	17	Take Charge Lady ($1,388,635)	$9,337,302
End Sweep, Dead	240	138	5	South Vigorous ($1,406,883)	8,706,427
Royal Academy, Ky.	395	158	19	Double Happiness ($655,798)	8,480,845
Gulch, Ky.	183	91	8	Nayef ($1,897,935)	8,478,339
Kris S., Dead	133	70	8	Symboli Kris S ($4,724,763)	8,085,603
Wild Again, Ky.	149	80	8	Milwaukee Brew ($1,590,000)	7,584,189
Woodman, Ky.	344	139	13	Hawk Wing ($1,143,720)	7,415,764
Cozzene, Ky.	139	70	7	Admire Cozzene ($2,149,552)	7,382,269
El Prado (Ire), Ky.	197	101	12	Medaglia d'Oro ($2,260,600)	7,264,951
A.P. Indy, Ky.	149	80	12	Aratama Indy ($566,460)	7,127,448
Kingmambo, Ky.	132	64	10	Mambo Twist ($775,075)	6,990,593
Jolie's Halo, Jpn	139	43	4	Sankin Halo ($479,234)	6,861,866
Broad Brush, Ky.	115	68	14	Farda Amiga ($1,248,902)	6,806,405
Black Tie Affair (Ire), Jpn	209	88	5	Evening Attire ($1,332,720)	6,682,187
Gone West, Ky.	159	65	5	Came Home ($1,624,500)	6,481,314
Storm Cat, Ky.	142	62	18	Storm Flag Flying ($967,000)	6,438,339
Mt. Livermore, Ky.	190	85	8	Orientate ($1,412,970)	6,404,422
French Deputy, Jpn	132	76	7	Left Bank ($626,146)	5,949,711
Rahy, Ky.	134	70	5	Grass World ($942,159)	5,946,535
Dynaformer, Ky.	186	88	15	Perfect Drift ($695,120)	5,891,680
Crafty Prospector, Ky.	158	83	4	Agnes Digital ($1,238,986)	5,815,239
Carson City, Ky.	197	101	11	Carson Hollow ($335,370)	5,775,524
Hennessy, Ky.	242	102	5	Wiseman's Ferry ($766,552)	5,642,951
Silver Deputy, Ky.	167	94	6	Divine Silver ($640,236)	5,575,683
Cryptoclearance, Ky.	216	100	4	Volponi ($2,389,200)	5,420,734
Theatrical (Ire), Ky.	128	51	8	Media Puzzle ($1,447,592)	5,419,346
Thunder Gulch, Ky.	251	88	10	Spain ($569,502)	5,359,025
Mr. Greeley, Ky.	198	114	10	Nonsuch Bay ($439,362)	5,197,096
Regal Classic, N.Y.	236	111	8	Regal Sanction ($318,400)	5,048,983
Our Emblem, Ky.	79	35	4	War Emblem ($3,455,000)	4,999,768
Saint Ballado, Dead	169	69	9	Kite Hill Wind ($512,994)	4,983,295
Unbridled's Song, Ky.	175	89	11	Agnes Sonic ($535,196)	4,958,884
Phone Trick, N.Y.	186	91	8	Caller One ($1,200,000)	4,957,368
Salt Lake, Ky.	207	106	3	Ocean Across ($456,398)	4,883,829
Housebuster, Va.	143	75	7	Electronic Unicorn ($1,043,292)	4,854,231
Smart Strike, Ky.	106	67	6	Portcullis ($562,535)	4,845,230
Gilded Time, Ky.	179	90	8	Mandy's Gold ($715,404)	4,832,021
Lear Fan, Ky.	110	53	8	Sarafan ($2,039,765)	4,820,485
Unbridled, Dead	131	69	8	Surya ($364,339)	4,774,611
Allen's Prospect, Md.	205	128	8	Your Out ($269,850)	4,736,397
Jade Hunter, Ky.	155	68	4	Azeri ($2,181,540)	4,735,114
Rubiano, Dead	151	90	6	Oregon Girl ($362,725)	4,724,820
Belong to Me, Ky.	197	103	9	Bulla Borghese ($242,782)	4,560,592
Tabasco Cat, Jpn	144	75	8	Snow Ridge ($399,990)	4,439,479
Not For Love, Md.	131	85	11	Sheila's Prospect ($322,814)	4,414,282
Twining, Ky.	173	100	5	Dreams Go Bye ($177,431)	4,351,752
Meadowlake, Ky.	133	77	5	Toho Medusa ($451,669)	4,264,901
Langfuhr, Ky.	145	65	5	Imperial Gesture ($1,143,600)	4,242,783
Forest Wildcat, Ky.	136	71	12	D'wildcat ($424,444)	4,233,095
Dixieland Band, Ky.	162	82	7	Bowman's Band ($333,800)	4,228,745
Danzig, Ky.	86	42	14	Magnaten ($1,501,296)	4,216,140
Pleasant Colony, Dead	98	48	6	Denon ($917,400)	4,176,545
Honour and Glory, Ky.	187	93	3	Name Value ($340,625)	4,156,484
Holy Bull, Ky.	157	74	4	Macho Uno ($519,600)	4,111,321
Deputy Minister, Ky.	134	56	3	Minister's Baby ($290,093)	4,081,416
Judge T C, N.Y.	154	79	9	The Judge Sez Who ($558,186)	4,059,689
Cherokee Run, Ky.	127	68	6	Kafwain ($535,848)	4,029,839
Glitterman, Ky.	164	104	8	Texas Glitter ($313,408)	3,999,573
Green Dancer, Dead	95	39	5	Eishin Preston ($1,763,126)	3,984,502
Pulpit, Ky.	67	34	4	Essence of Dubai ($1,805,000)	3,917,816
Summer Squall, Ky.	83	42	6	Summer Colony ($992,500)	3,895,120
Quiet American, Ky.	158	82	8	Allamerican Bertie ($619,235)	3,892,188
Boundary, Ky.	107	62	3	Saga Novel ($687,723)	3,859,660
Peaks and Valleys, Ky.	128	70	4	Dollar Bill ($496,850)	3,851,702
Two Punch, Md.	169	95	5	Jab ($208,223)	3,830,763

Leading Sires by Average Earnings per Runner Worldwide in 2002

Sire	Strs	Wnrs	Average
Harlan, Dead	44	24	$69,669
Our Emblem, Ky.	79	35	63,288
Kris S., Dead	133	70	60,794
Broad Brush, Ky.	115	68	59,186
Pulpit, Ky.	67	34	58,475
Relaunch, Dead	37	21	58,449
Cozzene, Ky.	139	70	53,224
Kingmambo, Ky.	132	64	52,959
Wild Again, Ky.	149	80	50,901
Jolie's Halo, Jpn	139	43	49,366
Danzig, Ky.	86	42	49,032
A.P. Indy, Ky.	149	80	47,835
Summer Squall, Ky.	83	42	46,929
Pleasant Tap, Ky.	75	38	46,922
Gulch, Ky.	183	91	46,425
Smart Strike, Ky.	106	67	45,710
Storm Cat, Ky.	142	62	45,340
French Deputy, Jpn	133	76	44,743
Bold n' Flashy, On.	29	14	44,742
Domasca Dan, On.	26	15	44,670

Leading Sires by Median Earnings per Runner Worldwide in 2002

Sire	Strs	Wnrs	Median
Smart Strike, Ky.	106	67	$21,985
Outflanker, Fl.	33	22	21,550
Valid Appeal, Dead	36	25	20,650
Lord At War (Arg), Dead	52	27	20,489
Lite the Fuse, Fl.	65	43	20,182
◆Coronado's Quest, Ky.	26	13	20,023
Meadow Monster, Md.	27	14	20,000
◆Swiss Yodeler, Ca.	27	16	19,880
Broad Brush, Ky.	115	68	19,740
A.P. Indy, Ky.	149	80	19,710
◆Elusive Quality, Ky.	39	23	19,200
I Can't Believe, On.	28	18	18,943
Claramount, Dead	46	32	17,890
Smoke Glacken, Ky.	84	52	17,685
Not For Love, Md.	131	85	17,475
Concorde's Tune, Fl.	76	49	17,204
Tabasco Cat, Jpn	144	75	17,179
Valid Expectations, Tx.	87	55	16,920
Wild Again, Ky.	149	80	16,826
Barbeau, Dead	39	22	16,774
Lost Soldier, Fl.	60	38	16,555
Dixie Brass, Dead	127	74	16,429
Rizzi, N.Y.	70	46	16,377

Leading Sires by Number of Winners Worldwide in 2002

Sire	Strs	Wnrs	Wnrs/Strs
Royal Academy, Ky.	402	164	40.8%
Woodman, Ky.	348	141	40.5%
Dehere, Jpn	289	139	48.1%
End Sweep, Dead	240	138	57.5%
Allen's Prospect, Md.	205	128	62.4%
Southern Halo, Jpn	282	127	45.0%
Numerous, Fr	241	127	52.7%
Mr. Greeley, Ky.	199	117	58.8%
Regal Classic, N.Y.	236	111	47.0%
Salt Lake, Ky.	207	106	51.2%
West by West, Tur	200	105	52.5%
Glitterman, Ky.	164	104	63.4%
Belong to Me, Ky.	197	103	52.3%
Hennessy, Ky.	242	102	42.1%
El Prado (Ire), Ky.	197	101	51.3%
Pentelicus, Dead	162	101	62.3%
Carson City, Ky.	197	101	51.3%
Cryptoclearance, Ky.	216	100	46.3%
Twining, Ky.	173	100	57.8%
Devil His Due, Ky.	185	99	53.5%
Two Punch, Md.	169	95	56.2%

Leading Sires by Number of Wins Worldwide in 2002

Sire	Strs	Wnrs	Wins
Allen's Prospect, Md.	205	128	247
Dehere, Jpn	289	139	240
Royal Academy, Ky.	402	164	239
End Sweep, Dead	240	138	235
Numerous, Fr	241	127	222
Woodman, Ky.	348	141	217
Southern Halo, Jpn	282	127	209
Carson City, Ky.	197	101	200
Twining, Ky.	173	100	191
Regal Classic, N.Y.	236	111	190
Salt Lake, Ky.	207	106	189
Glitterman, Ky.	164	104	185
El Prado (Ire), Ky.	197	101	183
Fortunate Prospect, Fl.	146	92	181
Mr. Greeley, Ky.	199	117	180
Devil His Due, Ky.	185	99	179
Cryptoclearance, Ky.	216	100	178
Notebook, Fl.	141	85	177
Rubiano, Dead	151	90	177
Belong to Me, Ky.	197	103	174
Marquetry, Ky.	171	90	166
Pentelicus, Dead	162	101	163
Phone Trick, N.Y.	186	91	163
West by West, Tur	200	105	162
Silver Deputy, Ky.	167	94	162
Dixie Brass, Dead	127	74	160
Not For Love, Md.	131	85	160
Press Card, Aust	141	79	159
Formal Dinner, Fl.	142	84	158
Hennessy, Ky.	242	102	157
Black Tie Affair (Ire), Jpn	209	88	156
Mountain Cat, Tur	181	93	155
High Brite, Ca.	145	84	154
Two Punch, Md.	169	95	154

Leading Sires by Number of Stakes Winners Worldwide in 2002

Sire	Strs	Wnrs	SWs
Roy, Arg	184	89	25
Southern Halo, Jpn	282	127	21
Royal Academy, Ky.	402	164	19
Storm Cat, Ky.	142	62	18
Dehere, Jpn	289	139	17
Dynaformer, Ky.	186	88	15
Broad Brush, Ky.	115	68	14
Danzig, Ky.	86	42	14
Woodman, Ky.	348	141	13
Candy Stripes, Fl.	177	82	12
El Prado (Ire), Ky.	197	101	12
Forest Wildcat, Ky.	136	71	12
A.P. Indy, Ky.	149	80	12
Not For Love, Md.	131	85	11
Unbridled's Song, Ky.	175	89	11
Carson City, Ky.	197	101	11

Leading Sires by Number of Graded Stakes Winners Worldwide in 2002

Sire	Strs	Wnrs	GSWs
Roy, Arg	184	89	14
Southern Halo, Jpn	282	127	14
Royal Academy, Ky.	402	164	10
Storm Cat, Ky.	142	62	10
Candy Stripes, Fl.	177	82	8
Thunder Gulch, Ky.	251	88	7
Theatrical (Ire), Ky.	128	51	7
Danzig, Ky.	86	42	7
Numerous, Fr	241	127	7
Dehere, Jpn	289	139	6
Mutakddim, Ky.	133	74	6
Kingmambo, Ky.	132	64	6
Mr. Greeley, Ky.	199	117	6
Spend a Buck, Dead	138	68	5
French Deputy, Jpn	133	76	5
Mr. Prospector, Dead	82	31	5
Dynaformer, Ky.	186	88	5

Leading Juvenile Sires by Progeny Earnings Worldwide in 2002

Worldwide earnings for stallions who stand or last stood in North America or had ten North American starters in 2002.

Sire, Where stands	Strs	Wnrs	SWs	Leading earner (earnings)	Progeny earnings
Storm Cat, Ky.	36	19	8	Storm Flag Flying ($967,000)	$2,540,238
End Sweep, Dead	66	29	2	Global Finance ($181,000)	1,768,081
◆Grand Slam, Ky.	58	23	1	Tiger Motion ($311,667)	1,403,880
◆Distorted Humor, Ky.	35	16	5	Awesome Humor ($309,115)	1,347,490
Cherokee Run, Ky.	40	22	2	Kafwain ($535,848)	1,297,329
Seattle Slew, Dead	25	12	2	Vindication ($680,950)	1,272,495
Langfuhr, Ky.	52	21	2	Wando ($362,377)	1,260,088
◆Awesome Again, Ky.	31	10	2	Toccet ($755,610)	1,258,620
◆Elusive Quality, Ky.	39	23	6	Elusive City ($169,053)	1,252,374
Dehere, Jpn	33	12	6	Outta Here ($404,260)	1,248,096
A.P. Indy, Ky.	38	14	3	Handpainted ($256,210)	1,106,275
Boston Harbor, Jpn	36	16	2	Wonderful Days ($288,896)	1,100,033
In Excess (Ire), Ca.	29	13	5	Icecoldbeeratreds ($353,800)	1,075,736
◆Tale of the Cat, Ky.	47	25	6	My Trusty Cat ($228,025)	1,074,868
Pulpit, Ky.	25	10	2	Sky Mesa ($416,576)	999,190
Carson City, Ky.	42	17	3	Hear No Evil ($174,590)	939,765
Silver Deputy, Ky.	25	10	2	Atago Taisho ($359,823)	908,500
Smart Strike, Ky.	24	11	2	Added Edge ($250,328)	867,561
Forest Wildcat, Ky.	43	18	4	Wild Snitch ($119,200)	839,617
Red Ransom, Ky.	45	15	2	Halibery ($155,867)	827,680
El Prado (Ire), Ky.	52	17	4	Julie's Prize ($102,052)	799,347
Saint Ballado, Dead	42	12	3	Truckle Feature ($125,300)	799,313
Formal Dinner, Fl.	57	27	1	Forest Picnic ($79,080)	792,850
◆Touch Gold, Ky.	32	9	1	Composure ($431,300)	781,094
Mt. Livermore, Ky.	33	9	1	Meiner Morgen ($346,208)	775,623
Wild Again, Ky.	25	10	2	Gigawatt ($176,095)	755,481
◆Swiss Yodeler, Ca.	27	16	3	Oberwald ($98,636)	748,718
◆Coronado's Quest, Ky.	26	13	3	Al ($131,573)	724,589
Belong to Me, Ky.	38	15	3	Miss Houdini ($175,800)	715,370
Montbrook, Fl.	27	12	1	Trust N Luck ($382,800)	703,801
Mountain Cat, Tur	40	19	1	Mountain Dawn ($162,864)	698,852
Suave Prospect, Fl.	27	15	2	Elegant Designer ($273,670)	697,968
Holy Bull, Ky.	36	12	1	Eishin Boone ($153,789)	689,878
Jules, Brz	42	19	3	Peace Rules ($209,990)	678,592
Rubiano, Dead	28	13	2	Ruby's Reception ($209,230)	674,177
Cozzene, Ky.	20	5	1	Silk Bravo ($500,258)	671,491
Lit de Justice, Ca.	34	14	1	I Testify ($92,160)	669,493
Not For Love, Md.	27	18	3	Coquettish ($98,520)	666,932
Gilded Time, Ky.	29	14	3	Elloluv ($242,700)	654,623
Capote, Ky.	26	11	3	Buffythecenterfold ($222,160)	646,074
Unbridled's Song, Ky.	34	14	3	Cafe Venetian ($156,448)	644,278
Mecke, Fl.	16	10	1	Supah Blitz ($246,330)	616,287
Hadif, Tx.	26	18	3	Action Tonight ($162,029)	613,397
Kingmambo, Ky.	34	13	2	Russian Rhythm ($176,662)	603,686
Devil His Due, Ky.	37	13	1	Spite the Devil ($124,815)	599,572
Honour and Glory, Ky.	32	15	1	One and Twenty ($173,520)	598,436
Out of Place, Ky.	38	14	0	Short Shadow ($93,153)	583,591
Unbridled, Dead	21	7	0	Santa Catarina ($302,580)	583,202
Mr. Greeley, Ky.	34	12	2	Whywhywhy ($284,060)	579,980
Woodman, Ky.	46	13	3	Lismore Knight ($246,800)	576,372
◆Indian Charlie, Ky.	39	13	1	Jazz Lady ($91,704)	575,843
◆Stormy Atlantic, Ky.	22	9	3	Atlantic Ocean ($234,780)	566,126
Roy, Arg	30	15	7	Lets Just Do It ($141,813)	559,626
Tactical Advantage, Dead	40	15	2	Crowned Dancer ($122,858)	556,444
Helmsman, Ca.	24	14	0	Chad's Hope ($137,510)	543,448
West Acre, Fl.	8	5	1	Ivanavinalot ($418,300)	541,799
Gold Fever, N.Y.	46	12	1	Arco's Gold ($224,460)	539,836
◆Favorite Trick, Ky.	32	12	1	Sum Trick ($82,531)	538,224
◆Concerto, Fl.	23	14	1	Collymore Hall ($170,507)	537,140
Gold Case, Ky.	30	15	2	Despreciado ($100,825)	534,994
Defrere, N.J.	20	8	1	Souris ($159,410)	528,890
Southern Halo, Jpn	53	16	3	Miss Listo ($79,984)	528,632
◆Souvenir Copy, Ky.	44	17	0	Long Term Wish ($78,154)	518,257
Storm Creek, Ky.	49	15	0	Sweet Storm Creek ($109,779)	515,386
Valid Wager, Ca.	24	11	3	Valid Video ($91,200)	514,794

Leading Juvenile Sires by Average Earnings per Runner Worldwide in 2002

Sire	Strs	Wnrs	Average
Storm Cat, Ky.	36	19	$70,562
Seattle Slew, Dead	25	12	50,900
◆Awesome Again, Ky.	31	10	40,601
Pulpit, Ky.	25	10	39,968
Mecke, Fl.	16	10	38,518
◆Distorted Humor, Ky.	35	16	38,500
Dehere, Jpn	33	12	37,821
In Excess (Ire), Ca.	29	13	37,094
Silver Deputy, Ky.	25	10	36,340
Smart Strike, Ky.	24	11	36,148
Cozzene, Ky.	20	5	33,575
Cherokee Run, Ky.	40	22	32,433
◆Elusive Quality, Ky.	39	23	32,112
Boston Harbor, Jpn	36	16	30,556
Hay Halo, Va.	11	8	30,499
Wild Again, Ky.	25	10	30,219
A.P. Indy, Ky.	38	14	29,113
Bold Badgett, Dead	13	6	29,097
Conquistador Cielo, Dead	17	6	28,834

Leading Juvenile Sires by Median Earnings per Runner Worldwide in 2002

Sire	Strs	Wnrs	Median
◆Coronado's Quest, Ky.	26	13	$20,023
◆Swiss Yodeler, Ca.	27	16	19,880
Concorde's Tune, Fl.	10	6	19,735
◆Elusive Quality, Ky.	39	23	19,200
Mecke, Fl.	16	10	18,665
Storm Cat, Ky.	36	19	17,067
◆Partner's Hero, Md.	25	14	16,000
Lite the Fuse, Fl.	12	7	14,714
Not For Love, Md.	27	18	14,250
Summer Squall, Va.	10	5	13,980
Bold Badgett, Dead	13	6	13,650
Seattle Slew, Dead	25	12	13,520
Smart Strike, Ky.	24	11	13,370
Carr de Naskra, Pens	10	6	13,290
Meadowlake, Ky.	19	11	13,200
Migrating Moon, Fl.	10	6	12,991
Helmsman, Ca.	24	14	12,725
◆Concerto, Fl.	23	14	12,670
Kipper Kelly, La.	13	8	12,570
Katahaula County, B.C.	19	14	12,555
Silver Deputy, Ky.	25	10	12,274
End Sweep, Dead	66	29	12,123

Leading Juvenile Sires by Number of Winners Worldwide in 2002

Sire	Strs	Wnrs	Wnrs/ Strs
End Sweep, Dead	66	29	43.9%
Formal Dinner, Fl.	57	27	47.4%
◆Tale of the Cat, Ky.	47	25	53.2%
◆Grand Slam, Ky.	58	23	39.7%
◆Elusive Quality, Ky.	39	23	59.0%
Pentelicus, Dead	47	23	48.9%
Cherokee Run, Ky.	40	22	55.0%
◆Double Honor, Fl.	40	21	52.5%
Langfuhr, Ky.	52	21	40.4%
Jules, Brz	42	19	45.2%
Mountain Cat, Tur	40	19	47.5%
Storm Cat, Ky.	36	19	52.8%
Not For Love, Md.	27	18	66.7%
Hadif, Tx.	26	18	69.2%
Patton, Pa.	52	18	34.6%
Forest Wildcat, Ky.	43	18	41.9%
◆Souvenir Copy, Ky.	44	17	38.6%
El Prado (Ire), Ky.	52	17	32.7%
Carson City, Ky.	42	17	40.5%
Southern Halo, Jpn	53	16	30.2%
Boston Harbor, Jpn	36	16	44.4%
◆Swiss Yodeler, Ca.	27	16	59.3%
◆Distorted Humor, Ky.	35	16	45.7%

Leading Juvenile Sires by Number of Wins Worldwide in 2002

Sire	Strs	Wnrs	Wins
End Sweep, Dead	66	29	38
Formal Dinner, Fl.	57	27	37
Cherokee Run, Ky.	40	22	35
◆Elusive Quality, Ky.	39	23	33
◆Tale of the Cat, Ky.	47	25	33
◆Grand Slam, Ky.	58	23	31
Storm Cat, Ky.	36	19	31
Suave Prospect, Fl.	27	15	29
Langfuhr, Ky.	52	21	28
◆Double Honor, Fl.	40	21	28
◆Distorted Humor, Ky.	35	16	28
Mountain Cat, Tur	40	19	27
Hadif, Tx.	26	18	27
Carson City, Ky.	42	17	26
Pentelicus, Dead	47	23	26
Forest Wildcat, Ky.	43	18	26

Leading Juvenile Sires by Number of Stakes Winners Worldwide in 2002

Sire	Strs	Wnrs	SWs
Storm Cat, Ky.	36	19	8
Roy, Arg	30	15	7
Dehere, Jpn	33	12	6
◆Elusive Quality, Ky.	39	23	6
◆Tale of the Cat, Ky.	47	25	6
In Excess (Ire), Ca.	29	13	5
◆Distorted Humor, Ky.	35	16	5
El Prado (Ire), Ky.	52	17	4
Forest Wildcat, Ky.	43	18	4
Katahaula County, B.C.	19	14	4
Vying Victor, B.C.	24	13	4
Danzig, Ky.	14	7	4
Southern Halo, Jpn	53	16	3
Woodman, Ky.	46	13	3
Capote, Ky.	26	11	3
Bold Badgett, Dead	13	6	3
Hadif, Tx.	26	18	3
A.P. Indy, Ky.	38	14	3
Eastern Echo, Md.	28	9	3
Sultry Song, Ky.	16	8	3
Carson City, Ky.	42	17	3
Belong to Me, Ky.	38	15	3
Saint Ballado, Dead	42	12	3
Gilded Time, Ky.	29	14	3
Cisco Road, Wa.	23	12	3
Not For Love, Md.	27	18	3
◆Coronado's Quest, Ky.	26	13	3
◆Swiss Yodeler, Ca.	27	16	3
Mercer Mill, Oh.	20	9	3
◆Stormy Atlantic, Ky.	22	9	3
Unbridled's Song, Ky.	34	14	3
Jules, Brz	42	19	3
◆Announce, Ky.	30	15	3
Valid Wager, Ca.	24	11	3
On Target, La.	23	7	3

Leading Juvenile Sires by Number of Graded Stakes Winners Worldwide in 2002

Sire	Strs	Wnrs	GSWs
Storm Cat, Ky.	36	19	5
Roy, Arg	30	15	4
◆Elusive Quality, Ky.	39	23	2
Hennessy, Ky.	47	13	2
◆Distorted Humor, Ky.	35	16	2
Boston Harbor, Jpn	36	16	2
Jules, Brz	42	19	2
Seattle Slew, Dead	25	12	2
Red Ransom, Ky.	45	15	2
Southern Halo, Jpn	53	16	2
Carson City, Ky.	42	17	2
Gilded Time, Ky.	29	14	2
Kingmambo, Ky.	34	13	2
Numerous, Fr	26	8	2
Dehere, Jpn	33	12	2

Leading Freshman Sires by Progeny Earnings
Worldwide in 2002

Worldwide earnings for stallions who stand or last stood in North America or had ten North American starters in 2002.

Sire, Where stands	Strs	Wnrs	SWs	Leading earner (earnings)	Progeny earnings
Grand Slam, Ky.	58	23	1	Tiger Motion ($311,667)	$1,403,880
Distorted Humor, Ky.	35	16	5	Awesome Humor ($309,115)	1,347,490
Awesome Again, Ky.	31	10	2	Toccet ($755,610)	1,258,620
Elusive Quality, Ky.	39	23	6	Elusive City ($169,053)	1,252,374
Tale of the Cat, Ky.	47	25	5	My Trusty Cat ($228,025)	1,074,868
Touch Gold, Ky.	32	9	1	Composure ($431,300)	781,094
Swiss Yodeler, Ca.	27	16	3	Oberwald ($98,636)	748,718
Coronado's Quest, Ky.	26	13	3	Al Jadeed ($131,573)	724,589
Indian Charlie, Ky.	39	13	1	Jazz Lady ($91,704)	575,843
Stormy Atlantic, Ky.	22	9	3	Atlantic Ocean ($234,780)	566,126
Favorite Trick, Ky.	32	12	1	Sum Trick ($82,531)	538,224
Concerto, Fl.	23	14	1	Collymore Hall ($170,507)	537,140
Souvenir Copy, Ky.	44	17	0	Long Term Wish ($78,154)	518,257
Skip Away, Ky.	37	12	2	Christmas Away ($107,805)	510,539
Deputy Commander, Ky.	48	10	0	Holiday Lady ($89,655)	507,912
King of Kings (Ire), Jpn	81	22	1	King's Chapel ($143,691)	467,638
Formal Gold, Ky.	28	15	0	Formal Dancer ($70,420)	463,868
Announce, Ky.	30	15	3	Indy Fire ($66,912)	458,323
Wild Rush, Ky.	35	10	0	Suzu Japan ($136,680)	458,160
Double Honor, Fl.	40	21	0	Honorable King ($46,920)	457,579
Banker's Gold, Ky.	24	12	1	Jenny's Prospector ($87,731)	452,711
Benchmark, Ca.	23	10	0	Martinblestme ($101,994)	435,089
Lucky Lionel, Fl.	24	13	0	Little Swimmer ($107,630)	421,578
Partner's Hero, Md.	25	14	1	Object of Virtue ($71,928)	405,846
Kiridashi, On.	21	10	1	Snake Pit ($124,905)	401,105
Dance Brightly, Ky.	39	8	0	Mr. Whitestone ($65,570)	376,510
Gentlemen (Arg), Ky.	22	9	1	Man Among Men ($74,040)	330,614
Cape Town, Ky.	26	8	0	Cape Good Hope ($90,050)	270,365
Northern Afleet, Fl.	18	9	0	Paris Adventure ($47,754)	248,988
Western Fame, Ca.	15	8	0	Tizalovelylady ($55,740)	246,634
Tomorrows Cat, N.Y.	21	6	1	Tomorrows Banquet ($74,296)	246,377
Ordway, Ky.	24	9	1	Ordinary Paula ($69,142)	242,326
Semoran, Fl.	22	13	0	Takeonefortheteam ($31,960)	230,336
Will's Way, Ky.	31	11	0	Lion Tamer ($35,600)	213,628
Swain (Ire), Ky.	21	5	1	Trillion Cut ($64,748)	210,780
Labeeb (GB), Ky.	11	2	1	Kabeeb ($182,398)	205,986
Wild Deputy, Ca.	18	8	1	Effectively Wild ($37,245)	199,083
Confide, Ky.	27	6	1	Confiding Winner ($67,020)	195,982
Subordination, Ky.	22	5	0	Goldies Legacy ($36,360)	192,491
Ghostly Moves, N.M.	9	7	1	Shemoveslikeaghost ($58,907)	188,699
Diligence, Fl.	23	6	0	Worker Man ($85,500)	182,955
Cyberspace, Fl.	8	4	0	Cyberdevil ($91,005)	182,476
Commanchero, Tx.	2	2	1	Most Feared ($166,020)	177,242
Anet, Ky.	22	5	1	My Own Groom ($73,723)	176,587
Storm Broker, Md.	17	10	0	Krebsie ($30,810)	176,465
Aggie Southpaw, Tx.	4	3	1	Call Me Lefty ($129,400)	169,976
Yoonevano, B.C.	4	1	1	Illusive Force ($159,948)	162,145
Proud and True, Fl.	19	5	0	Kryskaly ($42,040)	156,085
Acceptable, Ky.	14	6	0	Fostress ($46,550)	151,257
Snowbound, Az.	11	5	2	First Snowbound ($83,726)	151,022
Lasting Approval, Ky.	11	4	0	Four R Approval ($58,500)	141,766
Arch, Ky.	17	4	0	Honey Green ($53,631)	140,150
Dance Floor, Ca.	27	6	3	Lightmaster ($50,639)	129,319
Joyeux Danseur, Ca.	17	4	0	Attack Chance ($34,315)	127,486
Willowy Ambassador, Ky.	2	2	1	Hackendiffy ($116,750)	122,029
Yarrow Brae, Md.	12	3	0	Butiwillflysomeday ($36,350)	116,525
Haint, Ca.	11	5	0	Just Watch Me ($53,835)	114,681
Gold Token, N.Y.	10	3	0	Golden Damsel ($30,240)	109,299
Rage, N.Y.	5	4	0	Rageously ($38,830)	107,440
Traitor, Fl.	18	5	0	Gastonia ($27,670)	104,879
Swear by Dixie, Md.	7	5	0	Mark Aim Fire ($45,920)	101,423
Prince of the Mt., La.	8	3	1	Knight of the Mt. ($52,031)	97,496
Halory Hunter, N.Y.	22	4	0	Sweep Hunter ($25,474)	91,512
Western Echo, Pa.	11	6	0	Echo Lady ($22,180)	87,557
Parentheses, N.M.	3	2	1	Quote This ($62,764)	87,512

Leading Freshman Sires by Average Earnings per Runner Worldwide in 2002

Sire	Strs	Wnrs	Average
Awesome Again, Ky.	31	10	$40,601
Distorted Humor, Ky.	35	16	38,500
Elusive Quality, Ky.	39	23	32,112
Coronado's Quest, Ky.	26	13	27,869
Swiss Yodeler, Ca.	27	16	27,730
Stormy Atlantic, Ky.	22	9	25,733
Touch Gold, Ky.	32	9	24,409
Grand Slam, Ky.	58	23	24,205
Concerto, Fl.	23	14	23,354
Tale of the Cat, Ky.	47	25	22,870
Kiridashi, On.	21	10	19,100
Benchmark, Ca.	23	10	18,917
Banker's Gold, Ky.	24	12	18,863
Labeeb (GB), Ky.	11	2	18,726
Lucky Lionel, Fl.	24	13	17,566
Favorite Trick, Ky.	32	12	16,820
Formal Gold, Ky.	28	15	16,567
Western Fame, Ca.	15	8	16,442
Partner's Hero, Md.	25	14	16,234
Announce, Ky.	30	15	15,277
Gentlemen (Arg), Ky.	22	9	15,028
Indian Charlie, Ky.	39	13	14,765

Leading Freshman Sires by Median Earnings per Runner Worldwide in 2002

Sire	Strs	Wnrs	Median
Coronado's Quest, Ky.	26	13	$20,023
Swiss Yodeler, Ca.	27	16	19,880
Elusive Quality, Ky.	39	23	19,200
Partner's Hero, Md.	25	14	16,000
Concerto, Fl.	23	14	12,670
Kiridashi, On.	21	10	12,120
Tale of the Cat, Ky.	47	25	11,824
Storm Broker, Md.	17	10	10,410
Lucky Lionel, Fl.	24	13	9,866
Announce, Ky.	30	15	9,857
Formal Gold, Ky.	28	15	9,833
Banker's Gold, Ky.	24	12	9,823
Favorite Trick, Ky.	32	12	9,476
Gold Token, N.Y.	10	3	9,153
Semoran, Fl.	22	13	8,795
Stormy Atlantic, Ky.	22	9	8,785
Double Honor, Fl.	40	21	8,150
Souvenir Copy, Ky.	44	17	8,061
Benchmark, Ca.	23	10	8,025
Distorted Humor, Ky.	35	16	8,000
Northern Afleet, Fl.	18	9	7,967
Grand Slam, Ky.	58	23	7,844

Leading Freshman Sires by Number of Winners Worldwide in 2002

Sire	Strs	Wnrs	Wnrs/ Strs
Tale of the Cat, Ky.	47	25	53.2%
Elusive Quality, Ky.	39	23	59.0%
Grand Slam, Ky.	58	23	39.7%
King of Kings (Ire), Jpn	81	22	27.2%
Double Honor, Fl.	40	21	52.5%
Souvenir Copy, Ky.	44	17	38.6%
Swiss Yodeler, Ca.	27	16	59.3%
Distorted Humor, Ky.	35	16	45.7%
Formal Gold, Ky.	28	15	53.6%
Announce, Ky.	30	15	50.0%
Concerto, Fl.	23	14	60.9%
Partner's Hero, Md.	25	14	56.0%
Semoran, Fl.	22	13	59.1%
Lucky Lionel, Fl.	24	13	54.2%
Indian Charlie, Ky.	39	13	33.3%
Coronado's Quest, Ky.	26	13	50.0%
Banker's Gold, Ky.	24	12	50.0%
Favorite Trick, Ky.	32	12	37.5%
Skip Away, Ky.	37	12	32.4%
Will's Way, Ky.	31	11	35.5%

Leading Freshman Sires by Number of Wins Worldwide in 2002

Sire	Strs	Wnrs	Wins
Elusive Quality, Ky.	39	23	33
Tale of the Cat, Ky.	47	25	33
Grand Slam, Ky.	58	23	31
King of Kings (Ire), Jpn	81	22	28
Double Honor, Fl.	40	21	28
Distorted Humor, Ky.	35	16	28
Swiss Yodeler, Ca.	27	16	24
Lucky Lionel, Fl.	24	13	22
Souvenir Copy, Ky.	44	17	21
Announce, Ky.	30	15	20
Awesome Again, Ky.	31	10	19
Concerto, Fl.	23	14	19
Formal Gold, Ky.	28	15	18
Stormy Atlantic, Ky.	22	9	18
Coronado's Quest, Ky.	26	13	18
Partner's Hero, Md.	25	14	17
Skip Away, Ky.	37	12	17
Semoran, Fl.	22	13	16
Favorite Trick, Ky.	32	12	16
Indian Charlie, Ky.	39	13	14
Banker's Gold, Ky.	24	12	13
Wild Deputy, Ca.	18	8	13
Touch Gold, Ky.	32	9	13
Will's Way, Ky.	31	11	13
Deputy Commander, Ky.	48	10	12
Benchmark, Ca.	23	10	12
Ghostly Moves, N.M.	9	7	12
Wild Rush, Ky.	35	10	11
Storm Broker, Md.	17	10	11
Northern Afleet, Fl.	18	9	11
Gentlemen (Arg), Ky.	22	9	11
Cape Town, Ky.	26	8	10
Snowbound, Az.	11	5	10
Ordway, Ky.	24	9	10
Western Fame, Ca.	15	8	10
Kiridashi, On.	21	10	10
Dance Brightly, Ky.	39	8	9
Cyberspace, Fl.	8	4	9
Anet, Ky.	22	5	8
Confide, Ky.	27	6	8
Proud and True, Fl.	19	5	8
Halory Hunter, N.Y.	22	4	8
Notable Cat, Ok.	13	7	8
Rage, N.Y.	5	4	8

Leading Freshman Sires by Number of Stakes Winners Worldwide in 2002

Sire	Strs	Wnrs	SWs
Elusive Quality, Ky.	39	23	6
Tale of the Cat, Ky.	47	25	5
Distorted Humor, Ky.	35	16	5
Swiss Yodeler, Ca.	27	16	3
Stormy Atlantic, Ky.	22	9	3
Coronado's Quest, Ky.	26	13	3
Dance Floor, Ca.	27	6	3
Announce, Ky.	30	15	3
Awesome Again, Ky.	31	10	2
Skip Away, Ky.	37	12	2
Snowbound, Az.	11	5	2

Leading Freshman Sires by Number of Graded Stakes Winners Worldwide in 2002

Sire	Strs	Wnrs	GSWs
Distorted Humor, Ky.	35	16	2
Elusive Quality, Ky.	39	23	2
Awesome Again, Ky.	31	10	1
Touch Gold, Ky.	32	9	1
Stormy Atlantic, Ky.	22	9	1
Coronado's Quest, Ky.	26	13	1
Dance Floor, Ca.	27	6	1
Commanchero, Tx.	2	2	1
King of Kings (Ire), Jpn	81	22	1

Leading Broodmare Sires by Progeny Earnings Worldwide in 2002

Worldwide earnings for broodmare sires who stand or last stood in North America or had 25 North American starters in 2002.

Sire, Where stands	Strs	Wnrs	SWs	Leading earner (earnings)	Progeny earnings
Danzig, Ky.	409	176	21	Believe ($1,849,050)	$20,820,788
Mr. Prospector, Dead	474	218	28	No Reason ($1,298,823)	16,936,545
Nureyev, Dead	337	145	12	Gold Allure ($2,120,118)	16,104,929
Alydar, Dead	361	181	13	Diamond Biko ($1,791,071)	11,863,609
Affirmed, Dead	315	151	16	Narita Top Road ($2,434,223)	11,383,367
Seattle Slew, Dead	360	185	16	Astra ($758,000)	11,145,015
Caerleon, Dead	349	140	12	Preeminence ($1,634,737)	10,446,018
Deputy Minister, Ky.	316	153	17	Sarava ($665,040)	10,353,475
Miswaki, Ky.	328	161	23	Landseer (GB) ($678,088)	10,169,207
Sadler's Wells, Ire	397	148	19	Sakhee ($633,220)	10,085,583
Halo, Dead	370	194	18	Private Emblem ($550,940)	9,923,165
Lyphard, Pens	365	135	11	Rosado ($781,359)	9,201,284
Cox's Ridge, Dead	296	153	15	Orientate ($1,412,970)	8,788,083
Storm Cat, Ky.	208	112	8	Grass World ($942,159)	8,726,965
Nijinsky II, Dead	329	131	10	Rikiai Taikan ($505,375)	8,690,690
Private Account, Pens	328	170	14	Good Journey ($1,247,665)	8,575,741
Fappiano, Dead	252	123	15	Aratama Indy ($566,460)	8,466,285
Woodman, Ky.	356	142	16	Paian ($517,315)	8,134,986
Alleged, Dead	346	144	14	Sulamani ($1,037,003)	8,010,371
Clever Trick, Ky.	325	153	8	Came Home ($1,624,500)	7,951,669
Storm Bird, Pens	339	165	20	Come On Pekan ($345,253)	7,700,418
Vice Regent, Dead	291	146	10	Major Cafe ($451,728)	7,593,979
Pleasant Colony, Dead	231	134	9	Farda Amiga ($1,248,902)	7,479,452
Valid Appeal, Dead	285	170	12	Broad Appeal ($385,405)	7,443,937
Relaunch, Dead	339	190	8	Koolingar ($621,828)	7,153,434
Dixieland Band, Ky.	323	171	10	Sardonyx ($333,762)	6,878,597
Blushing Groom (Fr), Dead	227	103	7	Lady Pastel ($565,514)	6,576,295
Northern Dancer, Dead	129	56	4	Tap Dance City ($1,918,833)	6,393,545
Conquistador Cielo, Dead	280	141	15	Tokai Pulsar ($517,420)	6,376,092
Riverman, Dead	333	145	17	Yumeno Lucky ($272,882)	6,332,379
Green Dancer, Dead	353	150	16	T. H. Grace ($317,012)	6,284,727
Roberto, Dead	195	84	11	Electronic Unicorn ($1,043,292)	6,126,688
Spectacular Bid, N.Y.	243	127	12	Health Wall ($396,666)	6,070,759
Topsider, Dead	249	127	10	Kite Hill Wind ($512,994)	5,985,751
Irish River (Fr), Pens	314	144	9	Pregio ($411,827)	5,904,619
Bold Ruckus, Dead	224	113	8	Mysterious Affair ($295,073)	5,887,353
Crafty Prospector, Ky.	253	130	7	Icecoldbeeratreds ($353,800)	5,754,540
Afleet, Jpn	161	87	12	Sidewinder ($724,319)	5,749,043
Secretariat, Dead	343	149	7	Perfect Soul (IRE) ($280,020)	5,746,658
Slew o' Gold, Pens	196	99	4	El Camino ($458,625)	5,643,527
Forty Niner, Jpn	176	82	11	Inter Taiyo ($812,724)	5,582,672
Be My Guest, Pens	352	147	12	Rock of Gibraltar (IRE) ($1,353,921)	5,534,691
Sovereign Dancer, Dead	283	144	3	Disturbingthepeace ($452,640)	5,526,881
Naskra, Dead	167	85	9	Nobo True ($1,158,838)	5,524,040
Gold Meridian, Or.	44	24	2	Symboli Kris S ($4,724,763)	5,492,674
Lord At War (Arg), Dead	84	45	4	War Emblem ($3,455,000)	5,471,326
Gulch, Ky.	150	65	6	Media Puzzle ($1,447,592)	5,330,113
Alysheba, Sda	155	81	9	Grandera ($2,086,768)	5,260,163
Our Native, Dead	218	106	7	Evening Attire ($1,332,720)	5,227,806
Saratoga Six, Ky.	221	116	3	Dollar Bill ($496,850)	5,213,331
Strawberry Road (Aus), Dead	136	74	15	Vindication ($680,950)	5,185,815
Caro (Ire), Dead	172	75	6	Sarafan ($2,039,765)	5,180,085
The Minstrel, Dead	284	123	12	Lord Prevail ($375,115)	5,030,874
Ogygian, Jpn	146	76	8	Divine Silver ($640,236)	4,817,467
Cure the Blues, Dead	243	114	6	Nishino Moonlight ($277,670)	4,705,704
Chief's Crown, Dead	163	80	11	Agnes Digital ($1,238,986)	4,630,327
Silver Hawk, Ky.	183	88	8	Like a Hero ($408,910)	4,623,818
Wild Again, Ky.	258	111	8	Wild Spirit ($2,753,456)	4,543,123
Rahy, Ky.	128	70	11	Megahertz (GB) ($600,180)	4,528,977
Wolf Power (SAf), Dead	135	75	6	Milwaukee Brew ($1,590,000)	4,439,436
Devil's Bag, Ky.	222	92	7	Eishin Aiken ($472,890)	4,435,948
Star de Naskra, Dead	217	105	4	South Vigorous ($1,406,883)	4,387,215
Smarten, Pens	180	97	7	Full of Wonder ($357,580)	4,316,413
Manila, Tur	113	58	9	Eishin Champ ($861,688)	4,242,244
Seeking the Gold, Ky.	119	60	4	Riskaverse ($461,160)	4,171,426

Leading Broodmare Sires by Average Earnings per Runner Worldwide in 2002

Sire	Strs	Wnrs	Average
Gold Meridian, Or.	44	24	$124,834
Matsadoon, Dead	44	13	74,399
Lord At War (Arg), Dead	84	45	65,135
Rubiano, Dead	26	11	63,898
Easy Goer, Dead	56	25	59,805
Saros (GB), Dead	40	20	51,770
Danzig, Ky.	409	176	50,907
Monteverdi (Ire), Ven	41	19	49,821
Northern Dancer, Dead	129	56	49,562
Bailjumper, Dead	69	35	47,874
Nureyev, Dead	337	145	47,789
Homebuilder, La.	38	23	43,870
Always Fair, Dead	33	10	41,994
Storm Cat, Ky.	208	112	41,957
Snow Chief, Ca.	42	18	38,567
Strawberry Road (Aus), Dead	136	74	38,131
Silver Deputy, Ky.	71	31	38,021
Slewpy, Dead	106	51	38,016
Proper Reality, Ar.	57	35	37,971
Manila, Tur	113	58	37,542
Affirmed, Dead	315	151	36,138

Leading Broodmare Sires by Median Earnings per Runner Worldwide in 2002

Sire	Strs	Wnrs	Median
Concorde Bound, Dead	27	18	$17,310
Pine Bluff, Ky.	27	17	15,957
Broad Brush, Ky.	117	69	14,832
Personal Flag, N.Y.	91	58	14,659
Naked Sky, Dead	34	26	14,492
Carson City, Ky.	75	48	14,400
Jeblar, Dead	50	33	13,522
Storm Cat, Ky.	208	112	13,510
Valid Appeal, Dead	285	170	13,456
Seeking the Gold, Ky.	119	60	13,450
Big Burn, Pens	33	17	13,370
Yukon, Dead	61	35	12,935
Meadowlake, Ky.	136	78	12,790
Better Arbitor, Dead	26	17	12,625
Rahy, Ky.	128	70	12,559
American Standard, N.Y.	46	25	12,425
Mining, Jpn	114	60	12,172
Great Gladiator, On.	48	28	12,073
Alysheba, KSA	155	81	11,870
Bold Ruckus, Dead	224	113	11,861
Afleet, Jpn	161	87	11,839
Five Star Flight, Dead	26	14	11,777

Leading Broodmare Sires by Number of Winners Worldwide in 2002

Sire	Strs	Wnrs	Wnrs/ Strs
Mr. Prospector, Dead	474	218	46.0%
Halo, Dead	370	194	52.4%
Relaunch, Dead	339	190	56.0%
Seattle Slew, Dead	360	185	51.4%
Alydar, Dead	361	181	50.1%
Danzig, Ky.	409	176	43.0%
Dixieland Band, Ky.	323	171	52.9%
Private Account, Pens	328	170	51.8%
Valid Appeal, Dead	285	170	59.6%
Storm Bird, Pens	339	165	48.7%
Miswaki, Ky.	328	161	49.1%
Deputy Minister, Ky.	316	153	48.4%
Clever Trick, Ky.	325	153	47.1%
Cox's Ridge, Dead	296	153	51.7%
Affirmed, Dead	315	151	47.9%
Green Dancer, Dead	353	150	42.5%
Secretariat, Dead	343	149	43.4%
Sadler's Wells, Ire	397	148	37.3%
Be My Guest, Pens	352	147	41.8%
Vice Regent, Dead	291	146	50.2%
Riverman, Dead	333	145	43.5%
Nureyev, Dead	337	145	43.0%

Leading Broodmare Sires by Number of Wins Worldwide in 2002

Sire	Strs	Wnrs	Wins
Mr. Prospector, Dead	474	218	378
Halo, Dead	370	194	339
Relaunch, Dead	339	190	336
Valid Appeal, Dead	285	170	312
Alydar, Dead	361	181	305
Miswaki, Ky.	328	161	302
Seattle Slew, Dead	360	185	297
Danzig, Ky.	409	176	296
Cox's Ridge, Dead	296	153	283
Dixieland Band, Ky.	323	171	278
Deputy Minister, Ky.	316	153	272
Private Account, Pens	328	170	272
Sovereign Dancer, Dead	283	144	269
Vice Regent, Dead	291	146	267
Affirmed, Dead	315	151	265
Be My Guest, Pens	352	147	262
Crafty Prospector, Ky.	253	130	257
Secretariat, Dead	343	149	252
Alleged, Dead	346	144	251
Storm Bird, Pens	339	165	251
Clever Trick, Ky.	325	153	248
Riverman, Dead	333	145	244
Nureyev, Dead	337	145	242

Leading Broodmare Sires by Number of Stakes Winners Worldwide in 2002

Sire	Strs	Wnrs	SWs
Mr. Prospector, Dead	474	218	28
Miswaki, Ky.	328	161	23
Danzig, Ky.	409	176	21
Storm Bird, Pens	339	165	20
Sadler's Wells, Ire	397	148	19
Halo, Dead	370	194	18
Riverman, Dead	333	145	17
Deputy Minister, Ky.	316	153	17
Green Dancer, Dead	353	150	16
Seattle Slew, Dead	360	185	16
Affirmed, Dead	315	151	16
Woodman, Ky.	356	142	16
Strawberry Road (Aus), Dead	136	74	15
Cox's Ridge, Dead	296	153	15
Conquistador Cielo, Dead	280	141	15
Fappiano, Dead	252	123	15
Private Account, Pens	328	170	14
Alleged, Dead	346	144	14
Alydar, Dead	361	181	13
Be My Guest, Pens	352	147	12
The Minstrel, Dead	284	123	12
Valid Appeal, Dead	285	170	12
Nureyev, Dead	337	145	12
Spectacular Bid, N.Y.	243	127	12
Caerleon, Dead	349	140	12
Afleet, Jpn	161	87	12

Leading Broodmare Sires by Number of Graded Stakes Winners Worldwide in 2002

Sire	Strs	Wnrs	GSWs
Mr. Prospector, Dead	474	218	13
Seattle Slew, Dead	360	185	9
Cox's Ridge, Dead	296	153	9
Halo, Dead	370	194	8
Riverman, Dead	333	145	8
Affirmed, Dead	315	151	8
Miswaki, Ky.	328	161	8
Woodman, Ky.	356	142	8
Sadler's Wells, Ire	397	148	7
Storm Bird, Pens	339	165	6
Nureyev, Dead	337	145	6
Spectacular Bid, N.Y.	243	127	5
Danzig, Ky.	409	176	5
Wild Again, Ky.	258	111	5
Be My Guest, Pens	352	147	5
Strawberry Road (Aus), Dead	136	74	5

Leading Sires by Progeny Earnings in North America in 2002

Earnings in North America only for stallions represented by one starter in
North America in 2002, regardless of where the stallion stands or stood

Sire, Where stands	Strs	Wnrs	SWs	Leading earner (earnings)	Progeny earnings
El Prado (Ire), Ky.	176	90	10	Medaglia d'Oro ($2,260,600)	$6,808,668
Dehere, Jpn	147	76	10	Take Charge Lady ($1,388,635)	6,132,980
Wild Again, Ky.	123	67	6	Milwaukee Brew ($1,590,000)	6,040,549
End Sweep, Dead	216	130	4	Swept Overboard ($495,325)	5,824,048
Dynaformer, Ky.	159	79	12	Perfect Drift ($695,120)	5,613,618
A.P. Indy, Ky.	123	70	10	With Ability ($432,534)	5,455,439
Cryptoclearance, Ky.	206	96	4	Volponi ($2,389,200)	5,277,540
Mt. Livermore, Ky.	157	72	8	Orientate ($1,412,970)	5,269,643
Broad Brush, Ky.	111	66	12	Farda Amiga ($1,248,902)	5,250,671
Carson City, Ky.	184	96	10	Carson Hollow ($335,370)	5,145,530
Our Emblem, Ky.	73	31	4	War Emblem ($3,455,000)	4,880,389
Mr. Greeley, Ky.	185	108	8	Nonsuch Bay ($439,362)	4,783,464
Storm Cat, Ky.	104	45	11	Storm Flag Flying ($967,000)	4,726,279
Allen's Prospect, Md.	204	128	8	Your Out ($269,850)	4,706,905
Smart Strike, Ky.	98	63	6	Portcullis ($562,535)	4,664,392
Regal Classic, N.Y.	156	92	5	Regal Sanction ($318,400)	4,617,318
Gone West, Ky.	86	34	4	Came Home ($1,624,500)	4,609,600
Sadler's Wells, Ire	22	10	5	Beat Hollow (GB) ($1,437,150)	4,521,740
Not For Love, Md.	129	85	11	Sheila's Prospect ($322,814)	4,402,000
Unbridled, Dead	120	64	6	Surya ($364,339)	4,333,444
French Deputy, Jpn	116	67	6	Left Bank ($626,146)	4,304,850
Twining, Ky.	166	97	5	Dreams Go Bye ($177,431)	4,094,164
Judge T C, N.Y.	153	79	9	The Judge Sez Who ($558,186)	4,057,155
Forest Wildcat, Ky.	131	70	12	D'wildcat ($424,444)	4,001,377
Jade Hunter, Ky.	100	52	4	Azeri ($2,181,540)	3,985,924
Gilded Time, Ky.	158	83	5	Mandy's Gold ($715,404)	3,961,048
Tabasco Cat, Jpn	127	73	6	Snow Ridge ($399,990)	3,951,964
Pleasant Colony, Dead	79	42	5	Denon ($917,400)	3,927,736
Glitterman, Ky.	159	103	8	Texas Glitter ($313,408)	3,874,024
Silver Deputy, Ky.	151	87	5	Bare Necessities ($299,706)	3,796,842
Dixie Brass, Dead	127	74	4	Beautiful America ($241,363)	3,755,723
Belong to Me, Ky.	152	82	7	Miss Houdini ($175,800)	3,753,695
Quiet American, Ky.	146	79	7	Allamerican Bertie ($619,235)	3,751,301
Montbrook, Fl.	108	64	7	Trust N Luck ($382,800)	3,730,341
Notebook, Fl.	137	83	6	Booklet ($425,760)	3,660,868
Devil His Due, Ky.	181	98	5	Delray Dew ($201,260)	3,654,656
Saint Ballado, Dead	154	62	9	Saint Marden ($159,800)	3,615,415
Meadowlake, Ky.	125	75	5	Spring Meadow ($292,121)	3,615,016
Rubiano, Dead	132	83	6	Burning Roma ($350,237)	3,611,422
Peaks and Valleys, Ky.	123	68	3	Dollar Bill ($496,850)	3,594,550
Sky Classic, Ky.	142	66	10	First Quarter ($176,868)	3,577,116
Two Punch, Md.	165	94	5	Jab ($208,223)	3,570,258
Hennessy, Ky.	136	61	4	Wiseman's Ferry ($766,552)	3,545,379
Salt Lake, Ky.	174	95	3	Lake Lady ($224,000)	3,477,837
Black Tie Affair (Ire), Jpn	94	61	5	Evening Attire ($1,332,720)	3,463,859
Cherokee Run, Ky.	121	64	6	Kafwain ($535,848)	3,430,510
Holy Bull, Ky.	147	68	4	Macho Uno ($519,600)	3,418,251
Marquetry, Ky.	167	89	4	Darling Katey ($160,799)	3,394,931
Gulch, Ky.	114	64	5	Malmaison ($210,081)	3,374,311
With Approval, Ky.	166	78	6	Dust Me Off ($205,240)	3,367,145
Polish Numbers, Dead	149	80	8	Roman Dancer ($166,009)	3,347,984
Crafty Prospector, Ky.	138	74	3	Crafty C. T. ($415,075)	3,326,129
Woodman, Ky.	128	60	6	Chiselling ($405,760)	3,325,556
Langfuhr, Ky.	100	51	4	Imperial Gesture ($873,600)	3,323,848
Summer Squall, Ky.	75	38	6	Summer Colony ($992,500)	3,318,446
Dixieland Band, Ky.	128	68	5	Bowman's Band ($333,800)	3,317,962
In Excess (Ire), Ca.	116	63	8	Icecoldbeeratreds ($353,800)	3,307,524
Cure the Blues, Dead	120	70	4	Wake At Noon ($463,011)	3,303,054
Deputy Minister, Ky.	116	47	2	Minister's Baby ($290,093)	3,264,844
Runaway Groom, Ky.	161	83	6	Najran ($176,798)	3,232,604
Phone Trick, N.Y.	169	83	5	Day Trader ($286,175)	3,226,200
West by West, Tur	185	99	1	Rusty Spur ($180,610)	3,202,240
Unbridled's Song, Ky.	94	54	6	Buddha ($489,600)	3,186,655
Affirmed, Dead	65	30	5	The Tin Man ($598,020)	3,181,699
Numerous, Fr	134	70	1	Silver Nithi ($432,153)	3,155,855

Leading Sires by Average Earnings per Runner in North America in 2002

Sire	Strs	Wnrs	Average
Nureyev, Dead	32	15	$80,922
Harlan, Dead	44	24	69,669
Our Emblem, Ky.	73	31	66,855
Relaunch, Dead	37	21	58,449
Lear Fan, Ky.	57	34	54,514
Mr. Prospector, Dead	54	22	53,755
Gone West, Ky.	86	34	53,600
Pleasant Colony, Dead	79	42	49,718
Wild Again, Ky.	123	67	49,110
Affirmed, Dead	65	30	48,949
Smart Strike, Ky.	98	63	47,596
Broad Brush, Ky.	111	66	47,303
Storm Cat, Ky.	104	45	45,445
Domasca Dan, On.	26	15	44,670
A.P. Indy, Ky.	123	70	44,353
Summer Squall, Ky.	75	38	44,246
Distorted Humor, Ky.	31	15	41,955
Service Stripe, Ky.	27	16	41,877
Dehere, Jpn	147	76	41,721
Kingmambo, Ky.	57	29	41,460
Awesome Again, Ky.	31	10	40,601

Leading Sires by Median Earnings per Runner in North America in 2002

Sire	Strs	Wnrs	Median
Lord At War (Arg), Dead	48	25	$23,769
Smart Strike, Ky.	98	63	22,181
Danzig, Ky.	40	22	21,810
A.P. Indy, Ky.	123	70	21,060
Lite the Fuse, Fl.	64	43	20,737
Valid Appeal, Dead	34	24	20,650
Outflanker, Fl.	32	21	20,543
Meadow Monster, Md.	27	14	20,000
Swiss Yodeler, Ca.	27	16	19,880
Broad Brush, Ky.	111	66	19,740
I Can't Believe, On.	28	18	18,943
Claramount, N.Y.	46	32	17,890
Tabasco Cat, Jpn	127	73	17,845
Not For Love, Md.	129	85	17,575
Concorde's Tune, Fl.	76	49	17,204
Unbridled, Dead	120	64	17,140
Smoke Glacken, Ky.	81	49	16,790
Barbeau, Dead	39	22	16,774
Lost Soldier, Fl.	60	38	16,555
Virginia Rapids, Dead	51	29	16,432
Dixie Brass, Dead	127	74	16,429
Bold Badgett, Dead	54	36	16,392
Unbridled's Song, Ky.	94	54	16,360

Leading Sires by Number of Winners in North America in 2002

Sire	Strs	Wnrs	Wnrs/ Strs
End Sweep, Dead	216	130	60.2%
Allen's Prospect, Md.	204	128	62.7%
Mr. Greeley, Ky.	185	108	58.4%
Glitterman, Ky.	159	103	64.8%
West by West, Tur	185	99	53.5%
Devil His Due, Ky.	181	98	54.1%
Pentelicus, Dead	159	98	61.6%
Twining, Ky.	166	97	58.4%
Cryptoclearance, Ky.	206	96	46.6%
Carson City, Ky.	184	96	52.2%
Salt Lake, Ky.	174	95	54.6%
Two Punch, Md.	165	94	57.0%
Regal Classic, N.Y.	156	92	59.0%
Fortunate Prospect, Fl.	143	91	63.6%
El Prado (Ire), Ky.	176	90	51.1%
Marquetry, Ky.	167	89	53.3%
Silver Deputy, Ky.	151	87	57.6%
Mountain Cat, Tur	166	86	51.8%
Not For Love, Md.	129	85	65.9%
High Brite, Ca.	144	84	58.3%

Leading Sires by Number of Wins in North America in 2002

Sire	Strs	Wnrs	Wins
Allen's Prospect, Md.	204	128	247
End Sweep, Dead	216	130	220
Carson City, Ky.	184	96	189
Twining, Ky.	166	97	185
Glitterman, Ky.	159	103	184
Fortunate Prospect, Fl.	143	91	177
Devil His Due, Ky.	181	98	176
Notebook, Fl.	137	83	175
Salt Lake, Ky.	174	95	172
Cryptoclearance, Ky.	206	96	169
Rubiano, Dead	132	83	167
Mr. Greeley, Ky.	185	108	167
El Prado (Ire), Ky.	176	90	166
Marquetry, Ky.	167	89	164
Regal Classic, N.Y.	156	92	164
Dixie Brass, Dead	127	74	160
Not For Love, Md.	129	85	160
Press Card, Aust.	141	79	159
Formal Dinner, Fl.	136	82	156
West by West, Tur	185	99	155
Pentelicus, Dead	159	98	155
High Brite, Ca.	144	84	154
Two Punch, Md.	165	94	153
Silver Deputy, Ky.	151	87	152
Phone Trick, N.Y.	169	83	151
Valid Wager, Ca.	95	69	150

Leading Sires by Number of Stakes Winners in North America in 2002

Sire	Strs	Wnrs	SWs
Broad Brush, Ky.	111	66	12
Dynaformer, Ky.	159	79	12
Forest Wildcat, Ky.	131	70	12
Not For Love, Md.	129	85	11
Storm Cat, Ky.	104	45	11
Dehere, Jpn	147	76	10
Storm Boot, Ky.	158	80	10
A.P. Indy, Ky.	123	70	10
Carson City, Ky.	184	96	10
El Prado (Ire), Ky.	176	90	10
Sky Classic, Ky.	142	66	10
Saint Ballado, Dead	154	62	9
Judge T C, N.Y.	153	79	9
Katahaula County, B.C.	59	34	8
In Excess (Ire), Ca.	116	63	8
Polish Numbers, Dead	149	80	8
Allen's Prospect, Md.	204	128	8
Glitterman, Ky.	159	103	8
Mt. Livermore, Ky.	157	72	8
Mr. Greeley, Ky.	185	108	8
Quiet American, Ky.	146	79	7
Rare Brick, Tx.	93	63	7
Petersburg, Wa.	70	45	7
Colonial Affair, Jpn	91	47	7
Montbrook, Fl.	108	64	7
Bertrando, Ca.	126	63	7
Vying Victor, B.C.	111	64	7
Belong to Me, Ky.	152	82	7

Leading Sires by Number of Graded Stakes Winners in North America in 2002

Sire	Strs	Wnrs	GSWs
Mr. Prospector, Dead	54	22	5
Sadler's Wells, Ire	22	10	5
Storm Cat, Ky.	104	45	5
Dynaformer, Ky.	159	79	5
Theatrical (Ire), Ky.	72	34	5
French Deputy, Jpn	116	67	5
Mr. Greeley, Ky.	185	108	5
Thunder Gulch, Ky.	98	46	4
Forest Wildcat, Ky.	131	70	4
Gone West, Ky.	86	34	4
Broad Brush, Ky.	111	66	4
Affirmed, Dead	65	30	4

Leading Juvenile Sires by Progeny Earnings
in North America in 2002

Earnings in North America only for stallions with one North American starter in 2002, regardless of where the stallion stands.

Sire, Where stands	Strs	Wnrs	SWs	Leading earner (earnings)	Progeny earnings
Storm Cat, Ky.	16	7	2	Storm Flag Flying ($967,000)	$1,455,651
◆Distorted Humor, Ky.	31	15	4	Awesome Humor ($309,115)	1,300,602
Cherokee Run, Ky.	40	22	2	Kafwain ($535,848)	1,297,329
End Sweep, Dead	52	25	2	Global Finance ($181,000)	1,279,023
◆Awesome Again, Ky.	31	10	2	Toccet ($755,610)	1,258,620
Dehere, Jpn	29	11	5	Outta Here ($404,260)	1,230,556
Langfuhr, Ky.	43	20	2	Wando ($362,377)	1,180,947
A.P. Indy, Ky.	34	14	3	Handpainted ($256,210)	1,077,191
In Excess (Ire), Ca.	28	13	5	Icecoldbeeratreds ($353,800)	1,072,650
◆Elusive Quality, Ky.	37	21	5	Chimichurri ($148,340)	1,046,352
◆Tale of the Cat, Ky.	38	22	4	My Trusty Cat ($228,025)	1,022,215
Seattle Slew, Dead	20	8	1	Vindication ($680,950)	972,890
Smart Strike, Ky.	23	11	2	Added Edge ($250,328)	867,561
Forest Wildcat, Ky.	43	18	4	Wild Snitch ($119,200)	839,677
Carson City, Ky.	38	15	2	Hear No Evil ($174,590)	810,873
Formal Dinner, Fl.	57	27	1	Forest Picnic ($79,080)	792,850
Boston Harbor, Jpn	32	15	2	My Boston Gal ($194,537)	787,220
Pulpit, Ky.	22	7	2	Sky Mesa ($416,576)	771,323
◆Touch Gold, Ky.	31	8	1	Composure ($431,300)	769,506
◆Swiss Yodeler, Ca.	27	16	3	Oberwald ($98,636)	748,718
Saint Ballado, Dead	37	11	3	Truckle Feature ($125,300)	748,691
◆Grand Slam, Ky.	47	16	1	Big Score ($102,965)	748,218
Montbrook, Fl.	27	12	1	Trust N Luck ($382,800)	703,801
El Prado (Ire), Ky.	41	13	3	Julie's Prize ($102,052)	698,224
Mountain Cat, Tur	39	18	1	Mountain Dawn ($162,864)	693,244
Jules, Brz	36	18	1	Peace Rules ($209,990)	675,831
Not For Love, Md.	26	18	3	Coquettish ($98,520)	665,584
Suave Prospect, Fl.	26	14	2	Elegant Designer ($273,670)	661,492
Belong to Me, Ky.	34	14	2	Miss Houdini ($175,800)	637,323
Mecke, Fl.	16	10	1	Supah Blitz ($246,330)	616,287
Hadif, Tx.	26	18	3	Action Tonight ($162,029)	613,397
Honour and Glory, Ky.	30	14	1	One and Twenty ($173,520)	595,737
Devil His Due, Ky.	37	13	1	Spite the Devil ($124,815)	591,880
Gilded Time, Ky.	23	13	1	Elloluv ($242,700)	584,818
Unbridled, Dead	21	7	0	Santa Catarina ($302,580)	583,202
Lit de Justice, Ca.	29	12	0	I Testify ($92,160)	575,093
Mr. Greeley, Ky.	33	11	2	Whywhywhy ($284,060)	572,308
◆Stormy Atlantic, Ky.	22	9	3	Atlantic Ocean ($234,780)	566,126
Roy, Arg	26	15	2	Lets Just Do It ($141,813)	559,372
Tactical Advantage, Dead	39	15	2	Crowned Dancer ($122,858)	556,444
Wild Again, Ky.	20	6	1	Gigawatt ($176,095)	548,641
Rubiano, Dead	26	12	2	Ruby's Reception ($209,230)	547,008
◆Indian Charlie, Ky.	37	13	1	Jazz Lady ($91,704)	545,751
Helmsman, Ca.	23	14	0	Chad's Hope ($137,510)	543,448
West Acre, Fl.	8	5	1	Ivanavinalot ($418,300)	541,799
◆Concerto, Fl.	23	14	0	Collymore Hall ($170,507)	537,140
Gold Case, Ky.	30	15	2	Despreciado ($100,825)	534,994
Gold Fever, N.Y.	36	12	1	Arco's Gold ($224,460)	524,115
◆Souvenir Copy, Ky.	44	17	0	Long Term Wish ($78,154)	518,257
Storm Creek, Ky.	48	15	0	Sweet Storm Creek ($109,779)	515,386
Valid Wager, Ca.	24	11	3	Valid Video ($91,200)	514,794
Capote, Ky.	23	8	3	Buffythecenterfold ($222,160)	513,662
◆Favorite Trick, Ky.	31	12	1	Sum Trick ($82,531)	513,422
◆Skip Away, Ky.	36	12	2	Christmas Away ($107,805)	510,539
Out of Place, Ky.	36	13	0	Short Shadow ($93,153)	509,216
Defrere, N.J.	19	8	1	Souris ($159,410)	501,672
Dixie Brass, Dead	19	6	2	Beautiful America ($241,363)	501,046
Roar, Ca.	34	13	2	Roar Emotion ($156,600)	496,720
Leo Castelli, Dead	20	7	1	Leo's Last Hurrahy ($326,848)	486,094
Lord Carson, Ca.	25	11	2	Mt. Carson ($101,450)	484,810
Silver Deputy, Ky.	21	9	1	Posse ($184,415)	484,620
Pentelicus, Dead	47	23	1	Bases Are Loaded ($46,410)	481,687
Glitterman, Ky.	29	11	1	Champali ($125,874)	479,687
Conquistador Cielo, Dead	16	5	1	Lone Star Sky ($338,235)	471,837
◆Formal Gold, Ky.	28	15	0	Formal Dancer ($70,420)	463,868

Leading Juvenile Sires by Average Earnings per Runner in North America in 2002

Sire	Strs	Wnrs	Average
Storm Cat, Ky.	16	7	$90,978
Seattle Slew, Dead	20	8	48,645
Dehere, Jpn	29	11	42,433
◆Distorted Humor, Ky.	31	15	41,955
◆Awesome Again, Ky.	31	10	40,601
Mecke, Fl.	16	10	38,518
In Excess (Ire), Ca.	28	13	38,309
Smart Strike, Ky.	23	11	37,720
Pulpit, Ky.	22	7	35,060
Cherokee Run, Ky.	40	22	32,433
A.P. Indy, Ky.	34	14	31,682
Hay Halo, Va.	11	8	30,499
Conquistador Cielo, Dead	16	5	29,490
Bold Badgett, Dead	13	6	29,097
◆Elusive Quality, Ky.	37	21	28,280
Gone West, Ky.	12	1	28,279
Tethra, On.	10	4	27,937
Unbridled, Dead	21	7	27,772
◆Swiss Yodeler, Ca.	27	16	27,730
Langfuhr, Ky.	43	20	27,464
Lite the Fuse, Fl.	12	7	27,452
Wild Again, Ky.	20	6	27,432

Leading Juvenile Sires by Median Earnings per Runner in North America in 2002

Sire	Strs	Wnrs	Median
Storm Cat, Ky.	16	7	$23,123
◆Swiss Yodeler, Ca.	27	16	19,880
Concorde's Tune, Fl.	10	6	19,735
Mecke, Fl.	16	10	18,665
◆Partner's Hero, Md.	25	14	16,000
Smart Strike, Ky.	23	11	15,750
◆Elusive Quality, Ky.	37	21	15,413
◆Tale of the Cat, Ky.	38	22	15,050
Lite the Fuse, Fl.	12	7	14,714
Not For Love, Md.	26	18	14,500
Summer Squall, Ky.	10	5	13,980
◆Coronado's Quest, Ky.	22	10	13,680
Bold Badgett, Dead	13	6	13,650
Gilded Time, Ky.	23	13	13,400
Carr de Naskra, Pens	10	6	13,290
Helmsman, Ca.	23	14	13,230
Meadowlake, Ky.	19	11	13,200
Migrating Moon, Fl.	10	6	12,991
Dayjur, Ky.	16	10	12,706
◆Concerto, Fl.	23	14	12,670
End Sweep, Dead	52	25	12,603
Kipper Kelly, La.	13	8	12,570

Leading Juvenile Sires by Number of Winners in North America in 2002

Sire	Strs	Wnrs	Wnrs/Strs
Formal Dinner, Fl.	57	27	47.4%
End Sweep, Dead	52	25	48.1%
Pentelicus, Dead	47	23	48.9%
Cherokee Run, Ky.	40	22	55.0%
◆Tale of the Cat, Ky.	38	22	57.9%
◆Elusive Quality, Ky.	37	21	56.8%
Langfuhr, Ky.	43	20	46.5%
◆Double Honor, Fl.	39	20	51.3%
Patton, Pa.	52	18	34.6%
Forest Wildcat, Ky.	43	18	41.9%
Not For Love, Md.	26	18	69.2%
Jules, Brz	36	18	50.0%
Hadif, Tx.	26	18	69.2%
Mountain Cat, Tur	39	18	46.2%
◆Souvenir Copy, Ky.	44	17	38.6%
◆Grand Slam, Ky.	47	16	34.0%
◆Swiss Yodeler, Ca.	27	16	59.3%
Boston Harbor, Jpn	32	15	46.9%
Gold Case, Ky.	30	15	50.0%
Captain Bodgit, N.Y.	38	15	39.5%
◆Formal Gold, Ky.	28	15	53.6%

Leading Juvenile Sires by Number of Wins in North America in 2002

Sire	Strs	Wnrs	Wins
Formal Dinner, Fl.	57	27	37
Cherokee Run, Ky.	40	22	35
End Sweep, Dead	52	25	34
◆Elusive Quality, Ky.	37	21	31
◆Tale of the Cat, Ky.	38	22	30
Suave Prospect, Fl.	26	14	28
◆Distorted Humor, Ky.	31	15	27
Langfuhr, Ky.	43	20	27
◆Double Honor, Fl.	39	20	27
Hadif, Tx.	26	18	27
Mountain Cat, Tur	39	18	26
Pentelicus, Dead	47	23	26
Forest Wildcat, Ky.	43	18	26
Not For Love, Md.	26	18	25
Gold Case, Ky.	30	15	24
◆Swiss Yodeler, Ca.	27	16	24
Jules, Brz	36	18	22
◆Grand Slam, Ky.	47	16	22
Mister Jolie, Dead	21	11	22
Patton, Pa.	52	18	22
◆Lucky Lionel, Fl.	23	13	22
Carson City, Ky.	38	15	22
Katahaula County, B.C.	19	14	21
◆Souvenir Copy, Ky.	44	17	21
Boston Harbor, Jpn	32	15	21
In Excess (Ire), Ca.	28	13	21
Honour and Glory, Ky.	30	14	20
◆Announce, Ky.	30	15	20
Montbrook, Fl.	27	12	20
Pembroke, Ky.	33	15	20
Dehere, Jpn	29	11	20
Roy, Arg	26	15	20
Fortunate Prospect, Fl.	24	15	20
Gilded Time, Ky.	23	13	19
Colony Light, Fl.	18	13	19
You and I, Ky.	32	15	19
Valid Wager, Ca.	24	11	19
Storm Creek, Ky.	48	15	19
Sword Dance (Ire), Fl.	33	14	19
◆Concerto, Fl.	23	14	19
◆Awesome Again, Ky.	31	10	19

Leading Juvenile Sires by Number of Stakes Winners in North America in 2002

Sire	Strs	Wnrs	SWs
Dehere, Jpn	29	11	5
◆Elusive Quality, Ky.	37	21	5
In Excess (Ire), Ca.	28	13	5
◆Tale of the Cat, Ky.	38	22	4
Forest Wildcat, Ky.	43	18	4
◆Distorted Humor, Ky.	31	15	4
Vying Victor, B.C.	24	13	4
Katahaula County, B.C.	19	14	4
Sultry Song, Ky.	16	8	3
Hadif, Tx.	26	18	3
A.P. Indy, Ky.	34	14	3
Saint Ballado, Dead	37	11	3
Cisco Road, Wa.	23	12	3
Not For Love, Md.	26	18	3
Capote, Ky.	23	8	3
Bold Badgett, Dead	13	6	3
◆Announce, Ky.	30	15	3
Valid Wager, Ca.	24	11	3
On Target, La.	23	7	3
◆Swiss Yodeler, Ca.	27	16	3
Mercer Mill, Oh.	20	9	3
El Prado (Ire), Ky.	41	13	3
◆Stormy Atlantic, Ky.	22	9	3

Leading Juvenile Sires by Number of Graded Stakes Winners in North America in 2002

Sire	Strs	Wnrs	GSWs
◆Distorted Humor, Ky.	31	15	2
Boston Harbor, Jpn	32	15	2

Leading Freshman Sires by Progeny Earnings in North America in 2002

Earnings in North America only for stallions with one North American starter in 2002, regardless of where the stallion stands.

Sire, Where stands	Strs	Wnrs	SWs	Leading earner (earnings)	Progeny earnings
Distorted Humor, Ky.	31	15	4	Awesome Humor ($309,115)	$1,300,602
Awesome Again, Ky.	31	10	2	Toccet ($755,610)	1,258,620
Elusive Quality, Ky.	37	21	5	Chimichurri ($148,340)	1,046,352
Tale of the Cat, Ky.	38	22	4	My Trusty Cat ($228,025)	1,022,215
Touch Gold, Ky.	31	8	1	Composure ($431,300)	769,506
Swiss Yodeler, Ca.	27	16	3	Oberwald ($98,636)	748,718
Grand Slam, Ky.	47	16	1	Big Score ($102,965)	748,218
Stormy Atlantic, Ky.	22	9	3	Atlantic Ocean ($234,780)	566,126
Indian Charlie, Ky.	37	13	1	Jazz Lady ($91,704)	545,751
Concerto, Fl.	23	14	1	Collymore Hall ($170,507)	537,140
Souvenir Copy, Ky.	44	17	0	Long Term Wish ($78,154)	518,257
Favorite Trick, Ky.	31	12	1	Sum Trick ($82,531)	513,422
Skip Away, Ky.	36	12	2	Christmas Away ($107,805)	510,539
Formal Gold, Ky.	28	15	0	Formal Dancer ($70,420)	463,868
Announce, Ky.	30	15	3	Indy Fire ($66,912)	458,323
Deputy Commander, Ky.	46	10	0	Holiday Lady ($89,655)	455,651
Banker's Gold, Ky.	23	12	1	Jenny's Prospector ($87,731)	452,273
Hussonet, Chi	9	3	1	Seinne (CHI) ($228,906)	448,273
Double Honor, Fl.	39	20	0	Honorable King ($46,920)	446,339
Coronado's Quest, Ky.	22	10	1	Allspice ($76,800)	441,236
Benchmark, Ca.	23	10	0	Martinblestme ($101,994)	435,089
Lucky Lionel, Fl.	23	13	0	Little Swimmer ($107,630)	421,493
Partner's Hero, Md.	25	14	1	Object of Virtue ($71,928)	405,846
Kiridashi, On.	21	10	1	Snake Pit ($124,905)	401,105
Dance Brightly, Ky.	38	8	0	Mr. Whitestone ($65,570)	376,040
Gentlemen (Arg), Ky.	20	8	1	Man Among Men ($74,040)	275,612
Wild Rush, Ky.	33	8	0	Leagueofhisown ($40,120)	272,922
Cape Town, Ky.	25	7	0	Cape Good Hope ($90,050)	253,383
Western Fame, Ca.	15	8	0	Tizalovelylady ($55,740)	246,634
Tomorrows Cat, N.Y.	21	6	1	Tomorrows Banquet ($74,296)	246,377
Northern Afleet, Fl.	17	9	0	Paris Adventure ($47,754)	245,730
Ordway, Ky.	23	9	1	Ordinary Paula ($69,142)	241,122
Semoran, Fl.	22	13	0	Takeonefortheteam ($31,960)	230,336
Will's Way, Ky.	30	11	0	Lion Tamer ($35,600)	213,628
Wild Deputy, Ca.	18	8	1	Effectively Wild ($37,245)	199,083
Labeeb (GB), Ky.	8	2	1	Kabeeb ($182,398)	199,035
Ghostly Moves, N.M.	9	7	1	Shemoveslikeaghost ($58,907)	188,699
Confide, Ky.	26	5	1	Confiding Winner ($67,020)	188,494
Diligence, Fl.	22	6	0	Worker Man ($85,500)	182,955
Cyberspace, Fl.	8	4	0	Cyberdevil ($91,005)	182,476
Commanchero, Tx.	2	2	1	Most Feared ($166,020)	177,242
Anet, Ky.	22	5	1	My Own Groom ($73,723)	176,587
Storm Broker, Md.	17	10	0	Krebsie ($30,810)	176,465
Aggie Southpaw, Tx.	4	3	1	Call Me Lefty ($129,400)	169,976
Yoonevano, B.C.	4	1	1	Illusive Force ($159,948)	162,145
Subordination, Ky.	21	5	0	Goldies Legacy ($36,360)	159,329
Proud and True, Fl.	19	5	0	Kryskaly ($42,040)	156,085
Acceptable, Ky.	13	6	0	Fostress ($46,550)	151,086
Snowbound, Az.	11	5	2	First Snowbound ($83,726)	151,022
Lasting Approval, Ky.	11	4	0	Four R Approval ($58,500)	141,766
King of Kings (Ire), Jpn	13	4	0	Throne ($50,937)	137,117
Arch, Ky.	16	4	0	Honey Green ($53,631)	133,259
Willowy Ambassador, Ky.	2	2	1	Hackendiffy ($116,750)	122,029
Yarrow Brae, Md.	12	3	0	Butiwillflysomeday ($36,350)	116,525
Haint, Ca.	11	5	0	Just Watch Me ($53,835)	114,681
Gold Token, N.Y.	10	3	0	Golden Damsel ($30,240)	109,299
Rage, N.Y.	5	4	0	Rageously ($38,830)	107,440
Traitor, Fl.	18	5	0	Gastonia ($27,670)	104,879
Swear by Dixie, Md.	7	5	0	Mark Aim Fire ($45,920)	101,423
Prince of the Mt., La.	8	3	1	Knight of the Mt. ($52,031)	97,496
Halory Hunter, N.Y.	21	4	0	Sweep Hunter ($25,474)	90,856
Western Echo, Pa.	11	6	0	Echo Lady ($22,180)	87,557
Parentheses, N.M.	3	2	1	Quote This ($62,764)	87,512
Rodeo, N.Y.	14	2	0	Airialissue ($27,180)	84,522
Awad, Md.	13	2	0	Arab Miss ($30,360)	83,970

Leading Freshman Sires by Average Earnings per Runner in North America in 2002

Sire	Strs	Wnrs	Average
Distorted Humor, Ky.	31	15	$41,955
Awesome Again, Ky.	31	10	40,601
Elusive Quality, Ky.	37	21	28,280
Swiss Yodeler, Ca.	27	16	27,730
Tale of the Cat, Ky.	38	22	26,900
Stormy Atlantic, Ky.	22	9	25,733
Touch Gold, Ky.	31	8	24,823
Concerto, Fl.	23	14	23,354
Coronado's Quest, Ky.	22	10	20,056
Banker's Gold, Ky.	23	12	19,664
Kiridashi, On.	21	10	19,100
Benchmark, Ca.	23	10	18,917
Lucky Lionel, Fl.	23	13	18,326
Formal Gold, Ky.	28	15	16,567
Favorite Trick, Ky.	31	12	16,562
Western Fame, Ca.	15	8	16,442
Partner's Hero, Md.	25	14	16,234
Grand Slam, Ky.	47	16	15,920
Announce, Ky.	30	15	15,277
Indian Charlie, Ky.	37	13	14,750
Northern Afleet, Fl.	17	9	14,455
Skip Away, Ky.	36	12	14,182

Leading Freshman Sires by Median Earnings per Runner in North America in 2002

Sire	Strs	Wnrs	Median
Swiss Yodeler, Ca.	27	16	$19,880
Partner's Hero, Md.	25	14	16,000
Elusive Quality, Ky.	37	21	15,413
Tale of the Cat, Ky.	38	22	15,050
Coronado's Quest, Ky.	22	10	13,680
Concerto, Fl.	23	14	12,670
Kiridashi, On.	21	10	12,120
Lucky Lionel, Fl.	23	13	11,421
Banker's Gold, Ky.	23	12	11,345
Storm Broker, Md.	17	10	10,410
Announce, Ky.	30	15	9,857
Formal Gold, Ky.	28	15	9,833
Gold Token, N.Y.	10	3	9,153
Northern Afleet, Fl.	17	9	8,970
Semoran, Fl.	22	13	8,795
Stormy Atlantic, Ky.	22	9	8,785
Distorted Humor, Ky.	31	15	8,640
Favorite Trick, Ky.	31	12	8,400
Souvenir Copy, Ky.	44	17	8,061
Double Honor, Fl.	39	20	8,050
Benchmark, Ca.	23	10	8,025
Western Echo, Pa.	11	6	7,830
Western Fame, Ca.	15	8	7,306
Wild Deputy, Ca.	18	8	6,131
Will's Way, Ky.	30	11	5,725

Leading Freshman Sires by Number of Winners in North America in 2002

Sire	Strs	Wnrs	Wnrs/ Strs
Tale of the Cat, Ky.	38	22	57.9%
Elusive Quality, Ky.	37	21	56.8%
Double Honor, Fl.	39	20	51.3%
Souvenir Copy, Ky.	44	17	38.6%
Grand Slam, Ky.	47	16	34.0%
Swiss Yodeler, Ca.	27	16	59.3%
Distorted Humor, Ky.	31	15	48.4%
Formal Gold, Ky.	28	15	53.6%
Announce, Ky.	30	15	50.0%
Concerto, Fl.	23	14	60.9%
Partner's Hero, Md.	25	14	56.0%
Semoran, Fl.	22	13	59.1%
Lucky Lionel, Fl.	23	13	56.5%
Indian Charlie, Ky.	37	13	35.1%
Banker's Gold, Ky.	23	12	52.2%
Favorite Trick, Ky.	31	12	38.7%
Skip Away, Ky.	36	12	33.3%
Will's Way, Ky.	30	11	36.7%

Leading Freshman Sires by Number of Wins in North America in 2002

Sire	Strs	Wnrs	Wins
Elusive Quality, Ky.	37	21	31
Tale of the Cat, Ky.	38	22	30
Distorted Humor, Ky.	31	15	27
Double Honor, Fl.	39	20	27
Swiss Yodeler, Ca.	27	16	24
Grand Slam, Ky.	47	16	22
Lucky Lionel, Fl.	23	13	22
Souvenir Copy, Ky.	44	17	21
Announce, Ky.	30	15	20
Awesome Again, Ky.	31	10	19
Concerto, Fl.	23	14	19
Formal Gold, Ky.	28	15	18
Stormy Atlantic, Ky.	22	9	18
Partner's Hero, Md.	25	14	17
Skip Away, Ky.	36	12	17
Semoran, Fl.	22	13	16
Favorite Trick, Ky.	31	12	16
Indian Charlie, Ky.	37	13	14
Banker's Gold, Ky.	23	12	13
Wild Deputy, Ca.	18	8	13
Will's Way, Ky.	30	11	13
Deputy Commander, Ky.	46	10	12
Touch Gold, Ky.	31	8	12
Benchmark, Ca.	23	10	12
Ghostly Moves, N.M.	9	7	12
Coronado's Quest, Ky.	22	10	12
Storm Broker, Md.	17	1	11
Northern Afleet, Fl.	17	9	11
Ordway, Ky.	23	9	10
Western Fame, Ca.	15	8	10
Kiridashi, On.	21	10	10
Snowbound, Az.	11	5	10
Gentlemen (Arg), Ky.	20	8	10
Dance Brightly, Ky.	38	8	9
Cyberspace, Fl.	8	4	9
Wild Rush, Ky.	33	8	9
Rage, N.Y.	5	4	8
Anet, Ky.	22	5	8
Proud and True, Fl.	19	5	8
Halory Hunter, N.Y.	21	4	8
Cape Town, Ky.	25	7	8
Notable Cat, Ok.	13	7	8
Traitor, Fl.	18	5	7
Confide, Ky.	26	5	7
Diligence, Fl.	22	6	7
Acceptable, Ky.	13	6	7
Virtua Cop, P.R.	10	4	7
Capote's Prospect, Tx.	11	5	6
Western Echo, Pa.	11	6	6
Hussonet, Chi	9	3	6
Lasting Approval, Ky.	11	4	6
Tomorrows Cat, N.Y.	21	6	6
Swear by Dixie, Md.	7	5	6

Leading Freshman Sires by Number of Stakes Winners in North America in 2002

Sire	Strs	Wnrs	SWs
Elusive Quality, Ky.	37	21	5
Tale of the Cat, Ky.	38	22	4
Distorted Humor, Ky.	31	15	4
Swiss Yodeler, Ca.	27	16	3
Stormy Atlantic, Ky.	22	9	3
Announce, Ky.	30	15	3
Awesome Again, Ky.	31	10	2
Skip Away, Ky.	36	12	2
Snowbound, Az.	11	5	2

Leading Freshman Sires by Number of Graded Stakes Winners in North America in 2002

Sire	Strs	Wnrs	GSWs
Distorted Humor, Ky.	31	15	2
Elusive Quality, Ky.	37	21	1
Hussonet, Chi	9	3	1
Awesome Again, Ky.	31	10	1
Touch Gold, Ky.	31	8	1
Commanchero, Tx.	2	2	1
Stormy Atlantic, Ky.	22	9	1

Leading Broodmare Sires by Progeny Earnings in North America in 2002

Earnings in North America only for broodmare sires who had one North American starter in 2002, regardless of where stands.

Sire, Where stands	Strs	Wnrs	SWs	Leading earner (earnings)	Progeny earnings
Deputy Minister, Ky.	271	135	15	Sarava ($665,040)	$8,798,900
Cox's Ridge, Dead	258	139	13	Orientate ($1,412,970)	7,926,592
Mr. Prospector, Dead	250	134	13	With Ability ($432,534)	7,375,046
Halo, Dead	284	157	13	Private Emblem ($550,940)	7,130,406
Pleasant Colony, Dead	194	119	9	Farda Amiga ($1,248,902)	6,697,079
Private Account, Pens	246	137	9	Good Journey ($1,247,665)	6,678,245
Valid Appeal, Dead	273	166	11	Best of the Rest ($308,253)	6,633,863
Seattle Slew, Dead	224	123	10	Astra ($758,000)	6,448,788
Affirmed, Dead	221	114	12	Harlan's Holiday ($1,606,000)	6,392,278
Relaunch, Dead	311	182	6	Starrer ($310,000)	6,328,933
Dixieland Band, Ky.	280	158	8	Queen of Wilshire ($269,607)	5,858,167
Danzig, Ky.	187	100	11	Voodoo Dancer ($562,638)	5,766,363
Bold Ruckus, Dead	218	110	7	Mysterious Affair ($295,073)	5,605,648
Clever Trick, Ky.	278	136	5	Came Home ($1,624,500)	5,587,843
Vice Regent, Dead	242	127	9	Wild Whiskey ($155,550)	5,450,935
Crafty Prospector, Ky.	231	125	7	Icecoldbeeratreds ($353,800)	5,384,917
Miswaki, Ky.	221	116	13	Landseer (GB) ($372,000)	5,343,058
Alydar, Dead	221	132	6	Blue Burner ($256,100)	5,331,571
Lord At War (Arg), Dead	79	42	4	War Emblem ($3,455,000)	5,319,035
Fappiano, Dead	180	99	10	Transcendental ($265,516)	5,266,844
Storm Cat, Ky.	155	86	6	Buddha ($489,600)	5,088,846
Sovereign Dancer, Dead	239	130	3	Disturbingthepeace ($452,640)	4,969,184
Strawberry Road (Aus), Dead	121	64	12	Vindication ($680,950)	4,909,747
Storm Bird, Pens	204	116	14	Multiple Choice ($252,442)	4,836,439
Our Native, Dead	193	96	3	Evening Attire ($1,332,720)	4,603,943
Conquistador Cielo, Dead	224	119	10	My Cousin Matt ($307,159)	4,420,487
Secretariat, Dead	269	126	5	Perfect Soul (IRE) ($280,020)	4,419,597
Spectacular Bid, N.Y.	193	105	7	Bare Necessities ($299,706)	4,221,473
Saratoga Six, Ky.	175	97	1	Dollar Bill ($496,850)	4,129,561
Naskra, Dead	155	80	7	Perfect Drift ($695,120)	4,043,135
Smarten, Pens	166	90	6	Full of Wonder ($357,580)	3,995,508
Green Dancer, Dead	193	98	10	Alternate ($253,012)	3,975,920
Flying Paster, Dead	191	100	10	Bien Nicole ($340,610)	3,926,238
Wolf Power (SAf), Dead	127	72	4	Milwaukee Brew ($1,590,000)	3,903,789
Kris S., Dead	191	103	5	Ladies Din ($285,600)	3,900,863
Rahy, Ky.	101	61	9	Megahertz (GB) ($600,180)	3,890,543
Forty Niner, Jpn	138	69	9	Outta Here ($404,260)	3,864,491
Topsider, Dead	180	105	4	Pie N Burger ($147,200)	3,720,539
Nijinsky II, Dead	167	76	6	Bonapaw ($423,000)	3,607,740
Apalachee, Dead	185	91	3	Mulrainy ($380,234)	3,527,215
His Majesty, Dead	194	92	6	Parade Leader ($459,503)	3,481,808
Woodman, Ky.	148	62	5	Snow Ridge ($399,990)	3,472,388
Afleet, Jpn	136	76	8	Saint Marden ($159,800)	3,460,108
Copelan, Dead	167	90	3	Wrangler ($213,268)	3,417,479
Wild Again, Ky.	214	92	3	Dat You Miz Blue ($287,671)	3,412,420
Cure the Blues, Dead	169	89	5	Attest ($266,696)	3,381,309
Pirate's Bounty, Pens	202	102	6	Candid Glen ($303,240)	3,369,195
Mr. Leader, Dead	213	102	6	Scooter Roach ($208,794)	3,337,731
Alleged, Dead	156	75	5	Composure ($431,300)	3,312,293
Bailjumper, Dead	65	35	2	Medaglia d'Oro ($2,260,600)	3,289,165
Broad Brush, Ky.	108	66	6	Trial Prep ($237,434)	3,201,536
Cozzene, Ky.	131	56	6	Toccet ($755,610)	3,200,009
Great Above, Dead	160	80	8	Anglian Prince ($410,112)	3,026,224
Blushing Groom (Fr), Dead	88	54	3	Macho Uno ($519,600)	2,982,302
Devil's Bag, Ky.	167	73	4	Mountain Orchid ($206,154)	2,970,691
Well Decorated, Ky.	189	102	3	Melisma's Valley ($155,331)	2,970,571
Nureyev, Dead	83	39	5	Tates Creek ($661,512)	2,966,140
Damascus, Dead	154	75	3	Kudos ($468,735)	2,903,429
Lost Code, Dead	143	70	6	Calkins Road ($374,100)	2,894,193
Premiership, Fl.	160	83	5	Peekskill ($256,075)	2,893,207
Cutlass, Dead	141	80	3	Swept Overboard ($495,325)	2,888,354
Baldski, Dead	152	73	4	Jennasietta ($181,546)	2,863,547
Meadowlake, Ky.	124	74	4	Open Concert ($207,906)	2,852,520
Sir Harry Lewis, Eng	20	10	3	Volponi ($2,389,200)	2,843,804
Capote, Ky.	123	63	6	True Passion ($281,012)	2,828,680

Leading Broodmare Sires by Average Earnings per Runner in North America in 2002

Sire	Strs	Wnrs	Average
Easy Goer, Dead	36	16	$71,163
Lord At War (Arg), Dead	79	42	67,330
Saros (GB), Dead	40	20	51,770
Bailjumper, Dead	65	35	50,603
Homebuilder, La.	34	21	42,787
Silver Deputy, Ky.	62	30	40,916
Strawberry Road (Aus), Dead	121	64	40,576
Rahy, Ky.	101	61	38,520
With Approval, Ky.	68	34	37,389
El Gran Senor, Pens	59	28	36,857
Carson City, Ky.	71	47	35,758
Nureyev, Dead	83	39	35,737
Pleasant Colony, Dead	194	119	34,521
Badger Land, Dead	46	31	34,018
Blushing Groom (Fr), Dead	88	54	33,890
Steady Growth, Dead	31	16	33,165
Storm Cat, Ky.	155	86	32,831
Aloma's Ruler, Il.	34	16	32,743
Deputy Minister, Ky.	271	135	32,468
Seeking the Gold, Ky.	84	48	32,468
Danzig, Ky.	187	100	30,836
Wolf Power (SAf), Dead	127	72	30,738

Leading Broodmare Sires by Median Earnings per Runner in North America in 2002

Sire	Strs	Wnrs	Median
Concorde Bound, Dead	27	18	$17,310
Rahy, Ky.	101	61	17,270
Carson City, Ky.	71	47	15,784
Dayjur, Ky.	44	25	15,675
Broad Brush, Ky.	108	66	15,128
Seeking the Gold, Ky.	84	48	14,725
Personal Flag, N.Y.	89	58	14,659
Naked Sky, Dead	34	26	14,492
Gone West, Ky.	87	49	14,200
Storm Cat, Ky.	155	86	13,939
Steady Growth, Dead	31	16	13,756
Jeblar, Dead	50	33	13,522
Proper Reality, Ar.	51	32	13,442
Valid Appeal, Dead	273	166	13,380
Double Zeus, Md.	25	12	13,373
Big Burn, Pens	33	17	13,370
Meadowlake, Ky.	124	74	13,220
Mr. Prospector, Dead	250	134	13,158
Procida, Dead	65	43	13,100
American Standard, N.Y.	44	24	12,995
Yukon, Dead	61	35	12,935
El Raggaas, Phi	27	15	12,915
Pleasant Colony, Dead	194	119	12,686
Better Arbitor, Dead	26	17	12,625
Deputy Minister, Ky.	271	135	12,520

Leading Broodmare Sires by Number of Winners in North America in 2002

Sire	Strs	Wnrs	Wnrs/ Strs
Relaunch, Dead	311	182	58.5%
Valid Appeal, Dead	273	166	60.8%
Dixieland Band, Ky.	280	158	56.4%
Halo, Dead	284	157	55.3%
Cox's Ridge, Dead	258	139	53.9%
Private Account, Pens	246	137	55.7%
Clever Trick, Ky.	278	136	48.9%
Deputy Minister, Ky.	271	135	49.8%
Mr. Prospector, Dead	250	134	53.6%
Alydar, Dead	221	132	59.7%
Sovereign Dancer, Dead	239	130	54.4%
Vice Regent, Dead	242	127	52.5%
Secretariat, Dead	269	126	46.8%
Crafty Prospector, Ky.	231	125	54.1%
Seattle Slew, Dead	224	123	54.9%
Conquistador Cielo, Dead	224	119	53.1%
Pleasant Colony, Dead	194	119	61.3%

Leading Broodmare Sires by Number of Wins in North America in 2002

Sire	Strs	Wnrs	Wins
Relaunch, Dead	311	182	321
Valid Appeal, Dead	273	166	308
Halo, Dead	284	157	276
Cox's Ridge, Dead	258	139	264
Dixieland Band, Ky.	280	158	262
Crafty Prospector, Ky.	231	125	250
Sovereign Dancer, Dead	239	130	250
Mr. Prospector, Dead	250	134	249
Deputy Minister, Ky.	271	135	245
Vice Regent, Dead	242	127	242
Alydar, Dead	221	132	225
Miswaki, Ky.	221	116	225
Private Account, Pens	246	137	221
Clever Trick, Ky.	278	136	220
Secretariat, Dead	269	126	217
Bold Ruckus, Dead	218	110	215
Seattle Slew, Dead	224	123	212
Conquistador Cielo, Dead	224	119	208
Pleasant Colony, Dead	194	119	203
Affirmed, Dead	221	114	199
Flying Paster, Dead	191	100	191
Spectacular Bid, N.Y.	193	105	191
Mr. Leader, Dead	213	102	190
Topsider, Dead	180	105	186
Danzig, Ky.	187	100	184
Storm Bird, Pens	204	116	183
Well Decorated, Ky.	189	102	183
Pirate's Bounty, Pens	202	102	178
Saratoga Six, Dead	175	97	177
Kris S., Dead	191	103	171
Majestic Light, Dead	223	108	171
Naskra, Dead	155	80	169
Silent Screen, Dead	158	80	169
Phone Trick, N.Y.	176	86	166
Our Native, Dead	193	96	163
Tri Jet, Dead	167	84	163
Smarten, Pens	166	90	162
Apalachee, Dead	185	91	162
Copelan, Dead	167	90	162

Leading Broodmare Sires by Number of Stakes Winners in North America in 2002

Sire	Strs	Wnrs	SWs
Deputy Minister, Ky.	271	135	15
Storm Bird, Pens	204	116	14
Miswaki, Ky.	221	116	13
Halo, Dead	284	157	13
Mr. Prospector, Dead	250	134	13
Cox's Ridge, Dead	258	139	13
Affirmed, Dead	221	114	12
Strawberry Road (Aus), Dead	121	64	12
Danzig, Ky.	187	100	11
Valid Appeal, Dead	273	166	11
Green Dancer, Dead	193	98	10
Seattle Slew, Dead	224	123	10
Fappiano, Dead	180	99	10
Conquistador Cielo, Dead	224	119	10
Flying Paster, Dead	191	100	10

Leading Broodmare Sires by Number of Graded Stakes Winners in North America in 2002

Sire	Strs	Wnrs	GSWs
Cox's Ridge, Dead	258	139	7
Halo, Dead	284	157	6
Storm Bird, Pens	204	116	6
Nureyev, Dead	83	39	5
Affirmed, Dead	221	114	5
Seattle Slew, Dead	224	123	5
Mr. Prospector, Dead	250	134	5
Valid Appeal, Dead	273	166	4
Danzig, Ky.	187	100	4
Deputy Minister, Ky.	271	135	4

International Leading General Sires
by 2002 Progeny Earnings

Worldwide earnings for stallions represented by one starter in any of the following countries: United States, Canada, Puerto Rico, England, Ireland, France, Italy, Germany, United Arab Emirates, Saudi Arabia, Australia, Brazil, Argentina, Japan, and Hong Kong.

Sire, YOB, Sire	Loc	2002 Stud Fee	Strs	Wnrs	SWs/Stk Wins	Leading Earner (Earnings)	Progeny Earnings
SUNDAY SILENCE, 86, by Halo	Dead		415	159	16/23	=Gold Allure (Jpn) ($2,120,118)	$52,765,792
DANEHILL, 86, by Danzig	Ire	N/A	494	239	47/75	=Fine Motion (Ire) ($2,378,740)	23,829,879
BRIAN'S TIME, 85, by Roberto	Jpn	N/A	206	73	5/9	=Tanino Gimlet (Jpn) ($2,963,043)	21,028,122
TONY BIN, 83, by Kampala	Dead		205	72	4/4	=Telegnosis (Jpn) ($1,206,175)	20,704,040
AFLEET, 84, by Mr. Prospector	Jpn	$45,570	190	77	2/6	=Sterling Rose (Jpn) ($1,836,315)	16,094,472
FUJI KISEKI, 92, by Sunday Silence	Jpn	N/A	185	62	4/4	=Mitsuwa Top Lady (Jpn) ($896,340)	12,624,488
SADLER'S WELLS, 81, by Northern Dancer	Ire	N/A	256	99	29/42	High Chaparral (Ire) ($3,436,410)	12,361,999
FORTY NINER, 85, by Mr. Prospector	Jpn	N/A	140	72	3/3	=Biwa Shinseiki (Jpn) ($1,241,175)	11,772,796
SAKURA BAKUSHIN O, 89, by Sakura Yutaka O		N/A	149	58	2/3	=Shonan Kampf (Jpn) ($1,837,226)	11,017,434
DEHERE, 91, by Deputy Minister	Jpn	N/A	295	147	17/29	Take Charge Lady ($1,388,635)	10,568,351
DANCE IN THE DARK, 93, by Sunday Silence	Jpn	N/A	173	49	4/5	=Tsurumaru Boy (Jpn) ($1,853,442)	10,340,904
COMMANDER IN CHIEF, 90, by Dancing Brave	Jpn	N/A	158	43	4/5	=Hagino High Grade (Jpn) ($1,072,502)	10,271,845
ROYAL ACADEMY, 87, by Nijinsky II	Ky.	$20,000	405	173	19/27	=Double Happiness (Jpn) ($655,798)	8,869,080
LAST TYCOON (Ire), 83, by Try My Best	Jpn	N/A	259	80	5/6	=Arrow Carry (Jpn) ($953,963)	8,820,865
END SWEEP, 91, by Forty Niner	Dead		240	138	5/12	South Vigorous ($1,406,883)	8,706,427
GULCH, 84, by Mr. Prospector	Ky.	$50,000	183	91	8/11	Nayef ($1,897,935)	8,495,720
JADE ROBBERY, 87, by Mr. Prospector	UAE	N/A	166	52	1/2	=Yamakatsu Suzuran (Jpn) ($939,438)	8,453,489
SOCCER BOY, 85, by Dictus		N/A	73	22	4/6	=Narita Top Road (Jpn) ($2,434,223)	8,350,998
KRIS S., 77, by Roberto	Dead		133	70	8/12	Symboli Kris S ($4,724,763)	8,085,603
WARNING (GB), 85, by Known Fact	Dead		132	51	9/17	=Sunningdale (Jpn) ($1,460,063)	7,976,671
MACHIAVELLIAN, 87, by Mr. Prospector	Eng	$116,480	137	55	10/15	Street Cry (Ire) ($4,323,777)	7,804,231
WILD AGAIN, 80, by Icecapade	Ky.	$50,000	149	80	8/11	Milwaukee Brew ($1,590,000)	7,584,189
WOODMAN, 83, by Mr. Prospector	Ky.	$40,000	348	141	13/15	Hawk Wing ($1,143,720)	7,465,266
COZZENE, 80, by Caro (Ire)	Ky.	$60,000	139	70	7/9	=Admire Cozzene (Jpn) ($2,149,552)	7,398,133
EL PRADO (IRE), 89, by Sadler's Wells	Ky.	$30,000	197	101	12/16	Medaglia d'Oro ($2,260,600)	7,265,083
A.P. INDY, 89, by Seattle Slew	Ky.	$300,000	149	80	12/17	=Aratama Indy (Jpn) ($566,460)	7,127,448
KINGMAMBO, 90, by Mr. Prospector	Ky.	$200,000	132	64	10/15	Mambo Twist ($775,075)	6,990,593
JOLIE'S HALO, 87, by Halo	Jpn	N/A	139	43	4/5	=Sankin Halo (Jpn) ($479,234)	6,861,866
TIMBER COUNTRY, 92, by Woodman	Jpn	N/A	173	45	2/2	=Admire Don (Jpn) ($1,345,757)	6,806,782
BROAD BRUSH, 83, by Ack Ack	Ky.	(MF100,000)	115	68	14/18	Farda Amiga ($1,248,902)	6,806,405
BLACK TIE AFFAIR (Ire), 86, by Miswaki	Jpn	$11,392	209	88	5/9	Evening Attire ($1,332,720)	6,682,187
LAMMTARRA, 92, by Nijinsky II	Jpn	$22,785	128	40	3/3	=Meisho Ramses (Jpn) ($814,765)	6,609,962
GONE WEST, 84, by Mr. Prospector	Ky.	$125,000	159	65	5/12	Came Home ($1,624,500)	6,481,314
TOKAI TEIO, 88, by Symboli Rudolf (Jpn)		N/A	79	19	2/3	=Tokai Point (Jpn) ($1,776,336)	6,478,895
STORM CAT, 83, by Storm Bird	Ky.	$500,000	142	62	18/26	Storm Flag Flying ($967,000)	6,438,339
MT. LIVERMORE, 81, by Blushing Groom (Fr)	Ky.	$40,000	190	85	8/16	Orientate ($1,412,970)	6,404,422
MEJIRO RYAN, 87, by Amber Shadai		N/A	139	42	1/2	=Win Blaze (Jpn) ($994,089)	6,113,654
FRENCH DEPUTY, 92, by Deputy Minister	Jpn	$75,950	133	76	7/13	Left Bank ($626,146)	5,950,850
RAHY, 85, by Blushing Groom (Fr)	Ky.	$100,000	134	70	5/10	Grass World ($942,159)	5,947,618
DYNAFORMER, 85, by Roberto	Ky.	$50,000	187	89	15/26	Perfect Drift ($695,120)	5,898,405
TAMAMO CROSS, 84, by C B Cross		N/A	109	26	1/1	=My Sole Sound (Jpn) ($664,415)	5,871,309
CRAFTY PROSPECTOR, 79, by Mr. Prospector	Ky.	$25,000	158	83	4/8	Agnes Digital ($1,238,986)	5,815,239
CARSON CITY, 87, by Mr. Prospector	Ky.	$35,000	197	101	11/16	Carson Hollow ($335,370)	5,775,524
HENNESSY, 93, by Storm Cat	Ky.	$45,000	242	102	5/13	Wiseman's Ferry ($766,552)	5,642,951
SILVER DEPUTY, 85, by Deputy Minister	Ky.	$40,000	167	94	6/6	Divine Silver ($640,236)	5,575,823
BUBBLE GUM FELLOW, 93, by Sunday Silence	Jpn	N/A	104	36	2/3	=Appare Appare (Jpn) ($1,294,603)	5,564,930
CRYPTOCLEARANCE, 84, by Fappiano	Ky.	$20,000	216	100	4/8	Volponi ($2,389,200)	5,421,184
THEATRICAL (Ire), 82, by Nureyev	Ky.	$100,000	128	51	8/14	Media Puzzle ($1,447,592)	5,419,346
THUNDER GULCH, 92, by Gulch	Ky.	$80,000	251	88	10/13	Spain ($569,502)	5,359,025
MR. GREELEY, 92, by Gone West	Ky.	$25,000	199	117	10/16	Nonsuch Bay ($439,362)	5,213,731
HELISSIO, 93, by Fairy King	Jpn	N/A	112	30	2/5	=Helenus (Aus) ($966,148)	5,137,992
FUSAICHI CONCORDE, 93, by Caerleon	Jpn	N/A	100	29	2/3	=Balance of Game (Jpn) ($954,594)	5,088,255
REGAL CLASSIC, 85, by Vice Regent	N.Y.	$10,000	236	111	8/11	Regal Sanction ($318,400)	5,048,983
DANCING BRAVE, 83, by Lyphard	Dead		62	23	2/2	=T.M.Ocean (Jpn) ($553,155)	5,041,781
CAERLEON, 80, by Nijinsky II	Dead		105	35	8/14	=Marienbard (Ire) ($1,693,245)	5,004,602
OUR EMBLEM, 91, by Mr. Prospector	Ky.	$7,500	79	35	4/11	War Emblem ($3,455,000)	4,999,768
SAINT BALLADO, 89, by Halo	Dead		169	69	9/9	Kite Hill Wind ($512,994)	4,983,295
UNBRIDLED'S SONG, 93, by Unbridled	Ky.	(MF75,000)	175	89	11/14	Agnes Sonic ($535,196)	4,958,884
PHONE TRICK, 82, by Clever Trick	N.Y.	$25,000	186	91	8/12	Caller One ($1,200,000)	4,957,368
SALT LAKE, 89, by Deputy Minister	Ky.	$15,000	207	106	3/6	Ocean Across ($456,398)	4,883,829
WHITE MUZZLE (GB), 90, by Dancing Brave	Jpn	N/A	54	21	2/3	=Smile Tomorrow (Jpn) ($1,397,351)	4,879,988
HOUSEBUSTER, 87, by Mt. Livermore	Va.	$7,500	143	76	7/8	Electronic Unicorn ($1,043,292)	4,867,475
SCAN, 88, by Mr. Prospector	Jpn	N/A	113	36	0/0	=Meiner Presto (Jpn) ($331,324)	4,856,568
SMART STRIKE, 92, by Mr. Prospector	Ky.	$30,000	106	67	6/14	Portcullis ($562,535)	4,845,230
GILDED TIME, 90, by Timeless Moment	Ky.	$20,000	179	90	8/15	Mandy's Gold ($715,404)	4,832,021

Leading General Sire by Year

Year	General sire	Earnings	Year	General sire	Earnings	Year	General sire	Earnings
2002	Dehere	$9,337,302	1954	*Heliopolis	$1,406,638	1906	*Meddler	$151,243
2001	Danehill	13,542,612	1953	Bull Lea	1,155,846	1905	Hamburg	153,160
2000	Storm Cat	9,269,521	1952	Bull Lea	1,630,847	1904	*Meddler	222,555
1999	Storm Cat	10,383,259	1951	Count Fleet	1,160,847	1903	*Ben Strome	106,965
1998	Deputy Minister	8,526,094	1950	*Heliopolis	852,292	1902	Hastings	113,865
1997	Deputy Minister	8,581,511	1949	Bull Lea	991,842	1901	Sir Dixon	165,682
1996	Palace Music	5,231,734	1948	Bull Lea	1,334,027	1900	Kingston	116,368
1995	Sadler's Wells	5,862,410	1947	Bull Lea	1,259,718	1899	*Albert	95,975
1994	Broad Brush	5,397,181	1946	*Mahmoud	638,025	1898	Hanover	118,590
1993	Danzig	5,082,552	1945	War Admiral	591,352	1897	Hanover	122,374
1992	Danzig	6,932,569	1944	Chance Play	431,100	1896	Hanover	86,853
1991	Danzig	6,997,402	1943	*Bull Dog	372,706	1895	Hanover	106,908
1990	Alydar	6,661,455	1942	Equipoise	437,141	1894	*Sir Modred	134,318
1989	Halo	7,525,638	1941	*Blenheim II	378,981	1893	Himyar	249,502
1988	Mr. Prospector	9,575,605	1940	*Sir Gallahad III	305,610	1892	Iroquois	183,026
1987	Mr. Prospector	5,877,385	1939	*Challenger II	316,281	1891	Longfellow	189,334
1986	Lyphard	4,045,447	1938	*Sickle	327,822	1890	*St. Blaise	189,005
1985	Buckaroo	4,145,272	1937	The Porter	292,262	1889	*Rayon d'Or	175,877
1984	Seattle Slew	5,361,259	1936	*Sickle	209,800	1888	*Glenelg	130,746
1983	Halo	2,773,637	1935	Chance Play	191,465	1887	*Glenelg	120,031
1982	His Majesty	2,675,823	1934	*Sir Gallahad III	180,165	1886	*Glenelg	114,088
1981	Nodouble	2,499,946	1933	*Sir Gallahad III	136,428	1885	Virgil	73,235
1980	Raja Baba	2,483,352	1932	Chatterton	210,040	1884	*Glenelg	98,862
1979	Exclusive Native	2,872,605	1931	*St. Germans	315,585	1883	*Billet	89,998
1978	Exclusive Native	1,969,867	1930	*Sir Gallahad III	422,200	1882	*Bonnie Scotland	103,475
1977	Dr. Fager	1,593,079	1929	*Chicle	289,123	1881	*Leamington	139,219
1976	What a Pleasure	1,622,159	1928	High Time	307,631	1880	*Bonnie Scotland	135,700
1975	What a Pleasure	2,011,878	1927	Fair Play	361,518	1879	*Leamington	70,837
1974	T. V. Lark	1,242,000	1926	Man o' War	408,137	1878	Lexington	50,198
1973	Bold Ruler	1,488,622	1925	Sweep	237,564	1877	*Leamington	41,700
1972	Round Table	1,199,933	1924	Fair Play	296,102	1876	Lexington	90,570
1971	Northern Dancer	1,288,580	1923	The Finn	285,759	1875	*Leamington	64,518
1970	Hail to Reason	1,400,839	1922	*McGee	222,491	1874	Lexington	51,889
1969	Bold Ruler	1,357,144	1921	Celt	206,167	1873	Lexington	71,565
1968	Bold Ruler	1,988,427	1920	Fair Play	269,102	1872	Lexington	71,515
1967	Bold Ruler	2,249,272	1919	*Star Shoot	197,233	1871	Lexington	109,095
1966	Bold Ruler	2,306,523	1918	Sweep	139,057	1870	Lexington	120,360
1965	Bold Ruler	1,091,924	1917	*Star Shoot	131,674	1869	Lexington	56,375
1964	Bold Ruler	1,457,156	1916	*Star Shoot	138,163	1868	Lexington	68,340
1963	Bold Ruler	917,531	1915	Broomstick	94,387	1867	Lexington	54,030
1962	*Nasrullah	1,474,831	1914	Broomstick	99,043	1866	Lexington	92,725
1961	*Ambiorix	936,976	1913	Broomstick	76,009	1865	Lexington	58,750
1960	*Nasrullah	1,419,683	1912	*Star Shoot	79,973	1864	Lexington	28,440
1959	*Nasrullah	1,434,543	1911	*Star Shoot	53,895	1863	Lexington	14,235
1958	*Princequillo	1,394,540	1910	Kingston	85,220	1862	Lexington	9,700
1957	*Princequillo	1,698,427	1909	Ben Brush	75,143	1861	Lexington	22,425
1956	*Nasrullah	1,462,413	1908	Hastings	154,061	1860	Revenue	49,450
1955	*Nasrullah	1,433,660	1907	Commando	270,345			

Leading Juvenile Sire by Year

Year	Juvenile sire	Earnings	Year	Juvenile sire	Earnings	Year	Juvenile sire	Earnings
2002	Storm Cat	$2,540,238	1981	Hoist the Flag	680,753	1960	*My Babu	437,240
2001	Hennessy	1,766,695	1980	Raja Baba	807,335	1959	Determine	413,765
2000	Honour and Glory	1,436,584	1979	Mr. Prospector	529,665	1958	*Turn-to	463,280
1999	Storm Cat	1,570,026	1978	Secretariat	600,617	1957	Jet Jewel	360,402
1998	Storm Cat	1,686,995	1977	In Reality	432,596	1956	*Nasrullah	422,573
1997	Phone Trick	1,737,764	1976	Raja Baba	419,872	1955	*Nirgal	293,800
1996	Capote	2,756,558	1975	What a Pleasure	611,071	1954	*Nasrullah	625,692
1995	Storm Cat	1,281,030	1974	What a Pleasure	387,748	1953	Roman	550,966
1994	Woodman	1,303,362	1973	Raise a Native	311,002	1952	Polynesian	341,730
1993	Storm Cat	1,567,979	1972	Bold Ruler	541,990	1951	Menow	274,700
1992	Storm Cat	1,729,366	1971	First Landing	551,120	1950	War Relic	272,182
1991	Blushing Groom (Fr)	1,295,629	1970	Hail to Reason	473,244	1949	Roman	227,604
1990	Woodman	1,310,633	1969	Prince John	418,183	1948	War Admiral	346,260
1989	Mr. Prospector	1,514,223	1968	Bold Ruler	609,243	1947	Bull Lea	420,940
1988	Caerleon	953,353	1967	Bold Ruler	1,126,844	1946	*Mahmoud	283,983
1987	Mr. Prospector	1,566,919	1966	Bold Ruler	941,493	1945	*Sickle	183,510
1986	Rajab	950,335	1965	Tom Fool	592,871	1944	Case Ace	230,525
1985	Fappiano	1,232,408	1964	Bold Ruler	967,814	1943	*Bull Dog	178,344
1984	Danzig	2,146,530	1963	Bold Ruler	343,585	1942	*Bull Dog	221,332
1983	Alydar	1,136,063	1962	*Nasrullah	574,231			
1982	Olden Times	948,900	1961	Bryan G.	428,810			

Leading Freshman Sire by Year

Year	Freshman sire	Earnings	Year	Freshman sire	Earnings	Year	Freshman sire	Earnings
2002	Grand Slam	$1,403,880	1992	Forty Niner	$578,567	1982	Seattle Slew	$666,755
2001	Valid Expectations	1,397,911	1991	Capote	1,185,886	1981	Turn and Count	283,279
2000	Honour and Glory	1,436,584	1990	Woodman	1,310,633	1980	Foolish Pleasure	536,783
1999	Cherokee Run	1,369,126	1989	Secreto	584,023	1979	L'Enjoleur	201,116
1998	End Sweep	947,013	1988	Chief's Crown	760,842	1978	Mr. Prospector	309,168
1997	Gilded Time	730,106	1987	Crafty Prospector	349,405	1977	Roberto	359,285
1996	Salt Lake	850,954	1986	Sportin' Life	781,754	1976	Raja Baba	419,872
1995	Farma Way	818,043	1985	Fappiano	1,232,408	1975	Al Hattab	217,630
1994	Red Ransom	817,550	1984	Danzig	2,146,530			
1993	Seeking the Gold	939,642	1983	Alydar	1,136,063			

Leading Broodmare Sire by Year

Year	Broodmare sire	Earnings	Year	Broodmare sire	Earnings	Year	Broodmare sire	Earnings
2002	Danzig	$20,820,788	1981	Double Jay	$3,453,131	1960	Bull Lea	$1,915,881
2001	Mr. Prospector	11,430,437	1980	Prince John	3,423,135	1959	Bull Lea	1,481,291
2000	Mr. Prospector	10,390,642	1979	Prince John	2,856,004	1958	Bull Lea	1,646,812
1999	Mr. Prospector	11,124,523	1978	Crafty Admiral	2,298,048	1957	*Mahmoud	1,593,782
1998	Mr. Prospector	9,364,191	1977	Double Jay	2,696,490	1956	*Bull Dog	1,683,908
1997	Mr. Prospector	9,829,817	1976	*Princequillo	2,763,189	1955	*Sir Gallahad III	1,499,162
1996	Seattle Slew	9,105,905	1975	Double Jay	2,233,642	1954	*Bull Dog	1,780,267
1995	Seattle Slew	8,291,630	1974	Olympia	2,292,178	1953	*Bull Dog	1,941,345
1994	Nijinsky II	7,606,160	1973	*Princequillo	3,079,810	1952	*Sir Gallahad III	1,656,221
1993	Nijinsky II	7,179,266	1972	*Princequillo	2,717,859	1951	*Sir Gallahad III	1,707,823
1992	Secretariat	7,345,089	1971	Double Jay	2,053,235	1950	*Sir Gallahad III	1,376,629
1991	Northern Dancer	6,030,243	1970	*Princequillo	2,451,785	1949	*Sir Gallahad III	1,393,104
1990	*Grey Dawn II	6,211,259	1969	*Princequillo	2,189,583	1948	*Sir Gallahad III	1,468,648
1989	Buckpasser	10,111,605	1968	*Princequillo	2,104,439	1947	*Sir Gallahad III	1,458,309
1988	Buckpasser	7,593,450	1967	*Princequillo	2,302,065	1946	*Sir Gallahad III	1,529,393
1987	Hoist the Flag	5,516,181	1966	*Princequillo	2,007,184	1945	*Sir Gallahad III	1,020,235
1986	Prince John	4,468,468	1965	Roman	2,394,944	1944	*Sir Gallahad III	1,024,290
1985	Speak John	5,187,865	1964	War Admiral	2,028,459	1943	*Sir Gallahad III	703,301
1984	Buckpasser	5,111,391	1963	Count Fleet	1,866,809	1942	*Chicle	533,572
1983	Buckpasser	3,479,749	1962	War Admiral	1,654,396			
1982	Prince John	3,072,150	1961	Bull Lea	1,632,559			

Most Times as Leading General Sire (1830-2002)

16   Lexington (1861-'74, '76, '78)
8   Bold Ruler (1963-'69, '73)
   *Glencoe (1847, '49-'50, '54-'58)
5   Bull Lea (1947-'49, '52-'53)
   *Leviathan (1837-'39, '43, '48)
   *Nasrullah (1955-'56, '59-'60, '62)
   Sir Charles (1830-'33, '36)
   *Star Shoot (1911-'12, '16-'17, '19)
4   Glenelg (1884, '86-'88)
   Hanover (1895-'98)
   *Leamington (1875, '77, '79, '81)
   *Priam (1842, '44-'46)
   *Sir Gallahad III (1930, '33-'34, '40)
3   Boston (1851-'53)
   Broomstick (1913-'15)
   Danzig (1991-'93)
   Fair Play (1920, '24, '27)
Before 1860, leading sire was determined by number of wins.

Most Times as Leading Juvenile Sire (1942-2002)

6   Bold Ruler (1963-'64, '66-'68, '72)
   Storm Cat (1992-'93, '95, '98-'99, 2002)
3   Mr. Prospector (1979, '87, '89)
   *Nasrullah (1954, '56, '62)
   Woodman (1990, '94, '98)
2   *Bull Dog (1942-'43)
   Raja Baba (1976, '80)
   What a Pleasure (1974-'75)

Most Times as Leading Broodmare Sire (1942-2002)

12   *Sir Gallahad III (1939, 1943-'52, '55)
8   *Princequillo (1966-'70, '72-'73, '76)
5   Mr. Prospector (1997-2001)
4   Buckpasser (1983-'84, '88-'89)
   Bull Lea (1958-'61)
   Double Jay (1971, '75, '77, '81)
   Prince John (1979-'80, '82, '86)
3   *Bull Dog (1953-'54, '56)
2   Nijinsky II (1993-'94)
   Seattle Slew (1995-'96)

Most Times as Leading General Sire in Consecutive Years (1830-2002)

14   Lexington (1861-'74)
7   Bold Ruler (1963-'69)
5   *Glencoe (1854-'58)
4   Hanover (1895-'98)
   Sir Charles (1830-'33)
3   Boston (1851-'53)
   Broomstick (1913-'15)
   Bull Lea (1947-'49)
   Danzig (1991-'93)
   Glenelg (1886-'88)
   *Leviathan (1837-'39)
   *Priam (1844-'46)
2   Bull Lea (1952-'53)
   *Glencoe (1849-'50)

   *Nasrullah (1955-'56)
   *Nasrullah (1959-'60)
   *Sir Gallahad III (1933-'34)
   *Star Shoot (1911-'12)
   *Star Shoot (1916-'17)
Before 1860, leading sire was determined by number of wins.

Most Times as Leading Juvenile Sire in Consecutive Years (1942-2002)

3   Bold Ruler (1966-'68)
2   Bold Ruler (1963-'64)
   *Bull Dog (1942-'43)
   Storm Cat (1992-'93)
   Storm Cat (1998-'99)
   What a Pleasure (1974-'75)

Most Times as Leading Broodmare Sire in Consecutive Years (1942-2002)

9   Sir Gallahad III (1943-'52)
5   Mr. Prospector (1997-2001)
   *Princequillo (1966-'70)
4   Bull Lea (1958-'61)
2   Buckpasser (1983-'84)
   Buckpasser (1988-'89)
   *Bull Dog (1953-'54)
   Nijinsky II (1993-'94)
   Prince John (1979-'80)
   *Princequillo (1972-'73)
   Seattle Slew (1995-'96)

All-Time Leading Sires

The sire lists on the following pages do not include steeplechase statistics.

All-Time Leading Sires by
By Progeny Earnings Worldwide

Through December 31, 2002

Name, YOB, Sire	Where Stood	Earnings
Sunday Silence, 1986, by Halo	Jpn.	$337,908,157
Danehill, 1986, by Danzig	Ire., Jpn., Aus.	133,423,610
Mr. Prospector, 1970, by Raise a Native	U.S.	94,556,277
Danzig, 1977, by Northern Dancer	U.S.	92,833,879
Caerleon, 1980, by Nijinsky II	Ire.	89,575,624
Afleet, 1984, by Mr. Prospector	U.S., Jpn.	89,503,594
Sadler's Wells, 1981, by Northern Dancer	Ire.	88,529,050
Seattle Slew, 1974, by Bold Reasoning	U.S.	78,114,138
Woodman, 1983, by Mr. Prospector	U.S., Aus.	74,576,922
Nureyev, 1977, by Northern Dancer	Fr., U.S.	74,011,480
Storm Cat, 1983, by Storm Bird	U.S.	72,927,408
Crafty Prospector, 1979, by Mr. Prospector	U.S.	70,500,878
Last Tycoon (Ire), 1983, by Try My Best	Ire., Aus., Jpn.	68,096,206
Wild Again, 1980, by Icecapade	U.S.	66,283,876
Deputy Minister, 1979, by Vice Regent	U.S.	62,606,354
Miswaki, 1978, by Mr. Prospector	U.S.	61,057,172
Alydar, 1975, by Raise a Native	U.S.	60,556,180
Forty Niner, 1985, by Mr. Prospector	U.S. Jpn.	58,359,720
Dancing Brave, 1983, by Lyphard	Eng., Jpn.	57,627,213
Crystal Glitters, 1980, by Blushing Groom (Fr)	Fr., Jpn.	57,408,888
Cozzene, 1980, by Caro (Ire)	U.S.	57,153,533
Dixieland Band, 1980, by Northern Dancer	U.S.	56,714,006
Nijinsky II, 1967, by Northern Dancer	U.S.	55,220,808
Kris S., 1977, by Roberto	U.S.	55,187,621
Theatrical (Ire), 1982, by Nureyev	U.S.	55,107,000
Seeking the Gold, 1985, by Mr. Prospector	U.S.	54,289,837
Relaunch, 1976, by In Reality	U.S.	54,084,974
Conquistador Cielo, 1979, by Mr. Prospector	U.S.	53,611,487
Cure the Blues, 1978, by Stop the Music	U.S.	52,944,330
Broad Brush, 1983, by Ack Ack	U.S.	52,690,857
Pleasant Colony, 1978, by His Majesty	U.S.	52,344,343
Rahy, 1985, by Blushing Groom (Fr)	U.S.	52,296,598
Gulch, 1984, by Mr. Prospector	U.S.	51,157,258
Bravest Roman, 1972, by Never Bend	Jpn.	50,823,708
Lyphard, 1969, by Northern Dancer	Fr., U.S.	49,862,321
Hector Protector, 1988, by Woodman	Eng., Jpn.	49,333,768
Mt. Livermore, 1981, by Blushing Groom (Fr)	U.S.	48,817,814
Green Dancer, 1972, by Nijinsky II	Fr., U.S.	48,604,645
Gone West, 1984, by Mr. Prospector	U.S.	47,529,367
Affirmed, 1975, by Exclusive Native	U.S.	46,903,331
Vice Regent, 1967, by Northern Dancer	Can.	46,791,535
Valid Appeal, 1972, by In Reality	U.S.	46,673,609
Mogami, 1976, by Lyphard	Jpn.	46,011,889
Royal Academy, 1987, by Nijinsky II	Ire., Jpn., U.S.	45,578,369
Bold Ruckus, 1976, by Boldnesian	Can.	45,035,969
Halo, 1969, by Hail to Reason	U.S.	44,440,632
Private Account, 1976, by Damascus	U.S.	43,827,078
Riverman, 1969, by Never Bend	Fr., U.S.	43,582,499
Devil's Bag, 1981, by Halo	U.S.	42,928,442
Silver Hawk, 1979, by Roberto	U.S.	42,807,699
Mr. Leader, 1966, by Hail to Reason	U.S.	42,731,581
Phone Trick, 1982, by Clever Trick	U.S.	42,234,848

All-Time Leading Sires
by Number of Winners Worldwide

Through 2002

Name, YOB, Sire	Where Stood	Wnrs
Danehill, 1986, by Danzig	Ire., Jpn., Aus.	957
Mr. Prospector, 1970, by Raise a Native	U.S.	729
Woodman, 1983, by Mr. Prospector	U.S., Aus.	711
Mr. Leader, 1966, by Hail to Reason	U.S.	667
Sadler's Wells, 1981, by Northern Dancer	Ire.	657

Name, YOB, Sire	Where Stood	Wnrs
Night Shift, 1980, by Northern Dancer	Eng., U.S., Ire.	618
Last Tycoon (Ire), 1983, by Try My Best	Ire., Jpn., Aus., N.Z.	612
Miswaki, 1978, by Mr. Prospector	U.S.	597
Clever Trick, 1976, by Icecapade	U.S.	591
Danzig, 1977, by Northern Dancer	U.S.	580
Green Dancer, 1972, by Nijinsky II	Fr., U.S.	580
Caerleon, 1980, by Nijinsky II	Ire.	577
Royal Academy, 1987, by Nijinsky II	Ire., Jpn., U.S.	577
Alzao, 1980, by Lyphard	Ire., Aus.	576
Bluebird, 1984, by Storm Bird	Ire., Aus.	575
Valid Appeal, 1972, by In Reality	U.S.	560
Be My Guest, 1974, by Northern Dancer	Ire.	559
Crafty Prospector, 1979, by Mr. Prospector	U.S.	557
Dixieland Band, 1980, by Northern Dancer	U.S.	554
Sunday Silence, 1986, by Halo	Jpn.	551
Allen's Prospect, 1982, by Mr. Prospector	U.S.	542
Cure the Blues, 1978, by Stop the Music	U.S.	539
Riverman, 1969, by Never Bend	Fr., U.S.	536
Geiger Counter, 1982, by Mr. Prospector	Can., U.S., Aus.	535
Wild Again, 1980, by Icecapade	U.S.	529
Pirate's Bounty, 1975, by Hoist the Flag	U.S.	524
Runaway Groom, 1979, by Blushing Groom (Fr)	U.S.	523
Phone Trick, 1982, by Clever Trick	U.S.	517
Nijinsky II, 1967, by Northern Dancer	U.S.	505
Southern Halo, 1983, by Halo	Arg., U.S.	505
Irish River (Fr), 1976, by Riverman	Fr., U.S.	501
Conquistador Cielo, 1979, by Mr. Prospector	U.S.	500

All-Time Leading Sires
by Stakes Winners Worldwide

Through 2002

Name, YOB, Sire	Where Stood	SWs
Danehill, 1986, by Danzig	Ire., Jpn., Aus.	204
Sadler's Wells, 1981, by Northern Dancer	Ire.	199
Mr. Prospector, 1970, by Raise a Native	U.S.	179
Danzig, 1977, by Northern Dancer	U.S.	176
Nijinsky II, 1967, by Northern Dancer	U.S.	153
Northern Dancer, 1961, by Nearctic	Can., U.S.	146
Nureyev, 1977, by Northern Dancer	Fr., U.S.	136
Riverman, 1969, by Never Bend	Fr., U.S.	127
*Sir Tristram, 1971, by Sir Ivor	N.Z.	124
Caerleon, 1980, by Nijinsky II	Ire.	123
Southern Halo, 1983, by Halo	Arg., U.S.	115
Lyphard, 1969, by Northern Dancer	Fr., U.S.	114
Storm Cat, 1983, by Storm Bird	U.S.	107
Seattle Slew, 1974, by Bold Reasoning	U.S.	105
Vice Regent, 1967, by Northern Dancer	Can.	104
Alleged, 1974, by Hoist the Flag	U.S.	94
*Nasrullah, 1940, by Nearco	Ire., U.S.	93
Dixieland Band, 1980, by Northern Dancer	U.S.	92
Sir Ivor, 1965, by Sir Gaylord	Ire., U.S.	92
Blushing Groom (Fr), 1974, by Red God	U.S.	91
Roy, 1983, by Fappiano	Chi., Arg., U.S.	90
Habitat, 1966, by Sir Gaylord	Ire.	89
Nodouble, 1965, by *Noholme II	U.S.	89
Woodman, 1983, by Mr. Prospector	U.S., Aus.	89
Relaunch, 1976, by In Reality	U.S.	88
Alzao, 1980, by Lyphard	Ire., Aus.	87
Nearco, 1935, by Pharos	Eng.	87
Green Dancer, 1972, by Nijinsky II	Fr., U.S.	86
Miswaki, 1978, by Mr. Prospector	U.S.	86
Valid Appeal, 1972, by In Reality	U.S.	86

All-Time Leading Sires by Percentage of Stakes Winners Worldwide
Through 2002

Name, YOB, Sire	Where Stood	SWs
Northern Dancer, 1961, by Nearctic	Can., U.S.	22.6%
Bold Ruler, 1954, by *Nasrullah	U.S.	22.4%
*Nasrullah, 1940, by Nearco	Ire., U.S.	21.8%
Round Table, 1954, by *Princequillo	U.S.	20.5%
Hoist the Flag, 1968, by Tom Rolfe	U.S.	19.9%
*Sea-Bird, 1962, by Dan Cupid	U.S.	18.9%
Nearco, 1935, by Pharos	Eng.	17.9%
Nijinsky II, 1967, by Northern Dancer	U.S.	17.7%
Blushing Groom (Fr), 1974, by Red God	U.S.	17.4%
Danzig, 1977, by Northern Dancer	U.S.	17.1%
Kalamoun, 1970, by Zeddaan	Ire., Fr.	17.1%
Hyperion, 1930, by Gainsborough	Eng.	17.0%
Nureyev, 1977, by Northern Dancer	Fr., U.S.	16.9%
*Mahmoud, 1933, by *Blenheim II	Eng., U.S.	16.6%
Never Bend, 1960, by *Nasrullah	U.S.	16.5%
Tentam, 1969, by Intentionally	U.S.	16.1%
Roberto, 1969, by Hail to Reason	U.S.	16.0%
Philately, 1962, by *Princequillo	U.S.	16.0%
*Amerigo, 1955, by Nearco	U.S.	15.7%
Mill Reef, 1968, by Never Bend	Eng.	15.7%
Sea Aglo, 1971, by *Sea-Bird	U.S.	15.6%
Alycidon, 1945, by Donatello II	Eng.	15.5%
*Heliopolis, 1936, by Hyperion	U.S.	15.3%
*Ribot, 1952, by Tenerani	Ity., Eng., U.S.	15.2%
Nedayr, 1935, by Neddie	U.S.	15.1%
Vice Regent, 1967, by Northern Dancer	Can.	15.1%
Mr. Prospector, 1970, by Raise a Native	U.S.	14.9%
Bull Lea, 1935, by *Bull Dog	U.S.	14.9%
Tanerko, 1953, by Tantieme	Fr.	14.8%
Eight Thirty, 1936, by Pilate	U.S.	14.7%
*Herbager, 1956, by Vandale	U.S.	14.5%
Native Dancer, 1950, by Polynesian	U.S.	14.4%
In Reality, 1964, by Intentionally	U.S.	14.4%
Chop Chop, 1940, by Flares	Can.	14.4%
Pelouse, 1951, by Pavot	U.S.	14.3%
Dante, 1942, by Nearco	Eng.	14.2%
*Royal Charger, 1942, by Nearco	Ire., U.S.	14.2%
Nearctic, 1954, by Nearco	Can., U.S.	14.2%
Terrible Tiger, 1965, by *Amerigo	U.S.	14.2%

All-Time Leading Sires by Number of Graded/Group Stakes Winners Worldwide
Through 2002

Name, YOB, Sire	Where Stood	GSWs
Danehill, 1986, by Danzig	Ire., Jpn., Aus.	119
Sadler's Wells, 1981, by Northern Dancer	Ire.	116
Mr. Prospector, 1970, by Raise a Native	U.S.	109
Danzig, 1977, by Northern Dancer	U.S.	97
Nijinsky II, 1967, by Northern Dancer	U.S.	97
Southern Halo, 1983, by Halo	U.S.	86
*Sir Tristram, 1971, by Sir Ivor	N.Z.	82
Northern Dancer, 1961, by Nearctic	Can., U.S.	77
Nureyev, 1977, by Northern Dancer	Fr., U.S.	75
Roy, 1983, by Fappiano	Chi., Arg., U.S.	69
Riverman, 1969, by Never Bend	Fr., U.S.	67
Caerleon, 1980, by Nijinsky II	Ire.	66
Storm Cat, 1983, by Storm Bird	U.S.	66

Name, YOB, Sire	Where Stood	GSWs
Lyphard, 1969, by Northern Dancer	Fr., U.S.	64
Blushing Groom (Fr), 1974, by Red God	U.S.	58
Seattle Slew, 1974, by Bold Reasoning	U.S.	58
Alleged, 1974, by Hoist the Flag	U.S.	57
Ghadeer, 1978, by Lyphard	Brz.	57
Habitat, 1966, by Sir Gaylord	Ire.	56
Rainbow Quest, 1981, by Blushing Groom (Fr)	Eng.	53
Cipayo, 1974, by Lacydon	Arg.	48
Alydar, 1975, by Raise a Native	U.S.	46
Fitzcarraldo, 1981, by Cipayo	Arg.	46
*Vaguely Noble, 1965, by Vienna	U.S.	44
Sir Ivor, 1965, by Sir Gaylord	Ire., U.S.	44
Zabeel, 1986, by *Sir Tristram	N.Z.	44
Green Dancer, 1972, by Nijinsky II	Fr., U.S.	43
Roberto, 1969, by Hail to Reason	U.S.	42
Damascus, 1964, by Sword Dancer	U.S.	41
Egg Toss, 1977, by Buckpasser	Arg.	41
Affirmed, 1975, by Exclusive Native	U.S.	40
Elliodor, 1977, by Lyphard	SAf.	40
Irish River (Fr), 1976, by Riverman	Fr., U.S.	40
Bluebird, 1984, by Storm Bird	Ire., Aus.	39
Caro (Ire), 1967, by Fortino II	Fr., U.S.	39
Foveros, 1976, by Averof	SAf.	39
Marscay, 1979, by Biscay	Aus.	39
Mill Reef, 1968, by Never Bend	Eng.	39
Royal Academy, 1987, by Nijinsky II	Ire., Jpn., U.S.	39

All-Time Leading Broodmare Sires by Progeny Earnings Worldwide
Through 2002

Name, YOB, Sire	Where Stood	Earnings
Northern Taste (1971), by Northern Dancer	Jpn.	$363,538,443
Mr. Prospector (1970), by Raise a Native	U.S.	174,162,949
Nijinsky II (1967), by Northern Dancer	U.S.	166,625,981
Northern Dancer (1961), by Nearctic	Can., U.S.	148,230,057
Tosho Boy (1973), by Tesco Boy	Jpn.	147,237,862
Lyphard (1969), by Northern Dancer	Fr., U.S.	138,170,107
Danzig (1977), by Northern Dancer	U.S.	125,362,702
Secretariat (1970), by Bold Ruler	U.S.	119,035,499
Blushing Groom (Fr) (1974), by Red God	U.S.	116,662,307
Alydar (1975), by Raise a Native	U.S.	116,442,751
Seattle Slew (1974), by Bold Reasoning	U.S.	110,410,232
Vice Regent (1967), by Northern Dancer	Can.	98,609,283
Nureyev (1977), by Northern Dancer	Fr., U.S.	97,923,314
Tesco Boy (1963), by Princely Gift	Jpn.	97,658,786
Halo (1969), by Hail to Reason	U.S.	96,528,858
Bravest Roman (1972), by Never Bend	Jpn.	95,931,681
Damascus (1964), by Sword Dancer	U.S.	95,435,468
Riverman (1969), by Never Bend	Fr., U.S.	91,322,765
Raise a Native (1961), by Native Dancer	U.S.	89,506,693
Partholon (1960), by Milesian	Jpn.	85,324,241
In Reality (1964), by Intentionally	U.S.	84,976,983
*Grey Dawn II (1962), by *Herbager	U.S.	83,484,552
Roberto (1969), by Hail to Reason	U.S.	83,474,614
Graustark (1963), by *Ribot	U.S.	82,786,353
Caro (Ire) (1967), by Fortino II	Fr., U.S.	80,156,154
Sir Ivor (1965), by Sir Gaylord	Ire., U.S.	78,622,765
Mill George (1975), by Mill Reef	Jpn.	78,564,190
*Vaguely Noble (1965), by Vienna	U.S.	77,903,926
Affirmed (1975), by Exclusive Native	U.S.	77,180,070
Green Dancer (1972), by Nijinsky II	Fr., U.S.	75,413,351
Prince John (1953), by *Princequillo	U.S.	75,254,538
Buckpasser (1963), by Tom Fool	U.S.	72,228,851
Dancer's Image (1965), by Native Dancer	U.S., Ire., Fr., Jpn.	72,150,131
Faberge II (1961), by Princely Gift	Jpn.	72,083,465
Tom Rolfe (1962), by *Ribot	U.S.	70,446,075

All-Time Leading Broodmare Sires by Graded/Group Stakes Winners Worldwide
Through 2002

Name, YOB, Sire	Where Stood	Graded SWs
Mr. Prospector (1970), by Raise a Native	U.S.	104
Nijinsky II (1967), by Northern Dancer	U.S.	104
Northern Dancer (1961), by Nearctic	Can., U.S.	101
Habitat (1966), by Sir Gaylord	Ire.	98
Northfields (1968), by Northern Dancer	Ire., Aus., SAf.	95
Riverman (1969), by Never Bend	Fr., U.S.	79
*Sir Tristram (1971), by Sir Ivor	N.Z.	73
*Vaguely Noble (1965), by Vienna	U.S.	73
Lyphard (1969), by Northern Dancer	Fr., U.S.	73
Prince John (1953), by *Princequillo	U.S.	67
Sir Ivor (1965), by Sir Gaylord	Ire., U.S.	65
Buckpasser (1963), by Tom Fool	U.S.	64
Graustark (1963), by *Ribot	U.S.	63
Roberto (1969), by Hail to Reason	U.S.	61
Sovereign Edition (1962), by Sovereign Path	N.Z.	59
Green Dancer (1972), by Nijinsky II	Fr., U.S.	57
Mill Reef (1968), by Never Bend	Eng.	57
Nureyev (1977), by Northern Dancer	Fr., U.S.	57
Round Table (1954), by *Princequillo	U.S.	57
Alydar (1975), by Raise a Native	U.S.	56
Secretariat (1970), by Bold Ruler	U.S.	56
Blushing Groom (Fr) (1974), by Red God	U.S.	55
Damascus (1964), by Sword Dancer	U.S.	55
Raise a Native (1961), by Native Dancer	U.S.	54
Seattle Slew (1974), by Bold Reasoning	U.S.	53
Shirley Heights (1975), by Mill Reef	Eng.	53
Busted (1963), by Crepello	Eng.	51
Key to the Mint (1969), by Graustark	U.S.	51
Vain (1966), by Wilkes	Aus.	50
Bold Ruler (1954), by *Nasrullah	U.S.	49
Alleged (1974), by Hoist the Flag	U.S.	48
The Minstrel (1974), by Northern Dancer	U.S.	45

All-Time Leading Broodmare Sires by Stakes Winners Worldwide
Through 2002

Name, YOB, Sire	Where Stood	SWs
Mr. Prospector (1970), by Raise a Native	U.S.	241
Northern Dancer (1961), by Nearctic	Can., U.S.	226
Nijinsky II (1967), by Northern Dancer	U.S.	221
Habitat (1966), by Sir Gaylord	Ire.	208
Lyphard (1969), by Northern Dancer	Fr., U.S.	180
Raise a Native (1961), by Native Dancer	U.S.	176
Hyperion (1930), by Gainsborough	Eng.	175
*Princequillo (1940), by Prince Rose	U.S.	170
Prince John (1953), by *Princequillo	U.S.	169
*Nasrullah (1940), by Nearco	Ire., U.S.	159
*Vaguely Noble (1965), by Vienna	U.S.	156
Riverman (1969), by Never Bend	Fr., U.S.	156
Nearco (1935), by Pharos	Eng.	154
Damascus (1964), by Sword Dancer	U.S.	153
Secretariat (1970), by Bold Ruler	U.S.	153
Northfields (1968), by Northern Dancer	Ire., Aus., SAf.	148
*Sir Gallahad III (1920), by *Teddy	Fr., U.S.	147
Sir Ivor (1965), by Sir Gaylord	Ire., U.S.	146
Fleet Nasrullah (1955), by *Nasrullah	U.S.	145
In Reality (1964), by Intentionally	U.S.	145
Graustark (1963), by *Ribot	U.S.	141
*Mahmoud (1933), by *Blenheim II	Eng., U.S.	137
Buckpasser (1963), by Tom Fool	U.S.	137
*Sir Tristram (1971), by Sir Ivor	N.Z.	132
Roberto (1969), by Hail to Reason	U.S.	129
Blushing Groom (Fr) (1974), by Red God	U.S.	125
Round Table (1954), by *Princequillo	U.S.	124
Green Dancer (1972), by Nijinsky II	Fr., U.S.	123
Big Game (1939), by *Bahram	Eng.	122
*Court Martial (1942), by Fair Trial	Eng., U.S.	121
Nashua (1952), by *Nasrullah	U.S.	121
*Grey Dawn II (1962), by *Herbager	U.S.	120
Halo (1969), by Hail to Reason	U.S.	120
Mill Reef (1968), by Never Bend	Eng.	120

Leading 2002 Sires by State and Province

Earnings of horses reported as bred in states and provinces, regardless of where the stallions stand or stood. Limited to sires with 2002 progeny earnings of $5,000 or more by horses bred in that state or province.

Alabama

Sire, YOB, Sire	Strs	Wnrs	Wins	SWs	Leading Runner (earnings)	2002 Earnings
Royal Empire, 1994, by Forty Niner	14	5	10	1	Nell's Niner ($43,930)	$118,353
Schembechler, 1987, by Damascus	11	6	9	0	Azooma ($22,527)	86,896
Silver Element, 1986, by Silver Supreme	5	4	7	0	Poppa Canihave Him ($22,000)	61,714
Double Leader, 1978, by Mr. Leader	11	2	3	0	Leading Ruler ($27,515)	47,943
Reack Boldly, 1983, by Ack Ack	6	3	5	0	Blacksher ($25,060)	37,882

Arizona

Sire, YOB, Sire	Strs	Wnrs	Wins	SWs	Leading Runner (earnings)	2002 Earnings
Society Max, 1982, by Mr. Prospector	49	30	52	5	Coyote Lakes ($152,920)	$654,300
Benton Creek, 1993, by Septieme Ciel	35	19	34	3	Knoll Lake ($47,000)	326,512
Fool the Experts, 1983, by Crafty Drone	19	11	22	1	Monrow ($118,265)	260,832
Mr. Expo, 1990, by Explodent	14	9	19	1	Ex Post Facto ($28,070)	159,261
Dance Centre, 1983, by Mr. Prospector	29	13	22	1	Lake Garda ($36,196)	157,938

Arkansas

Sire, YOB, Sire	Strs	Wnrs	Wins	SWs	Leading Runner (earnings)	2002 Earnings
Stutz Blackhawk, 1977, by Mr. Prospector	49	26	54	1	Princess Jen ($146,800)	$634,102
Proper Reality, 1985, by In Reality	46	22	43	0	Senate Trial ($32,738)	390,207
Perfect, 1992, by Affirmed	20	8	14	1	Earth Shaker ($93,250)	275,539
Big Pistol, 1981, by Romeo	32	19	31	0	Shoot It ($30,739)	237,995
Temperence Hill, 1977, by Stop the Music	27	10	17	0	Dirty Mike ($58,876)	224,016

California

Sire, YOB, Sire	Strs	Wnrs	Wins	SWs	Leading Runner (earnings)	2002 Earnings
In Excess (Ire), 1987, by Siberian Express	108	59	97	8	Icecoldbeeratreds ($353,800)	$3,020,464
Flying Continental, 1986, by Flying Paster	129	72	132	4	Continental Red ($540,000)	2,554,638
High Brite, 1984, by Best Turn	109	71	122	1	Super High ($410,748)	2,337,594
Bertrando, 1989, by Skywalker	114	52	83	6	Leanessa ($137,422)	2,200,955
General Meeting, 1988, by Seattle Slew	77	34	67	1	Fit for a King ($201,166)	2,082,191

Colorado

Sire, YOB, Sire	Strs	Wnrs	Wins	SWs	Leading Runner (earnings)	2002 Earnings
Fuzzy, 1982, by It's Freezing	10	5	7	2	Moro Grande ($53,699)	$129,083
Kennedy Factor, 1988, by Meadowlake	13	8	16	0	Super Step ($17,941)	99,049
Personal Flag, 1983, by Private Account	1	1	3	1	Personal Beau ($78,834)	78,834
Music Master, 1981, by Marshua's Dancer	4	3	3	0	Music Lover ($29,156)	60,878
Verzy, 1982, by Vice Regent	8	3	4	0	Darn Tootin ($31,610)	53,887

Connecticut

Sire, YOB, Sire	Strs	Wnrs	Wins	SWs	Leading Runner (earnings)	2002 Earnings
Departing Prints, 1982, by Dactylographer	2	1	5	0	Nantucketeer ($76,658)	$79,088
Skywalker, 1982, by Relaunch	1	1	1	0	Simply Striking ($19,680)	19,680
Mixed Emotions, 1984, by Northern Prospect	3	1	2	0	Double the Cash ($15,645)	19,461

Florida

Sire, YOB, Sire	Strs	Wnrs	Wins	SWs	Leading Runner (earnings)	2002 Earnings
End Sweep, 1991, by Forty Niner	195	120	207	3	South Vigorous ($1,406,883)	$7,365,020
Notebook, 1985, by Well Decorated	132	82	171	6	Booklet ($425,760)	3,606,002
Montbrook, 1990, by Buckaroo	104	60	119	7	Trust N Luck ($382,800)	3,513,445
Fortunate Prospect, 1981, by Northern Prospect	140	89	171	3	Bold World ($295,350)	2,885,212
Valid Expectations, 1993, by Valid Appeal	79	51	98	2	Expected Flirt ($208,495)	2,712,335

Georgia

Sire, YOB, Sire	Strs	Wnrs	Wins	SWs	Leading Runner (earnings)	2002 Earnings
Roaring Camp, 1991, by Forty Niner	17	8	13	0	Roaring Jade ($38,240)	$210,189
American Standard, 1980, by In Reality	1	1	7	0	Bluesthestandard ($148,810)	148,810
Gold Alert, 1983, by Mr. Prospector	2	2	5	0	Thunder Alert ($56,806)	70,775
Reach for More, 1981, by I'm For More	11	4	7	0	More Tell ($30,459)	64,858
Grub, 1983, by Mr. Prospector	4	2	2	0	Georgia Glory ($30,750)	46,140

Idaho

Sire, YOB, Sire	Strs	Wnrs	Wins	SWs	Leading Runner (earnings)	2002 Earnings
Peterhof, 1979, by The Minstrel	9	5	8	1	Lookn Mighty Fine ($113,980)	$169,563
Jestic, 1987, by His Majesty	14	6	9	0	L'Effaceur ($117,600)	169,331
L. B. Jaklin, 1984, by Jaklin Klugman	17	8	12	0	Crooked Key ($45,660)	151,116
Eastern Echo, 1988, by Damascus	1	1	2	0	Lookn East ($102,120)	102,120
Synastry, 1983, by Seattle Slew	17	6	13	1	Quiet Syns ($22,664)	89,648

Illinois

Sire, YOB, Sire	Strs	Wnrs	Wins	SWs	Leading Runner (earnings)	2002 Earnings
Cartwright, 1990, by Forty Niner	78	49	78	4	Medlin Road ($107,640)	$1,307,243
Spy Signal, 1979, by Hoist the Flag	34	16	25	0	Paddy's Spy ($101,802)	426,107
Cherokee Run, 1990, by Runaway Groom	2	2	4	0	Kokomo King ($365,690)	418,490
Buckbean, 1985, by Buckfinder	15	10	22	1	Silver Bid ($131,693)	383,656
Classic Account, 1985, by Private Account	24	7	10	0	Jamoke ($88,440)	382,827

Indiana

Sire, YOB, Sire	Strs	Wnrs	Wins	SWs	Leading Runner (earnings)	2002 Earnings
Crown Ambassador, 1994, by Storm Cat	25	15	20	3	Pass Rush ($199,540)	$575,233
Jacquelyn's Groom, 1988, by Runaway Groom	16	6	9	0	One Eyed Jackie ($37,902)	183,348
Presidential Order, 1993, by Danzig	19	4	6	0	Indy Energy ($44,654)	165,964
Fit to Fight, 1979, by Chieftain	4	3	6	1	Fight for Ally ($98,760)	144,525
Senor Speedy, 1987, by Fast Gold	2	2	6	1	Senorita Ziggy ($133,095)	143,807

Iowa

Sire, YOB, Sire	Strs	Wnrs	Wins	SWs	Leading Runner (earnings)	2002 Earnings
Sharkey, 1987, by Sharpen Up (GB)	14	6	11	2	Sharky's Review ($215,983)	$407,976
Blumin Affair, 1991, by Dynaformer	31	19	23	0	Yoyo Jabo ($56,992)	348,658
Evansville Slew, 1992, by Slew City Slew	4	2	8	1	Cowboy Stuff ($264,820)	279,778
Commemorate, 1981, by Exclusive Native	38	17	24	0	Everybuddysbizness ($17,487)	227,727
Dazzling Falls, 1992, by Taylor's Falls	11	7	11	0	Dazzmataz ($43,396)	208,727

Kansas

Sire, YOB, Sire	Strs	Wnrs	Wins	SWs	Leading Runner (earnings)	2002 Earnings
Gold Ruler, 1980, by Mr. Prospector	19	12	22	3	Raise a Booger ($111,956)	$214,741
Big Splash, 1988, by Ziggy's Boy	10	4	5	2	Discreetly Irish ($30,780)	116,441
Speedy Nijinsky, 1980, by Nijinsky II	9	2	5	0	Mr. Crimson ($44,283)	75,516
Scarlet 'n Gray, 1986, by Secreto	6	3	6	1	C T King Oftheroad ($44,730)	69,206
A. M. Swinger, 1986, by Swing Till Dawn	9	4	7	0	Swinging Janie Gal ($33,414)	64,197

Kentucky

Sire, YOB, Sire	Strs	Wnrs	Wins	SWs	Leading Runner (earnings)	2002 Earnings
Gulch, 1984, by Mr. Prospector	164	82	133	4	Nayef ($1,897,935)	$7,903,064
Kris S., 1977, by Roberto	105	53	88	3	Symboli Kris S ($4,724,763)	7,121,220
Dehere, 1991, by Deputy Minister	146	74	138	9	Take Charge Lady ($1,388,635)	6,771,659
Woodman, 1983, by Mr. Prospector	214	91	148	5	Hawk Wing ($1,143,720)	6,349,796
Storm Cat, 1983, by Storm Bird	129	57	99	11	Storm Flag Flying ($967,000)	6,255,215

Louisiana

Sire, YOB, Sire	Strs	Wnrs	Wins	SWs	Leading Runner (earnings)	2002 Earnings
Bag, 1989, by Devil's Bag	108	48	78	5	Kool K. J. ($100,515)	$1,089,841
Zarbyev, 1984, by Nureyev	54	31	68	3	Zarb's Luck ($141,700)	991,253
Belek, 1986, by Irish Tower	46	31	66	4	Highhopesemilyluck ($79,440)	832,159
Zuppardo's Prince, 1976, by Cornish Prince	76	28	51	1	Mike's Sister ($73,200)	791,294
In a Walk, 1989, by Chief's Crown	41	21	44	1	Walk in the Snow ($331,380)	767,563

Maryland

Sire, YOB, Sire	Strs	Wnrs	Wins	SWs	Leading Runner (earnings)	2002 Earnings
Allen's Prospect, 1982, by Mr. Prospector	120	72	140	2	Your Out ($269,850)	$2,703,827
Not For Love, 1990, by Mr. Prospector	70	47	96	5	Sheila's Prospect ($322,814)	2,600,824
Two Punch, 1983, by Mr. Prospector	94	59	94	3	Willa On the Move ($197,550)	2,392,594
Polish Numbers, 1987, by Danzig	82	53	101	5	Ghostly Numbers ($140,730)	1,993,991
Press Card, 1990, by Fappiano	69	39	82	4	Shiny Sheet ($180,400)	1,464,842

Massachusetts

Sire, YOB, Sire	Strs	Wnrs	Wins	SWs	Leading Runner (earnings)	2002 Earnings
Sundance Ridge, 1986, by Cox's Ridge	10	6	12	4	Sunlit Ridge ($79,100)	$276,243
Senor Conquistador, 1991, by Conquistador Cielo	5	4	7	2	Jill's Layup ($58,400)	101,380
A. P Jet, 1989, by Fappiano	1	1	5	1	Jini's Jet ($99,790)	99,790
Concorde's Future, 1989, by Concorde Bound	6	4	11	0	Future Settlement ($31,720)	96,420
Scarlet Ibis, 1986, by Cormorant	2	1	5	1	Little Time ($92,084)	92,234

Michigan

Sire, YOB, Sire	Strs	Wnrs	Wins	SWs	Leading Runner (earnings)	2002 Earnings
Service Stripe, 1991, by Deputy Minister	19	14	42	5	Secret Romeo ($352,970)	$1,075,590
Smart Strike, 1992, by Mr. Prospector	1	1	5	1	Tenpins ($560,629)	560,629
Matchlite, 1983, by Clever Trick	49	24	33	1	I Match Too ($49,278)	439,033
Monetary Gift, 1978, by Gold and Myrrh	25	15	27	1	Monetary Star ($97,562)	428,885
Native Factor, 1987, by Foolish Pleasure	35	20	37	1	Sailing Sal ($90,254)	394,312

Minnesota

Sire, YOB, Sire	Strs	Wnrs	Wins	SWs	Leading Runner (earnings)	2002 Earnings
North Prospect, 1980, by Mr. Prospector	11	10	19	4	Crocrock ($74,121)	$303,073
A. P Jet, 1989, by Fappiano	1	1	4	1	J. P. Jet ($100,436)	100,436
Acaroid, 1978, by Big Spruce	7	3	5	0	Adroitly Superb ($35,387)	87,267
Squadron Leader, 1992, by Storm Bird	4	2	3	1	Aashu ($42,173)	84,911
Aferd, 1976, by Hoist the Flag	9	5	8	1	Winaferd ($22,482)	81,410

Mississippi

Sire, YOB, Sire	Strs	Wnrs	Wins	SWs	Leading Runner (earnings)	2002 Earnings
Blushing Star, 1993, by Blushing John	2	1	1	0	Lil' Nancy Dickens ($13,200)	$15,800
Gold Angle, 1990, by Globe	1	1	2	0	Question of Gold ($12,717)	12,717
Schembechler, 1987, by Damascus	2	1	1	0	Doc's Image ($6,970)	9,170
To a Wild Kris, 1992, by Kris S.	1	1	1	0	Charlie Riddell ($9,105)	9,105
Mc Carthy, 1980, by Son Ange	1	1	2	0	McCarthy's Baby ($8,703)	8,703

Missouri

Sire, YOB, Sire	Strs	Wnrs	Wins	SWs	Leading Runner (earnings)	2002 Earnings
Victorious, 1980, by Explodent	14	8	15	0	Page Two ($40,600)	$155,873
Palmister, 1990, by Nijinsky II	16	7	14	0	Said So ($31,300)	87,781
Metfield, 1988, by Seattle Slew	1	1	4	0	Fort Metfield ($49,098)	49,098
Gemini Dreamer, 1980, by Great Above	2	1	2	0	Worththewait ($46,560)	47,048
Czar Nijinsky, 1982, by Barrera	6	2	3	0	Elektrona ($19,053)	41,675

Montana

Sire, YOB, Sire	Strs	Wnrs	Wins	SWs	Leading Runner (earnings)	2002 Earnings
Black Mackee, 1976, by Captain Courageous	35	19	29	0	Jocko Miss ($49,984)	$207,059
Mr. Badger, 1979, by Mr. Leader	10	4	10	0	Badger Creek ($16,129)	56,069
Pendleton Ridge, 1987, by Cox's Ridge	5	4	5	0	Miss Spokane Creek ($12,800)	40,217
Personable Joe, 1988, by Seattle Slew	5	3	6	2	Flying Lady Cue ($11,523)	30,527
Lil Tyler, 1983, by Halo	2	1	2	0	What a Bargain ($28,055)	30,483

Nebraska

Sire, YOB, Sire	Strs	Wnrs	Wins	SWs	Leading Runner (earnings)	2002 Earnings
Verzy, 1982, by Vice Regent	41	20	45	4	Oglala Sue ($99,480)	$503,659
Lytrump, 1985, by Lypheor (GB)	32	19	35	4	High Dice ($47,063)	215,656
Yankee Fan, 1984, by Our Native	18	9	13	1	Kinetic Bend ($38,490)	115,532
Bengal Bay, 1989, by Woodman	15	9	11	0	Talk Too ($19,064)	101,756
Crafty Ridan, 1986, by Crafty Prospector	12	7	14	1	Gotta Ridan ($32,283)	101,463

New Jersey

Sire, YOB, Sire	Strs	Wnrs	Wins	SWs	Leading Runner (earnings)	2002 Earnings
Northern Idol, 1986, by Northrop	47	25	43	1	Whoop's Ah Daisy ($123,430)	$1,012,920
Evening Kris, 1985, by Kris S.	30	16	33	1	Jersey Giant ($144,899)	756,921
Private Interview, 1992, by Nureyev	34	19	30	1	Beatrix ($67,962)	675,817
Pappa Riccio, 1980, by Nashua	36	20	32	0	So Excited ($84,928)	610,608
Not For Love, 1990, by Mr. Prospector	13	7	14	3	Summer Swing ($129,000)	498,996

New Mexico

Sire, YOB, Sire	Strs	Wnrs	Wins	SWs	Leading Runner (earnings)	2002 Earnings
Jack Wilson, 1988, by Encino	36	19	40	5	Runmore Mema ($192,218)	$990,279
Prospector Jones, 1992, by Mr. Prospector	50	29	48	4	Ciento ($193,183)	865,884
Full Choke, 1980, by Full Pocket	27	14	33	2	Star Smasher ($227,360)	593,311
Devon Lane, 1993, by Storm Cat	36	17	22	2	Stormy Lane ($97,314)	437,341
Ghost Ranch, 1994, by Gone West	8	3	13	1	Espeedytoo ($321,094)	387,192

New York

Sire, YOB, Sire	Strs	Wnrs	Wins	SWs	Leading Runner (earnings)	2002 Earnings
Dixie Brass, 1989, by Dixieland Band	71	39	81	4	Beautiful America ($241,363)	$2,168,045
Cure the Blues, 1978, by Stop the Music	78	46	86	1	Dat You Miz Blue ($287,671)	2,146,734
Distinctive Pro, 1979, by Mr. Prospector	90	49	81	2	Grey Comet ($150,375)	2,073,499
Belong to Me, 1989, by Danzig	56	32	64	2	I'm All Yours ($98,282)	1,535,544
A. P Jet, 1989, by Fappiano	70	38	69	0	Bella Rouge ($111,200)	1,319,285

North Carolina

Sire, YOB, Sire	Strs	Wnrs	Wins	SWs	Leading Runner (earnings)	2002 Earnings
Above Normal, 1985, by Great Above	29	19	40	0	Lark's Impression ($87,978)	$468,292
Goldlust, 1982, by Mr. Prospector	5	2	5	0	Gold Summit ($23,734)	47,757
Tricky Tab, 1986, by Clever Trick	2	2	4	0	Backinthebusiness ($27,991)	42,227
Fit to Fight, 1979, by Chieftain	2	2	4	0	Sari's Son ($13,705)	25,455
Robin des Pins, 1988, by Nureyev	1	1	2	0	After After After ($20,334)	20,334

North Dakota

Sire, YOB, Sire	Strs	Wnrs	Wins	SWs	Leading Runner (earnings)	2002 Earnings
Sun Man, 1983, by Exclusive Native	1	1	4	1	Suntana ($57,587)	$57,587
Aferd, 1976, by Hoist the Flag	7	4	7	1	Stilaferd ($21,289)	55,056
Northern Prospect, 1976, by Mr. Prospector	1	1	5	0	Northern Ace ($41,075)	41,075
Key Image, 1977, by Key to the Kingdom	5	2	3	0	Chippewa Day ($7,988)	19,667
Storada, 1985, by Alleged	6	3	4	0	Duffel's Macrena ($10,476)	19,255

Ohio

Sire, YOB, Sire	Strs	Wnrs	Wins	SWs	Leading Runner (earnings)	2002 Earnings
Harlan, 1989, by Storm Cat	4	2	4	1	Harlan's Holiday ($1,606,000)	$1,678,648
Stalwars, 1985, by Stalwart	58	32	63	1	War Judge ($45,380)	660,844
Mercer Mill, 1994, by Forty Niner	37	21	38	3	Mercer's Cool Cat ($50,231)	485,615
Cryptoclearance, 1984, by Fappiano	8	5	14	2	Ashwood C C ($156,179)	360,516
Al Sabin, 1989, by Alydar	15	11	22	1	Lady Cherie ($133,325)	349,530

Oklahoma

Sire, YOB, Sire	Strs	Wnrs	Wins	SWs	Leading Runner (earnings)	2002 Earnings
Slewacide, 1980, by Seattle Slew	63	31	49	4	Mr Ross ($138,750)	$776,900
Here We Come, 1988, by Mr. Prospector	59	33	65	2	Rockchalk Jayhawk ($80,290)	731,466
Sunrise Shower, 1985, by *Grey Dawn II	32	23	40	1	Singin N D Shower ($44,178)	429,457
Fair American, 1989, by Mr. Prospector	29	17	33	0	Orienta ($30,590)	294,504
Coordinator, 1992, by Deputy Minister	31	10	24	2	Tulupai ($101,935)	275,504

Oregon

Sire, YOB, Sire	Strs	Wnrs	Wins	SWs	Leading Runner (earnings)	2002 Earnings
Abstract, 1993, by Danzig	25	17	41	4	Absolutism ($65,175)	$250,720
Cisco Road, 1990, by Northern Baby	43	24	44	4	Poncho Power ($17,870)	180,744
Can't Be Slew, 1989, by Seattle Slew	28	14	19	3	Revillew Slew ($64,680)	156,762
Crowning Season (GB), 1990, by Danzig	31	12	18	1	Hopeful Season ($30,720)	100,791
Corslew, 1990, by Seattle Slew	3	2	3	0	Lethal Grande ($62,080)	72,752

Pennsylvania

Sire, YOB, Sire	Strs	Wnrs	Wins	SWs	Leading Runner (earnings)	2002 Earnings
Relaunch, 1976, by In Reality	2	1	3	1	With Anticipation ($1,507,700)	$1,513,374
French Deputy, 1992, by Deputy Minister	5	5	8	0	Nobo Jack ($481,114)	1,102,337
Judge Smells, 1983, by In Reality	66	33	52	0	Bensalem ($90,078)	774,007
Allen's Prospect, 1982, by Mr. Prospector	30	24	49	1	Sumerset ($83,811)	702,444
Carnivalay, 1981, by Northern Dancer	24	16	34	1	Malvern Rose ($182,440)	673,562

South Carolina

Sire, YOB, Sire	Strs	Wnrs	Wins	SWs	Leading Runner (earnings)	2002 Earnings
Kokand, 1985, by Mr. Prospector	51	29	46	1	Controls Free ($68,540)	$690,075
Miner, 1993, by Forty Niner	17	7	11	0	American Prince ($114,190)	290,745
Signal, 1993, by Forty Niner	9	4	6	0	Early Signal ($34,503)	91,132
All of a Sudden, 1980, by *Ramsinga	5	4	11	0	Sparky Diamond ($71,060)	86,488
Ride the Storm, 1994, by Storm Cat	4	2	4	0	Intelligent Male ($43,480)	72,960

South Dakota

Sire, YOB, Sire	Strs	Wnrs	Wins	SWs	Leading Runner (earnings)	2002 Earnings
Tabib, 1994, by Storm Bird	9	5	9	0	I'm Homebound ($9,265)	$30,846
Atlantian, 1989, by Alydar	5	2	3	0	Airingout ($12,004)	21,767
Mr. O. P., 1986, by Naskra	9	3	4	0	Senor Mas ($6,810)	20,502
Proud Northern, 1978, by Northern Jove	2	2	3	0	Prairie Runner ($12,368)	13,828
Special Invention, 1990, by Taylor's Special	6	2	3	0	Cruel Jewel ($8,244)	13,548

Tennessee

Sire, YOB, Sire	Strs	Wnrs	Wins	SWs	Leading Runner (earnings)	2002 Earnings
Tethra, 1992, by Cure the Blues	1	1	2	0	Southern Sweet ($54,795)	$54,795
El Prado (Ire), 1989, by Sadler's Wells	1	1	1	0	Clever Crawford ($17,230)	17,230
Rockamundo, 1990, by Key to the Mint	1	0	0	0	Bin Rockin' ($15,929)	15,929
Blushing John, 1985, by Blushing Groom (Fr)	1	1	1	0	Smokey John ($12,932)	12,932
Smilin Singin Sam, 1991, by Smile	3	1	2	0	Sweet Sonata ($6,660)	12,762

Texas

Sire, YOB, Sire	Strs	Wnrs	Wins	SWs	Leading Runner (earnings)	2002 Earnings
Hadif, 1986, by Clever Trick	90	54	97	6	Action Tonight ($162,029)	$1,580,816
Naevus, 1980, by Mr. Prospector	90	55	104	0	Worldly Navy ($129,236)	1,261,438
Rare Brick, 1983, by Rare Performer	66	43	77	5	Rare Cure ($117,080)	1,000,063
Leo Castelli, 1984, by Sovereign Dancer	49	23	41	1	Leo's Last Hurrahy ($326,848)	871,255
Marked Tree, 1990, by Forty Niner	76	39	82	0	Marked Wish ($46,630)	862,563

Utah

Sire, YOB, Sire	Strs	Wnrs	Wins	SWs	Leading Runner (earnings)	2002 Earnings
Four Seasons (GB), 1990, by Sadler's Wells	27	6	9	0	Chory Four ($61,950)	$152,454
Regal Groom, 1987, by Runaway Groom	1	1	3	0	Lovehermadly ($23,247)	23,247
Navegante (Chi), 1978, by Tantoul	2	1	1	0	Nintyfiver ($10,093)	12,793
Regal Intention, 1985, by Vice Regent	1	1	2	0	Startinover ($10,813)	10,813
Tychonic (GB), 1990, by Last Tycoon (Ire)	1	1	1	0	Tychonic Lady ($10,395)	10,395

Virginia

Sire, YOB, Sire	Strs	Wnrs	Wins	SWs	Leading Runner (earnings)	2002 Earnings
Gilded Time, 1990, by Timeless Moment	4	2	6	1	Mandy's Gold ($715,404)	$733,908
Secret Hello, 1987, by Private Account	20	13	25	0	Plain Clothes ($74,616)	390,371
Magic Prospect, 1987, by Mr. Prospector	25	15	28	0	Miroslava ($62,171)	376,940
Rahy, 1985, by Blushing Groom (Fr)	8	3	9	1	Bop ($170,983)	374,159
Danzig, 1977, by Northern Dancer	4	1	1	0	Star El Dorado ($310,053)	320,971

Washington

Sire, YOB, Sire	Strs	Wnrs	Wins	SWs	Leading Runner (earnings)	2002 Earnings
Slewdledo, 1981, by Seattle Slew	94	51	90	5	Taiaslew ($126,916)	$1,308,800
Petersburg, 1986, by Danzig	69	45	89	7	Sabertooth ($194,725)	1,114,596
Game Plan, 1993, by Danzig	59	28	45	1	Game Well Planned ($67,850)	627,382
Jazzing Around, 1984, by Stop the Music	68	33	56	0	Encino Ump ($31,480)	510,764
Son of Briartic, 1979, by Briartic	66	39	64	0	Gifted Daughter ($52,200)	502,039

West Virginia

Sire, YOB, Sire	Strs	Wnrs	Wins	SWs	Leading Runner (earnings)	2002 Earnings
My Boy Adam, 1987, by Encino	58	31	51	2	Adams Tribe ($105,030)	$876,024
Weshaam, 1983, by Fappiano	37	17	27	1	Shesanothergrump ($114,474)	595,710
Feel the Power, 1982, by Raise a Native	28	14	20	0	Power of Faith ($41,710)	342,465
Eastover Court, 1991, by Seattle Slew	5	3	8	1	Confucius Say ($243,540)	330,263
Native Slew, 1985, by Raise a Native	20	5	6	1	Simon Slew ($74,581)	183,376

Wisconsin

Sire, YOB, Sire	Strs	Wnrs	Wins	SWs	Leading Runner (earnings)	2002 Earnings
Armed Truce, 1981, by Bold Forbes	1	1	3	0	Auat ($27,440)	$27,440
Bold James, 1984, by Bold Reason	2	2	4	0	Adios Amigo ($13,353)	19,604
Ledge of Night, 1990, by Alleged	1	1	1	0	Funky Cowboy ($13,016)	13,016
Classified Facts, 1993, by Seattle Slew	1	1	1	0	Classified Breeze ($6,110)	6,110
Spa Dancer, 1988, by Saratoga Six	1	1	1	0	Wanda the Witch ($5,335)	5,335

Puerto Rico

Sire, YOB, Sire	Strs	Wnrs	Wins	SWs	Leading Runner (earnings)	2002 Earnings
Goldgalliano (Ire), 1986, by Mr. Prospector	45	25	68	1	Biodynamics ($91,435)	$704,902
Sejm, 1987, by Danzig	30	13	38	1	Mediavilla R. ($381,166)	617,884
Eqtesaad, 1991, by Danzig	32	22	61	1	Don Piero ($80,360)	521,575
Sunshine Jimmy, 1987, by Judge Smells	24	13	30	3	La Machina ($112,682)	475,214
Royal Merlot, 1993, by Forty Niner	21	14	33	2	Hispanica ($129,084)	403,033

Canada

Alberta

Sire, YOB, Sire	Strs	Wnrs	Wins	SWs	Leading Runner (earnings)	2002 Earnings
Regal Remark, 1982, by Vice Regent	76	39	72	4	R Three ($50,791)	$919,443
Parlay Me, 1985, by Irish Tower	16	9	16	2	Parose ($283,790)	443,484
Brass Minister, 1988, by Deputy Minister	61	32	49	1	My Birthday Boy ($44,862)	416,741
Exclusive Era, 1979, by Exclusive Native	24	16	27	0	Exclusive Run ($176,416)	383,010
Highland Ruckus, 1985, by Bold Ruckus	26	20	33	2	Viva Ruckus ($86,610)	365,294

British Columbia

Sire, YOB, Sire	Strs	Wnrs	Wins	SWs	Leading Runner (earnings)	2002 Earnings
Vying Victor, 1989, by Flying Paster	93	51	85	7	Elana d'Amour ($204,882)	$1,708,147
Maudlin, 1978, by Foolish Pleasure	56	41	82	3	Lord Shogun ($161,400)	1,214,236
Free At Last, 1989, by Wild Again	82	64	98	2	Grey Tobe Free ($89,006)	1,038,816
Katahaula County, 1988, by Bold Ruckus	48	28	51	7	Cruising Kat ($179,633)	994,243
Alfaari, 1989, by Danzig	53	32	61	1	Jamaari Girl ($75,564)	890,248

Manitoba

Sire, YOB, Sire	Strs	Wnrs	Wins	SWs	Leading Runner (earnings)	2002 Earnings
Circulating, 1990, by Bold Ruckus	30	13	23	1	Dawn Edition ($91,175)	$234,816
Cognizant, 1981, by Explodent	11	3	5	0	Cayenne Pepper ($30,233)	95,072
Boanerges, 1995, by El Prado (Ire)	7	4	6	2	Beau Pip ($46,041)	92,426
Renegade Spirit, 1988, by Gate Dancer	5	3	6	1	Speedy Treat ($53,418)	78,975
Polka, 1986, by In Reality	11	6	7	0	Palapeine ($19,113)	74,510

Ontario

Sire, YOB, Sire	Strs	Wnrs	Wins	SWs	Leading Runner (earnings)	2002 Earnings
Regal Classic, 1985, by Vice Regent	68	41	74	3	Runaway Love ($227,566)	$2,624,826
War Deputy, 1991, by Deputy Minister	57	33	61	2	Forever Grand ($362,761)	2,205,502
Bold Executive, 1984, by Bold Ruckus	74	34	53	2	Sambuca On Ice ($249,965)	1,957,910
Tejabo, 1985, by Deputy Minister	52	21	39	3	T J's Lucky Moon ($644,212)	1,930,838
Ascot Knight, 1984, by Danzig	60	30	46	1	Yatsko ($138,868)	1,724,751

Quebec

Sire, YOB, Sire	Strs	Wnrs	Wins	SWs	Leading Runner (earnings)	2002 Earnings
Slew City Slew, 1984, by Seattle Slew	1	1	5	0	Nikita ($110,055)	$110,055
Langfuhr, 1992, by Danzig	2	0	0	0	Fuzzy Star ($57,344)	74,394
Salt Lake, 1989, by Deputy Minister	2	2	2	0	Granbury ($42,026)	53,716
Marquetry, 1987, by Conquistador Cielo	1	1	2	0	Starlit Marque ($41,670)	41,670
Thunder Gulch, 1992, by Gulch	1	1	2	0	Down Goes Frazier ($39,145)	39,145

Saskatchewan

Sire, YOB, Sire	Strs	Wnrs	Wins	SWs	Leading Runner (earnings)	2002 Earnings
Royal Quiz, 1984, by Real Emperor	12	10	14	3	Picture the Answer ($25,058)	$81,115
Stop the Stage, 1985, by Gold Stage	10	7	15	4	Top Stage Dancer ($25,424)	78,729
Insistent Beat, 1987, by Vice Regent	13	6	10	1	Bionic Beat ($17,727)	52,643
Arctic Blitz, 1986, by Son of Briartic	8	6	9	0	Princess Briartic ($12,930)	48,060
Satellite Signal, 1990, by Valid Appeal	7	5	11	1	Testy Two ($14,655)	41,602

Profiles of Leading Sires

2002—DEHERE, 1991 b. h., Deputy Minister–Sister Dot, by Secretariat. Bred in Kentucky by Robert E. Brennan's Due Process Stable. 9-6-2-0, $723,712. Champion two-year-old male in 1993. Trained by Reynaldo Nobles, swept Saratoga Race Course's three major juvenile races culminating with the Hopeful Stakes (G1); also won the Champagne Stakes (G1) at two. At three, won the Fountain of Youth Stakes (G2) but broke down before the Triple Crown races. Retired initially to Ashford Stud and sold to Japan in 1999. Through 2002, sire of 43 stakes winners (6%), including multiple Grade 1 winner Take Charge Lady, 2000 Puerto Rican champion imported two-year-old colt Mi Amigo Guelo, and Belle Du Jour, highweighted two-year-old filly on the 1999 Australian Free Handicap.

2001—DANEHILL, 1986 b. h., Danzig–Razyana, by His Majesty. Bred in Kentucky by Juddmonte Farms. 9-4-1-2, $321,064. Highweighted sprinter at three on European Free Handicap. Retired to Coolmore Stud, Ireland, in 1990. From 1991 through 2001, shuttled annually to Coolmore Australia; in 2002, covered mares on Southern Hemisphere schedule in Ireland. Stood in Japan in 1996. Leading sire in Australia six times; leading sire in France 2001, '02. Through 2002, sire of 202 stakes winners (12%) and 12 champions. Best runners: European highweights Rock of Gibraltar (Ire), Banks Hill (GB), Desert King, Mozart (Ire), Tiger Hill; Hong Kong Horse of the Year Fairy King Prawn; and Australian champions Dane Ripper, Danewin, Catbird, and Merlene. In 2001, set a single-season record with 48 stakes winners. Died May 13, 2003, at Coolmore.

2000, 1999—STORM CAT, 1983 dk. b. or br. h., Storm Bird–Terlingua, by Secretariat. Bred in Pennsylvania by W. T. Young Storage Inc., raced for W. T. Young. 8-4-3-0, $570,610. Won Young America Stakes (G1) and finished second by a nose to champion Tasso in 1985 Breeders' Cup Juvenile (G1). Entered stud in 1988 at Overbrook Farm in Kentucky for initial fee of $25,000; by 2002, stood for American high of $500,000. Through 2002, sire of 107 stakes winners (13%), including North American champion Storm Flag Flying, European highweight Giant's Causeway, and major American winners Tabasco Cat, Cat Thief, and Sharp Cat.

1998, 1997—DEPUTY MINISTER, 1979 dk. b. or br. h., Vice Regent–Mint Copy, by Bunty's Flight. Bred in Canada by Mr. and Mrs. Morton Levy's Centurion Farms. 22-12-2-2, $696,964. Canadian Horse of the Year 1981; Eclipse- and Sovereign Award-winning two-year-old male. Half-interest purchased by Kinghaven Farm midway through two-year-old season; purchased by Robert Brennan's Due Process Stable prior to 1982 season. Entered stud in 1984 at Windfields Farm Maryland; relocated in 1988 to Brookdale Farm in Kentucky. Sire of 71 stakes winners (8%) through 2002, including 12 millionaires. Best include Racing Hall of Fame member Go for Wand; two-time champion and filly triple crown winner Open Mind; 1993 champion juvenile male and leading sire Dehere; 1998 Breeders' Cup Classic (G1) winner Awesome Again. Broodmare sire of more than 75 stakes winners.

1996—PALACE MUSIC, 1981 ch. h., The Minstrel–Come My Prince, by Prince John. Bred in Kentucky by Mereworth Farm. Sold for $130,000 to Nelson Bunker Hunt at 1982 Keeneland July and raced for partnership of Hunt and Allen Paulson. 21-7-5-3, $918,700. Group 1 and Grade 1 turf stakes winner in England and North America. Stood one season at Hunt's Bluegrass Farm in Kentucky, then moved in 1988 to Paulson's Brookside Farm. Shuttled between Kentucky and New Zealand for several years before relocating permanently in 1991 to Australia, where he stands at Rangal Park Stud. Was 1996 leading U.S. sire due to one horse—Cigar, a two-time Horse of the Year and leading American money winner ($9,999,815). Also sire of several important Australasian runners, including 1992 champion stayer Naturalism; also sire of South Africa two-year-old champion Palace Line.

1995—SADLER'S WELLS, 1981 b. h., Northern Dancer–Fairy Bridge, by Bold Reason. Bred in Kentucky by Swettenham Stud and Partners. 11-6-3-0, $713,690. Winner of 1984 Irish Two Thousand Guineas (Ire-G1) and Eclipse Stakes (Eng-G1). Stands at Coolmore Stud in Ireland. Leading sire in England in 1990, 1992-2002, a modern-record 11 consecutive years; leading sire in France in '93, '99. Through 2002, sire of 14 champions and record-setting 211 stakes winners (15%), including 116 group or graded winners. Best include champions High Chaparral (Ire), Montjeu (Ire), Galileo (Ire), Northern Spur (Ire), Old Vic, Barathea (Ire).

1994—BROAD BRUSH, 1983 b. h., Ack Ack–Hay Patcher, by Hoist the Flag. Bred in Maryland by Robert E. Meyerhoff and raced three seasons for Meyerhoff. 27-14-5-5, $2,656,793. Winner of Santa Anita Handicap (G1), Suburban Handicap (G1), etc. Syndicated and entered stud in 1988 at Gainesway Farm in Kentucky. Through 2002, sire of 80 stakes winners (15%), including 2002 champion three-year-old filly Farda Amiga, 1994 Breeders' Cup Classic (G1) winner Concern, $4-million-earner Broad Appeal (in Japan), and 2001 North American Grade 1 winners Include and Pompeii.

1993, 1991–'92—DANZIG, 1977 b. h., Northern Dancer–Pas de Nom, by Admiral's Voyage. Bred in Pennsylvania by Derry Meeting Farm and William S. Farish. Sold for $310,000 to Henryk de Kwiatkowski at the 1978 Saratoga yearling sale. 3-3-0-0, $32,400. Undefeated New York allowance winner before injury ended his career. Entered stud in 1981 at Claiborne Farm. Through 2002, sire of 177 stakes winners (19%), including champions in U.S., Canada, Japan, England, France, Ireland, Spain, and United Arab Emirates. Best runners: 1984 two-year-old male champion Chief's Crown, two-time Breeders' Cup Mile (G1) winner Lure, and 1991 Canadian Triple Crown winner Dance Smartly. Through 2002, broodmare sire of 102 stakes winners, including 2000 Kentucky Derby (G1) winner Fusaichi Pegasus.

1990—ALYDAR, 1975 ch. h, Raise a Native–Sweet Tooth, by On-and-On. Bred in Kentucky by Calumet Farm. 26-14-9-1, $957,195. Won 1978 Blue Grass Stakes (G1), Florida Derby (G1), etc.; second to Affirmed in all three 1978 Triple Crown races. Entered stud in 1980 at Calumet Farm and became leading American freshman sire of 1983. Sired 77 stakes winners (11%) in 11 crops, with career progeny earnings of $60,604,510. Best runners include Horses of the Year Alysheba (1988) and Criminal Type ('90), North American champions Easy Goer, Turkoman, and Althea, and 1991 Kentucky Derby (G1) winner Strike the Gold. Broodmare sire of 118 stakes winners and earners of $119-million through 2002. Died at age 15 at Calumet on November 15, 1990, following a leg injury of suspicious cause.

1989, 1983—HALO, 1969 dk. b. or br. h., Hail to Reason–Cosmah, by Cosmic Bomb. Bred in Kentucky by John R. Gaines. Purchased for $100,000 by Charles Engelhard at 1970 Keeneland July yearling sale. 31-9-

8-5, $259,553. Won 1974 United Nations Handicap (G1). Sold for $600,000 to stand in England, but sale fell through upon discovery he was a cribber. Syndicated for $30,000 per share and retired in 1974 to Windfields Farm Maryland. In 1984, was sold based on $36-million valuation and moved to Stone Farm in Kentucky. Sire of 63 stakes winners (8%), including champion and Racing Hall of Fame member Sunday Silence, all-time leading sire in Japan; 1983 Kentucky Derby winner Sunny's Halo; and champions Glorious Song and Devil's Bag. Broodmare sire of more than 120 stakes winners. Pensioned in 1997 and died at Stone Farm on November 28, 2000, at age 31.

1988, 1987—MR. PROSPECTOR, 1970 b. h., Raise a Native–Gold Digger, by Nashua. Bred in Kentucky by Leslie Combs II. Sold for a sale-topping $220,000 at 1971 Keeneland July sale to Abraham I. "Butch" Savin, for whom he won the Gravesend and Whirlaway Handicaps and set a Gulfstream Park track record, six furlongs in 1:07⅗, in 1973. 14-7-4-2, $112,171. Retired in 1975 to Savin's Aisco Farm in Florida and was top freshman sire of '78. Moved to Claiborne Farm in Kentucky in 1981. Sired 179 stakes winners (15%) and 15 champions through 2002, including Gulch, Forty Niner, Conquistador Cielo, and Woodman. Broodmare sire of more than 240 stakes winners. Leading broodmare sire five times. Died of peritonitis at Claiborne Farm on June 1, 1999, at age 29.

1986—LYPHARD, 1969 b. h., Northern Dancer–Goofed, by *Court Martial. Bred in Pennsylvania by Mrs. J. O. Burgwin. Sold for $35,000 as a weanling at 1969 Keeneland November sale; resold as a yearling in Ireland for $38,000. 12-6-1-0, $195,427. Became one of Europe's top milers, winning 1972 Prix de la Foret and Prix Jacques le Marois while racing for Mrs. Pierre Wertheimer. Retired in 1973 and stood five seasons in France, where he was twice leading broodmare sire and subsequently was twice leading broodmare sire. For 1978 season, moved to Gainesway Farm in Kentucky and syndicated. Sired 115 stakes winners (14%) and eight champions, including Manila, Dancing Brave, and Three Troikas (Fr). Broodmare sire of 185 stakes winners through 2002. Pensioned at Gainesway in 1996.

1985—BUCKAROO, 1975 b. h., Buckpasser–Stepping High, by No Robbery. Bred in Kentucky by Greentree Stud. 18-5-5-1, $138,604. Won 1978 Saranac (G2) and Peter Pan (G3) Stakes. Retired to Greentree in 1980. Sold privately in 1985 to Gary and Stephen Wolfson and moved to Happy Valley Farm in Florida. Relocated in 1991 to Florida Stallion Station and again in '92 to Bridlewood Farm near Ocala. Leading sire of 1985 due largely to Horse of the Year and Kentucky Derby (G1) winner Spend a Buck, who received a $2-million bonus for winning the Jersey Derby (G3). Also sired millionaires Roo Art and Lite the Fuse among 29 stakes winners from 17 crops. Died of kidney failure on July 30, 1996, at the University of Florida School of Veterinary Medicine at age 21.

1984—SEATTLE SLEW, 1974 dk. b. or br. h., Bold Reasoning–My Charmer, by Poker. Bred in Kentucky by Ben Castleman. Sold at 1975 Fasig-Tipton Kentucky July sale for $17,500 to partnership of Mickey and Karen Taylor and Jim and Sally Hill. 17-14-2-0, $1,208,726. Champion at two, three, and four, Horse of the Year at three; in 1977, became first to win American Triple Crown while undefeated. Retired in 1979 to Spendthrift Farm in Kentucky but later relocated to Three Chimneys Farm; moved to Hill 'n' Dale Farm shortly before his death. Sired 105 stakes winners (10%) through

2002, including Horse of the Year and top sire A.P. Indy, champions Slew o' Gold, Vindication, Surfside, Swale, Capote, and Landaluce. First to sire winners of $5-million in a single season (1984). Noted sire of sires. Broodmare sire of Cigar; twice leading broodmare sire; broodmare sire of 109 stakes winners, including nine champions, through 2002. Died on May 7, 2002, at Hill 'n' Dale Farm in Kentucky, at age 28.

1982—HIS MAJESTY, 1968 b. h., *Ribot–Flower Bowl, by *Alibhai. Bred in Kentucky by Mr. and Mrs. John W. Galbreath. Full brother to Graustark. 22-5-6-3, $99,430. Only stakes victory was 1971 Everglades Stakes. Syndicated for $2-million valuation and retired in 1974 to his birthplace, Darby Dan Farm, where he remained throughout a 23-season stud career. Sired 59 stakes winners (9%) and champions in U.S., Italy, Canada, Panama, and Mexico. Best includes 1981 champion and dual-classic winner Pleasant Colony, 1991 grass champion Tight Spot, and $2-million earner Majesty's Prince. Maternal grandsire of leading international sire Danehill and 90 other stakes winners. Died at Darby Dan on September 21, 1995, at age 27.

1981—NODOUBLE, 1965 ch. h., *Noholme II–Abla-Jay, by Double Jay. Bred in Arkansas by Gene Goff. 42-13-11-5, $846,749. Two-time champion handicap horse, 1969-'70; known as "Arkansas Traveler" because he won stakes in seven states. Winner of 1969 Santa Anita Handicap, '70 Metropolitan Handicap, etc. Retired in 1971 and stood at four different farms from California to Florida before moving in '86 to Three Chimneys Farm in Kentucky. Sired 91 stakes winners (14%), including two-time Canadian Horse of the Year Overskate, Japan Cup (Jpn-G1) winner Mairzy Doates, and world record-setter Double Discount. Broodmare sire of 88 stakes winners through 2002. Pensioned in 1988. Died of colic at Three Chimneys Farm on April 26, 1990, at age 25.

1980—RAJA BABA, 1968 b. h., Bold Ruler–Missy Baba, by *My Babu. Bred in Kentucky by Michael G. Phipps. 41-7-12-9, $123,287. Modest stakes winner retired in 1974 to Hermitage Farm in Kentucky and sired 62 stakes winners (10%), including 1987 champion and Breeders' Cup Distaff (G1) winner Sacahuista, two-time Mexican Horse of the Year Gran Zar (Mex), and Canadian champion sprinter Summer Mood. Broodmare sire of more than 75 stakes winners of $64.7-million through 2002. Pensioned at Hermitage in 1987 and died October 9, 2002.

1979, 1978—EXCLUSIVE NATIVE, 1965 ch. h., Raise a Native–Exclusive, by Shut Out. Bred in Florida by Harbor View Farm. 13-4-4-3, $169,013. Won 1968 Arlington Classic Stakes but far better sire than racehorse. Entered stud in 1969 at Spendthrift Farm in Kentucky for a fee of $1,500. Eventually sired 66 stakes winners (13%), including Racing Hall of Fame members Affirmed and Genuine Risk—the former an American Triple Crown winner, the latter only the second filly to win the Kentucky Derby (G1). Syndicated in 1972 for $1.8-million. Broodmare sire of 97 stakes winners. Died of cancer at Spendthrift Farm on April 21, 1983, at age 18.

1977—DR. FAGER, 1964 b. h., Rough'n Tumble–Aspidistra, by Better Self. Bred in Florida by William L. McKnight's Tartan Farms. 22-18-2-1, $1,002,642. Horse of the Year in 1968. Set world record mile of 1:32⅕ at Arlington Park carrying 134 pounds. Syndicated for $3.2-million in 1968 and entered stud the next year at Tartan Farms in Florida, where he sired nine crops. His 35 stakes winners (13%) include 1978 champion sprinter Dr. Patches, '75 champion juvenile filly Dearly Precious, and '77 Canadian Horse of the Year L'Alezane. Broodmare sire of 98 stakes winners, including notable sires Fappiano and Quiet American. Inducted into the Racing Hall of Fame in 1971. Died at Tartan Farms on August 5, 1976, at age 12, from torsion of the large colon.

1976, 1975—WHAT A PLEASURE, 1965 ch. h., Bold Ruler–Grey Flight, by *Mahmoud. Bred in Kentucky by Wheatley Stable. 18-6-5-2, $164,935. Won Hopeful Stakes and ranked fourth on 1967 Experimental Free Handicap. Sold in 1968 to Howard Sams. Entered stud the following year at Sams's Waldemar Farm in Florida. Sired 50 stakes winners (10%), including Foolish Pleasure and Honest Pleasure, juvenile champions in 1974 and '75, respectively. Syndicated in 1976 for $8-million. Ranked twice as top juvenile sire by money won. Broodmare sire of 82 stakes winners, including champion juveniles Gilded Time and Tasso. Died of a heart attack at Waldemar Farm on March 13, 1983, at age 18.

1974—T. V. LARK, 1957 b. h., *Indian Hemp–Miss Larksfly, by Heelfly. Bred in California by Dr. Walter D. Lucas and raised in a half-acre paddock. Sold for $10,000 to Chase McCoy at 1958 Del Mar yearling sale. 72-19-13-6, $902,194. Champion grass horse of 1961 with victory over Kelso in Washington, D.C., International. Sold for $600,000 to syndicate headed by Preston Madden and retired in 1963 to Hamburg Place in Kentucky. First crop included world record-setter Pink Pigeon. Sired 53 stakes winners and 35% stakes horses from winners. Did not establish an enduring male line but became broodmare sire of Racing Hall of Fame filly Chris Evert. Died at Hamburg on March 6, 1975, at age 18.

1973, 1963-'69—BOLD RULER, 1954 dk. b. h., 1954, *Nasrullah–Miss Disco, by Discovery. Bred in Kentucky by Wheatley Stable. 33-23-4-2, $764,204. Racing Hall of Fame member, 1957 Horse of the Year. Retired to Claiborne Farm in 1959 and began his reign as perennial leading sire four years later. Became the dominant force in American breeding throughout the 1960s and '70s, leading by progeny earnings seven times in succession, eight times overall—more than any other 20th-century stallion. Also six times leading juvenile sire. Sired 43% stakes horses from starters, 82 stakes winners (22%), and 11 champions, among them Secretariat, Gamely, Wajima, and Bold Bidder. Broodmare sire of 119 stakes winners, although he never led in that category. Died of cancer at Claiborne on July 12, 1971, at age 17.

1972—ROUND TABLE, 1954 b. h., *Princequillo–*Knight's Daughter, by Sir Cosmo. Bred in Kentucky by Claiborne Farm. Sold privately in 1957 to Travis Kerr. 66-43-8-5, $1,749,869. Set or equaled 16 track, American, and world records. Horse of the Year in 1958, three-time champion grass horse, and world's leading money-earner at retirement. Entered stud in 1960 at Claiborne Farm. Made international impact, siring 83 stakes winners (21%) from 19 crops, including champions in England, Ireland, France, and Canada. Did not establish powerful male line, although several sons proved useful stallions. Broodmare sire of 125 stakes winners, including champions Outstandingly, De La Rose, and Bowl Game. Inducted into Racing Hall of Fame in June 1972. Pensioned in 1978 and died at Claiborne on June 13, 1987, at age 33.

1971—NORTHERN DANCER, 1961 b. h., Nearctic–Natalma, by Native Dancer. Bred in Canada by E. P. Taylor. 18-14-2-2, $580,647. Champion in Canada and U.S., won 1964 Kentucky Derby, Preakness Stakes. Entered stud in 1965 at Windfields Farm in Canada but later relocated to Windfields's Maryland division. Syndicated in 1970 for $2.4-million. Became one of the most sought-after commercial stallions of all time, with

numerous offspring selling at auction for $1-million and more. Leading sire in England four times. Leading U.S. broodmare sire in 1991. Former international leader by stakes winners, with 146—including 23 champions and noted sires Sadler's Wells, Nijinsky II, Danzig, Lyphard, Nureyev, and Storm Bird. Daughters produced 232 stakes winners (19 champions) through 2002. Inducted into the Racing Hall of Fame in 1976. Died of colic at Windfields in Maryland on November 16, 1990, at age 29. Buried at Windfields, Canada.

1970—HAIL TO REASON, 1958 br. h., *Turn-to–Nothirdchance, by Blue Swords. Bred in Kentucky by Bieber-Jacobs Stable. 18-9-2-2, $328,434. Champion at two. Sesamoid injury forced retirement in 1961 to Hagyard Farm in Kentucky. Syndicated for $1,085,000. Leading sire and juvenile sire of 1970, and also among leading sires in England and France. Sired 43 stakes winners (13%), including 1970 co-Horse of the Year Personality and fillies Trillion, Straight Deal, and Regal Gleam. Several sons became top sires, including two-time American leader Halo and 1972 Epsom Derby winner Roberto, both of whom kept his male line alive. Daughters produced millionaires Allez France, Triptych, Royal Glint, Colonial Waters, and 110 additional stakes winners. Died at Hagyard on February 24, 1976, at age 18.

1962, 1959-'60, 1955-'56—*NASRULLAH, 1940 b. h., Nearco–Mumtaz Begum, by *Blenheim II. Bred in Ireland by the Aga Khan. 10-5-1-2, $15,259. Champion at two in England and classic-placed at three but generally a disappointment due to tendency to sulk before and during races. Entered stud in 1944 at Great Barton Stud in England; sold and relocated the next year to Brownstown Stud in Ireland. Purchased in 1950 for approximately $400,000 by A. B. Hancock on behalf of an American syndicate and sent to Claiborne Farm in Kentucky for '51 breeding season. Sired 93 international stakes winners (22%) and established an enduring male line through Racing Hall of Fame son Bold Ruler and English-raced sons Red God and Grey Sovereign. Reigned five times as leading sire in America and once in England. Broodmare sire of 159 stakes winners. Suffered fatal heart attack at Claiborne on May 26, 1959, at age 19.

1961—*AMBIORIX, 1946 dk. b. h., Tourbillon–Lavendula, by Pharos. Bred in France by Marcel Boussac. 7-4-2-0, $25,165. Champion at two in France, winning Grand Criterium, and added the Prix Lupin at three before being narrowly beaten in the Prix du Jockey-Club (French Derby). Three-quarter brother to champion *My Babu. After failing to acquire *My Babu, A. B. Hancock purchased *Ambiorix in 1949 for syndication in America. Entered stud at Claiborne Farm in Kentucky the following year and ultimately sired 51 stakes winners (12%), including champion two- and three-year-old filly High Voltage. Leading sire of 1961 when runners included major winners Ambiopoise, Hitting Away, Make Sail, and Sarcastic. Also a successful broodmare sire, leading the list in England in 1963. Pensioned in 1972 and died at Claiborne in January 1975 at age 29.

1958, 1957—*PRINCEQUILLO, 1940 b. h., Prince Rose–*Cosquilla, by *Papyrus. Bred in England by American Laudy Lawrence. 33-12-5-7, $96,550. Imported to U.S. as a yearling, leased to Anthony Pelleteri at two, and claimed for $2,500 by future Racing Hall of Fame trainer Horatio Luro for Dimitri Djordjaze. Became a top stayer, with victories including the 1943 Jockey Club Gold Cup. Retired in 1945 to A. B. Hancock's Ellerslie Farm in Virginia for $250 fee. Moved two years later to Claiborne Farm in Kentucky. Racing Hall of Fame members Round Table and Hill Prince were among his 65 stakes winners (13%), and *Princequillo arguably was one of America's two greatest broodmare sires (along with *Sir Gallahad III) of the 20th century. Ranked eight times atop broodmare sire list; his daughters produced 170 stakes winners, including champions Secretariat, Mill Reef, Fort Marcy, Key to the Mint, and Bold Lad. Died at Claiborne on July 18, 1964, at age 24.

1954, 1950—*HELIOPOLIS, 1936 b. h., Hyperion–Drift, by Swynford. Bred in England by Lord Derby. 15-5-2-1, $71,216, stakes winner at two and three in England, third in 1939 Epsom Derby. Imported to America the following year by Charles B. Shaffer and finished last after sulking in his only U.S. start, an allowance race at Hialeah Park. Retired in 1941 to Shaffer's Coldstream Stud in Kentucky. Sold in 1951 to Henry Knight and relocated to Almahurst Farm. Among his 53 stakes winners (15%) were 1954 Belmont Stakes victor and champion High Gun, and champion fillies Grecian Queen, Parlo, Berlo, and Aunt Jinny. Died at Almahurst on April 2, 1959, at age 23.

1953, 1952, 1947–'49—BULL LEA, 1935 br. h., *Bull Dog–Rose Leaves, by Ballot. Bred in Kentucky by Coldstream Stud. 27-10-7-3, $94,825. Sold as a yearling for $14,000 to Calumet Farm. A moderately accomplished racehorse, he won the Widener Handicap and Blue Grass Stakes. Retired to Calumet in 1940 for a $750 fee and became one of the greatest American sires of all time. Sired 57 stakes winners (15%), including a record seven Racing Hall of Fame members—Citation, Armed, Coaltown, Bewitch, Two Lea, Real Delight, and Twilight Tear. In 1947, became first stallion with single-season progeny earnings of $1-million. Four-time leading broodmare sire of 105 stakes winners. Died and buried at Calumet on June 16, 1964, at age 29.

1951—COUNT FLEET, 1940 br. h., Reigh Count–Quickly, by Haste. Bred in Kentucky by Mrs. John D. Hertz. 21-16-4-1, $250,300. In the Hertz colors, won 1943 Triple Crown, taking Belmont Stakes by 25 lengths. Retired in 1944 to Stoner Creek Farm near Paris, Kentucky, where he remained for the next 30 years. Outstanding sire and even better broodmare sire, leading in the latter category in 1963 and ranking in the top five ten times. Among his 39 stakes winners (9%) were back-to-back Horses of the Year and Belmont Stakes winners Counterpoint (1951) and One Count ('52). Daughters produced 118 stakes winners and seven champions, including Racing Hall of Fame member Kelso. Pensioned in 1966. Count Fleet was inducted into the Racing Hall of Fame in 1961. He died at Stoner Creek on December 3, 1973, at age 33.

1946—*MAHMOUD, 1933 gr. h., *Blenheim II–Mah Mahal, by Gainsborough. Bred in France by the Aga Khan. 11-4-2-3, $86,439. Champion at three in England in 1936 when he won the Epsom Derby in record time. Entered stud at Newmarket in 1937. Purchased in 1940 by C. V. Whitney for about $85,000 and imported to stand at his Kentucky farm. Prior to his arrival, gray Thoroughbreds were spurned by many prominent American breeders, but *Mahmoud made the color acceptable. Sired 66 stakes winners, including U.S. champions Oil Capitol, The Axe II, and First Flight, and European champions *Majideh and Donatella. Leading broodmare sire of 1957 and among leaders throughout the 1960s. Daughters produced 139 stakes winners, including Racing Hall of Fame members *Gallant Man and Silver Spoon. Died at C. V. Whitney Farm on September 18, 1962, at age 29.

1945—WAR ADMIRAL, 1934 br. h., Man o' War–Brushup, by Sweep. Bred in Kentucky by Samuel D. Riddle and

raced for Glen Riddle Stable. 26-21-3-1, $273,240. Racing Hall of Fame runner is generally acknowledged as Man o' War's best son, both on the track and in the stud. Won 1937 Triple Crown and stood alongside Man o' War at Faraway Farm in Kentucky. Sire of 40 stakes winners (11%), including 1945 Horse of the Year Busher, champion Blue Peter, and the great racemares-broodmares Searching and Busanda. Twice leading broodmare sire of 113 stakes winners, including champions Buckpasser, Hoist the Flag, and Affectionately. Died on October 30, 1959, at age 25 and buried next to Man o' War at Faraway. Remains were exhumed, along with his sire's in the 1970s, and reinterred at the Kentucky Horse Park.

1944, 1935—CHANCE PLAY, 1923 ch. h., Fair Play–*Quelle Chance, by Ethelbert. Bred in Kentucky by August Belmont II. 39-16-9-2, $137,946. A handsome horse who resembled his sire, he raced for W. Averill Harriman's Log Cabin Stable and was considered best horse of the year in 1927. Retired in 1929, stood at farms from Kentucky to New York until purchased by Warren Wright, who made him one of first stallions to stand at Calumet Farm in Lexington. Sired 23 stakes winners (7%), including 1939 champion juvenile filly Now What and '45 Jockey Club Gold Cup winner Pot o' Luck. Pensioned in 1947 following heart attack. Euthanized at Calumet on July 6, 1950, at age 27 and buried in the farm's cemetery.

1943—*BULL DOG, 1927 b. or br. h., *Teddy–Plucky Liege, by Spearmint. Bred in France by Jefferson Davis Cohn. 8-2-1-0, $7,802. Stakes winner at three in France. Full brother to leading sire *Sir Gallahad III and half brother to top European sires Bois Roussel and Admiral Drake. Imported by Charles B. Shaffer in 1930 to stand at his Coldstream Stud in Kentucky. Top runners include champion two-year-olds Occupy and Our Boots and five-time leading American sire Bull Lea. Sired 52 stakes winners (15%) in 18 crops, and 27% of his starters were of stakes class. In 1953, he supplanted *Sir Gallahad III atop broodmare sire list and subsequently led that list three times. His daughters produced 89 stakes winners and four champions. Pensioned in 1948. Died at Coldstream on October 10, 1954, at age 27.

1942—EQUIPOISE, 1928 ch. h., Pennant–Swinging, by Broomstick. Bred in Kentucky by Harry Payne Whitney. 51-29-10-4, $338,610. First great racehorse to carry colors of Whitney's son, Cornelius Vanderbilt Whitney. Nicknamed the "Chocolate Soldier" because of his dark chestnut color and combative spirit, he was an American champion at ages two, four, and five. Entered stud at C. V. Whitney Farm in 1935. Sired just four crops and 74 foals, nine of whom won stakes (12%), including 1940 champion juvenile filly Level Best and 1942 Kentucky Derby and Belmont Stakes winner Shut Out. Broodmare sire of 1946 Triple Crown winner Assault. First foals were two-year-olds when he died of enteritis at age ten on August 4, 1938. Inducted into Racing Hall of Fame in 1957.

1941—*BLENHEIM II, 1927 br. h., Blandford–Malva, by Charles O'Malley. Bred in England by Lord Carnarvon. Sold as yearling to the Aga Khan for about $20,000. 10-5-3-0, $73,060. Injury forced retirement following victory in 1930 Epsom Derby. Stood in Europe for six seasons, siring 1936 Epsom Derby winner *Mahmoud, Italian champion Donatello II. Sold in 1936 for reported $250,000 to an American syndicate and sent to Claiborne Farm in Kentucky. Sire of more than 45 stakes winners, including 1941 American Triple Crown winner Whirlaway and 1943 champion handicap mare Markell. Broodmare sire of more than 120 stakes winners, including *Nasrullah and Kentucky Derby winners Ponder, Hill Gail, and Kauai King. Died at Claiborne on May 26, 1958, at age 31.

1940, 1933-'34, 1930—*SIR GALLAHAD III, 1920 b. h., *Teddy–Plucky Liege, by Spearmint. Bred in France by Jefferson Davis Cohn. 24-11-3-3, $17,009, Poule d'Essai des Poulains (French Two Thousand Guineas), match with *Epinard, etc. Full brother to leading sire *Bull Dog, half brother to top European sires Bois Roussel and Admiral Drake. Stood 1925 season in France, then sold for $125,000 to U.S. syndicate headed by A. B. Hancock. First important American stallion syndication. Stood at Claiborne Farm in Kentucky for remainder of career. First U.S. crop included 1930 Triple Crown winner Gallant Fox, and with two crops racing he led general sire list for the first of four times. Sired 56 stakes winners (10%), including three Kentucky Derby victors and several champions. Not a notable sire of sires but an all-time great broodmare sire, leading in that category 12 times. Died and buried at Claiborne on July 8, 1949, at age 29.

1939—*CHALLENGER II, 1927 b. h., Swynford–Sword Play, by Great Sport. Bred in England by the National Stud. 2-2-0-0 $10,930, Richmond S., Clearwell S., ranked third on English Free Handicap, one pound above future leading American sire *Blenheim II. Classic engagements canceled upon death of owner Lord Dewar under the rules then in force. Sold for reported $100,000 to William L. Brann and Robert Castle and imported to U.S. but injured in paddock accident before he could race again. Stood 17 seasons at Brann's Glade Valley Farm in Maryland, the first leading sire to spend his entire career outside Kentucky since *Sir Modred in 1894. Sired 34 stakes winners (11%), including future Racing Hall of Fame members Challedon and Gallorette. Died at Glade Valley on December 23, 1948, at age 21.

1938, 1936—*SICKLE, 1924 br. h., Phalaris–Selene, by Chaucer. Bred in England by Lord Derby. 10-3-4-2, $23,629, stakes winner at two, third in the 1927 Two Thousand Guineas. Half brother to the great racehorse and sire Hyperion, full brother to *Pharamond II. Stood one season in England before being imported under a lease agreement in 1930 by Joseph E. Widener, who eventually purchased him for a reported $100,000. Sent to Widener's Elmendorf Farm in Kentucky, where he replaced deceased Fair Play as the stud's leading stallion. Sired 22% stakes horses from foals, with 41 stakes winners (14%), including champions Stagehand, Star Pilot, and *Gossip II. Broodmare sire of 57 stakes winners, including 1951 Horse of the Year Counterpoint. Died on December 26, 1943, at Elmendorf at age 19.

1937—THE PORTER, 1915 b. h., Sweep–Ballet Girl, by St. Leonards. Bred in Kentucky by David Stevenson. Raced for Samuel Ross and later Edward McLean. 52-26-10-8, $89,249, Annapolis Handicap, etc. Stood barely 15 hands. From 1922-'31 stood at McLean Stud in Virginia. At age 16, purchased for $27,000 at McLean's 1931 dispersal by Mrs. John Hay Whitney and sent to Kentucky. Sired 11% stakes winners from foals, with the best of his 34 stakes winners being 1937 Santa Anita Handicap winner Rosemont, '37 Suburban Handicap winner Aneroid, and the top juvenile Porter's Mite. Died at Mare's Nest Farm in Kentucky on October 23, 1944, at age 29.

1932—CHATTERTON, 1919 ch. h., Fair Play–Chit Chat, by *Rock Sand. Bred in Kentucky by August Belmont II. 32-15-5-4, $26,565. Bred like Man o' War, by Fair Play out of *Rock Sand mare. Sold privately and raced for Frank J. Kelley. Multiple stakes winner in Midwest, though not a top runner. Stood 1924 in California but after Kelley's

death sent to Claiborne Farm in Kentucky. Remained there except for 1932 season when leased to Arrowbrook Farm in Illinois. His position atop list was due almost entirely to 1932 champion and Belmont Stakes winner Faireno. Also sired 1928 champion juvenile filly Current and nine other stakes winners. Died at Claiborne of kidney ailment on July 14, 1933, at age 14.

1931—*ST. GERMANS, 1921 b. h., Swynford–Hamoaze, by Torpoint. Bred in England by Lord Astor. 20-9-4-4, $44,793, Coronation Cup, Doncaster Cup, etc., second in Epsom Derby. Imported by Payne Whitney to stand at his Greentree Stud. Advertised "for private use only" in early years. He suffered from low fertility and averaged fewer than ten foals per crop, but those were highly successful. Best of 23 stakes winners (13%) was 1931 Horse of the Year Twenty Grand, winner of the Kentucky Derby and Belmont Stakes; two-time handicap champion Devil Diver; and 1936 Kentucky Derby-Preakness Stakes winner Bold Venture. Twenty Grand was sterile, and several prominent male-line descendants experienced fertility problems. Died at Greentree Stud on May 18, 1929, at age 18 following attack of enteritis.

1929—*CHICLE, 1913 b. h., Spearmint–Lady Hamburg II, by Hamburg. Bred in France by Harry Payne Whitney but raced in U.S. 10-3-0-2, $4,765. Had soundness problems but nonetheless won Champagne Stakes and Brooklyn Derby (now Dwyer Stakes). Entered stud in Kentucky at H. P. Whitney Farm for fee of $500. Fee later raised as high as $1,500. Bad tempered, kept muzzled as a stallion for safety of farm workers. Sired six stakes winners from first 13-foal crop and about 40 overall—including champion juveniles Whichone and Mother Goose. Leading broodmare sire of 1942. Died on May 20, 1939, at age 26, at C. V. Whitney Farm near Lexington.

1928—HIGH TIME, 1916 ch. h., Ultimus–Noonday, by Domino. Bred in Kentucky by Wickliffe Stud of Corrigan and McKinney. 7-1-0-1, $3,950, Hudson S., 3rd Great American S. Highly inbred to Domino, with three crosses in first three generations. Beautiful physical specimen, sold at auction as two-year-old for $8,500. Career limited by throat problems. Won Aqueduct's Hudson Stakes in track-record time for five furlongs. Retired at three to Haylands Stud in 1919 but was not well received by Kentucky breeders. In later years, changed ownership several times before settling at Dixiana Farm in Kentucky. Sired about 40 stakes winners, including Racing Hall of Fame champion gelding Sarazen and 1928 champion juvenile colt High Strung. Leading broodmare sire of 1940. Died at Dixiana on November 20, 1937, at age 21.

1927, 1924, 1920—FAIR PLAY, 1905 ch. h., Hastings–*Fairy Gold, by Bend Or. Bred in Kentucky by August Belmont II. 32-10-11-3, $86,950. Racing Hall of Fame runner had misfortune to come along in same crop as unbeatable Colin. Won 1908 Lawrence Realization. When betting was outlawed in New York, shipped to England, where heavy weight assignments and a deteriorating attitude led to a 6-0-0-0 record. Retired to Nursery Stud in 1910. When Belmont died in 1924, sold at age 20 on $100,000 bid to Joseph Widener. Renowned for producing stamina, the three-time leading sire got champions Chance Play and Mad Hatter but was immortalized as sire of Man o' War, through whom his male line survives today. Leading broodmare sire in 1931,'34, and '38. Died at age 24 in paddock at Elmendorf Farm in Kentucky on December 16, 1929.

1926—MAN O' WAR, 1917 ch. h., Fair Play–Mahubah, by *Rock Sand. Bred in Kentucky by August Belmont II. 21-

20-1-0, $249,465. Sold at auction as yearling for $5,000 to Samuel Riddle. Became one of the greatest racehorses of all time, winning Preakness and Belmont Stakes. Retired in 1921 to Hinata Stock Farm but soon moved to Faraway Farm, both in Kentucky. Instant success, led general sire list with only three crops racing. Top runners include future Racing Hall of Fame members War Admiral 'and Crusader as well as six other American champions. Also a great broodmare sire. As Riddle's private stallion, did not receive the best mares but nonetheless sired 64 stakes winners, 17% of foals. Died at age 30 at Faraway on November 1, 1947. Thousands attended funeral, which was nationally broadcast on radio and filmed for newsreels. Grave and larger-than-life bronze statue relocated in late 1970s to Kentucky Horse Park.

1925, 1918—SWEEP, 1907 br. h., Ben Brush–Pink Domino, by Domino. Bred in Kentucky by James R. Keene. 13-9-2-2, $59,998, champion at two in 1909 when he won the Futurity Stakes and added Belmont Stakes at three. Sold at 1913 Keene estate dispersal at Madison Square Garden for $17,500 to partnership of John Barbee, J. C. Carrick, and Andrew Stone. Led broodmare sire list twice and twice was leader by number of two-year-old winners. Sired more than 40 stakes winners. Top runners include 1918 champion juvenile Eternal and handicap star The Porter, leading sire of 1937. Died at age 24 from "indigestion" on August 15, 1931, at Glen-Helen Stud in Kentucky.

1923—THE FINN, 1912 bl. h., *Ogden–Livonia, by *Star Shoot. Bred in Kentucky by John E. Madden. 50-19-10-6, $38,965. Raced initially for Madden before being sold to H. C. Hallenbeck. Victories included Belmont and Withers Stakes as well as Metropolitan, Manhattan, and Havre de Grace Handicaps. Generally regarded as champion three-year-old colt of 1915. Madden later bought him back and in 1923 he was sold again, for $100,000 to W. R. Coe. Stood thereafter at Hinata Stock Farm in Kentucky. Sired Kentucky Derby winners Flying Ebony and Zev, the latter America's first racehorse to top $300,000 in earnings (1924). Died at Hinata on September 4, 1925, from "inflammation of the bowels," at age 13.

1922—*MCGEE, 1900 b. h., White Knight–Remorse, by Hermit. Bred in England by Lord Bradford. 53-24-14-5, $18,391, Fleetfoot H., etc. Only foal by an unraced stallion. Sold cheaply as yearling to Ed Corrigan and imported to U.S. Raced in Midwest, a minor stakes winner of 24 races. Primarily a sprinter—set American 5½-furlong record in 1903. Retired to Corrigan's Freeland Stud near Lexington, then sold in 1908 for $1,300 to Charles Moore. Relocated to nearby Mere Hill Stud where his 1909 fee was $50. Sired at least 20 stakes winners, most notably the great gelding Exterminator and Donerail, winner of 1913 Kentucky Derby at 91.45-to-1. His last foal was conceived in 1930 when *McGee was 30 years old. Prior to his death at Mere Hill on September 18, 1931, he was believed to be the oldest stallion in Kentucky.

1921—CELT, 1905 ch. h., Commando–*Maid Of Erin, by Amphion. Bred in Kentucky by James R. Keene. 6-4-1-1, $29,975. Lightly raced winner of 1908 Brooklyn Handicap, overshadowed by unbeaten stablemate Colin, another son of Commando. Stood initially at Castleton Stud, then leased for 1912 to stand at Hancock family's Ellerslie Stud in Virginia. Though lease expired in 1913, A. B. Hancock acquired him that fall for $20,000 at Keene's estate dispersal. Returned to Ellerslie to sire

a total of at least 29 stakes winners. In 1930, was top broodmare sire when Gallant Fox swept the Triple Crown. Died at age 14 in 1919.

1919, 1916-'17, 1911-'12—*STAR SHOOT, 1898 ch. h., Isinglass–Astrology, by Hermit. Bred in England by Maj. Eustace Loder. 10-3-1-3, $34,747, National Breeders' Produce S., etc. A good two-year-old, developed wind problems at three and was unplaced in two starts that season. Because he was from a family not noted for producing good sires, he was sold to America and entered stud in 1902 at Runnymede Farm in Kentucky, where he was an immediate success. Purchased privately by John Madden in 1912 and relocated to Hamburg Place. One of the most influential American-based stallions of his time; his sons included future Racing Hall of Fame members Grey Lag and Sir Barton. In 1916, had record 27 juvenile winners. Died of pneumonia at Hamburg on November 19, 1919, at age 21.

1915, 1913-'14—BROOMSTICK, 1901 b. h., Ben Brush–*Elf, by Galliard. Bred in Kentucky by Col. Milton Young. 39-14-11-5, $74,730, Travers S., etc. Young acquired *Elf for $250 in foal with Broomstick. Colt was sold privately to race for coal millionaire Samuel Brown. Racing Hall of Fame runner raced through age four. Retired in 1906 to Brown's Senorita Stud in Kentucky. Sold for $7,250 two years later at estate sale of his owner to H. P. Whitney. Eventually sired about 25% stakes winners from foals—nearly 60 in all–including the first New York handicap triple crown winner, Whisk Broom II; the first filly Kentucky Derby winner, Regret; 1911 Derby winner Meridian; and '12 Two Thousand Guineas winner *Sweeper. Died at C. V. Whitney Farm in Kentucky, on March 24, 1931, at age 30.

1910, 1900—KINGSTON, 1884 br. h., Spendthrift–*Kapanga, by Victorious. Bred in Kentucky by James R. Keene. 138-89-33-12, $140,195, First Special S., etc. Raced through age ten, primarily for Phil and Mike Dwyer. His 89 career victories remains an all-time record, and for about one year (1892-'93) he reigned as America's leading money earner. Entered stud in 1895 at Eugene Leigh's La Belle Farm in Kentucky for a $150 fee. Moved in a few years to Keene's Castleton Farm near Lexington, where he stood privately with leading sires Ben Brush and Commando. Represented by Futurity Stakes winners Ballyhoo Bey (1900) and Novelty ('10), as well as 1900 Belmont Stakes winner Ildrim. Died at Castleton on December 4, 1912, at age 28.

1909—BEN BRUSH, 1893 b. h., Bramble–Roseville, by Reform. Bred in Kentucky by Catesby Woodford and Ezekiel Clay. 40-25-5-5, $65,208. Small, plain, and tough, a superb racehorse, and Racing Hall of Fame member. Sold as yearling for $1,200 to Eugene Leigh and Ed Brown, and again at three for reported $25,000 to Mike Dwyer. Won 1896 Kentucky Derby and '97 Suburban Handicap. Sold to James R. Keene for stud duty at Castleton Farm in Kentucky. Following Keene's death in 1913, acquired for $10,000 by Kentucky Senator Johnson Camden and lived out his days at Camden's Hartland Stud near Versailles. Established noted male line that endured for decades. Best offspring include three-time leading American sire Broomstick and two-time leader Sweep. Died at age 25 on June 8, 1918.

1908, 1902—HASTINGS, 1893 br. h., Spendthrift–*Cinderella, by Tomahawk or Blue Ruin. Bred in Kentucky by Dr. J. D. Neet. 21-10-8-0, $16,340. Raced at two for Gideon and Daly. Upon dispersal of that stable at Sheepshead Bay in 1895, acquired for $37,000 by August Belmont II. Won 1896 Belmont Stakes, although generally not regarded as a top racehorse. Entered stud in 1898 at Belmont's Nursery Stud in Kentucky and was known for his savage disposition. Sire of champion filly Gunfire (1899), but by far his best was the 1905 colt Fair Play, the future sire of Man o' War. Died at Nursery Stud in 1917 at age 24 following an attack of paralysis.

1907—COMMANDO, 1898 b. h., Domino–Emma C., by *Darebin. Bred in Kentucky by James R. Keene. 9-7-2-0, $58,196. Coarse and heavily muscled, he did not resemble his handsome sire but was at least his equal on the racecourse. In James R. Keene's colors, won 1901 Belmont Stakes. The Racing Hall of Fame member retired to Keene's Castleton Stud in 1902 to take the place of Domino, who died at age six in 1897. Immediate success at stud but, like his sire, he died young. From three crops and 27 foals, sired ten stakes winners, among them Racing Hall of Fame members Peter Pan and Colin and influential sires Celt and Ultimus. Died of tetanus at Castleton in early March 1905 at age seven.

1906, 1904—*MEDDLER, 1890 b. h., *St Gatien–Busybody, by Petrarch. Bred in England by George Abington Baird. 3-3-0-0, $16,689, Dewhurst S., etc. By an Epsom Derby winner and out of an Epsom Oaks winner. Unraced after two-year-old season following the death of his owner, which, under rules in force at the time, voided his nominations to the three-year-old classics. Sold in 1893 for $76,000 to American William Forbes, who stood him initially at Neponset Stud in Massachusetts. Upon Forbes's death in 1897, sold to W. C. Whitney for $49,000 and moved to La Belle Stud in Kentucky. Sold at 1904 Whitney estate dispersal for $51,000. Represented by champion fillies Trigger, Tangle, and Tanya (winner of 1905 Belmont Stakes). When American racing was decimated by 1909 antiwagering legislation, relocated to France, where he died on April 17, 1916, at Haras de Fresnay-le-Buffard in Normandy at age 26.

1905—HAMBURG, 1895 b. h., Hanover–Lady Reel, by Fellowcraft. Bred in Kentucky by C. J. Enright. Sold for $1,250 as yearling to John E. Madden, who later named his famous breeding farm, Hamburg Place, for the Racing Hall of Fame member. 21-16-3-2, $60,380, Lawrence Realization, etc. Sold privately for $40,001 to Marcus Daly in 1898. Stood two seasons at Daly's Bitter Root Stud in Montana. After Daly's death in 1900, sold for $60,000 to W. C. Whitney, who sent him to La Belle Stud in Kentucky. At 1904 Whitney dispersal, sold for $70,000 to Whitney's son Harry Payne Whitney, who took him to Brookdale Stud in New Jersey. Sired Racing Hall of Fame filly Artful, champions Borrow, Hamburg Belle, Burgomaster, and Rosie O'Grady, and foundation mare Frizette. Died at Brookdale on September 15, 1915, at age 20.

1903—*BEN STROME, 1886 b. h., Bend Or–Strathfleet, by The Scottish Chief. Bred in England by the Duke of Westminster. 35-3-6-6, $2,975. Big (16.2 hands tall), good-looking, and beautifully bred, but a poor racehorse in England. Entered stud in 1894 at Thomas J. Carson's Dixiana Farm in Kentucky. When his first foals were yearlings, Dixiana advertised that a limited number of approved mares would be accepted by special contract, which meant at no cost. By 1904, his fee had jumped to $300, one of the highest in the country. Most noted as sire of Racing Hall of Fame member Roseben, but offspring also included juvenile champions Eugenia Burch and Highball. Died at Dixi-

ana in 1909 at age 23.

1901—SIR DIXON, 1885 br. h., *Billet–Jaconet, by *Leamington. Bred in Kentucky by Col. Ezekiel Clay. 29-10-7-7, $54,915. Sold for $1,125 as yearling to Green B. Morris, who resold him at three for $20,000 to Mike and Phil Dwyer. A high-strung, delicate type, he was unable to endure the tough campaigns favored by the Dwyers but nevertheless scored victories in the 1888 Belmont, Withers, and Travers Stakes. Stood his entire career at Clay's Runnymede Stud in Kentucky. Sired champions Butterflies, Blue Girl, Kilmarnock, and Running Water, and 1905 Kentucky Derby winner Agile. Died on March 23, 1909, at age 14 after breaking his right hip in a paddock accident.

1899—*ALBERT, 1882 b. h., Albert Victor–Hawthorn Bloom, by Kettledrum. Bred in England by Sir Richard Jardine. 6-1-1-0, $2,547. A racehorse of modest talents, won a minor stakes at Newcastle as a two-year-old. Imported as a stallion by Alfred Withers. Later spent most of his breeding career at the Adelbert Stud of Williams and Radford near Hopkinsville, Kentucky. Advertised for a $100 fee in 1896, with a reference to him as "the most uniform sire of winners in America—they mature early and make great campaigners." Not an outstanding sire, his best was probably 1899 juvenile champion Mesmerist and the good filly Hatasoo, an ancestress of many top racehorses. Believed to have died in 1907, because his last five foals arrived the following spring.

1898, 1895-'97—HANOVER, 1884 ch. h., Hindoo–Bourbon Belle, by *Bonnie Scotland. Bred in Kentucky at Col. Ezekiel Clay's Runnymede Farm. 50-32-14-2, $118,887, champion three-year-old, 1887 Belmont Stakes, etc. Sold as a yearling for $1,350 to Phil and Mike Dwyer. Won 17 consecutive races at two and three and ultimately retired with American earnings record. One of America's better all-time stallions, his best by far was Racing Hall of Fame member and leading sire Hamburg. Hanover was valued at $100,000 when he died on March 23, 1899, at McGrathiana Stud in Kentucky at age 15. Cause of death was said to be blood poisoning caused by a leg injury. He was originally buried at McGrathiana, but his skeleton was later exhumed for research and display.

1894—*SIR MODRED, 1877 b. h., Traducer–Idalia, by Cambuscan. Bred in New Zealand by Middle Park Stud. Among the foremost racehorses of his day in New Zealand, with victories in the Canterbury Derby, Canterbury Cup, and Metropolitan Stakes. Imported to California in 1885 by James Ben Ali Haggin. In 1894, became the first California-based stallion to lead the American sire list when his offspring won 137 races and $134,318. Notable offspring include champion Tournament, 1893 Belmont Stakes winner Comanche, 1890 Travers Stakes winner Sir John, and the outstanding fillies Gloaming and Lucania. Stood at Haggin's 44,000-acre Rancho del Paso near Sacramento, where he was pensioned for several seasons prior to his death due to infirmities of old age in June 1904 at age 27.

1893—HIMYAR, 1875 b. h., Alarm–Hira, by Lexington. Bred in Kentucky by Maj. Barak Thomas. 27-14-6-4, $11,650, Phoenix Hotel Stakes, etc. Finished second in 1878 as one of the heaviest favorites ever for the Kentucky Derby. High-strung, nervous, and hard to train, considered primarily a speed horse. Entered stud in 1882 at Thomas's Dixiana Farm near Lexington and got, among others, immortal racehorse and sire Domino and '98 Kentucky Derby winner Plaudit. In 1893, due largely to Domino, he established a single-season progeny earnings record of $259,252, which stood for 24 years. Died at age 30 on December 30, 1905, and was buried at Dixiana under a tombstone that reads: "Speed springs eternal from his ashes."

1892—IROQUOIS, 1878 br. h., *Leamington–Maggie B.B., by *Australian. Bred by Aristides Welch at Erdenheim Stud in Pennsylvania. 26-12-4-3, $99,707. Sold as a yearling to tobacco magnate Pierre Lorillard, who sent him to race in England. First American-bred winner of Epsom Derby and St. Leger Stakes; finished second in the Two Thousand Guineas. Wall Street briefly halted trading to celebrate news of his Derby triumph. Returned to U.S., he raced three times without success, probably because of pulmonary bleeding. Retired to stud at W. H. Johnson's Belle Meade Farm, where he died in 1899 at age 11. His offspring included champion Tammany.

1891—LONGFELLOW, 1867 br. h., *Leamington–Nantura, by Brawner's Eclipse. Bred, owned, and trained by John Harper. 16-13-2-0, $11,200. Standing a towering 17 hands, he was named for his long legs and not for the noted poet. One of the great racehorses of the 1870s, an injury forced his retirement to Harper's Nantura Stud near Midway, Kentucky. Sired more than 40 stakes winners, including Kentucky Derby winners Leonatus and Riley, 1886 Preakness winner The Bard, and champions Thora and Freeland. A dominant bay, it was said that all his foals but one were bay or brown. Died at Nantura on November 5, 1893, and was buried with a marker that reads: "King of Racers and King of Stallions."

1890—*ST. BLAISE, 1880 ch. h., Hermit–Fusee, by Marsyas. Bred in England by Lord Alington. 16-7-2-1, $41,066. Won 1883 Epsom Derby. Imported for $30,000 in 1885 by August Belmont I to stand at his Nursery Stud in Kentucky. Following Belmont's death, sold at auction in 1891 by Tattersalls of New York for a then-world record $100,000. Purchased on a solitary bid by Charles Reed of Tennessee. Not successful for Reed, sold at auction again in 1902 for $8,300 to James Ben Ali Haggin of Elmendorf Farm, Kentucky, but subsequently purchased privately by August Belmont II. At age 22, he returned to Nursery Stud to live out his days. Best runners include 1890 Futurity Stakes winner Potomac and '96 Preakness Stakes winner Margrave. Died in October 1909 at age 29.

1889—*RAYON D'OR, 1876 ch. h., Flageolet–Araucaria, by Ambrose. Bred in France by Haras de Dangu. 28-15-7-4, $110,207. Won from five to 18 furlongs, including 1879 St. Leger, and carried up to 132 pounds to victory. Imported in 1883 by W. L. Scott, who paid nearly $40,000 for him and stood him initially at his Algeria Stud in Pennsylvania. When Algeria dispersed in 1892, purchased by August Belmont II and moved to Nursery Stud in Kentucky. Sired many top runners, including Brooklyn Handicap winner Tenny, Futurity Stakes winner Chaos, and Banquet, winner of 62 races and $118,872. Died from "fever" on July 15, 1896, at Nursery Stud at age 20.

1888, 1886–'87, 1884—GLENELG, 1866 b. h., Citadel–*Babta, by Kingston. Imported in utero by R. W. Cameron, who earlier had imported four-time leading sire *Leamington. Foaled at Cameron's Clifton Farm in New York. 18-10-5-2, $23,340. Purchased as a yearling by August Belmont I for $2,000. Big, bad-tempered, and prone to colic, he nonetheless won the 1869 Travers Stakes and other important races. After his racing days, he was sold to Milton H. Sanford for $10,000. His many outstanding

runners include Racing Hall of Fame mare Firenze. Died on October 23, 1897, at age 31 at the farm of Tyree Bate in Castalian Springs, Tennessee.

1885—VIRGIL, 1864 dk. b. h., Vandal–Hymenia, by *Yorkshire. Bred in Woodford County, Kentucky, by Hyman C. Gratz. 10-7-2-1, $2,950, Sequel S. three times, etc. A beautiful, nearly black horse, owned during his racing days by Milton Sanford, primarily a sprinter in an era that prized stamina (although he won once at two miles). Initially had few opportunities as a stallion and was even broken to harness and used to pull a carriage. Sold cheaply in 1874. When his son Vagrant won the 1876 Kentucky Derby, Virgil was repurchased by Sanford. He subsequently sired Racing Hall of Fame member Hindoo (also a great sire) and unbeaten Tremont. Died at Quindaro Stud in Kentucky in 1893 at age 29.

1883—*BILLET, 1865 br. h., Voltigeur–Calcutta, by Flatcatcher. Bred in England by James Smith. 18-5-3-1, $3,983. Insignificant racehorse in England, racing most often in selling races. Imported to America in 1869 and stood several seasons in Illinois. After son Elias Lawrence established a Saratoga three-mile record in 1878, was moved to Runnymede Stud in Paris, Kentucky, where he remained until his death on January 17, 1889, at age 24. Top runners include Racing Hall of Fame member Miss Woodford, the first American Thoroughbred to top $100,000 in earnings, and 1901 leading sire Sir Dixon.

1882, 1880—*BONNIE SCOTLAND, 1853 b. h., Iago–Queen Mary, by Gladiator. Bred in England by William l'Anson. 4-2-1-0, $6,308. Lightly raced and never truly sound because of an injury as a foal, won Liverpool St. Leger and Doncaster Stakes. Imported to America in 1857, believed to have stood originally in Ohio before relocating to Gen. W. G. Harding's famous Belle Meade Stud near Nashville, Tennessee. Offspring include Racing Hall of Fame member Luke Blackburn, 1883 Belmont Stakes winner George Kinney, and champion Bramble. Died in his paddock at Belle Meade on February 2, 1880, at age 27.

1881, 1879, 1877, 1875—*LEAMINGTON, 1853 br. h., Faugh-a-Ballagh–mare by Pantaloon. Bred in England by Mr. Halford. 24-8-3-3, $33,446, Goodwood S., Tradesmen's Plate twice, etc. Imported in 1865 by R. W. Cameron of New York after standing six seasons in England. In U.S., stood first at Bosque Bonita Stud in Kentucky, later at Cameron's Clifton Stud on Staten Island, and finally at Aristides Welch's Erdenheim Stud near Philadelphia. Sire of Racing Hall of Fame members Longfellow and Parole, inaugural Kentucky Derby winner Aristides, and Iroquois, first American-bred winner of the Epsom Derby. Many of his best offspring were out of Lexington mares and were raced by the Lorillard brothers, George and Pierre, who dominated American racing during the 1870s and'80s. Died at Erdenheim on May 6, 1878, at age 25.

1878, 1876, 1861–'74—LEXINGTON, 1850 b. h., Boston–Alice Carneal, by *Sarpedon. Bred in Kentucky by Dr. Elisha Warfield. 7-6-1-0, $56,600, Great Post S., etc. Sold to Richard Ten Broeck as a three-year-old and in 1855 set an American four-mile record of 7:19¾. By then, he was going blind and was sold for $15,000 to R. A. Alexander of Woodburn Stud, Kentucky. He stood at that Midway farm his entire career except for an interlude in Illinois for his own safety during the Civil War. As with *Glencoe, a number of his offspring were utilized as Civil War mounts. His many outstanding runners include champions Kentucky, Asteroid, Norfolk, Duke of Magenta, Harry Bassett, Sultana, and Tom Bowling. Lexington's post-Civil War fee of $500 was unprecedented. His male-line survived into the 20th century, and numerous crosses of his name are still present in far branches of modern pedigrees. The unprecedented 16-time leading sire died on July 1, 1875, at age 25. His skeleton is in the possession of the Smithsonian Institution in Washington, D.C.

1860—REVENUE, 1843 b. h., *Trustee–Rosalie Somers, by Sir Charles. Bred in Virginia by statesman John M. Botts. 21-16-5-0. Son of a leading sire and champion racemare. Stood at Botts's farm in Virginia, where he sired the great Planet, widely viewed as the best American racehorse in the era preceding the Civil War, compiling a 31-27-4-0 record and surpassing Peytona as America's top earner with $69,700, a mark that stood for 20 years. In 1860, Revenue became the first stallion to lead an American sire list based on earnings ($49,450) rather than races won (the previously recognized standard), although he led by wins as well. He died in Virginia in September 1868 at age 25.

1859—*ALBION, 1837 bl. h., Cain or Actaeon–Panthea, by Comus or Blacklock. Bred in England; reportedly was a successful racehorse in America during the early 1840s. A reliable sire of winners during pre-Civil War years and later an outstanding broodmare sire. Died in 1859 at age 22 in Sumner County, Tennessee.

1858, 1854-'57, 1849-'50, 1847—*GLENCOE, 1831 ch. h., Sultan–Trampoline, by Tramp. Bred in England by Lord Jersey. 10-8-1-1, $33,459. Winner of 1834 Two Thousand Guineas, third in Epsom Derby. Stood one season in England, getting legendary broodmare Pocahontas. Imported in 1836 by James Jackson, who reportedly paid $10,000 for him. Swaybacked but otherwise handsome, he was much admired by breeders of the day. Stood from 1837-'44 in Alabama; 1845-'48 in Tennessee; and 1849-'57 in Kentucky as property of A. Keene Richards, an ardent secessionist who allegedly turned over many of his offspring for use as Confederate mounts during the Civil War. Sired the great mares Reel and Peytona, the latter America's leading money winner from 1845-'61 ($62,400), as well as top sons Star Davis and Vandal. Died of "lung fever" on August 25, 1857, at Blue Grass Park in Georgetown, Kentucky.

1853, 1851-'52—BOSTON, 1833 b. h., Timoleon–Sister to Tuckahoe, by Ball's Florizel. Bred in Virginia by John Wickham. 45-40-2-1, $51,700. Sold at two for $800 to Nathaniel Rives to satisfy a gaming debt. Racing Hall of Fame member won 30 four-mile heat races. Nicknamed "Old White Nose" for his distinctively blazed face, his vicious temper struck fear into the hearts of his handlers. Sire of Racing Hall of Fame member Lexington and his great rival, Lecomte (also known as Lecompte), as well as the great racemare Nina, dam of Planet. Died in 1850 at age 17 at Col. E. M. Blackburn's farm in Woodford County, Kentucky.

1848 (co-leader), 1843, 1837-'39—*LEVIATHAN, 1823 ch. h., Muley–Coxcomb's dam, by Windle. Bred in England by Mr. Painter. 19-15-3-0, $11,096, Dee S., etc. At 16 hands, large for his time. Imported in 1830 by James Jackson of Alabama. Not well received at first because of his enormous size. In 1838, became America's first $100,000 sire when his progeny won 92 races. At one time, his $75 fee was the highest in America. Stood in Tennessee, managed by Col. George Elliott. Died in Gallatin, Tennessee, in 1846, at age 23 from "inflammation of the bowels."

1848 (co-leader)—*TRUSTEE, 1829 ch. h., Catton–Emma, by Whisker. 11-4-3-3, $7,446, Claret S., etc. Third in 1832 Epsom Derby in first career start. Brother to 1835 Epsom Derby winner Mundig, half brother to 1843 Derby winner Cotherstone. Imported in 1835 by Commodore Robert Stockton, later senator from New Jersey. Not well received by American breeders and moved often during his stud career. Stood in New York between 1836-'41; Virginia in 1842; Kentucky in 1843-'44; Virginia in 1845-'46; and back to New York in 1847, where he remained until his death at age 27. Sire of Racing Hall of Fame filly Fashion, the great mare Levity, and leading 1860 American sire Revenue. Died in 1856 at West Farms, Westchester County, New York.

1846, 1844-'45, 1842—*PRIAM, 1827 b. h., Emilius–Cressida, by Whisker. Bred in England by Sir John Shelley. 16-14-1-1, $65,100. Winner of the 1830 Epsom Derby, Goodwood Cup. Considered the greatest English racehorse of his era. Imported in 1837 by Merritt and Co. for $15,000, then believed to be a record. Leading American sire four times. Sire of Epsom Oaks winners Crucifix, Miss Letty, and Industry before his importation. Sire in America of Margaret Wood, Little Trick, Lucy Long. Died in Tennessee in 1847 at age 20.

1841, 1840—MEDOC, 1829 ch. h., American Eclipse–Young Maid of the Oaks, by *Expedition. Bred in New York by James Bathgate. 5-4-1-0, $5,300. Greatest son of American Eclipse. Entered stud in Kentucky in 1835. His offspring won 61 races in 1840 and 51 races the following year. Sire of top four-miler Grey Medoc, Bob Letcher, Mary Morris, Picayune. Broke his near foreleg when he stepped in a hole during exercise in 1839 and died at age ten from the injury at Col. William Buford's farm in Woodford County, Kentucky.

1836, 1830-'33—SIR CHARLES, 1816 ch. h., Sir Archy–*Citizen mare, by *Citizen. Won 20 of 25 starts. Believed to have been bred in Virginia by W. R. Johnson. Ancestry of his dam questioned; some referred to her as a "cart mare" whose pedigree had been fabricated. Dominant in long heat races throughout the South. Beaten while lame in final start, 1822 match with American Eclipse for the national championship in Washington, D.C. Died on June 7, 1833, at age 17 at George Johnson's Earnscliffe Plantation, Virginia. Sired the great racemares Trifle, Bonnets o' Blue, and Rosalie Somers, and notable racehorse and sire Wagner.

1835—BERTRAND, 1821 b. h., Sir Archy–Eliza, by *Bedford. Bred in South Carolina by Col. John R. Spann. Won 13 of 16 starts. In 1826, he was sold to Hutchcraft and Co. and sent to Kentucky, where he stood his entire 12-season career, and was said to have covered between 175 and 200 mares per season. He is credited with vastly improving the Thoroughbred of the Bluegrass region. His best include John Bascombe, Richard Singleton, and Queen Mary. Died in Hopkinsville, Kentucky, in 1838 at age 17.

1834—MONSIEUR TONSON, 1822 b. h., Pacolet–Madam Tonson, by Top Gallant. Bred in Tennessee by Thomas Foxhall. Won 11 of 12 starts; only defeat was his first start as a two-year-old. William R. Johnson, the "Napoleon of the Turf" in America, bought him for $10,000. Stood initially in Virginia, later in North Carolina, and finally was sent to Kentucky where he died. Sire of South Carolina champion Argyle and many other winners.

Note: Prior to 1860, leading sires were based on races won rather than progeny earnings.

Stallion Syndications

In part because the definition of stallion syndication has changed over the decades, pinpointing the first syndication contract is difficult, if not impossible. However, the earliest syndication agreement comparable in form and intent to modern syndicates was that of Tracery in 1923. That agreement between the syndicators, the International Horse Agency and Exchange, and a group of 30 subscribers placed a value of $219,840 on the 1912 St. Leger winner, who was the sire of '23 Epsom Derby victor *Papyrus.

The principal idea behind that syndicate and all subsequent ones was to spread the risk of purchasing a very expensive breeding horse (and, in Tracery's case, returning him from Argentina). From the beginning of the Thoroughbred breeding industry in the late 17th century right up to the 20th century, Thoroughbred breeding was essentially a private affair, with rich aristocrats wholly owning stallions and breeding mostly their own mares to those sires.

As Thoroughbred breeding slowly became more commercial in the late 19th and early 20th centuries, a new method of financing was required, both to spread the risk of failure and to ensure that a stallion received an appropriate number and quality of mares. Syndication was the answer. In Tracery's case, spreading the risk was a wise strategy because the stallion died after only one season at stud in England.

In a modern syndicate agreement, individuals agree to purchase a specific percentage of ownership in a stallion—the percentage ownership is determined by the number of shares—with payment for that percentage interest usually spread in installments over several years. In return, the buyer of a syndicate share gains the right to breed one or more mares to that stallion each year without additional payments (except for agreed maintenance fees). The syndicate manager normally receives a specified number of free nominations each year as compensation.

The similarity to buying stock market shares is evident. The syndicate manager receives cap-

Chronology of Record Stallion Syndications

Stallion	Year	Price	Farm	Seller	Share price	No. shares
Tracery	1923	$219,400	Cobham Stud (Eng.)	Senor Unzue	$5,485	40
*Blenheim II	1936	$240,000	Claiborne Farm (Ky.)	H. H. Aga Khan	$30,000	8
Tehran	1945	$403,000	Barton Stud (Eng.)	Prince Aly Khan	$10,075	40
Stardust	1945	$451,360	Gilltown Stud (Ire.)	H. H. Aga Khan	$11,284	40
*Alibhai	1948	$500,000	Spendthrift Farm (Ky.)	Louis B. Mayer	$16,667	30
The Phoenix	1948	$619,920	Ballykisteen Stud (Ire.)	Fred Myerscough	$15,498	40
Nashua	1955	$1,251,200	Spendthrift (Ky.)	Estate of William Woodward Jr.	$39,200	32
Graustark	1966	$2,400,000	Darby Dan Farm (Ky.)	John W. Galbreath	$60,000	40
Raise a Native	1967	$2,625,000	Spendthrift Farm (Ky.)	Louis Wolfson and Leslie Combs	$75,000	35
Buckpasser	1967	$4,800,000	Claiborne Farm (Ky.)	Ogden Phipps (retained 16 shares)	$150,000	32
*Vaguely Noble	1969	$5,000,000	Gainesway Farm (Ky.)	Nelson Bunker Hunt and Dr. Robert Franklyn	$125,000	40
Nijinsky II	1970	$5,440,000	Claiborne Farm (Ky.)	Charles W. Englehard (retained 10 shares)	$170,000	32
Secretariat	1973	$6,080,000	Claiborne Farm (Ky.)	Meadow Stable	$190,000	32
Wajima	1975	$7,200,000	Spendthrift Farm (Ky.)	East-West Stable (retained 20 shares)	$200,000	36
What a Pleasure	1976	$8,000,000	Waldemar Farm (Ky.)	Waldemar (retained 16 shares)	$250,000	32
The Minstrel	1977	$9,000,000	Windfields Farm (Md.)	Robert Sangster, et al.	$250,000	36
Seattle Slew	1978	$12,000,000	Spendthrift Farm (Ky.)	Wooden Horse Investments (retained 20 shares)	$300,000	40
Alleged	1978	$16,000,000	Walmac-Warnerton Int'l. (Ky.)	Robert Sangster, et.al.	$400,000	40
Troy	1979	$16,500,000	Highclere Stud (Eng.)	Sir Michael Sobell and Arnold Weinstock	$412,500	40
Spectacular Bid	1980	$22,000,000	Claiborne Farm (Ky.)	Hawksworth Farm (retained 20 shares)	$550,000	40
Storm Bird	1981	$30,000,000	Ashford Stud (Ky.)	Robert Sangster, et.al.	$750,000	40
Conquistador Cielo	1982	$36,400,000	Claiborne Farm (Ky.)	Henryk de Kwiatkowski (retained 10 shares)	$910,000	40
Shareef Dancer	1983	$40,000,000	Dalham Hall Stud (Eng.)	Ashton Upthorpe Stud	$1,000,000	40
Lammtarra	1996	$42,000,000	Arrow Stud (Jpn.)	Dalham Hall Stud	$1,050,000	40
Fusaichi Pegasus	2000	†$60,000,000	Ashford Stud (Ky.)	Fusao Sekiguchi	$1,500,000	40

†Estimated value

ital to pay for a major capital asset, and shareholders gain the possibility of dividends from the share through sale of the nomination or value of the produce. Shares also may be sold later to other investors at a profit (or loss), just as in the stock market, although syndication agreements may place restrictions on the marketability of the shares.

Although the first clearly identifiable syndicate was English, Americans soon became active syndicators. Arthur B. Hancock Sr. of Claiborne Farm formed a four-man partnership in 1926 to purchase the high-class French miler *Sir Gallahad III for $125,000. When *Sir Gallahad III sired Triple Crown winner Gallant Fox in his first crop, making him leading sire for the first of four times, the syndication process gained impetus in America. In 1936, Hancock syndicated another leading sire, *Blenheim II, for a record price, $240,000. In his first crop, *Blenheim II sired Triple Crown winner Whirlaway.

The record returned to England in 1945 when the good young sires Stardust and Tehran were syndicated in rapid succession, but the record price returned to America in '48 when Leslie Combs II purchased *Alibhai from Louis B. Mayer as a replacement for Combs's first syndicated horse, *Beau Pere, who died before covering a mare.

Combs also syndicated Nashua, the first $1-million stallion, as a four-year-old in 1956. The record price remained in America until 1983 (except for a brief period in '79) when Sheikh Mohammed bin Rashid al Maktoum syndicated his Irish Derby (Ire-G1) winner, Shareef Dancer, for a reported $40-million.

That reported price signifies one of the problems with modern syndications. With values soaring to astronomical figures, stallion managers now often decline to publish the exact price per share or contact terms. Thus, the $60-million to $70-million figure for current record holder Fusaichi Pegasus is based on approximate figures released by the syndicate manager and private communications from syndicate members.

Leading Stud Farms by
2002 Stallion Progeny Earnings

Minimum of 20 starters for a farm's stallions in 2002, worldwide earnings. Includes all active stallions at each farm in 2002.

Rank	Name (State)	Stallion Earnings	Avg. Earnings	SWs/Strs	GSWs/Strs
1	Lane's End (Ky.)	$61,539,264	$30,862	4.61%	1.76%
2	Ashford Stud (Ky.)	42,423,574	19,677	3.57%	1.95%
3	Gainesway (Ky.)	34,269,190	31,239	4.74%	1.55%
4	Three Chimneys Farm (Ky.)	31,784,921	30,770	4.36%	1.74%
5	Claiborne Farm (Ky.)	29,200,331	29,555	4.35%	1.52%
6	Vinery Kentucky (Ky.)	27,355,964	22,350	3.02%	0.98%
7	Brookdale Farm (Ky.)	23,289,093	28,681	3.94%	1.60%
8	Hill 'n' Dale Farms (Ky.)	18,119,152	26,568	4.55%	2.64%
9	Overbrook Farm (Ky.)	16,874,174	27,572	5.88%	2.45%
10	Adena Springs Kentucky (Ky.)	16,284,955	29,555	4.17%	1.27%
11	Northview Stallion Station (Md.)	15,883,684	22,091	3.89%	0.42%
12	Ocala Stud Farm (Fla.)	15,400,006	21,969	2.71%	0.57%
13	Wafare Farm (Ky.)	13,397,556	18,080	2.43%	0.94%
14	Taylor Made Farm (Ky.)	12,596,697	26,298	4.59%	1.04%
15	Walmac Int'l. (Ky.)	12,310,964	19,206	2.03%	0.31%
16	Farnsworth Farms (Fla.)	12,118,851	18,169	1.95%	0.45%
17	Airdrie Stud (Ky.)	12,062,702	20,798	3.62%	1.21%
18	Margaux Farm (Ky.)	11,383,381	20,548	1.99%	0.36%
19	Pin Oak Stud (Ky.)	10,948,803	27,236	3.98%	1.00%
20	Harris Farms (Calif.)	10,185,060	16,375	1.93%	0.48%
21	Spendthrift Farm (Ky.)	10,133,877	22,223	3.95%	1.75%
22	Mill Ridge Farm (Ky.)	9,872,405	29,295	2.67%	1.48%
23	Darby Dan Farm (Ky.)	9,793,829	23,600	3.13%	1.20%
24	Crestwood Farm (Ky.)	9,682,412	21,233	4.61%	1.10%
25	Franks Farms, Southland Division (Fla.)	9,503,080	20,437	2.80%	0.65%
26	McMahon of Saratoga Thoroughbreds (N.Y.)	9,405,883	19,434	2.27%	0.83%
27	Blue Ridge Farm (Va.)	9,214,661	19,399	3.16%	0.63%
28	Country Life Farm (Md.)	8,848,911	21,426	3.39%	0.00%
29	Windfields Farm (Ont.)	8,827,528	19,444	1.54%	0.22%
30	Bridlewood Farm (Fla.)	8,622,734	17,350	3.22%	1.21%
31	Milfer Farm (N.Y.)	8,101,790	21,209	3.93%	1.31%
32	Jonabell Farm (Ky.)	8,012,367	28,213	3.52%	1.41%
33	Reigle Heir Farms (Pa.)	7,416,446	19,164	3.62%	0.78%
34	Murmur Farm (Md.)	6,763,264	28,658	2.12%	1.27%
35	Walnford Stud (N.J.)	6,315,559	15,218	4.10%	1.69%

Rank	Name (State)	Stallion Earnings	Avg. Earnings	SWs/Strs	GSWs/Strs
36	Questroyal Stud (N.Y.)	6,078,297	19,054	1.57%	0.31%
37	Lane's End Texas (Tex.)	5,835,863	24,418	2.09%	0.00%
38	Adena Springs South (Fla.)	5,728,439	21,216	2.96%	0.00%
39	Gainsborough Farm (Ky.)	5,724,583	22,807	6.37%	1.59%
40	Signature Stallions (Fla.)	5,700,860	18,272	1.92%	0.00%
41	Golden Eagle Farm (Calif.)	5,519,077	17,577	2.23%	0.00%
42	Sugar Maple Farm (N.Y.)	4,823,144	21,062	2.18%	0.00%
43	Valor Farm (Tex.)	4,748,839	16,319	5.50%	0.00%
44	Hidden Point Farm (Tex.)	4,741,925	16,465	1.74%	0.00%
45	Clear Creek Stud (La.)	4,455,101	11,512	2.84%	0.26%
46	Woodstead Farm (Wash.)	4,252,705	11,683	1.10%	0.27%
47	Walmac South (Fla.)	4,222,249	17,094	2.02%	0.00%
48	Glencrest Farm (Ky.)	4,093,768	15,162	2.96%	0.74%
49	Ternes Farm (B.C.)	4,043,514	16,709	7.44%	0.83%
50	Marablue Farm (Fla.)	3,572,259	16,164	2.71%	0.91%
51	T-Square Stud (Fla.)	3,564,973	15,915	1.79%	0.45%
52	Rising Hill Farm (Fla.)	3,545,830	16,647	1.41%	0.00%
53	El Dorado Farms (Wash.)	3,318,177	11,024	1.99%	0.33%
54	Blooming Hills Farm (Calif.)	2,956,593	11,242	1.52%	0.38%
55	Double Diamond Farm (Fla.)	2,934,942	13,715	1.87%	0.00%
56	Highcliff Farm (N.Y.)	2,928,675	14,427	1.97%	0.00%
57	Red River Farms (La.)	2,810,420	9,966	1.06%	0.00%
58	Victory Rose Thoroughbreds (Calif.)	2,764,558	10,393	2.26%	0.00%
59	Horizon Farm (Alb.)	2,747,840	13,023	3.79%	0.00%
60	Pin Oak Lane Farm, Pa. Division (Pa.)	2,730,228	13,449	0.00%	0.00%
61	Southwest Stallion Station (Tex.)	2,696,680	12,202	1.81%	0.00%
62	Rancho San Miguel (Calif.)	2,634,801	11,456	1.74%	0.00%
63	Rio Medina Ranch (Tex.)	2,606,820	12,905	1.98%	0.00%
64	Double S Thoroughbred Farm (Tex.)	2,585,652	8,505	1.32%	0.33%
65	Circle H Ranch (Calif.)	2,206,482	10,457	1.42%	0.47%
66	Hideaway Farms (Calif.)	2,131,368	9,960	1.87%	0.47%

Highest North American Stud Fees of 2003

Stallion	Farm	Location	Stud Fee
Storm Cat	Overbrook Farm	Lexington, Ky.	$500,000
A.P. Indy	Lane's End	Versailles, Ky.	300,000
Seeking the Gold	Claiborne Farm	Paris, Ky.	225,000
Kingmambo	Lane's End	Versailles, Ky.	200,000
Danzig	Claiborne Farm	Paris, Ky.	125,000
Fusaichi Pegasus	Ashford Stud	Versailles, Ky.	125,000
Giant's Causeway	Ashford Stud	Versailles, Ky.	125,000
Gone West	Mill Ridge Farm	Lexington, Ky.	125,000
Broad Brush	Gainesway	Lexington, Ky.	100,000
Deputy Minister	Brookdale Farm	Versailles, Ky.	100,000
Unbridled's Song	Taylor Made Farm	Nicholasville, Ky.	100,000
Rahy	Three Chimneys Farm	Midway, Ky.	80,000
El Prado (Ire)	Adena Springs Kentucky	Versailles, Ky.	75,000
Point Given	Three Chimneys Farm	Midway, Ky.	75,000
Pulpit	Claiborne Farm	Paris, Ky.	75,000
Theatrical (Ire)	Hill 'n' Dale Farms	Lexington, Ky.	75,000
Thunder Gulch	Ashford Stud	Versailles, Ky.	65,000
Cozzene	Gainesway	Lexington, Ky.	60,000
Dixieland Band	Lane's End	Versailles, Ky.	60,000
Forest Wildcat	Brookdale Farm	Versailles, Ky.	60,000
War Chant	Three Chimneys Farm	Midway, Ky.	60,000
Awesome Again	Adena Springs Kentucky	Versailles, Ky.	50,000
Coronado's Quest	Claiborne Farm	Paris, Ky.	50,000
Dynaformer	Three Chimneys Farm	Midway, Ky.	50,000
Forestry	Taylor Made Farm	Nicholasville, Ky.	50,000
Gulch	Lane's End	Versailles, Ky.	50,000
Lemon Drop Kid	Lane's End	Versailles, Ky.	50,000
Mr. Greeley	Spendthrift Farm	Lexington, Ky.	50,000
Touch Gold	Adena Springs Kentucky	Versailles, Ky.	50,000

Leading Stud Farms of 2002

LANE'S END—Location: Versailles, Kentucky. **Founded:** 1979. **Principals:** William S. Farish and Bill Farish. **Acreage:** 1,600. **Stallions for 2003:** A.P. Indy, Belong to Me, Came Home, Dixieland Band, Dixie Union, Fit to Fight, Gulch, King Cugat, Kingmambo, Lemon Drop Kid, Lil's Lad, Parade Ground, Pine Bluff, Pleasant Tap, Silver Ghost, Smart Strike, Stephen Got Even, Summer Squall. **Grade 1 or Group 1 winners of 2002 by Lane's End stallions:** Bulla Borghese, Jilbab, Malhub, Miss Houdini, Nayef, Portcullis, Summer Colony.

ASHFORD STUD—Location: Versailles, Kentucky. **Founded:** 1910. **Principals:** John Magnier and partners. **Acreage:** 1,500. **Stallions for 2003:** Bianconi, Black Minnaloushe, Fusaichi Pegasus, Giant's Causeway, Grand Slam, Hennessy, High Yield, Honour and Glory, Johannesburg, Louis Quatorze, Lure, Royal Academy, Stravinsky, Tale of the Cat, Thunder Gulch, Woodman. **Grade 1 or Group 1 winners of 2002 by Ashford stallions:** Bel Esprit, Chiselling, Hawk Wing, Hopetown (Arg), Shot of Thunder, Tully Thunder.

GAINESWAY—Location: Lexington. **Founded:** 1979. **Principal:** Graham Beck. **Acreage:** 1,680. **Stallions for 2003:** Bates Motel, Broad Brush, Cozzene, Formal Gold, K One King, Lear Fan, Luhuk, Mt. Livermore, Officer, Orientate, Sir Cat, Smoke Glacken, Strategic Mission, Subordination. **Grade 1 or Group 1 winners of 2002 by Gainesway stallions:** Dublino, Farda Amiga, Mongoose, Orientate, Sarafan.

THREE CHIMNEYS FARM—Location: Midway, Kentucky. **Founded:** 1973. **Principal:** Robert N. Clay. **Acreage:** 1,500. **Stallions for 2003:** Albert the Great, Atticus, Capote, Dynaformer, Point Given, Rahy, Silver Charm, War Chant, Wild Again. **Grade 1 or Group 1 winners of 2002 by Three Chimneys stallions:** Milwaukee Brew, Riskaverse, Sarava, Shine Again, Vindication.

CLAIBORNE FARM—Location: Paris, Kentucky. **Founded:** 1910. **President:** Seth Hancock. **Acreage:** 2,764. **Stallions for 2003:** Arch, Boundary, Coronado's Quest, Danzig, Devil's Bag, Go for Gin, Horse Chestnut (SAf), Monarchos, Ordway, Out of Place, Private Terms, Pulpit, Seeking the Gold. **Grade 1 or Group 1 winners of 2002 by Claiborne stallions:** Favorite Funtime, Sky Mesa.

VINERY KENTUCKY—Location: Lexington. **Founded:** 1987. **Principal:** Thomas Simon. **Acreage:** 462. **Stallions for 2003:** Brahms, Gilded Time, Langfuhr, Marquetry, More Than Ready, Red Ransom, Runaway Groom, Scorpion, Twining, Yonaguska. **Grade 1 or Group 1 winners of 2002 by Vinery Kentucky stallions:** Elloluv, Imperial Gesture, Mandy's Gold.

BROOKDALE FARM—Location: Versailles, Kentucky. **Founded:** 1983. **Principal:** Fred Seitz. **Acreage:** 375. **Stallions for 2003:** Crafty Prospector, Deputy Minister, Forest Wildcat, Silver Deputy, Will's Way, With Approval. **Grade 1 or Group 1 winners of 2002 by Brookdale stallions:** D'wildcat.

HILL 'N' DALE FARMS—Location: Lexington. **Founded:** 1980. **Principal:** John G. Sikura. **Acreage:** 525. **Stallions for 2003:** Buddha, Dance Brightly, El Corredor, Geri, Jade Hunter, Mongoose, Mutakddim, Theatrical (Ire), Vision and Verse. **Grade 1 or Group**

1 winners in 2002 by Hill 'n' Dale stallions: Astra, Azeri, El Charlatan, Media Puzzle.

OVERBROOK FARM—Location: Lexington. **Founded:** 1972. **Principal:** William T. Young. **Acreage:** 2,400. **Stallions for 2003:** Cape Canaveral, Cape Town, Carson City, Cat Thief, Editor's Note, Grindstone, Jump Start, Pioneering, Storm Cat, Tactical Cat. **Grade 1 or Group 1 winners in 2002 by Overbrook stallions:** Carson Hollow, Hold That Tiger, Raging Fever, Sophisticat, Storm Flag Flying.

ADENA SPRINGS KENTUCKY—Location: Versailles, Kentucky. **Founded:** 1989. **Principal:** Frank Stronach. **Acreage:** 1,850. **Stallions for 2003:** Alphabet Soup, Awesome Again, El Prado (Ire), Gold Case, Golden Missile, Touch Gold, Wild Rush. **Grade 1 or Group 1 winners of 2002 by Adena Springs Kentucky stallions:** Medaglia d'Oro, Toccet.

NORTHVIEW STALLION STATION—Location: Chesapeake City Maryland. **Founded:** 1989. **Principals:** Richard Golden, Allaire duPont, and Tom Bowman. **Acreage:** 400. **Stallions for 2003:** Awad, Concern, Crowd Pleaser, Diamond, Lion Hearted, Not For Love, Partner's Hero, Polish Miner, Tamayaz, Two Punch, Waquoit.

OCALA STUD FARM—Location: Ocala. **Founded:** 1956. **Principal:** J. Michael O'Farrell Jr. **Acreage:** 500. **Stallions for 2003:** Concerto, Concorde's Tune, Mecke, Montbrook, Notebook, Slew Gin Fizz, Sweetsouthernsaint, Trippi. **Grade 1 or Group 1 winners of 2002 by Ocala Stud Farm stallions:** Booklet.

WAFARE FARM—Location: Midway, Kentucky. **Founded:** 1984. **Principals:** Nathan Fox and Richard Kaster. **Acreage:** 325. **Stallions for 2003:** Acceptable, Barkerville, Canaveral, Catrail, Deerhound, Fast Play, Glitterman, Judge T C, Polish Navy, Richter Scale.

TAYLOR MADE FARM—Location: Nicholasville, Kentucky. **Founded:** 1976. **Principals:** Duncan, Ben, Frank, and Mark Taylor. **Acreage:** 1,600. **Stallions for 2003:** Artax, Exploit, Forestry, Our Emblem, Real Quiet, Storm Creek, Unbridled's Song. **Grade 1 or Group 1 winners of 2002 by Taylor Made stallions:** Buddha.

WALMAC INTERNATIONAL—Location: Lexington. **Founded:** 1936. **Principal:** John T. L. Jones Jr. **Acreage:** 1,097. **Stallions for 2003:** Confide, Evansville Slew, Favorite Trick, Gentlemen (Arg), Irgun, Lasting Approval, Leelanau, Minardi, Miswaki, Romanov (Ire), Salt Lake, Saratoga Six, Scatmandu, Sea of Secrets, Thunderello.

FARNSWORTH FARMS—Location: Morriston, Florida. **Founded:** 1956. **Principal:** Michael Sherman. **Acreage:** 700. **Stallions for 2003:** Adcat, Double Honor, Fortunate Prospect, Line in the Sand, Robyn Dancer, Sir Leon, Statesmanship, Suave Prospect.

AIDRIE STUD—Location: Midway, Kentucky. **Founded:** 1972. **Principal:** Brereton C. and Libby Jones. **Acreage:** 2,500. **Stallions for 2003:** Afternoon Deelites, Banker's Gold, Deputy Commander, Forest Camp, Include, Indian Charlie, Mazel Trick, Silver Hawk, Siphon (Brz), Slew City Slew, Stormin Fever, Yankee Victor, You and I. **Grade 1 or Group 1 winners in 2002 by Airdrie stallions:** Wonder Again, You.

Live Foal Report for 2002

The effects of mare reproductive loss syndrome (MRLS) were most visibly and starkly shown by the Jockey Club's Report of Live Foals for 2002. Nationally, the number of live foals as reported through December 31, 2002, slipped to 37,807 from 40,319 on the same date a year earlier. The end-of-year reports, representing more than 90% of all live foals reported by breeders, documented a 6.2% drop nationally. Also affected was the live-birth rate, which fell three percentage points, from 62% in 2001 to 59% in 2002.

Kentucky, which lost a portion of its 2001 foal crop and a significant number of its 2002 crop to MLRS in Central Kentucky, took the heaviest blow. In the report at the end of 2001, mares bred to Kentucky sires had produced 14,615 foals, with a live-foal rate of 70%. As of December 31, 2002, mares bred to Kentucky stallions had produced 12,276 live foals, a drop of 16%. The live-foal percentages also were hammered, dropping

a full ten percentage points to 60%.

Despite MLRS's effects, Kentucky remained the largest producer of live Thoroughbred foals, followed by Florida (4,517) and California (4,022). Reversing normal trends, both of the latter named states had higher percentages of live foals than Kentucky.

Stallions bred to the most mares commonly produce the most live foals, and Thunder Gulch, who was bred to a record 216 mares in 2001, had 137 live foals in 2002. Honour and Glory, who like Thunder Gulch stands at Ashford Stud near Versailles, Kentucky, covered the second-highest number of mares, 192, and was the second-leading sire by live foals, with 131. Breaking Ashford's domination on the list of leading foal producers was A. P Jet, who stood the 2002 breeding season at Sugar Maple Farm in Poughquag, New York. The son of Fappiano had 105 live foals from 133 matings, yielding a live-foal rate of 79%.

Leading Stallions by 2002 Foals

Stallion	Mares bred	Live foals	%	State	Stallion	Mares bred	Live foals	%	State
Thunder Gulch	216	137	63	KY	Unbridled's Song	107	73	68	KY
Honour and Glory	192	131	68	KY	Lord Carson	114	72	63	KY
A. P Jet	133	105	79	NY	Storm Cat	116	72	62	KY
Wheaton	140	101	72	FL	Golden Missile	105	71	68	KY
Louis Quatorze	162	100	62	KY	Leestown	85	71	84	LA
Maria's Mon	130	93	72	KY	Tiger Ridge	109	71	65	FL
Crafty Friend	132	92	70	KY	Alphabet Soup	96	70	73	KY
Bertrando	107	91	85	CA	Event of the Year	99	70	71	CA
Cee's Tizzy	105	91	87	CA	Foxtrail	103	70	68	Ont.
High Yield	170	91	54	KY	Malibu Moon	112	70	63	MD
Stormy Atlantic	129	91	71	FL	Old Trieste	118	70	59	KY
Swiss Yodeler	113	91	81	CA	Stravinsky	105	70	67	KY
Fusaichi Pegasus	150	89	59	KY	Kingmambo	98	69	70	KY
A.P. Indy	127	88	69	KY	Notable Cat	113	69	61	OK
Allen's Prospect	126	86	68	MD	Sky Classic	106	69	65	KY
Devil His Due	124	83	67	KY	Unbridled Jet	104	69	66	MD
Yankee Victor	117	83	71	KY	Awesome Again	104	68	65	KY
Royal Anthem	134	82	61	KY	Lite the Fuse	104	68	65	FL
Running Stag	114	82	72	FL	Royal Academy	119	68	57	KY
Slew Gin Fizz	116	82	71	FL	Storm Creek	103	68	66	KY
Afternoon Deelites	126	81	64	KY	Chief Seattle	109	67	61	KY
Mr. Greeley	124	81	65	KY	Grand Slam	120	67	56	KY
Artax	110	80	73	KY	Rubiano	99	67	68	KY
Saint Ballado	110	80	73	KY	Honor Grades	112	66	59	KY
Valid Expectations	107	79	74	TX	Mazel Trick	104	66	63	KY
Carson City	111	78	70	KY	Memo (Chi)	81	66	81	CA
Exploit	119	78	66	KY	Rahy	106	66	62	KY
King of Kings (Ire)	124	78	63	KY	Family Calling	101	65	64	FL
Bartok (Ire)	96	77	80	CA	Forestry	97	65	67	KY
Robyn Dancer	113	77	68	FL	Open Forum	117	65	56	FL
Charismatic	108	76	70	KY	Skip Away	121	65	54	KY
Silver Charm	113	76	67	KY	Vicar	103	65	63	KY
Straight Man	114	76	67	FL	Wild Rush	95	65	68	KY
Wild Zone	116	76	66	TX	Cryptoclearance	109	64	59	KY
Holy Bull	115	75	65	KY	Fly So Free	92	64	70	KY
Peaks and Valleys	113	75	66	KY	Gilded Time	104	64	62	KY
Halo's Image	105	74	70	FL	High Brite	79	64	81	CA
Stormin Fever	124	74	60	KY	Montbrook	87	64	74	FL
Tale of the Cat	107	74	69	KY	More Than Ready	95	64	67	KY
Yes It's True	105	74	70	FL	Siphon (Brz)	102	64	63	KY
Belong to Me	105	73	70	KY	Tomorrows Cat	102	64	63	NY
Double Honor	101	73	72	FL	Touch Gold	94	64	68	KY
Langfuhr	110	73	66	KY					

Live Foals by Stallions by State and Province in 2002

State	Stallions	Mares bred	Live foals	%	State	Stallions	Mares bred	Live foals	%
Alaska	1	1	0	0	New York	131	2,275	1,423	63
Alabama	20	95	55	58	Nebraska	42	357	159	45
Arkansas	71	573	317	55	Nevada	7	30	18	60
Arizona	71	465	267	57	Ohio	111	871	453	52
California	408	5,734	4,022	70	Oklahoma	234	1,947	1,016	52
Colorado	81	450	217	48	Oregon	53	450	267	59
Connecticut	3	7	4	57	Pennsylvania	114	979	546	56
Florida	291	7,249	4,517	62	South Carolina	24	231	117	51
Georgia	23	98	58	59	South Dakota	18	167	63	38
Hawaii	1	1	1	100	Tennessee	28	98	31	32
Iowa	68	748	403	54	Texas	426	3,624	1,979	55
Idaho	61	309	142	46	Utah	47	211	121	57
Illinois	133	1,291	658	51	Virginia	90	592	323	55
Indiana	103	820	379	46	Vermont	3	9	3	33
Kansas	31	199	91	46	West Virginia	56	663	350	53
Kentucky	447	20,604	12,276	60	Washington	125	1,357	823	61
Louisiana	198	2,227	1,305	59	Wisconsin	13	26	15	58
Massachusetts	23	113	48	42	Wyoming	18	56	25	45
Maryland	108	1,896	1,189	63	Puerto Rico	73	797	530	66
Maine	3	3	2	67	**Canada Province**				
Michigan	74	562	317	56	Alberta	85	847	446	53
Minnesota	30	253	138	55	British Columbia	81	824	473	57
Missouri	35	158	69	44	Manitoba	24	229	95	41
Mississippi	14	73	37	51	New Brunswick	1	1	1	100
Montana	48	273	93	34	Nova Scotia	2	5	3	60
North Carolina	23	66	35	53	Ontario	109	1,450	896	62
North Dakota	20	129	56	43	Quebec	5	16	4	25
New Hampshire	1	5	1	20	Saskatchewan	25	154	90	58
New Jersey	48	277	179	65	**Totals**	**4,540**	**64,184**	**37,807**	**59**
New Mexico	144	1,215	650	53					

Stallions With Live Foals in 2002

(As of December 31, 2002; minimum of ten mares bred)

Stallion	Mares bred	Fls	%	Stallion	Mares bred	Fls	%	Stallion	Mares bred	Fls	%
ALABAMA				Truce Maker	18	10	56	Demon's Crown	10	0	0
Casey On Deck	17	9	53	**CALIFORNIA**				Desert Secret (Ire)	16	10	63
Royal Empire	26	16	62	All Thee Power	14	13	93	Devon Lane	52	38	73
ARKANSAS				American Day	13	5	38	Din's Dancer	44	38	86
American General	12	7	58	Anziyan	36	26	72	Discover	13	10	77
A. V. Eight	31	13	42	Apollo	23	18	78	Distinctive Cat	41	30	73
Bold Anthony	39	29	74	Avenue of Flags	43	28	65	Dominated Debut	17	8	47
Caracey	13	5	38	Bartok (Ire)	96	77	80	Emerald Creme	18	10	56
Cinnamon Creek	53	32	60	Bay Street Star	35	21	60	Emerald Jig	13	5	38
Country Store	12	5	42	Beau Genius	40	33	83	Endow	10	4	40
Etbauer	22	17	77	Benchmark	78	54	69	Epic Honor	26	18	69
Gremlin Grey	12	1	8	Bertrando	107	91	85	Event of the Year	99	70	71
Harperstown	12	7	58	B. Hoedown	10	5	50	Fabulous Champ	30	23	77
Idabel	17	11	65	Bold Badgett	54	42	78	Falstaff	27	22	81
Olympic Prospector	23	11	48	Boomerang	11	5	45	Fargo	33	23	70
Southern Forest	12	6	50	Born Wild	39	26	67	Fine n' Majestic	21	14	67
Storm and a Half	77	47	61	Boulder Dam	10	4	40	Flying Continental	37	27	73
This Picture	34	14	41	Brave Romane	13	9	69	Flying Victor	44	30	68
Unbridled's Risk	16	10	63	Cactus Creole	10	7	70	For Really	23	18	78
ARIZONA				Candi's Gold	16	11	69	Free House	44	36	82
Barricade	49	33	67	Candyman Bee	12	11	92	Fruition	33	28	85
Benton Creek	34	26	76	Category Five	37	28	76	Future Storm	65	45	69
Buck Strider	34	20	59	Cee's Tizzy	105	91	87	Game Plan	48	31	65
Butler's Revenge	16	3	19	Cherokee Colony	14	8	57	General Meeting	59	36	61
Calumar	11	7	64	Chullo (Arg)	11	10	91	The Good Life	17	12	71
Chanate	45	34	76	Cold n Calculating	11	7	64	Haint	21	16	76
Chopin	25	13	52	Comet Shine	30	22	73	Half Term	16	5	31
Local Artist	18	7	39	Commitment	50	17	34	Helmsman	52	32	62
Racey Remarque	10	8	80	Corslew	19	14	74	High Brite	79	64	81
Relaunch a Tune	17	12	71	Country Light	17	7	41	Houston	25	22	88
Tax Collection	14	6	43	Crowning Storm	40	28	70	Hunter's Glory	13	7	54
				Dance Floor	64	49	77	Iam the Iceman	15	12	80
								Illinois Storm	30	17	57

Stallion	Mares bred	Fls	%
In Excess (Ire)	79	57	72
Iron Cat	18	15	83
Kahuna Jack	49	36	73
Kessem Power (NZ)	21	20	95
King of the Hunt	24	13	54
Kozak	19	13	68
Larry the Legend	40	35	88
Last Lion	26	16	62
Latin American	74	47	64
Lil Tyler	35	28	80
Lindsey's Roberto	17	10	59
Loyal Double	10	7	70
Lucayan Prince	26	19	73
Mach One	10	7	70
Majesterian	17	11	65
Makaleha	29	20	69
Makhraj	25	14	56
Malek (Chi)	42	28	67
Mantles Star (GB)	22	15	68
Matty G	18	11	61
Memo (Chi)	81	66	81
Mr. Broad Blade	10	8	80
Mr. Procrastinator	17	14	82
Mr Purple	23	19	83
Moscow Ballet	63	40	63
Mud Route	61	46	75
Muqtarib	25	20	80
My King (GER)	14	11	79
Native Storm	25	15	60
Newton's Law (Ire)	11	9	82
Northern Devil	21	17	81
Not Tricky	21	13	62
Old Topper	53	41	77
Ole'	23	16	70
Olympio	89	57	64
Paranoide (Arg)	18	13	72
Perfect Mandate	11	9	82
Pharisien (Fr)	11	8	73
Phone Roberto	25	17	68
Phone Saga	24	16	67
Phonetics	13	10	77
Proud Irish	46	41	89
Red	34	21	62
Rhythm	50	30	60
Rio Verde	33	29	88
River Flyer	13	9	69
Robannier	17	11	65
Royal Regatta (Ire)	11	9	82
Scherando	22	20	91
Score Quick	14	11	79
Seattle Bound	39	26	67
Seven Rivers	18	14	78
Siberian Summer	31	22	71
Silver Ray	12	9	75
Simply Majestic	12	7	58
Six Below	47	39	83
Slewpy	26	16	62
Slew the Bride	17	10	59
Slewvescent	24	20	83
Smokester	40	31	78
Smooth Runner	16	8	50
Stage Colony	13	11	85
State Performer	13	10	77
Strike Gold	15	10	67
Suggest	13	12	92
Surachai	35	22	63
Swiss Yodeler	113	91	81
Synastry	15	12	80
Tactical Heir	10	2	20
Tahoe City	17	12	71
Tinners Way	22	19	86
Town Caper	31	19	61
Trail City	52	40	77

Stallion	Mares bred	Fls	%
Tricky Creek	21	12	57
Truckee	51	39	76
Truly Met	17	6	35
Turkoman	74	42	57
Twin Spires	57	49	86
Tychonic (GB)	56	36	64
Unusual Heat	35	25	71
Valid Wager	71	57	80
Vaudeville	46	32	70
Ventriloquist	15	8	53
Via Lombardia (Ire)	20	17	85
Wanpum	19	9	47
Western Fame	39	33	85
What a Spell	11	6	55
Wild Deputy	33	22	67
Wild Gold	41	25	61

COLORADO

Stallion	Mares bred	Fls	%
Basic Rate	11	8	73
Cash Deposit	36	25	69
Coverallbases	26	11	42
Crafty Harold	16	7	44
Dash Ahead	10	6	60
Exploding Rainbow	11	3	27
Kennedy Factor	19	9	47
San Rafael Pass	13	0	0
Sinceilostmybaby	16	7	44
Smilin Singin Sam	36	19	53
Woody Win	10	8	80

FLORIDA

Stallion	Mares bred	Fls	%
Absent Russian	14	10	71
Adcat	39	23	59
Aloha Prospector	35	17	49
Anjiz	24	12	50
Appealing Skier	39	26	67
Badge	32	20	63
Believe It	14	7	50
Blue Ensign	12	5	42
Bon Point (GB)	29	16	55
Brief Ruckus	32	17	53
Byars	20	16	80
Capture the Gold	49	32	65
Carlisle Bay	14	8	57
Cimarron Secret	31	28	90
Classic Cat	26	13	50
Cloud Cover	28	17	61
Cohiba	32	20	63
Colony Light	48	38	79
Comeonmom	11	6	55
Commitisize	27	22	81
Concerto	51	28	55
Concorde's Tune	65	41	63
Conveyor	13	9	69
Crown Pleasure	12	6	50
Cyberspace	13	4	31
Dance Master	32	21	66
Darn That Alarm	19	13	68
David	13	10	77
Dawn Quixote	16	9	56
Diligence	43	27	63
Dixie Power	10	7	70
D. J. Cat	23	14	61
Dr. Caton	52	32	62
Double Honor	101	73	72
Dove Hunt	35	19	54
Eltish	45	32	71
Eskimo	15	9	60
Fabulous Frolic	61	43	70
Family Calling	101	65	64
Fast 'n Royal	14	11	79
Faygo	20	10	50
Forever Whirl	13	3	23
Formal Dinner	61	37	61

Stallion	Mares bred	Fls	%
Fortunate Move	13	5	38
Fortunate Prospect	55	38	69
Gold Alert	20	13	65
Greenwood Lake	67	43	64
Groomstick	22	19	86
Halos and Horns	29	17	59
Halo's Image	105	74	70
Hazaam	41	21	51
Hesabull	41	27	66
Holy Mountain	38	19	50
Hubble	14	5	36
Hunting Hard	56	20	36
Impeachment	25	17	68
Is It True	47	29	62
Island Whirl	27	18	67
Jeblar	25	15	60
Jules	50	37	74
Keep Dreaming	11	6	55
Kelly Kip	51	28	55
Kipper Kelly	43	23	53
Kissin Kris	64	47	73
Laubali	15	13	87
Limit Out	23	15	65
Line In The Sand	101	59	58
Lite the Fuse	104	68	65
Littlebitlively	70	47	67
Lost Soldier	99	59	60
Lucky Lionel	82	55	67
Lucky North	20	12	60
Lycius	57	32	56
Marco Bay	36	17	47
Master Bill	45	33	73
Meadow Flight	20	11	55
Mecke	29	16	55
Metfield	35	16	46
Migrating Moon	47	24	51
Miner's Mark	85	39	46
Minstrel Dancer	13	11	85
Mister Jolie	52	26	50
Montbrook	87	64	74
Montreal Red	22	14	64
Native Regent	24	19	79
Noactor	31	19	61
Northern Afleet	70	47	67
Northern Trend	15	9	60
Notebook	59	41	69
Ocala Slew	12	9	75
Oliver's Twist	16	8	50
Open Forum	117	65	56
Outflanker	60	43	72
Part the Waters	10	8	80
Pentelicus	49	39	80
Piccolino	18	12	67
Precocity	39	28	72
Premiership	20	12	60
Proud and True	45	27	60
Proudest Romeo	23	20	87
Quaker Ridge	42	26	62
Reality Road	17	10	59
Regal Humor	17	11	65
Reparations	26	18	69
Reprized	21	16	76
Rizzi	96	60	63
Robyn Dancer	113	77	68
Rocky Mountain	11	4	36
Running Stag	114	82	72
Sam's Sunny Hour	10	7	70
Sasha's Prospect	42	24	57
Seacliff	33	15	45
Semoran	53	29	55
The Silver Move	26	15	58
Skip Trial	28	16	57
Slew Gin Fizz	116	82	71

Stallion	Mares bred	Fls	%
Stack	13	12	92
Star of Valor	29	18	62
Statesmanship	11	7	64
Stormy Atlantic	129	91	71
Straight Man	114	76	67
Struggler (GB)	19	11	58
Suave Prospect	55	35	64
Successful Appeal	77	45	58
Sweetsouthernsaint	90	53	59
Sword Dance (Ire)	80	55	69
Tactical Advantage	61	36	59
Thats Our Buck	79	48	61
Thisnearlywasmine	13	5	38
Tiger Ridge	109	71	65
Time Bandit	30	18	60
Toolighttoquit	22	16	73
Top Account	63	32	51
Tour d'Or	72	55	76
Traitor	33	20	61
Twin Halo	10	7	70
Untuttable	31	23	74
Way West (Fr)	38	30	79
West Acre	43	21	49
Western Borders	29	15	52
Western Cat	49	27	55
Wheaton	140	101	72
Whitney Tower	27	13	48
Wild Escapade	37	24	65
Wild Event	69	40	58
Wild Wonder	87	57	66
Wind Whipper	61	36	59
Wised Up	42	32	76
Worldly Manner	65	29	45
World Stage (Ire)	69	7	10
Yes It's True	105	74	70
Zamindar	81	50	62

GEORGIA

Stallion	Mares bred	Fls	%
Roaring Camp	26	17	65
Sheikh Adel	11	4	36

IOWA

Stallion	Mares bred	Fls	%
At the Threshold	13	6	46
Buzz Saw	11	6	55
Cape Storm	32	19	59
Cat's Debut	10	3	30
Champagneforashley	13	10	77
Change Takes Time	21	12	57
Commemorate	23	14	61
De Guerin	10	7	70
Dignitas	20	10	50
Farragut	19	9	47
H. J. Baker	26	8	31
Honest Ensign	31	21	68
Humming	13	6	46
Kyle's Our Man	55	31	56
Lord Pleasant	12	5	42
Mercedes Won	32	22	69
Mocha Express	23	13	57
Night Runner	20	12	60
Parfaitement	11	9	82
Prospect Feature	13	7	54
Purdue King	22	13	59
Sharkey	32	20	63
Shotiche	20	13	65
Temujin	16	8	50
Tiger Talk	13	11	85
West Buoyant	24	11	46
Wild Invader	31	17	55
Yankee Fan	19	11	58

IDAHO

Stallion	Mares bred	Fls	%
Chisos	11	5	45
Coastal Voyage	15	5	33

Stallion	Mares bred	Fls	%
Firmlin	10	4	40
Hey Rob	15	6	40
Jestic	19	8	42
Kings Blood (Ire)	14	8	57
Present Value	18	3	17
Pro Chapeau	10	6	60
Renteria	21	13	62
Shergar's Best (Ire)	11	8	73
Thunderah	14	8	57

ILLINOIS

Stallion	Mares bred	Fls	%
Alaskan Frost	50	26	52
A Lee Rover	11	0	0
Allen Charge	21	8	38
Awesome Cat	33	16	48
Bold Revenue	17	7	41
Canyon Run	12	6	50
Cartwright	77	55	71
Charlie Barley	25	12	48
Cherokee Saga	10	7	70
City by Night	45	30	67
Classic Account	14	10	71
Classified Facts	22	10	45
Conte Di Savoya	22	12	55
Diazo	31	20	65
Double Niner	19	10	53
Electric Blue	18	7	39
Emancipator	12	3	25
Executive Order	20	8	40
Fact Book	15	5	33
Gogarty (Ire)	17	2	12
Goliard	30	5	17
Hannibal Cat	17	11	65
He's a Tough Cat	11	5	45
Jolly Blade	10	7	70
Let Him Go	15	5	33
Macaso	21	8	38
Mt. Magazine	22	8	36
Palmister	21	11	52
Presently	27	12	44
Seattle Morn	35	24	69
Shakeel	23	17	74
Smokin Mel	10	6	60
Spanish Drummer	37	19	51
U Folks	11	5	45
Unbridled Success	10	3	30
Unite	19	12	63
Unreal Zeal	67	37	55
Western Playboy	29	13	45
Wild Gambler	11	9	82
Zagor	17	11	65
Z Z Cat	27	13	48

INDIANA

Stallion	Mares bred	Fls	%
Ali Gaziba	21	4	19
Assembly Dancer	14	5	36
Bidding Proud	15	8	53
Bordagaray	10	2	20
Bravoure	12	1	8
Cat Power	41	17	41
Classy Prospector	16	11	69
Crown Ambassador	22	9	41
D. C. Tenacious	12	6	50
Fiscal	19	10	53
Gallant Step	13	5	38
Guys From Space	12	5	42
Hit the Roof	25	8	32
Indy Mood	41	15	37
Jacquelyn's Groom	22	19	86
Jungle Express	13	11	85
Magic Flagship	13	8	62
Mexican Bandit	10	7	70
Miswaki Bandit	10	4	40

Stallion	Mares bred	Fls	%
Moro Oro	25	16	64
Philadream	10	1	10
Presidential Order	25	11	44
Riflery	19	9	47
Seattle Rob	12	5	42
Sir Riddle	11	8	73
Swiss Trick	15	9	60
T. H. Fappiano	13	6	46
Tricon	24	8	33
Waki Warrior	26	17	65

KANSAS

Stallion	Mares bred	Fls	%
Gold Ruler	19	11	58
Groom's Image	10	2	20
Life Interest	11	6	55
Prospect North	17	4	24
So Ever Clever	12	7	58
Speedy Nijinsky	12	7	58
Torey Ridge	15	4	27

KENTUCKY

Stallion	Mares bred	Fls	%
Accelerator	85	46	54
Acceptable	34	18	53
Afternoon Deelites	126	81	64
Aggressive Chief	17	12	71
Aljabr	55	31	56
Allied Forces	41	27	66
Alphabet Soup	96	70	73
American Chance	72	47	65
Anees	87	47	54
Anet	40	23	58
Announce	43	30	70
Answer Lively	36	5	14
A.P. Indy	127	88	69
Arch	75	51	68
Artax	110	80	73
Atticus	55	32	58
Awesome Again	104	68	65
Bahri	47	29	62
Banker's Gold	63	39	62
Barkerville	19	11	58
Basic	16	5	31
Bates Motel	26	13	50
Behrens	52	33	63
Belong to Me	105	73	70
Bernstein	67	38	57
Best of Luck	88	54	61
Bianconi	102	58	57
Boston Harbor	82	49	60
Boundary	81	45	56
Bright Launch	52	25	48
Broad Brush	47	27	57
Brunswick	11	4	36
Caller I. D.	30	18	60
Canaveral	30	17	57
Cape Canaveral	82	60	73
Cape Town	85	59	69
Capote	42	24	57
Captain Bodgit	108	50	46
Carolina Kid	24	4	17
Carson City	111	78	70
Cat Creek Slew	16	3	19
Catienus	66	47	71
Catrail	63	25	40
Cat's Career	66	48	73
Cat Thief	93	59	63
Charismatic	108	76	70
Cherokee Run	90	58	64
Chester House	88	62	70
Chief Seattle	109	67	61
Chimes Band	39	21	54
Clever Trick	45	31	69
Cobra King	19	13	68

Stallion	Mares bred	Fls	%	Stallion	Mares bred	Fls	%	Stallion	Mares bred	Fls	%
Comic Strip	63	38	60	Gold Fever	74	51	69	Ordway	18	12	67
Commendable	58	33	57	Gold Legend	50	25	50	Our Emblem	31	22	71
Composer	41	21	51	Gold Tribute	53	21	40	Out of Place	98	61	62
Comstock Lode	41	18	44	Gone West	80	51	64	Parade Ground	80	49	61
Confide	47	35	74	Good and Tough	66	39	59	Party Manners	29	18	62
Conquistador Cielo	69	43	62	Grand Slam	120	67	56	Peaks and Valleys	113	75	66
Constant Demand	18	10	56	Grindstone	71	39	55	Pembroke	34	16	47
Coronado's Quest	74	53	72	Gulch	68	44	65	Perfect Vision	37	24	65
Count the Time	69	43	62	Halory Hunter	17	10	59	Peruvian	11	7	64
Cozzene	65	44	68	High Yield	170	91	54	Petionville	62	47	76
Crafty Friend	132	92	70	Hold for Gold	17	9	53	Phone Trick	71	36	51
Crafty Prospector	78	47	60	Holy Bull	115	75	65	Pine Bluff	84	52	62
Crimson Classic	13	5	38	Home At Last	16	11	69	Pioneering	98	61	62
Cryptoclearance	109	64	59	Honor Grades	112	66	59	Pistols and Roses	26	12	46
Dance Brightly	94	56	60	Honour and Glory	192	131	68	Pleasantprospector	11	5	45
Danzig	48	38	79	Horse Chestnut (SAf)	88	59	67	Pleasant Tap	86	58	67
Dare and Go	48	20	42	Ide	30	21	70	Polish Navy	68	34	50
Dayjur	23	15	65	Indian Charlie	73	41	56	Private Terms	53	29	55
Deerhound	21	11	52	In the Zone	14	3	21	Prized	48	18	38
Defensive Play	15	4	27	Intidab	13	8	62	Prospect Bay	36	22	61
Defrere	34	17	50	Irgun	58	43	74	Prospectors Gamble	15	8	53
Demidoff	36	7	19	Irish River (Fr)	20	3	15	Prudent Manner (Ire)	13	7	54
The Deputy (Ire)	86	46	53	Islefaxyou	31	14	45	Puerto Madero (Chi)	28	15	54
Deputy Commander	73	51	70	Jade Hunter	52	33	63	Pulpit	76	54	71
Deputy Minister	87	54	62	Jambalaya Jazz	45	21	47	Pyramid Peak	61	36	59
Devil His Due	124	83	67	Joyeux Danseur	49	26	53	Quiet American	59	35	59
Devil's Bag	64	48	75	Just a Cat	51	24	47	Rahy	106	66	62
Diesis (GB)	84	56	67	Kandaly	11	4	36	Real Quiet	99	59	60
Distant View	82	47	57	Kayrawan	20	11	55	Red Ransom	86	60	70
Distorted Humor	95	55	58	Kingmambo	98	69	70	Repriced	73	42	58
Dixieland Band	82	50	61	King of Kings (Ire)	124	78	63	Richter Scale	80	42	53
Dixieland Heat	64	28	44	K One King	46	24	52	Roar	59	35	59
Dixie Union	84	52	62	K. O. Punch	43	22	51	Rockamundo	11	5	45
Doneraile Court	95	51	54	Kris S.	55	26	47	Rod and Staff	18	7	39
Down the Aisle	59	31	53	Laabity	23	13	57	Romanov (Ire)	30	15	50
Dumaani	27	13	48	Labeeb (GB)	35	17	49	Royal Academy	119	68	57
Dusty Screen	19	8	42	Lac Ouimet	45	30	67	Royal Anthem	134	82	61
Dynaformer	98	60	61	Langfuhr	110	73	66	Rubiano	99	67	68
Eastern Echo	27	19	70	Lasting Approval	32	20	63	Runaway Groom	66	42	64
Editor's Note	59	30	51	Lear Fan	65	43	66	Run Softly	20	11	55
El Amante	34	17	50	Lemon Drop Kid	92	62	67	Sahm	37	19	51
El Angelo	12	4	33	Level Sands	25	11	44	Saint Ballado	110	80	73
Elnadim	43	22	51	Lil E. Tee	36	21	58	Salt Lake	69	47	68
El Prado (Ire)	86	56	65	Lil's Lad	73	44	60	Sandpit (Brz)	63	40	63
Elusive Quality	56	35	63	Lion Cavern	101	59	58	Saratoga Six	32	16	50
En Tete	13	3	23	Lit de Justice	32	18	56	Scatmandu	74	39	53
Evansville Slew	105	54	51	Lord Avie	66	39	59	Sea of Secrets	39	24	62
Expelled	42	21	50	Lord Carson	114	72	63	Seattle Sleet	25	11	44
Exploit	119	78	66	Louis Quatorze	162	100	62	Seattle Slew	63	35	56
Fastness (Ire)	13	7	54	Luhuk	68	31	46	Secreriner	26	10	38
Fast Play	41	19	46	Lure	52	9	17	Seeking the Gold	81	60	74
Favorite Trick	56	37	66	Mahogany Hall	17	8	47	Sefapiano	40	24	60
Fit to Fight	65	34	52	Maria's Mon	130	93	72	Senor Speedy	26	15	58
Flying Chevron	22	11	50	Marquetry	100	52	52	Service Stripe	57	22	39
Fly So Free	92	64	70	Mazel Trick	104	66	63	Shadeed	15	4	27
Fly Till Dawn	11	6	55	Meadowlake	93	50	54	Shawaf	37	15	41
Forestry	97	65	67	Menifee	70	50	71	Shuailaan	34	19	56
Forest Wildcat	78	51	65	Miesque's Son	53	29	55	Silic (Fr)	60	25	42
Formal Gold	80	46	58	Mighty	67	32	48	Silver Charm	113	76	67
Fort Chaffee	15	6	40	Military	40	27	68	Silver Deputy	82	44	54
Friendly Lover	85	57	67	Mr. Greeley	124	81	65	Silver Ghost	52	41	79
Frisk Me Now	19	11	58	Miswaki	71	39	55	Silver Hawk	57	41	72
Furiously	14	4	29	Mongol Warrior	10	6	60	Siphon (Brz)	102	64	63
Fusaichi Pegasus	150	89	59	More Than Ready	95	64	67	Sir Cat	59	34	58
General Royal	74	46	62	Mt. Livermore	84	56	67	Skip Away	121	65	54
Gentlemen (Arg)	80	42	53	Mutakddim	78	36	46	Sky Classic	106	69	65
Ghazi	34	13	38	Mystery Storm	31	13	42	Skywalker	62	46	74
Gilded Time	104	64	62	The Name's Jimmy	49	22	45	Slew City Slew	79	47	59
Glitterman	85	54	64	Northern No Trump	28	12	43	Slew o' Gold	23	6	26
Go for Gin	67	41	61	Northern Spur (Ire)	16	6	38	Smart Strike	76	49	64
Gold Case	96	62	65	Numerous	23	12	52	Smoke Glacken	94	52	55
Golden Gear	42	24	57	Nureyev	44	2	5	Southern Halo	81	43	53
Golden Missile	105	71	68	Old Trieste	118	70	59	Souvenir Copy	84	51	61

Stallion	Mares bred	Fls	%
Spinning World	84	47	56
Squadron Leader	11	6	55
Stalwart	31	17	55
State Craft	13	9	69
Stephen Got Even	95	59	62
Storm Boot	79	48	61
Storm Brewing	10	7	70
Storm Cat	116	72	62
Storm Creek	103	68	66
Stormin Fever	124	74	60
Stravinsky	105	70	67
Subordination	80	47	59
Sultry Song	34	24	71
Summer Squall	50	21	42
Swain (Ire)	73	37	51
Tactical Cat	77	50	65
Tale of the Cat	107	74	69
Tejano Run	65	32	49
Theatrical (Ire)	78	48	62
Thunder Gulch	216	137	63
Torrential	31	18	58
Touch Gold	94	64	68
Tough Call	14	7	50
Unaccounted For	55	33	60
Unbridled	85	60	71
Unbridled's Song	107	73	68
Valiant Nature	25	10	40
Vicar	103	65	63
Victory Gallop	86	58	67
Victory Speech	56	31	55
Wagon Limit	35	16	46
War Chant	78	54	69
Wavering Monarch	53	27	51
Wekiva Springs	47	30	64
Well Decorated	36	15	42
Westminster	14	5	36
Wild Again	64	29	45
Wild Rush	95	65	68
Wild Syn	18	8	44
Will's Way	36	24	67
With Approval	74	42	57
Wolf Power (SAf)	53	30	57
Woodman	102	60	59
Yankee Victor	117	83	71
You and I	65	32	49

LOUISIANA

Stallion	Mares bred	Fls	%
A Corking Limerick	18	9	50
Autocracy	12	10	83
Bag	32	26	81
Battle Launch	10	4	40
Belek	16	11	69
Bermuda Cedar	13	2	15
B. J's Mark	11	10	91
Buddy	16	4	25
Busterwaggley	14	5	36
Cachuma	12	4	33
Cafe Mocha	11	7	64
Carnovali	15	14	93
Charlie's Beau	11	4	36
City Nights (Ire)	14	11	79
Combat Ready	10	5	50
Contested Colors	12	7	58
Corwyn	49	30	61
Crowning Decision	11	4	36
Dancing Harlan	23	11	48
Deputy Diamond	67	54	81
Direct Hit	28	19	68
Doug's My Doc	10	6	60
Emphatic One	11	6	55
Esplanade Ridge	18	10	56
Excavate	31	25	81
Exceller Vice	11	6	55

Stallion	Mares bred	Fls	%
Far Out Wadleigh	14	7	50
Finest Hour	71	46	65
Forty Won	16	13	81
Gebbia	12	6	50
Gentle Kent	10	1	10
Giuseppe	11	5	45
Goodbye Doeny	43	31	72
Handkerchief (Arg)	13	2	15
Homebuilder	34	10	29
I'ma Hell Raiser	31	19	61
In a Walk	17	8	47
Jersey City	30	11	37
Jitterbug Chief	10	7	70
King of Tap	10	3	30
Lake Holme	29	14	48
Leestown	85	71	84
Like a Soldier	22	10	45
Lot o' Gold	10	2	20
Malagra	46	31	67
Many a Wish	17	8	47
Meena	10	6	60
Mr. Sparkles	36	19	53
Moonlight Dancer	20	11	55
My Friend Max	23	16	70
My Mike	13	12	92
Northern Niner	18	12	67
On the Sauce	26	20	77
Placid Fund	23	17	74
Prince of the Mt.	35	29	83
Pulling Punches	51	32	63
Rail	17	10	59
Right Jab	13	8	62
Savings	16	9	56
Scott's Scoundrel	23	6	26
Scottsville	14	4	29
Secret Odds	18	10	56
Sharp Frosty	26	19	73
Shelton	10	5	50
Slew the Surgeon	36	23	64
Smithfield	10	4	40
Spend a Buck	29	20	69
Spruce Bouquet	11	9	82
Stately Slew	22	5	23
Strategic Intent	17	6	35
Tirade	12	9	75
Trophy Hunter	49	30	61
Upping the Ante	20	13	65
Winter Halo	25	17	68
Wire Me Collect	36	27	75
Zarbyev	38	32	84
Zede	19	9	47
Zuppardo's Prince	25	15	60

MASSACHUSETTS

Stallion	Mares bred	Fls	%
Personal Matter	13	4	31
Safely's Mark	14	2	14
Sundance Ridge	11	7	64
Wee Thunder	17	8	47

MARYLAND

Stallion	Mares bred	Fls	%
Allen's Prospect	126	86	68
Ameri Valay	10	7	70
Another Reef	14	10	71
Awad	45	32	71
Carnivalay	52	25	48
Citidancer	55	21	38
Concern	40	24	60
Crowd Pleaser	89	58	65
Crypto Star	53	32	60
Deputed Testamony	15	10	67
Diamond	57	37	65
In Case	19	14	74
Larrupin'	42	22	52

Stallion	Mares bred	Fls	%
Lion Hearted	70	51	73
Malibu Moon	112	70	63
Meadow Monster	96	62	65
Not For Love	72	52	72
Ops Smile	33	22	67
Partner's Hero	56	39	70
Polish Numbers	55	36	65
Purple Passion	11	8	73
Rinka Das	22	11	50
Root Boy	12	8	67
Rubiyat	25	11	44
Secret Firm	24	17	71
Storm Broker	47	32	68
Swear by Dixie	14	8	57
Tamayaz	17	14	82
Two Punch	86	56	65
Unbridled Jet	104	69	66
Valley Crossing	27	20	74
Waquoit	33	20	61
Wayne County (Ire)	30	22	73
Yarrow Brae	65	48	74
Zignew	18	11	61

MICHIGAN

Stallion	Mares bred	Fls	%
Binalong	25	9	36
Cat in Town	13	10	77
Collateral Attack	17	2	12
Demaloot Demashoot	37	25	68
Flare Dancer	11	7	64
Grand Circus Park	18	17	94
Great Allegiance	11	7	64
Gulch It	11	10	91
Jacodra	11	8	73
Matchlite	27	17	63
Meadow Prayer	47	20	43
Native Factor	18	16	89
Pauliano	27	16	59
Predecessor	12	2	17
Quick and Dirty	16	0	0
Quiet Enjoyment	20	13	65
Research	20	11	55
Speedy Cure	12	7	58
Ulises	18	10	56

MINNESOTA

Stallion	Mares bred	Fls	%
Charging Through	11	8	73
Lakeshore Road	28	20	71
La Pete	10	7	70
North Prospect	24	12	50
Olaf	15	8	53
Quaker Hill	18	11	61
Quick Cut	39	20	51
Takur	15	9	60
Victor's Gent	10	5	50

MISSOURI

Stallion	Mares bred	Fls	%
American Tribute	17	11	65
Dark Hyacinth	12	9	75
Liginsky	13	5	38
Lucky South	17	1	6
Steel Robbing	14	5	36

MISSISSIPPI

Stallion	Mares bred	Fls	%
Golden Omen	17	10	59
Valid Victorious	14	6	43

MONTANA

Stallion	Mares bred	Fls	%
Autoroute	10	2	20
Fatih	16	5	31
Ghaza	14	4	29
Knight in Savannah	28	5	18
Matthews Keep	17	6	35
Nassau Square	10	1	10

Stallion	Mares bred	Fls	%
Ourcurtaincall	10	5	50
Perry Road	11	5	45
Stop the Fighting (Ire)	10	1	10
Strong Minded	15	6	40
Ultra Dawn	15	0	0

NORTH CAROLINA

Stallion	Mares bred	Fls	%
Chelsey Cat	16	13	81

NORTH DAKOTA

Stallion	Mares bred	Fls	%
Big Chinook	10	0	0
Bold Ribot	13	0	0
Castle Howard	13	6	46
Codys Key	16	11	69
Patriot Strike	13	3	23
Storada	11	7	64
Win Lose Or Draw	20	15	75

NEBRASKA

Stallion	Mares bred	Fls	%
Bengal Bay	16	10	63
Blumin Affair	52	28	54
Buzzer	24	3	13
Fighting Fantasy	12	9	75
Glenview	13	6	46
Hesaluckycat	16	2	13
Miracle Heights	33	22	67
More to Tell	15	7	47
O'Brannigan	14	12	86
Shawklit Player	11	6	55
Silver Launch	38	21	55

NEW JERSEY

Stallion	Mares bred	Fls	%
Bugatti Reef (Ire)	24	20	83
Close Up	24	14	58
Fort Wayne	13	8	62
Jack Livingston	14	9	64
Munch n' Nosh	17	11	65
My Prince Charming	17	10	59
Perfect	13	9	69
Private Interview	26	16	62
Tree	15	13	87

NEW MEXICO

Stallion	Mares bred	Fls	%
Adams Trail	21	11	52
Adios Mundo	16	7	44
Blind Man's Bluff	11	6	55
Catillac	15	11	73
Con Artist	15	11	73
Corwyn Bay (Ire)	25	10	40
Danzatore	26	17	65
Dee Lance	15	7	47
Desert God	16	10	63
Devil Begone	54	33	61
Devil Diamond	18	14	78
Digging In	17	13	76
Eishin Storm	15	11	73
Fair American	17	7	41
Ferrara	17	9	53
Ghostly Moves	28	17	61
Ghost Ranch	10	6	60
Gold Decorum	13	2	15
He's a Looker	17	8	47
Highland Park	29	14	48
Hoedown's Day	11	6	55
Hoolie	17	7	41
In Excessive Bull	80	56	70
Jack Wilson	12	10	83
Just a Tune	13	4	31
Old Chapel	11	4	36
Paramour	10	6	60
Parting the Sea	20	11	55
Patsyprospect	23	9	39
Poles Apart	15	8	53

Stallion	Mares bred	Fls	%
Prince of Fame	15	7	47
Prospector Jones	31	27	87
Retsina Run	15	10	67
R. Payday	16	7	44
Run Paul Run	11	4	36
Sadler Slew	27	13	48
Schizoid	11	5	45
Someplace Fast	12	0	0
Tap N Snap	22	10	45
Tricky Fun	15	11	73
Waki Bob	11	7	64
You Know How It Is	15	5	33

NEVADA

Stallion	Mares bred	Fls	%
The Danzig Kid	17	11	65

NEW YORK

Stallion	Mares bred	Fls	%
Abaginone	58	39	67
Adonis	43	32	74
Always Fair	14	10	71
American Standard	10	7	70
A. P Jet	133	105	79
Brushed On	38	19	50
Carry My Colors	11	6	55
Chequer	28	17	61
Claramount	18	14	78
Cozy Drive	20	15	75
Crimson Guard	11	5	45
Crusader Sword	25	14	56
Danzatame	41	28	68
Daygata	15	8	53
Distinctive Pro	57	46	81
Dixie Brass	55	36	65
Financial Matter	24	4	17
Goldminers Gold	26	19	73
Gold Token	35	22	63
Gone for Real	16	12	75
Gray Raider	12	7	58
Irish Conquest	18	12	67
Key Contender	47	27	57
Kingsboro	10	8	80
Let Goodtimes Roll	11	4	36
Malibu Wesley	40	23	58
Manlove	18	12	67
Mesopotamia	17	11	65
Mighty Magee	47	25	53
Millions	25	14	56
Nines Wild	29	12	41
Northernhemisphere	10	5	50
Obligato	15	10	67
Odyle	14	7	50
Optic Nerve	10	7	70
Personal Flag	73	47	64
Polish Pro	16	9	56
Preacherman	16	7	44
Precise End	93	59	63
Raffie's Majesty	28	20	71
Rage	13	11	85
Regal Classic	77	51	66
Reign Road	15	6	40
River Keen (Ire)	46	33	72
Rob 'n Gin	14	9	64
Rodeo	91	58	64
Satellite Sun	13	5	38
Scarlet Ibis	24	15	63
Sea Salute	30	13	43
Signal Tap	21	9	43
Silver Music	14	5	36
Slice of Reality	11	6	55
Spectacular Bid	22	13	59
Storm of Angels	41	18	44
Take Me Out	54	37	69
Tank's Number	15	12	80

Stallion	Mares bred	Fls	%
Tomorrows Cat	102	64	63
Treasure Cove	30	19	63
Tri Line	12	8	67
Western Expression	70	51	73
The Wicked North	24	10	42
Williamstown	41	30	73

OHIO

Stallion	Mares bred	Fls	%
Academy Award	63	35	56
Al Sabin	19	12	63
Camp Izard	11	1	9
Canvas	18	11	61
Coax Me Chad	22	13	59
Cool Quaker	19	3	16
Defense Witness	20	8	40
Devil's Luck	13	5	38
Flight Forty Nine	20	9	45
Forest Gazelle	13	5	38
French Legionaire	27	18	67
Gold Market	15	8	53
Hard Wire	13	9	69
I'll Raise You One	19	13	68
King of the Nile	10	1	10
Launch a Leader	18	12	67
Left Banker	10	7	70
Magnificent One	10	6	60
Mercer Mill	31	20	65
Noble Cat	22	17	77
Noon Prospect	13	10	77
Northern Symphony	16	7	44
Pacific Waves	15	9	60
Political Folly	17	8	47
Pride of Burkaan	19	10	53
Private School	36	12	33
Rhodes	12	8	67
Swift Crusader	19	9	47
Winthrop	26	19	73

OKLAHOMA

Stallion	Mares bred	Fls	%
Alamocitos	15	7	47
Alleged Risk	24	11	46
Alydot	11	3	27
Avies Copy	17	7	41
Backoff Dude	10	1	10
Bonus Time Cat	43	27	63
Burbank	33	19	58
Chief's Reward	23	13	57
Christmas Storm	11	7	64
Concorde Cal	10	5	50
Confederate Hero	11	5	45
Coordinator	79	45	57
Deodar	21	10	48
Dreamfield	16	7	44
Ecstatic Ride	15	0	0
Expense Account	22	13	59
Fashionable Enough	10	4	40
French Parliament	24	9	38
Full of Tricks	17	6	35
Ghost Tension	25	5	20
Goodbye Bob	15	6	40
Have Fun	26	15	58
Here We Come	35	23	66
Hestheman	11	2	18
Inca Chief	19	7	37
Indy Talent	18	14	78
Jungle Blade	10	2	20
King of Scat	54	35	65
Kipling	44	30	68
Lost Opportunity	22	10	45
Maddy's Waquoit	10	7	70
Magna	20	14	70
Minister's Mark	11	7	64
Mi Selecto	72	46	64

Stallion	Mares bred	Fls	%
Moro	12	10	83
Muldoon	25	15	60
My Liege	26	13	50
New Way	24	19	79
Night Ceremony	11	2	18
Notable Cat	113	69	61
Officer of Court	17	10	59
Peace Prize (Ire)	10	6	60
Perdition's Son	17	2	12
Proper Reality	17	10	59
Reel On Reel	14	9	64
Seattle Sun	11	6	55
Serves Em Right	12	5	42
Soviet State	12	5	42
Speak	24	13	54
Stauder	12	4	33
Storm Ruler	12	3	25
Sunrise Shower	10	10	100
Tarakam	26	12	46
Track Barron	17	8	47
Trouble Onthe Line	10	5	50
Undeniable	13	6	46
Unome	15	5	33
Wild Colony	20	9	45

OREGON

Stallion	Mares bred	Fls	%
Abstract	43	25	58
Airdrie Apache	24	23	96
Baquero	52	36	69
Cascadian	36	20	56
Crowning Season (GB)	12	8	67
Danjur	51	34	67
Gold Meridian	41	25	61
Superior Success	10	2	20
Tiffany Ice	12	7	58
True Confidence	39	29	74

PENNSYLVANIA

Stallion	Mares bred	Fls	%
Activist	23	15	65
Alyten	15	9	60
Attorney	30	15	50
Bankbook	12	7	58
Bombardier	16	8	50
Buck'sinthebank	13	10	77
Corporate Report	17	7	41
Count On Steve	10	4	40
De Niro	54	29	54
Deposit Ticket	41	29	71
Digamist	14	9	64
Fini Cassette	10	7	70
Flying Pidgeon	28	14	50
Foligno	15	9	60
Harry the Hat	26	16	62
Knockadoon	29	25	86
Obstructed	14	6	43
Patton	46	27	59
Pin Stripe	17	11	65
Pok Ta Pok	24	13	54
Power by Far	26	15	58
Power of Mind	23	9	39
Quarry	32	18	56
Roanoke	50	26	52
Sir Eric	12	7	58
Southern Rhythm	25	13	52
Tricky Mister	17	7	41
Two Plus	14	0	0
Western Echo	16	8	50

SOUTH CAROLINA

Stallion	Mares bred	Fls	%
Go West	19	13	68
Is Sveikatas	16	11	69
Kokand	59	31	53
Play Both Ends	12	10	83

Stallion	Mares bred	Fls	%
Ride the Storm	26	14	54
Signal	18	5	28
Stormville	12	3	25

SOUTH DAKOTA

Stallion	Mares bred	Fls	%
Alyone	10	1	10
Crafty Ridan	21	13	62
Gaelic Padraic	10	2	20
Get Me Out	10	6	60
Neff Lake	26	16	62
Storm of the Night	35	4	11

TENNESSEE

Stallion	Mares bred	Fls	%
Doppler	18	4	22
Moonlight Guy	10	2	20
Wild Hackett To	11	5	45

TEXAS

Stallion	Mares bred	Fls	%
Aggie Southpaw	12	5	42
Alleged Stardom	15	10	67
American Champ	33	23	70
Assault Cat	21	7	33
Boone's Mill	28	15	54
Bugatti	15	11	73
Capote's Prospect	27	14	52
Cat Strike	23	15	65
Cien Fuegos	26	13	50
Classic Look	12	3	25
Claudius	15	14	93
Clever Return	10	6	60
Cold Bid	11	8	73
Cold Hearted Man	11	5	45
Commanchero	33	16	48
Conquer	11	9	82
Country Side	11	5	45
Crafty	28	18	64
Devil's Rock	22	9	41
Devious Course	21	17	81
Diogenes	11	6	55
Dmitri	11	0	0
Eagle Station	11	7	64
Endless Queue	10	6	60
Excellent Secret	23	14	61
Fashion Find	26	15	58
Fire Maker	31	17	55
Foreign Holding	18	5	28
Gary Gumbo	10	9	90
Gold Regent	34	21	62
Gone East	14	8	57
Gringo Pilot	11	6	55
Hadif	43	27	63
Haymarket (GB)	22	10	45
Heather's Prospect	11	8	73
High Energy	12	5	42
Holzmeister	26	17	65
Hurlingham	10	4	40
Imtoocool	17	12	71
Irish Open	43	21	49
Island Born	10	4	40
Jan's Kinsman	10	4	40
Joe Who (Brz)	31	23	74
Karen's Cat	36	25	69
Kell's Sea Captain	10	4	40
Kentucky Jazz	11	9	82
Kicking Boot	15	6	40
Lacotte (Ire)	13	7	54
Lucky So n' So	34	10	29
Magic Cat	71	48	68
Majestic Twoeleven	20	15	75
Major Procida	10	3	30
Man From Eldorado	11	5	45
Manzotti	25	10	40
Marked Tree	45	22	49

Stallion	Mares bred	Fls	%
Marquet Watch	13	5	38
Meacham	15	11	73
Mr. Roberts	12	1	8
Miswaki Gold	12	9	75
Moving Shoulder	21	13	62
Myrmidon	14	6	43
Naevus	30	19	63
Night Beat	25	12	48
Olmos	11	4	36
Once a Sailor	16	10	63
Pancho Villa	74	45	61
Pele's Smile	13	8	62
Phone Fantasy	20	7	35
Political Whit	13	9	69
Pollock's Luck	34	19	56
Power Storm	18	10	56
The Prime Minister	31	19	61
Raise a Govenor	19	7	37
Raja's Best Boy	19	13	68
Rare Brick	23	14	61
Ray's Word	14	2	14
Relagate	10	4	40
River Squall	26	15	58
Ruhlmann	12	9	75
Sand Tunnel	12	0	0
San Romano	12	7	58
Seattle Pattern	14	6	43
Secret Claim	11	5	45
Seneca Jones	32	25	78
Siebe	10	2	20
Six Speed	12	6	50
Star Programmer	72	43	60
Sudden Storm	15	6	40
Sunny's Halo	80	44	55
Texas City	43	21	49
Totem and Taboo	13	7	54
Trancus	19	12	63
Trapp Mountain	14	6	43
Truluck	33	17	52
Tuesday's Special	17	11	65
Twilight Agenda	44	26	59
Under David's Wing	19	16	84
Valid Expectations	107	79	74
Waco Connection	13	10	77
Wajir	32	19	59
Wayne's Crane	20	13	65
Western Challenge (GB)	14	6	43
Western City	23	12	52
Western Trader	17	11	65
Why Change	16	10	63
Wild Zone	116	76	66
Zeeruler	14	6	43

UTAH

Stallion	Mares bred	Fls	%
Bustopher Jones	35	25	71
Isnad	12	9	75
Thunder Falcon	10	4	40
Wouldn't We All	12	9	75

VIRGINIA

Stallion	Mares bred	Fls	%
Ball's Bluff	21	13	62
Bring To Light	10	4	40
Chenin Blanc	14	10	71
Chief Protocol	20	17	85
Fred Astaire	19	9	47
Hay Halo	45	23	51
Husband	11	7	64
Musical River	10	4	40
Pleasant Dancer	13	7	54
Prenup	36	16	44
Rock Point	24	13	54
Secret Hello	45	26	58
Slavic	18	9	50

Stallion	Mares bred	Fls	%
Supremo	27	11	41
Tahoe (Fr)	10	1	10
Turn West	10	5	50
Two Smart	19	14	74

WASHINGTON

Stallion	Mares bred	Fls	%
Alnaab	11	5	45
Basket Weave	45	36	80
Beefchopper	22	17	77
Bull Inthe Heather	22	13	59
Cahill Road	60	45	75
Cathedral Bells	12	6	50
Cisco Road	20	13	65
Consigliere (GB)	13	8	62
Delineator	19	17	89
Demons Begone	40	28	70
Desert Wine	23	8	35
Detox	20	16	80
Dixieland Glo	18	2	11
Flying With Eagles	26	20	77
Former	11	8	73
Free At Last	44	32	73
He's Tops	25	21	84
Ihtimam	22	14	64
Individual Style	17	13	76
Jazzing Around	20	16	80
Jumron (GB)	20	14	70
Kansas City	14	8	57
Katowice	31	26	84
Kriskris (Ire)	11	3	27
La Saboteur	32	14	44
Lord Charmer	10	3	30
Matricule	31	22	71
Mr. Easy Money	20	13	65
Ore Grade	21	16	76
Personable Joe	36	24	67
Peterhof	13	5	38
Petersburg	28	17	61
Russellthemussell	11	6	55
Salty Shoes	10	8	80
Slewdledo	80	57	71
Snowbound	50	25	50
Son of Briartic	13	5	38
Stolen Gold	22	17	77
Storm Blast	24	16	67
Swing and Miss	30	9	30
Swiss Account	10	0	0
Taylor's Special	20	5	25
Tough Knight	25	19	76
Tropic Lightning	23	13	57

WEST VIRGINIA

Stallion	Mares bred	Fls	%
Citislipper	19	16	84
Eastover Court	58	31	53
Enough Reality	17	12	71
Gneiss	16	9	56
Jove Stone	13	5	38
Loach	11	3	27
Makin	54	29	54
My Boy Adam	59	38	64
Native Slew	18	10	56
Northern Wolf	12	3	25
Robb	27	13	48
Runaway Macho	14	3	21
Seeking the Crown	33	22	67
Slew O'Quoit	22	9	41
Standing On Edge	27	11	41
Storm Center	19	6	32
Tank	31	22	71
Tidehaven	10	5	50
Truculent Schular	30	15	50
Valid Indy	18	11	61

Stallion	Mares bred	Fls	%
Weshaam	27	13	48

PUERTO RICO

Stallion	Mares bred	Fls	%
Balcony	27	24	89
Bandit Bomber	10	3	30
Be Frank	12	9	75
Blustery	13	9	69
Cagey Bidder	10	9	90
Ceramal	14	5	36
Chicago Bound	10	0	0
Don Serafin	12	1	8
Eqtesaad	50	36	72
Fappiano's Star	56	38	68
Glitman	20	9	45
Goldwater	22	14	64
Greedy	18	12	67
Hard Charger	17	13	76
Johnny Jones	23	18	78
Laurentide	11	9	82
Macavity	30	22	73
M.D.'s Relampago	15	13	87
Nather	13	4	31
Once Ivor	15	8	53
Royal Merlot	36	31	86
Run Turn	18	12	67
Sejm	27	20	74
Shining Spring	15	6	40
Stake Procpect	16	12	75
Storm God	22	17	77
Sunshine Jimmy	19	12	63
Sutters Pond	10	8	80
Virtua Cop	21	18	86
Wonder Bird	27	24	89

ALBERTA

Stallion	Mares bred	Fls	%
Royal Empire	27	15	56
Banjo	29	13	45
Bashful Cloud	10	6	60
Battle Creek	13	5	38
Blazing Fire	20	12	60
Brass Minister	25	15	60
Cache In	11	8	73
Candid Cameron	10	8	80
Chapel Creek	25	13	52
Ciano Cat	55	29	53
Deputy Bodman	13	12	92
Desperately	15	7	47
Devonwood	44	35	80
Esteem	14	6	43
Exclusive Era	13	6	46
Fast Account	12	6	50
Go Gary Go	25	12	48
Ground Stroke	28	18	64
Hail the Ruckus	16	8	50
Incinderator	22	13	59
John the Magician	32	20	63
King's Nest	18	9	50
Lenado Road	13	7	54
Magic Prospect	27	14	52
Parlay Me	17	5	29
Ranger (Fr)	18	6	33
Rebmec	29	14	48
Rokeby (GB)	13	6	46
Royal Rumpus	10	2	20
Sir Ap	15	6	40
Vilzak	22	10	45
Weekend Guest	42	23	55
Yaak River	14	4	29

BRITISH COLUMBIA

Stallion	Mares bred	Fls	%
Alfaari	19	7	37
Alybro	12	9	75
Baron de Vaux	23	13	57

Stallion	Mares bred	Fls	%
Captain Collins (Ire)	11	6	55
Devil On Ice	18	10	56
Diamond Sword	10	2	20
Dixieland Brass	33	22	67
Feu d'Enfer	31	10	32
Katahaula County	48	30	63
King of Cats	12	5	42
Malmo	16	11	69
Musing	15	5	33
On Target	30	19	63
Orchid's Devil	18	12	67
Regal Intention	62	46	74
Regal Remark	18	13	72
Ringside	13	8	62
Silver Fox	32	22	69
Sky White	14	4	29
Stephanotis	44	27	61
Turbulent Kris	17	6	35
Vying Victor	56	38	68
Western Trick	22	13	59
Yoonevano	35	25	71

MANITOBA

Stallion	Mares bred	Fls	%
Act Smart	19	6	32
Boanerges	15	7	47
Buie	19	9	47
Circulating	19	14	74
His Excellence	25	12	48
Polka	14	6	43
Saratoga Express	14	1	7
Shrike	10	7	70
Sunset Ridge	11	1	9

ONTARIO

Stallion	Mares bred	Fls	%
Alydeed	37	25	68
Archers Bay	65	45	69
Ascot Knight	66	50	76
Birdonthewire	36	20	56
Bold Executive	56	33	59
Bold n' Flashy	90	57	63
Canyon Creek (Ire)	49	31	63
Compadre	51	30	59
Crown Attorney	57	32	56
Dr. Adagio	14	10	71
Elajjud	13	4	31
Foxtrail	103	70	68
Franc Coeur	14	9	64
Great Gladiator	39	10	26
Grey Counter	10	8	80
Highland Ruckus	92	47	51
I Can't Believe	36	21	58
Inspired Prospect	18	14	78
Kiridashi	55	41	75
Matter of Honor	18	12	67
My Imperial Slew	11	8	73
No Malice	12	1	8
Pete's Sake	13	8	62
Porto Foricos	42	23	55
Randy Regent	13	11	85
Regal Discovery	17	11	65
Synastry Express	12	10	83
Talkin Man	15	7	47
Tethra	47	26	55
War Deputy	12	8	67
Welbred Fred	12	10	83
Whiskey Wisdom	55	41	75
Wonneberg	26	15	58

SASKATCHEWAN

Stallion	Mares bred	Fls	%
Blowin de Turn	10	6	60
Clash of Steel	10	4	40
Pole Position	14	12	86
Royal Quiz	17	11	65
Shaheen	18	11	61

Report of Mares Bred for 2002

The Jockey Club's Report of Mares Bred for 2002 revealed that fewer stallions were standing in North America and that they were being bred to essentially the same number of mares as in the previous year. In 2002, the stallion population declined 5.1% to 3,860, from the 4,067 stallions reported active at the end of 2001. The number of mares bred declined modestly to 62,077 in 2002, down from 62,119 in 2001.

Thus, the average 2002 stallion book increased to 16.08 mares per stallion from 15.27. In 2001, the North American breeding industry had its first Thoroughbred stallion bred to more than 200 mares. Thunder Gulch, sire of 2001 Horse of the Year Point Given, was bred to 216 mares at Ashford Stud near Versailles, Kentucky, that year. In 2002, Report of Mares Bred revealed that two stallions, both standing at Ashford, were bred to more than 200 mares each.

While Thunder Gulch's 216 remains the record, Grand Slam was bred to 215 mares in 2002, and Giant's Causeway was bred to 213, according to reports filed by breeders through December 31, 2002. Those reports constitute more than 95% of all mares bred for the 2002 calendar year. Ashford, a division of Ireland's Coolmore, stood the top eight North American stallions by number of mares bred in 2002. In all, 93 stallions were bred to more than 100 mares each in 2002, up from 78 in the prior year.

Kentucky, struck hard by mare reproductive loss syndrome in 2001, had a significant decline in its stallion population, dropping 14.2%, from 429 in 2001 to 368 in '02. The number of mares bred slipped by 4.7%, from 20,962 in 2001 to 19,984. Kentucky remained the continent's leader by mares bred, followed by Florida (7,136), California (5,716), and Texas (3,323). California's number of stallions, 355, ranks only slightly behind Kentucky's total.

Leading Stallions by Mares Bred
(As of December 31, 2002)

Stallion, location	Mares bred	Stallion, location	Mares bred	Stallion, location	Mares bred	Stallion, location	Mares bred
Grand Slam, KY	215	Dixie Union, KY	118	Western Expression, NY	101	Not For Love, MD	88
Giant's Causeway, KY	213	Old Trieste, KY	117	Tiger Ridge, FL	101	Yankee Victor, KY	88
High Yield, KY	184	Southern Halo, KY	117	Trippi, FL	101	Exploit, KY	87
Louis Quatorze, KY	179	Smoke Glacken, KY	116	Touch Gold, KY	100	Chimes Band, NM	87
Tale of the Cat, KY	172	Forestry, KY	116	Pioneering, KY	100	Leestown, LA	87
Fusaichi Pegasus, KY	169	Gilded Time, KY	116	Storm Boot, KY	100	Indian Charlie, KY	86
Black Minnaloushe, KY	161	Judge T C, PA	115	Gentlemen (Arg), KY	100	Pulpit, KY	86
Stravinsky, KY	158	Stormin Fever, KY	115	Gulch, KY	100	Prime Timber, FL	85
Mr. Greeley, KY	150	Real Quiet, KY	114	Meadow Monster, MD	100	Theatrical (Ire), KY	85
Hennessy, KY	146	Yes It's True, FL	114	Kingmambo, KY	100	Stephen Got Even, KY	85
Thunder Gulch, KY	145	Adcat, FL	113	Concerto, FL	100	Silver Ghost, KY	84
Honour and Glory, KY	144	In Excess (Ire), CA	112	Gone West, KY	99	Notable Cat, OK	84
More Than Ready, KY	143	Saint Ballado, KY	111	Line In The Sand, FL	98	With Approval, KY	84
Mutakddim, KY	142	Forest Wildcat, KY	110	Lost Soldier, FL	98	Valid Belfast, LA	84
Royal Academy, KY	138	Brahms, KY	110	Numerous, NJ	98	Housebuster, VA	84
Bertrando, CA	135	Langfuhr, KY	109	Running Stag, FL	97	Grindstone, KY	84
El Corredor, KY	135	Montbrook, FL	109	Valid Expectations, TX	97	Crafty Prospector, KY	84
Aptitude, KY	133	Siphon (Brz), KY	109	Cee's Tizzy, CA	97	Bold n' Flashy, ON	84
Maria's Mon, KY	133	Silver Deputy, KY	108	A.P. Indy, KY	96	A. P Jet, NY	83
Straight Man, FL	131	Five Star Day, KY	108	Mi Selecto, OK	96	Crafty Friend, KY	83
Salt Lake, KY	130	Formal Gold, KY	107	Slew Gin Fizz, FL	96	Mecke, FL	83
Slew City Slew, KY	130	Charismatic, KY	106	Our Emblem, MD	95	Unusual Heat, CA	83
Broken Vow, KY	130	Skip Away, KY	106	Family Calling, FL	95	Twining, KY	83
Open Forum, TX	129	Service Stripe, KY	105	Favorite Trick, KY	95	Wild Event, FL	83
Unbridled's Song, KY	129	Swiss Yodeler, CA	105	Benchmark, CA	94	Sahm, KY	83
Stormy Atlantic, FL	128	Wild Rush, KY	105	Chester House, KY	94	Afternoon Deelites, KY	82
King of Kings (Ire), KY	127	Cryptoclearance, KY	105	Rahy, KY	94	Monarchos, KY	81
Forest Camp, KY	127	Albert the Great, KY	104	Snuck In, FL	93	Lite the Fuse, FL	81
Elusive Quality, KY	125	Mazel Trick, KY	104	Tejano Run, KY	93	Lord Carson, KY	81
Souvenir Copy, KY	125	Royal Anthem, KY	104	Artax, KY	93	King of Scat, OK	81
Tactical Cat, KY	124	Rodeo, NY	104	El Prado (Ire), KY	92	Seeking the Gold, KY	81
Tiznow, KY	124	Northern Afleet, FL	104	Mt. Livermore, KY	92	Richter Scale, KY	81
Storm Cat, KY	123	Point Given, KY	104	Silver Charm, KY	92	Runaway Groom, KY	80
Outflanker, FL	123	Vision and Verse, KY	103	Horse Chestnut (SAf), KY	91	Smart Strike, KY	80
Carson City, KY	123	Halo's Image, FL	103	Devil His Due, KY	91	War Chant, KY	80
Red Ransom, KY	122	Distorted Humor, KY	103	Deputy Commander, KY	90	General Royal, KY	80
City Zip, NY	121	Allen's Prospect, MD	102	Cartwright, IL	90	Gold Case, KY	80
Dance Brightly, KY	121	Banker's Gold, KY	102	Catienus, KY	89	Awesome Again, KY	80
Cat Thief, KY	120	Golden Missile, KY	102	Helmsman, CA	89	Cape Town, KY	80
Lemon Drop Kid, KY	120	Vicar, KY	102	Glitterman, KY	89	Event of the Year, CA	80
Marquetry, KY	119	Victory Gallop, KY	101	Dynaformer, KY	88	Diesis (GB), KY	80

Stallions and Mares Bred by State and Province
(As of December 31, 2002)

State	Stallions	Mares bred	State	Stallions	Mares bred	State	Stallions	Mares bred
Alabama	20	93	Missouri	28	140	Washington	89	1,090
Arkansas	71	634	Mississippi	14	72	Wisconsin	13	35
Arizona	60	503	Montana	38	231	West Virginia	60	878
California	355	5,716	North Carolina	16	55	Wyoming	10	29
Colorado	70	416	North Dakota	9	71	Puerto Rico	62	679
District of Columbia	1	21	Nebraska	28	298	Virgin Islands	1	2
Delaware	1	5	New Jersey	37	435	Unknown	31	97
Florida	260	7,136	New Mexico	135	1,402			
Georgia	24	114	Nevada	4	10	**Canada Province**		
Iowa	56	632	New York	141	2,554	Alberta	81	864
Idaho	45	254	Ohio	92	823	British Columbia	61	700
Illinois	110	1,172	Oklahoma	196	1,613	Manitoba	22	196
Indiana	99	825	Oregon	32	356	New Brunswick	1	1
Kansas	23	155	Pennsylvania	100	996	Northwest Territories	1	5
Kentucky	368	19,984	South Carolina	26	165	Nova Scotia	2	5
Louisiana	176	2,157	South Dakota	13	138	Ontario	92	1,445
Massachusetts	24	106	Tennessee	24	93	Prince Edward Island	1	14
Maryland	92	1,835	Texas	346	3,323	Quebec	7	16
Maine	2	3	Utah	18	107	Saskatchewan	23	155
Michigan	53	429	Vermont	5	11			
Minnesota	35	299	Virginia	56	484	**Totals**	**3,860**	**62,077**

Stallions Bred to Five or More Mares in 2002
(As of December 31, 2002)

Stallion	Mares bred	Stallion	Mares bred	Stallion	Mares bred	Stallion	Mares bred
ALABAMA		Barricade	17	Born Wild	16	Fine n' Majestic	46
		Benton Creek	38	Bouccaneer (Fr)	27	Flom's Prospector	11
Casey On Deck	14	Big Sky Chester	15	Boulder Dam	8	Flying Continental	57
Dantesque (Ire)	7	Bonus Bucks	9	Brave Romane	16	Flying Victor	28
Royal Empire	21	Buck Strider	40	Built for Pleasure	10	For Really	37
Schembechler	13	Cal Lite	6	Bustopher Jones	21	Free House	39
Special Coach	6	Chanate	27	Cactus Creole	16	Fruition	33
Troublesome Road	7	Chancery Court	12	Candi's Gold	51	Fun Devil	19
		Chopin	19	Category Five	34	Funontherun	6
ARKANSAS		Cordova	9	Cee's Tizzy	97	Future Storm	64
A. V. Eight	29	Delinsky	6	Character (GB)	8	Game Plan	66
American General	9	Desert Rival	14	Cherokee Colony	16	Garcon Gris	8
Bob's Prospect	8	E. W. Cat	10	Chimineas	11	General Gem	7
Bold Anthony	42	Individualist (GB)	8	Chullo (Arg)	16	General Meeting	62
Cinnamon Creek	35	Jestic	15	Comet Shine	35	Globalize	52
Cornish Snow	46	Local Artist	13	Comic Strip	61	Gold Knuckles	10
Croydon	11	Midnight Royalty	37	Commitment	38	Gold Pack	7
Delta Wolf	7	Perforce	11	Compelling Sound	7	Guarani	10
Enquire	17	Relaunch a Tune	22	Corslew	37	Haint	11
Etbauer	14	Reversal	18	Cromwell	12	Half Term	6
Explosive Ridge	8	Society Max	20	Crowning Storm	71	Helmsman	89
Forever Dancer	7	Strong Minded	7	Cutlass Reality	10	High Brite	68
Glorious Bid	15	T. G. Dewey	21	Dance Floor	49	Holding Court	21
Gremlin Grey	10	Truce Maker	10	Desert Classic	14	Hollycombe	18
Harperstown	9			Desert Secret (Ire)	22	Houston	22
I'am Cured	8	**CALIFORNIA**		Devon Lane	68	Huddle Up	7
Idabel	16	All Thee Power	14	Discover	15	Hunter's Glory	13
Kipling	54	Alymagic	6	Dismissed	11	Iam the Iceman	9
Late Act	10	American Day	6	Distinctive Cat	19	Illinois Storm	47
Mertzon	6	Anziyan	52	Dixie Dot Com	55	In Excess (Ire)	112
Proper Reality	15	Apollo	22	Dominique's Cat	67	Indy Film	11
Royal N Trouble	6	Arthur L.	6	Downtown Seattle	6	Iron Cat	26
Siberian Pine	11	Askmewhy	6	Dr. Giggles	6	Kahuna Jack	24
Smolderin Heart	33	Avenue of Flags	26	Dumaani	18	Kessem Power (NZ)	26
Southern Forest	11	B. Hoedown	8	Elegant Fellow	14	Kid Capote	10
Storm and a Half	63	Bartok (Ire)	32	Emerald Jig	9	King of the Hunt	6
This Picture	15	Battle Wise (Fr)	7	Endow	14	Kleven	7
Unbridled's Risk	12	Beau Genius	77	Epic Honor	17	Kris Kross	14
		Benchmark	94	Event of the Year	80	Lacey Evitan	6
ARIZONA		Bertrando	135	Fabulous Champ	21	Lake George	24
Amigo Menor (Ire)	8	Bienamado	28	Falstaff	14	Laramie's Deputy	24
Banuz (Arg)	8	Boomerang	11	Fargo	22	Larry the Legend	47

Stallion	Mares bred	Stallion	Mares bred	Stallion	Mares bred	Stallion	Mares bred
Last Lion	36	Slewvescent	45	Arrested	15	Lite the Fuse	81
Latin American	48	Smokester	32	B L's Appeal	38	Littlebitlively	59
Lil Tyler	22	Smooth Runner	18	Big Jewel	11	Lordhyexecutioner	6
Lindsey's Roberto	18	Snow Chief	8	Birdonthewire	57	Lost Soldier	98
Louisiana Slew	8	Soft Gold (Brz)	50	Brief Ruckus	14	Luciano P.	9
Loyal Double	13	Strike Gold	8	Bucksplasher	10	Lucky Lionel	54
Lucayan Prince	7	Summing	8	Byars	25	Lucky North	23
Mach One	7	Supermec	8	Capture the Gold	28	Magabird	14
Madraar	48	Surachai	31	Carlisle Bay	20	Marco Bay	17
Majesterian	8	Swiss Yodeler	105	Cimarron Secret	43	Master Bill	32
Makaleha	28	Synastry	20	Classic Cat	19	Mecke	83
Makhraj	23	T. U. Slew	29	Cloud Cover	31	Metfield	32
Malek (Chi)	31	Tactical Heir	10	Cloud Hopping	58	Middlesex Drive	45
Mantles Star (GB)	19	The Editor (GB)	6	Cobra King	29	Migrating Moon	31
Memo (Chi)	60	The Elfee Child	20	Cohiba	25	Miner's Mark	31
Menhal	17	Tinners Way	6	Colony Light	49	Minighosta	7
Mining for Money	6	Tom Cruiser	7	Commitisize	25	Mister Jolie	39
More Style	7	Town Caper	12	Concerto	100	Montbrook	109
Moscow Ballet	40	Trail City	28	Concorde's Tune	58	Montreal Red	8
Mr Purple	15	Tricky Creek	11	Crafty Dude	20	Mountain of Laws	6
Mr. Broad Blade	17	Truckee	37	Cyberspace	11	Native Regent	23
Mr. Expo	8	Turkoman	61	D. J. Cat	29	No Catch	6
Mr. Procrastinator	14	Twin Spires	43	Dance Master	41	Noactor	18
Mud Route	43	Tychonic (GB)	33	Darn That Alarm	16	Northern Afleet	104
Muqtarib	38	Unusual Heat	83	Dawn Quixote	26	Northern Trend	17
Naevus Star	9	Urgent Request (Ire)	6	De Hero	11	Notebook	70
Native Storm	22	Valid Wager	63	Delaware Township	73	Outflanker	123
Newton's Law (Ire)	14	Vaudeville	29	Diligence	57	Pass the Line	13
Nineeleven	22	Ventriloquist	9	Double Honor	73	Pentelicus	47
Northern Devil	17	Vermont	7	Dove Hunt	48	Piccolino	16
Old Topper	70	Vernon Castle	6	Dr. Caton	20	Precocity	30
Ole'	13	Via Lombardia (Ire)	19	Dr. Gigolo	8	Premiership	26
Olympio	53	Walter Willy (Ire)	10	Eltish	55	Prime Timber	85
Order	7	Western Fame	47	Exchange Rate	64	Proud and True	45
Paranoide (Arg)	8	What a Spell	12	Fabulous Frolic	56	Proudest Romeo	28
Paxos	15	Wild Deputy	22	Family Calling	95	Put It Back	61
Perfect Mandate	48	Wild Gold	26	Fast 'n Royal	15	Quaker Ridge	42
Peteski's Charm	7	Woody Win	9	Faygo	6	R. Cooper	20
Peyrano (Arg)	7	Zanferrier	14	Flame Thrower	74	Reality Road	20
Pharisien (Fr)	10	**COLORADO**		Forever Whirl	7	Reparations	9
Phone Roberto	19	A Man of Class	17	Formal Dinner	65	Reprized	36
Phone Saga	20	Alydarmer	6	Fortunate Move	15	Robyn Dancer	79
Phonetics	14	American Promise	8	Fortunate Prospect	56	Rocket Cat	10
Poteen	25	Annual Tradition	10	Friendly Lover	58	Running Stag	97
Pride of Slew	9	Basic Rate	11	Georgia Two	10	Salty Sea	10
Proud Irish	39	Cash Deposit	38	Gold Alert	21	Sam's Sunny Hour	7
Purdue's Double	7	Cathexis	11	Golden Gear	60	Seacliff	33
Pure Excess	6	Conquistador Deoro	12	Greenwood Lake	44	Semoran	27
Raz Lea	7	Coverallbases	10	Groomstick	19	Shanawi (Ire)	47
Red	27	Crafty Harold	17	Halo's Image	103	Sir Leon	9
Regal Affair	7	Dash Ahead	19	Halos and Horns	26	Skip Trial	25
Regent Act	8	Eishin Masamune (Jpn)	30	Hazaam	46	Slew Gin Fizz	96
Rhythm	54	Exploding Rainbow	11	Henriques	8	Slew the Message	9
Rio Verde	34	Gentle Ben's	7	Hesabull	16	Snuck In	93
River Flyer	12	Kennedy Factor	9	Hold On Chris	8	Songandaprayer	79
Royal Cat	25	My Memoirs (GB)	9	Holy Mountain	24	Stack	28
Royal Regatta (Ire)	8	Oliver's Twist	17	Hunting Hard	43	Star of Valor	14
Scherando	10	Percival	12	Impeachment	52	Stark Ridge	9
Score Early	8	Prince At Dawn	6	Intidab	9	Statesmanship	9
Score Quick	17	Sinceilostmybaby	12	Is It True	54	Stormy Atlantic	128
Seattle Bound	49	Sportin' Jack	7	Island Whirl	14	Straight Man	131
Seven Rivers	8	Tepee Creek	7	Jeblar	6	Struggler (GB)	15
Sharan (GB)	20	Top Villa	10	Jules	15	Suave Prospect	72
Sharp Victor	7	**DISTRICT OF COLUMBIA**		Keep Dreaming	35	Successful Appeal	58
Siberian Summer	34	Truly Met	21	Kelly Kip	69	Sweetsouthernsaint	77
Silver Ray	8	**FLORIDA**		Kipper Kelly	23	Sword Dance (Ire)	73
Simply Majestic	16	Adcat	113	Kissin Kris	78	Tactical Advantage	45
Six Below	35	Adhocracy	10	Lake Austin	34	Thats Our Buck	56
Slew of Angels	8			Lexicon	51	The Silver Move	33
Slew the Bride	10			Limit Out	26	Thisnearlywasmine	10
				Line In The Sand	98	Tiger Ridge	101

Stallion	Mares bred	Stallion	Mares bred	Stallion	Mares bred	Stallion	Mares bred
Time Bandit	31	U Folks	13	Smokin Mel	10	**KENTUCKY**	
Top Account	21	Wild Invader	32	Spanish Drummer	15	A P Valentine	60
Tour d'Or	76			Summer Cloud	11	A.P. Indy	96
Traitor	32	**IDAHO**		Unbridled Success	9	Acceptable	23
Trippi	101	Ascension	6	Unite	18	Afternoon Deelites	82
Twelve Relics	8	Carmen's Baby	20	Unreal Zeal	51	Albert the Great	104
Twin Halo	8	Chisos	14	Valid Vengeance	6	Aljabr	60
Untuttable	18	Coastal Voyage	8	Western Playboy	9	Alphabet Soup	38
Unzipped	6	Collateral	8	Wild Gambler	7	Anees	70
Way West (Fr)	52	Dr. Dan Eyes	8	Z Z Cat	8	Anet	36
Weekend Cruise	45	Hey Rob	12	Zagor	14	Announce	41
Wekiva Springs	16	Kings Blood (Ire)	16			Aptitude	133
West Acre	36	Mr. Publisher	8	**INDIANA**		Arch	58
Western Borders	31	Pirate's Gulch	7	Ali Gaziba	14	Artax	93
Western Cat	9	Pleasant Pope	6	Avalli	15	Atticus	29
Wheaton	50	Pro Chapeau	7	Bappa	12	Austin Powers (Ire)	7
Whitney Tower	6	Renteria	20	Bedivere	9	Austinpower (Jpn)	15
Wild Escapade	18	Silent Generation	9	Bidding Proud	8	Awesome Again	80
Wild Event	83	Starmaniac	22	Blase	18	Bahri	56
Wild Wonder	72	Thunderah	12	Board Member	13	Banker's Gold	102
Wind Whipper	62	Tricky Tower	8	Cat Power	50	Barkerville	16
Wised Up	41			Classy Prospector	18	Bartlettsunbridled	14
World Stage (Ire)	6	**ILLINOIS**		Colonel Bradley	9	Basic	11
Worldly Manner	30	Alaskan Frost	38	Colossus	8	Bates Motel	19
Yes It's True	114	Allen Charge	24	Conscience Clear	19	Behrens	70
Youmadeyourpoint	7	Awesome Cat	40	Crown Ambassador	44	Belong to Me	60
Zamindar	54	Ballard High	15	D. C. Tenacious	9	Bernstein	50
		Bold Revenue	16	Dewdle's Dancer	8	Bert's Bubbleator	15
GEORGIA		Canyon Run	14	El Angelo	19	Best of Luck	48
Fitz	6	Cartwright	90	Fast Ferdie	8	Bianconi	77
Golden Explosive	7	Catastrophic	15	Fiscal	20	Bird Brown (Brz)	6
Hurry to Dinner	7	Charlie Barley	16	Fort Stanton	9	Black Minnaloushe	161
Prospector Street	23	Cherokee Saga	7	Guys From Space	7	Boundary	53
Roaring Camp	17	City by Night	57	Indy Mood	27	Brahms	110
Sheikh Adel	9	Classi Envoy	6	Jacquelyn's Groom	41	Bright Launch	52
Yourplaceormine	6	Classic Account	18	Keynote	6	Broad Brush	50
Zalipour	11	Classified Facts	50	Launch a Leader	9	Broken Vow	130
		Conte Di Savoya	27	Le Casque Gris	10	Brunswick	14
IOWA		Crimson Classic	11	Meadowtime	8	Canaveral	28
Acaroid	8	Dave and Busters	16	Miswaki Bandit	11	Cape Canaveral	65
Another Good Deed	6	Denouncer	11	Monroan	10	Cape Town	80
Buzz Saw	10	Diazo	35	Moro Oro	16	Capote	71
Cape Storm	28	Electric Blue	18	Overnight Express	7	Captain Bodgit	71
Cat's Debut	12	Emigrant Peak	15	Presidential Order	17	Carolina Kid	47
Commemorate	13	Exetera	12	Prince Giustino	11	Carson City	123
Comstock Lode	10	Fitzhugh's Legacy	6	Radio Daze	10	Cat Thief	120
De Guerin	17	Fort Chaffee	13	Seattle Syn	12	Catienus	89
Deputy Slew	22	Fosh	8	Siberian Tiger	10	Catrail	15
Dignitas	37	Fractional	9	Sixto G	11	Charismatic	106
Dr. Danzig	7	Francis Nevil E.	6	Speedy Cure	6	Charles Bridge	8
Exclusivengagement	13	Hannibal Cat	15	Stylish Senor	9	Cherokee Run	69
Fappiano Road	8	He's a Tough Cat	9	Swiss Mirage	9	Chester House	94
Farragut	7	Let Him Go	12	Swiss Trick	16	Chief Seattle	69
Fugitive	7	Longliner	7	Timeraker	9	Clever Trick	53
H. J. Baker	16	Marte	24	Tracker	15	Commendable	69
Halory Hunter	40	Mt. Magazine	21	Tricon	17	Composer	45
Honest Ensign	20	Nooo Problema	9	Unbridled Man	17	Confide	76
Humming	16	Pirate Stronghold	9	Unloosened	15	Conquistador Cielo	50
Kyle's Our Man	52	Powerful Goer	14	Waki Warrior	31	Coronado's Quest	70
Mocha Express	21	Presently	12			Count the Time	33
Mr. Goldust	7	Primordial	10	**KANSAS**		Cozar	10
Night Runner	10	Prune	7	Admiral Indy	11	Cozzene	75
Omali's Buckaroo	9	Regal Code	8	Bleu Madura	8	Crafty Friend	83
Parfaitement	10	Rhythm Bound	6	Gold Ruler	28	Crafty Prospector	84
Political Whit	6	Rigging	13	Groom's Image	6	Cryptoclearance	105
Prospect Feature	8	River Basin	10	Island's Edge	7	Dance Brightly	121
Purdue King	27	S'No Business	10	Life Interest	9	Danzig	47
Sharkey	51	Sabona	20	Prospect North	13	Dayjur	67
Shotiche	7	Scoot the Moon	7	Reality's Conquest	7	Deerhound	18
So Private	7	Seattle Morn	51	So Ever Clever	12	Defrere	33
Temujin	11	Shakeel	8	Speedy Nijinsky	21	Demidoff	45
Tiger Talk	12	Sir Spellbinder	21	Torey Ridge	9		

Stallion	Mares bred	Stallion	Mares bred	Stallion	Mares bred	Stallion	Mares bred
Deputy Commander	90	King of Kings (Ire)	127	Roar	18	Vision and Verse	103
Deputy Minister	79	Kingmambo	100	Rod and Staff	16	Wagon Limit	39
Devil His Due	91	Kris S.	10	Romanov (Ire)	21	War Chant	80
Devil's Bag	59	L. B. Damned	7	Royal Academy	138	Wavering Monarch	53
Diesis (GB)	80	Laabity	12	Royal Anthem	104	Well Decorated	14
Distant View	37	Labeeb (GB)	50	Rubiano	62	Westminster	15
Distorted Humor	103	Lac Ouimet	39	Run Softly	9	Why Change	18
Dixie Union	118	Langfuhr	109	Runaway Groom	80	Wild Again	53
Dixieland Band	64	Lasting Approval	42	Sahm	83	Wild Rush	105
Dixieland Heat	78	Lear Fan	65	Saint Ballado	111	Wild Syn	10
Doneraile Court	49	Lemon Drop Kid	120	Salem Drive	7	Will's Way	22
Down the Aisle	45	Lil E. Tee	37	Salt Lake	130	With Approval	84
Dynaformer	88	Lil's Lad	23	Sandpit (Brz)	33	Wolf Power (SAf)	34
Ecton Park	79	Lion Cavern	61	Saratoga Six	29	Woodman	72
Editor's Note	66	Lit de Justice	17	Scatmandu	51	Yankee Victor	88
El Corredor	135	Lord Avie	23	Sea of Secrets	47	You and I	72
El Prado (Ire)	92	Lord Carson	81	Seattle Sleet	7	Zocor	6
Elusive Quality	125	Louis Quatorze	179	Seattle Slew	9		
En Tete	6	Luhuk	43	Secreniner	23	**LOUISIANA**	
England	7	Lure	39	Seeking the Gold	81	A Corking Limerick	6
Evansville Slew	76	Maria's Mon	133	Sefapiano	39	Astral Wood	7
Exploit	87	Marquetry	119	Service Stripe	105	Autocracy	18
Fast Play	42	Matty G	75	Shadeed	28	B. J.'s Mark	7
Favorite Trick	95	Mazel Trick	104	Silic (Fr)	53	Battle Launch	6
Fit to Fight	35	Meadowlake	72	Silver Charm	92	Belek	14
Five Star Day	108	Menifee	76	Silver Deputy	108	Believe It	13
Fly So Free	23	Miesque's Son	15	Silver Ghost	84	Blue Grass Magic	10
Flying Chevron	41	Mighty	35	Silver Hawk	48	Busterwaggley	15
Forest Camp	127	Military	36	Siphon (Brz)	109	Cachuma	8
Forest Wildcat	110	Minardi	75	Sir Cat	40	Cajun Flagman	6
Forestry	116	Miswaki	72	Skip Away	106	Carnovali	19
Formal Gold	107	Momsfurrari	7	Sky Classic	56	Change Takes Time	18
Frisk Me Now	24	Monarchos	81	Skywalker	50	Choosing Choice	30
Furiously	7	Mongol Warrior	9	Slew City Slew	130	City Nights (Ire)	12
Fusaichi Pegasus	169	More Than Ready	143	Slide to the Left	7	Combat Ready	10
General Royal	80	Mr. Greeley	150	Smart Strike	80	Constant Demand	17
Gentlemen (Arg)	100	Mt. Livermore	92	Smoke Glacken	116	Contested Colors	13
Geri	42	Mutakddim	142	Southern Halo	117	Corwyn	18
Ghazi	24	Nicholas	7	Souvenir Copy	125	Dancing Harlan	12
Giant's Causeway	213	Niganithat	10	St. Jovite	10	Dealing Richard	11
Gilded Time	116	Northern Spur (Ire)	11	Stalwart	19	Deputy Diamond	69
Glitterman	89	Old Kentucky Home	32	State Craft	14	Derby Wish	8
Go for Gin	35	Old Trieste	117	Stephen Got Even	85	Devil's Cry	7
Gold Case	80	Ordway	74	Storm Boot	100	Direct Hit	38
Gold Fever	36	Out of Place	78	Storm Cat	123	Disciple	8
Gold Spring (Arg)	12	Parade Ground	26	Storm Creek	59	Doeny Rain	6
Golden Missile	102	Peaks and Valleys	62	Stormin Fever	115	Doug's My Doc	9
Gone West	99	Pembroke	41	Strategic Mission	38	Esplanade Ridge	18
Grand Slam	215	Perfect Vision	26	Stravinsky	158	Fair Decor	9
Grindstone	84	Personal	6	Subordination	43	Far Out Wadleigh	9
Gulch	100	Peruvian	14	Sultry Song	51	Fenter	7
Hennessy	146	Petionville	62	Summer Squall	31	Festive	13
High Yield	184	Pikepass	68	Swain (Ire)	74	Fight Over	12
Hold for Gold	22	Pine Bluff	60	Tactical Cat	124	Finest Hour	53
Holy Bull	79	Pioneering	100	Tale of the Cat	172	Fly Cry	10
Home At Last	7	Pistols and Roses	16	Talk Is Money	57	Forty Won	27
Honor Grades	33	Pleasant Tap	63	Tejano Run	93	Gebbia	19
Honour and Glory	144	Pleasantprospector	7	The Call of Duty	7	Gift of Gib	11
Horse Chestnut (SAf)	91	Point Given	104	The Deputy (Ire)	57	Gold Tribute	79
Ide	39	Polish Navy	51	The Name's Jimmy	25	Goodbye Doeny	39
In the Zone	8	Prized	67	Theatrical (Ire)	85	Handkerchief (Arg)	8
Indian Charlie	86	Private Terms	69	Thousand Ores	8	Hi Plains Drifter	6
Irgun	19	Prospectors Gamble	28	Thunder Gulch	145	Homebuilder	48
Islefaxyou	24	Puerto Madero (Chi)	33	Tiznow	124	Huff	6
J P Hamer	11	Pulpit	86	Touch Gold	100	I'ma Hell Raiser	15
Jade Hunter	36	Pyramid Peak	53	Tough Call	12	Irish Bluff	9
Jambalaya Jazz	48	Quiet American	71	Turn Out	11	Jaunatxo	12
Joyeux Danseur	35	Rahy	94	Twining	83	Jersey City	29
K One King	20	Real Quiet	114	Unbridled's Song	129	Jitterbug Chief	9
K. O. Punch	23	Red Ransom	122	Valiant Nature	23	Jolie's Frolic	7
Kanjinsky	11	Repriced	45	Vicar	102	Lake Holme	22
King Cugat	71	Richter Scale	81	Victory Gallop	101	Leestown	87

Stallion	Mares bred
Like a Soldier	28
Llama Lover	6
Malagra	24
Man of the Night	6
Many a Wish	21
Middle Man	6
Mike's Little Man	6
Moonlight Dancer	12
Mr. Shawklit	16
Mr. Sparkles	24
Mutah	7
My Friend Max	13
My Mike	15
Nelson	9
No Budget	8
Northern Niner	14
On the Sauce	10
Out of the Crisis	23
Placid Fund	15
Planet Earth	14
Prince of the Mt.	47
Pulling Punches	64
Rail	32
Red Oak Rebel	7
Right Jab	7
Royal Strand (Ire)	11
Ruby Hill	14
Sanctuary	15
Say Guv	7
Scott's Scoundrel	19
Scottsville	7
Secret Odds	21
Sharp Frosty	22
Sky Raider	10
Slew the Surgeon	20
South Salem	17
Stately Slew	23
Super Native (Ire)	8
Thunder Breeze	12
Tirade	23
Toolighttoquit	21
Track Rebel	10
Trophy Hunter	14
Upping the Ante	12
Valid Belfast	84
Walnut Hall	10
Williams Sentiment	6
Winter Halo	24
Wire Me Collect	42
Worldly Ways (GB)	21
Zarbyev	47
Zede	14
Zuppardo's Prince	19

MASSACHUSETTS

Stallion	Mares bred
Eternal Orage	8
Personal Matter	6
Real Partner	7
Senor Conquistador	6
Silk Broker	7
Solid Hunch	6
Sundance Ridge	16
Wee Thunder	10

MARYLAND

Stallion	Mares bred
Aaron's Concorde	6
Allen's Prospect	102
Alster	12
Ameri Valay	10
Appealing Skier	52
Awad	28
Carnivalay	36
Cat Country	10
Citidancer	59
Concern	25
Crowd Pleaser	56
Crypto Star	37
Deputed Testamony	7
Diamond	50
Disco Rico	54
Dumyat	13
Eastern Echo	55
Hard Habitat	13
In Case	22
Innkeeper	7
Itaka	6
Jazz Club	60
Larrupin'	18
Lion Hearted	55
Malibu Moon	55
Meadow Monster	100
Mojave Moon	67
Mokhieba	8
Not For Love	88
One Golf Sierra	6
Ops Smile	20
Our Emblem	95
Partner's Hero	48
Polish Numbers	53
Purple Passion	12
Regal American	8
Rinka Das	11
Rubiyat	23
Secret Firm	10
Storm Broker	30
Swear by Dixie	23
Two Punch	74
Unbridled Jet	77
Valley Crossing	25
Waquoit	36
Wayne County (Ire)	19
Yarrow Brae	41

MICHIGAN

Stallion	Mares bred
Binalong	23
Cat in Town	8
Clock Radio	6
Collateral Attack	11
Couch King George	6
Creative	11
Daylight Savings	9
Demaloot Demashoot	50
Flare Dancer	6
Grand Circus Park	19
Grande Jette	9
Great Allegiance	12
Island Storm	7
Jacodra	6
Majesty's Imp	6
Matchlite	25
Mt. Ruritania	6
Native Factor	27
Ocala Slew	21
Pauliano	10
Puchilingui	7
Quick and Dirty	12
Quiet Enjoyment	19
Research	16
Royal Senoir	6
Sea Legs	6
Treasury	8
Ulises	7
Will Be Dancing	11

MINNESOTA

Stallion	Mares bred
Boundless	16
Come Summer	8
Creditworthy	9
Dixie Power	12
Dixie Road	8
Dynomania	7
Emailit	6
George Green	6
Lakeshore Road	35
North Prospect	16
Olaf	11
Pave the Way	7
Quaker Hill	13
Quick Cut	31
Shot of Gold	28
Silk Song	7
Texas Tuxedo	11
Victor's Gent	17
Wa Bert	9

MISSOURI

Stallion	Mares bred
American Tribute	16
Dixie Dancer	7
Isaypete	9
Kugelis	11
Liginsky	13
Lucky South	14
Quintillion (Ire)	7
Yoh May Kenta	7

MISSISSIPPI

Stallion	Mares bred
Blushing Star	7
Golden Omen	8
Valid Victorious	20
Warlaunch	6

MONTANA

Stallion	Mares bred
Callous Doughboy	7
Devil's Canyon	6
Double Dewars	14
Grey West	8
Khalsa	13
Mariner	7
Matthews Keep	8
Nassau Square	12
Ourcurtaincall	6
Perry Road	10
Personable Joe	36
Signoretto (Fr)	12
Son's Corona	19
Unbridled Desire	14
White Tie Tryst	7

NORTH CAROLINA

Stallion	Mares bred
Chelsey Cat	21

NORTH DAKOTA

Stallion	Mares bred
Codys Key	18
Kravis	6
Storada	10
Win Lose Or Draw	22

NEBRASKA

Stallion	Mares bred
Alyfoe	10
Bengal Bay	11
Blumin Affair	23
Box Buster	19
Dazzling Falls	22
Fortuoso	12
Glenview	17
Lytrump	8
Miracle Heights	27
More to Tell	15
Niner Bush	7
Not So Fast	12
O'Brannigan	9
Shawklit Player	19
Silver Launch	41
Yankee Fan	16

NEW JERSEY

Stallion	Mares bred
Bugatti Reef (Ire)	11
Caller I. D.	34
Deputy Warlock	22
E. K. Spatz	7
Evening Kris	20
Fort Wayne	6
G. P.'s Krugerrand	6
Imaginary Sword	9
Joker	10
Mr. Nugget	39
Munch n' Nosh	13
My Prince Charming	6
Nickle's Wind	6
Numerous	98
Perfect	14
Private Interview	40
Sailor's Warning	31
Sheryar	14
Tree	9

NEW MEXICO

Stallion	Mares bred
Adams Trail	19
Adios Mundo	17
Aledo	13
Alnaab	27
Blind Man's Bluff	8
Brave Lad	6
Brite Adam	13
Bull Inthe Heather	14
Call Me Cat	10
Caracal	40
Carmen's Glory	13
Chain of Command	10
Chimes Band	87
Con Artist	8
Copelan's Pache	25
Danzatore	29
Daytime Dancer	10
Dee Lance	14
Desert God	31
Devil Begone	23
Devil Diamond	15
Digging In	26
Dome	48
Eishin Seattle	7
Eishin Storm	22
Excess Is Good	7
Exclusive Dove	6
Expressman	7
Fair American	6
Ferrara	7
Ghost Ranch	11
Ghostly Moves	34
Gold Decorum	7
Gone Hollywood	11
Gun Bay	6
H. E. Miller	7
He's a Looker	17
Here Comes Charlie	10
Hezafastgold	7
Highland Park	26

Stallion	Mares bred	Stallion	Mares bred	Stallion	Mares bred	Stallion	Mares bred
Hitumwhenyacan	7	Halissee	20	Freedom Found	8	Ivory Dreams	13
Hoolie	20	Hard Circle	12	French Legionaire	20	Jim Nui	7
I Like to Win	12	Hidden Vice´	7	Gold Market	21	King of Scat	81
In Excessive Bull	44	Irish Conquest	12	Gold Meridian	27	Lost Opportunity	21
Jack Wilson	8	Its Acedemic	9	I'll Raise You One	10	Maghnatis	12
Just a Tune	7	Key Contender	29	Iroquois Park	28	Magna	9
Launch a Dream	10	King's Grant	6	Keep It Down	6	Major Henry	9
Le Grande Danseur	19	Kingsboro	13	Kingdom City	10	Master Robery	8
Lord John	8	Let Goodtimes Roll	7	Lake Superior	6	Mi Selecto	96
Major Procida	10	Lycius	47	Left Banker	13	Mister Deville	12
Mizaj	19	Malibu Wesley	23	Lived It Up	9	Moment of Crisis	7
Mountain Metal	9	Manlove	9	Magnificent One	15	Moro	14
Mr. Groush	20	Mesopotamia	18	Mahogany Hall	33	Muldoon	16
Night Fright	8	Mighty Magee	23	Mambo Game	10	My Liege	15
Not Tricky	29	Millions	36	Mercer Mill	65	Naroctive	8
Old Chapel	19	Nines Wild	10	Musical Dreamer	6	New Way	17
Paramour	11	Ormsby	42	Noble Cat	10	Notable Cat	84
Parentheses	19	Performing Magic	10	Noon Prospect	15	Officer of Court	16
Parting the Sea	19	Personal Flag	54	Northern Symphony	6	Peace Prize (Ire)	8
Patsyprospect	23	Phone Trick	78	Nunc Pro Tunc	9	Perdition's Son	13
Pragmatic	6	Polish Pro	11	Pacific Waves	7	Plentyofit	8
Prospector Jones	29	Preacherman	13	Polish Spray	9	Polar Ice Caps	7
R. Payday	20	Precise End	72	Political Folly	23	Preferences	6
Red Prairie	9	Radio Star	56	Pride of Burkaan	16	Prince Graustark	9
Retsina Run	14	Raffie's Majesty	35	Private School	11	Probable	8
Roglee	7	Rage	11	Railway Cat	16	Prospector's Music	48
Run Paul Run	10	Regal Classic	67	Rhodes	11	Quaker Quick	6
Sadler Slew	34	Reign Road	19	Spirit Voices	7	Raise a Rascal	7
Sandia Slew	7	River Keen (Ire)	34	Spunky Rascal	8	Red River Gorge	16
Schizoid	13	Rizzi	75	St l'Enjoleur	7	Reel On Reel	24
Sioux Maruk	7	Rob 'n Gin	25	Sun Master	13	Regalstaff	13
Someplace Fast	8	Rock and Roll	53	Winninginexcess	11	Revelrout	8
Storm Ashore	23	Rodeo	104	Winthrop	30	Rojo Dinero	7
Tap N Snap	23	Satellite Sun	15	Yeti	7	South Pass	6
Ticketless	6	Scarlet Ibis	9	Zero for Conduct	7	Speak	18
You Know How It Is	11	Sea Salute	30			Stauder	10
		Senor Speedy	21	**OKLAHOMA**		Sunrise Shower	10
NEW YORK		Signal Tap	30	Alamocitos	19	Taconic Road	9
A. P Jet	83	Silver Music	13	All Storm	7	Tarakam	7
Abaginone	21	Slice of Reality	7	Backoff Dude	7	Ti Valley	9
Adios My Friend	15	Spectacular Bid	25	Beat the Feet	8	Track Barron	13
Adonis	30	Storm of Angels	15	Black Mackee	6	Undeniable	13
All Gone	11	Take Me Out	49	Bluffy	9	Unome	12
American Chance	23	Testimonial	19	Bonus Time Cat	37	War Machine	17
American Standard	11	The Wicked North	9	Burbank	32	Western Challenge (GB)	11
Aristotle	23	Thriller	6	Chazerahy	15	Wild Colony	19
Badge	15	Thunder Puddles	8	Chief Kris	17	Wolf Touch	10
Brushed On	33	Thunder Rumble	13	Chief's Reward	15		
Carry My Colors	13	Tomorrows Cat	74	Coaxing Matt	7	**OREGON**	
Chequer	8	Treasure Cove	34	Concorde Cal	6	Abstract	46
City Zip	121	Tri Line	14	Confederate Hero	8	Airdrie Apache	20
Claramount	15	Trick Me	9	Coordinator	36	Bagshot	17
Comeonmom	12	Watch the Bird	16	Deodar	17	Baquero	32
Country Squire	8	Western Expression	101	Double Niner	10	Cascadian	39
Cozy Drive	18	Williamstown	34	Dreamfield	7	Danjur	39
Crimson Guard	12			Duxster	6	Ex Marks the Cop	14
Crusader Sword	28	**OHIO**		Ecstatic Ride	20	Klinsman (Ire)	24
Danzatame	18	Academy Award	48	Ensign Bering	7	Prince Stanley	7
David	19	Ago	22	Expense Account	24	Superior Success	8
Daygata	20	Al Sabin	11	Falkenham (GB)	10	Tiffany Ice	14
Deputy Cat	16	Alladin Rib	10	Fortunate Moment	7	True Confidence	46
Distinctive Pro	40	Allen Gorgeous	8	Full of Tricks	8		
Dunsinyne	6	Alota Gator Bait	7	Gamini	8	**PENNSYLVANIA**	
Executiveprivilege	6	Artic Chill	7	Garbu	8	Activist	16
Expensive Decision	7	Brolly	8	Ghost Tension	12	Afleetknowsasecret	7
Freud	46	Camp Izard	7	Golden Dodger	6	Alyten	6
Go West	18	Canvas	21	Harriman	11	Aquarian Prince	8
Gold Token	36	Coax Me Chad	15	Have Fun	21	Attorney	19
Goldminers Gold	25	Covered Wagon	6	Here We Come	38	Bankbook	8
Gone for Real	12	Donthelumbertrader	6	Inagroove	6	Big Steel	9
Good and Tough	45	Flight Forty Nine	17	Inca Chief	24	Bombardier	22
Gray Raider	16	Forest Gazelle	8	Indy Talent	27	Buck'sinthebank	10

Stallion	Mares bred	Stallion	Mares bred	Stallion	Mares bred	Stallion	Mares bred
Captain Capote	7	Royal Merlot	18	Country Side	9	Point in Time	6
Clash by Night	38	Run Turn	15	Crafty	13	Pollock's Luck	30
Coastal Storm	55	Sejm	30	Dancer's Ghost	11	Porto Varas	15
Corporate Report	9	Shining Spring	10	Desert Royalty	14	Power Storm	13
Count On Steve	11	Stake Procpect	11	Devious Course	7	Racing Rhinocerous	9
Dark Mystery	8	Storm God	28	Dome Mountain	7	Raise a Govenor	13
De Niro	16	Sunshine Jimmy	18	Eagle Station	19	Raja's Best Boy	16
Deposit Ticket	21	Tamhid	9	Eddie B Runs	7	Rare Brick	19
Digamist	14	Virtua Cop	36	El Amante	15	Regent Minister	13
Dusty Screen	11	Wonder Bird	21	Endless Queue	10	Relagate	10
Erland	10			Excellent Secret	6	Report On Rain	17
Fair Skies	7	**SOUTH CAROLINA**		Fashion Find	17	River Squall	28
Federal Trial	13	Is Sveikatas	13	Fiend	12	Roo Art	6
Fini Cassette	8	Just a Miner	16	Fire Maker	14	Ruhlmann	8
Fleg	6	Lad	8	Flaming Quest (GB)	8	Russian Connection	9
Flying Pidgeon	24	Play Both Ends	10	Fog Horn	9	Saxton	7
Foligno	9	Prime Legacy	8	Foreign Holding	10	Seattle Battle	10
Harry the Hat	31	Ride the Storm	9	Gary Gumbo	11	Seattle Pattern	15
Judge T C	115	Ring	15	Gen Stormin'norman	34	Secret Claim	19
Looks Good to Me	7	Roll Again	16	Gold Legend	67	Seeking a Home	36
Lord At Law	7	Signal	7	Gold Regent	26	Seneca Jones	42
Michael's Star	10	Sticks and Bricks	12	Goldmine (Fr)	7	Siebe	7
Mr. Explosive	12	Stormville	6	Gone East	13	Simon Lord Lovat	6
Mystic Replica	6	Valiant Lark	9	Gotzum	10	Slew You	6
Obstructed	12	Whisky Creek	6	Gracious Ghost	10	Socially Shaded	9
Ocean Splash	16			Grand Jewel	6	Southern Romance	13
Patton	57	**SOUTH DAKOTA**		Gringo Pilot	6	Star Programmer	70
Pin Stripe	12	Crafty Ridan	16	Groovy Jett	14	Sun Bull	11
Pok Ta Pok	20	Finn McCool	6	Hadif	31	Sunny's Halo	79
Power by Far	31	Get Me Out	10	Half Fast George	8	Texas City	40
Power of Mind	9	Letthebattlebegin	6	Haymarket (GB)	14	Texas Terror	7
Quarry	25	Mr. O. P.	7	Heather's Prospect	21	The Prime Minister	17
Rip Cat	11	Neff Lake	25	High Energy	8	Throw Down	11
Roanoke	31	Storm of the Night	40	High Street	9	Tory Hole	9
Saucy Token	10	Tabib	16	High Wire Acrobat	9	Totem and Taboo	9
Smart Guy	6			Holzmeister	18	Trancus	22
Spectaculardynasty	6	**TENNESSEE**		Hunter's Phone	9	Trapp Mountain	21
Turn West	19	Code Talker	6	Hurlingham	9	Trifecta Scott	8
Two Davids	9	Doppler	10	Ikari	24	Truluck	50
Valid Request	10	Head West	18	In the Headlights	6	Tuesday's Special	11
Western Echo	13	Moonlight Guy	10	Inevitable Hour	8	Twilight Agenda	17
Wild Kiss	6	Prince Nureyev	10	Irish Open	48	Tyler Wayne	7
				Itron	13	Uncle Abbie	36
PUERTO RICO		**TEXAS**		Joe Lin's Son	6	Under David's Wing	12
Abou El Abed	6	Aggie Southpaw	17	Joe Who (Brz)	13	Valid Expectations	97
Balcony	44	Alleged Stardom	9	Karen's Cat	60	Viva Deputy	10
Big Sal	10	American Brass	8	Kayrawan	14	Wajir	24
Billions	20	American Champ	21	Kentucky Jazz	19	Wake Up Alarm	9
Blustery	11	Ancient Quest	9	Kicking Boot	8	War	7
Casanova Star	16	Assault Cat	23	King of the Heap	20	Warfield	8
Chicago Bound	7	At Full Feather	14	Leafy	12	Western City	10
Don Guido	6	Aztec Native	6	Lil Honcho	10	Western Trader	15
Don Serafin	9	Band Dancer	6	Linear	10	Wild Zone	73
El Coloso	10	Bandwagon	8	Lucky So n' So	16	Won Song	13
El Jibaro	7	Ben's Ridge (GB)	11	Magic Cat	41		
El Justo	7	Big Lukey	6	Magic Chill	9	**UTAH**	
El Virazon	6	Biltmore	8	Majestic Tweeleven	19	Albright Avenue	6
Eqtesaad	47	Bionic Prospect	7	Man From Eldorado	9	Crystal Gazer	38
Fappiano's Star	42	Boone's Mill	37	Marked Tree	45	Delta Demon	7
Fiery Special	7	Capote's Prospect	35	Meacham	14	Simi Dancer	6
Fort La Roca	21	Carr Tech	9	Medifast	7	Thunder Falcon	13
Goldwater	23	Cat Strike	21	Miswaki Gold	9		
Greedy	7	Cat's Career	27	Moving Shoulder	12	**VIRGINIA**	
Johnny Jones	10	Cien Fuegos	11	Mystery Storm	40	Aaron's Gold	7
Just Typical	15	City Council (Ire)	6	Naevus	42	Akram	6
King's Crown	11	Claudius	18	Noble Savage (Ire)	12	Ball's Bluff	26
Lightning Al	10	Clever Return	18	Olmos	10	Chenin Blanc	10
Mr. Minister	10	Cold Hearted Man	7	Once a Sailor	11	Chief Protocol	9
Nather	8	Commanchero	51	Open Forum	129	Expelled	34
Once Ivor	9	Connecting Terms	12	Orbit's Revenge	11	Fred Astaire	19
Pair of Deuces	16	Conroe	7	Pancho Villa	56	Genuine Reward	9
Plano Pleasure	10			Pepper M.	9	Hay Halo	25

Stallion	Mares bred
He's Got Gall	8
Housebuster	84
Linkage	15
Mighty Forum (GB)	12
Musical River	6
One More Power	6
Prenup	28
Prospect Bay	35
Rock Point	12
Secret Hello	21
Slew the Deputy	6
Spartan Victory	6
Tom Cobbley	6
Two Smart	13

WASHINGTON

Stallion	Mares bred
Adventure Road	16
Altazarr	9
As the Bell Tolls	6
Basket Weave	40
Beefchopper	17
Cahill Road	57
Cisco Road	8
Commandperformance	6
Consigliere (GB)	8
Coz	6
Dave's Reality	6
Defensive Play	32
Delineator	25
Detox	17
Flagman Ahead	9
Flashy's Pretender	6
Flying With Eagles	25
Former	11
Free At Last	59
Gold Saga	10
He's Tops	16
I Am Not a Crook	8
Ihtimam	38
Individual Style	12
Jazzing Around	14
Jett Sett Joe	6
Jumron (GB)	6
Kansas City	9
Katowice	31
La Saboteur	29
Liberty Gold	35
Line Dance	8
Lord Charmer	10
Matricule	31
Midway Magistrate	19
Moon Up T. C.	6
Mr. Easy Money	13
Mula Gula	12
Ore Grade	21
Our Boy Harvey	19
Petersburg	27
Raisor's Edge	19
Rojo Warrior	6
Salty Shoes	6
Slewd	6
Slewdledo	76
Snowbound	50
Stolen Gold	13
Swing and Miss	37
Tahoe City	9
Tough Knight	12
Tropic Lightning	12

WISCONSIN

Stallion	Mares bred
Beeper	6
Bold James	7

WEST VIRGINIA

Stallion	Mares bred
Castine	56
Catastrophe	22
Citislipper	25
Creative Act	6
Eastover Court	78
Emancipator	20
Enough Reality	17
Explosive Red	17
Gneiss	16
Greenspring Willy	17
Johnbill	11
Jove Stone	15
Kokand	47
Legal Maneuver	6
Luftikus	75
Makin	52
Master's Honey	9
Medford	6
My Boy Adam	23
Native Slew	17
Our Valley View	15
Proper Texan	21
Robb	22
Runaway Macho	14
Satchmo's Band	16
Seeking the Crown	11
Shoot Again	8
Sprizzo	7
Standing On Edge	16
Storm Center	8
Strike Adduce	15
Tank	44
Ten Star Fleet	6
This Bulls for You	13
Tidehaven	10
Truculent Schular	26
Valid Indy	7
Van Go	9
Verification	6
Weshaam	15

WYOMING

Stallion	Mares bred
Hopedale O.	6

ALBERTA

Stallion	Mares bred
Banjo	15
Battle Creek	12
Blazing Fire	17
Brass Minister	24
Cache In	16
Cagey Lad	7
Chapel Creek	15
Ciano Cat	42
Cohoes Native	6
Cool Groom	6
Deal Breaker	9
Desperately	30
Devonwood	44
Esteem	11
Exclusive Era	27
Fast Account	16
Fatih	6
Go Gary Go	29
Ground Stroke	26
Hail the Ruckus	25
Hurricane Center	43
Incinderator	33
John the Magician	14

Stallion	Mares bred
Just a Cat	71
King's Nest	10
Lenado Road	9
Lover's Trust	13
Magic Prospect	29
Parlay Me	6
Quite Special	9
Ranger (Fr)	17
Rebmec	23
Regal Remark	25
Rokeby (GB)	7
Royal Rumpus	9
Silver of Silver	9
The Fed	7
Weekend Guest	29
Zuppardo's Future	7

BRITISH COLUMBIA

Stallion	Mares bred
Alfaari	25
Alybro	9
Baron de Vaux	18
Captain Collins (Ire)	16
Devil On Ice	17
Diamond Sword	8
Dixieland Brass	18
Easy Squeezy	7
Feu d'Enfer	24
Funboy	9
Katahaula County	37
King of Cats	9
Let's Go Blue	9
Light of Mine	13
Malmo	10
Mass Market	38
Musing	7
Net Asset	10
Nightofthegaelics	8
Northern Presence	6
Oka Revolt	6
On Target	23
Orchid's Devil	6
Persian Star	9
Regal Intention	51
Ringside	12
Royal Dixie	18
Seven Zero	12
Silver Fox	20
Sky White	7
Stephanotis	37
Tejabo	20
Turbulent Kris	10
Vying Victor	63
Wandering	12
Western Trick	12
Yoonevano	23

MANITOBA

Stallion	Mares bred
Act Smart	14
Akado	10
Boanerges	15
Buie	15
Callin Baton Rouge	14
Cognizant	11
Dargai	7
Gentle Kent	14
Gold Hat	9
His Excellence	18
My Man Tarzan	6
Polka	11
Shrike	18
Sunset Ridge	9
Super Rigger	6

ONTARIO

Stallion	Mares bred
Alydeed	58
Annihilate	6
Archers Bay	34
Ascot Knight	60
Ashbury	20
Bold Executive	73
Bold n' Flashy	84
Canyon Creek (Ire)	36
China Ruckus	7
Compadre	79
Cossack Fighter (GB)	9
Crown Attorney	49
Dr. Adagio	9
Elajjud	29
Foxtrail	61
Franc Coeur	7
Great Gladiator	21
Hierarch	8
Highland Ruckus	28
I Can't Believe	19
Inspired Prospect	10
Iskandar Elakbar	8
Kiridashi	41
Magic Walk	6
Matter of Honor	19
Minstrel Dancer	10
Not Impossible (Ire)	20
One Way Love	68
Parisianprospector	47
Perigee Moon	69
Pete's Sake	15
Porto Foricos	27
Randy Regent	7
Shelly's Charmer	15
Talkin Man	7
Tejano Red	7
Tempolake	7
Tethra	57
Trajectory	60
Umrigar	9
War Deputy	10
Welbred Fred	11
Whiskey Wisdom	64
Wild Irish Jigs	6
Wonneberg	20
Yellow Creek	7

PRINCE EDWARD ISLAND

Stallion	Mares bred
Be Frank	14

QUEBEC

Stallion	Mares bred
Oronero	7

SASKATCHEWAN

Stallion	Mares bred
Blowin de Turn	10
Castle Arms	10
Clash of Steel	7
McCallister's Risk	9
Optic Odyssey	8
Paskanell	6
Pole Position	16
Private Joe	9
Royal Quiz	7
Satellite Signal	10
Scratching Post	6
Shaheen	8
Slew Express	10
You've Got Action	17

BROODMARES

Broodmares of the Year

As awarded by the Kentucky Thoroughbred Owners and Breeders Association

2002—TOUSSAUD
Dk. b. or br. m. 1989, by El Gran Senor—Image of Reality, by In Reality
Breeder, Juddmonte Farms Inc. (Ky.). **Owner,** Juddmonte Farms Inc.
Dam of 6 foals, all starters, 5 winners, including **CHESTER HOUSE,** 6 wins, $1,944,545, 2000 Arlington Million-G1, etc.; **EMPIRE MAKER,** 4 wins, $1,885,800, 2003 Belmont S.-G1, Florida Derby-G1, etc.; **HONEST LADY,** 6 wins, $894,168, 2000 Santa Monica H.-G1, etc.; **CHISELLING,** 3 wins, $405,760, 2002 Secretariat S.-G1, etc.; **DECARCHY,** 6 wins, $590,462, 2002 Frank E. Kilroe Mile H.-G2, etc.

2001—TURKO'S TURN
Ch. m. 1992, by Turkoman—Turbo Launch, by Relaunch
Breeder, John F. Dolan (Ky.). **Owner,** The Thoroughbred Corp.
Dam of 4 foals, all winners, including **POINT GIVEN,** 9 wins, $3,968,500, 2001 Horse of the Year, 2001 champion three-year-old male, 2001 Preakness S. (G1), etc.

2000—PRIMAL FORCE
B. m. 1987, by Blushing Groom (Fr)—Prime Prospect, by Mr. Prospector
Breeders, Mr. and Mrs. Bertram R. Firestone (Ky.). **Owner,** Frank Stronach.
Dam of 7 foals, 4 starters, all winners, including **MACHO UNO,** 6 wins, $1,851,803, 2000 champion two-year-old male, 2000 Breeders' Cup Juvenile (G1), etc.; **AWESOME AGAIN,** 9 wins, $4,374,590, 1998 Breeders' Cup Classic (G1), etc.

1999—ANNE CAMPBELL
B. m. 1973, by Never Bend—Repercussion, by *Tatan
Breeder, Mill House (Ky.). **Owner,** Arthur B. Hancock III.
Dam of 13 foals, 10 starters, 7 winners, including **MENIFEE,** 5 wins, $1,732,000, 1999 Haskell Invitational H. (G1), etc.; **DESERT WINE,** 8 wins, $1,618,043, 1984 Californian S. (G1), etc.

1998—IN NEON
B. m. 1982, by Ack Ack—Shamara, by Dewan
Breeder, Clairmont Farm (Ky.). **Owner,** John Franks.
Dam of 7 foals, all starters, 6 winners, including **SHARP CAT,** 15 wins, $2,032,575, 1998 Beldame S. (G1), etc.; **ROYAL ANTHEM,** 6 wins, $1,876,876, 1998 Canadian International S. (Can-G1), etc.; **STAR RECRUIT,** 5 wins, $807,200, 1991 Alysheba S. (G3), etc.

1997—SLIGHTLY DANGEROUS
B. m. 1979, by Roberto—Where You Lead, by Raise a Native
Breeder, Alan Clore (Ky.). **Owner,** Juddmonte Farms.
Dam of 13 foals, 11 starters, 10 winners, including **COMMANDER IN CHIEF,** 5 wins, $1,311,514, 1993 champion three-year-old male in Eur, 1993 Epsom Derby (Eng-G1), etc.; **WARNING (GB),** 8 wins, $937,280, 1987 champion two-year-old in Eng, 1988 champion three-year-old in Eng, 1988 Queen Elizabeth II S. (Eng-G1), etc.; **YASHMAK,** 4 wins, $529,382, 1997 Flower Bowl Invitational H. (G1), etc.; **DUSHYANTOR,** 5 wins, $1,197,570, 1996 Great Voltigeur S. (Eng-G2), etc.; **JIBE,** 2 wins, $98,912.

1996—PERSONAL ENSIGN
B. m. 1984, by Private Account—Grecian Banner, by Hoist the Flag
Breeder, Ogden Phipps (Ky.). **Owner,** Ogden Phipps, Phipps Stable.

Dam of 7 foals, 6 starters, all winners, including MY FLAG, 6 wins, $1,557,057, 1995 Breeders' Cup Juvenile Fillies (G1), etc.; **MINER'S MARK,** 6 wins, $967,170, 1993 Jockey Club Gold Cup (G1), etc.; **TRADITIONALLY,** 5 wins, $495,660, 2001 Oaklawn H. (G1).

1995—NORTHERN SUNSET (Ire)
Ch. m. 1977, by Northfields—=Moss Greine (GB), by *Ballymoss
Breeder, Basil Brindly (Ire). **Owner,** Virginia Kraft Payson.
Dam of 13 foals, 12 starters, 11 winners, including **ST. JOVITE,** 6 wins, $1,604,439, 1992 Horse of the Year in Eur, 1991 champion two-year-old in Ire, 1992 Irish Derby (Ire-G1), etc.; **SALEM DRIVE,** 13 wins, $1,046,065, 1987 Bougainvillea H. (G2), etc.; **LAC OUIMET,** 12 wins, $817,863, 1986 Jim Dandy S. (G2), etc.; **L'CARRIERE,** 8 wins, $1,726,175, 1996 Saratoga Cup H. (G3).

1994—FALL ASPEN
Ch. m. 1976, by Pretense—Change Water, by Swaps
Breeder, Joseph M. Roebling (Ky.). **Owner,** John Magnier.
Dam of 14 foals, 13 starters, 12 winners, including **TIMBER COUNTRY,** 5 wins, $1,560,400, 1994 champion two-year-old male, 1995 Preakness S. (G1), etc.; **BIANCONI,** 3 wins, $134,520, 1998 Diadem S. (Eng-G2); **FORT WOOD,** 3 wins, $359,995, 1993 Grand Prix de Paris (Fr-G1), etc.; **NORTHERN ASPEN,** 5 wins, $253,678, 1987 Gamely H. (G1), etc.; **HAMAS (Ire),** 5 wins, $237,814, 1993 July Cup S. (Eng-G1), etc.; **COLORADO DANCER (Ire),** 3 wins, $203,389, 1989 Prix de Pomone (Fr-G2), etc.; **ELLE SEULE,** 3 wins, $101,478, 1986 Prix d'Astarte (Fr-G2); **MAZZACANO (GB),** 3 wins, $153,421, 1989 Goodwood Cup (Eng-G3); **PRINCE OF THIEVES,** 2 wins, $368,474.

1993—GLOWING TRIBUTE
B. m. 1973, by Graustark—Admiring, by Hail to Reason
Breeder, Paul Mellon, (Va.). **Owner,** John R. Gaines.
Dam of 11 foals, 10 starters, 9 winners, including **SEA HERO,** 6 wins, $2,929,869, 1993 Kentucky Derby (G1), etc.; **HERO'S HONOR,** 8 wins, $499,025, 1984 Bowling Green H. (G1), etc.; **GLOWING HONOR,** 6 wins, $296,450, 1988, 1989 Diana H. (G2), etc.; **WILD APPLAUSE,** 5 wins, $240,136, 1984 Diana H. (G2), etc.; **CORONATION CUP,** 3 wins, $172,181, 1994 Nijana S. (G3); **MACKIE,** 3 wins, $164,579, 1996 Busher S. (G3); **SEATTLE GLOW,** 4 wins, $69,023.

1992—WEEKEND SURPRISE
B. m. 1980, by Secretariat—Lassie Dear, by Buckpasser
Breeders, W. S. Farish III and W. S. Kilroy (Ky.). **Owners,** W. S. Farish III and W. S. Kilroy.
Dam of 13 foals, 12 starters, 8 winners, including **A.P. INDY,** 8 wins, $2,979,815, 1992 Horse of the Year, 1992 champion three-year-old male, 1992 Belmont S. (G1), etc.; **SUMMER SQUALL,** 13 wins, $1,844,282, 1990 Preakness S. (G1), etc.; **WELCOME SURPRISE,** 2 wins, $143,574, 2000 Dogwood S. (G3).

1991—TOLL BOOTH
B. m. 1971, by Buckpasser—Missy Baba, by *My Babu
Breeder, John M. Schiff (Ky.). **Owner,** Lazy Lane Farms.
Dam of 12 foals, all starters, 11 winners, including **PLUGGED NICKLE,** 11 wins, $647,206, 1980 champion sprinter, 1980 Florida Derby (G1), etc.; **CHRISTIECAT,** 11 wins, $799,745, 1992 Flower Bowl H. (G1), etc.; **KEY TO THE BRIDGE,** 7 wins, $289,747, 1988 Beaugay H. (G3); **TOLL FEE,** 7 wins, $333,917; **TOLL KEY,** 9 wins, $290,218; **IDLE GOSSIP,** 5 wins, $101,721; **TOKENS ONLY,** 4 wins, $50,455.

1990—KAMAR
B. m. 1976, by Key to the Mint—Square Angel,
by Quadrangle
Breeder, E. P. Taylor (Can). Owner, Heronwood Farm.
Dam of 9 foals, 8 starters, 7 winners, including KEY TO THE
MOON, 13 wins, $714,536, 1984 champion three-year-old
male in Can, 1984 Discovery H. (G3), etc.; GORGEOUS, 8
wins, $1,171,370, 1989 Ashland S. (G1), etc.; SEASIDE AT-
TRACTION, 4 wins, $272,541, 1990 Kentucky Oaks (G1);
HIAAM, 3 wins, $48,081, 1986 Princess Margaret S. (Eng-
G3).

1989—RELAXING
B. m. 1976, by Buckpasser—Marking Time, by To Market
Breeder, Ogden Phipps (Ky.). Owner, Ogden Phipps.
Dam of 12 foals, 9 starters, all winners, including EASY GOER,
14 wins, $4,873,770, 1988 champion two-year-old male,
1989 Belmont S. (G1), etc.; EASY NOW, 4 wins, $359,466,
1992 Go for Wand S. (G1), etc.; CADILLACING, 7 wins,
$268,137, 1988 Ballerina S. (G1), etc.

1988—GRECIAN BANNER
Dk. b. or br. m., 1974, by Hoist the Flag—*Dorine,
by =Aristophanes (GB)
Breeder, Ogden Phipps (Ky.). Owner, Ogden Phipps.
Dam of 7 foals, 5 starters, all winners, including PERSONAL
ENSIGN, 13 wins, $1,679,880, 1988 champion older female,
1996 Broodmare of the Year, 1988 Breeders' Cup Distaff
(G1), etc.; PERSONAL FLAG, 8 wins, $1,258,924, 1988
Suburban H. (G1), etc.

1987—BANJA LUKA
B. m. 1968, by Double Jay—Legato, by Dark Star
Breeder, Howard B. Keck (Ky.). Owner, Howard B. Keck.
Dam of 9 foals, all starters, 7 winners, including FERDINAND,
8 wins, $3,777,978, 1987 Horse of the Year, 1987 champion
older male, 1986 Kentucky Derby (G1), etc.; DONNA INEZ,
4 wins, $101,275; JAYSTON, 7 wins, $92,143; DANCING, 4
wins, $77,925; ANCIENT ART, 4 wins, $74,250; PLINTH, 3
wins, $65,980.

1986—TOO BALD
Dk. b. or br. m. 1964, by Bald Eagle—Hidden Talent,
by Dark Star
Breeder, H. F. Guggenheim (Ky.). Owner, North Ridge Farm.
Dam of 12 foals, 11 starters, all winners, including CAPOTE,
3 wins, $714,470, 1986 champion two-year-old male, 1986
Breeders' Cup Juvenile S. (G1), etc.; EXCELLER, 15 wins,
$1,674,587, 1978 Jockey Club Gold Cup (G1), etc.; VAGUELY
HIDDEN, 8 wins, $239,313, 1990 New Jersey Turf Classic
S. (G3); AMERICAN STANDARD, 5 wins, $180,120; BALD-
SKI, 7 wins, $103,214.

1985—DUNCE CAP II
Dk. b. or br. m. 1960, by Tom Fool—Bright Coronet,
by Bull Lea
Breeder, Greentree Stud Inc. (Ky.). Owner, Greentree Stud Inc.
Dam of 10 foals, 8 starters, all winners, including LATE
BLOOMER, 11 wins, $512,040, 1978 champion older female,
1978 Beldame S. (G1), etc.; JOHNNY APPLESEED, 4 wins,
$91,910, 1976 Louisiana Derby (G2); LATE ACT, 9 wins,
$661,089, 1985 Cliff Hanger H. (G3), etc.

1984—HASTY QUEEN II
Dk. b. or br. m. 1963, by One Count—Queen Hopeful,
by Roman
Breeder, A. E. Reuben (Ky.). Owners, Robert E. Courtney
and Robert B. Congleton.
Dam of 16 foals, 14 starters, 12 winners, including FIT TO
FIGHT, 14 wins, $1,042,075, 1984 Brooklyn H. (G1), etc.;
HASTY FLYER, 10 wins, $293,663, 1974 Round Table H.
(G3), etc.; HASTY TAM, 16 wins, $211,738; PLAYFUL
QUEEN, 5 wins, $101,837; MICHAEL NAVONOD, 6 wins,
$86,380; HASTY CUTIE, 8 wins, $63,639.

1983—COURTLY DEE
Dk. b. or br. m. 1968, by Never Bend—Tulle,
by War Admiral

Breeder, Donald Unger (Ky.). Owners, Helen Alexander,
David Aykroyd, and Helen Groves.
Dam of 18 foals, 17 starters, 15 winners, including ALTHEA,
8 wins, $1,275,255, 1983 champion two-year-old filly, 1984
Arkansas Derby (G1), etc.; ALI OOP, 7 wins, $174,020,
1976 Sapling S. (G1); KETOH, 3 wins, $173,550, 1985
Cowdin S. (G1); AQUILEGIA, 8 wins, $446,081, 1993 New
York H. (G2), etc.; TWINING, 5 wins, $238,140, 1994 Peter
Pan S. (G2), etc.; AISHAH, 6 wins, $169,340, 1990 Rare
Perfume S. (G2); NATIVE COURIER, 14 wins, $522,635,
1981 Bernard Baruch H. (G3), etc.; PRINCESS OOLA, 5
wins, $108,291.

1982—BEST IN SHOW
Ch. m. 1965, by Traffic Judge—Stolen Hour, by Mr. Busher
Breeder, Philip Connors (Ky.). Owners, Mr. and Mrs. Darrell
Brown.
Dam of 17 foals, 12 starters, 9 winners, including MALINOWSKI,
2 wins, 1975 champion two-year-old in Ire, 1976 Ladbroke
Craven S. (Eng-G3); BLUSH WITH PRIDE, 6 wins, $536,807,
1982 Kentucky Oaks (G1), etc.; GIELGUD, 1 win, $56,635,
1980 Champagne S. (Eng-G2); MONROE, 3 wins, $34,422,
1980 Ballyogan S. (Ire-G3).

1981—NATASHKA
Dk. b. or br. m. 1963, by Dedicate—Natasha, by *Nasrullah
Breeder, Greentree Stud Inc. (Ky.). Owner, W. S. Farish III.
Dam of 9 foals, 7 starters, all winners, including GREGORIAN,
4 wins, $194,912, 1980 Joe McGrath Memorial S. (Ire-G1),
etc.; TRULY BOUND, 9 wins, $382,449, 1980 Arlington-
Washington Lassie S. (G2), etc.; IVORY WAND, 5 wins,
$97,452, 1976 Test S. (G3); BLOOD ROYAL, 4 wins, $28,870,
1975 Jockey Club Cup (Eng-G3), etc.; ARKADINA, 2 wins,
$79,830, Athasi S. (Ire-G3).

1980—KEY BRIDGE
B. m. 1959, by *Princequillo—Blue Banner, by War Admiral
Breeder, Paul Mellon (Va.). Owner, Paul Mellon.
Dam of 11 foals, 8 starters, 7 winners, including FORT MARCY,
21 wins, $1,109,791, 1970 Horse of the Year, 1967, 1968,
1970 champion turf male, 1970 champion older male, 1967,
1970 Washington D.C. International S., etc.; KEY TO THE
MINT, 14 wins, $576,015, 1972 champion three-year-old
male, 1973 Suburban H. (G1), etc.; KEY TO CONTENT,
7 wins, $354,772, 1981 United Nations H. (G1), etc.; KEY
TO THE KINGDOM, 7 wins, $109,590, 1974 Stymie H.
(G3).

1979—SMARTAIRE
Dk. b. or br. m. 1962, by *Quibu—Art Teacher, by Olympia
Breeder, F. W. Hooper (Al.). Owners, Mr. and Mrs. James P.
Ryan.
Dam of 12 foals, all starters, 10 winners, including SMART
ANGLE, 7 wins, $414,217, 1979 champion two-year-old
filly, 1979 Frizette S. (G1), etc.; SMARTEN, 11 wins,
$716,426, 1979 American Derby (G2), etc.; QUADRATIC,
6 wins, $233,941, 1977 Cowdin S. (G2); SMART HEIRESS,
6 wins, $154,999.

1978—PRIMONETTA
Ch. m. 1958, by Swaps—Banquet Bell, by Polynesian
Breeder, John W. Galbreath (Ky.). Owner, John W. Galbreath.
Dam of 7 foals, 6 starters, all winners, including CUM LAUDE
LAURIE, 8 wins, $405,207, 1977 Beldame S. (G1), etc.;
PRINCE THOU ART, 3 wins, $167,902, 1975 Florida Derby
(G1); MAUD MULLER, 3 wins, $138,383, 1974 Gazelle H.
(G2), etc.; GRENFALL, 4 wins, $19,467, 1971 Gallinule S.
(Ire-G2), etc.

1977—SWEET TOOTH
B. m. 1965, by On-and-On—Plum Cake, by Ponder
Breeder, Calumet Farm (Ky.). Owner, Calumet Farm.
Dam of 13 foals, 10 starters, 8 winners, including OUR MIMS,
6 wins, $368,034, 1977 champion three-year-old filly, 1977
Coaching Club American Oaks (G1), etc.; ALYDAR, 14
wins, $957,195, 1978 Blue Grass S. (G1), etc.; SUGAR
AND SPICE, 5 wins, $257,046, 1980 Mother Goose S.
(G1), etc.

1976—*GAZALA II
Dk. b. or br. m. 1964, by Dark Star—*Belle Angevine, by =L'Amiral (Fr)
Breeder, Nelson Bunker Hunt (Fr). **Owner,** Nelson Bunker Hunt.
Dam of 10 foals, 8 starters, 6 winners, including **YOUTH,** 8 wins, $716,146, 1976 champion turf male, 1976 Prix du Jockey Club (Fr-G1), etc.; **MISSISSIPIAN,** 3 wins, $248,520, 1973 champion two-year-old in Fr, 1973 Grand Criterium (Fr-G1), etc.; **GONZALES,** 4 wins, $103,968, 1980 Irish St. Leger (Ire-G1), etc.; **SILKY BABY,** 2 wins, $51,351, 1981 Prix de Guiche (Fr-G3); **BEST OF BOTH,** 6 wins, $242,150.

1975—SHENANIGANS
Gr. m. 1963, by Native Dancer—Bold Irish, by Fighting Fox
Breeder, Stuart S. Janney Jr. (Md.). **Owner,** Locust Hill Farm.
Dam of 6 foals, all winners, including **RUFFIAN,** 10 wins, $313,428, 1974 champion two-year-old filly, 1975 champion three-year-old filly, 1975 Filly Triple Crown, 1975 Coaching Club American Oaks (G1), etc.; **ICECAPADE,** 13 wins, $256,468, 1973 William duPont Jr. H. (G2), etc.; **BUCKFINDER,** 9 wins, $230,513, 1978 William duPont Jr. H. (G2).

1974—COSMAH
B. m. 1953, by Cosmic Bomb—Almahmoud, by *Mahmoud
Breeder, Henry H. Knight (Ky.). **Owner,** John R. Gaines.
Dam of 15 foals, 10 starters, 9 winners, including **TOSMAH,** 23 wins, $612,588, 1963 champion two-year-old filly, 1964 champion three-year-old filly, 1964 champion handicap female, 1964 Beldame S., etc.; **HALO,** 9 wins, $259,553, 1974 United Nations H. (G1), etc.; **FATHERS IMAGE,** 7 wins, $173,318; **MARIBEAU,** 4 wins, $20,925.

1973—SOMETHINGROYAL
B. m. 1952, by *Princequillo—Imperatrice, by Caruso
Breeder, Mr. C. T. Chenery (Va.). **Owner,** Meadow Stable.
Dam of 18 foals, 11 starters, 11 winners, including **SECRETARIAT,** 16 wins, $1,316,808, 1972, 1973 Horse of the Year, 1972 champion two-year-old male, 1973 champion three-year-old male, 1973 champion turf male, 1973 Triple Crown, 1973 Kentucky Derby (G1), etc.; **SIR GAYLORD,** 10 wins, $237,404, 1961 Sapling S., etc.; **FIRST FAMILY,** 7 wins, $188,040, 1966 Gulfstream Park H., etc.; **SYRIAN SEA,** 6 wins, $178,245, 1967 Selima S., etc.

1972—*MOMENT OF TRUTH II
Ch. m. 1959, by =Matador (GB)—=Kingsworthy (Ire), by =Kingstone (GB)
Breeder, Mrs. M. Clarke (GB). **Owner,** Cragwood Estates.
Dam of 9 foals, all winners, including **CONVENIENCE,** 15 wins, $648,933, 1973 Vanity H. (G1), etc.; **NIGHT ALERT,** 3 wins, $121,248, 1980 Prix Jean Prat (Fr-G2), etc.; **INDULTO,** 27 wins, $466,789, 1966 Withers S., etc.; **PROLIFERATION,** 7 wins, $66,680; **PUNTILLA,** 3 wins, $64,255.

1971—IBERIA
Ch. m. 1954, by *Heliopolis—War East, by *Easton
Breeder, L. S. MacPhail (Md.). **Owner,** Meadow Stable.
Dam of 10 foals, all starters, all winners, including **RIVA RIDGE,** 17 wins, $1,111,497, 1971 champion two-year-old male, 1973 champion older male, 1972 Kentucky Derby, etc.; **HYDROLOGIST,** 10 wins, $277,958, 1970 Excelsior H., etc.; **POTOMAC,** 3 wins, $37,361.

1970—LEVEE
Ch. m. 1953, by Hill Prince—Bourtai, by Stimulus
Breeder, Claiborne Farm (Ky.). **Owner,** Whitney Stone.
Dam of 11 foals, 9 starters, 7 winners, including **SHUVEE,** 16 wins, $890,445, 1970, 1971 champion handicap mare, 1969 Filly Triple Crown, 1969 Coaching Club American Oaks, etc.; **ROYAL GUNNER,** 6 wins, $334,650; **NALEE,** 8 wins, $141,631, 1963 Black-Eyed Susan S., etc.; **A. T'S OLIE,** 6 wins, $82,211.

1969—ALL BEAUTIFUL
Ch. m. 1959, by Battlefield—Parlo, by *Heliopolis

Breeder, William duPont Jr. (Va.). **Owner,** Paul Mellon.
Dam of 12 foals, 11 starters, 9 winners, including **ARTS AND LETTERS,** 11 wins, $632,404, 1969 Horse of the Year, 1969 champion three-year-old male, 1969 champion handicap horse, 1969 Belmont S., etc.

1968—DELTA
B. m. 1952, by *Nasrullah—Bourtai, by Stimulus
Breeder, Claiborne Farm (Ky.). **Owner,** Claiborne Farm.
Dam of 10 foals, all starters, 9 winners, including **OKAVANGO,** 6 wins, $153,802, 1975 San Pasqual H. (G2), etc.; **DIKE,** 7 wins, $351,274, 1969 Wood Memorial S., etc.; **CANAL,** 33 wins, $280,358; **CABILDO,** 22 wins, $267,265; **SHORE,** 6 wins, $62,357.

1967—KERALA
B. m. 1958, by *My Babu—Blade of Time, by *Sickle
Breeder, Greentree Stud Inc. (Ky.). **Owner,** Mrs. Thomas M. Bancroft.
Dam of 13 foals, 9 starters, 8 winners, including **DAMASCUS,** 21 wins, $1,176,781, 1967 Horse of the Year, 1967 champion three-year-old male, 1967 champion handicap male, 1967 Preakness S., etc.

1966—JULIETS NURSE
Dk. b. or br. m. 1948, by Count Fleet—Nursemaid, by Luke McLuke
Breeder, Mrs. Roy Carruthers (Ky.). **Owner,** J. Graham Brown.
Dam of 13 foals, all starters, 11 winners, including **RUN FOR NURSE,** 22 wins, $253,145; **GALLANT ROMEO,** 15 wins, $202,401, 1966 Vosburgh H., etc.; **WOOZEM,** 7 wins, $163,083, 1966 Demoiselle S., etc.; **DUTIFUL,** 5 wins, $80,780.

1965—POCAHONTAS
Dk. b. or br. m. 1955, by Roman—How, by *Princequillo
Breeder, H. B. Delman (Ky.). **Owner,** Raymond Guest.
Dam of 9 foals, 5 starters, all winners, including **TOM ROLFE,** 16 wins, $671,297, 1965 champion three-year-old male, 1965 Preakness S., etc.; **LADY REBECCA,** 2 wins, $26,434, 1974 Prix Vanteaux (Fr-G3); **CHIEFTAIN,** 13 wins, $405,256, 1964 Governor's Gold Cup, etc.; ***WENONA,** 3 wins, Blandford S. (Ire), etc.

1964—MAID OF FLIGHT
Dk. b. or br. m. 1951, by Count Fleet—Maidoduntreath, by Man o' War
Breeder, Mrs. Silas B. Mason (Ky.). **Owner,** Mrs. Richard C. duPont.
Dam of 11 foals, 10 starters, 9 winners, including **KELSO,** 39 wins, $1,977,896, 1960, 1961, 1962, 1963, 1964 Horse of the Year, 1960 champion three-year-old male, 1961, 1962, 1963, 1964 champion handicap horse, 1960, 1961, 1962, 1963, 1964 Jockey Club Gold Cup, etc.

1963—MISTY MORN
B. m. 1952, by *Princequillo—Grey Flight, by *Mahmoud
Breeder, Wheatley Stable (Ky.). **Owner,** Mrs. H. C. Phipps.
Dam of 10 foals, 8 starters, 7 winners, including **SUCCESSOR,** 7 wins, $532,254, 1966 champion two-year-old, 1966 Champagne S., etc.; **BOLD LAD,** 14 wins, $516,465, 1964 champion two-year-old, 1964 Champagne S., etc.; **SUNRISE FLIGHT,** 11 wins, $380,995, 1963 Gallant Fox H., etc.; **BEAUTIFUL DAY,** 7 wins, $160,007; **BOLD CONSORT,** 6 wins, $38,147.

1962—TRACK MEDAL
Dkbbr. m. 1950, by *Khaled—Iron Reward, by *Beau Pere
Breeder, Rex C. Ellsworth (Ca.). **Owner,** Greentree Stud.
Dam of 10 foals, 8 starters, 6 winners, including **OUTING CLASS,** 6 wins, $229,759, 1962 Hopeful S., etc.; ***O'HARA,** 8 wins, $202,180, 1966 Sunset H.; **TUTANKHAMEN,** 12 wins, $157,530, 1962 Manhattan H.; **FOOL'S GOLD II,** 1 win, 1962 Musidora S. (Eng).

1961—STRIKING
B. m. 1947, by War Admiral—Baby League, by Bubbling Over

Breeder, Ogden Phipps (Ky.). **Owner**, Ogden Phipps.
Dam of 15 foals, 12 starters, 11 winners, including **HITTING AWAY**, 13 wins, $309,079, 1961 Dwyer H., etc.; **BATTER UP**, 7 wins, $166,504, 1962 Black-Eyed Susan S., etc.; **MY BOSS LADY**, 4 wins, $64,174; **GLAMOUR**, 6 wins, $60,775; **BASES FULL**, 3 wins, $17,627.

1960—SIAMA
B. m. 1947, by Tiger—China Face, by Display
Breeder, E. K. Thomas (Ky.). **Owner**, Harry F. Guggenheim.
Dam of 9 foals, 5 starters, all winners, including **BALD EAGLE**, 12 wins, $692,946, 1960 champion handicap male, 1959, 1960 Washington D.C. International, etc.; **ONE-EYED KING**, 15 wins, $266,281, 1960 Arlington H., etc.; **DEAD AHEAD**, 8 wins, $73,645.

1959—*KNIGHT'S DAUGHTER
B. m. 1941, by =Sir Cosmo (Ire)—=Feola (GB), by =Friar Marcus (GB)
Breeder, King George VI (GB). **Owner**, Claiborne Farm.
Dam of 7 foals, all starters, 6 winners, including **ROUND TABLE**, 43 wins, $1,749,869, 1958 Horse of the Year, 1957, 1958, 1959 champion turf male, 1958, 1959 champion older male, 1957 Hollywood Gold Cup, etc.; **MONARCHY**, 7 wins, $85,737; *LOVE GAME, 1 win.

1958—MISS DISCO
B. m. 1944, by Discovery—Outdone, by Pompey
Breeder, Alfred G. Vanderbilt (Md.). **Owner**, Mrs. H. C. Phipps.
Dam of 11 foals, 7 starters, all winners, including **BOLD RULER**, 23 wins, $764,204, 1957 Horse of the Year, 1957 champion three-year-old male, 1958 champion sprinter, 1957 Preakness S., etc.; **INDEPENDENCE**, 12 wins, $132,088; **NASCO**, 7 wins, $71,930.

1957—BELLE JEEP
B. m. 1949, by War Jeep—Model Beauty, by *Blenheim II
Breeder, Maine Chance Farm (Ky.). **Owner**, Maine Chance Farm.
Dam of 14 foals, 12 starters, all winners, including **JEWEL'S REWARD**, 7 wins, $448,592, 1957 champion two-year-old male, 1957 Champagne S., etc.; **TRIPLE CROWN**, 4 wins, $128,874, 1974 San Jacinto S. (G2), etc.; **LORD JEEP**, 11 wins, $64,504; **EVASIVE ACTION**, 3 wins, $47,004.

1956—SWOON
Ch. m. 1942, by Sweep Like—Sadie Greenock, by Greenock
Breeder, E. Gay Drake (Ky.). **Owner**, E. Gay Drake.
Dam of 10 foals, all starters, 8 winners, including **SWOON'S SON**, 30 wins, $970,605, 1956 American Derby, etc.; **DOGOON**, 28 wins, $220,360, 1954 Hawthorne Juvenile H., etc.

1955—IRON REWARD
B. m. 1946, by *Beau Pere—Iron Maiden, by War Admiral
Breeder, W. W. Naylor (Ca.). **Owner**, Rex Ellsworth.
Dam of 11 foals, 9 starters, 5 winners, including **SWAPS**, 19 wins, $848,900, 1956 Horse of the Year, 1956 champion handicap horse, 1955 Kentucky Derby, etc.; **THE SHOE**, 10 wins, $105,000, 1958 Cinema H., etc.; **LIKE MAGIC**, 10 wins, $87,872.

1954—TRAFFIC COURT
Dk. b. or br. m. 1938, by Discovery—Traffic, by Broomstick
Breeder, C. V. Whitney (Ky.). **Owner**, Clifford Mooers.
Dam of 3 foals, all winners, including **HASTY ROAD**, 14 wins, $541,402, 1953 champion two-year-old male, 1954 Preakness S., etc.; **TRAFFIC JUDGE**, 13 wins, $432,450, 1957 Suburban H., etc.

1953—GAGA
B. m. 1942, by *Bull Dog—Alpoise, by Equipoise
Breeder, A. C. Ernst (Ky.). **Owner**, Duval Headley.
Dam of 5 foals, all winners, including **TOM FOOL**, 21 wins, $570,165, 1953 Horse of the Year, 1951 champion two-year-old male, 1953 champion sprinter, 1953 champion

older male, 1953 Surburban H., etc.; **AUNT JINNY**, 5 wins, $106,020, 1950 champion two-year-old filly, 1950 Demoiselle S., etc.

1952—ACE CARD
B. m. 1942, by Case Ace—Furlough, by Man o' War
Breeder, Walter M. Jeffords (Pa.). **Owner**, Mrs. Walter M. Jeffords.
Dam of 12 foals, all starters, 11 winners, including **ONE COUNT**, 9 wins, $245,625, 1952 Horse of the Year, 1952 champion three-year-old male, 1952 Belmont S., etc.; **POST CARD**, 14 wins, $170,525; **MY CARD**, 7 wins, $98,404, 1963 Selima S.; **YILDIZ**, 7 wins, $90,475, 1951 Flamingo S., etc.

1951—*ALPENSTOCK III
Dk. b. or br. m. 1936, by =Apelle (Ity)—=Plymstock (GB), by =Polymelus (GB)
Breeder, Cliveden Stud (GB). **Owner**, Mereworth Farm.
Dam of 13 foals, 10 starters, 8 winners, including **RUHE**, 11 wins, $294,490, 1951 Blue Grass S., etc.; **STURDY ONE**, 13 wins, $202,970, 1951 Tanforan H., etc.; **ALLADIER**, 9 wins, $61,712, 1951 Breeders' Futurity.

1950—HILDENE
B. m. 1938, by Bubbling Over—Fancy Racket, by *Wrack
Breeder, Xalapa Farm (Ky.). **Owner**, Meadow Stable.
Dam of 13 foals, 12 starters, 9 winners, including **HILL PRINCE**, 17 wins, $422,140, 1950 Horse of the Year, 1949 champion two-year-old male, 1950 champion three-year-old male, 1951 champion older male, 1950 Preakness S., etc.; **FIRST LANDING**, 19 wins, $779,577, 1958 champion two-year-old male, 1958 Champagne S., etc.; **THIRD BROTHER**, 9 wins, $310,787; **MANGOHICK**, 23 wins, $115,115; **PRINCE HILL**, 8 wins, $98,300.

1949—EASY LASS
Bl. m. 1940, by *Blenheim II—Slow and Easy, by Colin
Breeder, Calumet Farm (Ky.). **Owner**, Calumet Farm.
Dam of 7 foals, all starters, 6 winners, including **COALTOWN**, 23 wins, $415,675, 1949 Horse of the Year, 1948 champion sprinter, 1949 champion older male, 1949 Washington Park H., etc.; **WISTFUL**, 13 wins, $213,060, 1949 champion three-year-old filly, 1949 Coaching Club of America Oaks, etc.; **ROSEWOOD**, 9 wins, $92,950; **FANFARE**, 9 wins, $46,140.

1948—OUR PAGE
B. m. 1940, by Blue Larkspur—Occult, by *Dis Donc
Breeder, Woodvale Farm (Oh.). **Owner**, Royce C. Martin.
Dam of 5 foals, all winners, **BULL PAGE**, 9 wins, $25,730, 1951 Horse of the Year in Canada, 1951 champion older horse in Canada, 1951 Canadian Championship S.; **NAVY PAGE**, 21 wins, $127,322, 1953 Jerome H., etc.; **SPORT PAGE**, 4 wins, $79,175; **BROTHER TEX**, 8 wins, $77,633; **PAGE BOOTS**, 3 wins, $51,635.

1947—POTHEEN
Dk. b. or br. m. 1928, by Wildair—Rosie O'Grady, by Hamburg
Breeder, H. P. Whitney (Ky.). **Owner**, Calumet Farm.
Dam of 12 foals, 11 starters, 9 winners, including **BEWITCH**, 20 wins, $462,605, 1947 champion two-year-old filly, 1949 champion older female, 1947 Washington Park Futurity, etc.; **POT O' LUCK**, 14 wins, $239,150, 1945 Jockey Club Gold Cup, etc.; **LOT O LUCK**, 9 wins, $46,950.

1946—BLOODROOT
B. m. 1932, by Blue Larkspur—*Knockany Bridge, by =Bridge of Earn (GB)
Breeder, Idle Hour Stock Farm (Ky.). **Owner**, Ogden Phipps.
Dam of 13 foals, 11 starters, 8 winners, including **ANCESTOR**, 26 wins, $237,956, 1959 champion steeplechaser, 1952 Discovery H., etc.; **BE FAITHFUL**, 14 wins, $189,040, 1947 Hawthorne Gold Cup H., etc.; **BRIC A BAC**, 13 wins, $103,225, 1945 San Juan Capistrano H., etc.; **BIMLETTE**, 4 wins, $28,065, 1946 Frizette S.

Leading Broodmares by Progeny Earnings

Worldwide leaders 1930-2002

Broodmare, YOB, Sire—Dam	Fls.	Strs.	Wnrs.	SWs	Progeny Earnings	Leading Earner	Earnings
Once Wed, 1984, Blushing Groom (Fr)—Noura	10	9	7	1	$18,374,614	T.M.Opera O	$16,200,337
Pacificus, 1981, Northern Dancer—Pacific Princess	11	10	7	3	$18,135,348	Narita Brian	$9,296,552
Dancing Key, 1983, Nijinsky II—Key Partner	11	11	7	3	$14,237,107	Dance Partner	$5,973,652
Katies (Ire), 1981, Nonoalco—Mortefontaine	14	11	10	5	$11,222,152	Hishi Amazon	$6,981,102
Solar Slew, 1982, Seattle Slew—Gold Sun (Arg)	11	6	6	2	$10,323,580	Cigar	$9,999,815
Ingot Way, 1981, Diplomat Way—Ingot	14	9	8	1	$10,222,330	Skip Away	$9,616,360
Campaign Girl, 1987, Maruzensky—Lady Shiraoki	3	2	2	1	$9,519,113	Special Week	$9,346,435
Floral Magic, 1985, Affirmed—Rare Lady	7	7	7	1	$9,414,301	Narita Top Road	$8,389,594
Cee's Song, 1986, Seattle Song—Lonely Dancer	11	8	5	2	$9,372,356	Tiznow	$6,427,830
Happy Trails, 1984, Posse—Roycon (GB)	9	8	7	2	$9,328,179	Shinko Lovely	$4,596,546
Mejiro Aurola, 1978, Remand—Mejiro Iris	10	6	5	2	$9,270,887	Mejiro Mc Queen	$7,618,803
Golden Sash, 1988, Dictus—Dyna Sash	8	6	3	1	$9,199,556	Stay Gold	$8,682,142
Dyna Carle, 1980, Northern Taste—Shadai Feather	9	9	8	1	$9,165,543	Air Groove	$6,832,242
Takeno Falcon, 1982, Philip of Spain—Cool Fair	9	8	5	1	$9,125,589	Hokuto Vega	$8,300,301
Tokai Natural, 1982, Nice Dancer—Tokai Midori	12	12	9	2	$9,031,908	Tokai Teio	$4,698,139
Tree of Knowledge (Ire), 1977, Sassafras (Fr)—Sensibility	10	7	5	2	$9,019,381	Taiki Blizzard	$5,523,549
Princess Reema, 1984, Affirmed—First Fling	12	11	9	2	$9,013,675	Meisho Doto	$8,088,202
Reru du Temps, 1982, Maruzensky—Kei Tsunami	8	6	4	2	$8,833,507	Mejiro Bright	$6,848,423
Sakura Clare, 1982, Northern Taste—Clare Bridge	11	7	5	2	$8,718,122	Sakura Chitose O	$5,178,760
Jood, 1989, Nijinsky II—Kamar	8	6	4	1	$8,591,495	Fantastic Light	$8,486,957
Powerful Lady, 1981, Maruzensky—Roch Tesco	15	9	8	2	$8,283,321	Winning Ticket	$3,359,368
Mejiro Beauty, 1982, Partholon—Mejiro Nagasaki	7	7	7	1	$8,163,350	Mejiro Dober	$6,240,681
White Narubi, 1974, *Silver Shark—Never Narubi	15	5	3	2	$8,155,897	Oguri Cap	$6,940,077
Legacy of Strength, 1982, Affirmed—Katonka	11	10	7	2	$8,139,940	Stinger	$3,467,289
Tenzan Otome, 1983, Maruzensky—Mombetsu Kachidoki	8	7	5	2	$8,020,189	Osumi Jet	$4,915,054
Croupier Lady, 1983, What Luck—Question d'Argent	9	9	6	1	$8,003,277	Genuine	$5,455,575
Urakawa Miyuki, 1981, *Habitony—Kemmaru Midori	9	8	6	1	$7,653,626	Nice Nature	$5,232,135
Sakura Hagoromo, 1984, Northern Taste—Clear Amber	9	7	7	1	$7,652,264	Sakura Bakushin O	$4,800,631
Never Ichiban, 1971, Never Beat—Miss Nanba Ichiban	14	9	6	1	$7,636,765	Daitaku Helios	$4,629,341
Bel Sheba, 1970, Lt. Stevens—Belthazar	13	13	11	5	$7,594,619	Alysheba	$6,679,242
Alp Me Please, 1981, Blushing Groom (Fr)—Swiss	7	6	2	1	$7,567,701	Mayano Top Gun	$7,463,557
Mountain Queen, 1982, Nizon—Yamaka Queen	12	8	6	1	$7,318,949	Kyoto City	$5,622,437
Chancey Squaw, 1991, Chief's Crown—Alliance	6	3	2	1	$7,120,200	Agnes Digital	$7,068,806
Bonnie's Poker, 1982, Poker—What a Surprise	11	9	6	1	$7,096,183	Silver Charm	$6,944,369
Lilac Point, 1979, Maruzensky—Kuri Katsura	10	7	4	1	$7,049,963	Rice Shower	$6,070,429
Sparkling Delite, 1985, Vice Regent—Sparkling Topaz	6	5	3	1	$6,896,314	Captain Steve	$6,828,356
Mysteries, 1986, Seattle Slew—Phydilla (Fr)	10	6	4	3	$6,816,984	Agnes World	$3,365,680
Once Double, 1967, Double Jay—Intent One	10	9	8	2	$6,770,102	John Henry	$6,591,860
Wakia, 1987, Miswaki—Rascal Rascal	4	4	4	1	$6,714,221	Silence Suzuka	$3,523,898
Lola Lola, 1985, Saint Cyrien—Bold Lady	7	7	5	1	$6,681,294	Sakura Laurel	$5,751,390
Crafty Wife, 1985, Crafty Prospector—Wife Mistress	10	9	8	1	$6,672,509	Big Shori	$2,984,808
Cocotte, 1983, Troy—Gay Milly	13	8	6	4	$6,636,821	Pilsudski (Ire)	$4,080,297
Songline, 1987, Western Symphony—Mcangus	7	3	1	1	$6,625,268	Sunline	$6,625,105
Glorious Song, 1976, Halo—Ballade	13	10	8	3	$6,575,951	Singspiel (Ire)	$5,952,825
Subtle Change, 1988, Law Society—Santa Luciana	7	6	4	2	$6,575,310	Manhattan Cafe	$4,164,517
Duplicit, 1985, Danzig—Fabulous Fraud	11	11	9	1	$6,525,054	Nishino Flower	$3,441,504
I Dreamed a Dream, 1987, Well Decorated—Hidden Trail	7	5	4	2	$6,509,032	Air Shakur	$4,943,099
The Last Word, 1987, Northern Taste—Gloria Wave	7	7	5	1	$6,504,489	Fast Friend	$5,896,693
Sanyo Arrow, 1988, Mr C B—Taniichi Power	6	4	2	1	$6,503,885	Wing Arrow	$6,273,733
Ameriflora, 1989, Danzig—Graceful Touch	5	4	4	2	$6,484,353	Grass Wonder	$5,987,405
Dyna Fairy, 1983, Northern Taste—Fancy Dyna	11	9	6	2	$6,468,692	Rosen Kavalier	$4,137,973
Warranty Applied, 1986, Monteverdi (Ire)—Implied Warranty	9	7	7	1	$6,417,727	Eishin Preston	$6,052,200
No Class, 1974, Nodouble—Classy Quillo	8	7	7	6	$6,408,741	Sky Classic	$3,320,398
Dyna Actress, 1983, Northern Taste—Model Sport	8	8	6	2	$6,398,056	Stage Champ	$4,077,863
Buper Dance, 1983, Lyphard—My Bupers	8	8	6	1	$6,336,237	Irish Dance	$2,355,600
North of Eden (Ire), 1983, Northfields—Tree of Knowledge (Ire)	14	9	7	4	$6,306,596	Paradise Creek	$3,401,416
Antique Value, 1979, Northern Dancer—Moonscape	11	10	9	3	$6,284,249	Vega	$2,105,918
Primal Force, 1987, Blushing Groom (Fr)—Prime Prospect	10	4	3	2	$6,282,719	Awesome Again	$4,374,590
Comaz, 1983, Danzig—Middlemarch	8	5	4	2	$6,273,855	Sterling Rose	$3,121,810
Silver Lane, 1985, Silver Hawk—Strait Lane	10	4	3	2	$6,250,207	Black Hawk (GB)	$5,750,386
Doff the Derby, 1981, Master Derby—Margarethen	12	10	9	6	$6,186,442	Osumi Tycoon	$2,842,458
Millracer, 1983, *Le Fabuleux—Marston's Mill	12	10	7	2	$6,175,726	Shinin' Racer	$1,915,140
Ubetshedid, 1980, King Pellinore—Ubetido	11	9	6	1	$6,067,705	Best Pal	$5,668,245
Dance Charmer, 1990, Nureyev—Skillful Joy	4	4	2	1	$6,048,561	Jungle Pocket	$5,466,240
Kuri Pussy, 1975, Arrow Express—Montaroch	13	8	6	1	$5,988,123	Matikanetannhauser	$4,522,666
Yamanin Policy, 1981, Blushing Groom (Fr)—Yamahouyuu (Jpn)	12	11	4	1	$5,945,152	Yamanin Zephyr	$4,957,983
Dominus Rose, 1981, Tosho Boy—Oferu	12	9	5	1	$5,919,242	Fujino Makken O	$3,735,159

Most Graded or Group Stakes Winners for a Broodmare
(1971-2002)

8   Fall Aspen (1976, Pretense—Change Water, by Swaps). 14 foals, 13 starters, 12 winners, 9 stakes winners, 8 graded/group stakes winners (Fort Wood [Fr-G1], Hamas [Ire] [Eng-G1], Timber Country [G1], Northern Aspen [G1], Colorado Dancer [Ire] [Fr-G2], Bianconi [Eng-G2], Elle Seule [Fr-G2], Mazzacano [GB] [Eng-G3])

7   Courtly Dee (1968, Never Bend—Tulle, by War Admiral). 18 foals, 17 starters, 15 winners, 8 stakes winners, 7 graded/group stakes winners (Ali Oop [G1], Althea [G1], Ketoh [G1], Aishah [G2], Aquilegia [G2], Twining [G2], Native Courier [G3])

6   Dahlia (1970, *Vaguely Noble—Charming Alibi, by Honeys Alibi). 13 foals, 11 starters, 8 winners, 6 stakes winners, 6 graded/group stakes winners (Dahar [G1], Dahlia's Dreamer [G1], Delegant [G1], Rivlia [G1], Wajd [Fr-G2], Llandaff [G2])

Glowing Tribute (1973, Graustark—Admiring, by Hail to Reason). 12 foals, 10 starters, 9 winners, 7 stakes winners, 6 graded/group stakes winners (Hero's Honor [G1], Sea Hero [G1], Glowing Honor [G2], Wild Applause [G2], Coronation Cup [G3], Mackie [G3])

5   Blessings (Fr) (1971, Floribunda—*Marabelle, by Miralgo). 17 foals, 11 starters, 8 winners, 6 stakes winners, 5 graded/group stakes winners (Bleding [Arg] [Arg-G1], Sings [Arg-G1], Blue Boss [Aus-G3], Blue Bles [Arg-G3], Flibless [Arg-G3])

Chaldee (1978, Banner Sport—Gevar, by Right of Way). 13 foals, 7 starters, 6 winners, 5 stakes winners, 5 graded/group stakes winners (Potrichal [Arg] [Arg-G1], Potrinner [Arg] [Arg-G1], Potrizaris [Arg] [Arg-G1], Potridee [Arg] [G1], Sun Banner [Arg-G3])

Coup de Folie (1982, Halo—Raise the Standard, by Hoist the Flag). 12 foals, 10 starters, 7 winners, 5 stakes winners, 5 graded/group stakes winners (Coup de Genie [Fr-G1], Exit to Nowhere [Fr-G1], Machiavellian [Fr-G1], Hydro Calido [Fr-G2], Ocean of Wisdom [Fr-G3])

Eight Carat (1975, *Pieces of Eight II—Klairessa [GB], by *Klairon). 10 foals, 5 starters, 5 winners, 5 stakes winners, 5 graded/group stakes winners (Marquise [NZ-G1], Our Diamond Lover [NZ-G1], Kaapstad [Aus-G1], Mouawad [Aus-G1], Octagonal [Aus-G1])

Halory (1984, Halo—Cold Reply, by Northern Dancer). 14 foals, 11 starters, 9 winners, 5 stakes winners, 5 graded/group stakes winners (Van Nistelrooy [Ire-G2], Halory Hunter [G2], Brushed Halory [G3], Key Lory [G3], Prory [G3])

*Lupe II (1967, Primera—Alcoa, by Alycidon). 10 foals, 9 starters, 8 winners, 5 stakes winners, 5 graded/group stakes winners (Lascaux [Fr-G2], Louveterie [Fr-G3], Legend of France [Eng-G3], Leonardo Da Vinci [Fr] [Eng-G3], L'Ile Du Reve [Eng-G3])

Princess Tracy (Ire) (1981, Ahonoora—Princess Ru, by Princely Gift). 10 foals, 9 starters, 7 winners, 5 stakes winners, 5 graded/group stakes winners (Tracy's Element [Aus] [SAf-G1], Danasinga [Aus-G1], Topasannah [SAf-G2], Cullen [Aus-G3], Towkay [Aus-G3])

Summoned (1978, Crowned Prince—Sweet Life, by *Pardao). 16 foals, 13 starters, 9 winners, 5 stakes winners, 5 graded/group stakes winners (Zeditave [Aus-G1], Alannon [Aus-G3], Pampas Fire [Aus-G3], Square Deal [Aus-G3], Zedagal [Aus-G3])

Most Stakes Winners for a Broodmare
(1930-2002)

9   Fall Aspen (1976, Pretense—Change Water, by Swaps). 14 foals, 13 starters, 12 winners, 9 stakes winners (Bianconi, Colorado Dancer [Ire], Elle Seule, Fort Wood, Hamas [Ire], Mazzacano [GB], Northern Aspen, Prince of Thieves, Timber Country)

Fallow (1957, *Worden—Galloway Queene, by Colombo). 16 foals, 11 starters, 12 winners, 9 stakes winners (Fact [Arg], Factory, Fairly [Arg], Fallowed, Far, *Farm, Farmer, Fazenda [Arg], *Fizz)

Grey Flight (1945, *Mahmoud—Planetoid, by Ariel). 15 foals, 15 starters, 14 winners, 9 stakes winners (Bold Princess, Bold Queen, Full Flight, Gray Phantom, Misty Day, Misty Flight, Misty Morn, Signore, What a Pleasure)

8   Astronomie (1932, Asterus—Likka, by Sardanapale). 10 foals, 9 starters, 8 winners, 8 stakes winners (Arbar, Arbele, *Asmena, Caracalla, Estremadur, Floriados, Marsyas II, Pharas)

Courtly Dee (1968, Never Bend—Tulle, by War Admiral). 18 foals, 17 starters, 15 winners, 8 stakes winners (Aishah, Ali Oop, Althea, Aquilegia, Ketoh, Native Courier, Princess Oola, Twining)

Retorica (1955, Snob—Rochelle, by Selim Hassan). 12 foals, 9 starters, 8 winners, 8 stakes winners (*Legent II, Leon II, Lioness, *Lirio, Llegador [Arg], Locomotor, *Lostalo, Ruizero [Arg])

7   Bold Pat (1975, Bold Destroyer—Bolerita, by Bolero). 14 foals, 13 starters, 12 winners, 7 stakes winners (A Bold Embrace, Arctic Pat, Bay Is O. K., Bold Fawn, Elegant Black, Milden's Girl, Pat's Bold Brat)

Dan's Dream (1961, Your Host—Rosella, by War Relic). 15 foals, 15 starters, 12 winners, 7 stakes winners (Costly Dream, Dream 'n Be Lucky, El Corazon, Go On Dreaming, Jesta Dream Away, Once Upon a Star, Royal Knightmare)

Donatella (1939, *Mahmoud—Delleana, by Clarissimus). 13 foals, 12 starters, 10 winners, 7 stakes winners (*Daumier, De Dreux, Delaroche, *Dominate II, *Donatellina II, Donna Lydia, Duccio)

Flying B. G. (1978, Barachois—Up Alone, by Solo Landing). 16 foals, 12 starters, 11 winners, 7 stakes winners (B. G.'s Drone, Burnone Gimmetwo, Draconic's B. G., Flying Drone, Soiree, Talent Connection, Texas Holdem)

Glowing Tribute (1973, Graustark—Admiring, by Hail to Reason). 12 foals, 10 starters, 9 winners, 7 stakes winners (Coronation Cup, Glowing Honor, Hero's Honor, Mackie, Sea Hero, Seattle Glow, Wild Applause)

Here's Lookn Adder (1983, Superbity—Sarah Blue Eyes, by Explodent). 12 foals, 9 starters, 9 winners, 7 stakes winners (Drumm Valley, Jessen, Just Lookn, Lookn At a Blurr, Lookn At Another, Peak Out, Takin It Deep)

Moccasin (1963, Nantallah—*Rough Shod II, by Gold Bridge). 9 foals, 8 starters, 7 winners, 7 stakes winners (Apalachee, Belted Earl, Brahms, Flippers, Indian, Nantequos, Scuff)

My Dear Girl (1957, Rough'n Tumble—Iltis, by War Relic). 15 foals, 14 starters, 13 winners, 7 stakes winners (Gentle Touch, In Reality, My Dear Lady, Really and Truly, Return to Reality, Superbity, Watchfulness)

7   Qui Royalty (1977, Native Royalty—Qui Blink, by Francis S.). 14 foals, 12 starters, 10 winners, 7 stakes winners (Appointed One, Bakharoff, Demonry, Emperor Jones, Majlood, Sum, Thyer)

Roar n' Honey (1965, Hezahoney—Rip 'n Roar, by Rippey). 14 foals, 12 starters, 11 winners, 7 stakes winners (Bar Tender, Dandy Man, My Favorite Gal, One That Got Away, Singh Honey, Sonny Says, St. Aubin)

Soumida (1953, Tehran—*Sou'wester, by Blue Peter). 10 foals, 7 starters, 8 winners, 7 stakes winners (Sarcelle, Senechal, Siska, Solidor, Solon, Sorana, *Soudard)

Toll Booth (1971, Buckpasser—Missy Baba, by *My Babu). 13 foals, 12 starters, 11 winners, 7 stakes winners (Christiecat, Idle Gossip, Key to the Bridge, Plugged Nickle, Tokens Only, Toll Fee, Toll Key)

Up the Flagpole (1978, Hoist the Flag—The Garden Club, by *Herbager). 11 foals, 10 starters, 10 winners, 7 stakes winners (Allied Flag, Flagbird, Fold the Flag, Long View, Prospectors Delite, Runup the Colors, Top Account)

6   Accra (1941, Annapolis—Ladala, by Ladkin). 11 foals, 11 starters, 10 winners, 6 stakes winners (Mandingo, Mongo, Nahodah, Nala, Neji, Songai)

Adriana (1944, Arjaman—Adriatica, by Janitor). 15 foals, 14 starters, 11 winners, 6 stakes winners (Ametta, Anatol, Andrea II, Appell, Aspiration, *Ataturk II)

Alta Mira (1948, *Don Bingo—Music Hall, by Snark). 9 foals, 9 starters, 9 winners, 6 stakes winners (Collin Baykey, Craig D., Donn Baykey, Ky. Miracle, Ky. Music, Son of Donn)

Annie Edge (Ire) (1980, Nebbiolo—Friendly Court, by Be Friendly). 12 foals, 11 starters, 8 winners, 6 stakes winners (Rimrod, Rory Creek, Seebe, Selkirk, Skillington, Syncline)

Apostille (1944, Astrophel—Polititia, by Comedy King). 8 foals, 6 starters, 6 winners, 6 stakes winners (Apostol, Bingo, Poisson Volant, Postboy, Postman, Virgule)

Banja Luka (1968, Double Jay—Legato, by Dark Star). 9 foals, 9 starters, 7 winners, 6 stakes winners (Ancient Art, Dancing, Donna Inez, Ferdinand, Jayston, Plinth)

Bargain (1943, Millero—Bonne Fille, by Bermejo). 7 foals, 7 starters, 6 winners, 6 stakes winners (Corbar, Dadiva, Moon Shine, Postwar, *Propina, Shilling)

Battle Creek Girl (1977, His Majesty—Far Beyond, by Nijinsky II). 19 foals, 17 starters, 15 winners, 6 stakes winners (Everhope, Parade Ground, Parade Leader, Speed Dialer, Tricky Creek, Wavering Girl)

Blessings (Fr) (1971, Floribunda—*Marabelle, by Miralgo). 17 foals, 11 starters, 8 winners, 6 stakes winners (Bleding [Arg], Blue Bles, Blue Boss, Flibless, Fritz, Sings)

Blue Denim (1940, Blue Larkspur—Judy O'Grady, by Man o' War). 15 foals, 14 starters, 11 winners, 6 stakes winners (Blue Prince, Green Baize, Piano Jim, Policeman Day, Suleiman, Tahiti)

Confirm (1977, Proudest Roman—Spanked, by Cornish Prince). 17 foals, 16 starters, 11 winners, 6 stakes winners (Autumn Glitter, Confirmed Dancer, Hollycombe, Ron Bon, Saratoga Sizzle, Yolanda)

Dahlia (1970, *Vaguely Noble—Charming Alibi, by Honeys Alibi). 13 foals, 11 starters, 8 winners, 6 stakes winners (Dahar, Dahlia's Dreamer, Delegant, Llandaff, Rivlia, Wajd)

Doff the Derby (1981, Master Derby—Margarethen, by *Tulyar). 12 foals, 10 starters, 9 winners, 6 stakes winners (Generous, Imagine, Osumi Tycoon, Strawberry Roan [Ire], Wedding Bouquet [Ire], Windy Triple K.)

Dumka (1971, Kashmir II—Faizebad [Fr], by *Prince Taj).

8 foals, 8 starters, 7 winners, 6 stakes winners (Dafayna, Dalsaan, Dayzaan, Dolka [Ire], Dolpour, Doyoun)

6   Eterna (1954, Atabor—Eme, by Lord Wembley). 9 foals, 7 starters, 7 winners, 6 stakes winners (El Califa, *El Fakir, El Faraon, Envidiada [Arg], Esporazo, Eternelle)

Floral Victory (1962, Victoria Park—La Belle Rose, by Le Lavandou). 17 foals, 15 starters, 13 winners, 6 stakes winners (Floral Dancer, Happy Victory, Nonparrell, Northern Ballerina, Snow Blossom, Victego)

Fun House (1958, The Doge—Recess, by Count Fleet). 9 foals, 9 starters, 9 winners, 6 stakes winners (Court Ruling, Funny Cat, Fun Palace, Good Manners, King's Palace, Yes Sir)

Gran Corrida (1961, Prince d'Or—Gay Ega, by Gay Boy). 14 foals, 7 starters, 6 winners, 6 stakes winners (A Esperar, Galopon, Grandeza Real, Grandor Real, Gran Real, Real Corrida)

*Green Valley II (1967, *Val de Loir—Sly Pola, by Spy Song). 15 foals, 14 starters, 13 winners, 6 stakes winners (Ercolano, Green Dancer, Pink Valley, Sir Raleigh, Soviet Lad, Val Danseur)

Hasty Queen II (1963, One Count—Queen Hopeful, by Roman). 16 foals, 14 starters, 12 winners, 6 stakes winners (Fit to Fight, Hasty Cutie, Hasty Flyer, Hasty Tam, Michael Navonod, Playful Queen)

Height of Fashion (Fr) (1979, Bustino—Highclere [GB], by Queen's Hussar). 12 foals, 10 starters, 8 winners, 6 stakes winners (Alwasmi, Mukddaam, Nashwan, Nayef, Sarayir, Unfuwain)

Il Mondo (1968, Promised Land—Nunzi Nunzi, by *Endeavour II). 13 foals, 13 starters, 8 winners, 6 stakes winners (Balimondo, Craftysmypapa, Mondanza, Mondo Lea, Mondolu, Turnin Doe)

Imperatrice (1938, Caruso—Cinquepace, by Brown Bud). 16 foals, 13 starters, 10 winners, 6 stakes winners (Imperial Hill, Imperium, Scattered, Speedwell, Squared Away, Yemen)

Kazanlik (1960, Ommeyad—Rose Supreme, by Supreme Court). 13 foals, 10 starters, 8 winners, 6 stakes winners (Boabdil, Darling Bud, Frances Jordan, Gay George, *Lark Rise II, Orient Rose)

Lapel (1935, Apelle—Lampeto, by Tetratema). 9 foals, 8 starters, 9 winners, 6 stakes winners (Carlist, Cassock, Durante, Golden Spur, Red Carnation, Val d'Assa)

Loudrangle (1974, Quadrangle—Lady Known as Lou, by Nearctic). 9 foals, 7 starters, 7 winners, 6 stakes winners (Dancing With Wings, No Louder, Ruling Angel, Slew of Angels, Tiffany Tam, Tilt My Halo)

Missy Baba (1958, *My Babu—*Uvira II, by Umidwar). 12 foals, 12 starters, 12 winners, 6 stakes winners (Chokri, Dromba, Gay Missile, Master Bold, Raja Baba, Sauce Boat)

Nas-Mahal (1959, *Nasrullah—*Love Game, by Big Game). 12 foals, 11 starters, 9 winners, 6 stakes winners (Beja, Celine, Craelius, Epidaurus, Tell, Turkish Trousers)

No Class (1974, Nodouble—Classy Quillo, by Outing Class). 8 foals, 7 starters, 7 winners, 6 stakes winners (Always a Classic, Classic Reign, Classy 'n Smart, Grey Classic, Regal Classic, Sky Classic)

Patsy Dru (1959, Alorter—Patsy, by Escadru). 17 foals, 17 starters, 15 winners, 6 stakes winners (Astaconda, Great Commander, Levant, Patsy's Reign, Prom Crasher, Shotgun Pat)

Phase (1939, Windsor Lad—Lost Soul, by Solario). 14 foals, 12 starters, 9 winners, 6 stakes winners (Narrator, Neasham Belle, Netherton Maid, None Nicer, No Pretender, Setting Star)

Picture Light (1954, *Court Martial—Queen of Light, by Borealis). 13 foals, 11 starters, 9 winners, 6 stakes winners (Dazzling Light, Father Christmas, Illuminous, Miss Pinkie, Photo Flash, Welsh Pageant)

6 **Polite Society** (1952, War Admiral—Doggin' It, by *Bull Dog). 12 foals, 12 starters, 12 winners, 6 stakes winners (Big Brigade, Blue Society, La Gentillesse, Long Position, Montjuich, Rising Market)

*Queen's Statute (1954, Le Lavandou—Statute, by Son-in-Law). 14 foals, 13 starters, 13 winners, 6 stakes winners (Court Royal, Dance Act, Down North, Epic Queen, Menedict, North of the Law)

Radiant Light (1953, Sayajirao—Wakening Light, by Eight Thirty). 13 foals, 6 starters, 7 winners, 6 stakes winners (Grand Slam, Mairona [CHI], Mediatore, Metapio, Morgan, *Morgana II)

Ripeck (1959, *Ribot—Kyak, by Big Game). 10 foals, 10 starters, 8 winners, 6 stakes winners (Anchor, Balinger, Bireme, Buoy, Fluke, *Kedge)

Stafaralla (1935, Solario—Mirawala, by Phalaris). 14 foals, 8 starters, 7 winners, 6 stakes winners (Anwar, Inshalla, Iran, Kerman, *Norooz, Tehran)

Sun Princess (1937, Solario—Mumtaz Begum, by *Blenheim II). 13 foals, 11 starters, 9 winners, 6 stakes winners (Alassio, *Flaneur II, Lucky Bag, *Royal Charger, Royal Justice, Tessa Gillian)

Tata (1938, Tresiete—Tacana, by Leteo). 6 foals, 6 starters, 6 winners, 6 stakes winners (Taia, Taimado, Taitao, Talon, Tatai, Tolpan)

Theresina (1927, Diophon—Teresina, by Tracery). 13 foals, 10 starters, 8 winners, 6 stakes winners (*Benane, Byculla, Eboo, *Nemrod, Tambara, Turkhan)

Tokamura (1940, Navarro—Tofanella, by Apelle). 16 foals, 3 starters, 12 winners, 6 stakes winners (Tanaka, Theodorica, Titano, Tommaso Da Modena, *Tommaso Guidi, *Toulouse Lautrec)

Vera Me (1979, Polar Night—Vera Jae, by Gaylord's Feather). 13 foals, 13 starters, 11 winners, 6 stakes winners (Amazonpassage, Heatherforyou, Jessica Jae, Mebazaar, Polar Barron, Steaksonme)

Verdura (1948, *Court Martial—Bura, by *Bahram). 12 foals, 11 starters, 11 winners, 6 stakes winners (Avon's Pride, Gratitude, Heathen, Highest Hopes, Patroness, Pharsalia)

Yakima Swinger (1974, Canadian Gil—Eternal Heeler, by Heeler). 12 foals, 11 starters, 11 winners, 6 stakes winners (Bucks for Bob, Hat Rock, Lyon Swinger, Rock On Merit, Sarajevo Merit, Slightly Sinister)

Zanzara (1951, Fairey Fulmar—Sunright, by Solario). 17 foals, 14 starters, 13 winners, 6 stakes winners (Duke Ellington, Enrico, Enticement, Farfalla, Matatina, Showdown)

Most Foals for a Broodmare
(1930-2002)

Broodmare, YOB, Pedigree	Foals	Starters	Winners	Wins	Earnings
*Betsy Ross II (1939, *Mahmoud—*Celerina, by *Teddy)	23	19	13	44	$152,943
Day Line (1963, *Day Court—Fast Line, by Mr. Busher)	21	17	14	42	$421,940
Wisp O'Will (1964, New Policy—Miss Willow, by Oil Capitol)	20	16	14	70	$894,640
Bold Bikini (1969, Boldnesian—Ran-Tan, by Summer Tan)	20	14	12	37	$974,619
Cequillo (1956, *Princequillo—Boldness, by *Mahmoud)	20	18	14	81	$1,031,646
Feather Bed (1961, Johns Joy—Silly Sara, by *Rustom Sirdar)	20	17	13	60	$305,357
Alanette (1962, Alarullah—Jaconet, by *Jacopo)	20	18	9	33	$128,897
Wind in Her Sails (1972, Mr. Leader—Bunch of Daisies, by Sir Gaylord)	20	13	12	44	$375,991
Such 'n Such (1974, Ack Ack—Long Stemmed Rose, by Jacinto)	20	16	11	46	$735,875
Capulet (1977, Gallant Romeo—Indaba, by Sir Gaylord)	20	16	10	55	$594,709
Wayward Miss (1936, Brumeux—Miss Contrary, by Cannobie)	20	16	4	26	$12,805
Bright Festive (1966, Festive—Bright Cirrus, by Solferino)	20	1	0	0	$0
Avra (1957, Vulgan—Golden Flight, by Gold Bridge)	19	11	3	5	$3,457
Miss Sandman (1974, Manacle—Sandby, by *Klairon)	19	18	8	15	$123,164
Akino Mairie (1973, Arrow Express—Tetsuno Arc , by Arctic Vale)	19	7	2	4	$527,746
Photo Flash (1965, *Match II—Picture Light , by *Court Martial)	19	16	8	20	$78,798
Blinking Owl (1938, *Pharamond II—Baba Kenny, by Black Servant)	19	16	15	66	$195,196
Tie a Bow (1979, Dance Spell—Bold Bikini, by Boldnesian)	19	13	7	33	$444,510
Extremadura (1954, British Empire—Lesina , by Pont l'Eveque)	19	6	8	21	$12,269
Miss Maverick (1960, Vilmorin—Top Table , by Big Game)	19	19	9	12	$51,573
Port Margaret (1951, Gustator—Port Beam , by Portlaw)	19	16	5	11	$15,986
Sarasail (1966, Hitting Away—*Sail Riona, by *Royal Charger)	19	9	1	1	$3,394
Dear Guinevere (1977, Fearless Knight—Brave and Free, by Warfare)	19	17	16	61	$1,435,291
Battle Creek Girl (1977, His Majesty—Far Beyond, by Nijinsky II)	19	17	15	80	$4,238,914
Gaelic Logic (1975, Bold Reason—Irish Party, by Irish Lancer)	19	15	12	31	$496,312
Nobile Decretum (1975, Noble Decree—Mid Evening, by Billings)	19	14	5	16	$292,887
Shocking Moment (1976, Info—Reneged's Belle, by Reneged)	19	16	14	60	$712,901
First Paula (1976, First Dawn—First Color, by Black Mountain)	19	13	5	45	$299,001
Gold Idol (1972, Don B.—Suzi Juris, by Imbros)	19	18	13	54	$382,085
Queen's Turf (1972, Round Table—Good Queen Bess, by Bold Ruler)	19	14	10	28	$316,412
My Room (1972, Bold Lad—Extra Place, by Round Table)	19	16	12	50	$520,454
Kadesh (1970, Lucky Mel—News Release, by Fleet Nasrullah)	19	15	14	45	$879,370
Heat of Holme (1970, *Noholme II—Heat Lamp, by Better Self)	19	16	12	49	$1,062,475
Brown Berry (1960, Mount Marcy—Brown Baby, by Phalanx)	19	17	13	49	$1,864,446
Ingenuity (1956, My Request—Resourceful, by Shut Out)	19	13	8	40	$205,902
Mid Evening (1957, Billings—Mideau, by *Bull Dog)	19	17	12	100	$572,999
Saygood (1967, Royal Ascot—Saybrook, by Brookfield)	19	13	10	44	$644,686
Delagoa (Fr) (1975, Targowice—Derna, by Sunny Boy)	19	12	9	20	$138,506

Steeplechase performances are not included in statistics

Most Consecutive Foals for a Broodmare
(1930-2002)

Broodmare, Year of Birth, Pedigree	Foals	Consecutive Foals
Bold Bikini (1969, Boldnesian—Ran-Tan, by Summer Tan)	20	19
Photo Flash (1965, *Match II—Picture Light , by *Court Martial)	19	19
Sarasail (1966, Hitting Away—*Sail Riona, by *Royal Charger)	19	19
Such 'n Such (1974, Ack Ack—Long Stemmed Rose, by Jacinto)	20	19
Gallant Lady (1930, *Sir Gallahad III—*Peroration, by Clarissimus)	18	18
Maxencia (Fr) (1977, Tennyson—Matuschka , by *Orsini II)	18	18
So What (1978, Iron Ruler—Merry Mama, by Prince John)	17	18
Trinity (1978, Logical—Trinidad, by Make Tracks)	18	18
Whitewood (1960, *Worden—Solarist , by Supreme Court)	18	18
*Ankole (1960, Crepello—Sun Path, by Hyperion)	17	17
*Danae II (1947, *The Solicitor II—Justitia , by Birthright)	17	17
Arch Miss (1977, Mississippian—Marble Arch, by Bold Lad)	17	17
Ayano Chanel (1975, Eastern Fleet—Erimo Chanel, by Tamanar)	18	17
Baroness Elsie (1925, Stedfast—Madame Esmond , by Radium)	15	17
Bee for Me (1966, Cyane—Tempted, by *Half Crown)	18	17
Duchess Rae (1966, Hitting Away—His Duchess, by *Blenheim II)	18	17
Extra Alarm (1973, Blazing Count—Deedee O., by Roman Bout)	17	17
Fibber (1981, No Robbery—Little True, by *Western Sky II)	17	17
Five Star's Sister (1976, Lt. Stevens—Whileaway, by Summer Tan)	18	17
Full Reign (1979, Secretariat—Hill River, by Hill Rise)	18	17
Jesster's Lady (1955, Cosmic Bomb—Elementary, by Count Fleet)	17	17
Joyce Grove (1946, Bois Roussel—Samovar, by Caerleon)	17	17
Maid to Measure (1960, Mark-Ye-Well—Bushleaguer, by War Admiral)	18	17
Norska (1982, Northfields—Gwendolyn, by Bagdad)	17	17
Orama (1932, Diophon—Cantelupe, by Amadis)	17	17
Queen Ambra (1977, Alhambra—King's Quote, by Bold Monarch)	17	17
Red Haste (1971, Red Monk—Plumed, by Alsab)	17	17
Ritas Gray (1968, Reneged—Close Play, by Shut Out)	17	17
Vali (1954, Sunny Boy—Her Slipper , by Tetratema)	18	17
Vital Match (1966, *Match II—Vitality Plus, by Never Say Die)	17	17
Wild Sketch (1966, Rambunctious—Sketch Artist, by Roman Artist)	17	17
Winter Garden (1958, Windfields—Rustic Charm, by Reaping Reward)	18	17
Wisp O'Will (1964, New Policy—Miss Willow, by Oil Capitol)	20	17

Most Wins by Broodmare's Offspring
(1930-2002)

Broodmare, YOB, Sire—Dam	Foals	Starters	Winners	Starts	Wins	Earnings
Slow and Easy (1922, Colin—*Shyness)	15	14	11	962	182	$287,417
*Adorable II (1925, Sardanapale—Incredule)	15	13	12	1,175	181	$164,936
Cotton Candy (1945, Stimulus—Sugar Bird)	13	12	12	1,109	178	$359,502
Transit (1926, *Chicle—*Traverse)	10	10	10	1,169	178	$308,632
*Clonaslee (1922, Orpiment—Bullet Proof)	18	17	16	1,170	176	$258,219
Sag Rock (1930, Rock Man—Atomin)	13	12	11	981	170	$237,689
Dame Mariechen (1931, High Time—Carrie Hogan)	14	14	14	1,149	167	$254,771
Pevensea (1935, Enoch—Truly Movin)	13	13	13	1,177	166	$167,298
Lady Excellent (1932, Nocturnal—Falco)	14	13	12	1,180	165	$185,899
Ginogret (1941, *Gino—Sunlygret)	12	12	12	982	164	$223,038
Alondra (1947, War Admiral—Lady Lark)	17	17	15	1,173	163	$496,993
Doggerel (1935, *Bull Dog—Shenanigan)	10	9	9	1,113	163	$200,484
Jemima Lee (1929, General Lee—Miss Jemima)	15	15	14	860	163	$219,609
Sassaby (1931, Broomstick—Saucy Sue)	9	9	9	1,112	163	$321,217
Agnes Ayres (1923, King James—Sweet Mary)	15	14	12	1,201	161	$364,151
Lady Floyd (1924, Sir Martin—Fruit Cake)	13	11	10	1,015	159	$151,435
Much Ado (1921, Ed Crump)	14	13	13	1,026	159	$93,168
Vanrose (1920, Vandergrift)	13	10	9	993	159	$123,744
Blame (1921, *Wrack—Censure)	11	10	9	1,153	157	$132,321
Balking (1935, Balko—Bodega)	11	11	10	853	156	$426,263
*Miss Turley (1924, Bachelor's Jap—Raftonia)	12	12	11	967	154	$74,273
New Melody (1952, Bimelech—Melodious)	13	13	13	961	154	$688,387
Mary Kelly (1926, Ormondale—Starina)	14	14	13	1,097	153	$136,548
Kind Annie (1938, Brilliant—*Chaucer Girl)	12	11	10	992	152	$273,962
Daunt (1925, Lucullite—Dauntless)	13	13	13	817	151	$230,505
Knightess (1929, *Bright Knight—Markiluna)	13	13	10	1,005	151	$175,222
Lucy T. (1933, Whichone—*Refugee Girl)	13	11	9	1,092	151	$254,071
Cariboo Lass (1928, *Marcus—Mary Fuller)	13	12	11	1,115	150	$126,034
Softie (1943, Flares—Sicklefeather)	16	15	13	1,073	150	$338,172
*Flamante (1926, Flamboyant—*Flaminia)	11	10	10	960	149	$210,627

Broodmare, YOB, Sire—Dam	Foals	Starters	Winners	Starts	Wins	Earnings
Maradadi (1930, Stimulus—Virginia L.)	18	18	13	1,065	**148**	$428,469
Vinnie (1948, Vincentive—Glorious Time)	15	14	11	851	**148**	$422,519
Accra (1941, Annapolis—Ladala)	11	11	10	646	**146**	$1,632,463
Happy Factor (1941, Benefactor—Miss Jemima)	13	10	10	940	**146**	$337,080
Lady Gallivant (1922, *Hourless—*Lady's Gauntlet)	11	10	10	1,049	**146**	$148,508
Hastily Yours (1936, John P. Grier—*Hastily)	14	12	11	1,080	**145**	$692,799
Mintairy (1927, Mint Briar—*Airy Fairy)	10	10	10	776	**145**	$195,913
Panoramic (1932, Chance Shot—Dustwhirl)	11	11	11	975	**144**	$686,387
Pennant Girl (1929, *Rire Aux Larmes—Flying Pennant)	14	14	10	848	**144**	$254,551
Royalite (1922, Lucullite—Royal Ensign)	9	8	8	853	**144**	$122,635
***Valdina Spirea** (1940, Canon Law—*Spiraea II)	14	14	13	1,157	**143**	$413,361
Cushion (1917, Nonpareil—Hassock)	12	9	9	617	**142**	$140,109
Predicament (1929, *Waygood—Precipitate)	15	13	13	1,024	**142**	$184,201
Brown Maiden (1933, Brown Bud—Tailor Maid)	10	10	10	1,165	**140**	$202,886
Miss Velocity (1957, Spy Song—Fairy Dancer)	18	17	17	1,174	**140**	$560,219
Scuttle (1928, Whiskaway—Sea Tale)	11	11	11	927	**140**	$199,437
Glacial (1926, *Hourless—*Snowcapt)	15	15	13	1,093	**139**	$199,418
Sis Tartan (1947, Port au Prince—Tartan Betsy)	10	10	9	824	**139**	$343,586
Sly Marie (1962, Neptune—*Marie Lou)	12	12	11	911	**139**	$523,325
Greedy Girl (1926, *Vulcain—Grasp)	12	10	10	817	**137**	$196,899
***Legend of the Lake** (1929, Dark Legend—Narrow Water)	10	10	7	766	**137**	$105,120
Nancy Clay (1923, *Wrack—Nancy Lee)	14	12	11	854	**137**	$163,667
Baffling Miss (1927, Baffling—Miss Merle)	4	4	4	764	**136**	$86,250
Dog Show (1940, *Bull Dog—Pomp and Glory)	16	15	15	892	**136**	$361,952
Annabell Lee (1926, *Volta—Compose)	12	11	11	774	**135**	$288,719
May Morning (1935, Pompey—Howdy)	9	9	9	1,087	**135**	$227,415
Nortell (1955, El Mono—Control Board)	12	12	12	864	**135**	$477,660

Most Winners for a Broodmare
(1930-2002)

Broodmare, YOB, Sire—Dam	Foals	Starters	Winners	SWs	Earnings
***Mindrum Maid** (1939, *Mahmoud—Imp)	17	17	**17**	0	$149,615
Miss Velocity (1957, Spy Song—Fairy Dancer)	18	17	**17**	0	$560,219
Arizona Jubilee (1964, Spotted Moon—The Frog Hook)	19	17	**16**	1	$271,893
***Clonaslee** (1922, Orpiment—Bullet Proof)	18	17	**16**	1	$258,219
Dear Guinevere (1977, Fearless Knight—Brave and Free)	19	17	**16**	1	$1,435,291
Lady Ambassador (1959, Hill Prince—Your Hostess)	17	17	**16**	1	$880,817
Northern Beauty (1955, Borealis—Fleeting Beauty)	18	15	**16**	2	$260,119
Pia Mia (1968, Pia Star—Surprise Lady)	18	18	**16**	3	$933,832
Sable Lady (1927, *Waygood—Kolinsky)	17	17	**16**	0	$180,004
Admittance (1946, Maeda—Stitches)	15	15	**15**	0	$208,098
Alondra (1947, War Admiral—Lady Lark)	17	17	**15**	2	$496,993
Amazer (1967, Mincio—*Alzara)	17	17	**15**	2	$1,916,353
Battle Creek Girl (1977, His Majesty—Far Beyond)	19	17	**15**	6	$4,238,914
Blinking Owl (1938, *Pharamond II—Baba Kenny)	19	16	**15**	0	$195,196
Bold Essence (1977, Native Charger—Cologne)	16	16	**15**	1	$1,018,048
Bold Pythian (1975, Bold Reason—Pythian)	18	18	**15**	0	$589,322
Bonnie Blade (1976, Blade—Promised Princess)	16	16	**15**	1	$1,047,846
Cherry Lady (1973, Bold Lad—Cherry Fool)	16	15	**15**	1	$773,746
Courtly Dee (1968, Never Bend—Tulle)	18	17	**15**	8	$3,446,275
Dancing Liz (1972, Northern Dancer—Crimson Queen)	16	16	**15**	1	$1,205,660
Day and a Half (1972, Time Tested—Jolly)	18	16	**15**	2	$942,371
Dog Show (1940, *Bull Dog—Pomp and Glory)	16	15	**15**	1	$361,952
Godzilla (1972, Gyr—Gently)	15	15	**15**	2	$4,353,027
Grecian Coin (1960, Royal Coinage—Greek Pillar)	17	15	**15**	0	$787,886
Maxencia (Fr) (1977, Tennyson—Matuschka)	18	16	**15**	2	$396,667
Mideau (1942, *Bull Dog—Wild Waters)	18	18	**15**	1	$509,729
Miss Cotton (1962, Swoon's Son—Always Movin)	16	16	**15**	4	$959,195
Newsun (1973, Penowa Rullah—Sunshine Bright)	16	16	**15**	2	$1,273,538
Our Patty (1933, Brown Bud—Perjury)	17	15	**15**	0	$141,309
Patsy Dru (1959, Alorter—Patsy)	17	17	**15**	6	$459,604
Pines Lady (1966, Pinebloom—Lady Peabody)	15	15	**15**	0	$497,559
Poker's Errand (1974, Poker—Gallant Lesina)	18	17	**15**	1	$621,568
Proof Enough (1969, Prove It—Theonia)	16	16	**15**	3	$910,495
Ribbon Duster (1973, Dust Commander—First Ribbon)	17	16	**15**	1	$595,664
Stepping High (1969, No Robbery—*Bebop II)	17	17	**15**	2	$1,377,143
Sweet Tulle (1978, Tom Tulle—Little Divy)	18	17	**15**	0	$272,105
Tattooed Miss (1960, Mark-Ye-Well—Mossy Number)	18	18	**15**	2	$375,182
Tweentzel Pie (1966, Four-and-Twenty—Peachywillow)	16	16	**15**	2	$633,905
Wolf Hands (1963, All Hands—Wolf Bait)	16	16	**15**	3	$462,595

Most Starts by Broodmare's Offspring
(1930-2002)

Broodmare, YOB, Sire—Dam	Foals	Starters	Winners	Starts	Earnings
Our Patty (1933, Brown Bud—Perjury)	17	15	15	1,275	$141,309
Mrs. Burke (1923, *Berrilldon—Pinkie)	12	11	11	1,248	$104,588
Admittance (1946, Maeda—Stitches)	15	15	15	1,217	$208,098
Mica (1924, Fair Play—Malachite)	9	8	8	1,215	$106,918
Tabset (1938, Upset Lad—McTab)	12	12	12	1,212	$194,434
Agnes Ayres (1923, King James—Sweet Mary)	15	14	12	1,201	$364,331
Lina Clark (1919, Delhi—Prism)	13	13	11	1,187	$115,562
Lady Excellent (1932, Nocturnal—Falco)	14	13	12	1,180	$185,899
Dark Victory (1929, *Traumer—Sun Vive)	11	11	10	1,179	$213,242
Pevensea (1935, Enoch—Truly Movin)	13	13	13	1,177	$167,298
*Adorable II (1925, Sardanapale—Incredule)	15	13	12	1,175	$164,936
Miss Velocity (1957, Spy Song—Fairy Dancer)	18	17	17	1,174	$560,219
Alondra (1947, War Admiral—Lady Lark)	17	17	15	1,173	$496,993
*Clonaslee (1922, Orpiment—Bullet Proof)	18	17	16	1,170	$258,219
Transit (1926, *Chicle—*Traverse)	10	10	10	1,169	$308,632
Brown Maiden (1933, Brown Bud—Tailor Maid)	10	10	10	1,165	$202,886
*Valdina Spirea (1940, Canon Law—*Spiraea II)	14	14	13	1,157	$413,361
Blame (1921, *Wrack—Censure)	11	10	9	1,153	$132,321
Respite (1922, Hilarious—Lucinda)	13	12	9	1,151	$134,844
Dame Mariechen (1931, High Time—Carrie Hogan)	14	14	14	1,149	$254,771
Galful (1940, Hadagal—Armful)	16	16	13	1,136	$183,184
Hurry Home (1921, *Omar Khayyam)	14	13	10	1,128	$105,900
Happy Seas (1939, *Happy Argo—Golden Billows)	12	10	9	1,120	$188,979
Cariboo Lass (1928, *Marcus—Mary Fuller)	13	12	11	1,115	$126,034
Doggerel (1935, *Bull Dog—Shenanigan)	10	9	9	1,113	$200,484
Miss Dora (1918, Jack Atkin)	14	10	9	1,112	$83,443
Asianna (1935, Wise Counsellor—Asia)	13	11	10	1,112	$185,443
Sassaby (1931, Broomstick—Saucy Sue)	9	9	9	1,112	$321,217
Cotton Candy (1945, Stimulus—Sugar Bird)	13	12	12	1,109	$359,502
Drystone (1929, Man o' War—*Keystone)	12	12	11	1,107	$189,932
Riva (1930, *Wrack—Celiva)	15	13	13	1,101	$195,657
Mary Kelly (1926, Ormondale—Starina)	14	14	13	1,097	$136,548
Glacial (1926, *Hourless—*Snowcapt)	15	15	13	1,093	$199,418
Lucy T. (1933, Whichone—*Refugee III)	13	11	9	1,092	$254,071
Paradox (1923, *Omar Khayyam—*Silent Queen)	13	12	11	1,092	$151,734
*Play Polly (1934, Chance Play—Hasten Polly)	14	14	10	1,091	$177,336
May Morning (1935, Pompey—Howdy)	9	9	9	1,087	$227,415
Beauty Slave (1922, Black Toney—*Padula)	14	13	10	1,081	$188,659
Hastily Yours (1936, John P. Grier—*Hastily)	14	12	11	1,080	$692,799
Softie (1943, Flares—Sicklefeather)	16	15	13	1,073	$338,172
*Soul Mate (1920, Argos—Affinity)	14	12	12	1,070	$110,177
Devil's Garden (1922, Colin—Garden of Allah)	15	14	11	1,065	$118,561
Maradadi (1930, Stimulus—Virginia L.)	18	18	13	1,065	$428,469
Fairy Day (1934, Man o' War—Ides)	12	12	11	1,064	$307,853
Audley Girl (1935, *Bright Knight—Princess Doreen)	13	12	11	1,061	$221,924
Blue Tack (1937, Hard Tack—Blue Eagle)	14	14	14	1,059	$220,827
Lady Gallivant (1922, *Hourless—*Lady's Gauntlet)	11	10	10	1,049	$148,508
Sky Susan (1940, Hadagal—Wise Susan)	17	16	14	1,048	$241,219
Sly Glance (1927, Fair Play—*Love-Blink)	13	13	9	1,048	$115,799

Oldest Broodmares to Produce a Winner
(1930-2002)

	Foals	Age produced 1st winner	Age produced last winner
Miss Jubilee (1951, Cassis—Bacchante, by Questionnaire)	5	31	31
Sumpinextra (1952, Super Duper—Ariels Elite, by Ariel)	10	19	30
Faila Suit (1957, Faila—Follow Suit, by Revoked)	9	12	28
Essayons (1955, Education—Little Lea, by Bull Lea)	11	17	27
Grades Great (1951, Free France—Spell Binder, by Equestrian)	9	23	27
Latamaha (1958, *Sir Ronald II—Judiciously, by Better Self)	13	14	27
Lovely Ann (1956, Flaming Fleet—Elisann, by Revoked)	14	13	27
Silent Marie (1950, Dr. Cattail—Wee Cutie, by Down Under)	8	23	27
Stay Together (1970, Kelley's Memory—Her Worship, by Golden Bull)	7	7	27
Suiturself (1951, Cloud Time—Miney, by Rolled Stocking)	8	12	27
Troublepeg (1960, Mr. Trouble—Pellene, by Revoked)	9	6	27

Oldest Broodmares to Produce a Stakes Winner
(1930-2002)

	Fls.	Age Prod. 1st SW	Age Prod. last SW	Stakes Winner
Mary's Fantasy (1973, Olympian King—Fantasy Dream, by Everett Jr.)	12	12	26	Perfect Fantasy
Beaconaire (1974, *Vaguely Noble—Ole Liz, by Double Jay)	14	6	25	Binya (Ger)
Brown Berry (1960, Mount Marcy—Brown Baby, by Phalanx)	19	8	25	Hours After
Conejo Bonita (1949, Trace Call—Downy Pillow, by Morvich)	10	25	25	Coneja's Con Man
Fairy Sprite (1953, Papa Redbird—Fairy Fleet, by Broadside)	11	15	25	Orphan Annye
Fire's Gem (1961, *Royal Gem II—Fire Fire Fire, by Attention)	13	22	25	Lassafras
Floral Victory (1962, Victoria Park—La Belle Rose, by Le Lavandou)	16	6	25	Floral Dancer
Green Finger (1958, Better Self—Flower Bed, by *Beau Pere)	17	12	25	Blandford Park
Heat of Holme (1970, *Noholme II—Heat Lamp, by Better Self)	18	4	25	Speed On Holme
Hill of Sheba (1964, Federal Hill—Sheba S., by Errard King)	13	17	25	Apart
Little Blush (1968, *Day Court—Beaukiss, by *Mahmoud)	14	7	25	Cartofel
Melanie's Girl (1958, Nashua—*Nebroda, by Nearco)	14	8	25	Hagley's Relic
Phanatam (1941, Mokatam—Phantom Fairy, by *Negofol)	12	25	25	Jacks Again
Sooni (1970, Buckpasser—Missy Baba, by *My Babu)	16	20	25	Black Cash
*Uvira II (1938, Umidwar —Lady Lawless , by Son-in-Law)	13	6	25	Francis U.
Coed (1965, *Ribot—Bushel-n-Peck, by *Khaled)	13	24	24	Blacksmith
Crim Potatoes (1968, Hilarious—Baby Beauful, by Beau Gar)	11	14	24	Zoddy's
Fatal Conflict (1961, *River War—Bridal Wreath, by Lochinvar)	10	17	24	Big Upheaval
Generals Sister (1960, Count Fleet—Cigar Maid, by Pavot)	13	6	24	General Silver
His Lady Fair (1958, Tom Fool—*Dangerous Dame, by *Nasrullah)	10	24	24	Diplomette
Honor an Offer (1975, Hoist the Flag—Bridget o' Brick, by Mr. Brick)	13	15	24	Imperial Gesture
I'm Nosey Too (1961, Jackstraw—Cherry Sak, by Nassak)	6	24	24	Pilot Lady Straw
Impish (1972, Majestic Prince—Lady Be Good, by Better Self)	14	12	24	Karly's Harley
Kind Gesture (1939, Zacaweista—Console, by *Under Fire)	12	24	24	Kind Col.
Lady in Red (1966, Prince John—Red Damask, by Jet Action)	10	24	24	Ragtime Rebel
Like a Charm (1964, Pied d'Or—*Albany Isle, by Jamaica Inn)	16	10	24	Vidid Gold
Marcia W. (1955, Blue Swords—Charwoman, by Discovery)	14	24	24	Red Deer Ruler
Miss Willow (1956, Oil Capitol—Pussy Willow, by *Bull Dog)	10	9	24	Willow Drive
Natalma (1957, Native Dancer—Almahmoud, by *Mahmoud)	14	4	24	Born a Lady
Northern Meteor (1975, Northern Dancer—Patelin, by Cornish Prince)	15	5	24	Meteor Miracle
Obey the Helm (1973, What a Pleasure—Lookout Billie, by Misty Flight)	13	6	24	Rose City Special
Painted Veil (1938, Blue Larkspur—Killashandra, by *Ambassador IV)	8	10	24	Tulyars Veil
Pia Mia (1968, Pia Star—Surprise Lady, by Discovery)	18	6	24	Mia's Hope
*Pluie d'Or II (1950, Sayani —Folie d'Or, by Vatellor)	7	24	24	Mamia
Queen San (1968, Middle Brother—Social Side, by Roman)	13	11	24	Ambridge Augie
Ribonette (1968, *Ribot—*Sweet Sovereign, by Grey Sovereign)	12	9	24	Taibhseach
Specious (1968, Prince John—*Sophist, by Acropolis)	14	6	24	Frappe
T Joe's Girl (1969, Pia Star—Fee Fee Girl, by Johns Chic)	14	8	24	Dales Derby Star
Winter Garden (1958, Windfields—Rustic Charm, by Reaping Reward)	18	24	24	Varykino
Xenia (1974, Majestic Prince—Mother Russia, by Vertex)	15	6	24	Tub Tosser

Most Millionaires Produced by a Broodmare

No. Millionaires	Broodmare	Millionaires
4	Dancing Key, 1983, m., Nijinsky II—Key Partner, by Key to the Mint	Air Dublin ($3,401,386), Air Gang Star ($1,259,625), Dance Partner ($5,973,652), Dance in the Dark ($3,459,758)
3	Antique Value, 1979, m., Northern Dancer—Moonscape, by Tom Fool	News Value ($1,246,690), Maquereau ($1,245,865), Vega ($2,105,918)
3	Happy Trails, 1984, m., Posse—Roycon (GB), by High Top	Happy Path ($1,038,106), Shinko Lovely ($4,596,546), Taiki Marshal ($1,910,894)
3	Legacy of Strength, 1982, m., Affirmed—Katonka, by Minnesota Mac	Legacy of Zelda ($1,256,666), Silent Happiness ($1,870,725), Stinger ($3,467,289)
3	Millracer, 1983, m., *Le Fabuleux—Marston's Mill, by In Reality	Fuji Kiseki ($1,319,239), Shinin' Racer ($1,915,140), Super License ($1,214,916)
3	Northern Sunset (Ire), 1977, m., Northfields—Moss Greine, by *Ballymoss	L'Carriere ($1,726,175), Salem Drive ($1,046,065), St. Jovite ($1,604,439)
3	Powerful Lady, 1981, m., Maruzensky —Roch Tesco , by Tesco Boy	Marubutsu Powerful ($1,100,278), Royal Touch ($2,795,933), Winning Ticket ($3,359,368)
3	Vega, 1990, m., Tony Bin —Antique Value, by Northern Dancer	Admire Boss ($1,101,340), Admire Don ($2,017,561), Admire Vega ($2,466,038)

AUCTIONS
History of Thoroughbred Auctions

By far the oldest brand name in Thoroughbred racing is Tattersalls, the English auction company founded by the eponymous Richard Tattersall at London's Hyde Park Corner in 1766. Tattersalls (the appropriate apostrophe was lost at some point in its history) remains the preeminent European auction house and has served as the model for Thoroughbred sales companies throughout the world.

Richard Tattersall expanded his position as the leading seller of Thoroughbreds by providing a dining room for Jockey Club members, and his descendants (who remained in charge of the company for more than 200 years) transferred its headquarters to Newmarket in 1870.

The first American to attempt to emulate Tattersalls's success was English-educated William Easton, who served as Tattersalls's American representative for the last quarter of the 19th century and in 1879 established his own company, the American Horse Exchange, which he later merged with Tattersalls of New York. Easton was the auctioneer at the famous dispersal of August Belmont I's breeding stock in 1891, when Charles Reed made the first $100,000 bid at auction to acquire leading sire *St. Blaise.

Several competitors for Easton's company emerged in the 1890s, principally Powers-Hunter and the Fasig Co. William B. Fasig began auctioneering in his native Cleveland in the early 1890s, and Easton soon invited him to join Tattersalls. The English company chose to sell its American division after the financial panic of 1893, and Fasig took control. In 1898, he took on a partner, Edward A. Tipton, giving the company its now-familiar name, Fasig-Tipton.

Fasig's assistant Enoch J. Tranter took control of the company when Fasig abandoned ship after another panic in 1907, and Tranter established the Saratoga yearling sale in '17. Saratoga has remained the backbone of Fasig-Tipton ever since, through the stewardship of Humphrey S. Finney, his son John M. S. Finney, and the current management led by D. G. Van Clief Jr.

The commercial breeding industry began in both England and the U.S. around the middle of the 19th century. William Blenkiron's Middle Park Stud was the first famously successful commercial breeding operation in England, sending a long succession of high-priced horses to the annual Tattersalls October yearling sale.

Robert A. S. C. Alexander was the key figure in establishing Thoroughbred breeding as a viable commercial endeavor in the U.S. through the foundation of his Woodburn Stud near Lexington in the 1850s. Though hampered by the Civil War, Woodburn held annual yearling sales at the Kentucky farm until 1890. Those sales drew buyers from all over the U.S., and its success—plus the presence of 16-time leading sire Lexington at Woodburn—effectively concentrated the breeding industry in the Bluegrass.

Several small sales companies sprung up in Kentucky over the decades but died just as quickly, primarily because most buyers were in the East. Once Woodburn's star faded, they rarely could be enticed to Kentucky to buy horses. Petroleum rationing during World War II prevented Kentucky breeders from shipping their horses to Saratoga in 1943, however, and Fasig-Tipton agreed to hold a sale in a tent on the grounds of Keeneland Race Course in Lexington. That sale included eventual 1945 Kentucky Derby winner Hoop, Jr.

Kentucky breeders liked the idea so much that by the next year they had formed their own cooperative company, Breeders' Sales Co., and purchased Fasig-Tipton's Lexington sales pavilion, which was dismantled and reconstructed at Keeneland. Breeders' Sales Co. merged with Keeneland in 1962 to become the sales division of the Keeneland Association.

Benefiting from the worldwide success of American-breds over the last 50 years, Keeneland has become the world's largest and most successful sales company. Keeneland sold the first $100,000 yearling, $130,000 Swapson in 1961; the first $1-million yearling, Canadian Bound at $1.5-million in '76; and the world-record-priced yearling, Seattle Dancer, at $13.1-million in '85.

Fasig-Tipton re-established itself in Kentucky in the 1970s, selling three Kentucky Derby (G1) winners in five years, including Triple Crown winner Seattle Slew, but its strategy differs from Keeneland's. While Keeneland's sales are based almost exclusively at its facility in Lexington, Fasig-Tipton spreads a wider net with sales at six locations in five states, often serving regional markets as well as national ones.

As the breeding industry has grown, regional markets have also begun to support their own sales organizations, most notably Ocala Breeders' Sales Co. in Florida. OBSC, founded in 1974, grew out of the two-year-old sales industry that began in the late 1950s when one of the first Florida breeders, Carl Rose, started selling his two-year-olds to trainers at Hialeah Park.

In the late 1980s, Barretts Equine Ltd. was formed to build a sales pavilion and to conduct sales on the Los Angeles County Fair Grounds in Pomona. Barretts's two-year-old sales were particularly successful when Japanese buyers were active in the market in the early 1990s.

—John P. Sparkman

Auction Review of 2002

Total receipts from North American Thoroughbred auctions declined for the second straight year in 2002. After receipts peaked at more than $1-billion in 2000, the combination of after-effects of the September 11, 2001, terrorist attacks, mare reproductive loss syndrome, and a sluggish economy pushed total receipts down 9.4% to $767,118,402 in 2002. On the plus side, while average for the 17,979 horses sold declined 17.1%, median increased 16.7%.

The second year of the new millennium was schizophrenic in the Thoroughbred marketplace. Sales of juveniles during the first half of the year held their own in terms of average but seemed to be disconnected from market trends. The summer yearling sales, with the exception of Fasig-Tipton Kentucky, were down markedly. The market began to revive slightly during the Keeneland September yearling sale, and the Keeneland November sale showed strong gains, but a mediocre market at the 2003 Keeneland January sale signaled that a sustained recovery might not yet have begun.

Yearlings

No market segment was more bipolar than the yearling sales of 2002. The high-profile summer selected sales were down sharply, in large part because the two largest buyers cut their spending by almost 40%. On the other hand, prices for more mainstream yearlings showed surprising strength at the Fasig-Tipton Kentucky selected yearling sale in July and during the second half of the Keeneland September yearling sale.

In the end, though, the market could not withstand the $37-million that perennial leading buyers John Ferguson Bloodstock and Demi O'Byrne did not spend, as shown by the following global figures:

- Number offered down 3.9% to 12,215;
- Number sold dropped 0.4% to 9,000;
- Total receipts declined 17.4% to $390,820,438;
- Average dipped 17.1% to $43,424; but
- Buy-back rate declined from 28.9% to 26.3%; and
- Median climbed sharply, by 16.7% to $10,500.

That substantial increase in median illustrated a reversal in one of the strongest trends of the Thoroughbred marketplace of the previous five years, when prices at the top of the market generally increased rapidly while prices in the middle and lower echelons stagnated or declined. Indeed, average prices for the top 10% of all yearlings sold declined by 27.3%. That decline was almost entirely due to the reduced spending of Ferguson, representing Sheikh Mohammed bin Rashid al Maktoum's Godolphin Racing, and

O'Byrne, who buys for Michael Tabor and John Magnier. Together, they spent $57.4-million for yearlings in 2002, almost $37-million less than in 2001.

O'Byrne paid $3,454,574 for the top-priced yearling of 2002, a son of Sadler's Wells out of Sharata, by Darshaan, at the Tattersalls Houghton sale in Newmarket. That purchase easily topped the $3.1-million that the Irish agent paid for a yearling colt by Storm Cat out of Tacha, by Mr. Prospector, at Keeneland July. The three highest-priced American yearlings were all by Storm Cat, including the year's top-priced filly, a daughter of Amelia Bearhart, by Bold Hour, at $2.8-million. Only 31 yearlings sold for $1-million or more on the international market, 21 short of the 52 such yearlings sold in 2001 and even farther off the record of 57 set in 2000.

Both O'Byrne and Ferguson said they could not find the type of yearlings with both excellent conformation and stallion pedigrees that would justify high bids. O'Byrne led all international buyers for the fourth time in the eight years, spending $32.4-million for 41 yearlings in 2002. In 2001, he spent $9-million more for three fewer horses. Taylor Made Sales Agency sold more yearlings for more money than any other consignor, with 334 sold for $44,785,800.

Two-Year-Olds

Since their heyday in the mid-1990s, when the market for two-year-olds in training kick-started the commercial breeding industry's recovery, the juvenile sales at times have seemed disconnected from the rest of the Thoroughbred business. That was never more true than in 2002, when both buyers and sellers seemed to be uncertain how the winds of industry trends were blowing. As a result, the 2002 juvenile market remained essentially unchanged from the year before, with about the same number of horses sold for slightly more money at slightly higher prices, as shown by the following global statistics:

- 4,057 horses offered, down 1%;
- 2,689 sold, ten more than in 2001;
- Total receipts of $129,926,434, up 2.3%;
- Average increased 1.9% to $48,318;
- Buy-back rate down slightly to 33.7%; and
- Median dropped 5% to $19,000.

The one surprise of 2002 was the sale of Atlantic Ocean for $1.9-million, a world record for a filly at a two-year-old auction, at the Barretts March sale. Purchased by the late Ahmed bin Salman's The Thoroughbred Corp., the Stormy Atlantic filly confirmed her ability with two stakes victories by the end of the year.

Unlike other segments, the juvenile market

displayed the same pattern seen in the previous few years of increases in average at the top of the market and stagnation or declines in the middle and lower echelons.

The two-year-old market is dominated by pinhookers—those who buy for resale—and, after a disastrous year in 2001 when they lost more than $14-million on paper, the pinhookers cut that paper loss in half. Most of those losses came at the very top and very bottom of the market, where gambles went awry. The buy-back rate continued to be a problem for pinhookers, since the return rate on the 65% of horses that they sold successfully was a healthy 50.5%. Robert N. Scanlon sold 2002's highest-priced colt, the Seeking the Gold colt Dawson Trail for $1-million, and led all consignors for the first time, selling 54 horses for $9,373,000. The Thoroughbred Corp. led the list of leading buyers of two-year-olds for the third time.

Weanlings

Central Kentucky's 2002 foal crop was decimated by mare reproductive loss syndrome, which led directly to a 23.5% decline in the number of weanlings offered at public sale. The reduced supply in turn led directly to substantial increases in average and median prices for weanlings at public auction. Going against weak 2001 figures, the weanling market posted these statistics in 2002:

- 2,031 weanlings offered, down 23.5%;
- 1,576 sold, an 18.2% decline;
- Total receipts of $49,062,617, down 6.6%;
- Average jumped 14.2% to $31,131; and
- Median soared 57.1% to $11,000.

The scarcity of weanlings benefited all echelons of the marketplace, but increases in average price were far stronger in the middle of the market than at either end. The stagnation at the top of the yearling market translated directly to modest gains for the top 20% of the weanling market, while the middle-market strength seen at the Keeneland September yearling sale was reflected by a doubling (or more) in value of middle-market weanlings.

The power of the middle and lower market also was reflected in returns by stud fee range, with stallions whose stud fees were below $20,000 performing best overall. However, no stud fee range reached the industry standard for profitability of 2.5 times stud fee, and accordingly average stud fees for new stallions declined 38% for 2003.

For the second straight year, the highest-priced weanling of the year was sold at Tattersalls Newmarket December sale, where Charlotte Weber's Live Oak Stud paid $2,955,582, a world record for a weanling filly, for a daughter of Giant's Causeway out of Urban Sea, by Miswaki. For the first time in four years, no $1-million weanlings were sold at American auctions. John Ferguson Bloodstock led all buyers, purchasing 14 weanlings for $3,351,279. Taylor Made Sales Agency led all American consignors of weanlings, selling 45 for $4,385,500.

Broodmares

The tumultuous events of 2001 most heavily affected the broodmare market that year. The biggest broodmare sales occurred after the September 11 terrorist attacks as war loomed in Afghanistan. The effects of mare reproductive loss syndrome sharply reduced the number of broodmares on offer in 2001, a year of recession and stock-market declines.

Thus, the 2002 broodmare market did not need to be very good to match 2001's figures, but it did better than that. By the time the Keeneland November breeding stock sale rolled around, the market had absorbed the lessons of the summer and fall yearling sales, consignors had readjusted their expectations, and the result was a substantially better sale than many participants had anticipated. Since Keeneland November is by far the biggest sale of broodmares, it was largely responsible for the following statistics for mixed sales in 2002:

- 6,236 mares offered, down 6.8% from 2001;
- 4,714 sold, down 5%;
- Total receipts of $192,012,919, up 2.4%;
- Average increased 7.8% to $40,732; and
- Median remained at the 2001 level of $6,500.

Those figures, though, do not do justice to the upsurge in confidence felt at Keeneland November, when the marketplace realized that money could still be made, as long as everyone acted reasonably.

The most interesting aspect of the November sale was that the market for broodmares was strongest at or near the top and significantly weaker farther down the scale. Thus, broodmare buyers clearly indicated the weakness at the top of the market for yearlings and weanlings was an anomaly that is unlikely to be repeated in the future. As a result, unlike every other segment of the marketplace, the most-expensive covering sires performed best in the broodmare market.

That emphasis on perceived quality was exemplified by the most-expensive mare of the year, Arthur B. Hancock's and Stonerside Stable's Bless, an unraced full sister to 2000 Kentucky Derby (G1) winner Fusaichi Pegasus, in foal to Storm Cat. Bless was one of 22 seven-figure mares sold in North America in 2002, four more than in 2001, but far off the record of 43 set in 2000. S. David Plummer, the market's leading buyer, purchased Bless and 26 other mares for $17,535,000 in the name of ClassicStar. Taylor Made Sales Agency led all consignors, selling 217 horses for $33,161,500.—*John P. Sparkman*

Highest-Priced Yearlings of 2002

Horse	Consignor	Buyer	Sale	Price
F., by Sadler's Wells—Sharata	Barronstown Stud	Demi O'Byrne	Tatt Hou.	$3,454,574
C., by Storm Cat—Tacha	Taylor Made Sales Agency, agent	Demi O'Byrne	Kee July	3,100,000
F., by Storm Cat—Amelia Bearhart	David and Ginger Mullins, agent	Eugene N. Melnyk	Kee July	2,800,000
C., by Storm Cat—Clear Mandate	Lane's End, agent	Demi O'Byrne	Kee Sept.	2,500,000
C., by Danzig—Aquilegia	Middlebrook Farm, agent	D. Wayne Lukas, agent	Kee Sept.	2,400,000
C., by Seeking the Gold—Gioconda	Three Chimneys Sales, agent	Demi O'Byrne	Kee Sept.	2,150,000
C., by Gone West—Colonial Play	Taylor Made Sales Agency, agent	Baden P. Chace, agent	Kee July	2,100,000
F., by Belong to Me—Tomisue's Delight	Lane's End, agent	John Ferguson Bloodstock	Kee July	2,000,000
F., by Indian Ridge—Maximova (Fr)	Haras d'Etreham	Gainsborough Stud Mgmt.	Deauville Aug.	1,967,400
F., by Sadler's Wells—Dazzling Park	Lodge Park Stud, Ireland	Shadwell Estate Co.	Tatt Hou.	1,809,539
C., by Gone West—Touch of Greatness	Three Chimneys Sales, agent	John Ferguson Bloodstock	Kee July	1,800,000
F., by Seeking the Gold—Desert Stormer	Eaton Sales, agent	Reynolds Bell, agent	Kee July	1,800,000
C., by Deputy Minister—Highest Glory	Middlebrook Farm, agent	John Ferguson Bloodstock	Kee Sept.	1,650,000
C., by Dixieland Band—Hidden Garden	Lane's End, agent	John Ferguson Bloodstock	Kee Sept.	1,600,000
C., by A.P. Indy—Bosra Sham	Lane's End, agent	John Ferguson Bloodstock	Kee Sept.	1,500,000
C., by Danzig—Catchascatchcan (GB)	Paramount Sales, agent for Castleton/Lyons	Demi O'Byrne	Kee Sept.	1,500,000
C., by Kingmambo—Mysterial	Calumet Farm	John Ferguson Bloodstock	Kee July	1,500,000
F., by Gone West—Daijin	Hill 'n' Dale Sales Agency, agent	Live Oak Plantation	Kee Sept.	1,450,000
C., by Pulpit—Marshesseaux	Hill 'n' Dale Sales Agency, agent	Kazuko Yoshida	Kee Sept.	1,400,000
F., by Gone West—Primedex	Lane's End, agent	Robert and Beverly Lewis and Overbrook Farm	Kee July	1,350,000
F., by Storm Cat—Sacahuista	Eaton Sales, agent	John G. Sikura	F-T Saratoga	1,300,000
C., by A.P. Indy—Ballerina Princess	Three Chimneys Sales, agent	B. Wayne Hughes	Kee July	1,250,000
F., by Thunder Gulch—Drina	Mill Ridge Sales, agent	Demi O'Byrne	Kee Sept.	1,200,000
C., by In the Wings (GB)—Park Special	Lodge Park Stud, Ireland	Demi O'Byrne	Tatt Hou.	1,110,398
C., by Hennessy—Altair	FitzGerald/Keogh Agency, agent	Demi O'Byrne	Kee Sept.	1,100,000
C., by Unbridled's Song—Roll Over Baby	Taylor Made Sales Agency, agent	Baden P. Chace, agent	Kee Jan.	1,100,000
C., by A.P. Indy—Wild Planet	Lane's End, agent	Reynolds Bell, agent	Kee Sept.	1,000,000
C., by Seeking the Gold—Mackie	Indian Creek, agent	Kazuko Yoshida	Kee Sept.	1,000,000
C., by Storm Cat—Scoop the Gold	Eaton Sales, agent	John Ferguson Bloodstock	Kee Sept.	1,000,000
C., by Storm Cat—Unbridled Wind	Mill Ridge Sales, agent	M. J. Dance	Kee Sept.	1,000,000
C., by Unbridled's Song—Wanda's Dream	Dromoland and Hartwell Farms, agent	Aaron and Marie Jones	F-T Saratoga	1,000,000
C., by Sadler's Wells—Groom Order	Ballygallon Stud	John Ferguson Bloodstock	Tatt Hou.	987,021
F., by Darshaan—Spinning The Yarn	Meon Valley Stud	Demi O'Byrne	Tatt Hou.	987,021
F., by Storm Cat—Now That's Funny	Paramount Sales, agent	Robert and Beverly Lewis	Kee Sept.	975,000
F., by Barathea (Ire)—Dayanata	Voute Sales, agent	Gainsborough Stud Mgmt.	Tatt Hou.	970,571
C., by Forestry—Alexandrina	Eaton Sales, agent	Robert Baker, D. Cornstein, and William L. Mack	F-T Saratoga	950,000
F., by Storm Cat—Lilac Garden	Taylor Made Sales Agency, agent	Chiefswood Stables and Robert Krembil	Kee Sept.	950,000
C., by Storm Cat—La Affirmed	Eaton Sales, agent	Overbrook Farm	Kee Sept.	925,000
F., by Machiavellian—Fair of the Furze	Airlie Stud	Shadwell Estate Co.	Tatt Hou.	921,220
C., by Sadler's Wells—Dedicated Lady	Camas Park Stud, Ireland	Demi O'Byrne	Tatt Hou.	904,769
C., by Grand Slam—Alaska Queen	Highclere Sales, agent	John C. Oxley	F-T Saratoga	900,000
C., by Honour and Glory—Ruby Wedding	Taylor Made Sales Agency, agent	Padua Stables	F-T Saratoga	900,000
F., by Unbridled—Solar Colony	Lane's End, agent	Brushwood Stable	Kee Sept.	900,000
C., by Machiavellian—Bella Colora	Meon Valley Stud	Demi O'Byrne	Tatt Hou.	863,643
C., by Machiavellian—Kithanga	Voute Sales, agent	Demi O'Byrne	Tatt Hou.	863,643
F., by Sadler's Wells—Arutua	Watership Down Stud	Demi O'Byrne	Tatt Hou.	863,643
C., by Sadler's Wells—Puck's Castle	Camas Park Stud	Demi O'Byrne	Goffs Orby	852,476
F., by Gone West—Multiply	Gracefield, agent	Shadwell Estate Co.	Kee Sept.	850,000
F., by Unbridled—Ivory Idol	Taylor Made Sales Agency, agent	JMJ Stables Corp.	Kee July	850,000
C., by Forestry—Broad Dynamite	Taylor Made Sales Agency, agent	West Wind Farm	Kee July	800,000
C., by Forestry—President's Girl	Bluewater Sales, agent	John C. Oxley	F-T Saratoga	800,000
C., by Seeking the Gold—Wandering Star	Middlebrook Farm, agent	Frank Stronach	Kee Sept.	800,000
C., by Unbridled's Song—Salty Gal	Clifton Farm	Toyomitsu Hirai	Kee Sept.	800,000
C., by Danehill—Born Beautiful	Lynn Lodge Stud, agent	BBA (England) & A. Stroud	Goffs Orby	795,645
F., by Danehill—Solar Crystal	Watership Down Stud	McKeever-St. Lawrence	Tatt Hou.	781,391
F., by Danehill—Solo de Lune	Britton House Stud	Demi O'Byrne	Tatt Hou.	781,391
C., by A.P. Indy—Watch Out	Paramount Sales, agent	John Ferguson Bloodstock	Kee Sept.	775,000
C., by Danehill—Sleepytime (Ire)	Bugley Stud	Gainsborough Stud Mgmt.	Tatt Hou.	756,716
C., by Inchinor (GB)—Sumoto	Watership Down Stud	Demi O'Byrne	Tatt Hou.	756,716
C., by Deputy Minister—Runup the Colors	Lane's End, agent	M. J. Dance	Kee Sept.	750,000
C., by Mt. Livermore—Tenga	Paramount Sales, agent	Brushwood Stable	Kee July	750,000
F., by Unbridled's Song—Dreamscape	Gainesway, agent	Robert and Beverly Lewis	F-T Saratoga	750,000
C., by Machiavellian—One So Wonderful	Killeen Castle Stud, Ireland	Shadwell Estate Co.	Tatt Hou.	740,266
C., by Sadler's Wells—Free At Last (GB)	Voute Sales, agent	Demi O'Byrne	Tatt Hou.	740,266
C., by Kingmambo—Mother of Pearl (Ire)	Paramount Sales, agent	John Ferguson Bloodstock	Kee Sept.	725,000
F., by Unbridled's Song—Desert Queen	Runnymede Farm, agent	R. N. Scanlon, agent	Kee Sept.	725,000
C., by Danehill—Marlene-D	Abbeville and Meadow Court Studs	John Warren Bloodstock	Goffs Orby	723,314
C., by Arch—Resurge	John R. Williams, agent	John Ferguson Bloodstock	Kee Sept.	700,000
C., by Unbridled's Song—Arctic Valley	Marshall W. Silverman, agent	Robert and Beverly Lewis	F-T Ky. July	700,000
F., by Silver Deputy—T. V. Countess	Eaton Sales, agent	Darby Dan Bloodstock	Kee July	700,000

Highest-Priced Weanlings of 2002

Horse	Consignor	Buyer	Sale	Price
F., by Giant's Causeway—Urban Sea	Irish National Stud	Live Oak Stud	Tatt Dec.	$2,955,582
C., by Sunday Silence—Dancing Key	Shadai Farm	Takaya Shimakawa	Japan July	2,791,667
C., by Sunday Silence—Fanjica (Ire)	Shadai Farm	Genichiro Tawara	Japan July	1,708,333
C., by Sunday Silence—See You Soon (Fr)	Northern Farm	Kiyoshi Nishikawa	Japan July	1,250,000
C., by Sunday Silence—Catalyst	Northern Farm	Riichi Kondo	Japan July	1,125,000
C., by Sunday Silence—Las Meninas (Ire)	Shadai Farm	Kiyoshi Nishikawa	Japan July	1,125,000
C., by Sunday Silence—Aubergade	Northern Farm	Makoto Kaneko	Japan July	1,000,000
C., by Sunday Silence—Ballet Queen	Northern Farm	Kiyoshi Nishikawa	Japan July	916,667
C., by Danehill—Al Theraab	Barton Stud	Demi O'Byrne	Tatt Dec.	837,415
C., by Seattle Slew—Zoe Montana	Taylor Made Sales, agent	John Ferguson Bloodstock	Kee Nov.	800,000
C., by Fusaichi Pegasus—Party Cited	Three Chimneys Sales, agent	John McCormack Bloodstock	Kee Nov.	725,000
C., by Fusaichi Pegasus—Queen Maud (Ire)	Shadai Farm	Hiroyoshi Usuda	Japan July	708,333
C., by Fusaichi Pegasus—Jeweled Crown	Paca Paca Farm	John McCormack Bloodstock	Japan July	675,000
F., by Giant's Causeway—Soha	Churchtown House Stud	Demi O'Byrne	Tatt Dec.	656,796
F., by Seattle Slew—Artful Pleasure	Eaton Sales, agent	John Ferguson Bloodstock	Kee Nov.	640,000
C., by Sunday Silence—Eternal Beat	Oiwake Farm	Kawacho Sangyo	Japan July	616,667
F., by War Chant—Bright Feather	Three Chimneys Sales, agent	Irving Cowan	Kee Nov.	610,000
C., by Sunday Silence—Jo Knows	Oiwake Farm	John Ferguson Bloodstock	Japan July	583,333
C., by Sunday Silence—Sermon Time	Northern Farm	Matsuura Bokujo	Japan July	583,333
C., by Sunday Silence—Wind in Her Hair (Ire)	Northern Farm	Makoto Kaneko	Japan July	583,333
C., by Sunday Silence—White Tornado	Northern Farm	Grandprix Co. Ltd.	Japan July	541,667
C., by Green Desert—Krisalya (GB)	Collin Stud	Lodge Park Stud	Tatt Dec.	525,437
C., by French Deputy—Sun Spring (Arg)	Northern Farm	Riichi Kondo	Japan July	525,000
F., by Sunday Silence—Princess Reema	Paca Paca Farm	Shadai Farm	Japan July	516,667
C., by Brian's Time—Bound to Dance	Hayata Farms	Nakamura Chikusan	Japan July	500,000
C., by El Condor Pasa—Prayer Wheel	Shadai Farm	Lucky Field Co. Ltd.	Japan July	500,000
C., by Storm Cat—Seeking Regina	Eaton Sales, agent	Bradley T'bred. Brokerage	Kee Nov.	500,000
C., by Sunday Silence—Ibuki Pink Lady	Kanaishi Stud	Nakamura Chikusan	Japan July	500,000
F., by A.P. Indy—England's Rose	Vinery	Brushwood Stable	Kee Nov.	485,000
F., by El Prado (Ire)—Tedarshana (GB)	Brereton C. Jones, agent	Olin B. Gentry, agent	Kee Nov.	480,000
F., by French Deputy—Kurokami	Symboli Stud	Makoto Kaneko	Japan July	466,667
F., by Sunday Silence—Oenothera	Yukiko Hosokawa	John Ferguson Bloodstock	Japan July	416,667
C., by Sunday Silence—Darrery	John Troy, agent	John Ferguson Bloodstock	Tatt Dec.	410,498
F., by Fusaichi Pegasus—La Chaposa (Per)	Paramount Sales, agent	William C. Schettine	Kee Nov.	410,000
F., by Sunday Silence—Risque Attache	Hidaka Taiyo Bokujo	Soda Noen Co. Ltd.	Japan July	408,333
F., by Sunday Silence—Buzen Candle	Northern Farm	Akira Makabe	Japan July	391,667
C., by Coronado's Quest—Sociable Duck	Lantern Hill Farm, agent	Philip DiLeo	Kee Nov.	390,000
C., by Jade Robbery—Turnback the Alarm	Oiwake Farm	Hisato Kubo	Japan July	383,333
C., by Unbridled's Song—La Gueriere	C. Bruce Hundley, agent	Dromoland and Hartwell Farms	Kee Nov.	380,000
F., by Seattle Slew—European Rose	Eaton Sales, agent	Kilboy Estate	Kee Nov.	375,000
F., by Thunder Gulch—Save Me the Waltz (Ire)	FitzGerald/Keogh, agent	Charles Gordon-Watson	Kee Nov.	375,000
C., by Grand Slam—Barb's Lass	Mill Ridge Sales, agent	Chestnut Valley Farm	Kee Nov.	370,000
C., by End Sweep—Nany's Appeal	Itaka Bokujo	Toru Okawa	Japan July	366,667
C., by Fusaichi Pegasus—Heraklia	Taylor Made Sales, agent	ClassicStar LLC	Kee Nov.	350,000
C., by Seattle Slew—Her Temper	Taylor Made Sales, agent	Paramount Sales, agent	Kee Nov.	350,000
C., by Singspiel (Ire)—Valeureuse	Shiraoi Farm	Seiho Tanaka	Japan July	345,833
C., by El Condor Pasa—Air Rag Doll	Shadai Farm	Keiko Tawara	Japan July	341,667
C., by Green Desert—Tamheed	Shiraoi Farm	P and P Co. Ltd.	Japan July	333,333
C., by Sunday Silence—From Beyond	Hidaka Taiyo Bokujo	K. I. Farm	Japan July	333,333
C., by Almutawakel (GB)—Atnab	Voute Sales, agent	Shadwell Estate Co.	Tatt Dec.	328,398
C., by Special Week—O. P. Cat	Northern Farm	Riichi Kondo	Japan July	325,000
C., by Yankee Victor—Far Away Kisses	Bluewater Sales, agent	Athens Woods LLC	Kee Nov.	320,000
C., by Bubble Gum Fellow—Tokio Querida	Northern Farm	Yoshio Komurasaki	Japan July	316,667
C., by Peintre Celebre—Infinie	Kazuo Nakamura	Big Red Farm	Japan July	316,667
F., by Danehill—Delilah (Ire)	Goldford Stud, agent	North Hills Management	Tatt Dec.	311,978
C., by Dance in the Dark—Arrow Again	Shadai Farm	Takeshi Osawa	Japan July	308,333
C., by Machiavellian—Popolaccio	Shiraoi Farm	Big Red Farm	Japan July	308,333
C., by Taiki Shuttle—Laila Alawi	Shadai Farm	Noboru Syudo	Japan July	308,333
F., by Dance in the Dark—Make a Wish	Shadai Farm	Keiko Tawara	Japan July	308,333
C., by Forty Niner—Splintercat, by Storm Cat	Jiro Matsuda	Ryoji Yagi	Japan July	304,167
C., by Special Week—Belle Saison	Shadai Farm	Kiyoshi Nishikawa	Japan July	304,167
C., by Agnes World—Lucky Pisces	Shadai Farm	Takao Watanabe	Japan July	300,000
C., by A.P. Indy—Michelle's Monarch	Lane's End, agent	Senaca LLC	Kee Nov.	300,000
C., by El Condor Pasa—Berry Rose	Northern Farm	Keiko Jurry Fujishima	Japan July	300,000
C., by End Sweep—Silent Prayer	Shadai Farm	Reiko Hara	Japan July	300,000
C., by Fuji Kiseki—Very Rhythmic	Shadai Farm	Kawacho Sangyo	Japan July	300,000
C., by Green Desert—Classique	Shiraoi Farm	IJS Co. Ltd.	Japan July	300,000
C., by Silver Charm—Impact Now	John J. Greely, agent	Robert and Beverly Lewis	Kee Nov.	300,000
C., by French Deputy—Gianotti	Shadai Farm	Takushi Hirai	Japan July	295,833
C., by Grand Lodge—Miniver	Airlie Stud	John Ferguson Bloodstock	Tatt Dec.	295,558

Highest-Priced Two-Year-Olds of 2002

Horse	Consignor	Buyer	Sale	Price
Atlantic Ocean, f., by Stormy Atlantic—Super Chef	Chapman Farms	The Thoroughbred Corp.	Barretts March	$1,900,000
Dawson Trail, c., by Seeking the Gold—Bounteous (Ire)	Robert Scanlon, agent	Demi O'Byrne	F-T Calder	1,000,000
Atswhatimtalknabout, c., by A.P. Indy—Lucinda K	M & H Training/Sales, agt.	B. Wayne Hughes	F-T Calder	900,000
To Teras, c., by Unbridled's Song—Whatamiss	Robert N. Scanlon, agent	Darby Dan Bloodstock	Kee April	850,000
Saranoia, c., by Seattle Slew—Sharp Call	Terry Oliver, agent	Michael Gill	F-T Calder	800,000
Pray for Aces, f., by Pulpit—Aces	Kirkwood Stables, agent for Claiborne Farm	John C. Oxley	Kee April	750,000
Kafwain, c., by Cherokee Run—Swazi's Moment	Sequel Bloodstock, agent	The Thoroughbred Corp.	F-T Calder	720,000
Stellar, f., by Grand Slam—Starr County	Niall Brennan, agent	Demi O'Byrne	Kee April	700,000
Admiralty Arch, c., by Arch—Mixed Appeal	Solitary Oak, agent	Demi O'Byrne	F-T Calder	660,000
Golden Penny, f., by Touch Gold—Penny's Growl	Bowling and Dodd, agent	Robert and Beverly Lewis	Kee April	650,000
Saphiria, f., by Touch Gold—Marshesseaux	Eddie Woods, agent	Demi O'Byrne	F-T Calder	650,000
Goal, c., by Gone West—Madame Sunshine	Sequel Bloodstock, agent	The Thoroughbred Corp.	Barretts March	600,000
Honest Answer, f., by Tale of the Cat—Cup of Honey	Sequel Bloodstock, agent	The Thoroughbred Corp.	Barretts March	600,000
Zavata, c., by Phone Trick—Pert Lady	Robert N. Scanlon, agent	Demi O'Byrne	F-T Calder	575,000
Scrimshaw, c., by Gulch—Rogue Girl	Robert N. Scanlon, agent	Robert and Beverly Lewis	Kee April	550,000
Tsumujikaze, c., by Storm Cat—Nannerl	Robert J. Harris, agent	Katsumi Yoshida	F-T Calder	550,000
Unnamed, c., by Storm Cat—Fontemar (Arg)	Robert N. Scanlon, agent	Patrick Biancone, agent	F-T Calder	550,000
Logician, c., by Tabasco Cat—Arbela	Niall Brennan, agent	J. Paul Reddam	Kee April	520,000
Truckle Feature, c., by Saint Ballado—Magic Gleam	Straightaway Farm, agent	James McIngvale	Ocala Calder	500,000
Polo Ridge, f., by Wild Rush—Cranberry Muffin	Hartley/De Renzo, agent	Eugene N. Melnyk	F-T Calder	475,000
Position One, c., by Carson City—Delagating	Jerry Bailey Sales Agency, agent for Bailey-Ellenberg	North Hills Management	F-T Calder	460,000
Monte Ocean, c., by Grand Slam—Spinner	William B. Harrigan, agent	Ever Union Shokai	F-T Calder	450,000
Velvet Robe, f., by Gone West—Verbasle	Leprechaun Racing, agent	Katsumi Yoshida	F-T Calder	450,000
Carthage, c., by Smoke Glacken—Halomatic	Kirkwood Stables, agent	B. Wayne Hughes	Kee April	440,000
U and I Win, f., by In Excess (Ire)—Video Menu	Havens Bloodstock, agent	Jim L. Ingalls	Barretts March	440,000
Hitchcock's Best, c., by Bates Motel—Chelly M.	Havens Bloodstock, agent	The Thoroughbred Corp.	Barretts March	410,000
American Boundary, c., by Boundary—Nameseeker	Wavertree Stables, agent	Team Valor	Kee April	400,000
Finance the Cat, c., by Storm Cat—Refinancing	Straightaway Farm, agent	John Patitucci	Ocala Calder	400,000
Political Risk, c., by A.P. Indy—Two Altazano	William B. Harrigan, agent	Lane's End Bloodstock	Kee April	400,000
Windsor Lodge, c., by Phone Trick—Chattahoochee	Hartley/De Renzo, agent	Eugene N. Melnyk	Ocala March	400,000
Buju, c., by Maria's Mon—Full Retreat	Wavertree Stables, agent	John C. Kimmel, agent	Kee April	385,000
Chimney Slew, c., by Seattle Slew—Heaven Knows Why	M. W. Miller, agent	D. Wayne Lukas	F-T Calder	380,000
Eishen Hampton, c., by Dynaformer—Sedona Berry	Niall Brennan, agent	Eishindo Co. Ltd.	Kee April	380,000
Fairly Valued, c., by Clever Trick—Mrs. Marcos	Nick de Meric, agent	C. T. Grether Inc.	Kee April	375,000
Supreme Cat, c., by Hennessy—Sweet Little Lies	Hoby & Layna Kight, agent	Tom Durant	F-T Calder	375,000
Glorys Price, c., by Storm Creek—Delicate Rose	Hoby & Layna Kight, agent	Mike Gill	Ocala Calder	360,000
Bullisomo, c., by Holy Bull—Painted Pink	Robert N. Scanlon, agent	Pegasus Bloodstock	F-T Calder	355,000
At Night, f., by Dayjur—Ra'a	Montepelier Thoroughbred and H. T. Stables, agent	The Thoroughbred Corp.	Barretts March	350,000
Bishop Court Hill, c., by Holy Bull—Just Cuz	Leprechaun Racing, agent	Eugene N. Melnyk	F-T Calder	350,000
Close to Reno, c., by Carson City—Tremolos	Niall Brennan, agent	Darby Dan Bloodstock	Kee April	350,000
Omega Code, c., by Elusive Quality—Tin Oaks	Hartley/De Renzo, agent	Wesley Ward	F-T Calder	350,000
Toho Sekito, c., by Silver Deputy—I Think Not	Robert N. Scanlon, agent	Fumio Koga	F-T Calder	350,000
Go for Four, c., by Gone West—Marina Duff (Ire)	M. W. Miller, agent	Omar Trevino	F-T Calder	350,000
With a Rush, c., by Wild Rush—Aubegris	Jerry Bailey Sales Agency, agent for Bailey-Ellenberg	McBride Bluegrass	F-T Calder	350,000
Ekolu Place, c., by Grindstone—Tropico Cielo	Terry Oliver, agent	Katsumi Yoshida	F-T Calder	340,000
Baron Karanotegami, c., by Coronado's Quest—Hitch	Robert N. Scanlon, agent	Karuizawa 1st Lady Co.	Kee April	335,000
Ranger Chance, c., by Boston Harbor—Northern Dynasty	Cleveland Wheeler, agent	Hardacre Farm and Amy Tarrant	Ocala Calder	330,000
Touch Silk, f., by Touch Gold—Silken Magic	Jerry Bailey Sales Agency, agent for Bailey-Ellenberg	NW Management	Barretts May	330,000
College Honor, c., by Double Honor—Camptown Miss	Farnsworth Farms, agent	William J. Condren	Ocala June	310,000
J. B. Hood, c., by French Deputy—Belle Boyd	Niall Brennan, agent	Robert L. Beck	F-T Calder	310,000
Lofty Call, c., by Deputy Commander—Reverse the Call	Jerry Bailey Sales Agency, agent for Bailey-Ellenberg	Great Diehl	F-T Calder	310,000
Penobscot Bay, c., by Is It True—Allison's Pride	Bowling and Dodd, agent	J. D. & Christine Brown	F-T Calder	310,000
Run Rayma Run, f., by Langfuhr—Jeanie's Gift	Eddie Woods, agent	Baden P. Chace, agent	F-T Calder	305,000
Bierstadt, c., by Hennessy—Tricky Game	William B. Harrigan, agent	James C. Spence	F-T Calder	300,000
Cafe Venetian, c., by Unbridled's Song—Astaire Case	Niall Brennan, agent	Ever Union Shokai	F-T Calder	300,000
Philadelphia Jim, c., by Mr. Greeley—Salsa Stacy	Cleveland Wheeler, agent	Mike Gill	Ocala Calder	300,000
Rappel, c., by Twining—Foxy Ridge	Kirkwood Stables, agent	Iron Horse Racing	F-T Calder	300,000
Saint Buddy, c., by Saint Ballado—Heart of America	Jerry Bailey Sales Agency, agent for Bailey-Ellenberg	NW Management	Barretts May	300,000
Southern Image, c., by Halo's Image—Pleasant Dixie	Bridlewood Farm	Mike Machowsky, agent	Ocala March	300,000
Eishen Kinder, c., by Belong to Me—Double Smooth	Niall Brennan, agent	Eishindo Co. Ltd.	Kee April	300,000
Kazekozo, c., by Pulpit—Alaskan Tide	Eisaman Equine Services	Katsumi Yoshida	F-T Calder	300,000
Charming Kris, f., by Kris S.—Too Cool to Fool	Asmussen Horse Center	Shadai Farm	Kee April	295,000
Marathon Man, c., by Capote—Dixie Maintenance	Wavertree Stables, agent	Robert and Beverly Lewis	Kee April	290,000
Cafe Floridian, c., by Grand Slam—Susie Ticket	Terry Oliver, agent	Ever Union Shokai	F-T Calder	290,000
Grab Your Heart, f., by Deputy Commander—Kelly Amber	Wavertree Stables, agt.	Shadai Farm	Kee April	290,000

Highest-Priced Broodmares and Broodmare Prospects of 2002

Horse, Age	Consignor	Buyer	Sale	Price
Bless (Storm Cat), 3	Stone Farm, agent for Arthur Hancock and Stonerside Stable	ClassicStar	Kee Nov.	$4,000,000
Desert Stormer (Kris S.), 12	Taylor Made Sales, agent for Norfields	Live Oak Stud	Kee Jan.	3,600,000
Fiji (GB) (Danehill), 8	Newgate Stud Farm	Brushwood Stable	Kee Nov.	3,100,000
Flat Fleet Feet (Storm Cat), 9	Three Chimneys Sales, agent	Eaton Sales, agent	Kee Nov.	2,300,000
Gourmet Girl (Fusaichi Pegasus), 7	Taylor Made Sales Agency, agent	Courtlandt Farm	Kee Nov.	2,250,000
Ela Athena (GB) (Giant's Causeway), 6	Michael C. Byrne, agent	Newsells Park Stud	Kee Nov.	2,000,000
Warrior Queen (A.P. Indy), 5	Eaton Sales, agent	BBA (Ireland)	Kee Nov.	2,000,000
Rose of Tara (Ire) (Storm Cat), 6	Glennwood Farm Voute Sales, agent	Chiefswood Stables	Kee Nov.	1,950,000
Kalookan Queen 6	Taylor Made Sales Agency, agent	Courtlandt Farm	Kee Nov.	1,850,000
Salty Gal (Broad Brush), 10	Clifton Farm	Live Oak Stud	Kee Nov.	1,750,000
Fabulously Fast (Giant's Causeway), 8	Three Chimneys Sales, agent	Newsells Park Stud	Kee Nov.	1,700,000
Hookedonthefeelin (Deputy Minister), 6	Hill 'n' Dale Sales Agency, agent	ClassicStar	Kee Nov.	1,525,000
Christmas in Aiken (Forestry), 10	Taylor Made Sales Agency, agent	Eaton Sales, agent	Kee Nov.	1,450,000
Velvet Moon (Daylami [Ire]), 11	Voute Sales, agent	Penfold Bloodstock	Tatt Dec.	1,436,741
Happyanunoit (NZ) (Giant's Causeway), 7	Mill Ridge Sales, agent	Newsells Park Stud	Kee Nov.	1,400,000
Last Resort (Mozart [Ire]), 5	Voute Sales, agent	John Ferguson Bloodstock	Tatt Dec.	1,354,642
Bright Feather (Giant's Causeway), 13	Three Chimneys Sales, agent	Overbrook Farm	Kee Nov.	1,300,000
The Seven Seas (Thunder Gulch), 6	Mill Ridge Sales, agent	Northwest Farms	Kee Nov.	1,300,000
Nannerl (Storm Cat), 15	Eaton Sales, agent	ClassicStar	Kee Nov.	1,250,000
On a Soapbox (Danzig), 6	Taylor Made Sales Agency, agent	Newsells Park Stud	Kee Nov.	1,250,000
Veil of Avalon (Giant's Causeway), 5	Dromoland Farm, agent	France Pur Sang	Kee Nov.	1,250,000
Pink Cristal (Grand Lodge), 6	Bugley Stud	Hugo Lascelles Bloodstock	Tatt Dec.	1,182,233
Nasty Storm, 4	Eaton Sales, agent	Frank Stronach	Kee Nov.	1,075,000
Brigitta (Ire) (Danehill), 5	Kiltinan Stud	De Burgh Bloodstock	Tatt Dec.	1,067,294
Molasses (Mozart [Ire]), 4	Haras de Fresnay-le-Buffard	McKeever-St. Lawrence	Tatt Dec.	1,026,244
Roll Over Baby (Unbridled's Song), 13	Taylor Made Sales Agency, agent	S. David Plummer	Kee Jan.	1,000,000
Starine (Fr), 5	Mill Ridge Sales, agent	Newsells Park Stud	Kee Nov.	1,000,000
Victoria Cross (Danehill), 19	Voute Sales, agent	John Magnier	Tatt Dec.	985,194
Golightly (Seeking the Gold), 5	David L. and Ginger Mullins, agent	Newsells Park Stud	Kee Nov.	950,000
Tedarshana (GB) (El Prado [Ire]), 8	Brereton C. Jones, agent	BBA (Ireland)	Kee Nov.	950,000
With Flair (Gone West), 6	Anderson Farms, agent for Sam-Son Farm	Summer Wind Farm	Kee Nov.	950,000
Langoustine (Aus) (Giant's Causeway), 4	Eaton Sales, agent	John Warren Bloodstock, agt.	Kee Nov.	900,000
Tap Your Heels (Forestry), 6	Fred Seitz, agent for Oldenburg Farm	Nesco II	Kee Nov.	900,000
Midnight Angel (Ger), 3	Union Stud	Newsells Park Stud	Tatt Dec.	820,995
Cedar Knolls (Seeking the Gold), 5	Three Chimneys Sales, agent	ClassicStar	Kee Nov.	800,000
Ocean Queen (Pulpit), 9	Newgate Stud Farm	Summer Wind Farm	Kee Nov.	800,000
Rings a Chime, 5	Taylor Made Sales Agency, agent	Stonerside Stable	Kee Jan.	800,000
Top Order (Saint Ballado), 6	Newgate Stud Farm	Wertheimer & Frere	Kee Nov.	775,000
Velvet Lady (GB) (Dr Fong), 5	Voute Sales, agent	John Ferguson Bloodstock	Tatt Dec.	738,896
Cleverly (Out of Place), 4	Claiborne Farm, agent	JMJ Stables Corp.	Kee Nov.	725,000
Fantasy Royale (Sadler's Wells), 4	Glenvale Stud, agent	Brushwood Stable	Tatt Dec.	722,476
Valley of Song (Machiavellian), 4	Loughbrown Stud and Martinstown Farm	De Burgh Bloodstock	Tatt Dec.	722,476
Fara's Team (Broad Brush), 17	Taylor Made Sales Agency, agent	ClassicStar	Kee Nov.	700,000
Highbury (Giant's Causeway), 5	Michael C. Byrne, agent	Swordlestown Stud	Kee Nov.	700,000
My Branch (Grand Lodge), 9	Kiltinan Stud	Blandford Bloodstock	Tatt Dec.	689,636
Ashford Castle (Tiznow), 8	Eaton Sales, agent	Newsells Park Stud	Kee Nov.	675,000
Brianda (Ire) (Gone West), 5	Taylor Made Sales Agency, agent	ClassicStar	Kee Nov.	675,000
Louve Mysterieuse (Giant's Causeway), 6	Taylor Made Sales Agency, agent	ClassicStar	Kee Nov.	650,000
Wichitoz (Cozzene), 5	Ashview Farm, agent	Wertheimer & Frere	Kee Nov.	650,000
Our Dani (In a Walk), 9	Lane's End, agent	Horse France	Kee Jan.	625,000
Tizso (Hennessy), 7	Hopewell Farm, agent	Diamond A Farms	Kee Nov.	625,000
Willa Joe (Ire) (Fusaichi Pegasus), 12	Hartwell Farm, agent	Summer Wind Farm	Kee Nov.	625,000
Above Perfection, 4	Taylor Made Sales and Darrell Vienna, agt.	ClassicStar	FT Ky. Nov.	610,000
La Gueriere (Louis Quatorze), 14	Wimborne Farm	ClassicStar	Wimborne Disp.	610,000
Mabrova (GB) (Green Desert), 15	Wertheimer & Frere	Horse France	Tatt Dec.	607,536
Cruising Haven (Unbridled's Song), 14	Nursery Place, agent	Gaines-Gentry T'breds., et al.	Kee Nov.	600,000
Regally Appealing (Unbridled's Song), 5	Taylor Made Sales Agency, agent	ClassicStar	Kee Nov.	600,000
Sweet Ludy (Ire) (Gone West), 6	Denali Stud, agent	Newsells Park Stud	Kee Nov.	600,000
Janet (GB), 5	David L. and Ginger Mullins, agent	Newsells Park Stud	Kee Nov.	575,000
L'amour (Alhaarth), 4	Voute Sales, agent	Hugo Lascelles Bloodstock	Tatt Dec.	574,697
Cayman Sunset (Ire) (Gulch), 5	Glennwood Farm Voute Sales, agent	Newsells Park Stud	Kee Nov.	550,000
Lady Lochinvar (Seeking the Gold), 9	Eaton Sales, agent	Larry and Marianne Williams	Kee Nov.	550,000
Lyphard Gal (Unbridled's Song), 12	Taylor Made Sales Agency, agent	ClassicStar	Kee Nov.	550,000
Red Cat (Kingmambo), 7	Gaillardia, agent	Haruya Yoshida	Kee Nov.	550,000
Knight's Baroness (Grand Lodge), 15	Voute Sales, agent	Charles P. Gordon-Watson	Tatt Dec.	525,437
Diane Suzanne (Point Given), 16	Three Chimneys Sales, agent	Payson Stud	Kee Nov.	525,000
Really Polish (A.P. Indy), 7	Lane's End, agent	Newsells Park Stud	Kee Nov.	500,000
Saudia (Theatrical [Ire]), 4	Newgate Stud Farm	Gracefield	Kee Nov.	500,000
Smokey Mirage (Giant's Causeway), 6	Taylor Made Sales Agency, agent	Audley Farm	Kee Nov.	500,000
Squall City (Deputy Minister), 5	Taylor Made Sales Agency, agent	ClassicStar	Kee Nov.	500,000

Chronological Review of Major 2002 Sales

	No. sold	Total	Chg	Average	Chg	Highest Price
January						
Keeneland January horses of all ages	937	$34,689,200	–12.5%	$37,022	+12.7%	$3,600,000
Ocala Breeders' Sales Co. winter mixed	494	4,231,900	–21.6%	8,567	+8.6%	160,000
Heritage Place winter mixed	82	285,550	+55.8%	3,482	+6.4%	26,000
Barretts Equine Ltd. winter mixed	460	3,257,800	–45.9%	7,082	–49.6%	72,000
February						
Fasig-Tipton Midlantic winter mixed	123	900,700	+0.4%	7,323	+18.4%	60,000
Ocala Breeders' Sales Co. selected two-year-olds in training	114	13,041,000	–7.7%	114,395	+10.2%	500,000
Thomas Sales Co. Horseman's Racing Bred winter mixed	38	67,625	–49.5%	1,780	–5.6%	6,200
Fasig-Tipton Kentucky winter mixed	248	2,829,100	+0.8%	11,408	+29.7%	190,000
Arkansas Thoroughbred Sales Co. winter mixed	79	412,200	–33.3%	5,218	+23.3%	48,000
Fasig-Tipton Florida select two-year-olds in training	139	29,479,000	+4.6%	212,079	+2.3%	1,000,000
March						
Barretts Equine March sale of select two-year-olds in training	73	10,950,000	+8.6%	150,000	+5.6%	1,900,000
Fair Grounds Sales Co. select two-year-olds in training	32	265,450	–31.7%	8,295	–46.6%	32,000
Ocala Breeders' Sales Co. select sale of two-year-olds in training	200	14,722,000	–2.9%	73,610	+4.8%	400,000
Adena Springs two-year-olds in training	40	945,500		23,638		80,000
Fasig-Tipton Texas two-year-olds in training	175	3,722,100	–17.2%	21,269	–8.7%	110,000
April						
Louisiana Thoroughbred Breeders Sales Co. spring mixed	110	292,150	–26.8%	2,656	–24.2%	20,000
Keeneland April two-year-olds in training	102	17,749,500	+19.1%	174,015	+6.3%	850,000
Ocala Breeders' Sales Co. spring two-year-olds in training	673	15,332,100	–15.1%	22,782	–13.6%	280,000
May						
Thomas Sales Co. Horseman's Racing Bred spring mixed	45	94,025		2,089		7,500
Barretts Equine spring sale of two-year-olds in training	271	7,507,000	+69.2%	27,701	+1.8%	330,000
C.T.H.S. (Ontario division) two-year-olds in training	23	381,742	–45.3%	16,597	–21.5%	46,217
Fasig-Tipton Midlantic two-year-olds in training	282	9,312,600	+9.2%	33,023	+3.8%	280,000
June						
American Equine Sales two-year-olds in training	36	483,400	+61.8%	13,428	+34.8%	39,000
San Antonio Rose classic mixed horse	62	118,950	–24.8%	1,919	–3.0%	12,500
Ocala Breeders' Sales Co. June two-year-olds in training and horses of racing age	249	4,609,500	+20.0%	18,512	+10.8%	310,000
Heritage Place spring mixed	24	45,850	+19.7%	1,910	–30.2%	6,000
Illinois Thoroughbred Breeders two-year-olds in training and horses of racing age	25	299,300	–57.5%	11,972	–28.6%	50,000
July						
Japan Racing Horse Association selected foal	186	45,329,996	+10.6%	243,710	+10.0%	2,791,667
Fasig-Tipton Midlantic two-year-olds in training and horses of racing age	108	1,610,600	–5.3%	14,913	–20.2%	102,000
Wimborne Farm dispersal	85	3,268,700		38,455		610,000
Keeneland July selected yearling	87	42,385,000	–32.9%	487,184	–31.4%	3,100,000
Fasig-Tipton Kentucky select yearling	325	31,790,000	+37.3%	97,815	+0.1%	700,000
Idaho Cup mixed	66	120,900		1,832		8,000
August						
Thomas Sales Co. Horseman's Racing Bred summer mixed	64	115,475		1,804		11,000
Louisiana Thoroughbred Breeders Sales Co. summer mixed	97	326,600	+2.2%	3,367	+5.4%	16,000
Fasig-Tipton Saratoga selected yearling	140	35,242,000	–43.5%	251,729	–34.7%	1,300,000
Stallion Access Champagne seasons and shares	35	1,145,500	+22.9%	32,729	+40.5%	205,000
Minnesota Thoroughbred Association horses of all ages	26	133,000	+43.2%	5,115	+153.3%	22,000
Fasig-Tipton New York Saratoga preferred yearling	108	5,345,500	+50.3%	49,495	+14.1%	300,000
California Thoroughbred Breeders Association Del Mar August yearling	98	4,289,500	–5.5%	43,770	+0.2%	250,000
Ruidoso Annual Thoroughbred yearling and mixed	187	1,257,100	+18.0%	6,722	–4.1%	70,000
L'Agence Francaise Deauville August yearling sale	371	26,530,356	–16.1%	71,510	–16.1%	1,967,400
Michigan Thoroughbred Owners and Breeders Association yearling	35	143,700	–1.4%	4,106	–43.7%	13,000
Ocala Breeders' Sales Co. select and open yearling sales	842	11,606,900	–4.9%	13,785	–8.1%	200,000
Indiana Thoroughbred Owners and Breeders Association horses of all ages	27	52,700	–50.9%	1,952	–23.6%	4,500
C.T.H.S. (Alberta division) summer yearling	142	670,503	–11.6%	4,722	–9.7%	20,435
Fasig-Tipton Texas summer yearling	261	2,702,500	–7.0%	10,354	–8.1%	85,000
American Equine Sales wine country yearling	108	650,600	+7.0%	6,024	–21.7%	40,000

	No. sold	Total	Chg	Average	Chg	Highest Price
September						
C.T.H.S. (Saskatchewan division) yearling	20	40,990	−31.3%	2,050	−21.0%	4,398
C.T.H.S. (Manitoba division) yearling	35	106,859	+9.0%	3,053	−6.6%	10,366
Washington Thoroughbred Breeders summer yearling	146	2,480,600	+1.6%	16,990	−2.6%	120,000
Fasig-Tipton Canada selected and open Canadian-bred yearling	313	5,209,008		16,642		103,656
Iowa Thoroughbred Breeders and Owners Association fall mixed	69	323,550	+11.8%	4,689	+21.5%	40,000
Keeneland September yearling	2,934	210,809,000	−17.1%	71,850	−18.2%	2,500,000
C.T.H.S. (British Columbia division) yearling and mixed	110	553,961	+27.8%	5,036	+25.4%	27,642
Oregon Thoroughbred Breeders' Association annual mixed	88	192,150	+16.2%	2,184	−1.0%	14,000
Midwest Regional mixed	101	218,200	−25.5%	2,160	−26.9%	25,000
Fasig-Tipton Midlantic Eastern fall yearling	530	8,840,400	−3.4%	16,680	−1.4%	150,000
October						
Breeders Sales Co. of Louisiana fall mixed	214	922,500	+32.4%	4,311	−9.1%	48,000
Tattersalls Ltd. Houghton yearling sale	124	46,064,887	+3.8%	371,491	+8.8%	3,454,574
Ocala Breeders' Sales Co. fall mixed	746	6,194,700	−0.3%	8,304	+12.0%	82,000
Barretts Equine October preferred yearling	215	2,721,900	+22.2%	12,660	+26.1%	165,000
Goffs Bloodstock Sales Ltd. Orby select yearling	349	37,565,316	−0.9%	107,637	+5.6%	852,476
C.T.H.S. (Alberta division) fall mixed	57	80,414	−5.4%	1,411	−20.3%	9,235
Keeneland October yearling	103	1,606,400	−68.5%	15,596	+3.5%	150,000
Washington Thoroughbred Breeders fall mixed	168	593,200	−34.7%	3,531	−8.2%	24,000
Fasig-Tipton Kentucky October yearling	519	6,381,400	+54.0%	12,296	−4.2%	300,000
Arizona Thoroughbred Breeders Association fall mixed	130	881,100	+8.9%	6,778	−5.4%	47,000
Heritage Place fall mixed	86	128,050	−53.7%	1,489	−31.1%	9,500
Arkansas Thoroughbred Sales Co. fall mixed	94	404,500	−11.5%	4,303	+39.3%	52,000
Barretts Equine fall mixed	423	3,176,600	+73.2%	7,510	+43.3%	145,000
November						
Fasig-Tipton Kentucky fall selected mixed	94	4,578,900	−29.5%	48,712	−17.5%	610,000
Keeneland November breeding stock	2,377	187,230,000	+4.3%	78,767	+9.9%	4,000,000
Tattersalls Ltd. December mixed sale	1,504	89,589,917	+13.5%	59,568	+4.4%	2,955,582
C.T.H.S. (Ontario division) winter mixed	124	471,100		3,799		28,886
December						
Fasig-Tipton Midlantic December mixed	378	2,478,600	−29.8%	6,557	−16.8%	103,000
Fasig-Tipton Texas mixed	207	665,600	+24.6%	3,215	−13.9%	30,000
Fasig-Tipton Kentucky December mixed	140	946,700	+78.2%	6,762	+54.0%	55,000

Histories of Major Sales

Following are the histories of several prominent Thoroughbred auctions in North America. The sales are listed by type of sale, with the order within each category determined by total sales.

Keeneland September Yearlings

Year	Offered	Sold	Gross	Chg	Average	Chg	High Price
2002	3,840	2,934	$210,809,000	−17.1%	$71,850	−18.2%	$2,500,000
2001	4,003	2,895	254,190,600	−12.9%	87,803	−0.3%	6,400,000
2000	4,302	3,313	291,827,100	+25.2%	88,085	+13.8%	6,800,000
1999	3,788	3,011	233,020,800	+37.2%	77,390	+30.3%	3,900,000
1998	3,528	2,860	169,811,800	+9.8%	59,375	+9.2%	2,100,000
1997	3,396	2,844	154,666,800	+12.7%	54,384	+16.3%	2,300,000
1996	3,649	2,936	137,233,800	+5.5%	46,742	+6.2%	1,400,000
1995	3,495	2,955	130,085,300	+24.4%	44,022	+18.4%	1,200,000
1994	3,264	2,812	104,552,900	+19.8%	37,181	+6.1%	625,000
1993	2,862	2,492	87,308,100	+11.3%	35,035	+23.0%	775,000
1992	3,188	2,754	78,427,400	+1.2%	28,478	−4.0%	400,000
1991	3,065	2,612	77,511,000	−10.7%	29,675	−0.5%	900,000
1990	3,310	2,909	86,756,500	+12.8%	29,823	−12.6%	535,000

First held in current format in 1960. From 1944 to '48, fall yearlings were part of a mixed sale format. In 1949, approximately half the yearlings were sold in a separate October sale and the remainder in a November breeding stock sale. In 1950, yearlings were in a separate session of breeding stock sale. In 1951, fall yearling sales were separated from breeding stock by least a week. Selected sessions were inaugurated in 1989.

Keeneland July Selected Yearlings

Year	Offered	Sold	Gross	Chg	Average	Chg	High Price
2002	146	87	$42,385,000	−32.9%	$487,184	−31.4%	$3,100,000
2001	132	89	63,212,000	−21.7%	710,247	+14.4%	4,000,000
2000	180	130	80,732,000	+5.1%	621,015	+6.7%	3,600,000
1999	181	132	76,815,000	+6.8%	581,932	+20.5%	3,000,000
1998	201	149	71,932,000	+15.0%	482,765	+35.0%	4,000,000
1997	236	175	62,565,000	+7.1%	357,514	+2.2%	1,500,000
1996	204	167	58,430,000	+25.8%	349,880	+41.6%	1,700,000
1995	225	188	46,450,000	+2.6%	247,074	+5.9%	1,250,000
1994	257	194	45,265,000	−8.3%	233,325	−1.2%	1,050,000
1993	251	209	49,350,000	+4.7%	236,124	−9.3%	1,050,000
1992	266	181	47,120,000	−35.8%	260,331	−18.8%	1,700,000
1991	300	229	73,443,000	−21.0%	320,712	+10.8%	2,600,000
1990	416	321	92,920,000	−19.9%	289,470	−4.7%	2,900,000

First held in 1943; not scheduled in 2003.

Fasig-Tipton Saratoga Selected Yearlings

Year	Offered	Sold	Gross	Chg	Average	Chg	High Price
2002	196	140	$35,242,000	−43.5%	$251,729	−34.7%	$1,300,000
2001	201	162	62,412,000	+49.0%	385,259	+26.0%	3,300,000
2000	173	137	41,901,000	+7.6%	305,847	+17.0%	4,200,000
1999	201	149	38,957,000	+13.8%	261,456	+23.7%	3,000,000
1998	220	162	34,246,000	+23.7%	211,395	+15.3%	1,700,000
1997	205	151	27,691,000	+1.4%	183,384	+13.5%	1,400,000
1996	220	169	27,311,000	+21.1%	161,604	+26.2%	630,000
1995	207	176	22,545,000	+21.4%	128,097	+32.5%	440,000
1994	241	192	18,566,000	+53.4%	96,698	+3.9%	520,000
1993	162	130	12,101,000	+0.5%	93,085	−4.2%	350,000
1992	152	124	12,046,000	−20.0%	97,145	−19.4%	525,000
1991	168	125	15,062,000	−54.3%	120,496	−42.5%	800,000
1990	219	157	32,923,000	+3.7%	209,701	−12.8%	1,500,000

First held in 1917. Not held in 1943-'45, because of World War II travel restrictions.

Fasig-Tipton Kentucky July Selected Yearlings

Year	Offered	Sold	Gross	Chg	Average	Chg	High Price
2002	536	325	$31,790,000	+37.3%	$97,815	+0.1%	$700,000
2001	381	237	23,148,000	−11.6%	97,671	+25.7%	625,000
2000	517	337	26,186,500	+17.9%	77,705	+3.6%	525,000
1999	361	296	22,211,000	+58.2%	75,037	+35.3%	525,000
1998	340	253	14,036,500	+43.9%	55,480	+5.3%	220,000
1997	238	185	9,751,000	−2.6%	52,708	+36.3%	290,000
1996	393	259	10,013,500	+52.2%	38,662	+4.0%	300,000
1995	227	177	6,580,500	+16.6%	37,178	+18.5%	200,000
1994	245	180	5,645,000	+24.1%	31,361	−0.8%	170,000
1993	173	144	4,550,500	+95.2%	31,601	−6.5%	147,000
1992	97	69	2,331,000	−35.0%	33,783	−0.1%	115,000
1991	154	106	3,585,000	−28.8%	33,821	−16.8%	140,000
1990	143	124	5,038,500	−44.5%	40,633	−12.3%	140,000

First held in 1972. Held at Newtown Paddocks since 1975.

Fasig-Tipton Calder Selected Two-Year-Olds in Training

Year	Offered	Sold	Gross	Chg	Average	Chg	High Price
2002	254	139	$29,479,000	+4.6%	$212,079	+2.3%	$1,000,000
2001	237	136	28,186,000	−16.3%	207,250	−4.0%	1,000,000
2000	264	156	33,690,000	+0.9%	215,962	+17.1%	1,950,000
1999	296	181	33,386,000	+26.9%	184,453	+33.9%	1,100,000
1998	302	191	26,303,000	+13.6%	137,712	+14.2%	1,000,000
1997	297	192	23,162,000	+1.7%	120,635	+16.1%	780,000
1996	309	219	22,765,000	+22.2%	103,950	+11.1%	875,000
1995	306	199	18,624,000	+39.0%	93,588	+31.3%	550,000
1994	276	188	13,403,000	+17.7%	71,293	+25.2%	390,000
1993	318	200	11,386,000	−8.0%	56,930	−3.9%	450,000
1992	292	209	12,376,000	+14.1%	59,215	−5.5%	350,000
1991	299	173	10,846,000	−24.6%	62,694	−17.2%	375,000
1990	269	190	14,383,000	+36.0%	75,700	+18.8%	625,000

First held in 1983.

Keeneland April Two-Year-Olds in Training

Year	Offered	Sold	Gross	Chg	Average	Chg	High Price
2002	178	102	$17,749,500	+19.1%	$174,015	+6.3%	$850,000
2001	146	91	14,898,000	−19.2%	163,714	+8.3%	775,000
2000	195	122	18,435,000	−0.7%	151,107	+0.1%	825,000
1999	179	123	18,560,000	+33.3%	150,894	+0.8%	2,000,000
1998	125	93	13,925,000	−3.5%	149,731	+52.6%	725,000
1997	210	147	14,427,000	+0.9%	98,143	−14.9%	900,000
1996	195	124	14,305,000	+20.6%	115,363	+11.8%	400,000
1995	169	115	11,865,000	+3.3%	103,174	+41.0%	700,000
1994	219	157	11,491,500	+69.0%	73,194	+15.2%	400,000
1993	136	107	6,800,500	—	63,556	—	300,000

First held in 1993.

Ocala Breeders' Sales Co. Calder Two-Year-Olds in Training

Year	Offered	Sold	Gross	Chg	Average	Chg	High Price
2002	175	114	$13,041,000	−7.7%	$114,395	+10.2%	$500,000
2001	188	136	14,124,000	−9.5%	103,853	−5.5%	900,000
2000	226	142	15,599,000	−5.2%	109,852	+6.8%	550,000
1999	204	160	16,454,000	+31.0	102,838	+25.2%	525,000
1998	193	153	12,564,000	+20.5	82,118	+20.5%	430,000
1997	184	153	10,428,000	+12.0%	68,157	+16.4%	300,000
1996	218	159	9,314,000	+19.5%	58,579	+6.7%	275,000
1995	181	142	7,794,500	+24.7%	54,891	+24.7%	270,000
1994	202	142	6,248,500	+9.4%	44,004	+14.0%	350,000
1993	200	148	5,712,000	+8.6%	38,595	+2.7%	325,000
1992	182	140	5,261,000	−1.5%	37,579	+2.7%	260,000
1991	218	146	5,341,000	−17.6%	36,582	−14.2%	135,000
1990	205	152	6,478,000	+18.3%	42,618	+23.0%	360,000

First in 1985 at Hialeah Park; held at Calder Race Course since '86.

Barretts Equine Ltd. Selected Two-Year-Olds in Training

Year	Offered	Sold	Gross	Chg	Average	Chg	High Price
2002	121	73	$10,950,000	+8.6%	$150,000	+5.6%	$1,900,000
2001	130	71	10,085,000	−41.7%	142,042	−21.1%	750,000
2000	170	96	17,287,000	−21.4%	180,073	−20.6%	2,000,000
1999	172	97	21,995,000	−3.2%	226,753	+30.8%	2,000,000
1998	200	131	22,711,000	−28.9%	173,366	−21.8%	1,000,000
1997	255	144	31,926,000	−3.3%	221,708	+7.4%	1,100,000
1996	233	160	33,016,000	+56.1%	206,350	+56.1%	900,000
1995	274	160	21,148,000	+57.4%	132,175	+61.3%	900,000
1994	240	164	13,440,000	+51.6%	81,951	+39.6%	700,000
1993	237	151	8,863,400	−7.5%	58,698	−5.1%	430,000
1992	280	155	9,584,000	−33.0%	61,832	−20.1%	370,000
1991	317	185	14,313,000	−12.8%	77,368	−7.6%	600,000
1990	270	196	16,405,000	—	83,699	—	700,000

First held in 1990.

Keeneland November Breeding Stock

Year	Offered	Sold	Gross	Chg	Average	Chg	High Price
2002	2,982	2,377	$187,230,000	+4.3%	$78,767	+9.9%	$4,000,000
2001	3,383	2,506	179,568,600	−41.0%	71,655	−22.9%	4,000,000
2000	4,367	3,277	304,549,800	−4.1%	92,936	+1.3%	4,900,000
1999	4,227	3,461	317,666,000	+20.0%	91,784	+17.2%	4,700,000
1998	4,312	3,379	264,657,700	+23.7%	78,324	+10.3%	7,000,000
1997	3,673	3,013	213,979,800	+25.4%	71,019	+17.6%	1,400,000
1996	3,451	2,826	170,691,800	+21.2%	60,400	+22.5%	2,600,000
1995	3,505	2,855	140,822,300	+16.3%	49,325	+1.6%	2,500,000
1994	2,932	2,494	121,056,900	+32.5%	48,539	+10.3%	2,700,000
1993	2,300	2,075	91,342,900	+24.6%	44,021	+16.6%	1,150,000
1992	2,324	1,942	73,337,200	−11.6%	37,764	−9.7%	1,100,000
1991	2,281	1,984	82,938,400	−18.0%	41,804	+5.8%	1,400,000
1990	3,061	2,558	101,107,700	−34.8%	39,526	−43.1%	2,300,000

First held in 1944.

Keeneland January Horses of All Ages

Year	Offered	Sold	Gross	% Chg	Average	% Chg	High Price
2003	1,600	1,185	$31,186,000	−10.1%	$26,317	−28.9%	$475,000
2002	1,135	937	34,689,200	−12.5%	37,022	+12.7%	3,600,000
2001	1,667	1,207	39,657,700	−34.9%	32,856	−33.1%	1,700,000
2000	1,605	1,241	60,951,200	+43.7%	49,115	+39.3%	5,000,000
1999	1,452	1,203	42,410,900	−20.2%	35,254	−23.1%	3,250,000
1998	1,378	1,160	53,164,800	+121.1%	45,832	+91.2%	3,400,000
1997	1,156	1,003	24,042,300	−20.6%	23,970	−21.0%	710,000
1996	1,220	997	30,263,400	+56.2%	30,354	+61.2%	1,800,000
1995	1,195	1,029	19,377,700	+29.5%	18,832	+7.0%	375,000
1994	948	850	14,960,600	+25.5%	17,601	+24.0%	210,000
1993	1,018	840	11,918,600	−37.5%	14,189	−36.4%	210,000
1992	952	855	19,066,000	−14.2%	22,299	+38.9%	650,000
1991	1,670	1,385	22,229,900	+9.9%	16,050	−33.1%	685,000
1990	983	844	20,234,200	−1.8%	23,974	+5.9%	2,100,000

First sale in 1956. Not held 1958-'60.

Highest-Priced Horses of All Time
American Top-Priced Yearlings
(With subsequent race record)

Key—Bold-faced caps: stakes winner. Bold-faced caps and lower case: stakes placed.

$13,100,000 **SEATTLE DANCER**, 1984 c., Nijinsky II–My Charmer, by Poker. Consignor: Warner L. Jones Jr.; Buyer: BBA (England), agent for Robert Sangster and partners. 1985 Keeneland July. 5 starts, 2 wins, $152,413, SW, Ire-G2.

$10,200,000 SNAAFI DANCER, 1982 c., Northern Dancer–My Bupers, by Bupers. Consignor: Crescent Farm; Buyer: Aston Upthorpe Stud, agent for Sheikh Mohammed bin Rashid al Maktoum. 1983 Keeneland July. Unraced.

$8,250,000 IMPERIAL FALCON, 1983 c., Northern Dancer–Ballade, by *Herbager. Consignor: Windfields Farm; Buyer: BBA (England), agent for Robert Sangster and partners. 1984 Keeneland July. 3 starts, 2 wins, $13,395.

$7,100,000 JAREER, 1983 c., Northern Dancer–Fabuleux Jane, by *Le Fabuleux. Consignor: Bruce Hundley, agent for Ralph C. Wilson Jr.; Buyer: Darley Stud Management. 1984 Keeneland July. 9 starts, 1 win, $5,591.

$7,000,000 LAA ETAAB, 1984 c., Nijinsky II–Crimson Saint, by Crimson Satan. Consignor: Tom Gentry; Buyer: Gainsborough Farm. 1985 Keeneland July. Unraced.

$6,800,000 TASMANIAN TIGER, 1999 c., Storm Cat–Hum Along, by Fappiano. Consignor: Lane's End, agent; Buyer: Demi O'Byrne. 2000 Keeneland September. 3 starts, 1 win, $10,665 in Ireland.

$6,500,000 AMJAAD, 1983 c., Seattle Slew–Desiree, by Raise a Native. Consignor: Spendthrift Farm, agent for Mr. and Mrs. Louis E. Wolfson and Mrs. Ethel D. Jacobs; Buyer: Darley Stud Management. 1984 Keeneland July. 4 starts, unplaced.

$6,400,000 **VAN NISTELROOY**, 2000 c., Storm Cat–Halory, by Halo. Consignor: Lane's End, agent for Stonerside Stable; Buyer: Demi O'Byrne. 2001 Keeneland September. 6 starts, 3 wins, $229,980 in England, Ireland, and North America, SW, Ire-G2.

$5,500,000 ALAJWAD, 2000, c., Storm Cat–La Affirmed, by Affirmed. Consignor: Eaton Sales, agent; Buyer: John Ferguson Bloodstock. 2001 Keeneland September. 1 start, 0 wins, $1,348.

$5,400,000 OBLIGATO, 1983 c., Northern Dancer–Truly Bound, by In Reality. Consignor: Windfields Farm; Buyer: BBA (Ireland), agent for Robert Sangster and partners. 1984 Keeneland July. 2 starts, unplaced.

$5,300,000 KING'S CONSUL, 1999 c., Kingmambo–Battle Creek Girl, by His Majesty. Consignor: Lane's End, agent; Buyer: John Ferguson Bloodstock. 2000 Keeneland September. 1 start, 1 win, $24,600 in England and North America.

$5,100,000 **WASSL TOUCH**, 1983 c., Northern Dancer–Queen Sucree, by *Ribot. Consignor: North Ridge Farm; Buyer: Darley Stud Management. 1984 Keeneland July. 6 starts, 3 wins, $30,168, SW.

$4,600,000 PARLANDO, 1983 c., Northern Dancer–Bubbling, by Stage Door Johnny. Consignor: Wild Oak Plantation; Buyer: BBA (Ireland), agent for Robert Sangster and partners. 1984 Fasig-Tipton Saratoga. Unraced.

$4,600,000 PROFESSOR BLUE, 1983 c., Northern Dancer–Mississippi Mud, by Delta Judge. Consignor: Lane's End; Buyer: BBA (England), agent for Stavros Niarchos. 1984 Keeneland July. 7 starts, placed, $5,171.

$4,400,000 MOON'S WHISPER, 1999 f., Storm Cat–East of the Moon, by Private Account. Consignor: Lane's End; Buyer: Shadwell Estate Co. Ltd. 2000 Keeneland September. Unraced.

$4,400,000 **Shah Jehan**, 1999 c., Mr. Prospector–Voodoo Lily, by Baldski. Consignor: Lane's End, agent; Buyer: Demi O'Byrne. 2000 Keeneland September. 20 starts, 2 wins, $158,457 in U.S., Ireland, England, and France, spl, G3.

$4,250,000 **EMPIRE GLORY**, 1981 c., Nijinsky II–Spearfish, by Fleet Nasrullah. Consignor: Glencoe Farm; Buyer: BBA (Ireland). 1982 Keeneland July. 6 starts, 2 wins, $35,420, SW, Ire-G3.

$4,250,000 FOXBORO, 1982 c., Northern Dancer–Desert Vixen, by In Reality. Consignor: North Ridge Farm; Buyer: BBA (England), agent for Robert Sangster and partners. 1983 Keeneland July. 1 start, unplaced.

$4,200,000 DISTINCTION, 1999 c., Seattle Slew–Omi, by Wild Again. Consignor: Double Diamond Farm; Buyer: David J. Shimmon. 2000 Fasig-Tipton Saratoga. 11 starts, 1 win, $41,878.

$4,100,000	**GALLANT ARCHER**, 1982 c., Nijinsky II–Belle of Dodge Me, by Creme dela Creme. Consignor: E. A. Seltzer and Parlina; Buyer: Aston Upthorpe Stud, agent for Sheikh Mohammed bin Rashid al Maktoum. 1983 Keeneland July. 16 starts, 5 wins, $294,477, SW, G3.
$4,000,000	**ELNAWAAGI**, 1983 c., Roberto–Gurkhas Band, by Lurullah. Consignor: Keswick Stables; Buyer: Darley Stud Management. 1984 Fasig-Tipton Saratoga. 11 starts, 4 wins, $23,607, SW.
$4,000,000	**FUSAICHI PEGASUS**, 1997 c., Mr. Prospector–Angel Fever, by Danzig. Consignor: Stone Farm, agent; Buyer: Fusao Sekiguchi. 1998 Keeneland July. 9 starts, 6 wins, $1,994,400, SW, G1.
$4,000,000	**SHOWLADY**, 1999 f., Theatrical (Ire)–Claxton's Slew, by Seattle Slew. Consignor: Brookside Farms; Buyer: John Ferguson Bloodstock. 2000 Keeneland September. 6 starts, 2 wins, $158,640, SW.
$4,000,000	**WARHOL**, 2000 c., Saint Ballado–Charm a Gendarme, by Batonnier. Consignor: Taylor Made Sales Agency, agent; Buyer: Demi O'Byrne. 2000 Keeneland July. 3 starts, placed in Ireland, $6,125.
$3,900,000	DUBAI TO DUBAI, 1998 c., Kris S.–Mr. P's Princess, by Mr. Prospector. Consignor: Harold Harrison; Buyer: John Ferguson Bloodstock. 1999 Keeneland September. 11 starts, 3 wins, $152,319 in U.S. and UAE.
$3,800,000	HOYER, 2000 c., Mr. Prospector–Destination Mir, by Cherokee Colony. Consignor: Lazy E Ranch; Buyer: John Ferguson Bloodstock. 2000 Keeneland September. Unraced.
$3,750,000	ALCHAASIBIYEH, 1983 f., Seattle Slew–Fine Prospect, by Mr. Prospector. Consignor: Spendthrift Farm; Buyer: Darley Stud Management. 1984 Keeneland July. 6 starts, placed, $2,098.
$3,700,000	**WARRSHAN**, 1986 c., Northern Dancer–Secret Asset, by Graustark. Consignor: Hermitage Farm; Buyer: Darley Stud Management. 1987 Keeneland July. 11 starts, 4 wins, $125,928, SW, Eng-G3.
$3,700,000	VIRTUOSA, 2000 f., Seeking the Gold–Escena, by Strawberry Road (Aus). Consignor: Denali Stud, agent for Falls Creek Farm; Buyer: Reynolds Bell, agent. 2000 Keeneland July. Unraced.

North American Top-Priced Weanlings

$2,500,000	**MAGIC OF LIFE**, 1985 f., Seattle Slew–Larida, by Northern Dancer. Consignor: Newstead Farm Trust. Buyer: British Bloodstock Agency (England). 1985 Newstead Farm Trust Dispersal. 9 starts, 4 wins, $254,841, SW, Eng-G1.
$2,300,000	GHASHTAH, 1987 f., Nijinsky II–My Charmer, by Poker. Consignor: Hermitage Farm. Buyer: Shadwell Estate Co. Ltd. 1987 Warner L. Jones Jr. Dispersal. Unraced.
$1,500,000	**KING CHARLEMAGNE**, 1998 c., Nureyev–Race the Wild Wind, by Sunny's Halo. Consignor: Ashford Stud, agent. Buyer: Demi O'Byrne. 1998 Keeneland November. 6 starts, 5 wins, $200,211, SW, Fr-G1, Eng-G3, Ire-G3.
$1,450,000	**Juniper**, 1998 c., Danzig–Montage, by Alydar. Consignor: Taylor Made Sales Agency, agent. Buyer: Demi O'Byrne. 1998 Keeneland November. 6 starts, 1 win, $37,214, spl, Eng-G2.
$1,400,000	WINTHROP, 1996 c., Storm Cat–Tinnitus, by Restless Wind. Consignor: John R. Gaines Thoroughbreds, agent. Buyer: Demi O'Byrne. 1996 Keeneland November. Unraced.
$1,400,000	RESTORATION, 1999 c., Sadler's Wells–Madame Est Sortie (Fr), by Longleat. Consignor: Eaton Sales, agent for Padua Stables. Buyer: M. W. Miller III, agent. 1999 Keeneland November. Unraced.
$1,300,000	NEW TRIESTE, 1999 c., A.P. Indy–Lovlier Linda, by Vigors. Consignor: John R. Gaines Thoroughbreds, agent. Buyer: Paul Shanahan. 1999 Keeneland November. 1 start, unplaced, $1,500.
$1,200,000	**Net Dancer**, 1989 f., Nureyev–Doubles Partner, by Damascus. Consignor: Bruce Hundley, agent for Ralph C. Wilson Jr. and Oxford Stable. Buyer: E. Hudson. 1989 Keeneland November. 13 starts, 2 wins, $46,225, spl.
$1,200,000	TIDE CAT, 1998 f., Storm Cat–Maytide, by Naskra. Consignor: John R. Gaines Thoroughbreds, agent. Buyer: Brad Martin, agent for 505 Farms. 1998 Keeneland November. Unraced.
$1,200,000	SHE'S A BEAUTY, 2000 f., Storm Cat–Now That's Funny, by Saratoga Six. Consignor: Gaines-Gentry Thoroughbreds. Buyer: Timothy Hyde. 2000 Keeneland November. 3 starts, placed, $1,772 in Ireland.
$1,175,000	**RAZEEN**, 1987 c., Northern Dancer–Secret Asset, by Graustark. Consignor: Hermitage Farm. Buyer: Darley Stud Management. 1987 Warner L. Jones Jr. Dispersal. 9 starts, 3 wins, $106,665, SW, Ind-G2.
$1,150,000	A. P. PETAL, 2000 f., A.P. Indy–Golden Petal, by Mr. Prospector Consignor: Taylor Made Sales Agency, agent. Buyer: B. Wayne Hughes. 2000 Keeneland November. Unraced.
$1,100,000	**WOROOD**, 1985 f., *Vaguely Noble–Farouche, by Northern Dancer. Consignor: Newstead Farm Trust. Buyer: British Bloodstock Agency (England). 1985 Newstead Farm Trust Dispersal. 16 starts, 3 wins, $82,067, SW, Fr.
$1,100,000	**HOLD THAT TIGER**, 2000 c., Storm Cat–Beware of the Cat, by Caveat. Consignor: Lane's End, agent for Ten Broeck Farm. Buyer: Demi O'Byrne. 2000 Keeneland November. 5 starts, 3 wins, $400,907, SW, Fr-G1.
$1,050,000	**SEASIDE ATTRACTION**, 1987 f., Seattle Slew–Kamar, by Key to the Mint. Consignor: Hermitage Farm. Buyer: Monty Hinton. 1987 Warner L. Jones Jr. Dispersal. 12 starts, 4 wins, $272,541, SW, G1.
$1,050,000	WILDCAT QUEEN, 2000 f., Storm Cat–Jetapat, by Tri Jet. Consignor: Brereton C. Jones, agent. Buyer: Bradley and Bowden, agent. 2000 Keeneland November. 1 start, 1 win, $20,400.
$1,000,000	SWISS DESERT, 1989 c., Danzig–Strictly Raised, by Raise a Native. Consignor: Bruce Hundley, agent for Kentucky Select Bloodstock and Kentucky Heritage Thoroughbred Breeding Partners. Buyer: Gainsborough Farm. 1989 Keeneland November. Unraced.
$1,000,000	BLISSFUL, 1996 f., Mr. Prospector–Angel Fever, by Danzig. Consignor: Stone Farm, agent. Buyer: J. B. & B. Stables. 1996 Keeneland November. 3 starts, unplaced, $3,240.
$1,000,000	LEMON TART, 1998 f., Deputy Minister–Lemon Dove, by Forty Niner. Consignor: Hill 'n' Dale Sales Agency, agent. Buyer: Brushwood Stable. 1998 Keeneland November. 4 starts, unplaced, $2,460.
$1,000,000	MALIBU KAREN, 1998 f., Seeking the Gold–Regent's Walk, by Vice Regent. Consignor: Claiborne Farm, agent for Edward A. Cox Jr. Buyer: B. Wayne Hughes. 1998 Keeneland November. 5 starts, placed twice, $18,490.
$1,000,000	PRINCESS ATOOSA, 1998 f., Gone West–Kooyonga (Ire), by Persian Bold. Consignor: Eaton Sales, agent. Buyer: Brushwood Stable. 1998 Keeneland November. Unraced.

North American Top-Priced Two-Year-Olds

$2,700,000	SWIFT SECRET, 2001 c., Sea of Secrets–Swift Spirit, by Tasso. Consignor: Sequel Bloodstock, agent. Buyer: Charles Fipke. 2003 Barretts March. Unraced.
$2,000,000	LA SALLE STREET, 1997 c., Not for Love–Three Grand, by Assert (Ire). Consignor: H. T. Stables, agent, for Cam Allard. Buyer: Demi O'Byrne. 1999 Keeneland April. 3 starts, placed, $3,420.
$2,000,000	MOROCCO, 1997 c., Brocco–Roll Over Baby, by Rollin On Over. Consignor: Sequel Bloodstock, agent. Buyer: The Thoroughbred Corp. 1999 Barretts March. 15 starts, 4 wins, $133,640.
$2,000,000	GOTHAM CITY, 1998 c., Saint Ballado–What a Reality, by In Reality. Consignor: Jerry Bailey Sales Agency. Buyer: David J. Shimmon. 2000 Barretts March. 2 starts, unplaced, $2,880.
$1,950,000	YONAGUSKA, 1998 c., Cherokee Run–Marital Spook, by Silver Ghost. Consignor: Niall Brennan Stables, agent. Buyer: Demi O'Byrne. 2000 Fasig-Tipton Florida February. 18 starts, 6 wins, $536,355, SW, G1.
$1,900,000	ATLANTIC OCEAN, 2000 f., Stormy Atlantic–Super Chef, by Seattle Slew. Consignor: Chapman Farms. Buyer: The Thoroughbred Corp. 2001 Barretts March. 11 starts, 5 wins, $508,820, SW, G3.
$1,650,000	HARMONY LODGE, 1998 f., Hennessy–Win Crafty Lady, by Crafty Prospector. Consignor: Eddie Woods, agent. Buyer: Eugene Melnyk. 2000 Fasig-Tipton Florida February. 13 starts, 6 wins, $298,820, SW, G3.
$1,400,000	WAR OFFICE, 2001 c., Tale of the Cat–Satin Sunrise, by Mr. Leader. Consignor: Robert N. Scanlon, agent. Buyer: Demi O'Byrne. 2003 Fasig-Tipton Florida February. Unraced.
$1,300,000	MINSTRESS, 1983 f., The Minstrel–Fleet Victress, by *King of the Tudors. Consignor: Newstead Farm Trust. Buyer: W. S. Farish. 1985 Newstead Farm Trust Dispersal. 19 starts, 5 wins, $147,399, SW.
$1,250,000	LOCHLIN SLEW, 1997 f., Seattle Slew–Lochlin, by Screen King. Consignor: M. W. Miller III, agent. Buyer: B. Wayne Hughes. 1999 Keeneland April. Unraced.
$1,250,000	LE CHAT, 1998 c., Storm Cat–Adorable Micol, by Riverman. Consignor: Hartley/De Renzo Thoroughbreds, agent. Buyer: John Moynihan, agent. 2000 Fasig-Tipton Florida February. 3 starts, 1 win, $28,470.
$1,200,000	TASK, 1996 f., Mr. Prospector–Department, by Secretariat. Consignor: Claiborne Farm and Nicole Perry Gorman. Buyer: Course Investment. 1998 Keeneland January. 3 starts, unplaced, $405.
$1,200,000	DANCE MASTER, 1997 c., Gone West–Nijinsky's Lover, by Nijinsky II. Consignor: Jerry Bailey Sales Agency. Buyer: Padua Stables. 1999 Barretts March. 19 starts, 4 wins, $196,455, SW, G2.
$1,100,000	SCATMANDU, 1995 c., Storm Cat–Princess Alydar, by Alydar. Consignor: Jerry Bailey Sales Agency, agent, for Bailey-Ellenberg Select. Buyer: John C. Kimmel, agent. 1997 Barretts March. 16 starts, 6 wins, $330,789, SW, G3.
$1,100,000	I'M PERSUADED, 1997 c., Deputy Minister–The Way We Were, by Avatar. Consignor: The Kindergarten Farm, agent. Buyer: Narvick International. 1999 Keeneland April. 7 starts, 1 win, $38,900.
$1,100,000	PRATHER, 1997 c., Brocco–Dazzling Dixie, by Dixieland Band. Consignor: Welcome Gate Farm, agent. Buyer: Aaron and Marie Jones. 1999 Fasig-Tipton Florida February. Unraced.

North American Top-Priced Broodmares

$7,000,000	MISS OCEANA, 1981, Alydar–Kittiwake, by *Sea-Bird. (Northern Dancer). Consignor: Newstead Farm Trust. Buyer: Foxfield. 1985 Newstead Farm Trust mixed sale.
$7,000,000	KORVEYA, 1982, Riverman–Konafa, by Damascus. (Woodman). Consignor: Claiborne Farm, agent. Buyer: Reynolds Bell Jr., agent. 1998 Keeneland November.
$6,000,000	PRICELESS FAME, 1975, Irish Castle–Comely Nell, by Commodore M. (Seattle Slew). Consignor: Highclere, agent for Joseph O. Morrissey. Buyer: Darley Stud Management. 1984 Fasig-Tipton Kentucky November.
$5,500,000	PRINCESS ROONEY, 1980, Verbatim–Parrish Princess, by Drone. (Danzig). Consignor: Stone Farm agent. Buyer: Wichita Equine. 1985 Keeneland November.
$5,400,000	LIFE'S MAGIC, 1981, Cox's Ridge–Fire Water, by Tom Rolfe. (Mr. Prospector). Consignor: Mel Hatley Racing Stables, agent. Buyer: Eugene V. Klein. 1986 Keeneland November.
$5,400,000	LADY'S SECRET, 1982, Secretariat–Great Lady M., by Icecapade. Consignor: D. Wayne Lukas, agent for Eugene V. Klein. Buyer: Fasig-Tipton Bloodstock, agent. 1987 Night of the Stars, Fasig-Tipton Kentucky November.
$5,250,000	PRODUCER, 1976, Nashua–*Marion, by Tantieme. (Northern Dancer). Consignor: Walnut Green, agent for Carelaine Stable. Buyer: BBA (England). 1983 Keeneland November
$5,000,000	MACKIE, 1993, Summer Squall–Glowing Tribute, by Graustark. (Mr. Prospector). Consignor: Eaton Sales, agent. Buyer: Britton House Stud. 2000 Keeneland January.
$4,900,000	JEWEL PRINCESS, 1992, Key to the Mint–Jewell Ridge, by Melyno (Ire). (Storm Cat). Consignor: Lane's End, agent. Buyer: John Magnier. 2000 Keeneland November.
$4,700,000	DANCE DESIGN (IRE), 1993, Sadler's Well–Elegance in Design (Ire), by Habitat. (A.P. Indy). Consignor: Eaton Sales, agent for Padua Stables. Buyer: Hugo Lascelles, agent. 1999 Keeneland November.
$4,700,000	CATCHASCATCHCAN (GB), 1995, Pursuit of Love–Catawba, by Mill Reef. (Danzig). Consignor: Claiborne Farm, agent. Buyer: Lyons Demesne. 2000 Keeneland November.
$4,600,000	IT'S IN THE AIR, 1976, Mr. Prospector–A Wind Is Rising, by Francis S. (Seattle Slew). Consignor: Hill 'n' Dale Sales Agency. Buyer: Darley Stud Management. 1984 Keeneland November.
$4,600,000	WINGLET, 1988, Alydar–Highest Trump, by Bold Bidder. (Storm Cat). Consignor: Lane's End, agent for Brookside Farms. Buyer: John Magnier. 1999 Keeneland November.
$4,600,000	MYHRR, 1997, Mr. Prospector–Miesque, by Nureyev. Consignor: Lane's End, agent. Buyer: Reynolds Bell Jr., agent. 2000 Keeneland November.
$4,500,000	TWO RINGS, 1970, Round Table–Allofthem, by Bagdad. (Nijinsky II). Consignor: Mint Lane Farm, agent for Kinghaven Farms. Buyer: Due Process Stable. 1983 Keeneland November.
$4,500,000	ESTRAPADE, 1980, *Vaguely Noble–Klepto, by No Robbery. Consignor: Blue Grass Farm, agent. Buyer: Allen E. Paulson. 1985 Keeneland November.

Record Prices, Mixed Accomplishment

Public interest in record prices paid for Thoroughbreds at public auction soared in the 1970s and '80s, when the record price for a yearling racing prospect exceeded $1-million. Yet there has always been a record-priced yearling ever since the first yearling was sold. Just when that may have been, no one can say with certainty, but the first really famous record-priced yearling was Sceptre, a lovely brown filly foaled in 1899 at the Duke of Westminster's Eaton Stud in England. Breeder and owner of *Ormonde, the greatest racehorse of the 19th century, and his grandson Flying Fox, winner of the Triple Crown in the year of Sceptre's birth, the Duke died late in 1899, forcing the dispersal of his bloodstock.

Sceptre, by the great Persimmon out of *Ormonde's full sister Ornament, by Bend Or, and with the looks to match her purple pedigree, came up for sale in 1900 at the Tattersalls Newmarket July sale, then one of the two most important auctions in England. Victorian England was scandalized when the gambler Robert Sievier outbid the late Duke's son and heir to acquire Sceptre for 10,000 guineas ($51,133 at the contemporary exchange rate).

Sceptre proved more than worth the price, though her racing career was somewhat scarred by the roller-coaster fortunes of Sievier, who won and lost fortunes betting on horses and cards for the two years he owned her. Sometimes training the great filly himself, Sievier could not resist attempting betting coups with Sceptre, running her in inappropriate races, such as the Lincolnshire Handicap against older males in her first start at three. Sceptre overcame such abuse, winning four of the five English classics of 1902 (she finished fourth in the Epsom Derby), and is still acclaimed as one of the greatest racemares of all time.

Sceptre's successors as world-record-priced yearlings have never achieved quite the same level of fame or accomplishment, but overall the race records of the 21 successive record-priced yearlings have been quite good. Of the 21 listed in the accompanying chart, five (including Sceptre) have become champions or classic winners, and four more won recognized stakes races. Thus, nine of the 21 record-priced yearlings listed, or 42.9%, were stakes winners, which is far superior to the breed average of about 3%.

On the other hand, only two, Sceptre and Majestic Prince, recaptured their purchase price in purse money on the racecourse, and there were certainly some very expensive total failures. Hustle On, who wrested the record away from the English (though he himself was American-bred only by virtue of his dam being imported while carrying him), never raced. His immediate successor, New Broom, could not win in nine starts, the same dismal record as the $1.6-million Hoist the King.

Perhaps the saddest tale of any record-priced yearling though, is that of Colonel Payne, the Fairway colt out of Golden Hair, by Golden Sun, purchased for 15,000 guineas ($78,278) by Dorothy Paget at Tattersalls Doncaster yearling sale in 1936. An eccentric English-born granddaughter of William C. Whitney, founder of the Whitney family's bloodstock empire, Paget generally refused to grant her horses a name until they had won a race, a practice then permissible under English rules. Colts that failed to meet her standards, she habitually had shot.

The Golden Hair colt ran with promise in his only outing at two, finishing third in the National Breeders' Produce Stakes, then the richest two-year-old race in England. Unfortunately, he proved to be the victim of his owner's eccentricities and never reappeared on the racecourse or anywhere else.—*John P. Sparkman*

Progression of Top-Priced Yearlings

Price	Year	Horse, Sex, Breeding	Sale	Consignor	Buyer	Race record
$13,100,000	1985	SEATTLE DANCER c., Nijinsky II–My Charmer	Keeneland July	Warner L. Jones Jr.	BBA England (agent for Robert Sangster)	5-2-1-1, $152,413 Gallinule S. (Ire-G2) etc.
10,200,000	1983	SNAAFI DANCER c., Northern Dancer–My Bupers	Keeneland July	Crescent Farm	Aston Upthorpe Stud (Sheikh Mohammed bin Rashid al Maktoum)	unraced
4,250,000	1982	EMPIRE GLORY c., Nijinsky II–Spearfish	Keeneland July	Glencoe Farm	BBA Ireland (agent for Robert Sangster)	6-2-2-2, $35,420, Royal Whip S. (Ire-G3) etc.
3,500,000	1981	BALLYDOYLE c., Northern Dancer–South Ocean	Keeneland July	Windfields Farm	BBA Ireland (agent for Robert Sangster)	4-1-1-0, $2,542
1,700,000	1980	LICHINE c., Lyphard–Stylish Genie	Keeneland July	Carelaine Farm, Getty, Riordan, Heerman, agent	BBA England (agent for Stavros Niarchos)	16-3-1-4, $71,527, Prix de Suresnes etc.
1,600,000	1979	HOIST THE KING c., Hoist the Flag–Royal Dowry	Keeneland July	Tom Gentry	Kazuo Nakamura	9-0-1-1, $6,977
1,500,000	1976	CANADIAN BOUND c., Secretariat–Charming Alibi	Keeneland July	Bluegrass Farm	Blue Meadows Farm, agent (Ted Burnett, John Sikura, and partners)	4-0-1-0, $4,769
625,000	1974	KENTUCKY GOLD c., Raise a Native–Gold Digger	Keeneland July	Spendthrift Farm	Wallace A. Gilroy	7-1-0-3, $5,950
600,000	1973	WAJIMA c., Bold Ruler–*Iskra	Keeneland July	Claiborne Farm	James A. Scully (agent for Zenya Yoshida and partners)	16-9-5-0, $537,837, Champion 3-year-old male, Travers S. (G1) etc.

Price	Year	Horse, Sex, Breeding	Sale	Consignor	Buyer	Race record
510,000	1970	CROWNED PRINCE c., Raise a Native–Gay Hostess	Keeneland July	Spendthrift Farm	Frank McMahon	4-2-0-0, $37,883, champion 2-year-old in England, Dewhurst S., etc.
250,000	1967	MAJESTIC PRINCE c., Raise a Native–Gay Hostess	Keeneland July	Spendthrift Farm	Frank McMahon	10-9-1-0, $414,200, Kentucky Derby, Preakness S., etc.
200,000	1966	BOLD DISCOVERY c., Bold Ruler–La Dauphine	Keeneland July	Spendthrift Farm	Frank McMahon	3-0-0-0, $0
170,000	1964	ONE BOLD BID c., Bold Ruler–Forgetmenow	Keeneland July	Warner L. Jones Jr.	Mrs. Velma Morrison	unraced
130,000	1961	SWAPSON c., Swaps–Obedient	Keeneland July	Spendthrift Farm	John M. Olin	31-8-3-5, $26,766
118,492 (15,000g)	1945	SAYAJIRAO c., Nearco–Rosy Legend	Tattersalls Doncaster	Sir Eric Ohlson	Gaekwar of Baroda	16-6-6-3, $96,647, champion (28,000g) 3-year-old in England, St. Leger S. etc.
78,278 (15,000g)	1936	Colonel Payne c., Fairway–Golden Hair	Tattersalls Doncaster	Viscount Furness	Dorothy Paget	1-0-0-1, $494, 3rd National Breeders' Produce S.
75,000	1928	NEW BROOM c., Whisk Broom II–Payment	Fasig-Tipton Saratoga	Mrs. T. J. Regan	C.V.B. Cushman	9-0-2-1, $275
60,000	1927	HUSTLE ON c., Hurry On–*Fatima II	Fasig-Tipton Saratoga	Himyar Stud	W. R. Coe	unraced
55,724 (14,500g)	1920	BLUE ENSIGN c., The Tetrarch–Blue Tit	Tattersalls Doncaster	Sledmere Stud	Lord Glanely	1-0-0-0, $0
53,492 (11,500g)	1919	WESTWARD HO c., Swynford–Blue Tit	Tattersalls Doncaster	Sledmere Stud	Lord Glanely	6-2-0-0, $3,989, Great Yorkshire S., 3rd St. Leger S.
51,133 (10,000g)	1900	SCEPTRE f., Persimmon–Ornament	Tattersalls Newmarket July	Estate of Duke of Westminster	Robert Sevier	25-13-4-4, $192,544 champion 3-year-old, champion older horse, Epsom Oaks etc.

Top-Priced Yearlings by Year

High-priced yearlings have a poor reputation in the Thoroughbred industry. Although statistics show that, on average, the higher the price paid for a yearling the better the racehorse, high-priced failures such as the $10.2-million Snaafi Dancer, who never raced, are remembered more readily than success stories such as the $2.9-million Horse of the Year A.P. Indy. Even the world's record-priced yearling, the $13.1-million Seattle Dancer, is regarded as a failure though he won at Group 2 level in Europe.

In the years since Fasig-Tipton first began selling yearlings at Saratoga, 24 of the 92 top-priced yearlings each year (there were six ties) have become stakes winners. That 26% strike rate is obviously far higher than the 3% average of stakes winners to foals for the breed.

Yearling buyers appear to have greatly improved their selection techniques over the last few decades. The record of top-priced yearlings for the first half of the 20th century was little better than that of the average horse. But in the 36 years since 1969 Kentucky Derby winner Majestic Prince sold for $250,000 at Keeneland July in 1967, 15 year-toppers have become stakes winners. —*John P. Sparkman*

Most Expensive North American Yearlings by Year

Year	Horse	Sex, Breeding	Price	Sale	Buyer	Race Record
2002	ONE COOL CAT	c., Storm Cat—Tacha	$3,100,000	Kee July	Demi O'Byrne	1-0-0-0, $662
2001	VAN NISTELROOY	c., Storm Cat—Halory	6,400,000	Kee Sept	Demi O'Byrne	6-3-1-1, $229,980, †† EBF Futurity S. (Ire-G2) etc.
2000	TASMANIAN TIGER	c., Storm Cat—Hum Along	6,800,000	Kee Sept	Demi O'Byrne	14-2-0-1, $67,201
1999	DUBAI TO DUBAI	c., Kris S.—Mr. P's Princess	3,900,000	Kee Sept	John Ferguson Bldstk.	11-3-1-2, $152,319
1998	FUSAICHI PEGASUS	c., Mr. Prospector—Angel Fever	4,000,000	Kee July	Fusao Sekiguchi	9-6-2-0, $1,994,400, Kentucky Derby (G1), etc.
1997	SASHA'S PROSPECT	c., Mr. Prospector—Missy's Mirage	2,300,000	Kee Sept	Padua Stables	10-1-0-0, $37,200
1996	PARGATA KING	c., Storm Cat—Alpargata	1,700,000	Kee July	Fusao Sekiguchi	1-0-0-0, $0
1995	CONSTANT WISH	f., Mr. Prospector—Daring Bidder	1,250,000	Kee July	Demi O'Byrne	unraced
1994	Golden Colors	f., Mr. Prospector—Winning Colors	1,050,000	Kee July	Pegasus Bloodstock	10-3-1-0, $509,963, 2nd Daily Hai Queen Cup
1993	GOLDEN LEGEND	c., Mr. Prospector—Reminiscing	1,050,000	Kee July	John R. Gaines, agt.	6-0-0-0, $5,700
1992	NUMEROUS	c., Mr. Prospector—Number	1,700,000	Kee July	Finney Bloodstock, agt.	18-4-2-2, $255,348, Derby Trial S. (G3) etc.
1991	JEUNE HOMME	c., Nureyev—Alydariel	2,600,000	Kee July	Morio Sakurai	20-4-5-3, $431,724, Citation H. (G2), etc.

Year	Horse	Sex, Breeding	Price	Sale	Buyer	Race Record
1990	A.P. INDY	c., Seattle Slew—Weekend Surprise	2,900,000	Kee July	BBA (Ire)	11-8-0-1, $2,979,815, Horse of the Year, champion 3yo male, Breeders' Cup Classic (G1), etc.
1989	NORTHERN PARK	c., Northern Dancer—Mrs. Penny	2,800,000	Kee July	Zenya Yoshida	30-4-7-4, $171,493, Grand Prix de Villeurbanne
1988	ROYAL ACADEMY	c., Nijinsky II—Crimson Saint	3,500,000	Kee July	Vincent O'Brien	7-4-2-0, $758,994, European Hwt. at 3, 7-9½ f., Breeders' Cup Mile (G1) etc.
1987	WARRSHAN	c., Northern Dancer—Secret Asset	3,700,000	Kee July	Darley Stud Mgt.	11-4-0-3, $125,928, Gordon S. (Eng-G3) etc.
1986	NORTHERN STATE	c., Northern Dancer—South Ocean	3,600,000	Kee July	Darley Stud Mgt.	4-1-0-0, $2,137
1985	SEATTLE DANCER	c., Nijinsky II—My Charmer	13,100,000	Kee July	BBA (Eng), agt. for Robert Sangster	5-2-1-1, $152,413, Gallinule S. (Ire-G2) etc.
1984	IMPERIAL FALCON	c., Northern Dancer—Ballade	8,250,000	Kee July	BBA (Eng)	3-2-0-0, $13,395
1983	SNAAFI DANCER	c., Northern Dancer—My Bupers	10,200,000	Kee July	Aston Upthorpe Stud	unraced
1982	EMPIRE GLORY	c., Nijinsky II—Spearfish	4,250,000	Kee July	BBA (Ire), agt. for Robert Sangster	6-2-2-2, $35,420, Royal Whip S. (Ire-G3) etc.
1981	BALLYDOYLE	c., Northern Dancer—South Ocean	3,500,000	Kee July	BBA (Ire), agt. for Robert Sangster	4-1-1-0, $2,542
1980	LICHINE	c., Lyphard—Stylish Genie	1,700,000	Kee July	BBA (Eng), agt. for Stavros Niarchos	16-3-1-4, $71,527, Prix de Suresnes etc.
1979	HOIST THE KING	c., Hoist the Flag—Royal Dowry	1,600,000	Kee July	Kazuo Nakamura	9-0-1-1, $6,977
1978	NUREYEV	c., Northern Dancer—Special	1,300,000	Kee July	BBA (Eng)	3-2-0-0, $42,522, champion miler in France, Prix Thomas Bryon (Fr-G3) etc.
1977	FOREIGN SECRETARY	c., Secretariat—Lady Victoria	725,000	Kee July	BBA (Ire)	11-3-1-1, $47,375
1976	CANADIAN BOUND	c., Secretariat—Charming Alibi	1,500,000	Kee July	Blue Meadows Farm, agt.	4-0-1-0, $4,769
1975	ELEGANT PRINCE	c., Raise a Native—Gay Hostess	715,000	Kee July	Franklin Groves	unraced
1974	KENTUCKY GOLD	c., Raise a Native—Gold Digger	625,000	Kee July	Wallace A. Gilroy	7-1-0-3, $5,950
1973	WAJIMA	c., Bold Ruler—*Iskra	600,000	Kee July	James A. Scully, agt. for Zenya Yoshida & partners	16-9-5-0, $537,837, champion 3-year-old male, Travers S. (G1) etc.
1972	Riboquill	c., *Ribot—Quill	230,000	Kee July	Cromwell Bloodstock	11-3-1-1, $46,875, 3rd Grand Prix de Deauville (Fr-G2)
1971	PASS	c., Buckpasser—*Casaque Grise	235,000	FT Sara	Marion duPont Scott	unraced
1970	CROWNED PRINCE	c., Raise a Native—Gay Hostess	510,000	Kee July	Frank McMahon	4-2-0-0, $37,883, champion two-year-old in Eng., Dewhurst S. etc.
1969	KNIGHTS HONOR	c., Round Table—Vestment	210,000	Kee July	Bert W. Martin	4-0-1-1, $1,670
1968	REINE ENCHANTEUR	f., *Sea-Bird—*Libra	405,000	Kee July	W. P. Rosso	7-1-1-5, $9,305
1967	MAJESTIC PRINCE	c., Raise a Native—Gay Hostess	250,000	Kee July	Frank McMahon	10-9-1-0, $414,200, Kentucky Derby, Preakness S., etc.
1966	BOLD DISCOVERY	c., Bold Ruler—La Dauphine	200,000	Kee July	Frank McMahon	3-0-0-0, $0
1965	ROYAL MATCH	f., *Turn-to—Cosmah	140,000	Kee July	Arnold Winick, agt.	unraced
1964	ONE BOLD BID	c., Bold Ruler—Forgetmenow	170,000	Kee July	Mrs. Velma Morrison	unraced
1963	LENSO	c., Swaps—*Blue Star II	85,000	Kee July	Leonard Sasso	5-0-0-1, $420
1962	GOLDEN GORSE	f., Swaps—*Auld Alliance	83,000	FT Sara	J. T. Skinner, agt.	2-0-0-2, $735
1961	SWAPSON	c., Swaps—Obedient	130,000	Kee July	John M. Olin	31-8-3-5, $26,766
1960	NASHOLIN	c., Nashua—*Pashmina	75,000	Kee July	N. McLeod	25-2-0-3, $7,955
1959	ROYAL DRAGOON	c., *Royal Charger—Grecian Queen	80,000	Kee July	C. G. Raible	9-1-2-1, $5,050
	GLOBEMASTER	c., *Heliopolis—No Strings	80,000	FT Sara	Penowa Farms	27-10-9-2, $355,423, Wood Memorial S., etc.
1958	PRINCE BLESSED	c., *Princequillo—Dog Blessed	77,000	Kee July	Kerr Stables	35-8-6-4, $255,805, Hollywood Gold Cup S. etc.
1957	LAW AND ORDER	c., *Nasrullah—In Bloom	65,000	Kee July	J. H. Rouse Farm, agt. for King Ranch	unraced
1956	*RISE 'N SHINE	c., Hyperion—Deodara	$87,000	FT Sara	Mrs. M. E. Lunn	43-4-2-1, $17,515
1955	TULSAN	c., *Nasrullah—In Bloom	80,000	Kee July	Forrest Lindsay Farm	25-2-2-3, $8,050
1954	NALUR	c., *Nasrullah—Lurline B	86,000	Kee July	F. J. Adams Syndicate	20-2-1-0, $6,575
1953	ROMAN BOAT	f., Roman—Boat	59,000	Kee July	Duntreath Farm	4-1-0-0, $1,950
1952	LADYBREATH	f., Roman—Miss Brief	46,000	Kee July	Chester Gates, agt.	7-1-0-0, $2,100
1951	PERFECTION	f., Bull Lea—Lady Lark	60,000	Kee July	C. S. Jones	31-3-4-4, $30,600, Playa del Rey S., etc.
1950	FARAHAAN	f., *Mahmoud—Aphaona	35,000	FT Sara	William Post	3-0-0-1, $725
1949	Unification	c., War Admiral—Summer Time	37,000	Kee July	William Helis	80-6-11-14, $24,015, 3rd Dominion Day H.
	OLD ROWLEY	c., Menow—Risk	37,000	Kee July	Moody Jolley, agt.	9-2-1-1, $5,275
1948	DESTINO	c., *Beau Pere—Sun Lady	52,000	FT Sara	King Ranch	7-0-4-1, $3,400

Year	Horse	Sex, Breeding	Price	Sale	Buyer	Race Record
1947	**Spotted Bull**	c., *Bull Dog—Spotted Beauty	45,000	Kee July	Jaclyn Stable	19-4-1-2, $12,850, 3rd Will Rogers H.
1946	LA CHICUELA	f., *Blenheim II—La Chica	54,000	Kee July	J. P. Smith	14-1-2-2, $4,100
	SILVER QUEEN	f., War Admiral—Danise M	54,000	Kee July	Maine Chance Farm	16-1-1-1, $3,650
1945	SIR GALLASCENE	c., *Sir Gallahad III—*Scenery II	46,000	Kee July	C. C. Tanner	54-1-5-3, $8,175
	BLUE FANTASY	f., Blue Larkspur—Risk	46,000	Kee July	Leslie Combs II, agt. for Elizabeth Nightingale Graham	unraced
1944	**COLONY BOY**	c., Eight Thirty—Heritage	46,000	Kee July	Leslie Combs II, agt. for Elizabeth Arden (Graham)	17-5-0-3, $39,750, Walden S., etc.
1943	PERICLES	c., *Blenheim II—Risk	66,000	FT Kee	William Helis	5-2-0-1, $5,200
1942	**BOY KNIGHT**	c., *Sir Gallahad III—Heloise	9,000	FT Sara	Crispin Oglebay	36-5-2-10, $44,145, Wilmington H., etc.
1941	BULRUSHES	c., *Bull Dog—Spur Flower	10,000	FT Sara	Ogden Phipps	196-25-40-33, $24,232
1940	REAPER'S BLADE	c., *Sickle—Friendly Gal	18,000	FT Sara	Brookmeade Stable	15-3-2-2, $3,425
1939	TOM-TOM	c., *Sir Gallahad III—Percussion	20,000	FT Sara	Manhasset Stable	unraced
	Lord Kitchener	c., *Blenheim II—Argosie	20,000	FT Sara	Samuel D. Riddle	38-4-5-7, $9,726, 3rd Travers S. etc.
1938	**Romanov**	c., *Ksar—Duration	22,000	FT Sara	Brookmeade Stable	28-2-3-3, $4,756, 3rd Lawrence Realization H.
1937	TEMULAC	c., *Sir Gallahad III—Marching Along	26,000	FT Sara	Calumet Farm	69-7-5-11, $6,732
1936	FARRELL	c., *Sir Gallahad III—Sari	18,000	FT Sara	Milky Way Farms	100-12-19-13, $9,999
1935	WINGED VICTORY	c., Victorian—Grief	13,000	FT Sara	Milky Way Farms	97-7-16-11, $7,130
1934	TEDDY BOY	c., *Teddy—Superstitious	11,500	FT Sara	Calumet Farm	32-1-3-5, $1,425
1933	**CALUMET DICK**	c., Gallant Fox—*Martha Snow	13,000	FT Sara	Calumet Farm	51-17-6-8, $72,515, Dixie H.
1932	THE TRIUMVIR	c., Pompey—Cowslip	14,500	FT Sara	Greentree Stable	176-12-15-15, $10,935
1931	CARRY THE NEWS	c., The Porter—Cypher Code	16,000	FT Sara	J. H. Whitney	20-1-3-6, $1,665
1930	TEXAS KNIGHT	c., *Sir Gallahad III—Fasnet	30,000	FT Sara	Three D's Stock Farm	82-8-5-11, $6,390
	GALA FLIGHT	f., *Sir Gallahad III—*Starflight	30,000	FT Sara	Griffin Watkins	25-3-0-4, $3,425
1929	**War**	c., Man o' War—Milky Way	45,000	FT Sara	Sagamore Stable	61-8-13-4, $8,280, 2nd Brookdale H.
1928	NEW BROOM	c., Whisk Broom II—Payment	75,000	FT Sara	C.V.B. Cushman	9-0-2-1, $275
1927	HUSTLE ON	c., Hurry On—*Fatima II	60,000	FT Sara	W. R. Coe	unraced
1926	TUSKEGEE	c., Black Toney—Humanity	35,000	FT Sara	E. M. Byers	43-10-7-8, $11,925 Belgrade Claiming S.
1925	WAR FEATHERS	c., Man o' War—*Tuscan Red	50,500	FT Sara	Hamilton Farms	7-1-10, $1,350
1924	BLASISTA	c., Eternal—*Aquamarine	16,000	FT Sara	William Zeigler Jr.	5-0-0-0, $0
1923	**FLYING EBONY**	c., The Finn—Princess Mary	21,000	FT Sara	G. A. Cochran	13-6-1-2, $62,420, Kentucky Derby, etc.
1922	THE TRAMP	c., The Finn—Kate Adams	12,500	FT Sara	Montfort Jones	1-0-0-0, $0
1921	COEUR DE LION	c., Fair Play—*Couronne de Laurier	8,600	FT Sara	Rancocas Stable	288-48-50-43, $33,165
1920	PIRATE GOLD	c., Rock View—Gold	14,000	FT Sara	Greentree Stable	157-20-34-20, $23,258
1919	SUN TURRET	c., Sunstar—Marian Hood	25,000	FT Sara	J.K.L. Ross	103-6-5-11, $3,855
1918	**Royal Jester**	c., Black Jester—*Primula II	14,500	FT Sara	J.K.L. Ross	33-1-9-7, $4,381, 2nd Earl Grey H., etc.
1917	*HURON	c., *Sweeper—Zuna	4,000	FT Sara	Joseph E. Widener	105-28-20-14, $17,131, Windon H., etc.
	THE SAINT	c., Sain—Nannette	4,000	FT Sara	Samuel D. Riddle	unraced

†† Through June 1, 2003

Leading Sires of Top-Priced Yearlings

Northern Dancer	7
Mr. Prospector	6
*Sir Gallahad III	6
Raise a Native	4
Storm Cat	4
*Blenheim II	3
Bold Ruler	3
*Nasrullah	3
Nijinsky II	3
Swaps	3

Leading Consignors of Top-Priced Yearlings

Arthur B. Hancock Sr.	12
Spendthrift Farm/ Leslie Combs II	9
Hermitage Farm/ Warner L. Jones	4
Lane's End	4
Windfields Farm	4
Claiborne Farm	3
Robert A. Fairbarn	3
Himyar Stud/Phil T. Chinn	3

Leading Buyers of Top-Priced Yearlings

British Bloodstock Agency (Ireland)	5
Demi O'Byrne	4
*Sheikh Mohammed bin Rashid al Maktoum	4
British Bloodstock Agency (England)	3
Greentree Stud	3
Maine Chance Farm/ Elizabeth Arden	3
Frank McMahon	3
Milky Way Farm	3

*Bought in the name of John Ferguson Bloodstock, Darley Stud Management, and Aston Upthorpe Stud

ORGANIZATIONS
Jockey Club

The Jockey Club, one of the Thoroughbred industry's most powerful organizations, derives much of its strength from its position as the registration agency for all North American Thoroughbreds and from an influential membership comprising most of the sport's leading breeders and owners. In its distant past, the Jockey Club also was a regulator of racing; today, it has utilized advancing computer technology to expand its role and influence.

The Jockey Club grew out of meetings in late 1893 in which leading owners addressed the question of how to reform an unruly and corrupt racing industry. Two years earlier, prominent owner Pierre Lorillard had founded the Board of Control, but it largely represented the interests of racetrack owners, many of whom also were leading owners of racehorses. Alarmed that the racetrack owners might reduce purses, James R. Keene and seven fellow owners and breeders met on December 23 and 27, 1893, in a New York hotel to form an organization that represented the interests of both racetracks and racehorse owners. The goals of the organization were "not only to encourage the development of the Thoroughbred horse, but to establish racing on such a footing that it may command the interests as well as the confidence and favorable position of the public."

The organization was formally incorporated on February 9, 1894, as the Jockey Club, taking its name from the foundation institution in England. John Hunter was the first chairman of the American organization.

Although the Jockey Club today maintains the *American Stud Book*, it did not set out in 1894 to fulfill that function. Since 1868, Col. Sanders D. Bruce had been publishing a stud book of American pedigrees, and the Jockey Club wrote to him that it "does not propose to publish a stud book, but to keep a record of foals in the interest and for the protection of racing." The parallel projects proved to be incompatible, however, and on May 17, 1897, the Jockey Club purchased the six volumes of the *American Stud Book* previously published by Bruce, plus all related works and copyrights, for $35,000.

One of the Jockey Club's original goals was to bring order to racing in New York and New Jersey, and it played a significant role in developing the rules of racing for the East Coast and eventually the entire United States. Its influence in that area waned as the system of state racing commissions developed in the 1930s and it lost a court case involving Jule Fink, but it remains the official registrar of racing silks in New York.

Maintaining the sport's integrity has been the thread that runs through the Jockey Club's history, and the organization has been at the forefront of precise identification of horses. The Jockey Club adopted the photographing of night eyes—the structure on the inside of the leg that to the horse is the equivalent of a fingerprint—as a method of identifying Thoroughbreds. In the 1970s, the Jockey Club adopted blood-typing as an identification tool, and, with the foal crop of 2001, began DNA testing as a definitive verification of parentage.

In July 1953, Jockey Club Chairman George D. Widener convened in New York a meeting of 18 owners, racing officials, and journalists to discuss a wide range of issues facing the industry. The following year, the meeting was moved to Saratoga Springs, New York, and now is known as the Jockey Club Round Table Conference on Matters Pertaining to Racing. Some topics discussed in recent years were marketing, technology, and medication.

The Jockey Club has developed the world's most extensive database of race records and pedigrees of Thoroughbreds. It has complete information for all North American racing from 1930 to the present. In recent years it has been able to work with other countries' registrars to obtain complete racing information and pedigrees from such countries as England, Ireland, France, Italy, Germany, Japan, Hong Kong, Australia, United Arab Emirates, Saudi Arabia, Brazil, and Argentina.

Lexington Office
821 Corporate Dr.
Lexington, KY 40503
Phone: (859) 224-2700
Fax: (859) 224-2710
Web site: *http://www.jockeyclub.com*

New York Office
40 East 52nd St.
New York, NY 10022
Phone: (212) 371-5970
Fax: (212) 371-6123

Officers
Chairman: Ogden Mills Phipps
Vice Chairman: William S. Farish
Secretary-Treasurer: James C. Brady
President: Alan Marzelli
Executive Vice President/Executive Director: Dan Fick
Executive Vice President, Finance and Administration: James S. J. Liao

Stewards

Helen C. Alexander	James C. Brady
Sherwood C. Chillingworth	Donald R. Dizney
William S. Farish	G. Watts Humphrey Jr.
Stuart S. Janney III	Ogden Mills Phipps
Peter G. Schiff	

Members

Josephine E. Abercrombie	Helen C. Alexander
Joseph L. Allbritton	John Ed Anthony
Charles Baker	John Barr
James E. Bassett III	Rollin Baugh
John A. Bell III	Reynolds Bell Jr.
James H. Binger	Edward S. Bonnie
Gary Biszantz	Lucy Boutin
Frank A. Bonsal Jr.	Nicholas F. Brady
James C. Brady	Michael C. Byrne
Larry Bramlage, D.V.M.	Thomas R. Capehart
Alexander G. Campbell Jr.	Alice H. Chandler
Charles J. Cella	George M. Cheston
Helen B. Chenery	Robert N. Clay
Sherwood C. Chillingworth	F. Eugene Dixon Jr.

Allan R. Dragone
Richard L. Duchossois
Allaire duPont
Edward P. Evans
William S. Farish
Hugh A. Fitzsimons Jr.
John K. Goodman
Arthur B. Hancock III
Seth W. Hancock
John C. Harris
John Hettinger
G. Watts Humphrey Jr.
Richard I. G. Jones
Peter F. Karches
Robert B. Lewis
Harry T. Mangurian Jr.
J. W. Y. Martin Jr.
Robert E. Meyerhoff
MacKenzie Miller
Charles Nuckols Jr.
John C. Oxley
John W. Phillips
Hiram C. Polk Jr., M.D.
David P. Reynolds
J. David Richardson, M.D.
J. Mack Robinson
Richard Santulli
Barry Schwartz
Viola Sommer
George Strawbridge Jr.
Shirley H. Taylor
Donald J. Valpredo
Joseph Walker Jr.
Wheelock Whitney
Martin Wygod
C. Steven Duncker
Donald R. Dizney

Jack J. Dreyfus Jr.
William duPont III
Robert S. Evans
William S. Farish Jr.
Richard L. Gelb
Martha F. Gerry
Louis L. Haggin III
Dell Hancock
Joseph W. Harper
Marquess of Hartington CBE
E. Edward Houghton
Stuart S. Janney III
Russell B. Jones Jr.
Gary Lavin
F. Jack Liebau
William C. MacMillen Jr.
Frank L. Mansell
James K. McManus
Leverett Miller
Kenneth Noe Jr.
J. Michael O'Farrell Jr.
John H. Peace
Ogden Mills Phipps
Carl Pollard
Reuben F. Richards
Jack K. Robbins, V.M.D.
Timothy H. Sams
Peter G. Schiff
Joseph V. Shields Jr.
Robert S. Strauss
Dwight Sutherland
Oakleigh B. Thorne
Daniel G. Van Clief Jr.
Charlotte C. Weber
David Willmot
William T. Young

Jockey Club Chairmen

Chairman	Term
John Hunter	March 1, 1894-January 24, 1895
August Belmont II	January 24, 1895-December 10, 1924
Frank K. Sturgis	December 30, 1924-November 3, 1930
William Woodward	November 3, 1930-January 12, 1950
George D. Widener	January 12, 1950-January 7, 1964
Odgen Phipps	January 7, 1964-January 12, 1974
Nicholas F. Brady	January 12, 1974-April 19, 1982
August Belmont IV	May 3, 1982-February 10, 1983
Ogden Mills Phipps	February 10, 1983-present

Jockey Club subsidiaries

Jockey Club Information Systems Inc.

The Jockey Club Information Systems Inc., incorporated in 1989, is a wholly owned subsidiary of Jockey Club Holdings Inc. All profits from its activities are reinvested in the Thoroughbred industry, helping to stabilize registration fees and finance industry projects. The organization has three divisions, Information Services, Cataloguing, and Software Sales and Consulting. In 2000, it launched equineline.com, (*http://www.equineline.com*), an Internet-based information and communication network. Through equineline, the Jockey Club sells information—pedigrees of horses, race records, sire progeny records, produce records of dams, etc.—online to customers. Under the equineline banner, the Lexington-based organization has launched management programs for horse owners and breeders, trainers, and farms.

Phone: (859) 224-2800 or 1-800-333-1778
Fax: (859) 224-2810

Web site: *http://www.tjcis.com*
Chairman and Chief Executive Officer: Carl E. Hamilton
Board Members: C. Steven Duncker, Robert S. Evans, Carl E. Hamilton, Alan Marzelli, John Phillips, and Ogden Mills Phipps

InCompass

InCompass, a wholly owned subsidiary of Jockey Club Holdings Inc., was created as part of the Jockey Club's corporate restructuring in November 2001. Formerly known as McKinnie Systems, Lexington-based InCompass provided recordkeeping and operational assistance to more than 60 client racetracks in 2003. Functions include attendance and wagering tracking, race entries, and horsemen's bookkeeper applications.

Phone: (859) 296-3000 or 1-800-625-4664
Fax: (859) 296-3010
Web site: *http://www.incompass-solutions.com*
Chairman: Alan Marzelli
President: David Haydon
Executive Vice President, Sales and Marketing: David Ruffra

Grayson-Jockey Club Research Foundation

Established in 1940 to raise funds for equine veterinary research, the Grayson Foundation was combined with the similarly chartered Jockey Club Research Foundation in 1989. The Lexington-based foundation, which solicits contributions from the Thoroughbred community, allocated $800,000 in research grants in 2002, raising its total contributions to nearly $8-million since the merger. In 2001 and '02, it contributed more than $250,000 for research into mare reproductive loss syndrome.

Phone: (859) 224-2850
Fax: (859) 224-2853
Web site: *http://home.jockeyclub.com/grayson.html*
E-mail: ebowen@jockeyclub.com

Chairman: John Hettinger
Vice Chairman: Gary Lavin, D.V.M.
Secretary-Treasurer: James S. J. Liao
President: Edward L. Bowen
Vice President of Development: Nancy C. Kelly
Board Members: Josephine Abercrombie, William Backer, Lucy Young Boutin, William Condren, Allan Dragone, Allaire duPont, William Farish Jr., John Goodman, Dell Hancock, Joseph W. Harper, Leverett Miller, Ogden Mills Phipps, Hiram Polk Jr., M.D., Jack Robbins, V.M.D., and Joseph V. Shields Jr.

The Jockey Club Foundation

Established in 1943, the Jockey Club Foundation provides confidential financial assistance to needy members of the Thoroughbred industry and their families. The New York-based foundation distributed more than $700,000 in 2002 and 2003.

Phone: (212) 521-5305
Fax: (212) 371-6123

Trustees: John Hettinger, C. Steven Duncker, D. G. Van Clief Jr.
Treasurer: James S. J. Liao
Executive Director: Nancy C. Kelly

National Thoroughbred Racing Association

With its founding in 1998, the National Thoroughbred Racing Association immediately became one of the industry's leading organizations. The NTRA originated in part from a "Guest Commentary" by Lexington advertising executive Fred Pope in the August 27, 1993, issue of THOROUGHBRED TIMES. Pope, an associate of Breeders' Cup founder John Gaines, suggested that horse owners pool their media rights—the images of their horses in races—and establish a major league of racing. With the funds generated from simulcasting the sport's leading races, the proposed owners' association—the National Thoroughbred Association—would market the sport to the American public.

The industry was not ready for Pope's idea in 1993, but three years later full-card simulcasting had exploded across the nation and provided a new stream of revenue for racing. Former Carter White House aides Hamilton Jordan and Tim Smith were hired by Pope and Gaines to sell the NTA concept to the Thoroughbred industry. Although not accepted by the racetracks, Pope's idea—that the sport needed a national presence and national marketing—gained momentum, and in March 1997 four industry organizations—Breeders' Cup Ltd., the Jockey Club, Keeneland Association, and Oak Tree Racing Association—put up $1-million each as seed money for a new organization to market the sport. In a short time, the new entity was named the National Thoroughbred Racing Association, and the efforts of the NTA were effectively folded into it. (The NTA formally merged into the NTRA in August 1998, and Pope was compensated for his intellectual property.)

Even with the backing of industry leaders, the NTRA was not a sure bet to be supported by racetracks and national organizations. Breeders' Cup President D. G. Van Clief Jr., serving as the NTRA's interim chief executive, and Jockey Club Executive Director Nick Nicholson traveled throughout the country to sell the concept of a national office to market racing to industry participants. They gained sufficient backing and a business plan was released in December 1997. The NTRA formally began operation on April 1, 1998. Its commissioner and chief executive officer was Smith, who, after leaving the White House, had served as deputy commissioner of the Professional Golfers' Association Tour and had helped to reorganize the Association of Tennis Professionals Tour.

The NTRA's first priority was marketing, and it produced an edgy, attention-grabbing national television advertisement featuring actress Lori Petty. Industry members, however, panned the ad, and the NTRA could not replicate its success through subsequent marketing campaigns, including spots that featured actor Rip Torn. In its first years, the NTRA ventured beyond marketing, opening subsidiary operations such as NTRA Services, NTRA Investments, NTRA Productions (for television production), and NTRA Charities. The NTRA became the producer of the Eclipse Awards, assuming a role formerly held by Thoroughbred Racing Associations.

By the end of 1999, several racetrack executives, including Magna Entertainment Corp.'s Frank Stronach and a group of Mid-Atlantic track owners, complained that the NTRA had veered away from its original mandate and had entered business enterprises where it was in competition with tracks, notably by operating a telephone-wagering hub in Oregon for Television Games Network. Some of the Mid-Atlantic tracks pulled out of the NTRA but returned later, while Stronach was appeased when more racetrack representation was added to the NTRA board of directors, including a seat for a Stronach representative. Also that year, NTRA transferred operation of the Oregon hub to TVG.

NTRA's continuing budget deficits contributed to a decision in 2000 to merge many of its operations with Breeders' Cup Ltd., and the merger took place on January 1, 2001. Smith remained as commissioner and Van Clief became the NTRA's vice chairman. By the end of 2001, many NTRA functions had been melded into the Breeders' Cup operation, with the NTRA increasingly focusing on lobbying and marketing of the Breeders' Cup championship day, which in 2001 was renamed the Breeders' Cup World Thoroughbred Championships. After the terrorist attacks of September 11, 2001, the NTRA raised $5-million for charitable efforts.

2525 Harrodsburg Rd.
Lexington, KY 40504
Phone: (859) 223-5444
Fax: (859) 223-3945
Web site: http://www.ntra.com
E-mail: ntra@ntra.com

Commissioner and Chief Executive Officer: Tim Smith
Vice Chairman: D. G. Van Clief Jr.
Deputy Commissioner and Chief Operating Officer: Greg Avioli

Directors: John Amerman, Alan Foreman, Craig Fravel, Bruce Garland, G. Watts Humphrey Jr., Bryan Krantz, Jim McAlpine, Tom Meeker, Terry Meyocks, Nick Nicholson, Ogden Mills Phipps, John Roark, Tim Smith, D. G. Van Clief Jr., John Van de Kamp

Thoroughbred Racing Associations

In January 1942, racing's representatives to the National Association of State Racing Commissioners convention perceived themselves to be in a war-related emergency and convened a meeting that March in Chicago. The object of the meeting initially was to pull together all elements of the industry into a single ruling organization.

The two-day meeting that began on March 19, 1942, would not yield an overall ruling body for the fractious and fragmented industry. However, at that meeting, 33 executives of 22 racetracks formed the Thoroughbred Racing Associations of the United States, with Hialeah Park President John C. Clark as its first president. The organization was formally incorporated on May 22, 1942. (The name subsequently was changed to the Thoroughbred Racing Associations of North America when Canada's tracks joined the organization.)

Representatives to the March 1942 meeting realized that they could not conduct racing throughout the war strictly as an entertainment vehicle, and the Turf Committee of America was formed to raise funds to support the war effort.

New challenges awaited in the postwar years; chief among them was the integrity of the sport. In 1946, at the behest of Federal Bureau of Investigation Director J. Edgar Hoover (an avid racing fan), the TRA formed the Thoroughbred Racing Protective Bureau. A former FBI agent, Spencer J. Drayton became the first director of the TRPB and instituted practices such as fingerprinting of all licensees, from hotwalkers to owners.

Drayton became the TRA's executive vice president in 1960, and his appointment resulted in the resignation of five racetracks. He retired in 1974, and since 1976, the TRA has had only two executive vice presidents, J. B. Faulconer and Christopher N. Scherf (since 1988).

In 1950, the TRA had begun to select its own end-of-year champions, which sometimes differed from those chosen by the *Daily Racing Form*, which established its poll in 1936. Faulconer was given the task of unifying the championships in 1971. Then president of Turf Publicists of America, Faulconer brought together the TRA, the *Daily Racing Form*, and the National Turf Writers Association to launch the Eclipse Awards that year. In the late 1990s, the National Thoroughbred Racing Association supplanted the TRA as the industry's representative to the Eclipse Awards.

420 Fair Hill Dr.
Elkton, MD 21921-2573
Phone: (410) 392-9200

Fax: (410) 398-1366
Web site: *http://www.tra-online.com*
e-mail: info@tra-online.com

President: Joseph W. Harper
Vice Presidents: Corey S. Johnson, Terence J. Meyocks
Secretary: Robert L. Bork
Treasurer: William I. Fasy
Executive Vice President: Christopher N. Scherf

Directors: Charles W. Bidwill III, Robert L. Bork, Thomas F. Carey III, Charles J. Cella, Sherwood C. Chillingworth, Joseph A. De Francis, C. Kenneth Dunn, Robert N. Elliston, Robert A. Farinella, William Gallo Jr., Bruce H. Garland, Andrew Ian Gaughan, Clifford C. Goodrich, Jeffrey Greco, Robert W. Green, Harold G. Handel, Joseph W. Harper, Phil Heard, Corey S. Johnsen, Bryan G. Krantz, Robert J. Kulina, Robert P. Levy, F. Jack Liebau, John R. Long, Jim McAlpine, Arthur L. McFadden, Terence J. Meyocks, Hugh M. Miner Jr., Jerry M. Monahan, Richard B. Moore, Howard M. Mosner Jr., Nick Nicholson, Richard E. Orbann, Louis J. Raffetto Jr., William M. Rickman Jr., Charles J. Ruma, Randall D. Sampson, Scott Savin, Steven P. Sexton, Christopher N. Scherf, Richard T. Schnaars, Barry K. Schwartz, Ronald A. Sultemeier, Stella F. Thayer, Alexander M. Waldrop, David S. Willmot, John C. York II

TRA Presidents

Term	President	Representing
1942-'43	John C. Clark	Hialeah
1944-'46	Henry A. Parr II	Pimlico
1947-'48	James E. Dooley	Narragansett
1949-'50	Donald P. Ross Sr.	Delaware
1951-'52	Alfred G. Vanderbilt	Belmont
1953-'54	John A. Morris	Jamaica
1955-'56	Amory L. Haskell	Monmouth
1957-'58	James D. Stewart	Hollywood
1959-'60	John G. Cella	Oaklawn
1961-'62	E. E. Dale Shaffer	Detroit Race Course
1963-'64	Robert P. Strub	Santa Anita
1965-'66	Edward P. Taylor	Ontario Jockey Club
1967-'68	Louis Lee Haggin II	Keeneland
1969-'70	John D. Schapiro	Laurel
1971-'73	James E. Brock	Ak-Sar-Ben
1973-'75	Frank M. Basil	New York Racing Association
1975-'76	Charles J. Cella	Oaklawn
1977-'78	Baird C. Brittingham	Delaware
1979-'80	Robert S. Gunderson	Bay Meadows
1981-'82	Lynn Stone	Churchill Downs
1983-'84	Morris J. Alhadeff	Longacres
1985-'86	James E. Bassett III	Keeneland
1987-'88	Gerard J. McKeon	New York Racing Association
1989-'90	Robert P. Levy	Atlantic City
1991-'92	Thomas H. Meeker	Churchill Downs
1993-'94	David M. Vance	Remington
1995-'96	Clifford C. Goodrich	Santa Anita
1997-'98	Harold G. Handel	New Jersey Sports and Exposition Authority
1999-2000	Stella F. Thayer	Tampa Bay Downs
2001-'02	Bryan G. Krantz	Fair Grounds
2003-'04	Joseph W. Harper	Del Mar

Thoroughbred Racing Protective Bureau

Modeled after the Federal Bureau of Investigation and initially staffed by former FBI agents, the Thoroughbred Racing Protective Bureau is the investigative and security arm of the Thoroughbred Racing Associations of North America. The TRPB was founded in January 1946 to protect the integrity of the sport.

420 Fair Hill Dr.
Elkton, MD 21921-2573
Phone: (410) 398-2261
Fax: (410) 398-1499

Web site: *http://www.trpb.com*
E-mail: trpbinfo@trpb.com

President and Treasurer: Paul W. Berube
Vice President and Secretary: James P. Gowen
Chairman: John E. Mooney
Vice Chairman: Bryan Krantz

Directors: Robert L. Bork, Charles J. Cella, Sherwood Chillingworth, Hugh M. Miner Jr., Nick Nicholson, Richard Schnaars, Stella F. Thayer

Equibase

Equibase Co. LLC, a general partnership of the Thoroughbred Racing Associations of North America (TRA) and the Jockey Club, is the official source of all racehorse past performances and racing data in North America. It was founded in 1991 because the racetracks and racing authorities at that time did not own their own database of racing performance, nor did they have free access to the information. Rather, the independent daily newspaper, *Daily Racing Form,* compiled and owned all racing records of horses starting in North America.

For decades previous, racetracks published an official program that was a thin booklet containing official betting numbers and such basic information as a horse's pedigree, owner, trainer, jockey, post position, morning-line betting odds, and colors of each owner's racing silks. Past performances were the exclusive province of the *Daily Racing Form.*

Equibase began operation in 1991 with its own chart callers for the purpose of creating past-performance lines that could be used in programs sold by racetracks. (The charts, a statistical description of a race and each horse's running position, are the raw materials of past-performance lines.) To help subsidize the start-up, each participating track pledged 25 cents from each program sold to be paid to Equibase. While some tracks began publishing magazine-sized official programs with Equibase past performances, a significant competitor to *Daily Racing Form* emerged when *Racing Times,* backed by publishing magnate Robert Maxwell, began operation. *Racing Times* purchased its past-performance lines from Equibase. *Racing Times* was making inroads into the *Racing Form*'s monopoly when Maxwell drowned off the Canary Islands in late 1991, and his empire collapsed in a scandal over misuse of pension funds.

The magazine-sized programs, which usually sold for about one-third of the price of the *Daily Racing Form,* gradually became popular with racegoers, which sharply reduced the *Daily Racing Form*'s circulation. In 1998, after years of negotiations between the two parties, Equibase became the sole data-collection agency, with the *Daily Racing Form* dropping its collection efforts and thereafter purchasing its racing information from Equibase. Today, Equibase provides information to more than 100 tracks and 1,100 simulcast outlets, as well as to the *Daily Racing Form, Sports-Eye,* several online resellers, and the industry's major interactive wagering services.

Since repaying all start-up costs in 1997, Equibase profits have been shared among the TRA and its limited-partner racetracks (66%) and the Jockey Club (33%) in the form of dividends. In 2002, Equibase distributed dividends of $1.8-million to its partners. Equibase employs 45 full-time employees, 90 full-time chart callers, and a number of part-time employees.

The company also serves the sport's fan base through its Web site, *http://www.equibase.com,* which offers a wide array of handicapping information and services geared toward every level of handicapper. Among the products available are race programs with handicapping information in easy-to-understand formats for new and existing fans. These pages were developed in conjunction with the National Thoroughbred Racing Association. The Equibase Virtual Stable, the exclusive notification service of the NTRA, delivers entry, workout, and result notices for horses fans wish to follow. Virtual Stable also features a race series notification service that allows fans to monitor the progress of leading contenders for the Triple Crown and Breeders' Cup races in the months leading up to those events.

In April 2002, Equibase hired John Ertmann as its first full-time president, and in July 2002 it purchased AXCIS Information Network Inc., a provider of electronic handicapping information, through its Track Master product.

821 Corporate Dr.
Lexington, KY 40503-2794
Phone: (859) 224-2860 or (800) 333-2211
Fax: (859) 224-2811
Web site: http://www.equibase.com

Chairman: Alan Marzelli
President and Chief Executive Officer: John C. Ertmann
Executive Vice President and Chief Operating Officer: Hank Zeitlin
Secretary: Christopher N. Scherf
Treasurer: James S. J. Liao
Management Committee: Sherwood Chillingworth, C. Steven Duncker, John C. Ertman, Craig Fravel, Alan Marzelli, Jim McAlpine, Terence J. Meyocks, Nick Nicholson, Ogden Mills Phipps, Hans J. Stahl, Steve Sexton, Ray Tromba, Michael Weiss

National Industry Organizations

American Academy of Equine Art
4089 Iron Works Parkway
Lexington, KY 40511
Ph: (859) 281-6031
Fax: (859) 281-6043
E-mail: julieb@aaea.net
Web site: http://www.aaea.net
President: Werner Rentsch

American Association of Equine Practitioners
4075 Iron Works Pkwy.
Lexington, KY 40511
Ph: (859) 233-0147
Fax: (859) 233-1968
E-mail: aeepoffice@aaep.org
Web site: http://www.aaep.org
President: Thomas R. Lenz, D.V.M.

American Farriers Assn.
4059 Iron Works Pkwy., Ste. 1
Lexington, KY 40511
Ph: (859) 233-7411
Fax: (859) 231-7862
E-mail: farriers@americanfarriers.org
Web site: http://www.americanfarriers.org
President: Craig Trnka

American Horse Council
1616 H Street NW, 7th floor
Washington, D.C. 20006
Ph: (202) 296-4031
Fax: (202) 296-1970
E-mail: ahc@horsecouncil.org
Web site: http://www.horsecouncil.org
President: James J. Hickey Jr.

American Horse Protection Assn.
1000 29th St. NW., Ste. T-100
Washington, D.C. 20007
Ph: (202) 965-0500
Fax: (202) 965-9621
Web site: http://www.ahpa.us

Animal Transportation Assn.
111 East Loop North
Houston, TX 77029
Ph: (713) 532-2177
Fax: (713) 532-2166
E-mail: info@aata-animaltransport.org
Web site: http://www.aata-animaltransport.org

Association of Racing Commissioners Int'l
2343 Alexandria Dr., Ste. 200
Lexington, KY 40504-3276
Ph: (859) 224-7070
Fax: (859) 224-7071
E-mail: lpowell@arci.com
Web site: http://www.arci.com
Chairman: William E. Jackson
President: Lonny T. Powell

Breeders' Cup Ltd.
P.O. Box 4230
Lexington, KY 40544-4230
Ph: (859) 223-5444
Fax: (859) 223-3945
E-mail: breederscup@breederscup.com
Web site: http://www.breederscup.com
President: D. G. Van Clief Jr.

Canadian Veterinary Medical Assn.
339 Booth St.
Ottawa, ON K1R 7K1 Canada
Ph: (613) 236-1162
Fax: (613) 236-9681
E-mail: info@canadianveterinarians.net
Web site: http://www.cvma-acmv.org

Grayson-Jockey Club Research Foundation
821 Corporate Dr.
Lexington, KY 40503
Ph: (859) 224-2850
Fax: (859) 224-2853
E-mail: ebowen@jockeyclub.com
Web site: http://www.jockeyclub.com
President: Edward L. Bowen

Horsemen's Benevolent and Protective Assn. (National)
4063 Iron Works Pkwy., Bldg. B, Ste. 2
Lexington, KY 40511-8905
Ph: (859) 259-0451
Fax: (859) 259-0452
E-mail: racing@hbpa.org
Web site: http://www.hbpa.org
Executive Director: Remi Bellocq
President: John Roark

Jockey Club of Canada
P.O. Box 156
Rexdale, ON M9W 5L2 Canada
Ph: (416) 675-7756
Fax: (416) 675-6378
E-mail: jockeyclub@bellnet.ca
Web site: http://www.jockeyclubcanada.com

Jockeys' Guild
P.O. Box 150
Monrovia, CA 91017
Ph: (866) 465-6257

E-mail: info@jockeysguild.com
President: Wayne Gertmenian

National Horse Carriers Assn.
2053 Buck Ln.
Lexington KY 40511
Ph: (859) 255-9406
Web site: http://www.nationalhorsecarriers.com
President: Robert D. Maxwell

National Steeplechase Assn.
400 Fair Hill Dr.
Elkton, MD 21921-2573
Ph: (410) 392-0700
Fax: (410) 392-0706
E-mail: steeplechs@aol.com
Web site: http://www.nationalsteeplechase.com
President: George Strawbridge Jr.

National Thoroughbred Racing Assn.
2525 Harrodsburg Rd., 5th Fl.
Lexington, KY 40504-3359
Ph: (859) 223-5444
Fax: (859) 245-6868
E-mail: ntra@ntra.com
Web site: http://www.ntra.com
Commissioner: Tim Smith

National Turf Writers Assn.
1244 Meadow Ln.
Frankfort, KY 40601
Ph: (502) 875-4864
E-mail: dliebman@bloodhorse.com
President: Jennie Rees

North American Pari-Mutuel Regulators Assn.
P.O. Box 446
Cheyenne, WY 82003
Ph: (888) 627-7250
Fax: (307) 777-3681
E-mail: flamb@state.wy.us
Web site: http://www.napraonline.com
President: Gene Olander
Executive Director: Frank Lamb

The Jockey Club
40 E. 52nd St.
New York, NY 10022
Ph: (212) 371-5970
Fax: (212) 371-6123
E-mail: comments@jockeyclub.com
Web site: http://www.jockeyclub.com
Chairman: Ogden Mills Phipps

Thoroughbred Club of America
P.O. Box 8098
Lexington, KY 40533-8098

Ph: (859) 254-4282
Fax: (859) 231-6131
President: Arnold Kirkpatrick

Thoroughbred Owners and Breeders Assn.
P.O. Box 4367
Lexington, KY 40544-4367
Ph: (859) 276-2291
Fax: (859) 276-2462
E-mail: TOBA@toba.org
Web site: http://www.toba.org
President: Dan Metzger

Thoroughbred Racing Assns. of North America
420 Fair Hill Dr., Ste. 1
Elkton, MD 21921-2573
Ph: (410) 392-9200
Fax: (410) 398-1366
E-mail: info@tra-online.com
Web site: http://www.tra-online.com
President: Joe Harper
Executive Vice President: Chris Scherf

Thoroughbred Racing Protective Bureau
420 Fair Hill Dr., Ste. 2
Elkton, MD 21921
Ph: (410) 398-2261
Fax: (410) 398-1499
E-mail: trpbinfo@trpb.com
Web site: http://www.trpb.com
President: Paul W. Berube

Triple Crown Productions
700 Central Ave.
Louisville, KY 40208-1200
Ph: (502) 636-4405
Fax: (502) 636-4554
E-mail: TripleCrown@KentuckyDerby.com
Web site: http://www.visatriplecrown.com
President: Thomas H. Meeker
Executive Vice President: Edward Seigenfeld

Turf Publicists of America
P.O. Box 90
Jamaica, NY 11417
Ph: (718) 641-4700
Fax: (718) 843-7673
E-mail: bzalubil@nyrainc.com
Web site: http://www.turfpublicists.com
President: Michele Blanco

United Thoroughbred Trainers of America
P.O. Box 7065
Louisville, KY 40257-0065
Ph: (502) 893-0025
Fax: (502) 893-0026

State and Provincial Racing Organizations

Alabama

Alabama Horsemen's Benevolent and Protective Assn.
1523 Indian Hills
Hartsdale, AL 35640
Ph: (256) 773-3592
Fax: (256) 773-3592
E-mail: alahbpa@aol.com
President: Skip Drinkard

Birmingham Racing Commission
2101 6th Ave. N., Ste. 725
Birmingham, AL 35203
Ph: (205) 328-7223
Chairman: Michael G. Kendrick

Arizona

Arizona Horsemen's Benevolent and Protective Assn.
P.O. Box 43636
Phoenix, AZ 85080
Ph: (602) 942-3336
Fax: (602) 866-3790
E-mail: azhbpa@uswest.net
President: Kevin Eikleberry

Arizona Racing Commission
1110 W. Washington, Suite 260
Phoenix, AZ 85007
Ph: (602) 364-1700
Fax: (602) 364-1703
E-mail: ador@racing.state.az.us
Executive Director: Geoffrey Gonsher
Chairman: Burton Kruglick

Arizona Thoroughbred Breeders Assn.
P.O. Box 41774
Phoenix, AZ 85080
Ph: (602) 942-1310
Fax: (602) 942-8225
E-mail: atba@worldnet.att.net
Web site: http://www.atba.net
President: Frank W. Covello

Arkansas

Arkansas Horsemen's Benevolent and Protective Assn.
P.O. Box 1670
Hot Springs, AR 71902
Ph: (501) 623-7641
Fax: (501) 623-1350
President: Bill Walmsley

Arkansas Racing Commission
P.O. Box 3076
Little Rock, AR 72203
Ph: (501) 682-1467
Fax: (501) 682-5273

E-mail: bob.cohee@dfa.state.ar.us
Executive Director: Bob Cohee
Chairman: Cecil Alexander

Arkansas Thoroughbred Breeders and Horsemen's Assn.
P.O. Box 21641
Hot Springs, AR 71903-1641
Ph: (501) 624-6328
Fax: (501) 623-5722
E-mail: atbha@direclynx.net
President: Cynthia Baker

California

California Assn. of Thoroughbred Racetracks
980 9th St., Ste. 1550
Sacramento, CA 95814-2735
Ph: (916) 449-6820
Fax: (916) 449-6830

California Equine Council
P.O. Box 40000
Studio City, CA 91604
Ph: (818) 768-7752
Fax: (818) 768-7752

California Horse Racing Board
1010 Hurley Wy., Ste. 300
Sacramento, CA 95825
Ph: (916) 263-6000
Fax: (916) 263-6042
E-mail: royw@chrb.ca.gov
Web site: http://www.chrb.ca.gov
Executive Director: Roy C. Wood Jr.
Chairman: Roger H. Licht

California Thoroughbred Breeders Assn.
P.O. Box 60018
Arcadia, CA 91066-6018
Ph: (626) 445-7800
Fax: (626) 574-0852
E-mail: info@ctba.com
Web site: http://www.ctba.com
President: Daniel Schiffer

California Thoroughbred Farm Managers Assn.
P.O. Box 321
Murrieta, CA 92564
Ph: (909) 677-6571
Fax: (909) 677-6446
E-mail: cboots@webtv.net
Web site: http://www.thoroughbredinfo.com/showcase/ctfma.htm
President: Leigh Ann Howard

California Thoroughbred Horsemen's Foundation
P.O. Box 660129
Arcadia, CA 91066-6251

Ph: (626) 446-0169
Fax: (626) 447-6251

California Thoroughbred Trainers
285 West Huntington
Arcadia, CA 91066
Ph: (626) 447-2145
Fax: (626) 446-0270
E-mail: caltrnrs@pacbell.net
Web site: http://www.thoroughbredinfo.com/show-case/CTT.htm
President: Leigh Ann Howard

Thoroughbred Owners of California
285 W. Huntington Dr.
Arcadia, CA 91007
Ph: (626) 574-6620
Fax: (626) 821-1515
E-mail: santaanita@toconline.com
Web site: http://www.toconline.com
Chairman: Jack B. Owens
President: John K. Van de Kamp

Colorado

Colorado Horse Racing Assn.
P.O. Box 460635
Aurora, CO 80046-0635
Ph: (303) 690-5919
Fax: (303) 766-5268
E-mail: coracing@aol.com
Executive Director: Shannon Rushton

Colorado Racing Commission
1881 Pierce St., Ste. 108
Lakewood, CO 80214
Ph: (303) 205-2990
Fax: (303) 205-2950
E-mail: racing@spike.dor.state.co.us
Executive Director: David C. Reitz
Chairman: Dr. Gene Naugle

Colorado Thoroughbred Breeders Assn.
4701 Marion St., Ste. 203
Denver, CO 80216
Ph: (303) 294-0260
Fax: (303) 294-0260
E-mail: ctba@worldnet.att.net
Web site: http://www.toba.org/state/coindex.html
President: F. A. Heckendorf

Delaware

Delaware Thoroughbred Racing Commission
2320 S. DuPont Hwy.
Dover, DE 19901
Ph: (302) 698-4599
Fax: (302) 697-4748
E-mail: johnwayne@.state.de.us
Executive Director: John F. Wayne
Chairman: Bernard J. Daney

Delaware Thoroughbred Horsemen's Association
777 Delaware Park Blvd.
Wilmington, DE 19804
Ph: (302) 994-2521, Ext. 284
Fax: (302) 994-3392
E-mail: dpha@aol.com
Executive Director: Robin Metz

Florida

Florida Horsemen's Benevolent and Protective Assn.
P.O. Box 1808
Opa Locka, FL 33055
Ph: (305) 625-4591
Fax: (305) 625-5259
E-mail: fhbpa@bellsouth.net
President: Linda Mills
Executive Director: Kent Stirling

Florida Division of Pari-Mutuel Wagering
1940 N. Monroe St.
Tallahassee, FL 32399-1035
Ph: (850) 488-9130
Fax: (850) 488-0550

Florida Thoroughbred Breeders' and Owners' Assn.
801 SW. 60th Ave.
Ocala, FL 34474-1827
Ph: (352) 629-2160
Fax: (352) 629-3603
E-mail: ftboa@aol.com
Web site: http://www.ftboa.com
President: Harold J. Plumley
Executive Vice President: Richard E. Hancock

Florida Thoroughbred Farm Managers
6998 NW. Highway 27, Ste. 106B
Ocala, FL 34482
Ph: (352) 401-3535
Fax: (352) 401-3533
E-mail: ftfm@atlantic.net
Web site: http://www.flfarmmanagers.com
President: Bobby Jones

Florida Turf Writers/Media Assn.
P.O. Box 374
Hallandale, FL 33008
Ph: (954) 680-8681
Fax: (954) 457-6497
E-mail: mtanner983@aol.com
President: Mike Tanner

Horse Protection Assn. of Florida
20690 NW. 130th Ave.
Micanopy, FL 32667
Ph: (352) 466-4366
Fax: (305) 466-4072
E-mail: director@hpaf.org
Web site: http://www.hpaf.org

Sunshine State Horse Council
P.O. Box 4158
North Fort Myers, FL 33918-4158
Ph: (727) 731-2999
E-mail: jean1sshc@aol.com
Web site: http://www.sshc.org
President: Vicki Lawry

Thoroughbred Owners of Florida
P.O. Box 2148
Hobe Sound, FL 33475
Ph: (800) 382-3892
Fax: (800) 382-656

Georgia

Georgia Thoroughbred Owners and Breeders Assn.
P.O. Box 987
Tyrone, GA 30290
Ph: (404) 886-6739
Fax: (770) 969-9035
E-mail: gtoba@mindspring.com
Web site: http://www.gtoba.com
President: Jack Damico

Idaho

Idaho Horsemen's Benevolent and Protective Assn.
P.O. Box 140143
Boise, ID 83714
Ph: (208) 939-0650

Idaho Racing Commission
P.O. Box 700
Meridian, ID 83680
Ph: (208) 884-7080
Fax: (208) 884-7098
E-mail: ardie.noyes@isp.state.id.us
Executive Director: Eugene O. Baker
Chairman: Dr. Michael Lineberry

Idaho Thoroughbred Assn.
5000 Chinden Blvd.
Boise, ID 83714
Ph: 208-375-5930
Fax: 208-375-5959
Web site: http://www.cyberhighway.net/~ita

Idaho Thoroughbred Breeders Assn.
3085 N. Cole Rd., Ste. 113
Boise, ID 83704
Ph: (208) 375-5930
Fax: (208) 375-5959
E-mail: ita@micron.net

Illinois

Chicago Horsemen's Benevolent and Protective Assn.
138 West Station St.
Barrington, IL 60010
Ph: (847) 382-3484
Fax: (847) 382-9579
President: Noel Hickey

Illinois Horsemen's Benevolent and Protective Assn.
P.O. Box 429
Caseyville, IL 62232-0429
Ph: (618) 345-7724
Fax: (618) 344-9049
President: Jim Watkins

Illinois Racing Board
100 W. Randolph St., Ste. 11-100
Chicago, IL 60601
Ph: (312) 814-2600
Fax: (312) 814-5062
Chairwoman: Lorna Propes

Illinois Thoroughbred Breeders and Owners Foundation
P.O. Box 336
Caseyville, IL 62232
Ph: (618) 344-3427
Fax: (618) 346-1051
E-mail: itboffp@apci.net
Web site: http://www.illinoisracingnews.com/itbof.htm
President: John D. Bauman

Indiana

Indiana Horse Council
225 S. East St. #738
Indianapolis, IN 46202
Ph: (317) 692-7115
Fax: (317) 692-7350
E-mail: inhorsecouncil@aol.com
Web site: http://www.indianahorsecouncil.org
President: Jack Haefling

Indiana Horsemen's Benevolent and Protective Assn.
4500 Dan Patch Cir.
P.O. Box 9317
Anderson, IN 46013
Ph: (317) 894-1520
Fax: (317) 894-1530
E-mail: inhbpa@aol.com
President: Dan Horrell

Indiana Racing Commission
150 W. Market St., ISTA Center, Ste. 530
Indianapolis, IN 46204
Ph: (317) 233-3119
Fax: (317) 233-4470
Executive Director: Joe Gorajec
Chairman: Richard Darko

Indiana Thoroughbred Owners and Breeders Assn.
P.O. Box 3753
Carmel, IN 46082-3753

Ph: (317) 462-0046
Fax: (317) 467-0396
E-mail: webmaster@itoba.com
Web site: http://www.itoba.com
President: Jerry C. Walker

Iowa

**Iowa Horsemen's Benevolent and
    Protective Assn.**
P.O. Box 163
Altoona, IA 50009
Ph: (515) 967-4804
Fax: (515) 967-4963
E-mail: iahbpa@aol.com
President: Leroy Gessman

Iowa Racing Commission
717 E. Court Ave., Ste. B
Des Moines, IA 50309
Ph: (515) 281-7352
Fax: (515) 242-6560
E-mail: irgc@irgc.state.ia.us
Chairwoman: Rita Sealock

**Iowa Thoroughbred Breeders and
    Owners Assn.**
1 Prairie Meadows Dr.
Altoona, IA 50009
Ph: (515) 957-3002
Fax: (515) 957-1368
E-mail: itboa@prairiemeadows.com
Web site: http://www.iowathoroughbred.com
President: Ray Shattuck

Kansas

Kansas Horse Council
P.O. Box 1612
Manhattan, KS 66505-1612
Ph: (785) 776-0662
Fax: (785) 770-8558
E-mail: kansashorsecouncil@yahoo.com
Web site: http://www.kansashorsecouncil.com
President: Joe Taylor

**Kansas Horsemen's Benevolent and
    Protective Assn.**
16585 SW. 90th Ave.
Zenda, KS 67159
Ph: (616) 243-6641
President: Ralph Lilja

Kansas Racing & Gaming Commission
3400 SW. Van Buren St.
Topeka, KS 66611-2228
Ph: (785) 296-5800
Fax: (785) 296-0900
E-mail: kracing@cjnetworks.com
Executive Director: Tracy T. Diel
Chairman: Gene Olander

Kansas Thoroughbred Assn.
215 Monroe Dr.
Fredonia, KS 66736-1262
Ph: (316) 378-4772
Fax: (316) 378-4772
E-mail: gejo@twinmounds.com
President: Dwight Daniels

Kentucky

Kentucky Horse Council
P.O. Box 11706
Lexington, KY 40577-1706
Ph: (800) 459-4677
Fax: (859) 299-9849
E-mail: anita.magan@mail.state.ky.us
Web site: http://www.kentuckyhorse.org
President: Anita Magan

**Kentucky Horsemen's Benevolent and
    Protective Assn.**
P. O. Box 9317
Louisville, KY 40209
Ph: (502) 363-1077
Fax: (502) 367-6800
E-mail: kyhbpalou@ntr.net
Web site: http://www.hbpa.org
President: Susan Bunning

Kentucky Racing Commission
4063 Iron Works Pkwy., Bldg B
Lexington, KY 40511-8434
Ph: (859) 246-2040
Fax: (859) 246-2039
E-mail: bernard.hettel@mail.state.ky.us
Executive Director: Bernard J. Hettel
Chairman: C. Frank Shoop

Kentucky Thoroughbred Assn.
4079 Iron Works Pkwy.
Lexington, KY 40511
Ph: (859) 381-1414
Fax: (859) 233-9737
E-mail: contact@kta-ktob.com
Web site: http://www.kta-ktob.com
President: R. Alex Rankin

**Kentucky Thoroughbred Farm Managers
    Club**
P.O. Box 4688
Lexington, KY 40544-4688
Ph: (859) 296-4279
E-mail: kyfarmclub@aol.com
Web site: http://www.ktfmc.org
President: Mike Owens

**Kentucky Thoroughbred Owners and
    Breeders**
4079 Iron Works Pkwy.
Lexington, KY 40511
Ph: (859) 259-1643
Fax: (859) 233-9737
E-mail: contact@kta-ktob.com

Web site: *http://www.kta-ktob.com*
President: R. Alex Rankin

Louisiana

Louisiana Horsemen's Benevolent and Protective Assn.
1535 Gentilly Blvd.
New Orleans, LA 70119
Ph: (504) 945-1555
Fax: (504) 945-1579
E-mail: lahbpa@aol.com
President: Oran Trahan

Louisiana Racing Commission
320 N Carrollton Ave., Ste. 2-B
New Orleans, LA 70119
Ph: (504) 483-4000
Fax: (504) 483-4898
Executive Director: Charles Gardiner
Chairman: Albert M. Stall

Louisiana Thoroughbred Breeders Assn.
P.O. Box 24650
New Orleans, LA 70184
Ph: (504) 947-4676
Fax: (504) 943-2149
E-mail: ltba@iamerica.net
President: Bryan Krantz

Maryland

Maryland Horse Breeders Assn.
P.O. Box 427
Timonium, MD 21094
Ph: (410) 252-2100
Fax: (410) 560-0503
E-mail: mdhobr@erols.com
Web site: *http://www.mdhorsebreeders.com*
President: R. Thomas Bowman

Maryland Horse Council
P.O. Box 233
Lisbon, MD 21765
Ph: (410) 489-7826
Fax: (410) 489-7828
E-mail: admin@mail.mdhorsecouncil.org
Web site: *http://www.mdhorsecouncil.org*

Maryland Million Ltd.
P.O. Box 365
Timonium, MD 21094
Ph: (410) 252-2100
Fax: (410) 252-0503
E-mail: info@mdhorsebreeders.com
Web site: *http://www.mdhorsebreeders.com/Million/Default.cfm*
President: Michael Pons

Maryland Racing Commission
500 N. Calvert St., Rm. 201
Baltimore, MD 21202-3651
Ph: (410) 230-6330
Fax: (410) 333-8308
E-mail: mhopkins@dllr.state.md.us
Chairman: Louis Ulman

Maryland Thoroughbred Horsemen's Assn.
6314 Windsor Mill Rd.
Baltimore, MD 21207
Ph: (410) 265-6842
Fax: (410) 265-6841
E-mail: mdhorsemen@erols.com
Web site: *http://www.mdhorsebreeders.com/MTHA/Index.cfm*
President: Richard Hoffberger

Massachusetts

Massachusetts Racing Commission
1 Ashburton Pl., Rm. 1313
Boston, MA 02108
Ph: (617) 727-2581
Fax: (617) 227-6062
E-mail: elizabeth.barry@state.ma.us
Chairman: Joseph Betro

New England Horsemen's Benevolent and Protective Association
P. O. Box 388
Revere, MA 02151
Ph: (617) 567-3900
Fax: (617) 569-3797
President: Manford Roos

Michigan

Michigan Horsemen's Benevolent and Protective Assn.
4800 S. Harvey
Muskegon, MI 49444
Ph: (231) 798-2250
Fax: (517) 552-0004
E-mail: mihbpa@aol.com
President: Robert Miller

Michigan Racing Commission
Office of Racing Commissioner
37650 Professional Center Dr., Ste. 105-A
Livonia, MI 48154-1100
Ph: (734) 462-2400
Fax: (734) 462-2429
E-mail: perroned9@michigan.gov
Commissioner: R. Robert Geake

Minnesota

Minnesota Horsemen's Benevolent and Protective Assn.
1100 Canterbury Rd.
Shakopee, MN 55379
Ph: (952) 496-6442
Fax: (952) 496-6443
E-mail: mnhbpa@pclink.com
Web site: *http://www.pclink.com/mnhbpa*
President: Tom Metzen Sr.

Minnesota Racing Commission
P.O. Box 630
Shakopee, MN 55379
Ph: (952) 496-7950
Fax: (952) 496-7954
E-mail: Richard.Krueger@state.mn.us
Executive Director: Richard Krueger
Chairman: Cindy Piper

Minnesota Thoroughbred Assn.
1100 Canterbury Rd.
Shakopee, MN 55379
Ph: (952) 496-3770
Fax: (952) 496-3672
E-mail: mtassoc@voyager.net
President: Craig Biorn

Mississippi

Mississippi Thoroughbred Owners and Breeders Assn.
107 Sundown Rd.
Madison, MS 39110
Ph: (601) 856-8293
President: Bruns Myers Jr.

Missouri

Missouri Equine Council
P.O. Box 608
Fulton, MO 65251
Ph: (800) 313-3327
E-mail: info@mo-equine.org
Web site: *http://www.mo-equine.org*
President: Sharon Marohl

Missouri Racing Commission
P.O. Box 1847
Jefferson City, MO 65102-1847
Ph: (573) 526-4080
Fax: (573) 526-1999
E-mail: afranks@mail.state.mo.us
Chairwoman: Betty Weldon

Montana

Montana Horsemen's Benevolent and Protective Assn.
139 New Dracut Hill Rd.
Vaughn, MT 59487
Ph: (406) 452-2135
Fax: 406 727-2663
President: R. C. Foster

Montana Racing Commission
1424 9th Ave.
Helena, MT 59620-0512
Ph: (406) 444-4287
Fax: (406) 444-4305
Executive Director: Sam Murfitt

Nebraska

Nebraska Horsemen's Benevolent and Protective Assn.
6406 South 150th Street
Omaha, NE 68137
Ph: (402) 438-4684
Fax: (402) 438-4793
E-mail: nebrhbpa@radiks.net
President: Donald Everett

Nebraska Racing Commission
P.O. Box 95014
Lincoln, NE 68509-5014
Ph: (402) 471-4155
Fax: (402) 471-2339
Chairman: Dennis Lee

Nebraska Thoroughbred Breeders Assn.
P.O. Box 2215
Grand Island, NE 68802
Ph: (308) 384-4683
Fax: (308) 384-9172
E-mail: NTBAI@KDSI.net
President: Jim Cranwell

New Hampshire

New Hampshire Horse Council
273 Poor Farm Rd.
New Ipswich, NH 03071
Ph: (603) 456-3230
E-mail: brookee171@hotmail.com
Web site: *http://www.nhhorsecouncil.com*
President: Christian Devereaux

New Hampshire Racing Commission
244 N. Main St.
Concord, NH 03301-5041
Ph: (603) 271-2158
Fax: (603) 271-3381
E-mail: pkelley@nhpmc.state.nh.us
Executive Director: Paul M. Kelley
Chairman: Timothy J. Connors

New Jersey

New Jersey Racing Commission
P.O. Box 088
Trenton, NJ 08625
Ph: (609) 292-0613
Fax: (609) 599-1785
Executive Director: Frank Zanzuccki
Chairman: John Tucker

Thoroughbred Breeders Cooperative
15 Hutchinson Rd.
Allentown, NJ 08501
Ph: (201) 488-4446
Fax: (201) 488-4213

Thoroughbred Breeders' Assn. of New Jersey
4444 N. Ocean Blvd.
Long Branch, NJ 07740

Ph: (732) 870-9718
Fax: (732) 870-9719
E-mail: duartej@njbreds.com
Web site: *http://www.njbreds.com*
President: Michael Harrison

New Mexico

New Mexico Horse Breeders' Assn.
P.O. Box 36869
Albuquerque, NM 87176-6869
Ph: (505) 262-0224
Fax: (505) 265-8009
E-mail: nmhba@worldnet.all.net
Web site: *http://www.nmhorsebreeders.com*
President: Paul Taylor Jr.

New Mexico Horse Council
P.O. Box 10206
Albuquerque, NM 87184-0206
Ph: (505) 345-8959
Fax: (505) 565-3223
E-mail: valcole@flash.net
Web site: *http://www.nmhorsecouncil.org*
President: Nancy Gage

New Mexico Racing Commission
300 San Mateo Blvd. NE., Ste. 110
Albuquerque, NM 87108-1519
Ph: (505) 841-6400
Fax: (505) 841-6413
E-mail: nmrc@state.nm.us
Chairman: Jack Cole

New York

Finger Lakes Horsemen's Benevolent and Protective Association
P.O. Box 25250
Farmington, N.Y. 14425
Ph: (585) 924-3004
Fax: (585) 924-1433
E-mail: flhbpa@frontier.net
President: Paul Steckel

New York State Horse Council
760 Webster Rd.
Webster, NY 14580-9559
Ph: (716) 872-3178
E-mail: kinggeo@westelcom.com
Web site: *http://www.nyshc.org*
President: George King

New York State Racing and Wagering Board
1 Watervliet Avenue Ext., Ste. 2
Albany, NY 12206-1668
Ph: (518) 453-8460
Fax: (518) 453-8490
E-mail: info@racing.state.ny.us
Chairman: Michael Hoblock Jr.

New York Thoroughbred Breeders
57 Phila St., 2nd Fl.
Saratoga Springs, NY 12866

Ph: (518) 587-0777
Fax: (518) 587-1551
E-mail: nytb@nybreds.com
Web site: *http://www.nybreds.com*
President: Gerald Nielsen

New York State Thoroughbred Breeding and Development
1 Penn Plaza, Ste. 725
New York, NY 10119
Ph: (212) 465-0660
Fax: (212) 465-8205
E-mail: nybreds@nybreds.com
Web site: *http://www.nybreds.com*

New York Thoroughbred Horsemen's Assn.
P.O. Box 170070
Jamaica, NY 11417
Ph: (718) 848-5045
Fax: (718) 848-9269
Web site: *http://www.nytha.com*
President: Richard Bomze

North Carolina

North Carolina Horse Council
P.O. Box 12999
Raleigh, NC 27605
Ph: (919) 821-1030
Fax: (919) 821-1415
E-mail: cindy@nchorsecouncil.com
Web site: *http://www.nchorsecouncil.com*
President: Glenn Petty

North Carolina Thoroughbred Breeders Assn.
2103 Orange Factory Rd.
Bahama, NC 27503
Ph: (919) 471-0131
Fax: (919) 286-9421
President: Robert Sanford

North Dakota

North Dakota Racing Commission
500 North 9th St.
Bismarck, ND 58501
Ph: (701) 328-4290
Fax: (701) 328-4300
Chairwoman: Ann Mahoney

Ohio

Ohio Horsemen's Benevolent and Protective Assn.
3684 Park St.
Grove City, OH 43123
Ph: (614) 875-1269
Fax: (614) 875-0786
E-mail: ohio-hbpa@iwaynet.net
Web site: *http://www.ohiohbpa@rrohio.com*
President: Gus George

Ohio Racing Commission
77 S. High St., 18th Fl.
Columbus, OH 43215-6108

Ph: (614) 466-2757
Fax: (614) 466-1900
E-mail: can@osrc.state.oh.us
Executive Director: Clifford A. Nelson II
Chairman: C. Luther Heckman

Ohio Thoroughbred Breeders and Owners Assn.
6024 Harrison Ave., Ste. 13
Cincinnati, OH 45248-1621
Ph: (513) 574-5888
Fax: (513) 574-2313
E-mail: gb.otbo@fuse.net
Web site: *http://www.otbo.com*
President: Dennis Heebink

Oklahoma

Oklahoma Horsemen's Benevolent and Protective Assn.
1 Remington Pl.
Oklahoma City, OK 73111
Ph: (405) 427-8753
Fax: (405) 427-7099
E-mail: okhbpa@earthlink.net
President: Joe Lucas

Oklahoma Racing Commission
2614 Villa Prom
Oklahoma City, OK 73107-2421
Ph: (405) 943-6472
Fax: (405) 943-6474
E-mail: ohrc@socket.net
Executive Director: Gordon L. Hare
Chairman: Jim Bowers

Oklahoma Thoroughbred Assn.
2000 SE. 15th St., Bldg. 450, Ste. A
Edmond, OK 73013
Ph: (405) 330-1006
Fax: (405) 330-6206
E-mail: info@otawins.com
Web site: *http://www.otawins.com*
President: David Brookins

Oklahoma Thoroughbred Breeders Assn.
R.R. 6, Box 164
Blanchard, OK 73010-9236
Ph: (405) 485-3030

Oregon

Oregon Horsemen's Benevolent and Protective Assn.
11919 N. Jantzen Ave.
Portland, OR 97217
Ph: (503) 285-4941
Fax: (503) 285-4942
E-mail: ohbpa@aol.com
President: Dave Benson

Oregon Racing Commission
800 NE. Oregon St. #11
Portland, OR 97232
Ph: (503) 731-4052
Fax: (503) 731-4053
E-mail: cmorgan@oregonvos.net
Executive Director: Steven W. Barham
Chairman: Stephen S. Walters

Oregon Thoroughbred Breeders Assn.
P.O. Box 17248
Portland, OR 97217
Ph: (503) 285-0658
Fax: (503) 285-0659
E-mail: otba@mindspring.com
Web site: *http://www.thoroughbredinfo.com/show case/otba.htm*
President: Bruce Loudon

Pennsylvania

Pennsylvania Equine Council
P.O. Box 21
Dallas, PA 18612
Ph: (888) 304-0281
E-mail: expo2002@hky.com
Web site: *http://www.pennsylvaniaequinecouncil.com*
President: Walter Jeffers

Pennsylvania Horse Breeders Assn.
701 E. Baltimore Pike, Ste. C-1
Kennett Square, PA 19348
Ph: (610) 444-1050
Fax: (610) 444-1051
E-mail: exsec@pabred.com
Web site: *http://www.pabred.com*
President: Ray Hamm
Executive Secretary: Mark McDermott

Pennsylvania Horsemen's Benevolent and Protective Assn.
P.O. Box 88
Grantville, PA 17028
Ph: (717) 469-2970
Fax: (717) 469-7714
E-mail: pahbpa@paonline.com
President: John Wames

Pennsylvania Horse Racing Commission
2301 N. Cameron St., Rm. 304
Harrisburg, PA 17110
Ph: (717) 787-1942
Executive Director: Benjamin H. Nolt Jr.
Chairman: Cayler H. Walker

Pennsylvania Thoroughbred Horsemen's Assn.
P.O. Box 300
Bensalem, PA 19020-0300
Ph: (215) 638-2012
Fax: (215) 638-2919
President: Lawrence Riviello

South Carolina

South Carolina Thoroughbred Owners and Breeders
Route 1, Box 19-A
Wando, SC 29492
Ph: (803) 432-3388
Fax: (803) 432-5777
President: Ted Hoover

South Dakota

South Dakota Commission on Gaming
118 W. Capitol Ave.
Pierre, SD 57501
Ph: (605) 773-6050
Fax: (605) 773-6053
E-mail: gaminginfo@state.sd.us
Executive Director: Larry Eliason
Chairman: John Wiles

Texas

Texas Horsemen's Benevolent and Protective Assn.
P.O. Box 142533
Austin, TX 78714
Ph: (512) 467-9799
Fax: (512) 467-9790
E-mail: wobanan@texashorsemen.com
Web site: *http://www.texashorsemen.com*
Executive Director: Tommy Azopardi

Texas Racing Commission
P.O. Box 12080
Austin, TX 78711-2080
Ph: (512) 833-6699
Fax: (512) 833-6907
E-mail: paula@txrc.state.tx.us
Executive Director: Paula C. Flowerday
Chairman: Terri Lacy

Texas Thoroughbred Assn.
P.O. Box 14967
Austin, TX 78761
Ph: (512) 458-6133
Fax: (512) 453-5919
E-mail: info@texasthoroughbred.com
Web site: *http://www.validinteractive.com/tta/*
President: John Adger

Vermont

Vermont Horse Council
P.O. Box 105
Montpelier, VT 05601-0105
Ph: (800) 722-1419
Fax: (802) 229-1150
E-mail: newsilk@together.net

Virginia

Virginia Horsemen's Benevolent and Protective Assn.
38 Garrett St.
Warrenton, VA 20186

Ph: (540) 347-0033
Fax: (540) 675-1103
E-mail: vhbpa@earthlink.net
Web site: *http://www.vhbpa.org*
President: Robin Richards

Virginia Racing Commission
10700 Horsemen's Rd.
New Kent, VA 23124
Ph: (804) 966-7400
Fax: (804) 966-7418
E-mail: bowker@vrc.state.va.us
Chairwoman: Robin Traywick Williams

Virginia Thoroughbred Assn.
38-C Garrett St.
Warrenton, VA 20186-3107
Ph: (540) 347-4313
Fax: (540) 347-7314
E-mail: vta@vabred.org
Web site: *http://www.vabred.org*
President: Deborah A. Easter

Washington

Northwest Horsemen's Benevolent and Protective Assn.
P. O. Box 40141
Spokane, WA 99202
Ph: (509) 536-5123
Fax: (509) 536-5145
President: Jay Healy

Washington Horsemen's Benevolent and Protective Assn.
3702 W. Valley Hwy., Ste. 210
Auburn, WA 98001
Ph: (206) 804-6822
Fax: (206) 804-6899
President: Larry Hills

Washington Racing Commission
6326 Martin Way, Ste. 209
Lacey, WA 98516
Ph: (206) 459-6462
Fax: (206) 459-6461
E-mail: whrc@whrc.state.wa.us
Chairman: Patrick LePley

Washington Thoroughbred Breeders Assn.
P.O. Box 1499
Auburn, WA 98071-1499
Ph: (253) 288-7878
Fax: (253) 288-7890
E-mail: maindesk@washingtonthoroughbred.com
Web site: *http://www.washingtonthoroughbred.com*
President: Jerry Woods

Washington Thoroughbred Farm Managers Assn.
P.O. Box 857
Enumclaw, WA 98022
Ph: (253) 288-7897

Fax: (253) 288-7890
E-mail: nancy@washingtonthoroughbred.com
Web site: *http://www.washingtonthoroughbred.com/
IndAddrs/WTFMA.htm*

West Virginia

Charles Town Horsemen's Benevolent and Protective Assn.
P.O. Box 581
Charles Town, W.V. 25414
Ph: (304) 725-1535
Fax: (304) 728-2113
E-mail: cthbpa@intrepid.net
President: Richard Watson

Mountaineer Park Horsemen's Benevolent and Protective Assn.
P. O. Box 358
Chester, WV 26034
Ph: (304) 387-9772
Fax: (304) 387-1925
E-mail: hbpa@raex.com
President: Charles Bailey

West Virginia Breeders Classics Ltd.
P.O. Box 1251
Charles Town, WV 25414
Ph: (304) 725-0709
Fax: (540) 687-6927
E-mail: wvbcmbn@erols.com
Web site: *http://www.wvbc.com*
President: Sam Huff

West Virginia Horsemen's Benevolent and Protective Assn.
P.O. Box 358
Chester, WV 26034
Ph: (304) 387-9772
Fax: (304) 387-1925
E-mail: hbpa@raex.com
President: Charles E. Bailey

West Virginia Racing Commission
106 Dee Dr.
Charleston, WV 25311
Ph: (304) 558-2150
Fax: (304) 558-6319
Chairman: George Sidiropolis

West Virginia Thoroughbred Breeders Assn.
P.O. Box 626
Charles Town, WV 25414
Ph: (304) 728-6868
Fax: (304) 724-7870
President: Cynthia O'Bannon

Wyoming

Wyoming Pari-Mutuel Commission
2515 Warren Ave., Ste. 301
Cheyenne, WY 82002

Ph: (307) 777-5887
Fax: (307) 777-6005
E-mail: flamb@state.wy.us
Executive Director: Frank R. Lamb

Canada

Alberta Division Canadian Thoroughbred Horse Society
225 17th Ave. SW. #401
Calgary, AB T2S 2T8 Canada
Ph: (403) 229-3609
Fax: (403) 244-6909
E-mail: cthsalta@telusplanet.net
Web site: *http://www.cthsalta.com*
President: Jim Thomson

Alberta Horse Racing
9707 110th St., #720
Edmonton, AB T5K 2L9 Canada
Ph: (780) 415-5432
Fax: (780) 488-5105
Web site: *http://www.thehorses.com*

British Columbia Division Canadian Thoroughbred Horse Society
17687 56A Ave.
Surrey, BC V3S 1G4 Canada
Ph: (604) 574-0145
Fax: (604) 574-5868
E-mail: cthsbc@axionet.com

British Columbia Horsemen's Benevolent and Protective Assn.
609 W. Hastings St. No. 888
Vancouver, BC V6B 4W4 Canada
Ph: (604) 647-2211
Fax: (604) 647-0095
President: Mel Snow

British Columbia Racing Commission
4720 Kingsway No. 2003
Burnaby, BC V5H 4N2 Canada
Ph: (604) 660-7400
Fax: (604) 660-7414
Chairman: Lorna Romilly

Canadian Racing Commission
P.O. Box 5904
LCD Merivale
Ottawa, ON K2C 3X7
Ph: (613) 946-1700
Fax: (613) 952-7466
E-mail: emassey@em.agr.ca
Executive Director: Elizabeth Massey

Eastern Canadian Thoroughbred Assn.
Longview Farm, RR 4
Ashton, ON K0A 1B0 Canada
Ph: (613) 257-5837
Fax: (613) 257-5837

E-mail: info@ecta-equine.ca
Web site: http://www.ecta-equine.ca
President: Mary Pappone

Horse Council of British Columbia
27336 Fraser Highway
Aldergrove, BC V4W 3N5 Canada
Ph: 604 856-4304
Fax: 604 856-4302
E-mail: administration@hcbc.ca
Web site: http://www.horsecouncilbc.com
President: Dr. Susan Thompson

Manitoba Division Canadian Thoroughbred Horse Society
Westdale Postal Outlet Box 46152
Winnipeg, MB R3R 3S3 Canada
Ph: (204) 832-1702
Fax: (204) 831-6735
E-mail: cthsmb@autobahn.mb.ca
President: Brent Hrymak

Manitoba Horse Council
200 Main St., Ste. 207
Winnipeg, MB R3C 4M2 Canada
Ph: (204) 925-5718
Fax: (204) 925-5737
E-mail: info@cthsmb.ca
Web site: http://www.escape.ca/~mhc

Manitoba Racing Commission
P.O. Box 46086 RPO Westdale
Winnipeg, MB R3R 3S3 Canada
Ph: (204) 885-7770
Fax: (204) 831-0942
E-mail: dwilliams@manitobahorsecomm.org
Executive Director: D. F. Williams
Chairman: David Miles

Newfoundland Equestrian Assn.
P.O. Box 372, Station C
Saint John's, NF A1C 5JB Canada
Ph: (709) 729-0826
E-mail: nea@webpage.ca
Web site: http://www.webpage.ca/nea
President: Chris Gallant

Ontario Division Canadian Thoroughbred Horse Society
P.O. Box 172
Rexdale, ON M9W 5L1 Canada
Ph: (416) 675-3602
Fax: (416) 675-9405
E-mail: cthsont@idirect.com
Web site: http://www.cthsont.com

Ontario Equestrian Federation
9120 Leslie St.; Ste 203
Richmond Hill, ON L4B 3J9 Canada
Ph: 905 (709) 6545
Fax: 905 (709) 1867
E-mail: horse@horse.on.ca
Web site: http:www.horse.on.ca

Ontario Horse Breeders Assn.
P.O. Box 520
Caledon, Ontario L0N ICO Canada
Ph: (519) 942-3527

Ontario Horsemen's Benevolent and Protective Assn.
135 Queens Plate Dr., Ste. 370
Toronto, ON M9W 6V1 Canada
Ph: (416) 747-5252
Fax: (416) 747-9606
E-mail: general@hbpa.com
President: Lawrence D. Regan

Ontario Racing Commission
20 Dundas Street West; 9th floor
Toronto, ON M5G2C2 Canada
Ph: (416) 327-0520
Fax: (416) 325-3478
E-mail: wendy.hoogeveen@cbs.gov.on.ca

Quebec Division Canadian Thoroughbred Horse Society
1684 McCullough
Dunham QC J0E 1M0 Canada
Ph: (514) 538-8172
Fax: (514) 538-8170

Saskatchewan Division Canadian Thoroughbred Horse Society
1229 Spadina Crescent W.
Saskatoon, SK S7M 1P4 Canada
Ph: (306) 242-9128
Fax: (306) 665-5829
E-mail: dturner@sk.sympatico.ca

Saskatchewan Horse Federation
2205 Victoria Ave.
Regina, SK S4P 0S4 Canada
Ph: (306) 780-9244
Fax: (306) 525-4009
E-mail: sk.horse@sasktel.net
Web site: http://www.saskhorsefed.com
President: Connie Dorsch

Puerto Rico

Puerto Rico Thoroughbred Breeders Assn.
P.O. Box 270281
San Juan, PR 00928-3081
Ph: (787) 725-8715
Fax: (787) 725-8606
E-mail: criadores@icepr.com

Mexico

Mexico Racing Commission
Fuente de Templanza No. 6, P. H.
Col. Tecamachalco,
Naucalpan, Edo. De Mexico
Mexico City 53950
Ph: 011(52) 5 293-0264
Fax: 011 (52) 5 294-7928
E-mail: cnccg@aol.com

Charitable Organizations

Bright Futures Farm
44793 Harrison Rd.
Spartansburg, PA 16434
Ph: (814) 827-8270
Fax: (814) 827-8278
E-mail: info@brightfuturesfarm.org
Web site: http://www.brightfuturesfarm.org

California Equine Retirement Foundation
34032 Kooden Rd.
Winchester, CA 92596
Ph: (909) 926-4190
Fax: (909) 926-4181
E-mail: cerf@pe.net
Web site: http://www.cerfhorses.org

Citizens for Animal Protection
P.O. Box 1496
Litchfield, CT 06759
Ph: (203) 699-8447
Fax: (203) 699-8447
E-mail: capinc@usa.net
Web site: http://www.geocities.com/
Petsburgh/Zoo/7966

Community Association for Riding
for the Disabled
4777 Dufferin St.
North York, ON M3H 5T3 Canada
Ph: (416) 667-8600
Fax: (416) 739-7520
E-mail: card.info@sympatico.ca
Web site: http://www.card.ca

Days End Farm Horse Rescue
15856 Frederick Rd.
Lisbon, MD 21765
Ph: (301) 854-5037
E-mail: defhr@erols.com
Web site: http://www.defhr.org

Don MacBeth Memorial Jockey Fund
P.O. Box 18470
Encino, CA 91416
Ph: (310) 550-4542
Fax: (818) 981-6914
E-mail: info@macbethfund.org
Web site: http://www.macbethfund.org

Equine Rescue League
P.O. Box 4366
Leesburg, VA 20177
Ph: (703) 771-1240
E-mail: bubbasays9@aol.com
Web site: http://www.equinerescueleague.org

Exceller Fund to Rescue Horses
4701 Spruce St.
Flower Mound, TX 75028
Ph: (972) 874-7486
E-mail: excellerfund@earthlink.net
Web site: http://www.excellerfund.org

Grayson-Jockey Club Research Foundation
821 Corporate Dr.
Lexington, KY 40503
Ph: (859) 224-2850
Fax: (859) 224-2853
E-mail: ebowen@jockeyclub.com
Web site: http://www.jockeyclub.com/grayson.html

Horses' Haven
P.O. Box 166
Howell, MI 48884
Ph: (517) 548-4880
E-mail: horsesmail@ismi.net; barbarabaker14@gte.net
Web site: http://www.ismi.net/horseshaven

Indiana Hooved Animal Humane Society
102 Spring Grove Ave.
Salem, IN 47167
Ph: (812) 883-8012
Fax: (812) 883-8175
E-mail: ihahs@earthlink.net
Web site: http://www.ihahs.org

Jockeys' Guild Disabled Riders Fund
P.O. Box 150
Monrovia, California 91017
Ph: (866) 465-6257
E-mail: info@jockeysguild.com

Kentucky Horse Park Foundation
4089 Iron Works Pike
Lexington, KY 40511
Ph: (859) 255-5727
Fax: (859) 254-7121
E-mail: khpf@mis.net
Web site: http://www.kyhorsepark.com/khp/foundation

Lone Star Equine Rescue
P.O. Box 627
Haslet, TX 76052
Ph: (409) 776-9396
Fax: (413) 803-0282
E-mail: info@lser.org
Web site: http://www.lser.org

Maryland Horsemen's Assistance Fund
6314 Windsor Mill Rd.
Baltimore, MD 21207
Ph: (410) 265-6843
Fax: (410) 265-6841

E-mail: mdassistance@erols.com
Web site: http://www.mdhorsemen.com

New Hampshire Equine Humane Assn.
27 Main St.
Goffstown, NH 03045
Ph: (603) 497-5900
E-mail: nhehainfo@aol.com
Web site: http://nheha.org

New Vocations Racehorse Adoption Program
3293 Wright Rd.
Laura, OH 45337-9706
Ph: (937) 947-4020
Fax: (937) 947-3201
E-mail: dot@horseadoption.com
Web site: http://www.horseadoption.com

Piedra Foundation
P.O. Box 1400
Bonsall, CA 92003
Ph: (760) 726-9206
Fax: (760) 726-9342
E-mail: tpf@piedra.org
Web site: http://www.piedra.org

Project Equus
P.O. Box 18030
Boulder, CO 80308-1030
Ph: (720) 565-2889
E-mail: equus@projectequus.org
Web site: http://www.projectequus.org

Race Track Chaplaincy of America
P.O. Box 91640
Los Angeles, CA 90009
Ph: (310) 419-1640
Fax: (310) 419-1642
E-mail: etorres@racetrackchaplaincy.org
Web site: http://www.racetrackchaplaincy.org
President: Don Dean
Executive Director: Dr. Enrique Torres

Recycle Racehorses
853 Raughley Hill Rd.
Harrington, DE 19952
Ph: (302) 398-4682
Fax: (302) 398-5196
E-mail: recycleracehs@yahoo.com
Web site: http://hollihorse.tripod.com/recycle/welcome.htm

ReRun
P.O. Box 96
Carlisle, KY 40311-0096
Ph: (859) 289-7786
Fax: (859) 289-7786
E-mail: rerunhorse@kih.net
Web site: http://www.rerun.org

Second Career Racehorses
25 S. Division
Grand Rapids, MI 49503
Ph: (616) 913-2790
Fax: (616) 913-2801
E-mail: scr@cybernet-usa.com
Web site: http://www.secondcareerracehorses.org

Shoemaker Foundation
P.O. Box 17026
Ingelwood, CA 90308-7026
Ph: (310) 419-1503
Fax: (310) 672-3899

The Jockey Club Foundation
40 East 52nd St.
New York, NY 10022
Phone: (212) 521-5305
Fax: (212) 371-6123
E-mail: nkelly@jockeyclub.com
Web site: http://home.jockeyclub.com/tjcf.html
Executive Director: Nancy C. Kelly

Thoroughbred Charities of America
P.O. Box 229
Middletown, DE 19709
Ph: (302) 378-7192
Fax: (302) 378-0535
E-mail: wendy@thoroughbredcharities.org
Web site: http://www.thoroughbredcharities.com
Chairman: Herb Moelis

Thoroughbred Retirement Foundation
450 Shrewsbury Plaza, Ste. 351
Shrewsbury, NJ 07702
Ph: (800) 728-1660
Fax: (802) 496-3276
E-mail: trfinc@msn.com
Web site: http://www.trfinc.org

United Pegasus Foundation
5671 Esplanade Avenue
Hemet, CA 92545
Ph: (909) 487 2770
Fax: (909) 487 0308
E-mail: unitedpegasus@yahoo.com
Web site: http://www.unitedpegasus.com

Winner's Circle Foundation
285 W. Huntington Dr.
Arcadia, CA 91007
Ph: (626) 574-6498
Fax: (626) 821-9091

Winners Federation
P.O. Box 46098
Chicago, IL 60646-0098
Ph: (847) 477-3551
Fax: (847) 982-6559
E-mail: winfed2002@yahoo.com
President: William E. Jackson

Sales Companies

Agence Francaise de Vente du Pur-Sang
32 Avenue Hocquart de Turtot No.51
Deauville, 14800 France
Ph: 33 2 31 81 81 00
Fax: 33 2 31 81 81 01
E-mail: af@deauville-sales.com
Web site: *http://www.deauville-sales.com*
President: Philippe Augier

American Equine Sales
4061 E. Castro Valley Blvd., Ste. 276
Castro Valley, CA 94552
Ph: (925) 600-8060
Fax: (925) 600-8061
E-mail: aes@mciworld.com
Web site: *http://www.thoroughbredinfo.com/show case/aes.htm*

Arizona Thoroughbred Breeders Assn.
P.O. Box 41774
Phoenix, AZ 85080
Ph: (602) 942-1310
Fax: (602) 942-8225
E-mail: atba@worldnet.att.net
Web site: *http://www.atba.net*
President: Frank Clovello

Arkansas Breeders' Sales Co.
P.O. Box 1665
Hot Springs, AR 71902
Ph: (501) 624-6336
Fax: (501) 623-5722

Arkansas Thoroughbred Sales Co.
P.O. Box 180159
Fort Smith, AR 72918-0159
Ph: (800) 752-8034
Fax: (501) 648-3980

Barretts Equine Ltd.
P.O. Box 2010
Pomona, CA 91769
Ph: (909) 629-3099
Fax: (909) 629-2155
E-mail: barrettseq@aol.com
Web site: *http://www.barretts.com*
President: Gerald F. McMahon

Breeders Sales Co. of Louisiana
P.O. Box 24650
New Orleans, LA 70184
Ph: (504) 947-4676
Fax: (504) 943-2149
E-mail: *ltba@iamerica.net*
President: Bryan Krantz

California Thoroughbred Breeders Sales
P.O. Box 60018
Arcadia, CA 91066-6018
Ph: (626) 445-7800
Fax: (626) 574-0852
E-mail: cookie@ctba.com
Web site: *http://www.ctba.com*
Sales Coordinator: Cookie Hackworth

Canadian Breeders Sales
P.O. Box 10 Station B
Etobicoke, ON M9W 5K9 Canada
Ph: (416) 674-1460
Fax: (416) 675-6430
Web site: *http://www.canadiansales.com*

Doncaster Bloodstock Sales Ltd.
Auction Mart Offices, Hawick
Roxburghshire, TD9 9NN England
Ph: 44 (1450) 372222
Fax: 44 (1450) 378017
E-mail: winners@dbsauctions.com
Web site: *http://www.dbsauctions.com*
Managing Director: Henry G. Beeby

Fair Grounds Sales Co.
1751 Gentilly Blvd. N.
New Orleans, LA 70152
Ph: (504) 944-5515
Fax: (504) 944-2511
Web site: *http//www.fgno.com/sales*

Fasig-Tipton Co.
2400 Newtown Pike
Lexington, KY 40583
Ph: (859) 255-1555
Fax: (859) 254-0794
E-mail: info@fasigtipton.com
Web site: *http://www.fasigtipton.com*
President: Walt Robertson
Executive Vice President and Chief Operating Officer: Boyd T. Browning Jr.

Fasig-Tipton Florida
21001 NW. 27th Ave.
Miami, FL 33056
Ph: (305) 626-3947
Fax: (305) 625-9242
E-mail: fasigtip@aol.com
Web site: *http://www.fasigtipton.com*
Director of Two-Year-Old Sales: Peter Penney

Fasig-Tipton Midlantic
356 Fair Hill Dr., Suite C
Elkton, MD 21921

Ph: (410) 392-5555
Fax: (410) 392-5556
Web site: *http://www.fasigtipton.com*
Sales Coordinator: Paget Bennett

Fasig-Tipton New York
40 Elmont Rd.
Elmont, NY 11003-0036
Ph: (516) 328-1800
Fax: (516) 328-1808
Web site: *http://www.fasigtipton.com*

Finger Lakes Thoroughbred Sales
P.O. Box 301
Shortsville, NY 14548-0301
Ph: (585) 289-8524
Fax: (585) 289-8524
E-mail: GVBA@nybreds.com
Web site: *http://www.nybreds.com*
President: Erica Waite

Goffs Bloodstock Sales Ltd.
Kildare Paddocks Kill
County Kildare, Ireland
Ph: 353 (45) 886600
Fax: 353 (45) 877119
E-mail: sales@goffs.ie
Web site: *http://www.goffs.com*
Chairman: Michael Osborne
Managing Director: Matt Mitchell

Heritage Place Sales Co.
2829 S. MacArthur Blvd.
Oklahoma City, OK 73128
Ph: (405) 682-4551
Fax: (405) 686-1267
E-mail: info@heritageplace.com
Web site: *http://www.heritageplace.com*
General Manager: Clayton Keys

Illinois Thoroughbred Breeders and Owners Foundation
P.O. Box 336
Caseyville, IL 62232
Ph: (618) 344-3427
Fax: (618) 346-1051
E-mail: itboffp@apci.net
Web site: *http://www.illinoisracingnews.com/ltbof.htm*
President: John Bauman

Iowa Thoroughbred Breeders and Owners Assn.
1 Prairie Meadows Dr.
Altoona, IA 50009
Ph: (515) 957-3002
Fax: (515) 957-1368
E-mail: itboa@PrairieMeadows.com

Web site: *http://www.iowathoroughbred.com/entry.html*
President: Ray Shattuck

Keeneland Association
4201 Versailles Rd.
Lexington, KY 40592-1690
Ph: (859) 254-3412
Fax: (859) 288-4348
E-mail: sales@keeneland.com
Web site: *http://www.keeneland.com*
President: Nick Nicholson
Director of Sales: Geoffrey G. Russell

Louisiana Thoroughbred Breeders Sales Co.
P.O. Box 789
Carencro, LA 70520
Ph: (337) 896-6152
Fax: (337) 896-6153
E-mail: ltbscl1@aol.com
Web site: *http://www.evangelinedowns.com/ltbsc.html*
President: Charles Ashy Sr.

Magic Millions Sales
28 Ascot Ct.
Bundall, QLD 9726 Australia
Ph: 61 (7) 5538 8933
Fax: 61 (7) 5531 7082
E-mail: info@magicmillions.com.au
Web site: *http://www.magicmillions.com.au*
Chairman: Gerry Harvey

Ocala Breeders' Sales Co.
P.O. Box 99
Ocala, FL 34478
Ph: (352) 237-2154
Fax: (352) 237-3566
E-mail: obs@obssales.com
Web site: *http://www.obssales.com*
Director of Sales: Tom Ventura

Ohio Thoroughbred Breeders and Owners Assn.
6024 Harrison Ave., Ste. 13
Cincinnati, OH 45248-1621
Ph: (513) 574-0440
Fax: (513) 574-2313
E-mail: gb.otbo@fuse.net
Web site: *http://www.otbo.com*
President: Dennis Heebink

Ontario Division Canadian Thoroughbred Horse Society
P.O. Box 172
Rexdale, ON M9W 5L1 Canada
Ph: (416) 675-3602
Fax: (416) 675-9405
E-mail: cthsont@idirect.com
Web site: *http://www.cthsont.com*

Oregon Thoroughbred Breeders Assn.
P.O. Box 17248
Portland, OR 97217
Ph: (503) 285-0658
Fax: (503) 285-0659
E-mail: otba@mindspring.com
Web site: *http://www.thoroughbredinfo.com/show-case/otba.htm*
Executive Director: Ursula V. Gibbons

Puerto Rico Breeders Sales Co.
P. O. Box 40957, Minillas Station
San Juan, Puerto Rico 00940
Ph: (787) 825-6444
Fax: (787) 825-6144

Ruidoso Horse Sales Co.
P.O. Box 909
Ruidoso Downs, NM 88346
Ph: (505) 378-4474
Fax: (505) 378-4788
E-mail: *ruihorse@zianet.com*
President: Lowell Neumayer

San Antonio Horse Sale Co.
6514 N. New Braunfels Ave.
San Antonio, TX 78209-3828
Ph: (210) 824-7552
Fax: (210) 824-7562
Sales Manager: Bart Sherwood

Tattersalls Ltd.
Terrace House
Newmarket, Suffolk, CB8 9BT Great Britain
Ph: 44 (1638) 665931

Fax: 44 (1638) 660850
E-mail: sales@tattersalls.com
Web site: *http://www.tattersalls.com*
Chairman: Edmond Mahony

Tattersalls (Ireland) Ltd.
Fairyhouse, Ratoath
County Meath, Ireland
Ph: 353 (1) 8864300
Fax: 353 (1) 8864303
E-mail: info@tattersalls.ie
Web site: *http://www.tattersalls.ie*
Chairman: Edmond Mahony

Tennessee Breeders Sales Co.
2474 Old Natchez Trace Rd.
Franklin, TN 37069-6302
Ph: (615) 373-8197

Thomas Sales Co.
10410 N. Yale Ave.
Sperry, OK 74073
Ph: (918) 288-7308
Fax: (918) 288-7330
E-mail: *thomas.sales@worldnet.att.net*
President: Robert Thomas

Washington Thoroughbred Breeders Assn.
P.O. Box 1499
Auburn, WA 98071-1499
Ph: (253) 288-7878
Fax: (253) 288-7890
E-mail: nancy@washingtonthoroughbred.com
Web site: *http://www.washingtonthoroughbred.com*
Sales and Research: Nancy Ross

Publicly Owned Companies With Thoroughbred-Industry Holdings

Boyd Gaming Corp.

A newcomer to the horse-racing industry, Boyd Gaming hit a home run when it purchased Delta Downs in Vinton, Louisiana, in 2001. Purses and wagering have increased substantially since the Las Vegas-based company opened its Delta Downs slots pavilion in early 2002. With the Boyd family controlling nearly half of the common stock, the company has 12 gaming properties in Nevada, Mississippi, Illinois, and Indiana, in addition to Louisiana. It is developing the Borgata casino hotel in Atlantic City, New Jersey, with MGM Mirage. Boyd Gaming owns the Stardust Hotel and Casino in Las Vegas and has two adjacent properties in Tunica, Mississippi, Sam's Town and Isle of Capri.

Headquarters: 2950 Industrial Road, Las Vegas, NV 89109-1150
Phone: (702) 792-7200
Web site: *http://www.boydgaming.com*
Chairman and CEO: William S. Boyd
President: Donald D. Snyder
Symbol, exchange: BYD, New York Stock Exchange
Employees: 4,225
2002 Revenues: $1.23-billion
2002 Net Profit: $40-million

Canterbury Park Holding Corp.

Canterbury Downs opened in 1985 outside Minneapolis, and—like several other tracks debuting in that era, such as Garden State Park and the Birmingham Turf Club—it struggled for survival as it failed to meet expectations for pari-mutuel handle and attendance. Ladbroke Racing bought the track in 1990 but closed it two years later. In late 1993, investor Irwin Jacobs bought the property and sold it a few months later to a group headed by Curtis A. Sampson, owner of a successful Minnesota telecommunications company. Randall Sampson, his son and an investor in the track, became president of the track. The elder Sampson spearheaded an initial public offering in 1994, and the track, with its name changed to Canterbury Park, reopened for live racing in 1995. Boosted by full-card simulcasting, Canterbury posted its first profit in 1997 and showed further gains when its card club opened in 2000. Canterbury Park Holding was one of *Forbes* magazine's top 200 small companies in 2000, ranking 88th.

Headquarters: 1100 Canterbury Road, Shakopee, MN 55379
Phone: (952) 445-7223
Web site: *http://www.canterburypark.com*
Chairman: Curtis A. Sampson
President and CEO: Randall D. Sampson
Symbol, exchange: ECP, American Stock Exchange
Employees: 681
2002 Revenues: $41.7-million
2002 Net Profit: $2.3-million

Churchill Downs Inc.

For more than a half-century, Churchill Downs has been America's best-known racetrack, but financial difficulties in the early 1980s almost led to a takeover. Warner Jones, a prominent breeder, stepped in and reorganized the company, bringing in lawyer Thomas Meeker as president and chief executive officer in 1984. In the intervening two decades, Churchill Downs Inc. has become a heavyweight within the racetrack industry, occupying top spots with Magna Entertainment Corp. and the New York Racing Association. Churchill's expansion began rather modestly, building Hoosier Park as a controlling partner and buying Ellis Park in western Kentucky. But the pace accelerated after Magna's Frank Stronach began his acquisitions in 1999, and Churchill bought Calder Race Course, Hollywood Park, and most recently Arlington Park. In 2003, Churchill officials indicated they never considered Ellis Park as part of their long-term strategic plan and put the track up for sale.

Headquarters: 700 Central Avenue, Louisville, KY 40208
Phone: (502) 636-4400
Web site: *http://www.churchilldownsincorporated.com*
Chairman: Carl F. Pollard
President and CEO: Thomas H. Meeker
Employees: 1,500

Symbol, exchange: CHDN, NASDAQ
2002 Revenues: $439.2-million
2002 Net Profit: $21-million

Gemstar-TV Guide International Inc.

Television Games Network, the racing industry's first national provider of televised races by cable and satellite signal, became a part of Gemstar-TV Guide International when Gemstar bought out TV Guide in 2002. In turn, Gemstar-TV Guide is 42% owned by Rupert Murdoch's News Corp. Gemstar developed the technology for VCR Plus+, which allows videotape recorder owners to enter a code for taping favorite television programs, and then licensed VCR Plus+ to television and VCR manufacturers. It entered into on-screen program listings and became a dominant player in the listings market when it bought TV Guide. The company owns SkyMall, a retailer whose catalog is found in most airline seat pockets. In early 2003, Gemstar-TV Guide restated its earnings for previous years and reported a $6.4-billion loss for 2002.

Headquarters: 135 N. Los Robles Ave., Suite 800, Pasadena, CA 91101
Phone: (626) 792-5700
Web site: *http://www.gemstartvguide.com*
Chief Executive: Jeff Shell
Employees: 2,700
Symbol, exchange: GMST, NASDAQ
2002 Revenues: $1-billion
2002 Net Loss: ($6.4-billion)

GTECH Holdings Corp.

The world's largest operator of lottery systems, GTECH Holdings Corp. has an interest in the racing industry from its one-third ownership of Turfway Park. A wholly owned GTECH subsidiary, Dreamport Inc., formally holds the ownership interest in the Northern Kentucky track. Dreamport is a part-owner of Suffolk Downs in East Boston, Massachusetts, and provides technological services to several pari-mutuel operations, including Harrington Raceway in Delaware. If Turfway's performance has proved to be disappointing, it is a small piece of GTECH, which supplies or operates lotteries for more than 80 customers in 44 countries.

Headquarters: 55 Technology Way, West Greenwich, RI 02817
Phone: (401) 392-1000
Web site: *http://www.GTECH.com*
Chairman: Emmett Paige Jr.
President: William B. Turner
Employees: 4,500
Symbol, exchange: GTK, New York Stock Exchange
2003 Revenues: $1.1-billion
2003 Net Profit: $83.6-million

Harrah's Entertainment Inc.

The world's third-largest casino company behind Park Place Entertainment Corp. and MGM Mirage, Harrah's Entertainment Inc. has been increasing its involvement in the pari-mutuel industry. By virtue of a loan to Turfway Park, Harrah's became a one-third owner of the Northern Kentucky track when Keeneland led a buyout of Jerry Carroll and his partners in January 1999. In August 2002, Harrah's announced that it was buying 95% of Louisiana Downs. The attraction was the impending arrival of slot machines at the Bossier City track in 2003. Harrah's said it planned significant improvements to the track and an investment in a slots facility. The company's total investment in Louisiana Downs, including the purchase price, was estimated at $183-million. Harrah's already had a Louisiana presence, owning and operating two riverboat casinos in Lake Charles.

Headquarters: One Harrah's Court, Las Vegas, NV 89119
Phone: (702) 407-6000
Web site: *http://www.harrahs.com*
Chairman: Philip G. Satre
President and CEO: Gary W. Loveman
Employees: 42,000
Symbol, exchange: HET, New York Stock Exchange
2002 Revenues: $4.14-billion
2002 Net Profit: $235-million

International Game Technology

International Game Technology became a player in the pari-mutuel industry with its 2001 purchase of Anchor Gaming, owner of United Tote Co. IGT acquired Anchor for more than $1.3-billion in stock, and the attraction was Anchor's slot-machine and lottery-related businesses. With the acquisition, IGT has become a dominant player in the slots industry, controlling about two-thirds of the United States market. The company was founded in 1980 by William "Si" Redd, and it has prospered with the growth of riverboat casinos and Native American casinos.

Headquarters: 9295 Prototype Drive, Reno, NV 89521
Phone: (775) 448-7777
Web site: *http://www.igt.com*
Chairman: Charles N. Matthewson
President and CEO: G. Thomas Baker
Employees: 6,200
Symbol, exchange: IGT, New York Stock Exchange
2002 Revenues: $1.85-billion
2002 Net Profit: $271.1-million

Magna Entertainment Corp.

Spun off from Frank Stronach-controlled Magna International in 1999, Magna Entertainment Corp. has quickly become the biggest player in the racetrack industry. Stronach's buying spree began with Santa Anita Park in 1999 and has grown to no fewer than 13 tracks, including ones that it leases. In addition to Santa Anita, Magna has acquired another top-level track, Gulfstream Park in South Florida, and in 2002 completed its purchase of Lone Star Park in the Dallas-Fort Worth metroplex for $80-million and assumption of $20-million in debt. Also in 2002, Magna added a Triple Crown track to its portfolio when it acquired controlling interest in Pimlico Race Course and Laurel Park. Although Magna has not been pushing hard for slot machines at its tracks, the company said it would move ahead with installing the machines at the Maryland tracks if approved by the state. Magna rolled out its XpressBet system for phone wagering, and in early 2003 unveiled HorseRacing TV, a cable-television network featuring races from the 13 Magna-owned or –affiliated tracks and 60 other racetracks.

Headquarters: 337 Magna Drive, Aurora, ON L4G 7K1, Canada
Phone: (905) 726-2462
Web site: *http://www.magnaent.com*
Chairman: Frank Stronach
President and CEO: Jim McAlpine
Employees: 4,300
Symbol, exchange: MECA, NASDAQ
2002 Revenues: $549.4-million
2002 Net Loss: ($14.4-million)

MAXXAM Inc.

A highly diversified company that has stirred controversy with its past acquisitions, MAXXAM Inc. offers a range of products from aluminum to lumber to live horse racing. Its principal source of revenues is Kaiser Aluminum, which filed for Chapter 11 bankruptcy in February 2002. The company also owns Pacific Lumber, which owns more than 2,000 acres of commercial timberlands in Humboldt County, California. In addition, MAXXAM owns commercial and residential properties in several states and Puerto Rico. Although its Sam Houston Race Park investment was a big loser initially, the track's financial picture has improved significantly with full-card simulcast wagering and savvy management.

Headquarters: 5847 San Felipe, Suite 2600, Houston, TX 77057
Phone: (713) 975-7600
Web site: None
Chairman and CEO: Charles E. Hurwitz
President: Paul N. Schwartz
Employees: 10,300
Symbol, exchange: MXM, American Stock Exchange
2002 Revenues: $446.6-million
2002 Net Loss: ($84-million)

MTR Gaming Group Inc.

Edson R. "Ted" Arneault thought he was simply helping a friend sell woebegone Mountaineer Park in 1992, but he ended up in the middle of a campaign to put video lottery terminals at West Virginia's racetracks. The effort succeeded, and Mountaineer became a hot property. MTR, of which Arneault owns approximately 14%, changed the name of the Chester facility to Mountaineer Racetrack and Gaming Resort to emphasize that it has both racing and 2,500 slot machines. In 2000, MTR was honored as one of *Forbes* magazine's 200 best small companies, ranking seventh. In 2002, MTR opened a hotel on the site and hosted its first graded race, the West Virginia Derby (G3). In 2002, it applied to build a new racetrack, Presque Isle Downs, near Erie, Pennsylvania. The company owns the Ramada Inn and Speakeasy Casino in Las Vegas and the Ramada Inn in Reno, Nevada.

Headquarters: Route 2 South, Chester, WV 26034
Phone: (304) 387-5712
Web site: *http://www.mtrgaming.com*
Chairman, President, and CEO: Edson R. "Ted" Arneault
Employees: 1,700
Symbol, exchange: MNTG, NASDAQ
2002 Revenues: $266.3-million
2002 Net Profit: $17.9-million

Penn National Gaming Inc.

From relatively modest beginnings as the owner of a regional racetrack near Harrisburg, Pennsylvania, Penn National Gaming has grown into the nation's seventh-largest publicly owned gaming company. Under Chairman and Chief Executive Officer Peter M. Carlino, son of the racetrack's principal owner, the company made profitable investments in off-track betting facilities in Central Pennsylvania, bought Pocono Downs and its off-track facilities, and then moved into gaming with its purchase of Charles Town Races in 1996. With extensive remodeling and slot machines, Charles Town has prospered and so has Penn National Gaming. It owns several casino properties and in 2002 agreed to purchase Hollywood Casino Co. for $780-million.

Headquarters: 825 Berkshire Blvd., Suite 200, Wyomissing, PA 19610
Phone: (610) 373-2400
Web site: *http://www.pennnational.com*
Chairman and CEO: Peter M. Carlino
President: Kevin DeSanctis
Employees: 5,180
Symbol, exchange: PENN, NASDAQ
2002 Revenues: $657.5-million
2002 Net Profit: $30.8-million

Scientific Games Corp.

Autotote Corp., a leading provider of pari-mutuel equipment and services, acquired Scientific Games Holdings Corp. in September 2000, and the combined company took the name Scientific Games Corp. A. Lorne Weill, who had been chairman and chief executive officer of Autotote since 1992, took over those positions in the new company. Scientific Games is a leading provider of instant lottery tickets, and Autotote controlled approximately 65% of the racetrack pari-mutuel market through 2002. In late 2002, the company gained wide attention when an employee and two of his friends conspired to fix a winning ticket, worth $3-million, for the Breeders' Cup Ultra Pick Six at Arlington Park. The three quickly were indicted and sentenced for wire fraud, and Autotote took steps to improve security in its pari-mutuel operations.

Headquarters: 750 Lexington Ave., 25th floor, New York, NY 10022
Phone: (212) 754-2233
Web site: *http://www.scientificgames.com*
Chairman and CEO: A. Lorne Weill
Employees: 2,750
Symbol, exchange: SGMS, NASDAQ
2002 Revenues: $455.3-million
2002 Net Profit: $52.1-million

Youbet.com Inc.

After a rocky start, interactive wagering company Youbet.com is making some headway in racetrack wagering over the Internet. A membership service with an Oregon wagering hub, Youbet.com reached an agreement with Television Games Network in 2001 that allowed Youbet.com clients to bet on races shown on TVG's cable and satellite programming. As part of the transaction, TVG acquired the right to purchase up to 51% of Youbet.com and in 2002 exercised options that gave it 16.6% of the online wagering company. Charles F. Champion became Youbet.com's president in 2002 and installed a new management team with a mandate to cut costs and increase revenues. In late 2002, the company achieved a positive cash flow for the first time in its history.

Headquarters: 5901 De Soto Ave., Los Angeles, CA 91367
Phone: (818) 668-2100
Web site: *http://www.youbet.com*
Chairman: David M. Marshall
President and CEO: Charles F. Champion
Employees: 76
Symbol, exchange: UBET, NASDAQ
2002 Revenues: $25.9-million
2002 Net Loss: ($9-million)

INTERNATIONAL

Review of the 2002 Racing Season

European racing in 2002 was built upon the rock-solid foundation established by Rock of Gibraltar (Ire), who was as dominant in his mile specialty as many of the teams fielded by his co-owner, Sir Alex Ferguson, manager of the Manchester United Football Club. But Rock of Gibraltar was by no means the only noteworthy runner in a season highlighted by a deep three-year-old division and the continuing on-course competition between the House of Maktoum and the Irish dynasty known as Coolmore.

Rock of Gibraltar, sired by Coolmore stallion Danehill, assured his place in the record books by scoring a record seven consecutive Group 1 victories between 2001 and '02, one more than the fabled Mill Reef accumulated in 1971 and '72. Bred by trainer Aidan O'Brien, his wife, and father-in-law, Rock of Gibraltar was an accomplished two-year-old, winning the Grand Criterium (Fr-G1) and Darley Dewhurst Stakes (Eng-G1), but he was overshadowed by stablemate Johannesburg, winner of the 2001 Breeders' Cup Juvenile (G1) at Belmont Park. The Rock, as he was popularly known, started the 2002 season at 9-to-1 in the Two Thousand Guineas (Eng-G1) while another stablemate, Hawk Wing, was favored at 3-to-2. Rock of Gibraltar took the lead with a furlong remaining in the one-mile classic and prevailed by a neck over a closing Hawk Wing. The Two Thousand Guineas field raced in two groups, and the winner's phalanx was regarded as having an advantage with a faster early pace over Hawk Wing's band.

While O'Brien-trained horses took the top two spots in the year's first classic for males, 14-to-1 Kazzia (Ger) landed the first filly classic, the One Thousand Guineas (Eng-G1), for the Maktoum family's Godolphin Racing. Another Godolphin runner, Marienbard, showed promise in winning the Jockey Club Stakes (Eng-G2) at the Newmarket meeting. Although the European season effectively begins with the English Guineas, the Maktoums staged their rich Dubai race meet in March, with Godolphin's Street Cry (Ire) impressively winning the $6-million Dubai World Cup (UAE-G1), the world's richest race. Sent to the United States, he won the Stephen Foster Handicap (G1) and was retired after sustaining an injury following his second-place finish to Left Bank in the Whitney Handicap (G1).

France staged the continent's next set of classics, but it was again an Irish triumph as O'Brien-trained Landseer (GB) prevailed at Longchamp in the Poule d'Essai des Poulains (Fr-G1), the Two Thousand Guineas equivalent. On the same May weekend, Godolphin's Grandera won the Singapore International Cup (Sin-G1), and O'Brien-trained High Chaparral (Ire) tuned up for the Epsom Derby (Eng-G1) with a victory in the Derrinstown Stud Derby Trial (Ire-G3) at Leopardstown. O'Brien had no Derby pretensions for Rock of Gibraltar, who next scored an easy victory in the Irish Two Thousand Guineas (Ire-G1) at the Curragh for his fourth consecutive Group 1 win. In the Irish One Thousand Guineas (Ire-G1), Luca Cumani-trained Gossamer (GB) made up for a poor effort in the English One Thousand and won by 4½ lengths. In France, the Niarchos family's Sulamani defeated Act One in the Prix du Jockey-Club (Fr-G1), the Derby equivalent.

For the Epsom Derby, O'Brien sent out the duo of 2.25-to-1 favorite Hawk Wing and 7-to-2 High Chaparral, and they overwhelmed their field. High Chaparral took the lead with a quarter-mile remaining and turned back Hawk Wing's challenge to win by two lengths, with Godolphin's Moon Ballad finishing another 12 lengths farther back in third. In the Epsom Oaks (Eng-G1), Godolphin's Kazzia went off as the 3.30-to-1 favorite and won by a half-length over O'Brien-trained Quarter Moon. High Chaparral proved that his Epsom victory was the true bill with a breezy 3½-length victory in the Irish Derby (Ire-G1) in late June, and Hawk Wing subsequently secured his only Group 1 win of the year in the Eclipse Stakes (Eng-G1) at Sandown.

Rock of Gibraltar returned to the races at Royal Ascot in mid-June and put together another trademark performance in the St. James's Palace Stakes (Eng-G1), quickening in the final quarter-mile, taking the lead with a furlong remaining, and easily holding off all challenges. In this case, his victim was stablemate Landseer. Godolphin also had a noteworthy Ascot meet, with Grandera triumphing in the Prince of Wales's Stakes (Eng-G1).

In July, Rock of Gibraltar tied Mill Reef's mark of six straight Group 1 wins with an easy win over Noverre in Goodwood's Sussex Stakes (Eng-G1), his first run against older horses. After a poor effort in the Epsom Oaks, Islington (Ire) came back to win the Nassau Stakes (Eng-G1) at Goodwood and the Aston Upthorpe Yorkshire Oaks (Eng-G1), both by impressive margins. Also in the European summer, other horses were making their marks. Godolphin's Marienbard found his groove at 1½ miles and scored two

Group 1 victories in Germany, the Deutschlandpreis at Dusseldorf and the Grosser Preis von Baden at Baden-Baden. Golan (Ire), winner of the 2001 Two Thousand Guineas, prevailed by a head over Nayef in the King George VI and Queen Elizabeth Stakes (Eng-G1) a few days after the death of his owner, Lord Weinstock. However, Nayef would come back to defeat Golan in the Juddmonte International Stakes (Eng-G1) at York.

In early September, Rock of Gibraltar etched his name in the record books when he traveled to Paris for the Prix du Moulin de Longchamp (Fr-G1), in which he was thoroughly tested on a Longchamp course rated as good. Advancing on the leaders with more than a furlong remaining, he grabbed the lead in the final 100 yards and prevailed by a half-length over Banks Hill (GB), with Gossamer another length back in third. It would be his final race in Europe; he finished a troubled second in the Breeders' Cup Mile (G1) and was retired to stud at Coolmore.

Before the Breeders' Cup came into existence, the European racing season traditionally wrapped up its championships with the Prix de l'Arc de Triomphe (Fr-G1) meet in early October at Longchamp. For some horses, the Arc is still the last major stop; for others, it is a stepping stone to the rich American event. Though unraced because of a virus after his two Derby triumphs, High Chaparral went off as the 2.20-to-1 favorite in the Arc, but he proved no match for Godolphin's Marienbard, who advanced to the lead in the final quarter-mile and turned back 7-to-2 Sulamani to win by three-quarters of a length. High Chaparral finished third. Also at the Arc meet, Domedriver (Ire) won the Prix Daniel Wildenstein de la Rochelle (Fr-G2) to earn a trip to Arlington Park for the Breeders' Cup Mile, which he won by three-quarters of a length over Rock of Gibraltar. Marienbard did not make the trip to America, but High Chaparral was at the top of his game and won the $2-million Breeders' Cup Turf (G1).

Among the year's two-year-olds, none stood out as Johannesburg had in 2001. Oasis Dream, owned by Juddmonte Farms' Khalid Abdullah, won a maiden race at Nottingham and the Shadwell Stud Middle Park Stakes (Eng-G1) to take the top spot on the end-of-year International Classifications.

Japan's richest races follow the Breeders' Cup by a few weeks, and Italian-born jockey Frankie Dettori scored two major victories, aboard Italian-trained Falbrav in the Japan Cup (Jpn-G1) and Eagle Cafe in the Japan Cup Dirt. Media Puzzle, trained in Ireland by Dermot Weld, won the Melbourne Cup (Aus-G1).

Richest International Races of 2002

Race (Grade)	Total Purse	Track, Country	Distance	Date	Winner	Value to Winner
Dubai World Cup (UAE-G1)	$6,000,000	Nad Al Sheba, United Arab Emirates	1¼m	03-23-2002	Street Cry (Ire)	$3,600,000
Japan Cup (Jpn-G1)	3,869,919	Nakayama, Japan	1⅜mT	11-24-2002	Falbrav	2,032,520
Arima Kinen	2,850,000	Nakayama, Japan	1 9/16mT	12-22-2002	Symboli Kris S.	1,500,000
Hong Kong Cup (HK-G1)	2,307,600	Sha Tin, Hong Kong	1¼mT	12-15-2002	Anabar	1,307,640
Tokyo Yushun (Japanese Derby)	2,288,000	Tokyo, Japan	1½mT	05-26-2002	Tanino Gimlet	1,200,000
Epsom Derby (Eng-G1)	2,077,602	Epsom, England	1½mT	06-08-2002	High Chaparral (Ire)	1,229,589
Takarazuka Kinen	2,076,033	Hanshin, Japan	1⅜mT	06-23-2002	Dantsu Flame	1,090,909
Tenno Sho (Autumn)	2,025,806	Nakayama, Japan	1¼mT	10-27-2002	Symboli Kris S.	1,064,516
Japan Cup Dirt	2,016,260	Nakayama, Japan	1⅛m	11-23-2002	Eagle Cafe	1,056,911
Dubai Duty Free S. (UAE-G1)	2,000,000	Nad Al Sheba, UAE	1⅛mT	03-23-2002	Terre a Terre	1,200,000
Dubai Sheema Classic (UAE-G1)	2,000,000	Nad Al Sheba, UAE	1½mT	03-23-2002	Nayef	1,200,000
Dubai Golden Shaheen (UAE-G1)	2,000,000	Nad Al Sheba, UAE	6f	03-23-2002	Caller One	1,200,000
UAE Derby (UAE-G2)	2,000,000	Nad Al Sheba, UAE	1¼m	03-23-2002	Essence of Dubai	1,200,000
Melbourne Cup (Aus-G1)	1,997,730	Flemington, Australia	2mT	11-05-2002	Media Puzzle	1,345,410
Tenno Sho (Spring)	1,962,500	Kyoto, Japan	2mT	04-28-2002	Manhattan Cafe	1,031,250
Hong Kong Vase (HK-G1)	1,794,800	Sha Tin, Hong Kong	1½mT	12-15-2002	Ange Gabriel	1,025,600
Hong Kong Mile (HK-G1)	1,794,800	Sha Tin, Hong Kong	1mT	12-15-2002	Ecclesiastical	1,025,600
Queen Elizabeth II Cup (HK-G1)	1,794,800	Sha Tin, Hong Kong	1¼mT	04-21-2002	Eishin Preston	1,025,600
Kikuka Sho (Japanese St. Leger)	1,692,063	Kyoto, Japan	1⅞mT	10-20-2002	Hishi Miracle	888,889
W. S. Cox Plate (Aus-G1)	1,630,670	Moonee Valley, Australia	1¼mT	10-26-2002	Northerly	1,090,713
International Cup (Sin-G1)	1,623,900	Kranji, Singapore	1¼mT	05-11-2002	Grandera	989,961
Queen Elizabeth II Commemorative Cup	1,583,333	Kyoto, Japan	1⅜mT	11-10-2002	Fine Motion	833,333
Prix de l'Arc de Triomphe (Fr-G1)	1,574,560	Longchamp, France	1½mT	10-06-2002	Marienbard	899,704
Mile Championship	1,495,000	Morioka, Japan	1mT	11-17-2002	Tokai Point	783,333
Yushun Himba (Japanese Oaks)	1,465,873	Tokyo, Japan	1½mT	05-19-2002	Smile Tomorrow	769,841
Sprinters S.	1,458,537	Niigata, Japan	6fT	09-29-2002	Believe	764,228
Yasuda Kinen	1,446,774	Tokyo, Japan	1mT	06-02-2002	Admire Cozzene	758,065

Race (Grade)	Total Purse	Track, Country	Distance	Date	Winner	Value to Winner
Satsuki Sho	1,399,242	Nakayama, Japan	1¼mT	04-14-2002	No Reason	734,848
NHK Mile Cup	1,379,528	Tokyo, Japan	1mT	05-04-2002	Telegnosis	724,409
Shuka Sho	1,362,097	Kyoto, Japan	1¼mT	10-13-2002	Fine Motion	717,742
Hong Kong Sprint (HK-G2)	1,282,000	Sha Tin, Hong Kong	5fT	12-15-2002	Easy Thrills	730,740
Oka Sho	1,279,545	Hanshin, Japan	1mT	04-07-2002	Arrow Carry	674,242
Golden Slipper S. (Aus-G1)	1,273,000	Rosehill, Australia	6fT	03-23-2002	Calaway Gal	763,800
Caulfield Cup (Aus-G1)	1,169,006	Caulfield, Australia	1½mT	10-19-2002	Northerly	620,950
Irish Derby (Ire-G1)	1,098,798	The Curragh, Ireland	1½mT	06-30-2002	High Chaparral (Ire)	678,466
King George VI and Queen Elizabeth Diamond S. (Eng-G1)	1,097,325	Ascot, England	1½mT	07-27-2002	Golan (Ire)	636,448
Irish Champion S. (Ire-G1)	1,082,510	Leopardstown, Ireland	1¼mT	09-07-2002	Grandera	615,259
Sapporo Kinen	1,033,898	Sapporo, Japan	1¼mT	08-18-2002	T.M. Ocean	542,373
Derby Italiano (Ity-G1)	1,021,303	Rome, Italy	1½mT	05-26-2002	Rakti	506,062
CBC Sho	1,008,264	Chukyo, Japan	6fT	12-15-2002	Sunningdale	528,926
Godolphin Mile (UAE-G2)	1,000,000	Nad Al Sheba, UAE	1m	03-23-2002	Grey Memo	600,000
Atto Mile (Can-G1)	1,000,000	Woodbine, Canada	1mT	09-08-2002	Good Journey	600,000
Stayers S.	1,000,000	Nakayama, Japan	2¼mT	11-30-2002	Hot Secret	524,590
Prix du Jockey Club (Fr-G1)	995,940	Chantilly, France	1½mT	06-02-2002	Sulamani	569,080
Mainichi Okan (Jpn-G2)	991,870	Nakayama, Japan	1⅛mT	10-06-2002	Magnaten	520,325
Sankei Sho All Comers	991,870	Niigata, Japan	1⅜mT	09-22-2002	Rosado	520,325
Kyoto Daishoten	991,870	Kyoto, Japan	1½mT	10-06-2002	Narita Top Road	520,325
Kinko Sho	976,000	Chukyo, Japan	1¼mT	05-25-2002	Tsurumaru Boy	512,000
Hanshin Daishoten	945,736	Hanshin, Japan	1⅞mT	03-17-2002	Narita Top Road	496,124
Hanshin Himba S.	942,149	Hanshin, Japan	1mT	12-15-2002	Diamond Biko	495,868
Hanshin Juvenile Fillies	934,426	Hanshin, Japan	7fT	12-01-2002	Peace of World	491,803
Sankei Osaka Hai	927,485	Hanshin, Japan	1¼mT	03-31-2002	Sunrise Pegasus	488,525
Swan S.	919,355	Kyoto, Japan	7fT	10-26-2002	Shonan Kampf	483,871
Copa Republica Argentina	905,738	Nakayama, Japan	1 9/16mT	11-03-2002	Sunrise Jaeger	475,410
Milers Cup	904,709	Hanshin, Japan	1mT	04-13-2002	Millennium Bio	449,880
Keio Hai Spring Cup (Jpn-G2)	890,625	Tokyo, Japan	7fT	05-12-2002	God of Chance	468,750
Tokai S.	876,984	Chukyo, Japan	1 7/16m	05-19-2002	Hagino High Grade	460,317
Grosser Preis von Baden (Ger-G1)	856,167	Baden-Baden, Germany	1½mT	09-01-2002	Marienbard	501,891
St. Lite Kinen	848,361	Niigata, Japan	1⅜mT	09-15-2002	Balance of Game	442,623
Kobe Shimbun Hai	841,463	Hanshin, Japan	1¼mT	09-22-2002	Symboli Kris S.	439,024
Kyoto Shimbun Hai	814,961	Kyoto, Japan	1⅜mT	05-03-2002	Fast Tateyama	415,197
Rose S.	811,475	Hanshin, Japan	1¼mT	09-15-2002	Fine Motion	426,230
T.V. Tokyo Hai Aoba Sho	808,594	Tokyo, Japan	1½mT	04-27-2002	Symboli Kris S.	626,750
Spring S.	802,326	Nakayama, Japan	1⅛mT	03-17-2002	Tanino Gimlet	418,605
New Zealand Trophy	784,091	Nakayama, Japan	1mT	04-06-2002	Taiki Lion	409,091
Revue S.	767,442	Hanshin, Japan	7fT	03-10-2002	Success Beauty	403,101
Flora S.	761,538	Tokyo, Japan	1¼mT	04-21-2002	Nishino Hanaguruma	400,000
Hakodate Kinen	705,172	Hakodate, Japan	1¼mT	07-21-2002	Yamanin Respect	370,690
Kitakyushu Kinen	699,145	Kokura, Japan	1⅛mT	07-14-2002	Top Protector	367,521
Ibis Summer Dash	693,220	Niigata, Japan	5fT	08-18-2002	Calstone Light O	364,407
Juddmonte International S. (Eng-G1)	689,445	York, England	1¼mT	08-20-2002	Nayef	399,878
Sekiya Kinen	687,395	Niigata, Japan	1mT	07-28-2002	Magnaten	361,345
Asahi Challenge Cup	687,395	Hanshin, Japan	1¼mT	09-07-2002	Tap Dance City	364,345
Centaur S.	687,395	Hanshin, Japan	6fT	09-08-2002	Believe	361,345
Keisei Hai Autumn H.	687,395	Niigata, Japan	1mT	09-08-2002	Breaktime	361,345
Victoria Derby (Aus-G1)	683,305	Flemington, Australia	1 9/16mT	11-02-2002	Helenus	445,480
Elm S.	682,203	Sapporo, Japan	1 1/16m	08-31-2002	Preeminence	355,932
Tanabata Sho	681,667	Fukushima, Japan	1¼mT	07-07-2002	Eagle Cafe	358,333
Niigata Kinen	681,667	Niigata, Japan	1¼mT	08-25-2002	Towa Treasure	358,333
Kokura Kinen	681,667	Hakodate, Japan	1¼mT	08-11-2002	Aratama Indy	358,333
Fukushima Kinen	681,667	Fukushima, Japan	1¼mT	11-17-2002	Win Blaze	358,333
Queen S.	670,833	Sapporo, Japan	1⅛mT	08-11-2002	Mitsuwa Top Lady	350,000
Mermaid S.	670,833	Hanshin, Japan	1¼mT	07-07-2002	Yamakatsu Suzuran	350,000
Keihan Hai	665,041	Kyoto, Japan	1⅛mT	11-23-2002	Sidewinder	349,593
Champion S. (Eng-G1)	661,864	Newmarket, England	1¼mT	10-19-2002	Storming Home	383,881
Aichi Hai	659,677	Chukyo, Japan	1¼mT	06-02-2002	Tokai Pulsar	346,774
Chunichi Shimbun Hai	659,677	Chukyo, Japan	1⅛mT	12-07-2002	My Sole Sound	346,774
Naruo Kinen	659,677	Hanshin, Japan	1¼mT	12-08-2002	Ibuki Government	346,774
Epsom Cup	657,677	Tokyo, Japan	1⅛mT	06-09-2002	Joten Brave	346,774
Sirius S.	654,472	Hanshin, Japan	7f	09-29-2002	Sterling Rose	341,463

Note: all distances approximate except for races in England and Ireland

Major International Races

Canada

Atto Mile Stakes

Grade 1, Woodbine, Ontario, three-year-olds and up, 1 mile, turf. Held September 9, 2001, with a gross value of $1,000,000. First held in 1997.

Year	Winner	Jockey	Second	Third	Strs	Time	1st Purse
2002	Good Journey, 6	P. Day	†Chopinina, 4	Nuclear Debate, 7	13	1:33.27	$600,000
2001	Numerous Times, 4	P. Husbands	Affirmed Success, 7	Quiet Resolve, 6	14	1:32.79	$600,000
2000	Riviera (Fr) 6	J. R. Velazquez	Arkadian Hero, 5	Affirmed Success, 6	13	1:33.18	$600,000
1999	Quiet Resolve, 4	R. C. Landry	Rob 'n Gin, 5	Jim and Tonic (Fr), 5	15	1:33.19	$630,000
1998	Labeeb (GB), 6	K. J. Desormeaux	Jim and Tonic (Fr), 4	Poteen, 4	11	1:33.00	$450,000
1997	Geri, 5	C. W. Antley	Helmsman, 5	Crown Attorney, 4	12	1:36.20	$300,000

1997-'98 Woodbine Mile S. 1999 Hawksley Hill (Ire) finished first, disqualified to fourth. † denotes female.

Breeders' Stakes

Not graded, Woodbine, Ontario, three-year-olds, foaled in Canada, 1½ miles, turf. Held August 11, 2001, with a gross value of $500,000. First held in 1889.

Year	Winner	Jockey	Second	Third	Strs	Time	1st Purse
2002	Portcullis	S. Callaghan	El Soprano	Mountain Beacon	10	2:29.80	$300,000
2001	†Sweetest Thing	J. S. McAleney	Flaming Sky	†Asia	6	2:29.90	$300,000
2000	Lodge Hill	M. E. Smith	Master Stuart	Scatter the Gold	7	2:28.97	$300,000
1999	†Free Vacation	L. L. Gulas	John the Drummer	American Falcon	13	2:28.45	$195,000
1998	†Pinafore Park	R. C. Landry	Patriot Love	Comet Kris	9	2:30.20	$180,000
1997	John the Magician	S. R. Bahen	†One Emotion	†Heaven to Earth	12	2:35.60	$175,860
1996	Chief Bearhart	M. Walls	Firm Dancer	Sealaunch	9	2:28.60	$171,120
1995	Charlie's Dewan	C. Perret	Mt. Sassafras	Dagda	13	2:26.40	$182,700
1994	Basquelan	J. M. Lauzon	Pagagar	Testalino	5	2:47.80	$149,739
1993	Peteski	C. Perret	Flashy Regent	English Toff	4	2:30.40	$237,549
1992	Blitzer	D. J. Seymour	†Classic Reign	Rodin	11	2:35.60	$180,000

1994 held at Fort Erie. † denotes female.

Canadian International Stakes

Grade 1, Woodbine, Ontario, three-year-olds and up, 1½ miles, turf. Held September 30, 2001, with a gross value of $1,500,000. First held in 1938.

Year	Winner	Jockey	Second	Third	Strs	Time	1st Purse
2002	Ballingarry (Ire), 3	M. Kinane	Falcon Flight, 6	Yavana's Pace, 10	8	2:31.68	$900,000
2001	Mutamam (GB), 6	R. Hills	Paolini (Ger), 4	Lodge Hill, 4	12	2:28.46	$900,000
2000	Mutafaweq, 4	L. Dettori	Williams News, 5	Daliapour (Ire), 4	12	2:27.62	$900,000
1999	Thornfield, 5	R. A. Dos Ramos	Fruits of Love, 4	Courteous (GB), 4	9	2:32.39	$936,000
1998	Royal Anthem, 3	G. L. Stevens	Chief Bearhart, 5	Parade Ground, 3	8	2:29.60	$630,000
1997	Chief Bearhart, 4	J. A. Santos	Down the Aisle, 4	Romanov (Ire), 3	6	2:29.00	$600,000
1996	Singspiel (Ire), 4	G. L. Stevens	Chief Bearhart, 3	Mecke, 4	7	2:33.20	$600,000
1995	Lassigny, 4	P. Day	Mecke, 3	Hasten To Add, 5	15	2:29.80	$653,250
1994	Raintrap (GB), 4	R. G. Davis	†Alywow, 3	Volochine (Ire), 3	9	2:25.60	$606,900
1993	Husband, 3	C. B. Asmussen	Cozzene's Prince, 6	Regency (GB), 3	11	2:36.40	$623,100
1992	Snurge (Ire), 5	R. T. Quinn	Ghazi, 3	Wiorno (GB), 4	14	2:39.00	$636,000

1992-'95 Rothmans Ltd. International S. 1992 Wiorno (GB) finished first, disqualified to third; 2002 Zindabad (Fr) finished third, DQ to sixth. † denotes female.

E. P. Taylor Stakes

Grade 1, Woodbine, Ontario, three-year-olds and up, fillies and mares, 1¼ miles, turf. Held September 30, 2001, with a gross value of $500,000. First held in 1956.

Year	Winner	Jockey	Second	Third	Strs	Time	1st Purse
2002	Fraulein (GB), 3	K. Darley	Alasha (Ire), 3	Volga (Ire), 4	6	2:10.03	$450,000
2001	Choc Ice (Ire), 3	J. P. Murtagh	Volga (Ire), 3	Spring Oak (GB), 3	13	2:03.01	$300,000
2000	Fly for Avie, 5	T. Kabel	Lady Upstage (Ire), 3	Innuendo (Ire), 5	6	2:02.78	$300,000
1999	Insight (Fr), 4	M. E. Smith	Cerulean Sky (Ire), 3	Midnight Line, 4	7	2:05.34	$300,000
1998	Zomaradah (GB), 3	G. L. Stevens	Tresoriere, 4	Griselda, 3	8	2:02.40	$273,600
1997	Kool Kat Katie (Ire), 3	O. Peslier	Mousse Glacee (Fr), 3	L'Annee Folle (Fr), 4	9	2:02.00	$206,460
1996	Wandering Star, 3	W. H. McCauley	Flame Valley, 3	Carling (Fr), 4	8	2:04.60	$204,120
1995	Timarida (Ire), 3	L. Dettori	Matiara, 3	Bold Ruritana, 5	13	2:03.60	$213,120
1994	Truly a Dream (Ire), 3	C. J. McCarron	Bold Ruritana, 4	Hero's Love, 6	9	2:01.60	$207,180
1993	Hero's Love, 5	E. Fires	Dance for Donna, 4	Lady Shirl, 6	7	2:14.40	$204,300
1992	Hatoof, 3	W. R. Swinburn	Urban Sea, 3	Hero's Love, 4	12	2:07.80	$210,960

Prince of Wales Stakes

Not graded, Fort Erie, Ontario, three-year-olds, foaled in Canada, 1 3/16 miles, dirt. Held July 22, 2001, with a gross value of $350,000. First held in 1929.

Year	Winner	Jockey	Second	Third	Strs	Time	1st Purse
2002	Le Cinquieme Essai	B. Bochinski	Bravley	Anglian Prince	12	1:56.53	$300,000
2001	Win City	C. Montpellier	†Dancethruthedawn	Brushing Bully	6	1:56.14	$210,000
2000	Scatter the Gold	T. Kabel	For Our Sake	Cool N Collective	7	1:56.01	$170,280
1999	†Gandria	C. Montpellier	Woodcarver	Euchre	8	1:56.23	$155,700
1998	Archers Bay	R. C. Landry	Nite Dreamer	One Way Love	6	1:55.20	$118,500
1997	Cryptocloser	W. Martinez	C. C. On Ice	Rabbit in a Hat	7	1:56.00	$117,660
1996	Stephanotis	M. Walls	Firm Dancer	Kristy Krunch	7	1:55.20	$121,620
1995	Kiridashi	L. Attard	Regal Discovery	Mt. Sassafras	6	1:55.00	$121,800
1994	Bruce's Mill	C. Perret	Basqueian	Parental Pressure	4	1:53.20	$87,296
1993	Peteski	D. Penna	Flashy Regent	Cheery Knight	8	1:54.40	$72,203
1992	Benburb	L. Attard	Alydeed	Judge Carson	6	1:57.40	$107,700

† denotes female.

Queen's Plate Stakes

Not graded, Woodbine, Ontario, three-year-olds, foaled in Canada, 1 1/4 miles, dirt. Held June 24, 2001, with a gross value of $1,000,000. First held in 1860.

Year	Winner	Jockey	Second	Third	Strs	Time	1st Purse
2002	T J's Lucky Moon	S. Bahen	Anglian Prince	Forever Grand	13	2:06.88	$600,000
2001	†Dancethruthedawn	G. Boulanger	Win City	Brushing Bully	10	2:03.78	$600,000
2000	Scatter the Gold	T. Kabel	I and I	For Our Sake	16	2:05.53	$600,000
1999	Woodcarver	M. Walls	†Gandria	Euchre	17	2:03.13	$300,000
1998	Archers Bay	K. J. Desormeaux	Brite Adam	Kinkennie	13	2:02.20	$300,000
1997	Awesome Again	M. E. Smith	Cryptocloser	Sovereign Storm	14	2:04.20	$255,420
1996	Victor Cooley	E. Ramsammy	Stephanotis	Kristy Krunch	13	2:03.80	$255,480
1995	Regal Discovery	T. Kabel	Freedom Fleet	Mt. Sassafras	14	2:03.80	$261,660
1994	Basqueian	J. M. Lauzon	Bruce's Mill	Parental Pressure	11	2:03.40	$276,420
1993	Peteski	C. Perret	Cheery Knight	Janraffole	11	2:04.20	$218,600
1992	Alydeed	C. Perret	Grand Hooley	Benburb	12	2:04.60	$228,900

† denotes female.

England

Derby Stakes

Group 1, Epsom, three-year-olds, colts and fillies, 1 1/2 miles and ten yards, turf. Held June 9, 2001, with a gross value of $1,379,900. First held in 1780.

Year	Winner	Jockey	Second	Third	Strs	Time	1st Purse
2002	High Chaparral (Ire)	J. Murtagh	Hawk Wing	Moon Ballad	12	2:39.45	$1,249,424
2001	Galileo (Ire)	M. J. Kinane	Golan	Tobougg	12	2:33.20	$800,342
2000	Sinndar	J. Murtagh	Sakhee	Beat Hollow (GB)	15	2:36.75	$918,981
1999	Oath	K. Fallon	Daliapour	Beat All	16	2:37.43	$990,671
1998	High-Rise (Ire)	O. Peslier	City Honours	Border Arrow	15	2:33.88	$978,679
1997	Benny the Dip	W. Ryan	Silver Patriarch	Romanov (Ire)	13	2:34.77	$971,448
1996	Shaamit	M. Hills	Dushyantor	Shantou	20	2:35.05	$804,894
1995	Lammtarra	W. Swinburn	Tamure (Ire)	Presenting	15	2:32.31	$805,687
1994	Erhaab	W. Carson	King's Theatre (Ire)	Colonel Collins	25	2:34.16	$717,662
1993	Commander in Chief	M. J. Kinane	Blue Judge	Blues Traveller (Ire)	16	2:34.51	$693,078
1992	Dr Devious (Ire)	J. Reid	St. Jovite	Silver Wisp	18	2:36.19	$649,473

Gold Cup

Group 1, Ascot Racecourse, four-year-olds and up, 2 1/2 miles, turf. Held June 21, 2001, with a gross value of $297,297. First held in 1807.

Year	Winner	Jockey	Second	Third	Strs	Time	1st Purse
2002	Royal Rebel, 6	J. Murtagh	Vinnie Roe, 4	Wareed, 4	15	4:25.64	$199,184
2001	Royal Rebel, 5	J. Murtagh	Persian Punch, 8	Jardines Lookout, 4	12	4:18.90	$172,432
2000	Kayf Tara, 6	M. J. Kinane	Far Cry, 5	Compton Ace, 4	11	4:24.53	$184,308
1999	Enzeli, 4	J. Murtagh	Invermark, 5	Kayf Tara, 5	17	4:18.85	$191,662
1998	Kayf Tara, 4	L. Dettori	Double Trigger, 7	Three Cheers, 4	16	4:32.36	$198,132
1997	Celeric, 5	P. Eddery	Classic Cliche, 5	Election Day, 5	13	4:26.19	$187,197
1996	Classic Cliche, 4	M. Kinane	Double Trigger, 5	Nononito, 5	7	4:23.20	$182,980
1995	Double Trigger, 4	J. Weaver	Moonax, 4	Admiral's Well, 5	7	4:20.25	$178,465
1994	Arcadian Heights, 6	M. Hills	Vintage Crop, 7	Sonus, 5	9	4:27.67	$169,666
1993	Drum Taps, 7	L. Dettori	Assessor, 4	Turgeon, 7	10	4:32.57	$166,410
1992	Drum Taps, 6	L. Dettori	Arcadian Heights, 4	Turgeon, 6	6	4:18.20	$198,590

King George VI and Queen Elizabeth Stakes

Group 1, Ascot Racecourse, three-year-olds and up, 1 1/2 miles, turf. Held July 28, 2001, with a gross value of $1,068,525. First held in 1951.

Year	Winner	Jockey	Second	Third	Strs	Time	1st Purse
2002	Golan (Ire), 4	K. Fallon	Nayef, 4	Zindabad, 6	9	2:29.70	$636,448
2001	Galileo (Ire), 3	M. J. Kinane	Fantastic Light, 5	Hightori, 4	12	2:27.71	$619,745

Year	Winner	Jockey	Second	Third	Strs	Time	1st Purse
2000	Montjeu (Ire), 4	M. J. Kinane	Fantastic Light, 4	Daliapour, 4	7	2:29.98	$654,023
1999	Daylami (Ire), 5	L. Dettori	Nedawi, 4	Fruits of Love, 4	8	2:29.35	$539,676
1998	Swain (Ire), 6	L. Dettori	High-Rise (Ire), 3	Royal Anthem, 3	8	2:29.60	$587,463
1997	Swain (Ire), 5	J. Reid	Pilsudski (Ire), 5	Helissio, 4	8	2:36.45	$490,509
1996	Pentire, 4	M. Hills	Classic Cliche, 4	Shaamit, 3	8	2:28.11	$457,867
1995	Lammtarra, 3	L. Dettori	Pentire, 3	Strategic Choice, 4	7	2:31.01	$445,877
1994	King's Theatre (Ire), 3	M. Kinane	White Muzzle (GB), 4	Wagon Master, 4	12	2:28.92	$408,813
1993	Opera House (GB), 5	M. Roberts	White Muzzle (GB), 3	Commander in Chief, 3	10	2:33.94	$409,307
1992	St. Jovite, 3	S. Craine	Saddlers' Hall (Ire), 4	Opera House (GB), 4	8	2:30.85	$497,878

Oaks Stakes

Group 1, Epsom, three-year-olds, fillies, 1½ miles and ten yards, turf. Held June 8, 2001, with a gross value of $503,663. First held in 1779.

Year	Winner	Jockey	Second	Third	Strs	Time	1st Purse
2002	Kazzia (Ger)	L. Dettori	Quarter Moon	Shadow Dancing	14	2:44.52	$297,009
2001	Imagine	M. J. Kinane	Flight of Fancy	Relish The Thought	14	2:36.70	$292,125
2000	Love Divine	T. Quinn	Kalypso Katie (Ire)	Melikah (Ire)	16	2:43.11	$288,823
1999	Ramruma	K. Fallon	Noushkey	Zahrat Dubai	10	2:38.72	$286,775
1998	Shahtoush	M. J. Kinane	Bahr (GB)	Midnight Line	8	2:38.23	$289,342
1997	Reams of Verse	K. Fallon	Gazelle Royale	Crown of Light	12	2:35.59	$297,432
1996	Lady Carla (GB)	P. Eddery	Pricket	Mezzogiorno	11	2:35.55	$309,279
1995	Moonshell (Ire)	L. Dettori	Dance a Dream (GB)	Pure Grain (GB)	10	2:35.44	$236,037
1994	Balanchine	L. Dettori	Wind in Her Hair (Ire)	Hawajiss	10	2:40.37	$223,758
1993	Intrepidity (GB)	M. Roberts	Royal Ballerina (Ire)	Oakmead (Ire)	14	2:34.19	$228,404
1992	User Friendly (GB)	G. Duffield	All At Sea	Pearl Angel (GB)	7	2:39.77	$269,851

One Thousand Guineas

Group 1, Newmarket, three-year-olds, fillies, 1 mile, turf. Held May 6, 2001, with a gross value of $431,850. First held in 1814.

Year	Winner	Jockey	Second	Third	Strs	Time	1st Purse
2003	Russian Rhythm	K. Fallon	Six Perfections	Intercontinental	19	1:38.43	$292,747
2002	Kazzia (Ger)	L. Dettori	Snowfire	Alasha (Ire)	17	1:37.85	$250,612
2001	Ameerat	P. Robinson	Muwakleh	Toroca	15	1:38.30	$250,473
2000	Lahan (GB)	R. Hills	Princess Ellen (GB)	Petrushka (Ire)	18	1:36.38	$221,517
1999	Wince	K. Fallon	Wannabe Grand (Ire)	Valentine Waltz (Ire)	22	1:37.91	$206,757
1998	Cape Verdi	L. Dettori	Shahtoush	Exclusive	16	1:37.86	$214,081
1997	Sleepytime	K. Fallon	Oh Nellie	Dazzle	15	1:37.66	$169,872
1996	Bosra Sham	P. Eddery	Matiya (Ire)	Bint Shadayid	13	1:37.75	$151,461
1995	Harayir	R. Hills	Aqaarid	Moonshell (Ire)	14	1:36.72	$178,983
1994	Las Meninas (Ire)	J. Reid	Balanchine	Coup de Genie	15	1:36.71	$166,127
1993	Sayyedati (GB)	W. R. Swinburn	Niche	Ajfan	12	1:37.34	$163,969
1992	Hatoof	W. R. Swinburn	Marling (Ire)	Kenbu (Fr)	14	1:39.45	$192,254

St. Leger Stakes

Group 1, Doncaster, three-year-olds, colts and fillies, 1¾ miles and 127 yards, turf. Held September 15, 2001, with a gross value of $544,381. First held in 1776.

Year	Winner	Jockey	Second	Third	Strs	Time	1st Purse
2002	Bollin Eric	K. Darley	Highest	Bandari	8	3:02.92	$374,640
2001	Milan (GB)	M. J. Kinane	Demophilos	Mr Combustible	10	3:05.10	$326,629
2000	Millenary	T. Quinn	Air Marshall	Chimes At Midnight	11	3:02.58	$315,018
1999	Mutafaweq	R. Hills	†Ramruma	Adair	9	3:02.75	$353,664
1998	Nedawi	J. Reid	†High and Low	Sunshine Street	9	3:05.61	$335,898
1997	Silver Patriarch	P. Eddery	Vertical Speed	The Fly (GB)	10	3:06.92	$295,420
1996	Shantou	L. Dettori	Dushyantor	Samraan	11	3:05.10	$271,692
1995	Classic Cliche	L. Dettori	Minds Music	Istidaad	10	3:09.74	$259,794
1994	Moonax	P. Eddery	Broadway Flyer	Double Trigger	8	3:04.19	$236,950
1993	Bob's Return	P. Robinson	Armiger	Edbaysaan	9	3:07.85	$292,567
1992	†User Friendly (GB)	G. Duffield	Sonus	Bonny Scot	7	3:05.48	$323,139

† denotes female.

Two Thousand Guineas

Group 1, Newmarket, three-year-olds, colts and fillies, 1 mile, turf. Held May 5, 2001, with a gross value of $431,850. First held in 1809.

Year	Winner	Jockey	Second	Third	Strs	Time	1st Purse
2003	Refuse To Bend	P. Smullen	Zafeen	Norse Dancer	20	1:37.98	$292,747
2002	Rock of Gibraltar (Ire)	J. Murtagh	Hawk Wing	Redback	22	1:36.50	$250,612
2001	Golan	K. Fallon	Tamburlaine	Frenchmans Bay	18	1:37.40	$250,473
2000	King's Best	K. Fallon	Giant's Causeway	Barathea Guest	27	1:37.77	$265,820
1999	Island Sands	L. Dettori	Enrique	Mujahid	16	1:37.14	$276,426
1998	King of Kings (Ire)	M. Kinane	Lend a Hand	Border Arrow	18	1:39.25	$286,219

Year	Winner	Jockey	Second	Third	Strs	Time	1st Purse
1997	Entrepreneur	M. Kinane	Revoque	Poteen	16	1:35.64	$213,832
1996	Mark of Esteem (Ire)	L. Dettori	Even Top (Ire)	Bijou d'Inde	13	1:37.59	$184,212
1995	Pennekamp	T. Jarnet	Celtic Swing	Bahri	11	1:35.16	$190,487
1994	Mister Baileys (GB)	J. Weaver	Grand Lodge	Colonel Collins	23	1:35.08	$194,491
1993	Zafonic	P. Eddery	Barathea (Ire)	Bin Ajwaad	14	1:35.32	$173,569
1992	Rodrigo de Triano	L. Piggott	Lucky Lindy	Pursuit of Love	16	1:38.37	$203,189

France

Poule d'Essai des Poulains (French Two Thousand Guineas)

Group 1, Longchamp, three-year-old colts, 1,600 meters, turf. Held May 13, 2001, with a gross value of $233,800. First run in 1883.

Year	Winner	Jockey	Second	Third	Strs	Time	1st Purse
2002	Landseer (GB)	M. Kinane	Medecis (GB)	Bowman	13	1:36.80	$176,111
2001	Vahorimix	C. Soumillon	Clearing	Denon	12	1:35.40	$133,600
2000	Bachir	L. Dettori	Berine's Son	Valentino	7	1:39.40	$140,100
1999	Sendawar	G. Mosse	Dansili (GB)	Kingsalsa	15	1:36.20	$162,600
1998	Victory Note	J. A. Reid	Muhtathir (GB)	Desert Prince (Ire)	12	1:34.50	$168,500
1997	Daylami (Ire)	G. Mosse	Loup Sauvage	Visionary	6	1:42.60	$175,700
1996	Ashkalani	G. Mosse	Spinning World	Tagula	10	1:37.60	$193,200
1995	Vettori	L. Dettori	Atticus	Petit Poucet (GB)	8	1:40.40	$210,920
1994	Green Tune	O. Doleuze	Turtle Island	Psychobabble (Ire)	7	1:37.40	$177,230
1993	Kingmambo	C. Asmussen	Bin Ajwaad	Hudo	10	1:39.10	$187,740
1992	Shanghai	F. Head	Rainbow Corner (GB)	Lion Cavern	9	1:38.20	$180,800

2002 Noverre finished first, DQ to 12th.

Poule d'Essai des Pouliches (French One Thousand Guineas)

Group 1, Longchamp, three-year-olds, fillies, 1,600 meters, turf. Held May 13, 2001, with a gross value of $233,800. First held in 1883.

Year	Winner	Jockey	Second	Third	Strs	Time	1st Purse
2002	Zenda (GB)	R. Hughes	Firth of Lorne	Sophisticat	17	1:37.30	$176,111
2001	Rose Gypsy	M. J. Kinane	Banks Hill (GB)	Lethals Lady (GB)	15	1:36.70	$133,600
2000	Bluemamba	T. Jarnet	Peony	Alshakr	11	1:40.20	$140,100
1999	Valentine Waltz (Ire)	R. Cochrane	Karmifira (Fr)	Calando	14	1:36.00	$162,600
1998	Zalaiyka	G. Mosse	Cortona	La Nuit Rose	14	1:35.70	$168,500
1997	Always Loyal	F. Head	Seebe	Red Camellia	7	1:40.20	$175,700
1996	Ta Rib	W. Carson	Shake the Yoke (GB)	Sagar Pride (Ire)	9	1:38.70	$193,200
1995	Matiara	F. Head	Carling (Fr)	Shaanxi	16	1:42.40	$210,920
1994	East of the Moon	C. Asmussen	Agathe	Belle Argentine	8	1:37.10	$177,230
1993	Madeleine's Dream	C. Asmussen	Ski Paradise	Gold Splash	8	1:36.40	$187,740
1992	Culture Vulture	T. R. Quinn	Hydro Calido	Guislaine (Fr)	9	1:37.00	$180,800

Prix de Diane (French Oaks)

Group 1, Chantilly, three-year-olds, fillies, 2,100 meters, turf. Held June 10, 2001, with a gross value of $385,858. First held in 1843.

Year	Winner	Jockey	Second	Third	Strs	Time	1st Purse
2002	Bright Sky	D. Boeuf	Dance Routine	Ana Marie	15	2:07.60	$260,302
2001	Aquarelliste	D. Boeuf	Nadia	Time Away	12	2:09.50	$220,490
2000	Egyptband	O. Doleuze	Volvoreta	Goldamix (Ire)	14	2:08.50	$203,420
1999	Daryaba	G. Mosse	Star of Akkar	Visionnaire (Fr)	14	2:16.10	$224,700
1998	Zainta	G. Mosse	Abbatiale	Insight (Fr)	11	2:11.20	$235,340
1997	Vereva	G. Mosse	Mousse Glacee (Fr)	Brilliance (Fr)	12	2:08.20	$240,520
1996	Sil Sila	C. Asmussen	Miss Tahiti	Matiya (Ire)	12	2:07.30	$269,080
1995	Carling (Fr)	T. Thulliez	Matiara	Tryphosa	12	2:07.70	$282,240
1994	East of the Moon	C. Asmussen	Her Ladyship	Agathe	9	2:07.90	$248,850
1993	Shemaka	G. Mosse	Baya	Dancienne	14	2:16.00	$260,582
1992	Jolypha	P. Eddery	Sheba Dancer (Fr)	Verveine	12	2:09.50	$259,770

Prix de l'Arc de Triomphe

Group 1, Longchamp, three-year-olds and up, 2,400 meters, turf. Held October 7, 2001, with a gross value of $1,470,000. First held in 1920.

Year	Winner	Jockey	Second	Third	Strs	Time	1st Purse
2002	Marienbard, 5	L. Dettori	Sulamani, 3	High Chaparral (Ire), 3	16	2:26.70	$899,704
2001	Sakhee, 4	L. Dettori	†Aquarelliste, 3	Sagacity, 3	17	2:36.10	$840,000
2000	Sinndar, 3	J. P. Murtagh	†Egyptband, 3	†Volvoreta, 3	10	2:25.80	$806,400
1999	Montjeu (Ire), 3	M. J. Kinane	El Condor Pasa, 4	Croco Rouge, 4	14	2:38.50	$654,000
1998	Sagamix, 3	O. Peslier	†Leggera (Ire), 3	Tiger Hill, 3	14	2:34.50	$724,000
1997	Peintre Celebre, 3	O. Peslier	Pilsudski (Ire), 5	†Borgia (Ger), 3	18	2:24.60	$677,600
1996	Helissio, 3	O. Peslier	Pilsudski (Ire), 4	Oscar Schindler, 4	16	2:29.90	$771,600
1995	Lammtarra, 3	L. Dettori	Freedom Cry (GB), 4	Swain (Ire), 3	16	2:31.80	$811,600
1994	Carnegie (Ire), 3	T. Jarnet	Hernando (Fr), 4	Apple Tree (Fr), 5	20	2:31.10	$754,440

Year	Winner	Jockey	Second	Third	Strs	Time	1st Purse
1993	†Urban Sea, 4	E. Saint-Martin	White Muzzle (GB), 3	Opera House (GB), 5	23	2:37.90	$879,050
1992	Subotica (Fr), 4	T. Jarnet	†User Friendly (GB), 3	Vert Amande, 4	18	2:39.00	$1,039,500

† denotes female.

Prix du Jockey-Club (French Derby)

Group 1, Chantilly, three-year-olds, colts and fillies, 2,400 meters, turf. Held June 3, 2001, with a gross value of $905,100. First held in 1836.

Year	Winner	Jockey	Second	Third	Strs	Time	1st Purse
2002	Sulamani	T. Thulliez	Act One	Simeon	15	2:25.00	$569,080
2001	Anabaa Blue	C. Soumillon	Chichicastenango	Grandera	14	2:27.90	$517,200
2000	Holding Court	P. Robinson	Lord Flasheart	Circus Dance	14	2:31.80	$359,750
1999	Montjeu (Ire)	C. Asmussen	Nowhere to Exit	Rhagaas	8	2:33.50	$395,500
1998	Dream Well (Fr)	C. Asmussen	Croco Rouge	Sestino (Ire)	13	2:29.30	$417,250
1997	Peintre Celebre	O. Peslier	Oscar	Astarabad	14	2:29.60	$433,500
1996	Ragmar	G. Mosse	Polaris Flight	Le Destin	15	2:27.20	$484,250
1995	Celtic Swing	K. Darley	Poliglote (GB)	Winged Love	11	2:32.80	$504,000
1994	Celtic Arms (Fr)	G. Mosse	Solid Illusion	Alriffa	15	2:31.30	$444,375
1993	Hernando (Fr)	C. Asmussen	Dernier Empereur	Hunting Hawk	11	2:27.20	$465,325
1992	Polytain	L. Dettori	Marignan	Contested Bid	17	2:30.30	$463,875

Prix Royal-Oak (French St. Leger)

Group 1, Longchamp, three-year-olds and up, 3,100 meters, turf. Held October 28, 2001, with a gross value of $95,270.

Year	Winner	Jockey	Second	Third	Strs	Time	1st Purse
2002	Mr Dinos, 3	D. Boeuf	†Sulk (Ire), 3	Clety, 6	7	3:38.50	$84,347
2001	Vinnie Roe, 3	P. J. Smullen	Generic, 6	Germinis, 7	13	3:37.80	$54,440
2000	Amilynx, 4	O. Peslier	San Sebastian, 6	Tajoun, 6	11	3:33.40	$51,280
1999	Amilynx, 3	O. Peslier	Tajoun, 5	Northerntown, 3	7	3:40.60	$65,200
1998	Tiraaz, 4	G. Mosse	†Erudite, 3	Asolo, 4	7	3:58.40	$72,840
1997	†Ebadiyla, 3	G. Mosse	†Snow Princess, 5	Oscar Schindler, 5	11	3:26.50	$67,160
1996	†Red Roses Story (Fr), 4	V. Vion	Moonax, 5	†Helen of Spain, 4	5	3:38.40	$77,840
1995	Sunshack (GB), 4	T. Jarnet	Shrewd Idea (GB), 4	†Sunrise Song, 5	7	3:16.20	$81,160
1994	Moonax, 3	P. Eddery	Always Earnest, 6	†Dalara, 3	7	3:28.90	$75,444
1993	Raintrap (GB), 3	P. Eddery	Mashaallah, 5	Sonus, 4	8	3:45.80	$70,324
1992	Assessor, 3	T. Quinn	†Always Friendly, 4	†Sought Out, 4	12	3:35.80	$83,160

† denotes female.

Ireland
Irish Derby

Group 1, the Curragh, three-year-olds, colts and fillies, 1½ miles, turf. Held July 1, 2001, with a gross value of $971,712. First held in 1866.

Year	Winner	Jockey	Second	Third	Strs	Time	1st Purse
2002	High Chaparral (Ire)	M. Kinane	Sholokhov	Ballingarry (Ire)	9	2:32.20	$678,466
2001	Galileo (Ire)	M. J. Kinane	Morshdi	Golan	12	2:27.10	$551,571
2000	Sinndar	J. P. Murtagh	Glyndebourne (Ire)	Ciro	11	2:33.90	$584,814
1999	Montjeu (Ire)	C. Asmussen	Daliapour	Tchaikovsky	10	2:30.10	$583,427
1998	Dream Well (Fr)	C. Asmussen	City Honours	Desert Fox	10	2:44.30	$592,554
1997	Desert King	C. Roche	Dr Johnson	Loup Sauvage	10	2:32.50	$601,322
1996	Zagreb	P. Shanahan	Polaris Flight	His Excellence	13	2:30.60	$546,276
1995	Winged Love	O. Peslier	Definite Article (GB)	Annus Mirabilis (Fr)	13	2:30.10	$556,247
1994	†Balanchine	L. Dettori	King's Theatre (Ire)	Colonel Collins	9	2:32.70	$515,040
1993	Commander in Chief	P. Eddery	Hernando (Fr)	Foresee	11	2:31.20	$524,676
1992	St. Jovite	C. Roche	Dr Devious (Ire)	Contested Bid	10	2:25.10	$591,093

† denotes female.

Irish One Thousand Guineas

Group 1, the Curragh, three-year-olds, fillies, 1 mile, turf. Held May 27, 2001, with a gross value of $245,903. First held in 1922.

Year	Winner	Jockey	Second	Third	Strs	Time	1st Purse
2002	Gossamer (GB)	J. Spencer	Quarter Moon	Starbourne	15	1:45.50	$198,135
2001	Imagine	J. A. Heffernan	Crystal Music	Toroca	16	1:41.10	$138,443
2000	Crimplene (Ire)	P. Robinson	Amethyst (Ire)	Storm Dream (Ire)	13	1:39.80	$133,195
1999	Hula Angel	M. Hills	Golden Silca	Dazzling Park	17	1:38.80	$151,446
1998	Tarascon	J. P. Spencer	Kitza (Ire)	La Nuit Rose	13	1:38.40	$120,461
1997	Classic Park	S. Craine	Strawberry Roan (Ire)	Caiseal Ros (Ire)	10	1:42.20	$128,119
1996	Matiya (Ire)	W. Carson	Dance Design (Ire)	My Branch	12	1:39.80	$131,497
1995	Ridgewood Pearl (GB)	C. Roche	Warning Shadows	Khaytada	10	1:43.90	$137,791
1994	Mehthaaf	W. Carson	Las Meninas (Ire)	Relatively Special	10	1:49.00	$127,067
1993	Nicer (Ire)	M. Hills	Goodnight Kiss	Danse Royale (Ire)	14	1:44.20	$174,235
1992	Marling (Ire)	W. Swinburn	Market Booster	Tarwiya	9	1:41.10	$196,988

Irish St. Leger Stakes

Group 1, the Curragh, three-year-olds and up, 1¾ miles, turf. Held September 15, 2001, with a gross value of $263,160.
First held in 1915.

Year	Winner	Jockey	Second	Third	Strs	Time	1st Purse
2002	Vinnie Roe, 4	P. Smullen	Pugin, 4	Ballingarry (Ire), 3	8	2:59.00	$171,824
2001	Vinnie Roe, 3	P. J. Smullen	Millenary, 4	Marienbard, 4	8	2:58.40	$153,159
2000	Arctic Owl, 6	D. Harrison	Yavana's Pace, 8	Mutafaweq, 4	8	3:02.20	$110,412
1999	Kayf Tara, 5	L. Dettori	Yavana's Pace, 7	Silver Patriarch, 5	5	3:12.50	$143,953
1998	Kayf Tara, 4	J. Reid	Silver Patriarch, 4	†Delilah (Ire), 4	7	3:05.70	$131,690
1997	Oscar Schindler, 5	S. Craine	Persian Punch, 4	†Whitewater Affair, 4	7	3:06.40	$132,223
1996	Oscar Schindler, 4	S. Craine	†Key Change, 3	Sacrament, 5	9	2:59.10	$137,349
1995	Strategic Choice, 4	T. R. Quinn	Moonax, 4	Oscar Schindler, 3	7	3:00.90	$141,290
1994	Vintage Crop, 7	M. J. Kinane	†Rayseka, 4	†Kithanga, 4	8	3:07.30	$133,045
1993	Vintage Crop, 6	M. J. Kinane	Assessor, 4	Foresee, 3	8	3:06.70	$123,262
1992	Mashaallah, 4	S. Cauthen	Snurge (Ire), 5	Drum Taps, 6	9	3:02.01	$163,314

† denotes female.

Irish Two Thousand Guineas

Group 1, the Curragh, three-year-olds, colts and fillies, 1 mile, turf. Held May 26, 2001, with a gross value of $245,903.
First held in 1921.

Year	Winner	Jockey	Second	Third	Strs	Time	1st Purse
2002	Rock of Gibraltar (Ire)	M. Kinane	Century City (Ire)	Della Francesca	7	1:47.30	$209,239
2001	Black Minnaloushe	J. P. Murtagh	Mozart (Ire)	Minardi	12	1:41.40	$138,443
2000	Bachir	L. Dettori	Giant's Causeway	Cape Town	8	1:39.80	$137,926
1999	Saffron Walden	O. Peslier	Enrique	Orpen	10	1:38.10	$151,379
1998	Desert Prince (Ire)	O. Peslier	Fa-Eq	Second Empire (Ire)	7	1:35.80	$169,717
1997	Desert King	C. Roche	Verglas (Ire)	Romanov (Ire)	12	1:38.30	$171,383
1996	Spinning World	C. Asmussen	Rainbow Blues (Ire)	Beauchamp King	10	1:38.80	$175,902
1995	Spectrum	J. Reid	Adjareli	Bahri	9	1:40.30	$187,592
1994	Turtle Island	J. Reid	Guided Tour	Ridgewood Ben	9	1:50.10	$169,989
1993	Barathea (Ire)	M. Roberts	Fatherland (Ire)	Massyar (Ire)	11	1:43.00	$175,777
1992	Rodrigo de Triano	L. Piggott	Ezzoud (Ire)	Brief Truce	6	1:41.00	$198,616

Kildangan Stud Irish Oaks

Group 1, the Curragh, three-year-olds, fillies, 1½ miles, turf. Held July 15, 2001, with a gross value of $244,168. First
run in 1895.

Year	Winner	Jockey	Second	Third	Strs	Time	1st Purse
2002	Margarula	K. Manning	Quarter Moon	Lady's Secret	12	2:37.40	$204,023
2001	Lailani (GB)	L. Dettori	Mot Juste (GB)	Karsavina (Ire)	12	2:30.50	$137,466
2000	Petrushka (Ire)	J. Murtagh	Melikah (Ire)	Inforapenny	10	2:31.20	$133,775
1999	Ramruma	K. Fallon	Sunspangled	Sister Bella (Ire)	7	2:33.00	$153,443
1998	Winona (Ire)	J. Murtagh	Kitza (Ire)	Bahr (GB)	9	2:39.80	$157,965
1997	Ebadiyla	J. Murtagh	Yashmak	Brilliance (Fr)	11	2:33.70	$170,988
1996	Dance Design (Ire)	M. Kinane	Shamadara	Key Change	6	2:29.70	$192,348
1995	Pure Grain (GB)	J. Reid	Russian Snows	Valley of Gold	10	2:33.60	$185,279
1994	Bolas (GB)	P. Eddery	Hawajiss	Gothic Dream	10	2:37.60	$171,295
1993	Wemyss Bight (GB)	P. Eddery	Royal Ballerina (Ire)	Oakmead (Ire)	11	2:35.00	$162,573
1992	User Friendly (GB)	G. Duffield	Market Booster	Arrikala	9	2:33.10	$212,040

United Arab Emirates

Dubai World Cup

Group 1, Nad al Sheba, three-year-olds and up, 2,000 meters, dirt. Held March 29, 2003, with a gross value of
$6,000,000. First held in 1996.

Year	Winner	Jockey	Second	Third	Strs	Time	1st Purse
2003	Moon Ballad	L. Dettori	Harlan's Holiday	Nayef	11	2:00.48	$3,600,000
2002	Street Cry (Ire), 4, 126	J. D. Bailey	Sei Mi, 6	Sakhee, 5	11	2:01.18	$3,600,000
2001	Captain Steve, 4, 126	J. D. Bailey	To the Victory, 5	Hightori, 6	12	2:00.47	$3,600,000
2000	Dubai Millennium, 4, 126	L. Dettori	Behrens, 6	Public Purse, 6	13	2:00.65	$3,600,000
1999	Almutawakel (GB), 5, 126	R. Hills	Malek (Chi), 6	Victory Gallop, 4	8	2:00.65	$3,000,000
1998	Silver Charm, 4, 126	G. L. Stevens	Swain (Ire), 6	Loup Sauvage, 4	9	2:04.29	$2,400,000
1997	Singspiel, 5, 126	J. D. Bailey	Siphon (Brz), 6	Sandpit (Brz), 8	12	2:01.91	$2,400,000
1996	Cigar, 6, 126	J. D. Bailey	Soul of the Matter, 5	L.Carriere, 5	11	2:03.84	$2,400,000

1996-'97 listed race.

English Triple Crown

Over its long history, the English Triple Crown has proved to be as elusive as its younger American cousin, perhaps even more so. Approaching its third century, the English Triple Crown has been won only 15 times, while the American Triple Crown has been won 11 times since 1875. The American Triple Crown has not had a winner since Affirmed in 1978, and the English drought extends slightly longer. Since Gainsborough became the 13th winner in 1918, only two more have followed: unbeaten *Bahram in 1935 and the brilliant Nijinsky II in '70.

The English Triple Crown for three-year-olds, dating from 1809, consists of the one-mile Two Thousand Guineas (Eng-G1) at Newmarket in May, the 1½-mile Epsom Derby (Eng-G1) at Epsom Downs in June, and the St. Leger Stakes (Eng-G1) at 1¾ miles and 127 yards at Doncaster Race Course in September. Over the years, there has been some variance in the distances of the three races, and alternative races were used during war years.

The St. Leger Stakes was named for the popular local sportsman Lt. Col. Anthony St. Leger. Alabaculia was the first winner of the St. Leger Stakes in 1776. Four years later, *Diomed, later imported to the United States, won the initial running of the Epsom Derby. The first Two Thousand Guineas was taken by Wizard in 1809, nine years after Champion became the first three-year-old to win both the Epsom Derby and the St. Leger Stakes. In 1813, Sir Charles Bunbury's Smolensko became the first to win the Two Thousand Guineas and the Epsom Derby.

Forty years later in 1853, West Australian became the first to win all three stakes. He was followed by Gladiateur (1865), Lord Lyon (1866), *Ormonde (1886), Common (1891), Isinglass (1893), Galtee More (1897), Flying Fox (1899), Diamond Jubilee (1900), *Rock Sand (1903), Pommern (1915), Gay Crusader (1917), Gainsborough (1918), *Bahram (1935), and Nijinsky II (1970).

In today's racing world, the English Triple Crown is a prize not pursued. The most recent horse with a chance to seize the crown, 1989 Two Thousand Guineas (Eng-G1) and Epsom Derby (Eng-G1) victor Nashwan, was withheld from the St. Leger Stakes (Eng-G1) by owner Sheikh Hamdan bin Rashid al Maktoum to point for the Prix de l'Arc de Triomphe (Fr-G1), in which he did not start because of injury.

Following are the 15 English Triple Crown winners:

WEST AUSTRALIAN—1850 b. h., Melbourne–Mowerina, by Touchstone. 10-9-1-0, $68,615. Known popularly as "the West," West Australian gave owner-breeder John Bowes his fourth and final Epsom Derby victory. Trained by John Scott, West Australian ran second in the Criterion Stakes to Speed the Plough and then beat his rival in the Glasgow Stakes as a two-year-old. At three, West Australian won the Two Thousand Guineas by a half-length over the Duke of Bedford's Sittingbourne and the Epsom Derby by a desperate neck over the same opponent. West Australian won the St. Leger easily, and at four won the Triennial Stakes and the Ascot Gold Cup. Though not widely regarded as a success at stud, he sired The Wizard, the 1860 Two Thousand Guineas winner, and his son *Australian sired Spendthrift, tail-male ancestor of the Man o' War male line that leads to Tiznow.

GLADIATEUR—1862 b. h., Monarque–Miss Gladiator, by Gladiator. 19-16-0-1, $236,537. French-bred and -owned Gladiateur shattered the notion that England's Thoroughbreds were superior when he won the 1865 Two Thousand Guineas, earning the gleeful nickname "Avenger of Waterloo" among the French. Trained at Newmarket by Tom Jennings, he added the Epsom Derby "in a canter" and the St. Leger. In between, he traveled to his native France and captured that country's greatest race at the time, the Grand Prix de Paris. At four, Gladiateur won the Gold Cup at Ascot by 40 lengths after reputedly trailing by 300 yards at one point. He was not a success at stud.

LORD LYON—1863 b. h., Stockwell–Paradigm, by Paragone. 19-15-3-1, $180,497. Leased to Richard Sutton, the second son of Sir Richard Sutton, and trained by James Dover, Lord Lyon dead-heated with Redan in the Champagne Stakes for two-year-olds at Doncaster and then won the Criterion and Troy Stakes at Newmarket. After winning the Two Thousand Guineas by one length over Monarch of the Glen, Lord Lyon completed the Triple Crown by beating Savernake by a head in the Epsom Derby and the same rival by inches in the St. Leger. The following year, Lord Lyon won the Ascot Biennial and the Stockbridge Cup. His most famous offspring were *Ormonde's rival Minting, winner of the 1886 Grand Prix de Paris, and '77 Oaks winner Placida.

ORMONDE—1883 b. h., Bend Or–Lily Agnes, by Macaroni. 16-16-0-0, $138,340. Considered by many as the finest Thoroughbred of the 19th century, the Duke of Westminster's *Ormonde was unbeaten in his 16-race career, despite developing a wind infirmity. At four in the Hardwicke Stakes, he bested Grand Prix de Paris winner Minting. *Ormonde sired just seven foals in his first season at stud in England, but that crop included Orme, a multiple major stakes winner and sire of 1899 Triple Crown winner Flying Fox. After a stint in Argentina, *Ormonde was purchased by William O'Brien Macdonough, an American, for $150,000 in 1893 and stood in California. From 1894 through 1905, *Ormonde sired just 17 foals, but 12 started and five, including Ormondale, won stakes races.

COMMON—1888 br. h., Isonomy–Thistle, by Scottish Chief. 5-4-0-1, $77,567. Owned by his breeder, Lord Allington, and Sir Frederick Johnstone, Common was a colt with dubious joints and thus was not raced at two by trainer John Porter. Common made his debut in the 1891 Two Thousand Guineas, and his profuse sweating prompted Prince Soltykoff to remark, "He's very well named." Uncommon on the Newmarket course, Common won easily. He won the Epsom Derby by two lengths in a downpour and subsequently won the St. James's Palace Stakes before finishing third in the Eclipse Stakes. In the final start of his only racing season, Common completed the Triple Crown by winning the St. Leger by one length. Common's progeny included 1898 One Thousand Guineas winner Nun Nicer and Mushroom, who became a successful stallion in Belgium.

ISINGLASS—1890 b. h., Isonomy–Deadlock, by Wenlock. 12-11-1-0, $279,231. Despite soundness problems that he passed on to his progeny, Isinglass lost only once for his owner, Col. Harry McCalmont, in a four-year career. Isinglass suffered the only loss in his three-year-old campaign when he was defeated by Raeburn in the Lancashire Plate at Manchester, giving the winner ten pounds over an inadequate distance. At four, Isinglass captured the Princess of Wales's Stakes, Eclipse Stakes, and Jockey Club Stakes. As a five-year-old, he won the 1895 Ascot Gold Cup and retired as the sport's all-time money winner. Isinglass stood at his owner's Cheveley Park Stud near Newmarket and sired three British classic winners as well as *Star Shoot, who was North America's leading sire five times and also was leading broodmare sire five times.

GALTEE MORE—1894 b. h., Kendal–Morganette, by Springfield. 13-11-1-0, $131,312. Galtee More, named after a peak in the Galtee Mountains, was owned by John Gubbins, who used his considerable inheritance from an uncle to open two stud farms, one of which housed Galtee More's sire, Kendal. Trained by Sam Darling, Galtee More won the Molecomb Stakes, the Rous Plate, and the Middle Park Plate as a two-year-old. At three in 1897, Galtee More completed the Triple Crown by taking the St. Leger by three-quarters of a length over the filly Chelandry. At the end of his racing career, Galtee More was sold by Gubbins to the Russian government, and the stallion subsequently was purchased by German interests. His most noteworthy progeny was Orchidee II, dam of Oleander, leading German sire in the 1930s and '40s. Galtee More's half brother Ard Patrick won the Epsom Derby in 1892.

FLYING FOX—1896 b. h., Orme–Vampire, by Galopin. 11-9-2-0, $194,867. A large colt with beautiful shoulders, Flying Fox became the Duke of Westminster's second Triple Crown winner despite a difficult temperament that most likely came from his aptly named dam. At two in 1898, Flying Fox won the New, Stockbridge Foal, and Criterion Stakes, and he finished second in both the Imperial Produce Stakes and the Middle Park Plate. Flying Fox was unbeaten at three and ended his career with a four-length victory in the Jockey Club Stakes. Flying Fox sired French classic winner Val d'Or, and his grandson *Teddy (by French Derby winner Ajax) became an important in-

The Influence of England's Triple Crown Worldwide

Although England's Triple Crown is the original and perhaps most difficult Triple Crown to win in the world, historically it has served as a model for racing programs around the globe. Virtually every major racing country has its set of Guineas, Derbys, and St. Legers, or their equivalents. As in most aspects of Thoroughbred racing, England, the birthplace of the Thoroughbred, established the pattern that the rest of the world adapted for its own local purposes, and the idea of a series of classic tests for three-year-olds is universal.

The Triple Crown in the United States evolved into the familiar Kentucky Derby (G1), Preakness Stakes (G1), and Belmont Stakes (G1) early in the 20th century, but several American racing jurisdictions in the 19th century attempted to establish Triple Crown series more closely modeled on the English pattern. For example, the Withers, Belmont, and Lawrence Realization Stakes were originally intended to be New York's version of the English series.

Other former English colonies such as Australia and New Zealand likewise established Guineas-Derby-St. Leger series, and those races still exist in Antipodean lands, though it has been many years since they have been a serious objective as a series for owners and trainers. As racing throughout the world has become more specialized, winning a Triple Crown over a variety of distances as wide as that in England has become increasingly difficult.

Argentina, historically the most important South American racing country, established its own series, the Polla de Potrillos (Arg-G1), Gran Premio Jockey Club (Arg-G1), and Gran Premio Nacional (Arg-G1) over 1,600 meters, 2,000 meters, and 2,500 meters, respectively, but went one better than the English. The Argentines also required their best three-year-olds to beat older horses in the 2,400-meter Gran Premio Carlos Pellegrini (Arg-G1) to win their Quadruple Crown. Twenty three-year-olds have captured the Argentine Triple Crown since 1902, with Refinado Tom (Arg) in '96 the most recent winner. Only ten horses, the last being the great *Forli in 1966, have completed the Quadruple Crown.

English fillies have an opportunity to win their version of the Triple Crown, though no filly has ever completed the Two Thousand Guineas (Eng-G1), Epsom Derby (Eng-G1), St. Leger (Eng-G1) triple. Two fillies, however, have won four of the five English classics, failing only to capture the Derby. Formosa in 1868 dead-heated in the Two Thousand and won the One Thousand Guineas, Epsom Oaks, and St. Leger. Sceptre won the One Thousand, Two Thousand, Oaks, and St. Leger in 1902 but was beaten into fourth place in the Derby by Ard Patrick.

Nine fillies have won a "fillies Triple Crown" consisting of the One Thousand Guineas, Oaks, and St. Leger:

1868 **Formosa**, ch. f., Buccaneer—Eller, by Chanticleer
1871 **Hannah**, b. f., King Tom—Mentmore Lass, by Melbourne
1874 **Apology**, ch. f., Adventurer—Mandragora, by Rataplan
1892 **La Fleche**, br. f., St. Simon—Quiver, by Toxophilite
1902 **Sceptre**, b. f., Persimmon—Ornament, by Bend Or
1904 **Pretty Polly**, ch. f., Gallinule—Admiration, by Saraband
1942 **Sun Chariot**, b. f., Hyperion—Clarence, by Diligence
1955 **Meld**, b. f., Alycidon—Daily Double, by Fair Trial
1985 **Oh So Sharp (GB)**, ch. f., Kris—Oh So Fair, by Graustark

fluence on North American bloodlines through full brothers *Sir Gallahad III and *Bull Dog.

DIAMOND JUBILEE—1897 b. h., St. Simon–Perdita, by Hampton. 16-6-5-1, $142,131. Owned by the Prince of Wales, Diamond Jubilee was described as "ferocious, with a nature more befitting the bullring than the racecourse." He was found to be a cryptorchid (and thus spared from gelding) after finishing unplaced in his first two starts at two. Diamond Jubilee's trainer, Richard Marsh, gave Diamond Jubilee's groom, 18-year-old Herbert Jones, a chance to ride the ridgling, and Diamond Jubilee won the Two Thousand Guineas by four lengths. He won the Epsom Derby by a half-length and the St. Leger by one length. After standing at stud in England, he was sold in 1906 to Las Ortegas Stud in Argentina, where he was the leading sire from 1914 through '16. Diamond Jubilee was a full brother to the outstanding racehorse Persimmon, winner of the Epsom Derby and the St. Leger in 1896.

*ROCK SAND—1900 br. h., Sainfoin–Roquebrune, by St. Simon. 20-16-1-3, $221,703. Although he hobbled along at a trot and canter, *Rock Sand would fully extend himself at a gallop once warmed up and never finished unplaced in his career. He won six stakes races as a two-year-old in 1902, and at three he won the St. James's Palace Stakes and Bennington Stakes in addition to the Triple Crown contests. He won the Hardwicke, Princess of Wales's, Lingfield Park Plate, First Foal, and the Jockey Club Stakes at four. Best known for his success as a broodmare sire, *Rock Sand sired Mahubah, dam of Man o' War. *Rock Sand's other leading daughters included Hour Glass, dam of Blue Glass and *Hourless, and Tea Biscuit, dam of Hard Tack. *Rock Sand's most accomplished sons were Tracery, winner of the St. James's Palace and the Eclipse Stakes and one of the leading sires in England for many years in the 1920s; Friar Rock, who won the 1916 Belmont Stakes and Suburban Handicap in the United States; and 1916 Preakness Stakes winner Damrosch.

POMMERN—1912 b. h., Polymelus–Merry Agnes, by St. Hilaire. 10-7-1-0, $75,165. A homebred of Solomon B. Joel, at two Pommern won the Richmond Stakes at Goodwood and the Imperial Produce Stakes at Kempton. Steve Donoghue was engaged to ride Pommern in his unusual three-year-old season. Pommern won the 1915 Two Thousand Guineas comfortably at Newmarket. With World War I raging across the English Channel in France, Epsom Downs was requisitioned by the military, and Pommern scored a two-length victory in the substitute for the Epsom Derby, the New Derby at 1½ miles on Newmarket's July Course. He then won the substitute for the St. Leger, the 1¾-mile September Stakes at Newmarket. In his only start at four, Pommern won the June Stakes at Newmarket. His best offspring were Adam's Apple, who won the 1927 Two Thousand Guineas; Pondoland, second in the 1922 Two Thousand Guineas; and Glommen, who won the Goodwood Cup.

GAY CRUSADER—1914 b. c., Bayardo–Gay Laura, by Beppo. 10-8-2-0, $53,530. Bred and owned by A. W. "Fairie" Cox, Gay Crusader was the first foal of his dam and from his sire's first crop. Trained by Alec Taylor, Gay Crusader was a small colt who developed sore shins in June of his two-year-old season. He made a late start that year, losing his debut before winning the Criterion Stakes. After finishing second in his three-year-old debut in the Column Produce Stakes, Gay Crusader won the 1917 Two Thousand Guineas by a head over Magpie, who also was trained by Taylor.

With Magpie exported to Australia, Gay Crusader won the Epsom Derby, which was delayed until July 31 because of World War I, by four lengths. He then won the September Stakes, the St. Leger substitute. Gay Crusader also won the Newmarket Gold Cup, Champion Stakes, and Lowther Stakes. A tendon injury ended his career before his first start as a four-year-old. At stud, his best were Hot Night, second in the 1927 Epsom Derby, and Hurstwood, third in the '24 Derby.

GAINSBOROUGH—1915 b. h., Bayardo–Rosedrop, by St. Frusquin. 9-5-2-1, $67,021. Lady Jane Douglas bred Gainsborough and became the first woman to own an Epsom Derby winner when the colt took the 1918 classic. Gainsborough gave his sire, Bayardo, a second straight Triple Crown winner. Gainsborough, who was twice champion sire, sired Hyperion, the 1933 Epsom Derby winner who went on to be England's leading sire six times. Gainsborough also sired 1932 Two Thousand Guineas winner Orwell and Solario, who was England's leading sire in 1937 and its leading broodmare sire in 1949 and '50. Gainsborough died in 1945 at the age of 30 and was buried at Gainsborough Stud, which was originally named Harwood Stud.

*BAHRAM—1932 br. h., Blandford–Friar's Daughter, by Friar Marcus. 9-9-0-0, $212,816. A large colt who grew to 16.2 hands, *Bahram was bred and raced in England by the Aga Khan. Unbeaten in nine career starts through his three-year-old season, *Bahram won the National Produce, Rous Memorial, Gimcrack, and Middle Park Stakes at two. In addition to sweeping the Triple Crown at three, he won the St. James's Palace Stakes. England's second-leading sire in 1940, he was sold for $160,000 to an American syndicate that included Alfred G. Vanderbilt, Walter P. Chrysler, James Cox Brady, and S. W. Labrot. *Bahram stood in Maryland and Virginia before being sold in 1945 to stand in Argentina. *Bahram's 25 stakes winners included 1940 St. Leger and Irish Derby winner Turkhan, '40 Irish Oaks winner Queen of Shiraz, and '42 Two Thousand Guineas winner Big Game, who became the leading sire in England in 1948, and the excellent sire Persian Gulf, winner of the '44 Coronation Cup.

NIJINSKY II—1967 b. h., Northern Dancer–Flaming Page, by Bull Page. 13-11-2-0, $667,220. Bred in Canada by E. P. Taylor and owned by Charles W. Engelhard, Nijinsky II was Northern Dancer's first international champion. He was a powerful, sickle-hocked colt who more closely resembled his dam than his diminutive sire. Trained by Vincent O'Brien, Nijinsky II was a champion in England and Ireland at two in 1969. He won the Two Thousand Guineas at odds of 4-to-7, the Epsom Derby at 11-to-8 odds, and the St. Leger at 2-to-7 odds, all under Lester Piggott. That year, Nijinsky II also won the Irish Sweeps Derby and the King George VI and Queen Elizabeth Stakes. His only defeats were in his final two starts, the Prix de l'Arc de Triomphe and Champion Stakes. At stud at Claiborne Farm in Kentucky, he was England's leading sire in 1986 and North America's leading broodmare sire in '93 and '94. Nijinsky II at one time was the all-time leading sire of stakes winners with 155, surpassing the record of his sire. Nijinsky II sired 11 champions, including 1987 North American Horse of the Year Ferdinand, '83 French champion Caerleon, two-time English champion Ile de Bourbon, and two undefeated winners of the Epsom Derby, Golden Fleece and Lammtarra.—*Bill Heller*

2002 International Classifications
Two-Year-Olds

Wt.	Horse	Sire–Dam, Broodmare sire	Trained	Sts	1st	2nd	3rd	Earnings
123	Oasis Dream	Green Desert—Hope, by Dancing Brave	GB	4	2	1	0	$169,167
122	Tout Seul	Ali-Royal—Total Aloof, by Groom Dancer	GB	7	5	2	0	487,958
121	Six Perfections (f)	Celtic Swing—Yogya, by Riverman	Fr	4	3	1	0	195,648
119	Elusive City	Elusive Quality—Star of Paris, by Dayjur	GB	4	1	0	1	169,053
	Tomahawk	Seattle Slew—Statuette, by Pancho Villa	Ire	5	1	3	0	174,816
118	Dalakhani	Darshaan—Daltawa, by Miswaki	Fr	3	3	0	0	183,151
	Somnus	Pivotal—Midnight's Reward, by Night Shift	GB	5	4	0	0	396,307
117	Airwave (f)	Air Express—Kangra Valley, by Indian Ridge	GB	5	3	1	0	191,373
	Hold That Tiger	Storm Cat—Beware of the Cat, by Caveat	Ire	5	3	0	1	330,907
	Zafeen	Zafonic—Shy Lady, by Kaldoun	GB	6	2	2	0	142,107
116	Brian Boru	Sadler's Wells—Eva Luna, by Alleged	Ire	3	2	1	0	213,550
	Chevalier	Danehill—Legend Maker, by Sadler's Wells	Ire	3	1	2	0	72,944
	Etoile Montante (f)	Miswaki—Willstar, by Nureyev	Fr	3	2	1	0	78,409
	Russian Rhythm (f)	Kingmambo—Balistroika, by Nijinsky	GB	4	3	1	0	176,662
	Trade Fair	Zafonic—Danefair, by Danehill	GB	3	1	0	2	54,627
115	Le Vie Dei Colori	Efisio—Mystic Tempo, by El Gran Senor	Ity	7	6	1	0	233,539
	Refuse To Bend	Sadler's Wells—Market Slide, by Gulch	Ire	2	2	0	0	189,753
114	Alberto Giacometti	Sadler's Wells—Sweeten Up, by Shirley Heights	Ire	2	2	0	0	97,751
	Al Jadeed	Coronado's Quest—Aljawza, by Riverman	GB	6	3	0	1	131,573
	Saturn	Marju—Delfinus, by Soviet Star	GB	4	2	0	0	32,348
	Soviet Song (f)	Marju—Kalinka, by Soviet Star	GB	3	3	0	0	208,721
113	Bahamian Dancer	Bering (GB)—Fantastic Flame, by Generous	GB	6	1	2	0	52,805
	Hanabad	Cadeaux Genereux—Handaza, by Be My Guest	Ire	5	1	0	1	7,184
	Powerscourt	Sadler's Wells—Rainbow Lake, by Rainbow Quest	Ire	4	1	3	0	90,051
	Summerland	Danehill—Summerosa, by Woodman	GB	6	2	1	1	70,254
	Van Nistelrooy	Storm Cat—Halory, by Halo	Ire	6	3	1	1	229,980
112	Danaskaya (f)	Danehill—Majinskaya, by Marignan	Ire	5	1	1	2	84,065
	Dublin	Carson City—Lustre, by Halo	GB	5	3	0	0	98,701
	Luvah Girl (GB) (f)	Alzao—Girl of My Dreams, by Marju	GB	5	2	2	0	89,172
	Mister Links	Flying Spur—Lady Anna Livia, by Ahonoora	GB	6	3	2	0	182,820
	Monsieur Bond	Danehill Dancer—Musical Essence, by Song	GB	6	2	2	1	82,262
	Peace Offering	Victory Note—Amnesty Bay, by Thatching	GB	3	2	0	0	44,439
	Spartacus	Danehill—Teslemi, by Ogygian	Ire	6	3	1	0	337,134
	Wunders Dream (f)	Averti—Pizzicato, by Statoblest	GB	8	4	2	0	172,422
111	Country Reel	Danzig—Country Belle, by Seattle Slew	GB	3	2	0	0	131,404
	Foss Way	Desert Prince—Lishaway, by Polish Precedent	GB	4	2	0	0	61,828
	Intercontinental (f)	Danehill—Hasili, by Kahyasi	Fr	3	2	0	1	61,779
	Makhlab	Dixieland Band—Avasand, by Avatar	GB	5	3	0	1	60,105
	Muqbil	Swain (Ire)—Istiqlal, by Diesis (GB)	GB	2	1	1	0	41,028
	Ontario	Storm Cat—Flying Fairy (GB), by Bustino	Ire	7	2	0	1	74,731
	Statue of Liberty	Storm Cat—Charming Lassie, by Seattle Slew	Ire	2	2	0	0	63,335
110	Alamshar	Key of Luck—Alaiyda, by Shahrastani	Ire	2	2	0	0	60,913
	Almushahar	Silver Hawk—Sayeddati (GB), by Shadeed	GB	2	2	0	0	141,688
	Casual Look (f)	Red Ransom—Style Setter, by Manila	GB	5	1	2	1	97,553
	Eagle Rise	Danehill—Evening Breeze, by Surumu	Ger	2	2	0	0	87,903
	Geminiani	King of Kings (Ire)—Tadkiyra (Ire), by Darshaan	GB	2	2	0	0	52,634
	Great Pyramid	Danehill—Offshore Boom, by Be My Guest	Ire	5	1	1	0	15,634
	Hurricane Alan	Mukaddamah—Bint Al Balad, by Ahonoora	GB	9	4	1	3	161,533
	Illustrator	Sadler's Wells—Illusory, by Kings Lake	GB	3	0	1	2	39,675
	Marino Marini	Storm Cat—Halo America, by Waquoit	Ire	6	2	1	1	117,993
	Marshall	Anabaa—Monitrice, by Groom Dancer	Fr	3	1	0	1	32,598
	New South Wales	In The Wings (GB)—Temora (Ire), by Ela-Mana-Mou	Ire	2	2	0	0	57,527
	Pakhoes	College Chapel—Park Charger, by Tirol	Ire	5	1	4	0	56,233
	Romantic Liason (f)	Primo Dominie—My First Romance, by Danehill	GB	3	2	0	1	70,356
	Yesterday (f)	Sadler's Wells—Jude, by Darshaan	Ire	6	2	1	1	70,471
	Zinziberine (f)	Zieten—Amenixa (Fr), by Linamix	Fr	7	3	3	0	207,574

Three-Year-Olds (Turf)
14 furlongs +

117	Bollin Eric	Shaamit—Bollin Zola, by Alzao	GB	6	1	2	3	$497,773
115	Highest	Selkirk—Pearl Kite, by Silver Hawk	GB	6	2	4	0	241,456
	Mr Dinos	Desert King—Spear Dance, by Gay Fandango	GB	8	4	2	1	218,102
110	Mamool	In the Wings (GB)—Genovefa, by Woodman	GB	4	1	0	0	99,015

11 furlongs +

126	High Chaparral (Ire)	Sadler's Wells—Kasora, by Darshaan	Ire	6	5	0	1	$3,436,860

Wt.	Horse	Sire–Dam, Broodmare sire	Trained	Sts	1st	2nd	3rd	Earnings
	Sulamani	Hernando (Fr)—Soul Dream, by Alleged	Fr	6	4	1	0	$1,037,003
123	Act One	In the Wings (GB)—Summer Sonnet, by Baillamont	Fr	3	2	1	0	360,474
	Hawk Wing	Woodman—La Lorgnette, by Val de l'Orne (Fr)	Ire	6	1	4	0	1,143,720
120	Islington (Ire) (f)	Sadler's Wells—Hellenic, by Darshaan	GB	7	4	0	1	594,316
	Next Desert	Desert Style—Night Petticoat, by Petoski	Ger	4	3	1	0	358,807
119	Kazzia (Ger) (f)	Zinaad—Khoruna, by Lagunas	GB	5	3	0	0	1,021,097
	Pearly Shells (f)	Efisio—Piffle, by Shirley Heights	Fr	6	5	1	0	249,080
	Symboli Kris S.	Kris S.—Tee Kay, by Gold Meridian	Jpn	10	5	2	3	4,724,763
118	Ballingarry (Ire)	Sadler's Wells—Flamenco Wave, by Desert Wine	Ire/USA	7	2	1	2	1,282,645
	Bandari	Alhaarth—Miss Audimar, by Mr. Leader	GB	5	3	0	1	309,173
117	Quarter Moon (f)	Sadler's Wells—Jude, by Darshaan	Ire	7	0	3	1	300,364
116	Ana Marie (f)	Anabaa—Marie de Ken, by Kendor	Fr	7	1	2	1	171,480
	Black Sam Bellamy	Sadler's Wells—Urban Sea, by Miswaki	Ire	6	2	1	0	211,357
	Margarula (f)	Doyoun—Mild Intrigue, by Sir Ivor	Ire	9	3	1	0	267,381
115	Balakheri	Theatrical (Ire)—Balanka (Ire), by Alzao	GB	5	2	0	1	185,557
	Fine Motion (f)	Danehill—Cocotte, by Troy	Jpn	6	5	0	0	2,378,740
	Rakti	Polish Precedent—Ragera, by Rainbow Quest	Ity	7	4	0	1	523,104
	Simeon	Lammtarra—Noble Lily, by *Vaguely Noble	GB	6	3	0	1	195,427
114	Dance Routine (f)	Sadler's Wells—Apogee, by Shirley Heights	Fr	7	3	2	0	217,781
	Dubai Destination	Kingmambo—Mysterial, by Alleged	GB	1	0	1	0	11,240
	Dupont	Zafonic—June Moon, by Sadler's Wells	GB	6	2	0	1	214,081
	Great Pretender	King's Theatre (Ire)—Settler, by Darshaan	Fr	7	1	1	1	106,175
	Nysaean	Sadler's Wells—Irish Arms, by Irish River (Fr)	GB	6	3	0	2	91,018
113	Systematic	Rainbow Quest—Sensation (GB), by Soviet Star	GB	9	7	1	0	192,751
112	Castle Gandolfo	Gone West—Golden Oriole, by Northern Dancer	Ire/USA	5	1	0	1	58,298
	Guadalupe (f)	Monsun—Guernica, by Unfuwain	Ger	7	2	2	1	421,372
	Lohengrin	Singspiel (Ire)—Carling (Fr), by Garde Royale	Jpn	9	5	0	1	1,028,776
	Salve Regina (f)	Monsun—Sacarina, by Old Vic	Ger	7	3	4	0	492,906
	Trumbaka (f)	In the Wings (GB)—Questina, by Rainbow Quest	Fr	7	1	4	0	85,233
111	Albanova	Alzao—Alouette, by Darshaan	GB	3	2	0	0	39,947
	Bustan	Darshaan—Dazzlingly Radiant, by Try My Best	GB	5	2	0	1	50,893
	Coshocton	Silver Hawk—Tribulation, by Danzig	GB	3	1	0	0	29,634
	Fisich	Halling—Sispre, by Master Willie (GB)	Ity	7	3	1	1	306,851
	Frankies Dream	Grand Lodge—Galyph, by Lyphard	GB	10	2	2	3	58,894
	Scott's View	Selkirk—Milly of the Vally, by Caerleon	GB	13	8	1	3	186,198
	Sulk (Ire) (f)	Selkirk—Masskana, by Darshaan	GB	7	0	2	1	131,215
110	Bernimixa (f)	Linamix—Bernique, by Affirmed	Fr	6	3	0	0	96,164
	Fight Your Corner	Muhtarram—Dame Ashfield, by Grundy	GB	3	1	0	0	101,443
	Legal Approach	Zafonic—Legaya, by Shirley Heights	GB	3	2	0	1	51,443
	Mellow Park (f)	In the Wings (GB)—Park Special, by Relkino	GB	5	2	0	0	83,156
	Millstreet	Polish Precedent—Mill Path, by Mill Reef	Ire	8	2	5	1	85,531
	Uriah (Ger) (f)	Acatenango—Ulanowa, by Kamiros	Ger	8	5	0	2	168,878
	9½ furlongs +							
123	Hawk Wing	Woodman—La Lorgnette, by Val de l'Orne (Fr)	Ire	6	1	4	0	$1,143,720
120	Bright Sky (f)	Wolfhound—Bright Moon, by Alysheba	Fr	7	2	3	1	488,014
	Islington (Ire) (f)	Sadler's Wells—Hellenic, by Darshaan	GB	7	4	0	1	594,316
	Moon Ballad	Singspiel (Ire)—Velvet Moon, by Shaadi	GB	7	3	2	1	642,387
119	Kazzia (Ger) (f)	Zinaad—Khoruna, by Lagunas	GB	5	3	0	0	1,021,097
	Symboli Kris S.	Kris S.—Tee Kay, by Gold Meridian	Jpn	10	5	2	3	4,724,763
117	Sholokhov	Sadler's Wells—La Meilleure, by Lord Gayle	Ire	7	0	2	0	412,586
116	Burning Sun	Danzig—Media Nox (GB), by Lycius	GB	7	2	2	2	112,411
	Riskaverse (f)	Dynaformer—The Bink, by Seeking the Gold	USA	7	2	2	0	461,160
115	Gold Allure	Sunday Silence—Nikiya, by Nureyev	Jpn	10	5	0	1	2,120,118
	No Reason	Brian's Time—Ambrosine, by Mr. Prospector	Jpn	9	3	1	0	1,298,823
	Turtle Bow (Fr) (f)	Turtle Island—Clara Bow, by Top Ville	Fr	10	5	2	0	319,516
	Zenda (Fr) (f)	Zamindar—Hope, by Dancing Brave	GB	6	2	2	0	371,500
114	Chiselling	Woodman—Toussaud, by El Gran Senor	USA	8	3	2	2	405,760
	Kaieteur	Marlin—Strong Embrace, by Regal Embrace	GB	6	2	2	0	148,920
	Khalkevi	Kahyasi—Khalisa (Ire), by Persian Bold	Fr	4	3	0	0	339,308
	Marotta (f)	Highest Honor (Fr)—Mistra, by Rainbow Quest	Fr	7	3	0	2	204,844
	Nysaean	Sadler's Wells—Irish Arms, by Irish River (Fr)	GB	6	3	0	2	91,018
	Orchard Park	Hennessy—Blue Begum, by With Approval	USA	7	5	0	1	613,310
113	Fraulein (GB) (f)	Acatenango—Francfurter, by Legend of France	GB	7	2	1	2	520,318
	Highdown	Selkirk—Rispoto, by Mtoto	GB	6	3	1	0	131,129
	Naheef	Marju—Golden Digger, by Mr. Prospector	GB	4	1	0	0	41,771
	Tau Ceti	Hernando (Fr)—Napoli, by Baillamont	Fr	7	2	0	0	86,159
112	Rawyaan	Machiavellian—Raheefa, by Riverman	GB	5	3	0	0	59,102
	Secret Singer	Singspiel (Ire)—Secret Dancer, by Fabulous Dancer	Fr	2	0	2	0	36,516
	Shaanmer	Darshaan—Fee des Mers, by Alzao	Fr	5	0	4	0	186,722

Wt.	Horse	Sire–Dam, Broodmare sire	Trained	Sts	1st	2nd	3rd	Earnings
	Sights on Gold	Indian Ridge—Summer Trysting, by Alleged	Ire	7	2	3	1	$104,833
111	Alasha (f)	Barathea (Ire)—Alasana, by Darshaan	GB	5	1	1	1	226,714
	Dublino (f)	Lear Fan—Tuscoga, by Theatrical (Ire)	Fr/USA	4	1	2	0	291,607
	Irresistible Jewel (f)	Danehill—In Anticipation, by Sadler's Wells	Ire	8	3	1	1	270,587
	Izdiham	Nashwan—Harayir, by Gulch	GB	5	2	1	2	63,480
	Louveteau	Bahri—Louveterie, by Nureyev	Fr	5	1	1	1	28,507
	Sohaib	Kingmambo—Fancy Ruler, by Half a Year	GB	5	1	2	2	80,899
	Without Connexion	Rainbow Quest—Flabbergasted, by Sadler's Wells	Fr	7	1	0	4	116,415
110	Caesarion	Danehill—Carelaine, by Woodman	Fr	6	2	1	1	74,250
	Jazz Beat (Ire)	Darshaan—Hint of Humour, by Woodman	Ire	6	1	2	0	144,638
	Megahertz (GB) (f)	Pivotal—Heavenly Ray, by Rahy	USA	7	5	1	0	600,180
	Mellow Park (f)	In the Wings (GB)—Park Special, by Relkino	GB	5	2	0	0	83,156
	Millstreet	Polish Precedent—Mill Path, by Mill Reef	Ire	8	2	5	1	85,531

7 furlongs +

Wt.	Horse	Sire–Dam, Broodmare sire	Trained	Sts	1st	2nd	3rd	Earnings
128	Rock of Gibraltar (Ire)	Danehill—Offshore Boom, by Be My Guest	Ire	6	5	1	0	$1,353,921
123	Where or When	Danehill Dancer—Future Past, by Super Concorde	GB	7	2	0	0	360,460
120	Landseer (GB)	Danehill—Sabria, by Miswaki	Ire	7	2	1	1	678,088
118	Gossamer (GB) (f)	Sadler's Wells—Brocade, by Habitat	GB	5	1	0	1	266,859
117	Sophisticat (f)	Storm Cat—Serena's Song, by Rahy	Ire	4	2	0	1	282,622
116	Dress to Thrill (Ire) (f)	Danehill—Trusted Partner, by Affirmed	Ire	6	5	0	0	506,918
	Medecis (GB)	Machiavellian—Renashaan, by Darshaan	Fr	8	2	3	0	177,568
	Redback	Mark of Esteem (Ire)—Patsy Western, by Precocious	GB	8	1	2	2	126,165
	Riskaverse (f)	Dynaformer—The Bink, by Seeking the Gold	USA	7	2	2	0	461,160
115	Bowman	Irish River (Fr)—Cherokee Rose (Ire), by Dancing Brave	Fr	7	2	0	1	85,529
	Johar	Gone West—Windsharp, by Lear Fan	USA	11	4	3	1	582,215
	Wonder Again (f)	Silver Hawk—Ameriflora, by Danzig	USA	8	4	1	1	323,840
	Zenda (Fr) (f)	Zamindar—Hope, by Dancing Brave	GB	6	2	2	0	371,500
114	Firebreak	Charnwood Forest (Ire)—Breakaway, by Song	UAE/GB	6	1	2	0	119,641
	Inesperado (Fr)	Zayyani (Ire)—Ile Mamou, by Ela-Mana-Mou	Fr	8	4	1	0	441,251
	Massigann	Selkirk—Masslama, by No Pass No Sale	Fr	5	3	1	0	55,153
	Orchard Park	Hennessy—Blue Begum, by With Approval	USA	7	5	0	1	613,310
	Regiment	Outflanker—Forever Full, by Full Out	USA	6	4	2	0	286,120
	Telegnosis	Tony Bin—Make a Wish, by Northern Taste	Jpn	7	2	2	0	1,206,175
113	Blatant	Machiavellian—Negligent (Ire), by Ahonoora	Ire	4	2	2	0	61,875
	Flying Dash (Ger)	Dashing Blade—Full Board, by Fabulous Dancer	USA	3	1	1	0	162,000
	Meshaheer	Nureyev—Race the Wild Wind, by Sunny's Halo	GB	6	1	0	2	52,875
	Miesque's Approval	Miesque's Son—Win Approval, by With Approval	USA	7	2	2	1	325,550
	Rouvres	Anabaa—Riziere, by Groom Dancer	Fr	3	3	0	0	122,751
	Zarewitsch	Night Shift—Zayraba, by Doyoun	Ger	6	4	1	0	123,990
112	Aramram	Danzig—Felawnah, by Mr. Prospector	GB	8	1	1	1	92,235
	Bel Esprit	Royal Academy—Bespoken, by Vain	Aus	6	2	3	0	260,394
	Finality	Dehere—Finally Found, by Lord Durham	USA	6	3	2	0	235,300
	Guys and Dolls	Efisio—Dime Bag, by High Line	GB	5	1	1	0	45,365
	Imtiyaz	Woodman—Shadayid, by Shadeed	UAE/GB	4	1	2	0	67,434
	Johannesburg	Hennessy—Myth, by Ogygian	Ire	3	0	1	0	11,691
	King of Happiness	Spinning World—Mystery Rays, by Nijinsky II	GB	4	1	1	0	45,400
	Mananan McLir	Royal Academy—St. Lucinda, by St. Jovite	USA	8	1	2	1	293,398
	Massalani	Ashkalani—Massatixa, by Linamix	Fr	2	1	0	0	17,927
	Quest Star	Broad Brush—Tinaca, by Manila	USA	13	2	4	4	261,655
	Rock Opera	Royal Academy—Star de Rahy, by Rahy	USA	7	3	1	2	211,680
	Shaanmer	Darshaan—Fee des Mers, by Alzao	Fr	5	0	4	0	186,722
	Snowfire (f)	Machiavellian—Hill of Snow, by Reference Point	GB	3	0	1	0	96,947
	Tashawak (f)	Night Shift—Dedicated Lady, by Pennine Walk (Ire)	GB	3	2	0	0	115,206
	War Zone	Danzig—Proflare, by Mr. Prospector	Fr	4	1	0	0	47,902
111	Alasha (f)	Barathea (Ire)—Alasana, by Darshaan	GB	5	1	1	1	226,714
	Century City (Ire)	Danzig—Alywow, by Alysheba	Ire/USA	8	3	2	1	256,533
	Dedication (f)	Highest Honor (Fr)—Dissertation, by Sillery	Fr	8	3	3	0	159,484
	Dublino (f)	Lear Fan—Tuscoga, by Theatrical (Ire)	Fr/USA	4	1	2	0	291,607
	Millennium Dragon	Mark of Esteem (Ire)—Feather Bride, by Groom Dancer	GB	8	2	1	0	65,181
	Mr. Mellon	Red Ransom—Mackie, by Summer Squall	USA	8	3	1	0	273,580
	Patrol	Lear Fan—Maid for Walking (GB), by Prince Sabo	USA	6	4	0	1	175,500
	Royal Gem	Royal Academy—Tiffany's Gem, by Effervescing	USA	6	3	0	2	201,760
	Salselon	Salse—Heady, by Rousillon	Ity	9	3	2	0	144,861
	Sohaib	Kingmambo—Fancy Ruler, by Half a Year	GB	5	1	2	2	80,899
110	Bernebeau	Green Tune—Princesse Bilbao, by Highest Honor (Fr)	Fr	4	1	1	0	40,501
	Devious Indian (Ire)	Dr. Devious (Ire)—Danseuse Indienne, by Danehill	Fr	8	3	0	3	79,411
	Doc Holiday (Ire)	Dr. Devious (Ire)—Easter Heroine, by Exactly Sharp	USA	4	1	3	0	135,310
	Dolores (f)	Danehill—Agnus, by In the Wings (GB)	GB	6	1	1	1	124,854
	Firth of Lorne (f)	Danehill—Kerrera, by Diesis (GB)	Fr	2	0	1	1	81,842

Wt.	Horse	Sire–Dam, Broodmare sire	Trained	Sts	1st	2nd	3rd	Earnings
	Golden Arrow	Rahy—Dabaweyaa (Ire), by Shareef Dancer	USA	10	2	3	3	$143,794
	Helenus	Helissio—Worldwide Elsie, by Java Gold	Aus	8	4	2	1	962,464
	Hero's Journey	Halling—Zahwa, by Cadeaux Genereux	GB	4	2	1	0	36,753
	Horeion Directa	Big Shuffle—Hosianna, by Surumu	Ger	7	1	2	2	77,096
	Little Treasure (f)	Night Shift—Luminosity, by Sillery	USA	6	4	0	1	212,964
	Love Regardless	Storm Bird—Circus Toons, by Wild Again	GB	7	2	1	0	74,252
	Masani	Indian Ridge—Masawa, by Alzao	Ire	7	2	1	2	71,872
	Megahertz (GB) (f)	Pivotal—Heavenly Ray, by Rahy	USA	7	5	1	0	600,180
	Sambaprinz	Big Shuffle—Samambaia, by Ti Amo	Ger	8	2	1	1	73,570
	Special Kaldoun	Alzao—Special Lady, by Kaldoun	Fr	6	2	0	1	61,228
	Stage Call (Ire)	Sadler's Wells—Humble Eight, by Seattle Battle	USA	2	0	1	0	28,260
	Twilight Blues	Bluebird—Pretty Sharp, by Interrex	GB	7	1	0	0	46,798

5 furlongs +

Wt.	Horse	Sire–Dam, Broodmare sire	Trained	Sts	1st	2nd	3rd	Earnings
115	Captain Rio	Pivotal—Beloved Visitor, by Miswaki	GB	5	1	1	0	$ 51,183
	Zipping	Zafonic—Zelda, by Caerleon	Fr	6	1	1	1	126,428
114	Feet So Fast	Pivotal—Splice, by Sharpo	GB	5	3	1	0	166,576
112	Slap Shot (f)	Lycius—Katanning, by Green Desert	Ity	7	1	4	1	129,105
111	Millennium Dragon	Mark of Esteem (Ire)—Feather Bride, by Groom Dancer	GB	8	2	1	0	65,181
110	Agnetha (f)	Big Shuffle—Aerleona, by Caerleon	Ire	9	1	1	2	92,614
	Ashdown Express	Ashkalani—Indian Express, by Indian Ridge	GB	8	1	1	3	69,224
	Choisir	Danehill Dancer—Great Selection, by Lunchtime	Aus	7	1	0	3	168,612
	Dominica (f)	Alhaarth—Dominio, by Dominion (GB)	GB	2	1	0	0	123,779
	Polar Way	Polar Falcon—Fetish, by Dancing Brave	GB	5	4	0	0	82,732
	Twilight Blues	Bluebird—Pretty Sharp, by Interrex	GB	7	1	0	0	46,798

Older Horses (Turf)

14 furlongs +

Wt.	Horse	Sire–Dam, Broodmare sire	Trained	Sts	1st	2nd	3rd	Earnings
119	Vinnie Roe	Definite Article (GB)—Kayu, by Tap On Wood	Ire	5	3	1	0	$ 391,496
118	Manhattan Cafe	Sunday Silence—Subtle Change, by Law Society	Jpn	3	1	0	0	1,052,215
117	Jungle Pocket	Tony Bin—Dance Charmer, by Nureyev	Jpn	4	0	2	0	826,680
116	Pugin	Darshaan—Gothic Dream, by Nashwan	Ire/GB	4	1	1	0	90,646
	Royal Rebel	Robellino—Greenvera, by Riverman	GB	3	1	0	0	191,311
115	Akbar	Doyoun—Akishka, by Nishapour	GB	3	1	1	0	59,146
	Narrative	Sadler's Wells—Barger, by Riverman	UAE/GB	7	3	1	0	231,031
	Warrsan	Caerleon—Lucayan Princess, by High Line	GB	11	2	5	0	118,295
114	Born King	Sunday Silence—Ballet Queen, by Sadler's Wells	Jpn	4	0	0	1	327,573
	Invermark	Machiavellian—Applecross, by Glint of Gold	GB	3	0	1	0	22,390
	Ringaskiddy	Slewvescent—Halo at Dawn, by Halo	USA	7	2	1	0	326,280
	Wareed	Sadler's Wells—Truly Special, by Caerleon	GB	2	1	0	1	86,161
113	Boreas	In The Wings (GB)—Reamur, by Top Ville	GB	7	2	3	0	264,062
	Give Notice	Warning (GB)—Princess Genista, by Ile de Bourbon	GB	5	2	1	0	190,513
	Jardines Lookout	Fourstars Allstar—Foolish Flight, by Fools Holme		6	1	0	1	114,002
112	Daliapour (Ire)	Sadler's Wells—Dalara, by Doyoun	GB	5	1	0	0	60,258
	Persian Punch	Persian Heights—Rum Cay, by Our Native	GB	10	2	2	2	144,519
	Pushkin	Caerleon—Palmeraie, by Lear Fan	Fr	10	2	2	1	142,114
111	King the Fact	Known Fact—Koluctoo's Robin, by Koluctoo Bay	Jpn	7	1	0	0	322,714
	Media Puzzle	Theatrical (Ire)—Market Slide, by Gulch	Ire	9	2	0	2	1,447,592
110	Cut Quartz	Johann Quatz (Fr)—Cutlass, by Sure Blade	Fr	7	1	0	2	89,604
	Hatha Anna	Sadler's Wells—Moon Cactus, by Kris	GB	4	0	0	0	20,004
	Miraculous	Linamix—Bernique, by Affirmed	Fr	11	2	2	2	92,075

11 furlongs +

Wt.	Horse	Sire–Dam, Broodmare sire	Trained	Sts	1st	2nd	3rd	Earnings
127	Marienbard	Caerleon—Marienbad, by Darshaan	GB	6	4	0	0	$1,693,245
126	Golan (Ire)	Spectrum—Highland Gift, by Generous	GB	4	1	1	0	832,503
125	Nayef	Gulch—Height of Fashion (Fr), by Bustino	GB	5	2	1	1	1,897,935
123	Califet	Freedom Cry (GB)—Sally's Room, by Kendor	Fr	9	3	2	0	209,425
122	Ange Gabriel	Kaldouneeves (Fr)—Mount Gable, by Head for Heights	Fr	7	4	2	1	1,329,893
	With Anticipation	Relaunch—Fran's Valentine, by Saros (GB)	USA	8	3	3	0	1,507,7000
121	Falcon Flight (Fr)	Persian Bold—Flying Circus, by Gay Mecene	USA	5	1	1	2	947,700
120	Boreal	Java Gold—Britannia, by Tarim	Ger	5	1	0	1	444,157
	Falbrav	Fairy King—Gift of the Night, by Slewpy	Ity	6	4	0	1	2,458,697
	Zindabad (Fr)	Shirley Heights—Miznah, by Sadler's Wells	GB	7	3	0	2	498,627
119	Anabaa Blue	Anabaa—Allez Les Trois, by Riverman	Fr	5	1	1	0	88,434
	Aquarelliste (f)	Danehill—Agathe, by Manila	Fr	9	3	1	1	621,215
	Denon	Pleasant Colony—Aviance (Ire), by Northfields	USA	7	2	2	0	917,400
	Sarafan	Lear Fan—Saraa Ree, by Caro (Ire)	USA	12	2	4	2	2,039,765
	The Tin Man	Affirmed—Lizzie Rolfe, by Tom Rolfe	USA	9	5	1	1	598,020
118	Ekraar	Red Ransom—Sacahuista, by Raja Baba	UAE/GB	4	0	1	1	302,545

Wt.	Horse	Sire–Dam, Broodmare sire	Trained	Sts	1st	2nd	3rd	Earnings
	Kutub	In The Wings (GB)—Minnie Habit, by Habitat	GB	3	0	0	0	$ 8,960
117	Mubtaker	Silver Hawk—Gazayil, by Irish River (Fr)	GB	2	1	1	0	85,270
	Tap Dance City	Pleasant Tap—All Dance, by Northern Dancer	Jpn	12	3	2	4	1,918,833
	Well Made	Mondrian—Well Known, by Konigsstuhl	Ger	7	3	1	0	274,040
116	Magnaten	Danzig—Magic Night (Fr), by Le Nain Jaune (Fr)	Jpn	7	3	0	0	1,501,296
	Millenary	Rainbow Quest—Ballerina, by Dancing Brave	GB	6	1	1	2	146,984
	Polish Summer	Polish Precedent—Hunt the Sun, by Rainbow Quest	Fr	7	2	2	0	249,941
	The Whistling Teal	Rudimentary—Lonely Shore, by Blakeney	GB	5	2	2	0	82,749
	Yavana's Pace (Ire)	Accordion—Lady in Pace, by Burslem	GB	10	1	1	4	381,077
115	Blazing Fury	Dynaformer—Blazing Kadie, by Our Native	USA	5	1	1	0	192,000
	Dantsu Flame	Brian's Time—Inter Pyrenees, by Sanquirico	Jpn	6	1	1	0	1,547,737
	Delta Form (Aus)	Marscay—Arborea (Aus), by Imperial Prince	USA	6	1	0	3	274,980
	Fair Mix	Linamix—Fairlee Wild, by Wild Again	Fr	8	4	0	1	105,672
	Indigenous	Marju—Seaport, by Averof	HK	9	0	0	2	407,055
	Man From Wicklow	Turkoman—Star of Wicklow, by Fast Play	USA	6	1	1	2	247,865
	Narrative	Sadler's Wells—Barger, by Riverman	UAE/GB	7	3	1	0	231,031
	Sligo Bay (Ire)	Sadler's Wells—Angelic Song, by Halo	USA	5	2	0	0	182,900
114	Blue Steller (Ire)	Barathea (Ire)—Banque Privee, by Private Account	USA	8	2	1	3	168,260
	Cetewayo	His Majesty—Aletta Maria, by Diesis (GB)	USA	9	3	2	1	443,375
	Coin Toss	Sunday Silence—Re Toss (Arg), by Egg Toss	Jpn	7	2	1	4	1,254,226
	Continental Red	Flying Continental—Sharp Looking Lady, by Glaros (Fr)	USA	10	2	4	2	540,000
	High Pitched	Indian Ridge—Place de l'Opera, by Sadler's Wells	GB	4	1	1	0	55,089
	Mr Combustible	Hernando (Fr)—Warg, by Dancing Brave	GB	1	0	0		1,448
	Tsurumaru Boy	Dance in the Dark—Tsurumaru Girl, by Soccer Boy	Jpn	9	4	2	1	1,853,442
113	Balto Star	Glitterman—Miss Livi, by Devil's Bag	USA	6	2	2	0	192,876
	Grammarian	Definite Article (GB)—Leaping Water (GB), by Sure Blade	USA	9	3	2	0	340,166
	Island House	Grand Lodge—Fortitude, by Last Tycoon (Ire)	GB	9	3	3	1	112,784
	Kim Loves Bucky	Green Dancer—Moondust Mink, by Great Above	USA	8	1	0	0	159,657
	Moon Queen (Ire) (f)	Sadler's Wells—Infamy (Ire), by Shirley Heights	USA	2	1	0	0	60,000
	Noroit	Monsun—Noble Princesse, by Windwurf (Ger)	Ger	5	0	1	1	123,604
	Rochester	Green Dancer—Central City (GB), by Midyan	USA	10	3	3	1	443,124
	St Expedit	Sadler's Wells—Miss Rinjani, by Shirley Heights	GB	3	1	2	0	90,823
	Sweetest Thing (f)	Candy Stripes—Escape Reality, by Lear Fan	Can	5	2	2	1	278,994
112	Don Eduardo	Zabeel—Our Diamond Lover, by Sticks and Stones	Aus	9	5	1	0	818,431
	Helene Vitality	Zabeel—Anna's Choice, by Vice Regal	HK	11	0	3	0	838,404
	Julie Jalouse (f)	Kris S.—Julie La Rousse (Ire), by Lomond	USA	6	2	0	1	179,117
	Keemoon (Fr) (f)	Goldneyev—Mahonie, by Kenmare	USA	3	0	1	0	50,000
	Lord Flasheart	Blush Rambler—Miss Henderson Co., by Silver Hawk	USA	5	0	0	3	71,880
	Rain Gauge	Kenvain—Turn to Rain, by Family Ties	Aus	12	3	1	4	242,308
	Smart Bet	Cossack Warrior—Quieter Still, by Almurtajaz	Sin	8	4	1	2	854,741
	Staging Post	Pleasant Colony—Interim (GB), by Sadler's Wells	USA	4	1	2	0	148,040
	Water Jump	Suave Dancer—Jolies Eaux, by Shirley Heights	GB	2	0	0	1	8,015
	Whitmore's Conn	Kris S.—Albonita, by Deputed Testamony	USA	9	3	2	0	210,100
111	Bonapartiste (Fr)	Kendor—Fab's Melody, by Devil's Bag	USA	2	0	0	1	24,000
	Firyal Pursuit	Midyan—Firyal, by Nonoalco	HK	10	1	0	3	720,292
	Matikane Kinnohosi	Seattle Slew—Alysbelle, by Alydar	Jpn	6	0	1	0	354,845
	Mot Juste (GB) (f)	Mtoto—Bunting, by Shaadi	GB/USA	7	1	1	2	151,700
	Sagittarius (GB)	Sadler's Wells—Ste Nitouche, by Riverman	Nor	2	0	1	0	24,088
	Tareno	Saddler's Hall—Triclaria, by Surumu	Ger	6	2	1	0	98,121
110	Aeskulap	Acatenango—Aerope, by Celestial Storm	Ger	1	0	1	0	14,675
	Border Arrow	Selkirk—Nibbs Point, by Sure Blade	GB	10	1	1	3	69,107
	Diamond Biko (f)	Sunday Silence—Stella Madrid, by Alydar	Jpn	8	3	3	0	1,791,071
	Dictum	Secret 'n Classy—Doretta, by Aspros	Ger	9	4	2	1	108,154
	Freemason	Grand Lodge—Sashed, by *Sir Tristram	Aus	16	2	3	2	297,414
	Hot Secret	Hunting Hawk—Suda Nadeshiko, by Tai Tehm	Jpn	7	1	1	1	858,604
	Ovambo	Namaqualand—Razana, by Kahyasi	GB	5	0	1	2	29,573
	Samum	Monsun—Sacarina, by Old Vic	Ger	4	0	1	1	69,740
	Sangreal	Celtic Swing—Grosvenor Gardens, by Grosvenor	Fr	6	0	1	1	41,360
	Valley Chapel	Selkirk—Valley Springs, by Saratoga Six	Nor	9	2	1	2	112,454
	Xtra	Sadler's Wells—Oriental Mystique (Ire), by Kris	GB	3	1	1	0	29,397

9½ furlongs +

Wt.	Horse	Sire–Dam, Broodmare sire	Trained	Sts	1st	2nd	3rd	Earnings
126	Grandera	Grand Lodge—Bordighera, by Alysheba	UAE/GB	8	3	1	1	$2,086,498
125	Nayef	Gulch—Height of Fashion (Fr), by Bustino	GB	5	2	1	1	1,897,935
124	Northerly	Serheed—North Bell, by Bellwater	Aus	7	5	0	0	2,253,966
122	Beat Hollow (GB)	Sadler's Wells—Wemyss Bight (GB), by Dancing Brave	USA	8	4	2	1	1,437,150
	Starine (Fr) (f)	Mendocino—Grissonnante, by Kaldoun	USA	4	1	2	0	820,600
121	Astra (f)	Theatrical (Ire)—Savannah Slew, by Seattle Slew	USA	5	3	1	1	758,000
	Best of the Bests	Machiavellian—Sueboog, by Darshaan	UAE/GB	7	2	0	2	272,687

Wt.	Horse	Sire–Dam, Broodmare sire	Trained	Sts	1st	2nd	3rd	Earnings
	Storming Home	Machiavellian—Try to Catch Me, by Shareef Dancer	GB	8	2	2	2	$ 579,080
120	Defier	Dehere—Lilande, by Marscay	Aus	5	3	1	0	533,274
	Falbrav	Fairy King—Gift of the Night, by Slewpy	Ity	6	4	0	1	2,458,697
	Noverre	Rahy—Danseur Fabuleux, by Northern Dancer	UAE/GB	7	0	3	2	694,258
119	Banks Hill (GB) (f)	Danehill—Hasili, by Kahyasi	Fr/USA	7	1	2	3	667,077
	Golden Apples (Ire) (f)	Pivotal—Loon, by Kaldoun	USA	7	3	3	0	1,111,680
	Sarafan	Lear Fan—Saraa Ree, by Caro (Ire)	USA	12	2	4	2	2,039,765
118	Bach (Ire)	Caerleon—Producer, by Nashua	Ire	5	1	1	0	76,404
	Eishin Preston	Green Dancer—Warranty Applied, by Monteverdi (Ire)	Jpn	7	1	2	0	1,763,126
	Indian Creek	Indian Ridge—Blue Water, by Bering (GB)	GB	7	1	1	0	172,269
	Rebelline (f)	Robellino—Fleeting Rainbow, by Rainbow Quest	Ire	3	3	0	0	224,294
	Ulundi (GB)	Rainbow Quest—Flit, by Lyphard	GB	3	1	0	0	93,407
	Anabar	Anabaa—Stop Fiddling, by Welsh Term (Ire)	HK	11	2	3	1	1,938,960
	Lonhro	Octagonal—Shadea, by Straight Strike	Aus	7	4	1	0	440,256
	Narita Top Road	Soccer Boy—Floral Magic, by Affirmed	Jpn	7	3	1	1	2,434,223
	Paolini (Ger)	Lando (Ger)—Prairie Darling, by Stanford	Ger	5	0	2	0	886,358
	Voodoo Dancer (f)	Kingmambo—Zuri, by Danzig	USA	7	3	3	1	562,638
116	Irish Prize	Irish River (Fr)—Cadeaux d'Amie, by Lyphard	USA	4	1	1	0	120,000
	Sakhee	Bahri—Thawakib (Ire), by Sadler's Wells	GB	3	1	1	1	633,220
	Skipping (GB)	Rainbow Quest—Minskip, by The Minstrel	USA	4	1	1	1	132,485
	Strut the Stage	Theatrical (Ire)—Ruby Ransom, by Red Ransom	Can	8	3	0	1	403,542
	Sunrise Pegasus	Sunday Silence—Higashi Brian, by Brian's Time	Jpn	5	2	0	1	1,129,838
	Sunstrach	Polar Falcon—Lorne Lady, by Local Suitor	Ity	7	1	2	2	205,419
	Wellbeing	Sadler's Wells—Charming Life (NZ), by *Sir Tristram	Fr	5	2	0	1	77,115
115	Dano-Mast	Unfuwain—Camera Girl, by Kalaglow	Den	6	3	1	1	388,885
	England's Legend (Fr) (f)	Lure—Mystery Tune, by Commanche Run	USA	3	1	0	1	160,000
	Indigenous	Marju—Seaport, by Averof	HK	9	0	0	2	407,055
	Janet (GB) (f)	Emperor Jones—Bid Dancer (Ire), by Spectacular Bid	USA	7	1	2	2	180,500
	Simoun	Monsun—Suivez, by Fioravanti	Ger	7	3	1	0	191,160
114	Air Shakur	Sunday Silence—I Dreamed a Dream, by Well Decorated	Jpn	6	0	2	0	735,516
	Blue Steller (Ire)	Barathea (Ire)—Banque Privee, by Private Account	USA	8	2	1	3	168,260
	Carnival Dancer	Sadler's Wells—Red Carnival, by Mr. Prospector	GB	3	0	0	0	36,455
	Old Comrade	Old Spice—Belgravia, by Ksar	Aus	13	3	3	1	745,780
	Owsley (f)	Harlan—Insipid, by Sham	USA	8	4	0	0	593,870
	Universal Prince	Scenic (Ire)—Biscay Bird, by Bluebird	Aus	5	0	0	1	107,489
	Volga (Ire) (f)	Caerleon—Verveine, by Lear Fan	USA	6	1	1	2	208,720
113	Chancellor	Halling—Isticanna, by Far North	GB	7	2	1	0	163,417
	Equerry	St. Jovite—Colour Chart, by Mr. Prospector	GB	4	1	0	1	96,666
	Execute	Suave Dancer—She's My Lovely, by Sharpo	Fr	6	2	1	0	97,367
	Housemaster	Rudimentary—Glenarff, by Irish River (Fr)	HK	6	1	0	1	191,7878
	Imperial Dancer	Primo Dominie—Gorgeous Dancer, by Nordico	GB	14	4	0	3	217,564
	Night Patrol	Storm Boot—Downtown Blues, by Seattle Song	USA	10	2	1	0	322,720
	Toho Shiden	Brian's Time—Blushingintherain, by Blushing Groom (Fr)	Jpn	4	0	0	0	231,451
112	Carnegie Express	Carnegie (Ire)—Honeymoon Express, by Star Way	Aus	8	6	1	0	572,631
	Desert Deer	Cadeaux Genereux—Tuxford Hideaway, by Cawston's Clown	GB	6	3	1	1	80,993
	Freefourinternet	Tabasco Cat—Dixie Chimes, by Dixieland Band	GB/USA	8	2	0	0	63,256
	Nazirali (Ire)	Kahyasi—Naziriya, by Darshaan	USA	5	1	1	0	158,400
111	Beekeeper	Rainbow Quest—Chief Bee, by Chief's Crown	GB	4	1	0	1	182,960
	Cagney (Brz)	Roy—Donnegalle, by Campero	USA	4	0	0	1	62,000
	Ice Dancer	Sadler's Wells—Tappiano, by Fappiano	Ire	2	1	0	0	33,279
	Mot Juste (GB) (f)	Mtoto—Bunting, by Shaadi	GB/USA	7	1	1	2	151,700
	Peu a Peu (Ger) (f)	Dashing Blade—Plains Indian, by Dancing Brave	USA	2	1	1	0	105,000
	Sobriety	Namaqualand—Scanno's Choice, by Pennine Walk (Ire)	HK	3	1	0	0	594,912
	Tareno	Saddler's Hall—Triclaria, by Surumu	Ger	6	2	1	0	98,121
110	Binary File	Nureyev—Binary (GB), by Rainbow Quest	GB	5	1	1	0	57,628
	Border Arrow	Selkirk—Nibbs Point, by Sure Blade	GB	10	1	1	3	69,107
	Dash For Cash	Secret Savings—Gulistan, by Rubiton	Aus	15	4	4	2	582,377
	Hawkeye (Ire)	Danehill—Tea House, by Sassafras (Fr)	GB	5	0	1	1	78,997
	Ibuki Government	Commander in Chief—Rosita, by Mill George	Jpn	5	1	2	0	640,014
	Kappa King	Kingmambo—Charming Ballerina (Ire), by Caerleon	USA	4	1	1	1	109,800
	Sensible	Sadler's Wells—Raisonnable, by Common Grounds	Fr	6	0	1	1	46,694
	Terre de L'home	Lomitas (GB)—Theresina, by Vision	Ger	5	2	0	0	43,744
	T.M. Ocean (f)	Dancing Brave—River Girl, by Rivlia	Jpn	4	1	0	0	553,155

7 furlongs +

Wt.	Horse	Sire–Dam, Broodmare sire	Trained	Sts	1st	2nd	3rd	Earnings
126	Keltos	Kendor—Loxandra, by Last Tycoon (Ire)	Fr	3	2	0	0	$ 197,078
124	Domedriver (Ire)	Indian Ridge—Napoli, by Baillamont	Fr	6	3	2	0	743,833
122	Good Journey	Nureyev—Chimes of Freedom, by Private Account	USA	5	4	0	1	1,247,665
121	Astra (f)	Theatrical (Ire)—Savannah Slew, by Seattle Slew	USA	5	3	1	1	758,000

Wt.	Horse	Sire–Dam, Broodmare sire	Trained	Sts	1st	2nd	3rd	Earnings
120	Forbidden Apple	Pleasant Colony—North of Eden (Ire), by Northfields	USA	6	0	2	3	$ 354,420
	Ladies Din	Din's Dancer—Ladies Double, by Kris S.	USA	3	2	0	1	285,600
119	Banks Hill (GB) (f)	Danehill—Hasili, by Kahyasi	Fr/USA	7	1	2	3	667,077
	Golden Apples (Ire) (f)	Pivotal—Loon, by Kaldoun	USA	7	3	3	0	1,111,680
	Nayyir	Indian Ridge—Pearl Kite, by Silver Hawk	GB	10	5	0	0	240,191
	Sunline (f)	Desert Sun (GB)—Songline, by Western Symphony	NZ	4	1	1	1	180,482
	Val Royal (Fr)	Royal Academy—Vadlava, by Bikala	USA	2	0	0	0	78,000
118	Hap	Theatrical (Ire)—Committed, by Hagley	USA	3	0	0	1	45,250
	No Excuse Needed	Machiavellian—Nawaiet, by Zilzal	GB	6	1	0	0	169,843
	Shogun Lodge	Grand Lodge—Pride of Tahnee, by Best Western	Aus	4	0	0	1	13,926
117	Affluent (f)	Affirmed—Trinity Place, by Strawberry Road (Aus)	USA	8	2	3	0	560,615
	Decarchy	Distant View—Toussaud, by El Gran Senor	USA	5	2	1	1	333,000
	Del Mar Show	Theatrical (Ire)—Prankstress, by Foolish Pleasure	USA	7	3	1	0	310,000
	Ecclesiastical	Bishop of Cashel—Rachael Tennessee, by Matsadoon	HK	7	3	1	0	2,783,652
	Green Fee	Green Dancer—Raska, by Rahy	USA	6	2	1	1	280,460
	Tates Creek (f)	Rahy—Viviana, by Nureyev	USA	8	5	2	0	661,512
	Tillerman	In The Wings (GB)—Autumn Tint, by Roberto	GB	7	2	1	1	167,516
	Touch of the Blues (Fr)	Cadeaux Genereux—Silabteni, by Nureyev	USA	9	1	2	0	305,350
	Voodoo Dancer (f)	Kingmambo—Zuri, by Danzig	USA	7	3	3	1	562,638
116	Admire Cozzene	Cozzene—Admire McArdy (Jpn), by Northern Taste	Jpn	7	3	2	0	2,149,552
	Electronic Unicorn	Housebuster—Lilac Garden, by Roberto	HK	5	1	2	0	1,043,292
	Irish Prize	Irish River (Fr)—Cadeaux d'Amie, by Lyphard	USA	4	1	1	0	120,000
	Nuclear Debate	Geiger Counter—I'm An Issue, by Cox's Ridge	USA	7	2	0	2	363,580
	Olden Times	Darshaan—Garah, by Ajdal	GB	1	0	0	1	27,589
	Strut the Stage	Theatrical (Ire)—Ruby Ransom, by Red Ransom	Can	8	3	0	1	403,542
	Tokai Point	Tokai Teio—Match Point, by Real Shadai	Jpn	10	2	1	1	1,776,336
115	Dantsu Flame	Brian's Time—Inter Pyrenees, by Sanquirico	Jpn	6	1	1	0	1,547,737
	Gateman (GB)	Owington (GB)—Scandalette, by Niniski	GB	10	2	2	3	103,308
	Janet (GB) (f)	Emperor Jones—Bid Dancer (Ire), by Spectacular Bid	USA	7	1	2	2	180,500
	Moon Solitaire (Ire)	Night Shift—Gay Fantastic (GB), by Ela-Mana-Mou	USA	6	1	1	2	325,420
	Redattore (Brz)	Roi Normand—Political Intrigue, by Deputy Minister	USA	5	1	2	1	309,940
	Reel Buddy	Mr. Greeley—Rosebud (GB), by Indian Ridge	GB	9	4	0	2	144,752
	Suggestive	Reprimand—Pleasuring, by Good Times	GB	7	2	1	1	85,664
	Terre a Terre (f)	Kaldouneeves (Fr)—Toujours Juste, by Always Fair	Fr	1	1	0	0	1,200,000
114	Babae (Chi) (f)	Barkerville—Betrayer, by Fain	USA	8	4	0	2	344,992
	Designed for Luck	Rahy—Fantastic Look, by Green Dancer	USA	3	1	0	1	75,000
	Poussin	Alzao—Paix Blanche, by Fabulous Dancer	Fr	5	0	1	1	43,480
	Quiet Resolve	Affirmed—Quiet Cleo, by No Louder	Can	7	2	2	0	283,647
	Show A Heart	Brave Warrior—Miss Sandman, by Regal Advice	Aus					
	Sneaky Visit	Snippets—Shingle Moss, by Twig Moss	HK	10	2	1	1	490,366
	Snow Dance (f)	Forest Wildcat—Northern Pageant, by Spectacular Bid	USA	7	1	3	1	281,687
	Special Ring	Nureyev—Ring Beaune, by Bering (GB)	USA	6	4	0	1	168,975
	Startac	Theatrical (Ire)—Tenga, by Mr. Prospector	USA	6	1	1	1	172,095
	Suances (GB)	Most Welcome (GB)—Prayer Wheel, by High Line	USA	4	2	0	0	290,000
	Tout Charmant (f)	Slewvescent—Charm a Gendarme, by Batonnier	USA	4	2	0	0	159,000
113	Falvelon	Alannon—Devil's Zephyr, by Zephyr Zing	Aus	6	0	2	1	188,421
	Island House	Grand Lodge—Fortitude, by Last Tycoon (Ire)	GB	9	3	3	1	112,784
	Night Patrol	Storm Boot—Downtown Blues, by Seattle Song	USA	10	2	1	0	322,720
	Pisces	Prized—Distaff Magic, by Fluorescent Light	USA	10	2	2	2	252,533
	Rikiai Taikan	Afleet—No No Never, by Nijinsky II	Jpn	7	0	1	1	505,375
	Slickly (Fr)	Linamix—Slipstream Queen, by Conquistador Cielo	GB	1	1	0	0	89,158
112	Altieri	Selkirk—Minya, by Blushing Groom (Fr)	Ity	8	4	1	0	224,643
	Cayoke (Fr)	Always Fair—Sarah Annita, by Pharly	Fr	10	2	1	2	105,509
	Daitaku Riva	Fuji Kiseki—Spring Never, by Sakura Yutaka O	Jpn	4	1	0	0	333,202
	Desert Deer	Cadeaux Genereux—Tuxford Hideaway, by Cawston's Clown	GB	6	3	1	1	80,993
	Excellerator	Marscay—Artless, by Dahar	Aus	6	2	1	2	316,024
	God of Chance	Cozzene—Team Colors, by Mr. Prospector	Jpn	6	1	1	0	612,189
	Grass World	Rahy—A Chance of Storm, by Storm Cat	Jpn	9	3	1	1	942,159
	Kachamandi (Chi)	Royal Danzig—Pura Tora, by Puro Toro	USA	15	2	2	4	171,956
	Magic Mission (GB) (f)	Machiavellian—Dream Ticket, by Danzig	USA	6	2	1	2	163,400
	Millennium Bio	Sunday Silence—Dolsk (GB), by Danzig	Jpn	6	3	0	2	1,142,872
	Morluc	Housebuster—Flashing Eyes, by Time to Explode	USA	5	2	2	0	163,095
	Nicobar (GB)	Indian Ridge—Duchess of Alba, by Belmez	USA	9	1	1	1	97,765
	Palace Line	Palace Music—Mamarrahca, by Pepenador	Sin	8	2	1	0	469,863
	Proudwings (f)	Dashing Blade—Peraja, by Kaiseradler	Fr	5	0	0	2	41,186
	Spinelessjellyfish	Skywalker—Silk Sand Sammy, by Desert Wine	USA	11	0	2	3	151,567
	Tamburlaine (Ire)	Royal Academy—Well Bought, by Auction Ring	GB	2	0	0	3	41,275
	Warningford	Warning (GB)—Barford Lady, by Stanford	GB	5	2	0	0	53,048
111	Amonita (GB) (f)	Anabaa—Spectacular Joke, by Spectacular Bid	USA	3	2	1	0	83,072

Wt.	Horse	Sire–Dam, Broodmare sire	Trained	Sts	1st	2nd	3rd	Earnings
	Breaktime	Danehill—Homareno Princess, by Prince of Birds	Jpn	6	1	2	0	$595,101
	Even the Score	Unbridled's Song—Ashtabula, by Rahy	USA	9	1	1	4	188,320
	Fields of Omagh	Rubiton—Finneto, by Cerreto	Aus	7	2	3	1	465,215
	Frenchmans Bay	Polar Falcon—River Fantasy, by Irish River (Fr)	GB	6	2	0	1	54,529
	Hoeberg	Maroof—Petrava (NZ), by Imposing	Sin	8	1	1	1	280,291
	Meisho Ramses	Lammtarra—Meisho Yaegaki, by Creator (GB)	Jpn	7	3	1	1	814,765
	North East Bound	D'Accord—North East Dancer, by Far North	USA	7	1	2	0	141,000
	Reine de Romance (Ire) (f)	Vettori—Romanche, by Galetto	USA	7	1	0	2	63,056
	Stylish (f)	Thunder Gulch—Miss Lenora, by Theatrical	USA	7	2	2	2	183,976
	Surya (f)	Unbridled—Wild Planet, by Nureyev	USA	6	4	0	1	364,339
	Thady Quill	Nureyev—Alleged Devotion, by Alleged	USA	4	0	1	0	28,400
	Tie the Knot	Nassipour—Whisked, by Whiskey Road	Aus	7	1	0	1	109,200
	Touch Down	Dashing Blade—Time to Run, by Sicyos	Ger	6	2	1	1	91,230
	Tough Speed	Miswaki—Nature's Magic, by Nijinsky II	GB	6	0	0	4	47,655
110	American Boss	Kingmambo—Redeemer, by Dixieland Band	Jpn	8	0	0	1	130,555
	Atlantis Prince	Tagula—Zoom Lens, by Caerleon	UAE/GB	5	1	1	0	33,387
	Band is Passing	Pass the Line—Fairforband, by Fairway Fortune	USA	4	2	1	0	193,543
	Baptize	Dynaformer—Screening Room, by Storm Cat	USA	5	1	0	0	49,800
	Blizz Bless	Lode—Bless the Bride, by Blushing Groom (Fr)	Sin	12	5	3	0	366,047
	Blue Moon (Fr) (f)	Lomitas (GB)—To the Rainbow, by Rainbow Quest	USA	4	1	1	0	153,780
	Calista (GB) (f)	Caerleon—Proskona, by Mr. Prospector	USA	4	3	1	0	278,750
	Chopinina (f)	Lear Fan—Lady Aloma, by Cozzene	Can	4	2	1	0	292,280
	Clearly a Queen	Lucky North—Cryptoqueen, by Cryptoclearance	USA	6	3	0	2	166,211
	Cornelius	Barathea (Ire)—Rainbow Mountain, by Rainbow Quest	GB	6	1	1	2	111,704
	Crawl	Dr Grace—Traipse, by Bletchingly	Aus	5	0	1	0	62,872
	Crazy Ensign (Arg) (f)	Firery Ensign—Crazy Fitz, by Fitzcarraldo	USA	9	1	2	2	161,520
	Diadella (f)	Diesis (GB)—Rabiadella, by Dynaformer	USA	2	1	1	0	109,650
	Dr. Kashnikow	El Gran Senor—One More Breeze, by Mythical Ruler	USA	8	1	2	2	201,905
	Duck Row	Diesis (GB)—Sunny Moment, by Roberto	GB	7	2	2	0	137,120
	Le Zagaletta	Last Tycoon (Ire)—Swiftsynd, by Swift Gun	Aus	7	0	2	2	74,876
	No Slip (Fr)	Exit to Nowhere—Slipstream Queen, by Conquistador Cielo	USA	3	1	0	0	91,500
	Seinne (Chi)	Hussonet—White Lady, by Worldwatch	USA	9	1	1	2	228,906
	Sir Nicholas	Cadeaux Genereux—Final Shot, by Darshaan	HK	8	2	2	0	739,842
	Smirk (GB)	Selkirk—Elfin Laughter, by Alzao	GB	8	2	2	1	138,455
	Tenzan Seiza	Tony Bin—Casey (GB), by Caerleon	Jpn	7	0	0	2	286,274
	Umistim	Inchinor (GB)—Simply Sooty, by Absalom	GB	9	2	2	0	86,369
	Up and Away	Le Glorieux (GB)—Ultima Ratio, by Viceregal	Ger	7	2	1	1	77,817
	Veil of Avalon (f)	Thunder Gulch—Wind in Her Hair (Ire), by Alzao	USA	2	1	0	0	60,000
	War Blade	Dashing Blade—Warluskee, by Dancing Brave	Ger	8	2	2	0	73,758
	White Heart (GB)	Green Desert—Barari, by Blushing Groom	USA	3	0	0	1	85,625

5 furlongs +

Wt.	Horse	Sire–Dam, Broodmare sire	Trained	Sts	1st	2nd	3rd	Earnings
119	Kyllachy	Pivotal—Pretty Poppy, by Song	GB	5	4	0	1	$ 284,370
118	Invincible Spirit	Green Desert—Rafha, by Kris	GB	5	2	0	0	241,704
117	All Thrills Too	St Covet—Red Slippers, by Citidancer (Ire)	HK	9	3	2	0	1,350,074
	Continent	Lake Coniston (Ire)—Krisia, by Kris	GB	13	2	3	0	422,477
	Malhub	Kingmambo—Arjuzah (Ire), by Ahonoora	GB	6	2	3	0	408,642
116	Bahamian Pirate	Housebuster—Shining Through, by Deputy Minister	USA	12	0	2	1	121,140
	Indian Prince	Indian Ridge—Lingering Melody, by Nordico	GB	5	0	0	2	40,591
	Nuclear Debate	Geiger Counter—I'm An Issue, by Cox's Ridge	USA	7	2	0	2	363,580
	Rubitano	Rubiton—Mrs. Soffel, by The Judge	Aus	8	3	1	1	343,875
	Shonan Kampf	Sakura Bakushin O—Shonan Grace, by Lucky Sovereign	Jpn	9	4	0	2	1,837,226
	Texas Glitter	Glitterman—Come on Texas, by Apalachee	USA	9	3	2	2	313,408
114	Malabar Gold	Unbridled—Stormy Spell, by Tsunami Slew	USA	6	2	1	2	179,605
	May Ball (f)	Cadeaux Genereux—Minute Waltz, by Sadler's Wells	GB	7	1	1	0	105,911
	Shibboleth	Danzig—Razyana, by His Majesty	USA	5	1	1	0	89,074
113	Astonished (GB)	Weldnaas—Indigo, by Primo Dominie	USA	7	2	2	0	121,395
	Believe (f)	Sunday Silence—Great Christine, by Danzig	Jpn	11	5	1	3	1,850,749
	Falvelon	Alannon—Devil's Zephyr, by Zephyr Zing	Aus	6	0	2	1	188,421
	Mistegic	Strategic—Volcanic Mist, by Volcanic Prince	Aus	6	1	0	3	116,978
	North Boy	Rory's Jester—North Bell, by Bellwater	Aus	5	2	0	0	335,505
	Orientor	Inchinor (GB)—Orient, by Bay Express	GB	7	0	1	1	34,253
	Three Points	Bering (GB)—Trazl, by Zalazl	GB	5	1	0	2	111,361
	Tiger Royal	Royal Academy—Lady Redford, by Bold Lad	Ire	10	4	1	0	145,650
	Volata	Flying Spur—Musianica, by Music Boy	HK	6	2	1	1	906,771
112	Air Thule (f)	Tony Bin—Ski Paradise, by Lyphard	Jpn	8	0	1	3	189,025
	Blu Air Force (Ire)	Sri Pekan—Carillon Miss, by The Minstrel	USA	3	1	0	0	69,360
	Charming City	Chief's Crown—Quarentieme, by Bletchingly	HK	8	2	0	2	800,931
	Crystal Castle	Gilded Time—Wayage, by Mr. Prospector	Fr	6	3	0	1	269,066

Wt.	Horse	Sire–Dam, Broodmare sire	Trained	Sts	1st	2nd	3rd	Earnings
	Danehurst (f)	Danehill—Miswaki Belle, by Miswaki	GB	7	3	1	1	$ 285,654
	El Cielo	El Prado (Ire)—Only Above, by Great Above	USA	3	0	1	1	27,234
	Palace Affair (f)	Pursuit of Love—Palace Street, by Secreto	GB	9	3	2	0	97,822
111	Boleyn Castle	River Special—Dance Skirt, by Caucasus	GB	4	2	1	0	90,893
	Mugharreb	Gone West—Marling (Ire), by Lomond	GB	7	1	3	0	50,439
	Tedburrow	Dowsing—Gwiffina, by Welsh Saint	GB	6	2	0	0	43,678
	The Trader	Selkirk—Snowing, by Tate Gallery	GB	6	1	0	0	32,965
	Vision of Night (GB)	Night Shift—Dreamawhile, by Known Fact	GB	4	0	2	0	33,356
110	Bishops Court	Clantime—Indigo, by Primo Dominie	GB	11	2	1	3	82,584
	Century Kid	Centaine—Zeffi, by Pompeii Court	Aus	8	2	0	1	98,541
	Joe's Son Joey	Fast Play—Flew By Em, by Air Forbes Won	Can	4	1	3	0	143,450
	Nobel Prize	Lode—Norma's Lady, by Unfuwain	Swe	9	5	1	1	104,399
	Rolly Polly (Ire) (f)	Mukaddamah—Rare Sound, by Rarity	USA	8	4	0	1	227,954
	Smokin Beau	Cigar—Beau Dada, by Pine Circle	GB	11	4	4	0	119,193
	Sudurka	Perugino—My Sparkling Star, by Copper Kingdom	Aus	7	2	0	1	258,125
	Testify	Pembroke—Vands, by Seattle Song	USA	6	1	0	1	92,807
	Troubles	Carolingian—Last Round Up, by Sovereign Dynasty	HK	2	0	0	0	90,766
	Vinaka	Volksraad—Shepherds Delight, by Famous Star	NZ	7	3	1	2	60,341
	Waltz in the Park	Bletchley Park—Corporate Dancer, by Corporate Raider	Sin	3	1	2	0	129,638

Three-Year-Olds (Dirt)

11 furlongs +

Wt.	Horse	Sire–Dam, Broodmare sire	Trained	Sts	1st	2nd	3rd	Earnings
120	Sarava	Wild Again—Rhythm of Life, by Deputy Minister	USA	4	2	2	0	$ 665,040
113	Jilbab (f)	A.P. Indy—Headline (GB), by Machiavellian	USA	5	2	1	1	319,300
111	Tarnished Lady (f)	Lord Avie—Tarnished Gold, by Cabrini Green	USA	14	3	4	3	225,150

9½ furlongs +

Wt.	Horse	Sire–Dam, Broodmare sire	Trained	Sts	1st	2nd	3rd	Earnings
124	War Emblem	Our Emblem—Sweetest Lady, by Lord At War (Arg)	USA	10	5	0	0	$3,455,000
121	Came Home	Gone West—Nice Assay, by Clever Trick	USA	8	6	0	0	1,624,500
	Medaglia d'Oro	El Prado (Ire)—Cappucino Bay, by Bailjumper	USA	9	4	3	0	2,260,000
120	Repent	Louis Quatorze—Baby Grace (Arg), by Cipayo	USA	5	2	2	0	840,000
119	Magic Weisner	Ameri Valay—Jazema, by Bold Forbes	USA	8	4	3	0	791,000
118	Farda Amiga (f)	Broad Brush—Fly North, by Pleasant Colony	USA	6	3	1	0	1,248,902
	Proud Citizen	Gone West—Drums of Freedom, by Green Forest	USA	5	1	1	1	526,083
117	Admire Don	Timber Country—Vega, by Tony Bin	Jpn	7	1	0	2	1,345,757
	Perfect Drift	Dynaformer—Nice Gal, by Naskra	USA	8	3	2	10	695,120
116	Allamerican Bertie (f)	Quiet American—Clever Bertie, by Timeless Native	USA	11	6	1	2	619,235
	Easyfromthegitgo	Dehere—Montera, by Easy Goer	USA	11	2	3	2	606,905
115	Gold Allure	Sunday Silence—Nikiya, by Nureyev	Jpn	10	5	0	1	2,120,118
114	Nothing Flat	Peaks and Valleys—Her Decision, by Judger	USA	11	2	4	1	345,900
113	Essence of Dubai	Pulpit—Epitome, by Summing	UAE/USA	7	3	1	1	1,805,000

7 furlongs +

Wt.	Horse	Sire–Dam, Broodmare sire	Trained	Sts	1st	2nd	3rd	Earnings
121	Came Home	Gone West—Nice Assay, by Clever Trick	USA	8	6	0	0	$1,624,500
	Medaglia d'Oro	El Prado (Ire)—Cappucino Bay, by Bailjumper	USA	9	4	3	0	2,260,000
120	Buddha	Unbridled's Song—Cahooters, by Storm Cat	USA	4	3	0	0	489,600
	Harlan's Holiday	Harlan—Christmas in Aiken, by Affirmed	USA	10	3	2	1	1,606,000
119	Sunday Break (Jpn)	Forty Niner—Catequil, by Storm Cat	USA	7	4	0	2	402,500
118	Farda Amiga (f)	Broad Brush—Fly North, by Pleasant Colony	USA	6	3	1	0	1,248,902
117	Booklet	Notebook—Crafty Bobbie, by Bob's Dusty	USA	7	3	1	0	425,760
	Imperial Gesture (f)	Langfuhr—Honor an Offer, by Hoist the Flag	UAE/USA	7	5	0	1	1,143,600
116	Easyfromthegitgo	Dehere—Montera, by Easy Goer	USA	11	2	3	2	606,905
	Take Charge Lady (f)	Dehere—Felicita, by Rubiano	USA	10	6	3	0	1,388,635
	You (f)	You and I—Our Dani, by Homebuilder	USA	9	4	2	1	883,805
114	Habibti (f)	Tabasco Cat—Miss Sobriety, by Temperence Hill	USA	7	0	3	1	171,851
	Labamta Babe	Skywalker—Bambina Linda (Arg), by Liloy (Fr)	USA	5	1	1	0	102,280
	Mayakovsky	Matty G—Joy to Raise, by Raise a Man	USA	4	1	0	0	174,000
	Siphonic	Siphon (Brz)—Cherokee Crossing, by Cherokee Colony	USA	3	0	2	1	70,800
113	Easy Grades	Honor Grades—Itsoeasy, by Easy Goer	USA	9	2	4	1	284,705
	Private Emblem	Our Emblem—Merion Miss, by Halo	USA	8	4	1	1	550,940
	Saarland	Unbridled—Versailles Treaty, by Danzig	USA	4	1	1	0	115,000
112	Sightseek (f)	Distant View—Viviana, by Nureyev	USA	5	4	1	0	261,978
	U S S Tinosa	Foxhound—Angel Puss, by Wolf Power (Saf)	USA	6	1	1	1	130,940
	Wiseman's Ferry	Hennessy—Emmaus, by Silver Deputy	USA	8	3	1	1	766,552
111	Azillion (Ire)	Alzao—Olivia, by Ela-Mana-Mou	USA	7	0	1	2	114,477
	Bella Bellucci (f)	French Deputy—Blue Avenue, by Classic Go Go	USA	6	3	0	2	213,265
	Lusty Latin	El Prado (Ire)—Scarlet Ann, by Afleet	USA	5	1	0	3	148,000
	Request for Parole	Judge T C—Madison's Quest, by Deputy Minister	USA	5	2	0	1	145,610
	Tracemark	Conquistador Cielo—Juta's Fame, by Danzig	USA	8	2	3	1	257,660
	Werblin	Unbridled's Song—Roll Over Baby, by Rollin On Over	USA	3	0	1	2	57,855

Wt.	Horse	Sire–Dam, Broodmare sire	Trained	Sts	1st	2nd	3rd	Earnings
	Yougottawanna	Candi's Gold—Chapel's Sister	USA	3	1	1	0	$ 133,675
110	Adoration (f)	Honor Grades—Sewing Lady, by Key to the Mint	USA	10	3	1	0	283,106
	Blue Burner	French Deputy—Haiati, by Alydar	USA	5	3	1	1	256,100
	Boston Common	Boston Harbor—Especially, by Mr. Prospector	USA	13	3	4	2	303,177
	Dust Me Off (f)	With Approval—Emma Loves Marie, by Wild Again	USA	6	2	0	0	205,240
	Ile de France (f)	Storm Cat—Cara Rafaela, by Quiet American	USA	7	1	2	1	86,600
	It'sallinthechase	Take Me Out—Limestone Landing, by Red Ryder	USA	6	0	0	2	98,000
	Like a Hero	Pleasant Colony—Like a Hawk, by Silver Hawk	USA	9	3	2	1	408,910
	Nonsuch Bay (f)	Mr. Greeley—Brighter than Gold, by Light Idea	USA	10	4	2	1	439,362
	Ocean Sound (Ire)	Mujadil—Ossana, by Tejano	USA	7	1	2	1	146,800
	Puzzlement	Pine Bluff—Taine, by Sir Ivor	USA	9	3	1	2	157,140

5 furlongs +

Wt.	Horse	Sire–Dam, Broodmare sire	Trained	Sts	1st	2nd	3rd	Earnings
120	Gygistar	Prospector's Music—Starr County, by Ogygian	USA	5	5	0	0	$ 395,400
	Thunderello	Montbrook—On the Square, by In Reality	USA	5	2	2	0	355,600
116	You (f)	You and I—Our Dani, by Homebuilder	USA	9	4	2	1	883,805
115	Officer	Bertrando—Sky Captive, by Septieme Ciel	USA	1	1	0	0	64,080
113	Carson Hollow (f)	Carson City—Lizeality, by Hold Your Peace	USA	7	5	1	0	335,370
	Listen Here	Gulch—Listen Now, by Storm Bird	USA	6	1	3	1	171,500
112	Cashier's Dream (f)	Service Stripe—Jerry's Sister, by Monetary Gift	USA	1	1	0	0	69,812
	Roman Dancer	Polish Numbers—Phalanopsis, by Cormorant	USA	4	2	1	0	166,009
	Spring Meadow (f)	Meadowlake—Go for it Lady, by Mr. Prospector	USA	13	3	4	2	292,121
111	Proper Gamble (f)	Prospectors Gamble—Bare It Properly, by Proper Reality	USA	6	3	1	1	321,475
110	Boston Common	Boston Harbor—Especially, by Mr. Prospector	USA	13	3	4	2	303,177
	Captain Squire	Flying Chevron—Dolly's Back, by At the Threshold	USA	8	3	2	2	324,100
	Cashel Castle	Silver Ghost—Desviacion, by Unreal Zeal	USA	3	2	1	0	111,966
	Ethan Man	Glitterman—Twilight Spectre, by Imp Society	USA	3	2	0	0	121,339
	French Riviera (f)	French Deputy—Actinella, by Seattle Slew	USA	4	3	0	0	110,200
	Lady George (f)	Lake George—Metro Link, by Kennedy Road	USA	5	1	0	1	88,659
	September Secret (f)	Our Emblem—Andrushka, by Giboulee	USA	3	2	0	0	95,580
	True Direction	French Deputy—Ms Paragon, by Tank's Prospect	USA	8	5	1	1	228,620

Older Horses (Dirt)

9½ furlongs +

Wt.	Horse	Sire–Dam, Broodmare sire	Trained	Sts	1st	2nd	3rd	Earnings
125	Volponi	Cryptoclearance—Prom Knight, by Sir Harry Lewis	USA	8	3	3	1	$2,389,200
124	Street Cry (Ire)	Machiavellian—Helen Street (GB), by Troy	UAE/USA	4	3	1	0	4,323,777
120	Evening Attire	Black Tie Affair (Ire)—Concolour, by Our Native	USA	9	5	1	0	1,332,720
119	Momentum	Nureyev—Imprudent Love, by Foolish Pleasure	USA	7	0	4	1	526,888
	Sky Jack	Jaklin Klugman—Sky Captive, by Skywalker	USA	5	2	1	0	556,900
118	Milwaukee Brew	Wild Again—Ask Anita, by Wolf Power (Saf)	USA	7	2	0	3	1,590,000
117	Agnes Digital	Crafty Prospector—Chancey Squaw, by Chief's Crown	Jpn	3	1	1	0	1,238,986
116	E Dubai	Mr. Prospector—Words of War, by Lord At War (Arg)	USA	3	1	0	0	315,000
	Macho Uno	Holy Bull—Primal Force, by Blushing Groom (Fr)	USA	6	2	0	1	519,600
	Summer Colony (f)	Summer Squall—Probably Colony, by Pleasant Colony	USA	8	4	2	1	992,500
115	Bosque Redondo	Mane Minister—Pima, by Cox's Ridge	USA	7	2	2	0	291,510
	Sei Mi	Potrillazo—Seine, by Logical	USA	6	0	5	1	1,224,740
113	Abreeze	Danzig—Priceless Pearl, by Alydar	USA	11	3	1	0	196,480
	Hail the Chief (GB)	Be My Chief—Jade Pet, by Petong	USA	6	3	1	0	458,590
	Kanetsu Fleuve	Paradise Creek—Rosita, by Mill George	Jpn	11	3	2	2	1,279,750
	Mongoose	Broad Brush—Salty Gal, by Cox's Ridge	USA	4	2	1	0	384,000
112	Hal's Hope	Jolie's Halo—Mia's Hope, by Rexson's Hope	USA	6	2	0	2	278,500
	Total Impact (Chi)	Stuka—Pebbles, by Manos de Piedra	USA	3	0	2	0	414,700
111	Tenpins	Smart Strike—Maid's Broom, by Deputy Minister	USA	7	5	0	1	560,629

7 furlongs +

Wt.	Horse	Sire–Dam, Broodmare sire	Trained	Sts	1st	2nd	3rd	Earnings
125	Azeri (f)	Jade Hunter—Zodiac Miss (Aus), by Ahonoora	USA	9	8	1	0	$2,181,540
124	Street Cry (Ire)	Machiavellian—Helen Street (GB), by Troy	UAE/USA	4	3	1	0	4,323,777
122	Left Bank	French Deputy—Marshesseaux, by Dr. Blum	USA	4	3	0	0	626,146
121	Congaree	Arazi—Mari's Sheba, by Mari's Book	USA	6	3	0	1	570,000
	Swept Overboard	End Sweep—Sheer Ice, by Cutlass	USA	5	1	0	1	495,325
120	Lido Palace (Chi)	Rich Man's Gold—Sonada, by Quick Decision	USA	7	3	2	1	1,015,764
119	Mizzen Mast	Cozzene—Kinema, by Graustark	USA	1	1	0	0	240,000
118	Spain (f)	Thunder Gulch—Drina, by Regal and Royal	USA	7	2	1	2	569,502
117	Agnes Digital	Crafty Prospector—Chancey Squaw, by Chief's Crown	Jpn	3	1	1	0	1,238,986
116	Eagle Cafe	Gulch—Net Dancer, by Nureyev	Jpn	12	2	1	0	1,611,007
	Macho Uno	Holy Bull—Primal Force, by Blushing Groom (Fr)	USA	6	2	0	1	519,600
	Mandy's Gold	Gilded Time—Manduria, by Aloma's Ruler	USA	13	5	3	3	715,404
	Pleasantly Perfect	Pleasant Colony—Regal State, by Affirmed	USA	8	4	2	0	479,880
	Raging Fever (f)	Storm Cat—Pennant Fever, by Seattle Slew	USA	10	4	4	1	595,160
115	Dancethruthedawn (f)	Mr. Prospector—Dance Smartly, by Danzig	Can	6	2	1	2	350,952
	Forest Secrets (f)	Forest Wildcat—Garden Secrets, by Time for a Change	USA	5	1	1	0	173,951

Wt.	Horse	Sire–Dam, Broodmare sire	Trained	Sts	1st	2nd	3rd	Earnings
	Red Bullet	Unbridled—Cargo, by Caro (Ire)	USA	5	1	1	0	$ 95,120
	Western Pride	Way West (Fr)—Strongerthanpride, by Proud Birdie	USA	5	1	1	0	334,640
114	Euchre	Personal Flag—Solid Eight, by Fit to Fight	USA	9	0	4	0	188,600
	Grey Memo	Memo (Chi)—B. Mozelle, by Snow Chief	USA	10	2	1	1	808,000
	Include	Broad Brush—Illeria, by Stop the Music	USA	4	1	0	1	127,000
	Kudos	Kris S.—Souq, by Damascus	USA	3	2	0	1	468,735
	Regent Bluff	Park Regent—Sally Belle, by Goodly	Jpn	9	1	1	1	1,245,735
	Wooden Phone	Pick up the Phone—Teaksberry Road, by High Honors	USA	1	1	0	0	120,000
113	Burning Roma	Rubiano—While Rome Burns, by Overskate	USA	9	2	1	2	350,237
	Gander	Cormorant—Lovely Nurse, by Sawbones	USA	8	2	2	1	306,000
	Miss Linda (Arg) (f)	Southern Halo—Miss Peggy, by Fitzcarraldo	USA	3	1	0	1	125,000
	Mongoose	Broad Brush—Salty Gal, by Cox's Ridge	USA	4	2	1	0	384,000
	Nobo True	Broad Brush—Nastique, by Naskra	Jpn	9	2	2	2	1,158,838
	Seeking Daylight	Seeking the Gold—Play All Day, by Steady Growth	USA	5	2	1	0	193,710
112	Atelier (f)	Deputy Minister—Aishah, by Alydar	USA	6	1	1	0	236,340
	Crafty Shaw	Crafty Prospector—Her She Shawklit, by Air Forbes Won	USA	10	4	1	1	348,445
	Express Tour	Tour d'Or—Express Fashion, by Private Express	UAE/USA	4	0	0	1	64,000
	Favorite Funtime (f)	Seeking the Gold—Promising Girl, by Youth	USA	4	2	0	0	222,000
	Mystic Lady (f)	Thunder Gulch—Diane Suzanne, by Compliance	USA	9	1	5	1	256,840
	Parade Leader	Kingmambo—Battle Creek Girl, by His Majesty	USA	7	1	3	1	459,503
	Starrer (f)	Dynaformer—To the Hunt, by Relaunch	USA	6	1	1	1	310,000
111	Dollar Bill	Peaks and Valleys—Saratoga Dame, by Saratoga Six	USA	9	1	3	2	496,850
	Pure Prize	Storm Cat—Heavenly Prize, by Seeking the Gold	USA	7	3	1	1	375,850
	Toho Emperor	Brian's Time—Rainbow Blue, by No Lute	Jpn	7	2	0	1	881,442
110	Aldebaran	Mr. Prospector—Chimes of Freedom, by Private Account	USA	8	1	6	0	428,800
	Ask Me No Secrets (f)	Seattle Slew—In On the Secret, by Secretariat	USA	4	2	0	1	180,628
	Bowman's Band	Dixieland Band—Hometown Queen, by Pleasant Colony	USA	9	2	5	0	333,800
	Cat's At Home	Tabasco Cat—Homewrecker, by Buckaroo	USA	8	2	1	1	273,904
	Kela	Numerous—Bolshoi Comedy, by Sovereign Dancer	USA	6	2	2	0	139,600
	Kiss a Native	Kissin Kris—Ronique, by Raise a Native	USA	3	0	1	0	95,000
	Printemps (Chi) (f)	Hussonet—Wrist, by Worldwatch	USA	5	0	1	3	143,225
	Reba's Gold	Slew o' Gold—Lovely Reba, by Herat	USA	11	3	2	2	320,642
	Royally Chosen (f)	In Excess (Ire)—Her Royalty, by King of Kings	USA	2	0	1	0	34,000
	Shiny Band (f)	Dixieland Band—Shiner, by Two Punch	USA	9	1	2	3	183,054
	Sir Bear	Sir Leon—Spicy Pearl, by Bet Big	USA	7	1	1	1	130,262
	Skoozi	Prince of Praise—Tweed View, by Imposing	UAE	5	1	1	0	260,710

5 furlongs +

Wt.	Horse	Sire–Dam, Broodmare sire	Trained	Sts	1st	2nd	3rd	Earnings
124	Orientate	Mt. Livermore—Dream Team, by Cox's Ridge	USA	10	6	1	0	$1,412,970
120	Xtra Heat (f)	Dixieland Heat—Begin, by Hatchet Man	USA	11	7	2	1	965,485
119	Crafty C.T.	Crafty Prospector—Andriana B., by Far North	USA	7	2	1	4	415,075
	Kalookan Queen (f)	Lost Code—Regal Realm, by Majestic Prince	USA	8	4	2	1	560,640
118	Caller One	Phone Trick—Baltic Sea, by Danzig	USA	2	1	0	0	1,200,000
	Snow Ridge	Tabasco Cat—Snow Forest, by Woodman	USA	6	4	1	0	399,990
117	Disturbingthepeace	Bold Badgett—Regal Riot, by Sovereign Dancer	USA	9	6	0	1	452,640
	Echo Eddie	Restless Con—Geri's Princess, by Siyah Kalem	USA	7	2	4	0	633,338
116	Raging Fever (f)	Storm Cat—Pennant Fever, by Seattle Slew	USA	10	4	4	1	595,160
115	Affirmed Success	Affirmed—Towering Success, by Irish Tower	USA	6	2	2	1	383,120
	Bonapaw	Sabona—Pawlova, by Nijinsky II	USA	9	5	0	0	463,000
	Squirtle Squirt	Marquetry—Lost the Code, by Lost Code	USA	2	0	1	0	45,000
114	Freespool	Geiger Counter—Broadtail, by Olden Times	USA	3	0	1	0	40,000
	Kona Gold	Java Gold—Double Sunrise, by Slew o' Gold	USA	3	1	0	0	128,340
113	Above Perfection (f)	In Excess (Ire)—Something Perfect, by Somethingfabulous	USA	3	3	0	0	182,717
	D'Wildcat	Forest Wildcat—D'Enough, by D'Accord	USA	10	3	2	1	424,444
	Explicit	Distant View—Elegant Victress, by Sir Ivor	USA	9	3	2	0	397,900
112	Ceeband	Chimes Band—Miss Sonrisa (Chi), by Domineau	USA	4	0	1	1	49,683
	Irguns Angel (f)	Irgun—November Morn, by Capote	USA	4	3	0	0	187,500
	Mellow Fellow	Belek—Lady Blockbuster, by Silent Screen	USA	9	4	0	3	279,525
	Shine Again (f)	Wild Again—Shiner, by Two Punch	USA	10	4	2	3	425,500
	Twilight Road	Cahill Road—Glory's Light, by Halo	USA	11	2	3	1	177,727
111	Binthebest	Binalong—Lady Tori, by Fappiano	USA	12	1	3	3	169,475
	Hot Market	Cee's Tizzy—Time to Plant, by Seattle Song	USA	10	4	2	1	261,040
	I Love Silver	Silver Ghost—Lost Love, by Lost Code	USA	6	0	1	0	83,540
	Nasty Storm (f)	Gulch—A Stark is Born, by Graustark	USA	8	2	0	3	167,304
	Secret Liaison	Housebuster—Pennant Winner, by Crafty Prospector	USA	4	3	1	0	137,600
110	Aldebaran	Mr. Prospector—Chimes of Freedom, by Private Account	USA	8	1	6	0	428,800
	Elaborate	Gilded Time—Jeanie's Gift, by Gulch	USA	4	0	0	2	33,324
	Gold Mover (f)	Gold Fever—Intentional Move, by Tentam	USA	9	4	3	0	503,032
	Victory Ride (f)	Seeking the Gold—Young Flyer, by Flying Paster	USA	5	2	0	2	143,366
	Wake At Noon	Cure the Blues—Sermon Time, by Silver Deputy	Can	11	6	0	2	463,011
	Wrangler	Carson City—Fighting Jet, by Copelan	USA	7	3	0	0	213,268

Cartier Awards

Established in 1991, the Cartier Awards are European racing's closest equivalent to the Eclipse Awards. Winners are determined by points earned in pattern races and votes of racing experts and Daily Telegraph *readers.*

Award of Merit

2002	Khalid Abdullah
2001	John Magnier
2000	Aga Khan
1999	Peter Walwyn
1998	Head family
1997	Sir Peter O'Sullevan
1996	Frankie Dettori
1995	John Dunlop
1994	Lord Hartington
1993	Francois Boutin
1992	Lester Piggott
1991	Henri Chalhoub

Horse of the Year

2002	Rock of Gibraltar (Ire)
2001	Fantastic Light
2000	Giant's Causeway
1999	Daylami (Ire)
1998	Dream Well (Fr)
1997	Peintre Celebre
1996	Helissio
1995	Ridgewood Pearl (GB)
1994	Barathea (Ire)
1993	Lochsong (GB)
1992	User Friendly (GB)
1991	Arazi

Millennium Award of Merit

2000	Queen Elizabeth II

Two-year-old filly

2002	Six Perfections
2001	Queen's Logic
2000	Superstar Leo
1999	Torgau (Ire)
1998	Bint Allayl
1997	Embassy (GB)
1996	Pas de Reponse
1995	Blue Duster
1994	Gay Gallanta
1993	Lemon Souffle (GB)
1992	Lyric Fantasy (Ire)
1991	Culture Vulture

Two-year-old colt

2002	Hold That Tiger
2001	Johannesburg
2000	Tobougg (Ire)
1999	Fasliyev
1998	Aljabr
1997	Xaar
1996	Bahamian Bounty
1995	Alhaarth
1994	Celtic Swing
1993	First Trump
1992	Zafonic
1991	Arazi

Three-year-old filly

2002	Kazzia (Ger)
2001	Banks Hill (GB)
2000	Petrushka (Ire)
1999	Ramruma
1998	Cape Verdi (Ire)
1997	Ryafan
1996	Bosra Sham
1995	Ridgewood Pearl (GB)
1994	Balanchine
1993	Intrepidity (GB)
1992	User Friendly (GB)
1991	Kooyonga (Ire)

Three-year-old colt

2002	Rock of Gibraltar (Ire)
2001	Galileo (Ire)
2000	Sinndar
1999	Montjeu (Ire)
1998	Dream Well (Fr)
1997	Peintre Celebre
1996	Helissio
1995	Lammtarra
1994	King's Theatre (Ire)
1993	Commander in Chief
1992	Rodrigo de Triano
1991	Suave Dancer

Stayer

2002	Vinnie Roe
2001	Persian Punch
2000	Kayf Tara
1999	Kayf Tara
1998	Kayf Tara
1997	Celeric
1996	Nononito
1995	Double Trigger
1994	Moonax
1993	Vintage Crop
1992	Drum Taps
1991	Turgeon

Sprinter

2002	Continent
2001	Mozart (Ire)
2000	Nuclear Debate
1999	Stravinsky
1998	Tamarisk
1997	Royal Applause (GB)
1996	Anabaa (Ire)
1995	Hever Golf Rose (GB)
1994	Lochsong (GB)
1993	Lochsong (GB)
1992	Mr Brooks (GB)
1991	Sheikh Albadou (GB)

Older horse

2002	Grandera
2001	Fantastic Light
2000	Kalanisi (Ire)
1999	Daylami (Ire)
1998	Swain (Ire)
1997	Pilsudski (Ire)
1996	Halling
1995	Further Flight
1994	Barathea (Ire)
1993	Opera House (GB)
1992	Mr Brooks (GB)
1991	Terimon

Special Award

2002	Tony McCoy
1994	Vincent O'Brien

Lord Derby Awards

Presented by the British Horse Race Writers and Photographers Association for overall excellence.

Service to International Racing

2002	Nick Clarke
2001	Pam Blatz-Murff
2000	Aga Khan
1999	Michael Osborne
1998	James E. "Ted" Bassett III
1997	Geoffrey Gibbs
1996	Flying Grooms
1995	Maj. Gen. Guy Watkins
1994	Robert Sangster
1993	Francois Boutin
	Niarchos family
1992	Maktoum family
1991	John Dunlop
1990	Louis Romanet
1989	Michael Byrne
1988	Richard Duchossois
1987	Yves Saint-Martin
1986	John Gaines
1985	Lord Derby
1984	Ivan Straker
1983	Paul Mellon
1982	Jean Romanet
1981	Joe Hirsch

Outstanding Achievement Award (George Ennor Trophy)

2002	Ian Balding
2001	Graham Rock
2000	Johnny Murtagh
1999	Peter Walwyn
1998	Capt. Tim Forster
1997	Sir Peter O'Sullevan
1996	Peter Easterby
1995	Lester Piggott
1994	Vincent O'Brien
1993	Dermot Weld

Outstanding Achievement Award (President's Trophy)

2002	Not awarded
2001	John Reid
2000	Ray Cochrane
1999	Jack Berry
1998	Not awarded
1997	Maj. Dick Hern
1996	Not awarded
1995	Jim Old Stable staff

International Trainer of the Year

2002	Demot Weld
2001	Aidan O'Brien
2000	Saeed bin Suroor

1999	Saeed bin Suroor
1998	Saeed bin Suroor
1997	Sir Michael Stoute
1996	Sir Michael Stoute
1995	Peter Chapple-Hyam
1994	John Dunlop
1993	John Dunlop
1992	Paul Cole
1991	Paul Cole
1990	Paul Cole
1989	Henry Cecil
1988	Luca Cumani
1987	Paul Cole
1986	Michael Stoute
1985	Clive Brittain
1984	Ian Balding
1983	Luca Cumani
1982	John Dunlop
1981	Ian Balding

Owner of the Year

2002	Sir Alex Ferguson
2001	Susan Magnier
	Michael Tabor
2000	Aga Khan
1999	Michael Tabor
1998	The Summit Partnership
1997	Peter Winfield
1996	Godolphin Racing
1995	Godolphin Racing
1994	Jeff Smith
1993	Robert Sangster
1992	Bill Gredley
1991	Prince Fahd Salman
1990	Sheikh Hamdan bin Rashid al Maktoum
1989	Sheikh Hamdan bin Rashid al Maktoum
1988	Jim Joel
1987	Louis Freedman
1986	Khalid Abdullah
1985	Lord Howard de Walden
1984	Eric Moller
1983	Robert Barnett
1982	Paul Mellon
1981	Aga Khan
1980	Pat Muldoon
1979	Snailwell Stud
1978	David McCall
1977	Queen Elizabeth II
1976	Daniel Wildenstein
1975	Carlo Vittadini
1974	Peter O'Sullevan
1973	Louis Freedman
1972	Lady Beaverbrook
1971	John and Jean Hislop
1970	Charles Engelhard and David McCall
1969	Earl of Rosebery
1968	Lord Allendale
1967	Jim Joel

Trainer of the Year

2002	Mark Johnston
2001	Aidan O'Brien
2000	John Oxx
1999	Henry Cecil
1998	Saeed bin Suroor
1997	Sir Michael Stoute
1996	Henry Cecil
1995	John Dunlop
1994	Mark Johnston
1993	Richard Hannon

1992	Richard Hannon
1991	Paul Cole
1990	Jack Berry
1989	Maj. Dick Hern
1988	David Chapman
1987	Henry Cecil
1986	Sir Michael Stoute
1985	Henry Cecil
1984	Roy Sheather
1983	John Dunlop
1982	David Chapman
1981	Guy Harwood
1980	Maj. Dick Hern
1979	Henry Cecil
1978	Michael Stoute
1977	Vincent O'Brien
1976	Henry Cecil
1975	Maj. Dick Hern
1974	Peter Walwyn
1973	Arthur Budgett
1972	Bruce Hobbs
1971	Ian Balding
1970	Vincent O'Brien
1969	Harvey Leader
1968	Sir Cecil Boyd-Rochfort
1967	Sir Noel Murless

Jockey of the Year

2002	Richard Hughes
2001	Michael Kinane
2000	Kevin Darley
1999	Richard Quinn
1998	Kieren Fallon
1997	Kieren Fallon
1996	Frankie Dettori
1995	Frankie Dettori
1994	Frankie Dettori
1993	Kevin Darley
1992	Michael Roberts
1991	Alan Munro
1990	Frankie Dettori
1989	Willie Carson
1988	Michael Roberts
1987	Steve Cauthen
1986	Pat Eddery
1985	Steve Cauthen
1984	Steve Cauthen
1983	Willie Carson
1982	Lester Piggott
1981	Lester Piggott
1980	Lester Piggott
1979	Joe Mercer
1978	Greville Starkey
1977	Willie Carson
1976	Brian Taylor
1975	Joe Mercer
1974	Pat Eddery
1973	Tony Murray
1972	Edward Hide
1971	Willie Carson
1970	Lester Piggott
1969	Geoff Lewis
1968	Sandy Barclay
1967	Doug Smith

National Hunt Owner of the Year
(awarded 1969-'73)

1973	Noel le Mare
1972	Mrs. John Rogerson
1971	Col. Bill Whitbread
1970	Bryan Jenks
1969	Edward Courage

National Hunt Trainer of the Year

2002	Henrietta Knight
2001	Martin Pipe
2000	Noel Chance
1999	Paul Nichols
1998	Martin Pipe
1997	Martin Pipe
1996	Jim Old
1995	Kim Bailey
1994	David Nicholson
1993	Nigel Twiston-Davies
1992	Mary Reveley
1991	Martin Pipe
1990	Martin Pipe
1989	Martin Pipe
1988	David Elsworth
1987	Nicky Henderson
1986	Nicky Henderson
1985	Capt. Tim Forster
1984	Jenny Pitman
1983	Michael Dickinson
1982	Michael Dickinson
1981	Peter Easterby
1980	Peter Easterby
1979	Peter Easterby
1978	Fred Winter
1977	Peter Easterby
1976	Tony Dickinson
1975	Gordon Richards
1974	Donald "Ginger" McCain
1973	Fulke Walwyn
1972	David Barons
1971	Fred Winter
1970	Arthur Stephenson
1969	Colin Davies
1968	Fred Rimell

National Hunt Jockey of the Year

2002	Tony McCoy
2001	Tony McCoy
2000	Tony McCoy
1999	Tony McCoy
1998	Tony McCoy
1997	Tony McCoy
1996	Tony McCoy
1995	Norman Williamson
1994	Aidrian Maguire
1993	Richard Dunwoody
1992	Peter Niven
1991	Peter Scudamore
1990	Peter Scudamore
1989	Peter Scudamore
1988	Chris Grant
1987	Peter Scudamore
1986	Péter Scudamore
1985	John Francome
1984	John Francome
1983	John Francome
1982	Peter Scudamore
1981	Bob Champion
1980	Jonjo O'Neil
1979	Tommy Carmody
1978	Jonjo O'Neill
1977	Tommy Stack
1976	Jeff King
1975	Tommy Stack
1974	Richard Pitman
1973	Ron Barry
1972	Bob Davies
1971	Graham Thorner
1970	Terry Biddlecombe

1969	Stan Mellor
1968	Brian Fletcher
1967	Josh Gifford

Stable Staff of the Year

2002	Tom Townsend
	Dave Goodwin
2001	Rodney Boult
	Peter Maughan
	Jimmy Scott
2000	George Charlton
	John Smillie
1999	Rachel Hume
	Robynne Watton
1998	Michael Leaman
	Geoff Snook
1997	Jack Nelson
	Eddie Watt
1996	Harry Buckle
	Ian Willows
1995	Sidney Outen
	John Sayers
1994	Vicki Harris
	Ron Thomas
1993	John Cullen
	Geoff Thompson
1992	Johnny East
	Bill Palmer
1991	Harvey Ewart
	Steven Rose
1990	Steve Fox
	Colin Nutter
1989	Brian Delaney
	Meg MacDonald
1988	Peter Heaney
	Kevin Murrell

1987	Alison Dean
1986	Glyn Foster
1985	Jimmy Swales
1984	Syd McGahey
1983	Raymond Campbell
1982	Linda McCauley
1981	Olga Nicholson
1980	Alan Welborne
1979	Jack Kidd
1978	Nigel Atkinson
1977	John Hallum
1976	Mervyn Heath
1975	John Vickers

Journalist of the Year (Clive Graham Trophy)

2002	Tom O'Ryan (*Racing Post*)
2001	Alan Lee (*The Times*)
2000	Alan Amies (Raceform)
1999	Alastair Down (*Racing Post*)
1998	Claude Duval (*The Sun*)
1997	Rodney Masters (*Racing Post*)
1996	David Ashforth (*Sporting Life*)
1995	Richard Evans (*The Times*)
1994	Alastair Down (*Sporting Life*)
1993	Paul Haigh (*Racing Post*)
1992	Jim McGrath (*Daily Telegraph*)
1991	John Sexton (Wolverhampton *Express and Star*)
1990	Tony Morris (*Racing Post*)
1989	Michael Seely (*The Times*)
1988	Geoff Lester (*Sporting Life*)
1987	Peter Goodall (Press Association)
1986	Peter O'Sullevan (BBC)
1985	Jim Stanford (*Daily Mail*)

1984	John Sharratt (Raceform)
1983	Bill Garland (Press Association)
1982	George Ennor (*Sporting Life*)
1981	Jonathan Powell (*Sunday People*)
1980	Michael Seely (*The Times*)
1979	Christopher Poole (*Evening Standard*)
1978	Tim Richards (*Daily Mirror*)
1977	Brough Scott (*Sunday Times*)
1976	Peter Willett (*Sporting Chronicle*)
1975	Peter Scott (*Daily Telegraph*)
1974	Tom Cosgrove (London *Evening News*)
1973	Richard Baerlein (*The Guardian/Observer*)
1972	Roger Mortimer (*Sunday Times*)
1971	Clive Graham (*Daily Express*) Peter O'Sullevan (*Daily Express*)
1970	George Stevens (Birmingham *Post & Mail*)
1969	Geoffrey Hamlyn (*Sporting Life*)
1968	John Lawrence (*Daily Telegraph*)
1967	Quintin Gilbey (*Sporting Chronicle*)

Photographer of the Year

2002	Ed Whitaker (*Racing Post*)
2001	Anne Grossick (free-lance)
2000	John Grossick (free-lance)
1999	Ed Whitaker (*Racing Post*)
1998	Alec Russell (free-lance)
1997	Mark Cranham (free-lance)

Major International Racetracks

Argentina

Hipodromo Argentino

Located in the Palermo district close to downtown Buenos Aires and familiarly known as Palermo, Hipodromo Argentino opened on May 7, 1876. Originally a harness racing facility offering just one Thoroughbred flat race daily, the track changed to full-time Thoroughbred racing on August 18, 1883, and was the first racetrack in Argentina to feature a totalizator. A sales pavilion, veterinary hospital and laboratory, equine institute, and museum complement the racetrack, which is home of the Gran Premio Nacional (Arg-G1), Argentina's equivalent of the Kentucky Derby (G1) and third race of the Argentine Triple Crown. Two of its most famous winners were *Yatasto in 1951 and *Forli in '66. Another major stakes race is the Polla de Potrillos (Arg-G1) (Argentine Two Thousand Guineas), the first race of the Triple Crown, in September. Racing is held over a 2,410-meter,* left-handed track with three chutes. (*See conversion table from metric to English distances in Reference section.)

Location: Ave. Del Libertador 4101, Capital Federal
Phone: 54 4778-2800
Fax: 54 4774-6807
E-mail: Palermo@satlink.com
Web site: http://www.palermo.com.ar/
Principal races: Comparacion (Arg-G1), Criadores (Arg-G1), De Honor (Arg-G1), De las Americas-Internacional (Arg-G1), Jorge de Atucha (Arg-G1), Nacional (Arg-G1), Pollo de Potrancas (Arg-G1), Santiago Luro (Arg-G1), Seleccion de Potrancas (Arg-G1)

Hipodromo de La Plata

The first racetrack in Argentina to hold evening race cards, Hipodromo de La Plata opened on September 14, 1884. Situated approximately 35 miles south of Buenos Aires, the track is in the city of La Plata in the province of Buenos Aires. The track's proximity to a railway station makes it easily accessible by public transportation. The left-handed, elliptical dirt track is 2,000 meters (approximately 1¼ miles) with two chutes. As many as 145 racing dates are held annually.

Location: La Plata, Pica de Buenos Aires
Phone: 54 (21) 211071
Fax: 54 (21) 42390
Principal races: Dardo Rocha Internacional (Arg-G1), Joachin V. Gonzalez Internacional (Arg-G1), Ciudad de La Plata Internacional (Arg-G1), Seleccion de Potrancas (Arg-G1)

San Isidro

Located 14 miles north of Buenos Aires on the edge of the Pampas, San Isidro Racecourse was founded on December 8, 1935, by the Jockey Club Argentino. San Isidro hosts the Gran Premio Carlos Pellegrini–Internacional (Arg-G1), the country's most important race, which is the final leg of the San Isidro Quadruple Crown. *Yatasto won the Carlos Pellegrini in 1952 before a record crowd of 104,810. *Forli accomplished the feat in 1966 and was then imported to the United States. A daily card consists of as many as 14 races, which begin in midafternoon and conclude at night under lights. Two overlapping, left-handed turf courses—the main one is 2,738 meters—have three different chutes.

Location: 504 Avenue Marquez, San Isidro 1642
Phone: 54 (11) 4743 4010
E-mail: jchsi@overnet.com.ar
Web site: http://www.hipodromosanisidro.com.ar/
Principal races: 25 de Mayo (Arg-G1), Carlos Pellegrini-Internacional (Arg-G1), Copa de Oro (Arg-G1), De Potrancas (Arg-G1), Estrellas Sprint (Arg-G1), Estrellas Distaff (Arg-G1), Estrellas Junior Sprint (Arg-G1), Estrellas Juvenile Fillies (Arg-G1), Estrellas Sprint (Arg-G1), Felix de Alzaga Unzue-Internacional (Arg-G1), Gran Criterium (Arg-G1), Jockey Club (Arg-G1)

Australia

Ascot

Located along the Swan River in the heart of Perth, capital city of Western Australia, Ascot features the Perth Cup (Aus-G2), first contested in 1879. In 1982, the track underwent a major renovation. It has a left-handed course of 2,000 meters with a 300-meter straight. Three different chutes are used to start Ascot's three major races, the Perth Cup, the Western Australian Turf Club Derby (Aus-G1) at 2,400 meters, and the Railway Stakes (Aus-G1) at 1,600 meters.

Location: Grandstand Road, Ascot, Western Australia 6104
Phone: 61 (8) 9277 0713
Fax: 61 (8) 9277 0710
Web site: http://www.waturf.org.au/
Principal races: Railway S. (Aus-G1), W.A.T.C. Derby (Aus-G1)

Canterbury

Canterbury Racecourse, located approximately seven miles southwest of Sydney's central business district, is easily accessible by public transportation and offers ample free parking. Its intimate 1,600-meter track affords spectators a close view of the 34 race cards conducted annually by the Sydney Turf Club. Racing is usually held on Thursday evenings, although there are occasional Saturday-evening programs, including the beginning of the rich Autumn Golden Slipper Festival. Programs of eight to ten races are held on the right-handed turf course. In July 2002, Sydney Turf Club officials announced that the Canterbury facility would not be sold for development. The 1,800-meter Canterbury Guineas (Aus-G1) for three-year-olds is the track's top race.

Location: King Street, Canterbury, New South Wales 2193
Phone: 61 (2) 9930 4000
Fax: 61 (2) 9930 4099
Web site: http://www.theraces.com.au/
Chairman: Bruce McHugh
Chief executive: Michael T. Kenny
Principal race: Canterbury Guineas (Aus-G1)

Caulfield Racecourse

Situated about five miles southeast of Melbourne, Caulfield Racecourse has a rich history that traces to August 5, 1876. In 1996, the Melbourne Racing Club (formerly the Victoria Amateur Turf Club) widened the track to 30 meters around the entire circumference and lengthened the straight by 43 meters. Affectionately known as "the Heath," Caulfield is home to the Caulfield Carnival each spring, which features three major stakes: the 2,400-meter Caulfield Cup (Aus-G1), the 1,600-meter Caulfield Guineas (Aus-G1) for

three-year-olds, and the 1,600-meter Vinery Australia Thousand Guineas (Aus-G1) for three-year-old fillies. The Autumn Carnival offers Victoria's richest race for two-year-olds, the AAMI Blue Diamond Stakes (Aus-G1) at 1,200 meters. Caulfield stages 20 dates of racing during the year.

Location: 22 Station Street, East Caulfield, Victoria 3145
Phone: 61 (3) 9257 7200
Fax: 61 (3) 9257 7210
E-mail: contact@melbourneracingclub.net.au
Web site: http://www.melbourneracingclub.net.au/
Chairman: Kevin A. Hayes
Chief executive: Peter J. Sweeney
Principal races: Caulfield Cup (Aus-G1), Caulfield Guineas (Aus-G1), Vinery Australia Thousand Guineas (Aus-G1), AAMI Blue Diamond Stakes (Aus-G1), Underwood Stakes (Aus-G1)

Doomben (Brisbane Turf Club)

Doomben Ltd., formerly the Doomben Park Recreation Grounds Ltd., was opened in 1933 by the Brisbane Amateur Turf Club, which subsequently changed its name to the Brisbane Turf Club. Called the Garden Racecourse, Doomben was used as a base by U.S. troops during World War II. The track underwent an extensive renovation in 1982 and now hosts 40 race dates, 25 of them on Saturdays, each year. Its major races include the Doomben 10,000 Stakes (Aus-G1), formerly the T. M. Ahern Memorial Stakes, and the Doomben Cup (Aus-G1) at 2,200 meters. Another highlight is the six-day Winter Racing Carnival. Doomben is adjacent to Eagle Farm Racecourse, the principal track in Brisbane, Queensland's capital. The track is approximately four miles from Brisbane's central business district and a short distance from Brisbane Airport.

Location: Hampden Street, Ascot, Queensland 4006
Phone: 61 (7) 3268 6800
Fax: 61 (7) 3868 1281
E-mail: btc@doomben.com
Web site: http://www.doomben.com/
Chairman: Ian Baxter
Chief executive: Sean Kelk
Principal races: Doomben Cup (Aus-G1), Doomben 10,000 Stakes (Aus-G1)

Eagle Farm

Located on the northern side of Brisbane in Ascot, Eagle Farm boasts a long history and excellent equine facilities. Its racing started on August 14, 1865, under the Queensland Turf Club, which was founded in 1863 by a group of 53 sportsmen. The training facilities include two turf tracks, a wood-fiber track, a sand track, two exercise rings, and an equine swimming pool. The main turf track is approximately 2,026 meters with a single chute. Horses race clockwise and must navigate a slight uphill climb heading for the finish line. During World War II, Eagle Farm was used as a military base by both Australian and United States troops. For those five years, the Queensland Turf Club held race meetings at Albion Park.

Location: Lancaster Road, Eagle Farm, QLD 4007
Phone: 61 (7) 3268 2171
Fax: 61 (7) 3868 2410
E-mail: info@qtc.org
Web site: http://www.qtc.org
Principal races: Brisbane Cup (Aus-G1), Queensland Derby (Aus-G1), Queensland Oaks (Aus-G1), Sires' Produce S. (Aus-G1), Stradbroke H. (Aus-G1), The T J Smith S. (Aus-G1)

Flemington

A breathtaking course with Melbourne's skyline as a backdrop, Flemington has been hosting racing since 1840, and the Melbourne Cup (Aus-G1), its famed stakes race at about two miles on the first Tuesday of November, is treated as a national holiday. On the morning of the Melbourne Cup, a service held at St. Francis's Church is followed by a carnival on Burke Street, Melbourne's central thoroughfare. Up to 100,000 spectators fill Flemington on Melbourne Cup day to celebrate the stakes first run in 1861. The winner of the first Melbourne Cup, Archer, was reported to have walked more than 500 miles from his stable in New South Wales to enter the race. In 1930, *Phar Lap won the race after surviving an attempt on his life while training at Flemington. He was hidden in the ensuing days, arrived at the track just minutes before post time, and won the race in a canter. The legendary runner is honored by a bronze statue outside an entrance into the track. Flemington also holds the Victoria Derby (Aus-G1), first run in 1855 and the oldest established race in Australia. The left-handed, 2,300-meter turf course has a 1,200-meter straight chute.

Location: 400 Epsom Road, Flemington, Victoria 3031
Phone: 61 (1300) 727 575
E-mail: customerservice@vrc.net.au
Web site: http://www.vrc.net.au/
Chairman: A. P. Ramsden
Vice chairman: R. M. Fitzroy
Principal races: Australian Cup (Aus-G1), Australian Guineas (Aus-G1), MacKinnon S. (Aus-G1), Lightning S. (Aus-G1), Melbourne Cup (Aus-G1), Victoria Derby (Aus-G1), Sires Produce S. (Aus-G1)

Moonee Valley

Located less than four miles from central Melbourne, Moonee Valley was founded by William Samuel Cox in 1883. The Cox Plate (Aus-G1), Australia's most important weight-for-age race, is run at Moonee Valley one week before the Melbourne Cup at Flemington. First run in 1922, the Cox Plate was won by *Phar Lap in '30 and '31. In a historic running of the Cox Plate in 1986, Bonecrusher edged fellow New Zealand champion Our Waverley Star by a neck. Moonee Valley offers a wide range of amenities, including a 1,000-seat dining room, glass-enclosed dining boxes, 20 bars, and electronic gaming machines, which were added in 1992. The 1,800-meter, left-handed course is more rectangular than oval, with very sharp turns and short straights, putting a high premium on agility and speed. It is intersected by a diagonal straight course. Inside the main course are hurdle and steeplechase courses.

Location: McPherson Street, Moonee Ponds, Victoria 3039
Phone: 61 (1800) 062 644
Fax: 61 (3) 9326 0090
E-mail: customerservice@mvrc.net.au
Web site: http://www.mvrc.net.au/
Principal races: W. S. Cox Plate (Aus-G1), Manikato S. (Aus-G1)

Morphettville

Located along the Anzac Highway in Adelaide, South Australia, Morphettville is run by the South Australian Jockey Club, Founded in 1860, Morphettville holds its principal meet in May, when it stages the South Australian Derby (Aus-G1), the South Australian Oaks, (Aus-G1), and the Adelaide Cup (Aus-G1). The 2,300-meter course has a short straight of nearly 400 meters. The track's grandstand was razed in 1976 and replaced

by a modern facility, and a multimillion-dollar renovation of the course itself was completed in 2002.

Location: Adelaide, South Australia 5001
Phone: 61 (3) 8294 2577
Fax: 61 (3) 8295 0136
Web site: http://www.sajc.com.au/
Chairman: Peter Lewis
Principal races: Adelaide Cup (Aus-G1), South Australian Derby (Aus-G1), South Australian Oaks (Aus-G1)

Randwick

Home of the Australian Jockey Club, Randwick has conducted racing since 1860, when the club relocated from Homebush. The inaugural running of the Australian Jockey Club St. Leger (Aus-G2) was held in 1841 at Homebush but was moved to Randwick when the track opened. The first AJC Derby (Aus-G1) was run in 1861. The Sydney Cup (Aus-G1) was first contested in April 1865. Randwick, which is close to Sydney, holds racing festivals in both the spring at the start of October and in the fall in April. The major stakes in the spring is the Metropolitan (Aus-G1) at 2,600 meters. The AJC Derby, Doncaster Handicap (Aus-G1), and Queen Elizabeth Stakes (Aus-G1) are contested in the fall. Randwick's 2,218-meter course with four chutes circles an infield lake and is considered one of the most demanding in Australia.

Location: Alison Road, Randwick, New South Wales 2031
Phone: 61 (2) 9663 8400
Fax: 61 (2) 9662 6292
Web site: www.ajc.org.au
Principal races: A.J.C. Australian Derby (Aus-G1), A.J.C. Australian Oaks (Aus-G1), Champagne S. (Aus-G1), Doncaster H. (Aus-G1), Sires' Produce S. (Aus-G1), Spring Champion S. (Aus-G1), Sydney Cup (Aus-G1),

Rosehill

Located about 14 miles west of Sydney, Rosehill frequently is called Sydney's garden course and is home to Australia's premier race for two-year-olds, the 1,200-meter Golden Slipper Stakes (Aus-G1), first contested in 1957. The beautifully landscaped track was constructed on the land of Australia's most historic agricultural property, Elizabeth Farm, and major festivals are held in both the spring and autumn. The about 2,000-meter course features a 400-meter straight. Races of 1,200 meters (approximately six furlongs) start in the center of the course and traverse a long bend into the straight. Training facilities include Equitrack, grass, sand, and cinder training tracks with stabling available adjacent to the track.

Location: Canterbury, New South Wales 2193
Phone: 61 (2) 9930 4090
Fax: 61 (2) 9930 4099
Web site: http://www.theraces.com.au/
Principal races: Golden Slipper S. (Aus-G1), George Ryder S. (Aus-G1), H. E. Tancred S. (Aus-G1), Rosehill Guineas (Aus-G1), Storm Queen/Ansett Australia S. (Aus-G1)

Victoria Park

Founded in 1879, Victoria Park is the South Australian capital city of Adelaide's second-oldest racetrack and the largest track in the country. Located less than a mile from the city center in the Adelaide City Parklands, Victoria Park has two turf courses, one 2,361 meters in circumference with a 601-meter straight, and an inner course of 1,961 meters with a 479-meter straight. Known as "the Course of Natural Beauty," the track also has a 1,000-meter straight. Victoria Park stages the Adelaide Guineas (Aus-G3), among other stakes races. Each December, it is host to Christmas Twilight, a race program that benefits the South Australia Variety Club.

Location: Wakefield Street, Adelaide, South Australia
Phone: 61(8) 8223 54667
Fax: 61 (8) 295 0136
Chairman: Peter Lewis
Chief executive: Steve Ploubidis
Principal race: Adelaide Guineas (Aus-G3)

Warwick Farm

Warwick Farm Racecourse, operated by the Australian Jockey Club, is located about 18 miles from Sydney and is renowned for its picnic atmosphere. Racing is conducted on an oblong, 1,937-meter oval with a straight of just 326 meters. The track has a chute for races between 1,000 and 1,400 meters, and it also has two short chutes for 1,600-meter and 2,400-meter races. Front-runners tend to do well because of Warwick Farm's sharp turns, which can force late closers very wide. The track opened in 1925 and resumed racing in 1952 after being closed through World War II. Its J. M. B. Carr Grandstand was built in 1982.

Location: Hume Highway, Warwick Farm, 2170
Phone: 61 (2) 9663 8400
Fax: 61 (2) 9662 1447
Web site: http://www.ajc.org.au/
Chairman: Bill Rutledge
Chief executive: Tony King
Principal races: George Main Stakes (Aus-G1), Chipping Norton Stakes (Aus-G1)

Brazil
Cidade Jardim

Just minutes from downtown São Paulo, Cidade Jardim offers year-round turf and dirt racing on left-handed courses. Cidade Jardim opened January 25, 1941, after Brazilian racing officials deemed Mooca, the track in the center of São Paulo, too small and too crowded. Today, Cidade Jardim is a sprawling facility that houses many important Brazilian racing authorities, including the *Stud-Book Brazileiro.* Cidade Jardim's main turf course is an about 2,000-meter oval with a dirt course of about 1,800 meters. Cidade Jardim also encompasses a training center with two dirt training tracks, a stud farm, and an exhibition center for cultural and scientific activities.

Location: Rua Bento Frias, 248 Sao Paulo
Principal races: Consagracao (Brz-G1), Derby Paulista (Brz-G1), Diana (Brz-G1), Jockey Clube de Sao Paulo (Brz-G1), Organizacao Sulamericana de Fomento ao Puro Sangue de Corrida (Brz-G1), Oswaldo Aranha (Brz-G1), Presidente da Republica (Brz-G1), Sao Paulo (Brz-G1)

La Gávea

With the Statue of Christ the Redeemer atop Corcovado Mountain in Rio de Janeiro serving as a dramatic backdrop, La Gávea is located adjacent to Lake Rodrigo de Freitas. An outer, 2,120-meter turf course rings a 2,036-meter dirt track with two separate turns out of the home straight. Though racing was conducted in Brazil as early as 1825, betting was not allowed until 1872. In that year, the Jockey Club Brazileiro was formed, which led to the opening of La Gávea. La Gávea's spring season in October and November features the Gran Premio Linneo de Paula Machado (Brz-G1), among other stakes. Racing is held year-round on Saturdays and Sundays.

Location: Rio de Janeiro

Principal races: Proprietarios do Cavalo de Corrida (Brz-G1), Brasil (Brz-G1), Cruzeiro do Sul (Brz-G1), Diana (Brz-G1), Jockey Club Club Brasileiro (Brz-G1), Linneo de Paula Machado (Brz-G1), Presidente da Republica (Brz-G1),

Taruma

Located ten minutes from downtown Curitiba, a city of 2.3-million people that is the capital of the state of Parana, Taruma races year-round under the ownership of Jockey Club do Parana. Opened on December 2, 1873, Taruma has a 1¼-mile track. Its biggest race, the 1¼-mile Gran Premio International Parana (Brz-G1), is run in December.

Location: Avenue Victor Ferreira do Amaral, Curitiba, Parana
Phone: 55 (41) 366-2121
Chairman: Cesar de Paula ou Alessandro Reichel
Principal race: Parana (Brz-G1)

Chile
Club Hipico de Santiago

Lush, beautiful, and close to the center of Santiago, Club Hipico de Santiago encompasses more than 200 acres and is full of gardens, lakes, tennis courts, and fountains. Members of the Chilean bourgeoisie created Club Hipico in 1869, and its first race was run on September 20,1870. Club Hipico is home to the oldest stakes race in South America, the El Ensayo (Chi-G1), first run in 1873 for three-year-old colts and fillies. The track stages as many as 16 races a day, usually on Mondays and Thursdays in January, February, and March, and on Sundays during other months.

Location: Avenida Blanco Encalada, Santiago
Phone: 56 (2) 6939600
Fax: 56 (2) 6837074
Principal races: El Ensayo (Chi-G1), Club Hipico de Santiago (Chi-G1), Las Oaks (Chi-G1), Polla de Pontrancas (Chi-G1), Polla de Potrillos (Chi-G1)

Hipodromo de Vina del Mar

Hipodromo de Vina del Mar is operated by the Valparaiso Sporting Club. Thirteen to 17 dates are held annually on Wednesdays and Fridays, and races range from four furlongs to 1½ miles. The two main turf courses and dirt training track can accommodate 600 horses. The Derby, the third leg of the Triple Crown, is contested at 1½ miles on turf.

Location: Los Castanos 404, Vina del Mar
Phone: 56 (32) 689393
Fax: 56 (32) 976700
E-mail: sporting@sporting.cl
Principal races: El Derby (Chi-G1), Copa de Plata Italo Traverso (Chi-G1)

Hipodromo Chile

Founded in 1904 by a group of 19 breeders, owners, and trainers, Hipodromo Chile is located ten minutes north of Santiago and near the Comodo Merino Benitez Airport. Racing is conducted on every other Wednesday and every Saturday year-round on a 1,645-meter, left-handed dirt track. A nearby sales complex, conducting two-year-olds in training sales in the spring and fall, complement the racing.

Location: 1715 Avenue Hipodromo Chile, Santiago
Phone: 56 (2) 7376700
Fax: 56 (2) 7375043
E-mail: hipodromo.chile@chilnet.cl
Chairman: Juan Cuneo Solari

Executive director: Luis Solar Feuereise
Principal races: Dos Mil Guineas (Chi-G1), Gran Criterium (Chi-G1), Gran Premio Hipodromo Chile (Chi-G1), Mil Guineas (Chi-G1), St. Leger (Chi-G1)

England

Aintree

Located a short distance from Liverpool, Aintree is home to the world's best-known steeplechase race, the Grand National, a 4½-mile marathon over 30 tall, testing fences in early April. The Grand National was first run at Aintree in 1839, when the striking bay Lottery won the third running of a race known then as the Grand Liverpool Steeplechase, which was held at another site in its first two years.

In the 1990s, animal-rights protests forced the taming of the 2¼-mile Grand National course's more terrifying fences. Most notable was the filling of Becher's Brook, named for Captain Martin Becher, who fell at its tall fence and tumbled into the creek after his mount allegedly was impeded by Lottery. The Chair, one of two obstacles on the 16-fence course that are jumped only once, stands 5'2" tall, and its landing side is higher than the takeoff side. As many as 40 horses can start in the Grand National, but in 2001 heavy rains, deep ground, and numerous mishaps led to only four horses finishing the course. Two of them, including 2000 winner Papillon, were remounted after losing their riders.

Location: Ormskirk Road, Aintree, Liverpool L9 5AS
Phone: 44 (151) 523 2600
Fax: 44 (151) 522 2920
E-mail: aintree@races.u-net.com
Web site: http://www.aintree.co.uk
Director of Operations: Alastair Warwick
Chief executive: Charles Barnett
Principal race: Grand National Steeplechase

Ascot

Host of the traditional Royal Meeting in June as well as racing throughout the year in both National Hunt and flat divisions, Ascot is owned by Queen Elizabeth II. Queen Anne marked the course out in Windsor Park, and racing began there in August 1711. The National Hunt course was added in 1965. The Royal Meeting begins with the queen and her royal party driving down the straight mile in horse-drawn carriages to the applause of the crowd, with the men sporting top hats and morning suits and the women wearing elegant hats. Traditionally, the first race is the Queen Anne Stakes (Eng-G1), and the races that follow offer a wide variety of competition from sprinters to stayers. No Ascot race is more demanding than the 2½-mile Ascot Gold Cup (Eng-G1), first run in 1807. The St. James's Palace Stakes (Eng-G1), the King George VI and Queen Elizabeth Stakes (Eng-G1), the King Edward VII Stakes (Eng-G2), the Queen Elizabeth II Stakes (Eng-G1), the Coronation Stakes (Eng-G1) for fillies, and the Meon Valley Stud Fillies' Mile (Eng-G1) are among Ascot's most definitive events. The flat course at Ascot is a right-handed triangular oval of 1¾ miles with two mile chutes. Ascot, which was previously held in a private trust, underwent a $140-million renovation in 2002.

Phone: 44 (1344) 622211
Fax: 44 (1344) 628299
E-mail: enquiries@ascot.co.uk
Web site: http://www.ascot.co.uk
Chief executive: Douglas Erskin-Crum

Principal races: Coronation S. (Eng-G1), Gold Cup S. (Eng-G1), King George VI and Queen Elizabeth S. (Eng-G1), Prince of Wales's S. (Eng-G1), Queen Elizabeth II S. (Eng-G1), St. James's Palace S. (Eng-G1)

Cheltenham

Located in the Cotswolds in west-central England, Cheltenham is a stunning racecourse that is host each March to the National Hunt Festival, which features the Cheltenham Gold Cup and Champion Hurdle Stakes, championship races for their respective divisions. The 2001 Cheltenham festival was canceled because of the foot-and-mouth disease outbreak that winter, but in most years the festival is standing room only. The first Gold Cup was held in 1819 as a three-mile flat race on Cleeve Hill, which overlooks the current course. When crowds grew to 50,000, a grandstand was constructed, but it was torn down when an anti-gambling sentiment swept the area in the 1820s. Racing was re-established at the current site in Prestbury Park in 1831, but there was no racing in Cheltenham from the 1840s through the '90s. Barry Bingham purchased the course, refurbished it, built a new grandstand and running rails, and launched the festival in 1902 as a two-day event. A third day was added in 1923. The Gold Cup was reinstituted the next year, and three years later the Champion Hurdle was added. Cheltenham has separate, left-handed steeplechase and hurdle courses, with a testing, uphill run to the finish post. Among the heroes of Cheltenham are Dorothy Paget's Golden Miller, who won five consecutive runnings of the Gold Cup (1932-'36), and trainer Michael Dickinson, who saddled the first five finishers in the 1983 Gold Cup.

Location: Prestbury Park, Cheltenham, Gloucestershire NP6 5YH
Phone: 44 (1242) 513014
Fax: 44 (1242) 224227
E-mail: cheltenham@rht.net
Web site: http://www.cheltenham.co.uk
Chairman: Lord Vestey
Chief executive: E. W. Gillespie
Principal races: Champion Hurdle S., Cheltenham Gold Cup

Doncaster

Home of the final leg of the English Triple Crown, the St. Leger Stakes (Eng-G1) in September, Doncaster has hosted racing since 1778. Doncaster runs flat and jump races on separate courses. The pear-shaped, left-handed main course is nearly two miles in circumference. The St. Leger meeting begins with the filly version of the St. Leger Stakes, the Park Hill Stakes (Eng-G3). The Doncaster Cup (Eng-G3), first run in 1766 and the oldest race still run by the Jockey Club, the Champagne Stakes (Eng-G2), May Hill Stakes (Eng-G3), and the Flying Childers Stakes (Eng-G2) for two-year-olds precede the St. Leger, the oldest of the English classics and named for popular local sportsman Lt. Col. Anthony St. Leger. Winners of the St. Leger Stakes include Hambletonian in 1795, Champion (the first horse to win the Epsom Derby and St. Leger Stakes) in 1800, and West Australian, who became the first Triple Crown winner 53 years later. Nijinsky II became the most recent English Triple Crown winner in 1970. The Racing Post Trophy (Eng-G1) is Doncaster's most significant juvenile race.

Location: The Grandstand, Leger Way, Doncaster DN2 6BB
Phone: 44 (1302) 320066
Fax: 44 (1302) 323271

E-mail: administration@doncasterracing.co.uk
Web site: http://www.doncaster-racecourse.com
Chairman: C. L. Wedd
Chief executive: Tim Betteridge
Principal races: Racing Post Trophy S. (Eng-G1), St. Leger S. (Eng-G1)

Epsom

Thoroughbreds have been racing at Epsom, 15 miles south of London in Surrey, for more than 350 years. In 1648, a party of Royalists held races there, and the first recorded race meet was in 1661 on Banstead Downs, which is part of Epsom Downs. The jewel of the racing year is the Epsom Derby (Eng-G1), which traditionally had been run on the first Wednesday in June but now has been moved successfully to the Saturday five weeks after the Two Thousand Guineas (Eng-G1) at Newmarket on the first Saturday of May. First run in 1780, one year after the initial running of the Epsom Oaks (Eng-G1), the 1½-mile Derby is the middle leg of the English Triple Crown. Epsom has other important stakes during its season, with meets beginning in April and concluding in September of each year. The major races include the Coronation Cup (Eng-G1) and the Diomed Stakes (Eng-G3). The course features a downhill run to the final turn, the world-famous Tattenham Corner, and an uphill pull to the finish.

Location: The Racecourse, Epsom Downs, Surrey KT18 5LQ
Phone: 44 (1372) 726311
Fax: 44 (1372) 748253
E-mail: epsom@rht.net
Web site: http://www.epsomderby.co.uk
Chief executive: S. H. Wallis
Principal races: Coronation Cup (Eng-G1), Derby S. (Eng-G1), Oaks S. (Eng-G1)

Goodwood

Located amid rolling countryside on Sussex Downs 60 miles southwest of London, Goodwood traces its history to the Duke of Richmond, who first hosted racing on his estate in 1802. The fifth Duke of Richmond improved the quality of racing at Goodwood by making it part of the English social circuit, a task made easier by the development of a railroad network to transport horses and racegoers to the estate. The about one-mile Sussex Stakes (Eng-G1), the about two-mile Goodwood Cup (Eng-G2), the six-furlong Richmond Stakes (Eng-G2), and the 1¼-mile Nassau Stakes (Eng-G1) for fillies and mares are the major races of the annual July meeting, though racing is also held in May, June, August, and October. Goodwood also is host of the Celebration Mile Stakes (Eng-G2) at the end of August. Goodwood has a skewered figure-eight, right-handed course with a six-furlong straight that allows horses to finish in front of Goodwood's restaurant atop the grandstand.

Location: Goodwood, Chichester, West Sussex PO18 0PS
Phone: 44 (1243) 755022
Fax: 44 (1243) 755025
E-mail: racing@goodwood.co.uk
Web site: http://www.goodwood.co.uk
Chairman: Duke of Richmond
Chief executive: R. N. Fabricius
Principal races: Nassau S. (Eng-G1), Sussex S. (Eng-G1)

Haydock

Located north of Liverpool, Haydock Park Racecourse was created as a direct successor to the nearby Old Golborne Heath course, home of the Newton Races, which flourished in the 1750s. Haydock conducted its first race in 1899. Haydock's 1⅚-mile track has a tight top bend, and the Sprint Cup Stakes (Eng-G1) is staged each September. A new grandstand was completed in 1982.

Location: Newton-Le-Willows, Merseyside WA12 0HQ
Phone: 44 (1942) 725963
Fax: 44 (1942) 270879
E-mail: haydockpark@rht.net
Web site: http://www.haydock-park.com
Chairman: W. T. Whittle
Chief executive: Adam Waterworth
Principal races: Haydock Sprint Cup S. (Eng-G1)

Newbury

Located west of London, Newbury has its own railway station just yards from the attractive left-handed racecourse. The course measures more than 1¾ miles with a slightly undulating straight mile ideal for galloping.

Fifteen days of flat racing extend from April through October, and steeplechase meets are conducted during the colder months. Its major flat races include the one-mile Juddmonte Lockinge Stakes (Eng-G1), and its premier race over fences is the Hennessy Cognac Gold Cup.

Newbury, which opened in 1905, resulted from a chance meeting between well-known trainer John Porter and King Edward VII. It quickly became known as one of the country's best courses, but the course has been pressed into other duties during wartime. Newbury was requisitioned during World War I and was used for troops, supplies, tank testing and repair, and as a prisoner of war camp. In World War II, the track became a major American base and prisoner of war camp.

Racing resumed on April 1, 1949, and now features elegant surroundings, including a sky-lighted "Long Bar" overlooking the track on the first floor and 41 private boxes. The New Grandstand, which opened to the public in November 2000, features several exhibition spaces as well as conference rooms for up to 1,000 delegates. The course also features an 18-hole, par 71 golf course and a 20-bay driving range. A leisure center with a swimming pool and gymnasium also are on the property.

Location: The Racecourse, Newbury, Berskhire RG14 7NZ
Phone: 44 (1635) 40015
Fax: 44 (1635) 528354
E-mail: info@newbury-racecourse.co.uk
Web site: http://www.newbury-racecourse.co.uk
Chairman: Sir David Sieff
Chief executive: Mark Kershaw
Principal races: Lockinge S. (Eng-G1)

Lingfield

Set on 300 acres in the Surrey countryside south of London, Lingfield Park is one of Great Britain's most modern racetracks, featuring year-round flat racing on its all-weather artificial-surface track.

Owned by Arena Leisure, Lingfield was the first of England's all-weather tracks, but its Equitrack surface increasingly drew complaints. In late 2001, the racecourse replaced Equitrack with Polytrack, a synthetic surface composed of polypropylene, polyester, Lycra, silica sand, and rubber, covered by a wax coating. The new surface, which cost $4.2-million, has been praised by jockeys and trainers. The all-weather track is 1¼ miles around, with a quarter-mile stretch and a quarter-mile chute for 1½-mile races. Lingfield also has a 1¼-mile, left-handed turf course with a 3½-furlong run-in and a 1⅝-mile steeplechase course.

Location: Lingfield, Surrey RH7 6PQ
Phone: 44 (1342) 834800
Fax: 44 (1342) 832833
E-mail: info@lingfieldpark.co.uk
Web site: http://www.lingfield-racecourse.co.uk
Principal race: Derby Trial S. (Eng-G3)

Newmarket

Newmarket is the headquarters of British racing, and its racecourse is a fitting complement to the training gallops to the east of the course. An observer once said: "Newmarket is one of the only places where a man can go racing; elsewhere he merely goes to the races, which isn't the same thing at all." Racing has been held at Newmarket, a Suffolk town 60 miles northeast of London, for more than 350 years. Newmarket's racing spans the entire British flat season, with the spring season featuring the year's first classics, the Two Thousand Guineas (Eng-G1) and One Thousand Guineas (Eng-G1), down its one-mile Rowley Mile Course on the first weekend in May. In the fall, the Champion Stakes (Eng-G1), Cheveley Park Stakes (Eng-G1), Middle Park Stakes (Eng-G1), and Dewhurst Stakes (Eng-G1) are contested across the flat, a ten-furlong straight that includes the Rowley course. Longer races, such as the rich Cesarewitch Handicap over 2¼ miles, require the use of a ten-furlong extension of the Rowley Mile in a backward, L-shape configuration that extends through the ancient "Devil's Dike." Between those spring and fall events, racing is conducted on the July Course, a straight that connects to the Rowley course. The July Cup (Eng-G1) is the major July stakes. Though Charles I decided Newmarket would be an ideal place to race his horses, his son, Charles II, created the course and the straight mile derives its name from his nickname, "Old Rowley." In 1665, he founded the Newmarket Town Plate, a race that is still contested in a different form. With its uphill finish and no turns, Newmarket provides a severe test of stamina.

Location: Westfield House The Links, Newmarket, Suffolk CB8 0TG
Phone: 44 (1638) 663482
Fax: 44 (1638) 663044
E-mail: newmarket@hrt.net
Web site: http://www.newmarketracecourses.co.uk
Chairman: Peter Player
Chief executive: Lisa Hancock
Principal races: Champion S. (Eng-G1), Cheveley Park S. (Eng-G1), Dewhurst S. (Eng-G1), July Cup S. (Eng-G1), One Thousand Guineas S. (Eng-G1), Two Thousand Guineas S. (Eng-G1)

Sandown Park

Only 14 miles south of central London, Sandown Park opened in 1875 and was the first totally enclosed racecourse in the country. The course was the brainchild of Lt. Col. Owen Williams, and his brother, Hwfa (pronounced "Hoofer"), was instrumental in Sandown Park's development, serving as chairman and clerk of the course for 50 years. The grandstand, rebuilt in 1973 for approximately $5-million, sits on a hill overlooking the racecourse. The right-handed, 1⅜-mile course includes a downhill run to the back straight and a substantial uphill pull to the homestretch. A five-furlong, uphill straight course runs through the main course.

Sandown Park's major stakes race is the 1¼-mile Eclipse Stakes (Eng-G1) in July. It was first run in 1886 and, at the time, was the country's richest stakes race. In the spring, Sandown features the Whitbread Gold Cup, the National Hunt season's final major race over steeplechase fences. Flat racing is held in short meets from late April through the beginning of October. A $33.4-million renovation of the grandstand was completed in early 2002.

Location: Esher, Surrey KT10 9AJ
Phone: 44 (1372) 463072
Fax: 44 (1372) 465205
E-mail: sandown@rht.net
Web site: http://www.sandown.co.uk
Principal races: Eclipse S. (Eng-G1)

York

Referred to by many as England's Ascot of the North, York is home to the popular Ebor Festival in mid-August at the Knavesmire, common land 20 minutes from the city of York that has featured racing since 1731. The wide horseshoe-shaped, two-mile, unenclosed course has a 4½-furlong straight after a left-handed turn. Two separate chutes are used for sprints of six and seven furlongs. York came to prominence in 1767 when the Gimcrack Club was founded to honor the champion Gimcrack, who won 26 races between 1764 and '71. The club members organized the York meeting to attract the best horses to the North, and by the 1840s the August meeting featured the Ebor Handicap, Yorkshire Oaks (Eng-G1), and the Gimcrack Stakes (Eng-G2). The Nunthorpe Stakes (Eng-G1) was added in 1903. In 1851, one of the most famous match races in Turf history pitted Epsom Derby winners The Flying Dutchman and Voltigeur, who had inflicted the former's only loss the previous year in the Doncaster Cup. More than 100,000 fans turned out to see the rematch, won by The Flying Dutchman. More than a century later, the Benson & Hedges Gold Cup (Eng-G1), now known as the Juddmonte International Stakes, was created to match two champions of the 1970s, Mill Reef and Brigadier Gerard. Mill Reef broke down before the race, but John Galbreath's Epsom Derby (Eng-G1) victor Roberto handed Brigadier Gerard his only career defeat and set a course record.

Location: York, North Yorkshire YO23 1EX
Phone: 44 (1904) 620911
Fax: 44 (1904) 611071
E-mail: info@yorkracecourse.co.uk
Web site: http://www.yorkracecourse.co.uk
Chief executive: J. L. Smith
Principal races: Gimcrack S. (Eng-G2), Juddmonte International S. (Eng-G1), Nunthorpe S. (Eng-G1), Yorkshire Oaks (Eng-G1)

France

Chantilly

Racing at Chantilly, a village approximately 20 miles north of Paris, is held every June in front of the palatial Les Grandes Ecuries (literally, "the big stables") and the Chateau de Chantilly. The palatial stables were built by the Prince de Condé, who believed he would be reincarnated as a horse. The estate includes a lavish stable that can house 250 horses. Chantilly, surrounded by woods, lakes, and 250 acres of greenery, also serves as France's principal training center, with as many as 100 trainers and 3,000 horses using its sand, all-weather, and turf training tracks. Chantilly's premier races are the

2,400-meter Prix du Jockey-Club (Fr-G1), first run in 1836 and popularly known as the French Derby, for three-year-olds, and the 2,100-meter (1�⅙-mile) Prix de Diane (Fr-G1) (French Oaks) for three-year-old fillies, begun in 1841.

Location: 16 Avenue du General Leclerc, BP 209, Chantilly 60631
Phone: 33 3 44 62 41 00
Fax: 33 3 44 57 34 89
Chief executive: Mathieu Vincent
Principal races: Prix de Diane (Fr-G1), Prix du Jockey-Club (Fr-G1), Prix Jean Prat (Fr-G1)

Deauville

Deauville, sometimes referred to as the Saratoga of France, held its first meet in 1864, the same year as Saratoga Race Course's first meet. It runs a short meeting in August, as Saratoga did for decades, and also features a major sale of yearlings, as does Saratoga. Deauville was founded by the Duke of Morny to cater to Parisian society vacationing on the Normandy coast. The setting allows horses to gallop on the beach or in the surf. There is also polo in the afternoons and the casino in the evenings for entertainment, as well as innumerable first-rate restaurants. Deauville offers a top-class, 1,600-meter stakes, the Prix du Haras de Fresnay-le-Buffard Jacques Le Marois (Fr-G1), and the 1,200-meter Prix Morny (Fr-G1) for two-year-olds. Deauville is a right-handed course of 2,200 meters with a 1,600-meter chute on one end and a short chute on the other. Another major stakes, the Grand Prix de Deauville (Fr-G2), is held on the last Sunday of the meeting.

Location: 45 Avenue Hocquart de Turtot, Deauville 14800
Phone: 33 2 31 14 20 00
Fax: 33 2 31 14 20 01
Chief executive: Yves Deshayes
Principal races: Prix du Haras de Fresnay-le-Buffard Jacques le Marois (Fr-G1), Prix Maurice de Gheest (Fr-G1), Prix Morny (Fr-G1)

Longchamp

Emperor Napoleon III traveled by boat on the Seine River to attend Longchamp's first day of racing on April 27, 1857, and he was joined at the Paris track by nearly 10,000 countrymen. Finishing second in the first of five races that afternoon was Miss Gladiateur, the dam of Gladiateur, who became a legend as the first French-bred horse to win the Epsom Derby. For Gladiateur's first start after the English classic, 150,000 racegoers turned out to watch him win the Grand Prix de Paris (now a Group 1 race) at Longchamp.

But the race for which Longchamp is best known is the Prix de l'Arc de Triomphe (Fr-G1), first contested in 1920. Horses from both England and Italy took on France's best, and the first winner was Comrade, owned and bred by Frenchman Evremond de Saint-Alary, trained in England by Peter Gilpin, and ridden by Australian jockey Frank Bullock. The 2,400-meter race on the first Sunday in October was an instant international success and has become Europe's championship race.

Other Longchamp stakes have longer histories. The Grand Prix de Paris was inaugurated in 1863 and for a century was France's most important race for three-year-olds. Following the modern trend, its distance was reduced from 3,000 meters to 2,000 meters in 1987. The first classics of each year, the 1,600-meter Poule

d'Essai des Poulains (Fr-G1) (French Two Thousand Guineas) and Poule d'Essai des Pouliches (Fr-G1) (French One Thousand Guineas) for three-year-olds and three-year-old fillies, respectively, are run in May. The Poule d'Essai des Poulains was first run in 1840, while the Poule d'Essai des Pouliches debuted in 1883. Longchamp's right-handed course has a long and testing homestretch with a slightly uphill finish.

Location: Route des Tribunes, Bois de Boulogne, Paris 75016
Phone: 33 1 44 30 75 00
Fax: 33 1 44 30 75 99
Chief executive: Gerard Grandchamp
Principal races: Grand Criterium (Fr-G1), Grand Prix de Paris (Fr-G1), Poule d'Essai des Poulains (Fr-G1), Poule d'Essai des Pouliches (Fr-G1), Prix de l'Abbaye de Longchamp (Fr-G1), Prix de l'Arc de Triomphe (Fr-G1), Prix du Moulin de Longchamp (Fr-G1), Prix Ganay (Fr-G1), Prix Marcel Boussac (Fr-G1),

Maisons-Laffitte

Secluded near the Saint-Germain forest just west of Paris and home to some 1,800 Thoroughbreds conditioned by more than 80 trainers, Maisons-Laffitte offers one of Europe's most pleasant settings for Thoroughbred racing. Its 2,000-meter straight course, rivaled only by the Rowley Mile at Newmarket in England, is complemented by both right- and left-handed courses to accommodate 35 racing dates from the end of March until the end of July and from early September through early December.

The Prix Robert Papin (Fr-G2) is the first major stakes for two-year-olds each year, while other juvenile stakes, such as the Criterium de Maisons-Laffitte (Fr-G2), are run later in the meet. Among the course's top races for two-year-old fillies is the Prix Miesque (Fr-G3), named for the outstanding filly who won two North American championships with her triumphs in the 1987 and '88 Breeders' Cup Mile (G1).

Miesque won the Prix Imprudence at Maisons-Laffitte immediately before her victory in the 1987 One Thousand Guineas (Eng-G1). Among the other champions who have raced at Maisons-Laffitte are *Sea-Bird, Nureyev, Arctic Tern, *Match II, Exbury, and Relko.

Set on more than 120 acres, Maisons-Laffitte is home to the Museum of the Racecourse, which was opened in 1990 and allows fans to review the history of racing by walking through magnificent rooms of an ancient castle.

Location: 1 Avenue de la Pelouse, Maisons-Laffitte 78600
Phone: 33 1 39 62 90 95
Fax: 33 1 39 62 76 08
Chief executive: Martial de Rouffignac
Principal races: Prix Robert Papin (Fr-G2), Prix Miesque (Fr-G3)

Saint-Cloud

The most frequently used Parisian track, Saint-Cloud hosts racing from February through July and from September through December. Its history extends to 1901 when the Societe du Demi-Sang was thrown out of Vincennes by the army and retreated to a strip of land owned by Edmond Blanc to continue racing. After World War I, the course was given to the Societe Sportive d'Encouragement, which supervised Thoroughbred racing at Maisons-Laffitte. The major stakes at Saint-Cloud is the Grand Prix de Saint-Cloud (Fr-G1), which began in 1904 under the name Prix du President de la Republique. *Sea-Bird, fellow Arc winners Rheingold and Sagace (Fr), and Epsom Derby winners Relko and Teenoso all won races at Saint-

Cloud, which also was the site of *Vaguely Noble's lone three-year-old defeat.

The inaugural running of the Criterium International (Fr-G1) was won by Act One in 2001. The new stakes was introduced after the distance of the Grand Criterium (Fr-G1) at Longchamp was changed from 1,600 meters to 1,400 meters. Saint-Cloud's left-handed, 2,200-meter course is dissected by a 600-meter straight.

Location: 1 Rue du Camp Canadien, Saint-Cloud 92210
Phone: 33 1 47 71 69 26
Fax: 33 1 47 71 37 74
Chief executive: Christian Leger
Principal races: Criterium de Saint-Cloud (Fr-G1), Criterium International (Fr-G1), Grand Prix de Saint-Cloud (Fr-G1)

Germany
Baden-Baden
Set among the foothills of the Black Forest nine miles northwest of Baden-Baden, Baden-Baden Racecourse was the idea of Edouard Bénazet, who offered visitors to the world-famous spa not only Thoroughbred racing but also a casino. When the casino closed in 1872, racing was taken over by the Internationale Club, which today supervises racing in short meets from May through June and from August through September. The nearby attractions include a casino, the vineyards of Rebland, Old Town, theaters, concerts and elegant boutiques. Baden-Baden hosts the Grosser Preis von Baden (Ger-G1) and the Grosser Mercedes-Benz Preis (Ger-G2). The three overlapping, left-handed courses at Baden-Baden are named Old Course, New Course, and Straight Course.

Location: Lichtentaler Allee 8, Baden-Baden, 76530
Phone: 49 7229-21120
Fax: 49 7221-211222
E-mail: club@baden-galopp.de
Web site: http://www.baden-galopp.de
Chairman: Hartmann Freiherr von Richthofen
Chief executive: Dr. Frank Joyeux
Principal race: Grosser Preis von Baden (Ger-G1)

Dusseldorf
Located in a hilly, wooded park on the edge of the Grafenberg Forest in Dusseldorf's Broich district, Dusseldorf Racecourse is the site of one of Germany's richest races, the Deutschland-Preis (Ger-G1), which is contested in late July. Other important stakes include the Henkel-Rennen (Ger-G2) (German One Thousand Guineas) in early May and the Grosser Preis von Dusseldorf (Ger-G3) in mid-October. The hilly, undulating right-hand track features a sharp bend.

Location: Rennbahnstrasse 20, Dusseldorf, 40629
Phone: 49 211-363466
Fax: 49 211-351752
Website: http://www.bbtt.com/drrv
Chairman: Peter Endres
Chief Executive: Detlef Meimann
Principal races: Deutschland-Preis (Ger-G1), Henkel-Rennen (Ger-G2)

Hamburg
Hamburg is the home of the Deutsches Derby (Ger-G1), a 2,400-meter race for three-year-olds first contested in 1869 under the management of the Hamburger Renn-Club. Hamburg's other major stakes include the Hansa-Preis (Ger-G2) at 2,100 meters, the Deutscher Herold-Preis (Ger-G3) at the same distance, and the 1,200-meter Holsten-Trophy (Ger-G3). The racetrack is about six miles from Hamburg and is accessible by the motorway to Berlin, the subway, and the bus. Racing is conducted from the end of June through early July over a right-handed turf course of approximately 2,000 meters.

Location: Rennbahnstr 96, Hamburg 22111
Phone: 49 4065 18229
Fax: 49 4065 56615
E-mail: deutsches-derby@t-online.de
Web site: http://www.galopp-derby.de
Chairman: Franz-Guenther von Gaertner
Chief executive: Guenther Gudert
Principal race: Deutsches Derby (Ger-G1)

Koln
Situated in the Cologne neighborhood of Weidenpesch, Koln Racecourse is a flat, right-handed track with a 2½-furlong straight. Top stakes at Koln include the Europa-Preis (Ger-G1), the Gerling-Preis (Ger-G2), the Mehl-Mulhens-Gennen (Ger-G2) (German Two Thousand Guineas), and the Union-Rennen (Ger-G2).

Location: Rennbahnstr 152, Koln 50737
Phone: 49 221-9745050
Fax: 49 221-9745055
Chairman: Baron Georg von Ullman
Chief executive: Benedikt Fassbender
Principal race: Europa-Preis (Ger-G1), Mehl-Mulhens-Rennen (Ger-G2)

Mulheim
Located in western Germany, Mulheim is host to the country's longest flat race, the 3,400-meter Silbernes Band der Ruhr. Mulheim is a right-handed track with a 2½-furlong straight. The Preis der Diana-Deutches Stuten-Derby (Ger-G1) (German Oaks) is contested in mid-June.

Location: Akazienallee 80-82, Mulheim/Ruhr 45478
Phone: 49 208-57001
Fax: 49 208-57005
Chairman: Bodo Scheibel
Chief executive: Michael Kunst
Principal race: Preis der Diana-Deutsches Stuten-Derby (Ger-G1)

Hong Kong
Happy Valley
Surrounded today by Hong Kong's towering buildings, Happy Valley was built on reclaimed marshland and has held racing since 1846. Training horses is not easy on the 31-square-mile island, now under the control of the People's Republic of China, but the rich purses attract horsemen whose runners are housed in high-rise stables. Overshadowed by Sha Tin, Happy Valley conducts a 60-day racing season that lasts from September through June.

Location: 2 Sports Road, Happy Valley
Phone: (852) 28951523
Fax: (852) 29668111
Web site: www.happyvalleyracecourse.com

Sha Tin
In 1959, Sir John Saunders, then chairman of the Royal Hong Kong Jockey Club, proposed creating a racetrack in Sha Tin Bay to alleviate overcrowding at Happy Valley. After three years of planning, the project of reclaiming 250 acres from the bay was begun. The 14,000 cubic feet of soil needed for the project was taken from the top of one of the nearby mountains, allowing development of that property and financing the cost of the track.

Working round the clock on a tight, three-year schedule, Sha Tin opened as planned on October 7, 1978, with an expansive grandstand that encompasses 16½ acres. A 1,900-meter turf course encircles an all-weather dirt track. Sha Tin's major races are the Hong Kong Derby for four-year-olds, run every February at the start of the Chinese New Year since 1990, the Hong Kong Cup (HK-G1), the Hong Kong Vase (HK-G1), the Hong Kong Mile (HK-G1), and the Hong Kong Sprint (HK-G1).

Location: Sha Tin, New Territories
E-mail: shatinracing@hongkong.com
Web site: www.shatinracetrack.com
Chief executive: Lawrence T. Wong
Principal races: Hong Kong Cup (HK-G1), Hong Kong Mile (HK-G1), Hong Kong Vase (HK-G1), QE II Cup (HK-G1), Hong Kong Sprint (HK-G1)

Ireland
The Curragh

According to legend, St. Bridget was offered as much of the Curragh plain as she could cover with her cloak. Unfurling the cloak from her shoulder, she threw it to cover the whole plain of Kildare. When she gathered her cloak up, the land was covered in the richest and deepest grass imaginable—ideal for training and racing Thoroughbreds. Match races have been held there for centuries. The first recorded one was in 1634 when the Earl of Ormond beat Lord Digby in a four-mile race. The first race recorded at the Curragh was in 1741, and the first Irish Derby (Ire-G1) was held in 1866. By 1921, all five Irish classic stakes were contested at the Curragh. Joining the Derby were the Irish Oaks (Ire-G1), the Irish St. Leger (Ire-G1), the Irish Two Thousand Guineas (Ire-G1), and the Irish One Thousand Guineas (Ire-G1). Located 30 miles west of Dublin, the Curragh offers race meets from mid-March to the beginning of November. The horseshoe-shaped, right-handed course is two miles in length with an uphill, straight run-in of three furlongs to the finish line.

Location: Tara Court, Dublin Road Naas, Co Kildare
Phone: 353 (45) 441205
Fax: 353 (45) 441442
E-mail: info@curragh.ie
Web site: http://www.curragh.ie
Chief executive: Paul Hensey
Principal races: Irish Derby (Ire-G1), Irish Oaks (Ire-G1), Irish One Thousand Guineas (Ire-G1), Irish St. Leger (Ire-G1), Irish Two Thousand Guineas (Ire-G1), Moyglare Stud S. (Ire-G1), National S. (Ire-G1), Phoenix S. (Ire-G1), Tattersalls Gold Cup (Ire-G1)

Leopardstown

Roughly six miles from Dublin, Leopardstown overcame a troubled past. Nine years after its opening in 1888, the five-furlong course was found to be only 4½ furlongs long. Capt. George Quin, who headed a syndicate that had purchased the course, constructed a new five-furlong course that was not well received. Finally, Richard "Boss" Croker, owner of 1907 Irish Derby and Epsom Derby winner Orby, purchased additional land and a larger course was constructed. Leopardstown was owned by Fred Clarke until he sold the track to the Irish Racing Board in 1967. Two years later, Leopardstown received an extensive facelift, reopening in 1971 with a new grandstand, an enclosed betting hall, new dining and bar facilities, and a new stable area. Another renovation in 1988 extended the grandstand and added 16 private boxes. Race meets are held at Leopardstown from mid-March through mid-November over a left-handed turf course of about 2,800 meters. Leopardstown's premier race is the Irish Champion Stakes (Ire-G1). Because of construction on an adjacent motorway, Leopardstown did not conduct five-furlong races in 2002. As a result, the Phoenix Stakes (Ire-G1), Phoenix Sprint Stakes (Ire-G3), and Flying Five Stakes (Ire-G3) were moved to the Curragh, and the Matron (Ire-G3) and Desmond Stakes (Ire-G3) were moved from the Curragh to Leopardstown.

Location: Foxrock, Dublin 18
Phone: 353 (12) 893607
Fax: 353 (12) 892634
E-mail: info@leopardstown.com
Web site: http://www.leopardstown.com
Chairman: Joseph Donnelly
Principal race: Irish Champion S. (Ire-G1)

Italy
Capannelle

Less than eight miles from the Colosseum in Rome, Capannelle opened in 1926. The grandstand, turf course, and interior dirt course are close to an ancient Roman aqueduct and are not far from St. Peter's Basilica in the Vatican. Race meets are held from March to mid-June and from September through November over right-handed turf and sand courses that are slightly uphill near the start and slightly downhill near the finish. National Hunt races also are conducted. Top stakes include the Premio Presidente della Repubblica (Ity-G1) for four-year-olds and up, the Derby Italiano (Ity-G1) for three-year-olds, and the Premio Roma (Ity-G1) for three-year-olds and older. Capannelle's training facilities include 2,600-meter turf and dirt tracks, another turf course inside them, and a 1,200-meter sand track around the stabling area.

Location: Via Appia Nuova 1255, Rome 00178
Phone: 39 (671) 6771
Fax: 39 (671) 677213
Chief Executive: Ing. Elio Pautasso
Principal races: Derby Italiano (Ity-G1), Premio Presidente della Repubblica (Ity-G1), Premio Roma (Ity-G1)

San Siro

Racing began at San Siro in 1888 on a racecourse designed by architect Giulio Valerio. In 1909, a training center was added to the facility located just north of downtown Milan. Today, some 200 acres of training grounds include two turf tracks, two sand tracks, and a nearby all-weather track. San Siro's racecourse consists of three right-handed, overlapping turf courses of 2,800, 2,000, and 1,800 meters. Race meets are held from mid-March through July and from September to mid-November. Its premier races are the Oaks d'Italia (Ity-G1) for three-year-old fillies, the Gran Criterium (Ity-G1) for two-year-olds, and the Gran Premio di Milano (Ity-G1) and the Premio del Jockey Club (Ity-G1) for three-year-olds and up.

Location: Via Ippodromo 100, Milan 201550
Phone: 39 (248) 216215
Fax: 39 (248) 201721
Chief executive: Alessandro Berardelli
Principal races: Gran Criterium (Ity-G1), Oaks d'Italia (Ity-G1), Premio di Capua (Ity-G1), Premio Jockey Club (Ity-G1), Gran Premio di Milano (Ity-G1)

Japan

Hanshin

The newest of the Japan Racing Association's four major tracks, Hanshin opened in 1949 and is about 12 miles from Osaka. Hanshin completed an extensive modernization in 1991 and races from March through June and in September and December. A lush, wide, right-handed turf course—slightly downhill in the backstretch and slightly uphill in the homestretch—encircles a dirt track.

On the second Sunday in April, Hanshin stages the 1,600-meter Oka Sho (Japan's equivalent of the one-mile One Thousand Guineas [Eng-G1]), named for the cherry blossom in bloom at that time each year. Other major stakes include the all-age Grand Prix Takarazuka Kinen (Jpn-G1) in mid-June and the Hanshin Sansai Himba Stakes in early December for two-year-old fillies.

Location: 1-1 Komano-cho, Takarazuka-shi, Hyogo 665-0053
Phone: 81-798-51-7151
Web site: http://www.jair.jrao.ne.jp/courses/jra/jra004.html
Principal races: Takarazuka Kinen (Jpn-G1), Oka Sho

Kyoto

Another of the major Japan Racing Association tracks, Kyoto Racecourse is located six miles south of Kyoto and stages racing in January, February, April, May, October, and November over a 1,900-meter, right-handed turf course that is uphill in the backstretch. Enclosed within the main course is a dirt course, an inner turf course, and a huge lake. A mammoth walking ring allows thousands of fans to see horses prepare for their race. The Spring Tenno Sho (Emperor's Cup) is a 3,200-meter endurance stakes for four-year-olds and older held on the last Sunday in April. In November, three major stakes are held on successive Sundays: the 3,000-meter Kikuka Sho (Japanese St. Leger) for three-year-olds, the final leg of the Japanese Triple Crown; the 2,400-meter Queen Elizabeth Cup, which is the concluding race of the Japanese filly triple crown; and the 1,600-meter Mile Championship.

Location: 32 Yoshijima, Watashibashima-machi, Fushimi-ku Kyoto, 612-8265
Phone: 81-75-631-3131
Web site: http://www.jair.jrao.ne.jp/courses/jra/jra003.html
Principal races: Spring Tenno Sho, Kikuka Sho, Queen Elizabeth Cup, Mile Championship

Tokyo

Home of Japan's premier race, the Japan Cup (Jpn-G1), Tokyo Racecourse at Fuchu, 15 miles west of Tokyo, was built in 1933. The 1,878-meter interior dirt course is based on the design of American courses but is uniquely fine-tuned to handle Japan's heavier precipitation. The track is packed firmly with a layer of mountain sand and covered with loose river sand, giving horses a spongy bottom underneath and a surface on top to absorb impact and ease stress on their legs. The undulating turf course is 2,116 meters. The Japan Cup, which is run left-handed on turf at 2,400 meters, begins on a 400-meter straight run that minimizes the impact of poor post position. On the same weekend, the $2-million Japan Cup Dirt is run. Because of extensive renovations, both races were held at Nakayama in 2002. The Japan Racing Association operates both Tokyo Racecourse and Nakayama, 12 miles east of Tokyo.

Location: 1-1 Hiyoshi-cho, Fuchu-shi, Tokyo 183-0024
Phone: 81-42-363-3141
Web site: http://www.jair.jrao.ne.jp/courses/jra/jra001.html
Principal races: Japan Cup (Jpn-G1), Keio Hai Spring Cup (Jpn-G2), Mainichi Okan (Jpn-G2)

New Zealand

Avondale

Operated by the Avondale Jockey Club, which was formed in 1889, Avondale is located near Auckland and hosts 14 racing dates during the year. The original left-handed course was just under a mile in circumference. It was enlarged to nine furlongs and converted to a right-handed course a few years later.

Location: Ash Street, 103 Avondale, Auckland
Phone: 64 (9) 828 3309
Fax: 64 (9) 828 3099
E-mail: avon.jc@extra.co.nz
Chairman: Graham Reddaway
Chief executive: Jim Patterson
Principal races: Avondale Gold Cup H. (NZ-G1), Avondale Guineas (NZ-G1)

Ellerslie

Several of New Zealand's 21 Group 1 races are held at Ellerslie, including the New Zealand Derby (NZ-G1) and the Easter Handicap (NZ-G1). The track, approximately five miles from New Zealand's largest city, Auckland, boasts an elegant grandstand and beautifully maintained grounds. Racing was first conducted about one mile from Ellerslie on January 5, 1842, but the present site was not used until May 25, 1874, a national holiday to observe Queen Victoria's birthday. Ellerslie's major stakes are held from December 26 through January 2 and during the first week in June. The main track is a 1,870-meter, right-handed turf course with a finishing straight of 380 meters that is slightly downhill.

Location: Greenlane, Auckland
Phone: 64 (9) 524 4069
Fax: 64 (9) 524 8680
E-mail: davel@ellerslie.co.nz
Web site: http://www.ellerslie.co.nz
Chairman: G. J. Clatworthy
Chief executive: D. J. Lloyd
Principal races: Auckland Cup (NZ-G1), Ellerslie Sires' Produce S. (NZ-G1), Easter H. (NZ-G1), New Zealand Derby (NZ-G1)

Hawke's Bay

Racing dates back to 1845 at Hawke's Bay, located near the cities of Napier and Hastings on the eastern shore of New Zealand's northern island. The four racing clubs using the racetrack, however, did not unite until 1989. Now, 14 dates are conducted annually. The highlight of the year is the Spring Carnival, which is held over five weeks in August and September and features the Kelt Capital Stakes (NZ-G1), the richest weight-for-age race in New Zealand. The Hawke's Bay Cup Handicap (NZ-G2), the country's second-oldest race, was first contested in 1860.

Location: Prospect Road, Box 1046, Hastings
Phone: 64 (6) 8734545
Fax: 64 (6) 8766488

E-mail: comeracing@hb-racing.co.nz
Web site: www.hb-racing.co.nz
Chairman: John McGifford
Principal races: Hawke's Bay Guineas (NZ-G3), Kelt Capital S. (NZ-G1)

Otaki Racecourse

Otaki Racecourse, located at the north end of Otaki on Kapiti island, has an 1,800-meter left-handed track and is home of the Otaki-Maori Racing Club. Organized racing has been held at Otaki since the 1850s, and the Otaki-Maori Racing Club dates from 1866. In September 2000, the Levin Racing Club, Wellington Race Club, and Masterson Racing Club joined with the Otaki Maori Racing Club to form Capital Racing. The four clubs, each of which had been facing financial difficulties before the 2000 agreement, combine to run 27 days a year at Otaki, which is easily accessible by railroad from Wellington, at the southern tip of New Zealand's northern island. The WFA Stakes (NZ-G1) is staged there.

Location: P.O. Box 13, Otaki
Phone: 64 (6) 364 8078
Fax: 64 (6) 364 8079
E-mail: otaki_maorirc@xtra.co.nz
Chief executive: Butch Castles
Principal race: WFA Stakes (NZ-G1)

Riccarton Park

The Canterbury Jockey Club was formed in 1854, and the following year began racing at Riccarton Park Racecourse, which is located ten minutes from the center of Christchurch, New Zealand's second-largest city, on the southern island. Among the races held at Riccarton are the New Zealand Two Thousand Guineas (NZ-G1), New Zealand One Thousand Guineas (NZ-G1), and the New Zealand Cup Handicap (NZ-G2).

Location: Racecourse Road, Riccarton, Christchurch
Phone: 64 (3) 342 8928
Fax: 64 (3) 342 6114
E-mail: enquiries@riccartonpark.co.nz
Web site: http://www.riccartonpark.co.nz/cjc/
Chief executive: Tim Mills
Principal races: New Zealand One Thousand Guineas (NZ-G1), New Zealand Two Thousand Guineas (NZ-G1)

Te Rapa

Located north of Hamilton on New Zealand's northern island, Te Rapa Racecourse is operated by the Waikato Racing Cup and conducts 18 days of racing annually. Flat racing is conducted on a left-handed, 1,800-meter track with two chutes. Te Rapa has an expansive galloping track, tree-lined paddocks, and a large grandstand. Among its major races are the Waikato Draught Sprint Stakes (NZ-G1), Whakanui Stud International Stakes (NZ-G1), and the Cambridge Stud Sir Tristram Fillies Classic Stakes (NZ-G2).

Location: P.O. Box 10050, Te Rapa, Hamilton
Phone: 64 (7) 849 8807
Fax: 64 (7) 849 1211
E-mail: info@waikatoracing.co.nz
Web site: http://www.waikatoracing.co.nz/
Chairman: D. C. Ellis
Chief executive: Tony Enting
Principal races: Waikato Draught Sprint Stakes (NZ-G1), Whakanui Stud International (NZ-G1)

Trentham

Located about 20 miles north of New Zealand's capital city, Wellington, Trentham was founded in 1870, not long after the city itself was built. Trentham's figure-eight steeplechase course is ringed by a wide, 2,000-meter turf course with a 450-meter home straight. Its major races include the Wellington Cup Handicap (NZ-G1), the Telegraph Handicap (NZ-G1), and the New Zealand Oaks (NZ-G1). Trentham was home of the country's top yearling sale for more than six decades. In its second year in 1928, the sale included a chestnut colt bought for 160 guineas. Named *Phar Lap, he was sent to Australia and made racing history. In 1988, the sale was shifted north, closer to the major breeding operations in the country.

Location: Racecource Road, Trentham UPPER HUTT
Phone: 64 (4) 528 9611
Fax: 64 (4) 528 4166
E-mail: maryanne.edwards@trentham.co.nz
Web site: http://www.racingwellington.paradise.net.nz
Chairman: R. Dixon
Chief executive: Mary-Anne Edwards
Principal races: New Zealand Oaks (NZ-G1), Telegraph H. (NZ-G1), Thorndon Mile H. (NZ-G1), Wellington Cup H. (NZ-G1)

Peru
Monterrico Race Track

Racing in Peru began in the 20th century at a small racetrack called Cancha Maiggo, and then was conducted at Santa Beatriz before the opening of the Monterrico Race Track in Lima on December 18, 1960. Racing is conducted year-round on Tuesday and Thursday evenings, Saturdays, and Sundays. The left-handed track has both a dirt track and a grass course. On December 8, 1997, Panama native Laffit Pincay Jr. and Peruvian-born Edgar Prado, Jorge Chavez, and Julio Pezua represented the United States in an international riders competition at Monterrico. Juan Jose Paule of Argentina and Peruvian Edwin Talaverano tied for first place in the three-race event. Monterrico's premier races form the Quadruple Crown. All of Peru's more than 40 graded races are run at Monterrico.

Location: Avenue El Derby, Santiago de Surco, Lima
Phone: 51 (1) 610-3000
Chairman: Herbert Moebius Castaneda
Principal races: Derby Nacional (Per-G1), Jockey Club del Peru (Per-G1)

Singapore
Singapore Racecourse

Singapore Racecourse at Kranji in the northern part of Singapore is the host of the Singapore Airlines International Cup (Sin-G1), a leg of the Emirates World Series. The stakes race is contested at 1¼ miles in May over the 2,000-meter, left-handed track. The race was canceled in 2003 because of the severe acute respiratory syndrome (SARS) outbreak. Another major stakes in the Singapore KrisFlyer Sprint (Sin-G3). With three training tracks, the track accommodates approximately 1,000 horses. Horses are stabled in either air-conditioned or naturally ventilated stalls in barns separated by large courtyards. The four-story grandstand can accommodate 30,000 people.

Location: 1 Turf Club Ave, Kranji, 738078
Phone: (65) 6879-1000

Fax: (65) 687-1010
Web site: www.turfclub.com.sg
President: Yu Pang Fey
Principal race: Singapore Airlines International Cup (Sin-G1)

South Africa
Clairwood

Clairwood, operated by the Gold Circle Racing and Gaming Group in Merebank, is host of the 2,000-meter Champions Cup (SAf-G1) in late July. A flat, left-handed track of approximately 2,500 meters in circumference, Clairwood features a 1,200-meter straight that is used for all sprints. The start for 1,400-meter races begins very close to the turn, often resulting in a scramble for good position early, especially in large fields.

Location: 89 Barrier Lane, Merewent, Merebank 4059
Phone: 27 (31) 469 1020
Fax: 27 (31) 309 8159
E-mail: clairwood@goldcircle.co.za
Web site: http://www.clairwood.co.za
Chief executive: Ken McArthur
Principal races: Champions Cup (SAf-G1), Gold Challenge S. (SAf-G1)

Greyville

Located in a complex that includes a championship golf course, Greyville has conducted racing just outside the city of Durban since 1844. In 1897, the Durban Turf Club took over the track's administration. The 2,000-meter Durban July Handicap (SAf-G1), the country's most prestigious race, is held on the first Saturday of the month and attracts crowds of up to 60,000. Other major stakes are the South African Guineas (SAf-G1) in May, the South African Fillies Guineas (SAf-G1), and the Daily News Two Thousand (SAf-G1). The right-handed, pear-shaped turf course of about 2,800 meters features tight turns and a straight of nearly 500 meters.

Location: 150 Avondale Rd, Greyville Box 40, Durban 4000
Phone: 27 (31) 309 4545
Fax: 27 (31) 309 2553
Principal races: Daily News Two Thousand (SAf-G1), Durban July H. (SAf-G1), Garden Province S. (SAf-G1), Gold Cup (SAf-G1), Premier's Champion S. (SAf-G1), South African Fillies Guineas (SAf-G1), South African Guineas (SAf-G1)

Scottsville

Located near Pietermaritzburg, Scottsville's racing dates back to April 3, 1886. Racing is held on 14 Saturdays, two holidays, and 17 weekdays throughout the year on a right-handed, oval turf course approximately 2,270 meters in circumference. Nearby training centers in Ashburton, Clairwood Park, and Summerveld accommodate 2,000 horses for some 50 trainers. Scottsville hosts the South African Fillies Sprint (SAf-G1) and the Golden Spur Stakes (SAf-G1). Like Clairwood, it is owned by the Gold Circle Racing and Gaming Group.

Location: 45 New England Road, PMB Box 40, Durban 4000
Phone: 27 (33) 345 3405
Fax: 27 (33) 345 4392
E-mail: scottsville@goldcircle.co.za
Web site: http://www.scottsville.co.za
Principal races: Allan Robertson Fillies Championship (SAf-G1), Gold Medallion (SAF-G1)

Turffontein

Only two miles south of Johannesburg, Turffontein has been home to racing since 1889, just one year after the first Thoroughbred race was held in the city. While maintaining its traditions, including a Royal Box, Turffontein has been thoroughly modernized. The grandstand, rebuilt in the 1970s, allows a panoramic view of the course, and the Ascot Bar and Lounge, Caradoc Room, and Lawn Enclosure give fans many alternatives for enjoying their day at the races. The course has its own water source, which allows for beautiful lawns, numerous flower gardens, meticulously maintained trees and shrubs, and a bird sanctuary. Racing is conducted mostly on Saturdays on a testing, uphill, right-handed turf course of 2,658 meters. Its single chute allows for a 1,200-meter straight. Turffontein also has a 2,000-meter grass training track and four sand training tracks. The South Africa Derby (SAf-G1), Champion Stakes (SAf-G1), and Horse Chestnut 1600 Stakes (SAf-G1), formerly the President's Cup, are three of Turffontein's biggest races.

Location: Turf Club Street, Turffontein 2190, Box 183, Johannesburg 2000
Phone: 27 (11) 681 5000
Fax: 27 (11) 683 3407
Principal races: Champion S. (SAf-G1), Empress Club S. (SAf-G1), Gold Bowl (SAf-G1), Horse Chestnut S. (SAf-G1), South Africa Derby (SAf-G1), South Africa Nursery (SAf-G1), Summer Cup (SAf-G1), Triple Crown 1600 (SAf-G1), Triple Tiara 1600 (SAf-G1)

United Arab Emirates
Nad al Sheba

Offering the world's richest race—the $6-million Dubai World Cup (UAE-G1)—and no betting on any of its races, Nad al Sheba Racecourse is located within the tiny sheikhdom of Dubai in the United Arab Emirates. First laid out in 1986 and resurfaced in 1997 before the third running of the World Cup, the 2,200-meter (1⅜-mile), left-handed dirt course has three chutes. A left-handed turf course inside the dirt course is composed of Bermuda hybrid grass, which thrives in hot and humid climates. Two-time North American Horse of the Year Cigar won the inaugural Dubai World Cup in 1996 to give the stakes instant credibility. Buttressing the 2003 Dubai World Cup on March 22 were the Dubai Duty Free Stakes (UAE-G1), the Dubai Golden Shaheen (UAE-G1), the Dubai Sheema Classic (UAE-G1), the UAE Derby (UAE-G2), and the Godolphin Mile (UAE-G2). The Dubai World Cup Committee pays a wide array of costs for visiting horses competing in Dubai, including roundtrip airfare, feed, bedding, and veterinary treatment.

Location: Millennium Grandstand First Floor, PO Box 36699, Dubai
Phone: 971 (4) 336 3737
Fax: 971 (4) 336 3727
E-mail: drc@emiratesracing.com
Web site: http://www.drc.co.ae
General Manager: Jerry Kilby
Principal races: Dubai Duty Free S. (UAE-G1), Dubai Golden Shaheen (UAE-G1), Dubai Sheema Classic (UAE-G1), Dubai World Cup (UAE-G1), Godolphin Mile (UAE-G2), UAE Derby (UAE-G2)

*See table of conversions from metric to English distances in Reference section on page 741.

International Sire Lists
Sires by Earnings by Country for Calendar Year 2002

Argentina

Sire	Strs	Wnrs	SWs	Leading Earner (Earnings)	Total Earnings
Roy	88	50	14	Ice Point ($126,942)	$818,389
Southern Halo	144	86	14	Flirteador ($39,295)	$770,980
Numerous	102	57	8	Miss Terrible (Arg) ($43,909)	$584,969
Ride the Rails	114	61	2	Rodion (Arg) ($35,162)	$500,350
Lode	92	46	6	Decencia (Arg) ($62,416)	$470,877
Candy Stripes	116	65	4	Persky (Arg) ($26,861)	$460,256
Equalize	128	61	2	Maximal ($17,123)	$417,669
Shy Tom	117	54	4	Renombrado Tom (Arg) ($30,270)	$388,243
Interprete	83	41	3	Insociable ($48,393)	$378,504
Hidden Prize	43	19	2	Second Reality ($213,729)	$370,751

Australia

Sire	Strs	Wnrs	SWs	Leading Earner (Earnings)	Total Earnings
Danehill	201	107	26	Ha Ha ($629,818)	$4,033,288
Zabeel	155	60	6	Don Eduardo ($818,431)	$2,756,531
Rhythm	31	15	3	Ethereal ($2,299,352)	$2,591,828
Royal Academy	167	83	9	Bel Esprit ($536,130)	$2,209,828
Scenic (Ire)	161	78	6	Universal Prince ($335,148)	$2,167,844
Desert Sun (GB)	34	16	3	Sunline ($1,559,478)	$1,945,330
Serheed	78	32	2	Northerly ($1,226,956)	$1,759,467
Dehere	122	70	7	Defier ($442,578)	$1,685,949
Grand Lodge	123	60	4	Shogun Lodge ($453,432)	$1,621,623
Strategic	109	43	5	Mistegic ($666,039)	$1,504,606

Brazil

Sire	Strs	Wnrs	SWs	Leading Earner (Earnings)	Total Earnings
Choctaw Ridge	158	79	7	Gregoriano (Brz) ($53,192)	$563,482
Minstrel Glory	188	99	4	Gatuno ($30,327)	$460,126
Ghadeer	149	68	5	Be Happy ($23,786)	$376,995
Clackson	120	52	4	Gigli (Brz) ($36,868)	$325,665
Roi Normand	95	43	5	Rizzolini ($29,830)	$313,973
Midnight Tiger	128	59	4	Napolitano ($22,009)	$303,650
Fast Gold	162	66	1	House of Lords ($11,706)	$297,737
Dodge	83	46	3	Lost Love ($68,983)	$292,643
Irish Fighter	146	70	1	Cachito Mio ($8,594)	$283,355
Tsunami Slew	103	51	3	Trancaferro ($43,083)	$274,916

Canada

Sire	Strs	Wnrs	SWs	Leading Earner (Earnings)	Total Earnings
Regal Classic	66	37	4	Runaway Love ($227,566)	$2,777,503
War Deputy	56	33	2	Forever Grand ($362,761)	$2,169,052
Tejabo	48	21	3	T J's Lucky Moon ($644,212)	$1,907,345
Bold Executive	66	29	2	Sambuca On Ice ($249,965)	$1,907,177
Ascot Knight	61	25	1	Yatsko ($138,868)	$1,832,397
Smart Strike	20	12	3	Portcullis ($463,830)	$1,628,220
Vying Victor	88	45	7	Elana d'Amour ($204,882)	$1,493,513
Open Forum	32	18	1	Open Concert ($207,906)	$1,388,613
Valid Expectations	26	16	0	Expected Flirt ($208,495)	$1,300,855
Tethra	35	13	2	Mighty Quinn ($224,927)	$1,228,251

England

Sire	Strs	Wnrs	SWs	Leading Earner (Earnings)	Total Earnings
Sadler's Wells	118	38	5	High Chaparral (Ire) ($1,168,504)	$3,006,898
Danehill	112	43	6	Rock of Gibraltar (Ire) ($752,931)	$2,454,706
Selkirk	79	33	7	Highest ($241,456)	$1,620,018

Sire	Strs	Wnrs	SWs	Leading Earner (Earnings)	Total Earnings
Pivotal	52	24	3	Somnus ($396,307)	$1,331,309
Green Desert	61	32	5	Invincible Spirit ($241,704)	$1,274,721
Spectrum	69	21	2	Golan (Ire) ($832,503)	$1,253,473
Machiavellian	54	17	3	Storming Home (GB) ($579,080)	$1,250,817
Grand Lodge	99	39	5	Grandera ($245,548)	$1,219,647
Indian Ridge	83	34	5	Nayyir ($223,559)	$1,217,328
Woodman	46	14	2	Hawk Wing ($940,229)	$1,205,241

France

Sire	Strs	Wnrs	SWs	Leading Earner (Earnings)	Total Earnings
Danehill	57	28	9	Banks Hill (GB) ($280,074)	$1,952,836
Sadler's Wells	70	22	10	Dance Routine ($217,781)	$1,483,847
Hernando (Fr)	26	16	3	Sulamani ($1,037,003)	$1,418,247
Caerleon	15	8	4	Marienbard ($895,132)	$1,260,480
Exit to Nowhere	80	30	4	Al Nowhere ($115,162)	$1,117,724
Linamix	72	29	5	Fair Mix ($105,672)	$1,091,650
Kendor	78	43	4	Maid of Dawkins ($120,469)	$1,071,829
Anabaa	64	30	3	Ana Marie ($171,480)	$1,024,114
Green Tune	77	36	2	Afalkayar ($54,816)	$983,762
Bering (GB)	87	40	3	Sarrasin ($83,556)	$886,985

Germany

Sire	Strs	Wnrs	SWs	Leading Earner (Earnings)	Total Earnings
Monsun	60	33	5	Salve Regina ($492,906)	$1,278,658
Big Shuffle	128	62	3	Sambaprinz ($73,570)	$921,065
Dashing Blade	125	49	6	War Blade ($73,758)	$863,390
Lomitas (GB)	89	51	7	Liquido ($98,095)	$755,464
Acatenango	79	46	5	Uriah (GER) ($78,878)	$616,090
Caerleon	4	1	1	Marienbard ($609,882)	$613,324
Platini	102	47	1	Harry Potter ($27,999)	$483,886
Goofalik	94	49	0	Askant ($41,789)	$420,088
Second Set (Ire)	58	27	5	Willingly ($51,601)	$397,583
Desert Style	2	1	1	Next Desert ($358,807)	$359,194

Hong Kong

Sire	Strs	Wnrs	SWs	Leading Earner (Earnings)	Total Earnings
Danehill	70	31	1	Jeune King Prawn ($827,787)	$6,308,554
Anabaa	9	5	1	Anabar ($1,938,960)	$2,717,244
Bishop of Cashel	1	1	1	Ecclesiastical ($2,696,302)	$2,696,302
Snippets	20	12	1	Sneaky Visit ($490,366)	$1,958,783
Last Tycoon (Ire)	23	10	0	Score ($346,406)	$1,818,173
Housebuster	12	7	1	Electronic Unicorn ($1,043,292)	$1,680,779
St Covet	3	3	1	Easy Thrills ($1,350,074)	$1,503,448
Chief's Crown	8	3	1	Charming City ($800,931)	$1,220,244
Marju	16	7	0	Northern Gold Ball ($417,433)	$1,192,032
Green Dancer	1	1	1	Eishin Preston ($1,102,520)	$1,102,520

Ireland

Sire	Strs	Wnrs	SWs	Leading Earner (Earnings)	Total Earnings
Sadler's Wells	75	30	8	High Chaparral (Ire) ($830,448)	$2,547,169
Danehill	45	19	5	Rock of Gibraltar (Ire) ($218,638)	$1,001,236
Grand Lodge	31	8	1	Grandera ($635,615)	$794,155
Spectrum	38	14	2	Marionnaud ($196,732)	$621,362
Storm Cat	14	8	4	Van Nistelrooy ($187,981)	$499,404
Danzig	8	5	3	Century City (Ire) ($236,501)	$428,113
Indian Ridge	26	6	2	Luminata ($144,895)	$406,663
Definite Article (GB)	16	5	1	Vinnie Roe ($234,735)	$340,835
Doyoun	11	4	1	Margarula ($267,381)	$336,044
Barathea (Ire)	29	8	3	Vinthea (Ire) ($104,867)	$321,288

Italy

Sire	Strs	Wnrs	SWs	Leading Earner (Earnings)	Total Earnings
Love the Groom	106	51	0	Maktub ($134,275)	$979,041
Sri Pekan	50	29	0	Madras ($62,685)	$765,798
Danehill	28	14	2	Spartacus ($145,800)	$747,270
Halling	17	9	3	Fisich ($303,585)	$697,382
Mukaddamah	42	24	1	Checkit ($88,621)	$671,133
Polish Precedent	11	5	1	Rakti ($523,104)	$608,312
Lycius	43	29	0	Slap Shot ($75,291)	$598,202
Roi Danzig	66	31	0	Tenero Giacomo ($129,906)	$592,649
Sadler's Wells	11	3	3	Ballingarry (Ire) ($188,396)	$584,202
Spectrum	38	22	0	Ravanello ($82,018)	$548,152

Japan

Sire	Strs	Wnrs	SWs	Leading Earner (Earnings)	Total Earnings
Sunday Silence	407	158	16	Gold Allure ($2,120,118)	$52,707,007
Brian's Time	207	73	5	Tanino Gimlet ($2,963,043)	$21,092,392
Tony Bin	205	72	4	Telegnosis ($1,206,175)	$20,670,775
Afleet	170	67	2	Sterling Rose ($1,836,315)	$15,783,214
Fuji Kiseki	142	45	3	Mitsuwa Top Lady ($896,340)	$12,081,934
Forty Niner	124	62	2	Biwa Shinseiki ($1,241,175)	$11,222,538
Sakura Bakushin O	149	58	2	Shonan Kampf ($1,837,226)	$11,017,434
Dance in the Dark	173	49	4	Tsurumaru Boy ($1,853,442)	$10,340,904
Commander in Chief	158	43	4	Hagino High Grade ($1,072,502)	$10,271,845
Jade Robbery	167	52	1	Yamakatsu Suzuran ($939,438)	$8,453,489

Saudia Arabia

Sire	Strs	Wnrs	SWs	Leading Earner (Earnings)	Total Earnings
Another Review	41	12	6	Ikhlaas ($80,726)	$235,155
Polar Run	16	4	2	Markhan ($72,702)	$156,084
Mirror Black	32	10	3	Waaslah ($28,554)	$113,707
Sharpitor	16	6	2	Bariyah ($33,325)	$84,948
Casteddu	5	3	1	Asfahaan ($42,403)	$77,408
Lycius	5	2	2	Usaylah ($61,494)	$75,448
Environment Friend	2	1	1	Jammaha ($72,676)	$72,676
Ezzoud (Ire)	1	1	1	Sahaaj ($67,450)	$67,450
Thoughtless	28	8	1	Almotammin ($29,433)	$67,151
Manific	18	6	5	Saaroom ($13,464)	$66,031

Puerto Rico

Sire	Strs	Wnrs	SWs	Leading Earner (Earnings)	Total Earnings
Goldgalliano (Ire)	45	25	1	Biodynamics ($91,435)	$704,902
Sejm	32	14	1	Mediavilla R. ($381,166)	$631,915
Eqtesaad	32	22	1	Don Piero ($80,360)	$521,575
Sunshine Jimmy	24	13	3	La Machina ($112,682)	$475,214
Royal Merlot	21	14	2	Hispanica ($129,084)	$403,033
Cagey Bidder	17	11	0	Gabriela A. ($48,098)	$315,686
Fappiano's Star	25	10	0	Starlet in Motion ($66,122)	$301,723
Lord Cardinal	26	11	0	Cayuco ($55,524)	$266,773
Once Ivor	25	13	0	Harry d'Angel ($44,074)	$245,683
Sneaky Solicitor	17	10	0	Salado's Kid ($58,674)	$244,059

United Arab Emirates

Sire	Strs	Wnrs	SWs	Leading Earner (Earnings)	Total Earnings
Machiavellian	25	10	3	Street Cry (Ire) ($3,657,162)	$4,082,712
Pulpit	1	1	1	Essence of Dubai ($1,350,000)	$1,350,000
Gulch	10	4	1	Nayef ($1,200,000)	$1,269,253
Phone Trick	1	1	1	Caller One ($1,200,000)	$1,200,000
Potrillazo	1	0	0	Sei Mi ($1,200,000)	$1,200,000
Kaldounevees (Fr)	1	1	1	Terre a Terre ($1,200,000)	$1,200,000
Bahri	1	1	0	Sakhee ($620,415)	$620,415
Memo (Chi)	1	1	1	Grey Memo ($600,000)	$600,000
Rahy	2	0	0	Noverre ($400,000)	$402,097
Zabeel	2	0	0	Helene Vitality ($400,000)	$400,000

Sovereign Awards

Inaugurated in 1975, four years after the Eclipse Awards were instituted, the Sovereign Awards honor the best horses and outstanding individuals in Canadian racing. Administered by the Jockey Club of Canada, Sovereign Awards are presented in ten horse categories, and a Canadian Horse of the Year is selected from the nine racing categories. In addition, a Broodmare of the Year award is presented.

Sovereign Awards are awarded to individuals in five categories: owner, breeder, trainer, jockey, and apprentice jockey. In addition, the E. P. Taylor Award of Merit, formerly known as the Man of the Year, is presented in most years. Sovereign Awards are presented in four media categories.

With Canada's highest-quality racing concentrated in Ontario, the Sovereign Awards commonly go to horses that have raced in that province.

The best of Canada have been honored with Eclipse Awards in the past. Most recently, 1997 Canadian Horse of the Year Chief Bearhart was voted an Eclipse Award as champion turf male. In 1991, Canadian Triple Crown winner and Canadian Horse of the Year Dance Smartly was honored with an Eclipse Award as champion three-year-old filly, and 1981 Canadian Horse

of the Year Deputy Minister won the champion juvenile male Eclipse Award for that season.

Sovereign recipients are selected by a panel of sportswriters, broadcasters, and racing officials across Canada. Horses need not be bred in Canada, but they must make at least three Canadian starts to be eligible for each year's awards.

2002 Sovereign Awards

Unlike some past years, few Canadian-based horses made successful cross-border forays to win major stakes races in the United States in 2002. But the racing season was a personal triumph for longtime owner and breeder Bruno Schickedanz, whose Wake At Noon won the Sovereign Awards for Horse of the Year, champion older male, and champion sprinter.

Trained by Abraham Katryan, Wake At Noon ran best at Woodbine, Ontario's principal racetrack. His early-season splurge of stakes victories—he won three stakes before May 1, including the Vigil Handicap (Can-G3)—and subsequent triumph in the Highlander Handicap (Can-G3) helped earn him the Horse of the Year title.

Other contenders for the overall title were undefeated champion two-year-old male Added

History of the Sovereign Awards

E. P. Taylor

Year	Award of Merit†	Owner	Breeder	Trainer	Jockey	Apprentice Jockey
2002	Not awarded	Stronach Stable	Sam-Son Farm	Roger Attfield	Patrick Husbands	Chantal Sutherland
2001	Not awarded	Sam-Son Farm	Sam-Son Farm	Bob Tiller	Patrick Husbands	Chantal Sutherland
2000	Mike Harris	Sam-Son Farm	Sam-Son Farm	Mark Frostad	Patrick Husbands	Cory Clark
1999	George Hendrie	Stronach Stables	Frank Stronach	Mark Frostad	Patrick Husbands	Ben Russell
1998	David Willmot	Stronach Stables	Frank Stronach	Michael Wright Jr.	David Clark	Helen Vanek
1997	Not awarded	Frank Stronach	Frank Stronach	Mark Frostad	Emile Ramsammy	Rui Pimentel
1996	Not awarded	Minshall Farms	Minshall Farms	Barbara Minshall	Emile Ramsammy	Neil Poznansky
1995	Charles Taylor	Frank Stronach	Kinghaven Farms	Danny Vella	Todd Kabel	Dave Wilson
1994	Jack Kenney	Frank Stronach	Kinghaven Farms	Danny Vella	Robert Landry	Dave Wilson
1993	Not awarded	Frank Stronach	Kinghaven Farms	Roger Attfield	Robert Landry	Constant Montpellier
1992	Col. Charles Baker	Knob Hill Stable	Knob Hill Stable	Philip England	Todd Kabel	Stanley Bethley
1991	Ernest Samuel	Sam-Son Farm	Sam-Son Farm	Jim Day	Mickey Walls	Mickey Walls
1990	James Wright	Kinghaven Farms	Kinghaven Farms	Roger Attfield	Don Seymour	Mickey Walls
1989	George C. Frostad	Kinghaven Farms	Kinghaven Farms	Roger Attfield	Don Seymour	Maree Richards
1988	Sandy Hawley	Sam-Son Farm	Sam-Son Farm	Jim Day	Sandy Hawley	Jim McAleney
1987	Larry Regan	Kinghaven Farms	Kinghaven Farms	Roger Attfield	Don Seymour	Jim McAleney
1986	D. G. Willmot	D. G. Willmot	D. G. Willmot	Roger Attfield	Larry Attard	Todd Kabel
1985	George Gardiner	Ernest Samuel	E. P. Taylor	Jim Day	Don Seymour	Nancy Jumpsen
1984	Jim Coleman	Ernest Samuel	Frank Stronach	Mike Doyle	Chris Loseth	Robert King
1983	Joe Thomas	B. K. Yousif	Mr. and Mrs. Russell Bennett	Bill Marko	Larry Attard	Robert King
1982	Jean-Louis Levesque	D. G. Willmot	D. G. Willmot	Bill Marko	Lloyd Duffy	Richard Dos Ramos
1981	Jim Bentley	Dave Kapchinsky	Tom Webb	Ron Brock	Erwin Driedger	Richard Dos Ramos
1980	Jack Stafford	Ernest Samuel	Mr. and Mrs. Marvin Hamilton	Gerry Belanger	Gary Stahlbaum	Valerie Thompson
1979	George C. Hendrie	James Shields	D. G. Willmot	Jim Day	Robin Platts	Ray Creighton
1978	Ron Turcotte	Conn Smythe	Jean-Louis Levesque	F. H. Merrill	Sandy Hawley	Ron Hansen
1977	E. P. Taylor	Bory Margolus	Conn Smythe	Red Smith	Avelino Gomez	Brad Smythe
1976	Jack Diamond	George Gardiner	E. P. Taylor	Lou Cavalaris	Chris Rogers	Chris Loseth
1975	E. P. Taylor	Jack Stafford	Bory Margolus	Gil Rowntree	Hugo Dittfach	Jeff Fell

†Formerly known as Man of the Year

Edge and champion turf male Portcullis. Trained by Mark Casse, Woodbine's leading trainer by 2002 wins, Added Edge made a successful U.S. debut in winning Aqueduct's Nashua Stakes (G3) on November 2. Portcullis won the concluding Canadian classic race, the Breeders' Stakes, as well as the Toronto Cup Handicap (Can-G3) and the Charlie Barley Stakes.

The Jockey Club of Canada, which administers the awards, for the first time did not release a breakdown of the Horse of the Year voting, saying that it wanted to spare the runners-up any embarrassment.

For the second consecutive year, the Jockey Club of Canada did not present the E. P. Taylor Award, which is named for the legendary Canadian breeder and racing-association leader.

Individuals honored with Sovereign Awards:

Sam-Son Farm, outstanding breeder. The racing and breeding operation founded by the late Ernest Samuel collected its third consecutive title as outstanding breeder. Now headed by Samuel's widow, Liza, and daughter, Tammy, Sam-Son sent out the winners of 26 races and the earners of $3,560,278. Among others, Sam-Son bred and raced stakes winners Dancethruthedawn and Portcullis.

Stronach Stable, outstanding owner. An industrialist and chairman of racetrack conglomerate Magna Entertainment Inc., Frank Stronach had developed a formidable racing and breeding operation in Canada and the United States. Stronach's horses dominated races at Woodbine, winning 58 races in 2002 and accumulating $3,638,926 in purses. The 2002 title gave Stronach his seventh Sovereign as outstanding owner.

Roger Attfield, outstanding trainer. Training principally for Kinghaven Farms, Attfield took home his sixth Sovereign as champion trainer, albeit his first since 1993. He was Woodbine's leading trainer by earnings with more than $4-million, and he trained champion older female Small Promises, a two-time stakes winner whom he co-owned with Kinghaven.

Patrick Husbands, outstanding jockey. The Barbados-born rider made history in 2002 when he won a record fourth straight Sovereign as outstanding jockey. He was a dominating force at Woodbine, winning 167 races and accumulating purse earnings of more than $9-million. Among his mounts was Added Edge in Aqueduct's Nashua.

Chantal Sutherland, champion apprentice jockey. Sutherland collected a second Sovereign in the apprentice category after a productive year in which she finished third in the Woodbine standings, behind Husbands and Todd Kabel. Although she lost her apprentice allowance in early August 2002, she ended the year with 135 wins and purse earnings of $5.9-million.

History of the Sovereign Awards

Year	Broodmare of the Year	Two-Year-Old Filly	Two-Year-Old Male	Three-Year-Old Filly	Three-Year-Old Male
2002	First Class Gal	Brusque	Added Edge	Lady Shari	Le Cinquieme Essai
2001	Dance Smartly	Ginger Gold	Rare Friends	Dancethruthedawn	Win City
2000	Primarily	Poetically	Highland Legacy	Catch the Ring	Kiss a Native
1999	Sharpening Up	Hello Seattle	Exciting Story	Gandria	Woodcarver
1998	Fleet Courage	Fantasy Lake	Riddell's Creek	Kirby's Song	Archers Bay
1997	Charming Sassafras	Primaly	Dawson's Legacy	Cotton Carnival	Cryptocloser
1996	Amelia Bearhart	Larkwhistle	Cash Deposit	Silent Fleet	Victor Cooley
1995	Sea Regent	Silken Cat	Gomtuu	Scotzanna	Peaks and Valleys
1994	Rainbow Connection	Honky Tonk Tune	Talkin Man	Alywow	Bruce's Mill
1993	Bold Debra	Term Limits	Comet Shine	Deputy Jane West	Peteski
1992	Ballade	Deputy Jane West	Truth of It All	Hope for a Breeze	Benburb
1991	Classy 'n Smart	Buckys Solution	Free At Last	Dance Smartly	Bolulight
1990	Shy Spirit	Dance Smartly	Rainbows for Life	Lubicon	Izvestia
1989	Passing Mood	Wavering Girl	Sky Classic	Blushing Katy	With Approval
1988	Polite Lady	Legarto	Mercedes Won	Tilt My Halo	Regal Intention
1987	Arctic Vixen	Phoenix Factor	Regal Classic	One From Heaven	Afleet
1986	Loudrangle	Ruling Angel	Blue Finn	Carotene	Golden Choice
1985	No Class	Stage Flite	Grey Classic	La Lorgnette	Imperial Choice
1984	Friendly Ways	Deceit Dancer	Dauphin Fabuleux	Classy 'n Smart	Key to the Moon
1983	Two Rings	Ada Prospect	Prince Avatar	Northern Blossom	Bompago
1982	Yonnie Girl	Candle Bright	Sunny's Halo	Avowal	Runaway Groom
1981	Native Flower	Choral Group	Deputy Minister	Rainbow Connection	Frost King
1980	Hangin Round	Rainbow Connection	Bayford	Par Excellance	Ben Fab
1979	Fitz's Fancy	Par Excellance	Allan Blue	Kamar	Steady Growth
1978	Fanfreluche	Liz's Pride	Medaille d'Or	La Voyageuse	Overskate
1977	Doris White	L'Alezane	Overskate	Northernette	Dance in Time
1976	Northern Minx	Northernette	Sound Reason	Bye Bye Paris	Norcliffe
1975	Reasonable Wife	Seraphic	Proud Tobin	Momigi	L'Enjoleur

Horses honored with 2002 Sovereign Awards were:

Horse of the Year
Older male, Sprinter

WAKE AT NOON, 1997 ch. h., Cure the Blues—Sermon Time, by Silver Deputy. 2002 record: 11-6-0-2, $463,001. Career: 36-16-5-4, $1,260,821. Owner-breeder: Bruno Schickedanz (Can.). Trainer: Abraham R. Katryan. In 2002, won Highlander H. (Can-G3), Vigil H. (Can-G3), Jacques Cartier S., Briartic H.; 3rd Kennedy Road S., Bold Venture H.

Two-year-old male

ADDED EDGE, 2000 ch. c., Smart Strike—Sweet Nostalgia, by Mr. Redoy. Career record: 4-4-0-0, $250,328. Breeder: Gulf Coast Farms Bloodstock LP (Ky.). Owners: Team Valor and Robert J. Wilson. Trainer: Mark E. Casse. In 2002, won Nashua S. (G3), Swynford S., Silver Deputy S.

Two-year-old filly

BRUSQUE, 2000 ch. f., Canaveral—Privileged Speech, by General Assembly. Career record: 7-3-1-1, $260,964. Breeder: Wind Hill Farm (Ky.). Owner and trainer: Ronald A. Woods. In 2002, won Mazarine Breeders' Cup S. (Can-G2).

Three-year-old male

LE CINQUIEME ESSAI, 1999 ch. c., Fastness (Ire)—Words of Royalty, by Regal Classic. 2002 record: 6-4-0-0, $412,410. Career: 8-4-1-0, $423,395. Breeder: W. J. Scott (Can.). Owner: William R. Scott. Trainer: Paul Nielsen. In 2002, won Prince of Wales S.

Three-year-old filly

LADY SHARI, 1999 dk. b. or br. f., Judge T C—Badgering Shari, by Badger Land. 2002 record: 11-3-0-2, $316,506. Career: 18-5-3-3, $592,716. Breeders: Robert H. and Bea Roberts (Ky.). Owners: Dominion Bloodstock, Derek Ball, and Hugh Galbraith. Trainer: David Cotey. In 2002, won Maple Leaf S. (Can-G3), Canadian Derby (Can-G3); 3rd La Lorgnette S., Star Shoot S.

Older female

SMALL PROMISES, 1998 gr. or ro. f., Carson City—Promiseville, by Alwasmi. 2002 record: 9-4-1-1, $242,334. Career: 16-7-1-1, $411,006. Breeders: Kinghaven Farms Ltd. and Tracy Attfield (Can.). Owners: Kinghaven Farms and Roger Attfield. Trainer: Roger Attfield. In 2002, won Algoma S., H. A. Hindmarsh S.; 2nd Maple Leaf S. (Can-G3).

Turf male

PORTCULLIS, 1999 b. g., Smart Strike—

History of the Sovereign Awards

Year	Older Female	Older Male	Turf Female†	Turf Male	Sprinter	Horse of the Year
2002	Small Promises	Wake At Noon	Chopinina	Portcullis	Wake At Noon	Wake At Noon
2001	Mountain Angel	A Fleets Dancer	Sweetest Thing	Numerous Times	Mr. Epperson	Win City
2000	Saoirse	One Way Love	Heliotrope	Quiet Resolve	One Way Love	Quiet Resolve
1999	Magic Code	Deputy Inxs	Free Vacation	Thornfield	Deputy Inxs	Thornfield
1998	Santa Amelia	Terremoto	Colorful Vices	Chief Bearhart	Deputy Inxs	Chief Bearhart
1997	Woolloomooloo	Chief Bearhart	Woolloomooloo	Chief Bearhart	Glanmire	Chief Bearhart
1996	Windsharp	Mt. Sassafras	Windsharp	Chief Bearhart	Langfuhr	Mt. Sassafras
1995	Bold Ruritana	Basqueian	Bold Ruritana	Hasten To Add	Scotzanna	Peaks and Valleys
1994	Pennyhill Park	King Ruckus		Alywow	King Ruckus	Alywow
1993	Dance for Donna	Cozzene's Prince		Hero's Love	Apelia	Peteski
1992	Wilderness Song	Rainbows for Life		Rainbows for Life	King Corrie	Benburb
1991	Avant's Gold	Sky Classic		Sky Classic	King Corrie	Dance Smartly
1990	Diva's Debut	Twist the Snow		Izvestia	Twist the Snow	Izvestia
1989	Proper Evidence	Steady Power		Charlie Barley	Mr. Hot Shot	With Approval
1988	Carotene	Play the King		Carotene	Play the King	Play the King
1987	Carotene	Play the King		Carotene	Play the King	Afleet
1986	Bessarabian	Let's Go Blue		Carotene	New Connection	Ruling Angel
1985	Lake Country	Ten Gold Pots		Imperial Choice	Summer Mood	Imperial Choice
1984	Sintrillium	Canadian Factor		Bounding Away	Diapason	Dauphin Fabuleux
1983	Eternal Search	Travelling Victor		Kingsbridge	Fraud Squad	Travelling Victor
1982	Eternal Search	Frost King		Frost King	Avowal	Frost King
1981	Glorious Song	Driving Home		Ben Fab	Eternal Search	Deputy Minister
1980	Glorious Song	Overskate		Overskate	La Voyageuse	Glorious Song
1979	La Voyageuse	Overskate		Overskate		Overskate
1978	Christy's Mount	Giboulee		Overskate		Overskate
1977	Reasonable Win	Norcliffe		Momigi		L'Alezane
1976	Momigi	Victorian Prince		Victorian Prince		Norcliffe
1975	Victorian Queen	Rash Move		Victorian Queen		L'Enjoleur

†1995 marks the first year the award for turf horse to be divided into male and female categories.

Dancer's Gate, by Gate Dancer. 2002 record: 10-6-0-1, $562,535. Career: 11-6-0-1, $565,859. Breeder-owner: Sam-Son Farm (Can.). Trainer: Mark R. Frostad. In 2002, won Breeders' S., Toronto Cup H. (Can-G3), Charlie Barley S.

Turf female
CHOPININA, 1998 gr. or ro. f., Lear Fan—Lady Aloma, by Cozzene. 2002 record: 4-2-1-0, $292,280. Career: 11-4-1-1, $386,626. Breeder-owner: Knob Hill Stable (Can.). Trainer: Alec Fehr. In 2002, 2nd, Atto Mile S. (Can-G1).

Broodmare of the Year
FIRST CLASS GAL, 1988 b. m., Geiger Counter—Postage Stamp, by Ack Ack. Race record: 32-5-9-7, $125,548. Bred by Anderson Farms (Can.); owned by A. W. Minshall. Through 2002, dam of 4 foals, 4 starters, 3 winners, 2 stakes winners, 1 graded stakes winner, 1 champion. Dam of One Way Love (Regal Classic), 2000 champion sprinter and older male, winner of 2000 Autumn H. (Can-G3), Vigil H. (Can-G3), etc.; Runaway Love (Regal Classic), winner of 2002 Steady Growth S., Shepperton S., 2000 Deputy Minister S.

Canadian Horse Racing Hall of Fame

Founded in 1976, the Canadian Horse Racing Hall of Fame recognizes the people and horses who have established the roots of Canadian racing. The Hall of Fame was originally a list of inductees until a permanent site was established in 1997 at the west entrance of Woodbine. Memorabilia include Sir Barton's Triple Crown trophy.

Horses (Year inducted)
Afleet (1992)
Arise (1983)
Awesome Again (2001)
Belle Geste (1990)
Bull Page (1977)
Bunty Lawless (1976)
Canadiana (1978)
Casa Camara (2000)
Chief Bearhart (2002)
Chop Chop (1977)
Ciboulette (1983)
Dance Smartly (1995)
Deputy Minister (1988)
Duchess of York (1976)
E. Day (1989)
Fanfreluche (1981)
Flaming Page (1980)
Frost King (1986)
Gallant Kitty (1977)
George Royal (1976)
Glorious Song (1995)
Horometer (1976)
Inferno (1976)
Izvestia (1999)
Joey (1976)
Kennedy Road (2000)
Kingarvie (1976)
Langcrest (1984)
La Prevoyante (1976)
Major Presto (1982)
Martimas (2001)
Mona Bell (2000)
Nearctic (1977)
New Providence (1982)
Nijinsky II (1976)
No Class (1997)
Northern Dancer (1976)

Northernette (1987)
Overskate (1993)
Runaway Groom (2001)
Shepperton (1976)
Sir Barton (1976)
Sky Classic (1998)
South Shore (2000)
Sunny's Halo (1986)
Terror (1996)
The Minstrel (1979)
Vice Regent (1989)
Victoria Park (1976)
Windfields (2002)
With Approval (1993)
Yellow Rose (1996)
Youville (1977)

Jockeys
Ted Atkinson (2002)
Larry Attard (2001)
Hugo Dittfach (1983)
Jeff Fell (1993)
Jim Fitzsimmons (1984)
Norman "Dude" Foden (2000)
David Gall (1993)
Avelino Gomez (1977)
Sandy Hawley (1986)
Charles "Chick" Lang (1990)
Herb Lindberg (1991)
Charles Littlefield (2000)
John Longden (1976)
Don MacBeth (1988)
Frank Mann (2000)
Richard "Dick" O'Leary (2000)
Robin Platts (1997)
John "Red" Pollard (1982)
Pat Remillard (1979)
Chris Rogers (1977)

William "Smokey" Saunders (1976)
Don Seymour (1999)
Ron Turcotte (1980)
R. B. "Bobby" Watson (1998)
Headley Woodhouse (1980)
George Woolf (1976)

Trainers
A. E. "Burt" Alexandra (2002)
Roger Attfield (1999)
Macdonald "Mac" Benson (2002)
James "Jim" Bentley (1981)
Charles Boyle (2001)
W. H. "Bill" Bringloe (2000)
Donald "Duke" Campbell (1984)
Lou Cavalaris Jr. (1995)
John Dyment Jr. (2001)
Morris Fishman (2001)
Harry Giddings (1985)
R. K. "Doc" Hodgson (2001)
Gord Huntley (1998)
Lucien Laurin (1978)
Barry Littlefield (2000)
Edward "Ted" Mann (1982)
Gordon "Pete" McCann (1980)
Frank Merrill Jr. (1981)
J. C. "Jerry" Meyer (1999)
John Nixon (2002)
John Passero (2000)
Gil Rowntree (1997)
F. H. "Fred" Schelke (2002)
Joseph "Yonnie" Starr (1979)
Austin Irwin "Butch" Taylor (1987)
J. J. "Johnny" Thorpe (2002)
John R. Walker (2000)
Arthur Warner (1984)
James White (1996)
Ed Whyte (2001)

REFERENCE
Rules of Racing

The following model rules were developed by the Association of Racing Commissioners International. Although individual states implement their own regulations for how racing is conducted in their jurisdictions, the model rules combine both time-tested concepts and new developments in the Thoroughbred sport. The following rules encompass the running of the race. Other Association of Racing Commissioners International model rules cover such matters as racing officials, medications, and pari-mutuel wagering, among others.

I. Entries and nominations
A. Entering
No horse shall be qualified to start unless it has been and continues to be entered.

B. Procedure
1. Entries and nominations shall be made with the racing secretary and shall not be considered until received by the racing secretary, who shall maintain a record of time of receipt of them for a period of one year.

2. An entry shall be in the name of the horse's licensed owner and made by the owner, trainer, or a licensed designee of the owner or trainer.

3. Races printed in the condition book shall have preference over substitute and extra races.

4. An entry must be sent in writing, by telephone, or facsimile machine to the racing secretary. The entry must be confirmed in writing should the stewards or the racing secretary so request.

5. The person making an entry shall clearly designate the horse so entered.

6. No alteration may be made in any entry after the closing of entries, but an error may be corrected with permission of the stewards.

7. No horse may be entered in more than one race (with the exception of stakes races) to be run on the same day on which pari-mutuel wagering is conducted.

8. Any permitted medication or approved change of equipment must be declared at time of entry.

C. Limitation as to spouses
No entry in any race shall be accepted for a horse owned wholly or in part by, or trained by, a person whose husband or wife is under license suspension at time of such entry; except that, if the license of a jockey has been suspended for a routine riding offense, the stewards may waive this rule.

D. Coupled entries
1. Two or more horses entered in a race shall be joined as a mutuel entry and single betting interest if they are owned or leased in whole or in part by the same owner or are trained by a trainer who owns or leases any interest in any of the other horses in the race.

2. No more than two horses having common ties through ownership or training may be entered in an overnight race. Under no circumstances may both horses of a coupled entry start to the exclusion of a single entry. When making a coupled entry, a preference for one of the horses must be made.

3. No entry shall be coupled in any race in which the gross purse is $1-million or more.

4. In all races in which paragraph D. 3. applies, the racing secretary shall have the authority to establish a mutuel field and coupled entries in any race with more than 14 starters.

E. Nominations
1. Any nominator to a stakes race may transfer or declare such nomination prior to closing.

2. Joint nominations and entries may be made by any one of joint owners of a horse, and each such owner shall be jointly and severally liable for all payments due.

3. Death of a horse, or a mistake in its entry when such horse is eligible, does not release the nominator or transferee from liability for all stakes fees due. No fees paid in connection with a nomination to a stakes race that is run shall be refunded, except as otherwise stated in the conditions of a stakes race.

4. Death of a nominator to a stakes race shall not render void any subscription, entry, or right of entry. All rights, privileges, and obligations shall be attached to the legal heirs of the decedent or the successor owner of the horse.

5. When a horse is sold privately or at public auction or claimed, stakes engagements shall be transferred automatically to its new owner, except when the horse is transferred to a person whose license is suspended or who is otherwise disqualified to race or enter the horse; then such nomination shall be void as of the date of such transfer.

6. All stakes fees paid toward a stakes race shall be allocated to the winner unless otherwise provided by the conditions for the race. If a stakes race is not run for any reason, all such nomination fees paid shall be refunded.

F. Closings
1. Entries for purse races and nominations to stakes races shall close at the time designated by the association in previously published conditions for such races. No entry, nomination, or declaration shall be accepted after such closing time; except in the event of an emergency or if an overnight race fails to fill, the racing secretary may, with the approval of a steward, extend such closing time.

2. Except as otherwise provided in the conditions for a stakes race, the deadline for accepting nominations and declarations is midnight of the day of closing, provided they are received in time for compliance with every other condition of the race.

G. Number of starters in a race
The maximum number of starters in any race shall be limited to the number of starting positions afforded by the association starting gate and its extensions. The number of starters may be further limited by the number of horses that, in the opinion of the stewards, can be afforded a safe, fair, and equal start.

H. Split or divided races
1. In the event a race is canceled or declared off, the association may split any overnight race for which post positions have not been drawn.

2. Where an overnight race is split, forming two or more separate races, the racing secretary shall give notice of not less than 15 minutes before such races are closed to grant time for making additional entries to such split races.

I. Post positions

Post positions for all races shall be determined by lot and shall be publicly drawn in the presence of a steward or steward designee.

J. Also-eligible list

1. If the number of entries for a race exceeds the number of horses permitted to start, the racing secretary may create and post an also-eligible list.

2. If any horse is scratched from a race for which an also-eligible list was created, a replacement horse shall be drawn from the also-eligible list into the race in order of preference. If none is preferred, a horse shall be drawn into the race from the also-eligible list by public lot.

3. Any owner or trainer of a horse on the also-eligible list who does not wish to start the horse in such race shall so notify the racing secretary prior to scratch time for the race, thereby forfeiting any preference to which the horse may have been entitled.

4. A horse that draws into a straightaway race from the also-eligible list shall start from the post position vacated by the scratched horse. In the event more than one horse is scratched, post positions of horses drawing in from the also-eligible list shall be determined by public lot.

5. A horse that draws into a nonstraightaway race from the also-eligible list shall start from the outermost post position. In the event more than one horse is scratched, post positions of horses drawing in from the also-eligible list shall be determined by public lot.

K. Preferred list

The racing secretary shall maintain a list of entered horses eliminated from starting by a surplus of entries, and these horses shall constitute a preferred list and have preference. The manner in which the preferred list shall be maintained and all rules governing such list shall be the responsibility of the racing secretary. Such rules must be submitted to the racing commission 30 days prior to the commencement of the race meeting and are subject to the approval of the commission.

II. Declarations and scratches

Declarations and scratches are irrevocable.

A. Declarations

1. A "declaration" is the act of withdrawing an entered horse from a race prior to the closing of entries.

2. The declaration of a horse before closing shall be made by the owner, trainer, or their licensed designee in the form and manner prescribed in these rules.

B. Scratches

1. A "scratch" is the act of withdrawing an entered horse from a contest after the closing of entries.

2. The scratch of a horse after closing shall be made by the owner, trainer, or their licensed designee, with permission from the stewards.

3. A horse may be scratched from a stakes race for any reason at any time up until 45 minutes prior to post time for that race.

4. No horse may be scratched from an overnight race without approval of the stewards.

5. In overnight races, horses that are physically disabled or sick shall be permitted to be scratched first. Should horses representing more than ten betting interests in the daily double or exotic wagering races, or horses representing more than eight betting interests in any other overnight race, remain in after horses with physical excuses have been scratched, then owners or trainers may be permitted at scratch time to scratch horses without physical excuses down to such respective minimum numbers for such races. This privilege shall be determined by lot if an excessive number of owners or trainers wish to scratch their horses.

6. Entry of any horse that has been scratched or excused from starting by the stewards because of a physical disability or sickness shall not be accepted until the expiration of three racing days after such horse was scratched or excused and the horse has been removed from the Veterinarian's List by the official veterinarian.

III. Weights

A. Allowances

1. Weight allowance must be claimed at time of entry and shall not be waived after the posting of entries, except by consent of the stewards.

2. A horse shall start with only the allowance of weight to which it is entitled at time of starting, regardless of its allowance at time of entry.

3. Horses not entitled to the first weight allowance in a race shall not be entitled to any subsequent allowance specified in the conditions.

4. Claim of weight allowance to which a horse is not entitled shall not disqualify it unless protest is made in writing and lodged with the stewards at least one hour before post time for that race.

5. A horse shall not be given a weight allowance for failure to finish second or lower in any race.

6. No horse shall receive allowance of weight nor be relieved extra weight for having been beaten in one or more races, but this rule shall not prohibit maiden allowances or allowances to horses that have not won a race within a specified period or a race of a specified value.

7. Except in handicap races that expressly provide otherwise, two-year-old fillies shall be allowed three pounds, and fillies and mares three years old and upward shall be allowed five pounds before September 1 and three pounds thereafter in races where competing against male horses.

B. Penalties

1. Weight penalties are obligatory.

2. Horses incurring weight penalties for a race shall not be entitled to any weight allowance for that race.

3. No horse shall incur a weight penalty or be barred from any race for having been placed second or lower in any race.

4. Penalties incurred and allowances due in steeplechase or hurdle races shall not apply to races on the flat, and vice versa.

5. The reports, records, and statistics as published by *Daily Racing Form*, Equibase, or other recognized publications shall be considered official in determining eligibility, allowances, and penalties, but may be corrected.

IV. Workouts

A. Requirements

A horse shall not start unless it has participated in an official race or has an approved timed workout satisfactory to the stewards. The workout must have occurred at a pari-mutuel or commission-recognized facility within the previous 30 days. A horse that has not started for a period of 60 days or more shall be ineligible to race until it has completed a timed workout approved by the stewards prior to the day of the race in which the horse is entered. The association may impose more stringent workout requirements.

B. Identification

1. Unless otherwise prescribed by the stewards or the commission, the official lip tattoo must have been affixed to a horse's upper lip or other identification method approved by the appropriate breed registry and the commission applied prior to its participation in workouts from the gate, schooling races, or workouts required for removal from the Stewards' List, Starter's List, Veterinarian's List, or Bleeder List.

2. The trainer or exercise rider shall take each horse scheduled for an official workout to be identified by the clocker or clocker's assistant immediately prior to the workout.

3. A horse shall be properly identified by its lip tattoo or other identification method approved by the appropriate breed registry and the commission immediately prior to participating in an official timed workout.

4. The trainer or trainer's designee shall be required to identify the distance the horse is to be worked and the point on the track where the workout will start.

C. Information dissemination

Information regarding a horse's approved timed workout or workouts shall be furnished to the public prior to the start of the race for which the horse has been entered.

D. Restrictions

A horse shall not be taken onto the track for training or a workout except during hours designated by the association.

V. Ineligible horses

A horse is ineligible to start in a race when:

1. It is not stabled on the grounds of the association or present by the time established by the commission;

2. Its breed registration certificate is not on file with the racing secretary or horse identifier, unless the racing secretary has submitted the certificate to the appropriate breed registry for correction;

3. It is not fully identified and tattooed on the inside of the upper lip or identified by any other method approved by the appropriate breed registry and the commission;

4. It has been fraudulently entered or raced in any jurisdiction under a different name, with an altered registration certificate or altered lip tattoo or other identification method approved by the appropriate breed registry and the commission;

5. It is wholly or partially owned by a disqualified person or a horse is under the direct or indirect training or management of a disqualified person;

6. It is wholly or partially owned by the spouse of a disqualified person or a horse is under the direct or indirect management of the spouse of a disqualified person, in such cases, it being presumed that the disqualified person and spouse constitute a single financial entity with respect to the horse, which presumption may be rebutted;

7. The stakes or entrance money for the horse has not been paid in accordance with the conditions of the race;

8. The losing jockey mount fee is not on deposit with the horsemen's bookkeeper;

9. Its name appears on the Starter's List, Stewards' List, or Veterinarian's List;

10. It is a first-time starter and has not been approved to start by the starter;

11. It is owned in whole or in part by an undisclosed person or interest;

12. It lacks sufficient official published workouts or race past performance(s);

13. It has been entered in a stakes race and has subsequently been transferred with its engagements, unless the racing secretary has been notified of such prior to the start;

14. It is subject to a lien that has not been approved by the stewards and filed with the horsemen's bookkeeper;

15. It is subject to a lease not filed with the stewards;

16. It is not in sound racing condition;

17. It has had a surgical neurectomy performed on a heel nerve that has not been approved by the official veterinarian;

18. It has been trachea tubed to artificially assist breathing;

19. It has been blocked with alcohol or otherwise drugged or surgically denerved to desensitize the nerves above the ankle;

20. It has impaired eyesight in both eyes;

21. It is barred or suspended in any recognized jurisdiction;

22. It does not meet the eligibility conditions of the race;

23. Its owner or lessor is in arrears for any stakes fees, except with approval of the racing secretary;

24. Its owner(s), lessor(s), and/or trainer have not completed the licensing procedures required by the commission;

25. It is by an unknown sire or out of an unknown mare; or

26. There is no current negative test certificate for Equine Infectious Anemia attached to its breed registration certificate, as required by statute.

VI. Running of the race

A. Equipment

1. No whip shall be used unless it has affixed to the end of it a looped leather "popper" not less than 1¼ inches in width and not over 3 inches in length, and is "feathered" above the "popper" with not less than three rows of leather "feathers," each "feather" not less than 1 inch in length. No whip shall exceed 31 inches in length. All whips are subject to inspection and approval by the stewards.

2. No bridle shall exceed two pounds.

3. A horse's tongue may be tied down with clean bandages, gauze, or tongue strap.

4. No licensee may add blinkers to a horse's equipment or discontinue their use without the prior approval of the starter, the paddock judge, and the stewards.

5. No licensee may change any equipment used on a horse in its last race in this jurisdiction without approval of the paddock judge.

B. Racing numbers

1. Each horse shall carry a conspicuous saddlecloth number corresponding to the official number given that horse on the official program.

2. In the case of a coupled entry that includes more than one horse, each horse in the entry shall carry the same number, with a different distinguishing letter following the number. As an example, two horses in the same entry shall appear in the official program as 1 and 1A.

3. Each horse in the mutuel field shall carry a separate number or may carry the same number with a distinguishing letter following the number.

C. Jockey requirements

1. Jockeys shall report to the jockeys' quarters at the time designated by the association. Jockeys shall

report their engagements and any overweight to the clerk of scales. Jockeys shall not leave the jockeys' quarters except to ride in scheduled races until all of their riding engagements of the day have been fulfilled, except as approved by the stewards.

2. A jockey who has not fulfilled all riding engagements who desires to leave the jockeys' quarters must first receive the permission of the stewards and must be accompanied by an association security guard.

3. While in the jockeys' quarters, jockeys shall have no contact or communication with any person outside the jockeys' quarters other than commission personnel and officials, an owner or trainer for whom the jockey is riding, or a representative of the regular news media, except with the permission of the stewards. Any communication permitted by the stewards may be conducted only in the presence of the clerk of scales or other person designated by the stewards.

4. Jockeys shall be weighed out for their respective mounts by the clerk of scales not more than 30 minutes before post time for each race.

5. Only valets employed by the association shall assist jockeys in weighing out.

6. A jockey must wear a safety vest when riding in any official race. The safety vest shall weigh no more than two pounds and be designed to provide shock-absorbing protection to the upper body of at least a rating of five as defined by the British Equestrian Trade Association (BETA).

7. A jockey's weight shall include his or her clothing, boots, saddle and its attachments, and any other equipment except the whip, bridle, bit or reins, safety helmet, safety vest, blinkers, goggles, and number cloth.

8. Seven pounds is the limit of overweight any horse is permitted to carry.

9. Once jockeys have fulfilled their riding engagements for the day and have left the jockeys' quarters, they shall not be readmitted to the jockeys' quarters until after the entire racing program for that day has been completed, except with permission of the stewards.

D. Paddock to post

1. Each horse shall carry the full weight assigned for that race from the paddock to the starting post, and shall parade past the stewards' stand, unless excused by the stewards. The post parade shall not exceed 12 minutes, unless otherwise ordered by the stewards. It shall be the duty of the stewards to ensure that the horses arrive at the starting gate as near to post time as possible.

2. After the horses enter the track, no jockey may dismount nor entrust his horse to the care of an attendant unless, because of accident occurring to the jockey, the horse, or the equipment, and with the prior consent of the starter. During any delay during which a jockey is permitted to dismount, all other jockeys may dismount and their horses may be attended by others. After the horses enter the track, only the jockey, an assistant starter, the official veterinarian, the racing veterinarian, or an outrider or pony rider may touch the horse before the start of the race.

3. If a jockey is injured on the way to the post, the horse shall be returned to the paddock or any other area designated by the stewards, resaddled with the appropriate weight, and remounted with a replacement jockey.

4. After passing the stewards' stand in parade, the horses may break formation and proceed to the post in any manner unless otherwise directed by the stewards. Once at the post, the horses shall be started

without unnecessary delay.

5. Horses shall arrive at the starting post in post-position order.

6. In case of accident to a jockey or his or her mount or equipment, the stewards or the starter may permit the jockey to dismount and the horse to be cared for during the delay, and may permit all jockeys to dismount and all horses to be attended to during the delay.

7. If a horse throws its jockey on the way from the paddock to the post, the horse must be returned to the point where the jockey was thrown, where it shall be remounted and then proceed over the route of the parade to the post. The horse must carry its assigned weight from paddock to post and from post to finish.

8. If a horse leaves the course while moving from paddock to post, the horse shall be returned to the course at the nearest practical point to that at which it left the course, and shall complete its parade to the post from the point at which it left the course, unless ordered scratched by the stewards.

9. No person shall willfully delay the arrival of a horse at the post.

10. The starter shall load horses into the starting gate in any order deemed necessary to ensure a safe and fair start. Only the jockey, the racing veterinarian, the starter, or an assistant starter shall handle a horse at the post.

E. Post to finish
1. The start

a. The starter is responsible for assuring that each participant receives a fair start.

b. If, when the starter dispatches the field, any door at the front of the starting-gate stalls should not open properly due to a mechanical failure or malfunction or should any action by any starting personnel directly cause a horse to receive an unfair start, the stewards may declare such a horse a nonstarter.

c. Should a horse, not scratched prior to the start, not be in the starting-gate stall, thereby causing it to be left when the field is dispatched by the starter, the horse shall be declared a nonstarter by the stewards.

d. Should an accident or malfunction of the starting gate or other unforeseeable event compromise the fairness of the race or the safety of race participants, the stewards may declare individual horses to be nonstarters, exclude individual horses from one or more pari-mutuel pools, or declare a "no contest" and refund all wagers except as otherwise provided in the rules involving multirace wagers.

2. Interference, jostling, or striking

a. A jockey shall not ride carelessly or willfully so as to permit his or her mount to interfere with, impede, or intimidate any other horse in the race.

b. No jockey shall carelessly or willfully jostle, strike, or touch another jockey or another jockey's horse or equipment.

c. No jockey shall unnecessarily cause his or her horse to shorten its stride so as to give the appearance of having suffered a foul.

3. Maintaining a straight course

a. When the way is clear in a race, a horse may be ridden to any part of the course, but if any horse swerves or is ridden to either side so as to interfere with, impede, or intimidate any other horse, it is a foul.

b. The offending horse may be disqualified if, in the opinion of the stewards, the foul altered the finish of the race, regardless of whether the foul was accidental, willful, or the result of careless riding.

c. If the stewards determine the foul was intentional or due to careless riding, the jockey may be held responsible.

d. In a straightaway race, every horse must maintain position as nearly as possible in the lane in which it starts. If a horse is ridden, drifts, or swerves out of its lane in such a manner that it interferes with, impedes, or intimidates another horse, it is a foul and may result in the disqualification of the offending horse.

4. Disqualification

a. When the stewards determine that a horse shall be disqualified for interference, they may place the offending horse behind such horses as in their judgment it interfered with, or they may place it last.

b. If a horse is disqualified for a foul, any horse or horses with which it is coupled as an entry may also be disqualified.

c. When a horse is disqualified for interference in a time-trial race, for the purposes of qualifying only, it shall receive the time of the horse it is placed behind plus one-hundredth of a second penalty or more exact measurement if photo-finish equipment permits, and shall be eligible to qualify for the finals or consolations of the race on the basis of the assigned time.

d. Possession of any electrical or mechanical stimulating or shocking device by a jockey, horse owner, trainer, or other person authorized to handle or attend to a horse shall be prima-facie evidence of a violation of these rules and is sufficient grounds for the stewards to scratch or disqualify the horse.

e. The stewards may determine that a horse shall be unplaced for the purpose of purse distribution and time-trial qualification.

5. Horses shall be ridden out

All horses shall be ridden out in every race. A jockey shall not ease up or coast to the finish without reasonable cause, even if the horse has no apparent chance to win prize money. A jockey shall give a best effort during a race, and each horse shall be ridden to win.

6. Use of whips

a. Although the use of a whip is not required, any jockey who uses a whip during a race shall do so only in a manner consistent with exerting his or her best efforts to win.

b. In all races where a jockey will ride without a whip, an announcement of such fact shall be made over the public address system.

c. No electrical or mechanical device or other expedient designed to increase or retard the speed of a horse, other than the whip approved by the stewards, shall be possessed by anyone or applied by anyone to the horse at any time on the grounds of the association during the meeting, whether in a race or otherwise.

d. Whips shall not be used on two-year-old horses before April 1 of each year.

e. Prohibited use of the whip includes whipping a horse:

i. On the head, flanks, or on any other part of its body other than the shoulders or hindquarters except when necessary to control a horse;

ii. During the post parade or after the finish of the race except when necessary to control the horse;

iii. Excessively or brutally, causing welts or breaks in the skin;

iv. When the horse is clearly out of the race or has obtained its maximum placing;

v. Persistently even though the horse is showing no response under the whip; or

vi. Striking another rider or horse.

7. Horse leaving the racecourse

If a horse leaves the racecourse during a race, it must turn back and resume the race from the point at which it originally left the course.

8. Order of finish

a. The official order of finish shall be decided by the stewards with the aid of the photo-finish camera, and in the absence of the photo-finish film strip, the video replay. The photo finish and video replay are only aids in the stewards' decision. The decision of the stewards shall be final in all cases.

b. The nose of the horse shall determine the placement of the horse in relationship to other horses in the race.

9. Returning after the finish

a. After a race has been run, the jockey shall ride promptly to the place designated by the stewards, dismount, and report to the clerk of scales to be weighed in. Jockeys shall weigh in with all pieces of equipment with which they weighed out.

b. If a jockey is prevented from riding to the designated unsaddling area because of an accident or illness to the jockey or the horse, the jockey may walk or be transported to the scales or may be excused from weighing in by the stewards.

10. Unsaddling

a. Only persons authorized by the stewards may assist the jockey with unsaddling the horse after the race.

b. No one shall place a covering over a horse before it is unsaddled.

11. Weighing in

a. A jockey shall weigh in at least at the same weight at which he or she weighed out, and if under that weight by more than two pounds, his or her mount shall be disqualified from any portion of the purse money.

b. In the event of such disqualification, all money wagered on the horse shall be refunded unless the race has been declared official.

c. No jockey shall weigh in at more than two pounds over the proper or declared weight, excluding the weight attributed to inclement weather conditions and/or of health and safety equipment approved by the stewards.

12. Dead heats

a. When two horses run a dead heat for first place, all purses or prizes to which first and second horses would have been entitled shall be divided equally between them; and this principle applies in dividing all purses or prizes whatever the number of horses running a dead heat and whatever places for which the dead heat is run.

b. In a dead heat for first place, each horse involved shall be deemed a winner and liable to penalty for the amount it shall receive.

c. When a dead heat is run for second place and an objection is made to the winner of the race and sustained, the horses that ran a dead heat shall be deemed to have run a dead heat for first place.

d. If the dividing owners cannot agree as to which of them is to have a cup or other prize that cannot be divided, the question shall be determined by lot by the stewards.

VII. Protests, objections, and inquiries

A. Stewards to inquire

1. The stewards shall take cognizance of foul riding and, upon their own motion or that of any racing official or person empowered by this chapter to object or complain, shall make diligent inquiry or investigation into such objection or complaint when properly received.

2. In determining the extent of disqualification, the stewards in their discretion may:

a. Declare null and void a track record set or equaled by a disqualified horse or any horses coupled with it as an entry;

b. Affirm the placing judges' order of finish and hold the jockey responsible if, in the stewards' opinion, the foul riding did not affect the order of finish; or

c. Disqualify the offending horse and hold the jockey blameless if in the stewards' opinion the interference to another horse in a race was not the result of an intentional foul or careless riding on the part of a jockey.

B. Race objections

1. An objection to an incident alleged to have occurred during the running of a race shall be received only when lodged with the clerk of scales, the stewards, or their designees, by the owner, the trainer, or the jockey of a horse engaged in the same race.

2. An objection following the running of any race must be filed before the race is declared official, whether all or some riders are required to weigh in or the use of a "fast official" procedure is permitted.

3. The stewards shall make all findings of fact as to all matters occurring during and incident to the running of a race, shall determine all objections and inquiries, and shall determine the extent of disqualification, if any, of horses in the race. Such findings of fact and determinations shall be final.

C. Prior objections

1. Objections to the participation of a horse entered in any race shall be made to the stewards in writing, signed by the objector, and filed not later than one hour prior to post time for the first race on the day that the questioned horse is entered. Any such objection shall set forth the specific reason or grounds for the objection in such detail so as to establish probable cause for the objection. The stewards upon their own motion may consider an objection until such time as the horse becomes a starter.

2. An objection to a horse entered in a race may be made on, but not limited to, the following grounds or reasons:

a. A misstatement, error, or omission in the entry under which a horse is to run;

b. The horse entered to run is not the horse it is represented to be at the time of entry, or the age was erroneously given;

c. The horse is not qualified to enter under the conditions specified for the race, or the allowances are improperly claimed or not entitled the horse, or the weight to be carried is incorrect under the conditions of the race;

d. The horse is owned in whole or in part, or leased or trained by a person ineligible to participate in racing or otherwise ineligible to own a racehorse as provided in these rules; or

e. The horse was entered without regard to a lien filed previously with the racing secretary.

3. The stewards may scratch from the race any horse that is the subject of an objection if they have reasonable cause to believe that the objection is valid.

D. Protests

1. A protest against any horse that has started in a race shall be made to the stewards in writing, signed by the protestor, within 72 hours of the race exclusive of nonracing days. If the incident upon which the protest is based occurs within the last two days of the meeting, such protest may be filed with the commission within 72 hours exclusive of Saturdays, Sundays, or official holidays. Any such protest shall set forth the specific reason or reasons for the protest in such detail as to establish probable cause for the protest.

2. A protest may be made on any of the following grounds:

a. Any grounds for objection as set forth in this chapter;

b. The order of finish as officially determined by the stewards was incorrect due to oversight or errors in the numbers of the horses that started the race;

c. A jockey, trainer, owner, or lessor was ineligible to participate in racing as provided in this chapter;

d. The weight carried by a horse was improper by reason of fraud or willful misconduct; or

e. An unfair advantage was gained in violation of the rules.

3. Notwithstanding any other provision in this article, time limitation on the filing of protests shall not apply in any case in which fraud or willful misconduct is alleged, provided the stewards are satisfied that the allegations are bona fide and verifiable.

4. No person shall file any objection or protest knowing the same to be inaccurate, false, untruthful, or frivolous.

5. The stewards may order any purse, award, or prize for any race withheld from distribution pending the determination of any protest. In the event any purse, award, or prize has been distributed to an owner or for a horse that by reason of a protest or other reason is disqualified or determined to be not entitled to such purse, award, or prize, the stewards or the commission may order such purse, award, or prize returned and redistributed to the rightful owner or horse. Any person who fails to comply with an order to return any purse, award, or prize erroneously distributed shall be subject to fines and suspension.

Preference Date System

Racing secretaries long have struggled with two problems: Not enough horses for a race in the track's condition book, which details prospective races for the meet, and too many horses for a specific race.

When a race has too few entries, the racing-office staff must make calls to trainers and solicit them to enter horses in the race. This process is widely known as "hustling," and a starter that is entered into such a race is often referred to a "hustled horse."

A race with too many entrants offers a different set of problems. Often, the race can be split. When other overnight races on the card are slow to fill, a racing

secretary may choose to split a popular race, a maiden special weight race for instance, into two or three or more separate races.

If splitting a race is not feasible, the racing secretary needs a system that determines the 12 eligible horses that will get starting positions. Racing offices long used the "star system," under which a horse denied a starting place in an oversubscribed race was given a star. A horse excluded twice from a race would get two stars. Under the star system, horses with the most stars received preference for the next race with the same conditions.

Many tracks now have changed to a "preference date system," which is similar to the star system but simpler to maintain. In the preference date system, the horses with the earliest preference date get into the race first.

As an example of how the preference date rules system is used, following are the preference date rules of Golden Gate Fields and Bay Meadows Race Course in Northern California:

Preference Date System

All horses whose foal certificates are registered with the racing secretary on the first day of entries will receive an entry date for that day. Thereafter, horses will receive entry dates for the day their foal certificates are registered with the racing secretary. Such entry dates will be good for any category.

1. In all races, winners are preferred.

2. Maidens will not be eligible to receive an entry date in any race until their papers are on file with the racing office at the time of the draw. Entry dates for maidens are good for any maiden race.

3. Horses which are drawn into races and horses on the also-eligible list which draw into races will receive a running date corresponding to the date on which they are to run, and lose all dates previously held.

4. Horses on the Veterinarian's, Stewards' or Starter's list cannot establish a date. They will not be permitted to enter until they have been approved to start. Horses placed on these lists will keep their dates if they ran in the particular race in which they made the list. Horses that are scratched and placed on a list will be given a scratch date for the day of that race.

5. In all cases, an entry date takes preference over a running date of the same day and a running date takes preference over a scratch date of the same day.

6. Horses drawn on the overnight (either in the race or on the also-eligible) which scratch will lose their date and acquire a scratch date corresponding to the day of the race, unless otherwise specified by the stewards. Any horse on the also-eligible list that is declared will retain its preference date if the scratch is not activated.

Other scratched horses will be treated in the following manner:

a. Runaway in the paddock—Entry date for day of race.

b. Runaway in the post parade—Entry date for day of race.

c. Flip in the gate prior to the start—Scratch date for day of race.

d. Scratched for insufficient works—Scratch date for day of race.

e. Scratched because of incorrect markings—Scratch date for day of race.

f. Ineligible to race in which drawn into—Scratch date for day of race.

g. Scratched because of breakdown in transportation to the track—Retains original date.

h. Scratched at the gate and not put on any list—Scratch date for day of race.

i. Entered in the wrong race by delegated agent or trainer—Scratch date for day of race.

j. Horse hurt in gate due to accident involving another horse—Retains original date.

k. Horse left behind the gate—Retains original date.

7. Horses that have established a date at the current meeting will lose that preference date should they race elsewhere.

8. Stakes races are not considered in the preference date system.

9. In no way does the claiming, ownership transfer, or trainer transfer of a horse affect the preference date.

10. Maidens, when entered in a winners' race, will retain original date.

11. Horses entered will initially receive an entry date corresponding to the date on which they are entered.

12. A same-owner entry cannot exclude a single entry except when race preferences indicate otherwise. Trainers must declare at time of entry if he or she has a same-owner or different-owner entry in the race. All same-owner entries must have a declared first and second choice at entry time.

How Jockeys Are Paid

Leading jockeys often will be paid upfront fees when they travel to ride a horse in a stakes race, but most jockeys are compensated according to a table of fees based on race purse and finish position of the horse they ride. The Association of Racing Commissioners International's model rules of racing contain a suggested fee table, although fees vary from one track or state to another. Following is the Association of Racing Commissioners International's model fee schedule as published in its 2003 rules of racing.

In the absence of a written agreement, the following jockey mount fees apply:

Purse	Winning Mount	2nd-Place Mount	3rd-Place Mount	Losing Mount
$599 and Under	$33	$33	$33	$33
$600-699	$36	$33	$33	$33
$700-999	10% Win Purse	$33	$33	$33
$1,000-1,499	10% Win Purse	$33	$33	$33
$1,500-1,999	10% Win Purse	$35	$33	$33
$2,000-3,499	10% Win Purse	$45	$40	$38
$3,500-4,999	10% Win Purse	$55	$45	$40
$5,000-9,999	10% Win Purse	$65	$50	$45
$10,000-14,999	10% Win Purse	5% Place Purse	5% Show Purse	$50
$15,000-24,999	10% Win Purse	5% Place Purse	5% Show Purse	$55
$25,000-49,999	10% Win Purse	5% Place Purse	5% Show Purse	$65
$50,000-99,999	10% Win Purse	5% Place Purse	5% Show Purse	$80
$100,000 & Up	10% Win Purse	5% Place Purse	5% Show Purse	$105

How to Handicap a Race

Handicapping a horse race is fun and intellectually challenging, and it also can be profitable. That does not mean you are destined to retire to a life of luxury if you learn how to handicap, but you can have winning afternoons and even winning years at the racetrack.

There is no feeling in the world quite like the one when you have correctly handicapped a race, a feeling that is tangibly rewarded if you bet your selection. Picking a winner evokes a feeling of pride, as well as bragging rights with your friends. Handicapping is an intellectual exercise, a skill that should improve as you become more experienced—as long as you are realistic.

Wagering at racetracks is pari-mutuel, which means bettors are competing against other bettors every single race. (See following section on pari-mutuel wagering and odds.) There is no single right way to handicap. But a good start is setting up a realistic framework.

Framework of reality

You are not going to win every race. Nobody does. No person has the magic answer to crank out winner after winner—not public handicappers, the expensive daily sheets, speed handicappers, system players, or your Aunt Tillie betting her favorite colors.

The reality of horse racing is that, year after year, at every track in North America, favorites in Thoroughbred racing win 25%-35% of the time. In other words, the betting public is wrong two out of three times. If you can correctly handicap vulnerable favorites, you will be able to identify overlays, which are horses whose odds are higher than they should be. Correctly finding one or two overlays can allow you to have a successful afternoon. An underlay is a horse whose odds are shorter than justified by past performances or physical condition.

A fundamental point here is that there is a difference between handicapping and wagering. Money management, deciding which races to bet and how to bet them, with a myriad of options available, is an entirely different ballgame. But, money management also is a skill you can hone. For now, remember, there are no rules saying you have to bet every race or even any race.

Reading past performance lines

The raw materials for handicapping any race are the past-performance lines, the statistical picture of each horse's previous starts. These past-performance lines can be found in *Daily Racing Form* or a program published by the track. The *Racing Form*, which is a newspaper, provides more information in its past-performance lines than the track program, which is printed in a magazine format.

To understand the past-performance lines, you

Track condition abbreviations

Thoroughbred racing is contested on dirt and turf, the latter also called grass. The abbreviations for track conditions:

Dirt	Turf
ft: fast	**hd:** hard
gd: good	**fm:** firm
sy: sloppy	**gd:** good
my: muddy	**yl:** yielding
	sf: soft

---

must first learn the abbreviations and terms in the accompanying boxes. You cannot handicap without reading and comprehending past-performance lines; doing so is easier than it appears.

The conditions for each race appear at the top of all the horses' past-performance lines, defining which horses are eligible. The race may be limited to fillies, two-year-olds, horses that have only won a certain number of races or a certain amount of money, or horses bred in a particular state. If it is a claiming race, the claiming, or purchase price is indicated.

The horses' names are listed in post-position order in the *Racing Form*. A track program lists the horses by the numbers they will be wearing on their saddlecloths in the race. That is the number you will use when placing a bet.

In case of an entry—when one betting number covers more than one horse because two horses have the same trainer or the same owner—horses will be designated as 1 and 1A. The horse closest to the rail will be 1, the other 1A. If there is a second entry in the same race, those two horses will be designated 2 and 2B. A single bet covers both horses in an entry.

Located just above the program numbers are the preliminary odds set by a racetrack employee to reflect how she or he believes the betting in that race will proceed. These are known as morning-line or program-line odds.

Now, let's examine a single past-performance line, that of 2002 Kentucky Derby (G1) winner War Emblem for the 2002 Preakness Stakes (G1) at Pimlico Race Course on May 18. (These past performances are courtesy of Equibase LLC, which provides past-performance information to both *Daily Racing Form* and track programs.)

Each horse's name is accompanied with specific information about that horse: color (dark bay or brown), age (3), sire (Our Emblem), dam (Sweetest Lady), sire of the dam (Lord At War [Arg]), where he was bred (Kentucky), and who bred him (Charles Nuckols Jr. & Sons). The letter L in parentheses after War Emblem's name indicates that he will be treated with an antibleeding medication in this race.

3-1 **WAR EMBLEM (L)**

8

Dk B/Br.c.3 Our Emblem - Sweetest Lady by Lord At War (ARG) **126**

Bred in KY by CHARLES NUCKOLS JR. & SONS

WHITE, green braces & stripes on white sleeve, green cap

Owner: THE THOROUGHBRED CORP.

Trainer: BOB BAFFERT

Jockey: VICTOR ESPINOZA

2002:	5	3	0	0	$2,205,000
2001:	3	2	0	0	$36,000
Life:	8	5	0	0	$2,241,000
Turf:	1	0	0	0	$0
Off Dirt:	0	0	0	0	$0

04May02	CD9	ft	1¼	$:47^{04}$	$1:36^{70}$	$2:01^{13}$	3	Ky Derby(G1)-2175k	96	5	$1^{1\,1/2}$	$1^{1\,1/2}$	$1^{1\,1/2}$	$1^{1\,1/2}$	1^{4}	EspinozaV	126	L	20.50	$WrEmblm126^{4}PrdCitizen126^{3/4}PrfctDrift126^{3\,1/2}$	pace, 3w, hand urging	18
06Apr02	Spt8	ft	1⅛	$:48^{30}$	$1:13^{03}$	$1:49^{92}$	3	IllDerby(G2)-500k	100	4	$1^{1\,1/2}$	$1^{1\,1/2}$	$1^{2\,1/2}$	1^{5}	$1^{6\,1/4}$	Sterling JrL	114	L	6.30	$WarEmblem114^{6\,1/4}Repent124^{4\,1/2}Fonz's117^{6\,1/2}$	ridden out	9
17Mar02	Spt8	ft	1	$:47^{06}$	$1:12^{46}$	$1:39^{22}$	3	Alw69570	88	1	1^{1}	$1^{1\,1/2}$	$1^{1\,1/2}$	1^{3}	$1^{10\,3/4}$	Juarez JrA	118	L	*.80	$WarEmblem118^{10\,3/4}ColorfulTour121^{3}BostonCommon115^{8}$	driving	6
17Feb02	FG9	ft	1$\frac{1}{16}$	$:46^{12}$	$1:11^{27}$	$1:43^{17}$	3	RisenStr(G3)-150k	80	3	3^{1}	4^{2}	$4^{1\,3/4}$	7^{6}	$6^{9\,3/4}$	TheriotJ	117	L	38.80	$Rpent122^{2\,1/4}Bb'sImage115^{3}Esyfromthegitgo122^{2\,1/4}$	ranged up 3w, faded	9
26Jan02	FG9	ft	1	$:47^{48}$	$1:12^{01}$	$1:37^{96}$	3	Lecomte-100k	86	3	2^{hd}	$1^{1/2}$	$1^{1/2}$	$2^{1/2}$	5^{2}	TheriotJ	117	L	12.40	$Esyfromthegitgo114^{ns}SkyTrce119^{3/4}It'sInthchse122^{1/4}$	faltered final 1/16th	11

Workouts: 14May02 CD 5 ft 1:03.20 b 20/26 30Apr02 CD 5 ft 1:00.40 b 7/34

(L) - Treated with furosemide; (L*) - First time using furosemide; (O) Off of furosemide

Copyright 2002 Equibase Company LLC

Underneath that information is a description of the owner's silks (white, green braces and stripes on white sleeve, green cap), the weight he will carry (126 pounds), and the names of the owner (The Thoroughbred Corp.), trainer (Bob Baffert), and jockey (Victor Espinoza).

The horse's race record is in the upper right. It contains the racing record for the current season and the previous year—number of starts, followed by wins, seconds, thirds, and earnings—a lifetime record, and the horse's record on turf and off dirt (wet) tracks. Before the Preakness, War Emblem had never raced on a wet track.

Beneath all that information are the horse's past performances. Each line is a summary of that horse's performance in a race, starting with the most recent race on top.

The past-performance line can be split into thirds. Let's start with the left one-third of War Emblem's last start, the Kentucky Derby:

04May02 CD9 ft 1¼ :47.04 1:36.70 2:01.13 3 Ky Derby(G1) 2175K

In order, this identifies War Emblem's most recent race, May 4, 2002, which was the ninth race at Churchill Downs (CD9). The track condition was fast (ft), and the distance of the race was 1¼ miles. Next are the fractions of that race. Equibase past-performance lines at this distance list only the time of the race leader after a half-mile (47.04 seconds), after one mile (one minute and 36.70 seconds), and the final time of the winner, two minutes and 1.13 seconds (2:01.13). War Emblem is three years old (3). *Daily Racing Form* gives additional fractions of the race, which can be useful in handicapping.

The name of the race was the Kentucky Derby (Ky Derby), and it is a Grade 1 stakes (G1), meaning that it was one of the 101 highest-ranked stakes races in the United States that year. Next is the purse of the race, $2,175,000 (2175K). The actual purse of the Kentucky Derby was $1,175,000, but War Emblem earned a $1-million bonus for winning both the Illinois Derby (G2) and Kentucky Derby. The bonus was added to the Derby purse, though the bonus was paid by the Illinois Derby's host track, Sportsman's Park, which sponsored the bonus to attract better horses to its signature race.

The next set of numbers reveals how the race was run and gives additional information on War Emblem.

96 5 $1^{1\,1/2}$ $1^{1\,1/2}$ $1^{1\,1/2}$ $1^{1\,1/2}$ 1^{4} EspinozaV 126 L

The first number, 96, was War Emblem's speed rating in the Derby. The higher the number, the better the race. (In general, any speed rating above 90 is considered very good.) The speed figure is an effort to give War Emblem's race an absolute rating so it can be compared to other races at other tracks and at other distances. Equibase employees are responsible for the speed ratings in track programs, while *Racing Form* speed ratings are compiled by Andrew Beyer.

The next number, 5, was War Emblem's post position, meaning he was the fifth horse out from the rail in the starting gate. The numbers with superscript figures tell how War Emblem ran his race. The first number indicates War Emblem was first after a half-mile by 1½ lengths ($1^{1\,1/2}$). He was again first by 1½ lengths at the second point of call of the race, after three-quarters of a mile. He was first by the same 1½ lengths at the third point of call after one mile, which is the top of Churchill's stretch. He still held a 1½-length lead at the stretch call, which is always one-eighth mile (one furlong) from the finish line. The final set of numbers indicates that War Emblem won the Kentucky Derby by four lengths (1^{4}). In summary, War Emblem led at every point of call and pulled away in deep stretch.

Next in the past-performance line is the jockey's name (EspinozaV) and the weight he carried, 126 pounds. All horses in the Kentucky Derby carry the same weight, although fillies get a five-pound break in the weights and carry 121 pounds. The capital letter L indicates War Emblem was treated with the diuretic furosemide, an antibleeding medication that for decades was known by the trade name Lasix. The veterinary formulation now is sold under the trade name Salix. Some horses improve dramatically the first time they are treated with the medication.

Now, let's look at the final third of the past-performance line.

20.50 $WrEmblem126^{4}$ $PrdCitizen126^{3/4}$ $PrfctDrift126^{3\,1/4}$

pace,3W,hand urging 18

The first number (20.50) is War Emblem's final odds, 20.50-to-1. The odds are followed by the names of the top three finishers, each with their weight carried and the distance they finished ahead of the horse immediately behind them. War Emblem finished four lengths in front of Proud Citizen, who finished second. In turn, Proud Citizen was three-quarters of a length in front of third-place finisher Perfect Drift, who finished 3¼ lengths ahead of the fourth-place finisher (Medaglia d'Oro). The summary of the finish is followed by a description of War Emblem's performance. He set the pace (pace), while racing three widths off the inside rail (3W), and won under hand urging, which means the jockey never used his whip. The final number, 18, indicates the number of horses in the race; the 2002 Kentucky Derby had 18 starters.

Beneath the horse's past-performance lines are its most recent workouts with the date, the racetrack or training center where the workout occurred, the time, whether the horse was breezing (not at full speed) or working handily (under urging from his rider), and how that workout compared with all the horses that worked the same distance that morning on that particular track. Workouts can be very important, especially for horses coming off layoffs and for first-time starters.

War Emblem showed:

Workouts: 14May02 CD 5 ft 1:03.20 b 20/26 30Apr02 CD 5 ft 1:00.40 b 7/34

On May 14 (14May02), four days prior to his start in the Preakness, War Emblem was given a workout at Churchill Downs (CD). He went five furlongs (5) on a fast track (ft) in 1:03.20 while breezing (b). It was meant to be an easy workout, and the rank (20/26) indicated that only six workouts at the distance were slower than his.

Before the Kentucky Derby on May 4, War Emblem had had a much faster workout at Churchill, going five furlongs in 1:00.40, which was the seventh-fasted of 34 horses (7/34) clocked at five furlongs on April 30. If a horse has the fastest workout of that morning at any distance, it is designated by a typographer's bullet in front of the workout information. Those workouts are commonly referred to as bullet workouts.

Both track program and *Daily Racing Form* past-performance lines provide a bare outline of a race. The full details are found in the charts, which are compiled by Equibase at North American tracks. The charts provide more detailed information on how the race was run and footnotes that describe each horse's trip in that race. Serious handicappers will frequently save all the charts from one track to provide details unavailable in the past-performance lines because of space limitations. (For more on how to read a chart, see "Handicapping a Sample Race.")

Three Schools of Handicapping

There are three main schools of handicapping, each posing different questions. Class asks: How much ability has this horse shown, and what has been the quality of its competition? Form asks: How has this horse performed most recently, and how is it likely to race today? Speed simply asks: How fast is this horse?

Handicappers have been arguing for decades over the relative importance of the three schools. An understanding of each will aid your handicapping.

Class

Class can be measured by the level of competition the horse has faced in its prior races. For this reason, past-performance lines should be read from the bottom line (least recent) to the top (most recent) to see how a horse is coming into today's race and whether it has previously

---

Types of bets

Win Your horse must finish first to collect.

Place Your horse must finish first or second.

Show Your horse must finish first, second, or third.

Quinella You bet two horses and they must finish first and second in either order.

Exacta You bet two horses and they must finish first and second in exact order.

Exacta box A multiple bet in which you select two or more horses and bet all combinations of them finishing first and second.

Exacta wheel You bet one horse to win and every other horse in the field to finish second.

Trifecta or triple You bet three horses and they must finish first, second, and third in exact order.

Trifecta box or triple box A multiple bet in which you select three or more horses and they must finish first, second, and third in any order.

Superfecta You bet four horses and they must finish first, second, third, and fourth in exact order.

Superfecta box You bet four or more horses and they must finish first, second, third, and fourth in any order.

Daily (or instant, late, or middle) double You must pick the winners of two consecutive races.

Pick three or pick four You must pick the winners of three or four consecutive races.

Pick six You must pick the winners of six consecutive races. There is usually a consolation payoff for those who pick five winners.

faced other horses in this race. (See box, "How to Improve Your Handicapping.") Let's say you are handicapping a race for $10,000 claimers. Horse A's last race was in an $8,000 claimer, which he won. He is now moving up to $10,000. But previously in his past-performance lines, he may have already run in $10,000 claiming races or for an even higher claiming price. How he previously performed at that level could be vital information in evaluating his chances when moving up to the $10,000 level today.

A second gauge of class is a horse's average earnings per start. Horse B has made $50,000 in his career from ten starts. Horse C has made $55,000 in his career from 25 starts. Horse B's average earnings per start, $5,000, is considerably higher than Horse C, whose average per start is $2,200. Be aware, though, that money does not mean everything. Earnings in races restricted to horses bred in one state—for example, those bred in New York or New Jersey—can inflate a horse's earnings and present a distorted picture of its ability to compete in the race you are handicapping.

A third way to measure class is by the number of wins a horse has or does not have. Chronic losers should be avoided. If a maiden has had ten or more starts without a win, stay away. If an allowance horse has had 15 starts or more with only one win, stay away. This strategy may not work every time, but in the long run you will save yourself a lot of money by avoiding horses that find a way to lose and frequently are over-bet because they often come close to winning.

Form

Horses are athletes, not machines. Even the best horses cannot maintain their highest level of performance for an extended period of time, which is why Cigar's 16-race winning streak in the mid-1990s was so remarkable.

Experienced horses tend to run in form cycles. They are either moving forward or backward. Many times, horses tip off which direction they are headed in a previous race, a workout, or both. If a horse had been performing very poorly for several races and then showed a sign of life by rallying from ninth to fourth, it may very well improve again in its next start and win.

If a horse that had been racing well throws in a poor performance, the handicapper must ask whether there was a legitimate excuse. Did the horse get overextended in a speed duel, get

---

Racing terms and comments

Here are some terms commonly used in racing news stories and chart footnotes. Additional terms can by found in the following section, Glossary of Racing Terms.

Apprentice A rider at the beginning of his career. Horses with apprentice jockeys carry five, seven, or ten pounds less than their rivals.

Bolted The horse made a sharp, sudden move to the extreme outside.

Bore in or bore out Instead of racing in a straight line, the horse veered inside or outside.

Boxed in The horse was trapped with nowhere to move.

Brushed The horse made light contact with another horse.

Dogs Pylons or traffic cones put around a course to protect the area on the inside near the rail. Horses that work around dogs cover more distance on turns. The symbol (d) is used to denote dogs were up in a workout.

Driving The horse was all out to win.

Entry Two or more horses are coupled in the wagering because of common ownership or, in some jurisdictions, the same trainer. You bet on one and collect if either member of the entry wins.

Field Two or more horses coupled as one betting entity. Just as in an entry, you get more than one horse and collect if any horse in the field wins.

Furlong One-eighth of a mile.

Furosemide A diuretic commonly used in American Thoroughbred racing to prevent or limit pulmonary bleeding. Trade name is Salix (formerly Lasix).

Gamely The horse showed courage while racing.

Greenly The horse showed inexperience by racing erratically.

Handily The horse won comfortably.

Hung The horse made an apparent winning move but then failed to sustain it.

Ridden out The jockey continued to ride the winning horse to the wire without undo urging.

Route A race of one mile or longer.

Saved ground The horse raced on the inside, thereby taking a shorter route around the track.

Sprint A race shorter than one mile.

Steadied The jockey had to physically stop his riding motion because of traffic problems.

Taken up The jockey had to restrain his horse severely, usually because of traffic problems or interference.

Unruly The horse acted up before the start.

Used up The horse expended all its energy by contesting the pace early in the race.

Willingly The horse continued to run its best without urging.

forced wide, or run into traffic? Did that problem cause the poor effort or simply disguise diminished form? Again, going through all the horse's past-performance lines will frequently provide clues. If a horse races wide in four of five starts, there is a likelihood it will do so again if it draws an outside post position.

You should expect young horses to improve. For example, in a seven-furlong maiden special weight race at Belmont Park on October 3, 2002, a field of 12 New York-bred two-year-olds went to post. Of the seven who had raced previously, Fly Our Flag, Sicilian Princess, and Katies Danza had had the most promising efforts.

Fly Our Flag had finished behind both Katies Danza and Sicilian Princess in separate races. Sicilian Princess was adding the antibleeding medication furosemide (Salix) after running second by a neck at 3.75-to-1 and fourth at 4.80-to-1 in her first two starts, respectively. Horses receiving the antibleeding medication for the first time frequently improve, sometimes dramatically, and she went off as the 8-to-5 favorite.

Katies Danza had been third at 36.25-to-1 in her debut. She then ran poorly on a sloppy track at Saratoga at 24.25-to-1 with Salix added, but in her prior start on a fast track she had dueled for the lead, fell back to fourth, 6½ lengths off the leader, and finished second by three lengths at 5.60-to-1, earning the rare comment at the end of her past-performance line: "Came again for place." It is rare to see any horse come back after losing the lead, let alone a two-year-old filly. She had shown great desire and was adding blinkers off a good workout. Nonetheless, she went off at 9.30-to-1, a decided overlay.

Among five first-time starters, Doubtful Diva had been training at Finger Lakes racetrack in western New York. While racing at Finger Lakes is not the same quality as Belmont, two-year-olds from Finger Lakes sometimes do well at Saratoga Race Course and Belmont. Doubtful Diva had had a three-furlong bullet workout, and, of greater importance, a bullet six-furlong workout of 1:15.80 prior to her debut for trainer John Progno, who had won with 18% of his 17 first-time starters that year.

The track selections were Katies Danza, Sicilian Princess, and Doubtful Diva, who went off at 49.25-to-1. Katies Danza broke sharply, took the lead heading into the far turn, opened a 2½-length lead, and then drifted out badly, allowing her to be caught by both Doubtful Diva, who won by 1½ lengths, and Sicilian Princess, who beat Katies Danza by three-quarters of a length for second. Doubtful Diva paid $100.50 for a $2 win ticket.

Speed

If every race went to the horse with the highest speed figure, racing would become quite boring and not much fun to bet on. Speed is part of the equation, not the answer. Speed must always be considered in context. If a horse is a front-runner with good, early speed, is he the lone speed in the race? Or will he be pressured? And, if so,

---

Five Ways to Improve Your Handicapping

1. Always handicap past performance lines from the bottom (least recent) to the top. This strategy will definitely give you an edge on other bettors who only handicap a horse's most recent few races. This process helps you to find potentially important information. Maybe two or more of the horses in this race competed against each other previously, and perhaps more than once.

2. Get and use as much pertinent information as you can. Read the analysis boxes in *Daily Racing Form* next to a horse's past-performance lines. Use the significant statistics that the *Form* provides underneath each horse's past-performance lines, such as a trainer's record with two-year-olds or with layoff horses or switching a horse from dirt to grass. Subscribe to THOROUGHBRED TIMES and peruse the sire statistics, especially for grass horses and two-year-olds. The more you learn, the better handicapper you become.

3. Improve your knowledge of odds, wet-track horses, and horses' ability to race on grass based on their breeding. When you study a race, write down what you think the final odds will be and then see how they compare with the actual final odds. For a turf race or a race on a wet track, write down who you think will perform well. Do the same thing with two-year-olds. Then see how they do. These are exercises that will only take you a couple minutes, and in time you will develop a better sense of the game.

4. Watch as many races as you can. Watch the replays of the prior day's races shown before the first race every day, or videotape the late-night recap shows on television that some tracks offer. If your track or off-track betting facility has a replay center where you can look up most horses' last race or several recent races, make use of it. Watch for horses that had trouble and legitimate excuses for a bad finish.

5. Cross out a horse's irrelevant past performance lines, such as grass races when handicapping a dirt race. With a stroke of pen or pencil, you can wipe out starts that are immaterial to today's race and concentrate on the pertinent starts.

how hard will he be pressed?

There is a world of difference between a horse running loose on the lead—running freely without pressure from other horses—and being pressed hard on the lead by one or more others. If there are three speed horses in race, has any one of them ever rated from just off the pace? If so, has that horse won when doing so? Maybe the horse has a past-performance line four races back with that same scenario.

This is another reason to go over a horse's past-performance lines from the bottom up. For example, a race might contain three speed horses—they usually break sharply from the gate and dictate the early pace of the race. Examine the three speed horses' opening quarter-mile and half-mile times in each of their races. If one of them routinely runs a quarter in :22 and a half in :45, while the other two show :23 and :46 splits, it is reasonable to assume the other two horses will not make the lead and therefore should be discarded.

If a horse has shown speed and tired under early pressure, make sure it will be pressured again in today's race. If not, it may be able to go gate to wire, which means leading from start to finish. Also, some speed horses must be on the lead to win, and watch out for those that will not extend themselves when they do not make the lead.

Always be sure to differentiate speed in sprints from speed in races at one mile or longer, which are known as route races. A front-runner in a longer race may be able to determine the early pace while running the first half-mile in 48 seconds. If entered in a sprint, the same horse might be required to run a :46 half-mile to be on the lead.

What is good speed?

Almost any Thoroughbred can go a furlong (one-eighth mile) in 12 seconds (:12) and two furlongs in :24. Maintaining or exceeding that rate an additional furlong or furlongs constitutes a sharp workout, be it three furlongs in :36, or four furlongs in :48. The farther the workout, the more impressive the move. Factor in that training tracks are slower than main tracks, so a good workout on a training track should be given greater consideration.

Changes

Change is good, sometimes. Change is worth noting all the time, be it equipment, the use of Salix, track surface, or a change in jockey, trainer, or both. The most common equipment change is the addition or removal of blinkers. Blinkers tend to keep a horse more focused because its field of sight has been narrowed. Subsequently, most horses adding blinkers show more early speed. Conversely, horses that have blinkers removed may show less speed. Again, it is important to check a horse's past-performance lines to see whether it had ever raced with (or

without) blinkers and how it performed.

Horses using Salix for the first time frequently improve greatly. Other horses improve the second time they use Salix, presumably because they become accustomed to its diuretic effects. Past performances in *Daily Racing Form* and some past-performance programs reveal how much of a difference Salix can make. For example, Live Doppler finished fourth by 18½ lengths in a one-mile, $25,000 maiden claimer at Aqueduct without Salix in on March 21, 2001. Treated with Salix a few hours before his next race under the same conditions and at the same distance, he finished second by 2½ lengths. It was the same track, same distance, and same level of competition, but a vastly different result.

A change from dirt to grass or vice versa can be a defining moment for many horses. Many times, there is absolutely no connection between a horse's form on dirt and grass. We need only think of Cigar, a superstar on dirt and just another horse on turf. When a horse has raced on dirt and is making its first grass start, check *Daily Racing Form* statistics for the trainer's record with first-time turf horses and read the *Form*'s analysis of the race, which frequently discusses that horse's grass pedigree.

Jockey changes can be important if there is a significant difference in the two riders' abilities. When a horse switches riders from a Gary Stevens to a Jerry Bailey, the impact is minimal because they are both Racing Hall of Fame jockeys. A switch from a jockey with a poor record to Bailey or vice versa is significant. When there is a rider switch, check the two riders' records.

Jockeys, just like horses, can perform at different levels on dirt and grass. Bailey is one of the top jockeys on dirt, but on grass he is in a class by himself. Other jockeys win less frequently in turf races. Usually, apprentices do better on dirt than on grass.

Layoffs

Once a horse has resumed racing after a layoff, there should not be long gaps between its races or in its workouts. These absences often are a sign of unsoundness. If a horse races well, shows no workouts for a month, and then races again, be wary. If there is a gap of more than a month between workouts, something most likely happened to stop this horse's training.

Use the statistics in the *Daily Racing Form* to see a trainer's percentage of winners with horses off significant layoffs. And go through the horse's past-performance lines from the bottom up to see if he has ever raced off similar layoffs. If he has raced off layoffs, how did he do?

Post positions

Post positions are extremely important in turf racing because most turf courses are inside the main dirt track, thus making the turns much

Types of Races

allowance race A race for which eligibility and weight to be carried are determined by the specific conditions of the race, such as number of career wins, earnings, or time since last win. The lowest-level allowance race is for horses that have not won one race other than maiden or claiming. At the highest level, allowance conditions are written for horses that have not won a specific amount of purse money in their career or within a specified period of time, such as $100,000 in the previous 12 months, or, for example, nonwinners of two races worth $40,000 (usually referring to the purse to the winner) since March 15. Allowance races are generally the second-best type of race on a card, behind stakes races.

claiming race A race for horses that can be purchased (claimed) immediately from that race for the price specified at the time of entry. The claimed horse becomes the new owner's property as soon as the starting gate opens, regardless if the horse finishes, but the previous owner collects any purse money earned by the claimed horse from that race. Claims must be entered before the race, usually ten to 15 minutes before post time depending on the state rules, and they can be made only by a person who has had a horse claimed at the same meeting or has received a claim certificate from the stewards. If more than one owner puts in a claim for the same horse, the disposition of the horse is determined by lot by the stewards. Claiming races are generally of lower class than allowance races. The lower the claiming price, the lower the class, and also the lower the purse.

futurity A stakes race, usually for two-year-olds, that is restricted to horses whose owners have made nomination payments shortly after the horse's birth and subsequently have made sustaining payments to maintain the horse's eligibility. As field sizes and quality of futurities dwindled in the 1980s, this type of race became relatively rare, and nominating conditions changed as a result. In 1972, for instance, the first payment for the Futurity Stakes (G1) at Belmont Park had to have been made by August 15, 1970, the year the horses were foaled. By 1990, the subscription deadline was May 1, 1990, for a race to be run in September 1990. Two years later, the Futurity became a stakes race, with nominations closing 17 days before the race.

handicap race A race, usually of stakes caliber, in which the racing secretary determines the amount of weight each horse will carry based on career record and current form. In theory, the handicapper seeks to assign weights so that all starters finish at the same time in a dead heat to win. Handicap races formerly placed high weight assignments on such champions as Kelso (won the 1964 Straight Face Handicap with 136 pounds) and Forego (won the 1977 Nassau County Handicap with 136 pounds), but few top-weight assignments now exceed 126 pounds.

maiden claiming race A race for nonwinning horses that can be purchased immediately from that race for a specified price (see claiming race).

maiden race A race for horses that have never won a race. Maiden races are either maiden special weight, with all horses assigned a specified weight, or maiden claiming. Additional conditions may apply, such as the race being restricted to state-breds.

optional claiming A race that is both a claiming race, for those horses entered to be claimed for a specific price, and an allowance race, for those whose owners do not enter them to be claimed.

overnight handicap A race where owners do not pay to enter their horses but are assigned weights by the racing secretary. These races generally offer some of the higher purses, on a par with the best allowance races but below stakes race purses.

restricted race A race whose starters are limited to those eligible under specified conditions, such as horses that were bred in the state where the race is held, were offered or sold at a specific sale, or by their previous winnings.

stakes race A race that is generally the highest quality of race offered by a track. For stakes, owners pay a fee to nominate and enter their horses in the starting gate, with the track putting up added money to make up the difference in the total purse. Stakes races are generally the richest races run at each track and attract the best horses on the grounds, plus horses coming in from other tracks or states when the purse money is high enough to attract shippers.

starter allowance An allowance race for horses that have started for a specified minimum claiming price within a specified time. For example, some starter allowances are restricted to horses that have started for a claiming price of $10,000 or less in the previous year. Conditions of the race, meaning the weight carried, are determined by allowances.

starter handicap A race similar to a starter allowance, except the horses are assigned weights by the track racing secretary, based on current ability and form rather than allowance conditions.

tighter. You can check how many winners are coming from each post position on the dirt track and grass course in the *Daily Racing Form* or program. Invariably, you will find that horses from the extreme outside posts have not done well on grass. For example, at the Pimlico 2001 spring meet from March 28 through May 6, post position eight was zero-for-13, post nine one-for-11 and post positions 10 through 12 produced no winners. You should factor that information into your handicapping. If a horse breaks from the 12 post, races wide, and rallies for fourth, it may do much better in its next start with a better post position.

On some dirt courses, races at seven furlongs and one mile may be more difficult for horses breaking from the first post position, immediately next to the rail. If a horse lacks early speed, it most likely will get caught behind faster pacesetters and will be trapped behind horses when ready to make a run at the leaders.

Trainer patterns

Trainers have patterns and proclivities, and you should be aware of them. Some are more adept with older horses, while others excel with two-year-olds. Some do equally well on grass and dirt, while others definitely do not. Some train their horses hard, and others train lightly and allow their horses to reach peak fitness by racing them. Some trainers can have their horses fit to race off long layoffs, but others never do.

Thanks to the innovations by *Daily Racing Form* over the last few years, much of that information is readily available to all handicappers in the trainer statistics at the bottom of each horse's past-performance lines. They will show each trainer's percentage of winners with horses coming off layoffs, first time on grass, first-time starters, first start after claiming a horse, stretching out from sprint to route, and other significant statistics. Trainers also can have winning and losing streaks. If a trainer has been

struggling but does well with a couple of horses, other horses in the barn may be ready to perform better, too.

Handicapping two-year-olds

Handicapping horses with established form is difficult enough. Handicapping a two-year-old maiden race loaded with first-time starters is even more daunting. Here are some clues. First-time starters with several good workouts—for example, four furlongs in :48 or :49 and five furlongs in 1:00 or 1:01—do as well as those with one blazing bullet workout at three furlongs, in :35⅘ or :36. Some trainers' horses usually improve dramatically in their second or third starts. New York-based trainer Nick Zito is a prime example. Some stallions are extremely proficient at siring precocious two-year-olds. Other sires' progeny do well in distance races or on turf. Again, going through available statistics will help your handicapping.

Weight

In general, the longer the race, the more important is the weight assignment. If trainers regarded weight as unimportant, they would not rush to use every hot apprentice that shows up with a five-pound weight allowance.

Weight can be overrated, but the significant factor is how a horse's weight in today's race relates to the assignments of the other horses. If two horses had been close to each other in their previous start at equal weights and now one of them carries three pounds more and the other five pounds less, that eight-pound swing could mean a difference in the outcome.

Final thought

In many ways, handicapping is comparable to a chess match. Many factors must be considered to forecast how a race will unfold and how those factors will affect the race's outcome. The process can be mind-twisting at first, but in time your handicapping will become more skillful and more fun. Good luck and good racing.—*Bill Heller*

Daily Racing Form/NTRA National Handicapping Championship

Steve Wolfson Jr., a Florida high school teacher with a formidable Thoroughbred-industry pedigree, won the fourth annual *Daily Racing Form*/NTRA National Handicapping Championship and the $100,000 first prize at Bally's Casino in Las Vegas on January 18, 2003.

The handicapping champion, 35, is the grandson of Louis Wolfson, whose Harbor View Farm campaigned 1978 Triple Crown winner Affirmed. His father, Steve Wolfson Sr., has been involved in the Thoroughbred industry as a breeder and owner. His uncle, Marty Wolfson, is a trainer on the South Florida circuit.

Wolfson, who teaches social studies and coaches cross-country in Port Orange, took the top spot among 213 handicapping championship finalists. His total from 30 $2 win and $2 place bets spread over eight tracks was $279.60. More than 45,000 players participated in 81 qualifying tournaments, during 2002.

The winner was presented an Eclipse Award as the champion handicapper during the Eclipse Award dinner.

Year	Winner	Residence	Winning Total
2003	Steve Wolfson Jr.	Port Orange, FL	$279.60
2002	Herman Miller	Oakland, CA	205.30
2001	Judy Wagner	New Orleans, LA	237.70
2000	Steve Walker	Lincoln, NE	305.40

9

WHITNEY H. - Grade 1
Purse $750,000 Guaranteed
Distance 1 1/8 Miles

EXACTA WAGERING
TRIFECTA WAGERING
PICK 3 WAGERING RACES 2-3-4

WEIGHT

9-2 1 LEFT BANK (L)

Ch.h.5 French Deputy - Marshesseaux by Dr. Blum — **118**
Bred in KY by JOHN YOUNGBLOOD & FLETCHER GRAY
Royal Blue, Orange Ball, Orange Stripes on Sleeves, Blue Cap, Orange Stripes

Owner: MICHAEL TABOR
Trainer: TODD A. PLETCHER
Jockey: JOHN R. VELAZQUEZ

2002:	3	2	0	0	$176,146
2001:	8	4	1	0	$524,200
ife:	23	14	2	0	$952,806
Turf:	0	0	0	0	$0
Off Dirt:	2	0	1	0	$8,200

04Jul02	Bel8	ft	7f	:21^{96} :44^{27} 1:20^{17} 3u	TomFoolH(G2)-150k	**99**	4	3	3½	3^{nk}	1½	16¼	VelazquezJ	121	Lbf	*1.60	LeftBank1216¼ AfirmedSuces1205¾ SumerNote1131¼	vigorous hand ride	6
27May02	Bel9	ft	1	:44^{79} 1:08^{64} 1:33^{34} 3u	MtropltH(G1)-750k	**88**	4	1^{hd}	2^{hd}	5^{4}	512½	5^{13}	VelazquezJ	121	Lbf	*2.20	SwptOverboard1174¾ Aldbaran1151½ CrftyC.T.1164¼	vied 4 wide, tired	10
11May02	Bel6	ft	6f	:22^{57} :45^{17} 1:09^{30} 3u	BoldRlrH(G3)-105k	**96**	4	3	3½	1^{hd}	1½	1^{1}	VelazquezJ	121	Lbf	*.35	LftBank121^{1} SlkySwep114½ SyFloridaSandy116^{9}	vied 3 wide, driving	4
24Nov01	Aqu8	ft	1	:45^{72} 1:09^{54} 1:33^{35} 3u	CigarMiH(G1)-350k	**99**	6	2^{hd}	2^{hd}	1½	12½	13¼	VelazquezJ	120	Lbf	*2.45	LeftBank1203¼ GraemeHall118^{hd} RedBullet1181¾	when roused, driving	9
27Oct01	Bel6	ft	6f	:22^{45} :44^{75} 1:08^{41} 3u	PnskBCSp(G1)-1000k	**97**	8	10	51¼	62¼	6^{4}	52½	VelazquezJ	126	Lbf	8.90	SquirtleSquirt124½ XtraHeat121^{nk} CalerOne126^{nk}	3 wide, good finish	14
22Sep01	Bel10	ft	7f	:22^{72} :44^{57} 1:20^{73} 3u	Vosburgh(G1)-300k	**101**	6	2	21½	22½	21½	1½	VelazquezJ	126	Lbf	3.75	LeftBank126½ SquirtleSquirt1239¾ BigEE126^{nk}	game outside, driving	6

20-1 2 SAINT VERRE (L)

B.c.4 Saint Ballado - Margot Verre by Tom Rolfe — **113**
Bred in FL by GEORGELINA GONZALEZ
Green and White Blocks, Green Sleeves, White Stripes, Green Cap

Owner: JOSEPH ALLEN
Trainer: H. ALLEN JERKENS
Jockey: JEAN-LUC SAMYN

2002:	3	1	1	0	$52,240
2001:	7	1	1	3	$66,560
Life:	14	4	2	3	$166,800
Turf:	4	0	1	1	$39,490
Off Dirt:	2	0	1	1	$13,958

05Jul02	Bel8	fm	Ⓣ1	:45^{23} 1:08^{34} 1:32^{24} 3u	PokerH(G3)-111k	**89**	6	1^{1}	1^{1}	1½	1^{hd}	22¼	SamynJ	112	Lb	18.30	Volponi1152¼ SaintVerre112^{nk} Navesink117¾	set pace, gamely	7
21Jun02	Bel7	ft	1	:44^{59} 1:08^{85} 1:34^{83} 3u	Alw50000	**88**	2	1^{1}	12½	1½	1½	11½	SamynJ	118	Lb	2.30	SntVre1181½ FrLvandHonor1184¾ MntIntrpid1175¼	strong pace, driving	8
08Jun02	Bel11	gd	Ⓣ7f	:23^{49} :45^{91} 1:22^{32} 4u	Alw49000	**89**	4	3	1^{hd}	1^{hd}	31½	66½	SamynJ	116	Lf	*3.05	QietOne1161½ PintofAmerica1162¾ Zning(GB)116^{nk}	vied inside, tired	11
26Aug01	Mth7	fm	Ⓣ1⅛	:47^{69} 1:10^{98} 1:47^{77} 3	Choice-75k	**89**	8	31½	42½	41½	4^{nk}	6^{3}	GuidryM	115	L	*1.30	OneEyedJoker1171½ Szep114^{hd} FirstSpear122½	close up,outside,wknd	8
06Aug01	Sar8	fm	Ⓣ1⅛	:48^{72} 1:12^{25} 1:47^{94} 3	HalOFmeH(G2)-150k	**89**	1	11½	1½	1^{hd}	2^{hd}	31¾	DayP	113	L	6.20	Bptize1221¼ StrtegicPartner120½ SintVere1133¼	stayed on stubbornly	7
29Jul01	Sar8	ft	1⅛	:46^{99} 1:10^{64} 1:49^{39} 3u	Alw46000	**94**	2	3^{2}	3^{2}	36½	3^{5}	1^{nk}	VelazquezJ	116	L	3.40	SaintVerre116^{nk} Unbridling120^{hd} Ubiquity1207½	came again outside	7

20-1 3 UNSHADED (L)

B.g.5 Unbridled - Shade the Flame by Caucasus — **114**
Bred in KY by SHAWNNA SORENSON
Yellow and Blue Diagonal Quarters, Yellow Sleeves, Two Blue Hoops, Yellow and Blue Cap

Owner: JIM TAFEL
Trainer: CARL A. NAFZGER
Jockey: JON K. COURT

2002:	6	0	2	0	$148,457
2001:	4	1	0	0	$75,790
Life:	16	5	3	3	$1,251,395
Turf:	0	0	0	0	$0
Off Dirt:	0	0	0	0	$0

06Jul02	PrM9	ft	1⅛	:46^{61} 1:10^{27} 1:47^{97} 3u	CmhsBCH(G3)-400k	**89**	10	86½	88¼	66½	72¾	22¼	CourtJ	115	BLbf	2.90	Mr.John1142¼ Unshaded1153¼ Fajardo113½	split horses late	10
15Jun02	CD10	ft	1⅛	:47^{50} 1:10^{88} 1:47^{84} 3u	SFosterH(G1)-833k	**89**	7	6^{6}	6^{6}	5^{4}	4^{5}	59½	CourtJ	115	Lbfm	11.90	StreetCry(IRE)1206½ DollarBill1142¼ Tenpins115^{ns}	duck in bmp start	8
18May02	CD5	ft	1	:46^{07} 1:11^{03} 1:36^{82} 3u	Aoc59800	**87**	3	4^{4}	3^{5}	34½	3^{nk}	2½	CourtJ	116	Lfm	*1.10	XCountry118½ Unshaded1165¾ Fraze'sFoly1237¾	angled 3w,outfinished	5
28Jul01	Sar6	ft	1⅛	:46^{78} 1:10^{34} 1:47^{94} 3u	WhitneyH(G1)-1008k	**94**	5	74¾	74¾	6^{5}	74¼	6^{5}	DayP	115	Lf	8.40	LdPalace(CHI)115^{2} AlbrthGreat124^{nk} Gndr113^{nk}	outside, no response	7
01Jul01	Bel8	ft	1¼	:46^{73} 1:35^{05} 2:00^{39} 3u	SuburbnH(G2)-500k	**93**	3	68½	67½	6^{10}	5^{12}	511¾	AlbaradoR	117	Lf	10.80	AlbrthGreat1232¼ LdPalace(CHI)115^{hd} Indde122^{7}	inside, no response	6
16Jun01	CD11	ft	1⅛	:46^{92} 1:10^{70} 1:47^{74} 3u	SFosterH(G2)-831k	**92**	8	67½	611½	6^{7}	5^{6}	55¼	AlbaradoR	118	Lfm	3.40	GuidedTour113½ CaptainSteve1232¾ Brahms1141¼	7-8w lane,no threat	8

5-2	
4	

LIDO PALACE (CHI) (S20%) (L) 119

Ch.h.5 Rich Man's Gold - Sonada (CHI)
by Quick Decision
Bred in CHI by HARAS FIGURON
Dark Blue, White Epaulets, White Hoops on Sleeves, Blue Cap, White Button

Owner: JOHN W. AMERMAN AND JERRY AMERMAN
Trainer: ROBERT J. FRANKEL
Jockey: JORGE F. CHAVEZ

2002:	2	0	1	0	$115,000
2001:	6	2	2	1	$1,240,000
Life:	18	10	7	2	$1,805,101
Turf:	1	0	1	0	$17,370
Off Dirt:	9	6	2	0	$432,731

06Jul02	Bel10	ft	$1\frac{1}{4}$	:48^{72}	1:37^{11}	2:00^{95}	3u	SuburbnH(G2)-500k	**91**	3	$3^{1\frac{1}{2}}$	3^{1}	2^{1}	$2^{1\frac{1}{2}}$	$2^{\frac{3}{4}}$	BaileyJ	119	Lb	2.65	EDubai116$^{\frac{3}{4}}$ LidoPalace(CHI)119^{1} MachoUno119$^{3\frac{3}{4}}$	3 wide, game finish	7
03Feb02	SA6	ft	$1\frac{1}{8}$	:47^{77}	1:11^{60}	1:48^{66}	4u	SnAntnoH(G2)-250k	**95**	4	$5^{2\frac{1}{2}}$	4^{2}	4^{2}	$4^{2\frac{3}{4}}$	4^{3}	BaileyJ	121	BLb	*.80	Rdtre(BRZ)116$^{\frac{1}{2}}$ Echre119$^{1\frac{1}{2}}$ Irshysareflying117^{1}	stalked btwn,no bid	7
24Nov01	Tok*(Jpn)	st	*$1\frac{5}{16}$			2:05^{90}	3u	The Japan Cup Dirt-1994k (G1)							$8^{13\frac{1}{2}}$	BaileyJ	126		2.50	Krfne121^{7} WngArw(JPN)126$^{\frac{1}{2}}$ MrdOpera(JPN)126$^{\frac{3}{4}}$	ridden and no extra	16
08Sep01	Bel9	ft	$1\frac{1}{8}$	:46^{66}	1:10^{28}	1:47^{42}	3u	Woodward(G1)-500k	**97**	3	3^{1}	3^{1}	$3^{\frac{1}{2}}$	$2^{\frac{1}{2}}$	1^{1}	BaileyJ	126	Lb	2.90	LdPalace(CHI)126^{1} AlbrthGreat126$^{\frac{1}{2}}$ Tznw126$^{8\frac{1}{4}}$	determinedly outside	5
28Jul01	Sar6	ft	$1\frac{1}{8}$	:46^{78}	1:10^{34}	1:47^{94}	3u	WhitneyH(G1)-1008k	**97**	3	5^{3}	5^{3}	4^{2}	$1^{\frac{1}{2}}$	1^{2}	BaileyJ	115	Lb	2.95	LdPalace(CHI)115^{2} AlbrthGreat124^{nk} Gndr113^{nk}	4 wide move, driving	7
01Jul01	Bel8	ft	$1\frac{1}{4}$	:46^{73}	1:35^{05}	2:00^{39}	3u	SuburbnH(G2)-500k	**99**	5	3^{1}	$2^{\frac{1}{2}}$	$2^{1\frac{1}{2}}$	$2^{1\frac{1}{2}}$	$2^{2\frac{1}{4}}$	FloresD	115	Lb	4.10	AlbrthGreat123$^{2\frac{1}{4}}$ LdPalace(CHI)115^{hd} Incde122^{7}	inside run, gamely	6

5-1	
5	

MACHO UNO (L) 118

Gr/Ro.c.4 Holy Bull - Primal Force
by Blushing Groom (FR)
Bred in KY by ADENA SPRINGS
Black, Gold Ball with Emblem, Two Red Hoops on Sleeves. Black Cap, Red Visor and Button

Owner: STRONACH STABLES
Trainer: JOSEPH F. ORSENO
Jockey: PAT DAY

2002:	3	2	0	1	$382,600
2001:	4	1	1	1	$563,400
Life:	11	6	1	3	$1,714,803
Turf:	0	0	0	0	$0
Off Dirt:	0	0	0	0	$0

06Jul02	Bel10	ft	$1\frac{1}{4}$	:48^{72}	1:37^{11}	2:00^{95}	3u	SuburbnH(G2)-500k	**90**	5	$5^{3\frac{1}{4}}$	$4^{2\frac{1}{2}}$	3^{1}	3^{3}	$3^{1\frac{3}{4}}$	StevensG	119	Lb	*1.10	EDubai116$^{\frac{3}{4}}$ LidoPalace(CHI)119^{1} MachoUno119$^{3\frac{3}{4}}$	game finish outside	7
01Jun02	Suf13	ft	$1\frac{1}{8}$	:46^{46}	1:10^{67}	1:50^{52}	3u	MassH(G2)-500k	**98**	2	$4^{3\frac{1}{2}}$	5^{3}	$5^{1\frac{3}{4}}$	$4^{1\frac{1}{2}}$	$1^{1\frac{3}{4}}$	StevensG	117	BLb	2.10	MachoUno117$^{1\frac{3}{4}}$ EveningAtire114^{nk} Include120$^{1\frac{1}{4}}$	altrd crs 1/8, in hand	9
23Mar02	GP9	ft	1^{70}	:46^{38}	1:11^{13}	1:41^{10}	4u	Alw46000	**91**	4	6^{4}	$7^{3\frac{3}{4}}$	$5^{2\frac{3}{4}}$	3^{3}	$1^{\frac{1}{2}}$	DouglasR	120	Lb	*.70	MachoUno120$^{\frac{1}{2}}$ HailTheChief(GB)120$^{4\frac{1}{4}}$ ProperMan116$^{8\frac{3}{4}}$	up final strides	8
27Oct01	Bel10	ft	$1\frac{1}{4}$	:47^{04}	1:35^{87}	2:00^{62}	3u	BCClasic(G1)-4000k	**98**	7	$9^{4\frac{3}{4}}$	$9^{3\frac{3}{4}}$	$6^{3\frac{3}{4}}$	4^{3}	$4^{4\frac{1}{2}}$	StevensG	122	Lbf	19.50	Tiznow126^{ns} Sakhee126$^{1\frac{3}{4}}$ AlberttheGreat126$^{2\frac{3}{4}}$	even finish	13
29Sep01	Tdn11	ft	$1\frac{1}{8}$	:47^{20}	1:10^{84}	1:48^{66}	3	OhioDrby(G2)-306k	**94**	4	$5^{2\frac{3}{4}}$	$5^{4\frac{1}{2}}$	$4^{3\frac{1}{2}}$	$2^{1\frac{1}{2}}$	$3^{\frac{3}{4}}$	StevensG	119	Lbf	*.20	WesternPride119$^{\frac{1}{2}}$ Wodmon113^{nk} MachoUno119^{4}	brushed,bid,outfinishd	6
03Sep01	Pha11	ft	$1\frac{1}{8}$	:48^{68}	1:12^{77}	1:49^{69}	3	PaDerby(G3)-500k	**95**	5	$4^{2\frac{1}{2}}$	$4^{3\frac{1}{2}}$	$4^{2\frac{1}{2}}$	3^{nk}	$1^{1\frac{1}{2}}$	StevensG	116	Lbf	*.90	MachoUno116$^{1\frac{1}{2}}$ UnbridledElaine119$^{\frac{1}{2}}$ TouchTone122$^{6\frac{3}{4}}$	outside, easily	6

4-5	
6	

STREET CRY (IRE) (L) 123

Dk B/Br.c.4 Machiavellian - Helen Street (GB)
by Troy (GB)
Bred in IRE by SHEIKH MOHAMMED BIN RASHID AL MAKTOUM
Royal Blue, White Chevrons on Sleeves, Blue Cap

Owner: GODOLPHIN STABLE
Trainer: SAEED BIN SUROOR
Jockey: JERRY D. BAILEY

2002:	3	3	0	0	$4173,777
2001:	3	1	2	0	$571,860
Life:	11	5	6	1	$5,000,392
Turf:	0	0	0	0	$0
Off Dirt:	0	0	0	0	$0

15Jun02	CD10	ft	$1\frac{1}{8}$	:47^{50}	1:10^{88}	1:47^{84}	3u	SFosterH(G1)-833k	**96**	4	$3^{1\frac{1}{2}}$	$4^{2\frac{1}{2}}$	$2^{\frac{1}{2}}$	1^{3}	$1^{6\frac{1}{2}}$	BaileyJ	120	L	2.10	StretCry(IRE)120$^{6\frac{1}{2}}$ DolarBil114$^{2\frac{1}{4}}$ Tenpins115^{ns}	driv,gathered up late	8
23Mar02	Nad*(Uae)	ft	*$1\frac{1}{4}$			2:01^{18}	4u	Dubai World Cup-6000k (G1)							$1^{4\frac{1}{4}}$	BaileyJ	126			StrtCry(IRE)126$^{4\frac{1}{4}}$ SiMi(ARG)126$^{4\frac{1}{4}}$ Skhe126$^{2\frac{1}{4}}$	ran clear, stayed well	11
28Feb02	Nad*(Uae)	ft	*$1\frac{1}{4}$			2:01^{25}	3u	Sh M b Ras A Mak Chl R III-95k (G2)							$1^{8\frac{1}{2}}$	DettoriL	128			StrtCry(IRE)128$^{8\frac{1}{2}}$ SttShinto128$^{\frac{1}{2}}$ RylTryst128$^{4\frac{1}{2}}$	clear 1f out, easily	7
31Oct01	Aqu8	ft	$1\frac{1}{8}$	:46^{54}	1:11^{97}	1:48^{62}	3	DiscvryH(G3)-109k	**91**	7	5^{4}	$5^{1\frac{1}{2}}$	3^{nk}	1^{hd}	2^{1}	FloresD	118	Lbf	*.85	EveningAtire111^{1} StretCry(IRE)118$^{1\frac{3}{4}}$ FreofLove115$^{\frac{3}{4}}$	wide both turns	7
24Mar01	Nad*(Uae)	ft	*$1\frac{1}{8}$			1:47^{04}	3	UAE Derby-2000k (G3)							2^{ns}	DettoriL	122			ExprsTr122^{ns} StrtCry(IRE)122^{6} LdPlc(CHI)128$^{3\frac{1}{2}}$	5th str, headed post	14
01Mar01	Nad*(Uae)	ft	*1			1:35^{14}	3u	UAE 2000 Guineas-250k							1^{2}	DettoriL	118			StrtCry(IRE)118^{2} Nvere118^{6} CntDubois(GB)118^{3}	led 1f out, ran on	8

(L) - Treated with Lasix; (L*) - First time using Lasix; (O) Off of Lasix; (S20%) - 20% Supplementary Nomination

Probable Favorites 6-4-1

Copyright 2002 Equibase Company LLC

Handicapping a Sample Race

Saratoga Race Course's 2002 Whitney Handicap (G1) provided a top-quality field and an intriguing challenge for handicappers. The Whitney's purse was $750,000, and its six starters had total career earnings of more than $10-million. The past performances for this race are on the preceding pages.

To make the handicapping challenge even more complicated, Racing Hall of Fame trainer H. Allen Jerkens entered a speed horse, Saint Verre, in the 1⅛-mile Whitney, which had been expected to feature Left Bank as the only early speed. Street Cry (Ire) was the Whitney's 123-pound highweight. Here is a look at the starters in post-position order, with their weights listed after their names.

1. **Left Bank** (118). Although regarded as a top sprinter, Left Bank had won his only start at 1⅛ miles, the Discovery Handicap (G3) in 2000 at Aqueduct. He had run fifth in the 2001 Breeders' Cup Sprint (G1), beaten 2½ lengths, and then had won the Cigar Mile Handicap (G1) by 3¼ lengths. He began his five-year-old season by winning the Bold Ruler Handicap (G3) at six furlongs but then faded to fifth in the one-mile Metropolitan Handicap (G1) after engaging in a suicidal early speed duel. In his start prior to the Whitney, he had won Belmont Park's seven-furlong Tom Fool Handicap (G2) by 6¼ lengths in a track-record 1:20.17 after sitting a close third early. Though he had blazing speed, Left Bank had not been the leader at the first point of call in his prior seven races, implying that he did not need to be on the lead to win. His career record was 14 wins in 23 starts, with earnings of $952,806.

2. **Saint Verre** (113). Saint Verre entered the Whitney without a career stakes victory although he twice had placed in grass stakes. His early speed was exceptional, and in his prior start on dirt he had won a mile allowance race in 1:34.83 while leading at every point of call.

3. **Unshaded** (114). The 2000 Travers Stakes (G1) winner had done little since that victory. Sidelined for almost nine months after the Travers win, the Unbridled gelding had won an allowance race in his return in May 2001 but was winless since then. He showed just two seconds in his next six starts and was soundly beaten by Lido Palace (Chi) twice and Street Cry once. The one-run closer would need a complete burnout on the front end to make an impact.

4. **Lido Palace (Chi)** (119). A two-time champion in his native Chile, Lido Palace was an immediate success in the United States in 2001, finishing second in the Hawthorne Gold Cup (G2) and Suburban (G2) Handicaps before

winning the Whitney and Woodward Stakes (G1). After skipping the Breeders' Cup Classic (G1), Lido Palace finished eighth of 16 in the Japan Cup Dirt. After a dull fourth in the San Antonio Handicap (G2) at Santa Anita Park on February 3, trainer Bobby Frankel gave Lido Palace a five-month rest. His return race, a second-place finish by three-quarters of a length to unpressured, front-running winner E Dubai in the Suburban at 1¼ miles, was a nice prep for the Whitney.

5. **Macho Uno** (118). The 2000 two-year-old male champion after his Breeders' Cup Juvenile (G1) victory, Macho Uno was making only his 12th career start in the Whitney. He had won six of those starts, but the light schedule implied that unsoundness tempered his talent. After finishing fourth in the 2001 Breeders' Cup Classic, he opened his 2002 season with an allowance victory before scoring a 1¾-length win in the Massachusetts Handicap (G2). Sent off the 1.10-to-1 favorite in the Suburban, Macho Uno ran third for much of the race and finished behind E Dubai and Lido Palace.

6. **Street Cry (Ire)** (123). Like Macho Uno, Street Cry had made only 11 starts prior to the Whitney, but his winter training in Dubai had been a factor in his light racing schedule. A promising two-year-old who finished third behind Macho Uno in the 2000 Breeders' Cup Juvenile, he made only one U.S. start in 2001, finishing second in the Discovery Handicap (G3). But he blossomed at four, winning the 2002 Dubai World Cup (UAE-G1) by an impressive 4¼ lengths under Jerry Bailey, who rode him in the Whitney. In his only U.S. start of 2002, he dominated the Stephen Foster Handicap (G1) at Churchill Downs, winning by 6½ lengths.

ANALYSIS: Before Saint Verre joined the Whitney field, Left Bank appeared likely to set an uncontested lead because none of the other prospective starters had the early speed to keep up with him. But, with Saint Verre in the race, the obvious question was whether Left Bank would challenge him in the early going. The key question, though, was whether Saint Verre would matter because Left Bank had shown he did not need to be on the lead to win. Street Cry possessed tactical speed and had been able to stay close to an honest pace in the Stephen Foster. Lido Palace also had displayed an ability to stay close to a legitimate pace. Macho Uno's Suburban effort had shown that he was not the equal of the top contenders, and Unshaded had little to recommend him against top-level competitors. How did the race turn out? Look at the chart and an analysis of the race on the next pages.

How to Read a Race Chart

A race chart is a comprehensive and easily understandable explanation of exactly how a race unfolded and how it was won or lost. Experienced handicappers often save charts of all races at tracks they play most often because the charts are the most definitive written description of a race.

The chart first lists the bare facts of the race: The Whitney Handicap was the ninth race at Saratoga Race Course on August 3, 2002; it was a Grade 1 race; it was run at 1⅛ miles for three-year-olds and up (older horses); and it had a $750,000 purse, with $450,000 to the winner and lesser amounts to the second- through fifth-place finishers.

The chart lists the runners in their finish order and provides considerable information about each horse. Following the horse's name is any race-day medication received, any equipment used, and the weight carried. For instance, all Whitney starters were treated with the diuretic furosemide (L), which reduces pulmonary bleeding, and all but Street Cry wore blinkers (b), which help a horse to concentrate during a race. Left Bank and Unshaded wore front bandages (f), and Saint Verre wore racing calks (c), which are cleated horseshoes.

The next figures indicate how the race was run in a numerical format. The first figure is the horse's post position, from the rail out. The start figure tells the order in which the horses

Whitney H.-Grade 1
Purse $750,000 Guaranteed

NINTH RACE	Stakes. Purse $750,000. 3-year-olds and up. 1⅛ Miles Dirt Track: Fast
Saratoga	
August 3, 2002	

Value of race: $750,000. Value to winner: $450,000; second: $150,000; third: $82,500; fourth: $45,000; fifth, $22,500. Mutuel Pool: $1,541,529.

P#	Horse	Wgt	M/Eqt	PP	St	¼	½	¾	Str.	Fin.	Jockey	Odds
1	Left Bank	118	Lbf	1	1	2^7	2^6	2^6	$1^{2\frac{1}{2}}$	$1^{1\frac{1}{4}}$	J R Velazquez	3.60
6	Street Cry (IRE)	123	L	6	3	$3^{1\frac{1}{2}}$	$4^{1\frac{1}{2}}$	3^{hd}	$2^{\frac{1}{2}}$	2no	J D Bailey	*1.00
4	Lido Palace (CHI)	119	Lb	4	5	4^1	$3^{\frac{1}{2}}$	$4^{2\frac{1}{2}}$	$3^{\frac{1}{2}}$	$3^{1\frac{1}{2}}$	J F Chavez	3.80
5	Macho Uno	118	Lb	5	4	6	6	6	$5^{2\frac{1}{2}}$	4^3	P Day	4.60
3	Unshaded	114	Lbf	3	6	$5^{\frac{1}{2}}$	5^{hd}	6	6	5^{nk}	J K Court	24.50
2	Saint Verre	113	Lbc	2	2	1^2	1^3	$1^{1\frac{1}{2}}$	5^3	6	J Samyn	36.25

OFF AT 5:26. Start: Good for all. Winner: Driving. Temp: 85°. Weather: Clear.
Time: :23.00, 45.94, 1:09.36, 1:34.19, 1:47.04.

Total W/P/S Pool: $1,541,529
Mutuel Payoffs

1—LEFT BANK	9.20	4.10	2.50	EXACTA 1-6 PAID	$20.40	Total Pool: $978,629
6—STREET CRY (IRE)		3.00	2.10	TRIFECTA 1-6-4 PAID	$52.00	Total Pool: $664,975
4—LIDO PALACE (CHI)			2.50			

Winner: Left Bank, ch. h., 5, by French Deputy—Marshesseaux, by Dr. Blum.
Trainer Todd A. Pletcher. Bred in Kentucky by John Youngblood and Fletcher Gray (Ky).

LEFT BANK came away in good order, was taken in hand and guided to the outside behind pacesetter SAINT VERRE on the first turn, stalked that rival from the outside on the backstretch, advanced on the second turn, took over and drew clear nearing the stretch, dug in resolutely when roused and remained clear to the wire under a drive. STREET CRY (IRE) was unhurried early on, took a spot at the inside into the first turn, rallied on the rail on the second turn, angled out into the stretch and finished gamely despite drifting out in deep stretch. LIDO PALACE (CHI) was unhurried early while wide, advanced three wide on the second turn, responded when roused and finished gamely outside. MACHO UNO was outrun early, rallied inside nearing the stretch and finished gamely. UNSHADED was outrun early, raced inside, came wide for the drive and had no response when roused. SAINT VERRE quickly opened a clear lead, set the pace, had no answer for the winner on the second turn and tired in the stretch.

Owners: (1) Michael B. Tabor; (6) Godolphin Racing, Inc.; (4) Amerman Racing Stables; (5) Stronach Stable; (3) James B. Tafel; (2) Joseph Allen

Trainers: (1) T A Pletcher; (6) S bin Suroor; (4) R J Frankel; (5) J F Orseno; (3) C A Nafzger; (2) H A Jerkens

Copyright © 2002 by Equibase Co. LLC

came out of the starting gate and can identify a horse that always breaks sharply or one that had difficulty at this crucial point in the race. The next figures are the points of call in the race. The points of call—where the Equibase chart caller describes the distances separating the runners—vary depending on the distance of the race. In a six-furlong race, for instance, the points of call are after one-quarter mile, one-half mile, and the stretch call, which is one-eighth mile from the finish. Races of a mile or longer add a point of call at three-quarters of a mile.

The superscript number with the running position indicates how far that horse was ahead of the next horse, and the finish number indicates the margin for the winner and the distances separating the other finishers. The horse's jockey is identified, and the final column is odds to one dollar, with the favorite indicated by an asterisk.

Below the running positions is information about weather and track conditions; the fractions and finish time of the race; the winner; and all betting payouts. Below that information is a narrative of how the race was run, written by the Equibase chart caller.

About the Whitney

The Whitney chart indicates that Saint Verre was no factor in the race's outcome and in fact may have assisted Left Bank to victory. While Saint Verre sprinted away to a daylight lead over Left Bank and set fairly quick fractions—:23.00 for the first quarter-mile, :45.94 for the half-mile, and 1:09.36 for three-quarters of a mile—Left Bank was running his own race, oblivious to Saint Verre and well ahead of Street Cry. Left Bank went after Saint Verre on the far turn, took the lead as Saint Verre slowed, and fought off Street Cry's challenge through the stretch to win by 1¼ lengths in the final time of 1:47.04, which equaled the track record. Lido Palace closed ground in late stretch to finish a nose behind Street Cry in third. Macho Uno closed from last place to be fourth, Unshaded never was a factor, and Saint Verre faded to last.

How Pari-Mutuel Wagering Began

Virtually all betting on horse races in North America, as in most countries, is conducted using the pari-mutuel wagering system. Unlike a casino, where bettors play against the house, racehorse bettors bet against each other, with the track holding the bets and, after taking out money for the track, purses, state taxes, etc., returning the money bet to the winning patrons after each race is run.

Unlike most traditions in North American horse racing, pari-mutuel wagering came from France rather than England. The system was devised in the mid-1860s by Pierre Oller, a Paris perfume merchant who had become disenchanted with the city's bookmakers.

Oller developed a variation of the auction pool, in which betting interests in individual horses were sold. Because fairly large sums of money were required to buy the winning interest in a favorite in the auction pools, they were not widely used by small-scale bettors. Oller's system allowed small wagers on all horses and quickly came into wide use in France. He called his wagering system perier mutuel, which means to wager among ourselves. Adopted in England, it became known as Paris mutuals, and finally pari-mutuel.

New York tracks used the pari-mutuel system (known then as Paris pools) in the early 1870s.

Col. M. Lewis Clark, the founder of Churchill Downs, observed the pari-mutuels in operation during a sojourn in Europe in the early 1870s and introduced the devices at his track in 1878. (Auction pools were used in 1875, 1876, and 1877, the first three years of Churchill's existence.)

Bookmakers soon made their appearance in both New York and Louisville, and the popularity of betting with bookmakers supplanted the pari-mutuel machines. Clark abandoned pari-mutuels in 1889 at the demand of bookmakers.

In 1908, however, anti-Churchill forces took over City Hall and banned bookmaking. Col. Matt Winn, then the track's general manager, rounded up six of the old pari-mutuel machines, refurbished them, and used them for betting on the 1908 Kentucky Derby. Pari-mutuel wagering on the Derby day program that year was $67,570 ($18,300 of that total on the Derby, won by Stone Street at 23.72-to-1 odds), with another $12,669 in auction pools.

The first machines sold only one denomination of ticket, $5 for the 1908 Derby program, but by 1911 Winn had commissioned new machines that offered $2, $5, and $10 tickets. By 1914, most American tracks had switched to the pari-mutuel system as antigambling sentiment led to bans against bookmaking.

Betting Odds and Payouts

Pari-mutuel betting odds are based on the percentage of the net wagering pool placed on each horse. For instance, a horse sent off at even money, or 1-to-1 odds, has attracted 50% of the net wagering pool.

The net wagering pool on which the odds are based is total wagering minus deductions broadly known as takeout—money taken out for state tax, horsemen's purses, the track's share, and other deductions. Total wagering is known as handle, which the track holds until after each race is run and then returns the net balance to winning bettors.

When devising a program betting line, also known as the morning line, a line maker generally will assign odds based on 125% of handle to account for takeout.

All tracks in North America show payouts after each race on their tote boards based on a $2 wager. To figure the exact odds, for instance, at which a horse went off in the win pool, subtract the $2 bet and divide by two. If a horse paid $4.70 to win, its winning odds were 1.35-to-1 ([$4.70-$2]/2=1.35).

Exact betting odds usually are rounded down to the nearest 10 cents, although some jurisdictions round to the next lowest 5 cents. Rounding is used so pennies and nickels are not used in paying off winning bettors. The money left over from rounding is known as breakage. Individual state laws determine how this breakage money is distributed at the end of the year.

Pari-mutuel Odds	Percentage of Handle	Payout
1-to-20	95.23%	$2.10
1-to-10	90.91	2.20
1-to-5	83.33	2.40
2-to-5	71.42	2.80
1-to-2	66.66	3.00
4-to-5	55.55	3.60
Even (1-to-1)	50.00	4.00
7-to-5	41.67	4.80
9-to-5	35.71	5.60
2-to-1	33.33	6.00
5-to-2	28.57	7.00
3-to-1	25.00	8.00
7-to-2	22.23	9.00
4-to-1	20.00	10.00
9-to-2	18.19	11.00
5-to-1	16.67	12.00
10-to-1	9.09	22.00
15-to-1	6.25	32.00
20-to-1	4.76	42.00
30-to-1	3.23	62.00
50-to-1	1.96	102.00
100-to-1	0.99	202.00

Distance Equivalents

Distances of races have been directly or indirectly derived from distances conventionally run in England, the cradle of Thoroughbred racing. Distances of English races are measured in the traditional English system of furlongs and miles. A furlong is 660 feet, or one-eighth of a mile, and a mile is comprised of eight furlongs.

France used the metric system instituted by Napoleon for its racing since the inception of racing in that country. As racing countries around the world have adopted the metric system of measurement, racing distances often have been changed to metric equivalents.

The following table includes equivalent distances for both systems.

Furlongs to Meters

Furlongs	Miles	Approx. meters	Exact meters
1.00	⅛	200	201.168
2.00	¼	400	402.336
3.00	⅜	600	603.504
4.00	½	800	804.672
4.50	⁹⁄₁₆	900	905.256
5.00	⅝	1,000	1,005.840
5.50	¹¹⁄₁₆	1,100	1,106.424
6.00	¾	1,200	1,207.008
6.50	¹³⁄₁₆	1,300	1,307.592
7.00	⅞	1,400	1,408.176

Furlongs	Miles	Approx. meters	Exact meters
7.50	¹⁵⁄₁₆	1,500	1,508.760
8.00	1	1,600	1,609.344
8.32	1&70 yds.	1,670	1,673.717
8.50	1¹⁄₁₆	1,700	1,709.928
9.00	1⅛	1,800	1,810.512
9.50	1³⁄₁₆	1,900	1,911.096
10.00	1¼	2,000	2,011.680
10.50	1⁵⁄₁₆	2,100	2,112.264
11.00	1⅜	2,200	2,212.848
11.50	1⁷⁄₁₆	2,300	2,313.432
12.00	1½	2,400	2,414.016
12.50	1⁹⁄₁₆	2,500	2,514.600
13.00	1⅝	2,600	2,615.184
13.50	1¹¹⁄₁₆	2,700	2,715.768
14.00	1¾	2,800	2,816.352
14.50	1¹³⁄₁₆	2,900	2,916.936
15.00	1⅞	3,000	3,017.520
15.50	1¹⁵⁄₁₆	3,100	3,118.104
16.00	2	3,200	3,218.688
16.50	2¹⁄₁₆	3,300	3,319.272
17.00	2⅛	3,400	3,419.856
18.00	2¼	3,600	3,621.024
19.00	2⅜	3,800	3,822.192
20.00	2½	4,000	4,023.360
21.00	2⅝	4,200	4,224.528
22.00	2¾	4,400	4,425.696
23.00	2⅞	4,600	4,626.864
24.00	3	4,800	4,828.032

Meters to Furlongs

Meters	Approx. furlongs	Approx. miles	Exact furlongs	Exact miles
200	1.00	1/8	0.9942	.1243
400	2.00	1/4	1.9884	.2485
600	3.00	3/8	2.9826	.3728
800	4.00	1/2	3.9768	.4971
900	4.50	9/16	4.4739	.5592
1,000	5.00	5/8	4.9710	.6214
1,100	5.50	11/16	5.4681	.6835
1,200	6.00	3/4	5.9652	.7456
1,300	6.50	13/16	6.4623	.8078
1,400	7.00	7/8	6.9594	.8699
1,500	7.50	15/16	7.4565	.9321
1,600	8.00	1	7.9536	.9942
1,670	8.32	1&70 yds.	7.9784	.9973
1,700	8.50	1 1/16	8.4506	1.0563
1,800	9.00	1 1/8	8.9477	1.1185
1,900	9.50	1 3/16	9.4448	1.1806
2,000	10.00	1 1/4	9.9419	1.2427
2,100	10.50	1 5/16	10.4390	1.3049
2,200	11.00	1 3/8	10.9361	1.3670
2,300	11.50	1 7/16	11.4332	1.4292
2,400	12.00	1 1/2	11.9303	1.4913
2,500	12.50	1 9/16	12.4274	1.5534
2,600	13.00	1 5/8	12.9245	1.6156
2,700	13.50	1 11/16	13.4216	1.6777
2,800	14.00	1 3/4	13.9187	1.7398
2,900	14.50	1 13/16	14.4158	1.8020
3,000	15.00	1 7/8	14.9129	1.8641
3,100	15.50	1 15/16	15.4100	1.9263
3,200	16.00	2	15.9071	1.9884
3,300	16.50	2 1/16	16.4042	2.0505

Meters	Approx. furlongs	Approx. miles	Exact furlongs	Exact miles
3,400	17.00	2 1/8	16.9013	2.1127
3,500	17.50	2 3/16	17.3984	2.1748
3,600	18.00	2 1/4	17.8955	2.2369
3,700	18.50	2 5/16	18.3926	2.2991
3,800	19.00	2 3/8	18.8897	2.3612
3,900	19.50	2 7/16	19.3868	2.4233
4,000	20.00	2 1/2	19.8839	2.4855
4,100	20.50	2 9/16	20.3810	2.5476
4,200	21.00	2 5/8	20.8781	2.6098
4,300	21.50	2 11/16	21.3752	2.6719
4,400	22.00	2 3/4	21.8723	2.7340
4,500	22.50	2 13/16	22.3694	2.7962
4,600	23.00	2 7/8	22.8665	2.8583
4,700	23.50	2 15/16	23.3636	2.9204
4,800	24.00	3	23.8607	2.9826

Countries and Measurements Used

Argentina	furlongs and meters
Australia	meters
Brazil	meters
Canada	furlongs
Chile	meters
England	furlongs
France	meters
Germany	meters
Hong Kong	meters
Ireland	furlongs
Italy	meters
Japan	meters
New Zealand	meters
United Arab Emirates	meters
United States	furlongs

Glossary of Common Racing and Breeding Terms

account wagering Betting by phone, in which a bettor must open an account with a track or an off-track agency. A synonym: phone betting.

acey-deucy Uneven stirrups, popularized by Racing Hall of Fame jockey Eddie Arcaro, who rode with his left (inside) iron lower than his right to achieve better balance on turns.

across the board A bet on a horse to win, place, and show. If the horse wins, the player collects three ways; if second, two ways (place and show); and if third, one way (show).

action 1) A horse's manner of moving. 2) A term meaning wagering.

added money Money added to the purse of a race by the racing association, a breeding fund, or other source. The association's money is added to the amount paid by owners in nomination, eligibility, entry, and starting fees. Added-money stakes became less common in the 1990s as more tracks went to guaranteed purses.

agent A person empowered to transact business for a stable owner or a jockey, or one empowered to sell or buy horses for an owner or a breeder.

airing Not running at best speed in a race; usually used in reference to a horse in an easy winning effort.

all-age race A race for two-year-olds and up.

all out When a horse extends itself to the utmost.

allowance race A race for which the racing secretary drafts certain conditions to determine weights to be carried based on the horse's age, sex, past performance, or a combination of all three.

allowances Reductions in weights to be carried, with the adjustments based on the conditions of the race or because an apprentice jockey is on a horse. Also, a weight reduction that female horses are entitled to when racing against males or that three-year-olds receive against older horses.

also-eligible A horse officially entered for a race but not permitted to start unless the field is reduced by scratches below a specified number.

also-ran A horse that does not finish first, second, or third.

American Horse Council A national association of individuals, organizations, and companies formed as a lobbying group to represent all breeds of the horse industry. Based in Washington, D.C., the AHC works on tax regulations, import and export rules, disease prevention and control, trails and recreation enhancement, and humane concerns. Founded in 1969, AHC was formed as an advocate of the entire American horse industry though started principally by Thoroughbred interests concerned about legislation that was being discussed in Congress that would have negatively affected racing and breeding.

American Stud Book Official book of foal registrations in North America maintained by the Jockey Club.

apprentice jockey Rider at the beginning of his career who has not ridden a certain number of winners within a specified period of time. Also known as a bug rider or bug boy, from the asterisk used in racing programs and past performances to denote the weight allowance such riders receive.

apprentice allowance Weight concession given to an apprentice rider: usually ten pounds until the fifth winner, seven pounds until the 35th winner, and five pounds for one calendar year from the 35th winner. More rarely, a three-pound allowance is allowed to a rider under contract to a specific stable or owner for two years from his or her first win. This rule varies from state to state. Apprentices do not receive an allowance when riding in a stakes race. All jockeys going from track to track must have a receipt from the clerk of scales from their track verifying the jockey's most recent total number of wins.

apron The (usually) paved area between the grandstand and the racing surface.

Association of Racing Commissioners International (RCI) Formerly the National Association of State Racing Commissioners (NASRC). Its office is based in Lexington.

asterisk Used with names of horses to denote they were imported into the United States. Practice preceded the use of country codes starting January 1, 1977.

auxiliary starting gate A second starting gate used when the number of horses in a race exceeds the capacity of the main starting gate.

average earnings index (AEI) A breeding statistic that compares racing earnings of a stallion's or mare's foals to those of all other foals racing at that time. An AEI of 1.00 is considered average, 2.00 is twice the average, 0.50 half the average, etc.

baby race A race for two-year-olds.

backstretch 1) Straight portion of the far side of the racing surface between the turns. 2) Generally, a racetrack's stable area, which often contains dormitories, a track kitchen, chapel, and recreation area for stable employees. It gained its name because most stable areas are located along the racetrack's backstretch.

bad doer A horse with a poor appetite, a condition that may be due to nervousness or other causes.

bandage Wrappings used on a horse's legs are three to six inches wide and are made of a variety of materials. In a race, they are used for support or protection against injury. Rundown bandages are used during a race to affix a pad under the fetlock to avoid injury due to abrasion when the fetlocks sink toward the ground during the weight-bearing portion of the canter. A horse may also wear standing bandages, thick cotton wraps used during shipping and while in the stall to prevent swelling, injury, or both, or to apply medication.

bar shoe A horseshoe closed at the back to help support the frog and heel of the hoof. It is often worn by horses with quarter cracks or bruised feet.

base The portion of the track that lies under the thick top layer, or cushion. The base provides support and drainage.

bat A jockey's whip.

battery A term for an illegal electrical device used by a jockey to stimulate a horse by electrical shock during a race. Also known as a machine or a joint.

bay A horse color that varies from a yellow tan to a bright auburn. The mane, tail, and lower portion of the legs are always black, except where white markings are present.

bearing in (or out) Deviating from a straight course. May be due to weariness, infirmity, inexperience, or the rider overusing the whip or reins to make a horse alter its course.

bell Signal sounded when the starter opens the gates or, at some tracks, to mark the close of betting.

Beyer number A handicapping tool, popularized by author Andrew Beyer, assigning a numerical value (speed figure) to each race run by a horse based on final time and track condition. This enables different horses running at different racetracks to be objectively compared.

bid in The act of buying back a horse that does not meet a minimum price at public auction. Synonym for buy-back, reserve not attained (RNA).

Big Red Refers to either of two famous chestnut-colored horses: Man o' War or Secretariat.

Bill Daly (on the) Taking a horse to the front at the start of a race and remaining there to the finish. Term stems from "Father Bill" Daly, a famous old-time horseman who developed many great jockeys.

birthdays All Thoroughbreds born in the Northern Hemisphere celebrate their birthday on January 1. In the Southern Hemisphere, all Thoroughbred birthdays are as follows: South America, July 1; South Africa, Australia, and New Zealand, August 1.

bit A stainless steel, rubber, or aluminum bar attached to the bridle; it is placed in the bar, the space between front and back teeth in the horse's mouth, and is one of the means by which a jockey exerts guidance and control. The most common racing bit is the D-bit, named because the rings extending from the bar are shaped like the letter D. Most racing bits are snaffled (snaffle bit), which means the metal bar is made up of two pieces, connected in the middle, which leaves it free to swivel. Other bits may be used to correct specific problems, such as bearing in or out.

black A horse color that includes the hair and the skin of the muzzle, flanks, mane, tail, and legs, unless white markings are present.

black type Boldface type, used in sales catalogs and stakes results, to distinguish horses that have won or placed in a stakes race. Sales companies today have eliminated the use of black type for stakes below a certain monetary level—$15,000 in 1985; $20,000 from 1986-'89; $25,000 beginning in 1990; $30,000 beginning in 2002; and $35,000 beginning in 2003. If a horse's name appears in boldface capital letters in a catalog or stakes results, the horse has won at least one black-type event. If the name appears in boldface type with capital and lower-case letters, the horse was second or third in at least one black-type event.

blaze A generic term describing a large, white vertical marking on a horse's face.

blind switch A circumstance in which a rider's actions cause him to be impeded during a race when moving into a space in which he finds himself blocked.

blinkers A cup-shaped device to limit a horse's vision and thus prevent it from swerving from objects or other horses on either side while racing. Blinker cups come in a variety of sizes and shapes to allow as little or as much vision as the trainer feels is necessary.

blister Counterirritant causing acute inflammation;

used to increase blood supply and blood flow and to promote healing in the leg.

bloodstock Horses of Thoroughbred breeding, especially such horses used for or considered in relation to racing.

bloodstock agent A person who advises or represents a buyer or a seller of Thoroughbreds at a public auction or a private sale. A bloodstock agent usually works on commission, often 5% of the purchase or sale price, and may also prepare a horse for sale.

blood typing A way to verify a horse's parentage. Blood typing was usually completed within the first year of a horse's life and was necessary before registration papers were issued by the Jockey Club. Beginning in 2001, the Jockey Club adopted DNA technology to verify horse's parentage.

blowout A short, timed workout, usually a day or two before a race, designed to sharpen a horse's speed. Usually three-eighths or one-half mile in distance.

blue hen Used to describe a great broodmare, the producer of a number of stakes winners and whose daughters, granddaughters, and great-granddaughters in turn produced important winners.

board Short for tote board, on which odds, betting pools, and other information are displayed.

boat race Slang for a fixed race.

bobble A bad step away from the starting gate, usually caused by the track surface breaking away from under a horse's hooves, causing it to duck its head or nearly go to his knees.

bolt Sudden veering from a straight course, usually to the outside rail.

bomb(er) A winning horse sent off at extremely high odds.

book 1) The group of mares being bred to a stallion in a given year. If a stallion attracts the maximum number of mares allowed by the farm manager, he has a full book. 2) A term used to describe a jockey's riding commitments with his agent.

bookie Short for bookmaker.

bookmaker A person who books bets.

bottom 1) Stamina in a horse developed over a long period of time. 2) Subsurface of a racing strip.

bottom line A Thoroughbred's breeding on the female side. It is the lower half of an extended pedigree diagram.

bounce A poor race run immediately after a career-best or near-best performance.

box 1) A wagering term denoting a combination bet whereby all possible numeric combinations are covered for certain horses. 2) A disadvantageous position in a race, behind and between horses. 3) A horse's stall.

boxed (in) To be trapped between, behind, or inside other horses.

brace (or bracer) Rubdown liniment used on a horse after a race or workout.

break 1) To train a young horse to wear a bridle and saddle, carry a rider, and respond to a rider's commands. Most often done when the horse is a yearling. 2) To leave from the starting gate.

breakage In pari-mutuel payoffs, which are rounded down to a nickel or dime, the pennies that are left over. Breakage may be used for any of a number of purposes. Depending upon a state's rules of racing, the money goes to the state, the track, purses, or benevolence programs.

breather Easing off on a horse for a short distance in a race to permit it to conserve or renew its strength.

bred A horse is considered to have been bred in the state or country where it was foaled.

breeder Owner of the dam at time of foaling unless the dam was under a lease or foal-sharing arrangement at the time of foaling. In that case, the person(s) specified by the terms of the agreement is (are) the breeder(s) of the foal.

breed-back rule Restriction imposed in some jurisdictions that for a mare's offspring to be eligible for state-bred bonuses, the mare, after foaling, must be bred to a stallion standing in that state.

Breeders' Cup Thoroughbred racing's year-end championship. Known as Breeders' Cup day, Breeders' Cup championship day, or beginning in 2001 as World Thoroughbred Championships, it consists of races conducted on one day at one of several major North American racetracks each year. The Breeders' Cup concept was developed by Lexington breeder John R. Gaines. The first Breeders' Cup races were run in 1984 at Hollywood Park in Inglewood, California. Breeders' Cup day now comprises eight races totaling $13-million in purses: $1-million Breeders' Cup Sprint, for three-year-olds and older at six furlongs; $1-million Breeders' Cup Juvenile Fillies, for two-year-old fillies at 1 1/16 miles; $2-million Breeders' Cup Distaff, for three-year-olds and older, fillies and mares, at 1 1/8 miles; $1-million Breeders' Cup Mile, for three-year-olds and older at one mile on turf; $1-million Breeders' Cup Juvenile, for two-year-olds at 1 1/16 miles; $1-million Filly and Mare Turf, for fillies and mares at 1 3/8 miles on turf; $2-million Breeders' Cup Turf, for three-year-olds and older at 1 1/2 miles on turf; $4-million Breeders' Cup Classic, for three-year-olds and older at 1 1/4 miles. The Classic was raised to $4-million from $3-million beginning with the 1996 running at Woodbine; the Distaff was increased from $1-million to $2-million in '98. The Filly and Mare Turf was added for 1999. The distances of some of the races have been changed over the years. The Distaff started as a 1 1/4-mile race before being shortened to 1 1/8 miles for the 1988 running. Both the Juvenile and Juveniles Fillies were held at one mile the first three years until changed to 1 1/16 miles in 1986. The $250,000 Breeders' Cup Steeplechase was run from 1986 through '93 and resumed in 2000. Breeders' Cup Ltd. also contributes funds to existing races, and each of those races has Breeders' Cup as part of its name, such as the Gamely Breeders' Cup Handicap (G1).

Breeders' Cup Ltd. Corporate entity that oversees the Breeders' Cup program. It is a not-for-profit organization based in Lexington.

breeding fund A state fund set up to provide bonuses for state-breds.

breeding right The right to breed one mare per year to a specific stallion. Breeding rights, as opposed to stallion shares, do not usually come with bonuses (money derived from extra seasons sold), nor are they assessed expenses.

breeze (breezing) Working a horse at a moderate speed, less effort than handily.

bridge jumper A person who wagers large amounts of money, usually on short-priced horses to show, hoping to realize a small but almost certain profit. The term comes from the structure these bettors may seek if they lose.

bridle A piece of equipment, usually made of leather or nylon, that fits on a horse's head; other equipment, such as a bit and the reins, are attached to it.

broken wind Abnormality of the upper or lower respiratory tract causing loss of normal air exchange, generally resulting in reduced performance.

broodmare A mare that has been bred and is used to produce foals.

broodmare sire The maternal sire; the sire of the dam.

Broodmare Sire Index The Broodmare Sire Index is an average of the Racing Index (RI) of all foals out of the sire's daughters that started at least three times. For BSI to be calculated, a broodmare sire must be represented by a minimum of 75 starters lifetime.

brush 1) During a race when two horses lightly touch each other. 2) Injury that occurs when one hoof strikes the inside of the opposite limb. 3) A type of obstacle used in steeplechase racing.

bullet work The best workout time for a particular distance on a given day at a track. Derived from the printer's bullet that precedes the time of the workout in listings. Also known as a black-letter work in some parts of the country.

bullring A small racetrack, usually less than one mile in circumference.

buy-back A horse put through a public auction that fails to reach a minimum (reserve) price set by the consignor and so is retained. The consignor must pay a fee to the auction company based on a percentage of the reserve to cover the auction company's marketing, advertising, and other costs. A synonym for reserve not attained (RNA).

calk A projection on the heels of a horseshoe, similar to a cleat, on the rear shoes of a horse to prevent slipping, especially on a wet track. Also known as a sticker.

(race) call Running position of horses in a race at various points.

cast A horse positioned on its side or back and wedged against a wall in such a way that it cannot get up.

chalk Wagering favorite in a race. Term dates from the days when on-track bookmakers would write current odds on a chalkboard and the horse that was bet the most used the most chalk.

chalk player Bettor who wagers on favorites.

champion Horse or individual determined to be the outstanding performer in his or her division in a specific year. In the United States, champions are determined by voting in the Eclipse Awards balloting.

chart A statistical picture of a race (from which past performances are compiled) showing the position and margin of each horse at designated points of call (depending on the distance of the race), as well as the horse's age, weight carried, owner, trainer, jockey, and the race's purse, conditions, payoff prices, odds, time, and other data. Before 1991, all charts were compiled by *Daily Racing Form*. From 1991 to '98, charts were compiled by both *Daily Racing Form* and Equibase; since mid-1998, charts

have been compiled exclusively by Equibase.

check(ed) When a jockey slows a horse due to other horses impeding its progress.

chestnut 1) A horse color that may vary from a red-yellow to golden-yellow. The mane, tail, and legs are usually variations of coat color, except where white markings are present. 2) Horny, irregular growths found on the inside of the legs. On the forelegs, they are just above the knees. On the hind legs, they are just below the hocks. No two horses have been found to have the same chestnuts, and so chestnuts may be used for identification. Also called night eyes.

chute Extension of backstretch or homestretch to permit a straight start in a race, as opposed to starting on or near a turn.

claiming Process by which a licensed person may purchase a horse entered in a designated race for a predetermined price. When a horse has been claimed, its new owner assumes title after the starting gate opens although the former owner is entitled to all purse money earned in that race. Sometimes called halter or haltered, for the act of putting a new halter on a claimed horse so that it can be led back to its new barn.

claiming box, claims box Box in which claims are deposited before the race.

claiming race A race in which each horse entered is eligible to be purchased at a set price. Claims must be made before the race and only by licensed owners or their agents who have a horse registered to race at that meeting or who have received a claim certificate from the stewards. A claiming race in which there is an option to have horses entered to be claimed for a stated price or not eligible to be claimed is an optional claiming race.

classic 1) A race of traditional importance, usually modeled on one of the five original English classic races, and often considered part of a triple crown. 2) Used to describe a distance. The American classic distance is 1¼ miles on dirt. The European classic distance is 1½ miles on turf.

clerk of scales An official whose chief duty is to weigh the riders before and after a race to ensure proper weight is or was carried.

climbing When a horse lifts its front legs abnormally high as it gallops, causing it to run inefficiently.

clocker Individual who times workouts and races.

closer A horse that runs best in the latter part of the race, coming from off the pace.

clubhouse turn Generally, the turn on a racing oval that is closest to the clubhouse facility; usually the first turn after the finish line.

colors (horse) Colors accepted by the Jockey Club are bay, black, chestnut, dark bay or brown, gray/roan, and white. In 1996, the Jockey Club started combining gray and roan, which had been separate colors previously.

colt An ungelded (entire) male horse four years old or younger.

commingle Combining mutuel pools from off-track sites with the host track.

company Class of horses in a race or the class of horses a runner usually keeps.

comparable index (CI) Indicates the average earnings of progeny produced from mares bred to one sire when these same mares are bred to other sires. A

CI of 1.00 is considered average, 2.00 is twice the average, and 0.50 half the average.

condition book(s) A series of booklets issued by a track's racing secretary setting forth conditions of races to be run at that track.

conditioner 1) A trainer. 2) A workout or race to enable a horse to attain fitness.

conditions The requirements for being able to enter a horse in a particular race as written by the track's racing secretary. Conditions may include age, sex, money or races won, weight carried, and the distance of the race.

conformation The physical makeup and bodily proportions of a horse.

connections Persons identified with a horse, such as owner, trainer, rider, and stable employees.

consolation double A payoff to holders of daily double tickets combining the winning horse in the first race of the double with a scratched horse in the second.

cooling out Restoring a horse to its normal body temperature, usually by walking, after it has become overheated during exercise or racing. All horses that are exercised and raced are cooled out.

coupled (entry) Two or more horses running as an entry in a single betting unit.

cover A single breeding of a stallion to a mare.

crop 1) The number of foals by a sire in a given year. 2) All horses collectively born in the same year. 3) A jockey's whip.

cup horse A term once used to describe horses competing at the highest level of the sport in races at a distance of two miles or more.

cuppy (track) A drying and loose racing surface that breaks away under a horse's hooves.

cushion Top portion of a racetrack.

cut down Horse suffering injuries from being struck by the shoes of another horse. Or, due to a faulty stride, a horse may cut itself down.

daily double Type of wager calling for the selection of winners of two consecutive races, usually the first and second.

Daily Racing Form A daily newspaper containing news, past performance data, and handicapping information. Founded in 1895, it is the successor of the *Morning Telegraph*. The *Morning Telegraph* was founded in 1833 and was closed during a strike by printers in 1972.

dam The female parent of a foal.

dam's sire (broodmare sire) The sire of a broodmare. Used in reference to the maternal grandsire of a foal.

dark A day when there is no racing at the track.

dark bay or brown A horse color that ranges from brown with areas of tan on the shoulders, head, and flanks, to a dark brown, with tan areas seen only in the flanks, muzzle, or both. The mane, tail, and lower portions of the legs are always black unless white markings are present.

dark horse Probably a good horse whose full potential is unknown before a race.

dead heat Two or more horses finishing a race in a tie.

dead track Racing surface lacking resiliency.

declared In the United States, a horse withdrawn from a stakes race in advance of scratch time. In Europe, a horse confirmed to start in a race.

deep stretch A position very close to the finish line in a race.

Derby A stakes event for three-year-olds, deriving its name from Lord Derby.

disqualification Change in order of finish by officials for an infraction of the rules.

distaffer A female horse.

distaff race A race for female horses.

distanced Horse so far behind the rest of the field of runners that it is out of contact and unable to regain a position of contention. A horse beaten more than 40 lengths.

dogs Rubber traffic cones (or a barrier) placed at certain distances out from the inner rail when the track is wet, muddy, soft, yielding, or heavy to prevent horses during the workout period from churning the footing along the rail.

dope 1) Any illegal drug. 2) Slang term for past performances: Readers of past performances are said to dope out a race.

dosage Although other dosage theories exist, the term is most commonly associated with the one interpreted by Dr. Steven Roman. A variation of Dr. Franco Varola's work on pedigree analysis, the system identifies patterns of ability in horses based on a list of prepotent sires, each of whom is designated a *chef-de-race*. The dosage system puts these sires into one of five categories: brilliant, intermediate, classic, solid, or professional, which are subjective judgments of speed and stamina. Sires can be listed in up to two *chef-de-race* categories. Each generation of sires is worth 16 points, divided by the number of sires; i.e., the immediate sire is worth 16 points while the four sires four generations back are worth four points apiece.

dosage index (DI) A mathematical reduction of the dosage profile to a number reflecting a horse's potential for speed or stamina. The higher the number, the more likely the horse is suited to be a sprinter. The average dosage index of all horses is about 4.00. The dosage index (DI) is derived from the dosage profile to reflect the ratio of speed to stamina in a pedigree. This is calculated by adding points from the two speed categories (brilliant and intermediate), plus half of those from the classic (middle) category, and dividing that total by the points from the two stamina categories (solid and professional), plus the other half of the classic points. The higher the DI, the more speed is supposedly present in the pedigree. A 4.00 DI is generally the cutoff where a horse is considered not likely to be competitive at the American classic distance of 1¼ miles.

driving A horse that is all out to win and under strong urging from its jockey.

drop down A horse meeting a lower class of rival than it had been running against previously.

dwelt Extremely late in breaking from the gate.

earmuffs A piece of equipment that covers a horse's ears to prevent it from hearing distracting sounds.

eased A horse that is gently pulled up during a race.

easily Running or winning without being pressed by rider or opposition.

Eclipse Award Thoroughbred racing's year-end awards, honoring the top horses and people in several categories. Named for the great 18th-century racehorse and sire Eclipse, who was undefeated in 18 career starts and sired the winners of 344 races. The Eclipse Awards are sponsored by the National Thoroughbred Racing Association, *Daily Racing Form*, and National Turf Writers Association. They were first awarded in 1971; previously, separate year-end champions were named by *Daily Racing Form* (beginning in 1936) and the Thoroughbred Racing Associations (beginning in 1950).

eligible Qualified to start in a race, according to conditions.

engagement 1) Stakes nomination. 2) Riding commitment.

entire An ungelded horse. In Europe, where geldings are not permitted to enter certain races, the race conditions might read: Entire colts and fillies.

entry Two or more horses with common ownership (in some cases, trained by the same trainer) that are paired as a single betting unit in one race or are placed together by the racing secretary as part of a mutuel field. Rules on entries vary from state to state. Also known as a coupled entry.

entry fee Money paid by an owner to enter a horse in a stakes race—and is what usually defines a race as a stakes. Entry fees are not required for overnight races and some invitational stakes races.

epistaxis Blood coming out of the horse's nostrils. See bleeder.

Equibase Co. A partnership between the Jockey Club and the Thoroughbred Racing Associations to establish and maintain an industry-owned, central database of racing records. Equibase past-performance information is used in track programs across North America. Formed in 1990, Equibase first collected data in '91. In 1998, it began supplying past performance information to *Daily Racing Form* and became the sole collector of racing data.

estrus (heat) Associated with ovulation; a mare usually is receptive to breeding during estrus. Referred to as horsing.

euthanize To end a horse's life because of a catastrophic injury or critical illness and to prevent further pain and suffering.

evenly Neither gaining nor losing position during a race.

exacta (or perfecta) A wager in which the first two finishers in a race, in exact order of finish, must be picked. Called an exactor in Canada.

exacta box A wager in which all possible combinations using a given number of horses are bet on.

exercise rider Individual who is licensed to exercise a horse during morning training hours.

exotic (wager) Any wager other than win, place, or show that requires multiple combinations. Examples of exotic wagers: trifecta, pick six, pick three.

Experimental Free Handicap A year-end assessment of the best North American two-year-olds of the season. It is put together by a panel of racing secretaries under the auspices of the Jockey Club and is based on performances in unrestricted races. Two lists are drawn up, one for males and one for females. Only the handicap for two-year-olds is called the Experimental Free Handicap; lists for older horses are free handicaps. First started by Walter Vosburgh in 1933. Race based on Experimental was run at Aqueduct from 1940 to '56 at six furlongs (Experimental Free Handicap

No. 1) and another from 1946 to '52 at 1⅟₁₆ miles (Experimental Free Handicap No. 2).

extended Running at top speed.

farrier Horseshoer, blacksmith.

fast (track) Footing that is dry, even, and resilient.

fault Weak points of a horse's conformation or character as a racehorse.

feather Light weight. Usually refers to the weight a horse is assigned to carry in a race.

fee 1) Amount paid to a jockey for riding in a race. 2) The cost of nominating, entering, or starting a horse in a stakes race.

field The horses in a race.

field horse (or mutuel field) Two or more starters running as a single betting unit (entry), when there are more starters in a race than positions on the totalizator board.

filly Female horse four years old or younger.

firm (track) A condition of a turf course corresponding to fast on a dirt track. A firm, resilient surface.

flag Signal manually held a short distance in front of the gate at the exact starting point of a race. In some jurisdictions, official timing starts when flag is dropped by the flagman to denote proper start.

flagman Person who drops the flag to signal the start of a race.

flak jacket Similar to a jacket worn by football quarterbacks, the jockey's flak jacket protects the chest, ribs, kidneys, and back from injury.

flat race Contested on level ground as opposed to a steeplechase race. Often used in the term, on the flat.

flatten out A very tired horse that slows considerably, dropping its head on a straight line with its body. Some horses, however, like to run with their heads lowered.

float 1) An equine dental procedure in which sharp points on the teeth are filed down. 2) The instrument with which the above procedure is performed.

floating Flat plate or wooden implement (float) dragged over the surface of a wet track to aid in draining water.

foal(ed) 1) A horse of either sex in its first year of life. 2) Can also denote the offspring of either a male or female parent. 3) To give birth.

Fontana safety rail An aluminum rail, in use since 1981, designed to help reduce injuries to horse and rider. It has more of an offset (slant) to provide greater clearance between the rail and the vertical posts as well as a protective cover to keep horse and rider from striking the posts.

founding sires The Darley Arabian, Byerly Turk, and Godolphin Arabian. Every Thoroughbred must trace its male line parentage to one of the three founding sires.

fractional time Intermediate times recorded in a race, as at the quarter-mile, half-mile, three-quarters, etc.

free handicap A race in which no nomination fees are required. More recently, and more commonly, a ranking of horses three years old and up by weight for a theoretical race or as an intellectual challenge.

front-runner A horse whose running style is to attempt to get on or near the lead at the start of the race and to continue there as long as possible.

frozen (track) The condition of a racetrack where any moisture present is frozen.

full brother, full sister Horses that share the same sire and dam.

furlong One-eighth of a mile, which is equal to 220 yards or 660 feet.

furosemide A medication used in the treatment of bleeders, commonly known by the trade name Salix, a diuretic. Although research has not determined definitively how furosemide reduces bleeding, it is widely believed that the diuretic effect reduces pressure within capillaries in the lungs.

futurity A race for two-year-olds in which the owners make a scheduled series of payments over a period of time to keep their horses eligible. Purses for these races vary but can be considerable.

gait The characteristic footfall pattern of a horse in motion. Thoroughbreds have four natural gaits: walk, trot, canter, and gallop. Thoroughbreds compete at a gallop.

gap An opening in the rail where horses enter and leave the course.

Garrison finish A close victory, usually from off the pace. Derived from Ed "Snapper" Garrison, a 19th-century rider known for his close finishes.

gate card A card, issued by the starter, stating that a horse is properly schooled in starting-gate procedures.

gelding A male horse of any age that has been neutered by having both testicles removed (gelded).

gentleman jockey Amateur rider, generally in steeplechases.

get Progeny of sire.

girth An elastic and leather band, sometimes covered with sheepskin, that passes under a horse's belly and is connected to both sides of the saddle.

good (track) A dirt track that is almost fast or a turf course slightly softer than firm.

grab a quarter Injury to the back of the hoof or foot caused by a horse stepping on itself (usually affects the front foot). Being stepped on from behind in the same manner usually affects the back foot. Very common in racing, the injury is usually minor.

graded race Established in 1973 to classify select stakes races in North America, at the request of European racing authorities, who had set up group races two years earlier. Grading of races is performed by a committee under the direction of the Thoroughbred Owners and Breeders Association. See graded stakes section elsewhere in this book.

grandsire The grandfather of a horse; father (sire) of the horse's dam or sire.

grass slip Used in some areas, permission to exercise a horse on the turf course. Also known as a turf card.

gray A horse color in which the majority of the coat is a mixture of black and white hairs. The mane, tail, and legs may be either black or gray unless white markings are present. Starting with foals of 1993, the color classifications gray and roan were combined as roan or gray.

Grayson-Jockey Club Research Foundation A privately financed charitable organization established in 1989, which combined the Grayson Foundation Inc. (begun in 1940) and the Jockey Club Research Foundation.

group race Designation of best races in countries outside North America. European authorities began designating races as Group 1, Group 2, and Group 3 in 1971. North American officials, under the direction of the Thoroughbred Owners and Breeders Association, began grading races in 1973.

guineas By definition, a guinea is 21 shillings, or in current usage a pound and a shilling. Thus, the guinea is equal to 1.05 pounds. Used by sales companies in England and Ireland to report sales since it includes the sales company's commission.

half brother, half sister Horses out of the same dam but by different sires. Horses with the same sire and different dams are not considered half siblings in Thoroughbred racing.

halter Like a bridle, but lacking a bit and reins. Used to handle horses around the stable and when they are not being ridden.

hand Four inches. A horse's height is measured in hands and inches from the top of the shoulder (withers) to the ground; that is, 15.2 hands is 15 hands, 2 inches, or a total of 62 inches. Thoroughbreds typically range from 15 to 17 hands.

handicap 1) Race for which the track handicapper assigns the weights to be carried. 2) To make selections on the basis of past performances.

handicap horse A horse that competes in handicap races.

handicapper 1) A person, usually the racing secretary, who assigns weights to horses. 2) A bettor that is making selections based on information of horses' performances from previous starts.

handily 1) Working in the morning with maximum effort. 2) A horse racing well within itself, with little exertion from the jockey.

handle Amount of money wagered in the pari-mutuels on a race, a program, during a meeting, or for a year.

hand ride Urging a horse with the hands and not using the whip.

hard (track) A condition of a turf course where there is no resiliency to the surface.

hardboot A Kentucky horseman.

hard-knocker A tough horse who makes a lot of starts.

harrow Implement or unit with pulling teeth, or tines, used to rake and loosen the upper surface of a track.

head A margin between horses. One horse leading another by the length of its head.

head of the stretch Beginning of the straight run to the finish line.

head to head Running on even terms.

heat 1) A race in which more than one running is required to decide the winner. Not used in flat racing today, though it was common in the 19th century. Still used occasionally in harness racing. 2) A breeding term for estrus in a mare.

heavy (track) Wettest possible condition of a turf course; not usually found in North America.

helmet A lightweight fiberglass cap worn by riders to prevent head injuries. It is required equipment and is not considered part of a jockey's riding weight.

high weight Refers to highest weight assigned or carried in a race.

highweight Horse assigned the highest weight on the Experimental Free Handicap, a division of the International Classification, or one of many Free Handicaps in individual countries, and often viewed as the equivalent of a champion in the absence of offficial championships.

homebred A horse bred by its owner.

homestretch Long section of racetrack closest to the stands.

hood A covering, usually nylon, that goes over a horse's head; blinkers or earmuffs may be attached to it.

hopped A horse that has been illegally stimulated with a drug.

horse When reference is made to sex, an ungelded male five years old or older.

Horsemen's Benevolent and Protective Association A national organization of horsemen, largely composed of owners, that has divisions at many racetracks in North America to help owners and trainers negotiate purses and other issues with track management.

hotwalker A person or automatic machine that walks horses to cool them out after workout or races.

hung A horse that does not advance its position in a race when called upon by its jockey.

icing 1) A physical therapy procedure, properly known as cryotherapy. 2) When a horse's leg or legs are placed in a tub of ice or ice packs are applied to the legs to reduce inflammation or swelling.

impost Weight carried by a horse or assigned to a horse.

inbreeding The mating of closely related individuals, resulting in a pedigree with at least one common ancestor duplicated on both sire and dam's side of the pedigree. In Thoroughbreds, horses with one or more duplicated ancestors within the first four or five generations are generally considered inbred, while duplications of ancestors in more distant generations are often referred to as "linebreeding."

infield Area enclosed by the inner rail of the racetrack.

in hand Running under moderate control, at less than top speed.

inquiry A review of the running of the race to check into a possible infraction of the rules, called by the stewards. Also, a sign flashed by officials on the tote board on such occasions. If lodged by a jockey, it is called an objection.

in the money A horse that finishes first, second, or third in a race.

Irish rail Movable rail.

isolation barn A facility used to separate horses to ensure that disease is not carried into the area.

jail Requirement that a claimed horse when it next runs in a claiming race must run for a claiming price 25% higher over the next 30 days.

Jockey Club Organization dedicated to the improvement of Thoroughbred breeding and racing. Incorporated February 9, 1894, in New York City, the Jockey Club serves as North America's Thoroughbred registry, responsible for the maintenance of the *American Stud Book*, a register of all Thoroughbreds foaled in the United States, Puerto Rico, and Canada; and of all Thoroughbreds imported into those countries fresh from jurisdictions that have a registry recognized by the Jockey Club and the International Stud Book Committee.

jockey fee Sum paid to rider for competing in a race.

Jockeys' Guild National organization of professional riders.

jockey's race A race whose outcome will hinge mostly on strategic thinking by the riders; one in which riders must pay close attention to pace to keep their horses fresh for a strong finish.

jog Slow, easy gait.

joint 1) Point of juncture of two bones and usually composed of fibrous connective tissue and cartilage. 2) Slang for an illegal electrical stimulation device.

jumper Steeplechase or hurdle horse.

juvenile Two-year-old horse.

key horse A horse used in multiple combinations in an exotic wager.

kilometer One thousand meters and equal to .62 of a mile.

lame A deviation from a normal gait due to pain in a limb or its supporting structures.

Lasix See Salix.

late double A second daily double offered during the latter part of the program.

lead Refers to the leading leg when a horse is racing in full stride. The lead leg is the one that reaches out the farthest and bears the full weight of the horse's impact. Horses usually race on the left, or inside, lead on the turn, and on the right, or outside, lead on straightaways. Changing leads refers to the horse's ability to switch from one leading leg to the other at the proper time.

leaky-roof circuit Minor tracks.

leg up To help a jockey mount a horse.

length A measurement approximating the length of a horse and used to describe the distances between horses in a race. A length is approximately eight feet.

listed race A stakes race just below a group race or graded race in quality.

lock Slang for a sure winner.

longe 1) A long rope fastened to a horse's head and held by a trainer, who causes the horse to move around in a circle. 2) A method of exercising a horse on a tether (longe line).

lug (bearing in or lugging out) Deviating from a straight course. May be due to weariness, infirmity, inexperience, or the rider overusing the whip or reins to make a horse alter its course.

maiden 1) A horse or rider that has not won a race. 2) A female that has never been bred.

maiden race A race for nonwinners.

mare Female horse five years old or older. Also, any female that has been bred regardless of age.

mare's month September. In theory, mares that have not run well during the summer often perform better in September.

mash Soft, moist mixture, hot or cold, of grain and other feed that is easily digested by horses.

massage Rubbing of various parts of the anatomy to stimulate healing.

match race A race between two horses.

medication list A list kept by the track veterinarian and published by the track showing which horses have been treated with legally prescribed medications.

meter The basic unit of length in the metric system. It is equal to approximately 39.37 inches. It takes 100 centimeters to make a meter and 1,000 meters to make a kilometer. To convert to inches, multiply by 39.37 (5 meters x 39.37 inches = 196.85 inches). To convert to yards, multiply by 1.1 (5 meters x 1.1 = 5.5 yards). Most European races are expressed in meters. A mile is approximately 1,600 meters, the distance at which the classic Poule d'Essai des Pouliches (Fr-G1) and the Poule d'Essai des Poulains (Fr-G1) are run. The Prix de l'Arc de Triomphe (Fr-G1) is 2,400 meters, or approximately 1½ miles; the Prix Eugene Adam (Fr-G2) is 2,000 meters, or approximately 1¼ miles. See Distance Conversion

Table elsewhere in this book.

middle distance Broadly, from one mile to 1¼ miles.

minus pool A negative mutuel pool created when a horse is so heavily played that, after deductions of state tax and commission, not enough money remains to pay the legally prescribed minimum on each winning bet. The racing association usually makes up the difference.

money rider A rider who excels in rich races.

monkey on a stick Type of riding with short stirrups popularized by riding great Todhunter Sloan shortly before 1900.

morning glory Horse that performs well in morning workouts but fails to reproduce that form in races.

morning line Probable odds on each horse in a race, as determined by a mathematical formula used by the track odds maker, who tries to gauge both the ability of the horse and the most likely final odds as determined by the bettors. Those odds now are known as the program-line odds because they appear in the track's official program.

mud calks Special cleats that help a horse gain traction on a muddy track.

muddy (track) Condition of a racetrack that is wet but has no standing water.

mudder Horse that races well on muddy tracks. Also known as a mudlark.

mutuel pool Short for pari-mutuel pool. Sum of the wagers on a race or event, such as the win pool, daily double pool, exacta pool, etc.

muzzle 1) Nose and lips of a horse. 2) A guard placed over a horse's mouth to prevent it from biting or eating.

name (of a Thoroughbred) Names of North American Thoroughbreds are registered by the Jockey Club. They can be no longer than 18 characters, including punctuation and spaces.

National Thoroughbred Association Started as concept of advertising agency executive Fred Pope in early 1990s, with backing from owner-breeder John R. Gaines. The NTA was based on the concept that owners possess rights to their horses' images for simulcasting purposes, with the owners banding together to form a major league of racing through the pooling of simulcasting rights. Hamilton Jordan and Tim Smith were brought in to help sell the concept in 1997, and the NTA initiative eventually led to a broader industry coalition, the formation of the National Thoroughbred Racing Association. NTA officially was folded into the NTRA in August 1998.

National Thoroughbred Racing Association A not-for-profit association created by a consensus of industry factions to market the sport. Founding members were Breeders' Cup Ltd., the Jockey Club, Keeneland Association, and Oak Tree Racing Association, with each putting up $1-million in seed money. Before officially launching the office, the National Thoroughbred Association became a founding member when it ceased its existence and was rolled into the NTRA. In 2000, the Thoroughbred Owners and Breeders Association retroactively became a founding member. The NTRA first proposed a business plan to the industry in August 1997. The NTRA officially opened for business on April 1, 1998. Its first commissioner was Tim Smith. D. G. Van Clief Jr. of Breeders' Cup Ltd. acted as interim chief executive officer of the NTRA in its formative stages. The NTRA formally merged many of its administrative functions with Breeders' Cup Ltd. on January 1, 2001.

National Museum of Racing and Hall of Fame Building in Saratoga Springs, New York, that houses a museum and a Racing Hall of Fame. The National Museum of Racing was founded in 1950. It had its first home in the old Canfield Casino, Congress Park, Saratoga Springs. It moved to its present site in 1955, the same year the Racing Hall of Fame was created.

near side Left side of a horse. Side on which a horse is mounted.

neck Unit of measurement. About the length of a horse's neck; a little less than one-quarter length.

nod Lowering of head. To win by a nod, a horse extends its head with its nose touching the finish line ahead of a close competitor.

nominator One who owns a horse at the time it is named to compete in a stakes race or makes it eligible to a stakes program such as the Breeders' Cup.

North American Pari-Mutuel Regulators Association Organization founded in 1997 as a splinter group from the Association of Racing Commissioners International due to philosophical differences in practices and policies. NAPRA's original members were Alabama, Arizona, Florida, Idaho, Kansas, Minnesota, Oklahoma, Oregon, Saskatchewan, South Dakota, Wisconsin, and Wyoming. Joining the organization by January 2002 were the Alberta Racing Corp., British Columbia, Canadian Pari-Mutuel Agency, Colorado, Florida Division of Pari-Mutuel Wagering, Kentucky, Manitoba, Maryland, Montana, New Mexico, North Dakota, Pennsylvania, and Virginia.

nose Smallest advantage a horse can win by. Called a short head in Britain.

nose band A leather strap that goes over the bridge of a horse's nose to help secure the bridle. A figure-eight nose band goes over the bridge of the nose and under the rings of the bit to help keep the horse's mouth closed. The figure-eight nose band keeps the tongue from sliding up over the bit and is used on horses that do not like having a tongue tie used.

Oaks A stakes event for three-year-old fillies.

objection Claim of foul lodged by rider, patrol judge, or other official after the running of a race. If lodged by an official, it is called an inquiry.

odds-on Odds of less than even money.

odds maker The individual who prepares the program line for a track.

official 1) Notice displayed when a race result is confirmed. 2) Used to denote a racing official.

off side Right side of horse.

off-track betting Wagering at legalized betting outlets usually run by the tracks, management companies specializing in pari-mutuel wagering, or, in New York, by independent corporations chartered by the state. Wagers at OTB sites are usually commingled with on-track betting pools.

on the bit When a horse is eager to run. Also known as in the bridle.

on the board Finishing among the first three.

on the muscle Denotes a fit horse.

on the nose Betting a horse to win only.

optional claiming A claiming race in which there is an option to have horses entered to be claimed for a stated price or not eligible to be claimed.

outcross When a horse has no inbreeding, especially within the first five generations.

out of the money A horse that finishes worse than third.

overcheck A strap that holds the bit in place.

overgirth An elastic band that goes completely around a horse and over the saddle, to keep the saddle from slipping.

over-reaching Toe of hind shoe striking the forefoot or foreleg.

overland, overland route Racing wide throughout, outside other horses.

overlay A horse going off at higher odds than it appears to warrant based on its past performances.

overnight A sheet published by the racing secretary's office listing the entries for an upcoming racing card.

overnight race A race in which entries close in a specific number of hours before running (such as 48 hours) and do not require an entry fee, as opposed to a stakes race for which nominations close weeks and sometimes months in advance and usually require a monetary payment for a horse to be eligible.

overweight Excess weight carried by a horse when the rider exceeds the required weight.

pacesetter The horse that is running in front (on the lead).

paddock Area where horses are saddled and paraded before being taken onto the track.

paddock judge Official in charge of paddock and saddling routine.

panel A slang term for a furlong.

pari-mutuel A form of wagering originated in 1865 by Frenchman Pierre Oller in which all money bet is divided and distributed to those who have winning tickets after taxes, takeout, and other deductions are made. Oller called his system perier mutuel, meaning mutual stake or betting among ourselves. As this wagering method was adopted in England, it became known as Paris mutuals, and soon after pari-mutuels.

parlay A multirace bet in which all winnings are subsequently wagered on a succeeding race.

part wheel Using a key horse or horses in different, but not all possible, exotic wagering combinations.

pasteboard track A lightning-fast racing surface.

past performances A horse's racing record, earnings, bloodlines, and other data, presented in composite form.

patrol judges Officials who observe the progress of a race from various vantage points around the track.

pattern race Synonym for a group race in Europe.

photo finish A result so close it is necessary to use the finish-line camera to determine the order of finish.

pick (number) A type of multirace wager in which the winners of all the included races must be selected. Pick three (sometimes called the daily triple), pick six, and pick nine are commonly used by tracks in the United States.

pill Small numbered ball used in a blind draw to decide post positions.

pinched back A horse forced back when racing in close quarters, particularly on turns.

pin firing Thermocautery used to increase blood flow to the leg and intended to promote healing.

pinhooker A person who buys a racehorse prospect with the intention of reselling it at a profit. Examples are weanling-to-yearling pinhookers and yearling-to-juvenile pinhookers.

pipe-opener Exercise at a brisk speed.

place Second position at finish.

place bet Wager on a horse to finish first or second.

placing judge Official who posts the order of finish in a race.

plate(s) 1) A prize for a winner. Usually less valuable than a cup. 2) Generic term for lightweight horseshoes, usually made of aluminum, that are used during a race.

plater Vernacular for a claiming horse.

pocket A position in a race with horses in front and alongside.

pole(s) Markers at measured distances around the track designating the distance from the finish. The quarter pole, for instance, is one-quarter mile from the finish line, not from the start.

pony Any horse or pony that leads the parade of the field from paddock to starting gate. A horse or pony that accompanies a horse to the starting gate. Also known as a lead pony.

post 1) Starting point for a race. 2) An abbreviated version of post position.

post parade Horses going from paddock to starting gate past the stands.

post position Position of stall in starting gate from which a horse starts.

preferred list Horses with prior rights to starting, usually because they have previously been entered in races that have not filled with the minimum number of starters or they have been excluded from races that drew an excess of entries.

prep (race) A workout (or race) used to prepare a horse for a future engagement.

program line Probable odds on each horse in a race, as determined by a mathematical formula used by the track odds maker, who tries to gauge both the ability of the horse and the likely final odds as determined by the bettors. These odds are published in the track's official program and formerly were known as the morning line.

prop When a horse suddenly stops moving by digging its front feet into the ground.

public trainer One whose services are not exclusively engaged by a single stable and who accepts horses from a number of owners.

pull up To stop or slow a horse during or after a race or workout.

purse The total monetary amount distributed after a race to the owners of the entrants finishing in the top positions, usually five. Some racing jurisdictions may pay purse money through other places.

quarantine barn 1) A United States Department of Agriculture structure used to isolate foreign horses for a short period of time to ensure they are not carrying a disease. The structure may be at a racetrack, an airport, or a specially designated facility. Horses must be cleared by a federal veterinarian before being released from quarantine. 2) Any facility used to keep infected horses away from the general equine population.

quarter crack A vertical crack between the toe and heel, usually extending into the coronary band.

quinella Wager in which the first two finishers must be picked in either order.

rabbit A speed horse running as an entry with another, usually a come-from-behind horse.

Racing Index Racing Index (RI) is based on the average earnings per start for all runners in the United States, Canada, England, Ireland, France, Italy, Germany, Puerto Rico, and the United Arab Emirates. RI is determined by calculating the average earnings per start, divided into males and females, of all starters in each individual country, and the average for each individual year is by definition 1.00. Median RI is much lower.

racing secretary Official who drafts conditions of races and assigns weights for handicap events.

rail The barrier on either side of the racing strip. Sometimes referred to as the fence.

rail runner Horse that prefers to run next to the inside rail.

rank A horse that refuses to settle under a jockey's handling in a race, running in a headstrong manner without respect to pace.

receiving barn Structure used to house horses shipping in for a race on a specific day. Horses trained on farms or at training centers often will be placed in the receiving barn until their races.

redboard 1) Old-time method of declaring a race official by posting a red flag or board on the tote board. 2) A mildly derogatory phrase used to describe someone who claims to have selected the winner, but always after the race.

refuse 1) When a horse will not break from the gate. 2) In jumping races, balking at a jump.

reins Long straps, usually made of leather, that are connected to the bit and used by the jockey to control the horse.

reserve A minimum price, set by the consignor, for a horse in a public auction.

reserve not attained A minimum price, or reserve, set by the consignor for a horse at a public auction that is not met by those who are bidding. RNA.

reserved 1) Held for a particular engagement or race. 2) Held off the pace.

ridden out A horse that finishes a race under mild urging; not as severe as driving.

ride short Using short stirrups.

ridgling (rig) A term describing either a cryptorchid (neither testicle descended) or a monorchid (only one testicle descended into the scrotum).

roan A horse color in which the majority of the coat is a mixture of red and white hairs or brown and white hairs. The mane, tail, and legs may be black, chestnut, or roan unless white markings are present. Starting with foals of 1993, the color classifications of gray and roan were combined as gray or roan.

rogue Ill-tempered horse.

route A race of long distance; broadly, a race at a distance of 1⅛ miles or more in North America.

router Horse that performs well at longer distances.

run-out bit A special type of bit to prevent a horse from bearing out (or in).

saddle A Thoroughbred racing saddle is the lightest saddle used, weighing less than two pounds.

saddlecloth A cotton cloth that goes under the saddle

to absorb sweat. It usually has the horse's program number on it and, often in major races, the horse's name.

saddlepad A piece of felt, sheepskin, or more usually, foam rubber, used as a base for the saddle.

Salix An antibleeder medication that had been named Lasix until the medication's manufacturer, Intervet, changed the name in 2001. Its generic name is furosemide, and it was first used in veterinary practice in 1967.

savage When a horse bites another horse or a person.

scale of weights Fixed weights to be carried by horses according to their age, sex, race distance, and time of year. See scale of weights table elsewhere in this book.

schooling Process of familiarizing a horse with the starting gate and teaching it racing practices. A horse also may be schooled in the paddock. In steeplechasing, to teach a horse to jump.

schooling list List of horses eligible to school at the starting gate before being permitted to race.

scratch To be taken out of a race before a horse starts. Trainers usually scratch horses due to adverse track conditions or a horse's health. A track veterinarian can scratch a horse at any time.

second call A secondary mount of a jockey in a race in case his primary mount is scratched.

second dam Grandmother of a horse. Also known as a grandam.

set A group of horses being exercised together.

set down 1) To be suspended, usually referring to a jockey. 2) When a jockey assumes a lower crouch in the saddle while urging the horse to pick up speed.

sex allowance Female horses (fillies and mares), according to their age and the time of year, are allowed to carry three to five pounds less when racing against males.

shadow roll A bulky piece of material, usually sheepskin or synthetic fabric, that is secured over the bridge of a horse's nose to keep it from seeing shadows on the track. Often used with horses that shy away from shadows on the track or jump them.

shank Rope or strap attached to a halter or bridle by which a horse is led.

shedrow Stable area; walking path within a barn.

sheets A handicapping tool assigning a numerical value to each race run by a horse to enable different horses running at different racetracks to be objectively compared. Two principal companies in this field are operated by Len Ragozin, the originator, and Jerry Brown.

short A horse in need of more workouts or racing to reach winning form.

show Third position at the finish.

show bet Wager on a horse to finish in the money; third or better.

shut off Unable to improve position due to being surrounded by other horses.

silks Jacket and cap worn by riders to designate owner of the horse, or at some smaller tracks, to designate post positions (e.g., yellow for post position one, blue for two, etc.).

Silky Sullivan A term sometimes used for a horse that makes a big run from far back. Named for the horse Silky Sullivan, who once made up 41 lengths to win a six-furlong race.

simulcast A simultaneous live television transmission

of a race to other tracks, off-track betting offices, or other outlets for the purpose of wagering.

sire 1) The male parent. 2) To beget foals. According to cataloging standards and standard usage, a stallion must sire a winner to be called a sire; he is a stallion until that time.

Sire Index (SI) Sire Index is an average of the Racing Index (RI) of all foals by a sire that have started at least three times. For SI to be calculated, a sire must be represented by a minimum of three crops and 25 starters lifetime.

slipped A breeding term meaning spontaneous abortion.

sloppy (track) A racing strip that is saturated with water and has standing water visible.

slow (track) A racing strip that is wet on both the surface and base.

snip Small patch of white hairs on the nose or lips of a horse.

socks Solid white markings extending from the top of the hoof to the ankles. Also called stockings.

soft (track) Condition of a turf course with a large amount of moisture. Horses' hooves sink deeply into the surface.

sophomores Three-year-old horses.

speed figure A handicapping tool in which a numerical value is assigned to a horse's performance.

speedy cut Injury to the inside of the knee or hock caused by a strike from another foot.

spit box A generic term describing a barn or area to which horses are taken for post-race testing. Tests may include saliva, urine, or blood.

spit the bit Or spit out the bit. A term referring to a tired horse that begins to run less aggressively.

split(s) Fractional times in a race in increments of one-eighth of a mile.

sprint Short race, less than one mile.

stakes A race for which the owner usually must pay a fee to run a horse. The fees can be for nominating, maintaining eligibility, entering, and starting; the track adds additional money to make up the total purse. Some stakes races are by invitation and require no payment or fee.

stakes-placed Finished second or third in a stakes race.

stakes horse A horse whose level of competition includes mostly stakes races.

stallion A male horse used for breeding.

stallion season The right to breed one mare to a specific stallion during one breeding season.

stallion share A lifetime right to breed one mare to a specific stallion each breeding season. Although generally limited to one mare per season per share, larger stallion books have in some cases allowed share owners to breed more than one mare each year. Stallion share owners are usually assessed a proportionate share of expenses and will also share in any bonuses.

stall walker Horse that moves about its stall constantly and frets rather than resting.

star 1) Any of a number of white markings on the forehead. (The forehead is defined as being above an imaginary line connecting the tops of the eyes.) 2) A type of credit a horse receives from the racing secretary if it is excluded from an overfilled race, giving it priority in entering future races.

starter 1) An official responsible for ensuring a fair start to the race. The starter supervises the loading of horses into the starting gate by assistant starters who collectively are known as a gate crew. The starter also has control of opening the gate. 2) A horse that is in the starting gate when the race begins, whether it runs or not.

starter race An allowance or handicap race restricted to horses that have started for a specific claiming price or less.

starting gate Partitioned mechanical device having stalls in which the horses are confined until the starter releases the stalls' front doors to begin the race.

stayer A horse that can race long distances successfully.

steadied A horse being taken in hand by its rider, usually when in close quarters.

step up A horse moving up in class to meet better competition.

steward Official of the race meeting responsible for enforcing the rules of racing.

steeplechase A race in which horses are required to jump a series of obstacles on the course. Steeplechase races in the United States are run over National Fences (artificial brush fences), natural brush fences, and timber fences. In England and Ireland, jump races are over hurdles and steeplechase fences.

stick A jockey's whip.

stirrups Metal D-shaped rings into which a jockey places his or her feet. They can be raised or lowered by shortening or lengthening the leather straps that connect the stirrups to the saddle. Also known as irons.

stockings Solid white markings extending from the top of the hoof to the knee or hock. Also called socks.

stone English system of weights is based on stones. A stone is equal to 14 pounds; thus, 126 pounds is nine stone.

(home) stretch Final straight; portion of the racetrack from the end of the final turn to the finish line.

stretch call Position of horses at the eighth pole, or one-eighth mile from the finish.

stretch runner Horse that runs fastest, relative to the pacesetters, nearing the finish of a race.

stretch turn Bend of track into the final straightaway.

stride Manner of going. Also, distance covered between successive imprints of the same hoof.

stripe A white marking running down a horse's face, starting under an imaginary line connecting the tops of the eyes.

stud 1) Male horse used for breeding. 2) A breeding farm.

stud book Registry and genealogical record of Thoroughbreds, maintained by the Jockey Club or Turf authority of the country in question.

subscription Fee paid by owner to nominate a horse for a stakes race or to maintain eligibility for a stakes.

substitute race Alternate race used on overnight sheets to replace a regularly scheduled race that does not fill or is canceled.

suckling A foal in its first year of life, while it is still nursing.

sulk When a horse refuses to extend itself.

swayback Horse with a prominent concave shape of the backbone, usually just behind the withers (saddle area). Lordosis.

tack Rider's racing equipment. Also applied to stable gear.

tail off Used to describe a fit horse losing its competitive edge.

takeout Commission deducted from mutuel pools that is shared by the track, horsemen (in the form of purses), and local and state governing bodies in the form of tax. Also called take.

taken up A horse pulled up sharply by its rider due to being in close quarters.

tattoo A permanent, indelible mark on the inside of the upper lip used to identify the horse.

teaser A male horse used at breeding farms to determine whether a mare is ready to receive a stallion.

teletimer Electronic means to time races, including fractional times at various points of call. The lead horse trips an electronic beam of light and the clockings are transmitted instantly to the tote board.

Thoroughbred A Thoroughbred is a horse whose parentage traces in male line to any of the three founding sires—the Darley Arabian, Byerly Turk, and Godolphin Arabian. The horse also must have satisfied the rules and requirements of the Jockey Club for inclusion in the *American Stud Book*, or it is registered in a foreign stud book recognized by the Jockey Club and the International Stud Book Committee.

Thoroughbred Horsemen's Association A representative group organized on local levels primarily in Mid-Atlantic states to represent the interests of owners in negotiations with tracks on purses and other issues. Started as an alternative to the Horsemen's Benevolent and Protective Association.

Thoroughbred Racing Associations An industry group founded in 1942 and comprising about 50 racetracks in North America.

tight Vernacular for fit and ready to race.

tightener 1) A race used to give a horse a level of fitness that cannot be obtained through morning exercise alone. 2) A leg brace.

timber topper Steeplechase horse racing over post-and-rail fences.

tongue tie Strip of cloth or cloth-like material used to stabilize a horse's tongue to prevent it from choking down in a race or workout or to keep the tongue from sliding up over the bit, rendering the horse uncontrollable. Also known as a tongue strap.

top line 1) A Thoroughbred's breeding on its sire's side. 2) The visual line presented by the horse's back.

totalizator An automated pari-mutuel system that dispenses and records betting tickets, calculates and displays odds and payoffs, and provides the mechanism for cashing winning tickets. Often shortened to tote.

tote board Structure in the racetrack infield where up-to-the-minute odds and other information are listed. It may also show the amounts wagered in each mutuel pool as well as information such as jockey and equipment changes. Also known as the board.

tout Person who professes to have, and sells, advance information on a race.

track bias A racing surface that favors a particular running style or position.

track condition Condition of the racetrack surface.

trial In Thoroughbred racing, a preparatory race created in tandem with a subsequent, more important stakes race to be run a few days or weeks hence. In Europe, a trial can refer to a vigorous morning workout with other horses under race-like conditions.

trifecta A wager in which the first three finishers must be selected in exact order. Called a triactor in Canada and a triple in some parts of the United States.

trifecta box A trifecta wager in which all possible combinations using a given number of horses are bet upon.

trip An individual horse's race, with specific reference to the difficulty (or lack of difficulty) the horse had during competition, such as whether the horse was repeatedly blocked or had an unobstructed run.

Triple Crown Used generically to denote a series of three important races. In the United States, the Kentucky Derby, Preakness Stakes, and Belmont Stakes make up the Triple Crown. In England, the Two Thousand Guineas, Epsom Derby, and St. Leger Stakes. In Canada, the Queen's Plate, Prince of Wales Stakes, and Breeders' Stakes.

turn down(s) Rear shoe that is turned down—from a half-inch to one inch at the ends—to provide better traction on an off-track. Illegal in most jurisdictions.

twitch A restraining device usually consisting of a stick with a loop of rope or chain at one end, which is placed around a horse's upper lip and twisted, releasing endorphins that relax a horse and curb its fractiousness while it is being handled.

underlay A horse at shorter odds than seem warranted by its past performances.

under wraps Horse under stout restraint in a race or workout to keep it from pulling away from the competition by too large a margin.

untried 1) Not raced or tested for speed. 2) A stallion that has not been bred.

unwind Gradually withdrawing a horse from intensive training.

valet A person employed by a racing association to clean and care for a jockey's tack and other riding equipment.

walkover A race in which only one horse competes.

washed out A horse that becomes so nervous that it sweats profusely. Also known as washy or lathered (up).

weanling A foal less than one-year-old that has been separated (weaned) from its dam.

weigh in (out) The certification by the clerk of scales of a rider's weight before (after) a race. A jockey weighs in fully dressed with all equipment except for his or her helmet, whip, and (in many jurisdictions) flak jacket.

weight for age An allowance condition in which each entrant is assigned a weight according to its age. Females usually receive a sex allowance as well.

wheel Betting all possible combinations in an exotic wager using at least one horse as the key.

white A horse color, extremely rare, in which all the hairs are white. The horse's eyes are brown, not pink, as would be the case for an albino.

wire The finish line of a race.

workout A fast gallop at a predetermined distance.

yearling A horse in its second calendar year of life, beginning January 1 of the year following its birth for horses born in the Northern Hemisphere.

yielding Condition of a turf course with considerable moisture. Horses sink into it noticeably.

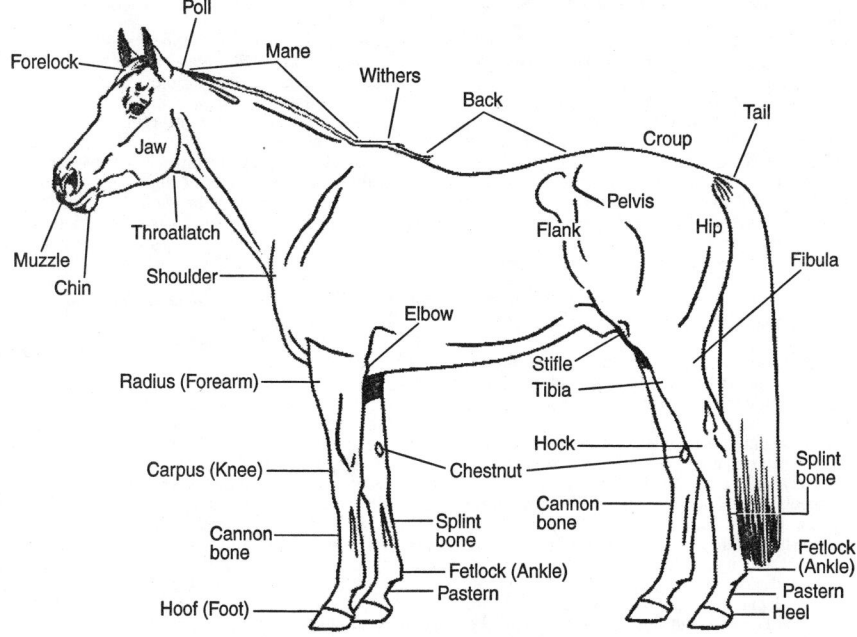

Conformation and Anatomy Terms

The following are words and expressions commonly used to describe Thoroughbred anatomy and conformation. This glossary contains many terms and definitions found in *The Media Guide to Equine Sport*, published by the American Association of Equine Practitioners.

angular limb deformity A limb that does not have correct conformation because of developmental problems in the angles of the joints.

anterior Toward the front.

back at the knee A leg that looks as though it has a backward arc, with its apex at the knee when viewed from the side.

cannon bone The third metacarpal (front leg) or metatarsal (rear leg), also referred to as the shin bone. The largest bone between the knee and ankle joints.

carpus A joint in the horse's front leg, more commonly referred to as the knee.

caudal Toward the tail.

coffin bone The third phalanx (P3). The major bone within the confines of the hoof. Also called the pedal bone.

conformation The physical makeup and bodily proportions of a horse; how the horse is put together.

coronary band Where the hair meets the hoof. Also called the coronet.

cow hocks Abnormal conformation in which the points of the hocks turn in.

cranial Toward the head.

curb A thickening of the plantar ligament of the hock.

deep flexor tendon Present in all four legs, but injuries most commonly affect the front legs. Located on the back (posterior) of the front leg between the knee and the foot and between the hock and the foot on the rear leg. The function is to flex the digit (pastern) and knee (carpus) and to extend the elbow on the front leg and extend the hock on the rear leg. Functions in tandem with the superficial flexor tendon.

digital The part of the limb below the ankle (fetlock) joint. Includes the long and short pastern bones and the coffin bone.

digital cushion The area beneath the coffin bone in the back of the foot that separates it from the frog. The digital cushion serves as a shock absorber for the foot.

distal Away from a reference point. Usually refers to the limbs.

distal sesamoidean ligaments Attach to the bottom of the sesamoid bones, passing down and attaching to the long and short pastern bones.

dorsal Up; toward the back or spine. Also used to describe the front of the lower limb below the knee (front) or hock (rear).

extensor tendon Extends the knee (carpus) joint, ankle joint, pastern, and foot and flexes the elbow. The muscles begin above the knee and attach to the coffin and pastern bones.

fault Weak points of a horse's conformation or its character as a racehorse.

fetlock Joint located between the cannon bone and the long pastern bone, also referred to as the ankle.

frog The V-shaped, pliable support structure on the bottom of the foot.

hock A large joint just above the shin bone in the rear

legs. Corresponds to the level of the knee of the front leg.

hoof The foot of the horse. Consists of several parts that play an integral role in supporting the weight of the horse.

inferior check ligament A direct continuation of the posterior (back) ligaments of the knee (carpus), located below the knee. Function is in support of the deep flexor tendon.

insensitive laminae The layer just under the wall of the hoof; similar to the human fingernail. It is an integral structure that helps attach the hoof wall to the underlying coffin bone.

joint Point of juncture of two bones and usually composed of fibrous connective tissue and cartilage.

joint capsule The saclike structure that encloses the ends of bones in certain joints; contains synovial fluid.

ligament A band of fibrous tissue that connects bones, supports and strengthens joints, and limits the range of motion. Some ligaments support certain organs.

medial Pertaining to the middle in anatomy, nearer the median plane (the vertical plane that bisects the body into right and left halves).

metacarpal The cannon bone, located between the knee and the fetlock joint in the front leg. The cannon bone of the front leg is the third metacarpal.

metatarsal Cannon bone in the hind leg.

musculoskeletal system Consisting of the bones, muscles, ligaments, tendons, and joints of the head, vertebral column, and limbs, together with the associated muscles, tendons, ligaments, and joints.

muzzle Nose and lips of a horse.

navicular bone A small, flat bone within the confines of the hoof that helps, along with the short pastern bone and the coffin bone, to make up the coffin joint.

open knee A condition of young horses in which the physis of the knee has not closed; an immature knee. Often used to describe the status of the physis immediately above the knee and is an indicator of long-bone growth in two-year-olds.

over at the knee A leg that looks as though it has a forward arc with its center at the knee when viewed from the side.

palmer Pertaining to the back of the front limb from the knee down.

parrot mouth A horse with an extreme overbite.

pastern Bones in the area between the fetlock joint and the hoof. The joint between the long and short pastern bones is called the pastern joint. Can also be used to describe the area of the limb or to describe a specific bone: long pastern bone. Technically known as the P1 (long) and the P2 (short).

physis The growth plate at the end of the long bones (such as the cannon bone) that lets the bone grow in length.

plantar Pertaining to the sole of the foot or back of the hind limb from the hock down.

plantar ligament The large ligament that is below and behind the hock joint.

poll The top of the head between the ears.

posterior Situated behind or toward the rear.

proximal Toward the body; the proximal cannon region is the upper portion of the cannon bone.

respiratory system Organ system responsible for gas exchange from nostrils to lungs.

sensitive laminae The area of the hoof that contains nerves and vessels.

sesamoid Two small bones (medial and lateral sesamoids) located above and at the back of the fetlock joint. Four common fractures of the sesamoids are apical (along the top of the bone), abaxial (the side of the sesamoid away from the ankle joint), midbody (sesamoid broken in half), and basilar (through the bottom) fractures. Fractures can be small chips or involve the entire bone. Surgical repair is often done by arthroscopy.

sickle hocks Forward deviation of the lower hind leg, from the hocks to the hoof, producing the appearance of a sickle when viewed from the side. Also known as curby hocks.

splint Either of the two small bones that lie along the sides of the cannon bone.

stifle The large joint above the hock is made up of the femur, patella, and tibia.

superficial flexor tendon Present in all four legs, but injuries most commonly affect the front legs. Located on the back (posterior) of the front leg between the knee and the foot and between the hock and the foot in the rear leg. Functions are to flex the digit (pastern) and knee (carpus), to extend the elbow on the front leg, and to extend the hock on the rear leg. Functions in tandem with the deep flexor tendon.

superior check ligament Fibrous band of tissue that originates above the knee and attaches to the superficial flexor tendon. Primary function is support of this tendon. Accessory ligament of the superficial flexor tendon.

suspensory ligament Originates at the back of the knee (front leg) and the back of the top part of the cannon bone (hind leg), attaching to the sesamoid bones. The lower portion of the ligament attaches the lower part of the sesamoid bones to the pastern bones. Its function is to support the fetlock. The lower ligaments that attach the sesamoid bone to the pastern bones are the distal sesamoidean ligaments.

synovial joint A movable joint that consists of articulating bone ends covered by articular cartilage held together with a joint capsule and ligaments and containing synovial fluid in the joint cavity.

synovial sheath The inner lining of a tendon sheath that produces synovial fluid. Allows ease of motion for the tendons as they cross joints.

tendon Cords of strong, white (collagen) elastic fibers that connect a muscle to a bone or other structure and transmit the forces generated by muscular contraction to the bones.

toe-in A conformation flaw in which the front of the foot angles inward and looks pigeon-toed, often causing the leg to swing outward during locomotion (paddling).

toe-out A conformation flaw in which the front of the foot faces out, often causing the leg to swing inward during locomotion (winging).

ventral Down; toward the belly.

vocal folds The membranes attached to the arytenoid cartilages in the larynx. Vibration produces vocalization.

white line When looking at the sole of the foot, the thin area between the insensitive outer hoof wall (insensitive laminae) and the inner sensitive laminae.

withers Area above the shoulder, where the neck meets the back.

Common Veterinary Terms

The following are commonly used veterinary terms. This glossary contains many terms and definitions found in the *Media Guide to Equine Sport*, published by the American Association of Equine Practitioners.

acupressure Utilizing stimulation on acupuncture points to treat an animal.

acupuncture A centuries-old therapy for treating an animal or human through the use of needles, electrical current, or moxibustion (heat and herbs) to stimulate or realign the body's electrical fields.

anhydrosis Inability to sweat in response to work output or increases in body temperature. A horse with this condition is also known as a nonsweater. Most are athletic horses, though frequently the condition appears in pastured horses not being ridden. Most commonly occurs when both the temperature and humidity are high. Clinical signs include inability to sweat, increased respiratory rate, elevated body temperature, and decreased exercise tolerance. The condition sometimes can be reversed if the horse is moved to a more temperate climate.

anterior enteritis Acute inflammation of the small intestine producing signs of abdominal distress, such as colic and diarrhea.

arthritis Inflammation of a joint. An increase in the amount of synovial fluid in the joint is a result of this inflammation.

arthroscope A thin tube containing a lens that is used for viewing areas inside a joint. Usually attached to a small video camera.

arthroscopic surgery Utilizing an arthroscope to perform surgery, eliminating the need to open the joint with a large incision to view the damaged area.

articular cartilage Cartilage that covers the ends of bones where they meet in a joint.

arytenoid cartilages Triangular cartilages in the upper part of the entrance to the larynx. Movements of the arytenoid cartilages control the diameter of the laryngeal opening.

ataxia Loss or failure of muscular coordination.

atrophy To waste away; usually used in describing muscles.

bleeder A horse that bleeds within its lungs when small capillaries that surround the lungs' air sacs (alveoli) rupture. The veterinary term is exercise-induced pulmonary hemorrhage. Blood may be seen coming out of the horse's nostrils, known as epistaxis, although it is typically discovered by an examination using a fiber-optic endoscope after exercise or racing. Hot, humid weather and cold conditions are known to exacerbate the problem. The most common preventive treatment currently available is the use of the diuretic furosemide (Salix). Less than one bleeder in 20 shows signs of epistaxis.

blister Counterirritant causing acute inflammation; used to increase blood supply and blood flow to promote healing in the leg.

bog spavin A filling with excess synovial fluid of the largest joint of the hock, called the tibial tarsal joint.

bone graft Utilizing bone taken from one part of the body to promote formation of bone in another region.

bone spavin Arthritis of the hock joint. A bone spavin that has progressed to the point that the arthritis can be seen externally is called a jack spavin.

bowed tendon A type of tendinitis. The most common injury to the tendon is a strain or bowed tendon, so named because of the appearance of a bow shape due to swelling. The most common site of injury is in the superficial flexor tendon between the knee and the ankle. Despite aggressive treatment with anti-inflammatory drugs, physical therapy, and rest, horses commonly reinjure the tendon when they return to strenuous training. Two surgeries are felt to aid horses to come back to racing: tendon splitting at the lesion site to release accumulated fluid and blood, and superior check ligament desmotomy. The latter surgery is designed to reduce forces on the tendon when the horse returns to training and racing.

breakdown When a horse suffers a potentially career-ending injury, usually to the leg.

broken wind Abnormality of the upper or lower respiratory tract causing loss of normal air exchange, generally resulting in reduced performance.

bronchodilator A drug that widens the airways in the lungs to improve breathing and to relieve muscle contraction or buildup of mucus.

bucked shins Inflammation of the covering of the bone (periosteum) of the front surface of the cannon bone to which young horses are particularly susceptible. Usually a condition of the front legs.

bursa A sac containing synovial fluid (a natural lubricant). Its purpose is to pad or cushion and thus facilitate motion between soft tissue and bone, most commonly where tendons pass over bones.

bursitis Inflammation in a bursa that results in swelling due to accumulation of synovial fluid. Capped elbow is inflammation of the bursa over the point of elbow (olecranon process of the ulna). Capped hock is inflammation of the bursa over the point of the hock (tuber calcis).

Bute Short for phenylbutazone, a nonsteroidal anti-inflammatory medication that is legal in many racing jurisdictions. Often known by the trade names Butazolidin and Butazone.

capillary refill time The amount of time it takes for blood to return to capillaries after it has been forced out, normally two seconds; usually assessed by pressing the thumb against the horse's gums. When the pressure is removed, the gum looks white but the normal pink color returns as blood flows into the capillaries.

capped elbow Inflammation of the bursa over the point of the elbow. Also known as a shoe boil.

capped hock Inflammation of the bursa over the point of the hock.

chiropractic The use of bone alignment to treat specific or general health problems.

chronic obstructive pulmonary disease Commonly known as COPD, a hyperallergenic response of the respiratory system that involves damage to the lung tissue, similar in many ways to human asthma. Affected horses may cough, develop a nasal discharge, and have a reduced tolerance for exercise. Respiratory rate is increased and lung elasticity is diminished.

chronic osselet Permanent buildup of synovial fluid in a joint, characterized by inflammation and thickening of the joint capsule over the damaged area. Usually accompanied by changes in the bone and cartilage.

clenbuterol A bronchodilator used for respiratory

ailments. It is not permissible for use on race day.

closed knees A condition when the cartilaginous growth plate above the knee (distal radial physis) has turned to bone. Indicates completion of long bone growth and is one sign of maturity.

Coggins test Used to identify antigens or antibodies against equine infectious anemia.

colic Often used broadly to describe abdominal pain, it is the leading cause of death in horses. Its causes include obstruction in the large colon; a twist in the intestine that shuts off the food passageway and blocks the blood supply; or gastric ulcers.

comminuted A fracture with more than two fragments.

compound A fracture in which the damaged bone breaks through the skin. Also known as an open fracture.

condylar A fracture in the knuckle (condyle) of the lower (distal) end of a long bone such as the cannon bone or humerus (upper front limb).

congenital Present at birth.

contagious equine metritis A venereal disease. Mares may have a profuse vaginal discharge. No symptoms of CEM may be obvious in stallions.

corticosteroids Hormones (class of steroid) that are either naturally produced by the adrenal gland or man-made. They function as anti-inflammatory hormones or as hormones that regulate the chemical stability (homeostasis) of the body. One common misconception is that a horse receiving corticosteroids experiences an increase in its natural abilities and therefore has an unfair advantage.

cough To expel air from the lungs in a spasmodic manner. Can be a result of inflammation or irritation to the upper airways (pharynx, larynx, or trachea) or may involve the lower airways of the lungs (deep cough).

cracked hoof A vertical split of the hoof wall. Cracks may extend upward from the bearing surface of the hoof or downward from the coronary band, as the result of a defect in the band. Varying in degrees of severity, cracks can result from injuries or concussion. Hooves that are dry or thin (shelly) or improperly shod are susceptible to cracking upon concussion. Corrective trimming and shoeing may remedy mild cracks, but in severe cases, when the crack extends inward to the sensitive laminae, more extensive treatment is required, such as using screws and wires to stabilize the sides of the crack.

cribber A horse that clings to objects with its teeth and sucks air into its stomach. Also known as a wind sucker.

cryptorchid A unilateral cryptorchid is a male horse of any age that has one testicle undescended. A bilateral cryptorchid is a male horse of any age that has both testicles undescended. The Jockey Club defines cryptorchid as a male horse of any age that has both testicles undescended.

cup Refers to the irregular occlusal surface of the tooth (the surfaces that meet when a horse closes its mouth) and is used as a visual method of determining age in a horse.

curb A thickening of the plantar ligament of the hock.

degenerative joint disease Any joint problem that has progressive degeneration of joint cartilage and the underlying (subchondral) bone. Occurs most frequently in the joints below the radius in the foreleg and femur in the hind leg. Some of the more common causes include repeated trauma, conformation faults, blood disease, traumatic joint injury, subchondral bone defects, osteochondritis dissecans (OCD) lesions, and excessive intra-articular corticosteroid injections. Also known as osteoarthritis or as developmental orthopedic disease (DOD).

desmitis Inflammation of a ligament. Often a result of tearing of any number of ligament fibrils.

deworming The use of drugs (anthelmintics) to kill internal parasites, often performed by administration of oral paste or liquid or by passing a nasogastric tube into the horse's stomach.

digestible energy The amount of energy a horse is able to digest from its feed.

DMSO Dimethyl sulfoxide, a topical anti-inflammatory. Its chief characteristic is its ability to penetrate the skin and therefore act as a vehicle for medications.

dorsal displacement of the soft palate A condition in which the soft palate, located on the floor of the airway near the larynx, moves up into the airway. A minor displacement causes a gurgling sound during exercise, while in more serious cases the palate can block the airway. This is sometimes known as choking down, but the tongue does not actually block the airway. The base of the tongue is connected to the larynx, of which the epiglottis is a part. When the epiglottis is retracted, the soft palate can move up into the airway (dorsal displacement). This condition can sometimes be managed with equipment such as a figure-eight noseband or a tongue tie. In more extreme cases, surgery might be required, most commonly a myectomy.

drench Liquid administered through mouth.

Eastern equine encephalomyelitis One of several different types of encephalomyelitis that are extremely contagious, causing sickness and death in horses by affecting the central nervous system. EEE is spread by mosquitoes and can affect humans. Can be prevented by annual vaccination.

endoscope An instrument used for direct visual inspection of a hollow organ or body cavity such as the upper airway or stomach. A fiber-optic endoscope comprises a long, flexible tube that has a series of lenses and a light at the end to allow the veterinarian to view and photograph the respiratory system through the airway. Other internal organs may be viewed through a tiny surgical opening. A video endoscope has a small camera at its tip.

entrapped epiglottis A condition in which the thin membrane lying below the epiglottis moves up and covers the epiglottis. The abnormality may obstruct breathing. It is usually corrected by surgery to cut the membrane if it impairs respiratory function.

enzyme-linked immunosorbant assay A test, commonly referred to as the ELISA test, that is used after a race to detect the presence of drugs in racehorses. Developed in the early 1990s by the University of Kentucky.

epiphysitis An inflammation in the growth plate (physis) at the ends of the long bones (such as the cannon bone). Symptoms include swelling, tenderness, and heat. Although the exact cause is unknown, contributing factors seem to be high caloric intake (either from grain or a heavily lactating mare) and a fast growth rate.

equine protozoal myeloencephalitis Commonly called EPM. A neurological condition in a horse caused by a parasite that infects the horse's central nervous system. The cause of EPM is *Sarcocystis neurona*, a small protozoan organism that is slightly larger than a bacterium. The host necessary to complete the organism's life cycle is the opossum.

equine viral arteritis A highly contagious disease that is characterized by swelling in the legs of all horses and swelling in the scrotum of stallions. EVA can cause abortion in mares and can be shed in the semen of stallions for years after infection.

exercise-induced pulmonary hemorrhage (EIPH) See bleeder.

fissure Longitudinal crack through only one surface of a bone.

float An equine dental procedure in which sharp points on the teeth are filed down.

founder See laminitis.

fracture A break in a bone.

furosemide A medication used in the treatment of bleeders, commonly known by the trade name Salix, a diuretic. Although research has not determined definitively how furosemide reduces bleeding, it is widely believed that the diuretic effect reduces pressure within capillaries in the lungs.

gastric ulcers Ulceration of a horse's stomach. Often causes symptoms of abdominal distress (colic) and general unthriftiness.

gravel Infection of the hoof resulting from a crack in the white line (the border between the insensitive and sensitive laminae). An abscess usually forms in the sensitive structures and eventually breaks through at the coronet as the result of the infection.

green osselet In young horses, a swelling in the fetlock joint, particularly on the front of the joint where the cannon and long pastern bones meet. This swelling is a result of inflammation and reactive changes of the front edges of these two bones and adjacent cartilage. If the green osselet does not heal, a chronic osselet might develop with a permanent buildup of synovial fluid in the joint and inflammation and thickening of the joint capsule over the damaged area with secondary bone changes following the initial inflammation.

heaves Emphysema.

heel crack A crack on the heel of the hoof. Also called a sand crack.

hematoma A blood-filled area resulting from injury.

hyaluronic acid A normal component of joint fluid. Also can be a man-made intra-articular medication used to relieve joint inflammation.

IM Abbreviation for intramuscular.

impaction A type of colic caused by a blockage of the intestines by ingested materials (constipation).

intra-articular Within a joint.

intramuscular An injection given in a muscle.

intravenous An injection given in a vein.

ischemia Deficiency of blood supply, which may be temporary or permanent. Caused by the shutting down of blood vessels.

IV Abbreviation for intravenous.

lactic acid Organic acid normally present in muscle tissue, produced by anaerobic muscle metabolism as a byproduct of exercise. An increase in lactic acid causes muscle fatigue, inflammation, and pain.

lame A deviation from a normal gait due to pain in a limb or its supporting structures.

laminitis An inflammation of the sensitive laminae of the foot. There are many factors involved, including changes in the blood flow through the capillaries of the foot. Many events can cause laminitis, including ingesting toxic levels of grain, eating lush grass, systemic disease problems, high temperature, toxemia, retained placenta, excessive weight-bearing as occurs when the opposite limb is injured, and the administration of some drugs. Laminitis usually manifests itself in the front feet, develops rapidly, and is life threatening. In mild cases, however, a horse can resume a certain amount of athletic activity. Also known as founder.

magnetic therapy Physical therapy technique using magnetic fields. The low-energy electrical field created by the magnetic field causes dilation of the blood vessels (vasodilation) and tissue stimulation. Magnetic therapy may be used on soft tissue to treat such injuries as tendinitis or bony (skeletal) injuries such as bucked shins.

mare reproductive loss syndrome In the spring of 2001, a severe outbreak believed to have been caused by Eastern tent caterpillars caused the loss in Central Kentucky of more than 500 late-term fetuses and newborn foals and almost 5,000 early-term fetuses. The economic loss to Central Kentucky's Thoroughbred industry from MLRS was estimated at more than $300-million.

metacarpal (fracture) Usually refers to a fracture of the cannon bone, located between the knee and the fetlock joint in the front leg. Also may refer to a fracture of the splint bone. The cannon bone of the front leg is the third metacarpal.

monorchid A male horse of any age that has only one testicle in his scrotum; the other testicle was either removed or is undescended.

nasogastric tube A long, flexible tube that reaches from the nose to the stomach.

navicular disease A degenerative disease that affects the navicular bone (small bone in the back of the foot), navicular bursa, and deep flexor tendon. Generally considered a disease of the front feet. Both front feet are often affected, but one will usually be more noticeable than the other.

neurectomy A surgical procedure in which the nerve supply to the navicular area is removed. The toe and remainder of the foot retain feeling. Sometimes referred to as posterior digital neurectomy or heel nerve. Also known as nerving.

oblique Fracture at an angle.

oiling Administration of mineral oil by nasogastric tube to relieve gas or to break a blockage. Preventive procedure commonly used before long van rides to prevent impaction and subsequent colic.

open knee A condition of young horses in which the physis of the knee has not closed; an immature knee. Often used to describe the status of the physis immediately above the knee and is an indicator of long bone growth in two-year-olds.

osteoarthritis A permanent form of arthritis with progressive loss of the articular cartilage in a joint.

osteochondritis dissecans A cartilaginous or bony lesion that is the result of a fragment of cartilage and its underlying bone becoming detached from an articular surface. The OCD lesions occur commonly in the knee joint and are associated with a failure in bone development.

pastern Bones located between the fetlock joint and the hoof. The joint between the long and short pastern bones is called the pastern joint. Can also be used to describe the area of the limb or to describe a specific bone: long pastern bone. Technically known as the P1 (long) and P2 (short).

periostitis Inflammation of the tissue (periosteum) that overlies bone. Periostitis of the cannon bone is referred to as bucked shins, while periostitis of the splint bone is called a splint, which may be expressed as a popped splint.

phenylbutazone A nonsteroidal anti-inflammatory medication that is legal in many racing jurisdictions. Trade names are Butazolidin and Butazone.

physis The growth plate at the end of the long bones (such as the cannon bone) that lets the bone grow in length.

pin firing Thermocautery used to increase blood flow to the leg and intended to promote healing.

pulled suspensory Suspensory ligament injury (suspensory desmitis) in which some portion of the fibers of the ligament have been disrupted and some loss of support of the distal limb may have occurred.

quarter crack A crack between the toe and heel, usually extending into the coronary band.

radiograph The picture or image on film generated by X rays.

ring bone Osteoarthritis of joints between the pastern bones (high ring bone) or just above the coronet (low ring bone).

roaring (laryngeal hemiplegia) A whistling sound made by a horse during inhalation while exercising. The condition is caused by a partial or total paralysis of the nerves controlling the muscles that elevate the arytenoid cartilages and thereby open the larynx. In severe cases, a surgical procedure known as tie-back surgery (laryngoplasty) is performed, in which a suture is inserted through the cartilage to hold it out of the airway permanently. Paralysis almost exclusively occurs on the left side and most frequently in horses over 16 hands tall.

run down Abrasion of the heel during stride.

saucer Stress fracture of the front of the cannon bone; the fracture can be straight or curved.

screw fixation A procedure in which steel-alloy screws are surgically inserted to hold together a fractured bone.

sesamoid Fracture of the sesamoid bone. Fractures can be small chips or involve the entire bone. Surgical repair is often done by arthroscopy.

sesamoiditis Inflammation of the sesamoid bones.

simple A fracture along a single line that does not penetrate the skin.

slab A bone fracture in a joint that extends from one articular surface to another. Most often seen in the third carpal bone of the knee.

slipped Spontaneous abortion.

splint A condition in which calcification occurs on the splint bone and causes a bump. This condition can occur in response to a fracture or other irritation to the splint bone. A common injury is a popped splint.

stress A fracture created by the repetitive stress placed on a bone, most often in athletic training. Usually seen in the front of the cannon bone as a severe form of bucked shins. Also seen in the tibia and causes a hard-to-diagnose hind-limb lameness.

synchronous diaphragmatic flutter A contraction of the diaphragm in synchrony with the heartbeat after strenuous exercise, giving the appearance of hiccups. Affected horses have a noticeable twitch or spasm in the flank area that may cause an audible sound, hence the term 'thumps.' Most commonly

seen in electrolyte-depleted or exhausted horses. The condition resolves spontaneously with rest.

synovitis Inflammation of a synovial structure, typically a synovial sheath.

tendinitis Inflammation of a tendon.

thermography Diagnostic technique utilizing instrumentation that measures temperature differences. Records the surface temperature of a horse. Unusually hot or cold areas may be indicative of some underlying pathology (deviation from the normal).

thoroughpin Swelling of the synovial sheath of the deep flexor tendon above the hock.

tie-back surgery A procedure (laryngoplasty) used to suture the arytenoid cartilage out of the airway.

toe crack A crack near the front of the hoof.

torsion A twist in the intestine.

toxemia Poisoning sometimes caused by the absorption of bacterial products (endotoxins) formed at a local source of infection.

tubing Inserting a nasogastric tube through a horse's nostril into its stomach for the purpose of providing oral medication.

twitch A restraining device usually consisting of a stick with a loop of rope or chain at one end, which is placed around a horse's upper lip and twisted, releasing endorphins that relax a horse and curb its fractiousness while it is being handled.

tying up Known as acute rhabdomyolysis, a form of muscle cramp that ranges in severity from mild stiffness to a life-threatening disease. A generalized condition of muscle-fiber breakdown usually associated with exercise. The cause of the muscle-fiber breakdown is uncertain. Signs include sweating, reluctance to move, stiffness, and general distress.

ultrasound 1) Diagnostic ultrasound: A technique that uses ultrasonic waves to produce images of internal structures. 2) Therapeutic ultrasound: A therapy to create heat and stimulate healing.

Venezuelan equine encephalomyelitis A highly contagious disease affecting the central nervous system that can cause illness or death in horses and humans. Abbreviated as VEE.

Western equine encephalomyelitis A highly contagious disease spread by mosquitoes that affects the central nervous system. WEE can cause death in horses two to three days after onset of clinical signs. The horse is considered a dead-end host. Can be prevented by annual vaccination. Also affects humans.

West Nile virus Encephalitis first reported in North America in 1999. Virus is harbored in birds and spread by mosquitoes to other birds, horses, and humans. Not all horses bitten by infected mosquitoes develop clinical signs, but mortality rate is 38% in those that do. Conditionally approved vaccine appears to prevent the disease.

wind puff Accumulation of synovial fluid in the fetlock-joint capsule. Also known as a wind gall.

wobbler syndrome Neurological disease clinically associated with general incoordination and muscle weakness. Can be caused by an injury to the spinal cord in the area of the cervical (neck) vertebrae or is associated with malformation or degeneration of the cervical vertebrae.

Xeroradiography A costly type of x-ray procedure using specially sensitized screens that give higher resolution on the edges of bone and better visualization of soft-tissue structures.

Essentials for Every Racing Library

THE FIRST, THE ORIGINAL RACING ALMANAC

An annual reference guide, the THOROUGHBRED TIMES RACING ALMANAC has all the facts, figures, and statistics on racing. Look for next year's edition in August of 2004.

$19.95 (plus $5.99 shipping and handling)

THE BEST BOOK WRITTEN ON THE HISTORY OF AMERICAN RACING

RACING THROUGH THE CENTURY brings to life the excitement, wonder, disappointment, riches, and exhilarating speed of Thoroughbred racing over the past one hundred years. The changing times. The characters and events. The economic and political climate of each era. This beautifully illustrated book will catapult you into the fast-paced world of racing.

$49.95 (plus $7.99 shipping and handling)

THOROUGHBRED TIMES BOOKS™

Visit us online at www.thoroughbredtimes.com or call toll free 888-738-2665 to order.
Thoroughbred Times, P.O. Box 8237, Lexington, KY 40533; (859) 260-9800

Quick Reference Index